THE STUDENT'S

ENGLISH-SANSKRIT DICTIONARY

D1871503

THE STUDENT'S
ENGLISH-SANSKRIT
DICTIONARY

By

VAMAN SHIVRAM APTE

GYAN

Published by

Gyan Publishing House
5, Ansari Road
Daryaganj, New Delhi-110002
Phone: 011-47034999, 9811692060
E-mail: books@gyanbooks.com

Distribution Network
gyanbooks.com
India, USA, Canada, UK, Australia, France

© Publisher

All rights reserved. No part of this work may be reproduced, stored, adapted, or transmitted in any form or by any means, electronic, mechanical, photocopying, micro-filming, recording or otherwise, or translated in any language, without the prior written permission of the copyright owner and the publisher.

ISBN : 978-81-212-6627-7 (PB)
First Published, 1893

2nd Impression 2022

Printed at: Gyan Press, Delhi.

The book is sold subject to the condition that it shall not, by way of trade or otherwise, be lent, resold, hired out, or otherwise circulated without the prior publisher's written consent.

THE STUDENT'S ENGLISH-SANSKRIT DICTIONARY
Author: VAMAN SHIVRAM APTE

THE STUDENT'S ENGLISH-SANSKRIT DICTIONARY.

BY

VAMAN SHIVRAM APTE, M. A.,

Author of the "Practical" and "Student's" Sanskrit-English Dictionaries, "Student's Guide to Sanskrit Composition" &c. &c.

LATE PRINCIPAL AND PROFESSOR OF SANSKRIT, FERGUSSON COLLEGE, POONA.

Reprint with corrections from the First Edition.

1893.

PREFACE.

When I prepared "The Student's Hand-Book of Progressive Exercises," Part II., I thought of adding to it a glossary of difficult words and expressions in the Exercises. When this was done, an idea occurred that the Glossary should be made to include all words of ordinary occurrence, such are as given in small School-Dictionaries. When the revision of the sheets thus written out commenced, and when they were put to a practical test, it was found that several words and expressions had still been left out. I, then, resolved to prepare an English-Sanskrit Dictionary as complete as possible, and the following pages are the result. The Dictionary has thus passed through different stages, and has assumed this form, far exceeding the limits which I had first assigned to it.

Much need not, I think, be said with regard to the necessity of a work like this. In these days of literary activity, when the attention of students is drawn more and more to the study of Sanskrit, it is necessary that all appliances should be ready before them to facilitate this study. There are one or two small Sanskrit-English Dictionaries, though not quite adequate to meet the wants of advanced students of Sanskrit, but there is no English-Sanskrit Dictionary such as will be within their easy reach. The Dictionaries of this description that I know of, are two in number:—one by Professor Monier Williams, and another by Mr. Anundoram Borooah of Calcutta. Both these Dictionaries, though valuable in themselves, are not accessible to the student, the prices being prohibitively high. But there are other considerations which make these works not quite adopted to his wants. Professor Monier Williams' Dictionary, having been compiled nearly 35 years ago, chiefly by inverting the then existing Sanskrit-English Dictionaries, is naturally open to the fault of being often not *practical*. As he says in the Preface to his Dictionary, he proceeded to translate Webster's Dictionary systematically into Sanskrit, omitting words, phrases &c. of which no classical equivalent could be found or suggested. The result has been that many of his synonyms appear more as coined words than classical expressions used by standard Sanskrit authors. With regard to words collected in Lexicons, such as Amarakosha, Medini, Sabdakalpadruma, there is no difficulty; but in the case of those words and expressions which can only be suggested by a careful study of the usage of the best authors, the work, in my humble opinion, falls short of one's expectations. Mr. Anundoram Borooah's work is eminently *practical*: it abounds with quotations from several standard authors; the renderings are generally happy, and the work has, at least, a classical appearance. The fondness for giving quotations has induced the writer to give several quotations for illustrating such words as गम्, इति, तत्, यद् &c., of the meanings of which there is no doubt nor is any confirmation needed. But one great defect of his otherwise very useful work is that it gives too few equivalents. He has pursued the course of referring one word to another, but this is, in some cases, carried to such an extent, that when a word, as directed, is referred to another, that again is referred to some other word of a synonymous nature, which in its turn is referred to another, till the reader returns to the original word, apparently without having his labours rewarded. A study of Mr. Borooah's work is a good treat for an advanced Sanskrit scholar, but will not, I believe, satisfy the student. From considerations like these I thought I should be doing some service to the Sanskrit reading public, if I compiled an English-Sanskrit Dictionary adapted to the wants of the student. The foregoing remarks are made not with the view of detracting from the high and acknowledged merits of the two works, but solely to indicate the line I have followed, and the object I have had in compiling this work.

Some words are now necessary as to the plan and scope of the Dictionary. When I resolved to make this Dictionary as complete as possible, consistently with its aim of being useful for the student, I took the latest edition of Webster's Complete Dictionary, and taking that as my basis, proceeded with the work of compilation. As I advanced, I found that several words, phrases and expressions and several senses of single words, could not be adequately represented in Sanskrit, so as to appear like Sanskrit, either because the words &c. were purely technical and referred to specific ideas in subjects, such as Chemistry, Botany, Medicine, Psychology, Law, Engineering &c., or were such as had no corresponding ideas in Sanskrit and were peculiar to the English language. Words of this nature are numerous in Webster's Dictionary, and I have omitted them, including also obsolete and rare words or senses of words. Several words of obvious signification, such as those formed by the prefixes, '*in*,' '*mis*,' '*pre*' '*un*,' are also omitted, as they may be easily formed from their second member. But the general terms of all sciences have been included, and of technical terms such as could be duly represented by Sanskrit equivalents actually existing in the language or by short, wieldy new combinations of words have been inserted. Of this description are words like Telegram, Democrat, Society, Literature, Address (of a letter) and several other words which have a peculiar sense in English and have to be translated by inventing equivalents. English, like many other languages, has so many expressions and idioms peculiar to itself, so many shades and nice distinctions of meaning, and so many new formations of words, progressing with the progress of the language, that it would be impossible to embrace them all in an English-Sanskrit Dictionary, even if it were the most comprehensive work ; much more so, in a work designed principally for students. Take the works Line, Pass, Strong. Webster gives 21 senses under 'Line,' 13 under 'Pass (*v. i.*)' and 20 under 'Strong.' Some of these are technical, and some are not *different* senses as such, but shades of meaning or particularities of use ; most of which may be translated by the words given for the general sense, (*see* the words). I have not thought it desirable, like Professor Monier Williams, to insert words the English explanation of which has to be systematically translated, in order to give some idea of their meaning. 'Indian-rubber' is translated by आतस्थितिस्थापकविशिष्टो भारतदेशीयवृक्षनिर्यासः ; 'Shuttle cock.' by लघुगुलिकाविशेषः यां विनोदार्थं दंडाहतां भूत्वा इतस्ततः प्रक्षिप्यते ; and many others of this nature, which can be translated by विशेषः 'a kind of tree, flower, fruit' &c. Such words may be retained by the student in their English form, or their meaning may be translated if he desire to have them in a Sanskrit garb. स्पंजः 'Sponge,' ड्यूकः 'Duke,' साबनं 'Soap,' लाटिनं 'Latinity,' (as given by Mr. Boroosh) may, I think, be very safely omitted even in a comprehensive Dictionary.

To turn now to the plan and arrangement of the work. The most striking feature of the arrangement is that a word in its different parts of speech, compound words derived from it, derivatives formed from it either regularly, by means of terminations (*e. g.* ed, ing, ly, ness &c.) or irregularly, have been given together, the derivatives being arranged in order under the root or primitive word, by means of small black dashes. The dashes are intended to at once strike the eye and to direct it to the word after it; and when the "Directions to the student" are remembered, there will, I believe, be no difficutly in referring words to the Dictionary. The principle of the arrangement is to give words according to the root-system; words regularly derived will, of course, be referred in their proper places; but words formed from the radical irregularly should also be referred under that radical. 'Abstemious,' should be referred under 'Abstain,' 'Perception' under, 'Perceive,' 'Death,' 'Dead,' under 'Die,' 'Strengh' &c., under 'Strong,' 'Would,' under 'Will,' and so on; where it is not likely for the student to know where such words are given, reference is made to those places; *e. g. see* Material, Sight. One of the greatest advantages of the system has been practically (whatever it may be theoretically) to effect a very large saving of space. To give the reader an idea of the vast saving effected by this system, it may be stated that, if the words in their different parts of speech and their compounds and derivatives were separately given, as in Monier Williams' Dictionary, they would cover nearly 800 pages of this size, or 1,000 of the size, style of printing, &c. of Monier Williams' Dictionary. Besides, by giving the words 'Dead' 'Death' under 'Die,' a considerable repetition of words is avoided. About 20 equivalents are given for 'Die,' and only a few are given for 'Dead'; the rest can be formed in the same way from the roots *immediately* above; if it were given in its usual place, all words would have to be given, or a reference made to 'Die.' My chief aim has been to give a good deal of matter in a small space, and this object is, I believe, considerably secured, as shown by the figures given above; and I have thus been enabled to give this book to the public at a cheap price.

The next point to be noticed is the number of equivalents that are given for a word. I believe that in an English-Sanskrit Dictionary, it is sufficient to give such words only as are of very frequent occurrence in Sanskrit authors. It cannot include *all* words in the language, and even if it could, it would be of no great use, since many of the words would be found to be very rarely used. The word 'Gold' has over 50 synonyms given for it in the different lexicons; 'Sun' has nearly a hundred. But it will easily be seen that, excepting some, the synonyms are either combinations of simple words, or are descriptive epithets. Of this class are the words वक्रपुच्छः, ललजिह्वः, रात्रिजागरः for 'Dog.' Mr. Borooah in his Dictionary has given only a few equivalents, in some instances, only one, where there were 5 most commonly used; Prof. Williams has very often given too many equivalents, grouping together common and rare, synonyms proper and epithets. In the former case the student will hardly have any room left for choosing his word, while in the latter, he will be at a loss to see which to choose. In giving equivalents in this Dictionary, whether for Substantives, Adjectives, Adverbs or Verbs, I have endeavoured to strike a middle course between these two courses, and, have kept one principle steadily in view: to give such words as are found frequently used in the works of standard authors. The equivalents are arranged in the order of their frequency of use; and the students, in his ordinary prose composition, would do well to make his selection from the first few equivalents enumerated. In the case of Verbs it has not been possible to maintain this principle with perfect accuracy in every case, but it is generally maintained. It is only in a few cases of substantives that I have gone the length of giving all words enumerated in the Amarakosha; and in the case of names of material substances, names of plants and trees that have been identified, and in a few others, all the words given in the Amarakosha have been here incorporated, care being taken to arrange them in the order of their usefulness. Similarly such Genders, Padas or Conjugations are given as will be found generally used; I have very rarely given all possible ones.

It has not been thought necessary to give the 3rd person singular, Present tense, nor all possible derivatives from simple words ; they will have, if necessary, to be made up according to the "Directions" afterwards given. In giving equivalents for a word in its different senses, it has also not been thought necessary to give the meanings in English, except where it was necessary to note a particular sense. One word in Sanskrit often represents several meanings in English, and to render them into Sanskrit, the Sanskrit word has to be repeated. This accounts for the repetition of some Sanskrit words under different meanings.

It will be noticed that there are several sentences given to illustrate the meanings of words, some of which are quotations from standard authors, as will be readily seen from the references given after them ; but many of the phrases and sentences that are translated, and are not supported by any authority, are taken from the "Student's Hand-Book of Progressive Exercises," Part II. I deemed it essential to illustrate, in some cases at least, the *construction* of the equivalents given, wherever it was peculiar in Sanskrit ; and I thought I could do this better if I gave sentences from classical authors instead of framing them myself. The quotations have become quite necessary in those cases where equivalents have been here suggested for the first time ; I thought I should produce my vouchers for a particular word that I suggested rather than leave the reader in doubt as to its genuineness. In a few cases the English or Sanskrit sentences are closely translated ; in a few others only such parts of the Sanskrit sentences are translated as are sufficient to illustrate the word intended to be illustrated, while in several cases, Sanskrit sentences alone are given, which might be readily understood by the student. On a reference to the names of works or authors drawn upon for quotations, it will be found that the list is not very comprehensive ; several large and useful works have been left out, and works falling in the range of classical literature excluded. But my principal aim in giving quotations has been to supply the student with good expressions from works *within his easy reach*, so that he might study, if necessary, the particular places referred to. Kálidása's works and Bána's Kâdambarî are more frequently drawn upon than the Râmâyana, the Mahâbhârata, the Naishadha or the Mahávîracharita.

An attempt has been made to avoid as much unnecessary repetition as was possible, without marring the usefulness of the work. A Dictionary is necessarily a work of repetition ; several words have to be unavoidably repeated, howsoever unwilling one might be to do so. I have thought it necessary to make reference under some words to preceding or succeeding parts of the Dictionary, chiefly with the view of avoiding repetition ; but in such cases a few equivalents are given, and the student is told to follow out the reference, if he want to know more about the word. Take, for instance, the words, Beguile, Cheat, Deceive, Delude, Defraud, Impose upon, Take in ; or Blame, Censure, Reprove, Reproach, Scold, Reprimand, Reprehend ; or Path, Road, Way: these words, whatever be their shades of meaning in English, are, when represented in Sanskrit, almost synonymous, and may be conveniently represented by the same words. If ten or fifteen equivalents under one of these words, say, Cheat, Censure, or Way, are given, it would be unnecessary to repeat all of them again under the synonymous words. In all such cases, therefore, references have been made to some general word under which are given all the equivalents. In a few cases the reference has been made, not for any equivalents, but for any expressions, phrases, idioms &c. that may have been given under the principal word. In no case will the student have to refer to the Dictionary *more than twice.*

In a work which professes to deal with the phrases and expressions of the English Language, the writer cannot afford to disregard the several small useful proverbs, mottoes, or other expressions which have become proverbial. I have, with this view, inserted, under some principal word therein, such proverbs &c., and have given exact or approximate equivalents wherever they existed in Sanskrit, and have in a few cases given my own translation of them. Of this nature are proverbs given under Bush, Handsome, Make, Oil, Race, Something, Suffer, Touch &c.

With regard to the method of writing the Sanskrit equivalents, an objection might possibly be raised. Throughout the work the usual practice of representing every anusvara in the body of a word by its corresponding nasals has been rejected and the anusvara sign is invariably used, where usually a nasal would stand. I have not been able to understand the principle on which scholars reject this system and betake themselves solely to the other ; though the anusvara system is most convenient in printing, and occasionally saves much misunderstanding. Besides, it is a practice generally followed in our old Manuscripts, and is sanctioned by Pàṇini as being optional. For these reasons I have scrupulously followed it in this Dictionary, but more especially because it is very convenient in printing. The rules of Sandhi, to make the words clearly intelligible, are not in all cases strictly observed.

It now remains for me to do the grateful duty of acknowledging my obligations to those that have assisted me in the preparation of the Dictionary in one form or another. Foremost among them stand the works of Mr. Boroоah and Prof. Williams, both of which I have most frequently consulted. Monier Williams' Dictionary, though inferior in several respects to Mr. Boroоah's, has several happy renderings of short words and expressions, especially where ideas, purely English, have to be clothed in a Sanskrit garb, and I have freely consulted his Dictionary for such renderings. I have also frequently referred to the learned Professor's valuable Sanskrit-English Dictionary ; for both of which my sincere thanks are due to him. But my acknowledgments are chiefly due to Mr. Boroоah, from whose work I have derived much substantial assistance, in the suggestion of equivalents for words or phrases, more particularly from his numerous quotations, and therein again, quotations from such works as were not accessible to me, or being accessible, I had no time at my disposal sufficient to go through them. I have also had to keep constantly by my side, the useful Sanskrit Lexicon—the Kosha of Amarasimha—made more useful by the edition published by the Department of Public Instruction, Bombay. In giving illustrative sentences from classical Authors, I have used annotations or translations wherever they existed, and have derived hints from them and have occasionally adopted their translation. My thanks are due to all annotators, editors or translators of such works. I have to thank sincerely Prof. R. G. Bhandarkar, M. A., Deccan College, Poona, who kindly proposed suitable equivalents for some difficult words and phrases which were referred to him. I have also to thank my friend, Mr. Ganesh Krishna Garde, L. M. & S., for having supplied me with accurate equivalents for some knotty and technical terms in Medicine, from books and sources which I had no time to reach, and which even if I had time to reach and use, I could not, unaided by him, turn to much practical account. Lastly, my thanks are due to several kind and obliging friends, who assisted me either in collecting materials for the Dictionary, or in carrying it through the Press.

In conclusion, I trust that the Dictionary will be useful, not only to those for whose use it is principally prepared, but to the general public also who may wish to avail themselves of appliances calculated to help the study of Sanskrit. It is my belief that, except for the translation of passages from purely technical subjects, such as Chemistry, Botany, Medicine, Philosophy &c., this Dictionary will be useful to all readers of Sanskrit for translating any passage dealing with ordinary subjects. None is more conscious than myself of the defects of the book, and of the mistakes or inaccuracies that might have crept into it, in spite of my vigilance ; and when a second edition is prepared, I shall endeavour, to the best of my ability, to make the Dictionary complete in itself. I shall be very happy to receive any suggestions that readers may have to make and shall be but too willing to adopt them, if I find them useful. With these prefatory remarks I leave the work to the indulgent judgment of the public.

Poona,
June 11th, 1884.

V. S. A.

PUBLISHER'S PREFACE TO THE SECOND EDITION.

The Publisher had hoped that the learned author would write a preface to this Edition; but unfortunately it was not to be. He was snatched away suddenly from amongst us by the cruel hand of death to the sincere regret of all lovers of Sanskrit learning. Therefore the present edition has had to suffer along with other works of his, the want of his finishing touch. However it is in some respect a consolation to think that Mr. Apte found time before his death to go carefully through the first Edition and to make the necessary corrections in it in the light of his riper studies.

DIRECTIONS TO THE STUDENT.

(To be studied before using the Dictionary.)

1. Words and their derivatives are arranged in the following order : first the radical or primitive word, in all its different parts of speech; then compound words, arranged in alphabetical order; (in the case of verbs, such words as Break off, Turn out, are given as -off, -out); and then the derivatives which are always distinguished by a black dash; those formed regularly being given first, and the irregular ones, written fully, after them (*see* Ambition, Humble, Young).

Note.—This order is not regularly observed in the first three letters, compound words and derivatives being, in a few cases, both distinguished by black dashes.

2. In giving the terminations by which derivatives are formed, the changes which the final and initial letters undergo, *e. g.* the dropping, doubling or assimilation of letters are assumed; the terminations being always given in their original form; *see* Cut, Hurry, Mature.

3. (*a*) A small black dash (–) marks the commencement of a new derivative. (*b*) A word preceded by a large black dash (—) indicates that the derivatives given after it, are from that word and *not* from the radical or primitive word; *see* Die, Dead. (*c*) A hyphen used in the middle of Sanskrit words indicates that each of the members separated by the hyphen is to be repeated with the word after it ; or that the word after the hyphen is to be taken as an alternative for the word immediately before it (to be, in some cases, decided by the context); *e. g.* in Have, *l.* 9, यथाकामं-स्वरुच्या-वृत् means यथाकामं वृत्, स्वरुच्या वृत्; in Practice, *l.* 3, नित्यवृत्तिः-चर्या-अनुष्ठानं means नित्यवृत्तिः, नित्यचर्या, नित्यानुष्ठानं. (*d*) A hyphen followed by a comma (-,) indicates that the word after it may stand by itself or may be joined with the word before it ; *e. g.* in Place, *l.* 1, प्र-,देशः means the word is either देशः, or प्रदेशः. (*e*) A comma followed by a hyphen (,-) indicates that the word after it may be compounded with the word preceding it; *e. g.* in Stage, *l.* 1, रंगः,-शाला means the word is either रंगः, or रंगशाला. (*f*) ° denotes that the word immediately before it which is separated by a comma, may be compounded with the words which it connects ; *e. g.* Prevent, *l.* 1 वृ c., नि-विनि°, means the root is also निवृ c. and विनिवृ c.

4. In the case of substantives, the nominative case, wherever it could at once indicate the gender, has been given ; the visarga thus indicates masculine gender, and anusvàra neuter gender. Where the nominative is not indicative of the gender, it is given as *m.*, *f.*, *n.*, as the case may be. All substantives ending in consonants have their genders specified as *m.*, *f.*, or *n.*

5. In the case of adjectives, the simple base only is given. The feminine of the majority of adjectives in अ ends in आ, and adjectives ending in ई, उ have generally the same base for all genders. In all such cases the simple base is given, the genders being formed regularly according to similar substantive bases. Irregular feminines are denoted in brackets (*f.*). Bases ending in तृ, नृ, सृ, from their feminine regularly in ती, नी, सी ; this is given in the first three letters, but afterwards discontinued.

6. (*a*) In the case of verbs, the Arabic figure denotes the conjugation to which the root belongs ; P denoting Parasmaipada, A Atmanepada, and U Ubhayapada (P & A) Roots of the tenth conjugation belong to both Padas, theoretically at least; and hence 10 is used for all roots of this conjugation, though the Parasmaipada, unless where otherwise specified, should be generally preferred for use. (*b*) c. denotes causal, and is formed from roots by making the same changes as in the 10th conjugation. Wherever it cannot be formed by this general rule, it is shown in brackets. (*c*) D. means Denominatives ; here the 3rd pers. singular Present tense is given throughout.

7. All the derivatives from a word are not always given when they may be easily supplied ; more especially, in the case of potential passive participles, formed by तव्य, य, अनीय, past participles, present participles, verbal nouns, abstract nouns from adjectives, and adverbs from adjectives. Where there was any peculiarity in the formation of these derivatives, they are given; but in many cases the student will have to supply the forms, according to rules given in grammars.

ABBREVIATIONS.

A.

Of Grammatical Terms &c.

A.	Atmanepada.
a.	Adjective.
abl.	Ablative.
acc.	Accusative.
adv.	Adverb.
Arith.	Arithmetic.
Bah.	Bahuvrihi.
c.	Causal.
circum.	Circumlocution.
comp.	Compound.
conj.	Conjunction.
D.	Denominative.
dat.	Dative.
deriv.	Derivative.
desid.	Desiderative.
ex.	Expressed.
f.	Feminine.
fig.	Figurative.
freq.	Frequentative.
gen.	Genitive, Generally (when followed by ex.)
gen. abs.	Genitive absolute.
ind.	Indeclinable.
inf.	Infinitive.
instr.	Instrumental.
interj.	Interjection.
lit.	Literal, literally.
loc.	Locative.
loc. abs.	Locative absolute.
m.	Masculine.
Math.	Mathematics.
n.	Neuter.
nom.	Nominative.
P.	Parasmaipada.
part.	Participle.
pass.	Passive.
pot.	Potential.
pot. pass. part.	Potential passive participle.
pl.	Plural.
pr.	Prefixed.
prep.	Preposition.
pron.	Pronoun.
pron. a.	Pronominal adjective.
q. v.	Quod vide, which see.
s.	Substantive.
sim. comp.	Similar compound.
Tat.	Tatpurusha.
U.	Ubhayapada (Parasmaipada and Atmanepada).
v.	Verb (transitive and intransitive).
v. i.	Verb intransitive.
voc.	Vocative.
v. t.	Verb transitive.

B.

Of the Names of Works.

N. B.—Where a Roman figure is followed by an Arabic figure; the former refers to the canto or chapter, and the latter, to the number of the verse; Arabic figures in the case of dramas &c. refer to the act or page.

Bh.	Bhartrihari, II denoting Nitishataka and III Vairagyashataka. (Bombay Edition.)
D. K.	Dashakumâracharita, I denoting the Purvapithika, and II the Uttarapithika, and the Arabic figure, the number of the story.
H.	Hitopadesha, the Arabic figures denoting the four parts in their order.
K.	Kumarasambhava.
Ka.	Kadambari (Bombay Edition.)
Kav.	Kavyadarsha.
Ki.	Kiratarjuniyam.
Li.	Lilavati.
M.	Malavikagnimitra (Bombay Edition.)
Mal.	Malatimadhava (Bombay edition)
Mah.	Mahabharata.
Me.	Meghuduta (Calcutta Edition.)
Mn.	Mallinath.
Mr.	Mrichchhakatika.
Mu.	Mudrarakshasa.
N.	Naishadha.
P.	Panchatantra, the Roman figure denoting the number of the Tantra and the Arabic, the number of the story (Bombay Edition.)
R.	Raghuvamsha.
Rat.	Ratnavali.
S.	Shakuntala.
S. B.	Shankar Bhashya.
Si.	Sisupalavadha.
S. K.	Siddhanta Kaumudi.
S. R.	Subhashitaratnabhandagaram.
U.	Uttararamacharita.
V.	Vikramorvashiyam
V. M.	Vyavahara Mayukha (Mr. Mandlik's Edition.)
Ve.	Venisamhara.
Vi.	Viracharita.
Y.	Yajnavalkya.

THE STUDENT'S ENGLISH-SANSKRIT DICTIONARY.

A.

A, An (As an article) not ex.; 'a man' नरः. 2 (One) एक. 3 (Indefinite) किं with चित्, चन or अपि. 4 With part., ex. by dat. or inf.; 'set out a-hunting' मृगयायै or मृगयां कर्तुं प्रतस्थे; 'fell a-weeping' क्रंदितुं प्रवृत्तः. 5 (Every) प्रति in comp., or by repetition of word; '100 Rs. a day' प्रतिदिनं or दिने दिने शतरूप्यकं. 6 (Species) विशेषः, भेदः, in comp.; 'dog is an animal' श्वा प्राणिविशेषः.

Abandon, *v. t.* त्यज् 1 P, हा 3 P, वि-उत्-सृज् 6 P, उज्झ् 6 P, अपास् 4 P, रह् 1 P, 10, मुच् 6 P. -ed, *a.* त्यक्त, हीन, मुक्त &c. 2 पापात्मन्, भ्रष्टचरित; 'he was a. to his fate' दैवाधीनः कृतः, यद्भावि तद्भवतु इत्युक्त्वा स परित्यक्तः. -ment, *s.* त्यागः, उत्सर्गः; 'a. of worldly connections' संन्यासः, विरक्ति *f.*

Abase, *v. t.* अभिभू 1 P, स्वस्थानात् निपत् c., अपकृष् 1 P, लघूकृ 8 U.-ment, *s.* अपकर्षः, अभिभवः, मानभंगः, अवज्ञानं.

Abash, *v. t.* लज्ज् c., ह्री c. (ह्रेपयति), त्रप् c. (त्रपयति). -ed, *a.* लज्जित, त्रपित, विलक्ष, व्रीडित, ह्रीपरिगत; 'with an a. countenance' त्रपाधोमुख (खी *f.*).

Abate, *v. t.* ह्रस् c., लघयति (D.), शम् c. (शमयति). 2 (price) न्यूनीकृ 8 U; अवसद् c. -*v. i.* क्षि pass., ह्रस् 1 P; प्र-उप-शम् 4 P. -ment, *s.* न्यूनीकरणं; ह्रासः, क्षयः.

Abbey, *s.* विहारः, मठः.

Abbot, *s.* मठाध्यक्षः, विहारस्य प्रधानपुरुषः. -Abbess, *s.* मठाध्यक्षा, विहारपालिनी.

Abbreviate, *v. t.* सं-प्रतिसं-हृ 1 P, संक्षिप् 6 P, समस् 4 P, ह्रस् c. -ion, *s.* संक्षेपः-पणं.

Abdicate, *v.* राज्यं or पदं त्यज् 1 P or अपास् 4 P or क्षिप् 6 P. -ion, *s.* पदत्यागः, अधिकारत्यागः स्वेच्छया परित्यागः.

Abdomen, *s.* उदरं, कुक्षिः.

Abduction, *s.* अपहरणं, अपहारः.

Aberration, *s.* भ्रंशः, च्युति *f.*, भ्रेषः, पथभ्रष्टता; 'a. of mind' चित्त-मति-भ्रमः.

Abet, *v. t.* प्रवृत् c., प्रोत्सह् c. 2 उपकृ 8 U, साहाय्यं कृ. -tor, *s.* प्रवर्तकः, प्रोत्साहकः.

Abeyance, *s.* विलंबः, व्याक्षेपः.

Abhor, *v. t.* गुप् desid. (जुगुप्सते), बध् desid. (बीभत्सते), (with abl.), गर्ह् 1, 10 A, विद्विष् 2 U. -rence, *s.* जुगुप्सा, बीभत्सः, गर्हा, विद्वेषः. -rent, *a.* जातविद्वेष. 2 विरुद्ध, अयुक्त, विपरीत.

Abide, *v. i.* वस् 1 P, स्था 1 P, वृत् 1 A. -*v. t.* (Wait for) प्रतीक्ष् 1 A, प्रतिपाल् 10. 2 (Endure) सह् 1 A, क्षम् 1 A, 4 P, तिज् desid. (तितिक्षते); 'a. by' स्था (loc.), अनुवृत्; कस्यान्यस्य वा वचसि मया स्थातव्यं (Ka. 156); 'I shall a. by your decision' तव निर्णयमनुवर्तिष्ये, निर्णयानुरोधेन वर्तिष्ये, निर्णये स्थास्यामि; 'a. s by his promise' प्रतिज्ञां-अभिसंधां-पालयति. -ing, *a.* स्थायिन् (नी *f.*); अनुवर्तिन्.

Abject, *a.* अधम, अप-नि-कृष्ट, कृपण, नीच, तिरस्कार्य, *See* Mean. -ness, *s.* अधमता, कार्पण्यं.

Abjure, *v. t.* सशपथं त्यज् 1 P. 2 प्रत्याख्या 2 P. -ation, *s.* सशपथः त्यागः.

Able, *a.* समर्थ, क्षम, शक्त; कर्मक्षम, अलंकर्मीण. 2 प्रबल, बलवत् (ती *f.*), शक्तिमत्. 3 पटु, निपुण; 'to be a.' शक् 5 P, पृ c., or पार् 10 U, उत्सह् 1 A, प्रभू 1 P, with inf.; अलं with inf. or dat. of noun; 'a. to protect' रक्षितुं-रक्षणाय-अलं, प्रभवति &c. -Ability, *s.* शक्ति *f.*, बलं, सामर्थ्यं. 2 पाटवं, वैचक्षण्यं; कर्मक्षमता. 3 धीशक्तिः, मत्युत्कर्षः, मति *f.*, बुद्धि *f.*; 'to the best (utmost) of one's a.' यथाशक्ति, यावच्छक्यं, सर्वप्रयत्नैः. -Ably, *adv.* निपुणं, कुशलतया.

Ablution, *s.* प्रक्षालनं, धावनं; स्नानं, मज्जनं.

Abnegation, *s.* प्रत्याख्यानं, संयमः, निग्रहः; 'self-a.' आत्मसंयमः, इंद्रियनिग्रहः. 2 अप-नि-ह्नवः.

ABOARD, *adv.* अधिनु ; 'go a.' नावमधिरुह् 1 P.

ABODE, *s.* गृहं, वेश्मन् *n.*, निवासः, निलयः, आलयः, वसति *f.*, *See* HOUSE. 2 पदं, आस्पदं, स्थानं, भाजनं; 'riches are the a. of calamities' संपदः पदं (आस्पदं) आपदां.

ABOLISH, *v. t.* विलुप् c., निरस् 4 U; खंड् 10. 2 नश् c., उत्सद् c., उच्छिद् 7 P. –ABOLITION, *s.* लोपः. 2 नाशः, उच्छेदः, निवर्तनं, खंडनं.

ABOMINATE, *v. t.* द्विष् 2 U, गर्ह् 1, 10 A; *See* ABHOR.–ION, *s.* गर्हा, विद्वेषः. 2 अशुद्धद्रव्यं, कुत्सास्पदं. –ABOMINABLE, *a.* द्वेष्य, गर्हणीय, गर्हित. 2 जुगुप्साकर (री *f.*).

ABORIGINES, *s.* आदिमवासिनः (pl.).

ABORTION, *s.* गर्भस्रावः-पातः; 'to cause a.' भ्रूणहत्यां कृ; 'causing a.' भ्रूणहत्या.–ABORTIVE, *a.* गर्भस्राविन् (णी *f.*), अपूर्णकाल. 2 अकालकृत, निष्फल मोघ, व्यर्थ (as an attempt.).

ABOUND, *v. i.* (with, in) संकॄ-पॄ pass., or by बहु, भूयिष्ठ, in comp.; भूयिष्ठवृक्षं वनं; बहुकौतुकः स देशः 'a. s in curiosities.' –ING, *a.* आढ्य, संकीर्ण, आकुल, प्राय, in comp. –ABUNDANT, *a.* बहुल, प्रभूत, प्रचुर, विपुल. भूरि. –LY, *adv.* बहुशः,अनेकवारं, विपुलं. –ABUNDANCE, *s.* बाहुल्यं, प्राचुर्यं.

ABOUT, *prep.* परि ; परि-इ 'go a.' &c. 2 देशीय (with numerals); 'a. five years old' पंचवर्षदेशीयः. 3 (Regarding) अधिकृत्य, प्रति, उद्दिश्य ; संबद्ध-अनुविद्ध-गत-विषये in comp.; 'I ask a. my friend' मित्रगतं पृच्छामि ; पराजयानुविद्धा आलापाः &c. 4 कृते, अर्थे, अर्थं, हेतोः. 5 परितः, अभितः, (acc.) ; समीपं, समीपे, पार्श्वतः, निकटे, (gen.). 6 (Nearly) with numerals उप, आसन्न, अदूर, in comp.; उपचतुराः 'a. four'. –*adv.* (Showing prospective fut.) ex. by fut. part., उन्मुख (खी *f.*), उद्यत, आसन्न, or desid.; अनुयास्यन् मुनितनयां (S. 1) 'a. to follow' &c.; जिघांस्यमानो नरः 'a. to be killed'; आसन्नमरणः 'a. to die'; आसन्नराज्यनाशः 'a. to lose the realm'. 2 प्राय, कल्प, in comp; 'it is a. noon' मध्याह्नप्रायः-कल्पः समयः; 'what are you a.' किं कर्तुमुद्यतोसि, किंकार्येव्यग्रोसि, किमारंभस्त्वं. 3 परितः, अभितः. 4 इतस्ततः, स्थानात्स्थानं.

ABOVE, *adv.* अधि or अभि pr.; उपरि, उपरिष्टात्, ऊर्ध्वं ; 'just a.' उपर्युपरि (acc.) –*a.* प्रागुक्त, पूर्वनिर्दिष्ट. –*prep.* उपरि (gen.); अति pr.; अधिक, उत्तर, विशिष्ट, (abl.); 'a. calculation' अतिसंख्य ; 'he stands a. all' स सर्वेषां मूर्ध्नि तिष्ठति; 'a. mentioned' पूर्वोक्त, प्रागुक्त ; 'to be a.' ऊर्ध्वं स्था 1 P, अभिभू 1 P, *See* EXCEL.

ABREAST, *adv.* पार्श्वापार्श्वि.

ABRIDGE, *v. t.* संक्षिप् 6 P, समस् 4 P, संग्रह् 9 P. –MENT, *s.* संक्षेपः, सारः, संग्रहः &c.

ABROAD, *adv.* विदेशे, देशांतरे. 2 बहिः (abl.). 3 (Widely) सर्वत्र, दूरं; 'casting a. his rays' दूरप्रसारितकरः (सूर्यः); 'live a.' प्रवस् 1 P; 'go a.' प्रसृ 1 P, बहुलीभू 1 P, प्रकाशतां गम् 1 P, प्रकाशीभू ; 'the dreadful vow became known a.' सा दारुणा प्रतिज्ञा लोके प्रसिद्धाभूत, लोके प्रकाशतां गता.

ABROGATE, *See* ABOLISH.

ABRUPT, *a.* विषम, (प्रपातः). 2 आकस्मिक (की *f.*), असंबंध, अकांड. –LY, *adv.* एकपदे, सहसा, अकस्मात्.

ABSCESS, *s.* विद्रधिः ; स्फोटः, व्रणः-णं.

ABSCOND, *v. i.* प्रच्छन्न *a.* भू 1 P, आत्मानं गुह् 1 U or प्रच्छद् 10, अंतर्धा pass. 2 पलाय् 1 A, व्यपसृप् 1 P, अपक्रम् 1 U, 4 P.

ABSENT, *a.* अवर्तमान, अविद्यमान, अनुपस्थित, स्थानांतरगत. 2 प्रोषित. 3 (In mind) हृदयेन असन्निहित, शून्यहृदय-मानस ; 'to be a.' स्थानांतरे वृत् 1 A, न उपस्था 1 U. –EE, *s.* अनुपस्थितः, प्रवासिन् *m.*, प्रोषितः.–ABSENCE, *s.* अनुपस्थिति *f.*, असन्निधिः, परोक्षं, परोक्षता. 2 (Non-existence) अभावः. 3 विरहः, वियोगः ; 'in one's a.' परोक्षे ; 'a. of mind' शून्यमनस्कता, शून्यहृदयत्वं, अनवधानं, विगतचेतनत्वं.

ABSOLUTE, *a.* संपूर्ण, पर्याप्त. 2 नित्य, परम. 3 (Not relative) केवल, मात्रक, अनन्यसंबद्ध. 4 परम, उत्तम, श्रेष्ठ. 5 अनियत, निर्यंत्रण, स्वाधीन ; 'a. king' सम्राज् *m.*, अधिराजः. –LY, *adv.* सर्वथा, सर्वशः, केवलं, एकांततः.

ABSOLVE, *v. t.* (पापात् &c.) मुच् 6 P or c., उद्धृ 1 P, 10 ; पापं-अपराधं क्षम् 1 A. –ABSOLUTION, *s.* पापमुक्ति *f.*, क्षमा. 2 मुक्ति *f.*, मोक्षः, निःश्रेयसं, अपवर्गः, निर्वाणं, श्रेयस् *n.*, कैवल्यं.

ABSORB, *v. t.* उत्-, शुष् c., निगॄ 6 P, आचम् 1 P, नि-आ-पा 1 P. 2 ग्रस् 1 A, आत्माधीन *a.* कृ 8 U; व्यापृ c., आसंज् c. –ED, *a.* नि-,मग्न, आसक्त, निरत, लीन, व्यापृत, पर, परायण, in comp. 2 निपीत. –ABSORPTION, *s.* निपानं, शोषणं; 'a. into the Supreme Soul' मोक्षः, निर्वाणं ; ब्रह्मणि लयः, ईश्वरसायुज्यं.

ABSTAIN, *v. i.* निवृत् 1 A (abl.) परि वि-वृज् 10 (acc.); 'has a. ed from eating flesh' निवृत्तमांसो जनकः (U. 4). 2 विरम् 1 P (abl.); 'a. from food' उपवस् 1 P. –ABSTINENCE, *s.* निवृत्ति *f.* 2 उपवासः, अल्पाहारः, आहारनियमः. 3 संयमनं, जितेंद्रियत्वं. —ABSTINENT, *a.* उपवासिन् (नी *f.*). 2 जितेंद्रिय, संयतात्मन्; वशिन्. —ABSTEMIOUS, *a.* मिताहार, अल्पाहारिन् (णी *f.*), अल्पाशन, मितभुज्. —NESS, *s.* मिताहारः, मितभोजनं, अल्पाहारः.

ABSTRACT, *v. t.* संक्षिप् 6 P, संह 1 P. 2 आदा 3 A, अप-अव-कृष् 1 P, अपह 1 P. —*s.* सारः, संग्रहः, संक्षेपः. —*a.* विभिन्न, केवल; अमूर्त. 2 आन्वीक्षिक (की *f.*), निगूढ. —EDLY, -LY, *adv.* विविक्तं. 2 केवलं, मात्रं. —ION, *s.* समाधिः, प्रणिधानं, ध्यानैकाग्रता. 2 अपहरणं, आदानं. 3 विभेदः, पृथक्करणं.

ABSTRUSE, *a.* गूढ, प्रच्छन्न. 2 निगूढ, दुर्ज्ञेय, गूढार्थ, असुबोध, दुर्बोध, गहन.

ABSURD, *a.* अनर्थक, अयुक्त, न्यायविरुद्ध, अनुपपन्न. —NESS, -ITY, *s.* आनर्थक्यं, अनुपपत्ति *f.*, असंगति *f.*; sometimes ex. by शशविषाणं, गगनपुष्पं, &c. —LY, *adv.* अविचारेण, अनुपपन्नं; 'do not talk so a.' कृतमेतादृशेन असंगतेन-अनर्थकेन-प्रलापेन.

ABUSE, *v. t.* वृथा-मृषा-अन्यायतः प्र-वि-नि-युज् 7 A, 10 or व्यय् 1 P. 2 अधि-आ-क्रुश् 10 A, भर्त्स् 10 A, आ-अधि-क्षिप् 6 P, अभिशंस् 1 P, अपवद् 1 U, अभिशप् 1 U, अपभाष् 1 A. —*s.* आक्रोशः, अपवादः, उपालंभः, अपभाषणं, निंदा, अधिक्षेपः, वाक्पारुष्यं, परुषोक्ति *f.* 2 कुप्रयोगः, अपव्ययः, अन्यायोपयोगः. —ABUSIVE, *a.* निंदक, आक्षेपरूक्ष, निंदागर्भ; 'a. word' निंदात्मकवचः, आक्षेपवचनं.

ABYSS, *s.* गभीरगर्तः, अगाधविलं, अतलस्पर्शं खातं.

ACADEMY, *s.* विद्यालयः. 2 विद्वत्परिषद् *f.*

ACCEDE, *v. i.* अनुमन् 4 A, अंगी-स्वी-कृ 8 U, अनुज्ञा 9 U. 2 सं-इ 2 P, संमिल् 6 P, सं-अभि-उपगम् 1 P.

ACCELERATE, *v. t.* त्वर् c. (त्वरयति), आशु संपद् c. or प्रवृत् c.

ACCENT, *s.* स्वरः. 2 आघातः, उच्चारणचिह्नं; 'human a. s' मानुषी गीः. —*v. t.* सस्वरमुच्चर् c. —ED, *a.* स्वरित, उदात्त.

ACCEPT, *v. t.* प्रतिग्रह् 9P, आदा 3 A, प्रतिपद् 4A, प्रति-इष् 6 P, स्वीकृ 8 U.—ABLE, *a.* ग्रहणीय, आदेय. 2 रुचिर, मनोरम, प्रिय. —ANCE, *s.* प्रतिपत्ति *f.*, प्रतिग्रहः, आदानं, स्वीकारः. —ATION, *s.* अर्थः, आशयः; 'usual a. of a word' शब्दस्य निरूढार्थः.

ACCESS, *s.* प्रवेशः, उपसर्पणं, अभि-उप-गमः; 'wishing to gain a. to the king' राजानं द्रष्टुकामः. —IBLE, *a.* सुलभ, सुखोपसर्प्य, अभि-,गम्य, सुगम, उपसर्पणीय (अवसरोपसर्पणीया राजानः S. 6), सुलभदर्शन; 'nothing is in-a. to desires' मनोरथानामगतिर्न विद्यते (K. v. 64).—ION, *s.* योगः, उपगमनं, मिलनं. 2 (to power) राजपदावाप्ति *f.*, राज्यप्राप्तिः, सिंहासनारोहणं. 3 आगमः, वृद्धि *f.*, उपचयः. —ARY, —ORY, *s.* सहकारिन् *m.*, प्रवर्तकः, पापसहायः.—*a.* अधिक; सहित, संयुक्त.

ACCIDENT, *s.* समापत्ति *f.*, दैवयोगः-गति *f.*, दैवघटनं; यदृच्छा; 'seen by a.' समापत्ति-यदृच्छादृष्ट. 2 आपद्-विपद् *f.*; अत्याहितं, उपप्लवः. 3 अप्रकृति *f.*, असहजो गुणः, विकृति *f.*; 'life is but an a.' विकृतिर्जीवितमुच्यते (R. VIII. 87); 'by a.' अकस्मात्, दैवेन, दैवात्, दैवगत्या. —AL, *a.* यादृच्छिक-आकस्मिक (की *f.*), काकतालीय, दैवायत्त. 2 अप्रकृत, असमवायिन् (नी *f.*), असहज, आहार्य. —ALLY, *adv.* दैवात्, दैवयोगेन, यदृच्छया, विधि-दैव-वशात्, समापत्त्या, अकस्मात्.

ACCLAMATION, *s.* धन्यवादः, प्रशंसाघोषः, जयशब्दः. 2 निःस्वनः, प्रणादः, उच्चैर्घोषः.

ACCLIVITY, *s.* उत्संगः.

ACCOMMODATE, *v. t.* युज् 10, *See* ADAPT; 'a. oneself to the will of' भावमनुप्रविश् 6 P (स्वामिनो भावं भृत्योऽनुप्रविशेत्). 2 वसतिस्थानेन उपकृ 8 U, उपकरणद्रव्याणि उपक्लृप् c. 3 संधा 3 U, प्रशम् c., (dispute &c.). —ION, *s.* संयोजनं, संधानं. 2 उपकरणद्रव्योपकल्पनं &c.

ACCOMPANY, *v. t.* अनु-इ 2 P, अनुया 2 P, परिवृ 5 U or c.; संयुज् 10; सह चर् or व्रज् 1 P, सं-इ, अनुसृ 1 P, सहचरो भू 1 P.—ED, *a.* सहित, अनुषक्त, समेत, परिवृत, परिवार, in comp.; by Bah. comp. with स or word indicating 'companionship'; वसंतसहायः-सवसंतः-वसंतद्वितीयः कामः 'Cupid a. by Spring.'

ACCOMPLICE, *s.* अनुषंगिन्; *See* ACCESSORY.

ACCOMPLISH, *v. t.* साध् 5 P or c., सिध् c. (साधयति); पूर् 10; समाप् c., अनुष्ठा 1 P, संपद् c., निर्वृत् c. —ED, *a.* सिद्ध, सं-,पूर्ण, संपन्न. 2 विशारद, निपुण, गुणवत् (ती *f.*), कृतिन् (नी *f.*). —MENT, *s.* सिद्धि-समाप्ति *f.*, निर्वृत्ति *f.*, निष्पत्ति *f.* 2 कृतार्थता, कृतकृत्यता. 3 गुणित्वं, निपुणता, वैचक्षण्यं, गुणः.

ACCORD, *v.i.* संवद् 1 P, संयुज् pass. 2 एकचित्तीभू 1 P, एकमनीभू. —*v. t.* *See* GIVE. —*s.* संमति *f.* स्वीकरणं. 2 ऐकमत्यं, एकचित्तता; 'with one a.' एकचित्तीभूय. 3 एकतालः (in music); 'of one's own a.' यदृच्छया, स्वयं, स्वेच्छातः, कामतः. —ANCE *s.* अनुसारः, सादृश्यं, अनुरोधः; 'in a. with his words' तद्वचनानुसारेण-नुरोधेन; oft. by the instr. or abl. of the noun itself; सचिवाज्ञया, मदादेशात्, &c. —ING, *prep.* यथा, अनुरूपं, अनु,

in comp. ; 'a. to seniority' अनुज्येष्ठं ; 'a. to desire' यथेष्टं, यथाभिमतं ; 'a. to one's power' यथाशक्ति.—INGLY, *adv.* इत्थं, तदनुरोधात्, तदनुसारेण, तथाच.

ACCOST, *v. t.* सं-अभि-आ-भाष् 1 A, अभिधा 3 U, समामंत्र् 10 A, संबुध् c.

ACCOUCHEUR, *s.* प्रसव-सूति-वैद्यः.

ACCOUNT, *s.* गणना, संख्यानं, विगणनं; 'balancing a. s' गणनां समीकृत्य. 2 मूल्यं, अर्घः. 3 गणना, मात्रा; 'of what a. is a king' राजेति का मात्रा-गणना. 4 वृत्तांतः, कथा, कथनं, उपाख्यानं ; 'to turn to a.' हितं साध् c., हितानुकूल *a.* कृ ; 'take into a.' समीक्ष् 1 A, गण् 10, (तेजसां हि न वयः समीक्ष्यते R. XI. 1). 5 कारणं, हेतुः, निमित्तं ; 'on a. of' ex. by the abl. or instr. ; हेतोः, निमित्तेन, अर्थं-र्थे ; 'on this a.' अतः, अतः कारणात् ; 'on no a.' न कथंचन ; 'on one's a.' कृते (gen.) ; 'on all a. s' सर्वथा.—*v. t.* मन् 4 A. 2 गण् 10 ; 'a. for' कारणं-निमित्तं-दृश् c. (with gen.). —ABLE, *a.* चिंत्यहेतुक, प्रतिसंख्येय. 2 परानुयोगायत्त. —ANT, *s.* गणकः, लेखकः, गणनाकृत् *m.*

ACCOUTRE, *v. t.* संनह् 4 P or c. —MENT, *s.* संनाहः, अलंकारः, भूषणं, प्रसाधनं, सज्जा.

ACCREDIT, *See* BELIEVE.

ACCRUE, *v. i.* उत्पद्-जन् 4 A, प्राप् pass. 2 प्रतिवृत् 1 A, गम् 1 P ; 'the fruit a. s to the agent' कर्तृगामि फलं.

ACCUMULATE, *v. t.* सं-प्र-चि 5 U, संग्रह् 9 P, राशीकृ 8 U, एकत्र कृ.—*v. i.* उपचि pass., वृध् 1 A, राशीभू. —ION, *s.* संचयः, समुदायः, राशीकरणं.

ACCURATE, *a.* यथार्थ, सूक्ष्म, सत्य, यथावृत्त ; विशुद्ध, *See* EXACT. —LY, *adv.* यथार्थतः-र्थं, सूक्ष्मतः, तत्त्वतः, सम्यक्, सत्यं. —ACCURACY, *s.* याथार्थ्यं, सत्यता, यथार्थता, सूक्ष्मता.

ACCURSED, *a.* ex. by हतक, अपसद, at the end of nouns, or by दग्ध pr. ; 'the a. fate' दैवहतकं, दग्धदैवं ; 'a. man' नरापसदः. 2 निंद्य गर्हणीय ; शापग्रस्त, अभिशप्त, आक्रुष्ट.

ACCUSE, *v. t.* अभियुज् 7 A, 10, अपवद् 1 A अभिशंस् 1P, अधिक्षिप् 6 P, दुष् c. (नार्हसि कामापराधैर्देवं दूषयितुं Ka. 235) ; घातकः अयं इति तमभियुयुजिरे 'they a. ed him of murder.' —ATION, *s.* अभियोगः, अपवादः, अधिक्षेपः, अभिशंसनं, दूषणं. —ER, *s.* अभियोक्तृ *m.*, अभियोगिन् *m.*

ACCUSTOM, *v. t.* अभ्यस् 4P, अभ्यासं-व्यवहारं कृ 8 U ; 'to be a. ed' अभ्यस्त-परिचित-*a.* भू 1 P.

ACE, *s.* एकबिंदुः. 2 अणुः, लवः.

ACERB, *a.* तुवर, कटु, अम्ल. —ATE, *v. t.* अम्लीकृ 8 U. —ITY, *s.* कटुता, अम्लता ; 'a. of temper' स्वभावपरुषता, रूक्षता.

ACHE, *s.* वेदना, पीडा, व्यथा ; 'head-a.' शिरोवेदना ; 'I have a strong head-a.' बलवती शिरोवेदना मां बाधते ; 'tooth a.' दंतवेदना. —*v. i.* पीड् pass., व्यथ् 1 A. *See* PAIN.

ACHIEVE, *v. t.* समाप् c., संपद् c., निर्वृत् c., *See* ACCOMPLISH. 2 प्राप् 5P, लभ् 1A. *See* GET. —MENT, *s.* निष्पत्ति *f.*, साधनं. 2 पराक्रमः, विक्रमः, अवदातं कर्म-चेष्टितं, विक्रांतचरितं.

ACID, *s.* अम्लः. —*a.* अम्ल, शुक्त. —ITY, *s.* अम्लत्वं-ता, शुक्तता. —ULATE, *v. t.* अम्लीकृ 8 U.

ACKNOWLEDGE, *v. t.* अभ्युपगम् 1 P, अभ्युप-इ 2 P, प्रतिपद् 4 A, अंगीकृ 8 U, स्वीकृ ; ग्रह् 9 P. —MENT, *s.* स्वीकारः, अभ्युपगमः, अंगी-स्वी-कारः, प्रतिपत्ति *f.* 2 (receipt) अभ्युपगमलेखः-पत्रं.

ACME, *s.* परा काष्ठा-कोटिः.

ACOUSTIC, *a.* श्रुतिविषयक, श्रवणसंबंधिन् (नी *f.*). —ACOUSTICS, *s.* ध्वनिविद्या-शास्त्रं.

ACQUAINT, *v. t.* बुध् c., ज्ञा c. (ज्ञापयति), निविद् c. (with dat.), गृहीतार्थ-परिगृहीतार्थ-*a.* कृ 8 U ; 'the queen was made a. ed with your immodesty' भवतोऽविनयमंतरेण परिगृहीतार्था कृता देवी (M. 4). 2 परिचयं कृ, अभ्यस् 4 P. —ANCE, *s.* परिज्ञानं ; परिचयः, ज्ञानं. 2 मित्रं, परिचितः; 'old a.' चिरंतनं मित्रं, चिरपरिचितः. 3 संसर्गः, संस्तवः. —ED, *a.* परिचित, अभ्यस्त; अभिज्ञ, अभ्यंतर (अनभ्यंतरे आवां मदनगतस्य वृत्तांतस्य S. 3).

ACQUIESCE, *v. i.* अनुमन् 4 A, अनुज्ञा 9 U, संमतिं दृश् c. —ENCE, *s.* सं-अनु-मति *f.*

ACQUIRE, *v. t.* अर्ज् 1 P, लभ् 1 A, समासद् c., अवाप् 5 P, प्रतिपद् 4 A, अश् 5 A, अधिगम् 1 P. *See* GET.—MENT,—ACQUISITION, *s.* अर्जनं, प्राप्ति *f.*, लाभः, अधिगमः. 2 गुणः, ज्ञानं.

ACQUIT, *v. t.* (पापात्-दोषात्) मुच् c., विमुच् c., निस्तृ c., शुध् c.; 'he was a. ted' स निर्दोषः कृतः, पापविमुक्तोऽमन्यत; 'a. oneself' कर्म निर्वह् c., आचर् 1 P; 'they a. ted themselves well' ते स्वकर्म साधु निरवाहयन्,-आचरन्. —AL, *s.* मुक्ति-शुद्धि-*f.*, मोचनं. —ANCE, *s.* निस्तारः; 'a. of debt' ऋणनिर्यातनं-परिशोधनं.

ACRID, ACRIMONIOUS, *a.* कटु, उग्र, तीक्ष्ण, अरुंतुद.—ACRIMONY, *s.* कटुता, तीक्ष्णता.

ACROSS, *prep.* पारं, तीरांतरं, in comp.; 'a. the ocean' सागरपारं. 2 व्यत्यस्त *a.*; 'with legs a.

व्यस्यस्तपाद *a.*; 'to come a.' लभ् 1 A, अधिगम् 1 P, *See* GET.

ACT, *v. i.* वृत् 1 A (आर्योऽस्मिन् विनयेन वर्ततां U. 6), व्यवहृ 1 P, आचर् 1 P, (with loc. of person); अयमाचरत्यविनयं तपस्विकन्यासु (S. 1) 'a. s rudely towards' &c. 2 चेष्ट् 1 A, विधा 3 U, कृ 8 U. 3 स्थानेऽधिकारं कृ. 4 फल् 1 P, गुणं आवह् 1 P; कार्यं कृ; 'fire a. s like water' अग्निर्जलायते; स कृष्णायते &c.; 'a. up to' अनुवृत् 1 A; अनुरुध् 4 A, स्था 1 P (शासने तिष्ठ भर्तुः V. 5). –*v. t.* नट् 10, निरूप् 10, अभिनी 1 P; प्रयुज् 10; oft. by denom.; 'a. ing the part of Lakshmi' लक्ष्मीभूमिकायां वर्तमाना (V. 3); नृपायते 'a. s the king'; 'a. the part of a dear friend towards your rivals' कुरु प्रियसखीवृत्तिं सपत्नीजने (S. 4). –*s.* कर्मन् *n.*, कृति *f.*, क्रिया, चरितं, चेष्टितं. 2 अंकः. 3 व्यवस्था, विधिः. –ION, *s.* क्रिया, व्यापारः, चेष्टितं &c.; प्रवृत्ति *f.*; कारणं. 2 अभियोगः, व्यवहारकार्यं, कार्यं, अर्थः. 3 संग्रामः, युद्धं, *See* FIGHT. 4 अंगविक्षेपः, हस्ताभिनयः; 'in a., thought and speech' कर्मणा मनसा वाचा, मनोवाक्कायकर्मभिः. –IONABLE, *a.* अभियोज्य, व्यवहार्य. –OR, *s.* कर्तृ *m.*; कारिन् *m*; कारकः, in comp. 2 नटः, नर्तकः, कुशीलवः, अभिनेतृ *m.*, शैलूषः. – ACTRESS, *s.* नटी, नर्तकी. –ACTIVE, *a.* उद्योगिन् (नी *f.*), कर्मोद्युक्त, अनलस, सोद्योग, सोत्साह, व्यवसायिन् (नी *f.*). 2 क्षिप्रकारिन् (णी *f.*), अतंद्र, क्षिप्रकर्मन्. 3 व्यायामशील, व्यायामिन् (नी *f.*). 4 उत्थानयोग्य, (उत्थानयोग्यं वपुः S. 2); 'a. voice' कर्तृवाच्यम्. –ITY, *s.* उद्योगिता, व्यवसायः क्षिप्रकारिता. 2 उत्साहः. 3 उत्थानयोग्यता. –LY, *adv.* सोद्योगं, सोत्साहं. –ACTUAL, *a.* वास्तविक (की *f.*), तथ्य, सत्य, वास्तव (वी *f.*), यथार्थ, परमार्थ. –LY, *adv.* साक्षात्, प्रत्यक्षं. 2 यथार्थतः, परमार्थतः, वस्तुतः, अर्थतः, वस्तुवृत्तेन; 'what a. took place' यद्यद् वृत्तं; oft. ex. by एव only.

ACTUATE, *v. t.* प्रेर् 10, प्रोत्सह् c., प्रवृत् c., प्रणुद् 6 P; *See* PROMPT.

ACUMEN, *s.* मतिसूक्ष्मता, विदग्धता.

ACUTE, *a.* नि-, शित, तीक्ष्ण; 'a. pain' दारुण-तीव्रवेदना. 2 सूक्ष्ममति, विदग्ध. –LY, *adv.* तीव्रं, तीक्ष्णं. –NESS, *s.* तीक्ष्णता, तेजस् *n.* 2 विदग्धता; 'a. of intellect' कुशाग्रबुद्धिः *f.*

ADAGE, *s.* सूत्रं, वचनं, वाक्यं, आभाणकः.

ADAMANT, *s.* वज्रः-ज्रं. 2 हीरकः,-मणिः, हीरं. –INE, *a.* वज्रमय (यी *f.*), वज्र in comp.

ADAPT, *v. t.* युज् 10, संधा 3 U; 'a. your conduct to circumstances' यथाकालं व्यवहर, कालानुवर्ती भव; 'has a. ed a portion of it to the stage' तस्यैकदेशः अभिनेयार्थः कृतः (U. 4). –ATION, *s.* संयोजनं, संविधानं. –ED, *a.* युक्त, योग्य पर्याप्त.

ADD, *v. t.* संकल् 10 (कलयति), परिगण् 10, परिसंख्या 2 P, सं-समा-युज् 10; 'he a. ed his army to the general's' सेनापतेः सेनया स्वबलं संयोजयामास; समाचि 5 U, संमिल् c. 2 अन्यच्च ब्रू 2 U, or कथ् 10 or अभिधा 3 U; 'a. to' वृध् c., पुष् 4 P, तन् 8 U; मलिनमपि हिमांशोर्लक्ष्म लक्ष्मीं तनोति (S. 1) 'a. s to her lustre'; there is this also to a. to my (grounds of) anger' एतदपि मे द्वितीयं संतापकारणं (Mr. 5); 'this is another evil to a. to the first' गंडस्योपरि पिटिका संवृत्ता (S. 2), अयमपरो गंडस्योपरि विस्फोटः (Mu. 5). –ITION, *s.* संमेलनं, संयोजनं, संयोगः. 2 परिगणनं, परिसंख्या, संकलनं. 3 (Something added) आधिक्यं; 'he is a valuable a. to our side' अस्मत्पक्षेऽयमनर्घ्यः सहायः संजातः. –ITIONAL, *a.* अपर, अधिक, अधिकतर.

ADDICT, *v. t.* (oneself) आ-नि-सेव् 1 A, भज् 1 U; आसंज् pass., आसक्त-निरत-*a* भू 1P, (loc.). –ED, *a.* आसक्त, प्रसक्त, निरत, निविष्ट, परायण, in comp. –EDNESS, –ION, *s.* आसक्ति-प्रसक्ति *f.*, निषेवणं, व्यसनं, निरति *f.*, परायणता.

ADDLE, *a.* असंपूर्ण, नष्ट, दुष्ट; 'a. headed-,pated' मूढ, नष्टधी, दुर्मति.

ADDRESS, *v. t.* आमंत्र् 10 A, सं-अभि-आ-भाष् 1 A, अभिधा 3 U, संबुध् c., आलप् 1 P; 'a. ed his mind to Súrya' सूर्यं मनसाध्यायत्; 'a. me as is wont with you' (मां प्रति) यथाभ्यस्तमभिधीयताम् (U. 1). 2 नाम ग्रह् 9 P; नामग्राहं वद् 1 P or आह्वे 1P. 3 प्राहि 5P, प्रेष् 10. –*s.* अभि-सं-भाषणं, संबोधनं &c. 2 वचनं, आलापः; 'mode of a.' आमंत्रणपदं; संज्ञायिते परिणये नैष समुदाचारः (S. 5) 'not the proper mode of a.'; 'of agreeable a.' मधुरालाप, प्रियंवद. 3 पटुता, दक्षता, नैपुण्यं. 4 (Of a letter) बाह्यनामन् *n.*; अदत्तबाह्यनामानं लेखं (Mu. 1) 'a letter without any a. upon it'; 'send the letter to my a.' दत्त-लिखित-मद्बाह्यनाम (मामुद्दिश्य) पत्रं प्रेषय. 5 (Place of residence &c.) नामधामविशेषाः.

ADDUCE, *v. t.* (proof, witness &c.) निर्दिश् 6 P, उपन्यस् 4 P, उपक्षिप् 6 P, उपानी 1 P; 'a. ing proofs' प्रमाणोपन्यासः.

ADEPT, *a.* निपुण, कुशल, प्रवीण, अभिज्ञ.

ADEQUATE, *a.* पर्याप्त, समर्थ, क्षम, तुल्य, योग्य,

-अनुरूप. -LY, *adv.* पर्याप्तं. -ADEQUACY, *s.* क्षमता, सामर्थ्यं, &c.

ADHERE, *v. i.* संज् pass., सज्ज् 1 P, संसक्त-अनु-षक्त- *a.* भू, संलग् 1 P, (loc.); अनुबंध् 9 P. 2 अवलंब् 1 A, पाल् 10, रक्ष् 1 P; 'a. s to his promise' प्रतिज्ञां पालयति-रक्षति. -ENCE, *s.* आसक्ति *f.*, आसंगः, अनुषंगः, अवलंबनं. -ENT, *s.* पक्षायः, पक्ष्यः, सपक्षः. 2 अनुषंगिन् *m.*, सहायः, अनुगामिन् *m.* -ADHESION, *s.* संसक्ति *f.*, आसंगः, आसक्तिः, अवलंबनं; संलग्नत्वं. -ADHESIVE, *a.* संलग्नशील.

ADIEU, *adv.* स्वस्ति (dat.).-*s.* आमंत्रणं, आप्रच्छनं; 'to bid a.' आप्रच्छ् 6 A, आमंत्र् 10 A; आमंत्रयस्व सहचरं (S. 3).

ADJACENT, *a.* आसन्न, समीप, समीपवर्तिन् (नी *f.*), सन्निकृष्ट, सन्निहित, निकटवर्तिन् (नी *f.*), निकट, पार्श्वस्थ.

ADJOIN, *v. t.* लग् 1 P, समीपे-निकटे-वृत् 1 A or स्था 1 P; *See* ADJACENT above.

ADJOURN, *v. t.* व्याक्षिप् 6 P, विलंब् c.; व्यवहारं त्यज् 1 P.

ADJUDGE, *v. t.* दा c. (दापयति). 2 निर्णयं कृ 8 U, निर्णीय समाप् c.

ADJUDICATE, *v. t.* निर्णी 1 P, *See* above.

ADJUNCT, *a.* संयुक्त, सहित. -*s.* अनुबंधः.

ADJURE, *v. t.* सशपथं समादिश् 6 P, शप् c.

ADJUST, *v. t.* समीकृ 8 U, समा-प्रतिसमा-धा 3 U, समायुज् 10, व्यवस्था c. (स्थापयति); (accounts) एकीकृ, संमिल् c. -MENT, *s.* समाधानं, समायोगः, एकीकरणं.

ADJUTANT, *s.* सहायः, सहकारिन् *m.*

ADMINISTER, *v. t.* प्रशास् 2 P, निर्वह् c., निर्वृत् c.; 'a. justice' धर्म-न्याय-विवेचनं कृ, न्यायं प्रणी 1 P, or प्रवृत् c.; 'a. an oath' शप् c. 2 दा 3 U, प्रतिपद् c. -ADMINISTRATION, *s.* शासनं, प्रवर्तनं, निर्वाहः; राज्यधुरा; 'during his a.' तस्मिन् राज्यं (प्रजाः) शासति. 2 धर्मविवेचनं. 3 प्रकृति *f.*, सचिवाः. 4 साचिव्यं, मंत्रित्वं. -ADMINISTRATIVE, *a.* शासनदक्ष, कार्यनिर्वाहकुशल. -ADMINISTRATOR, *s.* शासितृ *m.*, राज्यधुरंधरः. 2 प्रवर्तकः, प्रणेतृ *m.*

ADMIRAL, *s.* नौसाधनाध्यक्षः.

ADMIRE, *v. t.* प्रशंस् 1 P, श्लाघ् 1 A, स्तु 2 U. 2 विस्मयेन दृश् 1 P.-ABLE, *a.* श्लाघ्य, अद्भुत, प्रशंसनीय, अनुपम. -ABLY, *adv.* श्लाघ्यप्रकारेण, साधु, अद्भुतं.-ATION, *s.* प्रशंसा, श्लाघा. 2 विस्मयः, आश्चर्यं.-ER, *s.* प्रशंसकः, श्लाघिन् *m.*; 'a. of ladies' कामिन् *m.*, कामुकः.

ADMIT, *v. t.* प्रविश् c., अभ्यंतरीकृ 8 U; 'should be a. ed to all confidential matters' सर्वविश्रंभेष्वभ्यंतरीकरणीया (Ka. 101). 2 अंगी-स्वी-कृ, अभ्युपगम् 1 P, अभ्युपे 2 P; ग्रह् 9 P; 'a. of' ex. by adj. or noun denoting 'capability'; 'his remark a. s of no doubt' तस्य वचनं न संदेहास्पदं; 'her illness a. s of no delay' तस्या विकारो विलंबाक्षमः.-ADMISSION, *s.* प्रवेशनं, प्रवेशः. 2 अभ्युपगमः, अंगीकारः, प्रतिपत्ति *f.* -ADMISSIBLE, *a.* उपादेय, स्वीकरणीय, ग्राह्य.-ADMITTANCE, *s.* प्रवेशः-शनं.

ADMIX, *v. t.* संमिश्र् 10, संयुज् 7 U, 10, संकॄ 6 P.-TURE, *s.* मिश्रणं, संकरः.

ADMONISH, *v. t.* उपदिश् 6 P, अनुबुध् c., विज्ञा c. (ज्ञापयति), अनुशास् 2 P. 2 निर्भर्त्स् 10 A, उपालभ् 1 A, *See* CENSURE. -ER, *s.* उपदेशकः, अनुबोधकः.-ADMONITION, *s.* अनुबोधनं, उपदेशः, अनुशासनं; उपालंभः.

ADO, *s.* श्रमः, दीर्घायासः.

ADOLESCENCE, *s.* यौवनदशा, यौवनं. -ADOLESCENT, *a.* युवन् (यूनी *f.*), प्राप्तयौवन.

ADOPT, *v. t.* परिग्रह् 9 P, पुत्रीकृ 8 U. 2 ग्रह्, स्वीअंगी-कृ, अनुवृत् 1 A. -ED, *a.* परिगृहीत, स्वीअंगी-कृत; 'a. son' कृतकः पुत्रः, दत्रिमः सुतः, दत्तकः; 'a. daughter,' कृतिका दुहिता, अपत्यकृतिका. -ION, *s.* परिग्रहः, पुत्रीकरणं. 2 अंगी-स्वीकारः, अनुवर्तनं.

ADORE, *v. t.* आराध् c., नमस्यति (D.), नमस्कृ 8 U, अर्च् 1 P, or c., पूज् 10, उपस्था 1 U, उपास् 2 A. -ATION, *s.* पूजा, अर्चनं, नमस्कारः. -ER, *s.* पूजकः, उपासकः, आराधकः, भक्तः, अर्चकः.

ADORN, *v. t.* वि-,भूष् 10, अलंकृ 8 U, परिष्कृ, संस्कृ, मंड् 10, प्रसाध् c., शुभ् c. -ING, *s.* अलंकारः, भूषणं, प्रसाधनं, मंडनं.

ADRIFT, *adv.* इतस्ततः प्लवमान *a.* 2 अशरण-अनाथ-निरालंब-*a.*

ADROIT, *a.* निपुण, दक्ष, धूर्त, चतुर. -LY, *adv.* सनैपुण्यं, चतुरं &c. -NESS, *s.* नैपुण्यं, दक्षता, &c.

ADULATION, *s.* चाटूक्ति *f*, अतिप्रशंसा, श्लाघा. स्तुतिपूर्वकः अनुनयः, स्तवोक्तिः, अतिस्तुति *f.* -ADULATORY, *a.* चाटूक्तिपूर्ण, प्रशंसागर्भ, अतिप्रशंसायुक्त.

ADULT, *s.* प्रौढः, प्राप्तयौवनः, प्राप्तव्यवहारदशः, युवन् *m.*

ADULTERATE, *v. t.* अपद्रव्येण संमिश्र् 10, अशुद्धीकृ 8 U. -ION, *s.* दूषणं, मिश्रणं.

ADULTERY, *s.* व्यभिचारः; पारदार्यं, परभार्यालंघनं ; (of a woman) परपुरुषसंगति *f.*, पतिलंघनं. -ADULTERER, *s.* परस्त्रीगामिन् *m*, पारदारिकः भुजंगः, विटः, जारः. -ADULTERESS, *s.* व्यभिचा-

रिणी, जारिणी, पुंश्चली, परपुरुषसंगता, बंधकी. –ADULTERINE, *s.* जारजः.

ADUMBRATION, *s.* प्रतिच्छाया, प्रतिबिंबं. 2 पांडुलेख्यकरणं.

ADVANCE, *v. i.* प्र-उत्-चल् 1 P, प्र-अभि-या 2 P, अभिमुखं या, or -गम्-व्रज् 1 P, प्रगम्, प्रस्था 1 A; शत्रोरभिमुखं याति 'a. s against the enemy.' 2 वृध् 1 A, प्र-उप-चि pass., उन्नतिं या, उत्कर्षं या; 'a. ed some steps to receive' सादरमभिमुखदत्ताविरलपदः (Ka.95); 'a. ed in age' परिणतवयस्, वयोवृद्ध, प्रवयस्; 'a. ed in knowledge' ज्ञानवृद्ध.–*v. t.* उच्चल् c., पुरस्कृ 8 U, अग्रे नी 1 P. 2 वृध् c., परिपुष् 4 P. 3 उपक्षिप् 6 P, उपन्यस् 4 P, पुरो निधा 3 U. 4 प्राक् दा 3 U. –*s.* उच्चलनं, प्रगमनं, प्रयाणं. 2 उन्नति *f.*, क्रमशो वृद्धि *f.*, उत्कर्षः, वर्द्धनं; 'price of a book in a.' पुस्तकप्रकाशनात्पूर्वं दत्तं मूल्यं. –MENT, *s.* उत्कर्षः, उन्नति *f.*, अभ्युदयः, वृद्धि *f.*, आगमः, उपचयः; 'a. in knowledge' विद्यागमः; 'a. of learning' ज्ञानोत्कर्षः.

ADVANTAGE, *s.* लाभः, हितं, गुणः, फलं, अर्थः. 2 अवसरः, अवकाशः. 3 आधिक्यं, उत्कर्षः; taking a. of my weak point' मम छिद्रेण लब्धावकाशः; 'show or set off to a.' लक्ष्मीं-शोभां-तन् 8 U, *See* ADD; 'they had an a. over their enemy in bravery' शौर्ये ते शत्रुभ्योऽत्यरिच्यंत. –*v. t.* उपकृ 8 U, अनुग्रह् 9 P, लाभाय भू. –OUS, *a.* फलद, हितावह, लाभकर, हितकर (री *f.*). –OUSLY, *adv.* सफलं, सलाभं. 2 सावकाशं.

ADVENT, *s.* आगमनं, प्रवृत्ति *f.*; 'a. of spring' वसंतसमयावतारः, मधुप्रवृत्तिः. –ITIOUS, *a.* बाह्य, औपाधिक-आगंतुक (की *f.*), आहार्य.

ADVENTURE, *s.* साहसं, अद्भुतं कर्म. 2 दैवाधीनं कर्मचेष्टितं. 3 वृत्तांतः, चरितं, चेष्टा, चेष्टितं, क्रिया. –*v. i.* दैवाधीनं कर्म कृ 8 U. 2 साहसेन व्यवसो 4 P or प्रयत् 1 A. –ER, *s.* साहसिकः, साहसव्यवसायिन् *m.* –OUS, *a.* साहसिक (की *f.*), प्रगल्भ, निर्भय. 2 संदिग्ध, दैवायत्त.

ADVERB, *s.* क्रियाविशेषणं, अव्ययं.

ADVERSE, *a.* प्रतिकूल, विपक्ष, वैरिन् (णी *f.*), विपरीत, वाम, विरुद्ध, पराङ्मुख (खी *f.*). –ARY, *s.* शत्रुः, अरिः, *See* ENEMY. –ITY, *s.* विपद् *f.*, आपद् *f.*, विपत्ति *f.*, आपत्कालः, व्यसनं, दुःखं.

ADVERT (to), *v. i.* उदाहृ 1 P, अनुलक्ष् 10; अधिकृत्य-उद्दिश्य-वद् 1P or वच् 2 P. 2 अव-सं-ईक्ष् 1A, मनः समाधा 3 U, अवधा, अवधानं दा 3 U. –ENCE, *s.* अवधानं, अवहितता, मनोयोगः, अवेक्षा.

ADVERTISE, *v. t.* विज्ञा c. (ज्ञापयति), निविद् c., प्रकाश् c., बुध् c., वि-उद्-घुष् 10. –ER, *s.* प्रकाशकः, ज्ञापकः. –MENT, *s.* विज्ञापना, घोषणा.

ADVISE, *v. t.* उपदिश् 6 P, अनुशास् 2 P. 2 बुध् c., निविद् c., ज्ञा c. (ज्ञापयति). –*v. i.* विचर् c., आलोच् 10.–ABLE, *a.* उचित, योग्य, युक्त. 2 उपदेष्टव्य. –EDLY, *adv.* सुविचारतः, ज्ञानतः, बोधपूर्वं. 2 सावधानं, अवधानेन. –ER, *s.* उपदेशकः, उपदेष्टृ *m.* 2 सचिवः, अमात्यः, मंत्रिन् *m.* –ADVICE, *s.* उपदेशः, अनुशासनं, बोधनं. 2 समाचारः, वार्ता.

ADVOCATE, *v. t.* परार्थं वद् 1 P, पक्षं समर्थ् 10 or रक्ष् 1 P. –*s.* परार्थं वक्तृ *m*, पक्षसमर्थकः, वक्तृ *m.* 2 आश्रयः, रक्षकः, प्रतिपालकः.

ADZE, *s.* कुठारिका, तक्षणी.

AERIAL, *a.* *See* under AIR.

AFAR, *adv.* दूरात्, आरात्; दूरे-रं; 'a. off' दूरस्थ *a.*

AFFABLE, *a.* सुजन, सुशील. 2 मधुरालाप, प्रियवादिन् (नी *f.*). –AFFABILITY, *s.* मधुरालापता, सुशीलत्वं, सौजन्यं, प्रश्रयः. –AFFABLY, *adv.* चाटूक्त्या, मृदुवचनेन, सुजनवत्, सप्रश्रयं.

AFFAIR, *s.* कार्यं, व्यापारः, कर्मन् *n.*, अर्थः.

AFFECT, *v. t.* (To act upon) अभिभू 1 P, आकुलीकृ 8 U, उपहन् 2 P, विकृ, उपसृज् 6 P, संस्कृ; क्लेशलेशैरभिन्नं (S. 2) 'not a. ed by the slightest fatigue'; 'a. ed by a devil' वेतालोपहत; 'a. ed with many diseases' अनेकव्याध्युपसृष्ट; 'our position is not in the least a. ed (it does not a. us in the least)' न नः किंचिच्छिद्यते (S. B. 345). 2 (Pretend) Ex. by छद्म-छलं कृ, मिथ्या in comp., by कृतककृत्रिम-*a.* कृ; 'a. ing a quarrel or anger' कृतककलहं-कोपं-कृत्वा. 3 आकुलीकृ, आर्द्रीकृ, द्रु c.; अवकाशं-पदं-ग्रह् 9 P; 'my words a. ed his heart' मम वचसा तस्य हृदयं द्रवीभूतं, मम वचस्तस्य हृदये दृढं पदं लेभे. 4 मन् 4 A; 'he a. s learning' पंडितंमन्योऽसौ. –ATION, *s.* अहंकारः, आटोपः; मिथ्यागौरवं. 2 छद्मन् *n.*, *See* PRETEXT. 3 विलासः, अभिनयः, हावः.–ED, *a.* आकुल, अभिभूत, उपहत, विकृत. 2 मिथ्या in comp.; कृतक, कृत्रिम; 'by an a. courage' मिथ्याप्रतापमात्मन्यारोप्य. 3 अहंकारिन् (णी *f.*), मानिन् (नी *f.*), सदर्प.–EDLY, *adv.* साहंकारं, साटोपं.–ING, *a.* करुण, मर्मभेदिन् (नी *f.*). –INGLY, *adv.* करुणं. –ION, *s.* प्रेमन् *m. n.*, अनुरागः, स्नेहः, प्रणयः, प्रीति *f.*, वात्सल्यं, (with loc.). 2 धर्मः, संस्कारः, विकारः, अनुभावः, वृत्ति *f.*, भावः, विक्रिया, रागः.–IONATE, *a.* स्निग्ध, स्नेहशील, प्रणयिन् (नी *f.*), सप्रणय, सानुराग, वत्सल.–IONATELY, *adv.* सप्रेमं, सस्नेहं, स्निग्धं, सानुरागं.

AFFIANCE, *v. t.* प्रतिश्रु 5 P, वाचा दा 3 U.–*s.* वाग्दानं. 2 विश्वासः, श्रद्धा.

AFFIDAVIT, *s.* शपथपत्रं, सशपथं लिखितो लेखः.

AFFILIATE, *v. t.* संश्लिष् c., संयुज् 10.

AFFINITY, *s.* संबंधः, संपर्कः, योगः. 2 बंधुता-त्वं, सादृश्यं, साम्यं.

AFFIRM, *v. t.* प्रतिज्ञा 9 A, वद् 1 P, वच् 2 P, उपक्षिप् 6 P, उपन्यस् 4 P. 2 सनिश्चयं वद्, तथेति दृढं ब्रू 2U. 3 दृढीकृ 8U, निश्चित *a.* कृ, प्रमाणीकृ.—ATION, *s.* उक्ति *f*, दृढवचनं, प्रमाणीकरणं, सनिश्चयं वचनं. 2 प्रतिज्ञा, पक्षः.—ATIVE, *a.* स्वीकार-अंगीकार-द्योतक-सूचक; 'two negatives make one a.' द्वौ नञौ प्रकृतार्थं गमयतः. 2 पक्षानुकूल.

AFFIX, *s.* आगमः.—*v. t.* अनुबंध् 9 P, सं-आ-युज् 7U, 10.

AFFLICT, *v. t.* क्लिश् 9 P, दु 5P, परि-सं-तप् c., व्यथ् c. (व्यथयति), पीड् 10, बाध् 1 A, आयस् c.—ED, *a.* आर्त, दुःखित, अभिभूत, पीडित, आतुर. 'to be a. for' तम् 4 P, पर्युत्सुक *a.* भू.—ION, *s.* क्लेशः, बाधा, पीडा, कष्टं, व्यथा, दुःखं.—ING,—IVE *a.* क्लेशावह, व्यथाकर (री *f.*).

AFFLUENCE, *s.* समृद्धि *f.*, सधनता, धनबाहुल्यं.—AFFLUENT, *a.* समृद्ध, धनाढ्य, बहु-महा-धन; 'a. circumstances' सधनता, सुस्थिति *f.* 2 एकस्थानं प्रति प्रवाहक.—AFFLUX, *s.* एकस्थाने प्रवाहः.

AFFORD, *v. t.* दा 3 U. 2 (To be able) शक् 5 P, समर्थ-क्षम-*a.* भू 1 P.

AFFRAY, *s.* कलहः, द्वंद्वं, युद्धं.

AFFRIGHT, *v. t.* संत्रस् c., भी c. (भापयते-भीषयते), उद्विज् c.—*s.* भयं, सं-त्रासः, साध्वसं.

AFFRONT, *s.* अवज्ञा, निकृति *f.*, अपमानः, तिरस्कारः, मानभंगः.—*v. t.* (संमुखं-प्रत्यक्षं) अवज्ञा 9 U, अवमन् 4 A, अधिक्षिप् 6 P, तिरस्कृ 8 U.

AFFUSION, *s.* आसेकः.

AFLOAT, *a.* प्लवमान; 'a rumour is a.' वार्ता प्रसृता.

AFOOT, *adv.* पद्भ्याम्; 'set a.' प्रारभ् 1 A, *See* BEGIN; 'the army is a.' प्रचलितं सैन्यं; 'going a.' पादग, पादचारिन्.

AFORE, *adv.* अग्रे, पुरः, संमुखं. 2 पूर्वं, पुरा, गतकाले; 'a. said' पूर्वोक्त, प्रागुक्त.

AFRAID, *a.* भीत, भयान्वित, शंकान्वित; 'to be a.' त्रस् 1, 4 P, भी 3 P, (with abl.). 2 आ-शंक् 1 A, मन् 4 A.

AFRESH, *adv.* पुनरपि, अभिनवं.

AFTER, *prep.* अनु pr. to roots, पश्चात्; 'to go a.' अनुगम्, अनुसृ, 1 P. 2 (of time) परं, अनंतरं, ऊर्ध्वं, (with abl.); 'a. that,' तस्मात्परं, तत ऊर्ध्वं; 'a. one another' आनुपूर्व्येण, अनुपूर्वशः; 'a. 10 years' दशवर्षे व्यतीते; 'a. eating' भोजनानंतरं; पश्चात् (gen.), अनु in comp.; 'a. a few days' दिनेषु गच्छत्सु; by gerund, or पूर्वकं in comp.; (अनामयप्रश्नपूर्वकं S. 5); 'he waters tree a. tree' वृक्षं वृक्षं सिंचति; 'in a. time' आगामिकाले, उत्तरकाले. 3 अनुसारेण-सारतः, अनुरूपं; 'you write a. his hand' लेखने तस्यानुकरोषि; 'he is called a. his grandfather' स पितामहनाम्नाऽभिधीयते-आहूयते; *See* NAME. In comp. e. g. 'a.-ages,' ex. by उत्तर; 'a.-ages' उत्तरकालः; पुत्रपौत्राः; 'a.-inquiry,' उत्तरजिज्ञासा; 'a.-crop' शस्यस्य द्वितीयसंग्रहः; 'a.-life' आयुःशेषः, उत्तरवयस् *n.*; 'a. noon' *s.* अपराह्णः, पराह्णः, विकालः; (*a.*) अपराह्णतन (नी *f.*), वैकालिक (की *f.*); 'a. all' अंते, शेषे; 'a.-wards' पश्चात्, अनंतरं, ततः परं, परं.

AGAIN, *adv.* पुनः, भूयः; 'a. and a.' भूयो भूयः, वारंवारं; 'as much a.' द्विगुण *a.* 2 अपरं च, अन्यच्च, अपि च. 3 (With verbs) by प्रति pr.

AGAINST, *prep.* प्रति-अभि pr. to nouns; प्रतिवातं 'a. the wind' &c. 2 अभिमुखं, प्रतिमुखं, संमुखं, in comp. or with gen. 3 विरुद्धं, प्रतिकूलं, or by अतिक्रम्य; 'a. my order' मम शासनस्य विरुद्धं, शासनमतिक्रम्य-उल्लंघ्य; 'assist him a. his brother' भ्रातरि बद्धवैरस्य तस्य साहाय्यं कुरु. 4 अर्थे, अर्थं; आपदर्थे धनं रक्षेत् 'should lay by wealth a. (as a provision for) calamities.'

AGAPE, *a.* जृंभमाण; 'with eyes a. with astonishment' विस्मयोत्फुल्ललोचन.

AGE, *s.* युगं, कालः, समयः. 2 वयस् *n.*; 'a. of the world' कल्पः; 'old a.'; वृद्धत्वं, वार्धक्यं, वृद्धभावः, परिणतं वयः; 'come of a.' प्राप्तव्यवहार; 'of the same a.' समकालीन, समानवयस्क; 'of age' ex. by वर्षीय *a.* वर्षात्मक *a.*; '5 years of a.' पंचवर्षीय-वर्षात्मक; 'about 8 years of a.' अष्टवर्षदेशीय; 'a. of majority' यौवनदशा, यौवनावस्था; 'he reached the 16th year of his a.' षोडशवर्षवयोवस्थामस्पृशत्.—ED, *a.* वृद्ध, जीर्ण, पुराण.

AGENT, *s.* प्रतिहस्तः, प्रतिनिधिः. 2 (in grammar) कर्तृ *m.*; कारकः, कारः in comp. 3 हेतुः, कारणं, साधनं; शक्ति *f.*—AGENCY, *s.* कर्तृत्वं, निर्मातृत्वं; 'the action was done through his a.' तत्कर्तृका क्रिया, तस्य साहाय्येन संपादिता क्रिया. 2 कारणं. 3 नियोगिपदं, नियोज्यत्वं.

AGGLOMERATE, *v. t.* संचि 5 U, एकत्र-राशी-कृ 8 U.

AGGLUTINATE, *v. t.* संयुज् 10, संश्लिष् c., संलग्न *a.* कृ 8 U, संसंज् c.

AGGRANDIZE, *v. t.* वि-सं-प्र-वृध् c., आप्ये c., एध् c., स्फाय् c. (स्फावयति), उत्कृष् 1 P, उपचि 5 U.—MENT, *s.* विवृद्धि *f.*, उन्नति *f.*, अभ्युदयः, उत्कर्षः, उपचयः, उदयः.

AGGRAVATE, *v. t.* वृध् c., उपचि 5 U, प्रवृद्धिं नी 1 P. 2 प्रकुप् c., संक्षुभ् c., उद्दीप् c. -ION, *s.* वृद्धि *f.*, उपचयः. 2 प्रकोपनं-णं, उद्दीपनं.

AGGREGATE, *s.* संग्रहः, समाहारः, राशिः, समूहः, समुदायः.—*v. t.* संग्रह् 9 P, राशीकृ 8 U, संचि 5 U, एकत्र कृ. -ED, *a.* एकीकृत, समुदित, संचित, समाहृत. -ION, *s.* संग्रहणं, राशीकरणं. 2 समूहः, *See* (*s.*) above.

AGGRESS, *v. i.* (प्रथमं) आक्रम् 1 U, 4 P, लंघ् 1 A, 10, हिंसारंभं कृ 8 U. -ION, *s.* आ-अति-क्रमः, लंघनं. 2 प्रथमापकारः, हिंसारंभः. -IVE, *a.* प्रथमापकारिन् (णी *f.*); 'a. step' हिंसारंभः, प्रथमाक्रमः. -OR, *s.* प्रथमापकारकः, आक्रामकः.

AGGRIEVE, *v. t.* अर्द् 1 P or c., दुःखाकुलीकृ 8 U, *See* AFFLICT.

AGHAST, *a.* ससाध्वस, भयाभिभूत. 2 विस्मयाकुल, आश्चर्यचकित.

AGILE, *a.* लघु, चपल, लघुशरीर.

AGITATE, *v. t.* सं-वि-प्र-क्षुभ् c., आकुलीकृ 8 U, उद्विज् c.; धू 5, 9 U, प्रमंथ् 9 P, विलुड् c. (water). 2 Discuss, q. v.—ED, *a.* क्षुब्ध, विह्वल, आकुल, विक्लव, पारिप्लव. 2 प्रमथित, विलोडित; 'to be a.', क्षुभ् 4, 9 P, 1 A, विह्वल &c. भू. -ION, *s.* संक्षोभः, उद्वेगः, उपप्लवः, आकुलत्वं. 2 विलोडनं. 3 विचारणा, वादानुवादः. -OR, *s.* क्षोभकः.

AGNATE, *a.* संबंधिन् (नी *f.*), संबद्ध.

AGO, *adv.* पूर्वं, प्राक्, (with abl.); 'long a.' पुरा; 'not long a.' नातिचिरात्प्राक्, अनतिपूर्वं.

AGONY, *s.* व्यथा, यातना, वेदना, संतापः; 'in the a. es of death' मृत्युवेदनाभिभूत; 'sharp a.' तीव्रयातना-वेदना &c. -IZE, *v. i.* व्यथ् 1 A.—*v. t.* Afflict, q. v.

AGRARIAN, *a.* भूमिविषयक, क्षेत्रसंबंधिन् (नी *f.*).

AGREE, *v. i.* संमन् 4 A, तथा-एवं-मन्; 'I don't a. with you' नैवमहं मन्ये. 2 एकचित्तीभू, एकमत *a.* भू; 'birds in their nests a.' स्नेहभावैनैकत्र वसंति; 'they all a. on this point' अस्मिन्विषये सर्वेषां तेषामैकमत्यम्. 3 ग्रह् 9 P, स्वीकृ 8 U, अनुमन् 4 A, अनुज्ञा 9 U. 4 संकृप् c., समयं-संविदं-कृ, प्रतिपद् 4 A, अभ्युप-इ 2 P or गम् 1 P, प्रतिश्रु 5 P. 5 आरोग्याय क्लृप् 1 A, हिताय भू, हितमावह् 1 P; '(living in) Bombay does not a. with my health' मुंबापुरनिवासो ममारोग्याय न कल्पते. 6 Resemble, q. v. -ABLE, *a.* रम्य, सुख in comp. (सुखस्पर्शता शिलाविशेषस्य M. 4); मनोज्ञ, प्रिय, सूनृत, अभिमत, सुभग. 2 अनुरूप, योग्य, तुल्य, सदृश (शी *f.*) -ABLY, *adv.* यथासुखं. 2 अनुरूपं, अनुसारतः; 'a. to one's nature' स्वानुरूपं. -MENT, *s.* समयः, संविद् *f.* 2 ऐक्यं, संमति *f.*, ऐकमत्यं. 3 सादृश्यं, संवादः. 4 अभ्युपगमः, स्वीकारः, प्रतिपत्ति *f.*

AGRICULTURE, *s.* कृषि *f.*, कर्षणं; 'science of a.' कृषिकर्मविद्या. -AGRICULTURIST, *s.* कृषीवलः, कर्षकः, कृषिजीविन् *m.*, क्षेत्रिन् *m.* 2 वैश्यः, विश् *m.*

AGROUND, *adv.* तटस्थ *a.*, उत्तीर्ण.

AGUE, *s.* कंप-शीत-ज्वरः, विषमः; 'tertian a.' त्र्याहिकविषमः; 'quartan a.' चातुर्थिकविषमः.

AH, *interj.* आः, हंत, हा, अहो, अहह.

AHEAD, *adv.* अग्रे, पुरतः, पुरः. 2 अधोमुख, अवाक्शिरः.

AJAR, *adv.* अर्धविवृत *a.*

AID, *v. t.* उपकृ 8 U, साहाय्यं कृ (with gen.). —*s.* साहाय्यं, उपकारः. 2 सहायः, उपकारकः. -LESS, *a.* असहाय. *See* HELP.

AIL, *v. t.* पीड् 10; दु 5 P, तप् c.; 'what a. s thee' किं त्वां व्यथयति or का ते पीडा. -ING, *a.* पीडित, क्षुद्ररोगपीडित. -MENT, *s.* पीडा, आतंकः. 2 क्षुद्ररोगः-व्याधिः.

AIM, *v. t.* लक्ष्यीकृ 8 U, उद्दिश् 6 P, संधा 3 U; 'well a. ed arrow' साधुकृतसंधानः शरः (S. I). 2 आप् desid. (ईप्सति), आकांक्ष् 1 P, लभ् desid. (लिप्सते); 'a. ed at the crown' राजपदं लिप्सांचक्रे &c. 3 लक्ष्यं प्रति क्षिप् 6 P or अस् 4 P. —*s.* लक्ष्यं-क्षं, शरव्यं. 2 संधानं; 'taking a.' शरसंधानं कुर्वन्. 3 अभिप्रायः, आशयः, वांछा, कांक्षा, हेतुः, चिकीर्षितं; 'friend, where are you going without any definite a.' हला क्वानिर्दिष्टकारणं गम्यते (V. 2).

AIR, *s.* व्योमन् *n.*, आकाशः, नभस् *n.*, विहायस् *n.*; 'to take the a.' वातमासेव् 1 A; 'take a.' प्रकाशतां गम् 1 P. 2 वायुः, वातः, समीरणः. 3 तालः, रागः, मूर्छना. 4 रूपं, आकारः, मुद्रा; 'with a dignified a.' सगौरवाकारेण; 'a. of conceit' अवलेपमुद्रा; 'with the a. of one who is offended' निकृतमिवात्मानं संदर्श्य. 5 गति *f.*, विधिः, प्रकारः, रूपं; 'through a.' विहायसा, नभोवर्त्मना; 'to build castles in the a.' गगनकुसुमानि चि 5 U; 'a. balloon' आकाशयानं, व्योमयानं; 'a. bladder' वायुकोषः; 'a. hole' वातायनं, गवाक्षः, जालं; 'a. born', 'aerial', आकाशज; आकाशस्थ, नभःस्थ. -Y, *a.* वायव (वी *f.*), वायुमय (यी *f.*). 2 सुवात, प्रवात; 'a. place' प्रवातं; प्रवातशयनं 'a bed in an a. place (in the current of wind)'. 3 असार, फल्गु, खपुष्पवत् *ind.* -AERONAUT, *s.* वैमानिकः.

AKIN, *a.* सगोत्र, सनाभि, सजातिय. 2 सदृश (शी *f.*), समान, संबंधिन् (नी *f.*).

ALACK, *See* ALAS.

ALACRITY, *s.* औत्सुक्यं, उत्साहः. 2 शीघ्रत्वं, क्षिप्रता, अविलंबः.

ALARM, *s.* त्रासः, शंका, भयं, साध्वसं. 2 सान्नहनिकं. 3 भयध्वनिः, भयाक्रंदनं ; 'a. bell' भयसूचको घंटानादः. –*v. t.* प्राक् सूचनां दा 3 U. 2 भी c., संत्रस् c, उद्विज् c. –ED, *a.* भीत, उद्विग्न, भयार्त, चकित. –ING, *a.* भयावह, उद्वेगकर (री *f.*), त्रासजनन (नी *f.*), भयप्रद. –IST, *s.* भयोत्पादकः. –ALARUM, *s.* सान्नहनिकं, भयध्वनिः, प्रबोधनघंटा.

ALAS, *interj.* कष्टं, हा, हंत, हा धिक्, अहह, अहो बत. 2 अत्याहितं, अब्रह्मण्यं.

ALBEIT, *adv.* यद्यपि.

ALBUGO, *s.* शुक्लं ; चक्षूरोगः.

ALCHEMY, *s.* रसविद्या, रससिद्धि *f.*–ALCHEMIST, *s.* रसायनविद् *m.*, रसज्ञः.

ALCOHOL, *s.* मद्यसारः.

ALCOVE, *s.* कुंजः, पर्णशाला, निभृतस्थानं.

ALDERMAN, *s.* पुराध्यक्षः ; वृद्ध-गुरु-जनः.

ALE, *s.* यवसुरा-रं, मद्यं; 'a. house,' शुंडा, पानं ; 'keeper of an a. house' शौंडिकः.

ALERT, *a.* जागरूक, दक्ष, सावधान, अवहित, अतंद्र, उद्यमिन्-उद्योगिन् (नी *f.*). –NESS, *s.* जागरूकता, अवधानं, दक्षता.

ALGEBRA, *s.* बीजगणितं. –ICAL, *a.* बीजविषयक.

ALIEN, *a.* विदेशीय, अन्यदेशीय. 2 विरक्त ; विरुद्ध, भिन्न, अप्रस्तुत. –ATE, *v. t.* (affection) विघट् c., विश्लिष् c., विनश् c., विभिद् 7 P or c., विच्छिद् 7 P or c. 2 (person) विरंज् c., वि-अप-रक्त *a.* कृ 8 U. 3 पराधीन *a.* कृ, परस्वत्वे प्रतिपद् c. –ATION, *s.* विघटनं, विरागः, विरक्ति *f.*

ALIGHT, *v. i.* अवतॄ 1 P, उपविश् 6 P, अव-निपत् 1 P.

ALIKE, *a.* सदृश (शी *f.*), तुल्य, समान, सम.

ALIMENT, *s.* आहारः, भोजनं, पौष्टिकं. –AL, –ARY, *a.* पोषक, पुष्टिप्रद, शक्तिवर्धन (नी *f.*). –ATION, *s.* पोषणं, भरणं.

ALIVE, *a.* जीवत् (न्ती *f.*), सजीव, सचेतन ; 'I caught him a.' जीवग्राहमग्रहीषं (D. K. II. 4). 2 अभिज्ञ (with gen.), or विद् 2 P, *See* KNOW.

ALKALI, *s.* क्षारः, सर्जिका, *See* NATRON. –ALKALINE, *a.* क्षारस्वभाव, क्षारविशिष्ट.

ALL, *s.* सर्वं, अखिलं, साकल्यं. – *a.* सर्व-विश्व, *pron. a.*, अखिल, सकल, कृत्स्न, निखिल, समस्त ; 'not at a.' न किमपि, न मनागपि ; 'at a. times' सर्वदा; 'a. but' प्राय, कल्प, in comp.; 'a. but dead' मृतप्राय ; छिन्नप्राय 'a. but cut'; 'a. of a sudden' अकस्मात्, सहसा, सपदि, एकपदे; 'this is not a.' एतावतापि दोषो &c. न समाप्यते; 'a. I can' यथाशक्ति, यथासामर्थ्यं; 'this is a. I can do to serve you' एतावान्मे विभवो भवंतं सेवितुं (M. 2); 'by a. means' सर्वथा ; 'a.-in-a. of one's life' जीवितसर्वस्वं ; 'a. at once' युगपत् ; 'a. round' सर्वतः, सर्वदिक्षु, समंततः ; 'in a.' साकल्येन, पिंडीकृत्य, मिलित्वा ; 'give me 20 rupees in a.' एवं पिंडीकृत्य मह्यं विंशतिं रूप्यकान्देहि; सर्वे मिलित्वा सप्त वयं 'we are 7 in a.'; 'a.-bearing' सर्वसह ; 'a.-conquering' सर्वदमन, सर्वजय, सर्वंदम ; 'a.-destroying' सर्वंकष ; 'a.-knowing' सर्वज्ञ, सर्वविद् ; 'a.-pervading' सर्वव्यापिन् (नी *f.*), विश्वात्मन्, सर्वगत ; 'a. powerful' सर्वशक्तिमत् (ती *f.*).

ALLAY, *v. t.* प्र-उप-शम् c. (शमयति), नियम् c.; निर्वा c. (वापयति); 'a. ing of heat' निर्वापणं. 2 सांत्व् 10, तुष् c.–ER, *s.* शमकः, शांतिदः-करः. –MENT, *s.* प्रशमनं, सांत्वनं ; 'a. of hunger' क्षुत्प्रतीकारः.

ALLEGE, *v. t.* प्रतिज्ञा 9 A, वद् 1 P, दृढं ब्रू 2 U; 'the charges a. ed against me' मयि समारोपिता दोषाः. 2 छद्म कृ 8 U, व्यपदिश् 6 P, मिथ्या वद्. 3 उदाहृ 1 P. –ATION, *s.* प्रतिज्ञा, उक्ति *f.*, वचनोपन्यासः. 2 दोषारोपः, मिथ्याभियोगः. 3 व्यपदेशः, छद्मन् *n.*, व्याजः.

ALLEGIANCE, *s.* निष्ठा, भक्ति *f.*, अनुरागः; 'a. to the king' राजनिष्ठा.

ALLEGORY, *s.* रूपकं, दृष्टांतः. –ICAL, *a.* लाक्षणिक (की *f.*), रूपकमय (यी *f.*). –ICALLY, *adv.* दृष्टांततः, दृष्टांतेन. –IZE, *v. t.* दृष्टांतयति (D.), रूपकेण दृश् c.

ALLEVIATE, *v. t.* उप-प्र-शम् c., नियम् c., सांत्व् 10 ; निर्वा c. (वापयति), लघयति (D.), लघूकृ. –ION, *s.*उप-प्र-शमः, निर्वापणं ; 'a. of sorrow' दुःखनिर्वापणं. –IVE, *a.* शांतिद, शमक.

ALLEY, *s.* उद्यानपथः, वीथि-थी *f.* 2 दुर्गममार्गः, संबाधपथः.

ALLIGATE, *v. t.* सं-अनु-बंध् 9 P. –ION, *s.* संबंधः, संयोजनं.

ALLIGATOR, *s.* नक्रः, ग्राहः.

ALLITERATION, *s.* अनुप्रासः.

ALLOT, *v. t.* परिक्लृप् c., दा 3 U, विभज् 1 U. –MENT, *s.* विभागः, विभजनं. 2 अंशः, भागः.

ALLOW, *v. t.* अनुज्ञा 9 U, अनुमन् 4 A, अनुमुद् 1 A. 2 Give, q. v. 3 ग्रह् 9 P. *See* ADMIT. 4 उप-ईक्ष् 1 A, विषह् 1 A ; स कस्मादार्येणापक्रामन्नुपेक्षितः (Mu. 3); 'I a. my feet to be burnt' दह्यमानावपि चरणावुपेक्षे. 5 (for) न्यूनांकृ, न गण् 10.–ABLE, *a.* अनुज्ञेय, अनुमोद्य; 'a. mistake' क्षमार्होपराधः ; 'not a.' प्रति-नि-षिद्ध.

—ANCE, *s.* अनुज्ञा, अनुमति *f.*, अनुमोदनं. 2 वेतनं, निरूपितमूल्यं, वृत्ति *f.* 3 स्वीकारः; न्यूनीकरणं.

ALLOY, *s.* मिश्रणं, दोषः, न्यूनता. 2 अपद्रव्यं, कुप्यं, मिश्रधातुः. —ED, *a.* मिश्रित, दूषित ; 'un-a. pleasure' केवलं-दुःखासंभिन्नं-सुखं.

ALLUDE, *v. t.* उद्दिश्य-अधिकृत्य वद् 1 P or वच् 2 P or अभिधा 3 U; उद्दिश् 6 P, सूच् 10, लक्षीकृ ; अनुसंधा ; 'this story a. s to myself' इयं कथा मामेव लक्षीकरोति (S. 7). —ALLUSION, *s.* उद्देशः, उदाहरणं, कीर्तनं ; इंगितं, सूचनं; 'in a. to' अधिकृत्य, समुद्दिश्य.

ALLURE, *v. t.* हृ 1 P, आकृष् 1 P. वि-प्र-लुभ् c. —ING, *a.* प्रलोभक, हारिन् (णी *f.*), आकर्षक; 'a. things' प्रलोभनवस्तूनि. —MENT, *s.* प्र-विलोभनं ; वंचनं, विकारहेतुः, आकर्षणं.

ALLUVIUM, *s.* पुलिनं, नदीरयसमाहृता मृत्तिका. —ALLUVIAL, *a.* पुलिनमय (यी *f.*).

ALLY, *s.* मित्रं, सहायः, पक्ष्यः, सहकारिन् *m.* — *v. t.* संबंध् 9 P. 2 संधा 3 U; संयुज् 10, संश्लिष् c. —ALLIANCE, *s.* संधिः; 'friendly a.' सख्यं, मैत्री. 2 संबंधः, संपर्कः; 'matrimonial a.' विवाहसंबंधः.

ALMANAC, *s.* पंजिका, पंचांगं.

ALMIGHTY, *a.* सर्वशक्तिमत् (ती *f.*), अमितौजस् ; सर्वशक्, सर्वसमर्थ.

ALMOND, *s.* वातामफलं.

ALMONRY, *s.* भिक्षादानगृहं, भैक्ष्यशाला. —ALMONER, *s.* भिक्षादाने अधिकृतः.

ALMOST, *adv.* प्राय, भूयिष्ठ, कल्प, affixed to adj.; 'a. dead' मृतकल्प, मृतप्राय; 'when the night had a. worn away' क्षीणभूयिष्ठायां क्षपायां ; 'it is a. dawn now' अधुना प्रभातप्राया-कल्पा शर्वरी. 2 प्रायः, प्रायशः; 'a. all' प्रायः सर्वे. 3 (With num.) ex. by आसन्न, उप, in comp. ; उप-आसन्न-दशाः &c.

ALMS, *s.* भैक्ष्यं, भिक्षा, भिक्षादानं ; 'beg a.' भिक्षाटनं कृ 8 U, भिक्ष्-याच् 1 A; 'a.-giving' भिक्षादानं, त्यागः; 'a. house' अनाथगृहं, भिक्षागेहं; 'a. man' भिक्षुकः, भिक्षाशिन् *m.*

ALOE, *s.* सहा ; कुमारीरसोद्भवो बोलः.

ALOFT, *adv.* ऊर्ध्वं, उपरि; 'a. in the air' विहायसा, व्योमवर्त्मना.

ALONE, *a.* एक, अद्वितीय, एकाकिन् (नी *f.*). 2 एव, केवलं, मात्र in comp.

ALONG, *prep.* अनु in comp. or with acc.; or by instr.; 'a. the way' अनुमार्गं; 'a. the city of Ayodhyâ' अयोध्यानगरमिनु; 'a. a road' मार्गेण. 2 पुरः, अग्रे, पुरस्तात् ; 'a. with' सह, साधं, *See* WITH; 'all a.' आप्रथमं, प्रथमावधि; 'a. side' पार्श्वतः; समीपं-पे.

ALOOF, *adv.* दूरे, अंतरे, पृथक् ; 'standing a.' दूरस्थ; 'keep a.' पृथक् निधा 3 U, न गण् 10.

ALOUD, *adv.* उच्चैः, उच्च-तार-स्वरेण. 2 प्रकाशं, प्रकट-मुक्तकंठं (weep a.); 'call a.' शब्दायते (D.).

ALPHABET, *s.* वर्णमाला. —ICAL, *a.* वर्णक्रमानुसारिन् (णी *f.*). —ICALLY, *adv.* वर्णक्रमेण, वर्णानुसारेण.

ALREADY, *adv.* पूर्वं, पुरा, प्राक्, with एव; sometimes by एव alone; 'the moon has a. risen' उदित एव हिमरश्मिः.

ALSO, *adv.* अपि, च. 2 अपरंच, पुनश्च, अपिच. 3 तद्वत्.

ALTAR, *s.* वेदि-दी *f.*, चैत्यं, स्थंडिलं.

ALTER, *v. t.* अन्यथा कृ 8 U, विपर्यस् 4 P, विपर्यासं नी 1 P, परिवृत् c. 2 विकृ, विरूप् 10; 'a. ed in appearance' भिन्नाकार इव लक्ष्यमाण. —*v. i.* परिवृत् 1 A, अन्यथा-अन्यरूप *a.* भू; विपर्यासं या 2 P. —ATION, *s.* परि(री)वर्तः, विकारः, विकृति *f.*, विपर्यासः.

ALTERCATE, *v. i.* विवद् 1 A, कलहायते (D.). —ION, *s.* विवादः, कलहः, वाग्युद्धं.

ALTERNATE, *a.* Ex. by पर्याय in comp.; 'a. service' पर्यायसेवा. —*v. t.* परिवृत् c.; ex. by a verb with पर्यायेण. —ION, *s.* विपर्ययः, परिवृत्ति *f.*, पर्यायः. —IVE, *s.* विकल्पः, पक्षः, पक्षांतरं; gen. ex. by words like गतिः, शरणं &c.; 'there is no other a.' अन्या गतिर्नास्ति, अन्यच्छरणं नालोक्यते (Ka. 152). 2 विकल्पः, विभाषा (in grammar). —LY, *adv.* पर्यायेण, यथाक्रमं.

ALTHOUGH, *conj.* यद्यपि, अपि.

ALTITUDE, *s.* उच्चत्वं, उच्छ्रायः, उत्सेधः.

ALTOGETHER, *adv.* सर्वथा, सर्वतः, अशेषतः, साकल्येन. 2 सहित-संहत-एकीकृत-*a.* ; समं, एकीकृत्य.

ALUM, *s.* स्फटी, तुवरी, सौराष्ट्री, स्फाटिकी.

ALWAYS, *adv.* सदा, सर्वदा, अनिशं, सततं, सर्वकालं, निरंतरं, अनवरतं.

AMAIN, *adv.* प्रसभं, प्रसह्य, बलात्, सवेगं, जवेन.

AMALGAM, *s.* कांस्यं, मिश्रधातुः, पारदसंसृष्टधातुः. —ATE, *v. t.* संमिश्र् 10. 2 संयुज् 10, एकीकृ 8 U, संश्लिष् c. —ATION, *s.* धातुसंमिश्रणं. 2 संयोजनं, संयोगः, संमेलनं.

AMANUENSIS, *s.* लेखकः, लिपिकारः.

AMARANTH, *s.* अम्लानपुष्पं. 2 अम्लानः, महासहा.

AMASS, *v. t.* संचि 5 U, संग्रह् 9 P, संभृ 3 U, राशी-एकी-कृ 8 U. —MENT, *s.* संचयः, संग्रहः, &c.

AMATORY, *a.* कामिन् (नी *f.*), प्रेमशील, शृंगारप्रिय.

AMAZE, *v. t.* विस्मि c. (विस्माययति, विस्मापयते), विस्मयाकुल-साश्चर्य-*a.* कृ 8 U. —ED, *a.* विस्मापित, विस्मित, विस्मयाकुल, साश्चर्य. —MENT, *s.* विस्मयः, आश्चर्यं, विस्मयाकुलत्वं. — EDLY, *adv.* सविस्मयं; सा-

र्यं. -ING, *a.* विस्मयकारिन् (णी *f.*), विचित्र, अद्भुत. 2 अतिरिक्त; अति pr.

AMBAGES, *s.* वक्रोक्ति *f.*

AMBASSADOR, *s.* दूतः, राजदूतः, प्रणिधिः, संदेशहरः. -SHIP,-AMBASSAGE, *s.* दौत्यं, प्रणिधिकार्यं.

AMBER, *s.* तृणमणिः.

AMBIDEXTROUS, *a.* उभयहस्तकुशल.

AMBIENT, *a.* व्यापक; निपातिन् (नी *f.*), गामिन् in comp.

AMBIGUOUS, *a.* द्व्यर्थ, संदिग्धार्थ, अव्यक्त, अस्पष्ट, संदिग्ध. -LY, *adv.* अस्पष्टं, वक्रोक्त्या, द्व्यर्थतः. -NESS,-AMBIGUITY, *s.* वक्रोक्ति *f.*, संदिग्धार्थता, संदेहार्थः.

AMBIT, *s.* मंडलं, चक्रवालं, वर्तुलं.

AMBITION, *s.* स्पृहा, आकांक्षा. 2 कीर्तिस्पृहा, ऐश्वर्याकांक्षा, उच्चपदवांछा; 'a. to get a throne,' राज्यलोभः -तृष्णा. -AMBITIOUS, *a.* सस्पृह, साकांक्ष, ऐश्वर्येप्सु, यशस्काम; 'who, a. of your throne, has roused your envy' केनाभ्यसूया पदकांक्षिणा ते जनिता (K. III. 4). 2 (Of hopes) दूराधिरोहिन्-उत्सर्पिन् (णी *f.*). -LY, *adv.* ऐश्वर्याकांक्षया &c.

AMBLE, *v. i.* ललितं वल्ग् 1 P, द्रु 1 A; धोर् 1 P. -*s.* धोरितं. -ER, *s.* धोरितगामिन् *m.*

AMBROSIA, *s.* अमृतं, सुधा, पीयूषं. -AL, *a.* अमृतमय (यी *f.*), अमृततुल्य, (*s.*) in comp.

AMBULATE, *v. i.* विचर् 1 P, परिक्रम् 1 U, 4 P, इतस्ततश्चर्. -ION, *s.* परिक्रमः, पर्यटनं.

AMBUSH, AMBUSCADE, *s.* (पराबस्कंदनार्थं) निभृते स्थानं; निभृतावस्थिति *f.*; 'they all lay in a.' सर्वे एव ते निभृतं तस्थुः.

AMELIORATE, *v. t.* वृध् c., श्रेयस्-साधीयस् (सी *f.*)- कृ 8 U, समुन्नतिं नी 1 P, *See* IMPROVE.-ION, *s.* वर्धनं, समुन्नति *f.*, श्रेयस्त्वं.

AMEN, *adv.* ओम्, भवतु, एवमस्तु, तथास्तु.

AMENABLE, *a.* परानुयोगाधीन, अनुविधायिन् (नी *f.*), आज्ञाकर (री *f.*), आयत्त, वशं यात; 'a. to another's power' पराधिकारवशः.

AMEND, *v. t.* सं-वि-परि-शुध् c., समा-प्रतिसमा-धा 3 U; 'a. one's life' पापान्निवृत् 1 A, पापं त्यक्त्वा धर्ममाचर् 1 P. -*v. i.* शुध् 4 P; समाधा pass., भद्रतर *a.* भू. -MENT, *s.* संशोधनं; प्रतिसमाधानं. 2 दोषशोधनं &c. -AMENDS, *s.* प्रमार्जनं, निस्तारः, निष्कृति *f.*, शोधनं; 'to make a. for' प्रमृज् 2 P; शुध् c.; *See* ATONE.

AMENITY, *s.* रम्यता, मनोज्ञता.

AMERCE, *v. t.* *See* PUNISH.

AMIABLE, *a.* सुशील, सुप्रिय, सुजन. 2 प्रियदर्शन, रमणीय. -NESS, *s.* सौजन्यं, सद्भावः, सुशीलत्वं. -AMIABLY, *adv.* सुशीलतया, प्रीत्या, स्नेहभावेन.

AMICABLE, *a.* मैत्र (त्री *f.*), हित, स्नेहशील; मित्रभावेन; 'a. settlement' मित्रभावेन निर्णयः. -NESS, *s.* मित्रत्वं, सख्यं, सौहार्दं. -AMICABLY, *adv.* मित्रवत्, मित्रभावेन, सौहार्देन.

AMID,-ST, *prep.* मध्ये, अंतरे, अभ्यंतरे, (with gen.); मध्यगत-स्थित *a.*; 'a. these thoughts he was pierced by an arrow' एवं विचारयन् -एवं विचारनिमग्नः सन्-बाणेन हतः.

AMISS, *a.* दोषिन् (णी *f.*), अपराधिन् (नी *f.*). 2 अनुचित, अयोग्य.-*adv.* अनुचितं, अयुक्तं; 'take a.' *See* MISUNDERSTAND.

AMITY, *s.* मैत्री, स्नेहभावः, सख्य, संधिः.

AMMUNITION, *s.* युद्धसामग्री, युद्धोपकरणानि.

AMNESTY, *s.* (राजकृता) दोषक्षमा, दोषाद्विमोचनं.

AMONG,-ST, *prep.* मध्ये, अभ्यंतरे, (with gen.); ex. by loc. or gen. of noun; 'a. cows the black one gives much milk' गवां गोषु वा कृष्णा बहुक्षीरा (S. K.); काव्येषु नाटकं रम्यं &c.

AMOROUS, *a.* कामुक, प्रेमशील, रसिक, शृंगारप्रिय. 2 सविलास, सविभ्रम, ललित; 'a. sport' सविलासक्रीडा. -LY, *adv.* सकामं, सानुरागं; सविलासं, सविभ्रमं, ललितं.

AMOUNT, *v. i.* उपचि-संख्या-pass.; संपद् 4 A; 'a. ing to' संख्यक in comp.; 'a. to 100' शतसंख्य-संख्याक; 'they a. in all to 24 men' एवं पिंडीकृत्य चतुर्विंशतिर्नराः संपद्यंते; 'thus the families a. to 14' एवमेतान्येकत्र चतुर्दश कुलानि (Ka. 136); 'your whole speech a. s to this' एतावता-एवंच; एष तव वचसो निष्कर्षः -पिंडितार्थः; 'your exertions do not a. to even a hundredth part of mine' तव व्यवसायो ममोद्योगस्य शततमीमपि कलां न स्पृशति. -*s.* राशिः, परिमाणं, समुदायः, संख्या, समुच्चयः; 'by any a. of labour' महता श्रमेणापि; 'to the a. of 100' शतसंख्यं.

AMPHIBIOUS, *a.* स्थलजलचर. 2 द्विधागति.

AMPHITHEATRE, *s.* रंगः, रंगभूमि *f.*

AMPLE, *a.* विशाल, विपुल, बृहत् (ती *f.*), विस्तीर्ण, विस्तृत. 2 प्रचुर, प्रभूत, बहुल, यथेष्ट. -NESS, *s.* विशालता. 2 प्राचुर्यं. -AMPLY, *adv.* सविस्तरं, प्रचुरं, यथेष्टं; 'he was a. rewarded' तस्मै प्रभूतं पारितोषिकं दत्तं. -AMPLIFY, *v. t.* सविस्तरं -विस्तरेण -वर्ण् 10. 2 तन् 8 U, वृध् c., विस्तृ 9 U. -AMPLIFICATION,-AMPLITUDE, *s.* विस्तारः, वृद्धि *f.* 2 महत्त्वं, प्राचुर्यं.

AMPUTATE, *v. t.* अंगं छिद् 7 P or निकृत् 6 P. -ION, *s.* छेदः, कर्तनं.

AMULET, *s.* रक्षाकरंडः.

AMUSE, *v. t.* विनुद् c., रम् c., नंद् c.; 'a. oneself' विहृ 1 P, विलस् 1 P, क्रीड् 1 P.—MENT, *s.* विनोदः, विनोदनं, क्रीडा, केलि *f.*, विलासः, कौतुकं. —ING, *a.* विनोदिन् (नी *f.*), विनोदनशील, हृदयंगम, रम्य.

ANACHRONISM, *s.* कालगणनायां प्रमादः or भ्रमः.

ANALOGY, *s.* सादृश्य, समानता, संबंधः. —ICAL, —OUS, *a.* सदृश (शी *f.*), तुल्यरूप, समान, अनुरूप, संबंधिन् (नी *f.*), आनुषंगिक (की *f.*). —LY, *adv.* सादृश्येन, औपम्येन.

ANALYZE, *v. t.* व्याकृ 8 U, विभज् 1 U, विच्छिद् 7 P, विभिन्न *a.* -खंडशः -पृथक् -कृ, विश्लिष् c. —ANALYSIS, *s.* विभागः, व्यवच्छेदः, विभेदः, व्याकरणं. 2 सारः.

ANARCHY, *s.* अशासनं, अनीश्वरता, राजविप्लवः, अराजकता; 'when the country is in a.' अराजके जनपदे.

ANATHEMA, *s.* अभिशापः, शापः, आक्रोशः. —TIZE, *v. t.* शप् 1 U, आक्रुश् 1 P.

ANATOMY, *s.* पृथक्करणं, विच्छेदः. 2 शरीरव्यवच्छेदविद्या-शास्त्रं. —IZE, *v. t.* (शरीरं) व्यवच्छिद् 7 P, पृथक् कृ. 2 विवृ 5 U, व्याख्या 2 P. —IST, *s.* व्यवच्छेदकः.

ANCESTOR, *s.* पूर्वपुरुषः; a.s पूर्वजाः (pl.), पितरः (pl.), पितृलोकः.—ANCESTRAL, *a.* पितृक, पैतृक (की *f.*); 'a. property' पित्र्यं रिक्थं. —ANCESTRY, *s.* पितरः, पितृश्रेणी. 2 वंशः, अन्वयः.

ANCHOR, *s.* नौबंधनकीलः-लं, लांगलं. — *v. t.* कीलेन बंध् 9 P, स्थिरीकृ, गतिं निरुध् 7 U or प्रतिहन् 2 P.

ANCHORITE, *s.* यतिः, आरण्यकः, संन्यासिन् *m.*, वनवासिन् *m.*, वानप्रस्थः.

ANCIENT, *a.* पुराण, पुरातन (नी *f.*), पूर्व, प्राक्कालीन, प्राक्तन, प्राचीन. —*s.* (a. s) वृद्धाः-प्राचीनपुरुषाः (pl.). 2 ध्वजः, पताका. 3 पताकिन् *m.*—LY, *adv.* पुरा, पूर्वं, पूर्वकाले. —NESS, *s.* प्राचीनता, पुरातनत्वं, &c.

AND, *conj.* च repeated after each word joined, or after all. In the case of nouns, ex. by Dvandva comps.; 'the Sun and the Moon' आदित्यचंद्रौ. 2 (With adjectives) gen. ex. by Karm. comps.; अलसलुलितमुग्धानि अंगकानि; (with numerals) by a comp. with अधिक, उत्तर; '100 a. 8' अष्टाधिकं-अष्टोत्तरं शतं. 3 (In the case of verbs) ex. by the use of gerunds; 'go a. tell him' गत्वा तस्मै कथय; sometimes by वा in questions; जात अस्ति ते माता स्मरसि वा तातं (U. 4). 4 अपि च, अन्यच, किं च. 'A. then' अथ, तदनु, ततः; 'a. yet,' तथापि, or ex. by च-च (असुलभा सकलेंदुमुखी च सा किमपि चेदमनंगविचेष्टितं V. 2).

ANECDOTE, *s.* कथा, उपाख्यानं, आख्यायिका.

ANENT, *prep.* उद्दिश्य, अधिकृत्य, विषये in comp.

ANEW, *adv.* पुनः, पुनरपि. 2 अभिनवं.

ANGEL, *s.* देवदूतः, ईश्वरप्रेष्यः, स्वर्गदूतः, 'you are my a.' त्वं मे प्रियतमा, प्राणप्रेयसी. — IC,-ICAL *a.* दिव्य, देवदूतोपम, अमानुष (षी *f.*).

ANGER, *s.* क्रोधः, कोपः, अमर्षः, रोषः, मन्युः.—*v. t.* प्रकुप् c., क्रुध् c. — ANGRY, *a.* जातामर्ष, रुष्ट, सामर्ष, सरोष, कोपिन् (नी *f.*), कुपित, क्रुद्ध, समन्यु; 'to be a.' कुप्-क्रुध्-रुष्- 4 P, (with dat.). —ANGRILY, *adv.* सकोपं, सरोषं, कोपात् &c.

ANGLE, *s.* अस्रः, कोणः. — *v. i.* बडिशेन मत्स्यान् ग्रह् 9 P, उद्धृ-हृ 1 P. — ER, *s.* मत्स्यवेधकः. — ING, *s.* मत्स्यग्रहणं. — ANGULAR, *a.* कोणविशिष्ट, अस्रोपेत.

ANGUISH, *s.* परितापः, पीडा, बाधा, वेदना, यातना, आतंकः; 'a. of mind' मनस्तापः.

ANHELATION, *s.* उच्छ्वसनं, हृदयकंपः, वेपथुः.

ANIMADVERT, *v. i.* निंद् 1 P, उपालभ् 1 A; *See* CENSURE. 2 परीक्ष् 1 A, चर्चां कृ. —ANIMADVERSION, *s.* निंदा, उपालंभः. 2 परीक्षणं, चर्चा.

ANIMAL, *s.* जंतुः, प्राणिन् *m.*, जीविन् *m.*, जीवः, जन्मवत् *m.* 2 पशुः, मृगः, तिर्यच् *m.* —*a.* प्राणिसंबंधिन् &c. 2 चेतन; 'a. food' मांसाहारः; 'a. pleasures' विषयाः, विषयसुखानि; 'a. passions' (carnal) षड् रिपवः-इंद्रियाणि; 'a. kingdom' प्राणिवर्गः.—CULE, *s.* क्षुद्रजंतुः.

ANIMATE, *v. t.* जीव् c., समा-आ-श्वस् c., प्राण् c. 2 प्रोत्सह् c., जीवं संचर् c., उत्तिज् c., उद्युज् 10, पराणुद् c.—ED, *a.* सजीव, चेतन, चर, प्राणिन्. 2 प्रोत्साहित, आश्वासित. 3 प्रफुल्ल, प्रोत्साहनप्रेरित, सारवत् (ती *f.*); 'a. by passion' मदोल्लसित, समद. —ION, *s.* जीवसंचारणं, जीवप्रदानं. 2 प्रोत्साहनं, प्रफुल्लता, उल्लासः. —OR, *s.* प्राणदः, प्रोत्साहकः &c.

ANIMOSITY, *s.* द्वेषः, वैरं, विरोधः, मात्सर्यं.

ANISE, *s.* छत्रा, सालेयः.

ANKLE, *s.* गुल्फः, घुटिका.

ANKLET, *s.* नूपुरः-रं, मंजीरं.

ANNALS, *s.* वार्षिकवृत्तांतः, वार्षिकवृत्तेतिहासः. 2 पुरावृत्तकथा, चरित्राख्यानं. —ANNALIST, *s.* चरित्रलेखकः.

ANNEX, *v. t.* संयुज् 10, अनुबंध् 9 P, उपाधा 3 U; 'Oudh was a. ed to the British territory' अवधदेश आंग्लराज्यांगं कृतः,-राज्येन संयोजितः. 2 अंते निर्दिश् 6 P; 'a list of names is a. ed' नामावली लेखांते दत्ता, नामानि लेखांते निर्दिष्टानि.

-ATION, *s.* संयोजनं, अनुबंधनं; 'a thing annexed' अनुबंधः. -ED, *a.* संयोजित, उपाहित.

ANNIHILATE, *v. t.* उत्-समुत्-छिद् 7 P, उन्मूल् 10, अव-उत्-सद् c., नश् c., विलुप् c. -ION, *s.* उच्छेदः, क्षयः, अवसादनं, विलोपः, विनाशः; प्रलयः (of the world).

ANNIVERSARY, *a.* सांवत्सरिक-वार्षिक (की *f.*).-*s.* सांवत्सरिको विधिः; 'a. of birth' जन्मदिवसः; 'a. of death' मृततिथिः.

ANNOTATE, *v. t.* टीकां-भाष्यं-लिख् 6 P (with gen.), व्याख्या 2 P, व्याचक्ष् 2 A. -ION, *s.* टीका, व्याख्यानं, भाष्यं, टिप्पनी. -OR, *s.* टीकाकारः, टीका-भाष्य-कृत् *m.*

ANNOUNCE, *v. t.* आख्या 2 P or c., निविद् c., विघुष् 10, प्रकाश् c. -ER, *s.* आख्यायकः, संदेशहरः. -MENT, *s.* ख्यापनं, निवेदनं, विघोषणा. 2 वार्ता, समाचारः, संदेशः.

ANNOY, *v. t.* बाध् 1 A, पीड् 10, दु 5 P, *See* AFFLICT. -ANCE, *s.* पीडा, व्यथा, क्लेशः, बाधा, दुःखं; 'a source of a.' कंटकः.-ER, *s.* पीडा-व्यथा-करः.-ING, *a.* बाधक, दुःखप्रद.

ANNUAL, *a.* वार्षिक-सांवत्सरिक-आब्दिक (की *f.*); प्रति°. -LY, *adv.* प्रतिवर्षं, प्रतिसंवत्सरं, वर्षे वर्षे.

ANNUITY, *s.* वार्षिकं वेतनं.

ANNUL, *v. t.* वि-अव-लुप् c., निरस् 4 U, निरर्थक *a.* कृ. -MENT, *s.* लोपः.

ANNULAR, *a.* मंडलाकार, वलयाकार.

ANNULET, *s.* क्षुद्रवलयः-यं.

ANODYNE, *s.* शूलघ्नं.

ANOINT, *v. t.* लिप् 6 P, दिह् 2 U, अंज् 7 P, समालभ् 1 A. 2 अभिषिच् 6 P; 'a. ed as king' राज्येभिषिक्तः. -ER, *s.* अभिषेचकः, विलेपकः.-ING, *s.* विलेपनं, अभ्यंजनं, अभिषेकः-षेचनं, समालंभः.

ANOMALY, *s.* विधि-नियम-विरोधः, अनियमः, व्यभिचारः. -OUS, *a.* विधि-नियम-विरुद्ध, अविधि. -OUSLY, *adv.* अनियमतः, विधिविरुद्धं.

ANON, *adv.* सपदि, शीघ्रं, झटिति; 'ever and a.' मुहुर्मुहुः.

ANONYMOUS, *a.* अविदित-अनिर्दिष्ट-लेखकनामन्, नामसंज्ञा-हीन. -LY, *adv.* नाम विना, नामनिर्देशं विना.

ANOTHER, *a.* अन्य-इतर-पर-अपर, *pron. a.*; or अंतरं in comp.; नगरांतरं 'a. city;' 'in a. place' अन्यत्र; 'in a. manner' अन्यथा; 'at a. time' अन्यदा; 'a. day' अन्येद्युः, परेद्युः; 'one after a.' अनुपूर्वशः, एकैकशः.

ANSWER, *v. i.* उत्तरं दा 3 U or प्रतिपद् 4 A, प्रतिवच् 2 P, प्रतिभाष् 1 A.; he a. ed in the affirmative' बाढं-तथा-इति स प्रत्युवाच. 2 संवद् 1 P, अनुरूप-तुल्य-भू. 3 प्रतिभूः स्था 1 P, प्रातिभाव्यं स्वीकृ, उत्तरं दा 3U.-*v. t.* (a question) कथ् 10, ब्रू 2 U, उत्तरं दा (with gen.); 'a. my letter' मम लेखस्योत्तरं प्रहिणु-प्रेषय. 2 Refute, q. v. 3 कॢप् 1 A (dat.), उपयुक्त *a.* भू; 'this will a. my purpose' अनेन मे प्रयोजनं भवेत्, इदं मे इष्टसिद्धये कल्पेत. -*s.* उत्तरं, प्रतिवचनं, प्रत्युक्ति *f.*, प्रतिवाच् *f.*, प्रत्युत्तरं. -ABLE, *a.* परानुयोगाधीन, प्रष्टव्य.

ANT, *s.* पिपीलिका.-HILL, *s.* वल्मीकः-कं, वामलूरः, कूलकः.

ANTAGONIST, *s.* प्रतिपक्षः, विपक्षः, शत्रुः, वैरिन् *m.*, *See* ENEMY. -IC, *a.* विरुद्ध, विरोधिन् (नी *f.*). -ANTAGONISM, *s.* विरोधः, वैरं.

ANTARCTIC, *a.* दक्षिणकेंद्रीय. -*s.* दक्षिणकेंद्रं.

ANTECEDENT, *a.* पूर्वगामिन् (नी *f.*), पूर्वगत. -*s.* पूर्वचरितं-वृत्तं. 2 पूर्वगामी शब्दः-शब्दसमूहः.

ANTEDILUVIAN, *a.* विश्वप्रलयात् प्राग् वर्तमान, अतिपुराण.

ANTELOPE, *s.* कृष्णसारः, हरिणः, एणः, मृगः, कुरंगः.

ANTERIOR, *a.* प्राक्तन (नी *f.*), पूर्व.

ANTHEM, *s.* ईश्वरस्तुति *f.*, स्तुतिरूपं गीतं.

ANTHROPOPHAGI, *s.* क्रव्याशिनः (pl.), राक्षसाः.

ANTIC, *s.* भंडः, वैहासिकः. -*a.* भंडसदृश (शी *f.*), अयोग्य, असंगत.

ANTICHAMBER, *s.* उपशाला.

ANTICIPATE, *v. t.* पूर्व-प्रागेव-ज्ञा 9 U or निरूप् 10 or ग्रह् 9 P. 2 अग्रतः अनुभू 1 P or भुज् 7 A, पूर्वास्वादनं कृ. -ION, *s.* पूर्वमेव ज्ञानं, पूर्वभुक्ति *f.*, पूर्वास्वादनं.

ANTIDOTE, *s.* विषघ्नोऽगदः, प्रतिविषं; 'a. against anxiety' चिंताविषघ्नोऽगदः, 'dealer in a. s' विषवैद्यः, जांगुलिकः. 2 प्रतिकारः. -AL, *a.* विषघ्न (घ्नी *f.*).

ANTIMONY, *s.* स्रोतोंजनं, यामुनं, सौवीरं.

ANTIPATHY, *s.* विरोधः, वैरं, द्वंद्वभावः, विद्वेषः; 'natural a.' शाश्वतिको विरोधः.

ANTIPHONY, *s.* प्रतिध्वनिः, प्रतिगानं.

ANTIPODES, *s.* प्रतिलोमं; 'living in a' प्रतिलोमाः.

ANTIQUARY,-RIAN, *s.* प्राक्कालीनविषयकोविदः-पंडितः.-*a.* प्राक्कालीन, प्राक्तन (नी *f.*).

ANTIQUATED, ANTIQUE, *a.* प्राचीन, पुरातन-प्राक्तन (नी *f.*), पुराण; (style) अप्रचलित, लुप्तप्रयोग (भाषासरणिः). -ANTIQUITY, *s.* Ancients, q. v. 2 प्राक्कालः, पूर्वकालः. 3 पुरातनत्वं, प्राक्कालीनत्वं.

ANTISEPTIC, *a.* पूतिनाशक.

ANTITHESIS, *s.* प्रातपक्षता, विरोधः, अर्थवैपरीत्यं.

ANTITYPE, *s.* मूलमूर्ति *f.*, आदर्शः.

ANTLER, *s.* हरिणशृंगं, मृगविषाणं. -ED, *a.* शृंगवत् (ती *f.*), विषाणिन् (नी *f.*).

ANUS, *s.* गुदं, अपानं, पायुः.

ANVIL, *s.* शूर्मः-र्मी, स्थूणा.

ANXIETY, *s.* चिंता, उत्कंठा, औत्सुक्यं, व्यग्रता, मनस्तापः, चित्तोद्वेगः, आकुलत्वं, उत्कलिका, रणरणकः. –ANXIOUS, *a.* व्याकुलित, उद्विग्न, उत्कंठित, चिंतापर, व्यग्र. 2 उत्सुक, ईप्सु, सकाम; 'he thus passes a. nights' एवमुद्विग्नस्य यांति रजन्यः; 'to be a. (for)' उत्कंठ् 1 A, उत्सुकायते (D.), उत्तम् 4 P; 'he is a. to see you near' उत्कंठते युष्मत्सन्निकर्षस्य (U. 6.). 3 चिंताप्रद, उद्वेगकर (री *f.*) –LY, *adv.* सोद्वेगं, सोत्कंठं, सचिंतं.

ANY, *a.* Ex. by चित्, चन, or अपि with the forms of किम्; 'a. man' कोपि नरः; 'a. woman' काचित्स्त्री &c., 'at a. time' कदाचित्. 2 (Any whosoever) Ex. by forms of यत् with the above; यः कश्चनागच्छतु 'let a. come'; 'I may be a. one' यो वा को वा भवाम्यहं; 'a. how' कथंचित्, येन केन प्रकारेण, यथा कथंचित्; 'a. longer' पुनः, इतः-अतः-परं; 'a. where' कुत्रापि, क्वचिदपि; 'a. thing' ईषदपि, स्तोकमपि.

APACE, *adv.* सत्वरं, शीघ्रं, *See* QUICKLY.

APART, *adv.* पृथक्; वि-प्र-गत *a.*; 'having knees a.' प्रज्ञुः. 2 निभृतं, रहसि, विजने, एकांते, विविक्ते. 3 दूरे. 4 स्वगतं, जनांतिकं. 'a. from this consideration', 'this consideration a.' इदं कारणं विहाय-त्यक्त्वा, एतदर्थभिन्न *a.*; 'excellence of virtues a., a woman must have modesty at least' गुणसंपत्स्त्रिया मा नाम भवतु, शालीनता पुनरवश्यं स्यादेव. –MENT, *s.* कोष्ठः, शाला, कक्षा, आवासः, सौधं; 'inner a. s' अंतःपुरं, अंतर्वेश्मन् *n.*

APATHY, *s.* औदासीन्यं, उदासीनता, वैराग्यं. –ETIC, *a.* उदासीन. 2 वीतस्पृह-राग, निःस्पृह, निरीह, निरपेक्ष. 3 निरुत्साह.

APE, *s.* वानरः, कपिः, प्लव (वं) गः. 2 अनुकारिन् *m.* –*v. t.* वानरवत् अनुकृ 8 U (gen.). –APISH, *a.* कापेय (यी *f.*), वानरोपम.

APEPSY, अजीर्णं.

APERIENT, *s.* रेचकं, रेचनं.

APERTURE, *s.* छिद्रं, रंध्रं, सूक्ष्मं द्वारं.

APETALOUS, *a.* दलहीन, निष्पत्र, निर्दल.

APEX, *s.* शिखा, चूडा, अग्रं; शिरस् *n.*, मस्तकं.

APHORISM, *s.* सूत्रं, वचनं.

APIARY, *s.* करंडः, आधारः, समुद्गकः.

APIECE, *adv.* एकैकशः, पृथक् पृथक्, एकैकं.

APOCRYPHAL, *a.* संदिग्धप्रमाण.

APOLOGY, *s.* क्षमाप्रार्थना, क्षमायाचना, स्वदोषस्वीकारः. 2 व्यप-अप-देशः; छद्मन् *n.* –IST, *s.* स्वदोषस्वीकारिन् *m.*, व्यपदेष्टृ *m.* –IZE, *v. i.* क्षमां याच् 1 A or प्रार्थ् 10 A, स्वदोषं स्वीकृ-अंगीकृ 8 U. 2 व्यपदिश् 6 P, व्यपदेशं-छद्म-कृ. –APOLOGETIC, *a.* व्यपदेशक.

APOLOGUE, *s.* उपकथा, उपाख्यानं.

APOPHLEGMATIC, *a.* कफनाशन (नी *f.*).

APOPHTHEGM, *s.* सूत्रं, वचनं, नीतिवचनं.

APOPLEXY, *s.* अंगविकृति *f.*, संन्यासः.

APOSTATE, *s.* स्वधर्मत्यागिन् *m.*, स्वधर्मभ्रष्टः-च्युतः, पतितः. –APOSTACY, *s.* स्वधर्मत्यागः, धर्मभ्रंशः, परधर्माश्रयः. –APOSTATIZE, *v. i.* स्वधर्मात् भ्रंश् 1 A, 4 P or पत् 1 P, परधर्ममाश्रि 1 U.

APOSTLE, *s.* ईश्वरप्रेरितः, ईश्वरदूतः.

APOSTROPHE, *s.* संबोधनं. –IZE, *v. t.* संबुध् c., आमंत्र् 10 A.

APOTHECARY, *s.* औषधानां विक्रेतृ *m.*, भेषजविक्रयिन् *m.*

APPALL, *v. t.* सं-वि-त्रस् c., भी c., उद्विज् c., व्याकुलीकृ 8 U; 'he was a. ed with fear' भयेन विवर्णीभूतः; 'a. ing sight' महात्रासजनकं स्थानं.

APPARATUS, *s.* उपकरणं, सामग्री.

APPAREL, *s.* वेशः-षः, वस्त्रं, परिधानं, आभरणं. –*v. t.* वस् c., प्रावृ 5 U, संव्ये 1 P.

APPARENT, *a.* व्यक्त, अभिव्यक्त, स्फुट, स्पष्ट, प्रत्यक्ष, प्रकाश, आविर्भूत. 2 मिथ्या *ind.*, अवास्तव (वी *f.*); 'a. praise' व्याजस्तुति *f.* 3 बाह्य, बहिः in comp.; 'to make a.' आविष्कृ, स्पष्टी-प्रकटीकृ. –LY, *adv.* व्यक्तं, स्पष्टं &c. 2 बहिः; 'a wise man acts a. agreeably' विद्वान् जनो बहीं रमणीयं व्यवहरति (Mal. 1).

APPARITION, *s.* आभासः, छाया, आकारः. 2 वेतालः, पिशाचः.

APPEAL, *v. i.* पुनर्विचारं प्रार्थ् 10 A. 2 प्रमाणीकृ 8 U, प्रमाणयति (D.); or by प्रमाणं; 'I a. to your lordship in this case' अत्र विषयेऽत्रभवंतं प्रमाणीकरोमि, अत्रभवान् प्रमाणं. –*s.* पुनर्विचारप्रार्थना; प्रमाणीकरणं.

APPEAR, *v. i.* उदि 2 P, उद्गम् 1 P, प्रकाश् 1 A, प्रादुर्भू 1 P, आविर्भू. 2 उपस्था 1 U, सन्निधा pass. 3 प्रतिभा 2 P, अवभास् 1 A, दृश् pass., लक्ष् pass.; so as to a. dead' मृतमिवात्मानं संदर्श्य; 'the witness did not a.' साक्षी नोपतस्थौ. –ANCE, *s.* उदयः, प्रादुर्भावः, आविर्भावः. 2 उपस्थिति *f.* 3 आकारः, आकृति *f.*, रूपं; 'good in a.' शोभनाकृति, सुदृश्य, प्रेक्षणीय. 4 आभासः, छाया, आभा; your story has an a. of truth' तव कथा सत्येव प्रतिभाति-अवभासते. 5 अनुमानं.

APPEASE, *v. t.* सां(शां)त्व् 10, प्र-उप्-शम् c. (शमयति), तुष् c., प्रसद् c., अनुनी 1 P; to be a.

ed ' प्रसद् 1 P, प्रशम् 4 P.–ING, *s.* सांत्वनं, प्र-उप-शांति *f.*, प्रसादनं, अनुनयः.

APPELLATION, *s. See* NAME.–APPELLATIVE, *a.* अभिधायिन् (नी *f.*). 2 सामान्य.

APPEND, *v. t.* अनुबंध् 9 P, उपाधा 3 U, आसंज् c. –AGE, *s.* अनुबंधः; उपाहितभागः. 2 उपकरणं. –ED, *a.* संयोजित, उपाहित. –IX, *s.* परिशिष्टं, शेषसंग्रहः.

APPERTAIN, *v. i. See* BELONG. –APPERTENANCE, *s.* अनुबंधः, उपकरणं, उपस्करः, सामग्री.

APPETITE, *s.* कामः, रागः, अभिलाषः, इच्छा, रुचि *f.* 2 बुभुक्षा, क्षुधा-धू *f.*; ' sensual a. ' विषयरुचिः. विषयोपरागः.

APPLAUD, *v. t.* प्रशंस् 1 P, श्लाघ् 1 A, अभिनंद् 1 P, स्तु 2 U. 2 उपगै 1 P.–APPLAUSE, *s.* प्रशंसा, श्लाघा, स्तुति *f.* 2 प्रशंसावाचः (pl.), धन्यवादः; ' he rose to speak amidst loud a. ' उच्चैः प्रशंसावाच उदीरयत्सु श्रोतृषु स वक्तुमुदतिष्ठत्.–APPLAUSIVE, *a.* श्लाघान्वित; स्तुतिमय (यी *f.*).

APPLE, *s.* आताम्रक्षः,-फलं. 2 (Of the eye) तारा, कनीनिका; ' a. of discord भेद-कलह-बीजं.

APPLY, *v. t.* संयुज् 10, न्यस् 4 P, ऋ c. (अर्पयति). निविश् c., निधा 3 U, आरुह् c.; ' a. your shoulder to the wheel ' चक्रमंसेन उत्तंभय; ' a. ing the hand to my shoulder ' अंसे हस्तं निवेश्य &c. 2 विधा 3 U; प्रयुज् 7 A, 10; ' they do not a. the word विषय to happiness ' सुखार्थे विषयशब्दं न प्रयुंजते, -शब्दस्य प्रयोगो न दृश्यते. 3 आश्रि 1 U; याच् 1 A, अर्थ् 10 A. 4 (Oneself to) अनुष्ठा 1 P, मनः-चित्तं-समाधा, or बंध् 9 P, अभियुज् pass. (एते वयं स्वकर्मण्यभियुज्यामहे Mu. 3). – *v. i.* लग् 1 P, सं-अनु-बंध् 9 P. 2 प्रयुज् pass., उपपद् 4 A; oft. by गम् 1 P, इ 2 P; ' this our title does not a. to any one else ' द्वितीयगामी न हि शब्द एष नः (R. III. 49); राम इत्ययं शब्द उच्चारित एव मामगात् (R. XI. 73); विषय in comp.; ' the word ईश्वर not a. ing to anybody else ' ईश्वर इत्यनन्यविषयः शब्दः (V. 1). 3 (to, for) याच् 1 A, प्र-अभि-अर्थ् 10 A; ' a. ed for further orders' कोपरो नियोगोनुष्ठीयतामिति प्रार्थयामास–APPLIANCE, *s.* उपायः, उपकरणं, सामग्री.–APPLICATION, *s.* योजनं, विधानं, प्रयोगः, संप्रयोगः, निवेशनं, न्यासः, अर्पणं. 2 मनोनियोगः, चित्तासक्ति *f.*, अभ्यसनं, अध्यवसायः, अभिनिवेशः, आसक्ति *f.*, अनुष्ठानं. 3 उपयोगः, प्रयोजनं. 4 संबंधः; ' a. of this speech to Râma' अस्य वचनस्य रामगामी संबंधः. 5 प्रार्थना. –APPLICABLE, *a.* लगत् (न्ती *f.*), प्रयोज्य. 2 संगत, संबद्ध.–APPLICANT, *s.* प्रार्थयितृ *m.*, अर्थिन् *m.*, याचकः, प्रणयिन् *m.*

APPOINT, *v. t.* युज् 7 U, 10, स्था c. (स्थापयति), निधा 3 U. 2 अधिकृ, नियुज् 7 A (with loc.) य इमामाश्रमधर्मे नियुंक्ते (S. 1); व्यादिश् 6 P. 3 निर्दिश् 6 P, निरूप् 10; ' a. ed lesson ' निर्दिष्टपाठः ; ' a. ed time ' कृतः कालावधिः, कृतसंकेतः, समयः. –MENT, *s.* नियोगः, अधिकारः, पदं. 2 नियमः, विधिः, आज्ञा, शासनं. 3 उपकरणं. 4 निरूपणं, स्थापनं. 5 समयः, संकेतः ; ' keep your a. ' समयमनुरुध्यस्व-वर्तस्व ; ' Queen, let us keep (to) our a. ' देवि सामयिका भवामः (M. 1.).

APPORTION, *See* DIVIDE.

APPOSITE, *a.* युक्त, यथार्थ, संगत. –LY, *adv.* स्थाने, यथार्थतः.

APPOSITION, *s.* समानाधिकरणं, एकान्वयः.

APPRAISE, *v. t.* (goods) (मूल्यं) निरूप् 10, निर्धृ 10. –ER, *s.* मूल्यनिरूपकः.

APPRECIATE, *v. t.* (गुणागुणं) ज्ञा 9 U, अवगम् 1 P, ग्रह् 9 P, विविच् 7 P; ' appreciator of merits ' गुणग्रहीता, गुणज्ञः, मर्मज्ञः. 2 बहु मन् 4 A. – ION, *s.* गुणग्रहणं, गुणागुणज्ञानं-विवेचनं.

APPREHEND, *v. t.* ग्रह् 9 P, परामृश् 6 P, आसिध् 1 P, आक्रम् 1 U, 4 P, धृ 1 P. 2 आ-वि-परि-शंक् 1 A. 3 मन् 4 A, शंक् 1 A; तर्क् 10, ऊह् 1 U, अनुमा 3 A. 4 अव-अधि-गम् 1 P, उपलभ् 1 A. –APPREHENSION, *s.* ग्रहणं, आसेधः; आ-वि-परिशंका, अनुमानं, तर्क, मति *f.*, बुद्धि *f.*; 'of quick a.' तीक्ष्णमति; ' of dull a. ' मंदधी, स्थूलबुद्धि. –APPREHENSIVE, *a.* आशंकमान, शंकित; ' a. of danger ' भयमाशंकमानः.

APPRENTICE, *s.* शिल्पविद्याशिष्यः, अंतेवासिन् *m.*, शिष्यः. –SHIP, *s.* सेवाकालः.

APPRISE (of) *See* INFORM.

APPROACH, *v. t.* उप-समुप-अभि-गम् 1 P, °इ-या 2 P, °सृ-सृप् 1 P; समीपं-निकटे गम् (with gen.). –*v. i.* उप-समुपा-स्था 1 U, °गम्; प्रत्यासद् 1 P. –*s.* आगमः, अवतारः, उपस्थिति *f.*; ' a. of night ' दोषागमः, रजन्युपस्थितिः. 2 संनिकर्षः, आसन्नता. 3 प्रवेशः, उपसर्पणमार्गः. –ING, *a.* आसन्न; ' his death a. ' आसन्नमरणे तस्मिन्; संनिकृष्ट, समुपस्थित. –ABLE, *a.* उपसर्पणीय, समुपगम्य.

APPROPRIATE, *v. t.* आत्मसात् कृ 8 U, स्वाधीनस्वायत्त.–*a.* कृ. 2 प्र-विनि-उप- युज् 7 A, 10, उपक्लृप् c. –*a.* उपपन्न, संगत, उचित, युक्त; ' a. to the occasion ' प्रस्तावसदृशं. 2 स्वकीय. –LY, *adv.* उपपन्नं, युक्तं, स्थाने, यथार्थतः. –ION, *s.* आत्मसात्करणं; विनियोगः, उपकल्पनं.

APPROVE, *v. t.* अनुमुद् 1 A, अनु-सं-मन् 4 A, प्रशंस् 1 P, अभि-प्रति-नंद् 1 P, रुच् 1 A ; एतयोर्विवाद एव मे न रोचते (M. 1) ' I do not a. of their very quarrel '; ' I do not a. of your speech ' न ते वचोऽभिनंदामि (S. 2). 2 प्रमाणयति (D.), विभू c. -AL, s. अनुमोदनं, अभिनंदनं; संमति f., प्रशंसा; ' he got the a. of his mother ' मात्रानुमोदितः. -ED, a. संमत, प्रशस्त &c., परीक्षित. -APPROBATION, s. सं-अनु-मति f. 2 साधु-धन्य-वादः, प्रशंसा.

APPROXIMATE, v. t. उपनी 1 P, उपस्था c. (स्थापयति). -v. i. समीपं-निकटं-वृत् 1 A, आसन्न a. भू, See APPROACH. 2 Resemble, q. v. -a. समीप, आसन्न, संनिकृष्ट; ' a. to 10 ' आसन्नदशाः. -ION, s. आसन्नता, उपगमः &c.

APRIL, s. चैत्रः, मधुमासः, वैशाखः.

APRON, s. (मलनिवारणार्थं) कटिप्रच्छदः, मलवस्त्रं.

APROPOS, adv. अनुरूपं, यथा in comp.

APT, a. उचित, योग्य, युक्त. 2 Ex. by शील in comps., प्राय: with pot. pass. part.; ' youths are a. to forget ' युवानो विस्मरणशीलाः; ' lazy boys are a. to be bad boys ' अलसैर्बालकैः प्रायो दुर्वृत्तैर्भवितव्यं; ' over-affection is a. to suspect evil ' अतिस्नेहः पापशंकी (S. 4); आलु in comp.; ' a. to take pity ' दयालुः; ' a. to break ' भंगुर. 3 दक्ष, कुशल, अभिज्ञ, See SKILFUL. 4 त्वरित. चपल, उत्सुक. -ITUDE, s. योग्यता, पात्रता, औचित्यं. 2 °शीलता, स्वभावः, शीलं. -LY, adv. यथोचितं, यथोपपन्नं, स्थाने, चातुर्येण, सकौशलं. -NESS, s. योग्यता; कौशलं, पाटवं. 2 शक्ति f., सामर्थ्यं.

AQUATIC, a. जल in comp., जलोद्भव, वारिचर; ' a. animal ' जलजंतुः, यादस् n. 2 जलचर, जलज, वारिज.

AQUEDUCT. s. जलप्रणाली, जलमार्गः, परीवाहः.

AQUEOUS, a. जलमय (यी f.), अम्मय, सजल, अनूप.

AQUILINE, a. शुकसदृश (शी f.); वक्र, कुंचित; ' having an a. nose ' शुकनासः.

ARABLE, a. कर्षणीय, कृषियोग्य.

ARBITER, s. मध्यस्थः; निर्णेतृ m., प्रमाणपुरुषः. 2 ईशः, प्रभुः. -ARBITRATE, v. विचर् c., निर्णी 1 P; मध्यस्थतां गृहीत्वा निर्णी or परिच्छिद् 7 P. -ION, s. मध्यस्थकृतनिर्णयः; विचारणं, निर्णयः. 2 माध्यस्थ्यं. -OR, s. मध्यस्थः, निर्णेतृ m., विचारकः.

ARBITRARY, a. स्वेच्छाचारिन् (णी f.), कामचारिन्, स्वच्छंद, स्वैरवृत्त. 2 अनियंत्रण, उद्दाम. 3 चपल, अविहित. -LY, adv. स्वेच्छया, स्वकामतः, स्वैरं, निर्यंत्रणं.

ARBOUR, s. लतागृहं, निकुंजः-जं, पर्णशाला.

ARC, s. वृत्तखंडं, धनुस् n.

ARCADE, s. छत्रपथः-मार्गः, गूढमार्गः.

ARCH, s. खंडमंडलं, वृत्तखंडं ; ' a. of heaven ' नभोमंडलं. 2 तोरणः-णं. -v. t. मंडलीकृ; तोरणरूपेण निर्मा 3 A, गोलाकारेण आच्छद् 10 ; a. ed सतोरण, न्यस्ततोरण; भुग्न, कुंचित, वक्र, तोरणाकार. -a. विदग्ध, धूर्त, चतुर; मुख्य, श्रेष्ठ, उत्तम, प्रधान, अग्रणी; ' a. fiend ' पिशाचाग्रणीः; ' a. angel ' प्रधानदूतः; ' a. bishop ' मुख्यो धर्माध्यक्षः.

ARCHAISM, s. प्राचीन-आर्ष-प्रयोगः.

ARCHAIOLOGY, s. पुराणवस्तुशास्त्रं.

ARCHER, s. धन्विन् m., धानुष्कः, इषुधरः, निषंगिन् m., धनुर्धरः. -Y, s. धनुर्विद्या, शराभ्यासः, धनुर्वेदः.

ARCHETYPE, s. मूलरूपं, आदर्शः.

ARCHITECT, s. स्थपतिः, शिल्पिन् m ; ' man is the a. of his own fortune ' लोके गुरुत्वं विपरीततां वा स्वचेष्टितान्येव नरं नयंति (H. 2). -URE, s. शिल्पं, वस्तुनिर्माणकौशलं, निर्माणशिल्पं.

ARCHIVES, s. ग्रंथरक्षागारं. 2 पुरावृत्तं.

ARCTIC, a. उत्तर, उदीचीन, उत्तरकेंद्रीय.

ARDENT, a. उत्तप्त, प्रचंड, उत्कट, उत्सुक, कुतूहलिन्, उत्साहिन् (नी f.), व्यग्र ; ' a. love ' निरतिशयोनुरागः ; ' a. looks ' सतृष्णा दृष्टिः. - LY, adv. उत्कटं, सतृष्णं, सानुरागं. -ARDOUR, s. उत्तापः, अत्यंतता, निरतिशयः, अतिरेकः, उत्कटता, उत्साहः, व्यग्रता, कुतूहलं, औत्सुक्यं.

ARDUOUS, a. दुष्कर, यत्नसाध्य, दुःसाध्य, सु-अति-दुष्कर. 2 प्रांशु, दुरारोह, उच्च.

AREA, s. फलं ; ' a. of a field ' क्षेत्रफलं. 2 अंगणं-नं ; ' inner a. ' प्रकोष्ठः.

ARENA, s. रंगः, रंगभूमि f., मल्लभूः.

ARGENT, a. राजत (ती f.), रौप्य (प्यी f.).

ARGUE, v. i. तर्क् 10, ऊहापोहं कृ 8 U, विचर् c., विवेचनं कृ. 2 विवद् 1 A, वादे उत्तरप्रत्युत्तरं कृ. -v. t. प्रमाणेन -तर्केण सिध् c. (साधयति), प्रमाणयति (D.), युक्तिवादेन सिध् c. ; युक्त्या तर्क् 10, ऊह् 1 A. -ER, s. तर्किन् m., विचारकः, वादिन् m. -ARGUMENT, s. युक्ति f., उपपत्ति f. 2 पक्षः, प्रमाणं, हेतुः, न्यायः, वितर्कः ; 'a wrong a.' पक्षाभासः, हेत्वाभासः. 3 वादानुवादः, विवादः, वाक्कलहः. 4 विषयः, अनुक्रमणिका. -ATIVE, a. तार्किक (की f.), तर्कानुबद्ध. न्यायानुसारिन् (णी f.), उपपत्तिमत् (ती f.). 2 वादशील, विवादप्रिय. -LY, adv. सोपपत्तिकं, सवितर्कं, युक्तिवादेन.

ARID, a. शुष्क, आतपाक्रांत; ' a. soil ' मरुः, मरुस्थलं-ली.

ARIGHT, adv. युक्तं, यथातथं, यथास्थानं, सम्यक्, यथार्हं.

ARISE, v. i. उत्था 1 P ; उत्पद् 4 A, उत्-प्र-सं-भू 1 P, प्रजन् 4 A, प्रवृत् 1 A ; उदि 2 P, उद्गम् 1 P; आविः-प्रादुः-भू, विनिः-प्र-सृ 1 P ; ' a. ing from ' ex. by ज, भव, उद्भव, प्रभव, in comp. ; स्मरजा पीडा ' torment a. ing from love ' ; यौवन-

प्रभवं तमः &c. ; oft. by उत्थ, समुत्थ ; नयनसमुत्थं ज्योतिः.

ARISTOCRACY, *s.* कुलीन-विशिष्ट-जनाः. 2 शिष्टजनसत्ताकं राज्यं.—ARISTOCRATIC, *a.* कुलीन. अभिजात.

ARITHMETIC, *s.* अंकविद्या-गणितं, परिकर्मन् *n.* —IAN, *s.* अंकविद्याज्ञः, गणकः.

ARK, *s.* नौ *f.*, तरणी, पोतः. 2 आधारः, कोषः.

ARM, *s.* बाहुः, भुजः, भुजा, दोस् *m. n.*; 'fore-a.' प्रकोष्ठः. 2 शाखा. 3 नदीवंकः, वक्रं. 4 शक्ति *f.*, बलं, वीर्यं; 'got by one's own a.' स्वभुजवीर्येण लब्धं, भुजोपार्जितं. —*v. t.* सन्नह् c., सज्जीकृ 8 U, अस्त्रैः संयुज् 10, सायुध *a.* कृ. —*v. i.* सन्नह् 4 U, सज्जीभू 1 P. —s अस्त्रं, शस्त्रं, आयुधः-धं, शस्त्रास्त्रं. 2 विग्रहः, रणसमयः, संग्रामः, युद्धं; 'taking up a.' युद्धारंभः; 'passage of a.' अस्त्रविद्या. —ED, सायुध, सन्नद्ध, सज्ज; 'a. with a sword' सखड्गः. —LESS, *a.* अभुज, अशस्त्र, अनायुध. —PIT, —HOLE, *s.* कक्षाक्षः, बाहुमूलं, भुजकोटरः-रं, दोर्मूलं. —LET, केयूरः-रं, अंगदः-दं. 2 क्षुद्रबाहुः, उपशाखा.

ARMADA, *s.* बृहन्नौसाधनं.

ARMAMENT, *s.* बलं, सज्जीकृतं बलं, युद्धोपकरणानि.

ARMISTICE, *s.* युद्धविरति *f.*, संधिः, युद्धनिवर्त्तनं (नियतकालं यावत्).

ARMOUR, *s.* वर्मन् *n.*, कवचः-चं, कंचुकः, सन्नाहः, तनुवारं, तनुत्रं-त्राणं. 'a. for the head' शिरस्त्राणं. —ER, *s.* शस्त्रकारः, अस्त्रकारः. —Y, *s.* आयुधागारं, शस्त्रगृहं. 2 शस्त्रसमूहः.

ARMY, *s.* सेना, सैन्यं, बलं, वाहिनी, चमूः, अनीकं, पृतना, दंडः-डं; 'full a.' चतुरंगं बलं, अक्षौहिणी.

AROMA, *s.* गंधः, आमोदः, परिमलः. —TIC, *a.* सुरभि, सुगंधि. 2 सुरभित; a. s सुगंधिद्रव्याणि. —TIZE, *v. t.* वास् 10.

AROUND, *prep.* परितः, अभितः, (with acc.). —*adv.* समंततः, सर्वतः, विष्वक्, समंतात्.

AROUSE, *v. t.* (From sleep) जागृ c., प्रबुध् c. 2 उत्-प्रोत्-सह् c., उत्तिज् c., उत्था c. (उत्थापयति); उद्बुध् c., जन् c. (जनयति).

ARRAIGN, *v. t.* *See* ACCUSE.

ARRANGE, *v. t.* रच् 10, घट् c., वि-उह् 1 U; संविधा 3 U, विनि-अस् 4 U, स्था c. (स्थापयति); 'well a. ed' सुघटित; 'a. in order' यथाक्रमं रच्, संविधा c. &c. 2 (Settle) उपक्लृप् c., निर्णी 1 P; 'I have a. ed to pay his debts' तस्य ऋणं कथं प्रतिदेयमिति मया निर्णीतं-आलोचितं. —MENT, *s.* रचना, विन्यासः. संविधा. व्यूहनं. क्रमेण स्थापनं, परिपाटि-टी *f.*, क्रमः; 'a. of plot' वस्तुरचना, संविधानकं; सरणि-णी *f.* 2 निर्णयः; 'all a. s for his reception are complete' सर्वास्तत्संभावनासंविधा उपकल्पिताः.

ARRANT, *a.* अत्यंत, भृश, अति pr. 2 अतिनिंद्य, अतिदुष्ट, निकृष्ट.

ARRAY, *s.* व्यूहः, रचनं, विन्यासः, क्रमः, श्रेणि-णी *f.*, पंक्ति *f.* 2 वेषः, आभरणं, परिच्छदः. —*v. t.* क्रमेण रच् 10, सज्जीकृ 8 U. 2 भूष् 10, अलंकृ; वस्त्रेण आच्छद् 10; 'he was richly a. ed' स महार्घवस्त्रभूषितः-वस्त्राणि पर्यधत्त.

ARREAR, *s.* अवशिष्टदेयं, ऋणशेषं, अशोधितो भागः; 'clear up all a. s' सर्वमवशिष्टदेयं परिशोधय; 'his pay remained in a. s' यथावसरमदत्तत्वात्तस्य वेतनं समुचितं.

ARREST, *v. t.* निरुध् 7 U, ग्रह् 9 P. आसिध् 1 P. बंध् 9 P, धृ 1 P, 10; ऋणहेतोः राजाज्ञया धृ 10. 2 निवृत् c., स्तंभ् 9 P or c. (निवर्तयामास नृपस्य दृष्टिं (R. II. 28); 'the Chitrakuta mountain a. s my eye' बध्नाति मे चक्षुश्चित्रकूटः (R. XIII. 47); 'a. attention' अनन्यमनः *a.* कृ 8 U, अनन्यचित्त *a.* कृ. —*s.* निरोधः, आसेधः, ग्रहणं, धरणं, बंधनं.

ARRIVE, *v. i.* प्र-संप्र-अनुप्र-आप् 5 P, आ-समा-सद् 1 P, अभि-उपा-गम् 1 P, उपस्था 1 U, प्रपद् 4 A (यौवनदशां प्रपेदे). —AL, *s.* आगमनं, उपस्थिति *f.* &c.

ARROGANCE, *s.* औद्धत्यं, दर्पः, अभिमानः. अहंकारः, गर्वः, मदः. अवलेपः, प्रागल्भ्यं, उत्सेकः, आटोपः. —ARROGANT, *a.* उद्धत, दृप्त, अहंकारयुक्त, प्रगल्भ, समद, गर्वित, अवलिप्त, उत्सिक्त, मानिन् (नी *f.*); 'a. lady' मानिनी प्रमदा. —LY, *adv.* उद्धतं, सावलेपं, सदर्पं &c.

ARROGATE, *v. t.* सगर्वं-अन्यायेन-ग्रह् 9 P or स्वायत्तीकृ 8 U or आदा 3 A. —ION, *s.* अन्यायग्रहणं, उपधा.

ARROW, *s.* शरः, बाणः, सायकः, इषुः, कांडं, भल्लः, नाराचः, मार्गणः, शिलीमुखः, विशिखः. —Y, *a.* बाणवत् (ती *f.*) &c.; बाणाकार.

ARSENAL, *s.* आयुधागारं, शस्त्रगृहं. 2 शस्त्रास्त्रसमूहः.

ARSENIC, *s.* मल्लः, फेनाश्मन् *m.*; मनःशिला.

ART, *s.* शिल्पं, शिल्पविद्या, कला, व्यवसायः; नाट्यकला 'a. of dancing'. 2 कल्पना, विद्या (science). 3 निपुणता, युक्ति *f.*, कौशलं; साधनं; 'a. s of life' जीवनसाधनानि. 4 व्याजः, कपटं. माया, वैदग्ध्यं, चातुर्यं. —FUL, *a.* चतुर; 'a. look' चतुरो दृष्टिक्षेपः; विदग्ध, मायावत् (ती *f.*). 2 शिल्पेन कृत. 3 निपुण, कुशल. —FULNESS, *s.* चातुर्यं, वैदग्ध्यं. &c.—LESS, *a.* ऋजु, अमाय, अकृतक, अकृत्रिम, अव्याज; 'a. ly lovely body' अव्याजमनोहरं वपुः (S. 1.). —LESSNESS, *s.* सरलता, अमायिता, अकृतकता, आर्जवं.—ARTIFICE *s.* उपायः, छलं, छद्मन् *n.*, व्यपदेशः, कपटं, व्याजः.—ARTIFICER, *s.* शिल्पिन् *m.*, कर्मशिल्प-कारः. 2 कर्तृ *m.*, निर्मातृ *m.* —ARTIFICIAL, *a.* कृत्रिम, कृतक; सव्याज. 2 शिल्पनिर्मित; 'a. mountain' क्रीडापर्वतः. –ARTIZAN, ARTIST, *s.* शिल्पिन् *m.*, चित्रकरः. 2 पंडितः. निपुणः.

ARTERY, *s.* धमनी, रक्तवाहिनी.

ARTICLE, *s.* द्रव्यं, वस्तु *n.*, सामग्री. 2 विषयः, पदं, भागः. 3 समयः, समयपत्रं.

ARTICULATE, *a.* स्पष्ट, परिस्फुट, व्यक्त. –*v. t.* स्पष्टं-स्फुटं-उच्चर् c. or उदीर् 10. 2 ग्रंथ् 9 P, संयुज् 10, संधा 3 U. –NESS, *s.* स्पष्टता, स्फुटता ; 'a. in uttering syllables' वर्णोच्चारणे स्पष्टता: 'utters articulate sounds' परिस्फुटाक्षरां गिरमुदीरयति (Ka. 13). –ION, *s.* उच्चारणं &c. 2 संधानं.

ARTILLERY, *s.* अग्न्यस्त्राणि; युद्धास्त्राणि.

As, *conj.*, *adv.* Ex. by वत्, इव; मातृवत्-मातरमिव-परदारान्पश्य. 2 यथा, यद्वत्, अनुरूपं-पेण; यथा in comp. (यथोक्तं कथय); 'as-so' यथा-तथा with or without एव; 'as-as' यथैव-तथैव (यथैव शांता तथैव सीता दशरथस्य प्रिया (U. 4); 'as-since-therefore' तथा-तथा, यतः-ततः, यत्-तत्; 'as for instance.' यथा (यथा महानसे), or तथाहि. 2 (On account of) ex. by abl. or instr. of noun. 3 (While) यावत्-तावत् ; or by pres. part. ; 'as he was going, he thought' गच्छन् स इत्थं मनसि चकार ; 'as high as' दघ्न (घ्नी *f.*), मात्र, in comp. ; 'water as high as the knee' जानुदघ्नं जलं ; ऊरुमात्रा भित्तिः &c. ; 'as soon as' यावत्-तावत् ; or loc. abs. constr. with मात्र or एव ; 'as he had spoken' उक्तवत्येव तस्मिन् ; 'as before.' यथापुरा, यथापूर्वं, पूर्ववत् ; 'as far as' यावत् with acc., आ with abl. or in comp., (आसमुद्रक्षितीशानां) ; 'as if,' 'as it were' इव ; oft. by मन् 4 A ; 'as if the city had been a large tank' नगरं महाकासारं मन्यमानः ; 'as follows' इति (इति वक्तुं प्रचक्रमे). or ex. by यथा-यत् at the beginning of narratives ; 'it is as follows' तद्यथा ; 'as to,' 'as for' तु, तावत्, इति, अधिकृत्य, उद्दिश्य ; 'as for merits, he has none' गुणास्तावत्तस्य नैव विद्यंते ; 'as for doing it quickly it is easy' शीघ्रमिति सुकरं (निभृतमिति तु चिंतनीयं S. 3); 'as well as' च-च ; 'as many as' 'as much as' यावत् (ती *f.*)-तावत् (ती *f.*); 'as yet' अद्यापि, अद्य यावत्. 4 (Connecting words in apposition) ex. by इति; स बंधुरिति मतः, बंधुर्मतः ; 'as a father he respects me' पितेति मां स मानयति.

ASCEND, *v. i.* उदि 2 P, उद्गम् 1 P. –*v. t.* आ-अधि-रुह् 1 P, आ-अधि-क्रम् 1 U, 4 P, (with acc.) ; 'a. ed the throne' राजपदमवाप, सिंहासनमारुरोह. –ANT, *a.* आधिरोहिन् (णी *f.*). 2 प्रधान, प्रबल, उत्तम. –*s.* उच्चता, उच्छ्रायः. 2 प्राधान्यं, प्राबल्यं, प्रभुत्वं ; 'his stars are in the a.' तस्य जन्मग्रहाः उच्चसंश्रयाः. –ANCY, *s.* प्रभुत्वं, प्राधान्यं, प्राबल्यं. –ASCENT, *s.* आरोहणं, उद्गमः, उदयः, समुत्थानं, अधिरोहणं. 2 अधिरोहणमार्गः, सोपानं; 'difficult of a.' दुरारोह.

ASCERTAIN, *v. t.* ज्ञा 9 U, ज्ञा desid. (जिज्ञासते), निरूप् 10, उपलभ् 1 A. 2 निर्णी 1 P, अवनिर्-धृ 10, निश्चि 5 U, व्यवसो 4 P ; 'I shall a. accurately (the truth) about her' तत्त्वत एनामुपलप्स्ये (S. 1.) ; 'for a. ing time' वेलोपलक्षणार्थं (S. 4.) ; –MENT, *s.* निरूपणं, अवनिर्-धारणं, निर्णयः.

ASCETIC, *s.* यतिः, योगिन् *m.*, तापसः, तपस्विन् *m.*, मुनिः, वानप्रस्थः, संन्यासिन् *m.* –ISM, *s.* वैराग्यं, संन्यासः.

ASCRIBE, *v. t.* निक्षिप् 6 P, अध्या-आ-रुह् c., (रोपयति), कारणत्वेन संबंध् 9 P; 'a. the defeat to my weakness' मम दौर्बल्यात् पराजयः संभूतः, दौर्बल्यं पराभवस्य कारणं, इति वदंति; 'a. every thing to Fate' दैवायत्तं सर्वमिति वदंति ; 'to whom shall I a. the blame' कस्मिन् दोषं निक्षिपामि, कं दोषपक्षे स्थापयामि ; पापं कर्म च यत्परैरपि कृतं तत्तस्य संभाव्यते (Mr. I) 'is a. ed to him' &c.

ASHAMED, *a.* ह्रीण, ह्रीत, लज्जमान, त्रपान्वित, लज्जित, व्रीडित, त्रपित, (with instr.) ; 'to be a.' लज्ज् 6 A. ह्री 3 P, त्रप् 1 A.

ASHES, *s.* भस्मन् *n.*, भसितं, पांशुः, भूति *f.*; 'to reduce to a.' भस्मावशेष *a.* कृ 8 U, भस्मी-भस्मसात्-कृ ; 'to be reduced to a.' भस्मी-भू 1 P ; 'reducing to a.' भस्मीकरणं. –ASHY, *a.* पांशुवर्ण, धूसर ; 'a. pale' विवर्णवदनः. 2 भस्मलिप्त, भस्मीकृत.

ASHORE, *adv.* तीरे, तटे, उत्तीर, तटस्थ *a.*

ASIDE, *adv.* एकपार्श्वे ; पार्श्वतः. 2 निभृतं, एकांते; जनांतिकं, अपवार्य 'a. to one's self' आत्मगतं, स्वगतं.

ASK, *v. t.* याच् 1 A, अर्थ् 10 A, भिक्ष् 1 A. 2 अनुयुज् 7 A, प्रच्छ् 6 P, (all governing two acc.) –ING. *s.* प्रार्थना, याचना. 2 अनुयोगः, पृच्छा.

ASKANCE, ASKEW, ASLANT, *adv.* तिर्यक्, साचि ; 'looking a.' साचिविलोकिन्-अपांगदर्शिन् (नी *f.*).

ASLEEP, *a.* सुप्त, शयित, निद्रित, निद्रालस ; 'he fell a.' स निद्रावशं गतः ; 'fast a.' गाढसुप्तः, गाढनिद्रावशं गतः.

ASLOPE, *adv.* प्रवण *a.*; प्रवणं.

ASPECT, *s.* रूपं, आकारः, आकृति *f*; 'a gloomy a.' विषण्णाकृतिः; 'he had a cheerful a.' तस्य

वदनं हर्षोत्फुल्लं बभौ. 2 अवस्था, दशा ; 'all things wore a different a.' सर्वं विभिन्नावस्थायामवर्तत, विपर्यासं यातं. 3 अवस्थानं; 'my house has a northerly a.' उदगभिमुखं मे गृहं. 4 दर्शनं, निरीक्षणं, संबंधः.

ASPERITY, *s.* तीव्रता, रौक्ष्यं, तैक्ष्ण्यं, कर्कशता. 2 विषमता, असमानत्वं.

ASPERSE, *v. t.* अधिक्षिप् 6 P, परिवद् 1 U, *See* CENSURE. 2 सिच् 6 P, उक्ष् 1 P. –ION, *s.* आक्षेपः, निंदा &c. 2 सेकः, प्रोक्षणं.

ASPIRE, *v. i.* स्पृह् 10 (with dat.). आ-अभि-कांक्ष् 1 U, आप् desid. (ईप्सति), प्रार्थ् 10 A, अभिलष् 1, 4 P. –ING, *a.* –ANT, *s.* आकांक्षिन्-अभिलाषिन् (णी *f.*), ईप्सु ; 'a. to the throne' राजपदाभिलाषी ; 'a. to the fame of a poet' कवियशःप्रार्थी (R. I. 3) ; जनोयमुच्चैःपदलंघनोत्सुकः (K. V. 64). –ATION, *s.* स्पृहा, आकांक्षा, ईप्सा, अभिलाषः, लालसा; 'high a.' महाकांक्षा; 'these are, indeed, high a. s' दूरारूढाः-दूराधिरोहिण्यः खलु एता आकांक्षाः.

ASPIRATE, *s.* महाप्राणः.

ASS, *s.* गर्दभः, खरः, रासभः; 'a. headed' मंदधी, खरबुद्धि. –ASININE, *a.* रासभीय, खरसंबंधिन् (नी *f.*). [सहस्रवेधि *n.*

ASSAFŒTIDA, *s.* हिंगु *n.*, जतुकं, बाह्लीकं, रामठं,

ASSAIL, *v. t.* *See* ATTACK; 'the character of the king is a. ed' दोषैर्नृपः स्पृश्यते (Mr. 9). –ANT, *s.* अभियोक्तृ *m.*, आक्रामकः.

ASSASSIN, *s.* घातकः, हंतृ *m.*, उपांशुघातकः, प्राणहारकः. –ATE, *v. t.* हन् c. (घातयति), मृ c., व्यापद् c., निभृतं हन् 2 P, वध-हत्यां-कृ (with gen.). –ATION, *s.* वधः, घातः, उपांशु-निभृत-वधः.

ASSAULT, *v. t., s.* *See* ATTACK.

ASSAY, *s.* परीक्षा, निकषः. 2 प्रारंभः, प्रथमा प्रवृत्ति *f.* –*v. t.* परीक्ष् 1 A, प्रयत् 1 A, *See* ATTEMPT.

ASSEMBLE, *v. i.* समागम् 1 P, संमिल् 6 P, समुद्-समा-समभि-इ 2 P, संनिपत् 1 P, संगम् 1 A, एकीभू, एकत्र इ, संकुलीभू. –*v. t.* c. of roots above; समा-समुपा-हृ 1 P, एकत्र कृ 8 U. –ASSEMBLY, *s.* सभा, सदस् *f.*, *n.*, समाजः, संसद् *f.*, परिषद् *f.*; 'a. house' सभागृहं, गोष्ठीस्थानं; 'a. hall' आस्थानमंडपः-गृहं, आस्थानी-नं; 'a. room' इंद्रकं, आस्थानं. –ASSEMBLAGE, *s.* समूहः, संघातः, समाहारः, समुच्चयः, वृंदं, चयः, समुदायः, निवहः, समवायः, गणः, ओघः, संघः, ग्रामः in comp.; 'a. of kings' राजकं.

ASSENT, *v. i.* अनुज्ञा 9 U, अनुमन् 4 A. 2 ग्रह् 9 ,P अंगीकृ 8 U, स्वीकृ, अभ्युप-गम् 1 P, ॰इ 2 P. –*s.* संमति *f.*, अनुमति *f.*, अनुज्ञा, अनुमोदनं. 2 अंगीकारः, अभ्युपगमः.

ASSERT, *v. t.* प्रतिपद् c., *See* AFFIRM. –ION, *s.* वचनं ; प्रतिज्ञा, पूर्वपक्षः.

ASSESS, *v. t.* देयं करं निरूप् 10 or निर्धृ 10 or दा c. (दापयति). –MENT, *s.* करनिर्धारणं; राजस्वग्रहणं. 2 करः, बलिः, शुल्कः-ल्कं, राजस्वं. –OR, *s.* सभ्यः, सभासद् *m.* 2 कर-शुल्क-ग्राहिन् *m.*

ASSETS, *s.* विभवः, संपद् *f.*

ASSEVERATE, *v. i.* सप्रतिज्ञं-सशपथं-वद् 1 P.–ION, *s.* शपथपूर्वकं वचनं, दृढोक्ति *f.*

ASSIDUITY, ASSIDUOUSNESS, *s.* व्यवसायः, उद्यमः, तत्परता, अभियोगः, उद्योगः, मनोयोगः, प्रसक्ति *f.* –ASSIDUOUS, *a.* उद्यमिन्-व्यवसायिन्-उद्योगिन् (नी *f.*); तत्पर, सोद्योग, प्रसक्त, परायण, अभियोगवत् (ती *f.*). –LY, *adv.* तत्परतया, साभियोगं, सोद्योगं. अविरतं. प्रसक्तं, प्रयत्नतः.

ASSIGN, *v. t.* निरूप् 10, निर्दिश् 6 P. 2 प्र-उप-क्लृप् c., निर्णी 1 P. 3 नियुज् 7 A, 10, स्था c. (स्थापयति). 4 दा 3 P, ऋ c. (अर्पयति). 5 Ascribe, q. v. –ATION, *s.* द्रव्यसमर्पणं-दानं. 2 संकेतः, अभिसारः; 'place of a.' संकेतस्थानं. –EE, *s.* प्रतिनिधिः, प्रतिपुरुषः, नियोगिन् *m.* –MENT, *s.* निर्देशः, समर्पणं. दानं, उपकल्पनं.

ASSIMILATE, *v. t.* सदृशी-एकी-कृ 8 U; 'a. food' परिपाकं नी 1 P, परिणम् c. (णमयति). –ION, *s.* समीकरणं. 2 समता, साम्यं, ऐक्यं. 3 परिपाकः, परिणामः, पक्वता.

ASSIMULATE, *See* PRETEND.

ASSIST, *v. t.* उपकृ 8 U, साहाय्यं-उपकारं-कृ (gen.); अनुग्रह् 9 P. –ANCE, *s.* उपकारः; साहाय्यं, साहित्यं. –ER,–ANT, *s.* सहायः, उपकर्तृ *m.*, उपकारिन् *m.*, साहाय्यकर्तृ *m.* 2 उप in comp. ; 'a. master' उपगुरुः.

ASSIZE, *s.* न्यायसभा. 2 अर्घपरिमाणं. –*v. t.* अर्घ-मूल्यं-निरूप् 10 or संख्या c. (ख्यापयति). –ER, *s.* मूल्यनिरूपकः.

ASSOCIATE, *v. i.* संसर्गं-संगतिं-समागमं-कृ 8 U; संवस् 1 P, संमिल् 6 P, सहवासं कृ, संगममनुव्रज् 1 P; 'deer a. with deer' मृगा मृगैः संगममनुव्रजंति. –*v. t.* संयुज् 7 U, 10, संश्लिष् c., संगम् c. (गमयति). –*s.* वयस्यः, मित्र, सहचरः, अनुषंगिन् *m.*, सजुस् *m.*, सहवासिन् *m.*–ION, *s.* संगमः, संसर्गः, संगः, समागमः, साहचर्यं, संयोगः, संश्लेषः ; 'a. of the good with the good' सतां सद्भिः संगः (U. 2). 2 सभा, समाजः, पंक्ति *f.*. परिषद् *f.*

ASSORT, *v. t.* यथाक्रमं स्था c. (स्थापयति) or रच् 10 or विन्यस् 4 U ; पृथक् कृ 8 U. –MENT, *s.* विन्यासः, पृथक्करणं, रचना.

ASSUAGE, *v. t.* प्र-उप-शम् c. (शमयति), तुष् c., शां-सां-त्व् 10.–*v. i.* प्र-उप-शम् 4 P.–ASSUASIVE, *a.* शांतिप्रद, शामक.

ASSUME, *v. t.* ग्रह् 9 P, धृ 10, आदा 3 A. 2 Arrogate, q. v. 3 ग्रह्, सिद्ध *a.* मन् 4 A; प्रमाणं विना वद् 1 P; 'a. ing to be true' तत्सत्यमिति गृहीत्वापि ; 'a. ed silence' कृतकं-मिथ्या-मौनं. –ING, *a.* *See* ARROGANT.–ASSUMPTION, *s.* ग्रहणं, धारणं. 2 कल्पना; 'on the a. that he is a fool' स मूर्ख इति मत्वा. 3 प्रतिज्ञा; प्रमेयं.

ASSURE, *v. t.* प्रति-इ c., प्रतीतिं कृ 8 U, विश्वस् c. 2 दृढीकृ, संस्तंभ् 9 P or c., सुनिश्चित *a.* कृ. (Oneself) प्रति-इ 2 P, विश्वस् 2 P; निश्चयेन कथ् 10; सनिश्चयं-दृढं-वद् 1 P. –ANCE, *s.* विश्वासः, प्रत्ययः, दृढः प्रत्ययः, प्रत्याशा. 2 साहसं, प्रागल्भ्यं. 3 विश्वासकारणं, प्रत्ययहेतुः. 4 योगक्षेमः, अभयवचनं. –ED, *a.* असंदिग्ध, सुनिश्चित, असंशय, दृढ. –EDLY, *adv.* नियतं, नूनं, खलु, असंशयं ; 'I a. feel,' 'I feel a. ed' इति मे निश्चयः, दृढं मन्ये.

ASTERISM, *s.* नक्षत्रं, तारा, तारकं-का.

ASTERN, *adv.* नौपश्चिमभागं प्रति.

ASTHMA, *s.* श्वासः, श्वासरोगः. –TIC, *a.* श्वासरोगपीडित.

ASTONISH, *v. t.* विस्मि c. (विस्मापयति, विस्मापयते), विस्मयं जन् c. (जनयति), विस्मयाकुलीकृ 8 U, चकित *a.* कृ –ED, *a.* विस्मित, विस्मयाकुल, चकित; 'to be a.' विस्मि 1 A, विस्मयवशं गम् 1 P. –ING, *a.* विस्मयकर (री *f.*), अद्भुत, साश्चर्य. –MENT, *s.* विस्मयः, आश्चर्यं, चमत्कारः.

ASTOUND, *v. t.* विमुह् c., विस्मयाकुल *a.* कृ 8 U, व्याकुलीकृ, जडीकृ; 'a. ed with fear' साध्वसजडीकृतः.

ASTRAY, *adv.* उत्पथं; 'who goes a.' उन्मार्गगामिन् (नी *f.*), पथभ्रष्ट, भ्रांत, विपथगामिन् ; 'to lead a.' उत्पथं-उन्मार्गं-नी 1 P.

ASTRIDE, *adv.* प्रगतजंघं स्थित *a.*, पादौ पृथक् कृत्वा स्थित *a.*

ASTRINGENT, *a.* रूक्ष, कषाय. 2 संकोचनशील. –*s.* स्तंभकं.

ASTROLOGY, *s.* ज्योतिषं, नक्षत्रविद्या, दैवज्ञविद्या. –ER, *s.* गणकः, दैवज्ञः, ज्योतिषिकः, कार्तांतिकः, दैवचिंतकः, मौहूर्तिकः, सांवत्सरिकः. –ICAL, *a.* ज्योतिष (षी *f.*), नक्षत्र in comp.

ASTRONOMY, *s.* ज्योतिःशास्त्रं, ज्योतिषं, खगोलविद्या. –ER, *s.* ज्योतिर्विद् *m.*, ज्योतिःशास्त्रज्ञः, ज्योतिषिकः, खगोलविद्याभिज्ञः. –ICAL, *a.* ज्योतिष (षी *f.*), नाक्षत्रिक (की *f.*), खगोलविद्याविषयक.

ASTUTE, *a.* विदग्ध, चतुर, निपुण, कार्यदक्ष.

ASUNDER, *adv.* पृथक्, विरलं, विगत-भग्न *a.*; oft. by वि ; 'throw a.' विक्षिप् 6 P; 'burst a.' विदीर्ण &c.

ASYLUM, *s.* आश्रमः. 2 आश्रयः, शरणं, संश्रयः, गति *f.* ; 'seek a. with' आ-समुपा-श्रि 1 U.

AT, *prep.* (Denoting *time* or *place*) by loc. of noun ; 'a. Kás'i' काश्यां ; 'a. that time' तस्मिन्काले. 2 In other senses, by instr. or abl. ; oft. by gerund, or loc. abs. ; 'a. this' इदं श्रुत्वा ; 'a. his arrival' संप्राप्ते तस्मिन् ; 'a. his advice' तस्योपदेशेन; 'a. what price' कियता मूल्येन ; 'a. first' प्रथमं ; 'a. last' अंततः ; 'at once' युगपत्, समं ; 'a. all' मनागपि, किमपि.

ATHEIST, *s.* नास्तिकः, अनीश्वरवादिन् *m.*, निरीश्वरः. –ICAL, *a.* नास्तिकवृत्ति. –ATHEISM, *s.* नास्तिक्यं ; ईश्वरनिंदा.

ATHLETE, *s.* मल्लः, मल्लयोद्धृ *m.* –ATHLETIC, *a.* मल्ल, बाहुवीर, बलवत् (ती *f.*), संनद्धशरीर ; 'a. exercise, sports' व्यायामः.

ATHWART, *prep.* विलोमं ; व्यत्यस्तं ; पारं, प्रति pr.

ATMOSPHERE, *s.* गगनं, आकाशः-शं अंतरि (री)-क्षं, नभस् *n.* 2 शून्यं. –ICAL, *a.* आंतरीक्ष (क्षी *f.*), वायव (वी *f.*), आकाशीय.

ATOM, *s.* परमाणुः, अणुः, कणः, लवः, लेशः ; 'a. ic theory' परमाणुवादः. –ICAL, *a.* परमाणुमय (यी *f.*), सूक्ष्म. 2 अणुविषय,-अणुविषयक.

ATONE, *v. i.* प्रायश्चित्तं कृ 8 U, निष्कृतिं कृ, प्रायश्चित्तेन परिशुध् c. ; प्रमृज् 2 P ; उपचारातिक्रमं प्रमार्ष्टुमयमस्माकमारंभः (M. 4) 'to a. for the slighting of prostration' &c. 2 अनुनी 1 P, संधा 3 U, प्रशम् c. (शमयति). –MENT, *s.* प्रायश्चित्तं, निष्कृति *f.* 2 प्रमार्जनं.

ATONIC, *a.* अग्निनाशक, अतेजस्विन् (नी *f.*).

ATRAMENTOUS, *a.* *See* BLACK.

ATROCIOUS, *a.* घोर, बीभत्स (of things); अतिपापिन् (नी *f.*), अतिदुर्वृत्त, पापिष्ठ, नृशंस. –NESS, –ATROCITY, *s.* नृशंसता, बीभत्सता, घोरता. 2 अतिपापं, घोरकर्मन् *n.*

ATROPHY, *s.* क्षयः, क्षयरोगः, अन्नचभावः.

ATTACH, *v. t.* आसञ्ज् c., अनुरंज् c., संबंध् c.; 'I a. great importance to public censure' लोकापवादो बलवान्मतो मे (R. XIV. 40); 'a. friends to you by virtue' सदाचरणेनात्मनि मित्राण्यासंजय-अनुरंजय. 2 आसिध् 1 P, आक्रम् 1 U, 4 P, धृ 10. 3 Ascribe, q. v. –*v. i.* संबंध् 9 P, अनुषक्त *a.* भू 1 P. –ED, *a.* अनुरक्त, आसक्त, सं-प्र-सक्त. 2 भक्तिमत् (ती *f.*), सानुराग, अविरक्त, (with loc.); 'to be a.' आसंज्-अनुरंज्-pass.; 'subjects are firmly a. to the king' देवे सुदृढमनुरक्ताः प्रजाः

(Mu. 1); 'fondly a.' बद्धगाढानुराग. -MENT, *s.* अनुरागः, अभिनिवेशः, आसक्ति *f.*, प्रीति *f.*, भक्ति *f.*, प्रसक्ति *f.*, आसंगः (all with loc.). 2 आसंधः, ग्रहणं.

ATTACK, *v. t.* अभिद्रु 1 P, अवस्कंद् 1 P, आक्रम् 1 U, 4 P, अभियुज् 7 A; आपत् 1 P, अभिप्रया 2 P, प्रतिरुध् 4 A; आसद् c. 2 आ-परा-हन् 2 U; (an opinion &c.) परामृश् 6 P, प्रत्यवस्था 1 A (with loc.); 'a. ed by a disease' व्याधिग्रस्तः, रोगाक्रांतः. -*s.* अभियोगः, अवस्कंदः-दनं, आपातः, आक्रमः.

ATTAIN, *v.* (to) प्राप् 5 P, प्रति-प्र-आ-पद् 4 A, लभ् 1 A, अधिगम् 1 P, आ-समा-सद् c., अश् 5 A; 'easy to a.' सुलभ *a.*; 'difficult to a.' दुराप *a.*, दुष्प्राप *a.* -MENT, *s.* अधिगमः, लाभः, अवाप्ति *f.*, प्राप्ति *f.*, समासादनं.

ATTAINDER, *s.* कलंकः, अपयशस् *n.* 2 आधर्षणं, अभियोगः.

ATTAINT, *v. t.* आधृष् c., अभियुज् 7 A. 2 Stain, q. v.

ATTEMPER, *v. t.* यथांशतः मिश्र् 10 or संयुज् 10. 2 नियम् 1 P, शम् c. (शमयति).

ATTEMPT, *v. t.* प्रयत् 1 A, घट् 1 A, उपक्रम् 1 A, आरभ् 1 A, उद्यम् 1 P, प्रवृत् 1 A, चेष्ट् 1 A, व्यवसो 4 P (शामीलतां छेत्तुं व्यवस्यति S. 1). 2 Attack, q. v. -*s.* यत्नः, प्रयत्नः, उद्यमः, आरंभः, प्रयासः, उपक्रमः, प्रवृत्ति *f.*, उद्योगः.

ATTEND, *v. t.* उपस्था 1 U, संनिधा 3 U, आ-समागम् 1 P; 'a. the meeting' संसदि संनिहितो भव; 'a. school' शालां गच्छ. 2 अनु-इ-या 2 P, परिवृ c., सह गम्; 'good luck a. s our lord in every respect' सर्वथा स्पृशंति नः स्वामिनमभ्युदयाः (Rat. I.) 3 (on, upon) उप-पर्युप-स्था 1 A, उप-आस् 2 A, उपचर् 1 P, उपसेव् 1 A, श्रु desid. (शुश्रूषते), (with acc.). 4 (to words) श्रु 5 P, आकर्ण् 10; 'a. to me' मद्वचनं शृणु; 'a. now' सावधानो भव, अवधीयतां; (duty &c.) अवधा 3 U, मनः-दा, निधा, 3U, मनो युज् 10, (with loc.); अवेक्ष् 1 A. 5 विलंब्-प्रतीक्ष् 1 A. -ED, *a.* समेत, परिवृत, समन्वित, अनुयात, सहित, स in comp; 'a. by maid-servants' सखीगणपरिवृता, सखीपरिवारा. -ANCE, *s.* उपस्थानं, संनिधानं; शुश्रूषा, उपचारः, उपासनं, सेवा. -ANT, *a.* आनुषंगिक (की *f.*), सहगामिन् (नी *f.*), सहचारिन् (णी *f.*). -*s.* अनुचरः, सेवकः, अनुयायिन् *m.*, परिचरः; 'a group of a. s' अनुयायिवर्गः, परिच्छदः, परिवारः, परिबर्हः. -ATTENTION, *s.* आसक्ति *f.*, अभिनिवेशः, अवधानं, मनोयोगः, अवेक्षा, अप्रमादः, अप्रमत्तता. 2 अनुष्ठानं, उपसेवनं, परायणता; 'a. to one subject' एकाग्रता, निविष्टचित्तता, 'pay a.' अवधानं दा (with loc.). -ATTENTIVE; *a.* अवहित, सावधान, दत्तावधान, समाहित, अप्रमत्त, आसक्त, अभिनिविष्ट; 'closely a.' एकाग्र, अनन्यवृत्ति, एकतान, सादर, दक्षिण (to ladies); 'in-a. to houses &c.' गृहदारनिरपेक्ष; a. ly *adv.* सावधानं, अवहितं &c.

ATTENUATE, *v. t.* क्षै c. (क्षपयति), तनूकृ 8 U, क्षीणी-कृशी-कृ.-ED, *a.* कृश, क्षीण, तनु, क्षाम, अपचित (अपचितं गात्रं). -ION, *s.* कृशता, क्षामता, कृशांगत्वं.

ATTEST, *v. t.* साक्ष्यं दा 3 P; (साक्ष्येण) प्रमाणीकृ 8 U, व्यंज् 7 P, प्रकटीकृ, दिश् 6 P. 2 साक्षिणं कृ, साक्ष्ये आह्वे 1 P.-ATION, *s.* साक्ष्यं, प्रमाणं, प्रत्यक्षप्रमाणं.

ATTIRE, *s.* वेषः, वेशः, वस्त्रं, परिधानं, आभरणं, परिच्छदः, नेपथ्यं, अलंकारः; 'richly attired' गृहीतमहार्घवेषः, उदार-आर्य-नेपथ्यः. -*v. t.* (वस्त्रेण) आच्छद् 10, वेष्ट् 1 A, संव्ये 1 P. 2 भूष् 10, *See* ADORN; 'a. oneself' वस् 2 A; 'a. ing business' नेपथ्यविधानं.

ATTITUDE, *s.* संस्थिति *f.*, संस्थितं, भावः, अवस्था, वृत्ति *f.*, आकारः; 'hostile a.' वैरभावः, विपक्षवृत्तिः.

ATTORNEY, *s.* परकार्यसाधकः, प्रतिपुरुषः,-हस्तकः.

ATTRACT, *v. t.* आ-समा-कृष् 1 P, अनुकृष् (in grammar); आवृज् 10, अभिप्रणी 1 P, विमुह् c., वि-प्र-लुभ् c.-ION, *s.* आ-समा-कर्षणं, आवर्जनं; अनुकर्षः-र्षणं. 2 प्र-वि-लोभनं. -IVE, *a.* आकर्षक, आकर्षणशील, मनोहर, चित्तापहारिन्-हारिन् (णी *f.*). 2 मोहक, प्रलोभक.

ATTRIBUTE, *v. t.* *See* ASCRIBE; 'a. ing to themselves false greatness' आत्मन्यारोपितालीकाभिमानाः (Ka. 108). *s.* धर्मः, उपाधिः, गुणः. 2 विशेषणं. -IVE, *a.* वाच्य, विशेषक-ण.

ATTRITION, *s.* घर्षणं, पेषणं, क्षयः. 2 अनुतापः, अनुशयः.

ATTUNE, *v. t.* तालोपेत *a.* कृ 8 U. 2 एकतालं कृ, तुल्यस्वरं-तौर्यत्रिकं-कृ.

AUBURN, *a.* पिशंग (गी *f.*), गौर (री *f.*), कापिश, पांडुवर्ण.

AUCTION, *s.* घोषणपूर्वको द्रव्यविक्रयः. -EER, *s.* सघोषणं विक्रेतृ *m.*

AUDACIOUS, *a.* प्रगल्भ, निर्भय. 2 साहसिक, निर्लज्ज, धृष्ट, प्रतिभानवत् (ती *f.*).-NESS,-AUDACITY, *s.* धृष्टता, प्रागल्भ्यं, साहसं, प्रतिभानं. 2 निर्लज्जत्वं.

AUDIBLE, *a.* स्फुट, श्रवणक्षम, श्राव्य, कर्णगोचर, श्रोत्रग्राह्य.-AUDIBLY, *adv.* स्फुटं; 'in-a.' अस्फुटं, निःशब्दं; 'began to sob i.' निःशब्दं रोदितुमारेभे (Ka. 135).

AUDIENCE, *s.* समाकर्णनं, श्रवणं, निशमनं. 2 दर्शनं; 'have an a.' दर्शनं लभ् 1 A; (राजदर्शनं लेभे);

'I wish to be favoured with an a.' दर्शनानुग्रहमिच्छामि (M. 4); 'give a.' कर्ण दा 3 P, *See* ATTEND (to). 3 प्रेक्षकाः, श्रोतृवर्गः, श्रोतारः. 4 सभा, परिषद् *f.*, रंगः (आलिखित इव सर्वतो रंगः S. 1); 'a. chamber' दर्शनगृहं.

AUDIT, *v. t.* (गणितं) शुध् c., अनुसंधा 3 U, परीक्ष् 1 A. –*s.* गणितशोधनं-परीक्षणं &c. –OR, *s.* श्रोतृ *m.* 2 गणितशोधकः-परीक्षकः. –ORY, *s.* *See* AUDIENCE.

AUGHT, *s.* किमपि, किंचन, किंचित्.

AUGMENT, *v. t.* वृध् c., एध् c., आप्यै c., प्रचुरीकृ 8 U, उपचि 5 U.–*v. i.* वृध्-एध् 1 A, उपाधि pass., प्यै 1 A.–*s.* वृद्धि *f.* 2 आगमः. –ATION, *s.* वृद्धि *f.*, वर्धनं. 2 उपचयः, ऋद्धि *f.*, समुन्नति *f.*

AUGUR, *s.* शकुनज्ञः, निमित्तज्ञः, पूर्वलक्षणज्ञः. –*v. i.* शुभाशुभं परीक्ष् 1 A or आलोच् 10. 2 अनुमा 3 A, शंक् 1 A; 'this does not a. well for the success of your undertaking' तव कार्यसिद्धेर्नैतच्छुभलक्षणं. –Y, *s.* निमित्तज्ञानं, शकुनज्ञानं. 2 शकुनं, अजन्यं, पूर्वलक्षणं, निमित्तं.

AUGUST, *a.* महनीय, अत्युत्कृष्ट, अतिमहत् (ती *f.*), महामहिमन्; ऐश्वर (री *f.*), प्रतापवत्; 'a. queen' आरूढप्रतापा राज्ञी. –*s.* श्रावणः, नभस्यः नभस् *m.* –NESS, *s.* महाप्रतापः, ईश्वरत्वं.

AUNT, *s.* पितृस्व(ष्व) सृ *f.*, मातृस्व(ष्व) सृ *f.*, पितृव्या, मातुलानी, मातुला-ली.

AURICLE, *s.* कर्णशष्कुली.–AURICULAR, *a.* कार्णिक (की *f.*), श्रावण (णी *f.*). 2 कर्ण-उपकर्णं कथित, जपित, गुप्त.

AURORA, *s.* उषस् *f.*, अरुणः.

AUSPICE, *s.* शकुनं, निमित्तं, पूर्वलक्षणं; a. s अनुग्रहः, आश्रयः, प्रसादः. –AUSPICIOUS, *a.* शिव, शुभ, शिवं-शुभं-कर, मांगलिक (की *f.*), कल्याण (णी *f.*), मंगल, भद्र; 'a. time' लग्नवेला, शुभलग्नं. 2 श्रीयुक्त, सौभाग्यवत् (ती *f.*). 3 प्रसन्न, अनुग्राहिन् (णी *f.*). –LY, *adv.* शुभक्षणे; सौभाग्येन, क्षेमेण. –NESS, *s.* कल्याणं, मंगलं, मांगल्यं, सौभाग्यं, भद्रं, क्षेमः-मं, शुभं.

AUSTERE, *a.* तीव्र, उग्र (तपः), निष्ठुर, कर्कश, कठोर, निर्दय, कठिन; (in taste) शुष्क, रूक्ष, कटु. –ITY, *s.* उग्रता, कठोरता &c; 'religious a.' तपस् *n.*, कृच्छ्रं.

AUTHENTIC,–AL, *a.* अकृत्रिम, तथ्य, प्रमाणयुक्त; अकल्पित, सत्य.–ATE, *v. t.* सप्रमाण *a.* कृ 8 U, प्रमाणीकृ.–ITY, *s.* सप्रमाणता, सत्यता, प्रामाण्यं. –ALLY, *adv.* सप्रमाणं, प्रमाणानुसारेण.

AUTHOR, *s.* कारः-कृत् in comp.; 'a. of Gadâdhari' गदाधरीकारः-कृत्; ग्रंथकारः. 2 कृत् *m.*, प्रणेतृ *m.*, लेखकः. 2 प्रवर्तकः, आरंभकः, उत्पादकः, जनकः, संपादयितृ *m.* –SHIP, कर्तृत्वं, प्रवर्तकता.

AUTHORITY, *s.* प्रभुत्वं, प्रभावः, शक्ति *f.* 2 अधिकारः, प्रभुत्वं. 3 ऐश्वर्यं, आधिपत्यं, आज्ञा, शासनं, नियोगः. 4 प्रमाणं, आप्तवचनं, निदर्शनं; 'Pâṇini is an a. in this respect' अत्र विषये पाणिनिः प्रमाणं. 5 प्रामाण्यं, विश्वसनीयता. 6 गुरुत्वं, गौरवं. 7 अधिकारिन् *m.*, नियोगिन् *m.*, अधिकृतः पुरुषः, प्रभुः. –ATIVE, *a.* सप्रमाण, शासनानुरूप, वैधिक (की *f.*); a. ly, *adv.* शासनेन; सप्रमाणं.

AUTHORIZE, *v. t.* प्रमाणीकृ 8 U, सप्रमाण *a.* कृ. 2 अधिकृ, नियुज् 7 A, 10. 3 अनुज्ञा 9 U, अनुमन् 4 A; 'a. ed person' अधिकृतः पुरुषः.

AUTOBIOGRAPHY, *s.* आत्मवृत्तकथनं, आत्मचरितरचनं.

AUTOCRAT, *s.* सम्राज् *m.*, अधिराजः, अनियंत्रितशासनः.–AUTOCRACY, साम्राज्यं, आधिराज्यं.

AUTOGRAPH, *s.* स्वहस्तलेखः. –*a.* स्वहस्तलिखित.

AUTOMATON, *s.* स्वयं चलद् यंत्रं.

AUTUMN, *s.* शरद् *f.* –AL, *a.* शरत्कालीन, शारदीय, शारद (दी *f.*). 2 शरदिज

AUXILIARY, *a.* सहायभूत, उपकारक, सहकारिन् (णी *f.*). –*s.* सहायः, उपकारकः, सहकारिन् *m.*

AVAIL, *v. t.* उपकृ 8 U, अनुग्रह् 9 P; gen. ex. by instr. with अर्थ, गुण &c.; 'what a. s thy weeping, child' वत्स किं रुदितेन. 2 प्र-उप-युज् 7 A, 10; 'a. ing himself of the opportunity' गृहीतावसरः. –*v. i.* सफल *a.* भू, हितायफलाय-भू; लाभाय-भू. –*s.* प्रयोजनं, उपयोगः, गुणः. 2 फलं, हितं, लाभः, अर्थः; 'of no a.' निष्फल, व्यर्थ &c. –ABLE, *a.* प्रयोज्य. 2 सफल, हितावह. 3 प्राप्य, लभ्य; 'not a.' दुर्लभ, असुलभ, अनुपलभ्य.

AVENT-GUARD, *s.* सेनामुखं, रणशिरस् *n.*

AVARICE, *s.* लोभः, लालसा, जिघृक्षा, विप्सिहा.–AVARICIOUS, *a.* लोभिन् (नी *f.*), धनलुब्ध, अर्थपर, मितंपच, लुब्ध, कृपण. –LY, *adv.* अतिलोभेन, कृपणवत्. –NESS, *s.* कृपणत्वं, कार्पण्यं, अतिलोभः, लुब्धता.

AVAUNT, *interj.* अपेहि, अपसर.

AVENGE, *v. t.* प्रतिकृ 8 U, प्रति(ती)कारं कृ, (with gen.); वैरानृण्यं गम् 1 P (with loc. of offender). 2 निर्यत् 10, शुध् c.; 'a. a wrong' वैरनिर्यातनं-वैरसाधनं-कृ. 3 दंड् 10, प्रतिहिंस् 7 P. –ER, *s.* प्रतिकर्तृ *m.*, प्रतिहिंसकः, वैरशोधकः.

AVENUE, *s.* द्वारं, मार्गः; वीथि *f.*; तरुपंक्ति-वृक्ष-श्रेणी *f.*

AVER, *v. t.* सप्रतिज्ञं-सशपथं वद् 1P, दृढं वच् 2 P.

AVERAGE, *a.* सामान्य, मध्यम. –*s.* मध्यमावस्था, मध्यस्थता; 'on an a.' सामान्यतः, स्थूलप्रमाणेन.

AVERSE, *a.* पराङ्मुख (खी *f.*), विरक्त, प्रतिकूल, विपरीत, द्वेषिन् (णी *f.*). 2 अननुकूल, वाम; 'fate being a.' प्रतिकूलतां उपगते विधौ; 'a. to giving intelligence' प्रवृत्तिदानपराङ्मुखः; 'to be a.'

(to) अपावृत् 1 A, विरंज् pass. -NESS, AVERSION, *s.* विरागः, अप्रीति *f.*, द्वेषः, विमति *f.*, प्रतिकूलता, विरक्ति *f.*; पराङ्मुखता, (with loc.). 2 त्रासः, भयं.

AVERT, *v. t.* सं-परि-हृ 1 P, विनि-अप-नि-वृ c., नि-व्या-अप-वृत् c., अपानुद् 6 P; 'with the face a. ed' विमुख-पराङ्मुख (खी *f.*).

AVIARY, *s.* पंजरं, वीतंसः, विटंकः, पक्षिशाला.

AVIDITY, *s.* Avarice, q. v. 2 अतिस्पृहा, कौतूहलं.

AVOCATION, *s.* कार्यं, व्यापारः, वृत्ति *f.*, कर्मन् *n.* 2 आकर्षणं.

AVOID, *v. t.* परिहृ 1 P, वि-परि-वृज् 10, प्रोज्झ् 6 P, हा 3 P, त्यज् 1 P. -ANCE,-ING, *s.* त्यागः, वर्जनं, परिहारः,-हरणं.

AVOUCH, *v. t.* सनिश्चयं-सशपथं-वद् 1 P. 2 परार्थं वद्, निर्व्यूह् 1 U.

AVOW, *v. t.* प्रकाशं-स्पष्टं-वद् 1 P. 2 स्वीकृ 8 U, अंगीकृ, अभ्युपगम् 1 P. -EDLY, *adv.* स्पष्टं, प्रकाशं, प्रकटं.

AWAIT, *v. t.* प्रति-ईक्ष् 1 A (तवागमनं प्रतीक्षते), प्रतिपाल् 10, उद्दृश् 1 P. 2 प्रत्यासद् 1 P, लग्न *a.* संपद् 4 A; उपस्था 1 U, आपत् 1 P, (with gen.): 'destruction (death) a. s those that are born' विपदुत्पत्तिमतामुपस्थिता (R. VIII. 83).

AWAKE, *v. i.* वि-प्र-बुध् 4 A, निद्रां त्यज् 1 P, विनिद्र *a.* भू, जागृ 2 P. -*v. t.*,AWAKEN, जागृ c., बुध् c., निद्रां भंज् 7 P. 2 जन् c. (जनयति), उत्तिज् c., उत्था c. (उत्थापयति). -*a.* जाग्रत् (ती *f.*), उन्निद्र, प्रबुद्ध, प्रजागर, जागरूक.

AWARD, *v. t.* दा 3 P. 2 दा c. (दापयति). -*s.* निर्णयः; विचारः, आज्ञा.

AWARE, *a.* विज्ञापित, सावधान. 2 वेदिन्-ज्ञ in comp.; or by ज्ञा 9 U, *See* KNOW.

AWAY, *a.* परोक्ष, अविद्यमान, अनुपस्थित ; दूरस्थ. -*adv.* अलं, कृतं (instr.). 2 अपेहि, अपसर.

AWE, *s.* साध्वसं, भयं, त्रासः, आदरः, संभ्रमः, आदरप्रयुक्तं भयं; 'I approach the king with a.' चकितं नृपस्य पार्श्वमुपैमि (M. 1); 'stand in a. of' भी 3 P, त्रस् 1, 4 P. -*v. t.* भी c., त्रस् c., संभ्रमेण आकुलीकृ 8 U; 'a. ed, struck with awe' संभ्रांत, विस्मयाकुल; भयाकुल, भयविह्वल, ससाध्वस. -AWFUL, *a.* घोर, दारुण, भीषण, भैरव (वी *f.*) (of things). 2 अतितेजस्विन् (नी *f.*). महातेजस्, आदरणीय, पूज्य; 'how a. is royal greatness' अहो दुरासदो राजमहिमा (M. 1). 3 प्रशांतगंभीर (अरण्यश्रीः). -LY, *adv.* सभयं, अत्यंतं. -NESS, *s.* तेजस् *n.*; दारुणता, घोरता.

AWHILE, *adv.* किंचित्कालं, मुहूर्तं, क्षणं यावत्.

AWKWARD, *a.* अकुशल, अदक्ष, अक्षिप्र, अपटु. 2 (Manners) ग्राम्य; विरूप, स्थूल. -NESS, *s.* अदक्षता; ग्राम्यता &c.

AWL, *s.* आरा, चर्मप्रभेदिका.

AWN, *s.* शूकं, किंशारुः.

AWNING, *s.* वितानं, आच्छादानं.

AWRY, *adv.* तिर्यक्, साचि, जिह्मं. 2 विपरीतं, प्रतिलोमं. प्रतिकूलं.

AXE, *s.* टंकः, परशुः, कुठारः, परश्वधः.

AXIOM, *s.* तत्त्वं, सिद्धांतः. 2 वचनं, सूत्रं. -ATIC, *a.* (*s.*) in comp.

AXIS, *s.* अक्षरेखा, अक्षः, ध्रुवः.

AXLE, *s.* अक्षाग्रं.

AY, *adv.* तथेति, एवं, आम्, नूनं.

AYE, *adv.* सदा, सर्वदा, अजस्रं.

AZURE, *a.* नील, नील-आकाश-वर्ण.

B.

BABBLE, *v. i.* जल्प् 1 P, प्रलप् 1 P. 2 रहस्यभेदं कृ 8 U. -ING, *s.* जल्पः, प्रलपितं. -ER, *s.* जल्पकः, वाचाटः, वाचालः, प्रलापिन् *m.*, वावदूकः.

BABE, BABY, *s.* शिशुः, शावकः, दारकः (रिका *f.*), स्तनंधयः. -HOOD, *s.* बाल्यं, शैशवं, बालभावः. -ISH, *a.* बालिश, बालेय.

BABEL, *s.* संकरः, कोलाहलः, संकीर्णनादः.

BABOON, *s.* वानरः, कपिः, मर्कटः.

BACCHANALIAN, *s.* मद्यपानासक्तः, मद्यप्रियः, पानरतः.

BACHELOR, *s.* अकृतदारपरिग्रहः, अकृतोद्वाहः, अविवाहितः.

BACK, *s.* पृष्ठं, पृष्ठदेशः; 'lying on the b.' उत्तानशयः; 'behind one's b.' परोक्षे-क्षं. -*adv.* प्रति. अपा. नि, परा, with verbs; पुनर्निवृत् 1 A 'come b.,' 'give b.' प्रतिदा 3 U. -*prep. See* BEFORE. -*v. t.* अनुमुद् 1 A, समर्थ् 10, रक्ष् 1 P. 2 (horse), आ-अधि-रुह् 1 P. 3 पश्चानुद् 6 P, *See* DRIVE. -BITE, *v. t.* परोक्षे अधिक्षिप् 6 P, परिवद् 1 U, असूयति (D.) with dat.; पृष्ठमांसं अद् 2 P or खाद् 1 P (with gen.). -BITER, *s.* पिशुनः, पृष्ठमांसादः, परिवादरतः. -BITING, *s.* पैशुन्यं, परि(री) वादः. -BONE, *s.* पृष्ठवंशः, कशेरुका. -DOOR, *s.* पक्षद्वारं, पक्षकं. -GAMMON, *s.* चर्मपट्टिकाक्रीडा. -GROUND, *s.* पश्चाद्भूमि *f.*; 'throw into the b.' (lit.) दृष्टिपथान्निवार् 10, निभृते स्था c. (स्थापयति) ; (fig.) 'Urvas'i throws Lakshmi into the b.' उर्वशी प्रत्यादेशः श्रियः (V. 1); रतेरपि न्हीपदमादधाति (K. III. 57). -ROOM, *s.* अंतर्गृहं, अंतः-उप-शाला. -SIDE, *s.* पृष्ठभागः-देशः. -SLIDE, *v. i.* स्वधर्मात् भ्रंश् 1 A, 4 P or च्यु 1 A. -STAIRS, *s.* उप-प्रच्छन्न-सोपानं;

'b. influence' प्रच्छन्न-सामर्थ्य-गुणः. –WARD, *a.* पराङ्मुख (खी *f.*), अतीतकाल. 2 मंदधी-मति, मंद, (of a boy). 3 अनिच्छु, प्रतीप. –WARDS, *adv.* परा, प्रति, with verbs; पृष्ठतः, पृष्ठभागे-देशे. 2 पश्चात्, प्रतीपं; गतागतं; 'move b. and forward' गतागतं-गमनागमनं-कृ 8 U.

BACON, *s.* शूकरमांसं.

BAD, *a.* निंदित, गर्ह्य. 2 अशुभ, अभद्र. 3 असार, निर्गुण, अहित; gen. ex. by दुः, वि, कु, किं, कत्, अप, prefixed; 'a b. man' दुर्जनः; दुर्दैवं &c.; कुपथः 'a b. way'; कुमतिः; किंसखा 'a b. friend'; अपयशः 'b. fame', infamy; कदश्वः 'a b. horse.' –LY, *adv.* Gen. Ex. by दुर्, कु; 'b. prepared' कुनिर्मित; 'smells b.' दुर्गंधः अस्य; 'b. bitten' तीव्रं-बलवत्-असुखं-दष्ट; 'b. off' दुःस्थित, कष्टापन्न, दुर्गत. –NESS, *s.* Ex. by (*a.*); 'b. of result' कुपरिणामः; दुराचारः. 2 दुर्जनता, दुष्टता. 3 निःसारता, निर्गुणता, अभद्रता.

BADGE, *s.* चिह्नं, लक्षणं.

BAFFLE, *v. t.* व्यर्थी-मोघी-कृ 8 U, खंड् 10, भंज् 7 P, प्रति-वि-हन् 2 P. 2 पराभू 1 U, पराजि 1 A; 'b. ed in efforts' भग्नोद्यमः; 'the scene b. s description' वर्णनविषयातिक्रांतं तत्स्थानं. –ED, *a.* खंडित, भग्नाश, मोघाश; पराजित.

BAG, *s.* पुटः-टं, प्रसेवः, स्यूतः, कोषः; 'leather b.' चर्मभस्त्रिका. –*v. t.* स्यूते निधा 3 U.

BAGGAGE, *s.* सामग्री, उपकरणं, साधनं; 'bag and b.' सर्वमपि गृहीत्वा, किमपि नावशेष्य.

BAGATELLE, *s.* क्षुद्रविषयः, अगुर्वर्थः.

BAGNIO, *s.* स्नानागारं. 2 वेश्यावासः, वेश्यालयः.

BAIL, *s.* प्रतिभूः, लग्नकः, प्रातिभाव्यं; 'admitted to b.' प्रतिभूदानेन मुक्तः. – *v. t.* लग्नकं दा 3 U, दत्त्वा मुच् c.

BAILIFF, *s.* आसेध्दृ *m.*, ग्राहकः.

BAIRN, *s.* *See* BABE.

BAIT, *s.* आमिषं; 'b. fixed to a fish-hook' बडिशयुतं पिशितं. 2 प्र-वि-लोभनं. –*v. t.* प्र-विलुभ् c. 2 आमिषं दा 3 U (with dat.); आमिषं बडिशे निधा 3 U or यु 2 P or निविश् c.; 'this is surely a b. to catch me' मां वशीकर्तुं नूनमिदमामिषं प्रकल्पितं. 3 (horses) विश्रम् c.; भुज् c. – *v. i.* भोजनार्थं विश्रम् 4 P.

BAKE, *v. t.* (कंदौ) पच् 1 P, तप् c., भ्रस्ज् 6 P. – ED, *a.* पक्व; 'b. brick' पक्वेष्टिका; कंदुपक्व.–ER, *s.* कांदविकः; आपूपिकः. – HOUSE, *s.* आपाकः; कंदु *m. f.*

BALANCE, *s.* तुला, मापनः; 'beam of a b.' तुलादंडः-यष्टि *f.* 2 शेषं, अवशेषः; 'what is the b. against me' मया देयः (द्रव्य-)शेषः कियान्वर्तते. 3 विवेचनं; विगणनं, समतोलनं. 4 तुल्यता, समानभारता. – *v. t.* तुल् 10 (तुलयति); 'b. accounts' समीकृ 8 U, शुध् c. 2 (In thought) विविच् 7 P; विकृप् c. – ED, *a.* तुलित. 2 तुल्यभार; समीकृत.

BALCONY, *s.* वरंडः, प्रग्रीवः. वितर्दि-र्दी *f.*

BALD, *a.* वि-अ-केश (शी *f.*), मुंड, खलति. 2 अनावृत, नग्न, असंस्कृत. 3 असभ्य, अशिष्ट, अलंकारहीन.

BALDRICK, *s.* मेखला, कांची, रस (श) ना. 2 राशिमंडलं, ज्योतिश्चक्रं.

BALE, *s.* भांडं, भारः; द्रव्यपोटलिका. –FUL, *a.* सशोक, क्लेशार्त, दुःखित. 2 प्राणहर (री *f.*), विनाशिन् (नी *f.*), *See* DEADLY.

BALK, *v. t.* *See* BAFFLE. – *s.* सेतुः, सेतुबंधः.

BALL, *s.* कंदुकः (for playing); गोलः-लं, वर्तुलं, मंडलं; 'eye-b.' तारा. 2 नृत्यक्रीडा; 'b. room' नृत्यस्थानं.

BALLAD, *s.* गीतं, गीति *f.*, गानं; 'b. singer' गायकः.

BALLAST, *s.* पोतस्थैर्यद्रव्यं.

BALLOON, *s.* विमानं, आकाश-व्योम-यानं.

BALLOT, *s.* गुटि(लि)का.

BALM, *s.* गुग्गुलः, वृक्षनिर्यासः. 2 प्रशमः, शांतिः *f.* –Y, *a.* सुरभि. 2 तापहर (री *f.*) शांतिद, उपशमक.

BALSAM, *s.* विलेपनं, अभ्यंजनं. –IC, *a.* स्निग्ध, चिक्कण.

BAMBOO, *v.* वेणुः, वंशः, कीचकः (sounding b.).

BAMBOOZLE, *See* CHEAT.

BAN, *s.* घोषणं. 2 अभिशापः, आक्रोशः. 3 नि-प्रतिषेधः. – *v. t.* अभिशप् 1 U, प्रतिषिध् 1 P.

BAND, *s.* बंधः, पाशः, बधनं. 2 समूहः, श्रेणी. 3 दलं, गुल्मः-ल्मं (of troops). 4 तूर्यसमूहः, वादित्रगणः. – *v.* संमिल् 6 P, संयुज् 10, *See* ASSEMBLE.

BANDAGE, *s.* बंधः, बंधनं, पट्टः, आवेष्टनं.

BANDIT, *s.* दस्युः, चोरः, स्तेनः.

BANDY, *v. t.* इतस्ततो विक्षिप् 6 P. 2 विनि-मे 1 A; 'b. words' वाचा उत्तरं दा 3 U. –LEGGED, *a.* प्रज्ञु, प्रगतजानु.

BANE, *s.* गरः-रं, विषं. 2 (fig.) नाश-अनर्थ-मूलं, क्षयकारणं, विनाशहेतुः, आधिः; वामाः कुलस्याधयः (*S.* 4.) 'are a b. to the family.' – FUL, *a.* विषान्वित, सविष, विनाशिन् (नी *f.*), विनाशन (नी *f.*).

BANG, *v. t.* प्रहृ 1P, तड् 10, अभि-प्रति-हन् 2P. –*s.* आघातः, प्रहारः, कराघातः.

BANGLE, *s.* वलयः-यं, कंकणं.

BANISH, *v. t.* वि-निर्-वस् c., प्रव्रज् c. 2 निराकृ 8 U, निः-उत्-सृ c., अपानुद् 6 P, निरस् 4 P; 'the thought was b. ed from his mind' सा चिंता मनसो निरस्ता.–MENT, *s.* विवासनं, निर्वासनं, प्रव्रा-(व्र) जनं. 2 निराकरणं, निरसनं.

BANK, *s.* तीरं, कूलं, तटः-टी, रोधस् *n.*, कच्छः; 'the other b.' पारं ; 'sand b.' सैकतं. 2 धनागारं.

-v. t. कूलेन परिविश् 1 A or c. -ER, s. धनागारपतिः; श्रेष्ठिन् m., कुसीदिकः.

BANKRUPT, s. ऋणदान-ऋणशोधन-अक्षमः, सर्वस्वच्युतः, परिक्षीणः, निर्धनः. -CY, s. परिक्षीणता, ऋणशोधनाक्षमता, &c.

BANNER. s. ध्वजः, पताका, केतनं, वैजयंती, केतुः.

BANQUET, s. विशिष्टभोजनं, स्वाद्वन्नभोजनं. -v. t. मिष्टान्नैः भुज् c. or संतृप् c. -v. i. विशिष्टान्नं भुज् 7 A or भक्ष् 10; 'the horses were b. ing upon the grass' अश्वास्तृणं यथेष्टं भक्षयंत आसन्.

BANTER, v. t. भर्त्स् 10 A, निंद् 1 P अधिक्षिप् 6 P. 2 अव-वि-उप-हस् 1 P. -s. निंदा, अधिक्षेपः, अवहासः, &c.

BANTLING, s. *See* BABY.

BANYAN, s. वटः, न्यग्रोधः.

BAR, s. अर्गलं-ला, अर्गलाबंधः. 2 प्रत्यूहः, अंतरायः. 3 शलाका (of a cage.) 4 दंडः; 'iron b.' लोहदंडः, लोहपिंडः. 5 सैकतं. 6 न्यायसभा. -v. t. नि-प्रति-रुध् 7 U, नि-प्रति-षिध् 1 P, निराकृ 8 U, निरस् 4 P, निवृ c. or निवार् 10. 2 अर्गलेन बंध् 9 P.

BARB, s. कर्णः, शूलाग्रं. 2 अश्वतनुत्रं. -ED, a. कर्णिन् (नी f.).

BARBARIAN, s. ग्राम्यः, असभ्यः. 2 म्लेच्छः; यवनः, किरातः. 3 विदेशीन् m., वैदेशिकः.

BARBAROUS, a. वैदेशिक (की f.). 2 अशिष्ट, असभ्य, अश्लील. 3 निष्ठुर, क्रूर, निर्दय. -LY, *adv.* क्रूरवत्, निष्ठुरवत्, श्वापदवत्, पशुवत्. -BARBARITY, s. निष्ठुरता, नृशंसता, क्रौर्यं, असभ्यता, अशिष्टता.

BARBER, s. नापितः. क्षौरिकः, क्षुरिन् m.; 'b.'s wife' नापिती; 'b.'s business' नापित्यं.

BARD, s. वंदिन् m., वैतालिकः.

BARE, a. अनावृत. शून्य. 2 केवल, मात्र in comp.; 'on the b. ground' अव्यवधानायां भूमावेव (ka. 151). 3 विवस्त्र; 'b. footed' पादुकाहीन, अनावृतपाद; 'b. headed' अनावृतशिरस्; 'b. faced' निर्लज्ज, धृष्ट; 'thread b.' (clothes) जीर्णानि वासांसि. -v. t. नग्नीकृ 8 U, विवस्त्रीकृ; उच्छद् 10. 2 अपहृ 1 P, अपनी 1 P, उत्कृष् 1 P. -LY, *adv.* मात्रं, केवलं. 2 कथमपि, कष्टेन, कृच्छ्रेण. -NESS, s. शून्यता, विवस्त्रता. 2 क्षीणता, दैन्यं.

BARGAIN, s. संविद् f., समयः, अभ्युपगमः, 'a b. was struck' इति समयः कृतः; 'buy the horse, it is a good b.' स्तोकमूल्येन लभ्यतेयमश्वः क्रीणीहि तावदेनं; 'in the b.' अपि, अपरंच. 2 पणः, विपणः, क्रयविक्रयनियमः. -v. t. पण् 1 A, व्यवहृ 1 P.

BARGE, s. केलिनौका. 2 तरालुः, वहित्रं. -MAN, s. नाविकः, पोतवाहः.

BARK, s. त्वच् f., वल्कं, वल्कलः-लं. 2 पोतः, क्षुद्रनौः, तरीः. -v. i. बुक्क् 1 P., 10; 'dogs b. at the moon' श्वानः शशिनं वीक्ष्य बुक्कयंति; भष् 1 P. -v. t. त्वचं-वल्कं-अपनी 1 P or निष्कृष् 1 P. -ING, s. बुक्कनं, भषणं. -Y a. वाल्कल (ली f.), त्वङ्मय (यी f.).

BARLEY, s. यवः, प्रवेटः; 'b. broth' यवसुरा-रं; 'b. corn' यवः; 'unripe b.' कुल्माषं; 'b. water' उदमंथः.

BARM, s. सुरा-मद्य-मंडः.

BARN, s. कुशूलः, धान्यगारं, धान्यसंग्रहस्थानं.

BAROMETER, s. आकाशतोलनयंत्रं.

BARRACK, s. सैन्यावासः, सैन्यागारं. -v. t. सैन्यागारे स्था c. (स्थापयति) or निवस् c.

BARREL, s. दीर्घगोलाकारं काष्ठपात्रं. 2 (Of guns) नाडि-डी f., नालि-ली f.

BARREN, a. वंध्य (lit. and fig.). 2 व्यर्थ, मोघ, निष्फल. 3 (Ground) अनुर्वर, अशस्यप्रद, मरुस्थलं-ली. 4 शून्य, रिक्त. -NESS, s. वंध्यत्वं. 2 वैयर्थ्यं, शुष्कता.

BARRICADE, s. प्राकारः, वप्रः-प्रं, प्राचीरं. -v. t. विप्रति-रुध् 7 U, *See* OBSTRUCT.

BARRIER, s. वृति f., वप्रः-प्रं, प्राकारः. 2 सीमन् f., सीमा, पर्यंतः-तं. 3 विघ्नः, प्रत्यूहः, अंतरायः, व्याघातः.

BARRISTER, s. उत्तरवादिन् m., परार्थं वक्तृ m.; स्मृतिशास्त्रकुशलः.

BARROW, s. शूकरः. 2 उन्नतभूभागः.

BARTER, s. विनिमयः, प्रतिदानं, परि (री) वर्तः. -v. t. विनि-मे 1 A, परिवृत् c.; 'b. ed for 5 cows' पंचगु (गृहं &c.). -v. i. भांडविनिमयेन वाणिज्यं कृ 8 U, व्यवहृ 1 P.

BASE, a. नीच, अनार्य, खल, दुष्ट, कदर्य, जघन्य, अधम, नि-अप-कृष्ट. 2 विजात, हीनजाति, अनभिजात, अकुलीन. 3 कृपण. 4 (Notes) धीर, गंभीर; 'b. metal' कुप्यं. -s. अधोभागः, मूलं, तलं, उपस्तंभः. 2 मूर्धन् m., भूमि f. 3 वास्तु n.; पोटः; 'based on' ex. by मूल in comp.; 'delusion b. ed on ignorance' अज्ञानमूलका भ्रांतिः. -LY, *adv.* नीचतया, अधमं &c. -LESS, a. निर्मूलक, निराधार, अमूल. -NESS, s. अधमता, अनार्यता, निकृष्टता; अकुलीनता, वैजात्यं; गांभीर्यं.

BASHFUL, a. ह्रीमत्-लज्जावत् (ती f.), सव्रीड, त्रपित, सलज्ज, शालीन, सत्रप, विनीत, भीरु. -LY, *adv.* सलज्जं, सत्रपं, सव्रीडं; 'his face b. bent down' लज्जावनतमुखः, त्रपाधोमुखः. -NESS, s. लज्जा, त्रपा, ह्रीः, व्रीडा, शालीनता, विनयः, भीरुता.

BASIL, s. तुलसी, कुठेरकः, पर्णासः.

BASIN, BASON, s. भांडं, द्रोणी. 2 जलाशयः, तडागः, कासारः. 3 आलवालं, आधारः, आवापः, आवालं. 4 खातं.

BASIS, s. मूलं; योनि f.; आधारः.

BASK, *v. t.* सूर्यातपं नि-आ-सेव् 1 A ; 'b. s in the morning sun' बालातपं निषेवते.

BASKET, *s.* मंजूषा, पि (पे) टकः, करंडः, कंडोलः. -MAKER, *s.* वैणवः, वैदलकारः. -WORK, *s.* वैदलं.

BASS, *s. See* BASE. 2 कटः ; 'b. relief' प्रतिच्छाया.

BASTARD, *a.*, *s.* जारज, कुंड, कुलटोत्पन्न; कौलटेय, कानीन, विजन्मन्, दासीपुत्रः (त्री *f.*), विजात.

BASTE, *v. t.* लगुडेन तड् 10 or प्रहृ 1 P or आहन् 2 U. 2 सिव् 4 P.- BASTINADE, *s.* लगुडाघातः, गदाप्रहारः, ताडनं.

BASTILE, *s.* प्राकारयुक्तं दुर्गं.

BASTION, *s.* वप्रः-प्रं.

BAT, *s.* जतुका, अजिनपत्रा, परोष्णी, तैलपायिका. 2 यष्टि *f.*, गदा, लगुडः.

BATCH, *s.* गणः, संघः, समूहः.

BATE, *See* ABATE.

BATH, *s.* स्नानागारं, स्नानकुंडं, अवगाहनस्थानं.

BATHE, *v. i.* स्ना 2 P, मस्ज् 6 P, (loc.); गाह् 1 A, वि-अव-गाह् (with acc.). -*v. t.* स्ना c. (स्नास्न-पयति); प्रक्षल् 10, धाव् 10; अभिषिच् 6 P, निमस्ज् c. (मज्जयति). -ING, *s.* स्नानं, निमज्जनं, अवगाहनं, अभिषेकः. -*a.* स्नानीय; 'b. cloth' स्नानीयवस्त्रं.

BATHOS, *s.* नीचता. 2 गांभीर्यं.

BATING, *prep. See* EXCEPT.

BATLET, *s.* रजकप्रयुक्तः काष्ठमुद्गरः.

BATOON, *s.* दंडः, गदा, यष्टि *f.*, लगुडः.

BATTALION, *s.* गुल्मः-ल्मं, वाहिनी, सैन्यदलं.

BATTEN, *v. i.* आप्यै 1 A, स्फाय् 1A ; 'the wolf b. s on the lamb' अजा (मांस) भक्षणेनात्मानमाप्याययति; उदरं भृ 3 U.-*v. t.* प्यै c., संवृध् c., पीन *a.* कृ 8 U.

BATTER, *v. t.* मृद् 9 P, चूर्ण 10, मंथ् 9 P, निष्पिष् 7 P; प्रभंज् 7 P.-Y, *s.* मर्दनं, पेषणं. 2 कामानश्रेणी.

BATTLE, *s.* युद्धं, रणः-णं, समरः, संग्रामः, संख्यं, प्रधनं, आहवः, आजि *f.*; समिति *f.*, युध् *f.*, 'b. array' व्यूहः, सैन्यविन्यासः ; 'b. axe' परशुः; 'b. cry' सिंहनादः, क्ष्वेडितं; 'b. field' रण-समर-&c. भूमि *f.*, रणांगणं.- *v. i.* युध् 4 A. - MENT, *s.* सच्छिद्रः प्राकारः, भित्ति *f.*

BAUBLE, *s.* अल्पमूल्यं आभरणं, अल्पार्घं क्रीडनकं.

BAWD, *s.* कुट्टिनी, दूती, शंभली. -RY, *s.* दूतीकार्यं ; कुट्टिनीकर्मन् *n.* -Y, *a.* गर्हित, अशुद्ध, अविनीत, नीच; 'bawd-house' वेश्याश्रमः, वेशः.

BAWL, *v. i.* आ-उत्-क्रुश् 1 P, उच्चैः-तारस्वरेण शब्दायते (D.); रट् 1 P, नर्द् 1 P, उद्घुष् 10.-ER, *s.* आ-उत्-क्रोष्टृ *m.*, उद्घोषकः.- ING. *s.* उत्क्रोशः, उद्घोषणं.

BAY, *a.* पिंग, पिंगल. - *v. i. See* BARK. -*s.* खातं, वंकः ; 'turn to b.' 'stand at b.' शत्रोरभिमुखं स्था 1 P ; 'b. salt.' समुद्रलवणं, सैंधवं.

BAYONET, *s.* निस्त्रिंशः, गुलिकाप्रक्षेपणीसंसक्ता छुरिका.

BAZAR, *s.* आपणः-णं, पण्यवीथिका-वीथी, विपणि-णी *f.*, हट्टः, निषद्या.

BE, *v. i.* भू 1 P, अस् 2 P, वृत् 1 A, विद् 4 A; 'b. it so' भवतु, एवं-तथा-अस्तु. - BEING, *s.* भावः, अवस्था, वृत्ति *f.*, अस्तित्वं, सत्ता. 2 भूतं, सत्वः-त्वं ; 'rational b.' सचेतनः, प्राणिन् *m.*; 'corporal b.' शरीरिन् *m.*, देहिन् *m.* ; 'Supreme B.' परमेश्वरः, परमात्मन् *m.* 2 जन्मन् *n.*, संभवः, उत्पत्ति *f.* -*a.* सत् (ती *f.*), वर्तमान ; 'b. that' यतः, यस्मात् ; ex. by abl. or instr. of nouns.

BEACH, *s.* (समुद्र-) तीरं, कूलं, वेला, तटं-टी.- Y, *a.* तटयुक्त, कूलमय (यी *f.*).

BEACON, *s.* आकाशदीपः, महोल्का.

BEAD, *s.* गुली, गुटिका ; 'a string of b. s' माला; हारः ; 'a rosary of b.s ; ' जप-अक्ष-माला ; 'telling b. s' जपमालां गण् 10.-MAN, *s.* जपकरणे नियुक्तो जनः.

BEADLE, *s.* राजदूतः , दंडधरः.

BEAK, *s.* चंचु *f.*, चंचूः, मुखं, तुंडः-डं.-ED, *a.* चंचुमत् (ती *f.*), तुंडयुक्त.

BEAM, *s.* तुला, स्थूणा ; 'of a balance' दंडः, यष्टि *f.* ; 'of a carriage' धुर् *f.* 2 किरणः, अंशुः; *See* RAY. -*v. i.* प्रोत्-वि-लस् 1 P, स्फुर् 6 P ; 'a face b. ing with joy' मुदा विलसदाननं. -LESS, *a.* निष्प्रभ, निस्तेजस्. -Y, *a.* भास्वत् (ती *f.*), भासुर, देदीप्यमान, अंशुमत्.

BEAN, *s.* माषः, शिंबिकः.

BEAR, *v. t.* वह् 1 P, नी 1 P. 2 धृ 1 P, आलंब् 1 A, भृ 3 U (राज्यभारमुवाह-बभार). 3 सह् 1 A, मृष् 4 P, 10, क्षम् 1 A. 4 प्रसू 2 A ; उत्पद् c., जन् c. (जनयति) ; 'Satyavati bore two sons to the king' नृपेण सत्यवत्यां पुत्रौ जातौ,-उत्पादितौ, नृपः सत्यवत्यां पुत्रावजीजनत्; the same sense ex. in स नैषधस्य सुतायां पुत्रमुत्पादयामास (R. XVIII. 1) 'he had a son by the daughter' &c. 5 (Cherish) भृ 3 U, धृ 1 P ; 'I b. no malice to you' तवोपरि द्वेषं न धारयामि, or न त्वं मम द्वेषपात्रं-स्थानं ; 'he bore himself bravely on the occasion' तस्मिन्नवसरे तेन साधु आचरितं, धीरं विक्रांतं ; 'b. witness' साक्ष्यं दा 3 P (with gen.) ; 'b. company' सहचरः (री *f.*) भू 1 P ; 'b. name' नाम भृ 3 U, or धृ 10 ; व्यपदेशं भज् 1 A; (एवंव्यपदेशभाजिनः U. 6); 'b. fruit' सफलीभू, फल् 1 P; 'b. in mind' चित्ते अवधृ 10, मनसि कृ, अनुस्मृ 1 P. -*s.* ऋक्षः, भल्लूकः, भालुकः.

—BORN, *a.* जात, उत्पन्न, प्रसूत, संभूत; 'to be b.' जन् 4A; उत्पद् 4 A; प्रसू pass., उद्भू 1 P, संभू; was b. in the form of a dwarf' वामनरूपेण जातः-अवतीर्णः. —back, *v. i.* परा-प्रति-नि-वृत् 1 A.—down, *v. t.* अपाकृ 8 U; पराजि 1 A, निपत् c.; 'bore down all opposition' सर्वमंतरायमपाकुर्वन्. —on, *v. i.* *See* APPLY. —out, *v. t.* (fig.) दृढयति (D.); समर्थ् 10.—up, *v.* उद्वह् c., उत्तंभ् c., as in झटिति घटनोत्तंभितामिव (U. 3). 2 सह् 1A; 'b. under grief' दुःखप्रतिकारं कुरु, शोकवशं मा गमः. —ER, *s.* वाहः, हरः, वाहकः, in comp, वार्ताहरः 'b. of news'. —ING, *s.* अवस्थानं, स्थिति *f.* 2 वृत्ति *f.*, वर्त्तनं, आचरणं, रीति *f.* —BIRTH, *s.* जन्मन् *n.*, उद्भवः, संभवः, उत्पत्ति *f.*, जनि *f.*, उत्पादनं, प्रसूति *f.*; 'rich from his b.' गर्भेश्वरः; 'high or noble b.' कुलं, कुलीनता, अभिजातता, अभिजनः, कुले जन्म. 2 वंशः, कुलं, अन्वयः. 3 योनि *f.*, मूलं; 'pride of b.' कुलाभिमानः; 'blind from b.' जात्यंध, जन्मांध, जन्वंध. —DAY, *s.* जन्मदिवसः-दिनं. —PLACE, *s.* जन्मस्थानं-भूमि *f.* —RIGHT, *s.* जन्मतो लब्धोधिकारः; पैतृकं स्वत्वं.

BEARD, *s.* श्मश्रु *n.*, कूर्चं; मुखरोमन् *n*; 'wearing long b.s.' दीर्घकूर्चाः (pl.). 2 शूकं, किंशारुः. 3 फलं, कर्णः. —*v. t.* न्यक्कृ 8 U, समक्षं अवज्ञा 9 U or निर्भर्त्स् 10 A or अधिक्षिप् 6 P. —ED, *a.* सश्मश्रु; श्मश्रुल, कूर्चधर &c. —LESS, *a.* श्मश्रुहीन; अजात-अनुद्भिन्न-श्मश्रु. 2 अप्राप्तव्यवहार.

BEAST, *s.* पशुः, मृगः, जंतुः; 'b. of prey' श्वापदः; 'b. of burden' धुर्यः, धुरीणः; 'b. in the form of man' नरपशुः. —IAL, —LY, *a.* पशुतुल्य; जघन्य, पशुशील.

BEAT, *s.* आघातः, प्रहारः; ताडनं. 2 स्पंदनं, स्फुरणं. —*v. t.* तड् 10, प्रह 1 P, तुद् 6 P, अभिहन् 2 P, आहन् 2 A, (आहतायां प्रयाणभेर्यां). 2 (defeat) विध्वंस् c., भंज् 7 P, पराजि 1 A, पराभू 1 U. 3 आलुड् c., चूर्ण् 10. —*v. i.* स्पंद्-कंप्-वेप्-1 A, स्फुर् 6 P; 'b. very fast' धमधमायते (D.). —down निपत् c.; (price) न्यूनीकृ. —into ताडनेन कृ or निर्मा 3 A; 'I shall b. thee into a good boy' ताडयित्वा ताडयित्वा त्वामहं विद्वांसं करिष्यामि.—off विद्रु c., प्रतिहन्. —about the bush, (lit.) वनं ग्रह 9 P, आलुड 10; (fig.) अप्रस्तुतमालप् 1 P.

BEATIFY, *v. t.* परमानंदं दा 3 U. 2 अमरेषु गण् 10, स्वर्गीयलोकमध्ये आरुह् c. —IC, *a.* अपवर्गद, मोक्षप्रद.

BEATITUDE, *s.* मोक्षः, मुक्ति *f.*, निःश्रेयसं, अपवर्गः, निर्वाणं, परमा गतिः, कैवल्यं; 'desirous of b.' मुमुक्षुः.

BEAU, *s.* सुवेशः, सुभगंमन्यः.

BEAUTY, *s.* सौंदर्यं, चारुता, लावण्यं, शोभा, कांति *f.*, रूपं, रमणीयता, अभिख्या, मनोज्ञत्वं, श्रीः, लक्ष्मीः. —BEAUTIFY, *v. t.* शुभ् c., भूष् 10, अलंकृ 8U. —BEAUTIFUL, BEAUTEOUS, *a.* सुंदर (री *f.*), रम्य, रमणीय, कांत, मनोज्ञ, सुरूप, लावण्यवत् (ती *f.*), रुचिर, शोभन, चारु (र्वी *f.*), मंजुल; oft., by सु in comp.; सुमुखं-सुस्थलं. —LY, *adv.* साधु, सुंदरं, सुष्ठु, सु in comps.

BEAVER, *s.* शिरस्त्राणभागः.

BECALM, *v. t.* निर्वात *a.* कृ 8 U, प्रशम् c. (शमयति); *See* CALM.

BECAUSE, *conj.* इति, हि (not at the beginning of a statement); यतः, यत्; more oft. ex. by कुतः, कस्मात् with abl.; by abl. or instr.; 'b. he is liable to the charge of inequality and cruelty' (नेश्वरो जगतः कारणमुपपद्यते) कुतः वैषम्यनैर्घृण्यप्रसंगात्; 'b. of' ex. by instr. or abl.; हेतोः, कारणात्; 'b. of this' इति हेतोः.

BECK, *s.* संज्ञा; संकेतः. —ON, *v. t.* शिरसा-हस्तेन संज्ञां-संकेतं दा 3 U. 2 संज्ञया आह्वे 1 P.

BECOME. *v. i.* भू 1 P, संपद् 4 A; वृत् 1A, जन् 4 A; in majority of adjectives ex. by nouns with गम्, प्राप् &c.; 'became dejected' विषादं गतः, विषण्णो बभूव; 'b. s hated' द्वेष्यतां याति; 'became amazed' विस्मयमापेदे; 'b. ing curious' समुपजातकुतूहलः; 'what became of the queen Sita' सीतादेव्याः किं वृत्तं (U. 2), किमभवत्. —*v. t.* युज् pass., उपपद् 4 A, (with loc.); gen. ex. by अनुरूप, सदृश (शी *f.*), उचित, उपपन्न (all with gen.); 'does this b. thy matted hair' किमिदं जटानामनुरूपं, युक्तं-सदृशं &c. —ING, *a.* उचित, अनुरूप, युक्त, उपपन्न; 'it is b.' सांप्रतं. —INGLY, *adv.* यथोचितं, यथार्हं, युक्तं, अनुरूपं.

BED, *s.* शय्या, शयनं, तल्पः-ल्पं, संस्तरः, शयनीयं; 'leave the b.' मुंच शय्यां; 'confined to b.' 'b. rid' शय्यागत, शय्याग्रस्त; 'polluter of other's b.' पारतल्पिकः, परतल्पगः; 'go to b.' स्वप् 2 P, शी 2 A; 'b. chamber,' 'b. room' शयनागारं, शयनगृहं, वासगृहं; 'b. clothes' शय्योपस्करः; 'b. sheet' शयनास्तरणं, उत्तरच्छदः; 'b. stead' पर्यंकः, खट्वा, मंचः. 2 (of a river) मध्यं, स्यपथः. 3 फलकः. —BEDDING, *s.* शय्योपकरणं, शयनसामग्री.

BEDASH, BEDAGGLE, *See* STAIN.

BEDAUB, *See* DAUB.

BEDECK, BEDIZEN, *v. t.* विभूष् 10, *See* ADORN.

BEDEW, *v. t.* आर्द्रीकृ 8 U, क्लिद् c., प्रोक्ष् 1 P, सिच् 6 P.

BEDIM, *v. t.* मलिनीकृ 8 U, कलुषीकृ; 'eyes b. ed with tears' बाष्पप्रकरकलुषां दृष्टिं (S. 6).

BEDLAM, *s.* उन्मत्तानां निवासः, वातुलालयः. —*a.*, —ITE, उन्मत्त, वातुल.

BEE, *s.* अलिः, भ्रमरः, द्विरेफः, शिलीमुखः, भृंगः, मधुकरः, षट्पदः; 'honey b.' सरघा, मधुमक्षिका; 'b. hive' मधुकोषः; 'bees-wax' मधुजं, शिक्थं.

BEEF, *s.* गोमांसं.

BEER, *s.* यवसुरा-रं, यवमद्यं.

BEETLE, *s.* पिंगकपिशा. 2 मुद्गरः.

BEFALL, *v. t.* आ-समा-पत् 1 P; 'such incidents b. worldly persons' आपतंति हि संसारपथमवतीर्णानामेतं वृत्तांताः (Ka. 175); उपस्था 1 U, उपनम् 1 P (with gen.); कस्यात्यंतं सुखमुपनतं दुःखमेकांततो वा; संपद् 4 A, घट् 1 A.

BEFIT, *v. t.* *See* BECOME.

BEFOOL, *v. t.* व्यामुह् c., विभ्रम् c. (भ्रमयति).

BEFORE, *prep.* (Time) प्राक्, पूर्वं, अर्वाक्, (with abl.). 2 (Place) पुरः, पुरतः, अग्रे, अग्रतः, पुरस्तात्, (with gen.); समक्षं, साक्षात्, प्रत्यक्षं.—*adv.* (place) *See* above. 2 (Time) पूर्वं in comp.; 'not heard b.' अश्रुतपूर्वं. —*conj.* यावत् न-तावत्; 'study your lesson b. he comes' यावदसौ नागच्छति तावत्पाठमधीष्व; एकस्य दुःखस्य न यावदंतं गच्छामि तावद्द्वितीयं समुपस्थितं मे; 'b. hand' प्रागेव, पूर्वमेव, प्रथममेव, अग्रे; 'b. mentioned' पूर्वोक्त, प्रागुक्त; 'as b.' यथा पुरा, यथापूर्वं; पूर्ववत्; 'in times gone b.' पुरा, गतकाले.

BEFOUL, *v. t.* दुष् c. (दूषयति); *See* STAIN.

BEFRIEND, *v. t.* अनुग्रह् 9 P; उपकृ 8 U, साहाय्यं कृ (with gen.).

BEG, *v. i.* भिक्ष् 1 A, भिक्षाटनं कृ 8 U, भिक्षां याच् 1 A. —*v. t.* अंजलिं बद्ध्वा-पादयोः पतित्वा विज्ञा c. (ज्ञापयति) or निविद् c. 2 याच् 1 A; अभि-प्र-अर्थ् 10 A; 'b. s. to say' विज्ञापयति; 'b. favour of' प्रसद् c., अनुनी 1 P. —GING, *s.* याचा, प्रार्थना. 2 भिक्षा, भिक्षाटनं. —BEGGAR, *v. t.* दरिद्रीकृ 8 U, सर्वस्वं हृ 1 P; 'b. s description' वर्णनातीत. *s.* -प्रार्थकः, अर्थिन् *m.*, भिक्षुः, याचकः, दरिद्रः. —LY, *a.* निर्धन, कृपण. 2 नीच, अपकृष्ट. —Y, *s.* दैन्यं, कार्पण्यं, दारिद्र्यं, भैक्ष्यं.

BEGET, *v. t.* जन् c. (जनयति), उत्पद् c.; प्रसू 2 A, सृज् 6 P. —TER, *s.* जनकः, उत्पादकः, जनयितृ *m.*

BEGIN, *v. t.* आ-प्रा-रभ् 1 A; प्र-उप-क्रम् 1 A, प्रस्तु 2 U, (प्रस्तूयतां भोः), प्रवृत् 1 A; 'the wind began' वातोभिसरोभूत्. —NER, *s.* आरब्धृ *m.*, नवच्छात्रः, —NING, *s.* आरंभः, उपक्रमः. 2 आदि *m.*; 'having no b.' अनादि. 3 मूलं, योनि *f.*, प्रभवः; 'b. with' आदि-आद्य- in comp.; 'in the b.' आदौ; 'from the b.' आमूलात्, आदितः; 'god has neither b. nor end' अनाद्यनंत ईश्वरः.

BEGIRD, *v. t.* परिवेष्ट् 1 A or c., अव-बध् 7 U, आ-परि-वृ 5 U; वलय, रसना, in comp.; समुद्ररसना-उदधिवलया-पृथ्वी 'earth begirt by sea'.

BEGONE, *interj.* अपेहि, अपसर, अपयाहि.

BEGREASE, *v. t.* वसया लिप् 6 P, or स्निग्धीकृ 8 U.

BEGRIME, *See* SOIL.

BEGRUDGE, *See* ENVY, *v. t.*

BEGUILE, *v. t.* विनुद् c., अतिवह् c. (of time) (कथाभिर्दिवसमत्यवाहयत्). 2 व्यामुह् c., वंच् 10, विप्रलभ् 1 A, आकृष् 1 P; प्र-वि-लुभ् c.

BEHALF, (on or in) अर्थे, अर्थे, हेतोः, कारणात्, कृते (with gen.).

BEHAVE, *v. i.* आचर् 1P, वृत् 1 A, व्यवहृ 1 P; *See* ACT. 2 वृत्तिं कृ 8 U, अनुष्ठा 1 P; 'well b. ed' सदाचारः. —BEHAVIOUR, *s.* आचारः, वृत्ति *f.*, व्यवहारः, चेष्टितं, चरितं, आचरणं.

BEHEAD, *v. t.* शिरः (*n.*) छिद् 7 P or कृत् 6 P. —ING, *s.* शिरच्छेदः; 'worthy of b.' शीर्षच्छेद्यः.

BEHEST, *See* COMMAND (*s.*).

BEHIND, *prep.* पश्चात्, पृष्ठतः, (with gen.); अनु (with acc.); 'concealing his body b. the creepers' लतांतरित-लताव्यवहितविग्रहः; 'he is far b. (backward)' मंदः, मंदधीः; 'b. the scenes' नेपथ्ये. —*adv.* पृष्ठतः; 'from b.' पश्चादेत्य, पृष्ठेनागत्य. 2 अवरतः, अधस्तात्. 3 दूरे, दूरतः; 'b. part' पश्चाद्देशः, पृष्ठं, नितंबः.

BEHOLD, *v. t.* दृश् 1 P, ईक्ष् 1 A; *See* SEE. —EN, *a.* उपकारज्ञ, कृतोपकारेण पराधीन. —ER, *s.* प्रेक्षकः, दर्शकः, द्रष्टृ *m.*

BEHOOF, *s.* अर्थः, फलं, वृद्धि *f.*, लाभः.

BEHOVE, *v. t.* Ex. by pot. pass. part., pot. mood, or अर्ह् 1 P; 'it b. s thee to assist me' त्वया मम साहाय्यं कर्तव्यं, साहाय्यं कर्तुमर्हसि &c., *See* BECOME, *v. t.*

BELABOUR, *v. t.* *See* BEAT.

BELAY, *v. t.* प्रति-उप-रुध् 7 U.

BELCH, *v. t.* उद्वम् 1 P, उद्गॄ 6 P. —ING, *s.* उद्वमनं, उद्गिरणं, उद्गारः.

BELEAGUER, *See* BESIEGE.

BELIE, *v. t.* असत्यं आरुह् c. (रोपयति); मिथ्याभियोगं कृ 8 U; परि-अप-वद् 1 A.

BELIEVE, *v. t.* विश्वस् 2 P (with loc.), श्रद्धा 3 U (with loc. of person and acc. of thing); प्रति-इ 2 P, (with acc.). 2 संभू c., तर्क् 10, मन

4 A. -ER, *s.* विश्वासिन् *m.*, श्रद्धालुः, श्रद्धान्वितः. -BELIEF, *s.* विश्वासः, विश्रंभः, प्रत्ययः. 2 श्रद्धा, आस्तिक्यबुद्धि *f.* 3 मति *f.*, बुद्धि *f.*; 'it is my b.' इति मे मतिः मतं, इत्यहं मन्ये.

BELIKE, *adv.* अपि नाम, किंस्वित्.

BELL, *s.* घंटा; 'small b.' किंकिणी; 'b. metal' कांस्यं, पीतलोहं; 'b. clapper' घंटावादकः.

BELLE, *s.* सुंदरी, रूपवती स्त्री; सुभगंमन्या.

BELLIGERENT, *a.*, *s.* बद्धसमर; योधनशील, युयुत्सु.

BELLOW, *v. i.* नद् 1 P, निनद्. गर्ज् 1 P, रस् 1 P, रट् 1 P, नर्द् 1 P. -ING, *s.* गर्जितं, निनादः, गर्जनं, रसितं.

BELLOWS, *s.* भस्त्रा, दृति *f.*, भस्त्री, चर्मप्रसेविका.

BELLY, *s.* उदरं, जठरं, तुंदं, कुक्षिः; 'b. ache' उदरशूलः-लं; 'b. full' आकंठं; उदरपूरणं (*s.*); 'b. bound' आनद्ध; बद्धोदर; 'b. god' उदरंभरिः, औदरिकः; 'b. worm' क्रिमिः; कृमिः.

BELONG, *v. i.* अस् 2 P, विद् 4 A, भू 1 P, with gen.; or by an adj. from noun; 'this book belongs to me' ममेदं पुस्तकं, or मदीयमेतत् पुस्तकं, 'b. ing to Râma' रामसकाशवर्तिन्; 'b. ing to spring' वासंतिक (की *f.*); 'b. ing to the king;' राजकीय. 2 संबंध् pass.; 'this does not b. to you' नायं तव व्यापारः.

BELOVED, *a.* प्रिय, इष्ट, दयित, वल्लभ; 'b. person' दयितजनः, &c.

BELOW, *prep.* अधः, अधस्तात्, तले, (with gen.). 2 ऊन in comp. 3 अयोग्य, अनर्ह, अननुरूप, असदृश (शी *f.*); 'the gods are b. Hari' अनु हरिं सुराः (S. K.) -*adv.* अधः, अधस्तात्; अधोभागे-लोके (in hell). 2 नीचे, अवरतः. 3 इह, इह लोके.

BELT, *s.* मेखला, रस (श) ना, कांची. -*v. t.* मेखलारूपेण परिवृ 5 U or परिवेष्ट् 1 A.

BEMANGLE, *See* MANGLE.

BEMIRE, *v. t.* पंकेन मलिनयति (D.) or दुष् c. (दूषयति).

BEMOAN, *See* LAMENT.

BENCH, *s.* पीठं; फलकः; 'b. of justice' धर्मासनं, व्यवहारासनं.

BEND, *v. t.* नम् c. (न-ना-मयति), अव-आ-नम् c. (नमयति), नम्रीकृ 8 U, आवृज् 10, वक्रीकृ, भुज्-, वि-आ-, 6 P; 'bent under the load of breasts' कुचभारानमिता, स्तनभरेण नम्रतामानीता, स्तनभारेणावर्जिता; 'b. the brow' भ्रूभंगं कृ; 'he bent his mind again to his task' स पुनरपि स्वकार्ये मनो न्यदधात्-बबंध-न्यवेशयत्; 'b. to one's will' वशीकृ. -*v. i.* आ-अव-प्र-नम् 1 P, नम्र-लीन- *a.* भू 1 P; 'trees b. down under the load of fruits' भवंति नम्रास्तरवः फलागमैः (S. 5) -BENT, *a.* आनमित; ना-न-मित, आभुग्न; प्रवण, प्रह्व, आवर्जित; 'b. on' कृतनिश्चय, सुनिश्चय, कृतसंकल्प, विहितप्रतिज्ञ; 'eagerly b. on (killing) each other' परस्परवधोद्यतौ. -*s.* नति *f.*, वक्रता, जिह्मता. 2 वंकः, पुटभेदः. 3 शीलं, वांछा, निश्चयः, प्रवृत्ति *f.*, अभिनिवेशः. -ING, *s.* नति *f.*, नमनं, अवनमनं.

BENEATH, *prep*, *adv.* *See* BELOW.

BENEDICTION, *s.* आशिस् *f.*, आशीर्वादः; नांदी (in dramas); आशास्यं, धन्यवादः. 2 स्तवः, स्तुति *f.* -BENEDICTORY, *a.* मांगलिक (की *f.*); 'b. stanza' नांदीश्लोकः; नांदी.

BENEFACTION, *s.* उपकारः, उपकृतं, हितं.

BENEFACTOR, *s.* उपकर्तृ *m.*, उपकारिन् *m.*, हितकृत् *m.*, उपकारकः, हित-प्रिय-करः.

BENEFICE, *s.* धर्मशिक्षकवृत्ति *f.*

BENEFICENCE, *s.* उपकारशीलता, परोपकारः; उपकारः, हितं, दया, कृपा, त्यागिता.

BENEFICENT, *a.* दान-त्याग-शील, परोपकारिन् (णी *f.*), उपकारपर. 2 (things) हितकर (री *f.*), हितकारिन्, हितावह.

BENEFICIAL, *a.* हित, हितावह, उपकारक, लाभजनक; कल्याणकारक, सुखप्रद.

BENEFIT, *s.* उपकारः, हितं, अनुग्रहः. 2 फलं, लाभः; 'for public b.' प्रजार्थं.-*v. t.* उपकृ 8 U, अनुग्रह् 9 P, हितं कृ, लाभं दा 3 U.

BENEVOLENCE, *s.* परहितेच्छा, परोपकारिता, दया, कृपा, उदारता. —BENEVOLENT, *a.* हितैषिन् (णी *f.*), उपकारपर, परोपकारशील, दयालु, परहितेच्छु.-LY, *adv.* परहितेच्छया, कृपया, दयापूर्वं.

BENIGHT, *v. t.* तमसा आच्छद् 10.-ED, *a.* तमोवृत, नैशतमसाक्रांत; (fig.) अज्ञानतमोवृत.

BENIGN, BENIGNANT, *a.* दयालु, प्रेमपर, सदय, सुखप्रद, कृपालु.-ITY, *s.* दया, प्रीति *f.*, कृपा, अनुग्रहः, दयालुत्वं.

BENISON, *s.* आशिस् *f.*, आशीर्वादः.

BENUMB, *v. t.* जडयति (D.), जडीकृ 8 U, स्तंभ् 9 P.

BEQUEATH, *v. t.* मृत्युसमये इच्छापत्रेण दा 3 U or ऋ c. (अर्पयति), or प्रतिपद् *c.*-BEQUEST, *s.* रिक्थप्रदानं.

BEREAVE, *v. t.* विनाकृ 8 U, वियुज् 10, (with instr. for 'of'); 'b. ed of Madana' मदनेन विनाकृता. 2 अपनी 1 P, भ्रंश् c., 'to be b. ed' परिहा pass., वियुज् pass.-ED, BEREFT, *a.* रहित, हीन, वियुक्त, हत-गत in comp.-MENT, *s.* विप्रयोगः, वियोगः; विरहः.

BERRY, *s.* गुली, गुटिका.

BESCATTER, *See* SCATTER.

BESEECH, *v. t.* अनुनी 1 P, प्रसद् c., विनयेन याच् 1 A or प्रार्थ् 10A.-ER, *s.* प्रार्थकः, याचकः, अर्थिन् *m.*

BESEEM, -LY, *See* BECOME.

BESET, *v. t.* रुध् 7 U, आकुलीकृ 8U, आक्रम् 1 U, 4 P, संबाध् 1 A, उपपीड् 10, अभिभू 1 P. -*a.* आकुल, अभिभूत; 'b. with difficulties or dangers' संकटाकुल, अनर्थसंबाध, विपदभिभूत.

BESHREW, *v. t.* अमंगलं प्रार्थ् 10 A.

BESIDE, *prep.* पार्श्वे, समीपं -पे; अभितः, परितः (acc.); निकटं-टे (gen.). 2 असंबद्ध *a.*; 'b. oneself with joy' आनंदपरवशः, आनंदेन विगतचेतन इव भूत्वा; 'this is b. the question' अप्रास्ताविकं-अप्रासंगिकं- एतत्, अप्रकृतं.

BESIDES, *prep.* Ex. by भिन्न, व्यतिरिक्त, अपर, इतर, in comp., or with abl. -*adv.* अपरंच, अन्यच्च, किंच, अपिच, अधिकं.

BESIEGE, *v. t.* रुध् 7 U, अव-उप-रुध्, परिवेष्ट् 1 A or c., आक्रम् 1 U, 4 P.-ER, *s.* अव-उप-रोधकः.-ING, *s.* उप-अव-रोधः, रोधनं.

BESLAVE, *v. t.* वशीकृ 8 U, दम् c. (दमयति).

BESMEAR, *v. t.* वि-आ-अनु-लिप् 6 P, अंज् 7 P, दिह् 2 U.-ED, *a.* लिप्त, अक्त, दिग्ध; विषदिग्धः शरः 'b. with poison'; रक्ताक्तः 'b. with blood'.

BESOM, *s.* मार्जनी, शोधनी.

BESORT, *v. i.* युज् pass., उपपद् 4 A.

BESOT, *v. t.* मुह् c., जडीकृ 8 U.-TED, *a.* मूढबुद्धि, मूढात्मन्.

BESPANGLE, *v. t.* वलयैः अनुव्यध् 4 P or उप-शुभ् c. or भूष् 10.

BESPATTER, *v. t.* मलेन सिच् 6 P, मलिनयति (D.), कलुषयति (D.).

BESPEAK, *v. t.* सूच् 10, दृश् c., कथ् 10, *See* INDICATE; आकृतिरेवानुमापयत्यमानुषतां (Ka. 132) 'b. s its being superhuman.'

BESPECKLE, BESPRINKLE, *See* SPECKLE, SPRINKLE.

BEST, *a.* प्रशस्ततम, उत्तम, श्रेष्ठ, परम, परार्ध्य; 'to the b. of one's capacity or power' यथाशक्ति, यावच्छक्यं; 'to the b. of one's belief' यथामति; 'b. of' ex. by रत्न or वर in comp.; स्त्रीरत्नं, मुनिवरः.

BESTAIN, *See* STAIN.

BESTEAD, *v. t.* लाभाय भू 1 P, हिताय क्लृप् 1 A.

BESTIAL, *See* under BEAST.

BESTIR, (oneself) चेष्ट् 1 A, घट् 1 A, प्रयत् 1 A, उद्यमं कृ 8 U, व्यवसो 4 P.

BESTOW, *v. t.* दा 1P, 3 U, प्रदा, प्रतिपद् c., (with dat.) विन्यस् 1 P (with loc.). 2 प्रयुज् 7 A, 10, निक्षिप् 6 P; 'b. ing wealth on proper persons' वित्तस्य पात्रे व्ययः; 'great care seems to be b. ed on this picture' इदमालेख्यं प्रयत्नतः-सुनिपुणं-निर्मितमिति अनुमीयते; 'b. oneself' सेव् 1 A, आस्था 1 A, मनो निविश् c. -AL, *s.* दानं, प्रतिपादनं. -ER, *s.* दातृ *m.*, प्रदः in comp.

BESTRAUGHT, *a.* व्यग्र, चिंताकुल; *See* ANXIOUS.

BESTREW, *v. t.* आस्तृ-स्तृ 5-9 U.

BESTRIDE, *v. t.* पादौ पृथक् कृत्वा आ-अधिरुह् 1 P or अधिक्रम् 1 U, 4 P.

BESTUD, *v. t.* अनुव्यध् 4 P, खच् 10.

BET, *s.* पणः, प्रतिज्ञा. -*v. t.* पण् 1 A (with gen. of thing staked); शतस्य पणते (S. K.).

BETAKE, (oneself to) *v. t.* आश्रि 1 U, अंगीकृ 8 U; अरण्यवासमंगीचकार 'betook himself to forest residence'.

BETEL, *s.* (tree) तांबूली, पुन्नागवल्ली, नागलता; 'b. box' तांबूलकरंकः, पूगपात्रं; 'b. nut' पूगं, तांबूलं; 'b. box bearer' तांबूलकरंकवाहिन् (नी *f.*).

BETHINK, *v. t.* अनुध्यै. 1 P, विमृश् 6 P; *See* THINK.

BETIDE, *v. t.* आपत् 1 P, उपस्था 1 U, (gen.), *See* BEFALL; 'may woe b. him' अभद्रं तस्य भूयात्.

BETIMES, *adv.* प्रभाते, प्रातः, प्रत्यूषे. 2 यथासमयं, वेलायां, यथावसरं.

BETOKEN, *v. t.* सूच् 10, दृश् c., *See* INDICATE.

BETRAY, *v. t.* शत्रुकरेषु ऋ c. (अर्पयति), विश्वासघातेन ऋ c. 2 भिद् 7 U; 'b. ed the secret' रहस्यं बिभेद. 3 Indicate, q. v. 4 वंच् 10; *See* CHEAT; 'b. themselves' आत्मस्वरूपं प्रकटयंति. -ER, *s.* विश्वासघातकः; वंचकः.

BETRIM, *v. t.* भूष् 10, अलंकृ 8 U.

BETROTH, *v. t.* (वाचा) दा 3 U, प्रतिपद् c., प्रतिश्रु 5 P, (dat.). -AL, *s.* वाग्दानं, वाक्प्रदानं.

BETRUST, *See* ENTRUST.

BETTER, *a.* श्रेयस् (सी *f.*), भद्रतर, गरीयस्, प्रशस्ततर, साधीयस्; 'b. than' वरं-न; 'better death than disgrace (I prefer death to disgrace)' वरं मृत्युर्न पुनरपमानः. 2 (In health) ex. by विशेषः; 'I am b. to-day' अस्ति मे विशेषोऽद्य (S. 3). -*adv.* वरं, श्रेयः, भद्रतरं, अधिकतरं, अधिकं. 2 (With verbs) ex. by तरां; 'he cooks b. than Râma' रामात्पचतितरां. -*s.* श्रेष्ठता, प्रमुखत्वं, वर्चस्वं; 'get the b. of' अभिभू 1P, अतिरिच् pass., *See* EXCEL. -*v. t.* वृध् c.; कृ with (*a.*) -BETTERS, गुरुजनः, गुरवः (pl.).

BETWEEN, BETWIXT, *prep.* मध्ये, अभ्यंतरे, अंतरे, मध्यस्थाने; oft. ex. by gen. of nouns; देशयोरंतरं 'distance b. the two countries'; 'b. joy and sorrow (tears)' शोकानंदमध्यवर्तिनी (Ka. 318).

BEVERAGE, *s.* पानं, पेयं, पानीयं; 'b. of the Gods' अमृतं.

BEVY, *s.* गणः, संघः, समवायः.

BEWAIL, *v. t.* विलप् 1 P, शुच् 1 P, *See* LAMENT.–ING, *s.* शोकः, विलापः, परिदेवनं.

BEWARE, *v. i.* सावधान-अप्रमत्त-अवहित-*a.* भू 1 P; 'b. of your enemies' शत्रुविषये सावधानो भव; 'b. lest you will be seduced by pleasures' सावधानो भव नीचेंद्रियविषयैः प्रलोभ्येथाः; or तथा प्रयतेथा यथानाक्षिप्यसे विषयैः (Ka. 109).

BEWEEP, BEWET, *See* WEEP, WET.

BEWILDER, *v. t.* आकुलीकृ 8 U, विक्लवीकृ, व्या-सं-मुह् c., संभ्रम् c. (भ्रमयति), जडीकृ. –ED, *a.* विक्लव, आकुलीभूत, आ-व्या-कुल, विमूढ, विह्वल, संभ्रांत; 'b. what to do' किंकर्तव्यतामूढः, प्रतिपत्तिमूढः. –MENT, *s.* संभ्रमः, वैक्लव्यं, संमोहः, व्याकुलत्वं.

BEWITCH, *v. t.* मुह् c., सं-वि-परि°, वशीकृ 8 U, मद् c. (मनो मदयंति ये Mal. 2); मंत्रेण वशीकृ. 2 मनो हृ or आकृष् 1 P. –ING, *a.* मोहन (नी *f.*), हारिन् (णी *f.*). –MENT, *s.* मोहनं, मोहः, वशीकरणं, माया, आकर्षणं.

BEWRAY, *See* BETRAY.

BEYOND, *prep.* परतः (with abl.), अतिक्रम्य, अतीत्य, (with acc.); 'b. the forest is the Kailâsa' तदरण्यमतिक्रम्य कैलासगिरिः (Ka. 121); 'Oh! Change b. belief' अहो विश्वासातिक्रांतो (अविश्वास्यः) दशाविपर्यासः; 'b. comprehension' अगम्य, दुर्ज्ञेय, दुर्बोध; 'b. expectations' मनोरथानामभूमिः (S. 7); gen. ex. by अति pr.; अधिकं; 'b. measure' अतिमात्रं; 'b. human power' अतिमानुषं; 'b. this continent' द्वीपांतरे; 'lives b. his means' आयाधिकं व्ययं करोति. –*adv.* दूरे, पारे-रं; 'go or pass b.' अतिक्रम् 1 U, अति-इ 2 P.

BIAS, *s.* स्पृहा, अभिलाषः. 2 शीलं, भावः. 3 पक्षपातः, पक्षपातित्वं. 4 प्रोत्साहनं, प्रवर्तनं. –*v. t.* प्रवृत् c., प्रणुद् 6 P, प्रोत्सह् c. 2 साचीकृ 8 U; दुष् c. (दूषयति).

BIBBER, *s.* मद्यपायिन् *m.*, सुरापः, मद्यपः.

BIBLIOGRAPHY, *s.* पुस्तकविद्या.

BIBLIOMANIA, *s.* दुर्लभपुस्तकसंग्रहणोन्मादः or -व्यग्रता.

BIBULOUS, *a.* जलशोषक.

BICKER, *v. i.* कलहं कृ 8 U, विवद् 1 A, वाग्युद्धं कृ. –ING, *s.* कलहः, विवादः, कलिः. 2 डिंबाहवः.

BID, *v. t.* आ-व्या-दिश् 6 P, आज्ञा c. (ज्ञापयति). 2 मूल्यं ख्या c. (ख्यापयति) or उद्घुष् 10. 3 निमंत्र् 10 A; 'b. welcome' स्वागतं वद् 1 P, or व्याह् 1 P; 'b. adieu or farewell' आमंत्र् 10A, आप्रच्छ् 6 A; 'b. defiance' धृष् 5 P, आह्वे 1 A. –DER, *s.* क्रेतृ *m.* –DING, *s.* आज्ञा, आदेशः, शासनं. 2 मूल्यख्यापनं, अर्घघोषणा.

BIDE, *v. t.* स्था 1 P, वृत् 1 A. –*v. t.* प्रतीक्ष् 1A. 2 सह् 1 A.

BIDENTAL, *a.* द्विदत् (ती *f.*), द्विरद.

BIENNIAL, *a.* द्विवार्षिक (की *f.*), द्विवर्षीण, द्वैवर्षिक.

BIER, *s.* शवयानं, कटः, खाटः-टी.

BIFOLD, *a.* द्विगुण, द्वैध (धी *f.*).

BIFORMED, *a.* द्विरूप.

BIFURCATE, *v. t.* द्विधा कृ 8 U, विभिद् 7 P or c. –ED, *a.* द्व्यग्र. 2 विश्लेषित, द्विधा कृत.

BIG, *a.* महाकाय, बृहत्काय (of animate creatures); महाप्रमाण, अतिप्रमाण, स्थूल, विपुल, बृहत् (ती *f.*), पृथु (थुः, थ्वी *f.*). 2 Pregnant, q. v. 3 संकुल, पूर्ण, संकीर्ण, आकीर्ण; 'as b. as' परिमाण, परिमित, मात्र, in comp.; बिल्वमात्र 'b. as Bilwa.' –NESS, *s.* स्थूलता, वैपुल्यं &c. 2 परिमाणं, प्रमाणं.

BIGAMY, *s.* (एककाले) द्वीपत्नीकरणं; द्विभर्तृकरणं. –IST, *s.* द्विपत्नीकः; द्विभर्तृका.

BIGOTRY, *s.* स्वमतासक्ति *f.*, स्वमताग्रहः, सनिर्बंधं स्वमतालंबनं.–BIGOTED, *a.*, BIGOT, *s.* निर्बंधशील, (अविचार्य) स्वमतरक्षिन् (णी *f.*), निर्बंधेन स्वमतावलंबिन्.

BILBO, *See* SWORD.

BILE, *s.* पित्तं, मायुः. –OUS, पैत्तिक (की *f.*), मायुमय (यी *f.*).

BILINGUOUS, *a.* द्विजिह्व.

BILK, *See* CHEAT.

BILL, *s.* पत्रं, लेखः. 2 चंचु (चू) *f.*, तुंडं. –*v. t.* *See* KISS, or EMBRACE.

BILLET, *s.* पत्रं, लेखः, लेख्यं. 2 काष्ठखंडं. –*v. t.* सैन्यानि वस् c.

BILLION, *s.* खर्वः.

BILLOW, *s.* महोर्मि *f.*, कल्लोलः, तरंगः. –*v. i.* तरंगायते (D.). –Y, *a.* कल्लोलमालाकुल, प्रचलदूर्मिमालाकुल; तरंगित.

BIN, *s.* कुशूलः, धान्यकोष्ठः.

BINARY, *a.* द्विगुण. द्वैध (धी *f.*).

BIND, *v. t.* बंध् 9 P, (lit. & fig.); नि-सं-यम् 1 P; 'bound by affection' स्नेहनिबद्धः; नियंत्र् 10; 'I am not bound by these rules' नाहमेभिर्विधिभिर्नियंत्रितोस्मि. 2 आनह् 4 P, पिनह्; 'b. together' सं-बंध्, संश्लिष् c.; ग्रंथ् 9 P, संह् 1 P, संयुज् 7 U, 10; 'b. oneself' प्रतिज्ञा 9 U, प्रतिश्रु 5P; 'b. by oath' शप् c.; 'b. on' ex. by pot. pass., part., or अर्ह् 1 P; 'the protection of your wife is b. ing on you' त्वया भार्यापोषणम-

वरयमेव कर्तव्यं. -ING, *s.* बंधः, बंधनं, वेष्टनं, पट्टः, आवरणं. -BOUND, *a.* बद्ध, निबद्ध, संयत, नियंत्रित, आनद्ध; 'you are b. to obey my orders' त्वया ममादेशा अनुरोद्धव्या एव, आदेशाननुरोद्धुमर्हसि ; 'where are you b.' कुत्र गंतुं कृतनिश्चयोसि-कुत्र गंतुकामोसि.

BINACULAR, *a.* द्विनेत्र, द्विनयन.

BIOGRAPHY, *s.* चरितं, जीवनवृत्तांतः. -ER, *s.* वृत्तांतलेखकः-आख्यातृ *m.*, चरितनिवेदकः.

BIPARTITION, *s.* द्विधाकरणं.

BIPED, *s.* द्विपाद् *m.*, or द्विपदः.

BIRCH, *s.* भूर्जः, मृदुत्वचः, प्रतिविषा. -EN, *a.* भूर्जमय (यी *f.*), भूर्जनिर्मित.

BIRD, *s.* विहगः, विहंगः,-गमः, पक्षिन् *m.*, खगः, शकुंतः, पतत्रिन् *m.*, गरुत्मत् *m.*, द्विजः, पत्रिन् *m.*, शकुंतिः, अंडजः, पतंगः, शकुनिः; 'bird's eye-view' उच्चस्थानादालोकनं, स्थूलदर्शनं, असूक्ष्मदृष्टिः.

BISCUIT, *s.* अपूपः, पिष्टकः, पूपः.

BISECT, *v. t.* समांशद्वयेन विभज् 1 U, द्विखंडीकृ 8 U, द्विधा छिद् 7 P.

BISHOP, *s.* धर्माध्यक्षः. -RIC, *a.* धर्माधिकारः.

BIT, *s.* खलीनः-नं, कविका. 2 खंडः, लवः, भागः; 'not a b.' न मनागपि, न स्तोकांशेनापि; गंधः (क्रियायाः गंधमात्रस्यापि अनुप्रवेश इह नोपपद्यते S. B. 74). 3 पिंडः, ग्रासः. -*v. t.* खलीनेन नियंत्र् 10.

BITCH, *s.* शुनी, कुक्कुरी, सरमा.

BITE, *v. t.* दंश् 1 P ; 'bit off a large piece' दंतैर्महाखंडं संदष्टवान्-चर्वितवान् ; उत्पट् 10, चर्व् 1 P, खाद् 1 P. 2 शीतेन पीड् 10. 3 अधिक्षिप् 6 P, *See* CENSURE. 4 पीड् 10, अर्द् 1 P, 10. -*s.* दंशः, दंशनं. 2 दंतपदं, दशनांकः. -ING, *s.* दंशनं ; 'b. of conscience' मनसोनुतापः. -*a.* दंशक. 2 पीडाकर (री *f.*).

BITTER, *a.* कटु, तिक्त. 2 (Touching) मर्मभिद्-छिद्. 3 उग्र, निठुर, परुष, तीक्ष्ण, कठोर. -LY, *adv.* निठुरं, परुषं. 2 अत्यंतं. 3 प्रमुक्तकंठं (weeping b.). -NESS, *s.* कटुता, शुक्तता, तीक्ष्णता. 2 दुःखातिरेकः, उग्रशोकः; 'in b. of soul' दुर्मनायमानचित्त *a.*, समन्युना चेतसा. 3 कठोरता, परुषता, निठुरता. 4 मात्सर्यं, पैशुन्यं.

BITUMEN, *s.* शिलाजतु *n.*, गिरिपुष्पकं, गैरेयं, गिरिजं, अश्मजं, अर्थ्यं.

BIVALVE, *a.* द्विकोष.

BLAB, *v. i.* रहस्यं भिद् 7 P. -BER, *s.* रहस्यभेदकः.

BLACK, *a.* कृष्ण, श्याम, कृष्णवर्ण, काल. 2 निष्प्रभ, तिमिर, असित, नील, मेचक. 3 (fig.) निंद्य, घोर, दारुण; 'b. deed' अपयशोमलिनं कर्म; 'b. guard' दुर्वृत्तः, दुराचारः, अधमः, खलः. -*s.* कृष्णः, कृष्णवर्णः; 'clothed in b.' नीलवस्त्रः. -EN, *v. t.* कृष्णकृ 8 U, श्यामी-नीलीकृ. 2 दुष् c. (दूषयति), कलंकयति (D.) *See* STAIN. -ISH, *a.* ईषत्कृष्ण, आनील. -NESS, *s.* कृष्णिमन् *m.*, श्यामत्वं, नीलता, कालिमन् *m.*, तमस् *n.*, तिमिरं. -SMITH, *s.* कर्मकारः, लोहकारः, अयस्कारः.

BLADDER, *s.* मूत्राशयः, वस्ति *m.*, *f.*

BLADE, *s.* (Of a sword) धारा, पत्रं, फलं. 2 (Of grass) दलं, कांडं, अंकुरः. 3 स्कंधास्थि *n.*

BLAIN, *s.* स्फोटः, व्रणः-णं.

BLAME, *v. t.* निंद् 1 P, गर्ह् 1, 10 A, उपालभ् 1 A; दोषं क्षिप् 6 P or आरुह् c. (रोपयति), *See* CENSURE; 'I am not to b.' नाहमपराधी, न ममायं दोषः. -*s.* दोषः, अपराधः. 2 गर्हा, आक्षेपः, उपालंभः, निंदा, जुगुप्सा; 'lays the b. on another' अन्यस्मिन्दोषं क्षिपति. -ABLE, *a.* निंद्य, निंदनीय, गर्हणीय, गर्ह्य, वाच्य; 'he is not b. or to blame' स न दोषास्पदं-दोषपात्रं. -ER, *s.* निंदकः, परिवादकः, अधिक्षेपकः. -LESS *a.* अनिंद्य, निर्दोष, निष्कलंक, विशुद्ध (pure). -LESSNESS, *s.* अनिंद्यता, अनवद्यता (अहो अनवद्यता रूपस्य M. 2), अवाच्यता, दोषाभावः.

BLANCH, *v. t.* शुक्लीकृ 8 U, धवलीकृ. 2 निस्तुषयति (D.), त्वचं निष्कृष् or अपनी 1 P. 3 Avoid, q. v.

BLAND, *a.* मृदु, कोमल, मसृण, सौम्य, श्लक्ष्ण; 'b. in speech' प्रियंवद. -ISH, *v. i.* शां(सां)त्व् 10, चाटूक्तिभिः तुष् c., अनुनी 1 P, उपच्छंद् 10. -ISHMENT, *s.* विलासः, विभ्रमः. 2 प्रियवाक्यं, चाटूक्ति *f.*, मधुरभाषितं, उपच्छंदनं, अनुनयः.

BLANK, *a.* शुभ्र, शुक्ल; 'b. with fear' भयविवर्णः-विवर्णाननः. 2 शून्य, रिक्त, लेखारहित. 3 एकांत, अत्यंत; 'b. despair' एकांततो नैराश्यं. 4 अनुप्रास-यमक-हीन (verse). -*s.* लेखाशून्यं पत्रं. 2 शून्यता; रिक्तं, शून्यं.

BLANKET, *s.* कंबलः, उर्णायुः, रल्लकः.

BLASPHEME, *v. t.* ईश्वरं निंद् 1 P or अवमन् 4 A or अभिशप् 1 U. -OUS, *a.* ईश्वरनिंदक, पाषंडीय. -Y, *s.* पाषंडता, ईश्वरनिंदा.

BLAST, *s.* वात्या, वातः, वायुवेगः, प्रभंजनः, झंझानिलः. 2 ध्मानं (of horns). 3 विनाशः, क्षयः, अपायः. -*v. t.* विनश् c., विहन् 2 P, म्लानीकृ 8 U, विशृ c., क्षै c. (क्षपयति); 'b. ed by lightning' अशनिहतः. -ER, *s.* विनाशकः.

BLAZE, *v. i.* ज्वल् 1 P, प्र-उत्°-, दीप् 4 A, सं-उत्-प्र-°; 'b. ing' उज्ज्वल, प्रदीप्त, देदीप्यमान, भास्वर, *See* BRIGHT; 'b. abroad' प्रकाश् c., प्रख्या c. (ख्यापयति). -*s.* प्रभा, अर्चिस् *f.*, *n.*, दीप्ति *f.*, ज्वाला; 'b. of light' रश्मि-अंशु-जालं.

BLAZON, *v. t.* भूष् 10, अलंकृ 8 U. 2 प्रख्या c. (ख्यापयति), प्रकाश् c., उद्घुष् 10.

BLEACH, *v. t.* निर्णिज् 3 U, धाव् 1 P, 10, धवली-

कृ 8 U. -ED, *a.* धौत, निर्णिक्त. -ER, *s.* धावकः, वस्त्रनिर्णेजकः.

BLEAK, *a.* अतिशीत (winter) ; शिशिर, हैमंत (ती *f.*), हिमशीत. 2 (fig.) निरानंद, असुभग.

BLEAR-EYED, *a.* क्लिन्नाक्ष, चुल, चिल, पिल्ल; 'b. eye' चुल्लः &c.

BLEAT, *v. i.* रेभ् 1 A, मेंमें शब्दं कृ 8 U, उ 1 A. -ING, *s.* रेभणं, मेषरुतं, उरभ्रनादः.

BLEED, *v. t.* रक्तं-रुधिरं &c. (blood) मुच् c. or स्रु c. or मोक्ष् 10, with gen. of person or part bled; 'they b. the wound' क्षतेः रक्तमोक्षणं कुर्वंति. -*v. i.* रक्तं-रुधिरं स्रु 1 P, or मुच् 6 P, or प्रवह् 1 P ; 'his hand b. s' तस्य हस्ताद्रुधिरं स्रवति ; 'b. ing profusely' रुधिरप्राग्भारनिस्यंदिन् (Mal. 5) ; 'to b. for one's country' स्वदेशार्थे जीवितं त्यज् 1 P. -ER, रक्तस्रावकः-मोचकः. -ING, *s.* रक्तस्रावः, रक्तमोक्षणं, रक्तस्रुति *f.*, रुधिरक्षरणं.

BLEMISH, *s.* दोषः, कलंकः, छिद्रं ; 'un-b. ed' निष्कलंक, निर्दोष. 2 अपयशस् *n.*, अकीर्ति *f.* -*v. t.* मलिनयति (D.), कलंकयति (D.), दुष् c. (दूषयति).

BLENCH, *v. i.* सहसा संकुच् 1 P. 2 सहसा अपसृ 1 P or अपक्रम् 1 U, 4 P or निवृत् 1 A ; पराङ्मुख (खी *f.*) भू 1 P.

BLEND, *v. t.* मिश्र् 10, संयुज् 10, एकत्र कृ 8 U ; 'to be b. ed' संकॄ pass. ; संमिल् 6 P, एकीभू 1 P. -ED, *a.* संमिश्र, व्यामिश्र, संकीर्ण, संसृष्ट, मिश्रीकृत. 2 एकरूप, एकीभूत.

BLESS, *v. t.* Gen. ex. by Imperative or Benedictive of verb ; 'I b. that you may get a son' पुत्रं लभस्व or लप्सीष्ठाः. 2 आशास् 2 A, आशिषं दा 3 U ; वितॄ 1 P (with loc.) ; त्वयि वितरतु भद्रं (U. 3) 'b. you with auspicious good.' 3 सुखिन् (नी *f.*)-धन्य *a.* कृ 8 U; 'was b. ed with a son' सुतलाभेन कृती बभूव. -ED, *a.* धन्य, महाभाग, कल्याण (णी *f.*), मंगल, सुखिन्, सुखभाज् ; 'of b. memory or name' सुगृहीतनामन् *a.* (म्नी *f.*), पुण्यश्लोक. -EDNESS, *s.* धन्यता, कृतार्थता. 2 परमानंदः, परमसुखं ; परं पदं, अपवर्गः. -ING, *s.* आशिस् *f.*, आशीर्वादः, आशीर्वचनं. 2 वरः. हितं. उपकारः, कुशलं, धन्यत्वं ; लाभः, सुखं.

BLIGHT, *v. t.* विफलीकृ 8 U, नश् c., *See* BLAST ; 'schemes of policy b. ed by opposing fate' विगुणविधियोगात्रयाः फलैर्हीनाः (Mu. 6). -*s.* नाशः, क्षयः.

BLIND, *a.* अंध ; 'born b.' जन्मांधः ; 'b. following the b.' अंधपरंपरा ; 'b. of one eye' अक्ष्णा काणः. 2 अज्ञान, हतज्ञान. -*v. t.* अंधीकृ 8 U, अंधयति (D.); 'b. ed by rage' क्रोधांधः; कामांधः, &c. -*s.* तिरस्कारिणी, व्यवधानं, यवनिका. 2 छद्मन् *n.*, कपटं. -FOLD, *v. t.* वस्त्रेण नयने पिधा 3 U or बंध् 9 P or अवरुध् 7 U ; b. ed बद्धनेत्र, अवरुद्धनयन. -LY, *adv.* अंधवत्, असमीक्ष्य, रभसा, साहसेन. -NESS, *s.* अंधता. 2 अज्ञानं, मोहः.

BLINK, *v. i.* निमील् 1 P, निमिष् 6 P. -*s.*, -ING, निमि (मे) षः, दृष्टिनिपातः, निमीलनं.

BLISS, *s.* परमसुखं, सुखातिशयः, प्रहर्षः, धन्यता, अत्यंतसुखं. 2 अपवर्गः; *See* BEATITUDE. -FUL, *a.* आनंदमय (यी *f.*), धन्य, सानंद, परमसुखभाज् ; सुखावह. -FULLY, *adv.* परमानंदपूर्वकं, सानंदं, ससुखं. -LESS, *a.* सुखहीन-रहित, निरानंद.

BLISTER, *s.* त्वक्स्फोटः, शोफः; व्रणः-णं, 'b. on the foot' पादस्फोटः, विपादिका. 2 स्फोटजननः उपनाहः. -*v. t.* स्फोटं उत्पद c.

BLITHE, BLITHESOME, *a.* हृष्ट, प्रमुदित, सानंद, प्रसन्नवदन. -LY, *adv.* सहर्षं, सानंदं, हृष्टमनसा. -NESS, *s.* प्रहर्षः, आह्लादः, आनंदः.

BLOAT, *v. t.* श्वि c., आप्यै c., पीनीकृ 8 U. -*v. i.* स्फाय् 1 A, श्वि 1 P, आप्यै 1 A. -ED, *a.* शून पान, स्फीत, आप्यायित.

BLOCK, *s.* काष्ठं; शिला (of stone) ; 'b. of snow' शिलीभूतं हिमं, घनं हिमं. 2 वध्यशिला-काष्ठं. 3 उपरोधः, प्रत्यूहः, अंतरायः. 4 पिंडः, भारः. -up, *v. t.* नि-,अव-,प्रति-,रुध् 7 U, स्तंभ् 9 P, प्रतिबंध् 9 P, आवृ 5 U, (आवृत्य पंथानमजस्य तस्थौ R. VII. 31). -ADE, *v. t.* रुध् 7 U, *See* BESIEGE. -*s.* उप-अव-रोधः, परिवेष्टनं. -HEAD, *s.* मृत्पिंडबुद्धिः, स्थूलधीः, मूढः, दुर्बुद्धिः, मूर्खः.

BLOOD, *s.* रक्तं, रुधिरं, शोणितं, लोहितं, अस्रं, असृज् *n.*; 'shed b.' रुधिरार्पणेन जीवितं त्यज् 1 P; 'take one's b.' हन् 2 P. 2 गोत्रं, वंशः, कुलं; 'of whole b.' सोदर, सोदर्य, सगर्भ ; सनाभि ; 'of noble b.' कुलीन, अभिजात ; 'of royal b.' राजकुलप्रसूत. 3 (Temper) शीलं ; 'hot-b. ed' तीव्रकोप, सुलभकोप ; 'b. rising to the cheeks' कोपप्रदीप्ताननः. -*v. t.* रक्तेन लिप् 6 P or अंज् 7 P. -LESS, *a.* रक्तहीन. 2 रक्तस्रावं विना. -LETTER, *s.* रक्तस्रावकः, रुधिरमोक्षकः. -RED, *a.* रक्त-लोहित-वर्ण. -SHED, *s.* रक्तस्रावः-पातः, नृहत्या. -SHOT, *a.* रक्तपूर्ण, शोणिताक्त. -THIRSTY, *a.* रुधिरप्रिय ; जिघांसु, वधोद्यत. -VESSEL, *s.* रक्तवाहिनी, नाडी, शिरा, असृग्वहा, धमनी. -Y, *a.* रक्तमय (यी *f.*), रक्ताक्त. 2 क्रूर, मारात्मक, नृशंस ; 'a b. battle it was' तस्मिन् युद्धे महारक्तस्रावोऽभूत्.

BLOOM, *s.* *See* BLOSSOM below ; 'b. of youth' यौवनभरः, नवयौवनं; 'in the b. ing youth' प्रथमे वयसि, नवयौवने. 2 रागः (कपोलरागः). -*v. i.*

फुल्ल् 1 P, विकस् 1 P, स्फुट् 6 P. 2 वृध् 1A, एध् 1 A.

BLOSSOM, *s.* पुष्पं, कुसुमं, मुकुल:-लं, प्रसव:, पल्लव:, प्रवाल:. —*v. i.* स्फुट् 6 P, प्रफुल्ल् 1 P, भिद् pass.; विकस् 1 P, मुकुलै: संनद्ध *a.* भू. —ED, —ING, *a.* स्फुटित, प्रफुल्ल, विकसित, भिन्न, विकच, स्फुटितकुसुम; स्मित.

BLOT, *s.* कलंक:, दोष:, लक्ष्मन् *n.*, अपयशस् *n.* 2 लोप:, व्यामर्ष:. —*v. t.* मलिनयति (D.), दुष् c. (दूषयति), कलंकयति (D.), कृष्णीकृ 8 U. 2 अदर्शीकृ; 'b. out' विनश् c., उच्छिद् 7 P, विलुप् c., व्यामृज् c., व्यामृश् c.; 'b. ing paper' मसीशोषक:, °कं पत्रं.

BLOTCH, *s.* किलासं, सिध्मं; स्फोट:, विस्फोट:, व्रण:-णं, सिध्मन् *n.*; 'having b. es' किलासिन्, सिध्मल. —*v. t.* मलिनयति (D.).

BLOW, *s.* आ-अभि-घात:, प्रहार:; पातनं, निर्घात:; 'Oh! the hard b. of Fate' अहह दारुणो दैवनिर्घात: (U. 2); 'b. with the fist' मुष्टिघात:-प्रहार:; 'to strike a b.' मुष्टिना तड् 10 or हन् 2 P or प्रह् 1 P or अभि- आ- हन् 2 P; युध् 4 A, युद्धार्थं संमिल् 6 P. 2 स्फुटनं, विकास:, फुल्लनं. —*v. i. See* BLOSSOM; oft. by स्मि 1 A; 'b. n Pâtala flower' स्मितपाटलं. 2 वा 2 P, वह् 1 P, प्रवह्. 3 श्वस् 2 P, उच्छ्वस्, विनिश्वस्. —*v. t.* उद्-हन् 2 P, उद्-धू 9 U, उत्-क्षिप् 6 P, वह्. 2 उत्-, श्वि c., स्फाय् c. (स्फावयति).; 'dust b. n by wind' अनिलोद्धतं रज:. 3 (As an instrument) ध्मा 1 P, मुखमारुतेन पूर् 10, (स्नानशंखानामापूर्यमाणानां Ka. 16); 'b. hot and cold' निग्रहानुग्रहौ (युगपत्) प्रकटयति (D.). —away, उद्-हन्, उद्धू, उत्क्षिप्. —out, निर्वा c. (निर्वापयति). —up, वि-उत्-धू, सहसा उन्मूल् 10. —upon, बीज् 10. —ING, *s.* विकास:, व्याकोश:, स्फुटता, प्रोत्फुल्लता. 2 नाद:; ध्मानं. —PIPE, *s.* धमनी; वेणुधमनी.

BLUBBER, *s.* तिमिमेदस् *n.* —*v. i.* अतिरोदनात् उच्छूनमुख *a.* (खी *f.*) भू. —ED, *a.* उच्छून, स्फीत.

BLUDGEON, *s.* लगुड:, गदा.

BLUE, *a.* नील, श्याम. —*s.* नील:, नीलिमन् *m.*, नीलवर्ण:. —ISH, *a.* आनील, ईषन्नील.

BLUFF, *a.* स्थूल; *See* BIG. 2 रूक्ष, परुष, उग्र.

BLUNDER, *s.* प्रमाद:, स्खलितं दोष:. —*v. i.* प्रमद् 4 P, स्खल् 1 P, भ्रम् 1, 4 P. —ER, *s.* प्रमादिन् *m.*, स्खलनशील:. —ING, *a.* प्रमादिन् (नी *f.*), प्रमत्त, अनवधान, अदक्ष. —INGLY, *adv.* सप्रमादं, स्खलनपूर्वं.

BLUNT, *a.* धाराहीन, अतीक्ष्ण, कुंठित, निस्तेजस्. 2 स्थूल, घन; मंद, अविदग्ध. 3 सरल, अजिह्म, ऋजुप्रकृति. 4 रूक्ष, परुष, कर्कश, असभ्य. —*v. t.* कुंठीकृ 8 U, तीक्ष्णतां विलुप् c.; कृ with (*a.*); तेजो हृ 1 P. 2 न्यूनीकृ, शम् c. (शमयति). —LY, *adv.* सरलतया, अजिह्मं; परुषोक्त्या, सपारुष्यं; अविदग्धं. —NESS, *s.* अतीक्ष्णता, स्थूलता, पारुष्यं, &c.

BLUR, *s.* कलंक:, मलं, दूषणं. —*v. t.* मलिनयति (D.), मलेन लिप् 6 P.

BLURT, *v. t.* असमीक्ष्य-अविचार्य-वद् 1 P.

BLUSH, *v. i.* लज्जां नट् 10, ह्री 3 P, लज्ज् 6 A, त्रप् 1 A; व्रीडया-त्रपया-अधोमुख *a.* (खी *f.*) भू 1 P. 2 अरुणाभू, लोहितायते (D.). —*v. t.* अरुणीकृ 8 U. —*s.* अरुणिमन् *m.*, रक्तिमन् *m.*, कपोलराग:. 2 लज्जा, व्रीडा, त्रपा, ह्री:; 'put to b.' ह्री c. (ह्रेपयति). —ING, *a.* प्रफुल्ल, विकसित; 'bears b. honors' संमानरूपाणि विकसितकुसुमानि धारयति, संमानरूपपुष्पभरेणानत:. 2 (Blushful) लज्जित, सव्रीड, सत्रप, लज्जावनत, ह्रीपरिगत, त्रपाधोमुख (खी *f.*).

BLUSTER, *v. i.* गर्ज् 1 P, तुमुलं-कोलाहलं कृ 8 U, उच्चै: आरट् 1 P, उत्क्रुश् 1 P. 2 विकत्थ् 1 A, श्लाघ् 1 A. 3 तर्ज् 10 A, भर्त्स् 10 A. —ER, *s.* कलहकार:, दांभिक:, विकत्थिन् (नी *f.*); आत्मश्लाघापर:. —*s.*, —ING, *s.* गर्जनं, तुमुलं, कोलाहल:; उच्चै: आरटनं, उत्क्रोश:.

BOA-CONSTRICTOR, *s.* अजगर:, शयु:, वाहस:.

BOAR, *s.* वराह:, किरि:-र:, शू(सू) कर:, कोल:, घृ(गृ)ष्टि:, पोत्रिन् *m.*, किटि:, दंष्ट्रिन्-घोणिन्-स्तब्धरोमन् *m.*, क्रोड:, भूदार:. —ISH, *a.* वाराह (ही *f.*). 2 असभ्य, ग्राम्य.

BOARD, *s.* फलक:-कं; भोजनासनं, काष्ठखंडं. 2 ग्रास:, भोजनं, आहार:. 3 सभा, परिषद् *f.*, समाज:, गण:, वर्ग:. 4 नौकातलं-पृष्ठं; 'to go on b. a ship' पोतं आ-अधि-रुह् 1 P; 'on b.' नौकारूढ *a.*, नौतले. 5 अष्टापदं, शारिफलं. —*v. t.* बलात् नावं आरुह् 1 P. 2 फलकै: आस्तृ-स्तॄ 5, 9 U. —ER, *s.* निरूपितमूल्येन भोक्तृ *m.*

BOAST, *v. i.* विकत्थ् 1 A, दृप् 4 P, (with instr.) नात्मना दृप्यति; आत्मानं श्लाघ् 1 A, गर्वं वह् 1 P (with gen.); (मुधा यौवनगर्वं वहसि M. 4). —ER, *s.* आत्मश्लाघिन् *m.*, विकत्थनशील:, शूरंमन्य:. —FUL, *a.* आत्मश्लाघापर, विकत्थन, दृप्त, गर्वित, अवलिप्त. —FULLY, *adv.* गर्वेण, सदर्पं, विकत्थनपूर्वं. —ING, *s.* आत्मश्लाघा, अहंकारोक्ति *f.*, दर्प:, विकत्थनं, गर्व:. —INGLY, *adv.* सगर्वं, सदर्पं.

BOAT, *s.* नौ:, तरी:, तरणि-णी *f.*; 'a small b.' उडुपं, नौका, प्लव:, कोल:; 'b. man,' *s.* नाविक:, पोतवाह:, औडुपिक:; 'b. swain,' *s.* मुख्यनाविक:, कर्णधार:.

BOB, *v. t.* तड् 10; *See* BEAT. 2 Crop, q. v. —*v. i.* इतस्ततो लुठ् 6 P, 1 A, स्फुर् 6 P, चंच् 1 P.

BOBBIN, *s.* तंतुकीलः, कपालनाडिका.

BOBTAIL, *s.* छिन्नपुच्छधारिन् *m.*

BODE, *v. t.* शुभाशुभं सूच् 10 ; आविद् c., कथ् 10 प्राक् शंस् 1 P, *See* PREDICT ; 'absence of delay b. s future success' अव्याक्षेपो भविष्यंत्याः कार्यसिद्धेर्हि लक्षणं (R. x. 6) ; 'b. s evil to the country' जनपदस्य अनिष्टशंसि-सूचकं, अशुभचिह्नं-लक्षणं. –MENT, *s.* शुभाशुभलक्षणं ; पूर्वचिह्नं, निमित्तं.

BODICE, *s.* कंचुकः, चोलः, कूर्पासकः-कं.

BODKIN, *s.* सूचि-ची *f.* 2 छुरिका, वेधनिका, कृपाणिका.

BODY, *s.* शरीरं, कायः, देहः, विग्रहः, अंगं, वपुस् *n.*, कलेवरं, तनु-नू *f.*, गात्रं ; 'dead b.' शवः-वं, कुणपः. 2 (Some b.) कः-का-किम्-अपि-चित्-चन ; जनः, लोकः. 3 पदार्थः, वस्तु *n.* 4 समवायः, समूहः, संघातः, वृंदं, समाजः, समुदायः ; 'in a b.' समेत *a.*, संहत *a.*, एकत्र मिलित *a.* 5 समागमः, श्रेणी. 6 कांडः-डं, स्कंधः ; 'b. of the house' गर्भः, अभ्यंतरं, उदरं ; 'b. of troops' सैन्यदलं ; 'b. guard' आसन्नपरिचारकः-रिका, परिवारगणः. –BODILESS, *a.* अ (अन्) in comp. with (*s.*); अनंग, &c. –BODILY, *a.* शारीरिक-दैहिक-कायिक (की *f.*) ; gen. (*s.*) in comp. ; 'b. pain' शरीरवेदना, देहक्लेशः &c. –*adv.* सशरीरं, सांगं. 2 साकल्येन.

BOG, *s.* अनूपः, कच्छभूः, पंकः. –BOGGY, पंकिल, आनूप (पी *f.*).

BOGGLE, *v. i.* वि-आ-शंक् 1 A, संदिह् 2 U, विकृप् 1 A. –ER, *s.* शंकितमतिः, शंकाशीलः.

BOIL, *v. t.* पच् 1 P, उत्क्वथ् 1 P, श्रा 2 P. –*v. i.* क्वथ् pass., तप्-पच् pass. ; 'b. ing with anger' कोपपरीतमानसः, संतप्तचित्तः. 2 फेनायते (D.), –*s.* व्रणः-णं, स्फोटः, विस्फोटः, पिटकः, पिट (टि)-का, गंडः. –ED, *a.* उख्य, पक्व, स्थालीपक्व. 2 श्राण, शृत. –ER, *s.* स्थाली, पिठरः-रं ; उखा.

BOISTEROUS, *a.* गर्जनकारिन् (णी *f.*) ; प्रचंड, उत्कट ; 'b. noise' कोलाहलः, तुमुलरवः, उच्चैराक्रोशः. 2 कलह-तुमुल-कारिन् (णी *f.*) ; 'b. laugh' अट्टहासः. –LY. *adv.* प्रचंडं, उत्कटं, कोलाहलेन. –NESS, *s.* प्रचंडता, &c.

BOLD, *a.* शूर, साहसिक (की *f.*), साहसपर. 2 (Of things) साहसाभास, साहसं, (इति वचनं साहसमात्रं S. B. 79). 3 (Rude) धृष्ट, निर्लज्ज, अविनीत. 4 प्रगल्भ, निर्विशंक, निर्भय, निर्भीक. 5 सुप्रकाश, स्पष्ट; 'he made b. to say' स निर्भयमुवाच ; 'to be b.' धृष् 5 P. –LY, *adv.* साहसेन, निर्भयं, प्रगल्भं ; धृष्टतया. –NESS, *s.* साहसं, शौर्यं. 2 धृष्टता, अविनयः. 3 प्रगल्भता, निर्भयता.

BOLE, *s.* स्कंधः, प्रकांडः.

BOLL *s.* नाडि डी *f.* ; कांडः-डं.

BOLSTER, *s.* उपधानं, उपबर्हः ; बंधः; आलंबः. –*v. t.* (up) संस्तंभ् 9 P, समालंब् 1 A.

BOLT, *s.* अर्गलाबंधः, अर्गलं, कालकं, कीलः-लं. 2 शूलः-लं, शंकुः, शरः. –*v. t.* अर्गलेन रुध् 7 U or पिधा 3 U or बंध् 9 P ; कीलयति (D.). 2 तितउना शुध् c. or चल् c. –*v. i.* (away, out) सहसा-अलक्षितं निर्गम्-निःसृ 1 P, or अपक्रम् 1 U, 4 P, or अपया 2 P.

BOMB, *s.* अग्न्यस्त्रं. –ARD, *v. t.* अग्न्यस्त्रेण अवमृद् 9 P, or विद् 9 U, 10, or चूर्ण् 10.

BOMBAST, *s.* दर्पवचनं, अतिशयोक्ति *f.*, असारं वाक्यं, निःसारा उक्तिः. –IC, –ICAL, *a.* असार ; दर्पध्मात.

BOND, *s.* बंधः, बंधनं, पाशः, जालं ; (fig. also) ; निगडाः (pl.) ; 'b. of love' प्रेमबंधः-पाशः. 2 संश्लेषः, संहति *f.*, संधिः, संबंधः. 3 प्रतिज्ञापत्रं-लेख्यं, समयपत्रं. 4 समयः, नियमः, संविद् *f.* –AGE, *s.* बंधनं, दासत्वं ; 'died in b.' कारागृहे-दासावस्थायां मृतः ; 'bond-maid' दासी, चेटी ; 'bond-man' दासः, भृत्यः, किंकरः.

BONE, *s.* अस्थि *n.* ; 'set a b.' त्रुटितास्थि संधा 3 U. –LESS, *a.* अस्थिहीन, निरस्थि. –Y, *a.* अस्थिमय (यी *f.*). 2 अस्थिमत् (ती *f.*), अस्थिपूर्ण.

BONFIRE, *s.* जयसूचकः अग्निः.

BONNET, *s.* स्त्रीधृतं शिरोवेष्टनं, शिरस्कं.

BONNY, *a.* सुंदर (री *f.*); रूपवत् (ती *f.*); *See* BEAUTIFUL. 2 हृष्ट, सुप्रीत, प्रमुदित. 3 हृष्टपुष्ट, सुललित.

BOOBY, *s.* मंदबुद्धिः, मूढः, मूर्खः.

BOOK, *s.* पुस्तकं, ग्रंथः ; 'part of a b.' अध्यायः, पर्वन् *n.* ; 'b. case' ग्रंथाधारः, ग्रंथकुटी ; 'b. mate' सहाध्यायिन् *m.* ; 'b. worm' ग्रंथवाचनासक्तः . – *v. t.* लेख्ये आरुह् c. –ISH, *a.* पुस्तकपठनासक्त; व्यवहारविसंवादिन् (नी *f.*), अव्यवहार्य.

BOON, *s.* वरः, प्रसादः, अनुग्रहः. –*a.* हृष्ट, विलासिन् (नी *f.*), उदार, प्रमुदित.

BOOR, s. ग्राम्यः जनः, ग्रामिकः, वृषलः. –ISH, *a.* ग्राम्य, अशिष्ट, असभ्य.

BOOT, *v. t.* or *s.* *See* AVAIL. –*s.* उपानह् *f.*, पादुका, पादत्रं. –LESS, *a.* निष्फल, व्यर्थ, निरर्थक, मोघ, निर्गुण.

BOOTH, *s.* पटमंडपः, उपकार्या, पटभवनं.

BOOTY, *s.* लोप्त्रं, लुंठितं, लुंठनं, लोत्रं.

BORAX, *s.* रसशोधनः, बिडं.

BORDER, *s.* पर्यंतः-तं, प्रांतः; परिसरभूमि *f.*, उत्संगः, उपांतः. 2 (Of a garment) अंचलः, दशा. 3 समंतः, सीमा, सामंतं. 4 तीरं, कूलं, तटं (of a river); 'b. of a forest' वनांतः. –*v. i.* (on, upon) Ex. by वृत् 1A, स्था 1 P, with (*s.*); जनस्थानपर्यंतानि दीर्घारण्यानि (U.2) 'large forests b. ing on Janasthâna'; 'his age b. s on 20' विंशतिपर्यंतवयोवस्थां स्पृशति,

विंशतिवर्षदेशीयोसौ. 2 कल्प, प्राय, in comp.; 'his condition b. s on poverty' तस्य दशा दारिद्र्या-त्किंचिदूना, दारिद्र्यकल्पा. —*v. t.* प्रांतयति (D.), प-र्यंतं कृ 8 U; पर्यंते निविश् c.; 'garment b. ed with silk' निर्मितकौशेयप्रांतं वसनं. —ING, *a.* प्र-त्यंत, पर्यंतस्थ, निकटस्थ.

BORE, *s.* छिद्रं, रंध्रं. 2 वेधनी. 3 सुषिरं, छिद्रव्यासः. —*v. t.* व्यध् 4 P, छिद्रं कृ 8 U. —ER, *s.* वेधकः.

BOREAL, *a.* उदीचीन, उत्तर.

BOREAS, *s.* उत्तरवायुः.

BORROW, *v. t.* ऋणं कृ 8 U or प्रार्थ् 10 A or ग्रह् 9 P. 2 अन्यस्माद् ग्रह् or आदा 3 A, or लभ् 1 A. —ER, *s.* ऋणकर्तृ-ग्रहीतृ *m.*, ऋणयाचकः.

BOSOM, *s.* वक्षस् *n.*, उरस् *n.*, क्रोडं, वक्षःस्थलं. 2 गर्भः, अभ्यंतरं. 3 हृदयं, चित्तं, मनस् *n.*; 'b. friend' हृदयंगमः सखा, प्रियसुहृद्. 4 स्तनः, कुचः, वक्षोजः.

BOSS, *s.* गंडः. —ED, *a.* गंडानुविद्ध.

BOTANY, *s.* उद्भिद्विद्या, ओषधिशास्त्रं, वनस्पतिशास्त्रं. —IST, *s.* ओषधिशास्त्रज्ञः.

BOTCH, *s.* व्रणः-णं, स्फोटः. 2 छिद्रं, दोषः. —*v. t.* जीर्णवस्त्राणि सिव् 4 P, सूच्या संधा 3 U.

BOTH, *pron. a.* उभौ, उभे; उभय-द्वि in comp.; उ-भयं, द्वयं; 'b. sides' उभयपक्षौ; 'on b. sides' उभयतः; 'in b. ways' उभयथा; 'in b. places' उभयत्र. 2 Ex. by च-च, तथा; 'does b. good and bad' शुभं चाशुभं च विदधाति.

BOTHER, *v t.* क्लिश् 9 P, पीड् 10, बाध् 1 A.

BOTTLE, *s.* काचकूपी-पात्रं-भाजनं. —*v. t.* काचकूप्यां निविश् c.

BOTTOM, *s.* तलं, अधोभागः; 'examine it to the b.' आमूलं-तलं परीक्षस्व तत्; 'you are at the b. of this plot' अस्य कपटप्रबंधस्य त्वं मूल-प्रधान-का-रणं, त्वं प्रधानः प्रवर्तकः. 2 दरी, उपत्यका, निम्नभूः, पादः. 3 मलं, शेषं, अवशेषं. —*v. i.* (upon) आलंब् 1 A, मूल in comp. —LESS, *a.* अगाध, अतलस्पर्श.

BOUGH, *s.* शाखा, विटपः.

BOUNCE, *v. i.* प्रपत् 1 P, अभि-उत्-प्लु 1 A, सत्वरं-सवेगं-धाव् 1 P or पलाय् 1 A. 2 स्वन्-ध्वन् 1 P. 3 Boast, q. v. —*s.* ध्वनिः, अकस्मादाघातः.

BOUND, *s.* प्लुति *f.*, प्लुतं, वल्गनं. 2 मर्यादा, सीमन् *f.*, सीमा, प्रांतः, पर्यंतः, अंतः. 3 प्रतिघातः, उत्पतनं. —*v. t.* Ex. by सीमा, प्रांत; 'b. ed on the south by the ocean' अस्य दक्षिणा सीमा सागरः; 'b. ed by dales on all sides' दरीपरिगतः; *See* BORDER. 2 नियम् 1 P, निग्रह् 9 P. —*v. i.* उत्प्लु 1 A, वल्ग् 1 P. —up, उत्पत् 1 P. —LESS, *a.* अनंत, अमित, निःसीम, निरवधि. —BOUNDARY, *s.* सीमा, सीमन् *f.*, मर्यादा, पर्यंतः, प्रांतः, अवधिः.

BOUNTEOUS, BOUNTIFUL, *a.* वदान्य, उदार, मुक्त-हस्त, दान-त्याग-शील. —LY, *adv.* अतित्यागेन, उदा-रवत्, मुक्तहस्तं. —BOUNTY, —NESS, *s.* औदार्यं, वदा-न्यता, मुक्तहस्तता, त्यागिता. 2 प्रदानं, पारितोषिकं. 3 कृपा, अनुग्रहः, प्रसादः.

BOUQUET, *s.* कुसुमस्तबकः, पुष्पगुच्छः.

BOURN, *See* BOUNDARY.

BOUT, *s.* वारः; 'drinking b.' संपीति *f.*

BOW, *v. i.* नम् 1 P, प्रणम् (acc. or dat.); अभि-वद् c., अभिवंद् 1 A, प्रह्वीभू; चरणयोः पत् 1 P. 2 अंगीकृ 8 U, अभ्युप-इ 2 P, °गम् 1 P; oft. by प्र-माणं; 'I b. to your decision' आर्यमिश्राः प्रमाणं (M. 1) or भवतो निर्णयो मे प्रमाणं. —*v. t.* अव-आ-वि-नम् c. (नमयति), प्रह्वी-नम्रीकृ; 'b. ing the head down' प्रणम्य शिरसा; 'b. ed down with age' जरानमितकायः; 'b. ing down the head on the ground' अवनितलनिवेशित-लोल-शिरस् *a.*; 'b. ed in silence' अलक्षितं लयं गच्छत्. —*s.* प्रणामः, प्रणति *f.*, नमस्कारः. 2 धनुस् *n.*, चापः-पं, कार्मुकं, शरासनं, कोदंडं, इष्वासः, शरावापः; 'b. man' ध-न्विन् *m.*, धनुष्मत् *m.*, धनुर्धरः, धनुर्भृत् *m.*, धानुष्कः, निषंगिन् *m.*; 'b. string' *s.* ज्या, मौर्वी, गुणः, शिं-जिनी; 'b. shot' बाणगोचरं, शरपथः-विषयः. —*in-terj.* नमः (with dat.).

BOWELS, *s.* अंत्राणि (pl.). 2 (fig.) अभ्यंतरं, गर्भः.

BOWER, *s.* कुंजः-जं, लतामंडपः. 2 कुटीरः, पर्णशा-ला. —*v. t.* परिवेष्ट् 1 A, परिवृ 5 U or c. —Y, *a.* कुंजवत् (ती *f.*), लतापरिच्छन्न.

BOWL, *s.* पात्रं, भाजनं, शरावः. 2 गुलिका. 3 विषं. —*v. i.* गुलिकाभिः क्रीड् 1 P.

BOX, *s.* पेटिका, समुद्गकः, संपुटः, पिटकः, मंजूषा. 2 मुष्टिप्रहारः-घातः, पाणिघातः. —*v. i.* मुष्टीमुष्टि प्रहृ 1 P; बाहूबाहवि युध् 4 A or तड् 10; मल्लयुद्धं कृ 8 U. —*v. t.* मुष्टिना प्रहृ or तड्. 2 संपुटके निधा 3 U. —ER, *s.* मल्लयोधः, बाहुयोधिन् *m.* —ING, *s.* मल्लयुद्धं, बाहु-युद्धं, बाहूबाहवि *ind.*

BOY, *s.* बालः-लकः, शिशुः, कुमारः-रकः, दारकः. —HOOD, *s.* बाल्यं, कौमारं, शैशवं, बालभावः. —ISH, *a.* बालिश, बालेय. 2 शिशुयोग्य; बालसदृश (शी *f.*), बालभावसुलभ; 'b. nature' बालभावः, शिशुत्वं, बालिशता.

BRABBLE, *See* QUARREL.

BRACE, *s.* युग्मं, युगं, युगलं, द्वयं, युगुलं. 2 बंधः-धनं, चर्मबंधः. —*v. t.* बंध् 9 P. 2 दृढीकृ 8 U, संस्तंभ् 9 P or c., शक्ति-बलं-वृध् c.

BRACELET, *s.* कंकणं, कटकः-कं, आवापकः, पारि-हार्यः, हस्तसूत्रं, वलयः-यं; करभूषणं; 'marriage b.' विवाहकौतुकं.

BRACKET, *s.* नागदंतः. 2 अर्धचंद्रद्वयं.

BRACKISH, *a.* क्षार, क्षाररसयुक्त.

BRAG, *v. i.* विकत्थ्-, श्लाघ् 1 A; *See* BOAST. –*s.* आत्मश्लाघा, विकत्थनं, वृथास्तुति *f.* –INGLY, *adv.* साहंकारं, आत्मश्लाघापूर्वं. –BRAGGART (BRAGGADOCIO), *s., a.*, विकत्थनशील:, आत्मश्लाघिन् *m.*, आत्मश्लाघापर:, पिंडीशूर:.

BRAHMAN, *s.* ब्राह्मण:, विप्र:, द्विज:, द्विजन्मन् *m.* अग्रजन्मन् *m.*, भूसुर:, भूदेव:; 'a pseudo b.' ब्राह्मणब्रुव:. –ICAL, *a.* ब्राह्म (ह्मी *f.*); ब्राह्मणजातीय.

BRAID, *s.* कबरी, वेणि-णी *f.*, धम्मिल्ल:, केशबंध:-पाश:.–*v. i.* वेणीकृ 8 U, वेण्यारूपेण केशान् संग्रंथ् 9 P or रच् 10. 2 संग्रंथ्, वे 1 P, संश्लिष् c., संसिव् 4 P.

BRAIN, *s.* मस्तिष्कं, मस्तिकं, गोर्दं. 2 बुद्धि *f.*, मति *f.* –LESS, *a.* बुद्धिहीन, निर्बुद्धि. –PAN, *s.* कपाल:-लं, शिरोस्थि *n.* –SICK, *a.* मूढमति, भ्रांतचित्त, संभ्रांत.

BRAKE, *s.* गुल्मगहनं, कंटकवनं. 2 कंटकखलीनं, खलीन:-नं.

BRAMBLE, *s.* कंटक:, कंटकगुल्म:, गोक्षुर:.

BRAN, *s.* तुष:, धान्यत्वच् *f.*, बुसं, कडंगर:.

BRANCH, *s.* शाखा, विटप:. 2 अंगं, शाखा, एकदेश:-भाग:. 3 उपनदी, अल्पसरित् *f.* 4 अपत्यं, कुलसंतानं; वंश:. –*v. i.* शाखारूपेण विभिद् pass., or भिद् pass. 2 सविस्तरं वद् 1 P; 'the family b. ed into 8 parts' निश्चोष्टधा विप्रससार वंश: (R. XVI. 3). –Y, –ING, *a.* शाखिन् (नी *f.*), शाखामय (यी *f.*), शाखासनाथ; विस्तीर्ण, विस्तारयुक्त.

BRAND, *s.* अलातं, उल्का, दग्धकाष्ठं. 2 कलंक:, अंक:, लांछनं, अपकीर्तिचिह्नं. –*v. t.* तप्तलोहेन अंक् 10 or चिह्न् 10; 'b. ed with disgrace' अपयशोंकित:, उपक्रोशमलीमस:. –ED, *a.* तप्तलोहेन चिह्नित, दुष्कीर्तिचिह्नांकित.

BRANDISH, *v. t.* परि-भ्रम् c. (भ्रमयति), विधू 5, 9 U.

BRANDY, *s.* सुरा, आसवं, वारुणी, सीधु *f.*

BRANGLE, *s.* कलह:, व्याक्रोश:.

BRASS, *s.* पित्तलं, आरकूट:-टं, रीति-ती *f.* –Y, *a.* पित्तलमय (यी *f.*). –BRAZEN, *a.* (fig.) निर्लज्ज, धृष्ट, निरपावरण. –BRAZIER, *s.* ताम्र-कांस्यकार:. –EFFLORESCENCE, *s.* रीतिपुष्पं, पुष्पकेतु, पुष्पकं, कुसुमांजनं.

BRAT, *s.* शिशु:, बाल:, बटु:.

BRAVE, *v. t.* भर्त्स् 10 A, तर्ज् 10 A. 2 धृष् 5 P; आ-समा-ह्वे 1 A. –*a* वीर, शूर, विक्रांत, धीर, पराक्रमवत् (ती *f.*), वीर्य-विक्रम-शालिन् (नी *f.*), साहसिक (की *f.*); उदार, तेजस्विन् (नी *f.*); 'fortune favours the b.' साहसे श्री: प्रतिवसति. –*s.* शूरंमन्य:. 2 समाह्वानं. –LY, *adv.* सधैर्यं, निर्भयं, सविक्रमं, शूर-वीर-वत्. –RY, *s.* वीर्यं, शौर्यं, धैर्यं, परा-वि-क्रम:, साहसं. 2 (BRAVADO) विकत्थनं, आत्मश्लाघा.

BRAVO, *interj.* साधु, साधु साधु. –*s.* घातक:, आततायिन् *m.*

BRAWL, *s.* कलि:, कलह:, विवाद:, द्वंद्वं, विप्रतिपत्ति *f.* –*v. i.* विवद् 1 A, कलहं कृ 8 U, कलहायते (D.).

BRAWN, *s.* शूकरमांसं. 2 स्नायु:; बाहु:. –Y, *a.* मांसल; दृढांग (गी *f.*); संनद्धशरीर.

BRAY, *v. i.* चीत्कारशब्दं कृ 8 U, आरट् 1 P. –*v. t.* चूर्ण् 10, पिष् 7 P. –*s.*, –ING, *s.* ची(चि) त्कार:, खरनाद:.

BREACH, *s.* छिद्रं, रंध्रं. 2 भंग:, भेदनं; अतिक्रम:, लंघनं; 'b. of promise' प्रतिज्ञाभंग:; आज्ञाभंग:. 3 भेद: (सुहृद्भेद:); 'b. in a wall' संधि:, सुरंगा.

BREAD, *s.* अपूप:, पिष्टक:, कांदवं. 2 अन्नं, आहार:.

BREADTH, *s.* *See* under BROAD.

BREAK, *v. t.* भंज् 7 P (fig. also), खंड् 10. 2 क्षुद्-पिष् 7 P, चूर्ण् 10, मृद् 9 P. 3 अतिक्रम् 1 U, 4 P, उल्लंघ् 1 A, 10, अतिचर् 1 P; विलुप् c. 4 भिद् 7 U, विघट् c. (घटयति); विदृ 9 P, 10, स्फुट् c., (as heart); 'b.- fast' पारणां निर्वृत् c., प्रातराशं-कल्यवर्तं सेव् 1 A; 'b. wind' गुदरवं कृ 8 U, पर्द् 1 A ; 'b. the way for' अपसृ 1 P, अप-इ 2 P, अपक्रम्. 5 विनश् c., उच्छिद् 7 P. –*v. i.* भिद्-दृ-भंज्- pass., त्रुट् 6, 4 P, स्फुट् 6 P (स्फुटति हृदयं), दल् 1 P. 2 प्रभा 2 P; 'the day broke' उषा: समागता, प्रभाता रजनी, दृष्टं दिनमुखं. 3 क्षि pass., अवसद् 1 P, विशॄ pass., भ्रंस् 1 A, जॄ 4, 9 P. –*s.* विच्छेद:, निवृत्ति *f.*, विराम:, भंग:; 'b. of day' प्रभातं, उष:काल:, अरुणोदय:; 'the story has suffered a b.' विच्छेदमाप कथाप्रबंध: (Ka. 239). –down, चूर्ण् 10; (*v. i.*) *See* FAIL. –in upon, प्रसह्य-सहसा-प्रविश् 6 P. –into, विनी 1 P, दम् c. (दमयति). –into, (a house) संधिं कृत्वा प्रविश्. –loose, प्रमुच्, विमुच् pass.; 'the elephant broke loose from the post' आलानस्तंभं भंक्त्वा निर्जगाम. –off, भंज्, भंगं कृ 8 U; (*v. i.*) अकस्मात् विरम् 1 P, त्यज् 1 P, निवृत् 1 A. –open, बलात्-सहसा-उद्घट् c. or अपवृ 5 U. –out, (*v. i.*) उद्भू 1 P, उत्पद् 4 A, प्रादुर्भू, उदि 2 P. 2 निर्गम् 1 P. –through, निर्भंज्, अपानुद् 6 P, निरस् 4 P; *See* DISPEL. –up, (*v. t.*) *See* BREAK (*v. i.*) 'the party broke up' सभ्या: स्वं स्वं स्थानं प्रतिजग्मु:. –upon, आहन् 2 A; 'the dawn broke upon his eyes' तस्याक्ष्णो: प्रभातमासीत् (S. 2). –with, विवद् 1 A, कलहं कृ. –ER, *s.* भंजक:, भेदक:. –FAST, *s.* प्रातराश:, कल्यवर्त:.

BREAST, *s.* उरस् *n.*, क्रोडं, वक्षस् *n.* 2 स्तन:, पयोधर:, वक्षोज:, कुच:, (of human beings). 3 हृदयं, अंत:करणं, चित्तं, मनस् *n.*; 'b. high' वक्षोदघ्न

(श्री *f.*); 'b. plate' कवचं, उरस्त्राणं; 'b. work' वक्षःप्रमाणः प्राकारः.

BREATHE, *v. i.* श्वस् 2 P; प्राण् 2 P. 2 अन् 2 P, जीव् 1 P, वृत् 1 A. 3 निर्गम् 1 P, विप्रकृ pass. 4 आ-प्र-उत्-समा-श्वस्; 'b. deep' दीर्घ-स्थूलंस्थूलं निश्वस्; 'b. freely' उच्छ्वस्; 'b. the last' *See* DIE. —*v. t.* (out) उद्गॄ 6 P, अव-प्र-सं-कॄ 6 P. 2 प्रवा 2 P. —BREATH, *s.* श्वासः, निश्वासः, उच्छ्वसितं. 2 प्राणाः (pl.); प्राणायामः 'holding the b.'; असवः (pl.). 3 विरामः, उपशमः. 4 उद्गारः. 5 मंदानिलः, मृदुवातः; 'in the same b.' एकावसरे, समकालमेव. —ING, *s.* श्वासः, श्वसितं. 2 स्पृहा, इच्छा; 'b. through nose' नासिकंधनः; 'b. hole' वातायनं, गवाक्षः. —LESS, *a.* प्राणहीन, निरुच्छ्वास, विचेतन. 2 मृत, उत्क्रांतवायु; यष्टप्राण.

BREECH, *s.* पश्चाद्भागः, नितंबः, कटिदेशः. —ES, *s.* कटिवस्त्रं, शाटकः.

BREED, *v. t.* जन् c. (जनयति), उत्पद् c., प्रसू 2 A. 2 पुष् 1, 4, 9 P or c., संवृध् c. 3 विनी 1 P. —*v. i.* वृध् 1 A, प्रजन्-उत्पद् 4 A. 2 गर्भवती भू, *See* CONCEIVE; 'b. ing season' गर्भधारणकालः, उत्पत्तिसमयः. —*s.* वंशः, कुलं, जाति *f.* 2 अपत्यं, प्रजा. 3 समुत्पन्नः शावकगणः, शिशुजातं. —BRED, *a.* जनित; संवर्द्धित; विनीत; 'well b.' सुविनीत, सदाचार; 'ill b.' दुर्विनीत, दुराचार. —ER., *s.* जनकः, पोषकः, विनेतृ *m.* —ING, *s.* पोषणं, पालनं, संवर्द्धनं. 2 शिक्षणं, विनयः. 3 सभ्यता, सुशीलता; 'of good b.' सुविनीत, सुशील. 4 गर्भधारणं, गर्भाधानं.

BREEZE, *s.* मृदुपवनः, मंदानिलः. 2 वातः, अनिलः, *See* WIND; 'agreeable b.' सुखस्पर्शः-सुखः-वायुः. —Y, *a.* वातवत् (ती *f.*), वातैरुपवीजित.

BREVIARY, *s.* संहिता, संग्रहः. 2 स्तोत्रसंग्रहः.

BREVITY, *s.* संक्षेपः, समासः, संहारः, संग्रहणं.

BREW, *v. t.* (यवसुरां) पच् 1 P or क्वथ् 1 P. 2 प्रचित् 10, प्रक्लृप् c. —AGE, *s.* निष्क्वाथः. —ERY, *s.* यवसुरापचनस्थानं.

BRIBE, *s.* उत्कोचः, उपायनं. —*v. t.* उत्कोचं दा 3 U, उत्कोचदानेन वशीकृ 8 U. —RY, *s.* उत्कोचदानं-ग्रहणं. 2 उत्कोचदानादानापराधः.

BRICK, *s.* इष्टका, सुधा; 'burnt b.' पक्वेष्टका; 'b. bit' इष्टकाशकलं; 'b. kiln' आपाकः, पचनस्थानं; 'b. layer' लेपकः, सुधाजीविन् *m.*; 'b. work' इष्टकानिर्मितं.

BRIDAL, *s.* विवाहोत्सवः, उद्वाहकर्मन् *n.* —*a.* वैवाहिक (की *f.*), विवाहयोग्य.

BRIDE, *s.* वधूः, नववधूः; पाणिगृहीता, नवोढा. 2 कन्या, कुमारी. —GROOM, *s* वरः, परिणेतृ *m.*, परिग्रहीतृ *m.*, पाणिग्राहकः; 'bride and b.' वधूवरं-रौ. —MAID, *s.* जन्या.

BRIDGE, *s.* सेतुः, धरणं, संवरः. 2 आली-ली *f.*, धरणः (small); 'make a b.' सेतुं निर्मा 3 A, or कृ 8 U, or बंध् 9 P; 'fort b.' संक्रमः; 'b. of the nose' नासावंशः. —*v. t.* सेतुना बंध् 9 P, संवृ 5 U.

BRIDLE, *s.* वल्गा; रश्मिः; 'giving the b. to the passions' रागाधीनः, रागवशः. 2 निग्रहः, संयमः. —*v. t.* वल्गासनाथ *a.* कृ, रश्मिभिः यम् 1 P. 2 निग्रह् 9 P, नि-सं-यम्; *See* CONTROL; 'by un-b. ed tongue' निर्यंत्रणया वाचा.

BRIEF, *a.* स्वल्प, अचिर, अल्पकाल, क्षणिक (की *f.*), अचिरस्थायिन् (नी *f.*); संक्षिप्त, परिमित, संहृत, अदीर्घ, संकुचित; 'to be b.' किं बहुना 2 संग्रहः, संक्षेपः. 3 सारपत्रं. —LY, *adv.* संक्षेपतः, संक्षेपेण, समासतः, समासेन. 2 अचिरेण, आशु, क्षिप्रं. —NESS, *s.* संक्षेपः, समासः, संहारः, परिमितता.

BRIER, BRIAR, *s.* गोक्षुरः, कंटकगुल्मः. —Y, *a.* कंटकावृत.

BRIGADE, *s.* चमूः, वाहिनी, सैन्यदलं, गुल्मः-ल्मं. —IER, *s.* वाहिनीपतिः, चमूपतिः.

BRIGAND, *s.* दस्युः, चौरः.

BRIGHT, *a.* उज्ज्वल, प्रदीप्त, भासुर, रुचिर, तेजस्विन् (नी *f.*), भास्वत् (ती *f.*), भ्राजमान, प्रभावत्, दीप्तिमत् देदीप्यमान. 2 विशद, निर्मल, शुचि. 3 विश्रुत. —EN, *v. t.* प्र-उत्-द्युत् c., प्र-उत्-दीप् c., उद्भास् c, भ्राज् c., विराज् c. 2 विमलयति (D.), विशदीकृ 8 U. —*v. i.* विमलीभू 1 P, प्रसद् 1 P, प्रसादं गम् 1 P, विशदीभू, (दिशः प्रसेदुः R. III. 14). 2 शुभ्-द्युत् 1 A; *See* SHINE. —LY, *adv.* उज्ज्वलं, विमलं, तेजसा, कांत्या. —NESS, *s.* तेजस् *n.*, औज्ज्वल्यं; द्युतिः, रुचिः, कांतिः, प्रभा, दीप्तिः, शोभा, (all fem.); भासुरत्वं, तेजस्विता; 'b. of intellect' प्रदीप्ता प्रज्ञा.

BRILLIANCE, BRILLIANT, *See* BRIGHT.

BRIM, *s.* कंठः, प्रांतः, मुखं, धारः, कर्णः; 'to the b.' आमुखं, आकंठं. 2 (of a river) तीरं, तटः-टं. 3 अंचलः, दशा (of a cloth). —FUL, *a.* परिपूर्ण, आकर्णपूर्ण; ex. by मय (यी *f.*), निर्भर; 'b. of joy' हर्षनिर्भरः.

BRIMSTONE, *s.* गंधकः. —Y, *a.* गंधकपूर्ण-विशिष्ट.

BRINDLE, *s.* चित्रता, चित्रांगत्वं, शबलत्वं. —ED, *a.* शबल, चित्रित, कल्माषित.

BRINE, *s.* लवणजलं. 2 बाष्पः, अश्रु *n.*, अस्रं.

BRING, *v. t.* आनी 1 P, आ-उपा-हृ 1 P, आवह् 1 P. 2 प्राप् c., आगम् c. (गमयति). 3 अनुनी 1 P, आकृष् 1 P. 4 जन् c. (जनयति), उत्पद् c.; ex. by प्रभू 1 P, जन् 4 A; 'poverty b. s one to shame' दारिद्र्याद् ह्रियमेति (Mr. 1); 'b. to end' समाप् c., निर्वृत् c., अवसो 4 P; 'brought by the setting sun' सूर्योढः; 'b. to ruin' नश् c., नाशकारणं भू; 'b. word' निविद्

c., वार्ता आख्या 2 P; 'b. action' अभियुज् 7 A. –about, (to pass) साध् 5 P, 10; घट् c. (घटयति), संपद् c., आवह् 1 P; क्लृप् 1 A, संपद् 4A, (with dat.). –down, नि-अव-पत् c., अपकृष्, अभिभू. –forth, *See* BEGET. –forward, उपन्यस् 4 P, उदाहृ 1 P, उपक्षिप् 6 P, उपानी, पुरस्कृ. 2 अग्रे-पुरः-आनी, प्रसू c. –on, आवह् 1 P, or with dat.; 'disgrace b. s on despair' परिभवः निर्वेदमावहति, निर्वेदाय (भवति); oft. by प्रभू, जन्; 'avarice b. s on anger' लोभात् क्रोधः प्रभवति-जायते &c. –out, प्रकाश् c., प्रकटीकृ. –together, समा-नी, समुपाहृ; *See* ASSEMBLE. –under, आनम् c. (नमयति); 'b. one's power' वशं नी, दम् c. (दमयति), अभिभू. –up, संवृध् c, पोषणं-पालनं-कृ 8 U (with gen.); पुष्10.

BRINK, *s.* तीरं, तटः-टं. कूलं. 2 प्रांतः, अंतः, पर्यंतः; धारा, उत्संगः, परिसरः, कंठः.

BRISK, *a.* चपल, त्वरित, क्षिप्र, अविलंब. 2 प्रबल, ससार, तीव्र; 'b. shower' धारासंपातः –LY, *adv.* सत्वरं, क्षिप्रं, आशु. –NESS, *s.* तेजस् *n.*, सारः, सत्त्वं.

BRISTLE, *v. i.* पुलकित-रोमांचित-कंटकित *a.* भू 1 P; 'his body b. ing with joy' हर्षरोमांचितपुलकित-तनुः; हृष् 4 P (of hair). –*s.* शूकः-कं, दृढलोमन् *n.* 2 शूकरलोमन् *n.* –ING, *a.* हृषित, पुलकित, रोमांचित.

BRITTLE, *a.* भंगुर, भिदुर, सुखभेद्य, सुभंग.

BRIZE, *s.* दंशः; गोमक्षिका.

BROACH, *s.* शूलः, शंकुः; कीलः-लं. –*v. t.* अपावृ 5 U. 2 निविद् c., प्रकाश् c., कथ् 10. 3 छिद् 10.

BROAD, *a.* विस्तीर्ण, पृथु, विपुल, विस्तृत, विशाल, परिणाहवत् (ती *f.*), आयत; '10 yojanas b.' दशयोजनमायता (नगरी). 2 असभ्य, अश्लील, गर्हित; 'b. day-break' सुप्रभातं; स्पष्टे जाते प्रत्यूषसि (Ka. 26); 'b. day light' प्रखरतेजसि सवितरि; 'b. awake' प्रबुद्ध, उन्निद्र; 'b. breasted' व्यूढोरस्कः; विशालवक्षस्. –NESS, BREADTH, *s.* विस्तारः, परिणाहः, आयामः, विशालता, पृथुता; 'five fingers in b.' पंचांगुलं (दारु).

BROCADE, *s.* कार्मिकवस्त्रं.

BROGUE, *s.* प्राकृतभाषा, अपभ्रंशः.

BROIDER, *v. t.* चित्र् 10, सूच्या वस्त्रे पुष्पादिकं सिव् 4 P. –Y, *s.* सूचिकर्मन् *n.*

BROIL, *v. i.* तप्-पच्-pass. –*v. t.* भ्रस्ज् 6 P; (fig.) संक्षुभ् c, प्रकुप् c., उद्दीप् c. –*s.* कलहः, द्वंद्वं, कलिः, तुमुलं.

BROKER, *s.* निरूपितमूल्येन कार्यनिर्वाहकः. –AGE, *s.* कार्यनिर्वाहणार्थं दत्तं द्रव्यं.

BRONZE, *s.* *See* BRASS.

BROOCH, *s.* वक्षोभूषणं, उरामणिः.

BROOD, *v. i.* (lit.) (अंडानां) उपरि-सद् 1 P. निविश् 6 P; (fig.) नि-ध्यै 1 P, पुनः पुनर् आलोच् 10; चिंताव्यग्र *a.* भू. –*s.* प्रजा, संतति *f.*, अपत्यं. 2 समसुत्पन्नः शावकगणः, अपत्यजातं.

BROOK, *s.* कुसरित् *f.*, स्रोतस् *n.*, क्षुद्रनदी, क्षुद्र-अल्प-सरित्. –*v. t.* सह् 1 A, क्षम् 1 A, मृष् 4 P, 10.

BROOM, *s.* संमार्जनी, शोधनी. 'b. stick-staff' मार्जनीदंडः; दीर्घ-कृश-यष्टिः.

BROTH, *s.* सूपः, यू(जू)षं.

BROTHEL, *s.* वेशः, वेश्यालयः, गणिकागृहं.

BROTHER, *s.* भ्रातृ *m.*, सोदरः, सहोदरः, सोदर्यः. 2 बंधुः, सहकारिन् *m.*, संसर्गिन् *m*; 'spiritual brethren' एकगुरवः. –HOOD, *s.* भ्रातृभावः,-त्वं, सौभ्रात्रं. 2 साहचर्यं, बंधुता, संसर्गः, समाजः. –LY, *a.* भ्रात्रीय, भ्रातृसदृश (शी *f.*); 'b. in law,' *s.* श्यालः, देवृ *m.*, देवरः (husband's brother.).

BROW, *s.* कटकः, उत्संगः; *See* EDGE. 2 भ्रूः, भ्रूलता; 'knit the b. s' भ्रूभंगं कृ 8 U, भ्रुकुटिं बंध् 9 P, भ्रूकुटिरचनां कृ. 3 ललाटं; वदनं, आननं. –BEAT, *v. t.* भ्रूभंगेण-कटाक्षेण-तर्ज् 10, or निरीक्ष् 1 A. –BOUND, *a.* किरीटिन् (नी *f.*).

BROWN, *a.* कपिश, पिशंग (गी *f.*), पिंगल, कपिल, श्याव. –ISH, *a.* ईषत्कपिश, आपिंगल. –NESS, *s.* कपिशः, पिंगलवर्णः.

BROWSE, *v. t.* अद् 2 P, चर्व् 10, लंघ् 1 A, (पल्लवान् लंघितुमागच्छति M. 4), भक्ष् 10, संदंश् 1 P. –*s.*, –ING, *s.* किसलयः-यं, नवपल्लवः-वं; नवतृणं, शाद्वलं.

BRUISE, *v. t.* अपकृ 8 U, क्षण् 8 P, प्रहारेण हिंस् 7 P. 2 मृद् 9 P, पिष् 7 P. –*s.* क्षतं, अपकारः, प्रहारः, आघातः. 2 पिष्टितव्रणः.

BRUIT, *s.* ध्वनिः. 2 वार्ता, जनप्रवादः. –*v. t.* ख्या c. (ख्यापयति), घुष् 10.

BRUNETTE, *s.* श्यामा, श्यामवर्णा.

BRUNT, *s.* भारः; 'b. of battle' रणधुरा; संघट्टः, प्रथमाक्रमः; प्रहारः, आघातः.

BRUSH, *s.* आघर्षणी; लोममयी मार्जनी or शोधनी. 2 तूलिका, शलाका, वर्तिका. 3 संघट्टः, समाघातः. –*v. t.* मृज् 2 P, घृष् 1 P, घर्षणेन शुध् c. 2 मृदु तड् 10, लघुगत्या स्पृश् 1 P. –*v. i.* (by) लघु घृष्. 2 अपधाव् 1 P, विसृप् 1 P. –WOOD, *s.* गुल्मः, जंगलं. –Y, *a.* लोमश.

BRUTE, *s.* पशुः, तिर्यंच् *m.* 2 नृपशुः, दुर्वृत्तः, क्रूराचारः. –*a.* अ-वि-चेतन, अज्ञान. 2 क्रूर-कर्मन्, असभ्य. –AL. –ISH, *a.* नृशंस, क्रूर, पशु in comp.; *See* CRUEL. 2 पशुशील, पाशव (वी *f.*), पशुसदृश (शी *f.*), पशुतुल्य. –ALLY, *adv.* पशुवत्; निर्दयं, अतिक्रौर्येण.

BUBBLE, *s.* बुद्बुदः, डिंबिका. 2 (fig.) असारं वस्तु,

माया, वंचकः, मोहः, मायाजालं. -*v. i.* बुद्बुदायते (D.) -*v. t. See* CHEAT.

BUBBY, *s. See* BREAST.

BUCK, *s.* हरिणः, मृगः. 2 वस्त्रधावनार्थं जलं. 3 सुभगंमन्यः.

BUCKET, *s.* अरघट्टः, उदंचनं, घटीयंत्रं. 2 पात्रं, द्रोणी, सेचनी-नं.

BUCKLE, *s.* कुडुपः, गंडकः. -*v. t.* कुडुपेन बंध् 9 P; 'to be b. ed to' परायण-आसक्त *a.* भू 1 P. -ER, *s.* फलकः-कं, चर्मन् *n.*

BUCKRAM, *s.* स्थूलपट्टं-पटः.

BUD, *s.* कलिका, कोरकः-कं, मुकुलः-लं, कुड्मलः; जालं, कोशः-षः, प्ररोहः, अंकुरः, पल्लवः-वं. -*v. t.*, -ED, *See* under BLOSSOM.

BUDGE, *v. i.* प्रचल् 1 P, अपसृ 1 P, नि-परा-वृत् 1 A, त्यज् 1 P.

BUDGET, *s.* शाणपुटः, दृति *f.* 2 कोषः, संग्रहः, संचयः. 3 आयव्ययगणना, °पत्रं.

BUFF, *s.* महिषचर्मन् *n.* 2 पांडुवर्णः.

BUFFALO, *s.* महिषः; 'she-b.' महिषी; 'b. milk' माहिषं पयः.

BUFFET, *s.* मुष्टिप्रहारः, कराघातः, चपेटिका. 2 कुशूलः. -*v. t.* मुष्टिना तड् 10 or प्रह 1 P.

BUFFOON, *s.* विदूषकः, वैहासिकः, भंडः. -ERY, *s.* परिहासः, हास्यं, नर्मन् *n.*

BUG, *s.* मत्कुणः, उद्दंशः; 'b. bear' महाभयास्पदं, भयहेतुः.

BUGLE, *s.* काहलः-ला, व्याधशृंगं-विषाणं. 2 शृंगं, विषाणं.

BUILD, *v. t.* निर्मा 3 A or c. (मापयति), प्रकॢप् c., विधा 3 U, विरच् 10; 'b. upon' समालंब् 1 A, आ-समा-श्रि 1 U. -ER, *s.* निर्मातृ *m.*, विधायकः. 2 स्थपतिः, शिल्पिन् *m.*, दारुकर्मन् *m.* -ING, *s.* निर्माणं, विधानं. 2 भवनं, गृहं, हर्म्यं.

BULB, *s.* कंदः-दं, गोलमूलं. -OUS, *a.* कंदिन् (नी *f.*), कंदविशिष्ट. 2 कंदाकृति.

BULGE, *v. i.* बहिर्लंब् 1 A, उदराकारेण प्रलंब्.

BULK, *s.* प्रमाणं, परिमाणं, मात्रा. 2 स्थूलता, बृहत्त्वं. 3 प्रधान-अधिक-भागः, भूयस् *m.* -Y, *a. See* BIG.

BULL, BULLOCK, *s.* वृषः, वृषभः, बलीवर्दः, ऋषभः, अनडुह् *m.*, उक्षन् *m.*, ककुद्मत् *m.* 2 वाग्दोषः, महास्खलितं, सुस्पष्टो वचनविरोधः.

BULLET, *s.* सीसकगुलिका.

BULLETIN, *s.* शारीरस्थितिज्ञापकं पत्रं.

BULLION, *s.* हिरण्यं; रूप्यं.

BULLY, *s.* पिंडीशूरः, शूरंमन्यः; दांभिकः, कलहकारिन् *m.* -*v. t.* तर्ज् 10, भर्त्स् 10 A; आह्वे 1 A.

BULWARK, *s.* वप्रः-प्रं, प्राकारः. 2 आश्रयः, शरणं, संश्रयस्थानं, आलंबः, रक्षणसाधनं.

BUM, *s.* नितंबः, कटिप्रोथः.

BUMP, *s.* स्फोटः, गंडः, शोफः. -*v. i.* श्वि 1 P. 2 BEAT, q. v.

BUMPER, *s.* अतिपूर्णं पात्रं; चषकः; 'b. crops' अतिप्रचुरः शस्यागमः; 'b. house' जनाकीर्णं प्रेक्षागृहं.

BUMPKIN, *s.* वृषलः, जानपदः, ग्राम्यजनः.

BUNCH, *s.* गुच्छः, स्तबकः. 2 पिंडः, गंडः. 3 ग्रंथिः, शेखरः-रं. 4 पोट्टली, संघातः, संहतद्रव्यं. -*v. i.* (out) पिंडीभू 1 P.

BUNDLE, *s.* भारः, कूर्चः, पोटलिका, गुच्छः, संघातः; 'b. of goods' भांडकं. -*v. t.* (up) गुच्छीकृ 8 U, एकत्र समाहृ 1 P.

BUNG, *v. t.* छिद्रं निरुध् 7 U or पिधा 3 U. -HOLE, *s.* पात्रच्छिद्रं, पात्रधारा.

BUNGLE, *v. i.* अदक्षतया कार्यं निर्वह् c., प्रमद् 4 P, स्खल् 1 P. -*s.* प्रमादः, स्खलितं, दोषः. -ER, *s.* अदक्षः, प्रमादिन् *m.*, अनिपुणः. -INGLY, *adv.* सप्रमादं, प्रमादतः, अदक्षतया.

BUNTER, *See* HARLOT.

BUOY, (up) *v. t.* उत्तंभ् 9 P, उद्धृ 1P, 10, आलंब् 1 A. 2 प्लु c. -ANCY, *s.* लघुता, लाघवं, प्लवनशीलता.

BURDEN, *s.* भारः, भरः, धुर् *f.* (राज्यधुरा); 'beast of b.' धुर्यः, धुरीणः. 2 ध्रुवकं, अनुपदं. 3 पीडाकर *a.* (री *f.*), पीडाहेतुः, भारभूत *a.* -*v. t.* भारं न्यस् 4 P or निविश् c. -ED, *a.* भाराक्रांत, आरोपितभार. -SOME, *a.* दुर्वह, दुर्भर, दुरुद्वह. 2 पीडाकर, दुःखावह.

BUREAU, *s.* आधारः. 2 लेखनस्थानं, लेखनसाधनाधारः.

BUREAUCRATIC, *a.* अनियंत्रितशासन.

BURGH, *s.* नगरं, पुरं. -ER, BURGESS, *s.* नगरजनः; पौरः. 2 नगरप्रतिनिधिः, पुरप्रतिनिधिः. -ERSHIP, *s.* नगरजनाधिकारः, पौराधिकारः.

BURGLAR, *s.* संधिचौरः, गृहभंगकृत् *m.*, कुड्यच्छेदिन् *m.*, संधिच्छेदकः. -Y, *s.* भित्तिचौर्यं, गृहभंगः.

BURGOMASTER, *s.* नगराध्यक्षः.

BURLESQUE, *a.* परिहासकर (री *f.*), हासजनन (नी *f.*), परिहास्य. -*s.* परिहासः, भांडं, नर्मन् *n.* -*v. t. See* LAUGH.

BURLY, *a. See* BIG.

BURN, *v. t.* दह् 1 P, शुष् 1 P, ज्वल् c. (ज्वलयति), तप् 1 P or c., उष् 1 P, दीप् c. -*v. i.* ज्वल् 1 P, दह् pass., तप् 4 A, दीप् 4 A; 'b. after' उत्कंठ् 1 A, स्पृह् 10; 'b. out' शम् 4 P; 'b. up' निर्दह्. -ER, *s.* दाहकः, तापकः, दीपकः. -ING, *s.* दाहः, दहनं, शोषः, तापः, ज्वलनं; 'b. ground' श्मशानं. -*a.* दाहक, तापक. 2 चंड, प्रखर; 'b. glass' सूर्यकांतः, सूर्योपलः.

BURNISH, *v. t.* प्रमृज् 2 P (प्रमृष्टं चामीकरं); तिज् c., परिष्कृ 8 U. -ER, *s.* तेजकः, धावकः.

BURROW, *s.* बिलं, विवरं, गर्तः -र्ता. -*v. i.* बिले-गर्ते-वस् 1 P.

BURSAR, *s.* धनाध्यक्षः, कोषाधिपतिः. -Y, *s.* कोषः, धनागारं.

BURST, *v. i.* स्फुट् 6 P, दल् 1 P, वि-दॄ-शॄ-pass., भिद्-भंज् pass.; 'b. in pieces' शकलीभू, खंडशो भिद् pass.; 'b. into tears' सहसा रोदितुमारेभे, सहसा प्रावर्ततास्रुधारा. -*v. t.* भिद्-भंज् 7 P, स्फुट् c., दॄ 9 P, 10, शकलीकृ 8 U, दल् c. (दलयति); 'she b. herself' हृदयस्फोटनेन मृता. -*s.* स्फोटनं, विदलनं, भंगः, भेदः; 'there was a b. of applause' संभूय प्रशंसागिरः उदतिष्ठन्; 'b. of laughter' अट्टहासः, उच्चैर्हासः.

BURTHEN, *s.* *See* BURDEN.

BURY, *v. t.* निखन् 1 P, निगुह् 1 U, (श्मशाने-भूमौ) निधा 3 U, स्था c. (स्थापयति), निक्षिप् 6 P; निरुह् 1 P; 'this buried the king into sorrow' एतेन (वचसा) राजा दुःखमग्नो-दुःखोदधिमग्न इव-बभूव. -ING, *s.* निखननं, श्मशाने स्थापनं; 'b. ground' श्मशानं, प्रेतावासः, परेतभूमि *f.*, पितृवनं, पितृसद्मन् *n.*

BUSH, *s.* गुल्मः-ल्मं, क्षुपः, स्तंबः; 'why do you beat about the b.' अप्रस्तुतं किमिति अनुसंधीयते, (निरर्थकं किमिति वनमालोडयसि); 'a bird in the hand is worth two in the b.' ध्रुवाणि परित्यज्य अध्रुवनिषेवणं नेष्टं, अध्रुवाद् ध्रुवं वरं, वरं तत्कालोपनता तित्तिरिः न पुनर्दिवसांतरिता मयूरी, or वरमद्य कपोतो न श्वो मयूरः. -Y, *a.* गुल्मावृत, निबिड; गाढ, अविरल. 2 घन, स्थूल; लोमश.

BUSS, *See* KISS.

BUST, *s.* ऊर्ध्वकायप्रतिमा-प्रतिकृति *f.*

BUSINESS, *s.* कार्यं, अर्थः, कृत्यं, कर्मन् *n.*, व्यवसायः, व्यवहारः; व्यापारः; नियोगः (duty). 2 अर्थः, प्रयोजनं; 'what b. had you to talk with him' तेन सहालापेन किं तव कार्यमासीत्. 3 वृत्ति *f.*, जीविका; 'a man of b.' कार्यकुशलः, दृष्टकर्मन् *m.* —BUSY, *a.* व्यापृत (with loc.); कार्यसमाकुल, कार्यव्यग्र; 'with what work are you b.' कस्मिन्कार्ये व्यापृतोसि, किमारंभस्त्वं; कार्योद्युक्त, सोद्योग, अतंद्रित, अनलस, व्यग्र. -*v. t.* व्यापृ c., कार्ये नियुज् 10 or अधिकृ 8 U. -BODY, *s.* पराधिकारचर्चकः. -LY, *adv.* अतंद्रितं, सोत्साहं, मनोभिनिवेशेन, औत्सुक्येन, व्यग्रतया.

BUSTLE, *s.* संभ्रमः, आकुलत्वं, त्वरा, व्यग्रता. 2 कोलाहलः, तुमुलरवः. -*v. i.* कार्यव्यापृतत्वाद् इतस्ततो धाव् 1 P or गम् 1 P or चेष्ट् 1 A, or व्यवसो 4 P. -ER,-ING, *s.*, *a.* चपलप्रकृतिः, व्यवसायिन् *m.*

BUT, *prep.* अन्य, इतर, ऋते with abl., विना; विहाय, मुक्त्वा (acc.). -*adv.* एव, केवलं, मात्रं. -*conj.* तु, पुनः, (not at beginning); in 'not only but' अपि takes the place of '*but*'; न केवलं रूपे शिल्पेप्यद्वितीया मालविका (M. 2); 'b. for' (=If it were not) यदि न; 'all b.' *See* ALMOST; 'next b. one' एकांतर *a.*

BUTCHER, शौ(सौ)निकः, आखेटकः, मांसिकः, विशसितृ *m.* -*v. t.* विशस् 1 P, निषूद् 10, हन् 2 P. -Y, *s.* वधः, हननं, विशसनं. 2 सूना, वधस्थानं.

BUT-END, *s.* घनाग्रं, स्थूलाग्रं.

BUTT, *s.* लक्ष्यं, शरव्यं. 2 उपहासास्पदं, परिहासभूमि *f.* 3 आशयः, अभिप्रायः. 4 पात्रं; (सुरा-) भाजनं-भांडं. -*v. t.* शिरसा-शृंगेण-आहन् 2 U.

BUTTER, *s.* नवनीतं, नवोद्धृतं; दधिजं, किलाटः; 'clarified b.' घृतं, सर्पिस् *n.*, आज्यं; 'b. man' नवनीतविक्रयिन् *m.*; 'b. milk' (*s.*) तक्रं, अरिष्टं, कालशेयं, दंडाहतं, गोरसः; 'b. of last day's milk' हैयंगवीनं. -*v. t.* नवनीतेन लिप् 6 P.; (fig.) चाटूक्तिभिः प्रसद् c. or अनुनी 1 P.

BUTTERFLY, *s.* चित्रपतंगः.

BUTTOCK, *s.* नितंबः, कटिप्रोथः; जघनं, श्रोणि-णी *f.*

BUTTON, *s.* गंडः, कुड्मपः; 'b. hole' गंडाधारः. -*v. t.* गंडेन बंध् 9 P.

BUTTRESS, *s.* वप्रः-प्रं, आधारार्थं कृतः प्राकारः. 2 आश्रयः, आधारः.

BUXOM, *a.* सानंद, प्रफुल्लवदन, हृष्ट. 2 सरस, सविलास, ललित. -LY, *adv.* सानंदं, सरसं, ललितं. -NESS, *s.* लीला, लालित्यं, विलासः.

BUY, *v. t.* क्री 9 U; 'b. off' मूल्यदानेन परिक्री. -ER, *s.* क्रेतृ *m.*, क्रयिकः; क्रयिन् *m.*

BUZZ, *v. i.* गुंज् 1 P, विरु 2 P. -*s.*, -ING, गुंजितं, गुंजारवः, कलरवः.

BY, *prep.* Gen. ex. by instr. of noun; रामेण हतः, बाणेन हतः, &c. 2 (Near) उप in comp., or समीपे-निकटे-पार्श्वे with gen.; 'b. her father' उपजनकं, पितुः पार्श्वे-समीपे; 'by this time' अनेन समयेन; 'day b. day' अनुदिवसं-दिनं, दिने दिने; 'b. god' ईश्वरं साक्षीकृत्य-ईश्वरसमक्षं; 'b. and b.' अचिरात्; अचिरेण, क्रमशः, शनैः शनैः; 'b. the b.' अपरंच; 'b. degrees' क्रमशः; 'b. hundreds' शतशः; 'one b. one' एकैकशः, आनुपूर्व्येण; 'b.-end' स्वार्थः, स्वहितं; 'b. oneself' रहसि, निभृतं, रहः; 'b.-gone' अतीत, अतिक्रांत, गत; 'b.-path' विमार्गः; विपथः, उपमार्गः, गूढपथः; 'b.-law' उपव्यवस्था, उपविधिः; 'b.-name' उपाधिः; 'b.-stander' पार्श्वस्थः, प्रेक्षकः, समीपस्थः; 'b.-word' उपहासास्पदं.

C.

CABAL, *s.* गूढमंत्रणा, कुविचारणा. -*v. i.* निभृतं मंत्र्

10 A, कूटार्थे संमिल् 6 P. -LER, s. कुमंत्रणकृत् m., गूढमंत्रिन् m., भेदकरः.

CABALA, s. गूढशास्त्रं, गुप्तविद्या. —CABALIST, s. गूढशास्त्रज्ञः. -IC, a. निगूढार्थ, गुप्तार्थ.

CABBAGE, s. शाकं, हरितकं.

CABIN, s. कुटि-टी f., शाला, कोष्ठः. 2 नौकाभ्यंतरे कोष्ठः. 3 वेश्मन् n., कुटीरः. 4 Tent, q. v. -ET, s. वेश्मन् n., कक्षांतरं, उपरोधकं. 2 शिष्टसभा, धीसचिवसभा; गूढमंत्रणं. 3 रत्नकोष्ठः. 4 समुद्गकः, संपुटः; *See* BOX.

CABLE, s. नौरज्जु f. -ED, a. रज्जुबद्ध.

CACHEXY, s. दोषत्रयं, त्रिदोषं.

CACHINATION, s. अट्टहासः, प्रहासः.

CACKLE, CACKLING, s. कूजनं, हंसरुतं; अव्यक्तरवः. 2 जल्पितं, प्रलापः. -v. i. कूज् 1 P, अव्यक्तं रु 2 P. -ER, s. कूजकः.

CADAVEROUS, a. शवतुल्य, शवसवर्ण.

CADENCE, s. पातः, च्युति f. 2 स्वरः, विरावः, निन्हादः; स्वरसंक्रमः, स्वरावरोहः.

CADET, s. अनुजः, अवरजः.

CADGER, s. आपणिकः.

CÆSURA, s. विच्छेदः, विरामः.

CAGE, s. पंजरः-रं, पिंजरं, वीतंसः. 2 Prison, q. v. -v. t. पंजरे रुध् 7 U or बंध् 9 P.

CAIRN, s. उपल-पाषाण-राशिः, शिलासमुच्चयः, प्रस्तरचिति f.

CAITIFF, s. खलः, शठः, दुर्वृत्तः; *See* WICKED.

CAJOLE, v. t. लल् 10, उपच्छंद् 10. 2 CHEAT, q. v. -RY, s. चाटूक्ति f. 2 वंचनं, छलं, &c.

CAKE, s. पूपः, पिष्टकः, अपूपः. -v. i. पिंडीभू 1 P.

CALAMITY, s. विपद् f., आपद् f., व्यसनं, अनर्थः, उपद्रवः, दुःखं, संकटं, अत्याहितं. 2 उत्पातः, दैवी आपद्. -OUS, a. विपद्ग्रस्त, व्यसनोपेत, विपदापन्न, दुर्गत, विधुर.

CALAMUS, s. वेत्रः, वेणुः.

CALASH, s. केलिरथः, क्रीडायानं.

CALCAREOUS, a. शार्करीय.

CALCINE, v. t. भस्मीकृ 8 U.

CALCULATE, v. t. गण् 10, परिसं-सं-ख्या 2 P, संकल् 10. 2 निरूप् 10; चिंत् 10, प्रक्लृप् c. -ED, a. गणित, संख्येय. 2 युक्त, पर्याप्त, उचित, अलं with inf. -ION, s. गणनं-ना, संख्यानं. -OR, s. गणकः.

CALCULOUS, a. शिला-अश्म-मय (यी f.).

CALCULUS, s. अश्मरी, मूत्रकृच्छ्रं.

CALDRON, s. पिठरः रं, उखा, कुंडं, स्थाली.

CALEFY, v. t. तप् 1 P.

CALENDAR, s. पंजी, पंजिका.

CALENDS, s. प्रतिपद् f.; प्रथमदिवसः.

CALF, s. गोवत्सः, वत्सः, तर्णकः. 2 जंघापिंडः, पिंडिका.

CALIBRE, s. छिद्रं; छिद्रव्यासः. 2 परिमाणं. 3 प्रकारः, जाति f.

CALICO, s. चित्रितकार्पासपटः.

CALIGATION, *See* DARKNESS.

CALIGRAPHY, s. शोभनलेखनकला-शिल्पं.

CALIX, s. पुष्पगर्भः, पुष्पकोशः.

CALL, v. t. ह्वे 1 P, आह्वे, शब्दायति (D.), आकृ c. 2 अभिधा 3 U, आख्या 2 P, आह्वे, चक्ष् 2 A, नाम कृ 8 U; कृत् 10; 'c. ed her by the name of Pârvati' तां पार्वतीति नाम्ना जुहाव (बंधुजनः) (K. I. 26), तस्याः पार्वतीति नाम चकार; वच् 2 P, उदाहृ 1 P, ब्रू 2 U. 3 नि-आ-मंत्र् 10 A; 'c. by name' नामग्राहमाह्वे, संबुध् c.; 'c. to mind' स्मृ 1 P, मनसि कृ 8 U; 'c. to account' किं किं कृतमिति प्रच्छ् 6 P or अनुयुज् 7 A or अनुसंधा 3 U; 'c. to witness' साक्षिणं कृ, तमेव (अग्निं) चाधाय विवाहसाक्ष्ये (R. VII. 20). -s. आह्वानं; पृच्छा; निमंत्रणं; संबोधनं. 2 प्रयोजनं. 3 अभिगमः; नियोगः; 'I have many c. s upon me to-day' मयाद्य कर्तव्या बहवो नियोगाः संति. -back, प्रत्यादिश् 6 P, निवृत् c.; खंड् 10, निरस् 4 P. -for, अर्ह् 1 P; 'this matter c. s for consideration' अयमर्थो विचारणामर्हति; or अत्र विचारणया प्रयोजनं; अपेक्ष् 1 A. -forth, प्रोत्सह् c., उद्युज् 10; प्रकटीकृ, प्रकाश् c. -out, पठ् 1 P; उत्क्रुश् 1 P. 2 तारस्वरेण-उच्चैः आह्वे, घुष् 10. -upon, on, अर्थ् 10 A, याच् 1 A. 2 द्रष्टुं गम् 1 P, अभिगम्. -up, (from sleep) प्रबुध् c. -ED, a. आहूत. 2 अभिहित, उक्त, उदाहृत; gen. ex. by नाम *ind.*, नामन्, अभिधान, आख्या, अभिधा, संज्ञा, नामधेय, in comp.; 'a boy c. Râma,' रामो नाम, रामनामा, रामसंज्ञः, &c. बालः. -ING s. *See* (s.). 2 वृत्ति f., जीवनसाधनं, उपजीविका; व्यवसायः.

CALLOUS, a. कठिन, घन. 2 कठोर, निर्दय, कर्कश; 'c. to contempt' तिरस्कारमगणयन्, तिरस्कारानभिज्ञः. 3 निर्लज्ज, धृष्ट; अविनीत. -NESS, s. काठिन्यं, निर्दयता, &c. -CALLOSITY, s. किणः, त्वग्दृढता.

CALLOW, a. अजातपक्ष, पक्षहीन.

CALM, a. प्र-उप-शांत, निश्चल, प्रसन्न, स्तिमित, अनुत्तरंग, अक्षुब्ध, निष्कंप, निर्वात, अव्याकुल; 'to be c.' शम् 4 P, प्रसद् 1 P; 'heart, be c.' हृदय प्रसीद, मा उत्ताम्य. -s. निर्वातः, शांति f.; प्रसादः, विश्रामः. 2 शांतता, स्तिमितता; ex. by (a.). -v. t. उप-प्र-शम् c. (शमयति), उप-परि-सांत्व् 10; तुष् c., प्रसद् c. 2 लघूकृ 8 U, अपनी 1 P. -LY, *adv.* निश्चलं, अक्षोभं, शांत्या, प्रशांतं. -NESS, s. प्र-उप-शांति f., निर्विकारता, प्रसादः, अव्याकुलता, असंभ्रमः. 2 निर्वातत्वं, अक्षोभः, स्तिमितता.

CALORIFIC, a. तापकर (री f.); तापजनक.

CALVE, v. i. वत्सं सू 2 A; प्रजन् 4 A.

CALUMNIATE, *v. t.* परि-अप-वद् 1 U; निर्भर्त्स् 10 A, निंद् 1 P, अपभाष् 1 A; मिथ्या अभियुज् 7 A, 10; आ-अधि-क्षिप् 6 P. -OR, *s.* परिवादरतः, परिवादिन् *m.*, निंदकः, अभ्यसूयकः, अभिशापकः, पिशुनः, आक्षेपकः. —CALUMNY, *s.* परिवादः, पैशुन्यं, अभ्यसूया, अलीकप्रवादः, मिथ्याभिशापः, पिशुनवचनं, आक्षेपः, नियाभियोगः. -OUS, *a.* पिशुन, कलंकमय (यी *f.*). -OUSLY *adv.* सापवादं, परिवादेन, साभ्यसूयं.

CALX, *s.* चूर्णं, भस्मन् *n.* 2 रीतिपुष्पं.

CAMBRIC, *s.* अंशुकं, दुकूलं.

CAMEL, *s.* उष्ट्रः ; क्रमेलकः, मयः, महांगः ; 'young c.' करभः ; 'she-c.' उष्ट्री.

CAMISADO, *s.* रात्रियुद्धं.

CAMOUS, *a.* चिपिट.

CAMP, *s.* शिबिरं, निवेशनस्थानं, निवेशः. 2 सैन्यनिवासः. -*v. t.* सैन्यं निविश् c.

CAMPAIGN, *s.* समरभूमि *f.*, -स्थलं. 2 युद्धकालः, युद्धप्रवृत्ति *f.*

CAMPHOR, *s.* कर्पूरः-रं, घनसारः, सिताभ्रः, हिमवालुका, चंद्रः, सोमः. -ATED, *a.* कर्पूरसंमिश्र-संसृष्ट.

CAN, *v. i.* शक् 5 P, प्रभू 1 P, or समर्थ-क्षम-शक्त *a.* भू, with inf. of verb; *See* ABLE; oft. by ईश् 2 A; पृ 10. 2 In pass. ex. by pot. pass. part.; 'c. be done' करणीय *a.*, कार्य, &c; 'I cannot but go' मयावश्यं गंतव्यमेव. -*s.* कंसः, भाजनं, धातुपात्रं, चषकः.

CANAL, *s.* कुल्या, प्रणाली.

CANCEL, *v. t.* अव-वि-लुप् 6 P or c., व्या-अप-निर्-मृज् 2 P; निरस् 4 P, खंड् 10, निवृत् c.

CANCER, *s.* कर्कटः, कर्कः. 2 कुलीरः. 3 मांसार्बुदं; तनुव्रणः, विस्फोटः. -ATE, *v. i.* व्रणीभू 1 P.

CANDENT, *a.* *See* HOT.

CANDID, *a.* निष्कपट, निर्व्याज, सरल, स्फुट-स्पष्ट-वादिन् (नी *f.*), ऋजु, निर्मल, शुद्धात्मन्, निर्व्यलीक; शुचि. -LY, *adv.* निष्कपटं; स्फुटं, निर्व्याजं. -NESS, -CANDOUR, *s.* निष्कापट्यं, निर्व्याजता; आर्जवं, सरलता, अमाया, दाक्षिण्यं, निर्व्यलीकता, शौचं.

CANDIDATE, *s.* अर्थिन् *m.*, याचकः, प्रार्थकः, पदान्वेषिन् *m.*

CANDIFY, *v. t.* धवलीकृ 8 U, शर्क्रीकृ.

CANDLE, *s.* दीपः, दीपिका, वर्ति-र्ती *f.* -HOLDER, *s.* दीपहस्तः-वाहः. -STICK, *s.* दीपपादपः, दीप-शिखावृक्षः .

CANDY, *v. t.* घनी-खंडी-सांद्री-कृ 8 U, स्त्यै c. -*v. i.* स्त्यै 1 A, घनीभू 1 P. -*s.* शर्करा, सितोपला, खंडमोदकः.

CANE, *s.* वेतसः, वेत्रः, वेणुः, वंशः, वानीरः. 2 वेत्रयष्टि *f.* -दंडः ; 'sugar-c.' इक्षुः; 'seat of c.' वेत्रासनं; 'made of c.' वैणव (वी *f.*), वैदल (ली *f.*). -*v. t.* वेत्रेण तड् 10 or हन् 2 P or प्रहृ 1 P.

CANINE, *a.* कुक्कुरीय, श्वन् in comp.

CANKER, *s.* विद्रधिः; व्रणः. 2 फलनाशी कीटः. 3 कलंकः; विषं. 3 दूषणं, विलयनं, विनाशः. -*v. t.* विनश् c., विली c., दुष् c. (दूषयति). -*v. i.* विली 4 A, दुष् 4 P.

CANNIBAL, *s.* नृभुज् *m.*, पिशिताशः -शनः, पुरुषादः, क्रव्याशिन् *m.* -ISM, *s.* क्रव्याशित्वं, &c.

CANNON, *s.* गुलिप्रक्षेपणी लोहनाडि-डी *f.* -BALL, *s.* आग्नेयास्त्रं, रणगुलि *f.*

CANOE, *s.* लघुनौका, उडुपं, प्लवः, कोलः.

CANON, *s.* विधिः, नियमः ; शास्त्रं, व्यवस्था. 2 पौरोहितधर्मशास्त्रं. 3 धर्मपुस्तकसंहिता. -ICAL, *a.* वैधिक (की *f.*), नियमानुसारिन् (णी *f.*). -ICALLY, *adv.* विधिवत्, यथाविधि,-शास्त्रं. -IZE, *v. t.* सिद्धजनमध्ये आरुह् c. (रोपयति) or गण् 10 or संख्या 2 P.

CANOPY, *s.* वितानं, उल्लोचः, आच्छादनं, पिधानं. -*v. t.* वितानीकृ 8 U, वितानेन आच्छद् 10.

CANOROUS, *a.* सुस्वर, मधुरस्वन.

CANT, *s.* परिभाषा, कल्पितसंज्ञा. 2 अपभाषा. 3 वाक्छलं, दंभोक्ति *f.*, दांभिकवचनं. -*v. i.* परिभाष् 1 A. 2 दांभिकतया वद् 1 P. -ATION, *s.* गानं, गीतं. -ER, *s.* अर्थवल्गितं. 2 दांभिकः, धर्मध्वजिन् *m.* -ICLE, *s.* उपगानं.

CANTHARIDES, *s.* विस्फोटकीटकः.

CANTHUS, *s.* अपांगः-गं, नेत्रपर्यंतः.

CANTLE, CANTLET, *s.* खंडः, भागः.

CANTO, *s.* सर्गः, पर्वन् *n.*, परिच्छेदः ; अध्यायः, स्कंधः, (of different compositions).

CANTON, *s.* चक्रं ; भूभागः, प्रदेशः. -*v. t.* खंडशो विभज् 1 P. 2 आवासं क्लृप् c. -MENT, *s.* सैन्यावासः, शिबिरं.

CANVASS, *v. t.* Beg, q. v. 2 परि-ईक्ष् 1 A, विचर् c., निरूप् 10 ; अनुसंधा 3 U. -*s.* स्थूलपटः, शाणं. 2 वातवस्त्रं. -ER, *s.* प्रार्थकः.

CAP, *s.* शिरस्त्राणं, शिरस्कं, शिरोवस्त्रं, शिरोवेष्टनं. -*v. t.* पिधा 3 U; *See* COVER. -*v. i.* अभिवादनार्थं शिरस्त्रमुन्मुच् 6 P or आनम् c. or अपनी 1 P.

CAPABLE, *a.* समर्थ, शक्त, क्षम, योग्य, उचित ; gen. ex. by शक्य with inf., or pot. pass. part.; 'c. of being defeated' पराजेतुं शक्यः, पराजेतव्यः, 'Râma is not c. of such atrocity' नेदृशं नृशंसचरितं रामेण कर्तुं शक्यते, रामे संभाव्यते; 'c. person' पात्रं, गुणवत् (ती *f.*); 'to be c.' शक् 5 P, उत्सह् 1 A, क्लृप् 1 A (with dat.). -CAPABILITY, *s.* सामर्थ्यं, शक्ति *f.*, पात्रता, योग्यता.

CAPACIOUS, *a.* विशाल, उरु, प्रसृत; *See* BROAD. 2 विपुल, प्रचुर.

CAPACITATE, *v. t.* उपयुक्त-क्षम *a.* कृ 8 U.

CAPACITY, *s.* धारणशक्ति *f.*. ग्रहणसामर्थ्यं (lit. & fig.); 'c. for all knowledge' अशेषविद्याग्रहणसामर्थ्यं. 2 बलं, शक्ति *f.*, सामर्थ्यं. पात्रता, योग्यता. 3 परिमाणं, विस्तारः. 4 (Relation) gen. ex. by इति or रूपेण; 'he served the king in the c. of a servant' सेवकरूपेण राजानं सिषेवे; अवस्था, भावः, वृत्ति *f.*, विषयः; विधेयविषये सभवान्नियुंक्ते (Mal. 1) 'employs me in the c. of a servant.'

CAP-A-PIE, *adv.* नखशिखांतं, सर्वांगं.

CAPARISON, *s.* आस्तरणं; अश्वसज्जा-प्रसाधनं, अश्वालंकाराः (pl.). –*v. t.* विभूष् 10, अलंकारैर्भूष्.

CAPCASE, *s.* समुद्गकः, संपुटः.

CAPE, *s.* भूशिरस् *n.*, अंतरीपः-पं. 2 स्कंधप्रावरणं, ग्रीवाप्रच्छदः.

CAPER, *s.* *See* LEAP.

CAPILLAMENT, *s.* केशरः-रं, किंजल्कः.

CAPILLARY, *a.* केशोपम; सूक्ष्म, केश in comp.; 'c. attraction' केशाकर्षणं.

CAPITAL, *a.* श्रेष्ठ, परम, मुख्य, प्रधान, विशिष्ट, वरिष्ठ, उत्तम, उत्कृष्ट; 'c. punishment' उत्तमसाहसं, देहदंडः, प्राणदंडः; 'c. crime' वधार्ह पातकं; वधदंडर्घ्यं पापं. –*s.* राजधानी. 2 मूलं, मूलद्रव्यं. 3 शीर्षं, अग्रं. –IST, *s.* द्रव्यवत् *m.*, कोटीश्वरः. –LY, *adv.* उत्तमसाहसेन; प्राणदंडेन. 2 परमं, श्लाघ्यप्रकारेण, विशिष्टतया.

CAPITATION, *s.* एकैकशः परिगणनं; मस्तकसंख्या.

CAPITULATE, *v. i.* शत्रुहस्ते आत्मानं ससमयं सम्-ऋ c. (अर्पयति), शत्रोरधीन *a.* भू, वशं गम् 1 P. 2 संक्षेपतः लिख् 6 P or कथ् 10. –ION, *s.* समयपूर्वकं समर्पणं; वशीभवनं, शत्रुकरार्पणं.

CAPRICE, *s.* कामचारः, चापल्यं, मनोलौल्यं; 'c. of fortune' दैवविलसितं-विजृंभणं; दैवस्य कामचारः (Mu. 2). —CAPRICIOUS, *a.* कामचारिन् (णी *f.*), चपल, चंचलप्रकृति, लोल-चल-चित्त, लोल, अस्थिर, स्वैरवृत्त, स्वैरिन्. –LY, *adv.* लोलचेतसा, चापल्येन; कामतः, स्वैरं, कामचारेण. –NESS, *s.* चापल्यं, लोलता, कामचारिता, &c.

CAPSULE, *s.* बीजकोषः, पुटः-टं. –AR, *a.* पुटाकार.

CAPTAIN, *s.* सेनानीः, गुल्मपतिः, दंडनायकः. 2 पोताध्यक्षः. 3 नायकः, नेतृ *m.*, मुखरः, अग्र-पुरो-गः.

CAPTATION, *s.* लोकरंजनं, जनश्लाघासेवनं.

CAPTIOUS, *a.* दोषैकदृश्, छिद्रान्वेषिन् (णी *f.*); विवादशील. 2 भ्रांतिकर (री *f.*). –LY, *adv.* विवादेच्छयैव, छिद्रान्वेषिवत्. –NESS, *s.* छिद्रान्वेषिता; विवादशीलता.

CAPTIVATE, *v. t.* मुह् c., ग्रह् 9 P; हृ 1 P; विलुभ् c. (eye, ear, &c.); 'c. s the eye' विलोभयति चक्षुः. 2 दासीकृ 8 U, बंदीकृ, वशीकृ, दम् c. (दमयति). –ING, *a.* मनोहर, चित्तहारिन् (णी *f.*), मनोज्ञ, हृदयग्राहिन् (णी *f.*), हारिन्, मोहिन्. –ION, *s.* बंदी-दासी-करणं, &c.

CAPTIVE, *s.* बंदी, बंदि *f.*; कारागतः ; 'made c.' (taken prisoner) बंदीकृत, बंदिग्राहं गृहीत. 2 दासः. –*a.* बंदीकृत, दासीकृत, शत्रुवश, कारास्थ. –ITY, *s.* बंधनं, बंदित्वं, कारावासः. 2 दासत्वं, दासभावः.

CAPTOR, *s.* जेतृ *m.*, बंदीकर्तृ *m.*

CAPTURE, *v. t.* ग्रह् 9 P, बंदी-दासी-कृ 8 U; (a fort) भंज् 7 P, लंघ् 10, आक्रम् 1 U, 4 P. –*s.* ग्रहः, ग्रहणं; लोप्त्रं, लोत्रं; 'c. of a fort' दुर्गलंघनं; 'c. of cattle' गोग्रहः, धेनुहरणं.

CAR, *s.* रथः, वाहनं, चक्रयानं, प्रवहणं; 'heavenly c.' विमानं; 'war c.' स्यंदनः.

CARACOLE, *s.* तिर्यक्प्लुतं, वक्र-कुटिल-गति *f.* –*v. i.* तिर्यक् प्लु 1 A, or वल्ग् 1 U.

CARAVAN, *s.* सार्थः, संघः; 'leader of c.' सार्थवाहः. –SARY, *s.* पथिकावासः, पांथनिवासस्थानं.

CARBUNCLE, *s.* विस्फोटः; वल्मीकं. 2 पद्मरागः.

CARCANET, *s.* मुक्तावलि *f.*, मणिमाला.

CARCASS, *s.* शवः-वं, कुणपः, मृतं शरीरं.

CARD, *s.* पत्रं; क्रीडापत्रं. 2 ऊर्णामार्जनी. –*v. t.* ऊर्णां संमृज् 2 P or घृष् 1 P. –ER, *s.* ऊर्णामार्जकः.

CARDAMOM, *s.* एला, निष्कुटि-टी *f.*, पृथ्वीका, चंद्रवाला, बहुला; 'small c.' उपकुंचिका, तुत्था, कोरंगी, त्रिपुटा, त्रुटि-टी *f.*

CARDINAL, *a.* प्रधान; *See* CAPITAL, *a.*; 'c. point' दिग्भागः. –*s.* धर्माध्यक्षः.

CARE, *s.* चिंता, औत्सुक्यं, उद्वेगः; *See* ANXIETY. 2 यत्नः, प्रयत्नः, आदरः, मनोयोगः; 'brought up with c.' प्रयत्नसंवर्धितः, सादरं परिपालितः. 3 सूक्ष्मता, निपुणता; 'searching with c.' निपुणमन्विष्य; 'thinking with c.' सुनिपुणं विमृश्य. 4 रक्षा; अवेक्षा; 'leave under the c. of' *See* CHARGE. 5 अप्रमादः, सावधानता, अवधानं; 'have a c. what you do' यत्कर्तव्यं तद्विमृश्य-समीक्ष्य-कुरुत. –*v. i.* अव-अप-ईक्ष् 1 A, चिंत् 10, मनो धा 3 U; oft. ex. by the several nouns above; 'I do not c. now' अधुनाहं वीतचिंतः; 'I c. very much for your protection' तव रक्षणे बलवान्ममादरः. 2 गण् 10, (न तृणमपि गणयति शत्रुं), आदृ 6 A (न त्यागमाद्रियते); ईक्ष् 1 A, (the sense being clear); न कामवृत्तिर्वचनीयमीक्षते (K. v. 82) 'a self-willed person c. s not for blame'. –take c. रक्ष् 1 P, अव-ईक्ष् 1 A (श्वश्रां दुहितरमवेक्षस्व जानकीं U. 1), चिंत् 10 (तातस्त्वां चिंतयिष्यति). 2 लल् 10; संवृध् c., पा c. (पालयति), विनी 1 P. 3 अप्रमत्त-सावधान-*a.* भू 1 P, अवधा 3 U, 'let c. be taken of each character' प्रतिपात्रमाधीयतां यत्नः (S. 1); 'do not c. to think' सावधानेन चेतसा

विचारयति, इति विचारं नादियंते.—FUL, *a.* Anxious, q. v. 2 अप्रमत्त, सावधान, अभियुक्त, अवहित, दक्ष. —FULLY, *adv.* सावधानं, प्रयत्नतः, अप्रमत्तं, सादरं, निपुणं.—LESS, *a.* प्रमत्त, अनवधान, निरपेक्ष, निरवधान, असमीक्ष्यकारिन् (णी *f.*); 'to be c. in' प्रमद् 4 P (with abl.), स्वाधिकारात्प्रमत्तः (Me. 1). —LESSLY, *adv.* सप्रमादं, अनवधानेन, &c.

CAREER, *s.* चर्या; धावनं. 2 गति *f.*, क्रमः, चलनं, चरितं; 'c. in life' जीव-लोक-यात्रा; 'during his c.' तस्मिन् (भुवं) शासति.—*v. i.* वेगेन धाव् 1 P.

CARESS, *v. t.* परामृश् 6 P, आलिंग् 1 P, परिरभ् 1 A; *See* CLASP. 2 लल् 10.—*s.* परिरंभः-णं, लालनं, आलिंगनं, परिष्वंगः.

CARET, *s.* काकपदं, हंसपादाकृति चिह्नं.

CARGO, *s.* पोतभारः, पोतस्थं द्रव्यं-भांडं.

CARICATURE, *s.* हासजनकं चित्रं; हास्यचित्रं. —*v. t.* चित्रेण हास्यास्पद नी 1 P; हास्यप्रकारेण चित्र् 10. —IST, *s.* हास्यप्रतिमाकृत् *m.*

CARIOUS, *a.* गलित, क्षीण, पूयपूर्ण. —CARIES, CARIOSITY, *s.* अस्थिक्षयः-शोषः.

CARK, *v. i.* चिंताकुल *a.* भू 1 P.

CARLE, *s.* दुर्वृत्तः; *See* WICKED.

CARMINATIVE, *a.* वायुनाशिन् (नी *f.*), अग्निद, अग्निवर्धक.

CARMINE, *s.* ऋतुजरंगः.

CARNAGE, *s.* वधः, विशसनं, संहारः, हत्या.

CARNAL, *a.* कायिक-शारीरिक (की *f.*). 2 ऐहिक (की *f.*). 3 विषयिन् (णी *f.*), विषयासक्त, विषयोपसेविन् (नी *f.*); 'c. pleasure' विषयसुखं; 'c. desires' विषयवासनाः; 'c. union' संभोगः, अभिगमः. —ITY, *s.* विषयासक्ति *f.*, विषयोपसेवा, कामुकता. —LY, *adv.* कामुकवत्.

CARNATION, *s.* मांसवर्णः; लोहितवर्णः.

CARNIVOROUS, *a.* क्रव्याद्, मांसभुज्, पिशिताशन, क्रव्यभोजन.

CARNOSITY, *s.* गंडः; मेदोग्रंथिः.

CAROCHE, *s.* क्रीडारथः, चातुरं.

CAROL, *s.* हर्ष-आनंद-गीतं. 2 स्तोत्रं, भक्तिगीतं.—*v. t.* हर्षेण गै 1 P; उपगै, स्तु 2 U.

CAROUSE, *v. i.* अतिपानं कृ 8 U, पानोत्सवं कृ, अतिपानेन क्षीब *a.* भू.—*s.*, —AL, *s.* अतिपानं, पानोत्सवः. —ER, *s.* पानरतः, अतिपायिन् *m.*

CARP, *s.* शफरी, प्रोष्ठः-ष्ठी. —*v. i.* (at) छिद्रं अन्विष् 4 P; दोषं दृश् 1 P or निरूप् 10, निंद् 1 P; *See* CENSURE.—ER, *s.* छिद्रान्वेषिन् *m.*, दोषैकदृश् *m.* —ING, *s.* गर्हा, निंदा, छिद्रान्वेषः.

CARPENTER, *s.* तक्षकः, सूत्रधारः, रथकारः, स्थपतिः, त्वष्टृ *m.*, तक्षन् *m.* —CARPENTRY, *s.* दारुकर्मन् *n.*, तक्षकक्रिया, तक्षशिल्पं.

CARPET, *s.* कुथः-था, आस्तरणं; 'brought on the c.' प्रस्तुत, उपक्षिप्त.

CARRION, *s.* पूतिमांसं, अखाद्यमांसं; कुणपः.—EATER, *s.* कुणपभुज् *m.*

CARRY, *v. t.* वह् 1 P, नी 1 P, भृ 3 U, हृ 1 P; 'c. ed a dog on his shoulder' स्कंधे-धेन श्वानमुवाह. 2 साध् 5 P or c.; 'c. a fort' दुर्गं लंघ् 1 A, 10 or भंज् 7 P, or वशीकृ 8 U; 'the enemy c. ed the day' शत्रवो जयमापुः; 'c. one's point' अभीष्टं लभ् 1 A, प्रतिज्ञां पूर् 10; 'c. oneself' आचर् 1 P; *See* ACT; 'c. arms' शस्त्राणि ग्रह् 9 P; सैनिकवृत्तिं आस्था 1 A. —away, —off, अपवह्, अपनी, अपहृ; अप-उद्ह् 1 U, अपकृष् 1 P. —on, प्रवृत् c., प्रणी, विधा 3 U; 'c. on war' युद्धं-संग्रामं कृ, विग्रह् 9 P. —out, अनुष्ठा 1 P, कृ 8 U, साध् 5 P or c. —through, पारं नी; 'c ing through all difficulties' आपदां पारं नयनं. —CARRIAGE, *s.* वाहनं, यानं, रथः, प्रवहणं, शकटः-टं; 'closed c.' कर्णीरथः, प्रवहणं, डयनं; 'c. road' रथ्या; 'c. horse' रथ्यः. 2 आचरणं, व्यवहारः, गति *f.*, चरितं, चेष्टा. 3 निर्वाहः, प्रणयनं. —CARRIER, *s.* वाहकः, हरः, in comp. 2 भांडवाहनजीविन् *m.*

CART, *s.* शकटः-टं, शकटिका, वाहनं, प्रवहणं, यानं. —*v. t.* शकटेन वह् 1 P. 2 शकटे निधा 3 U. 'Carter', 'c. man' शाकटिकः, शकटवाहः; 'c. horse' शकटवाहनः; धुर्यः, धुरीणः; 'c. load' शाकटं, शलाटः, शाकटो भरः; 'c. rut' शकटचिह्नं पदवी-पद्धति *f.*; 'c. wright' शकटकारः.

CARTEL, *s.* युद्धाह्वानपत्रं.

CARTILAGE, *s.* कोमलास्थि *n.* —CARTILAGINOUS, *a.* तरुणास्थिविशिष्ट.

CARTOON, *s.* चित्रितपटः, विचित्रमालेख्यं, हास्योत्पादकं चित्रं.

CARUNCLE, *s.* गंडः, मांसपिंडः.

CARVE, *v. t.* कृ 6 P, तक्ष् 1, 5 P, उत्कृ, (उत्कीर्णा इव वासयष्टिषु V. 3); उल्लिख् 6 P. 2 कृंत् 6 P, छिद् 7 P; क्लृप् c.; विभज् 1 U; 'c. out (a plan)' युज् 10; प्रक्लृप् c.; प्रतियुज् 10; चिंत् 10, निरूप् 10. —ER *s.* तक्षकः, कारुः, त्वष्टृ *m.*, तष्टृ *m.* 2 परिकल्पकः.

CASCADE, *s.* प्रपातः, प्रस्रवणं, वारिप्रवाहः, निर्झरः, उत्सः.

CASE, *s.* अवस्था, भावः, दशा, स्थिति *f.*, वृत्ति *f.*; 'what is the c. with him' किं तस्य वृत्तं. 2 पदं. 3 अर्थः. 4 कार्यं, पक्षः. 5 पुटः, पिधानं, कोषः, आवेष्टनं. 6 भांडं, आधारः. 7 स्थानं, स्थलं. 'In c.' यदि, चेत्; 'this being the c.' एवं सति-गते; 'in this c.' अत्र, अत्र विषये; 'in the c. of' gen. ex. by gen., or विषये in comp.; 'in the c. before us,' 'in the present c.' प्र-

स्तुतविषये, प्रकृते; ' if such be the c.' यद्येवं, तेन हि; ' in both c. s' उभयथा, उभयपक्षे. –*v. t.* भांडे निधा 3 U or निविश् c. 2 पिधा 3 U, आवृ 5 U.

CASEMENT, *s.* गवाक्षः, वातायनं, जालं.

CASH, *s.* टंकः, मुद्रा, नाणकं. –KEEPER, –IER *s.* टंकाधीशः, रक्षकः.

CASHIER, *v. t.* अधिकाराद् भ्रंश् c. or च्यु c. or निरा-कृ 8 U or अपास् 4 P.

CASK, *s.* भांडं, भाजनं, पात्रं.

CASKET, *s.* समुद्गकः, भांडं, मंजूषा, करंडकः, संपुटः-टकः.

CASQUE, *s.* शिरस्त्राणं, शिरस्कं.

CAST, *v. t.* क्षिप् 6 P, प्र-वि-°; अस् 4 P, मुच्-सृज्-6 P, पत् c. 2 (about) विगण् 10, आकल् 10, चिंत् 10, विचर् c. 3 विलाप्य संधा 3 U; ' c. glance ' दृशं क्षिप्, दृष्टिं-चक्षुः &c. दा 3 P (कृष्णसारे ददचक्षुः S. I); ' c. skin ' कंचुकं विमुच्; ' c. lots ' गुटिकां पत् c.; ' why c. pearls before swine ' किमिदमत्रं खरसूकराणां. –*s.* क्षेपः; पातः. 2 मूर्ति *f.*; घटनना ; ' c. of characters ' भूमिकासंविभागः. –aside, अपाकृ 8 U, निराकृ. –away, अपास्, परित्यज्, उत्क्षिप्. –down, अव-वि-सद् 1 P, म्लै 1 P; विषण्ण *a.* भू 1 P ; ' with a face c. ' खिन्न-विषण्ण-वदनः ; ' c. look ' अधोदृष्टि *f.* 2 निपत् c., अधः क्षिप्. –forth, उत्सृज्, उद्वम् 1 P, उद्गॄ 6 P. –off, विमुच्; अप-निर्-अस्. –out, अपाकृ, निःसृ c., निष्कस् c., प्रत्यादिश् 6 P. –AWAY, *s.* त्याज्यः ; अपाकियः. –LING, *s.* गर्भपतितः, गर्भच्युतः.

CASTE, *s.* वर्णः, जाति *f.*, कुलं ; ' of the same c. ' सवर्णः; ' low c. ' हीनवर्णः, नीचः, निकृष्टजातिः ; ' high c. ' उत्तमवर्णः; ' mixture of c. s ' वर्णसंकरः; ' low c. man ' अंत्यजः; ' loss of c. ' जातिभ्रंशः; ' out of c. ' अपसदः, चांडालः, जातिहीनः; ' c. man ' सजातीयः.

CASTIGATE, *v. t.* दंड् 10 ; तड् 10. –ION, *s.* कशाघातः, तीव्रप्रहारः ; दंडः, निग्रहः.

CASTLE, *s.* दुर्गं, कोटः. –CASTELLAN, *s.* दुर्गाधिपतिः. –CASTELLATED, *a.* दुर्गाकार.

CASTOR-OIL, *s.* एरंडतैलं.

CASTRATE, *v. t.* वृषणौ कृत् 6 P or उत्पट् 10 or छिद् 7 P. –ED, *a.* छिन्नमुष्क, निर्वृषण. –ION, *s.* मुष्क-वृषण-छेदः, पुंस्त्वहरणं.

CASTREL, *s.* श्येनः.

CASUAL, *a.* अतर्कित, अचिंतित; आकस्मिक-आपातिक-आगंतुक-दैविक (की *f.*), दैवायत्त. –LY, *adv.* अचिंतितं, दैवात, समापत्त्या, दैवयोगात्. –TY, *s.* दैवयोगः-घटना, संगति *f.*, समापत्ति *f.* 2 अदृष्टं, आकस्मिकी आपद्.

CASUIST, *s.* धर्माधर्मविचारकः. –RY, *s.* धर्माधर्मविचारणा. 2 विवेचनविद्या.

CAT, *s.* मार्जारः, बिडालः, ओतुः, आखुभुज् *m.*; 'cat o'-nine-tails ' नवरज्जुयुक्ता चर्मयष्टिः.

CATACLYSM, *s.* पृथ्वीप्लावः, भूतसंप्लवः.

CATALEPSIS, *s.* अपस्मारः ; महामयः.

CATALOGUE, *s.* परिसंख्या, परिगणना; ' c. of names' नामावलि-ली *f.*

CATAPLASM, *s.* प्रलेपः, उपनाहः.

CATARACT, *s.* निर्झरः, प्रपातः, प्रस्रवणं, उत्सः. 2 नेत्रपटलं, मंथः, शुक्रः; काचः.

CATARRH, *s.* अभिष्यंदः. 2 श्लेष्मन् *m.*, कफः, (variety of c.). –AL, *a.* अभिष्यंदिन्-कफिन् (नी *f.*), श्लेष्मल.

CATASTROPHE, *s.* परिणामः, निर्वाहः, निर्वहणं. 2 आपद् *f.*; *See* CALAMITY.

CATCH, *v. t.* धृ 1 P, 10, ग्रह् 9 P, बंध् 9 P (in a net &c.). 2 परामृश् 6 P, अवलंब् 1 A. 3 प्रलुभ् c., आकृष्-हृ- 1 P; ' the house caught fire ' ज्वलनमुपगतं-अग्निदीप्तं-गेहं; ' caught cold ' शीताकुलो बभूव, पीनसोपहतः, अभिष्यंदाकुलः; ' c. in the act ' (red-handed) कर्मगृहीत, रूपाभिग्राहित, लोप्त्रेण गृहीतः ; ' Sir, you are c. ' भो निगृहीतोऽसि (U. 4); ' c. in his own words ' स्ववचनेनैव गृहीतः-निरुत्तरीकृतः. –at, अवलंब् 1A, आश्रि 1 U.–up, अपहृ 1 P, अपनी 1 P. –*s.* तालकं. 2 लाभः, फलं. 3 पर्यायगीतं. –ER, *s.* ग्राहकः, जालिकः. 2 वागुरा, जालं. –ING, *a.* संपर्कीय, संचारक. 2 हारिन् (णी *f.*).

CATECHISM, *s.* प्रश्नोत्तरं, सप्रश्नोत्तरः पाठः. –CATECHIZE, *v. t.* प्रश्नोत्तरद्वारेण-क्रमेण-अधि-इ c. (अध्यापयति) or उपदिश् 6 P or प्रच्छ् 6 P. –CATECHIST, –CHISER, *s.* प्रश्नोत्तरविधिना अध्यापकः-पाठकः.

CATECHU, *s.* खदिरसारः.

CATECHUMEN, *s.* नवशिष्यः-छात्रः.

CATEGORY, *s.* पदार्थः. 2 समानवर्गः, अधिकरणं. –ICAL, *a.* सुव्यक्त, स्पष्टार्थ; नियत, व्य.क्त. –ICALLY, *adv.* स्पष्टं, सुव्यक्तं.

CATENATION, *s.* संबंधः, अन्वयः, परस्परान्वयः. 2 शृंखलात्वं, दामता; परंपरा.

CATER, *v. i.* भोजनादि परि-उप-क्लृप् c.

CATERPILLAR, *s.* कोषकारः-वासिन् *m.*

CATES, *s.* स्वाद्वन्नं; विशिष्टान्नं.

CATHARTIC, *s.* रेचकं, रेचनं, उदरशोधनं.

CATHEDRAL, *s.* महामंदिरं, महती पूजाशाला.

CATHOLIC, *a.* सर्वसामान्य-साधारण (णी *f.*), सार्वलौकिक (की *f.*). –ISM, *s.* साधारण्यं, सार्वलौकिकता.

CATTLE, *s.* गावः (pl.), गोकुलं, पशुसमूहः, गोव्रजः; ' c. for draught ' धुर्यः, धुरीणः; ' keeper of c.' गोपालः, पशुपालः.

CAUL, *s.* शिरोवेष्टनं. 2 अंत्रावेष्टनं. 3 गर्भावेष्टनं.

CAUSE, *s.* कारणं, (oft. with loc. of effect, दैवं नृणां वृद्धौ कारणं), निदानं, बीजं, हेतुः, निमित्तं, मूलं, योनि *f.* 2 कार्यं, प्रयोजनं. 3 स्थानं, अवसरः, पदं. 4 उत्पादकः, प्रवर्तकः. 5 अर्थः, पक्षः, कार्यं ; 'material c.' समवायिकारणं ; उपादानकारणं, प्रकृतिः; 'efficient (instrumental) c.' निमित्तकारणं ; 'primary c.' बीजं, मूल-कारण-कारणं. —*v. t.* Ex. by causal of verbs ; 'c. to fall' पातयति; गमयति, &c. 2 उत्पद् c., जन् c. (जनयति): कृ 8 U ; oft. ex. by dat. of nouns with or without भू, अस् ; यतस्तौ स्वल्पदुःखाय (भवतः) (P. I. 1); *See* TEND (to); also ex. by संभव, जन्य, ज, in comp.; स्मरजा पीडा 'torment c. ed by Cupid', &c. —AL, *a.* हेतुक, हेतुमत् (ती *f.*). —*s.* णिच् (of verbs). —ATION, *s.* कारणत्वं, हेतुता. —ATIVE, *a.* उत्पादक, जनयितृ (त्री *f.*). —ER, *s.* कारकः, उत्पादकः, प्रवर्तकः. —LESS, *a.* अकारण, निष्कारण, निर्निमित्त, and sim. comps. —LESSLY, *adv.* अकारणं, अहेतुकं, निर्निमित्तं, निष्प्रयोजनं.

CAUSEWAY, *s.* सेतुः, धरणं.

CAUSTIC, *a.* दाहक, तिग्म, प्रखर. 2 अरुंतुद, मर्मस्पृश्-छिद्.

CAUTERIZE, *v. t.* दह् c. —CAUTERY, *s.* दाहः; तप्तलोहेन मांसदाहः.

CAUTION, *s.* दक्षता, सावधानता, अप्रमादः, समीक्षा, अवेक्षा, अवधानं. 2 प्रातिभाव्यं, आधिः. 3 प्रत्यादेशनं, प्राक् सूचना or उपदेशः, प्राक् प्रबोधनं. —*v. t.* प्राक् सूच् 10; प्रत्यादिश् 6 P, प्राक् प्रबुध् c.; 'c. ed me against the approaching danger' उपस्थितापद्विषये सावधानो भव इति मामुपादिशत्. —CAUTIOUS, *a.* सावधान, दक्ष, अप्रमत्त: समीक्ष्य-विमृश्य-कारिन् (णी *f.*); अवहित. —LY, *adv.* सावधानं, अवेक्षया, &c. —NESS, *s.* अप्रमादः, दक्षता.

CAVALCADE, *s.* सादियात्रा, अश्वारोहश्रेणी.

CAVALIER. *s.* अश्वारोहः, सादिन् *m.*, तुरगिन् *m.*; 'to treat c. ly' अवमन् 4 A, सावलेपं अवज्ञा 9 U. —C. S, —CAVALRY, *s.* तुरगबलं; अश्वारोहवर्गः, आश्विकं, सादिगणः.

CAVATE, *v. t.* खन् 1 P.

CAVE, CAVERN, *s.* गुहा, दरी, गह्वरं, कंदरः-रा, विवरः-रं.

CAVEAT, *s.* प्राक्सूचनं; निषेधः.

CAVIL, *v. i.* मिथ्या निंद् 1 P; दोषं ग्रह् 9 P; छिद्रं अन्विष् 4 P; मिथ्या विवद् 1 A ; मिथ्या अभियुज् 7 A, 10. —*s.* विवादः, वाग्युद्धं, मिथ्याविवादः, विप्रतिपत्ति *f*; मिथ्याभियोगः. —LER, *s.* विवादशीलः. —LING, *a.* अपवादक, दोषग्राहिन् (णी *f.*), छिद्रान्वेषिन्.

CAVITY, *s.* रंध्रं, छिद्रं, विवरं, बिलं, खातं. 2 पुटः-टं; खं; 'c. of hands' अंजलिपुटः.

CEASE, *v. i.* विरम् 1 P, निवृत् 1 A, विश्रम् 4 P, (with abl.) ; शम् 4 P, प्र-उप° ; 'this said, he c. ed' इत्युक्त्वोपशशाम; 'c. ed to be opulent' निर्धनोभूत्; 'c. to exist' लयं-क्षयं-गम् 1 P, नश् 4 P. 3 गम्, वि-अप्-निर्-°, अपया 2 P. —*v. t.* (c.) of roots above. —ING, —CESSATION, *s.* विरामः, उप-प्र-शमः, निवृत्ति *f.*, विरति *f.*, विच्छेदः. —LESS, *a.* अनवरत, निरंतर, सतत, नित्य; अविच्छिन्न. —LESSLY, *adv.* निरंतरं, अनवरतं, नित्यं, &c.

CECITY, *s.* अंधता, तिमिरं.

CEDAR, *s.* देवदारुः.

CEDE, *v. t.* उत्सृज् 6 P, दा 3 U, वितृ 1 P, परित्यज् 1 P. 2 अभ्युपगम् 1 P, वशं या 2 P. —CESSION, *s.* प्रदानं, वितरणं, विसर्जनं.

CEILING, *s.* वितानं, अंतःपटलं, पटलं, अंतच्छादनं.

CELEBRATE, *v. t.* प्रशंस् 1 P, उपगै 1 P, स्तु 2 U, कृत् 10, प्रथ् 10, प्रख्या c. (ख्यापयति), वर्ण् 10. 2 (As a ceremony) यथाविधि अनुष्ठा 1 P; पा c. (पालयति), आचर् 1 P, अभिनंद् c. (महोत्सवेन मज्जन्माभिनंदितवान् Ka. 137); निर्वृत् c. (प्रस्थानकौतुकं निर्वर्तयितुं S. 4), निर्वह् c.' —ED, *a.* प्रथित, वि-प्रख्यात, प्रसिद्ध, विश्रुत; लब्धवर्ण. 2 अनुष्ठित; 'c. in song' उपगीत. —ION, *s.* अनुष्ठानं, पालनं, &c. 2 स्तुति *f.*, वर्णनं, कीर्तनं, प्रशंसा. —CELEBRITY, *s.* यशस् *n.*; कीर्ति-ख्याति-विश्रुति-प्रसिद्धि *f.*, प्रतिष्ठा.

CELERITY, *s.* वेगः, जवः, त्वरा.

CELESTIAL, *a.* दिव्य, अमर्त्य, स्वर्गीय, दिविज; 'c. world' स्वर्लोकः, द्यो *f.*; 'c. damsel' अप्सरस् *f.* 2 (fig.) परम, उत्कृष्ट.

CELIBACY, *s.* अनुद्वाहः, अदारपरिग्रहः, अविवाहः; 'he led a life of c.' अकृतदारः स आयुरत्यवाहयत्.

CELL, *s.* बिलं, रंध्रं, छिद्रं. 2 कुटी, कक्षः-क्षा, कुटीरः. 3 मठः, आश्रमः. —CELLULAR, *a.* सूक्ष्मरंध्रपूर्ण.

CELLAR, *s.* भूमिगृहं, गुप्ति *f.*

CELSITUDE, *s.* *See* HEIGHT.

CEMENT, *s.* लेपः, सुधा. 2 बंधनं, दृढीकरणं, संधिः. —*v. t.* संश्लिष् c., संधा 3 U, संयुज् 10. —ATION, *s.* संयोगः, संश्लेषः, संधानं.

CEMETERY, *s.* श्मशानं, परेतभूमि *f.*, पितृकाननं-वनं, प्रेतावासः.

CENOTAPH, *s.* चैत्यं.

CENSER, *s.* धूपपात्रं-भाजनं.

CENSOR, *s.* गुणदोषविवेचकः, पापापापनिर्णेतृ *m.* 2 दंडप्रणेतृ *m.*, नीतिशास्तृ *m.* —CENSORIOUS, *a.* दोषैकदृश्, अपवादक, निंदक; दोषदर्शिन् (नी *f.*), निंदाशील. —LY, *adv.* सापवादं, निंदापूर्वकं. —NESS, *s.* निंदा, छिद्रान्वेषिता, अपवादप्रियता.

CENSURE, *v. t.* निंद् 1 P, उपालभ् 1 A, निर्भर्त्स् 10 A, गर्ह् 1, 10 A, परि-अप-वद् 1 U, धिक्कृ 8 U,

तिरस्कृ, दुष् c. (दूषयति), आ-अधि-क्षिप् 6 P; कुत्स् 10. –*s.* निंदा, उपालंभः, निर्भर्त्सना, गर्हणं, निर्वादः, वाच्यता, वचनीयता, अप-परी-वादः, आक्षेपः. –ABLE, *a.* निंद्य, उपालभ्य, गर्हणीय, वाच्य, &c. –ER, *s.* निंदकः, उपालंभकः, अप-परि-वादकः, आक्षेपकः.

CENT, *s.* शतं; '3 per c.' त्रिकं शतं; पंचकं शतं वृद्धिर्देया 'interest at 5 per c.' –CENTENARIAN, *s.* शतायुस् *m.* –CENTENARY, *s.* शतकं, शतं. –*a.* शतक, शत्य. –CENTENNIAL, *a.* शताब्द, शतवर्ष. –CENTESIMAL, *a.* शततम (मी *f.*). –CENTIPEDE, *s.* शतपदी, कर्णजलौकस्. –CENTUPLE, *s.* शतगुणः. –CENTUPLICATE, *v. t.* शतगुणीकृ 8 U. –CENTURY, *s.* वर्षशतं, शतवर्षं. 2 शतं, शतकं. –CENTURIAN, *s.* योधशताधीशः.

CENTRE, *s.* मध्यः-ध्यं, मध्यभागः. 2 उदरं, गर्भः. 3 केंद्रं.–*v. t.* एकत्र कृ 8 U, समाहृ 1 P. –*v. i.* संमिल् 6 P, सं-इ 2 P, एकत्र समागम् 1 P, एकीभू; 'all eyes were c. ed on him' नेत्रव्रजास्तस्मिन्निपेतुः (R. VI. 7); त्वयि तु परिसमाप्तं बंधुकृत्यं प्रजानाम् (S. 5); 'is c. ed in you' &c. 2 आश्रि 1 U, आ-अव-लंब् 1 A. –CENTRAL, –CENTRICAL, *a.* मध्य, मध्यम, मध्यस्थ, मध्यगत, मध्यवर्तिन् (नी *f.*). –LY, *adv.* मध्ये, मध्यस्थाने.

CEPHALAGY, *s.* शिरोवेदना.

CERATED, *a.* सिक्थलिप्त,-सिक्थमय (यी *f.*).

CEREBRUM, *s.* मस्तिष्कं, गोर्दं. –CEREBRAL, *a.* मस्तिष्कसंबंधिन् (नी *f.*).

CERECLOTH, CEREMENT, *s.* सिक्थाक्तं वस्त्रं.

CEREMONY, *s.* विधिः, संस्कारः; 'marriage c.' परिणयविधिः. 2 नियमः, आह्निकाचारः, नित्यकर्मन् *n.*, नित्यकृत्यं; 'c. es of religion' वर्णाश्रमधर्मः (as opposed to शाश्वतधर्मः); 'occasional c.' नैमित्तिकं कर्म. 3 शिष्टाचारः, सभ्याचारविधिः. –AL, *a.* वैधिक-नैयमिक-व्यावहारिक (की *f.*). –*s.* व्यवहारः, आचारः, विधिः, नियमः &c.; 'sacrificial c.' यज्ञकर्म; इष्टि *f.* –OUS, *a.* अतिसभ्य, अत्यादरयुक्त, अत्यादृत, अत्यनुनयिन् (नी *f.*). –OUSLY, *adv.* परमादरेण, अतिप्रश्रयेण, सप्रश्रयं, सादरं. –OUSNESS, *s.* अत्यादरः, अतिसौजन्यं, अतिप्रश्रयः.

CERTAIN, *a.* Ex. by चित्-चन & अपि with forms of किं. 2 निश्चित, ध्रुव, असंदिग्ध, असंशय, निःसंशय; अवश्य, नियत; 'I feel c.' इति मे निश्चयः, दृढं मन्ये, 'it is c.' नात्र संशयः, नूनं, खलु. 3 अमोघ, अनिष्फल, अवंध्य. 4 सविशेष, विशिष्ट. –LY, *adv.* (for c.) नियतं, ध्रुवं, खलु, असंशयं, नूनं, नाम; 'oh c.' (as a reply), अथ किं, कः संदेहः, कोऽत्र संशयः. –NESS, –TY, –CERTITUDE, *s.* ध्रुवत्वं, ध्रुवं, निश्चयः, असंशयः, निर्णयः, नियमः; 'leaves c. es' ध्रुवाणि परित्यजति.

CERTIFY, *v. t.* विज्ञा c. (ज्ञापयति). 2 प्रमाणीकृ 8 U, सप्रमाणं कथ् 10; दृढीकृ. –CERTIFICATE, *s.* प्रमाण-निर्णय-पत्रं, आगमः, आगमपत्रं, निदर्शनपत्रं.

CERULEAN, *a.* नील, आकाशवर्ण.

CERUMEN, *s.* कर्णमलं, तोक्मं.

CESS, *s.* करः, शुल्कं, राजस्वं. –*v. t.* राजस्वं दा c. or ग्रह् 9 P.

CHAFE, *v. i.* प्रकुप्-क्रुध्-रुष् 4 P, संतप् pass., क्षोभं या 2 P, क्षुभ् 4 P, 1 A. –*v. t.* बाध् 1 A, प्रकुप् c., संतप् c., क्षुभ् c. 2 निर्घृष् 1 P, घर्षणेन तप् c. –*s.* रोषः, मन्युः, क्षोभः, प्रकोपः.

CHAFF, *s.* तुषः, बुष-सं, कडंगरः. –LESS, *a.* निस्तुष. –Y, *a.* बुसमय (यी *f.*).

CHAFFER, *v. i.* पण् 1 A, क्रयविक्रयं कृ 8 U, व्यवहृ 1 P.

CHAGRIN, *v. t.* उद्विज् c., संतप् c., क्लिश् 9 P, व्यथ् c. (व्यथयति). –*s.* मन्युः, व्यथा, संतापः, क्लेशः.

CHAIN, *s.* शृंखला-लं, निगडः, बंधनं (lit. and fig.); 'a golden c.' कनकसूत्रं. 2 परंपरा, पंक्ति *f.*, श्रेणी, माला; 'c. work' शृंखलारूपं विरलकर्म. –*v. t.* निगडेन-शृंखलया-बंध् 9 P, निगडयति (D.). –ED, *a.* निगडित, शृंखलानिबद्ध, संयत, संदानित.

CHAIR, *s.* विष्टरः, आसनं, पीठं ; 'arm c.' आसंदी. –MAN, *s.* अध्यक्षः, सभापतिः, नायकः.

CHAISE, *s.* रथः, यानं, वाहनं.

CHALDRON, *s. See* CALDRON.

CHALICE, *s.* पात्रं, भाजनं, शरावः, कंसः.

CHALK, *s.* कठिनी, खटि(डि)का, शुक्लशिला-धातुः, सितोपलः ; 'red c.' गैरेयं, शिलाजतु *n.* –*v. t.* (out) निर्दिश् 6 P, प्रकॢप् c., चित्र् 10, निरूप् 10. 2 (lit.) कठिनीखंडेन लिख् 6 P.

CHALLENGE, *v. t.* धृष् 5 P, आह्वे 1 A, युद्धार्थं आकृ c., प्रत्यर्थ् 10 A, स्पर्ध् 1 A. 2 अभियुज् 7 A, 10, दोषं ग्रह् 9 P; निषिध् 1 P. –*s.* आह्वानं, समराह्वानं, अभिग्रहः. –ER, *s.* समाह्वातृ *m.*, अभियोक्तृ *m.*

CHALYBEATE, *a.* लोहसंसृष्ट, अयोगुणविशिष्ट.

CHAMBER, *s.* कोष्ठः, शाला, आगारं, आवासः, कक्षः, वेश्मन् *n.*; 'bed-c.' शय्यावेश्म, शयनागारं, वासगृहं; 'inner c.' कक्षांतरं, उपरोधकं; 'upper c.' चंद्रशाला, शिरोगृहं. –LAIN, *s.* कंचुकिन् *m.*; शयनाधिकृतः, अंतःपुरवर्तिन् *m.*, महत्तरः; 'female c.' महत्तरिका. –MAID, *s.* शयनपरिचारिका, अंतःपुरदासी.

CHAMELEON, *s.* कृकलासः, सरटः.

CHAMOIS, *s.* वातप्रमीः.

CHAMP, *v. t.* चर्व् 1 P, परि-सं-दंश् 1 P.

CHAMPION, *s.* योधः, वीरः, विक्रांतः, भटः. 2 रक्षकः, रक्षितृ *m.*, गोप्तृ *m.*

CHANCE, *s.* दैवं, दैवयोगः-घटना-गति *f.* 2 संशयः, संदेहपदं-वस्तु *n.*; 'try your c.' आत्मनो दैवपरी-

क्षणं कुरु; 'to try the c. of a battle' रणसंशये आत्मानं पातयितुं; 'birth in a noble family is the work of c.' दैवायत्तं कुले जन्म (Ve. 3); 'depend on c.' दैवपरः, यदृच्छिक:; 'by c.' दैवात्, दैववशात्-योगात्, अकस्मात्, असमर्थितं. 3 संभवः. 4 अवसरः, अवकाशः. —*v. i.* दैवात्-अकस्मात्-आपत् 1 P or समापद् 4 A or उपस्था 1 U or वृत् 1 A; oft. ex. by यदृच्छया, दैवात्, with verbs; 'c. ed to see two Kinnaras' किन्नरमिथुनं यदृच्छयाद्राक्षीत् (Ka. 119); 'I c. ed to see her' सा दैवान्मम लोचनपथं याता; 'whom I c. ed to see' समापत्तिदृष्टः.

CHANCELLOR, *s.* प्रधानधर्माधिकारिन् *m.*, अध्यक्षः.

CHANDELIER, *s.* दीपवृक्षः, दीपाधारः.

CHANDLER, *s.* वार्तावहः, वि(वै)वधिकः.

CHANGE, *s.* परि(री)वर्तः, परिवर्तनं, परिवृत्ति *f.*, विपर्ययः, (प्रवहणविपर्ययः); विकारः, विकृति *f.*, विक्रिया (of feelings &c.); 'oh, what a c. in the site of the ground' अहो अनवस्थितो भूसंनिवेशः (U. 2); विपरिणामः, विपर्यासः, विवर्तः. 2 अल्पार्घमुद्रा. 3 श्रेष्ठिचत्वरं. 4 विभेदः, वैचित्र्यं. 5 निवर्तनं. —*v. i.* परिवृत् 1 A; 'in this c. ing world' परिवर्तिनि संसारे; अन्यथा-अन्यरूप *a.* भू, अंतर affixed to nouns; 'the colour of the water c. ed in a moment' जलं क्षणेनैव वर्णांतरमुपागमत्; विपर्यासं या 2 P, विपर्यस् 4 P, विकृ pass. or विकारं या. —*v. t.* परिवृत् c., विकृ 8 U; 'nature can't be c. ed' स्वभावो दुरतिक्रमः; विपर्यस् c., अन्यथाकृ; oft. ex. by (*s.*) with कृ, or अन्य-भिन्न *a.* कृ. 2 विनि-नि-मे 1 A, प्रतिदा 1 P, 3 U; 'to be c. ed into' ex. by भावेन परिणम् 1 U, भावमापद् 4 A; 'milk is c. ed into curds' क्षीरं दधिभावेन परिणमते (S. B. 475); न हि वायुर्दधिभावमापद्यते (S. B. 476); 'he has c. ed his evil course of life' पापाचरणान्निवृत्तोऽसौ; 'c. ing his clothes' वेषपरिवर्तनं विधाय. —ABLE, —FUL, *a.* लोल, चपल, अधीर, अस्थिर; नैकभावाश्रय, अनित्य, चल, अस्थायिन् (नी *f.*). —LING, *s.* कृत्रिमपुत्रः, पुत्रप्रतिनिधिः.

CHANNEL, *s.* स्रोतस् *n.* 2 प्रणाली, कुल्या, खातं. 3 नदीपात्रं-गर्भः. 4 संकटं; संकट-संकीर्ण-पथः. —*v. i.* खन् 1 P, कुल्याः कृ 8 U.

CHANT, *v. t.* गै 1 P, पठ् 1 P. —*s.* गीतं, गानं, स्तोत्रं. —ER, *s.* गातृ *m.*, गायकः.

CHANTICLEER, *s.* कृकवाकुः, उषाकलः, ताम्रचूडः.

CHAOS, *s.* संकरः, संकुलं, संकीर्णता, व्यस्तता. —CHAOTIC, *a.* संकीर्ण, संकुल, अस्ताव्यस्त.

CHAP, *s.* बटुः, माणवकः. 2 गर्तः, छिद्रं, रंध्रं; 'c. s' आस्यं, वदनं. —*v. i.* (शीतवशात्) विभिद् pass., त्रुट् 4, 6 P, विदॄ pass., स्फुट् 6 P.

CHAPE, *s.* बंधनी, ग्रहणी.

CHAPEL, *s.* देवायतनं, देवालयं.

CHAPLAIN, *s.* पुरोहितः; कुलगुरुः, कुलाचार्यः.

CHAPLET, *s.* *See* GARLAND.

CHAPTER, *s.* अध्यायः; परिच्छेदः, स्कंधः, उल्लासः, उच्छ्वासः, प्रकरणं (of various compositions).

CHAR, *v. t.* अंगारीकृ 8 U, ईषद् दह् 1 P. 2 Do, q. v.

CHAR-WOMAN, *s.* दिनिकाचेटी, सैरंध्री.

CHARACTER, *s.* अक्षरं, वर्णः. 2 निसर्गः, प्रकृति *f.*, स्वभावः. 3 शीलं, चारित्र्यं, सौजन्यं. 4 कीर्ति *f.*, यशस् *n.*, गौरवं; 'he obtained the c. of a dull boy' मंदमतिरसाविति स विख्यातो बभूव. 5 रूपं, लक्षणं, चिह्नं, अभिज्ञानं; 'assuming the c. of an astrologer' कार्तांतिको नाम भूत्वा. 6 गुणः, विशेषः. 7 भूमिका; 'chief c.' प्रधानपुरुषः, नायकः. —ISTIC, *s.* स्वभावः, लक्षणं, चिह्नं, विशेषः, विशेषणं, विशिष्टलिंगं. —*a.* स्वभावानुरूप, स्वाभाविक (की *f.*). —IZE, *v. t.* विशिष् c., संलक्ष् 10; विशेषणं दा 3 U. 2 गुणदोषविवेचनं कृ 8 U.

CHARADE, *s.* सर्वतोभद्रः.

CHARCOAL, *s.* अंगारः-रं, दग्धकाष्ठं.

CHARGE, *v. t.* अवस्कंद् 1 P, अभिद्रु 1 P; *See* ATTACK. 2 Accuse, q. v. 3 आदिश् 6 P, शास् 2 P, आज्ञा c. (आज्ञापयति). 4 मूल्यं प्रार्थ् 10 A; 'you will be c. ed 8 Rupees' अष्टरूपकं त्वया देयं भविष्यति. 5 निक्षिप् 6 P, सम्-ऋ c. (अर्पयति), न्यस् 4 P; नियुज् 7 A, 10; योग्यसचिवे न्यस्तः समस्तो भरः (Rat. 1) 'a competent minister is c. ed with the whole responsibility.' 6 भारं न्यस् or निविश् c.; 'c. ed with water' जलपूर्णः-गर्भः (मेघः). —*s.* निक्षेपः, न्यासः; 'give in c. of' हस्ते निक्षिप्; सम्-ऋ c.; अयं जनः कस्य हस्ते समर्पितः, एषा हस्ते वो निक्षेपः (S. 4); इमां देवीहस्ते निक्षिपता (Rat. 1). 2 रक्षणं, अवेक्षा, गुप्ति *f.* 3 आदेशः, आज्ञा, शासनं. 4 नियोगः, अधिकारः. 5 अभियोगः, मिथ्यादोषः, दोषारोपः; 'lays a crime to one's c.' कस्मिंश्चिदपि दोषमारोपयति. 6 अवस्कंदः, आक्रमः, संघट्टः, अभिसंपातः. 7 भारः. 8 व्ययः. 9 मूल्यं, अर्घः. —ER, *s.* युद्धाश्वः, वारकीरः. 2 पात्रं, भाजनं.

CHARIOT, *s.* रथः, स्यंदनः. —EER, *s.* सारथिः, सूतः, सव्येष्टृ *m.*, नि-, यंतृ *m.*

CHARITY, *s.* भूतानुकंपा, दीनवत्सलता, दयालुत्वं, कृपा. 2 दानं, भिक्षादानं, त्यागः; 'out of c.' पुण्यार्थे. —ABLE, *a.* दीनवत्सल, दानशील, धर्मात्मन्, दरिद्रपालक. 2 सदय, कृपालु, दयार्द्र, अनुकंपारत. 3 अनसूयक

परदोषसहन. -ABLY, *adv.* सदयं, सानुकंपं; अनसूयया, अमत्सरं.

CHARLATAN, *s.* छद्मवैद्यः, मिथ्याचिकित्सकः. 2 छद्मिन् *m.*, मायिन्-कपटिन् *m.*, छाद्मिकः. -ICAL, *a.* दांभिक-छाद्मिक (की *f.*). -RY, *s.* मिथ्याचिकित्सा; छलं, छद्मन् *n.*, माया, वंचनं.

CHARM, *s.* गारुडं, मंत्रः. 2 रक्षाकरंडः. 3 मनोरमत्वं, चित्ताकर्षकत्वं, रामणीयकं, मनोज्ञता, शोभा, कांति *f.*, श्रीः. 3 प्र-वि-लोभनं. -*v. t.* मंत्रैर्वशीकृ 8 U, अभिचर् c. 2 परि-वि-मुह् c., हृ 1 P; 'I was c. ed by the melody of thy song' तव गीतरागेण हृतोस्मि (S. 1). -ER, *s.* गारुडिकः, जांगुलिकः. 2 मायिन् *m.*, मोहिन् *m.*, कुहककारः. 3 प्रिया, मुग्धा (of women). -ING, *a.* रमणीय, रम्य, मनोरम, सुभग, कमनीय, चेतोहर, कांत, हारिन्. -INGLY, *adv.* मनोरमं, सुभगं, चारुतया.

CHART, *s.* वेलापटः.

CHARTER, *s.* शासनपत्रं.

CHARY, *a.* परिमित, सावधान, अमुक्तहस्त.

CHASE, *v. t.* अनुधाव्-अनुसृ-अनुगम् 1 P, मृग् 10 A. 2 (away) निरस् 4 P, अपानुद् 6 P, विधू 5, 9 U, निराकृ 8 U, विद्रु c. -*s.* मृगया, आखेटः. 2 अनुसरणं, अनुधावनं; 'gave c.' अन्वसरत्. 3 जांगलं. -ER, *s.* अनुधावकः, मृगयुः.

CHASM, *s.* रंध्रं, बिलं, विवरं, दरी, गर्तः.

CHASTE, *a.* (Of a woman) सती, कुलवधूः, कुलस्त्री, अपांसुला, पतिव्रता, विशुद्धशीला, एकपत्नी. 2 विशुद्ध, निर्मल. 3 जितेंद्रिय, निष्काम, अव्यभिचारिन् (णी *f.*). -CHASTITY, *s.* सतीत्वं, चारित्र्यं, पातिव्रत्यं. 2 विशुद्धि *f.*, शुचिता. 3 इंद्रियनिग्रहः, ब्रह्मचर्यं, जितेंद्रियत्वं.

CHASTISE, CHASTEN, *v. t.* दंड् 10, अनुशास् 2 P. -ER, *s.* दंडप्रणेतृ *m.*, शास्तृ *m.* -MENT, *s.* शासनं, निग्रहः, दंडः.

CHAT, *v. t.* विश्रब्धं आलप् 1 P or संभाष् 1 A or संलप्; वृथाकथां कृ 8 U. -*s.* संलापः, संकथा, संभाषणं, विश्रंभालापः, वृथाकथा.

CHATTELS, *s.* अस्थावरद्रव्यं, विभवः.

CHATTER, *s.* किलकिलारावः. 2 विप्रलापः, जल्पितं, वृथालापः, प्रजल्पः. -*v. i.* प्रजल्प्-प्रलप् 1 P. 2 किलकिलरवं कृ 8 U, कूज् 1 P; 'with c. ing teeth' दंतैर्दंतान्निष्पीड्य, दंतवीणां वादयन्. -ER, *s.* जल्पकः, वाचालः, वावदूकः.

CHAW, *v. t.* चर्व् 1 P, परि-सं-दंश् 1 P.

CHEAP, *a.* अल्पमूल्य, अल्पार्घ, सुलभ, सुखक्रेय. -EN, *v. t.* मूल्यं-अर्घं-न्यूनीकृ 8 U or अल्पीकृ; अर्घतः पत् c. -LY, *adv.* अल्पीयसा मूल्येन, अल्पार्घेण, सुलभं.

CHEAT, *v. t.* वंच् 10, प्रतृ c., विप्रलभ् 1 A, अति-अभि-संधा 3 U; छल् 10, शठ् 10, मुह् c. -*s.* वंचनं, कपटं, प्रतारणं, कैतवं, माया, भ्रमः, मोहः. 2 वंचकः, धूर्तः, प्रतारकः, कितवः, कपटिन् *m.* -ING, *s.* प्रतारणं, अतिसंधानं, वंचनं, &c.

CHECK, *v. t.* नि-सं-यम् 1 P, प्रतिबंध् 9 P, प्रतिहन् 2 P, वार् 10; निग्रह् 9 P, निरुध् 7 U, नि-प्रति-षिध् 1 P, विष्टंभ् 9 P. -*s.* प्रतिबंधः, प्रत्यूहः; संरोधः, प्रतिषेधः, निग्रहः, संयमः, निवारणं, निरोधः.

CHEEK, *s.* कपोलः, गंडः, गल्लः, करटः (of elephants); 'broad c. s' गंडभित्ती; मांसलकपोलौ; 'c. bone' कपोलफलकः.

CHEER, *s.* हर्ष-(द्योतक)निस्वनः, जयध्वनिः-शब्दः. 2 स्थैर्यं, धैर्यं, स्थिरता; 'be of good c.' or 'c. up' समाश्वसिहि, धैर्यं निधेहि हृदये. 3 आहारः, भोजनं.-*v.t.* आ-समा-श्वस् c. सांत्व् 10. 2 प्रहृष् c., मुद् उल्लस् c., आनंद् c. 3 प्रोत्सह् c., प्रेर् c. 4 प्रसद् c., स्थिरीकृ 8 U (भवतीभ्यामेव स्थिरीकर्तव्या शकुंतला S. 4). -*v. i.* (up) आ-समा-श्वस् 2 P; हृष् 4 P. -FUL, *a.* सहर्ष, प्रफुल्ल, सानंद, हृष्ट, प्रसन्न, आनंदित, उल्लासित. -FULNESS, *s.* प्रसन्नता, प्रसादः, उल्लासः, हर्षः, आनंदः, आह्लादः, प्रमोदः. -LESS, *a.* विषण्ण, निरानंद.

CHEESE, *s.* किलाटः, दधिजं, मथजं; 'c. curds' दधि *n.*, क्षीरजं. -MONGER, *s.* दधिजविक्रयिन् *m.*

CHEMISTRY, *s.* रसक्रिया, रसतंत्र-विद्या. -CHEMIST, *s.* रसज्ञः, रसतंत्रविद् *m.*

CHEQUER, *v. t.* चित्र् 10, कर्बुरीकृ 8 U, शबलीकृ. -ED, *a.* कर्बुरित, शबल, कल्माष, चित्र.

CHERISH, *v.t.* लल् 10, पुष् 1,4,9 P, पा c. (पालयति), संवृध् c., भृ 3 U. 2 धृ 10, बंध् 9 P; 'c. ed hatred towards him' तस्मिन् द्वेषं बबंध. 3 भज् 1 U, उपास् 2 A, निविश् c.; ध्यै 1 P; 'c. ing Hari in his heart' हरिं मनसा ध्यायन्. 4 Love, q. v; 'c. those (hearts) that hate thee' विद्विषोप्यनुनय (Bh. I. 77). -ER, *s.* पोषकः, संवर्धकः, पालकः.

CHERUB, *s.* स्वर्ग-दिव्य-दूतः. -IC, *a.* दिव्य.

CHESS, *s.* चतुरंगं; 'c. board' अष्टापदं, शारिफलं; 'c. man' शारः, शारिः.

CHEST, *s.* *See* BREAST.

CHEVALIER, *s.* सादिन् *m.*, अश्वारोहः, महावीरः.

CHEW, *v. t.* चर्व् 1 P, संदंश् 1 P; 'c. the cud' रोमंथं अभ्यस् 4 P, रोमंथायते (D.). -ING, *s.* रोमंथः, चर्वणं.

CHICANE, *s.* कपटं, छलं, व्यपदेशः, मिथ्यापत्ति *f.* -ER, *s.* मिथ्याविवादिन् *m.* -ERY, *s.* वाक्छलं, मिथ्यावादः, पक्षाभासः; अनृतवाच् *f.*

CHICKEN, *s.* कुक्कुटशावः; 'c. hearted' भीरु, कातर.

CHICK-PEAS, *s.* चणकः.

CHIDE, *v. t.* निर्भर्त्स् 10 A, तर्ज् 10 A, निष्ठुरमभिधा 3 U. 2 निंद् 1 P; अधिक्षिप् 6 P; *See* CENSURE.

—*v. i.* उत्क्रुश् 1 P; विवद् 1 A, विप्रवद् 1 U, कलहं कृ 8 U. —ER, *s.* निंदकः.

CHIEF, *a.* प्रधान, अग्रिम, मुख्य, परम, उत्तम, प्रमुख, अग्र्य, विशिष्ट; वर-पुंगव-इंद्र-ऋषभ-in comp. —*s.* प्रधानपुरुषः, अधिपतिः, नायकः, ईशः, अग्रिमः, ईश्वरः, पुरोगः, अध्यक्षः, अधिष्ठातृ *m.*, मुखरः; 'military c.' सेनापतिः, सेनाध्यक्षः, चमूपतिः. —LY, *adv.* प्रधानतः, विशेषेण-षतः, मुख्यशः-तः. —TAIN, *s.* मुखरः, नायकः, पतिः, ईश्वरः. 2 गणपतिः, सामंतः.

CHILBLAIN, *s.* पादस्फोटः, क्षतं.

CHILD, *s.* बालः-लकः, शिशुः, अर्भकः, दारकः, अपत्यं, सूनुः, पुत्रः; वत्सः-त्सा, जातः-ता, (terms of endearment). 2 संतानः, प्रजा, संतति *f.*, अपत्यं, प्रसूति *f.*; 'to be with c.' *See* PREGNANT; 'c. bearing' प्रसवः; 'beyond c. bearing' विगतार्तवा, निष्कला; 'capable of c.' सरजस्का ; 'c. bed' प्रसवावस्था, प्रसूतिकालः ; 'c. birth' प्रसवः, जननं. —HOOD, *s.* बाल्यं, शैशवं, कौमारं-रकं, बालभावः, बालावस्था. —ISH, *a.* बालिश, बालेय, बालोचित, बाल in comp. —ISHLY, *adv.* बाल-शिशु-वत्, शिशुतुल्यं. —LESS, *a.* निरपत्य, असंतान, अपुत्र, निरन्वय, निर्वंश, पुत्ररहित, अप्रजस् & sim. comp. ; 'a c. woman' वंध्या, अशिश्वी. —LIKE, *a.* शिशुतुल्य, बालानुरूप, बालोपम.

CHILL, *a.* शीतल, शीत, शिशिर. —*s.* शैत्यं, शीतं, हिमं. 2 स्वेदविष्टंभः. —*v. t.* शीतीकृ 8 U, तेजोहीन *a.* कृ, उत्साहं ध्वंस् c. —Y, *a.* ईषच्छीत, आशिशिर.

CHIME, *v. i.* संवद् 1 P, अनुगुण-अनुरूप-*a.* भू 1 P. —*v. t.* वद् c., वादित्राणि तड् 10. —*s.* एकतानः, तालैक्यं, स्वरसंवादः. 2 घंटानादः.

CHIMERA, *s.* असंभवकल्पना, मनोरथसृष्टि *f.*, शशविषाणं; वृथा-मिथ्या-वासना. —CHIMERICAL, *a.* मनोरथसृष्ट, काल्पनिक (की *f.*), भावनाकल्पित, अमूलक.

CHIMNEY, *s.* धूमनिर्गमः, धूमनाली-रंध्रं. 2 चुल्लि-ल्ली *f.*, अग्निकुंडं; 'c. piece' चुल्लिशीर्ष-शिला.

CHIN, *s.* चिबुकं, हनु *m.*, *f.*

CHINA-CLOTH, *s.* चीनांशुकं.

CHINE, *s.* पृष्ठं, कशेरुका.

CHINK, *s.* छिद्रं, रंध्रं. 2 क्वणितं, रावः. —*v. i.* स्फुट् 6 P, विदृ pass. 2 शिंज् 1, 2 A; क्वण् 1 P, स्वन् 1 P.

CHIP, *s.* खंडः-डं, शकलः-लं, लवः, विदलं, तष्टं. —*v. t.* तक्ष् 1, 5 P; खंडीकृ 8 U; 'c. axe' तक्षणी. —CHIPPINGS, *s.* तष्टानि, खंडानि.

CHIROGRAPHY, —ER, *See* WRITING, WRITER.

CHIROMANCER, *s.* हस्तरेखाविद्याज्ञः.

CHIRP, *v. i.* विरु 2 P, कूज् 1 P. —ING, *s.* विरावः, कूजितं, रुतं.

CHISEL, *s.* व्रश्चनः, तक्षणी, टंकः. —*v. t.* व्रश्च् 6 P, तक्ष् 1, 5 P.

CHIT, *s. See* BOY. —CHAT, *s.* जल्पनं, विश्रंभालापः, विश्रंभकथा.

CHIVALRY, *s.* शौर्यगुणः, सुविक्रमः, सुवीर्यं, पौरुषं, धामन् *n.* —OUS, *a.* धामवत् (ती *f.*), सुविक्रांत, महावीर्य.

CHOICE, *s. See* under CHOOSE.

CHOIR, *s.* गायक-संगायक-गणः, गायकचक्रं.

CHOKE, *v. t.* प्रति-नि-रुध् 7 U, स्तंभ् 9 P. 2 कंठं संपीड् 10, गलं ग्रह् 9 P, श्वासावरोधं कृ 8 U, श्वासं निरुध्. —ED, *a.* कलुष, (कंठः स्तंभितबाष्पवृत्तिकलुषः S. 4); निरुद्धश्वास.

CHOLER, *s.* पित्तं. 2 क्रोधः, अमर्षः; *See* ANGER. —IC, *a.* क्रोधिल, क्रोधन, चंड, कोपिन् (नी *f.*); 'c. constitution' पित्तप्रकृतिः, कोपशीलता.

CHOLERA, *s.* विसू(षू)चिका, महामारी.

CHOOSE, *v. t.* वृ 5 U, वृ 9 U, ग्रह् 9 P (the sense being clear). 2 अभिलष् 1. 4 P, मनो बंध् 9 P; रुच् 1 A; इष् 6 P. 3 निरूप् 10, नियुज् 7 A, 10. —CHOICE, *s.* वरणं, वरः, ग्रहणं; अभिलाषः, मनोबंधः; 'c. of a husband' स्वयंवरः; 'of one's c.' यथेप्सितं, यथाकामं, यथेष्टं, स्वेच्छया. 2 उत्तमभागः, उत्तमांशः. 3 विकल्पः; कामः, रुचि *f.*; 'you have no c. in this matter' स्वरुच्या वर्तितुं न शक्नोषि. —*a.* सर्वोत्तम, विशिष्ट, उत्कृष्ट, परम, सार-विशेष-रत्न in comp.; 'c. food.' भोजनविशेषः, विशिष्टान्नं; 'c. girl' स्त्रीरत्नं. —LESS, अविकल्प.

CHOP, *v. t.* खंडशः छिद् 7 P, कृत् 6 P, शकलीकृ 8 U; *See* CUT. —*s.* खंडः-डं, शकलः-लं; 'c. house' पाकशाला. —CHOPS, *s.* आस्यं, वदनं.

CHORD, *s.* गुणः, तंत्रीः. 2 ज्या, जीवा.

CHORION, *s.* गर्भकोशः, गर्भवेष्टनं.

CHORISTER, *s.* गायकः, चारणः, किन्नरः.

CHORUS, *s.* ध्रुवः-वकः, अनुपदं. 2 गायकगणः.

CHOUSE, *v. t. See* CHEAT.

CHOWRIE, *s.* चामरं, रोमगुच्छः.

CHRISTEN, *v. t.* नाम कृ 8 U or दा 3 U. *See* CALL.

CHROMATIC, *a.* वर्णसंबंधिन् (नी *f.*). 2 ग्रामीण.

CHRONIC, *a.* कालिक (की *f.*), दीर्घस्थायिन् (नी *f.*), अविसर्गिन् (णी *f.*).

CHRONICLE, *s.* इतिहासः, पुरावृत्ताख्यानं, वृत्तविवरणं. —*v. t.* अभिलिख् 6 P, वृत्तांतं लिख्; यथाक्रमं रच् 10. —ER, *s.* पुरावृत्तरचकः, इतिहासलेखकः.

CHRONOLOGY, *s.* कालनिर्णयविद्या. 2 कालक्रमेण पुरावृत्तविवरणं. —IST, *s.* कालगणकः-ज्ञः, पुरावृत्तरचकः. —ICAL, *a.* कालानुसारिन् (णी *f.*), कालक्रमानुसारिन्; 'in c. order' आनुपूर्व्येण, अनुपूर्वशः; कालानुसारेण.

CHRONOMETER, *s.* कालमापनं, घटी, यामनाली.

CHRYSALIS, *s.* कोषकारः, कोशस्थः.

CHRYSOLITE, *s.* चंद्रकांतः.

CHUB-FACED, *a.* स्थूलास्य.

CHUCK, *s.* कुक्कुटीशावः. 2 (-ling) प्रिये-वत्से, वत्सजात (voc.). 3 चपेटिका, ईषत्प्रहारः, लघ्वाघातः.

CHUCKLE, *v. i.* अंतः विहस् 1 P or स्मि 1 A, आनंदं भज् 1 U.

CHUFF, *s.* ग्रामिकः, स्थूल-जड-बुद्धिः, असभ्यः. -Y, *a.* ग्राम्य, स्थूल, असभ्य.

CHUM, *s.* वयस्यः; प्रियसुहृद् *m.*

CHURCH, *s.* देवतायतनं, देवालयं, धर्ममंदिरं, भजनगृहं. 2 धर्मः; 'c. yard' श्मशानं, पितृवनं, प्रेतभूमि *f.*

CHURL, *s.* ग्राम्यजनः, ग्रामजः, वृषलः. 2 अविनीतः, असभ्यः; वामशीलः. 3 कृपणः, कदर्यः. -ISH, *a.* अशिष्ट, अश्लील, ग्राम्य, अविनीत, असभ्य. 2 खल, कदर्य, दुराचार. -NESS, *s.* अविनयः, असभ्यता, &c.

CHURN, *v. t.* मथ् 1 P, मंथ् 9 P, (with two acc.); 'the ocean was c. ed for nectar' अमृतमंबुनिधिर्ममंथे; समा-आ-लुड् 1 P, or c. -ING, *s.* मंथनं, मंथः; 'c. stick,-handle' मंथनदंडः, मथिन् *m.*, मंथानः; 'c. rope' मंथनरज्जु *f.* 'c. ing stick' मंथः, मंथदंडः, वैशाखः; 'a pot used for c. ing' गर्गरी, मंथनी.

CHYLE, *s.* अन्नरसः, धातुपः. -OUS, *a.* अन्नरसमय (यी *f.*).

CICATRICE, *s.* सिध्मन् *n.*, रूढक्षतं. —CICATRIZE, *v. t.* क्षतं रुह् c. or शुष् c.; 'c. ed' रूढ, शुष्क, रोपित. -ATION, *s.* व्रणरोपणं, व्रणशोषणं.

CINCTURE, *s.* मेखला, रशना, कांची.

CINDER, *s.* अंगारः-रं, भस्मन् *n.*, अग्न्युच्छिष्टं.

CINNABAR, *s.* रक्तपारदः.

CINNAMON, *s.* दारुगंधः, दारुसिता, सुगंधित्वच् *f.*

CINQUE, *s.* पंचकं, पंचन् in comp.

CIPHER, *s.* शून्यं, बिंदुः, खं. 2 अक्षरं, वर्णः. 3 बीजाक्षरं; गूढाक्षरं. 4 अंकः. -*v. t.* अंकविद्यां अभ्यस् 4 P or शिक्ष् 1 A. 2 गूढाक्षरैर्लिख् 6 P. -ING, *s.* अंकविद्या, गणनविद्या, गणितं.

CIRCLE, *s.* मंडलं, वृत्तं, चक्रं, वलयः-यं, गोलः-लं; 'c. of friends' मित्रचक्र-मंडलं; 'c. of people' परिषद् *f.*; 'being in the c. of her friends' सखीमध्यगता; तापसपरिषदाबद्धमंडला प्रतीक्षते (Ka. 40) 'formed into, or sitting in, a c.' &c. 2 परिधिः, परिणाहः; 'area of a c.' फलं; 'segment of a c.' वृत्तखंडं. -*v. t.* परिवृ 5 U, परिवेष्ट् 1 A or c., परि-इ 2 P. -*v. i.* चक्रवत्-मंडलाकारेण-परिवृत् 1 A or परिभ्रम् 1, 4 P. — CIRCULAR, *a.* वर्तुल, वृत्त, मंडलाकार, चक्राकृति, गोल. -LY, *adv.* चक्रवत्, मंडलरूपेण.

CIRCUIT, *s.* परिभ्रमणं, पर्यटनं; आ-वि-वर्तः, आवृत्ति *f.* 2 मंडलं, परिधिः, परिणाहः. -*v. i.* (to make a c.) परिभ्रम् 1, 4 P, परि-इ 2 P, परिवृत् 1 A. -OUS, *a.* वक्र, कुटिलगामिन् (नी *f.*), अतिदीर्घ.

CIRCULATE, *v. t.* प्रचल् c., प्रसृ c., परिवृत् c., प्रवृत् c.; 'who c. ed false reports all around' समंतात् प्रवृत्तबीभत्सकिंवदंतीकाः (पौरजानपदाः) (U. 4). -*v. i.* आ-वि-परि-वृत् 1 A, प्रचर्-चल्-1 P, प्रसृ 1 P. -ION, *s.* परिभ्रमणं, परिवर्तनं, प्रसरः, प्रचारः, चलनं, व्यावर्तः; 'c. of blood' रुधिराभिसरणं, रक्तवहनं. -ING, *a.* परिवर्तिन् (नी *f.*), व्यावर्तक.

CIRCUMAMBIENT, *a.* परिगत, व्यापक, परिवेष्टक.

CIRCUMAMBULATE, *v. t.* परि-इ 2 P, परिभ्रम् 1, 4 P, परिगम् 1 P, प्रदक्षिणीकृ 8 U. -ION, *s.* परिभ्रमणं, पर्यटनं, प्रदक्षिणा.

CIRCUMCISE, *v. t.* त्वचं छिद् 7 P or कृत् 6 P; 'c. ed man' बंडः-ठः, दुश्चर्मन् *m.*

CIRCUMDUCT, *v. t.* लुप् 6 P; *See* BAFFLE. -ION, *s.* लोपः; मोघीकरणं.

CIRCUMFERENCE, *s.* परिधिः, मंडलं, परिवेशः-षः, परि(री)णाहः; 'c. of a wheel' नेमि *f.*, प्रधिः, नीव्रः.

CIRCUMFLUENT,—FLUOUS, *a.* परिस्यंदिन् (नी *f.*), परिस्रुत, परिगलित. —CIRCUMFLUENCE, *s.* परिस्रवः, परिस्यंदनं.

CIRCUMFUSE, *v. t.* परि-समा-द्रु c., समाक्रम् 1 U, 4 P, व्याप् 5 P, वि-अश् 5 A. -ILE, *a.* व्यापक.

CIRCUMJACENT, *a.* उपांतिक, पर्यंतस्थ.

CIRCUMLOCUTION, *s.* वक्रोक्ति *f.*, वाक्यविस्तरः; अत्युक्ति *f.*, अतिशयोक्ति *f.* —CIRCUMLOCUTORY, *a.* वक्र, बहुवाक्य, सवाक्यविस्तर.

CIRCUMNAVIGATE, *v. i.* पोतेन परिभ्रम् 1, 4 P, समंततः प्लु 1 A, तॄ 1 P.

CIRCUMROTATION, *s.* चक्रावर्तः, परिवर्तः, आवृत्ति *f.* —CIRCUMROTATORY, *a.* आवर्तमान, परिवर्तिन् (नी *f.*).

CIRCUMSCRIBE, *v. t.* परिमा 3 A, सं-नि-यम् 1 P, संवृ 5 U, संकुच् c. —CIRCUMSCRIPTION, *s.* संकोचः, संयमः.

CIRCUMSPECT, *a.* समीक्ष्यकारिन् (णी *f.*), विमृश्यकारिन्, सावधान, अवहित, अप्रमत्त, दक्ष. -ION, *s.* समीक्ष्य-विमृश्य-कारित्वं, अप्रमादः, अवधानं, दक्षता. -LY, *adv.* समीक्ष्य, सुविमृश्य, सावधानं.

CIRCUMSTANCE, *s.* दशा, अवस्था, स्थिति *f.*, भावः, वृत्ति *f.* 2 वृत्तं, वृत्तांतः; 'c. s as they happened' यथावृत्तः वृत्तांतः. 3 विषयः, वस्तु *n.*, अर्थः. 4 संबंधः; 'under these c. s' एवंगते-सति; 'in good c. s' सुस्थ-सुस्थित-*a.*; 'in bad c. s' दुर्गत-दुर्दशापन्न-दुःस्थित *a.*; 'under any c. s' यद्वा तद्वा भवतु; येन केनापि प्रकारेण; 'according to c. s' यथास्थितं, यथासंभवं, यथावसरं, यथाकालं. -ED, *a.* स्थित, अवस्थित, भूत, स्थ in comp. — CIRCUMSTANTIAL, *a.* सविस्तर, विस्तीर्ण. 2 अप्रकृत, आगंतुक (की *f.*), आहार्य; अप्रत्यक्ष (प्रमाणं). -LY, *adv.* यथावृत्तं, सविस्तरं, &c.

CIRCUMVALLATE, *v. t.* परिखादिना परिवेष्ट् 1 A or उपरुध् 7 U. -ION, *s.* समंतादुपरोधनं, परिखानिर्माणं.

CIRCUMVENT, *See* CHEAT.

CIRCUMVEST, *v. t.* परिव्ये 1 P, परिधा 3 U.

CIRCUMVOLVE, *v. t. See* REVOLVE.

CIRCUS, *s.* क्रीडारंगः, क्रीडांगनं, क्रीडाचक्रं.

CIST, *s.* कोशः, पुटः, आवेष्टनं.

CISTERN, *s.* जलकुंडं, जलाशयः, तोयाधारः.

CIT, *s.* नागरिकः, पृथग्जनः, नागरजनः.

CITADEL, *s.* दुर्गं, कोटः-टि *f.*

CITE, *v. t.* उपनी 1 P, उपन्यस् 4 P, उपक्षिप् 6 P, अवतॄ c. 2 आह्वे 1 P, अभियुज् 7 A, 10. -ATION, *s.* आह्वानं, अभियोगः. 2 अवतारण, उपन्यस्तवाक्यं, अवतरणं.

CITRON, *s.* जंबीरः, जंभीरः, जंभः-भलः, बीजपूरः, फलपूरः.

CITY, *s.* पुरं-री, नगरं-री, पत्तनं, पुर् *f.* — CITIZEN, *s.* पौरः, पुरवासिन् *m.*, नगरजनः, पौरजनः, पौरलोकः; 'c. s and villagers' पौरजानपदाः. -LIKE, *adv.* आर्यवत्, नागरिकवृत्त्या, पौरवत्. -SHIP, *s.* पौरत्वं, पौराधिकारः.

CIVET, -CAT, *s.* गंधमार्जारः.

CIVIC, *a.* पौर (री *f.*).

CIVIL, *a.* दक्षिण, सादर, प्रियंवद, सानुनय; अनुकूल; सुशील. 2 पौर (री *f.*), पुर in comp.; 'c. war' प्रकृतिक्षोभः, जनप्रकोपः. -ITY, *s.* दाक्षिण्यं, प्रश्रयः, आदरः, सौजन्यं, अनुरोधः, अनुवृत्ति *f.*, सुशीलता. -LY, *adv.* सादरं, सप्रश्रयं. —CIVILIZE, *v. t.* विनी 1 P, शिष्टाचारान् शिक्ष् c. or शास् 2 P, आर्यपदवीं आरुह् c. (रोपयति), उन्नम् c. (नमयति), उत्कर्ष-उन्नतिं-नी. -ATION, *s.* सभ्यता, आचारशिष्टता. -ED, *a.* शिष्टाचारापन्न, आर्यवृत्त, शिष्ट, सभ्य, विनीत.

CLACK, *s.* वावदूकता, अतिजल्पनं. -*v. i.* अतिभृशं जल्प् 1 P.

CLAD, *See* under CLOTHE.

CLAIM, *v. t.* स्वीय-आत्मीय- *a.* इति प्रतिपद् c. or याच् 1 A or ब्रू 2 U or वच् 2 P; 'he c. s that property' तद्धनं मदीयमिति स भाषते or प्रतिपादयति; 'c. s reverence' संमानमर्हामीति प्रतिपादयति; ममेति उक्त्वा ग्रह् 9 P; अभिमानं कृ 8 U, स्वत्वं ज्ञा c. (ज्ञापयति), अभिमन् 4 A. 2 (have a c. to) अर्ह् 1 P. -*s.* अधिकारः, अभियोगः, अभिमानः, स्वत्वप्रतिपादनं, प्रार्थना; 'false c.' मिथ्याभियोगः; 'laying c. to learning' विद्याभिमानः. -ANT, *s.* अर्थिन् *m.*, अभियोक्तृ *m.*, प्रार्थयितृ *m.*

CLAM, *v. t.* सांद्रीकृ 8 U; श्यानीकृ. -MY, *a.* श्यान, सांद्र, घन.

CLAMBER, *v. t.* आयासेन अध्यारुह् 1 P.

CLAMOUR, *v. i.* उत्-आ-क्रुश् 1 P, उच्चैः घुष् 10, आरट् 1 P. -*s.* आ-उत्-क्रुशः, महारवः, उच्चैर्घोषः, जनरवः. -OUS, *a.* महास्वन, मुखर, बहुघोष, घोषकर (री *f.*).

CLAMP, *v. t.* कीलेन संयुज् 10 or संबंध् 9 P. -*s.* इष्टकाराशिः.

CLAN, *s.* गणः. 2 वंशः, कुलं, गोत्रं, वर्गः, संघः, शाखा, जाति *f.*

CLANDESTINE, *a.* निभृत, रहस्य, प्रच्छन्न, गूढ; 'c. marriage' चोरिकाविवाहः. -LY, *adv.* निभृतं, गुप्तं, रहः.

CLANG, *v. i.* क्वण्-स्वन्-1 P, शिंज् 1, 2 A. -*s.* शिंजितं, क्वणितं; तुमुलरवः, शस्त्रघोषः.

CLANK, *s.* शिंजितं, क्वणितं.

CLAP, *v. t.* करतालं दा 3 U or वद् c. 2 अकस्मात् संहन् 2 P, संघट्ट् c.; न्यस् 4 P. 3 करतालेन प्रशंस् 1 P; 'c. wings' उत्क्षिप् 6 P. -*s.*, -ING, *s.* करतालवादनं, तालः. 2 प्रशंसाशब्दः. 3 मेघगर्जितं-नादः, वज्रनिर्घोषः, मेघस्तनितं. 4 ध्वनिः; क्वणितं, संघातशब्दः. -PER, *s.* घंटावादकः, घंटाताडनी.

CLARIFY, *v. t.* सं-वि-शुध् c., विमलीकृ 8 U, पू 9 U. -*v. i.* विमलीभू 1 P, प्रसद् 1 P.

CLARINET, *s.* वेणुः, वंशः.

CLARION, *s.* तूर्यः; काहलः.

CLASH, *v. i.* विरुध् 7 U, विसंवद् 1 P, विप्रतिपद् 4 P, विवद् 1 A. 2 संघट्ट् 1 A, आहन् 2 U. -*s.* समाघातः, संघट्टः, विरोधः, विसंवादः, विप्रतिपत्ति *f.* -ING, *a.* परस्परविरोधिन् (नी *f.*), विरुद्धार्थ, विसंवादिन्.

CLASP, *v. t.* आश्लिष् 4 P, समा-आ-लिंग् 1 P, परिष्वंज् 1 A, परिरभ् 1 A, उपगुह् 1 U, आपीड् 10; 'c. to the bosom' वक्षसा परिरभ्, क्रोडीकृ 8 U. 2 कुडुपेन बंध् 9 P or पिनह् 4 P. 3 परिवेष्ट् 1 A, परिनिधा 3 U; 'c. the hands' हस्तौ समानी 1 P, अंजलिं बंध्. -*s.* आश्लेषः, आलिंगनं, परिरंभः, परिष्वंगः. 2 कुडुपः, गडः.

CLASS, *s.* वर्गः, छात्रसमूहः, सहाध्यायिगणः. 2 श्रेणि-णी *f.*, गणः (of verbs); समूहः, संघः; समाहारः. 3 जाति *f.* (kind); 'of the c. of beasts' पशुजातीयः. 4 वर्णः, जातिः, वर्गः; 'people of the lower c. es' अवरवर्णाः, अंत्यजातीयाः; 'of the same c.' वर्ग्यः, वर्गीयः, सवर्णः. -*v. t.*, -IFY, *v. t.* वर्गक्रमेण विन्यस् 4 P, यथावर्गं रच् 10, वर्गीकृ 8 U, गणीकृ, गणशः व्यस्. -CLASSICAL, *a.* संस्कृत, श्रेष्ठ, प्रथमवर्गीय. -CLASSIFIER, *s.* गणकारः; व्यासः.

CLATTER, *v. i.* क्वण्-स्वन्-1 P; झणझणायते (D.).

2 प्रलप्-जल्प्-1 P. —s. क्वणितं, ध्वनिः, तुमुलरवः.

CLAVATED, a. ग्रंथिल, जटिल.

CLAUSE, s. पदं, अंगं, अधिकरणं. 2 वाक्यं. 3 नियमः.

CLAW, s. नखः-खं, नखरः-रं. —v. t. नखैः विद् 9 P, 10 or आहन् 2 U.

CLAY, s. मृद् f., मृत्तिका. 2 पंकः, जंबालः, कर्दमः; 'made of c.' मृण्मय (यी f.). —v. t. पंकेन लिप् 6 P or दिह् 2 U. —ISH, a. पंकिल, कार्दम (मी f.).

CLEAN, a. शुचि, पवित्र, वि-परि-शुद्ध, विमल, निर्मल, धौत (वासः). 2 विमलात्मन्, निर्दोष, अनघ. 3 श्लक्ष्ण, मसृण. —v. t. See CLEANSE, below. —adv. साकल्येन, अशेषेण, आमूलं, सर्वांशेन. —LY, a. निर्मल, पवित्रदेह. —adv. शुचि, निर्मलं. —LINESS, s. शौचं, शुद्धि f., निर्मलता. —NESS, s. शुचिता, पवित्रत्वं, निर्मलता, &c.

CLEANSE, v. t. शुध् c., पू 9 U. 2 प्रक्षल् 10, प्र-संमृज् 2 P or c., धाव् 1 P, 10, निर्-अव-निज् 3 U, पवित्रीकृ 8 U. —ER, s. शोधकः, पावकः.

CLEAR, a. वि-निर्-अ-मल, प्रसन्न, शुद्ध, अच्छ, विशद, स्वच्छ. 2 स्पष्ट, सुप्रकाश, परिस्फुट, व्यक्त. 3 (fig.) विशद, निश्चित; निष्कालुष्य, निःसंदेह; oft. by निर्-अ-pr.; 'c. sky' अनभ्र-निरभ्र-नभः; 'c. from debt' अनृण, ऋणमुक्त; 'c. forest' निष्कंटकं-असंबाधं-वनं; 'a c. sum' अभग्न, निरवशेष, निरुद्धार. —v. t. 'make c.' विशदीकृ 8 U, विवृ 5 U, व्याख्या 2 P. 2 शुध् c., प्रसद् c., विमलीकृ, मृज् 2 P. 3 मुच् 6 P or c.; by निर् pr.; 'c. ed the forest of its thorns' अरण्यं निष्कंटकं चकार; निःक्षत्रियां पृथ्वीं चकार &c.; 'c. from obstacles' विघ्नानपनी 1 P, निर्विघ्न a. कृ; 'c. a doubt' (शंकां) छिद् 7 P, निरस् 4 P, अपनी; 'c. debt' (ऋणं) शुध् c., अपाकृ; निस्तॄ c.; 'c. oneself' आत्मानं निर्दोषं कृ; 'c. up a business &c.' समाप् c., संपूर् 10, निःशेषीकृ; 'c. the throat' उत्कासनं कृ. —v. i. (up) प्रसद् 1 P, प्रसादं गम् 1 P or ग्रह् 9 P, निरभ्रीभू (as sky); दिशः प्रसेदुः (R. III. 14), गंगा रोधःपतनकलुषा गृह्णतीव प्रसादं (V. 1). —LY, adv. व्यक्तं, स्पष्टं, स्फुटं. 2 प्रसन्नं, विशदं. 3 भिन्नार्थं, स्पष्टार्थं. —NESS, s. प्रसादः, वैशद्यं, वैमल्यं, स्वच्छता, शुद्धि f. 2 स्पष्टता, व्यक्तता, स्फुटता.

CLEAVE, v. i. संज् pass., आ-वि-सं-अनु°, लग् 1 P, संलग्नीभू. 2 विदॄ pass., दल् 1 P, स्फुट् 6 P. —v. t. विदॄ 9 P, 10; वि-निर्-भिद् 7 P, दल् c. (दलयति), विपट् 10. —ER, s. भेदकः. 2 मांसच्छेदिका. —CLOVEN, a. विदीर्ण, स्फुटित, विभिन्न; 'c. hoofed' द्विशफ.

CLEFT, s. दरी, भंगः, संधिः, छिद्रं, रंध्रं.

CLEMENT, CLEMENCY, See KIND, -NESS.

CLENCH, CLINCH, v. t. (the fist) मुष्टिं बंध् 9 P; 'a blow with the fist c. ed' मुष्टिप्रहारः-संघातः. 2 बद्धमुष्टिना संग्रह् 9 P or पीड् 10. 3 दृढीकृ 8 U, स्थिरीकृ.

CLERGY, s. पुरोहितवर्गः, धर्माध्यापकवर्गः. —MAN, s. पुरोहितः, धर्मशासकः, धर्मप्रवक्तृ m. —CLERICAL, a. याजकीय, धर्मोपदेशविषय.

CLERK, s. लिपिकारः, लेखकः, कायस्थः. 2 पुरोहितः, धर्माध्यापकः. 3 पंडितः, कृतविद्यः, विद्वस् m. —SHIP, s. कायस्थकर्मन् n.

CLEVER, a. चतुर, दक्ष, विचक्षण, विदग्ध, पटु, मतिमत् (ती f.), निपुण, कुशल, प्रवीण, विशारद, पेशलमति. —LY, adv. चतुरं, सपाटवं. —NESS, s. चातुर्यं, वैचक्षण्यं, पाटवं, नैपुण्यं, बुद्धिमत्ता, मतिप्रकर्षः.

CLEW, CLUE, s. सूत्रकोषः. 2 सूत्रं, संधानं; मार्गदर्शकः.

CLIENT, s. आश्रितः, अधीनः, पक्ष्यः, श्रावकः.

CLIFF, s. प्रपातः, भृगुः, अतटः.

CLIMATE, CLIME, s. प्रकृति f. 2 देशः, प्रदेशः, दिश् f.

CLIMAX, s. पराकाष्ठा, पराकोटि f., अतिभूमि f.; 'anxiety reaching its c.' अतिभूमिं गतेन रणरणकेन (U. 1); 'the jealousy of her love reached its c.' दुरारूढः प्रणयोऽसहनः (V 4); सारः (a figure), उत्तरोत्तर उत्कर्षः.

CLIMB, v. t. आ-अधि-रुह् 1 P, अधिक्रम् 1 U, 4 P. —v. i. उपरि गम् 1 P. —ER, s. आ-अधिरोहिन् m., आरोढृ m. 2 (plant) प्रतति-ती f., वल्लरी, वल्लि-ली f.

CLINCH, s. श्लेषः, द्व्यर्थवाक्यं.

CLING, v. i. संज् 1 P, आ-प्र-स°, सज्ज् 1 U; (निवसने कः सज्जति S. 4), लग् 1 P, सं-परि°; 'c.-ing to my neck at the time of going' गमनसमये कंठे लग्ना (Mal. 2), आ-अव-लंब् 1 A, अनुबंध् 9 P; 'c. to hope' आशां न त्यज् 1 P, आशामवलंब्.

CLINIC, CLINICAL, a. शय्यागत, शयनग्रस्त.

CLINK, v. i. शिंज् 1, 2 A, विरु 2 P, क्वण् 1 P. —s. शिंजितं, क्वणितं, किंकिणीशब्दः. 2 नादः, शब्दः.

CLIP, v. t. छिद् 7 P; See CUT. 2 दृढं परिष्वंज् 1 A, उपगुह् 1 U. 3 संहृ 1 P, ह्रस् c., संक्षिप् 6 P. —PER, s. वंचकः. 2 मुंडिन् m. —PING, s. खंडः, विदलं, तक्षं.

CLOAK, s. कंचुकः, प्रावारः-रकः, अवगुंठनं. —v. t. प्रावृ 5 U, आच्छद् 10, अवगुंठ् 10.

CLOCK, s. घटी, घटिका, यामनाली. —MAKER, s. घटीकारः. —WORK, s. घटीकर्मन् n.

CLOD, s. लोष्ठः-ष्ठं, मृत्खंडः, मृत्पिंडः. 2 पिंडः; 'c.-pated', 'c. poll' जडः, मृत्पिंडबुद्धिः, स्थूलमतिः. —DY, a. लोष्ठपूर्ण-मय (यी f.).

CLOG, v. t. उप-नि-रुध् 7 U, प्रतिबंध् 9 P, स्तंभ् 9

P. 2 निगडेन बंध् 9 P, शृंखलयति (D.) –*s.* पाशः, निगडः, बंधनं, शृंखला. 2 विघ्नः, प्रत्यूहः, अंतरायः. –GY, *a.* प्रतिरोधिन् (नी *f.*), विघ्नकर (री *f.*).

CLOISTER, *s.* मठः, विहारः. –AL, *a.* विविक्तसेविन् (नी *f.*). –ER, *s.* मुनिः, मठवासिन् *m.*, संन्यासिन् *m.*

CLOSE, *v. t.* अपि-पि-धा 3 U, संवृ 5 U; आ-निमील् 1 P or c. (eyes &c.); निमिमील नरोत्तमप्रिया (R. VIII. 37) 'c. ed her eyes in death'. 2 निर्वृत् c., संपद् c., समाप् c., अवसो 4 P. 3 आवेष्ट् 1 A or c., आच्छद् 10, प्रावृ, अवरुंध् 10; 'c. hands' हस्तौ बध् 9 P; पाणिपुटं कृ; 'c. in' परिवेष्ट् 1 A. परिवृ 5 U. –*v. i.* संमिल् 6 P, संगम् 1 A, संयुज् pass. 2 निमील् 1 P, मुकुलीभू 1 P (lotuses &c.). 3 अवासित-समाप्त-*a.* भू, निवृत् 1 A, निष्पद्-समाप्-pass. –round, समंततः परिवेष्ट् 1 A or c., पारिवृ 5 U or c. –with, *See* AGREE. 2 संघट्ट् 1 A; बाहूबाहवि युध् 4 A. –*s.* अवसानं, अत्ययः, परिणामः, अंतः, विरामः, क्षयः. 2 निष्पत्ति *f.*, सिद्धि *f.*, समाप्ति *f.*, 'c. of day' दिनात्ययः, सायाह्नः.–*a.* पिहित, संवृत, निमीलित. 2 बद्ध, समंततो निरुद्ध (prisoner &c.). 3 गाढ, अशिथिल, दृढ, घन; 'c. fisted' अमुक्तहस्तः, बद्धमुष्टिः. 4 अविरल, सांद्र, निबिड, गहन, निरंतर. 5 आसन्न, समीपस्थ, निकटवर्तिन् (नी *f.*), समीप, निकट. 6 विविक्त, गुप्त. 7 आसक्त, अभिनिविष्ट, एकाग्र; 'c. application to S'âstras' शास्त्राभिनिवेशः. 8 निर्वात; अभ्रित; 'it is c. to-day' निर्वातं-अभ्रितं-नभः. 9 संकट, संकुचित, अविस्तृत, संबाध; 'c. fight' रणसंकुलं, तुमुलयुद्धं. 10 दृढसौहृद, सुपरिचित. 11 कृपण. 12 (concise) संक्षिप्त.–*adv.* अंतिकं, समीपं-पं, निरंतरं; निकटे; 'c. to the ear' कर्णांतिकं; 'c. by' अनतिदूरं, नातिदूरं.–LY, *adv.* निभृतं, गुप्तं, रहसि. 2 निरंतरं, अविरलं, सन्निकृष्टं. 3 प्रयत्नतः, मनोभिनिवेशेन, चित्तासक्त्या. 4 गाढं, दृढं, &c. –NESS, *s.* समीपता, सन्निकर्षः, सन्निधिः. 2 रहस् *n.*, गुप्ति *f.* 3 घनता, &c. 4 निर्वातता, &c.

CLOSET, *s.* कोष्ठः, कुटि-टी *f.*, निभृतागारं, वेश्मन् *n.* –*v. t.* कुट्यां गुप् 1 P or निविश् c.

CLOSURE, *s.* पिधानं, वेष्टनं, प्रावरणं.

CLOT, *s.* पिंडः, घनता, गुटिका, गुल्मः; 'c. of blood' घनशोणितं; 'c. of hair' जटा. –*v. i.* सांद्रीभू, घनीभू, पिंडीभू, जट् 1 P, श्यै 1 A. –TED, –TY, *a.* पिंडीभूत, घनीभूत, श्यान.

CLOTH, *s.* वस्त्रं, वासस् *n.*, वसनं, चेलः-लं, पटः, परिधानं, अंबरं; 'fine c.' अंशुकं; 'old, tattered, c.-es' कर्पटः, जीर्णवस्त्रं, चीरं; 'unbleached c.' अनाहतं, निष्प्रवाणि, तंत्रकं, नवांबरं. — CLOTHE, *v. t.* (oneself) वासः &c. परिधा 3 U or ग्रह् 9 P; वस् 2 A; 'c. ing herself' गृहीतवसना. 2 (वस्त्रेण) आच्छद् 10, परिच्छद्, संव्ये 1 P; वस् c., परिधा c. (धापयति), वेष्ट् 1 A. –ED, CLAD, *a.* (in) वसान, परिदधत् (ती *f.*), (*s.*) in comp. 2 संवीत, आवृत, आच्छादित; परिच्छन्न; सवासस्, अनग्न. –IER, *s.* पटकारः, वस्त्रनिर्मातृ *m.* –ING, *s.* परिधानं, आच्छादनं, परिच्छदः, वासस् *n.*, वसनं; 'food and c.' ग्रासाच्छादनं.

CLOUD, *s.* मेघः, घनः, अभ्रं, जीमूतः, स्तनयित्नुः, वलाहकः, मुदिरः, धूमयोनिः, and combinations of words for 'water' (q. v.) with 'giving' or 'bearing', जलदः, तोयवाहः, पयोधरः, जलमुच्, वारिदः, &c.; 'a c. of dust' धूलिपटलं; 'c.-capped' अभ्रंलिह, अभ्रंकष-लिख. –*v. t.* प्रच्छद् 10, आवृ 5 U. 2 तिमिरेण आच्छद्. –ED, *a.* मेघावृत, अभ्रित, अभ्राच्छादित; तमोवृत, दुर्दिनग्रस्त. –LESS, *a.* निरभ्र, अमेघ, &c. –Y, *a.* साभ्र, मेघाकीर्ण, समेघ; 'it is c. weather to-day' दुर्दिनमद्य. 2 तमोवृत, तिमिराच्छन्न, अंधकारयुक्त.

CLOUGH, *s.* कंदरः-रा, दरि-री *f.*

CLOVE, *s.* (Tree) लवंगवृक्षः. 2 (Spice) लवंगं, देवकुसुमं.

CLOVER, *s.* त्रिपर्णं, त्रिपत्रं.

CLOUT, *s.* चीरं, कर्पटः, कंथा. –*v. t.* जीर्णवस्त्राणि संधा-समाधा 3 U.

CLOWN, *s.* ग्राम्यः, ग्रामिकः, कृषीवलः, वृषलः, जानपदः, पृथग्जनः, असभ्यो जनः. –ISH, *a.* अशिष्ट, ग्राम्य, असभ्य, ग्रामीण. –ISHLY, *adv.* ग्राम्यवत्, अशिष्टं.

CLOY, *v. t.* उद्विज् c.; पिंडखर्जूरैरुद्वेजितस्य (S. 2) 'c. ed with eating dates;' अतितृप्तिं जन् c. (जनयति).

CLUB, *s.* यष्टि *f.*, लगुडः, गदा, परिघः; 'armed with a c.' याष्टीकः, यष्टिधरः. 2 गणः, समाजः, मेलकः. 3 पंक्ति *f.*; सहभोजिनां संसर्गः. 4 अंशः, भागः; 'c. foot' स्थूलचरणः.

CLUE, *See* CLEW.

CLUMP, *s.* गुच्छः, संचयः, षंडः, निचयः, गुल्मः, स्तंबः.

CLUMSY, *a.* अचतुर, अदक्ष, अकुशल, असुंदर, ग्राम्य, स्थूल. –LY, *adv.* अदक्षं, दाक्ष्यं विना, अचतुरं, अपाटवं. –NESS, *s.* अचातुर्यं, अपाटवं, &c.

CLUSTER, *s.* गुल्मः, गुच्छः, स्तंबः, स्तबकः. 2 संघः, गणः, समूहः, निवहः, ओघः, चयः, समुदायः. –*v. i.* एकत्र मिल् 6 P, एकीभू 1 P, पिंडीभू. –*v. t.* संचि 5 U, एकीकृ 8 U, पिंडीकृ, समाहृ 1 P.

CLUTCH, *v. t.* ग्रह् 9 P, धृ 1 P, 10; आक्रम् 1 U, 4 P. 2 मुष्टिं बंध् 9 P. –*s.*, ग्रहः, ग्रहणं; मुष्टिबंधः. 2 हस्तः, पाणिः, नखं; 'rescued from the c. es of death' मृत्युमुखान्मुक्तः.

CLUTTER, *s.* कोलाहलः, तुमुलरवः.

COACERVATE, *See* COLLECT.

COACH, *s.* रथः, प्रवहणं, यानं, वाहनं, शकटः-टिका; 'travels by c.' रथेन संचरति; 'a c. and four' चतुरश्वं यानं; 'c. box' सूतासनं; 'c. ful' पूर्णरथः, शाकटं; 'c. horse' रथ्यः; 'c. house' रथशाला; 'c. maker' रथकारः; 'c. man' सूतः, सारथिः, यंतृ *m.*

COACTION, *s.* प्रमाथः, बलात्कारः. —COACTIVE, *a.* प्रमाथिन् (नी *f.*), बलान्वित, सबल.

COADJUTOR, *s.* सहायः, सहकारिन् *m.*

COAGULATE, *v. i.* घनीभू 1 P, श्यै 1 A. —*v. t.* श्यै c., घनीकृ 8 U, संहन् 2 P. —ION, *s.* शीनता, संहति *f.*, घनीभावः, श्यानत्वं.

COAL, *s.* अंगारः -रं; 'c. black' अंगारसवर्ण, अतिकृष्ण.

COALESCE, *v. i.* संमिल् 6 P, संगम् 1 A; एकीभू, संयुज्-संधा-संश्लिष् pass. —COALITION, *s.* संयोगः, संश्लेषः, मेलनं, संधिः.

COARSE, *a.* स्थूल (cloth &c.); घन, नीरंध्र; अविरल, निबिडस्यूत. 2 असभ्य, अश्लील, ग्राम्य, अशिष्ट. 3 अवाच्य, नीच, निकृष्ट, गर्ह्य; 'c. food' मंदाहारः. —NESS, *s.* स्थूलता, ग्राम्यता, अश्लीलता, &c.

COAST, *s.* तीरं, तटः -टं, वेला. 2 सीमा. 3 देशः, प्रदेशः. —*v. i.* उपतीरं नावा संचर् 1 P, नौकां वह् c.

COAT, *s.* कंचुकः, उत्तरीयं, प्रावारः -रकः, निचोलः. 2 पटलं, आच्छादनं, पुटं, आवेष्टनं. 3 लो(रो)मन् *n.* (of animals). —*v. t.* आच्छद् 10, अवगुंठ् 10, आ-सं-वेष्ट् 1 A or c. 2 अनुव्यध् 4 P; विलिप् 6 P, छुर् 10. —ING, *s.* पटलं, पुटं, आच्छादनं, आवेष्टनं. 2 लेपः, छुरणं.

COAX, *v. t.* चाटूक्त्या सांत्व् 10, अनुनी 1 P, उपच्छंद् 10, लल् 10. —ER, *s.* चाटुकारः. —ING, *s.* चाटुवचनं, चाटु *m. n.*, उपच्छंदनं.

COBBLE, *v. t.* जीर्णपादुकाः सूच्या समाधा-संधा 3 U. 2 अपाटवं किंचित्कर्म कृ 8 U. —ER, *s.* पादुकासंधातृ *m.*; अनिपुणः शिल्पी.

COBRA, *s.* नागः, फणिन् *m.*; *See* SNAKE.

COBWEB, *s.* जालं, सूत्रजालं. 2 संतानः; 'c. of speech' वाग्जालं.

COCK, *s.* कुक्कुटः, शिखिन् *m.*, ताम्रचूडः, नखायुधः, कृकवाकुः; 'c.'s comb' शिखा, चूडा; 'c.-sparrow' चटकः. 2 प्रणाली, जलयंत्रं. 3 पुंगवः, मुखरः, नायकः. 4 तृणोत्करः; 'weather c.' वायुध्वजज्ञापकः; 'c. and bull story' मृषा-वृथा-कथा; 'c. crowing' कुक्कुटरवः; प्रभातकालः; 'c. fight,' 'c. match' प्राणिद्यूतं, ताम्रचूडयुद्धं; समाह्वयः; 'c. pit' कुक्कुटयुद्धस्थानं. —*v. t.* उन्नम् c. (नमयति), उत्क्षिप् 6 P, उच्छ्रि 1 U. —*v. i.* सलीलं चर्-चल् 1 P. 2 दृप् 4 P.

COCKATRICE, *s.* अजगरः.

COCK-BOAT, *s.* उप-क्षुद्र-नौका.

COCK-SWAIN, *s.* क्षुद्रनौकापतिः.

COCKER, *v. t.* *See* FONDLE.

COCKLE, *s.* शुक्ति *f.*

COCKLOFT, *s.* चंद्रशाला, शिरोगृहं.

COCKNEY, *s.* नगर-पुर-वासिन् *m.*; प्राकृतजनः.

COCOA-NUT, *s.* नारिकेलः-रः, कौशिकफलं; (tree) तृणद्रुमः, शिरःफलः, नालिकेरः-लः, नारि(डि)केरः-केलिः, नारीकेलः-ली, लांगली.

COCOON, *s.* कोशः-षः.

COCTION, *See* DECOCTION.

COD, *s.* बीजकोषः, पुटः.

CODDLE, *v. t.* ईषत्-शनैः पच् 1 P or क्वथ् 1 P. 2 निपुणं संवृध् c. or पुष् 1, 9 P, 10.

CODE, *s.* संहिता; 'c. of laws' धर्म-स्मृति-शास्त्रं, स्मृति *f.*

COEFFICACY, *s.* सहकारिता, संयोगिता.

COEFFICIENT, *s.* मानं.

CO-EQUAL, *a.* समानपदस्थ, स-सह-धर्मन्, समानभाव. —ITY, *s.* समानावस्था; तुल्यभागः, सहधर्मः, तुल्यपदत्वं.

CO-ERCE, *v. t.* सं-नि-यम् 1 P, निरुध् 7 U, निग्रह् 9 P, नियंत्र् 10; *See* COMPEL also. —ION, *s.* निग्रहः, संयमः; नियंत्रणं. —IVE, *a.* नियामक; प्रतिरोधिन् (नी *f.*).

CO-EVAL, *a.* सम-एक-कालीन; समान-तुल्य-वयस्क, सवयस्. —*s.* वयस्यः, स-तुल्य-वयस् *m.*

CO-EXIST, *v. i.* समं-एकत्र वृत् 1 A or भू 1 P, एककाले भू or जीव् 1 P. —ENCE, *s.* एककालावस्थानं, सहवर्तनं, सहजीवनं. —ENT, *a.* सहवर्तिन्-जीविन् (नी *f.*).

CO-EXTEND, *v. i.* समं विस्तॄ pass. or व्याप् 5 P. —CO-EXTENSION, *s.* अभिव्याप्ति *f.*; समविस्तारः.

COFFER, *s.* धनभांडं, कोषः-शः, मुद्राधारः.

COFFIN, *s.* शवाधारः, शवभाजनं. —*v. t.* शवभाजने निधा 3 U.

COG, *v. t.* Flatter, q. v.; 'c. a die' कूटाक्षं कृ 8 U; 'c. a wheel' नेमिं सदंतां कृ. —*s.* नेमिदंतः.

COGENT, *a.* बलवत् (ती *f.*), प्रबल; निरुत्तर. —LY, *adv.* निरुत्तरं. —COGENCY, *s.* बलं, सामर्थ्यं, प्रभावः, शक्ति *f.*

COGGLESTONE, *s.* चूर्णखंडः.

COGITATE, *v. t.* चिंत् 10, ध्यै 1 P, विचर् c., विमृश् 6 P, आलोच् 10, वितर्क् 10. —ION, *s.* चिंता, विचारः, आलोचनं, विमर्शः, वितर्कः.

COGNATE, *a.* सजाति, एकजातीय, सगोत्र, संबंधिन् (नी *f.*), तुल्य-समान-प्रभव. —ION, *s.* बंधुता, ज्ञातिभावः, संबंधः, सजातीयत्वं.

COGNITION, *s.* ज्ञानं, प्रज्ञानं.

COGNIZABLE, *a.* ज्ञेय, बोध्य. 2 विचार्य, अनुसंधेय.

COGNIZANCE, *s.* विचारणं, अनुसंधानं, चर्चा; अनुयोगः. 2 चिह्नं, लक्षणं, संज्ञा, लिंगं; 'take c. of' अनुसंधा 3 U, विचर् c., अनुयुज् 7 A, ज्ञा 9 U, अवेक्ष् 1 A.

COHABIT, *v. i.* संवस् 1 P; अभिगम् 1 P (with another's wife), संभोगं कृ 8 U.

COHERE, *v. i.* संसंज्-संयुज्-संहन्-संश्लिष्-pass. 2 युज् pass. –ENCE, *s.* संसक्ति *f.*, संश्लेषः, संयोगः. 2 संबंधः, संगति *f.*, अन्वयः, संदर्भः, अविरोधः. –ENT, *a.* संसक्त, संश्लिष्ट, संहत, संलग्न. 2 संगत, अविरुद्ध, संबद्ध, अनुरूप, सान्वय. –COHESION, *s.* संसक्ति *f.*, संयोगः, संश्लेषः, संलग्नता. –COHESIVE, *a.* सांद्र, संलग्नशील, स्निग्ध.

COHOBATE, *v. t.* पुनः संधा 3 U.

COHORT, *s.* सैन्यदलं-गुल्मं.

COIF, *s.* मुकुटः, शिरस्कं, शिरोवेष्टनं.

COIL, *s.* मंडलं, व्यावर्तनं, आवेष्टनं; गुणः (of a rope). 2 तुमुलं, व्यस्तता; 'mortal c.' नश्वरदेहः. –*v. t.* मंडलीकृ 8 U, वर्तुलीकृ, पुटीकृ; व्यावृत् c., आ-परिवेष्ट् c.

COIN, *s.* मुद्रा, नाणकं, टंकः; 'copper c.' पणः; 'I paid him in his own c.' यथैव स मयि व्यवाहरत्तथैवाहं तस्मिन्नाचरं. –*v. t.* मुद्रयति (D.), मुद्रया अंक् 10. 2 सृज् 6 P, क्लृप् c., निर्मा 3 A. –AGE, *s.* मुद्रा; कल्पना, सृष्टि *f.* –ER, *s.* मुद्राकारः; कल्पकः.

COINCIDE, *v. i.* एकीभू 1 P, संगम् 1 A, सं-सन्निपत् 1 P, संधा-संयुज्-pass. 2 संमन् 4 A, एकचित्तीभू; *See* AGREE. 3 अनुरूप *a.* भू, युज् pass., अनुवृत् 1 A, संवद् 1 P, तुल्य-समान-*a.* भू. –ENCE, *s.* संनिपातः, संगमः; संयोगः. 2 संमति *f.*, ऐकमत्यं, संधिः, एकचित्तता. 3 संवादः, अनुरूपता, आनुगुण्यं. 4 दैवयोगः -घटनं; 'by an unlucky c.' दुर्दैवात्. –ENT, *a.* संपातिन् (नी *f.*). 2 समकालीन. 3 अविरुद्ध, अनुरूप, संवादिन्.

COITION, *s.* मैथुनं, सुरतं, रतिक्रिया.

COKE, *s.* अर्धदग्धांगारोच्छिष्टं.

COLANDER, *s.* चालनी, शोधनी, तितउः.

COLATION, *s.* शोधनं, चालनं.

COLD, *a.* शीत, शिशिर, हिम, शीतल, तुषार, अघर्म; 'c. rayed' (moon) हिमांशुः, शीतकरः, &c.; 'c. season' हिमागमः, शिशिरः, शीतकालः. 2 (fig.) अनादरयुक्त, विरक्त, निःस्नेह, निरुत्साह, उदासीन; 'gave me a c. welcome' निरुत्साहं स्वागतं मां व्याजहार, मत्संभावनायां तेन औदासीन्यं दर्शितं; 'in c. blood' प्रकोपनं विना; पूर्वसंकल्पेन. –*s.* शीतं, शैत्यं; शिशिरः, हिमः. 2 प्रतिश्यायः; 'suffering from c.' शीतार्त. –LY, *adv.* शीतं, शैत्येन. 2 निरुत्साहं, विरक्तं, उदासीनतया. –NESS, *s.* शीतता, हिमता, शैत्यं. 2 अनादरः, निःस्नेहता, विरागः, विरक्ति *f.*, औदासीन्यं.

COLIC, *s.* शूलः-लं, उदर-जठर-व्यथा-शूलं. –*a.* उदरव्यथाजनक.

COLLAPSE, *v. i.* क्षयं-लयं-गम् 1 P, अवसद् 1 P. 2 संहृ-गृ-pass.; संकुच् 1 P; सं-सन्नि-पत् 1 P. –*s.* संकोचः. 2 संहारः, क्षयः, लयः, अवसादः. 3 सन्निपातः, शक्तिपातः, लयः.

COLLAR, *s.* ग्रैवं-वेयं, कंठभूषणं, माला. 2 कंठपाशः. –BONE, *s.* ग्रीवास्थि *n.*, जत्रु *n.*

COLLATE, *v. t.* समवलोक् 10, परीक्ष् 1 A; उपमा 3 A, संशुध् c. 2 वृत्तिं प्रदा 3 U. –ION, *s.* संपरीक्षणं, संशोधनं, उपमानं. 2 कल्यवर्तः, प्रातर्भक्ष्यः फलादिसंभारः, प्रातराशः. 3 वृत्तिप्रतिपादनं.

COLLATERAL, *a.* आनुषंगिक-प्रासंगिक (की *f.*), असरल. 2 भिन्नशाख, उपलोम. 3 समानोदक, सपिंड. 4 पार्श्वापार्श्विगत. –LY, *adv.* पार्श्वापार्श्वि; असरलं, वक्रं, प्रसंगतः.

COLLEAGUE, *s.* सहायः, सहकारिन् *m.*, समानव्यापारः, एकविषयिन् *m.*

COLLECT, *v. t.* चि 5 U, अव-वि-सं-नि-°, समानी 1P, संग्रह् 9 P, समाहृ 1 P, संभृ 3 U, समाक्षिप् 6 P, पिंडीकृ 8 U, राशीकृ, एकत्र कृ. 2 अनुमा 3 A, ऊह् 1 A, अवगम् 1 P; 'c. ed his mind into itself' चित्तं समादधौ; 'c. oneself' संज्ञा-चेतनां-लभ् 1 A or आ-प्रति-पद् 4 A, चेतः-मनः-समाधा 3 U. –*v. i.* संमिल् 6 P, समागम् 1 P; *See* ASSEMBLE. –ION, *s.* गणः, संघः, समवायः, निवहः, चयः, समूहः, ओघः, समुच्चयः, समाहारः, समुदायः, वृंदं. –IVE, *a.* समवेत, संहत, समाहृत, गणीभूत, समवायिन् (नी *f.*), एकीकृत. –IVELY, *adv.* एकीभूय, संभूय; संघशः, साकल्येन. –OR, *s.* संग्राहकः, संचेतृ *m.* 2 करग्राहकः.

COLLEGE, *s.* विद्यालयः-यं, पाठशाला. 2 मठः, विहारः. 3 गणः, समाजः, जनसमूहः. –COLLEGIAN, *s.* विद्यार्थिन् *m.*, छात्रः; विद्यालयप्रविष्टः.

COLLET, *See* COLLAR.

COLLIDE, *v. i.* सं-समा-हन् 2 U, संघट्ट् 1 A or c.; संमृद् 9 P. –COLLISION, *s.* संघट्टः, समाघातः, प्रतिघातः, संमर्दः, संघर्षणं.

COLLIGATION, COLLIMATION, *s.* संबंधः; संधानं.

COLLOCATE, *v. t.* सं-प्रति-स्था c. (स्थापयति), निधा 3 U, न्यस् 4 P, निविश् c. 2 नियुज् 7 A, 10. –ION, *s.* स्थापनं, निवेशनं.

COLLOCUTION, *s.* संभाषणं, कथाप्रसंगः, कथायोगः, संवादः, संकथा.

COLLOGUE, *See* FLATTER.

COLLOP, *s.* मांसखंडः-लवः.

COLLOQUY, *s.* संलापः, संकथा, संभाषणं, संवादः. –AL, *a.* आलापविषय, भाषणप्रयुक्त; 'c. style' संलापोचिता भाषासरणिः.

COLLUDE, *v. i.* पक्षपातं-कूटं कृ 8 U; वंच् 10, कूट-

योगं कृ. —COLLUSION, *s.* पक्षपातः, कूटसंविद् *f.*; प्रतारणा, शाठ्यं, कपटं.

COLLY, *s.* अंगारमलं-किट्टं. —*v. t.* अंगारेण कृष्णीकृ 8 U. —ED, *a.* अंगारमलिन, मलीमस, कृष्ण. —ER, *s.* अंगारखनकः-विक्रेतृ *m.* —Y, *s.* अंगारोत्पत्तिस्थानं.

COLLYRIUM, *s.* अंजनं, कज्जलं, नेत्ररंजनं.

COLON, *s.* द्विबिंदुः. 2 महदंत्रं.

COLONEL, *s.* गुल्मपतिः, सैन्यदलाध्यक्षः, वाहिनीपतिः.

COLONY, *s.* अधिनिवेशः; वासितः प्रदेशः. 2 गणः, संघः; *See* COLLECTION. —IST, *s.* अधिवासिन् *m.*, अधिनिवेशिन् *m.* —IZE, *v. t.* अधिवस् 1 P, अधिनिविश् 6 P, अध्यास् 2 A, (with acc.).

COLOSSUS, *s.* बृहत्प्रतिमा, भीमविग्रहा मूर्तिः. —COLOSSAL, *a.* बृहत्काय, अतिमानुषाकार, भीमविग्रह.

COLOUR, *s.* वर्णः, रागः, रंगः. 2 वर्णकः-का, लेपः; 'change c.' विवर्णीभू; 'ruddy c. ed face' लोहिताननं; 'without c.' पांडु, विवर्ण. 3 अप-व्यपदेशः, छद्मन् *n.*, छलं, व्याजः. 4 पताका, ध्वजः, केतुः. —*v. t.* रंज् c., वर्ण् 10, चित्र् 10. 2 व्यप-अप-दिश् 6 P, आच्छद् 10, शम् c. (शमयति). 3 सत्यवदाभास् c., सत्याभास *a.* कृ 8 U, सत्यसन्निभ *a.* कृ. —*v. i.* रंज् pass. 2 लज्जाया अरुणवदन *a.* भू, व्रीडित *a.* भू, लज्ज् 6 A. —ING, *s.* रंजनं; 'art of c.' चित्रकर्मन् *n.*, आलेख्यकरणं, आलेख्यविद्या. 2 वर्णनं; अलंकारः. —IST, *s.* वर्णिन् *m.*, रंजकः. —LESS, *a.* अवर्ण, विवर्ण, वर्णहीन. —COLORATE, *a.* सराग, रागयुक्त. —COLORIFIC, *a.* वर्णद.

COLT, *s.* अश्वशावः, किशोरः. 2 चपलः, प्रमत्तः. —ISH, *a.* चपल, तरल, चंचल, लोल.

COLTER, *s.* हलदंतः, फालदंतः.

COLUMBARY, *s.* कपोतागारं, विटंकः.

COLUMN, *s.* स्तंभः, यूपः, स्थाणुः, स्थूणा. 2 सूचिव्यूहः; सैन्यभागः. 3 पत्रभागः, धारा; 'c. of smoke' धूमराशिः, धूमोत्पीडः.

COMATE, *s.* सहायः, सहवासिन् *m.*

COMATOSE, *a.* अतिनिद्रातुर.

COMB, *s.* प्रसाधनी, कंकतः -तिका, केशमार्जनी. 2 कुक्कुटचूडा-शिखा. 3 दर्वी. —*v. t.* प्रसाध् c., मृज् 2 P, विजटीकृ 8 U. —MAKER, *s.* कंकतकृत् *m.*

COMBAT, *s.* युद्धं, संग्रामः, समरं; *See* BATTLE; 'single c.' द्वंद्वयुद्धं; 'hand-to-hand-c.' बाहूबाहवि, बाहुयुद्धं; 'mingled c.' (melee) तुमुलं, रणसंकुलं. —*v. i.* युध् 4 A, विग्रह् 9 P, विवद् 1 A. —*v. t.* प्रतियुध्, प्रतिरुध् 7 U, प्रतिबंध् 9 P. 2 खंड् 10, निरस् 4 P, निराकृ 8 U; 'c. one's passions' संयम् 1 P, निग्रह् 9 P. —ANT, *s.* योधः, योद्धृ *m.*, भटः, वीरः.

COMBINE, *v. t.* संयुज् 7 U, 10, संश्लिष् c., संधा 3 U, संमिश्र् 10, एकीकृ 8 U. —*v. i.* मिल् 6 P, संगम् 1 P, संगम् 1 A; संहत-समवेत *a.* भू, एकीभू; संयुज्-संधा-संहन्-संसृज्-pass.; 'all things c. ed to ruin him' सर्वमेव तस्य नाशायाकल्पत; 'having c. ed' संभूय, मिलित्वा. —ATION, *s.* संहति *f.*, संयोगः, संसर्गः, संधिः, संघातः, संगः, सहायता, संश्लेषः, व्यतिकरः, समवायः; (of letters) संधिः; 'working by c.' संभूय समुत्थानं; 'in c. with his brothers' भ्रातृसंघातवान् (राजा).

COMBUSTIBLE, *a.* दाह्य, दाहग्राहक; ज्वलनार्ह, दहनशील. —*s.* दाह्यः पदार्थः.

COMBUSTION, *s.* दाहः, दहनं, ज्वलनं, ओषः.

COME, *v. i.* आगम् 1 P, आया 2 P, आ-इ 2 P; उपस्था 1 U, आव्रज् 1 P, आ-अभि-पद् 4 A; 'c. what may' यद्भावि तद्भवतु; 'c. harm, c. good' यद्भावि तद्भवतु शुभमशुभं वा. —about, संवृत् 1A, संभू, आपत् 1P. —back, निवृत्, प्रत्यागम्. —at, or by, *See* GET. —down, अवतृ 1 P, अवरुह् 1 P, अवपत् 1 P. —down upon, (सहसा-रभसा) अवस्कंद् 1 P, आपत् 1P, अभिद्रु 1 P, आक्रम् 1 U, 4 P. —forth, निर्गम्, निःसृ 1 P. —into, प्रविश् 6 P; 'c. into trouble' विपदाभिभू, आपद्ग्रस्त *a.* भू. —near, *See* APPROACH. —of, *See* ARISE. —off, out, निष्क्रम्; निर्गम्, उदि 2 P; 'came out successful' जयी बभूव. 2 प्रवृत्, संपद्, निवृत्, अवसो pass. —over, आश्रि 1 U. —short, न्यूनीभू. —to, सकाशं आगम्-याइ,°प्राप् 5 P; *See* AMOUNT; 'c. to life' उज्जीव् 1 P; 'came to nothing' तस्य कोऽपि परिणामो नासीत्, निष्फलं-निर्गुणं-बभूव; 'c. to pass' आपत्, समापद्, संवृत्; 'c. to oneself' प्रकृतिमापद् 4 A, संज्ञां-चेतनां-लभ् 1 A or प्रतिपद्, प्रकृतौ स्था. —up to, समुपागम्, समाया, समुपसृ-सृप्. —up with, आसद् c., प्राप्. —upon, आ-समा-पत्, उपस्था, आक्रम्. —ING, *s.* आगमनं. —*a.* (to come) आगामिन् (नी *f.*); 'on the c. Monday' आगामिनि सोमवासरे; भाविन्, उत्तर; 'time to c.' उत्तरकालः; 'c. generations' पुत्रपौत्राः; उत्तरकालीना जनाः.

COMEDY, *s.* भाणः, प्रहसनं, हर्षप्रधानं नाटकं. —IAN, *s.* नटः, कुशीलवः, नर्तकः, वैहासिकः. 2 प्रहसनकृत् *m.*

COMELY, *a.* चारु, सुंदर (री *f.*), सुरूप; *See* BEAUTIFUL. —NESS, *s.* सौंदर्यं; *See* BEAUTY.

COMET, *s.* धूमकेतुः, केतुः, उत्पातः, उल्का.

COMFIT, COMFITURE, *s.* मिष्टान्नं, मोदकः.

COMFORT, *v. t.* समा-आ-श्वस् c., सान्त्व् 10. 2 संतुष् c., आनंद् c., हृष् c., सुखं दा 3 U, सुखिन्-*a.* कृ 8 U; 'c. yourself' समाश्वसिहि. —*s.* आश्वासनं, सान्त्वनं; संतोषणं. 2 सुखं, सुस्थता, सौख्यं, स्वास्थ्यं, निर्वृति *f.* —ABLE, *a.* सुखकर (री *f.*), सुखद; सुखशायितं प्रष्टुं (S. 4) 'to ask whether she had a c. sleep.' 2 आश्वासक, शांतिद, क्लेशापह, श्रमविनोदक. —ABLY, *adv.* सुखं, यथासुखं ; निकामं ; 'I can't sleep c. even at night' रात्रावपि निकामं शयितव्यं नास्ति (S. 2). -ER, *s.* आश्वासकः, संतोषदः, शोकापहर्तृ *m.*, सांत्ववादः. -LESS, *a.* निरानंद, सुखरहित, संतोषहीन.

COMIC, COMICAL, *a.* हासजनक, हासकर (री *f.*), हास्योत्पादक. 2 अपरूप, असंगत. -ALNESS, *s.* हास्यता, कौतुकं ; अपरूपता.

COMMAND, *v. t.* आज्ञा c. (आज्ञापयति), आदिश् 6 P, व्या-सं-समा-°, विधा 3 U, शास् 2 P, नियुज् 7 A, 10. 2 अधिष्ठा 1 P, अध्यास् 2 A ; ईश् 2 A, प्रभू, (with gen.); 'Râkshasas c.-ed by 2 chieftains' नायकाभ्यामधिष्ठिता राक्षसाः. 3 नियम् 1 P, निग्रह् 9 P; *See* CONTROL. 4 आत्मवशं नी 1 P, स्वायत्तीकृ 8 U. 5 अवलोक् 10; 'sitting at a window c. ing (the view of) a well' दीर्घिकावलोकनगवाक्षगता (M. 1); 'good forms c. respect' आकृतिविशेषेष्वादरः पदं करोति (M. 1); पदं हि सर्वत्र गुणैर्निधीयते (R. III. 62) 'c. notice or attention'. -*s.* आदेशः, निदेशः, शासनं, नियोगः. 2 अधिकारः, प्रभुत्वं, आधिपत्यं, अधिष्ठातृत्वं; 'has Râkshasas under his c.' तस्यादेशमनुवर्तमाना राक्षसाः or स राक्षसानामधिपतिः-नायकः-अधिष्ठाता; 'under one's c.' वशीकृत, स्वाधीन; 'to the c. of the army' सैनापत्ये; 'bring under one's c.' आत्मवशं नी, स्वाधीन *a.* कृ; 'though I have no c. over language' तनुवाग्विभवोपि सन् (R. I. 9); 'who has perfect c. over language' यं वाग्वश्येवानुवर्तते (U. 1). -ANT, -ER, *s.* आज्ञापकः, आदेष्टृ *m.* 2 पतिः, अध्यक्षः, नायकः, नीः in comp.; 'c. of an army' चमूपतिः, सेनानीः, सेनाध्यक्षः. -MENT, *s.* आज्ञा, विधिः, सूत्रं. 2 चोदना, शास्त्र-धर्म-आज्ञा.

COMMEMORATE, *v. t.* स्मरणार्थं उत्सवं कृ 8 U or आचर् 1 P; संकृत् 10, संस्मृ c., वर्ण् 10. -ION, *s.* उत्सवकरणं, स्मरणोत्सवः; 'in c. of' स्मरणार्थं, समुद्दिश्य. -IVE, *a.* स्मारक, स्मरणकृत.

COMMENCE, *v.* आ-प्रा-रभ् 1 A, प्र-उप-क्रम् 1 A, प्रवृत् 1 A, व्यवसो 4 P. 2 अनुष्ठा 1 P, प्रस्तु 2 U. -MENT, *s.* आरंभः, उपक्रमः, प्रस्तावः, मुखं, आदि *m.* 2 आमुखं, प्रस्तावना (in dramas). 3 अनुष्ठानं, प्रवृत्ति *f.*, प्रवर्तनं; 'from the c.' आमूलात्, आदितः.

COMMEND, *v. t.* प्रशंस् 1 P, स्तु 2 U, श्लाघ् 1 A, कृत् 10, वर्ण् 10. 2 सम्-ऋ c. (अर्पयति), हस्ते निक्षिप् 6 P, अधीन *a.* कृ 8 U; 'thy speech does not c. itself to me' त्वद्वचो नाभिनंदामि (S. 2). -ABLE, *a.* प्रशंस्य, श्लाघ्य, स्तुत्य. -ATION, *s.* श्लाघा, प्रशंसा, स्तुति *f.* -ATORY, *a.* श्लाघासूचक, प्रशंसाकर (री *f.*), स्तुतिद्योतक. -ER, *s.* प्रशंसकः, स्तावकः.

COMMENSURATE, *v. t.* अनुरूप-अनुगुण-*a.* कृ 8 U. 2 अपवृत् c. -*a.*, -COMMENSURABLE, *a.* अनुरूप, अनुगुण, सदृश (शी *f.*), सम, तुल्य. 2 सापवर्त.

COMMENT, *v. i.* व्याकृ 8 U, व्याचक्ष् 2 A, विवृ 5 U, भाष्यं लिख् 6 P. 2 निरूप् 10, चर्चां कृ, परीक्ष् 1 A, अनुसंधा 3 U. -ARY, *a.* टीका, व्याख्या, वृत्ति *f.*, भाष्यं. 2 निरूपणं, परीक्षणं, चर्चा. -ATOR, -ER, *s.* भाष्यकृत्-कारः, व्याख्यातृ *m.*, टीकाकारः-कृत्.

COMMENTITIOUS, *a.* कृत्रिम, कल्पित.

COMMERCE, *s.* वाणिज्यं, क्रयविक्रयः, निगमः. 2 व्यवहारः, संगमः-ति *f.*, संसर्गः. -*v. i.* वाणिज्यं कृ 8 U, पण् 1 A, व्यवह् 1 P. -IAL, *a.* वाणिज्य-विषयक-संबंधिन् (नी *f.*); 'c. people' वाणिज्यपरायणा नराः.

COMMINATION, *s.* *See* CURSE, THREAT.

COMMINGLE, *v. t.* संयुज् 7 U, 10, संमिश्र् 10, एकीकृ 8 U, संकॄ 6 P; *See* UNITE.

COMMINUTE, *v. t.* चूर्ण् 10. पिष् 7 P, क्षुद् 7 U. -ION, *s.* चूर्णनं, पेषणं, क्षोदः.

COMMISERATE, *v. t.* दय् 1 A (with gen.), अनुकंप् 1 A. -ION, *s.* दया, अनुकंपा, करुणा. -IVE, *a.* करुणात्मक, अनुकंपाशील, सदय, दयार्द्र.

COMMIT, *v. t.* कृ 8 U, आचर् 1 P, अनुष्ठा 1 P, विधा 3 U. 2 (Entrust) ऋ c. (अर्पयति), न्यस् 4 P, निक्षिप् 6 P. 3 नियुज् 7 A, 10, समादिश् 6 P, प्रतिपद् c.; 'c. to memory' कंठस्थ *a.* कृ; अभ्यस् 4 U; 'c. to prison' कारागारं प्रविश् c, आसिध् 1 P; 'c. to writing' अभिलिख् 6 P; लेख्य-पत्रं आरुह् c. (पत्रमारोप्य दीयतां प्रत्यवेक्षितं कर्म S. 6); पत्रे निविश् c. (पत्रे निवेशितमुदाहरणं प्रियायाः V. 2), पत्रे ऋ c. -TAL, *s.* आचरणं, करणं, अनुष्ठानं. -TEE, *s.* कार्यसंपादिका सभा, नियुक्तजनाः. -MENT, *s.* आसेधः, निरोधः, काराप्रवेशनं. —COMMISSION, *s.* आचरणं, करणं. 2 समर्पणं, निक्षेपः, न्यासः. 3 नियोगः, व्यापारः, अधिकारः. 4 आज्ञा-शासनपत्रं, आदेशः. 5 परार्थ-विक्रयः. 6 नियुक्तजनाः; 'c. in the army' सेनायां पदं. -*v. t.* नियुज् 7 A, 10, आदिश् 6 P, अधिकृ 8 U. -ER, *s.* नियोगिन् *m.*, अधिकारिन् *m.*

COMMIX,-TURE, *See* MIX,-TURE.

COMMODE, *s.* स्त्रीमस्तकाभरणं.

COMMODIOUS, *a.* उचित, उपयुक्त, योग्य. 2 सोपकरण, यथायुक्त-योग्य. -LY, *adv.* युक्तं, योग्यं. -NESS, *s.* योग्यता, औचित्यं. &c.

COMMODITY, *s.* पण्यं, द्रव्यं, क्रयवस्तु *n.*, भांडं.

COMMON, *a.* साधारण(णी *f.*). सामान्य. सर्वीय. सार्वलौकिक(की *f.*). 2 प्राकृत, ग्राम्य ; 'c. man' प्राकृतः, पृथग्जनः, वृषलः. 2 प्रसिद्ध, व्यावहारिक (की *f.*), बहुशः कृत-दृष्ट. 4 बहुस्वामिक. 5 सुलभ ; 'c. report' जनप्रवादः ; 'c. food' गणान्नं, सहभोजनं ;

'c. road' प्रचारः ; 'in c.' सामान्येन; 'who have made c. cause with us' अस्माभिः सहैककार्योणां (Mu. 2). –*s.* प्रचारः, सर्वसाधारणं क्षेत्रं. –ALTY, *s.* प्रजा, लोकाः, अवरवर्णाः. –LAW, *s.* देशाचारः, देशव्यवहारः-विधिः. –LY, *adv.* सामान्यतः, प्रायः, साधारण्येन, बहुशः. –PLACE, *a.* प्रसिद्ध, प्राकृत. –WEALTH, *s.* प्रजाधीनं राज्यतंत्रं, प्रजाप्रभुत्वं ; 'c. (of ants)' समूहः, स्वतंत्रो गणः.

COMMORANCY, *s.* वासः, वसति *f.*

COMMOTION, *s.* क्षोभः, विप्लवः ; प्रकोपः, कलहः.

COMMUNE, *v. i.* संभाष् 1 A, संमंत्र् 10 A, संवद् 1 P, व्यवह 1 P ; व्यासादयो देवादिभिः प्रत्यक्षं व्यवहरंति (S. B. 313) 'c. directly with Gods.' –ION, *s.* संभाषणं ; संवादः. 2 व्यवहारः. 3 संसर्गः, संगः, संगमः. –ITY, *s.* समाजः, जनसमूहः, प्रजाजनः, जनता, गणः. 2 सामान्यं, साधारण्यं ; ऐक्यं, साम्यं.

COMMUNICATE, *v. t.* कथ् 10, निविद् c., आख्या 2 P, आचक्ष् 2 A, (with dat. of person), विवृ 5 U, प्रकाश् c., वद् 1 P, विज्ञा c. (ज्ञापयति), संदिश् 6 P. 2 वितॄ 1 P (with loc.), दा 3 U, प्रतिपद् c. (with dat.). –*v. i.* संगम् 1 A, समागम्, संयुज् pass.; 'c. ing with Sindhu' सिंधुनदेन संगत-संगच्छमान. 2 संलप् 1 P, संवद् 1 P, संभाष् 1 A; व्यवह 1 P. 3 संचर् 1 P. –ION, *s.* कथनं, निवेदनं, विज्ञापनं ; संदेशः, लेखः, लेख्यं. 2 दानं, वितरणं. 3 संगमः, संसर्गः, संव्यवहारः. 4 संकथा, संलापः, संवादः. 5 सामान्यपथः. 6 संचारः. –IVE, *a.* संप्रदान-संवादशील ; 'not c.' मितवाक्, वाग्यत.

COMMUTE, *v. t.* परिवृत् c., विनिमे 1 A, विपर्यस् 4 P or c., प्रतिदा 3 U. –ATION, *s.* परिवर्तनं, विनिमयः. 2 विक्रिया, विपरिणामः, विपर्ययः ; 'c. of a curse' उच्छापः.

COMPACT, *a.* सुसंहत, निबिड, घन, सांद्र, दृढ, अनंतर, अविरल. –*s.* नियमः, समयः, संविद् *f.*, अभ्युपगमः, प्रतिश्रवः ; 'a written c.' नियमपत्रं; 'make a c.' संविदमभ्युपगम् 1 P, प्रतिश्रु 5 P. –*v. t.* संहन् 2 P, संधा 3 U, संश्लिष् c., घनीकृ 8 U. –LY, *adv.* दृढं, निबिडं, घनं. –NESS, *s.* संहति *f.*, निबिडता, &c.

COMPANION, *s.* सखि *m.*, सहचरः, मित्रं, वयस्यः, सहायः, सजुस् *m.* ; 'with Madhu for a c.' मधुसहायः, मधुद्वितीयः ; 'c. of the king' (in love matters) नर्मसुहृद्-सचिवः ; 'c. of youth' बालसहचरः ; 'c. at school' सहाध्यायिन् *m.* ; 'c. in arms' सहयोद्धृ *m.*; 'c. in joy & sorrow' समदुःखसुखः ; 'boon c.' सहपायिन् *m.*, सहभोजिन् *m.* –SHIP, *s.* साहचर्यं, साहाय्यं, संसर्गः, संगति *f.*

COMPANY, *s.* साहचर्यं, संगति *f.*, समागमः, संसर्गः, संवासः, सहवसति *f.* 2 जनसमूहः, परिषद् *f.*, समाजः ; दलं, वृंदं, गणः, पंक्ति *f.*, वर्गः ; 'c. of soldiers' सैन्यदलं-गुल्मः; 'c. of traders' श्रेणी, नैगमाः; 'not admissible into c.' अपांक्तेयः; 'keep or bear c. with' सह वस्-चर्-1 P, संगमनुव्रज् 1 P; *See* ASSOCIATE.

COMPARE, *v. t.* तुल् 10 (तुलयति), उपमा 3 A ; 'c. ed with the moon' शशांकेन तुलितं ; समीकृ 8 U, सदृशीकृ. 2 एकत्र परीक्ष् 1 A, संप्रधृ 10. —COMPARATIVE, *a.* आनुषंगिक (की *f.*), तुलनया निर्णीत, उपमाजन्य ; oft. by अपेक्षया in comp. –LY, *adv.* 'as c. ed with' तुलनया, औपम्येन, उपमानेन, अपेक्षया ; 'I like mango as c. ed with a Jambu fruit' जंबुफलाद्-जंबुफलापेक्षया आम्रं मेऽधिकतरं रोचते; 'the merits of Râma c.' अन्यापेक्षया रामस्य गुणाः. –COMPARISON, *s.* तुला, तुलना, उपमा-मानं, सादृश्यं, औपम्यं; 'without c.' अतुल, अनुपम; 'standard of c.' उपमानं; 'subject of c.' उपमेयं.

COMPARTMENT, *s.* शाला, कोष्ठः, कक्षः-क्षा. 2 छेदः, भागः, अंशः.

COMPASS, *s.* विषयः, गोचरः; 'within the c. of the eye' नयनगोचरस्थ. 2 मंडलं, परिधिः, परिणाहः, विस्तारः, परिमाणं, पर्यंतः. 3 परिमितता, अनतिक्रमः. 4 दिङ्निर्णययंत्रं. –*v. t.* परिगम् 1 P, परि-इ 2 P, परिवेष्ट् 1 A or c., परिवृ 5 U. 2 अधिगम् 1 P, लभ् 1 A; *See* GET. 3 घट् c. (घटयति), साध् 5 P or c., संपद् c., निष्पद् c.

COMPASSION, *s.* दया, अनुकंपा, कृपा, घृणा, करुणा, अनुक्रोशः ; 'feel or have c. for' अनुकंप् 1 A, अभ्युपपद् 4 A, दयां कृ or दृश् c. (loc.), दय् 1 A (gen.). –ATE, *a.* सदय, करुणार्द्र, सानुकंप, सानुक्रोश, कृपालु, दयालु, सकरुण, दयाशील. –ATELY, *adv.* सदयं, सानुकंपं, कृपया.

COMPATERNITY, *s.* धर्मपितृत्वं.

COMPATIBLE, *a.* अनुगुण, अनुरूप, अविरुद्ध, उपयुक्त; *See* CONSISTENT. –COMPATIBILITY, *s.* अविरोधः, योग्यता, अनुरूपता, अविसंवादः.

COMPATRIOT, *s.* स्वदेशजः, एकदेशनिवासिन् *m.*

COMPEER, *s.* वयस्यः, समानपदस्थः.

COMPEL, *v. t.* Ex. by causal of verbs with बलाद्, बलेन, or एव; 'I shall c. you to go' त्वां गमयिष्याम्येव or बलाद् गमयिष्यामि; 'c. s payment' बलाद् दापयति &c. ; 'c.s me to ask' बलादनिच्छंतमपि मां प्रश्नकर्मणि नियोजयति (Ka. 134) ; sometimes ex. by अवश्यं with pot. pass. part ; 'you will be c. ed to stay here' त्वयात्रावश्यं स्थातव्यं; or by प्रेर् c., प्रवृत् c. — COMPULSORY, *a.* अवश्य-क ; 'it is not c. on you to go' गमनं न तेऽवश्यकं. 2 बलवत् (ती *f.*), बलिन् (नी *f.*). –LY, *adv.* बलात्, अवश्यं, बलेन, अनि-

च्छत् *a.* (ती-न्ती *f.*). —COMPULSION, *s.* बलात्कारः, प्रसभं, साहसं, बलं; 'by c.' बलात्, बलेन, प्रसभं, प्रसह्य, हठात्.

COMPEND, COMPENDIUM, *s.* संक्षेपः, संग्रहः, संहारः, सारः. —COMPENDIOUS, *a.* संक्षिप्त, संगृहीत, अविस्तीर्ण, परिमित, सारभूत. —LY, *adv.* संक्षेपेण, संक्षेपतः, समासतः, अविस्तरेण. —NESS, *s.* संक्षेपः, अविस्तरः.

COMPENSATE, *v. t.* परितुष् c., निष्कृतिं दा 3 U, प्रत्युपकृ 8 U, (of persons); अपाकृ, शुध् c., निस्तॄ c. —ION, *s.* प्रतिफलं, निष्कृति *f.*, निस्तारः, पारितोषिकं. —IVE, *a.* क्षति-हानि-पूरक.

COMPETE, *v. i.* स्पर्ध् 1 A, संघृष् 1 P, विजि desid. (जिगीषते); oft. ex. by अहमहमिका, अहमहमिकया प्रणामलालसाः (Ka. 81) 'c.-ing with one another to salute first.' —ENCE,-ENCY, *s.* योग्यता, सामर्थ्यं, शक्ति *f.*, औचित्यं, कार्यक्षमता. 2 वृत्त्युचितं द्रव्यं; 'bare c.' ग्रासाच्छादनमात्रं. —ENT, *a.* योग्य, उचित, समर्थ, शक्त, क्षम, पर्याप्त, कार्यक्षम, कार्यनिर्वाहक्षम. 2 परिमित, अनाधिक. —ITION, *s.* स्पर्धा, अहमहमिका, संघर्षः, विजिगीषा. —ITOR, *s.* प्रतिस्पर्धिन् *m.*, प्रत्यर्थिन् *m.*, प्रतिपक्षः, प्रतियोगिन् *m.*

COMPILE, *v. t.* संकल् 1 P, 10 (कलयति), सं-समाहृ 1 P, आलोड् 10, संग्रह् 9 P; उद्धृत्य समाहृ. —ATION, *s.* संकलनं, संग्रहः, सारः. —ER, *s.* समाहर्तृ *m.*, संग्रहीतृ *m.*, व्यासः, संकलयितृ *m.*

COMPLACENCE,-CY, *s.* प्रसादः, संतोषः, प्रीति *f.* 2 सौजन्यं, अनुवृत्ति *f.*, दाक्षिण्यं. —COMPLACENT, *a.* प्रसन्न, सुसंतुष्ट, सुप्रीत. 2 सुशील, दक्षिण. —LY, *adv.* प्रसादेन, प्रीत्या, सानंदं.

COMPLAIN, *v. i.* Ex. by verbs of 'telling' gen. with सशोकं, सविलापं; आ-अधि-क्षिप् 6 P; 'c. ed of her brother's rudeness to her father' भ्रातुरविनयमधिकृत्य पित्रे ऽकथयत्, or भ्रातुरविनयाचरणं पित्रे न्यवेदयत्; 'c. ed to me of partiality' पक्षपातमधिकृत्य मां सविलापं विज्ञापयामास; 'how can I do what you c. of' यत्त्वं मय्यारोपयसि तत्कथमहं कुर्यां. 2 विलप् 1 P, शुच् 1 P, परिदेव् 1 A, आक्रंद् 1 P, आक्रुश् 1 P. 3 अभियुज् 7 A, 10, राजकुले निविद् c. (in law). 4 पीड् pass. अनुभू 1 P; 'has been c.ing of ill-health' आमयपीडितः. —ANT, *s.* अभियोक्तृ *m.*, अर्थिन् *m.*, अभियोगिन् *m.*, वादिन् *m.*, पिशुनः. —ER, *s.* परिदेवकः, विलापिन् *m.* —COMPLAINT, *s.* अभियोगः. 2 विज्ञापना (सविलापा); दुःखनिवेदनं, विलपनं, परिदेवनं; 'breathed out this doleful c.' इमानि परिदेविताक्षराणि सकरुणमुदीरयामास. 3 व्याधिः, पीडा, रोगः, आमयः.

COMPLAISANCE, *s.* दाक्षिण्यं, अनुवृत्ति *f.*, अनुनयः, प्रश्रयः, अनुरोधः. —COMPLAISANT, *a.* दक्षिण, अनुनयिन्-अनुरोधिन् (नी *f.*), अनुकूल, सप्रश्रय. —LY, *adv.* सानुनयं, सानुरोधं.

COMPLEMENT, *s.* पूरणं, परिपूरकं. 2 कोटि *f.* 3 संपूर्णता, सामग्र्यं.

COMPLETE, *v. t.* समाप् c., संपद् c., साध् c., अवसो c. (साययति), निर्वह् c., संपॄ c. (पूरयति) or संपूर् 10, निर्वृत् c. —*a.* संपूर्ण, समाप्त, अवसित, सिद्ध, संपन्न, निर्वृत्त. 2 संपूर्ण, निखिल, अखिल, समस्त, समग्र, अशेष, अन्यून. 3 पक्व, परिणत; 'c. army' चतुरंगबलं. —ION, *s.* समापनं, निर्वर्तनं, संपादनं. 2 सिद्धि *f.*, समाप्ति *f.*, निर्वृत्ति *f.* 3 परिणामः, परिपाकः. 4 पूरणं, परिपूरकं. —LY, *adv.* संपूर्णं; निःशेषं, पर्याप्तं, निरवशेषं, अशेषतः, सर्वथा. 2 आमूलं, कार्त्स्न्येन. —NESS, *s.* संपूर्णता, निःशेषता.

COMPLEX, *a.* संकीर्ण, मिश्रित, विषम, संमिश्र, मिश्र, संकुल. 2 नानार्थक, असरल, बह्वर्थ. —ITY, *s.* संकरः, मिश्रता, संकुलता.

COMPLEXION, *s.* वर्णः, मुखरागः; 'of a pale c.' विवर्णः, पांडुवदनः. 2 आकारः, स्वरूपं. 3 प्रकृति *f.*, शरीरभावः. —AL, *a.* प्रकृतिसंबंधिन् (नी *f.*).

COMPLICATE, *v. t.* संमिश्र् 10, संकीर्ण-संकुल-*a.* कृ 8 U, प्र-सं-कॄ 6 P, संकरी-संकुली-कृ. —ION, *s.* संकुलीकरणं, संकीर्णता, संमिश्रता.

COMPLICE, *s.* पापसहायः. —ITY, *s.* पापसहायता, सहकारिता.

COMPLIMENT, *s.* अभिनंदनवचस् *n.*, नमस्कारः; 'presents c. s' अभिनंद्य ब्रवीति; 'give my c. s to Chyavana' च्यवनाय मां प्रणिपातय (V. 5), मदीयो नमस्कारो वाच्यः; श्वश्रूजनं सर्वं विज्ञापय प्रापितमत्प्रणामः (R. XIV. 60). 2 प्रश्रयवाच् *f.*, चाटूक्ति *f.*, प्रशंसा, श्लाघा, प्रशंसोक्ति *f.*; 'high c.' उच्चैर्वादः; स्तुति *f.* —*v. t.* *See* PRAISE. 2 मधुरगिरा-चाटूक्त्या सांत्व् 10. —ARY, *a.* उपचार in comp.; 'c. saying' उपचारपदं; प्रियवादिन् (नी *f.*), स्तुतिमय (यी *f.*); 'c. present' उपायनं. —ER, *s.* प्रियवादिन् *m.*, चाटुकारः.

COMPLOT, *v. i.* गूढं मंत्र् 10 A, कूटसंविदं कृ 8 U. —*s.* गूढ-कु-मंत्रणा, कूटसाहित्यं. —TER, *s.* कूटसहायः.

COMPLY, *v. i.* अनुविधा 3 U, अनुरुध् 4 A, अनुवृत् 1 A. 2 अनु-सं-मन् 4 A, अनुज्ञा 9 U, स्वीकृ 8 U, प्रति-परि-ग्रह् 9 P, प्रतीष् 6 P, अभ्युपगम् 1 P; क्रियतामस्याः प्रणयपरिग्रहः (Ka. 145) 'c. with her request.' —ANCE, *s.* अनुवृत्ति *f.*, अनुविधायित्वं, अनुरोधः, अनुसारः. 2 स्वीकारः, संमति *f.*, अभ्युपगमः, परिग्रहः; 'in c. with your orders' त्वच्छासनानुरोधात्-नुसारेण. —ANT, *a.* अनुविधायिन् (नी *f.*), अनुवृत्तिकुशल-शील, अनुरोधिन् (नी *f.*), वचने स्थित. —ER, *s.* अनुरोधिन् *m.*, परिग्रहिन् *m.*

COMPONENT, *a.* or *s.* घटक, साधक, रचक; 'c. part' घटकावयवः, अंगं, भागः, साधनं.

COMPORT, *v. i.* Behave, q. v. 2 युज्-उपपद्-pass. —ABLE, *a.* योग्य, उचित. —MENT, *s.* आचारः, व्यवहारः, चेष्टितं.

COMPOSE, *v. t.* (of books &c.) प्रणी 1 P, विरच् 10, बंध् 9 P, निबंध्, संग्रंथ् 9 P. 2 विन्यस् 4 P, संधा 3 U, संक्लृप् c., संविधा, निर्मा 3 A. 3 घट् c. (घटयति), निर्मा, क्लृप् c.; or gen. ex. by आत्मक, रूप, मय (यी *f.*) in comp.; 'the body c. ed of 5 elements' पंचभिर्निर्मितो देहः, पंचभूतात्मको देहः. 4 (Calm) स्थिरीकृ 8 U, शम् c. (शमयति), प्रसद् c., संस्तंभ् c., पर्यवस्था c. (स्थापयति); 'does not yet c. (collect) himself' नाद्यापि पर्यवस्थापयत्यात्मानं (U. 3). 5 (a dispute &c.) संधा 3 U, प्रशम् c., (प्रशमयसि विवादं S. 5). —ED, *a.* शांत, प्रसन्न, अव्याकुल, अनुद्विग्न, स्थिरीकृत, समाहित. 2 विरचित, निर्मित, निबद्ध; 'c. in verse, or music' श्लोक-स्वर-बद्ध; 'c. of' घटित, आत्मक- (त्मिका *f.*), रूप in comp. —EDLY, *adv.* असंभ्रमं, प्रशांतचेतसा, निरुद्वेगं. —ER, *s.* रचकः, प्रणेतृ *m.*, निबंद्धृ *m.* —ITION, *s.* रचना, प्रणयनं, निर्माणं, निबंधनं. 2 विन्यासः, संधानं, प्रशमनं. 3 समसनं, मिश्रणं, संयोगः, संधिः, संघातः. 4 ग्रंथः, प्र-नि-बंधः.—URE, *s.* स्थैर्यं, शमः, प्रसादः, असंभ्रमः, अक्षोभः. 2 संधानं, संयोगः, मिश्रणं, निर्माणं.

COMPOTATION, *s.* सहपानं, संपीति *f.*

COMPOUND, *v. t.* संयुज् 10, संमिश्र् 10, संधा 3 U, समस् 4 P, संश्लिष् c. 2 (a dispute) संधा, समाधा, प्रशम् c. (शमयति). —*v. i.* ऋणशोधनेन आनृण्यं गम् 1 P; 'was glad to c. for his escape with the loss of it' तन्नाशेनापि मुक्तिरभवदिति हृष्टो बभूव. —*a.*, —ED, *a.* संयुक्त, यौगिक (की *f.*), संसृष्ट, संमिश्र, सामासिक, साधित; 'c. word' समासः. —*s.* मिश्रणं, संकरः; मिश्रितद्रव्यं, योगः. 2 परिसरभूमि *f.*, प्रांगणं (नं). —ER, *s.* मिश्रणकृत्-समाधातृ *m.*; 'c. of medicines' औषधयोगविद् *m.*

COMPREHEND, *v. t.* बुध् 1 P, विद् 2 P, ज्ञा 9 U, ग्रह् 9 P, परिग्रह्, उपलभ् 1 A, अवगम् 1 P, ऊह् 1 A; विभू c., अवधृ 10. 2 व्याप् 5 P, अंतर्गण् 10, अंतर्भू c., परिग्रह् 9 P, आकल् 10, समाविश् c. —COMPREHENSIBLE, *a.* ग्राह्य, वेद्य, अवधारणीय, विभाव्य, धीगम्य; 'easily c.' सुबोध; 'not c.' दुर्बोध, दुर्ग्रह, दुर्गम, दुर्ज्ञेय. —COMPREHENSION, *s.* ग्रहणं, बोधः. 2 धी *f.*, मति *f.*, बुद्धि *f.*, अवधारणा, मेधा; 'power of c.' ग्रहणसामर्थ्यं, आकलनशक्तिः. 3 प्रतिसंहारः, व्याप्ति *f.*, समावेशः, अंतर्भावः. —COMPREHENSIVE, *a.* व्यापक, बहुविस्तीर्ण, व्यापिन् (नी *f.*), बहुग्रह. 2 साक्षेपिक (की *f.*). —LY, *adv.* समासतः, संक्षेपेण. 2 व्यापकत्वेन. —NESS, *s.* व्यापकत्वं. 2 संक्षेपः, समस्तता.

COMPRESS, *v. t.* संवृ 5 U, संकुच् 1 P, संहन् 2 P, संपीड् 10, संहृ 1 P. —IBLE, *a.* संकोचनीय. —IBILITY, *s.* संकोचक्षमता, संहरणीयता. —ION, *s.* संकोचः-चनं, संहति *f.*, संपीडनं; संवरणं.

COMPRISE, *v. t.* व्याप् 5 P, अंतर्गण् 10, परिग्रह् 9 P, समाविश् c., अंतर्भू c.; 'to be c. ed in' अंतर्गम् 1 P, अंतर्भू 1 P, or by आत्मक, गर्भ, in comp.

COMPROBATION, *s.* प्रमाणं, साक्ष्यं, संमति *f.*

COMPROMISE, *v. t.* आपुष् 10. 2 संशये पत् c., संशयस्थ *a.* कृ 8 U. —*s.* आपोषः-षणं. 2 मध्यस्थावलंबननियमः.

COMPROVINCIAL, *a.* एकदेशीय, एकदेशज.

COMPTROL, *v. t.* अधिष्ठा 1 P, पर्यव-ईक्ष् 1 A. —LER, *s.* कार्याधिकृतः, पर्यवेक्षकः, कार्यद्रष्टृ *m.*

COMPULSION, —SORY, *See* under COMPEL.

COMPUNCTION, *s.* अनुशयः, अनुतापः, पश्चात्तापः. —COMPUNCTIOUS, *a.* अनुशयार्त, अनुतापिन् (नी *f.*).

COMPUTE, *v. t.* गण् 10, सं-परिसं-ख्या 2 P, संकल् 10. —ATION, *s.* गणनं-ना, संख्यानं. —ER, *s.* गणकः.

COMRADE, *See* COMPANION.

CON, *v. t.* अधी 2 A, अभ्यस् 4 U.

CONCATENATE, *v. t.* (अविच्छेदं) संयुज् 10, संश्लिष् c., अनुबंध् 9 P, संधा 3 U. —ION, *s.* अविच्छेदसंयोगः, निरंतरः संश्लेषः, अनुबंधः. 2 माला, परंपरा, श्रेणी, पंक्ति *f.*

CONCAVE, *a.* पुटाकार, उत्तान, उदराकार. —ITY, *s.* उत्तानता, पुटः, गर्भः.

CONCEAL, *v. t.* गुह् 1 U, प्रच्छद् 10, अपवृ 5 U or c., अंतर्धा 3 U; पिधा 3 U, संवृ, नि-अप-ह्नु 2 A (feelings &c.); गुप् 1 P or 10; 'c. oneself' 'to be c. ed' अंतर्-इ 2 P; 'c. ing the body (oneself) behind a bush' विटपांतरितविग्रहः (Ka. 152); ली 4 A (मातुर्निलीयते कृष्णः S. K.). —ED, *a.* गूढ, प्रच्छन्न, निभृत, गुप्त, निलीन. —MENT, *s.* गूहनं, प्रच्छादनं, नि-अप-ह्नवः, गोपनं, संवरणं; 'in c.' निभृतं, रहः, गुप्तं, छन्नं.

CONCEDE, *v. t.* अनुमन् 4 A, प्रदा 3 U, अनुज्ञा 9 U, वितृ 1 P; 'c. ed the point to him' तस्याभिप्रेतमन्वमन्यत. 2 अंगीकृ 8 U, अभ्युपगम् 1 P, प्रतिपद् 4 A. —CONCESSION, *s.* प्रदानं, वितरणं; त्यागः. 2 क्षमा. 3 अंगीकारः, प्रतिपत्ति *f.*, अभ्युपगमः.

CONCEIVE, *v. i.* गर्भं धृ 1 P, 10 or आधा 3 U, गर्भवती-आपन्नसत्वा-ससत्वा-अंतर्वत्नी भू 1 P. —*v. t.* विभू c., बुध् 1 P, अवधृ 10, अवगम् 1 P, ग्रह् 9 P, आलोच् 10, ज्ञा 9 U. 2 मन् 4 A, चिंत् 10, ध्यै 1 A. 3 संभू c., क्लृप् c. (नरपतेर्भूषणविक्रयं को नाम संभावयेत् Mu. 5). 4 धृ, वह् 1 P; *See* BEAR; 'I c. no hatred against you' त्वयि मे द्वेषबुद्धिर्नास्ति, न तुभ्यमसूयामि. –CONCEPTION, *s.* गर्भाधानं, गर्भधारणं. 2 विभावना, बोधः, ग्रहणं, अवधारणं. 3 विचारः, कल्पना, भावना, बुद्धि *f.*, मति *f.*, संकल्पः. —CONCEIT, *s.* अभिमानः, अवलेपः, दर्पः, अहंकारः, गर्वः; 'self-c.' स्वाभिमानः. 2 कल्पना, भावना, चिंता, विचारः. 3 मति *f.*, बुद्धि *f.*, मतं. –ED, *a.* दृप्त, अवलिप्त, अभिमानिन् (नी *f.*). उद्धत, आत्ममानिन्, सगर्व; 'c. of learning' पंडितंमन्यः. –EDLY, *adv.* साभिमानं, सगर्वं. –EDNESS, *s.* मानिता, अहंकारः, सगर्वता.

CONCENTRE, *v. t.* एकीकृ 8 U, *See* below; 'c. ed all in self' आत्मपरायणः, आत्मन्येव निविष्टचेतोवृत्तिः.

CONCENTRATE, *v. t.* समाहृ 1 P, समुपाचि 5 U, एकीकृ 8 U. 2 समाधा 3 U (as mind); अनन्यमनस्क-एकाग्र-*a.* भू; 'my affections are c. ed in her' सा मे स्नेहस्यैकायनीभूता (M. 2). –ED, *a.* एकतान, अनन्यवृत्ति, एकाग्र, एकायन, एकसर्ग, एकाग्र्य, एकायनगत. –ION, *s.* एकीकरणं, एकत्र समाहरणं. 2 एकाग्रता, समाधिः, अनन्यमनस्कता.

CONCENTRIC,-CAL, *a.* एक-समान-केंद्र.

CONCERN,-MENT, *s.* अर्थः, व्यापारः, विषयः, कार्यं, संबंधः. 2 चिंता, उद्वेगः, औत्सुक्यं. 3 गौरवं, गुरुता, माहात्म्यं. 4 अवेक्षा, प्रणयः, अनुरागः, मनोयोगः, मनोभिनिवेशः. 5 चर्चा, व्यापारः. विचारः. –*v. t.* संबंध् 9 P, उद्दिश् 6 P, आश्रि 1 U; 'this does not c. you' नायं तव व्यापारः. 2 अवेक्ष् 1 A. 3 Afflict, q. v. 4 (Oneself about) व्यापृ 6 A, आत्मानं व्यापृ c., व्यापृत *a.* भू, चर्चां कृ ; 'I am not c. ed in the least in this business' अनेन कर्मणा न मे कोपि संबंधः. –ING, *prep.* संबंधिन् (नी *f.*)-विषय in comp. ; उद्दिश्य, अधिकृत्य, आश्रित्य.

CONCERT, *s.* एकतानः-लः, संगीतं; 'c. hall' संगीतशाला. 2 संप्रधारणा, संमंत्रणं, कार्यविमर्शः, संवादः. 3 सहकारिता, संभूयकारित्वं, चित्तैक्यं, एकभावः.–*v. t.* संमंत्र् 10 A, संप्रधृ 10, कार्याणि चिंत् 10 or विमृश् 6 P, संवद् 1 P. 2 संभूय-एकत्र-कृ 8U. 3 घट् c.(घटयति). कृप् c., चिंत् 10; 'well c. ed plan' सुघटितः-सुचिंतितः-प्रयोगः.

CONCH, *s.* शंखः, कंबुः, दरं.

CONCILIATE, *v. t.* अनुरंज् c., आराध् 10, प्रसद् c., तुष् c., लल् 10, सांत्व् 10. 2 संधा 3 U, अनुनी 1 P. –ION, *s.* अनुरंजनं, सांत्वनं, प्रसादनं. 2 सामन् *n.*, संधानं. –OR, *s.* अनुरंजकः. 2 संधानकर्तृ *m.*, मध्यस्थः. –ORY, *a.* आराधक, सामन् in comp.; सामोपचाराः 'c. means'.

CONCISE, *a.* संक्षिप्त, संहत, सामासिक (की *f.*). –LY, *adv.* संक्षेपेण, संक्षेपतः, अविस्तरेण, समासतः; 'a c. worded message' लघुसंदेशपदा सरस्वती (R. VIII. 77). –NESS, *s.* संक्षिप्तता, संहारः, अविस्तरः. –CONCISION, *s.* कर्तनं, छेदनं, उच्छेदः.

CONCITATION, *s.* उत्तेजनं, प्रोत्साहनं, उत्थापनं.

CONCLAVE, *s.* समाजः, सभा, परिषद् *f.* 2 गूढ-सभा-समाजः. 3 कक्षांतरं.

CONCLUDE, *v. t.* समाप् c., निर्वृत् c., अवसो 4 P, निष्पद् c., संपद् c., साध् c., संपूर् 10. 2 अनुमा 3 A, विभू c., ऊह् 1 A, तर्क् 10. 3 निर्णी 1 P, निश्चि 5 U, अवधृ 10, व्यवसो 4 P; 'c. a treaty' संधिं कृ 8 U or विधा 3 U. –*v. i.* विरम् 1 P, निवृत् 1 A; प्र-उप-शम् 4 P; 'when he had c. ed' वचस्यवसिते तस्य. –CONCLUSION, *s.* समाप्ति *f.*, निष्पादनं, सिद्धि *f.*, निष्पत्ति *f.*, निवृत्ति *f.* 2 अवसानं, अंतः, परिणामः, उपसंहारः. 3 अनुमानं, ऊहनं, अनुमिति *f.* 4 निर्णयः, अवधारणं, फलं, उत्तरं. 5 सिद्धांतः, राद्धांतः, उत्तरपक्षः, निगमनं (in logic). —CONCLUSIVE, *a.* अखंडय, अनिरस्य, निरुत्तर, समर्थ. 2 निर्णायक, संशयच्छेदिन् (नी *f.*), निश्चायक. –LY, *adv.* सनिश्चयं, निश्चितं, संशयच्छेदितया.

CONCOCT, *v. t.* पच्-क्वथ् 1 P, तप् c. 2 चिंत् 10, घट् c. (घटयति), प्रकृप् c., निरूप् 10. –ION, *s.* क्वाथः. 2 पाकः, पाचनं. –IVE, *a.* पाचक.

CONCOMITANT, *a.* आनुषंगिक (की *f.*), समवायिन् (नी *f.*), सभेत, समन्वित; सहवर्तिन्, सहकारिन्. –*s.* सहचारिन् *m.*, सहवर्तिन् *m.*, संगिन् *m.* –LY, *adv.* समवेतं, सहितं, सह, संभूय. –CONCOMITANCE, *s.* संयोगः, समन्वयः, अनुषंगः, समवायः.

CONCORD, *s.* ऐक्यं, एकता; चित्तैक्यं, अविसंवादः, अविप्रतिपत्ति *f.*, अविरोधः; 'c. of hearts' ऐक्यं हृदययोः, एकचित्तता. 2 प्रीति *f.*, प्रणयः, संधिः. 3 समयः, संविद् *f.*, नियमः. 4 अनुषंगः, अन्वयः, समन्वयः. 5 तालैक्यं, स्वरैकता. –ANCE, *s.* एकता, सादृश्यं, ऐक्यं. –ANT, *a.* अनुरूप, अनुगुण, सदृश(शी *f.*), अविरुद्ध, संवादिन् (नी *f.*).

CONCOURSE, *s.* संधिः, संगमः. 2 (of people) (जन-) समूहः, संघातः, निवहः, ओघः, गणः.

CONCREMENT, *s.* पिंडः, राशिः. घनता, संहति *f.*, संघातः.

CONCRETE, *v. t.* राशीकृ 8 U, पिंडीकृ, एकीकृ, घनीकृ, संहन् 2 P. –*v. i.* राशीभू 1 P, पिंडीभू, घनीभू, संहन् pass. –*s.* पिंडः, ओघः, घनचयः. 2 घनद्रव्यं, श्यानद्रव्यं. –*a.* घन, राशीभूत, संहत, श्यान, पिंडीभूत. 2 अविविक्त, अकेवल, समवेत, आन्वित. –ION, *s.* घनीकरणं; संहति *f.*, संघातः. 2 पिंडः, लोष्टः, संहतद्रव्यं.

CONCUBINE, *s.* उपपत्नी, उपस्त्री, गणिका, वारस्त्री, वेश्या ; 'c. shut up' अवरोधस्त्री. –AGE, *s.* उपस्त्रीगमनं, वेश्यासेवा.

CONCUPISCENCE, *s.* कामः, अभिलाषः, रताभिरुचि *f.* –CONCUPISCENT, *a.* कामुक, कामिन् (नी *f.*), रतार्थिन्.

CONCUR, *v. i.* एकत्र मिल् 6 P, संगम् 1 A, संभू1P, संपत् 1 P, समागम् 1 P. **2** संभूय-एकीभूय-कृ 8 U. **3** संमन् 4 A, तथा मन् ; अभ्युपगम्, एकचित्तीभू ; *See* AGREE. –RENCE, *s.* सं-अनु-मति *f.*, संमतं, इच्छा. **2** मतैक्यं, एकचित्तता. –RENT, *a.* एकचित्त, संप्रतिपन्न, संवादिन् (नी *f.*). **2** अनुषंगिन् (णी *f.*); संभूय-सह-कारिन् (णी *f.*). –RENTLY, *adv.* संमतिपूर्वं, अनुमत्या. **2** सममेव, युगपत्.

CONCUSSION, *s.* संघट्टः, विकंपः, विधुवनं, संक्षोभः.

CONDEMN, *v. t.* Censure, q. v. **2** दंड् 10, दंडं आदिश् 6 P or कृ 8 U; 'c. to death' वधदंडमादिश् ; 'he was c. ed to be hanged' शूलमारोप्यतामसाविति दंड आदिष्टः. **3** अपराधिन् *a.* (नी *f.*) स्था c. (स्थापयति), अपराधं निर्णी 1 P ; 'c. to pay' दा c. (दापयति). –ATION, *s.* दंडनं, दंडाज्ञा. **2** अपराधनिर्णयः. **3** निंदा, गर्हा, दूषणं. –ATORY, *a.* निंदक, अपवादक. –ER, *s.* दंडप्रणेतृ *m.*, निंदकः.

CONDENSE, *v. t.* संहन् 2 P, घनीकृ 8 U, सांद्रीकृ, श्यै c. **2** संक्षिप् 6 P. –*v. i.* सांद्री-घनी-भू, संहन् pass., श्यै 1 A. –*a.*,-ED, *a.* घन, सांद्र, निबिड, श्यान ; संक्षिप्त. **2** स्थूल, अविरल. –ATION, *s.* घनीकरणं. –ITY, *s.* घनता, निबिडता, &c.

CONDESCEND, *v. i.* प्रसद् 1 P, अर्ह् 1 P, (followed by inf.) ; *See* PLEASE ; 'the king c.-ed to speak with his servant' प्रसन्नो भूत्वा, दक्षिणतया, गौरवं-अभिमानं-अपास्य, भृत्येन सहाभाषत ; 'c. to look at me' मयि दृष्टिप्रसादं कुरु. **2** अनुवृत् 1 A, अनुमन् 4 A, अनुज्ञा 9 U. –ING, *a.* प्रसादाभिमुख (खी *f.*), प्रसन्न, अस्तगर्व, त्यक्तगौरव. –INGLY, *adv.* अगर्वं, प्रसन्नतया, नम्रतया. –CONDESCENSION, *s.* प्रसादः, दाक्षिण्यं, दर्पत्यागः, गौरवत्यागः, नम्रता.

CONDIGN, *a.* यथार्ह, अनुरूप, समुचित, योग्य. –LY, *adv.* यथार्हं, यथोचितं. –NESS, *s.* योग्यता, औचित्यं.

CONDIMENT, *s.* व्यंजनं, उपस्करः.

CONDISCIPLE, *s.* सतीर्थः, एकगुरुः.

CONDITION, *s.* दशा, अवस्था, भावः, स्थिति *f.*, वृत्ति *f.*, गति *f.*; 'in this c.' एवंविध *a.*, एवंभूत *a.*; oft. ex. by त्व & ता affixed; दरिद्रता, दुर्गतत्वं, &c. **2** समयः, नियमः, प्रतिज्ञा, अभिसंधिः; संकेतः; 'on this c.' अनेन समयेन. **3** अर्थः, आस्पदं, पदं; अधिकारः, भावः. **4** गुणः, उपाधिः, विशेषणं, प्रकृति *f.* –AL, *a.* समययुक्त, सोपाधिक (की *f.*), सनियम, नियत; संकेतार्थ. –ALLY, *adv.* समयपूर्वकं, सप्रतिज्ञं, समयपुरःसरं. –ED, *a.* स्थित, वर्तिन् (नी *f.*), स्थ in comp.; 'well c.' सुस्थित, सुस्थ.

CONDOLE, *v. i.* समदुःख *a.* भू 1 P, (अन्यं) अनुशुच् 1 P, शोकार्तं समदुःखेन सान्त्व् 10. –ENCE, *s.* समदुःखता, अनुशोचनं; शोकः, संपरिदेवनं. –ER, *s.* समदुःखभागिन् *m.*

CONDONE, *v. t.* क्षम् 1 A, प्रशुध् c., प्रमृज् 2 P. –ATION, *s.* क्षमा, अपराधक्षमा, प्रमार्जनं.

CONDUCE, *v. i.* (to) आवह् 1 P; (महदपि राज्यं न मे सौख्यमावहति P. I. 1), भू with dat., क्लृप् 1 A, संपद् 4 A, (dat.). **2** वृध् c., संपद् c., उत्पद् c., प्रवृत् c. –IVE, *a.* आवह, कर (री *f.*), जनक, in comp.; 'c. to happiness' सुखावह, हितकर, &c.

CONDUCT, *v. t.* नी 1 P, प्राप् c. (ननु मां प्रापय पत्युरंतिकं K. IV. 32), गम् c. (गमयति), वह् 1 P. **2** विधा 3 U, निर्वह् c. प्रवृत् c., प्रणी. **3** (oneself). वृत् 1 A, व्यवहृ 1 P, आचर् 1 P; *See* ACT; 'c. oneself properly' सदाचारेण वृत्, सदाचारं प्रतिपद् 4 A; 'well c. ed' साधुवृत्त, सदाचार. **4** परि-अनुचर् 1 P, अनुया 2 P, मार्गं दृश् c. or आदिश् 6 P. –*s.* निर्वाहणं, निर्वाहः, प्रणयनं. **2** वृत्ति *f.*, वृत्तं, आचारः, व्यवहारः, कर्मन् *n.*, चरितं, चेष्टितं, आचरणं. **3** परिचरः, मार्गदर्शकः. –OR, *s.* नायकः, अग्रगः, नेतृ *m.*, अग्रणीः; (of heat &c.) प्रवाहकः. **2** निर्वाहकः, प्रणेतृ *m.*

CONDUIT, *s.* प्रणाली, जलनिर्गमः. **2** कुल्या.

CONE, *s.* सूचि-ची *f.*, शिखा. **2** शंकुः. –CONIC, –CONICAL, *a.* सूच्याकार, शंक्वाकृति.

CONFABULATE, *See* CONVERSE.

CONFECT, *v. t.* उपस्कृ 8 U, स्वादु *a.* कृ. –ION, *s.* उपस्करः, मिष्टान्नं, मोदकः. –IONERY, *s.* मोदकविक्रयस्थानं. –IONER, *s.* आपूपिकः, भक्ष्यकारः.

CONFEDERATE, *v. t.* संधा 3 U, संयुज् 7 U, 10, एकत्र कृ 8 U. –*v. i.* संघट्ट् 1 A, संयुज् pass., संधिं कृ. –*a.* संधिबद्ध, सुश्लिष्ट, कृतसंधि, संयुक्त, संघातवत् (ती *f.*). –*s.* सहायः, सहकारिन् *m.*, सहयोगिन् *m.* –ION, *s.* संधानं; संयोजनं. –CONFEDERACY, *s.* संधिः, साहित्यं, संघातः, संयोगः.

CONFER, *v. t.* (upon) वितृ 1 P (with loc.), प्रतिपद् c., दा 3 U, 1 P (with dat.); 'I shall c. upon you 100 grants of land' त्वां शासनशतेन योजयिष्यामि (P. I. 1). **2** आवह् 1 P, दा, उत्पद् c. **3** Compare, q. v.; 'c. a favour' प्रसादं कृ 8 U, अनुग्रह् 9 P; 'c.-ing pleasure' सुखद, सुखावह. –*v. i.* संभाष् 1 A, संलप् 1 P, संवद् 1 P. **2** संमंत्र् 10 A, संचित् 10, विचर् c. –ENCE, *s.* संवादः; संकथा, संभाषणं. **2** मंत्रणं. **3** उपमानं. **4** मेलकः, समाजः. –RER, *s.* दातृ *m.*, द or प्रद in comp.

CONFESS, *v. t.* स्वीकृ 8 U, अंगीकृ, प्रतिपद् 4 A, अभ्युपगम् 1 P, अभ्युप-इ 2 P. **2** विवृ 5 U, सूच् 10,

प्रकाश् c., ख्या c. (ख्यापयति). 3 (आचार्याय-गुरवे) पापानि निविद् c. or कथ् 10. -EDLY, *adv.* असंशयं, व्यक्तं, प्रतिपत्तिपूर्वकं. -ION, *s.* अंगीकार:, संप्रतिपत्ति *f.*, अभ्युपगम:, ग्रहणं. 2 ख्यापनं, प्रकाशनं. 3 पापनिवेदनं. -OR, *s.* स्वीकर्तृ *m.*; ख्यापक:.

CONFIDE, *v. i.* विश्वस् 2 P, प्रति-इ 2 P, श्रद्धा 3 U; 'she was made to c. in a false man' असत्यसंधे जने पदं कारिता (S. 4). -*v. t.* निक्षिप् 6 P, न्यस् 4 P (with loc.), सम्-ऋ c. (अर्पयति); 'have you kept the secret c. ed to you' अपि रक्ष्यते रहस्यनिक्षेप: (V. 2). -ANT, *s.* विश्वास-विश्रंभभूमि *f.*, सखि *m.*, वयस्य:. 2 (of a woman) सखी, वयस्या, आलि-ली *f.*-ENCE, *s.* विश्वास:, विश्रंभ:, प्रत्यय:; श्रद्धा. 2 निश्चय:, दृढप्रत्यय:, दृढज्ञानं, असंशय:; 'enter into c.' विश्वासं गम् 1 P or व्रज् 1P; 'raising of c.' विश्वासोपगम:; 'inspire with c.' विश्वासं नी 1 P, विश्वस् c.; 'take into c.' विश्रंभस्थाने मन् 4 A; 'self- c.' प्रगल्भता, प्रागल्भ्यं, धृष्टता; 'an object of c.' विश्वासभूमि:, विश्रंभस्थानं-भाजनं. -ENT, *a.* विश्वासिन् (नी *f.*), विश्वासप्रतिपन्न, विश्वस्त, जातप्रत्यय, विश्रब्ध. 2 निश्चित, असंदेह, छिन्नसंशय; 'he is c. of success' जयं निश्चितं (ध्रुवं) मन्यते. 3 प्रगल्भ, धृष्ट, निर्विशंक, साहसिन्. -ENTIAL, *a.* विश्वस्त, विश्रब्ध; आप्त (आप्तजन:); 'c. talk' विश्रंभालाप: ; 'c. matter.' विश्वासकार्यं. 2 गुप्त, अप्रकाश्य, संवरणीय. -ENTIALLY, *adv.* विश्रब्धं; गुप्तं. -ING, *a.* विश्वासापन्न, विश्वासभाज्, विश्वस्त, जातप्रत्यय, विश्रब्ध, अविशंकमान, नि:शंक. -INGLY, *adv.* विश्रब्धं, सप्रत्ययं, निर्विशंकं, नि:संदेहं.

CONFIGURATION, *s.* आकार:, रूपं, मूर्ति *f.*, विग्रह:, आकृति *f.*

CONFINE, *s.* सीमा, पर्यंत:, प्रांत:, समंत:, परिसरभूमि *f.* -*v. i.* पर्यंते-निकटे-स्था 1 P or वृत् 1 A. -*v. t.* नि-अव-रुध् 7 U, आसिध् 1 P, नि-सं-यम् 1 P, निग्रह् 9 P, बंध् 9P, निबंध्. 2 (oneself to) न व्यति-इ 2 P or उल्लंघ् 1 A, 10, नातिचर् 1 P. 3 संह् 1 P, संकुच् 1 P. -ED, *a.* संयत, निरुद्ध. निबद्ध. 2 संकट, संकुचित; 'c. in the bowels' बद्धकोष्ठ: ; 'c. to bed' शयनग्रस्त; (of a woman) प्राप्तप्रसवकाला. -MENT, *s.* संयम:, निरोध:, निग्रह:, बंधनं, कारागृहं; 'c. of bowels' विड्ग्रह:, आनाह:, मलावरोध:; 'c. of a woman' प्रसवकाल:, प्रसवावस्था.

CONFIRM, *v. t.* दृढीकृ 8 U, द्रढयति (D.), संस्तंभ् c. 2 स्थिरीकृ, दृढप्रमाणं दा 3 U, प्रमाणीकृ, सुस्थिर-दृढं- *a.* कृ. -ATION, *s.* दृढीकरणं, संस्तंभनं, सत्यापनं, प्रमाणीकरणं. -ED, *a.* दृढीकृत, प्रमाणीकृत, स्थिरीकृत. 2 दृढ, स्थिर, रूढ, प्ररूढ; 'a c. fool' प्रतिनिविष्टमूर्ख:; 'c. friendship' प्ररूढ: संसर्ग:, रूढसौहृदं.

CONFISCATE, *v. t.* सर्वस्वं अपहृ 1 P or आच्छिद् 7 P or दंड् 10, नि:स्व *a.* कृ 8 U; 'let his property be c. ed' अस्य सर्वस्वहरणमादिश्यतां. -ED, *a.* राजापहृत; हृतसर्वस्व, नि:स्वीकृत. -ION, *s.* सर्वस्वहरणं, सर्वस्वदंड:, सर्वस्वापहार:.

CONFLAGRATION, *s.* दाह:, ज्वलनं, दीपनं; 'forest c.' दावानल:, दव:, दाव:, अरण्यवह्नि:.

CONFLICT, *s.* विरोध:, (स्मृत्योर्विरोध:); द्वंद्वं, कलह:, वैरं; विप्रतिपत्ति *f.*, विसंवाद:. 2 युद्धं, संग्राम:, विग्रह:. 3 संघट्ट:, समाघात:, अभिसंपात:. -*v. i.* युध् 4 A, विवद् 1 A, विग्रह् 9 P; 'mutually c. ing S'âstras' परस्परं विवदमानानां शास्त्राणां (H. 1); विप्रतिपद् 4 A, परस्परं विरुध् pass., विसंवद् 1 P. -ING, *a.* विप्रतिपन्न, विरुद्ध, परस्परविरोधिन् (नी *f.*), विसंवादिन्.

CONFLUENCE, CONFLUX, *s.* संगम:, संभेद:, तोयव्यतिकर:, वेणि *f.* 2 संयोग:, समागम:, संमिलनं. 3 Concourse, q. v. -CONFLUENT, *a.* संमेलक, संप्रवाहक.

CONFORM, *v. i.* (to) अनुवृत् 1 A, अनुसृ 1 P, अनुरुध् 4 A, प्रमाणीकृ 8 U, (इति सुजनचरितं प्रमाणीकुरु M. 3), अनुविधा 3 U. 2 युज् pass., सदृश-तुल्य-*a.* भू, उपपद् 4 A, संवद् 1 P. -*v. t.* अनुरूप-सदृश *a.* (शी *f.*) कृ, समीकृ. -ABLE, *a.* अनुरूप, सदृश, तुल्य, अनुगुण, समान, संवादिन् (नी *f.*). 2 अनुविधायिन् (नी *f.*), अनुरोधिन्, अनुकूल. 3 योग्य, उपपन्न. -ABLY, *adv.* अनुसारेण-सारत:, अनुरोधात्, अनुरूपं, यथा in comp. -ITY, *s.* अनुरोध:, अनुवृत्ति *f.* 2 अनुरूपता, आनुगुण्यं, सादृश्यं, अनुसार:; 'in c. with' अनुसारेण, अनुरूपं, &c. 3 योग्यता, युक्तता. -IST, *s.* धर्मानुसारिन् *m.*, प्रवृत्तधर्मानुवर्तिन् *m.*

CONFOUND, *v. t.* भ्रांत्या मन् 4 A; 'c. s falsehood with truth' सत्यमनृतमिति भ्रांत्या मन्यते; oft. by संदिह् 2 U; धूमैर्जालविनि:सृतैर्वडभय: संदिग्धपारावता: (V. 3) 'the pigeons c. ed with volumes of incense' &c.; *See* MISTAKE. 2 आकुलीकृ 8 U, मुह् c., वि-सं-क्षुभ् c., संभ्रम् c. (भ्रमयति). 3 संकृ 6 P, विक्षिप् 6 P, संमिश्र् 10, संकुलीकृ. 4 विलुप् c., विनश् c.; 'c. by argument' निरुत्तरीकृ. -ED, *a.* मोहित, आकुल, संभ्रांत, विहस्त, व्यग्र, विक्षिप्त. 2 संकीर्ण, संमिश्रित, संकुल. 3 दैवोपहत; लुप्तज्ञान. -ER, *s.* मोहक:, मोहन:. -ING, *a.* भ्रांतिजनक, संदेहोत्पादक, मोहिन् (नी *f.*).

CONFRATERNITY, *s.* सौभ्रात्रं ; भ्रातृत्वं, साहित्यं.

CONFRONT, *v. t.* अभिमुखी-संमुखीकृ 8 U, अभिमुखयति (D.), समक्षं उपानी 1 P. 2 संमुखीभू 1 P, सं-अभि-मुखं स्था 1 P or गम् 1 P or वृत् 1 A. 3 Compare, q. v. -ATION, *s.* संमुखस्थापनं; संमुखागमनं.

CONFUSE, *v. t.* वि-सं-भ्रम् c., आकुलीकृ 8 U, मुह् c.; *See* CONFOUND; 'to be c. ed' मुह् 4 P, आकुलीभू. –ED, *a.* मोहित, संभ्रांत, आकुल. 2 अस्पष्ट, अव्यक्त, क्रमहीन. –EDLY, *adv.* संकुलं, अक्रमेण, ससंभ्रमं, संकीर्णतया, अस्ताव्यस्तं. 2 अस्पष्टं, संदिग्धतया. –CONFUSION, *s.* संभ्रमः, वैक्लव्यं, व्याकुलत्व, व्यग्रता, विभ्रवः, मोहः. 2 वैलक्ष्यं, व्रीडा, लज्जा. 3 संकरः, संक्षोभः, व्यतिकरः, संकुलं. 4 अक्रमः, अस्पष्टता, क्रमभंगः, अस्ताव्यस्तता. 5 विनाशः, निग्रहः, लोपः.

CONFUTE, *v. t.* खंड् 10, प्रत्याक्षिप् 6 P, निरस् 4 U, प्रत्याख्या 2 P, निरा-अपा-कृ 8 U; निरुत्तरीकृ (of persons). –ATION, *s.* खंडनं, निराकरणं, निरसनं, प्रत्याख्यानं.

CONGE, *s.* प्रणामः, नमस्कारः. 2 आमंत्रणं, अनुज्ञाग्रहणं, आप्रच्छनं.

CONGEAL, *v. t.* घनीकृ 8 U, संहन् 2 P, श्यै c., पिंडीकृ; संचि 5 U. –*v. i.* घनीभू 1 P, श्यै 1 A, पिंडीभू, संहन् pass., शीतीभू. –CONGELATION, *s.* शीतिभावः, संहति *f.*, घनीभावः, घनीकरणं.

CONGENIAL, *a.* एकजातीय, सजाति. 2 समानशील, एकस्वभाव, सधर्मन्. 3 सुखावह, हितकर (री *f.*), अनुरूप, अनुगुण, अनुकूल, सदृश (शी *f.*); 'c. to health' आरोग्यावह, स्वास्थ्यकर. –ITY, *s.* समानशीलता, सधर्मता, सजातित्वं. 2 आनुरूप्यं, आनुगुण्यं.

CONGENITE, *a.* सहज, एककालोत्पन्न.

CONGER, *s.* जलव्यालः.

CONGERIES, *s.* राशिः, संचयः, ओघः, पुंजः, स्तोमः.

CONGEST, *v. t.* राशीकृ 8 U, संचि 5 U, पिंडीकृ, घनीकृ. –ION, *s.* (of blood) रक्तावष्टंभः, असृक्चयः, रक्तसंचयः.

CONGLOBATE, *a.* एकपिंडीभूत. –*v. t.* गोलीकृ 8 U, एकपिंडीकृ.

CONGLOMERATE, *v. t.* राशीकृ 8 U, संचि 5 U, संभृ 3 U, एकपिंडीकृ, समाक्षिप् 6 P. –ION, *s.* समुपचयनं, एकीकरणं. 2 एकराशिः, एकपिंडः.

CONGLUTINATE, *v. t.* संयुज् 10, संश्लिष् c., संधा 3 U; संरुह् c. (रोपयति) (of wounds). –*v. i.* pass. of roots above. –ION, *s.* संयोगः, संधिः,, संधानं. 2 संरोपणं.

CONGRATULATE, *v. t.* अभिनंद् 1 P or c., (तापसीभिरभिनंद्यमाना S. 4); gen. ex. by दिष्ट्या with वृध् 1 A or c., (चित्ररथहंसौ दिष्ट्या वर्धयितुं Ka. 365); दिष्ट्या सुतमुखदर्शनेन आयुष्मान्वर्धते (S. 7) 'you are to be c. ed upon seeing your son's face', or 'I c. you upon seeing' &c. –ION, *s.* धन्यवादः, अभिनंदनं, दिष्ट्या वर्धनं. –ORY, *a.* अभिनंदक, धन्यवादसूचक.

CONGREGATE, *v. t.* समाचि 5 U, समाहृ 1 P; *See* COLLECT. –*v. i.* संमिल् 6 P, सं-इ 2 P; *See* ASSEMBLE. –ION, *s.* सभा, परिषद् *f.*, संसद् *f.*, समाजः. 2 समवायः, निवहः, गणः, समाहारः, समुदायः. –IONAL, *a.* सामाजिक (की *f.*), सभ्य.

CONGRESS, *s.* सभा, परिषद् *f.*, संसद् *f.*, मेलकः, समाजः, सदस् *f. n.* 2 संघट्टः, समाघातः.

CONGRUOUS, *a.* योग्य, उचित, संगत, अविरुद्ध, अनुगुण, अनुरूप, सदृश (शी *f.*), संबद्ध. –LY, *adv.* युक्तं, अनुरूपं, संगतं. –CONGRUITY, CONGRUENCE, *s.* संगतता, अनुरूपता, युक्तता, सादृश्यं; oft. ex. by क्व-क्व; 'what c. is there between this (youthful) age and this restraint of passions' क्वेदं वयः क्वेयमिंद्रियाणामुपशांतिः (Ka. 135).

CONJECTURE, *v. t.* तर्क् 10, अनुमा 3 A, 2 P, ऊह् 1 A; उत्प्रेक्ष् 1 A, (किमुत्प्रेक्षसे कुतस्त्योयमिति U. 4). –*s.* तर्कः, वितर्कः, ऊहः-हनं, अनुमानं; 'your c. is clear (you have rightly c. ed)' प्रसन्नः-उपपन्नः-न्ते तर्कः. –AL, *a.* आनुमानिक (की *f.*). –ALLY, *adv.* अनुमानेन, सवितर्कं, अनुमानपूर्वकं.

CONJOIN, *v. t.* संयुज् 7 U, 10, संश्लिष् c., संधा 3 U; 'c. ed in bonds of friendship' मित्रभावेन वर्तमानाः, परस्परानुरक्ताः. –*v. i.* संयुज्-संश्लिष्-संधा pass. –ED, CONJOINT, *a.* संहत, संयुक्त, संश्लिष्ट, संबद्ध. –LY, *adv.* समं, सहितं, संहत *a.*, संभूय.

CONJUGAL, *a.* वैवाहिक (की *f.*); oft. ex. by दंपती; 'c. love' दंपत्योः प्रेम; 'c. fidelity' अव्यभिचारः; सतीत्वं, पातिव्रत्यं.

CONJUGATE, *v. t.* रूपाणि आख्या 2 P. –ION, *s.* गणः; '1st c.' भ्वादिगणः.

CONJUNCT, *a.* संयुक्त, संश्लिष्ट; 'a c. consonant' संयोगः, योगः. –ION, *s.* संयोगः, योगः, संश्लेषः, ससर्गः, समागमः, संगमः, संगः. 2 समुच्चयः; 'c. of planets' संगमः; 'lunar c.' अमावास्या, अमा. –IVE, *a.* संयुक्त, संश्लिष्ट, यौगिक (की *f.*). –URE, *s.* योगः, संयोगः, संधिः. 2 अवसरः, समयः, प्रस्तावः.

CONJURE, *v. t.* मुह् c., मंत्रैर्वशं नी 1 P; मायां कृ 8 U, अभिचर् 1 P. 2 सशपथं आदिश् 6 P, शप् c.; 'I c. thee by my life (soul)' शापितासि मम जीवितेन (Mal. 8); अभ्यर्थ् 10 A, सशपथं संबुध् c. 3 (in mind) अनु-सं-स्मृ 1 P; चिंत् 10. –*v. i.* सशपथं एकमत्यं-कूटं-कृ 8 U, संशप् 1 U. –ATION, *s.* माया, इंद्रजालं, कुहकः, मंत्रः. 2 शापनं. 3 सशपथः संकल्पः, संशपनं. –ER, *s.* इंद्र-ऐंद्र-जालिकः, मायिन् *m.*, आहितुंडिकः, कुहककृत् *m.*, कुहकाजीवः.

CONNATE, *a.* सहज, एककालोत्पन्न, सहजात.

CONNATURAL, *a.* सहज; एकस्वभाव.

CONNECT, *v. t.* संबंध् 9 P, अनुबंध्; संयुज् 7 U, 10, संश्लिष् c., संधा 3 U, व्यतिषंज् 1 P, संनह् 4 P,

संयु 2 P. -ED, *a.* संयुक्त, संबद्ध, अन्वित, सान्वय. 2 अविच्छेद, अविरत, अविच्छिन्न; 'a c. narrative' कथाप्रबंध:. -ION, *s.* संयोग:, अनुषंग:, संसर्ग:, संग:; 'in c. with' अनुबध्य, उद्दिश्य, अधिकृत्य. 2 संबंध:, संपर्क:, अन्वय:. संदर्भ:, समन्वय:. 3 बंधु:, बांधव:, ज्ञाति:; 'to have c. with' संगम् 1 A, अभिगम् 1 P.

CONNIVE, *v. i.* (at) कामत: उपेक्ष् 1 A, ज्ञानं निह्नु 2 A. 2 क्षम् 1 A, सह् 1 A. 3 अक्षि संकुच् 1 P. -ANCE, *s.* उपेक्षा, ज्ञानापह्नव:, कामत: उपेक्षा. 2 क्षमा. 3 अक्षिसंकोचनं.

CONNOISSEUR, *s.* गुणज्ञ:, परीक्षक:, अभिज्ञ:.

CONNUBIAL, *a.* वैवाहिक (की *f.*); दंपती in comp.; 'c. love' दंपतीस्नेह:.

CONQUER, *v. t.* जि 1 P, वि-परा-जि 1 A, अभि-परा-भू 1 P. 2 निग्रह् 9 P, नि-सं-यम् 1 P, दम् c. (दमयति), वशीकृ 8 U, स्वायत्तीकृ; 'one who has c.-ed his passions' जितेंद्रिय:, संयतेंद्रिय:, वशी, दांत:, संयमी. -ABLE, *a.* जेय, अभिभवनीय. -OR, *s.* जेतृ *m.*, विजेतृ, जयिन् *m.*, जित् in comp.; विश्वजित् 'c. of the world'. -CONQUEST, *s.* जय:, विजय:, वशीकरणं, अभिभव:, जयनं, स्वायत्तीकरणं. 2 जितप्रदेश:.

CONSANGUINEOUS, *a.* एकशरीर, एकपिंड; सपिंड, सगोत्र. -CONSANGUINITY, *s.* सगोत्रता, सपिंडता; एकशरीरान्वय:, संबंधित्वं.

CONSCIENCE, *s.* सदसद्विचारशक्ति *f.*, संज्ञानं; oft. ex. by मनस् *n.*, अंत:करणं; 'biting of c.' पश्चात्ताप:, मनस्ताप:. —CONSCIENTIOUS, *a.* निर्व्याज, अमाय, शुद्धमति, न्यायपरायण, ऋजुप्रकृति. 2 पुण्यात्मन्, पुण्यशील, न्यायवर्तिन् (नी *f.*). -LY, *adv.* शुद्धमनसा, निर्व्याजं, शुद्धभावेन. -NESS, *s.* मतिशुद्धि *f.*; शुचिता, पुण्यशीलत्वं.

CONSCIONABLE, *a.* न्याय्य, योग्य, यथार्थ. -CONSCIONABLY, *adv.* यथार्थं, धर्मत:, न्यायेन.

CONSCIOUS, *a.* Ex. by ज्ञ, विद् or अभिज्ञ in comp., or by verbs for 'know' q. v.; 'not c. of pain' वेदनानभिज्ञ; 'I am perfectly c. of my defects' स्वदोषान् दृढं खलु जाने. 2 सचेतन, सतर्क, ज्ञानिन् (नी *f.*), प्रतिबोधवत् (ती *f.*); 'to be c. of' ज्ञा 9 P; विभू c., (नात्मानमपि विभावयति S. 4), चित् 10 A; *See* KNOW. -LY, *adv.* ज्ञानात्, बुद्धिपूर्वं, ज्ञानत:, कामत:. -NESS, *s.* ज्ञानं, उपलब्धि *f.*, चेतना, चैतन्यं, संज्ञा, वेदनं, अनुभव:, बोध:, प्रतिबोध:.

CONSCRIPT, *s.* नवयोद्धृ *m.* -*a.* लिखितनामन्.

CONSECRATE, *v. t.* (an idol) प्रतिष्ठा c (प्रतिष्ठापयति); पवित्रीकृ 8 U, संस्कृ, अभि-अनु-मंत्र् 10 A, (वामदेवानुमंत्रितोऽश्व: U. 2). 2 अभिषिच् 6 P, प्रोक्ष् 1 P. 3 उप-प्र-विनि-युज् 7 A, 10, निक्षिप् 6 P, वि-उत्-सृज् 6 P, उपक्लृप् c. -*a.*,-ED, संस्कृत, प्रतिष्ठापित, विनियोजित, उपकल्पित. -ER, *s.* संस्कर्तृ *m.*, प्रतिष्ठापक:. -ION, *s.* संस्कार:, प्रतिष्ठापनं. 2 उत्सर्ग:, विनियोग:, उपयोग:.

CONSECUTION, *s.* क्रम:, अनुक्रम:, प्रबंध:, अन्वय:, परंपरा, श्रेणी, माला. —CONSECUTIVE, *a.* क्रमागत, अनुपूर्व; अविरत, निरंतर, सप्रबंध, संतत. -LY, *adv.* क्रमेण, यथाक्रमं, यथापूर्वं; अविरतं, अविच्छेदं. -NESS, *s.* आनुपूर्व्य, अविच्छेद:, प्रबंध:, संततता.

CONSENT, *v. i.* संमन्-अनुमन् 4 A, अनुमुद् 1 A, अनुज्ञा 9 U; ग्रह् 9 P, स्वीकृ 8 U; *See* AGREE. -*s.* संमति *f.*-तं, अनुमति *f.* -तं, अनुज्ञा, अनुमोदनं. 2 मतैक्यं, एकचित्तता, ऐक्यं. 3 इच्छा, काम:; 'against one's c.' अनिच्छया, संमतिव्यतिरेकेण, बलात्, बलेन; 'c. in writing' संमतिपत्रं; 'take the c. of' अनुमन् c., (भूयोपि सखीजनमनुमानयिष्यामि S. 3). -IENT, *a.* एकमत, एकचित्त, संमत. -INGLY, *adv.* संमत्या; कामत:, संमतिपूर्वं.

CONSENTANEOUS, *a.* *See* FIT.

CONSEQUENCE, *s.* फलं, परिणाम:, उदर्क:, उत्तरं, उत्तरफलं. 2 गौरवं, महिमन् *m.*, गुरुता, प्रतिष्ठा, प्रभाव:; 'of no c.' निरर्थक, यत्किंचन. 3 सिद्धि *f.*; कार्यं, प्रयोजनं, निमित्तं. 4 अनुमानं, ऊहनं, अभ्यूह:; 'in c. of this' अत:, अस्मात्कारणात्, अस्माद्धेतो:, अनेन हेतुना; 'as a c. of thy efforts' तव यत्नसामर्थ्यात्; 'immediate c.' सांदृष्टिकं; 'necessary c.' कार्यवश:; 'visible c.' दृष्टार्थ:. —CONSEQUENT, *a.* आनुषंगिक (की *f.*), अनुवर्तिन् (नी *f.*); oft. ex. by फलं; 'c. upon his coming' तदागमनफलं.-*s.* अनुषंग:, फलं, परिणाम:. -IAL, *a.* आनुषंगिक, अनुवर्तिन्. 2 मानिन्, सगर्व; *See* ARROGANT.-LY, *adv.* इति हेतो:, अत:, तन्निमित्तेन, तदनुसारेण; तदर्थं, इति, अनेन हेतुना, अस्मात्कारणात्.

CONSERVE, *v. t.* संरक्ष् 1 P, पा c. (पालयति), संधृ 10, गुप् 1 P. 2 संधा 3 U, उपस्कृ 8 U. -*s.* मिष्टं, मोदक:; संचितं, उपस्कर:, व्यंजनं. -ATION, *s.* रक्षा संरक्षणं, पालनं, गुप्ति *f.*, क्षेम:. -ATIVE, *a.* संरक्षक, पालक. 2 नवविद्वेषिन् (णी *f.*), स्थितिपालक.-ATOR, *s.* रक्षक:, पालक:. -ATORY, *s.* रक्षास्थानं, आधार:, रक्षणस्थानं-शाला.

CONSIDER, *v. t.* विचर् c., विमृश् 6 P, आ-समा-पर्या-लोच् 10, वि-सं-चिंत् 10, समीक्ष् 1 A, (न धर्मवृद्धेषु वय: समीक्ष्यते K. v. 16); ध्यै 1 P, संदृश् 1 A, अवधृ 10, अवेक्ष्. 2 मन् 4 A, संभू c., तर्क् 10, समर्थ् 10, विगण् 10, आकल् 10, (स्वशोमपि पावनमाकलयंति Ka. 108). 3 परीक्ष्, निरूप् 10, अवेक्ष्, अनुसंधा 3 U, वि-विच् 3, 7 U. 4 पूज् 10, अर्च् 10, मन् c., प्रत्युपकृ; सं-परि-तुष् c. -ABLE, *a.* अस्तो-

क, गुरु, अनल्प, प्रचुर, भूरि, महत् (ती *f.*). 2 मान्य, आर्य, पूज्य. –ABLY, *adv.* अतीव, भूरि, अति-सु-pr., भृशं, अनल्पं, अत्यंतं. –ATE, *a.* समीक्ष्य-विमृश्य-कारिन् (णी *f.*). 2 कृतावधान ; आदृत, दत्तादर, अप्रमत्त, अवहित. –ATELY, *adv.* समीक्ष्य, विमृश्य, अवेक्ष्या, अप्रमत्तं, अवधानतः, सावधानं. –ATION, *s.* विचारः, विचारणा, आलोचना, विमर्शः, समीक्षा, चिंता. 2 विवेचनं, निरूपणं, चर्चा, परीक्षणं. 3 आदरः, अपेक्षा, अवेक्षा. 4 कारणं, निमित्तं, हेतुः. 5 गौरवं, गुरुता, प्रतिष्ठा. 6 पूजा, संभावना, आदरः. 7 प्रतिफलं, पारितोषिकं; 'in c. of' अपेक्षया in comp., समीक्ष्य, आलोच्य, विचार्य; प्रथममिति प्रेक्ष्य भगवतैकोपराधो मर्षयितव्यः (S. 4) 'in c. of its being the first' &c.

CONSIGN, *v. t.* निक्षिप् 6 P, न्यस् 4 U, दा 3 U, 1 P, ऋ c. (अर्पयति), प्रतिपद् c.; 'c. to the flames' अग्निसात्कृ 8 U. 2 उप-प्र-विनियुज् 7 A, 10. –MENT, *s.* अर्पणं, न्यसनं, प्रतिपादनं.

CONSIST, *v. i.* (of, in) Ex. by रूप, आत्मक, मय (यी *f.*) in comp.; 'Ojas c. s in abundance of compounds' समासभूयस्त्वरूपं त्वं नाम ओजः; 'body's ornament c. s in true knowledge' सत्यज्ञानात्मकं शरीरभूषणं; *See* COMPOSE. 2 संवृत् 1 A, संस्था-संभू 1 P. –ENCE, *s.* घनता, सांद्रता, श्यानता. 2 स्थिरता, दृढता. 3 अविरोधः, आनुरूप्यं. –ENCY, *s.* संगतता, संवादः, अविरोधः, आनुरूप्यं. 2 स्थिरता, अचापल्यं. –ENT, *a.* अविरुद्ध, सदृश (शी *f.*), योग्य, अनुरूप, संवादिन् (नी *f.*); 'his conduct is c. with his words' तस्याचरणं (कर्म) वचसा न विवदते. वचसो न विरुद्धं, वचसा न विसंवदति; 'in-c.' विसंवादिन्, विरुद्ध; परार्थमुद्यमभृतः स्वार्थाविरोधेन (Bh. I. 74) 'c. ly with their own interests.' 2 स्थिर, अचपल, अलोल. 3 दृढ, घन, सांद्र, श्यान. –ENTLY, *adv.* अविरुद्धं, अविरोधेन, अनुसारतः. –ING, *a.* Ex. by मय (यी *f.*), आत्मक (आत्मिका *f.*) in comp.; 'c. for the most part' ex. by भूयिष्ठ affixed ; 'assembly c. of learned men' अभिरूपभूयिष्ठा परिषद् (S. 1).

CONSISTORY, *s.* पुरोहितसभा.

CONSOCIATE, *See* ASSOCIATE.

CONSOLE, *v. t.* आ-समा-श्वस् c., सां (शां) त्व् 10, विनुद् c., अभ्युपपद् 4 A, (रतिमभ्युपपत्तुमातुरां K. IV. 25). 2 शोकमपह 1 P, सुस्थ-प्रकृतिस्थ-*a.* कृ 8 U. –ATION, *s.* आश्वासः-सनं, सांत्वनं, विनोदनं, समाश्वासनं. –ATORY, *a.* सांत्वनशील, आश्वासिन् (नी *f.*), शोकापहारक, शांतिद, सुखावह. –ER, *s.* आश्वासकः, विनोदकः.

CONSOLIDATE, *v. t.* संहन् 2 P, एकीकृ 8 U, घनीकृ, संस्था c. (स्थापयति). –*v. i.* घनीभू, स्थिरीभू, संहन् pass. –ION, *s.* घनीकरणं-भवनं, संहति *f.*, संस्थापनं, समाहरणं, एकीकरणं.

CONSONANT, *s.* व्यंजनं; 'conjunct c.' संयोगः, योगः. –*a.* अविरुद्ध, अनुसारिन् (णी *f.*), अनुरूप, योग्य, अनुगुण. –LY, *adv.* अनुसारेण, अनुरूपं. –CONSONANCE, *s.* अविरोधः, अनुसारः, अनुरोधः, आनुरूप्यं.

CONSONOUS, *a.* एकताल, एकस्वर.

CONSORT, *s.* Husband or wife, q. v. 2 सहवासिन् *m.*, संगिन् *m.* –*v. i.* सह वस् or चर् 1 P; संगम् 1 A, संयुज् pass.; 'well c. ed' सुसंगत. –ION, *s.* साहित्यं, साहचर्यं, संसर्गः.

CONSPICUOUS, *a.* व्यक्त, सुप्रकाश, सुस्पष्ट, पुरःस्फुरत् (ती-न्ती *f.*), प्रत्यक्ष. 2 उत्कृष्ट, निरतिशय, प्रमुख, विशिष्ट. –LY, *adv.* स्पष्टं, व्यक्तं; विशिष्टतया. –NESS, *s.* व्यक्तता, स्पष्टता, विशिष्टता, उत्कृष्टता.

CONSPIRE, *v. i.* उपजप् 1 P, कूटं रच् 10, कुसाहित्यं कृ 8 U, कूटार्थं संशप् 1 U. 2 संमिल् 6 P, अनुकूल *a.* भू; 'all things c. ed to make him happy' सर्वं तस्य सुखायाकल्पत-अभवत्. –ACY, *s.* उपजापः, कपटप्रबंधः, कुसाहित्यं, कुमंत्रणा; 'c. against the king' राजद्रोहः, द्रोहः. –ATOR, *s.* उपजापकः, कुसंसर्गिन् *m.*, संशप्तकः, शपथबद्धः. 2 राजद्रोहिन् *m.* 3 विश्वासघातकः.

CONSTABLE, *s.* दंड-यष्टि-धरः; राजपुरुषः.

CONSTANT, *a.* स्थिर, दृढ, अचल, निश्चल. 2 शाश्वत (ती *f.*), सतत, प्रसक्त, अविरत, अनवरत, नित्य, सनातन (नी *f.*), निरंतर; 'c. wife' सती, पतिव्रता. –LY, *adv.* सततं, अनवरतं, अविरतं, अभीक्ष्णं, नित्यं, अनिशं, अजस्रं, सर्वदा, सर्वकालं. –CONSTANCY, *s.* स्थैर्यं, स्थिरता, निश्चलता, दृढता. 2 अभिनिवेशः, निर्बंधः. 3 सातत्यं, अविरामः, नैरंतर्यं. 4 दृढा भक्तिः, दृढसौहृदं.

CONSTELLATION, *s.* राशिः, राशिनक्षत्रं ; तारासमूहः, भगणः.

CONSTERNATION, *s.* संत्रासः, भीति *f.*, व्याकुलत्वं, साध्वसं, उद्वेगः, संभ्रमः.

CONSTIPATE, *v. t.* अवरुध् 7 U, अवष्टंभ् 9 P, बंध् 9 P, पिनह् 4 P. 2 निबिडीकृ 8 U. –ION, *s.* मलावरोधः, मलावष्टंभः, विड्ग्रहः, गुदग्रहः, बद्धकोष्ठः.

CONSTITUTE, *v. t.* रच् 10, निर्मा 3 A, विधा 3 U; gen. ex. by आत्मक, रूप, मय (यी *f.*) in comp., or by भू 1 P, अस् 2 P; 'we c. thy army' तव सैन्यं वयं स्मः; 'what c. s greatness' महिमा केन जायते; *See* COMPOSE. 2 संस्था c. (स्थापयति), प्रतिष्ठा c.; नियुज् 7 A, 10, समादिश् 6 P. –ION, *s.* रचना, घटना, निर्माणं. 2 अवस्था, दशा, रूपं, वृत्ति *f.*, भावः. 3 व्यवस्था; विधियंत्रणं, नियमः. 4 राजनीति *f.*, राज्यव्यवस्था. 5 प्रकृति *f.*, स्वभावः, शरीरावस्था; जन्म-प्रकृति-स्वभावः; 'of a sickly c.' जन्म-

रोगिन्, अशक्त, प्रकृतिदुर्बल. -IONAL, *a.* विध्यनुसारिन्, व्यवस्थानुरूप. 2 प्रकृति in comp. -IONALLY, *adv.* विध्यनुसारेण,व्यवस्थानुपूर्वं. -CONSTITUENT, *a.* घटक, रचक; 'c. parts' घटकावयवाः, घटकाः, अंगानि. 2 वास्तव (वी *f.*), सारभूत; 'c. members of a state' राज्यांगानि. -*s.* Ex. by *a.* 2 नियोजकः.

CONSTRAIN, *v. t.* बलात्कृ c., प्रवृत् c., प्रेर् c.; gen. ex. by causal of verbs; *See* COMPEL. 2 नि-अव-रुध् 7U, नियंत्र् 10, नि-सं-यम् 1P; 'c. ed silence' बलाद्धृतं मौनं; 'c. ed to be silent' नियंत्रितवाक्, यंत्रितकथ. -CONSTRAINT, *s.* बलं, बलात्कारः; 'by c.' बलात्, बलेन, अनिच्छत् *a.*, प्रसह्य. 2 अवश्यकता. 3 यंत्रणा, निरोधः, अवरोधः; 'c. of modesty' ह्रीयंत्रणा.

CONSTRICT, CONSTRINGE, *v. t.* संकुच् 1 P, आकुंच् c., संहृ 1 P. -ION, *s* संकोचः, आकुंचनं, संहरणं.

CONSTRUCT, *v. t.* निर्मा 3 A, 2 P or c. (मापयति), रच् 10, विधा 3 U, घट् c. (घटयति), प्रक्लृप् c., कृ 8 U. -ION, *s.* रचना, निर्माणं, विधानं, &c. 2 अन्वयः, संबंधः, पदयोजना-नं. 3 अर्थः, आशयः; 'do not put a bad c. upon his words' तस्य वचसि दुराशयं मा कल्पय-आरोपय. -IVE, *a.* निर्मातृ, प्रकल्पक, निर्माण or विधान in comp.; निर्माणचातुर्यं 'c. skill' &c.

CONSTRUE, *v. t.* अन्वयं कथ् 10, अर्थं व्याख्या 2 P, युज् 10; तत्परत्वेनैव वेदांतवाक्यानि योजयंति (S. B. 91) 'c. as referring to it'; 'to be c. ed' संबंध् pass., (इदं पदमेवं न संबध्यते).

CONSTUPRATION, *s.* कन्यादूषणं, धर्षणं, बलात्काराभिगमः.

CONSUBSTANTIAL, *a.* एकशरीर, एकमूर्ति.

CONSULT, *v.* संमंत्र् 10 A, संवद् 1 P or c., संभाष् 1 A. 2 विमृश् 6 P, चिंत् 10, विचर् c.; 'you must c. public good also' जनहितमपि तावत् त्वया मनसि कार्यमेव-अवेक्षणीयं; 'do not c. your private good' स्वहितपरायणो मा भूः; 'let astrologers be c. ed' सांवत्सरिकैः संवाद्यताम्; 'you have given this order, having c. ed (with) my very heart' मम हृदयेन सह संमंत्र्यादिष्टवानसि (Mu. 1); 'c. with oneself' मनसा विचर् c., आत्मगतं चिंत्. 3 निरूप् 10, समीक्ष् 1 A, आ-पर्या-लोच् 10; 'in c.-ing a horoscope' जन्मपत्रिकां विमृशन्, पत्रिकावलोकनेन शुभाशुभं पर्यालोचयन्. -ATION, *s.* मंत्रणा-णं, विचारणं; विमर्शः, विचारः; आलोचनं, संवादः; 'private c.' गूढमंत्रणं. -ATIVE, *a.* संमंत्र्य; मंत्रणयोग्य.

CONSUME, *v. t.* क्षि c. (क्षपयति), विनश् c.; 'c. by fire' निर्दह् 1 P. 2 उपयुज् 7 A, 10, उपयुज्य-उपभुज्य-निरवशेषीकृ 8 U. -*v. i.* क्षि pass., नश् 4 P, अवसद् 1 P, परिहा pass. -ER, *s.* नाशकः; विनियोजकः. -CONSUMPTION, *s.* क्षयः, शोषः, यक्ष्मन् *m.* 2 नाशः, क्षयः, अवसादः. 3 उपयोगः, उपभोगः, व्ययः, विनियोगः. -CONSUMPTIVE, *a.* क्षयिन्-क्षयरोगिन् (णी *f.*).

CONSUMMATE, *v. t.* समाप् c.; *See* COMPLETE. -*a.* संपूर्ण, निखिल, अन्यून. 2 परम, उत्कृष्ट, अग्रणीः; 'a c. rogue' शठाग्रणीः. -ION, *s.* समापनं, निष्पत्ति *f.* सिद्धि *f.* 2 उत्कर्षः, परमा गतिः.

CONTACT, *s.* सं-,स्पर्शः, संपर्कः, संसर्गः, संयोगः, आसंगः, व्यतिकरः, परामर्शः; 'in close bodily c.' अंगांगि *ind.*

CONTAGION, *s.* स्पर्शः, स्पर्शसंचारः. -CONTAGIOUS, *a.* स्पर्शजन्य, स्पर्शसंचारिन् (णी *f.*), संसर्गज, संपर्कीय; 'a c. disease' मारी.

CONTAIN, *v. t.* धृ 1 P, 10, आदा 3 A, परिग्रह् 9 P, धा 3 U, भृ 3 U; 'c. ing' ex. by धर-धारिन्-भृत् in comp.; 'c. ing water' तोयभृत्; oft. ex. by गर्भ, पूर्ण, आत्मक in comp.; अंबुगर्भः मेघः, शुकगर्भकोटरं; अमृतपूर्णं पात्रं, &c. 2 निवार् 10, संयम् 1 P, निग्रह् 9 P; 'he could not c. his great joy' गुरुः प्रहर्षः प्रबभूव नात्मनि (R. III. 17). -ED, *a.* धृत, अंतर्गत, अंतर्भूत, अंतर्गणित; वर्तिन् (नी *f.*), स्थ in comp. -ER, *s.* आधारः, धारिन्-भृत् in comp.; 'the relation between c. and contained' आधाराधेयभावः.

CONTAMINATE, *v. t.* दुष् c. (दूषयति), लिप् 6 P, कलंकयति-मलिनयति (D.). -ED, *a.* भ्रष्ट, दूषित, कलंकित, अपवित्र. -ION, *s.* दूषणं, कलंकः; अशौचं, भ्रष्टता, भ्रंशकारणं.

CONTEMN, *v. t.* अवमन् 4 A, अवज्ञा 9 U, अवधीर् 10 A, तिरस्कृ 8 U, अवगण् 10, न आदृ 6A, उपेक्ष् 1 A, लघूकृ, तृणाय मन्, परिभू 1 P. -ER, *s.* अवमंतृ *m.*, तिरस्कर्तृ *m.* —CONTEMPT, *s.* अवज्ञा, अवमानः-मानना, अवधीरणा, तिरस्कारः, अवगणना, अनादरः, परिभवः, उपेक्षा, अवहेलनं-ना. -IBLE, *a.* अवमंतव्य, तिरस्कार्य. 2 क्षुद्र, निकृष्ट, नीच; 'to make oneself c.' आत्मानं तिरस्कारास्पदं कृ, अवज्ञाभाजनं भू. -UOUS, *a.* अवमानिन् (नी *f.*), उपेक्षक, परिभाविन्, परिभावुक (की *f.*); सावज्ञ, सावमान. -UOUSLY, *adv.* सावज्ञं, सावमानं, उपेक्षया, सतिरस्कारं.

CONTEMPLATE. *v.* चिंत् 10; ध्यै 1 P; मनसा विचर् c., विमृश् 6 P. 2 निरूप् 10, निर्वर्ण् 10, अवेक्ष् 1 A, संदृश् 1 A, आलोच् 10, आलोक् 1 A, 10. 3 संकॢप् c., भू c. -ION, *s.* ध्यानं, चिंता, भावना, आलोचनं, विचारणा, विमर्शः; 'to be or have in c.' अभिप्र-इ 2 P, उद्दिश् 6 P. -IVE, *a.* ध्यानपर, चिंताशील, & sim. comp.; भावितात्मन्, चिंताविष्ट, समाधिस्थ. -OR, *s.* ध्यातृ *m.*

CONTEMPORARY, *a.* or *s.* समकालीन, एककालीन समानकाल; 'c. of that time' तदानींतन (नी *f.*); 'a c. poet' वर्तमानकविः (M. 1).

CONTEND, *v. i.* संयत् 1 A, विग्रह् 9 P, कलहायते (D.), विरुध् 7 U, प्रतिकृ 8 U, विवद् 1 A, युध् 4 A, स्पर्ध् 1 A. 2 वाग्युद्धं कृ, प्रत्यवस्था 1 A, (अपरे प्रत्यवतिष्ठंते S. B. 57). 3 यत्-चेष्ट् 1 A.–ER, *s.* विपक्षः, प्रतियोद्धृ *m.*, विवादिन् *m.*, प्रतियोगिन् *m.*, प्रतिपक्षः. –ING, *a.* विरोधिन् (नी *f.*); विवदमान, कलहशील. –CONTENTION, *s.* विवादः, विग्रहः, कलहः, कलिः, विप्रतिपत्ति *f.*, वाग्युद्धं, विप्रलापः; 'point (bone) of c.' विवादविषयः-वस्तु *n.* 2 संघर्षः, स्पर्धा. –CONTENTIOUS, *a.* कलहप्रिय, विवादिन्, विरोधिन्, कलह-विवादशील.

CONTENT, *a.* सं-,परि-,तुष्ट, तृप्त, निःस्पृह, वितृष्ण, प्रीत, प्रशांत, हृष्ट; 'to be c.' तुष् 4 P, तृप् 4 P, सं-परि-°; 'is c. with even little' स्वल्पकेनापि तुष्यति; 'poor and c. is rich and rich enough' संतोष एव पुरुषस्य परं निधानं. –*v. t.* तुष् c., तृप् c., सं-परि-°, नंद् c., प्री 9 P; 'c. s the eyes' कृतार्थयति चक्षुः. –*s.*, –MENT, *s.* सं-,परि-,तोषः, तृप्ति *f.*, प्रीति *f.*, अस्पृहा, वितृष्णा, धृति *f.*, कामनिवृत्ति *f.*; 'water to the heart's c.' प्रकामजलं. 2 (c. s) घनफलं (गोलस्य); पूरकं, अंतर्गतं; 'c. s of a letter' लेखार्थः; 'if so, I shall know its c. s' तेन ह्यस्य गृहीतार्थो भवामि (V. 2); 'table of c. s' सूचीपत्रं, अनुक्रमणिका. –ED, *a.* तुष्ट, तृप्त, प्रीत, &c.; 'keep c.' अनुरंज् c., प्री 9 P. –EDLY, *adv.* प्रीत्या, संतोषेण, तुष्ट्या.

CONTERMINOUS, *a.* सीमावासिन् (नी *f.*), समीप-निकट-वर्तिन्, पर्यंतस्थ.

CONTERRANEOUS, *a.* एकदेशज, सदेशज.

CONTEST, *v. i.* युध् 4 A, विवद् 1 A. –*v. t.* प्रतिकूलयति (D.), प्रति-वि-रुध् 7 U; *See* CONTEND. –*s.* कलहः, कलिः, विवादः, वाग्युद्धं, विप्रलापः, विप्रतिपत्ति *f.*; 'subject of c.' वादबीजं, विवादास्पदं, वादविषयः. –ED, *a.* वादग्रस्त, वादविषयीभूत; 'un-c. possession' अपरवोज्झितो भोगः (V. M. 11).

CONTEXT, *s.* अन्वयः, संदर्भः, संबंधः, प्रकरणं (S. B.); प्राज्ञस्याहि प्रकरणं विततं वर्तते &c. –*a.* संश्लिष्ट, संधित, संयुक्त. –URE, *s.* संस्थिति *f.*, विन्यासः.

CONTIGUITY, *s.* सन्निकर्षः, सन्निधिः, सन्निधानं, समीपता, नैकट्यं. —CONTIGUOUS, *a.* सन्निकृष्ट, समीप, सन्निहित, संलग्न, आसन्न, समीपस्थ, समीप-निकट-वर्तिन् (नी *f.*); 'c. ground' पर्यंतभूमि *f.*, परिसरः –LY, *adv.* समीपं-पे, संनिकृष्टं, परिसरे.

CONTINENT, *a.* जितेंद्रिय, संयत, संयमिन् (नी *f.*); यतमैथुन, ऊर्ध्वरेतस्, निवृत्तकाम, वशिन्, दांत. 2 परिमित. –*s.* वर्षः-र्षं; 'c. of India' भरतवर्षः; महाद्वीपः-पं. –AL, *a.* महाद्वीपीय, वर्षीय. –CONTINENCE, *s.* संयमः, इंद्रियनिग्रहः, दमः, जितेंद्रियत्वं, वशित्वं.

CONTINGENCY, *s.* दैवयोगः-घटनं, दैवं, यदृच्छा. 2 अतर्कितोपनतः वृत्तांतः; oft. ex. by words for 'doubtful' q. v. —CONTINGENT, *a.* अनिश्चित, संदिग्ध, दैवायत्त, दैववश, आगंतुक-आपातिक (की *f.*); अतर्कितोपनत, असमर्थितोपनत. –*s.* भागः, अंशः. 2 सैन्यदलं. –LY, *adv.* दैवात्, दैववशात्, यदृच्छया, अतर्कितं.

CONTINUE, *v. t.* प्रवृत् c., प्रसंज् c., प्रस्तु 2 U or c., निर्वह् c. 2 प्रतन् 8 U, दीर्घीकृ 8 U. –*v. i.* प्रवृत् 1A; gen. ex. by आस् 2 A, स्था 1 P, with present part., or not 'cease' q. v.; 'he c. ed to quarrel' कलहं कुर्वन्नास्त, कलहं कुर्वन्न व्यरमत्. –AL, –OUS, *a.* प्रसक्त, निरंतर, अविरत, अविच्छिन्न, संतत, सतत, नित्य, सनातन, अश्रांत; 'a c. story' कथाप्रबंधः. –ALLY, –OUSLY, *adv.* नित्यं, सर्वदा, सततं, अनवरतं, अविश्रांतं, &c. –ANCE, –ATION, –ITY, *s.* प्रबंधः, प्रसक्ति *f.*, अविरामः, अविच्छेदः, सातत्यं, संतानं, अनुबंधः; 'c. of sorrow' शोकानुबंधः; 'c. in life' स्थिति *f.*, अवस्थानं, जीवितं; 'continuation (of a story)' शेषः, उत्तरभागः-खंडः, परिशेषः; श्रेणी, अनुक्रमः. –ATOR, *s.* प्रवर्तकः, निर्वाहकः, उत्तरसाधकः.

CONTORT, *v. t.* आकुंच् c., वक्रीकृ 8 U, कुटिलीकृ; 'having the features c. ed' विकृताकारः. –ION, *s.* आकुंचनं, वक्रता, वैरूप्यं, विकृति *f.*

CONTOUR, *s.* आकारः, रूपं. 2 परि(री)णाहः, परिधिः; 'covering the c. s of the breasts' स्तनयुगपरिणाहाच्छादिन् (S. 1).

CONTRABAND, *a.* नि-प्रति-षिद्ध; धर्मविरुद्ध.

CONTRACT, *v. t.* संकुच् 1P, संकोचं नी 1 P, आकुंच् c., संहृ 1 P, समाकृष् 1P, संक्षिप् 6 P, संपीड् 10, ह्रस् c.; 'the body being c. ed through fear' भयसंपिंडितांगत्वात् (Ka. 34); 'c. ing the eye' अक्षिसंकोचेन. 2 अधिगम् 1 P, उपगम्; 'I c. ed friendship with him' तेन सह मित्रत्वं उपगतः, सख्यमबध्नां; 'c. acquaintance' परिचयं कृ; 'c. debt' ऋणं कृ, ऋणग्रस्त *a.* भू; 'c. a disease' व्याधिना अभिभू pass.; 'c. marriage' विवाहं कृ, दारान्परिग्रह् 9 P. –*v. i.* आ-सं-कुच् pass., संकोचं-या-इ-गम्, संहृ-संपीड्-संक्षिप् pass. 2 समयं कृ 8 U, पणं-संविदं-कृ, प्रतिपद् 4 A, संविद् 2 P. –*s.* समयः, संविद् *f.*, नियमः, पणः, अभ्युपगमः; 'written c.' नियमपत्रं; 'a sale c.' क्रयपत्रं; 'marriage c.' वाग्दानं, वाग्निश्चयः. –ED, *a.* आकुंचित, संक्षिप्त, संहृत, संपिंडित. 2 संकट, निरायत, संबाध. –ION, *s.* संकोचः-चनं, आकुंचनं, समाकर्षः, संपीडनं, संवृति *f.* 2 संक्षेपः-पणं.

—OR, *s.* कृतसंविद् *m.*, नियमकृत् *m.*, पणकर्तृ *m.*

CONTRADICT, *v. t.* विरुध् 7 U, प्रति-नि-षिध् 1 P, प्रत्याख्या 2 P, पराहन् 2 P, प्रतीपायते (D.); 'c. oneself' विप्रवद् 1 U, विसंवद् 1 P. —ION, *s.* विरोधः, प्रतिषेधः, प्रत्याख्यानं, विपक्षता, प्रतिबंधः. प्रतिकूलता. 2 प्रतिवादः, वचनविरोधः. 3 विप्रलापः. विरोधोक्ति *f.* 4 असंगति *f.*, विसंवादः, विरुद्धता. —ORY, *a.* विरुद्ध, विरोधिन् (नी *f.*), विपरीत, विरुद्धार्थ, प्रतीप, विसंवादिन्; परस्परविरुद्ध-विरोधिन्. 2 परस्परपराहत, संकुल, क्लिष्ट.

CONTRADISTINGUISH, *v. t.* विरुद्धगुणैः विशिष् 7 P or c. —CONTRADISTINCTION, *s.* विपरीतता, व्यतिरेकः, विपक्षता.

CONTRAPOSITION, *s.* संमुखस्थिति *f.*; प्रतिष्ठापनं.

CONTRARY, *a.* (in direction) संमुखागत, प्रतीप; gen. ex. by प्रति pr.; 'c. wind' प्रतिवातः. प्रतीपपवनः. 2 प्रतिकूल, विरोधिन् (नी *f.*). प्रति-वि-लोम. प्रतीप, विपरीत, विरुद्ध, विपक्ष, वैरिन्; oft. by इतर in comp.; 'the c. of true' सत्येतर. —*s.* विपर्ययः, विपरीतं, विपर्यासः, व्यतिक्रमः. 2 प्रतिपक्षः; 'c.-wise,' 'on the c.' प्रत्युत, पुनः, परंतु; 'to the c.' विपरीततया. —*adv.* —LY, *adv.* विपरीतं, विरुद्धं, प्रतिकूलं; 'c. to usage' आचारविरुद्धं, &c. —CONTRARIETY, *s.* वैपरीत्यं, विरोधः, विपर्ययः, प्रतिकूलता, विपक्षता, व्यत्ययः, व्यतिक्रमः.

CONTRAST, *v. t.* अंतरं-भेदं-दृश् c. or वर्ण् 10, परस्परविपर्ययेण उपमा 3 A. —*v. i.* विपर्यस् 4 P, विरुध् pass., विरुद्ध *a.* भू. —*s.* अंतरं, भेदः, विशेषः; oft. by क्व-क्व; क्व कंदमूलफलाशी शांतो मुनिजनः क्वायं रागप्रायः प्रपंचः (Ka. 151). 2 विरोधः, प्रतिपक्षता, व्यतिरेकः, व्यत्ययः, वैलक्षण्यं.

CONTRAVALLATION, *s.* परिखा, प्रतिकूपः.

CONTRAVENE, *v. t.* प्रति-वि-रुध् 7 U, व्याहन् 2 P, निषिध् 1 P; *See* OPPOSE. —CONTRAVENTION, *s.* व्याघातः, निषेधः, वि-प्रति-रोधः, प्रतिबंधः.

CONTRIBUTE, *v. t.* स्वं स्वं अंशं दा 3 U. 2 (to) उपकृ 8 U, प्रवृध् c., कृप् 1 A (with dat.); *See* CONDUCE. —ARY, *a.* एकराजाधीन. —ION, *s.* अंश-भाग-दानं. 2 अंशः, भागः, दत्तांशः, उद्धारः. —OR, *s.* अंशदातृ *m.* 2 साहाय्यकारिन् *m.*, उपकर्तृ *m.*, प्रवर्धकः.

CONTRITE, *a.* अनुशोकार्त, अनुशयपीडित, जातानुताप. —ION, *s.* पश्चात्तापः, अनुशयः, अनुतापः. —LY, *adv.* सानुशयं.

CONTRIVE, *v. t.* चिंत् 10, निर्मि 5 U, निर्णी 1 P, उह् c., क्लृप् c., युज् 7 U, 10, निरूप् 10, घट् c. (घटयति), संपध् 10, विधा 3 U. —*v. i.* उपायं चिंत्, उपायं युज्. —ANCE, *s.* उपायः, प्रयुक्ति *f.*, साधनं, कल्पना, योजना, अप-व्यप-देशः, उपायचिंतनं, कृति *f.* —ER, *s.* उपायज्ञः, उपायचिंतकः.

CONTROL, *v. t.* यम् 1 P, सं-नि-°, दम् c. (दमयति), वशं नी 1 P, जि 1 P, आवृ 5 U, वशीकृ 8 U, नि-विनि-ग्रह् 9 P, (passions &c.); निरुध् 7 U. 2 शास् 2 P, ईश् 2 A (gen.); कथंचिदीशा मनसां बभूवुः (K. III. 34) 'could hardly c. their mind'; नियंत्र् 10; 'un-c.ed speech' अनियंत्रिता वाणी; 'un-c.ed weeping' निरर्गलाः प्रलापाः; 'with passions c. ed' जितेंद्रियः, संयमी, वशी. —*s.* संयमः, निग्रहः, निरोधः, नियंत्रणा, दमनं; 'self-c.' आत्मसंयमः, निग्रहः, इंद्रियजयः, वशित्वं. 2 अधिकारः, वशः, प्रभुत्वं; 'under the king's c.' राजाधीन, नृपायत्त; 'mental c.' अंतर्यमनं, मनोदंडः. —LER, *s.* शास्तृ *m.*, अध्यक्षः, अधिकारिन् *m.*, अधिष्ठातृ *m.*, ईशः, प्रभुः.

CONTROVERSY, *s.* वादः, विचारः, विवादः, वादानुवादः, विप्रतिपत्ति *f.*, वितर्कः, वादयुद्धं, हेतुवादः. —AL, *a.* विवादसंबंधिन् (नी *f.*), वितर्किन्, (*s.*) in comp. —ALIST, *s.* वादिन् *m.*, तार्किन् *m.*, तार्किकः.

CONTROVERT, *v. t.* प्रत्याख्या 2 P, अधरीकृ 8 U, निरस् 4 U, निराकृ, खंड् 10. 2 विवद् 1 A, विचर् c. —ED, *a.* वादग्रस्त, विवादविषयीभूत. —IST, *s.* वादिन् *m.*, नैयायिकः, विवादकृत् *m.*, तार्किकः.

CONTUMACIOUS, *a.* धृष्ट, दुर्विनीत, दृप्त, सगर्व. 2 प्रतीप, प्रतिकूल, दुःशील. —LY, *adv.* सदर्पं, धृष्टतया. —CONTUMACY, *s.* धृष्टता, दुर्विनीतता; प्रतीपता, दुःशीलता.

CONTUMELY, *s.* अवज्ञा, निष्ठुर-परुष-वचनं, निष्ठुरता, निंदा, तिरस्कारः, अवमानना. —OUS, *a.* परुष, निष्ठुर, निंदक, अवमानिन् (नी *f.*). 2 सावज्ञ.

CONTUSE, *v. t.* मृद् 9 P, क्षुद् 7 U, पिष् 7 P; क्षण् 8 P, चूर्ण् 10. —ION, *s.* मर्दनं, निष्पेषः, क्षतं.

CONUNDRUM, *s.* प्रहेलिका, प्रवह्लिका.

CONVALESCENCE, *s.* स्वास्थ्यं, निरामयः, रोगोपशमः, प्रकृतिलाभः. —CONVALESCENT, *a.* निरामय, वीतरोग, प्रकृतिस्थ, नीरुज.

CONVENE, *v. t.* समाह्वे 1 P, साह्वानं एकत्र कृ 8 U, समानी 1 P; *See* ASSEMBLE. —*v. i.* संमिल् 6 P, सं-इ 2 P, एकत्र भू.

CONVENIENCE, *s.* सुखं, सोपकारत्वं, सुस्थता. 2 योग्यता, पात्रता; उचितसाधनं. 3 अवसरः: अवकाशः: 'in-c. ed by the shutting of the lotus' अंभोजविनिमीलनदुःस्थितः (Rat. 2); 'when it suits your c.' यथावसरं, अवसरं प्राप्य, कार्यांतरांतरायमंतरेण. —CONVENIENT, *a.* सुखकारक; उचित, अनुकूल, उपयुक्त; 'c. building' उचितसाधनयुक्तं भवनं; उपपन्न, यथाकाम, यथारुचि, यथोचित. —LY. *adv.* युक्तं, यथासुखं, यथावकाशं, यथावसरं; 'when may I c. ly see you' अन्यकार्यातिपातनंतरेण-कार्यांतराविरोधेन-भवान् कदा मया द्रष्टव्यः.

CONVENT, *s.* मठः, विहारः.

CONVENTICLE, *s.* सभा, समाजः, मेलकः. 2 गूढसभा.

CONVENTION, *s.* समयः, संविद् *f.*, नियमः, संकेतः. 2 सभा, संसद् *f.* 3 रूढि *f.*, लोकसंमति *f.*, आचारः. -AL, *a.* लौकिक (की *f.*), लोकसंमत, निरूढ, रूढ, सांकेतिक (की *f.*); 'c. usage' जनरूढिः, लोकाचारः. -ALISM. *s.* रूढि *f.*, आचारविधिः.

CONVERGE, *v. i.* संनि-नि-पत् 1 P, एकस्थानं-एककेंद्रं-प्रतिया 2 P, (with loc.), पंथानः सिद्धिहेतवस्त्वय्येव निपतंति (R. x. 26); 'c. to thee alone.' -ENCE, *s.* समवायः, संनिपातः. -ENT, *a.* एककेंद्राभिमुख (खी *f.*), संनिपातिन् (नी *f.*).

CONVERSE, *v. i.* सं-आ-लप् 1 P, संभाष् 1 A, संवद् 1 P, संवच् 2 P. 2 संसर्गं कृ 8 U, संवस् 1 P, संगम् 1 A, संव्यवह 1 P. -*s.* संलापः, संकथा, संभाषणं, संवादः. 2 संसर्गः, व्यवहारः, संगमः. 3 विपर्ययः, विपरीतं, व्यत्यासः, व्यतिक्रमः. -ANT, *a.* निपुण, चतुर, कुशल, विचक्षण, अभिज्ञ; कोविद, ज्ञ, विद्, in comp.; पटु, विशारद; 'c. with law' स्मृतिज्ञः; 'not c. with love matters' अनभ्यंतरे मदनगतस्य वृत्तांतस्य (S. 3). -ANCE, -ANCY, *s.* नैपुण्यं, पाटवं, चातुर्यं, विदग्धता, &c. -ATION, *s.* आ-सं-लापः, संभाषणं, संकथा, संवादः; कथायोगः, विश्रंभालापः. 2 आचारः, व्यवहारः, वृत्ति *f.* -LY, *adv.* विपर्ययेण, व्यतिक्रमेण, व्यत्ययेन, प्रतीपं.

CONVERT, *v. t.* विकृ 8 U, अन्यथा कृ, परिवृत् c.; oft. ex. by सात्; 'c. to ashes' भस्मसात्कृ; *See* REDUCE. 2 स्वधर्मं ग्रह् c.; स्व-पक्षं-मतं ग्रह् c.; 'to be c. ed' परधर्म-पक्षं-मतं-ग्रह् 9 P, स्वधर्मं &c. त्यज् 1 P. 3 प्र-उप-विनि-युज् 7 A, 10. 4 पापाद् विरम् c. (रमयति) or निवृत् c., कुमार्गं त्यज् c. -*v. i.* अन्यथा भू 1 P, भावांतरं या 2 P or प्राप् 5 P. 2 स्वधर्मं-पक्षं-मतं-त्यज् 1 P, परधर्मं &c. ग्रह् 9 P or आश्रि 1 U or अवलंब् 1 A or स्वीकृ. 3 पापाद्विरम् 1 P or निवृत् 1 A. -*s.* परधर्माश्रितः, परपक्ष-मत-अवलंबिन् *m.*, स्वधर्म-पक्ष-मत-त्यागिन् *m.* -CONVERSION, *s.* विकारः, विक्रिया, विकृति *f.*, परिवर्तः, विपर्ययः, भावांतरप्रापणं; 'c. to ashes' भस्मसात्करणं, भस्मीभवनं. 2 परधर्माश्रयः, परधर्म-पक्ष-मत-अवलंबनं, स्वधर्म-&c. त्यागः. 3 पापनिवृत्ति *f.*, कुमार्गत्यागः.

CONVEX, *a.* न्युब्ज, कूर्मपृष्ठाकार, आभोगवत् (ती *f.*). -ITY, *s.* न्युब्जता, आभोगः.

CONVEY, *v. t.* वह्-नी-हृ- 1 P, गम् c. (गमयति), प्राप् c., संचर् c. 2 ऋ c. (अर्पयति), दा 3 U. 3 (sense) गम् c., प्रतिपद् c., सूच् c. -ANCE, *s.* यानं, प्रवहणं, वाहनं, रथः. 2 नयनं, प्रापणं, समर्पणं; 'deed of c.' समर्पणपत्रं, क्रयलेख्यं. -ER, *s.* वाहकः, वाहिन् in comp.

CONVICT, *v. t.* अपराधं निर्णी 1 P, अपराधिन् *a.* (नी *f.*) स्था c. (स्थापयति), आधृष् c. -*s.*, -*a.*, -ED, *a.* निर्णीतापराधः, निश्चितदोषः, आधर्षितः, दृष्टदोषः. -ION, *s.* अपराधस्थापनं, अपराधनिर्णयः, दोषनिश्चयः, आधर्षणं.

CONVINCE, *v. t.* प्रति-इ c., प्रतीतिं कृ 8 U, उरीकर्तुं आनी 1 P, अभिज्ञा c. (ज्ञापयति); 'he was c. ed of his mistake' स्वभ्रममुद्दिश्य तस्य प्रतीतिः समजनि or अयं भ्रम एवासीदिति तस्य निश्चयो जातः; ताः स्वचारित्र्यमुद्दिश्य प्रत्याययतु मैथिली (R. xv. 73) 'c. them of her purity.' 2 संदेहं निराकृ or निरस् 4 U or अपनुद् 6 P. -ED, *a.* जातनिश्चय-प्रत्यय, छिन्नसंशय; 'I am c. that' &c. इति मे निश्चयः, इत्यसंदेहपदं. -ING, *a.* निर्णायक, प्रत्ययजनक, संशयच्छेदिन् (नी *f.*), निश्चायक. -CONVICTION, *s.* विश्वासः, प्रत्ययः, निश्चयः निर्णयः, दृढप्रत्ययः, दृढं मतं.

CONVIVIAL, *a.* उत्सवसंबंधिन् (नी *f.*), औत्साविक (की *f.*); 'a c. party' तुल्यभोजनं, सपीति *f.*

CONVOKE, *v. t.* समाह्वे 1 P, समाह्व 1 P, आह्वानेन एकत्र कृ 8 U. -CONVOCATION, *s.* समाह्वानं; समाह्वानविधिः. 2 सभा, समाजः, संसद् *f.*

CONVOLVE, *v. t.* आ-समा-वृत् c.

CONVOY, *v. t.* रक्षणार्थं अनुव्रज्, अनुगम् 1 P, अनु-परि-सं-सह-चर् 1 P. -*s.* पथि रक्षकः, सहचरः, परि-अनु-चरः.

CONVULSE, *v. t.* सं-वि-क्षुभ् c., कंप् c. 2 आकृष् 1 P, आकुंच् c., अप-तन् c., वि-आ-क्षिप् 6 P. -ION, *s.* सं-वि-क्षोभः, कंपः. 2 आक्षेपः, अपतानकः, आकर्षः. -IVE, *a.* आकर्षक, आक्षेपकर (री *f.*), विक्षेपिन् (णी *f.*); 'c. speech' गद्गदवाच् *f.*, गद्गदं; 'in a c. fit' आक्षेपाभिभूत.

CONY, *s.* शशः, शशकः.

COO, *v. t.* कूज् 1 P, कु 2 P, 1 A, वि-, रु 2 P.

COOK, *v. t.* पच् 1 P, श्रा 2 P or c. (श्रपयति), श्री 9 P; 'c. food' अन्नं संस्कृ 8 U, सिध् c. (साधयति), सिद्ध *a.* कृ; 'c. ing pot' पाकपात्रं, स्थाली; 'c. ed food' ओदनः-नं, सिद्धौदनः, सिद्धमन्नं. -*s.* पाचकः, सूपकारः, बल्लवः, सूदः. -ED, *a.* पक्व, सिद्ध, शृत, श्राण. -ERY, पाककला-विद्या; पाकसिद्धि-निष्पत्ति *f.* 2 पचनं, पाकः. -ROOM, *s.* पाकशाला, महानसः-सं.

COOL, *a.* शीतल, शीत, शिशिर, शीतस्पर्श, आर्द्र; (fig.) सुख, मृदु, सुखस्पर्श, कोमल; अनुष्ण, अतिग्म (rays). 2 प्रशांत, अनुद्वेग, धीर, अव्यग्र, असंभ्रांत, अव्याकुल. 3 वीतराग; *See* COLD. -*s.* शीतं, शीतलता; 'in the c. of evening' प्रशांते-अनुष्णे संध्यासमये. -*v. t* शीतलीकृ 8 U, आर्द्रयति (D.), निर्वा c. (वापयति), आर्द्रीकृ, तापं हृ 1 P; अन्यादृशा एव तेय निर्वापयति शरीरस्पर्शः (Mal. 6); शरीरनिर्वापणाय (S. 3). 2 (down) प्र-उप-शम् c.

(शमयति), विरम् c. 3 शिथिलीकृ, शिथिलयति (D.). —*v. i.* शीतलीभू 1 P, शीतीभू, शीतलायते (D.). 2 शिथिलीभू, शिथिलायते (D.); 'she will not let her love for you c. down' न सेतोगतमनुरागं शिथिलयति (V. 2). 3 प्र-उप-शम् 4 P, विरम् 1 P. —ING, *a.* तापहर, निर्वापक, शांतिद, शीतल, सुखद. —LY, *adv.* असंभ्रमं, शांतचेतसा, अव्यग्रं, शांतं, निरुद्वेगं. 2 प्रकोपनं विना, बुद्धिपुरःसरं. —NESS, *s.* शीतलता, आर्द्रता ; 'c. of affection' विरागः, विरक्ति *f.*, अनुरागशिथिलता.

COOP, *s.* भाजनं, काष्ठभांडं. 2 वीतंगः, पंजरः-रं. —*v. t.* (up) (पंजरे) निरुध् 7 U, बंध् 9 P, संयम् 1 P, नियंत्र् 10.

CO-OPERATE, *v. i.* संभूय कृ 8 U, साहाय्यं दा 3 U, अन्येन सार्धं प्रयत् 1 A or व्यवसो 4 P or चेष्ट् 1 A. —ION, *s.* सहकारिता, सहोद्योगः, साहाय्यं, संभूय व्यवसायः.—IVE, *a.* सहकारिन् (णी *f.*), सहोद्योगिन्.—OR, *s.* सहकारिन् *m.*, संभूयकारिन् *m.*, सहोद्योगिन् *m.*

COPARCENER, *s.* समांशिन् *m.*, संसृष्टः-ष्टिन् *m.*, अंशहरः, रिक्थाधिकारिन् *m.*, दायादः.—COPARCENARY, *s.* संसृष्टि *f.*, संसृष्टिता, समांशिता.

COPARTNER, *s.* समांशिन् *m.*, अंशभाज् *m.*, संभूयकारिन् *m.* —SHIP, *s.* समांशिता ; संभूय समुत्थानं.

COPE, *v. i.* (with) युध् 4 A, विग्रह् 9 P, विरुध् 7 U, अभिपत् 1 P (with acc.); यंता गजस्याभ्यपतद्गजस्थं (R. VII. 37). 2 स्पर्ध् 1 A, संघृष् 1 P, अभिभू 1 P; *See* COMPETE. —*s.* शिरस्त्राणं, मस्तकाच्छादनं.

COPING, *s.* प्राकारशीर्ष-शृंगं.

COPIOUS, *a.* प्रचुर, भूयिष्ठ, बहु, विपुल, प्रभूत, पुष्कल, भूरि, बहुल. —LY, *adv.* बहु, भूरि, बहुशः, प्रचुरं. अति-सु-pr. —NESS, *s.* बाहुल्यं, प्राचुर्यं, विपुलता, &c.

COPPER, *s.* ताम्रं, ताम्रकं, शुल्बं, द्व्यष्टं, वरिष्टं, उदुंबरं ; 'c. coin' पणः ; 'c. plate' ताम्रपत्रं-पट्टं-पटः; 'c. smith' ताम्रकारः, ताम्रिकः, ताम्रकुट्टकः, शौल्बिकः. —Y, *a.* ताम्र (म्री *f.*), ताम्रमय (यी *f.*).

COPPERAS, *s.* तुत्थं, मलीमसं.

COPPICE, COPSE, *s.* गुल्मावृतं स्थानं, जंगलं, तरुगहनं.

COPULATE, *v. i.* मैथुनं-संगं-कृ 8 U, अभिगम् 1 P, संगम् 1 A. —*v. t.* संयुज् 7 P, 10, संधा 3 U. —ION, *s.* मैथुनं, सुरतं, संभोगः, व्यवायः, रतिक्रिया. 2 संसर्गः, संपर्कः, संयोगः. —IVE, *a.* संयोग-संसर्ग-कारिन् (णी *f.*). 2 उभयान्वयिन्.

COPY, *s.* प्रतिलेखः, प्रतिलिपि *f.*, हस्तलेखः, लिपिः. 2 मूलं. 3 एकग्रंथः, एकपुस्तकं. 4 अनुकरणं; 'c. right' मुद्रणस्वामित्वं-स्वत्वं, मुद्रणाधिकारः. —*v. t.* प्रतिलिपिं कृ 8 U, लिख् 6 P. 2 अनुकृ (with gen.). —ER, —IST, *s.* लिपिक(का)रः, लेखकः, अक्षरचणः, अक्षरचंचुः. 2 अनुकारिन् *m.* 3 शब्दचोरः.

COQUET, *v. i.* विलस् 1 P, विभ्रम् 1, 4 P, हावं-विलासं-कृ 8 U, ललिताभिनयं कृ. —RY, *s.* विलासः, विभ्रमः, हावः, लीला, ललिताभिनयः. —COQUETTE, *s.* विलासिनी, विलासवती, कामिनी, लीलावती.

CORAL, *s.* विद्रुमः, प्रवालः.

CORD, *s.* रज्जु *f.*, दामन् *n.*, पाशः, शुल्बं, गुणः, सूत्रं, वटी. —*v. t.* रज्ज्वा बंध् 9 P or यंत्र् 10. —AGE, *s.* रज्ज्वादिसामग्री. —ED, *a.* पाश-रज्जु-बद्ध.

CORDIAL, *a.* दीपक, अग्निवर्द्धक; धातुपोषक. 2 दृढसौहृद, गाढपरिचय, सुशील (of persons); दृढ, गाढ, घन. —*s.* अग्निवर्धनं, रुचकं, दीपकः-कं. —ITY, *s.* सौहार्दं, सुशीलता, सौजन्यं, मित्रभावः, मैत्र्यं, सख्यं. —LY, *adv.* सौहार्देन, सुशीलवत्.

CORE, *s.* अंतरं, गर्भः, अंतर्भागः, हृदयं.

CORIANDER, *s.* धानी, धानेयः. 2 (seed) छत्रा, धान्यकं, वितुन्नकं, कुस्तुंबरु *n.*

CORK, *s.* पिधानं, कूपीछिद्रपिधानं.

CORMORANT, *s.* घस्मरः, औदरिकः, कुक्षिंभरिः, गृध्नुः.

CORN, *s.* धान्यं; 'growing c.' शस्यं. 2 किणः, कदरः. 3 अन्नं, आहारः, जीवनसाधनं; 'c. mill' धान्यपेषणी. —Y, *a.* शृंगवत् (ती *f.*).

CORNEA, *s.* शुक्लमंडलं.

CORNER, *s.* कोणः, अस्रः ; 'c. of the eye' अपांगः-गं, नयनोपांतः; 'c. of the mouth' सृक्कन् *n.* 2 विविक्तस्थानं, निर्जनदेशः; 'c. stone' प्रधान-कोणप्रस्तरः; 'c. wise' कोणाकोणि, अस्रास्रि.

CORNET, *s.* आश्विकनायकः. 2 आवेष्टनं, कोशः-षः.

CORNICE, *s.* प्राकारशीर्षं-शृंगं.

CORNUTED, *a.* (man) बंधकीभार्यः.

COROLLARY, *s.* अनुमानं; अपवाहः, उपसिद्धांतः, उपलक्ष्यः.

CORONAL, *s.* मुकुटं, किरीटः.

CORONATION, *s.* अभिषेकः, राज्याभिषेकः.

CORONER, *s.* अपमृत्युकारणनिरूपकः.

CORONET, *s.* मुकुटं, किरीटः.

CORPORAL, *a.* कायिक-शारीरिक-दैहिक (की *f.*), शारीर (री *f.*); 'c. punishment' देह-शरीर-दंडः. —ITY, *s.* देहवत्त्वं, शरीरवत्ता. —LY, *adv.* शरीरेण, देहतः.

CORPORATE, *a.* कृतसंसर्ग, संभूयकारिन् (णी *f.*), संघातवत् (ती *f.*), संसृष्ट. —ION, *s.* 'a c. body' श्रेणि-णी *f.*, समाजः.

CORPOREAL, *a.* देहिन् (नी *f.*), शरीरिन् (णी *f.*), वपुष्मत् (ती *f.*), सदेह, सशरीर.

CORPS, *s.* अनीकं, सैन्यदलं-गुल्मः, दंडः.

CORPSE, *s.* शवः-वं, कुणपः, प्रेतं, मृतशरीरं.

CORPULENT, *a.* स्थूल, स्थूलकाय, पीन, पीवर, मेदस्विन् (नी *f.*), मांसल; 'having a c. belly' तुंदिन्, तुंदवत् (ती *f.*), तुंदिल, बृहत्कुक्षि, पिचंडिलं.

—CORPULENCE, *s.* पीनता, स्थूलता, मेदस्विता, पृथूदरता.

CORPUSCLE, *s.* अणुः, कणः, लवः, लेशः.

CORRECT, *v. t.* वि-परि-सं-शुध् c., निर्दोष *a.* कृ 8 U, प्रतिसमा-समा-धा 3 U; 'instantly c. ing himself' सपदि स्ववचः समादधत् ; प्रमृज् 2 P; 'c. one's bad conduct' पापान्निवृत् 1 A, कुमार्गं त्यज् 1 P. 2 अनुशास् 2 P, दंड् 10. 3 प्रतिकृ, अपा-निरा-कृ. —*a.* शुद्ध, निर्दोष, अभ्रांत. 2 सत्य, तथ्य, यथार्थ, अवितथ, यथातथ ; 'c. in conduct' साधुवृत्त, निर्दोषाचरण. —ION, *s.* शोधनं, शुद्धि *f.*; समाधानं. 2 शासनं, दंडः-डनं, निग्रहः. —IVE, *a.* शोधक. 2 प्रतिकारक, अपह-हर-in comp. —*s.* प्रतिकारः, समाधानं. —LY, *adv.* शुद्धं, निर्दोषं. 2 सत्यं, यथातथं, यथावत्, साधु. —NESS, *s.* शुद्धि *f.*, शुद्धत्वं-ता, निर्दोषता; सत्यता, तथ्यता, यथार्थता. —OR, *s.* शोधकः. प्रतिकर्तृ *m.* 2 शास्तृ-शासितृ *m.*; दंडप्रणेतृ *m.* —CORRIGIBLE, *a.* शोधनीय; दंडनीय; समाधेय.

CORRELATION, *s.* परस्परसंबंधः, अन्योन्यान्वयः, व्यतिकरः. —CORRELATIVE, *a.* परस्परसंबद्ध, इतरेतरसंबंधिन् (नी *f.*).

CORRESPOND, *v. i.* (with) पत्रेण संवादं कृ 8 U, पत्रलेखनेन संवद् 1 P or व्यवह् 1 P. 2 (to) संवद् 1 P, अनुरूप-सदृश (शी *f.*) *a.* भू 1 P; युज्-उपपद्-pass. ; *See* RESEMBLE; 'his face c. s to that of Sitâ' अस्य मुखं सीताया मुखेन संवदति (U. 4). —ENCE, *s.* पत्रसंवादः, पत्रविनिमयः. 2 संवादः, अनुरूपता, सादृश्यं. 3 संबंधः, संसर्गः, संपर्कः. —ENT,-ING, *a.* अनुरूप. युक्त, सदृश, तुल्य, संगत, संवादिन्. —*s.* पत्रेण संवादिन् *m.* 2 नियोगिन् *m.*, प्रतिपुरुषः.

CORRIDOR, *s.* गूढ-छन्न-पथः.

CORRIVAL, *s.* प्रतिपक्षः, प्रतिस्पर्धिन् *m.*, प्रतियोगिन् *m.* —RY, *s.* प्रतिस्पर्धा, संघर्षः, प्रतियोगिता.

CORROBORATE, *v. t.* दृढीकृ 8 U, समर्थ् 10, दृढयति (D.), प्रमाणीकृ, प्रमाणं दा 3 U, उपोद्बल् 10. —ION, *s.* दृढीकरणं, प्रमाणीकरणं, समर्थनं, उपोद्बलनं, प्रमाणं.

CORRODE, *v. t.* क्षि 5 P or c, क्रमशः-लवशः-खाद् 1 P or नश् c. or विली c. —ENT, *a.* नाशक, क्षयकर (री *f.*). —CORROSION, *s.* क्रमशो विलयनं or नाशनं, क्षयः. —CORROSIVE, *a.* विलयन, नाशक. 2 तीव्र, तिग्म, प्रखर, अरुंतुद, मर्मस्पृश्.

CORRUGATE, *v. t.* (त्वचं-चर्म) संकुच् 1 P, आकुंच् c., संहृ 1 P. —ION, *s.* त्वगाकुंचनं, चर्मसंकोचः ; संकोचनं.

CORRUPT, *v. t.* दुष् c. (दूषयति), भ्रंश् c., नश् c., विकृ 8 U or c., मलिनयति (D.), कलुषयति (D.), अवपत् c.; 'the mind is c. ed in youth' यौवनारंभे कालुष्यमुपयाति बुद्धिः (Ka. 103); 'c. a woman' दुष् c., चारित्र्यं नश् c., सतीत्वाद् भ्रंश् c., धृष् 10. 2 पूतीकृ. 3 उत्कोचं दा 3 U, उत्कोचदानेन वशीअनुकूली कृ. —*v. i.* दुष् 4 P; पूतीभू 1P. —*a.* दूषित, कलुष, पतित, दुष्ट, भ्रष्ट, कलुषित. 2 दुष्टमति, दुराचार, पापचेतस्, अंतर्दुष्ट, दुरात्मन्, दुराशय, पापबुद्धि. 3 पूति, पूतिगंधि, दुर्गंध. —ION, *s.* दूषणं, पातनं, शीलभ्रंशनं. 2 उत्कोचग्राहित्वं, धनभेद्यत्वं. 3 दुष्टता, दौरात्म्यं, भ्रष्टता, अंतर्दुष्टता, दौर्जन्यं. 4 अपभ्रंशः, अपशब्दः, अपभ्रष्टशब्दः. 5 पूति *f.*, पूतता, दुर्गंधः. —ER,-IVE, *a.* दूषक, नाशक. —LY. *adv.* दुष्टं, दुष्टतया; सदोषं.

CORSAIR, *s.* समुद्रीयदस्युः.

CORSE, *s.* *See* CORPSE.

CORSET, *s.* चोलः-ली, कूर्पासकः, कंचुकः.

CORSLET, *s.* वक्षस्त्राणं, कवचः-चं.

CORTICAL, *a.* त्वङ्मय (यी *f.*), त्वाच (ची *f.*).

CORUSCATE, *v. i.* स्फुर् 6 P, द्युत् 1 A; *See* SHINE. —ION, *s.* स्फुरणं, स्फुरितं. —CORUSCANT, *a.* उज्ज्वल, भासुर.

COSINE, *s.* ज्या.

COSMETIC, *a.* कांतिवर्धक, शोभाजनन (नी *f.*), शोभाप्रद. —*s.* अंगरागः.

COSMICAL, *a.* जगत्संबंधिन् (नी *f.*).

COSMOGONY, *s.* विश्वोत्पत्ति *f.*, जगत्सृष्टि *f.*

COSMOGRAPHY, *s.* जगद्विवरणं-वर्णनं.

COSMOPOLITE,-POLITAN, *s.* विश्वस्थायिन् *m.*, सर्वत्रवासिन् *m.*, जगन्मित्रं.

COST, *s.* मूल्यं, अर्घः, अर्हा. 2 व्ययः; 'even at the c. of one's life' प्राणव्ययेनापि; 'high c.' बहुमूल्यं; oft. by instr. of noun, (आत्मानं सततं रक्षेद्दारैरपि धनैरपि). 3 धनव्ययः. —*v. t.* मूल्येन ग्रह् 9 P or क्री 9 U ; 'what does it c.' कियता मूल्येन विक्रीयते तत्; 'the house c. me 1000 Rs.' सहस्ररूपकेण मया गृहं क्रीतं; 'the marriage ceremony c. me much' बहुधनव्ययेन निष्पादितो विवाहविधिः ; 'his obstinacy c. him dear' दुराग्रहात्तस्य अत्यहितमभवत् ; व्ययेन साध् 10; 'will c. the lives of' प्राणनाशं-व्ययं-आवहेत्. —LY, *a.* महार्घ, महार्ह, बहुमूल्य.

COSTIVE, *a.* आनद्ध, बद्धकोष्ठ, अवरुद्धमल, विड्ग्रहिन्. —NESS, *s.* मलावरोधः, मलावष्टंभः, आनाहः, विड्-गुद-ग्रहः.

COSTUME, *s.* वेशः, नेपथ्यं ; *See* DRESS.

COSUFFERER, *s.* समदुःखः, समदुःखभाज् *m.*

COT, *s.* खट्वा, मंचः, पर्यंकः. 2 दोला, प्रेंखा. 3 Cottage, q. v.

COTERIE, *s.* एकविषयजनसंसर्गः-गणः.

COTQUEAN, *s.* स्त्रीकर्म-व्यापृतः.

COTTAGE, *s.* उटजः-जं, पर्णकुटि-टी *f.*, पर्णशाला, का-

यमानं, कुटीरः; 'c. girl' उटजनिवासिनी बालिका. -ER, COTTER, COTTIER, s. कुटीरस्थः, उटजवासिन् m.; ग्रामीणः.

COTTON, s. कार्पासः, तूलः, पिचुः, पिचुलः; 'made of c.' कार्पास a.; 'c. cloth' तूलांबरं, फालं, कार्पासं, बादरं; 'c. plant' कार्पासी. -Y, a. तूलसंबंधिन् (नी f.), कार्पासिक (की f.), (s.) in comp.

COUCH, s. शयनं, शय्या, पर्यंकः, खट्वा, मंचः; See BED. -v. i. शी 2 A, संविश् 6 P. 2 अधःपत् 1 P, नि-पत्. -v. t. शी c., सं-नि-विश् c. 2 परिग्रह् 9 P, समाविश् c. 3 आच्छद् 10, ग्रंथ् 9 P; 'c. ed in sweet words' मधुरवाग्ग्रथितः (लेखः); 'c. fellow' सहशायिन् (नी f.). -ANT, a. शय, शायिन्.

COUGH, s. कासः, काशः, उत्कासः, क्षवथुः; 'suffering from c.' कासिन्. -v. i. कास् 1 A, क्षु 2 P. -ER, s. उत्कासिन्-काशिन् m.

COULTER, s. फालदंतः, कृंतत्रं.

COUNCIL, s. सभा, संसद् f., सदस् f., n.; 'c. room' (chamber of c.) मंत्रणसभा, मंत्रगृहं. -LOR, s. सभासद् m., सदस्यः, &c.

COUNSEL, s. मंत्रणा, विचारः-रणा, विवेचनं, विमर्शः, चिंतनं. 2 उपदेशः, मंत्रः, मंत्रितं, अनुशासनं. 3 उपायः. 4 Barrister, q. v. -v. t. उपदिश् 6 P, मंत्र् 10, अनुशास् 2 P. -LOR, s. मंत्रिन् m., सचिवः, अमात्यः, धीसचिवः. 2 उपदेशकः, उपदेष्टृ m., बुद्धिसहायः. -LORSHIP, s. साचिव्यं, मंत्रिपदं.

COUNT, v. t. गण् 10 (lit. and fig.); संकल् 10, संख्या 2 P. 2 मन् 4 A. -v. i. मन्-गण्-pass.; 'c. on, upon' अवलंब् 1 A, आश्रि 1 U, विश्वस् 2 P, प्रति-इ 2 P; 'I do c. upon your help' त्वं साहाय्यं करिष्यसीति गणयाम्येव; 'c. ing upon your promise' तव वचनमवलंब्य, त्वद्वचनप्रत्ययात्. -s. गणनं, गणना, संख्या-ख्यानं. 2 अभियोगविषयः, भाषापादं. -LESS, a. असंख्य, अगण्य, संख्यातीत, अनंत, गणनातीत.

COUNTENANCE, s. मुखं, आननं, वदनं, आस्यं, वक्त्रं. 2 आकारः, आकृति f., रूपं. 3 आश्रयः, अनुग्रहः, साहाय्यं, उपकारः. 4 आनुकूल्यं, अनुमोदनं. -v. t. अनुग्रह् 9 P, उपकृ 8 U, साहाय्यं दा 3 U, आनुकूल्यं दृश् c.; अनुमन् 4 A, अनुमुद् 1 A; See ENCOURAGE also. -ER, s. उपकारकः, सहायः, अनुग्रहीतृ m., अनुमोदकः.

COUNTER, s. गणनाफलकः. 2 (गणनार्थं) मुद्रा, काकिणी, कपर्दः-र्दिका. -adv. प्रतिकूलं, विरुद्धं, विपरीतं, प्रतिलोमं; gen. by प्रति pr.; 'c. design' प्रत्युपायः; 'c. poison' प्रतिविषं.

COUNTERACT, v. t. मोघी-निष्फली-कृ 8 U, निवार् 10, प्रतिकृ, प्रतिहन् 2 P, प्रति-वि-रुध् 7 U. -ION, s. प्रतिक्रिया, प्रति(ती)कारः, प्रतियोगः, प्रति-व्याघातः.

COUNTERBALANCE, v. t. तुलया धृ 1 P, तुल्यभार a. कृ 8 U, समीकृ, प्रतितुल् 10.

COUNTERBUFF, v. t. प्रति-अभि-हन् 2 P. -s. प्रतिघातः.

COUNTERCHANGE, v. t. परस्परं परिवृत् c., विनि-मे 1 A. -s. परिवर्तः, विनिमयः, व्यतिकरः.

COUNTERCHECK, s. प्रतिबंधः, प्रतिरोधः.

COUNTEREVIDENCE, s. विरुद्धसाक्ष्यं; प्रतिकूलप्रमाणं.

COUNTERFEIT, a. कृत्रिम, कृतक, कपटिन् (नी f.), छाद्मिक (की f.); gen. ex. by कपट, छद्म, कूट in comp.; 'c. seal' कपटमुद्रा; कूटशासनं, छद्मवेशः, &c. -v. t. छद्म-कपटं-कृ 8 U, अनुकृ; कृ with कपट-कूट in comp.; 'c. a seal' कपटमुद्रां कृ; 'c. a document' कूटलेखं कृ; 'c. ing sleep' प्रसुप्तलक्षणः, लक्षसुप्तः, मिथ्यासुप्तः; See FEIGN. 2 विप्रलभ् 1 A; See CHEAT. -s. कूटं, कपटं, छद्मन् n., व्याजः. 2 कूटलेखः. -ER, s. कूटकृत् m., कूटलेख्यकारः. 2 वंचकः, प्रतारकः. -LY, adv. सकपटं, सकूटं, मिथ्या, छद्मना.

COUNTERMAND, v. t. प्रत्यादिश् 6 P, विपरीताज्ञां दा 3 U. -s. प्रत्यादेशः, विपरीताज्ञा.

COUNTERMARCH, v. i. प्रतिया 2 P, प्रतीपं या. -s. प्रतियानं, प्रतीपयात्रा.

COUNTERMARK, s. प्रतिलक्षणं, प्रतिचिह्नं.

COUNTERMINE, s. प्रतिसुरंगा. -v. t. प्रतिसुरंगां कृ 8 U.

COUNTERPANE, s. शयनास्तरणं, शय्याप्रच्छदः.

COUNTERPART, s. प्रतिरूपं, प्रतिमा, प्रतिबिंबं, प्रतिमूर्ति f.; (अहो चेष्टाप्रतिरूपिका कामिनी मनोवृत्तिः S. 1).

COUNTERPLEA, s. प्रत्युत्तरं; प्रत्यभियोगः.

COUNTERPOISE, COUNTERVAIL, v. t. See COUNTERBALANCE. -s. तुल्यभारता, समतोलनं.

COUNTRY, s. प्र-, देशः, विषयः, राष्ट्रं; दिश् f., आशा. 2 ग्रामः, जनपदः, (opposed to नगरं, पुरं); 'c. folk' जानपदाः, ग्राम्याः; 'c. life' जानपदवृत्तिः, ग्रामवसतिः; 'native c.' जन्मभूमि f., स्वदेशः; 'c. man' स्वदेशीयः, एकदेशस्थः, देशबंधुः; जानपदः, ग्राम्यजनः, ग्रामीणः; 'c. parson' जानपदाचार्यः, ग्रामगुरुः.

COUNTY, s. देशभागः, मंडलं, चक्रं.

COUPLE, s. युग्मं, युगलं, यमकं, युगं, द्वयं, द्वितयं; 'c. of animals' मिथुनं, द्वंद्वं; 'a married c.' वधूवरौ, दंपती, जायापती. -v. t. संयुज् 7 U, 10, संश्लिष् c., संगम् c. (गमयति), योक्त्रयति (D.). -v. i. मैथुनं कृ 8 U, स्त्रीपुरुषवत् संगम् 1 A or संमिल् 6 P.

COUPLET, s. श्लोकः; पंक्तिद्वयं; 'a c. formed by two verses' युग्मकं.

COURAGE, s. धैर्यं, शौर्यं, विक्रमः, पराक्रमः, वीर्यं, उत्साहः, पौरुषं, तेजस् n., धामन् n., प्रतापः. 2 निर्भी-

कता, धृष्टता, साहसं; 'lose c.' धैर्यहीन *a.* भू 1 P, सत्त्वात्परिभ्रंश् 1 A, 4 P; 'do not lose c.' धैर्यं निधेहि हृदये (Mal. 5); 'take c.' आ-समा-श्वस् 2 P; 'summon c.' धैर्यं आस्था 1A, धैर्यं अवलंब् 1 A or अवष्टंभ् 9 P, धैर्यावष्टंभं कृ 8 U; 'inspire c.' आ-समा-श्वस् c. -OUS, *a.* शूर, वीर, विक्रांत, धीर. 2 अभीरु, धृष्ट, साहसिक (की *f.*). -OUSLY, *adv.* सवीर्यं, सविक्रमं, वीर-शूर-वत्. -OUSNESS, *See* (*s.*).

COURIER, *s.* वार्ताहरः; दूतः, वैवधिकः.

COURSE, *s.* गति *f.*, प्रसरः, प्र-, क्रमः. 2 रयः, प्रवाहः (of water &c.). 3 मार्गः, पथिन् *m.*, पदवि-वी *f.* 4 व्यवहारः, वृत्ति *f.*, आचरणं, चरित्रं. 5 क्रमः, अनुक्रमः, आनुपूर्व्यं, परंपरा. 6 रजस् *n.*, पुष्पं, आर्तवं (of women). 7 विधिः, प्रकारः, रीति *f.*; 'the law must have its c.' यथाशास्त्रमस्य निर्णयेन भवितव्यमेव; 'in c. of conversation' कथाप्रसंगेन, कथायोगेन; 'in c. of time' कालक्रमेण, गच्छता कालेन, दिनेषु गच्छत्सु, गच्छति काले; 'a woman in c.' रजस्वला, ऋतुमती, मलिनी, पुष्पवती; 'of c.' अवश्यमेव, नियतं, नूनं, खलु, नाम with एव; 'c. of an arrow' बाणगोचरः, शरपथः; 'c. of study' अध्ययनक्रमः-मार्गः; 'mathematical c.' गणिताध्ययनक्रमः; 'c. of acting' क्रियाविधिः, अनुष्ठानं; 'proper c. of conduct' सुमार्गः; 'there being no other c.' गत्यंतराभावात्, अनन्यगतिक *a.*; 'race c.' चर्याभूमिः; 'in the c. of' मध्ये, अंतरे; 'a house in the c. of erection' निर्मीयमाणं भवनं; 'the c. of nature' सृष्टिक्रमः. -ER, *s.* जवनः, जविन् *m.*, वारकीरः.

COURT, *s.* चत्वरः-रं, अंगनं-णं, प्रांगणं, अजिरं. 2 राजकुलं, राजसभा, आस्थानी-नं (assembly room); राजगृहं-मंदिरं. 3 अनुनयः, अनुवृत्ति *f.*, आराधनं; भजनं, दाक्षिण्यं. 4 (Judge) अधिकरणिकः, अक्षदर्शकः, धर्माधिकारिन् *m.*; (Judges) धर्माध्यक्षाः, प्राड्विवाकाः (pl.); 'c. of justice' अधिकरणं, व्यवहारमंडपः, न्याय-धर्म-सभा. 5 राजपरिजनः-परिवर्हः-परिवारः; 'c. favour' राजप्रसादः, राजानुग्रहः; 'c. minion' राजवल्लभः-प्रियः; 'c.-yard' अंगनं, चत्वरं, अजिरं, प्रकोष्ठः, प्रांगणं, गृहांगणं. -*v. t.* आराध् 10, अनुनी 1 P, अनुरंज् c., भज् 1 A. 2 याच् 1 A, प्र-अभि-अर्थ् 10 A. 3 विवाहार्थं प्रार्थ् or सेव् 1 A. -EOUS, *a.* दक्षिण, विनीत, सविनय, सुजन, सप्रश्रय, सानुनय, सभ्य, प्रियंवद; 'c. words' सूनृता वाणी. -EOUSLY, *adv.* सप्रश्रयं, दक्षिणतया, सानुनयं, विनयेन. -ESY, *s.* दाक्षिण्यं, विनयः, प्रश्रयः, सौजन्यं, अनुरोधः, अनुवर्तनं; 'a title of c.' उपचारपदं. 2 प्रणामः, आमंत्रणं, आप्रच्छनं. -IER, *s.* राजभृत्यः, राजवल्लभः, राजसभासद् *m.*, सभिकः, सभ्यः. -LIKE, *a.* शिष्ट, शिष्टाचार, सभ्य. -LY, *a.* सुजन, शिष्ट, सभ्य, दक्षिण, सुशील. -SHIP, *s.* आराधनं, अनुरंजनं, अनुनयः, प्रसादनं. 2 उपासना, विवाहार्थं प्रार्थना.

COURTEZAN, *s.* गणिका, वेश्या, पण्यस्त्री, पण्यांगना, वारस्त्री-योषित्; बंधकी, पुंश्चली.

COUSIN, *s.* पितृव्यपुत्रः (त्री *f.*), मातुलपुत्रः (त्री *f.*), पितृष्वसेयः (यी *f.*), मातृष्वसेयः (यी *f.*), according to different relations. 2 ज्ञातिः, बांधवः.

COVE, *s.* वंकः, खातं.

COVENANT, *s.* समयः, नियमः, संविद् *f.*, पणः. -*v. i.* *See* CONTRACT. -ER, *s.* नियमबद्धः, सामयिकः.

COVER, *v. t.* प्र-समा-आ-च्छद् 10, प्रा-सं-आ-वृ 5 U, स्थग् 10, पिधा 3 U, निगुह् 1 U, व्यवधा 3 U, अवगुंठ् 10. 2 आ-,स्तृ 5 U, स्तॄ 9 U, व्याप् 5 P, आवेष्ट् 1 A or c., नि-आ-चि 5 U; 'a c. ed path' छन्न-गूढ-पथः. -*s.* आवरणं, आच्छादनं, पुटं, व्यवधानं, वेष्टनं, अवगुंठनं, पिधानं. 2 कोशः-षः, वेष्टनं. 3 प्रावारः, प्रच्छदपटः, आच्छादनवस्त्रं. 4 अप-व्यप-देशः, छद्मन् *n.*, व्याजः, छलं, माया, कपटं; 'c. of a well' वि(वी)-नाहः; 'c. of a carriage' रथगोपनं-आवरणं. -ING, *s.* आच्छादनं, आवरणं, &c. 2 तिरस्करिणी, व्यवधानं. 3 परिधानं, प्रावारः, वासस् *n.*, आच्छादनवस्त्रं. 4 अंतर्धा, व्यवधा, अंतर्धिः, अपवारणं, तिरोधानं. -LET, *s.* उत्तरच्छदः, शय्याप्रच्छदपटः.

COVERT, *a.* गूढ, प्रच्छन्न, गुप्त; 'a c. expression' व्यंगोक्ति *f.* 2 निर्वात. -*s.* गह्वरं, गह्वरं. 2 संश्रयः, आश्रयस्थानं.

COVET, *v. t.* लुभ् 4 U, गृध् 4 P, स्पृह् 10 (with dat.); कम् 10 A, अभिलष् 1, 4 P, अतिमात्रं इष् 6 P. -OUS, *a.* लुब्ध, लोलुप, गृध्नु, अभिलाषिन् (णी *f.*), ईप्सु, अतृप्त, सतृष्ण. 2 (Of wealth) धनलुब्ध, धनार्थिन्, अर्थपर, धनपरायण. -OUSLY, *adv.* सलोभं, लोभेन. -OUSNESS, *s.* लोभः, लिप्सा, तृष्णा, लालसा, स्पृहा, अभिलाषः, अतिस्पृहा, लौल्यं. 2 धनलोभः, अर्थतृष्णा.

COVEY, *s.* पक्षिगणः; शावकसमूहः.

COVIN, *s.* कूटसमयः-संविद् *f.*

COW, *s.* गो *f.*, धेनु *f.*; माहेयी, सौरभेयी, उस्रा; शृंगिणी, अर्जुनी, रोहिणी; एकहायनी, द्विहायनी, त्रिहायणी, चतुर्हायणी 'a c. one year old, 2 years old, and so on'; 'barren c.' वशा, वंध्या; 'mild one' अचंडी, सुकरा; 'bringing forth many calves' बहुसूतिः, परेष्टुका; 'producing calves every year' समांसमीना; 'an excellent c.' गोमतल्लिका, गोतल्लजः; 'c. dung' गोमयः-यं, शकृत् *n.*; 'c. herd' गोपः, आभीरः, गोपालः; 'c. house or pen' व्रजः, गोष्ठं, गोशाला. -*v. t.* भी c., त्रस् c.

COWARD, *s.* कापुरुषः, भीरुः, अशूरः, कातरः, क्लीबः, भीतः, शौर्यहीनः; 'a boasting c.' गेहेशूरः, गेहेनर्दिन् *m.* -ICE, *s.* भीरुता, कातर्यं, अपौरुषं, कापुरुष-

त्वं, अवीर्यं, अविक्रमः, क्लीवता. -LY, *a.* भीरु, निर्वीर्य, कातर; *See* (*s.*). -*adv.* सकातर्यं, भीरुवत्, कापुरुषवत्.

COWER, *v. i.* अवनतकाय-प्रणतशरीर -*a.* भू 1 P, प्रह्लीभू, निभृतं-अलक्षितं या 2 P or गम् 1 P, कायमवनमय्य गम्.

COWL, *s.* फणाकृति शिरोवेष्टनं.

COWRIE, *s.* काकिनी-णी, कपर्दिका, वराटकः.

COXCOMB, *s.* दंभिन् *m.*, दांभिकः, आत्माभिमानिन् *m.*, आत्मविकत्थनः, दृप्तः. 2 चूडा, शिखा. -RY, *s.* दंभः, आत्माभिमानः, दर्पः. गर्वः.

COY, *a.* अप्रगल्भ, सलज्ज, लज्जावत् (ती *f.*), विनीत, सव्रीड, शालीन. 2 अल्पभाषिन् (णी *f.*), मितवाच्. -*v. i.* लज्ज् 6 A, त्रप् 1 A, ह्री 3 P. -LY, *adv.* लज्जया, सव्रीडं, सत्रपं, सलज्जं. -NESS, *s.* लज्जा, व्रीडा, त्रपा; अप्रागल्भ्यं.

COZEN, *v. t.* वंच् 10; *See* CHEAT. -AGE, *s.* प्रतारणा, वंचनं; माया, भ्रमः, मोहः. -ER, *s.* वंचकः, कितवः, मायिन् *m.*

CRAB, *s.* कुलीरः, कर्कटः-टकः.

CRABBED, *a.* कर्कश, परुष, निष्ठुर. 2 वामशील, प्रतीप, दुःशील. 3 विषम, दुर्ज्ञेय, गूढ, निगूढार्थ. -NESS, *s.* निष्ठुरता, प्रतीपता, वैषम्यं, दुःशीलं.

CRACK, *v. t.* भंज् 7 P, खंड् 10, विद् 9 P, 10, स्फुट् c., भिद् 7 P; 'c. a joke' परिहासं कृ. 2 (अकस्मात्) ध्वन् c., आस्फल् 10, स्वन् c. -*v. i.* स्फुट् 6 P, वि-, दल् 1 P, भंज्-भिद्- pass.; 'a c. ed sound' अपस्वरः, विस्वरः. 2 विकत्थ् 1 A. 3 महारवेण स्वन्-क्वण्-ध्वन् 1 P, सहसा महारवं कृ 8 U. -*s.* छिद्रं, रंध्रं, संधिः, भंगः. 2 स्फोटनं, भेदनं. 3 विरावः, ध्वनिः, क्वणितं; 'c. brained' वातुल, उन्मत्त, भ्रांतचित्त.

CRACKLE, *v. i.* स्वन्-रट् 1 P, पटपटायते (D.). -*s.* स्वनितं, रटितं, पटपटशब्दः.

CRADLE, *s.* दोला, प्रेंखा, प्रेंखोलनं ; (शिशु) खट्वा ; 'from the c.' आशैशवात्; 'a child in the c.' स्तनंधयः, शिशुः. 2 (fig.) निवासभूमि *f.*, आवासः. -*v. t.* दोलायां शी c., दोलामारोप्य चल् c.

CRAFT, *s.* कला, शिल्पं; कौशलं. 2 व्यापारः, वृत्ति *f.*, व्यवसायः. 3 चातुर्यं, कौशलं, वैदग्ध्यं ; हस्तकौशलं, नैपुण्यं. 4 शाठ्यं, धूर्तता, कौटिल्यं, कपटं. 5 नौः, तरिः; 'c.s man' शिल्पिन् *m.*, कारुः, कर्मकारः. —CRAFTY, *a.* धूर्त, शठ, कुटिल, विजिह्म, कितव, कपटिन्. 2 चतुर, विदग्ध. -LY, *adv.* छलेन, सकैतवं, धूर्ततया ; चतुरं, विदग्धतया.

CRAG, *s.* शृंगं, कूटः-टं, शिखरः-रं. -GED, -GY, *a.* विषम, अत्युसम, शृंगिन् (णी *f.*).

CRAM, *v. t.* प्रक्षिप् 6 P, बलात् निविश् c. 2 अतिभोजनेन तृप् c. or संतुष् c. 3 अतिभृशं पृ c. or पूर् 10; स्वस्तिवायनमोदकैः कुक्षिं पूरयित्वा (M. 4) 'having c. ed the belly' &c.; 'c. ed with food' अतितृप्तः. 4 आकृष् 6 P, निरुध् 7 U, संबाध् 1 A; 'c. ed with people' जनाकीर्ण, जनसंकुल-संबाध.

CRAMP, *v. t.* संकुच् 1 P, स्तंभ् 9 P or c., नि-प्रतिरुध् 7 U, संबाध् 1 A. 2 (अंगं) आकृष् 1 P, उद्वेष्ट् c., उपहन् 2 P. 3 कील् 10 ; 'we are much c. ed in this place' अतीव दुःस्थिता वयमत्र. -*s.* स्तंभः, संकोचः-चनं, निरोधः, संक्षेपः. 2 उद्वेष्टनं, व्यासः, आक्षेपः, गात्रोपघातः; 'a c. in the calf of the leg' पिंडिकोद्वेष्टनं. 3 कीलः, लोहग्रहणी, बंधनकीलः (c. iron).

CRANE, *s.* बकः, कह्वः, सारसः; बलाका, बिसकंठिका (female c.). 2 भारोत्तोलनयंत्रं.

CRANIUM, *See* SKULL.

CRANK, *s.* वक्रमार्गः. 2 वक्रोक्ति *f.*, वक्रभाषितं.

CRANNY, *s.* छिद्रं, रंध्रं, संधिः.

CRASH, *s.* महाशब्दः, महानिनादः, कोलाहलः, महारवः. -*v. t.* भंज् 7 P, भिद् 7 P, मृद् 9 P, पिष् 7 P. -*v. i.* (परुषरवेण) ध्वन्-स्वन् 1 P, परुषं रु 2 P.

CRATCH, *s.* गवादनी, द्रोणि-णी *f.*

CRAUNCH, *v. t.* चर्व् 1 P, संदंश् 1 P.

CRAVAT, *s.* ग्रैवेयकं, ग्रीवावेष्टनं.

CRAVE, *v. t.* (सविनयं) याच् 1 A, प्र-अभि-अर्थ् 10 A; 'c. favour' प्रसद् c., अनुनी. 2 वांछ् 1 P, इष् 6 P, अभिलष् 1, 4 P, लभ् desid. (लिप्सते); *See* WISH. -ING, *s.* लालसा, स्पृहा, अभिलाषः, अतिकांक्षा, औत्सुक्यं, उत्कंठा, तृष्णा; 'c. for food' बुभुक्षा; 'c. for drink' पिपासा, तृष्णा.

CRAVEN, *s.* (c. hearted) कापुरुषः, भीरुः; *See* COWARD.

CRAW, *s.* पक्षिजठरः, पक्वाशयः.

CRAWL, *v. i.* सृप् 1 P, वि-प्र-सं°, उरसा गम् 1 P, मंदगत्या चल् 1 P. -*s.* गुप्ति *f.*; पोतोदरं.

CRAYON, *s.* वर्तिका, तूलिका.

CRAZE, *v. t.* भंज् 7 P, खंड् 10; *See* BREAK. 2 चूर्ण् 10, निष्पिष् 7 P. 3 ज्ञानं हन् 2 P, वातुलीकृ 8 U, मुह् c., संभ्रम् c. (भ्रमयति). -ED, -CRAZY, *a.* वातुल, बुद्धिविकल, हतज्ञान, उन्मत्त, भ्रांतचित्त. 2 जीर्ण, जर्जर, जर्जरीभूत. -EDNESS, *s.* बुद्धिवैकल्यं, वातुलता, उन्मादः, चित्तभ्रमः. 2 जीर्णता.

CREAK, *v. i.* कर्कशशब्दं कृ 8 U, परुषं विरु 2 P or स्वन् 1 P. -*s.* कर्कशशब्दः-ध्वनिः.

CREAM, *s.* शरः, क्षीरजं, शार्करः-रकः, क्षीरमंडं. 2 उत्तमांशः, सारः-रं, सारांशः. -*v. i.* शरं बंध् 9 P, फेनायते (D.). -*v. t.* शरं अपनी 1 P. -Y, *a.* शरमय (यी *f.*), शरोपम.

CREASE, *s.* वलि *f.*, वस्त्रभंगः, पुटचिह्नं.

CREATE, *v. t.* सृज् 6 P, निर्मा 3 A, जन् c. (जनयति), उत्पद् c., कृ 8 U, विधा 3 U, प्र-सं-क्लृप् c. 2 पदे-अधिका-

रै-नियुज् 7A, 10 or अभिषिच् 6P; 'a thing c. ed' भूतं.—ION, *s.* सर्गः, जननं, सृष्टि*f.*, निर्माणं, विधानं, प्रकल्पनं, भावना; 'a c. of the mind' मानसी सृष्टिः, मनःकल्पितं. 2 उत्पन्नं, भूतं. 3 विश्वं, निखिलजगत् *n.*, सृष्टि *f.*, सर्वभूतानि. —IVE, *a.* जनक, कल्पक, उत्पादक, निर्माण-रचना in comp.; 'c. genius' निर्माणशक्तिः. —OR, *s.* स्रष्टृ *m.*, निर्मातृ *m.*, उत्पादकः, जनकः. 2 ब्रह्मा, आत्मभूः, परमेष्ठी, पितामहः, विधाता, विश्वसृज्, धाता, प्रजापतिः, जगत्कर्ता, स्रष्टा, विधिः, वेधाः, स्वयंभूः, चतुराननः, विरिंचिः, कमलयोनिः, अब्जभूः. —URE, *s.* भूतं, जंतुः, जीविन्-प्राणिन् *m.*, देहिन् *m.* 2 प्रियः, वत्सः, जातः. 3 आश्रितः, उपजीविन् *m.*, लब्धोदयः; 'he is your c.' स त्वत्तो लब्धोदयः, त्वदुपजीवी.

CREDENCE, *s.* विश्वासः, प्रत्ययः, प्रमाणं; 'worthy of c.' विश्वास्य, प्रमाणं; 'to give c.' विश्वस्-प्रती 2 P.

CREDENTIALS, *s.* विश्वासपत्रं, प्रत्ययपत्रं.

CREDIBLE, *a.* विश्वसनीय, श्रद्धेय, विश्वास्य, प्रामाणिक (की *f.*). —CREDIBILITY, *s.* विश्वास्यता, विश्वासपात्रता, प्रामाण्यं. —CREDIBLY, *adv.* सप्रमाणं, श्रद्धेयतया, विश्वसनीयतया.

CREDIT, *s.* विश्वासः, प्रत्ययः, विश्रंभः; 'worthy of c.' विश्रंभभाजनं, विश्वासपात्रं. 2 प्रशंसा, श्लाघा, कीर्तिख्याति *f.*, प्रतिष्ठा, यशस् *n.*, स्तुति *f.*, स्तवः. 3 (In commerce) विश्वासः; कालिका; 'buying on c.' उद्धारः. 4 प्रामाण्यं, विश्वास्यता. —*v. t.* विश्वस्-प्रती 2P, सत्य *a.* मन् 4 A. 2 प्रमाणीकृ 8 U. —ABLE, *a.* श्लाघ्य, प्रशस्य, कीर्ति-गौरव-कर (री *f.*), स्तुत्य. —ABLY, *adv.* श्लाघ्यप्रकारेण, स्तुत्यर्हं; सगौरवं. —OR, *s.* उत्तमर्णः, ऋणदातृ *m.*, धनिकः.

CREDULOUS, *a.* श्रद्धालु, विश्वासशील, विश्वासिन् (नी *f.*), विश्रंभप्रवण, अशंकिन्. —NESS,-CREDULITY, *s.* विश्वासशीलता, अशंका, श्रद्धालुता.

CREED, *s.* धर्मः. 2 स्वीकृतमतं-पक्षः.

CREEK, *s.* वंकः, वक्रं, खातं. —Y, *a.* वंकवत् (ती *f.*), वक्र.

CREEP, *v. i.* सृप् 1 P, वि-सं-प्र°, मंदगत्या चल्-मंदं प्रसृ 1 P. 2 अलक्षितं प्रविश् 6 P. 3 शनैः प्रवृत् 1 A. —ER, *s.* लता, वल्ली, वल्लरी, व्रतति-ती *f.*; 'a branching c.' वीरुध् *f.*, गुल्मिनी, उलपः, प्रतानिनी. 2 सर्पिन्-उरोगामिन् *m.* —ING, *s.* विसर्पः-र्पणं, विसरः. —INGLY, *adv.* सर्पवत्, मंदगत्या; शनैःशनैः.

CREMATION, *s.* दाहः, दहनं.

CREPITATE, *See* CRACK.

CREPUSCLE,—SCULAR, *See* EVENING.

CRESCENT, *s.* अर्धचंद्रः, अर्धेंदुः, चंद्रार्धं. —*a.* 'c.-shaped' अर्धचंद्राकार. 2 वर्धमान, वर्धिन् (नी *f.*).

CRESSET, *s.* आकाशदीपः.

CREST, *s.* चूडा, शिखा, शेखरः, मौलिः; मुकुटं, किरीटः. 2 (Of a cock) चूडा, शिखा. 3 शिखरः-रं, मूर्धन् *m.* (of mountains); 'c. fallen' भग्न, भग्नदर्प, आत्तमान, विषण्ण; 'c. jewel' चूडामणिः, शिरोरत्नं-मणिः, शिखामणिः. —ED, *a.* शिखिन् (नी *f.*), चूडावत् (ती *f.*). 2 अवतंसित, किरीटिन्.

CRETACEOUS, *a.* कठिनीसंसृष्ट, कठिनीधर्मन्.

CREVICE, *s.* रंध्रं, छिद्रं, विवरं, बिलं, संधिः, गर्तः-र्ता.

CREW, *s.* नाविकाः, पोतवाहाः (pl.), नाविकगणः. 2 गणः, संघः, जनसमूहः.

CRIB, *s.* गवादनी, द्रोणि-णी *f.* 2 गोष्ठं, व्रजः. 3 शिशुदोला. —*v. t.* Confine, q. v.

CRIBBLE, *s.* चालनी, शोधनी, तितउः.

CRICK, *s.* कर्कशशब्दः. 2 मन्यास्तंभः.

CRICKET, *s.* झिल्लिका, भृंगारी, झीरुका, चीरी. 2 गुलिकाक्रीडा.

CRIME, *s.* अपराधः, पापं, दोषः, पातकं, पापकर्मन् *n.*, दुरितं; 'a heinous c.' घोर-महा-पातकं.—CRIMINAL, *a.* or *s.* अपराधिन् (नी *f.*), पापिन्, सपाप, पातकिन्, कृतापराध, पापकर्मन्, सदोष, दुष्कृतिन्; दंड्य, दोषग्रस्त; 'c. act' पापक्रिया; 'c. law' दंडविधिः-शासनं. —LY, *adv.* सापराधं, सदोषं. 2 दंडविधिन्यायेन, दंडविधिवत्. —ITY, *s.* सपापता, अपराधिता, सदोषत्वं.—CRIMINATE, *v. t.* दोषीकृ 8 U, सापराध-सदोष *a.* कृ, दोषेण लिप् 6 P. 2 अभिशंस् 1 P, अभियुज् 7 A, 10. —ION, *s.* अभियोगः, दोषीकरणं, दोषारोपणं, अभिशंसनं. —ORY, *a.* अभिशंसक; सदोष.

CRIMP, *a.* भंगुर, भिदुर. 2 असंगत, विरुद्ध, अयुक्त. —*v. t.*,-CRIMPLE, संकुच् 1P, पुटीकृ 8U, चूर्ण् 10.

CRIMSON, *a.* शोण, रक्त, अरुण, लोहित. —*s.* शोणः, रक्तिमन् *m.*, रक्तवर्णः, अरुणिमन् *m.*, लोहितः; 'covered with c.' अरुणित, पाटलित. —*v. t.* अरुणीकृ 8 U, अरुणयति-शोणयति-लोहितयति (D.).

CRINCUM, *s.* वलि *f.*, पुटः; संकोचः.

CRINGE, *v. i.* अंजलिं बंध् 9 P; साष्टांगपातं प्रणम् 1P or अनुनी 1 P; 'c. at the feet' अधश्चरणावपातं कृ 8 U (Bh. I. 31). —*s.*, —ING, *s.* अंजलिकर्मन् *n.*, अष्टांगपातः; श्ववृत्ति *f.* —*v. t.* *See* CONTRACT.

CRINIGEROUS, *a.* रोमवत् (ती *f.*); रोमोपम.

CRINKLE, *s.* वलि *f.*, पुटः, भंगः. —*v. i.* पुटीभू 1 P, व्यावृत् 1 A. —*v. t.* पुटीकृ 8 U, व्यावृत् c.

CRIPPLE, *a.* or *s.* पंगु (गु *f.*), विकल, विकलांग (गी *f.*); पादविकल; गतिहीन; श्रोण. —*v. t.* विकलयति (D.), विकलीकृ 8 U, व्यंगीकृ. 2 (fig.) दुर्बलीकृ. —NESS, *s.* पंगुता, अंगवैकल्यं.

CRISIS, *s.* संकटं, संकटवेला, संदेहसमयः; शुभाशुभलग्नं. 2 व्याधिसीमा. —CRITICAL, *a.* संदिग्ध; 'c. time' कार्यसंकटं, संकटसमयः, कार्यनिर्वहणकालः; 'at c' times' उपस्थितेषु दुर्गेषु.

Crisp, *a.* आकुंचित, बंधुर, भंगवत् (ती *f.*). 2 भंगुर, भिदुर, भिदेलिम. –*v. t.* (केशान्) रच् 10, भंगुरीकृ 8 U, आकुंच् c.; 'c. ing-iron, -pin' केशयमनकील:; 'c. ed tresses' घूर्णकुंतला:, वलीभूता: अलका:. –ature, *s.* केशाकुंचनं.

Criterion, *s.* लक्षणं, चिह्नं. लिंगं, संज्ञा. 2 निकष:.

Critic, *s.* गुणदोषविचारक:-निरूपक:, गुणागुणज्ञ:; विज्ञ:. गुणग्राहिन् *m.*, गुणदोषविवेचक:. 2 (cavilling c.) दोषैकदृश्-छिद्रान्वेषिन् *m.* –al, *a.* गुणदोषविचारयुक्त, गुणागुणज्ञ; गुणदोषग्राहिन् (णी *f.*), गुणदोषविवेचक. 2 दोषदर्शिन्, छिद्रान्वेषिन्. –ally, *adv.* सूक्ष्मं, सूक्ष्मतया, निपुणं. 2 गुणदोषपरीक्षया. 3 संकटसमये. –ise, *v. t.* गुणदोषविचारं-विवेचनं-कृ 8 U, गुणदोषान् निरूप् 10 or परीक्ष् 1 A or वि-विच् 3, 7 U. 2 छिद्राणि अन्विष् 4 P, or दृश् 1 P. –ism, Critique, *s.* गुणागुणपरीक्षा. गुणदोषविवेचनं-परीक्षणं-निरूपणं. 2 छिद्रान्वेषणं.

Croak, *v. i.* आरट् 1 P, विरु 2 P. 2 (As a crow) कै 1 P, ध्वांक्ष् 1 P. –*s.* आरटनं; भेकरव:, काकरव:.

Croceous, *a.* कुंकुमाक्त, गौर (री *f.*).

Crock, *s.* किट्टं, कज्जलं. –*v. t.* कृष्णीकृ 8 U, कज्जलेन लिप् 6 P. –ery, *s.* मृद्भांडानि (pl.); कौलालकं; मार्तिकं.

Crocodile, *s.* नक्र:, कुंभीर:, मकर:, ग्राह:, अवहार: (a kind of c.).

Croft, *s.* वाटिका; वाट:. वृति *f.*

Crone, *s.* स्थविरा, जरती, वृद्धा, जरठा.

Crony, *s.* चिरमित्रं, प्रियमित्रं-सुहृद् *m.*

Crook, *s.* दंड:; कुंचिताग्रयष्टि *f.*; आकर्षणी; 'by hook or c.' येन केन प्रकारेण; यथाकथंचित्; 'c. back' कुब्ज:, न्युब्ज:, गडुल:-र:. –*v. t.* आकुंच् c., वक्रीकृ 8 U, कुटिलीकृ, नम् c. –ed, *a.* वक्र, कुटिल, जिह्म, अराल; नामित, आकुंचित, भुग्न, न्युब्ज; 'c. bodied' विकृताकार:; 'c. armed' कुंप:, कु-कू-णि:, विकर:; 'c. nature' वक्रभाव:, कौटिल्यं; 'c. minded' कुटिलमति, जिह्मचेतस्, प्रतीप, अनृजुप्रकृति; 'c. with age' जरानतकाय, जरापरिणत. –edly, *adv.* वक्रं, कुटिलं, कुटिलगत्या, जिह्मं, साचि, तिर्यक्; 'going c.' जिह्मग:, कुटिलगति:. –edness, *s.* वक्रता, कुटिलता, जिह्मता. 2 विरूपता, विकृति *f.*

Crop, *s.* शस्यं, शस्यसंग्रह:, कृषिफलं; 'c. s' शस्यक्षेत्राणि. 2 अग्रं, शिखा. –*v. t.* (शस्यं) चर् 1 P, अद् 2 P, भक्ष् 10, चर्व् 1 P. 2 छिद् 7 P, लू 9 U, शस्यं लू or संग्रह् 9 P. –*v. i.* (up) आविर्भू 1 P, प्रादुर्भू, सहसा उद्गम् 1 P; 'c. eared' छिन्नकर्णाग्र, लूनकर्ण; 'c. ful' परिपूर्णोदर, अतितृप्त.

Crore, *s.* कोटि-टी *f.*

Cross, *v. t.* तॄ 1 P (lit. and fig.), सं-उत्°, लंघ्, उत्-, 1 A, 10, अति-इ 2 P, अतिक्रम् 1 U, 4 P, आक्रम्; 'these thoughts c. ed my mind' एते संकल्पा मम प्रादुरासन् or आसीत्-सम भूत्-मे मनसि (Ka.); 'he c. ed my sight' मम दर्शनपथमागत: (S. 3), नयनविषयमवतीर्ण:. 2 वि-प्रति-इध् 7 U, व्याहन् 2 U, प्रतिबंध् 9 P. 3 व्यति-अस् 4 U; 'with the arms c. ed' व्यत्यस्तभुज:; स्तनविनिहितहस्तस्वस्तिकाभिवंधुभि: (Mal. 4); 'c. legged' व्यत्यस्तपाद: ; 'to c. the legs' व्यत्यस्तपादाभ्यां आस् 2 A. 4 (In love) खंड् 10 ; खंडिता नारी 'c. ed or defeated in love'. –*s.* कूश:. 2 शूल:-लं. 3 प्रतिरोध:, विघ्न:, प्रत्यूह:, व्याघात:, प्रतिबंध:. 4 व्यस्तरेखाद्वयं, स्वस्तिकचिह्नं, स्वस्तिकं. –*a.* व्यत्यस्त, तिरश्चीन, साचिस्थित. 2 वि-प्रति-लोम, विरुद्ध, वाम, प्रतीप, प्रतिकूल. 3 दु:शील, पिशुन, दुरात्मन्, वक्रस्वभाव, जिह्मप्रकृति, वामशील; 'c. road' उपपथ:, उपमार्ग:; चतुष्पथं, शृंगाटकं; 'c.-examine' विविधं परीक्ष् 1 A or अनुयुज् 7 A; 'c. grained' प्रतीप, विलोम, विरुद्ध; 'to be c.' प्रतीपं गम् 1 P, प्रतीपायते (D.); 'c. multiplication' वज्राभ्यास:; 'c. threads' पूरणं. –ly, *adv.* तिर्यक्, व्यत्यस्तं, साचि. 2 प्रतीपं. प्रतिकूलं, विरुद्धं. 3 पिशुनतया. –ness, *s.* वक्रता, अमृजुता, जिह्मस्वभाव:, पैशुन्यं.

Crotch, *s.* अंकुश:, आकर्षणी, वडिश:.

Crotchet, *s.* कामचार:, लहरी, मनोलौल्यं, स्वैरिता.

Crouch, *v. i.* पत् 1 P (पादयो:); पादयोर्लुठ् 4 A, नम्रीभू 1 P, कायं नम् c. 2 चाटूक्त्या अनुनी 1 P or प्रसद् c.; *See* Cringe.

Crow, *s.* काक:, वायस:, ध्वांक्ष:, मौकुलि:; 'carrion c.' कुणपभुज्, द्रोणकाक:; 'c. bar' लोहदंड:. –*v. i.* विरु 2 P, नद् 1 P. 2 विकत्थ् 1 A; *See* Boast.

Crowd, *s.* समूह:, संघ:, वृंदं, गण:; *See* Collection; 'c. of people' जनसंमर्द:, संकुलं, जनौघ:, लोकसंघ:, बहुजनमेलक:. –*v. i.* 'to be c. ed' सं-आ-कॄ pass., परिवृ pass., संकुल-समाकुल-*a.* भू; 'house c. ed with people' जनाकीर्ण-जनसंकुलं गृहं; 'the place was very much c. ed' तस्मिन् स्थाने महान् जनसंमर्द आसीत्. –*v. t.* आ-सं-कॄ 6 P, परिवृ c. or पूर् 10, व्याप् 5 P, संकुलीकृ 8 U. 2 संमृद् 9 P. सबाध् 1 A. संकुलीकृ.

Crown, *s.* मुकुटं, किरीट:-टं. 2 राज्यं, राजपदं, राजत्वं; 'placed on the c.' राजपदमारोपित:, राज्येभिषिक्त:. 3 राजन् *m.*, शासितृ *m.* 4 (Of the head) चूडा, शिखा, मौलि:. 5 अग्रं, शिखा, शिखरं, शीर्षकं, शिरस् *n.*, शृंगं, अग्रभाग:. 6 स्रज् *f.*, माला. 7 रूप्यमुद्रा. –*v. t.* राज्ये अभिषिच् 6 P, मुकुटं परिधा c. (धापयति). 2 संपद् c., समाप् c., निष्पद् c.; 'c.

ed kings' मूर्धाभिषिक्ताः-मूर्धाभिषिक्ताः-राजानः; 'to c. all' इदं च तत्र विशिष्टतमं जातं; 'to be c. ed' फल् 1 P, सफलीभू; 'his efforts were c. ed with success' सर्वेऽस्य प्रयत्नाः सफलतां ययुः-फलिताः.

CRUCIBLE, CRUSET, *s.* मु(मू)षा-षी, तैजसावर्तनी.

CRUDE, *a.* अपक्व, अपरिणत, असिद्ध, असंस्कृत, आम. 2 अजीर्ण. 3 असंपूर्ण, असमाप्त; अपूर्णकाल, आकालिक (की *f.*); 'c. form' प्रातिपदिकं, असिद्धं रूपं.-LY, *adv.* अपूर्णकाले. -NESS, *s.* अपक्वता, आमता, अपाकः, अपरिणामः.

CRUEL, *a.* नृशंस, क्रूर, निष्ठुर, निष्करुण, निर्दय, निर्घृण, कठिनहृदय, क्रूरकर्मन्. -LY, *adv.* निष्करुणं, निर्दयं, निष्ठुरं, &c. -TY,-NESS, *s.* नृशंसता, निष्ठुरता, निर्दयत्वं, क्रूरता, निर्घृणता; 'c. to animals' प्राणिहिंसा.

CRUISE, *s.* समुद्रे परिभ्रमणं, पर्यटनं. -*v. i.* परिभ्रम् 1, 4 P, इतस्ततो भ्रम्.

CRUMB, CRUM, *s.* खंडः, लवः, शकलः-लं. 2 उच्छिष्टं, अन्नशेषः, पिष्टकशकलं. -CRUMMY, *a.* कोमल, मृदु.

CRUMBLE, *v. i.* चूर्णीभू 1 P, विशॄ pass., शकलीभू; पत् desid. (पिपतिषति). 2 विनश् 4 P, क्षि pass., अवसद् 1 P.-*v. t.* चूर्ण् 10, क्षुद् 7 U, निष्पिष् 7 P, मृद् 9 P, शकलीकृ 8 U; खंडशो विद् 10. 2 विनश् c., अवसद् c. -ING, *a.* जीर्ण, अवसन्न, विशीर्ण.

CRUMP, *a.* कुब्ज, न्युब्ज, वक्र.

CRUMPLE, *v. t.* संकुच् 1 P, संपुट् 10; *See* CONTRACT. 2 चूर्ण् 10, संमृद् 9 P.

CRUPPER, *s.* पुच्छबंधः.

CRUSH, *v. t.* संमृद् 9 P or c., संपीड् 10, निष्पिष् 7 P, क्षुद् 7 U, मंथ् 9 P, निर्दल् 1 P, 10, चूर्ण् 10; 'c. under the foot' पादतलेन-पादाघातेन-मृद्, पादभरेण आक्रम् 1 U, 4 P. 2 विध्वंस् c., विनश् c., उच्छिद् 7 P. -*s.* मर्दनं, निष्पेषः. 2 जनसंमर्दः, संकुलं. -ING, *a.* प्रमाथिन् (नी *f.*); 'c. defeat' सर्वनाशकरः पराजयः.

CRUST, *s.* त्वच् *f.*, बाह्यपटलं, वल्कं, बाह्यवेष्टनं. 2 घनभागः, बाह्यभागः. -*v. t.* घनपटलेन वेष्ट् c. or आवृ 5 U or आच्छद् 10; बाह्यतः घनीकृ 8 U. -*v. i.* घनपटलं बंध् 9 P, घनीभू; संहतीभू. -ACEOUS, *a.* कवचिन् (नी *f.*), वल्कवत् (ती *f.*), पटलवत्. -Y, *a.* घनपटलयुक्त, सपटल. 2 प्रतीप, परुष; निष्ठुर, पिशुन.

CRUTCH, *s.* अवलंबनार्थं दंडः; आधारदंडः.

CRY, *v. i.* क्रुश् 1 P, विलप् 1 P, रुद् 2 P, परि-देव् 1 A, 10, बाष्पं मुच्-विसृज् 6 P or पत् c. 2 (of crows &c.) वाश् 4 A, विरु 2 P; नद् 1 P, रट् 1 P. 3 वि-बद-घुष् 10, प्रकाश् c., प्रख्या c. (ख्यापयति); 'c. ing in the wilderness' अरण्यरुदितं. 4 तारस्वरेण-उच्चैः वद् 1 P or भाष् 1 A, आ-वि-क्रुश् 1 P, आ-, क्रंद् 1 P. -*s.* क्रंदनं, रुदितं, रोदनं, आक्रोशः, विलापः, परिदेवनं. 2 ध्वनिः, स्वनः, स्वरः, शब्दः, नादः; 'c. of distress' आर्तनादः, करुणस्वनः; रुतं, विरावः, (gen. of animals). 3 उत्क्रोशः, घोषणं, उच्चैर्घोषः, कोलाहलः. -down, अपवद् 1 P, अवगण् 10, अवमन् 4 A, अपलप्. -out, उत्क्रुश्, उच्चैः-तारस्वरेण-घुष्. -up, प्रशंस् 1 P, कृत् 10. -ER, *s.* घोषकः, प्रकाशकः, घोषणाकृत् *m.*

CRYSTAL, *s.* स्फटिकः, सितोपलः, सितमणिः, स्फटिकाश्मन् *m.* -*a.* 'c. like' स्फटिकाभ; विमल, स्वच्छ. -LIZE, *v. t.* स्फटिकरूपेण घनीकृ 8 U or घनीभू.

CUB, *s.* शावः-वकः, पोतः, कलभः, वत्सः, शिशुः, किशोरः-रकः.

CUBE, *s.* घनः; 'c. root' घनमूलं, घनपदं.-CUBICAL, *a.* घनाकार; 'c. contents' घनफलं.

CUBIT, *s.* हस्तः, किष्कुः; अरत्नि *m., f.* (with the last finger stretched).

CUCKOLD, *s.* बंधकीभार्यः; जारिणीपतिः and sim. comp.; 'c. maker' *See* ADULTERER.

CUCKOO, *s.* कोकिलः, पिकः, परभृतः, पुंस्कोकिलः (male c.); 'female c.' अन्य-पर-पुष्टा, परभृता, अन्यभृता, कोकिला.

CUCUMBER, *s.* चर्भटिका, चर्भटः, कर्कटी, उर्वारु *f.*, इ(ई)र्वारु-लु *f.*

CUD, *s.* चर्व्यः, आहारः.

CUDDLE, *v. i.* अंके-निकटे स्वप् 2 P or शी 2 A.

CUDGEL, *s.* लगुडः, यष्टि *f.*, दंडः, काष्ठं, गदा; 'c.-play' गदायुद्धं, दंडादंडि. -*v. t.* लगुडेन प्रहृ 1 P or आहन् 2 U or तड् 10; 'giving a sound c. ing' लगुडप्रहारैः जर्जरीकृत्य; 'c. your memory' स्मृतिं प्रबोधय तावत्.

CUE, *s.* संज्ञा, इंगितं, सूचना; सूत्रं. 2 अंचलः. 3 छंदः, भावः.

CUFF, *s.* मुष्टिप्रहारः, मुष्ट्याघातः. 2 पिप्पलांचलः.-*v. t.* मुष्टिना-पाणिना-तड् 10 or प्रहृ 1 P or आहन् 2 U; मुष्टीमुष्टि युध् 4 A.

CUIRASS, *s.* कवचः-चं, उरस्त्राणं. 2 कूर्पासः; निचोलकः.

CUISH, *s.* ऊरुत्राणं, ऊरुवर्मन् *n.*

CULINARY, *a.* पाक in comp.; 'c. skill' पाकसिद्धिज्ञानं.

CULL, *v. t.* उद्धृ 1 P, वृ 5 U; समा-हृ; एकत्र कृ 8 U; 'c. passages' चूर्णिकां कृ.

CULLION, *s.* जाल्मः, धूर्तः, शठः.

CULLY, *s.* वेश्याजितः; सुखप्रतार्यः.

CULM, *s.* नालं, कांडं.

CULMINATE, *v. i.* उच्चस्थानं प्राप् 5 P; 'the sun is c. ing' नभसो मध्यमध्यास्ते रविः; (fig.) परां कोटिं-काष्ठां-गम् 1 P, अतिभूमिं गम्; पाताभिमुखीभू, क्षयिष्णु -*a.* भू. -ION, *s.* परा कोटिः, परा काष्ठा.

CULPABLE, *a.* सदोष, सापराध, निंदार्ह, दोषिन् (णी *f.*), अपराद्ध, वाच्य, निंद्य, दूषणीय. -NESS, CULPABILITY, *s.* सदोषता, अपराधिता, वाच्यता.

CULPRIT, *s.* See CRIMINAL.

CULTIVATE, *v. t.* कृष् 1 P (land &c.). 2 वृध् c., उप-प्र-चि 5 U, परि-अनु-शील् 10, अभ्यस् 4 P, आ-सेव् 1 A, अनुष्ठा 1 P, भज् 1 U; 'c. friendship with the good' सतां मैत्रीं प्रचिनु-अभ्यस्य. -ION, CULTURE, *s.* कृषि *f.*, कर्षणं, कृषिकर्मन् *n.* 2 अनुशीलनं, अभिवृद्धि *f.*, संवर्धनं, प्रबोधनं. 3 उन्नति *f.*, उत्कर्षः; 'c. of the mind' प्रबोधः, प्रबुद्धता; 'men of c.' प्रबुद्धमनसः-संस्कारवंतः- जनाः, व्युत्पन्नाः; 'c. of learning' विद्याभिवृद्धिः; ज्ञानोन्नतिः, &c. -OR, *s.* कृषीवलः, कर्षकः, क्षेत्रिन् *m.* 2 अनुष्ठायिन् *m.*, परिशीलयितृ *m.*, संवर्धकः.

CULVER, See DOVE.

CUMBER, *v. t.* बाध् 1 A, क्लिश् 9 P; कष्ट-दुःखं आवह् 1 P, अतिभारो भू. -*s.* क्लेशः, कंटकः, शल्यं, अतिभारः. -SOME, CUMBROUS, *s.* कष्ट-दुःख-कर (री *f.*), क्लेशप्रद, अतिभारभूत. -CUMBRANCE, *s.* अतिभारः, शल्यभूतः, भारभूतः. 2 उपरोधः, प्रतिबंधः, प्रत्यूहः.

CUMIN, *s.* जीरकः, जरणः, कणा, अजाजी; 'black c.' सुषवी, कारवी, पृथ्वी, पृथुः, काला, उपकुंचिका.

CUMULATE, See ACCUMULATE.

CUNNING, *a.* विदग्ध, धूर्त, चतुर. 2 मायिन् (नी *f.*), वंचनशील, विप्रलंभक, कपटिन्. -*s.* विदग्धता, धूर्तता, चातुर्यं, नैपुण्यं, पटुता. 2 कपटं, माया, वंचनं. शाठ्यं, व्याजः, कैतवं, छलं. -LY, *adv.* चातुर्येण, विदग्धतया, धूर्ततया, सव्याजं.

CUP, *s.* पात्रं, चषकः-कं, भाजनं, काचपात्रं. 2 पुटः, कोशः-षः; 'fond of the c.' पानासक्तः; 'taste the c. of misery' दुःखभाग् भू. -*v. i.* आचूषणयंत्रेण रक्तं मुच् c. or मोक्ष् 10; 'c.-board' लघुकोष्ठः; 'c. ing glass' रक्तचूषणयंत्रं; 'dry c. ing' घटिकया अलाब्वा वा आचूषणं.

CUPID, *s.* मदनः, स्मरः, कामः, अनंगः, कंदर्पः, मन्मथः, मनसिजः, कुसुमबाणः, पंचशरः, मारः, प्रद्युम्नः, मीनकेतनः, कुसुमेषुः, मकरध्वजः, पुष्पधन्वा, आत्मभूः, अनन्यजः, चित्तजन्मन् and sim. comp. -ITY, *s.* लोभः, गृध्नुता, अतिलोभः-स्पृहा, लालसा, अतितृष्णा, लाभलिप्सा. 2 कामुकता.

CUPOLA, *s.* तोरणशृंगं, प्रासादशीर्षं.

CUR, *s.* शुनकः; See DOG. -RISH, *a.* भर्शील, दुष्ट.

CURATE, *s.* उपयाजकः, पुरोहितप्रतिनिधिः.

CURATOR, *s.* अवेक्षकः, अधिकारिन् *m.*, अध्यक्षः; 'c. of a depot' ग्रंथशालाधिकारी.

CURB, *v. t.* आवृ 5 U, सं-नि-यम् 1 P, नियंत्र् 10, प्र-नि-ग्रह् 9 P, अव-नि-रुध् 7 U, संहृ 1 P; 'c. the horses' प्रगृह्णंतां वाजिनः (S. 1); See CONTROL also. -*s.* मुखयंत्रणं, मुखशृंखला-लः. 2 यंत्रणं, संयमः, निरोधः, &c.

CURD, CURDLE, *v. i.* दधिरूपेण घनीभू, श्यै 1 A. -*v. t.* घनीकृ 8 U, श्यै c., संहन् 2 P. -*s.* दधि *n.*; पयस्यं, द्रप्सः-प्सं. -Y, -ED, *a.* दधिमय (यी *f.*). 2 घनीभूत, श्यान, संहत.

CURE, *v. t.* (disease) कित् desid. (चिकित्सति-ते), प्र-उप-शम् c. (शमयति), साध् c., प्रतिकृ 8 U, समाधा 3 U; (persons) सुस्थ-प्रकृतिस्थ-नीरोग-*a.* कृ; gen. ex. by निर्-गत-वीत in comp.; 'Râma was c. ed of his fever' रामो ज्वरोपशमना-न्नीरोगः कृतः, प्रकृतिस्थः संजातः; 'c. ed of wounds' निर्व्रणः कृतः; निर्विषः, &c. -*s.* चिकित्सा, उपशमः, प्रती(ति)कारः, रोगोपशमः. 2 सुस्थता, स्वास्थ्यं. 3 भेषजं, औषधं. -ABLE, *a.* साध्य; 'in-c. by physicians' भिषजामसाध्यं (R. VIII. 93); शमनीय, प्रतिकार्य. -ATIVE, *a.* रोगहर, रोगघ्न (घ्नी *f.*), व्याधिशमक, शांतिद. -ER, *s.* चिकित्सकः. -LESS, *a.* असाध्य, दुरुपचार.

CURIOSITY, *s.* कुतूहलं, कौतूहलं, जिज्ञासा, कौतुकं, कुतुकं; oft. ex. by desid. nouns; 'c. to see' दिदृक्षा. 2 (Object of c.) अपूर्ववस्तु *n.*, दुर्लभद्रव्यं, उत्कृष्टद्रव्यं. —CURIOUS, *a.* कुतूहलिन् (नी *f.*), जिज्ञासु, कौतुकाक्रांतचित्त, कुतुकाविष्ट, सकौतुक; 'my heart is c. to know' जिज्ञासाक्रांतहृदयोऽस्मि; oft. by desid.; 'c. to ascertain' उपलिप्सुः. 2 अपूर्व, अदृष्टपूर्व, अद्भुत, चित्र, दुष्प्राप, दुर्लभ; दर्शनीय. 3 सूक्ष्म, विज्ञ, निपुण, विचक्षण, सूक्ष्मदर्शिन्. -LY, *adv.* कुतूहलेन; सूक्ष्मं, अद्भुतं, चित्रं.

CURL, *s.* चूर्णकुंतलः, अलकः, कुरलः; 'hair thick with c. s' कुंतलाकीर्णाः शिरोरुहाः. 2 तरंगः, ऊर्मि *f.* -*v. t.* (केशान्) आकुंच् c., व्यावृत् c.; रच् 10. 2 तरंगयति (D.). -*v. i.* जिह्मीभू, वक्रीभू, आकुंच् pass., व्यावृत् 1 A. 2 तरंगायते (D.). -ED, -ING, *a.* कुटिल, अराल, कुंचित; 'c. mass of smoke' धूमस्योत्पीडः (U. 3).

CURMUDGEON, See MISER.

CURRENT, *a.* प्रचलित, प्रचल, सर्वसंमत; 'languages c. in India' भरतखंडे प्रचलिता भाषाः. 2 वर्तमान, विद्यमान; 'c. year' वर्तमानसंवत्सरः; 'c. report' जनप्रवादः; 'c. moment' आयातः. 3 सर्वसाधारण, लोकप्रसिद्ध-विश्रुत. -*s.* स्रोतस् *n.*, प्रवाहः, रयः, वेगः, धारा, ओघः; 'c. of opinion' साधारणमतौघः. -LY, *adv.* साधारणतः, सामान्यतः, लौकिकतया; 'c. known' लोकप्रसिद्ध. -CURRENCY, *s.* प्रचलनं, प्रचारः, प्रसरणं; 'to gain c.' प्रचलित *a.* भू, प्रसृ 1 P, व्यवहृ c. pass., सर्वसंमत *a.* भू; 'a report gained c.' इति जनप्रवादः प्रसृतः. 2

प्रवाहः, प्रसरः. 3 सुखोच्चार्यता. 4 प्रचलितमुद्रा.

CURRIER, *s.* चर्मकारः, पादूकृत् *m.*

CURRY, *v. t.* (favour) अतिचाटूक्त्या प्रसादं संपद् c. or आराध् 10. 2 (a horse) अश्वदेहं मृज् 2 P. 3 (leather) परिष्कृ 8 U, शुध् c. 4 Beat, q. v.; 'c. comb' अश्वदेहमार्जनी.

CURSE, *v. t.* शप् 1 U, अभिशंस् 1 P, शापं दा 3 U (with dat.), आक्रुश् 1 P ; गर्ह् 1, 10 A. –*s.* शापः, अभिशापः, आक्रोशः. 2 कंटकः, आधिः ; 'a c. to the family' कुलस्याधिः, कुलांगारः, कुलपांसुलः; 'a c. on thy folly' धिक् त्वां मूढ. –ED, *a.* शप्त, आक्रुष्ट; *See* ACCURSED.

CURSORY, *a.* क्षिप्र, असूक्ष्म, त्वरित ; अनिपुण, अनवहित, स्थूल ; 'even at a c. glance' स्थूलदृष्ट्यापि. –LY, *adv.* शीघ्रं, स्थूलदृष्ट्या, अनिपुणं.

CURT, *a.* ह्रस्व, संक्षिप्त. –LY, *adv.* संक्षेपेण. –NESS, *s.* संक्षेपः, संहारः, संक्षिप्तता. –CURTAIL, *v. t.* ह्रस् c., संक्षिप् 6 P; संहृ 1 P; अवच्छिद् 7 P, अल्पीकृ 8 U.

CURTAIN, *s.* ज(य)वनिका, तिरस्करिणी, व्यवधानं, आवरणपटः; 'behind the c.' नेपथ्ये; 'c. lecture' शय्यानुशासनं ; 'bed c.' मशहरी, मशकहरी. –*v. t.* आवरणेन प्रच्छद् 10, व्यवधा 3 U.

CURVE, *v. t.* नम् c., अव-आ-नम् c., आकुंच् c., वक्रीकृ 8 U, कुटिलीकृ, आवृज् 10. –*s.* नति *f.*, आवर्जनं, वक्रता, आकुंचनं, अंचनं. 2 वक्ररेखा. –*a.* आनत, वक्र, कुटिल, आभुग्न, जिह्म; *See* CROOKED. –ATED, *a.* आभुग्न, वक्र, &c. –ATION, *s.* आकुंचनं, आवर्जन, वक्रीकरणं. –ATURE, *s.* वक्रता, वक्रिमन् *m.*, कुटिलता, आनति *f.*, वक्रीभावः.

CURVET, *v. i.* प्लु 1 A, वल्ग् 1 P. –*s.* प्लुतं, वल्गनं.

CUSHION, *s.* उपधानं, उपबर्हः, पीठोपधानं.

CUSP, *s.* अर्धेंदुशिखा, अर्धचंद्राग्रं. –ATED, *a.* सूच्यग्र, निशिताग्र.

CUSTODY, *s.* रक्षा, अवेक्षणं, रक्षणं, पालनं, गुप्ति *f.*; *See* CHARGE. 2 निरोधः, बंधनं, कारानिरोधः, आसेधः.

CUSTOM, *s.* आचारः, संप्रदायः, व्यवहारः, रीति *f.*, अनुसारः, क्रमः. 2 करः, शुल्कं, राजस्वं; 'c. house' शुल्कस्थानं; 'the officer of c. s' शौल्किकः. –ARY, *a.* आचारिक-व्यावहारिक (की *f.*), प्रचलित, लोकसिद्ध, लौकिक (की *f.*); gen. by आचार in comp.; 'to take flowers as is c.' आचारपुष्पग्रहणार्थं (M. 4); आचारलाजाः, &c. –ARILY, *adv.* यथाव्यवहारं, संप्रदायानुसारेण, प्रायशः, यथाचारं. –ER, *s.* ग्राहकः, क्रेतृ *m.*, नित्यक्रायिन् *m.*

CUT, *v. t.* लू 9 U, छिद् 7 P, कृत् 6 P, दो 4 P, व्रश्च् 6 P, छो 4 P. 2 भिद् 7 U, खंड् 10 ; 'c. ing to the quick' मर्मच्छिद्-भिद्, मर्माणि कृंतत्; 'c. a hole through' व्यध् 4 P, निर्भिद्, समुत्कृ 6 P ; 'c. a figure' प्रतिष्ठां-कीर्तिं-लभ् 1 A; 'c. short' संहृ 1 P, संक्षिप् 6 P ; न्यूनीकृ 8 U ; 'to c. the matter short' किं बहुना ; 'c. ing short my speech' मद्वचनमाक्षिप्य ; 'c. to, or in, pieces' खंडशः-लवशः-छिद्. –*v. i.* उद्भिद् pass., उत्पद् 4 A, स्फुट् 6 P. –*s.* छेदः, प्रहारः, आघातः. 2 कुल्या, खातं. 3 खंडः-डं, भागः, दलं, लवः, लेशः. 4 सरलमार्गः, अर्वमार्गः. 5 रीति *f.*, रूपं, मार्गः, पद्धति *f.*; 'c.-purse' ग्रंथिभेदकः, चोरः; 'c.-throat' कंठच्छेदकः; प्राणघातकः, घातकः; (*a.*) मारात्मक, वधोद्यत. –down, अवच्छिद्, कर्तित्वा निपत् c. –off, निकृत्, व्यवच्छिद्. 2 उच्छिद्, उन्मूल् 10, विनश् c. 3 विलुप् c., अपनी 1 P. 4 विच्छिद्, अव-नि-रुध् 7 U, खंड् 10, निवार् 10. –out, उत्कृत् c. 2 परि-सं-कॢप् c. (मनसा); निरूप् 10, चित्र 10, युज् 10. 3 अतिक्रम् 1 U, 4 P, अतिशी 2 A; *See* Excel. –TER, *s.* छेदकः, छेत्तृ *m.*, छिद् in comp.; 'wood-c.' काष्ठच्छिद्. –TING, *s.* छेदनं, कर्तनं, &c. 2 खंडः-डं, शकलः-लं, दलं. –*a.* तीव्र, तीक्ष्ण, मर्मभेदिन् (नी *f.*), मर्मस्पृश्-छिद्, अरुंतुद.

CUTANEOUS, *a.* त्वाच (ची *f.*), त्वक्संबंधिन् (नी *f.*), त्वच् in comp.; 'c. disease' त्वग्रोगः.

CUTICLE, *s.* बाह्यत्वच् *f.*, बाह्यचर्मन् *n.*

CUTLASS, *s.* खड्गः; कृपाणी.

CUTLER, *s.* छुरिकाकारः, शस्त्रकारः.

CYCLE, *s.* चक्रं, आ-परि-वृत्ति *f.*, पर्यायः; कालचक्रं.

CYLINDER, *s.* गोलः, वर्तुलं. –CYLINDRICAL, *a.* वर्तुल, गोलाकार.

CYMBAL, *s.* झल्लकं, झल्लरी.

CYNIC, *s.* मनुष्यद्वेषिन् *m.* –AL, *a.* सदावक्र, कुटिलशील, दुरात्मन्, वक्रभाव ; निंदाशील.

CYNOSURE, *s.* ध्रुवः ; ज्योतीरथः.

D.

DAB, *v. t.* सिक्तद्रव्येण लघु तड् 10. –*s.* लघ्वाघातः, निषेकः. 2 लघुपिंडः. 3 क्षिप्तपंकः.

DABBLE, *v. t.* सिच् 6 P, प्रोक्ष् 1 P, लिप् 6 P. – *v. i.* जले-पंके-क्रीड् 1 P; 'd. ing in books' पल्लवग्राहि पांडित्यं (H. 1), शास्त्रचुंबनं. –ER, *s.* जलक्रीडः; शास्त्रचुंबकः.

DAGGER, *s.* कृपाणः, छुरिका, कर्तरी, असिपुत्रिका; 'at d.s drawn' सदाबद्धवैर *a.*

DAGGLE, *v. t.* मलेन दुष् c. (दूषयति), पंकेन लिप् 6 P.

DAILY, *See* under DAY.

DAINTY, *a.* स्वादु, रुचिर, सुरस, मिष्ट. 2 ललित, कोमल, मृदु, सूक्ष्म. 3 अतिविनीत, अतिसभ्य. –*s.* मिष्टविशिष्ट-भोजनं, स्वाद्वन्नं, भोजनविशेषः. –LY, *adv.* स्वादुतया, ललितं, कोमलं. –NESS, *s.* स्वादुता; कोमलता, लालित्यं, विलासः, विभ्रमः.

Dairy, *s.* दुग्धशाला, दधिमंथनगृहं; 'd. maid' गोपकन्या, आभीरी, गोदोहिनी.

Dale, *s.* दरी, कंदरः, उपत्यका.

Dally, *v. i.* विलस् 1 P, विभ्रम् 1, 4 P, क्रीड् 1 P, रम् 1 A, विहृ 1 P. **2** Delay, q. v. **-ance**, *s.* विलासः, विभ्रमः, क्रीडा, विहारः, कामचेष्टा.

Dam, *s.* सेतुः, जलावरणं, धरणः. **2** मातृ *f.*, जननी, अंबा, प्रसूः. **-***v. t.* (up) (सेतुना) जलं निरुध् 7 U or संस्तंभ् 9 P.

Damage, *s.* हानि *f.*, अपकारः, अपायः, नाशः, ध्वंसः. **2** (of things in use) क्षयः, क्षति *f.*, उपक्षयः, अपचयः. **3** निष्कृति *f.*, प्रतिफलं, क्षतिपूरणं. **-***v. t.* नि-अप्-कृ 8 U, क्षि c., नश् c., दुष् c. (दूषयति). **2** हिंस् 7 P, क्षण् 8 P.

Damask, *s.* चित्रदुकूलं. **-***v. t.* Variegate, q. v.

Dame, *s.* आर्या, भवती (in addressing). **2** स्त्री, गृहिणी; 'old d.' वृद्धा स्त्री, पुरंध्री.

Damn, *v. t.* दंड् 10; *See* Condemn. **2** नरकदंडं आदिश् 6 P, नरके निपत् c. **3** गर्ह् 1, 10 A; *See* Censure. **-able**, *a.* गर्ह्य, निंद्य. **2** नरकदंडार्ह. **-ation**, *s.* निरय-नरक-वासः; नरकदंडः, नरकयातना, विनिपातः, अनंतदंडः-यातना.

Damp, *a.* क्लिन्न, स्तिमित, आर्द्र, जलसिक्त, उन्न; 'to be d.' क्लिद् 4 P. **2** विषण्ण, म्लान, अवसन्न, भग्नोत्साह. **-***s.* क्लेदः, जलावसेकः, स्तेमः. **2** बाष्पः, धूमः. **3** विषादः, म्लानता, उत्साहभंगः. **-***v. t.* क्लिद् c., उंद् 7 P, आर्द्रीकृ 8 U. **2** भंज् 7 P, खंड् 10, ध्वंस् c., भग्नाश *a.*-कृ, भंगं-ध्वंसं-कृ; 'do not d. his energy' तस्योत्साहभंगं मा कृथाः; 'd. ed by defeat' पराजयेन भग्नोत्साहः. **-ish**, *a.* आक्लिन्न, ईषदार्द्र. **-ness**, *s.* आर्द्रता, क्लिन्नता.

Damsel, *s.* कन्या, बाला, कुमारी, बालिका, युवति-ती *f.*; 'd.'s child' कानीनः (नी *f.*); 'celestial d.' अप्सरस् *f.*, स्वर्गस्त्री-योषित्.

Dance, *v. i.* नृत् 4 P, नट् 1 P; 'who always d. s attendance' यः अहर्निशमुपरचितांजलिः (अधिदैवतमिव) स्तौति (Ka. 109); or merely सांजलि उपस्था 1 A or उपास् 2 A. **-***v. t.* नृत् c., संचल् c. **-***s.* नृत्यं, लास्यं, तांडवं, नाट्यं, पादन्यासः. **-er**, *s.* नटः, नर्तकः, कुशीलवः, शैलूषः; 'male d. in a female dress' भ्र(भ्रु)कुंसः, भ्रूकुंसः. **-ing**, *s.* नाट्यं, नृत्यं; 'd. girl' नर्तकी; 'd. house-school' नृत्यशाला; 'd. master' नाट्याचार्यः.

Dandle, *v. t.* अंके निधाय लल् 10.

Dandriff, *s.* मज्जा; दारुणं.

Dandy, *s.* सुवसनः, सुभगंमन्यः; दांभिकः.

Danger, *s.* भयं, भीति *f.*, शंका, संदेहः, संशयः. **2** आपद्-विपद् *f.*, अपायः, अनर्थः, व्यसनं, संकटं, दुर्गं, कृच्छ्रं, कष्टः-ष्टं; 'd. to life' जीवितसंशयः; 'the hour of d.' आपत्समयः; 'money is in d. of being lost' द्रव्यापहरणस्य भयं वर्तते; 'without any d.' अकुतोभय *a.*; 'brought into d.' संशयित; 'attended with d.' संदिग्ध, संशयदोलारूढ. **-***v. t.* संशये पत् c., संशयस्थ *a.* कृ 8 U. **-ous**, *a.* संकट, संबाध, विषम. **2** भयावह, भयंकर, भीतिप्रद, भयहेतुक; oft. by (*s.*) in comp. **3** संदिग्ध, शंकाक्रांत, संशयापन्न, विपज्जनक; 'a d. man' अविश्वास्यः, घातुकः. **-ously**, *adv.* भयपूर्वकं; 'my brother is d. ill' मम भ्राता जीवितसंशये वर्तते.

Dangle, *v. i.* दुल् 1 P, लुट् 6 P, चंच् 1 P, लंब् 1 A; 'd. ing at the feet' पादलग्न, चरणलोल.

Dapple, *v. t.* चित्र् 10, कर्बुरीकृ 8 U, कल्माषयति (D.). **-ed**, *a.* चित्र, कर्बुर, कल्माषित, शबल.

Dare, *v. i.* धृष् 5 P, उत्सह् 1 A; साहसं कृ 8 U, शक् 5 P. **-***v. t.* आह्वे 1 A, धृष् c. **-***s.* आह्वानं, योधसंरावः. **-ing**, *s.* साहसं, धार्ष्ट्यं, धैर्यं, प्रगल्भता, निर्भीकता. **-***a.* साहसिक (की *f.*), निर्विशंक, धृष्ट, शूर, प्रगल्भ, निर्भय. **-ingly**, *adv.* धृष्टं, साहसेन; प्रगल्भं, निर्भयं. **-ingness**, *s.* साहसं, धृष्टता, &c.

Dark, *a.* अंधकारमय (यी *f.*), तिमिरावृत, तमोवृत, तामस (सी *f.*), तमस्विन् (नी *f.*), निष्प्रभ, सतिमिर, सांधकार. **2** कृष्ण, श्याम, नील. **3** अस्पष्ट, गूढ, दुर्बोध. **4** पाप, दुष्ट, खल, गर्ह्य, निंद्य; 'd. in soul' तमोवृत्ति, पापात्मन्; 'd. thoughts' पापसंकल्पाः. **-***s.*, **-ness**, *s.* अंधकारः, तमस् *n.*, तमिस्रा-स्रं, ध्वांतं, तिमिरं; 'quality of (tendency to) d.' तमोगुणः; 'slight d.' अवतमसं; 'pitchy (blinding) d.' अंधंतमः, सूचिभेद्यं तमः; 'in the d.' रजनीतिमिरे; 'all-pervading d.' संतमसं. **2** गूढं, रहस्यं; 'I am still in the d. about the matter' तस्यार्थस्याहमद्याप्यनभिज्ञः, न किमपि वेद्मि. **-en**, *v. t.* अंधकारयति (D.), तिमिरेण आवृ 5 U, तिमिरेण आच्छद् 10. **2** (fig.) कलुषयति-कलंकयति (D.), दुष् c. (दूषयति); 'face d. ed with fury' कोपकलुषिताननं. **-***v. i.* अंधीभू 1 P. **-ish**, *a.* ईषत्कृष्ण, आनील. **-ly**, *adv.* सांधकारं, अस्पष्टं, अव्यक्तं, गूढं. **-some**, *a.* निष्प्रभ, तमोवृत.

Darling, *a.* प्रिय, प्रियतम, दयित; ex. by जात, तात. **-***s.* स्नेहपात्रं, वत्सः, जातः, दयितः.

Darn, *s.* वस्त्रसंधिः. **-***v. t.* जीर्णवस्त्राणि सिव् 4 P, or संधा 3 U.

Dart, *s.* अस्त्रं, शल्यं, शंकुः. **2** बाणः; *See* Arrow. **-***v. t.* मुच्-क्षिप् 6 P, अस् 4 P, पत् c., विसृज् 6 P, (with loc.). **-***v. i.* जवेन-सहसा-सवेगं-उत्था 1 P, or पलाय् 1 A. **2** सहसा उदि 2 P or आविर्भू 1 P. **3** स्फुर् 6 P, विलस् 1 P; 'd. on' रभसा-जवेन प्रचल् 1 P or आपत् 1 P or अभिद्रु 1 P.

Dash, *v. t.* रभसा प्रक्षिप् 6 P or पत् c., आ-प्रस्था-

हन् 2 U ; 'd. ed her head against a rock' प्रस्तरे तस्याः शिरः आजघ्ने. 2 मृद् 9 P, प्रभंज् 7 P, खंडशः कृ 8 U, चूर्ण् 10, विद् 10; 'the ship was d. ed to pieces' पोतः खंडशो भग्नः,-सहस्रधा विदीर्णः,-(प्रतिघातेन) शकलीकृतः. 3 अवकृ 6 P ; उक्ष् 1 P, सिच् 6 P. 4 संमिश्र् 10. 5 विनश् c., व्यामृज् 2 P or c., विलुप् c. –v. i. (against) आपत् 1P, आ-समा-हन्. 2 शकलीभू 1 P, विद्-प्रभंज् pass.; 'd. off' जवेन पलाय् 1 A or अपसृ 1 P. –s. संघट्टः, समाघातः, अभिघातः, निष्पेषः, संमर्दः. 2 प्रहारः, आघातः, आक्रमः. 3 प्रागल्भ्यं, धीरता, उत्साहः.

DASTARD,-LY, *See* COWARD,-LY.

DATA, s. स्वीकृतानि तत्त्वानि; उपन्यासः.

DATE, s. खर्जूरः -री. 2 कालः, तिथि m., f. ; कालावधिः, लेखनदिवसः-तिथिः-दिनं; 'out of d.' व्यवहारातिक्रांत. –v. t. दिनं-तिथिं-लिख् 6P.–v. i. (from) आरभ् 1 A (with abl.); विशिष्टकालादारभ्य प्रवृत् 1 A.

DAUB, v. t. लिप् 6 P, अंज् 7 P, दिह् 2 U. –s. लेपः, विलेपनं. 2 कुचित्रं, कदालेख्यं. –ER, s. लेपकः. 2 अकुशलचित्रकरः. –Y, a. श्यान, सांद्र.

DAUGHTER, s. कन्या, दुहितृ f., तनया, पुत्रिका, आत्मजा, सुता, पत्री, नंदिनी; oft. ex. by Patronymics; 'd. of Parvata' पार्वती; 'd. of Janaka' जानकी; 'd.-in-law' स्नुषा, वधूः.

DAUNT, v. t. त्रस् c., भी c., उत्साहं-धैर्यं-भंज् 7 P, भग्नाश a. कृ 8 U, धैर्यं स्खल् c. –LESS,(UND.-ED), a. निर्भीक, निर्भय, अजातशंक, अभीत, अस्खलितधैर्य. –LESSNESS, s. अभयं, विशंकता.

DAW, s. द्रोणकाकः.

DAWDLE, v. विलंब् 1 A; कालं हृ 1 P or क्षिप् 6 P.

DAWN, s. उषस् f., n., प्रत्यूषः, प्रभातं, विभातं, दिनमुखं, अरुणोदयः; 'it is d.' प्रभाता रजनी. 2 उदयः; 'd. of liberty' स्वातंत्र्योदयः ; 'belonging to the d.' उषस्य, प्रभातीय, (s.) in comp. –v. i. आविर्भू 1 P, उद्भिद् pass., उद्गम् 1 P, प्रभा 2 P; 'before the day d. ed' अप्रभातायां शर्वर्यां; 'the day d. ed' प्रभाता रजनी.

DAY, s. दिनं, दिवसः, वासरः, अहन् n., वारः; 'a lunar d.' तिथि m., f.; 'd. by d.' दिने दिने, अनुदिवसं, प्रत्यहं; 'by d.' दिवा; 'the next d.' परेद्युः; 'the d. before' पूर्वेद्युः; 'another d.' अन्येद्युः; 'the other d.' अचिरं; 'd. and night' अहर्निशं, अहोरात्रः; दिवारात्रं, नक्तंदिवं; 'all d. long' अहर्निशं, रात्रिंदिवं, दिवानिशं-रात्रं; 'till this d.' अद्य यावत्; 'the d. after to-morrow' परश्वः; 'he gained the d.' तस्मिन् दिने स विजयी बभूव; 'd.-break' *See* DAWN; 'd. labour' व्रातं, दैनिकं कर्म; 'd. labourer' व्रातीनः; 'd. light' सूर्यप्रकाशः, दिनज्योतिस् n.; 'd. star' प्रभातनक्षत्रं; 'd. time' दिनकालः, दिनसमयः; 'being in the d.' दिवातन (नी f.); 'during d.' दिवा. –DAILY, a. दैनिक-प्रत्यह्निक-आह्निक (की f.), दैनंदिन (नी f.); 'd. business' आह्निकं, नित्यकर्म. —adv. प्रति in comp. with 'day'; प्रत्यहं, प्रतिदिनं ; दिने दिने, अहरहः, &c.

DAZZLE, v. t. (the eye) चक्षुषः तेजः प्रतिहन् 2 P (Ka. 43) ; नेत्रं प्रतिहन्. –ING, a. दुष्प्रेक्ष्य, दुर्निरीक्ष्य; 'of d. splendour' प्रभाविशेषोदयदुर्निरीक्ष्यः (R. VI. 5); नेत्रप्रतिघातिन्, (विजित्य नेत्रप्रतिघातिनीं प्रभां K. v. 20).

DEAD, *See* under DIE.

DEAF, a. बधिर, श्रोत्रविकल, अकर्ण, एड ; 'd. and dumb' एडमूकः. –EN, v. t. बधिरयति (D.), कर्णं उपहन् 2 P, बधिरीकृ 8 U; 'd. ing all directions with cries of alas' हाहानिनादैर्दिशो बधिरयंतः. –LY, adv. बधिरवत् ; अश्रुतिपूर्वं. –NESS, s. बधिरता, एडता, श्रवणाक्षमता.

DEAL, s. बाहुल्यं, प्राचुर्यं ; 'a good d. of' बहु, प्रचुर, भूरि, विपुल ; 'a good d. of corn' बहुधान्यं; 'a good d.' (adv.) अत्यंतं, बहु, भृशं, गाढं, अति or सु pr.; सुतरां, अतिकृश, &c. 2 देवदारु n. –v. t. विभज् 1 U, परिक्लृप् c., पृथक् पृथग् विन्यस् 4 U. 2 विकृ 6 U, व्यस् 4 P; 'd. blows' मुष्टिना प्रह 1 P, आघातं-प्रहारं-कृ 8 U. –v. i. (in) पण् 1 A, व्याप् 6 A; क्रयविक्रयं कृ, व्यवह् 1 P ; 'he does not d. in missiles' नास्य व्यवहारोऽस्त्रेषु (U. 5). –with, आचर् 1 P, वृत् 1 A, व्यवहृ. 2 प्रतिकृ 8 U ; निरुध् 7 U ; स्पर्ध् 1 A; *See* CONTEND. 3 विधा 3 U, वशीकृ, विनी 1 P ; 'easy to d.' विधेयः, वश्यः. –ER, s. वणिज् m., आपणिकः, विपणिन् m., क्रयविक्रयिन् m. 2 व्यवहारिन्-व्यापारिन्-व्यवसायिन् m.; 'd. in wood' काष्ठव्यवहारकः. –ING, s. वाणिज्यं, निगमः, विपणः, क्रयविक्रयः. 2 व्यवहारः, व्यवसायः, आचरणं, व्यापारः, चेष्टितं, क्रिया, कर्मन् n., वृत्ति f., वर्तनं. 3 संव्यवहारः, संसर्गः, संगमः.

DEAR, a. बहुमूल्य, महार्घ-र्ह, महामूल्य. 2 प्रिय, दयित, वल्लभ, अभिमत, इष्ट, कांत, अभीप्सित ; 'd. friend' हृदयंगमः सखा ; 'as d. as one's life' प्राणप्रियसम. 3 (As a term of endearment) दयित, कांत, जात, वत्स, प्रिय; 'd. Jânakî' प्रिये जानकि; वत्स राम, &c. –adv., –LY, बहुमूल्येन, महार्घेण. 2 अत्यंतं; सुप्रियं, सुप्रीत्या, अति-सु-pr. 3 अहो, बत, हा, हंत, अहह. –NESS, s. प्रियता, अभीष्टता, प्रीति f. 2 बहुमूल्यं, महार्घता, महार्घः.

DEARTH, s. दुर्भिक्षं, दुष्कालः ; 'd. felt' नीवाकः, प्रयामः. 2 अभावः, अप्राप्ति f., विरहः, दुर्लभता.

DEATH, *See* under DIE.

DEBAR, *v. t.* नि-प्रति-षिध् 1 P, निवार् 10, निरुध् 7 U. 2 निराकृ 8 U, निरस् 4 U.

DEBARK, *v. i.* उत्तॄ 1 P, नौकाया अवतॄ. –*v. t.* अवतॄ c.

DEBASE, *v. t.* Ex. by कृ 8 U with 'Base' q. v.; अपकृष् 1 P, स्वपदात् पत् c. or भ्रंश् c. or च्यु c.; लघूकृ, अवज्ञा 9 U. –MENT, *s.* अपकर्षः, अभिभवः, पदच्यावनं, लघूकरणं, अवमानना, अवज्ञा. 2 अप-निकृष्टता, अधोगति *f.*, नीचस्थिति *f.*

DEBATE, *s.* वि-,वादः, वादप्रतिवादः, वादयुद्धं, विचारः, वितर्कः, हेतुवादः. –*v. t.* विचर् c., वितर्क् 10; *See* ARGUE. –*v. i.* विवद् 1 A, विप्रलप् 1 P, वाक्कलहं-वादयुद्धं-कृ 8 U. –ER, *s.* वादिन् *m.*, वितर्किन्-विवादकृत्-हेतुवादिन् *m.* –FUL, *a.* वादप्रिय, विवादशील, वादार्थिन्.

DEBAUCH, *v. t.* दुष् c. (दूषयति), नश् c., सत्पथात् च्यु c. or भ्रंश् c.; 'd. a girl.' (कन्यां) दुष् c., धृष् c., सतीत्वाद् भ्रंश् c., क्षतयोनिं कृ. –*s.* कामावेशः; विषयोपभोगः, विषयनिरति *f.* –EE, *s.* विषयिन् *m.*, विषयासक्तः, कामासक्तः, विषयोपभोगरतः. 2 दुराचारः, दुष्टचरितः, खंडितवृत्तः. –ER, *s.* दूषकः, नाशकः, –ERY, *s.* विषयासक्ति *f.*, कामासक्तता, विषयोपभोगः, व्यसनं, विषयित्वं.

DEBENTURE, *s.* प्रतिज्ञापत्रं, नियमलेखः.

DEBILITATE, *v. t.* तेजो हृ 1 P or नश् c., क्षै c. (क्षपयति), दुर्बलीकृ 8 U, क्षीणीकृ. –ED, *a.* दुर्बल, क्षीण, कृश, अशक्त, क्षाम. –DEBILITY, *s.* दौर्बल्यं, शक्तिहीनता, क्षामता, कार्श्यं, तेजोहानि *f.*, शक्तिक्षयः, शक्तिपातः, अशक्तता.

DEBIT, *v. t.* देयधनभागे लिख् 6 P.

DEBONAIR, *a.* सभ्य, शिष्ट, सुशील, सुविनीत, आर्य. –LY, *adv.* सभ्यवत्, सुविनीतं.

DEBT, *s.* ऋणं; 'pay off or discharge a d.' ऋणं दा 3 U or शुध् c., अनृणतां-आनृण्यं गम् 1 P; 'he paid off the d. of his master by his life' स्वासुभिर्भर्तुरानृण्यं गतः (M. 5); 'discharge of d.' ऋणशोधनं-निस्तारः, ऋणमोक्षः; 'involved in d.' ऋणग्रस्त, ऋणिन् (नी *f.*); 'run into or incur d.' ऋणं कृ, ऋणं ग्रह् 9 P; 'free from d.' अनृण. –OR, *s.* ऋणिन् *m.*, अधमर्णः.

DECADE, *s.* दशकं; 'd. of years' दशवर्षं.

DECADENCY, *s.* क्षयः, अवपातः, अवसादः.

DECAGON, *s.* दशास्रं, दशभुजः.

DECAMP, *v. i.* कटकं-शिबिरं-त्यज् 1 P, कटकनिवेशाद् अपसृ 1 P or अपक्रम् 1 U, 4 P, सहसा पलाय् 1 A or अपक्रम्. –MENT, *s.* कटकत्यागः, अपसरणं, पलायनं; अपगमनं.

DECANT, *v. t.* काचपात्रे स्रु c. or निक्षिप् 6 P. –ER, काचपात्रं, कूपी.

DECAPITATE, *See* BEHEAD.

DECAY, *v. i.* क्षि pass., क्षयं-लयं-या-इ 2 P, जॄ 4 P, शॄ pass., ह्रस् 1 P, अवसद् 1 P; गल् 1 P, नश् 4 P, म्ली 4 A, क्षै-म्लै-ग्लै 1 P, ध्वंस् 1A; 'with d.-ed leaves' प्रपर्ण:-शीर्णपर्णः-(वृक्षः). –*v. t.* Causal of roots above. –*s.* क्षयः, अवसादः, जीर्णता, ह्रासः, प्रलयः, नाशः, अपचयः, क्षामता, ग्लानि *f.* –ING, *a.* क्षयिन् (णी *f.*), क्षीयमाण, विशीर्यमाण.

DECEASE, *v. i.* मृ 6 A, उपरम् 1 P; *See* DIE. –*s.* मरणं, मृत्युः, निधनं; तनुत्यागः, उपरमः, संस्थानं. –ED, *a.* Dead, q. v.

DECEIVE, *v. t.* वंच् 10, प्रतॄ c., प्रलुभ् c., भ्रम् c. (भ्रमयति), मुह् c.; *See* CHEAT; 'you are much d. ed (in thinking so)' महाभ्रमोयं तव. –ER, *s.* वंचकः, प्रतारकः, कितवः, मायिन् *m.*, धूर्तः, शठः. —DECEIT, –DECEPTION, *s.* प्रतारणा, कपटं, छद्मन् *n.*, छलं, वंचनं-ना, कैतवं, माया, विप्रलंभः, कूटं, अतिसंधानं, उपधिः. 2 मोहः, भ्रमः. –FUL, -DECEPTIVE, *a.* कपटपर, वंचक, धूर्त, वंचनशील, कपटिन्, मायिन्, छाद्मिक, शठ, कितव. 2 भ्रमकारिन्, मोहिन्, भ्रांतिजनक, मोहोत्पादक. –FULLY, *adv.* सव्याजं, छद्मना, मायया, सकपटं, छलेन.

DECEMBER, *s.* सहस्यः, मार्गशीर्षपौषौ.

DECENNIAL, *a.* दशवार्षिक (की *f.*), दशवर्षीय-ण, दशवर्षस्थायिन्.

DECENT, *a.* विनीत, सविनय, समर्याद, शिष्ट, सभ्य. 2 युक्त, उचित, योग्य, उपपन्न, शिष्टाचारानुरूप, साधुसंमत. –LY, *adv.* सविनयं, सभ्यतया; युक्तं, यथातथं, यथोचितं. –DECENCE,-CY, *s.* विनयः, सभ्यता, मर्यादा, लज्जा, शालीनता. 2 औचित्यं, युक्तता, उपपत्ति *f.*, यथार्थता.

DECHARM, *v. t.* मंत्रं प्रतिकृ 8 U.

DECIDE, *v.* निर्णी 1 P, व्यवसो 4 P, निश्चि 5 U, परिच्छिद् 7 P, अव-सम-धृ 10; 'd. a case' कार्यं निर्णी, व्यवहारं दृश् 1 P or अवेक्ष् 1 A; 'perplexed so as not being able to d.' अपरिच्छेदाकुल (S. 5). 2 निष्पद् c., साध् c. –ED, *a.* निश्चित, ध्रुव, दृढ, स्थिर; स्थिरो निश्चयः 'd. or firm resolution'; असंदिग्ध, नियत, व्यवस्थापित. –EDLY, *adv.* असंशयं, नूनं, नियतं; *See* CERTAINLY. –ER, *s.* निर्णेतृ *m.*, निश्चायकः; प्रमाणपुरुषः. –DECISION, *s.* निर्णयः, निश्चयः, व्यवसायः, संप्रधारणं, परिच्छेदः. 2 (Final result) निर्णयः; निष्पत्ति *f.* —DECISIVE, *a.* संशयच्छिद्, निर्णायक, असंदिग्ध, निश्चयकारिन्; निश्चायक; 'said in a d. ly stern tone' परिच्छेदनिष्ठुरमाह स्म (Ka. 277). –LY, *adv.* सनिश्चयं, असंदिग्धं, सनिर्णयं; दृढं, स्थिरतया.

DECIDUOUS, *a.* पातुक, पतनशील, क्षयिन्, अस्थायिन्. –NESS, *s.* अवपातः, विध्वंसः, पतनशीलता. 2 अस्थायित्वं.

DECIMAL, *a.* दशक, दशगुणित.–*s.* दशांशः. –DECIMATE, *v. t.* दशमांशं ग्रह् 9 P; दशमं पुरुषं दण्ड् 1 P.

DECIPHER, *v. t.* (a letter &c.) निर्-अनु-वच् c., (गूढाक्षराणि) व्याख्या 2 P, स्पष्टीकृ 8 U, व्या-कृ, विशदीकृ. –ER, *s.* व्याख्यातृ *m.*, विवरणकृत् *m.* –ING, *s.* व्याख्यानं, स्पष्टीकरणं.

DECK, *v. t.* अलं-कृ 8 U, भूष् 10, मंड् 10; *See* ADORN. 2 आच्छद् 10, आस्तॄ 9 U. –*s.* नौतलं, नौकापृष्ठं.

DECLAIM, *v. i.* (against) अपभाष् 1 A, निंद् 1 P, आक्षिप् 6 P; *See* ABUSE. 2 सालंकारं ब्रू 2 U, वाक्तांडवं कृ 8 U. –ER, DECLAMATOR, *s.* वावदूकः, वागीशः. 2 निर्भर्त्सकः, निंदकः. –DECLAMATION, *s.* सालंकारं वचनं, शब्दपांडित्यं; वाक्चातुर्यं, वाक्तांडवं.

DECLARE, *v. t.* वद् 1 P, कथ् 10, ख्या 2 P, आ-प्र-ख्या c. (ख्यापयति), प्र-काश् c., प्रकटीकृ 8 U, उद्-घुष् 10, नि-आ-विद् c., अभिधा 3 U. 2 उदीर् c., उच्चर् c., कृत् 10; स्मृ 1 P (in scriptures). –*v. i.* स्वमतं-अभिप्रायं-निविद् c. or ज्ञा c.; 'd. for' अवलंब् 1 A, आश्रि 1 U; ' the army d. ed against its king' स्वराजानं परित्यज्य प्रतिपक्षं समालंबत सैन्यं. –ATION, *s.* प्रख्यापनं, प्रकाशनं, आख्यानं, ज्ञापनं, कीर्तनं, निवेदनं. 2 उक्ति *f.*, वचनं, भाषणं, प्रतिज्ञा, उपन्यासः. –ATORY, *a.* ख्यापक, ज्ञापक, निवेदक, वाचक, सूचक, अभिधायक. –EDLY, *adv.* स्पष्टं, व्यक्तं, प्रतिज्ञापूर्वकं.

DECLINE, *v. i.* क्षयं-ह्रासं-या-इ 2 P or गम् 1 P, अवसद् 1 P, क्षि pass.; स्रंस् 1 A, ध्वंस् 1 A, अपचि-विशॄ-pass. 2 त्यज् 1 P, विचल् 1 P, निवृत् 1 A, भ्रंश् 1 A, 4 P. 3 परिणम् 1 P, आ-अव-नम्, अस्तं गम् 1 P, अस्तमवलंब् 1 A; अनेन समयेन परिणतो दिवसः (Ka. 47) 'the sun had d. ed' &c. –*v. t.* प्रत्याख्या 2 P, प्रत्याचक्ष् 2 A, प्रत्यादिश् 6 P, अपाकृ 8 U, परिवृज् 10. 2 आ-अव-नम् c. (नमयति), अपकृष् 1 P, आवृज्. 3 शब्दरूपाणि आख्या or कथ् 10.–*s.* ह्रासः, क्षयः, परिणति *f.*, पातः, अवसादः, ध्वंसः, अपचयः, अस्तः ; ' in the d. of life, in d.-ing years ' पश्चिमे वयसि, परिणतवयसि. 2 देहक्षयः, क्षयरोगः. –ATION, *s.* भ्रंशः, क्षयः, च्युति *f.*, &c. 2 वक्रता, अवनमनं, आवर्जनं. 3 क्रांति *f.*, अपगमः. –DECLENSION, *s.* विभक्तिरूपाणि, शब्दविकारः. 2 क्षयः.

DECLIVITY, *s.* अवसर्पिणी भूमिः, उत्संगः. –OUS, DECLIVOUS, *a.* प्रवण, अवसर्पिन्.

DECOCT, *v. t.* क्वथ् 1 P, पच् 1 P. –ION, *s.* क्वाथः, कषायः,-यं, निर्यासः.

DECOLLATION. *s.* शीर्षच्छेदः.

DECOMPOSE, *v. t.* पृथक् कृ 8 U, व्या-कृ, वि-ली c., विद्रु c.–ITION, *s.* पृथक्करणं, व्याकरणं, विश्लेषः, विलयः.

DECOMPOUND, *v. t.* पुनर्मिश्र् 10. 2 Decompose, q. v.

DECORATE, *v. t.* भूष् 10, प्रसाध् c., अलंकृ 8 U, मंड 10. –ION, *s.* प्रसाधनं, मंडनं, भूषणं, अलंकारः, परिष्कारः, आभरणं. 2 आकल्पः, वेषः, नेपथ्यं, प्राति(परि)कर्मन् *n.* –OR *s.* प्रसाधकः, विभूषकः.

DECOROUS, *a.* विनीत, सविनय; युक्त, उचित; *See* DECENT. –DECORUM, *s.* विनयः, मर्यादा, सभ्यता, शिष्टाचारः, सुरीति *f.*, सौजन्यं. 2 युक्तता, औचित्यं.

DECORTICATE, *v. t.* त्वचं निष्कुष् 1 P, निस्त्वचीकृ 8 U, निर्वल्कयति (D.).

DECOY, *v. t.* कपटेन आकृष् 1 P, वि-, मुह् c., प्रलुभ् c., प्रतॄ c.; *See* CHEAT. 2 पाशे बंध्-ग्रह् 9 P.

DECREASE, *v. i.* परिक्षि pass., ह्रासं गम् 1 P or या-इ 2 P, अवसद् 1 P, ह्रस् 1 P, अल्पीभू 1 P, न्यूनीभू, अपचि pass. –*v. t.* ह्रस् c., अल्पीकृ 8 U, न्यूनीकृ, लघयति (D.), ऊन् 10, अपचि 5 U. –*s.*,-DECREMENT, *s.* ह्रासः, क्षयः, अपचयः, अवसादः, न्यूनता-त्वं, अल्पत्वं.

DECREE, *v. t.* आदिश् 6 P, आज्ञा c. (ज्ञापयति), शास् 2 P. 2 दा c. (दापयति), प्रक्लृप् c. विधा 3 U, दातुं निर्णी 1 P. –*v. i.* व्यवस्थाद्वारेण निर्णी, शासनं कृ, व्यवस्थां-विधिं-कृ; विचर् c., तीर् 10. –*s.* व्यवस्था, शासनपत्रं, व्यवस्थापत्रं, विधिः, राजाज्ञा; आ-निदेशः, आज्ञा, शासनं.

DECREPIT, *a.* जराक्रांत, जरातुर, जीर्ण, जरापरिणत. –UDE, (d. age), *s.* जरा, वार्धक्यं, जीर्णावस्था, जरावस्था.

DECRESCENT, *a.* क्षयिन्, क्षीयमाण, क्षयिष्णु.

DECRETAL, *s.* विधिसंहिता.

DECRY, *v. t.* अप-परि-वद् 1 U, निंद् 1 P, आक्षिप् 6 P, अपलप् 1 P. –AL, *s.* परिवादः, आक्षेपः, अपलपनं.

DECUMBENT, *a.* शयान, संविष्ट, निषण्ण, उपविष्ट.

DECUMBENCE, *s.* शयनं, शय्योपवेशनं.

DECUPLE, *a.* दशगुण.

DEDICATE, *v. t.* उत्सृज् 6 P, निक्षिप् 6 P, प्र-वि-नियुज् 7 A, 10. 2 प्रतिष्ठा c. (-ष्ठापयति), संस्कृ 8 U, उपक्लृप् c.; (books) सम्-ऋ c. (अर्पयति), निविद् c. –ION, *s.* उत्सर्गः, विनियोगः, प्रतिष्ठा, संस्कारः; समर्पणं, निवेदनं.

DEDUCE, *v. t.* अनुमा 2 P, 3 A, ऊह् 1 A, अपवह् 1 P, निर्णी 1 P, उपलक्ष् 10. –IBLE, *a.* आनुमानिक (की *f.*), ऊहनीय. –MENT,–DEDUCTION, *s.* अनुमानं, अनुमिति *f.*, ऊहनं, ऊहा, अपवाहः. –DEDUCTIVE, *a.* आनुमानिक (की *f.*). –LY, *adv.* अनुमानेन.

DEDUCT, *v. t.* वियुज् 10, अवच्छिद् 7 P, उद्हृ 1 P, व्यवकल् 10, ऊन् 10. -ION, *s.* वियोजनं, उद्धारः, व्यवकलनं, उद्धृतांशः.

DEED, *s.* कर्मन् *n.*, कार्य, क्रिया, कृत्यं, चेष्टितं. 2 लेखप्रमाणं, लिखितं; 'sale d.' विक्रयपत्रं; 'title d.' आगमः. 3 तत्त्वं, अर्थः, वस्तु *n.*

DEEM, *v. t.* मन् 4 A, गण् 10, अवगम् 1 P, संभू c.

DEEP, *a.* गभीर, गंभीर, अगाध, गहन, गाढ. 2 (of sound) मंद्र, धीर, गंभीर, मांसल, घन. 3 of colours) घन; 'd. red' घनारुण, सुरक्त. 4 निम्न, नीच. 5 गहन, दुर्बोध, निगूढार्थ, अगम्य. 6 गभीरबुद्धि, दूरदृष्टि, विदग्ध; 'd. darkness' अंध-घोरं-तमः, संतमसं; 'she is d. in love' दूरगतमन्मथा सा (S. 3); 'd. sigh' दीर्घनिश्वासः; 'd. love' दृढबद्धं प्रेम, गाढानुरागः; 'water knee-d.' जानुदघ्नं-मात्रं-द्वयसं जलं. -*s.* Sea, q. v.; 'd. of night' निशीथः; घोररात्रि *f.* -EN, *v. t.* गंभीरीकृ 8 U, घनीकृ, वृध् c. -LY, *adv.* गाढं, घनं, दीर्घं; अत्यंतं, अतीव, नितरां, निर्भरं, भृशं; 'sighing d.' दीर्घं निश्वस्य; 'd. sorry' शोकमग्न, अतिदुःखित; 'd. rooted' बद्धमूल. -NESS,-DEPTH, *s.* गांभीर्यं, गाढता, घनता, अगाधता; 'd. of meaning' अर्थतो गौरवं (Mal. 1), अर्थगौरवं. 2 उदरं, गभीरस्थानं; 'the d. of lower regions' पातालोदरं. 3 वेधः, वेधनं. 4 मध्यं.

DEER, *s.* मृगः, हरिणः, कुरंगः, कुरंगमः, वातायुः, अजिनयोनिः; पृषत् *m.*, कृष्णसारः, रुरुः, शंबरः, रोहिषः, वातप्रमीः (varieties of d.).

DEFACE, *v. t.* विनश् c., उच्छिद् 7 P, विलुप् 6 P or c., व्या-अप-मृज् 2 P. 2 विकृ 8 U, विरूप् 10, दुष् c. (दूषयति). -ER, *s.* दूषकः, विनाशकः. -MENT, *s.* लोपः, उच्छेदः, दूषणं, नाशनं.

DEFALCATE, *v. t.* न्यूनीकृ 8 U, ह्रस् c., अवच्छिद् 7 P, ऊन् 10. -ION, *s.* ह्रासः, अवच्छेदः, न्यूनता, अपचयः.

DEFAME, *v. t.* परि-अप-वद् 1 U, अपभाष् 1 A, आक्षिप् 6 P, गुणान्-अपलप् 1 P, अभिशंस् 1 P. -ATION, *s.* परि-अप-वादः, आक्षेपः, अपभाषणं, निंदा, अभिशंसनं. -ATORY, *a.* परिवादक, गुणापवादक, अकीर्तिकर (री *f.*), आक्षेपगर्भ. -ER, *s.* परिवादिन् *m.*, गुणापवादकः, आक्षेपकः, निंदकः.

DEFAULT, *s.* अपराधः, दोषः; व्यतिक्रमः, अननुष्ठानं, लोपः. 2 अभावः, असंभवः, अप्राप्ति *f.*; 'in d. of fine' अदत्ते दंडे, दंडदानाभावे. -ER, *s.* अपराधिन् *m.*, नियमलंघिन्, नियमव्यतिक्रामिन् *m.*

DEFEASANCE, *s.* लोपः, व्यतिक्रमः, नियमभंगः-लोपः.

DEFEASIBLE, *a.* लोपनीय.

DEFEAT, *v. t.* परा-जि 1 A, परा-परि-भू 1 U, जि 1 P, भंज् 7 P; वि-द्रु c., पराहन् 2 P, (d. completely). 2 मोघीकृ 8 U, व्याहन् 2 P, विहन्; *See* BAFFLE. -*s.* पराजयः, परिभवः, पराभवः, अभिभवः, भंगः. 2 व्याघातः, भंगः, प्रध्वंसः.

DEFECATE, *v. t.* मलं हृ 1 P, शुध् c., निर्मलीकृ 8 U. -*a.* निर्मल, शोधित, हृतमल. -ION, *s.* शोधनं, मलहरणं.

DEFECT, *s.* विकारः, दोषः, छिद्रं, वैकल्यं, न्यूनता; 'bodily d.' अंगविकारः, व्यंगता. 2 अभावः, विरहः. -IVE, *a.* विकारवत्, दोषयुक्त, सदोष, विकल; अंगहीन. 2 असंपूर्ण, असमग्र, अपर्याप्त, न्यून.

DEFECTION, *s.* त्यागः, उत्सर्गः, भ्रंशः, च्युति *f.*

DEFEND, *v. t.* रक्ष् 1 P, पा 2 P, त्रै 1 A, परित्रै, पा c. (पालयति) (with abl.); *See* PROTECT. 2 (In law) उत्तरं दा 3 U, पक्षं समर्थ् 10. -ANT, *s.* प्रत्यर्थिन् *m.*, प्रतिवादिन् *m.*, अभियुक्तः. -ER, *s.* रक्षकः, गोप्तृ *m.*, त्रातृ-रक्षितृ *m.*, पालकः, पः in comp. -DEFENSIVE, *a.* रक्षक, पालक, निवारक, आत्मरक्षक. -*s.* आत्मरक्षा, स्वपरित्राणं, शत्रुनिवारणं.—DEFENCE, *s.* रक्षा, गुप्ति *f.*, रक्षणं, त्राणं, पालनं. 2 उत्तरं, प्रत्युत्तरं; व्यपदेशः.-LESS, *a.* अशरण, अरक्षित, अनाश्रय, अनाथ. 2 निरायुध, शस्त्रहीन.

DEFER, *v. t.* विलंब् c., व्याक्षिप् 6 P. 2 (अन्यस्मिन्) निक्षिप् 6 P, न्यस् 4 P, सम्-ऋ c. (अर्पयति). -*v. i.* विलंब् 1 A, कालं क्षिप् or हृ 1 P, चिर(रा)यति (D.). 2 (to) अनुवृत् 1 A, अनुपा c. (पालयति), आदृ 6A, सादरं आश्रि 1 U, अनुरुध् 4 A. -ENCE, *s.* अनुरोधः, अनुवर्तनं, बहुमानः, आदरः, प्रश्रयः. 2 नम्रता, विनयः, वशता. -RING, *s.* कालयापनं, कालहरणं, विलंबः, व्याक्षेपः.

DEFICIENT, *a.* न्यून, ऊन, असंपूर्ण, विकल; often ex. by अल्प-हीन-रहित in comp.; 'd. in water' अल्पजल; 'd. in intellect' अल्पधी, बुद्धिहीन; 'd. in any organ' हीनांग, विकलेंद्रिय, विकलांग, अपोगंड, पो(पौ)गंड. -DEFICIENCE, -CY, *s.* न्यूनता, हीनता, अल्पता, अभावः, विरहः, वैकल्यं, अपूर्णता. 2 दोषः, छिद्रं.

DEFILE, *v. t.* दुष् c. (दूषयति), मलिनीकृ 8 U, मलिनयति-कलुषयति-आविलयति (D.); 'd. a virgin' कुमारीं दुष् c., आधृष् c.; 'a d. ed virgin' क्षतयोनिः. -*v. i.* दंडव्यूहेन प्रया 2 P or अपसृ 1 P. -*s.* संबाधपथः, संकटमार्गः, दुर्मार्गः, संचारः. -ER, *s.* दूषकः.-MENT, *s.* दूषणं. 2 मालिन्यं, कलंकः.

DEFINE, *v. t.* लक्षणं व्याख्या 2 P; उप-, लक्ष् 10, परिच्छिद् 7 P, निरूप् 10, निर्वच् 2 P. 2 निर्दिश् 6 P, निर्णी 1 P, निश्चि 5 U, निर्धृ 10. 3 चिन्ह् 10, परिमा 3 A.-ER, *s.* लक्षणव्याख्यातृ *m.*, निर्वक्तृ *m.* -ITE, *a.* नियत, निर्णीत, निश्चित, निर्दिष्ट; 'without any d. object' अनिर्दिष्टकारणं. 2 परिमित, समर्याद,सावधिक. -ITELY, *adv.* नियतं, व्यक्तं, सनिर्णयं, सपरिच्छेदं. -TION, *s.* व्याख्या, परिच्छेदः, लक्षणं, निर्वचनं, निर्दे-

शः; 'my anguish transcends d.' मम विकारः परिच्छेदातीतः (Mal. 1). -ITIVE, *a.* नियत, निर्णायक, स्थिर; अवश्यक.

DEFLAGRATION, *s.* दाहः, दाहनं, ज्वलनं.

DEFLECT, *v. i.* भ्रंश् 1 A, 4P, च्यु 1 A, विचल् 1 P, अप-व्या-वृत् 1A. -*v. t.* व्यावृत् c. -ION, *s.* भ्रंशः, च्युति *f.*, विचलनं, विमार्गगमनं. 2 उत्क्रमः, भ्रेषः.

DEFLOUR, *v. t.* चारित्र्यं नश् c. or हृ 1 P, धृष् c., क्षतयोनिं कृ 8 U, दुष् c. (दूषयति); 'a virgin d.-ed' क्षता, क्षतयोनिः. 2 शोभां हृ or नश् c. -ER, *s.* कुमारीदूषकः, सतीत्वनाशकः.

DEFLUXION, *s.* निस्यंदः, क्षरणं, स्रवणं.

DEFOLIATION, *s.* पत्रापगमः, पर्णमोक्षः. 2 पत्रच्युतिसमयः.

DEFORM, *v. t.* विरूप् 10, विकृ 8 U, व्यंगीकृ, विरूपीकृ. -ED, *a.* विरूप, विकृत, पोगंड, कु-अप-रूप, विकृतांग-व्यंग (गी *f.*); 'd. features' विकृताकारः. -ITY, *s.* वैरूप्यं, विरूपता, कुरूपता, व्यंगता, विकृति *f.*

DEFRAUD, *v. t.* वंच् 10, प्रवृ c.; *See* CHEAT. 2 छलेन-कपटेन-अपहृ 1 P. -ATION, *s.* कपटापहरणं. -ER, *s.* वंचकः, प्रतारकः.

DEFRAY, *v. t.* (Expenses) दा 3 U, अपाकृ 8 U, शुध् c.; धनव्ययं-व्ययशोधनं-स्वीकृ 8 U; 'to be d.-ed' शुध् 4 P; एकस्य मूल्येन व्ययः शुध्यति, सर्वा व्ययशुद्धिः संपद्यते (P. v. 8). -ER, *s.* व्ययशोधकः. -ING,-MENT, *s.* व्ययशोधनं-शुद्धि *f.*

DEFT, *a.* विनीत, दक्ष, चतुर, विदग्ध.

DEFUNCT, *a.* मृत, विपन्न; *See* DEAD. 2 (fig.) त्यक्तव्यापार, निश्चेष्ट. -ION, *s.* मरणं, मृत्युः, देहत्यागः.

DEFY, *v. t.* तृणीकृ 8 U, अवज्ञा 9 U, अवमन् 4 A, अनादृ 6 A. लघूकृ, तृणाय मन्, परिभू 1 P, अवगण् 10; 'I d. a king' राजेति कियती-का मम मात्रा; 'I d. you to find a mistake in my writing' मम लेखे स्खलितं कथं त्वं दर्शयसीति प्रेक्षे तावत्; 'a disease which d. ed medical skill' वैद्ययत्नपरिभाविनं गदं (R. XIX. 53). 2 युद्धार्थं आह्वे 1 A, अभियुज् 7 A, धृष् 5 P. -ANCE, *s.* समाह्वानं, युद्धाह्वानं, योधसंरावः. 2 अवज्ञा, अवगणना; 'in d. of' अवमत्य, तृणीकृत्य, अनादृत्य; ex. by gen. or loc. abs. -ANT, *a.* उद्धत, सदर्प, सावज्ञ; अवमानिन्; 'in a d. tone' उद्धतं, सदर्पं, सावज्ञं. -ER, *s.* समाह्वातृ *m.*, अभियोक्तृ *m.*

DEGENERATE, *v. i.* (कुलाचारात्) च्यु 1 A, भ्रंश् 1 A, 4 P, दुष् 4 P. -*a.* क्षीणपुण्य, नष्टधर्मन्, परिभ्रष्ट, अपकृष्ट, कुलाचारभ्रष्ट. -NESS, -DEGENERACY, *s.* क्षीणपुण्यत्वं, कुलाचारभ्रंशः, कुलमर्यादातिक्रमः. - 2 अपकर्षः, नीचावस्था, अपकृष्टदशा.

DEGRADE, *v. t.* (पदात् or अधिकारात्) अपकृष् 1 P, भ्रंश् c., च्यु c., अवरुह् c. (रोपयति), नीचपदं प्राप् c. 2 अवमन् c., लघूकृ 8 U, मूल्यं लघयति (D.) or ह्रस् c.; 'd. ed from office' अधिकारभ्रष्ट, पदभ्रष्ट, भ्रष्टाधिकार, पदावरोपित. -ATION, *s.* पद-अधिकार-भ्रंशः, अपकर्षः, पदच्युति *f.*, पदलोपः. 2 अवमानना, लघूकरणं, मानभंगः. 3 अपकृष्टता, अधोगति *f.*, नीचावस्था, अपकृष्टस्थिति *f.* -ING, *a.* लाघवकारिन्, अयशस्कर (री *f.*).

DEGREE, *s.* पदं, स्थानं, पदवि-वी *f.*, आस्पदं. 2 दशा, स्थिति *f.*, अवस्था. 3 उपाधिः, उपपदं. 4 कुलं, वंशः, अन्वयः. 5 प्रमाणं, परिमाणं. 6 गणः, वर्गः. 7 भागः, अंशः. 8 कोटि *f.*, काष्ठा; 'the highest d.' परा कोटिः-काष्ठा, अतिभूमिः. 9 क्रमः, अनुक्रमः, आवृत् *f.*, परिपाटि-टी *f.*, आनुपूर्व्य-र्वी, पर्यायः, तारतम्यभावः; 'in the highest d.' निरतिशयं, एकांततः; 'in some d.' किंचित्, कियताप्यंशेन, ईषत्; 'not in any d.' न केनाप्यंशेन; 'by d. s' क्रमेण, क्रमशः, शनैःशनैः, प्रतिपदं.

DEIFY, *v. t.* देवत्वमारुह् c. (आरोपयति), देवं कृ 8 U; 'to be deified' देवीभू 1 P, देवत्वं इ 2 P, देवत्वमापद् 4 A. -DEIFORM, *a.* देवाकार, देवरूप. -DEIFICATION, *s.* ईश्वरसायुज्यं, ब्रह्मणि लयः, देवत्वप्राप्ति *f.* 2 देवत्वं, देवकरणं.

DEIGN, *v.* अर्ह् 1P, प्रसद् 1P, with inf.;'d. to look at me' मयि दृष्टिप्रसादं कुरु; *See* PLEASE. 2 प्रसादपूर्वं दा 3 P, अनुग्रह् 9 P. 3 अनुज्ञा 9U, अनुमन् 4 A.

DEISM, *s.* ईश्वरवादः, आस्तिक्यं. -DEIST, *s.* आस्तिकः, ईश्वरवादिन् *m.*

DEITY, *s.* देवता, दैवतं, देवः; *See* GOD.

DEJECT, *v. t.* विषद् c., निर्विद् c., विषादं उत्पद् c., म्लानीकृ, धैर्यं त्यज् c. -ED, *a.* विषण्ण, निर्विण्ण, विषादापन्न, अवसन्न, दीन, म्लान, खिन्न; 'd. in mind' दीनमनस्, दुर्मनायमान, उद्विग्न, विमनस्, धैर्यच्युत; 'to be d.' विषद् 1 P, विषादं गम् 1 P, दुर्मनायते (D.), धैर्यं त्यज् 1 P. -EDLY, *adv.* सविषादं, सोद्वेगं, विषण्णं. -EDNESS, -ION, *s.* विषादः, वैमनस्यं, निर्वेदः, अवसादः, उद्वेगः, निषण्णता, दीनता, म्लानि *f.*, ग्लानि *f.*, खेदः, दौर्मनस्यं.

DEJECTURE, *s.* अवस्करः, पुरीषं.

DELATE, *v. t.* वह् 1 P, आनी 1 P. 2 Accuse, q. v.

DELAY, *v. t.* विलंब् c., व्याक्षिप् 6 P, अतिपत् c. 2 निरुध् 7 U, धृ 1 P, विष्टंभ् 9 P.-*v. i.* विलंब् 1 A, चिर(रा)यति (D.), कालं या c. (यापयति) or क्षिप् 6 P or हृ 1 P; 'why d. then' ततः किं विलंब्यते (U. 1). 2 विकृष् c., विचर् c. -*s.* विलंबः, व्याक्षेपः, कालातिपातः, कालयापनं, कालहरणं, कालक्षेपः. 2 व्याघातः, अंतरायः, विलंबहेतुः. 3 दीर्घसूत्रता; 'without d.' अविलंबितं, अविलंबं, अविलंबेन, अवि-

ई-रात्-रेण; 'd. is dangerous' दीर्घसूत्री विनश्यति. -ER, s. कालक्षेपकः.

DELECTABLE, a. रम्य, कमनीय, मनोज्ञ, आह्लादक, मनोरम-हर, रुचिर. -DELECTATION, s. आनंदः, आह्लादः, प्रमोदः, हर्षः.

DELEGATE, v. t. नियुज् 7 A, 10, व्यादिश् 6 P, प्रेर् c. (with acc. of person); न्यस् 4 P, नि-क्षिप् 6 P, ऋ c. (अर्पयति), प्रतिपद् c. -s. प्रतिनिधिः, नियोगिन् m., नियोज्यः, प्रतिपुरुषः. अधिकृतः पुरुषः. -ION, s. नियोजनं, प्रेरणं. निक्षेपः, &c.

DELETE, v. t. अप-व्या-मृज् 2 P, विलुप् c., विनश् c., उच्छिद् 7 P. -ION, s. व्यामर्षः, लोपः, उच्छेदः. -DELETERIOUS, a. विनाशक, घातिन्, हिंस्र. घातुक.

DELF, s. मृद्भांडं, मृण्मयद्रव्यं, कौलालकं.

DELIBERATE, v. i. विचर् c., चिंत् 10, विमृश् 6 P, संमंत्र् 10 A, विक्लृप् c.; *See* CONSIDER. -a. कामतः-विचारपूर्वकं-कृत, विमृश्य कृत. 2 विमृश्यकारिन्, स्ववहित, असाहसिक, अप्रमत्त. -ION, s. विचारः-रणं-रणा, चिंता, मंत्रणं-णा, विमर्शः, समीक्षा, वितर्कः, विवेचनं, चर्चा. -IVE, a. विचारशील, विचारिन्, विमर्शिन्. -LY, adv. जानत् with अपि or एव, बुद्धिपुरःसरं, कामतः, विचारपूर्वकं. 2 विमृश्य, समीक्ष्य, अवधानेन, असहसा, अप्रमत्तं.- NESS, s. समीक्ष्य- विमृश्य-कारित्वं, अप्रमादः, सावधानता, अवेक्षा.

DELICATE, a. मधुर, स्वादु, मिष्ट. 2 ललित, चारु, शोभन. 3 (Soft) मृदु, कोमल, सुकुमार, तनु, श्लक्ष्ण, लघु, प्रतनु, विरल, पार,-पेलव ; 'd. of person' कोमलांग (गी f.), मृदुशरीर; 'a d. woman' तन्वी, तन्वंगी, पेलवांगी. 4 विशिष्ट, उत्कृष्ट, उत्तम. 5 सभ्य, विनीत, शिष्ट; 'of a d. constitution' प्रकृतिकोमल, जन्मरोगिन्. -LY, adv. ललितं, सुकुमारं; मृदुतया. -DELICACY, s. माधुर्यं, स्वादुता, सौरस्यं. 2 लालित्यं, लावण्यं. 3 सौकुमार्यं, मार्दवं, पेलवता, तनुता. 4 आदरः, विनयः, शिष्टाचारः, सुशीलता, सौजन्यं. 5 प्रकृतिदुर्बलता. 6 स्वाद्वन्नं, भोजनविशेषः, विशिष्टान्नं.

DELICIOUS, a. स्वादु, मिष्ट, रुचिकर (री f.), मधुर, सुरस, आस्वादवत्. 2 (Of beauty &c.) मनोरम-हर, मधुर, कमनीय, रमणीय, हारिन्, चित्ताकर्षिन्. -LY, adv. स्वादु, मधुरं, मनोरमं. -NESS, s. स्वादुता, माधुर्यं, रम्यता, &c.

DELIGHT, s. आह्लादः, आ-प्र-मोदः, सुखं, हर्षः, प्रीति f.. प्र-सं-मदः, उल्लासः, शर्मन्, आनंदः, संतोषः, तृप्ति f., मुद्-दा f.; 'takes no d. in sports' नाभिनंदति केलिकलाः (Mal. 3); 'thrill of d.' पुलकः, रोमांचः ; 'thrilling with d.' आनंदपुलकिततनुः. 2 आनंदनं, आनंददः, हर्षकरः, आनंदहेतुः. -v. i., 'to be d. ed' मुद् 1 A, हृष् 4 P, आनंद् 1 P, ह्लाद् 1 A, रम् 1 A, प्री 4 A, सं-परि-तुष् 4 P, उल्लस् 1P. -v. t. सुखयति (D.); causal of roots above. -ED, a. सानंद, प्रीत, सहर्ष, मुदान्वित, हृष्ट, आह्लन्न, आनंदित, प्रमुदित, सोल्लास, आह्लादित, उल्लसित, साह्लाद. -FUL, a. प्रमोदिन्. प्रामोदिक (की f.), आनंदमद, हर्षजनन (नी f.), आह्लादक, आनंदक, सुखद; रुचिर, कांत, रम्य, रमणीय, मनोहर-रम. -FULLY, adv. सानंदं, सहर्षं, साह्लादं; रम्यं, कांतं.

DELINEATE, v. t. वर्ण् 10; *See* DESCRIBE. 2 आलिख् 6 P, चित्र् 10, चित्रे निविश् c. -ED, a. चित्रलिखित. चित्रगत, आलिखित, वर्णित. -ION, s. आलिखनं, वर्णनं. 2 आलेख्यं. चित्रं, चित्रारंभः.

DELINQUENCY, s. दोषः-अपराधः, पापं, दुष्कर्मन् n., पापचरितं, अपक्रिया, दुष्कृति f. -DELINQUENT, s. पापिन्-पापकृत्-अपराधिन् m., सदोषः, कृतापराधः.

DELIQUIUM, s. विलयनं, द्रवः.

DELIRIUM, s. चित्तभ्रमः, चैतन्यनाशः, ज्ञानभ्रांति f. -DELIRIOUS, a. भ्रांतचित्त, नष्टचेतन, चैतन्यरहित.

DELIVER, v. t. मुच् c., वि-प्र-मोक्ष् 10, उद्-हृ-धृ 1 P, निस्तॄ c., रक्ष् 1 P. परि-त्रै 1 A. 2 सम्-ऋ c. (अर्पयति), न्यस् 4 P, प्रतिपद् c., प्र-दा 3 U, 1 P, संक्रम् c., आरुह् c. (रोपयति), हस्ते निक्षिप् 6 P, हस्तं प्राप् c., हस्तगत-गामिन् a. कृ 8 U, (तस्य वसुधामपि हस्तगामिनीमकरोत् R. VIII. 1); 'shall d. it into his hand (to him)' इमं अस्य हस्ते प्रापयिष्यामि (S. 3); 'd. ed charge of office' स्वाधिकारं अन्यहस्ते न्यक्षिपत्. 3 उद्-ईर् c., उच्चर् c., उदाहृ 1 P, व्याहृ, वद् 1 P. 4 (Of a message) निविद् c., कथ् 10, आख्या 2 P, आचक्ष् 2 A, शंस् 1 P. 5 (Give back) उत्सृज् 6 P, प्रतिदा. निर्यत् c., (हस्तन्यासं निर्यातय V. 5); 'd. a woman' प्रसवं कृ c., सू c.; 'to be d. ed of' प्रसू 2 A, जन् c. (जनयति), उत्पद् c.; 'was d. ed of a son' सा पुत्रं प्रासूत. -ANCE, s. मोचनं, मोक्षः, मुक्ति f., उद्धारः, परित्राणं, रक्षणं, निस्तारणं, मोक्षणं, विमुक्तिः-मोचनं. -ER, s. मोचकः, रक्षकः, त्रातृ m., मुक्तिदातृ m., तारकः, उद्धर्तृ m. 2 निवेदकः, आख्यायकः. -Y, s. मुक्ति f.; *See* DELIVERANCE, above. 2 अर्पणं, निक्षेपणं, प्रतिपादनं, संक्रामणं, न्यसनं, प्रदानं. 3 उच्चारणं, उदीरणं, व्याहारः-रणं; 'a fluent d.' अस्खलितभाषणं, अप्रतिहतभाषणौघः-वाक्सरणिः. 4 निवेदनं, विज्ञापनं, विज्ञप्ति f., कथनं. 5 उत्सर्गः, निर्यातनं, वितरणं. 6 प्रसवः, प्रसूति f., गर्भमोचनं; 'd. bed' अरिष्टशय्या; 'a woman near her d.' आसन्न-प्राप्त-प्रसवा ; 'place of d.' अरिष्टं, सूतिकागृहं.

DELL, s. दरी, गुहा, कंदरः.

DELUDE, v. t. मुह् c., वंच् 10, प्रलुभ् c., आकृष् 1 P, वि-सं-भ्रम् c. (भ्रमयति); *See* CHEAT also. -ER, s. मोहकः, वंचकः, प्रतारकः, मायिन् m. -DELUSION, s. मोहः, भ्रमः, आभासः, माया, मति-

भ्रमः, इंद्रजालं, विवर्तः; 'the world is all a d.' विश्वमिदं मायामयं, असारं, विवर्त एव. 2 वंचनं, प्रतारणा, प्रलोभनं, कपटं. —DELUSIVE,-DELUSORY, *a.* मायामय (यी *f.*), असार, मायिन्, मोहक, ऐंद्रजालिक (की *f.*), मोहिन्, मोह-भ्रांति-जनक.

DELUGE, *s.* आप्लावः, संप्लवः, जलप्रलयः, भूतसंप्लवः, तोयविप्लवः; 'universal d.' प्रलयः, महासंप्लवः, संवर्तः. क्षयः, कल्पांतः. 2 धारासंपातः, वारिपूरः, अविरलधारासारः, अतिवृष्टि *f.* 3 उत्पातः, आकस्मिकी आपद्. —*v. t.* प्लु c., आ-सं°, निमस्ज् c. (मज्जयति).

DELVE, *v. t.* खन् 1 P, नि-अव°; उर्वी भिद् 7 P. —*s.* खातं, विवरं, बिलं, गर्ता-र्तः. —ER, *s.* खनकः, खनित्रृ *m.*

DEMAGOGUE, *s.* प्राकृतजननायकः, प्रजानायकः.

DEMAIN, DEMESNE, *s.* स्वाधीना भूमिः.

DEMAND, *v. t.* प्रच्छ् 6 P. अनुयुज् 7 A, ज्ञा desid. (जिज्ञासते); 'd. ed his name' किं तव नामेति पप्रच्छ; 'd. a boon' वरं वृ-वृ- 5, 9 U. 2 Claim, q. v. 3 अर्ह् 1 P; oft. by pot. pass. part.; 'Oh Goddess, Godâvari, the matter d. s thy care (attention)' भगवति गोदावरि तत्र त्वया सावधानया भवितव्यं (U. 3); अयमर्थो विक्षामर्हति 'd. s consideration'; 'this offence d. s an atonement of serious expense' भूरिद्रव्यव्ययेनायं दोषः प्रमार्ष्टुं शक्यः, भूरिधनव्ययसाध्यप्रायश्चित्तः दोषः. —*s.* प्रश्नः, अनुयोगः, पृच्छा, जिज्ञासा. 2 अभियोगः, प्रार्थना, याचना; 'on d.' दातुं पृष्टः सन्. —ANT,-ER, *s.* प्रार्थयितृ *m.*, याचितृ *m.*, अभियोक्तृ *m.*, अर्थिन् *m.*

DEMARKATION, *s.* सीमा-मर्यादा-परिच्छेदः.

DEMEAN (oneself), *v. i.* वृत्तिं अनुष्ठा 1 P, चेष्ट् 1 A, वृत् 1 A, व्यवहृ 1 P; *See* ACT. —OUR, *s.* वृत्ति *f.*, आचरणं, आचारः, चेष्टितं, व्यवहारः.

DEMENTATE, *v. t.* उन्मद् c., संज्ञां अपहृ 1 P. —*a.* उन्मत्त, नष्टसंज्ञ, मूढचित्त.

DEMERIT, *s.* अगुणः, दोषः, न्यूनता.

DEMI, अर्ध, सामि *ind.* in comp.

DEMI-GOD, *s.* नरदेवः, विद्याधरः, यक्षः, गंधर्वः, उपदेवता, देवयोनिः.

DEMI-MAN, *s.* अर्धपुरुषः-नरः, किन्नरः.

DEMISE, *s.* मृत्युः, मरणं, उपरति *f.* 2 समर्पणं, विधिवत् प्रदानं. —*v. t.* मृत्युपत्रेण प्रदा 3 U.

DEMISSION, *s.* अवपातः, अवसादनं, अपकर्षणं.

DEMOCRACY, *s.* प्रजाप्रभुत्वं, प्रजासत्तात्मकं राज्यं, प्रजातंत्रं. —DEMOCRAT, *s.* प्रजातंत्रवादिन् *m.*, प्रजापक्षानुकूलः, प्रजाप्रभुत्वानुग्राहकः, प्रजापक्षावलंबिन् *m.* —TICAL, *a.* सार्वलौकिक (की *f.*), प्रजातंत्रीय.

DEMOLISH, *v. t.* विनश् c., उच्छिद् 7 P, अवसद् c., ध्वंस् c., प्र-वि-°; उन्मूल् 10, उत्पट् 10. —ER, *s.* विनाशकः, उच्छेदकः. —DEMOLITION, *s.* विनाशः, उच्छेदः, प्र-वि-ध्वंसः, उन्मूलनं, उत्पाटनं, अवसादनं.

DEMON, *s.* दानवः, असुरः, रक्षस् *n.*, राक्षसः, दैत्यः, दनुजः, दैतेयः, सुरद्विट्, भूतः, पिशाचः, रात्रि(त्रिं)चरः, निशाचरः, यातुधानः. —IAC, *s.* भूताविष्टः, वेतालोपहतः. —*a.*, —IACAL, *a.* राक्षस (सी *f.*), पैशाच (ची *f.*), आसुर (री *f.*), (*s.*) in comp. —OLOGY, *s.* भूतपिशाच-विद्या.

DEMONSTRATE, *v. t.* साध् c., सिध् c. (साधयति), प्रदृश् c., प्रतिपद् c., उपपद् c., प्रमाणयति (D.); निर्णी 1 P, निर्दिश् 6 P. —ION, *s.* साधनं, सिद्धि *f.*, उपपत्ति *f.*, प्रतिपादनं. 2 निर्णयः, प्रामाण्यं, सिद्धांतः; 'ocular d.' प्रत्यक्षप्रमाणं, चाक्षुषज्ञानं-प्रमाणं. —IVE, *a.* दर्शक, निर्देशक, निर्णायक, प्रतिपादक, सिद्धांतकरण. —IVELY, *adv.* सिद्धिपूर्वं, सप्रमाणं, सुव्यक्तं, सोपपत्तिकं. —OR, *s.* निर्देशकः, प्रतिपादकः, प्रदर्शकः.

DEMORALIZE, *v. t.* धर्माद्-आचाराद्-भ्रंश् c. or च्यु c., आचारं दुष् c. (दूषयति). भ्रष्टीकृ 8 U, दुर्वृत्त *a.* कृ. —ATION, *s.* आचारभ्रष्टता, धर्मच्युति *f.*, धर्म-आचार-विप्लवः. अपकर्षः.

DEMULCENT, *a.* शामक, शांतिद. 2 स्निग्ध, चिक्कण.

DEMUR, *v. i.* शंक् 1 A, वि-आ°; विचर् c., विकृप् c.; विलंब् 1 A, मनसा दोलायते (D.); सवितर्कं व्याक्षिप् c. —*s.* आशंका, संदेहः, वितर्कः, विचारणं, विकल्पः; 'without d.' अविचारितं, अविलंबं.

DEMURE, *a.* विनीत, अतिनम्र, गंभीर, धीर, शांत, सलज्ज, सव्रीड, अवनत; 'with d. looks' सव्रीडवदन. —LY, *adv.* सलज्जं, सव्रीडं, धीरं, सविनयं. —NESS, *s.* विनयः, नम्रता, गांभीर्यं, त्रपा, लज्जा, व्रीडा, ह्रीः.

DEN, *s.* बिलं, विवरं, गुहा, गह्वरं, कंदरः, कुहरं.

DENGUE, *s.* संधिकसंनिपात.

DENIZEN, *s.* नि-,वासिन् *m.*, ओकस् in comp.; 'd.s of heaven' दिवौकसः, &c. 2 पौरः, नागरः, नगरजनः, स्वतंत्रजनः.

DENOMINATE, *v. t.* वद्-भण्-गद्-आह्वे 1 P, व्यपदिश् 6 P. अभिधा 3 U, वच् 2 P, ख्या 2 P; *See* CALL also. —ION *s.* नामन् *n.*, अभिधानं, संज्ञा, आख्या. —IVE, *a.* अभिधायिन्, आख्यायक; (in grammar) नामधातुः. —OR, *s.* नामकृत्-नामदातृ *m.* 2 हरः, हारः, छेदः; 'of the same d.' समच्छेद; 'reduced to the same d.' सवर्णित.

DENOTE, *v. t.* निर्दिश् 6 P, सूच् 10, उपलक्ष् 10, वच् 2 P, अभिधा 3 U, द्युत् c., गम् c. (गमयति); oft. ex. by अर्थ in comp.; *See* MEAN; 'the word क्षेत्र here d. s body' अत्र क्षेत्रशब्दः शरीरार्थः-र्थं:. —ATION, *s.* निर्देशः, सूचनं; अभिधा-धानं, उपलक्षणं. —ING, —ATIVE, *a.* सूचक, दर्शक, वाचक, अभिधायक, गमक.

DENOUEMENT, *s.* कार्यं, निर्वहणं, निष्ठा.

DENOUNCE, *v. t.* (अमंगलं or अनिष्टं) प्रकाश् c.,

ख्या c. (ख्यापयाति), आ-नि-विद् c., कथ् 10. 2 प्रकाशं तर्ज् 10 A, भर्त्स् 10 A, अभिशप् 1 U, अभिशंस् 1 P, निंद् 1 P, गर्ह् 1, 10 A, आ-क्रुश् 1 P. -ER, s. अनिष्टावेदकः. 2 अधिक्षेपकः, निंदकः. -MENT, -DENUNCIATION, s. अनिष्टख्यापनं-प्रकाशनं. 2 निर्भर्त्सना-नं, आक्रोशः, अभिशंसनं, निंदा, गर्हा.

DENSE, a. घन. निविड. सांद्र, अविरल, निरंतर, अनंतर, गाढ. गहन. 2 सुसंहत. दृढ, पीवर. -ITY, s. घनता, सांद्रता, आनतर्यं; पीवरता.

DENT, s. प्रहार-आघात-चिह्नं.

DENTAL, a. दंत्य; 'a d. letter' दंत्यं.

DENTED, DENTATED, a. दंतुर, भंगुर, अनुक्रकच.

DENTIFRICE, s. दंतशोधनं-धावनं.

DENTIST, s. दंतवैद्यः-चिकित्सकः.

DENTITION, s. दंतोद्भेदः, दंतवृद्धि f.

DENUDE, DENUDATE, v. t. नग्नीकृ 8 U, विवस्त्रीकृ, विवस्त्रयति (D.), वस्त्रं अपहृ 1 P, शून्यीकृ; निर् in comp.; 'a tree d. ed of leaves' निष्पत्री वृक्षः, निष्पत्रीकृतः; निर्द्रुमं वनं.

DENY, v. t. अपलप् 1 P, अपवद् 1 P, न स्वीकृ-अंगीकृ 8 U, निषिध् 1 P, प्रत्याख्या 2 P, नि-अप-ह्नु 2A, प्रत्यादिश् 6P. -AL, s. अप-नि-ह्नवः, प्रत्यादेशः. निषेधः. अस्वीकारः, प्रत्याख्यानं, अपलापः; 'self-d.' आत्मसंयमः, आत्मनिग्रहः. -ER. s. नि-ह्नोतृ m., अपलापिन् m., प्रत्यादेशकः.

DEOBSTRUCT, v. t. निर्विघ्नीकृ 8 U. विघ्नान् हृ or अपनी 1 P.

DEODAND, s. देवोपहारः.

DEODORIZE, v. t. दुर्गंधं हृ or अपनी 1 P.

DEPAINT, *See* PAINT.

DEPART, v. i. प्रस्था 1 A, प्रया 2 P, वि-निर्-गम् 1 P, अपक्रम् 1 U, 4 P, अपया, अप-इ 2 P, अपगम्, अपसृ-सृप् 1 P; 'whose life has d. ed' वि-गत-जीवितः. 2 प्र-इ, देहं उत्सृज् 6 P, विपद् 4 A, मृ 6A, संस्था 1 A; *See* DIE.-v. t. त्यज् 1P, हा 3 P, उत्सृज्. -ED, a. अपगत. व्यपेत; 'not d. from the meaning' अर्थादनपेत. अर्थ्यं. 2 प्रेत, मृत, दिवंगत, संस्थित. विपन्न. -MENT, s. भागः, विच्छेदः. प्र-वि-भागः. 2 विषयः. प्रकरणं, अंगं. 3 अधिकारः, नियोगः, कर्मन् n., व्यापारः. 4 देशः, विषयः, मंडलं.-URE, s. अपगमः, अपयानं, प्रस्थानं, प्रयाणं. अपसरणं, अपसृति f., निर्गमः. अपक्रमः. 2 देहत्यागः. संस्थिति f., मरणं, उपरति f.

DEPEND, v. i. अवलंब् 1 A, प्रलंब्. 2 अव-आ-लंब्, आश्रि 1 U, संश्रि; निबंधन, तंत्र, अधीन, आयत्त, वश, in comp.; 'every thing d. s on fate' सर्वं दैवाधीनं-यत्तं; मम प्राणास्त्वदाशानिबंधनाः (M. 4); oft. by अपेक्ष् 1 A, व्यपेक्ष्; *See* below. 3 अनु-उपजीव् 1 P. 4 (rely) विश्वस् 2 P (with loc.); सम्-ऋ c. (अर्पयति); 'I d. upon you alone' त्वय्येव मे विश्वासः; 'd. upon it, I shall starve myself to death' मया प्रायोपवेशनं कृतं विद्धि (P. IV. 1); 'd. upon it' असंशयं, नियतं, नूनं, खलु. 5 संबंध्-, प्र-अनु-संज् pass., समनु-इ 2 P. -ANCE, ENCE, s. अवलंबनं, आश्रयः, संश्रयः, निष्ठा, तंत्रता, निबंधनं, अधीनता; 'mutual d.' परस्परनिबंधनं, अन्योन्याश्रयः. 2 पराधीनता, परवशता, परवत्ता, पारतंत्र्यं, परायत्तत्वं. 3 विश्वासः, प्रत्ययः. 4 संबंधः, अनुषंगः, समन्वयः, संपर्कः. -ENCY, s. आयत्तता, अधीनता, &c. 2 अधीनः प्रदेशः, अन्यतंत्रं राज्यं. -ANT,-ENT, a. प्रलंब. 2 अधीन, आयत्त, आश्रित, अवलंबिन्, वश, संबद्ध, निघ्न-तंत्र in comp. 3 (d. on another) पराश्रित, पराधीन. परतंत्र, परायत्त, परवश, परवत्; 'd. on a cause' निमित्तमभ्यपेक्षः स्नेहः (Mal.1). -s. उप-अनु-जीविन् m., आश्रितः, परायत्तो जनः, भृत्यः, परिवारः.

DEPICT, v. t. आलिख् 6 P, वर्ण् 10, निर्दिश् 6 P.

DEPILATION, s. लो(रो)महरणं, उल्लुंचनं. -DEPILATORY, a. केशनाशक, लोमहारिन्.

DEPILOUS, a. अकेश, रो(लो)महीन.

DEPLETE, v. t. शून्यीकृ 8 U, रिच् c., निः-शिष् c. -ION, s. अवक्षयः. निःशेषता, रिक्तता, शून्यत्वं, शून्यीकरणं.

DEPLORE, v. t. शुच् 1 P, विलप् 1 P, परिदेव् 1 A, परिदिव् 10 A; *See* LAMENT. -ABLY, adv. शोच्यप्रकारेण, शोचनीयं. -ER, s. परिदेवकः, अनुशोचकः.

DEPLUME, v. t. पक्षान् उत्पट् 10 or उद्-हृ 1 P, निष्पक्षीकृ 8 U. -ATION, s. पक्षोत्पाटनं.

DEPONE, v. i. सशपथं वद् 1 P or कथ् 10; शपथपूर्वं उपक्षिप् 6 P or उपन्यस् 4 U. -ENT, s. साक्षिन् m. 2 अकर्तरि क्रिया.

DEPOPULATE, v. t. निर्जनीकृ 8 U, विजनीकृ, नरशून्य a. कृ; उपपीड् 10, बाध् 1 A, समुच्छिद् 7 P. -ION, s. निर्जनीकरणं. 2 उपप्लवः, उच्छेदः. उपपीडनं, बाधा. -OR, s. उच्छेदकः, उपपीडकः, विप्लवकारिन् m.

DEPORT, v. t. प्रव्रज् c., निः-प्र-वि-वस् c., देशांतरं गम् c. (गमयति). -v. i. (oneself) आचर्-व्यवहृ 1 P, वृत् 1 A; *See* ACT. -ATION, s. प्र-वि-वासनं, प्रव्राजनं. -MENT, s. वृत्ति f., आचरणं, चेष्टितं, व्यवहारः, वृत्तं.

DEPOSE, v. t. (राज्यात् or अधिकारात्) अवरुह् c. (रोपयति), भ्रंश् c., पत् c., च्यु c. -v. i. साक्ष्यं दा 3 U, वद् 1 P, वच् 2 P, कथ् 10. -ITION, s. साक्ष्यं, साक्ष्यदानं. 2 (Deposal) राज्यभ्रंशः-च्युति f., राज्यावरोपणं, अधिकारच्युतिः-भ्रंशः.

DEPOSIT, v. t. निक्षिप् 6 P, न्यस् 4 P, निधा 3 U, आधा, ऋ c. (अर्पयति), आधीकृ 8 U. -s. न्यासः,

निक्षेपः, आधिः, उपनिधिः. 2 किट्टं, शेषः, खलं, कालुष्यं, मलः-लं. -ARY, s. निक्षेपग्राहकः, न्यासधारिन् m. 2 विश्वासस्थानं-पात्रं-भूमि f. -OR, s. निक्षेपिन् m., न्यासकर्तृ m. -ORY, s. आधारः, आशयः, निधानं, निधिः, भाजनं, आगारं, संग्रहस्थानं.

DEPOT, s. आगारं, शाला, स्थानं, आलयः; 'book-d.' पुस्तकालयः, ग्रंथशाला; 'military d.' युद्धसामग्र्यागारं.

DEPRAVE, v. t. दुष् c. (दूषयति), भ्रंश् c., मलिनीकृ 8 U. कलुषयति (D.). -ED, a. दुराचार, भ्रष्ट, दुष्ट, खंडितवृत्त, दुरात्मन्, पापचेतस्, दुर्वृत्त, भ्रष्टशील, कलुषाचार. -EDNESS,-ITY, s. दुष्टता, भ्रष्टता, दुष्टभावता, दौरात्म्यं, दुराचारता, दौर्जन्यं, कालुष्यं, दुर्वृत्तता.

DEPRECATE, v. t. (प्रार्थनापूर्वकं) निवार् 10, व्यावृत् c., मा भूदिति याच् 1 A. 2 अनुशुच् 1 P. -ION, s. निवारणार्थं प्रार्थना-स्तवः. -IVE,-ATORY, a. अनिष्टनिवारक.

DEPRECIATE, v. t. अर्घतः पत् c., अवमन् 4 A, लघूकृ 8 U. लघु मन्, मूल्यं न्यूनीकृ, अवक्षिप् 6 P, अपलप् 1 P, अपकृष् 1 P. -ION, s. लघूकरणं, अवमानना, अपकर्षः, अपलापः.

DEPREDATE, v. t. अपहृ 1 P, लुंट्-लुट् 1 P, 10, उपद्रु 1 A, उपद्रुत्य ग्रह् 9 P. -ION, s. उपप्लवः, अपहरणं, लुंठनं, लोप्त्रग्रहणं. -OR, s. विप्लवकारिन् m., अपहारकः.

DEPREHEND, *See* APPREHEND.

DEPRESS, v. t. अवनम् c. (नमयति), पत् c., अपकृष् 1 P, अवपीड् 10, निम्नीकृ 8 U, अवसद् c., भ्रंश् c., अवगाह् 1 A. 2 विषादं नी 1 P, विषद् c., विषण्णीकृ; 'd. ed behind' पश्चादवगाढा (S. 3); 'd.-ed in spirits' विषण्ण, म्लान, मुक्तावयव, खिन्नचित्त; *See* DEJECTED. -ION, s. पातः, अवनमनं, अपकर्षः-र्षणं. 2 विषादः, खिन्नता, अवसादः, उद्वेगः, दौर्मनस्यं, म्लानि f.; 'd. of spirits' सत्वभ्रंशः.

DEPRIVE, v. t. अपनी 1 P, अपहृ 1 P, (with gen. of person); भ्रंश् c., च्यु c. (with abl.); वियुज् 7 A, 10, विनाकृ 8 U (with instr. of the object deprived). -ATION, s. हरणं, अपचयः, क्षयः, लोपः, हानि f., नाशः. -ED, a. हृत, अपहृत, हीन, वियुक्त, भ्रष्ट, विरहित, विनाकृत (gen. in comp.); वीत-लुप्त-निर् in comp.; 'd. of wealth' निर्धन, लुप्तवित्त; 'd. of authority' भ्रष्टाधिकार, पदभ्रष्ट; 'to be d.' हा pass., परिहा, वियुज् pass.

DEPURE, DEPURATE, *See* PURIFY.

DEPUTE, v. t. नियुज् 7 A, 10, ईर् c., प्रेष् c., प्रहि 5 P, समादिश् 6 P (of a person); निक्षिप् 6 P, न्यस् 4 P (of business). -ATION, s. नियोजनं, प्रेरणं, प्रेषणं. 2 नियुक्ताः-समादिष्टाः (pl.), नियोगिगणः, नियुक्तजनाः. -Y, s. प्रतिनिधिः, प्रतीहस्तः-स्तकः, नियोगिन् m., नियुक्तः, प्रतिपुरुषः.

DERACINATE, *See* ERADICATE.

DERANGE, v. t. विपर्यस् 4 U, विक्षिप् 6 P, क्रमं-व्यवस्थां-भंज् 7 P or उपहन् 2 P, विक्षुभ् c., संकॄ 6 P, आकुलीकृ 8 U. -ED, a. व्यस्त, अनवस्थित, भग्नक्रम, अव्यवस्थित, विक्षिप्त, संकीर्ण; 'd. in mind' उन्मत्त, भ्रांतचित्त. -MENT, s. व्युत्क्रमः, प्रक्रमभंगः, अव्यवस्था, व्यस्तता, अक्रमः, विसूत्रता, वैलक्षण्यं; 'd. of mind' मतिभ्रमः, चित्तविप्लवः, मतिविपर्यासः.

DERELICTION, s. त्यागः, उत्सर्गः, उपेक्षा.

DERIDE, v. t. वि-उप-अव-हस् 1 P, उपहासास्पदीकृ 8 U, अवज्ञा 9 U, भर्त्स् 10 A, गर्ह् 1, 10 A; 'to be d. ed' उपहास्यतां गम् 1 P, उपहासास्पदं भू 1 P; 'are d. ed by all' सर्वजनस्योपहास्यतामुपयांति (Ka. 108). -ER, s. उपहासकः, अवक्षेपकः. -INGLY, adv. अवहासेन, उपहासपूर्वं, सोपहासं. -DERISION. s. उप-अव-हासः, अवमानना, धिक्कारः, अवज्ञा, गर्हणं, निर्भर्त्सनं. -DERISIVE, a. सोपहास, अवहासगर्भ, अवहासिन्; उपहास्य, गर्ह्य.

DERIVE, v. t. निस्कृष् 1 P, उद्-भू c., जन् c. (जनयति), उत्पद् c. 2 प्राप् 5 P, लभ् 1 A; (get, q. v.). 3 व्युत्पद् c., निर्वच् 2 P, 10. व्युत्पत्तिं वद् 1 P. -ED, a. उत्पन्न, उद्भूत; oft. ex. by प्र-,भव-मूल-उद्भव-ज in comp.; 'the race d. ed from the sun' सूर्यप्रभवो वंशः; 'to be d. ed' उत्पद् 4 A, प्रभू 1 P, जन् 4 A, उद्-भू, निर्गम् 1 P. -ATION, s. व्युत्पत्ति f., निर्वचनं, शब्दोत्पत्ति f., शब्दयोनि f. 2 प्रभवः, उद्भवः, योनि f., मूलं, निर्गमः. -ATIVE, a. व्युत्पन्न; यौगिक (की f.); 'd. suffixes' तद्धितप्रत्ययाः. -s. साधितः शब्दः, व्युत्पन्नः शब्दः.

DEROGATE, v. t. अल्पीकृ 8 U, न्यूनीकृ, लघयति (D.); *See* DEPRECIATE. -ION, s. लघूकरणं, अपमानः, गौरवन्यूनता, अवमानना, लाघवं. -ORY, a. अननुरूप, अकीर्तिकर, लाघवकारिन्, असदृश (शी f.), अयशस्कर (री f.).

DERVISE, s. संन्यासिन् m. (महंमदीयः).

DESCANT, v. i. सविस्तरं व्याख्या 2 P, वि-वृ 5 U, विस्तरेण वर्ण् 10. 2 गै 1 P, वर्ण् 10. -s. वचनं, वादः, प्रवादः, भाषितं. 2 गीतं.

DESCEND, v. i. अवतॄ-अवरुह्-अवपत् 1 P, निपत्, च्यु 1 A, भ्रंश् 1 A, 4 P. 2 आ-अभि-गम् 1 P, प्रविश् 6 P. 3 (upon) अभिद्रु 1 P, अभिधाव् 1 P, आक्रम् 1 U, 4 P; *See* ATTACK. 4 (from) उत्पद् 4 A, प्र-उद्-भू 1 P, जन् 4 A; *See* DERIVE. 5 वंश-कुल-क्रमेण आगम् 1 P or या 2 P, परंपरया प्राप् pass.; 'd. into details' सविस्तरं वर्ण् 10, विस्तरशः वद् 1 P, प्रपंचयति (D.). -v. t. Causal of roots (1) above. -ANT, s. वंश्यः, वंशजः, अपत्यं, संतति f., प्रसूति f., संतानः; 'd. s' पुत्रपौत्राः,

कुलसंततिः, वंशः, अन्वयः, कुलं; 'male d.' पुत्रसंतानः. -ED, *a.* अवतीर्ण, अधोगत; 'lineally d.' कुलक्रमागत, वंशपरंपराप्राप्त, क्रमायात, पितृप्राप्त; 'to be d.' उत्पद्, जन्, प्रभू 1 P; gen. by derivative affixes; 'd. from Puru' पौरवः. -ENT, *a.* अवरोहिन्, अधोगामिन्. -DESCENT, *s.* अवतरणं, अवपातः, अवरोहः-हणं, अवतारः. 2 आक्रमः, अवस्कंदः, अभिद्रवणं. 3 जन्मन् *n.*, उत्पत्ति *f.*, वंशः, उद्भवः, कुलं; 'of noble d.' कुलीन, कुलोत्पन्न, महाकुलप्रसूत, अभिजात, अभिजनवत्. 4 संतति *f.*, अन्वयः, आवलिली *f.*, संतानः-नं. 5 वंशक्रमागमः, अन्वयागमः. 6 अवसर्पिणी भूमिः, प्रवणस्थानं.

DESCENSION, *s.* अवपातः, अधोगमनं. अधःपतनं.

DESCRIBE, *v. t.* वर्ण् 10, निर्दिश् 6 P, वि-वृ 5 U, कृत् 10, कथ् 10, निरूप् 10, वच् 2 P, व्याख्या 2 P; 'her splendour can't be d. ed' तस्याः श्रीर्वचनानामविषया. 2 (Draw) लिख् 6 P. -DESCRIPTION, *s.* वर्णनं-ना, निर्देशः, व्याख्यानं, कथनं, निरूपणं, विवरणं. -DESCRIPTIVE, *a.* निर्देशक, वाचक, अभिधायिन्, निर्देशिन्. 2 वर्णनपर.

DESCRY, *v. t.* दूरात् आलोक् 1 A, 10 or दृश् 1 P or ईक्ष् 1 A; निर्वर्ण् 10, आलक्ष् 10. 2 ज्ञा 9 U, अवगम् 1 P; *See* KNOW.

DESECRATE, *v. t.* दुष् c. (दूषयति), अपवित्रीकृ 8 U, पुण्यत्वं लुप् c., संस्कारहीन *a.* कृ. -ION, *s.* दूषणं, संस्कारदूषणं, अपवित्रीकरणं.

DESERT, *s.* मरुः, मरुस्थलं-ली, वालुकाप्रदेशः, धन्वन् *m.* 2 गुणः, पुण्यं, योग्यता, पात्रत्वं, पुण्यापुण्यं, अर्हत्वं. -*a.* निर्जन, निर्मानुष (षी *f.*), वन्य, खिल, निर्जल, शून्य, आरण्यक. -*v. t.* त्यज् 1 P, हा 3 P, उत्-वि सृज् 6 P, रह् 10 (रहयति), अपव्यध् 4 P. -*v. i.* सेनां त्यक्त्वा पलाय् 1 A. -ER, *s.* त्यागिन्-सेनात्यागिन् *m.*, परावर्तकः, रणपराङ्मुखः, पलायिन् *m.* -ION, *s.* त्यागः, उत्सर्गः; सेनात्यागः, निर्गमनं, अपक्रमणं. -LESS, *a.* निर्गुण, अनर्ह, अयुक्त, अपात्र.

DESERVE, *v. t.* अर्ह् 1 P, अर्ह-उचित-योग्य *a.* in comp.; oft. by pot. pass. part. -ED, *a.* योग्य, उचित, अर्ह. -EDLY, *adv.* उचितं, योग्यं, न्यायतः. -ER,-ING, *a.* अर्हत्, गुणवत्, अर्ह, उचित, योग्य, पात्र; 'd. of' ex. by pot. pass. part.; 'd. of pity' अनुकंप्य, &c. -*s.* गुणः, पात्रता, योग्यता, अर्हत्वं.

DESICCATE, *v. t.* शुष् c., आचम् 1 P. -*v. i.* शुष् 4 P. -ION, *s.* शोषणं, परिशोषः. -IVE, *a.* शोषक. -DESSICANTS, *s.* व्रणशोषकाः.

DESIDERATE, *See* DESIRE. -IVE, *a.* इच्छार्थक, सन्नंत. -DESIDERATUM, *s.* अभीष्टवस्त्वभावः.

DESIGN, *v. t.* परि-सं-कृप् c., अनुसंधा 3 U, व्यवसो 4 P, अभि-प्र-इ 2 P, उद्दिश् 6 P; चिंत् 10, घट् c. (घटयति), मनः-मतिं कृ 8 U. 2 प्र-विनि-युज् 7 A, 10. 3 आलिख् 6 P, सूत्रपातं कृ. -*s.* अभिप्रायः, अर्थः, आकांक्षा, उद्देशः, संकल्पः, आशयः, हेतुः, चिकीर्षितं, प्रयोजनं, कार्यं. 2 उपायः, चिंता, कल्पना, घटना, विधानं, व्यवसायः. 3 आलिखनं, सूत्रपातः, संस्कारः. -EDLY, *adv.* कामतः, यथाकामं, इच्छातः, बुद्धिपुरःसरं. -ER, *s.* चिंतकः, परिकल्पकः. 2 आलेखकः, सूत्रपातकः. -ING, *a.* उपजापिन्, मायिन्, छलिन्, वंचनशील, प्रतारक; विदग्ध, कपटपटु, धूर्त. -LESS, *a.* निरर्थक, निष्प्रयोजन.

DESIGNATE, *v. t.* उप,-लक्ष् 10, अप-व्यप-दिश् 6 P, निर्दिश्, सूच् 10, वृत् c., अभिधा 3 U, निर्वच् 2 P, गम् c. (गमयति). 2 नियुज् 7 A, 10, परि-सं-कृप् c. -ION, *s.* लक्षणं, उपलक्षणं, चिह्नं, विशेषणं, अभिधानं, संज्ञा, आख्या, नामन् *n.*

DESIRE, *v. t.* इष् 6 P, वांछ् 1 P, कम् 10 A, स्पृह् 10 (with dat.), ईह् 1 A, आकांक्ष् 1 U, अभिलष् 1, 4 P; oft. ex. by desid. of roots. 2 अर्थ् 10 A, याच् 1 A, वृ 5 U. -*s.* इच्छा, अभिलाषः, कामः, ईहा, आकांक्षा, समीहितं, आशा, इष्टं, ईप्सितं, मनोरथः, स्पृहा, अभीष्टं; 'according to one's d.' यथाकामं, यथेष्टं, स्वेच्छातः, स्वच्छंदं, स्वरुच्या; 'ardent d.' लालसा, औत्सुक्यं, उत्कंठा, लोभः, तृष्णा. -ABLE, *a.* स्पृहणीय, काम्य. 2 इष्ट, प्रशस्त, श्रेयस्. -OUS, *a.* सस्पृह, वांछिन्, इच्छु, ईप्सु; oft. by desid. forms; 'd. to speak' विवक्षुः; 'd. to take' जिघृक्षुः; पिपासुः; or by काम or मनस् in comp. with inf.; 'd. to take' आदातुकामः-मनाः.

DESIST, *v. i.* विरम् 1 P, निवृत् 1 A, विश्रम् 4 P, (with abl.); *See* CEASE. -ANCE, *s.* विरामः, निवृत्ति *f.*, विश्रामः.

DESK, *s.* लिखनफलकः, लेखनाधारः.

DESOLATE, *a.* निर्मानुष (षी *f.*), निर्जन, शून्य, विविक्त, वसतिहीन, विजन. 2 उच्छिन्न, जीर्ण, उद्ध्वस्त, उत्सन्न. 3 असहाय, निराश्रय, अगतिक, अनाथ. -*v. t.* उच्छिद् 7 P, अवसद् c., निर्जनीकृ 8 U; उत्पीड् 10, शून्यीकृ, प्रबाध् 1 A. -ION, *s.* उच्छेदः, अवसादनं, वसतिनाशः, निर्जनीकरणं. 2 शून्यता, निर्जनत्वं, विविक्तता.

DESPAIR, *v. i.* निराश *a.* भू 1 P, आशां हा 3 P, नैराश्यं गम्-व्रज् 1 P, विषद् 1 P, भग्नाश *a.* भू; 'd. ed. of success' जयविषये निराशोऽभूत्. -*s.* नैराश्यं, निराशता, आशाहीनता, वैक्लव्यं, विषादः; 'being in d.' त्यक्ताश, गताश. -DESPERATE, *a.* निराश, आशातीत, त्यक्ताश, आशाहीन. 2 जीवितनिरपेक्ष, आततायिन्, निर्भय, साहसिक (की *f.*). 3 निष्प्रतीकार, उग्र, संरब्ध, साहसद्योतक, अत्यंत; 'a d. act' साहसं, आततायिता. -LY, *adv.* जीवितनिरपेक्षं, प्रसह्य, उग्रं, उन्मत्तवत्. 2 अति-सु- pr.; अत्यंतं, भृशं. -NESS,

साहसिकता, उन्मादः, संरंभः, जीवितनिरपेक्षता. -DESPERADO, *s.* साहसिन् *m.*, साहसिकः, आततायिन् *m.*, वधोद्यतः.

DESPATCH, *v. t.* (सत्वरं) प्रेष् c, प्रहि 5 P, प्रस्था c. (स्थापयति), विसृज् 6 P. 2 शीघ्रं-झटिति संपद् c.; त्वर् c. (त्वरयति), आशु संविधा 3 U. 3 हन् 2 U, व्यापद् c.; *See* KILL. -*s.* त्वरा, शीघ्रता, शीघ्रकारित्वं, अदीर्घसूत्रता. 2 पत्रं, राजलेखः-लेख्यं, वाचिकपत्रं. 3 धावकः, प्रजविन् *m.*, वार्ताहरः, दूतः. -FUL, *a.* त्वराशील, शीघ्रकारिन्, अविलंबिन्, अदीर्घसूत्र.

DESPISE, *v. t.* अवज्ञा 9 U, तिरस्कृ 8 U, अवमन् 4 A, परिभू 1 P, अवधीर् 10; *See* CONTEMN. -ER, *s.* अवमंतृ *m.*, अवज्ञातृ *m.*, निंदकः. -INGLY, *adv.* सावज्ञं, सावमानं. -DESPICABLE, *a.* अवमान्य, अवज्ञेय, गर्ह्य, निंद्य, नीच, निकृष्ट, अधम, तुच्छ, कुत्सित, क्षुद्र.

DESPITE, *s.* द्वेषः, जुगुप्सा, मात्सर्यं, ईर्ष्या, अभ्यसूया, असूया. 2 प्रतिरोधः, प्रतिकारः; 'in d. of' (prep.) अनादृत्य, अवगणय्य, or gen. abs.; 'd. the (presence of the) teacher' पश्यतोपि गुरोः; *See* 'in spite of' under SPITE. -FUL, *a.* द्वेषिन्, सासूय, अभ्यसूयक, मत्सरिन्, द्रोहबुद्धि. -FULLY, *adv.* सद्वेषं, सद्रोहं, ईर्ष्यया. -FULNESS, *s.* मात्सर्यं, असूया, दौर्जन्यं, द्रोहः, द्रोहबुद्धि *f.*

DESPOIL, *v. t.* हृ 1 P, अपहृ; *See* DEPRIVE; 'd.-ed of everything' हृतसर्वस्व. -ER, *s.* अपहारकः. -DESPOLIATION, *s.* अपहरणं.

DESPOND, *v. i.* निर्विद् 4 A, नैराश्यं-निर्वेदं-विषादं-गम् 1 P or आपद् 4 A, विषद् 1 P, आशां त्यज् 1 P, अंगानि मुच् 6 P. -ENCY, *s.* निर्वेदः, विषादः, नैराश्यं, उद्वेगः, अवसादः, विषण्णता. -ENT,-ING, *a.* निर्विण्ण, विषण्ण, निराश, त्यक्ताश, म्लान, उद्विग्न; 'do not take a d. view' मा भवानंगानि मुंचतु (V. 2). -INGLY, *adv.* सविषादं, सनिर्वेदं.

DESPOT, *s.* प्रजापीडकः, लोकोपप्लवकः. 2 अधीश्वरः, सम्राज् *m.*, सार्वभौमः, चक्रवर्तिन् *m.* -IC,-ICAL, *a.* स्वतंत्र, निष्प्रतिबंध, अनियंत्रण, अनियत, निर्यंत्रण. -ICALLY, *adv.* स्वैरं, स्वेच्छातः, कामचारेण. -ISM, *s.* प्रजापीडनं, निष्ठुरशासनं, प्रजोपप्लवः, स्वेच्छाचारित्वं, स्वेच्छाप्रभुत्वं; निर्यंत्रणा राज्यसरणिः.

DESPUMATE, *v. i.* उत्सिच् pass., फेनायते (D.).

DESSERT, *s.* (भोजनांते) फलाहारः.

DESTINE, *v. t.* (Destinate) निरूप् 10, परि-प्र-क्लृप् c., निर्दिश् 6 P, नियुज् 7 A, 10, समुपस्था 1 U, (न जाने भोक्तारं कमिह समुपस्थास्यति विधिः S. 2); oft. ex. by pot. pass. part., with or without अवश्यं, नूनं; 'he is d. ed to be a king' अनेनावश्यं राज्ञा भवितव्यं; 'man is d. ed to die' मनुष्या नश्वराः; 'who is able to avoid what is d.-ed for him' लिखितमपि ललाटे प्रोज्झितुं कः समर्थः; तथा भवितव्यतया च तस्य तस्य वस्तुनः (Ka. 143) 'every thing being d. ed to occur' &c. -ATION, *s.* ईप्सितं स्थानं, इष्टः प्रदेशः, निरूपित-निर्दिष्ट-स्थानं. 2 उपयोगः, प्रयोजनं, उद्देशः; अर्थः, अभिप्रायः. -Y, *s.* दैवं, भवितव्यता, नियति *f.*, भाग्यं, भागधेयं; विधातृ *m.*, विधिः, दिष्टं, अदृष्टं, प्राक्तनं.

DESTITUTE, *a.* निर्धन, अर्थहीन, निराश्रय, दुर्गत, अशरण, दीन, अकिंचन, दुःस्थित. 2 (of) हीन, रहित, वर्जित, शून्य, वियुक्त, हत, विहीन, परिहीण, with instr. or in comp.; gen. by निर्-अ-वि- in comp.; 'd. of courage' धैर्यहीन, ज्ञानशून्य, &c.; निरुत्साह 'd. of energy'; 'd. of hands and feet' अपाणिपाद. -ION, *s.* दैन्यं, धनाभावः, अकिंचनत्वं, दारिद्र्यं, निराश्रयता. 2 हीनत्वं, राहित्यं, शून्यत्वं, अभावः, विरहः, वियोगः.

DESTROY, *v. t.* नश् c., प्र-नि॰; अव-उत्-सद् c., ध्वंस् c., प्र-वि॰; विलुप् c., क्षै c. (क्षपयति), क्षि 5 P or c., संहृ 1 P, उत्-निर्-दल् c., उच्छिद् 7 P, प्रतिहन् 2 P. 2 (persons &c.) हन् 2 P, निषूद् 10, व्यापद् c., मृ c.; 'to be d. ed' वि-,-नश् 4 P, ध्वंस् 1 A. क्षयं या-इ 2 P, or गम् 1 P, प्र-वि-ली 4 A. -ER, *s.* नाशकः, हंतृ *m.*, निषूदनः, घातिन् *m.*, अंतकः, ध्वंसकः, हन्-अपह in comp.; 'd. of Vritra' वृत्रहा, वृत्रनिषूदनः; 'd. of every thing' कृतांतः. -DESTRUCTIBLE, *a.* नश्वर, विध्वंसिन्, भंगुर, क्षयिन्. -DESTRUCTION, *s.* नाशः, विनाशः, प्रणाशः; प्र-, वि-,ध्वंसः, क्षयः, उच्छेदः, संहारः; उद्दलनं, उत्पाटनं. 2 निषूदनं, घातः, वधः; 'd. of the whole world' प्रलयः, प्रत्यवहारः, कल्पांतः, संवर्तः. -DESTRUCTIVE, *a*, विनाशिन्, क्षयकर (री *f.*), घातिन्, अंतकर, घातुक, अपह-घ्न (घ्नी *f.*) in comp.; 'd. to life' जीवितापह, प्राणहर, निधनकारिन्.

DESUETUDE, *s.* विरति *f.*, निवृत्ति *f.*, विच्छेदः, विरामः, प्रवृत्तिविच्छेदः.

DESULTORY, *a.* असतत, उच्छृंखल, अस्थिर, लोल, अनियत, चंचल, अनवस्थित, अव्यवस्थित.

DETACH, *v. t.* विश्लिष् c., विभिद् 7 P, विच्छिद् 7P, वियुज् 7 A, 10 पृथक् कृ 8 U; *See* SEPARATE. -ED, *a.* वियुक्त, विभिन्न, विच्छिन्न; असंसक्त, असंलग्न, गतसंग, विश्लिष्ट, असंगत. -MENT, *s.* विभागः, वियोगः, विच्छेदः, विश्लेषः, विभेदः. 2 सैन्यदलं, गुल्मः-ल्मं.

DETAIL, *s.* विस्तरः, विस्तारः; वाग्विस्तरः, प्रपंचः. 2 वृत्तांताख्यानं; 'in d.' or 'd. ed' सविस्तर (*a.*), विस्तरेण, विस्तरतः-शः, सविस्तरं. -*v. t.* सविस्तरं-विस्तरेण-वर्ण् 10 or आख्या 2 P or कथ् 10, प्रपंचयति (D.).

DETAIN, *v. t.* धृ 1 P, निरुध् 7 U; जामातृयज्ञेन वयं निरुद्धाः (U. 1) 'd. ed by reason of' &c.

2 निवार् 10, निग्रह् 9 P. 3 (In custody) आसिध् 1 P, बंध् 9 P, निरुध्. —DETENTION, *s.* धरणं, निग्रहः, संरोधः, निरोधः. 2 आसेधः, प्रति-नि-रोधः, बंधनं, बलात्कारेण धरणं.

DETECT, *v. t.* निरूप् 10, ज्ञा 9 U, अनुसंधा 3 U, अधि-अव-गम् 1 P; दृश् 1 P, उपलभ् 1 A, आसद् c. 2 धृ 1 P, प्रकाश् c., व्यंज् 7 P; 'd. ed in a crime' दृष्टदोष; निर्णीतापराध. —ION, *s.* ज्ञानं, निरूपणं, अनुसंधानं, उपलंभः, अवगमनं. —IVE, *a.* (Officer) चरः, चारः, प्रणिधिः; अपसर्पः; *See* SPY.

DETER, *v. t.* (समर्थ) निवृत् c., निवार् 10, विरम् c. (रमयति), भी c., निरुध् 7U; *See* PREVENT. —MENT, *s.* निवर्तनं, निवारणं.

DETERGE, *v. t.* शुध् c., मलं अपनी 1 P, परिमृज् 2 P. —ENT, *a.* शोधन (नी *f.*), परिमार्जक.

DETERIORATE, *v. i.* क्षि-हा pass., ह्रस् 1P, क्षयं गम् 1 P; दुष् 4 P, भ्रंश् 4 P, 1 A, अपकृष् pass. —*v. t.* अपकृष् 1 P, दुष् c. (दूषयति), विकृ 8 U, ह्रस् c. —ION, *s.* क्षयः, अपचयः, विकारः, विकृति *f.*, ह्रासः, भ्रष्टता. 2 अपकर्षः, दूषणं.

DETERMINE, *v. t.* निश्चि 5 U, स्था c. (स्थापयति), संक्लृप् c., निरूप् 10, निर्णी 1 P, निर्-अव-धृ 10, निर्दिश् 6 P, लक्ष् 10, परिच्छिद् 7 P. 2 निरूप्, अनुसंधा 3 U, निर्णी (a dispute &c.). —*v. i.* व्यव-अव-सो 4 P, निश्चयं कृ 8 U; 'd. ed to go' गमने कृतसंकल्प, गंतुं व्यवसित. —ATE, *a.* स्थिर, दृढ, निर्धारित, निश्चित, निर्णीत, नियत, सिद्ध, व्यवस्थित. 2 निश्चायक, निर्णायक. 3 (of persons) कृतनिश्चय, दृढसंकल्प, व्यवसित. —ATELY, *adv.* सनिश्चयं, सनिर्णयं, नूनं. —ATION, *s.* निश्चयः, निर्णयः, संकल्पः, निर्धारणं, व्यवसायः, विचारः, निरूपणं, परिच्छेदः, अवधारणं-णा. 2 अभिनिवेशः, अध्यवसायः, निर्बंधः. —ATIVE, *a.* निर्णायक, निर्धारक. —ED, *a.* निश्चित, निर्णीत, सिद्ध, नियत, व्यवस्थित, परिच्छिन्न, अवधारित. 2 (of persons) स्थिरनिश्चय, दृढ-कृत-संकल्प, अभिनिविष्ट, कृतनिश्चय. —EDLY, *adv.* स्थिरचेतसा, दृढं, दृढनिश्चयेन. —ER, *s.* निर्णयकृत् *m.*, निर्णेतृ *m.*

DETEST, *v. t.* विद्विष् 2 U, गर्ह् 1, 10 A, गुप् desid. (जुगुप्सते) (with abl.); *See* ABHOR. —ABLE, *a.* जुगुप्सित, गर्हित, निंद्य, गर्हणीय, विद्वेष्य. —ATION, *s.* गर्हा, जुगुप्सा, घृणा, विद्वेषः. —ER, *s.* द्वेषिन् *m.*, विद्वेष्टृ *m.*

DETHRONE, *v. t.* राज्याद् भ्रंश् c. or च्यु c. or अवपत् c. or अवरुह् c. (रोपयति). —MENT, *s.* राज्यभ्रंशः-च्युति *f.*

DETONATE, *v. i.* सहसा स्तन् 1P or ध्वन् 1 P. —ION, *s.* स्तनितं, आकस्मिकध्वनिः.

DETORT, *See* PERVERT.

DETRACT, *v.* अपकृष्-अपनी 1 P. 2 अपलप् 1 P, अपवद्-भाष्-1 A, अधिक्षिप् 6 P, निंद् 1 P, असूयति (D.) (with dat.); मूल्यं न्यूनीकृ 8 U; लघूकृ; *See* DEPRECIATE. —ION, *s.* अपकर्षः, लघूकरणं, ह्रासः. 2 असूया, अप-परि-वादः, आक्षेपः, गुणनिंदा, पैशून्यं, परदोषाविष्करणं, मात्सर्यं. —OR, *s.* अपवादकः, अधिक्षेपकः, निंदकः, असूयकः, परिवादरतः. —ORY, *a.* अपवादिन्, निंदक, अभ्यसूयक; पिशुन.

DETRIMENT, *s.* हानि *f.*, अपकारः, क्षति *f.*, नाशः, अपायः, बाधा, विरोधः. —AL, *a.* हानिकर (री *f.*), विरोधिन्, अपायकारक.

DETRUDE, *v. t.* अवपत् c., अधःक्षिप् 6 P, भ्रंश् c. —DETRUSION, *s.* अवपातनं.

DETRUNCATE, *v. t.* अवच्छिद् 7 P, निकृत् 6 P, वि-लू 9 U. —ION, *s.* अवच्छेदः, निकर्तनं.

DEUCE, *s.* द्वयं, द्विकं. 2 पिशाचः, भूतः.

DEVASTATE, *v. t.* उच्छिद् 7 P, उत्-अव-सद् c.; उपपीड् 10, वि-उप-द्रु 1 A, प्रबाध् 1 A, निर्जनीकृ 8 U. —ION, *s.* उच्छेदः, उपद्रवः, प्रबाधनं, विनाशः, निर्जनीकरणं.

DEVELOP, *v. t.* पुष् 1, 4, 9 P, प्र-उप-चि 5 U, प्र-सं-वृध् c.; 'she d. ed her lovely limbs' पुपोष लावण्यमयान् विशेषान् (K. I. 25); also प्रचीयमानावयवा (R. III. 7), उपचितांगी. 2 विकस् c., विस्तृ c., उद्भिद् c.; तस्य (कार्योपक्षेपस्य) विस्तारमिच्छन् (Mu. 4) 'wishing to d. it'. —*v. i.* प्र-उप-चि pass., उद्भिद् pass., क्रमशः विकस् 1 P, क्रमेण प्र-सं-वृध् 1 A. —MENT, *s.* प्रचयः, उपचयः, संवर्धनं; विस्तारः, विकासः, उद्भेदः.

DEVERGENCE, *See* DIVERGENCE.

DEVIATE, *v. i.* अति-व्यति-इ 2 P, अतिक्रम् 1 U, 4 P, अति-व्यभि-चर् 1 P; 'did not d. even an inch from the beaten path' क्षुण्णाद्वर्त्मनो रेखामात्रमपि न व्यतीयुः (R. I. 17); अप-या-इ 2P, चल् 1 P, प्र-वि-°; च्यु 1 A, भ्रंश् 4 P, 1 A, (with abl.). —ION, *s.* अतिक्रमः, विचलनं, च्युति *f.*, भ्रेषः, भ्रंशः, व्यभिचारः, त्यागः; 'd. from the right path' उत्पथयानं, विमार्गगमनं.

DEVICE, *s.* उपायः, युक्ति *f.*, प्रयोगः, कल्पना, साधनं. 2 अप-व्यप देशः, छलं, माया, छद्मन् *n.*, कैतवं, व्याजः. 3 लक्षणं, चिह्नं, अंकः. 4 निर्माणशक्ति *f.*, कल्पनाचातुर्यं.

DEVIL, *s.* भूतः, वेतालः, पिशाचः; 'I shall not raise a d. for my own destruction' नाहमात्मविनाशाय वेतालोत्थापनं करिष्यामि.

DEVIOUS, *a.* वक्र, कुटिल, जिह्म. 2 मर्यादातिक्रामिन्, व्यभिचारिन्.

DEVISE, *v.* चिंत् 10, उप-सं-क्लृप् c., निरूप् 10, युज् 7 U, 10, आ-पर्या-लोच् 10, घट् c. 2 इच्छापत्रेण प्रदा 3 U. —*s.* इच्छापत्रेण रिक्थदानं. —ER, *s.* धनाधिका-

रिन् *m.* —ER, *s.* उपायज्ञः, परिकल्पकः, प्रयोजकः.

DEVOID (of), *a. See* DESTITUTE (of).

DEVOIR, *s.* स्वकर्तव्यं, कर्तव्यता, धर्मः. 2 सत्कारः, आदरः, पूजा, संमानः.

DEVOLVE, *v. t.* निक्षिप् 6 P, न्यस् 4 P, संक्रम् c., सम्-ऋ c. (अर्पयति), आरुह् c. (रोपयति); 'having d. ed their property upon their sons' पुत्रसंक्रान्तलक्ष्मीकाः (U. 1); गुणवत्सुतरोपितश्रियः (R. VIII. 11). 2 प्रपत् c., प्रस्रु-प्रवह् c. —*v. i.* आगम् 1 P, आया 2 P, पत् 1 P, संक्रम् 1 U, 4 P; न्यस्-निक्षिप्-सम् c. pass.; 'after his death the kingdom d. ed upon his eldest son' मृते तस्मिंस्तस्य ज्येष्ठपुत्रो राजपदभाग्बभूव. 2 अधः पत् 1 P, अवपत्. —DEVOLUTION, *s.* निक्षेपणं, समर्पणं, संक्रामणं.

DEVOTE, *v. t.* प्र-विनि-युज् 7 A, 10, सम्-ऋ c. (अर्पयति), निक्षिप् 6 P, उत्सृज् 6 P, सं-उप-क्लृप् c. 2 (Oneself to) आसंज्-अनुरंज्-pass., मनः युज् or बंध् 9 P or अभिनिविश् c., आसक्त-अभिनिविष्ट *a.* भू (all with loc.); भज् 1 U, आसेव् 1 A. 3 नाशाय क्लृप् c.; *See* DOOM. —ED, *a.* सक्त, आ-प्र-व्या-सक्त; नि-, रत, अभिनिविष्ट, समाहित, पर-तत्पर-परायण in comp. 2 भक्त, दृढभक्ति, अनुरक्त, अनुरागिन्; 'd. to the king' राजनिष्ठ, नृपासक्तचित्त; 'a d. wife' एकपत्नी, पतिव्रता, साध्वी, सती; 'a d. husband' भार्यानिरतः, पत्नीसेवी; 'a d. friend' स्थिरप्रेम मित्रं, रूढसख्यः सुहृद्. —EDLY, *adv.* चित्तैकाग्रतया, भक्त्या, निष्ठया, अभिनिविष्टं, मनोभिनिवेशेन, मनोयोगेन, सुसमाहितं. —EDNESS, *s.* आसक्ति *f*, भक्ति *f.*, अभिनिवेशः, परायणता. —EE, *s.* तापसः, यतिः, योगिन् *m.*, तपस्विन् *m.*, मुनिः, व्रती. 2 भक्तजनः, प्रणयिजनः, उपासकः, भक्तः. —ION, *s.* अभियोगः, अभिनिवेशः, अनुरागः, सेवा, उपासना, प्रसक्ति *f.*, आसक्ति *f.*, भक्तिः, निरति *f.*, परायणता. 2 नियमः, धर्मक्रिया, तपस् *n.* 3 ईश्वरभक्तिः-सेवा; 'self-d.' आत्मोत्सर्गः-परित्यागः; 'd. to a husband' पातिव्रत्यं, पतिसेवा; 'to perform d. s' तपश्चर् 1 P or तप् 4 A, तपस्यति (D.). —IONAL, *a.* धर्मपर, धर्मनिष्ठ, भजनशील. 2 धर्मक्रियाविषयक, तपोमय (यी *f.*).

DEVOUR, *v. t.* भक्ष् 10, अद् 2 P, खाद् 1 P, ग्रस् 1 A, गॄ 6 P. 2 उपयुज् 10, उपयोगेन विनश् c. —ER, *s.* भक्षकः, खादकः.

DEVOUT, *a.* धार्मिक, धर्म-परायणशील, धर्मनिष्ठ, धर्मात्मन्, भक्त, ईश्वरनिरत, पुण्यशील, प्रयतात्मन्, पुण्यात्मन्. —LY, *adv.* भक्त्या, भक्तिपूर्वकं, भक्तिपुरःसरं, श्रद्धान्वितं. —NESS, *s.* धार्मिकता, धर्मात्मता, ईश्वरनिष्ठता, भक्ति *f.*

DEW, *s.* नीहारः, अवश्यायः, तुषारः, प्रालेयं, हिम-रात्रिख-जलं. —*v. t.* नीहारेण सिच् 6 P or प्रोक्ष् 1 P; 'd. drop' तुषारकणः-बिंदुः-शीकरः, and sim. comps. —Y, *a.* तुषारमय (यी *f.*), अवश्यायावसिक्त; तुषारकणोपम.

DEXTEROUS, *a.* कुशल, निपुण, पटु, दक्ष, लघुहस्त, करदक्ष. —LY, *adv.* निपुणं, दक्षतया, सपाटवं, हस्तलाघवेन. —DEXTERITY, *s.* दक्षता, पटुता, नैपुण्यं, हस्तकौशलं, हस्तलाघवं.

DEXTRAL, *a.* दक्षिण, अपसव्य, दक्षिणपार्श्वस्थ.

DIABETES, *s.* मधुमेहः, प्रमेहः, बहुमूत्ररोगः.

DIABOLICAL, *a.* पैशाच (ची *f.*), पिशाचोपम. 2 घोर, दारुण, पापिष्ठ, अतिघोर-पाप, अतिनिंद्य.

DIACOUSTICS, *s.* ध्वनिविद्या.

DIADEM, *s.* मुकुटं, किरीटः-टं, मौलिः, उष्णीषः-षं, शिरोवेष्टनं; 'd. ed' किरीटिन्, किरीटधारिन्.

DIAGNOSIS, *s.* रोगनिर्णयः-निरूपणं, रोगनिदानं; मीमांसा, चिकित्सा.

DIAGNOSTIC, *s.* रोगलक्षणं-चिह्नं.

DIAGONAL, *s.* कर्णः, श्रुति *f.* —LY, *adv.* कोणाकोणि, कर्णाकर्णि.

DIAGRAM, *s.* चित्रं.

DIAL, *s.* शंकुयंत्रं, सूर्यघटी.

DIALECT, *s.* प्राकृतभाषा, भाषा (as opposed to संस्कृत). 2 भाषणं, वचनं, उक्ति *f.*

DIALECTIC, *s.* तर्कः, न्यायः, हेतुविद्या, आन्वीक्षिकी विद्या. —AL, *a.* तार्किक (की *f.*), न्यायिन्. —IAN, *s.* तार्किकः, नैयायिकः, न्यायविद् *m.*

DIALOGUE, *s.* संलापः, संवादः, संकथा, संभाषणं, प्रश्नोत्तरं, कथोपकथनं. —DIALOGIST, *s.* संवादकः, उत्तरप्रत्युत्तरदायकः.

DIAMETER, *s.* व्यासः, विष्कंभः. —DIAMETRICALLY, *adv.* विपरीतं, प्रतिकूलं, अत्यंतं, एकांततः.

DIAMOND, *s.* वज्रः-ज्रं, हीरं, हीरकः; 'd. cutter' हीरकारः-मार्जकः.

DIAPASON, *s.* स्वराष्टकं, स्वरग्रामः.

DIAPER, *s.* चित्रितं क्षौमं. —*v. t.* क्षौमं चित्र् 10 or कर्बुरीकृ, &c.

DIAPHANIC, *a.* स्वच्छ, विशद; *See* CLEAR.

DIAPHORETIC, *a.* स्वेदन (नी *f.*), स्वेदजनक, घर्मोत्पादक; 'd. medicine' स्वेदनं.

DIAPHRAGM, *s.* शरीरमध्यदेशः.

DIARRHOEA, *a.* अतिसारः, प्रवाहिका; ग्रहणी-, रुज् *f.*

DIARY, *s.* दिनपत्रिका, दैनिकवृत्तपुस्तकं.

DIATRIBE, *s.* अधिक्षेपः, कुत्सात्मको लेखः.

DIBBLE, *s.* लघुखनित्रं.

DICTATE, *v. t.* आज्ञापूर्वकं कथ् 10, आदिश् 6 P, आज्ञा c. (ज्ञापयति). 2 सूच् 10, प्रोत्सह् c., प्रचुद् 10, प्रेर् c.; 'd. ed by good motives' सदाशयप्रेरित. —*s.* आज्ञा, आदेशः, शासनं. 2 चोदनं-ना, प्रेरणं-णा. —ION, प्रोत्साहनं. 2 आज्ञापनं, आज्ञापूर्वकं कथनं. —OR, *s.* एकाधिपतिः, अनन्याधीनः शास्ता, अ-

नियंत्रण: प्रभुः. 2 आदेशकः, शासितृ *m.* —ORIAL, *a.* अवलिप्त; *See* ARROGANT.

DICTION, *s.* भाषा, वाणी, वाक्सरणि *f.*, वचोविन्यासः.

DICTIONARY, *s.* कोशः-षः, शब्दसंग्रहः, अभिधानं.

DICTUM, *s.* वचनं, आदेशः, विधिः, नियमः.

DIDACTIC,–AL, *a.* उपदेशपर, प्रबोधक.

DIE, *s.* अक्षः, पाशकः, देवनः; 'a loaded d.' कूटाक्षः. —DICE, (pl.) अक्षाः, &c. –*v. i.* अक्षैः दिव् 4 P, ग्लह् 1 P. –ER, *s.* अक्षधूर्तः, अक्षदेविन् *m.*, धूर्तः, कितवः. –ING, *s.* द्यूतं, अक्षक्रीडा; 'd. board' अष्टापदं, शारिफलं; 'd. box' अक्षाधारः; 'the die is cast' कृतं दैवाधीनं (अप्रतिविधेयं) कर्म, अधुना यद्भावि तद्भवतु.

DIE, *v. i.* मृ 6 A, प्राणान्-असून्-जीवितं त्यज् 1 P or उत्सृज् 6 P or हा 3 P, पंचत्वं या 2 P or गम् 1 P, उपरम् 1 P; परासु-गतासु- *a.* भू 1 P, देहं-तनुं त्यज्, प्र-इ 2 P, विपद् 4 A, संस्था 1 A, प्रमी pass. 2 विनश् 4 P, प्रली 4 A, ध्वंस् 1 A, क्षि pass., अवसद् 1 P. 3 म्लै 1 P, विशॄ pass. —DEAD, *a.* मृत, उपरत, संस्थित, प्रेत, परेत, परासु, गतासु, विपन्न, गतप्राण, विचेतन, प्राणहीन, प्रमीत. 2 निश्चल, निश्चेष्ट, जड, निस्तेजस्, निःसत्व, असार, निष्फल. 3 सुप्त, स्तब्ध (as of limbs); 'd. body' शवं, मृतशरीरं; कुणपः; 'd. language' अप्रचलिता भाषा; 'd. sleep' घोर-गाढ-निद्रा; 'd. loss' परिपूर्णा-सकला हानिः; 'd. letter' लुप्तार्थं वचनं; 'd. soul' निरभिमानः आत्मा. –*s.* (Of night) मध्यरात्रः, निशीथः, अर्धरात्रः. 2 मध्यं; *See* DEPTH. –EN, *v. t.* दुर्बलीकृ 8 U, शिथिलीकृ, तेजो हृ 1 P, नश् c., म्लानीकृ. –*v. i.* म्लै 1 P, शिथिलीभू. –LY, *a.* प्राणापहारक, जीवितापह, मारात्मक, निधनकारिन्, प्राणांतक, प्राणहारिन्, प्राणनाशक, जीवितघ्न (घ्नी *f.*). 2 अशाम्य; 'd. enmity' आमरणांतिकं वैरं, अशाम्यं वैरं; 'd. poison' हाला(ल)हलं विषं. –*adv.* मृतवत्; प्राणांतिकं; 'd. wounded' भिन्नमर्मन्; 'd. pale' प्रेतसवर्ण. –NESS, *s.* दौर्बल्यं, निःसत्वता, जडत्वं, स्तंभः; वैकल्यं, विरक्ति *f.*, शिथिलता. —DEATH, *s.* मरणं, मृत्युः, उपरमः, निधनः-नं, अंतः, पंचत्वं-ता, संस्थिति *f.*, कालधर्मः, दिष्टांतः, प्रलयः, अत्ययः, नाशः, प्राणनाशः, तनुत्यागः, &c. 2 यमः, कालः, कृतांतः. 3 वधः, घातः, व्यापादनं; 'he was pelted to d.' सलोष्ठघातं हतः; 'he was sentenced to d.' तस्य प्राणदंड आदिष्टः; 'to put to d.' हन् 2 P, व्यापद् c., वधं आदिश् 6 P; 'a violent d.' अपमृत्युः; अपघातः; 'angel of d.' यमदूतः; 'd. by fasting' प्रायः, प्रायोपवेशनं; 'd. bed' मृत्युशय्या. –LESS, *a.* अमर, अनश्वर, अमर्त्य, चिरस्थायिन्.

DIET, *s.* आहारः, अन्नं, भोजनं, भक्ष्यं. 2 पथ्यं, पथ्यान्नं, पथ्याशित्वं. 3 राजसभा, शिष्टसभा. –*v. t.* पुष् c., भृ 3 U. 2 पथ्यं निर्दिश् 6 P.

DIFFER, *v. i.* भिद् pass., प्र-वि-°; विशिष् pass., (न कारणात्स्वाद्बिभिदे कुमारः R. v. 35); gen. ex. by (*s.*); 'they two do not d.' न तयोर्भेदः, विशेषः, &c. 2 अन्यथा मन् 4 A, न संमन्, विवद् 1 A, भिन्नमत *a.* भू, विप्रतिपद् 4 A, (एवं हि विप्रतिपन्नाः प्राणियत्तां प्रति श्रुतयः S. B. 702); 'I d. from you' मम मतं त्वन्मताद्भिन्नं. 3 वि-प्रति-रुध् pass. –ENCE, *s.* भेदः, विशेषः, अंतरं, (with gen.). 2 पार्थक्यं, इतरत्वं, भिन्नत्वं, व्यतिरेकः; 'that makes no d.' तेन न कोपि विशेषो जायते. 3 विरोधः, वैपरीत्यं, विपर्ययः, वैलक्षण्यं. 4 विप्रतिपत्ति *f.*, मतिभेदः, विसंवादः, वैमत्यं; कलिः, कलहः, विवादः. 5 असाम्यं, असादृश्यं; 'd. in quantity' वैषम्यं. –ENT, *a.* भिन्न, वि-प्र-भिन्न, इतर-अन्य-पर-*pron. a.*, व्यतिरिक्त, विपरीत, पृथक्, विशिष्ट, (with abl.); अंतर in comp.; 'she is not d. from my body (myself)' अव्यतिरिक्तेयमस्मच्छरीरात् (Ka. 151); 'a d. sense' अर्थांतरं. 2 असदृश (शी *f.*), असमान, विषम, असम. 3 विविध, नानाप्रकार, नाना in comp.; तत्तत् *pron. a.*, 'd. S'âstras' तानि तानि शास्त्राणि; 'in a d. way' अन्यथा, भिन्नप्रकारेण. –ENTIAL, *a.* भेदकर (री *f.*), विशेषक. –ENTLY, *adv.* अन्यथा, इतरथा, भिन्नरूपेण; अन्यप्रकारेण, पृथक्.

DIFFICULT, *a.* असुकर, दुश्चर, कठिन, दुष्कर, दुःसाध्य, कष्ट. 2 गहन, विषम, दुर्बोध, असुगम, कष्टज्ञेय, गूढार्थ, दुर्ज्ञेय. 3 (With inf.) ex. by दुर्, दुःख, कष्ट, in comp.; 'd. to get' दुष्प्राप, दुराप, कष्टसाध्य; दुरारोह, दुःखच्छेद्य, &c.; 'a d. case' सशल्योर्थः; 'a d. road' दुर्गसंचा(च)रः, संक्रमः; 'a d. place' विषमस्थानं, दुर्गं, दुर्गमस्थलं. –LY, *adv.* दुःखेन, कष्टेन, कृच्छ्रेण, कष्टं, आयासेन, दुर् pr. –Y, *s.* असौकर्यं, वैषम्यं, काठिनता, दुष्करत्वं, कष्टता, दुःसाध्यता. 2 आयासः, वैक्लव्यं, विरोधः. 3 कृच्छ्रं, संकटं, विघ्नः, आयासः, दुर्गं, दुःखं, विरोधः, क्लेशः, बाधा, कष्टः-ष्टं. 4 विषमपदं, असुबोधं-दुर्बोधं पदं, असुगमं स्थानं; 'without d.' अनायासेन, सुखं; 'with d.' कथमपि, कथं कथमपि, कथंचित्, दुःखेन, कृच्छ्रेण; 'a commentary explaining the d. es' विषमपदविमर्शिनी टीका; 'beset with d. es' सशल्य, सकंटक; 'overcoming d. es' दुर्गलंघनं.

DIFFIDENCE, *s.* अविश्वासः, अप्रत्ययः, आ-, शंका. 2 (In oneself) अप्रगल्भता, विनयः, ह्रीः, लज्जा. —DIFFIDENT, *a.* अविश्वासिन्, शंकाशील, अप्रत्यय, साशंक; 'the mind feels d. of itself' आत्मन्यप्रत्ययं चेतः (S. 1). 2 अप्रगल्भ, अधृष्ट, विनीत, ह्रीमत्, लज्जावत्. –LY, *adv.* अप्रगल्भं, साशंकं, लज्जया, सविनयं.

Diffract, *v. t.* वियुज् 7 A, 10, विश्लिष् c.

Diffuse, *v. t.* प्रसृ c., वि-परि-स्तॄ c., विसृप् c., प्रचर् c., विकॄ 6 P, तन् 8 U, अभि-प्र-वृष् c. 2 प्र-लु c., विद्रु c., प्रक्षिप् 6 P. 3 (Itself) व्याप् 5 P, विसृ-विसृप् 1 P, विस्तॄ pass., व्यश् 5 A, सर्वत्र गम् 1 P or प्रविश् 6 P. —*a.* वितत, सविस्तर, विस्तृत, असंक्षिप्त, विस्तीर्ण, सप्रपंच. —**ly**, *adv.* सविस्तरं, विस्तरेण, विस्तरशः, प्रपंचेन, असंक्षेपतः, असमासेन. —**ion**, *s.* प्रसारः, प्र-वि-सरः, विस्तारः, अभिवृद्धि *f.*, वितति *f.*, प्रचारणं, प्रसरणं. —**ive**, *a.* वि-प्र-सारिन्, व्यापक, व्यापिन्, प्रसरणशील. —**iveness**, *s.* विस्तारः, विस्तृति *f.*, व्यापकत्वं. 2 वाग्विस्तारः, प्रपंचः, वाक्यविस्तरः.

Dig, *v. t.* खन् 1 P; 'd. down' (भूमिं) अवदॄ 10, भिद् 7 P; 'd. in' निखन्. 2 निर्भिद्, छिद् 10, व्यध् 4 P. —**ger**, *s.* खनकः, खनितृ *m.*

Digest, *v. t.* (जठरे) जॄ c. (जरयति), पच् 1 P, परिपाकं नी 1 P, परिणम् c. (णमयति), दह् 1 P. 2 क्रमेण-यथाक्रमं-विन्यस् 4 U or रच् 10 or ग्रंथ् 9 P or लिख् 6 P. 3 मनसा विचर् c. or चिंत् 10. 4 Suffer, q. v. —*v. i.* जॄ 4 P, पच् pass., परिणम् 1 P. —**er**, *s.* पाचकं, जारणं, अग्निवर्धनं, रोचनं, रोचकं. —**ion**, *s.* पाकः, वि-परि-पाकः. पचनं, परिणामः. 2 जठराग्निः, जठरानलः, अग्निः; 'slowness of d.' अग्निमांद्यं; 'having a good d.' प्रदीप्ताग्निः. —**ive**, *a.* पाचन (नी *f.*), पाचक, अग्निवर्धक, परिपाकिन्.

Dight, See **Adorn**.

Digit, *s.* कला, लेखा, रेखा. 2 अंकः.

Dignity, *s.* महिमन् *m.*, माहात्म्यं, औदार्य. 2 अनुभावः, प्रतापः, तेजस् *n.*, प्रौढि *f.*, प्रौढत्वं-ता. 3 प्रतिष्ठा, गौरवं, पदं, उत्कृष्ट-परम-पदं, उत्कर्षः, उन्नति *f.*, आभिजात्यं, प्रतिपत्ति *f.*, ओजस्विता, उच्चत्वं, कुलीनता; 'd of style' ओजस् *n.* 4 मानः, अभिमानः, गर्वः, दर्पः; 'd. of expression' प्रौढत्वं वचसां. —**Dignify**, *v. t.* संमन् c., सत्कृ 8 U, पूज् 10. 2 उत्कृष्टपदे नियुज् 7 A, 10, परमपदं प्राप् c., उत्कर्षं नी 1 P. —**ed**, *a.* महानुभाव, अनुभाववत्, गंभीर, ओजस्विन्, प्रौढ; महाप्रताप; 'd. in mien' गंभीराकृति. 2 मानिन्, महाशय, महेच्छ. 3 उत्कृष्टपदनियुक्त, प्रतिपत्तिमत्, परमपदारूढ. —**Dignitary**, *s.* मान्यजनः, शिष्टजनः, कुलीनपुरुषः.

Digress, *v. i.* प्रस्तुतं न अनुसंधा 3 U, अप्रस्तुतं वद्-भण् 1 P or वच् 2 P, प्रकृतं-कथायोगं त्यज् 1 P; 'you are d. ing' न त्वया प्रस्तुतमनुसंधीयते. 2 उत्क्रम् 1 U, 4 P, विचल् 1 P, प्रच्यु 1 A, भ्रंश् 1 A, 4 P; See **Deviate**. —**ion**, *s.* प्रकृतत्यागः, अप्रस्तुतानुसंधानं; प्रसंगः, प्रासंगिकं वचनं; 'enough of d.' अलं प्रासंगिकेन or प्रसंगेन, प्रकृतमेवानुसंधीयतां. 2 उत्क्रमः, विचलनं, भ्रंशः, च्युति *f.*, त्यागः. —**ive**, *a.* अनन्वित, अप्रस्तुत, अप्रकृत, असंगत, असंबद्ध.

Dike, *s.* सेतुः, सेतुबंधः, पिंडलः, धरणः, कूलकः-कं. 2 कुल्या, परिखा, खातं, प्रणालः-ली.

Dilacerate, See **Tear**.

Dilapidate, *v. i.* जॄ 4 P, विनश् 4 P, क्षि-उच्छिद्-pass., अवसद् 1 P. —*v. t.* उच्छिद् 7 P, अवसद् c., प्रध्वंस् c., क्षि c., विनश् c.; See **Destroy**. —**ion**, *s.* क्षयः, ध्वंसः, नाशः, उच्छेदः, अवसादः.

Dilate, *v. t.* विस्तॄ c., वितन् 8 U, प्र-वि-सृ c., दीर्घीकृ 8 U. 2 (upon) प्रपंचयति (D.), सविस्तरं विवृ 5 U or व्याचक्ष् 2 A, अति-विवृ. —*v. i.* वितन्-विस्तॄ-विवृ pass., आयतीभू, दीर्घीभू. —**ed**, *a.* वितत, आयत; उत्फुल्ल, विकसित. —**ion**, *s.* विस्तारः, वितति *f.*, विस्तरणं, विवृति *f.*; विकासः-सनं, उत्फुल्लता.

Dilatory, *a.* दीर्घसूत्रिन्, दीर्घसूत्र, विलंबिन्, मंद, मंथर, चिरक्रिय, अक्षिप्रकारिन्. —**ly**, *adv.* सविलंबं, मंदं-मंदं, कालक्षेपेण. —**ness**, *s.* दीर्घसूत्रता, विलंबः, कालक्षेपः, मांद्यं, कार्यजडता.

Dilemma, *s.* उभयसंभवः, विकल्पः.

Diligent, *a.* उद्योगिन्, व्यवसायिन्, उद्युक्त, सोद्योग, उद्यमिन्, अनलस, अभिनिविष्ट, उद्यम-व्यवसाय-पर, उद्योगतत्पर. 2 (Of things), अनवरत, सतत, नित्यप्रवृत्त, प्र-आ-सक्त, अभ्यस्त, प्रसित, अविच्छिन्न. —**ly**, *adv.* प्रयत्नतः, सोद्योगं, सोद्यमं; अनवरतं, प्रसक्तं. —**Diligence**, *s.* उद्यमः, अध्यव-व्यव-सायः, उद्योगः, अभियोगः, अभिनिवेशः, प्रयत्नः, अभ्यासः, प्रसक्ति *f.*, उत्साहः. 2 सातत्यं, अविच्छेदः, अविरामः, नैरंतर्य.

Dill, *s.* सालेयः, मधुरिका.

Dilute, *v. t.* जलेन मिश्र् 10 or संसृज् 6 P, विली c., तनूकृ 8 U, क्षीणीकृ; मिश्रणेन शक्तिं तनूकृ. —**ion**, *s.* जलसंसर्गः, जलमिश्रणं; तनूकरणं. —**Diluent**, *s.* विलयनं, तनूकरणं.

Dim, *a.* मंदद्युति, मंदप्रभ, मलिनकांति, मलिन, निष्प्रभ, निस्तेजस्, सतिमिर. 2 अप्रकाश, अव्यक्त, अस्पष्ट, दुरालोक, दुर्दृश; 'seeing d.-ly' हतदृष्टि, अस्पष्टदृश्; 'of d. understanding' मंदमति, जड-स्थूल-धी-बुद्धि, &c. —*v. t.* अंधीकृ 8 U, अस्पष्टीकृ, कलुषीकृ, निष्प्रभीकृ, मलिनयति (D.). —**ly**, *adv.* अस्पष्टं, अव्यक्तं, निष्प्रभं, मलिनं. —**ness**, *s.* तिमिरं, अस्पष्टता, तेजोहानि *f.*, दुरालोकता, मालिन्यं, अस्पष्टता. 2 स्थूलमतिता, बुद्धिमांद्यं.

Dimension, *s.* प्रमाणं, परिमाणं, मात्रा, मानं, विस्तारः.

Diminish, *v. t.*, *v. i.* See **Decrease**. —**Diminution**, *s.* न्यूनीकरणं, ह्रासः, क्षयः, अपचयः, अवसादः, हानि *f.* —**Diminutive**, *a.* अल्पकाय, क्षुद्र, अल्प, स्तोक, सूक्ष्म, लघु. 2 अल्पार्थ (प्रत्ययः); 'कन् is a d. termination' अल्पार्थे कन्.

Dimity, *s.* दृढं कार्पासवस्त्रं.

Dimple, *s.* कपोलभंगः, गंडतरंगः, कपोलोर्मि *f.*; ऊ-

मिः, भंगुरता, दंतुरता, भंगः, तरंगः. –DIMPLY, *a.* भंगुर, ऊर्मिमत्, दंतुर.

DIN, *s.* कलकलः, निनादः, कोलाहलः, तुमुलरवः, निःस्वनः, उच्चघोषः, तुमुलं. –*v. t.* (श्रवणपुटं) जर्जरीकृ 8 U, कर्णौ उपहन् 2 P or जर्जरयति (D.); *See* STUN.

DINE, *v. i.* भुज् 7 A, आहारं-भोजनं-सेव् 1 A or निर्वृत् c., शरीरस्थितिं कृ 8 U or क्लृप् c. –*v. t.* भुज् c., अश् c. –DINNER, *s.* भोजनं, आहारः, अशनं; *See* FOOD. 2 उत्सवः, जग्धि *f.*, भोजनोत्सवः.

DING, *v. t.* शब्दायते (D.), नद्-स्वन्-कण् 1 P; 'ding dong' घंटानादः-शब्दः, किंकिणीरवः-शब्दः-नादः, सततनादः.

DINGLE, *See* DALE.

DINGY, *See* BLACK.

DINT, *s.* प्रहारः, आघातः, अभिघातः. 2 बलं, प्रभवः, सामर्थ्यं; 'by d. of' बलेन, प्रभावेण, सामर्थ्यात्, योगेन. –*v. t.* प्रहारेण अंक् 10 or चिह्न् 10.

DIOCESAN, *s.* प्रधानधर्माध्यक्षः.

DIORTHESIS, *s.* वक्रांगचिकित्सा.

DIP, *v. i.* नि,-मस्ज् 6 P (with loc.) ; अव-वि-गाह् 1 A, प्र-नि-विश् 6 P, आप्लु 1 A, (acc.). 2 व्याप्र 6 A, व्यापृत *a.* भू. –*v. t.* अवगाह् c., मस्ज् c. (मज्जयति), प्रविश् c. 2 सिच् 6 P, क्लिद् c., आर्द्रीकृ 8 U; 'd. in a business' ईषद् व्याप्र or प्रवृत् 1 A ; 'd. into books' चुंब् 1 P ; अल्पशः अधि-इ 2 A. –*s.* निमज्जनं, अवगाहः, प्रवेशः. 2 अवपातः, नम्रता, आनति *f.*

DIPTHERIA, *s.* मांससंतानिका.

DIPHTHONG, *s.* स्वरद्वयं, संयुक्तस्वरः, संध्यक्षरं.

DIPLOMA, *s.* पदवी-अधिकार-दायकं पत्रं.

DIPLOMACY, *s.* सामन् *n.*, नीति *f.*, दौत्यकर्मन् *n.* 2 राजदूतमंडलं-समूहः. –DIPLOMATICAL, *a.* दूतकार्यविषय. –DIPLOMATIST, *s.* सामप्रयोगज्ञः, राजनीतिकुशलः, दौत्यकार्यनिपुणः, सामकुशलः.

DIRE,–FUL, *a.* दारुण, घोर, उग्र, तीव्र. 2 भीषण, क्रूर, भयानक, रौद्र. –NESS, *s.* दारुणत्वं, घोरता, रौद्रता.

DIRECT, *v. t.* संधा 3 U, लक्ष्यीकृ 8 U, उद्दिश् 6 P, प्रेर् c., अधिकृत्य क्षिप् 6 P, (a missile &c.); 'd. attention or mind' मनो नियुज् 7 A, 10, मनः समाधा or बंध् 9 P or आसंज् c. or निक्षिप्. 2 शास् 2 P, विनियम् 1 P, प्रणी 1 P, निर्वह् c., अधिष्ठा 1 P, अवेक्ष् 1 A. 3 आ-निर्-उप-दिश्, प्रदृश् c. 4 नियुज्, आदिश्, आज्ञा c. (ज्ञापयति), प्रचुद् 10. 5 विधा 3 U, प्र-युज्. 6 (A letter &c.) *See* ADDRESS. –*a.* ऋजु, अवक्र, सरल, अकुटिल, अविलोम, अजिह्म, अनुलोम; 'd. descendants' अनुलोमाः, अनुलोमवंशजाः. 2 क्रमागत, अविप्रकृष्ट. 3 व्यक्त, स्पष्ट, सुस्पष्ट-व्यक्त, प्रत्यक्ष, साक्षाद् *ind.* –ION, *s.* शासनं, नियोगः, निर्देशः, आज्ञा, आदेशः. 2 संधानं, उद्देशः, प्रेरणं. 3 प्रणयनं, प्रशासनं, विनियमनं, अधिष्ठातृत्वं, अधिष्ठानं, अवेक्षा-क्षणं. 4 दिश् *f.*, दिशा, आशा, काष्ठा, ककुभ् *f.*, हरित् *f.* 5 Address, q. v. –IVE, *a.* निर्देशक, सूचक. –LY, *adv.* सपदि, सद्यः, अचिरात् , तत्क्षणात्, अविलंबितं, शीघ्रं, आशु. 2 स्पष्टं, प्रत्यक्षं, सुव्यक्तं, अगूढतया, भिन्नार्थं. 3 अनुलोमं, सरलतया. –OR, *s.* शासितृ-अधिष्ठातृ *m.*, अनुशासकः, अध्यक्षः, अधिकारिन् *m.*, अवेक्षकः, निर्वाहकः. –ORY, *s.* विधिसंहिता. 2 नामधामसूचकं पुस्तकं.

DIREPTION, *s.* अपहरणं, अपहारः, लुंठनं.

DIRGE, *s.* करुणगीतं, करुणरससंगीतं.

DIRK, *See* DAGGER.

DIRT, *s.* मलः-लं, पंकः, कर्दमः, जंबालः-लं, कल्कं, किट्टं. –Y, *a.* मलिन, समल, मलीमस, पंकिल, कलुष, आविल, मलदूषित, सकर्दम. 2 नीच, कुत्सित, खल, गर्ह्य. –*v. t.* मलिन-पंकिल-दुष् c. (दूषयति) or लिप् 6 P, मलिनीकृ 8 U, मलिनयति-आविलयति (D.).

DIRUPTION, *See* ERUPTION.

DISABLE, *v. t.* अनुपयुक्त *a.* कृ 8 U, विहस्तीकृ, (रुजा विहस्तचरणां देवीं M. 4); अशक्त-असमर्थ *a.* कृ. 2 अवसद् c., विकलीकृ, उपहन् 2 P, दुर्बलीकृ. –DISABILITY, *s.* अशक्ति *f.*, असामर्थ्यं, अक्षमता, अयोग्यता; अनुपयोगः.

DISABUSE, *v. t.* भ्रमं निरस् 4 U or उच्छिद् 7 P or अपनी 1 P or हृ 1 P or अपाकृ 8 U, भ्रांतिर्मुच् 6 P.

DISACCUSTOM, *v. t.* अभ्यासं लुप् c.

DISADVANTAGE, *s.* अहितं, अलाभः, अपकारः, अनर्थः, अनिष्टं, अपायः, हानि *f.*, पीडा, बाधा; 'at a d.' विषमावस्थ *a.*, असमवस्थ *a.* –OUS, *a.* अहितकर (री *f.*), प्रतिकूल, आहित, अनुपकारक, विरोधिन्, अपायावह, क्षतिकारक. –OUSLY, *adv.* आहितं, अनिष्टं, सापकारं.

DISAFFECT, *v. t.* विरंज् c., अपरागं उत्पद् c., उपजप् 1 P. –ED, *a.* वि-अप-रक्त, विप्रिय, असंतुष्ट, अप्रीत, अननुरक्त. –ION, *s.* विरागः, असंतोषः, विरक्ति *f.*, अभक्ति *f.*

DISAFFIRMANCE, *s.* प्रत्याख्यानं, प्रत्यादेशः; प्रत्यावर्तनं.

DISAGREE, *v. i.* न संमन् 4 A, विवद् 1 A, भिद् pass., विरुध् pass., असदृशीभू; *See* DIFFER. –ABLE, *a.* अनभिमत, अप्रिय, अनिष्ट, अहित, अप्रीतिकर (री *f.*), अरुचिर, अनाह्लादक. 2 विरुद्ध, प्रतिकूल. –MENT, *s.* विसंवादः, विवादः, भेदः, विप्रतिपत्ति *f.*, विमति *f.*; *See* DIFFERENCE.

DISALLOW, *v. t.* न अनुज्ञा 9 U, निषिध् 1 P, निद् 1 P. 2 प्रत्याख्या 2 P, प्रत्यादिश् 6 P; *See* DENY. –ANCE, *s.* प्रत्याख्यानं, निषेधः; निवारणं, निरसनं.

DISANIMATE, *See* DISCOURAGE.

DISANNUL, *See* ABOLISH.

DISAPPEAR, *v. i.* अंतर्-तिरः-धा pass., अंतर्-इ 2 P, तिरोभू 1 P, अदृश्य *a.* भू. 2 नश् 4 P, क्षयं-नाशं-या 2 P, प्र-वि-ली 4 A, प्र-वि-ध्वंस् 1 A; 'the pigeons having d. ed' चक्षुर्विषयातिक्रांतेषु, नयनपथातीतेषु, अदृष्टिगोचरेषु, कपोतेषु. -ANCE, *s.* अंतर्धानं, तिरोधानं, अदर्शनं; नाशः, लयः, &c.; better ex. by (*v. i.*).

DISAPPOINT, *v. t.* आशां भंज् 7 P or प्रति-वि-हन् 2 P or विफलीकृ or मोघीकृ 8 U or खंड् 10; विप्रलभ् 1 A; 'he was d. ed in his request' तस्य यच्ञा मोघी बभूव, स भग्नाशो बभूव; 'd. ed in love' खंडितप्रणय, खंडित. -ED, *a.* भग्नाश, मोघाश, भग्नोद्यम, अकृतार्थ, प्रतिहत, मनोहत, प्रतिबद्ध. -MENT, *s.* आशाभंगः, प्रणयवैफल्यं, विफलीकरणं, नैराश्यं, विप्रलंभः.

DISAPPROVE, *v. t.* निंद् 1 P, गर्ह् 1, 10 A, न प्रशंस् 1 P; not 'approve' q. v. -DISAPPROBATION, *s.* निंदा, असंमति *f.*, विरागः, अप्रीति *f.*, विमति *f.*, अनभिनंदनं.

DISARM, *v. t.* अस्त्राणि अपहृ 1 P or अपनी 1 P, निरायुधीकृ 8 U, निःशस्त्रीकृ. 2 (fig.) शम् c. (शमयति), सांत्व् 10. -ED, *a.* निरायुध, निःशस्त्र; 'd. of anger' शांतरोष, क्षीणमन्यु.

DISARRANGE, *v. t.* क्रमं भंज् 7 P, व्यस् 4 U, संकॄ 6 P, संकुलीकृ 8 U. -MENT, *s.* अक्रमः, क्रमभंगः, व्यस्तता.

DISARRAY, *v. t.* अपनह् 4 P, उच्छद् 10, विवस्त्रीकृ 8 U. 2 क्रमं भंज् 7 P. -*s.* व्यूहभंगः, विजलः, समुत्पिंजः.

DISASTER, *s.* आपद्-विपद् *f.*, व्यसनं, उपप्लवः, विपत्ति *f.*, उपद्रवः, अत्याहितं, अनर्थः. -*v. t.* पीड् 10, बाध् 1 A, उपप्लु 1 A, उपद्रु 1 P. -DISASTROUS, *a.* विपद्युक्त, दुर्भाग्य, दुरंत; अनर्थावह, दारुण, घोर.

DISAVOW, -AL, *See* DENY, DENIAL.

DISBAND, *v. t.* युद्धव्यापाराद् मुच् 6 P or c., सैन्यभंगं कृ 8 U. 2 मुच्, विमोक्ष् 10. -*v. i.* युद्धव्यापारात् मुच् 6 P.

DISBARK, *v. t.* नौकायाः अवतॄ c.

DISBELIEVE, *v. t.* Not 'believe' q. v. -ER, *s.* नास्तिकः, अविश्वासिन् *m.* -DISBELIEF, *s.* अप्रत्ययः, अविश्वासः.

DISBEND, *See* RELAX.

DISBRANCH, *v. t.* निःशाखीकृ 8 U, शाखां लू 9 U.

DISBURDEN, *v. t.* भारं अवतॄ c. or अपनी 1 P, निर्भार-रिक्तभार-*a.* कृ 8 U; 'd. one's mind' मनोगतं अन्यस्मै आख्या 2 P; 'the afflicted should d. their grief' कर्तव्यानि दुःखितैर्दुःखनिर्वापणानि (U. 3).

DISBURSE, *v. t.* व्यय् 10 P (व्ययति), उत्-सृज् 6P, वि-नियुज् 7 A, 10, व्ययीकृ 8 U. -MENT, *s.* व्ययः, उत्सर्गः, विनियोगः, त्यागः; 'receipt and d. आयव्ययौ.

DISCARD, *v. t.* अपास् 4 U, अवधू 5, 9 U, अपक्षिप् 6 P, निराकृ 8 U, अवसृज् 6 P, अपहा 3 P; निःसृ c., अपनुद् 6 P.

DISCERN, *v. t.* वि-विच् 3, 7 P, विचर् c., परिच्छिद् 7 P, निर्णी 1 P, परीक्ष् 1 A. 2 निर्वर्ण् 10, दृश् 1 P, ईक्ष् 1 A, आलोक् 1 A, 10, आलक्ष् 10, विभू c. -ER, *s.* विवेचकः, ईक्षितृ *m.* -IBLE, *a.* दृश्य, दृष्टिगोचर, विभाव्य, प्रत्यक्ष. -ING, *a.* सूक्ष्मदर्शिन्, दीर्घ-दूर-दृष्टि, विवेकिन्, परिणामदर्शिन्, विचारशील. -INGLY, *adv.* सविवेकं, सविचारं, सपरिच्छेदं. -MENT, *s.* विवेकः, विवेचनं, परिच्छेदः, विचारः-रणा, परीक्षा, दूरदृष्टि *f.*, अवबोधः, विज्ञानं.

DISCERPTION, *s.* व्यवच्छेदः, विभेदनं, विदारणं.

DISCHARGE, *v. t.* (A load &c.) भारं अवतॄ c. or अपनी 1 P. 2 उद्-गॄ 6 P, उद्दॄ c., प्रमुच् 6 P, उच्चर् 10, उत्सृज् 6 P, प्लु c., उद्वम् 1 P. 3 (Arrow &c.) मुच्, अस् 4 P, विसृज्, क्षिप् 6 P, प्रेर् c. निपत् c.; 'd. a gun' लोहनाडीस्थं आग्नेयं चूर्णं ज्वल् c. 4 (अधिकारात् or पदात्) निःसृ c., अपकृष् 1 P, अवरुह् c. (रोपयति), निष्क्रस् c., निराकृ 8 U, अपास् 4 U, च्यु c., भ्रंश् c. 5 (Duty) कृ, अनुष्ठा 1 P, विधा 3 U, निष्पद्-संपद् c., निर्वह् c., आचर् 1 P. 6 (Debt) (ऋणं) शुध् c., निर्यत् 10, निराकृ, निस्तॄ c., विनी, आनृण्यं गम् 1 P. 7 मुच्, मोक्ष् 10, विसृज्. 8 (As a river) अवतॄ 1 P, द्रु 1 P; सागरं वर्जयित्वा कुत्र वा महानद्यवतरति (S. 3) 'will d. itself &c'. -*v. i.* मुच् pass.; स्रु 1 P. -*s.* भारावतरणं. 2 उद्गारः, प्लावः, विसर्गः, उद्वमनं, उच्चारणं, उदीरणं. 3 क्षेपण, मोक्षः. 4 अवरोपणं, अधिकारभ्रंशनं, पदच्युति *f.*-भ्रंशः. 5 अनुष्ठानं, निर्वाहः, विधानं, संपादनं. 6 आनृण्यं, ऋणशोधनं-निस्तारः. 7 मोक्षः, मुक्ति *f.*, मोचनं.

DISCIPLE, *s.* शिष्यः, छात्रः, अंतेवासिन् *m.*, विद्यार्थिन् *m.*

DISCIPLINE, *v. t.* विनी 1 P, शिक्ष् c., शास् 2 P, आध-इ c. (अध्यापयति). 2 नियम् 1 P, विनियम्, शास्, दंड् 10, दम् c. (दमयति). 3 व्यायम्; अभ्यस् 4 U. -*s.* विनयः, अनुशासनं, शिक्षा-क्षणं, अध्यापनं, अभ्यासः. 2 नियमः, व्यवस्था, विधिः, शासनं, नीति *f.* 3 दंडः, निग्रहः, दमनं, शिष्टि *f.*, विनियमः-मनं; 'military d.' युद्धाभ्यासः, युद्ध-रण-शिक्षा; 'd. in arms' शस्त्राभ्यासः.

DISCLAIM, -ER, *See* DENY, DENIER.

DISCLOSE, *v. t.* विवृ 5 U, प्रकाश् c., व्यंज् 7 P, प्रकटीकृ 8 U, स्पष्टीकृ, भिद् 7 P or c., निविद् c., ख्या c. (ख्यापयति); 'd. ing secrets' रहस्यभेदः. -URE, *s.* विवृति *f.*, प्रकाशनं, निवेदनं, भेदः.

DISCOLOUR, *v. t.* वर्णांतरं ग्रह् c., कलुषी-मलिनीकृ 8 U, विवर्ण् 10, कृष्णीकृ. -ATION, *s.* वैवर्ण्यं, कालुष्यं, मालिन्यं.

DISCOMFIT, *v. t.* वि-प्र-ध्वंस् c., व्यूहं भंज् or भिद् 7 P (as an army); पराजि 1 A, विद्रु c.; *See* DEFEAT, BAFFLE. -URE, *s.* भंगः, व्यसनं, पराजयः, पराभवः.

DISCOMFORT, *v. t.* पीड् 10, व्यथ् c., बाध् 1 A; *See* AFFLICT. -*s.* अस्वास्थ्यं, दुःखं, पीडा, व्यथा, क्लेशः, बाधा.

DISCOMMEND, *See* CENSURE.

DISCOMPOSE, *v. t.* क्षुभ् c., व्यामुह् c., संभ्रम् c. (भ्रमयति), आकुलीकृ 8 U, बाध् 1 A. -ED, *a.* आकुलित, क्षुब्ध, व्याकुल, कातर, व्याकुलचित्त, अनवस्थित, व्यग्र, भ्रांत, पारिप्लव, विक्लवचित्त. -URE, *s.* क्षोभः, आकुलत्वं, व्यग्रता, वैक्लव्यं, उद्वेगः, अस्वास्थ्यं, अस्थिरता.

DISCONCERT, *v. t.* खंड् 10, मोघीकृ 8 U, प्रति-व्याहन् 2 P; *See* BAFFLE. 2 Discompose, q. v.

DISCONFORMITY, *s.* विरोधः, विरुद्धता, असादृश्यं, असंगति *f.*, विसंवादः, विप्रतिपत्ति *f.*

DISCONNECT, *See* SEPARATE. -ION, *s.* विश्लेषः असंगति *f.*, वियोगः.

DISCONSOLATE, *a.* खिन्न, विषण्ण, दीन, उद्विग्न, म्लान; *See* DEJECTED. -LY, *adv.* सविषादं, सखेदं, सोद्वेगं.

DISCONTENT, *a.* असंतुष्ट, अतृप्त. -*s.* असंतोषः, अतृप्ति *f.*, अप-वि-रागः, विरक्ति *f.*, अप्रीति *f.* -*v. t.* असंतोषं उत्पद् c. or जन् c.

DISCONTINUE, *v. t.* त्यज् 1 P, विच्छिद् 7 P, विरम् c. (रमयति), निवृत् c., उज्झ् 6 P, विलुप् c. -*v. i.* वि-उप-रम् 1 P, निवृत् 1 A, (with abl.); *See* CEASE. -ANCE, -ATION, *s.* विच्छेदः, विरामः, निवृत्ति *f.*; उपशमः, भंगः, अंतरायः.

DISCORD, *v. i.* विसंवद् 1 P, विभिद्-न युज्-विरुध्-pass. -*s.*,-ANCE, *s.* भेदः, भिन्नता, विसंवादः, मतभेदः, विरोधः, विमति *f.*, वैमत्यं, वैपरीत्यं, वैलक्षण्यं; 'd. of sound' स्वरविरोधः, अपस्वरः. -ANT, *a.* विषम, प्रतिकूल, विरुद्ध, विसंवादिन्, परस्परविरुद्ध, विभिन्न, असंगत, विपरीत; 'd. sound' विस्वरः, अपस्वरः, कर्कशध्वनिः,

DISCOUNT, *v. t.* भागं उद्-हृ 1 P. -*s.* उद्धारः, उद्धृतभागः.

DISCOUNTENANCE, *v. t.* न अनुग्रह् 9 P, न उपकृ 8 U, न अनुमुद् 1 A.

DISCOURAGE, *v. t.* उत्साहभंगं कृ 8 U, अव-वि-सद् c., विषादं जन् c., विषण्णीकृ, धैर्यं ध्वंस् c., मनः or आशाः भंज् 7 P. 2 Deter, q. v. -ED, *a.* भग्नोत्साह, हताश, भग्नोद्यम, विषण्ण, अवसन्न, खिन्न, निरुत्साह, मनोहत, प्रतिबद्ध, भग्नाश, धैर्यच्युत, स्खलितधैर्य. -ING, *a.* विषादजनक, धैर्यध्वंसिन्. -MENT, *s.* धैर्यध्वंसः, उत्साहभंगः, आशा-उद्यम-भंगः; विषादः, अवसादः, खिन्नता, धैर्यच्युति *f.*-स्खलनं.

DISCOURSE, *v. i.* संवद् 1 P, संभाष् 1 A, समालप् 1 P. 2 भाष् 1 A, वद्-गद् 1 P, अधिकृत्य वच् 2 P. -*s.* संवादः, संभाषणं, संकथा, संलापः. 2 वचनं, भाषणं, उक्ति *f.*, वचस् *n.*; *See* CONVERSE,-ATION. -ER, *s.* वादिन् *m.*, वक्तृ *m.* -IVE, *a.* तार्किक (की *f.*), ऊहिन्, तर्कविषय.

DISCOURTEOUS, *a.* असभ्य, अशिष्ट, अविनीत, दुःशील, अनार्य. -NESS,-DISCOURTESY, *s.* अविनयः अनार्यता, असभ्यता; मर्यादातिक्रमः, अशिष्टाचारः.

DISCOVER, *v. t.* विवृ 5 U, दृश् c., प्रकाश् c., आविष्कृ 8 U, स्पष्टीकृ, व्यक्तीकृ, प्रकटीकृ, व्यंज् 7 P, ज्ञा c. (ज्ञापयति), आ-नि-विद् c. 2 निरूप् 10, ज्ञा 9 U, उपलभ् 1 A, निर्णी 1 P. 3 समा-आ-सद् c., प्राप् 5 P, विद् 6 U, दृश् 1 P, अधिगम् 1 P, इ-या 2 P. -ER, *s.* निर्णेतृ-अधिगंतृ *m.*, निरूपकः. -Y, *s.* प्रकाशनं, विवरणं. 2 ज्ञानं, अवगमः, दर्शनं, निर्णयः, उपलब्धि *f.*, समासादनं, निरूपणं, प्राप्ति *f.*

DISCREDIT, *v. t.* न विश्वस् 2 P, न प्रति-इ 2 P, अविश्वास्य *a.* मन् 4 A, प्रामाण्यं लघयति (D.). 2 कलंकयति (D.), अकीर्तिं आवह् 1 P, दुष् c. (दूषयति), मलिनीकृ 8 U, मलिनयति (D.). -*s.* अपयशस् *n.*, अपकीर्ति *f.*, दूषणं, कलंकः, अप्रतिष्ठा, अकीर्तिः; 'bring d. on' दुष् c., मलिनयति; (यदा मेधाविनी शिष्योपदेशं मलिनयति M. 1). -ABLE, *a.* अकीर्तिकर-अयशस्कर (री *f.*), गर्हित, कलंककर, दूषणीय, गर्ह्य, निंद्य.

DISCREET, *a* समीक्ष्य-विमृश्य-कारिन्, विचक्षण, स्ववहित, विचारशील, सावधान, दीर्घ-दूर-दृष्टि. 2 (Of acts) साधु, श्रेयस्. -LY, *adv.* विमृश्य, समीक्ष्य, विचार्य. —DISCRETION, *s.* विवेकः, विमृश्यकारित्वं, समीक्षणं, विचक्षणता, विचारः, विज्ञता. 2 स्वातंत्र्यं, स्वाधीनता; 'having reached the years of d.' प्राप्तव्यवहारदश. 3 विकल्पः, कामः, रुचि *f.*, छंदः; 'at d.' विना समयेन; 'this matter is left to your d.' यथा भवानुचितं मन्यते तथा क्रियतां; स्वरुच्या-कामतः-वर्ततां भवान्; 'at one's own d.' स्वच्छंदं, स्वेच्छया, स्वरुच्या, कामतः. -ALLY, *adv.* स्वेच्छानुसारेण, यथाकामं. -ARY, *a.* स्वाधीन, वैकल्पिक-यादृच्छिक (की *f.*), स्वेच्छानुवर्तिन्.

DISCREPANT, *a.* विभिन्न, विरुद्ध, विपरीत, अ-वि-संगत, विसंवादिन्, विरोधिन्, प्रतिकूल. -DISCREPANCE, -CY, *s.* विभेदः, विरोधः, विप्रतिपत्ति *f.*, असंगति *f.*, विसंवादः, वैलक्षण्यं, वैपरीत्यं.

DISCRETE, *a.* विभिन्न, विविक्त. 2 अवधारणार्थक.

DISCRIMINATE, *v. t.* वि-विच् 3, 7 P, वि-शिष् 7 P or c., परिच्छिद् 7 P, विज्ञा 9 U, विज् 3 U, विचर् c. 2 लक्ष् 10, परीक्ष् 1 A, सं-अव-ईक्ष्. -ION, *s.*

विवेकः, परिच्छेदः, विज्ञानं, विचारणं-णा; विशेषः, अवधारणा; 'd. of proper and improper' पात्रापात्रविचारणा; 'd. of right and wrong' सदसद्विवेकः. -ING, -IVE, *a.* विशेषज्ञ, गुणदोषविद्, विवेकिन्, परिच्छेदक.

DISCURSIVE, *a.* नानाविषय, अनेकप्रसंग; अस्थिर, चंचल, अनवस्थित. 2 तार्किक (की *f.*), ऊहिन्.

DISCUS, *s.* चक्रं.

DISCUSS, *v. t.* विचर् c., पर्यालोच् 10, वितर्क् 10, विमृश् 6 P, परीक्ष् 1 A, निरूप् 10, अनुसंधा 3 U; 'd. in detail, at length, exhaustively' प्रपंचयति (D.), प्रपंचं कृ 8 U, सविस्तरं-विस्तरेण-वर्ण् 10. -*v. i.* विवद् 1 A, वादे व्याप्टृ 6 A. -ION, *s.* विचारणा, वितर्कः, परीक्षा, निरूपणं, विमर्शः, वादविवादः, पर्यालोचनं; 'to turn to the subject under d.' प्रकृतं-प्रस्तुतं-अनुसृ 1 P or अनुवृत् 1 A or अनुसंधा; 'subject under d.' प्रस्तावः, प्रस्तुत-प्रकृत-विषयः, प्रस्तुतं, प्रकृतं; 'result of d.' मथितार्थः.

DISCUSSIVE, DISCUTIENT, *a.* शोथघ्न (घ्नी *f.*), शोथहृत्, दुष्टधातुनाशक.

DISDAIN, *v. t.* अवमन् 4 A, अवज्ञा 9 U, अवगण् 10, तिरस्कृ 8 U; *See* CONTEMN. -*s.* औद्धत्यं, सावज्ञावलेपः, अवमानः-नना, अवहेलना; *See* CONTEMPT. -FUL, *a.* सावज्ञ, सावलेप, अवमानिन्; उद्धत, अवलिप्त, सावमान.

DISEASE, *s.* रोगः, गदः, व्याधिः, आमयः, उपतापः, रुजा, रुज् *f.*, विकारः, पीडा, क्लेशः, अस्वास्थ्यं. -*v. t.* रोगेण व्यथ् c. or पीड् 10 or क्लिश् 9 P. -ED, *a.* व्याधिग्रस्त, रोगोपसृष्ट, रोगार्त, सरोग, सरुज, सामय, आतुर, विकृत, अस्वस्थ.

DISEMBARK, *v. i.* पोतात्-नौकायाः अवतॄ 1 P or अव-रुह् 1 P. -*v. t.* अवतॄ-रुह् c. -ATION, *s.* अवरोहणं, उत्तरणं.

DISEDGE, *See* BLUNT.

DISEMBARRASS, *See* CLEAR.

DISEMBITTER, *v. t.* तिक्तत्वं-कटुत्वं-अपनी 1 P, मधुरीकृ 8 U, सुरस *a.* कृ.

DISEMBODIED, *a.* अशरीर, देहहीन, कायहीन, and sim. comps.

DISEMBOGUE, *v. i.* निर्गम्-निः-सृ 1 P; समुद्रं अवतॄ 1 P or प्रविश् 6 P or प्रसु-द्रु 1 P (of a river). -*v. t.* सलिलं सागरे निर्गम् c., &c.

DISEMPLOY, *See* DISCHARGE.

DISENABLE, *See* DISABLE.

DISEMBROIL, *v. t.* उद्वेगात्-संभ्रमाद्-मुच् c. or उद्-हृ 1 P.

DISENCHANT, *v. t.* प्रतिकृ 8 U, मंत्रवशाद् उद्-हृ 1 P.

DISENCUMBER, *v. t.* प्रतिबंधान् अपनी 1 P or अपनुद् 6 P, निर्विघ्नीकृ 8 U, निष्प्रत्यूह *a.* कृ.

DISENGAGE, *v. t.* वियुज् 7 A, 10, विश्लिष् c. 2 मुच् 6 P or c., मोक्ष् 10, उद्-हृ 1 P; 'd. the mind' मनो निवृत् c. -*v. i.* मुच् pass., निवृत् 1 A, विश्रम् 4 P; आत्मानं निवृत् c. -ED, *a.* मुक्त, उद्धृत, उत्तीर्ण. 2 लब्धक्षण, प्राप्तावकाश, प्राप्तावसर, अव्यापृत, कार्यरहित-शून्य, कार्यविरत, निर्व्यापार. -MENT, *s.* मोक्षणं, &c. 2 अवसरः, क्षणः, अवकाशः.

DISENTANGLE, *v. t.* Disengage, q. v. 2 वियुज् 7 A, 10, विश्लिष् c.

DISENTHRAL, *v. t.* दास्याद् मुच् 6 P or c. or मोक्ष् 10.

DISENTRANCE, *s.* मूर्च्छनात्प्रबुध् c.

DISESTEEM, *v. t.* अवमन् 4 A, अवज्ञा 9 U; *See* CONTEMN. -*s.* अनादरः, अवमानः, अवज्ञा, उपेक्षा.

DISFAVOUR, *v. t.* न अनुग्रह् 9 P, न उपकृ 8 U, न अनुमुद् 1 A. -*s.* अकृपा, अननुग्रहः, अप्रसादः, अनुपकारः, पराङ्मुखता, विरक्ति *f.*, अप-वि-रागः, अप्रीति *f.*, असंतोषः.

DISFIGURE, *v. t.* विरूप् 10, विरूपीकृ 8 U, विकृ 8 U, व्यंगयति (D.), विकलीकृ, विप्रकृ c., (रूपं प्रसाधनैर्विप्रकार्यते S. 4). -ED, *a.* वि-कु-अप-रूप, विकृताकार, विकृत, व्यंग (गी *f.*). -MENT, *s.* विरूपता, वैकल्यं, व्यंगता, विप्रकारः.

DISFRANCHISE, *v. t.* पौरत्वं-पौराधिकारं-हृ 1 P or विलुप् c.

DISGORGE, *v. t.* उद्-गॄ 6 P, उद्वम् 1 P, विच्छर्द् 10. -MENT, *s.* उद्गारः, उद्वमनं, वमथुः, प्रच्छर्दिका.

DISGRACE, *s.* अपमानः, अव-वि-मानना, परि-अभिभवः, निकृति *f.*, अ-अप-कीर्ति *f.*, अ-अप-यशस् *n.*, कलंकः, दूषणं. 2 कलंकास्पदं, अवमानहेतुः; 'a d. to the family' कुलांगारः, कुलपांसुलः. -*v. t.* अप-अव-मन् c., कलंकयति (D.), अकीर्ति-अयशः-कृ; परि-अभि-भू 1 P, दुष् c. (दूषयति); गर्ह् 1, 10 A, सावज्ञं निर्भर्त्स् 10 A. 2 Degrade, q. v. -FUL, *a.* अयशस्कर (री *f.*), कलंककर (री *f.*); गर्हित, अपमानहेतुक, लज्जाकर (री *f.*), अवमानजनक; निंद्य, दूषणीय. -FULLY, *adv.* गर्हितं; लज्जाकरं, सापमानं. -IOUS, *a.* अप्रसन्न, अननुकूल.

DISGUISE, *v. t.* कपटवेशेन-वेशांतरेण-गुह् 1 U or आच्छद् 10, 'd. ed as' वेष-रूप-धारिन् in comp.; 'd. ed as ascetics' तपस्विव्यंजनोपेताः, तापसच्छद्मना, तापसरूपधारिणः, &c. 2 (Oneself) वेषांतरं-वेषपरिवर्तनं कृ 8 U or विधा 3 U, अन्यवेषं परिधा 3 U, वेषं परिवृत् c.; 'd. ing himself differently' वेषांतरं विधाय, परिहितान्यवेषः; 'd. ed himself with a lion's skin' सिंहचर्मपरिच्छन्नः बभूव.

2 अप-नि-ह्नु 2 A, गुप् 1 P, 10, गुह् ; *See* CONCEAL. –*s.* कपट-छद्म-वेषः, वेषांतरं, आकारगोपनं; विडंबनं, अभिनयः. 2 छद्मन् *n.*, छलं, व्याजः, अप-व्यप-देशः, लक्षं. –ED, *a.* कपट-छद्म-वेषिन्, कपटवेष, कपटरूप; रूप-वेष, &c., in comp.; 'd. praise' व्याजस्तुति *f.*

DISGUST, *v. t.* उद्वेगं-निर्वेदं उत्पद् c., अरुचिमुत्पद् c., उद्विज् c. ; निर्विद् c. –*s.* जुगुप्सा, उद्वेगः, घृणा, निर्वेदः; अरुचि *f.*, विरक्ति *f.*, बीभत्सं; 'in d.' सनिर्वेदं. –ING,-FUL, *a.* बीभत्स, अरुचिर, कुत्सित, गर्ह्य, उद्वेगकर (री *f.*), जुगुप्सावह; 'to be d. ed with' उद्विज् 6 A (with abl.) ; निर्विद् pass., निर्विण्ण *a.* भू (with instr.), बाध् desid. (बीभत्सते) (with abl.).

DISH, *s.* शरावः, पात्रं, भाजनं. 2 भोजनं; आहारविशेषः.

DISHABILLE, *a.* विवस्त्र, कुचेल, अकृताभरण. –*s.* लघुवासस् *n.*

DISHEARTEN, *See* DISCOURAGE.

DISHEVELLED, *a.* प्र-वि-कीर्ण, पर्याकुल, स्रस्त; 'having d. hair' मुक्त-स्रस्त-केश.

DISHONEST, *a.* अशुचि, असरल, अनृजु, सव्याज, जिह्म, कुटिल, कापटिक (की *f.*), छाद्मिक (की *f.*), शठ, धूर्त, सव्यलीक; 'a d. woman' असती, भ्रष्टा, व्यभिचारिणी. –LY, *adv.* अन्यायेन, कपटेन, कुटिलं, धूर्ततया, सव्याजं, छलेन. –Y, *s.* अशुचित्वं, कापट्यं, कौटिल्यं, माया, &c.

DISHONOUR, *v. t.* Disgrace, q. v. 2 अवमन् 4 A, अवज्ञा 9 U, अवधीर् 10, अनादृ 6 A; *See* CONTEMN; 'd. a maiden' दुष् c. (दूषयति), सतीत्वाद् भ्रंश् c. –*s.* अपमानः, अनादरः, अयशस् *n.*, अकीर्ति *f.*, कलंकः, अप्रतिष्ठा. –ABLE, *a.* अनार्य, कलंककर (री *f.*); *See* DISGRACEFUL.

DISHUMOUR, *s.* स्वभाववक्रता, वक्रशीलता, प्रकृतिकर्कशत्वं, प्रतीपता.

DISINCLINE, *v. t.* विरंज् c., विरागं जन् c.; or उत्पद् c. –ATION, *s.* अस्पृहा, निरीहत्वं, विरागः, विरक्ति *f.*, द्वेषः, अनीहा, विमुखता, अनिच्छा, अरुचि *f.*, अप्रीति *f.* –ED, *a.* विरक्त, वि-पराङ्-मुख (खी *f.*), अनिच्छु, निरीह, निःस्पृह.

DISINFECTANT, *s.* विषघ्नं.

DISINGENUOUS, *a.* अनुदार, अदक्षिण, असरल; *See* DISHONEST.

DISINHERIT, DISHERIT, *v. t.* रिक्थाधिकाराद् भ्रंश् c., पैतृकं धनं लुप् c.–ED, *a.* अनधिकार, पैतृकधनहीन. –ING, *s.* पैतृकरिक्थच्छेदः-लोपः.

DISINTEGRATE, *v. t.* वियुज् 10, संहतिं भिद् 7 P, विश्लिष् c.; *See* SEPARATE. –ION, *s.* वियोगः, विश्लेषः, संहतिभेदः.

DISINTER, *v. t.* (शवं) उत्खन् 1 P.

DISINTERESTED, *a.* निःस्पृह, उदासीन, निर्मम, निष्काम, मुक्तसंग, निःसंग, अपक्षपातिन्, निरीह, आत्महितनिरपेक्ष, निष्कारण; 'a d. friend' निष्कारणो बंधुः.–LY, *adv.* निर्ममं, स्वार्थनिरपेक्षं, निःस्पृहं. –NESS, *s.* निरीहता, निःसंगता.

DISJOIN, DISJOINT, *v. See* SEPARATE. 2 (Disjoint) विसंधा 3 U, संधिं भंज् 7 P or त्रुट् c. 3 व्यवच्छिद् 7 P, अवकृत् 6 P. –ED, *a.* असंश्लिष्ट, असंहत, असंगत, असंबद्ध, अनन्वित, असंलग्न.

DISJUNCT, *a.* वियुक्त, विश्लिष्ट, असंलग्न, विभिन्न. –ION, *s.* वियोगः, विश्लेषः, विभेदः, असंगतता, असंधानं. –IVE, *a.* वियोगिन्.

DISK, *s.* बिंबं, मंडलं, परिवेषः, परिधिः. 2 चक्रं.

DISLIKE, *s.* अरुचि *f.*, विरागः, विरक्ति *f.*, विमुखता, द्वेषः; *See* DISINCLINATION. –*v. t.* द्विष् 2 U, विरज् pass. (with loc.), न रुच् 1 A, न अभिनंद् 1 P, न इष् 6 P. –ED, *a.* अप्रिय, अनिष्ट, विद्विष्ट, अनीप्सित.

DISLIKEN, *v. t.* असमीकृ 8 U, अतुल्यीकृ.

DISLOCATE, *v. t.* संधेः चल् c. or च्यु c., संधिं त्रुट् c. or भंज् 7 P, विसंधा 3 U. –ION, *s.* संधित्रोटनं, संधिभंगः, विसंधानं, संधिच्युति *f.*

DISLODGE, *v. t.* अप-निः-सृ c., निरस् 4 P, निष्कस् c.; *See* DRIVE. 2 वि-प्र-वस् c., निर्वस् c., गृहाद्बहिष्कृ 8 U. –*v. i.* अपसृ 1 P, स्थानांतरं गम् 1 P, स्थानांतरे निविश् 6 P.

DISLOYAL, *a.* भक्तिहीन, राजद्रोहिन्, राजापथ्यकारिन्, अराजनिष्ठ, अप-वि-रक्त, असंतुष्ट. –LY, *adv.* भक्तिहीनतया, राजद्रोहेण, अपरागेण. –TY, *s.* राजद्रोहः, अभक्ति *f.*, अप-वि-रागः, राजापथ्यकारिता, असंतोषः.

DISMAL, *a.* उदासीन, अप्रसन्न, सशोक, सखेद, निरानंद, निरुल्लास. 2 उग्र, दारुण, घोर, रौद्र (द्री *f.*), भैरव (वी *f.*), भयप्रद, भयानक. –LY, *adv.* उग्रं, भयानकं. –NESS, *s.* दारुणता, उग्रता; औदासीन्यं.

DISMANTLE, *v. t.* वस्त्रं अपहृ 1 P, विवस्त्रीकृ 8 U. 2 उपकरणादिकं हृ, उपस्करादि अपनी 1 P.

DISMASK, *v. t.* कपटवेशं अवतॄ c.

DISMAST, *v. t.* कूपकं भंज् 7 P.

DISMAY, *s.* सं-,त्रासः, साध्वसं, भयं, भीति *f.*, उद्वेगः, सविस्मयः त्रासः, आकुलत्वं; कातर्यं; 'filled with d.' पर्याकुल, संभ्रांतचित्त. –*v. t.* संत्रस् c., विस्मयं-साध्वसं उत्पद् c., भयेन उपहन् 2 P, उद्विज् c.; *See* DAUNT.

DISMEMBER, *v. t.* अंगानि विघट् c. (घटयति) or पृथक् कृ 8 U, अवयवशः छिद् 7 P; विभज् 1 U, विश्लिष् c., वियुज् 7 A, 10.–MENT, *s.* अंगव्यवच्छेदः, अवयवशः विभागः, विश्लेषः, भंगः.

DISMISS, *v. t.* विसृज् 6 P or c., प्रस्था c. (स्थापयति), संप्रेष् c., गंतुं अनुज्ञा 9 U or आदिश् 6 P. 2 (From office &c.) अधिकारात्-पदात् च्यु c. or

भ्रंश् c. or अवरुह् c.; *See* DISCHARGE; 'd. ed from office' अधिकारच्युत-भ्रष्ट, भ्रष्टाधिकार. 3 अपास् 4 P, हा 3 P, उत्सृज्, अपनी 1 P, अपनुद् 6 P, त्यज् 1 P, दूरीकृ 8 U, निरा-अपा-कृ, मुच् 6 P; 'd. all anxiety' सर्वथा वीतचिंतो भव, औत्सुक्यमपाकुरु. 4 प्रत्याख्या 2 P, प्रत्यादिश् 6 P. -ION, -AL, *s.* प्रस्थापनं, विसर्जनं. 2 पदाद् अवरोपणं; अधिकारभ्रंशः-च्युति *f.*, पदहानि *f.* 3 निराकरणं; प्रत्यादेशः, त्यागः, &c.

DISMOUNT, *v. i.* (अश्वात्-अश्वपृष्ठात्) अवतॄ-अवरुह् 1 P. -*v. t.* Causal of roots above.

DISOBEY, *v. t.* (Orders) भंज् 7 P, उल्लंघ् 1 A, 10, अतिक्रम् 1 U, 4 P, अतिचर् 1 P; प्रतीपं गम् 1 P, न अनुष्ठा 1 P, न अनुवृत् 1 A, न अनुरुध् 4 A; (persons) आज्ञां भंज्, &c.; 'he was never d.-ed' तस्याज्ञा कदापि नोल्लंघिता, &c. -DISOBEDIENCE, *s.* आज्ञाभंगः, आज्ञालंघनं, शासनव्यतिक्रमः, अननुष्ठानं, प्रतीपाचरणं, अननुरोधः. -DISOBEDIENT, *a.* प्रतीपाचार, निदेशलंघिन्, अविधायिन्, अननुवर्तिन्, अवश, प्रतीप; not 'obedient' q. v.

DISOBLIGE, *v. t.* अप्रियं आचर् 1 P, अपराध् 4, 5 P (with gen. or loc.), असंतोषं उत्पद् c., प्रतिकूलं-विप्रियं आचर् or अनुष्ठा 1 P. -ATION, अप्रियं, अपराधः, विप्रियं. -ING, *a.* अननुरोधिन्, अननुकूल, असंतोषकर (री *f.*).

DISORDER, *s.* आकुलत्वं, तुमुलं, विप्लवः, वैक्लव्यं, संभ्रमः, पर्याकुलता. 2 अक्रमः, क्रमभंगः, अव्यवस्था, व्यस्तता, संकरः, संक्षोभः, व्यतिक्रमः. 3 रोगः, पीडा, व्याधिः, आमयः, अस्वास्थ्यं; 'd. of the stomach' जठरामयः, अन्नविकारः; 'd. in the army' समुत्पिंजः, पिंजलः, अत्यंतमाकुलं. -*v. t.* आकुलीकृ 8 U, व्यस् 4 U, व्यामुह् c., संभ्रम् c. (भ्रमयति). 2 पर्यस्, संक्षुभ् c., क्रमं भंज् 7 P, संकरीकृ 8 U, संकुलीकृ. 3 पीड् 10, व्यथ् c., अस्वस्थ *a.* कृ. -ED, *a.* विपर्यस्त, भग्नक्रम, व्यस्त, व्यत्यस्त, संकुल, संकीर्ण, अव्यवस्थित; 'd. in mind' आकुल, संभ्रांत, व्यग्र-मूढ-चित्त. 2 अस्वस्थ, पीडित, आतुर, व्याध्युपसृष्ट, रुग्ण, रुजार्त. -LY, *a.* अव्यवस्थित; *See* above. 2 अनवस्थित, नियमविरुद्ध, अवश, अनियत, उद्दाम, उच्छृंखल, अविधेय. -*adv.* अक्रमं, क्रमभंगेन; ससंभ्रमं. 2 अविधितः, विधि-नियम-विरुद्धं.

DISORGANIZE, *See* DISORDER.

DISOWN, *v. t.* प्रत्याख्या 2 P, प्रत्याचक्ष् 2 A; *See* DENY.

DISPARAGE, *v. t.* परिभू 1 P, उपेक्ष् 1 A, अपकृष् 1 P, अवज्ञा 9 U; *See* CONTEMN. 2 मूल्यं न्यूनीकृ 8 U, अवमन् 4 A, लघूकृ, अपलप् 1 P; *See* DEPRECIATE. 3 अयोग्यविशेषेहि संबंध् 9 P, अयोग्यसंयोगेन अपकृष्. -MENT, *s.* अवज्ञा, तिरस्कारः, अवमानना, परिभवः, उपेक्षा; अभ्यसूया, परीवादः, गुणापकर्षः, गुणापलापः. 2 अयोग्यसंबंधः. -ER, *s.* निंदकः, अवमानिन् *m.*

DISPARITY, *s.* असाम्यं, विषमता, वैषम्यं, भेदः, असमानता, असंगतता, असंगति *f.*

DISPART, *v. t.* विभज् 1 U, द्विधा भिद् 7 P, वियुज् 7 A, 10.

DISPASSION, *s.* विरागः, प्रशांति *f.*, अक्रोधः; निरीहता, औदासीन्यं, निःसंगता. -ATE, *a.* वीतराग, शांत, असंभ्रांत, उदासीन, अक्रोधन, निरीह, निःसंग, विरक्त, मुक्तसंग, समचित्त, अपक्षपातिन्. -ATELY, *adv.* शांतचेतसा, समबुद्ध्या, असंभ्रमं, अपक्षपातेन.

DISPATCH, *See* DESPATCH.

DISPEL, *v. t.* अप-परा-नुद् 6 P, निर्-अप-अस् 4 U, निराकृ 8 U, प्रति-अप-निः-सृ c., अपनी 1 P, अपऊह् 1 U, अपाकृ, उच्छिद् 7 P, हृ 1 P, नश् c., विभिद् 7 P, वि-प्र-ध्वंस् c., अव-उत्-सद् c., हन् 2 P (gen. in comps.).

DISPENSARY, *s.* औषधशाला, रोगचिकित्सास्थानं.

DISPENSE, *v. t.* विधा 3 U. प्रणी 1 P, निर्वह् c., प्रवृत् c.; 'd. er of laws' राजशासनानां प्रवर्तयिता. 2 विभज् 1 U, पृथक् पृथग् विन्यस् 4 U, or विधा or वितॄ 1 P, परिकॢप् c. 3 (with) Ex. by न कार्यं or न प्रयोजनं; 'I d. with your services' तव सेवया न मे किमपि कार्यं-प्रयोजनं; उपेक्ष् 1 A, त्यज् 1 P, अवसृज् 6P. -ATION, *s.* विभजनं, विभागः, प्रणयनं, वितरणं, भागकल्पनं, परिकल्पनं. 2 व्यवस्थाभंगानुज्ञा, नियमलंघनानुमति *f.* 3 ईश्वरस्य नरेण संव्यवहारः. -ATOR, *s.* विभजकः, विभागकल्पकः. -ER, *s.* प्रवर्तकः, प्रणेता, निर्वाहकः.

DISPEOPLE, *v. t.* निर्जनीकृ 8 U.

DISPERSE, *v. t.* अप-वि-कॄ 6 P, विक्षिप् 6 P, इतस्ततः विद्रु c. or गम् c.; वि-प्र-सृ c., पर्यस् 4 U, दिशि दिशि गम् c.; *See* DISPEL. -*v. i.* अप-सृ 1 U or विद्रु 1 P; *See* BREAK UP. -ER, *s.* विद्रावयितृ *m.*, उच्छेदकः; अपहः, नाशकः, हरः, in comp. -ION, *s.* विद्रावणं, विक्षेपः, विकिरणं.

DISSPIRIT, *See* DISCOURAGE.

DISPLACE, *v. t.* (स्वस्थानात्) विचल् c., अप-निः-सृ c., निरस् 4 U, भ्रंश् c., च्यु c., निराकृ 8 U, अपास्. 2 Discharge, q. v. -MENT, *s.* स्थाननाशः-भ्रंशः, स्वस्थानात्-चलनं-च्युति *f.*

DISPLANT, *v. t.* उन्मूल् 10, उच्छिद् 7 P, उत्पट् 10. 2 निर्वस् c., स्थानाद् भ्रंश् c. or निरस् 4 U.

DISPLAY, *v. t.* दृश् c., प्रकाश् c., व्यंज् 7 P, विवृ 5 U, आविष्कृ 8 U, प्रकटीकृ, स्फुटीकृ. 2 वितन् 8 U, विस्तॄ c., प्रस् c., विकस् c., विलस् c.; 'd. itself' उद्-वि-जृंभ् 1 A. -*s.* उल्लासः, विकासः, प्रकाशनं, दर्शनं, व्यक्ति *f.*, विवरणं, आविष्करणं, विजृंभणं, विजृं-

भितं, विलासः, विलसितं ; 'd. of genius' मतिविलासः ; 'd. of ignorance' अज्ञानविजृंभितं.

DISPLEASE, *v. t.* विप्रियं-अनिष्टं-कृ 8 U, असंतोषं-कोपं-जन् c., प्रतिकूलं आचर् 1 P, कुप् c., रुष् c., अपराध् 4, 5 P (with gen. or loc.), वि-अप-रंज् c. -ED, *a.* असंतुष्ट, जातामर्ष, कृतरोष, अप्रसन्न, रुष्ट, कुपित, अप-वि-रक्त. -ING, *a.* अप्रिय, असंतोषजनक, कोपावह. -URE, *s.* असंतोषः, क्रोधः, अप्रसादः, अप-वि-रागः ; *See* ANGER.

DISPLODE, *See* EXPLODE.

DISPLUME, *v. t.* पक्षान् उद्-हृ 1 P or उत्पट् 10.

DISPORT, *v. See* AMUSE, PLAY. -*s.* विहारः, क्रीडा, केलि *f.*, विलासः.

DISPOSE, *v. t.* विन्यस् 4 U, रच् 10, संविधा 3 U. विनियुज् 7 A, 10, व्यूह् 1 U, क्रमेण स्था c. (स्थापयति). 2 विनि-प्र-युज्, निक्षिप् 6 P, दा 3 P, वितृ 1 P. 3 प्र-उप-क्लृप् c. 4 प्रवृत् c., प्रयुज् 10, प्रोत्सह् c. -of, विनि-उप-प्र-युज् ; 'how have you d. ed of my money' मम द्रव्यस्य कथं त्वया विनियोगः कृतः ; 'd. of goods' विक्री 9 A ; 'd. of time' क्षै c. (क्षपयति), नी 1 P, या c. ; 'd. of a girl' (विवाहे) दा, वितृ, प्रतिपद् c. 2 (Perform) समाप् c., अवसो 4 P. -AL, *s.* विन्यासः, रचना, व्यवस्थापनं, परिपाटि-टी *f.* 2 विनियमः. 3 समर्पण, वितरणं, विनियोगः, परिकल्पनं, प्रविभागः. 4 अधिकारः, वशः-शं, अधीनता, आयत्तता ; 'I am at your d.' अहं त्वदधीनोस्मि ; 'this matter is at your d.' अयमर्थस्त्वदायत्तः, अत्र भवान् प्रभवति ; 'divine d.' परमेश्वरेच्छा, नियतिः. -ED, *a.* विन्यस्त, व्यवस्थित, रचित. 2 (Inclined) ex. by शील in comp., or काम with inf. ; 'd. to quarrel' कलहशील, कलहकाम ; 'd. to fall' पातुक, पतयालु ; 'd. to go' गंतुकाम ; 'well-d.' सुस्वभाव, स्निग्ध, सस्नेह. -ER, *s.* प्रदातृ *m.*, विनियोगकृत् *m.* 2 विनियंतृ *m.*, अधिष्ठातृ *m.*, शासितृ *m.* -ITION, *s.* Disposal, q. v. 2 भावः, स्वभावः, शीलः-लं, प्रकृति *f.*; 'good d.' सद्भावः, साधुशीलत्वं, सौजन्यं, सुशीलं. 3 प्रवृत्ति *f.*, प्रवणता, शीलता-आलुता in comp. -URE, *s.* अधिकारः, शक्ति *f.*, विनियोगसामर्थ्यं. 2 अवस्थानं.

DISPOSSESS, *v. t.* अधिकारात्-स्वत्वाद्-भ्रंश् c. or निराकृ 8 U, स्वत्वं हृ 1 P; 'd. ed of one's right' हृताधिकार, अधिकारभ्रष्ट.

DISPRAISE, *See* CENSURE.

DISPREAD, *v. t.* नानादिक्षु विद्रु c., बहुधा वि-क्षिप् 6 P.

DISPROPORTION, *s.* वैषम्यं, असमता, अननुरूपता, असंगतता, अयोग्यता. -*v. t.* अयुक्तं संबंध् 9 P or संयुज् 7 U, 10. -ED,-ATE, *a.* विषम, अननुरूप, असम, अयोग्य, अतुल्यगुण, अतुल्य, अनुपयुक्त, असंगत, असंवादिन्. -ATELY, *adv.* अननुरूपं, असमं, अयुक्तं. -ATENESS, *s.* वैषम्यं; *See* (*s.*)

DISPROVE, *v. t.* प्रत्याख्या 2 P, निराकृ 8 U, निरस् 4 U, खंड् 10, बाध् 1 A; *See* CONFUTE. -DISPROOF, *s.* खंडनं, निरसनं, बाधः-धा, निराकरणं, प्रत्याख्यानं. 2 अनिर्णयः, अनिश्चयः, अप्रमाणं.

DISPUTE, *v.* विवद् 1 A, कलहायते (D.), विप्रतिपद् 4 A, विप्रलप् 1 P, वितर्क् 10; 'what are you d.ing about' किमर्थं विवदध्वे, किंवः विवादवस्तु. 2 विचर् c.; गुरोराज्ञा अविचार्या 'not to be d. ed' विकृप् c. -*s.* विवादः, कलहः, वादः, विप्रलापः, विप्रतिपत्ति *f.*, वितर्कः, वाग्युद्धं, वादयुद्धं, वितंडा; 'subject under d.' विवादवस्तु, विवादास्पदं ; 'it is a d. ed point' वादग्रस्तोर्थः. -ANT,-ER, *s.* तर्किन् *m.*, विवादी, हेतुवादी, नैयायिकः; तार्किकः; 'a d. might ask' ex. by ननु (followed by अत्रोच्यते or उच्यते), or अत्र कश्चित् प्रत्यवतिष्ठेत. -ATION, *s.* वादः, तर्कः; *See* (*s.*). -ATIOUS, *a.* कलहशालि, वादप्रिय, विवादार्थिन्, कलहप्रिय-काम.

DISQUALIFY, *v. t.* अक्षम-अयोग्य *a.* कृ 8 U, अपाकृ. -ICATION, *s.* निर्गुणः, प्रत्यूहः, अपात्रता, अक्षमता.

DISQUIET, *v. t.* आकुलीकृ 8 U, बाध् 1 A, संपीड् 10, क्षुभ् c., उद्विज् c., मुह् c. -*s.*,-NESS,-UDE, *s.* चिंता, उद्वेगः, आकुलत्वं, व्यग्रता, संभ्रमः, बाधा, औत्सुक्यं, वैक्लव्यं, क्षोभः, व्यामोहः, अनिर्वृति *f.* -ED, *a.* उद्विग्न, अनिर्वृत, क्षुब्ध, संभ्रांत, आकुल, व्यग्र, मूढ.

DISQUISITION, *s.* विचारः, परीक्षा, विवेचनं, विमर्शः, निरूपणं.

DISREGARD, *v. t.* उपेक्ष् 1 A, अवधीर् 10, अवज्ञा 9 U, अवमन् 4 A, अवगण् 10, तिरस्कृ 8 U, धिक्कृ, न श्रु 5 P, न आदृ 6 A, न अपेक्ष् 1 A. -*s.* उपेक्षा, अनादरः, अवधीरणा, अवज्ञा, अनपेक्षा, अनवधानं, निरपेक्षता. -FUL, *a.* निरपेक्ष, अनवधान, मंदादर, उपेक्षक, अवमानिन्. -FULLY, *adv.* निरपेक्षं, उपेक्षया, अनपेक्ष्य.

DISRELISH, *s.* अरुचि *f.*, विरागः, विरक्ति *f.*, विमुखता, अप्रीति *f.*, विद्वेषः. -*v. t.* विद्विष् 2 U, न रुच् 1 A.

DISREPUTE, -ATION, *s.* अ-अप-कीर्ति *f.*, अयशस् *n.*, अप्रतिष्ठा, वाच्यता, अपमानः. -ABLE, *a.* अकीर्तिकर (री *f.*), अनार्य, गर्हित, अयशस्कर, कलंककर, निंद्य, दूषणीय.

DISRESPECT, *v. t.* न आदृ 6 A, अवमन् 4 A, उपेक्ष् 1 A, अवज्ञा 9 U, अवगण् 10, न मन् c. ; *See* CONTEMN. -*s.* अवज्ञा, अनादरः, अवमानः, अवधीरणं-रणा, उपेक्षा, परिभवः, तिरस्कारः. -FUL, *a.* सावज्ञ, उपेक्षक, परिभाविन्, अवमानिन्.

DISROBE, *v. t.* विवसनीकृ 8 U, वस्त्रं अपकृष् 1 P, विवस्त्रयति (D.).

DISRUPTION, *s.* भंगः, विदारणं, भेदः.

DISSATISFY, *v. t.* असंतोष-अतृप्ति-उत्पद् c. or जन् c. (जनयति); न संतुष् c., न तृप् c.; अप-वि-रंज् c. -ED, *a.* अतृप्त, विरक्त, वितुष्ट, असंतुष्ट, अपरक्त. DISSATISFACTION, *s.* अतृप्ति *f.*, असंतोषः, विरक्ति *f.*, अप-वि-रागः.

DISSECT, *v. t.* (अंगानि) व्यवच्छिद् 7 P, निकृत् 6 P, पृथक् कृ 8 U. 2 सूक्ष्मं विचर् c. or परीक्ष् 1 A. -ION, *s.* व्यवच्छेदः, अंगच्छेदः. 2 सूक्ष्मपरीक्षणं. -OR, *s.* व्यवच्छेदकः.

DISSEMBLE, *v. t.* अप-व्यप-दिश् 6 P, नि-अप-ह्नु 2 A; *See* CONCEAL. -ER, *s.* छाद्मिकः, दांभिकः, व्यपदेशकः, छद्म-कपट-वेशिन् *m.* -ING, *s.* अपह्नवः, प्रतारणा, गोपनं, अपलापः, छद्मन् *n.*, दंभः, कपटं.

DISSEMINATE, *v. t.* वि-प्र-कृ 6 P, प्रसृ c., विस्तृ c., प्रचर् c., निवप् 1 P. -ION, *s.* प्रसारः, प्रसरणं, विस्तारः, प्रचारणं. -OR, *s.* प्रचारकः, प्रसारकः.

DISSENT, *v. i.* विवद् 1 A, विसंवद् 1 P, न संमन् 4 A, अन्यथा मन्, अन्यमत *a.* भू. -*s.* वैमत्यं, असंमति *f.*, मतिभेदः, विमतिः, विसंवादः, विरोधः, विप्रतिपत्ति *f.* -ER, *s.* भिन्नमतावलंबिन् *m.* 2 साधारणधर्मविरोधिन् *m.* -IENT, *a.* विमत, भिन्नमत, असंवादिन्; 'without one d. voice' सर्वेषामैकमत्येन.

DISSENSION, *s.* भेदः, कलहः, कलिः, विरोधः, विप्रतिपत्ति *f.*, विवादः; 'seeds of d.' कलहबीजं; 'sowing d.' उपजापः, भेदः; 'a sower of d.' उपजापकः, भेदकः; 'family d. s' गृहच्छिद्रं-रंध्रं, अंतर्भेदः.

DISSERTATION, *s.* विवरणं, वचनं, प्रबंधः, निबंधः.

DISSERVE, *v. t.* अपकृ 8 U, न उपकृ, हिंस् 7 P. -ICE, *s.* अपकारः, क्षति *f.*, अपायः, हानि *f.*

DISSEVER, *v. t.* वियुज् 7 A, 10, विच्छिद् 7 P, विक्षिप् c.

DISSIDENT, *a.* विमत, भिन्नमत.

DISSIMILAR, *a.* भिन्न, असदृश (शी *f.*), विरुद्ध, असम, विजातीय, विषम. -ITY, *s.* असादृश्यं, भेदः, वैषम्यं, अंतरं, विजातीयत्वं.

DISSIMULATION, *s.* छलं, कपटं, छद्मन् *n.*, माया; *See* PRETEXT.

DISSIPATE, *v. t.* वि-प्र-कॄ 6 P, विक्षिप् 6 P, अपास् 4 P; *See* DISPEL. 2 व्यय् 10 P (व्यययति), अपचि 5 U, क्षै c. (क्षपयति). -ED, *a.* प्रकीर्ण, निर्धूत, अपास्त. 2 दुराचार, व्यसनासक्त, नष्टचरित्र, भ्रष्टशील, दुर्वृत्त, खंडितवृत्त. -ION, *s.* विकिरणं. 2 धनव्ययः, द्रव्योत्सर्गः, अपव्ययः. 3 व्यसनिता, भ्रष्टशीलता, दुर्वृत्तता.

DISSOCIATE, *See* SEPARATE.

DISSOLVE, *v. t.* विली c., विद्रु c. 2 भिद् 7 P or c., वियुज् 7 A, 10, भंज् 7 P, विनश् c., विलुप् c., उच्छिद् 7 P; विघट् c.; 'd. a meeting' सभां विसृज् 6 P or c.; 'd. friendship' सौहृदं भिद् or त्रुट् c. or विघट् c.; 'd. a compound' समासं विग्रह् 9 P. -*v. i.* ली 4 A, वि-प्र°, (लवणं जले विलीयते); विद्रु 1 P, गल् 1 P, क्षर् 1 P, द्रवीभू 1 P. -ABLE, -DISSOLUBLE, *a.* विद्राव्य, क्षरणशील, विलयनशील. -ENT, *a.* विलयन (नी *f.*), विद्रावक. -DISSOLUTE, *a.* तरल, अनवस्थित, उद्दाम, उच्छृंखल, निर्यन्त्रण. 2 दुराचार, भ्रष्टशील, भोगासक्त, व्यसनिन्, दुर्वृत्त, विषयिन्, कामुक, विषयनिरत, इंद्रियसुखनिरत-तत्पर. -LY, *adv.* कामुकवत्, विषयासक्त्या. -NESS, *s.* विषयासक्ति *f.*, दुर्वृत्तता, भोगासक्तिः. -DISSOLUTION, *s.* विलयनं, द्रवीकरणं-भवनं. 2 प्रलयः, नाशः, क्षयः, विध्वंसः, उच्छेदः. 3 भंगः, वियोगः, निवृत्ति *f.*, विग्रहः, विच्छेदः, विघटनं.

DISSONANCE, *See* DISCORD.

DISSUADE, *v. t.* निवार् 10, निवृत् c., व्यावृत् c., (नैयमस्माद् व्यवसायाच्छक्यते व्यावर्तयितुं Ka. 172); नियम् 1 P, (सुतां शशाक मेना न नियंतुमुद्यमात् K. v. 5); नि-प्रति-षिध् 1 P, (उ मेति मात्रा तपसो निषिद्धा K. I. 26); प्रत्यादिश् 6 P. -ER, *s.* निवारकः, निवर्तयितृ *m.*, निषेधकः, प्रत्यादेष्टृ *m.* -DISSUASION, *s.* निवर्तनं, नियमनं, प्रत्यादेशः, निषेधः-धनं, निवारणं. -DISSUASIVE, *a.* व्यावर्तक, निषेधक, प्रत्यादेशक. -*s.* निवृत्तिहेतुः.

DISSYLLABLE, *s.* द्व्यक्षरं, द्व्यक्षरः शब्दः.

DISTAFF, *s.* तर्कु *m. f.*, तर्कुटी.

DISTANCE, *s.* (Space) अध्वन् *m.*, भूमि *f.*; 'by what d. separated' कियताध्वना विच्छिन्न. 2 अंतरं, अंतरालं, व्यवधानं. 3 विप्रकर्षः, दूरता, असान्निध्यं, दूरं; 'from a d.' दूरात्, आरात्; 'at a d.' दूरे-रं, दूरतः; 'at the d. of a mile' अर्धक्रोशमात्रायां (Ka. 74). 4 दुरासदत्वं, अनालापः, दुर्धर्षता, संवृतशीलत्वं. -*v. t.* दूरीकृ 8 U, अपसृ c. 2 Excel, q. v. -DISTANT, *a.* दूरस्थ, अंतरवर्तिन्, दूर, विप्रकृष्ट, असन्निकृष्ट, दवीयस्; 'a d. relation' विप्रकृष्टो बांधवः. 2 दुरासद, दुर्धर्ष; अगम्य; अनालापिन्.

DISTASTE, *s.* अरुचि *f.*, विरक्ति *f.*, विरागः, वितृष्णा, अप्रीति *f.*, अननुरागः, विद्वेषः. -*v. t.* न रुच् 1 A (with dat.). -FUL, *a.* अस्वादु, अरुचिकर (री *f.*), अप्रिय, अनिष्ट.

DISTEMPER, *s.* Disease, q. v. 2 व्यथा, क्लेशः, बाधा, तापः, अनिर्वृति *f.* 3 दुःशीलं, कुस्वभावः, असद्भावः; दुर्दशा. -*v. t.* पीड् 10, बाध् 1 A, क्लिश् 9 P, उपहन् 2 P. -ED, *a.* व्याधिग्रस्त, आतुर, रुग्ण, पीडित, आर्त, आकुल.

DISTEND, *v. t.* वितन् 8 U, विस्तृ c., श्वि c., आध्मा

1 P, स्फाय् c. (स्फावयति); 'd. ed with wind' वातपूरित, वातोच्छून, मारुताध्मात. –DISTENSION, *s.* विस्तारः, स्फीति *f.*, आध्मानं, पूरणं.

DISTICH, *s.* श्लोकः, द्विचरणं ; द्विपदं.

DISTIL, *v. i.* क्षर् 1 P, स्रु 1 P, स्यंद् 1 A, च्युत्-श्च्युत्- 1 P. –*v. t.* स्रु c., स्यंद् c., सृज्-मुच्- 6 P, अवपत् c. 2 (Spirit) संधा 3 U, निष्कृष् 1 P, आ-अभि-सु 5 P. –LATION, *s.* क्षरणं, स्रवणं, निस्यंदः, स्रवः, स्रवः. 2 अभिषवः, मद्यसंधानं, मद्यनिष्कर्षः. –ER, *s.* शौंडिकः, सुराजीविन् *m.*, सुराकारः. –LERY, *s.* संधानी, मद्यनिष्कर्षशाला, शुंडा.

DISTINGUISH, *v. t.* वि-विच् 3, 7 P or c., परि-च्छिद् 7 P, विभिद् 7 P, विशिष् 7 P or c., विभज् 1 U, विशेषं कथ् 10. 2 विभू c., लक्ष् 10, विज्ञा 9 U, अभि-ज्ञा. 3 (Oneself) उत्कर्ष-कीर्ति-प्रतिष्ठां-लभ् 1 A, विख्यात *a.* भू 1 P. –ED, *a.* विविक्त, परिच्छिन्न; विभिन्न. 2 लक्षित, चिह्नित, विज्ञात. 3 विशिष्ट, विश्रुत, प्रसिद्ध; विशेष in comp.; अतिथिविशेषः 'a d. guest'; 'men are d. from the lower animals by knowledge' नराणां तिरश्चां च प्रतिबोध एव विशेषः. —DISTINCT, *a.* भिन्न, विविक्त, विशिष्ट, व्यतिरिक्त, पृथग्विध, अन्य-इतर-(*pron. a.*), पृथक् *ind.* 2 स्पष्ट, परिस्फुट, व्यक्त, सुप्रकाश. –ION, *s.* विशेषः, भेदः, प्र-वि-भेदः, अंतरं, पृथक्त्वं, भिन्नता. 2 परिच्छेदः, विवेकः, विवेचनं, विचारः-रणा. 3 प्रतिष्ठा, गौरवं, वर्णः, ख्याति *f.*, विशिष्टता, उत्कर्षः, प्रमुखत्वं, परमपदं. –IVE, *a.* विशेषक, सविशेष, परिच्छेदक; 'a d. mark' विशेषचिह्नं, विशिष्टलिंगं. –IVELY, *adv.* सविशेषं, विशेषेण, पृथक् पृथक्. –LY, *adv.* पृथक्, विभिन्नं. 2 व्यक्तं, सुस्पष्टं, स्पष्टार्थं, भिन्नार्थं, परिस्फुटं. –NESS, *s.* भिन्नता. 2 व्यक्ति *f.*, स्पष्टता, भिन्नार्थत्वं.

DISTORT, *v. t.* आकुंच् c., साचीकृ 8 U, वक्रीकृ. 2 विरूप् 10, वि-कृ, व्यंगीकृ, कदाकारीकृ. 3 परिवृत् c., दुष् c. (दूषयति). –ION, *s.* साचीकरणं, वक्रता, परिवर्तनं. 2 विरूपकरणं, विकृति *f.*, आकुंचनं, वैरूप्यं, व्यंगता, कुरूपता.

DISTRACT, *v. t.* आकुलीकृ 8 U, व्यामुह् c., संभ्रम् (भ्रमयति), उन्मद् c., विक्षिप् 6 P, अप-वि-कृष् 1 P, संक्षुभ् c. 2 विदृ 10, खंड् 10, विभिद् 7 P, विदल् c. (दलयति). –ED, *a.* विक्षिप्त, मोहित, व्यग्र, विधुर, आकुल, मूढ, विह्वल, संक्षुब्ध, भ्रांत, उन्मत्त; 'of a d. mind' भ्रांतचित्त, वातुल; 'to be d.' मुह् 4 P, उन्मद् 4 P. –EDLY, *adv.* मूढचेतसा, व्यग्र, उन्मत्तवत्, ससंभ्रमं. –ION, *s.* भ्रमः, आकुलत्वं, विह्वलता, व्या-, मोहः, क्षोभः, व्यग्रता, उन्मादः. 2 विभेदः, विदारणं.

DISTRAIN, *v. t.* ऋणहेतोः बंध् 9 P or निरुध् 7 U.

DISTRESS, *s.* दुःखं, शोकः, क्लेशः, कष्टं, पीडा, दुर्गति *f.*, वैक्लव्यं, आर्ति *f.* 2 आपद् *f.*, विपद् *f.*, व्यसनं, वि-उप-प्लवः ; 'cry of d.' आर्तरवः-क्रंदितं. –*v. t.* पीड् 10, व्यथ् c., क्लिश् 9 P, बाध् 1 A, दुःखयति (D.), संतप् c., खिद् c. –ED, *a.* व्यथित, आर्त, दुःखित, पीडित, कष्टापन्न, कृच्छ्रगत, दुर्गत, विपन्न, विधुर, दीन, क्लेशभाज्. –FUL,-ING, *a.* शोकावह, कष्टप्राय, क्लेशद, पीडा-क्लेश-कर (री *f.*); दुःखमय (यी *f.*), खेदक.

DISTRIBUTE, *v. t.* विभज् 1 U, वंट् 10, वि-अंश् 10, विभागशः दा 3 P or परिकॢप् c., यथाभागं विसृज् 6 P or विन्यस् 4 U or निक्षिप् 6 P; 'd. food' अन्नं परिविष् 10. –ER, *s.* विभागकल्पकः, विभक्तृ *m.*, अंशदः; 'd. of food' परिवेष्टा. –ION, *s.* विभागः, संप्रविभागः, विभागकल्पना, व्यंशनं, वंटनं.

DISTRICT, *s.* देशविभागः, प्रांतः, मंडलं, चक्रं, प्रदेशः.

DISTRUST, *v. t.* आ-परि-शंक् 1 A, न विश्वस् or प्रति-इ 2 P. –*s.* अविश्वासः, अप्रत्ययः, आशंका. –FUL, *a.* साशंक, शंकाशील, अप्रत्ययिन्, अविश्वासिन्. –FULLY, *adv.* साशंकं, अविश्वासेन.

DISTURB, *v. t.* आकुलीकृ 8 U, धू 5, 9 U, उपरुध् 7 U, क्षुभ् c., बाध् 1 A ; *See* AGITATE. 2 भंज् 7 P, प्रतिबंध् 9 P, भिद् 7 P, विहन् 2 P, विच्छिद् 7 P; 'd. sleep' निद्राभंगं कृ ; 'd. studies' अध्ययनविघ्नमाचर् 1 P ; 'able to d. penance' तपोभेदायालं. 3 (Mind) व्यामुह् c., आकुलीकृ, आकुलयति (D.), संभ्रम् c., वि-कृ. –ANCE, *s.* क्षोभः, सं-वि-क्षोभः, विप्लवः, विमर्दः, पीडा. 2 प्रतिबंधः, प्रत्यूहः, अंतरायः, विघ्नः, विच्छेदः, भंगः, बाधा, भेदः ; 'd. of concentration' समाधिभेदः ; 'popular d.' प्रकृतिक्षोभः, कोपः ; 'cause of d.' विकारहेतुः. 3 मोहः, आकुलता, व्यग्रता, वैक्लव्यं, संभ्रमः. –ER, *s.* क्षोभकृत् *m.*, विघ्नकरः.

DISUNITE, *v. t.* वियुज् 7 A, 10, विश्लिष् c.; *See* SEPARATE. –*v. i.* वियुज्-विश्लिष्-विभिद् pass. –DISUNION, *s.* वियोगः, विश्लेषः, विभेदः, विच्छेदः.

DISUSE, DISUSAGE, *s.* अव्यवहारः, विलोपः, विरामः ; व्यवहारनिवृत्ति *f.*, अप्रचारः, आचारलोपः; 'fallen into d.' विलुप्त, लुप्तव्यवहार. –*v. t.* व्यवहाराद् विरम् c. or निवृत् c.

DITCH, *s.* परिखा, खातं, गर्तः-र्तं, उपकुल्या, प्रणालः-ली, प्रतिकूपः. –*v. t.* परिखन् 1 P, गर्तां कृ 8 U. –ER, *s.* खातकारः, आखनिकः.

DITTO, *adv.* तथा ; 'says d.' तथैव ममाभिप्राय इति वदति. –*a.* पूर्वोक्त, प्राग् लिखित, प्रागुक्त.

DITTY, *s.* गीतं, गीति *f.*, गीतिका, गानं, गानखंडः.

DIURETIC, *a* मूत्रवर्धक.

DIURNAL, *a.* आह्निक-दैनिक (की *f.*), दैनंदिन (नी *f.*); *See* DAILY.

DIUTURNAL, *a.* चिरकालिक (की *f.*), चिरस्थायिन्.

DIVAN, s. शिष्टसभा. 2 इंद्रकं, मंचयुक्तः प्रकोष्ठः, आस्थानं-नी. 3 मंचः.

DIVARICATE, v. i. द्विधा भू 1 P, द्विखंडीभू, द्विधा विभिद् pass. –v. t. द्विधा कृ 8 U, द्विधा भिद् 7 P.

DIVE, v. i. वि-अव-गाह् 1 A, निमस्ज् 6 P, प्रविश् 6 P, प्लु 1 A; 'd. ing into books' ग्रंथपरायण, ग्रंथमग्न-निविष्ट. –ER, s. विगाहकः, निमंक्तृ m.; 'river d.' नदीष्णः, जलेवाहः.

DIVERGE, v. i. (एककेंद्राद्) विचल् 1 P, च्यु 1 A, व्युत्क्रम् 1 U, 4 P, भ्रंश् 1 A, 4 P; *See* DEVIATE, also. 2 Differ, q. v. –ENCE, s. विचलनं, च्युति f., केंद्रापसरणं, भ्रेषः, भ्रंशः. 2 भेदः, विरोधः. –ENT, a. केंद्रविचल. 2 विभिन्न, विरुद्ध.

DIVERSE, (DIVERS), a. अनेक, विविध, नानारूपप्रकार-विध, नाना *ind.* 2 भिन्न, इतर-अन्य- (*pron. a.*), असम, विपरीत, पृथक् *ind.*; 'd. coloured' नानावर्ण, चित्र, कर्बुर, कल्माषित. –ITY, s. पृथक्त्वं, नानाविधत्वं, भिन्नता, नानात्वं, विभेदः, असादृश्यं, असाम्यं, वैषम्यं. 2 वैचित्र्यं, विचित्रता. –LY, *adv.* अनेकधा, नानाविधं, नानारूपेण, नाना. —DIVERSIFY, v. t. चित्र् 10, नानारूप a. कृ 8 U, शबलीकृ; *See* VAREGATE. –ED, a. कर्बुरित, नानाप्रकार, शबल, कल्माषित, चित्र, चित्रित. –ICATION, s. विचित्रता, विविधत्वं, विभेदः.

DIVERT, v. t. विनुद् c., रंज् c., नंद् c., रम् c. (रमयति); 'd. oneself' वि-हृ 1 P, क्रीड् 1 P. 2 व्या-वृत् c., आ-वि-कृष् 1 P, भ्रंश् c., संचर् c., संक्रम् c., आक्षिप् 6 P, प्र-वि-चल् c., च्यु c.; 'I shall d. his thoughts' एवं तावदाक्षिपामि (Mal. 9), अन्यतः संचारयामि (U. 1). –ING, a. विनोदक, हासजनक, नर्मप्राय, क्रीडापर. –DIVERSION, s. विनोदः-दनं, विहारः, क्रीडा, विलासः, केलि f., खेला, विभ्रमः. 2 मनोरंजनं, मनोविनोदनं. 3 विकर्षणं, भ्रंशनं, च्यावनं, आक्षेपणं.

DIVEST, v. t. हृ 1 P, अपनी 1 P; *See* DEPRIVE. 2 विवस्त्रीकृ 8 U, उच्छद् 10, वस्त्रं अपनी or उत्कृष् 1 P. –URE, s. अपहरणं; विवस्त्रीकरणं.

DIVIDE, v. t. विभिद् 7 P, विच्छिद् 7 P; वि-युज् 7 A, 10, विश्लिष् c., पृथक् कृ 8 U, शकलीकृ. 2 प्र-,सं-, विभज् 1 U, परिक्लृप् c.; 'd. ed in half' अर्धे विच्छिन्नं (S. 1); 'd. into 2, 3, parts' &c. द्विधा-,त्रिधा-,कृ; द्रव्यागामवयवशो विभज्यमानानां (S. B. 533) 'when d. ed into parts' &c. 3 (In Math.) भज्, विभज्, हृ 1 P; 'd. ing by the remainder' शेषेण हत्वा-विभज्य. –v. i. विश्लिष् 4 P, विभिद्-विच्छिद् pass., द्विधा भू 1 P. 2 दल् 1 P, स्फुट् 6 P; 'they were d. ed in opinion' ते भिन्नमता आसन्, द्वैधीभूताः; 'a house d. ed against itself' अंतर्भेदाकुलं गृहं. –ER, s. विभेदकः, विच्छेदकः, विभागकल्पकः. –DIVIDEND, s. भागः, अंशः, उद्धारः, लाभः. 2 भाज्यः. –DIVISOR, s. हरः, हारः, भाजकः, ह(हा)रकः. –DIVISION, s. विच्छेदः, विभेदः, खंडनं, पृथक्करणं, वियोगः, विश्लेषः, दलनं. 2 भिन्नता, विभक्तता. 3 विभागः, अंशनं, विभागपरिकल्पनं, उद्धारः. 4 भागः, खंडः, एकदेशः, विभागः. 5 भागहरः, हरणं, भाजनं; 'd. of an army' गुल्मं, दलं. –DIVISIBLE, a. विभाज्य, विच्छेद्य, विभेद्य.

DIVINE, a. दिव्य, दैव (वी f.), देव (वी f.), ऐश्वर (री f.), अमानुष (षी f.), अपार्थिव (वी f.). 2 ईश्वरतुल्य. –s. पुरोहितः, धर्मोपदेशकः, श्रोत्रियः. –v. t. लक्षणानि or शकुनानि परीक्ष् 1 A, शुभाशुभं आलोच् 10 or कथ् 10 or प्रदृश् c. 2 (Guess) ऊह् 1 A, अनुमा 3 A, 2 P, अवगम् 1 P, तर्क् 10. –ATION, s. शकुनपरीक्षणं, लक्षणपरीक्षणं, भविष्यसूचनं. 2 अनुमानं, तर्कः. –ER, s. दैवज्ञः, शकुनपरीक्षकः, निमित्तज्ञः. 2 अनुमातृ m. –ITY, s. दैवत्वं, दिव्यता, देवतानुभावः. 2 देवता ; *See* GOD. 3 परमार्थविद्या, श्रुतिविद्या, ईश्वरविषयं शास्त्रं. –LY, *adv.* दैववत्, दिव्यरूपेण.

DIVORCE, v. t. त्यज् 1 P, निराकृ 8 U, निरस् 4 U; विवाहं लुप् c. or भिद् 7 P. –s., –MENT, s. त्यागः, निराकरणं, विवाहलोपः, प्रत्यादेशः; विवाहोच्छेदः.

DIVULGE, v. t. प्रकाश् c., प्र-ख्या c. (ख्यापयति), वि-वृ 5 U, भिद् 7 P or c. –ER, s. प्रकाशकः, भेदकः. –ING, s. प्रकाशनं, विवरणं, भेदः.

DIVULSION, s. विवरणं, उत्पाटनं.

DIZZY, a. भ्रमित, घूर्णमान. 2 भ्रमकारक, भ्रमकर (री f.), भ्रमोत्पादक. 3 चपल, प्रमत्त, अनवहित. –NESS, s. घूर्णनं, घूर्णि f., भ्र(भ्रा)मरं, भ्रमः, भ्रमि f.

DO, v. t. कृ 8 U, विधा 3 U, संपद् c., अनुष्ठा 1 P, निर्वृत् c. आचर् 1 P, निर्वह् c., प्र-णी 1 P, प्रतिपद् 4 A, (किमधुना प्रतिपत्स्ये). 2 जन् c. (जनयति), उत्पद् c., साध् c.; 'd. one's best' यथाशक्ति कृ. 3 (Standing for verb) ex. by the verb or by circum.; 'speak as you are accustomed to d.' यथाभ्यस्तमभिधीयतां (U. 1). 4 (As emphatic) ex. by एव, नूनं, खलु, किल; आजगाम किल, तिष्ठत्येव, &c. –v. i. आचर् 1 P, व्यवहृ 1 P, वृत् 1 A; 'd. unto others' अन्येषु व्यवहर, वर्तस्व. 2 भू 1 P, अस् 2 P, स्वस्थ-कुशलिन्-a. भू; 'how do you d.' अपि कुशलं भवतः, कस्ते वृत्तांतः ; 'asks you how you d.' त्वां सुखं-कुशलं पृच्छति; 'd. well' सुस्थित a. भू; देवीं सुखं प्रष्टुमागता (M. 4) 'to ask if she was d.ing well &c.' 3 (At the end of a speech); 'I have done' अवसितवचनोऽस्मि; साधयामि; 'this carelessness will not d.' ईदृशं प्रमादित्वं न मया क्षंतव्यं or न ते हिताय कल्प्यते; 'that will d. now' अलमलं, वि-

रम, इत्यलं; 'this will d. as water for washing the feet' इदं पादोदकं भविष्यति (S. 1); 'it will d. just as well for you' एवमपि तव समीहितं सिद्धमेव. -away, विनश् c., लुप् c.; 'd. away with' अलं, कृतं (with instr.); 'have done with your importunity' अलं निर्बंधेन. 2 Kill, q. v.; अपह 1 P (life &c.). -with, Ex. by किं, किं कार्यं, or प्रयोजनं with instr.; 'what can you d. with such a servant' ईदृशेन भृत्येन किं तव कार्यं; 'what have we to d. with watching the movements of our master' किमस्माकं स्वामिचेष्टानिरूपणेन (H. 2). 2 प्र-उप-युज् 10, व्याप्टृ c. -without, Dispense with, q. v. -ER, s. कर्तृ m., कारकः-करः-कारः, कृत्-in comp.; संपादकः, निर्वर्तयितृ m., निर्वाहकः. -ING, s. करणं, विधानं, संपादनं; 'of one's own d.' आत्मकृत, स्वयंकृत. 2 (D. s) चरितं, चेष्टितं, कार्यं, व्यापारः. 3 व्यवहारः, आचारः, प्रवृत्ति f.

DOCILE, a. विनेय, अनुविधायिन्, विधेय, वश्य, अधीन, आयत्त, शिक्ष्य. -DOCILITY, s. विनेयता, वश्यता.

DOCK, s. छिन्नपुच्छं. 2 नौकागारं, नावाश्रयः. -v. t. (पुच्छं) छिद् 7 P, लू 9 U, कृत् 6 P.

DOCKET, s. सूचिपत्रं, अर्थिनामावली. 2 अंकपटः, अंकपत्रं.

DOCTOR, s. भिषज् m., वैद्यः, चिकित्सकः, अगदकारः, जीवदः, रोगहारिन् m. 2 पंडितः, व्युत्पन्नः, शास्त्रज्ञः; ex. by आचार्य in comp. 3 शिक्षकः, आचार्यः, गुरुः. -v. t. Treat, q. v. -SHIP, s. आचार्यपदं, गुरुपदं.

DOCTRINE, s. मतं. 2 तत्त्वं, न्यायः. 3 पथिन् m., पथ in comp.; मार्गः. 4 (System) वादः; 'd. of evolution' परिणामवादः; प्रधानकारणवादः, अनीश्वरवादः, &c.; 'received d. s' संप्रदायः, आम्नायः.

DOCUMENT, s. लेख्यं, लेखः, पत्रं, पत्रकं, लेख्यपत्रं. -ARY, a. (s.) in comp.; 'd. evidence' लेख्यप्रमाणं.

DODECAGON, s. द्वादशास्रं, द्वादशकोणः.

DODGE, v. t. वंच् 10, प्रतृ c.; *See* CHEAT. -v. i. छलेन अपक्रम् 1 U, 4 P, विपरिवृत् 1 A. -s. छलं, कपटोपायः, शाठ्यं, कपटं.

DOE, s. मृगी, हरिणी, एणी, पृषती, कुररी.

DOFF, v. t. (वस्त्रं) अपनी 1 P, अवतॄ c., उन्मुच् 6 P.

DOG, s. श्वन् m., कुक्कुरः, सारमेयः, शुनकः; कौलेयकः, भषकः, मृगदंशकः; 'd.-cheap' अतिस्वल्पमूल्य; 'd. days' अत्युष्णकालः; 'mad d.' अलर्कः; 'go to the d.s' विनश् 4 P, परिक्षि pass.; 'hunting d.' विश्वकद्रुः. -v. t. (कुक्कुरवत्) अनुसृ 1 P, पश्चा धाव् 1 P, अन्विष् 4 P, अनुसृत्य पीड् 10. -GISH, a. श्वशील, श्ववृत्ति, श्वभाव.

DOGGED, a. कठिन, निष्ठुर, वक्रभाव. 2 प्रतिनिविष्ट, साग्रह. निर्बंधपर.

DOGGEREL, a. विषम; 'd. verses' कुकाव्यं.

DOGMA, s. मतं, तत्त्वं, नियमः, व्यवस्था, विधिः, आदेशः. -TIC, -TICAL, a. स्वमताभिमानिन्, निर्देशक; वैधिक (की f.). -ALLY, adv. दृढनिश्चयपूर्वं, सधर्षं, साहसेन, सनिर्बंधं. -TISM, s. स्वमताभिमानः, सधर्षं, स्वमतावलंबनं, दृढोक्ति f. -TIZE, v. t. सधर्ष-सगर्वं स्वमतं संस्था c. (स्थापयति) or वद् 1 P.

DOLE, s. अंशः, भागः, विभागः, छेदः, उद्धारः. 2 पारितोषिकं. -v. t. विभज् 1 U, विभागशः दा 3 U, वितॄ 1 P, उत्-सृज् 6 P. -FUL, -SOME, a. सशोक, दुःखपूर्ण, सकरुण, शोकाकुल, उद्विग्न, विधुर, आकुल, विह्वल, आर्त. -FULLY, adv. सशोकं, सदुःखं, सविषादं. -FULNESS, s. शोकः, दुःखं, विषादः, खेदः, उद्वेगः, परिदेवनं.

DOLL, s. शालभंजिका, पांचालिका, पांचाली, कुरुंटी, पुत्रिका; 'ivory d.' दंतपांचालिका.

DOLOUR, s. शोकः, क्लेशः, खेदः, आर्ति f. -OUS, a. सशोक, शोकार्त, उद्विग्न, आकुल, विधुर. -IFIC, a. पीडा-व्यथा-कर (री f.).

DOLPHIN, s. स्थूलमीनः, मत्स्यभेदः.

DOLT, s. स्थूल-मंद-बुद्धिः, मूढः, मूर्खः, जडः -ISH, a. मूढ, स्थूल-मति-धी. -ISHLY, adv. मूढवत्, स्थूलवत्.

DOMAIN, s. राष्ट्रं, विषयः, प्रदेशः. 2 राज्यं, स्वामित्वं. 3 रिक्थं, स्वभूमि f.

DOME, s. अर्धगोलाकृति शृंग-शिखरं.

DOMESTIC, a. ग्राम्य, ग्राम-गृह- in comp.; ग्रामसिंहः 'd. lion'; 'd. pigeon' गृहकपोतः. 2 गृहज, गृह्य, गृहजात, गृह in comp.; 'd. quarrels' गृहकलहाः, गृहच्छिद्राणि; 'd. duties' कुलाचारः; 'd. dissension' अंतर्भेदः. 3 गृहप्रिय, गृहवासासक्त. 4 देशीय, देश in comp. -s. गृहदासः, किंकरः, प्रेष्यः, भृत्यः, सेवकः, परिचरः. 2 गृहवासिन् m. -ATE, v. t. विनी 1 P, दम् c. (दमयति), गृहे पुष् c. or संवृध् c. -ATED, a. गृहपुष्ट, दांत, ग्राम्य.

DOMICILE, s. गृहं, आ-नि-वासः, आलयः, वसति f. -ED, a. कृतावास, कृताधिष्ठान.

DOMINANT, a. प्रबल, प्रधान, प्रकृष्ट, श्रेष्ठ, प्रभविष्णु, सातिशय, वरीयस्.

DOMINATE, v. i. शास् 2 P; प्रभू 1 P, ईश् 2 A (with gen.), अधिष्ठा 1 P, अध्यास् 2 A. 2 अतिरिच् pass.; प्रकृष्ट a. भू. -ION, s. शासनं, प्रभुत्वं, आधिपत्यं, राज्यं, अधिकारः.

DOMINEER, v. t. सगर्वं शास् 2 P, or ईश् 2 A (with gen.), कदर्थ् 10, पीड् 10, उपमृ 1 A. -ING, *a.* उद्धत, अवलिप्त, अतिदृप्त, उत्सिक्त, मदोद्धत.

DOMINICAL, *a.*, *s.* भट्टारकवासरः.

DOMINION, *s.* अधिकारः, ऐश्वर्यं, प्रभुत्वं, शासनं, आधिपत्यं. 2 राज्यं. विषयः, देशः, राष्ट्रं.

DOMINO, *s.* दीर्घप्रावारः. 2 शलाका.

DON, *s.* सुजनः, आर्यः, शिष्टजनः.

DONARY, *s.* धर्मार्थं दत्तं-दानं.

DONATION, *s.* दानं, उपायनं, वितरणं, उपहारः, त्यागः, विश्राणनं ; *See* GIFT.

DONOR, *s.* दातृ *m.*, दायिन् *m.* ; त्यागशीलः. -DONEE, *s.* प्रतिग्रहितृ *m.*

DONKEY, *s.* खरः, रासभः, गर्दभः, चक्रीवत् *m.*, बालेयः.

DOODLE, *s.* अल्पबुद्धिः, जडः, दुर्मतिः, मंदः.

DOOM, *v. t.* दंड् 10, दंडाज्ञां कृ 8 U. 2 निक्षिप् 6 P, सम्-ऋ c. (अर्पयति). 3 निर्दिश् 6 P, सं-प्र-क्लृप् c.; 'how he was d. ed to die' कथं तस्यांतो भविष्यति. 4 निर्णी 1 P, निश्चि 5 U, विचर् c. ; 'he is d. ed to death' अस्य वधो निश्चितः, वधदंडः आज्ञप्तः; 'his fate is d. ed' अपरिहार्योऽस्य नाशः.-*s.* दंडाज्ञा, दंडनं, दंडः. 2 निर्णयः, निश्चयः, विचारः-रणा. 3 नियति *f.*, भवितव्यता, दिष्टं, विधिः ; *See* FATE. 4 अंतः, नाशः, क्षयः, लयः. -DOOMSDAY, *s.* विचारदिवसः.

DOOR, *s.* द्वारं (fig. also); द्वार् *f.*, प्रति(ती)हारः; 'leaf of a d.' कपाटः-टं-टी, अररः-रं-री. 2 मुखं, प्रवेशः ; 'from d. to d.' गृहाद् गृहं; 'in-d. s' गृहे, गृहस्थित *a.*; 'out of d. s' गृहाद्बहिः, स्थानांतरगत *a.*; 'principal d.' महा-सिंह-द्वारं; 'next d.' अनंतर *a.*, प्रातिवेशिक *a.*, निकटस्थ. कल्प in comp., ईषदून; 'private d.' प्रच्छन्नद्वारं; अंतर्द्वारं; 'd.-keeper' द्वाःस्थः, द्वारपालः, द्वाररक्षकः, प्रतीहारः, दौवारिकः; 'd. sill' द्वारपिंडी, देहलिली *f.*, गृहावग्रहणी.

DORMANT, *a.* निद्रित, शयितृ, सुप्त. 2 अलक्षित, प्रच्छन्न, गुप्त, निलीन, गूढ.

DORMITORY, *s.* शय्या-शयन-गृहं, निद्राशाला, शयनागारं.

DORSAL, *a.* पृष्ठसंबंधिन्.

DOSE, *s.* मात्रा; 'in one d.' एकयैव मात्रया.

DOT, *s.* बिंदुः, शून्यं, खं. -*v. t.* बिंदुना अंक् 10 or चिह्न् 10.

DOTE, (upon), *v. i.* अत्यंतं अभिलष् 1, 4 P, भृशं स्निह् 4 P (with loc.). 2 वृद्धत्वाद् मुह् 4 P, बालिशबुद्धि *a.* भू 1 P. -AGE, *s.* अत्यंतानुरागः, अतिप्रेमन् *m.*, *n.* 2 बुद्धिवैकल्यं, बुद्धिलोपः-भ्रंशः, बालिशता, मतिक्षीणता, जरावैक्लव्यं. 3 जरा, जरावस्था. -ARD, *s.* क्षीणबुद्धिः, हतज्ञानः, अतिवृद्धः, बालिशः.-ING, *a.* अत्यनुरक्त. -INGLY, *adv.* सातिस्नेहं, अनुरागातिरेकेण.

DOUBLE, *a.* द्विगुण, द्वैध (धी *f.*), द्विप्रकार ; द्वि in comp., उभय (*pron. a.*). 2 Deceitful, q. v.; 'having a d. meaning' द्व्यर्थ (वाक्यं); d. meaning' द्व्यर्थता; 'd. dealing' द्वैधीभावः, शाठ्यं, कपटं, छलं, माया; 'd.-tongued' द्विजिह्व, अनृतवाच्-वादिन्. -*s.* द्विगुणं, द्विकं. 2 छलं, कपटं, माया. 3 विपरिवर्तनं. -*v. t.* द्विगुणीकृ 8 U, गुणीकृ, द्विगुणयति (D.). 2 पुटीकृ, पुटयति (D.); 'd. the fist' मुष्टिं बंध् 9 P. -*v. i.* द्विगुणीभू 1 P. 2 विपरि-वृत् 1 A. 3 मायां-छलं-कृ. -NESS, *s.* द्वैगुण्यं, द्वित्वं, उभयत्वं. -DOUBLY, *adv.* द्विः, द्विगुणं, द्विधा, द्विविधं, उभयतः-था.

DOUBLET, *s.* उरोवस्त्रं, उरःपरिधानं.

DOUBT, *v. i.* आ-वि-शंक् 1 A, विकल्प् 1 A, संदिह् 2 U, संशी 2 A, विचर् c., मनसा दोलायते (D.).-*v. t.* न विश्वस् or न प्रति-इ 2P, आशंक्.-*s.* संशयः, संशीति *f.*, संदेहः, शंका, वितर्कः, आशंका, विकल्पः; 'my mind is still in d.' मनस्तु मे संशयमेव गाहते; 'without any d.', 'undoubtedly' असंदेहं, असंशयं, निराशंकं, निःसंशयं, संदेहं विना; अत्र कः संदेहः (in replies). 2 अस्थैर्यं, अनिर्णयः, आंदोलनं, चित्तविभ्रमः. 3 शंका, अविश्वासः, अप्रत्ययः. 4 कृच्छ्रं, विषमं, बाधा, शल्यं, विषमपदं; 'case of d.' संदेहपदं; 'in d.' सशंक-संदेहान्वित-दोलायमान- *a.* -FUL, *a.* संदिग्ध, शंकनीय, साशंक, शंकान्वित, संशयापन्न, ससंशय; संशयित, संदेहाकुल, संशयावृत, विकल्प्य; संदेहपदं, शंकास्थानं. 2 संदिग्धार्थ, अस्पष्ट; 'to make d.' संदिह् c. -FULLY, -INGLY, *adv.* ससंदेहं, साशंकं, सविकल्पं. -LESS, *a.* निराशंक, निःसंदेह, असंशय. -*adv.*, -LESSLY, निःसंशयं, असंशयं, विना संदेहेन, निःशंकं.

DOUCEUR, *s.* पारितोषिकं, उपायनं, उत्कोचः. 2 सौजन्यं, सुशीलता, सद्भावः.

DOUGH, *s.* गुंडिका, जलसंसृष्टाः सक्तवः.

DOUGHTY, *a.* शूर, वीर; *See* BRAVE.

DOUSE, *v. t.* जले निमस्ज् c. (मज्जयति). 2 निर्वा c. (वापयति).

DOVE, *s.* कपोतः, पारावतः, कलरवः; 'female d.' कपोतिका; 'd.-cot or house' कपोतपालिका, विटंकः-कं; 'd. tail' काष्ठसंधिः, दारुसीवनं.

DOWAGER, *s.* विधवा, गतभर्तृका.

DOWDY, *s.* विरूपिणी; दुर्वसना.

DOWER, DOWRY, *s.* शुल्कं, यौतकं, युतकं, वाहनिकं; स्त्रीधनं. -ED, *a.* यौतकवती, शुल्किनी. -LESS, *a.* यौतक-शुल्क-हीन.

DOWLAS, *s.* स्थूलवस्त्रं, स्थूलपट्टं.

DOWN, *s.* कोमलरोमन् *n.* 2 तूलं, कोमलपक्षः ; 'd. of goose' हंसतूलं ; तृणलोम (of plants). 3 निर्धनपर्वतः. 4 निम्नं, निम्नप्रदेशः ; 'the road having ups and d.s' नतोन्नतभूमिभागो मार्गः ; 'ups and d. s' पातोत्पाताः; 'there are ups and d. s. in our condition (in life) as in the course of the wheel' नीचैर्गच्छत्युपरि च दशा चक्रनेमिक्रमेण (Me. 112). -*prep.* अधः, अधस्तात् (with gen.); gen. ex. by अनु in comp.; 'd. the current' अनुस्रयं; 'd. to' यावत् (with acc.), पर्यंतं in comp.; 'd. to the present day' अद्य यावत्. -*adv.* अधः, अधस्तात्, नीचैः, नीचे; gen. ex. by अव-नि-अधः pr. to roots; 'bent d.' अवनत, नीचैः प्रणत; 'to come d.' अव-नि-पत् 1 P; 'd. with the tyrant' निपात्यतां-उच्छेद्यतां-असौ प्रजापीडकः; 'd.-cast' अधोमुख (खी *f.*), अवनतदृष्टि, विषण्ण, अधोदृष्टि, दीनवदन, म्लान, खिन्न; 'd.-fall' विनि-अव-पातः, विनाशः, क्षयः, उच्छेदः, विध्वंसः, लयः; 'd.-hearted' खिन्न-दीन-चेतस्, म्लान, विषण्ण; 'd.-hill' प्रवणभूमि *f.*, उपत्यका; 'd. lying' प्रातप्रसवकाला; (*s.*) शयनसमयः; 'd.-right' अवक्र, अकुटिल, स्पष्ट, सुव्यक्त, असंदिग्ध, प्रत्यक्ष; (*adv.*) अवक्रं, अकुटिलं, सरलं, अधोधः; व्यक्तं, प्रत्यक्षं, सुस्पष्टं, भिन्नार्थं, सर्वतः, साकल्येन, सु-अति pr. -WARD, *a.* प्रवण, पतनशील, अधस्तन (नी *f.*), अधोगामिन्, पतयालु, पातुक. -*adv.* (downwards) अव pr., अधः, अवाक्, अधस्तात्. -Y, *a.* मृदुलोमवत्. 2 मृदु, कोमल, सुकुमार, सुखस्पर्श.

DOWSE, *s.* चपेटिका, तलप्रहारः, चपेटाघातः. -*v. t.* Dip, q. v.

DOZE, *v. i.* निद्रा 2 P, स्वप् 2 P. -ING,-Y, *a.* निद्रालस, निद्राशील.

DOZEN, *a.*, *s.* द्वादशन्, द्वादशसंख्याक.

DRAB, *a.* कपिश, कपिल. -*s.* कपिशवर्ण. 2 कुलटा, बंधकी, व्यभिचारिणी, पुंश्चली.

DRABBLE, *v. t.* पंकेन लिप् 6 P or दिह् 2 U.

DRAFF, *s.* उच्छिष्टं, शेषं, भुक्तावशेषं, मलं, किट्टं. -ISH,-Y, *a.* मलिन, असार, फल्गु.

DRAFT, *v. t.* लिख् 6 P.

DRAG, *v. t.* आकृष् 1 P, हृ 1 P; 'd. away, off' अप-अव-कृष्; 'd. out' निष्कृष्, निर्हृ, उत्पद् 10; 'd. s on his life' कथमपि-कृच्छ्रेण-प्राणधारणां करोति, जीवितमतिवाहयति. -*v. i.* कृष् pass. 2 विलंब् 1 A, चिर(रा)यति (D.). -*s.* रथः, चक्रयानं, केलिरथः. 2 आकर्षणी; 'd.-net' आकर्षकजालं-पाशः.

DRAGGLE, *v. i.* पंके लुट् 6 P, लोठनाद् मलिनीभू 1 P. -*v. t.* पंकेन दुष् (दूषयति); 'd. tail' (*a.*) मलिनवसन, अपरिष्कृत.

DRAGON, *s.* नागः, व्यालः, पन्नगः, सपक्षो नागः.

DRAGOON, *s.* अश्वारोहः, सादिन् *m.*

DRAIN, *s.* निर्गमः, रेचनं; (for water) जलनिर्गमः, परी(रि)वाहः, प्रणालः-ली, प्रणालिका, जलोच्छ्वासः. -*v. t.* (क्रमशः) निर्गम् c. (गमयति), अपवह् c., निःसृ c., लु c. 2 शुष् c., आ-पा 1 P, क्षै c. (क्षपयति), रिच् c., रिक्तीकृ 8 U.

DRAKE, *s.* हंसः, कादंबः, कलहंसः.

DRAM, *s.* अल्पभागः, मात्रा. 2 सुरा, वारुणी, मदिरा.

DRAMA, *s.* नाटकं; 'science of d.' नाट्यं. -DRAMATIC,-AL, *a.* नाटकीय, नाटकविषय. -ALLY, *adv.* नाटकरूपेण प्रयोगतः. -DRAMATIST, *s.* नाटकानां प्रणेतृ *m.*, नाटककारः.

DRAP, *s.* वस्त्रं, वसनं, चेलः-लं; *See* CLOTH. -ER, *s.* वस्त्र-पट-विक्रयिन् *m.* -ERY, *s.* वस्त्रव्यवहारः. 2 वस्त्रं, पटः, वासस् *n.* 3 प्रच्छदपटः, परिच्छदः.

DRAW, *v. t.* कृष् 1 P, आ-सम-कृष्, वह् 1 P, नी 1 P; 'a carriage d. n by horses' अश्वोढः रथः. 2 निष्कृष्, संहृ 1 P, (प्रजाभ्यो धनं संहरति), निर्दुह् 2 U. 3 आ-अभि-लिख् 6 P, वर्ण् 10. 4 (Water) उद्-अंच् 1 U, पर्युदंच्. 5 लु c., मोक्ष् 10. 6 समाकृष्, लुभ् c.; 'd. n by merits' गुणलुब्ध. 7 अनुनी 1 P, आराध् c. 8 लभ् 1 A, ग्रह् 9 P, आदा 3 A; 'the day is fast d. ing to a close' परिणतप्रायमहः; 'd. curtains' जवनिकां संवृ 5 U; 'd. a sword' खड्गं कोशाद् निःसृ c. or आकृष्; 'd. in air' प्राण् 2 P, श्वस् 2 P; 'd. the breast' नि-पा 1 P, धे 1 P. -*v. i.* कृष्-आकृष्-pass. संकोचं-इ-या 2 P. 3 पूयं-पाकं जन् c. (जनयति) or उत्पद् c. -away, अपकृष्, अपनी, अपहृ. -back, प्रत्याहृ, प्रतिसंहृ, प्रत्यानी. 2 (*v. i.*) अपक्रम् 1 U, 4 P, अपसृ 1 P, अपया 2 P, परा-नि-वृत् 1 A, पलाय् 1 A. -down, उत्पद् c., जन् c., आवह् 1 P; 'you have d. n down ruin upon yourself with your own hands' त्वया स्वहस्तनांगाराः कर्षिताः (P. I. 3). -in, संहृ, विकृष्, प्रत्याहृ; 'd. in the reins' प्रगृह्यंतां रश्मयः. -near, प्रत्यासद् 1 P; उपसृप् 1P, उपागम् 1 P, उपस्था 1U; *See* APPROACH; (प्रत्यासीदति स्नानसमयः Ka. 47). -off, अप-वि-कृष्, अपहृ, अपनी; 'd. off the cloud' निवार्यतां जलदः (Mr. 5). 2 लु c., मुच् 6 P or c. (as liquids). 3 (*v. i.*) अपसृ 1 P; *See* Draw back. -on, आनी, आकृष्. 2 उत्पद् c., आवह् 1 P. 3 (*v. i.*) उपस्था, उपागम्, प्रत्यासद्. -out, निष्कृष्, निर्हृ, सं-हृ, निर्दुह्. 2 तन् 8 U, विस्तृ c., दीर्घीकृ 8 U, वितर्तीकृ. 3 निर्गम् c. (गमयति), उद्-भू c. 4 (Army) व्यूहेन रच् 10; सैन्यं व्यूह् 1 U. -together, समाकृष्, संग्रह्, समानी. -up, उत्कृष्, उद्-हृ-धृ 1 P, उत्तुल् 10. 2 लिख् 6 P, विरच् 10, निबंध् 9 P. 3 उन्नम् c. (नमयति); 'the goat drew himself up' अज उदस्थौ, शनैर्वपुरुदनमयत्. 'Drawback' प्रत्यूहः, अंतरायः. 2 हानि *f.*, अपचयः, अपायः. 3 उद्धारः; 'd.-bridge' जंगम-चल-सेतुः

—ER, *s.* कर्षकः. 2 चलसमुद्गकः, संपुटः, निष्कर्षणी; 'd. s' जंघावारः. —ING, *s.* आकर्ष:-र्षणं. 2 चित्रं, आलेख्यं, प्रतिरूपं; चित्रफलकः, प्रतिमानं. 3 चित्रकर्मन् *n.*, चित्रविद्या; 'd. room' दर्शनगृहं, सभाजनकोष्ठः.

DRAUGHT, *s.* पानं; 'a d. of water' गंडूषमात्रं जलं. 2 संग्रहः, सारः. 3 आलेखनं, चित्रारंभः, पांडुलेख्यं. 4 चित्रं, आलेख्यं, प्रतिमा-मानं. 5 परि(री)वाहः, जलनिर्गमः, जलोच्छ्वासः, प्रणालः-ली. 6 आकर्षणं; 'a d. horse' रथ्यः, शाकटः, शाकटीनः; 'd. board' अष्टापदं, शारिफलं; अष्टापदक्रीडा, शारिक्रीडा; 'a piece at d.' शा(सा)रिः, नयः, शा(सा)रः; जतुपुत्रकः; 'moving a piece at d.' परि(री)णायः. —DRAUGHTSMAN, *s.* लेखकः, चित्रकरः.

DRAWL, *v. i.* चिरेण-मंदं मंदं-वाक्यानि उच्चर् c. or उदाहृ 1 P. —ING, *s.* मंदोच्चारणं.

DRAY,-MAN, *See* under CART.

DREAD, *s.* भीति *f.*, त्रासः, भयं, साध्वसं. —*v. t.* भी 3 P, त्रस् 1, 4 P, उद्विज् 6 A, (with abl.). —ED, *a.* भयहेतुः, त्रासस्थानं. —*a.*,-FUL, *a.* दारुण, भयप्रद, भीम, भयंकर (री *f.*), त्रासावह, भीषण, भयानक, घोर, उग्र, भैरव (वी *f.*), रौद्र (द्री *f.*). —FULLY, *adv.* दारुणं, उग्रं, भीमं. —LESS, *a.* निर्भय, त्रासहीन.

DREAM, *s.* स्वप्नः, स्वापः, स्वप्नदर्शनं. 2 स्वप्नसृष्टि *f.*, मिथ्यावासना, असंभवकल्पना, आभासः, वृथावासना; 'bad d.' दुःस्वप्नः; 'speak in a d.' उत्स्वप्नायते (D.). —*v. t.* स्वप्ने दृश् 1 P. —*v. i.* स्वप्नं दृश्, स्वप्नायते (D.). 2 चिंत् 10, भू c, मनसा क्लृप् c., चित्ते आकल् 10 (कलयति). 3 वृथावासनां कृ 8 U, असंभवकल्पनां कृ. —ER, *s.* स्वप्नदर्शिन् *m.* 2 दुर्वासनाकृत् *m*, असंभवकल्पनाकृत् *m.* 3 उन्मत्तः. —Y, *a.* स्वप्नोपम, स्वप्नवत् *ind.*; असार.

DREARY, *a.* घोर, निर्जन, शून्य, जीर्ण. 2 निरानंद, दुरालोक, दुर्दर्शन, निष्प्रभ. —NESS, *s.* निर्जनत्वं, घोरता, शून्यत्वं.

DREDGE, *v. t.* आकृष् 1 P. —*s.* आकर्षणी.

DREGS, *s.* खलं, मलः-लं, उच्छिष्टं, शेषं, किट्टं, अवकरः, संकरः, असारः; 'he belongs to the d. of society' नीच-अधम-तमोयं पुरुषः. —DREGGIST, *a.* मलिन, समल.

DRENCH, *v. t.* क्लिद् c., प्रोक्ष् 1 P, सिच् 6 P, जलेन द्रु c. or स्ना c. (स्ना-स्न-पयति); 'd. ed with sweat' स्वेदसलिलस्नात. —*s.* पानं, पेयं.

DRESS, *s.* वेशः-षः, नेपथ्यं, वस्त्रं, परिच्छदः, वासस् *n.*, वसनं, परिधानं. 2 आकल्पः, परिकर्मन् *n.*, आभरणं, प्रसाधनं, भूषणं, अलंकारः, संस्कारः, परिष्कारः, मंडनविधिः. —*v. t.* प्रसाध् c., अलंकृ 8 U, परिष्कृ, मंड् 10, भूष् 10; प्रा-वृ 5 U, वस्त्रेण आच्छद् 10 or परिवेष्ट् c., संव्ये 1 P, वस्त्रं परिधा c. (धापयाति). 2 (Oneself) वस् 2 A, वस्त्रं परिधा 3 U. 3 उपकृप् c., संस्कृ, विधा 3 U, सज्जीकृ; 'd. food' (अन्नं) पच् 1 P, श्रा c. (श्रपयति), संस्कृ, श्री 9 U, सिद्धीकृ; 'd. hair' केशान् रच् 10 or विन्यस् 4 P; 'd. leather' चर्म परिष्कृ; 'd. wounds' क्षतं निर्णिज् 3 U or प्रक्षल् 10. —ED, *a.* परिच्छन्न, वस्त्रवेष्टित, सवेश, संवीत, प्रावृत, प्रसाधित, मंडित, भूषित, अलंकृत, सवासस्, वस्त्रान्वित, कृतनेपथ्य, कृतपरिकर्मन्, रचितवेष-आकल्प; 'well d.' सुवेश; 'd. as' ex. by वेश-वासस् in comp.; 'd. as a sage' मुनिवेशः, मुनिवेशधारी; 'd. in black' नीलांबर. 2 पक्व, सिद्ध, संस्कृत, श्राण, श्रपित, शृत; 'half d.' आपक्व. 3 निर्णिक्त. —ER, *s.* प्रसाधकः, आच्छादकः, आकल्पकः. 2 अन्नफलकः. —ING, *s.* वस्त्रपरिधानं, नेपथ्यविधानं, अंगसंस्कारः, परिकर्म. 2 पाकनिष्पत्ति *f.*, अन्नसंस्कारः, पाकसिद्धि *f.* 3 विलेप:-पनं, उपनाहः; 'd. room' नेपथ्यं, प्रसाधनागारं, वस्त्रपरिधानस्थानं.

DRIB, *v. t.* अवच्छिद् 7 P, उद्धृ 1 P, अन्यायेन स्वायत्तीकृ or आत्मसात्कृ 8 U.

DRIBBLE, *v. i.* कणशः स्यंद् 1 A, बिंदुक्रमेण पत् 1 P, शनैः क्षर् 1 P or स्रु 1 P or गल् 1 P. —*v. t.* कणशः स्रु c. or गल् c. —DRIBBLET, *s.* कणः, लवः, लेशः, कणिका, अल्पभागः; 'in d. s' बिंदुक्रमेण; कणशः, अल्पाल्पं.

DRIFT, *s.* भावः, तात्पर्यं, आशयः, अभिप्रायः, उद्देशः, प्रवृत्ति *f.*, आकांक्षा. 2 वेगः, रयः. 3 राशिः, संचयः, पुंजः, निकरः; 'd. of snow' हिमसंहति *f.*, हिमानी. 4 संपातः, वर्षः. —*v. i.* प्रवह् 1 P, जलस्रोतसा नी-वह् pass. 2 विप्लु 1 A, (विप्लवेतेह नौरिव H. 3). 3 वायुवेगेन पुंजीभू 1 P. —*v. t.* प्रवह् c., प्रेर् c., प्रचुद् 10, प्रणुद् 6 P or c. 2 संपत् c., राशीकृ 8 U, संहन् 2 P, पुंजीकृ.

DRILL, *s.* वेधनी-निका, आ-स्फोटनी. 2 व्यायामः, अस्त्रशिक्षा, शस्त्राभ्यासः. —*v. t.* व्यध् 4 P, छिद्र् 10, समुत्कृ 6 P. 2 युद्धविद्यां शिक्ष् c., शस्त्राभ्यासं कृ c.; रणशिक्षां दा 3 P.

DRINK, *v. t.* पा 1 P; 'd. up' आचम् 1 P, आपा, शुष् c. —*s.* पानं, पानीयं, पयस् *n.*, पेयं. 2 सुरा, मद्यं. —*v. i.* जलं पा or सेव् 1 A; 'd. together' सं-पा, सपीतिं कृ 8 U; 'd. (to) the health of' स्वास्थ्याय or शुभं भूयादिति प्रार्थनापूर्वकं पा. —ER, *s.* पातृ *m.*, पायिन् *m.*, पानरतः, पानासक्तः. —ING, *s.* पानं, आचमनं, पीति *f.*; 'd. vessel' पानपात्रं-भाजनं, चषकः, सरकः; 'd. together' सपीति *f.*, तुल्यपानं. —DRUNK, DRUNKEN, *a.* मत्त, क्षीव, समद, मदोन्मत्त, उपोढमद, मदोदग्र; 'to be d.' मद् 4 P; 'to make d.' मद् c. 2 सिक्त, क्लिन्न. —ARD, *s.*

पानरतः, पानासक्तः, पानशौंडः, मधुपः, मद्यपः. —ENNESS, s. मदः, मत्तता, क्षीवता, उन्मादः.

DRIP, v. i. कणशः-बिंदुक्रमेण-क्षर्-गल-स्रु 1 P or स्यंद् 1 A; 'd. ing garment' जलनिस्यंदि वस्त्रं. —v. t. कणशः स्रु c. or गल् c. —s. पटलप्रांतः-तं, वलीकः-कं, नीध्रं. —PING, s. क्षरणं, स्रवणं, गलनं, स्यंदनं, निस्यंदः. 2 मांसवसा, मांसस्नेहः-रसः; 'd. pan' रसधारिणी.

DRIVE, v. t. चर्-स्रु c., नुद् 6 P or c., प्र-णुद्; प्रेर् c.; (fig.) प्रवृत् c., प्रोत्सह् c., उत्त्विज् c., उद्युज् 10. 2 वह् c., कृष् 1 P, नी 1 P, प्र-चुद् 10 (fig. also); 'd. n to do this rash act' चापलाय प्रचोदितः (R. I. 9); 'd. a nail' कीलं प्रविश् c. —v. i. रथेन गम्-चल-चर् 1 P. 2 सं-अप-वह् pass., चल् c. pass., नुद्-कृष-नी pass.; 'a sharp d. ing shower' अविरलवारिधारासंपातः (U. 6), पटुधारासारः (V. 4). 3 आपत् 1 P, अभिद्रु 1 P, संघट्ट् 1 A. —s. रथेन संचरणं or विहारः. —at. उद्दिश् 6 P, अभि-प्र-इ 2 P; अधिकृत्य-उद्दिश्य-वद् 1 P; 'what are you d. ing at' किमुद्दिश्य भवान्भाषते. —away,-off, निर्-अप-अस् 4 U, अपवह् c., निर्-अप-सृ c., निरा-अपा-कृ 8 U, अपानुद्, निर्धू 5, 9 U; हृ 1 P, अप-परि-हृ, अप-ऊह् 1 U. —out, निर्वस् c., निष्कस् c., बहिष्कृ, निर्गम् c., विवस् c., नि-अप-सृ c. —ER, s. प्रेरकः, वाहकः. 2 यंतृ m., रथवाहकः; प्राजितृ m., सूतः, नियंता, क्षत्तृ m., सारथिः, सव्येष्टा, दाक्षिणस्थः. —ING, s. प्रेरणं, प्रचोदनं, निराकरणं, &c. —DROVE, s. कदंबकं, यूथं, गणः, कुलं, संघः. 2 पशुसमूहः.

DRIVEL, s. लाला, सृणि(णी)का, स्यंदिनी, द्राविका. —v. i. लालां पत् c. or निःसृ c. or स्रु c. 2 बुद्धिविकल a. भू 1 P, जडीभू, हतज्ञान a. भू. —LER, s. लालास्रावकः. 2 मूर्खः, बालिशः, जडः, मूढः, हतज्ञानः.

DRIZZLE, v. i. मंदं मंदं वृष् 1 P, शीकरायते (D.). —v. t. शीकरं वृष्. —ING, s. शीकरवर्षः-पातः (a d. shower). —DRIZZLY, a. शीकरयुक्त, तुषारविशिष्ट.

DROLL, s. भंडः, वैहासिकः, विदूषकः. —a. हासकर (री f.), उपहास्य, विनोदिन, असंबद्ध. —v. i. परिहासं उत्पद् c. —ERY, s. परिहासः, हास्यं, विहासः, विनोदः, नर्मालापः.

DROMEDARY, s. क्रमेलः-लकः, एककुकुद m.

DRONE, s. (dronish) अलसः, निरुद्योगः, आलस्यशीलः, तंद्रालुः, निरुत्साहः.

DROOP, v. t. अवनम् c. (नमयति); नम्रीकृ 8 U; See BEND. —v. i. अव-वि-सद् 1 P, म्लै 1 P. ग्लै 1 P, स्रंस् 1 A, गल् 1 P. क्लम् 1, 4 P; ध्वंस् 1 A, क्षि-मुच्-pass., शिथिलीभू 1 P, अव-आ-नम् 1 P; 'let not your spirits d. (flag)' मा भवानंगानि मुंचतु (V. 2); 'I slept with d.-ing limbs' मुक्तैरवयवैरशयिषि (D. K. II. 2); 'the vine is d. ing with its load' फलभारानमिता द्राक्षालता; 'the whole frame d. s down' स्रंसते देहबंधः (U. 3). —ING, a. अवसन्न, म्लान, क्लांत, स्रस्त, शिथिल, स्रंसिन्. 2 आ-अव-नत, आवर्जित, नम्रीभूत, नमित.

DROP, s. बिंदुः, पृषत् n., लवः, विप्रुष् f., पृषतः, कणिका, कणः, शीकरः; 'd. by d.' बिंदुक्रमेण, कणशः; 'small d. s make a pool' जलबिंदुनिपातेन क्रमशः पूर्यते घटः (H. 2). 2 कर्णावतंसः; लोलकः, कुंडलं. —v. t. कणशः स्रु c. or पत् c. or स्यंद् c.; 'd. ing rut' मदं क्षरंतः. मदनिस्यंदिनः (गजाः); 'd. ing nectar' अमृतस्रुत्, सुधास्यंदिन्. 2 अव-,नि-,पत् c., स्रंस् c., भ्रंश् c., च्यु c., मुच् 6 P, विसृज् 6 P, निविश् c. 3 सं-हृ 1 P, अपास् 4 P, त्यज् 1 P, निवृत् 1 A (with abl.); 'I shall d. congratulatory lines regarding you in my letters' मदीयेषु लेखेषु त्वामुद्दिश्य सभाजनाक्षराणि पातयिष्यामि (M. 5); 'let this matter (story) be d. ed' संह्रियतामियं कथा (Ka. 169). —v. i. स्रु 1 P, च्युत्-श्चुत् 1P, क्षर् 1 P, गल् 1 P, स्यंद् 1 A. 2 स्रंस्-च्यु- 1 A, भ्रंश् 1 A, 4 P; नि-,पत्; 'd. ing on his knees' जानुभ्यामवनीं गत्वा, क्षितितलनिहितजानुः. 3 नि-,अव-,पत् 1 P, अवसद् 1 P, मुर्छ् 1 P; See DROOP; 'I feel ready to d.' अवसन्नप्रायाणि मे गात्राणि, सीदंति मे अंगानि. 4 (in) सहसा-अतर्कितं-गम् 1 P or आगम्.

DROPSY, s. (generally) शोफः, शोथः. 2 जलोदरं, जठरामयः, उदरी; 'dropsied honour' केवलं स्थूलः-महाप्रमाणः-मानः.

DROSS, s. मंडूरं, सिंहाणं(नं), लोहमलं, सिंघाणं. 2 मलं, खलं, किट्टं; See DREGS. —Y, a. समल.

DROUGHT, s. अवग्र(ग्रा)हः, अनावृष्टि f., अवर्षणं, जलशोषः, वृष्टिविघातः, वर्षनिरोधः. —Y, a. जलशून्य, शुष्क, निरुदक, निर्वृष्टि.

DROWN, v. t. ब्रु c.; आ- सं-परि-ब्रु c. 2 जले निमस्ज् c. (मज्जयति) or प्रविश् c. 3 जलमज्जनेन व्यापद् c. or मृ c. 4 निरोधा 3 U, तिरयति (D.); 'd. s my voice with his cries' केकाभिस्तिरयति मे वचनं (Mal. 9). —v. i., 'to be d. ed' नि-मस्ज् 6 P, निमज्जनेन मृ 6 A or नश् 4 P or व्यापद् 4 A; 'd. ed in the sea' पयोराशौ निमग्नः; 'd. ed in reflection' चिंतामग्न. —ING, s. मज्जनं, आप्लावः, प्लावनं.

DROWSE, v. i. नि-द्रा 2 P, स्वप् 2 P, स्वप् desid. (सुषुप्सति). —DROWSY, a. निद्रालु, तंद्रिल, निद्रालस, निद्राशील, अलस. —NESS, s. तंद्रा, निद्रालुत्वं, आलस्यं, निद्रा, निद्राशीलत्वं, शयालुता.

DRUB, v. t. वेत्रेण तड् 10 or प्र-हृ 1 P.

DRUDGE, *v. i.* अविरतं-अतिक्लेशेन-आयस् 1, 4 P or परिश्रमं कृ 8 U, शारीरायासेन व्रातं कृ. –*s.* व्रातीनः, अविरतायासिन् *m.*, अतिक्लेशेन निकृष्टकर्मकारिन् *m.*, हीनवृत्तिः –RY, *s.* अविरतायासः, शारीरक्लेशः, नित्यश्रमः,नित्यक्लेशः, निकृष्टकर्माभियोगः, व्रातं.

DRUG, *s.* औषधं, भेषजं, अगदः, भैषज्यं, जायुः. –*v. t.* औषधादिना मिश्र् 10 or संसृज् 6 P. –DRUGGIST, *s.* औषधविक्रायिन् *m.*, भेषजकारः.

DRUGGET, *s.* स्थूलपटः, स्थूलशाटकः, वराशिः.

DRUM, *s.* पटहः, दुंदुभिः, डिंडिमः, भेरी, आनकः. 2 कर्णोदरं, कर्णदुंदुभिः. –*v. i.* पटहं तड् 10. 2 स्पंद् 1 A. –MER, *s.* पटहताडकः. –DRUMSTICK, *s.* कोणः, शारिका.

DRY, (up) *v. i.* शुष् 4 P, शोषं या 2 P or गम् 1P, आश्यै 1 A, नीरसीभू 1 P, शुष्कीभू. –*v. t.* शुष् c., शोषं नी 1 P, आश्यै c., रसं अपनी or हृ 1 P, शुष्कीकृ 8 U; 'she dried rice in the sun' तंडुलान्सूर्यातपे दत्तवती. 2 (up) आचम् 1 P, (आचामति स्वेदलवान् मुखे ते R. XIII. 20) ; उच्छुष् c., आ-नि-पा 1 P. –*a.* शुष्क, निर्जल, नीरस, अक्लिन्न, वान. 2 असार, निःसार, निःसत्व, अरस, नीरस, फल्गु, विरस, तुच्छ. 3 उदकार्थिन्, तृषित, तृषार्त; 'd. soil' मरुः, मरुस्थलं-ली; 'd. ground' स्थलं; 'd.-eyed' निरश्रुनयन; 'd. nurse' शिशुपालिका, अंकपाली; 'd. shod' शुष्कचरण *a.* –ER, *s.* शोषकः-णः. –ING, *s.* शोषः, शोषणं, शुष्कीकरणं. –LY, *adv.* शुष्कं, नीरसं, अरसिकतया. –NESS, *s.* शोषः, शुष्कता, निर्जलत्वं, अरसिकत्वं.

DUAL, *a.* द्विसंख्य, द्विवाचक, द्विक; 'the d. number' द्विवचनं. –ITY, *s.* द्वैतं, द्वित्वं, द्वैधं.

DUB, *v. t.* नवपदे नियुज् 7 A, 10, नवपदवीं दा 3 U or आरुह् c. (रोपयति).

DUBIOUS, *a.* अस्पष्ट, अव्यक्त, संदिग्धार्थ. 2 संदिग्ध, अनिश्चित; *See* DOUBTFUL. –LY, *adv.* ससंशयं, साशंकं, अस्पष्टं, अव्यक्तं.

DUCK, *s.* कलहंसः, कादंबः, चक्रवाकः, हंसः, प्लवः, वरटः. 2 तिर्यक्क्षिप्तः प्रस्तरः. 3 दयितः-ता, प्रियः-या, वत्सः-त्सा. –*v. i.* मस्ज् 6 P, अवगाह् 1 A; मस्तकं नम् c. –*v. t.* जले अवगाह् c. or आप्लु c. or मस्ज् c. (मज्जयति). –ER, *s.* आप्लावकः, मंक्तृ *m.* –ING, *v.* मज्जनं, अवगाहः, आप्लवनं. –LING, *s.* हंसशावकः-शिशुः.

DUCT, *s.* प्रणालः-ली, मार्गः, संक्रमः, कुल्या. 2 शिरा, नाडि-डी *f.*, धमनी.

DUCTILE, *a.* विनेय, विधेय, वश्य. 2 आनम्य, मृदु, कोमल, उद्वर्तनयोग्य. –DUCTILITY, *s.* वश्यता; आनम्यता; सुखोद्वर्तनीयता.

DUDGEON, *s.* अमर्षः, कोपः; *See* ANGER. 2 असिपुत्रिका, कृपाणिका.

DUE, *a.* देय, दातव्य, परिशोध्य; ex. by pot. pass. part., or अर्ह् 1 P; 'respect is d. to our elders' पूज्या हि गुरवः; 'the debt d.' परिशोध्यं ऋणं. 2 अनुरूप, युक्त, उचित, योग्य, यथार्ह, यथा in comp.; 'in d. time' समये, यथासमयं; यथाविधि, &c. 3 (Owing to) ex. by कारणं, हेतुः; 'your failure is d. to your carelessness alone' प्रमाद एव तवासिद्धेः कारणं-हेतुः, प्रमादात् तवासिद्धिः प्राभूत्. –*s.* देयं, परिशोध्यं, ऋणं. 2 प्राप्यं, ग्राह्यं, प्रातव्यं, योग्यांशः. 3 कर्तव्यं, अवश्यं कार्यं. 4 करः, शुल्कः-ल्कं, राजग्राह्यो भागः, राजस्वं. 5 अधिकारः. –DULY, *adv.* यथातथं, यथोचितं, यथार्हं, उचितं, सम्यक्. 2 यथासमयं, समये, यथावसरं.

DUEL, *s.* द्वंद्वं, द्वंद्वयुद्धं, मल्लयुद्धं, नियुद्धं, बाहुयुद्धं. –*v. i.* द्वंद्वयुद्धं कृ 8 U, द्वंद्वं कृ. –LER, –LIST, *s.* द्वंद्वमल्ल-योद्धृ *m.*, द्वंद्वकृत् *m.*

DUG, *s.* स्तनः, पयोधरः.

DULCET, *a.* सुरस, स्वादु, मधुर, मिष्ट; 'd. to the ear' सुखश्रव, सुस्वर, श्रुतिमनोहर. –DULCIFY, *v. t.* मधुरीकृ 8 U, स्वादूकृ.

DULCIMER, *s.* वल्लकी, विपंचिका.

DULL, *a.* मंद, मूढ, जड, मंद-स्थूल-बुद्धि-मति; 'd.-witted' दुर्मति, जडमति, मंदधी. 2 निष्प्रभ, विषण्ण, निस्तेजस्, निरुत्साह, क्लांत, म्लान, मंदच्छाय, मलिन, मंदद्युति. 3 अतीक्ष्ण, धाराहीन, अतेजस्, कुंठ. 4 अलस, मंथर, जड, मंदगति, मंद, अनुष्ण, शीतक, तुंदपरिमृज. 5 स्थूल, घन. 6 अरस, अरसिक. 7 कष्टकर (री *f.*), विषम, निरानंद; 'd. of hearing' विकलकर्ण; 'a d. day' दुर्दिनं, तमोवृतं नभः. –*v. t.* जडीकृ 8 U, मुह् c., कुंठ् 10, अतीक्ष्णीकृ, घनीकृ, निष्प्रभीकृ, तेजो हृ 1 P; वि-षद् c., म्लानीकृ, उत्साहं भंज् 7 P. –NESS, *s.* मांद्यं, जाड्यं, मूढता; अतीक्ष्णता, आलस्यं, तेजोमांद्यं, निष्प्रभता, अतेजस् *n.*, &c.

DUMB, *a.* मूक, जड, जडवाच्, वाग्रहित, वाक्शक्तिहीन, अनालाप, अवाच्. –LY, *adv.* मूकवत्, निःशब्दं; तूष्णीं, वाग्व्यतिरेकेण. –NESS, *s.* मूकता, वाक्स्तंभः, जाड्यं, वाग्राहित्यं.

DUMPISH, *a.* विषण्ण, दीन, उद्विग्न.

DUMPS, *s.* विषादः, उद्वेगः, म्लानि *f.*

DUMPY, *a.* ह्रस्वस्थूल.

DUN, *a.* कपिश, श्याव-म, पिंगल, कृष्ण. –*s.* सनिर्बंधं ऋणप्रार्थना.

DUNCE, *s.* स्थूलबुद्धिः, दुर्मेधस् *m.*, अज्ञः, अनभिज्ञः, मूढः, मूढमतिः, जडः, जडधीः.

DUNG, *s.* पुरीषं, विष्ठा, शकृत *n.*, शमलं, विष् *f.*, अप(व)स्करः, गूथं, वर्चस्कः-स्कं, उच्चारः; 'd.-hill' शकृन्निचयः, अवकरनिकरः; (*a.*) हीनजाति, अधम, नीच. –*v. t.* पुरीषेण लिप् 6 P or अंज 7 P.

DUNGEON, *s.* कारा, कारागृहं-वेश्मन् *n.*, बंधनागारं, अंधकूपः.

DUPE, *v. t.* वंच् 10; प्रतॄ c.; *See* CHEAT.—*s.* सुखप्रतार्यः, सुखेन वंचनीयः.

DUPLICATE, *a.* द्विगुण ; 'a d. copy' प्रतिलिपिः, प्रतिरूपं. —*v. t.* द्विगुणीकृ 8 U, पुटीकृ, पुटयति (D.). —ION, *s.* द्विगुणीकरणं, पुटीकरणं. —URE, *s.* पुटः-टं, भंगः; व्यावर्तनं.

DUPLICITY, *s.* कपटं, छलं, माया; द्वैधीभावः; *See* FRAUD.

DURABLE, *a.* स्थायिन्, चिरस्थायिन्, दीर्घकाल, अविनाशिन्, स्थिर, ध्रुव, अक्षय, अनपाय. —DURABLY, *adv.* स्थिरं, ध्रुवं, अनपायेन. —DURABILITY, *s.* स्थिरता, अक्षयता, चिरस्थायित्वं.

DURANCE, *s.* आसेधः, निरोधः, बंधनं, कारानिरोधः.

DURATION, *s.* स्थायित्वं, अवस्थिति *f.*, स्थिति *f.* 2 ध्रुवता, स्थिरता, अविरामः, अविच्छेदः, सातत्यं. 3 परिमाणं; 'of long d.' दीर्घस्थायिन्, स्थायिन्; 'of short d.' अस्थायिन्, क्षणभंगुर, क्षणिक.

DURING, *prep.* यावत्, मध्ये, अंतरे in comp.; ex. by loc., or loc. abs.; 'd. youth' यौवनदशायां; 'd. Das'aratha's reign' दशरथे महीं शासति; 'd. life' यावज्जीवं-वेन; oft. by आ with abl.

DUSK, *s.* संध्या, प्रदोषः, संध्याकालः-समयः; 'time of d.' सायंतनः समयः, संध्याकालः, सायंकालः. —*a.*,-Y, —ISH, *a.* ईषत्तामस (सी *f.*), ईषत्तिमिरावृत, ईषत्कृष्ण, सतमस्कल्प, आकृष्ण, आनील. —ILY, *adv.* अस्पष्टं, ईषत्तमसा. —INESS, *s.* ईषदंधकारः, ईषत्तिमिरं.

DUST, *s.* धूलि-ली *f.*, रजस् *n.*, रेणु *m.*, *f.*, पांशुः-सुः क्षोदः, चूर्णं. 2 संकरः, अवकरः-स्करः, उच्छिष्टं; 'd. of flowers' परागः; 'fragrant d.' पिष्टातः, पटवासः; 'd. of gold' कांचनभूः; 'd. coloured' धूलिधूसर. —*v. t.* रेणुं अपमृज् 2 P, नीरजीकृ 8 U, निर्धूलीकृ; 'd. hole-bin' संकरनिचयस्थानं; 'd.-man' खलपूः, धूलिमार्जकः, रजोवाहकः. —ED, *a.* नीरजीकृत, हतपांशु, संमृष्ट. —ER, *s.* मार्जनपटः, नक्तकः, रेणुसंमार्जकः. —Y, *a.* पांसुल, धूलिधूसर, रेणुदूषित-रूक्ष.

DUTY, *s.* धर्मः, कर्तव्यं. 2 कर्मन् *n.*, कृत्यं, कार्यं, नियमः, व्रतं. 3 नियोगः, अधिकारः, पदं, आस्पदं; 'one who has done his d.' कृतकृत्यः, कृती; 'morning duties' प्रातःकृत्यानि; 'having heavy d.' धुर्यः, धूर्वहः, धुरीणः. 4 करः, शुल्कः-ल्कं; तार्यं, तारिकं (for boats). 5 आदरः, भक्ति *f.*, मानः. —DUTEOUS,-DUTIFUL, *a.* भक्त, आज्ञाधारक, अनुविधायिन्, आज्ञापालक, आदृत, धर्मज्ञ, भक्तिमत्, वश्य, ज्ञातधर्मन्; *See* OBEDIENT. —LY, *adv.* भक्तवत्, भक्त्या. —NESS, *s.* भक्ति *f.*, आज्ञानुवर्तनं, वश्यता, सेवा, शुश्रूषा, अनुरोधः.

DWARF, *s.* वामनः, खर्वः, ह्रस्वः, ह्रस्वकायः. —*v. t.* ह्रस् c., खर्वीकृ 8 U. —ISH, *a.* खर्व, वामन, ह्रस्व, अतुंग, खर्वाकार, वामनमूर्ति.

DWELL, *v. i.* वस् 1 P, नि-प्रति-वस्, आ-अधि-वस् (with acc.), वृत् 1 A, स्था 1P. 2 अध्यास् 2 A, आश्रि 1 U, निषेव् 1 A; 'd. upon' विस्तरेण वर्ण् 10; प्रपंचयति (D.), सविस्तरं निरूप् 10; 'd. abroad' प्रवस्; 'd. together' एकत्र- सं-वस्. —ER, *s.* निवासिन् *m.*, वासिन्, वासकृत् *m.*, स्थ-वर्तिन् in comp. —ING, *s.* नि-आ-वासः, वसति *f.*, निलयः, आलयः, वसतिस्थानं, गृहं, आयतनं, आगारं, भवनं, आवसथः, ओकस् *n.*; *See* HOUSE; 'd. house or place' वासगृहं-स्थानं.

DWINDLE, *v. i.* *See* DECREASE; 'the number of members d. ed down to four' सभासदां संख्या तथा क्षीणाभूद् यथा चत्वार एव अवशिष्टाः.

DYE, *s.* रंगः, वर्णः, रागः; 'red d.' लाक्षा. —*v. t.* रंज् 10, वर्ण् 10, कुंकुमादिना अंज् 7 P. —ED, *a.* रक्त, रंजित, सराग, कषायित, वर्णित; 'd. red' अरुणित. —ER, *s.* रंजकः, वस्त्ररागकृत् *m.*

DYKE, *See* DIKE.

DYNASTY, *s.* वंशः, कुलं, अन्वयः, आवलि-ली *f.*, श्रेणी; 'of solar d.' सूर्यवंश्यः.

DYSENTERY, *s.* प्रवाहिका, अतिसारः, प्रस्कंदिका, आमातिसारः, संग्रहणी.

DYSPEPSIA, *s.* अजीर्ण-र्णि *f.*, मंदाग्निः, अन्नविकारः, अपाकः.

DYSPNŒA, *s.* श्वासावरोधः, श्वासस्तंभः.

E.

EACH, *a.* सर्व, सकल; gen. ex. by प्रति-अनु in comp., or by repetition of word; दिने दिने, प्रतिदिनं, &c.; 'all went away, e. to his own house' एकैकः स्वं स्वं गृहं निर्जगाम; 'e. one' एकैक *a.*, एकैकशः, पृथक् पृथक्; 'e. other' अन्योन्यं, इतरेतरं, परस्परं.

EAGER, *a.* (Of persons) उत्सुक, लालस, लोलुप, अत्याकांक्षिन्, व्यग्र, सोत्कंठ, आसक्त, रत, सोत्साह. 2 गाढ, प्रबल, उत्कट, प्रचंड, सातिशय; तीव्र, तीक्ष्ण; oft. by उत्तप् 4 P, (उत्ताप्यति मे हृदयं तद्दर्शनाय Ka. 349). —LY, *adv.* सस्पृह, सतृष्णं; सोत्कंठं, कुतूहलात्, अतिवांछया, उत्कटं. —NESS, *s.* लालसा; औत्सुक्यं, उत्साहः, अतिस्पृहा-वांछा, उत्कटता, व्यग्रता, कुतूहलं, कौतुकं.

EAGLE, *s.* गरुत्मत् *m.*, उत्क्रोशः; *See* GARUDA; 'e. eyed' सूक्ष्मदृष्टि.

EAR, *s.* कर्णः, श्रोत्रं, श्रुति *f.*, श्रवणं; श्रवः, शब्द-

ग्रहः; 'outer e.' श्रुतिमंडलं-वेष्टनं; 'lobe of e.' कर्णपालि *f*.; 'root of e.' कर्णमूलं, कर्णजाहं; 'tip of e.' श्रवणपालि-ली *f*.; 'having the e. s pricked' स्तब्धकर्ण; 'give e.' attend to, q. v.; 'he has his lord's e.' स भर्तुर्विश्रंभस्थानं-विश्वासभूमिः; 'e.-ache' कर्णशूलः-लं; 'e.-drop' कर्णपूरः; 'e.-lap' कर्णपालिः, कर्णशष्कुली; 'e. pick' कर्णकंडूयनकः; 'e.-ring' कर्णावतंसः, कुंडलं; कर्णभूषणं, कर्णिका, उत्तंसः; 'e.-shot' कर्ण-श्रवण-गोचरः-विषयः; 'be within e.-shot' श्रवणगोचरे तिष्ठ; 'e.-wax' कर्णमलं, पिंजूषः; 'e.-witness' श्रुतसाक्षी; 'e.-wig' कर्णकीटः-लुका. 2 शीर्षकं; कणिशं, मंजरी.

EARLY, *a.* आद्य, प्रथम, पूर्व. 2 अचिर, सद्यस्क, प्रत्यग्र, अभिनव, नूतन. 3 अकाल, अपूर्णकाल, आकालिक (की *f*.), अनवसर- परिणत or पक्व. 4 प्रातःकालीन, पूर्वाह्णतन-प्रगेतन (नी *f*.), वि-प्र-भातीय, उषस्य, औषस (सी *f*.), प्रभात-प्रातः in comp. —*adv.* प्रातर्, प्रत्युषसि, प्रत्यूषे; विभाते, प्रातःकाले, प्रभाते, व्युष्टे, प्रगे; 'e. in the morning' महति प्रत्यूषे; 'getting up e.' लघुलघूत्थित. 2 सद्यः, शीघ्रं, सत्वरं, आशु, सपदि. 3 पूर्वं, अग्रे, प्राक्. —NESS, *s.* पूर्वत्वं, अग्रत्वं. 2 प्रत्यग्रता, अचिरत्वं. 3 अकालता, अकालपरिणति *f*. 4 सुप्रभातं. 5 क्षिप्रता, अविलंबः, शीघ्रता.

EARN, *v. t.* अर्ज् 10, उपार्ज्, उपादा 3 A, आप् 5 P; लभ् 1 A, निर्विश् 6 P; *See* GET. 2 अर्ह् 1 P; 'e. livelihood' वृत्तिं कॢप् c. or सं-पद् c. —INGS, *s.* उपार्जितं, वेतनं, लभ्यांशः.

EARNEST, *a.* उद्युक्त, कृतोद्यम; *See* EAGER; 'e. desire' गाढाभिलाषः, अतिस्पृहा, कुतूहलं. 2 निविष्ट, एकाग्र, समाहित, आसक्त, एकतान, एकायन, एकसर्ग, एकाग्र्य, अनन्यासक्त, एकाग्रचित्त, अभिनिविष्ट, अनन्यविषय, उद्योगिन्; आसक्तचित्त, अनन्यवृत्ति, निविष्टमनस् (of persons). 3 अपरिहासशील. —*s.* अपरिहासः, अलाघवं; 'I am in e.' न परिहसामि, नायं परिहासस्य समयः; 'take in e.' परमार्थेन ग्रह् 9 P, (परिहासविजल्पितं वचः परमार्थेन न गृह्यतां S. 2). 2 सत्यकारः; सत्याकृति *f*., सत्यापनं-ना. 3 पूर्वभुक्ति *f*. 4 उपन्यासः, निक्षेपः, आधिः. —LY, 'in e.' *adv.* समाहित-निविष्ट-चेतसा, यत्नतः, सोद्योगं, एकाग्रमनसा, अभिनिवेशेन, उत्सुकं, सोत्साहं; 'e. desirous' अत्यभिलाषिन्, गाढाभिलाष. 2 अपरिहासेन, परमार्थतः, अलाघवं. —NESS, *s.* एकाग्रता, उत्कटता, औत्सुक्यं, अभिनिवेशः, चित्तासक्ति *f*., उत्साहः, अभियोगः, उद्योगः.

EARTH, *s.* मही, पृथिवी, पृथ्वी, वसुधा, उर्वी, वसुंधरा, धरा, धरित्री, मेदिनी, वसुमती, धरणी, अवनिः-नी, भूः, भूमिः, क्षो(क्षौ)णिः-णी, क्षितिः, अचला, अनंता, रसा, विश्वंभरा, स्थिरा, काश्यपी, सर्वंसहा, कुः, इला, ज्या, गोत्रा, क्ष्मा, क्षमा, भूतधात्री, रत्नगर्भा, जगती. 2 मृद् *f*., मृत्तिका. —*v. i.* भूमौ बिलं कृत्वा निवस् 1 P. *v. t.* भूमौ निविश् c. or निधा 3 U or निक्षिप् 6 P; 'e.-born' भूमिज, महीज; 'e.-ling' भूजंतुः, मर्त्यः, पामरः; 'e.-quake' कंपः-चलनं in comp. with (*s*.); क्ष्माचलितं, भूकंपः, &c.; 'e. worm' भूजंतुः; नीचजनः, अधमः. —EN, *a.* मृण्मय (यी *f*.), मार्त्तिक (की *f*.); 'e. ware' मृद्भांडं, कौलालकं, मार्त्तिकं. —LY, *a.* पार्थिव (वी *f*.), सांसारिक (की *f*.), ऐहिक (की *f*.), मर्त्य; नश्वर; विनाशधर्मन्; 'e.-minded' संसारासक्तचित्त; विषयोपभोगरत. —Y, *a.* पार्थिव, भौम (मी *f*.), मार्त्तिक.

EASE, *s.* सुखं, सौख्यं, विश्रामः, निर्वृति *f*., निरुद्वेगता, स्वास्थ्यं, स्वस्थता; 'I am at e.' लब्धं स्वास्थ्यं मया; अहं निर्वृतः, वीतचिंतः; 'this my soul is completely at e.' जातो ममायं विशदः प्रकामं अंतरात्मा (S. 4); 'at one's e.' यथाकामं, पर्याप्तं, यथेच्छं, प्रकामं, सुखेन, सुख in comp., अकुतोभयं, निर्वृत्या; 'sleeping at e.' सुखसुप्त. 2 सौकर्यं, अनायासः, सुकरत्वं, सुखं, लीला. —*v. t.* लघयति (D.), लघूकृ 8 U, प्र-उपशम् c. (शमयति), सां(शां)त्व् 10; हृ 1 P, अपनी 1 P; 'e. from griefs, burden &c.' दुःखात् &c. मुच् c., दुःखं-भारं-अपनी, उद्धृ, &c. —EASY, *a.* सुकर, अयत्नसाध्य, अनायास, सुखसाध्य. 2 सुबोध, सुगम, अविषम; अगहनं; gen. ex. by सुख or सु in comp.; अज्ञः सुखमाराध्यः; बालानां सुखबोधाय, &c.; 'e. of utterance, सुखोच्चार्य; 'e. style' सुगमा भाषासरणिः; 'e. to get' सुलभ, सुखलभ्य, &c.; 'e. in going' सुखचार; 'e. case' निःशल्योर्थः. 3 निर्वृत, सुस्थ, निश्चिंत, स्वस्थ, सुखिन्, निरुद्वेग, शांत, वीतचिंत, निर्वृतिमत्, विशद; 'e. circumstances' सुस्थिति, द्रव्यानुकूल्यं; 'heart, be not un-e.' हृदय मा उत्ताम्य (S. 1). 4 अनुकूल, अनुरोधिन्, अनुविधायिन्. —LY, *adv.* अनायासेन, सुखं, सुखेन, अयत्नेन, लीलया, अश्रमेण, सुकरं, अक्लेशं, सौकर्येण; सु or सुख in comp. 2 निरुद्वेगं, निश्चिंतं, स्वास्थ्येन. 3 सावकाशं, यथावसरं. —NESS, *s.* सौकर्यं, अनायासः, सुखसाध्यता. 2 सुगमत्वं, अवैषम्यं. 3 शांति *f*., स्वास्थ्यं, अक्लेशः, सुखं. 4 अनुरोधः, आनुकूल्यं, अनुवर्तनशीलता.

EASEL, *s.* चित्राधारः, चित्रफलकं.

EASEMENT, *s.* मलविसर्गः. 2 परभूम्यावधिकारः.

EAST, *s.* पूर्वदिश् *f*., पूर्वा, प्राची, पूर्वाशा, ऐंद्री. 2 पूर्वदेशः, पौरस्त्यजनपदः. —*a.*,-ERLY,-ERN, *a.* पूर्व, प्राच् (ची *f*.), पौरस्त्य, प्राच्य, प्राचीन, पूर्वदेशीय, पूर्वदिक्स्थ; प्राङ्मुख; 'the mountain is e. of the sea' समुद्राद् गिरिः पूर्वः; 'the e. mountain' उदयः, उदयगिरिः-शैलः-अचलः, पूर्वाचलः. —ERLY, —WARD, *adv.* पूर्वेण, पूर्वस्यां दिशि, पुरः, पूर्वं, प्राक्, पुरस्तात्, पूर्वदेशे.

EAT, *v. t.* अद् 2 P, जक्ष् 2 P, ग्रस् 1 A, खाद् 1 P,

अश् 9 P, भक्ष् 10, भुज् 7 A, घस् 1 P, प्सा 2 P, आस्वाद् 1 A, गॄ 6 P, चर्व् 1 P, अभ्यवहृ 1 P, प्रत्यवसो 4 P; 'e. one's own words' स्ववचनमसत्यं-अवितथ्यं-कृ 8 U, स्ववचनेन विसंवद् 1 P; 'e., drink and be merry' अश्नीतपिबता, खादतमोदता. -ABLE, s. भक्ष्यं, भोज्यं, अभ्यवहार्यं, खाद्यं, भोज्यवस्तु-द्रव्यं. -ER, s. खादकः, भक्षकः, भोक्तृ m., आशिन् m., अशन-भुज् in comp.; अद-भद् in comp.; 'flesh-e. s' मांसाशिनः, पिशिताशनाः; 'dead-body-e.' कुणपभुज्; क्रव्याद्, मांसादः, &c. -ING, s. भक्षणं, खादनं, अशनं, आस्वादनं, भोजनं, &c.; 'e. together' सहभोजनं, जग्धि f.; 'e.-house' सिद्धान्नविक्रयशाला.

EAVES, s. पटलप्रांतः, वलीकः-कं, नीध्रं, वल(इ)भि-भी f.; 'e.-dropper' निभृतश्रवणेच्छुः, प्रच्छन्नश्राविन् m.

EBB, s. क्षीयमाणा वेला, वेलापरिवर्तनं-परावर्तः, परा वेला. 2 (fig.) क्षयः, हानि f., अपचयः, व्यसनं, नाशः, परिवर्तः; 'e. and flow' व्यसनोदयौ. -v. i. क्षि pass., ह्रासं-लयं-गम् 1 P; (वेलावत्) परावृत् 1 A; *See* DECAY.

EBONY, s. कोविदारः, चमरिकः, कुद्दालः, युगपत्रकः.

EBRIETY, s. मदः, मत्तता, उन्मादः.

EBRIOSITY, s. उन्मादशीलता, क्षीवता.

EBULLITION, s. उत्सेचनं, उत्सेकः; उद्रेकः, फेनायितं, फेनोद्गमः. 2 अंतःक्षोभः, अंतर्वेगः, चित्तवैक्लव्यं-व्याकुलता, अंतस्तापः.

ECCENTRIC, a. सामान्येतर, विषम, विलक्षण, लोकबाह्य, लोकाचारविरुद्ध, विपथगामिन्, व्यभिचारिन्, उत्क्रांतमर्याद, उत्सूत्र. 2 केंद्रभ्रष्ट-च्युत. -ITY, s. वैषम्यं, उत्सूत्रता, वैलक्षण्यं, सामान्यविरोधः, लोकाचार-व्यवहार-विरोधः.

ECCLESIASTIC, s. पुरोहितः, आचार्यः, धर्माध्यापकः. -a.,-AL, a. धर्मोपदेशविषय, पौरोहित्यसंबंधिन्.

ECHO, s. प्रतिशब्दः-ध्वनिः-स्वनः-रवः-नादः-वचनं-गर्जनं, अनुरसितं-नादः, प्रतिश्रुत्-ति f.-v. i. प्रतिस्वन्-ध्वन्-रस्-नद्-स्तन् 1 P, प्रति-ह्व 2 P, अनुनद्-रस, कृ 8 U with (s.). -v. t. Causal of roots above; 'e.-ing the caves' कंदरभुवः प्रतिध्वानयन्-प्रतिध्वानिताः कुर्वन्.

ECLAT, s. प्रतिष्ठा, शोभा, गौरवं; आडंबरः. 2 स्तुति f., कीर्ति f., ख्याति f., प्रशंसा.

ECLECTIC, a. उद्धारक.

ECLIPSE, s. ग्रहः, ग्रहणं, ग्रासः, उपरागः, उपसर्गः, उपप्लवः, ग्रहपीडनं. -v. t. ग्रस् 1A, प्र-आ-च्छद् 10, तिमिरयति (D.), ग्रह् 9 P, उपसृज् 6 P, उपरञ्ज् 1 A, उपरंज् c. 2 (fig.) प्र-आ-,छद्, (गुणवत्तरपात्रेण छाद्यंते गुणिनां गुणाः P. I. 10); प्रत्यादिश् 6 P; 'Urvas'i e. s Lakshmi, proud of her beauty' उर्वशी प्रत्यादेशो रूपगर्विताया: श्रियः (V. 1). -ED, a. उपरक्त, उपसृष्ट, ग्रस्त, उपप्लुत, सोपप्लव, ग्रहपीडित. 2 तमोवृत, प्रच्छन्न, मलिनप्रभ. 3 प्रत्यादिष्ट, प्रत्याख्यात.

ECLIPTIC, s. क्रांतिवृत्तं-मंडलं, रविमार्गः.

ECONOMY, s. निर्वाहः-हणं, प्रणयनं, नयः, नीति f.; 'e. of the house' गृहकार्यनिर्वाहः, गार्हस्थ्यं. 2 परिमित-मित-व्ययः, स्वल्प-विवेक-व्ययः, अमुक्तहस्तत्वं. 3 विन्यासः, विरचनं, प्रकल्पनं, संविधानं. 4 (Political) अर्थशास्त्रं, राजनीतिः-शास्त्रं. -IC,-ICAL, a. मित-स्वल्प-व्यय, अमुक्तहस्त. 2 कार्यनिर्वाहसंबंधिन्. -ICALLY, adv. मित-स्वल्प-व्ययेन, अमुक्तहस्तं. -IST, s. मितव्ययिन् m., अमुक्तहस्तः. 2 अर्थशास्त्रज्ञः, राजशास्त्रविद् m., नीतिज्ञः. -IZE, v. t. मितं व्यय् 10 (व्यययति), स्वल्पशः विनि-प्र-युज् 7 A, 10. -v. i. मितव्ययेन गृहकार्याणि निर्वह् c. or प्रणी 1 P.

ECSTASY, s. हर्षोन्मादः, आनंदभरः, प्रहर्षः, प्रमदः, अत्यानंदः, संमोहः, उन्मादः. -ED, a. हर्षोन्मत्त,-पुलकित, हर्षमूढ-जड. -ECSTATIC,-AL, a. उन्मादिन्, संमोहिन्, परमानंदप्रद, मोहक.

ECUMENICAL, a. सर्वसाधारण (णी f.).

EDACIOUS, *See* GREEDY.

EDDY, s. आवर्तः, भ्रमः-मि f., भ्रमरकः.

EDENTATED, a. निर्दशन, नीरद.

EDGE, s. धारा, अग्रं, कोटि-अश्रि f., पालि-ली f., अणिः-णी. 2 उपांतः, सीमा, प्रांतः, परिसरः, पर्यंतः, उत्संगः; समंतः. 3 अंचलः, दशाः pl. (of garments), 4 तेजस् n., तीक्ष्णता, निशितता; 'e. of a brook' कच्छः, कूलं, तीरं, तटं; 'two or double e.-ed' द्विधार, उभयतस्तीक्ष्ण; कार्यद्वयसाधक; 'setting the teeth on e.' दंतहर्षः. -v. t. प्रांतयति (D.), पर्यंतेन सनाथीकृ 8 U. 2 शो 4 P, तिज् c., तीक्ष्णीकृ. -ED, a. कोटिमत्, धारासनाथ, तीक्ष्ण, सधार; 'sharp e.' तीक्ष्णाग्र, निशितधार. -LESS, a. अतीक्ष्ण, धाराहीन.

EDIBLE, a. खाद्य, भक्ष्य, भोज्य.

EDICT, s. शासनं, राजाज्ञा, राजशासनं; 'written e.' आज्ञा-शासन-पत्रं.

EDIFICE, s. भवनं, सदनं, हर्म्यं, मंदिरं, गृहं, प्रासादः, सौधं.

EDIFY, v. t. उत्कृष् 1 P, उन्नी 1 P, उन्नतिं-उत्कर्षं प्राप् c. 2 ज्ञानं वृध् c., शिक्ष् c., उपदिश् 6 P, मोहं-भ्रांतिं-नश् c. or निरस् 4 U. -ED, a. प्राप्तज्ञान, निरस्तमोह, उपदिष्ट. -ICATION, s. ज्ञानप्राप्ति-वृद्धि f., उपदेशः, शिक्षणं. -ING, a. उपदेशक, ज्ञानवर्धक.

EDIT, v. t. शोधयित्वा प्रकाश् c., शुध् c. 2 लिख् 6 P. -ION, s. प्रकाशनं, शोधनं, प्रकटीकरणं. 2 आवृत्ति f. -OR, s. प्रकाशकः. 2 लेखकः.

EDUCATE, v. t. विनी 1 P, शास् 2 P, अनुशास्, प्रबुध् c., शिक्ष् c., अधि-इ c. (अध्यापयति), संस्कृ 8 U;

उपदिश् 6 P. 2 विद्यादानेन पा c. (पालयति) or संवृध् c. or पुष् c. -ED, *a.* कृत-गृहीत-उपात्त-लब्ध-विद्य, शिक्षित प्रबुद्ध; संस्कृतबुद्धि, विनीत, व्युत्पन्न, कृताभ्यास, लब्ध ज्ञान. -ION, *s.* विनयः, शिक्षा-क्षणं, अध्यापनं, अनुशासनं, संस्कारः, विद्यादानं-ग्रहणं-प्राप्ति *f.*, व्युत्पत्ति *f.*, उपदेशः. 2 पोषणं, संवर्धनं. -OR, *s.* विनेतृ *m.*, शिक्षकः, प्रबोधकः.

EEL *s.* जलव्यालः. अंधाहिः.

EFFABLE, *a.* कथनीय, निर्वचनीय; वाच्य; 'in-e.' अनिर्वचनीय; 'in-e. joy' कोपि आनंदः, किमपि सुखं.

EFFACE, *v. t.* अप-प्र-व्या-उद्-निर्-मृज् 2 P or c., विनश् c., उच्छिद् 7 P, विलुप् 6 P or c., उद्-हृ 1 P, उन्मूल् 10. -*v. i.* उच्छ्वस् 2 P. -MENT, *s.* अपामार्जनं, लोपः, व्यामर्षः; 'e. of colours' वर्णिकोच्छ्वासः (S. 6).

EFFECT, *s.* कार्यं, नैमित्तिकं; उत्पन्नं, निष्पन्नं, सिद्धि *f.* 2 फलं, परिणामः, फलोदयः, उत्तरफलं, अंतः. 3 अर्थः, प्रयोजनं, गुणः, फलं, प्रभावः. 4 अभिप्रायः, आशयः. 5 निष्पत्ति-सिद्धि-*f.*; 'of no e.' निष्फल, निष्प्रयोजन, निर्गुण; 'to take e.' फल् 1 P, मूर्च्छ् 1 P, (छाया न मूर्च्छति मलोपहतप्रसादे दर्पणतले S. 7); 'to take no e.' ex. by कुंठ, (वज्रं तपोवीर्यमहत्सु कुंठं K. III. 12); 'to this e.' इति, एतदभिप्राय *a.*; 'to what e.' किमर्थं, केन हेतुना; 'to destroy the e. of' निष्फली-मोघी-कृ 8 U; 'in e.' अर्थतः, वस्तुतः, तत्वतः. 6 (E. s.) विभवः, द्रव्याणि, धनसामग्री, रिक्थं. -*v. t.* कृ 8 U, विधा 3 U, सं-निः-पद् c., साध् 5 P or c., निर्वृत् c., निर्वह् c. 2 जन् c., उत्पद् c. -IVE, *a.* कार्यसाधक, फलवत्, निष्पादक, संपादक, फलोत्पादक; 'e. speech' हृदयग्राहि वचः. -UAL, -EFFICACIOUS, *a.* फलोत्पादक, गुणावह, अमोघ, अभ्यर्थ, गुणवत्, सिद्धिकर (री *f.*), कार्यसाधक, सफल. 2 प्रबल, समर्थ, सप्रभाव, क्षम, अलंतम. -UALLY, *adv.* अमोघं, सफलं, निष्पत्तिपूर्वं, अभ्यर्थं. 2 प्रभावेण, सामर्थ्येन. -UATE, *v. t.* कृ, संपद् c., &c.

EFFEMINATE, *a.* क्लीब, दुर्बल, सुकुमार. 2 स्त्रैण (णी *f.*), स्त्रीधर्मन्, स्त्रीवदाचारिन्, स्त्रीप्रकृति, स्त्रीगुणविशिष्ट; स्त्रीभाव; 'an e. man' क्लीबः, कापुरुषः, गेहेशूरः. -*v. t.* क्लीबीकृ 8 U, दुर्बली-निष्पुरुषी-कृ. -LY, *adv.* क्लीबवत्, नारी-स्त्री-वत्, स्त्रीधर्मानुसारेण. -EFFEMINACY, *s.* क्लीबता, दौर्बल्यं, स्त्रीत्वं, स्त्रैणं, स्त्रीधर्माचरणं, सौकुमार्यं, मृदुता.

EFFERVESCE, *v. i.* बुद्बुदायते (D.), फेनायते (D.), उत्सिच् pass., उच्छूनीभू, फेनिलीभू. -ENCE, *s.* फेनोद्गमः, उत्सेचनं, बुद्बुदायितं, फेनिलता, उच्छूनीभावः, मंडोद्गमः. 2 उत्तापः, संक्षोभः; आलोडनं. -ING, *a.* फेनिल, फेनायमान.

EFFICACY, *s.* प्रभावः, बलं, सामर्थ्यं, गुणः, शक्ति *f.*, तेजस् *n.*, क्षमता, अमोघता, सफलता, फलोत्पादकत्वं. -OUS, *a.* प्रबल, समर्थ; *See* EFFECTUAL.

EFFICIENT, *a.* कार्यसाधक, कार्यसिद्धिक्षम, कार्योपयुक्त, विचक्षण, कर्मक्षम, अलंकर्मीण, निपुण; *See* EFFECTUAL also. -LY, *adv.* अमोघं, सिद्धिपूर्वं, निपुणं, विचक्षणतया. -EFFICIENCY, *s.* कार्यक्षमता, कार्यसिद्धिक्षमता, नैपुण्यं, वैचक्षण्यं.

EFFETE, *a.* जीर्ण, दुर्बल, निःशक्ति, क्षीण, निःसत्व, क्षीणशक्ति. 2 वंध्य, निष्फल, मोघ.

EFFIGY, *s.* प्रतिमा, मूर्ति-प्रतिकृति *f.*, प्रतिरूपं.

EFFLORESCENCE, *s.* पुष्पोत्पादनं, प्रस्फोटनं. 2 दद्रुः.

EFFLUENCE, *s.* प्रवाहः, निर्गमः, प्रस्रवः, निःस्रवणं.

EFFLUVIUM, EFFLUVIA, *s.* उद्गारः, वासः. 2 दुर्गंधः, पूतिगंधः.

EFFLUX, EFFLUXION, *s.* प्रवाहः, निस्रावः, ओघः, निःसारः-सरणं, निर्गमः.

EFFORT, *s.* प्र,-यत्नः, उद्यमः, व्यवसायः, आयासः, चेष्टा, चेष्टितं; 'to make e. s' उद्यम् 1 P; *See* ATTEMPT.

EFFRONTERY, *s.* धाष्टर्यं, वैयात्यं, निर्लज्जत्वं, प्रागल्भ्यं, प्रतिभानं.

EFFULGENT, *a.* दीप्तिमत्, तैजस (सी *f.*), उज्ज्वल, सुप्रभ, तेजस्विन्. -EFFULGENCE, *s.* तेजस् *n.*, दीप्ति-कांति *f.*, प्रभा; रुच् *f.*, शोभा; *See* BRIGHTNESS.

EFFUSE, *v. t.* प्र-निः-सृ c., प्रमुच् 6 P, उत्-वि-सृज् 6 P, पत् c., नि-अव-सिच् 6 P. -ION, *s.* उत्सर्गः, निषेकः, स्रावः, मोक्षणं, अवपातनं.

EGG, *s.* अंडं, पेशि-शी *f.*, कोषः-शः; 'lay e. s' अंडमोक्षणं कृ 8 U, अंडानि सू 2 A; 'e. on' प्रोत्सह् c.; *See* PROMPT.

EGLANTINE, *s.* अरण्यजपा-वा.

EGOTISM, *s.* अहंकारः, आत्मश्लाघा-स्तुति *f.*, आत्माभिमानः, ममता. -EGOTIST, *s.* आत्मश्लाघिन्-अहंकारिन्-आत्माभिमानिन् *m.*, विकत्थनशीलः. -IC, -ICAL, *a.* अहंकारिन्, दृप्त, गर्वित; *See* ARROGANT. -ICALLY, *adv.* सदर्पं, आत्मश्लाघापूर्वं.

EGREGIOUS, *a.* अत्यंत, असाधारण (णी *f.*), विशिष्ट, प्रख्यात, प्रसिद्ध, उत्तम, प्रमुख; oft. by अति pr.; 'an e. rogue' सुप्रसिद्धः शठः; अतिमूर्खता, &c. -LY, *adv.* अत्यंतं, अतीव, भृशं, अतिमात्रं, सातिशयं.

EGRESS, *s.* निर्गमः, निष्क्रमः, निर्याणं, निःसरणं, अपसारः, निर्गति *f.*

EIGHT, *a.* अष्टन्, अष्टकं; 'in e. ways' अष्टधा; 'e. times' अष्टकृत्वः; 'e.-fold' अष्टगुण.

EIGHTEEN, *a.* अष्टादशन्.

EIGHTY, *a.* अशीति *f.*

EITHER, *pron.*, *a.* अन्यतर; 'on e. side' उभयतः. -*conj.* (-or) वा-वा; or वा singly.

EJACULATE, *v. i.* सहसा उदीर् 10 or उच्चर् c.,

प्रार्थनां उदाहृ 1 P. 2 उद् 6 P, उत्क्षिप् 6 P. –ION, *s.* उद्गारः, आक्रंदनं, सहसा उदीरणं, उच्चारणं.

EJECT, *v. t.* निरस् 4 U, निराकृ 8 U, निःसृ c.; *See* DRIVE AWAY, DISCHARGE. 2 उत्क्षिप्-उद्गॄ 6 P. –ION, *s.* निःसारणं, निराकरणं, निष्कासनं; अधिकाराद् भ्रंशनं.

EJULATION, *s.* विलपनं, परिदेवनं, आर्तनादः, आक्रंदनं.

EKE, *v. t.* वृध् c., विस्तॄ c., प्रथ् c., तन् 8 U.

ELABORATE, *v. t.* महाश्रमेण साध् c., or निष्पद् c. or निर्मा 3 A or विधा 3 U or प्रक्लृप् c. –ED, *a.* बहुश्रमसिद्ध, महाप्रयत्नकृत-विरचित-प्रकल्पित. –LY, *adv.* महायत्नेन, बहुश्रमेण, महायासेन. –ION, *s.* बहुश्रमेण निर्माणं.

ELAPSE, *v. i.* व्यति-इ 2 P, अतिक्रम् 1 U, 4 P, व्यतिक्रम्, गम् 1 P; 'days having e.-ed' दिनेषु गच्छत्सु.

ELASTIC, *a.* स्थितिस्थापक, प्रकृतिप्रापक. –ITY, *s.* स्थितिस्थापकता-त्वं.

ELATE, *v. t.* उत्सिच् 6 P, दृप् c., आध्मा 1 P; दर्पेण उद्-श्वि c. or उद्-हन् 2 P; *See* PUFF. 2 प्रहृष् c., प्रनुद् c., उल्लस् c. –*a.*,-ED, *a.* दर्पाध्मात, उद्धत, गर्वित, उत्सिक्त, मदोद्धत, दृप्त, गर्वोच्छून. 2 प्रहृष्ट, प्रमुदित, सोल्लास, हृष्टचित्त. –ION, *s.* गर्वः, दर्पः, औद्धत्यं, प्रहर्षः, चित्तोल्लासः.

ELBOW, *s.* कूर्परः, कफ(फो)णि *m. f.* 2 वंकः, पुटभेदः. –*v. t.* कूर्परेण आहत्य बहिष्कृ 8 U.

ELDER, *a.* ज्यायस्, वरीयस्, अग्रज, पूर्वज, वर्षीयस्, वयोज्येष्ठ; 'e. brother' अग्रजः, अग्रजन्मा, ज्यायान् भ्राता. –*s.* गुरुः, वृद्धः; 'e. s, elderly persons' गुरुजनः, गुरवः, आर्यजनः, वृद्धाः.

ELDEST, *s.* ज्येष्ठ, वर्षिष्ठ, वरिष्ठ, श्रेष्ठ, सर्वज्येष्ठ.

ELECT, *v. t.* वृ 5 U or 10 (वरयति), वृ 9 U. 2 ग्रह् 9 P, आदा 3 A, स्वीकृ 8 U. 3 नियुज् 7 A, 10, निरूप् 10, निर्वच् c., 'self-election' स्वयंवरः 'self-e. ed bride' स्वयंवरवधूः; 'e. ed him as her husband' पतित्वे तं वरयामास.–*a.*,-ED, *a.* नियुक्त, निरूपित, वृत, निर्वाचित; व्यावृत्त; 'a person e.' नियोज्यः, नियोगिन् *m.*, निर्वाचितः. –ION, *s.* नियोजनं, वरणं, निर्वाचनं, वृति *f.* –IVE, *a.* जननियुक्त; 'e. right' वरणाधिकारः; 'e. municipality' जननियुक्तसभ्या ग्रामपालिका. –OR, *s.* नियोजकः, निर्वाचकः, वरणाधिकारविशिष्टः; 'body of e. s, electoral body' नियोजकगणः.

ELECTER, ELECTRUM, *s.* कांस्यं, मिश्रधातुः.

ELECTRIC, *a.* वैद्युत (ती *f.*), विद्युन्मय (यी *f.*), विद्युद्विषय. –ITY, *s.* तडित्-विद्युत्-वैद्युतशक्ति *f.*

ELECTUARY, लेह्यं, अवलेहः.

ELEEMOSYNARY, *a.* दरिद्रार्थ, दरिद्रोपकारिन्.

ELEGANT, *a.* चारु, ललित, सुंदर, सुरूप, लावण्यवत्, श्रील, अग्राम्य, सुभग. 2 (As composition) सुरस, ललित, चारु. –LY, *adv.* सविलासं, चारु, ललितं. –ELEGANCE,–CY, *s.* चारुता, सौंदर्यं, विलासः, लावण्यं, शोभा, विभ्रमः, लालित्यं; 'e. of words' पदलालित्यं.

ELEGY, *s.* करुणरसं गीतं, शोकगानं-गीति *f.*

ELEGIAC, *a.* करुणामय (यी *f.*), शोकप्रधान.

ELEMENT, *s.* भूतं, बीजं, मूलं, मूलवस्तु *n.* 2 तत्त्वं. 3 अवयवः, भागः, अंशः. 4 आरंभः, उपक्रमः, मूलतत्त्वं, बीजभूतं ज्ञानं. 5 वस्तुमात्रं; 'out of his e.' अस्थाने. –ARY, *a.* भौत (ती *f.*), भौतिक (की *f*).–ARY, *a.* अव्याकृत, शुद्ध, निरवयव. 2 मूल in comp., प्रारंभक.

ELEPHANT, *s.* गजः, हस्तिन्-करिन् *m.*, मातंगः, मतंगजः, कुंजरः, नागः, वारणः, इभः, द्विरदः, द्वि-अनेक-पः, दंती, दंतावलः, स्तंबेरमः; 'she-e.' करिणी, करेणु *f.*-शुका, वशा, धेनुका; 'a young e.' कलभः, करिशावकः; 'e. driver' हस्तिपः-पकः, आधोरणः, महामात्रः, निषादिन् *m.*; 'wild e.' वनगजः, वन्यः करी; 'furious or rutting e.' मदोत्कटः, मदकलः, प्रभिन्नः, गर्जितः, मत्तः; 'e. out of rut' उद्वांतः; निर्मदः; 'head of a herd of e.s' यूथनाथः, यूथपः; 'herd of e.s' हास्तिकं, गजता, गजयूथं; 'war-e.s' गजघटा; 'e. s of the quarters' दिग्गजाः; 'frontal globe of an e.' कुंभः; 'e.'s fore-head' ललाटं, अवग्रहः; 'his eyeball' इ(ई)षि(षी)-का, अक्षिकूटकं; 'corner of his eye' निर्याणं; 'root of his ear' चूलिका; 'his withers' आसनं, स्कंधदेशः; 'his side' पार्श्वभागः, पक्षभागः; 'the temple-juice' मदः, दानं; 'water emitted from the trunk' वमथुः, करशीकरः; 'his roaring' बृंहितं, गर्जितं; 'the whip to strike him' तोत्रं, वेणुकं; 'binding-post' आलानं; 'binding chains' शृंखलं, अंदुकः, निगडः; 'caparisoning of an e.' कल्पना, सज्जना; 'coloured housings' प्रवेणी, आस्तरणं, वर्णः, परिस्तो(स्तो)मः, कुथः.

ELEPHANTIASIS, *s.* श्लीपदं, शिलीपदं.

ELEVATE, *v. t.* उन्नम् c. (उन्नमयति), उच्छ्रि c., उद्यम् 1 P, उत्कृष् 1 P; उत्था c. (उत्थापयति), उच्छ्वि 1 P, अधिरुह् c. (रोपयति), उन्नति-उत्कर्षं-नी or कृ 8 U; 'e. to a high office' उत्तमपदे नियुज् 7 A, 10, उत्कृष्टपदं प्राप् c. –ED, *a.* अधिरोपित, उन्नीत; उत्तमपदनियुक्त. 2 उच्छ्रित, उत्तुंग, उन्नत, सोच्छ्राय; *See* HIGH.–ION, *s.* उन्नति *f.*, उत्कर्षः; उच्छ्रायः, उत्थापनं, अधिरोपणं, उच्चपदप्रापणं, उदयः. 2 उत्सेधः, उत्तुंगता, उच्छ्रयः, उन्नतस्थानं; *See* HEIGHT.

ELEVEN, *a.* एकादशन्. –ELEVENTH, *a.* एकादश (शी *f.*); 'what is the use of doing things at the e. hour' प्रोद्दीप्ते भवने तु कूपखननं प्रत्युद्यमः कीदृशः (Bh. II. 88).

ELF, *s.* वेतालः, भूतः, पिशाचः, अपदेवता. -ISH, *a.* पैशाच (ची *f.*).

ELF-LOCK, *s.* जटा, सटा.

ELICIT, *v. t.* निर्गम् c. (गमयति), निष्कृष् 1 P, उद्धृ c., निःसृ c., प्रकाश् c., अपवह् 1 P or c., आविष्कृ 8 U, निर्णी 1 P, ज्ञा 9 U or c. (ज्ञापयति). -ATION, *s.* निष्कर्षणं, निर्गमनं, &c.

ELIDE, *v. t.* लुप् 6 P or c. -ELISION, *s.* लोपः.

ELIGIBLE, *a.* वरणीय, नियोज्य, ग्राह्य, आदेय.

ELIMINATE, *v. t.* नश् c., निष्कस् c., विलुप् 6 P or c., निराकृ 8 U. -ION, *s.* लोपः, नाशः, आहरणं, अपनयनं.

ELIXIR, *s.* रसायनं, तेजोवर्धनं.

ELLIPSE, *s.* अंडवृत्तं, उपवृत्तं-मंडलं. -ELLIPTIC, *a.* अंडाकार, अंडाकृति.

ELLIPSIS, *s.* न्यूनपदं, अध्याहारः, समर्थपदलोपः. 2 पद-वाक्य-आकांक्षा; 'supplying an e.' आकांक्षापूरणं. -ELLIPTICAL, *a.* न्यूनपद; अध्याहार्य, अभ्यूहनीय.

ELOCUTION, *s.* वाक्शक्ति *f.*, वक्तृत्वं, वाक्पटुता, वाग्मिता. 2 व्याहारः, वाणी.

ELONGATE, *v. t.* दीर्घीकृ 8 U, आयम् 1 P; वितन् 8 U. -ED, *a.* आयत, आयामवत्, लंबाकृति, वितत. -ION, *s.* दीर्घीकरणं, प्रतानं, वितति *f.*, आयति *f.*

ELOPE, *v. i.* अलक्षितं पलाय् 1 A or अपसृप् 1 P. -MENT, *s.* गूढ अपसर्पणं, पलायनं.

ELOQUENT, *a.* वाग्मिन्, वागीश, वाग्विदग्ध, वक्तृ, वाक्पटु, शब्दचतुर. -LY, *adv.* वाग्विभवेन, शब्दचातुर्येण, वाक्पटुतया. -ELOQUENCE, *s.* वाक्पाटवं-शक्ति *f.*, वाग्मिता, वाग्विभवः, वक्तृत्वं.

ELSE, *a.* अन्य-इतर-अपर-*pron. a.*, भिन्न, व्यतिरिक्त; 'what e.' किमन्यत्, अथ किं; 'who e.' कोऽपरः. -*conj.* न(नो)चेत्, अन्यथा, इतरथा; एतद्विना, एतद्व्यतिरेकेण; 'e. where' अन्य-इतर-पर-त्र, स्थानांतरे, भिन्न-अन्य स्थाने.

ELUCIDATE, *v. t.* व्याख्या 2 P, व्याकृ 8 U, वि-वृ 5 U, स्पष्टी-विशदी-कृ; *See* EXPLAIN. -ION, *s.* व्याख्यानं, स्पष्टीकरणं, विवरणं. -OR, *s.* व्याख्यातृ *m.*, प्रकाशकः, विवरणकृत् *m.*

ELUDE, *v. t.* कौशलेन परिहृ 1 P; वृज् 10, छलेन अपसृप्-निर्गम् 1 P or पलाय् 1 A (with abl.); 'e.ing the senses' इंद्रियागोचर; 'it e.s grasp' ग्रहीतुं न शक्यते. -ELUSION, *s.* छलेन परिहरणं; अलक्षितं अपसरणं or निर्गमः. -ELUSIVE, *a.* निर्गमपर, परिहारिन्. -ELUSORY, *a.* छलिन्, मायिन्.

ELYSIUM, *s.* वैकुंठं, स्वर्गः, नंदनं, आनंदस्थानं. -ELYSIAN, *a.* परमानंदप्रद, स्वर्गीय.

EMACIATE, *v. t.* कृशीकृ 8 U, क्षै c. (क्षपयति), क्लिश् 9 P, ग्लै c. (ग्ल-ग्ला-पयति), शुष् c., क्षीण *a.* कृ. -*v. i.* क्षि-ग्लै 1 P, शुष् 4 P, विशॄ-क्षि-pass., कृशीभू. -ED, *a.* क्षीण, क्षीणशरीर-शक्ति, कृश, क्षाम, ग्लान, क्षीण-शुष्क-मांस; अपचित; 'e. by hunger' क्षुत्क्षामकंठ. -ION, *s.* कृशता, क्षामता, क्षीणता, कार्श्यं, शरीरशोषणं, मांसक्षयः, अपचयः.

EMANATE, *v. i.* उत्पद् 4 A, निर्गम् 1 P, निःसृ 1 P, उत्-प्र-भू 1 P, जन् 4 A, निःस्रु 1 P, प्रवृत् 1 A. -ION, *s.* उत्पत्ति *f.*, उद्भवः, प्रभवः, उद्गमः, निर्गमः, प्रवृत्ति *f.* -IVE, -EMANANT, *a.* उद्भूत, उत्पन्न, जात, ज, जन्य, प्रभव in comp.

EMANCIPATE, *v. t.* मुच् 6 P or c., वि-निर्°; मोक्ष् 10, उद्धृ 1 P, निस्तॄ c., विसृज् 6 P. -ION, *s.* विमोचनं, मोक्षः, मुक्ति *f.*, उद्धारः, निस्तारः. 2 मुक्ति *f.*, मोक्षः; *See* BEATITUDE. -OR, *s.* मोचकः, मोक्षकः.

EMASCULATE, *v. t.* वृषणौ छिद् 7 P or कृत् 6 P, पुंस्त्वं हृ 1 P, षंढी-क्लीबी-कृ 8 U. -ED, *a.* हतवीर्यः, हतपुंस्त्वः, छिन्नवृषणः, मुष्कशून्यः, षंडः-ढः, क्लीबः, नपुंसकः. -ION, *s.* वृषणच्छेदः, पुंस्त्वहरणं.

EMBALE, *v. t.* भांडं कृ 8 U, एकत्र कृ.

EMBALM, *v. t.* रक्ष् 1 P; तैले निक्षिप् 6 P, क्षयाद्रक्ष. 2 सुरभीकृ 8 U, आमोदेन पूर् 10, वास् 10.

EMBANK, *v. t.* सेतुना-वप्रेण-बंध् 9 P. -MENT, *s.* सेतु-वप्र-बंधः, मृत्तिकाचयः, वप्रः.

EMBAR, *v. t.* निरुध् 7 U, निषिध् 1 P.

EMBARGO, *s.* निषेधः. वाणिज्यकर्मनिषेधः, अवरोधः.

EMBARK, *v. t.* नौकायां नि-प्र-विश् c. or निधा 3 U. -*v. i.* नावं or पोतं आ-अधि-रुह् 1 P or प्रविश् 6 P. 2 व्या-पृ 6 A, अभियुज् pass. (with loc.); प्रारभ् 1 A (with acc.). -ATION, *s.* नौकारोहणं-रोपणं-प्रवेशनं. 2 व्यापारः, अभियोगः, प्रारंभः, उपक्रमः.

EMBARRASS, *v. t.* आकुलयति (D.), वि-व्या-मुह् c., व्यग्रीकृ 8 U, संभ्रम् c. (भ्रमयति), आकुलीकृ ; 'I am really c. ed' सत्यमाकुलीभूतोस्मि (S. 2). 2 बाध् 1 A, क्लिश् 9 P, उपरुध् 7 U, अभिभू. -ED, *a.* आ-व्या-कुल, व्यग्र, मोहित, संभ्रांत, मूढ. 2 बाधित, उपरुद्ध; क्लिष्ट, अभिभूत ; 'in e. circumstances' आपन्न, दुःस्थ, कृच्छ्रगत, दुर्गत; 'e. smile' विलक्षस्मित. -MENT, *s.* व्याकुलता, व्यग्रता, संभ्रमः, व्यामोहः, आकुलत्वं, क्लेशः, बाधः-धा, दुःखं, उपरोधः.

EMBASSY, *s.* दौत्यं, दूतधर्मः-क्रिया ; 'sent on an e.' दूतः, दौत्येन प्रस्थापितः.

EMBATTLE, *v. t.* व्यूह् 1 U or c., व्यूहेन रच् 10 or सज्जीकृ 8 U or व्यव-स्था c. (स्थापयति), व्यूहरचनां कृ. -ED, *a.* सन्नद्ध, सज्जीकृत, व्यूहेन रचित.

EMBEDDED, *a.* निहित, निविष्ट, न्यस्त.

EMBELLISH, *v. t.* भूष् 10, अलंकृ 8 U, मंड् 10, शुभ् c., भ्राज् c., परिष्कृ, प्रसाध् c. -MENT, *s.* प्रसा-

भनं, भूषणं; *See* ORNAMENT. 2 नेपथ्यं, आहार्यं, वेशः, आकल्पः.

EMBERS, *s.* भसितं, भस्मन् *n.*; अंगारशेषं; अंगाराच्छिष्टं.

EMBEZZLE, *v. t.* छलेन आत्मसात्कृ 8 U, स्वकीयं कृत्वा उप-विनि-युज् 7 A, 10; ग्रस् 1 A. -MENT, *s.* छलेन अपहारः or उपयोगः or आत्मसात्करणं, ग्रसनं; अप-नि-ह्नवः.

EMBITTER, *v. t.* तिक्तीकृ 8 U. 2 प्रकुप् c., उद्-दीप् c., कलुषीकृ. 3 क्लिश् 9 P, दु 5 P.

EMBLAZON, *v. t.* विभूष् 10, मंड् 10.

EMBLEM, *s.* लक्षणं, लांछनं, केतनं, केतुः, व्यंजनं, संज्ञा, ध्वजः, चिह्नं, लिंगं, पताका. -ATIC,-ATICAL, *a.* लाक्षणिक (की *f.*), व्यंजक, बोधक, लिंगिन्, सूचक, द्योतक.

EMBODY, *v. t.* सशरीर *a.* कृ 8 U, शरीरेण युज् 10 or सनाथीकृ. 2 संग्रह् 9 P, समाहृ 1 P, एकी-एकत्र-कृ. -IED, *a.* मूर्त, शरीरबद्ध, देहवत्, मूर्तिमत्, शरीरिन्; 'the e. spirit' शरीराभिमानी आत्मा. -MENT, *s.* शरीरिता, देहवत्त्वं, मूर्तिमत्ता. 2 मूर्ति *f.*, करुणस्य मूर्तिरथवा शरीरिणी विरहव्यथा (U. 3) 'the e. of pathetic sentiment &c.' 3 संग्रहः, सन्निपातः, समाहारः, एकीकरणं.

EMBOLDEN, *v. t.* प्रोत्सह् c., आश्वस् c., निर्भय *a.* कृ.

EMBOSS, *v. t.* गंडाकारेण परिष्कृ 8 U or उपशुभ् c.

EMBOW, *v. t.* भुज् 6 P; *See* BEND.

EMBOWEL, *v. t.* अंत्राणि अपनी or निर्हृ 1 P.

EMBOWERED, *a.* कुंजसनाथ, निकुंजित.

EMBRACE, *v. t.* आलिंग् 1 P, आश्लिष् 4 P; परि-, ष्वंज् 1 A, उपगुह् 1 U; *See* CLASP. 2 स्वी-अंगीकृ 8 U; ग्रह् 9 P, आदा 3 A, अभ्युपगम् 1 P. 3 परिग्रह्, व्याप् 5 P, प्रतिसंह् 1 P, समाविश् c. 4 परिवृ 5 U, परिवेष्ट् 1 A or c. -*s.* सं-आ-श्लेषः, आलिंगनं, परिरंभः, उपगूहनं, परिष्वंगः.

EMBRASURE, *s.* प्राकारच्छिद्रं, जालकं.

EMBROCATE, *v. t.* (औषधीयजलेन) लिप् 6 P, अंज् 7 P; मृद् 9 P, घृष् 1 P, संवह् c. -ION, *s.* मर्दनं, लेपनं, संवाहनं. 2 विलेपः-पनं, उपदेहद्रव्यं.

EMBROIDER, *v. t.* सूच्या पुष्पादिकं सिव् 4 P or चित्र् 10, कार्मिकवस्त्रं कृ 8 U; 'an e.-ed cloth' चित्रितं-कार्मिकं-वस्त्रं. -ER, *s.* कार्मिकवस्त्रकृत् *m.*, सूचिकर्मोपजीविन् *m.* -Y, *s.* सूचिकर्मन् *n.*, शिल्पं.

EMBROIL, *v. t.* संक्षुभ् c., आकुलीकृ 8 U, संकॄ 6 P, संकुलीकृ; विरागं उत्पद् c. -MENT, *s.* संक्षोभः, सांकर्यं, संभ्रमः, आकुलत्वं.

EMBRYO, EMBRYONE, *s.* गर्भः, भ्रूणः; 'in e.' गर्भच्छत्र, गर्भावस्थायां वर्तमान ; (fig.) अपरिणत, अपरिपक्व. 2 आ-प्रा-रंभः, उपक्रमः.

EMEND, *See* AMEND. -ATOR, *s.* शोधकः, समाधातृ *m.*

EMERALD, *s.* मरकतं, गारुत्मतं, अश्मगर्भः, हरिन्मणिः; 'e.-like' मारकत (ती *f.*), मरकतसदृश (शी *f.*).

EMERGE, *v. i.* (सलिलात्) उन्मस्ज् 6 P, उत्था 1 P, निर्गम्-निःसृ 1 P; त्यज् 1 P. 2 आविर्भू 1 P, उदि 2 P, निर्भा 2 P, दृष्टिगोचर *a.* भू, दृश् pass., प्रकाशतां गम्, &c. -ENCE,-CY, *s.* संकटं, विपत्समयः, आपद् *f.*, आकस्मिकसंभवः. 2 अवसरः, प्रस्तावः, प्रयोजनं, आवश्यकत्वं; 'according to e.' यथाप्रयोजनं, यथावसरं, प्रसंगवशात्. -ENT, *a.* उन्मज्जत्. 2 आकस्मिक (की *f.*), अकस्मादुद्भूत, अन्यावश्यक (की *f.*), अपरिहार्य. -EMERSION, *s.* उत्थानं, उन्मज्जनं; त्यागः. 2 आविर्भावः, उदयः, &c.

EMERY, *s.* उन्नमलोहं.

EMETIC, *s.* वमनं, वांतिकृद् औषधं. -*a.*, -AL, *a.* वांतिकर (री *f.*).

EMINENT, *a.* उत्कृष्ट, विशिष्ट, प्रमुख, उत्तम, परम, श्रेष्ठ, प्रवर, वरेण्य, प्रधान. 2 विश्रुत, लब्धप्रतिष्ठ-वर्ण, महायशस्क, सुविख्यात, प्रख्यात; 'of e. qualities' गुणाढ्य. 3 उच्च, उन्नत, उच्छ्रित. -LY, *adv.* अत्यंतं, भृशं, अतिशयेन, अत्यर्थं, अति pr. -EMINENCE, *s.* उन्नतभूमि *f.*, उच्छ्रायः, उच्चस्थानं, उत्सेधः, उच्चभूभागः. 2 उत्कर्षः, विशिष्टता, परमपदं, श्रेष्ठत्वं, ख्याति *f*, प्रतिष्ठा, उन्नति *f.*, प्रकर्षः, गौरवं.

EMISSARY, *s.* दूतः, वार्ताहरः, संदेशहरः. 2 चरः, चारः, गूढदूतः, अपसर्पः, प्रणिधिः, स्पशः.

EMIT, *v. t.* वि-निर्-मुच् 6 P, निःक्षिप् 6 P, उदीर् c., निः-सृ c., उत्-वि-सृज् 6 P, उद्-गॄ 6 P, उद्वम् 1 P, निर्गम् c. (गमयति); निःस्रु c., मोक्ष् 10. -EMISSION, *s.* उद्गारः, विमोचनं, उत्सर्गः, स्रावः, उदीरणं, उद्वमनं. 2 (Of semen) रेतः-क्षरणं-स्खलनं, वीर्यनिषेकः, रेतःस्रुति *f.*, निषेकः.

EMMET, *s.* पिपीलिका.

EMMEW, *v. t.* पंजरे निरुध् 7 U.

EMOLLIATE, *See* SOFTEN.

EMOLLIENT, *s.* अभ्यंजनं, विलेपनं, स्नेहनं. -*a.* स्निग्ध, स्नेहन (नी *f.*), चिक्कण. 2 शांतिद, सुखावह.

EMOLUMENT, *s.* लाभः, फलं, आगमः, प्राप्ति *f.*, आयः, उदयः.

EMOTION, *s.* विकारः, विकृति *f.*, भावः, रागः, चित्तविकारः, विक्रिया, मनोधर्मः-वृत्ति *f.* 2 उत्तापः, चित्तक्षोभः, मनस्तापः, अंतर्वेगः, आकुलता, आवेगः, संक्षोभः ; 'under e.' अन्यथावृत्ति *a.*; 'e. of sorrow' शोकावेगः. 3 रसः, भावः ; 'e. of love' शृंगाररसः. -AL, *a.* भाव-विकार-विशिष्ट, विकारशील.

EMPALE, *v. t.* Encircle, q. v. 2 शूले आरुह् c. (रोपयति) or निविश् c. -MENT, *s.* शूलारोपणं ; 'deserving e.' शूल्य.

EMPEROR, *s.* सम्राज् *m.*, अधिराजः, अधीश्वरः, चक्रवर्तिन् *m.*, सार्वभौमः, मंडलेश्वरः, राजाधिराजः. —EMPRESS, *s.* अधि-महा-राजाधि-राज्ञी.

EMPHASIS, *s.* अवधारणं, गुरूच्चारणं. —EMPHASIZE, *v. t.* गौरवेण उच्चर् c., दृढयति (D.). —EMPHATIC, *a.* दृढ, निश्चित; गौरवेण उच्चारित, अवधारणीय. —ALLY, *adv.* सुदृढं, सनिश्चयं, सावधारणं, सपरिच्छेदं.

EMPIRE, *s.* आधिराज्यं, साम्राज्यं, आधिपत्यं, ऐश्वर्यं, ईशत्वं, प्रभुत्वं. 2 राष्ट्रं, राज्यं, विषयः.

EMPIRIC, *s.* दुश्चिकित्सकः, छद्म-कु-वैद्यः. 2 परीक्षकः. —*a.*,—AL, *a.* अज्ञानसिद्ध, आयुर्वेदविरुद्ध, छाद्मिक (की *f.*); प्रयोगैकविषय, प्रयोगसिद्ध. —ALLY, *adv.* आयुर्वेदविरुद्धं, अविधया, अज्ञानानुसारेण, प्रयोगज्ञानमात्रेण. —ISM, *s.* दुश्चिकित्सा, &c.

EMPLASTIC, *a.* चिक्कण, सांद्र, लेप्य.

EMPLOY, *v. t.* नियुज् 7 A, 10 ; अधिकृ 8 U, विधा 3 U, व्याप् c., प्रवृत् c.; 'e. as a messenger' प्रतिशास् 2 P. 2 प्र-उप-युज्, उपभुज् 7 U, सेव् 1 A, व्यवहृ c., अभ्यस् 4 P. —EE, *s.* नियोज्यः, अधिकृतः. —ER, *s.* प्र-नि-योजकः, प्रवर्तकः, व्यापारयितृ *m.*, अधिकारिन्-स्वामिन् *m.* —MENT, *s.* नियोगः, व्यापारः, व्यवसायः, उद्योगः, कार्यं, कार्ययोगः; जीविका, व्यवहारः, वृत्ति *f.*; 'his e. was to chop wood' काष्ठच्छेदनवृत्तिरसौ; 'out of e.' निर्वृत्ति, क्षीणवृत्ति, निर्व्यापार. 2 प्रयोगः, उपयोगः, व्यवहारः. 3 अधिकारपदं, पदं.

EMPOISON, *v. t.* तीक्ष्णरसं-विषं-दा 3 U, विषप्रयोगेण नश् c. 2 विषेण दिह् 2 U or अंज् 7 P.

EMPORIUM, *s.* वाणिज्यस्थानं, निषद्या.

EMPOWER, *v. t.* अधिकृ 8 U, नियुज् 7 A, 10, क्षमतां-अधिकारं-दा 3 U.

EMPTY, *a.* शून्य, परिशून्य, शून्यगर्भ, रिक्त. 2 विरस, निःसार, असार, फल्गु, निःसत्व; 'e.-headed' मंदधी, अल्पबुद्धि, दुर्मति; 'an e. vessel makes most noise' अर्धो घटो घोषमुपैति नूनं. —*v. t.* रिच् 7 U, शून्यी-रिक्ती-कृ 8 U. 2 सारं हृ 1 P, निःसत्त्वीकृ. 3 तोयं पत् c.; अव-तॄ 1 P, स्रु 1 P, विश् 6 P; (कुत्र वा सागरं वर्जयित्वा महानद्यवतरति S. 3) 'e. s itself' &c. —NESS, *s.* रिक्तता, शून्यता ; निःसारता, &c.

EMPURPLE, *v. t.* अरुणी-लोहिती-कृ 8 U.

EMPYREAL, *a.* आग्नेय-तेजोमय (यी *f.*).

EMPYREAN, *s.* उत्तमस्वर्गः, वैकुंठं, तेजोलोकः.

EMULATE, *v. t.* स्पर्ध् 1 A, प्रतिस्पर्ध्, संघृष् 1 P (with instr.); विजि desid. (विजिगीषते), अभिभवितुं यत् 1 A or उद्यम् 1 P, अहमहमिकया यत्; *See* COMPETE. —ION, *s.* स्पर्धा, विजिगीषा, संघर्षः, अहमहमिका. —IVE,-EMULOUS, *a.* प्रतिस्पर्धिन्, विजिगीषु, जयेच्छु. —*s.* विजिगीषुः, सपत्नः, प्रतिस्पर्धिन् *m.*

EMULSION, *s.* पायसं, पयस्यं.

EMUNCTORY, *s.* शरीरमलपथः, देहमलनिर्गमः.

ENABLE, *v. t.* Gen. cx. by शक्य ; 'this will e. you to go back' अनेन तव परावर्तनं शक्यं ; शक्ति-सामर्थ्यं-दा 3 P, समर्थ-क्षम-शक्त *a.* कृ 8 U.

ENACT, *v. t.* कृ 8 U, विधा 3 U, निष्पद् c. 2 व्यव-स्था c. (स्थापयति), विधिं-व्यवस्थां-कृ, प्रशास् 2 P, शासनं कृ ; 'it is e. ed as follows' अयं विधिः क्रियते, एवं व्यवस्थाप्यते. 3 नट् 10, अभिनी 1 P, निरूप् 10. —MENT, *s.* विधिः, शासनं, व्यवस्था, शासनपत्रं.

ENAMOURED, *a.* सानुराग, आसक्त, अनुरक्त, बद्धभाव, कामासक्त (with loc.) ; 'the king was e. of her' नृपस्तस्यां बद्धभावः, आसक्तानुरागः, प्रीतिं बबंध; 'to be e.' अनुरंज्-आसंज् pass., आसक्त &c. भू.

ENCAGE, *v. t.* पंजरे निरुध् 7 U or बंध् 9 P.

ENCAMP, *v. t.* (सैन्यं) निविश् c., समावस् c. —*v. i.* निविश् 6 P, समावस् 1 P. —MENT, *s.* निवेशनं, सनावासः. 2 शिविरं, निवेशः.

ENCAVE, *v. t.* कंदरे प्रच्छद् 10 or गुह् 1 U.

ENCIENTE, *See* PREGNANT.

ENCHAFE, *v. t.* संतप्-प्रकुप्-दुष् c.

ENCHAIN, *v. t.* निगडैः बंध् 9 P, निगडयति (D.), खिलीकृ 8 U, अव-नि-रुध् 7 U. 2 आकृष् 1 P, हृ 1 P, निरुध्.

ENCHANT, *v. t.* मंत्रैर्वशीकृ 8 U or मुह् c., अभिचर् c., अभिमंत्र् 10. 2 (fig.) हृ 1 P, आकृष् 1 P, विलुभ् c. ; 'I was quite e.-ed with thy ravishing melody' तवास्मि गीतरागेण हारिणा प्रसभं हृतः (S. 1). —ER, *s.* वि-, मोहकः, ऐंद्रजालिकः, मायिन् *m.* ; 'e. of snakes' व्यालग्राही, अ(आ)हितुंडिकः. —ING, *a.* मनोहर, मोहिन्, हारिन्. —MENT, *s.* माया, योगः, इंद्रजालं, मोहः, कुहकः, अभिचारः. —ENCHANTRESS, *s.* मायिनी, मोहिनी, योगिनी.

ENCHASE, *v. t.* प्रणि-धा 3 U, प्रतिबंध् 9 P, अनुव्यध् 4 P, खच् 10 (खचयति).

ENCIRCLE, *v. t.* परि-वृ 5 U, परिवेष्ट् 1 A or c., परिगम् 1 P, परि-इ-या- 2 P, वलयति-मंडलयति (D.), वलय-रसना in comp. 2 EMBRACE, q. v.

ENCLOSE, *v. t.* आ-परि-वृ 5 U, परिवेष्ट् 1 A or c. 2 नि-सं-अव-रुध् 7 U. 3 प्राचीरेण परिवेष्ट् or आवृ or अवरुध्, परिक्षिप् 6 P. 4 आवेष्ट्, आ-सं-छद् 10, पि-धा 3 U, कोशे निविश् c., कोशस्थ *a.* कृ 8 U. —ED, *a.* परिवृत, परिवेष्टित, परिक्षिप्त. 2 अवरुद्ध, सावरण, प्राकारावृत. 3 कोशस्थ, पिहित, परिच्छन्न, आवेष्टित, कोशांतर्गत. —URE, *s.* वृति *f.*, आवरणं, प्राकारः, प्राचीरं, आवेष्टनं, अवरोधकं, वरणः. 2 वाटः-टी. 3 अंतर्गतपत्रं.

ENCOMIUM, *s.* प्रशंसा, श्लाघा, स्तुति *f.*, स्तवः, स्तुति-

वाक्यं, वर्णनं, गुणप्रशंसा. –ENCOMIAST, *s.* गुणप्रशंसकः, स्तुतिपाठकः. –IC,-ICAL, *a.* स्तुतिमय (यी *f.*); श्लाघामय, प्रशंसाकर (री *f.*).

ENCOMPASS, *v. t.* परि-इ 2 P, व्याप् 5 P, परिच्छद् 10, परिक्षिप् 6 P, संवल् 1 A, सं-वलयति (D.); *See* ENCIRCLE, –MENT, *s.* परिवेष्टनं, परिगमः, परिवृति *f.*

ENCORE, *v. t.* प्रशंसासूचनार्थं पुनः इति उत्क्रुश् 1 P, पुनरुक्तां प्रार्थ् 10 A.

ENCOUNTER, *v. t.* अभि-इ 2 P,-गम् 1 P, समागम्, मिल् 6 P, समा-इ, समासद् c., संमुखं-अभिमुखं-गम्, संमुखीभू. 2 विग्रह् 9 P, प्रतियुध् 4 A, संघट्ट् 1 A, समाहन् 2 P. 3 प्राप् 5 P, अभिभू pass.; 'e. difficulties' आपदं प्राप्नुवंति, आपदाभिभूयंते; 'he e.-ed many dangers' तस्य बहूनि संकटान्यापतितानि. –*s.* समागमः, संगः-गमः, संमिलनं, दर्शनं, समासादनं. 2 विग्रहः, संग्रामः, समाघातः, संपरायः, संप्रहारः, संआ-घातः; *See* BATTLE; 'close e.' संघट्टः.

ENCOURAGE, *v. t.* प्रोत्सह् c., आ-समा-श्वस् c., प्रेर् c., प्रवृत् c., उत्तिज् c., आशां वृध् c. –ER, *s.* आश्वासकः, प्रवर्तकः. –ING, *a.* आश्वासिन्, प्रोत्साहक, उत्तेजन (नी *f.*), आश्वासक. –MENT, *s.* प्रोत्साहनं, आश्वासनं, उत्तेजनं, धैर्यवर्धनं. 2 साहाय्यं, अनुग्रहः, उपकारः, आनुकूल्यं, आश्रयः, अभ्युपपत्ति *f.*

ENCROACH, *v. i.* आक्रम् 1 U, 4 P, अन्यायतः ग्रह् 9 P, अन्यायेन प्रविश् 6 P, अधर्मतः ग्रह् or आत्मसात्कृ. –MENT, *s.* अन्यायेन ग्रहणं, अधर्मतः आक्रमणं-ग्रहणं.

ENCRUST, *v. t.* घनपटलेन आच्छद् 10 or परिवेष्ट् 1 A or c., बहिर्भागे घनीकृ 8 U. –ED, *a.* सपटल, घनीभूत. –ATION, *s.* बाह्यपटलं, बहिरावेष्टनं.

ENCUMBER, *v. t.* प्रतिबंध् 9 P, उप-नि-रुध् 7 U, भारेण आक्रम् 1 U, 4 P or क्लिश् 9 P, भाराक्रांत *a.* कृ 8 U; 'e. ed with debt' ऋणभारग्रस्त. –ED, *a.* भाराक्रांत, भारग्रस्त. 2 बाधित, उपरुद्ध, प्रतिबद्ध, &c. –ENCUMBRANCE, *s.* भारः, भारभूतः. 2 प्रतिबंधः, उपरोधः, प्रत्यूहः, विघ्नः, अंतरायः. 3 ऋणभारः.

ENCYCLICAL, *a.* वर्तुल, चाक्रेय (यी *f.*); 'e. letter' चक्रं, बहुसाधारणपत्रं.

ENCYCLOPŒDIA, *s.* विद्याचक्रं-कोषः; 'e. of learning' विद्यासागरः, ज्ञानोदधिः.

END, *s.* अंतः, प्रांतः, पर्यंतः-तं, अवधिः, सीमा, अंतरं. 2 अत्ययः, शेषः-षं, क्षयः, अवसादः, अंतः, अवसानं, पर्यवसानं, परिणामः; 'pleasing at the e.' परिणामरमणीय; 'of good e.' सुखोदर्क. 3 समाप्ति-निष्पत्ति-निर्वृत्ति-सिद्धि- *f.* 4 विरामः, विच्छेदः, निवृत्ति *f.*, उपशमः. 5 निधनं, मरणं, अत्ययः, विनाशः, देहक्षयः. 6 फलं, परिणामः, उत्तरफलं. 7 आशयः, हेतुः, अभिप्रायः, अर्थः, उद्देशः, कार्यं, तात्पर्यं; 'to no e.' निरर्थकं; 'e. of the world' कल्पांतः, प्रलयः, प्रत्याहारः, क्षयः, संवर्तः; 'put an e. to' समाप् c., त्यज् 1 P, उत्सृज् 6 P, नश् c.; 'e. of a garment' अंचलः, दशाः pl.; 'hear my speech to the e.' शृणु मे वाचमशेषं वचः (M. 4). –*v. t.* समाप् c., अवसो 4 P, सं-निः-पद् c., निर्वृत् c., संवृ 10; oft. by अंत in comp. –*v. i.* अवसो pass., समाप्-निष्पद् pass.; शम् 4 P, विरम् 1 P, विगम् 1 P, अपया 2 P, निष्क्रम् 1 U, 4 P; oft. by (*s.*) above; 'it will e. in good' कल्याणोदर्कं भविष्यति (U. 4); 'roots e. ing in vowels' अजंता धातवः; सागरांता मही, &c. –ING, *s.* अंतः, अंत्यं अक्षरं. –*a.* अंत्य. –LESS, *a.* अनंत, अपार, अशेष, निर्मर्याद, निरवधि. 2 निरंतर, अविरत, अविच्छिन्न, सतत, अतिदीर्घ, अनवरत. –LESSLY, *adv.* अत्यंतं, अविरतं, सततं,&c. –LESSNESS, *s.* आनंत्यं, अविरति *f.*, अविच्छेदः, &c.

ENDANGER, *v. t.* संशये पत् c. or क्षिप् 6 P, संशयस्थ-संदेहदोलास्थ *a.* कृ 8 U; *See* DANGER.

ENDEAR, *v. t.* प्रिय *a.* or प्रीतिपात्रं कृ 8 U; 'e. oneself' प्रीतिपात्रं-भाजनं-भू. –ING, *a.* प्रियकर (री *f.*), प्रीतिकर. –MENT, *s.* प्रीति *f.*, प्रणयः, प्रेमन् *m.*, *n.*, प्रेम-स्नेह-कारणं-हेतुः; 'a word of e.' प्रियवाक्यं. 2 विलासः, विभ्रमः, हावः, शृंगारचेष्टा.

ENDEAVOUR, *v. i.* प्र-यत् 1 A, घट् 1 A, उद्यम् 1 P; 'e ing for others' परार्थघटकाः, परार्थमुद्यमभृतः. –*s.* व्यापारः, व्यवसायः, प्रयत्नः, आयासः; *See* ATTEMPT.

ENDORSE, *v. t.* पृष्ठे (स्वनाम) लिख् 6 P; लेखस्य पृष्ठेभिलिखेदत्वा दत्वा धनं ऋणी (Y. II.). 2 दृढयति (D.), दृढीकृ, प्रमाणीकृ 8 U.

ENDOW, *v. t.* वृत्तिं दा 3 U, प्रतिष्ठा c. (प्रतिष्ठापयति). 2 युज् 10; संपन्न *a* कृ 8 U; oft. by 'e. ed'. –ED, *a.* युक्त, संपन्न, विशिष्ट, अन्वित, उपेत, उपपन्न, शालिन्, gen. in comp. or with instr. –MENT, *s.* वृत्ति *f.*, वृत्ति-शुल्क-दानं; प्रतिष्ठा; अग्रहारदानं. 2 निबंधः. 3 गुणः, शक्ति *f.*; 'intellectual e. s' बुद्धिगुणाः, मतिविभवः-प्रकर्षः.

ENDUE, *See* ENDOW.

ENDURE, *v. t.* सह् 1 A, विषह्, क्षम् 1 A, तिज् desid. (तितिक्षते), मृष् 4 P, 10. 2 भुज् 7 A, धृ 10. 3 शक् 5 P, वृ 10, उत्सह्; *See* ABLE. –*v. i.* स्था 1 P, चिरं स्था; 'as long as the sun and the moon e.' यावच्चंद्रदिवाकरौ. –ANCE, *s.* सहिष्णुता, सहनशीलता. 2 क्षमा, तितिक्षा, सहनं, मर्षणं, क्षांति *f.* 3 धैर्यं, उत्साहः; 'e. of austerities' दमः. 4 स्थिति *f.*, स्थायित्वं. –ER, *s.* सोढृ *m.*, क्षंतृ *m.*, सहः in comp. –ING, *a.* स्थायिन्, चिरस्थायिन्, अविनाशिन्, शाश्वत; 'miseries are of an e. character' आयतस्वभावानि दुःखानि (Ka. 175). 2 सहिष्णु, सहनशील, तितिक्षु, सहन, क्षमिन्.

ENEMY, *s.* शत्रुः, अरिः, रिपुः, वैरिन् *m.*, अरातिः, द्विट्, प्रति-वि-पक्षः, परिपंथी, अमित्रः, द्वेष्टा *m.*, अपकर्ता, सपत्नः, दुर्हृद्, परः, प्रत्यर्थी, द्विषन्, द्वेषणः, अहितः, शात्रवः, अभिघाती; 'an e. in the rear' पार्ष्णिग्राहः. —INIMICAL, *a.* विरुद्ध, शात्रव (वी *f.*), द्वेषिन्, वैरिन्, अहित, विपक्ष, विरोधिन्, अननुकूल. —LY, *adv.* रिपुवत्, सवैरं, शत्रुबुद्ध्या. —ENMITY, *s.* वैरं, शत्रुता, शत्रुभावः, विद्वेषः, विपक्षता, सापत्न्यं, द्वंद्वभावः, विरोधः.

ENERGY, *s.* शक्ति *f.*, प्रभावः, वीर्यं, तेजस् *n.*, सत्वं, पौरुषं, उत्साहः, उद्योगः, अतंद्रिता, उद्यमः, व्यवसायः, कर्मयोगः. —ENERGETIC, *a.* उद्योगिन्, उद्यमिन्, व्यवसायिन्, सोत्साह, कर्मयुक्त, सोद्योग, अनलस, अतंद्रित, उत्साहवत्. 2 वीर्यवत्, तेजस्विन्. —ALLY, *adv.* सोत्साहं, सोद्योगं, सयत्नं, शक्त्या.

ENERVATE, ENFEEBLE, *v. t.* दुर्बलीकृ 8 U, क्षीणीकृ, तेजः-शक्ति-हृ 1 P. —ED, *a.* क्षीणशक्ति, हतवीर्य, क्षीणबल, दुर्बल, शिथिलबल. —ION, —ING, *s.* वीर्यक्षयः, शक्ति-तेजो-हानि *f.*, क्षीणता, अपचयः, क्षामता.

ENFORCE, *v. t.* बलात् कृ c.; *See* COMPEL; 'e.-ed to pay' दापित. 2 दृढीकृ 8 U, दृढयति (D.), सबल *a.* कृ, स्थिरीकृ. 3 (Rules &c.) प्रवृत् c., बलेन प्रणी 1 P or निर्वह् c. —MENT, *s.* (बलेन) प्रवर्तनं, प्रणयनं. 2 दृढीकरणं; दृढप्रमाणं.

ENFRANCHISE, *v. t.* बंधनात् मुच् 6 P or c. or मोक्ष् 10. 2 स्वतंत्रीकृ 8 U, स्वतंत्राधिकारं दा 3 U. —MENT, *s.* दास्यविमोचनं, बंधनमोक्षः. 2 पौराधिकारदानं.

ENGAGE, *v. t.* आकृष् 1 P, अनुरंज् c., आराध् c., हृ 1 P. 2 व्या-पृ c., प्रयुज् 10, विनियुज्. 3 नियुज्, अधिकृ 8 U, वृ 10 (वरयति). 4 (A word) प्रतिश्रु 5 P, प्रतिज्ञा 9 U, नियमपत्रेण (आत्मानं) बंध् 9 P. 5 सं-प्रति-युध् 4 A आक्रम् 1 U, 4 P, समाहन् 2 P. 6 वाचा दा 3 U or प्रतिश्रु; विवाहसंबंधं-वाग्निश्चयं-कृ. —*v. i.* (To be e. ed in;) व्याप्टृ 6 A, निरत-आसक्त *a.* भू 1 P. प्रवृत् 1 A, (with loc.); सेव् 1 A, आस्था 1 A (with acc.). 2 संयुध्, युद्धं कृ. 3 आरभ् 1 A, व्यव-सो 4 P, उपक्रम् 1 A. 4 प्रति-ज्ञा, प्रति-श्रु, परिपण 1 A, अभ्युपगम् 1 P. —ED, *a.* व्यापृत, सव्यापार, प्रवृत्त, कार्यनिष्ठ, कर्मयुक्त, उद्यमासक्त; gen. ex. by पर, निरत, मग्न, आसक्त, तत्पर, परायण, in comp; 'e. in contemplation' ध्यानपर-निरत, &c 2 प्रति-ज्ञात-श्रुत, संविदित, कृतसंकेत; 'e. to be married' वाग्दत्त, प्रतिज्ञा विवाहित. —ING, *a.* मनोहर, हृदयग्राहिन्, हारिन्, आकर्षक, मोहिन्; चित्ताकर्षिन्. —INGLY, *adv.* मनोहारितया. —MENT, *s.* व्यवसायः, प्रवृत्ति *f.*, व्यवहारः, कर्मन् *n.*, व्यापारः, कार्यं. 2 युद्धं, संग्रामः, रणाभियोगः; *See* BATTLE. 3 प्रतिज्ञा, संकेतः, संविद् *f.*, नियमः, समयः, पणः, व्यवस्था, अभ्युपगमः, प्रतिश्रुतं वचः; 'keep an e.' समयं पा c. (पालयति) or अनुरुध् 4 A or अनुवृत् 1 A; 'let us keep our e.' सामयिका भवामः (M. 1); 'has kept his e.' विहितप्रतिज्ञः; 'marriage e.' वाग्निश्चयः, विवाहप्रतिज्ञा; 'I have many e s to-day' मया बहवः संकेताः-समयाः-अद्य पालनीयाः.

ENGENDER, *v. t.* उत्पद् c., प्रसू 2 A, उद्-भू c., जन् c.; *See* BEGET.

ENGINE, *s.* यंत्रं, उपकरणं, साधनं; 'military e.' युद्धोपकरणं.

ENGINEER, *s.* यंत्रकारः, यंत्रकलाभिज्ञः, वास्तुविद्याविशारदः. —ING, *s.* यंत्रकारस्य व्यापारः. 2 वास्तुविद्या, यंत्रशास्त्रं.

ENGIRD, ENGRIDLE, *See* ENCIRCLE.

ENGRAFT, *v. t.* (अन्यस्थानादानीय) निविश् c., संयुज् 10, संलग्नीकृ 8 U.

ENGRASP, *v. t.* ग्रह् 9 P, धृ 1 P, 10.

ENGRAVE, *v. t.* मुद्र् 10, उत्कृ 6 P, तक्ष् 1, 5 P, त्वक्ष् 1 P; 'with the name e. ed on the ring' मणिबंधनोत्कीर्णनामधेयं (S. 6). —ER, *s.* तष्ट्-त्वष्टृ *m.*, तक्षन् *m.* —ING, *s.* तक्षणं. 2 मुद्रा.

ENGROSS, *v. t.* अभिभू 1 P, एकाग्र-अनन्यविषय- *a.* कृ, आकुलीकृ 8 U; better by 'e. ed'. 2 सर्वं ग्रह् 9 P, पूर्वं ग्रह् or क्री 9 U, साकल्येन आत्मसात्कृ. —ED, *a.* निविष्ट, अभिनिविष्ट, आसक्त, अनन्यविषय, एकाग्र; ex. by परायण, निमग्न, पर, in comp.; 'e. in grief' शोकपरायण. —ER, *s.* पूर्वक्रेतृ *m.*

ENGULF, *v. t.* जलावर्ते निक्षिप् 6 P, आवर्तेन ग्रस् 1 A.

ENHANCE, *v. t.* वृध् c., उपचि 5 U, अधिक *a.* कृ 8 U. —MENT, *s.* वृद्धि *f.*, वर्धनं, उपचयः.

ENIGMA, *s.* प्रहेलिका, गूढप्रश्नः, प्रश्नदूती, प्रवह्लिका. —ENIGMATICAL, *a.* गूढार्थ, अस्पष्टार्थ, दुर्ज्ञेय, अभिप्रायार्थ, वक्र, गूढ. —LY, *adv.* गूढं, अस्पष्टं, वक्रोक्त्या, अभिप्रायार्थं.

ENJOIN, *v. t.* शास् 2 P, आदिश् 6 P, विधा 3 U; 'e. ed by Scriptures' शास्त्रविहित. 2 नियुज् 7 A, 10, उपदिश्; प्र-चुद् 10.

ENJOY, *v. t.* उप-सं-भुज् 7 U, अनुभू 1 P, आस्वाद् 1 A, अश् 5 A; निर्विश् 6 P, (निर्विश्यतां सुंदरि यौवनश्रीः R. VI. 50). 2 (Be delighted by) मुद् 1 A, रम् 1 A, नंद् 1 P, (अन्येषामभ्युदयेन मोदस्व, &c.); 'let us e. this festive holiday in playing' अनध्यायमहोत्सवे खेलंतः संनादयामः (U. 4). 3 सुखेन उपभुज् or सेव् 1 A. —ABLE, *a.* भोग्य, उपभोग्य. 2 सुभग, रम्य, रमणीय, सुखद, मनोरम, कमनीय. —MENT, *s.* उप-सं-भोगः, अनुभवः, आस्वादः-

दनं, निर्वेशः, सुखास्वादः ; 'objects of e.' विषयाः. 2 सुखं, आनंदः, हर्षः, संतोषः, प्रमोदः, सौख्यं.

ENKINDLE, *See* KINDLE.

ENLARGE, *v. t.* विस्तृ c., वि-प्र-तन् 8 U, प्र-सृ c., प्रथ् 10, विशालीकृ 8 U. 2 वृध् c., एध् c., आप्यै c., वृद्धिं नी 1 P, स्फाय् c. (स्फावयति). -*v. i.* वृध् 1 A, विस्तृ-उपचि-वितन् pass., स्फाय् 1 A, प्यै 1 A, प्ररुह् 1 P, वृद्धिं इ 2 P. 2 (Upon) प्रपंचयति (D.), विस्तरेण-सविस्तरं-वद् 1 P or अभिधा 3 U or वर्ण् 10. -MENT, *s.* वृद्धि *f.*, विस्तारः, वर्धनं, स्फीति *f.*, बृहणं. 2 विपुलता, प्रपंचः, वाग्विस्तरः.

ENLIGHTEN, *v. t.* (ज्ञानेन) वि-प्र-काश् c., उद्भास् c., दीप् c., प्रति-प्र-बुध् c., उपदिश् 6 P, विमलीकृ 8 U, संस्कृ, व्युत्पद् c. -ED, *a.* प्रतिबुद्ध, संस्कृतचित्त, व्युत्पन्न, प्राप्तज्ञान, ज्ञानोद्दीपितचित्त, प्रतिबोधवत्. -MENT, *s.* ज्ञानोद्दीपनं, प्रबोधः-धनं ; संस्कारः, प्रवृत्ति *f.*, ज्ञानागमः, चित्तप्रबोधनं.

ENLIST, *v. t.* नामावलिपत्रे नाम लिख् 6 P or आरुह् c. (रोपयति). 2 (Soldiers) सैन्यमध्ये आरुह् c., युद्धकर्मणि व्या-पृ c. or प्रवृत् c., अस्त्राणि ग्रह् c. 3 आकृष् 1 P, आत्मसात्कृ 8 U, स्वपक्षे आनी 1 P or कृ ; 'having got a certificate e. ing him among Gods' अमरगणनालेख्यमासाद्य (R. VIII. 95).

ENLIVEN, *v. t.* हृष् c., ह्लाद् c., उल्लस् c. 2 उत्साहं जन् c. (जनयति), आश्वस् c., प्रोत्सह् c., उत्तिज् c. -ING, *a.* उत्साह-हर्ष-जनक.

ENNOBLE, *v. t.* उन्नम् c. (उन्नमयति), उत्कर्ष-उन्नतिं नी 1 P, उत्-श्रि c., उत्कृष् 1 P or c., प्रतिष्ठां प्राप् c. 2 कुलीनपदे नियुज् 7 A, 10, उच्चपदं आरुह् c. (रोपयति) or आप् c., संमन् c. -MENT, *s.* उत्कर्षः, उन्नति *f.*, प्रतिष्ठा, उच्चपदावाप्ति *f.*

ENNUI, *s.* ग्लानि *f.*, क्लांति *f.*, अवसादः, श्रमः.

ENORMOUS, *a.* असाधारण, अतिमात्र, अलौकिक (की *f.*), अपरिमित, अनंत. 2 महाप्रमाण, अतिबृहत्, अतिमहत्; 'e. in body' बृहत्कायः, भीम-महा-काय. 3 घोर, दारुण, अतिनिंद्य, सुदुष्ट, पापिष्ठ. -LY, *adv.* अतिमात्रं, सातिशयं, अत्यंतं, भृशं; सु-अति-pr. -ENORMITY, *s.* घोरता, दारुणता, &c. 2 घोर-महा-पातकं, महापराधः, अतिपापं.

ENOUGH, *a.* यथेष्ट, बहुल, प्रचुर, पर्याप्त. 2 समर्थ, क्षम, उचित, उपयुक्त; oft. by अलं with inf. or dat., (तस्यालमेषा क्षुधितस्य तृप्त्यै R. II. 39). -*adv.* अलं, कृतं, (with instr.); 'e. of prolixity' अलमतिविस्तरेण. 2 यथेष्टं, प्रचुरं, पर्याप्तं; 'to be e. for' कृप् 1 A (with dat.); 'rich e.' भूयसा वित्तवान्; with adverbs by एव or भूयसा; सम्यगेव, भूयसा युक्तं, &c.; 'be good e. to grant my request' मम प्रार्थनामनुमंतुं प्रसीदतु भवान्. -*s.* पर्याप्ति *f.*, प्राचुर्यं, बाहुल्यं, यथेष्टत्वं; having e. for maintenance' अलंजीविक.

ENQUIRE,-Y, *See* INQUIRE,-Y.

ENRAGE, *v. t.* प्रकुप् c. क्रुध् c., रुष् c., संरभ् c. (संरंभयति). कोपं-रोषं-नी 1 P; कोपं उद्दीप् c. or इंध् 7 A. -ED, *a.* कुपित, क्रुद्ध, उद्धमन्यु, प्रकोपित, कोपाकुल, संरब्ध, जातामर्ष; 'to be e.' क्रुध्-कुप्-रुष् 4 P (with dat).

ENRAPTURE, ENRAVISH, *v. t.* अतिहर्षेण मुह् c. or जडीकृ 8 U, अतिमात्रं हृष् c. or उल्लस् c. -ED, *a.* हर्षजड-मोहित, संप्रहृष्ट, अत्युल्लासित, हर्षोन्मत्त, परमानंदित; 'to be e.' अत्यंतं हृष् 4 P, हर्षेण मुह् 4 P or जडीभू. -MENT, *s.* हर्षोन्मादः, परमानंदः, हर्षमोहः.

ENRICH, *v. t.* धनिन्-सधन-आढ्य-द्रव्यसंपन्न-*a.* कृ 8 U; समृध् c., धनं वृध् c. or आप्यै c. or स्फाय् (स्फावयति). 2 Adorn, q. v.

ENROLL, *v. t.* Enlist, q. v. -ER, *s.* नामलेखकः. -MENT, *s.* नामलिखनं, नामारोपणं.

ENROOTED, *a.* रूढ-बद्ध-मूल.

ENSANGUINE, *v. t.* शोणितेन लिप् 6 P.

ENSCONCE, *See* CONCEAL.

ENSHRINE, *v. t.* सुप्रतिष्ठितस्थाने निविश् c. or रक्ष् 1 P.

ENSIFORM, *a.* खड्गाकार.

ENSIGN, *s.* पताका, ध्वजः, केतनं, केतुः, वैजयंती. 2 चिह्नं, लिंगं, लक्षणं. 3 (E.-bearer) ध्वजिन्-पताकिन् *m.*

ENSLAVE, *v. t.* दासीकृ 8 U, (fig. also), वशीकृ ; दास्ये नियुज् 7 A, 10 or बंध् 9 P. -MENT, *s.* दास्यं, दासभावः, बंधनं.

ENSNARE, *v. t.* पाशेन-जालेन-बंध् 9 P, पाशे पत् c., जालबद्ध *a.* कृ 8 U, जाले धृ 1 P, 10.

ENSUE, *v. i.* समापद् 4 A, प्रवृत् 1 A, उत्पद् 4 A, जन् 4 A, सं-उद्-न-भू 1 P, प्रसंज् pass. 2 अनुगम् 1 P, अनु-इ 2 P, पश्चात् आगम् 1 P. -ING, *a.* आगामिन्, भाविन्; अनागत, उत्तरकालीन, उत्तर-पर-in comp.; 'on the e. day' परेद्युः, आगामिनि दिवसे.

ENSURE, *v. t.* निश्चित *a.* कृ 8 U, स्थिरी-दृढी-कृ; 'diligence will e. you speedy success' उद्यमयोगाददूरवर्तिनीं सिद्धिमवगच्छ.

ENTAIL, *v. t.* आवह् 1 P, उत्पद् c., जन् c. (जनयति). 2 (रिक्थं) प्र-दा 3 U. -*s.* क्रमागतरिक्थं. 2 क्रमागमविधिः.

ENTANGLE, *v. t.* संश्लिष् c., संग्रंथ् 9 P, संलग्नीकृ 8 U, आकुली-संकीर्णी-कृ. 2 संबंध् 9 P, संमिश्र् 10; better by 'e. ed.' -ED, *a.* सक्त, आ-सं-सक्त, लग्न, सं-परिलग्न, आ सं-परि-श्लिष्ट ; कुरबकशाखापरिलग्नं च वल्कलं (S.1); शाखास्वसक्तमार्गा (S. 2), &c. 2 संकीर्ण, संकुल,

ग्रंथिल. 3 आकुंचित, व्यावर्तित; 'c. hair' जटा, जटाजूटः; 'having c. hair' जटिल, जटावत्; 'c. in a net' जालबद्ध. -MENT, s. संश्लिष्टता, जटिलत्वं. ग्रंथिलत्वं. 2 संकरः, व्यतिकरः, संकुलता.

ENTER, v. विश् 6 P, नि-प्र-आ°; गाह् 1 A, आगम् 1 P, आया 2 P, पदं कृ 8 U or निधा 3 U; 'a thought e. ed into his head' कश्चित्कल्पस्तस्य चेतसि प्रादुर्बभूव; 'curiosity e. ed his heart' कुतूहलेन तस्य चेतसि पदं कृतं; 'e. into conversation' भाषणनिमग्न a. भू 1 P; 'e. into alliance' संधिं कृ; 'e. into another's views' परमतं ग्रह् 9 P, अन्यभावमनुप्रविश्, अन्यमतं स्वीकृ or अनुमन् 4 A; 'e. on a course' कार्यं प्रारभ् 1 A, कार्ये प्रवृत् 1 A. 2 (A name) लिख् 6 P, निविश् c., समारुह् c. (रोपयति). -ENTRANCE, s. प्रवेशः-शनं, &c. 2 द्वारं; See DOOR. -ENTRY, s. द्वारं, गमनागमनमार्गः. 2 लिखनं, पत्रारोपणं.

ENTERPRISE, s. साहसं, आश्चर्यकर्मन् n., अद्भुतकार्यं, दुष्कर्म. 2 उद्यमः, व्यवसायकार्यं, प्रवृत्ति f., उद्योगः, चेष्टितं, आरंभः, व्यवसायः. 3 उत्साहः, धैर्यं. -v. t., See BEGIN. -ING, a. उद्योगिन्, व्यवसायिन्, सोद्योग. 2 धीर, उत्साहिन्, सोत्साह. 3 साहसिक (की f.), दुष्करकार्ये प्रवर्तक.

ENTERTAIN, v. t. पूज् 10, संमन् c., अर्च् 1 P, 10, संभू c., सत्कृ, आतिथ्यं कृ 8 U; 'e. with food' भोजनदानेन तृप् c. or तुष् c. 2 विनुद् c., रम् c. (रमयति), अतिवह् c. 3 धृ 1 P, 10, ग्रह् 9 P; See BEAR; 'e. a hope' आशां आस्था 1 U or अवलंब् 1 A; 'do not e. doubts' मा ते संशयोऽभूत्. -ER, s. विनोदकः, सत्कारिन् m., आतिथेयः. -MENT, s. पूजा, सत्कारः, आतिथ्यं, अतिथिसेवा-पूजनं. 2 विनोदः-दनं. 3 उत्सवः; 'musical c.' गानोत्सवः; संभोजनं, &c.

ENTHRAL, v. t. दासी-वशी-कृ 8 U.

ENTHRONE, v. t. सिंहासने उपविश् c., राज्ये अभिषिच् 6 P.

ENTHUSIASM, s. उत्साहः, उत्कटता, औत्सुक्यं, तीक्ष्णता, व्यग्रता, चंडता, उन्मादः. 2 (Religious e.) धर्मोन्मादः, भक्ति-श्रद्धा-उन्मादः, अतिश्रद्धोन्मादः. -ENTHUSIAST. s. भक्तिव्यग्रः, श्रद्धोन्मत्तः. 2 उत्साहिन् m. -IC, -ICAL, a. उत्साहवत्, सोत्साह; अत्यंत, उत्कट, प्रचंड, उत्सुक, व्यग्र, तीक्ष्ण, उद्युक्त; उन्मत्त; 'e. devotion' निरतिशया भक्तिः, निशातिरेकः. -ICALLY, adv. अत्यनुरागेन, अत्यंतं.

ENTHYMEME, s. लुप्तावयवः पक्षः or हेतुः.

ENTICE, v. t. वि-आ-कृष् 1 P, हृ 1 P, मुह् c., प्र-विलुभ् c., दुष्कृतौ प्रवृत् c. -MENT, s. आकर्षणं, प्र-विलोभनं, मोहः, वंचनं. -ER, -ING, See ALLURER, -ING.

ENTIRE, a. कृत्स्न, समग्र, अखंड, सकल, सर्व, अखिल, समस्त, संपूर्ण, निखिल, निःशेष, अशेष, अन्यून, अभिन्न, सावंत. 2 सरल, ऋजु, अभेद्य, अहार्य (धनादिना). -LY, adv. अखंडं, साकल्येन, अशेषं, कृत्स्नशः, सर्वतः, निखिलेन. 2 (Solely) एक in comp.; एव, सर्वथा; 'depending e. on water' जलैकायत्त. -NESS, -TY, s. समग्रता, साकल्यं, संपूर्णता, अखंडत्वं, अन्यूनता. 2 अभेद्यता, अहार्यता, आर्जवं.

ENTITLE, v. t. नाम कृ 8 U, अभिधा 3 U; See CALL. 2 अधिकारं दा 3 P, अधिकृ 8 U; ex. by अर्ह् 1 P, or pot. pass. part.; 'he is e. ed to respect' मानमर्हति, मान्यः, पूज्यः; 'persons e. ed to a share' अंशाधिकारिणः, अंशभाजः, अंशार्हाः; 'e. ed to praise' प्रशंसार्ह, प्रशंसापात्रं.

ENTITY, s. सत्वं, अस्तित्वं, भावः, सत्ता.

ENTOMB, v. t. श्मशाने निखन् 1 P or निधा 3 U or स्था c. (स्थापयति); 'e. ed in despair' नैराश्योपहत.

ENTRAILS, s. अंत्राणि (pl.), पुरीतत् n.

ENTRANCE, v. t. (Put in a trance) मुह् c., मूर्च्छां प्राप् c. -ED, a. मूढ, मूर्च्छापन्न, प्रलीन. 2 उन्मत्त, हर्षोन्मत्त.

ENTRAP, See ENSNARE.

ENTREAT, v. t. अभि-प्र-अर्थ् 10 A, अनुनी 1 P, विनयेन-सांजलि-याच् 1 A or अर्थ्, प्रसद् c., सविनयं निविद् c. -ING, a. सानुनय, सविनय, सांजलि. -Y, s. प्रार्थनं-ना, अभ्यर्थना, याचना, विनति f., अर्थिता, अनुनयः; सांजलिप्रार्थना.

ENTRUST, v. t. निक्षिप् 6 P, आ-समा-रुह् c. (रोपयति), निविश् c., न्यस् 4 U, न्यासीकृ 8 U (with loc.); प्रतिपद् c., दा 3 U, ऋ c. (अर्पयति) (with dat.).

ENTWINE, v. t. ग्रंथ् 9 P, उद्-ग्रंथ्, गु(गुं)फ् 6 P, विरच् 10; See ENCIRCLE also.

ENUCLEATE, v. t. वि-परि-शुध् c., स्पष्टीकृ 8 U.

ENUMERATE, v. t. परि-कृत् 10; परि-,संख्या 2 P, कथ् 10; परि-वि-गण् 10, यथाक्रमं ख्या or निर्दिश् 6 P. -ION, s. परि-,संख्यानं, गणनं-ना, परिकीर्तनं, आख्यानं, कथनं, एकैकशः निर्देशः.

ENUNCIATE, v. t. लक्षणं-स्वरूपं-कथ् or वर्ण् 10; उच्चर् c., उदीर् c., उदाहृ 1 P, कृत् 10, घुष् 10, निविद् c., विज्ञा c. (ज्ञापयति). -ION, s. उच्चारणं, उदीरणं, उदाहरणं, परिसंख्यानं, प्रकीर्तनं, विज्ञापनं; स्वरूपवर्णनं-ना. -IVE, a. व्यापक, उच्चारक.

ENVELOP, v. t. अवगुंठ् 10, आ-परि-वेष्ट् 1 A or c., आ-परि-वृ 5 U or c., आ-परि-सं-छद् 10, पिधा 3 U, 2 कोशे निधा or निविश् c. -s. कोशः-षः, आवेष्टनं, पिधानं, पुटः, आच्छादनं, अवगुंठनं. 2 प्रावारः, प्रच्छदपटः.

ENVENOM, *v. t.* विषेण दिह् 2 U or अंज् 7 P or लिप् 6 P; सविष *a.* कृ 8 U. –ED, *a.* सविष, विषदिग्ध, विषाक्त.

ENVIRON, *v. t.* परिवेष्ट् 1 A or c., परिक्षिप् 6 P; *See* ENCIRCLE. –(E. s) *s.* परिसर:, उपांत:, अभ्यास:, उपपुरं, नगरोपांत:-तं.

ENVY, *v. t.* असूयति (D.), ईर्ष्य् 1 P (with dat.); परोत्कर्षं न सह् 1 A or मृष् 4 P, 10, परद्रव्यं अभिलष् 1, 4 P or लुभ् 4 P; स्पर्ध् 1 A; 'I e. you your prosperity' त्वदुत्कर्षमसहिष्णुरहं. 2 (In a good sense) स्पृह् 10 (with dat.) –*s.* असूया, अभ्यसूया, ईर्ष्या, मात्सर्यं, मत्सर:, अक्षांति *f.*, असहिष्णुता; अमर्षणं; परधनाभिलाष:. –ABLE, *a.* स्पृहणीय, आकांक्षणीय. 2 ईर्ष्यणीय, लोभ्य. –ER, *s.* असूयक:, मत्सरिन् *m.*, ईर्ष्यिन् *m.* –OUS, *a.* ईर्ष्यिन्, सेर्ष्य, समत्सर, परोत्कर्षासहन, असूयक, मत्सरिन्, साभ्यसूय (with loc.); असहिष्णु in comp.; 'e. of other's happiness' परसुखासहिष्णु; oft. ex. by पुरोभाग in comp.; 'e. of each other's fame' (प्राय: समानविद्या:) परस्परयश:पुरोभागा: (M. 1). –OUSLY, *adv.* सेर्ष्यं, साभ्यसूयं, समत्सरं, सासूयं.

ENVOY, *s.* दूत:, संदेश-वार्ता-हर:, निसृष्टार्थ:; राजप्रतिनिधि:.

EPAULET, *s.* स्कंधाभरणं, अंसालंकार:.

EPHEMERAL, *a.* क्षणभंगुर, क्षणविध्वंसिन्, क्षणिक (की *f.*). 2 ऐकाह्निक (की *f.*).

EPIC, *s.* वीरचरितवर्णनं, महाकाव्यं, वीरपुरुषेतिहास:.

EPICENE, *a.* स्त्रीपुल्लिंग, साधारणलिंग.

EPICURE, EPICUREAN, *a.* उदरपरायण; भोजनलंपट, उदरंभरि, लोलुप; विषयासक्त, इंद्रियसुखनिरत, विषयिन्. –EPICURISM, *s.* विषयसेवा, विषयासक्ति *f.*, इंद्रियसुखानुराग:.

EPICYCLE, *s.* प्राकृचक्रं, परिधि:.

EPIDEMIC,-AL, *a.* व्यापक, सर्वग, बहुजनसाधारण (णी *f.*); संचारिन्; 'e. disease' मार:-री, महामारी. –*s.* जनपदोद्ध्वंस:.

EPIDERMIS, *s.* बाह्यत्वच *f.*, बाह्यचर्मन् *n.*

EPIGLOTTIS, *s.* उप-प्रति-अलि-जिह्वा, घंटिका.

EPIGRAM, *s.* क्षुद्रकविता, लघुकाव्यं.

EPILEPSY, *s.* अपस्मार:, भ्रामरं. –EPILEPTIC, *a.* अपस्मारिन्, भ्रामरिन्; 'an e. fit' अपस्माराक्रम:.

EPILOGUE, *s.* उपसंहार:.

EPISCOPACY, *s.* धर्माध्यक्षता, धर्माध्यक्षाधिकार:.

EPISODE, *s.* उपाख्यानं, उपकथा, प्रासंगिकवाक्यं, आख्यानं-कथा. –IC,-ICAL, *a.* प्रासंगिक (की *f.*), अप्रस्तुत, अप्रकृत.

EPISPASTIC, *a.* स्फोटजनक.

EPISTLE, *s.* पत्रं, लेख:, लेख्यं; 'epistolary correspondence' पत्रेण संवाद:.

EPITAPH, *s.* मृत्युलेख:, चैत्योपलिपि *f.*, स्मरणमंडनं.

EPITHALAMIUM, *s.* विवाहगीतं.

EPITHEM, *s.* प्रलेप:, उप-नाह: देह.

EPITHET, *s.* विशेषणं, उपाधि:.

EPITOME, *s.* संक्षेप:, सार:, संग्रह:, समाहार:, समसनं. –IZE, *v. t.* संक्षिप् 6 P, समस् 4 U. संग्रह् 9 P, संहृ 1 P. –IZER,–IST, *s.* संक्षेप्तृ *m.*, संग्रहकर्तृ *m.*

EPOCH, *s.* काल:, युगं, अवधि:, निर्णितकाल:. 2 विशिष्टकाल:. 3 शाक:, शक:.

EPODE, *s.* उपगीतं-गानं.

EPOPEE, *See* EPIC.

EQUABLE, *a.* समान, निर्विकार, समचित्त-वृत्ति-भाव.

EQUAL, *a.* सम, समान, तुल्य, सदृश (शी *f.*), प्रतिमसंकाश-in comp.;(with instr. or gen.of person); *See* LIKE; 'to whom gold and a clod of earth are e.' समलोष्टकांचन: ; the point of equality being in the instr. or loc.; समुद्रेण समो गांभीर्ये,-र्येण; 'to consider e.' तुलया धृ 1 P. 2 अनवर. 3 समवृत्ति-चित्त, निर्विकार. 4 पर्याप्त, अलं with inf. or dat.; क्लृप् 1 A (with dat.); 'he is e. to the task' तत्कार्यं साधयितुमलं स:; रक्षणाय कल्पते, &c. –*s.* समानपदस्थ:, तुल्यपदभाज् *m.* 2 सवयस्क:, सवयस्य:, तुल्यवयस्; oft. by (*a.*). –*v. t.* तुल् 10 (तुलयति), (प्रासादास्त्वां तुलयितुमलं Me. 65), समीतुल्यी-कृ 8 U; oft. ex. by (*a.*); 'none can e. me in bravery' न कोपि शौर्येण मम समान:. –ITY, *s.* साम्यं, समानता, तुल्यता, सादृश्यं, &c. –IZE, *v. t.* समीकृ 8 U. तुल् 10. –LY, *adv.* समं, सदृशं, समानं. तुल्यं.

EQUANIMOUS, *a.* समचित्त-भाव-वृत्ति, निर्विकार. –EQUANIMITY, *s.* समवृत्तिता-चित्तता, समभाव:, समानवृत्ति *f.*

EQUATION, *s.* समीकरणं, साम्यं.

EQUATOR, *s.* भूकक्षा, परिधि:, निरक्ष: ; 'celestial e.' व्योमकक्षा. –IAL, *a.* निरक्ष in comp.; 'e. region' निरक्षदेश:.

EQUERY, *s.* मंदुरा, अश्व-वाजि-शाला. 2 अश्वपाल:.

EQUIANGULAR, *a.* समकोण, समानास्त्र.

EQUESTRIAN, *a.* अश्वीय, आश्विक(की *f.*). –*s.* आश्विक:, अश्वारोह:.

EQUIDISTANT, *a.* समानांतर.

EQUILATERAL, *a.* समभुज.

EQUILIBRIUM, *s.* तुल्यता, समता, साम्यं. 2 तुल्यभारता, समतोलनं, समानभरत्वं ; 'to be in e.' तुल्य *a.* भू, तुलया धृ pass., समानभार *a.* भू.

EQUINOX, *s.* विषुवं, विषुवत् *n.*; 'the vernal e.' महाविषुवं, हरिपदं ; 'the autumnal e.' विषुपदं, जलविषुवं. –EQUINOCTIAL, *a.* विषुवीय ; 'e. line' विषुवद्वृत्तं, विषुमंडलं ; 'e. point' अयनं.

EQUIP, *v. t.* सज्जीकृ 8 U, सर्वोपकरणानि प्र-उप-क्लृप् c. or उपपद् c. or समाहृ 1 P, उपकरणैः समायुज् 7 U, 10 ; 'e. with arms' सन्नह् c. ; 'e. with cloths' वस्त्रैः संव्ये 1 P or भूष् 10. -AGE, *s.* उपकरणं, साधनं, संभारः, सामग्री, उपस्करः. 2 परिबर्हः, परिवारः. 3 सज्जा, परिच्छदः, सन्नाहः, सज्जना, कल्पना, आकल्पः. 4 वाहनं, विमानं, प्रवहणं. -MENT, *s.* सज्जा, संभारः, सज्जीकरणं, साधनं.

EQUIPOISE, *v. i.* समीकृ 8 U, तुलया धृ 1 P. -*s.* Equilibrium, q. v.

EQUIPOLLENT, *a.* तुल्यबल-शक्ति-सामर्थ्य.

EQUIPONDERANT, *a.* समभार-तोल, तुल्यपरिमाण.

EQUITY, *s.* न्यायः, धर्मः, अपक्षपातः, न्याय्यता, सर्वसमता. -ABLE, *a.* न्यायपरायण-वर्तिन्, अपक्षपातिन्, समदर्शिन्, सर्वसमन्यायिन्. 2 न्याय्य, यथान्याय, पक्षपातरहित, सर्वसाधारण. -ABLENESS, *s.* न्याय्यता, अपक्षपातः. -ABLY, *adv.* न्यायतः, यथान्यायं, पक्षपातं विना.

EQUIVALENT, *a.* सम, तुल्य ; *See* EQUAL. 2 तुल्यार्थक, समार्थ, तुल्यबल-शक्ति; तुल्य-सम-मूल्य, समार्घ. -*s.* तुल्यद्रव्यं-वस्तु *n.*, तुल्यमूल्यं वस्तु, प्रतिफलं. 2 तुल्यार्थः शब्दः, पर्यायः.

EQUIVOCAL, *a.* द्व्यर्थ, संदिग्धार्थ, वक्र, अस्पष्टार्थ, अव्यक्त. -LY, *adv.* वक्रोक्त्या, भंग्या, अस्पष्टं, संदिग्धार्थेन, अव्यक्तं. -NESS, *s.* संदिग्धार्थः, द्व्यर्थता, अर्थसंदेहः, वक्रता, अस्पष्टता.

EQUIVOCATE, *v. i.* वक्रं-अस्पष्टार्थं-वद् 1 P, वाक्यभेदं कृ 8 U. -ION, *s.* वक्रवचनं, वक्रोक्ति *f.*, वाक्यभेदः, वाक्छलं, अप-व्यप-देशः.

EQUIVOQUE, *s.* कूटोक्ति-अर्थापत्ति *f.*, वक्रभाषितं.

ERA, *s.* कालः, शाकः, ध्रुवः कालः. 2 विशिष्टकालः.

ERADIATE, *v. i.* किरणान् क्षिप्-मुच् 6 P, परिस्फुर् 6 P.

ERADICATE, *v. t.* उत्-निर्-मूल् 10 ; उच्छिद् 7 P, उत्सद् c., उत्पट् 10, वि-ध्वंस् c., आमूलं उद्धृ 1 P or उत्खन् 1 P, व्यप-रुह् c. (रोपयति). -ION, *s.* उन्मूलनं, उच्छेदः, उत्पाटनं, व्यपरोपणं. -OR, *s.* उन्मूलयितृ *m.*, उच्छेदिन् *m.*

ERASE, *v. t.* व्या-अप-मृज् 2 P, विलुप् c., व्यामृश् 6 P. 2 उच्छिद् 7 P, विनश् c., उन्मूल् 10. -URE, *s.* व्यामर्शः, लोपः, उच्छेदः, विनाशः.

ERE, *prep.*, *adv.* पूर्वं, प्राक्, (with abl.) ; 'e. this' अतः पूर्वं; 'e. long' अचिरात्-रेण; 'e. now' नातिचिरं, नातिचिरात्प्राक् ; 'e. while' किंचित्पूर्वं ; *See* BEFORE.

ERECT, *a.* उन्नत, उच्छ्रित, अनत, ऊर्ध्व, उत्तान, अजिह्म ; gen. ex. by उत् in comp. ; 'with the neck e.' उद्ग्रीव, उत्कंधर; 'with the hair e.' पुलकित, रोमांचित. -*v. t.* स्था c. (स्थापयति), प्रति-सं-अधि°, अधिरुह् c. 2 निर्मा 3 A, रच् 10, विरच्, निखन् 1 P, (निचखान जयस्तंभान् R. IV. 36). 3 उत्था c., उत्त्री 1 P, उच्छ्रि c., उन्नम् c. (उन्नमयति), उद्गम् c., उद्यम् 1 P, उत्क्षिप् 6 P, उद्धृ 1 P. -ION, *s.* प्रतिष्ठापनं, संस्थापनं. 2 निर्माणं, विरचनं. 3 उत्थापनं, उत्क्षेपः, उच्छ्रयः, उन्नमनं, उन्नति *f.*, उद्गमनं ; 'e. of the hair' पुलकः, पुलकोद्गमः, रोमोद्गमः, रोमहर्षणं, रोमांचः.

ERODE, *See* CORRODE.

EROTIC, *a.* कामप्रिय, कामिन्, कामुक.

ERR, *v. i.* विभ्रम् 1, 4 P, अपराध् 4, 5 P, उत्पथं या 2 P, उन्मार्गेण गम् 1 P or प्रवृत् 1 A ; स्खल् 1 P, प्रमद् 4 P, सत्पथाद् भ्रंश् 1 A, 4 P or च्यु 1 A or विचल् 1 P, व्युत्क्रम् 1 U, 4 P, व्यतिचर् 1 P. -ANT, *a.* परिभ्रमिन्, भ्रमणकारिन्. -ATIC, *a.* भ्रमणशील, जंगम, चर. -ING, *a.* भ्रांत, उन्मार्गप्रवृत्त, सत्पदभ्रष्ट-च्युत, उत्पथगामिन्, प्रमादिन्. -ERRONEOUS, *a.* भ्रांतिमूलक, प्रामादिक (की *f.*), भ्रमात्मक ; मिथ्या-मृषा-in comp.; 'e. notion' मिथ्याग्रहः. 2 अनृत, असत्य, अशुद्ध, अयथार्थ, अतथ्य, वितथ. -LY, *adv.* मिथ्या, मृषा, अयथार्थं, असत्यं, भ्रांत्या, प्रमादेन, सप्रमादं. -ERROR, *s.* भ्रमः, भ्रांति *f.*, मतिविभ्रमः, मोहः, व्यामोहः, मिथ्यामति *f.* 2 दोषः, अपराधः, प्रमादः, स्खलितं, पापं. 3 उन्मार्गगमनं, व्यतिक्रमः, उत्पथः, मार्गभ्रंशः ; 'in e.' भ्रांत, प्रमत्त, सदोष, अपराद्ध.

ERRAND, *s.* संदेशः, संदेशवाच् *f.*, वाचिकं ; शासनं, आदेशः. 2 दौत्यं, दूतकार्यं-कर्तव्यं ; 'send on an e.' प्रतिशास् 2 P, आदिश् 6 P, दौत्येन प्रेष्-प्रेर् c. ; 'sending on an e.' प्रतिशासनं.

ERRATUM, *s.* अशुद्धं.

ERRHINE, *a.* नस्य, क्षुत्कर (री *f.*).

ERST, *adv.* पुरा, पूर्वं, प्राक्, पूर्वकाले.

ERUCT, *v. t.* उद्गम् 1 P, उद्-गॄ 6 P. -ATION, *s.* उद्गारः, उद्गमः-मनं.

ERUDITE, *a.* व्युत्पन्न, संस्कृतचित्त, पंडित, कृतविद्य, विद्याभिज्ञ. -ION, *s.* पांडित्यं, ज्ञानं, विद्या, व्युत्पत्ति *f.*

ERUGINOUS, *a.* ताम्रकलंकरूप, ताम्रगुणविशिष्ट.

ERUPTION, *s.* निःसरणं, निर्गमः, उद्भेदः, उद्गिरणं, स्फोटनं, उद्गारः, उत्क्षेपः ; 'e. on the skin' दद्रुः, विस्फोटः. 2 कोठः, पिटिका, कोठोद्गमः. -ERUPTIVE, *a.* उद्भेदिन्, स्फोटनविशिष्ट.

ERYSIPELAS, *s.* उदर्दः, दद्रुः.

ESCALADE, *v. t.* लंघ् 1 A, 10, अवस्कंद् 1 P ; निश्रेण्या आरुह् 1 P. -*s.* दुर्गलंघनं, अवस्कंदः-दनं.

ESCAPE, *v. t.* मुच्-विमुच् pass., त्रै-रक्ष्-pass., (with abl.) ; 'e. ed death' मरणाद्विमुक्तः ; 'e. ed censure' दोषाद्विमुक्तः. 2 सं-निः-उत्-तॄ 1 P; लंघ् 1 A, 10, पारं इ-या-2 P or गम् 1 P. 3 परिहृ 1 P, त्यज् 1 P ; 'it e. ed his notice' स तत्रा-

लक्षयत्; 'he has e. ed one danger to fall into another' (*Cf.* e. ed Scylla to fall into Charybdis) बंधनभ्रष्टो गृहकपोतश्बिलाया मुखे पतितः (M. 4). -*v. i.* अप-निः-क्रम् 1 U, 4 P, अपसृ 1 P, अपसृप् 1 P, निर्गम् 1 P, परा-इ 2 P, पलाय् 1 A, अप-या 2 P, अपधाव् 1 P, अलक्षितं-निभृतं-गम्; 'he narrowly e. ed' कथं कथमपि मुक्तः; 'e. ed with his life' पलायनेन जीवितं रक्षितवान्. -*s.* पलायनं, निर्गमः, अपक्रमः-मणं, निष्क्रमः, अपसर्पणं, अपयानं. 2 निस्तारः, मुक्ति *f.*, मोक्षः, त्राणं, क्षेमलाभः.

ESCHEAT, *v. i.* राजसाद्-भू 1 P, (संतत्यभावात्) राजगामि भू, राजस्वतां आपद् 4 A, राजानं गम् 1 P. -*s.* राजसाद्भूतं क्षेत्रादि.

ESCHEW, *See* AVOID.

ESCORT, *s.* परि-अनु-चराः, रक्षापुरुषाः (pl.); परिवारः, रक्षकगणः, रक्षिवर्गः; 'send her with a good e.' सुरक्षितां तां प्रेषय. 2 रक्षणं, शरणं, रक्षा, अनुव्रजनं. -*v. t.* (रक्षार्थं) अनुगम् 1 P, सह-इ 2 P, अनुव्रज् 1 P, प्रतिरक्ष् 1 P, (ऋषिप्रतिरक्षितां S. 4), परि-अनु-चर् 1 P.

ESCULENT, *a.* खाद्य, भक्षणीय. -*s.* खाद्यं, भक्ष्यं.

ESCUTCHEON, *s.* कुलचिह्नपत्रं.

ESOPHAGUS, *s.* अन्नवाहि स्रोतस् *n.*

ESOTERIC, *a.* गूढ, अलौकिक (की *f.*); विशिष्ट.

ESPALIER, *s.* लताकुंजः, वृक्षजालं.

ESPECIAL, *a.* उत्तम, विशिष्ट, प्रधान, परम, मुख्य. 2 सविशेष, विशेष in comp.; 'e. qualification' विशेषगुणः. -LY, *adv.* विशेषेण-षतः,प्रधानतः, मुख्यशः.

ESPIONAGE, *s.* गूढावेक्षणं, चारवृत्ति *f.*, गूढप्रचारः. 2 चारप्रयोगः.

ESPLANADE, *s.* समः क्रीडाप्रदेशः, समीकृतं क्रीडास्थानं.

ESPOUSE, *v. t.* परिग्रह् 9 P, वि-उद्-वह् 1 P, परिणी 1 P, वृ 5 U, 10 (वरयति). 2 अंगी-स्वी-कृ 8 U, परिग्रह्, उरी-उररी-कृ, अवलंब् 1 A, आश्रि 1 U. 3 रक्ष् 1 P, अनु-पा c. (पालयति). संवृध् c. 4 वाचा दा 3 U or प्रति-ज्ञा 9 U. -AL, *s.* परिग्रहणं, उद्वाहः, परिणयनं. 2 वाग्दानं, वाग्निश्चयः. 3 स्वीकारः, ग्रहणं, अनुपालनं; अवलंबनं, आश्रयः; 'e. of a cause' पक्षपरिग्रहः-पातः, पक्षावलंबनं.

ESPY, *v. t.* (दूरात्) आलोक् 1 A, 10, निरूप् 10, ईक्ष् 1 A, निर्वर्ण् 10.

ESQUIRE, *s.* कंचुकवाहः, सान्नाहनिकः. 2 श्री pr., आर्यः, श्रीमत् in comp.

ESSAY, *v. t.* आरभ् 1 A, परीक्ष् 1 A, उपक्रम् 1 A, व्यवसो 4 P; *See* ATTEMPT. -*s.* परीक्षणं, प्रयत्नः, आरंभः, उद्योगः, उपक्रमः. 2 नि-प्र-बंधः, लेख्यं. -IST, *s.* निबंधलेखकः.

ESSENCE, *s.* सारः-रं, मूलं, अधिभूतं, मूलवस्तु *n.*; 'vital e. of body' शरीरधातवः (pl.). 2 सारः, निष्कर्षः, निर्गलितार्थः, पिंडितार्थः, भावः, निष्कृष्टार्थः. 3 Perfume, q. v. —ESSENTIAL, *a.* सारवत्, सारभूत, ससार. 2 आवश्यक, अत्यावश्य, गुरु, महत्; oft. ex. by अप-ईक्ष् 1 A; 'sprinkling of water is e. to the growth of sprouts' अंकुरवृद्धिर्जलसेकमपेक्षत एव. -*s.* तत्वं, मूलतत्वं, मूलं. 2 परमार्थः, गुवैर्थः. 3 (E. s of judicature) व्यवहारमातृकाः. -LY, *adv.* अवश्यं, तत्वतः, सारतः.

ESTABLISH, *v. t.* सं-प्रति-स्था c. (स्थापयति), अधिष्ठा c.; 'one whose rule is newly e. ed' अचिराधिष्ठितराज्यः (M. 1); प्रतिष्ठितं प्रकृतिषु 'well e.-ed' &c. 2 उप-प्रति-पद् c., समर्थ् 10; निर्णी 1 P, स्थिरी-दृढी-प्रमाणी-कृ 8 U, सं-स्तंभ् 9 P or c., निगम् c. (गमयति), सिद्धांतयति (D.). 3 व्यव-स्था c., प्रकृप् c., वि-धा 3 U. -MENT, *s.* संस्थापनं, स्थिरीकरणं. 2 प्रतिपादनं, उपपत्ति *f.*, निगमनं. 3 भृत्यादिवर्गः.

ESTATE, *s.* अवस्था, दशा; *See* CONDITION. 2 संपद् *f.*, धनं, रिक्थं, दायः; भूमि *f.*, विभवः, संपत्ति *f.*, द्रव्यं, वित्तं. 3 पदं, स्थानं. 4 वर्गः, गणः.

ESTEEM, *v. t.* बहु मन् 4 A or c., संमन्, पूज् 10, आ-दृ 6 A. 2 गण् 10, वि-भू c. -*s.* बहु-सं-मानः, आदरः, पूजा, मान्यत्वं. 2 मतं, मति *f.* -ESTIMABLE, *a.* मान्य, पूज्य, अर्घ्य, पूजार्ह.

ESTIMATE, *v. t.* निरूप् 10, वि-भू c., निर्णी 1 P, विगण् 10, सं-परिसं-ख्या 2 P, संकल् 10, निश्चि 5 U, अर्घ-मूल्यं निरूप् or निर्णी. -*s.* गणना-नं, परिसंख्यानं; मूल्यनिरूपणं, अर्घगणना; 'rough e.' स्थूल-आकारमानं. 2 मतं; 'in the popular e.' लोकमतेन. -ION, *s.* गणना-नं. 2 बहुमानः, मानः, आदरः, संमानः. -OR, *s.* गणकः, संख्यातृ *m.*

ESTIVAL, *a.* निदाघ-ग्रीष्म-संबंधिन्.

ESTRADE, *s.* समभूमि *f.*, समस्थानं-स्थलं.

ESTRANGE, *v. t.* अप-वि-रंज् c., विश्लिष् c., भिद् 7 P or c., विरागं उत्पद् c., स्नेहं भिद् or छिद् 7 P or विघट् c. (घटयति). 2 दूरीकृ 8 U, विच्छिद्, विश्लिष् c., वियुज् 7 A, 10. -ED, *a.* विरक्त, विश्लेषित, भेदित, जातविराग, निवृत्तस्नेह, अपरक्त, अपरागिन्. 2 दूरीकृत, विच्छिन्न, वियोजित. -MENT, *s.* विरक्ति *f.*, अप-वि-रागः, स्नेहनिवृत्ति *f.*, स्नेहच्छेदः-भेदः-विरामः. 2 वियोगः, विच्छेदः, विरहः, विश्लेषः, दूरीभावः, पृथग्भावः.

ESTUARY, *s.* समुद्रवेकः, पुटभेदः.

ESTUATE, *v. i.* फेनायते (D.), उत्सिच् pass.

ET CÆTERA, (&c.) Ex. by आदि, आद्य, प्रभृति in comp.; 'horses, asses, &c.' अश्वरासभादयः, गुडादि, &c.

ETCH, *v. t.* लिख् 6 P, चित्र् 10.

ETERNAL, *a.* नित्य, शाश्वत (ती *f.*), अनंत, सनातन (नी *f.*), अनादि, अनाद्य, संतत, सतत, अनाद्यनंत, शाश्वतिक (की *f.*), निरंतर, अविसर्गिन्, अमर, अनपाय, अविच्छिन्न, अक्षय. –LY, *adv.* नित्यं, शश्वत्, सदा, निरंतरं. अविरतं, सर्वकालं, अनंतं. –ETERNITY, *s.* नित्यता, आनंत्यं, सनातनत्वं. 2 अनंतकालः.

ETESIAN, *See* ANNUAL.

ETHER, *s.* आकाशः-शं. 2 तेजोवहः, हिमद्रवः. –ETHEREAL, *a.* आकाशीय, नभस्-आकाश- in comp., वैहायस (सी *f.*). 2 तैजस (सी *f.*).

ETHICS, *s.* नीतिविद्या-शास्त्रं, नीति *f.*, आचारनीतिः. –ETHIC, ETHICAL, *a.* नीतिविषय-शास्त्रीय. –ALLY, *adv.* नीत्यनुसारेण.

ETHNIC,-AL, *a.* अन्य-भिन्न-देशीय.

ETHNOLOGY, *s.* नृवंशविद्या.

ETIQUETTE, *s.* आ-उप-चारः, विनयरीति *f.*,-विधिः सदाचाररीतिः, सौजन्यं, सभ्यता, शिष्टाचारः.

ETYMOLOGY, *s.* व्युत्पत्ति *f.*, व्युत्पादनं, शब्दसाधनं, शब्दव्युत्पत्तिविद्या. –ICAL, *a.* व्युत्पत्तिविषय; 'e. sense' यौगिकोर्थः. –IST, *s.* शब्दव्युत्पत्तिकुशलः. –IZE, *v. t.* व्युत्पद् c.

EULOGY, *s.* प्रशंसा, स्तुति *f.*, स्तवः, श्लाघा, वर्णनं, गुणस्तुतिः-श्लाघा-वर्णना. –IZE, *v. t.* प्रशंस् 1 P, स्तु 2 U; *See* PRAISE. –ISTIC, *a.* स्तुतिमय (यी *f.*), प्रशंसाकर (री *f.*). –IST, *s.* प्रशंसकः, स्तुतिपाठकः, वंदिन् *m.*

EUNUCH, *s.* षं(शं)ढः-ढः, क्लीबः, नपुंसकः, पोगंडः, पंडः, तृतीय(या)प्रकृतिः. 2 वर्षवरः, स्थापत्यः, कंचुकिन् *m.*, सौविदः, सौविदल्लः.

EUPHEMISM, *s.* मंगलभाषितं.

EUPHONY, *s.* सुस्वरः-शब्दः-स्वनः, सुश्लिष्टस्वरत्वं, अकर्कशता. 2 संयोगः, संधिः. –IC,-IOUS, *a.* सुस्वर, सुश्राव्य, सुखश्रव, श्रुतिसुख, अकर्कश, सुश्लिष्टस्वन.

EUPHORBIA, *s.* समंतदुग्धा, सीहुंडः, वज्रः, स्नुह् *f.*, स्नुही, गुडा.

EVACUATE, *v. t.* परित्यज् 1 P, वि-हा 3 P, उत्-विसृज् 6 P. 2 रिच् 7 P, शून्यीकृ 8 U; 'e. bowels' शुध् c., मलशुद्धिं कृ 8 U. –ION, *s.* परित्यागः, उत्सर्गः. 2 (Of bowels) मलशुद्धि *f.*, मलोत्सर्गः, मलोचारः, उच्चारः, विरेचनं.

EVADE, *v. t.* शाठ्येन परि-हृ 1 P, वक्रोक्त्या परिहृ, अप-लप् 1 P, अप-नि-ह्नु 2 A, अप-व्यप-दिश् 6 P. –*v. i.* शाठ्येन पलाय् 1 A or अप-सृप् 1 P or अपधाव् 1 P, व्यपदेशं कृ 8 U, वाक्छलं कृ. –EVASION, *s.* अप-व्यप-देशः, छद्मन् *n.*, छलं, कपटं, निह्नवः, छलेन परिहरणं. 2 वक्रोक्ति *f.*, वाक्छलं, अपलापः, कपटवचनं, कैतवोक्तिः. 3 Escape, q. v.—EVASIVE, *a.* सकपट, छलिन्, छलान्वित, व्यपदेशिन्, अपह्नवकारिन्. 2 वक्र, कुटिल, जिह्म; 'e. answer' वक्रोत्तरं; 'when he made e. replies' यदा वाक्यभेदान् बहूनकथयत् (Mu. 2). –LY, *adv.* सानिह्नवं, वाक्छलेन, वक्रोक्त्या, प्रस्तुतं परिहृत्य.

EVANESCENT, *a.* क्षणिक, क्षणभंगुर, अशाश्वत (ती *f.*). 2 अदृश्य, परोक्ष, अंतर्हित, अप्रत्यक्ष.

EVAPORATE, *v. i.* बाष्पीभू 1 P, बाष्परूपेण उद्गम् 1 P or नश् 4 P, बाष्पायते (D.), आतपेन शुष् 4 P. 2 (fig.) विनश्, विली 4 A, अंतर्धा pass., वि-द्रु 1 P. –*v. t.* बाष्पीकृ 8 U, आतपेन शुष् c., उच्छुष् c., बाष्परूपेण नश् c. or उद्गम् c. (गमयति). –ED, *a.* आतपशुष्क, शोषितरस. –ION, *s.* बाष्पीभवनं-करणं, बाष्पभावः, शोषणं.

EVE, *s.* पूर्वप्रदोषः. 2 Evening, q. v.; 'to be on the e. of taking place' उपस्था 1 P, प्रत्यासद् 1 P; *See* APPROACH.

EVEN, *a.* सम (in all senses); 'e. ground' समप्रदेशः-स्थलं-पाटः-भूमि *f.*; 'e.-handed' समक्रिय, समदर्शिन्; 'e.-minded' समचित्त-भाव, समवृत्ति. 2 समरेख, अवक्र, ऋजु. –*v. t.* समीकृ 8 U. –*adv.* अपि; 'e. though' 'e. if' यद्यपि; 'e. now' अद्यापि; 'e. so' एवमेव, एवं, तथैव, अथ किं; 'e. as' यथा, यथैव. –LY, *adv.* समं, तुल्यं; सम, तुल्य in comp. –NESS, *s.* समता, साम्यं, तुल्यता, एकरूपता, निर्विकारता, &c.

EVENING, EVEN, *s.* संध्या, संध्यासमयः, सायंकालः, त्रि-वै-कालः, दिनावसानं, प्रदोषः, रजनीमुखं, सायाह्नः; 'in the e.' सायं; 'good e. to you' शुभस्ते प्रदोषः (भूयात्). –*a.* सायंतन (नी *f.*), प्रादोषिक (की *f.*), वैकालिक (की *f.*), सायंकालीन.

EVENT, *s.* वृत्तं, व्यतिकरः, वृत्तांतः, घटना, संभवः, संगतं; 'in the e. of' यदि, चेत्. 2 परिणामः, फलं, अनुवृत्तं, उद्वृत्तं, उत्तरं फलं. –FUL, *a.* विख्यात, बहुवृत्तविशिष्ट. –UAL, *a.* अंतिम, अंत्य. 2 आनुषंगिक (की *f.*), अनुवर्तिन्, अनुसारिन्. –UALLY, *adv.* अवशेषे, अंते, अंततः.

EVER, *adv.* कदा-चन-चित्, कदापि; कर्हिचित्, जातु; 'not e.' न कदाचन, न जातु, &c. 2 नित्यं, अहर्निशं; सदा, सर्वदा; 'for e.' शश्वत्, निरंतरं; अजस्रं, शाश्वतीः समाः; oft. by एकांत, अत्यंत in comp.; 'disappeared for e.' अत्यंतविलुप्तदर्शन; 'lost for e.' एकांतनष्ट; 'gone for e.' असन्निवृत्त्यै गत, अत्यंतगत; 'e. more' पुनः, इतः परं; 'e. and anon' वारंवारं, काले काले, मुहुर्मुहुः, मुहुः; 'e. since' यतः प्रभृति; 'e. so little' मनाक्-ईषत्-कियत्-किंचित्-अपि. With adj. ex. by नित्य, सदा, &c. in comp.; 'e. blooming' नित्यपुष्प; 'e. green' सततहरित, अम्लानपर्ण; 'e. lasting' नित्यस्थायिन्, नित्य, अक्षय्य, अमर; *See* ETERNAL; 'e. moving' सदा-नित्य गति.

EVERT, *v. t.* विपर्यस् 4 U, विनश् c.

EVERY, *a.* Ex. by प्रति-अनु- in comp.; 'e. day' प्रतिदिवसं; प्रतिवर्ष, अनुदिनं, &c.; oft. by repeating the word; 'in e. place' स्थाने स्थानें; दिवसे दिवसे 'e. day' &c.; 'at e. discussion' वादे वादे. 2 सर्व, विश्व, सकल; *See* EACH; 'knowing e. thing' सर्वज्ञः; 'suffering e. thing' सर्वंसहा (पृथ्वी); 'e. one' 'e. body' सर्वः, सर्वजनः, प्रत्येकः, एकैकः; एकैकशः, पृथक् पृथक्; 'e.-day' (*a.*) प्रात्यहिक (की *f.*); 'e. thing' सर्वं; 'e. other' एकैकं परित्यज्य अन्य-अपर; 'in e. way' सर्वथा; 'e. where' विष्वक्, सर्वतः, सर्वत्र, यत्र तत्र; 'e. time' यदा यदा; 'on e. side' सर्वतः, विश्वतः, समंततः.

EVICT, *v. t.* निःसृ c., निराकृ 8 U, बहिष्कृ, अधिकारात्-स्वत्वात्-भ्रंश् c. or च्यु c.

EVIDENCE, *s.* साक्ष्यं, प्रमाणं, प्रामाण्यं, निदर्शनं; 'written e.' लेखप्रमाणं, साधनपत्रं; 'ocular e.' प्रत्यक्षप्रमाणं, चाक्षुषज्ञानं. –*v. t.* प्रमाणीकृ 8 U, प्रमाणेन साध् c. or वि-भू c. or उप-पद् c.

EVIDENT, *a.* स्पष्ट, सुस्पष्ट, स्फुट, परिस्फुट, व्यक्त, विशद, प्रकाश, प्रत्यक्ष, प्रकट; 'make e.' प्र-काश् c., आविष्कृ 8 U, स्पष्टीकृ, वि-वृ 5 U, विशदीकृ; 'to be e.' स्पष्टीभू 1 P, &c. –LY, *adv.* स्पष्टं, स्फुटं, व्यक्तं, प्रत्यक्षं, नाम, oft. with एव.

EVIL, *a.* दुष्ट, पाप, खल, कुत्सित, असाधु, निंद्य, अधम, पापिन्, असत्, गर्ह्य, गर्हित, वाच्य; gen. ex. by दुर्, कु, अप, असत्, पाप in comp.; 'e.-intentioned' पापाशय, दुर्बुद्धि; 'e. passions' दुर्विकाराः; 'e. eye' कुदृष्टि *f.*, पापदृष्टिः; 'e. course' कुपथः-मार्गः, असत्पथः; 'e.-conducted' दुराचार, अपकर्मन्, दुर्वृत्त; 'e. doer' दुर्वृत्तः, कुकर्मन् *m.*; पापकर्मा, दुष्कृतिन् *m.*, पापकृत् *m.*; 'e.-minded' दुरात्मन्, पापमति-बुद्धि, दुष्टमति, कुमति, दुर्मति, दुर्बुद्धि, पापाशय; 'good or e. acts' शुभाशुभकर्माणि; 'e. speaking' दुरालापः, पिशुनवाक्यं; 'e.-tongued' दुर्मुख, मुखर, अबद्धमुख, कद्वद. –*s.* अनिष्टं, अहितं, अशुभं, अपायः, अभद्रं, अरिष्टं, दुःखं. 2 दुर्गति *f.*, दुरवस्था, व्यसनं, आ-वि-पद् *f.*, कष्टं, अत्याहितं. 3 अपकारः, अपायः, हिंसा, क्षतं-ति *f.* 4 पापं, पापाचरितं, दुष्कर्म, कुकृत्यं, अधर्मः, दुष्टकृत्यं, दौरात्म्यं, दोषः, दुराचारः, दुष्कृति *f.*; 'Oh! An e. has befallen'! अब्रह्मण्यं, अत्याहितं, हा धिक्, कष्टं.

EVINCE, *v. t.* निर्दिश् 6 P, प्रकाश् c., सूच् 10, दृश् c., स्पष्टी-व्यक्ती-प्रकटी-कृ 8 U, व्यंज् 7 P or c., द्युत् c. –IBLY, *adv.* स्पष्टं, असंशयं, व्यक्तं. –IVE, *a.* दर्शक, सूचक, द्योतक.

EVISCERATE, *v. t.* निरंत्रीकृ 8 U.

EVITABLE, *v. t.* परिहार्य, हेय, वर्जनीय, अनावश्यक (की *f.*), परिहरणीय.

EVOKE, *v. t.* आ-ह्वे 1 P, आ-समा-कृष् 1 P. 2 उत्पद् c., जन् c. (जनयति); प्र-बुध् c., प्रोत्सह् c., उत्तिज् c.; 'his speech e. ed laughter' तस्य वचः प्रहासाय बभूव, उपहासास्पदं जातं. –EVOCATION, *s.* आह्वानं. 2 Appeal, q. v.

EVOLVE, *v. t.* वि-वृ 5 U, उद्भिद् c. 2 वि-स्तॄ c., प्र-सृ c., वितन् 8 U. –EVOLUTION, *s.* उद्भेदः, विवरणं. 2 विस्तारः-रणं, प्रसारणं. 3 परंपरा, श्रेणी. 4 मूललाभः. 5 परिणामः; 'theory of e.' परिणामवादः.

EVULSION, *s.* उत्पाटनं, उत्कर्षणं, अवलुंचनं.

EWE, *s.* मेषी, एडका, उरणी, अविला; 'e.'s milk' अविसोढं, अविदूसं.

EWER, *s.* कमंडलुः, कुंभः, उदकपात्रं.

EXACERBATE, *v. t.* प्र-कुप् c., उत्तिज् c., क्रोधं उद्दीप् c.; *See* ENRAGE. –ION, *s.* प्रकोपणं-नं, क्रोधोद्दीपनं.

EXACT, *a.* यथार्थ, यथातथ, ऋत, सत्य. २ शुचि, निर्दोष, शुद्ध. 3 अवहित, अप्रमत्त; oft. by विशेष in comp.; स्थलविशेषः, नरविशेषः 'e. place', 'e. man &c.' 4 सूक्ष्म, विशिष्ट. 5 निर्विशेष, समान. –*v. t.* बलेन ग्रह् 9 P or आदा 3 A, बलाद् ग्रह् or निष्कृष् 1 P or आ-हृ c., दा c. (दापयति); oft. by causal. 2 बाध् 1 A, अर्द् c., उपपीड् 10. –ION, *s.* बलाद् ग्रहणं or आदानं, निष्कर्षः, दापनं. 2 उपद्रवः, विप्लवः, बाधा, बाधनं, उपपीडा. –LY, *adv.* यथार्थतः, यथावत्, यथातथं, तत्त्वतः, सम्यक्, सत्यं, सूक्ष्मतया. 2 नाधिकं न न्यूनं; oft. by एव; 'e. so' एवमेव, अथ किं, तथैव; 'they two are e. alike' नास्ति किमपि तयोरंतरं. –NESS, *s.* याथार्थ्यं, सत्यता, तत्त्वता. 2 सूक्ष्मता. 3 अवधानं, अप्रमादः.

EXAGGERATE, *v. t.* अतिशयेन-अत्युक्त्या वर्ण् 10 or कथ् 10; संवृध् c. (Mr. 9), विस्तॄ c. –ION, *s.* अत्युक्ति *f.*, अतिशयोक्तिः, अतिवर्णनं, वाग्उपचयः, संवर्धनं.

EXALT, *v. t.* उन्नम् c. (नमयति), नी 1 P or प्राप् c., उन्नी 1 P, उच्छ्रि c., उत्कृष् 1 P; उच्चपदं प्राप् c. or अधिरुह् c. (रोपयति), उत्कृष्टपदे नियुज् 7 A, 10. –ATION, *s.* उन्नति *f.*, उच्छ्रायः, उन्नमनं, उत्कर्षः, उच्चपदारोपणं; 'self-e.' आत्मोत्कर्षः. –ED, *a.* उन्नत, उच्छ्रित, उत्कृष्ट, परम, उच्चैः; 'e. place' उच्चैःपदं; 'e. rank' गौरवपदं; *See* ELEVATE.

EXAMINE, *v. t.* परीक्ष् 1 A, निरूप् 10, अनुसंधा 3 U, विचर् c., विमृश् 6 P, अवेक्ष्, आ-पर्या-लोच् 10. 2 निर्णी 1 P, निश्चि 5 U, परिच्छिद् 7 P. 3 अनुयुज् 7 A, प्रच्छ् 6 P; मृग् 10 A, अन्विष् 4 P, चर्चां कृ 8 U, ज्ञा desid. (जिज्ञासते). 4 निरीक्ष्, समीक्ष्,

परीक्ष्, निरूप्, दृश् 1 P, आ-अव-लोक् 1 A, 10. -ATION, s. परीक्षा-क्षणं, विचार:-रणं-णा, निरूपणं, अनुसंधानं, अनुयोग:, प्रश्न:. 2 निरीक्षणं, आलोचनं, संदर्शनं, अवेक्षा; 'judicial e.' व्यवहारदर्शनं. -ER, s. परीक्षक:, विचारक:, अनुयोक्तृ m., प्राश्निक:.

EXAMPLE, s. उदाहरणं, निदर्शनं, दृष्टांत:; 'for e.' यथा, तथाहि. 2 आदर्श:, प्रमाणं; 'follow an e.' अनुकृ 8 U, प्रमाणं मन् 4 A, वर्त्म अनुगम् 1 P. पदमनुविधा 3 U, (पदमनुविधेयं च महतां). -EXEMPLARY, a. प्रमाणी-आदर्शी-भूत, दृष्टांतयोग्य, प्रमाणयोग्य. 2 प्रशस्य, श्लाघ्य; अनुकरणीय-करणार्ह. -LY, adv. प्रमाणवत्, प्रमाणमिव, दृष्टांतरूपेण, अनुकरणीयतया. —EXEMPLIFY, v. t. उदाहृ 1 P, दृष्टांतेन स्पष्टीकृ 8 U or प्रकाश् c. or प्र-दृश् c. -ICATION, s. उदाहरणं, निदर्शनं, उदाहरणेन स्पष्टीकरणं.

EXANIMATE, a. निर्जीव, विचेतन. 2 निरुत्साह, भग्नोत्साह.

EXASPERATE, v. t. प्रकुप् c., संक्षुभ् c., रुष् c., क्रुध् c., सं-रभ् c. (रंभयति), क्रोधं उद्दीप् c. -ED, a. प्रकोपित, संरब्ध, जातामर्ष, इद्धमन्यु, प्रदीप्तक्रोध, संक्षुब्ध, प्रक्षोभित. -ION, s. प्रकोपणं-नं, संरंभ:, क्रोधोद्दीपनं.

EXCAVATE, v. t. उत्खन् 1 P, निर्भिद् 7 P or c., विदॄ 10. -ION, s. विदारणं, उत्खननं. 2 खातं, गर्त:-र्तं, रंध्रं, बिलं, सुषिरं; 'e. underneath the ground' सुरंगा. -or, s. खनक:, खातकृत् m.

EXCEED, v. t. अति-इ 2 P, अति-क्रम् 1 U, 4 P; स सत्कारो मनोरथानामप्यभूमि: (S. 7) 'e. ed even my expectations'; अतिचर्-गम् 1 P, लंघ् 1 A, 10; *See* BEYOND also. 2 अति-शी 2 A, अति-भू 1 P; *See* EXCEL. -ING, a, अतिशायिन्, अतिरिक्त, अधिक, अतिरेकिन्. 2 अत्यंत, परम, पर, भूरि, सु pr., अति pr.; 'e. man's power' अतिमानुष; 'e. written orders' आज्ञापत्रमुल्लंघयन्. -INGLY, adv. अत्यंतं, नितांतं, एकांतत:, अत्यर्थं, निर्भरं, प्रगाढं, सुतरां, नितरां, प्र-नि-कामं, सातिशयं, अतिमात्रं, अतीव, अति-सु-pr. —EXCESS, s. उत्कर्ष:, गाढता, बाहुल्यं, प्राचुर्यं, उत्सेक:, अतिशय:, उपचय:, आधिक्यं, अतिरेक:, उद्रेक:. 2 पौनरुक्त्यं, पुनरुक्तता. 3 मर्यादातिक्रम:, अतिक्रम:, अत्याचार:, असंयम:, अपरिमितता. -IVE, a. अत्यंत, अत्यधिक, अत्यर्थ, अतिमात्र, प्र-, गाढ, पर, परम, सातिशय, निर्भर, उत्कट, नितांत, अपरिमित, एकांत, अतिरिक्त, अतिगुरु, तीव्र; gen. by सु-अति-pr. -IVELY, adv. अत्यंतं, सु-अति- pr., तीव्रं, बलवत्; *See* above.

EXCEL, v. t. अतिशी 2 A, दूरी-अध:-अधरी-कृ 8 U, विशिष् c.; अतिरिच्-विशिष्-pass. (with abl. of person); अतिक्रम् 1 U, 4 P, अति-इ 2 P; oft. by जि 1 P, अभि-परा-भू 1 P, तिरस्कृ, धिक्कृ, प्रत्याख्या 2 P, प्रत्यादिश् 6 P. -LENCE, s. विशिष्टता, उत्कर्ष:, प्रकर्ष:, आतिशय:, श्रेष्ठता, उत्तमता, संपद् f., 'e. of beauty' रूपसंपद्. 2 गुणोत्कर्ष:, गुणविशिष्टता-प्रकर्ष:. 3 गुण:, गुणवत्ता, परभाग:, उत्कृष्टगुण:. -LENCY, s. उत्कर्ष:, &c. 2 देव:, महाराज:-भाग:. -LENT, a. विशिष्ट, उत्कृष्ट, उत्तम, श्रेष्ठ, परम, अग्र, वरेण्य, प्रशस्यतम, प्रवर, गुणवत्, सारवत्, गुणोपेत; oft. by वरविशेष-in comp., and by words like ऋषभ:, पुंगव:, व्याघ्र:, सिंह:, शार्दूल:, इंद्र:, प्रकांड:, उद्द:, तल्लज:, मतल्लिका, मचर्चिका, in comp.; पात्रविशेष: 'e. receptacle'; 'e. cow' गोमतल्लिका, गोतल्लज:, गवोद्द:, गोप्रकांड:, &c.; 'e. man' पुरुषर्षभ:, पुरुषसिंह:, &c. -LENTLY, adv. सुष्ठु, उत्तमं, सु pr.

EXCEPT, v. t. वृज् 10, परिवृज्, अप-वि-हा 3 P, त्यज् 1 P, अपास् 4 U, मुच् 6 P. 2 व्यावृत् c. (a rule &c.), संकुच् 1 P or c. -*prep.*, -ING, वर्जयित्वा, विहाय, मुक्त्वा, अंतरा-अंतरेण (with acc.), विना (with acc., instr., and abl.), ऋते (with abl.); oft. by वर्जं, व्यतिरिक्तं in comp.; गौतमीवर्जमितरा निष्क्रांता: (S. 4). 2 यदि न. -ION, s. वर्जनं, विवर्जनं, हानं, त्याग:, अपासनं; with the e. of; *See* (*prep.*) above. 2 अपवाद:, व्यभिचार:; 'rules have e.-s' उत्सर्गा: सापवादा:; 'as general rules are limited (in scope) by e. s' अपवादैरिवोत्सर्गा: कृतव्यावृत्तय: (K. II. 27); 'that saying has no e. s' अव्यभिचारि तद्वच: (K. v. 36), इति लोकवाद: न विसंवादमासादयति (Mallinâtha); 'counter-e.' प्रतिप्रसव:, (तृजकाभ्यां कर्तरीत्यस्य प्रतिप्रसव: S. K.). 3 वर्जनीयं, वर्ज्यं. 4 दोष:, बाधा, अपवाद:; 'take e.' दोषं ग्रह् 9 P, (नात्र दोषं ग्रहीष्यति कुलपति: S. 3); *See* OBJECT. -IONABLE, a. बाध्य, परिहरणीय, वर्ज्य. -IONAL, a. असाधारण (णी f.), असामान्य, अपवादभूत, अलौकिक (की f.); 'e.-ly sharp' अनन्यसाधारणं पटु:.

EXCERPT, v. t. उद्-हृ 1 P, निर्हृ, संकल् 10 (कलयति); 'e. passages' चूर्णीकृ 8 U. -ION, s. उद्धार:, उद्धृतभाग:, निर्हार:, चूर्णि:.

EXCHANGE, v. t. वि-,नि-मे 1 A, प्रतिदा 1 P, 3 U, (तिलेभ्य: प्रतियच्छति माषान्), प्रतिपण् 1 A, व्यति-हृ 1 P, परिवृत् c.; 'e. civilities' सत्कारविनिमयं कृ; 'by e. ing clothes' वेषपरिवर्तनेन-व्यतिहारेण; अन्योन्यसंभिन्नदृशां (Mal. 1) 'who e. ed glances with each other'. -s. विनिमय:, परि(री)वर्त:, परिवृत्ति f., परिवर्तनं, नैमेय:, नि(वि)मय:, परिदानं, प्रतिदानं-पणनं, व्यतिहार:; oft. by अन्योन्य or प्रति in comp.; 'e. of favours' अन्योन्योपकार:; 'e. of looks' अन्योन्यदृष्टिपात:, परस्परालोकनं;

'e. of blows' प्रतिघातः ; 'in e. for' विनिमयेन, व्यतिहारेण, प्रतिदानेन. 2 भांड-द्रव्य-विनिमयः. 3 श्रेष्ठिचत्वरं.

EXCHEQUER, *s.* राजधनागारं, राजस्वकोषः ; 'chancellor of the e.' कोषाधीशः, कोषावेक्षकः.

EXCISE, *v. t.* राजदेयकरं-शुल्कं-निरूप् 10 or निर्धृ 10 or स्था c. (स्थापयति). -*s.* राजस्वं, करः, शुल्कं. -MAN, *s.* करनिरूपकः, शुल्काधिकारिन् *m.*, कराध्यक्षः, शुल्कग्राहः.

EXCISION, *s.* उच्छेदः, कर्तनं, उत्पाटनं, उद्धरणं, विनाशः.

EXCITE, *v. t.* उत्तिज् c., प्रकुप् c., सं-वि-क्षुभ् c., उत्-सं-तप् c., उद्-दीप् c., उद्युज् 10, उत्था c. (उत्थापयति), प्रोत्सह् c., प्रचुद् 10, वृध् c., प्रवृत् c., संधुक्ष् 10 (feelings &c.). 2 जन् c. (जनयति), उत्पद् c., प्रबुध् c.; 'my curiosity is the more e. ed' इदमधिकतरमुपजनितं मे कौतुकं (Ka. 134); 'with anger e. ed' संजातामर्ष, उद्दीपितकोप ; oft. by dat. with or without भू ; 'his speech e.-ed laughter' तद्वचो हासाय बभूव ; *See* LEAD to. -ABLE, *a.* कोपन, उत्तेजनीय, सुलभकोप, क्रोधिल, शीघ्रकोपिन्. -ATION, -MENT, *s.* उत्तेजनं, उत्तापः, उत्थापनं, प्रकोपः, उद्दीपनं, संतापः-पनं, सं-,वि-, क्षोभः, संरंभः, चित्तोद्वेगः, चित्तोत्तापः, मनस्तापः, कोपोद्दीपनं. -ED, *a.* संरब्ध, प्रकोपित, क्षुब्ध, उत्तेजित, जातरोष, इद्धमन्यु, संतप्त ; सं-वि-क्षोभित; 'in an e. mood' क्रोधाविष्टेन ; रोषवशं गत. 2 उत्पन्न, जात, जनित. -ER, *s.* उद्दीपकः, उत्तेजकः, संक्षोभकः.

EXCLAIM, *v. i.* आ-उत्-क्रुश् 1 P, उच्चैः घुष् 10, तारस्वरेण वद् 1 P, आ-रट् 1 P, उच्चैः उदीर् c. -EXCLAMATION, *s.* उत्क्रोशः, आरटनं, घोषणं-णा, उच्चैः स्वरः, उद्गारः ; 'e. of joy' हर्षानस्वनः, हर्षोद्गारः.

EXCLUDE, *v. t.* नि-प्रति-षिध् 1 P, नि-अव-रुध् 7 U, नि-वृ c., व्या-वृत् c., (तुशब्दः पूर्वपक्षं व्यावर्तयति S. B.), बाध् 1 A, निरस् 4 U. 2 बहिष्कृ 8 U, निःसृ c., निष्कस् c., निराकृ, अपानुद् 6 P, व्यतिरिच् 7 P or c. 3 वृज् 10, त्यज् 1 P, वि-अप-हा 3 P, मुच् 6 P, अपास् 4 U. -EXCLUSION, *s.* निषेधः, व्यावर्तनं, व्यावृत्ति *f.*, व्यतिरेकः, बाधः-धः. 2 निराकरणं, निःसारणं. 3 वर्जनं, व्युदासः, हानं ; 'to the e. of' विहाय, मुक्त्वा, अतिक्रम्य, उज्झित्वा. -EXCLUSIVE, *a.* व्यावर्तक, निषेधक, निवारक, बाधक. 2 अनन्यसाधारण (णी *f.*); अनन्यसामान्य, अनन्यभुक्त ; 'e. of' विहाय, वर्जयित्वा, मुक्त्वा, हित्वा, रहित-हीन-in comp.; *See* EXCEPT. -LY, *adv.* अनन्यसाधारणं, केवलं, अन्यव्यतिरेकेण ; 'I am e. thy servant' अहं तवानन्यसाधारणो दासः (M. 4). -NESS, *s.* अनन्यसामान्या भुक्तिः.

EXCOGITATE, *v. t.* चिंत् 10, परिकॢप् c.; *See* CONSIDER. -ION, *s.* चिंतनं, परिकल्पनं.

EXCOMMUNICATE, *v. t.* (समाजात्) बहिष्कृ 8 U, निराकृ, अपास् 4 U, भ्रंश् c., च्यु c., अपांक्तीकृ; 'one e. ed' अपांक्तेयः, बहिष्कृतः. -ION, *s.* बहिष्कारः, अपांक्तेयत्वं.

EXCORIATE, *v. t.* त्वचं-चर्म-उल्लिख् 6 P or निघृष् 1 P or कृत् 6 P or छिद् 7 P, निस्त्वचीकृ 8 U. -ION, *s.* त्वक्छेदः-भेदः, चर्मक्षति *f.*-विदारणं-उल्लिखनं-पीडनं.

EXCORTICATION, *s.* निस्त्वचीकरणं.

EXCRESCENCE, *s.* गंडः, विस्फोटः, शोफः; 'fleshy e.' अधिमांसं, मांसपिंडः.

EXCRETE, *v. t.* उत्सृज् 6 P, उच्चर् c., निःसृ c., मलोत्सर्गं कृ 8 U. -ION,-EXCREMENT, *s.* विष्ठा, उच्चारः, शकृत् *n.*, पुरीषं, गूथं; *See* DUNG; 'e. and urine' विण्मूत्रं, मूत्रपुरीषं. -AL, *a.* उच्चरित, अवस्कृत, उत्सृष्ट.

EXCRUCIATE, *v. t.* अत्यंतं व्यथ् c. (व्यथयति) or बाध् 1 A or संतप् 1 P or c., प्र-मंथ् 9 P. -ING, *a.* मर्मच्छिद्-स्पृश्, अरुंतुद, प्रमाथिन्, अतिव्यथाकर (री *f.*), अतितीव्र, नितांतकठिन. -ION, *s.* तीव्रतिग्म-वेदना, अतियातना.

EXCULPATE, *v. t.* (दोषात्-अपराधात्) वि-परि-शुध् c.; वि-,मुच् 6 P or c., निर्दोषीकृ 8 U, दोषं परि-प्रमृज् 2 P or क्षल् 10; 'he e. ed himself' आत्मानं दोषमुक्तं चकार. -ED, *a.* निर्दोष, निरपराध, दोषमुक्त, विशुद्ध. -ION, *s.* दोषशोधनं-मुक्ति *f.*, अपराधक्षालनं-मार्जनं, &c. -ORY, *a.* दोषप्रमार्जक-मोचक, दोषक्षालन (नी *f.*).

EXCURSION, *s.* पर्यटनं, भ्रमणं, विहारः, विहरणं. 2 पथत्यागः-भ्रंशः, मार्गातिक्रमः, विचलनं, उत्क्रमः. 3 अभिद्रवः, आक्रमः, आपातः.

EXCURSIVE, *a.* भ्रमणशील, त्यक्तमार्ग. 2 सर्वतो धाविन्.

EXCUSE, *v. t.* क्षम् 1 A, मृष् 1 P, 10, सह् 1 A, तिज् desid. (तितिक्षते). 2 दोषाद् मुच् c. or शुध् ; 'e. a person' दोषं-अपराधं-क्षम् (with gen.); 'e. a fine' दंडं अवसृज् 6 P or मुच् 6 P; 'e. oneself' अप-व्यप-दिश् 6 P, उत्तरं दा 3 U, अपदेशं-छद्म-कृ 8 U, आत्मानं विमुच् c.; 'e. ing myself on the ground of head-ache' शिरःशूलस्पर्शनमपदिशन् (D. K. II. 2); 'e. me' प्रसीदतु भवान्. -*s.* अप-व्यप-देशः, उत्तरं, निमित्तं, छलं, छद्मन् *n.*, विमोचनहेतुः. 2 दोषक्षालनं, पापशोधनं, क्षमाप्रार्थना; oft. by हेतुः; 'under the e. of illness' अस्वास्थ्यहेतोः, अनामयापदेशेन. -LESS, *a.* निरुत्तर. 2 अक्षंतव्य.

EXECRATE, *v. t.* शप् 1 U, आक्रुश् 1 P, गर्ह् 1,

10 A, अभिक्रम् 1 P. -ION, *s.* शापः, आक्रोशः, अभिशंसनं. -EXECRABLE, *a.* गर्ह्य, गर्हणीय, अधम, नीच; *See* ACCURSED.

EXECUTE, *v. t.* अनुष्ठा 1 P, सं-निः-पद् c., कृ 8 U, वि-धा 3 U, आ-चर् 1 P, निर्वह् c., साध् 5 P or c., निर्वृत् c. ; 'e. thy business' स्वनियोगमशून्यं कुरु. 2 हन् 2 P, व्या-पद् c., प्राणदंडं-देहदंडं-आदिश् 6 P, दंड् 10; 'he was ordered to be e.-ed' तस्य वध-देह-दंड आदिष्टः, वध्यतामसौ इति आदिष्टः. -ION, *s.* अनुष्ठानं, आचरणं, विधानं, करण, संपादनं, निष्पत्ति-सिद्धि *f.*, निर्वाहः-हणं. 2 घातः, हननं, हत्या, व्यापादनं, वधः; 'place of e.' वध्यस्थानं-भूमि *f.*; 'sentence of e.' प्राणदंडः, उत्तमसाहसं. -IONER, *s.* घातकः, मातंगः, दंडपाशिकः, वध्यपुरुषः, वधाधिकृतः. -IVE, *a.* निर्वाहक, निष्पादक, विधायक, कार्यक्षम, अनुष्ठाननियुक्त, कार्यनिर्वाहक. -OR, *s.* मृतलेखाधिकारिन् *m.*, (मृतस्य) उत्तरसाधकः.

EXEGESIS, *s.* विवरणं, व्याख्यानं, व्याकरणं. -EXEGETICAL, *a.* विवरणकृत्, प्रकाशक.

EXEMPT, *v. t.* मुच् 6 P or c., मोक्ष् 10, वि-अव-सृज् 6 P, वृज् 1 P, 10 ; 'e. from fine' दंडादानं क्षम् 1 A ; 'e. from taxes' करादानं अनुज्ञा 9 U. -*a.*,-ED, *a.* मुक्त, वर्जित, हीन, रहित; oft. by अ, निर्, वि, वीत, गत, in comp.; 'e. from pride' गतावलेप, वीतदर्प, अगर्व, &c.; 'e. from avarice' निर्लोभ, वितृष्ण, लोभरहित, &c. 2 अनायत्त, अवश. -ION, *s.* मुक्ति *f.*, मोक्षः, वर्जनं, रहितत्वं, मोचनं, अभावः; oft. by अ or अन् in comp.; अनवलेपः 'e. from pride,' दंडाभावः 'e. from fine,' &c.

EXEQUIES, *See* OBSEQUIES.

EXERCISE, *s.* प्रयोगः, व्यापारः, अनुष्ठानं, आचरणं. 2 अभ्यासः, निषेवणं, अभ्यस्तता, आवृत्ति *f.*, चर्या. 3 व्यवसायः, उद्यमः, चेष्टा, उद्योगः. व्यापारः ; 'bodily e.' व्यायामः, परिश्रमः ; 'materials for taking e.' व्यायामोपकरणानि; 'military e.' रणशिक्षा, शस्त्राभ्यासः, युद्धाभ्यासः; 'shooting e.' शराभ्यासः, उपासनं ; 'usual e.' नित्यकृत्यं. -*v. t.* उप-प्र-युज् 7 A, 10, व्या-पृ c. 2 अभ्यस् 4 U; (सदा) आचर् 1 P, अनुष्ठा 1 P, आ-नि-सेव् 1 A, अनु-परि-शील् 10; आ-यस् c., व्या-यम् c.; 'e. soldiers' शिक्ष् c., रणशिक्षां दा 3 U; 'e. oneself' व्यायम् 1 P, उद्यम्, व्यव-सो 4 P, चेष्ट् 1 A ; व्यायामं-शारीरश्रमं-कृ 8 U. -*v. i.* परिश्रमं-व्यायामं-कृ; 'e. ed with an iron club' अयोदंडेन श्रममकरोत् (Ka. 76).

EXERT, *v. t.* नि-प्र-उप-युज् 7 A, 10, व्या-पृ c., प्रवृत् c.; 'e. oneself' प्रयत् 1 A, चेष्ट् 1 A, उद्यम् 1 P, व्यव-सो 4 P, प्रवृत् 1 A; 'e. one's utmost' यावच्छक्यं प्रयत्. -ION, *s.* व्यवसायः, उत्साहः, चेष्टा, व्यापारः, चेष्टितं, कर्मयोगः, यत्नः, उद्यमः, उद्योगः; *See* ATTEMPT. 2 आयासः, श्रमः, परिश्रमः, कायक्लेशः-आयासः.

EXFOLIATE, *v. i.* परिपुट् 6 P, विगल् 1 P.

EXHALE, *v. t.* उद्-गृ 6 P, उच्छ्वस् 2 P, निश्वस्, उत्क्षिप् 6 P, उद्वम् 1 P, निर्मुच् 6 P, उदीर् c., निर्गम् c. (गमयति), प्र-वा 2 P, निष्कृ 6 P, उद्गम् c. 2 (As water) आ-पा 1 P, उच्छुष् c., आचम् 1 P, बाष्पीकृ 8 U; 'trees e. ing fragrance' परिमलोद्गारिणः वृक्षाः. -ATION, *s.* उद्गारः, निश्वासः, उच्छ्वासः, उच्छ्वसितं, निर्गमः, उद्गमनं, उत्क्षेपः. 2 बाष्पः, धूमिका, धूमः. 3 बाष्पोद्गमनं, धूमोद्गारः.

EXHAUST, *v. t.* उत्-सं-शुष् c., आ-पा 1 P. 2 शून्यीकृ 8 U, निःशेषीकृ, सर्वसारं हृ 1 P, विरिच् 7 P or c. 3 क्षि 1 P, क्षै c. (क्षपयति), नश् c., व्ययं-क्षयं-कृ, अप-चि 5 U ; 'his wealth was e. ed in performing meritorious deeds' धर्मकर्माणि कुर्वतस्तस्य धनक्षयः संजातः (P. v. 1); 'who had e.-ed his whole treasure in gifts (charity)' निःशेषविश्राणितकोषजातं (R. v. 1). 4 खिद् c., क्लम् c. (क्लमयति), श्रम् c., अव-सद् c., ग्लै c. (ग्ला-ग्लपयति); 'I feel e. ed' क्लांतोस्मि, अवसन्नानि मे गात्राणि. -ED, *a.* शोषित, विरिक्त, निःशेषीकृत. 2 क्षीण, अपचित. 3 श्रांत, क्लांत, खिन्न, अवसन्न, ग्लान. -ION, *s.* शोषणं. 2 क्षयः, परिक्षयः, नाशः, व्ययः; अपचयः. 3 खेदः, श्रमः, क्लमः, ग्लानि *f.*, अवसादः, श्रांति-क्लांति *f.* -LESS, *a.* अक्षय, अनाश्य, अक्षय्य, अविनाशिन्.

EXHIBIT, *v. t.* प्र-दृश् c., प्रकाश् c., निर्दिश् 6 P, प्रकटीकृ 8 U, प्रकटयति (D.), व्यंज् 7 P or c., व्यक्तीकृ, आविष्कृ, प्र-सृ c. 2 (On the stage) प्रयुज् 7 A, 10, अभिनी 1 P; *See* ACT. -ER, *s.* प्रदर्शकः, प्रकाशकः. -ION, *s.* प्रदर्शनं, व्यंजनं, आविष्करणं, &c. 2 वृत्तिसाधनं, वृत्ति *f.* 3 अभिनयः, आविर्भावः. -IONER, *s.* वृत्तिभुज् *m.*

EXHILARATE, -ION, *See* DELIGHT.

EXHORT, *v. t.* सोत्सुकं याच् 1 A or प्रार्थ् 10 A, उप-दिश् 6 P, अनु-शास् 2 P, प्र-सं-बुध् c. 2 आ-समा-श्वस् c., प्रोत्सह् c., प्र-चुद् 10, प्रवृत् c., उद्युज् 10. -ATION, *s.* उपदेशः, उपदेशवचनं, सोत्सुकप्रार्थना, प्रबोधनवाक्यं. 2 प्रोत्साहनं, प्रेरणं, प्रचोदनं, उत्तेजनं, प्रबोधनं, समाश्वासनं, प्रवर्तनं. -ATIVE, -ATORY, *a.* प्रबोधक, उपदेशक. -ER, *s.* उपदेशकः, प्रबोधकः.

EXHUME, *v. t.* (शवं) उत्खन् 1 P. -ATION, *s.* उत्खननं.

EXIGENCE, -CY, *s.* आवश्यकत्वं, अपरिहार्यत्वं, अवश्यप्रयोजनं-कार्यं. 2 अवसरः, प्रस्तावः, समयः, कालः. 3 आपद्-विपद् *f.*, संकट-कष्ट-समयः-कालः, विपत्समयः, कृच्छ्रं, कष्टः-ष्टं, दुर्गति *f.*

EXILE, *v. t.* प्र-निर्-वि-वस् c., प्र-व्रज् c.; (स्वदेशात्)

निःसृ c., अपाकृ 8 U, बहिष्कृ. –*s.* वि-प्र-वासः-सनं, प्रव्राजनं. 2 प्रव्रजनं, दूरसंस्थिति *f.*, विवासनावधिः ; 'to go into e.' प्रव्रज् 1 P.

EXIST, *v. i.* भू 1 P, वृत् 1 A, विद् 4 A, अस् 2 P; जन् 4 A, उत्पद् 4 A. 2 जीव् 1 P, प्र-अन् 2 P. 3 स्था 1 P, प्रवृत्, आस् 2 A. –ENCE, *s.* अस्तित्वं, सत्ता, सत्त्वं, अवस्था, भावः, सद्भावः, संभवः, वर्तनं. 2 जीवितं, जीवनं, वृत्ति *f.*, प्राण-असु-धारणं ; 'worldly e.' संसारः, भवः. –ENT, *a.* सत्, विद्यमान, वर्तमान, जीविन् ; 'self-e.' आत्मभूः, स्वयंभूः.

EXIT, *s.* निष्क्रमः-मणं, निर्याणं ; अपक्रमः, अपगमः, निर्गमः. 2 (In dramas) निष्क्रांत *a.* ; 'exeunt omnes' निष्क्रांताः सर्वे.

EXONERATE, *v. t.* EXCULPATE, q. v. 2 भारं अपनी 1 P or अवतॄ c.

EXORABLE, *a.* अनुनेय, प्रसादनीय, सांत्वनीय ; 'not e.' निरनुक्रोश.

EXORBITANT, *a.* अमर्याद, अमित, अपरिमित, अतिरिक्त, सातिशय, अतिमात्र, अत्यधिक ; *See* EXCESSIVE. –EXHORBITANCE,-CY, *s.* अतिरेकः, मर्यादातिक्रमः, उद्रेकः, आधिक्यं.

EXORCISE, *v. i.* (भूतं) दूरीकृ 8 U, निःसृ c., भूतावेशाद् मुच् c. –EXORCISM, *s.* भूतापसारणं.

EXORDIUM, *s.* प्रस्तावः, वाङ्मुखं, आमुखं, मुखबंधः, उपोद्घातः.

EXOTERIC, *a.* साधारण (णी *f.*).

EXOTIC, *a.* विदेशीय, विदेशज, अन्यदेशोद्भव, वैदेशिक (की *f.*).

EXPAND, *v. t.* विस्तॄ c., प्र-वृध् c., वि-तन् 8 U, प्र-विसृ c.; 'e. itself' व्याप् 5 P, व्यश् 5 A. 2 वि-वृ 5 U, प्र-नि-काश् c., प्रपंचयति (D.). 3 (As flowers &c.) विकाश् c., वि-कस् c., भिद् 7 P or c., स्फुट् c., वि-स्फुर् c. (स्फारयति). –*v. i.* वि-प्र-सृ 1 P, प्र-,वृध् 1 A, pass. of roots above. 2 विकस् 1 P, स्फुट् 6 P, फुल्ल् 1 P, भिद् pass.; *See* BLOSSOM; विस्फुर् 6 P; 'whose boyhood gradually e. ed into youth (manhood)' क्रमाद्यौवनभिन्नशैशवः (R. III. 32); 'with his eyes e. ed through joy' हर्षोत्फुल्लनयनः. 3 विजृंभ् 1 A. —EXPANSE, *s.* प्र-वि-तानः, प्रसरः, विस्तारः, आभोगः, (आभोगस्तपोवनस्य S 1); 'in the e. of ocean' विस्तीर्णे सागरे; 'in this e. of universe' महति जगज्जाले. –ION, *s.* विस्तारः, प्रसारः, विततिः *f.*, प्रसरः, विस्तरः, प्रसरणं, व्याप्ति *f.* 2 प्रपंचः, विवरणं. –IVE, *a.* व्यापक, वि-प्र-सारिन्, विस्तारिन्; विसत्वर, विसमर.

EXPATIATE, *v. i.* Enlarge (upon), q. v. 2 परिभ्रम् 1, 4 P.

EXPATRIATE, *See* EXILE.

EXPECT, *v. t.* अपेक्ष् 1 A, उद्-दृश् 1 P; आशंस् 1 A, उदीक्ष्; प्रति-पा c. (पालयति); प्रति-इष् 6 P, प्रतीक्ष् (wait for); 'I am e. ing my brother' मम भ्रातुरागमनं प्रतीक्षे; वर्त्म अवलोकयामि (Ka. 220); सखि एष त्वां प्रतीच्छति (V. 2). –ANT, *a.* अपेक्षिन्, अपेक्षक, प्रत्याशिन्, आकांक्षिन्, सप्रत्याश. –ATION, *s.* अपेक्षा, आशा, प्रत्याशा, उदीक्षणं, आशंसा, प्रतीच्छा, प्रतीक्षा-क्षणं. –ED, *a.* अपेक्षित, आकांक्षित, समर्थित, तर्कित; 'un-e. call' अतर्किताह्वानं.

EXPECTORATE, *v. t.* (श्लेष्माणं) उद्-गॄ 6 P or निःसृ c., निष्ठिव् 1, 4 P. –ION, *s.* निष्ठ्यूति *f.*, निष्ठीवनं, श्लेष्मोद्गारः.

EXPEDIENT, *a.* युक्त, उचित, योग्य, उपपन्न, उपयुक्त, हित, हितावह. –*s.* उपायः, कल्पः, साधनं, गति *f.*, उपक्रमः, उपकरणं, योगः, गुणः; षड् गुणाः 'six e. s.' –LY, *adv.* युक्तं, उपपन्नं, यथोचितं. –EXPEDIENCY,-CE, *s.* औचित्यं, युक्तता, उपपत्ति *f.*, उपयोगः, हितावहत्वं.

EXPEDITE, *v. t.* त्वर् c. (त्वरयति), शीघ्रं संपद् c. or प्रवृत् c. or साध् c. or वि-धा 3 U. 2 शीघ्रं प्रेष् c. or प्रेर् c. –ION, *s.* त्वरा, शीघ्रता, क्षिप्रता, जवः, वेगः, अविलंबः, शीघ्रनिर्वाहणं, क्षिप्रकारित्वं. 2 यात्रा, प्रयाणं, प्रस्थानं, यानं, अभिषेणनं, अवपातः; 'to send an e.' सैन्यं प्रस्था c. (स्थापयति). 3 Enterprize, q. v. –IOUS, *a.* त्वरित, शीघ्र-क्षिप्र-कारिन्, सत्वर, अदीर्घसूत्र, अविलंबित, द्रुत, लघु. –IOUSLY, *adv.* शीघ्रं, सत्वरं, द्रुतं, &c.

EXPEL, *v. t.* Exile, q. v. 2 निष्कस् c., बहिष्कृ 8 U, अपा-निरा-कृ, निःसृ c., अपध्वंस् c., निर्धू 5, 9 U; *See* DRIVE, DISPEL. 3 (From society) अपपात्रयति (D.), अपांक्तीकृ 8 U. –LED, *a.* निष्कासित, अवकृष्ट, अपध्वस्त, निर्धूत, धिक्कृत. –EXPULSION, *s.* अपसारणं, निष्कासनं, निराकरणं; विवासनं, प्रव्राजनं.

EXPEND, *v. t.* व्यय् 10 (व्यययति), उत्-विसृज् 6 P, त्यज् 1 P, विनि-युज् 7 A, 10, प्र-उपयुज्. 2 क्षि 1 P, क्षै c. (क्षपयति), अप-चि 5 U, क्षयं-व्ययं-कृ 8 U. —EXPENSE, EXPENDITURE, *s.* व्ययः, विसर्गः, उत्सर्गः, त्यागः, विनियोगः; धनत्यागः-व्ययः, अर्थोत्सर्गः. 2 क्षयः, अपचयः, अपहारः. –IVE, *a.* बहुमूल्य, महार्ह-र्घ, बहुव्यय; बहुव्ययसाध्य, महामूल्य. –IVELY, *adv.* बहुव्ययेन, बहुमूल्येन.

EXPERIENCE, *v. t.* अनुभू 1 P, उप-भुज् 7 U, अश् 5 A, प्राप् 5 P, आसद् c., ज्ञा 9 U, विद् 2 P, परीक्ष् 1 A. 2 Suffer, q. v. –*s.* अनुभवः, परीक्षणं, वेदनं, प्रतीति *f.*, ज्ञानं, बोधः, भोगः, भुक्ति *f.* 2 बहुदर्शित्वं, अनुभवजन्यं ज्ञानं, बुद्धिपरिपाकः. 3 अभ्यासः, आचरणं. –ED, *a.* बहुदर्शिन्-, अनुभविन् (*f.* नी), बहुदृश्वन् (*f.* री); परिणतप्रज्ञ, पक्वबुद्धि, बहुदृष्ट, सानुभव;

'I am an e. teacher (of the art)' दत्तप्रयोगोस्मि (M. 1). —EXPERIMENT, *s.* प्रयोगः, परीक्षा-क्षणं, अनुभवः. —*v. t.* परीक्ष् 1 A, अनुभू 1 P; प्रयुज् 7 A, 10. —AL, *a.* अनुभवलब्ध-प्राप्त, अनुभूतिमूल. 2 परीक्षक, परीक्षार्थं कृत. —ALLY, *adv.* परीक्षणार्थं, अनुभूत्यर्थं. 2 परीक्षापूर्वं, अनुभवेन-भवात्. —ER,—ALIST, *s.* परीक्षकः.

EXPERT, *a.* दक्ष, प्रवीण, पटु, विज्ञ, निपुण, चतुर; विद्ज्ञ in comp.; विचक्षण, विशारद; *See* SKILFUL. —LY, *adv.* सपाटवं, सकौशलं. —NESS, *s.* पाटवं, कौशलं, नैपुण्यं, दक्षता, लाघवं, विज्ञता, विदग्धता, &c.

EXPIATE, *v. t.* वि-सं-परि-शुध् c., निष्कृ 8 U, निराकृ, शम् c. (शमयति), अपानुद् 6 P, प्रमृज् 2 P or c., प्रायश्चित्तेन पू 9 U or मुच् c. or शुध् c., पापनिष्कृतिं कृ. —ION, *s.* शोधनं, पावनं; प्रायश्चित्तं, पापनिष्कृति *f.* -नाशनं-विशुद्धि *f.* -क्षालनं-मार्जनं, शुद्धिः. —ORY, *a.* पावन, पापनाशक-शन, अघमर्षण (णी *f.*), विशोधक, पापघ्न (घ्नी *f.*).

EXPIRE, *v. t.* निश्वस् 2 P, श्वासं उत्क्षिप् 6 P or निर्गम् c. (गमयति). 2 उद्-गॄ 6 P; *See* EXHALE. —*v. i.* प्राणान् हा 3 P or त्यज् 1 P, मृ 6 A, उत्क्रांतवायु *a.* भू, उपरम् 1 P, संस्था 1 A; *See* DIE. 2 समाप् pass., अवसो pass., निवृत् 1 A, विरम्, अवसद् 1 P, क्षि pass. —ATION, —Y, *s.* प्राणत्यागः ; निश्वासः-सनं, उपरमः. 2 निवृत्ति *f.*, समाप्ति *f.*, विरामः, अत्ययः, क्षयः, अंतः, अवसानं, शेषः, विच्छेदः. —ING, *a.* कंठगतप्राण, आसन्नमृत्यु, मुमूर्षु.

EXPLAIN, *v. t.* व्या-ख्या 2 P, व्याचक्ष् 2 A, निरूप् 10, विवृ 5 U, द्युत् c., व्यंज् 7 P or c., स्फुटी-विशदी-कृ 8 U, व्या-कृ, प्र-वच् 2 P, प्रकाश् c., स्पष्टीकृ, प्रबुध् c. 2 वर्ण् 10, कथ् 10, प्रवद् 1 P, प्रकृत् 10. —ER, *s.* व्याख्यातृ *m.*, प्रकाशकः, प्रवक्तृ *m.*, वादिन् *m.*—EXPLANATION, *s.* व्याख्यानं, विवरणं, व्याकरणं, प्रकाशनं, स्पष्टीकरणं, विवृति *f.*, निरूपणं. 2 समाधानं, शोधनं. —EXPLANATORY, *a.* अर्थव्यंजक-द्योतक-प्रकाशक, वाचक, विवरणकृत्.

EXPLETIVE, *s.* पादपूरणं, वाक्यालंकारः.

EXPLICATE, *See* EXPLAIN.

EXPLICIT, *a.* स्पष्ट, व्यक्त, परिस्फुट, भिन्नार्थ, सुप्रकाश. —LY, *adv.* व्यक्तं, स्फुटं, स्पष्टं.

EXPLODE, *v. i.* महाशब्देन विदृ-विभिद् pass., महाशब्दपूर्वं स्फुट् 6 P, or विदल् 1 P. —*v. t.* कर्कशनिस्वनेन निंद् 1 P or असंतोषं दृश् c. or सूच् 10. 2 निरस् 4 U, खंड् 10, विलुप् c., अपा-कृ 8 U. —EXPLOSION, *s.* सशब्दभंगः-स्फोटनं, महाशब्दपूर्वं विदारणं. —EXPLOSIVE, *a.* शीघ्रदाह्य, विदारणशील.

EXPLOIT, *s.* पराक्रमः, अवदातं कर्म, आश्चर्य-अद्भुत-कर्म, विक्रमः, विचेष्टितं.

EXPLORE, *v. t.* अन्विष् 4 P, निरूप् 10, मृग् 10 A, निरीक्ष् 1 A, अनुसं-धा 3 U, मार्ग् 10. —ATION, *s.* अन्वेषणं, निरूपणं, मार्गणं, जिज्ञासा. —ER, *s.* अन्वेष्टृ *m.*

EXPORT, *v. t.* विदेशं नी 1 P or प्र-हि 5 P, बहिर्देशं प्रेर् c. or वह् 1 P or c. —*s.* निर्गतं द्रव्यं-भांडं. —ATION, *s.* विदेशनयनं, निर्गमनं.

EXPOSE, *v. t.* (lit.) उच्छद् 10, अपा-वृ 5 U, विवस्त्रीकृ 8 U, प्रकाश् c., प्रदृश् c. 2 व्यक्तीकृ, प्रत्यक्षीकृ, आविष्कृ, सत्यस्वरूपं आविष्कृ; *See* EXPLAIN also. 3 (Make liable) पदं नी 1 P or कृ 8 U, स्थानं-आस्पदं कृ; 'e. ed yourself to trouble' भवतात्मा क्लेशस्य पदमुपनीतः (S. 1); 'e. ed to the charge of cowardice' कातर इति वाच्यतां गतः-,दोषपात्रं जातः; 'e. ed to hundreds of calamities' व्यसनशतशरव्यतामुपगताः (Ka. 107); 'e. to contempt' तिरस्कारस्थानं कृ; 'e. to the sun' आतपे दा 3 U or शुष् c., आतपाय उज्झ् 6 P; 'e. for sale' क्रयार्थं प्र-सृ c. —ED, *a.* अनाच्छादित, अनावृत, &c.; 'e. for sale' क्रय्य. —ITION, *s.* विवरणं, व्याख्यानं, प्रकाशनं, स्पष्टीकरणं.—ITOR, *s.* विवृतिकारः, वृत्तिकारः, व्याख्यातृ *m.*, अर्थप्रकाशकः. —URE, *s.* विवृति *f.*, प्रदर्शनं, प्रकाशनं, व्यक्तीकरणं, स्वरूपाविष्करणं; 'e. to heat' आतपलंघनं (S. 3).

EXPOSTULATE, *v. i.* प्रत्यादिश् 6 P, (अपथात्) व्यावृत् c., निवारयितुं-निर्यंतुं उद्यम् 1 P or प्रयत् 1 A; *See* DISSUADE. —ION, *s.* प्रत्यादेशः, निवर्तनवाक्यं, निषेधः, निवारणं, प्रबोधवचनं.

EXPOUND,-ER, *See* EXPLAIN,-ER.

EXPRESS, *a.* व्यक्त, स्फुट, परिस्फुट, सुप्रकाश, भिन्नार्थ, असंदिग्ध; 'in e. terms' भिन्नार्थं, स्पष्टं. 2 विशिष्ट. —*s.* (Messenger) जंघाकारिकः, जांघिकः. 2 जंघालः, अतिजवः, प्रजविन्-वेगिन् *m.*, जवनः, त्वरितः, तरस्विन् *m.* —*v. t.* व्यंज् 7 P or c., आविष्कृ 8 U, प्रदृश् c., सूच् 10, द्युत् c., प्रकटीकृ, निर्दिश् 6 P, लक्ष् 10, प्रकटयति (D.). 2 वच् 2 P; उच्चर् c., उदीर् c., कथ् 10, शंस् 1 P, वद् 1 P, उदाहृ 1 P, व्याहृ, आ-नि-विद् c., ख्या 2 P, प्रकाश् c., बुध् c., ज्ञा c. (ज्ञापयति). अभि-धा 3 U; 'e. oneself' मनोगतं शंस्, वाचं उदीर्; 'e. by gesticulation' नट् 10, निरूप् 10, सूच्, अभिनी 1 P. 3 निष्पीड् 10, निष्कृष् 1 P, निर्दुह् 2 U, निर्हृ 1 P. —ION, *s.* व्यंजनं, प्रकाशनं, बोधनं, आ-नि-वेदनं, ज्ञापनं, आविष्करणं, कथनं, उदाहारः-हरणं. ख्यापनं. 2 निष्पीडनं, निष्कर्षणं. 3 वदनं, आस्यं; 'he had a smiling e.' हास्यवदन आसीत्; 'wore an angry e.' कुपित इव बभौ. 4 वचनं, उक्ति *f.*; वाक्यं, पदं, शब्दः, वचस् *n.*, वाच् *f.*; 'authoritative e.' आप्तवचनं, प्रमाणं. 5 रीति *f.*, मार्गः, पद्धति-सरणि *f.* —LY, *adv.* स्पष्टं, व्यक्तं, परिस्फुटं, भिन्नार्थं. —IVE, *a.* व्यंजक, वा-

चक, सूचक, द्योतक, अभिधायक, गमक, दर्शक. 2 सार्थ, साकूत, पूर्णार्थ, अर्थवत्. -IVELY, *adv.* सार्थं, साकूतं. 2 स्पष्टं, सुव्यक्तं, भिन्नार्थं, परिस्फुटं, व्यंजकतया. -IVENESS, *s.* व्यंजकत्वं, अर्थवत्ता, साकूतता.

EXPUGN, *v. t.* (दुर्गं) लंघ् 1 A, 10, वशीकृ 8 U, आक्रम् 1 U, 4 P, वि-जि 1 A.

EXPUNGE, *v. t.* वि-,लुप् c., व्या-अप-मृज् 2 P or c., व्यामृश् 6 P or c., उच्छिद् 7 P, विनश् c. -EXPUNCTION, *s.* वि-,लोपः, व्यामर्षः, उच्छेदः, नाशः.

EXPURGATE, *v. t.* पू 9 U, शुध् c, पवित्रीकृ 8 U. -ION, *s.* पावनं, शोधनं. -ORY, *a.* पावक-न.

EXQUISITE, *a.* अत्युत्तम; विशिष्ट, उत्कृष्ट, परम; *See* CHOICE; 'c. beauty' अतिमनोहरं-अतिरम्यं-लावण्यं; 'e. delight' परमानंदः. 2 सूक्ष्म. 3 तीक्ष्ण, तीव्र, उग्र (of pain). -LY, *adv.* परमं, उत्तमं, अति-परम- in comp. -NESS, *s.* विशिष्टता, उत्तमता, &c.

EXSICCATE, *v. t.* शुष् c., उच्छुष् c.; *See* DRY. -ION, *s.* उच्छोषणं, शोषः. -IVE, *a.* शोषक.

EXTANT, *a.* विद्यमान, उपलब्ध, वर्तमान.

EXTEMPORARY, -RANEOUS, *a.* तत्क्षणकृत, अचिंतितपूर्व, अयत्नकृत, अकल्पितपूर्व. 2 प्रस्तावोपयुक्त, समयोचित. -LY, -EXTEMPORE, *adv.* पूर्वचिंतां विना, अयत्नपूर्वं, पूर्वकल्पनां विना.

EXTEND, *v. t.* तन् 8 U, वि-प्र-°; विस्तृ-स्तॄ 5, 9 U or c., प्र-सृ c., आ-यम् 1 P, वृध् c., दीर्घीकृ 8 U, प्रथ् 10. 2 प्रदा 3 U, वितॄ 1 P. -*v. i.* वितन्-विस्तॄ pass., व्याप् 5 P; प्र-रुह् 1 P, आयम् pass., प्र-स-सृप् 1 P, प्रथ्-वृध् 1 A, वृत् 1 A; 'the age of man e. ed to 10,000 years' दशसहस्रवर्षायुषो नरा आसन्; 'e. as far as' ex. by आ with abl. or in comp.; 'whose sovereignty of the earth e. ed as far as the sea' आसमुद्रक्षितीशानां (R. I. 5). -EXTENSION, *s.* विस्तारः, वितति *f.*, विस्तृति *f.*, आयामः, प्रसारणं, प्रसरः, व्याप्ति *f.*, विस्तीर्णता. 2 वृद्धि *f.*, प्रपंचः, विपुलता. -EXTENSIVE, *a.* विस्तीर्ण, विपुल, प्रचुर, विशाल, पृथु, आयत, असंबाध, महत्. 2 व्यापक, व्यापिन्. -LY, *adv.* बहुशः, प्रचुरं, अतीव, अतिमात्रं, बाहुल्येन, भूयसा. -NESS, *s.* विस्तारः, &c. -EXTENT, *s.* विस्तारः, आयामः, आभोगः, विशालता, आयति *f.*, परिणाहः. 2 परिमाणं, प्रमाणं; 'the city is 100 yojanas in e.' विस्तीर्णा योजनशतं (पुरी); 'to a great e.' अतिमात्रं, अतीव; 'to some e.' कियताप्यंशेन, स्तोकं, ईषत्, मनाक्; 'to such e.' एतावत्, इयत्; 'to the fullest e.' सर्वांशेन, सर्वथा; 'to what e.' कियत्प्रमाणं, कियत्पर्यंतं.

EXTENUATE, *v. t.* Emaciate, q. v. 2 लघयति (D.), ऊन् 10, ह्रस् c., अल्पीकृ 8 U, लघूकृ, शम् c. (शमयति); प्रक्षल् 10, प्रमृज् 2 P (a crime &c.). -ION, *s.* उपशमः, लघूकरणं. 2 पापमार्जनं-प्रक्षालनं.

EXTERIOR, *a.* बाह्य, बहिःस्थ, बहिर्भव; gen. ex. by बहिः in comp. -*s.* बाहिराकारः, बाह्याकारः, बाह्यरूपं. 2 बाह्यभागः, बहिर्देशः-भागः.

EXTERMINATE, -ION, *See* ERADICATE,-ION.

EXTERNAL, *a.* बाह्य, बहिर्भव, बहिःस्थित-वर्तिन्, बहिः in comp.; 'without e. aid' विना बाह्यसाधनं, बाह्योपाधिं विना. -LY, *adv.* बहिः, बाह्यतः.

EXTINGUISH, *v. t.* निर्वा c. (वापयति); प्र-उप-शम् c. (शमयति) (as thirst &c.). 2 वि-नश् c., वि-लुप् c., अव-उत्-सद् c., उच्छिद् 7 P. -ED, EXTINCT, *a.* शांत, निर्वापित, निर्वाण. 2 नष्ट, उच्छिन्न, लुप्त, निर्गत, क्षीण, अवसन्न, निवृत्त; 'his family became e.' स निर्वंशो जातः; 'almost e.' निर्वाणभूयिष्ठ; 'to become e.' शम् 4 P, निर्वा 2 P. -MENT, EXTINCTION, *s.* निर्वाणं, निर्वापणं. 2 उच्छेदः, विलोपः, विनाशः, संहारः, क्षयः; 'final e.' निर्वाणं; मोक्षः; 'e. of family' कुलोच्छेदः, निर्वंशता.

EXTIRPATE, *See* ERADICATE.

EXTOL, *v. t.* वर्ण् 10, कृत् 10, प्रशंस् 1 P, श्लाघ् 1 A, स्तु 2 U, प्र-वि-ख्या 2 P; *See* PRAISE. -LER, *s.* प्रशंसकः, स्तावकः.

EXTORT, *v. t.* बलात्-अन्यायेन आदा 3 A or ग्रह् 9 P, दा c. (दापयति), आहृ c., निष्कृष् 1 P, बाधित्वा ग्रह्; बाध् 10, उपपीड् 10. -ER, -IONER, *s.* बलेन परस्वापहारकः, बाधकः, औपधिकः, उपपीडकः, उपद्रविन् *m.* -ION, *s.* बलादादानं, अन्यायेन परस्वापहरणं, उपद्रवः, बाधः-धा, बलात्कारः, विप्लवः. 2 हठः, बलं; 'by e.' बलात्, अन्यायेन, प्रसभं, प्रसह्य.

EXTRA, *a.*, *s.* अधिक, अतिरिक्त, अति pr.; (in comp.) ex. by व्यतिरिक्त, भिन्न, अधिक, अतिरिक्त.

EXTRACT, *v. t.* निष्कृष् 1 P, आकृष्, निः-उद्-हृ 1 P, उद्-ग्रह् 9 P; निर्दुह् 2 U, निष्कुष् 9 P, निः-सं-पीड् 10 (by squeezing); निर्गम् c. (गमयति), उत्पद् c. -*s.* रसः, निर्यासः, निर्यूहः, कषायः, निष्कर्षः, उद्धारः. 2 सारः, संग्रहः, संक्षेपः, उद्धृतभागः, निष्कर्षः, पिंडितभागः. -ION, *s.* निष्कर्षः-र्षणं, उद्धरणं, निर्हरणं. 2 कुलं, वंशः, उत्पत्ति *f.*, अन्वयः, जन्मन् *n.*, संभवः, उद्भवः; 'of high e.' अभिजात, महाकुल, कुलीन; 'of royal e.' राजवंश्य, राजकुलप्रसूत.

EXTRA-JUDICIAL, *a.* व्यवहारविषयातिक्रांत.

EXTRA-MUNDANE, *a.* अतिसंसार, लोकबाह्य.

EXTRANEOUS, *a.* बाह्य, बहिर्भव. 2 भिन्न, असंगत, व्यतिरिक्त, विदेशीय, असंबद्ध.

EXTRAORDINARY, *a.* असाधारण (णी *f.*), लोकोत्तर, असामान्य, अलोकसामान्य, अपूर्व, अद्भुत, चित्र, अदृष्टपूर्व, विलक्षण, आश्चर्य. -LY, *adv.* अपूर्वं, अद्भुतं,

चित्रं. -NESS, *s.* वैलक्षण्यं, आश्चर्यत्वं, लोकोत्तरता.

EXTRAVAGANT, *a.* अतिव्ययपर, अतिमुक्तहस्त, व्ययशील, अमितव्यय, अतिव्ययिन्. 2 अनियंत्रण, अमर्याद, अपरिमित, मर्यादातिक्रामिन्, उत्क्रांतमर्याद. -LY, *adv.* अतिव्ययेन, मुक्तहस्तेन. 2 अतिमात्रं, सातिशयं, अमितं. -EXTRAVAGANCE, *s.* अति-अमित-व्ययः, मुक्तहस्तः, धनोत्सर्गः, व्ययापरिमितता. 2 मर्यादातिक्रमः, अतिक्रमः, अतिशयः, अमितता, अत्याचारः, नियमोल्लंघनं.

EXTRAVASATED, *a.* शिरा-नाडि-बहिर्गत. -EXTRAVASATION, *s.* (Of blood!) रक्तमोक्षणं, रक्तनिर्गमः.

EXTREME, *a.* पर, परम, निरतिशय, अत्यंत, महत्, अति pr.; 'e. limit'; परमावधिः. 2 बाह्य. 3 अंत्य, अंतिम, शेष in comp. -*s.*, -ITY, *s.* परा कोटिः-काष्ठा, अत्यंतता, अतिभूमि *f.*, परमावधिः, अतिशयः. 2 अंतः-तं, पारः, पर्यंतः, अग्रं, प्रांतः, सीमा, अवधिः, उत्तमावधिः; 'this is the e. of delightful things' इयं प्रीतिजननानां सीमांतलेखा-परिसमाप्तिः-अवसानभूमिः (Ka. 124); 'e. s are ever bad' अति सर्वत्र वर्जयेत्. 3 विषमावस्था, आतिकृच्छ्रं, अत्यंतक्लेशः-दुःखं, दुःस्थिति *f.*, दुर्दशा, कष्टावस्था. -LY, *adv.* अत्यंतं. अतिभृशं; *See* EXCEEDINGLY.

EXTRICATE, *v. t.* उद्धृ 1 P, मुच् 6 P or c., मोक्ष् 10, परि-,त्रै 1 A, रक्ष् 1 P, सं-उत्-निः-तॄ c. -ION, *s.* उद्धारः, विमोचनं, मुक्ति *f.*, मोक्षः-क्षणं, निस्तारः, त्राणं, रक्षणं.

EXTRINSIC,-AL, *a.* बाह्य, बहिर्भव, असहज, आगंतुक (की *f.*). -ALLY, *adv.* बाह्यतः, असहजं.

EXTRUDE, *v. t.* उत्सृ c.; *See* DRIVE.

EXTUBERANCE, *s.* अधिमांसं, गंडः, स्फोटः, श्वयथुः.

EXUBERANT, *a.* प्रचुर, बहुल, समृद्ध, स्फीत, परिपूर्ण, उद्रिक्त, आतिरिक्त, भूरि, पुष्कल, उत्सिक्त. -LY, *adv.* प्रचुरं, बहुशः, बाहुल्येन. -EXUBERATE, *v. i.* प्रचुरीभू 1 P, वृध् 1 A, समृध् 5 P. -EXUBERANCE, *s.* प्राचुर्यं, समृद्धि *f.*; स्फीति *f.*, उद्रेकः, उपचयः, वृद्धि *f.*, अतिशयः, आधिक्यं; 'in e. of joy' हर्षनिर्भरं.

EXUDE, *v. i.* प्र-स्नु 2 P, स्विद् 1 A, 4 P; स्वेद इव प्र-स्नु 1 P or निस्यंद् 1 A. -*v. t.* (स्वेदं) निःस्नु c. or निःसृ c. 2 उद्-गॄ 6 P, उद्वम् 1 P, निष्ठिव् 1, 4 P. -ATION, *s.* प्रस्नवः, स्वेदः, स्वेदस्रावः. 2 स्रवः-वणं, स्यंदनं, निर्यासः, स्रावः. 3 निष्ठीवनं, उद्गारः, उद्वमनं.

EXULCERATE, *v. t.* व्रणं उत्पद् c., क्षतं कृ 8 U; क्षण् 8 P. -ION, *s.* व्रणोत्पत्ति *f.*, क्षतोत्पादनं.

EXULT, *v. i.* प्र-मुद् 1 A, उल्लिच् pass, अत्यंतं आनंद् 1 P or हृष् 4 P or उल्लस् 1 P. -ANT, *a.* उत्सिक्त, प्रमुदित, परमहृष्ट, उल्लसित, सगर्व, उन्मत्त, सदर्प. -ATION, *s.* प्रमोदः, उत्सेकः, उल्लासः, परमानंदः, परमाह्लादः, परमहर्षः, मदः, गर्वः, अवलेपः. -INGLY, *adv.* सप्रमोदं, सोल्लासं, सोत्सेकं, सगर्वं, सदर्पं.

EXUSTION, *s.* निर्दहनं, भस्मीकरणं.

EYE, *s.* चक्षुस् *n.*, वि-,लोचनं, नेत्रं, नयनं, अक्षि *n.*, दृश् *f.*, दृष्टि *f.*, ईक्षणं-णा, दृशा. 2 (View) दृष्टिः; 'in the e. s of the public' लोकदृष्ट्या. 3 रंध्रं, छिद्रं. 4 Bud, q. v.; 'corners of the e.' अपांगः-गं. नयनोपांतः; 'mind's e.' ज्ञानचक्षुः, मनोमयं ज्ञानं; 'before one's e. s' समक्षं, साक्षात्, प्रत्यक्षं-क्षतः; oft. by पश्यत्; 'before my very e. s' पश्यतोपि मम; 'in my e. s' मम दृष्ट्या, मां प्रति. -*v. t.* निरीक्ष् 1 A, आ-अव-लोक् 1 A, 10, दृश् 1 P; *See* SEE; 'e. pupil' तारा, कनीनिका, तारका; 'e. beam' नयन-दृष्टि-पातः; 'e.-drop' नेत्रजलं, बाष्पबिंदुः, अश्रु *n.*; 'e.-brow' भ्रूः, भ्रूलता; 'e.-glass' उपनेत्रं-नयनं; 'e.-lash' पक्ष्मन् *n.*; 'e.-let, e.-hole' गवाक्षः, छिद्रं, रंध्रं; 'e.-lid' नेत्र-नयन-च्छदः; 'e. reach (shot)' चक्षुर्विषयः, नयनगोचरः-रं, दृक्पथः; 'e.-sore' अक्षिशूलं, चक्षुःपीडा; आक्षिगतः, द्वेष्यः; 'I am an e.-sore to him' अक्षिगतोहमस्य; 'e.-wink' नयनसंज्ञा-संकेतः, कटाक्षः; 'e. witness' प्रत्यक्षसाक्षिन् *m.*, दर्शिन् *m.*, साक्षाद्द्रष्टृ *m.* -LESS, *a.* चक्षुर्हीन, अनयन, दृष्टिविकल. 2 अच्छिद्र.

F.

FABLE, *s.* कथा, आख्यायिका, उपाख्यानं, काल्पितकथा, पुरावृत्ताख्यानं, प्रबंधकल्पना. -*v.* मनसा कृप् c. or रच् 10 or सृज् 6 P. -FABULOUS, *a.* ऐतिहासिक (की *f.*), कथानिबद्ध, आख्यानकीर्तित. 2 अलीक, मनःकल्पित, मनसा सृष्ट, काल्पनिक (की *f.*), कृत्रिम. -FABULIST, *s.* कथारचकः, ऐतिहासिकः.

FABRIC, *s.* भवनं, गृहं, हर्म्यं, मंदिरं, प्रासादः, धामन् *n.*, शाला. 2 निर्माणं, रचनं. 3 ऊति *f.*, पटाकारः. 4 Cloth, q. v. —FABRICATE, *v. t.* निर्मा 3 A or 2 P or c. (मापयति), विरच् 10, कृ 8 U, कॢप् c., वि-धा 3 U, सृज् 6 P. 2 मनसा सृज् or कॢप् c., कपटेन-मिथ्या कॢप् c.; 'to f. evidence' कूटप्रमाणं निर्मा, कपटसाक्ष्यं कृ; *See* COUNTERFEIT. -ION, *s.* कपटरचना, अलीकं, कृत्रिमनिर्माणं, मनःकल्पना, कूटं. 2 निर्माणं, कल्पना-नं, रचना. -OR, *s.* निर्मातृ *m.*, रचकः. 2 कूटकृत् *m.*

FACE, *s.* मुखं, वदनं, आननं, वक्त्रं, आस्यं, तुंडं. 2 तलं, पीठं, पृष्ठं. 3 अवस्था, स्थिति *f.*, दशा; 'before one's f.' अग्रे, अग्रतः, पुरतः, समक्षं, प्रत्यक्षं, संमुखं-खे; 'long f.' विषण्णवदनं; 'f. to f.' मुखामुखि, संमुखं; 'in the f. of' अनादृत्य, अविगणय्य; *See* 'in spite of'; 'in the f. of so many difficulties' एवंविधान्यपि कृच्छ्राण्यविगणय्य; 'turn away the f.' विमुखीभू; 'stand f. to f.' संमुखी-अभिमुखी-भू. -*v. t.* संमुखयति-अभिमुखयति (D.); प्रतिमुखी-संमुखी-अभिमुखी-भू 1 P (with gen.), संमुखं स्था 1 P, अभिमुखं गम् 1 P; पर्यव-स्था 1 A. 2 संमुख-अभिमुख-प्रतिमुख- *a.* भू 1 P, or by मुख-अभिमुख in comp.; 'a house f.-ing the east' पूर्वाभिमुखं गृहं; 'stand f.-ing the east' प्राङ्मुखस्तिष्ठ; 'one who boldly f. s the enemy' अभ्यमित्र्यः; अभ्यमित्रीणः-यः. -ED, *a.* (*s.*) in comp.; 'moon-f.' चंद्रानना, इंदुमुखी. 2 पटाच्छन्न, अधिवस्त्रान्वित. -LESS, *a.* निर्मुख, आननहीन.

FACET, *s.* कणः, मुखं.

FACETIOUS, *a.* विनोदिन्, परिहासशील, नर्मप्राय, सरस, रसवत्, हास्योत्पादक, नर्म in comp. -LY, *adv.* सरसं, विनोदार्थं, परिहासपूर्वं. -NESS, *s.* परिहासशीलता.

FACILE, *a.* सुकर, सुसाध्य, अनायास; *See* EASY. 2 अनुकूल, अनुवर्तिन्. -ITY, *s.* Ease, q. v. 2 लाघवं; 'f. of hand' हस्तलाघवं, क्षिप्रता, सहजता. —FACILITATE, *v. t.* सुकर *a.* कृ 8 U, विघ्नान् अपनी 1 P or नश् c., निर्विघ्नीकृ; better ex. by words for 'Easy' q. v.; 'this will f. their communication' अनेन तेषामन्योन्यव्यवहारोऽयत्नसाध्यो भवेत्-सुकरो भवेत्. -ED, *a.* निर्विघ्न, हतप्रत्यूह, सुकरीकृत.

FACSIMILE, *s.* प्रतिलिपि *f.*, प्रतिरूपं.

FACT, *s.* तथ्यं, यथार्थता, सत्यं, तत्त्वं, भूतार्थः; 'it was a statement of f. s' भूतार्थव्याहृतिः सा (R. x. 33). 2 वृत्तं, वस्तु *n.*, अर्थः, कर्मन् *n.*; 'in fact' वस्तुतः, तत्त्वतः; 'as a matter of f.' वस्तुवृत्तेन, परमार्थतः, तत्त्वतः.

FACTION, *s.* दलं, पक्षः, शाखा. 2 भेदः, विरोधः, विप्रतिपत्ति *f.*, द्वंद्वं, द्वैधं, पक्षभेदः. —FACTIOUS, *a.* कलहप्रिय, भेदकारिन्, उपजापिन्, उपजापक, भेदिन्. 2 पाक्ष (क्षी *f.*). -LY, *adv.* सोपजापं. -NESS, *s.* उपजापः, भेदकारिता.

FACTITIOUS, *a.* कृत्रिम, कृतक, कल्पित, रचित, शिल्पनिर्मित.

FACTOR, *s.* नियोगिन् *m.*, प्रतिनिधिः; 'three is a f. of six' षट् त्रिभिर्भाज्याः.

FACTORY, *s.* शिल्प-कर्म-शाला-गृहं, पण्यनिर्माणस्थानं.

FACTOTUM, *s.* सर्वकर्मकरः.

FACULTY, *s.* शक्ति *f.*, क्षमता, प्रभावः, सामर्थ्यं. 2 अधिकारः. 3 गणः, समाजः.

FADE, *v. i.* म्लै-ग्लै 1 P, वि-शॄ pass., निर्गल् 1 P, विच्छायतां गम् 1 P, विवर्णीभू 1 P. 2 अवसद् 1 P, जॄ 4 P, नश् 4 P, क्षि pass., ध्वंस् 1 A, प्र-ली 4 A, अप-चि pass. -*v. t.* Causal of roots above. 2 तेजो हृ 1 P, वर्णं नश् c. or विलुप् c., विवर्णीकृ 8 U. -ED, *a.* नष्ट, क्षीण, अपचित. 2 म्लान, विवर्ण, विच्छाय, गतवर्ण, वीतराग. -ING, *s.* म्लानि *f.*, क्षयः, ध्वंसः, अवसादः, हानि *f.*; 'f. of colours' वर्णोच्छेदः, वर्णहानिः, वर्णिकोच्छ्रासः.

FAG, *s.* दासः, निरंतरायासिन् *m.*, श्रांतिनः. -*v. i.* Drudge, q. v.

FAG-END, *s.* अंतः, अवसानसमयः. 2 शेषः-षं, उच्छिष्टं, अवशेषः.

FAGOT, *s.* काष्ठानि (pl.); दारुखंडः, काष्ठभारः, इंधनदारु *n.*

FAIL, *v. i.* अव-वि-सद् 1 P, ध्वंस् 1 A, नश् 4 P, विलुप् pass., क्षि pass.; 'whose talent f. s not in difficulties' संकटेष्वविषण्णधीः. 2 भग्नाश *a.* भू 1 P; (of efforts) व्या-प्रति-हन् pass., व्यर्थ-मोघ *a.* भू, न सिध् 4 P, विफलीभू. 3 प्रमद् 4 P (with abl.), (स्वाधिकारात् प्रमत्तः Me. 1); विस्मृ 1P, उपेक्ष् 1 A, न आदृ 6 A. 4 न्यूनीभू, क्षि-अपचि pass. 5 विसं-वद् 1 P; 'f. s to give the fruit' फले विसंवदति (V. 2); 'a good appointment was made to f. by Fate' रमणीयोऽवधिर्विधिना विसंवादितः (S. 6). -*v. t.* त्यज् 1 P, हा 3 P; 'whose courage does not f. him' यस्य धैर्यं न हीयते, न स्खलति; 'f. ing male issue' पुत्राभावे; 'his memory f. ed him' तस्य स्मृतिलोपः संजातः. -*s.* उपेक्षा, अननुष्ठानं; 'without f.' अवश्यं, नियतं, नूनं, सुनिश्चितं, असंदेहं. -ING, *s.* दोषः, अपराधः, अगुणः, छिद्रं, न्यूनता, वैकल्यं. -*a.* मोघ, व्यर्थ; 'un-f. source' अक्षयः प्रभवः. -URE, *s.* अभावः, विरहः, लोपः, हानि *f.*, न्यूनता, वैकल्यं. 2 भंगः, अनिष्पत्ति *f.*, असिद्धि *f.* 3 अवसादः, क्षयः, ध्वंसः, नाशः, भ्रंशः, उच्छेदः, ह्रासः, क्षीणता, लोपः; 'f. of issue' संततिच्छेदः. 4 उपेक्षा-क्षणं, अननुष्ठानं, प्रमादः, उपात्ययः, अतिपातः, व्यतिक्रमः, लोपनं.

FAIN, *adv.* प्रकामं, सकामं, सानंदं; *See* GLADLY.

FAINT, *a.* अवसन्न, दीन, दुर्बल, अशक्त, शिथिलबल, निःसत्त्व, विह्वल, म्लान, ग्लान, क्लांत, खिन्न, तांत, विषण्ण; श्लथांग (गी *f.*), मुक्तगात्र, स्रस्तांग. 2 अस्पष्ट, अस्फुट, मंद. 3 (As colours) पांडु, विवर्ण, मंदप्रभ, मंदच्छाय; oft. by ईषत् or आ pr.; 'f. red' आरक्त, ईषद्रक्त; 'f.-hearted' भीरु, कातर, कापुरुष. -*v. i.* मुर्छ् 1 P, मुह् 4 P, मोहं-मूर्छां-गम् 1 P or प्राप् 5 P, चेतनां-संज्ञां-हा 3 P, नष्टचेतन-लुप्तसंज्ञ-*a.* भू 1 P. 2 ग्लै-म्लै 1 P, स्रंस् 1 A, वि-अव-सद् 1 P, क्लम् 1, 4 P, तम् 4 P. 3 प्र-ली 4 A, नश् 4 P, क्षि pass. -ING, *s.* मूर्छा, मोहः, प्र-सं-मोहः, चैतन्यसंज्ञा-लोपः-नाशः, प्रलयः, चेतनानाशः. -LY, *adv.* स्तोकं, अल्पं, ईषत्, मनाक्; मंदं, अल्पबलेन. -NESS, *s.* म्ला-ग्ला-नि *f.*, अवसादः, क्षीणता; वैवर्ण्यं, &c.

FAIR, *a.* चारु, सुंदर (री *f.*), शोभन ; *See* BEAUTIFUL; ex. by सु in comp.; 'the f. sex' स्त्रीजनः. 2 सम, न्याय्य, युक्त, उचित, धर्म्य, यथान्याय, न्यायवर्तिन्, शुचि, ऋजु, निर्व्याज, निष्कपट; विमलात्मन्, शुद्धधी; 'a f. fight' धर्मयुद्धं. 3 विमल, निर्मल, शुद्ध, विशद, स्वच्छ; गौर, शुभ्र (complexion); अनभ्र, निरभ्र, वितिमिर; 'f. day or weather' सुदिनं. 4 अनुकूल, प्रसन्न. 5 मध्यम; 'he soon bids f. to prosper' तेनाचिरादभ्युदयभाजा भवितव्यमित्यनुमीयते. —*s.* मेला, मेलकः, यात्रा, समाजः; हट्टः, निषद्या, निगमः. —*adv.*, —LY, *adv.* न्यायेन, यथान्यायं, धर्मतः, धर्मेण, निष्कपटं, न्याय्यं, यथार्हं. —NESS, *s.* सौंदर्यं, चारुता, श्रीः, शोभा. 2 (Fair dealing) सारल्यं, शुचिता, न्याय्यता, आर्जवं, अव्याजः, समता, अमाया. 3 विमलता, शुद्धि *f.*, प्रसादः.

FAITH, *s.* विश्वासः, प्रत्ययः, विश्रंभः. 2 श्रद्धा, भक्ति *f.*, निष्ठा, आस्तिक्यबुद्धि *f.* 3 अव्याजः, ऋजुता, सत्यता, विश्वास्यता. —FUL, *a.* विश्वास्य, विश्वसनीय, विश्रब्ध. 2 सत्यसंध, सत्यप्रतिज्ञ-व्रत; 'f. to promise' पालितसंगर, प्रतिज्ञापालक. 3 अनुरक्त, भक्त, दृढभक्ति, भक्तिमत्; 'a f. wife' साध्वी, एकपत्नी, पतिव्रता, सती, सुचरित्रा; 'a f. friend' दृढसौहृद-दृढप्रेम-मित्रं. 4 यथार्थ, सत्य. 5 श्रद्धालु, श्रद्धधान, प्रत्ययिन्, विश्वासिन्. —FULLY, *adv.* दृढभक्त्या, भक्तिपूर्वं, सानुरागं, निष्ठया; अव्याजं, ऋजुभावेन, निष्कपटं. —FULNESS, *s.* विश्वास्यता. 2 भक्ति *f.*, दृढाभक्तिः, अनुरक्ति-आसक्ति *f.*; आर्जवं, निष्कापट्यं. 3 प्रतिज्ञापालनं, सत्यसंधता. 4 सत्यता. —LESS, *a.* अविश्वास्य. 2 अभक्त, विश्वासघातक, भक्तिहीन, अननुरक्त. 3 असत्यसंध, भग्नप्रतिज्ञ, विसंवादिन्. 4 अविश्वासिन्, अप्रत्ययिन्, अश्रद्धधान. 5 व्यभिचारिन्; असती, असाध्वी, भग्नचारित्र्या (as a woman). —LESSNESS, *s.* अविश्वासः, अप्रत्ययः, अश्रद्धा. 2 विश्वासभंगः-घातः, अभक्तिः. 3 प्रतिज्ञाभंगः, समयव्यतिक्रमः, असत्यसंधता, व्रतलोपनं.

FALCATED, *a.* वक्र, दात्राकृति.

FALCHION, *s.* वक्रखड्गः, निस्त्रिंशः, चंद्रहासः, कृपाणः.

FALCON, *s.* श्येनः, शशादनः, पत्रिन् *m.*, खगांतकः, —ER, *s.* श्येनपालकः-पोषकः, श्येनाजीवः. —RY, *s.* श्येनपालनं-शिक्षा-पोषणं.

FALL, *v. i.* च्यु 1 A, गल् 1 P, स्रंस् 1 A, पत् 1 P, नि-अव°, भ्रंश् 1 A, 4 P; 'fell under his displeasure' तस्याकृपापात्रं-कोपास्पदं-बभूव. 2 मृ 6 A, नश् 4 P, वि-प्र-ध्वंस् 1 A, प्र-ली 4 A, प्राणैः वियुज् pass. 3 अवसद् 1 P, क्षि-अपचि pass., न्यूनीभू 1 P, ह्रस् 1 P; 'a cow f. s beneath his paw' गौस्तस्य नखपंजरे पतति, नखराक्रांता भवति; 'when the wind fell' शांते पवने. 4 दृ 1 P, प्रविश् 6 P, अवतॄ 1 P, (गंगा सागरं प्रविशति-अवतरति); 'f. foul of' संघट्ट् 1 A, आक्रम् 1 U, 4 P; वि-वद् 1 A; 'f. to the ground' ध्वंस्, (ध्वंसितस्ते उत्साहवृत्तांतः S. 2), विनश्. —*s.* पातः, पतनं, च्युति *f.*, ध्वंसः, भ्रंशः, स्रंसनं, अधः-निपतनं, अव-नि-पातः; 'in rapid f. descend' जवेन निपतंति. 2 स्थानभ्रंशः-च्युतिः, अपकर्षः, पदनाशः-भ्रंशः-च्युतिः. 3 प्र-वि-ध्वंसः, सं-उप-परि-क्षयः, अवसादः; 'rise and f.' पातोत्पाताः. 4 ह्रासः, अपचयः, न्यूनीभावः. 5 निर्झरः, प्रस्रवणं; प्रपातः, वारिप्रवाहः. 6 पातुक-प्रवण-भूमि *f.*; 'f. of snow' तुषारवर्षः, हिमच्युति *f.*; 'f. of rain' धारासंपातः, धारासारः, आसारः. —away, ग्लै-ग्लै 1 P, निर्गल्, प्र-ली, नश्. 2 स्वधर्मात् भ्रंश् or च्यु. —back, परावृत् 1 A, अप-स-सृ 1 P, अव-स्था 1 A. —in with, संगम् 4 A, अभ्युपगम् 1 P; *See* AGREE. 2 आसद् c., सहसा दृश् 1 P. —into, नि-अंतः-पत्; 'f. into vice' दुर्मार्गगामिनो भवंति ; 'f. into misfortune' विपद्ग्रस्ता भवंति. —off, च्यु, भ्रंश्. 2 अपसृ 1 P, पलाय् 1 A, वियुज् pass. 3 स्वधर्मं त्यज् 1 P, पत्. 4 ह्रासं गम् 1 P, क्षि-अपचि-संहृ-pass., ह्रस्. —on, -upon, आक्रम्, अभिद्रु, आपत्, अवस्कंद् 1 P. —out, विवद् 1 A, विप्रति-पद् 4 A, कलहं कृ 8 U. —short, न्यूनीभू, ह्रस्, क्षि-संहृ-pass.; 'his arrow fell short of its aim' स लक्ष्यच्युतसायकोभूत् ; 'words f. short in describing your greatness' तव महिमानमुत्कीर्त्य वचः संह्रियते (R. x. 32). —to, प्र-उप-क्रम् 1 A, प्रारभ् 1 A; 'they fell to blows' परस्परप्रहारमारेभिरे. —under, (power) वशं इ 2 P, अधीन *a.* भू. 2 अंतर्भू, अंतर्गण् pass.

FALLACY, *s.* वंचना, भ्रमः, मोहः, भ्रांति *f.*, मिथ्याज्ञानं, हेत्वाभासः, पक्षाभासः, मिथ्याहेतुः. —OUS, *a.* भ्रमजनक, भ्रांतिमत्, मोहिन्, मायिन् ; असत्य, अविश्वास्य, मिथ्या in comp. ; 'a f. argument' हेत्वाभासः. —OUSLY, *adv.* मिथ्या, सव्याजं, मायया.

FALLIBLE, *a.* पतन-स्खलन-शील, भ्रमशील, भ्रमाधीन, मोहशील, भ्रम-स्खलन-पात्रं. 2 भ्रमकारिन्, मोहिन्, मोहजनक. —FALLIBILITY, *s.* भ्रमपात्रता, मोहशीलता, स्खलनशीलं.

FALLOW, *a.* अकृष्ट, अहल्य, अप्रहत, खिल. 2 वंध्य, निष्फल, विफल, अनुप्तशस्य. 3 ईषद्रक्त, आरक्त, श्वेतरक्त.

FALSE, *a.* असत्य, अनृत, वितथ, अतथ्य, अयथार्थ, अलीक, मृषा-मिथ्या-in comp.; 'f. speech' मृषोद्यं. 2 कृत्रिम, कृतक, कल्पित, कूट-कपट-छद्म-in comp. ; 'f. balance' कूटतुलामानं ; 'f. ascetic' छद्मतापसः, बकव्रतः ; 'f. witness' कूट-मिथ्या-साक्षी ; 'f. accusation' मिथ्याभियोगः, अभिशापः, अभ्याख्यानं, मिथ्याभिशंसनं. 3 कापटिक (की *f.*), विश्वासघातिन्, मंत्र-रहस्य-भेदिन् ; 'f. to one's promise' लुप्तप्रतिज्ञ, असत्यसंध, भग्नप्रतिज्ञ-व्रत. 4 मा-

यिन्, दंभिन्, दांभिक-छाद्मिक (की *f.*). 5 मोघ, व्यर्थ, निरर्थक, वृथा-मिथ्या-in comp. —HOOD, *s.* अनृतं, असत्यं, वितथं, अलीकं, मृषोद्यं, कैतवं. 2 असत्यभाषणं, मिथ्या-मृषा-वादः, कैतवोक्ति *f.*, मिथ्याभिधानं, अनृतवादः. 3 असत्यता, अलीकता, अयथार्थता, अनृतता. —LY, *adv.* मृषा, मिथ्या, अन्यथा, असत्यं, अनृतं ; 'speaking f.' अनृतवादिन्. —NESS, *s.* असत्यता, &c. 2 कूटता, कापट्यं, व्याजः, छद्मन् *n.*, कैतवं. 3 विश्वासभंगः-घातः. —FALSIFY, *v. t.* मिथ्या कृ 8 U, कूटं-कपटं-कृ ; 'a. f. ed document' कूट-कृत्रिम-लेखः. 2 खंड् 10, निरा-अपा-कृ, अधरीकृ, वितथीकृ, प्रत्या-ख्या 2 P, निरस् 4 U. 3 अतिक्रम् 1 U, 4 P, अतिचर् 1 P, भिद् 7 P, उल्लंघ् 1 A, 10, वि-,लुप् 6 P or c. —*v. i.* असत्यं-अनृतं-वद् 1 P. —ER, *s.* कूटकृत् *m.*, कूटकः. 2 खंडनकृत्-प्रत्याख्यातृ *m.* —ICATION, *s.* कूटकरणं-रचना, मिथ्याकरणं.

FALTER, *v. i.* (स्वरेण) स्खल् 1 P, स्वरभंगेन or सगद्गदं-वद् 1 P; 'makes thy words f.' स्खलयाति वचनं ते (Mal. 3); 'f. ing with tears' बाष्पगद्गदं; 'a f. ing step' स्खलिता गतिः; प्रस्थानविक्लवगतेः (S. 5); 'whose step f. s &c'. 2 प्रचल् 1 P, कंप् 1 A, वेप् 1 A, प्रस्खल्. —ING, *s.* स्खलनं, स्वरभंगः-भेदः, गद्गदवाच् *f.*, स्खलद्वाक्यं. —INGLY, *adv.* गद्गदगिरा, स्खलद्वाचा, स्वरभंगेन, सगद्गदं.

FAME, *s.* यशस् *n.*, कीर्ति *f.*, ख्याति *f.*, विश्रुति *f.*, प्रसिद्धि *f.*, प्रतिष्ठा, प्र-वि-ख्यातिः, संप्रथा. —ED, —OUS, *a.* ख्यात, प्रथित, विश्रुत, प्र-वि-ख्यात, प्रसिद्ध, यशस्विन्, यशस्वत्, कीर्तिमत्, कीर्तित, लोकविश्रुत, महायशस्क, लब्धप्रतिष्ठ-वर्ण.

FAMILIAR, *a.* परिचित, संस्तुत, अभिज्ञ; ज्ञ-विद्-कुशल-in comp.; अभ्यंतर, (अनभ्यंतरे आवां मदनगतस्य वृत्तांतस्य S. 3). 2 सुविदित, सुज्ञात, लोकसिद्ध, प्राकृत, लौकिक (की *f.*), सुप्रसिद्ध, सुप्रकाश. 3 विश्रब्ध, विश्रंभ in comp. 4 निरादर, निर्गौरव, आदरहीन, निःप्रश्रय. —ITY, *s.* सु-, परिचयः; परिज्ञानं, संस्तवः; 'long f.' चिरपरिचयः; 2 सु-दृढ-संसर्गः, आसंगः, संसक्ति *f.* 3 अतिपरिचयः, अनादरः; 'f. breeds contempt'. अतिपरिचयादवज्ञा (भवति). —IZE, *v. t.* परिचयं कृ 8 U or c., अभ्यस् 4 U or c.; oft. by (*a.*); परिचितविविक्तेन मनसा (S. 5) 'with a mind f. ed to seclusion.' —LY, *adv.* सुपरिचितवत्, सुविश्रब्धं. 2 प्रायः, प्रायशः, लौकिकतया. 3 अनादरेण, निर्गौरवं.

FAMILY, *s.* कुलं, वंशः, जाति *f.*, गोत्रं. 2 कुटुंबं, पुत्रकलत्रादि, गृहजनः. 3 अन्वयः, संतानः-नं, संतति *f.*; 'members of a f.' कुटुंबिनः; 'head of a f.' कुटुंबी, कुलपतिः; 'of a good f.' कुलीन, महाकुल, अभिजात, कुल in comp.; 'his wife is in the f. way' आपन्नसत्त्वा-गर्भवती-जाता; 'of royal f.' राजवंश्य, राजकुलप्रसूत; 'f. dispute' गृहच्छिद्र, अंतर्भेदः; 'a f. man (diligently caring for the f.)' अभ्यागारिकः, उपाधिः, कुटुंबव्यापृतः.

FAMINE, *s.* दुर्भिक्षं, अनशनं, दुष्कालः, प्रयामः, नीवाकः, आहाराभावः, अनाहारसमयः; 'f.-stricken' दुर्भिक्षपीडित.

FAMISH, *v. t.* (क्षुधया) पीड् 10, अवसद् c., क्षीणी-कृशी-कृ 8 U; 'f. ed with hunger' क्षुत्क्षाम, क्षुत्क्षामकंठ. —*v. i.* अनशनाद् अवसद् 1 P or क्षि pass., क्षाम-कृशांग-*a.* भू. —ED, *a.* क्षुत्क्षाम, क्षुधार्त, क्षुत्पीडित, बुभुक्षित. —MENT, *s.* बुभुक्षा, अनाहारः, अन्नाभावः, क्षुत्पीडा, क्षुत्क्षामता.

FAN, *s.* तालवृंतः-वृंतकं, व्यजनं, वीजनं, व्यजः. —*v. t.* वीज् 10, उप-अनु-सं°; व्यजनेन विधू 5, 9 U; (fig.) उद्-दीप् c., संधुक्ष् 10.

FANATIC,—AL, *a.*, *s.* धर्मोन्मत्त, अतिश्रद्धाव्यग्र; उन्मत्त, भ्रांतबुद्धि. —ALLY, *adv.* उन्मत्तवत्, अतिश्रद्धया. —ISM, *s.* धर्मोन्मादः, भक्त्युत्कर्षः, अतिभक्तिव्यग्रता. 2 उन्मादः, उन्मत्तता.

FANCY, *s.* वासना, भावना, कल्पना, भावना-कल्पनाशक्ति *f.* 2 बुद्धि *f.*, मति *f.*, संकल्पः. 3 मनोलौल्यं, कामचारः, बुद्धिचापल्यं, चापलं, लहरी, तरंगः, छंदः. 4 रुचि *f.*, अभिरुचिः, कामः; 'to have or take a f. for' स्पृह् 10 (with dat.) or ex. by काम-मनः with inf.; स्पृहयामि खलु दुर्ललितायास्मै (S. 7); 'took a f. to hunt' मृगयां कर्तुंमना बभूव. —*v. t.* मन् 4 A, तर्क् 10, सं-वि-भू c. ; चिंत् 10, मनसा क्लृप् c., चित्ते-मनसि-कृ, आलोच् 10. 2 रुच् 1 A, अभिनंद् 1 P; 'f. ing oneself to be learned' पंडितंमन्य, पंडितमानिन्; 'doing what one f. es' कामचारिन्. —FANCIFUL, *a.* मानस (सी *f.*), काल्पनिक-मानसिक (की *f.*), मनःकल्पित, भावित, मनोरथसृष्ट-कल्पित, भावनोत्पादित, वासनाकल्पित, संकल्पज, मायामय (यी *f.*). 2 (Of persons) चलचित्त, लोलमति, कामचारिन्, चपलबुद्धि, मनोलौल्यवत्, स्वैरिन्, स्वैरवृत्त. 3 अनर्थकवासनाकृत, असंभवकल्पक. —LY, *adv.* कामचारेण, मनोलौल्यात्, स्वैरं; चापल्येन. —NESS, *s.* चलचित्तता, लोलमतिः, कामचारिता, मनोलौल्यं, बुद्धिचापल्यं, स्वैरिता.

FANE, *See* TEMPLE.

FANG, *s.* दंष्ट्रा, दशनः-नं, रदः, रदनः, दंतः; 'f. of a serpent' विषदंतः, आशी. —ED, *a.* दंष्ट्रिन्, दंतिन्. —LESS, *a.* भग्नदंष्ट्र, निर्दशन, निर्दंत.

FANTASM, *s.* आभासः, माया, मनोरथसृष्टि *f.* —FANTASTIC, *a.* Fanciful, q. v. 2 विषम, असंगत, अपरूप, विलक्षण.

FAR, *a.* दूर (with abl. or gen.), विप्रकृष्ट; *See* DISTANT; 'f. from comfort' सुखादपेत. —*adv.* दूरं-

रे, आरात् (with abl.), त्रिदूरतः. 2 अत्यंतं, भृशं, अतीव, सु-अति pr.: 'f. away' दूरे, सुदूरे; 'from f.' दूरात्, दूरतः (एव); 'how f.' कियद्दूरं, कियत्यध्वनि; कियत्प्रमाणं, कियर्यतं, कियतांशेन; 'f. off' दूर, दूरस्थ, दूरवर्तिन्, दूरस्थायिन्; 'as f. as' ex. by आ with abl. or in comp.; 'as f. as the sea' आसमुद्रात् or आसमुद्रं; oft. by यावत् (with acc.) or पर्यंत in comp; 'so far as', 'as f. as' इति; *See* under As; 'not f. from the tree' तस्य वृक्षस्य नातिदूरे; 'by f.' भूयसा; 'your statement is not f. from the truth' भूतार्थकल्पं तव वचः; 'f. gone in love' दूरगतमन्मथा (S. 3). In comp. ex. by अति, बहु, दूर; 'f.-extended' बहुविस्तीर्ण; 'f.-famed' प्रथितयशस्, उरुकीर्ति; 'f.-fetched' क्लिष्ट, यत्नकृत, असुगम, अमुकर; 'f.-reaching' दूराधिरूढ; 'f.-seeing', 'f.-sighted' दूरदर्शिन्, दीर्घदृष्टि, दूरदृष्टि.

FARCE, *s.* प्रहसनं, दुर्मल्लिका. —FARCICAL, *a.* उपहास्य, हासकर (री *f.*), हास्योत्पादक; असंगत, अपरूप, हासजनक.

FARE, *s.* अन्नं, आहारः, भक्ष्यं, भोजनं. 2 तार्यं, आता(त)रः, तारिकं, तरपण्यं-मूल्यं. —*v. i.* भू 1 P, वृत् 1 A, अस् 2 P, स्था 1 P; को वृत्तांतस्तत्रभवत्याः (M. 4) 'how f.s it with her ladyship'; 'f. ing well' सुस्थ, सुस्थित; 'f. ing ill' दुःस्थित, दुर्गत. —FAREWELL, *interj.* स्वस्ति, भद्रं (भूयात्) with dat.; 'bid f.' आमंत्र् 10 A, आप्रच्छ् 6 A.

FARINA, *s.* परागः, रजस् *n.*, पुष्परेणुः.

FARINACEOUS, *a.* धान्यमय, गोधूमचूर्णमय (यी *f.*).

FARM, *s.* क्षेत्रं, कृषिक्षेत्रं, क्षेत्रभूमि *f.*; 'f. house' क्षैत्रिकगृहं, क्षेत्रपतिगृहं; 'f. yard' क्षेत्रवाटः-टिका. —ER, *s.* क्षेत्रपतिः, क्षेत्रपालः, क्षैत्रिकः, क्षेत्राजीवः, क्षेत्रिन् *m.*, कर्षकः, कृषीवलः, कृषिकः. —ING, *s.* कृषि *f.*, कार्षिकर्मन् *n.*

FARRAGO, *s.* सन्निपातः, प्रकीर्णकं, संमिश्रणं. —FARRAGINOUS, *a.* संकीर्ण, संमिश्रित, सन्निपतित.

FARRIER, *s.* अश्ववैद्यः-चिकित्सकः. 2 अश्वपादत्रकारः. —Y, *s.* अश्वचिकित्सा.

FARROW, *s.* शूकरापत्यगणः.

FARTHER, *a.* दूरतर, दवीयस्. 2 अपर; 'the f. end' पारः, अपरप्रांतः. —*adv.* दूरतरं, अधिकदूरं. 2 अग्रे, अग्रतः, पुरः, पुरतः.

FARTHEST, *a.* दविष्ठ, दूरतम, सुदूर. —*adv.* सुदूरं, अतिदूरं-रे.

FARTHING, *s.* ताम्रमुद्रा; 'not even a f.' न काकिणी अपि, न किमपि.

FASCIA, *s.* बंधनं, वेष्टनं, पट्टः.

FASCINATE, *v. t.* मुह् c., अभिमंत्र् 10 A, अभिचर् c., मंत्रद्वारेण वशीकृ 8 U. 2 हृ 1 P, आकृष् 1 P, प्र-वि-लुभ् c., ग्रह् 9 P, रम् c. (रमयति). —ING, *a.* मोहिन्, हारिन्, हृदयग्राहिन्, मनोहर, चित्ताकर्षिन्, हृदयंगम. —ION, *s.* मोहः-हनं, सं-परि-वि-मोहनं, अभिचारः, अभिमंत्रणं, माया, इंद्रजालं, वशक्रिया. 2 आकर्षः, चित्तापहारः, चित्तविलोभनं.

FASHION, *s.* रीति *f.*, प्रकारः, विधिः, विधः, मार्गः; 'f. of dress' भूषाप्रकारः. 2 रूपं, आकारः, आकृति *f.*, मूर्ति *f.*, संस्थानं. 3 लोकाचारः, संप्रदायः, लोकमार्गः-रीतिः, लोकव्यवहारः, लौकिकव्यवहारः, लौकिकाचारः. —*v. t.* निर्मा 3 A, 2 P, वि-रच् 10, वि-धा 3 U, घट् c. (घटयति), सं-परि-क्लृप् c, तक्ष् 1, 5 P, त्वक्ष् 1 P. 2 युज् 7 U, 10, सं-समा-धा. —ABLE, *a.* लौकिक-व्यावहारिक (की *f.*), लोकाचारानुरूप, लोकव्यवहारानुसारिन्, लोकमार्गानुयायिन्. —FASHIONABLY, *adv.* लोकाचारानुरूपं, लोकरीतिवत्.

FAST, *a.* दृढ, गाढ, स्थिर, अचल, स्थावर, निश्चल, स्थायिन्, दृढबद्ध; 'f. friend' दृढसौहृदः; 'f. sleep' गाढनिद्रा, सुनिद्रा. 2 द्रुतगामिन्, त्वरितगति, शीघ्र, जविन्, जववत्, शीघ्रगति. —*adv.* दृढं, गाढं, स्थिरं; in comp. ex. by दृढ or सु; 'f. bound' सु-दृढबद्ध; 'f. rooted' बद्धमूल, सुरूढ; 'f. asleep' सुखसुप्त, गाढनिद्रां गत. 2 शीघ्रं, आशु, सत्वरं, क्षिप्रं, त्वरितं; 'not so f.' अलमलमीदृश्या त्वरया. —*v. i.* उप-वस् 1 P, आहाराद् निवृत् 1 A; 'f. to death' प्रायोपवेशनं कृ 8 U, अनशनेन मृ 6 A. —*s.*, —ING, *s.* उपवासः, अनशनं, अनाहारः, लंघनं, उपोषणं, आक्षपणं, प्रायः; 'f. ing to death' प्रायोपवेशनं. —ER, *s.* सोपवासः, कृतोपवासः. —NESS, *s.* दृढता, स्थिरता. 3 दुर्गं, कोटः. —FASTEN, *v. t.* बंध् 9 P, सं-नि°, निनह् 4 U, ग्रंथ् 9 P (together); संयुज् 7 U, 10, सं-श्लिष् c., सं-धा 3 U, योक्त्रयति (D.). 2 नि-धा 3 U, सं-वृ 5 U, निरुध् 7 U, अर्गलेन बंध्. 3 दृढीकृ 8 U, स्थिरीकृ, संस्तंभ् 9 P or c. —ING, *s.* बंधनं-नी, ग्रंथिः. 2 संधिः, कुडुपः.

FASTIDIOUS, *a.* दुस्तोषणीय, दुर्ललित, दुराराध्य. 2 सावज्ञ, अवमानिन्, उपेक्षक; 'a f. critic' दोषैकदृक्. —LY, *adv.* सावमानं, दुराराध्यतया.

FAT, *a.* पीन, पीवर, पुष्ट, मांसल, आप्यान, स्थूल, स्फीत; मेदस्विन्, पुष्टांग (गी *f.*), स्थूलदेह; 'f. land' उर्वरा. —*s.* मेदस् *n.*, वसा(शा), वपा, मांससारः-स्नेहः. —*v. t.*, —TEN, *v. t.*, आ-प्यै c., स्फाय् c. (स्फावयति), संवृध् c., पीवरीकृ 8 U, परिपुष् c. —*v. i.* आ-प्यै 1 A, पीनीभू, संवृध् 1 A, स्फाय् 1 A, उपबृंह् 1 P. —NESS, *s.* मेदस्विता, पीनता, स्थूलता, मेदोवृद्धि *f.*, स्फीति *f.* —TY, *a.* मांसल, मेदस्विन्.

FATE, *s.* दैवं, भाग्यं, भागधेयं, दिष्टं, अदृष्टं, कर्मन् *n.*, नियति *f.*, प्राक्तनं, भवितव्यता; personified f.' वि-

धि:, विधाता, कृतांत:, काल: ; 'it is our f. to do wrong' पापाचरणं दैवायत्तं-दैवाधीनं. 2 मृत्यु:, नाश:, क्षय:, अंत: ; गति *f.*, परिणाम: ; 'he met with a sad f.' शोचनीय:-कष्ट:-तस्य अंत: समजायत ; 'what was Sitā's f.' सीतादेव्या: किं वृत्तं (U. 2); 'such has been the f. of your birth' ईदृशस्ते निर्माणभाग: परिणत: (U. 4) ; 'ill-f.' दुर्दैवं, मंदभाग्यं, दैवदुर्विपाक:-विपर्यय:-विपर्यास:. -ED, *a.* नियत, दैवनियुक्त, निर्दिष्ट, भवितव्य ; 'whose f. time has come' प्राप्तकाल: ; 'ill-f.' दैवोपहत, दुर्दैव, मंदभाग्य ; 'well-f.' भाग्यवत्, धन्य, ससौभाग्य. —FATAL, *a.* प्राणहर, प्राणनाशक, जीवितापह, अंतकर, प्राणघातिन्, मृत्युजनक, दुर्विपाक, मर्मभेदिन्. 2 दैव (वी *f.*), नियत, दैवयुक्त, आवश्यक (की *f.*). -ISM, *s.* दैवपरता, दैवाधीनता. -IST, *s.* दैवपर:, दैवायत्त:, दैवपरायण:, दैवाधीन:, यद्भविष्य:, दैवप्रमाणक:. -ITY, *s.* प्राणहरत्वं ; नियति:, भवितव्यता, अवश्यकत्वं. -LY, *adv.* सनाशं, प्राणांतिकं ; 'f. wounded' तथा क्षतो यथाऽसंदिग्धो मृत्यु:.

FATHER, *s.* पितृ *m.*, जनक:, जनितृ-जनयितृ *m.*, जन्मद:, तात: ; 'f. and mother' पितरौ, मातापितरौ, मातरपितरौ. 2 गुरु:, पूज्य: ; 'f. in-law' श्वशुर: ; 'f. land' जन्म-पैतृक-भूमि *f.* -*v. t.* स्वीकृ 8 U, परिग्रह् 9 P. 2 आ-रुह् c. (रोपयति), निविश् c., (with loc.). -HOOD, *s.* पितृभाव:-धर्म:, पितृत्वं. -LESS, *a.* अपितृक, तात-पितृ-हीन, अनाथ. -LY, *a.* तात-पितृ-तुल्य, पितृनिर्विशेष; gen. by comp.; 'f. affection' पितृवात्सल्यं. -*adv.* पितृवत्, तातरूपेण.

FATHOM, *v. t.* (तलं or वेधं) परीक्ष् 1 A, निरूप् 10, मा 3 A or c. (मापयति), व्यध् 4 P; 'f. another's thoughts' मन: परीक्ष् or गाह् 1 A or निरूप्. -*s.* व्याम:, व्यायाम:. -LESS, *a.* अगाध, अतलस्पर्श, अनवगाह्य, अगम्यतल.

FATIGUE, *s.* आयास:, क्लम:, श्रम:, अवसाद:, खेद:, परिश्रम:, क्लेश:, ग्लानि-क्लांति-श्रांति *f.*, तंद्रा; 'inured to f.' श्रमसहिष्णु, जितश्रम. -*v. t.* खिद् c., आयस् c., अवसद् c., क्लम् c. or श्रम् c. (क्ल-श्र-मयति), क्लिश् 9 P, ग्लै c. (ग्ल-ग्ला-पयति). -ED, *a.* श्रांत, क्लांत, खिन्न, ग्लान, अवसन्न, श्रमार्त, सश्रम, जातखेद-श्रम; 'to be f.' श्रम् 4 P, क्लम् 1, 4 P, आयस् 1, 4 P, खिद् pass.

FATUOUS, *See* FOOLISH.

FAULT, *s.* दोष:, छिद्रं, अगुण:, अपराध:, पापं, प्रमाद:, स्खलितं, वाच्यं, वाच्यता; 'find f. with' दोषं ग्रह् 9 P, निंद् 1 P, उपा-लभ् 1 A, दुष् c. (दूषयति), (नात्र कुलपतिर्दोषं ग्रहीष्यति S. 3); 'chase, though found f. with' दृष्टदोषापि मृगया (S. 2); 'f. finder' दोषदृश्, दोषैकदृश्, छिद्रान्वेषिन्, दोषग्राहिन्, निंदक, पुरोभागिन्. -Y, *a.* सदोष, सापराध, दोषवत्, दोषिन्, निंद्य, वाच्य, अवद्य, निंदार्ह. 2 अशुद्ध, असत्य, अयथार्थ, वितथ, अनृत, मिथ्या-अपpr.; 'f. conclusion' पक्षाभास:, अपसिद्धांत:. -LESS, *a.* अ-निर्-दोष, अनवद्य, निरपराध, दोषहीन, अपाप, अनघ, अकल्मष, निष्कलंक, विशुद्ध, निर्मल, पवित्र. 2 सत्य, यथार्थ, अवितथ.

FAUN, *s.* वनदेवता.

FAVOUR, *v. t.* अनुग्रह् 9 P, उपकृ 8 U, प्रसादं-उपकारं-कृ 8 U or दृश् c., साहाय्यं दा 3 P, अभ्युपपद् 4 A; often by (*s.*); 'not inclined to f.' प्रसादपराङ्मुख; 'I wish to be f. ed with the mention of it' कथनेनानुग्राह्यमात्मानमिच्छामि (Ka. 134). 2 अनु-पा c. (पालयति), अनु-मन् 4 A, अनु-मुद् 1 A, अनुकूलयति (D.). 3 आश्रि 1 U, आ-अव-लंब् 1 A, स्वीकृ, अंगीकृ. -*s.* अनुग्रह:, प्रसाद:, आनुकूल्यं, कृपा, प्रीति *f.*, स्नेह: ; 'he is in the king's f.' स नृपप्रसादपात्रं-भाजनं. 2 आ-सं-श्रय:, साहाय्यं, अनुपालनं, अभ्युपपत्ति *f.*, आधार:. 3 हितं, उपकृतं-कार:, प्रियं, सुकृतं. 4 अनुज्ञा, अनुमति *f.*; 'in f. of' पक्षे (with gen.); 'I am speaking in your f.' अहं त्वदनुकूलं ब्रवीमि, त्वत्पक्षं समर्थये ; 'ask a f.' प्र-सद् c., उपकारं प्रार्थ् 10 A ; 'seek the f. of' आराध् c., अनुरंज् c. -ABLE, *a.* अनुकूल, प्रसन्न, हितकारिन्, हितकाम, अनुग्रहपर, हित, हितबुद्धि, उपकारक ; 'f. to' आवह, उत्पादक in comp. -ABLY, *adv.* सानुग्रहं, सानुकूल्यं, प्रसन्नतया. -ITE, *s.* प्रिय:, प्रीति-स्नेह-पात्रं-भाजनं, वल्लभ:. -*a.* प्रिय, दयित, अभीष्ट, इष्ट, दयिततम, हृद्य, वल्लभ. -ITISM, *s.* पक्षपातिता, पक्षानुग्रह:.

FAWN, *s.* मृगशाव:-वक:, मृगपोत:-शिशु:, हरिणवत्स:, कुरंगक:. -*v. i.* (upon) चाटुवचनै: आराध् c. or तुष् c., साष्टांगपातं सांत्व् 10 or उप-लल् 10, उपच्छंद् 10, छंदं अनुवृत् 1 A or अनुरुध् 4 A. -ER, *s.* चाटुकार:, सांत्ववाद:. -ING, *s.* उपलालनं, चाटूक्तिभि: आराधनं, उपच्छंदनं, चाटुवचनं. -INGLY, *adv.* चाटूक्त्या, स्तुतिपूर्वं.

FAY, *See* FAIRY.

FEALTY, *s.* अनुराग:, भक्ति *f.*, निष्ठा, प्रभुभक्ति:.

FEAR, *v.* भी 3 P, उद्विज् 6 A, सं-वि-त्रस् 1, 4 P, (with abl.). 2 वि-,आ-,शंक् 1 A, तर्क् 10. 3 भयार्त *a.* भू, त्रस्, भी ; 'do not f.' मा भैषी:. -*s.* भयं, भी:, भीति *f.*, सं-,त्रास:, साध्वसं, आशंका, दर:-रं ; 'put in f. *See* FRIGHTEN ; 'through f.' भयात्, भीत्या. -FUL, *a.* भयंकर, भयावह, भयप्रद, भीषण, भयानक, दारुण, भीम, रौद्र (द्री *f.*), उग्र, भैरव (वी *f.*), घोर, भीष्म, प्रतिभय. 2 (Afraid) भीत, सभय,ससाध्वस, भयार्त, भीरु, शंकित, साशंक, त्रस्त. -FULLY, *adv.* सभयं, सत्रासं, भयेन. 2 दारुणं, घोरं, उग्रं. -LESS, *a.* अभय, निर्भय, अभीत, नि:शंक,

निर्भीक, निर्विशंक, अभीरु, अकुतोभय ; साहसिक (की *f.*), प्रगल्भ, साहसिन्. –LESSLY, *adv.* निर्भयं, निःशंकं, साहसेन.

FEASIBLE, *a.* साध्य, शक्य, करणीय, संभाव्य, सुकर, उपपाद्य.

FEAST, *s.* उत्सवः (lit. & fig.), महः, पर्वन् *n.*, उद्धर्षः; 'f. to the eyes' नयनोत्सवः. 2 संभोजनं, विशिष्टान्नसंभारः, सहभोजनं. –*v. i.* प्रकामं भक्ष् 10; 'f. ing on grass' तृणं प्रकामं भक्षयन्. 2 उत्तमान्नेन तृप् 4 P or संतुष् 4 P. –*v. t.* भोजनविशेषैः संतृप् c. or संतुष् c. 2 (fig.) आनंद् c., प्रमुद् c.; नयनाभ्यां पा 1 P.

FEAT, *s.* अवदातं कर्म, अद्भुतं कर्म, आश्चर्यकर्म; चेष्टितं, कर्म, क्रिया.

FEATHER, *s.* पिच्छं, पक्षः, गरुत् *m.*, पत्रं, वाजः, पर्णं; 'peacock's f.' बर्हः-र्हं; 'f. of arrows' पुंखः, पत्रं, वाजः; 'f. bed' मृदुशय्या, कोमलशयनं; 'he thinks it a f. in his cap' स तदात्मनो विशिष्टगौरवपदं मन्यते. –ED, *a.* पक्षयुक्त, सपक्ष, पक्षिन्, गरुत्मत्, पत्रिन्, पतत्रिन्. –Y, *a.* पक्षतुल्य-समान.

FEATURE, *s.* रूपं, आकृति *f.*, आकारः, लक्षणं; 'inauspicious f. s' अभद्रलक्षणानि, अमंगलाकारः. 2 वदनाकृतिः, मुखरेखा, वदनाकारः. 3 (Sign) चिह्नं, लक्षणं, लिंगं.

FEBRIFACIENT, *a.* ज्वरोत्पादक.

FEBRIFUGE, *a.* ज्वरघ्न (घ्नी *f.*), ज्वरनाशक-निवारक. –*s.* ज्वरापहं औषधं.

FEBRILE, *a.* सज्वर, ज्वरित, ज्वरार्त.

FEBRUARY, *s.* माघः, फाल्गुनः, तपस्यः.

FECES, *s.* मलं, पुरीषं, विष् *f.*, उच्चारः, अप(व)स्करः, विष्ठा; *See* DUNG. 2 खलं, उच्छिष्टं, शेषं. –FECAL, *a.* विण्मय-मलमय (यी *f.*), अशुद्ध, अमेध्य. –FECULENT, *a.* समल, कलुष, अमेध्य, मलदूषित, खलिन्.

FECUND, *a.* बहुप्रज, बह्वपत्य. 2 अवंध्य, बहुफलप्रद, उर्वर (as soil). –FECUNDATE, *v. t.* सफलीकृ 8 U; रेतः सिच् 6 P. –FECUNDITY, *s.* सफलता, अवंध्यत्वं, प्रसवनं, फलवत्त्वं, स्फीति *f.*

FEDERAL, FEDERATE, *a.* संहत, संघातवत्, सामयिक-सांघातिक (की *f.*) कृतसंधि, संयुक्त, संधिसंश्लिष्ट.

FEE, *s.* शुल्कः-ल्कं, वेतनं, प्रतिफलं, उपायनं, निस्तारः, पारितोषिकं; 'monthly f.' मासिकं; 'f. simple' स्वाधीना-स्वतंत्रा-भूमिः.

FEEBLE, *a.* दुर्बल, अशक्त, शक्तिहीन, निर्बल, क्षीणशक्ति, अल्पशक्ति, अल्पबल-वीर्य-सत्त्व, क्षीण, अवसन्न, क्षाम, असमर्थ, शिथिलबल, निःसत्त्व. –NESS, *s.* दौर्बल्यं, क्षीणता, अल्पबलं, अल्पवीर्यं, तेजोहानि *f.*, वीर्यहानिः, असामर्थ्यं, अवसादः, अशक्ति *f.*, शक्तिक्षयः, सत्वनाशः, निःसत्वता. –FEEBLY, *adv.* दुर्बलतया, अल्पशक्त्या, मंदं.

FEED, *v. t.* भुज् c., अश् c., अन्नदानेन आप्यै c. or परि-पुष् c. 2 पुष् 1, 9 P or c.; सं-भृ 3 U, पा c. (पालयति), अन्नेन संवृध् c. or संतृप् c. or संतुष् c. 3 चर् c. 4 उपक्लृप् c., उपस्था c. (स्थापयति). –*v. i* (on) भक्ष् 10, अद् 2 P; *See* EAT; oft. by अशन, भुज्, in comp. ; पिशिताशनः, हुतभुक्, &c. 2 (Grass) चर् 1 P. –*s.* भक्ष्यं, भोज्यं. –ER, *s.* भोजयितृ *m.*, अन्नदाता, आशयिता. 2 पोषकः, उपकल्पकः. 3 भक्षकः, भोजिन् *m.*, अत्ता, भोक्ता, आशिन् *m.*; अद्-भुज्-आशिन्-अशन in comp. –ING, *s.* अन्नदानं, पालनं, पोषणं, भरणं. 2 भक्षणं, खादनं, भोजनं, अशनं.

FEEL, *v. t.* अनुभू 1 P, वि-भू c., (पादचारमपि न व्यभावयत् R. XI. 10), ज्ञा 9 U, उपलभ् 1 A, विद् 2 P, 10 A ; 'f. certain' दृढं ज्ञा, प्रति-इ 2 P; 'I felt his remarks much' तस्य वचो मम हृदयमर्माणि अस्पृशत्-अभिनत्. 2 (Think) मन् 4 A, गण् 10, आकल् 10; *See* CONSIDER; 'are felt by the mind as pleasant' मधुरतराण्यापतंति मनसः (K. 103). 3 स्पृश् 6 P, परामृश् 6 P, आलभ् 1 A, स्पर्शेन परीक्ष् 1 A or निरूप् 10; 'f. ing the pulse' नाडीं स्पृष्ट्वा. –*v. i.* (आत्मानं) गण्, मन्. 2 (for) अनुकंप् 1 A, समदुःख *a.* भू; 'I f. sorry for you' अहं तव कृते दुःखाकुलोस्मि; 'felt proud of his company' तत्समागमेनारूढगौरवमिवात्मानं मेने; 'I f. easy now' लब्धं मयेदानीं स्वास्थ्यं (S. 4); 'I f. better' अस्ति मे विशेषः (S. 3). –ER, *s.* स्पर्शशृंगं; 'it was intended as a f.' साधारणलोकमतज्ञानाय इदं प्रयुक्तमासीत्. –ING, *s.* अनुभवः, अनुभूति *f.*, संवेदनं, बोधः, ज्ञानं, उपलंभः, उपलब्धि *f.*, उपागमः, चैतन्यं, चेतना; संज्ञा. 2 स्पर्शः, परामर्शः, संपर्कः, स्पर्शजं ज्ञानं. 3 वृत्ति *f.*, रसः, भावः, रागः, विकारः, चित्त-मनो-वृत्तिः, मनोविकारः-धर्मः; 'f. of anger' कोपवृत्तिः. 4 कृपा, दया, अनुकंपा, करुणा, समदुःखिता; 'a man of f.' सहृदयः, सचेताः; 'what man of f. is not affected at heart' सचेतसः कस्य मनो न दूयते (K. v. 48). –*a.* चेतन, चेतनायुक्त, चैतन्य-बोध-विशिष्ट. 2 रसवत्, रागिन्, भाविक, सरस. –INGLY, *adv.* सरसं, सरागं, ज्ञानपूर्वं, स्वानुभूतिपूर्वं. 2 सदयं, सानुकंपं.

FEIGN, *v. t.* मनसा क्लृप् c. or सृज् 6 P. 2 कपटव्याज-छद्म-कृ 8 U; अप-दिश् 6 P; 'f. ing illness' शरीरास्वास्थ्यमपदिश्य; oft. ex. by कृतक, कृत्रिम, or कपट-व्याज-छद्म-मिथ्या in comp. ; 'he f. ed himself to be dead' आत्मानं मृतवत्संदर्शयामास; 'f. ing anger' कृतकं कोपं कृत्वा; 'f. ing sleep' प्रसुप्तलक्षण, व्याजसुप्त, लक्षसुप्त. –ED, *a.* व्याज-कपट-

छद्म-मिथ्या in comp.; कूटार्थ, काल्पित, कृतक, कृत्रिम; 'f. quarrel' कृतककलहः; 'a f. dress' कपटवेशः; 'f. sleep' व्याजनिद्रा; 'a f. ascetic' छद्मतापसः. -EDLY,-INGLY, *adv.* मिथ्या, सकपटं, सव्याजं, छद्मना. -ER, *s.* कापटिकः, छद्मिन् *m.*, प्रतारकः; 'f. of illness' आतुरलिंगी.

FEINT, *See* PRETEXT.

FELICITY, *s.* सुखं, श्रेयस् *n.*, परमसुखं, परमानंदः, धन्यता, सौभाग्यं, कल्याणं, प्रहर्षः; 'f. of expression' वचसां प्रौढत्वं (Mal. 1). 2 (Eternal f.) अपवर्गः, मोक्षः, निःश्रेयसं, परमा गतिः, परमपदं, मुक्ति *f.*, कैवल्यं, निर्वाणं, श्रेयस्, अमृतं. 3 सहजता, अकृत्रिमता, अनाहार्यत्वं. -OUS, *a.* श्रेयस्कर (री *f.*), अतिकल्याण, परमसुखिन्, धन्य, सुभग. —FELICITATE, *v. t.* अभिनंद् 1 P or c., दिष्ट्या वृध् c.; *See* CONGRATULATE. -ION, *s.* अभिनंदनं, धन्यवादः, कल्याणवचनं.

FELINE, *a.* मार्जारीय, बैडाल (ली *f.*).

FELL, *s.* चर्मन् *n.*, अजिनं, दृति *f.*, कृत्ति *f.* -*a.* निष्ठुर, क्रूर, दारुण, उग्र. -*v. t.* नि-अव-पत् c., अवकृत् 6 P, अवच्छिद् 7 P, नि-अव-भंज् 7 P, प्रहन्य पत् c., शद् c. (शातयाति). -ER, *s.* निपातकः, छेत्तृ *m.*

FELLOW, *s.* सहायः, मित्रं, सहचरः, अनुषंगिन् *m.*, सजुस् *m.*, सहवर्तिन् *m.*, वयस्यः. 2 समपदभाज् *m.*, तुल्यपदस्थः, सवयस्कः. 3 जनः, पुरुषः; 'this f. is bold' धृष्टोऽसौ जनः. 4 सजातीयः, सजातिः. 5 यमः, यमकः, एकतरः, युग्मकः. 6 कापुरुषः, माणवकः, जाल्मः; 'my good f.' भद्र, सौम्य. In comp. words ex. by सम-सह; 'f.-being, -creature' समानजातिः-जातीयः, सजातीयः, समभूतं ; 'f.-citizen' एकनगरस्थः, एकग्रामीणः ; 'f.-citizenship' पौरसख्यं, पौरसाहित्यं; 'f. countryman' स्वदेशजः, स्व-एक-देशीयः; 'f.-feeling' सहानुभूतिः, समदुःखत्वं, समभावः, भूतानुकंपा ; 'f.-student,-scholar' सहाध्यायः, सतीर्थः, सहाध्यायिन् *m.*, सहपाठकः; 'f.-labourer,-worker' सहकारी, संभूयकारी, सहकर्मी; 'f.-servant' सहभृत्यः, एकप्रभुः; 'f.-soldier' सहयोद्धा; 'f. sufferer' सम-सह-दुःखः-खी, समदुःखभाक, सहभोगी; 'f.-traveller' सहयायी, सहगामी; 'f. of a body' पारिषद्यः, पांक्तेयः, श्रेण्यभ्यंतरः. -SHIP, *s.* साहाय्यं, साहित्यं, संसर्गः, संगः-गमः, संघातः, संयोगः, साहचर्यं, सख्यं, मैत्री, समागमः. 2 वृत्ति *f.* 3 पारिषद्यपदं.

FELLY, *See* CIRCUMFERENCE.

FELON, *s.* साहसिकः, घोरपातकः, आततायिन् *m.*, महापापिन्-पातकिन् *m.*, महापराधिन् *m.* -OUS, *a.* आततायिन्, जिघांसु, वधोद्यत. 2 दुराचार, दुष्ट, पापिष्ठ, दुर्वृत्त, अतिनिंद्य. -Y, *s.* महापापं-पातकं, महापराधः, साहसं, आततायिता, घोरपापं.

FELT, *s.* ऊर्णा, और्णकं, ऊर्णायुः, कंबलः.

FEMALE, *s.* स्त्री, नारी; *See* WOMAN. -*a.* Ex. by the suffixes आ, ई, or वधू in comp.; 'f. sparrow' चटका; हरिणी, सिंही, चक्रवाकवधूः, &c.; 'f. friend' वयस्या, सखी, सहचरी, आलिः; 'f. apartments' अवरोधगृहं, शुद्धांतः, अंतःपुरं; 'a f. form' स्त्रीरूपं, स्त्रीसंस्थानं ; 'a f. dress' स्त्रीनेपथ्यं-वेषः.

FEMININE, *a.* स्त्रैण (णी *f.*), स्त्रीजातीय, स्त्रीधर्मन्. 2 कोमल, मृदु, पेलव, सुकुमार. 3 (In gram.) स्त्री ; 'this word is masculine or f.' अयं शब्दः पुंसि स्त्रियां वा.

FEN, *s.* अनूपः, अनूपभूः, कच्छभूः, पंकः, कर्दमः. -FENNY, *a.* जलाढ्य, सजल, पंकिल.

FENCE, *s.* वृति *f.*, आवरणं, प्राकारः, प्राचीरं, वेष्टनं, वरणः, शा(सा)लः. 2 रक्षा-क्षणं, गुप्ति *f.* -*v. t.* वृत्या रक्ष् 1 P or आ-परि-वृ 5 U or c. or परिवेष्ट् c. or अव-नि-रुध् 7 U. -*v. i.* दंडयुद्धं अभ्यस् 4 U or शिक्ष् 1 A. 2 मुष्टियुद्धं कृ 8 U, दंडादंडि युध् 4 A. -ER, *s.* असि-गदा-योधः, दंडयोद्धृ *m.* -ING, *s.* यष्टिदंड-युद्धं, आयुध-शस्त्र-विद्या. -LESS, *a.* अरक्षित, अनावृत.

FENDER, *s.* अंगारगुप्ति *f.* 2 वरूथः, रथगुप्तिः.

FENNEL, *s.* शा-सा-लेयः, छत्रा, मधुरिका.

FERACIOUS, *See* FECUND.

FERINE, *See* BEASTLY.

FERMENT,-ATION, *s.* मंडः-डं, अभिषवः, फेणः-नः, किण्वः-ण्वं, सुरामंडः, कारोत्तरः, नग्नहूः (*m.*). 2 अंतःक्षोभः-तापः-दाहः-उत्सेकः-वेगः, उत्तापः. -*v. t.* आकुलीकृ 8 U, अंतः क्षुभ् c., उत्सिच् 6 P or c., उत्तप् c., अंतर्वेगं उत्पद् c., अंतः तप् c. -*v. i.* फेनायते (D.), उत्सिच् pass., अंतः क्षुभ् 4 P or तप् 4 A, अंतस्तापं या 2 P. 2 क्षुभ्, उत्तप्.

FEROCIOUS, *a.* रौद्र (द्री *f.*), उग्र, क्रूर, अतिक्रूर, दारुण, क्रूरकर्मन्, मारात्मक, साहसिक (की *f.*); *See* GRIM, DREADFUL, also. -NESS, -FEROCITY, *s.* रौद्रता, क्रौर्यं, उग्रता, &c.

FERREOUS, *a.* लौह (ही *f.*), आयस (सी *f.*), लौहमय (यी *f.*), अयोधर्मन्.

FERRET, *s.* बभ्रुः, नकुलः.

FERRUGINOUS, *a.* लोहमलयुक्त.

FERRULE, *s.* लोहवलयः-यं, लौहरक्षणी.

FERRY, *s.* तरः, तरणस्थानं, घट्टः; 'f. boat' तरनौः, त(ता)रणः-णि *f.*, तरीः, तरालुः, उडुपः, वहित्रं; 'f.-man' तरनायकः, नाविकः, तारकः, तारणः. -*v. t.* (over) नावा तॄ 1 P or पारं गम् 1 P.

FERTILE, *a.* शस्यप्रद, उर्वर, बहुफलप्रद, बहुशस्यद, अवंध्य, स्फीत; 'f. in produce' समृद्धशस्य. 2

(Fig.) निर्माणकुशल, कल्पक, संविधायक. –ITY, –NESS, *s.* फलवत्ता, फलदता, सफलता, अवंध्यत्वं, स्फीति *f.* –IZE, *v. t.* सफल-फलप्रद-*a.* कृ 8 U, फलदीकृ, आप्यै c., स्फीतिकृ.

FERULE, FERULA, *s.* वेत्रं, दंडकाष्ठं.

FERVENT, *a.* चंड, उत्सुक, तीक्ष्ण, सातिशय, उग्र, सोत्साह, आसक्त, व्यग्र, उत्कट, उत्तप्त, उद्युक्त, सोद्योग; 'f. in piety' भक्तिव्यग्र, अतिभक्त. –LY, *adv.* सोत्साहं, साशंसं, सोत्सुकं, व्यग्रतया, औत्सुक्येन, उत्कटतया. –FERVENCY, *s.* व्यग्रता, उत्साहः, औत्सुक्यं, उत्कटता, तीक्ष्णता, चंडता, आसक्ति *f.*, मनोनिर्बंधः.

FERVID, *a.* प्रचंड, तीव्र, तीक्ष्ण, उत्तप्त, सातिशय, प्रखर, तिग्म, उग्र. –FERVOUR, *s.* प्र-,चंडता, तीव्रता, तीक्ष्णता, उत्तापः, उत्कटता, व्यग्रता; 'religious f.' अतिभक्ति *f.*, भक्तिव्यग्रता, श्रद्धोन्मादः.

FESTAL, *a.* औत्सविक (की *f.*).

FESTER, *v. i.* पूय् 1 A, पूतीभू, पक्व *a.* भू, सपूय *a.* भू.

FESTIVAL, *s.* उत्सवः, महः, पर्वन् *n.*, क्षणः, उद्धर्षः, उद्धवः, यात्रा, अभ्युदयः; 'public or general f.' यात्रोत्सवः.

FESTIVE, *a.* आनंदप्रद, सोत्सव, हर्षेण, सानंद, उत्सव in comp.; 'f. day' उत्सवदिनं. –ITY, *s.* उत्सवः, समुत्सवः, उत्सवकालः. 2 प्रमोदः, हर्षः, आनंदः, आह्लादः.

FESTOON, *s.* माला, हारः, स्रज् *f.*

FETCH, *v. t.* आहृ 1 P, उपा-आ-नी 1 P, उपा-दा 3 A. 2 निष्कृष् 1 P, उत्पद् c., स्रु c.; 'f. a deep sigh' दीर्घं निश्वस् 2 P; 'what price does the book f.' कियता मूल्येन तत्पुस्तकं विक्रीयते; 'f. up' उद्-धृ 1 P, 10; आ-सद् c.; *See* OVERTAKE. –*s.* कपटं, व्याजः, अपदेशः, उपायः.

FETE, *v. t.* तृप् c., तुष् c. –*s.* उत्सवः.

FETID, *a.* पूतिगंधि, पूत, असुगंधि, उग्रगंध, दुर्गंध.

FETOR, *s.* दुर्गंधः, पूति-उग्र-गंधः.

FETTER, *s.* निगडः-डं, बंधनं, पाशः, शृंखला-लं. –*v. t.* निगडेन बंध् 9 P, संयम् 1 P, यंत्र् 10, निगडयति (D.). –ED, *a.* निगडित, पाशबद्ध, संयत, शृंखलित, संदानित.

FETUS, *s.* गर्भः, भ्रूणः, पिंडः, कललं-लं, गर्भस्थः शिशुः.

FEUD, *s.* कलहः, कलिः, विग्रहः विरोधः, विपक्षता, द्वंद्वं, युद्धं; 'family f.' गृहच्छिद्रं, गृहरंध्रं, अंतर्भेदः.

FEUDATORY, *s.* सामंतः.

FEVER, *s.* ज्वरः (lit. & fig.), तापः, देहदाहः-तापः; 'inflammatory f.' दाहज्वरः; 'typhoid f.' संनिपातज्वरः, त्रिदोषसंनिपातः; 'ardent f.' तापोल्बणः; 'relapsing f.' मुक्तानुबंधी, संततः. –*v. t.* उत्-सं-तप् c., ज्वर् c. (ज्वरयति). –ISH, *a.* ज्वरार्त, ज्वरग्रस्त, ज्वरातुर, ज्वरपीडित, ज्वरित, सज्वर, ज्वरिन्. 2 ज्वरोत्पादक, ज्वरजनक.

FEW *a.* अल्प, कतिपय, स्तोक, परिमित, मित, अप्रचुर, अबहु; 'a f.' कतिचित्, स्तोकाः, कतिपयाः. –NESS, *s.* अल्पत्वं, स्तोकत्वं.

FIAT, *s.* आज्ञा, निर्देशः, शासनं, नियोगः, व्यवस्थापत्रं.

FIB, *See* FALSEHOOD.

FIBRE, *s.* तंतुः, सूत्रं, गुणः, तंत्रं. 2 केस(श)रः-रं, अंशुः, पक्ष्मन् *n.* 3 शिरा, नाडी, स्नसा; 'f. of a lotus' मृणालः-लं-ली, बिसं. –ED, –OUS, *a.* तंतुमत्, सूत्रिन्, केसरिन्, तंतुमय (यी *f.*), शिराल.

FICKLE, *a.* चपल, चंचल, लोल, तरल, चल, अस्थिर, अनवस्थित, अधीर; (of persons only) चलचित्त, चंचलहृदय, लोलबुद्धि, नैकभावाश्रय, प्रकृतितरल, लोल-चंचल-मति, अस्थिरबुद्धि. –NESS, *s.* चापल्यं, तरलता, लोलता, चांचल्यं, अधीरता, अस्थिरता, चलचित्तता, मनोलौल्यं.

FICTION, *s.* कल्पना, रचना, सृष्टि *f.*; मनःकल्पनासृष्टिः, मानसी सृष्टिः. 2 मिथ्याकथा, कल्पिता कथा. –FICTITIOUS, *a.* कृतक, कृत्रिम, कल्पित, असत्य, मृषार्थक, कूटार्थ, कपट-मिथ्या-कूट in comp. –LY, *adv.* मिथ्या, सकपटं, मृषा, सकूटं, सव्याजं.

FIDDLE, *s.* शा(सा)रंगी, पिनाकी. –*v. t.* सारंगीं वद् c.; 'f. stick' शारिका, कोणः, घर्षरिका.

FIDELITY, *s.* भक्ति *f.*, आसक्तता, अनुरागः, निष्कपटत्वं, विश्वास्यत्वं, स्वामि-प्रभु-निष्ठा-भक्तिः, अभेद्यता; 'f. to a husband' पातिव्रत्यं, पतिसेवा, सतीत्वं, चारित्र्यं.

FIDGET, *v. i.* चपल-चंचल-*a.* भू. –*s.* चापल्यं, चंचलता. –Y, *a.* चपल, चंचल, लोल, अशांत, अधीर; *See* FICKLE.

FIE, *interj.* धिक् (with acc.), sometimes with gen.

FIEF, *s.* क्षेत्रं, भूमि *f.*, क्षेत्रभूमिः.

FIELD, *s.* क्षेत्रं, भूमि *f.*, वप्रः-प्रं; 'a collection of f. s' कैदारकं, कैदार्यं, क्षैत्रं, कैदारिकं; 'f. of battle' रणभूमिः, रणाजिरं, रणांगनं-णं, रणं, समरभूमिः; 'f. marshal' सेनापतिः, बलाध्यक्षः, चमूपतिः, दंडनायकः, सेनानीः; 'f. sports' वनक्रीडा, अरण्य-मृगया-विहारः; 'the general took the f.' सेनानीर्युद्धाय प्रवृत्तः; 'they lost the f.' तस्मिन्युद्धे पराजिग्यिरे. 2 अवसरः, प्रसरः, स्थानं, विषयः.

FIEND, *s.* पिशाचः, राक्षसः, भूतः, वेतालः; *See* DEMON also. –ISH, –LIKE, *a.* पिशाचतुल्य, अतिदारुण, पैशाच (चा *f.*), राक्षस (सी *f.*), आसुर (री *f.*), अतिक्रूर.

FIERCE, *a.* उग्र, क्रूर, घोर, रौद्र (द्री *f.*), दारुण, भीषण, भैरव (वी *f.*); *See* DREADFUL, GRIM also. 2 तीक्ष्ण, तीव्र, चंड, प्रखर, परुष, निष्ठुर (of voice &c.). 3 संरब्ध, कोपज्वलित, क्रोधेद्ध, कोपा-

कुल, समन्यु, कोपोद्दीपित, क्रोधव्यंजक. –LY, *adv.* तीक्ष्णं, तीव्रं, उग्रं, क्रूरं, घोरं, चंडं, निष्ठुरं; सक्रोधं, संरंभेण. –NESS, *s.* क्रूरता, उग्रत्वं, रौद्रता. **2** तीक्ष्णता, चंडता. **3** संरंभः, अतिमन्युः, कोपोन्मादः, क्रोधातिशयः.

FIERY, *See* under FIRE.

FIFE, *s.* वेणुः, वंशः. –ER, *s.* वांशिकः, वेणुवादकः.

FIFTEEN, *a.* पंचदशन्; 'f.-th' पंचदश (शी *f.*).

FIFTY, *a.* पंचाशत् ; 'f.-th' पंचाश (शी *f.*), पंचाशत्तम (मी *f.*).

FIG, *s.* (Tree) अंजीरः, न्यग्रोधः, उदुंबरः ; (fruit) न्यग्रोधं, उदुंबरं, or ex. by फलं in comp.; 'I care a f. for you' न त्वां तृणायापि मन्ये-गणयामि.

FIGHT, *v. i.* युध् 4 A, विग्रह् 9 P, संप्र-हृ 1 P, संग्रामं आरभ् 1 A, वैरायते (D.), प्रति-आ-युध् (with acc.) ; 'f. a cause' कार्यार्थं युध्. –*s.*, –ING, *s.* युद्धं, रणः-णं, आयोधनं, समरः-रं, विग्रहः; *See* BATTLE. –ER, *s.* योद्धृ *m.*, युयुत्सुः.

FIGMENT, *s.* कल्पना, मिथ्या-कल्पित-कथा, मानसी सृष्टिः.

FIGURANTE, *s.* नर्तकी, लासिका.

FIGURE, *s.* आकारः, रूपं, आकृति *f.*, मूर्ति *f.* **2** कायः, देहः, विग्रहः, अंगं, गात्रं, वपुस् *n.*, (Body q. v.). **3** मूर्तिः, प्रतिमा, प्रतिरूपं-कृति *f.* **4** अंकः. **5** अलंकारः; 'f. of speech' वाक्यालंकारः. **6** रूपकं, आरोपः, लक्षणा, उपलक्षणं-णा, उपचारः. **7** प्रतिष्ठा, गौरवं, यशस् *n.*, वर्णः, कीर्ति *f.* ; *See* FAME.–*v. t.* वि-धा 3 U, विरच् 10, निर्मा 3 A, सं-परि-कॢप् c. **2** वर्ण् 10, चित्र् 10, लिख् 6 P, वि-आ°, रूप् 10, चित्रीकृ 8U, कर्बुरीकृ. **3** (To oneself) वि-भू c., चिंत् 10, कॢप् c., विगण् 10. –FIGURATE, *a.* साकार, रूपवत्, मूर्तिमत्, सरूप. —FIGURATIVE, *a.* सालंकार. **2** लाक्षणिक-औपचारिक (की *f.*), उपलक्षित; 'f. use' उपचारः. –LY, *adv.* सालंकारं, सोपलक्षणं; 'to be used f.' उपचर् pass. (with loc.) ; अचेतनेपि कूले चेतनवदुपचारदर्शनात्, तस्माचेतनवदुपचर्यते (S. B. 99, 100).

FILAMENT, *s.* केश(स)रः-रं, तंतुः, सूत्रं, पक्ष्मन् *n.*, अंशुः; 'f. of a lotus' मृणालः-लं, बिसं, किंजल्कः.

FILCH, *v. t.* मुष् 9 P, चुर् 10, अप-हृ 1 P. –ING, *s.* स्तेयं, अपहारः, चौर्यं, मोषणं.

FILE, *s.* पंक्ति *f.*, आवलि-ली *f.*, श्रेणि-णी *f.*; 'f. of an army' दंडव्यूहः, सैन्यश्रेणिः, बलविन्यासः. **2** सूत्रं, गुणः, ततुः. **3** लेख्यश्रेणी, लेख्यपत्रसमूहः. **4** व्रश्चनः, पत्रपरशुः.–*v. t.* यथाक्रमं रच् 10 or श्रेण्यां आरुह् c. **2** घृष् 1 P, मृज् 2 P. –*v. i.* व्यूहेन प्र-या 2 P.

FILIAL, *a.* पुत्रानुरूप, पुत्रयोग्य, पुत्रीय; gen. पुत्र in comp.; 'f. duty' पुत्रधर्मः; 'f. affection' पितृवात्सल्यं, पितृभक्ति *f.* –LY, *adv.* पुत्रवत्, पुत्रधर्मानुरूपं. –FILIATION, *s.* पुत्रत्वं, पुत्रीकरणं.

FILINGS, *s.* लोहचूर्णं-किट्टं, लोहजं.

FILL, *v. t.* पृ-पूृ 3 U, भृ 3 U, आ-नि-सं-चि 5 U, प्र-आ-सं-पूर् 10, आ-सं-कॄ 6 P, व्याप् 5 P, व्यश् 5 A, आवृ 5 U; better ex. by 'f. ed'; 'it f.-ed my heart with terror' तेन मम हृदयं भयसंकुल बभूव. **2** मधुरीकृ 8 U, बहुलीकृ, संपुलीकृ. –*s.* Ex. by यथेच्छं, पर्याप्तं आतृप्ति, प्र-नि-कामं; 'drank his f.' यथेच्छमपिबत्; नीवारौदनमंडं पर्याप्तमाचामति (U. 4) 'drinks his f. &c.' –ED, *a.* पूरित, पूर्ण, सं-परि-पूर्ण, आ-सं-कीर्ण, संकुल, आ-समा-कुल, व्याप्त, नि-सं-चित, आवृत, संभृत, आविष्ट, गर्भ in comp.

FILLET, *s.* पट्टः, बंधनं, वेष्टनं, बंधः (केशानां).

FILLIP, *s.* अंगुलिप्रहारः-घातः-ताडनं, छोटिका.

FILLY, *s.* किशोरी, बालतुरगी-वाजिनी-घोटिका.

FILM, *s.* पटलं, सूक्ष्मतंतुः, सूक्ष्मत्वच् *f.*, पुटः-टं; 'f. of the eye' अक्षिपटलं, अंतर्धानं. –Y, *a.* पटलावृत, सपटल.

FILTER, *v. t.* शुध् c., संमृज् 2 P, पू 9 U. –*v. i.* निर्गल् 1 P, निस्यंद् 1 A, निःसृत्य शुध् 4 P.

FILTH, *s.* मलः-लं, कालुष्यं, मालिन्यं, अव(व)स्करः, कल्कं, खलं, पंकः, कर्दमः. –Y, *a.* मलिन, कलुष, समल, मलीमस, मलदूषित, पंकिल, पंकिन्. **2** अशुद्ध, अमेध्य, अपवित्र. **3** कुत्सित, निंद्य, गर्ह्य, दूषणीय, कु-कद् pr.

FIN, *s.* पक्षः, देहधिः, वाजः (मत्स्यानां); 'f.-footed' जालपादः-द्. –LESS *a.* पक्षहीन-रहित.–FINNY, *a.* सपक्ष, पक्षविशिष्ट.

FINAL, *a.* अंतिम, अंत्य, अंत-शेष in comp., पश्चिम, चरम. **2** निःसंदेह, परिच्छिन्न, सुनिश्चित, अविकल्प, सुनिर्णीत. **3** अपरिवर्तनीय, अप्रतिकार्य. –LY, *adv.* अंततः, अंते, शेषे. **2** निरुत्तरतया, सपरिच्छेदं.

FINANCE,-S, *s.* आयः, करः, बलिः, धनागमः, शुल्कं, राजस्वं; 'his financial condition is prosperous' परिस्फीतं तस्य कोशजातं. –FINANCIER, *s.* कोशाध्यक्षः, धनाधिकारिन् *m.*

FIND, *v. t.* आप् 5 P, लभ् 1 A, अधिगम् 1 P, विद् 6 U, आ-समा-सद् c., दृश् 1 P; इ-या 2 P, (acc.), प्रतिपद् 4 A. **2** (F. out) बुध् 1 P, ज्ञा 9 U, अवगम् 1 P, अव-इ 2 P, वि-भू c.; निरूप् 10, अनुसंधा 3 U, उपलभ्, अन्विष् 4 P; निर्णी 1 P, निश्चि 5 U, अव-निर्-धृ 10; 'they found him guilty' सोपराधीति ते निर्णिन्युः, तैः सोपराधी स्थापितः. **3** उप-संकॢप् 10, चिंत् 10. **4** व्या-ख्या 2 P, व्या-कृ 8 U, व्यक्तीकृ. –ING, *s.* अधिगमः, अवाप्ति *f.* **2** निर्णयः.

FINE, *a.* सूक्ष्म, तनु, श्लक्ष्ण, अस्थूल, विरल; 'f. cloth' सूक्ष्मवस्त्रं, अंशुकं, सुवासः *n.* **2** तीक्ष्ण, तीव्र, कुशाग्रीय, मार्मिक. **3** पेलव, सुकुमार, कोमल, मृदु. **4** विशुद्ध, विमल, निर्मल. **5** परम, उत्तम, उत्कृष्ट, विशिष्ट. **6** सुंदर, कांत, शोभन, वाम, चारु, रूपवत्, सुभग, gen. by सु

in comp.; 'of f. teeth' सुदती; 'having f. eyes' सु-वाम-लोचना; 'a f. day' सुदिनं; 'f. art' कला; 'f.-fingered' लघुहस्त; 'it is a f. proposal' उदार:-प्रथम:-कल्प:. —*s.* दंड:, अर्थ-धन-दंड:; 'liable to f.' दंड्य; 'in fine' अंततः, शेषे, एतावता, एवं च. —*v. t.* दंड् 10 (two acc.), दंडं दा c. (दापयति) with instr. of giver. 2 शुध् c., पू 9 U, मलं ह or अपकृष् 1 P. —LY, *adv.* सूक्ष्मं, विरलतया. 2 चारु, सुष्ठु, सुंदरं, सु pr. —NESS, *s.* सूक्ष्मता, विरलता, तीक्ष्णता, &c. 2 कांति *f.*, शोभा, चारुता, लावण्यं. —FINERY, *s.* शोभा, आडंबर:, बाह्यशोभा. 2 अलंकार:, मंडनं, भूषणं, प्रसाधनं, आभरणं, परिकर्मन् *n.*, परिष्कार:; 'fond of f.' प्रियमंडन, अलंकारप्रिय.

FINGER, *s.* अंगुलि-ली *f.*, करशाखा; 'fore-f.' तर्जनी, प्रदेशि(श)नी; 'middle f.' मध्यमा; 'third f.' अनामिका; 'last f.' कनिष्ठा, कनिष्ठिका, कनीनीनिका; 'f.-ring' अंगुलीयं, अंगुली(री)यकं, ऊर्मिका; 'three f. s in breadth' त्र्यंगुलं (दारु). —*v. t.* अंगुल्या स्पृश् or परामृश् 6 P.

FINICAL, *a.* अतिसूक्ष्म, एकांतकोमल-पेलव, अत्युत्कृष्ट.

FINISH, *v. t.* समाप् c., सं-पू c.-पूर् 10, निर्वृत् c., अवसो 4 P, निः-सं-पद् c., साध् 5 P or c.; अंतं गम् 1 P, निः-शिष् c., निःशेषीकृ 8 U, पारं गम्. 2 संस्कृ 8 U, परिष्कृ, यत्नतः साध्. —*s.*, —ING, *s.* समाप्ति *f.*, अंत:, निर्वृत्ति *f.*, सिद्धि *f.*, अंतगमनं, &c.

FINITE, *a.* प्रमेय, परिच्छेद्य, निरूपणीय, नियत, समर्याद, परिमित, सांत; 'not f.' अनंत. —LY, *adv.* समर्यादं, नियतं.

FIR-TREE, *s.* देवदारु *m.*, *n.*, शक्रपादप:, पारिभद्रक:, भद्रदारु, द्रुकिलिमं, पीतदारु, दारु, पूतिकाष्ठं.

FIRE, *s.* अग्नि:, वैश्वानर:, ज्वलन:, अनल:, पावक:, कृशानु:, वह्नि:, दहन:, जातवेदा:, हुताशन:, शिखी, हुतभुक्, हुतवह:, बर्हि:, शुष्मा, कृष्णवर्त्मा, तनूनपात्, उषर्बुध:, शिखावान्, हव्यवाहन:, हिरण्यरेता:, चित्रभानु:, विभावसु:, शुक्र:, शुचि:, कृपीटयोनि:. 2 तेजस् *n.*, सत्वं, उत्साह:; 'on f.' अग्नि-हुतवह-परीत, अग्निदीप्त; 'submarine f.' वाडव:, और्व:, वडवानल:; 'set on f.' दह् c., दीप् c., अग्निं विसृज् 6 P (with loc.); अग्निना ज्वल् c. or दह् c.; 'take f.'; *See* under CATCH. —*v. t.* दह् 1 P, ज्वल् c., इंध् 7 A, अग्निसात्कृ 8 U. 2 उत्तिज् c., उद्दीप् c., प्रोत्सह् c., प्रचुद् 10, संक्षुभ् c., प्रेर् c., संधुक्ष् 10. —*v. i.* दीप् 4 A, ज्वल् 1 P, दह् pass. 2 लोहगोलान् प्रक्षिप् 6 P or विसृज् 6 P. 'F.-arms' आग्नेयास्त्राणि; 'f.-brand' अग्निकाष्ठं, अंगार:-रं, अलातं, उल्का, उल्मुकं; 'f.-fly' पतंग:, शलभ:, खद्योत:, ज्योतिरिंगण:, प्रभाकीट:; 'f.-pan' *See* HEARTH; 'f.-place' चुल्लि-ल्ली *f.*, अश्मंतं, उध्मानं, उद्धानं, अधिश्रयणी, अंति(दि)का; 'f.-proof' अदाह्य; 'f.-side' अग्निस्थानं, &c. (f. place); (f.-side comforts गृहसुखानि); 'f.-wood' इंधनं, इध्मं, दारुकाष्ठं; 'f.-works' अग्निक्रीडा,-द्रव्याणि. —FIERY, *a.* आग्नेय (यी *f.*), तेजस्विन्, अग्निमय (यी *f.*). 2 सुलभकोप, शीघ्रकोपिन्, क्रोधन, क्रोधिल, कोपशाल, संरंभिन्. 3 उग्र, तीक्ष्ण, प्र-,चंड, तीव्र.

FIRM, *a.* दृढ, स्थिर, निश्चल, अचल, अविचलित, अस्खलित, धीर, अकंपित, अक्षुब्ध, धृतिमत्, व्यवस्थित; 'f. step' अस्खलिता गति:. 2 गाढ, घन, दृढ, अशिथिल, अविरल, सांद्र, सुसंहत, दृढसंधि; 'of a f. mind' स्थिरधी, स्थिर-निश्चल-मति, दृढात्मन्; 'f. in friendship' दृढसौहृद, गाढसख्य. —*s.* वणिग्जनसंसर्ग:, समवाय:, संभूय समुत्थानं. —LY, *adv.* दृढं, गाढं, घनं, स्थिरं, धीरं, निश्चलं, &c.; 'f. rooted' बद्ध-रूढ-मूल; 'f. devoted' दृढभक्ति; 'f. joined' दृढबद्ध, दृढसंधि. —NESS, *s.* दृढता, स्थैर्यं, द्रढिमन् *m.*, धैर्यं, धृति *f.*; अक्षोभ:, अस्खलनं, अकंप:. 2 संहति *f.*, घनता, संधि:.

FIRMAMENT, *s.* आकाश:-शं, नभोमंडलं, नभस्तलं; व्योमन् *n.*, गगनं-णं, खं, अंतरीक्षं, तारा-उडु-पथ:, खगोल:; *See* SKY also. —AL, *a.* वैहायस (सी *f.*), आंतरीक्ष (क्षी *f.*), आकाशीय, नभःस्थ.

FIRST, *a.* प्रथम, आद्य, आदिम, पूर्व, अग्रिम, प्राक्तन (नी *f.*). 2 मुख्य, प्रमुख, प्रधान, अग्र्य, प्रवर, श्रेष्ठ, वरेण्य, अग्रणी, अग्रेसर, वर in comp.; *See* PRINCIPAL; 'f. half' पूर्वार्ध:; 'f. part of day' पूर्वाह्ण:; 'f. part of night' पूर्वरात्र:; 'for the f. time' प्रथमं; 'from the f.' प्रथमावधि, आप्रथमं; 'f. of all, in the first place' प्रथमंआदौ-तावत्; 'f.-born' अग्रज:, पूर्वज:, अग्रजन्मन् *m.*, ज्येष्ठ:, अग्र्य:, अग्रिम:; 'f.-fruits' प्रथम-आदि-अग्र-फलं, प्रथमोत्पन्नं; 'f.-rate' श्रेष्ठ, उत्कृष्ट, विशिष्टतम, परम, उत्तम. —*adv.*, —LY, *adv.* प्रथमं, पूर्वं, प्राक्, आदौ, अग्रे, पुरस्तात्.

FISCAL, *a.* धनसंबंधिन्.

FISH, *s.* मत्स्य:, मीन:, झष:, वैसारिण:, अंडज:, विसार:, शकुलिन् *m.*, पृथुरोमन् *m.* —*v. i.* मत्स्यान् ग्रह् 9 P or धृ 1 P or बंध् 9 P. 2 अनुसृ 1 P; 'f.-basket' मत्स्याधानी, कुवेणी; 'f.-hook' बडिशंशा-शी, मत्स्यवेधनं; 'f.-ing net' जालं, आनाय:, कुपिनी; 'f.-market' मीनाविक्रयस्थानं; 'f.-monger' मत्स्यविक्रयिन्; 'f.-pond' मीनाश्रय:, मत्स्यालय:, मत्स्यपूर्णं, सर:; 'f.-spawn' मत्स्यांडं; 'f. woman' मत्स्यविक्रेत्री. —ER, —ERMAN, *s.* धीवर:, कैवर्त:, दास:-श:, जालिक:, मत्स्याजीव:, मत्स्योपजीविन् *m.*, मात्स्यिक:, निषाद:. —ERY, —ING, *s.* धीवरकर्मन् *n.*, मत्स्यबंधनं-ग्रहणं.

FISSILE, *a.* भिदुर, भिदेलिम.

FISSURE, *s.* छिद्रं, रंध्रं, संधिः, भंगः, विदलः-लं, भेदः; (in the ground) बिलं, गर्तः-र्ता, विवरं. –*v. t.* वि-दृ 10, विदल् c. (दलयति).

FIST, *s.* मुष्टि *m. f.* -ष्टी; 'fisticuffs' 'blows with the f.' मुष्टिघातः-प्रहारः-युद्धं, मुष्टीमुष्टि-युद्धं; 'doubling or clenching the f.' मुष्टिबंधः-संग्राहः, खटः. –*v.* मुष्टीमुष्टि युध् 4 A, मुष्टिना तड् 10 or प्र-हृ 1 P.

FISTULA, *s.* नाडि-डी-लि-ली *f.*, नाडीव्रणं, नाडीक्षतं; 'f. in anus' भगंदरः.

FIT, *a.* योग्य, क्षम, न्याय्य, अनुरूप, उपपन्न, युक्त, उचित, यथार्ह, समुचित, यथायोग्य, संगत; oft. by अर्ह or pot. pass. part.; 'to be f. for' कृप् 1 A (with dat.), युज्-उपपद् pass.; अर्ह, उचित-योग्य-*a.* भू; 'f. to do a work' कर्मक्षम, अलंकर्मीण. –*v. t.* युज् 7 U, 10, समा-सं-धा 3 U, योग्य-युक्त *a.* कृ 8 U; 'f. an arrow' बाणं सं-धा; *See* FIX; 'this ill f. s thee' नैतदनुरूपं भवतः; 'f. out' सज्जीकृ सन्नह् c., उपकरणैः उपक्लृप् c., or संयुज् or उपस्कृ; 'fit up' Decorate, q. v. –*v. i.* युज्-उपपद्-pass., श्लिष् pass., युक्त *a.* भू; 'this f. s well' सुश्लिष्टमेतत् (Mal. 1), सुसंगतमिदं. –*s.* आक्रमः, आवेशः, अवतारः, अभिभवः; 'f. of anger' कोपावेशः; 'f. of fever' ज्वराक्रमः, ज्वराभिभवः. 2 मूर्छा, भ्रमि *f.*, भ्रामरं. –FUL, *a.* चल, चपल, चंचल, अनित्य, विषम, लोल, अस्थिर. –LY, *adv.* युक्तं, उचितं, सम्यक्, यथार्हं, सांप्रतं, स्थाने. –NESS, *s.* युक्तता, योग्यता, क्षमता, पात्रता, उपयोगिता, उपपत्ति *f.*, संगति *f.*, पर्याप्ति *f.*, याथार्थ्यं, देशरूपं.

FITCH, *s.* चणकः.

FIVE, *a.* पंचन्, पंचक, पंचतय; 'in f. ways' पंचधा;, 'f. times' पंचकृत्वः; 'f. fold' पंचगुण *a.* –FIFTH, *a.* पंचम (मी *f.*).

FIVES, *s.* कंदुकक्रीडा.

FIX, *v. t.* स्था c. (स्थापयति), प्रति-सं-°; नि-धा 3 U, निरुह् c.; 'f. your dwelling there' तत्र वसतिं कुरु, तत्स्थाने निवस. 2 स्थिरीकृ 8 U, दृढीकृ 3 (F. upon) निर्णी 1 P, निश्चि 5 U, अव-धृ 10, निरूप् 10, सं-परि-क्लृप् c., निर्दिश् 6 P, नियुज् 7 A, 10. 4 बंध् 9 P (lit. & fig.), युज्, आसंज् c., निविश् c.; 'did not f. her love on him' तस्मिन्न बबंध भावं (R. VI. 36); 'f. the eyes' दृष्टिं निविश् c., लक्षं बंध्, अनन्यदृष्ट्या-अनिमेषण-स्तिमित-लोचनेन-दृश् 1 P; 'with his eyes f.ed on my face' मन्मुखासक्तदृष्टिः; व्याप् c., उमामुखे व्यापारयामास विलोचनानि (K. III. 67); 'f. an arrow' सं-धा 3 U, (धनुष्यमोघं समधत्त बाणं K. III. 66); 'f. the mind' मनः-चित्तं-निविश् c., or युज् or बंध् or आ-धा, एकाग्र *a.* भू; तेन उपदेशेन मम चेतसि दृढं पदं चक्रे 'the advice is firmly f.ed &c.'; 'I am in a f.' चक्रांतरस्थित इवास्मि. –ED, *a.* व्यवस्थित, स्थिरीकृत, स्थापित, प्रतिष्ठित, निरूढ. 2 नियत, निश्चित, ध्रुव, स्थिर, दृढ, निश्चल, अचल; *See* FIRM. 3 सक्त, आ-सं-सक्त, सं-परि-लग्न; निविष्ट, बद्ध. 4 स्थावर, अजंगम, ध्रुव; 'firmly f.' दृढबद्ध, बद्धमूल, प्रतिष्ठित, रूढमूल; 'having the gaze f.' 'with a f. look' आसक्त-बद्ध-दृष्टि, स्तिमित-अनिमेष-लोचन; 'having the mind f. (on one thing)' एकाग्रचित्त, अनन्यमनस्क, निविष्ट-आसक्तमनस्; एकतान, अनन्यवृत्ति, एकाग्र, एकायन, एकसर्ग, एकाग्र्य, एकायनगत; 'of f. resolution' दृढनिश्चय-संकल्प, धीर-स्थिर-मति, स्थिरधी. –EDLY, *adv.* दृढं, स्थिरं, ध्रुवं, &c.: स्थिरदृष्ट्या, अनिमेषेण, स्तिमितं, एकाग्रतया, &c. –EDNESS, *s.* Firmness, q. v. –ITY, *s.* स्थिरता, स्थैर्यं, निष्ठा; 'the mind devoid of f. rambles' मनो निष्ठाशून्यं भ्रमति (Mal. 1). –TURE, *s.* स्थावरद्रव्यं.

FLAG, *s.* ध्वजः, केतुः, पताका; 'f.-staff' ध्वजदंडः-यष्टिः-स्तंभः. 2 (Stone) शिलापट्टः-प्रस्तरः. –*v. i.* अवसद् 1 P, ग्लै-म्लै 1 P, ध्वंस् 1 A, अपाच-क्षि-pass. 2 (Of persons) शिथिलबल-अवसन्न-भग्नोत्साह-*a.* भू, अंगानि मुच् 6 P; *See* DROOP. –*v. t.* शिलाभिः आस्तृ 5 U. –GY, *a.* शिथिल, क्षीण, अवसन्न, श्लथ.

FLAGELLATE, *v. t.* कशया तड् 10 or प्र-हृ 1 P or आहन् 2 U. –ION, *s.* कशाघातः, कशाप्रहारः.

FLAGEOLET, *s.* वंशः, वेणुः.

FLAGITIOUS, *a.* घोर, दारुण, अतिदुष्ट, अतिदुर्वृत्त, अति-महा-पापिन्, अतिनिंद्य. –NESS, *s.* महा-अति-पापं-पातकं, अतिदुष्टता, घोरता, दौरात्म्यं.

FLAGON, *s.* पानपात्रं-भाजनं, पृटग्रीवः, कंसः-सं.

FLAGRANT, *a.* घोर, दारुण, अतिदुष्ट, अतिनिंद्य, पापिष्ठतम. 2 सर्वज्ञात, लोकप्रसिद्ध, सुप्रकाश, सुव्यक्त, पुरःस्फुरत्. –FLAGRANCY, *s.* घोरता, अतिदुष्टता; सुव्यक्तता.

FLAIL, *s.* मुसलः-लं, कंडनी.

FLAKE, *s.* हिम-तुषार-लवः-कणः, हिमतूलं, तुषार-हिमघनः. 2 शकलः-लं, लवः, कणः, अल्पभागः. 3 फलकः, संस्तरः. –*v. i.* शकलीभू 1 P. –Y, *a.* सशकल.

FLAMBEAU, *s.* उल्का, अलातं, उन्मुकं.

FLAME, *s.* ज्वाला, शिखा, अर्चिस् *f.*, *n.*, कीलः-ला, अग्निज्वाला-जिह्वा; 'in f. s' ज्वलत्, हुतवहपरीत, दह्यमान. –*v. t.* ज्वल् c., दीप् c., दह् c. –*v. i.* ज्वल् 1 P, दीप् 4 A, दह् pass. –ING, *a.* उज्ज्वल, प्रदीप्त, अर्चिष्मत्, उज्ज्वल, ज्वलित, ज्वलत्; 'f. fire' ज्वालाभिः. –Y, *a.* शिखा-ज्वाला-मय (यी *f.*), शिखिन्.

FLAMINGO, *s.* मरालः, राजहंसः.

FLANK, *s.* पार्श्वः-र्श्वं, पक्षः, कुक्षिः, उत्संगः, पार्श्व-पक्ष-भागः, पार्श्वांगं. –*v.* पार्श्वतः रक्ष् or गुप् 1 P. 2 पार्श्वतः अभिद्रु 1 P. 3 स्पृश् 6 P, निकटे-पार्श्वे-वृत् 1 A; *See* BORDER.

FLANNEL, *s.* ऊर्णांशुः, और्णपटं.

FLAP, *v. t.* वि-धू 5, 9 U, 6 P, उत्क्षिप् 6 P, चल् c., आ-स्फल् c. –*v. i.* आस्फल् 1 P, विधू-उत्क्षिप्-pass. –*s.* प्रालंबः, लोलकः. 2 (f. ing) आस्फालनं, विधूननं, विधुवनं, उत्क्षेपः-पणं; 'f. ing of ears' कर्णतालः.

FLARE, *v. i.* लोलशिखया ज्वल् 1 P. –*s.* लोलशिखा, कंपितज्वाला.

FLASH, *v. i.* स्फुर् 6 P, दीप् 4 A, वि-लस् 1 P, विद्युत् 1 A, सहसा प्रकाश् 1 A or ज्वल् 1 P, अचिरं प्र-भा 2 P. 2 विद्युद्वेगेन-अकस्माद्-उदि 2 P or आविर्भू 1 P or उत्पद् 4 A. –*s.* स्फुरणं, स्फुरितं, विलासः, सहसा दीप्ति *f.*, आभासः, विभ्रमः, अचिर-क्षण-प्रभा, प्रभाकंपः, क्षणद्युति *f.*, अचिरद्युतिः. –Y, *a.* क्षणप्रभ, तैजस (सी *f.*). 2 असार, नीरस, फल्गु, निःसत्त्व.

FLASK, *s.* काचपात्रं-भाजनं, पानपात्रं, पुटग्रीवः.

FLAT, *a.* सम, समस्थ, समरेख, सपाट, अभुग्न. 2 निम्न, अनुच्च, नत, अनुन्नत. 3 असार, नीरस, फल्गु, विरस, रस-स्वाद-हीन, निस्तेजस्, निःसत्त्व. 4 स्पष्ट, स्फुट, व्यक्त, अवक्र, असंदिग्ध, सुव्यक्त, परिस्फुट. 5 अवानि गत, दंडवत् क्षित; 'he laid himself f. on the ground' भूमौ दंडवत्पतितः; 'f. surface' समपृष्ठं; 'f. roof' पृष्ठं; 'f.-nosed' अवनाट, अवटीट, अवभ्रट, नत-चिपिट-नासिक. –*s.* समभूमि *f.*, समस्थली, समस्थानं, पाटः. 2 निम्नभूमिः. 3 सैकतं, पुलिनं. 4 पत्रं, फलकः-कं. 5 मंदः, अनुदात्तः, मंद्रः. –LY, *adv.* समं. 2 स्फुटं, सुव्यक्तं, अवक्रं, असंदेहं. –NESS, *s.* समता, निम्नता, असारत्वं, &c. –TEN, *v. t.* समीकृ 8 U. 2 आ-अव-नम् c. (नमयति), नम्रीकृ, निम्नीकृ. 3 रसं हृ 1 P, नीरसीकृ–*v. i.* समीभू, नम्रीभू.

FLATTER, *v. t.* सं-अभि-परि-स्तु 2 U, प्र-शंस् 1 P, चाटुवचनैः-स्तुत्या-सांत्व् 10 or संतुष् c. or उप-लल् 10 or प्र-लुभ् c. or आकृष् 1 P, उपच्छंद् 10. 2 चाटूनि वच्-ब्रू 2 P, प्रियं वद् 1 P. 3 अनु-नी 1 P, आ-राध् c., मिथ्या प्रशंस् or श्लाघ् 1 A. 4 मिथ्या आशां उत्पद् c. or वृध् c. –ER, *s.* चाटुकारः, संस्तावकः, सांत्ववादिन् *m.*, प्रशंसकः, प्रियंवदः, चाटुवादी, मिथ्याशंसकः. –ING, *a.* स्तुतिमय (यी *f.*), परितोषक, प्रीतिकर (री *f.*), प्रशंसामय.–INGLY, *adv.* चाटूक्त्या, अतिप्रशंसापूर्वं, सांत्वनपूर्वं. –Y, *s.* संस्तावः, स्तुति *f.*, स्तवः, चाटु *m. n.*, चाटूक्ति *f.*, अतिप्रशंसा, सांत्वनं-ना, उपलालनं, मधुर-प्रिय-वचनं, सांत्ववादः, मिथ्याप्र 'सा, व्याजस्तुतिः, चाटुवादः. 2 अनुनयः, आराधनं, संतोषणं.

FLATULENT, *a.* वात-वायु-ग्रस्त, बद्धवात, वातफुल्ल, वायुपूर्ण, वातुल. –FLATULENCE, –CY, *s.* वायुः, वातः, वायुफुल्लता, अंत्राध्मानं, वातिकत्वं.

FLATUS, *s.* वातः, वायुः, अंत्रवायुः.

FLAUNT, *v. i.* सावलेपं चल्-चर् 1 P, सदर्पं-उद्धतं-विकटं-परिक्रम् 1 U, 4 P. –ING, *a.* उद्धतगति, विलासाढ्य, मंदगामिन्, दर्शनीयमानिन्, सुभगंमन्य; 'a f. gait' विकटा-धीरोद्धता-गतिः.

FLAVOUR, *s.* आ-,स्वादः, रसः, रुचि *f.* –*v. t.* सरस-*a.* कृ 8 U. –ED, *a.* सरस; 'well-f.' सुरस, स्वादु, सुस्वाद. –LESS, *a.* अरस, नीरस, विरस, अस्वादु. –OUS, *a.* मिष्ट, स्वादु, सुरस.

FLAW, *s.* दोषः, छिद्रं, रंध्रं, वैकल्यं, न्यूनता; 'seeking or finding f. s' रंध्रान्वेषिन्, छिद्रान्वेषिन्, दोषैकदृक्. 2 चंडवातः, प्रभंजनः; *See* HURRICANE. 3 भंगः, संधिः, भेदः, रंध्रं, छिद्रं; 'f. in a jewel' पुलकः, खंडः.–*v. t.* छिद् 10, व्यध् 4 P.–LESS, *a.* निर्दोष; *See* FAULTLESS. 2 निश्छिद्र, नीरंध्र. –Y, *a.* सरंध्र, सच्छिद्र, सदोष.

FLAX, *s.* क्षुमा, अतसी, उमा; शणं; 'f.-comb' उमामार्जनी. –EN, *a.* क्षौम-औम (मी *f.*).

FLAY, *v. t.* चर्म अपनी or निर्हृ 1 P or उल्लिख् 6 P or निष्कृष् 1 P, निस्त्वचयति (D.), निस्त्वचीकृ 8 U, त्वक्ष् 1 P. –ER, *s.* त्वग्विदारकः, चर्मनिष्कर्षकः. –ING, *s.* चर्मनिष्कर्षणं, निश्चर्मीकरणं.

FLEA, *s.* मक्षिका, मत्कुणः, देहिका, तल्पकीटः. –*v. t.* देहिकाः अपनी 1 P.

FLEDGED, *a.* संजातपक्ष, गरुत्मत्, सपक्ष, पक्षयुक्त.

FLEE, *v. i.* पलाय् 1 A, अपक्रम् 1 U, 4 P, वि-प्र-द्रु 1 P, परा-इ 2 P, अपधाव् 1 P, अप-निर्-गम् 1 P, अप-स-सृप् 1 P. 2 त्यज् 1 P, परिहृ 1 P, वृज् 10.

FLEECE, *s.* मेषलो(रो)मन् *n.* –*v. t.* (लोम) छिद् 7 P or लू 9 U. 2 अपहृ 1 P; 'f. ed' हृतसर्वस्व. –CY, *a.* बहुलोमन्, लोमश, लोमावृत.

FLEER, *v. t.* अव-उप-हस् 1 P, तिरस्कृ 8 U, अवमन् 4 A, अव-ज्ञा 9 U; *See* CONTEMN. –*s.* उप-अव-हासः, तिरस्कारः, अवहेलना, अवज्ञा.

FLEET, *s.* नौसमाजः-साधनं, पोतावलि *f.*, युद्धनौसमूहः.–*v. i.* द्रुतं-शीघ्रं-प्रसृप् 1 P or गम् 1 P, वेगेन चल् 1 P, त्वर् 1 A.–*a.* वेगवत्, शीघ्र-त्वरित-लघु-गति, प्रजविन्, अतिरंहस्, जवन (नी *f.*), शीघ्रगामिन्, महाजव; 'f. as the wind' वायुगति, वायुवेग; 'f. as thought' मनोजव. –ING, *a.* क्षणिक, क्षणभंगुर, अध्रुव, क्षणस्थायिन्; *See* FICKLE. –LY, *adv.* द्रुतं, शीघ्रं, लघु, सत्वरं, जवेन, वेगेन, रंहसा. –NESS, *s.* वेगः, प्र-,जवः, रंहस् *n.*, त्वरितगति *f.*

FLESH, *s.* मांसं, आमिषं, पिशितं, क्रव्यं, तरसं, पललं; 'dried f.' वल्लूरं-रा, उत्तप्तं, शुष्कं मांसं. 2 शरीरं, विषयसेवा, विषयासक्ति *f.*; 'f. diet or meat' मां-

साहार: ; 'f.-colour' मांसवर्णः-रागः, लोहित: ; 'f.-monger' मांसविक्रयिन्. -LESS, *a.* अमांस, अपुष्ट, मांसहीन. -LY, *a.* शारीरिक-दैहिक (की *f.*), विषयिन्, सांसारिक-ऐहिक (की *f.*,). -Y, *a.* मांसल, पुष्ट, पीन, पीवर, मेदस्विन् ; *See* FAT.

FLEXIBLE, *a.* आ-,नम्य, कुंचनीय, नमन-कुंचन-शील, कोमल, मृदु, आयम्य. 2 अनुनेय.

FLEXION, FLEXTURE, *s.* आ-,नति *f.*-नमनं ; भंगः, आ-अव-कुंचनं, वक्रता, वक्रिमन् *m.*

FLEXUOUS, *a.* वक्र, कुटिल, जिह्म, भंगुर.

FLICKER, *v. i.* चल् 1 P, चंचलतया ज्वल् 1 P, लोलशिखया ज्वल्, चंचलीभू 1 P. 2 पक्षौ आ-स्फल् c. -ING, *a.* चल, चंचल, अस्थिर, लोल. -*s.* चंचलशिखा, चलनं, चांचल्यं.

FLIMSY, *a.* असार, फल्गु, सारहीन, निर्बल, निःसत्त्व, अल्पबल, क्षीणशक्ति. -NESS, *s.* असारता.

FLINCH, *v. i.* विमुखी-पराङ्मुखी-भू 1 P, विचल् 1 P, नि-परा-वृत् 1 A, (abl.) ; पलाय् 1 A, त्यज् 1 P, त्यक्त्वा निर्गम् 1 P or अप-सृ 1 P, मुखं परा-वृत् c. -ING, *s.* निवर्तनं, विमुखता, विचलनं, विमुखीभवनं.

FLING, *v. t.* (सहसा-बलेन) क्षिप् 6 P, अस् 4 P, मुच् 6 P, वि-सृज् 6 P, पत् c., ईर् c.; 'f. away or off' अपक्षिप्, निरा-कृ, अपास्, अप-हा 3P; 'f. open' सहसा or बलाद् अपावृ 5 U. -*s.* क्षेपः-पणं, पातः-तनं, प्रक्षेपः.

FLINT, *s.* अरणिः, अग्निग्रावन् *m.*, अग्निप्रस्तरः. -Y, *a.* अग्निप्रस्तरमय (यी *f.*). 2 कठिनहृदय, पाषाणहृदय.

FLIP, *s.* आघातः, प्रहारः, आस्फालनं.

FLIPPANT, *a.* वाचाल, वावदूक, निःसार, वाक्चंचल. 2 चपल, अस्थिर, लोल, चंचल. -LY, *adv.* वाक्चापल्येन. -FLIPPANCY, *s.* वाक्चापल्यं, वावदूकता; निःसारता. 2 प्रगल्भता, लौल्यं, चापल्यं.

FLIRT, *v. t.* सहसा क्षिप् 6 P. -*v. i.* अव-हस् 1 P, अधिक्षिप् 6P. 2 वि-भ्रम् 1, 4 P, विलस् 1 P, विलासं-विभ्रमं-दृश् c. 3 चल *a.* भू 1 P, स्पंद् 1 A, कंप् 1 A, स्फुर् 6 P. -*s.* आकस्मिकक्षेपः. 2 विलासिनी, लीलावती, चपला, प्रगल्भा. -ATION, *s.* लीला, हेला, विभ्रमः, विलासः, हावः, खेला, प्रेमलीला. 2 स्पंदनं, स्फुरणं; हृदयकंपः.

FLIT, *v. i.* लघु चल् 1 P, द्रुतं वि-प्र-सृप् 1 P, स्थानात्स्थानं गम् or चल् 1 P, इतस्ततो भ्रम् 1, 4 P. 2 प्र-उत्-डी 1, 4 A, व्योम्नि विसृप्, चपलीभू. -TING, *s.* भ्रमणं, चलनं, लघु सर्पणं.

FLITCH, *s.* वल्लूरं, शूकरोत्तरं.

FLITTER, *s.* चीरं, कर्पटः, वस्त्रखंडः-डं.

FLITTERMOUSE, *s.* जतुका, अजिनपत्रा.

FLOAT, *v. i.* प्लु 1 A; तॄ 1 P. 2 भास् 1 A.-*v. t.* प्लु c., वह् c. -*s.* प्लवः, उडुपः, कोलः, वहित्रं, तरणी, तरीः.

FLOCCULENT, *a.* सांद्र, घनीभूत, श्यान.

FLOCK, *s.* यूथं, संघः, निवहः, समूहः, कुलं, गणः; *See* MULTITUDE; 'f. of cattle' पाशवं, पशुकुलं, गोवृंदं-कुलं; 'f. of sheep' अविकुलं, आविकं; 'f. of sheep and goats' अजाविकं; 'in f. s' गणशः, संघशः. -*v. i.* (Together) संघशः-गणशः-समागम् 1 P or मिल् 6 P or संनि-पत् 1 P, एकत्र मिल्, एकीभू.

FLOG, *v. t.* कशया-वेत्रेण-तड् 10 or आ-हन् 2 U or दंड् 10 or प्र-हृ 1 P. -GING, *s.* कशाघातः, कशाप्रहारः; 'deserving f.' कश्य.

FLOOD, *s.* पूरः, ओघः; स्रोतस् *n.*, प्रवाहः, रयः. 2 आप्लवः, संप्लवः, तोयाविप्लवः, जलप्रलयः, जलोपप्लवः; 'universal f.' महाप्रलयः, भूतसंप्लवः, संवर्तः. 3 प्राचुर्यं, बाहुल्यं, पूरः, ओघः; 'f. of tears' बाष्पपूरः-ओघः-वर्षः, अश्रुपातः-वर्षः ; 'f.-gate' द्वारं, निर्गममार्गः, परि(री)वाहः, जलद्वारं, जलनिर्गमः. -*v. t.* प्लु c., आ-सं-परि-°, परिवह् c. ; 'with her eyes f.-ed with tears' अश्रुपरिप्लुतेक्षणा; 'a f.ed river' आप्लुतोदका-परिवाहिणी-नदी.

FLOOK, *s.* हलदंतः.

FLOOR, *s.* भूमि *f.*, भूपृष्ठं, तलं, भूतलं, गृहभू-भूमिः *f.*, गृहपीठः, वास्तु *m. n.*, गृहमूलं, वेश्मभूः. 2 (Story) भूमिः, कोष्ठः; 'a palace having 7 f. s' सप्तभूमिकः प्रासादः; 'the upper f.' उपरिभूमिः. 3 फलकास्तरणं, फलकसंस्तरः, फलकः-कं. -*v. t.* फलकैः आ-स्तृ 9U or आच्छद् 10. 2 नि-पत् c., भूमौ क्षिप् 6P.

FLOP, *v. t.* आ-स्फल् c.

FLORAL, *a.* कौसुम (मी *f.*), पुष्प in comp.

FLORID, *a.* रक्त, रक्त-अरुण-वर्ण. 2 अलंकृत, उज्ज्वल, अलंकारशोभित, सालंकार. -ITY,-NESS, *s.* (कपोल)-रागः, अरुणिमन्-रक्तिमन् *m.* 2 वागलंकारः, सालंकारत्वं, अलंकारशोभा.

FLORIFEROUS, *a.* पुष्पोत्पादक, पुष्पप्रद.

FLORILEGE, *s.* पुष्पचयः-संगः.

FLORIST, *s.* मालाकारः, पुष्पविद्याज्ञः.

FLOTA, *See* FLEET.

FLOTILLA, *s.* लघुनौसमूहः.

FLOUNCE, *v. i.* अंगानि विक्षिप् 6 P or इतस्ततः चल् c. -*s.* आकस्मिकः अंगविक्षेपः.

FLOUNDER, *v. i.* इतस्ततः क्षिप् pass., लुठ् 1 A, 6 P, वि-लुठ् 1 A. 2 वि-परि-भ्रम् 1, 4 P.

FLOUR, *s.* गोधूमचूर्णं, चूर्णं, क्षोदः, पिष्टं, गुंडिका, सक्तवः (pl.).

FLOURISH, *v. i.* सं-जन् 4 A सं-भू 1 P; 'when Panini f. ed' यदा पाणिनिः समजायत. 2 वृद्धिं-उन्नतिं-गम् 1 P, सं-ऋध् 4, 5 P, एध् 1 A, सं-विवृध् 1 A, प्र-उप-चि pass., स्फाय् 1 A. -*v. t.* वृध् c. 2 चित्र् 10, पुष्पादिना अलंकृ 8 U or शुभ् c. or

रंज् c. 3 भ्रम् c. (भ्रमयति), घूर्ण् c. —s. आडंबरः, शोभा, अलंकारः, मंडनं. 2 निः-,स्वनः (of trumpets). 3 दर्पवाक्यं, गर्वोक्ति f. 4 भ्रमणं, उद्भ्रमः. —ING, a. समृद्ध, सुस्थित, सुस्थ, वर्धिष्णु, उदयिन्, उपचीयमान.

FLOUT, *See* CONTEMN.

FLOW, v. i. प्र-,स्रु 1 P; प्र-नि-अभि-स्यंद् 1 A, क्षर् 1 P, गल् 1 P, सृ 1 P, प्रवह् 1 P, री 4 A, द्रु 1 P; 'f. ing with tears' बाष्पजलनिस्यंदिन्; 'f. ing with nectar' सुधास्यंदिन्, अमृतस्रुत्; प्र-,स्नु 2 P; 'f. ing (of milk)' प्रस्नवः. 2 प्र-सृप् 1 P, प्र-सृ, प्रवृत् 1 A, प्र-गम्-चल् 1 P, प्र-या 2 P. 3 जन् 4 A, उत्पद् 4 A, उद्-प्र-सं-भू 1 P, प्रवृत्. 4 स्रंस् 1 A, शिथिलीभू, श्लथ-वितत-गलित a. भू. —s. स्रवः, स्रवणं, स्रुति f., स्रावः, क्षरणं, गलनं, प्रवृत्ति f., अभि-नि-स्यं-(ष्यं)दः-दनं. 2 प्रवाहः, स्रोतस् n., ओघः, प्लवः, वेगः, रयः, धारः-रा; वेला, पद्धति f. 3 समुद्रवेला, वेला; 'f. of tears' अश्रुपातः-प्रवाहः, बाष्पवर्षः, धाराश्रु n.; 'f. of words' वागोघः. अप्रतिहता वाक्सरणिः-पद्धतिः. —ING, a. प्रस्रुत, स्यंदिन्, विसारिन्, स्रवत्. 2 अप्रतिहत, अस्खलित; 'a f. delivery' अस्खलितभाषणपद्धतिः. —INGLY, adv. अस्खलितवाक्येन, अप्रतिहतं, द्रुतं, अविलंबितं.

FLOWER, s. पुष्पं, कुसुमं, प्रसूनं, सुमं, सूनं, सुमनस् f. (pl.). 2 अवतंसः, ललामभूतः, अलंकारः, तिलकभूतः ; 'Râma is the f. of his class' स्ववर्गललामभूतो रामः. 2 सारः, उत्कृष्ट-श्रेष्ठ-भागः, उत्तमांशः, सारांशः; 'f. of age' यौवनं; 'f. of youth' नवयौवनं; 'being in the f. of youth' आरूढयौवनारंभ, प्रौढयौवन. —v. i. फुल्ल् 1 P, विकस् 1 P, स्फुट् 6 P, भिद् pass. 2 मंडायते-फेनायते (D.). —v. t. पुष्पादिना अलंकृ 8 U or शुभ् c. —ED, a. कुसुमित, पुष्पित, कुसुमसनाथ. 2 विकसित, फुल्ल, स्फुटित. —ING, a. पुष्पवत्, कुसुमवत्, कुसुमित, प्रफुल्ल, स्फुटितपुष्प. 2 पुष्पद. —LESS, a. अकुसुम, कुसुमहीन. —Y, a. पुष्प-कुसुम-मय (यी f.), सपुष्प, सकुसुम, पुष्पशालिन्; gen. ex. by (s.) in comp.; 'f. arrows' कुसुमशराः. 2 सालंकार, अलंकृत, अलंकारयुक्त, मंडित.

FLUCTUATE, v. i. इतस्ततः चल् 1 P or घूर्ण् 1 A, लुल् 1, 6 P, विलुठ् 1 A, 6 P. 2 दोलायते (D.), विकृप् 1 A, संदिह् 2 U; विचल, अस्थिर-चंचल-a. भू 1 P. —ING, a. दोलायमान, अस्थिर, चंचल, अनवस्थित, लोल, तरल, चल. —ION, s. अस्थैर्यं, चलता, अप्रतिष्ठा, चांचल्यं, विकल्पः, संदेहः, अनवस्थिति f., आंदोलनं.

FLUE, s. धूममार्गः-पथः.

FLUENT, a. अस्खलितवाच्, अस्खलद्वाक्य, वाक्पटु, द्रुतत्वरित-वाच् (of persons); अनर्गल, अप्रतिहतौघ, अविश्रांत, अस्खलित, द्रुत, अप्रतिहत, अनवरत. —LY, adv. अस्खलितवाचा, द्रुतवाक्येन, अस्खलितं, द्रुतं, अप्रतिहतं, वाग्विभवेन. —FLUENCY, s. वाक्पटुत्वं, वाक्चापल्यं, वाग्विभवः, ओघः, अनर्गलता, अप्रतिहतत्वं.

FLUID, s. द्रवः, रसः, द्रववस्तु n. —a. द्रव, विलीन, द्रुत; *See* LIQUID. —ITY, s. द्रवता, विलयः

FLUMMERY, s. मिथ्याप्रशंसा-स्तुति f.

FLUNKY, s. दासः, चेटः, नीचकर्मकरः.

FLURRY, *See* AGITATE.

FLUSH, v. t. अरुणीकृ 8 U, अरुणयति (D.), रंज् c., रक्तीकृ; 'with her face f. ed with anger' कोपारुणितानना. 2 उत्सिच् c., दृप् c., दर्पेण आ-ध्मा 1 P, उद्धतीकृ. —v. i. अरुणीभू, रक्तीभू, लोहितायते (D.), रंज् pass.; अरुणवदन-लोहितानन-a. भू. —s. अरुणिमन् m., रक्तिमन् m., रक्तता, रागः, कपोल-वदन-रागः. 2 प्रफुल्लता, बाहुल्यं, समृद्धि f. —a. सतेजस्क, प्रौढ, तेजस्विन्. 2 समृद्ध, धनसंपन्न. 3 मुक्तहस्त, अतिव्ययपर. —ED, a. अरुणित; रक्त, लोहित. 2 उद्धत, दृप्त, दर्पाध्मात, उत्सिक्त, गर्वित, सावलेप.

FLUSTER, v. t. पानादिना मद् c. or मुह् c. —s. चित्तभ्रमः, उन्मादः, मोहः, व्याकुलता.

FLUTE, s. वेणुः, मुरली, वंशः. —v. i. 'Blow a f.' (वेणुं) मुखमारुतेन पूर् 10 or वद् c., ध्मा 1 P; 'f.-player' वैणविकः, वेणुध्मः, वांशिकः.

FLUTTER, v. i. पक्षौ वि-धू 5, 9 U, 6 P or आस्फल् c. or उत्क्षिप् 6 P or विचल् c. 2 इतस्ततः चल् 1 P or धाव् 1 P or प्र-सृ 1 P. 3 कंप् 1 A, स्फुर् 6 P, उच्छ्वस् 2 P, स्पंद् 1 A, क्षुभ् 4 P. —v. t. संक्षुभ् c., आकुलीकृ 8 U, स्पंद् c., कंप् c., स्फुर् c. —s. विधुवनं, आस्फालनं, उत्क्षेपणं. 2 विकंपः, स्फुरणं, स्पंदनं, उच्छ्वसनं. 3 सं-,क्षोभः, संभ्रमः, सं-आ-वेगः, चित्तवेगः-भ्रमः. —ING, s. पक्षास्फालनं, पक्षचालनं. —a. विचल, कंपमान; 'f. in the breeze' अनिलोद्धत, पवनाक्षिप्त, पवनाधूत.

FLUVIAL, a. नदीसंबंधिन्.

FLUX, s. संगमः, संघातः, समागमः, संमर्दः, 2 (Fluxion) प्रवाहः, प्र-,स्रवः, क्षरणं, गलनं, स्पंदनं. —v. t. वि-द्रु c., वि-ली c. —IBLE, a. द्राव्य, गलनीय.

FLY, s. मक्षिका, वर्वणा, नीला; 'f.-flap' अवचूलकः, रोमगुच्छः ; 'f.-leaf' मलपृष्ठं. —v. i. उद्-,डी 1, 4 A, उत्-पत् 1 P, खे विसृप् 1 P, आकाशेन या 2 P or गम् 1 P. 2 अप-या 2 P, वि-प्र-द्रु 1 P, पलाय् 1 A; *See* FLEE. 3 त्वरितं-शीघ्रं गम् or चल् 1 P or विसृप् or अतिक्रम् 1 U, 4 P. —v. t. त्यज् 1 P, परिहृ 1 P, वृज् 10. 2 आकाशे निक्षिप् 6 P or विसृप् c. or विसृ c.; 'f. at' आ-अभि-पत्, आ-अभि-द्रु, आ-अभि-प्र-धाव् 1 P; 'let f.' मुच् 6 P, उत्पत् c., विसृज् 6 P. —ING, s. डयनं, विसर्पणं, उत्पतनं; 'f. up and down' डीनावडीनं. —a. खविसर्पिन्, आकाशगति, आकाशगामिन्, डयमान, नभोगति; 'f.

bridge' चलसेतुः, जंगमसेतुः. —FLIGHT, *s.* पलायनं, विद्रावः, अपयानं, अपक्रमः-मणं, आगमः; 'to put to f.' विद्रु c.; 'put to f.' विद्रुत, विद्रावित, कांदिशीक. **2** (Of birds) डयनं, डीनं, उड्डयनं, उत्पतनं, उद्गमनं; 'downward f.' अवडीनं. **3** पक्षिमाला-श्रेणी. **4** मति-बुद्धि-विलासः; 'f. of steps' सोपानपंक्ति-श्रेणि-णी *f.*, सोपानपरंपरा; 'f. of an arrow' शरपातः. —Y, *a.* चलबुद्धि, भ्रांत-लोल-मति; अस्थिर, लोल; *See* FICKLE.

FOAL, *s.* किशोरः, अश्वशावः-वकः, बालघोटकः,अर्बरीषः.

FOAM, *s.* फेनः-णः. **2** मंडः, उत्सेकः; 'snowy f.' हिमधवलं, फेनपटलं. —*v. i.* फेनायते-मंडायते (D.), फेनं उत्पद् c. or निर्गम् c. (गमयति), उत्सिच्-उत्पीड् pass. —Y, *a.* फेनिल, फेनल, फेनयुक्त, फेनिन्.

FOB, *s.* घटीपिधानं-कोशः. —*v. t.* Cheat, q. v.

FOCUS, *s.* केंद्रं. —*v. t.* एकत्रीकृ 8 U.

FODDER, *s.* घासः, यवसं, पशुभोजनं, तृणादि.

FOE, *s.* शत्रुः, अरिः, रिपुः; *See* ENEMY.

FŒTUS, *See* FETUS..

FOG, *s.* कुहेडिका, कुहा, धूमि(मि-लि)का, कुज्झटिका, कुज्झटि-टी *f.* —GY, *a.* कुहावृत, धूमल, सधूमिक, कुज्झटिकाच्छन्न, धूमिकावृत-मय (यी *f.*).

FOIBLE, *s.* छिद्रं, दोषः, अपराधः, न्यूनता, हीनता, वैकल्यं, अगुणः.

FOIL, *v. t.* परा-भू 1 P, परा-जि 1 A; भंज् 7 P, व्या-प्रति-हन् 2 P, खंड् 10, परास् 4 U, मोघी-विफली-कृ 8 U. **2** Blunt, q. v. —*s.* भंगः, व्याघातः; पराभवः. **2** मिथ्याखड्गः, निर्धारखड्गः. **3** पत्रं; 'golden f.' स्वर्णपत्रं. **4** प्रभावर्धकं, कांति-शोभा-वर्धकं. —ED, *a.* (Of persons) भग्नोद्यम, खंडिताश, हताश, अकृतार्थ; *See* DISAPPOINTED. **2** (Of efforts &c.) भग्न, प्रतिहत, मोघीभूत, खंडित.

FOIN, *s.* यष्टि-खड्ग-आघातः. —*v. t.* यष्टिना प्रहृ 1 P or तड् 10.

FOIST, *v. t.* कपटेन लिख् 6 P or निविश् c., मिथ्या क्लृप् c., कृत्रिम *a.* कृ 8 U.

FOISTINESS, *s.* पूतिगंधिता.

FOLD, *v. t.* पुटी-गुणी-कृ 8 U, व्यावृत् c., संपीड् 10, पुटयति (D.); 'f.ed thrice' त्रिगुणीकृत; 'f.-ing his hands together' हस्तौ समानीय (R. II. 64), अंजलिं बद्ध्वा, कृतांजलिः, सां(प्रां)जलिः. **2** संवृ 5 U, पि-धा 3 U; आ-वेष्ट् c., आच्छद् 10. **3** Embrace, q. v.; 'f. ing her in his arms' भुजाभ्यां तामापीड्य. **4** व्रजे निरुध् 7 U or निविश् c. —*s.* पुटः-टं, भंगः, व्यावृत्ति *f.*, व्यावर्तनं; चूणः, वलिभंगः-पुटः, ऊर्मि *f.* **2** व्रजः, अवरोधः, शाला, गोष्ठं; 'cattle-f.' गोव्रजः; 'sheep-f.' मेषगोष्ठः-गोस्थानं, व्रजाजिरं. **3** (In comp.) ex. by गुण; 'eight-f.' अष्टगुण; 'f. ing doors' द्विपक्षद्वारं.

FOLIAGE, *s.* पल्लवः-वं, किसलयः-यं, पर्णं, दलं, पत्रं (gen. used in pl.); पल्लवगुच्छः-चयः.

FOLIATE, *a.* पर्णावृत, सदल.

FOLIO, *s.* पुस्तकपत्रं, पृथु-विशाल-पत्रं.

FOLK, *s.* जनः, जनसमूहः, जनता, लोकः; 'old f.' वृद्धजनः, वृद्धाः.

FOLLOW, *v. t.* अनु-गम्-व्रज्-सृ 1 P, अनुबंध् 9 P, अनु-इ-या 2 P, अनुचर् 1 P, अनुक्रम् 1 U, 4 P. **3** सेव् 1 A, अनुष्ठा 1 P, आ-स्था 1 A; अनुवृत् 1 A, आश्रि 1 U, पुरस्कृ 8 U, अनुवि-धा 3 U, अनुरुध् 4 A, अनुसृ; 'f. (in) the footsteps of the great' महतां पदमनुविधेयं; 'f. ing the path' पदवीं प्रतिपद्य; 'f. ing a middle course' पुरस्कृतमध्यमक्रमः (R. VIII. 9); 'one misfortune f. s another' दुःखं दुःखानुबंधि (V. 4), विपद्विपदमनुबध्नाति (Ka. 73). **3** उपास् 2 A, भज् 1 U, आश्रि, परिचर्; श्रु desid. (शुश्रूषते). —*v. i.* उत्पद् 4 A, प्राप्-आपद्-सिध्-अनुमा-pass.; परिच्छिन्नस्तावज्जीव इति प्राप्नोति (S. B. 651); 'it f. s therefore &c.'; 'what f. ed is understood' परस्तादवगम्यते (S. 1); (in conversations) ततस्ततः 'what f. ed next'; 'as f. s' तद्यथा, तद्यथानुश्रूयते; or merely एवं, इति, उक्तप्रकारेण, इत्थं. —ER, *s.* अनुयायिन्-गामिन्-वर्तिन्-सारिन् *m.* **2** परिजनः, सेवकः, अनु-उप-जीविन् *m.*, अनुगः, अनुचरः, अनुयातृकः, अनुगतिकः, परिवारः, सहचरः, सहायः. **3** आश्रितः, भक्तः, अनुषंगिन् *m.* —ING, *a.* इदं-एतद् *pron. a.*; 'the f. story' एषा-इयं-कथा; पश्चात् कीर्त्यमान, अनुग, अनुयायिन्. —*s.* अनुसरणं-यानं-गमनं-वृत्ति *f.*-रोधः-वर्तनं.

FOLLY, *s. See* under FOOL.

FOMENT, *v. t.* (उष्णोदकादिना) सं-सिच् 6 P, लिप् 6 P, अंज् 7 P, दिह् 2 U; स्विद् c. **2** उद्दीप् c., प्र-सं-वृध् c., उत्तिज् c., प्रोत्सह् c., उत्तॄ c., प्रकुप् c., प्रवृत् c.; 'f. disputes' उप-जप् 1 P, भेदं वृध् c., भेदबीजं वप् 1 P. —ATION, *s.* प्र-, स्वेदनं, घर्मानुलेपनं, द्रवस्वेदः. **2** उद्दीपनं, संवर्धनं, उत्तेजनं, प्रवर्तनं. —ER, *s.* उपजापकः, भेदकरः.

FOND, *a.* वत्सल, अनुरागवत्, सानुराग, अनुरक्त, प्रणयिन्, अनुरागिन्. **2** रुचिन्, अभिलाषिन्, आसक्त, रक्त, रत, पर, तत्पर, gen. in comp. **3** मूढ, मुग्ध, अत्यनुरक्त; 'f. of' ex. by शील, लालस, काम, प्रिय, in comp.; oft. by ईह् 1 A, कांक्ष् 1 U, अभिलष् 1, 4 P, भज् 1 U, सेव्-रुच् 1 A; 'f. of sport' क्रीडाप्रिय; 'f. of chase' मृगयाशील; 'f. of change' अवस्थांतरमीहमान; 'f. of drinking' पानासक्त, पानव्यसनिन्. —LY, *adv.* सानुरागं, सप्रेम-मं; अतिस्नेहेन, अविवाक्यत्येन. —NESS, *s.* अनुरागः, आसक्ति *f.*, रति *f.*, प्रीति *f.*, प्रणयः, स्नेहः; 'ingenious

f. for the mate' कांतानुवृत्तिचातुर्यं; प्रेमन् *m., n.,* वात्सल्यं; अभिरुचि *f.,* कामः, इच्छा, ईहा.

FONDLE, *v.t.* उप-लल् 10, अंके-पा c. (पाल्यति), क्रीडीकृ 8 U, आलिंग् 1 P, परिष्वंज् 1 A, आ-सं-पीड् 10; 'f. ed too much' दुर्ललित. –ING, *s.* उप-,लालनं, आलिंगनं, भुजापीडनं, परिष्वंगः. 2 प्रेम-स्नेह-पात्रं-भाजनं, स्नेहभूमि *f.*

FOOD, *s.* अन्नं, आहारः, भोजनं, भोज्यं, भक्ष्यं, खाद्यं, खादनं, भक्षणं, अभ्यवहार्यं, भक्तं, विघसः, ग्रासः, अशनं, अंधस् *n.*; 'cooked f.' ओदनः-नं; 'f. and raiment' ग्रासाच्छादनं, अन्नवस्त्रं; 'forbidden f.' अभक्ष्य.

FOOL, *s.* मूर्खः, मूढः, निर्बुद्धिः, अज्ञः, जडः, मंदः, अबुधः, अप्राज्ञः, प्रज्ञाहीनः, स्थूल-जड-धीः, अल्प-धीः-मतिः, मंद-धीः-मतिः, अनात्मज्ञः, बर्बरः; 'make a f. of' उपहासास्पदं कृ 8 U, विडंब् 10, (एवं प्रार्थयिता विडंब्यते S. 2). –*v. t.* मुह् c., वि-प्र-लुभ् c., वंच् 10; *See* CHEAT; 'f -hardy' अतिसाहसिक, व्यामूढ, अविमृश्यकारिन्, अविमृश्य प्रगल्भ, प्रमत्तवीर, प्रमत्त. –ERY, *s.* प्रहसनं, विडंबना. 2 बालिश्यं, मूर्खक्रिया, बालिशता, मूर्खता, व्यामोहः. –ISH, *a.* मूर्ख, मूढ, बालिश, अनात्मज्ञ, दुर्मति, दुर्मेधस्, वैधेय, बालिशमति, निर्बुद्धि, जड, स्थूलधी, प्रज्ञा-बुद्धि-हीन; *See* (*s.*). 2 निरर्थक, अविमृश्यकृत-दत्त. –ISHLY, *adv.* मूढतया, अज्ञानेन, मूर्खवत्, मूढवत्, मौर्ख्येण. –ISHNESS, –FOLLY, *s.* मौर्ख्यं, जाड्यं, मोहः, मंदमतिता, मूर्खता, मूढता, बालिश्यं, बालिशता, दुर्बुद्धिता, अज्ञानं, निर्बुद्धित्वं, ज्ञानाभावः, अनात्मज्ञत्वं.

FOOT, *s.* पादः, पदं, चरणः-णं, अंघ्रिः. 2 तलं, अधोभागः, मूलं; उपस्थः. 3 (In metre) चरणः, पदं. 4 पत्ति-पदाति-समूहः-गणः. –*v. t.* पादेन प्रहृ 1 P or तड् 10 or आहन् 2 U; 'f. of a mountain' उपत्यका, पादः; 'set one's f. in' पदं कृ 8 U (lit. and fig.); आश्रमे पदं करिष्यसि (S. 4), कुतूहलेन प्रश्नाशया हृदि पदं कृतं (Ka. 133); 'walk on f.' पद्भ्यां चर्-व्रज् 1 P, पादचारी भू; 'walking on f.' पादगः, पादचारः, पदातिः; 'water for the feet' पाद्यं; पादोदकं; 'set on f.' प्रवृत् c., उपक्रम् 1 A, प्रारभ् 1 A; 'f.-board' चरणफलकः; 'f.-boy' चेटः, भृत्यः, बालसेवकः, युवप्रेष्यः; 'f.-bridge' संक्रमः, संक्रमसेतुः; 'f.-fall' चरणपातः, पादन्यासः, स्खलनं; 'f.-fight' पदाति-पादग-युद्धं; 'f.-licker' पीठमर्दः, चरणसेवकः; 'f.-man' चेटः, सेवकः, प्रेष्यः, परिचरः, किंकरः; 'f.-mark-print' पाद-पद-चिह्नं, पदपंक्ति *f.,* पदवी, पद्धति *f.*; पादमुद्रा; 'f.-pace' पादन्यासः, चरणक्रमः-पातः; 'f.-path' संसरणं, चरणवीथि *f.,* पथिकमार्गः, पद्या; 'f.-soldier' पदातिः, पत्तिः, पादातिः-तिकः, प(पा)दातः, पादचारः, प(पा)दगः, पदाजिः, पद्गः, पदिकः; 'f.-step' पादन्यासः, पद-चरण-निक्षेपः-पातः, पदं, पदपंक्ति *f.* (f.-print); पद्धतिः, मार्गः, वर्त्मन् *n.,* पदवि-वी *f.,* लक्ष्मं; 'f.-stool' पादपीठं, चरणपीठं, पादासनं. –ING, *s.* पदं, स्थानं, भूमि *f.,* स्थलं, आस्पदं, पदवि-वी, सरणि *f.* 2 वास्तु *m., n.,* मूलं, उपष्टंभः. 3 आश्रयः, अवलंबनं, आधारः. 4 स्थिति *f.,* वृत्ति *f.,* अवस्था, भावः, दशा; 'f. of equality' समता, तुल्यभावः. –LESS, *a.* पादहीन, अचरण.

FOP, *s.* दर्शनीयमानिन् *m.,* वेषाभिमानी, दंभी, सुवेशमानी, छेकः, रूपगर्वितः. –PISH, *a.* दंभिन्.

FOR, *prep.* (On account of) Ex. by instr. or abl.; अर्थं-र्थे, हेतुना, हेतोः, कृते, कारणात्, निमित्तात्, निमित्तं, in comp.; 'for his deliverance' मोक्षनिमित्तं, मुक्तिहेतोः, &c. 2 (Purpose) by dat. or by अर्थं-अर्थे in comp. 3 (For the sake of) अर्थं, कृते (with gen.), or by dat. 4 (In exchange for) प्रति, स्थाने, विनिमयेन; तिलेभ्यः प्रतियच्छति माषान्, or तिलविनिमयेन &c. 5 (Considering) अपेक्ष्य, प्रतीक्ष्य, आलोच्य, इति कृत्वा, अपेक्षया in comp. 6 (Towards) प्रति, उद्दिश्य, (with acc.); संमुखं, अभिमुखं, in comp. 7 (Regarding) तावत्, उद्दिश्य; कृते; 'f. myself, rest secure' मद्विषये तावद्वीतचिंतो भव, मामुद्दिश्य न चिंता कार्या. 8 (Showing price) by instr.; त्रिरूप्यकेण क्रीतः 'bought f. 3 Rs.' 9 (Duration) by acc.; 'for 10 days' दशदिवसं; 'f. how many years' कियंति वर्षाणि; oft. by यावत् or पर्यंतं, आ with abl.; 'f. life' यावज्जीवं, आजीवितांतात्. 10 (On the side of) पक्षे; 'they are f. war' विग्रहमनुमोदंते, विग्रहमुपदिशंति. 11 (As if) वत् or इव. 12 (According to) यथा, अनुरूपं, अनुसारेण, in comp.; 'f. all' ex. by अनादृत्य (with acc) or loc. abs.; 'f. all his wealth' विद्यमानेपि महाकोशे, महाकोशमनादृत्य; 'f. a long time' चिरं, चिरकालं, चिराय; 'out of love f. me' मद्गतप्रीत्या; 'f. the most part' भूयिष्ठ in comp., प्रायः, प्रायेण; 'f. once' सकृदेव. –*conj.* हि (not at beginning of assertions); यतः, यस्मात्कारणात्, यत्, यस्मात्, इति, हेतोः, अनेन हेतुना.

FORAGE, *s.* यवसं, घासः, तृणादि. 2 पाथेयं, भोजनसंभारः, खाद्यसामग्री. 3 खाद्यान्वेषणं, खाद्यार्थं परिभ्रमणं; प्रसरणं. –*v. i.* बलात् खाद्यद्रव्यं आ-हृ 1 P, भोजनार्थं परिभ्रम् 1, 4 P. –ING, *s.* भोजनान्वेषणार्थं परिभ्रमणं-प्रसरणं.

FORBEAR, *v.* विरम् 1 P, निवृत् 1 A, (with abl.), परिहृ 1 P, वृज् 10, त्यज् 1 P. 2 विलंब् 1 A. 3 सह् 1 A, क्षम् 1 A, मृष् 4 P, 10, तिज् desid. (तितिक्षते). 4 सं-नि-यम् 1 P, निग्रह् 9 P, आ-वृ 5 U, निरुध् 7 U; 'he could not f. expressing his joy, or laughter' संतोषं-हासं-निग्रहीतुं न पारयामास. -ANCE, *s.* क्षमा, तितिक्षा, क्षांति *f.*, सहनं, सहिष्णुता, मर्षणं, सहनशीलता. 2 निवृत्ति *f.*, विरामः, विरति *f.*, वर्जनं, त्यागः, परिहारः. 3 संयमः, दमः, यमः, निग्रहः. -ING, *a.* तितिक्षु, सहिष्णु, सहनशील, क्षमिन्, सहन, क्षंतृ, क्षमितृ.

FORBID, *v. t.* प्रति-नि-षिध् 1 P or c., प्रत्या-ख्या 2 P, प्रत्यादिश् 6 P, निरा-अपा-कृ 8 U. 2 निरुध् 7 U, नि-वृ c. or वार् 10; 'God f.' शांतं पापं or (इति) शांतं, प्रतिहतममंगलं. -DING, -DANCE, *s.* नि-प्रतिषेधः, प्रत्याख्यानं, प्रत्यादेशः. 2 निवारणं, निरोधः. -DING, *a.* घृणावह, बीभत्सजनक, अनिष्ट.

FORCE, *s.* बलं, शक्ति *f.*, सामर्थ्यं (fig. also); 'the f. of this word' अस्य शब्दस्य शक्तिः &c. 2 प्रभावः; वीर्यं, शौर्यं, वि-परा-क्रमः, ऊर्जस् *n.*, प्रतापः, प्राबल्यं, गौरवं. 3 बलात्कारः, प्रसभः, साहसं, बलं, प्रमाथः, आवेशः; 'f. of passion' रागावेशः. 4 आवेगः, आपातः, अभिभवः. 5 सिद्धि *f.*, फलं, निष्पत्ति *f.*; 'put or bring into f.' प्रवृत् c. 6 सैन्यं, बलं, सेना, अनीकः-कं, पृतना, अनीकिनी, चमूः, वाहिनी, ध्वजिनी, चक्रं, वरूथिनी. -*v. t.* Ex. by causal of verbs, with बलात् or बलेन, or प्रवृत् c.; *See* COMPEL; 'he was f. ed to admit that &c.' इति अभ्युपगमनं अवश्यकं मेने. 2 प्रेर् c., प्रणुद् 6 P, समाकृष् 1 P, प्रचुद् 10, प्रोत्सह् c. 3 धृष् c., बलाद् अभिगम् 1 P, बलात्कारं कृ 8 U; 'f. an entrance' बलेन प्रविश् 6 P; 'f. a town' पुरं लंघ् 1 A, 10 or भंज् 7 P or बलात् प्रविश्. -ED, *a.* यत्नकृत, यत्नपूर्व, असहज, कृत्रिम, क्लिष्ट (as meaning). -FORCIBLE, *a.* प्रबल, समर्थ, क्षम, शक्तिमत्, बलवत्, सप्रभाव; अमोघ, अनिष्फल, प्रभविष्णु. 2 गौरवेण उक्त or प्रतिपादित, दृढ, तीक्ष्ण. 3 बलेन कृत, बलात्कृत, साहसिक (की *f.*), बल in comp.; 'f. consent' बलानुमोदनं. -FORCIBLY, *adv.* (by force) बलेन, बलात्, प्रसभं, प्रसह्य, बलात्कारेण, हठात्. 2 सगौरवं, दृढतया.

FORCE-MEAT, *s.* मिश्रान्नं, उपस्करः, व्यंजनं.

FORCEPS, *s.* सदंशकः-शिका.

FORD, *s.* तीर्थं, तरणस्थानं-स्थलं, घट्टः. -*v. t.* पद्भ्यां तॄ 1 P or पारं गम् 1 P. -ABLE, *a.* अल्पजल, सुतर, सुप्रतर; 'the rivers having become f.' सुखोत्तारतामापन्नास्वापगासु (Ka. 326).

FORE, *a.* अग्र, पूर्व, अग्रगामिन्; gen. ex. by अग्र, पूर्व in comp.; 'f.-fathers' पूर्वजाः, पितरः, पूर्वे-पूर्वाः, वृद्धाः; 'f.-finger' प्रदेशिनी, तर्जनी; 'f.-foot' अग्रपादः; 'f.-head' ललाटं, भालं, ललाट-भाल-पट्टं, अलि(ली)कं, गोधिः; 'f.-land' अंतरीपः-पं, टदग्रभूः-भूमिः; 'f.-lock' ललाटकेशः-हहः; 'f.-man' अध्यक्षः, अधिष्ठातृ *m.*, अधीशः; 'f.-mentioned-named-said-spoken' प्रागुक्त, पूर्वोक्त, पूर्वकथित; 'f.-mast' अग्रकूपकः; 'f.-most' प्रधान, उत्कृष्ट, परम; 'f.-noon' पूर्वाह्णः,-कालः; 'f.-part' अग्रभागः, पूर्व-आदि-प्रथम-भागः; 'f.-rank' अग्र-प्रधान-पदं; 'f.-tooth' अग्रदंतः, राजदंतः; 'f.-ward' मनामुखं, रणशिरस् *n.*

FOREARM, *s.* प्रकोष्ठः, अग्रभुजः-हस्तः-बाहुः. -*v. t.* पूर्वं सन्नह् 4 P or c. or सज्जीकृ 8 U.

FOREBODE, *v. t.* आ-,सूच् 10, प्राक् आ-विद c., पूर्वं कथ् 10; (अनिष्टं) पूर्वं ज्ञा 9 U or अव-गम् 1 P, अनु-मा 3 A; *See* BODE; 'the tawny lightning f. s a hurricane' वाताय कपिला विद्युत् (S. K.). -ER, *s.* अनिष्टावेदकः, अनिष्टसूचकः. -ING, *s.* अनिष्टसूचनं-ज्ञानं-दर्शनं.

FORECAST, *v. t.* पूर्वं-अग्रे-चिंत् 10 or निरूप् 10 or निर्दिश् 6 P or अनुसं-धा 3 U. -*s.* पूर्वकल्पना-विवेकः, अग्रनिरूपणं, पूर्वचिंतनं, दीर्घदृष्टि *f.*

FORECLOSE, *v. t.* प्रतिबंध् 9 P, प्रति-नि-षिध् 1 P. -URE, *s.* प्रतिबंधः, प्रतिषेधः.

FORE-DETERMINE, *v. t.* अग्रे-पूर्वं-निर्णी 1 P or निश्चि 5 U.

FOREDOOM, *v. t.* पूर्वं निर्दिश् 6 P or वि-चर् c.

FORE-FEND, *See* FORBID.

FOREGO, *v. t.* त्यज् 1 P, हा 3 P, उत्-वि-सृज् 6 P; 'I shall f. my name' स्वनामत्यागं करोमि (P. 1); 'a foregone conclusion' पूर्वनिर्णीतः-प्रागेवसिद्धः-सिद्धांतः.

FOREIGN, *a.* विदेशीय, वैदेशिक-पारदेशिक (की *f.*), विदेशज, विदेशिन्, अन्य-भिन्न देशज-देशीय-देशोद्भव, पारदेश्य, विदेशादागत, बहिर्देशोद्भव; 'a f. country' विदेशः, परदेशः, देशांतरं. 2 बाह्य, बाहिर्भव, अप्रस्तुत, अप्रकृत; 'this is f. to our present inquiry' अप्रकृतमेतदस्मिन् विषये. -ER, *s.* वैदेशिकः, पारदेशिकः, अन्यदेशीयः-देशजः; *See* (*a.*). -NESS, *s.* बाह्यता, भिन्नता; अप्रकृतता, असंबंधः.

FORE-IMAGINE, *v. t.* पूर्वं-अग्रे-चिंत् 10 or मन् 4 A.

FORE-JUDGE, *v. t.* पूर्वं अवेक्ष् 1 A विचर् c. or निर्णी 1 P.

FORE-KNOW, *v. t.* पूर्वं ज्ञा 9 U or बुध् 1 P, or विद् 2 P, (know, q. v.); प्रदृश् 1 P, अग्रे निरूप् 10. -LEDGE, *s.* अग्र-पूर्व-ज्ञानं, भविष्यज्ज्ञानं, अग्रनिरूपणं, अग्र-पूर्व-दृष्टि *f.*

FORENSIC, *a.* व्यावहारिक (की *f.*), व्यवहारानुबद्ध.

FORE-ORDAIN, *v. t.* अग्रे-पूर्वं-निर्दिश् 6 P or नियुज् 7 A, 10 or वि-धा 3 U.

FORERUN, *v. i.* पूर्वं-पुरः-अग्रे-सृ or गम् or धाव् 1 P or वृत् 1 A or या-इ 2 P. -NER, *s.* अग्रेसरः, पुरो-गः-गामिन् *m.*, अग्र-गः-गामी, अग्रवर्ती, अग्रगतः, पूर्वपुरुषः.

FORE-SAY,-SPEAK, प्राक्-पूर्व-वद् 1 P or कथ् 10.

FORESEE, *v. t.* पूर्वं दृश् 1 P or ज्ञा 9 U, भावि-अनागतं-दृश् or अवेक्ष् 1 A, अग्रे निरूप् 10; gen. ex. by भाविन्; 'I f. my ruin' जानामि भाविनं नाशं. –FORESIGHT, *s.* दूरदर्शित्वं-ता, दूर-दीर्घ-दृष्टि *f.*, अग्रनिरूपणं, दूरदर्शनं.

FORESHOW, *See* FOREBODE.

FOREST, *s.* वनं, अरण्यं, काननं, विपिनं, अटवि-वी *f.*, गहनं, कांतारः-रं; 'a large f.' अरण्यानी; 'growing in f.' वन्य, आरण्य,-क, वनोद्भव, अरण्यज-जात, वन or अरण्य in comp. –ER, *s.* वनेचरः, वनवासिन् *m.*, आरण्यकः, आटविकः, वनस्थः, वनचारी, वनचरः-वर्ती, वनौकस् *m.*, अरण्यसद् *m.* 2 अरण्यरक्षकः, वनपालकः.

FORESTALL, *v. t.* पूर्वं ग्रह् 9 P or आदा 3 A, पूर्वग्रहणेन मार्घीकृ 8 U; *See* ANTICIPATE. 2 पूर्वं क्री 9 U.

FORETASTE, *v. t.* पूर्वं अनुभू 1 P or आस्वाद् 1 A or भुज् 7 A. –*s.* पूर्वानुभवः, पूर्व-अग्र-ज्ञानं, पूर्वास्वादः, पूर्व-अग्र-भुक्ति *f.*

FORETELL, *v. t.* पूर्वं कथ् 10, भावि-भविष्यद्-वद् 1 P or वच् 2 P; प्रदृश् c., अनागतं निविद् c.; *See* PREDICT. –ER, *s.* भविष्यद्वादिन् *m.*, भाविदर्शकः, अनागतनिवेदकः, दैवज्ञः.

FORETHINK, *v. t.* पूर्वं चिंत् 10 or विमृश् 6 P. –FORETHOUGHT, *s.* अग्र-पूर्व-चिंता, पूर्वविमर्शः-विवेकः, प्रसमीक्षा-क्षणं, दूर-दीर्घ-दृष्टि *f.*, पूर्वविचारणं-णा.

FORETOKEN, *v. t.* पूर्वं सूच् 10. –*s.* पूर्वलक्षणं-चिह्नं-लिंगं, भाविलक्षणं.

FOREWARN, *v. t.* पूर्वं सूच् 10 or प्रबुध् c., अग्रे उपदिश् 6 P or ज्ञा c. (ज्ञापयति); 'to be f. ed is to be forearmed' पूर्वप्रबोधनं पूर्वसन्नाहतुल्यं. –ING, *s.* पूर्वप्रबोधः-धनं, पूर्वोपदेशः.

FORFEIT, *v. t.* दंड् pass., भ्रंश् 1 A, 4 P, च्यु 1 A, परि-हा pass., (with abl.); 'f. s his kingdom' राज्यात्परिभ्रंशते; 'f. s. his right' स्वत्वं तस्माच्चिवर्तते; oft. ex. by हीन-हृत in comp.; 'you will f. all your wealth' हृतसर्वस्वो भवेः, सर्वस्वं दंडयेथाः. –*s.* दंडः, धन-अर्थ-दंडः. –ED, *a.* दंडित, भ्रष्ट, च्युत, हीन; 'who has f. ed his right' स्वत्वभ्रष्टः, च्युताधिकारः; हृतसर्वस्वः, &c. –URE, *s.* हानि *f.*, च्युति *f.*, भ्रंशः, अपहारः, अपवर्तनं, नाशः, दंडदानं.

FORGE, *v. t.* घट् c. (घटयति), रच् 10, निर्मा 3 A, वि-धा 3 U, क्लृप् c. 2 मिथ्या-कूटेन-कृ 8 U, कपट-कूट in comp.; 'f. s a letter' कूट-कपट-लेखं प्रयुंक्ते; *See* COUNTERFEIT. –*s.* निर्माणस्थानं; अग्निकुंडं, उध्मानं. –ER, *s.* कूट-कारः-कृत् *m.*, कपट-लेखकारिन् *m.* –ERY, *s.* कूट-कपट-लेखकरणं, कूट-कपट-करणं, कूटरचना. –ING, *s.* घटना, घटनं, रचना-नं; कूटनिर्माणं, &c.

FORGET, *v. t.* विस्मृ 1 P, न स्मृ; स्मृतेः-स्मरणाद्-भ्रंश् 1 A, 4 P or अप-इ 2 P (of what is forgotten). –FUL, *a.* विस्मरणशील, लुप्त-नष्ट-स्मृति; अनवहित, प्रमत्त. –FULNESS, *s.* विस्मृति *f.*, विस्मरणं, स्मृतिलोपः, स्मृतिनाशः-भ्रंशः-हानि *f.*, विस्मरणशीलता, अनवधानं.

FORGIVE, *v. t.* क्षम् 1 A (with acc. of person also), मृष् 4 P, 10, सह् 1 A, तिज् desid. (तितिक्षते) (with acc. of fault). 2 मुच् 6 P, अव-सृज् 6 P, त्यज् 1 P, (as a debt). –NESS, *s.* क्षमा, तितिक्षा, क्षांति *f.*, सहिष्णुता, मर्षणं; 'f. of sin' पाप-दोष-मुक्ति *f.*-मार्जनं. –ING, *a.* क्षमिन्, सहिष्णु, क्षमावत्, क्षमाशील, तितिक्षु, क्षमायुक्त, क्षंतृ, क्षमितृ.

FORK, *s.* कंटकः, शूलं. –*v. i.* विभिद् pass., द्विशिखीभू 1 P, द्विधा भिद् pass. –ED, –Y, *a.* द्विशिख, द्व्यग्र; 'having a f. tongue' द्विजिह्व; 'f. lightning' विद्युल्लता.

FORLORN, *a.* त्यक्त, दीन, विधुर, अनाथ, अनाश्रय, गति-शरण-हीन, अ-निः-शरण, अ-निः-सहाय, निरवलंब, निराधार, निराश्रय, अगतिक.

FORM, *s.* रूपं, आकारः, आकृति *f.*; संस्थानं; वपुस् *n.*, मूर्ति *f.*, (Body, q. v.). 2 तंत्रं, मार्गः, पद्धति *f.*, प्रकारः, रीति *f.*, विधा-धः, विधिः, भेदः; 'f. of government' राज्यतंत्र-पद्धतिः. 3 विधिः, नियमः, स्थिति *f.*, व्यवस्था, आचारः, क्रमः, मर्यादा, व्यवहारः, संस्कारः; 'in due f.' यथाविधि, विध्यनुसारेण, विधिवत्. 4 रचना-नं, विन्यासः. 5 सहाध्यायिवर्गः, छात्रपंक्ति *f*, गणः. 6 दीर्घपीठं-आसनं. –*v. t.* निर्मा 2 P, 3 A, रच् 10, कृ 8 U, वि-धा 3 U, उत्पद् c., घट् c. (घटयति), क्लृप् c.; 'f. plans' उपायान् चिंत् 10 or मनसा क्लृप् c.; 'the cords that f. ed the net' याभिः रज्जुभिर्जालं निर्मितं. –AL, *a.* अत्याचारसेविन्, नियमनिष्ठ, अत्यादरयुक्त, सभ्याचारविशिष्ट. 2 नैयमिक-वैधिक (की *f.*), नियमानुसारिन्, व्यवहारानुरूप, आचारानुगत, आचारानुसारिन्, विध्यनुरूप; आचार in comp.; 'just perform the f. salutation' आचारं तावत्प्रतिपद्यस्व. 3 यथार्थ, विशिष्ट. –ALIST, *s.* नियममात्रसेविन् *m.* –ALITY, *s.* आचारः, उपचारः, यथाविधि वर्तनं; अत्यादरः; 'a title of f.' उपचारपदं; 'enough of f.' अलमत्यादरेण. –ALLY, *adv.* सोपचारं, अत्यादरेण, सभ्याचारपूर्वं, अत्यादरपूर्वं. 2 यथाविधि, विधिवत्, नियमानुसारेण. –ATION, *s.* घटना-नं, निर्माणं, विधानं, रचना, कल्पना-नं, उत्पादनं, उद्भवः, सृष्टि *f.* –ED, *a.* घटित, निर्मित, कृत, रचित, क्लृप्त, मय in comp.; 'f. of gold' हेमघटित, सुवर्णमय, &c.; *See* COMPOSED.

2 रूप-आकार-आकृति-in comp.; 'f. like a conch' शंखाकृति; 'well-f.' सुरूप. -LESS, *a.* निराकार, अरूप.

FORMER, *a.* पूर्व, प्रथम, अग्रिम, आद्य, आदिम, पूर्वकालीन, प्राक्कालीन, प्राचीन, गतकालीन, पुराण, पुरातन. -LY, *adv.* प्राक्, प्राक्काले, भूत-गत-काले, पुरा, पूर्वे, परात्कल्पे, पूर्वकाले; 'as f.' यथापूर्वं, पूर्ववत्; 'f. stated' प्रागुक्त, पूर्वोक्त; 'f. heard' श्रुतपूर्व.

FORMIDABLE, *a.* दारुण, भयावह, भीषण, भयानक, भयजनक, भयप्रद, भैरव (वी *f.*), घोर, उग्र, प्रतिभय, रौद्र (द्री *f.*). 2 (Great) प्रबल, महत्, अतिघोर. -NESS, *s.* भयानकत्वं, भीषणता, भैरवं.

FORMULA, *s.* सूत्रं, विधिः, नियमः, व्यवस्था, स्थिति *f.* -FORMULATE, *v. t.* विधि-सूत्र-रूपेण रच् 10 or व्यव-स्था c. (स्थापयति).

FORNICATE, *v. i.* व्यभि-चर् 1 P, वेश्यां सेव् 1 A or अभिगम् 1 P. -ION, *s.* व्यभिचारः, जारकर्मन् *n.*, वेश्यागमनं-सेवा, वेश्यासंभोगः. -OR, *s.* व्यभिचारिन् *m.*, जारः. -FORNICATRESS, *s.* Harlot, q. v.

FORSAKE, *v. t.* त्यज् 1 P, हा 3 P, उत्-वि-अपसृज् 6 P, उज्झ् 6 P, रह् 10 (रहयति). -ER, *s.* त्यागिन् *m.*, त्यक्तृ *m.* -ING, *s.* त्यागः, उत्सर्गः.

FORSOOTH, *adv.* नूनं, नाम, किल, खलु, यत्सत्यं, सत्यमेव.

FORSWEAR, *v. t.* सशपथं त्यज् 1 P or प्रत्या-ख्या 2 P or अप-नि-ह्नु 2A. -*v. i.* मिथ्या शप् 1U, कूट-मिथ्याशप्. -ER, *s.* असत्यशपथः, मिथ्याशपथकारिन् *m.*

FORT, FORTRESS, *s.* दुर्गं, कोटः, कोटि *f.*; 'governor of a f.' दुर्गाध्यक्षः, कोटपालः.

FORTE, *s.* विशिष्ट-श्रेष्ठ-गुणः, प्रधानगुणः.

FORTH, *adv.* बहिः, अग्रे, पुरतः; with verbs, ex. by निर्, उत्, प्र pr. 2 प्रभृति, आरभ्य; 'from this time f.' अद्य-अतः-प्रभृति, अद्यारभ्य; 'f.-coming' आगामिन्, आसन्न, उपस्थित. -FORTHWITH, *adv.* सपदि, झटिति, द्रागेव, सद्यः, अचिरात्-रेण, आशु, अविलंबितं, तत्क्षणात्.

FORTIFY, *v. t.* दृढीकृ, स्थिरीकृ 8 U, द्रढयति (D.), सं-स्तंभ् 9 P or c. 2 सुगुप्त-सुरक्षित-*a.* कृ, परिखया आपरि-वृ 5 U or परिवेष्ट् c. -ICATION, *s.* गुप्ति *f.*, परिखा, प्राचीरं, दुर्गं, कूटः, कोटः, प्राकारपरिखादि.

FORTITUDE, *s.* धैर्यं, सत्त्वं, धीरता, मनःस्थैर्यं. 2 वीर्यं, शौर्यं, विक्रमः, साहसं, पौरुषं.

FORTNIGHT, *s.* पक्षः, मासार्धं, अर्धमासः.

FORTUITY, *s.* दैवयोगः-घटना, दैवं, समापत्ति *f.* -OUS, *a.* दैवायत्त, दैवाधीन, अचिंतित, अतर्कितोपनत, आकस्मिक (की *f.*). -OUSLY, *adv.* Accidentally, q. v.

FORTUNE, *s.* दैवं, भाग्यं, भागधेयं, विधिः, अदृष्टं, भवितव्यता; *See* FATE. 2 ऋद्धि *f.*, श्रीः, लक्ष्मीः, ऐश्वर्यं, संपद् *f.*, संपत्ति *f.*, धनं. 3 शुभं, कल्याणं, भद्रं, शिवं, सौभाग्यं, मंगलं, पुण्योदयः; 'bad f.' दुर्दैवं, दुर्-मंद-भाग्यं, दैवदुर्विपाकः; 'tell f.' शुभाशुभं कथ् 10 or चिंत् 10 or निरूप् 10 or आलोच् 10; 'f.-teller' दैवज्ञः, गणकः, कार्तांतिकः, दैवचिंतकः; 'a female f.-teller' विप्रश्निका, ईक्षणिका, दैवज्ञा; 'f.-telling' शुभाशुभदर्शनं. -ATE, *a.* भाग्यवत्, महाभाग, सुभाग्य, सुभग, धन्य, सौभाग्यवत्, दैवशालिन्, पुण्यवत्, कृतिन्, श्रीमत्, पुण्यभाज्. 2 शुभ, कल्याण, शिव, मंगल, भद्र. -ATELY, *adv.* दैवात्, दैवयोगात्, दिष्ट्या, सौभाग्येन, भाग्य-दैव-वशात्.

FORTY, *a.* चत्वारिंशत् *f.* -FORTIETH, *a.* चत्वारिंश (शी *f.*)-शत्तम (मी *f.*).

FORWARD, *a.* अग्रिम, आदिम, अग्रस्थ, पुरोगामिन्. 2 अपूर्णकाल, आकालिक (की *f.*). 3 धृष्ट, प्रगल्भ, निर्लज्ज, प्रतिभानवत्, सप्रतिभ, अविनीत. 4 उद्यत, व्यग्र, उद्युक्त, प्रत्युत्पन्न, अविलंबित. -*v. t.* सं-प्र-वृध् c., उपकृ 8 U, पुरस्कृ, प्र-वृत् c., समुद्युज् 10, साहाय्यं कृ, उन्नतिं नी 1 P, अनुग्रह् 9 P. 2 प्रेर् c., प्र-चुद् 10, प्र-हि 5 P. 3 Accelerate, q. v. -*adv.* (f. s) अग्रतः, पुरतः, पुरः, अग्रे, पुरस्तात्, सं-अभि-मुखं; 'this day f.' अद्य प्रभृति; 'to go backward and f.' गतागतं कृ; *See* FORTH. -NESS, *s.* उत्साहः, अविलंबः, उद्योगः. 2 प्रागल्भ्यं, निर्लज्जता, धाष्टर्यं, अतिप्रसंगः, अविनयः, प्रतिभानं.

FOSSE, *s.* खातं, परिखा.

FOSSIL, *a.* शिलाजात. -*s.* धातुः; शिलाभवं, धातुद्रव्यं; उत्खातद्रव्यं. -IST, *s.* धातुविद्याज्ञः.

FOSTER, *v. t.* पुष् 1, 9 P; पा c. (पालयति), प्र-सं-वृध् c., भृ 3U, लल् 10. 2 (Love, hatred, &c.) धृ 10, वह् 1 P, बंध् 9 P; 'f.-brother' धात्रेयः, धात्रीपुत्रः; 'f.-child' पोष्यपुत्रः (त्री *f.*), पराचितः, परिस्क(ष्क)न्दः, परिस्क(ष्क)न्नः; परजातः, परैधितः; 'f.-father' पालकपिता, प्रतिपालकः, धर्मतातः; 'f.-mother' धात्री, उपमाता, प्रतिपालिका, अंकपालिका, मातृका, धात्रेयी.

FOUL, *a.* मलिन, समल, अशुचि, कलुष, मलदूषित, मलीमस, आविल, अशुद्ध, अपवित्र, अमेध्य, पंकिल. 2 कुत्सित, कश्मल, गर्ह्य, निंद्य, दुष्ट. 3 अवाच्य, अशिष्ट, अश्लील (language). 4 कूट, कपट, पाप, in comp.; 'f. means' कपटप्रबंधः; 'even by f. means' दुरितैरपि (R. VIII. 2); 'f. play' दुरितं, पापं; 'f. weather' दुर्दिनं; 'f. quality' रजोगुणः; 'f. smell' पूतिगंधः, दुर्गंधः; 'fall f. of' उपरि पत् 1 P, परस्परं आ-हन् 2 U or संघट्ट् 1 A; 'f.-mouthed' दुर्मुख, वाग्दुष्ट, कटुवाच, मुखर, परिवादिन्. -*v. t.* मलिनयति-कलुषयति-आविलयति (D.), दुष् c. (दूषयति). -LY, *adv.* अतिदुष्टं, घोरं, मलिनं. -NESS, *s.* मालिन्यं, गर्ह्यता, &c.

FOUND, *v. t.* स्था c. (स्थापयति), प्रति-सं-अव-

रुह् c. (रोपयति), निर्मा 3 A or c. (मापयति), बंध् 9 P, प्रवृत् c., आरभ् 1 A; मूल, निबंधन, निष्ठा, in comp.; 'attachment f. ed on love' प्रेममूलाभावनिबंधना-रतिः; 'f. ed on ignorance' अज्ञानज, अज्ञानमूल-लक, अविद्याकल्पित. -ATION, s. प्रतिष्ठापनं, संस्थापनं; निर्माणं. 2 वास्तु m., n., पोटः, ग्रहप्रतिष्ठा, गृहमूलं, भित्तिमूलं, वेश्मभूः. 3 (Fig.) मूलं, आधारः, उपष्टंभः. -ER, s. संस्थापकः, प्रवर्तकः, आरंभकः, आदिकर्तृ m., प्रतिष्ठापकः, कर्ता, प्रयोजकः. -v. i. जलमज्जनेन नश् 4 P, जले मस्ज् 6 P. -LING, s. अपविद्धबालकः, उत्सृष्टापत्यं.

FOUNDERY, s. संधानी, कुप्यशाला.

FOUNT, FOUNTAIN, s. निर्झरः, उत्सः, प्रस्रवणं, वारिप्रवाहः. 2 मूलं, योनि f., प्रभवः, हेतुः, आदिहेतुः. 3 धारायंत्रं (artificial f.).

FOUR, a. चतुर्, चतुष्टय; 'f. times' चतुः; 'in f. ways' चतुर्धा; 'f.-cornered' चतुरस्र-श्र; 'f.-fold' चतुर्गुण; 'f.-footed' चतुष्पाद्, चतुष्पाद; 'f. score' अशीति f. —FOURTH, a. चतुर्थ (र्थी f.), तुर्य, तुरीय. -s. चतुर्थभागः, पादः, चतुर्थांशः; तुरीयः, तुर्यः, तुर्यांशः; 'a rupee and one f.' सपादरूपकः. -LY, adv. चतुर्थस्थाने. —FOURTEEN, a. चतुर्दशन्. -TH, a. चतुर्दश (शी f.).

FOWL, s. खगः, पक्षिन् m., शकुनः; See BIRD. 2 कुक्कुटः, ताम्रचूडः, चरणायुधः. -v. i. पक्षिणो ग्रह् or बंध् 9 P or धृ 1 P. -ER, s. शाकुनिकः, व्याधः, शकुनिलुब्धः, जालिकः, लुब्धकः, पक्षिग्राहकः, जीवांतकः. -ING, s. पक्षिग्रहणं-वधः-घातः.

FOX, s. शृगालः, कि(खि)खिः, खिंकिरः, भूरिमायः, गोमायुः; See JACKAL; 'f.-hunt' शृगालानुसरणं; 'f.-like' विदग्ध, धूर्त, बहुमाय.

FRACTION, s. भिन्नं, भागः, अपूर्णांकः, राशिभागः. -AL, a. अपूर्ण, भागिक (की f.), भागिन्.

FRACTIOUS, a. कलहकारिन्, शीघ्रकोप; वामशील.

FRACTURE, s. भंगः, भेदः, विदारणं, त्रोटनं, विभंगः, विभेदः. -v. t. भंज् 7 P, भिद् 7 P, त्रिट्ट 10; See BREAK.

FRAGILE, a. भंगुर, भंगशील, भिदुर, भिदेलिम, सुखभेद्य, सुभंग; विनश्वर, क्षयिन्. -ITY, s. भंगुरता, क्षयिता, भिदुरता.

FRAGMENT, s. खंडः-डं, शकलः-लं, भागः, अंशः, दलं, भिन्नं; 'in a thousand f. s' सहस्रधा. -ARY, a. अपूर्ण, भागिन्, खंडयुक्त.

FRAGRANT, a. सुरभि, सुगंधि, सुवास, आमोद-परिमलवह, सुवासिक, सामोद, परिमलोद्गारिन्, गंधयुक्त, गंधवत्; तिक्त, कषाय. -LY, adv. सवास, सामोदं, सगंधं. -FRAGRANCE, s. आमोदः, परिमलः, सौरभं, सौरभ्यं, गंधः, वासः, सुवासः, सुगंधः.

FRAIL, a. भंगुर, नश्वर, ध्वंसिन्, अनित्य, अस्थायिन्, क्षयिन्, सद्यःपातिन्, क्षणभंगुर-विध्वंसिन्. -NESS, -TY, s. भंगुरता, नश्वरत्वं, क्षयिता, &c. 2 दोषः, स्खलितं, प्रमादः.

FRAME, v. t. वि-,रच् 10, वि-धा 3 U, क्लृप् c., कृ 8 U, घट् c. (घटयति), संवि-धा, समा-धा, निर्मा 2 P, 3 A. 2 निबंध् 9 P. 3 सदृशीकृ; 'f. in the mind' मनसा चिंत् 10 or क्लृप् c., चित्ते कृ. -s. निर्माणं, रचनं-ना, घटनं-ना. 2 आधारः, उपष्टंभः; आवरणं, कोशः, आवेष्टनं. 3 शरीरं, देहः, गात्रं, वपुस् n., कायः, अंगं; 'f. of body' देहबंधः; 'of a hardy f.' वज्रदेहिन्, सिंहसंहनन. 4 भावः, वृत्ति f., स्थिति f., दशा, अवस्था; 'joyous f. of mind' आनंदवृत्तिः. 5 आकारः, रूपं, आकृति f., रीति f., संस्थानं.

FRANCHISE, s. पौरजनाधिकारः. 2 मुक्ति f., मोचनं, स्वाधीनता. -v. t. मुच् 6 P.

FRANGIBLE, See FRAGILE.

FRANK, a. निष्कपट, सरल, ऋजुमति-बुद्धि, उदार, निर्व्याज, स्पष्ट-स्फुट-वादिन्, असंवृत, अवक्र, अमाय, निर्व्यलीक, दक्षिण, अगूढभाव ; अकपट, अव्याज, अमायिन् ; 'f.-hearted' विमलात्मन्, उदारधी; शुद्धांतःकरण. -LY, adv. निर्व्याजं, निष्कपटं, अमायया, सरलं. -NESS, s. अमाया, ऋजुता, निष्कापट्यं, औदार्य, दाक्षिण्यं, सारल्यं, अकापट्यं, &c.

FRANK-INCENSE, s. कुंदुरः-रुः, कुंदुः-दः, मुकुंदः, पालंकी.

FRANTIC, a. उन्मत्त, मदविक्षित, व्यस्तचित्त, संरब्ध; 'f. with rage' क्रोधोन्मत्त, कोपोन्मादिन्. -ALLY, adv. उन्मत्तवत्, सोन्मादं, ससंरंभं. -NESS, s. उन्मादः, व्यामोहः, चित्तविभ्रमः, उन्मत्तता, वातुलता, चित्तविभ्रमः.

FRATERNAL, a. भ्रात्रीय, भ्रातृसंनिभ, भ्रात्रनुरूप. -LY, adv. भ्रातृवत्, सोदरवत्.

FRATERNITY, s. भ्रातृत्वं, सौभ्रात्रं. 2 समाजः, संसर्गः, साहित्यं, बंधुता. -FRATERNIZE, v. i. भ्रातृवत् संमिल् 6 P or संयुज् pass. or एकीभू or सन्निपत् 1 P.

FRATRICIDE, s. भ्रातृघातकः, भ्रातृघातिन् m. 2 भ्रातृवधः-हत्या-घातः.

FRAUD, s. कपटः-टं, छलं, कैतवं, माया, व्याजः, कूटं, वंचनं-ना, उपधिः, प्रतारणं-णा, विप्रलंभः, छद्मन् n., दंभः, कुसृति f., निकृति f. —FRAUDULENT, a. कपटिन्, सव्याज, शठ, धूर्त, मायिन्, वंचक, प्रतारक, विप्रलंभक, कापटिक-छाद्मिक (की f.), कपट in comp.; 'a f. plan' कपटप्रबंधः. -LY, adv. छलेन, सकपटं, सव्याजं, मायया, धूर्तवत्, सव्याजं, सकैतवं.

FRAUGHT, a. धुर्य, धुरीण, भाराक्रांत. 2 आ-सं-परिपूर्ण, आकीर्ण, आ-सं-कुल, गर्भ-आवह-in comp.; 'f. with danger' अनर्थावह.

FRAY, s. कलहः, कलिः, युद्धं, द्वंद्वं.

FREAK, s. कामचारः, चापल्यं-लं, मनोलौल्यं, छंदः-दस् n., लहरी; तरंगः, विलासः, विभ्रमः, लीला, स्वैरिता.

—*v. t.* चित्रीकृ 8 U, चित्र् 10. —ISH, *a.* चपल, लोल, चलचित्त, लोलमति, स्वैरिन्, कामचारिन्.

FRECKLE, *s.* जडुलः, कालकः, पिप्लुः.

FREE, *a.* अमर्याद, मर्यादातिक्रांत, विनय-हीन-शून्य, प्रगल्भ, धृष्ट, अविनीत. 2 आत्म-स्व-तंत्र, स्वाधीन, अनधीन, अनायत्त, अपराधीन, स्वेच्छाचारिन्, स्वच्छंद, स्वैरिन्, निरवग्रह, अपावृत, अ-वि-वश. 3 मुक्त, विमुक्त, निर्मुक्त, विमोचित. 4 निर्यंत्रण, अबद्ध, अनिरुद्ध, वि-उत्-शृंखल, अनर्गल, निरर्गल, 5 निर्विघ्न, निष्प्रत्यूह, अप्रतिहत, निरवरोध, असंबाध. 6 निश्चिंत, शांतचित्त, विशद, स्वस्थ. 7 मुक्तहस्त, त्यागशील, व्ययपर. 8 अयतवाच्, असंवृत, अनियंत्रितकथ. 9 मूल्यं विना. 10 सर्वसाधारण-सामान्य; 'f. from' ex. by निर्-अ in comp. or by गत, वीत, हीन, रहित, वर्जित, शून्य, मुक्त, mostly in comp.; 'f. from pride' निरवलेप; अनृण, वीतस्पृह, चिंताहीन, &c.; 'f. choice' स्वेच्छा, स्वरुचि *f.*; 'f. course' प्रसरः. —*v. t.* मुच् 6 P or c., वि-निर्-°, वि-सृज् 6 P or c., मोक्ष् 10; gen. ex. by निर् or अ pr. to nouns; 'f. from obstacle' विघ्नान् अपनी or हृ 1 P, निर्विघ्नीकृ 8 U; 'f. from debt' अनृण *a.* कृ, ऋणं अपाकृ or निस्तॄ c.; 'I f. ed him from doubt' तं निर्मुक्तसंदेहमकरवं, तस्य संदेहमपानयम्. 'F.-agency' 'f.-will' स्वेच्छा, यदृच्छा, स्वातंत्र्यं, स्वाच्छंद्यं, स्वैरता, स्वकामः; 'f.-booter' दस्युः, साहसिकः, प्रसह्यचौरः; 'f.-booting' प्रसभं अपहारः, साहसं; 'f.-born' जात-जन्म-स्वतंत्र, जात्या स्वायत्त, जन्मनैव अपरायत्त, कुलीनजाति, अदासज; 'f.-hearted,-minded' *See* FRANK; 'f.-hold' निष्करभूमि *f.*, स्वाधीना भूः; 'f.-holder' स्वाधीनक्षेत्रस्वामिन् *m.*; 'f.-liver' कुक्षिंभरिः, औदरिकः; 'f.-man' स्वतंत्रः, अपरायत्तः, स्वाधीनः, अदासः; 'f.-spoken' स्फुटवादिन्, स्पष्टवाच्, अगूढभाव; 'f.-thinker' नास्तिकः, अनीश्वरवादिन् *m.*; 'f.-woman' स्वाधीना, स्वैरिणी, स्वैरचारिणी. —DOM, *s.* स्वतंत्रता, अवशता, स्वातंत्र्यं. 2 मोक्षः-क्षणं, वि-,मुक्ति *f.*, मोचनं. 3 निर्यंत्रणं-णता, निर्विघ्नता. 4 अविनयः, मर्यादातिक्रमः, प्रागल्भ्यं. 5 विरहः, अभावः, राहित्यं, हानि *f.*, मुक्तिः; 'f. of will or thought' स्वेच्छा, स्वहृच्छयानुवर्तनं, कामचारः, स्वाच्छंद्यं. —LY, *adv.* स्वेच्छया, स्वैरं, स्वच्छंदतः; कामतः, अयाचितं. 2 बहुशः, बाहुल्येन, मुक्तहस्तं, भूयसा. 3 यथेच्छं, नि-प्र-कामं, पर्याप्तं, यथेप्सितं, आतृप्ति. 4 निर्विघ्नं, निर्यंत्रणं, अनिवारितं. 5 मूल्यं विना. —NESS, *s.* निर्विघ्नता, निष्कापट्यं, वाग्यतत्वं, त्यागशीलता, &c.

FREEZE, *v. i.* शिलीभू 1 P, घनीभू, संहन् pass., स्त्यै 1 A, संहतीभू, स्त्यानीभू, पिंडं बंध् 9 P. —*v. t.* शिली-घनी-कृ 8 U, संहन् 2 P, जडयति (D.), जडीकृ, स्त्यै c., शीलीकृ; 'a frozen mass of ice' शिलीभूतं हिमं, हिमपिंडः.

FREIGHT, *s.* नौभांडं, नौभारः, पोतद्रव्याणि, नाविकं. 2 तरः, आतरः, तरपण्यं, तारिकं, तार्यं. —*v. i.* (द्रव्याणि) नावि निविश् c. or नि-धा 3 U, द्रव्यैः पूर् 10.

FRENETIC, *See* FRANTIC.

FRENZY, *s.* उन्मादः, चित्तविभ्रमः-विभ्रवः, उन्मत्तता, आवेशः. —ED, *a.* उन्मत्त, भ्रांतचित्त, आविष्ट.

FREQUENT, *a.* नित्य, अनवरत, सतत, अभीक्ष्ण, बहुशः घटमान or वर्तमान; better ex. by 'f.-ly.' —*v. t.* सेव् 1 A, नित्यं आधि 1 U, सततं भज् 1 U or अभिगम् 1 P, जुष् 6 A; सततं गम् &c.; *See* below. —ATIVE, *s.* यङ्लुगंतं, यङंतं. —LY, *adv.* पुनः पुनः, मुहुर्मुहुः, भूयोभूयः, नित्यं, असकृत्, वारंवारं, अभीक्ष्णं, सततं, बहुशः, अनेकशः, बहुवारं, प्रायः, प्रायेण, प्रायशः, शश्वत्. —FREQUENCE, -CY, *s.* पौनःपुन्यं, सातत्यं अभीक्ष्णता, नित्यता, अविरामः, समभिहारः, अविच्छेदः.

FRESCO, *s.* शीतता. 2 भंडोदकचित्रं.

FRESH, *a.* नव, अभिनव, नूतन, नवीन; प्रत्यग्र, अविशीर्ण, अम्लान, अशुष्क (of flowers only); 'f. age' नवं-प्रथमं-वयः; 'f. wound' आर्द्रक्षतं. 2 पेय, आस्वाद्य, अलवण. 3 शीतल, शिव, सुख (of breezes). 4 सरस, अश्रांत, अक्षतवीर्य, अक्लांत, अक्षीणतेजस्; 'a f. man' नवशिष्यः-छात्रः, प्राथमकल्पिकः, शैक्षः (just initiated). —EN, *v. t.* नवीकृ 8 U, सरसीकृ, (पुनर्नवीकृताः स्मः S. 5). —LY, *adv.* सद्यः, नवं, प्रत्यग्रं. 2 शीतलं, सुखं. —NESS, *s.* नवता, नूतनता, अम्लानता, अक्षीणता. 2 तेजस् *n.*, वीर्यं, सरसत्वं, अक्लांति-अश्रांति *f.* 3 अलवणता. 4 नवरक्तवर्णः.

FRET, *v. i.* क्षुभ् 4 P, पीड् pass., व्यथ् 1 A, दुर्मनायते (D.), अंतः सं-परि-आ-तप् 4 A, शुच् 1 P, क्लिश् pass., उद्विज् 6 A, आत्मानं तप् c. or क्षुभ् c. 2 घर्षणेन क्षि pass., संघृष् pass. —*v. t.* संतप् c., क्षुभ् c.; व्यथ् c. (व्यथयति), पीड् 10, बाध् 1 A, क्लिश् 9 P. 2 घृष् 1 P, घर्षणेन तप् c. —*s.* (Of sea) क्षोभः, वीचिपरिलोठनं. 2 (F.-fulness) चित्तव्यथा, आत्मपीडा-क्लेशः, उद्वेगः, मनस्तापः, मनःक्षोभः, अशांति *f.*, दुर्मनायितं. 3 प्रतीपता, वक्रभावः. —FUL, *a.* आत्मतापिन्, शीघ्रकोपिन्, दुर्मनस्, चंड, शीघ्रक्षुब्ध-संतप्त. 2 वक्रप्रकृति, प्रतीप, वक्रभाव, दुष्प्रकृति, वामशील, जिह्मस्वभाव. —FULLY, *adv.* सचित्तक्षोभं, मनस्तापेन.

FRETTY, *a.* व्यत्यस्तरेखारूपेण तष्ट.

FRIABLE, *See* FRAGILE.

FRIAR, *s.* योगिन् *m.*, मुनिः, यतिः, सन्यासी, तपस्वी. —Y, *s.* मठः, आश्रमः, विहारः.

FRICTION, *s.* घर्षणं, संघर्षः, आ-अभि-घर्षः-र्षणं, आ-वि-घट्टनं, परस्परघर्षणं-मर्दनं.

FRIDAY, *s.* शुक्र-भृगु-वारः-वासरः.

FRIEND, *s.* मित्रं, सखि *m.*, सुहृद् *m.*, स्निग्धः, प्रणयिन् *m.*, हितः, सहायः, सजुस् *m.*, संगिन् *m.*, वय-

ह्य:, बंधु:; (term of address) भद्र:-द्रा; 'an old f.' चिरमित्रं; 'a true f.' सन्मित्रं. -*v. t.* उपकृ 8 U, अनुग्रह् 9 P. -LESS, *a.* मित्र-बंधु-हीन, असहाय, अनाथ, अशरण; *See* FORLORN. -SHIP, *s.* सख्यं, मित्रत्वं; मैत्री, मैत्र्यं, बंधुता, सौहार्दं, सौहृदं, स्नेह:, प्रणय:, प्रीति *f.*, प्रेमन् *m.*, *n.*, अनुराग:. 2 साहाय्यं. -FRIENDLY, *a.* स्निग्ध, सदय, हितकाम, हितैषिन्, स्नेहशील, सानुराग, सुहृदय, सप्रणय. 2 हित, अनुकूल, अनुग्राहिन्, उपकारक, हितकर; सुखावह, कल्याणकर (री *f.*); 'on f. terms' स्नेहवृत्त्या, मित्रभावेन; 'f. disposed' हितबुद्धि; 'f. dispute' प्रणयकलह:, प्रीतिकलह:. -*adv.* मित्रवत्, हितवत्, स्निग्धं, प्रियं. -NESS, *s.* हितेच्छा, हितकामना, हितबुद्धि *f.*, अनुकूलता, मित्रत्वं, प्रणय:, स्नेहशीलता.

FRIEZE, *s.* स्थूलपट्ट-शाटक:, वराशि:.

FRIGATE, *s.* महायुद्धनौका.

FRIGHT, *s.* भयं, त्रास:, संत्रास:, शंका, साध्वसं, भीति *f.*, उद्वेग:, दरं; 'take f.' सं-उत्-त्रस् 1, 4 P, उत्त्रस्त-चकित-*a.* भू. -*v. t.*,-EN, *v. t.* भी c. (भापयते-भीषयते), सं-उत्-त्रस् c., उद्विज् c. -ED, *a.* भीत, त्रस्त, भयार्त; भयाकुल, चकित, ससाध्वस, जातशंक, शंकित, भयाविष्ट. -FUL, *a.* भीम, विकट, कराल, दारुण, भीषण, घोर, भैरव (वी *f.*), रौद्र (द्री *f.*), भयानक, भयावह, उग्र, भयंकर; 'f. in appearance' करालवदन, भीम-रौद्र-दर्शन, उग्रदर्शन. -FULLY, *adv.* दारुणं, घोरं, उग्रं.

FRIGID, *a.* शीत, शिशिर, हिम, जड. 2 निरुत्साह, नि:स्नेह; *See* COLD. -ITY, *s.* हिमं, शैत्यं, जडता. 2 विराग:, स्नेहाभाव:. -LY, *adv.* शीतलं, शिशिरं, नि:स्नेहं.

FRINGE, *s.* अंचल:-लं, दशा: (*f.* pl.), वस्तय: (*m. f.*); 'like a f. rent from the robe of heaven' छिन्ना इवांबरपटस्य दशा: (Mr. 5). -*v. t.* प्रांतयति (D.); 'f. ed with gold' सुवर्णमंडितप्रांतं (वस्त्रं).

FRIPPERY, *s.* चीराणि (pl.), जीर्ण-चीर-वस्त्रं, वस्त्रखंडा:, कर्पटा:. 2 निष्प्रयोजनद्रव्यं, उच्छिष्टं.

FRISK, *v. i.* क्रीड् 1 U, इतस्तत: रम् 1 A or नृत् 4 P or प्लु 1 A, खेल् 1 P, वि-हृ 1 P. -Y, *a.* हृष्ट, प्रहृष्ट, प्रफुल्ल, सानंद.

FRITH, *s.* संकटं, संभेद:.

FRITTER, *v. t.* खंडश: कृत् 6 P; खंड् 10, शकलीकृ 8 U; 'f. away' खंडश:-अल्पश:-न्यूनीकृ or क्षीणीकृ or क्षि c. (क्षपयति); 'f. away time' अल्पश: (मुधा) वेलां क्षि c. -*s.* खंड:-डं, शकल:-लं.

FRIVOLOUS, *a.* लघु, अगुरु, अनर्थक, तुच्छ, यत्किंचन, चपल, चपल-लघु-वृत्ति, लघुकर्मन्. -NESS,-FRIVOLITY, *s.* लाघवं, लघुवृत्तिता-त्वं, लघुता, यत्किंचनकारिता, चापलं, चपलं कर्म, निरर्थकव्यापार:.

FRIZ, FRIZZLE, *v. t.* कुंच् c., व्यावृत् c.

FRO, *adv.* (In 'to and f.') इतस्तत:; 'going to and f.' गमनागमनं.

FROCK, *s.* उत्तरीयं, कंचुक:.

FROG, *s.* भेक:, दर्दुर:, मंडूक:, वर्षाभू:, शा(सा)लूर:, प्लव:, प्लवग:, प्लवंगम:, वर्षाघोष:; "she-f." मंडूकी.

FROLIC, *v. i.* क्रीड् 1 U, विलस् 1 P, विहृ 1 P, खेल् 1 P, रम् 1 A, विभ्रम् 1, 4 P. -*s.* केलि *f.*, विलास:, क्रीडा, विहार:, वि-भ्रम:, लीला, खेला, क्रीडाकौतुकं. -SOME, *a.* केलि-विलास-प्रिय, विलासिन्, क्रीडा-खेलापर, उल्लासिन्, विहारिन्, केलिकर; परिहासशील.

FROM, *prep.* Gen. ex. by abl., when denoting source or place. 2 (Of cause) by abl. or instr., (only by instr., the noun being *f.*); 'f. curiosity' कुतूहलात्-लेन; 'f. its fragrance' सुरभितया. 3 (Of persons) by abl., or सकाशात् with gen.; रामस्य सकाशात् 'f. Râma.' 4 (Of time) by आ with abl. or in comp.; 'f. the beginning' आमूलात्; आजन्मन:, आजन्म; gen. by आरभ्य or प्रभृति, with abl.; तद्दर्शनादारभ्य or प्रभृति; 'f. this day' अद्यप्रभृति, अद्यारभ्य; 'f. above' उपरिष्टात्, ऊर्ध्वात्; 'f. day to day' दिनेदिने, दिनादिनं; 'f. below' अधस्तात्, अधोभागात्; अध:स्थानात्; 'f. behind' पश्चादेत्य, पृष्ठत:, पृष्ठत आगत्य; 'f. hence' अत:, इत:; 'f. afar' दूरत:, दूरात्; 'f. without' बहिर्देशात्; 'f. within' अभ्यंतरात्, अंत:प्रदेशात्.

FRONT, *s.* अग्रं, अग्रभाग:-देश:, मुखं, मूर्धन् *m.*; 'f. door or gate' मुखं, नि:सरणं. 2 वदनं, आस्यं, मुखं, आननं. 3 शिरस् *n.*, ललाटं; 'in f. of' पुर:, पुरत:, अग्रे, अग्रत:, पुरस्तात्, प्रत्यक्षं, समक्षं, साक्षात्, अभि-सं-मुखं-खे, (with gen.); 'f. of war' रणधुरा, रणशिर:-मूर्धा; 'f. of army' सेनामुखं, सेनाग्रं, अग्रानीकं (f. ranks); 'in the f.' अग्रे, मूर्ध्नि, धुरि, शिरसि; 'to place in the f.' पुरस्कृ, अग्रणीकृ, अग्रेसरीकृ. -*v.* संमुखं-खे स्था 1 P or वृत् 1 A, संमुखी-अभिमुखी-भू; oft. by मुख or अभिमुख in comp.; 'a house f. ing the east' प्राङ्मुखं-प्राच्यभिमुखं-गृहं. -AGE, *s.* अग्र-पूर्व-भाग:, मुखं. -AL, *a.* लालाटिक (की *f.*), ललाट in comp. -*s.* ललाटपट्टं; 'f. of an elephant' कुंभ:, गंड:. -LESS, *a.* धृष्ट, निर्लज्ज, निस्त्रप. -LET, *s.* ललाटपट्टं.

FRONTIER, *s.* सीमा-मन् *f.*, उपांत:, पर्यंत:, प्रांत:, समंत:, सामंत:-तं. -*a.* 'Dwelling on the f.' सामंत (ती *f.*), सीमावर्तिन्, पर्यंतस्थ, प्रांतनिवासिन्; *See* BORDER.

FRONTISPIECE, *s.* मुखप्रतिमा-चित्रं; 'f. of a house' गृहमुखं, गृहाग्रभाग:.

FROST, *s.* तुषार:, तुहिनं, हिमं, अवश्याय:, नीहार: ;

प्रालेयं, मिहिका ; 'f.-bitten' हिमसिक्त, तुषार-शीत-उपहत. -Y, *a.* हिम, तुषार, हिम-तुषार-वत्.

FROTH, *s.* फेनः-णः, मंडः-डं, उत्सेचनं ; *See* FERMENT. -*v. i.* फेनायते-मंडायते (D.), उत्सिच् pass. -Y, *a.* फेनिल, फेनमय (यी *f.*), फेनिन्. 2 असार, लघु, निःसार, निःसत्व, अंतःशून्य.

FROUZY, *a.* पूतिगंधि, उग्रगंध.

FROWARD, *a.* अदम्य, आविनेय, अतिलालित, दुर्ललित, उच्छृंखल, दुर्दांत. 2 प्रतीप, प्रतिकूल, वक्रस्वभाव, विलोम, वामशील, प्रतीपाचार. -LY, *adv.* वक्रभावेन, प्रतिकूलं. -NESS, *s.* प्रतीपता, वामता, वक्रभावः, अदम्यता.

FROWN, *s.* भ्रूभंगः, भ्रू(भ्रु)कुटि-टी *f.*, भ्रूभेदः-क्षेपः-संकोचः. -*v. i.* भ्रुकुटिं बंध् 9 P or रच् 10 or कृ 8 U, भ्रूभंगेन दृश् 1 P, भ्रुवौ संकुच् 1 P; 'Oh he just f. s at myself' अये मय्येव भ्रुकुटीधरः संवृत्तः (U. 5). -ING, *a.* नत-आकुंचित-भ्रू, सभ्रूभंग. -INGLY, *adv.* सभ्रूभंगं, भ्रूक्षेपेण, भ्रुकुटिं बद्ध्वा, सभ्रूक्षेपं.

FRUCTIFY, *v. t.* बहुफलदीकृ 8 U, सफलीकृ, स्फीतीकृ, सफलयति (D.). -FRUCTUOUS,-FRUCTIFEROUS, *a.* (बहु)फलद, फलिन्, फलदायिन्.

FRUGAL, *a.* मित-अल्प-व्यय-व्ययिन्, स्वल्प-परिमित-व्यय, अमुक्तहस्त, कृपण, व्ययविमुख. -ITY, *s.* मितव्ययिता, मित-स्वल्प-व्ययः, अमुक्तहस्तत्वं, कृपणत्वं. -LY, *adv.* अमुक्तहस्तं, मित-स्वल्प-व्ययेन, अल्पव्ययपूर्वं, कृपणं.

FRUIT, *s.* फलं (lit. and fig.); श (स)स्यं, प्रसवः, उत्पन्नं. 2 परिणामः, उत्तरफलं, कर्मफलं. 3 (Progeny) अपत्यं, संतानः-नं, संतति *f.*, प्रजा, प्रसूति *f.*; फलं. 4 अर्थः, लाभः, फलागमः, फलप्राप्ति *f.*; 'dry f.' वानं; 'unripe f.' शलाटु; 'bear f.' फल् 1 P, फलं बंध् 9 P or दा 3 U, सफलीभू, पच् pass., (सद्य एव सुकृतां हि पच्यते कांक्षितं R. XI. 50); 'f.-bearer' फलदातृ *m.*, फलदः; 'f.-bearing' फलद, फलेग्रहि, फलभृत्, फलदायिन्, फलिन्, फलशालिन्; 'f.-garden' फलवाटः-टिका; 'f.-season or time' फलकालः-समयः, फलावचयकालः; 'f.-stalk or stem' शस्यमंजरी, प्रसवबंधनं, वृंतं; 'f.-tree' फलदः वृक्षः, वनस्पतिः, फलग्राहिन् *m.* -AGE, *s.* फलोच्चयः, फलभारः-गुच्छः, फलागमः. -ERER, *s.* फलविक्रयिन् *m.* -ERY, *s.* फलानि. 2 फलस्थानं. -FUL, *a.* फलवत्, फलद, फलिन्, सफल, फलित, अवंध्य, अमोघ, बहुफलद, फलिन, फलेग्रहि. 2 बहुप्रज, प्रजनिष्णु, बह्वपत्य, बहुप्रजोपेत. 3 उत्पादक, जनक; आवह-प्रभवः-मूलं-कारणं in comp. -LESS, *a.* निष्फल, वि-अ-फल, निरर्थक, व्यर्थ, मोघ, वंध्य, अनर्थक, निष्प्रयोजन, निर्गुण, अनुपयुक्त, फलहीन, अवकेशिन्. -LESSLY, *adv.* व्यर्थं, निरर्थकं, मुधा, वृथा, मोघं, निष्फलं. -LESSNESS, *s.* वैयर्थ्यं, अनुपयोगः, व्यर्थता, वैफल्यं. -FRUITION, *s.* उप-,भोगः, भुक्ति *f.*, अनुभवः, आस्वादः; सुखोपभोगः, फलास्वादः, सुखानुभवः, सुखास्वादः.

FRUMENTACEOUS, *a.* गोधूममय (यी *f.*).

FRUSTRATE, *v. t.* विफली-निष्फली-मोघी-कृ 8 U, प्रति-व्या-हन् 2 P, भंज् 7 P, खंड् 10, वृथा-मुधा-कृ; *See* BAFFLE. -*a.* Fruitless, q. v. -ED, *a.* प्रति-व्या-हत, मोघीकृत, वृथाभूत; 'f. in attempts or hopes' भग्नोद्यम, व्यर्थप्रयत्न, भग्नसंकल्प; भग्नाश, अकृतार्थ, मोघाश, खंडिताश, प्रतिहत, प्रतिबद्ध. -ION, *s.* भंगः, व्याघातः, विफलीकरणं, खंडनं. -IVE, -ORY, *a.* व्याघातिन्, भंजक, वृथाकारिन्.

FRUTESCENT, *a.* गुल्मावृत.

FRY, *s.* क्षुद्रमत्स्यसंघः, मत्स्यसंघातः, पोताधानं. 2 मीनांडं. -*v. t.* भ्रस्ज् 6 P or c. (भर्जयति), पच् 1P, भृज्ज् 1 A. -ING, *s.* भर्जनं, पचनं; 'f.-pan' पिठरः-रं, भृज्जनं, भ्राष्ट्रः, भर्जनपात्रं, अंबरीषं; ऋजीषं, पिष्टपचनं; (for liquor) स्वेदनी, कंदु-दू *m.-f.* -ED, *a.* भ्रष्ट, भर्जित, कंदुपक्व; 'f. grain' धानाः (*f.*, pl.), भ्रष्टयवाः, लाजाः (*m.* pl.).

FUDDLE, *v. t.* मद् c., मदेन मुह् c. -*v. i.* मद् 4 P. -ER, *s.* पानासक्तः, पानरतः.

FUEL, *s.* इंधनं, एधस् *n.*, एधः, इध्मं, समिध् *f.*, समिंधनं; 'add f. to the flames' *See* under OIL.

FUGACIOUS, *a.* पलायनशील, पलायनपर; अस्थिर, चपल, लोल.

FUGITIVE, *s.* कृतपलायनः, पलायिन् *m.*, कांदिशीकः. -*a.* प्रपलायिन्, पलायनपर-शील. 2 चपल, तरल, चंचल, अस्थिर.

FULCRUM, *s.* आधारः, उपस्तं(ष्ट)भः, आलंबः, आश्रयः.

FULFIL, *v. t.* सं-परि-पूर् 10, साध् 5 P or c., निर्वह् c., निः-सं-पद् c., समाप् c., निर्वृत् c., सफलीकृ 8 U, निस्तॄ c., तीर् 10; 'f. a promise' प्रतिज्ञां निर्वह् c. or तीर् or शुध् c. or पा c. (पालयति) or अप-वृज् 10; gen. in pass. constr. ex. by पूर्ण, कृत, आप्त, लब्ध, in comp.; 'whose desires are f. ed' समवाप्त-लब्ध-मनोरथः-कामः, कृतार्थः, पूर्णमनोरथः-कामः, कृती; 'who has f. ed his promise' पूर्णप्रतिज्ञः, पालितसंगरः, सत्यप्रतिज्ञः, सत्यव्रतः-संधः. -LER, *s.* निर्वाहकः, साधकः, पूरयितृ *m.* -MENT, *s.* पूरणं, सिद्धि *f.*, निष्पत्ति *f.*, साधनं, निर्वाहः; 'f. of desires' कृतार्थता, कामसिद्धिः, इच्छापूरणं, इष्टावाप्तिः.

FULGENT, *a.* उज्ज्वल, दीप्ति-द्युति-मत्; *See* BRIGHT. -FULGENCY, *s.* तेजस् *n.*, प्रभा, कांति-दीप्ति-द्युति *f.*

FULL, *a.* (of) सं-परि-पूर्ण, आ-सं-कीर्ण, आ-संकुल, संभृत, व्याप्त, निर्भर, पूरित, मय (यी *f.*) in comp. 2 अशेष, अन्यून, सकल, निखिल, कृत्स्न, समग्र, अविकल, अखंड, संपूर्ण; 'f. year' पूर्णवर्षं; 'f. speed' पूर्णवेगः ; 'f. 8 months old' पूर्णाष्टमास. 3 परिणत, परिपक्व, पक्व, कठोर,

प्रौढ, संपन्न. **-s.** पूर्णता, साकल्यं; 'in f.' सविस्तरं, साकल्येन. **-adv.** कृत्स्नशः, सर्वथा, साकल्येन, अशेषतः-षेण, पूर्णं; 'f.-blown' प्रफुल्ल, विकच, विकसित, प्रस्फुट, प्रस्फुटित; 'f.-bodied' स्थूलकाय, सन्नद्धांग, पुष्टदेह; 'f.-bosomed' पीनस्तन (नी *f.*), पीनकुचकुड्मल; 'f.-fed' पुष्टांग, हृष्टपुष्ट; 'f.-grown' प्रवृद्ध, प्रौढ, कठोर, परिणत, प्ररूढ; गतशैशव, प्राप्तयौवन, यौवनारूढ, समारूढयौवनारंभ (of men); 'f.-growth' प्रौढि *f.*, प्रौढता, प्रवृद्धि *f.*; 'f.-laden' पूर्णभार, सुभाराक्रांत; 'f. moon' पूर्णेंदुः, सकलेंदुः; 'f. moon day' पौर्णिमा, पूर्णिमा, राका. **-ER,** *s.* रजकः, निर्णेजकः. **-LY,** *adv.* अशेषेण, सविस्तरं, अशेषतः, सर्वशः-था, साकल्येन, कृत्स्नशः, निरवशेषं, विस्तरेण-रशः, पूर्णतया. **-NESS,** *s.* पूर्णता, निर्भरता, पूर्ति *f.*, संभारः. 2 बाहुल्यं, प्राचुर्यं. 3 परिणामः, परिपाकः, सिद्धि *f.*, प्रौढि *f.*, संपद् *f.*

FULMINATE, *v. t.* विकटं रस् or स्तन् 1 P, स्फूर्ज् 1 P. **-v. t.** वज्रनिर्घोषेण इव प्रेर् c. or उदीर् c. **-ION,** *s.* स्फूर्जनं, वज्र-मेघ-निर्घोषः, स्तनितं.

FULSOME, *a.* गर्हित, कुत्सित, गर्ह्य, बीभत्सजनक, विरस. **-NESS,** *s.* विरसता, गर्ह्यता.

FUMBLE, *v. i.* परामृश् 6 P, समालभ् 1 A, अदक्षं कार्यं वि-धा 3 U. **-ING,** *a.* संभ्रांतं परामृशत्, अदक्षतया कार्यविधायिन्. **-s.** अदक्षं कार्यविधानं.

FUME, *s.* धूमः-मिका, बाष्पः, धूपः. 2 धूमोद्गारः. 3 क्रोधः, संरंभः. **-v. t.** धूमयति (D.), धूप् 1 P (धूपायति). **-FUMIGATE,** *v. t.* धूप् 10, धूप् 1 P (धूपायति), धूपेन वास् 10 or भू c.; 'a thing f. ed' वासितं, भावितं. **-v. i.** धूमायते (D.), बाष्पं उद्गॄ 6 P. 2 Angry, to be, q. v. **-ION,** *s.* वासनं, भावनं, अधिवासनं. **-FUMY,** *a.* सधूम, सधूप.

FUN, *s.* परि(री)हासः, नर्मन् *n.*, क्रीडा, खेला, केलि *f.*, प्रहसनं, क्रीडाकौतुकं; 'said in f.' नर्मभाषितं, नर्मालापः. **-FUNNY,** *a.* हासजनक, विनोदनशील, रसिक, कौतुककारिन्, नर्म-परिहास- in comp. 2 उपहास्य, अपरूप.

FUNCTION, *s.* व्यापारः, कर्मन् *n.*, कार्यं, कृत्यं, चेष्टा, क्रिया, चेष्टितं, व्यवसायः, व्यवहारः, वृत्ति *f.*, प्रवृत्तिः. 2 नियोगः, अधिकारः, पदं. 3 आचरणं, अनुष्ठानं, करणं. 4 गुणः, धर्मः स्वभावः. 5 इंद्रियं, शक्ति *f.*, कर्मेंद्रियं. **-ARY,** *s.* नियोगिन् *m.*, अधिकारी, कार्यनिर्वाहकः, नियुक्तः, अधिकृतः.

FUND, *s.* संचयः, पुंजः, राशिः, समुदायः, निचयः, संयोगः, संनिपातः; *See* COLLECTION. 2 मूलधनं, नीवि-वी *f.* **-v. t.** सं-चि 5 U, संग्रह् 9 P, पुंजीकृ 8 U, राशीकृ.

FUNDAMENT, *s.* गुदं, पायुः, अपानं, मलद्वारं. 2 अधोभागः, तलं.

FUNDAMENTAL, *a.* प्रधान, सार, सारभूत, गुर्वर्थ, मौलिक, मूल in comp.; 'f. cause' मूलकारणं; 'f. principle' मूलतत्त्वं. **-s.** प्रधान-मूल-तत्त्वं, मूलं, तत्त्वं, सारः.

FUNERAL, *s.* और्ध्वदेहिकक्रिया, अंत्येष्टि *f.*, प्रेतकार्यं-कृत्यं, प्रेतनिर्हारः, अंत्यक्रिया, उत्तरक्रिया-कर्म, और्ध्वदेहिकं, श्राद्धादि कर्म **-a.** और्ध्वदेहिक, और्ध्वदैहिक (की *f.*), better by (*s.*); 'f. pile' चिता, चिति-ती *f.*, चित्या.

FUNGUS, *s.* विड्जं, गोमयजं, शिलीध्रं, शा(सा)लेयः, शीतशिवः, छत्रा, मधुरिका, मिसि-शि-सी-शी-*f.*, मिश्रेया.

FUNICLE, *s.* क्षुद्ररज्जु *f.*, क्षुद्रगुणः, सूत्रं.

FUNNEL, *s.* धूममार्गः-पथः-द्वारं. 2 नाली, प्रणाली-लिका, नाडि-डी *f.*

FUR, *s.* रो(लो)मन् *n.*, तनूरुहः-हं, पशुलोम; 'f. on the tongue' कुलुकं, मलं. **-RED,** *a.* लोमावृत, लोमान्वित. 2 समल.

FURBISH, *v. t.* तिज् c., निः-तप् c., प्रमृज् 2 P or c., धाव् 10, परिष्कृ 8 U. **-ED,** *a.* निर्धौत, प्रमृष्ट, निष्टप्त. **-ER,** *s.* तेजकः, मार्जकः, निर्णेजकः; 'f. of weapons' शस्त्रमार्जः, असिधावकः. **-ING,** *s.* धावनं, परिष्कारः, तेजनं.

FURCATED, *a.* द्व्यग्र.

FURL, *v. t.* सं-वेष्ट् c., सं-वृ 5 U, संपुटीकृ 8 U, सं-हृ 1 P.

FURLONG, *s.* नल्वः.

FURMENTY, *s.* क्षीरान्नं, परमान्नं, पायसं.

FURNACE, *s.* अग्निकुंडं, अधिश्रयणी, अंति(दि)का, उष्मानं; 'a portable f.' *See* HEARTH.

FURNISH, *v. t.* (उपकरणैः) संयुज् 10 or सनाथीकृ 8 U; (उपस्करं) उप-क्लृप् c., उप-पद् c., सं-भृ 3 U, वि-धा 3 U; gen. ex. by स or सनाथ in comp.; 'f. ed with arrows' सशरं धनुः; मणिशिलापट्टसनाथं लतागृहं (V. 2) 'f. ed with a marble slab'; 'to f. with arms' शस्त्रास्त्रैः संनह् 4 P or सज्जीकृ. **-ED,** *a.* सं,-युक्त, समन्वित, उपेत, उपपरि-कृत, सनाथ, संभृत, स in comp. 2 सोपस्कर, सोपकरण, उपस्करादियुक्त. 3 सन्नद्ध, सज्जीकृत., **-FURNITURE,** *s.* उपस्करः, उपकरणं, परिच्छदः सामग्री, सज्जा, संभारः, उपचारः, परिबर्हः; 'on sofas with all f.' उपचारवत्सु मंचेषु (R. VI. 1); परिबर्हवंति वेश्मानि (R. XIV. 15); 'household f.' गृहोपस्करः, पारिणाह्यं.

FURROW, *s.* सीता, हलिः, लांगलमार्गः-पद्धति *f.*, हलरेखा. 2 रे(ले)खा, सुषिरं. 3 वदनरेखा, वलि-ली *f.* **-v. t.** (हलेन) कृष् 1 P, (लांगलेन) लिख् 6 P or रेखाः कृ 8 U. **-ED,** *a.* सीत्य, कृष्ट, हल्यवत्.

FURTHER, *a.* दूरतर, दूरस्थ, दवीयस्. 2 अधिक, अपर, अधिकतर, पर. **-adv.** दूरतरं, अधिकदूरं, अग्रे-

प्रतः, पुरतः, अग्रेतरां, पुरस्तात्; 'a little f. on' स्तोकांतरं, अग्रतः, किंचिदग्रे; 'f. and f.' अधिकाधिकं, उत्तरोत्तरं. 2 अपरं, अन्यच्च, अपरं च, किं च, अपि च, अपरं तु. –v. t. प्र-सं-वृध् c., अनुग्रह् 9 P, उपकृ 8 U, त्वर् c. (त्वरयति), पुरस्कृ, प्रवृत् c., साहाय्यं दा 3 U, उत्कृष् 1 P, उन्नतिं-उत्कर्षं-नी 1 P. –ANCE, s. सं-प्र-वर्धनं, प्रवर्तनं, अभि-प्र-वृद्धि f., अनुग्रहः, उपकारः, साहाय्यं, उत्कर्षः. –ER, s. उपकारकः, प्रवर्धकः. –MORE, *See* (*adv.*).

FURTHEST, *a.* दविष्ठ, दूरतम. –*adv.* सुदूरं, दविष्ठं.

FURTIVE, *a.* चौर्येण गृहीत, अपहृत, छलापहृत, निभृतं कृत. –LY, *adv.* चौरवत्, उपांशु, रहसि, निभृतं, छलेन.

FURY, *s.* मत्तता, उन्मत्तता, चंडता, उग्रता, औत्कट्यं. 2 संरंभः, कोपः, क्रोधः, रोषः, आवेशः, अमर्षः. 3 महावेगः, अत्यंतवेगः-जवः, बलं, आपातः. 4 चंडी, दुर्गा. —FURIOUS, *a.* प्र-,चंड, तीव्र, उग्र, प्रबल, महावेगवत्. 2 उन्मत्त, मत्त, मदोत्कट, मदकल, समद, उदग्रमद, उन्मादसंरब्ध, उत्कट. 3 कोपाकुल, संरब्ध, क्रोधाविष्ट, कोपपरीत, रोषण, इद्धकोप, जातामर्ष. –LY, *adv.* उग्रं, चंडं; महावेगेन, संरंभेण. –NESS, *s.* संरंभः, उग्रता, उन्मादः, कोपाकुलत्व.

FUSCOUS, *a.* आकृष्ण, आनील.

FUSE, *v. t.* वि-द्रु c., वि-ली c., जलसात् कृ 8 U. 2 एकरूप *a.* कृ, संमिश्र् 10, सायुज्यं कृ, संयुज् 10, सदृशीकृ. –*v. i.* वि-द्रु 1 P, वि-ली 4 A, द्रवीभू, गल्-क्षर् 1 P. 2 सदृशीभू, सायुज्यं प्राप् 5 P, एकरूप *a.* भू. –IBLE, *a.* द्राव्य, विलयनीय, द्रवशील, क्षरणशील. –ION, *s.* द्रावः, विलयनं, विलयः, द्रवत्वं, क्षरणं. 2 एकरूपता, सदृशीभावः, एकभावः, संमिश्रणं, संकरः, संयोगः.

FUSS, *s.* आडंबरः, तुमुलं, कोलाहलः, संभ्रमः. –Y, *a.* संभ्रमकारिन्.

FUST, *s.* स्तंभः, स्तंभदंडः. 2 उग्र-पूति-गंधः, दुर्गंधः. –FUSTY, *a.* पूति, पूतिगंधि, उग्रगंध. –NESS, *s.* पूति *f.*, दुर्गंधः.

FUSTIAN, *s.* स्थूलशाटकः, वराशिः, स्थूलपट्ट-वस्त्र-कार्पासं. 2 अतिशयोक्ति *f.*, गर्वोक्तिः, दर्पवचनं, सदर्पो वाचायुक्तिः. –*a.* स्थूलकार्पासिक (की *f.*). 2 अतिगर्वित, दर्पाध्मात, सगर्व.

FUTILE, *a.* निरर्थक, मोघ, व्यर्थ, निर्गुण. 2 असार, लघ्वर्थ, निःसार, निःसत्त्व, फल्गु, तृणप्राय, तुच्छ. –ITY, *s.* मोघता, लाघवं, असारता, &c.

FUTURE, *a.* भविष्यत्, उत्तर, अनागत, आगामिन्, भाविन्, उत्तरकालीन, श्वस्तन (नी *f.*); 'f. time' अनागतवेला, उत्तरकालः, आयति *f.* 2 पारलौकिक-पारत्रिक-आमुष्मिक (की *f.*), अमुत्रत्य, परलोकगत. –*s.*, –ITY, *s.* भावि-उत्तर-कालः, भविष्यत्-आगामि-कालः, भाविन् *n.*, अनागतं, अनागत कालः, आयति *f.*, उदर्कः; 'past, present and f.' समतीतं च भवच्च भावि च (R. VIII. 78); 'ignorant of the f.' अश्वस्तनविद्, उदर्कानभिज्ञ.

G.

GABARDINE, *s.* वराशिः, स्थूलशाटकः.

GABBLE,-ER, *See* BABBLE,-ER.

GABEL, *s.* करः, राजस्वं, शुल्कः-ल्कं, बलिः.

GABLE, *s.* गृह-प्रासाद-शिखरं.

GAD, *s.* बाणाग्रं, शूलाग्रं; अग्रं, कर्णः. 2 कीलः, लोहकीलः. –*v. i.* अट् 1 P, परिभ्रम् 1, 4 P. –DING, *s.* परि-,अटनं-भ्रमणं.

GAD-FLY, *s.* दंशकः, गोमक्षिका, दंशः-शी, वनमक्षिका.

GAFFER, *s.* वृद्धजनः; अशिष्टाचारः.

GAG, *s.* मुखबंधनी-पिधानं, रोधनं. –*v. t.* मुखं बंध् 9 P or निरुध् 7 U or पि-धा 3 U.

GAGE, *s.* पणः, आधिः, परिपणनं. 2 मानं, प्र-परि-माणं. 3 मापनयंत्रं. 4 आह्वानं. –*v. i.* पण् 1 A, प्रति-ज्ञा 9 U, अंगीकृ 8 U, प्रतिपद् 4 A, सशपथं प्रतिज्ञा.

GAGGLE, *v. i.* कलं कृ 2 P; कूज् 1 P.

GAIN, *v. i.* लभ् 1 A, अर्ज् 1 P or c., आप् 5 P, आ-समा-सद् c.; *See* GET; 'g. ground' उप-चि pass., प्रवृध् 1 A; प्ररुह् 1 P; 'g. over' साध् c., वशं नी 1 P (धनदानादिना); अनुरंज् c., ग्रह् 9 P; 'g. over to one's side' स्वपक्षं ग्रह् c; 'g. a battle' युद्धे जयं लभ्; 'g. the day' जयं प्राप्, विजयिन् *a.* भू; 'g. upon one's steps' समासद् c.; *See* OVERTAKE. –*v. t.* क्रमशः प्रसृप् or प्रगम् 1 P. –*s.* लाभः, प्राप्ति *f.*, फलं, आयः, अर्थः, उपार्जं, फलोदयः, अर्जनं. –ER, *s.* अर्जकः; प्राप्तलाभः; फलप्रापकः. –FUL, *a.* फलद; लाभजनक, अर्थोत्पादक. –LY, *adv.* दक्षं, चतुरं, सपाटवं.

GAINSAY, *v. t.* विरुध् 7 U; प्रति-प्रत्यभि-षिध् 1 P, प्रत्या ख्या 2 P, प्रत्यादिश् 6 P, अपवद् 1 U, अपलप् 1 P, अधरीकृ 8 U, निरा-कृ, बाध् 1 A, निरस् 4 U. –ER, *s.* अपवादकः, निषेधकः.

GAIRISH, *a.* अतिशोभन, रूपगर्वित. –NESS, *s.* अतिशोभा, रूपगर्वः, दंभः.

GAIT, *s.* गति *f.*, गमनं, गतं, चारः; 'graceful in g.' हंसगति, चारुगामिन्.

GALA, *s.* उत्सवः, उत्सवदिवसः, पर्वदिनं.

GALAXY, *s.* सुरनदी, आकाशगंगा, स्वर्गंगा, वियद्गंगा. 2 सुवस्तुमंडलं.

GALE, *s.* वातः, वायुः, पवनः; 'strong g.' वात्या, वाताली, चंडवातः, जवानिलः, वेगानिलः, प्रकंपनः, ध्राजि *f.*

GALL, *s.* क्षतं, विषं; दंशः; (fig.) पीडा, दुष्टभावः, संबाधा. 2 पित्तं, मायुः. 3 कटुता, तिग्मता, कठोरता, अरुंतुदत्वं. -*v. t.* चर्म घृष् 1 P or कुष् 1 P. 2 सं-परि-तप् c., पीड् 10, बाध् 1 A, क्लिश् 9 P, अर्द् 1 P, मर्माणि कृत् 6 P or भिद् 7 P. -*v. i.* आत्मानं तप् c. -ING, *a.* परुष, मर्मच्छिद्-भिद्, अरुंतुद.

GALLANT, *a.* शोभन, सुभगदर्शन; सभ्य, सभ्याचार, सुशील; दक्षिण; अत्युपचारपर-दक्ष. 2 वीर, शूर, विक्रांत, महावीर्य; *See* BRAVE. -*s.* वल्लभः, रमणः, कामुकः, कामिजनः, कामिन् *m.*, नायकः, दयितः. 2 जारः, विटः, उपपतिः. 3 सभ्याचारः, सुजनः; अत्युपचारशीलः-परः. -RY, *s.* दाक्षिण्यं; कामचेष्टा, शृंगारविलसितं, अत्युपासना, अत्युपचारः. 2 वीर्यं, शौर्यं, धामन् *n.*, विक्रमः, पौरुषं. 3 उदारता, माहात्म्यं. -LY, *adv.* सविक्रमं, सवीर्यं, शूर-वीर-वत्. 2 रमणवत्.

GALLERY, *s.* मंचाः (pl.), मंचसनाथः कोष्ठः. 2 छन्नपथः-मार्गः. 3 अलिंदः-दकः.

GALLINACEOUS (fowl), *s.* कुक्कुटः, ताम्रचूडः, चरणायुधः.

GALLINULE, *s.* दात्यूहः, कालकंठकः.

GALLOP, *v. i.* वल्ग् 1 P, द्रुतगत्या चल् or धाव् 1 P, द्रु 1 A. -*s.* द्रुतं, वल्गितं, प्लवनं.

GALLOWS, *s.* वधस्तंभः, वध्यशिला-काष्ठं; वध-घातस्थानं, वध्यस्थलं; 'met his death on the g.' शूलमारोपितः.

GALOCHE, *s.* काष्ठपादुका, पादुका.

GALVANIZE, *v. t.* विद्युच्छक्त्या आकृष् 1 P or उपहन् 2 P.

GAMBLE, *v. i.* दिव् 4 P (अक्षैः अक्षान् वा); अक्षैः क्रीड् 1 P. -ER, *s.* द्यूतकारः, देवितृ *m.*, द्यूतकृत् *m.*, धूर्तः, अक्षदेविन् *m.*, कितवः, अक्षधूर्तः. -ING, *s.* द्यूतं, दुरोदरं, पणः, अक्षवती, अक्षक्रीडा-द्यूतं, कैतवं, देवनं, द्यूतसेवा ; 'g.-house' द्यूतशाला-सभा; 'he who keeps a g.-house' सभिकः, द्यूतकारकः.

GAMBOL, *v. i.* क्रीड् 1 P, नृत् 4 P, इतस्ततः वल्ग् 1 P, द्रु 1 A. -*s.* नृत्यं, क्रीडा, लास्यं, लीला, केलि *f.*, खेला.

GAME, *s.* क्रीडा, खेला, केलि *f.*, लीला, विलासः, परि-(री)हासः. 2 वन्यपक्ष्यादि, जांगलः, वन्यपक्षिन् *m.* 3 मृगया. 4 संकल्पः, व्यवसायः; कल्पना, संदिग्धव्यवसायः. -*v. i.* क्रीड् 1 P, दिव् 4 P; 'G.-cock' चरणायुधः, योधकुक्कुटः; 'g.-keeper' वन्यपक्षिपालकः; 'g.-leg' पंगुपादः. -ING, *s.* द्यूतं. -STER, *s.* धूर्तः; *See* under GAMBLE. -SOME, *a.* क्रीडा-लीला-पर, विलासशील, विलासिन्, परिहासशील, उल्लासिन्, परिहासिन्, विनोदिन्, नर्मालापिन्.

GAMMON, *s.* वल्लूरं, उत्तप्तं, सूकरशुष्कमांसं. 2 चर्मपट्टशारि-क्रीडा. 3 Deceit, q. v. -*v. t.* सूकरमांसं लवणीकृ 8 U. 2 Cheat, q. v.

GAMUT, *s.* ग्रामः.

GANDER, *s.* हंसः, चक्रांगः, चक्रवाकः, चक्रः; श्वेतगरुत् *m.*, मानसौकस् *m.*, राजहंसः (white).

GANESH, *s.* गणेशः, गणपतिः, विनायकः, विघ्नेशः, विघ्नराजः, द्वैमातुरः, गणाधिपः, एकदंतः, हेरंबः, लंबोदरः, गजाननः, गजास्यः, गजदंतः.

GANG, *s.* गणः, संघः, निवहः; *See* COLLECTION.

GANGES, *s.* गंगा, मंदाकिनी, वियद्गंगा, स्वर्णदी, सुरदीर्घिका, जाह्नवी, जह्नुतनया-कन्या, भागीरथी, अमरापगा, सुरनदी, त्रिस्रोतस् *f.*, त्रिपथगा.

GANGLION, *s.* शिरास्फोटः.

GANGRENE, *s.* पूतिमांसं; मांसपाकः; कोथः. -*v. i.* कोथीभू 1 P, पूतीभू.

GANGWAY, *s.* आरोहावरोहपथः.

GAOL,-ER, *See* JAIL,-ER.

GAP, *s.* छिद्रं, भंगः, विच्छेदः, भेदः, रंध्रं, छेदः, विवरं, गर्तः-र्ता.

GAPE, *v. i.* वि-प्र-जृंभ् 1 A ; जभ्-जंभ् 1 A, मुखं व्यादा 3 A. 2 वि,-दल् 1 P, स्फुट् 1 P. -*s.*,-ING, *s.* जृंभः-भा, जृंभणं, जृंभिका, जृंभितं, हमंन् *n.*, हाफिका, मुखव्यादानं. -ING, *a.* जृंभिन्, जृंभित, व्यात्तमुख.

GARB, *s.* वेशः-षः, वस्त्रं, वसनं, वासस् *n.*, परिधानं, प्रसाधनं; 'putting on the g. of virtue' धर्मकंचुकप्रवेशिनः (S. 5).

GARBAGE, *s.* उच्छिष्टं, मलं.

GARBLE, *v. t.* साचीकृ 8 U; सत्यं गुह् 1 U, विकृ, वक्रीकृ.

GARDEN, *s.* उद्यानं, उपवनं; 'g. near a house' गृहारामः, निष्कुटः, गृहवाटिका ; 'pleasure-g.' क्रीडोपवनं, आरामः, प्रमदवनं, आक्रीडः; 'flower-g.' पुष्पवनं-वाटः-वाटिका, कुसुमाकरः ; 'fruit-g.' फलवृक्षवाटिका; 'vegetable g.' शाकवाटिका, शाकशाकटं, शाकशाकिनं; 'g.-wall' उद्यानपरिसरः-प्राकारः. -ER, *s.* उद्यानपालकः-रक्षकः, मालाकारः, मालिकः, मालिन् *m.* -ING, *s.* उद्यानकर्मन् *n.*, उद्यानसेवनं-कर्षणं, फलोत्पत्तिकर्म.

GARGLE, *v. i.* (जलं) आचम् 1 P, उप-स्पृश् 6 P, जलेन मुखं मृज् 2 P or धाव् 1 P. -*s.* आचमनीयं, आचाम्यं.

GARLAND, *s.* माला, स्रज् *f.*, माल्यं, आपीडः; शेखरः, हारः; 'g. worn in the hair' गर्भकः; 'g. hanging from the crest' प्रभ्रष्टकं, शिखालंबि माल्यं; 'g. worn straight' प्रालंबः-बिका; 'worn sideways' वैकक्षिकं; 'g. of pearls' हारः, मुक्तावली, मौक्तिकसरः.

GARLIC, *s.* ल(र)शुनं, रसोनः-नकः, महौषधं, गृंजनं, अरिष्टः, महाकंदः, सोनहः.

GARMENT, *s.* वस्त्रं, वासस् *n.*, वसनं, पटः, परिधानं, परिच्छदः, अंबरं, प्रच्छादनं; वेशः-षः; 'under or lower g.' अंतरीयं, अधोंशुकं, उपसंव्यानं, परिधानं, अधोवासः-रसनं; 'upper g.' उत्तरीयं, प्रावा(व)रः, उत्तरासंगः, बृहतिका, संव्यानं; 'g. as a protection from wind and cold' नीशारः.

GARNER, *s.* कुशू(सू)लः, धान्यागारं, धान्यकोष्ठः, कंडोलः-लकः, पिटः. –*v. t.* कंडोले निविश् c. or नि-धा 3 U.

GARNISH, *v. t.* भूष् 10, मंड् 10, अलंकृ 8 U, परिष्कृ, शुभ् c. –*s.*,–MENT,–GARNITURE, *s.* प्रसाधनं, भूषणं, अलंकारः, मंडनं, आभरणं; उपकरणानि (pl.), सज्जा.

GARRET, *s.* शिरोगृहं, चंद्रशाला, अट्टः, अट्टालः.

GARRISON, *s.* दुर्गरक्षकाः (pl.); दुर्गसैन्यं-बलं; रक्षिणः-रक्षकाः (pl.); रक्षिवर्गः. –*v. t.* रक्षापुरुषैः युज् 10, (दुर्गे) रक्षिणः निविश् c. or स्था c. (स्थापयति).

GARRULOUS, *a.* अतिवक्तृ, वावदूक, बहुभाषिन्-वादिन्, वाचाल, वाचाट, जल्पाक, मुखर. –NESS, GARRULITY, *s.* वाचालता, वावदूकता, अतिवादः, बहुभाषित्वं, अतिजल्पनं.

GARTER, *s.* पादावरणबंधनी, जंघाबंधनी.

GARUDA, *s.* गरुडः, गरुत्मत् *m.*, तार्क्ष्यः, वैनतेयः, खगेश्वरः, नागांतकः, विष्णुरथः, सुपर्णः, पन्नगाशनः, भुजगदारणः, भुजगरिपुः.

GAS, *s.* वायुः. –EOUS, *a.* वायुरूप.

GASH, *s.* दीर्घच्छेदः, दीर्घ,-गंभीर-क्षतं.

GASOMETER, *s.* वायुमापनयंत्रं.

GASP, *v. i.* कृच्छ्रेण श्वस् or अन् 2 P, दुःखेन श्वस्, स्थूलस्थूलं निश्वस्. –*s.* उच्छ्वासः, निश्वासः, कृच्छ्रोच्छ्वासः, कष्टश्वासः.

GASTRIC, *a.* जाठर (री *f.*), उदरीय, जठरीय, उदर-जठर in comp.; 'g. juice' जठराग्निः.

GASTRONOME, *s.* औदरिकः, उदरंभरिः, कुक्षिंभरिः, उदरपरायणः; *See* GLUTTON. –GASTRONOMY, *s.* उदरपरायणता, उदरसेवा.

GATE, *s.* द्वारं, प्रतिहारः, द्वार् *f.*; 'g.-way' तोरणः-णं, गोपुरं; निर्गमः, द्वारपथः; for other comps. *See* DOOR.

GATHER, *v. t.* चि 5 U, सं-अव-प्र-आ-°; समा-हृ 1 P, समा-नी 1 P, संग्रह् 9 P, सं-भृ 1, 3 U, एकीकृ 8 U; *See* COLLECT; 'g. flowers' पुष्पाणि चि or लू 9 U. **2** ज्ञा 9 U, अनु-मा 3 A, 2 P, ऊह् 1 A, अवगम् 1 P. **3** उद्-वृ 5 U, उद्धृ 1 P. –*v. i.* संगम् 1 A, सं-इ 2 P, संमिल् 6 P, सन्नि-पत् 1 P, एकत्र मिल्, एकस्थ *a.* भू 1 P, एकीभू. **2** उपचि pass., प्रवि-वृध् 1 A, एध् 1 A. **3** पूयं बंध् 9 P, पूय् 1 A. –*s.* पुटः, चूणः. –ER, *s.* अवचायिन् *m.*, संग्राहकः; 'g. of taxes' शौल्किकः, करग्राहकः. –ING, *s.* चयः, अव-सं-चयः, संग्रहणं. **2** समूहः, गणः, संघः, समागमः, निवहः, संघातः; जनसमूहः, लोकनिवहः-संघः.

GAUDY, *a.* उज्ज्वल, शोभन, नानावर्ण, चित्र; 'having a g. dress' उज्ज्वलवेशधारिन्, आर्य-उदारनेपथ्यभृत्. –*s.* FESTIVAL, q. v. –NESS, *s.* अतिशोभा, औज्ज्वल्यं, चित्रता, नानावर्णता.

GAUGE, *See* MEASURE.

GAUNT, *a.* क्षाम, कृश, क्षीण, शुष्कमांस, क्षुत्क्षाम, कृश-क्षीण-देह.

GAUNTLET, *s.* हस्तत्राणं; 'throw down the g.' युद्धार्थं आह्वे 1 A; 'take up the g.' युद्धाह्वानं स्वीकृ or उरीकृ 8 U.

GAWK, *s.* मूर्खः; *See* FOOL. **2** Cuckoo, q. v.

GAWKY, *a.* स्थूल-दीर्घ-देह, स्थूल.

GAY, *a.* प्रमोदिन्, प्रहृष्ट, आनंदित, उल्लासित, प्रमुदित, सानंद, प्रफुल्ल, अनुत्सुक, सोल्लास. **2** विलासिन्, परिहासशील, विनोदन-शील-पर, केलिपर. **3** Gaudy, q. v. –GAIETY, *s.* प्रमोदः, उल्लासः, प्रहर्षः, आनंदः, आह्लादः. **2** उत्सवः; *See* FESTIVAL. –GAILY, *adv.* सहर्षं, सोल्लासं, सानंदं, प्रफुल्लतया. **2** उज्ज्वलं, शोभनं.

GAZE, *v. i.* निर्-ईक्ष् 1 A, निर्वर्ण् 10, निध्यै 1 P, बद्ध-स्थिर-दृष्ट्या दृश् 1 P or आलोक् 1 A, 10; दृष्टिं or लक्षं बंध् 9 P (loc.); 'g. ing up to heaven' नभोदत्तदृष्टि; 'g. ing in all directions' दिक्षु दृष्टिं क्षिप्त्वा. –*s.* निरीक्षणं, निर्वर्णनं, आ-अव-लोकनं; दृष्टि *f.*, प्रेक्षणं, दर्शनं; बद्ध-स्थिर-अनिमेष-दृष्टिः; 'with a fixed g.' अनिमेषनयन-बद्धदृष्टि *a.*

GAZETTE, *s.* वार्ताहरः, वार्तापत्रं.

GEAR, *s.* उपकरणं, सामग्री, सज्जा, प्रसाधनं. **2** कार्यं, व्यापारः; 'out of g.' विलग्न, असंगत, असंबद्ध.

GELATINOUS, *a.* सांद्र, शीन, श्यान, संलग्नशील.

GELD, *v. t.* वृषणौ छिद् 7 P or कृत् 6 P or उत्पट् 10. –ING, *s.* छिन्नमुष्कः (अश्वः).

GELID, *a.* अतिशीत, हिम, शिशिर.

GEM, *s.* रत्नं, मणि *m. f.* **2** Bud, q. v. –*v. t.* रत्नैः शुभ् c. –MED, *a.* रत्नखचित, मणिभूषित, रत्नानुविद्ध. –MY, *a.* मणिमय (यी *f.*), रत्नभासिन्, रत्नोज्ज्वल.

GEMMATE, *a.* मुकुलित, बद्धपल्लव.

GEMINI, *s.* मिथुनं, द्वंद्वं, युगुलं, युगं, युग्मं, द्वयं, यमकं-लं; यमौ, यमजौ -लौ. –GEMINATE, –GEMINOUS, *a.* द्विगुण, द्विरावृत्त, द्विक; यम, यमज-ल.

GENDER, *s.* लिंगं, प्रकृति *f.* –*v. t.* Beget, q. v. –*v. i.* Copulate, q. v.

GENEOLOGY, *s.* वंशावलि-ली *f.*, वंशक्रमः, वंशश्रेणी-परंपरा-वृक्षः; oft. ex. by वंशः, अन्वयः. –ICAL, *a.* (*s.*) in comp. –IST, *s.* अन्वयज्ञः, वंशक्रमज्ञः, वंशावलिरचकः.

GENERAL, *a.* सामान्य, साधारण, सर्वजनीय-न,सार्वत्रिक-सार्वलौकिक-औत्सर्गिक-(की *f.*), सर्व-बहु-सामान्य, व्यापक, सर्वव्यापिन्, अविशेषक, प्रायिक, सर्वत्र प्रचलित; 'a g. rule' उत्सर्गः; 'a g. practice' लोकाचारः, जनरूढि *f.*, जनव्यवहारः, लोकः; 'against g. practice' लोकविरुद्धं; 'g. opinion' बहुमतं; 'g. reader' चुंबकः. –*s.* सेनापतिः, सेनाध्यक्षः, चमूपतिः, सेनानीः, बलाध्यक्षः-नायकः. –ITY, *s.* बहुतरभागः, मुख्यांशः, प्रधानभागः; better by 'g. ly'; 'the g. of beasts' प्रायः सर्वे पशवः. 2 सामान्यता, साधारण्यं. –IZE, *v. t.* जातीः निर्दिश् 6 P, जातिशः गणीकृ 8 U, साधारणधर्मं प्रदृश् *c.*, वर्गीकृ. 2 सामान्यतः वद् 1 P, उत्सर्गरूपेण कथ् or निरूप् 10. –IZATION, *s.* जातिनिर्देशः, गणीकरणं, सामान्यधर्मकथनं, सामान्यवादः. –LY, *adv.* 'in g.' प्रायः, प्रायेण, प्रायशः, सामान्यतः, बहुशः, भूयसा, भूयिष्ठं, साधारण्येन; oft. ex. by हि. –NESS, *s.* व्यापकत्वं, सामान्यता. –SHIP, *s.* सैनापत्यं, सेनाध्यक्षत्वं. 2 रणकौशलं, युद्धनैपुण्यं, बलविन्यासकौशलं.

GENERATE, *v. t.* उत्पद् *c.*, प्र-सू 2, 4 A, आवह् 1 P, सं-उद्-भू *c.*, जन् *c.* (जनयति); *See* CAUSE also. –ION, *s.* उत्पादनं, प्रसवः, जननं, जन्मन् *n.*, उत्पत्ति *f.*, प्रसूति *f.*; संभवः, उद्भवः. 2 अन्वयः, कुलं, वंशः, जाति *f.*, संतानः, संतति *f.* 3 पुरुषाः, पुरुषपरंपरा, वंशश्रेणी ; 'former g. s.' पूर्वे पुरुषाः ; 'a pair, one g. removed from the creator' स्रष्टुरेकांतरं (द्वंद्वं) (S. 7). 4 समकालीनपुरुषाः. –IVE, *a.* उत्पादक, जनक ; 'g. organ' उपस्थः ; योनि *f.* –OR, *s.* जनयितृ *m.*, जनकः, उत्पादकः,जन्मप्रदः-दाता.

GENERIC,-AL, *a.* जातिगत, सामान्य, साधारण, व्यापक, वर्गीय; 'g. property' जातिधर्मः-लक्षणं-स्वभावः, जातित्वं, सामान्यधर्मः-लक्षणं. –ALLY, *adv.* जातिमुद्दिश्य, सामान्यतः.

GENEROUS, *a.* उदार, वदा(द)न्य, त्यागशील, अवदात, दानशील, दानरत, दानशौंड, स्थूललक्ष्य, बहुप्रद. 2 महात्मन्, उदारधी-चेतस्, महामनस्, उदारचरित, महेच्छ, महाशय. 3 कुलीन, महाकुल, अभिजात. –NESS, –GENEROSITY, *s.* औदार्यं, त्यागिता, त्यागः, दानशीलं, वदान्यता. 2 उदारात्मता, महात्मता, माहात्म्यं.

GENIAL, *a.* सुखप्रद, आनंदद, सुखावह, रम्य, रमणीय, मनोहर-रम, रुचिर, प्रसन्न, सुखकर (री *f.*), उत्साहवर्धक, जीवद. 2 प्रसवकारिन्, जनक. 3 प्रसन्नचित्त, सोल्लास, उदार. –LY, *adv.* प्रसन्नं, सानंदं, सहर्षं, सोल्लासं, प्रफुल्लं. –NESS, *s.* रम्यता, उल्लासः, प्रसादः, प्रसन्नता.

GENICULATED, *a.* ग्रंथिल.

GENITAL, *a.* जननसंबंधिन्, जनन in comp.; 'g. organ' जननेंद्रियं, उपस्थः, योनि *f.*, शिश्नं.

GENITIVE, *s.* षष्ठी विभक्तिः.

GENITOR, *See* GENERATOR.

GENIUS, *s.* धीशक्ति *f.*, मति *f.*, बुद्धि *f.*, धीः, मतिबुद्धि-प्रभावः-सामर्थ्यं, मतिप्रकर्षः. 2 धीसंपन्नः, धीमत् *m.*, धीशक्तियुतः, गुणवत् *m.* 3 कल्पना-निर्माण-शक्तिः. 4 प्रकृति *f.*, स्वभावः, शीलं. 5 लक्षणं, विशेषचिह्नं, वृत्ति *f.*, स्वधर्मः. 6 भूतः, पिशाचः, वेतालः ; *See* DEMON; 'dramatic g.' नाट्यशक्तिः-कल्पना; 'good g.' सुदैवं; 'evil g.' दुर्दैवं.

GENTEEL, *a.* विनीत, दक्षिण, सभ्य, सुजन, सुशील, आर्य, आर्य-साधु-वृत्त, शिष्टाचार, आर्यचरित, सदाचार. 2 कुलीन, अभिजात, कुलोत्पन्न. 3 चारु, ललित, सुभग. –LY, *adv.* आर्यवत्, सुजनवत्. –NESS,–GENTILITY, *s.* विनयः, दाक्षिण्यं, आर्यता, सौजन्यं, सुशीलता, सभ्यता, साधुता. 2 आभिजात्यं, कुलोत्कर्षः. 3 लालित्यं, चारुता.

GENTIAN, *s.* किरातः, चिर(रा)तिक्तः, भूनिंबः, हिमकः, किराततिक्तः, अनार्यतिक्तः.

GENTILE, *a.*, *s.* अन्य-भिन्न-देशीय, देवार्चक. 2 सगोत्र, गोत्रज, ज्ञातीय.

GENTLE, *a.* भद्र, कल्याण (णी *f.*), शिव, सुख. 2 कोमल, मृदु, मसृण, अपरुष, सुकुमार, अचंड, मृदुल, मंद, सौम्य; 'a g. laugh' मंदस्मितं, ईषद्धासः ; 'g. breeze' मंदानिलः, मृदुपवनः; 'g. means' सामोपचारः, सामन् *n.*, मृदूपायः; 'g. words' प्रिय-मृदुवचनं. 3 महाकुल, कुलीन, अभिजात, सुजन्मन्, साधु-आर्य-वंशज, कुल in comp.; 'a girl of g. blood' कुलकन्यका, कुलप्रसूता. 4 (In addressing) अयि, भद्र, सौम्य, आर्य; 'g. lightning' अयि विद्युत्; 'g. folk' आर्यमिश्राः, आर्याः, साधुजनाः. 5 शांत, दांत. –NESS, *s.* मृदुता, कोमलता, सौम्यता, सौकुमार्यं, मंदता; 'g. of manners' आचारसौजन्यं, आर्यवृत्तिः. –GENTLY, *adv.* मृदु, सदयं, अजातव्यथं, यथासुखं; 'shall rub g.' यथासुखं संवाहयामि (S. 3). 2 मंदं मंदं, शनैः शनैः, शनैः, अपरुषं, अचंडं. 3 निभृतं, अलक्षितं, मंदं. —GENTLEMAN, *s.* आर्यः, सुजनः, साधुजनः, आर्यवृत्तः, कुलीनः; सुविनीतः, महाजनः, आर्य-कुलीन-जनः, भद्रः, महानुभावः; oft. by श्री in comp. –LIKE,-LY, *a.* सभ्य, विनीत, शिष्ट, सुशील, आर्य; 'g. manner' आर्यवृत्तिः, सौजन्यं; 'in a g. manner' नागरिकवृत्त्या (S. 5).

GENTRY, *s.* विशिष्टजनाः, आर्याः, आर्यलोकाः-जनाः, कुलीनवर्गः-जनाः, सुजनता.

GENUFLECTION, *s.* जानुभ्यां आनतिः *f.*, जानुनतिः.

GENUINE, *a.* अकृतक, अकृत्रिम, अकल्पित, निर्व्याज, निर्व्यलीक, अकपट, निष्कपट, अवितथ, सत्य, यथार्थ. –LY, *adv.* सत्यं, निष्कपटं, निर्व्याजं. –NESS, *s.* सत्यता, यथार्थता, निर्व्याजत्वं, अकृत्रिमता.

GENUS, *s.* जाति *f.*, गणः, वर्गः.

GEOGRAPHY, *s.* भूगोलविद्या-शास्त्रं, भूपृष्ठविद्या. –ER, *s.*

भूगोलशास्त्रज्ञः, भूवृत्तविद्याज्ञः. -ICAL, *a.* भूगोलशास्त्रविषयक.

GEOLOGY, *s.* भूतत्त्वं, भूगर्भशास्त्रं, भूतत्त्वविद्या. -ICAL, *a.* भूतत्त्वविषयक. -IST, *s.* भूतत्त्वज्ञः.

GEOMETRY, *s.* ज्यामिति *f.*, रेखागणना-गणितं, भूमितिः. -IC,-ICAL, *a.* (*s.*) in comp.; 'g. proof' रेखागणितेन उपपत्तिः. -ICIAN, *s.* भूमितिज्ञः.

GERM, *s.* अंकुरः, अभिनवोद्भिद् *m.* 2 बीजं, मूलं, योनि *f.*, आदिः, प्रभवः, बीजकारणं. —GERMINATE, *v. i.* उद्भिद् pass., प्ररुह् 1 P, स्फुट् 6 P, विकस् 1 P. -ING, *a.* उद्भिद्-द्-ज्ज, अंकुरित. -ION, *s.* उद्भेदः, स्फुटनं.

GERMANE, *a.* सनाभि, संपर्किन्, संपृक्त.

GESTICULATE, *v. i.* अंगानि विक्षिप् 6 P or संचल् c. -*v. t.* अभि-नी 1 P, नि-,रूप् 10, सूच् 10, नट् 10; *See* ACT. -ION, *s.* अभिनयः, अंगविक्षेपः, चेष्टा, सूचना, अंगहारः, हावः, संकेतसूचनं. -OR, *s.* अंगविक्षेपकः.

GESTURE, *s.* चेष्टा, व्यापारः, इंगितं, भावः, अभिनयः, विलासः, विभ्रमः, अंगविक्षेपः, हावः, हस्तादिचालनं.

GET, *v. t.* लभ् 1 A, आप् 5 P, अर्ज् 1 P or c., आ-समा-सद् c., विद् 6 U, प्रति-आ-पद् 4 A, अश् 5 A, अधिगम् 1 P, ग्रह् 9 P, आ-दा 3 A. 2 (To be produced) जन् 4 A, उत्पद् 4 A, सं-उद्-भू 1 P, प्र-सू 2, 4 A, (with genitive of person); 'I have got a pain in my teeth' दंतपीडा मे उत्पन्ना-जाता. 3 धृ 1 P, 10, भृ 3 U; धा 3 U; 'I have got that book with me' तत्पुस्तकं मत्सकाशे वर्तते; *See* BEAR also. 4 (Cause) ex. by causal; 'g. it done by him' तं तत्कारय; oft. by अनुनी 1 P, प्रोत्सह् c., प्रवृत् c.; 'g. ahead' अग्रेसरीभू; 'g. clear of' मुच् pass.; 'g. rid of' आत्मानं मुच् c., (with abl.); by निर् in comp.; 'g. abroad' प्रसृ-प्रसृप् 1 P, बहुलीभू 1 P; *See* under ABROAD. -among, मध्ये प्रविश् 6 P or गम्. -at, प्राप्, आगम्, आ-या 2 P, उप-स्था 1 U. -away, अपसृ 1 P, अप-इ 2 P, अपक्रम् 1 U, 4 P; चल् 1 P, अप-या-गम्; 'g. away, you fool' अपेहि रे मूर्ख. -back, प्रतिलभ्, प्रत्या-दा, &c. -beyond, तॄ 1 P, अति-इ, अतिक्रम्. -down, अवतॄ, अवरुह् 1 P, अधो गम्, नि-अव-पत् 1 P; (*v. t.*) अवतॄ c., अवरुह् c., &c. -in, प्रविश् 6 P. -into, पत्; संकटे पतितः 'got into troubles'; आरुह् 1 P (a car &c.); 'he got into debt' ऋणग्रस्तो बभूव; 'g. ing into deep mud' पंकपूर्णमासाद्य. -off, (*v. i.*) निः-सृ, निर्गम्, अप-या, अपक्रम्, निस्तॄ. 2 अवतॄ, अवरुह्; (*v. t.*) निरस् 4 U, अप-नी 1 P. -on, प्रवृत् 1 A, प्रचल्, प्र-सृ; 'they long got on well' चिरं ते सुखेन अवर्तंत or कालं निन्युः. -out, निर्गम्, अप-इ, निः-सृ. 2 त्यज् 1 P, मुच् 6 P; 'g. out of bed now' अधुना मुंच शय्यां. -over, -through, संतॄ; पारं-अंतं-गम्, अतिक्रम्, निस्तॄ, तीर् 10; आरुह्. 2 समाप् c.; *See* COMPLETE. -together, संधि 5 U; समा-नी, संग्रह्; *See* COLLECT. -up, उत्-स्था; प्रबुध् 4 A, शयनं त्यज् 1 P or मुच्; (*v. t.*) सज्जीकृ 8 U, विरच् 10; उपकॢप् c. -upon, अधि-आ-रुह्. -TER, *s.* प्रापकः, लब्धृ *m.*, अर्जकः. -TING, *s.* लाभः, अवाप्ति *f.*, अर्जनं, अधिगमः-मनं, आगमः, आसादनं.

GEWGAW, *s.* क्रीडनकं, अल्पमूल्यं द्रव्यं or आभरणं. -*a.* निःसार, बहिरेव मनोहर.

GHASTLY, *a.* प्रेत-शव-तुल्य, विवर्ण, शवसरूप-सवर्ण. 2 कराल, विकट, भीम, उग्र, दारुण, भयानक, भीमदर्शन, करालवदन, घोराकृति. -NESS, *s.* प्रेतसारूप्यं, वैवर्ण्यं; विकटत्वं, दारुणत्वं.

GHEE, *s.* घृतं, आज्यं, हविस् *n.*, सर्पिस् *n.*, तनूनपं.

GHOST, *s.* भूतः, पिशाचः, वेतालः, निशाचरः, प्रेतनरः. 2 आत्मन् *m.*; 'give up the g.' मृ 6 A; *See* DIE. -LIKE, *a.* प्रेत-भूत-सरूप, प्रेततुल्य. -LY, *a.* भूतविषयक-संबंधिन्. 2 पारत्रिक (की *f.*), आत्मविषय, पारमार्थिक (की *f.*).

GIANT, *s.* महापुरुषः, विकटविग्रहः, बृहच्छरीरः, भीमविग्रहः, बृहत्कायः, अतिशक्त्युपेतः, राक्षसः. 2 दैत्यः, दानवः; *See* DEMON. -*a.*,-LIKE, *a.* अतिस्थूल, प्रकांडदेह, स्थूलप्रमाण, अतिमहत्, बृहत्काय, महाशरीर, विकट. -ESS, *s.* राक्षसी, बृहच्छरीरा. -GIGANTIC, *a.* अतिमानुष (षी *f.*), राक्षसपरिमाण, भीमविग्रह, अतिमहत्-बृहत्, स्थूलकाय, विकट.

GIBBER, *v. i.* *See* BABBLE. -ISH, *s.* असंबद्धवचनं, प्रलापः, प्रजल्पितं, मृषार्थकं वाक्यं -*a.* मृषार्थकं, अनर्थकं.

GIBBET, *s.* वध्यकाष्ठं-शिला. वध-घात-स्थानं. -*v. t.* वधं आदिश् 6 P, उद्-बंध् 9 P.

GIBBOUS, *a.* न्युब्ज, वक्र, आभोगवत्, बिंबाकार.

GIBE, *See* ABUSE.

GIDDY, *a.* भ्रमिन्, भ्रामररोगिन्, विभ्रांत, भ्रमणशील; better ex. by भ्रम् 1, 4 P. 2 भ्रमकारिन्, मत्त, उन्मादिन्. 3 (Fig.) चपल, चंचल, लोल, अस्थिर; *See* FICKLE. 4 उद्धत, उन्मत्त, उत्सिक्त, गर्वित. -LY, *adv.* अविचार्य, लौल्यात्, चापल्येन. -NESS, *s.* भ्र-(भ्रा)मरं, भ्रमः-मि *f.*, घूर्णनं, घूर्णि *f.* 2 चापल्यं, लौल्यं, अस्थैर्य, &c.

GIFT, *See* under GIVE.

GIG, *s.* भ्रमरं. 2 लघुयानं-रथः. 3 क्षुद्र-लघु-नौका.

GIGGLE, *v. i.* मूर्खवत् हस् 1 P.

GILD, *v. t.* स्वर्णेन रंज् c., हेमरसेन-द्रवेण लिप् 6 P, सुवर्णयति (D.); बाह्यतेजसा रंज् c. 2 प्रकाश् c., विद्युत् c., विराज् c. -ING, *s* स्वर्णरंजनं, स्वर्णच्छदः.

-ED,-GILT, *a.* सुवर्णित, हेमरसखचित, स्वर्णमंडित, स्वर्णप्रतिबद्ध. 2 रंजित, विराजित.

GILL, *s.* श्वासेंद्रियं, अधोगंडः.

GIMCRACK, *s.* क्रीडनकं, क्रीडावस्तु *n.*

GIMLET, *s.* वेधनिका, आस्फोटनी.

GIN, *s.* Liquor, q. v. 2 पाशः, उन्माथः, कूटयंत्रं, बंधनं, वागुरा.

GINGER, *s.* आर्द्रकं, शृंगवेरं, गुल्ममूलं; 'dry g.' शुंठि-ठी *f.*, विश्वं-श्वा *f.*, नागरं, विश्वभेषजं, महौषधं; 'g. beer or wine' आर्द्रकासवं, आर्द्रकमद्यं-पानं; 'g.-bread' आर्द्रकपिष्टकः.

GINGERLY, *adv.* असहसा, सावधानं, शनैः.

GINGLE, *See* JINGLE.

GIPSY, *s.* यक्षिणी, विप्रश्निका, ईक्षणिका.

GIRAFFE, *s.* चित्रोष्ट्रः.

GIRD, *v. t.* परि-अधि-वेष्ट् c., परि-वृ 5 U or c. 2 आ-बंध् 9 P, परि-धा 3 U, सं-पि-नह् 4P; 'g. round the body' शरीरं प्रावृ or आच्छद् 10, परि-बंध् or परि-धा; 'g. up one's loins' परिकरं बंध्; 'girt by the (golden) lightning, as by a yellow garb' विद्युत्प्रभारचितपीतपटोत्तरीयः (Mr. 5). -*s. See* CRAMP. -ED,-GIRT, *a.* बद्ध, आनद्ध, परिवेष्टित, परिवृत; वलय-मेखला-रसना in comp.; 'sea-g. earth' समुद्ररसना-उदधिवलया-पृथ्वी.

GIRDLE, *s.* मेखला, रश(स)ना, कांचि-ञ्ची *f.*, सतकी, सारसनं (of women); कटिसूत्रं, कटिवलयं, कक्ष्या-क्षा, परिकरः, काटिबंधनी, शृंखलः-ला-लं (of men). 2 वेष्टनं, परि-आ-वेष्टनं, मंडलं, वलयः-यं, चक्रवालं. 3 राशिचक्रं. -*v. t.* परि-वेष्ट् c., परि-वृ 5 U, मेखलया बंध् 9 P; *See* GIRD.

GIRL, *s.* कन्या, बाला, बालिका, कुमारी, दारिका, वासूः, *See* DAUGHTER also; 'one born from a g.' कानीनः, कन्यकाजातः. -HOOD, *s.* बालभावः, बाल्यं, कुमारीत्वं. -ISH, *a.* कन्यानुरूप, बालेय.

GIRTH, *s.* वरत्रा, नध्री, वध्री; दू(चू)ष्या, कक्षा-क्ष्या.

GIST, *s.* फलितार्थः, निष्कर्षः, भावः, फलितं, परमार्थः, पिंडितार्थः.

GIVE, *v. t.* दा 1 P, 3 U, ऋ c. (अर्पयति), प्रति-पद् c., दद् 1 A, विश्रण् 10, उत्-वि-सृज् 6 P, (with dat. of person); निक्षिप् 6 P, संक्रम् c. (with loc.); त्यज् 1 P, दिश् 6 P. 2 (Produce) ex. by भू 1 P, संपद् 4 A, जन् 4 A; '3 repeated 2 times g. s 6' द्विरावृत्तास्त्रयः षड् भवंति-संपद्यंते; 'g. chase' अनुसृ-अनुधाव् 1 P; 'g. ear' अव-धा 3 U, कर्णं दा, श्रु 5 P; 'g. ground' अपक्रम् 1 U, 4 P; अपसृ, परा-नि-वृत् 1 A; त्यक्त्वा गम् 1 P; 'g. one's self up to' सेव् 1 A, भज् 1 A; आसंज् pass., आसक्त-निरत-निविष्ट-*a.* भू, (with loc.); 'g. offence' अपराध् 4, 5 P, विप्रियं-प्रति-कूलं-कृ 8 U or आचर् 1 P; 'g. utterance' उदीर् 10, उच्चर् c., उदाहृ 1 P. -away, (in marriage) प्रतिपद् c., उत्सृज्, प्र-दा. 2 विश्रण्, दानेन क्षै c. (क्षपयति). -back, प्रतिदा, प्रति-ऋ c., निर्यत् 10. -forth, प्रथ् 10, प्रकाश् c., निविद् c., ख्या c. (ख्यापयति). -in, अनुमन् 4 A, अनुमुद् 1 A; स्वाग्रहं त्यज्. -off, Abandon, q. v. -out, निविद् c., प्रकाश् c., घुष् 10, प्रथ् 10, प्र-ख्या c. 2 मुच् 6 P, विसृज्, उद्वम् 1 P, उद्-गॄ 6 P, निःसृ c.-over, त्यज्, उत्सृज्; निवृत् 1 A, विरम् 1 P, (with abl.). 2 असाध्य *a.* इति मत्वा त्यज्; आशां त्यज्; (*v. i.*) शम् 4 P, पत् 1 P; 'when the winds g. over' शांते पवने. -up, त्यज्, हा 3 P, उत्-वि-सृज्. 2 निवृत्, वि-रम्; 'g. up for lost' नष्टप्राय *a.* मन् 4 A. -way, शम् 4 P, निवृत्, विरम्, शिथिलीभू. 2 भंज् pass., अवसद् 1 P; 'the cord gave way' रज्जुर्भग्ना; 'the wall gave way' भित्तिरवसन्ना. 3 अव(प)सृ, अप-इ, मार्गं दा or त्यज्, अपक्रम्, अप-या. 4 वशं गम्-इ-या, अधीन-वश-आयत्त *a.* भू; 'do not g. way to grief' शुचो वशं मा गमः, शोकाधीनो मा भूः, वैक्लव्यं मावलेवस्व. -ER, *s.* दातृ *m.*, त्यागिन् *m.*; gen. ex. by दायक, द, प्रद, दायिन्, in comp.; 'g. of milk' पयोदायिनी, दुग्धप्रदा, &c. -ING, *s.* दानं, विसर्जनं, उत्सर्गः, त्यागः, वितरणं, अर्पणं, प्रतिपादनं, विश्राणनं. -GIFT, *s.* दानं, प्रतिपादनं; *See* above. 2 दानं, उपहारः, उपायनं, उपदा, प्रीतिदानं, प्राभृतं, प्रदेशनं. उपग्राह्यं; 'one deserving a g.' दक्षिणीय, दक्षिणार्ह, दक्षिण्य; 'marriage-g.' यौतकं, सुदायः. 3 गुणः, शक्ति *f.* -ED, *a.* उपेत, सं-उप-पन्न, विशिष्ट, युक्त, अन्वित, शालिन् in comp. 2 गुणोपेत, गुणसंपन्न, गुणिन्, गुणवत्.

GLACIAL, *a.* हिमरूप, हैम (मी *f.*), हिम.

GLACIER, *s.* हिमानी, हिमसंहति *f.*

GLACIS, *s.* प्रवण-निम्न-भूमि *f.*

GLAD, *a.* प्र-,सं-,हृष्ट, आनंदित, प्रीत, सानंद, प्रमुदित, तुष्ट, सोल्लास, उल्लसित, प्रसन्न. 2 हर्षजनक, हर्ष-आनंद-कर (री *f.*); नंदक, रमणीय, प्रमोदिन्; 'I am g.' हंत, दिष्ट्या. -DEN, *v. t.* आ-,नंद् c., प्री 9 P, 10; *See* DELIGHT. -DENING, *a.* हर्षद, प्रीतिप्रद, हर्षकर, प्रमोदिन्. -LY, *adv.* सहर्षं, सानंदं, सप्रमोदं, हृष्टमनसा, संतोषेण, प्रीत्या, साह्लादं. -NESS, *s.* हर्षः, प्रमोदः, आह्लादः, संतोषः, प्रीति *f.*, उल्लासः, चित्त-प्रसादः, तुष्टि *f.* -SOME, *See* (*a.*).

GLADE, *s.* वन-गुल्म-पथः-मार्गः, तरुगहनमार्गः.

GLADIATOR, *s.* असिक्रीडकः, आसिकः, मल्लः. -GLADIATURE, असिक्रीडा-युद्धं.

GLAIR, *s.* अंडशुक्लं.

GLANCE, *s.* दृष्टिपातः, ईक्षणं, वीक्षितं, नयनपातः-वि-

क्षेपः, दृक्पातः, आलोकितं; 'side-long g.' नयनोपांतविलोकितं, साचिविलोकितं, अपांगदर्शनं-दृष्टि *f.*, कटाक्षः; 'at the very first g.' सकृद्दृष्टिपातेन, प्रथममेव; 'good at the first g.' आपाततो रमणीय, आपातरमणीय. 2 अर्धवीक्षणं, ईषद्दृष्टिः. 3 स्फुरितं, स्फुरणं, द्युति *f.* **–*v. i.*** दृष्टिं क्षिप् 6 P, चक्षुः-दृष्टिं-दा 3 U or पत् c. (with loc.); 'g.-ing at the antelope' कृष्णसारे ददच्चक्षुः (S. 1). 2 लघु निर्घृष् 1 P, लघु हत्वा अति-इ 2 P. 3 (जवेन) परिस्फुर् 6 P or विलस् 1 P. **–INGLY,** *adv.* लघु, ईषत्, अल्पमात्रं, स्तोकं. 2 दृक्पातेन, तिर्यक्, साचि, कटाक्षेण.

GLAND *s.* अधिमांसं, मांसपिंडः, पिंडः.

GLANDERS, *s.* क्षयथुः.

GLARE, *s.* तेजस् *n.*, दीप्ति *f.*, द्युति *f.*, प्रखर-अतितेजः, अतिप्रभा-द्युतिः-दीप्तिः, नेत्रप्रतिघातिनी प्रभा. 2 उग्रदृष्टि *f.*, क्रोधेद्धदृष्टिः **–*v. i.*** संदीप् 4 A, प्रद्युत् 1 A, उज्ज्वल् 1 P, अतितेजसा स्फुर् 6 P or दृष्टिं प्रतिहन् 2 P or संतप् c.; दीप् freq. (देदीप्यते). 2 उग्रदृष्टिं पत् c., कोपेन दृश् 1 P or ईक्ष् 1 A. **–ING,** *a.* संदीप्त, उज्ज्वल, अतिभास्वत्, देदीप्यमान. 2 सुस्पष्ट, सुप्रकाश, प्रत्यक्ष, पुरःस्फुरत्. **–INGLY,** *adv.* सुस्पष्टं, सुप्रकाशं.

GLASS, *s.* काचः, स्फटिकः, क्षारः. 2 (Cup) चषकः-कं, काचपात्रं-भाजनं. 3 आदर्शः, दर्पणः, मुकुरः. **–*a.*** काचमय (यी *f.*), काचनिर्मित, काच in comp.; 'g.-blower' काचधमकः; 'g.-grinder' काचपरिष्कारकः; 'g.-house' काचनिर्माणशाला-स्थानं; 'g.-man' काचविक्रयिन् *m.*; 'g.-work' काचनिर्माणं-कर्म. **–LIKE,** *a.* काचोपम, काचतुल्य. **–Y,** *a.* स्फटिकोपम, काचवत्स्वच्छ, काचविमल, स्फटिकप्रभ, स्फाटिक (की *f.*), सुप्रसन्न. 2 श्लक्ष्ण, स्निग्ध. **–GLAZE,** *v. t.* काचयति (D.), काचेन आच्छद् 10. 2 श्लक्ष्णीकृ 8 U, स्निग्धीकृ, श्लक्ष्णयति (D.). **–*s.*** स्निग्धता, श्लक्ष्णता. **–GLAZIER,** *s.* काचसंधातृ *m.*, काचबंधकः.

GLAUCOUS, *a.* घनश्याम, मेघनील, समुद्रवर्ण.

GLEAM, *v. i.* परि-,स्फुर् 6 P, विलस् 1 P, क्षणमात्रं प्रकाश् 1 A or उज्ज्वल् 1 P; *See* SHINE also. **–*s.*** प्रभा, कांति *f.*, तेजस् *n.*, औज्ज्वल्यं. 2 स्फुरणं, स्फुरितं, क्षणप्रभा-कांतिः, अचिरप्रभा, क्षणज्योतिस् *n.* 3 रश्मिः, करः, किरणः, अंशुः; 'not a g. of hope' न आशालवोपि. **–Y,** *a.* क्षण-अचिर-प्रभ, चलद्युति, कंपितप्रभ, क्षणद्योतिन्.

GLEAN, *v. t.* (bits &c.) उंछ् 6 P, शिल् 6 P, उद्-ग्रस् 9 P or c., अवशेषं चि 5 U or संग्रह् 9 P. 2 संकल् 10, संग्रह्, उद्ध 1 P. **–*s.*** धान्यशेषः, शेषधान्यसंचयः. **–ER,** *s.* उंछशीलः-वृत्तिः, उंछनकृत् *m.* 2 संग्रहीतृ *m.* **–ING,** *s.* उंछः, शिलं, उंछशिलं, कणं. 2 संग्रहः, संकलनं, उद्धारः.

GLEBE, *s.* मृद् *f.*, मृत्तिका; स्थलं-ली, भूमि *f.*

GLEE, *See* DELIGHT.

GLEET, *s.* इक्षु-मधु-मेहः, मेहविकारः.

GLEN, *s.* दरी, कंदरः-रा; अद्रिद्रोणी, उपत्यका.

GLIB, *a.* वाक्चपल, त्वरित-द्रुत-वाच्; चपल, लोल. 2 पिच्छिल, मसृण, स्निग्ध, श्लक्ष्ण, चिक्कण. **–*v. t.*** Castrate, q. v. 2 श्लक्ष्णीकृ 8 U. **–LY,** *adv.* चपलतया, वाक्चापल्येन. 2 श्लक्ष्णं. **–NESS,** *s.* वाक्चापल्यं, चापल्यं 2 श्लक्ष्णता, मसृणता.

GLIDE, *v. t.* सृप् 1 P, सं-वि-प्र°, प्र-वि-सृ 1 P; मंदं इ-या 2 P or गम् 1 P, शनैः प्रसृ or चल् 1 P; अलक्षितं-निभृतं गम् or या or अति-इ; *See* STEAL. 2 वह् 1 P, स्रु 1 P, स्यंद् 1 A, री 4 A. **–ING,** *s.* संसर्पः-र्पणं, स्रवणं, निस्यंदः-दनं.

GLIMMER, *v. i.* मंदं मंदं ज्वल् 1 P or दीप् 4 A; मंदप्रभया-अचिरप्रभया प्रकाश् 1 A or द्युत् 1 A or स्फुर् 6 P. **–*s.*, GLIM,** *s.* मंदप्रभा-तेजस् *n.*, मंद-अचिर-द्युति *f.*-दीप्ति *f.*, स्फुरणं, स्फुरितं. **–ING,** *a.* मंदप्रभ-द्युति-तेजस, ईषत्स्फुरित, पांडुद्युति-किरण, मंदच्छाय. 2 मंद, असुप्रकाश, अव्यक्त, अस्पष्ट.

GLIMPSE, *s.* क्षण-मुहूर्त-दर्शनं; ईषद्दृष्टि *f.*, अर्धवीक्षणं, अल्पो दृक्पातः. 2 क्षण-अचिर-प्रभा; *See* GLEAM.

GLISTEN, GLISTER, *v. i.* स्फुर् 6 P, प्रकाश् 1 A, द्युत् 1 A. **–ING,** *a.* मसृण, चिक्कण, श्लक्ष्ण, स्निग्ध.

GLITTER, *v. i.* द्युत्-प्रकाश् 1 A; भास् 1 A, भा 2 P; स्फुर् 6 P; *See* SHINE. **–*s.*** दीप्ति-द्युति-रुचि-कांति *f.*, प्रभा, तेजस् *n.*, ज्योतिस् *n.*, वर्चस् *n.*, आभा. **–ING,** *a.* प्रभावत्, उज्ज्वल, भासमान, विद्योतिन्, भासुर.

GLOAT, *v. i.* संतृप् 4 P, संतुष् 4 P; आत्मानं संतृप् c. or संतुष् c., लोभाद् निरीक्ष् 1 A or निर्वर्ण् 10.

GLOBE, *s.* गोलः-लं; वर्तुलः-लं; मंडलं; चक्रं. 2 भूमंडलं, भूगोलः, क्षितिमंडलं-तलं. **—GLOBATE,-GLOBULAR,** *a.* वर्तुल, गोलाकार, गोलाकृति, वृत्त, निस्तल, मंडलाकार, गोल. **–LY,** *adv.* मंडलरूपेण, मंडलवत्, गोलाकारेण. **–GLOBULE,** *s.* बिंदुः, लघुगोलः, गोलकः.

GLOMERATE, *v. t.* मंडलीकृ 8 U, गोलीकृ, पिंडीकृ.

GLOOM, *s.* अंधकारः, तमस् *n.*, तमिस्रं-स्रा, तिमिरं, ध्वांतं; अवतमसं, ईषत्तमः (partial g.). 2 निष्प्रभत्वं, विषादः, छाया. **–*v. t.*** Darken, q. v. **–GLOOMY,** *a.* सतिमिर, तमोवृत, सांधकार, तिमिरावगुंठित. 2 दुर्दर्शन, मलिनप्रभ, अप्रभ, निष्प्रभ, निरालोक, मलिन. 3 विषण्ण, दीन, अवसन्न, सविषाद, निरानंद, म्लान, खिन्न, उद्विग्न. **–LY,** *adv.* निष्प्रभं, सांधकारं. 2 सविषादं, सखेदं, सोद्वेगं. **–NESS,** *s.* निष्प्रभत्वं, &c. 2 विषादः, दैन्यं, अवसादः, चित्तोद्वेगः, खेदः, म्लानता, उद्वेगः.

GLORY, *s.* कीर्ति *f.*, यशस् *n.*, ख्याति *f.*, विश्रुति *f.*, महिमन् *m.*, प्रतापः, ओजस्विता. 2 श्रीः, तेजस् *n.*,

शोभा, द्युति *f.*; 'g. of youth' यौवनश्रीः. 3 माहात्म्यं, गौरवं, प्रतिष्ठा, पूजा, मानः. 4 प्रशंसा, स्तुति *f.*, श्लाघा, स्तवः, स्तुतिवाक्यं. 5 रत्नं, अवतंसः, तिलकः, ललामं. 6 Absolution, q. v.; 'vain g.' अहंकारः, विकत्थनं-ना, दर्पः, गर्वः, आत्मश्लाघा; 'g. to you, Oh king' जयतु जयतु देवः; 'g. of victory' जयोदाहरणं. -*v. i.* अत्यंतं प्रमुद् 1 A or आनंद् 1 P, उल्लस् 1 P; 'you g. in disobeying your father' पितुरवज्ञानं आत्मगौरवं मन्यसे. 2 विकत्थ् 1 A, दृप् 4 P, आत्मानं श्लाघ् 1 A; 'I do g. in that name' तन्नामधारी कृतिनमात्मानं मन्ये खलु. —GLORIFY, *v. t.* उत्-सं-कृत् 10, प्रशंस् 1 P, श्लाघ्, स्तु 2 U; गुणान् वर्ण् 10 or कृत् or प्रकाश् c., कीर्तिं गै 1 P. 2 स्वर्गं आरुह् c., परमपदं प्राप् c. -ICATION, *s.* गुणवर्णनं-ना, प्रशंसा, स्तुतिवादः, गुणकीर्तनं, यशःख्यापनं. —GLORIOUS, *a.* यशस्वत्, कीर्तिमत्, महायशस्, प्रथित, विश्रुत, ख्यात, यशस्विन्, उदग्रयशस्. 2 कीर्तिकर-यशस्कर (री *f.*), श्लाघावह, प्रशस्य. 3 तेजस्विन्, महत्, महोज्ज्वल, श्रीमत्, प्रतापवत्, महोदय, अतिशोभन, ओजस्विन्, सुप्रभ, वर्चस्विन्. 4 विशिष्ट, परम, उत्तम, उत्कृष्ट, प्रशस्ततम, श्रेष्ठ. -LY, *adv.* सप्रतापं, कीर्तियुक्तं, परमं, उत्कृष्टं.

GLOSS, *s.* टीका, टिप्पनी, भाष्यं, व्याख्यानं, वृत्ति *f.*, विवरणं. 2 बाह्यशोभा-कांति-रुचि *f.*, बहिराभा, कृत्रिमच्छवि *f.*, कल्पितशोभा. -*v. t.* टीकया व्या-ख्या 2 P or वि-वृ 5 U; भाष्यं लिख् 6 P. 2 बाह्यतः शुभ् c.; स्निग्धी-मसृणी-कृ 8 U; बाह्यशोभां दा 3 U or उत्पद् c. -Y, *a.* स्निग्ध, चिक्कण, श्लक्ष्ण, मसृण. 2 बाह्यप्रभ, बाह्यतः शोभित, आपातरुचिर, बहीरमणीय.

GLOSSARY, *s.* कोशः-षः, शब्दसंग्रहः-कोशः, निघंटुः, अभिधानं, समाम्नायः; पशुसमाम्नायः 'g. of words relating to beasts.' -IST, *s.* कोशलेखकः; संकलयितृ *m.*

GLOTTIS, *s.* प्रति-अलि-उप-जिह्वा.

GLOVE, *s.* करच्छदः, हस्तत्राणं-परिधानं, हस्ताच्छादनं.

GLOW, *s.* तापः, आतपः, दाहः, उष्मन् *m.*, दीप्ति-द्युति *f.*, तेजस् *n.*, उत्तापः. 2 रक्तता, रक्तिमन् *m.*, रागः, अरुणिमन् *m.* -*v. i.* दीप् 4 A, प्रकाश् 1 A, ज्वल् 1 P, तप् 1 P, 4 A, दह् pass.; अरुणीभू 1 P, रंज् pass., रक्तीभू; 'g. ing with rage' क्रोधेद्ध, रोषसंतप्त, प्रदीप्तक्रोध; ज्वलन्निव ब्रह्ममयेन तेजसा (K. v. 30) 'as if g. ing with Brahmanic lustre.' -ING, *a.* सं-,प्र-,दीप्त, ज्वलित, उत्तप्त, देदीप्यमान, उज्ज्वल, चंड; रक्त, अरुण; 'in g. colours' उज्ज्वलरूपेण, हृदयहारितया, हृदयंगमं, मनोरमं; 'with g. eyes' दीप्ताक्ष *a.* -INGLY, *adv.* तेजसा, उत्तापेन, चंडं, दीप्त्या. —GLOW-WORM, *s.* खद्योतः, ज्योतिरिंगणः, प्रभाकीटः.

GLOZE, *See* FLATTER.

GLUE, *s.* संश्लेषणद्रव्यं, लेपः. -*v. t.* सं-धा 3 U. संश्लिष् c., संयुज् 7 U, 10, संलग्नीकृ 8 U. -Y, *a.* श्यान, सांद्र, चिक्कण.

GLUM, *a.* प्रतीप, वाम-वक्र-शील.

GLUT, *v. t.* भक्ष् 10, ग्रस् 1 A, निगॄ 6 P; अतिमात्रं तृप् c., अत्यंतं पूर् 10, सौहित्यं जन् c. (जनयति). -*s.* अतितृप्ति *f.*, अतिसौहित्यं, निर्वेदः. 2 अतिरेकः, उद्रेकः, अतिबाहुल्यं, प्राचुर्यं.

GLUTINATE, *v. t.* लेपेन संश्लिष् c. or संयुज् 7 U, 10.

GLUTINOUS, *a.* श्यान, सांद्र, चिक्कण, स्निग्ध, संलग्नशील.

GLUTTON, *s.* औदरिकः, उदरंभरिः, घस्मरः, आद्यूनः, कुक्षिंभरिः, अत्याहारिन् *m.*; *See* below. -OUS,-ISH, *a.* औदरिक (की *f.*), अत्याहारिन्, बहुभोजिन्, अत्याहारप्रिय, भक्षक, घस्मर, अद्मर, आद्यून, कुक्षिंभरि, उदरंभरि, गृध्नु, लोलुप-भ, अतिलुब्ध, अतृप्त. -OUSLY, *adv.* अत्याहारेण, लोलुपतया. -Y, *s.* अत्याहारः, घस्मरता, गृध्नुता, जिह्वालौल्यं, अतृप्ति *f.*, औदरिकता.

GNARL, *v. i.* गर्ज् 1 P.

GNARLED, *a.* ग्रंथिल, ग्रंथि-पर्व-विशिष्ट.

GNASH, *v. t.* (The teeth) दंतैर्दंतान् निष्पीड् 10 or विघट्ट् c. or घृष् 1 P, निष्पिष् 7 P or सं-दंश् 1 P, क्ष्विड् 1 P. -ING, *s.* दंतनिष्पेषः-घर्षणं, क्ष्वेडनं.

GNAT, *s.* मशकः, दंशः, प्राचिका, वनमक्षिका.

GNAW, *v. t.* दंश् 1 P, चर्व् 1 P or c., अल्पशः भक्ष् 10 or खाद् 1 P; चर्वणेन कृत् 6 P. -ING, *s.* चर्वणं, दंशनं.

GNOMON, *s.* शंकुः; कीलः-लकः.

GO, *v. i.* गम् 1 P, या-इ 2 P, व्रज् 1 P, चल्-चर् 1 P, पद् 4 A, ऋ 1, 3 P; सृ 1, 3 P; क्रम् 1 U, 4 P; (as water) वह् 1 P, प्लु 1 P, स्यंद् 1 A. 2 (Fare) वृत् 1 A, स्था 1 P; 'how g. es it with her' कस्तस्या वृत्तांतः. 3 (As prospective future) ex. by fut. part., मनः or काम with inf. or desid. forms; *See* ABOUT; 'g. astray' भ्रम् 1, 4 P; उत्पथं या, सन्मार्गात् च्यु 1 A or भ्रंश् 1 A, 4 P; उत्क्रम्, अति-व्यभि-चर्; 'g. on foot' पद्भ्यां व्रज्; 'g. on horse-back' अश्वेन संचर्; 'as the story g. es' किल; 'g. for nothing' (go to dogs) विफलीभू; 'g. to bed' शय्यां भज्-सेव् 1 A; 'she is far gone in love' दूरगतमन्मथा सा (S. 3), अतिभूमिं गतोऽस्या अनुरागः; 'g.-between' मध्यस्थः, मध्यपुरुषः; (female g.) शंभली, कुट्टिनी; सुरतदूती; 'g.-by' निर्गमः, पलायनं, व्यपदेशः; 'g.-cart' क्रीडाशकटः. -about, परिगम्-इ &c. 2 यत् 1 A, उद्यम् 1 A, व्यव-सो 4 P, आरभ् 1 A, उपक्रम् 1 A. 3 अनु-ष्ठा, वि-धा 3 U; *See* EXECUTE. -away, अप-इ, अपसृ-क्रम्-गम्-या-सृप्, प्र-इ,

स्था 1 A. –between, मध्ये स्था or वृत्, अंतः-इ. –by,अति-इ, समीपतः गम्. 2 अनुगम्, अनुवृत्, अनुरुध् 4 A, अनु-सृ; 'he g. es by the name of' इति ख्यातः or ज्ञातः; उमाख्यां सुमुखी जगाम (K. I. 26) 'went by the name of' &c. –down, अधो गम्. 2 अस्तं गम्-या; (fig.) नाशं-क्षयं-या; प्र-ली 4 A, ध्वंस् 1 A. –forth,-forward, निर्गम्, निःसृ-क्रम्, प्रसृ, प्र-स्था, प्र-या. –in, प्र-आ-विश् 6 P, अंतर्गम्-या. 2 (for) संमन् 4 A, उरी-अंगी-कृ 8 U, प्रति-पद् 4 A. –off, अपगम् &c. 2 प्र-इ, मृ 6 A; परलोकं या. –on, प्र-वृत्, प्रगम्-या-सृप्. 2 प्र-स्तु 2 U, प्रारभ् 1 A; 'g. on with your study' प्रवर्ततां-प्रस्तूयतां-अध्ययनं. –out, निर्गम्, निःसृ, &c., बहिर्गम्. 2 (Of light) निर्वा 2 P or c. pass.; शम् 4 P. –over, वच् c., अधि-इ 2 A; (to one's self) अनुवच् c. 2 परि-ईक्ष् 1 A. 3 आक्रम्, लंघ् 1 A, 10. 4 अन्यपक्षं सं-आ-श्रि 1 U; स्वपक्षाद् भ्रंश् 1 A, 4 P. –round, परि-इ-गम्; प्रदक्षिणीकृ. –through, अनुभू, उपागम्, वि-धा, अनु-ष्ठा, कृ, निर्वह् c.; सेव् 1 A, आचर्. 2 पारं गम्, समाप् c.; अव-सो 4 P. 3 प्र-निर्-विश्, निभिद् 7 P; भित्त्वा निर्गम्; व्यध् 4 P. –to, up to, उपसृ-इ-गम्-या, उप-स्था, प्रति-पद् &c. 2 (*Interj.*) धिक्, अपेहि, अपसर. –up, उद्-इ, उत्पत्, ऊर्ध्वं गम्. –ER, *s.* गामिन्-गंतृ *m.*, चरः, यायिन् *m.* in comp. –ING, *s.* गमनं, यानं, सरणं, चलनं, व्रजनं, गति *f.*, अयनं, &c.

GOAD, *s.* अंकुशः, सृ(शृ)णि *f.* –*v. t.* अंकुशेन तुद् 6 P or प्रचुद् 10. 2 प्रचुद्, प्रणुद् c., प्रोत्सह् c., प्रेर् c., प्रवृत् c., उद्युज् 10, उत्तिज् c.

GOAL, *s.* अंतः, अंतस्थानं, अवधिः, अवसानभूमि *f.*; 'g. of ambition' आशावधिः. 2 आशयः, अभिप्रायः, उद्देशः.

GOAT, *s.* अजः, छागः, छगलकः, बस्तः, शुभः; 'she-g.' अजा, छागी; 'g.-herd' अजाजीवः, जाबालः, अजपालः-लकः, छागपोषकः; 'a flock of g. s' आजकं. –ISH, *a.* अजगंध.

GOBBLE, *v. t.* सत्वरं ग्रस् 1 A or भक्ष् 10.

GOBLET, *s.* चषकः-कं, पानपात्रं-भाजनं, कंसः-सं.

GOBLIN, *s.* भूतः, वेतालः, पिशाचः, राक्षसः, निशाचरः, रात्रि(त्रिं)चरः.

GOD, *s.* देवः, सुरः, अमरः, निर्जरः, विबुधः, सुपर्वा, सुमनाः, त्रिदिवेशः, दिवौकाः, आदितेयः, दिविषद्, लेखः, अदितिनंदनः, आदित्यः, ऋभुः, अस्वप्नः, अमर्त्यः, अमृतांधाः, बर्हिर्मुखः, क्रतुभुक्, गीर्वाणः, दानवारिः, वृंदारकः, दैवतः-तं; 'great g.' परमेश्वरः, परमात्मा; 'goddess' देवी, भगवती, सुरांगना, देवपत्नी; in comp. words ex. by धर्म; 'g.-father' धर्मपिता; so धर्ममाता, धर्मपुत्रः-त्री, धर्मकन्या-सुता, &c. –LESS, *a.* निरीश्वर, नास्तिक, अनीश्वरवादिन्. –LESSNESS, *s.* मिथ्यादृष्टि *f.*, नास्तिकता. –LIKE, *a.* देवतुल्य-रूप, देवोपम, दिव्य. –LY, *a.* धार्मिक (की *f.*), धर्मनिष्ठ-परायण, पुण्यशील, पुण्यात्मन्, ईश्वरभक्त-पूजक. –LINESS, *s.* धर्मसेवा, पुण्यशीलता, ईश्वरभक्ति *f.*, श्रद्धा, &c. –SHIP, *s.* देवत्वं, देवभावः. –GODSEND, *s.* ईश्वरप्रेरित *a.* द्रव्यं, ईश्वरप्रसादः, सौभाग्यं, लक्ष्मीदत्तं.

GOGGLE, *v. i.* नयने विक्षिप् 6 P or लुल् c.; 'g. eye' लोलनयनं; 'g.-eyed' लोलनयन, वक्र-तिर्यक्-दृष्टि.

GOITRE, *s.* गडुः.

GOLD, *s.* सुवर्णं, स्वर्णं, कनकं, कांचनं, हेमन् *n.*, चामीकरं, जातरूपं, हिरण्यं, हाटकं, तपनीयं, शातकुंभं, गांगेयं, भर्मन् *n.*, कर्बुरं, महारजतं, रुक्मं, कार्तस्वरं, जांबूनदं, अष्टापदः-दं; 'g. for ornaments' शृंगिः, शृंगीकनकं; 'g.-beater or drawer' सुवर्णोद्वर्तनकृत् *m.*; 'g.-dust' कांचनभूः, कनकरागः; 'g.-smith' स्वर्ण-सुवर्ण-कारः, कलादः, नाडिंधमः. रुक्मकारकः; 'g.-thread' कनकसूत्रं. –*a.*, –EN, *a.* हैम (मी *f.*), सौवर्ण (र्णी *f.*), (*s.*) in comp., or by मय (यी *f.*) affixed to (*s.*).

GOLF, *s.* कंदुकक्रीडा-लीला.

GONORRHÆA, *s.* शुक्रदोषः.

GOOD, *a.* भद्र, साधु, प्रशस्त, प्रशस्य, शुभ, कल्याण (णी *f.*), सत्, वर, शोभन, गुणवत्, निर्दोष; oft. by सु or सत् in comp. 2 धर्मशील, साधु-आर्य-वृत्त, सदाचार, सच्चरित, सुकृतिन्, पुण्य, पुण्यात्मन्, पुण्यशील, धार्मिक (की *f.*). 3 योग्य, उचित, युक्त, उपयुक्त, हित; gen. ex. by pot. pass. part. 4 सुजन, हितकाम, प्रियकारिन्, उपकारक, हित, प्रियकर. 5 अन्यून, अदूषित, अक्षत, संपूर्ण. 6 बहु, प्रचुर, महत्, अनल्प, भूरि, सु or अति pr.; 'a g. fellow' भद्रः, सौम्यः; 'my g. sir' भद्र, सौम्य; 'g. quality' गुणः, सद्गुणः; 'g. wishes' आशिस् *f.*, आशीर्वादः-वचनं; 'g. and bad' शुभाशुभ; 'so g. as' अनुग्रहपूर्वकं, कृपया; 'for g.' अत्यंतं, असन्निवृत्त्यै; 'a g. deal' भृशं, अतीव, सु or अति pr.; 'g. morning to you' (अपि) शुभस्ते प्रभातकालः; 'it will be g. for you' तव कल्याणाय भवेत्, कल्याणमावहेत्; 'is g. unto weariness' आयासजनकमेव, श्रममात्रदायकं; 'g. for nothing' निरुपयोग, निर्गुण, निष्फल; 'as g. as' समं –*s.* उपकारः, उपकृति *f.* 2 हितं, भूति *f.*, भद्रं, शुभं, कल्याणं, कुशलं, श्रेयस् *n.*, क्षेमं; oft. by अर्थः; 'for the g. of the people' प्रजार्थं, लोकहिताय, प्रजाभूतये, &c. 3 उपयोगः, लाभः, फलं; oft. ex. by किं, अर्थः, अलं, with inst.; 'what is the g. of seeing her' किं तया दृष्टया S. 2), कोर्थस्तस्या दर्शनेन; 'what g. do you get by weeping' अलं परिदेवनेन. 4 सुकृतं, पुण्यं, धर्मः, सुचरित, साधुवृत्तं, सदाचारः; 'to do g.' उपकृ 8 U; हितं-कल्याणं-कृ; क्षेमं आवह् 1 P; 'g. and evil (bad) ' शुभाशुभं, हिताहितं. -*interj.* साधु, सुष्ठु, सम्यक्, बाढं, कामं, भवतु, तथास्तु, तथेति; युज्यते, अनुमतं मम (V. 2). 'G.-breeding' साधुता, सौजन्यं, विनयः, सभ्यता, 'possessed of g.-breeding' सुशील, सुविनीत, सुजन, अभिजात; 'g.-conditioned' सुस्थ, सुस्थित; 'g. fortune or luck' *See* FORTUNE ; 'g.-humour' सद्भावः, उल्लासः, चित्तप्रसादः, उल्लासवृत्ति *f.*, आनंदः, प्रमोदः; 'g.-nature' सद्भावः, सुस्वभावः, सौजन्यं, सुशीलता ; सुप्रकृति *f.*; 'g.-humoured or g.-natured' हृष्टचित्त, प्रसन्नचित्त, सोल्लस, सानंद, सुस्वभाव, सुशील, सुप्रकृति, सुजन, सद्भाववत्, साधुशील, धर्मात्मन्, पुण्यात्मन्, सुहृदय; 'g.-looking' दर्शनीय, सुरूप, सुदर्शन, सुभग, प्रियदर्शन, प्रेक्षणीय, रम्याकार, सुवदन; 'g.-manners' विनयः, विनीतता, मर्यादा, सुनीति-रीति *f.*; सभ्यता, शिष्टाचारः, सुशीलता, सौजन्यं, सु-सत्-चरित्रं, सदाचारः, साधुवृत्तं; 'g.-sense' विवेकः, ज्ञानं, प्रज्ञता, प्रबुद्धता, प्रबोधः, सौजन्यं, सद्भावः, सुशीलता; 'g.-will' हितेच्छा, हितकाम्या, प्रीति *f.*, प्रियता, अनुकूलता, भक्ति *f.*, अनुरागः. -LY, *a.* चारु, सुंदर (री *f.*), सुरूप, सुदृश्य, प्रेक्षणीय, लावण्यवत्, रम्य, रमणीय, मनोरम-हर, रुचिर. 2 अनल्प, महत्, प्रचुर, बहु, अल्पेतर. -NESS, *s.* साधुता, प्रशस्तता, गुणवत्ता, श्रेष्ठता, विशिष्टता. 2 साधुशीलता, सदाचारता, धार्मिकत्वं. 3 सुशीलता, दया, कृपालुत्वं, सद्भावः, सौजन्यं, सुजनता; 'tendency to g.' सत्त्वगुणः.

GOODS, *s.* द्रव्यं, द्रव्यराशिः, विभवः, सामग्री, वस्तुजातं, द्रव्याणि-वस्तूनि (pl.). 2 भांडकं, भांडसमुदायः, पण्यं, भांडानि (pl.); 'house-hold g.' गृहोपस्करः, गृहोपकरणानि.

GOOSE, *s.* हंसः (सी *f.*), चक्रांगः (गी *f.*), वरटः-टा; कलहंसः (सी *f.*); *See* GANDER; 'ruddy g.' चक्रवाकः (की *f.*), चक्रः, रथांगः, कोकः, द्वंद्वचरः. 2 Fool, q. v.

GORBELLIED, *a.* महोदर, बृहत्कुक्षि, तुंदिन्, स्थूलोदर; *See* CORPULENT.

GORE, *s.* रक्तं, शोणितं, रुधिरं, असृज् *n.*, लोहितं. 2 रक्तगुल्मः, रक्तपिंडः. 3 संधितवस्त्रखंडः. -*v. t.* व्यध् 4 P, निर्भिद् 7 P, छिद् 7 P, वि-दृ 10, क्षण् 5 P, उल्लिख् 6 P. -ED, *a.* छिन्नत्वक्, क्षतभिन्न. -Y, *a.* रक्ताक्त, असृग्दिग्ध. 2 रुधिरप्रिय, मारात्मक.

GORGE, *s.* कंठः, गलः. 2 रंध्रं, दुर्गमार्गः, संकट-संबाधपथः, संचारः, संकटं, गिरिकंदरः. -*v. t.* उद्-ग्रस् 1 A, गॄ 6 P. 2 (One's self) कुक्षिं पूर् 10, अत्यंतं तृप् c., अन्नादिना परिपॄ 3 P.

GORGEOUS, *a.* शोभन, उज्ज्वल, अतिशोभन, विभ्राजमान, तेजस्विन्, सुप्रभ, एकांतरमणीय-चारु, महाप्रभ-दीप्ति, विचित्र, -LY, *adv.* अतितेजसा, उज्ज्वलं.

-NESS, *s.* औज्ज्वल्यं, अति-प्रभा-तेजस् *n.*, सुप्रभा.

GORGET, *s.* ग्रीवा-गल-त्राणं.

GORMAND,-IZER, *See* GLUTTON.

GOSLING, *s.* हंसशिशुः-शावकः.

GOSSIP, *s.* वावदूकः, प्रलापिन् *m.*, जल्पकः. 2 पानमित्रं, सहपायिन् *m.* 3 वार्ता, जनप्रवादः, जल्पः, जल्पितं, प्रलापः, प्रजल्पः, वृथाकथा-संलापः. -*v. i.* प्रजल्प् 1 P, प्रलप् 1 P.

GOUGE, *v. t.* (नयनं) उत्पट् 10, उद्धृ 1 P.

GOURD, *s.* अ(आ)लाबु-बू *f.*, तुंबि-बी *f.*, लाबु-बू *f.*, तुंबा. 2 (Vessel of g.) कमंडलुः; 'bitter g.' इक्ष्वाकु *f.*, कटुतुंबी.

GOURMAND, *See* GLUTTON.

GOUT, *s.* वातरक्तं, वातशोणितं. -Y, *a.* वातग्रस्त, वातरोगोपहत, वातरोगिन्, वातकिन्.

GOVERN, *v. t.* प्र-शास् 2 P, परि-पा c. (पालयति), ईश् 2 A (with gen.); गुप् 1 P, तंत्र् 10 A, नियम् 1 P; *See* RULE. 2 वि-धा 3 U, वि-नी 1 P, निग्रह् 9 P, सं-नि-यम्, आ-वृ 5 U, वशीकृ 8 U, दम् c. (दमयति), सं-हृ 1 P, नि-यंत्र् 10; *See* CONTROL. 3 (In grammar) अनु-इ 2 P, वि-धा; 'g. ed by another' परायत्त, पराधीन, परतंत्र, विधेय. -MENT, *s.* नियमनं, सं-नि-यमः, निग्रहः. 2 शासनं, परिपालनं; 'during the g. of Rāma' रामे महीं शासति. 3 प्रभुत्वं, ईशत्वं, ऐश्वर्यं, आधिपत्यं, स्वामित्वं. 4 राज्यं. 5 (Rulers) राजन् *m.*, प्रभुः, ईशः, राजमंत्रिणः-सचिवाः; 'g. affairs' राज्यकार्याणि; 'form of g.' राज्यरीति-पद्धति *f.* -OR, *s.* शासितृ *m.*, शासकः, ईशः, अधिपतिः, अधिष्ठातृ *m.*, अधिपः, अधिकृतः. 2 (Of a province) भोगपतिः. -ORSHIP, *s.* आधिपत्यं, प्रभुत्वं.

GOWN, *s.* शाटः-टी, शाटकः, कटिवस्त्रं; 'girl's g.' अधोरुकं, चंडातकः-कं.

GRAB, *s.* ग्रहः, धरणं, संग्रहः.

GRABBLE, *v.* स्पृश्-परामृश् 6 P, 2 भूमौ देहं क्षिप् 6 P.

GRACE, *s.* प्रसादः, अनुग्रहः, दया, कृपा, अनुकंपा, आनुकूल्यं. 2 सौंदर्यं, श्रीः, चारुता, शोभा, लावण्यं; *See* BEAUTY. 3 गुणः, भूषणं. 4 क्षमा, पापमार्जनं-निष्कृति *f.* 5 (As a title) देवः-वी, अत्र-तत्रभवान्-भवती. -*v. t.* अलंकृ 8 U, शुभ् c., भूष् 10, उद्-द्युत् c. (जाति पुनरप्युद्योतयोस्संग U. 4); सं-मन् c. सं-भू c.; 'g. the ceremony with your presence' संनिधानेन इमं विधिं संमानयतु-अलंकरोतु-भवान्. -FUL, *a.* ललित, चारु, सुंदर (री *f.*), सुभग, लावण्यवत्, मुग्ध, सविलास; 'g. movement' मुग्धचेष्टा, विलासः, विभ्रमः, ललितं, हेला, लीला, हावः, विब्बोकः, शृंगारचेष्टा-क्रिया; 'g. speech' वाग्विलासः; 'g. gait' खेलगति *f.*, विलासगतं. -FULLY, *adv.* सविलासं, ललितं, सुंदरं, चारुतया. -FULNESS, *s.*

लावण्यं, श्रीः, शोभा, लालित्यं, मुग्धता ; *See* BEAUTY. –LESS, *a.* रूपहीन. 2 निर्लज्ज, दुराचार, दुर्वृत्त, अतिदुष्ट, दुष्टभाव. —GRACIOUS, *a.* प्रसन्न, सदय, दयाशील, अनुकूल, अनुकंपिन्, दयालु, अनुकंपाशील, अनुग्राहिन्, कृपालु, सानुक्रोश, हितबुद्धि, सानुकंप; 'to be g.' प्रसद् 1 P, अनु-कंप् 1 A. –LY, *adv.* सानुग्रहं, सदयं, सानुकंपं, दयया, कृपया, प्रसन्नतया, सप्रसादं. –NESS, *s.* प्रसादः, अनुकंपा, दयालुत्वं, अनुग्रहः, दया, कृपा, &c.

GRADATION, *s.* क्रमः, आनुपूर्व्यं, पर्यायः, अनुक्रमः; परंपरा, समन्वयः, परिपाटि-टी *f.*; 'in regular g.' यथाक्रमं, क्रमशः, अनुपूर्वशः, पर्यायेण.

GRADE, *s.* श्रेणि-णी *f.*, प्रकारः, वर्गः, परिपाटि-टी *f.*, क्रमः, परंपरा, आनुपूर्व्यं. 2 पदं, अवस्था, आस्पदं पदवि-वी *f.*, कोटि *f.*, काष्ठा (highest g.). —GRADUAL, *a.* क्रमिक, आनुक्रमिक, अनुपूर्व, उत्तरोत्तर; better ex. by 'g. ly'. –LY, *adv.* क्रमशः, शनैः शनैः, क्रमतः, क्रमेण, यथाक्रमं, अनुक्रमं, अल्पाल्पशः, उत्तरोत्तरं, प्रति-अनु-पदं, पदे पदे, अनुपूर्वशः, आनुपूर्व्येण. —GRADUATE, *v. t.* क्रमचिह्नैः अंक् 10. 2 उपपदं प्राप् 5 P. –*s.* उपपद-उपाधि-पद-युक्तः. –ION, *s.* क्रमचिह्नांकनं. 2 Gradation, q v.

GRAFT, *v. t.* (fig.) निविश् c., नि-धा 3 U.

GRAIN, *s.* धान्यं, शस्य, व्रीहिः, स्तंबकरिः, बीजरुहः, जीवसाधनं. 2 बीजं. 3 कणः-णिका, लवः, लेशः, अणुः. 4 काष्ठरेखा-शिरा; 'fried g.' लाजाः, भ्रष्टयवाः; पृथुकः, चिपिटकः; 'against the g.' प्रतिलोमं, विरुद्धं, विप्रतीपं, निरुत्साहं, कथमपि; 'with the g.' अनुलोमं; 'chaffless g.' धान्यास्थि. –Y, *a.* धान्यशस्य-मय (यी *f.*).

GRAMINEOUS, *a.* तृणमय (यी *f.*), शाद्वल.

GRAMINIVOROUS, *a.* तृण-शष्प-भोजिन्, तृणभुज्.

GRAMMAR, *s.* व्याकरणं, व्याकरणशास्त्रं-विद्या, शब्दशास्त्रं. –IAN, *s.* वैयाकरणः, व्याकरणज्ञः, शब्दशास्त्रविद् *m.* –GRAMMATICAL, *a.* व्याकरणविषय, व्याकरणानुसारिन्; gen. (*s.*) in comp.

GRANARY, *s.* कुशूलः, धान्यकोष्ठः, धान्यागारं, कंडोलः, पिटः.

GRAND, *a.* महत्, बृहत्, गुरु. 2 उत्तम, प्रधान, मुख्य, अग्र, अग्र्य, विशिष्ट. 3 सुप्रभ, भव्य, प्रतापवत्, तेजस्विन्, उज्ज्वल; 'g.-child' पौत्रः-त्री; 'g.-daughter' पौत्री, पुत्रसुता, दौहित्री; 'great g.-daughter' प्रपौत्री; 'g.-father' पितामहः, मातामहः (maternal); 'great g.-father' प्रपितामहः, प्रमातामहः ; 'g.-mother' पितामही, मातामही; वृद्धा. स्थविरा; 'g.-nephew' भ्रातृपौत्रः, स्वसृपौत्रः (त्री *f.*); 'g.-son' पौत्रः, पुत्रसुतः, नप्तृ *m.*, दौहित्रः, पुत्रिकासुतः; 'great g.-son' प्रपौत्रः, &c.; 'great great g.-son' परप्रपौत्रः. –LY, *adv.* वैभवेन, तेजसा, ऐश्वर्येण, महाप्रतापेन, उज्ज्वलं, सुप्रभं, उत्कृष्टं, परमं, श्रेष्ठतया. –NESS, –GRANDEUR, *s.* महत्त्वं, महिमन् *m.* 2 माहात्म्यं, औदार्यं, उत्कर्षः, श्रेष्ठता, प्राधान्यं. 3 वैभवं, तेजस् *n.*, विभूति *f.*, प्रतापः, शोभा, उज्ज्वलता, प्रभावः, ऐश्वर्यं, संपद् *f.* –GRANDEE, *s.* कुलीनः, कुलीनजनः, अभिजनः, महाजनः.

GRANDILOQUENT, *a.* गर्वितवाच्, सदर्पवादिन्. –GRANDILOQUENCE, *s.* अतिशयोक्ति *f.*, दर्पवाक्यं, सालंकारं वचनं, दर्पाध्मातं वचनं.

GRANGE, *s.* क्षेत्रं, क्षेत्रभूमि *f.*

GRANIVOROUS, *a.* शस्याद, शस्यभक्षक.

GRANT, *v. t.* वितॄ 1 P, दा 3 U, 1 P, प्रति-पद् c.; *See* GIVE. 2 अनुमन् 4 A, अनु-ज्ञा 9 U, अनु-मुद् 1 A. 3 ग्रह् 9 P, अंगीकृ 8 U, उरीकृ, स्वीकृ, प्रतिपद् 4 A, अभ्युपगम् 1 P, अभ्युप-इ 2 P; 'I g.', 'g. ed' gen. ex. by कामं followed by तु, तथापि or पुनः; or by imp.; 'well it is g. ed' भवतु, एवमस्तु, गृहीतमिदं. –*s.* प्रदानं, दानं, उत्सर्गः, दायः, विहापितं, उपायनं; *See* GIFT; 'g. of property' निबंधः; 'royal g.' (gifts of land, &c.) शासनं, पट्टः, शासनपत्रं; 'a written g.' लेख्यपत्रं. –EE, *s.* प्रतिग्रहीतृ *m.*, दानभोगिन् *m.*, आदाता. –OR, *s.* दातृ *m.*

GRANULE, *s.* कणिका, लवः, बीजकं, अणुः. –GRANULAR, *a.* बीजाकार, बीजमय (यी *f.*), कणमय. —GRANULATE, *v. t.* घनीकृ 8 U, संहतीकृ; सूक्ष्मकणान् बंध् 9 P. –ION, *s.* पोथकी.

GRAPE, *s.* द्राक्षा, मृद्वीका, गोस्तना-नी, स्वाद्वी, मधुरसा; (fruit) द्राक्षाफलं, &c.; 'g.-stone' द्राक्षाबीजं, अष्ठीला, आष्ठि *f.* –GRAPERY, *s.* द्राक्षावाटिका.

GRAPHIC, *a.* स्पष्ट, अर्थवत्, सुलिखित, सुचित्रित, सुनिर्दिष्ट.

GRAPNEL, *s.* क्षुद्रलंगरः. 2 आकर्षणी.

GRAPPLE, *v. t.* धृ 1 P, 10, संग्रह् 9 P, आकृष् 1 P; नि-सं-बंध् 9 P, संश्लिष् c. –*v. i.* युध् 4 A, संघट्ट् 1 A, बाहूबाहवि or हस्ताहस्ति युध्; अभिसं-पत् 1 P. –*s.* संग्राहः, धरणं. 2 बाहुयुद्धं. 3 आकर्षणी.

GRASP, *v. t.* ग्रह् 9 P, धृ 1 P, 10, (fig. also), आकल् 10, आकृष् 1 P, मुष्टिना ग्रह्; अवलंब् 1 A, परामृश्-स्पृश् 6 P. 2 ग्रस् 1 A, आक्रम् 1 U, 4 P; आ-घ्रा 1 P, आ-अव-लिह् 2 U; 'g.-ed by death' कालग्रस्त; 'g. ed by a tiger' व्याघ्राघ्रात, &c.; 'he quickly g. ed what I meant' मदाशयं झटिति गृहीतवान्. 3 (at) ग्रह् desid. (जिघृक्षति), हृ desid. (जिहीर्षति); आप् desid. (ईप्सति), लंघ् 1 A, 10; *See* ASPIRE. –*s.* ग्रहः-हणं, धरणं, परामर्शः, मुष्टिग्राहः, संग्राहः, हस्तग्राहः, आक्रमः, ग्रसनं; gen. ex. by गोचरः, वशः, विषयः, मुखं; 'is within the g. of death'

मृत्योर्मुखे वर्तते, कालालीढः, मृत्युगोचरं गतः, &c.; 'and this g. over every (kind of) learning' इदं च अशेषविद्याग्रहणसामर्थ्यं (Ka. 96); 'firmness of g.' दृढमुष्टिता, निबिडमुष्टिः.

GRASS, *s.* तृणं, शस्यं, शादः; 'young g.' शष्पं, बालतृणं, घासः; 'meadow g.' य(ज)वसः; 'sacrificial g.' दर्भः, कुशः-शं; 'g.-green' शादहरित, शाद्वल; 'g.-hopper शल(र)भः; 'g.-plot' शाद्वलं, तृणभूमि *f.* -Y, *a.* तृणावृत, बहुतृण, तृणपूर्ण, सतृण, बहुघास, शाद्वल, घास-तृण-मय (यी *f.*). 2 हरित, शादहरित.

GRATE, *s.* चुल्लि-ल्ली *f.*, अधिश्रयणी; *See* FIRE-PLACE. 2 लोहजालं. -*v. t.* घृष् 1 P, निष्पिष् 7 P, मृद् 9 P, संघट्ट् c. 2 बाध् 1 A, पीड् 10, व्यथ् c. (व्यथयति), संतप् c.; मर्माणि छिद् 7 P or स्पृश्-तुद् 6 P. 3 घर्षणेन चूर्ण् 10, पिष्, क्षुद् 7 P. 4 लोहजालेन गुज् 10; 'g. the teeth' दंतैर्दंतान् निष्पिड् or घृष्. -ING, *a.* कर्कश, परुष, निष्ठुर, खर, कटु, मर्मस्पृश्-छिद्, अरुंतुद; 'g. to the ear' श्रवणकटु. -*s.* अन्योन्यघर्षणं, कर्कशध्वनिः. 2 लोहजालं, लोहशलाकासनाथः गवाक्षः. -INGLY, *adv.* कर्कशं, निष्ठुरं, कटु.

GRATEFUL, *a.* सुखकर (री *f.*), रम्य, रमणीय, आनंदावह, सुखावह, हृद्य, सुभग, मनोरम. 2 कृतज्ञ, कृतवेदिन्, उपकृतिज्ञ, कृतविद्, उपकारज्ञ. -LY, *adv.* कृतज्ञतया. 2 सुभगं, रम्यतया. -NESS,-GRATITUDE, *s.* कृतज्ञता, उपकारस्मरणं, उपकृतज्ञता, कृतवेदित्वं.

GRATER, *s.* घर्षणी, घर्षणयंत्रं.

GRATIFY, *v. t.* तुष् c., सं-परि°, आनंद् c., प्री 10, तृप् c., प्रमुद् c., हृष् c, रम् c., आह्लाद् c.; *See* DELIGHT also. 2 अनु-वृत् 1 A, अनुरुध् 4 A, लल् 10, प्र-सद् c., आराध् c., अनुरंज् c., सांत्व् 10. 3 शम् c. (शमयति), पॄ c. or पूर् 10, साध् c., निर्वृत् c.; 'having all desires g. ed' पूर्णकाम, कृतार्थ, कृतिन्, सिद्धार्थ, निवृत्तकाम; 'g. ed at heart' प्रीत-हृष्ट-चित्त. -ICATION, *s.* सं-,परि-,तोषः, आनंदः, तृप्ति *f.*, तुष्टि *f.*, प्रीति *f.*, सुखं, हर्षः, आह्लादः, प्रमोदः. 2 आराधनं, अनुरोधः, अनुवर्तनं, प्रसादनं, तर्पणं, तोषणं. 3 शांति *f.*, शमनं, सिद्धि *f.*, साधनं, पूरणं, निर्वर्तनं; 'g. of desire' मनोरथसिद्धिः, इष्टसाधनं; 'g. of another's whim' छंदोनुवृत्ति *f.*-वर्तनं. -ING, *a.* सं-परि-तोषक, तुष्टि-प्रीति-द, सुखावह, आनंदप्रद, सुख-प्रीति-कर (री *f.*).

GRATIS, *adv.* विना मूल्येन, धर्मार्थं, निर्मूल्यं.

GRATUITOUS, *a.* अमूल्यवत्, निर्मूल्य, मूल्यं विना दत्त, कामतः दत्त. 2 अमूलक, निष्कारण, निर्निमित्त, अहेतुक. -LY, *adv.* निर्मूल्यं.

GRATUITY, *s.* प्रदानं, उपायनं; *See* GIFT.

GRATULATE, *See* CONGRATULATE.

GRAVE, *a.* गुरु, महत्, अलघु. 2 ग(गं)भीर, धीर, अचपल. 3 (Sound) मंद, घन, गंभीर, धीर, मंद्र, मंथर; 'g. matter' गुर्वर्थः. -*s.* प्रेत-शव-स्थानं; समाधिः, श्मशानं, अवटः. 'g.-clothes' प्रेतवासस् *n.*, शववस्त्रं; 'g.-stone' चित्यं, चैत्यं, समाधिप्रस्तरः. -*v. t.* तक्ष् 1, 5 P, त्वक्ष् 1 P. -LY, *adv.* गंभीरतया, धीरं, सगौरवं, गांभीर्येण. 2 मंद्रं, धीरं, गंभीरं. -NESS, *s.* गुरुता-त्वं, गौरवं, महत्त्वं. -GRAVITY, *s.* गुरुत्वं, भारः. 2 गौरवं, गुरुत्वं-ता, महिमन् *m.*, गांभीर्यं; अलाघवं, धीरता, मंद्रता. 3 आकर्षणशीलता, आकर्षणशक्ति *f.* —GRAVITATE, *v. i.* आकृष् pass., अधः गम् or पत् 1 P. -ION, *s.* आकर्षणं, अधःपतनशीलता.

GRAVEL, *s.* शर्करा, वालुका, शिला-पाषाण-खंडः-चूर्णं. 2 (Disease) अश्मरी, मूत्रकृच्छ्रं, मूत्रशर्करा. -*v. t.* शर्करावृत *a.* कृ 8 U. 2 मुह् c., सं-वि-भ्रम् c. (भ्रमयति). -LY, *a.* सशर्कर, शार्करित, शर्करावृत, शार्करावत्, शार्करीय.

GRAVEOLENT, *a.* दुर्गंध, पूतिगंधि.

GRAVID, *See* PREGNANT.

GRAVY, *s.* मांससारः, मांसजूषं.

GRAY, *a.* आपांडु, धूसर, पांशुवर्ण, आशुक्ल. 2 शुक्ल, धवल, श्वेत, पक्व, पलित (hair); 'g. beard' जीर्णकूर्चं; 'g. head' पलितं शिरः; 'g.-haired' पलित, धवल-शुक्ल-केश; 'g.-headed' पलितशिरस्. 3 जीर्ण, परिणत, पक्व, वृद्ध. -*s.* धूसरः, धूसर-पांशु-वर्णः. -ISH, *a.* आपांडु, पांडुर, आधूसर; 'g. with dust' धूलिधूसर. -NESS, *s.* धूसरता, पलितता, केशधावल्यं, पक्वता, जीर्णता.

GRAZE, *v. t.* चर् c., तृणं भुज् c. or खाद् c. 2 निर्घृष् 1 P, लघु तड् 10, लघुप्रहारेण अति-इ 2 P. -*v. i.* चर् 1 P, तृणं खाद् 1 P or भक्ष् 10 or भुज् 7 A; 'a place g. ed by cattle' आशितंगवीनं. -ER, *s.* तृणभक्षकः. -ING, *s.* चरणं; 'g. ground' गोचरः, गोप्रचारः. -GRAZIER, *s.* गोचारकः, पशुपालः, गोपालकः.

GREASE, *s.* वसा, मेदस् *n.*, वपा, मांसस्नेहः-सारः. 2 स्नेहः, तैलं, घृतं. -*v. t.* वसया-स्नेहेन लिप् 6 P or अंज् 7 P or दिह् 2 U. -Y, *a.* मेदस्विन्, वसामय (यी *f.*), चिक्कण, प्र-,स्निग्ध, वसाक्त, स्नेहाभ्यक्त, सस्नेह, वसा-स्नेह-युक्त.

GREAT, *a.* महत्, गुरु, बृहत्, विशाल, विपुल, विस्तीर्ण, उरु, पृथु, स्थूल, महाप्रमाण. 2 (In number) बहु, भूरि, प्रचुर, बहुल, बहुसंख्याक. 3 उत्कृष्ट, उत्तम, परम, विशिष्ट, विश्रुत, श्रेष्ठ, लब्धप्रतिष्ठ, प्रसिद्ध, महायशस्क. 4 महेच्छ, महाशय, महात्मन्, उदार, उदारचित्त. 5 प्रधान, मुख्य, परम, अग्र्य, गुरु. 6 अत्यंत, अतिमात्र, गाढ, आधिक, भृश, परम, एकांत, नितांत, अतिरिक्त;

oft. by महत्, सु, अति, in comp.; 'to a g. distance, सुदूरं, अतिदूरं; 'to a g. degree' भृशं, अतिमात्रं, अत्यंतं, निर्भरं, गाढं. -LY, *adv.* भृशं, अत्यंतं, सातिशयं, सु-नि-तरां, एकांततः, परं, बलवत्, गाढं, परमं, सु-अति-अतिशय in comp.; *See* EXCEEDINGLY; oft. ex. by कोटि *f.*, काष्ठा; 'he was g. delighted' आनंदस्य परां कोटिं-काष्ठां-अधिगतवान्. -NESS, *s.* महत्त्वं, माहात्म्यं, महिमन् *m.*, गुरुत्वं; विपुलता, विशालता, &c. 2 विस्तारः, परिमाणं. 3 विभुति *f.*, उत्कर्षः, विशिष्टता, परमता, आधिक्यं, प्रतिष्ठा, गौरवं. 4 वैभवं, शोभा, ऐश्वर्यं; *See* GRANDEUR; 'g. of mind' औदार्यं, माहात्म्यं; 'g. of rank' कुलीनता, आभिजात्यं, कुलोत्कर्षः.

GREAVES, *s.* जंघा-उरु-त्राणं, मंक्षुक्षणं.

GREED, *s.* लोभः, गृध्नुता, अतिस्पृहा, लौल्यं, लुब्धता, अत्यभिलाषः, अतिलिप्सा, अत्याकांक्षा, लोलुपत्वं, अतृप्ति *f.*, अपरितोषः. 2 (Of food) अत्याहारः, घस्मरता, अद्मरता, उदरंभरित्वं. —GREEDY, *a.* लुब्ध, लोलुप, लोलुभ, गृध्नु, लोभाविष्ट, अत्यभिलाषिन्, अत्याकांक्षिन्, सतृष्ण, अतितृष्णाकुल, अतिलोभिन्. 2 आहारलुब्ध, अत्याहारप्रिय, घस्मर, अद्मर, अतिभोजिन्, बहुभुज्, औदारिक, उदरंभरि, कुक्षिंभरि, बहुभक्षक; 'to be g.' गृध् 4 P, लुभ् 4 P. -LY, *adv.* अतिलोभेन, सलोभं, सतृष्णं, लोलुपतया, जिह्वालौल्यात्, अत्यभिलाषेण, अतिस्पृहया. -NESS, *s.* लोभः; *See* (*s.*).

GREEN, *a.* हरित, हरित्, हरिद्वर्ण; प(पा)लाश. 2 नव, प्रत्यग्र, अभिनव. 3 अपरिपक्व, अपरिणत; 'g.-headed' अपरिणतप्रज्ञ, अपक्वधी. -*s.* हरिद्वर्णः, हरितः, हरित् *m.*, पालाशवर्णः. 2 हरितस्थानं, शाद्वलं, शाद्वलस्थली, तृणावृता भूमिः; 'g.-leaved' हरित्पर्ण; 'g.-room' नेपथ्यशाला; 'g.-sward' हरितभूमिः, तृणावृतं स्थानं, हरितकं, शाकादि. -ISH, *a.* ईषद्धरित, हरिदाभ, ईषत्पलाश. -NESS, *s.* हरितत्वं, पलाशत्वं. 2 अपरिणतत्वं, अपरिपाकः, अपक्वता.

GREET, *v. t.* अभिनंद् 1 P or c., सभाज् 10, वंद् 1 A, अभिवद् c. (A), अर्च् 1 P, 10, सं-भू c., सत्कृ 8 U, पूज् 10; नमस्कृ, प्रणम् 1 P; 'g. in return' प्रतिनंद्, प्रत्यभि-वद् c. -ING, *s.* प्रणामः, प्रणति *f.*, अभिवंदनं, अभिनंदनं, नमस्कारः, अभिवादः-वादनं, कुशलवादः-प्रश्नः.

GREGARIOUS, *a.* यूथचारिन्, संघचारिन्.

GREY, *See* GRAY.

GRICE, *s.* शूकरशावकः-शिशुः.

GRIDELIN, *s.* श्वेतारुणः.

GRIEVE, *v. t.* दु 5 P, पीड् 10, बाध् 1 A, क्लिश् 9 P, व्यथ् c. (व्यथयति), उप-सं-परि-तप् c., आयस् c., उद्विज् c., दुःखयति (D.), शुच् c., खिद् c., 'it g. s me to see you in this condition' एतदवस्थं त्वां वीक्ष्य दुःखितोस्मि. -*v. i.* शुच् 1 P, व्यथ् 1 A, दुर्मनायते (D.), उत्तम् 4 P, उत्कंठ् 1 A, पीड्-खिद्-क्लिश्-दु-तप् pass., दुःखायते (D.), उद्विज् 6 A, उत्सुक-उत्क-*a.* भू. -ANCE, *s.* दुःखं, क्लेशः, कष्टं, बाधा, पीडा, पीडाहेतुः, दुःखमूलं-बीजं-कारणं. -ED, *a.* दुःखित, दून, पीडित, व्यथित, संतप्त, शोकार्त, दुःखाकुल, शोकातुर, खेदित, क्लिष्ट, उद्विग्न, आतुर, आर्त, कष्टाप्त, उत्सुक, उत्क. -INGLY, *adv.* सशोकं, सोद्वेगं, सदुःखं. -OUS, *a.* दुःखकर-व्यथाकर-कष्टकर (री *f.*), पीडावह, क्लेशप्रद, पीडाजनक, शोच्य, शोचनीय, दुस् pr. 2 घोर, उग्र, दारुण, महत्, गुरु. -OUSLY, *adv.* घोरं, दारुणं. सशोकं; 'g. hurt' बलवत् पीडित, घोरक्षत, &c. -GRIEF, *s.* शोकः, दुःखं, शुच् *f.*, क्लेशः, खेदः, सं-परि-तापः, व्यथा, मन्युः, पीडा, अ-आर्ति *f.*, उद्वेगः, आधिः, वेदना, मनस्तापः, चित्तव्यथा, औत्सुक्यं, उत्कंठा.

GRILL, *See* FRY.

GRIM, *a.* उग्र, दारुण, घोर, भयानक, रौद्र (द्री *f.*), विकृत, विकट. 2 (In appearance) उग्रदर्शन, घोराकृति, रौद्ररूप, कदाकार, दुर्दर्शन, कु-अप-रूप. -LY, *adv.* उग्रं, घोरं, विकटं. -NESS, *s.* घोरता, रौद्रता, &c.

GRIMACE, *s.* वदनविकारः-विकृति *f.*; मुख-वक्त्र-भंगः, मुखविरूपता, वक्रमुखं, विकृतास्यं.

GRIME, *s.* मलः-लं; *See* DIRT. -*v. t.* मलिनयति (D.), दुष् c. (दूषयति).

GRIN, *v. i.* सस्मितं दंतान् दृश् c.; कु-स्मि 1 A or हस् 1 P, विकृतं-मुखविकारेण हस् or स्मि. -*s.* कुस्मितं, कुहासः, विकृतहासः-स्मितं, दंतदर्शनं. -NER, *s.* कु-विकृत-हासिन् *m.*, विकृतहासः.

GRIND, *v. t.* पिष् 7 P, क्षुद् 7 P, मृद् 9 P, चूर्ण् 10, चूर्णीकृ 8 U; चूर्णपेषं पिनष्टि; 'g. s to powder'. 2 (As a gem) उल्लिख् 6 P, उल्लिह् 2 U; संस्कारोल्लिखितः-शाणोल्लीढः-मणिः 'a gem ground on a polishing or touch-stone'; घर्षणेन नि-शो 4 P or उत्तिज् c. 3 घृष् 1 P; 'g. ing the teeth in rage' रोषाद् दंतैर्दंतान्विनिष्पिष्य. 4 उप-द्रु 1 A, बाध् 1 A, पीड् 10, अर्द् 1 P or c.; 'ground by heavy taxes' करभारेण चूर्णित-पीडित, &c. -ER, *s.* पेषकः. 2 (g.-stone) पेषणं-णी, पेषणयंत्रं. 3 चर्वणदंतः, दंष्ट्रा. -ING, *s.* पेषणं, चूर्णीकरणं, संमर्दनं, घर्षणं, उल्लिखनं; 'g. stone' पेषणं-णी, पेषणशिला, शाणः, निकषशिला.

GRIPE, *v. t.* ग्रह् 9 P, मुष्टिना ग्रह् or धृ 1 P; *See* GRASP. 2 पीड् 10, सं-नि°. 3 मुष्टिं बंध् 9 P. -*s.* मुष्टिग्राहः, हस्तग्रहः, संग्राहः, दृढग्रहः, मुष्टिबंधः, मुष्टि *m.*, *f.* 2 निष्पीडनं. 3 (g. s) अंत्रशूलं-वेदना, उदरशूलं-व्यथा. -ER, *s.* ग्राहकः. 2 पीडकः, बाधक.

GRISLY, *a.* उग्रदर्शन, करालवदन, विकटाकार, घोर-

कृति, भीमविग्रह, उग्र, घोर, दारुण, भयानक, क्रूर, कराल, भयावह.

GRIST, *s.* गोधूमचूर्णं, पिष्टधान्यं.

GRISTLE, *s.* तरुणास्थि *n.*, कोमलास्थि.

GRIT, *s.* Gravel, q. v. -GRITTY, *a.* सशर्कर, शर्करिल, शर्करामय (यी *f.*).

GRIZZLE, *s.* धूसर-पांशु-वर्णः. -GRIZZLY, *a.* ईषद्धूसर, आपांडुवर्ण.

GROAN, *v. i.* दुःखवशात् क्रण्-स्वन् 1 P or नद् 1 P or रु 2 P or आक्रुश् 1 P, सशब्दं निश्वस् 2 P, आर्तरवं-दीर्घनादं-कृ 8 U. -*s.* दीर्घनिश्वासः, आर्तरवः-नादः, सनिश्वासं क्रणितं, सीत्कारः, ससीत्कारं परिदेवनं.

GROCER, *s.* वणिज् *m.*, नैगमः; *See* MERCHANT. -Y, *s.* वाणिज्यं, वणिक्कर्मन् *n.*

GROG, *See* LIQUOR.

GROIN, *s.* ऊरुसंधिः.

GROOM, *s.* परिचारकः, भृत्यः, किंकरः; (strictly) अश्वपालः-रक्षकः-सेवकः.

GROOVE, *s.* रेखा, प्रणाली. 2 सुषिरं, दीर्घसुषिरं.

GROPE, *v. i.* अंधकारे परा-मृश् 6 P, तमसि निरूप् 10 or अन्विष् 4 P or परीक्ष् 1 A.

GROSS, *a.* स्थूलकाय, बृहत्, पीन, पीवर, मेदस्विन्. 2 घन, स्थूल, असूक्ष्म; 'g. measurement' स्थूलमानं. 3 गाढ, निबिड, निरंतर, अविरल, सांद्र. 4 अश्लील, ग्राम्य, नीच, अवाच्य, अशिष्ट, असभ्य, गर्ह्य, निंद्य, अशुद्ध, कुत्सित, नि-अप-कृष्ट, अपवित्र, मलीमस, अमेध्य, अयशस्कर (री *f.*). 5 जड, मूढ, मंद. 6 अविनीत, अमर्याद. 7 अत्यंत, अतिमात्र, महत्, सु-अति pr.; 'g. fault' महापराधः; 'g. body' स्थूल-जड-देहः; 'g. darkness' संतमसं, अंधं तमः. -*s.* स्थूलांशः, प्रधानभागः, प्रधानांशः, साकल्यं, सामग्र्यं, समासः; 'in the g.' स्थूलमानेन, साकल्येन. -LY, *adv.* स्थूलं, घनं, असभ्यं, गर्हितया, नीचं; अत्यंतं, अतिमात्रं, अति-सु pr.; 'g. corrupted' अतिदुष्ट. -NESS, *s.* स्थूलता, पीनता; निबिडता, अशिष्टता, ग्राम्यत्वं, अविनयः, अमर्यादा, अत्यंतता, अतिरेकः, गाढता, आधिक्यं.

GROT, GROTTO, *s.* कुहरं, गह्वरं, गुहा, कंदरः, शैलविवरं; 'natural g.' देवखातं, देवखातबिलं; 'artificial g.' क्रीडाकुटीरः, कृत्रिमकंदरः.

GROTESQUE, *a.* वि-अप-रूप, विलक्षण, हास्यरूप, कदाकार, असंगताकार; हास्य, असंगत, असंबद्ध, विषम. -LY, *adv.* असंगतं, विलक्षणतया, हास्यरूपेण.

GROUND, *s.* भूमि *f.*, भूः, क्षिति *f.*, मही, धरणी, पृथ्वी; *See* EARTH. 2 भूतलं-पृष्ठं-पीठं. 3 स्थलं, स्थली. 4 उपष्टंभः, वास्तु *m. n.*, गृहभूमिः-प्रतिष्ठा. 5 आधारः, मूलं, कारणं, निमित्तं, हेतुः, निदानं, प्रयोजनं. 6 मृत्तिका, मृद् *f.*, क्षेत्रं; 'gain g.' उप-चि pass., प्र-वृध् 1 A, एध् 1 A, वृद्धिं गम् 1 P; 'lose g.' क्षि-अपचि-pass., ह्रासं गम्; शनैः परा-नि-वृत् 1 A. -*v. t.* मूलं न्यस् 4 P or प्रतिष्ठा c. (प्रतिष्ठापयति); oft. by मूल in comp.; 'devotion g. ed on faith' श्रद्धामूला भक्तिः. 2 आरंभं-उपक्रमं शिक्ष् c. or अधि-इ c. (अध्यापयति); 'well g. ed in grammar' स्वधीतव्याकरणः; 'g.-floor' गृहतलं, कुट्टिमं, अधःकोष्ठः; 'g.-work' मूलकर्मन् *n.*, प्रारंभः, उपक्रमः, मूलं. -LESS, *a.* निर्मूल, निष्कारण, अहेतुक, अनिमित्त, निराधार, अमूलक; मिथ्या in comp. -LESSLY, *adv.* निष्कारणं, मिथ्या. -LESSNESS, *s.* अकारणं, निर्मूलत्वं.

GROUNDS, (pl.) *See* DREGS.

GROUND-SIL, *s.* देहली, गृहावग्रहणी.

GROUP, *s.* संघः, निवहः, समुदायः; गणः; *See* MULTITUDE; 'in g. s' गणशः, संघशः. -*v. t.* एकीकृ 8 U, वर्गी-गणी-कृ, सं-चि 5 U; (Collect, q. v.).

GROVE, *s.* उपवनं, वनराजि-जी *f.*, वृक्षवाटिका, वनांतः; *See* FOREST also.

GROVEL, *v. i.* नीचतया भूमौ पत् 1 P or सृप् 1 P, अधमवत् आचर् 1 P, धूलिं स्पृश् 6 P. -ING, *a.* नीच, अपकृष्ट, अधम, तुच्छ, अतिक्षुद्र.

GROW, *v. i.* स्फुट् 6 P, विकस् 1 P, फुल्ल् 1 P, उद्भिद् pass. (generally of plants). 2 रुह् 1 P, ऋध् 4, 5 P, एध् 1 A; पुष् 4 P, वृध् 1 A, उपाचि pass., स्फाय् 1 A, प्यै 1 A, वृद्धिं या-इ 2 P. 3 सं-,जन् 4 A, भू 1 P; 'the beard having begun to g.' उद्भिद्यमानश्मश्रुराजितया (Ka. 29). 4 जन्, उत्पद् 4 A; उद्-इ 2 P, भू, उत्-सं-प्र.° 5 विस्तृ pass., व्याप् 5 P; 'g. up' संवृध्, एध्, प्रौढीभू; 'bad boys g. to be bad men' कुबालाः कुनरा एव निष्पद्यंते-भवंति; 'he was grown up', 'he grew up to man's estate (majority)' यौवनपदवीमारूढः, समारूढयौवनारंभः, प्रौढः, प्राप्तयौवनः, यौवनदशामापेदे, अतीत-गत-शैशवः; 'g. old' जृ 4 P. -*v. t.* वृध् c., रुह् c. -ING, *a.* वर्धमान, उपचीयमान, वर्धिष्णु. 2 रोहिन्, रुह, रुह्, भव, उद्भव, प्रभव, ज, जात, उत्थ, समुत्थ, भू, in comp.; 'growing in size' प्र-उपचीयमान-अवयव. -GROWTH, *s.* वृद्धि, आगमः, वर्धनं, उपचयः, ऋद्धि *f.*, स्फीति *f.*, अभ्युदयः, विस्तारः. 2 उत्पत्ति *f.*, सं-प्र-भवः, जननं, जन्मन् *n.* 3 प्रौढि *f.*, प्रवृद्धता.

GROWL, *v. i.* भष् 1 P, गर्ज् 1 P, रै 1 P, घुर्घुररवं कृ 8 U. -*s.* भषणं, गर्जितं, घुर्घुररवः.

GRUB, *See* DIG. -*s.* कीटः, कृमिः, कोशस्थः. 2 वामनः, खर्वः, ह्रस्वः.

GRUDGE, *v.* ईर्ष्य् 1 P, द्रुह् 4 P, असूयति (D.), (with dat.); न सह् 1 A, न मृष् 4 P, 10; *See* ENVY. 2 अकामतः-अनुत्साहं-अनिच्छया-कृ 8 U or दा 3 U or ग्रह् 9 P. 3 परि-देव् 1 A, परिदिव

10 A, विलप् 1 P; *See* COMPLAIN. —*s.* असूया, मत्सरः, मात्सर्यं, ईर्ष्या. 2 वैरं, वैरभावः, विद्वेषः, चिर-दीर्घ-द्वेष-वैरं. —INGLY, *adv.* असूयया, साभ्यसूयं, सेर्ष्यं. 2 अकामतः, अनिच्छया, अनुत्साहं, कृच्छ्रेण, दुःखेन.

GRUEL, *s.* यवागूः, उष्णिका, श्राणा, विलेपी, तरला; 'sour g.' आरनालकं, सौवीरं, कुल्माषाभिषुतं, अवंती-सोमं, धान्याम्लं, कुंजलं, कांजिकं.

GRUFF, *a.* कर्कश, परुष, निष्ठुर, रूक्ष, कठोर, कटु, कर्कशस्वभाव. 2 (Voice) गंभीर, मंद्र.

GRUMBLE, *v. i.* खिद् pass., असंतोषाद् विलप् 1 P or परिदेव् 1 A or परिदिव् 10 A, विषण्ण-*a.* भू 1 P, न तुष् 4 P, विषद् 1 P. 2 गर्ज् 1 P, स्तन् 1 P. —ING, *s.* विलापः, विलपनं, परिदेवनं-देवितं, असंतोषोद्गारः, विषादः. 2 गर्जनं, स्तनितं, गंभीरनादः-ध्वनिः-शब्दः.

GRUME, *See* CLOT.

GRUNT, *v. i.* गर्ज् 1 P. —*s.*,—ING, *s.* गर्जितं, शूकर-नादः-गर्जितं. —LING, *s.* बालशूकरः;, शूकरशावकः.

GUARANTEE, *s.* प्रत्ययः, विश्वासः, प्रातिभाव्यं. 2 प्रतिभूः, लग्नकः, बंधकः. —*v. t.* Ex. by (*s.*); प्राति-भाव्यं दा 3 U, प्रतिभूः स्था 1 P; 'I g. you the security of your property' त्वद्वित्तरक्षणेहं प्रतिभूस्तिष्ठामि.

GUARD, *v. t.* सं-,पारि,-रक्ष् 1 P; पा 2 P; पा c. (पाल-यति), त्रै 1 A, अव् 1 P, गुप् 1 P; *See* PROTECT. 2 वृ c., वार् 10, नि°; 'g. against' अव-धा 3 U; सावधान-अवहित-*a.* भू ; *See* BEWARE. —*s.* रक्षा, रक्षणं, गुप्ति *f.*, गोपनं, पालनं, त्राणं. 2 रक्षकः, रक्षिन् *m.*, रक्षिवर्गः, रक्षाधिकृतः, सैनिकः, परिचरः; वारणं, त्राणं, त्रं, in comp.; 'finger-g.' अंगुलित्रं, तनुत्राणं, &c.; 'arm-g. in shooting' गोधा, तलं, ज्याघात-वारणं; 'on one's g.' सावधान-अप्रमत्त-अवहित-*a.*; 'off one's g.' प्रमत्त *a.*; 'g.-room' रक्षकनिवासः, उद्घाटः. —ED, *a.* रक्षित, त्राण-त्र, &c. 2 (g.-ful) अवहित, सावधान, स्ववहित, समीक्ष्यकारिन्, समीक्ष्यकृत्. —EDLY, *adv.* सावधानं, विमृश्य, अवधानेन, स्ववहि-तं. —ER, *s.* पालकः, रक्षकः, गोप्तृ *m.*, त्रातृ *m.*, पालः-लकः in comp. —IAN, *s.* रक्षकः, रक्षिता, गो-प्ता, नाथः; 'orphan's g.' पितृस्थानीयः; 'g. deity' लोकपालः, दिक्पालः. —IANSHIP, *s.* पाल-कपदं, रक्षा, रक्षणं.

GUERDON, *See* REWARD.

GUESS, *v. t.* ऊह् 1 A; अनु-मा 3 A, 2 P; आशंक् 1 A, तर्क् 10. —*s.* वि-,तर्कः, ऊहा, अभ्यूहः-हनं; अनुमानं, अनुमिति *f.*, शंका; 'your g. is plain' प्रसन्नस्ते तर्कः.

GUEST, *s.* अतिथिः, अभ्यागतः, प्राघूर्णकः, प्राघुणकः आगंतुः, आवेशिकः, गृहागतः, आगंतुकः; 'friendly to g. s' आतिथेय (यी *f.*).

GUIDE, *v. t.* नी 1 P, पंथानं-मार्गं (way, q. v.) दृश् c. or आ-उप-दिश् 6 P. 2 प्र-अनु-शास् 2 P, निर्-उप-दिश्, विनि-यम् 1 P, प्र-णी 1 P, वि-धा 3 U; अधिष्ठा 1 P. —*s.* अध्वदर्शिन् *m.*, पुरोगः, मुखरः, मार्गोपदेशकः, नेतृ *m.*, नायकः, मार्गदर्शकः, उपदे-शकः, निर्देशकः. 2 शास्ता, अध्यक्षः, अधिष्ठाता. —ANCE, *s.* नयः, नीति *f.*, मार्गदर्शनं, अध्वोपदेशः. 2 अनुसरणं, अनुवर्तनं.

GUILD, *s.* श्रेणि-णी *f.*, निगमः, वणिक्समाजः-संसर्गः. 2 संघातः, समाजः, गणः.

GUILE, *s.* माया, कपटः-टं, छलं, व्याजः, कैतवं, शाठ्यं, छद्मन् *n.*; *See* FRAUD. —FUL, *a.* मायिन्, वंचनशील, शठ, धूर्त, कापटिक (की *f.*), सव्याज, वंचक, मायान्वित, कितव. —FULLY, *adv.* सव्याजं, सकपटं, छद्मना, मायया. —LESS, *a.* निष्कपट, अकप-ट, अव्याज, अनुपधि, सरल, निर्व्यलीक, विमलात्मन्; *See* FRANK. —LESSLY, *adv.* अमायया; निष्कप-टं, निर्व्याजं, &c.

GUILT, *s.* अपराधः, दोषः, पापं, पातकं, अघं, एनस् *n.*, पापकर्म, दुष्कृति *f.*, आगस् *n.*, दुरितं. 2 सदोष-ता, पापत्वं, अपराधिता. —LESS, *a.* निरपराध, अनप-राधिन्, अनागस्, अपाप, निष्पाप; अकृतदोष, निर्दोष, अनघ, शुद्ध, पाप-दोष-हीन. —LESSLY, *adv.* निरप-राधं, पापं-दोषं-विना. —Y, *a.* पापिन्, अपराधिन्, सापराध, अपराद्ध, सपाप, पापकर्मन्, सदोष, कृतागस्, कृतापराध, दोष-पाप-वत्, पातकिन्, दुष्कृतिन्, पापात्म-न्, पाप.

GUINEA-WORM, *s.* स्नायुकः.

GUISE, *s.* वेशः-षः, वस्त्रं, परिधानं, रूपं, आकारः, छद्मन् *n.*; *See* DISGUISE.

GUITAR, *s.* वीणा, वल्लकी, विपंची; सारंगी, पिनाकी; 'seven-stringed g.' परिवादिनी.

GULF, *s.* अखातं, समुद्रवंकः, पुटभेदः. 2 अगाधं-अतल-स्पर्शं-खातं, रंध्रं. 3 Whirlpool, q. v.

GULL, *v. t.* वंच् 10, प्रतॄ c.; *See* CHEAT. —*s.* सुप्रतार्यः, सुखं वंचनीयः. 2 जलकुक्कुटः, विष्किका; 'g.-catcher' वंचकः, प्रतारकः. —ERY, *s.* प्रतारणा, वंचनं-ना, छलं, कपटं.

GULLET, *s.* गलः, गलस्रोतस् *n.*, निगरणः.

GULLY, *s.* प्रणालः-ली, कुल्या, जलमार्गः, परि(री)वाहः.

GULOSITY, *s.* अतिभोजनं, घस्मरता, अत्याहारः.

GULP, *v. t.* नि-गॄ 6 P, ग्रस् 1 A. 2 उद्-गॄ, उत्क्षिप् 6 P. —*s.* निगरणं, ग्रसनं. 2 उद्गिरणं, उद्गमः-मनं.

GUM, *s.* निर्यासः, रसः. 2 (Of tooth) दंतमांसं, दंतमूलं. 3 श्यान-सांद्र-द्रव्यं; 'g.-boil' दंतव्रणः-विस्फोटः. —MY, *a.* श्यान, सांद्र, निर्यासमय (यी *f.*),

GUN, *s.* लोहभुषि *f.*, गुलि-गुलिका-प्रक्षेपिणी, लोहनाडिः-डी *f.*; अग्न्यस्त्रं; 'g.-powder' आग्नेयचूर्णं.

GURGE, *See* WHIRLPOOL.

GURGLE, *v. i.* घर्घररवं कृ 8 U, गद्गदं नद् 1 P, (कुहरेषु गद्गदनदद्गोदावरावारय: U. 2).

GUSH, *v. i.* निष्पत् 1 P; बहुशः स्रु 1 P or नि-स्यंद् 1 A or क्षर् 1 P; वेगात् निः-सृ 1 P or प्रवृत् 1 A; तस्यास्तु मद्दर्शनादेव आबद्धधारमश्रु प्रावर्तत (D. K. II. 3) 'tears g. ed forth from her eyes in torrents &c.', उद्बाष्पे नयने जाते. -*s.* जलप्रपातः, उत्पीडः, वेगेन निःसरणं, प्रवृत्ति *f.*

GUST, *s.* चंडवातः, वात्या, प्रकंपनः, जवानिलः, वायुवेगः, तीव्र-प्रबल-वातः-वायुः. 2 रुचि *f.*, आस्वादः, रसः. -FUL, *a.* सरस, रुचिर. -LESS, *a.* विरस, अस्वादु. -Y, *a.* पवनक्षिप्त, वातुल, वातमय (यी *f.*).

GUT, *s.* अंत्रं, पुरीतत् *n.*; शिरा, अंतर्नाडी. 2 उदरं, जठरः-रं. -*v. t.* अंत्राणि बहिष्कृ 8 U or निष्कृष् 1 P. 2 सर्वस्वं अपहृ 1 P.

GUTTER, *s.* जलमार्गः, परि(री)वाहः, प्रणालः-ली.

GUTTLER, *See* GLUTTON.

GUTTURAL, *a.* कंठ्य, कंठस्थ-स्थानीय.

GUZZLE, *v. t.* अतिमात्रं पा 1 P or ग्रस् 1 A or नि-गृ 6 P.

GYMNASIUM, *s.* व्यायामभूमि *f.* -शाला. -GYMNASTIC, *a.* व्यायामशील-पर-सेविन्. 2 व्यायामसंबंधिन्; 'g. s' व्यायामः, व्यायामविद्या, मल्लक्रीडा.

GYRATE, *See* REVOLVE.

GYRE, *s.* मंडलं, आवृत्ति *f.*, चक्रगति *f.*

GYVES, *s.* निगडः-डं, शृंखला-लं, पाशः, बंधनं.

H.

HA, *interj.* हा, अहो, अयि, बत, हंत.

HABERDASHER, *s.* क्षुद्रपण्यविक्रयिन् *m.*

HABERGEON, *s.* वक्षस्त्राणं, उरश्छदः.

HABILIMENT, *See* DRESS.

HABIT, *s.* Dress, q. v. 2 शीलं, भावः, प्रकृति *f.*, स्थिति *f.*, वृत्ति *f.*, अवस्था, दशा, स्वभावः. 3 अभ्यासः, नित्यप्रवृत्तिः, आचारः, नित्यक्रिया, व्यवहारः, रीति *f.*, प्रचारः, क्रमः, आवृत्तिः, अनुशीलनं; 'in the h. of' शील or वृत्ति in comp.; 'in the h. of stealing' चौर्यवृत्ति; मृगयाशील, &c; 'bad h.' व्यसनं, दुर्गुण; 'having bad h.s' दुर्वृत्त, दुराचार, पापवृत्ति, भ्रष्टचरित्र. -*v. t.* Dress, q. v. -ABLE, *a.* वासक्षम, वसतियोग्य. -ATION, *s.* वासः, धामन् *n.*, वसति *f.*, आलयः, गृहं, गेहं, आगारं; *See* HOUSE. -UAL, *a.* अभ्यासज, नित्य, सतत, अनुशीलित, आभ्यासिक-व्यावहारिक-स्वाभाविक (की *f.*); 'a h. drunkard' नित्यपानासक्तः; 'a h. worker' क्रियावान्, कर्मसु उद्यतः, कार्मः, कर्मशीलः. -UALLY, *adv.* नित्यं, सततं, यथाभ्यासं, यथारीति, यथाव्यवहारं. -UATE, *v. t.* अभ्यस् 4 U, अनुशील् 10, शिक्ष् c., परिचि c., अभ्यस्त-परिचित-*a.* कृ 8 U; 'h. ed to distress' ज्ञातदुःख, परिचितक्लेश; दुःखशील, दुःखाभिज्ञ.

HACK, *v. t.* खंडशः कृत् 6 P or छिद् 7 P, बहुलवशः व्रश्च् 6 P or विद्ृ 10, व्यवच्छिद्. -*s.* प्रहारः, छेदः, आघातः. 2 पण्याश्वः, कदश्वः, जीर्णः अश्वः, सर्वप्रयोज्यः-सर्वसाधारणः-अश्वः. 3 हीनवृत्तिः, नीचकर्मकारिन् *m.*, व्रातीनः, सर्वप्रयोज्यः, पण्यः.

HACKLE, *s.* उमामार्जनी-शोधनी.

HACKNEY, *s. See* HACK (*s.*). 2 पण्यस्त्री, सर्वोपभोज्या. -*v. t.* हीनकर्मणि नियुज् 7 A, 10; 'h.-coach' पण्यवाहनं, पण्य-साधारण-रथः. -ED, *a.* जीर्ण, साधारण, बहुप्रयुक्त, सर्वसाधारण.

HADES, *s.* पाताललोकः, पातालं, अधोलोकः-भुवनं.

HAFT, *See* HANDLE.

HAG, *s.* जरती, स्थविरा, कुरूपिणी. -HAGGARD, *a.* परिकृश, क्षाम, क्षीण, क्षाम-शुष्क-वदन, रूक्ष, उग्रदर्शन. 2 जरठ, स्थविर.

HAGGLE, *v. i.* क्रयविक्रयकाले विलंब् 1 A or विवद् 1 A.

HAIL, *interj.* नमः, स्वस्ति, (with dat.); oft. ex. by जि 1 P; जयतु जयतु देवः 'h. to your Majesty'; कुशलं भूयात्, अभिवादये. -*s.* शिलावृष्टि *f.*, करकानिपातः; 'h.-stone' करका, वर्षोपलः, वर्षशिला, पयोघनः, घन-मेघ-कफः; 'h.-storm' करकासारः, शिलावर्षः. -*v. i.* उपलान् वृष् 1 P or निपत् c., करकासारं पत् c. -*v. t.* वंद् 1 A, अभिवद् 10 A, संबुध् c., आमंत्र् 10 A, आ-अभि-भाष् 1 A, आ-ह्वे 1 P. 2 (fig.) प्रीत्या-मुदा-अंगीकृ 8 U; अभिनंद् 1 P.

HAIR, *s.* केशः, कचः, बालः, चिकुरः, कुंतलः; 'h. on the head' शिरोरुहः, मूर्धजः, शिरसिजः. 2 (Of the body gen.) रो(लो)मन् *n.*, तनूरुहः-हं, तनुजः; 'quantity of h.' कैश्यं, कैशिकं. 3 केश(स)रः; 'whole collection of h.' केशकलापः-पक्षः-हस्तः-पाशः; 'h. hanging on the forehead' भ्रमरकाः; 'lock of h.' काकपक्षः, शिखंडकः; 'matted h.' जटा, सटा; 'a braid of h.' कबरी, केशवेशः; 'curled h.' अलकः, चूर्णकुंतलः; 'braided h.' वेणि-णी *f.*, धम्मिल्लः; 'crest-h.' शिखा, चूडा, केशपाशी; 'clean h.' चीरिण्यः, शिरस्यः; 'h.-broom or brush' केशमार्जनी-शोधनी; 'h.-dressing' केशरचना-संस्कारः; 'even a h.'s breadth' रेखामात्रमपि; 'a h.-breadth escape' कथमपि लब्धा मुक्तिः. -LESS, *a.* अकेश, केशहीन, विकेश. -Y, *a.* लोमश, लोमावृत, प्रचुर-बहु-लोमन्, लोममय (यी *f.*), लोमवत्, लोमपूर्ण, केशव, केशवन्, केशिक.

HALBERDIER, *s.* प्रासिकः, शार्ङ्गकः.

HALCYON, *s.* मत्स्यरंगः. –*a.* शांत, निरुद्वेग, निराकुल, प्रसन्न, अक्षुब्ध, निर्वात.

HALE, *a.* सुस्थ, नीरोग, कल्य, निरामय, नीरुज्-ज, आधिव्याधिरहित. –*v. t.* आकृष् 1 P; *See* PULL.

HALF, *a.* अर्ध, सामि in comp. ; 'h. done' सामिकृतं. –*s.* अर्धः-र्धं, अर्धभागः, अर्धांशः; in comp. ex. by अर्ध; अर्धांगं, पूर्वार्धः, &c.; 'a year and a h.' सार्धवत्सरः; 'h. eaten' अर्धभुक्त; अर्धविवृत, अर्धच्छिन्न, &c.; 'h.-brother' वैमात्रेयः, सापत्नः, अन्योदर्यः, वैमात्रः; 'h.-blood' भिन्नोदर, भिन्नगर्भ, अन्योदर्य; 'h. dead' मृतकल्प-प्राय, मरणोन्मुख, आसन्नमृत्यु, मुमूर्षु, कंठगतप्राण; 'h.-hearted' निरुत्साह, उत्साहहीन, आस्थारहित; 'h. moon' अर्धेंदुः, चंद्रार्धः; 'h.-sister' वैमात्रेयी, वैमात्री, अन्योदर्या; 'h. starved' क्षुधावसन्नप्राय, क्षुत्क्षामकल्प; 'h. way' अर्धमार्गे-पथे, मध्यमार्गे; 'h. year' अर्धवर्ष; 'h. yearly' षाण्मासिक-आर्धवार्षिक (की *f.*); 'h. a bread is better than no loaf' सर्वनाशे समुत्पन्ने अर्धं त्यजति पंडितः or अर्धेन कुरुते कार्यं.

HALLOO, *interj.* हंहो, अहो, अरे, अये, भोभोः. –*v. t.* उच्चैः शब्दायते (D.), दूराद् उत्क्रुश्-आह्वे 1 P or उद्-घुष् 10.

HALLOW, *v. t.* पवित्रीकृ 8 U, पूज् 10, मह् 1 P, 10, अर्च् 1 P, 10. 2 संस्कृ, प्रोक्ष् 1 P, अभिषिच् 6 P.

HALLUCINATION, *s.* मतिविभ्रमः; माया, मोहः, भ्रमः, व्यामोहः, वंचना, इंद्रजालं.

HALM, *s.* पलालः-लं, तृणं.

HALO, *s.* प्रभा-तेजो-मंडलं, परिवेषः-शः, परिधिः, द्युति-दीप्ति-मंडलं-चक्रं-माला; 'h. crown of silver light' रजतधवलप्रभामंडलं; 'with a h. of brilliant lustre' स्फुरत्प्रभामंडल *a.*

HALSER, *s.* नौगुणः-रज्जु *f.*

HALT, *v. i.* निविश् 6 P, अव-स्था 1 A, प्रयाणभंगं कृ 8 U, अध्वमध्ये स्था. 2 विरम् 1 P, विश्रम् 4 P. 3 लंग् 1 P. –*a.* पंगु, गतिविकल, श्रोण. –*s.* निवेशः, अवस्थिति *f.*, अवस्थानं, प्रयाणभंगः, यानविवृत्ति-विरति *f.*, विश्रामः; 'h. ing place' निवेशस्थानं. 2 लंगनं.

HALTER, *s.* पाशः, गुणः, रज्जु *f.*, कंठपाशः. –*v. t.* कंठपाशेन बंध् 9 P or संयम् 1 P.

HAM, *s.* जंघा, प्रसृता. 2 वल्लूरं-रः. 3 मंदिरः.

HAMADRYAD, *s.* वन-तरु-देवता.

HAMLET, *s.* ग्रामः, क्षुद्रग्रामः, कुग्रामः, पल्लि-ल्ली *f.*

HAMMER, *s.* मुद्गरः, घनः, अयोघनः, द्रुघणः-नः. –*v. t.* बलेन-ताडनेन-प्रविश् c. 2 मुद्गरेण तड् 10 or प्र-हृ 1 P. –*v. i.* सोद्योगं यत् 1 A or परिश्रम् 4 P. –ING, *s.* मुद्गराघातः.

HAMMOCK, *s.* प्रेंखा, दोला, प्रेंखोलनं.

HAMPER, *s.* पेटिका, पेटकः, करंडः, पिटः, कंडोलः. –*v. t.* प्रति-नि-रि-रुध् 7 U, प्रति-रि-हन् 2 P, कुंठ् 10, बाध् 1 A, विघ्नयति (D.), स्तंभ् 9 P. प्रतिबंध् 9 P. –ED, *a.* कुंठित-निरुद्ध-गति, प्रतिहत, निरुद्ध, बाधित, कुंठित, प्रतिबद्ध.

HAMSTRING, *s.* मंदिरशिरा.

HAND, *s.* हस्तः, पाणिः, करः, शयः, पंचशाखः, भुजादलः. 2 पार्श्वः, भागः, पक्षः. 3 करणं, विधानं, चेष्टा, क्रिया, व्यापारः. 4 वशः-शं, अधिकारः, शक्ति *f.*, प्रभुत्वं. 5 कर्तृ *m.*, कारः-कारकः in comp.; कर्मकरः. 6 प्रदेशिनी, सूचिनी; कीलः; सूचि *f.* 7 लिपि *f.*, लिबि *f.*, अक्षरसंस्थानं, लिखितं; 'h. to hand' हस्ताहस्ति, बाहूबाहवि, मुष्टीमुष्टि; 'h. to h. fight' नियुद्धं, बाहुयुद्धं; 'on the one h.-on the other h.' एकतः-अन्यतः, इतः-इत, एकंच-अपरंच; oft. by च-च; 'on the other h.' विपर्यये, प्रत्युत, तु, तावत्; 'if on the other h.' अथ, यदि; 'on all h. s' सर्वथा, सर्वत्र; 'at h.' प्रत्यासन्न, समीपवर्तिन्, आसन्न, संनिहित, समीपं-पे; 'in h.' हस्ते, हस्तगत, हस्तवर्तिन्, करतलगत; 'subject in h.' प्रकृत, प्रस्तुत; 'h. in h.' एकत्र, समवायसंबंधेन; सह, सहितं, समं, संभूय; 'to give a helping h.' हस्तावलंबं दा 3 U; 'given a helping h.' दत्तहस्तावलंब; 'living from h. to mouth' उत्पन्नभोजिन्; दुर्गत, कृच्छ्रगत; 'on h.' अनुपयुक्त, अभ्यागत; (of books &c.) अविक्रीत; 'sword in h.' खड्गहस्त, कृपाणपाणि; 'off-h.' आशु, अविचार्य, अविलंबं; आकस्मिक-प्रत्युत्पन्न-अचिंतितपूर्व-*a.*; 'out of h.' सपदि, तत्क्षणात्; 'to take in h.' आरभ् 1 A, प्रस्तु 2 U, उपक्रम् 1 A; 'lend a h.' उपकृ 8 U, अनुग्रह् 9 P, साहाय्यं कृ; 'lay h. s on' धृ 1 P, ग्रह्, आधृष् c., परामृश्-स्पृश् 6 P; 'to have a h. in' सहकारिन् *a.* भू, सहायः भू; 'have or get the upper h.' अभि-भू, प्र-भू, अतिरिच् pass.; 'under-h.' निभृत, छलेन, सकपट; 'clap the h. s' करतालं वद् c.; 'to support with the h.' करेण अव-आ-लंब् 1 A, हस्तावलंबं दा; 'the open or extended h.' चपेटः, चर्पटः, प्रहस्तः, प्रतलः; 'hollow of the h.' करपुटं, हस्तकोषः; 'two open h.s joined together' संहततलः, प्रतलः; 'folded h.' प्रसृतिः; 'folded h. s joined' अंजलिः; 'clenched h.' मुष्टि *m. f.*; 'h. with the fist clenched' रत्निः. –*v. i.* हस्ते-करे-निक्षिप् 6 P or दा 3 U or कृ c. (अर्पयति); 'h. down' परंपरया-क्रमेण-संचर् c. or संक्रम् c.; 'to be h. ed down' परंपरया आगम् 1 P; उप-,संक्रम् 1 U, 4 P, (यानि भगवतः कृशाश्वात्कौशिकमृषिमुपसंक्रांतानि U. 1); (in sacred texts) आ-समा-म्ना pass.; 'h.-book' हस्तमेयं पुस्तकं, लघुग्रंथः; 'h.-cuff' हस्तपाशः-निगडः, करबंधनं;

(*v. t.*) पाशेन हस्तौ बंध् 9 P or संयम् 1 P or यंत्र् 10; 'h.-kerchief' करवस्त्रं; 'h.-maid' चेटी, दासी, परिचारिका; 'h.-mill' हस्तचालिता पेषणी; 'h.-weapon' हस्तायुधं, करशस्त्रं; 'h.-writing' लिखितं, लिपि-बि *f.*, अक्षरसंस्थानं; 'one's own h.-writing' हस्तलेखः, स्वहस्ताक्षरं. -FUL, *s.* मुष्टि *m. f.*; 'a h. of grass' तृणमुष्टिः. 2 अल्प-स्तोक-संख्या, oft. by अल्प-स्तोक-*a.* -HANDICRAFT, *s.* शिल्पं, हस्तलाघवं, हस्त-शिल्पं-कर्म, शिल्पविद्या; 'h. s-man' शिल्पिन् *m.*, शिल्पकारः, कर्मकरः. -HANDIWORK, *s.* हस्तकृतं कर्म. —HANDY, *a.* दक्ष, लघुहस्त, करदक्ष, सुप्रयोगवत्, कुशल, निपुण, चतुर, पटु, क्षिप्रकारिन्. 2 सुखनेय, लघुभार, अदुर्वह. 3 आसन्न, निकट, प्रत्युत्पन्न. -LY, *adv.* हस्तलाघवेन, दक्षतया, सपाटवं, युक्त्या, चतुरं, दाक्ष्येण. -NESS, *s.* दक्षता, हस्तलाघवं, करदक्षता, कौशलं, चातुर्यं, नैपुण्यं.

HANDLE, *s.* मुष्टि *m. f.*, दंडः, कर्णः, वारंगः, तलः-लं. 2 (Of swords) त्सरुः, सरुः. 3 (Of ploughs) ईषादंडः; 'to give h.' अवसरं-अवकाशं-दा 3 U; 'serve as a h.' उपकरणीभू 1 P. -*v. t.* (A subject) विचर् c., विमृश् 6 P, निरूप् 10, परीक्ष् 1 A, पर्यालोच् 10; *See* EXAMINE. 2 प्रयुज् 7 A, 10; वृत् 1 A, व्यव-हृ 1 P, आचर् 1 P (with loc.). 3 प्र-णी 1 P, वि-धा 3 U, निर्वह् c. 4 हस्तेन स्पृश्-परामृश् 6 P or आ-समा-लभ् 1 A.

HANDSEL, *s.* प्रथमव्यवहारः-विक्रयः.

HANDSOME, *a.* कांतिमत्, सुंदर (री *f.*), रूपवत्, सुरूप, चारु, शुभ, शोभन, कांत, वाम, सुगात्र (त्री *f.*), सुदृश्य, सु in comp.; *See* BEAUTIFUL. 2 विपुल, यथेष्ट, प्रचुर. 3 उदार, वदान्य, स्थूललक्ष्य; 'h. is that h. does' आचारसौष्ठवमेव परमार्थतः सौष्ठवमित्युच्यते. -LY, *adv.* चारुतया, शोभनं, सु pr. -NESS, *s.* कांति *f.*, रूपं, लावण्यं, शोभा.

HANG, *v. t.* बंध् 9 P, नि-धा 3 U, अनु-वि-संज् (षंज्) 1 P, आ-अव-लंब् c., आंदोलयति (D.); 'hung by a loop' काचित, शिक्यित. 2 उद्-बंध्, उद्बध्य व्या-पद् c. or हन् c. (घातयति). 3 आ-अव-नम् c. (नमयति), नम् c., नम्रीकृ 8 U, नम्रतां नी 1 P; *See* BEND; 'with his lotus-like face hung down' अवनतमुखपुंडरीकः; 'h.-ing the head' अवनतमुख-शिरस्, नतमूर्धन्. 4 आ-च्छद् 10, वि-भूष् 10, प्र-साध् c., मंड् 10, अलंकृ 8 U, परिष्कृ. -*v. i.* प्र-अव-लंब् 1 A, लुल् 1 P, लुट् 6 P, 1 A, चंच् 1 P, दोलायते (D.), प्रेंख् 1 P, उद्-बध् pass.; 'h. between' त्रिशंकुरिवांतरा तिष्ठ (S. 2). 2 (Stick) आसंज् pass., लग् 1 P, अनुबंध् pass., संलग्नीभू 1 P. 3 (On, upon) अव-लंब्, आ-श्रि 1 U, उप-अनु-जीव् 1 P; *See* DEPEND; 'thereby h. s a tale' तदनुविद्धा काचिदाख्यायिका वर्तते; 'h. over' उपक्रम् 1 P, उप-स्था 1 U, प्रत्यासद् 1 P. -ER, *s.* उद्बंधकः; 'h. on' आश्रितः, पादसेविन् *m.*, पीठमर्दः, अनु-उप-जीवी, पराधीनः, परपिंडादः. -ING, *s.* उद्बंधनं. 2 परिच्छदः, वसनं; जवनिका, प्रच्छदपटः, चित्रयवनिका. -HANGMAN, *s.* घातकः, दंडपाशिकः, वध्यपुरुषः.

HANK, *s.* काष्ठवलयः. 2 Cheat, q. v.

HANKER, *v. i.* अभिलष् 1, 4 P, स्पृह् 10, वांछ् 1 P, उत्कंठ् 1 A; लुभ् 4 P; *See* LONG; oft. by उत्क, उत्सुक, पर्युत्सुक, पर, तत्पर, परायण, in comp. -ING, *s.* अतिस्पृहा, उत्कंठा, औत्सुक्यं, अत्यभिलाषः.

HAP, *s.* दैवं, दैवयोगः-घटना, यदृच्छा. -LESS, *a.* अधन्य, मंदभाग्य, दुर्दैव. -LY, *adv.* दैवात्, दैवयोगात्, दैववशात्.

HAPHAZARD, *a.* असमीक्ष्य, अविचार्य; दैवायत्त, दैवाधीन.

HAPPEN, *v. i.* वृत् 1 A, भू 1 P, घट् 1 A; संवृत्, सं-भू, सं-समा-पद् 4 A, स्था 1 P, आ-सं-पत् 1 P, प्रसंज् pass. 2 अकस्मात्, यदृच्छया, दैवात्, दैववशात् with verbs; *See* CHANCE.

HAPPY, *a.* सुखिन्, प्रीत, हृष्ट, सानंद, सुखित, सुखभाज्, प्रमुदित, आह्लन्न, निर्वृत, निश्चिंत, तृप्त, संतुष्ट. 2 भाग्यवत्, शुभान्वित, शुभंयु, समृद्ध, श्रीमत्, निरापद्, कुशलिन्, निर्वृतिमत्, क्षेम; धन्य, कृतिन्, कृतार्थ; 'h. is it for me that &c.' इदमेव तावन्मम परमभाग्यं मन्ये. 3 शुभ, शिव, कल्याण (णी *f.*), मंगल, पुण्य, भद्र, भव्य, आनंदप्रद, भावुक, प्रशस्त; 'a h. result' सुफलं, कल्याणोदर्कः. -LY, *adv.* सुखेन, सुखं, निर्विघ्नं, स्वास्थ्येन, यथासुखं. 2 दिष्ट्या, दैवात्, अकस्मात्, यदृच्छया, दैववशात्, सौभाग्येन, पुण्योदयात्. -NESS, *s.* सुखं, सौख्यं, आनंदः, धन्यता, हर्षः, कृतार्थता, शर्मन् *n.*, संतोषः, निर्वृति *f.*, श्रीः, संपद् *f.*, पुण्योदयः. 2 कल्याणं, भद्रं, क्षेमः-मं, शिवं, स्वास्थ्यं, कुशलं.

HARANGUE, *s.* उच्चैः वचस् *n.*, तारस्वरेण भाषणं, सालंकारं वचनं. -*v. i.* सालंकारं-सदर्पं-वद् 1 P or भाष् 1 A. -ER, *s.* वागीशः, प्रवचनपटुः, वाक्पटुः.

HARASS, *v. t.* अर्द् 1 P or c., व्यथ् c. (व्यथयति), पीड् 10, क्लिश् 9 P, दु 5 P, सं-परि-तप् c., उपहन् 2 P, विप्र-कृ 8 U, नि-कृ, उपद्रु 1 A, बाध् 1 A, प्रतिरुध् 7 U. 2 खिद् c., श्रम् c., क्लम् c., आयस् c., ग्लै c. (ग्ल-ग्ला-पयति). -ER, *s.* पीडकः, उपद्रावकः, खेदकः, आयासकः. -ING, *a.* दुःख-क्लेश-कर (री *f.*), पीडाप्रद, क्लेशावह.

HARBINGER, *s.* अग्रे(प्र)सरः, अग्रदूतः, अग्र-पुरोगः-गामी; वार्ताहरः, संदेशहरः (of news); 'h. of spring' वसंताग्रदूतः; 'antecedent good omens are the h. s of the coming happiness'

आवेदयंति प्रत्यासन्नमानंदं अग्रजातानि शुभानि निमित्तानि (Ka. 65).

HARBOUR, *s.* खातं, क्रोडः, नौकाश्रयः. 2 शरणं, गति *f.*, आश्रयः, संश्रयः, अवकाशः, वासस्थानं. —*v. t.* वस् c., आश्रयं-वासस्थानं-दा 3 U, मन्त्र 8 U. 2 धृ 1 P, 10, मनसि कृ or उपलभ् 1 A or ग्रह् 9 P or नि-धा 3 U. 3 आश्रि 1 U, निवस् 1 P. —AGE, *s.* आश्रयः; *See* (*s.*). —LESS, *a.* निराश्रय, अगतिक, अशरण.

HARD, *a.* दृढ, घन, संहत, कठिन, दृढसंधि, कठोर, कर्कश, कीकस; 'becoming h. (solid)' कठिनतामापद्यमान. 2 उग्र, दारुण; निर्घृण, निर्दय, क्रूर, नृशंस, निष्ठुर, कठोर; 'oh h. fate' अहो दारुणो दैवदुर्विपाकः, अहो वामता-वक्रता-विधेः, अहो वक्रो विधिः क्रीडितं. 3 (Lesson) दुर्बोध, असुगम, दुर्ज्ञेय, गहन. 4 क्लेशावह, दुःखद, व्यथा-पीडा-कर (री *f.*), क्लेशिन्. 5 (Sound) कर्कश, कठोर, रूक्ष, परुष. 6 अननुकूल, वाम, विरुद्ध, प्रतिकूल, प्रतीप, वक्र. 7 असुकर, दुष्कर, कष्ट, दुःसाध्य, कठिन, दुर्-दुःख-कष्ट in comp.; *See* DIFFICULT. 8 शुक्त, अम्ल. —*adv.* प्रयत्नतः, आयासेन, सोद्योगं, बलेन, बलवत्, सोत्साहं, प्रसभं, तीक्ष्णं, सप्रयत्नं, सोद्यमं. 2 दुःखेन, कष्टेन, कृच्छ्रेण, प्रयासेन, दुर् pr. 3 त्वरितं, शीघ्रं; 'h.-pressed by hunger' क्षुधया नितरां-बलवत्-पीडित, प्रबलक्षुधावसन्न; 'h. by' समीपे-पं, अनतिदूरं-रे, निकटं-टे, उपांते, आरात्; 'h.-drinker' पानरतः, अतिपानासक्तः; 'h.-earned' कष्टोपार्जित, श्रमेण लब्ध; 'h.-featured' दुर्मुख, कदाकार; 'h.-fisted' दृढ-बद्धमुष्टि, अमुक्तहस्त, व्ययपराङ्मुख; 'h.-hearted' कठोर, नृशंस, क्रूर, निर्दय, निर्घृण, कठोर-कठिन-हृदय, पाषाण-वज्र-हृदय, अयोहृदय, वज्रमय (यी *f.*), निरनुक्रोश; 'h.-ware' लोहभांडानि (pl.). —EN, *v. t.* कठिनीकृ 8 U, दृढीकृ, घनीकृ, कृ with (*a.*). —LY, *adv.* कथं कथमपि, कष्टेन, दुःखेन, कष्टं, कृच्छ्रेण, नैव. —NESS, *s.* काठिन्यं, दृढता, कठोरता, निष्ठुरता, दुर्बोधता, दुष्करत्वं, उग्रता, &c. —SHIP, *s.* कष्टः-ष्टं, क्लेशः, दुःखं, पीडा, बाधा, काय-देह-क्लेशः, कृच्छ्रं, आयासः, खेदः. —HARDY, *a.* साहसिन्, प्रगल्भ, शूर, वीर, धीर, निर्भय, प्रतिभानवत्, साहसिक (की *f.*), विक्रांत, निःशंक. 2 दृढ-कठिन-देह-शरीर-काय; 'of a h. frame' सिंहसंहनन, वज्रदेह. —HOOD, *s.* वीर्यं, शौर्यं, साहसिकता, प्रागल्भ्यं, साहसं; धृष्टता, प्रतिभा, निर्लज्जता. —NESS, *s.* शौर्यं, वीर्यं, देहकाठिन्यं.

HARE, *s.* शशः, शशकः; 'h.-brained' अविमृश्यकारिन्, चपलबुद्धि, भ्रांतचित्त, साहसपर.

HAREM, *s.* अवरोधः-धनं, शुद्धांतः, अंतःपुरं, अवरोधगृहं, स्त्रीगृहं; 'women of the h.' अवरोधः, परिग्रहः, अंतःपुरं.

HARK, *interj.* ननु, शृणु, आकर्णय, अवधीयतां.

HARLEQUIN, *s.* वैहासिकः, भंडः, विदूषकः.

HARLOT, *s.* वेश्या, पण्यस्त्री, वारस्त्री-योषित्-योषा, पण्यांगना, गणिका, वारांगना, रूपाजीवा; बंधकी, पुंश्चली, कुलटा. —RY, *s.* वेश्यावृत्ति *f.*, वेश्यासेवा.

HARM, *s.* क्षति *f.*, हिंसा, अपायः, नाशः, पीडा, बाधा, अपचयः, अपकृति *f.*, विरोधः, अपकारः, हानि *f.*, उपद्रवः. 2 दोषः, अपराधः, पापं, नियमव्यतिक्रमः. —*v. t.* दु 5 P, क्लिश् 9 P, अर्द् 1 P or c., हिंस् 7 P, उपद्रु 1 P, पीड् 10, बाध् 1 A, अपकृ 8 U, आहन् 2 P, द्रुह् 4 P (with dat.), क्षण् 1 P, वि-प्र-कृ. —FUL, *a.* हिंस्र, अपकारिन्, उपद्रविन्, हिंसक, अपकारक, हिंसात्मक, क्षतिकारक; घातुक, शरारु, शारुक (animals). —LESS, *a.* अनपकारिन्, अहिंस्र, निरुपद्रव, अहिंसक, अघातुक. 2 निर्दोष, निरपराध, निष्पाप. —LESSNESS, *s.* अहिंसा, अद्रोहः, अनपकारः, हिंसात्यागः. 2 निरपराधता.

HARMONY, *s.* तालैक्यं, स्वरैक्यं, स्वरसंगः, एकतालः-नः; 'the triple h.' तौर्यत्रिकं. 2 कलता, श्राव्यता, स्वरमाधुर्यं, सुस्वरता. 3 संवादः, अविरोधः, ऐक्यं, एकता, संगः, संयोगः, आनुलोम्यं, सादृश्यं; 'h. of thought or mind' चित्तैक्यं, संमति *f.*, एकचित्तता, मतसंवादः. 4 स्नेहभावः, प्रीति *f.*, मैत्र्यं, स्नेहः. —IC,-ICAL, *a.* एकताल-न, सम-एक-स्वर, सुस्वर. —IZE, *v. t.* सदृशीकृ 8 U. 2 स्वरैक्यं-तालैक्यं-उत्पद् c. —*v. i.* सदृशीभू 1 P, एकी-तुल्यी-भू, सं-वद् 1 P, न विरुध् pass. —OUS, *a.* एकताल-न, एक-सम-स्वर, एकस्वन, संगतस्वर-स्वन, एकलय. 2 मधुरस्वर-स्वन, सुस्वर, सुखश्रव, श्रोत्राभिराम, श्राव्य, श्रुतिसुख, कल, श्रवणसुभग. 3 संवादिन्, सदृश (शी *f.*), अविरुद्ध, अनुगुण, अनुरूप. —OUSLY, *adv.* एकस्वरेण-स्वनेन. 2 मधुरस्वरेण-स्वनेन, कलं, मधुरं, सुस्वरं. 3 चित्तैक्येन, अविरोधेन.

HARNESS, *v. t.* सज्जीकृ 8 U, सन्नह् 4 P or c., सज्ज *a.* कृ. 2 (रथे) युज् 7 U, 10, नि-आ-सम्°. —*s.* सज्जा, सन्नाहः, प्रसाधनं, परिच्छदः, आभरणं. 2 अश्वसज्जा.

HARP, *s.* वल्लकी, वीणा, सारंगी, विपंची. —*v. i.* वीणां वद् c.; 'praise by h.ing' उपवीणयति (D.); 'h. on' पुनरुक्त्या-पौनःपुन्येन-वद् 1 P, प्रपंचयति (D.). —ER, *s.* वीणावादकः.

HARPOON, *s.* तिमिवेधनी. —ER, *s.* तिमिवेधकः.

HARRIDAN, *s.* वृद्धवेश्या, जरती गणिका.

HARROW, *v. t.* अत्यंतं पीड् 10 or तुद् 6 P, संतप् c., प्रबाध् 1 A; *See* GRIEVE. 2 लोष्टानि भिद् 7 P or विद् 10. —*s.* कोटि(टी)शः, लोष्टभेदनः. —ING, *a.* हृदयं-मर्म-च्छिद्, अरुंतुद, हृदिस्पृश्, अतिदुःखावह.

HARRY, *See* HARASS.

HARSH, *a.* कर्कश, परुष, रूक्ष, निष्ठुर, कठोर, उग्र, कठिन, क्रूर, कटु; 'h. to the touch' असुखद, दुःखस्पर्श, रूक्ष; 'h. to the taste' शुक्त, कषाय;

'h. to the ear' विस्वर, कर्णकटु, दुःश्राव्य, परुष, कर्कश. **-LY**, *adv.* निष्ठुरं, परुषं, रूक्षं, कौर्येण, उग्रं. **-NESS**, *s.* पारुष्यं, कर्कशत्वं, रूक्षता, काठिन्यं.

HARSLET, *s.* शूकरांत्राणि (pl.).

HART, *s.* मृगः, हरिणः, एणः, कुरंगः-गमः.

HARUM-SCARUM, *a.* प्रमादिन्, असावधान, साहसिन्.

HARVEST, *s.* लवः, शस्यसंग्रहकालः, शस्यलवन-संचय-समयः. **2** शस्यानि, संगृहीत-लून-शस्यं. **-***v. t.* शस्यं लू 9 U or संग्रह् 9 P or सांच 5 U ; 'h.-lord' प्रधानः शस्यसंग्राहकः; 'h.-man' शस्यसंग्राहकः-छेत्ता.

HASH, *See* HACK.

HASTE, *s* त्वरा, वेगः, जवः, तूर्णि *f.*, संभ्रमः, शीघ्रता, क्षिप्रता, तरस् *n.*, रभसः-सं, त्वरित-आशु-गति *f.*-गमनं. **-***v. i.*, **-EN**, 'make h.' त्वर् 1 A, सत्वरं-आशु-गम् or चल् or धाव् 1 P ; 'h. towards' अभिद्रु 1 P. **-***v. t.*,**-EN**, त्वर् c. (त्वरयति). **-HASTY**, *a.* सत्वर, त्वरित, क्षिप्र, तूर्ण, शीघ्र, त्वरावत्, द्रुत, अविलंबिन्, आशुकारिन्. **2** साहसिन्, अविमृश्य-असमीक्ष्य-कारिन् or-कृत्. **3** शीघ्रकोपिन्, सुलभकोप. **-HASTILY**, *adv.* शीघ्रं, क्षिप्रं, सत्वरं, अविलंबं, त्वरितं, आशु, झटिति, द्रुतं. **2** सहसा, सरभसं, ससंभ्रमं, वेगेन. **3** कोपेन, संरंभेण.

HAT, *s.* शिरस्त्राणं, मस्तकावेष्टनं, शिरोभूषणं.

HATCH, *v. t.* उत्पद् c., उद्भू c., जन् c., निर्गम् c. **2** घट् c. (घटयति), चिंत् 10, निरूप् 10 ; *See* CONTRIVE. **-***s.* पक्षिशावकगणः. **2** चिंतनं, घटनं-ना. **3** नौमुखं.

HATCHEL, *s.* अतसीमार्जनी-शोधनी.

HATCHET, *s.* परशुः, कुठारः, वृक्षादनी, परश्वधः, वृक्षभेदी; 'h. for cutting stones' टं(तं)कः, पाषाणदारणः.

HATE, *v. t.* वि-,द्विष् 2 U, गुप् desid. (जुगुप्सते) (with abl.), गर्ह् 1, 10 A, नि-प्र-, कुत्स् 10 A, द्रुह् 4 P (with dat.), अभिद्रुह् (with acc.). **-***s.* **-HATRED**, *s.* वि-,द्वेषः, जुगुप्सा, गर्हा, कुत्सा, घृणा, अप्रीति *f.* **-ER**, *s.* द्वेष्टृ *m.*, द्विष्-द्वेषिन् *m.*, द्वेषणः. **-FUL**, *a.* विद्विष्ट, गर्हित, घृणार्ह, गर्ह्य, विद्वेष्य, अक्षिगत, कुत्सित.

HAUGHTY, *a.* उद्धत, उत्सिक्त, मत्त, सगर्व, गर्वित, मानिन्, मानवत्, दृप्त, सदर्प, साटोप, साहंकार, अवलिप्त, मदोद्धत, मदोदग्र; 'to be h.' दृप् 4 P. **-LY**, *adv.* सगर्वं, सदर्पं, सावलेपं, उद्धतं. **-NESS**, *s.* उत्सेकः, दर्पः, औद्धत्यं, गर्वः, मदः, अहंकारः, अवलेपः, मानः, अभिमानः, आटोपः, प्रागल्भ्यं.

HAUL, *v. t.* कृष् 1 P, हृ 1 P, आनी c. **-***s.* आकर्षः, हरणं.

HAULM, HAUM, *s.* पलालः-लं.

HAUNCH, *s.* जघनं, नितंबः, कटि-टी *f.*, प्रोथः, श्रोणिणी *f.* **2** उत्संगः, अंकः.

HAUNT, *v. t.* सदा-नित्यशः (Frequently, q. v.) आ-श्रि 1 U or सेव् 1 A or अभिगम् 1 P; जुष् 6 A, उपसृज् pass.: आक्रम् 1 U, 4 P; 'h. ed by devils' भूतोपसृष्ट, पिशाचसेवित-जुष्ट. **-***s.* नित्यस्थानं, नित्यागमनस्थानं; आश्रयः, निलयः.

HAUTEUR, *s.* दर्पः, गर्वः, आटोपः; *See* HAUGHTINESS.

HAVE, *v. t.* Ex. by भू 1 P, अस् 2 P, वृत् 1 A, विद् 4 A (with gen. of possessor); धृ 1 P, 10, धा 3 U, भृ 3 U; 'I h. two sons' मम पुत्रौ स्तः-विद्येते, &c.; 'he had many sons by Gangâ' गंगायां स बहून् पुत्रानुदपादयत्. **2** (With inf.) by pot. pass. part. ; 'I h. to go' मया गंतव्यं. **3** प्राप् 5 P, लभ् 1 A, आ-सद् c.; *See* GET; 'h. one's own way' स्वातंत्र्यमवलंब् 1 A, यथाकामं-स्वेच्छया-वृत्, कामचारीभू. **4** (Make) Ex. by causal of verbs; 'I would h. you go' त्वं गच्छेरित्यहमिच्छामि or त्वां गमयेयं. **-ING**, *a.* Ex. by the terminations वत्, मत्, मिन्, इन्, विन्, वल, &c. or by उपेत, धारिन्, युक्त, अन्वित, सनाथ, उपपन्न, भृत् in comp.; or by Bah. comp.; 'h. three eyes' त्रिलोचनः; धनवत्, रजस्वल, गुणोपेत, &c. **-***s.* भोगः, भुक्ति *f.*, स्वत्वं, सत्ता, अधिकारः, वशः-शं, धरणं.

HAVEN, *See* HARBOUR.

HAVOC, *s.* प्रमाथः, निर्दलनं, निर्मथनं, विनाशः, वि-प्र-ध्वंसः, संहारः, उच्छेदः, महाप्रलयः, महाविप्लवः, संक्षयः. **-***v. t.* उच्छिद् 7 P; *See* DESTROY.

HAWK, *s.* श्येनः, पत्रिन् *m.*, शशादनः, कपोतारिः, खगांतकः, 'h.-eyed' सूक्ष्म-दूर-दृष्टि. **2** उत्कासनं, श्लेष्मोत्क्षेपः. **-***v. i.* उत्कास् 1 A, श्लेष्माणं उत्क्षिप् 6 P. **2** पक्षिणः ग्रह् 9 P or धृ 1 P. **-***v. t.* घोषणापूर्वं विक्री 9 A. **-ER**, *s.* श्येनपालकः-पोषकः.

HAY, *s.* शुष्क तृणं-शष्पं-घासः; 'make h. while the sun shines' अनुकूलेऽवसरे स्वकार्यसिद्धिं कुरु, इष्टसिद्धिं संपादय; 'h.-cock or-stack' शुष्कतृणराशिः-उत्करः-चिति *f.*; 'h.-market' तृणविक्रयस्थानं.

HAZARD, *s.* संकटं, संशयः, शंका, संदेहः, विकल्पः. **2** दैवं, दैवयोगः-घटना, दैवगति *f.*; 'h. of life' जीवितसंशयः; 'at any h.' समुपस्थितेपि संशये. **-***v. t.* संकट-संशये-निक्षिप् 6 P or पत् c., संशयस्थ-संदेहदोलास्थ-दैवाधीन-*a.* कृ 8 U; 'he who h. s his life' संशयितजीवितः. **-OUS**, *a.* संदिग्ध, संशयस्थ, संशयाक्रांत, सांशयिक (की *f.*), ससंदेह, दैवाधीन, दैववशग; 'a h. position' संशयस्थानं, शंकास्पदं.

HAZE, *s.* धूमिका, कुज्झटिका, कुहेडिका. **-HAZY**, *a.* सधूमिक, सांधकार, साभ्र, कुज्झटिकाच्छन्न. **2** अस्पष्ट, अव्यक्त; संकुल, संकीर्ण.

HAZEL, *a.* ईषत्कपिशवर्ण, आताम्र.

HE, *pron.* सः, एषः, असौ, अयं.

HEAD, *s.* शिरस् *n.*, शीर्षं, शीर्षकं, मूर्धन् *m.*, मस्तकः-कं, मौलि *m. f.*, वरांगं, उत्तमांगं, मुंडः-डं. 2 अग्रणीः, अध्यक्षः, धौरेयः, धुर्यः, धूर्वहः, धुरीणः, पुरोगः, पतिः, नायकः, अधिपः-पतिः, मुखरः, श्रेष्ठः, अधिष्ठातृ *m.*, मुख्य-प्रधान in comp. 3 विषयः, पदं, स्थानं, अधिकरणं. 4 अग्रं, शिरस्, चूडा, शिखरं. 5 मूलं, प्रभवः, उद्गमः, उद्भवः, आदिहेतुः. 6 मति *f.*, बुद्धि *f.*, धीः; 'to be placed at the h. of' धुरि कीर्तनीय-or प्रतिष्ठापयितव्य-*a.*; 'h. merchant' श्रेष्ठिन् *m.*, विट्पतिः; 'the h. of a family' कुलपतिः, कुटुंबभारवाहकः; 'at the h.' ex. by आदि-प्रमुख in comp. or धुरि-मूर्धनि-स्था. &c.; 'with Indra at their h.' इंद्रादयः-इंद्रप्रमुखाः (देवाः); 'he stands at the h. of all' स सर्वेषां धुरि-मूर्धनि-तिष्ठति; 'h. over ears in debt' ऋणराशौ निमग्न or ऋणग्रस्त; 'to get a-h. of' अतिक्रम् 1 U, 4 P, अतिरिच् pass., अभिभू; 'make h. against' प्रत्यवस्था 1 A, विरुध् 7 U, प्रतिकूलयति (D.). —*v. t.* नी 1 P, अधिष्ठा 1 P, अग्रे-मूर्धनि-पुरः-गम् or स्था 1 P; 'h. ed by Vasish*th*a' वशिष्ठाधिष्ठिताः; gen. ex. by प्रमुख-पुरोग-पुरस्सर- in comp.; 'h.-ache' शिरोवेदना, शीर्षव्यथा-पीडा, शिरः-शूलं-रोगः; *See* ACHE; 'h.-band' शिरोवेष्टनं-बंधनं, ललाटपट्टः; 'h.-dress' शिरोभूषणं, किरीटः-टं, मुकुटं; 'h.-land' अंतरीपः-पं, भूशिरः, भूनासिका; 'h.-long or h. foremost' अवाक्शिरस्, अधोमुख-अवाङ्मुख (खी *f.*), अवाञ्च्, साहसिक, सरभस, साहसिन्, क्षिप्र-अविमृश्य-कारिन्-कृत; प्रवण, पातुक, पतयालु; (*adv.*) अवाक्, अधोमुखेन, सोत्पातं, सवेगं; 'h.-most' अग्रच, प्राग्रच, प्रमुख, मुख्य, वर, वरेण्य, उत्तम, प्रधान, in comp.; 'h.-piece' शिरस्त्रं, शिरस्त्राणं, शिरस्कं; 'h. s-man' घातकः, वधाधिकृतः, वध्यपुरुषः, मृतपाः; 'h.-strong' दुर्दांत, अप्रतिविधेय, अवश्य, दुर्दम, उच्छृंखल, अविधेय, प्रमत्त, अस्थिर, चंचल. —LESS, *a.* मस्तकहीन, अशिरस्. —Y, *a.* साहसिन्, साहसिक, क्षिप्रकारिन्. 2 संरंभिन्, शीघ्र-सुलभ-कोप, अमर्षण.

HEAL, *v. t.* शम् c. (शमयति), साध् c., समुत्था c. (समुत्थापयति), व्याधेः मुच् c.; *See* CURE; 'to h. a wound' व्रणं वि-रुह् c. (रोपयति); 'sore-h.-ing oil' व्रणविरोपणं तैलं (S. 4). 2 समा-सं-प्रतिसमा-धा 3 U, शम् c. —*v. i.* रुह् 1 P. 2 प्र-, शम् 4 P. —ER, *s.* रोगहरः, चिकित्सकः. —ING, *s.* उप-शमः-शांति *f.*, रुक्प्रतिक्रिया, चिकित्सा, प्रतीकारः, समुत्थानं. 2 विरोपणं-रोहणं. —*a.* शांतिद, रोगहर, शांतिकर (री *f.*), विरोपण.

HEALTH, *s.* कुशलं, अरोगः, सुस्थता, वार्तं, रोगाभावः, निरामयत्वं, सुस्थिति *f.*, आरोग्यं, स्वास्थ्यं, अनामयं, कल्यत्वं-ता, शरीरसुखं, अरोगिता. 2 प्रकृति *f.*, शरीरावस्था. शरीरस्थितिः-प्रकृतिः; 'of a delicate h.' प्रकृतिकोमल-दुर्बल; 'he is in good h.' सुस्थोसौ, कुशलमस्य. —FUL, —Y, *a.* आरोग्यवत्, अरोगिन्, नीरोग, नीरुज-जू, स्वस्थ, व्याधिरहित, निरामय, वार्त, सुस्थ, कल्य, कुशलिन्, निर्व्याधि; 'became as h. as before' पूर्ववत् प्रकृतिस्थः समजायत. 2 आरोग्य-सुख-कर (री *f.*), पथ्य, हित, स्वास्थ्यजनक, सुखावह. —FULNESS, *See* (*s.*).

HEAP, *s.* राशिः, नि-सं-चयः, चिति *f.*, निकरः, स्तोमः, पुंजः, गणः, ओघः, संभारः; *See* COLLECTION. —*v. t.* राशीकृ 8 U, सं-आ-प्र-चि 5 U, एकीकृ, समाक्षिप् 6 P, सं-भृ 3 U, पिंडीकृ, आ-समा-स्तृ 5 U; *See* COLLECT; 'why do you h. accusations (calumnies) upon us' किमस्मान् संभृतदोषैरधिक्षिपथ (S. 5).

HEAR, *v. t.* श्रु 5 P, समा-आ-कर्ण् 10, निशम् 4 P or c. (निशामयति); 'h. cases' व्यवहारान् दृश् 1 P, कार्याणि अवेक्ष् 1 A or विचर् c. or अनुसं-धा 3 U. —*v. i.* वार्तां श्रु; 'I have not heard from him for a long time' चिरं तद्वार्ता मया न श्रुता. —ER, *s.* श्रोतृ *m.*, श्रावकः, आकर्णयिता. —ING, *s.* श्रवणं, श्रुति *f.*, आकर्णनं, निशामनं. 2 (In law) दर्शनं, अवेक्षणं, अनुसंधानं; 'the organ of h.' श्रवणेंद्रियं, श्रोत्रं; 'within h.' श्रवणगोचरे, श्रुतिपथवर्तिन्. —HEARSAY, *s.* जनश्रुति *f.*, कर्णपरंपरा, जनवादः-प्रवादः, किंवदंती; 'know it by h.' इति कर्णपरंपरया श्रुतं.

HEARKEN, *See* HEAR.

HEARSE, *s.* प्रेत-शव-यानं-वाहनं.

HEART, *s.* हृदयं, हृद् *n.* 2 (The substance) बुक्का, अग्रमांसं, बुक्काग्रमांसं. 3 (Mind) चित्तं, मनस् *n.*, चेतस् *n.*, मानसं, हृदयं, अंतःकरणं, आत्मन् *m.*, अंतरात्मा, स्वांतं. 4 उरस् *n.*, वक्षस् *n.*, वक्षःस्थलं. 5 मर्मन् *n.* 6 स्नेहः, प्रणयः, रागः, भावः. 7 उदरं, गर्भः, अभ्यंतरं, अंतर in comp. 8 सत्त्वं, धैर्यं, पौरुषं, तेजस् *n.*; 'take h.' आ-समा-श्वस् 2 P; धैर्यं, अवलंब् 1 A or अवष्टंभ् 9 P; 'learn or get by h.' कंठस्थ *a.* कृ 8 U, अभ्यस् 4 P; 'keep in the h.' चित्ते कृ, अवधृ 10; 'out of h.' दीन-खिन्न-चित्त; 'at h.' अंतः; 'with all one's h.', 'h. and soul' प्रकामं, कामं, सोत्साहं, सर्वात्मना; 'he has applied himself to the work h. and soul' सर्वात्मना तस्मिन्कर्मणि स व्यापृतः; 'to one's h.'s content' यथेच्छं, पर्याप्तं, आचित्ततोषं, कामं, प्रकामं, निकामं, इष्टं, यथेष्टं सातं; 'from the h.' निर्व्याजं, सोत्साहं, निर्व्यलीकं; 'h.-ache' हृदयसंतापः, मनोव्याधिः, हृदयव्यथा-पीडा-वेदना, मनस्तापः, मानसी व्यथा; 'h.-broken' भग्नमानस, अंतर्भिन्न, भिन्नहृदय; 'h.-burn'

हृदयवेदना, मनस्तापः; ह्लासः, अम्लपित्तं; 'h.-ease' हृदयस्वास्थ्यं-सुखं, चित्तशांति-निर्वृति *f.*; 'h.-felt' अव्याज, निर्व्याज, वास्तविक (की *f.*), अकृत्रिम; 'h.-breaking,-rending,-wounding' मर्मभिद्-स्पृश्-च्छिद्, हृदय-मर्म-भेदिन्-च्छेदिन्, हृदिस्पृश्, अरुंतुद, चित्तोद्वेगजनक; 'h.-robbing' मनोहर, चित्तहारिन्; 'h.-sick' दुर्मनस्, उद्विग्नचित्त, खिन्न-विषण्ण-हृदय; *See* DEJECTED; 'h.-struck,-wounded' विद्धमर्मन्, क्षत-विद्ध-हृदय; 'h.-whole' अक्षत-अभिन्न-हृदय. –LESS, *a.* निर्वीर्य, निस्तेजस्; भीरुहृदय, निस्सत्त्व, निष्पौरुष, क्लीब. 2 निर्दय, क्रूर, कठोरहृदय, निर्घृण. –LESSLY, *adv.* निर्वीर्यं, क्लीबवत्. 2 निर्दयं, क्रूरतया. –LESSNESS, *s.* अपौरुषं, क्लीबता, निर्वीर्यत्वं. 2 निर्दयत्वं, कठोरता. —HEARTY, *a.* सरल, निर्व्यलीक, निष्कपट, निर्व्याज, शुद्धांतःकरण; *See* FRANK. 2 अकृत्रिम, अकृतक, सोत्साह, उत्सुक, सोल्लास, सस्नेह, हृद्य; हृदयंगम, स्नेहनिर्भर; 'a h. friend' हृदयंगमः सखा. 3 वीर्यवत्, सपौरुष; कल्य, सुस्थ. –LY, *adv.* निर्व्यलीकं, निष्कपटं, निर्व्याजं. 2 सोल्लासं, सोत्साहं, प्रकामं, सर्वात्मना, संतुष्टचेतसा, कामतः, सानंदं, साह्लादं, चित्तसंतोषेण. 3 सवीर्यं. –NESS, *s.* सारल्यं, अकृत्रिमता, अव्याजत्वं; उत्साहः, औत्सुक्यं, वीर्यं, तेजस् *n.*, पौरुषं.

HEARTH, *s.* अग्निकुंडं, चुल्लि-ल्ली *f.*, अंतिका, अंदिका, उद्धानं, उध्मानं, अधिश्रयणी. अश्मंतं. 2 (Portable fire-place) अंगारधानिका, अंगारशकटी, हसनी, हसंती.

HEAT, *v. t.* तप् c., परि-प्र-सं°; उद्-,दीप् c.; ज्वल् c., संधुक्ष् 10; दह् 1 P. –*s.* तापः, सं-उत्-परि-तापः, दाहः; उष्णता, ऊष्मः, तिग्मता, प्रखरत्वं, उ-उष्मन् *m.*, चंडता. 2 आतपः, घर्मः, निदाघः; 'affected by h.' उष्णालु; 'expose to the sun's h.' सूर्यातपं दा 3 U. 3 (Summer) ग्रीष्मः, निदाघः, घर्मकालः, उष्णकालः, निदाघसमयः. 4 उत्तापः, संक्षोभः, चंडता, तीक्ष्णता, तीव्रता, उग्रता, व्यग्रता. 5 संरंभः, मदः, क्रोधः, उद्दीपनं, संधुक्षणं; आवेशः, आक्रमः; 'in the h. of excitement' रोषावेशेन. 6 कपोलरागः; 'h. of youth' यौवनगर्वः-दर्पः, यौवनोन्मादः, तारुण्यमदः. –ING, *s.* तापनं, दीपनं. –*a.* तापक, दीपन.

HEATH, *s.* जंगलभूमि *f.*, वनभूमिः. 2 प्रचारः.

HEATHEN, *s.* मूर्ति-प्रतिमा-पूजकः-उपासकः-अर्चकः. –*a.*,-ISH, *a.* प्रतिमापूजकानुरूप. 2 Barbarous, q. v. –ISM, *s.* मूर्तिपूजा-अर्चनं-उपासना.

HEAVE, *v. t.* उन्नम् c. (नमयति), उन्नी 1 P, उच्छ्रि 1 U, उद्-हृ-धृ 1 P, उद्यम् 1 A, उत्था c. (उत्थापयति), उत्क्षिप् 6 P, उत्तुल् 10; 'h. a sigh' निश्वस् 2 P, दीर्घं निश्वस्; 'h. ing deeply' दीर्घ-स्थूलस्थूलं-निश्वस्य. –*v. i.* स्पंद् 1 A, स्फुर् 6 P, कंप् 1 A, वेप् 1 A. 2 निश्वस्, कृच्छ्रेण उच्छ्वस् 3 उत्सृप् 1 P, प्र-लुठ् 6 P, 1 A, लुल् 1 P, तरंगायते (D.), उन्नम् 1 P. –*s.* उन्नमनं, उत्क्षेपः, उत्तोलनं, उद्धरणं. –ING, *s.* स्पंदनं, स्फुरणं, कंपनं, वेपथुः. 2 निश्वासः, कृच्छ्रेण उच्छ्वासः, दीर्घनिश्वासः. 3 उत्सर्पणं, प्रलोठनं, लोलनं, उन्नमनं. –*a.* स्पंदमान, उत्सर्पिन्, लोल.

HEAVEN, *s.* दिव् *f.*, द्यो *f.*, स्वर्गः, त्रिदिवः-वं, सुरलोकः, त्रिदशालयः, त्रिविष्टपं, नाकः, स्वर् *ind.*; 'h. of Vishnu' वैकुंठं; 'this is a h. on earth' भूस्वर्गायमाणमेतत्स्थलं, स्थानांतरगतः स्वर्गः (V. 2). 2 आकाशः-शं, नभस् *n.*, गगनं-नं; *See* SKY. 3 God, q. v.; परमेश्वरः, विधिः, ईश्वरः; 'h. and earth' द्यावापृथिव्यौ, द्यावाभूमी, रोदसी-स्यौ, द्यावाक्षमे; 'h.-born' दिविज, स्वर्गीय, स्वर्गोत्पन्न. –LY, *a.* दिव्य, स्वर्गीय, अपार्थिव (वी *f.*), स्वर्ग्य, त्रिदिवस्थ, दिविष्ठ; 'h. body' नक्षत्रं; 'h. voice' आकाशवाणी, अशरीरिणी वाक्; 'h. nymph' सुरांगना, स्वर्योषित्, दिव्यांगना. 2 परम, उत्तम. –WARDS, *adv.* स्वर्गाभिमुखं, अभिगगनं.

HEAVY, *a.* गुरु, भारवत्. 2 गाढ, दीर्घ, गुरु, तीक्ष्ण, महत्, तीव्र, अत्यंत, उग्र, दारुण, उचंड, महा-सु-अति in comp.; 'h. shower' महासारः, अतिवृष्टिः. 3 आकुल, क्षुब्ध; 'h. sea' सागरक्षोभः, क्षुब्धसागरः, ऊर्मिमालाकुलः सागरः. 4 अवसन्न, खिन्न, दीन, चिंताकुल, विषण्ण. 5 मंद, स्थूल, जड, मंथर, अलस, मंद-धी-मति, जड-स्थूल-बुद्धि-धी; 'h.-headed' मंद-स्थूल-धी; 'h.-laden' गुरुभाराक्रांत, सुभारवत्. –LY, *adv.* गुरुभारेण, गुरुतया. 2 भृशं, तीव्रं, बलवत्, अत्यंतं, सु-अति pr.; *See* EXCEEDINGLY. 3 सविषादं, मंदं, शनैःशनैः. –NESS, *s.* गुरुता, गुरुत्वं, भारः; गरिमन् *m.*, विषादः, दैन्यं, मांद्यं, स्थूलता, &c.

HEBETATE, *v. t. See* BLUNT, DULL.

HECATOMB, *s.* शतबलिदानं.

HECTIC, *a.* संतत, अविरत. 2 ज्वरसूचक, अंतर्दाहसूचक.

HECTOR, *s.* विकत्थिन् *m.*, आत्मश्लाघी, पिंडीशूरः, शूरंमन्यः. 2 कलहकारः, भर्त्सकः. –*v. i.* विकत्थ् 1 A, प्रगल्भ् 1 A; *See* BOAST. 2 तर्ज्-भर्त्स् 10 A.

HEDGE, *s.* वृति *f.*, प्राचीरं, प्राकारः, आवरणं, वेष्टनं, आवारः, क्षेत्रावरोधकं, क्षेत्रवेष्टनं; 'h.-born' अंत्यज, हीनजाति-वर्ण, अधम-नीच-जातीय; 'h.-hog' शल्यः, शल्यकंठः; 'h.-sparrow' कलविंकः, चटकः. –*v. t.* वृत्या परिवेष्ट् c. or आवृ 5 U or अवरुध् 7 U.

HEED, *v. t.* आदृ 6 A, अवेक्ष् 1 A, गण् 10, मन् c., अभिनंद् 1 P; सेव् 1 A. 2 अव-धा 3 U, मनो दा 3 U, सावधान *a.* भू, श्रु 5 P; *See* HEAR. –*s.* अवधानं, अवेक्षा, सावधानता, मनोयोगः; 'take h.' सावधानो भव. –FUL,-LESS, *a. See* CAREFUL,-LESS.

HEEL, *s.* पार्ष्णि *m. f.*, पादतलं-मूलं; 'to be at one's h. s' पार्ष्णिं ग्रह् 9 P, अनुसृ, पदं अनुगम् 1 P; 'I shall be close upon your h. s' अहमनुपदमागत एव (S. 3); 'to take to or show h. s'

पलाय् 1 A, अपक्रम् 1 U, 4 P; 'betake to h. s' जंघाबलमवलंब् 1 A; 'h. s over head' अवाक्शिरस् a., ऊर्ध्वपाद a. –v. i. एकपार्श्वे पत् 1 P or परिवृत् 1 A or प्र-लंब् 1 A.

HEFT, s. उद्योगः, यत्नः, उत्साहः. 2 मुष्टि m. f., त्सरुः.

HEIFER, s. वत्सतरी, वत्सा ; 'h. one year old' एकहायनी ; so द्विहायनी, त्रिहायणी.

HEIGH-HO, *interj.* हंहो, अहो, भो भोः, रे रे.

HEIGHT, *See* under HIGH.

HEINOUS, a. घोर, दारुण, अतिनिंद्य, गर्ह्यतम, अतिदुष्ट, महत्, अतिपापिन्, अतिघोर, पापिष्ठ. –LY, adv. घोरं, दारुणं. –NESS, s. घोरता, दारुणत्वं.

HEIR, s. दायादः, रिक्थहरः, अंशहरः-हारिन् m., रिक्थभागी, रिक्थिन् m., धनाधिकारी, उत्तराधिकारी, अंशभाक्, अंशी; 'sole h.' समग्रधनभाक्; 'h.-apparent' युवराजः; 'h.-loom' क्रमायातं जंगमद्रव्यं. –ESS, s. धनाधिकारिणी, &c. –LESS, a. दायादशून्य हीन. –SHIP, s. धनाधिकारित्वं.

HELIOTROPE, s. सूर्यकमलं, श्रीहस्तिनी.

HELL, s. नरकः, निरयः, नारकः, दुर्गति f. 2 पातालं, रसातलं, अधोलोकः, अधोभुवनं ; 'h.-tortures' कारणा, यातना, तीव्रवेदना ; 'river of h.' वैतरणी. –ISH, a. नारक (की f.), नरकीय, नारकीय (यी f.), नरकस्थ. 2 Cruel, q. v. 3 अतिनिंद्य, दुष्टतम.

HELM, s. कर्णः, केनिपातः-तकः, अरित्रं. 2 Helmet, q. v.; 'placed at the h. of (royal) affairs' राज्यधुरायां स्थापित. –HELMSMAN, s. कर्णधारः, नाविकः.

HELMET, s. शिरस्त्रं, शिरस्कं, शिरोभूषणं, शिरस्त्राणं, शीर्षकं-ण्यं.

HELP, s. साहाय्यं, उपकारः, उपकृतं-कृति f., साहित्यं, अनुग्रहः, आनुकूल्यं. 2 गति f., आश्रयः, शरणं; 'help! help!' परित्रायध्वं, परित्रायध्वं. –v. t. साहाय्यं कृ 8 U, सहायः भू, अनुग्रह् 9 P, उपकृ (gen.); न हि दीपौ परस्परस्योपकुरुतः (S. B. 420); तान्यपि तत्त्वज्ञानायोपकुर्वंति (S. B. 447) 'h. a right understanding'. 2 संवृध् c., प्रवृत् c., पुरस्कृ, उद्युज् 10; 'h. ed him on his legs' उत्थातुं तस्य साहाय्यं चकार; 'God h. s those who h. themselves' दैवमुद्यमायत्तं, विना पुरुषकारेण दैवं न सिध्यति; दैवं पुरुषकारेण साध्यसिद्धिनिबंधनं; न स्वयं दैवमादत्ते पुरुषार्थमपेक्षते (S. R. 104); 'can't h.' का गतिः, किमन्यच्छरणं; 'to h. himself to a mouthful' ग्रासग्रहणेन आत्मानं तर्पयितुं; 'a h. ing hand' हस्तावलंबः-बनं; दैवेनेत्थं दत्तहस्तावलंबे प्रारंभे (Rat. 1); 'he could not h. laughing' हासं निग्रहीतुं न शशाक; 'I cannot h. going' मयावश्यं गंतव्यं; 'to h. at table' परिविष् 10. –ER, s. उपकारकः, उपकर्तृ m., सहायः. –FUL, a. उपयोगिन्, सहाय, उपकारक, साहाय्यकारिन्. –LESS, a. अनाथ, निराश्रय, अगतिक, अशरण, गतिहीन, निरवलंब, असहाय. 2 अप्रतिकार्य, अपरिहार्य, अप्रतिविधेय, निरुपाय; 'we are simply h. in that matter' तस्मिन्विषये अस्माकमन्या गतिरेव नास्ति. –HELPMATE, s. सहधर्मिणी. 2 सहायः, सहकारिन् m.

HELVE, s. दंडः, मुष्टि m. f.

HEM, s. अंचलः, वसनप्रांतः, वस्त्रयः-दशाः (pl.). 2 उत्कासनं. –v. t. अंचलं सिव् 4 P. 2 (in) परिवेष्ट् 1 A or c., परि-वृ 5 U or c., निरुध् 7 U.

HEMICRANIA, s. अर्धावभेदकः.

HEMICYCLE, s. गोलार्धं.

HEMIPLEGY, s. पक्षाघातः, पक्षवायुः.

HEMISPHERE, s. गोलार्धं, अर्धगोलः.

HEMISTICH, s. श्लोकार्धं, अर्धश्लोकः.

HEMORRHAGE, s. रक्त-रुधिर-स्रावः, रक्तक्षरणं.

HEMORRHOIDS, s. अर्शस् n., गुदकीलः.

HEMP, s. शणं, भंगा, मातुलानी. –EN, a. शाण (णी f.), शण in comp.

HEN, s. कुक्कुटी; 'h.-hearted' भीरु, भीरुहृदय, कातर, कापुरुष; 'h.-house' कुक्कुटपालिका; 'h.-pecked' स्त्रीवश, स्त्रीविधेय, स्त्रीजित, स्त्रीवश्य, स्त्रीवशवर्तिन्, भार्याटक; 'h.-roost' कुक्कुटालयः.

HENCE, adv. इतः, अस्मात् स्थानात्. 2 अतः, एतस्मात् कारणात्, तस्मात्; अत एव. 3 (From h.) अतः परं, अतः-इतः-परं-ऊर्ध्वं; अद्यप्रभृति; 'hence!' अपेहि, अपयाहि, अपसर; 'h.-forth,-forward' अतः-इतः-परं-ऊर्ध्वं, अद्यप्रभृति, अद्यारभ्य, अद्यावधि.

HEPTAGON, s. सप्तभुजा-सप्तकोणा-आकृतिः.

HERALD, s. घोषकः, बंदिन् m., राजदूतः. 2 (fig.) अग्रदूतः, प्रथमवार्ताहरः, अग्रेसरः. –HERALDRY, s. वंशावलीज्ञानं.

HERB, s. ओषधि-धी f., शाकः, शाकलता, हरितकं. –HERBAGE, s. तृणं, शस्यं, घासः, यवसं. –HERBAL, s. वृक्षायुर्वेदः.

HERCULEAN, a. भगीरथ in comp.; 'h. efforts' भगीरथप्रयत्नाः. 2 अतिप्रबल, अतिशक्तिमत्.

HERD, s. यूथं, गणः, संघः, वृंदं, कदंबः, कुलं, समूहः, व्रजः, निवहः; 'h. of cattle' गोकुलं, पाशवं, गोवृंदं, गोत्रा; 'h. of oxen' औक्षणं; 'h. of calves' वात्सकं; 'h. of elephants' हास्तिकं. –v. i. यूथेन चर् 1 P, यूथशः संमिल् 6 P or संगम् 1 A, एकीभू, एकत्र भू or मिल्. –HERDSMAN, s. गोरक्षकः, गोपालः, गोपः, गोधुक्, आभीरः, गोसंख्यः, बल्लवः.

HERE, adv. अत्र, इह (gen. in this world). 2 इह लोके; ex. by demon. pron.; 'h. comes your mother' एषागच्छति ते माता; 'h. am I' अयमस्मि. -*Interj.* भो भोः; 'h. and there' इतस्ततः; अंतरांतरा, असमग्रं, असंपूर्णं; 'h. about' इतो नातिदूरे, इह समीपे; 'h.-after' इतः परं-ऊर्ध्वं, अतः, परतः, परस्तात्, अनंतरं, पश्चात्, उत्तरतः, उत्तरत्र, अग्रे, उपरिष्टात्, अतः परं; (in the next world) परत्र, अमुत्र, परलोके; (*s.*) उत्तरकालः, पर-भावि-आगामि-कालः; 'h.-at' अत्रांतरे, अथ; 'h.-by' अनेन, तस्मात्; 'h.-in' अत्र, अत्र-स्थाने-विषये; 'h.-before' इतः पूर्वं, पूर्वकाले, पुरा, प्राक्, अतीत-गतकाले; 'h.-upon' ततः, अनंतरं, तदुपरि, तच्छ्रुत्वा.

HEREDITARY, *a.* पितृपैतामह (ही *f.*), पित्र्य, पैतृक (की *f.*), पारंपरीण-य, परंपरागत, परंपराप्राप्त, क्रमायात, क्रमागत, कुलक्रमागत, अन्वयागत; 'h. disease' संचारी रोगः; 'h. servant' मूलभृत्यः, मौलः; 'h. succession' क्रमागतत्वं. -LY, *adv.* कुलक्रमेण, वंशक्रमेण, परंपरया, पारंपर्येण.

HEREDITAMENT, *s.* दायः, रिक्थाधिकारः.

HERESY, *s.* पाषंडमार्गः, नास्तिकता, मिथ्यादृष्टि *f.*; विधर्मः, विधर्मसेवा, परधर्माश्रयः, अपथं, विपथः. —HERETIC, *s.* पाषं(खं)डः, नास्तिकः, विधर्मसेविन् *m.*, परधर्मावलंबी, देवनिंदकः, उपधर्मसेवी, स्वधर्मभ्रष्ट:-च्युतः, पतितः. -AL, *a.* धर्मविरुद्ध, विपथ-विधर्मगामिन्. -ALLY, *adv.* पाषंडवत्, नास्तिकवत्.

HERITAGE, *s.* दायः, पैतृकं धनं, रिक्थं, पैतृकद्रव्याधिकारः.

HERMAPHRODITE, *s.* स्त्रीपुरुषलक्षणान्वितः.

HERMETICALLY, *adv.* सुदृढं, गाढं.

HERMIT, *s.* यतिः, तापसः, तपस्विन् *m.*, मुनिः, आरण्यकः, वन-अरण्य-वासी, वानप्रस्थः, वैखानसः. -AGE, *s.* आश्रमः, उटजः-जं, पर्णशाला.

HERNIA, *s.* अंत्रवृद्धि *f.*; अंत्रस्रंसः.

HERO, *s.* वीरः, शूरः, भटः, विक्रांतपुरुषः, प्र-महा-वीरः, जेतृ *m.*, रथिन् *m.*, अतिरथः, शौटीरः. 2 (In dramas &c.) नायकः, कथापुरुष; 'h. s of Râmâyana' रामायणकथापुरुषाः or -नायकाः. -IC,-ICAL, *a.* वीर, शूर, प्रवीर, विक्रांत, वीर्यवत्, अमितौजस्, महावीर्य; 'a h. deed' पराक्रमः, विक्रमः, अवदातं कर्म. 2 वीर-चरित्र-विषयक, वीररसप्रधान. -ICALLY, *adv.* सविक्रमं, सवीर्यं, शूरवत्. -ISM, *s.* वीर्यं, शूरत्वं, शौर्यं, परा-वि-क्रमः, धामन् *n.*, ओजस् *n.*, रणोत्साहः, पौरुषं, साहसं, वीर्यवत्त्वं, शौटीर्यं. -HEROINE, *s.* नायिका.

HERON, *s.* बकः, सारसः, लोहपृष्ठः, क्रौंचः.

HERPES, *s.* *See* ITCH.

HESITATE, *v. i.* वि-आ-शंक् 1 A, दोलायते (D.), विचर् c., विकृप् 1 A or c., विलंब् 1 A, चिर-(रा)यति-आंदोलयति (D.); *See* DOUBT also. 2 Falter, q. v. -INGLY, *adv.* संशय्य, सविकल्पं, ससंशयं, साशंकं. 2 स्खलनपूर्वकं. -ION, *s.* शंका, संशयः, विकल्पः, आ-वि-परि-शंका, विचारः, संदेहः, वितर्कः, द्वापरः, अनिर्णयः, विचिकित्सा. 2 (In speaking) स्खलनं, स्वरभेदः-भंगः, स्खलद्वचनं, गद्गदवाच् *f.*

HETEROCLITE, *a.* विधिविरुद्ध, निपातित.

HETERODOX, *a.* भिन्न-मत-धर्मन्, धर्मविरुद्ध, विपरीत, विधर्मिन्, वैधर्मिक (की *f.*), अपथवर्तिन्-गामिन्. -Y, *s.* विधर्मः, भिन्नमतं-धर्मः.

HETEROGENEOUS, *a.* भिन्न, विजातीय, पृथग्विध, भिन्नजातीय, विरुद्ध; *See* DIFFERENT.

HEW, *v. t.* छिद् 7 P, कृत् 6 P, लू 9 U; *See* CUT. -ER, *s.* छेदकः, छेदिन् *m.*, छिद् in comp. -HEWN, *a.* छिन्न, दात, वृक्ण, लून, कृत्त, दित, छात.

HEXAGON, *s.* षट्कोणः, षडस्रः.

HEXAMETRE, *s.* षट्पदी चरणः.

HEY, *interj.* अहो, ननु, हाहा.

HEYDAY, *interj.* नमः, स्वस्ति (with dat.); अहो, भोः. -*s.* उल्लासः, प्रमोदः, हर्षः, मुदा, परिहासः; 'h. of youth' नवं-प्रथमं-यौवनं.

HIATUS, *s.* भंगः, भेदः, छेदः, विच्छेदः.

HIBERNAL, *a.* हैमंत (ती *f.*), हैमंतिक (की *f.*).

HICCOUGH, HICCUP, *s.* हिक्का, हिध्मा. -*v. i.* हिक्क् 1 U.

HIDE, *s.* चर्मन् *n.*, अजिनं, दृतिः, कृत्ति *f.*, पशुचर्म-त्वच् *f.*; 'h.-bound' दृढमुष्टि, कृपण; अवश्य, अविनय, कठोर, कठिन. -*v. t.* प्रच्छद् 10, गुह् 1 U, गुप् 1 P, अंतर्धा 3 U, तिरोधा, स्थग् 10, अपवृ c.; *See* CONCEAL. -*v. i.* गुह्-गुप् pass., गुप्त-निलीन-*a.* भू 1 P, नि-ली 4 A, तिरोभू, तिरोधा pass.; 'h. s behind the bushes' विटपांतरितस्तिष्ठति-भवति. -HID, -HIDDEN, *a.* गूढ, गुप्त, प्रच्छन्न, छादित, अंतर्हित, तिरोहित, अंतरित, अपवारित, निभृत, स्थगित, लीन, निलीन. -ING, *s.* गोपनं, गुप्ति *f.*, प्रच्छादनं, स्थगनं, तिरोधानं; 'h.-place' निभृत-गूढ-स्थानं, गुप्तिः, निभृतं.

HIDEOUS, *a.* बीभत्स, विकृत, घोर, भीषण, कराल, उग्रदर्शन, कराल-मुख-वदन, कदाकार, भीम-घोर-दर्शन-आकृति, उग्र-घोर-रूप, दुर्दर्शन; 'Oh! this is indeed a h. spectacle' हंत बीभत्समेवाग्रतो वर्तते (Mal. 5). -LY, *adv.* उग्रं, घोररूपेण, बीभत्सं. -NESS, *s.* घोरता, करालता, उग्रता.

HIE, *v. i.* त्वर् 1 A, सत्वरं गम् 1 P.

HIERARCH, *s.* पुरोहितेश्वरः, आचार्यवरः. -Y, *s.* आचार्याधिपत्यं, धर्माध्यापकप्रभुत्वं.

HIEROGLYPH,-IC, *s.* गूढाक्षरं, बीजाक्षरं.

HIGGLE, *v. i.* पण् 1 A, व्यव-हृ 1 P. 2 Haggle, q. v.

HIGH, *a.* उच्च, उन्नत, उच्छ्रित, समुच्छ्रित, सोच्छ्राय, तुंग, प्रांशु, उदग्र, उत्तुंग, उद्धत, उत्तम, ऊर्ध्व. 2 उत्तम,

विशिष्ट, मुख्य, श्रेष्ठ, परम, अग्र्य, महा-प्रधान- in comp.; *See* PRINCIPAL. 3 प्रचंड, तीक्ष्ण, तीव्र, बलवत्, तरस्विन्, प्रबल; *See* STRONG. 4 उदात्त, उत्ताल; 'a h. tone' उदात्तः, उच्च-तार-स्वरः, तारः. 5 (Of h. rank) विशिष्ट, उत्कृष्ट, उत्कृष्ट-विशिष्ट-पदस्थ, उत्तम-परम-पदभाज्, लब्धप्रतिष्ठ, प्रतिपत्तिमत्, सगौरव. 6 (Of h. family) कुलीन, महाकुल, अभिजात, अभिजनवत्, कुलज, महाकुलप्रसूत. 7 गर्वोद्धत, दर्पाध्मात, सावलेप, गर्वित, अवलिप्त, उत्सिक्त. 8 गहन; 'h. water' प्रवृद्धा वेला; 'it is h. noon' (नभसः) मध्यमलंकरोति भानुः; 'h. and low' उच्चावच, अधरोत्तर, उत्तमाधम, उन्नतानत, नतोन्नत, निम्नोन्नत; 'h.-er and h.-er' अधिकाधिकं, उत्तरोत्तरं; 'h. price' महामूल्यं; 'h. ground' उन्नतभूः; 'as h. as' मात्र (त्री *f.*), द्वयस (सी *f.*), दघ्न (घ्नी *f.*) in comp.; 'he has a h. opinion of you' स त्वां बहु मन्यते. —*adv.* उच्चैः, उच्चं, अति-सु pr.; ऊर्ध्वं, उपरि, उत्तमं, परमं; 'on h.' ऊर्ध्वं, उपरि; 'from on h.' उपरिष्टात्; 'the sea runs h.' बलवत्क्षुब्धः सागरः. 'H.-birth' कुलीनता, कुलोत्कर्षः, आभिजात्यं; 'h.-blest' अतिपुण्यवत्, महाभाग, अतिधन्य, परमसुखभाज्; 'h.-blown' अत्युच्छून, अतिस्फीत; 'h.-born' कुलीन, महाकुलजात-प्रसूत, अभिजात, सुजात, अभिजनवत्, सद्वंश्य, श्रेष्ठ-उत्तम-कुलोद्भव; 'h.-bred' कुलीन, शिष्टाचार, सुजन, सुशील, सद्भावविशिष्ट, सौजन्योपेत, सदाचार, साधुवृत्त; 'h.-built' सोच्छ्राय, उच्च; 'h.-day' उत्सवदिनं, उद्धर्षदिवसः; 'h-fed' अतिपुष्ट, हृष्टपुष्ट; 'h.-flying' अपरिमित; 'h.-hand' औद्धत्यं, गर्वः, उद्दामत्वं, निर्यंत्रणत्वं; 'h.-handed' उद्धत, सगर्व, उद्दाम, अनियंत्रण, उच्छृंखल, स्वैरिन्; 'h.-hung' ऊर्ध्वबद्ध; 'h.-land' अधित्यका, उन्नतभूमि *f.*; (*a.*) पर्वतीय, उन्नत; h.-lander' पर्वतीयः, पर्वतवासिन् *m.*; 'h.-mettled' महासत्त्व, उरुसत्त्व, ओजस्विन्, अदीनचित्त, तेजस्विन्; गर्वित, अतिमदान्वित; 'h.-minded' महात्मन्, महामनस्क, उदार-धी-चेतस्-चरित, महेच्छ, महाशय; 'h.-principled' साधुचरित्र, पुण्यात्मन्, पुण्यशील; 'h.-priest, पुरोहिताध्यक्षः; 'h.-prized' महामूल्य, महार्घ, बहुमत; 'h.-red' घनारुण, अतिरक्त; 'h.-road, -street,-way' राजमार्गः-पथः, महापथः-मार्गः, घंटापथः, संसरणं, रथ्या, विशिखा, प्रतोली; 'h.-seasoned' सुवासित; 'h.-spirited' महा-उरु-सत्त्व, अदीनवृत्ति, ओजस्विन्, ऊर्जित, महेच्छ; 'a h.-spirited speech' ऊर्जिताश्रयं वचनं (KI. II. 1); 'h. treason' राजद्रोहः, राजापथ्यकारित्वं; 'h.-wrought' यत्नसंस्कृत, प्रयत्नपरिष्कृत; 'h.-wayman' परिपंथिन् *m.*, दस्युः, वाटपाटच्चरः, पादाविकन्नः. —EST, *a.* उच्चैस्तम, तुंगतम, उत्तम, परम. —LY, *adv.* उच्चैः. 2 भृशं, अत्यंतं, नितांतं, परमं, परं, अतीव, अति-सु pr.; *See* EXCEEDINGLY; 'h. pleased' परमानंदभाज्, हर्षकाष्ठां गत. —NESS, *s.* देवः (वी *f.*), अत्रतत्र-भवत् (ती *f.*). —HEIGHT, *s.* उच्छ्रायः, उच्छ्र्यः, उत्सेधः, आरोहः, उन्नयः, तुंगता, उच्चता; उत्कर्षः, उन्नति *f.* 2 उच्चस्थानं, उत्सेधः, उन्नतभूभागः, गिरिः, पर्वतः. 3 शिखरं, अग्रं, शृंगं, शिखा, चूडा. 4 (परा) काष्ठा, कोटिः; अतिभूमिः, परमावधिः, उत्तमावधिः; 'being in the h. of joy' आनंदकोटिमधिगत. 5 कुलोत्कर्षः, परमपदं, श्रेष्ठत्वं, विशिष्टता; 'the h. of winter' शिशिरमध्यं, कठोरीभूतः शिशिरः. —EN, *v. t.* उन्नी 1 P, उत्कृष् 1 P. 2 वृध् c., उपचि 5 U, श्वि c., स्फाय् c. (स्फावयति); *See* ADD to.

HILARITY, *s.* आनंदः, उल्लासः, प्रमोदः, कौतुकं, आह्लादः, उत्सवः; *See* DELIGHT.

HILL, *s.* गिरिः, पर्वतः, अद्रिः, शैलपादः; 'h. near a mountain' पादः, प्रत्यंतपर्वतः. —OCK, *s.* वप्रः, उन्नतभूभागः; वामलूरः, वल्मीकः-कं, नाकुः, मृत्तिकाचयः. —Y, *a.* पर्वतमय (यी *f.*), सपर्वत, पर्वतीय, उन्नतानत, विषम.

HILT, *s.* त्सरुः, मुष्टि *m. f.*, खड्गमुष्टिः.

HIND, *s.* मृगी, हरिणी, कुरंगी, एणी, पृषती. 2 ग्राम्यजनः, ग्रामिकः, वृषलः.

HINDER, *a.* पश्चिम, जघन्य, पश्चात् in comp., चरम, अपर, अवर; 'h. part' पश्चाद्भागः, पृष्ठदेशः-भागः, पृष्ठं, नितंबः, पश्चिमभागः.

HINDER, *v. t.* नि-विनि-वार् 10 or वृ c., नि-प्रति-षिध् 1 P, रुध् 7 U, नि-उप-अव-सं-प्रति°, स्तंभ् 9 P, बाध् 1 A, वि-प्रति-हन् 2 P, प्रतिबंध् 9 P. —ANCE, *s.* प्रतिषेधः, निवारणं, प्रतिबंधः, विघ्नः, अंतरायः, प्रत्यूहः, प्रतिरोधः, व्याघातः, बाधा, विष्टंभः. —ER, *s.* निवारकः, प्रतिबंधकः, विघ्नकृत् *m.*

HINGE, *s.* कीलं, द्वारसंधिः-ग्रंथिः. —*v. i.* (upon) अवलंब् 1 A, अपेक्ष् 1 A; *See* DEPEND.

HINT, *s.* इंगितं, आकूतं, सूचना, संज्ञा, भावः, संकेतः, आशयः. 2 उपन्यासः, उपक्षेपः. —*v. t.* इंगितेन सूच् 10, उपन्यस् 4 U, सूच्, उपक्षिप् 6 P, उद्दिश् 6 P, साकूतं निर्दिश् or उपन्यस्.

HIP, *s.* कटि-टी *f.*, नितंबः, श्रोणि-णी *f.*, कटः, प्रोथः, जघनं, श्रोणिफलकं.

HIPPOPOTAMUS, *s.* करियादस् *n.*

HIRE, *v. t.* वेतनेन-मूल्यदानेन नि-प्र-युज् 7 A, 10 or व्या-पृ c. or उप-भुज् 7 P or सेव् 1 A or ग्रह् 9 P, परिक्री 9 A, भट् 1 P or c., भृतिं दा 3 U; 'h. labourers' कर्मकरान् उपनी 1 A or कर्मणि व्यापृ c.; 'a h. ed labourer' भृतिभुज्, भरण्यभुज्, भृतकः; 'a person h. ed' कृत-कल्पित-वेतनः. —*s.* वेतनेन ग्रहणं or व्यापारणं, वेतनदानं. 2 भृति *f.*, भृत्या,

भरण्यं, वेतनं, भाटकं, मूल्यं, कर्मण्या, विधा, भर्मन् *n.*, निर्वेशः, पणः, निष्क्रयः; 'for h.' पण्य, वेतनेन ग्राह्य, साधारण; 'a woman for h.' पण्यांगना, पण्यस्त्री; 'a teacher for h.' भृतकाध्यापकः. –LING, *s.* 'worker for h.' भृतकः, भृतिभुक्, भरण्यभुक्, वैतनिकः; कर्मकरः, भृत्यः.

HIRSUTE, *a.* लोमश, प्रचुरलोमन्.

HISS, *v. i.* फूत्कारं कृ 8 U or उद्-गॄ 6 P, सीत्कारं कृ, सर्पवत् श्वस् 2 P; 'h. off' सीत्कारेण असंतोषं सूच् 10 or दृश् c. –*s.*,–ING, *s.* फूत्कारः, सीत्कारः, सर्पश्वासः-नादः.

HIST, *adv.* तूष्णीं भव, वाचंयम. *a.* भव.

HISTORY, *s.* इतिहासः, पुरावृत्तं, पुराभूतं, पुराणोपाख्यानं, उपाख्यानं, चरित्रवर्णनं. 2 वृत्तांतः, उदंतः, समाचारः, वार्ता. –IC,–ICAL, *a.* ऐतिहासिक (की *f.*), पुरावृत्तविषयक, पौराणिक (की *f.*). –ICALLY, *adv.* इतिहासानुसारेण. –HISTORIAN,–HISTORIOGRAPHER, *s.* इतिहास-पुरावृत्त-लेखकः-रचकः, पुराणरचकः, चरित्रलेखकः, ऐतिहासिकः.

HISTRIONIC,-AL, *a.* नाटकीय, रंग-नाट्य-योग्य, रंगानुरूप.

HIT, *v. t.* प्र-हृ 1 P, तड् 10; अभि-नि-आ-हन् 2 P, तुद् 6 P, व्यध् 4 P. 2 (Upon) (दैवात्) आ-सद् c., प्राप् 5 P, अधिगम् 1 P, लभ् 1 A; 'arrows h. a moving mark' इषवः सिध्यंति लक्ष्ये चले (S. 2). –*v. i.* संघट्ट् 1 A, समा-प्रति-हन्, अभि-सं-पत् 1 P. –*s.* प्रहारः, आघातः, ताडनं, घातः. 2 दैवघटना, संगति *f.*, दैवं.

HITCH, *v. t.* ग्रह् 9 P, धृ 1 P, 10, आकृष् 1 P. –*v. i.* ग्रह्-धृ -pass. 2 HOP, q. v. –*s.* अंतरायः, प्रत्यूहः; *See* OBSTACLE.

HITHE, *s.* घट्टः, तरस्थानं.

HITHER, *adv.* अत्र, इह, इतः. –MOST, *a.* आसन्नतम, नेदिष्ठ, अत्यंतिक. –WARD, *adv.* इतः, अत्र. –HITHERTO, *adv.* अद्ययावत्, आवर्तमानकालात्, अद्यावधि, एतत्कालपर्यंतं.

HIVE, *s.* मधुकोषः, करंडः, छत्रकः, चषालः. –*v. t.* मधुकोषे निधा 3 U or निविश् c.

HOAR, *a.* धवल, शुभ्र, सित, श्वेत, शुक्ल; *See* WHITE; 'h.-frost' तुषारः, अवश्यायः; *See* FROST.

HOARD, *s.* संचयः, निचयः, निवहः, पुंजः, राशिः, गणः, संघः, संग्रहः, निधिः; *See* MULTITUDE. –*v. t.* संचि 5 U, संग्रह् 9 P, समा-हृ 1 P, राशीकृ 8 U, पुंजीकृ.

HOARSE, *a.* रूक्ष, परुष, कर्कश; भग्न, सगद्गद. –LY, *adv.* रूक्षस्वरेण, स्वरभंगेन, सगद्गदं. –NESS, *s.* भंगः, भेदः, रूक्षता; स्वरभंगः-रूक्षता.

HOARY, *a.* सित, धवल, श्वेत, शुक्ल, गौर (री *f.*), शुभ्र. 2 पलित, पक्व-पलित-केश.

HOAX, *s.* वंचनं-ना, प्रतारणं-णा, छलं, कपटं, विप्रलंभः. –*v. t.* वंच् 10, प्र-तॄ c., विप्र-लभ् 1 A.

HOB, *s.* वृषलः, ग्राम्यः, जानपदः.

HOBBLE, *v. i.* *See* LIMP.

HOBBY, *s.* प्रियवस्तु-द्रव्यं, चिरकाम्यं; निर्बंधः, अभीष्टमनोरथः, लहरी, छंदः. अभिरुचि *f.*; 'h.-horse' क्रीडाश्वः, क्रीडाद्रव्यं, क्रीडनकं.

HOBGOBLIN, *s.* भूतः, पिशाचः, वेतालः, राक्षसः; *See* DEMON, DEVIL.

HOCUS-POCUS, *s.* मंत्रतंत्रं, कुहकः, इंद्रजालं.

HOD, *s.* लेपाधारः, सुधाभाजनं.

HODGE-PODGE, *s.* संकरः, सन्निपातः, नानाद्रव्यसमूहः, प्रकीर्णकं.

HOE, *s.* खनित्रं, अवदारणः, स्तंबघ्नः. –*v. t.* खनित्रेण खन् 1 P, भूमिं भिद् 7 P, अव-दॄ 10.

HOG, *s.* वराहः, किरिः, शू(सू)करः; *See* BOAR; 'village h.' विट्चरः, ग्राम्यः; 'h.-herd' शूकरपालः-पोषकः; 'h.-sty' शूकरस्थानं-वासः. –GISH, *a.* शूकरोपम, शूकरीय, वाराह (ही *f.*), सूकरगुणविशिष्ट.

HOGO, *s.* अति-तीक्ष्ण-स्वादः.

HOG-WEED, *s.* शोथघ्नी, पुनर्नवा, शोथजित् *f.*

HOIDEN, *s.* पुंश्चली, बंधकी, स्वैरिणी, प्रगल्भा.

HOIST, *v. t.* उन्नम् c. (नमयति), उद्गम् c., उच्छ्रि c., उद्यम् 1 A, उन्नी 1 P, उद्-धृ-हृ 1 P, उत्तुल् 10, उत्था c. (उत्थापयति).

HOLD, *v. t.* धृ 1 P, 10, अव-लंब् 1 A, आ-दा 3 A, ग्रह् 9 P, परामृश् 6 P, हस्तेन धृ or अवलंब्. 2 स्तंभ् 9 P, नि-अव-रुध् 7 U, बलाद् धृ. 3 (Possess) भृ 3 U, आ-धा 3 U; *See* HAVE. 4 (Contain) धृ, परिग्रह्, आ-धा, समाविश् c., भृ, आ-दा. 5 पा c. (पालयति), रक्ष् 1 P, न त्यज् 1 P. 6 (As a festival) अनुष्ठा 1 P, सेव् 1 A, पा c. (पालयति), कृ 8 U, सं-पद् c., निर्वह् c., वि-धा, यथाविधि कृ, अभिनंद् c. 7 मन् 4 A, गण् 10; *See* CONSIDER; 'I h. them of no account' का-किंपर्ता-मात्रा तेषां मत्पुरतः, तानहं तृणाय मन्ये or तृणीकरोमि; 'h. an opinion' मतं अवलंब् or आश्रि 1 U, मन्; 'h. one's tongue' जिह्वां धृ or रक्ष्; 'h. your tongue' वाचंयमो भव, वाचं नियच्छ, तूष्णीं-जोषं-आस्स्व; 'h. a meeting' सभां मिल् c. or समा-ह्वे 1 P; 'a meeting was held' परिषद् मिलिता; 'h. in esteem' बहु मन्; 'h. in contempt' अवगण्, अवमन्, तृणीकृ, तृणाय मन्; 'h. a council' सभां निमंत्र् 10 A or आह्वे; 'h. a consultation' संमंत्र्, मंत्रणां कृ; 'I h. you responsible for this act' अस्य त्वयोत्तरं दातव्यं. –*v. i.* स्था 1 P, स्थिरीभू, सं-स्था 1 A; चिरस्थायीभू, स्थायीभू. 2 अनुबंध् 9 P or pass.; सं-संज् pass., संलग्नीभू, आलंब् 1 A. 3 विरम् 1 P, निवृत् 1 A (with abl.);

आत्मानं संयम् 1 A or निग्रह्, परिह् 1 P, त्यज्; 'hold, hold !' विरम विरम, मा मा एवं, मा तावत्. 4 अधीन- *a.* भू, आश्रि, अव-आ-लंब्. 5 (As a rule) गम्, न व्यभिचर् 1 P; 'this rule h. s everywhere' सर्वगामी-अव्यभिचारी-अयं नियमः. **–***s.* धरणं, धृति *f.*, ग्रहः-हणं, अवलंबः-बनं, हस्तेन ग्रहणं-धरणं; 'letting go the h.' मुक्त-स्रस्त-हस्त, मुक्तग्रह. 2 कारा, कारागृहं, कारागारं, बंधनस्थानं, गुप्ति *f.* 3 आधारः, आ-अव-लंबः-बनं, उपस्तंभः, आश्रयः. 4 दुर्गं, कोटः. 5 मुष्टि *m. f.*, वारंगः. 6 आस्पदं, पदं, अधिकारः, वशः-शं; 'red colour takes a firm h. on a white cloth' रागः शुक्लपटे स्थायीभवति (P. I. 1); 'had a h. on the mind of the people' स लोकस्य मन आददे (R. IV. 8); 'the advice took no h. on (her) mind' तस्यैंतरं चेतसि नोपदेशः (R. VI. 66). –back, नि-वृ c., वार् 10, संहृ 1 P, निग्रह्, विक्लृप् 1 A, विचर् c.; *See* HESITATE. –forth, दृश् c., पुरो निधा. –in, निग्रह्, प्रतिसंहृ, नि-सं-यम्. –off, विलंब् 1 A, विक्लृप्. –on, प्रवृत् c., न विरम्, न मुच् 6 P, न त्यज्, उद्वह् 1 P, निर्वह् c. –out, प्रसृ c., वितन् 8 U, दीर्घीकृ. 2 दृश् c., उपन्यस् 4 U, उपक्षिप् 6 P, उप-स्था c. (स्थापयति); (*v. i.*) चिरं यावत्सह् 1 A or युध् 4 A or प्रतिकृ. –together, संबंध् pass., संश्लिष् 4 P, संलग् 1 P. –up, उन्नम् c. (नमयति), उद्यम्, उच्छ्रि 1 U or c., ऊर्ध्वीकृ. 2 उत्तंभ्, अवष्टंभ्, आ-अव-लंब्, भृ, धृ. **–ER,** *s.* धारकः, धारयितृ *m.*, ग्राहकः, धरः-आधारः-in comp. **–ING,** *s.* धरणं, ग्रहणं, &c. **–***a.* धारिन्, धर in comp.; oft. by हस्त in comp.; 'h. a sword' कृपाणपाणिः. **–HOLDFAST,** *s.* ग्राहकः, ग्रहणी, बंधनी, कुड्यः. 2 दृढ-बद्ध-मुष्टिः, अमुक्तहस्तः.

HOLE, *s.* विवरं, बिलं, छिद्रं, रंध्रं, सुषि(षि)रं, कुहरं, निर्व्यथनं, रोकं, वपा, सुषि *f.*; श्वभ्रं, गर्तः-र्ता, अवटः (in the ground). 2 कंदरः-रं-रा, गुहा, गह्वरं, दरी, खातं (of mountains). 3 (Of garments &c. or fig.) रंध्रं, छिद्रं; 'a rat digs a h. and a snake uses it' एकः परिश्रमं करोति, अन्यस्तत्फलमुपभुंक्ते; 'picking h. s (in the character &c.) of others' छिद्रान्वेषिन्, दोषैकदृश्, पुरोभागिन्, रंध्रानुसारिन्; 'full of h. s' अनेकरंध्र, बहुविवर.

HOLLOW, *a.* रिक्त-शून्य-गर्भ, अंतःशून्य, शून्यमध्य-उदर; उदराकृति, सुषिर, पुटाकार. 2 असार, निःसत्त्व, निःसार, फल्गु, शून्य. 3 मोघ, निरर्थक, निष्फल. 4 असत्य, वितथ, मिथ्या, in comp. 5 ग(गं)भीर, मंद्र, मंद. **–***s.* (Of trees) कोटरः-रं, क्रोडः, निष्कुहः. 2 विवरं, गुहा, बिलं, कुहरं, अवटः; *See* HOLE. 3 गर्भः, उदरं, अभ्यंतरं, क्रोडं. 4 खातं, खातभूः, गर्तः-र्ता. 5 दरी, कंदरः, अद्रिद्रोणी, कंदरभूः. 6 कुल्या, प्रणाली; 'h. of the hand' पुटः, करपुटः-कोषः; 'h. of the navel' नाभिगर्ता, नाभ्यावर्तः; 'ground full of h. s' उत्खातिनी भूमिः (S. 1); 'natural h.' देवखातं; 'h. of the ear' ऋषभः; 'h. s in the buttocks' जघनकूपकौ, गर्तौ. **–***v. t.* उत्खन् 1 P, पुटीकृ 8 U. **–NESS,** *s.* शून्यता, असारता, असत्यता, &c.

HOLY, *a.* पुण्य, पवित्र, परिपूत, साधु, शुचि, विमल; पुण्यात्मन्, शुचिव्रत, धार्मिक (की *f.*), धर्म-पुण्यशील, धर्मात्मन्, शुद्धमति; 'h. study' वेदाध्ययनं; 'h. wisdom' ब्रह्मज्ञानं; 'h. writing' श्रुतिः, वेदाः, निगमः; 'h. land' पुण्यभूमिः; 'h. place of pilgrimage' तीर्थं, क्षेत्रं, पुण्यस्थानं-तीर्थं. **–LY,** *adv.* पुण्यं, पवित्रतया, शुचिवत्. **–NESS,** *s.* पवित्रता, पुण्यता, शुचिता, वैमल्यं, पुण्यशीलता, धार्मिकत्वं; 'his or her h.' भगवान्, भगवती. **–HOLIDAY,** *s.* पुण्याहं, पुण्यदिनं. 2 अनध्यायः, अनध्यायदिवसः-महोत्सवः. 3 उत्सवः, पर्वन् *n.*, उद्धर्षः, उत्सव-उद्धर्ष-दिनं; 'h. people' यात्राजनः.

HOMAGE, *s.* नमस्कारः, अभिवंदनं, प्रणामः, प्रणति *f.*, पूजा, अर्चनं, उपासना, प्रणिपातः, सेवांजलिः; सेवा, आदरः, प्रभुभक्ति *f.*; 'pay or do h.' प्रणम् 1 P, वंद् 1 A, प्रणिपत् 1 P; *See* BOW.

HOME, *s.* गृहं, वासः, वासस्थानं-भूमि *f.*, स्वगृहं, स्व-निज-गेहं-देशः-वासः-स्थानं-भवनं; *See* HOUSE; 'devoted to h.' गृहासक्तचित्त. **–***adv.* गृहं, गृहं प्रति; 'the words went h. to his heart' तद्वचः तस्य हृदयमर्मास्पृशत्; 'touching h.' मर्मस्पृश्-भिद्; 'goes h. to me' मामेव लक्षीकरोति (S. 7); 'h.-born' गृहजात; 'h.-bound' गृहगामिन्; 'h.-bred' गृहज-जात, गृह्य; 'h.-made' गृहनिर्मित, गृहोत्पन्न; 'h.-sick' गृहविरहार्त; 'h.-stall,-stead' गृहं, वासः; वेश्मभूः, वास्तु *m. n.* **–LESS,** *a.* निरालय, निराश्रय, निर्गृह. **–LY,** *a.* गृह्य, गृहज. 2 ग्राम्य, ग्रामीण-य, अशिष्ट, प्राकृत, असभ्य, अश्लील, असंस्कृत. **–***adv.* ग्राम्यवत्, असभ्यतया, अशिष्टप्रकारेण. **–WARD,** *adv.* गृहाभिमुखं, अभिगृहं.

HOMICIDE, *s.* नृहत्या, मनुष्यवधः. 2 (Person) मनुष्यघातिन् *m.*, नृहंतृ *m.*, मनुष्यघातकः. **–AL,** *a.* नृघातिन्.

HOMILY, *s.* धर्मवाक्यं.

HOMOGENEAL, HOMOGENEOUS, *a.* समानजाति-जातीय, स-एक-जाति, सवर्ण, एक-स-धर्मन्, समानभाव, एक-स-जातीय; 'h. vowels' सवर्णाः.

HOMOLOGOUS, *a.* तुल्य-सम-परिमाण.

HOMONYM, *s.* भिन्नार्थः शब्दः; 'a collection of h. s' भिन्नार्थवर्गः. **–OUS,** *a.* भिन्नार्थ, अनेकार्थ.

HONE, *s.* शाणः, शाणाश्मन् *m.*

HONEST, *a.* शुचि, ऋजु, सरल, अमायिन्, दक्षिण, अ-

कुटिल, अजिह्म, शुद्धमति-भाव, शुद्धात्मन्, अकपट, निष्कपट, निर्व्याज, निर्व्यलीक, अव्याज, विमलात्मन्, दंभहीन, न्याय्य, न्याय्याचार, सच्चरित, न्यायवर्तिन्, साधुवृत्त-शील, साधु, प्रांजल, सत्यवृत्त, सत्यशील, सत्यवादिन्. 2 अवितथ, सत्य, अकृत्रिम, अकृतक; *See* FRANK also; 'h. gains' न्यायार्जितं; 'h. statement' निर्व्याजं वचनं. -LY, *adv.* सरलं, न्यायेन, न्यायतः, शुचितया, निष्कपटं, निर्व्याजं, अमायया, निर्व्यलीकं. -Y, *s.* शुचिता, आर्जवं, निष्कापट्यं, सारल्यं, अकौटिल्यं, दाक्षिण्यं, अमाया, अकपटं, अव्याजः, शुद्धभावः, वैमल्यं, निर्व्यलीकता, अजिह्मता, सत्यता, अकृतकता; 'h. is the best policy' भावशुद्धिः एव साधिष्ठा आचारसरणिः, सारल्यं सत्तमो मार्गः.

HONEY, *s.* मधु *n.*, क्षौद्रं, माक्षिकं, सारघं; 'h. of flowers' पुष्पासवं, पुष्परसः-सारः, कुसुममधु; 'h.-bee' मधुमक्षिका, सरघा; 'h.-comb' मधुकोशः, करंडः; 'h.-moon' आनंदमासः; 'h.-tongued' मधुरभाषिन्, मधुरवाच्. -*v. t.* मधुरीकृ 8 U. -*v. i.* उपलल् 10; *See* FAWN. -ED, *a.* मधुमधुर, सुधास्यंदिन्, मधुर.

HONOR, *v. t.* पूज् 10, अर्च् 1 P, 10, मन् c., संभू c., सत्कृ 8 U, पुरस्कृ, मह् 1 P, 10, आदृ 6 A. 2 सेव् 1 A, श्रु desid. (शुश्रूषते), आराध् c.; 'h. ed the invitation' निमंत्रणमाद्रियत, सगौरवं स्वीचकार. 3 अनुग्रह् 9 P, प्रसद् 1 P (with loc.). -*s.* मानः, संमानः, पूजा, अर्चनं, अर्हणा, संभावना, आदरः, सत्कारः. 2 सेवा, शुश्रूषा, आराधनं. 3 ख्याति *f.*, कीर्ति *f.*, यशस् *n.*, प्रतिष्ठा, गौरवं, प्रतिपत्ति *f.*, उत्कर्षः, उत्कृष्ट-प्रधान-पदं, उन्नति *f.*; कुलीनता, आभिजात्यं, प्राधान्यं, श्रेष्ठत्वं; 'your or his h.' अत्र-तत्र-भवान्; भवत्. -ABLE, *a.* पूज्य, मान्य, माननीय, पूजार्ह, आदरणीय. 2 सु-प्र-विख्यात, विश्रुत, सुप्रसिद्ध, प्रतिपत्तिमत्, महायशस्. 3 यशस्कर-कीर्तिकर (री *f.*), प्रतिष्ठावह, श्लाघ्य, प्रशस्य, मानद, गौरवान्वित. 4 कुलीन, अभिजात, महाकुल, उदारचित्त-चरित; *See* NOBLE. 5 शुचि, न्याय्याचार, सच्चरित, साधुवृत्त, पुण्यात्मन्, शुचिव्रत; *See* HONEST. -ARY, *a.* मानद, कीर्तिकर, यशस्कर, प्रशस्य. 2 अलाभकर, मानमात्रदायिन्. -HONORABLY, *adv.* समानं, सगौरवं, श्लाघ्यप्रकारेण, प्रशंसापूर्वं, सुयशसा, प्रतिष्ठापूर्वं. 2 शुचिवत्, धार्मिकतया, ऋजुतया, सरलतया, न्यायतः.

HOOD, *s.* फणा-णः, फटा, स्फोटा; 'expands the h.' फणां कुरुते (S. 6); 'expanded h.' भोगः. 2 फणाकृति शिरस्कं. -*v. t.* शिरस्त्राणेन पिधा 3 U or प्रावृ 5 U.

HOODWINK, *v. t.* (नयने) वस्त्रेण पिधा 3 U or आच्छद् 10 or आवृ 5 U.

HOOF, *s.* खुरः, शफः-फं, क्षुरः, विखः, निघृष्वः. -ED, *a.* खुरिन्, खुरयुक्त, शफयुक्त.

HOOK, *s.* आकर्षणी, ग्रहणी, धरणी; 'fish-h.' बडिशं-शा-शी, मत्स्यवेधनी; 'h. for elephants' अंकुशः, श्रु(सृ)णि *f.* -*v. t.* बडिशेन धृ 1 P or ग्रह् 9 P. -ED, *a.* वक्र, कुटिल, कुंचित, अंकुशाकार, जिह्म; *See* CROOKED.

HOOP, *s.* चक्रं, वलयः-यं. 2 क्रीडाचक्रं. -*v. t.* लोहवलयैः युज् 10. 2 उच्चैः घुष् 10.

HOOT, *s.* घु(घू)त्कारः. 2 धिक्कारः, उच्चैः अप्रशंसासूचनं, दीर्घघोषः. -*v. i.* घूत्काररवं कृ 8 U, उच्चैः आरट् 1 P or घुष् 10, दीर्घं रु 2 P; 'h. at' उच्चैः अवज्ञां-धिक्कारं-सूच् 10.

HOP, *v. i.* प्लु 1 A, वल्ग् 1 U, एकपादेन नृत् 4 P. -*s.* प्लुतं, वल्गितं, प्लवः, एकपादेन नृत्यं.

HOPE, *v. t.* आशंस् 1 A, उत्-प्रति-अप-ईक्ष् 1 A, स्पृह् 10, प्रत्याकांक्ष् 1 P, वांछ् 1 P, आशां धृ or वह् 1 P; in implied questions, gen. ex. by अपि, कच्चित् or अपि नाम; 'I h. this lotus-leaf breeze pleases you' अपि सुखायते ते नलिनीपत्रवातः (S. 3); अपि नाम रामभद्रः पुनरपीदं वनमलंकुर्यात् (U. 2), कच्चिन्मृगीणामनघा प्रसूतिः (R. v. 7); 'I h. not' न खलु; न खलु तामभिक्रुद्धो गुरुः (V. 3) 'I h. the preceptor did not get angry with her'; 'I scarcely h. ed to see you here' न खलु मे आसीदाशंसा यदत्र भवंतं प्रेक्षिष्ये. -*s.* आशा, प्रत्याशा, आशंसा, आकांक्षा, अपेक्षा, प्रतीक्षा, उदीक्षणं; स्पृहा, मनोरथः, वांछा, इच्छा, आशाबंधः. 2 (Giving h.) आश्वासनं, आश्वासः; 'having h. s fulfilled' पूर्णाश; 'a vain h.' वृथाभिलाषः, मोघाशा; 'h.-ing against h.' अतीव दुरापेतं. -FUL, *a.* आशान्वित, आशावत्, आशायुक्त, आशाबद्ध, स्पृहयालु, अपेक्षिन्, सप्रत्याश, आशाविष्ट. 2 (Giving hopes) आशाजनन (नी *f.*), आशाकारिन्. -FULLY, *adv.* साशंसं, सप्रत्याशं. -LESS, *a.* निराश, आशातीत, आशाहीन, हताश, त्यक्ताश, निरपेक्ष. -LESSLY, *adv.* नैराश्यात्, सनैराश्यं.

HORAL, HORARY, *a.* मौहूर्तिक (की *f.*).

HORDE, *s.* महान् गणः, बृहत्संघः, महौघः, स्तोमः; *See* MULTITUDE.

HORIZON, *s.* क्षितिजं, दिङ्मंडलं, दिक्चक्रं, अंबरांतः; चक्रं, मंडलं; 'the eastern h.' प्राची-ऐंद्री-दिक्, प्राचीमूलं. —HORIZONTAL, *a.* सम, दिगंतसम, अनुप्रस्थ; 'h. plane' समभूभागः, समा भूमिः. -LY, *adv.* समं, अनुप्रस्थं.

HORN, *s.* शृंगं, विषाणः-णं, कूणिका; 'h. of a buffalo' गवलं. 2 काहलः-ला, शंखः. 3 चंद्राग्रं, चंद्रशिखा. -ED, *a.* शृंगिन्, विषाणिन्, शृंगयुक्त-विशिष्ट. 2 शृंगाकार, शृंगाकृति. -Y, *a.* शार्ंग (र्गी *f.*). 2 कठिन; *See* HARD.

HORNET, *s.* वरटा, बृहद्दंशः.

Horologue, *s.* घटी, कालमापनयंत्रं.

Horoscope, *s.* जन्मपत्रिका, जन्मपत्रं, जन्मयोगपत्रं.

Horror, *s.* त्रासः, संत्रासः, साध्वसं, भयकंपः, भयसंहर्षः. 2 बीभत्सता, रौद्रता, घोरता, भैरवं, भयानकं, भीष्मं, भीषणं. —**Horrific**, *a.* भीषण, उग्र, भयानक, भयावह. —**Horrid**, **Horrible**, *a.* घोर, दारुण, भीम, भयानक, उग्र, भीषण, कराल, विकट; *See* **Fearful**. —**ly**, *adv.* घोरं, दारुणं, रौद्रं, उग्रतया; बीभत्सतया. —**Horrify**, *v. t.* Frighten, q. v. —**ed**, *a.* साध्वसोपहत, भीत, संत्रस्त, भयसंहृष्ट.

Horripilate, *v. t.* पुलकयति-कंटकयति-रोमांचयति (D.), रोमाणि उद्गम् c. or उद्-हृष् c. —**ed**, *a.* पुलकित, कंटकित, सपुलक, रोमांचित. —**ion**, *s.* पुलकः, रोमांचः, रोमहर्षः-र्षणं, रोमोद्गमः-द्गतत्वं, पुलकोद्भेदः, उद्धर्षणं.

Horse, *s.* अश्वः, तुरगः, तुरंगः-गमः, हयः, सप्तिः, वाजिन् *m.*, वाहः, अर्वन् *m.*, घोटकः, वीतिः; गंधर्वः, सैंधवः; 'a well-bred h.' आजानेयः, कुलीनः, भूमिरक्षकः, सिंधुवारः; 'a well-trained h.' साधुवाही, विनीतः; 'a white h.' कर्कः; 'a bay h.' उकनाहः, कियाहः; 'a fleet h.' जवनः, जवाधिकः; 'a pack-h.' पृष्ठ्यः, स्थौरी, स्थोरी; 'a h. for a sacrifice' ययुः, अश्वमेधीयः; 'a chariot-h.' रथ्यः; 'h.'s pace' गतिः, धारा; (namely) आस्कंदितं 'full gallop'; धो(धौ)रितकं, धोरितं 'trot or ambling'; रेचितं 'cantering'; वल्गितं 'vaulting'; प्लुतं 'bounding or capering'; 'his nose' घोणा, प्रोथः-थं; 'tail hair' बालधिः, बालहस्तः; 'his tail' पुच्छः-च्छं, लूमं, लांगूलं; 'a number of h.'s आश्वं, अश्वीयं; 'relating to a h.' अश्वीय, आश्विक (की *f.*); 'h.-soldiers' आश्वं, आश्विकं, अश्वारोहगणः; 'h.-back' अश्वपृष्ठं; 'go on h.-back' अश्वेन गम् or चर् 1 P; 'going on h.-back' तुरंगयायिन्, सादिन्; 'h.-bean' मुद्गः, माषः, शिंबा; 'h.-breaking' अश्वशिक्षा-दमनं-विनयः; 'h.-breaker' अश्वविनेता-शिक्षकः; 'h.-dealer' अश्वव्यापारी, हयज्ञः; 'h.-driving' अश्वसारथ्यं, रथवाहनकौशलं; 'h.-laugh' अट्टहासः, अतिहासः, अतिहसितं, आच्छुरितं; 'h.-man' अश्वारोहः, तुरंगस्थः, सादिन् *m.*, तुरगी, हयारूढः, अश्वारूढः; 'h.-manship' अश्वारोहणकौशलं-विद्या, अश्वविद्या, अश्वहृदयं; 'h.-shoe' अश्वपादत्रं; 'h.-trappings' आदानं, अश्वपरिष्टोमः, अश्वास्तरणं; 'h.-whip' कशा, अश्वताडनी, प्रतिष्कषः-शः, चर्मदंडः; (*v. t.*) कशया तड् 10 or प्र-हृ 1 P.

Horticulture, *s.* उद्यानविद्या, उद्यानपालनं. —**ist**, *s.* उद्यानविद्याज्ञः.

Hose, *s.* और्णं पादत्राणं. —**Hosier**, *s.* और्णपादत्रविक्रयिन् *m.*

Hospitable, *a.* आतिथेय (यी *f.*), सत्कारशील, अतिथिपूजक, आतिथ्यकारिन्. —**Hospitably**, *adv.* सादरं, सप्रश्रयं, सबहुमानं, आतिथेयसत्कारेण, सत्कारआतिथ्य-पूर्वं; 'to receive h.' सत्कृ 8 U, पूज् 10, सं-भू c.

Hospital, *s.* आतुरशाला, रुग्णागारं, आरोग्यचिकित्सा-शाला, रुजोपायशाला.

Hospitality, *s.* आतिथ्यं, आतिथ्यकर्मन् *n.*, अतिथिसत्कारः-पूजा-सेवा-क्रिया; सत्कारः, सत्क्रिया, सत्कृति *f.*, उपचारः, पूजा, सेवनं.

Host, *s.* गणः, संघः, समूहः, ओघः, निवहः; *See* **Multitude**. 2 चमूः, सेना, अनीकं, वरूथिनी. 3 गृहिन् *m.*, भोजनदायिन् *m.*, निमंत्रणकृत्, निमंत्रकः, आतिथ्यकृत्. —**age**, *s.* विश्वासस्थानं, शरीरबंधकः; 'retaining 4 hares as h. s' चतुरः शशकान् विश्वासस्थाने धृत्वा (P. I. 8). —**ess**, *s.* गृहिणी, भोजनदात्री, आतिथ्यकारिणी.

Hostel, **Hostelry**, *s.* पथिकाश्रमः, उत्तरण-गृहं-शाला.

Hostile, *a.* विपक्ष, विरुद्ध, वैरिन् प्रत्यर्थिन्, प्रतिकूल, विपरीत, विद्वेषिन्, अहित, प्रतिरोधिन्; 'a h. invasion' शत्रुविग्रहः, शत्रुयानं; 'to be h.' विरुध् 7 U, द्विष् 2 U; पर्यव-स्था 1 A, प्रतिकूलयति-वैरायते (D.), विपक्षी-प्रत्यर्थी-भू. —**ly**, *adv.* शत्रुवत्, विपक्षवत्. —**ity**, *s.* विपक्षता, वैरं, शत्रुता, वैरभावः, विरोधः, प्रतिद्वंद्वं, विद्वेषः; 'in a state of constant h.' सदाबद्धवैर *a.*; 'natural h.' स्वभाव-जाति-वैरं, शाश्वतिकः विरोधः. 2 विग्रहः, युद्धं, संग्रामः, युद्धभावः.

Hostler, *s.* अश्वपालकः.

Hot, *a.* उष्ण, आतपाक्रांत, आतपवत्, तप्त, सं-उत्-तप्त, सोष्ण; प्रखर, उग्र, तिग्म, चंड, खर, तीव्र, तीक्ष्ण. 2 ग्रीष्म, नैदाघ (घी *f.*), घर्म in comp. 3 शीघ्रसुलभ-कोपिन्, क्रोधिन्, संरंभिन्. 4 साहसिन्, तीक्ष्णकर्मन्; 'h. weather or season' ग्रीष्मः, निदाघः, घर्म-ग्रीष्म-उष्ण-कालः; 'to make h.' तप् c.; 'to be h.' तप् 1 P, 4 A, उष्णीभू; 'h.-bed' उष्णस्थलं, (fig.) क्षेत्रं; 'h.-blooded or -headed' चंडप्रकृति-शील, संरंभिन्, शीघ्रकोपिन्, उत्तप्त, प्रचंड, तीक्ष्णकर्मन्, साहसिक, साहसिन्. —**ly**, *adv.* तीक्ष्णं, तीव्रं, प्रचंडं, उग्रं, उष्णं; सोत्तापं; व्यग्रं, सोत्साहं, सोत्कटं. —**ness**, *s.* उष्णता, तापः, प्रखरता, उग्रता, चंडता, तिग्मता, औष्म्यं, निदाघः, घर्मता. 2 उत्तापः, तीक्ष्णता, संरंभः, व्यग्रता; 'h. of temper' शीघ्रकोपित्वं, चंडता.

Hotel, *s.* पथिकाश्रमः, भोजनगृहं.

Hotspur, *s.* संरंभिन् *m.*, साहसिकः.

Hough, *s.* जंघास्थिशिरा.

Hound, *s.* विश्वकद्रुः, मृगदंशकः, आखेटिकः, मृगयाकुक्कुरः.

Hour, *s.* घटी, घटिका, नाडिका; 'h.-drum'

नाडिकाविच्छेदघटह:. 2 (H.s) काल:; 'at all h. s' सदा, सर्वदा; 'in an evil h.' अशुभे लग्ने-मुहूर्ते; 'an h. and a half' अर्धयाम:. -LY, *a.* प्रतिघटिकं *adv.*

HOURI, *s.* दिव्यांगना, स्वर्गकन्या, दिव्ययोषित्.

HOUSE, *s.* गृहं, गेहं, अ(आ)गारं, सदनं, वेश्मन्-सद्मन् *n.*, निकेतनं, मंदिरं, वास:, आ-नि-वास:, भवनं, आयतनं, नि-आ-लय:, ओकस्-धामन् *n.*, वसति *f.*, निवासस्थानं, आवसथ:, उदवसितं, निकाय्य:, निशांतं, व(प)स्त्यं; 'body of a h.' गर्भागारं, वासगृहं. 2 कुलं, अन्वय:, वंश:. 3 गृहजन:, कुटुंबं, परिवार:; 'h.-breaker' कुडयच्छेदिन् *m.*, भित्ति-संधि-चौर:, कपाटघ्न:, गृहभेदक:; 'h.-dog' गृहकुक्कुर:; 'h.-door' गृहद्वारं; 'h.-hold' परिवार:, कुटुंबं-बकं, परिजन:, गृहपरिजन:-परिवार:; (*a.*) गृह्य, ex. by गृह in comp.; 'h.-hold duties' गृहकार्याणि, गृहाचारा:; 'h.-hold gods' कुलदेवता:; 'h.-holder' गृहिन् *m.*, गृहस्थ:, गृहपति:, गृहमेधी, कुटुंबी, गेही; 'h.-hold stuff' गृहोपस्कार:, गृहसामग्री; 'h.-keeper' गृहस्वामिन् *m.*, गृही, गृहाधिकारी, कुटुंबी; 'a female h.-keeper' गृहिणी, कुटुंबिनी; 'h.-keeping' गृहव्यापार:-कार्यं-कर्म; 'h.-maid' दासी, गृहदासी-मार्जनी; 'h.-room' वासस्थानं, वेश्म; 'h.-warming' गृहप्रवेश:; 'h.-wife' गृहिणी, गेहिनी, गृहकार्यकुशला-दक्षा, गृहमेधिनी; 'h.-wifery' गृहकार्यकुशलता-नैपुण्यं, गृहकर्मानुष्ठानं, परिमितव्यय:. -LESS, *a.* गृहहीन-शून्य, निरालय, अशरण, निराश्रय, निर्गृह.

HOUSING, *s.* परिस्तो(स्त्रो)म:, सज्जा, कल्पना, कुथ:, आस्तर:, प्रसाधनं.

HOVEL, *s.* उटज:-जं, कुटीर:, कुटी, पर्णशाला, तृणकुटी.

HOVER, *v. i.* परित: विसृप् 1 P or डी 1 A, आकाशे व्यावृत् 1 A or विसृप् or विचल् 1 P, परिभ्रम् 1, 4 P; 'h. about' मंडले चर् 1 P, (दीपस्योपरि मंडले चरति Mr. 3); मंडलाकारेण भ्रम्. 2 (fig.) विशंक् 1 A, विक्लृप् 1 A, विचर् c. -ING, *s.* परिभ्रमणं, मंडलावृत्ति *f.*

HOW, *adv.* कथं, केन प्रकारेण-रूपेण. 2 कियत् (in 'how long,' 'how far'); 'h. much' कियत्; 'h. many' कति (pl.); 'h. long' कियच्चिरं, कियंतं कालं; 'h. many kinds' कतिविधा:; 'h. many times' कतिकृत्व:; 'h. now' ननु, ननु भो:; 'h. far' कियद्दूरं, कियदवधि; 'h. much more-less' किमुत, किं पुन:, किमु; 'h. else' अथ किं; with *adj.* ex. by अहो; 'h. pleasing' अहो मधुरं; अहो पापं, &c.

HOWDAH, *s.* वरंडक:.

HOWEVER, HOWSOEVER, *adv.* यथातथा, येनकेन प्रकारेण; (with *adj.*) by अपि, or by नाम with imp. of verb; 'h. industrious a man may be' दीर्घव्यवसायोपि नर:, करोतु नाम व्यवसायं नर: (H. 2). -*conj.* (Howbeit) किंतु, अपि तु, तु, परंतु, तथापि, पुन:.

HOWL, *v. i.* आक्रंद् 1 P, उत्क्रुश् 1 P, उच्चै: रस्-रद् 1 P, गर्ज् 1 P, दीर्घ वि-रु 2 P, रै 1 P. -*s.*, -ING, *s.* उत्क्रोश:-शनं, आक्रंदनं, दीर्घरुतं, आरटनं, र(रा)व:, दीर्घरव:, गर्जनं, रसितं; 'h. of dogs' भषणं, बुक्कनं, रायणं.

HUB, *s.* नाभि *f.* 2 त्सरु:. 3 लक्ष्यं, शरव्यं.

HUBBUB, *s.* कोलाहल:, कलकल:, तुमुलं, तुमुलरव:-नाद:, संकीर्णनाद:.

HUCKLEBONE, *s.* श्रोण्यस्थि *n.*

HUCKSTER, *s.* क्षुद्रपण्यविक्रयिन्-विक्रेतृ *m.* -*v. i.* क्षुद्रपण्यानि वि-क्री 9 A.

HUDDLE, *v. t.* पिंडीकृ 8 U, सं-कॄ 6 P, संमिश्र् 10, संकुलीकृ, संपिंडयति (D.). 2 संक्षुभ् c.; ससंभ्रमं वि-धा 3 U or कृ. -*v. i.* संकुलीभू 1 P, संमिश्री-संकरी-भू, संकॄ pass., पिंडीभू. -*s.* संकुलं, संकर:, संक्षोभ:, संकीर्णता.

HUE, *s.* राग:, रंग:, वर्ण:, छाया, छवि *f.* 2 आक्रोश:; 'h. and cry' कलकल:, कोलाहल:, जनरव:, संहूति *f.*

HUFF, *v. t.* विस्तॄ c., श्वि c., वृध् c. 2 सदर्पं निर्भर्त्स् or तर्ज् 10 A. -*v. i.* श्वि 1 P, स्फाय् 1 A, वृध् 1 A. 2 दृप् 4 P, विकत्थ् 1 A, प्रगल्भ् 1 A. -*s.* कोप:, रोष:, संरंभ:; *See* ANGER. 2 दर्प:, औद्धत्यं, निर्भर्त्सनं. 3 उद्धत:, दर्पाध्मात:, दांभिक:, विकत्थन:. -ER, *s.* दांभिक:, शूरंमन्य:, विकत्थन:. -ISH, *a.* Angry, Arrogant, q. v.

HUG, *v. t.* आलिंग् 1 P, आ-सं-श्लिष् 4 P, परिष्वंज् 1 A, बाहुभ्यां पीड् 10; *See* CLASP. -*s.* आश्लेष:, परिष्वंग:, आलिंगनं, उपगूहनं.

HUGE, *a.* महत्, बृहत्, स्थूल, विशाल, विपुल, गुरु, बृहत्परिमाण, अतिमहत्-बृहत्. 2 (In body) स्थूलकाय-देह, बृहच्छरीर, महाकाय, विपुलांग (गी *f.*). -LY, *adv.* अतिमहत्, अत्यंतं, अतिमात्रं. -NESS, *s.* अतिबृहत्त्वं, स्थूलता, विशालता.

HULK, *s.* जीर्णनौका.

HULL, *s.* (पोतस्य) स्थूलभाग:. 2 पुट:-टं, कोश:-ष:, त्वच् *f.*, आवेष्टनं, तुष: (of grain).

HUM, *v. i.* गुंज् 1 P, वि,-रु 2 P, हुंकृ 8 U, अस्पष्टं निस्वन् 1 P or ध्वन् 1 P. -*s.*,-MING, *s.* गुंजनं, गुंजितं, कलरव:-स्वर:, वि,-रुतं-राव:, झंकार:, हुंकार:, हुंकृतं, अस्पष्टध्वनि:-निस्वन:-नाद:, कलकल:.

HUMAN, *a.* मानुष (षी *f.*), पौरुषेय (यी *f.*), मनुष्यजातीय, मानवीय-न; gen. ex. by मनुष्य or नर in comp.; 'in h. accents' मनुष्यवाचा; 'uttered h. accents' मानुषीं गिरमुदीरयामास; 'h.

nature' मानुष्यकं, पुरुषत्वं, नरस्वभावः; 'h. form' मानुषी तनुः, नररूपं; 'a h. brute' नरपशुः; 'h. kind' मनुष्य-नृ-जाति *f.*, मनुष्यवर्गः. -IZE, *v. t.* वि-नी 1 P, शिष्टाचारं-सभ्यरीतिं शिक्ष् c. or शास् 2 P. -LY, *adv.* नरवत्, मानुषप्रकारेण. —HUMANE, *a.* दयालु, कृपालु, सदय, परहितकाम, परोपकारशील, अनुकंपिन्, करुणा-दया-शील, दयावत्, करुणार्द्र, दयार्द्र, परहितैषिन्, आपन्न-दीन-अनुकंपिन्; *See* KIND. -ITY, *s.* दया, करुणा, कृपा, दयालुता, आपन्नानुकंपा, दीनवात्सल्यं, दयाशीलता, परहितेच्छा. 2 मानुष्यं-ष्यकं, मनुष्यता, मानुषता, मानवत्वं. 3 मनुष्याः, मनुष्यवर्गः-जातिः. -LY, *adv.* सदयं, सकरुणं, परहितेच्छया, सानुकंपं.

HUMBLE, *a.* नीच, अपकृष्ट, अधम. 2 क्षुद्र, अल्पमति. 3 (In good sense) नम्र, विनीत, निरभिमान, विनत, सविनय, निरहंकार, अनुद्धत, दर्प-गर्व-अभिमान-हीन-रहित, नम्रचेतस्, विनयिन्, विनयशील-वृत्ति. 4 निःस्व, दरिद्र, दीन, दुर्गत, निर्धन, आपन्न; 'in h. days' आपत्समये, दरिद्रावस्थायां, आपदि; 'the friends of h. days' आपत्कालीनमित्राणि; 'to eat h. pie' मानं पृष्ठे कृ 8 U. -*v. t.* अव-नम् c. (नमयति), प्रह्वयति (D.), (सपदि विनयः प्रह्वयति मां U. 6); अभि-परा-भू 1 P, दर्प-गर्व-भंज् 7 P or हृ 1 P, नि-अव-पत् c., अप-कृष् 1 P, नम्रीकृ; 'thus completely h. ing the kings' इति राज्ञां शिरसि वामपादमाधाय (R. VII. 70); 'h.-bee' भ्रमरः; *See* BEE. -ED, *a.* अभिभूत, भग्नदर्प, आत्त-गर्व-गंध, हृतगर्व; आनत, नम्रीकृत, पातित, अपकृष्ट. -ING, *s.* दर्प-मान-भंगः, अभिभवः. -NESS, *s.* नीचता, अपकृष्टता, क्षुद्रता. 2 विनयः, नम्रता, अनहंकारः, अनभिमानः, अगर्वः, निरभिमानता, नम्रशीलता. -HUMBLY, *adv.* नीचैः, क्षुद्रतया, कृपणं. 2 सविनयं, नम्रतया, नम्रं, निरभिमानं, गर्वं विना, अनुद्धतं, नम्रचेतसा.

HUMBUG, *v. t.* प्रतॄ c., वंच् 10; *See* CHEAT. -*s.* प्रतारणं-णा, वंचना, कपटः-टं, छलं.

HUMDRUM, *a.* विरस, जड, मंद, फल्गु. -*s.* मूढः, स्थूलधीः.

HUMERUS, *s.* प्रगंडः.

HUMID, *a.* आर्द्र, क्लिन्न, उन्न, सरस, तिमित. -ITY, *s.* आर्द्रता, क्लेदः, तेमः, सरसता.

HUMILIATE, *v. t.* गर्वं हृ 1 P or भंज् 7 P, अभिभू 1 P, अपकृष् 1 P; *See* HUMBLE. -ING, *a.* दर्प-मान-हर. -ION, *s.* गर्व-दर्प-भंगः, अवमानना, मान-भंगः-हानि *f.*, अभिभवः, अपकर्षः; दमनं; नियमनं.

HUMILITY, *s.* विनयः, शालीनता, अगर्वः, अदर्पः, नम्रता, अनभिमानः, अनहंकारः, अनौद्धत्यं.

HUMOUR, *s.* भावः, वृत्ति *f.*, मनोवृत्तिः, स्वभावः, शीलः-लं, प्रकृति *f.*; 'good h.' सद्भावः, सुशीलता, सौजन्यं; 'bad h.' वक्रभावः, दुःशीलं; 'joyous h.' आनंदवृत्तिः. 2 छंदः, छंदस् *n.*, मनोलौल्यं, बुद्धिचापल्यं, लहरी, चित्ततरंगः, चापलं. 3 क्लेदः, तेमः, आर्द्रता; स्नेहः, जलावसेकः. 4 रसः, जलं, धातुः (of the body); 'disorder of the three h. s' दोषत्रयं, त्रिदोषं. 5 वैदग्ध्यं, रसिकता, रसः, सारस्यं, वैचित्र्यं. -*v. t.* (a person) चित्तवृत्तिं अनुवृत् 1 A, (अहं तावत्स्वामिनश्चित्तवृत्तिमनुवर्तिष्ये S. 2), छंदेन or छंदः(दं)अनुवृत्, भावं अनुरुध् 4 A or अनुप्र-विश् 6 P; (inclinations) अनुवृत्, अनुरुध्, अनुप्र-विश्. 2 अनुरंज् c., संतुष् c., आराध् c., प्र-सद् c., भज् 1 U, उपलल् 10, उपच्छंद् 10. -ING, *s.* अनुवर्तनं, अनुरोधः, छंदोनुवृत्तिः, भावानुप्रवेशः. -IST, *s.* वैहासिकः, हासकरः, विदूषकः, भंडः, परिहासशीलः, नर्मसचिवः. 2 रसज्ञः. -OUS, *a.* हासकर (री *f.*), परिहासवत्, विनोदिन्, सरस, रसवत्, रसिक, हास्य, परिहासशील; विनोदनशील; oft. by परिहास or नर्म in comp.; 'a h. speech' परिहासः, परिहासजल्पितं, नर्मालापः, नर्मभाषितं. -OUSLY, *adv.* सरसं, विनोदार्थं, परिहासपूर्वं. -SOME, *a.* वक्रभाव-शील, दुःशील, दुष्प्रकृति. 2 चलचित्त, लोलमति, चलप्रकृति-भाव; *See* FICKLE.

HUMP, *s.* ककुद् *f.*, ककुदः-दं (fig. also), अंसकूटः (of bulls); गडुः, स्थगुः; 'having a h.' ककुद्मत्, ककुद्मिन्; 'h.-backed' कुब्ज, गडुल-र, कुब्जक, वक्रपृष्ठ, न्युब्ज.

HUNCH, *s.* गडुः. 2 पिंडः. -*v. t.* अरत्निना तड् 10 or प्रहृ 1 P; 'h.-backed' Hump-backed, q. v.

HUNDRED, *a.* शतं; शतसंख्यक; 'by h. s' शतशः; 'in h. ways' शतधा; 'h.-fold' शतगुण *a.*; 'the life of man extends to h. years' शतायुर्वै पुरुषः. -*s.* शतं. -TH, *s.* शततम (मी *f.*).

HUNGER, *s.* क्षुधा, क्षुध् *f.*, बुभुक्षा, जिघत्सा, अशनाया, अशनायितं; 'h.-starved' क्षुत्क्षाम, क्षुधावसन्न. -*v. i.* क्षुध् 4 P (with dat.), भुज् desid. (बुभुक्षति-ते). 2 Long, q. v. -HUNGRY, *a.* क्षुधित, क्षुधार्त, क्षुधार्दित, क्षुत्पीडित, क्षुधातुर, जिघत्सु, बुभुक्षु, क्षुधाव्याकुल, बुभुक्षित, अन्नार्थिन्, अशनायित; 'h. and thirsty' क्षुत्पिपासित. 2 अवसन्न, क्षीण, क्षाम, कृश.

HUNKS, *s. See* MISER.

HUNT, *v.* मृग् 10 A, मृगयां कृ 8 U, (मृगयायां) अनुधाव् 1 P, अनुहृ 1 P, अनुवृत् 1 A, अनुबंध् 9 P. 2 अन्विष् 4 P, निरूप् 10. -*s.*,-ING, *s.* मृगया, आखेटः, मृगव्यं, आच्छोदनं, पापर्द्धि *f.* 2 अनुसरणं, अन्वेषणं, मार्गणं, अनुधावनं; लाभेच्छा, लिप्सा; 'h.-dress' मृगयावेषः; 'h.-dog' विश्वकद्रुः, मृगयाकुक्कुरः. -ER, HUNTSMAN, *s.* व्याधः, लुब्धकः, मृगयुः, आखेटकः, मृगवधाजीवः; जीवांतकः, शाकुनिकः (of birds); वागुरिकः, जालिकः (with nets).

HURDLE, *s.* काष्ठावरणं.

HURL, *v. t.* (तरसा-सवेगं) क्षिप् 6 P, वि-सृज्-मुच् 6 P,

प्रास् 4 U, ईर् c., प्रेष् c., प्रह 1 P; 'h. down' नि-अव-पत् c., अव-भ्रंश् c., अधःक्षिप्. –*s.* क्षेपः-पणं, पातनं. 2 तुमुलं, कोलाहलः. –ING, *s.* क्षेपणं; 'h. of stones' शिलावर्षः-आसारः.

HURLY-BURLY, *s.* तुमुलं, कोलाहलः, तुमुलरवः. कलकलः.

HURRAH, *interj.* जय-हर्ष-निस्वनः-शब्दः-नादः.

HURRICANE, *s.* प्रकंपनः, महावातः, अतिवातः, प्रभंजनः, वात्या, प्रचंडवातः, वेगानिलः, वाताली, वात्यावेगः, चक्रवातः, जवानिलः, झंझावातः (with showers).

HURRY, *v. i.* त्वर् 1 A, शीघ्रं गम् 1 P,ससंभ्रमं गम्. –*v. t.* त्वर् c. (त्वरयति). 2 सत्वरं आकृष् 1 P or प्रणुद् 6 P, or प्रेर् c.; शीघ्रं सं-नि:-पद् c. or वि-धा 3 U or साध् 5 P. –*s.* त्वरा, संभ्रमः, रभस् *n.*, रभसः, व्यग्रता, वेगः, आकुलत्वं, आ-सं-वेगः, त्वरितगति *f.*; 'why are you in such a h.' किमसि संभ्रांतेव (U. 3); 'in a h.' संभ्रांत, व्याकुल, व्यग्र. –ED, *a.* त्वरित, शीघ्र; 'a h. speech' निरस्तं वचः, त्वरितोदितं. –EDLY, *adv.* शीघ्रं, त्वरितं, सत्वरं, ससंभ्रमं, सरभसं, व्यग्रं.

HURT, *v. t.* क्षि 5 P, तुद् 6 P, हिंस् 7 P, अर्द् 1 P or c., बाध् 1 A, व्यथ् c. (व्यथयति), द्रुह् 4 P, क्षण् 8 P, पीड् 10, अपकृ 8 U, विप्र-कृ, दु 5 P; 'does not h. one's reputation' यशः न क्षिणोति (R. II. 40). –*s.* क्षतं, हिंसा, अपकारः, अपकृति *f.*, बाधा, पीडा, व्यथा. 2 अपायः, क्षयः, हानि *f.*, नाशः. –FUL, *a.* पीडाकर (री *f.*), अपायावह, हिंसात्मक, बाधक, अपकारिन्, अहित-हानि-क्षति-कर. 2 हिंस्र, घातुक, शरारु. –FULLY, *adv.* हिंसापूर्वं, सापकारं. –LESS, *a.* अक्षत. 2 अहिंस्र, अनपकारिन्, अनुपद्रविन्.

HURTLE, *v. i.* संघट्ट् 1 A, अभिसं-पत् 1 P. 2 सरभसं निष्क्रम् 1 U, 4 P or निर्गम् 1 P. 3 Echo, q. v.

HUSBAND, *s.* पतिः, भर्ता, उपयंता, परिणेता, परिग्रहीता, विवोढा; कांतः, दयितः, धवः, नाथः, स्वामी; इष्टः, प्रियतमः, प्राणेशः, हृदयेशः, (poetical words); 'h. and wife' दं(जं)पती, जायापती, भार्यापती; 'h.'s brother' देवरः, देवा, देवलः; 'a second h.' दिधिषुः; 'h.'s sister' ननांदृ; 'h.'s brother's wife' यातृ; 'sister's h.' श्यालः, श्यालकः, आवुत्तः, भगिनीपतिः. –*v. t.* परिमितं व्यय् 10 (व्यययति), न विक्षिप् 6 P, परिमितव्ययं कृ 8 U. 2 कृष् 1 P, 6 U. –LESS, *a.* विधवा, अनाथा, पतिहीना, गतभर्तृका, निर्णाथा. –RY, *s.* कृषि *f.* कृषिकर्मन् *n.*, कर्षणं, कृषिविद्या, वैश्यवृत्ति *f.*, हलभृति *f.* 2 परिमितव्ययः, गृहकर्मनिर्वाहविद्या. –HUSBANDMAN, *s.* कृष(षि)कः, कर्षकः, कृषीवलः, क्षेत्रिकः, हालिकः; *See* FARMER. 2 वैश्यः, विश् *m.*, ऊरुजः, ऊरव्यः, अर्यः, भूमिस्पृश् *m.*

HUSH, *interj.* तूष्णीं भव, शांतं, वाचंयम-*a.* भव, निःशब्दो भव. –*v. i.* शम् 4 P, प्र-उप-शम्, तूष्णीं भू, मौनीभू. –*v. t.* शम् c. (शमयति), निभृतं समा-धा 3 U; *See* CONCEAL also.

HUSK, *s.* तुषः, त्वच् *f.*, कोशः, पुटः-टं, आवेष्टनं. 2 बुषं-सं, कडंगरः. –*v. t.* निस्तुषयति-निस्त्वचयति (D.), त्वचं हृ 1 P, निस्तुषीकृ 8 U. –ED, *a.* निस्तुष, त्वग्हीन. 2 सतुष, त्वग्युक्त. –Y, *a.* सतुष, तुषवत्. 2 रूक्ष, कर्कश; 'in h. tones' रूक्षस्वरेण, बाष्पवृत्तिकलुषं.

HUSSAR, *s.* *See* CAVALIER.

HUSSY, *s.* बंधकी, पापा, दुष्टा स्त्री.

HUSTLE, *v. t.* Drive away, q. v. 2 संबाध् 1 A, संक्षुभ् c.

HUT, *s.* उटजः-जं, पर्णशाला, कुटीरः, तृणकुटी, कायमानं.

HUTCH, *s.* कुशू(सू)लः, धान्यकोष्ठः.

HUZZA, *s.* जयध्वनिः, हर्षनादः-स्वनः.

HYBRID, *a.* संकीर्णजाति, संकीर्ण, संकरजात, मिश्रज.

HYDRA, *s.* जलव्याल.

HYDRAULICS, *s.* चलज्जलविज्ञानं.

HYDROCELE, *s.* कोष-मुष्क-वृद्धि *f.*, फल-कोष-शोफः.

HYDROCEPHALUS, *s.* मस्तिष्कशोथः, शिरोग्रहः.

HYDROGRAPHY, *s.* समुद्रवेलादिविवरणं.

HYDROMEL, *s.* जलसंसृष्टं मधु.

HYDROPATHY, *s.* जलोपचारः, जलप्रयोगचिकित्सा.

HYDROPHOBIA, *s.* जलसंत्रासः; अलर्काभिभवः, आलर्कं.

HYDROPSY, *See* DROPSY.

HYEMAL, *a.* हैमंत (ती *f.*), शीतकालीन.

HYENA, *s.* तरक्षुः-क्षः, तर्क्षुः.

HYGROMETER, *s.* क्लेदमापकः.

HYMENEAL, *a.* विवाहीय, वैवाहिक-उद्वाहिक (की *f.*).

HYMN, *s.* स्तोत्रं, सूक्तं, गेयं, गानं, गीतं, स्तुतिगीतं; 'a chanter of h. s' उद्गातृ *m.*, सुम्नयुः. –*v. t.* गै 1 P, वर्ण् 10, गानद्वारेण स्तु 2 U or प्रशंस् 1 P; 'h. praises' उपवीणयति (D.).

HYP, *s.* *See* DEJECTION.

HYPERBOLE, *s.* अतिशयोक्ति *f.*, अत्युक्तिः, वाग्उपचयः, सत्यातिक्रमः. –IC, –ICAL, *a.* अत्युक्तिपूर्व, सत्यातिक्रामिन्. –IZE, *v. t.* अत्युक्त्या वर्ण् 10 or कथ् 10.

HYPERBOREAN, *a.* उत्तर, उदच्, उदीचीन, उत्तरीय.

HYPERCRITIC, *s.* एकांततः गुणदोषनिरूपकः or छिद्रान्वेषिन् *m.*, दोषैकदृश् *m.*

HYPOCHONDRIA, *s.* पित्तोन्मादः, वायुकोपः. 2 विषादः, उद्वेगः, अवसादः. –CAL, *a.* पित्तोन्मादिन्, विषण्ण.

HYPOCRITE, *s.* दांभिकः, दंभिन् *m.*, कपटी, कापटिकः, कुहकवृत्तिः, छद्म-कपट-वेशी; 'a religious h.' धर्मध्वजी, लिंगवृत्तिः, बकवृत्तिः-व्रतः, आर्यरूपः-लिंगी, छद्मतापसः, बैडालव्रतः. –ICAL, *a.* दंभिन्, कपटिन्, छाद्मिक-कापटिक-दांभिक (की *f.*), छद्म-कपट- in comp.; 'a h. sage' छद्मतापसः, कपटव्रती, मुनिवेषधारी. –ICALLY, *adv.* सदंभं, सकपटं, सव्याजं;

दांभिकवत्, छद्मना. —HYPOCRISY, *s.* दंभः, दांभिकता, कपटधर्मः, धर्मोपधा, बकव्रतं, धर्मध्वजमात्रं, लिंगवृत्ति *f.*, कुहकवृत्तिः, छाद्मिकता, कापट्यं, सव्याजता, आर्यरूपता.

HYPOTENUSE, *s.* कर्णः, श्रुति *f.*

HYPOTHECATE, *v. t.* आधि गृहे गुप् 1 P; 'a h.-ed article' गोप्याधिः.

HYPOTHESIS, *s.* उपन्यासः, प्रतिज्ञा, संकेतः, समयः. —HYPOTHETIC,-AL, *a.* उपन्यस्त, सांकेतिक (की *f.*), सोपन्यास, कल्पित. —ALLY, *adv.* सोपन्यासं, ससंकेतं, ससमयं, प्रतिज्ञाक्रमेण.

HYSTRICS, (Hysteria) *s.* वातोन्मादः; हर्षमूर्च्छा, हर्षमोहः; मोहः, मूर्च्छा. —HYSTERIC,-AL, *a.* हर्षमूर्च्छाल, मूर्च्छावत्; मोहोपहत, मूढ, मुग्ध.

I.

I, *pron.* अहं; oft. ex. by अयं जनः (referring to persons of any number or gender).

ICE, *s.* तुषार-हिम-संघातः, हिमसंहति *f.*, संहत-घनीकृतजलं, हिमं; *See* SNOW also; 'i.-berg' हिमपर्वतः-राशिः, हिमसंघातः, तुषारराशिः. —*v. t.* हिमीकृ 8 U, हिमेन शीतीकृ. —ICY, 'i.-cold', *a.* हिम, हिम्य, हैम (मी *f.*), तुषारवत्. 2 हिमशिशिर-शीतल; जड, शीत, शिशिर. 3 निरुत्साह, निःस्नेह, वीतराग. —ICICLE, *s.* हिमकणः-बिंदुः.

ICHNEUMON, *s.* नकुलः, बभ्रुः, अंगूषः.

ICHOR, *s.* पूयरक्तं.

ICONOCLASM, *s.* प्रतिमाभंगः.

ICONOGRAPHY, *s.* प्रतिमालिखनं.

ICONOLOGY, *s.* प्रतिमाविद्या.

IDEA, *s.* मति *f.*, बुद्धि *f.* 2 मतं, अभिप्रायः, आशयः, मनोगतं, भावः. 3 कल्पः, संकल्पः, कल्पना, भावना, वासना, बोधः; 'with the i. that' ex. by बुद्ध्या in comp. or इति कृत्वा. —IDEAL, *a.* मनःकल्पित, मानस (सी *f.*), काल्पनिक-मानसिक (की *f.*), चित्तोद्भावित; मनसिज, मनोभव. —*s.* मनोरथसृष्टि *f.*; oft. ex. by परम; 'i. of beauty' परमलावण्यं. —ISM, *s.* बाह्यशून्यवादः. —LY, *adv.* मनसा, कल्पनया, भावनापूर्वं.

IDENTICAL, *a.* तद् (*pron. a.*) with एव, अनन्य, अनन्यरूप, निर्विशेष, अभिन्न, अव्यतिरिक्त, अभिन्नरूप, सम, समान, निरस्तभेद, आत्मन्-रूप- in comp.; 'i. with the world' जगदात्मक, विश्वरूप; 'becoming i. with Brahman' ब्रह्मसायुज्यं प्राप्तः, ब्रह्मलीनः. —LY, *adv.* अभिन्नं, समं, निर्विशेषं. —IDENTIFY, *v. t.* समीकृ 8 U, तुल्यीकृ, अनन्यीकृ. 2 तदेव इति प्रति-पद् c. or वि-भू c. or अभि-ज्ञा 9 U, तुल्यत्वेन परिच्छिद् 7 P. —*v. i.* समीभू. —ICATION, *s.* समीकरणं, एकरूपता, सायुज्यं, अभिज्ञानं, विभावनं; 'i. with Brahman' ब्रह्मसायुज्यं, ब्रह्मभूयं. —IDENTITY, *s.* ऐक्यं, साम्यं, संवादः, निर्विशेषः, अभेदः, अनन्यता, तादात्म्यं, सारूप्यं, सरूपता, आत्मता, सायुज्यं; 'i. of thoughts' चित्तैक्यं, एकचित्तता; 'i. of class' सावर्ण्यं, सजातित्वं; 'i. of hand' वर्णसंवादः.

IDIOM, *s.* वाक्पद्धति-रीति *f.*, वाग्व्यवहारः, वाक्संप्रदायः, विशिष्टस्वरूपं. —ATIC, *a.* Ex. by (*s.*).

IDIOSYNCRASY, *s.* देहस्वभावः, जातिस्वभावः.

IDIOT, *s.* जडः, मूर्खः, अनात्मज्ञः, मूढः, वैधेयः, बालिशः, अज्ञः, निर्बुद्धिः. —IC, *a.* जड, मूढ, मूर्ख, हतज्ञान, बुद्धिविकल. —IDIOCY, *s.* मूढता, मूर्खता, जाड्यं, अज्ञता, बालिशता; *See* FOOL,-ISH, FOLLY.

IDLE, *a.* अलस, कर्मविमुख-कार्यपराङ्मुख (खी *f.*), कर्मद्वेषिन्, आलस्यशील, अनुद्योगशील. 2 अव्याहृत, निरुद्योग, निर्व्यवसाय, कर्म-कार्य-शून्य-रहित, निर्व्यापार, निरुद्यम, निश्चेष्ट; उदासीन, निरुत्साह. 3 निरर्थक, निष्प्रयोजन, व्यर्थ, मोघ; 'it were i. to talk of friend or foe in Govinda' गोविंदविषये मित्रामित्रकल्पनं व्याघातः, व्याहतं एव; 'to be i.' उदास् 2 A; 'i. talk' वृथालापः, वृथाकथा. —*v. t.* (time) उदास्, कालं मुधा क्षै c. (क्षपयति) or नी 1 P or अतिवह् c., कालं हृ 1 P or क्षिप् 6 P, कालक्षेपं कृ 8 U, अलस-निर्व्यापार-*a.* भू. —ER, *s.* निर्व्यापारः, कालक्षेपकः, कार्यद्विटः, मुखनिरीक्षकः. —NESS, *s.* आलस्यं, कार्यद्वेषः, कार्यविमुखता, उदासीनता. 2 अनुद्योगः, अव्यापारः, कार्यशून्यता, कालक्षेपः-पणं. —IDLY, *adv.* आलस्येन, अलसवत्. 2 निरुद्योगं, निर्व्यापारं. 3 निरर्थकं, व्यर्थं, वृथा, मुधा.

IDOL, *s.* (देव-) प्रतिमा-मानं, मूर्ति *f.*, दैवतं, देवता, देवताविग्रहः, प्रतिकृति *f.* 2 (Fig.) आराध्यदेवता; 'attendant on an i.' देवलः, देवाजीवः-वी. —IDOLATER, (Idolatrous), *s.* मूर्ति-प्रतिमा-पूजकः-अर्चकः-उपासकः, देवतार्चकः, प्रतिमासेविन् *m.* —IDOLATRY, *s.* प्रतिमा-मूर्ति-पूजा-अर्चनं, देवतार्चनं, प्रतिमासेवा, देवतोपासना, मूर्तिसेवा-उपासनं. —IDOLATRIZE, *v. i.* प्रतिमां पूज् 10 or अर्च् 1 P, 10. —IDOLIZE, *v. t.* देवतां इव आराध् c., देववत् पूज्, or भज् 1 U; एकांततः प्री-अनुरंज्-pass., अत्यंतानुरक्त-*a.* भू, अतिप्रेम कृ 8 U.

IDONEOUS, *a.* *See* FIT.

IF, *conj.* यदि, चेत् (not at beginning); 'if so' यद्येवं, एवं स्थिते; 'if not' नोचेत्, अन्यथा, यदि न; 'as if' इव.

IGNEOUS, *a.* अग्निमत्, आग्नेय-अग्निमय (यी *f.*).

IGNIS-FATUUS, *s.* मिथ्याग्निः, मिथ्यादीप्ति *f.*, दीप्त्याभासः.

IGNITE, *v. t.* ज्वल् c., दीप् c., सं-इंध् 7 A, संधुक्ष् 10, दह् 1 P, तप् c. —*v. i.* ज्वल् 1 P, दीप् 4 A, सं-इंध् pass. —ION, *s.* दीपनं, ज्वलनं, इंधनं.

IGNOBLE, *a.* अकुलीन, हीनजाति-वर्ण, नि-अप-कृष्ट, नीच, अधम, जघन्य, अनार्य; *See* BASE. 2 अकीर्तिकर-लज्जाकर (री *f.*). —IGNOBLY, *adv.* अनार्यवत्, नीच-अधम-वत्.

IGNOMINY, *s.* Disgrace, q. v. 2 अपकर्षः, अवज्ञा, अपमानः, कलंकः, अप्रतिष्ठा, तिरस्कारः, परिभवः. —IOUS, *a.* अपकीर्ति-लज्जा-कलंक-कर (री *f.*), गर्ह्य, कलंकावह, वाच्य.

IGNORE, *v. t.* न ज्ञा 9 U, न स्वीकृ 8 U. —ANCE, *s.* अज्ञानं, अविद्या, ज्ञानाभावः, अबोधः, मोहः. 2 ज्ञानहीनता, अनभिज्ञता, अज्ञता, अनभिज्ञानं, निर्बुद्धित्वं; 'difference imagined by i.' अविद्याकल्पितभेदः. —ANT, *a.* अज्ञ, अवेदिन्, अज्ञान, अनभिज्ञ, oft. ex. by not 'know', q. v. 2 अप्राज्ञ, अविज्ञ, अपंडित, दुर्बुद्धि, निर्बुद्धि, अ-निर्-बोध, विद्या-ज्ञान-प्रज्ञा-बोध-हीन-शून्य-रहित, दुर्मति, अविद्वस्. —ANTLY, *adv.* अज्ञानतः, अज्ञानेन, अज्ञान-अबोध-पूर्वं.

IGUANA, *s.* गोधा, गौधारः.

ILIAC, *a.* आंत्रिक (की *f.*), अंत्र in comp.; 'i. pain' अंत्रशूलं, शूलव्याधिः-रोगः.

ILL, *a.* दुष्ट, पाप, असत्, असाधु, गर्ह्य, खल, कुत्सित, अभद्र, अमंगल, अशुभ, gen. ex. by दुर्, कु, अप, वि, कद् pr.; *See* BAD; oft. by अ in comp. 2 अस्वस्थ, अस्वस्थ-असुस्थ-शरीर, असुस्थ, असुस्थित, व्याधित, सामय, रोगिन्; gen. ex. by आर्त, ग्रस्त, आतुर, पीडित in comp.; 'i. with fever' ज्वरार्त, ज्वरपीडित. —*s.* दुष्टता, खलता, असाधुता. 2 पापं, दुराचारः, अधर्मः, दुर्वृत्तं, दोषः, अपराधः. 3 अनिष्टं, अशुभं, अमंगलं, अकुशलं, अभद्रं, दुःखं, दुर्गति *f.*, आपद्-विपद् *f.*, व्यसनं, उत्पातः, अनर्थः, अरिष्टं, अनिष्टपातः, कष्टः-ष्टं, अपायः. 4 अपकारः, अपकृति *f.*, अहितं, अपायः, क्षति-हानि *f.*, क्षयः, अपचयः. 5 रोगः, व्याधिः, आमयः, पीडा, उपतापः, अस्वास्थ्यं; *See* DISEASE. —*adv.* असाधु, अनार्यं, असम्यक्, दुष्टं. 2 दुःखेन, कष्टेन, कृच्छ्रेण; in comp. words, ex. by दुर्, कु, अप, वि, कद्, अ, दुष्ट, पाप; 'i.-advised' अपरीक्षित, अविमृश्य कृत; 'i.-affected' वि-अप-रक्त, द्रोहबुद्धि, अहितैषिन्; 'i.-arranged,-ordered,-regulated' दुष्क्रम, दुर्विरचित, अव्यवस्थित; 'i.-behaved,-bred,-natured' अविनीत, दुःशील, दुर्वृत्त, कुशील, अविनय, दुर्विनीत, अशिष्ट, असभ्य, दुराचार, पाप, कुप्रवृत्ति, विनयानेत; 'i.-breeding' अविनयः, दुःशीलता, असभ्यता, विनयप्रमाथः, दुर्वृत्ति *f.*, दुराचारः; 'i.-conditioned' दुर्गत, दुःस्थित; 'i.-dressed' दुर्वासस्, कुप्रावृत; 'i.-fame' अयशः, अपकीर्ति *f.*, अप्रतिष्ठा; 'i.-fated' दुर्भाग्य, मंदभाग्य, दुर्दैव, दैवोपहत, दुर्दैवग्रस्त-उपहत; 'i.-favoured,-formed,-shaped' अप-कु-रूप, कदाकार, दुर्दर्शन; 'i.-fitted' अयोग्य, अनर्ह, अनुचित; 'i.-gotten' अन्यायार्जित; 'i.-grounded' अमूलक; 'i.-judged' अविमृश्य-अविचार्य-कृत, अनालोचित; 'i.-judging' विवेकशून्य, निर्विवेक; 'i.-looking' दुर्दर्शन, कुरूप; 'i.-luck' दुर्दैवं, दुर्भाग्यं, मंदभाग्यं, दैवविपर्यासः-दुर्विपाकः, दुर्जातं, अनिष्टं; *See* (*s.*); 'i.-nature,-temper' दुःशीलं, दुष्प्रकृति *f.*, वक्रभावः-शीलं, वामशीलं, भावप्रतीपता, वामशीलता, स्वभाववक्रता; 'i.-natured,-tempered' दुष्प्रकृति, वक्र-वाम-शील, दुष्ट-खल-स्वभाव, कटु-कर्कश-प्रतीप-स्वभाव, कु-दुः-शील; 'i.-omened' अशुभसूचक, अनिष्टशंसिन्, अनिष्टलक्षण; 'i.-sounding' अपस्वर, विकु-स्वर, कटु; 'i.-timed' अकाल, अप्राप्तकाल, अप्राप्तावसर, अनवसर, आकालिक (की *f.*); 'i.-treat' विप्र-अप-नि-कृ 8 U, उपद्रु 1 A, पीड् 10, अर्द् 1 P or c., खलीकृ; 'i.-treatment' अपकारः, पीडा, अर्दनं; *See* (*s.*); 'i.-turn' अपकारः, पापं, अप्रियं, अहितं, हिंसा, द्रोहः; 'i.-will' दुष्टभावः-बुद्धिः, द्रोहः, द्वेषः, मात्सर्यं, असूया. —NESS, *s.* रोगः, व्याधिः, आमयः, रुजा, अस्वास्थ्यं, पीडा, बाधा, आर्ति *f.*, क्लेशः, उपतापः, दुःखं, विकारः, विकृति *f.*; 'dangerous i.' जीवितसंशयः, सन्निपातः.

ILLAPSE, *s.* सहसा प्रवेशः or आक्रमणं. —*v. i.* सहसा प्रविश् 6 P or पत् 1 P.

ILLATIVE, *a.* आनुमानिक (की *f.*). —LY, *adv.* अनुमानेन, अपोहेन.

ILLEGAL, *a.* नियम-विधि-विरुद्ध, शास्त्र-स्मृति-व्यवहार-न्याय-विरुद्ध, स्मृत्यपेत, अधर्म्य, अन्याय्य, न्यायधर्म-रोधिन्, अविधि. —ITY, *s.* विधि-धर्म-शास्त्र-नियमविरोधः, अन्याय्यता, अधर्म्यता, अव्यवस्था, नियम-व्यवस्था-विधि-भंगः. —LY, *adv.* नियम-विधि-विरुद्धं.

ILLEGIBLE, *a.* दुर्वाच्य, अव्यक्ताक्षर, अस्पष्टाक्षर, अस्पष्ट-अव्यक्त-वर्ण.

ILLEGITIMATE, *a.* अन्याय्य, विधिविरुद्ध; *See* ILLEGAL. 2 विजात, जारजात, जारज, असतीप्रसूत, अनौरस, विजन्मन्, जारोत्पन्न. 3 कृत्रिम, कृतक, कल्पित; 'an i. child' अनौरसः-सी, जारजः-जा, दासीपुत्रः, कौलटेयः-यी, कौलटेरः-री, बंधकी-उपपत्नी-सुतः-ता, बंधुलः, कौलटिनेयः-यी. —LY, *adv.* विजन्मना; अधर्मेण. —ILLEGITIMACY, *s.* विजन्मन् *n.*, वैजात्यं, अनौरसत्वं.

ILLIBERAL, *a.* अनुदार, कृपण, कृपणबुद्धि-चेतस्-स्वभाव, (lit. and fig.); अत्याग-अदान-शील, अवदान्य. —ITY, *s.* अत्यागः, अवदान्यत्वं, अनौदार्यं, कार्पण्यं, नीचता, दीनता.

ILLICIT, *a.* प्रति-नि-षिद्ध, अधर्म्य, अन्याय्य, नियम-धर्म-विरुद्ध, व्यवहारविरोधिन्.

ILLITERATE, *a.* अशिक्षित, अप्रबुद्ध, असंस्कृत, अव्यु-

त्यत्र, विद्या-ज्ञान-हीन, निरक्षर, अनक्षर, असंस्कृतचित्त.

ILLIMITED,-ABLE, *a.* निरवधि; अनंत, अमेय, असीम, अमित, अमर्याद; *See* ENDLESS.

ILLOGICAL, *a.* अयुक्तिसिद्ध, न्यायविरुद्ध-विपरीत, अन्यायानुसारिन्, अन्याय्य, अतार्किक (की *f.*); 'i. conclusion' अपसिद्धांत:, अविनिगम:. -LY, *adv.* न्यायविरुद्धं.

ILLUDE, *v. t.* वंच् 10, मुह् c., प्रलुभ् c.; *See* CHEAT. -ILLUSION, *s.* माया, प्रपंच:, इंद्रजालं, अलीकता, अविद्या; *See* DELUSION. -ILLUSIVE,-ILLUSORY, *a.* मायिन्, अलीक, ऐंद्रजालिक; *See* DELUSIVE.

ILLUME, ILLUMINE, ILLUMINATE, *v. t.* द्युत् c., प्रकाश् c., उद्भास् c., उद्दीप् c., वि-,राज् c., भ्राज् c., उज्ज्वल् c. 2 (पत्राणि) रंज् c. -ION, *s.* उद्भासनं, द्योतनं, प्रकाशनं, उज्ज्वलनं, दीप्ति-द्युति *f.*, भ्राजिष्णुता. 2 (i. s) दीपालि *f.*, दीपमाला-समूह:, दीपोत्सव:. 3 पत्ररंजनं. -OR, *s.* द्योतक:, प्रकाशक:, दीपक:. 2 पत्ररंजक:.

ILLUSTRATE, *v. t.* व्या-ख्या 2 P, व्या-चक्ष् 2 A, स्पष्टीकृ 8 U, विवृ 5 U; उदा-हृ 1 P, निदृश् c., निदर्शनेन व्या-ख्या, व्यक्ती-विशदी-कृ, चित्रेण स्पष्टीकृ, प्रकाश् c., द्युत् c., शुभ् c., दीप् c , चित्रादिना शुभ् c. -ION, *s.* उदाहरणं, दृष्टांत:, निदर्शनं, व्याख्या-ख्यानं, प्रकाशनं, निरूपणं. -IVE, *a.* प्रकाशक, दार्ष्टांतिक (की *f.*). -OR, *s.* प्रकाशक:, निदर्शक:, व्याख्यातृ *m.*

ILLUSTRIOUS, *a.* विश्रुत, ख्यात, प्रथित, प्रसिद्ध, महायशस्क; *See* FAMOUS. 2 विशिष्ट, उत्तम, उत्कृष्ट, परम, प्रमुख, महत्. -LY, *adv.* विश्रुतं, प्रथितयशसा, विशिष्टतया. -NESS, *s.* विश्रुति-ख्याति *f.*

IMAGE, *s.* प्रतिमा, मूर्ति *f.*, प्रतिकृति *f.*-मूर्ति:-मानं-रूपं, प्रतिच्छंदकं. 2 प्रतिबिंबं, बिंबं, छाया, प्रतिच्छाया, प्रतिच्छंद:-दकं; 'this youth is the complete i. of Râma' रामस्याकृतिरस्मिन् शिशौ संपूर्ण प्रतिबिंबिता (U. 4). 3 Idea, q. v.; 'iron i.' लोहप्रतिमा, स्थूणा, सू(शू)र्मी. -*v. t.* मनसा क्लृप् c. or चित्र् 10, प्रतिबिंबयति (D.) ; 'i. various shapes' तैस्तैराकृतिविशेषैरनुगता: (Mr. 5). -ERY, *s.* मन:-कल्पना-सृष्टि *f.*-संकल्प:, भावना, वासना. 2 उपलक्षणं, लक्षणा. 3 आभास:, आडंबर:, अनुकार:.

IMAGINE, *v. t.* मनसा क्लृप् c., सं-परि°; सं-वि-भू c., सृज् 6 P, ध्यै 1 P. 2 मन् 4 A, गण् 10, चिंत् 10, तर्क् 10, उत्प्रेक्ष् 1 A, बुध् 1 P, अव-इ 2 P, अवगम् 1 P, उपलभ् 1 A. -ABLE, *a.* संभाव्य, चिंतनीय, बोधगम्य; 'with all i. ease' मनसोऽप्यगोचरीभूतया-मनसाप्यकल्प्यमानया-लीलया. -ARY, *a.* मन:कल्पित, वासना-भावना-सृष्ट, मनोरथसृष्ट, मानस (सी *f.*), काल्पनिक (की *f.*), संकल्पज. 2 अमूलक, असत्य, मायामय (यी *f.*). -ATION, *s.* भावना-नं, कल्पना-नं, संकल्प:, वासना, मन:कल्पना. 2 (Faculty of i.) कल्पना-तर्क-शक्ति *f.*, भावना, उपलब्धि *f.* -ATIVE, *a.* कल्पक, विभावक, भावनापर, कल्पनाशील.

IMBECILE, *a.* दुर्बल, अशक्त, क्षीणबल; *See* FEEBLE. 2 (In mind) न्यूनबुद्धि, अल्प-विकल-मति, बालिश, कृपणबुद्धि. -ITY, *s.* दौर्बल्यं, न्यूनबुद्धिता, बालिशत्वं.

IMBIBE, *v. t.* नि-पा 1 P, आ-पा, शुष् c. 2 (Fig.) अधिगम् 1 P, मनसा ग्रह् 9 P or आकल् 10 (कलयति) or उपलभ् 1 A.

IMBRUE, *v. t.* सिच् 6 P, लिप् 6 P, उक्ष् 1 P, क्लिद् c.; अंज् 7 P, दिह् 2 U; 'i. ed with blood' रक्ताक्त, रक्तक्लिन्न.

IMBUE, *v. t.* अभिरंज् c. 2 शास् 2 P, उपविश् 6 P, शिक्ष् c.

IMITATE, *v. t.* अनुकृ 8 U (oft. with gen.), अनुगम्-सृ 1 P, अनु-इ-या 2 P, अनुवृत् 1 A, अनुविधा 3 U, अनुवद् 1 P, अनुहृ 1 P, विडंब् 10. -ION, *s.* अनुकार:-करणं, अनुकृति *f.*, विडंबनं, अनुवृत्ति *f.*, अनुसरणं. 2 उपमानं, प्रतिरूपं, सादृश्यं. -IVE, *a.* अनुकरणशील, अनुकारिन्, अनुगामिन्. -OR, *s.* अनुकर्तृ *m.*, अनुकारक:, अनुयायिन्-अनुकारिन् *m.*, अनुगतिक:.

IMMACULATE, *a.* निष्कलंक, निर्मल, अकल्मष, अनघ, निर्दोष, विमल.

IMMANENT, *a.* अंतर्भव, अंतरस्थ.

IMMATERIAL, *a.* अमूर्त, निरवयव, अशरीरिन्, अमूर्तिमत्. 2 लघु, अगुरु, अगुर्वर्थ, यत्किंचित्, निष्प्रयोजन, अनावश्यक (की *f.*), निरर्थक. -ISM, *s.* निराकारवाद:. -IST, *s.* निराकारवादिन् *m.* -ITY, *s.* अमूर्तता, अशरीरता. -LY, *adv.* निरर्थकं, निष्प्रयोजनं.

IMMATURE, *a.* अपक्व, अपरिणत, असंपूर्णकाल, असिद्ध, अप्राप्तकाल, आकालिक (की *f.*). -LY, *adv.* अपक्वं, अपरिणतं, अप्राप्तकालं, अतिशीघ्रं, परिणामकालात् प्राक्. -ITY,-NESS, *s.* अपाक:, अपरिपाक:, अपरिणाम:, अप्रौढता, अप्राप्तकालता.

IMMEASURABLE, *a.* अमेय, अमित, अपरिमाण, दुर्मेय, महत्, बहु, अति pr.

IMMEDIATE, *a.* अनंतर, अव्यवहित, निरंतर, अव्यवधान. 2 तात्कालिक (की *f.*), सद्यस्क, अचिर, शीघ्र; better by 'i. ly'. 3 सन्निहित, उपस्थित, आसन्न, निकट. -LY, *adv.* सद्य:, सपद्येव, समनंतरमेव, सपदि; तत्क्षणात्, तत्काले, सद्य एव, झटिति, द्राक्, आशु, अविलंबितं, अचिरादेव; oft. by एव or मात्र; 'i. after he had spoken' तस्मिन्नुक्तवत्येव; मुक्तमात्रे सायके &c.

IMMEDICABLE, *a.* दुरुपचार, अचिकित्स्य.

IMMEMORABLE, *a.* अस्मर्तव्य.

IMMEMORIAL, *a.* अस्मार्त, स्मरणातिक्रांत, अतिप्राचीन, अनादि; 'i. succession' अनादिपरंपरा; 'from times i.' अनादिकालात्, अस्मार्तकालात्.

IMMENSE, *a.* अत्यंत, अपरिमेय, अतिमात्र, अनंत, अपरिमाण, अमित, अतिमर्याद, दुर्मेय; महत्, बृहत्, सु-अति-महत्, अतिमृहत्. -LY, *adv.* अत्यंतं, अतिमात्रं. -ITY, *s.* आनंत्यं, अमितता, अपरिमाणत्वं, महत्त्वं, सुमहत्त्वं.

IMMERGE, IMMERSE, *v. t.* अवगाह् c., निमस्ज् c. (मज्जयति), आप्लु c., जले प्रविश् c. -ED, *a.* मग्न, नि-अभिनि-विष्ट, व्यापृत, लीन, आसक्त, निष्ठ-पर-तत्पर- in comp.; *See* FIXED, INTENT. -IMMERSION, *s.* निमज्जनं, अवगाहः-हनं, आप्लावः, स्नानं, अभिषेकः. 2 मग्नता, निष्ठा, तत्परता, अभिनिवेशः.

IMMETHODICAL, *a.* क्रमहीन, क्रमविरुद्ध, अव्यवस्थित. -LY, *adv.* क्रमविरुद्धं, अक्रमेण.

IMMIGRATE, *v. i.* देशांतरं अधिवस् 1 P or आध्यास् 2 A (with acc.). -ION, *s.* देशांतराधिवासः, देशत्यागः. -IMMIGRANT, *s.* देशांतराधिवासिन् *m.*

IMMINENT, *a.* उपस्थित, आसन्न, संनिकृष्ट, उपनत, निकट-आसन्न-वर्तिन्; 'a drought is i.' अनावृष्टिः संपद्येत लग्ना (P. I. 7). 2 आत्ययिक (की *f.*), जीवितसंशयावह; 'he stood in i. peril of death' महति जीवितसंशये अवर्तत.

IMMIT, *v. t. See* PLACE.

IMMOBILE, *a.* स्थिर, निश्चल, अचल, निष्कंप.

IMMODERATE, *a.* अमित, अपरिमित, अमर्याद, अत्यंत, अतिमात्र, अत्यधिक, सु-अति- pr. -LY, *adv.* अतिमात्रं, अत्यंतं, सु-अति- pr. -ION, *s.* अमर्यादा, मर्यादातिक्रमः, अत्याचारः, अतिरेकः, अतिशयः.

IMMODEST, *a.* वियात, निर्लज्ज, निस्त्रप, अविनीत, प्रगल्भ, धृष्ट, लज्जा-व्रीडा-त्रपा-हीन. 2 अश्लील, गर्ह्य, अवाच्य, अशुद्ध, अशुचि. 3 असाधु, असद्वृत्त, पांसुल, व्यभिचारिन्. -LY, *adv.* निर्लज्ज, प्रगल्भं, धृष्टवत्, अश्लीलं. -Y, *s.* वैयात्यं, अविनयः, प्रागल्भ्यं, धृष्टता, निर्लज्जत्वं.

IMMOLATE, *v. t.* (यज्ञे) हन् 2 P, विशस् 1 P, उपहारीकृ 8 U, हत्वा उत्सृज् 6 P, बलिं दा 3 U or कृ, आलभ् 1 A, सं-ज्ञा c. (ज्ञपयति); 'i. oneself' प्रेतेन सह आत्मानं दह् 1 P, सह गम्. -ION, *s.* उपहारीकरणं, उपहारः, बलिदानं, आलंभः, संज्ञपनं, उत्सर्गार्थं वधः or विशसनं.

IMMORAL, *a.* असाधु, दुश्चरित्र, दुर्वृत्त, दुराचार, पापकर्मन्, व्यभिचारिन्, व्यसनिन्, पापिन्; दुष्ट, धर्मविरुद्ध, अपुण्य, अशुचि, पाप. -ITY, *s.* असाधुता, दुर्वृत्तता; व्यसनं, अधर्मः, पापं, पापचरितं, दुश्चरितं, व्यभिचारः. -LY, *adv.* धर्मविरुद्धं, दुराचारेण.

IMMORTAL, *a.* अमर, अमर्त्य, जरामरणरहित, अक्षय, अजर, निर्जर, अनश्वर, अविनाशिन्, नित्य, सनातन (नी *f.*), अनंत, शाश्वत (ती *f.*), सदास्थायिन्. -ITY, *s.* अमरता-त्वं, अनश्वरता, आनंत्यं, नित्यता. -IZE, *v. t.* अमरी-अक्षयी-कृ 8 U; better by (*a.*). -LY, *adv.* अजरं, अक्षयं, अनश्वरं, शाश्वतं.

IMMOVEABLE, *a.* अचल, स्थिर, स्थावर, अचर, अजंगम.

IMMUNITY, *s.* मुक्ति *f.*, मोक्षः. 2 अभावः, विरहः, न्यूनता, राहित्यं; oft. by अ or निर् pr.; 'i. from danger' अभयं, निर्भयत्वं.

IMMURE, *v. t.* नि-अव-रुध् 7 U, बंध् 9 P, संयम् 1 P, कारायां गुप् 1 P. 2 परिवृ 5 U, परिवेष्ट् 1 A or c.

IMMUTABLE, *a.* अव्यय, निर्विकार, नित्य, अविक्रिय, विकाराक्षम, स्थिर, निर्विकल्प, अपरिवर्तनीय. -IMMUTABILITY, *s.* अविकारः, नित्यता, अव्ययः.

IMP, *s.* पिशाचः, भूतः; *See* DEVIL, DEMON.

IMPACT, *s.* संस्पर्शः, संपर्कः, समा-प्रति-घातः, संघट्टः.

IMPAIR, *v. t.* ह्रस् c., अप-चि 5 U, क्षि 1, 5 P or c., नश् c., विलुप् c., लघूकृ 8 U, ऊन् 10, उप-हन् 2 P, दुष् c. (दूषयति), अल्पीकृ, विकलीकृ, क्षीणीकृ. 2 तेजः-बलं-हृ 1 P, दुर्बलीकृ. -ED, *a.* ह्रसित, क्षीण, विकल, अपचित, उपहत, विशीर्ण, लुप्त, न्यूनी-विकली-कृत; 'i. in strength' क्षीणबल, निःसत्व. -ING, *s.* क्षयः, ह्रासः, अपचयः, अवसादः; वैकल्यं, न्यूनता, लोपः.

IMPALPABLE, *a.* अस्पृश्य, अग्राह्य, स्पर्शाव्यक्त, इंद्रियागोचर, अव्यक्त, अतिसूक्ष्म.

IMPARITY, *s.* वैषम्यं, भेदः, असाम्यं.

IMPART, *v. t.* दा 3 U, 1 P, प्रति-पद् c., सम्-ऋ c. (अर्पयति), निक्षिप् 6 P, संक्रम् c., ग्रह् c., वि-तॄ 1 P (with loc.), संसृज् 6 P; सुवर्णविकारा अर्पांतो न सुवर्णमात्मीयेन धर्मेण संसृजंति (S. B. 431) 'do not i. to gold their properties'. 2 नि-आ-विद् c., कथ् 10, प्रकाश् c., वि-ज्ञा c. (ज्ञापयति), ख्या 2 P or c. 3 संचर् c., संक्रम् c.

IMPARTIAL, *a.* अपक्षपातिन्, समक्रिय, समदर्शिन्, समवृत्ति-भाव, उदासीन, मुक्तसंग, सर्वसम, पक्षपातहीन, न्यायवर्तिन्, न्याय्य, धर्म्य. -ITY, *s.* अपक्षपातः, धर्मः, समता, निःसंगता, औदासीन्यं, न्याय्यता. -LY, *adv.* न्यायेन, निःसंगं, अपक्षपातेन.

IMPARTIBLE, *a.* अविभाज्य, अवंटनीय.

IMPASSABLE, *a.* अगम्य, अलंघ्य, दुस्तर, दुर्गम, दुस्तार्य, गहन, संबाध, संकट.

IMPASSIBLE, *a.* अ-निः-चेतन, सुखदुःखाक्षम.

IMPASSIONED, *a.* अनुरक्त, अनुरागवत्, रागान्वित, बद्धभाव, सानुराग, प्रीत्याकृष्ट, आसक्तचित्त. 2 सरस, रसिक, रागयुक्त, रागिन्; 'what an i. strain' अहो रागपरिवाहिणी गीतिः (S. 5).

IMPATIENT, *a.* (For) उत्सुक, व्यग्र, सोत्कंठ, प्रसित, उत्क; *See* EAGER. 2 (Of) असह, असहन, अक्षमिन्, असहिष्णु, अक्षम. 3 अधीर, कालहरणाक्षम, अमर्षण, अतितिक्षु. -LY, *adv.* अधीरं, सोत्सुकं, व्यग्रं,

सावेगं, अक्षांत्या. –IMPATIENCE, *s.* अधीरता, औत्सुक्यं, व्यग्रता, उत्कंठा, अक्षमा, असहत्वं.

IMPAWN, *v. t. See* PLEDGE.

IMPEACH, *v. t.* अभियुज् 7 A, 10, अभिशंस् 1 P, अपवद् 1 U, आधृष् c. –ER, *s.* अभियोगिन्-योक्तृ *m.* –MENT, *s.* अभियोगः, अभिशंसनं.

IMPECCABLE, *a.* अपाप, निर्दोष.

IMPEDE, *v. t.* रुध् 7 U, प्रतिबंध् 9 P, वि-प्रति-हन् 2 P, नि-वृ c., स्तंभ् 9 P or c., बाध् 1 A, कुंठयति (D.). –IMPEDIMENT, *s.* विघ्नः, प्रत्यूहः, अंतरायः, व्याघातः, उपरोधः, प्रतिबंधः; *See* OBSTACLE.

IMPEL, *v. t.* नि-प्र-उद्-युज् 10, प्रवृत् c., प्रोत्सह् c., उत्तिज् c., प्रेर् c., नुद् 6 P or c., प्रणुद्, प्रचुद् 10, कृष् 1 P; *See* DRIVE. –LENT, *s.* प्रवर्तकः, प्रेरकः, प्रोत्साहकः, प्रचोदकः.

IMPEND, *v. i.* आ-प्र-लंब् 1 A, उपरि लंब्. 2 उन्नम् 1 P, समा-पत् 1 P, प्रत्या-सद् 1 P, उप-स्था 1 U, उपागम् 1 P, निकटे-समीपं-वृत् 1 A or स्था; 'an untimely storm i. s' उन्नमत्यकालदुर्दिनं (Mr. 5); 'a drought is closely i. ing' अनावृष्टिः संपद्यते लग्ना (P. I. 7). –ENT,-ING, *a.* उपस्थित, आसन्न, निकटवर्तिन्, उपनत, उन्नमत्.

IMPENETRABLE, *a.* अभेद्य, अच्छेद्य, अप्रवेश्य, गहन, दुर्गम. 2 कठिन, वज्रमय (यी *f.*); 'darkness i. by the sun' अभानुभेद्यं तमः.

IMPENITENT, *a.* अननुशयिन्, अननुतापिन्, खेद-पश्चात्ताप-हीन, अननुतप्त. –IMPENITENCE, *s.* अननुतापः; अननुशयः, अखेदः; कठिनता, कठोरता.

IMPERATIVE, *a.* आज्ञापक, आदेशक, नियोजक, विधायक, प्रचोदक. 2 अविचार्य, अवश्यकर्तव्य, अनुपेक्ष्य; 'i. mood' लोट्, आज्ञार्थः. –LY, *adv.* अवश्यमेव.

IMPERCEPTIBLE, *a.* अस्पष्ट, अव्यक्त, अविभाव्य, अगोचर, अगम्य; 'i. to the senses' इंद्रियागोचर, इंद्रियातीत, अतींद्रिय; 'i. to the eye' अप्रत्यक्ष, परोक्ष, नयनागोचर; 'i. difference' अतिसूक्ष्मः भेदः. –IMPERCEPTIBLY, *adv.* अव्यक्तं, अगोचरं, अलक्षितं, निभृतं.

IMPERFECT, *a.* अपूर्ण, अपरिणत, असंपन्न, अपक्व, असमाप्त, असमग्र. 2 न्यून, विकल, लुप्त, हीन, सदोष, सच्छिद्र, ऊनावयव, विकलेंद्रिय, विकलांग; 'i. memory' विकला स्मृतिः; 'i. comparison' लुप्तोपमा. 3 (I. tense) लङ्. –ION, *s.* दोषः, छिद्रं, रंध्रं, अगुणः, दूषणं; कलंकः, वैकल्यं, न्यूनता, हानि *f.*, क्षति *f.*, अपर्याप्ति *f.* –LY, *adv.* असंपूर्णं, असम्यक्, विकलं.

IMPERFORATE, *a.* नीरंध्र, अच्छिद्र.

IMPERIAL, *a.* महेश्वरीय,महाराज-अधिराज-in comp.; 'i. rule' आधिराज्यं, चक्रवर्तित्वं.

IMPERIL, *v. t. See* ENDANGER.

IMPERIOUS, *a.* आज्ञापकः. 2 दृप्त, उद्धत, धृष्ट, अवलिप्त, सावलेप; 'in an i. tone' सावलेपं, तर्जयंत्या गिरा, उद्धतं, साटोपं. –NESS, *s.* दर्पः, अवलेपः उत्सेकः, औद्धत्यं; *See* PRIDE.

IMPERISHABLE, *a.* अनश्वर, अक्षय-य्य, अक्षयिन्, अविनाशिन्, अव्यय, अजर, अक्षर.

IMPERMEABLE, *a.* अप्रवेश्य, अभेद्य.

IMPERSONAL, *a.* अकर्तृक, अकर्तृवाच्य; ex. by भावः; 'i. verb' भाववाच्यं.

IMPERSONATE, *v. t.* चेतनवत् उपचर् 1 P (with loc.). 2 Feign, q. v.; 'i. ed Râma' गृहीतरामरूपः-वेशः.

IMPERTINENT, *a.* वियात, अशिष्ट, प्रगल्भ, धृष्ट, अविनीत, दुः-कु-शील. 2 अप्रस्तुत, अप्रकृत, अप्रासंगिक (की *f.*); असंगत, असंबद्ध, निष्प्रयोजन, अनर्थक. 3 पराधिकारचर्चक, अव्यापारेषु व्यापारं कुर्वत्. –LY, *adv.* आविनयेन, धृष्टतया, प्रगल्भं, अप्रस्तुतं. –IMPERTINENCE, *s.* अविनयः, प्रागल्भ्यं, धृष्टता, अशिष्टता, वैयात्यं. 2 अप्रस्तुतत्वं, असंबंधः, अनन्वयः, असंगतता.

IMPERTURBABLE, *a.* अक्षोभ्य, निर्विकार, समवृत्तिबुद्धि; अपारिप्लव.

IMPERVIOUS, *a.* दुर्भेद्य, दुष्प्रवेश्य, अभेद्य. 2 गहन, निबिड, अगम्य, संकट, संबाध, नीरंध्र.

IMPETUOUS, *a.* तीव्र, चंड, तीक्ष्ण, उग्र, प्रबल, अविमृश्य कृत, वेगवत्, सरभस. 2 संरंभिन्, साहसिन्, अमर्षण, साहसिक (की *f.*), असमीक्ष्यकारिन्, तीक्ष्णकर्मन्. –LY, *adv.* वेगेन, महावेगेन, सवेगं, उग्रं, ससंरंभं, तीक्ष्णं, साहसेन, सरभसं, तरसा. –NESS, –IMPETUOSITY, *s.* वेगः, सं-आ-महा-वेगः; चंडता, संरंभः, तीव्रता, साहसं, अमर्षता, रभस् *n.*, रभसः.

IMPETUS, *s.* वेगः, सं-आ-वेगः, गति-शक्ति *f.*; (fig.) प्रेरणा, प्रचोदना, प्रोत्साहनं.

IMPINGE, *v. t.* आहन् 2 U (usually A), समापत् 1 P, संघट्ट् 1 A.

IMPIOUS, *a.* अभक्त, अधार्मिक (की *f.*), अपुण्यशील, अधर्मिन्; दुष्ट, पापिष्ठ, असाधु. –NESS,-IMPIETY, *s.* अभक्ति *f.*, अधर्मः, पापं, दुष्कृतं, धर्मलोपः, देवनिंदा, धर्महीनता, असाधुता, दुष्टता.

IMPLACABLE, *a.* अहार्य, अचल, अशाम्य, अशमनीय, अतोषणीय, अनाराध्य, अप्रसाद्य, असांत्वनीय. 2 दीर्घअति-द्वेषिन्; 'i. hatred' आमरणांतिकं वैरं, दीर्घद्वेषः, बद्धवैरं.

IMPLANT, *v. t.* नि-धा 3 U, विलिख् 6 P, निरुह् c., प्रति-नि-ष्ठा c. (-ष्ठापयति), प्रतिवप् 1 P, निखन् 1 P; 'as if i. ed in the heart' प्रत्युप्तेव...अंतर्निखातेव च (Mal. 5); 'so many are the thorns of anxiety i. ed in the heart' तावंतोपि विलिख्यंते हृदये शोकशंकवः (H. 4).

IMPLEMENT, *s.* उपकरणं, साधनं, उपस्करः, सामग्री, द्रव्यं, पात्रं, यंत्रं.

IMPLICATE, *v. t.* संबंध् 9 P, संश्लिष् c., लिप् 6 P, संसृज् 6 P, संक्रम् c.; 'he is i. ed in many crimes' अनेकपापैर्लिप्यते, अनेकदोषास्तास्मिन् संक्रांताः. –ION, *s.* संबंधः, संसर्गः, समन्वयः, अनुषंगः.

IMPLICIT, *a.* निर्विवाद, अवैकल्पिक-असांशयिक (की *f.*); विचारानपेक्ष, अवितर्कित, अनाशंकित, अविचारित; 'better by i. ly.' –LY, *adv.* अवितर्क, अनाशंकं, असंशयपूर्व, अविचार्य, निःशंकं, निर्विवादं, निर्विकल्पं.

IMPLORE, *v. t.* प्र-अभि-अर्थ् 10 A, याच् 1 A, सविनयं-सांजलि-याच्, अनुनी 1 P, आराध् c., प्र-सद् c. –INGLY, *adv.* बद्धांजलि *a.*, पादयोः पतित्वा, सप्रणिपातं, सविनयं.

IMPLY, *v. t.* सूच् 10, ध्वन् c., वच् desid. (विवक्षति), भंग्या व्यंज् c., उप-लक्ष् 10, बुध् c. 2 (As meaning) प्रति-इ c., द्युत् c., गम् c., अभि-धा 3 U; *See* MEAN; 'these senses are i. ed' एते अर्थाः प्रतीयंते (S. B. 33); oft. by अर्थ, गर्भ in comp.; 'words i. ing censure' निंदार्थं वचः. –ED, *a.* विवक्षित, प्रतीत, उपलक्षित, भंग्या सूचित, ध्वनित; 'i. sense' ध्वनिः, फलितं, फलित-ध्वनित गर्भित-अर्थः. –ICATION, *s.* विवक्षा, उपलक्षणं-णा, भंगी *f.*, व्यंजना, अनुमानं.

IMPOLITE, *a.* अशिष्ट, असभ्य, ग्राम्य, दुर्मर्याद, असुजन, दुःशील, अनार्य, अविनीत, अदक्षिण.

IMPOLITIC, *a.* अनीतिज्ञ, नयानभिज्ञ, अबुध, अनिवेचक, अविज्ञ, असमीक्ष्यकारिन्, अमतिमत्. 2 अहित, सापकार, अनर्थावह, अनिष्टकर (री *f.*), असमीक्ष्यकृत, न्यायविरुद्ध. –ALLY, *adv.* असमीक्ष्य, अनीतिज्ञवत्, अविचार्य. –IMPOLICY, *s.* दुर्णयः, अनयः, अनीति *f.*

IMPONDERABLE, IMPONDEROUS, *a.* अगुरु, लघु, निर्भार.

IMPORT, *v. t.* (देशांतरात्) आनी or आहृ or आवह् 1 P. 2 सूच् 10, बुध् c., उद्दिश् 6 P, द्युत् c.; *See* IMPLY, MEAN. 3 गुरुतया संबंध् 9 P or अवलंब् 1 A. –*s.* (I.s) विदेशीयपण्यानि, विदेशजद्रव्याणि, बहिर्देशागतवाणिज्यद्रव्याणि. 2 अर्थः, भावः, अभिप्रायः, आशयः, उद्देशः, विवक्षा; 'of like i.' तुल्यार्थ, समानार्थ. 3 गुरुत्वं, गौरवं. –ANCE, *s.* महत्त्वं, गुरुत्वं, गुरुता, गौरवं, प्रभावः, गरिमन्-महिमन् *m.* 2 उत्कर्षः, उन्नति *f.*, प्रतिष्ठा, प्रतिपत्ति *f.*, गौरवपदं; परम-उच्च-पदं. 3 अभिमानः, दर्पः. –ANT, *a.* महत्, गुरु, अलघु, गुर्वर्थ, बह्वर्थ, बहु-गुरु-प्रभाव, परम; 'i. object' गुर्वर्थः. –ANTLY, *adv.* गुरुतया, परमं. –ATION, *s.* देशांतरादानयनं. 2 आनीतद्रव्याणि.

IMPORTUNE, *v. t.* निर्बंधेन प्रच्छ् 6 P or प्रार्थ् 10 A or याच् 1 A, अनु-निर्-बंध् 9 P, अनु-रुध् 7 U, अतिप्रार्थनया उद्विज् c. or आवस् c.; 'being i. ed &c.' निर्बंधपृष्टः स जगाद सर्वं (R. XIV. 32); पुनः पुनश्चानुबध्यमाना (Ka. 69). –ACY, –ITY, *s.* निर्बंधः, अतिनिर्बंधः, अतियाचना-प्रार्थना, नित्यप्रार्थना, आग्रहः. –ATE, *a.* निर्बंधशील-पर, आग्रहिन्, अतियाचक-प्रार्थक; 'i. demand' अतिनिर्बंधः. –ATELY, *adv.* साग्रहं, निर्बंधेन, पुनःपुनः, सनिर्बंधं.

IMPOSE, *v. t.* निक्षिप् 6 P, नि-विश् c., न्यस् 4 U, नि-आ-धा 3 U, आ-समा-रुह् c. (रोपयति), स्था c. (स्थापयति), नियुज् 7 A, 10; 'i. upon' वंच् 10, विप्र-लभ् 1 A; *See* CHEAT. –ING, *a.* गांभीर्यद्योतिन्, गुरुप्रभाव, विस्मयावह, अद्भुत, विस्मापक, भव्य, प्रकांड, महातेजस्. –ITION, *s.* न्यासः, आरोपः-पणं, स्थापनं, निवेशनं. 2 करः, शुल्कः-ल्कं. 3 छलं, कपटं, दंभः; *See* FRAUD.

IMPOSTOR, *s.* धूर्तः, दांभिकः, वंचकः, प्रतारकः, कितवः. 2 (In religion) धर्मध्वजिन् *m.*, लिंगवृत्तिः; *See* HYPOCRITE.

IMPOSTURE, *s.* वंचना-नं, छद्मन् *n.*, दंभः, कपटं, माया, विप्रलंभः, अतिसंधानं, प्रतारणा; *See* FRAUD.

IMPOSSIBLE, *a.* अशक्य, असाध्य, असंभव, अकरणीय, दुष्कर; gen. ex. by न शक् pass. – IMPOSSIBILITY, *s.* अशक्यता, असाध्यता. 2 असाध्यं, असंभवः; oft. ex. by शशविषाणं-श्रृंगं, खपुष्पं, गगनकुसुमं.

IMPOST, *s.* करः, शुल्कः-ल्कं; बलिः, राजस्वं, राजभागः.

IMPOSTHUME, *s.* विद्रधिः.

IMPOTENT, *a.* निर्बल, दुर्बल, अशक्त, निःसत्व; *See* FEEBLE. 2 क्लीब, पुंस्त्वहीन, नपुंसक, निष्पौरुष. 3 निष्फल, निरर्थक, व्यर्थ, वृथा-मुधा- in comp. –LY, *adv.* दुर्बलं निर्वीर्यं, निःसत्वं. –IMPOTENCY, *s.* दौर्बल्यं, निःसत्वं, वीर्याभावः, क्लीबता, अपौरुषं, पुंस्त्वाभावः, वैक्लव्यं.

IMPOUND, *v. t.* गोष्ठे नि-अव-रुध् 7 U or रक्ष् 1 P.

IMPOVERISH, *v. t.* निर्धनीकृ 8 U, दरिद्रीकृ, धनं नश् c. or क्षि c. 2 वीर्य-शक्ति-हृ 1 P or नश् c. –ED, *a.* निर्धन, क्षीणधन, परिक्षीण, गतविभव, नष्टार्थ, दरिद्रीकृत, अकिंचन, गत-प्रचलित-विभव; *See* POOR. –MENT, *s.* दारिद्र्यं, धननाशः-क्षयः, परिक्षीणता.

IMPRACTICABLE, *a.* असाध्य, अशक्य, दुष्कर, असंभव, अनुपपाद्य, अकार्य.

IMPRECATE, *v. t.* शप् 1 U, आ-क्रुश् 1 P, गर्ह् 1, 10 A, अभिशंस् 1 P. –ION, *s.* शापः, आक्रोशः-शनं, अभिशंसनं, गालि *f.* –ORY, *a.* आक्रोशक, अनिष्टावेदिन्, शापगर्भ.

IMPREGNABLE, *a.* अजय्य, अलंध्य, दुर्जय, दुराक्रम, अनाक्रम्य. 2 गहन, दुर्गम, अगम्य.

IMPREGNATE, *v. t.* सिच् 6 P, नि-आ-°, प्रक्षिप् 6 P; व्याप् 5 P or c., व्यश् 5 A, पूर् 10. 2 (Make pregnant) रेतः सिच्, गर्भं ग्रह् c. or उत्पद् c., ससत्वां कृ; *See* PREGNANT. –ED, *a.* सिक्त, व्याप्त,

पूर्ण-गर्भ- in comp. 2 आपन्नसत्त्वा, गर्भवती. –ION, s. सेकः, निषेकः, गर्भाधानं.

IMPRESS, v. t. नि-धा 3 U, न्यस् 4 U, निविश् c.; पदं ग्रह् c., निष्ठा c. (निष्ठापयति), चित्तनिष्ठ- a. कृ 8 U; संस्कृ; (हृदये) पदं कृ, स्थानं लभ् 1 A (in the mind). 2 अंक् 10, चिह्न् 10, मुद्र् 10; *See* below. 3 हृ 1 P, आकृष् 1 P; *See* ATTRACT. –s. मुद्रा, अंकः, चिह्नं, लक्षणं. –ED, a. मुद्रित, अवगाढ, अंकित; निवेशित, निष्ठ–स्थ- in comp.; 'i. in the mind' हृदयस्थ, चित्तनिष्ठ; 'deeply i. on the ground' अवगाढा (भूमौ) (S. 3). –ION, s. अंकनं, चिह्नं, मुद्रा, अंकः. 2 संस्कारः, चित्तसंस्कारः. 3 अनुभवः, बुद्धि f., मति f., मतं. 4 परिणामः, उत्पन्नं, संस्कारजन्यं फलं; oft. ex. by अंतरं, अवकाशः, पदं with लभ् or ग्रह्; तदलब्धपदं हृदि शोकघने (R. VIII. 91), लेभेंतरं चेतसि नोपदेशः (R. VI. 66) 'made or left no i. on the heart &c'. 5 आघातचिह्नं, छेदः. –IVE, a. हृदयहारिन्, हृदयंगम, चित्ताकर्षिन्, हृदयस्पृश्.

IMPRINT, v. t. मुद्र् 10, अंक् 10, न्यस् 4 U; *See* IMPRESS.

IMPRISON, v. t. कारायां-कारागृहे-निक्षिप् 6 P or बंध् 9 P or निरुध् 7 U. 2 बंदिग्राहं ग्रह् 9 P, आसिध् 1 P, बंदीकृ 8 U. –MENT, s. कारावासः, कारानिरोधः, काराबंधनं-प्रवेशः, निरोधः-धनं, बंधनं, आसेधः, प्रग्रहः, बंदीकरणं.

IMPROBABLE, a. असंभव, अघटनीय, दुर्घट, अनुपपन्न; 'it is i.' नैतदुपपद्यते, संभवति or घटते. –IMPROBABILITY, s. असंभवः, अनुपपत्ति f., असंगति f.

IMPROBITY, s. अशुचिता, अनृजुता, असारल्यं, कापट्यं, कौटिल्यं, शाठ्यं, जिह्मता, खलता; *See* FRAUD.

IMPROMPTU, a. आकस्मिक (की f.), अयत्नपूर्व, अचिंतितपूर्व. –adv. पूर्वचिंतां विना.

IMPROPER, a. अयुक्त, अनुचित, अनुपपन्न, अनर्ह; oft. by कु-अ pr.; 'i. union' असंगतिः, कुयोगः. –LY, adv. अयुक्तं, असम्यक्, अस्थाने, अनुचितं, अनुपपन्नं; 'acting i.' अकृत्यकारिन्. –IMPROPRIETY, s. अनौचित्यं, अन्यायः, अयुक्तता, अनुपपत्ति f. 2 (Of conduct) अविनयः, कुचरितं, अमर्यादा, दुश्चरितं, अकार्यं, अपचारः, मर्यादातिक्रमः.

IMPROVE, v. t. उत्कृष् 1 P or c., संस्कृ 8 U, उन्नतिं-श्रेयस्त्वं-नी 1 P or प्राप् c., उप-चि 5 U, भद्रतर-श्रेयस्-a. कृ; शुध् c., प्रमृज् 2 P or c., प्रतिसंसमा-धा 3 U (as faults). –v. i. सं-वि-अभिवृध् 1 A, उपचि pass., वृद्धिं-उन्नतिं-उत्कर्षं-इ-या 2 P or गम् 1 P or प्राप् 5 P, श्रेयस्-भद्रतर-a. भू; 'has i. ed in health' अस्ति विशेषः; 'to i. in knowledge' विद्यां अर्ज् 1 P or अधिगम् or आप्. –MENT, s. वृद्धि f., अभि-प्र-वृद्धिः, उत्कर्षः, उन्नति f., उपचयः, उदयः, अभ्युदयः, आगमः, आधिक्यं, बृंहणं. 2 श्रेयस्त्वं, भद्रतरत्वं, वरीयस्त्वं. 3 शोधनं, प्रतिसमाधानं; 'i. in knowledge' विद्यागमः, ज्ञानोपचयः; 'i. in health' विशेषः.

IMPROVIDENT, a. अदीर्घदृष्टि, अदूरदर्शिन्; *See* IMPRUDENT. –LY, adv. असमीक्ष्य, अविमृश्य. –IMPROVIDENCE, s. अदीर्घ-अदूर-दृष्टि f.

IMPRUDENT, a. अनयज्ञ, अनीतिमत्, अविज्ञ, अविचक्षण, अनीतिज्ञ, अनभिज्ञ, अमतिमत्; अदीर्घ-अदूरदृष्टि, अविमृश्य-असमीक्ष्य-कारिन्, अदूरदर्शिन्, अविवेकिन्, निर्विवेक, असावधान. 2 (Of acts) अविमृश्यकृत, अनवहित; better by 'i.-ly'. –LY, adv. अविमृश्य, असमीक्ष्य, अविचार्य, अनालोचितं, अदीर्घदृष्ट्या, निर्विवेकं, अविज्ञवत्, अविवेकितया, साहसेन, सावेगं, ससंरंभं. –IMPRUDENCE, s. अदीर्घ-अदूर-दृष्टि f., अपूर्वचिंता, असमीक्षा-क्षणं, अविमर्शः, अविवेकः, अविचारः. 2 अविनयः, दुर्णीति f., दुर्णयः.

IMPUDENT, a. धृष्ट, वियात, प्रगल्भ, निर्लज्ज, अविनीत, दुर्विनीत, निष्त्रप, लज्जा-त्रपा-व्रीडा-हीन, प्रौढ, प्रतिभावत्. –LY, adv. धृष्टवत्, प्रगल्भं, निर्लज्जं, वैयात्येन, धार्ष्ट्येन. –IMPUDENCE, s. धृष्टता, धार्ष्ट्यं, वैयात्यं, प्रागल्भ्यं, अविनयः, अलज्जा, निर्लज्जता, प्रतिभा-भानं.

IMPUGN, v. t. प्रत्या-ख्या 2 P, विरुध् 7 U, निरा-कृ 8 U, अधरीकृ, प्रत्यादिश् 6 P; *See* CONTRADICT. 2 अपवद् 1 A, विपरीतं वद्, निंद् 1 P, दोषं ग्रह् 9 P.

IMPULSE, s. प्रवर्तनं, प्रणोदनं, प्रवृत्ति f., प्रचोदनं-ना, प्रोत्साहनं-ना; 'sudden i.' आकस्मिकी प्रवृत्तिः, वेगः, सं-आ-वेगः. 2 हेतुः, कारणं, निमित्तं, प्रयोजनं. –IMPULSIVE, a. प्रवर्तक, प्रणोदक, प्रोत्साहक, प्रचोदक. 2 आवेगशील, सहसाप्रवर्तिन्, वेगानुवर्तिन्, संरंभिन्; 'pray, don't grow i.' सहसा-आकस्मिकवृत्त्या कर्मणि प्रवर्तितुं नार्हसि. –LY, adv. सहसा, आकस्मिकप्रवृत्त्या.

IMPUNITY, s. दंडाभावः, दंडमुक्ति f. 2 अनपायः, अनपकारः, अक्षति f., अहानि f., अनाशः, अहिंसा, अपीडा; 'with i. (to oneself)' अपकारं विना, स्वयमक्षतेन, आत्महानिं विना.

IMPURE, a. अशुद्ध, अशुचि, अपवित्र, अनिर्मल, समल, अमेध्य. 2 गर्ह्य, निंद्य, कश्मल, कुत्सित. 3 पांसुल, व्यभिचारिन्. –LY, adv. अपवित्रं, अशुचिवत्. –ITY, –NESS, s. अशुचित्वं, अमेध्यता. 2 मलः-लं, अशौचं, कालुष्यं, किट्टं, मालिन्यं, अपद्रव्यं; *See* DIRT. 3 गर्ह्यता, निंद्यता. 4 पांसुलता, लांपट्यं, व्यभिचारः.

IMPUTE, v. t. आरुह् c. (रोपयति), संबंध् 9 P, कॢप् c., प्रसंज् c., निक्षिप् 6 P; *See* ASCRIBE. 2 अपपरि-वद् 1 U, आ-अधि-क्षिप्, निंद् 1 P; *See* CENSURE. –ATION, s. (Act) आरोपः-पणं, कल्पना, संबंधः, प्रसंगः; 'i. of a crime' दोषकल्पना, दोषारोपः. 2 अभियोगः, अभिशंसनं. 3 आरोपः, आ-अधि-

क्षेपः, दूषणं, अपवादः, कलंकः, परि(री)वादः; *See* CALUMNY.

IN, *prep.* Gen ex. by loc.; अंतरे, मध्ये, in comp.; with verbs by नि pr. 2 (Denoting instrument, manner, time, direction) ex. by instr.; 'i. great intimacy' महता स्नेहेन; 'i. six days' षडहेन; 'i. a short time' अचिरेण, अचिरात्; 'i. breadth' विस्तारेण; 'drives i. a chariot' रथेन याति-चरति; 'i. a joyful mood' आनंदेन; 'i. order' क्रमेण, क्रमशः; 'i. small quantities' अल्पशः; 'i. the same manner' तद्वत्, तथैव; 'i. as much as' यतः, यस्मात्, यत्, oft. by abl. or instr. of abstract nouns; *See* BECAUSE; 'i. as much as it arises from ignorance' अविद्यामूलत्वात्.

INABILITY, *s.* असामर्थ्यं, दौर्बल्यं, अशक्ति *f.*

INABSTINENCE, *s.* असंयमः, अनिग्रहः.

INACCESSIBLE, *a.* अगम्य, दुर्गम, दुरासद, दुष्प्राप, दुरारोह, गहन, विषमस्थ.

INACCURATE, *a.* अयथार्थ, अनृत, अतथ्य, अशुद्ध. -LY, *adv.* अयथार्थं, अन्यथा.

INACTION, INACTIVITY, *s.* आलस्यं, अनुद्योगः, निर्व्यापारत्वं, कार्यद्वेषः, औदासीन्यं.

INACTIVE, *a.* अलस, निर्व्यापार, निरुद्यम, अव्यवसाय; *See* IDLE; 'to be i.' उदास् 2 A.

INADEQUATE, *a.* अक्षम, अयोग्य, असमर्थ, अपर्याप्त, अनुचित, अननुरूप.

INADMISSIBLE, *a.* अग्राह्य, अनुपादेय; 'i. into society' अपांक्तेय, अपांक्त.

INADVERTENT, *a.* अनवधान, प्रमादिन्, प्रमत्त, उपेक्षक, निरवेक्ष, असमीक्ष्य-सप्रमादं-कृत. -LY, *adv.* सप्रमादं, निरवेक्षं, अनवधानात्, असमीक्ष्य, असावधानं. -INADVERTENCE, *s.* प्रमादः, उपेक्षा, अनवेक्षा, अनवधानं.

INALIENABLE, *a.* अविच्छेद्य, अनन्यहार्य.

INAMORATA,-INAMORATO, *s.* *See* LOVER.

INANE, *a.* रिक्त, शून्य, अ-निः-सार.

INANIMATE, *a.* अ-वि-चेतन, प्राणहीन, निर्जीव.

INAPPLICABLE, *a.* अनुपयोज्य, अनुपपन्न, अयोग्य, अनुचित.

INAPPLICATION, *s.* आलस्यं, अनुद्योगः, कार्यनिवृत्ति *f.*, अप्रवृत्ति *f.*, अमनोयोगः, अनभिनिवेशः.

INAPPOSITE, INAPPROPRIATE, *a.* अयोग्य, असंगत, अप्रस्तुत, विरुद्ध.

INAPPREHENSIVE, *a.* निःशंक, अकुतोभय, वीतभय.

INAPTITUDE, *s.* अपात्रता, अयोग्यता.

INAPTLY, *adv.* अस्थाने, असंगतं.

INARTICULATE, *a.* अव्यक्त, अस्पष्ट, अस्फुट, अव्यक्त-पद-वर्ण-अक्षर. -LY, *adv.* अस्पष्टं, अव्यक्तं; गद्गदवाचा.

INARTIFICIAL, *a.* अकृत्रिम, सहज.

INATTENTIVE, *a.* अनवधान, निरपे(वे)क्ष, अनासक्त, उपेक्षक, मंदादर, प्रमत्त, प्रमादिन्, अनवहित, अनिविष्टचित्त, शून्यहृदय. -LY, *adv.* सप्रमादं, अनवधानेन, प्रमादतः, असमीक्ष्य, अविमृश्य, निरपेक्षं. -INATTENTION, *s.* अनवधानं, अनपे(वे)क्षा, उपेक्षा, अनादरः, अननुरागः, अमनोयोगः, प्रमादः, शून्यहृदयत्वं.

INAUDIBLE, *a.* अश्राव्य, कर्णागोचर; 'i. weeping' निःशब्दरोदनं.

INAUGURATE, *v. t.* अभिषिच् 6 P, अधिकारे निविश् c. 2 प्रति-ष्ठा c. (प्रतिष्ठापयति), संस्कृ 8 U, उपक्रम् c., आ-रभ् c. (रंभयति). -ION, *s.* अभिषेकः, प्रतिष्ठापनं, संस्कारः; उपक्रमः.

INAURATE, *See* GILD,-ED.

INAUSPICIOUS, *a.* अशुभ, अमंगल, अभद्र, अकल्याण (णी *f.*). -LY, *adv.* अशुभं, अशुभलग्ने.

INBORN, INBRED, *a.* सहज, नैसर्गिक-स्वाभाविक (की *f.*), स्वभावज, अंतर्भव.

INCALCULABLE, *a.* अगण्य, संख्यातीत.

INCANDESCENT, *a.* प्रज्वलन, उत्तप्त, अत्युष्ण. -INCANDESCENCE, *s.* अत्युष्णता, उष्णता.

INCANTATION, *s.* मंत्रः, अभिचारः, योगः, मंत्रप्रयोगः, माया; 'to use i. s' मंत्रैः वशीकृ 8 U or मुह् c., अभिमंत्र् 10 A, अभिचर् c.

INCAPABLE, *a.* अक्षम, असमर्थ, अशक्त, अपर्याप्त, अनुचित, अयोग्य.

INCAPACIOUS, *a.* अपृथु, अविपुल, अविशाल, संकट, संबाध.

INCAPACITY, *s.* असामर्थ्यं, अशक्ति *f.*, अनर्हता, अयोग्यता, अपात्रता. 2 मेधाभावः, बुद्धिहीनता.

INCARCERATE,-ION, *See* IMPRISON,-MENT.

INCARNATE, *a.* मूर्त, मूर्तिमत्, देहवत्, शरीरिन्, शरीरबद्ध, देहिन्, सशरीर. 2 अवतारिन्, मनुष्यरूपधारिन्, गृहीतदेह, मनुष्यरूपेण अवतीर्ण. -ION, *s.* अवतारः; शरीरधारणं, देहग्रहणं, मूर्तिमत्ता, सशरीरता; better by (*a.*); *See* EMBODY also.

INCASE, *v. t.* भांडे नि-धा 3 U or निविश् c. 2 पि-धा, आवृ 5 U, आ-परि-वेष्ट् c., परि-आ-च्छद् 10.

INCAUTIOUS, *a.* असमीक्ष्य-अविमृश्य-कारिन्, साहसिन्. 2 अनवधान, प्रमादिन्, प्रमत्त. -INCAUTION, *s.* प्रमादः, असमीक्षा; *See* INATTENTION.

INCENDIARY, *s.* गृह-अगार-दाहिन् *m.* -INCENDIARISM, *s.* गृहदाहः.

INCENSE, *s.* धूपः, तुरुष्कः, पिंडकः, सिह्लः, यावनः (olibanum); यक्षधूपः, सर्जरसः, रालः, सर्वरसः; 'artificial i.' वृकधूपः, कृत्रिमधूपकः. -*v. t.* धूप् 1 P, 10, धूपेन वास् 10. 2 उत्तिज् c., उद्दीप् c., सं-

धुक्ष् 10, क्षुभ् c, क्रुध् c., प्रकुप् c.; *See* ENRAGE. –INCENSORY, *s.* धूपपात्रं-भाजनं.

INCENTIVE, *s.* प्रलोभनं, प्रचोदनं, प्रवर्तनं, उत्तेजनं, प्रोत्साहनं; प्रेरणं, प्रणोदनं, उद्बोधकं. 2 कारणं, निमित्तं, प्रयोजनं, हेतुः. –*a.* प्रवर्तक, प्रचोदक, &c.

INCEPTION, *s.* प्रारंभः, उपक्रमः.

INCERTITUDE, *s.* विकल्पः, शंका, अनिर्णयः.

INCESSANT, *a.* सतत, अविरत, अनवरत, अविच्छिन्न, अविश्रांत, प्रसक्त. –LY, *adv.* अनवरतं, सततं, अजस्रं, अविच्छेदं, अश्रांतं, सर्वदा, प्रसक्तं, निरंतरं, अभीक्ष्णं.

INCEST, *s.* व्यभिचारः, अगम्यगमनं; oft. by गमनं; 'i. with a mother' मातृगमनं; स्वसृगमनं, &c. –UOUS, *a.* अगम्यगामिन्, व्यभिचारिन्; 'i. son' गुरुतल्पगः; मातृगामी.

INCH, *s.* अंगुलः; 'not even an i.' न रेखामात्रमपि, नाल्पमपि; 'by i. es' अल्पाल्पं, अल्पशः.

INCHASTITY, *s.* व्यभिचारः; असतीत्वं, पांसुलता (of women).

INCHOATE, *a.* उपक्रांत, अचिरप्रारब्ध. 2 असंपूर्ण. –ION, *s.* उपक्रमः, प्रारंभः.

INCIDENT, *s.* वृत्तं, वृत्तांतः, व्यतिकरः, प्रसंगः, संगति *f.*, घटना. 2 उपाख्यानं, प्रासंगिककथा. –AL, *a.* प्रासंगिक-आनुषंगिक-आगंतुक-आकस्मिक-आपतिक,-नैमित्तिक (की *f.*), आहार्य, आगंतु, अप्रस्तुत, अप्रकृत; 'i. cause' आगंतुकारणं, कार्यनिमित्तं. –ALLY, *adv.* प्रसंगतः, प्रसंगवशात्, यदृच्छया, कथाप्रसंगेन, कार्यकारणतः, दैवात्, आगंतुकतया.

INCINERATE, *v. t.* भस्मसात्कृ 8 U, भस्मीकृ.

INCIPIENT, *a.* आरब्ध, उपक्रांत; प्रथम, अग्र, पुरोगामिन्.

INCISE, *v. t.* छिद् 7 P, कृत् 6 P, तक्ष् 1, 5 P; *See* CUT. –ION, *s.* छेदः, कर्तनं, क्षतं, भेदः.

INCITE, *v. t.* प्रवृत् c., प्रोत्सह् c., प्रेर् c., प्रचुद् 10, प्रणुद् 6 P or c., उद्युज् 10; (anger &c.) उद्दीप् c., उत्तिज् c., संधुक्ष् 10. 2 आ-समा-श्वस् c. –ATION,–MENT, *s.* प्रोत्साहनं, प्रचोदनं, प्रवर्तनं, प्रेरणं, उत्तेजनं. 2 Incentive, q. v.

INCLEMENT, *a.* निठुर, कर्कश, निर्घृण, निर्दय. 2 (Of weather) उग्र, कठोर, रूक्ष, असौम्य, तीक्ष्ण, तीव्र, प्रचंड. 3 वातवृष्टिमत्. –INCLEMENCY, *s.* अदया, अकारुण्यं, रूक्षता, कटुता.

INCLINE, *v. i.* नम् 1 P, अव-आ-,नम्रीभू 1 P. 2 प्रवण-*a.* भू; 'favourably i. ed towards her by (her) penance' तपसा तत्प्रवणीकृतः (K. IV. 42); gen. ex. by शील in comp.; 'i. ed to favour' अनुग्रहशील; or by इष् 6 P, वांछ् 1 P; by मनस् or काम with inf. form, or by desid. forms. –*v. t.* आ-अव-नम् c. (नमयति), आवृज् 10, नम्रीकृ. 2 प्रवणीकृ, प्रवृत् c., नि-उद्-युज् 10, प्रोत्सह् c., प्रेर् c.; *See* INCITE. –*s.* उत्सर्पिणी or अवसर्पिणी भूमिः, प्रवणा भूमिः. –ATION, *s.* प्रवृत्ति *f.*, प्रवाहः, प्रावण्यं; gen. ex by शीलता-त्वं or आलुता-त्वं in comp. or by desid. forms; 'i. to fall' पतनशीलता, पतयालुता, पिपतिषा. 2 भावः, अभिलाषः, इच्छा, कामः, छंदः, छंदस् *n.*, रुचि *f.*, चित्तप्रवृत्तिः; 'following one's own i.' कामचारिन्, स्वच्छंद, स्वैरवृत्त, कामचार, स्वैर, स्वैरिन्. 3 आ-,नति *f.*; 'i. of a planet's orbit to the ecliptic' परमापमः. –ED, *a.* नत, आवर्जित. 2 प्रवर्तित, प्रवण, in comp., शील or आलु in comp. or by desid. forms.

INCLUDE, *v. t.* परिग्रह् 9 P, अंतर्गण् 10, समाविश् c., अंतः कल् 10, परिसमाप्-अभिव्याप्- 5 P, प्रतिसं-हृ 1 P; gen. ex. by अंतर् with भू-गम्-पत् 1 P or वृत् 1 A (with nom. of what is included). 2 आ-धा 3 U, धृ 10, आ-दा 3 A, गर्भ in comp. –ED, *a.* अंतर्भावित, अंतर्गणित; परिगृहीत, अंतर्भूत, अंतर्गत, अंतर्वर्तिन्, समाविष्ट, सहित, अवांतर, गर्भित, अभिव्याप्त; गर्भ in comp.; 'i. space' अंतरालः-लं, अभ्यंतरं; 'those persons i.' तानितरान् समाकलय्य, तैरैः सह. –ING,-INCLUSIVE, *a.* परिग्राहिन्, अभिव्यापक; oft. by सह, or सहित *a.*; 'both days i.' उभाभ्यामपि दिनाभ्यां सह, उभयदिनसहितं; 'then enter a hermit with two others (three i. himself)' ततः प्रविशत्यात्मनातृतीयो वैखानसः (S. 1). –INCLUSIVELY, *adv.* साकल्येन, अशेषेण, सहितं. –INCLUSION, *s.* अंतर्भावः, अंतर्गणना-नं, समावेशः-शनं, परिग्रहः, अभि-,व्याप्ति *f.*, प्रतिसंहारः.

INCOGNITO, *a.*, *adv.* प्रच्छन्न, अलक्षित, प्रच्छन्न-गुप्त-रूप; प्रच्छन्नं, गुप्त-अलक्ष्य-रूपेण, निभृताकारेण.

INCOHERENT, *a.* असंगत, असंबद्ध, अनन्वित. –LY, *adv.* असंगतं, अनन्वयं. –INCOHERENCE, *s.* असंबंधः, असंगति *f.*, अनन्वयः, असंदर्भः.

INCOMBUSTIBLE, *a.* अदाह्य, दुर्दाह्य.

INCOME, *s.* आयः, उदयः, आगमः, धनागमः, अर्थप्राप्ति *f.*, धनोदयः.

INCOMMENSURATE, *a.* अतुल्य, असमान; अननुरूप; अपर्याप्त, न अलं.

INCOMMODE, *v. t.* पीड् 10, क्लिश् 9 P, आयस् c.; 'don't i. yourself' अलमायासेन. –INCOMMODIOUS, *a.* अनुपयुक्त, अयोग्य. 2 क्लेश-पीडा-कर (री *f.*), असुखद, उपरोधिन्.

INCOMMUNICATIVE, *a.* वाग्यत, मितवाच्, मितकथ, भाषणविरक्त, संलापविमुख (खी *f.*).

INCOMPARABLE, *a.* अतुल, अनुपम, अद्वितीय, निरुपम, अप्रतिम, अप्रतिरूप, अनुपमेय.

INCOMPASSIONATE, *a.* निर्घृण, क्रूर, नृशंस, निर्दय; *See* CRUEL.

INCOMPATIBLE, *a.* *See* INCONSISTENT.

INCOMPETENT, *a.* अशक्त, असमर्थ, अयोग्य. अकर्मक्षम, अनलंकर्मीण. -LY, *adv.* अयोग्यं, अक्षमवत्. -INCOMPETENCE,-CY, *s.* अक्षमता, असामर्थ्यं, कार्याक्षमता, अपर्याप्ति *f.*

INCOMPLETE, *a.* अपूर्ण, असमाप्त, अनिष्पन्न, सावशेष. 2 विकल, न्यून, लुप्त, हीनांग, न्यूनावयव, लुप्तावयव, असमग्र. -LY, *adv.* अपूर्णं, सावशेषं, अपर्याप्तं; वैकल्येन, असमस्तं. -NESS, *s.* अपूर्णता, असमाप्ति *f.* 2 वैकल्यं, न्यूनता.

INCOMPLEX, INCOMPOSITE, *a.* अमिश्रित, असंकीर्ण, शुद्ध.

INCOMPREHENSIBLE, INCONCEIVABLE, *a.* अज्ञेय, अगम्य, दुर्बोध, अचिंत्य, अविभाव्य, अग्राह्य, अबोधगम्य, अतर्क्य, अधीगम्य, बोधातीत; इंद्रियातीत, अतींद्रिय, इंद्रियागोचर.

INCONCLUSIVE, *a.* अनिर्णायक, अप्रमाण, अनिश्चायक. -LY, *adv.* अप्रमाणं, प्रमाणं विना, अनिर्णायकत्वेन.

INCONGRUOUS, *a.* असंगत, विरुद्ध, असंबद्ध, अनुपपन्न. -NESS,-INCONGRUITY, *s.* विरोधः, असंगति *f.*, अनुपपत्ति *f.*; oft. by क-क; *See* CONGRUOUS.

INCONSIDERATE, *a.* असमीक्ष्य-अविमृश्य-कारिन्, अविवेकिन्, अविमर्शिन्, साहसिन्, प्रमत्त, असावधान; ‘an i. deed’ साहसं. -LY, *adv.* अविमृश्य, असमीक्ष्य, अविचार्य, सहसा, निर्विवेकं, सरभसं, अनालोचितं, निरवधानं, प्रमादतः, साहसेन. -NESS, *s.* अविमर्शः, अविवेकः, असमीक्ष्यकारित्वं, अविचारणा, असमीक्षा.

INCONSISTENT, *a.* असंगत, विरुद्ध, विरोधिन्, असंबद्ध, अनन्वित, विसंवादिन्, विगीत, विपरीत; परस्परविरोधिन्-विरुद्ध, परस्परपराहत, संकुल, पूर्वापरविरुद्ध, क्लिष्ट; oft. ex. by विसंवद् 1 U, विरुध् pass., विप्रवद्; *See* CONSISTENT also. -LY, *adv.* विरोधेन, विरुद्धं, विसंवादेन, परस्परविरुद्धं. -INCONSISTENCE,-CY, *s.* असंगति *f.*, असंबंधः, अनन्वयः, विरोधः, वैपरीत्यं, विभेदः, असादृश्यं, विसंवादः, विप्रतिपत्ति *f.*, परस्परविरोधः, विरोधोक्ति *f.*

INCONSOLABLE, *a.* अशरण, निर्विनोद, शोकाकुल.

INCONSONANT, *a.* *See* INCONSISTENT.

INCONSTANT, *a.* अस्थिर, अदृढ; चल, चंचल; तरल, लोलमति, चलचित्त. -INCONSTANCY, *s.* अस्थैर्यं, तरलता, चंचलत्वं; *See* FICKLE,-NESS.

INCONTAMINATE, *a.* अकलंक, अदूषित, पवित्र.

INCONTESTABLE, INCONTROVERTIBLE, *a.* निर्विवाद, अविचार्य, अप्रत्याख्येय, निःसंदेह, सुनिश्चित.

INCONTINENT, *a.* असंयत, अवशिन्, अजितेंद्रिय, व्यभिचारिन्.-INCONTINENCE, *s.* असंयमः, अदमः, अयमः, अजितेंद्रियत्वं, व्यभिचारः, लांपट्यं, इंद्रियादमः.

INCONVENIENT, *a.* अनुपयुक्त, अनुचित, अपर्याप्त, अयोग्य; अहित, असुखकर-क्लेशकर-(री *f.*); क्लेशद, दुःखावह, उपरोधक, दुःखद. -INCONVENIENCE, *s.* अयोग्यता, अनौचित्यं, अनुपयोगः, अपर्याप्ति *f.* 2 क्लेशः, असुखं, उपरोधः, पीडा, आयासः, आयास-क्लेश-हेतुः-कारणं. -*v. t.* उप-रुध् 7 U; बाध् 1 A, पीड् 10; *See* CONVENIENCE.

INCONVERSANT, *a.* अनभिज्ञ, अविज्ञ; अनभ्यंतर.

INCORPORATE, *v. t.* संमिश्र् 10, संहन् 2 P, संयुज् 7 U, 10, संसृज् 6 P, संश्लिष् c., एकीकृ 8 U. -*v. i.* एकीभू, संसृज्-संयुज्-pass. -ION, *s.* संयोगः, संश्लेषः, संमिश्रणं, संसर्गः.

INCORPOREAL, *a.* अशरीरिन्, विदेह, निरवयव.

INCORRECT, *a.* अशुद्ध, अशुचि, सदोष, दोषवत्. 2 असत्य, अयथार्थ, वितथ; ‘i. in conduct’ दुर्वृत्त, दुराचार. -LY, *adv.* मिथ्या, अन्यथा, अतथ्यं, अयथार्थं; अशुद्धं. -NESS, *s.* अशौचं, अशुद्धता, असत्यता, &c.

INCORRIGIBLE, *a.* अशोध्य, असमाधेय, शिक्षातीत, असाध्य, अप्रतिसमाधेय.

INCORRUPT, *a.* अदुष्ट, शुचि, पवित्र, शुद्ध. -NESS, *s.* शुचिता, शुद्धता.

INCORRUPTIBLE, *a.* अनाश्य, अदूष्य, अक्षय.

INCREASE, *v. i.* वृध् 1 A, वि-सं-प्र-परि°, एध् 1 A, सं-ऋध् 4, 5 P, स्फाय् 1 A, आ-प्यै 1 A, वृद्धिं या-इ 2 P or गम् 1 P or प्राप् 5 P, प्र-उप-चि pass., मुर्छ् 1 P, (मुमूर्छ सहजं तेजो हविषेव हविर्भुजां R. x. 79), प्ररुह् 1 P. 2 विस्तॄ-वितन्-pass., वि-प्र-सृ 1 P. -*v. t.* वृध् c., एध् c., ऋध् c., आप्यै c., स्फाय् c. (स्फावयति), आगम् c., बृंह् c., वृद्धिं नी 1 P, प्ररुह् c., प्र-उप-चि 5 U. 2 विस्तॄ c., वितन् 8 U, प्रसृ c. -*s.* वृद्धि-स्फीति-समृद्धि *f.*, उप-प्र-चयः, वर्धनं, आप्यायनं, बृंहणं, उन्नति *f.*, विस्तारः, आधिक्यं. -ING, *a.* वर्धिष्णु, प्रचीयमान, प्ररोहिन्; *See* GROW.

INCREDIBLE, *a.* अश्रद्धेय, अविश्वास्य, प्रत्ययातीत, विश्वासानर्ह, अतिप्रत्यय-विश्वास, अप्रमाणभूत.

INCREDULOUS, *a.* अश्रद्धालु, अप्रत्ययिन्, शंकाशील, अविश्वासशील. -LY, *adv.* साशंकं, अप्रत्ययेन. -INCREDULITY, *s.* अप्रत्ययः, अश्रद्धा, अविश्वासः.

INCREMENT, *See* INCREASE (*s.*).

INCRIMINATE, *v. t.* अभियुज् 7 A, 10; *See* ACCUSE.

INCUBATE, *v. i.* अव-स्था 1 A, अंडानामुपरि संविश् 6 P, अंडानि पुष् 1, 9 P. -ION, *s.* अंडपोषणं.

INCUBUS, *s.* कुस्वप्नः, दुःस्वप्नः.

INCULCATE, *v. t.* अनु-,शास् 2 P, उपदिश् 6 P, (चित्ते) निविश् c.; शिक्ष् c.; *See* IMPRESS.

INCULPATE, *v. t.* *See* CENSURE.

INCUMBENT, *a.* अवलंबिन्; आश्रित, उपरिस्थ. 2 अवश्यक; oft. ex. by pot. pass. part. or अर्ह् 1 P. -*s.* अधिकृतः, नियोज्यः, वृत्तिभुज् *m.*, वृत्तिभोगिन्-धारिन् *m.*

INCUR, *v. t.* भज् 1 U, आश्रि 1 U, आप् 5 P, लभ् 1 A; आवह् 1 P, उत्पद् c.; gen. ex. by इ-या- 2 P, गम् 1 P &c. with object, by pot. pass. part., अर्ह् 1 P or अर्ह, योग्य, भाजनं, पात्रं, in comp.; 'he i. s blame' वाच्यतां याति, दोषभाजनं-दोषभाक्-दोषपात्रं-भवति; 'i. s debt' ऋणं करोति; 'you will only i. sin' पापमेवाश्रयेथाः; 'i. s a penalty' दंड्यो भवति, दंडमर्हति.

INCURABLE, *a.* असाध्य, अशमनीय, दुरुपचार, अप्रतिकार्य, अपरिहार्य, असमाधेय, निरुपाय.

INCURIOUS, *a.* अनुत्सुक, अजिज्ञासु, अकुतूहलिन्.

INCURSION, *s.* अवस्कंदः-दनं, अभिद्रवः, उपप्लवः, आक्रमः, अभिप्रयाणं, अभिग्रहः; 'to make i. s' अवस्कंद् 1 P, अभिद्रु 1 P; *See* ATTACK. –INCURSIVE, *a.* उपप्लविन्, उपद्रविन्.

INCURVATE, *v. t.* नम् c., आवृज् 10, भुज् 6 P, आकुंच् c. –ION, *s.* आ-,नति *f.*, आकुंचनं.

INDEBTED, *a.* ऋणिन्, ऋणग्रस्त-बद्ध. 2 उपकृत, अनुगृहीत, कृतोपकार; 'I am i. to fortune' दैवेनानुगृहीतोस्मि.

INDECENT, *a.* ग्राम्य, अश्लील, अवाच्य, अश्राव्य. 2 अविनीत, विनयशून्य-रहित, निर्मर्याद, अतिक्रांतमर्यादविनय; अशिष्ट, असभ्य, शिष्टाचारविरुद्ध. 3 अयुक्त, अन्याय्य, लज्जाकर (री *f.*), निंद्य, निर्लज्ज. –LY, *adv.* गर्हितं, अश्लीलतया, अविनयेन, अमर्यादं, अयुक्तं. –INDECENCY, *s.* अश्लीलता, ग्राम्यता. 2 अविनयः, अमर्यादा, अशिष्टता, मर्यादातिक्रमः. 3 अयुक्तता, अनुपपत्ति *f.*, निंद्यता, गर्ह्यता, अन्यायः, कुरीति *f.*, अनीति *f.*, अनयः, कुशीलं, अपचारः.

INDECISION, *s.* संदेहः, अनिर्णयः, अनिर्धारणं, विकल्पः, संशयः, अनिश्चयः, वितर्कः, आशंका, द्वापरः. 2 विकल्प-वितर्क-शीलता, संदिग्ध-अस्थिर-मतित्वं, चलचित्तता, लौल्यं, चंचलता.

INDECISIVE, *a.* संदिग्ध, अनिर्णीत, अनिश्चित, सविकल्प, अनिर्णायक. 2 विकल्प-वितर्क-संदेह-शील, अस्थिरसंदिग्ध-लोल-मति,-धी,-बुद्धि,-चित्त, अनवस्थित, चलचित्त, दोलायमानचित्त; *See* FICKLE. –LY, *adv.* अनिश्चितं, ससंदेहं.

INDECLINABLE, *a.* अव्यय, अविकार्य, अविभक्तिक; 'an i. word' अव्ययः-यं, निपातः.

INDECOROUS, INDECORUM, *See* INDECENT.

INDEED, *adv.* नूनं, खलु, किल, नाम, वस्तुतः, परमार्थतः, सत्यं, तत्त्वतः, अर्थतः, ध्रुवं, तावत्, हि, एव.

INDEFATIGABLE, *a.* अक्लांत, अश्रांत, अविषण्ण, महोत्साह, बहुश्रमक्षम, अनिर्विण्ण; *See* ASSIDUOUS.

INDEFENSIBLE, *a.* अरक्षणीय, अप्रतिपादनीय, अनुत्तर.

INDEFINITE, *a.* अनियत, अनिश्चित, अनिर्दिष्ट, अलक्षित.

INDELIBLE, *a.* अक्षर, शाश्वत (ती *f.*), अनाश्य, अलोप्य, अक्षय्य, अमार्ष्ट्य.

INDELICATE, *a.* ग्राम्य, अश्लील. 2 अविनीत, अशिष्ट, असभ्य, अयुक्त; *See* INDECENT.

INDEMNIFY, *v. t.* (क्षतिं) पूर् 10, निष्कृ 8 U, निस्तॄ c., अपाकृ, प्रतिकृ, शुध् c., प्रमृज् 2 P or c., क्षेमं प्रतिवि-धा 3 U. –INDEMNITY, *s.* क्षति-हानिपूरणं, क्षतिनिष्कृति *f.*-निस्तारः, अपकारशुद्धि *f.*, प्रतिफलं, क्षेमप्रतिविधानं, योगक्षेमः; 'a paper granting i.' अभयपत्रं, दंडाभयपत्रं.

INDENT, *v. t.* दंतुरीकृ 8 U, भंगुरीकृ; अनुक्रकचं छिद् 7 P or अंक् 10. –ATION, *s.* भंगः, छेदः, भंगुरीकरणं. –ED, *a.* दंतुर, दंतुरित, भंगुर, सभंग, अनुक्रकच, –URE, *s.* प्रतिज्ञा-नियम-पत्रं.

INDEPENDENT, *a.* स्वाधीन, अनायत्त, स्वायत्त, स्वतंत्र, आत्मायत्त, आत्मतंत्र, अनाश्रित, अपरायत्त, अ-विवश, अपरतंत्र. 2 स्वैरिन्, स्वच्छंद, स्वैरवृत्ति, स्वैर, स्वैरकाम-चारिन्, यादृच्छिक (की *f.*), निर्यंत्रण, अनियंत्रण, स्वेच्छाचारिन्; *See* FREE; 'i. of' विमुच्य, विहाय, विना; *See* EXCEPT; निरपेक्ष, अनपेक्ष, in comp., बाह्यनिमित्तनिरपेक्षमपि स्वाश्रयं कार्यं भवति (S. B. 508) 'i. of external causes' &c. –LY, *adv.* स्वातंत्र्येण, स्वैरं, स्वेच्छया, स्वच्छंदं, अनायत्तं, यदृच्छया, यथेष्टं, यथाकामं, स्वतंत्रं, अन्यनिरपेक्षं. –INDEPENDENCE, *s.* स्वातंत्र्यं, आत्माधीनता, अपरवशता, अपारतंत्र्यं, स्वाच्छंद्यं, स्वैरता, यदृच्छा.

INDESCRIBABLE, *a.* अकथ्य, अतिकथ, वाग्विभवातिवृत्त, वर्णनातीत, वर्णनाविषय, अवर्णनीय, अनिर्वाच्य; oft. by कः-का-किं-with अपि; काप्यभिख्या तयोरासीत् (R. I. 46) 'an i. splendour' &c.; 'the splendour of that pair is simply i.' किं कथ्यते श्रीरुभयस्य तस्य (K. VII. 78).

INDESTRUCTIBLE, *a.* अक्षय्य, अनश्वर, अनाश्य, अविनाशिन्, अजर, अक्षयिन्.

INDETERMINATE, *a.* अनियत, अनिर्दिष्ट, अनिर्णीत, संदिग्ध, सविकल्प, अलक्षित; अपरिमित. –ION, *s.* Indecision, q. v.

INDEX, *s.* सूचि(ची)पत्रं, सूचि-ची *f.*, निघंटुः, अनुक्रमणिका. 2 प्रदेशि(शि)नी, दर्शकः. 3 (Indicative of) ex. by ज्ञापक-सूचक-गमक-*a.*, तदेव गमकं पांडित्यवैदग्ध्ययोः (Mal. 1) 'that only is the i. of wisdom and skill'; *See* INDICATE.

INDIA, *s.* भारतं, भ(भा)रतवर्षं, जंबुद्वीपः. –INDIAN, *a.* भारतीय, भारतदेशीय.

INDICATE, *v. t.* सूच् 10, द्युत् c., वि-अंज् 7 P or c., गम् c. (गमयति), प्र-निर्-दिश् 6 P, प्र-दृश् c., बुध् c., प्रकटीकृ 8 U, आविष्कृ, निरूप् 10, प्रकाश् c., ज्ञा c. (ज्ञापयति), नि-आ-विद् c., लक्ष् 10, निर्वच् 2 P or c., अभि-धा 3 U, अवगम् c., प्रति-इ c. (प्रत्याययति), पिशुनयति (D.). –ION, *s.* लक्षणं, चिह्नं, लिंगं, व्यंजनं, सूचना, रूपं, अभिज्ञानं; आकूतं, आकारः, इं-

गितं. 2 (Act) प्रकाशनं, निर्देशः, प्रदर्शन. -IVE, -ORY, *a.* दर्शक, गमक, सूचक, व्यंजक, द्योतक, वाचक, ज्ञापक, निर्देशक, बोधक, पिशुन; 'i. of equal love' तुल्यानुरागपिशुनं (V. 2); 'i. mood' स्वार्थः.

INDICT, *v. t.* अभियुज् 7 A, 10, अपवद् 1 A. -MENT, *s.* अभियोगः, अभिशंसनं, अभियोगपत्रं.

INDIFFERENT, *a.* सामान्य, मध्यम, विगुण. 2 समभाव, समबुद्धि, समदृष्टि. समदर्शिन, समपक्ष, तटस्थ, अपक्षपातिन्, निःसंग, मुक्तसंग. 3 निरपेक्ष, अनपेक्ष, निरादर, अनभिलाष, निरभिलाष, निरीह, निस्पृह, विरक्त, निरुत्सुक, अव्यग्र; 'to remain or be i.' उदास् 2 A or उप-ईक्ष् 1 A, किमित्युदासते भरताः (Mal.1); (in good sense) माध्यस्थ्यं अवलंब् 1 A, माध्यस्थ्यमिष्टेप्यवलंबतेर्थे (K. I. 52). -LY, *adv.* निरपेक्षं, निरुत्सुकं, निरभिलाषं. 2 मध्यमतया, सामान्यतः. -INDIFFERENCE, *s.* औदासीन्यं, माध्यस्थ्यं, विरक्ति *f.*, वैराग्यं, अनभिलाषः, अनपेक्षा, अनीहा, अस्पृहा, निःस्पृहता, निरीहता, निःसंगता, ताटस्थ्यं. 2 प्रमादः, उपेक्षा, अमनोयोगः, अनवेक्षा, अनवधानं, अनादरः. 3 समभावः, अपक्षपातः, असंगः.

INDIGENT, *a.* दीन, दरिद्र, अधन, दुर्गत, निःस्व, अकिंचन; *See* POOR. -LY, *adv.* दीनवत्, सकार्पण्यं, सदैन्यं. -INDIGENCE, *s.* दैन्यं, दारिद्यं, निर्धनता, दुर्गति *f.*, दुःस्थिति *f.*, निःस्वता, अकिंचनत्वं.

INDIGENOUS, *a.* स्वदेशोद्भव, स्वदेशीय, स्वदेशजात.

INDIGESTION, *s.* अजीर्णं, अपाकः, अग्निमांद्यं, मंदाग्निः, अन्नविकारः, अन्नापरिपाकः. -INDIGESTIBLE, *a.* दुष्पच, दुर्जर, अजर्य.

INDIGNANT, *a.* कोपाकुल, इद्धमन्यु, समन्यु, सरोष, संरंभिन्, कुपित, अतिक्रुद्ध, अतिरुष्ट, जातामर्ष, संजातकोप, दीप्तकोप. -LY, *adv.* सरोषं, सकोपं, सामर्षं, सक्रोधं. -INDIGNATION, *s.* मन्युः, संरंभः, कोपः, रोषः, क्रोधः, अमर्षः, रुष् *f.*, प्रतिघः, क्रुध् *f.*, गुरुकोपः.

INDIGNITY, *s.* अप(व)मानः, परिभवः, अवज्ञा, अनादरः, उपेक्षा, अवधीरणं-णा, तिरस्कारः, धिक्कारः; *See* DISGRACE, INSULT, also.

INDIGO, *s.* नीलं; (plant) नीली, काला, क्लीतकिका, ग्रामीणा, मधुपर्णिका, रंजनी, श्रीफली, तुत्था, द्रोणी, दोला, नीलिनी, मेला, तूणी.

INDIRECT, *a.* अनृजु, वक्र, कुटिल, जिह्म, परोक्ष; 'i. tax'; परोक्षकरः; 'i. hint' वक्रोक्ति *f.*, भंगिभाषणं, वक्रभणितं, भंग्युक्तिः, भंगि-गी *f.* -LY, *adv.* भंग्युक्त्या, वक्रोक्त्या. 2 वक्रं, कुटिलं, अनृजु, असरलं, तिर्यक्, तिरस्.

INDISCERNIBLE, *a.* अप्रत्यक्ष, अव्यक्त, अदृष्टिगोचर.

INDISCREET, *a.* अविमृश्य-असमीक्ष्य-कारिन्, अविचक्षण, अदूरदर्शिन्, अविवेचक, अनीतिज्ञ, अमतिमत्, विवेकहीन-शून्य, अनवहित. -LY, *adv.* अविमृश्य, असमीक्ष्य, अविचार्य, निर्विवेकं, अविचार-असमीक्षा-पूर्वं. -INDISCRETION, *s.* अविवेकः, अविचारः-रणा, असमीक्षा; अविज्ञता, अविमर्शः, असमीक्ष्यकारिता-त्वं; अनवधानं, प्रमादः, अनपेक्षा.

INDISCRIMINATE, *a.* अविविक्त, निर्विशेष, अपरिच्छिन्न, अपृथक्कृत. 2 संकुल, संकीर्ण, अव्यवस्थित. -ING, -IVE, *a.* अविवेकिन्, अविशेषज्ञ, निर्विवेक. -ION, *s.* अविवेकः, अविचारः-रणा, अपरिच्छेदः, अविज्ञानं. -LY, *adv.* अविविक्तं, निर्विशेषं. 2 संकुलं, संकीर्णं, अक्रमेण, क्रमं विना.

INDISPENSABLE, *a.* अवश्य, अपरित्याज्य, अपरिहार्य, अवश्यकार्य; 'an i. duty' नित्यकर्म.

INDISPOSE, *v. t.* विरंज् c., विमुखीकृ 8 U, अरुचि-विरक्ति-उत्पद् c. or जन् c., प्रतिकूल-*a.* कृ; न प्रवृत् c. 2 अस्वास्थ्यं जन् c. -ED, *a.* विरक्त, विमुख-पराङ्मुख (खी *f.*), अनिच्छु, अननुकूल, द्वेषिन्, प्रतिकूल, अप्रवृत्त, अनभिलाषिन्. 2 अस्व(सु)स्थ, अस्व(सु)स्थशरीर; 'severely i.' बलवदस्वस्थशरीर. -ITION, *s.* विरक्ति *f.*, विरागः, अरुचि *f.*, विमुखता, अनिच्छा, अनीहा, अप्रवृत्ति *f.*, अस्पृहा, प्रतिकूलता. 2 अस्वास्थ्यं, असुस्थता, शरीरास्वास्थ्यं.

INDISPUTABLE, *a.* *See* INCONTESTABLE.

INDISSOLUBLE, *a.* अभेद्य, दुर्भेद्य, अलंघ्य; सुदृढ, दृढबद्ध, सुसंहत. 2 अद्राव्य, अक्षरणीय.

INDISTINCT, *a.* अव्यक्त, अस्फुट, अस्पष्ट, अप्रकाश, अप्रत्यक्ष. 2 संकुल, संकीर्ण; 'an i. speech' म्लिष्टं, अविस्पष्टं. -LY, *adv.* अव्यक्तं, अस्पष्टं. -NESS, *s.* अव्यक्ति *f.*, अस्पष्टता.

INDITE, *v. t.* लिख् 6 P.

INDIVIDUAL, *s.* व्यक्ति *f.*, पुरुषः, एकजनः, अवयवः. -*a.* व्यक्तिगत, अव्यापक, अव्यापिन्, एक. -ITY, *s.* व्यक्तिता, अव्यापकत्वं, व्यक्तिः. 3 पृथक्त्वं, पार्थक्यं, ममता. -LY, *adv.* एकैकशः, प्रत्येकशः, एकैकं, प्रत्यवयवं, अवयवशः, पृथक् पृथक्.

INDIVISIBLE, *a.* अविभाज्य, अभेद्य, अनंश्य, निरवयव.

INDOCILE, *a.* अविनेय, अवश्य, अविधेय, अवशग, दुर्दम, दुर्दांत, अनधीन, अनायत्त, स्वैरिन्, स्वच्छंद.

INDOCTRINATE, *v. t.* *See* ADVISE.

INDOLENT, *a.* तंद्रिल, अलस, तंद्रालु, मंद, निरुद्यम, उद्योगविरक्त, कार्यद्वेषिन्, कार्यविमुख (खी *f.*), निश्चेष्ट, निरुत्साह, जड, मंदक्रिय. -LY, *adv.* निरुद्यमं, अलसवत्, मंदतया. -INDOLENCE, *s.* तंद्रा, आलस्यं, तंद्रि-द्री *f.*, मंदता, जाड्यं, अनुद्योगः, कार्यविमुखता, अनुत्साहः, कार्यद्वेषः.

INDOMITABLE, *a.* दुर्दम, दुर्दांत, अदम्य, अघृष्य. 2 अदीन-अकृपण-चेतस्, अत्युत्साहवत्, दृढसत्त्व.

INDUBITABLE, *a.* असंदिग्ध, सुनिश्चित, अनाशंक्य, निःसंशय; *See* CERTAIN.

INDUCE, *v. t.* अनु-नी 1 P, प्रवृत् c., उद्-नि-युज् 10, प्रचुद् 10, प्रोत्सह् c., प्रेर् c.; *See* INCITE. 2 आ-

कृष् 1 P, प्र-वि-लुभ् c., हृ 1 P; oft. ex. by causal forms. 3 उत्पद् c., जन् c. (जनयति), सं-उद्-भू c., आवह् 1 P. 4 प्रबुध् c. -MENT, s. प्रोत्साहनं, प्रवर्तनं, अनुनयः; प्रचोदनं. 2 कारणं, हेतुः, निमित्तं, प्रलोभनं; *See* INCENTIVE. -INDUCTION, s. अनुमानं; अपवाहः. -INDUCTIVE, a. आनुमानिक (की f.).

INDUCT, v. t. धर्माधिकारे नियुज् 7 A, 10. -ION, s. प्रतिष्ठापनं.

INDULGE, v. i. आ-संज् pass., आसक्त-निरत- a. भू 1 P (with loc.); सेव् 1 A, भज् 1 U. -v. t. उप-,लल् 10, उपच्छंद् 10; अनुग्रह् 9 P, तृप् c., तुष् c.; अनु-वृत् 1 A, अनुरुध् 4 A, अनुवि-धा 3 U, अनुप्रविश् 6 P, पूर् 10. 2 अनु-ज्ञा 9 P, अनु-मुद् 1 A, अनु-मन् 4 A, क्षम् 1 A, 4 P, उपेक्ष् 1 A, न विरुध् 7 U, न संयम् 1 P, न निग्रह् 9 P, न निषिध् 1 P. -ENCE, s. आसक्ति f., निरति f., सेवा, आसंगः; शीलता-आलुता- in comp. 2 अदमः, अनिषेधः, असंयमः, अनिग्रहः, अप्रतिरोधः. 3 तोषणं, तर्पणं, अनुवर्तनं, लालनं, उपच्छंदनं, अनुरोधः, अनुविधानं, अनुवृत्ति f., अनुवृत्तं, छंदोनुवृत्तं. 4 प्रसादः, अनुग्रहः; अनुज्ञा, अनुमति f. -ENT, a. सदय, अनुग्रहशील, अनुग्राहिन्, अनुकूल, अनुकंपक, करुणात्मक. 2 छंदोनुवर्तिन्, छंदानुरोधिन्, अनुविधायिन्. -ENTLY, adv. सानुरोधं, छंदोनुरोधिन, सदयं, सानुग्रहं, सकारुण्यं.

INDURATE, v. t. घनीकृ 8 U, दृढीकृ, संहन् 2 P. -v. i. घनीभू. -ION, s. घनीकरणं, काठिन्यं, घनीभावः, घनता.

INDUSTRY, s. उद्यमः, उद्योगः, व्यवसायः, अध्यवसायः, उत्साहः, यत्नः, अभियोगः, चेष्टा, क्रिया, कार्याभिनिवेशः, कर्मशीलता, कार्यप्रसक्ति-प्रवृत्ति f., अभ्यासः, अनालस्यं, परिश्रमः, आ-प्र-यासः, सोद्योगता. -IOUS, a. उद्यमिन्, उद्योगिन्, व्यवसायिन्, सोद्यम, सोद्योग, सोत्साह, अनलस, कार्यासक्त, कर्मशील, कर्मनिष्ठ, कर्मासक्त, कर्मशूर, क्रियापरायण, अतंद्रित, उद्युक्त, उद्यत, कर्मप्रसित. -IOUSLY, adv. सोद्यमं, सोद्योगं, सोत्साहं, सप्रयत्नं, प्रसक्तं, अभिनिवेशेन.

INEBRIATE, v. t. मद् c., मदं उत्पद् c. -ED, a. मत्त, क्षीव, मदोन्मत्त, उन्मद. -ION, s. मदः, मादः, उन्मादः, क्षीवता.

INEFFABLE, a. *See* INDESCRIBABLE.

INEFFECTIVE, INEFFECTUAL, a. निष्फल, विफल, व्यर्थ, मोघ, निरर्थक, निष्प्रयोजन. 2 निर्बल, असमर्थ, अक्षम, असिद्धिकर (री f.), निष्प्रभाव, अवीर्यवत्; *See* FRUITLESS. -LY, adv. निष्फलं, व्यर्थं, मुधा, वृथा, निरर्थकं; निर्बलं. -INEFFICACY, s. अप्रभावः, अक्षमता, अशक्ति f., असामर्थ्यं, शक्तिहीनता, वैफल्यं, मोघत्वं, व्यर्थता, अनर्थकत्वं. -INEFFICACIOUS, a. अप्रभाव, अक्षम, असमर्थ, तेजोहीन, अप्रबल. 2 मोघ, व्यर्थ, अकिंचित्कर (री f.), विफल, निष्फल. -INEFFICIENT, a. अनुपयुक्त, कार्याक्षम, अनलंकर्मीण, अयोग्य, अकार्यसाधक. 2 अप्रबल.

INELASTIC, a. स्थितिस्थापकत्वहीन.

INELEGANT, a. अशोभन, अश्लील, अप्रशस्त, अविनीत; *See* INDECENT. -INELEGANCE, s. अलावण्यं; अशोभा, &c.

INELOQUENT, a. वागपटु, अवाग्मिन्.

INEPT, a. अयोग्य, अनुचित, अनर्ह. 2 मूढ, मूर्ख, बालिश.

INEQUALITY, s. वैषम्यं, असाम्यं, विषमता, विभेदः, असादृश्यं, भिन्नता.

INEQUITABLE, a. अन्याय्य, अधर्म्य, न्यायविरुद्ध.

INERT, a. जड, निश्चेष्ट, अचेष्ट, अचल, गतिहीन, निश्चल, अचेतन. 2 अनुयोगिन्, मंद, तंद्रिल, जड, अलस. -LY, adv. मंदं, जडवत्. -NESS, s. जाड्यं, अचेष्टा, अनुयोगः, मंदता, आलस्यं, कार्यविमुखता. -INERTIA, s. निश्चलता, जाड्यं.

INESTIMABLE, a, अनर्घ-र्घ्य, अमूल्य, अत्युत्कृष्ट.

INEVITABLE, a. अपरिहार्य, अवश्यभाविन्, अहार्य, अवारणीय, अनिवार्य, नियत, भवितव्य, अवश्यक, आनुषंगिक (की f.). -INEVITABLY, adv. अवश्यं, नियतं, ध्रुवं, एकांत in comp., (एकांतविध्वंसिषु विंडेषु R. II. 57).

INEXCUSABLE, a. अक्षम्य, असोढव्य, अमर्षणीय. 2 निरुत्तर, अनिवार्यदोष, निर्व्यपदेश.

INEXHAUSTIBLE, a. अक्षय, अक्षयिन्, अविनाश्य, अविध्वंसिन्, अनंत, अव्यय.

INEXORABLE, a. निष्ठुर, निरनुरोध, अनाराध्य, अनम्य, अननुनेय, निरनुक्रोश, निर्दय, कठिन-पाषाण-हृदय, कठोरचित्त.

INEXPEDIENT, a. अनुचित, अयोग्य, अनर्ह, अनुपपन्न.

INEXPERIENCE, s. अननुभवः, अपक्वबुद्धित्वं, अपरिणतमतित्वं, व्यवहारानभिज्ञता, अबहुदर्शित्वं. -ED, a. अपक्वबुद्धि, अपरिणतप्रज्ञ, अनभिज्ञ, व्यवहारानभिज्ञ, अल्पदृश्वन्, अबहुदर्शिन्.

INEXPERT, a. अकुशल, अनिपुण, अविदग्ध, अपटु, अदक्ष.

INEXPIABLE, a. अशोध्य, प्रायश्चित्ताक्षम, अनिष्करणीय.

INEXPLICABLE, a. अव्याख्येय, अगम्यार्थ, दुर्बोध, गहन, अबोध्य, दुर्गम.

INEXPRESSIBLE, a. अनभ्रुद्य, अकथ्य; *See* INDESCRIBABLE.

INEXTINGUISHABLE, a. अशाम्य, अनिर्वाप्य.

INEXTRICABLE, a. दुस्तर, अनुद्धार्य.

INFALLIBLE, a. अमोघ, अव्यर्थ, निश्चित. 2 अभ्रमाधीन, प्रमादाक्षम, अस्खलनशील, अस्खलित-मति-बुद्धि, भ्रमानर्ह. -INFALLIBILITY, s. अभ्रांति f., प्रमादाक्षमता, अप्रमादित्वं.

INFAMY, s. अ-अप-यशस् n., दुष्कीर्ति f., अकीर्तिः, अप्रतिष्ठा, वाच्यता, कलंकः, अपकर्षः. -OUS, a. अ-

यशस्कर (री *f.*), निंद्य, वाच्य, कलंकावह, गर्ह्य, अतिदुष्ट, गर्हणीय. 4 (Of persons) दुष्कीर्तिमत्, अयशस्विन्, अपयशस्क, ख्यातगर्हण, अभिशस्त. -OUSNESS, *See* (*s.*).

INFANT, *s.* बालः, शिशुः, बालकः, स्तनंधयः, स्तनपः-पाः, अर्भकः, दारकः, डिंभः, क्षीरपाः, स्तन-क्षीर-पायिन्, उत्तानशयः; (all *f.* also). 2 व्यवहारायोग्य, अप्राप्तव्यवहारदश; 'i. state.' बालावस्था. -*a.*,-ILE, -IVE, *a.* बालयोग्य, बालकीय, (*s.*) in comp. -INFANCY, *s.* बाल्यं, शैशवं, शिशु-बाल-भावः, बाल्यावस्था, शिशु-बाल-कालः. 2 प्रथम-बाल-अवस्था, आरंभः, प्रारंभः. -INFANTICIDE, *s.* बालहत्या, शिशुवधः-हत्या. 2 बालहन् *m.*, बालघातकः.

INFANTRY, *s.* पत्तयः, पदातयः, पदातिकाः (pl.), पदातिबलं, पादातं, पत्तिसैन्यं.

INFATUATE, *v. t.* मुह् c., मद् c., बुद्धि-ज्ञानं हन् 2 P or लुप् c. -ED, *a.* मूढ, वि-सं-परि-मूढ, विमोहित, हत-नष्ट-बुद्धि-ज्ञान, नष्ट-लुप्त-संज्ञ, बुद्धिभ्रष्ट, मोहोपहत, उन्मत्त; 'i. by lust' कामांध, काममूढ. -ING, *a.* मोहिन्, मोहकारिन्, मोहन. -ION, *s.* मोहः, वि-सं-मोहः, मूढता, मूर्खता, बुद्धि-ज्ञान-लोपः-भ्रंशः-नाशः, विवेकहानि *f.*-लोपः.

INFEASIBLE, *a.* असाध्य, दुष्कर, असंभाव्य, अनिष्पादनीय.

INFECT, *v. t.* (अन्यस्मिन्) संचर् c., संक्रम् c., (रोगेण) संसृज् 6 P, रोगाक्रांत-*a.* कृ 8 U. 2 दुष् c. (दूषयति), भ्रंश् c.; *See* CORRUPT. -ED, *a.* रोगदूषित-संसृष्ट-आक्रांत, संचार-संपर्क-संसर्ग-दुष्ट or -दूषित. 2 दुष्ट, दूषित, भ्रष्ट. -ION, *s.* संचारः, संक्रमः, संसर्ग-संचार-संपर्क-स्पर्श-दोषः, रोगसंचारः-संसर्गः-संपर्कः. 2 दोषः, दूषणं. -IOUS,-IVE, *a.* संचारिन्, संसर्गिन्, स्पर्शसंचारिन्, संसर्गीय, सांसर्गिक (की *f.*).

INFECUND, *a.* वंध्य, निष्फल; *See* FRUITLESS.

INFELICITY, *s.* असुखं, अकुशलं, अक्षेमः, दुःखं; आपद्-विपद् *f.*

INFER, *v. t.* अनु-मा 3 A, 2 P, सं-भू c., उन्नी 1 P, ऊह् 1 A, तर्क् 10, अपवह् 1 P, अवगम् 1 P; 'his dignity may be i. ed from his form' संभावनीयानुभावास्याकृतिः (S. 7); 'her very form leads (me) to i. her being superhuman' आकृतिरेवानुमापयत्यमानुषतां (Ka. 132). -ABLE, *a.* अनुमेय, आनुमानिक (की *f.*), तर्कसाध्य-गम्य. -ENCE, *s.* (Process) अनुमिति *f.*, युक्ति *f.*, अपोहनं, परामर्शः. 2 (Result) अनुमानं, अपोहः, अपवाहः, तर्कः, अभ्यूहः; तर्कनिर्णयः-सिद्धांतः. -ENTIAL, *a.* आनुमानिक-आनुषंगिक (की *f.*), अनुमान-तर्क-सिद्ध.

INFERIOR, *a.* ऊन, न्यून, अल्पीयस्. 2 नीच, हीन, नि-अप-कृष्ट, अवर, अधर, जघन्य, अधम, अनुत्तम; *See* MEAN. 3 अधःस्थ, निम्न, अधर, नीचस्थ, अधस्तन (नी *f.*). 4 गौण (णी *f.*), अप्रधान, उपसर्जन, अमुख्य; oft. by कु or दुर् pr.; 'of an i. caste' हीनजाति-वर्ण, दुर्वर्ण, कुकुल; 'i. in rank' अवरपदभाक्; 'i. in age' कनीयस्, अवरज, अनुज; 'it will be clear who is i. and who is superior' अधरोत्तरव्यक्तिर्भविष्यति (M. 1); gen. ex. by परिहा pass. with abl. for 'to'; 'she is not i. to Sachî in majestic dignity' ओजस्वितया न परिहीयते शच्याः (V. 3). -*s.* अवरपदभाक्, हीनपदस्थः, अवरः. -ITY, *s.* न्यूनता, ऊनता, हीनता, अधरता, अवरत्वं, अपकर्षः, अप्राधान्यं, गौणता.

INFERNAL, *a.* नारक (की *f.*), नरकीय, नरकस्थ, निरयगत. 2 आसुर (री *f.*), राक्षस (सी *f.*); 'i. regions' नरकः, निरयः; पातालं, अधोभुवनं, नागलोकः, प्रेतलोकः, बलिसद्मन् *n.* -*s.* नरकवासिन् *m.*, नरकस्थः.

INFERTILE, *a.* *See* FRUITLESS.

INFEST, *v. t.* बाध् 1 A, उप-रुध् 7 U, उप-स्रु 1 A, उप-द्रु 1 P, उपपीड् 10, उपसृज् 6 P, क्लिश् 9 P. -ED, *a.* उपसृष्ट, बाधित. 2 (नित्यं) सेवित, जुष्ट, आश्रित; 'i. by wild animals' श्वापदजुष्ट.

INFIDEL, *s.* नास्तिकः, अश्रद्धालुः, धर्मनिंदकः, अनीश्वरवादिन् *m.*, पाषंडः. -*a.* अश्रद्दधान, नास्तिकवृत्ति, अनीश्वरवादिन्, अविश्वासिन्, मिथ्यादृष्टि. -ITY, *s.* नास्तिकता, अनीश्वरवादः, देव-धर्म-निंदा, शास्त्राश्रद्धा. 2 अभक्ति *f.*, व्यभिचारः, विवाहसमयभंगः. 3 विश्वासघात-भंगः.

INFINITE, *a.* अनंत, अमेय, अमित, अपरिमित, अपार, निर्मर्याद, निरवधि, निःसीम, अपर्यंत; 'an i. number' परार्ध्यं. -ITUDE,-Y, *s.* आनंत्यं, अनंतता, अपारता, सीमाभावः, असीमता. -LY, *adv.* अमितं, अनंतं, अत्यंतं, अतीव, अतिमात्रं.

INFINITESIMAL, *a.* अतिसूक्ष्म, अत्यंतसूक्ष्म.

INFINITIVE, *s.* सामान्य-साधारण-रूपं, the technical name being तुमुन्.

INFIRM, *a.* दुर्बल, क्षीण, अशक्त, अवसन्न, क्षीणबल-सत्त्व-शक्ति; *See* FEEBLE. 2 अस्थिर, स्खलित, अधीर, अदृढ; 'the step being i.' नातिस्थिरचरणसंचारस्य (Ka. 35). 3 जीर्ण, जरापरिणत, जरातुर, जरठ. -ITY, *s.* दौर्बल्यं, अशक्ति *f.*, वीर्य-शक्ति-हानि *f.* 2 दोषः, छिद्रं, विकारः, अपराधः, वैकल्यं, अगुणः. 3 व्याधिः, रोगः, आमयः. -INFIRMARY, *s.* आतुरशाला, रुग्णालयः.

INFIX, *v. t.* *See* FIX.

INFLAME, *v. t.* दीप् c., सं-उत्-प्र॰ ज्वल् c., तप् c., दह् 1 P, सं-इंध् 7 A. 2 उत्तिज् c., प्रोत्सह् c., उद्दीप् c. (as feelings); 'will only serve to i. his grief' संदीपना एव दुःखस्य (विनोदनोपायाः) (U. 3); प्रकुप् c., रुष् c.; *See* ENRAGE, EXCITE; 'i. ed with wrath' इद्धमन्यु, कोपज्वलित.

मदीत; 'i. ed with pride' समिद्धदर्प; 'to be i.-ed' ज्वल् 1 P, दीप् 4 A, दह्-इंध्-pass. -INFLAMMABLE, *a.* दाह्य, ज्वलनशील, आशुज्वलनीय, दाहात्मक. -INFLAMMATION, *s.* तापनं दीपनं, दाहनं. 2 तापः, दाहः, श्रेषः. 3 (In medicine) पाकः; 'i. of the eyes' नेत्रपाकः; अस्थिपाकः, &c. -INFLAMMATORY, *a.* तापक, दीपक, दाहक, दीपन, दाहिन्, तापकारिन्. 2 दाहयुक्त-विशिष्ट, सदाह, सताप, दाह in comp.; 'i. fever' दाहज्वरः.

INFLATE, *v. t.* ध्मा 1 P, श्वि c., स्फाय् c. (स्फावयति), विस्तॄ c., उद्-हन् 2 P; उत्सिच् 6 P or c., उन्मद् c.; 'i. with air' वातेन पॄ c. or पूर् 10, उच्छूनीकृ 8 U. -ED, *a.* ध्मात, स्फीत, शून, उत्सिक्त, उद्धत, उन्मत्त; 'i. with pride' दर्पाध्मात, मदोद्धत, गर्वोद्धत; 'i. with air' वातफुल्ल, वातपूरित-पूर्ण. -ION, *s.* आध्मानं, वातपूरणं.

INFLECT, *v. t.* नम् c., आवृज् 10, भुज् 6 P, कुंच् c. 2 विकृ c., रूपाणि आ-ख्या 2 P; 'the word is not i. ed' तच्छब्दस्य विभक्त्यादिविकारा न जायंते. -ION, *s.* आ-,नति *f.*, आवर्जनं. 2 विकारः, रूपं, विभक्त्यादिकार्यं, कार्यं, विभक्ति *f.*

INFLEXIBLE, *a.* अनम्य, अनावर्ज्य. 2 दृढ, काठिन, संहत; *See* HARD. 3 दृढ-स्थिर-संकल्प-मति-निश्चय, धीर. 4 कठोर, कठिणहृदय, निरनुरोध, निरनुक्रोश, क्रूर. -INFLEXIBLY, *adv.* सुदृढं, दृढनिश्चयपूर्वं, निर्विकल्पं, कठोरं, निरनुरोधं. -INFLEXIBILITY, *s.* अनम्यता, काठिन्यं, संहननं, कठोरता, धैर्यं, दृढसंकल्पत्वं.

INFLICT, *v. t.* प्र-णी 1 P, प्रवृत् c., प्रयुज् 7 A, 10, आचर् 1 P, वि-धा 3 U, कृ 8 U, पत् c., आ-नि-धा; 'to i. pain on' दुःखे पत् c. or दुःखस्य पदं नी 1 P; oft. ex. by कृ or दा 3 U; 'i. punishment' दंडं कृ or दा. -ION, *s.* प्रणयनं, विधानं, प्रवर्तनं, दानं, करणं; 'i. of punishment' दंडप्रणयनं, दंडाधानं.

INFLUENCE, *s.* बलं, प्रभावः, शक्ति *f.*, सामर्थ्यं, वशः-शं, गुणः, प्रतापः. 2 प्रतिष्ठा, गौरवं, वर्णः, अधिकारः, उत्कर्षः, पद-स्थान-गौरवं-माहात्म्यं; 'under the i. of' वश, वश्य, विधेय, अधिष्ठित, आयत्त, अधीन, तंत्र, &c. in comp.; 'under the i. of sleep' निद्रावशविधेय; 'through the i. of love' कामाधीनत्वात्; 'planetary i.' ग्रहावेशः. -*v. t.* अधि-ष्ठा 1 P; प्र-भू 1 P, ईश् 2 A (with gen.); वशीकृ 8 U. 2 प्रवृत् c., प्रेर् c., प्रोत्सह् c., प्र-नि-युज् 10, नी 1 P, आकृष् 1 P, हृ 1 P; 'a fool has his mind i. ed by the convictions of others' मूढः परप्रत्ययनेयबुद्धिः (M. 1); 'to be i. ed by' वशं गम् 1 P, विकृ pass., आयत्त-*a.* भू; 'not i. ed by anger or passions' अनायत्तो रोषस्य, अवशो विषयाणां (Ka. 45).—INFLUENTIAL, *a.* प्रतिष्ठापन्न, सप्रताप, लब्धवर्ण, प्रतिष्ठित, सगौरव; महत्, गुरु, प्रबल, प्रभाववत्; 'an i. meeting' लब्धप्रतिष्ठनराणां समाजः. -LY, *adv.* सप्रतापं, सप्रभावं, सगौरवं.

INFLUX, *s.* आगमः, अंतःप्रवाहः-स्रवणं.

INFOLD, *v. t.* वेष्ट् 1 A or c., आच्छद् c., पि-धा 3 U, कोशे नि-धा. 2 Clasp, q. v.

INFORM, *v. t.* वि-ज्ञा c. (ज्ञापयति), नि-आ-विद् c., शंस् 1 P, कथ् 10, आ-ख्या 2 P or c., बुध् c., संदिश् 6 P, श्रु c., अवगम् c. (गमयति); *See* TELL. 2 (Against) आ-ह्वे 1 A, अभियुज् 7 A, 10, अभिशंस्, आधृष् c. -ANT, *s.* विज्ञापकः, आ-नि-वेदकः; ख्यापकः. -ATION, *s.* निवेदनं, विज्ञापनं, बोधनं, ख्यापनं. 2 वार्ता, प्रवृत्ति *f.*, उदंतः, वृत्तांतः, समाचारः. 3 वि,-ज्ञानं, बोधः, प्रबुद्धता, अवगमः. 4 अभियोगः, अभिशंसनं. -ER, *s.* सूचकः, पिशुनः, कर्णे(र्णे)जपः.

INFORMAL, *a.* अविधि, नियम-विधि-रीति-विरुद्ध, उत्सूत्र. -ITY, *s.* अविधिः, नियम-विधि-विरोधः-भंगः, अव्यवस्था, उत्क्रमः, अनियमः, अरीति *f.* -LY, *adv.* विधि-नियम-विरुद्धं, अयथाविधि.

INFRACTION, *s.* भंगः, अति-व्यति-क्रमः, लंघनं, उल्लंघनं.

INFREQUENT, *a.* असतत, अनभीक्ष्ण, विरल, अनित्य. -LY, *adv.* अनित्यं, अबहुशः, कदाचित्.

INFRINGE, *v. t.* उत्-,लंघ् 1 A, 10, भंज् 7 P, अति-व्यति-क्रम् 1 U, 4 P, अतिचर् 1 P, लुप् c., व्याहन् 2 P. 2 भंज्, खंड् 10, भिद् 7 P. -MENT, *s.* लंघनं, उल्लंघनं, भंगः, अति-व्यति-क्रमः, लोपः, व्याघातः.

INFURIATE, *v. t.* Enrage, q. v. -*a.* संरब्ध, कोपाकुल, क्रोधांध; *See* FURIOUS.

INFUSCATE, *v. t.* *See* DARKEN.

INFUSE, *v. t.* निषिच् 6 P, संमिश्र् 10, संसृज् 6 P, समा-नि-आ-धा 3 U, प्र-नि-क्षिप् 6 P, आ-नि-प्र-विश् c. 2 कथ् 1 P; 'does not i. strength into their understanding' न तयोर्ज्ञाने शक्तिं करोति (U. 2); 'i. into the mind' उपदिश् 6 P, चित्ते निविश् c.; 'i. with perfumes' भू c., वास् 10. -ION, *s.* निषेकः, आधानं, प्रक्षेपः-पणं, निवेशनं, संमिश्रणं. 2 फांटः, हिमं (cold i.); निर्यासः, निर्यूहः, क्वाथः. 3 वासनं, भावनं.

INGEMINATE, *a.* पुनःपुनः कृत. -*v. t.* पुनःपुनः कृ 8 U, द्विगुणीकृ.

INGENIOUS, *a.* चतुर, विदग्ध, प्रवीण, दक्ष, पटु, विचक्षण, उपायज्ञ, विज्ञ, युक्तिमत्, कल्पक, निपुण, तीक्ष्ण-सूक्ष्म-बुद्धि. 2 सुप्रयुक्त, युक्तिकृत. -LY, *adv.* चतुरं, सपाटवं, युक्त्या, निपुणवत्, सुप्रयोगेण. -NESS, -INGENUITY, *s.* युक्ति *f.*, सुप्रयोगः, कल्पना, चातुर्यं, वैदग्ध्यं, पाटवं, दाक्ष्यं, कल्पकशक्ति *f.*, मतिसूक्ष्मता.

INGENUOUS, *a.* निष्कपट, निर्व्याज, अमाय, शुद्धमति, अजिह्म; *See* FRANK, HONEST. 2 उदार, अभि-

जात, महानुभाव. -LY, *adv.* निष्कपटं, अमायया. -NESS, *s.* निष्कापट्यं, अमाया, अव्याजः, सारल्यं, आर्जवं, विमलात्मता, शुद्धभावः. 2 औदार्यं, महानुभावः, आभिजात्यं.

INGLORIOUS, *a.* *See* INFAMOUS.

INGOT, *s.* पिंडः; 'i. mould' तू(तु)लिका, ईषि(षी)का.

INGRAFT, *v. t.* प्रतिवप् 1 P, प्रति-नि-खन् 1 P; *See* ENGRAFT also.

INGRATE, *a.* कृतघ्न (घ्नी *f.*), अकृतज्ञ, अकृतवेदिन्. -INGRATITUDE, *s.* कृतघ्नता, अकृतज्ञता, उपकारविस्मरणं-नाशनं, अकृतवेदित्वं.

INGRATIATE, *v. t.* प्रसादभाजनं भू 1 P, आराध् c., प्रसद् c., अनुरंज् c., उपलल् 10, अनुग्रहं प्राप् 5 P.

INGREDIENT, *s.* अंगं, साधनं, भागः, अंशः, घटकः, घटकावयवः, उपकरणं.

INGRESS, *s.* प्रवेशः, प्रवेशनं, प्रवेशद्वारं-मार्गः.

INHABIT, *v. t.* वस् 1 P, नि-प्रति-°, (with loc.); आ-अधि-वस्, अध्यास् 2 A, आश्रि 1 U, सेव् 1 A, जुष् 6 A, अधि-ष्ठा 1 P (all with acc.); 'thickly i. ed' जनाकीर्ण. -ABLE, *a.* वासयोग्य, निवासार्ह, वासक्षम; आजीव्य. -ANT, *s.* नि-,वासिन्-स्थायिन् *m.*, स्थः in comp.; oft. by derivatives; 'a merchant i. of Kauśâmbî' कौशांबीयो वणिक्; आयोध्यिकः, अत्रत्यः, तत्रत्यः, &c.

INHALE, *v. t.* श्वस् 2 P, नि-पा 1 P, अंतः ग्रह् 9 P; वायुना पूर् 10.

INHARMONIOUS, *a.* विस्वर, कर्कशस्वन, असंगत.

INHERE, *v. i.* निवस् 1 P, नि-ष्ठा 1 P, अंतः वृत् 1 A or जन् 4 A or भू 1 P. -ENCE, *s.* निष्ठा, संस्था, अंतर्वृत्ति *f.*, अधिष्ठानं, अनुषंगः. -ENT, *a.* निष्ठ in comp.; अंतर्जात, अंतर्वर्तिन्, निरूढ, अनुषंगिन्, समवायिन्. 2 निज, सहज, स्वभावज, स्वाभाविक-नैसर्गिक (की *f.*), प्रकृतिस्थ. -ENTLY, *adv.* प्रकृत्या, स्वभावतः.

INHERIT, *v. t.* अन्वयागमेन-कुलक्रमेण-प्राप् 5 P, परंपरया प्राप्, अधिकारीभू 1 P, पैतृकाधिकारं लभ् 1 A. -ANCE, *s.* रिक्थलाभः, अंश-दाय-प्राप्ति *f.*, पैतृकरिक्थप्राप्तिः. 2 दायः, रिक्थं, पैतृकं, पैतृकं धनं or रिक्थं, औद्धारिकं, क्रमागतधनं. 2 उत्तराधिकारः, रिक्थाधिकारः. 4 दायभागः. -ED, *a.* क्रमागत, परंपरागत-प्राप्त, क्रमायात, पैतृक (की *f.*), पितृप्राप्त, अन्वयागत. -OR, *s.* दायादः, रिक्थाधिकारिन् *m.*; *See* HEIR.

INHIBIT, *v. t.* *See* FORBID.

INHOSPITABLE, *a.* आतिथ्यविमुख (खी *f.*), अनातिथेय (यी *f.*), असत्कारशील, सत्कारद्वेषिन्. -INHOSPITALITY, *s.* अतिथ्यनादरः, आतिथ्यविमुखता, असत्कारः.

INHUMAN, *a.* अमनुष्यधर्मन्. 2 क्रूर, नृशंस, निर्दय, निर्घृण, निष्ठुर, कठोरहृदय; *See* CRUEL. -ITY, *s.* क्रौर्यं, निर्दयता, नैष्ठुर्यं. -LY, *adv.* निर्दयं, निष्ठुरं, निष्करुण, क्रूरवत्.

INHUME, *v. t.* भूमौ निखन् 1 P or नि-धा 3 U or निविश् c. or निक्षिप् 6 P. -ATION, *s.* निखननं, भूमौ निवेशनं.

INIMICAL *a.* पारिपंथिन्, वैरिन्, अहित, प्रत्यर्थिन्, विरोधिन्, विपक्ष, द्वेषिन्, प्रतिकूल; *See* under ENEMY. -LY, *adv.* अहितबुद्ध्या, शत्रुभावेन, शत्रुवत्, शत्रु-द्रोह-बुद्ध्या, प्रतिकूलं, विरुद्धं, सवैरं.

INIMITABLE, *a.* असाधारण (णी *f.*), अननुकार्य, अनुपमेय, अप्रतिम, अनुपम, अद्वितीय, अनन्यसाध्य-शक्य.

INIQUITY, *s.* अन्यायः, दौर्जन्यं, दुरात्मता, दुर्वृत्तता, खलता, अधर्मः, अन्याय्यता. 2 पापं, कुकर्मन् *n.*, दुराचारः, अपचारः-कर्म, दुष्कर्म, महापराधः- -OUS, *a.* अन्याय्य, अधर्म्य, दुष्ट, खल, पापिष्ठ, पाप, धर्मापेत, अन्यायिन्, अधार्मिक (की *f.*); (of persons only) दुरात्मन्, दुर्जन, दुर्वृत्त, दुराचार, कुकर्मन्. -OUSLY, *adv.* अन्यायेन, अधर्मेण, खलवत्, दुष्टवत्.

INITIAL, *a.* प्रथम, पूर्व, अग्रिम, आदिम, आद्य, प्राथमिक (की *f.*), आदि in comp. -*s.* आद्याक्षरं, आदिवर्णः, प्रथमाक्षरं.

INITIATE, *v. t.* आरभ् 1 A, उपक्रम् 1 A, प्र-स्तु 2 U. 2 प्रथमतत्त्वानि उपनी 1 A, अभिमंत्र् 10 A, उपदिश् 6 P, दीक्ष् 1 A, (संस्कारपूर्वं) प्रविश् c. -ED, *a.* दीक्षित, कृतसंस्कार, उपनीत, कृतदीक्ष, अभिमंत्रित. 2 कृतविद्योपक्रम, विद्याप्रविष्ट, कृतप्रवेश. -ION, *s.* आरंभः, उपक्रमः, प्रथमशिक्षा-उपदेशः, विद्यातत्त्वोपदेशः, दीक्षा, संस्कारः, अभिमंत्रणं, उपनयः, विद्याप्रवेशः. 2 दीक्षाकरणं. -IVE, *s.* आरंभः, उपक्रमः. -*a.*, -ORY, *a.* आद्य, आरंभक, उपक्रमकारिन्.

INJECT, *v. t.* अंतः प्रविश् c. or निक्षिप् 6 P. -ION, *s.* अंतःक्षेपणं.

INJUDICIOUS, *a.* अविवेकिन्, अविचक्षण, विचार-विवेक-शून्य, विचारहीन, असमीक्ष्यकारिन् or -कृत्; *See* INDISCREET,

INJUNCTION, *s.* शासनं, आज्ञा, आ-नि-देशः, नियोगः; 'sacred i.' विधिः, कल्पः, चोदना; 'scriptural i.' शास्त्रचोदना, धर्मसूत्रं, शास्त्राज्ञा.

INJURE, *v. t.* पीड् 10, नि-अप-कृ 8 U, दु 5 P, हिंस् 7 P (a strong term); सं-,बाध् 1 A, अर्द् 1 P or c., क्षण् 8 P, क्षि 1, 5 P or c., दुष् c. (दूषयति), व्यथ् c. (व्यथयति), द्रुह् 4 P (with dat.), अपराध् 4, 5 P (with loc. or gen.). -ER, *s.* अपकर्तृ *m.*, पीडकः, हिंसकः, अपकारकः, द्रोहिन् *m.* -IOUS, *a.* पीडाकर-अनिष्टकर-हानिकर-अहितकर (री *f.*), अहित, बाधक, अपकारक, हिंसक, द्रोहिन्; घातक, घातुक, हिंसात्मक, हिंस्र, हिंसालु, शरारु, नृशंस. -IOUSLY, *adv.* सापकारं, सापायं, हिंसा-क्षतिपूर्वं. -Y, *s.* पीडा, अपकारः, अपकृति *f.*, अपक्रिया, अपायः, हिंसा, अहितं, अनिष्टं, हानि *f.*, निकृतिः; अन्यायः, द्रोहः, अपराधः. 2 क्षति *f.*, क्षतं, बाधा. 3 नाशः, क्षयः, अपचयः.

INJUSTICE, *s.* अन्यायः, अधर्मः, अनीति *f.*, दुर्णीतिः, न्याय-धर्म-विरोधः, अनयः.

INK, *s.* मसि-सी(मषि-षी) *f.*, मेला, गोला; 'red i.' अलक्तः, अलक्तरसः; 'i.-stand' मसीपात्रं, मस्याधारः, मसिकूपी-भाजनं-धानी, मेलांधुकः, वार्दलः; 'bring i. and paper' मसीभाजनं पत्रं चोपनय (Mu. 1). -*v. t.* मस्या लिप् 6 P or दुष् c. (दूषयति). -Y, *a.* मसीलिप्त, मसीवर्ण-दूषित.

INKLING, *s.* यत्किंचिदवबोधनं, ईषज्ज्ञानं, इंगितं, किंचिद्बोधनं.

INLAND, *a.* देशीय, दैशिक-आभ्यंतरिक (की *f.*), देश in comp. 2 देशमध्यवर्तिन्, देशमध्यस्थ. -ER, *s.* देशमध्यवासिन् *m.*

INLAY, *v. t.* प्रतिबंध् 9 P, (यदि मणिस्त्रपुणि प्रतिबध्यते P. I. 1), प्रतिवप् 1 P, प्रणि-धा 3 U, अनु-व्यध् 4 P, खच् 10 (खचयति), छुर् 6 P or c.

INLET, *s.* द्वारं, प्रवेशः, प्रवेशद्वारं-मार्गः. 2 पुटभेदः, समुद्रवंकः.

INLY, *adv.* अंतर्; अन्तरस्थ *a.*

INMATE, *s.* निवासिन् *m.*, सहवर्तिन् *m.*; gen. परिजनः, भृत्यवर्गः.

INMOST, *a.* अत्यभ्यंतर, अत्यंतर्भूत; gen. ex. by उदरं, गर्भः, अंतर् in comp.; 'i. heart' हृदयोदरं; 'i. soul' अंतरात्मन् *m.*

INN, *s.* पथिकाश्रमः, मठः, उत्तरणस्थानं. 2 स्मृतिशास्त्रज्ञवासः. 3 शुंडा, पानस्थानं, मदिरागृहं-शाला; 'i.-keeper' पथिकाश्रमपतिः, शौंडिकः.

INNATE, *a.* सहज, स्वभावज, निज, स्वाभाविक-नैसर्गिक (की *f.*), निसर्गज, प्रकृतिस्थ. -LY, *adv.* स्वभावतः, निसर्गतः.

INNAVIGABLE, *a.* अनौगम्य.

INNER, *a.* अंतरस्थ, अंतर्भूत, अंतर्गत, अंतरवर्तिन्, अंतरीय, आंतर-आभ्यंतर (री *f.*); oft. by अंतर, अंतर्, गर्भ, उदर in comp.; 'i. apartments' अंतर्गृहं, भवनोदरं, वासगृहं.

INNERMOST, *a.* See INMOST.

INNOCENT, *a.* निरपराध, अकृतापराध, अदोष, अपाप, निष्पाप, अनघ, अनागस्, निर्मल, निर्दोष, शुचि, निष्कलंक, अनवद्य. 2 मुग्ध, मुग्धस्वभाव; अहेतुक, अनिमित्त, निष्कारण; 'i. smile' अनियतस्मितं, अनिमित्तहासः. 3 निरुपद्रव, अनुपद्रविन्, अद्रोहिन्, अहिंस्र, अघातुक, अनपकारिन्. 4 शुद्धमति, निर्मलचित्त, निष्कपट, निर्व्याज, सरल, अकृत्रिम, निर्व्यलीक. -LY, *adv.* निरपराधं, दोषं-पापं-विना, शुचि, निष्कपटं. -INNOCENCE,-CY, *s.* निरपराधता, शुचिता, निर्दोषता, अनघता, दोषमुक्ति *f.*; निष्कापट्यं, सारल्यं, &c.

INNOCUOUS, *a.* अहिंस्र, अहिंसक, अनुपद्रविन्, अनपकारिन्, अद्रोहिन्, अघातुक. -LY, *adv.* अनपकारं, अहिंसापूर्वं, अहिंसया. -NESS, *s.* अहिंसा, अनपकारः, अद्रोहः, अक्षति *f.*

INNOVATE, *v. t.* नूतनरीतिं-व्यवहारं-संप्रदायं-स्था c. (स्थापयति) or प्रवृत् c. or क्लृप् c., देशाचारं परिवृत् c. -ION, *s.* नूतनमार्गप्रवर्तनं, नवाचारस्थापनं, देशाचारपरिवर्तनं. 2 नूतना रीतिः, नवरीतिः-व्यवहारः, नवाचारः, नूतनमार्गः-पद्धति-सरणि *f.*, रीत्यंतरं. -OR, *s.* नवमार्गप्रवर्तकः, नवरीतिस्थापकः.

INNOXIOUS, *a.* See INNOCUOUS.

INNUENDO, *s.* भंगि-गी *f.*, वक्रोक्ति *f.*, व्यंग्योक्तिः, भंग्युक्तिः, छेकोक्तिः, वक्र-भंगि-भाषितं.

INNUMERABLE, *a.* असंख्य, गणनातीत, संख्यातीत, अगण्य, असंख्येय.

INOCULATE, *v. t.* (अन्यस्मिन् स्थाने) निविश् c., संक्रम् c., संचर् c. -ION, *s.* निवेशनं, संचारणं.

INODOROUS, *a.* निर्गंध, गंधहीन.

INOFFENSIVE, *a.* अक्लेशद, अनुपद्रविन्, अबाधक, अद्रोहशील, निरपराध; अपीडाप्रद, अहिंस्र; See INNOCENT, INNOCUOUS. -NESS, *s.* अहिंसा, अद्रोहः, अनपकारः, हिंसाविरति *f.*, अनपकारिता, अद्रोहशीलता.

INOPERATIVE, *a.* अकार्यसाधक, अकिंचित्कर (री *f.*).

INOPPORTUNE, *a.* अप्राप्तकाल, अनवसर, असमयोचित, अस्थान, अयोग्य, अप्रस्तावयोग्य, असमयानुरूप, अ(आ)कालिक (की *f.*). -LY, *adv.* अकाले, अस्थाने, अप्राप्तकालं, अनवसरं, अयथाकालं. -NESS, *s.* अनवसरः, असमयः, अकालिकत्वं.

INORDINATE, *a.* अत्यंत, उद्रिक्त, अतिरिक्त, अमित, अपरिमित, अतिमात्र, अमर्याद. -LY, *adv.* अत्यंतं, अतिमात्रं, नि-सु-तरां, सातिशयं, अतीव. -NESS, *s.* उद्रेकः, अतिरेकः, अत्यंतता, अमितत्वं; See EXCESS, EXCESSIVE, &c.

INORGANIC, *a.* निर्जीव, अप्राणिन्, जड.

INQUEST, *s.* विचारः-रणा, व्यवहारदर्शनं. 2 अपमृत्युविचारणा.

INQUIETUDE, *s.* अशांति *f.*, अस्वास्थ्यं, उद्वेगः, वैक्लव्यं, आकुलता, चित्तवेदना, मनस्तापः.

INQUIRE, (of, after) *v. t.* प्रच्छ् 6 P, अनुयुज् 7 A. 2 अन्विष् 4 P, मृग् 10 A, गवेष् 10, ज्ञा desid. (जिज्ञासते). 3 (into) अव-परि-ईक्ष् 1 A विचर् c., विमृश् 6 P, चर्च् 6 P, 10 A, निरूप् 10, अनुसं-धा 3 U, परिच्छिद् 7 P, निर्णी 1 P, निश्चि 5 U; 'i. about one's health' सुखं-कुशलं-प्रच्छ्, (देवीं सुखं प्रष्टुमागता M. 4). -ER, *s.* प्रष्टृ *m.*, पृच्छकः, अनुयोक्ता, जिज्ञासुः, अन्वेषकः. 2 परीक्षकः, निरूपकः, विचारकः, निर्णेता. -Y, *s.* अनुयोगः, पृच्छा, प्रश्नः. 2

जिज्ञासा, अन्वेषणं, मार्गणं. 3 परीक्षा-क्षणं, अनुसंधानं, निरूपणं, विचार:-रणा, निर्णय:, चर्चा, विमर्श:, निश्चय:, विवेचनं; 'i. about one's well-being (health)' अनामय-कुशल-प्रश्न:.

INQUISITION, *s.* परीक्षणं, विचार:; *See* above. 2 धर्मविचारणसभा.

INQUISITIVE, *a.* जिज्ञासु, प्रश्न-पृच्छन-शील, कुतूहलिन्, कौतुकवत्, कौतुकाविष्ट, अनुसंधान-अन्वेषण-शील. 2 ज्ञानेप्सु. -LY, *adv.* सकौतुकं, कुतूहलात्, जिज्ञासापूर्वं, कुतूहलेन. -NESS, *s.* कु(कौ)तूहलं, कौतुकं, जिज्ञासा, विपृच्छिषा, ज्ञानेच्छा, अन्वेषणशीलता, अनुसंधानेच्छा.

INQUISITOR, *s.* परीक्षक:, विचारक:, निरूपक:. 2 धर्मविचारसभासद् *m.* -IAL, *a.* अतिपरीक्षक-निरूपक, अतिचर्चक. -IALLY, *adv.* अतिचर्चया, अतिपरीक्षापूर्वं.

INRAIL, *v. t.* शंकुपंक्त्या परिवेष्ट् c. or आ-वृ 5 U.

INROAD, *s.* अवस्कंद:-दनं, आपात:, आक्रमणं, उपप्लव:, उप-अभि-द्रव:, अभिनिर्याणं; 'to make i. s' अवस्कंद् 1 P, अभिद्रु 1 P; *See* ATTACK.

INSALUBRIOUS, *a.* अनारोग्य, अक्षेमकर (री *f.*), अक्षेम्य, अहित.

INSALUTARY, *a.* अहित, अक्षेम्य, अहित-अनिष्ट-अक्षेम-असुख-कर (री *f.*).

INSANE, *a.* उन्मत्त, भ्रांतचित्त, उन्मादिन्, सोन्माद, हत-नष्ट-विक्षिप्त-बुद्धि, वातुल, हतज्ञान, भ्रष्टबुद्धि. -LY, *adv.* सोन्मादं, उन्मत्तवत्. -NESS, INSANITY, *s.* उन्माद:, चित्तभ्रम:, बुद्धिभ्रंश:-नाश:, चित्तविप्लव:.

INSATIABLE, INSATIATE, *a.* अतोषणीय, अतृप्त, अतर्पणीय, दुस्तोष. 2 अतिलुब्ध, अतिलंलुप; *See* GREEDY.

INSCRIBE, *v. t.* अभिलिख् 6 P, पत्रे-लेख्ये-निविश् c. or ऋ c. (अर्पयति) or न्यस् 4 U or आरुह् c. 2 वर्णः अंक् 10 or चिह्न् 10. 3 Dedicate, q. v. -ED, *a.* अभिलिखित, पत्रारूढ, न्यस्ताक्षर, लेख्यारोपित; 'writing i. ed on a Bhûrja leaf' भूर्जपत्रगतान्यक्षराणि. -INSCRIPTION, *s.* लेख:, लेख्यं, लिखितं. 2 पाषाण-शिला-लेख:.

INSCRUTABLE, *a.* अतर्क्य, दुर्गाह्य, अचिंत्य, दुर्बोध, अलंघ्य, बोधातीत, गहन, दुर्ज्ञेय, अज्ञेय, अगाध. -INSCRUTABLY, *adv.* परमगहनं, दुर्ज्ञेयतया.

INSCULP, *v. t.* तक्ष् 1, 5 P.

INSECT, *s.* कृमि:, कीट:, क्रिमि:, नील(लां)गु:. -INSECTIVOROUS, *a.* कीटभोजिन्, कृमिभुज्.

INSECURE, *a.* शंकान्वित, संशय-संदेह-स्थ, सशंक, भयान्वित, संशय-शंका-आपन्न, भययुक्त, अनुरक्षित, अक्षेम. -ITY, *s.* भयं, शंका, अक्षेम:-मं, भयशंका-संशय:.

INSENSATE, *a.* मूढ, निर्बुद्धि, हतज्ञान, अचेतन; *See* FOOL.

INSENSIBLE, *a.* अ-वि-गत-नष्ट-चेतन, सुप्त, स्पर्शानभिज्ञ, सुप्त-नष्ट-इंद्रिय, प्र-,मूढ, लुप्तसंज्ञ, नि:संज्ञ, नष्टचेष्ट-संज्ञ, संज्ञा-चेष्टा-चैतन्य-हीन-रहित, प्रलीन, मूर्च्छित. 2 अगोचर, दुर्लक्ष्य, अलक्ष्य, इंद्रियागोचर, इंद्रियातीत, अतींद्रिय. 2 अनार्द्रचित्त, कृपा-दया-हीन, राग-रस-हीन, निर्दय, निष्कृप. 4 जड, कुंठ, मूढ, मूर्ख. 5 (Unaware) अनभिज्ञ, अज्ञ; ex. by not 'Know' q. v.; 'i. to pain' अवेदनाज्ञ, दु:खानभिज्ञ. -NESS,-INSENSIBILITY, *s.* प्रमोह:, प्रलय:, मूर्च्छा, संज्ञा-चेतना-चैतन्य-हानि *f.* -नाश:, अचैतन्यं, अचेतना, इंद्रियसुप्ति *f.* -नाश:, स्पर्शाज्ञानं, अचेतनत्वं, नष्टचेष्टता. 2 रागभाव-हीनता, दयाहीनता. 3 जडता, जाड्यं, जडिमन् *m.* 4 अनभिज्ञता, अबोध:, अज्ञानं. -INSENSIBLY, *adv.* अलक्ष्यं; क्रमेण, शनै:, शनै: शनै:, क्रमश:.

INSEPARABLE, *a.* अवियोज्य, अविभेद्य, समवायिन्, नित्यसहवर्तिन्; 'i. relation' समवायसंबंध:. -INSEPARABLY, *adv.* नित्यसंबंधेन, समवायसंबंधेन.

INSERT, *v. t.* नि-आ-प्र-विश् c., पर्याकल् 10, नि-धा 3 U, अंत: स्था c. (स्थापयति), or न्यस् 4 P; 'i. in writing' अभिलिख् 6 P, लेख्ये आरुह् c. (रोपयति) or सम्-ऋ c. (अर्पयति). -ION, *s.* निवेश:-शनं, निधानं, आ-प्र-वेशनं.

INSIDE, *s.* अभ्यंतरं, अंतरं, उदरं, गर्भ:, क्रोडं, अंतर्भाग:; 'the i. of a house' अंतर्गृहं, भवनोदरं; 'i. of a tree' तरुक्रोडं, कोटरं. -*adv.* अभ्यंतरे, गर्भे, अंतरे, अंत:.

INSIDIOUS, *a.* सव्याज, सकपट, छलिन्, मायान्वित, कापटिक (की *f.*); *See* FRAUDULENT. -LY, *adv.* समायं, सकपटं, सव्याजं, छलेन. -NESS, *s.* कापट्यं, मायित्वं, सव्याजता.

INSIGHT, *s.* ज्ञानं, परिज्ञानं, परिचय:, प्र-नि-वेश:, निरीक्षणं.

INSIGNIA, *s.* लक्षणं, चिह्नं, लिंगं, व्यंजनं, लांछनं, लक्ष्मन् *n.*

INSIGNIFICANT, *a.* निरर्थक, अनर्थक, अर्थहीन-शून्य; not 'Significant' q. v. 2 अगुरु, लघु, अल्पप्रभाव, अकिंचित्कर (री *f.*). 3 तुच्छ, क्षुद्र, नीच, अल्पक, कदर्य, अपकृष्ट, तृणप्राय, नि:सत्त्व; oft. by किं-का-in comp.; कापुरुष: 'i. man'. -LY, *adv.* निरर्थकं, अर्थं विना. 2 लघुतया, लाघवेन, अगौरवेण. -INSIGNIFICANCE,-CY, *s.* अनर्थकत्वं, वैयर्थ्यं, अर्थाभाव:, आनर्थक्यं. 2 लाघवं, अगौरवं, लघिमन् *m.*, अल्पत्वं. 3 क्षुद्रता, अपकर्ष:, तुच्छता.

INSINCERE, *a.* सव्याज, सकपट, कितव, कापटिक-छाद्मिक-(की *f.*), वक्र, मायिन्, कुटिल, कृतक, कृत्रिम, असत्य, वितथ, अलीक, अनृत, मृषार्थक, मिथ्या-मृषा-in comp.; *See* FALSE, DECEITFUL. -ITY, *s.* कापट्यं, असारल्यं, कौटिल्यं, छद्मन् *n.*, दंभ:, माया, जिह्मता, असत्यता, अलीकता, कृत्रिमता. -LY, *adv.* सकपटं,

सव्याजं, असरलं, असत्यं, अयथार्थं, मृषा, मिथ्या.

INSINUATE, *v. i.* मंदं मंदं विसृप् 1 P or प्रविश् 6 P or अंतर्गम् 1 P. –*v. t.* भंग्या आक्षिप् 6 P or सूच् 10, वक्रोक्त्या उपन्यस् 4 U or उद्दिश् 6 P or उपक्षिप् . 2 सामोपचारैः लल् 10 or सांत्व् 10 or आराध् c. or अनुरंज् c. or परानुग्रहं प्राप् 5 P. –ING, *a.* लालन-सांत्वन-शील. 2 वक्रोक्त्या सूचक. –ION, *s.* वक्रोक्ति *f.*, कटाक्षाक्षेपः, भंगिभाषणं, छेकोक्तिः, भंग्युक्तिः, व्यंग्योक्तिः, वक्रभणितं-भाषितं-वाक्यं. 2 लालनं, शनैः परानुग्रहसंपादनं.

INSIPID, *a.* अ-वि-रस, नीरस, रसहीन, अस्वादु, लवणहीन. 2 असार, निःसार, निःसत्त्व, फल्गु, निस्तेजस्. –ITY,-NESS, *s.* वैरस्यं, नीरसता, अस्वादुता, अरसता, असारता, फल्गुता.

INSIST, *v. i.* ग्रहं न मुच् 6 P, निर्बंधेन वद् 1 P or कथ् 10, अतिनिर्बंधेन अव-स्था 1 A or अवलंब् 1 A, दृढोक्त्या वद् or सूच् 10; 'I i. ed on his following me' त्वयावश्यमहमनुसर्तव्य इति निर्बंधेन तमवदम्; 'i. ed on her demands' प्रार्थनाविषये स्वं ग्रहं न मुमोच; *See* IMPORTUNE.

INSOCIABLE, *a.* संसर्गविमुख (खी *f.*), असंलापिन्, अनालाप-असंसर्ग-शील.

INSOLATE, *v. t.* सूर्यकिरणैः व्याप् c.

INSOLENT, *a.* दृप्त, गर्वित, मत्त, उद्धत, मदोद्धत, अवलिप्त, उत्सिक्त. 2 धृष्ट, अविनीत, प्रतिभावत्, वियात, निर्लज्ज, प्रगल्भ, सावहेल, अमर्याद. –LY, *adv.* सदर्पं, सावलेपं, सगर्वं, धृष्टतया, सधर्षं, प्रगल्भं, अविनयेन, सावहेलं, अमर्यादं. –INSOLENCE, *s.* औद्धत्यं, अवलेपः, दर्पः, गर्वः, उत्सेकः. 2 वैयात्यं, अविनयः, प्रागल्भ्यं, धाष्टर्यं, प्रतिभानं, धृष्टता.

INSOLUBLE, *a.* अद्राव्य, अभेद्य, अविलयनीय.

INSOLVENT, *a.* परिक्षीण, गतविभव, निर्धन, ऋणशोधनाक्षम.

INSPECT, *v. t.* ईक्ष् 1 A, सं-परि-अव-निर्-वि-°, निरूप् 10, दृश् 1 P, आ-अव-लोक् 1 A, 10, आलोच् 10, अनुसं-धा 3 U.–ION, *s.* निरीक्षणं, अवेक्षणं, निरूपणं, दर्शनं, आलोकनं. 2 अनुसंधानं, कार्यदर्शनं. 3 अध्यक्षता, अधिकारः, अवेक्षा. –OR, *s.* द्रष्टृ *m.*, निरूपकः, निरीक्षकः. 2 अध्यक्षः, अधिकारिन् *m.*, अवेक्षकः, कर्माधिकारी, कार्यद्रष्टा, कार्याध्यक्षः, कार्याधीशः. –ORSHIP, *s.* अध्यक्षता, कार्याधीशता.

INSPERSION, *s.* अभिषेकः, प्रोक्षणं.

INSPIRE, *v. i.* श्वसिन पृ c. or पूर् 10, श्वस् 2 P, प्राणं आकृष् 1 P. 2 निविश् c., नि-धा 3 U, उपनि-धा, उत्पद् c., जन् c. (जनयति), प्रबुध् c., उपन्यस् 4 U, उपक्षिप् 6 P. 3 आश्वस् c., उत्तिज् c., प्रेर् c., प्रोत्सह् c., संचर् c., उद्युज् 10, प्रवृत् c., धैर्य-तेजः-उत्पद् c.; 'divine speech suddenly i. ed' आकस्मिकप्रत्यवभासां देवीं वाचं (U. 2); 'i. ed life into him' तं सोच्छ्वासमकरोत्; 'i. ed with a passion for Rambhâ' रंभायां बद्धभावः, बद्धानुरागः, कृतप्रणयः; 'i. with confidence' विश्वस् c., विश्वासं नी 1 P or जन् c.; 'i. s with awe' भयं जनयति (प्रथमोपगतस्य Ka. 43). –ATION, *s.* श्वसितं, श्वसनं, उच्छ्वासः, श्वासः, प्राणः, श्वास-प्राण-ग्रहणं, श्वासेन पूरणं. 2 निवेशनं, आधानं, जननं, उत्पादनं. 3 अवभासः, आकस्मिकोद्भवः, ईश्वरप्रेरणा-सूचना-प्रबोधः, ईश्वरप्रेरितं ज्ञानं, दैवज्ञानं. –ED, *a.* निवेशित, जनित, उत्पादित, निहित. 2 प्रेरित, संचारित, ईश्वरप्रेरित-संचारित-प्रबोधित, आकस्मिकप्रत्यवभास. 3 आश्वासित, जातविश्वास, प्रोत्साहित, उत्तेजित; oft. by जात in comp.; 'thus i. with confidence' एवं जातविश्वासः, जातभयः, &c.

INSPIRIT, *v. t.* उत्तिज् c., प्रोत्सह् c., आश्वस् c., उल्लस् c., प्रहृष् c., जीव् c., जीवं-तेजः-धैर्यं आ-धा 3 U or उत्पद् c. or दा 3 U. –ING, *a.* उत्तेजक, प्रोत्साहक, आश्वासक, उत्साहप्रद.

INSPISSATE, *v. t.* घनी-सांद्री-कृ 8 U, संहन् 2 P. –*a.*,-ED, *a.* घनीभूत, घन, सांद्र, संहत, निबिड. –ION, *s.* घनता, सांद्रता, गाढता.

INSTABILITY, *s.* अस्थैर्यं, चंचलता, चापल्यं, अनवस्था, अस्थायित्वं, अनित्यता.

INSTALL, *v. t.* यथाविधि प्रतिष्ठा c. (प्रतिष्ठापयति), अधिकारे नियुज् 7 A, 10, अधिकारारूढ-पदस्थ-*a.* कृ 8 U, अभिषिच् 6 P (with loc.); 'i. as heir apparent' यौवराज्याभिषेकं कृ, यौवराज्ये अभिषिच्. 2 संस्कृ, अभि-अनु-मंत्र् 10 A. –ATION, *s.* प्रतिष्ठापनं, अभिषेकः, नवाधिकार-प्रवेशनं-प्रतिष्ठा, संस्कारः, पदस्थापनं, राज्याभिषेकः. –ED, *a.* प्रतिष्ठापित, प्रतिष्ठित, अभिषिक्त, कृताभिषेक, कृतसंस्कार, कृत-लब्ध-प्रतिष्ठ, नवाधिकारप्रवेशित, अधिकार-पद-आरूढ.

INSTALMENT, *s.* भागः, अंशः, ऋणभागः; 'by i. s' अंशांशतः, विभागशः, भागतः.

INSTANCE, *s.* उदाहरणं, निदर्शनं, दृष्टांतः, उदाहारः. 2 पदं, स्थलं, विषयः, स्थानं. 3 प्रस्तावः, समयः, अवसरः. 4 प्रार्थना-नं, निर्बंधः, प्रेरणा; 'at his i.' तत्प्रेरितः; 'for i.' तथाहि, यथा, दृष्टांतरूपेण; 'as for i.' तद्यथा; in the first i.' प्रथमतः, प्रथमं, प्रथमसमये. –*v. t.* दृष्टांतरूपेण कथ् 10, निदृश् c., दृष्टांतयति (D.).

INSTANT, *a.* सद्यः in comp., तात्कालिक-सायस्क (की *f.*), अनंतरकालीन, अव्यवहितकाल, क्षिप्र, शीघ्र, अचिर. 2 निर्बंध-आग्रह-शील, अतियाचक-प्रार्थक. 3 वर्तमान; 'i. death' सद्योमृत्युः; 'bearing an i. fruit' सद्योविपाक. –*s.* क्षणः, पलं, निमि(मे)षः, मात्रा; 'the present i.' आपातः; 'in an i.' क्षणात्, क्षणेनैव, निमेष-क्षण-मात्रेण, एकपदे; 'for an i.' क्षणमात्रं, क्षणं; 'the i.' ex. by एव, मात्र in comp., or यावत्-तावत्; 'at that (very) i.' तत्काले एव,

तत्क्षणे; ‘every i.’ प्रति-अनु-क्षणं, क्षणे क्षणे; ‘the next i.’ क्षणांतरं; ‘from the i. of birth’ जातमात्र-*a.* —ANEOUS, *a.* क्षणस्थायिन्, अचिर, तात्कालिक-तत्क्षणिक (की *f.*), क्षणिक. —ANEOUSLY, *adv.* क्षणेणपात्, एकपदे, सद्यः, तत्काले, तत्क्षणे; *See* below. —LY, *adv.* सपदि, द्राक्, तत्क्षणं-णे-णेन, झटिति, सद्य एव, क्षण-निमेष-मात्रेण, क्षणेन, क्षणाद् एव, अंजसा.

INSTATE, *v. t.* पदं आ-रुह् c. (रोपयति), प्रति-ष्ठा c. (-ष्ठापयति), प्रविश् c.

INSTAURATION, *s.* प्रतिष्ठापनं, प्रतिसमाधानं.

INSTEAD (of), *prep.*, *adv.* (Before nouns) ex. by स्थाने, स्थले, भूमौ, विनिमयेन, in comp.; ‘i. of my brother’ भ्रातृस्थाने; तिलविनिमयेन, &c.; (before participles) ex. by loc. abs. with pot. pass. part.; ‘i. of saying *on Purushottama*’ पुरुषोत्तमे इति भणितव्ये (V. 3); ‘i. of studying, why do you play’ अध्ययने आरब्धव्ये किमिति क्रीडसि; ‘be not sorry i. of being glad’ हर्षस्थाने अलं विषादेन (V. 2).

INSTEEP, *v. t.* वास् 10, भू c., सिच् 6 P or c., आप्लु c.

INSTEP, *s.* पिचं(चिं)डिका, पिंडि-डी *f.*, पिंडिका.

INSTIGATE, *v. t.* प्रोत्सह् c., उत्तिज् c., उद्-नि-युज् 10, प्रेर् c., प्रचुद् 10, प्रवृत् c., प्रणुद् c., उद्दीप् c., उत्था c. (उत्थापयति), प्ररुच् c. —ION, *s.* प्रोत्साहनं-ना, प्रेरणं-णा, प्रचोदनं-ना. —OR, *s.* प्रोत्साहकः, प्रवर्तकः, उत्तेजकः, प्रेरकः.

INSTIL, *v. t.* लवशः-अल्पाल्पं-निषिच् or निक्षिप् 6 P, शनैः शनैः प्र-नि-विश् c. or उपदिश् 6 P or शास् 2 P.

INSTINCT, *s.* सहजज्ञानं, अशिक्षितबोधः, स्वाभाविक-नैसर्गिक-सहज-बुद्धि *f.*, स्वाभाविकज्ञानं; ‘natural i.’ सहजावबोधः. —*a.* उत्तेजित, उद्दीपित, उद्दीप्त. —IVE, *a.* सहज, सहजज्ञानसिद्ध, प्रकृतिसिद्ध, सहजात, स्वाभाविक-नैसर्गिक (की *f.*), स्वभावप्रेरित. —IVELY, *adv.* अंतःप्रवृत्त्या, स्वयं, स्वत एव, स्वभावतः, सहजावबोधेन.

INSTITUTE, *v. t.* प्रारभ् 1 A, उपक्रम् 1 A, प्रवृत् c., प्रस्तु 2 U; स्था c. (स्थापयति), प्रति-व्यव-सं°. 2 प्र-परि-क्लृप् c., वि-धा 3 U, आ-निर्-दिश् 6 P, प्रचुद् 10, शास् 2 P. —*s.* व्यवस्था, स्थिति *f.*, विधिः, नियमः, कल्पः, सूत्रं, शास्त्रविधानं-मर्यादा-निदर्शनं, नियोगः, चोदना; ‘religious i. s’ धर्मशास्त्रं; ‘i. s of Manu’ मनुसंहिता, मनुस्मृतिशास्त्रं. —ION, *s.* स्थापनं, कल्पनं, विधानं. 2 विधिः, नियमः, रीति *f.*, मार्गः; *See* (*s.*). 3 शाला, आलयः, मंदिरं, सभा; श्रेणि-णी *f.*, संसर्गः, संस्थानं, समाजः; ‘religious i.’ धर्मसंस्थानं-शाला; ‘educational i.’ विद्यालयः, ज्ञानमंदिरं. —OR, *s.* संस्थापकः, प्रवर्तकः, आरंभकः.

INSTRUCT, *v. t.* अनु-, शास् 2 P, शिक्ष् c., उपदिश् 6 P, अधि-इ c. (अध्यापयति), पठ् c., विनी 1 P. 2 बुध् c., ज्ञा c. (ज्ञापयति), नि-आ-विद् c., सूच् 10. 3 आ-निर्-सं-दिश्, आ-ज्ञा c., नियुज् 7 A, 10, प्रचुद् 10. —ION, *s.* उपदेशः, शिक्षा-क्षणं, विनयनं, अध्यापनं, शासनं, बोधनं. 2 विधिः, नियमः, सूत्रं, कल्पः. 3 आज्ञा, नि-आ-देशः, शासनं, नियोगः. —IVE, *a.* उपदेशक, उपदेशप्रद, बोधावह, बोधकर (री *f.*), बोधक. —OR, *s.* शिक्षकः, गुरुः, उपाध्यायः, उपदेशकः, अध्यापकः, उपदेष्टृ *m.*, आचार्यः. —INSTRUCTRESS, *s.* उपदेष्ट्री, आचार्या, उपाध्याया-यी, अध्यापिका.

INSTRUMENT, *s.* यंत्रं, साधनं; कार्यसाधनं, उपकरणं, सामग्री, उपस्करः, द्रव्यं. 2 कारणं, करणं, हेतुः, निमित्तं, निमित्तकारणं. 3 कारकः, साधकः, कर्ता, कारकहेतुः. 4 लेखः, लेख्यं, पत्रं, लेखपत्रं; ‘serving as the i. of others’ परोपकरणीकृत-भूत; ‘where such persons become helping i. s’ यंत्रोपकरणीभावमायात्येवंविधो जनः (U. 3); ‘musical i.’ वादित्रं, वाद्यं, तूर्यं, आतोद्यं; ‘a wind-i.’ सुषिरं, शंखः; ‘stringed i.’ तंत्रीः; तंतुवाद्यं; ‘martial i.’ रणवाद्यं. —AL, *a.* Ex. by साधनं, कारणं, हेतुः, निमित्तं; ‘he was i. in elevating me’ स ममोन्नतौ कारणं-हेतुः; साधक, साधन-कारण-भूत, साधनी-कारणी-भूत, उपकारक. 2 वाद्यज, वाद्यसंभूत, वाद्योत्पन्न. 3 करणं, तृतीयाविभक्तिः. —ALITY, *s.* कारणत्वं, कर्तृत्वं, करणत्वं, साधनत्वं; *See* THROUGH. —ALLY, *adv.* कारणतः, निमित्ततः.

INSUBORDINATE, *a.* अविधेय, अवश, अवशवर्तिन्, अनायत्त, अविनीत, अनुपसर्जन, अगौण (णी *f.*). —ION, *s.* अविनयः, अविधेयता, शासन-आज्ञा-भंगः-व्यतिक्रमः, अवशता, अगौणता.

INSUBSTANTIAL, *a.* अ-निः-सार, निःसत्त्व, अवास्तविक (की *f.*).

INSUFFERABLE, *a.* असह्य, दुःसह, अक्षंतव्य.

INSUFFICIENT, *a.* अपर्याप्त, न्यून, अयथेष्ट, अल्प, अप्रचुर, हीन, क्षीण, अनलं *ind.* 2 अनुचित, अक्षम, अयोग्य. —LY, *adv.* अनलं, अप्रचुरं, अपर्याप्तं. 2 अनुचितं, अयोग्यं. —INSUFFICIENCY, *s.* न्यूनता, अपर्याप्ति *f.*, अल्पत्वं, अबाहुल्यं, हीनता, अप्राचुर्यं. 2 अक्षमता, अनौचित्यं.

INSULAR, *a.* द्वीपीय, द्वीप्य, द्वीपसंबंधिन्. 2 जलपरिगत-परिवृत-वेष्टित.

INSULATE, *v. t.* पृथक् कृ 8 U; पृथग् विन्यस् 4 P; *See* SEPARATE. —ED, *a.* अन्यविश्लिष्ट, पृथक् स्थित, अनन्यसंलग्न-संसक्त. —ION, *s.* अन्यावियोगः-विश्लेषः, पृथक् स्थिति *f.*

INSULT, *s.* अवमानना, निकृति *f.*, मानभंगः, अवज्ञा; परिभवः-भूति *f.*, अप(व)मानः, तिरस्कारः, परिवादः, दुर्वचस् *n.*, खलोक्ति *f.*; अनादरः, भर्त्सना, धर्षणं, आ-अव-क्षेपः; ‘add i. to injury’ क्षते क्षारं प्रक्षिप् 6 P.

–*v. t.* निक्कृ 8 U, अव-अप-मन् 4 A or c., अव-ज्ञा 9 U, तिरस्कृ, परिभू 1 P, आ-अव-धृष् c., निंद् 1 P, गर्ह् 1, 10 A, आ-अधि-क्षिप् 6 P, आक्षर् c., अप-परि-वद् 1 U, कुत्स् 10 A, लघूकृ. –ING, *a.* अपमानकारिन्, अवमानिन्, परिभाविन्, निंदार्थ. –INGLY, *adv.* सावज्ञं, सावमानं.

INSUPERABLE, *a.* दुरतिक्रम, अलंघ्य, दुस्तर, अनतिक्रमणीय, दुरत्यय, दुरारोह, दुर्जय.

INSUPPORTABLE, *a.* दुःसह, असह्य, निःसह, दुरुद्वह, दुर्वह.

INSUPPRESSIBLE, *a.* दुर्निग्रह, दुर्निवार.

INSURE, *v. t.* रक्ष् 1 P, प्रतिवि-धा 3 U, सत्यीकृ 1 U, योगक्षेमं कृ or वि-धा, नाशात् निवार् 10. –ANCE, *s.* योगक्षेमः, क्षेमविधानं-करणं, सत्यापनं, रक्षणं.

INSURGENT, *s.* राजद्रोहिन् *m.*, राजविरोधी, राजापथ्यकारी, प्रजाविप्लव-प्रकृतिक्षोभ-कारी.

INSURMOUNTABLE, *a. See* INSUPERABLE.

INSURRECTION, *s.* राजविद्रोहः, राजप्रकोपः, नृपाभिद्रोहः, प्रकृति-प्रजा-क्षोभः-कोपः, राज्योपप्लवः, उपप्लवः, उपद्रवः. –ARY, *a.* राजविरुद्ध-प्रतीप-विपरीत, उपद्रविन्.

INSUSCEPTIBLE, *a.* अग्राहक, अविकारिन्, ग्रहणाक्षम.

INTACT, *a.* अखंड, अविकल, अभेद्य.

INTANGIBLE, *a.* अस्पृश्य, स्पर्शागोचर, अस्पर्शवेद्य, दुरालभ.

INTEGRAL, INTEGER, *s.* पूर्णांकः, अभिन्नः. रूपं. –*a.* पूर्ण, अविकल, समग्र, अभिन्न, अखंड, अन्यून, सांग. 2 पूरित, पूर्ण. –INTEGRATE, *v. t.* संपूर् 10. –INTEGRITY, *s.* अवैकल्यं, साकल्यं, पूर्णता, अभिन्नभावः, अभेदः, अखंडता. 2 शुचिता, आर्जवं, सारल्यं, वैमल्यं; *See* HONESTY; 'of strict i.' अभेद्य, अहार्य.

INTEGUMENT, *s.* वेष्टनं, आ-परि-°; पटलं, कंचुकः, पुटः-टं, कोशः-षः, आच्छादनं, आवरणं.

INTELLECT, *s.* मतिः, बुद्धिः, प्रज्ञा, धीः, धि(धी)षणा, मनीषा, प्रेक्षा, शेमुषी, उपलब्धिः, चित्, संविद्, प्रतिपद्, ज्ञप्तिः, चेतना (all *f.*); 'retentive i.' मेधा, धारणावती धीः. –UAL, *a.* Ex. by (*s.*) in comp.; बुद्धिविषयक, मानसिक (की *f.*); 'i. gain' ज्ञानोत्कर्षः, मानसोन्नति *f.* 2 बुद्धिमत्, धीमत्, मनीषिन्; 'i. faculty' धीशक्ति *f.*, निष्क्रमः; 'possessing i. qualities' धीगुणसंपन्न. –UALLY, *adv.* धिया, बुद्धिपूर्वं.

INTELLIGENCE, *s.* मति *f.*, ज्ञानं, बुद्धिचातुर्यं, वैदग्ध्यं, मेधा; *See* INTELLECT. 2 वार्ता, उदंतः, वृत्तांतः, प्रवृत्ति *f.*, समाचारः, 3 संदेशः, वाचिकं. –ER, *s.* वार्ताहरः, वार्तावहः, संदेशहरः, आख्यायकः, वैवधिकः. —INTELLIGENT, *a.* मति-बुद्धि-धी-मत्, प्रज्ञावत्, मेधाविन्, सज्ञान, प्राज्ञ, सुधी. 2 चतुर, कुशल, निपुण, विज्ञ, विदग्ध, निपुणमति. –LY, *adv.* चतुरं, सवैदग्ध्यं, सनैपुण्यं, विज्ञवत्, सुबुद्धिपूर्वं, बुद्धिचातुर्येण. –INTELLIGIBLE, *a.* स्पष्ट, सुगम, बोधगम्य, भिन्नार्थ, सुबोध, सुव्यक्त, सुग्राह्य, बुद्धिगम्य-ग्राह्य. –INTELLIGIBLY, *adv.* स्पष्टं, सुव्यक्तं, भिन्नार्थं, स्पष्टार्थं.

INTEMPERATE, *a.* असंयत, असंयमिन्, असंयमशील, अतिमर्याद, अयतवृत्ति, असंयताचार, असंयतेंद्रिय, अमितभोगिन्; (in eating) अतिभोजिन्, अत्याहारिन्, अयताहार; *See* GLUTTON; (in drinking) अतिपानासक्त, अतिपायिन्, पानप्रसक्त. 2 (Of things) अमित, अपरिमित, अमर्याद, अनियत, अयत, अपरिमाण, उद्रिक्त, अतिरिक्त, अत्यधिक. –LY, *adv.* असंयमेन, अमर्यादं, अपरिमितं, अतिशयेन, नियमातिक्रमेण. –INTEMPERANCE, *s.* असंमयः, अदमः, अनिग्रहः, नियमातिक्रमः, अजितेंद्रियत्वं, अनियतवृत्ति *f.*, अत्याचारः; अतिभोजनं, अत्याहारः, अमिताहारः; अतिपानं, पानप्रसक्ति *f.* 2 उद्रेकः, अमर्यादा, अमितत्वं, आधिक्यं, अनियमः, मर्यादातिक्रमः, अतिशयः, अतिरेकः.

INTEND, *v. t.* अभिप्र-इ 2 P, परि-सं-क्लृप् c., इष् 6 P, ईह् 1 A, उद्दिश् 6 P, मनः-मतिं-कृ 8 U (with dat.), कृ desid. (चिकीर्षति-ते), मनसा चिंत् 10 or उद्दिश्; oft. ex. by desid. forms, or by मनः-काम with inf. form; 'what do you i. to do' किं कर्तुमनाः. —INTENTION, *s.* अभिप्रायः, संकल्पः आशयः, उद्देशः, इच्छा, कामः, चिकीर्षा, आकांक्षा, आकूतं, बुद्धि-मति *f.*, भावः, मतं, इंगितं. 2 अर्थः, कार्यं, प्रयोजनं. 3 विवक्षा; 'purity of i.' भाव-चित्त-शुद्धि *f.*; 'change of i.' बुद्धिभेदः; 'avowed i.' प्रकटिताशयः; 'with what i.' किमुद्दिश्य, किमभिप्रेत्य, किं फलमपेक्ष्य. –AL, *a.* मति-बुद्धि-ज्ञान-पूर्व, बुद्धि-संकल्प-कृत, काम्य, कामकृत, सांकल्पिक-ऐच्छिक (की *f.*). 2 अभिप्रेत, अर्थवत्. –ALLY, *adv.* मति-बुद्धि-ज्ञान-पूर्वं, मतिपुरःसरं, कामतः, ज्ञानतः, बुद्ध्या, साभिप्रायं, मनः-इच्छा-पूर्वकं, यथाकामं. –ED, *a.* Ex. by आशय, बुद्धि, मति in comp.; 'well-i.' सदाशय; 'evil-i.' दुराशय, दुष्टमति, पापबुद्धि.

INTENSE, *a.* प्रचंड, तीव्र, उग्र, तिग्म, प्रखर, अत्यंत, घन, गाढ, प्रबल, तीक्ष्ण, परम, महत्, गुरु, अतिमात्र, भृश, नितांत; gen. by सु or अति pr. –IFY, *v. t.* वृध् c., प्रकर्षं नी 1 P, better by कृ with (*a.*). –ITY, -NESS, *s.* चंडता, तीव्रता, अत्यंतता, गाढता, प्रकर्षः, उत्कर्षः, गरिमन् *m.*, अतिशयः, उद्रेकः, अतिभूमि *f.*, पराकोटिः-काष्ठा; 'i. of application' अत्यंताभिनिवेशः, व्यासंगः. –IVE, *a.* प्रकर्षकर-वृद्धिकर (री *f.*). –LY, *adv.* अत्यंतं, तीव्रं, तीक्ष्णं, नितांतं, अतीव, बलवत्, सु-अति pr.

INTENT, *s.* Intention, q. v.; 'to all i. s' सर्वथा. –*a.* एकाग्र, एकनिष्ठ, सुसमाहित, अनन्यमानस, अनन्यविषय, एकतान-चित्त-प्रयत्न; *See* FIXED; आसक्तचित्त,

आसक्त, व्यापृत, निरत, नियत, व्यग्र, निष्ठित, समाहित, नि-आ-अभिनि-विष्ट, अभियुक्त; oft. by पर, तत्पर, निष्ठ, परायण in comp.; 'i. on evil' दुष्टपरायण; अध्ययनपर, &c. -LY, *adv.* एकाग्रचित्तेन, अनन्यमनसा, एकाग्रतया, निष्ठापूर्वं, साभिनिवेशं, आसक्तचेतसा, मनोयोगेन; 'look or hear i.' लोचनैः or कर्णैः पा 1 P. -NESS, *s.* एकाग्रता, एकनिष्ठता, अनन्यचित्तता, आसक्ति *f.*, अभिनिवेशः, तत्परता, निष्ठा, मनोयोगः.

INTER, *v. t.* भूमौ-श्मशाने निखन् 1 P or निक्षिप् 6 P or नि-धा 3 U.

INTERCALAR,-Y, *a.* अधिक, निवेशित; 'i. month' अधिकमासः, मलमासः, मलिम्लुचः. -INTERCALATE, *v. t.* अधिकमासं-दिवसं निविश् c.

INTERCEDE, *v. i.* अंतर् गम् 1 P or स्था 1 P, मध्ये स्था or गम्, मध्यस्थो भू, सं-धा 3 U, मध्यस्थतां ग्रह् 9 P, मध्यस्थवृत्तिं आ-स्था 1 U or आश्रि 1 U, माध्यस्थ्यं कृ 8 U; (परार्थं) प्रार्थ् 10 A, अनुनी 1 P, आराध् c., वद् 1 P. -ER,-INTERCESSOR, *s.* मध्यस्थः, मध्यस्थपुरुषः, परार्थं प्रार्थकः, परार्थवादिन् *m.* -INTERCESSION, *s.* माध्यस्थ्यं, मध्यस्थता, संधानं, परार्थप्रार्थनं-ना, परार्थवादः-निवेदनं.

INTERCEPT, *v. t.* रुध् 7 U, विच्छिद् 7 P, वियुज् 7 A, 10, प्रतिबंध् 9 P; *See* OBSTRUCT. -ER, *s.* रोधकः, विघ्नकरः. -ION, *s.* रोधः, विच्छेदः, प्रतिबंधः, विघ्नः, भंगः.

INTERCHANGE, *v. t.* परस्परं विनि-मे 1 A or परिवृत् c., व्यति-हृ 1 P. -*s.* विनिमयः, परिवर्तः, व्यतिहारः, परिवृत्ति *f.*, आदानप्रदानं; *See* EXCHANGE. -ABLE, *a.* परिवर्तनीय, परस्परानुगामिन्.

INTERCLUDE, *v. t. See* INTERCEPT.

INTERCOMMUNE, *v. See* ASSOCIATE. -ITY, *s.* अन्योन्यव्यवहारः.

INTERCOMMUNION, *v. i.* सह भुज् 7 A or अश् 9 P.

INTERCOURSE, *s.* संगः, समागमः, संगति *f.*, संसर्गः, संगमः, संपर्कः, साहचर्यं, साहित्यं, संघट्टनं; अन्योन्यसंसर्गः, आलापः, संवादः, परिचयः; 'sexual i.' मैथुनं, रतिक्रिया, सुरतं, स्त्रीभोगः; 'social i.' लोकव्यवहारः-संसर्गः.

INTERCUTANEOUS, *a.* त्वगंतर्भूत.

INTERDICT, *v. t.* नि-प्रति-षिध् 1 P, निवार् 10, प्रत्याख्या 2 P, प्रत्या-दिश् 6 P; *See* FORBID. -*s.*, -ION, *s.* निषेधः, निवारणं, प्रत्याख्यानं, निरोधः, बाधा. 2 शापः, आक्रोशः. -ORY, *a.* निषेधक, निवारक.

INTEREST, *s.* अर्थः, हितं, लाभः, कल्याणं, श्रेयस् *n.*, भूति *f.*, क्षेमः-मं; 'in my i. s' मदर्थे-र्थं. 2 आदरः, स्नेहः, रागः, अवेक्षा, अनुरागः, स्पृहा, अपेक्षा. 3 पक्षपातः, संगः; 'without any i.' मुक्त-वीतसंग *a.* 4 वृद्धि *f.*; वार्द्धुष्यं; 'simple i.' सरलवृद्धिः; 'compound i.' चक्रवृद्धिः; 'i. at five per cent.' पंचकेन शतेन, पंचकशतं, पंचोत्तरं शतं. 5 भागः, अंशः, अधिकारः, उद्धारः. 6 रसः, विनोदकत्वं, मनोहरता, हृदयंगमता; दृष्टं कथारसस्याक्षेपसामर्थ्यं (Ka. 346) 'you have seen how the i. (i. ing nature) of the story diverted (me) from my topic'; 'take or feel i.' आदृ 6 A; 'looking to one's own i.' स्वार्थदृष्टि *f.*, स्वार्थपरता, स्वार्थलिप्सा. -*v. t.* अनुरंज् c., स्नेहं-अनुरागं-उत्पद् c., अनुरक्त-सानुराग-*a.* कृ 8 U. 2 वि-नुद् c., मनः-चित्तं-रंज् c. or विनुद् c., हृदयं गम् 1 P or आकृष् 1 P or हृ 1 P, मनो हृ. 3 भागं-अंशं दा 3 U or लभ् 1 A or आप् 5 P; संबंध्-अनुषंज्-pass. -ED, *a.* अनुरक्त, जातानुराग, जातस्नेह. 2 पक्षपातिन्, संगिन्, सपक्षपात. 3 आसक्त, निविष्ट, निरत. 4 भागिन्, अंशिन्. 5 संबद्ध, लाभालाभसंबद्ध. 6 स्वार्थपर, स्वार्थदर्शिन्, स्वलाभासक्त, स्वहितपरायण-तत्पर, स्वलाभापेक्ष, स्वहितैषिन्, स्वार्थलिप्सु. -ING, *a.* विनोदिन्, मनोहर, सरस, चित्ताकर्षिन्, हृदयंगम, हृदयहारिन्-ग्राहिन्, विनोदिन्, चित्तरंजक.

INTERFERE, *v.i.* मध्ये स्था or पत् 1 P, परकार्येषु व्यापृ 6 A, परकार्याणि निरूप् 10 or चर्च् 6 P, 10 A; 'if it should not i. with other duties' न चेदन्यकार्यातिपातः (S. 1); 'he who i. s with matters not his own' अव्यापारेषु व्यापारं यः करोति (P. 1). 2 परस्परं संघट्ट् 1 A or विरुध् 7 U. -ENCE, *s.* माध्यस्थ्यं, परव्यापार-परकार्य-चर्चा, परकार्यनिरूपणं; चर्चा, निरूपणं. 2 परस्परसंघट्टः, समाघातः.

INTERFLUENT, *a.* मध्यस्रविन्.

INTERFUSED, *a.* मध्यप्रसारिन्, मध्यप्रसृत.

INTERIM, *s.* कालाभ्यंतरं, कालांतरालं, मध्य-अंतर्गतकालः; 'in the i.' अत्रांतरे, कालाभ्यंतरे.

INTERIOR, *a.* अंतरस्थ, अंतर्गत, अंतर्भूत, अंतःस्थ, अंतर्वर्तिन्, आंतर-आभ्यंतर (री *f.*), अंतर् in comp. -*s.* अंतर्भागः, उदरं, गर्भः, अभ्यंतरं, हृदयं, अंतर् in comp.; 'the i. of a house' गर्भागारं, वासगृहं, भवनोदरं, अंतर्भवनं.

INTERJACENT, *a.* मध्यवर्तिन्, मध्यस्थित.

INTERJECT, *v. t.* मध्ये-अंतः-क्षिप् 6 P or प्रविश् c. -ION, *s.* अंतःक्षेपः-पणं. 2 उद्गारः.

INTERLACE, *v. t.* संमिश्र् 10, संश्लिष् c.

INTERLARD, *v. t.* मध्ये-अंतर्-निविश् c. 2 संमिश्र् 10.

INTERLAY, *v. t.* मध्ये नि-धा 3 U or नि-विश् c.

INTERLEAVE, *v. t.* अंतः-मध्ये पत्रं निविश् c.

INTERLINEAR, *a.* पंक्तिद्वयमध्ये लिखित.

INTERLOCUTION, *s.* संलापः, संवादः, संकथा, संभाषणं. -INTERLOCUTOR, *s.* संभाषकः, संवादकः, उत्तरप्रत्युत्तरकृत् *m.* -TORY, *a.* संवाद-संकथा-रूप, संवादात्मक, संकथासंबंधिन्.

INTERLOPE, *v. i.* अन्यायेन (पराधिकारं) प्रविश् 6 P

or आक्रम् 1 U, 4 P. -ER, *s.* अन्यायेन प्रवेशकः, आगंतुकः.

INTERLUDE, *s.* मध्यरंगः; विष्कंभः-भकः.

INTERLUNAR,-Y, *a.* अमा, अमावास्या in comp.

INTERMARRY, *v. i.* परस्परं विवह् 1 P or दारान् परिग्रह् 9 P or परिणी 1 P. -AGE, *s.* परस्परविवाहः, प्रत्युद्वाहः, विवाहव्यवहारः.

INTERMEDDLE, *v. i.* परकार्याणि निरूप् 10 or चर्च् 6 P, 10 A, पराधिकार-परकार्य-चर्चां कृ 8 U; *See* INTERFERE. -ER, *s.* पराधिकारचर्चकः-निरूपकः.

INTERMEDIATE, INTERMEDIAL, *a.* अंतर्-मध्यवर्तिन्, मध्य, मध्यस्थित, व्यवहित, अंतरालस्थित, अंतर-अंतराल-in comp.; 'i. space' अंतरं, अभ्यंतरं, अंतरालं; 'i. time' कालांतरं. -LY, *adv.* मध्ये, अंतराले, अभ्यंतरे.

INTERMINABLE, *a. See* INFINITE.

INTERMINGLE, INTERMIX, *v. t.* संमिश्र् 10, संकॄ 6 P, संसृज् 6 P, संपृच् 2 A, 7 P, संमिल् c.; संकुली-संकीर्णी-कृ 8 U, मिश्रीकृ. -*v. i.* संमिश्रीभू 1 P, संमिल् 6 P. -ED, *a.* सं-व्या-मिश्र, मिश्रित, संकीर्ण, संसृष्ट, संपृक्त. -INTERMIXTURE, *s.* संमिश्रणं, संकरः, संसर्गः, संपर्कः, संयोगः, संमिलनं.

INTERMIT, *v. i.* विरम् 1 P, निवृत् 1 A (with abl.); शम् 4 P, विच्छिद् pass. -*v. t.* निवृत् c., विरम् c. or शम् c. (र-श-मयति), विच्छिद् 7 P, त्यज् 1 P; *See* CEASE. -TENT,-INTERMISSIVE, *a.* सविराम, सविच्छेद; 'i. fever' मुक्तानुबंधी ज्वरः.- INTERMISSION, *s.* विरामः, विरति *f.*, निवृत्ति *f.*, विच्छेदः, उपशमः; 'without i.' निरंतरं, अनवरतं, अविरतं, अविच्छेदं.

INTERMONTANE, *a.* पर्वतमध्यवर्तिन्.

INTERMUNDANE, *a.* जगन्मध्यवर्तिन्.

INTERMURAL, *a.* प्राकारांतर्वर्तिन्.

INTERNAL, *a.* अंतर् in comp.; अंतर्गत, अंतःस्थ, आभ्यंतर-आंतर (री *f.*), गर्भस्थ; 'i. soul' अंतरात्मा; 'i. anguish' अंतःशोकः, अंतर्दाहः; *See* INSIDE. -LY, *adv.* अंतर्, अंतरं, अभ्यंतरे.

INTERNATIONAL, *a.* (देशानां) परस्परव्यवहारसंबंधिन्.

INTERPOLATE, *v. t.* सकपटं नि-विश् c. or निक्षिप् 6 P, मिथ्या कृप् c. or अभिलिख् 6 P. -ION, *s.* कपटेन निवेशनं, मिथ्याकल्पनं; मिथ्याकल्पितं, निवेशितलेखः.

INTERPOSE, *v. t.* मध्ये निक्षिप् 6 P, अंतर्-धा 3 U, व्यव-धा, मध्ये-अंतः-स्था c. (स्थापयति) or नि-प्रविश् c. -*v. i.* मध्ये स्था 1 P or वृत् 1 A or गम् or पत् 1 P, अंतर्-इ 2 P, मध्ये प्रविश् 6 P; मध्यस्थतां ग्रह् 9 P, माध्यस्थ्यं अवलंब् 1 A. -ER, *s.* मध्यस्थः, मध्यवर्तिन् *m.*, मध्यस्थायी. -ITION, *s.* मध्यस्थता, माध्यस्थ्यं; व्यवधानं, मध्यवर्तित्वं, अंतरायः.

INTERPRET, *v. t.* युज् 10 (words, &c.); व्याख्या 2 P, वि-वृ 5 U, व्याचक्ष् 2 A, अर्थं प्रकाश् c. or व्या-ख्या or वि-वृ or व्याकृ 8 U; *See* CONSTRUE, EXPLAIN. 2 भाषांतरेण वद् 1 P or कथ् 10 or व्याहृ 1 P. -ATION, *s.* (पदानां) योजना; व्याख्या, व्याख्यानं, विवरणं, निरूपणं, अर्थबोधनं-प्रकाशनं, विचारः; 'i. of a dream' स्वप्नार्थः, स्वप्नविचारः-निरूपणं. 2 अर्थः, व्याख्या, टीका, भाष्यं. 3 भाषांतरं. -ER, *s.* व्याख्यातृ *m.*, विवरणकृत् *m.*, अर्थप्रकाशकः-बोधकः. 2 भाषाद्वयज्ञः. 3 भाष्य-वृत्ति-कारः, टीकाकृत् *m.*

INTERREGNUM, *s.* अराजत्वं, अनायका-अराजकाराज्यस्थितिः.

INTERROGATE, *v. t.* प्रच्छ् 6 P, अनुयुज् 7 A, परीक्ष् 1 A. -ION, *s.* पृच्छा, प्रश्नः, अनुयोगः. -IVE,-ORY, *a.* प्रश्नरूप, प्रश्नार्थक, प्रश्नात्मक. -IVELY, *adv.* प्रश्नरूपेण-क्रमेण, अनुयोगतः, प्रश्नार्थरूपेण. -OR, *s.* प्रष्टृ *m.*, पृच्छकः, अनुयोक्तृ *m.* -ORY, *s.* प्रश्नः, अनुयोगः.

INTERRUPT, *v. t.* प्रति-बंध् 9 P, प्रति-वि-हन् 2 P, उप-नि-रुध् 7 U, भंज् 7 P, विच्छिद् 7 P, खंड् 10, बाध् 1 A, भिद् 7 P, विघ्नयति (D.); (speech &c.) आक्षिप् 6 P; 'do not i. him' मैनमंतरा प्रतिबध्नीतं (S. 6). -ION, *s.* अंतरायः, प्रतिबंधः, उपरोधः, विच्छेदः, भंगः, भेदः, व्याघातः, विघ्नः; 'i. in sleep' निद्राभंगः. -EDLY, *adv.* सविच्छेदं, सभंगं. -ER, *s.* विच्छेद-भंग-कारिन् *m.*, विघ्न-व्याघातकृत् *m.*

INTERSECT, *v. t.* परस्परं-अंतरा-छिद् 7 P. -ION, *s.* परस्परच्छेदः.

INTERSPERSE, *v. t.* इतस्ततः प्र-क्षिप् 6 P or संसमा-कॄ 6 P or संमिश्र् 10. -ED, *a.* संमिश्र, संकीर्ण. -ION, *s.* संमिश्रणं, वि-सं-किरणं.

INTERSTELLAR, *a.* तारागणमध्यवर्तिन्.

INTERSTICE, *s.* छिद्रं, रंध्रं, संधिः, विच्छेदः, अंतरं, अंतरालः-लं, अवकाशः, विवरं; 'without i.s' निरंतर. नीरंध्र, निश्छिद्र, निबिड, घन, अविरल; 'having i.s' सच्छिद्र, सांतराल, विरल.

INTERTEXTURE, *s.* संग्रंथनं. परस्परव्यूति *f.*

INTERTWINE, INTERTWIST, *v. t.* ग्रंथ् 9 P, सं-तन्, परस्परं कुंच् c. or व्यावृत् c., उत्क्षच् 10, परस्परं ग्रंथ् or संयुज् 7 U, 10, संमिश्र् 10; 'with hair i. ed with the tendrils of creepers' लताप्रतानोद्ग्रथितैः केशैः (R. II. 8); अनुव्यध् 4 P, सं-व्ये 1 U; शैवलेनानुविद्धं (सरसिजं) (S. 1) 'i. ed with moss.'

INTERVAL, *s.* अंतरं, अंतरालं, अभ्यंतरं ; अवकाशः, मध्यस्थानं, व्यवधानं, व्यवायः. 2 अवधिः, मध्य-अभ्य-

तर-कालः, अवकाशः. 3 विरामः, विच्छेदः, निवृत्ति *f.*, उपशमः; 'in the i.' अंतराले, अंतरा; 'at i. s' काले काले, अंतरा अंतरा, (प्रजानुरागहेतोश्चांतरांतरा दर्शनं ददौ Ka. 58); रम्यांतरः कमलिनीहरितैः सरोभिः (S. 4) 'pleasant at i. s &c.'; 'without i. s' निरंतर, निरंतराल.

INTERVENE, *v. i.* मध्ये-अंतर्-गम् 1 P or भू 1 P or स्था 1 P or वृत् 1 A, अंतर्या 2 P or उप-स्था. 2 अंतर्-इ 2 P, व्यव-धा pass. –ING, *a.* मध्यवर्तिन्, मध्यस्थायिन्, व्यवहित, अंतरित, अंतरागत, मध्ये स्थित; 'i. period' अंतरालं, अभ्यंतरकालः. –INTERVENTION, *s.* मध्यस्थता, माध्यस्थ्यं, व्यवधानं, अंतर्गमनं, मध्यवर्तनं, मध्ये स्थिति *f.*

INTERWEAVE, *v. t. See* INTERTWINE.

INTERVIEW, *s.* दर्शनं; सन्निपातः, संगमः, समागमः, अन्योन्य-परस्पर-दर्शनं; 'he had an i. with the king' स नृपदर्शनं लेभे, राजदर्शनं कारितः.

INTESTATE, *a.* अकृतमृत्युलेख.

INTESTINE, *a.* अबाह्य; *See* INTERNAL. 2 अविदेशज, देशीय; गृह in comp.; 'i. quarrels' गृहच्छिद्रं-भेदः, अंतर्भेदः. –*s.* अंत्रं, पुरीतत् *n.*; नाडि-डी-लि-ली *f.*

INTIMATE, *a.* गाढ, रूढ, प्र-वि-रूढ, दृढ, दृढबद्ध, घन. 2 (Of persons) सुपरिचित, रूढसौहृद, बद्धसख्य, प्रणयिन्, प्रियतम, हृदयंगम, सुसंसर्गिन्, संस्तुत, दृढगाढ-सौहृद. 3 Internal, q. v.; 'strangers made i.' बाह्या अभ्यंतरीकृताः (P. I. 9). –*s.* दृढसुहृद् *m.*, दृढमित्रं, सुहृत्तमः, प्रियवयस्यः. –*v. t.* (भंग्या) सूच् 10, संदिश् 6 P, उपन्यस् 4 U, उपक्षिप् 6 P; साकूतं कथ् 10. –ION, *s.* सूचना, संदेशः, उपक्षेपः; इंगितं, आकूतं. –LY, *adv.* दृढं, गाढं; दृढसौहृदेन-संसर्गेण, सुपरिचितं, दृढमित्रवत्; दृढ, गाढ in comp. –INTIMACY, *s.* गाढसौहृदं, सुपरिचयः, दृढसंसर्गः-संयोगः, संस्तवः,अतिमित्रता-प्रणयः-सख्यं,अत्यासंगः,अतिपरिचयः.

INTIMIDATE, *v. t.* त्रस् c., भी c. (भीषयते-भापयते), सभयं निवृत् c. 2 भर्त्स् 10 A, तर्ज् 1 P, 10 A. 3 Dishearten, q. v. –ION, *s.* भीषका, भीषा, भीषणं, भयदर्शनं, भर्त्सनं, तर्जनं.

INTO, *prep.* मध्ये, अंतर्, अंतरे; gen. by loc., or by acc. with verbs of motion; 'converted i. water' जलसात्कृत; 'made i. one mass' एकपिंडीकृत-भूत.

INTOLERABLE, *a.* असह्य, असहनीय, दुःसह, अक्षंतव्य, दुर्विषह.

INTOLERANT, *a.* अक्षमिन्, असहन, अमर्षण, असहिष्णु, अक्षम. 2 परमतासहिष्णु, परमतासूयक, अन्यमतासह. –INTOLERANCE, *s.* अमर्षणं, अतितिक्षा, अक्षमा, असहिष्णुता.

INTONE, *v. t.* गंभीरं वद् 1 P or वच् 2 P, गंभीरस्वरं उदीर् c. or उदाह 1 P. –ATION, *s.* स्वरः, लयः, वर्णोच्चारणं; स्वरभेदः.

INTORT, *v. t. See* CONTORT.

INTOXICATE, *v. t.* मद् c., उत्-प्र-°, मदं उत्पद् c., मत्तीकृ 8 U; (fig.) उत्सिच् c., उद्-हन् 2 P, आ-ध्मा 1 P, मुह् c. –ED, *a.* मत्त, प्र-उत्-मत्त, क्षीव, मदोन्मत्त, उन्मद, मदोदग्र, मदान्वित, शौंड, मदोद्धत; 'to be i.' मद् 4 P, मदेन स्पृश् pass., क्षीव् 1, 4 P. –ING, *a.* उन्मादक, मादक, उन्मादिन्. –ION, *s.* मदः, मादः, उन्मादः, क्षीवता, शौंडता, मत्तता.

INTRACTABLE, *a.* दुर्दम, दुर्दांत, अदम्य, अविधेय, अवश्य, अविनेय, दुर्निग्रह, दुराधर्ष, दुःशास्य, अनिवार्य, प्रतीप, उच्छृंखल.

INTRANSIENT, *a.* अभंगुर, चिरस्थायिन्.

INTRANSITIVE, *a.* अकर्मक.

INTRENCH, *v. t.* परिखया रक्ष् 1 P or परिवेष्ट् c. or परि वृ 5 U, परिखां खन् 1 P. 2 आक्रम् 1 U, 4 P. –MENT, *s.* परिखा, परिक्रिया.

INTREPID, *a.* निर्भय, निःशंक, शूर, साहसशील, प्रगल्भ. –ITY, *s.* वीर्यं, प्रतिभा, प्रतिभानं, शौर्यं, निर्भयत्वं, पौरुषं, विक्रमः. –LY, *adv.* वीरवत्, सविक्रमं, सप्रतिभं; *See* BOLD,-LY, &c.

INTRICATE, *a.* विषम, दुर्ग्राह्य, संकुल, गहन, दुर्बोध, गूढ, अस्पष्टार्थ. 2 वक्र, असरल, जिह्म कुटिल. –LY, *adv.* विषमं, असरलं, कुटिलं. –NESS, –INTRICACY, *s.* वैषम्यं, गहनता, गूढता. 2 वक्रता, कौटिल्यं, असारल्यं.

INTRIGUE, *s.* उपजापः, कूटप्रबंधः, कपटप्रबंधः, कूटयुक्ति *f.*, कु-कपट-संकल्पः-प्रयोगः; 'love-i.' व्यभिचारकर्म, कामचरितं. –*v. i.* उपजप् 1 P, उपजापं रच् 10, कूटप्रबंधं प्रयुज् 7 A, 10, कूटप्रयोगं रच्. –ER, *s.* उपजापकः, कपटप्रबंधयोजकः.

INTRINSIC,-AL, *a.* अंतरस्थ, अंतर्गत, सहजवर्तिन्, स्वभावज, आंतर-आभ्यंतर (री *f.*). 2 सत्य, यथार्थ, वास्तविक (की *f.*), अकृत्रिम, स्वाभाविक-सांसिद्धिक (की *f.*). –ALLY, *adv.* वस्तुतः, तत्त्वतः, यथार्थतः, स्वभावतः.

INTRODUCE, *v. t.* प्रविश् c., दर्शनं कृ c. 2 (Insert) प्र-नि-आ-विश् c. 3 परिचयं उत्पद् c. or जन् c. (जनयति); 'i. me to your friend' तव मित्रेण मम परिचयमुत्पादय. 4 प्रवृत् c., प्रचर्-ल् c., प्रति-ष्ठा c. (-ष्ठापयति), प्रारभ् 1 A, प्रस्तु 2 U, उपक्रम् 1 A. 5 आनी 1 P, आवह् 1 P, आगम् c. (गमयति). –ER, *s.* प्रवेशकः. 2 प्रवर्तकः, प्रतिष्ठापकः, प्रारंभकः. –INTRODUCTION, *s.* प्रवेशनं; परिचयकरणं. 2 प्रवर्तनं, प्रचारणं, प्रतिष्ठापनं, निवेशनं; आनयनं. 3 मुखबंधः, आमुखं, प्रस्तावना (of plays); प्रस्तावः, आरंभः, उपन्यासः, वाङ्मुखं, उपोद्घातः, उदाहारः, उपक्रमः, वचनारंभः. –INTRODUCTORY, –INTRODUCTIVE, *a.* प्रावेशिक (की *f.*), आरंभक,

प्राथमिक (की *f.*), प्रथम; उपोद्घात or प्रस्तावना in comp.; 'as an i. portion' उपोद्घातरूपेण, प्रस्तावनाद्वारा. 2 प्रस्तावनारूप; पारिभाषिक (की *f.*).

INTROMIT, *v. t.* प्रविश् c.

INTROSPECTION, *s.* अंतर्दर्शनं, अंतरालोकनं.

INTROVERT, *v. t.* अंत: परिवृत् c.

INTRUDE, *v. i.* अनाहूत-*a.* प्र-आ-विश् 6 P or आगम् 1 P, सधर्षं प्रविश् or आक्रम् 1 U, 4 P, अनधिकारपूर्वं प्रविश्. –ER, *s.* आगंतुकः, अनाहूतप्रवेशकः. –INTRUSION, *s.* आगंतुकभावः, अनाहूतप्रवेशः-शनं. –INTRUSIVE, *a.* धृष्ट, आगंतुक, प्रगल्भ, सधर्ष; परचर्चाशील.

INTUITION, *s.* सहजावबोधः, सहजज्ञानं, अंतर्ज्ञानं. —INTUITIVE, *s.* सहजोपलब्ध, अंतर्ज्ञानोपलभ्य, अविचारपूर्वं उपलब्ध. 2 सहजज्ञ, अंतर्ज्ञानिन्. –LY, *adv.* सहजज्ञानेन; अंतर्ज्ञानेन, प्रमाणनिरपेक्षं.

INTUMESCE, *v. i.* श्वि 1 P; *See* SWELL. –ENCE, *s.* शोथः, शोफः.

INTURBIDATE, *v. t.* कलुषीकृ 8 U, आविलयति (D.); *See* CONFUSE.

INTWINE, INTWIST, *v. t.* ग्रंथ् 9 P, गु(गुं)फ् 6 P, रज्जु 10; *See* INTERTWINE.

INUMBRATE, *v. t.* छायया आ-प्र-च्छद् 10.

INUNCTION, *s.* अभ्यंजनं, विलेपनं.

INUNDATE, *v. t.* जलेन आप्लु c. or व्याप् 5 P. –ED, *a.* आप्लावित, आ-सं-प्लुत, जलाप्लावित, जलव्याप्त, जलमय (यी *f.*). –ION, *s.* आप्लावः, जलौघः, तोयजल-विप्लवः-प्रलयः-उपप्लवः, जलवृद्धि *f.*; *See* DELUGE.

INURBANITY, *s.* अशिष्टता, असभ्यता.

INURE, *v. t.* अभ्यस् 4 U or c., शिक्ष् c., परिचयं कृ 8 U; परिचित-*a.* भू. 2 कठिनी-दृढी-कृ. –ED, *a.* अभ्यस्त, ज्ञात, परिचित; अभिज्ञ in comp.; 'i. to fatigue' जितश्रम; 'i. to seclusion' परिचितविविक्त.

INURN, *v. t.* समाधौ नि-धा 3 U or निक्षिप् 6 P.

INUTILITY, *s.* अनुपयोगः, वैफल्यं, व्यर्थता, मोघता, वैयर्थ्यं.

INVADE, *v. t.* अभि-द्रु 1 P, आक्रम् 1 U, 4 P, अवस्कंद् 1 P, अभिप्र-या 2 P, आपत् 1 P, उप-द्रु 1 A or c.; *See* ATTACK. –ER, *s.* आक्रामकः, उपप्लविन् *m.*; gen. ex. by 'Enemy' q. v. –INVASION, *s.* आक्रमः-मणं, अवस्कंदः, अभिद्रवः, उपप्लवः, अभिप्रयाणं, अभियोगः, आपातः.

INVALID, *a.* दुर्बल, अशक्त, अप्रभाव, निस्तेजस्, व्यर्थ, विफल. 2 अप्रमाण, निष्प्रमाण, लघुप्रमाण. –*s.* रोगिन् *m.*, रुग्णः, आतुरः. –ATE, *v. t.* मोघी-व्यर्थी-कृ 8 U, विफलीकृ, लुप् 6 P or c., अधरीकृ. –ITY, *s.* निर्बलता, अनिष्पत्ति *f.*, व्यर्थता, मोघता. 2 अप्रामाण्य.

INVALUABLE, *a.* अनर्घ, अनर्घ्य, अमूल्य, मूल्यातीत, अतिमूल्य, अत्युत्कृष्ट.

INVARIABLE, *a.* नित्य, सतत, अविकार्य, निर्विकार, स्थिर, नियत, अचल, एकांत; नायमेकांतो नियमः (S. B. 273) 'not an i. rule.' –INVARIABLY, *adv.* एकांततः, नित्यं, नियतं.

INVECTIVE, *s.* आ-अधि-क्षेपः, निर्भर्त्सना, निंदा, निंदावाक्यं, दुरुक्ति *f.*, अप-परि-वादः, गर्हा. –*a.* निंदक, अपवादक, निंदात्मक.

INVEIGH, (against) *v. i.* आ-अव-अधि-क्षिप् 6 P, निंद् 1 P, गर्ह् 1, 10 A, अभिशंस् 1 P; *See* ABUSE, CENSURE.

INVEIGLE, *v. t.* प्र-वि-लुभ् c., मुह् c., चाटूक्त्या आकृष् 1 P or प्रलुभ् c. or निपत् c., वंच् 10. –ER, *s.* प्र-वि-लोभकः, मोहकः, आकर्षकः. –ING,-MENT, *s.* प्र-वि-लोभनं; आकर्षणं, मोहः, वंचना, प्रतारणा.

INVENT, *v. t.* क्लृप् c., निर्मा 3 A, 2 P, सृज् 6 P, वि-धा 3 U, घट् c. (घटयति), रच् 10. 2 मनसा युज् 10 or चिंत् 10 or क्लृप् c. 3 मिथ्या क्लृप् c. –ED, *a.* क्लृप्त, निर्मित, रचित, घटित. 2 मनःसृष्ट, मनःकल्पित, मिथ्याकल्पित, काल्पनिक (की *f.*), कृतक, कृत्रिम. –ION, *s.* कल्पना-नं, रचना-नं, निर्माणं, घटनं. 2 कृति *f.*, सृष्टि *f.*, कल्पितं, कल्पना, निर्मितकला. 3 कल्पना, युक्ति *f.*, उपायज्ञानं. 4 मिथ्याकल्पनं, कूटरचना, मनःसृष्टिः; 'one's own i.' स्वकपोलकल्पितं. –IVE, *a.* कल्पक, योजक, उपायज्ञ, कल्पनाचतुर, निर्माणकुशल, चतुर, युक्तिमत्. –OR, *s.* कल्पकः, स्रष्टृ *m.*, निर्माता, चिंतकः, योजकः.

INVENTORY, *s.* (गृहोपस्करादेः) परिसंख्या, परिगणना, संख्यापत्रं.

INVERT, *v. t.* विपर्यस् 4 U or c., परि-वि-व्यति-अस्, परिवृत् c., विपर्यासं-विपर्ययं-नी 1 P; *See* ALTER, CHANGE. 2 अधोमुखीकृ 8 U; विलोमीकृ. –ED, –INVERSE, *a.* व्यत्यस्त, विपर्यस्त, व्यस्त, पर्यस्त, विपरीत, वि-प्रति-लोम, प्रतीप, व्युत्क्रांत. –LY, *adv.* विपर्ययेण, वि-प्रति-लोमतः, व्यत्यासेन, व्युत्क्रमेण. –INVERSION, *s.* विपर्यासः, विपर्य(र्या)यः, व्युत्क्रमः, व्यत्यासः, पर्यासः, प्रातिलोम्यं, व्यत्ययः; व्यस्तता, विपरीतता.

INVEST, *v. t.* परि-धा c. (धापयति), आच्छद् 10, प्रावृ 5 U, संवेष्ट् c., वस् c., सं-व्ये 1 P. 2 अलंकृ 8 U, मंड् 10, भूष् 10. 3 संयुज् 7 U, 10, संपन्न-युक्त-विशिष्ट-*a.* कृ; *See* ENDOW. 4 उपरुध् 7 U, पर्यवष्टंभ् 9 P. 5 (Money) लाभार्थं विनियुज् 7 A, 10; 'i. with power' अधिकारं प्रविश् c. or नियुज्; प्रति-स्था c. (स्थापयति), संस्कृ, अभिषिच् 6 P. –ITURE, *s.* अभिषेकः, संस्कारः, प्रतिष्ठापनं, पदस्थापनं, अधिकारदानं; 'i. with the sacred thread' उपनयः-यनं.

-MENT, *s.* परिधानं, वस्त्रं. 2 उपरोधः, अवष्टंभः. 3 लाभार्थं धनविनियोगः.

INVESTIGATE, *v. t.* अव-परि-सं-ईक्ष् 1 A, निरूप् 10, अनुसं-धा 3 U, विचर् c., विमृश् 6 P, निर्णी 1 P, निश्चि 5 U, निर्धृ 10, आलोच् 10. 2 अन्विष् 4 P, मृग् 10 A; *See* EXAMINE. -ION, *s.* अवेक्षणं, निरूपणं, अनुसंधानं, विचारः-रणा-णं, विमर्शः, निर्णयः, निश्चयः; चर्चा, अन्वेषणं, अनुयोगः, जिज्ञासा; 'under i.' निरूप्यमाण. -OR, *s.* अवेक्षकः, निरूपकः, विचारकः, अनुसंधातृ *m.*, निर्णेतृ.

INVETERATE, *a.* बद्ध-रूढ-मूल, सुदृढ, गाढ, प्ररूढ, दृढ, स्थिर, चिर-बहु-कालिक (की *f.*), चिरस्थायिन्; 'i. enemy' गाढ-बद्ध-वैरः शत्रुः; 'i. enmity' बद्धवैरं. -INVETERACY, *s.* बद्धवैरं, वैरानुबंधः; बद्धमूलता, विरूढता, स्थिरता, अभिनिविष्टता.

INVIDIOUS, *a.* द्वेषजनन (नी *f.*), मत्सरावह, ईर्ष्या-असूया-कर (री *f.*). 2 मत्सरिन्, समत्सर, ईर्ष्यालु. -LY, *adv.* समत्सरं, साभ्यसूयं, सेर्ष्यं.

INVIGORATE, *v. t.* बलं-तेजः-शक्तिं वृध् c. or दा 3 U or उप-चि 5 U, आप्यै c., पुष् 1, 9 P or c.; दीप् c. -ING, *a.* बलवर्धन (नी *f.*), तेजस्कर (री *f.*), पुष्टिद, वीर्यप्रद, उत्साहदायिन्. -ION, *s.* बल-तेजो-वर्धनं, पुष्टिकरणं. 2 बल-तेजो-वृद्धि *f.*

INVINCIBLE, *a.* अजय्य, दुर्जय, दुरासद, अधृष्य, अदम्य.

INVIOLABLE, *a.* अलंघ्य, अनतिक्रमणीय, अभेद्य, भंगायोग्य. 2 अबाध्य, अनपकार्य, अवध्य (as a herald). -NESS, *s.* अलंघ्यता, अवध्यभावः.

INVIOLATE, *a.* अभिन्न, अभग्न, अलंघित, अक्षत, अदूषित, अखंड, अभंग.

INVISIBLE, *a.* अदृश्य, परोक्ष, दुर्दर्श, अंतर्हित, तिरोहित, अंतरित, दर्शनातीत, नयनविषयातीत, दृगगोचर, दृष्टचविषय, अलक्ष्य, अचाक्षुष (षी *f.*) (evidence &c.); 'to be i.' अंतर्-तिरः-धा pass., तिरोभू 1 P, अंतर्-इ 2 P. -NESS, *s.* परोक्षता, अप्रत्यक्षता, अदर्शनं, तिरोधानं, अंतर्धानं, अविषयः, परोक्षं. -INVISIBLY, *adv.* अप्रत्यक्षं, परोक्षं, असमक्षं, अलक्ष्यं, असाक्षात्, अदृष्टरूपेण; निभृतं, अलक्षितं.

INVITE, *v. t.* आ-नि-अभि-मंत्र् 10 A, आ-समा-ह्वे 1 P, अभ्यर्थ् 10 A, आकृ c., आवह् c. 2 आकृष् 1 P, हृ 1P, प्र-वि-लुभ् c. -ATION, *s.* निमंत्रणं, आह्वानं, आवाहनं, अभ्यर्थना. -ING, *a.* चित्ताकर्षिन्, मोहिन्, मनोहर.

INVOICE, *s.* आवाहपत्रं, बीजकं.

INVOKE, *v. t.* आ-ह्वे 1 P, आ-अभि-मंत्र् 10 A, आ-वद् 1 P, संबुध् c., आवह् c., आकृ c., नाम ग्रह् 9 P or स्मृ 1 P; अर्थ् 10 A, अभिवंद् 1 A; 'i. blessings on' आशास् 2 A. -INVOCATION, *s.* आह्वानं, आमंत्रणं, आवाहनं, नामग्रहणं, प्रार्थनं-ना.

INVOLUNTARY, *a.* अकाम्य, अनिच्छापूर्व, अबुद्धि-अज्ञान-पूर्व, अनैच्छिक (की *f.*), अस्वेच्छाजात. 2 अकाम, अनिच्छु. -LY, *adv.* अकामतः, अकाम-अनिच्छा-अमति-पूर्वं, अनिच्छया, असंतोषेण, अबोध-अज्ञान-पूर्वं.

INVOLVE, *v. t.* अवगुंठ् 10, आवृ 5 U, आ-वेष्ट् 1 A, or c., आच्छद् 10. 2 परिग्रह् 9 P, अंतर्गण् 10, समाविश् c.; *See* INCLUDE. 3 अभिभू 1 P, ग्रस् 1 A; 'i. ed in difficulty' विपद्ग्रस्त. 4 संबंध् 9 P, संश्लिष् c., संयुज् 7 U, 10, संसञ्ज् 6 P, लिप् 6 P, संक्रम् c.; *See* IMPLICATE. -ED, *a.* आवेष्टित, अवगुंठित, आवृत, आच्छन्न. 2 अंतर्गत, परिगृहीत, समाविष्ट, अंतर्भूत, गर्भ in comp. 3 अभिभूत, ग्रस्त. 4 संबद्ध, संश्लिष्ट, संसृष्ट, संसक्त, अनुषक्त, संयुक्त, लिप्त; 'i. in crimes' पापलिप्त, दोषग्रस्त. 5 ध्वनित, फलित; 'i. meaning' फलितं, फलितार्थः, ध्वनिः. -INVOLUTION, *s.* आवेष्टनं, आवरणं. 2 जटिलत्वं, व्यतिकरः, संकीर्णता, अन्योन्यसंश्लेषः, परस्परसंसक्ति *f.* 3 (In Math.) संवर्गीकरणं; 'i. to the third power' सदृशत्रयसंवर्गः.

INVULNERABLE, *a.* अभेद्य-अवेध्य-देह, वज्रदेह-शरीर, क्षताक्षम.

INWARD, *a.* अंतर्वर्तिन्, अंतःस्थित, अंतरस्थ, अंतर्भव; oft. by अंतर् in comp. -*adv.*, -LY, *adv.* अंतः, अभ्यंतरे; 'i. corrupted' अंतर्दुष्ट. 2 मनसा, चित्तेन, हृदये; सुनिभृतं. -INWARDS, *s.* अंत्राणि (pl.).

INWEAVE, *v. t. See* INTERTWINE.

INWRAP, *v. t.* आवेष्ट् 1 A or c.; *See* INVOLVE(1).

INWROUGHT, *a.* खचित, प्रणिहित, प्रतिबद्ध, छुरित.

IOTA, *s.* अणुः, लवः, कणः, कणिका, बिंदुमात्रं.

IRASCIBLE, *a.* चंडकोप, क्रोधशील, सुलभकोप, शीघ्रकोपिन्, क्रोधिल, संरंभिन्, चंडस्वभाव. -NESS, *s.* क्रोधशीलता, सुलभकोपः, चंडता, पित्तस्वभावः-प्रकृति *f.*

IRATE, *a.* क्रुद्ध, कुपित, रुष्ट.

IRE, *s.* रोषः, क्रोधः, कोपः. -FUL, *a.* क्रुद्ध, रुष्ट; *See* ANGRY.

IRIS, *s.* इंद्रधनुस् *n.* 2 तारामंडलं. 3 गोलोमी, श्वेतदूर्वा.

IRK, *v. t.* पीड् 10, आयस् c., खिद् c.; *See* AFFLICT. -SOME, *a.* दुःख-खेद-कर (री *f.*), दुःखद, क्लेशावह, क्लेशद, आयासहेतुक, कष्ट; 'how i. are the toils of state' राज्यं हि नाम (राज्यशासनश्रमाः) महदप्रीतिस्थानं (Mu. 3).

IRON, *s.* लोहः-हं, अयस् *n.*, आयसं, कालायसं, कृष्णायसं, पिंडं, तीक्ष्णं, शस्त्रकं, अश्मसारः, लौहं; 'green sulphate of i.' धातुशेखरं, कासी(शी)सं; 'rust of i.' मंडूरं, सिंहाणं, अयोमलं, 'tipped with i.' आयोग्र, लोहाग्र; 'sulphuret of i.' ताप्यं; 'wrought i.' कुशी. 2 बंधनं, शृंखला-लः-लं, लौहबंधनं. -*v. t.* शृंखलया बंध् 9 P or संयम् 1 P. -*a.* लौह (ही *f.*), लोहमय-अयोमय (यी *f.*), लोहनिर्मित, आयस (सी *f.*), लोहात्मक, लोह or अयस् in comp.; 'of an i. constitution' वज्रदेह, सिंहसंहनन; 'i.-bar' फालः, लोहपिंडः; 'i.-filings' लोहचूर्णं, लोहजं; 'i.-fisted' लोह-वज्र-मुष्टि; 'i.-foundery' संधानी, कुप्यशाला; 'i.-hearted' अयो-वज्र-हृदय, कठिन-पाषाण-हृदय; 'i.- mold' लोहांकः, लोहचिह्नं; 'i.-monger' लोहकारः, अयस्कारः, अयोकारः, लोहकारकः. -Y, *a. See* (*a.*) above.

IRONY, *s.* सोल्लुंठः-ठनं, सोत्प्रासः, व्याजस्तुति *f.*, निंदा, व्याजोक्ति *f.*, विपरीतलक्षणा, उपरोधः; 'it was a strange i. of fate in the case of Rāma' रामस्यापि दैवदुर्नियोगः कोपि यत् &c. (U. 4). -ICAL, *a.* (*s.*) in comp.; 'i. speech' सोल्लुंठवचनं, सोल्लुंठनोक्तिः; 'i. speaker' सोल्लुंठनवादिन्. -ICALLY, *adv.* सोत्प्रासं, सोल्लुंठनेन, व्याजोक्त्या.

IRRADIATE, *v. t.* प्रकाश् c., द्युत् c., दीप् c., राज् c. -ION, *s.* प्रकाशनं, द्योतनं, प्रदीपनं. 2 (Irradiance) उद्द्योतः, दीप्ति *f.*, प्रभा, कांति-द्युति *f.*, तेजस् *n.*

IRRATIONAL, *a.* विवेकरहित-वर्जित-हीन, अचेतन, अविवेक, ज्ञान-बुद्धि-हीन, निर्बोध, अव्युत्पन्न, चिच्छक्तिरहित; पशुधर्मन्. 2 न्याय-युक्ति-विरुद्ध, अन्याय्य, अयुक्तिसिद्ध, अतार्किक (की *f.*). -ITY, *s.* बुद्धिहीनता, अन्याय्यता. -LY, *adv.* न्यायविरोधेन, अयुक्तिवादेन.

IRRECONCILABLE, *a.* असंधेय, अशाम्य. 2 असंगत, विगीत, परस्परविरुद्ध, परस्परपराहत; *See* INCONSISTENT. -NESS, *s.* असंगति *f.*, परस्परविरोधः.

IRRECOVERABLE, *a.* अपुनःप्राप्य, पुनरलभ्य, असमाहार्य. -IRRECOVERABLY, *adv.* अनुद्धार्यतया; 'it is i. gone' असन्निवृत्त्यै तदतीतमेव (S. 6).

IRREFRAGABLE, *a.* अखंड्य, अबाध्य, अप्रत्याख्येय, दृढ-स्थिर-प्रमाण.

IRREGULAR, *a.* अनियत, विधि-नियम-विरुद्ध, अयथाविधि, अविधि, उत्सूत्र, विधिघ्न (घ्नी *f.*); (as words) अपवादक, निपातित; 'these are put down as i. forms' एते निपात्यंते (S. K.). 2 क्रमहीन-रहित-शून्य-विरुद्ध, अव्यवस्थित, अपर्याय, उच्छृंखल. 3 (In conduct) उत्क्रांतमर्याद, व्यभिचारिन्, विपथ-अपथ-गामिन्, दुराचार, कुचरित, अमर्याद. 4 विषम, असम; 'i. in shape' विरूप, कदाकार. -ITY, *s.* अविधिः, विधि-नियम-विरोधः-भंगः, अनियमः, उत्सूत्रता, निपातः-तनं. 2 अक्रमः, उत्क्रमः, व्यतिक्रमः, अपर्यायः, अपरिपाटि-टी *f.* अव्यवस्था. 3 व्यभिचारः, विपथगमनं, अमर्यादता, अनाचारः, दुर्वृत्तता. 4 वैषम्यं. -LY, *adv.* विधि-नियम-विरुद्धं, अविध्यनुरूपं, अयथाविधि, क्रमविरुद्धं; अनियमेन, अनियतवेलं, अविधितः; अक्रमेण.

IRRELATIVE, *a.* असंबंधिन्, असंग, निःसंग.

IRRELEVANT, *a.* अप्रस्तुत, अप्रकृत, असंबद्ध, (अ) प्रासंगिक (की *f.*), अनन्वित, प्रस्तुतबाह्य, असंगत. -LY, *adv.* अप्रकृतं, अप्रस्तुतं, असंबद्धं. -IRRELEVANCY, *s.* अप्रकृतता, अनन्वयः, असंबंधः, असंगति *f.*, अप्रस्तावः.

IRRELIGION, *s.* अधर्मः, अपूजा, अभक्ति *f.*, धर्मलोपः, देवनिंदा, पापता. -IRRELIGIOUS, *a.* अधार्मिक (की *f.*), अधर्मनिष्ठ, विधर्म, धर्म-भक्ति-हीन; अपुण्य, दुष्ट, पापिन्. -LY, *adv.* अधर्मेण, दुष्टवत्.

IRREMEDIABLE, *a.* अप्रतिविधेय, अप्रतिकार्य, निरुपाय, अशक्यप्रतिकार, उपायातीत, अचिकित्स्य, दुःसाध्य.

IRREMOVABLE, *a.* अपरिहार्य, अनपानेय; स्थिर, अचल.

IRREPARABLE, *a.* असमाधेय, असाध्य; अप्रतिकार्य, अशक्यप्रतिकार. -IRREPARABLY, *adv.* अप्रतिविधेयं; 'the act i. damaged his reputation' तेन कर्मणा तस्य यशस्तथा क्षीणं यथा तत्प्रतिसंधानमशक्यं.

IRREPREHENSIBLE, *a.* अनिंद्य, अदूषणीय, निर्दोष.

IRREPRESSIBLE, *a.* अनिवार्य, दुर्निवार, दुर्निग्रह.

IRREPROACHABLE, *a.* अनिंद्य, अगर्ह्य, अनवगीत; *See* FAULTLESS.

IRRESISTIBLE, *a.* अनिवार्य, दुर्निवार, अप्रतिकार्य, अनवग्रह, दुर्निग्रह, दुर्धर, अप्रतिहत. -IRRESISTIBLY, *adv.* दुर्निवारं, अनवग्रहं.

IRRESOLUTE, *a.* अस्थिर-चल-लोल-मति-चित्त-बुद्धि, चलवृत्ति, चंचलधी, विकल्पशील, संशयात्मन्, अधीर, तरलमनस्. -LY, *adv.* अस्थिरचेतसा, चंचलवृत्त्या, लोलबुद्ध्या, अधीरं. -NESS, -IRRESOLUTION, *s.* अस्थैर्यं, विकल्पशीलता, लोलमतित्वं, चलचित्तता, चंचलबुद्धि *f.*, लोलमति *f.*, अनवस्थिति *f.*, चापल्यं.

IRRESPECTIVE. (of) *a.* अनपेक्ष्य, अगणयित्वा, अव्यपेक्ष्य, विहाय (with acc.); अनपेक्ष, निरपेक्ष, निर्व्यपेक्ष in comp.; *See* INDEPENDENT (of). -LY, *adv.* अनपेक्षं, निरपेक्षं.

IRRESPONSIBLE, *a.* अननुयोगाधीन, अप्रष्टव्य, अनुच्छाधीन.

IRRESTRAINABLE, *a. See* IRRESISTIBLE.

IRRETRIEVABLE, *a. See* IRREPARABLE, IRRECOVERABLE.

IRREVERENT, *a.* अनादरिन्, परिभाविन्, उपेक्षक, अवज्ञाकारिन्. -LY, *adv.* सावज्ञं, सावमानं, अनादरेण. -IRREVERENCE, *s.* अवमानः, अवज्ञा, अनादरः, तिरस्कारः, परिभवः.

IRREVERSIBLE, *a.* अपरिवर्तनीय, अलोप्य, अखंड्य.

IRREVOCABLE, *a.* अनन्यथाकरणीय.

IRRIGATE, *v. t.* अव-सिच् 6 P, जलेन आर्द्र c. or अभ्युक्ष् 1 P, अभिवृष् 1 P. -ION, *s.* सेकः, जलस्रावनं, अभ्युक्षणं.

IRRIGUOUS *a.* जलाढ्य, सजल, जलपूर्ण, अनूप, बहूदक, जलसिक्त.

IRRITATE, *v. t.* कुप् c., क्रुध् c., रुष् c.; *See* ENRAGE. -ION, *s.* प्रकोपः, क्रोधः, रोषः, कोप-रोष-कारणं-हेतुः. 2 उत्तापः, उत्तेजनं, संतापः, दाहः; 'i. of the throat' कासः, क्षवथुः. -ING, -IVE, *a.* संतापक; कोपावह. -IRRITABLE, *a.* क्रोधन, कोपन, कोपशील, सुलभकोप, शीघ्रकोपिन्, चंडप्रकृति-स्वभाव. -IRRITABILITY, *s.* चंडस्वभावः-प्रकृति *f.*, शीघ्रकोपित्वं.

IRRUPTION, *s.* *See* INROAD.

ISCHURY, *s.* मूत्रावष्टंभः, मूत्रकृच्छ्रं.

ISLAND, ISLE, *s.* द्वीपः-पं, अंतरीपं -*a.* द्वीप्य, द्वीपस्थ, द्वैप (पी *f.*). -ER, *s.* द्वीपवासिन् *m.*, द्वीपस्थः.

ISOCHRONAL, *a.* समकालीन.

ISOLATE, *v. t.* वि-युज् 7 A, 10, विच्छिद् 7 P, विश्लिष् c.; *See* SEPARATE. -ED, *a.* वियुक्त, अन्यविश्लिष्ट, अनन्यसंसक्त, गतसंग. -ION, *s.* विच्छेदः, विश्लेषः, असंगः, पृथक्त्वं.

ISOSCELES, *a.* समद्विभुज.

ISSUE, *v. i.* निर्गम् 1 P, अप-इ 2 P, निर्-या 2 P, निःसृ 1 P, निष्क्रम् 1 U, 4 P. 2 स्रु 1 P, निः-प्र-°; क्षर् 1 P, गल् 1 P, स्यंद् 1 A. 3 उत्-प्र-भू 1 P, प्रजन् 4 A, उत्पद् 4 A, प्रवृत् 1 A; *See* ARISE. 4 निष्पद्, निर्वृत्, समाप् pass. -*v. t.* निःसृ c., प्रचर्-ल् c., निर्गम् c. (गमयति), बहिर्गम् c. 2 प्रकाश् c., प्र-ख्या c. (ख्यापयति), घुष् 10. -*s.* निर्गमः, निःसरणं, निर्याणं, निष्क्रमणं. 2 फलं, परिणामः, उदर्कः, अंतः, उत्तरफलं, उत्पन्नं; *See* END. 3 संतति *f.*, प्रजा, अपत्यं, संतानः-नं. 4 रक्तातिसारः, स्रावः; 'matter at i.' विवादवस्तु, विचार्यविषयः. -LESS, *a.* निरपत्य, निर्वंश, निःसंतान, अप्रजस्, निरन्वय.

ISTHMUS, *s.* संयोगभूमि *f.*

IT, *pron.* Ex. by *m. f.* or *n.* form of pronouns, corresponding to the noun ; sometimes not ex. at all; 'what is i. that you want' किमपेक्ष्यते त्वया; 'i. is good to study' अध्ययनं प्रशस्यं.

ITCH, *s.* कंडु-डू *f.*, खर्जूः, कंडूया; (dry) कच्छु-च्छू *f.*, पामा, पामन् *f.*, विचर्चिका. 2 कंडूयनं. 3 अत्यभिलाषः, अतिस्पृहा, इच्छातिरेकः. -*v. i.* कंडूयति-ते (D.). 2 अत्यंतं इष् 6 P or अभिलष् 1, 4 P, गृध् 4 P. -Y, *a.* कंडूल, पामन, कच्छुर.

ITEM, *s.* विषयः, अर्थः, पदं, अधिकरणं, भिन्नभागः.

ITERATE, *v. t.* पुनः पुनः वद् 1 P or वच् 2 P. 2 पुनः पुनः कृ 8 U. -ION, *s.* पुनरुक्ति *f.*, पौनरुक्त्यं, पुनर्वचनं, पुनःकरणं. -IVE, *a.* पुनर्वादिन्, पुनःकारिन्.

ITINERANT, *a.* भ्रमणशील, अटमान, परिभ्रमिन्, भ्रमणकारिन्, अवनिचर.

ITINERARY, *s.* प्रवासवृत्तांतलेखः.

ITINERATE, *v. i.* *See* TRAVEL.

IVORY, *s.* गज-हस्ति-दंतः, दंतः (the sense being clear). -*a.* (*s.*) in comp.; 'i. doll' दंतपांचालिका.

IVY, *s.* तरुरोहिणी, वृक्षलता.

J.

JABBER, *v. i.* प्रजल्प् 1 P, प्रलप् 1 P, अव्यक्तं-अस्पष्टं-वद् 1 P, त्वरितं वच् 2 P. -ER, *s.* वाचालः-टः, वावदूकः, जल्प(ल्पा)कः. -ING, *s.* जल्पः, प्रलापः, प्रजल्पः, अस्पष्टं वचनं.

JACK, *s.* पनसः. 2 वृक्षः, उपस्तंभः, आधारः; 'j.-fruit' पनसं.

JACKAL, *s.* शृ(सृ)गालः, गोमायुः, जंबू(बु)कः, क्रोष्टृ *m.*, फेरवः, भूरिमायः, शिवा, मृगधूर्तकः, वंचु-(च)कः, फेरुः.

JACKANAPES, *s.* वानरवृत्ति *f.*, मर्कटशीलं.

JACKASS, *s.* गर्दभः, रासभः, खरः.

JACKDAW, *s.* काकः, द्रोणकाकः, द्रोणः.

JACKET, *s.* कूर्पासकः, कंचुकः, निचोलः.

JACK-KETCH, *s.* घातकपुरुष, उद्बंधकः.

JACK-PUDDING, *s.* भंडः, विदूषकः, वैहासिकः.

JADE, *s.* कदश्वः, अश्वकः. 2 पुंश्चली, बंधकी, कुलटा, भ्रष्टा, असती, असाध्वी. -*v. t.* खिद् c., क्लम् c., श्रम् c., आयस् c., अवसद् c. -*v. i.* श्रम् 4 P, क्लम् 1, 4 P, आयस् 1, 4 P, अवसद् 1 P, खिद् pass. ग्लै 1 P. -ED, *a.* क्लांत, श्रांत, खिन्न, श्रमार्त, ग्लान. -JADISH, *a.* दुष्ट, पापीयस्, कुत्सित, कु-कद्-दुर्-pr.

JAG, *s.* भंगः, दंतः, छेदः. -*v. t.* भंगुरी-दंतुरी-कृ 8 U, क्रकचरूपेण छिद् 7 P. -GED, -GY, *a.* दंतुर, अनुक्रकच, भंगुर, क्रकचाकार.

JAIL, *s.* कारा, कारागृहं, कारागारं, कारावेश्मन् *n.*, बंधनागारं, बंधनालयः, बंधन-निरोध-स्थानं, बंदिशाला, गुप्ति *f.* -ER, *s.* काराध्यक्षः, बंदिपालः, काराधिपतिः, कारागृहावेक्षकः.

JAM, *s.* मिष्टान्नं, स्वाद्वन्नं, संधितं. -*v. t.* संपीड् 10, संबाध् 1 A, संमृद् 9 P, क्लिश् 9 P. -MED, *a.* संपीडित, संबाध, संकुल, संकट.

JANGLE, *v. i.* वि-वद् 1 A, विप्र-लप् 1 P, विमति-पद् 4 A, कलहं कृ 8 U. -*v. t.* Rattle, q. v. -*s.*, -ING, *s.* विवादः, विप्रलापः, वाक्कलहः, वाग्युद्धं.

JANITOR, *s.* द्वाःस्थः, द्वारपालः, प्रति(ती)हारः.

JANTY, *a.* चपल, लघु-चल-स्वभाव, सरस.

JANUARY, *s.* पौषमाघं.

JAR, *s.* घटः-टी, कुंभः, कलशः-शी-शं; (earthen) मृद्भांडं, मृण्मयं पात्रं; कुटः, निपः; 'a large j.' मणिकः, अलिं(लं)जरः. 2 कर्कशध्वनिः-शब्दः, संघर्षणध्वनिः, कटु-परुष-स्वनः. 3 कलहः, विसंवादः. 4 संघट्टः, समाघातः, परस्पराघातः. -*v. i.* संघट्ट् 1 A, समाहन् 2 P. 2 कर्कशं ध्वन्-स्वन् 1 P. 3 विवद् 1 A, कलहायते (D.), विप्र-लप् 1 P. -RING, *a.*

कर्णकर्कश, परुष, कटु, कर्कशशब्दकारिन्. 2 परस्पर-विरुद्ध; *See* INCONSISTENT.

JARGON, *s.* प्रलपितं, अनर्थकं वचनं, अनर्थकवागुपचयः; संकीर्णवाच् *f.*

JASMINE, *s.* भूपदी, श(शी)तभीरुः, मल्लिका, आस्फोटा (wild); मागधी, गणिका, यूथिका, अंबष्ठा; अतिमुक्तः, पुंड्रकः; वासंती, माधवी, सुमनाः, मालती, जाति-ती *f.*, सप्तला, नवमल्लिका-मालिका; माघ्यं, कुंदः-दं (different species).

JASPER, *s.* सूर्यकांतः.

JAUNDICE, *s.* कामला-लः, पांडुः, पांडुरोगः. -ED, *a.* कामलोपहत, पांडुग्रस्त. 2 साचीकृत, सन्यात् परिवर्तित.

JAUNT, *v. i.* विहारार्थं परिभ्रम् 1, 4 P or पर्यट् 1 P. -*s.* विहारः, पर्यटनं.

JAVELIN, *s.* शूलः-लं, शल्यं, शंकुः, प्रासः, शक्ति *f.*, अस्त्रं, कुंतः.

JAW, *s.* हनु *m. f.* 2 वक्त्रं, मुखं; 'lower j.' पीचं, कुंजः, चिबुकं, चिबुः; 'locked j.' हनुग्रहः; 'j.-tooth' दंष्ट्रा; 'fallen in the j.s of death' मृत्योर्मुखे पतितः, मृत्युदंष्ट्रांतर्गतः. 3 भर्त्सना, वाक्पारुष्यं, तर्जनं, आक्रोशः. -*v. i.* तर्ज् 1 P, 10 A, भर्त्स् 10 A, आक्रुश् 1 P. -ED, *a.* हनुमत्, हनुविशिष्ट.

JAY, *s.* चाषः-सः, किकीदिविः, किकिदिवः-विः, किकीदिवीः-वः, किकिः, दिवः.

JEALOUS, *a.* मत्सरिन्, समत्सर, सासूय, साभ्यसूय, सेर्ष्य, परोत्कर्षासहन, परसुखद्वेषिन्; *See* ENVIOUS. 2 प्रेमसंशयिन्-शंकाशील, प्रीत्याशंकिन्; 'a j. husband' परपुरुष-व्यभिचार-जार-शंकित; 'a j. wife' परस्त्रीशंकिनी. 3 कृतादर, आदृत, साभिमान, सावधान, अनुपेक्षक. -LY, *adv.* समत्सरं, सेर्ष्यं, सासूयं, साभ्यसूयं; साभिमानं. -NESS, -Y, *s.* मत्सरः, मात्सर्यं, असूया, ईर्ष्या, अभ्यसूया, सापत्न्यं, परोत्कर्षद्वेषः. 2 शंकाशीलता, व्यभिचारशंका, प्रेम-प्रीति-शंका. 3 सावधानता, अभिमानापेक्षा.

JEER, *v. i.* उप-अव-हस् 1 P, अव-आ-क्षिप् 6 P, अव-ज्ञा 9 U, तिरस्कृ 8 U, गर्ह् 1, 10 A, अवहासास्पदीकृ. -*s.* उप-अव-हासः, अवक्षेपः, अवज्ञा. -INGLY, *adv.* सोपहासं, सावक्षेपं; सावज्ञं.

JEJUNE, *a.* शुष्क, रूक्ष, नीरस, विरस, निःसार, निःसत्व.

JELLY, *s.* श्यान-सांद्र-द्रव्यं.

JEOPARDY, *s.* संशयः, संदेहः, शंका; 'j. of life' जीवितसंशयः, प्राणसंदेहः. -JEOPARD, *v. t.*, -IZE, *v. t.* संशये पत् c., संशयस्थ-संशयित-*a.* कृ 8 U; 'one who j.es his life' संशयितजीवितः; *See* DANGER also.

JERK, *v. t.* (सहसा) चल् c., वि-धू 6 P, 5, 9 U; लघु-सहसा तड् 10 or प्रह् 1 P, अकस्मात्-सवेगं-क्षिप् 6 P. -*s.* चालनं, लघुप्रहारः, लघ्वाघातः, लघु-आकस्मिक-क्षेपः.

JERKIN, *s.* *See* JACKET.

JESSAMINE, *s.* *See* JASMINE.

JEST, *s.* परि(री)हासः, नर्मन् *n.*, हास्यं, विनोदोक्ति *f.*, प्रहसनं, विनोदभाषणं, परिहासोक्तिः, नर्मालापः; 'truce to (fie upon) your j.s' धिक्प्रहसनं (U. 4.), अलं परिहासेन; 'uttered in j.' परिहासजल्पितं; 'made a j. of the matter' तमर्थं परिहासमिव मेने. 2 खेला, क्रीडा, केलि *f.*, कौतुकं; 'in j.' परिहासेन, परिहासपूर्वं. -*v. i.* परिहस् 1 P, विनोद-परिहास-वाक्यं वद् 1 P or उदीर् c.; क्रीड् 1 P. -ER, *s.* वैहासिकः, परिहासयितृ *m.*, परिहास-विनोदकारिन् *m.*, भंडः, चाटुपटुः; 'king's j.' विदूषकः, नर्मसचिवः. -INGLY, *adv.* परिहासपूर्वं, सपरिहासं, सविनोदं.

JET, *s.* जलोत्क्षेपः. 2 कृष्णप्रस्तरः; 'j.-black' घनकृष्ण, अतिकृष्ण. -TY, *a.* कृष्णवर्ण.

JEWEL, *s.* मणि *m. f.*, रत्नं; 'j. of a woman' स्त्रीरत्नं; 'j.-house' मणिशाला, रत्नागारं; 'j.-mine' रत्नाकरः, रत्न-मणि-खनि *f.*-भूमि *f.* -LED, *a.* रत्नवत्, मणि-रत्न-मय (यी *f.*), रत्नसनाथ, मणि-रत्न-खचित, रत्नानुविद्ध. -LER, *s.* रत्नाजीविन् *m.*, मणिकारः, रत्नकारः. -JEWELRY, *s.* रत्नानि (pl.), रत्नादिकोशः-षः.

JIFFY, *s.* निमेषः, क्षणः.

JIG, *s.* नृत्यविशेषः. 2 वंचना, व्याजः, छलं.

JILT, *s.* प्रतारिका, चपला, वंचिका, संकेतलंघिनी. -*v. i.* प्रेमसंकेतं लंघ् 1 A, 10, प्रेमविषये वंच् 10, or प्रतॄ c., खंड् 10.

JINGLE, *v. i.* शिंज् 2 A, 10, क्वण् 1 P, वि-रु 2 P, झणझणायते (D.), कलं स्वन् 1 P. -*s.*, -ING, *s.* शिंजितं, शिंजा, झणत्कारः, झणझणस्वनः, क्वणितं, क्वणनं, कलरवः.

JOB, *s.* कार्यं, कृत्यं, व्यापारः, क्रिया. 2 लघु-क्षुद्र-नीचक्रिया. 3 स्वार्थपरं कार्यं, आत्मवृद्ध्यर्थं कर्म. -*v. i.* क्षुद्रकर्माणि कृ 8 U, स्वार्थमुद्दिश्य कार्यं कृ. 2 पण् 1 A. -BER, *s.* क्षुद्रकर्मकारिन् *m.*, परार्थं क्रयविक्रयकारी, स्वार्थप्रवर्तकः, क्रयविक्रयी. -BING, *s.* क्षुद्रकर्मव्यवसायः, स्वार्थप्रवृत्ति *f.*

JOCKEY, *s.* अश्वज्ञः, हयज्ञः, अश्वविद् *m.*, अश्वकोविदः, अश्वविद्याविशारदः. -*v. t.* अश्वज्ञ इव प्रतॄ c. or वंच् 10. -ISM, *s.* अश्वविद्या-शिक्षा.

JOCOSE, JOCULAR, *a.* हास्यकर (री *f.*), विनोदिन्, हास्यावह, विनोदात्मक, सरस, हास्यगर्भ, सकौतुक; (of persons) परिहासशील, परिहासक, विनोद-नर्मालाप-पर, कौतुकिन्. -LY, *adv.* परिहासेन, परिहासपूर्वं, सकौतुकं, विनोदार्थं, रसिकवत्. -NESS, -ITY, *s.* परिहासशीलता, रसिकता, विनोदः, कौतुकं, उल्लासः, हर्षः, प्रमोदः.

JOCUND, *a.* प्र-,हृष्ट, प्र-,मुदित, आनंदवृत्ति. -ITY, *s.* उल्लासः, प्रहर्षः, आनंदः; *See* GLAD.

JOG, (on) *v. i.* मंदं मंदं प्रसृप् 1 P or चल् 1 P or सृ 1 P. -*v. t.* अरत्निना तड् 10, ईषत् चल् c. -*s.* ईषदाघातः, ईषत्प्रहारः-चालनं; 'j.-trot' गज-मंद-गति *f.*, मंदप्रयाणं.

JOIN, *v. t.* युज् 7 U, 10, सं-आ-°, संसंज् 1 P, यु 2 P, संश्लिष् c., सं-धा 3 U, संबंध् 9 P, संहन् 2 P, एकत्र कृ 8 U, संग्रंथ् 9 P, योक्त्रयति (D.), घट् c. (घटयति), संपृच् 2 A, 7 P. **2** (Go to) समुपा-गम् 1 P, सं-इ 2 P, संमिल् 6 P, संगम् 1 A; pass. of roots above (with instr.); 'j. hands' अंजलिं बंध् 9 P, प्रां(सां)जलि-*a.* भू, हस्तौ समा-नी 1 P; 'j. ed their hands in marriage' विवाह-विधिना ताभ्यां अन्योन्यपाणिग्रहणं कारयामास, वधूवरं संगमयांचकार. -ED, *a.* युक्त, युत, संयुक्त, संयुत, संश्लिष्ट, संहत, सं-समा-सक्त, लग्न, संलग्न, संबद्ध, संश्क्त, संहित, सहित, संगत, समेत, मिलित, घटित. -ER, *s.* तक्षकः, रथकारः, सूत्रधारः, तष्टृ *m.*, तक्षन् *m.*, काष्ठ-तक्ष् *m.*, वर्धकिः. -ERY, *s.* काष्ठतक्षणं. -ING, *s.* सं-,योगः, संधिः, संसर्गः, संधानं, संश्लेषः, संघातः, सं-गमः, संसक्ति *f.* —JOINT, *s.* संधिः, पर्वन् *n.*, ग्रंथिः, कांडः-डं, अस्थिग्रंथिः-संधिः; 'out of j.' विलग्न, वि-संधि. -*a.* संयुक्त, समवेत, एककार्यव्यापृत, संहत. **2** असंविभक्त, अविभक्त, साधारण (णी *f.*), सामान्य, सह in comp.; संघातवत्, संभूयकारिन्; 'j. proprietor' सहाधिकारी; 'j. family property' संसृष्टिधनं; 'members of a j. family' संसृष्टाः, संसृष्टिनः; 'with j. labour' संभूयश्रमेण, सर्वेषां यत्नेन; 'j.-stock company' संभूयसमुत्थानं; 'j.-heir' भागी, संविभागी, समांशहरः, समांशी. -*v. t.* संधियुक्त-*a.* कृ; ex. by (*s.*). -ED, *a.* संधिविशिष्ट, ग्रंथिल, संधि-ग्रं-थि-युक्त, पर्ववत्. -LY, *adv.* समं, सह, संभूय, संयोगे-न, सहितं, समवायेन, एकीभूय, एकचित्तीभूय, युगपत्. -JOINTURE, *s.* विधवाधनं; स्त्रीधनं.

JOKE,-ER, *See* JEST,-ER.

JOLE, *s.* गंडः, कपोलः.

JOLLY, *a.* प्र-,हृष्ट, सानंद, उल्लसित, प्रमोदिन्, हृष्ट-प्रीत-हृदय; परिहासशील, विनोदिन्, विलासिन्, विनोदशील. -ITY, *s.* उल्लासः, आनंदः, प्र-,हर्षः, प्रमोदः, उत्सवः. -NESS, *s.* विनोदपरता, प्रहासः.

JOLT, *v. t.* संक्षुभ् 9 P or c. -*v. i.* क्षुभ् 1 A, 4 P. -*s.*,-ING, *s.* संक्षोभः, उद्घातः, आकस्मिकक्षेपः.

JOLTHEAD, *s.* स्थूलबुद्धिः, मूर्खः, मूढः; *See* FOOL.

JOSTLE, *v. t.* स्कंधताडनेन निराकृ 8 U or निः-सृ c. or निर्-धू 6 P, 5, 9 U or निरस् 4 U; परस्परं समा-हन् 2 P or संघृष् 1 P or संमृद् 9 P, अभिसं-पत् 1 P; संघट्ट् 1 A. -ING, *s.* परस्परसमाघातः-घर्षणं, अन्यो-न्यसंमर्दः, अभिसंपातः.

JOT, *s.* कणः, लवः, अणुः, लेश-लव-कण-बिंदु-मात्रं, तिलमात्रं. -*v. t.* (स्मरणार्थं) लिख् 6 P or अंक् 10. -TING, *s.* अभिलिखितं.

JOURNAL, *s.* वार्ता-वृत्त-समाचार-पत्रं-पत्रिका. -IST, *s.* वृत्तपत्रप्रकाशकः-लेखकः.

JOURNEY, *s.* प्रयाणं, प्रस्थानं, प्रवासः, यात्रा, देशभ्रमणं-पर्यटनं, अध्वन् *m.*, मार्गः, अध्व-मार्ग-गमनं-क्रमणं, 'on account of the fatigues of j.' अध्वसंजात-खेदात्; उत्थाय पुनरवहत् (Ka. 299) 'resumed his j.' &c.; 'it is only a week's j.' सप्ताहग-म्योऽध्वा; 'to return from a j.' प्रवासाद् उपा-नि-वृत् 1 A; 'may the j. be pleasant to you' शिवा-स्ते पंथानः संतु. -*v. i.* प्र-या 2 P, मार्गेण गम् or व्रज् or चर् 1 P or या, पर्यट् 1 P, परिभ्रम् 1, 4 P, वह् 1 P; दिवा रात्रौ चावहत् (Ka. 301); 'to j. abroad' प्रवस् 1 P. -ER, *s.* अध्वगः, पथिकः, पांथः, यात्रिकः. -JOURNEYMAN, *s.* वैतनिकः; हस्तकर्मकारः.

JUBILANT, *a.* जयघोषं कुर्वाण, जयध्वनिकारिन्.

JUBILEE, *s.* प्रहर्षः, महोत्सवानंदः, महोत्सवः, उत्सव-कालः.

JUDGE, *s.* प्राड्विवाकः, अ(आ)धिकरणिकः, अक्षदर्शकः, धर्माध्यक्षः, धर्माधिकारिन् *m.*, न्यायाध्यक्षः, निर्णेतृ *m.*, दंडनायकः. **2** (In general) अभिज्ञः, गुणदोषज्ञः, विशेषज्ञः, परीक्षकः, परिच्छेदकः, विवेकिन् *m.*, गुणग्राही, रसज्ञः, तद्विद् *m.* -*v.* वि-विच् 3, 7 U, परिच्छिद् 7 P, वि-ज्ञा 9 U, विभू c., विचर् c., निर्णी 1 P, निश्चि 5 U, अव-निर्-धृ 10, अव-परि-ईक्ष् 1 A, तीर् 10, अनुसं-धा 3 U. **2** वितर्क् 10, विमृश् 6 P, विगण् 10, विक्लृप् c., मनसा विचर् or विविच्, मन् 4 A; 'it is for you to j. whether &c.' एतद्विषये भवान् प्रमाणं; 'j. me by my acts' फलेन मद्गुणदोषनिर्णयः क्रियतां; 'to j. ill or wrongly' मिथ्या क्लृप् c. or संभू c. or मन्. -MENT, *s.* विवेकः, परिच्छेदः, विचारः-रणा, विज्ञानं, विभावनं, निर्धारणा, निर्णयः, निश्चयः, संकल्पः, अवधारणं-णा. **2** (Judicial decision) निर्णयः, विचारः, निर्णयपादः, आधर्षणं, तीरणं, दंडाज्ञा. **3** अनुभवः, तर्कः, ज्ञानं, अनुमानं. **4** मति *f.*, बुद्धि *f.*, मतं, अभिप्रायः, संकल्पः, बोधः; 'according to one's j.' यथामति, यथाबुद्धि. **5** (Divine j.) ईश्वराज्ञा, ईश्वरविधिः, नियमः-शासनं; 'j.-day' विचारदिनं; 'j.-hall' न्यायसभा, विचार-धर्म-सभा; 'j.-seat' व्यवहारासनं, न्यायासनं, धर्मासनं. -JUDICATORY, *s.* धर्म-विचार-न्याय-सभा, व्यवहारमंडपः, धर्माधिकरणं. **2** न्यायप्रणयनं. -JUDICATURE, *s.* न्यायाधिकारः, व्यवहारदर्शनाधिकारः; *See* JUDICATORY above. -JUDICIARY, *a.* विचारक, व्य(व्या)वहारिक (की *f.*). —JUDICIAL, *a.* व्यवहारविषयक, व्यवहार in comp.; 'j. proceeding' व्यवहारदर्शनं, व्यवहारः, न्यायविचारः. -LY, *adv.* व्यवहारानुसारेण, यथा-

व्यवहारं, न्यायानुरूपं. —JUDICIOUS, *a.* (Act) समीक्ष्य-विमृश्य-कृत, न्याय्य, धर्म्य, समंजस, उचित,यथा-न्याय, सविवेक, युक्त, योग्य. 2 (Persons) विमृश्य-समीक्ष्य-कारिन्, विवेकिन्, नीतिमत्, परिच्छेदक, नयज्ञ, प्राज्ञ, विवेकदृश्वन्, विशेषज्ञ, सदसद्दर्शिन्. —LY, *adv.* युक्तं, समंजसं, यथान्यायं, उचितं, सम्यक्. 2 सविवेकं, सपरिच्छेदं, सुविमृश्य, सुविचार्य, प्राज्ञ-विज्ञ-वत्.

JUG, *s.* कुंभः, कलशः, कंसः, उदकपात्रं; *See* JAR.

JUGGLE, *v.* मुह् c., छल् 10, वंच् 10, दृष्टिं मुह् c. or बंध् 9 P, मायां-कुहकं-इंद्रजालं-कृ 8 U. —*s.*,—ING, —RY, *s.* माया, कुसृति *f.*, दृष्टिमोहः-बंधः, इंद्रजालं, कुहका-कं, इंद्रिय-दृष्टि-मोहः, हस्तलाघवं-चापल्यं. 2 वंचना, छलं, कूटता, प्रतारणा. —ER, *s.* ऐंद्रजालिकः, मायिन् *m.*, मायाकारः, मायाजीवी, कुहकजीवी, कौसृतिकः, अ-(आ)हितुंडिकः.

JUGULAR, *a.* कंठस्थ, कंठ्य.

JUICE, *s.* रसः, द्रवः, सारः, निर्यासः, आसवः; 'j. issuing from the elephant's temples' मदः, दानं, मदवारि. —LESS, *a.* नीरस, अरस, विरस, असार, सारहीन-शून्य, शुष्क, पिंडीर. —Y, *a.* रसमय (यी *f.*), रसपूर्ण, सरस, बहुरस, रसाढ्य, सार-रस-वत्.

JUJUBE, *s.* बदरी, कर्कंधु-धू *m. f.*, कोलि *f.*, कोलाली; (fruit) बदरं, कोलं, कुवलं, फेनिलं, सौवीरं, घोंटा.

JULY, *s.* आषाढश्रावणं.

JUMBLE, *v. t.* संकॄ 6 P, संमिश्र् 10, संक्षिप् 6 P, संकुली-संकरी-कृ 8 U. —*v. i.* संकॄ pass., संकरी-संकुली-भू 1 P. —*s.* संकरः, सं-,मिश्रणं, संक्षोभः, संकुलता, संनिपातः.

JUMP, *v. i.* प्लु 1 A, वल्ग् 1 U, स्कंद् 1 P; 'j. about' नृत् 4 P; 'j. over' लंघ् 1 A, 10; 'j. up' उत्प्लु, उत्पत् 1 P; 'j. with' Agree, q. v. —*s.*,-ING, *s.* प्लवनं, उत्पतनं, वल्गितं, प्लुतं-ति *f.*, प्लवः, आस्कंदः, झंपः-पा. —ER, *s.* प्लवकः, झंपिन् *m.*

JUNCTION, *s.* सं-,योगः, संगमः, संमिलनं, संगति *f.*, समागमः, संश्लेषः, संधिः, संसर्गः, संघातः, संसक्ति *f.*, संपर्कः; 'j. of rivers' संभेदः, संगमः. 2 संधिस्थानं.

JUNCTURE, *s.* वेला, समयः; कष्टकालः-समयः, संकटवेला. 2 संधिः, ग्रंथिः.

JUNE, *s.* ज्येष्ठाषाढकं.

JUNGLE, *s.* गुल्मावृतं स्थानं.

JUNIOR, *a.* कनीयस्, अवर, अवरज, यवीयस्, अवरपदभाज्.

JUNKET, *s.* निभृतोत्सवः. 2 मिष्टान्नं, मोदकः.

JUNTA, JUNTO,*s.* सभा, समाजः, गूढसंसर्गः, कुसंसर्गः.

JURIDICAL, *a.* व्य(न्या)वहारिक (की *f.*); *See* JUDICIAL.

JURISCONSULT, *s.* स्मृतिशास्त्रज्ञः, धर्मशास्त्रकोविदः.

JURISDICTION, *s.* अधिकारः, व्यवहारदर्शनाधिकारः, न्यायप्रभुत्वं.

JURISPRUDENCE, *s.* धर्मशास्त्रं, स्मृतिशास्त्रं, व्यवहार-विद्या-ज्ञानं-शास्त्रं, विधिः; 'a head of j.' व्यवहारविषयः-पदं.

JURIST, *s.* धर्मशास्त्रकोविदः, स्मृतिज्ञः.

JURY, *s.* सभ्याः; प्रमाणपुरुषगणः.

JUST, *a.* (Of persons) न्यायवर्तिन्, न्यायिन्, न्यायशील-पर, साधुवृत्ति, ऋजु, विमलात्मन्, निष्कपट, निर्व्याज, शुचि, न्यायपरायण, धार्मिक-सात्त्विक (की *f.*). 2 न्याय्य, धर्म्य, यथान्याय, न्यायानुसारिन्, सत्य, तथ्य, योग्य, युक्त, यथार्थ, उचित, सम्यञ्च्. 3 सम, समवृत्ति, निःपक्षपात, समदर्शिन्. 4 संपूर्ण, अविकल, अन्यून. —*adv.* अंतिकं-के, समीपं, निकटे. 2 प्रायः, प्रायशः; oft. by भूयिष्ठ, कल्प, प्राय in comp., or by desid.; *See* ABOUT. 3 सद्यः, अचिरादेव, नातिचिरात्, प्राक्; oft. by एव, मात्र in comp.; 'j. now' अधुनैव; 'it is j. proper' उचितमेव; 'j. dead' सद्योमृत; 'j. born' जातमात्र. 4 युक्तं, सम्यक्, यथार्थं, यथावत्. 5 तावत्; 'j. come here' इतस्तावदागम्यतां; 'j. so' एवमेव, तथैव, एवमेतत्, अथ किं, युक्तं, युज्यते; 'j. as', 'j. like' इव, यद्वत्, or निर्विशेष in comp.; 'stay j. as in your own house' स्वगृहनिर्विशेषमत्र वस; 'bred j. like one's own children' स्वपुत्रनिर्विशेषं संवर्द्धित. 6 कष्टेन, कृच्छ्रेण. —LY, *adv.* निर्व्याजं, निर्व्यलीकं, सारल्येन. 2 यथान्यायं, न्यायेन, धर्मेण, न्यायतः, धर्मतः, यथाधर्मं, न्यायानुसारेण, सम्यक्, यथावत्. 3 सत्यं, अवितथं, यथार्थं, अर्थतः, यथावत्, यथातथं, यथार्हं, उपपन्नं, यथोचितं, युक्तं, स्थाने, यथायोग्यं, अंजसा.—NESS, *s.* न्याय्यता, यथार्थता, योग्यता, औचित्यं, युक्तता; साम्यं, अपक्षपातः. —JUSTICE, *s.* धर्मः, न्यायः, नयः, नीति *f.*, न्यायिता, ऋजुता, साधुता. 2 न्याय्यता, युक्तता, योग्यता, यथार्थता, सत्यता, युक्ति *f.*, याथार्थ्यं. 3 साम्यं, समदर्शित्वं, अपक्षपातः, सर्वसमता. 4 न्याय्यदंडः, योग्यदंडः-शिक्षा, अपराधानुरूपो दंडः. 5 धर्माध्यक्षः; प्राड्विवाकः; *See* JUDGE; 'court of j.' न्याय-धर्म-सभा, व्यवहारमंडपः.—SHIP, *s.* धर्माधिकारः, न्यायाध्यक्षत्वं. —JUSTICIARY, *s.* Judge, q. v. —JUSTIFY, *v. t.* न्याय्य-*a.* इति प्रति-पद् c. or प्रदृश् c.; शुध् c., दोषं निराकृ 8 U or निवार् 10 or शुध् c. or मृज् 2 P, दोषाद् मुच् 6 P or c. —ABLE, *a.* निवार्यदोष, शोधनीय, शुद्धिक्षम. —ICATION, *s.* शुद्धि *f.*, शोधनं, दोषशुद्धिः, दोषमुक्ति *f.*,-मार्जना, दोषप्रतीकारः, विमोचनहेतुः, अप-व्यप-देशः. —ER, *s.* शोधकः, दोषनिवारकः.

JUSTLE, *v. See* JOSTLE.

JUT, *v. i.* प्रलंब् 1 A, बहिर्वृत् 1 A or स्था 1 P. —*s.* प्रलंबनं, आभोगः, प्रालंबः.

JUVENILE, *a.* तरुण, अल्पवयस्क, युवन्, कौमार (री *f.*), अभिनववयस्. —ITY, *s.* यौवनं, तारुण्यं, कौमारं, यौवनावस्था, तारुण्यभावः.

JUXTAPOSITION, *s.* सान्निध्यं, संनिधिः, संस्थिति *f.*, सन्निकर्षः, संसर्गः, नैकट्यं, उपश्लेषः.

K.

KAW, *v. i.* कै 1 P, ध्वां(ध्रां)क्ष् 1 P. –*s.* काकरवः-रुतं.

KEEL, *s.* नौतलं.

KEEN, *a.* तीक्ष्ण, शित, निशित, शात, निशात, शितधार, तीक्ष्णाग्र; तीव्र, तिग्म, प्रखर. 2 व्यग्र, उच्चंड, उत्सुक, उत्कट, कुतूहलिन्; *See* EAGER. 3 सूक्ष्म, कुशाग्र-ग्रीय, विदग्ध. 4 उग्र, कटु, अरुंतुद, मर्मस्पृश्, तिग्म (words); 'k. words' वाग्विषुः, वागसिः; 'k.-eyed' 'k.-sighted' सूक्ष्ममति, तीक्ष्ण-सूक्ष्म-बुद्धि, कुशाग्रमति-बुद्धि, दूरदर्शिन्. –LY, *adv.* तीक्ष्णं, तीव्रं, उग्रं, प्रखरतया. –NESS, *s.* तीक्ष्णता, तीव्रता. 2 व्यग्रता, उच्चंडता, कौतूहलं, अत्युत्साहः. 3 सूक्ष्मता, विदग्धता, कुशाग्रमतित्वं, बुद्धिसूक्ष्मता. 4 कटुता, तिग्मता, उग्रता.

KEEP, *v. t.* रक्ष् 1 P, पा 2 P, पा c. (पालयति), गुप् 1 P, त्रै 1 A, अव् 1 P. 2 धृ 1 P, 10; धा 3 U, नि-आ-°, निविश् c., स्था c. (स्थापयति), न्यस् 4 U. 3 रुध् 7 U, नि-अव-उप-°,धृ, बंध् 9 P, निवार् 10, प्रति-नि-षिध् 1 P, नि-सं-यम् 1 P. 4 (As cattle) निरूप् 10, पा c., रक्ष्. 5 (As a secret) न प्रकाश् c. or भंज् 7 P or भिद् 7 P, गुप्, रक्ष्. 6 (Observe) आचर् 1 P, अनु-ष्ठा 1 P, वि-धा, कृ, सेव् 1 A, भज् 1 U, आश्रि 1U, आ-स्था 1U, आ-अव-लंब् 1A. 7 शुध् c., निर्वह् c., अप-वृज् 10, पूर् 10, तॄ 1 P, साध् 5 P or c., पा c. (पालयति) (as a promise). 8 भृ 1 P, 3 U, पुष् c., पा c.; (as servants) व्यापृ c., सेवायां नियुज् 7 A, 10, वेतनं-भृति-दा 3 U; 'to k. bad hours' वेलातिक्रमेण स्वप् 2 P; 'to k. in mind' हृदये-मनसि-कृ, अव-धृ; 'k. company with' संगम् 1 A, सं-इ 2 P, सह वस् or चर् 1 P, संवस्; *See* ASSOCIATE. –*v. i.* स्था, वृत् 1 A, आस् 2 A, न विरम् 1 P or निवृत् or विश्रम् 4 P, with pres. part. (when followed by p. p. &c.); 'he kept weeping' रुदन्नास्त, रुदन्नोपरराम; 'k. going up and down' आरोहावरोहं कुर्वन्नास्त्व. 2 संसंज्-संश्लिष्-अनुबंध्-pass., लग् 1 P. 3 वस् 1 P. –*s.* रक्षा-क्षणं, पालनं, गुप्ति *f.* 2 अवस्था, दशा, स्थिति *f.*, वृत्ति *f.*, भावः. 3 भृति *f.*, पोषणं. 4 दुर्गं, कोटः. 5 काराबंधनं, निरोधः, गुप्तिः. –back,-from, निग्रह् 9 P, संयम्, संह् 1 P, निवृ c.; (*v. i.*) निवृत्, विरम्. –in, गुह् 1 U, आच्छद् 10, अंतर्धा, संवृ 5 U. –off, निवार्, निवृत् c., निरुध्, प्रति-नि-हन् 2 P, प्रतिकृ, व्यप-ऊह् 1 U, परिह् 1 P; (*v. i.*) निवृत्, विरम्; *See* CEASE. –on, *See* Keep (*v. i.*) above; प्रवृत्, प्रारब्धं सं-पद् c. –out, व्यावृत् c., प्रतिषिध्; *See* EXCLUDE. –to, अनुवृत्, अनुसृ 1 P, अनुरुध् 4 A, परिरक्ष्, परिपा c. (पालयति); *See* Keep (*v. t.*) above. –under, वशीकृ, वशं नी 1 P, स्वायत्तीकृ. –up, प्रवृत् c., पा c.; (*v. i.*) जागृ 2 P; न दम् or श्रम् 4 P. –ER, *s.* रक्षकः, पालकः, रक्षितृ *m.*, रक्षिन् *m.*, गोप्ता, पः-पालः in comp. –ING, *s.* रक्षा, अवेक्षा, पालनं, गुप्तिः. 2 सादृश्यं, अविरोधः, संगति *f.*, आनुरूप्यं; 'in k. with' अनुरूप-संवादिन्-सदृश-योग्य-*a.*

KEEP-SAKE, *s.* स्मृतिदानं; स्नेहाभिज्ञानं.

KEG, *s.* काष्ठभांडं.

KELTER, *s.* *See* ORDER.

KEN, *s.* गोचरः-रं, विषयः; नयनविषयः-पथः, बुद्धिविषयः. –*v. t.* दूरादालोक् 1 A, 10 or ईक्ष् 1 A or दृश् 1 P. 2 परि-ज्ञा 9 U, अवगम् 1 P.

KENNEL, *s.* श्वशाला, श्वगृहं, कुक्कुरालयः. 2 श्वगणः. 3 जलमार्गः, प्रणालः-ली. –*v. i.* श्वगृहे वस् 1 P.

KERCHIEF, *s.* आवरणं, वेष्टनं, आभरणं; 'hand-k.' हस्तप्रावारकः, नक्तकः; 'neck.' ग्रीवावेष्टनं, कंठवस्त्रं.

KERNEL, *s.* बीजं, गर्भः, अस्थि *f.*, अष्ठीला, फलबीजं-गर्भः, सारभूतं द्रव्यं. 2 मध्यः-ध्यं, गर्भः, उदरं, हृदयं, अभ्यंतरं. –LY, *a.* बीजाकार, बीजपूर्ण.

KETTLE, *s.* कटाहः, पिठरः-रं, स्थाली, उखा, कुंडं; 'k.-drum' भेरि-री *f.*, दुंदुभिः, डिंडिमः.

KEY, *s.* अंकुटः, कुंचिका, ताली, उद्घाटकः-कं. 2 व्याख्या, निर्वचनं, टीका; 'k.-hole' कुंचिका-छिद्रं; 'k.-stone' संधान-संयोग-प्रस्तरः.

KIBE, *s.* पादस्फोटः, विपादिका.

KICK, *v. t.* पादेन-लत्तया-प्रह् 1 P or तड् 10 or आ-हन् 2 U, लत्ताप्रहारं कृ 8 U; पादं-पार्ष्णिं-खुरं-क्षिप् 6 P. –*s.* पाद-लत्ता-प्रहारः, पादाघातः, पार्ष्णि-खुर-क्षेपः, खुराघातः.

KID, *s.* छागशावः-शावकः, अजशिशुः, अजपोतः, छागशिशुः. 2 काष्ठभारः.

KIDNAP, *v. t.* (बालकं-दासं) चुर् 10, अपहृ 1 P or बलाद् हृ. –PER, *s.* बालस्तेयकृत् *m.* –PING, *s.* बालस्तेयं, बालापहारः.

KIDNEY, *s.* वृक्कः-क्का, गुर्दः; 'k.-bean' मुद्गः, माषः, शिंबा, शिंबिकः-का.

KILL, *v. t.* हन् 2 P, व्यापद् c., मृ c., सूद् 10, निषूद्, नश् c., प्र-मी 9 U or c. (मापयति), हिंस् 7 P, तृह् 6, 7 P, वि-शस् 1 P, पंचत्वं-परलोकं गम् c. (गमयति) or नी 1 P; शद् c. (शातयति), निपत् c., नि-कृत् 6 P, अप-नी, क्षि 5 P or c. –ER, *s.* हंतृ *m.*, घातकः, नाशकः, निषूदनः, अंतकः; gen. हन् or घातिन् in comp.; 'k. of Vritra' वृत्रहन्; 'k. of Madhu' मधुसूदनः. –ING, *s.* हत्या, वधः, हननं, घातः, मारणं, नाशः, निषूदनं, हिंसा-सनं, आलंभः, विशसनं, व्यापादनं, प्रमापणं, निबर्हणं, निकारणं, विशारणं, प्रवासनं, परासनं, संज्ञपनं, निर्मथनं, निस्तर्हणं,

क्षपणनं, परिवर्जनं, निर्वापणं, प्रमथनं, क्रथनं, उज्जासनं, पिंजः, विशरः, उन्माथः.

KILN, *s.* पाकपुटी, आपाकः.

KIMBO, *a.* वि-अव-भुग्न, वक्र, कुटिल.

KIN, *See* KINDRED; 'of k.' सजातीय, सगोत्र.

KIND, *a.* दयालु, सदय, कृपाकुल, कृपालु, अनुकंपिन्, सानुकंप, सकरुण, करुणात्मन्, दया-करुणा-शील, करुणार्द्र, दयार्द्र, स्निग्ध, कृपा-दया-घृणा-वत्, कारुणिक (की *f.*); प्रियकर (री *f.*), हित, प्रियैषिन्, हितैषिन्, हितकाम, हितबुद्धि, उपकार-पर-शील, उपकारिन्, सुहृदय, अनुकूल, सुशील, प्रसन्न, प्रीत. 2 मधुर, प्रिय; 'k. to the poor' दीनानुकंपिन्, दीनवत्सल; 'k. office' उपकारः; 'k. act' सुकृतं; 'k. words' प्रियवचनं; 'speaking k. words' प्रियंवद, प्रियवादिन्; 'k. present' प्रीतिदानं. —*s.* जाति *f.*, गणः, वर्गः. 2 विशेषः, भेदः, प्रकारः, जातिः, रूपं, विधा, in comp.; 'of many k. s' बहुविध; 'of various k. s' विविध, नानारूप-विध, नाना *ind.*; 'of this k.' एवंविध, एवंरूप; 'of all k. s' सर्वप्रकार; 'Jâti is a k. of flower' जातिः कुसुमविशेषः-भेदः. —LY, *a.* सौम्य, मृदु, कोमल, स्निग्ध, प्रिय. 2 अनुकूल; समानशील. —*adv.* सदयं, सकरुणं, दयया, कृपया, प्रीत्या, सस्नेहं, सानुकंपं, सानुग्रहं; प्रियं, हितेच्छया, सुशीलवत्, सुजनवत्; 'speaking k.' प्रियवादिन्; 'k. disposed' हितबुद्धि, अनुरक्त. —NESS, *s.* प्रसादः, अनुग्रहः, कृपा, दया, अनुकंपा, करुणा, प्रीति *f.*, स्नेहः, कृपालुता, दयालुता, हितेच्छा, कृपाशीलता, सुशीलं, सौजन्यं, प्रेमन् *m. n.*, आनुकूल्यं. 2 उपकारः, उपकृतं-ति *f.*, प्रियं, सुकृतं-तिः, हितं. —KINDLINESS, *s.* सौम्यता, स्निग्धता; सौजन्यं, सुशीलता.

KINDLE, *v. t.* प्र-उत्-सं-दीप् c., इंध् 7 A, ज्वल् c., तप् 1 P or c. 2 उत्तिज् c., संधुक्ष् 10, प्रोत्सह् c.; प्रकुप् c., रुष् c.; 'with glances k. ed with anger' क्रोधेद्धैर्दृष्टिपातैः (Rat. 1). —*v. i.* ज्वल् 1 P, दीप् 4 A, तप् 4 A.

KINDRED, *a.* सजातीय, सगोत्र, सनाभि, सवर्ण, सवंशीय, सकुल्य, संबंधीय. 2 समान, सम-तुल्य-गुण, सधर्मन्, अनुगुण. —*s.* बंधुता, ज्ञातित्वं, ज्ञातिभावः, सगोत्रता, सजातित्वं, संबंधः, सपिंडता. 2 (Relatives) बंधवः, ज्ञातयः, बांधवाः, सगोत्राः, सकुल्याः, गोत्रजाः, संबंधिनः (pl.); बंधुजनः, बंधु-ज्ञाति-वर्गः, बंधु-बांधव-गणः.

KING, *s.* राजन् *m.*, नृपः, नरपतिः, नृपतिः, भूपतिः, भूपः, भूपालः, नरेंद्रः; and comp. of ईशः, अधीशः, पतिः, इंद्रः, पः, पालः, भृत् or भुज् with 'Man' and 'Earth' q. v.; अवनिपः, क्षोणीपालः, भूभृत्, महीभुक्, क्षितिपतिः; 'supreme or great k.' महाराजः, अधिराजः, सम्राज्, अधीश्वरः, मंडलेश्वरः; 'k. of k. s' राजराजः, राजाधिराजः, सार्वभौमः, चक्रवर्ती; 'k. of beasts' मृगेंद्रः, मृगाधिपः, पशुपतिः; 'k.-craft' राजनीति *f.*,-नयः, राज्यचातुर्यं; 'k.'s-evil' गंडमाला. —DOM, *s.* राज्यं, राष्ट्रं, विषयः. 2 आधिपत्यं, ऐश्वर्यं, प्रभुत्वं, स्वामित्वं. 3 जाति *f.*, वर्गः, गणः; 'animal k.' प्राणिवर्गः-जातिः. —LESS, *a.* अराजक, अनायक, राज-नृप-हीन. —LIKE,-LY, *a.* राजकीय. 2 राजानुरूप, राजयोग्य, राजार्ह, राजसदृश (शी *f.*), नृपोचित, राज in comp. —SHIP, *s.* राजत्वं, प्रभुत्वं, ऐश्वर्यं, आधिपत्यं, नृपत्वं, राजपदं, राजाधिकारः.

KINSFOLK, *See* KINDRED (*s.*).

KINSMAN, *s.* बंधुः, बांधवः, ज्ञातिः, सकुल्यः, सजातिः-तीयः, सगोत्रः, सनाभिः, गोत्रजः, बंधुजनः.

KIRK, *s. See* CHURCH.

KISS, *v. t.* चुंब् 1 P, निस् 2 A; 'k. the lip' अधरं पा 1 P, अधररसं पा; 'k. on the head' शिरसि आ-समा-उपा-घ्रा 1 P. —*s.* चुंबनं, चुंबितं, अधरपानं. —ER, *s.* चुंबकः.

KIT, *s.* उपकरणसमुदायः, उपस्करः, उपकरणसामग्री, संभारः. 2 महाकूपी. 3 लघुसारंगी.

KITCHEN, *s.* महानसं, रसवती, सूदशाला, पाक-शाला-स्थान-गृहं; 'k.-garden' शाकशाकिनं, शाकशाकटं, शाकवाटिका; 'k.-maid' पाकचेटी; 'k.-work' पाककार्यं, पाकनिष्पत्ति *f.*; 'superintendent of the k.' पौरोगवः.

KITE, *s.* चिल्लः-ल्ला, आतापि(यि)न् *m.* 2 चिल्लाभासः, चिल्लासदृशं क्रीडनकं.

KITTEN, *s.* मार्जारशावः-वत्सः-शिशुः.

KNAB, *v. t.* दंश् 1 P, दंतैः ग्रह् 9 P or धृ 1 P.

KNACK, *s.* कौशलं, चातुर्यं, वैदग्ध्यं, पाटवं; हस्त-कौशलं-लाघवं; *See* SKILL. 2 क्रीडनकं, क्रीडावस्तु-द्रव्यं.

KNAG, *s.* ग्रंथिः, पर्वन् *n.* 2 Peg, q. v. —GED, -GY, *a.* ग्रंथिल, पर्ववत्.

KNAP, *s.* Knob, q. v. 2 उन्नतभूभागः, उत्सेधः. —*v. i.* Snap, q. v.

KNAVE, *s.* धूर्तः, कितवः, जाल्मः, वंचकः, शठः, प्रतारकः, कूटकारः, दांभिकः. —ISH, *a.* धूर्त, कितव, शठ, जाल्म, वंचक, प्रतारक, धूर्तशील, कपटिन्. —ISHLY, *adv.* सकपटं, सव्याजं, शठवत्, धूर्ततया. —ISHNESS,-RY, *s.* धूर्तता, शाठ्यं, कैतवं, माया, व्याजः, छलं, कपटं.

KNEAD, *v. t.* (कराभ्यां) मृद् 9 P or c., संपीड् 10, चूर्ण् 10, पिष् 7 P. —ING, *s.* मर्दनं, पीडनं; 'k.-trough' द्रोणि-णी *f.*

KNEE, *s.* जानु *n.*, ऊरुपर्वन् *n.*, अष्ठीवत् *m. n.*, ऊरुसंधिः; 'go or fall on the k. s' जानुभ्यां (अवनौ) गम् or पत् 1 P; 'k.-deep' जानुदघ्न (घ्नी *f.*),-द्वयस (सी *f.*),-मात्र (त्री *f.*); 'k.-pan' जानुफलकं.

KNEEL, *v. i.* जानुभ्यां (अवनौ) गम् or पत् 1 P or नम् 1 P, (क्षितितले) जानुनी नि-धा 3 U or न्यस् 4 U or निविश् c. or नम् c.

KNELL, *s.* प्रेतघंटा.

KNICK-KNACK, *s.* क्रीडनकं, क्रीडाद्रव्यं-वस्तु.

KNIFE, *s.* कर्तरिका, छुरिका, छुरी, कृपाणी, कृपाणिका, असिपुत्री-पुत्रिका, शस्त्री, असिधेनुः-नुका.

KNIGHT, *s.* सादिन् *m.*, योधः, भटः.

KNIT, *v. t.* सं-,ग्रंथ् 9 P, सिव् 4 P, निषिव्. 2 संबंध् 9 P, सयुज् 7 U, 10, संश्लिष् c., व्यतिषंज् 1 P, संहन् 2 P; व्यतिषजति पदार्थान् (Mal. 1) 'k. s objects together'; 'k. the eyebrows' भ्रुकुटिं बंध्, भ्रुवौ संकुच् 1 P or भिद् 7 P; *See* FROWN. –*a.* ग्रथित, स्यूत, संश्लिष्ट, व्यतिषक्त; 'well-k.' संहत सुसंहत, दृढसंधि. –TING, *s.* सूत्रश्लेषः-ग्रथनं; 'k.-needle' दीर्घसूचि-ची *f.*

KNOB, *s.* पिंडः, गंडः; ग्रंथिः, पर्वन् *n.*, संधिः (in wood). –BED, –BY, *a.* सपिंड, पिंडिन्, ग्रंथिल, सगंड.

KNOCK, *v. t.* समा-आ-हन् 2 U, तड् 10, प्रह् 1 P; 'k. on the head' मस्तकं तड्, मस्तकाघातेन व्यापद् c.; (fig.) मोघीकृ 8 U, विफलीकृ, भंज् 7 P. –*v. i.* द्वारं तड् or प्रह्..–*s.* आघातः, अभिघातः, प्रहारः, ताडनं, पातः, हति *f.*; 'k. with a stick' वेत्राघातः; 'k. with the fist' मुष्टिघातः-प्रहारः. –against, अभि-प्रति-आ-हन्, संघट्ट् 1A, अभिसं-पत् 1 P; 'k. ed her head against a rock' दृषदं शीर्षेण आजघ्ने. –down, नि-अव-पत् c., आघातेन-प्रहारेण-निपत् c. or भ्रंश् c. –off, सत्वरं-लघु-संपद् c. or साध् 5 P. 2 विरम् 1 P, निवृत् 1 A. –out, प्रहारेण निर्गम् c. (गमयति) or निः-सृ c. or बहिष्कृ 8 U; 'k. out the brains' मस्तिष्कं निष्पिष् 7 P. –up, खिद् c., आयस् c., अवसद् c., श्रम् c. or क्लम् c. (श्र-क्ल-मयति); (*v. i.*) श्रम् 4 P, क्लम् 1, 4 P; खिद् pass., अवसद् 1 P, ग्लै-म्लै 1 P; 'k. ed up by the journey' अध्वसंजातखेदः, नितांतं परिश्रांतः. –ER, *s.* प्रहर्तृ *m.*, ताडयिता. 2 द्वारमुद्गरः, द्वारताडनी.

KNOLL, *v. i.* घंटां वद् c. or तड् 10. –*s.* क्षुद्रपर्वतः, उन्नतभूभागः, वप्रः-प्रं.

KNOT, *s.* ग्रंथिः, बंधनं, ग्रंथिका, बंधः, गंडः; (of garments) नीवि-वी *f.*; (in wood) पर्वन् *n.*, संधिः. 2 संधिः, संयोगः, संश्लेषः, संबंधः. 3 मंडलं, समूहः, गणः, वर्गः, संघः, चक्रं, निवहः. 4 (Of trees) षंडः, गुच्छः, स्तबकः, गुल्मः-ल्मं, स्तंबः, कांडः. –*v. t.* ग्रंथिं बंध् 9 P, ग्रंथ् 9 P, संश्लिष् c.; 'k. ed hair' वेणी; 'k. ed wound' रूढग्रंथिः व्रणः (U. 2). –TED, –TY, *a.* ग्रंथिल, ग्रंथिमत्, पर्वसंधि-मय (यी *f.*), पर्ववत्. 2 विषम, गूढ, दुर्ज्ञेय, दुर्बोध, गहन, गूढार्थ; 'k. point' ग्रंथिः, विषमपदं.

KNOW, *v. t.* ज्ञा 9 U, विद् 2 P, बुध् 1 P, अवगम् 1 P, अव-इ 2 P, अभि-ज्ञा, परिचित-*a.* भू 1 P. 2 अनु-भू, वि-भू c., उपलभ् 1 A, ग्रह् 9 P; 'how should a dependent k. of sincere happiness (pleasure)' परायत्तः प्रीतेः कथमिव रसं वेत्तु पुरुषः (Mu. 3). –ER, *s.* ज्ञातृ *m.*, ज्ञानिन् *m.*, वेत्ता; ज्ञः-अभिज्ञः in comp. –ING, *a.* विज्ञ, ज्ञानिन्; gen. ex. by विद्, ज्ञ or अभिज्ञ in comp.; 'k. Dharma' धर्मविद्, धर्मज्ञः. –INGLY, *adv.* ज्ञानपूर्वं, कामतः, बोध-मति-बुद्धि-पूर्वं, जानत्-*a.* with अस्. –LEDGE, *s.* (Act) ज्ञानं, परि-वि-ज्ञानं, बोधः-धनं, वेदनं, अवगमः, उपलंभः, उपलब्धि *f.* 2 (Learning) ज्ञानं, विद्या, विद्वत्ता, पांडित्यं, व्युत्पन्नता, वैदुष्यं. 3 अभिज्ञानं, परिचयः; 'spiritual k.' आत्मज्ञानं-विद्या, परमार्थज्ञानं, अध्यात्मविद्या, परमार्थः, ब्रह्मविद्या, परमार्थबोधः; 'acquiring k.' विद्यार्जनं, विद्यागमः, ज्ञानप्राप्ति *f.*; 'eager after k.' ज्ञानेच्छु, जिज्ञासु; 'thirst after k.' जिज्ञासा, ज्ञानलिप्सा, ज्ञानेच्छा; 'according to one's k.' यथाज्ञानं; 'for the right k. of words and their meaning' वागर्थप्रतिपत्तये (R. I. 1); 'without the k. of' अविज्ञाप्य, अनिवेद्य, अगोचरं-रेण, परोक्षं-क्षे; 'with the k. of' गोचरं-रेण, प्रत्यक्षं, साक्षात्, समक्षं; 'to come to the k. of' श्रुति-कर्ण-पथं या-इ 2 P or गम् 1 P; 'k. is power' बुद्धिर्यस्य बलं तस्य (P. I. 8). –KNOWN, *a.* ज्ञात, विदित, अवगत, बोधित, उपलब्ध, अनुभूत, विभावित. 2 ख्यात, विश्रुत, प्रसिद्ध, वि-प्र-ख्यात, विज्ञात; 'to make k.' वि-ज्ञा c. (ज्ञापयति), नि-आ-विद् c., बुध् c.; 'to become k.' ज्ञा- प्रति-इ pass.; 'be it k. to your honors' एवमत्रभवंतो विदांकुर्वंतु; 'be it k.' ज्ञातं-विदितं-अस्तु; 'became k. by that name' तदाख्यया (भुवि) पप्रथे (R. XV. 101), तदाख्यां जगाम.

KNUCKLE, *s.* अंगुलिपर्वन् *n.*-संधिः-ग्रंथिः; पर्व, संधिः, ग्रंथिः. –*v. i.* वशीभू 1 P, वशं गम् 1 P or इ-या 2 P. –ED, *a.* संधि-पर्व-विशिष्ट, ग्रंथिल.

KNURL, *s.* ग्रंथिः, गंडः. –ED, *a.* ग्रंथिल.

L.

LABEL, *s.* पत्रं, अंकपत्रं, बीजकं, लेपपत्रं. –*v. t.* लेपपत्रं आसंज् c. or अनुबंध् 9 P.

LABIAL, *a.* ओष्ठ्य.

LABIO-DENTAL, *a.* दंतो(तौ)ष्ठ्य.

LABOR (LABOUR), *s.* श्रमः, परिश्रमः, प्र-आ-यासः, क्लेशः, कष्टं, दुःखं. 2 उद्यमः, उद्योगः, व्यापारः, व्यवसायः, चेष्टा, प्र-,यत्नः, उत्साहः. 3 प्रसूतिकालः-समयः, प्रसवकालः, प्रसवावस्था; 'pain of l.' प्रसूति-प्रसव-वेदना-यातना-व्यथा; 'bodily l.' व्रातं, देह-काय-क्लेश-आयासः-श्रमः; 'unpaid l.' विष्टि *f.*, आज्ञूः; 'got by one's l.' स्वकष्टार्जित. –*v. i.* परिश्रमं-आयासं-कृ 8 U, श्रम् 4 P, प्र-,यत् 1 A, व्यव-सो 4 U, चेष्ट् 1 A, उद्-

श्रम् 1 P, प्रवृत् 1 A, आयस् 1, 4 P, यत्नं कृ, शरीरायासं कृ. 2 खिद्-क्लिश्-पीड् pass., व्यथ् 1 A. 3 प्रसवावस्थायां वृत्, (आसन्नप्रसवा or प्राप्तप्रसववेदना सा स्त्री); 'l. under' बाध्-अभिभू- आक्रम्-पीड्-उपहन्-pass., 'l. ing under hundreds of anxieties' चिंताशतैर्बाध्यमान-अभिभूत; अतिभाराक्रांत &c.; 'l.-ing under a disease' रोगपीडित, रुग्णार्त. —*v. t.* महाश्रमेण-प्रयत्नेन-साध् 5 P or सं-पद् c. or क्लृप् c. or वि-धा 3 U or कृ or अनु-ष्ठा 1 P. 2 कृष् 6 U. —ED, *a.* श्रम-यत्न-कष्ट-सिद्ध, यत्न-श्रम-पूर्व, प्रयत्नकृत. —ER, *s.* कृतश्रमः, कर्मिन् *m.*, व्यवसायिन् *m.*, कार्मः. 2 कर्मकरः, कर्मकारः, भृतकः, वैतनिकः, भृतिभरण्य-भुज् *m.* 3 कृषकः, कृषीवलः; *See* FARMER. —LABORIOUS, *a.* श्रम-आयास-कष्ट-साध्य, कष्ट-आयास-प्रद, पीडाकर (री *f.*), दुःखसाध्य, कष्ट. 2 आयासिन्, कृतश्रम, श्रम-उद्योग-कर्म-शील, उद्यमिन्, उद्योगिन्, सोद्यम, सोद्योग, सोत्साह; *See* INDUSTRIOUS. —LY, *adv.* श्रमेण, श्रम-आयास-पूर्वं, आ-प्र-यासेन, सयत्नं, सोद्योगं, सोद्यमं, सोत्साहं; कष्टेन, कृच्छ्रेण. —NESS, *s.* श्रमसाध्यता. 2 उद्योगः, उद्यमः, व्यवसायः, उद्योगशीलता. —LABORATORY, *s.* रसक्रियास्थानं, रससंस्कारशाला. 2 उद्योग-शिल्प-शाला-गृहं.

LABYRINTH, *s.* अतिगहनः प्रदेशः, दुस्तरं or सुगहनं स्थानं, अशक्यनिर्गमः प्रदेशः, गहनं. —IAN, *a.* गहन, सुदुस्तर.

LAC, *s.* ला(रा)क्षा, अलक्तः-क्तकः, जतु *n.*, यावः, द्रुमामयः. 2 लक्षं.

LACE, *s.* सूत्रं, तंतुः, गुणः. 2 सूत्रजालं, जालाभरणं, जालरूपं, वस्त्राभरणं. —*v. t.* सूत्रेण बंध् 9 P, or संयुज् 7 U, 10 or संश्लिष् c. 2 जालाभरणैः भूष् 10 or अलंकृ 8 U.

LACERATE, *v. t.* दॄ 9 P, 10, निर्भिद् 7 P, व्यवच्छिद् 7 P, वि-पट् 10, कृत् 6 P; *See* TEAR. —ION, *s.* विदारः-रणं, निर्भेदः, विपाटनं. 2 भेदः, छिद्रं, संधिः.

LACHRYMAL, *a.* अश्रुप्रवाहिन्, अश्रूत्पादिन्. 2 अश्रुसंबंधिन्. —LACHRYMATORY, *s.* अश्रुपात्र-भाजनं. —LACHRYMOSE, *a.* सास्र, बाष्पाकुल.

LACK, *v.* न धा 3 U or धृ 1 P or भृ 3 U; gen. ex. by हीन, रहित, वर्जित, शून्य in comp., or अ or निर् pr.; 'l. s wisdom' निर्बुद्धिः, अज्ञानः, बुद्धिहीनः, &c. —*s.* अभावः, हीनता, न्यूनता, विरहः, शून्यता. 2 प्रयोजनं; 'l.-lustre' निष्प्रभ, अतेजस्, मंदच्छाय, मलिनकांति; 'l.-brain' निर्बुद्धिः, मतिहीनः, मूढः, मूर्खः.

LACK-A-DAY, *interj.* अहो, हत, हा, अहह, बत.

LACK-A-DAISICAL, *a.* ध्यानपर-मग्न, चिंताकुल, उत्कंठित, विषण्ण.

LACKER, LACQUER, *See* LINE.

LACKEY, *s.* चेटः, दासः, भृत्यः, पाणिग्राहः, पार्श्वानुचरः.

LACONIC,-AL, *a.* संक्षिप्त, लघु, अल्प-मित-शब्दक, अविस्तीर्ण, सांक्षेपिक (की *f.*); 'l. message' लघुसंदेशपदा सरस्वती. 2 अल्प-मित-भाषिन्. —ALLY, *adv.* संक्षेपेण, संक्षेपतः, अविस्तरेण, मितोक्त्या. —ISM,-LACONISM, *s.* लाघवं, लघूक्ति *f.*, संक्षेपोक्तिः, मितवाक्यं-भाषणं.

LACTARY, *s.* क्षीरस्थानं, गोदुग्धस्थानं.

LACTATION, *s.* क्षीर-दुग्ध-दानं.

LACTEAL, LACTEAN, LACTIOUS, *a.* क्षीरिन्, क्षीर-दुग्ध-मय (यी *f.*), पायस (सी *f.*). 2 अन्नरसवाहिन्.

LACTIFEROUS, *a.* दुग्ध-क्षीर-वाहिन्.

LACTOMETER, *s.* दुग्धमापनयंत्रं, दुग्धमापनी.

LAD, *s.* बालः-लकः, बटुः, दारकः, कुमारः-रकः, शिशुः, किशोरः, माणवकः.

LADDER, *s.* नि(निः)श्रेणि-णी *f.*, निश्रयि(य)णी, अधिरोहिणी, सोपानपथः, सोपानपरंपरा-पद्धति *f.*

LADE, *v. t.* *See* LOAD.

LADING, *s.* नौभारः, पोतस्थद्रव्यं.

LADLE, *s.* दर्वि-र्वी *f.*, कंबि-बी *f.*, खजाका; 'wooden l.' तर्दूः, दारुहस्तकः; 'sacrificial l.' स्रुवः-वा, स्रुच् *f.*, चमसः-सी. —FUL, *s.* कंबि-दर्वी-पूरकं-मात्रं.

LADRONE, *s.* दस्युः, जाल्मः, कितवः.

LADY, *s.* (As a title) देवी; 'your or her ladyship' अत्रभवती, तत्रभवती, भवती. 2 गृहिणी, स्वामिनी, भार्या. 3 आर्या, वनिता, कुलांगना, कुलस्त्री, कुलवधूः, भाविनी, कुलजा; 'l.-bird,-fly, -cow' इंद्रगोपः, शक्रगोपः, इंद्र-शक्र-कीटः; 'l.-love' प्रिया, कांता, प्रणयिनी, कामिनी, दयिता; 'l.'s maid' प्रसाधिका, वस्त्रपरिकल्पिका. —LIKE, *a.* शिष्ट, सभ्य, सुविनीत, आर्यवृत्ति. 2 पेलव, कोमल, मृदु, सुकुमार.

LAG, *v. i.* मंदायते (D.) चिर(रा)यति (D.), विलंब् 1 A, मंदं मंदं चल्-र् 1 P. —*s.* अंत्यजाः, हीनजनाः (pl.); हीनवर्णः. —*a.*,-LAGGARD, *a.* मंद, मंदकर्मन्, विलंबिन्, चिरक्रिय, मंदायमान.

LAGOON *s.* अनूपः, कच्छः, कच्छभूः, जलसनाथः प्रदेशः

LAIC,-AL, *a.* *See* under LAY.

LAIR, *s.* (श्वापदानां) आ-नि-लयः, शयनस्थानं, वासस्थानं, गुहा, बिलं.

LAITY, *s.* *See* under LAY.

LAKE, *s.* सरस् *n.*, कासारः, ह्रदः, सरसी, तडागः-गं, तटाकः-कं; पद्माकरः, सरोवरः, जलाधारः, जलाशयः.

LAMB, *s.* मेषशावः-वकः, अजाशिशुः, मेषवत्सः-पोतः, अविपोतः. —KIN, *s.* क्षुद्रमेषशिशुः, अविपोतकः.

LAMBATIVE, *a.* लेह्य. —*s.* लेहः, अवलेहः-हं.

LAMBENT, *a.* इतस्ततः वेपमान, लोल, कंपमान, तरल, चंचल.

LAME, *a.* खंज, पंगु (गू *f.*), खोड-ल-र, विकलगति, व्यंग; 'l. of a leg' पादेन खंज. 2 (Fig.) दुर्बल,

विकल, सच्छिद्र, न्यून. -LY, *adv.* खंजवत्. 2 विकलं. -NESS, *s.* खंजता, पंगुता, गतिवैकल्यं. 2 वैकल्यं, दुर्बलता, न्यूनता, सच्छिद्रता.

LAMEL, LAMELLA, *s.* कवचः, आवेष्टनं, पटलं.

LAMENT, *v.* विलप् 1 P, रुद् 2 P, आ-,क्रंद् 1 P, अनु-,शुच् 1 P, परि-देव् 1 A, परिदिव् 10 A, क्रुश् 1 P, वि-आ-अभि-° ; 'they l. ed his departure' तद्गमनमन्वशोचन्, तद्गमनमुद्दिश्य अक्रोशन्, &c. -ABLE, *a.* शोच्य, शोचनीय, शोकविषय, शोकास्पदं, शोकार्ह. -ATION, *s.* विलापः, रोदनं, परिदेवना-नं, परिदेवितं, शोकः, शुच् *f.*, विलपनं, रुदितं, आ-वि-क्रोशः, आ-,क्रंदनं, क्रंदितं. -ED, *a.* शोचित; 'the l. Krishna' शोकास्पदीभूतः or स्वर्ग-परलोक-वासी कृष्णः. -ER, *s.* शोचकः, परिदेवकः.

LAMINA, *s.* कवचः-चं, शल्कं, पत्रं, फलकः-कं. -LAMINATED, *a.* सपत्र, फलकिन्.

LAMP, *s.* प्र-,दीपः, दीपकः, दीपिका, दशाकर्षः, दोषास्यः;-'l.-black' कज्जलं, दीपकिट्टं; 'l.-light' दीपप्रभा-प्रकाशः; 'l.-stand' दीपवृक्षः-पादपः-आधारः.

LAMPOON, *s.* निंदालेखः, अवगीतं, निंदार्थो लेखः. -*v. t.* लेखैः निंद् 1 P or आक्षिप् 6 P or अव-गै 1 P. -ER, *s.* निंदकः, अवगायकः, आक्षेपकः.

LANATE,-ED, *a.* लोमश, लोमविशिष्ट.

LANCE, *s.* प्रासः, कुंतः, शूलः-लं, शल्यं, शक्ति *f.*, तोमरः. -*v. t.* प्रासेन व्यध् 4 P or निर्भिद् 7 P. -ER, *s.* प्रासिकः, कौंतिकः, शाक्तीकः, शक्तिधरः-ग्रहः, शूलधरः. -ING, *s.* (gums) लेखनं.

LANCET, *s.* शलाका.

LANCH, *v. t.* *See* CAST.

LANCINATE, *See* LACERATE, TEAR.

LAND, *s.* (Opposed to sea) स्थलं; 'proceeded by l.' प्रतस्थे स्थलवर्त्मना (R. IV. 60); 'the way by l.' स्थलमार्गः-वर्त्म. 2 भूः, भूमि *f.*, प्र-,देशः, विषयः, राष्ट्रं. 3 मृद् *f.*, मृत्तिका. 4 क्षेत्रं, क्षेत्रभूमिः; 'arable l.' कृष्ट-सत्य-भूमिः; 'barren l.' मरुः, मरुस्थलं-ली, धन्वन् *m.*; 'marshy l.' कच्छभूः, अनूपभूमिः; 'waste or fallow l.' खिला-अप्रहता-भूमिः; 'gift of l.' भूमिदानं; 'l.-animal' स्थलचरजंतुः, भूमिचरजंतुः; 'l.-fight' स्थलयुद्धं; 'l.-force' स्थलसैन्यं, स्थलयोधाः; 'l.-holder' भू-क्षेत्र-स्वामिन् *m.*, क्षेत्रपतिः; 'l.-lord,-lady' भू-क्षेत्र-स्वामी-मिनी, गृहपतिः, गृहेश्वरः-री; 'l.-locked' भूवेष्टित, भूमिपरिगत; 'l.-lotus' स्थलारविंदं, स्थलकमलिनी; 'l.-mark' सीमाचिह्नं, स्थल-भूमि-सीमा, सीमालिंगं; 'l.-owner' भूस्वामी, क्षेत्रपतिः-स्वामी; 'l.-seape' नयनगोचरीभूतः भूप्रदेशः or भूभागः, दृष्टिगत-दृष्टिगोचर-प्रदेशः; भूभागः, प्र-,देशः; 'l.-tax' भू-क्षेत्र-करः; 'l.-waiter' शौल्किकः. -*v. t.* (पोतात्-नावः) अवतॄ c., अव-रुह् c. (रोपयति); उत्तॄ c., स्थले निविश् c. -*v. i.* अवतॄ 1 P, अवरुह् 1 P, उत्तॄ ; निविश् 6 P. -ED, *a.* अवतीर्ण, नौकावरूढ, नौकोत्तीर्ण. 2 भूमिसंपन्न, क्षेत्रवत्, भूमिधन; भू in comp.; 'l. property' भूमिद्रव्यं, भूमिः, क्षेत्रं, स्थावरद्रव्यं; 'l. proprictors' भूस्वामिनः. -ING, *s.* उत्तरणं; 'l.-place' तरस्थानं, तरः, तरणस्थानं, घट्टः-ट्टी.

LANE, *s.* संकट-संबाध-पथः-मार्गः, कुपथः.

LANGUAGE, *s.* भाषा, वाणी, वाच् *f.* 2 वचनं, वचस् *n.*, वाक्यं, उक्ति *f.*, वाणी, व्याहारः, वाक्, निगदः, भाषणं, भाषितं, आलापः, भारती. 3 भाषासरणि-पद्धति *f.*, वाग्व्यापारः; वचोविन्यासः; 'abusive l.' वाक्पारुष्यं, खलोक्तिः, आक्षेपवचः; आक्षरणं; 'dignity of l.' वचसां प्रौढता.

LANGUID, *a.* परि-,म्लान, क्लांत, ग्लान, लुलित, अवसन्न, शिथिल, विषण्ण, खिन्न, श्रांत, स्रस्त, विश्लथ, मुक्त; अलस, मंद, शिथिल-क्षीण-बल, श्लथांग-स्रस्तांग (गी *f.*); *See* DROOP. -LY, *adv.* म्लान-ग्लान-वत्, सविषादं, अलसवत्, मंदं, क्लांतमनसा, मुक्तगात्रैः. -NESS, -LANGUOR, *s.* ग्लानि *f.*, म्लानि *f.*, अवसादः, शिथिलता, क्लांति *f.*, ग्ला(म्ला)नता, मुक्तावयवता; मांद्यं, बलशैथिल्यं, गात्रलंसः, अंगश्लथः, तंद्रा-द्रि *f.*, आलस्यं, जडता, जाड्यं, कार्यविमुखता.

LANGUISH, *v. i.* अवसद् 1 P, परि-,क्लम् 1, 4 P, परि-,म्लै-ग्लै 1 P, स्रंस् 1 A, गल् 1 P, शिथिलीभू 1 P, क्षि-विशॄ-खिद्-pass.; ध्वंस् 1 A. 2 (With love) उत्तम् 4 P, उत्कंठ् 1 A, उत्सुक-*a.* भू. -ING, *a.* म्लायत्, क्षीयमाण, स्रंसिन्, मुक्त. 2 उत्सुक, उत्कंठित, कामालस; 'with her l. looks' अलसेक्षणा, कामालसदृष्टिः, कामार्द्रदृष्टिः. -INGLY, *adv.* अवसादेन, अलसवत्. 2 सोत्कंठं, सोत्सुकं; कामालसदृष्ट्या. -MENT, *s.* अवसादः, ग्लानता; *See* LANGUOR. 2 औत्सुक्यं, उत्कंठा, उत्सुकता.

LANIARY, *s.* घात-वध-स्थानं. 2 चर्वणदंतः, अग्रदंतः.

LANIER, *s.* चर्मबंधः, वरत्रा.

LANIFEROUS, *a.* रोमोत्पादिन्, लोमोद्भवकारिन्.

LANK, *a.* कृश, क्षाम, क्षीण, क्षीणमांस-शरीर; *See* LEAN. 2 दीर्घतनु, दीर्घदेह. 3 श्लथ, शिथिल. -NESS, *s.* कृशता, कार्श्यं, क्षामता, &c. -Y, *a.* कृशदीर्घ, दीर्घक्षाम.

LANTERN, *s.* प्रच्छन्नदीपः, सावेष्टनो दीपः, आवृतदीपिका; दीपः, दीपिका; 'l.-jawed' क्षीणवदन.

LANUGINOUS, *a.* लोमश, लोममय (यी *f.*).

LAP, *s.* उत्संगः, अंकः, क्रोडं. 2 अंचलः-लं; वस्त्रांतः, दशाः-वस्तयः (pl.); 'to place on the l.' क्रोडीकृ 8 U. -*v. t.* पुटीकृ, व्यावृत् c. 2 आ-परि-वेष्ट् 1 A or c.; अवगुंठ् 10, आ-परि-वृ 5 U, कोशे नि-धा 3 U. 3 लिह् 2 U, आ-अव-सं°; आ-स्वाद् 1 A; 'l.-

dog' अंके पालनीयः कुक्कुरः; 'l.-ful' अंकपूर्णं-कं.
LAPIDARIOUS, *a.* शिला-प्रस्तर-मय (यीं *f.*).
LAPIDARY, *s.* मणिकारः, रत्नाजीवः. 2 रत्न-मणि-चिछद् *m.*
LAPIS-LAZULI, *s.* वैदूर्यं, असितोपलः, नीलोपलः.
LAPPET, *s. See* LAP (2).
LAPSE, *s.* क्रमः, गति *f.*, प्रवाहः, प्रवृत्ति *f.*, अत्ययः, अतिक्रमः; 'after a l. of time' अथ दिनेषु गच्छत्सु, कालक्रमेण, गच्छता कालेन. 2 स्खलितं, प्रमादः, भ्रमः. 3 स्खलनं, पातः, भ्रंशः, च्युति *f.*, पतनं. —*v. i.* क्रमशः या 2 P or गम् 1 P or सृप् 1 P; शनैः शनैः अति-इ 2 P or अतिक्रम् 1 U, 4 P. 2 भ्रंश् 1 A, 4 P, च्यु 1 A, पत् 1 P, विचल् 1 P, व्युत्क्रम्. 3 स्खल् 1 P, प्रमद् 4 P, भ्रम् 1, 4 P. 4 संक्रम्, अपवृत् 1 A. —ED, *a.* पतित, भ्रष्ट, &c. 2 परहस्तगत, संक्रांत, अपवृत्त; 'a l. suit' नियतवेलातीतं कार्यं.
LAPWING, *s.* टिट्टिभः-भकः, कांयष्टिकः.
LAR, *s.* कुल-गृह-देवता.
LARBOARD, *s.* नौवामभागः.
LARCENY, *s.* चौर्यं, स्तेयं; *See* THEFT.
LARD, *s.* शूकरवसा-मेदस् *n.* 2 शूकरमांसं, वल्लूरं. —*v. t.* शूकरमेदसा पू 3 U or c. 2 वि-सं-मिश्र् 10. 3 आ-प्यै c.; पुष् 1, 9 P or c.
LARDER, *s.* भक्ष्यमांसागारं, भोजनागारं.
LARGE, *a.* (In size) विशाल, पृथु, बृहत्, स्थूल, विपुल, महत्, गुरु, उरु, पृथुल, आयत, विस्तीर्ण. 2 (Of l. body) महाकाय, स्थूल-विकट-शरीर, पृथुबृहत्-शरीर; पीन, पीवर. 3 (In number) महत्, गुरु, पुष्कल, विपुल, प्रभूत, प्रचुर, बहु, बहुल, भूरि; 'of l. soul' महात्मन्; 'of l. nature' उदारधी, महात्मन्, अकृपणचेतस्. 4 (In age) वृद्ध, वयोधिक; 'larger boy' वर्षीयान् बालः; 'at l.' अपराधीनं, स्वेच्छया, स्वेच्छाचारेण, निर्यंत्रणं, निरवग्रहं, निरवरोधं; सविस्तरं, विस्तरेण, विस्तरशः. —LY, *adv.* बहु, भूरि, अतीव, विपुलं, प्राचुर्येण, सु-अति-pr. —NESS, *s.* स्थूलता, बृहत्त्वं, वैपुल्यं, प्राचुर्यं, महत्त्वं, बाहुल्यं; महाकायता, शरीरबृहत्त्वं, पीनता, पीवरता. 2 आयामः, विस्तारः.
LARGESS, *s.* दानं, वितरणं, पारितोषिकं, उपायनं, उपहारः; *See* GIFT.
LARK, *s.* भा(भ)रद्वाजः, व्याघ्राटः, भारयः.
LARUM, *s.* आसन्नभयसूचना-घोषणा.
LARVA, *s.* कीटः, कीटडिंभः.
LARYNX, *s.* कंठनालः-ली, कृकः.
LASCAR, *s.* नाविकः, पोतवाहः.
LASCIVIOUS, *a.* कामुक, कामिन्, रतार्थिन्, कामासक्त, रतिसुखासक्त, भोगासक्त, लंपट, लोलंपट, कामप्रवण; *See* LUSTFUL. 2 कामहेतुक, काममूलक. —LY, *adv.* कामुकवत्, लंपटवत्, भोगासक्त्या. —NESS, *s.* कामुकत्वं, भोगासक्ति *f.*, रतासक्तिः, व्यवायेच्छा, लांपट्यं.
LASH, *s.* कशा, प्रतिष्कशः-षः, चर्मरज्जु *f.*, चर्मबंधः. 2 कशाघातः-ताडनं-प्रहारः. 3 वाग्असिः, परुषवचनं. —*v. t.* कशया आहन् 2 U or तड् 10 or प्रहृ 1 P. 2 वि-धू 5, 9 U, 6 P, विचल् c., इतस्ततः क्षिप् 6 P or चल् c. 3 वाग्बाणैः भिद् 7 P or तड्, वागसिना प्रहृ; तीक्ष्णं निंद् 1 P; 'l.ed into fury' वाग्बाणैः उत्तेजितक्रोधः; शिलातलप्रतिघातोत्पतनफेनिलानामपां (Ka. 133); 'l.ed into foam by striking' &c.; जर्जरितजलतरंगविततनीहारं (Mal. 9) 'so as to l. the water into snowy foam'. 4 रज्ज्वा बंध् 9 P; 'worthy of being l.ed' कश्य, कशार्ह.
LASS, *s.* तरुणी, कन्या, बाला, कुमारिका, दारिका.
LASSITUDE, *s.* खेदः, क्लमः, ग्लानि *f.*; *See* LANGUIDNESS.
LASSO, *s.* पाशः, पादबंधः-रज्जुः *f.*
LAST, *a.* अंत्य, अंतिम, अवर, अवरतम, चरम, पश्चिम; शेष-अंत- in comp. 2 गत, अतीत, चरम, पूर्व, भूत. 3 जघन्य, अधम, अपकृष्ट. 4 परम, उत्तम, अत्यंत; 'l. night' गतायां रात्रौ; 'the l. year' गत-अतीत-संवत्सरः, परुत् *ind.*; 'l. but one' उपांत्य, उपांतिक; 'l.-born' अवरज; 'at l.' अंते, अंततः; 'l. part' शेषभागः; 'l. part of the night' उत्तररात्रः, चरमयामः; 'l. half' उत्तरार्धः, पश्चार्धः, परार्धः, 'the year before l.' परारि *ind.*; 'to the l.' शेषे यावत्. —*adv.* अंते, शेषे, अंततः, अवरं, चरमं, अवरतः. —*v. i.* अव-स्था 1 A, स्था 1 P; oft. by अवधि: in comp.; 'l. ing for many days' चिरस्थायिन्, एष ते जीवितावधिः प्रवादः (U. 1) 'will l. through life'; 'this will l. as food for four months' एतेन (अस्माकं) मासचतुष्टयस्य भोजनं भविष्यति; 'the bloom of youth l. s for a few days' कतिपयदिवसस्थायिनी यौवनश्रीः (Bh. II. 2). —ING, *a.* स्थायिन्, चिर-दीर्घ-कालस्थायिन्; अनपायिन्, नित्य, स्थिर, ध्रुव, अक्षय, शाश्वत (ती *f.*), अजर, चिरंतन (नी *f.*). —LY, *adv.* अंते, अंततः, चरमतः, शेषे, अवरतः.
LATCH, *s.* अर्गला-लं, विष्कंभः, अर्गलाबंधः, तालकं, द्वारबंधनी; 'the postern door was on the l.' अर्गलानिरुद्धं पक्षद्वारं.
LATCHET, *s.* पादुकाबंधनी.
LATE, *a.* विलंबेन आगत or प्राप्त; कालातीत, वेलातीत, समयातीत, अतिक्रांतकाल, अतिकाल, अतीतकाल-समय. 2 अवसित, परिणत, अवसन्न. 3 नूतन, अचिर, प्रत्यग्र, अभिनव, आधुनिक (की *f.*), नातिपुराण, सद्यस्कालीन. 4 अतीत, गत, व्यतीत, भूत; प्राक्तन-पूर्वतन (नी *f.*), पौर्विक (की *f.* 'at a

l. hour of the day' परिणते दिवसे, अवसन्नप्राय अह-नि; 'at a l. hour of the night' क्षीणभूयिष्ठायां क्ष-पायां; 'at a l. period of life' परिणते वयसि. -*adv.* विलंबेन, विलंबात, वेलातिक्रमेण, अतिकालं-सम-यं, चिरेण, चिरात्, चिरकालेन-लात्; 'to be l.' वेला-तिक्रमं कृ 3 U, चिर(रा)यति (D.); 'why are you l.' किमिति चिरायितं त्वया; 'l. in life' परिणतवयसि, *See* above; 'too l. in the day' अतिपराह्णे; 'too l. in the evening' अतिसायं. 2 अकाले, असमये. -LY, 'of late', *adv.* इदानींतने काले, नातिचिरात्प्राक्, आधुनिकसमये; अचिरं. -NESS, *s.* कालातीतता, कालातिक्रमः; परिणामः, परिणति *f.* -LATER, *a.* उत्तर, अपर, पर, उत्तरकालीन, पाश्चात्य. -*adv.* (on) उत्तरं, उत्तरोत्तरं, पश्चात्, उत्तर-पर-काले.

LATENT, *a.* नि-,लीन, गूढ, छन्न, गुप्त, अदृष्ट, अप्रत्यक्ष, अप्रकाश, अप्रकट, अदृश्य, अंतर्हित, निभृत; 'a l. disease' धातुस्थः-शरीरांतर्गतः-रोगः.

LATERAL, *a.* पार्श्वीय, पार्श्वस्थ, पार्श्विक (की *f.*). -LY, *adv.* पार्श्वभागे, पार्श्वतः, पार्श्वे.

LATH, *s.* सूक्ष्मकाष्ठ-दारु, तनुफलकः-कं.

LATHE. *s.* कुंदः-दं, भ्रमः-मि *f.*, चक्रं.

LATHER, *s.* अंजनफेनः, मार्जनतैलफेनः.

LATIFOLIOUS, *a.* पृथु-विशाल-पर्ण.

LATITUDE, *s.* अक्षः. 2 (Celestial) विक्षेपः. 3 विस्तारः, विस्तृति *f*, प्रथिमन् *m.*, आयति *f.* 4 अनि-यंत्रणं, स्वातंत्र्यं, नियमोपेक्षा, नियमातिक्रमः, शैथिल्यं; 'degree of l.' अक्षांशः; 'l. of a planet' पतनं; 'parallel of l.' अक्षांशवृत्तं. —LATITUDINARI-AN, *a.* शिथिल, अनियंत्रण, निर्यंत्रण. -*s.* मतस्वातं-त्र्यावलंबिन् *m.*, निर्बंधहीनः. -ISM, *s.* मतशैथिल्यं, विचारस्वातंत्र्यं, अनियंत्रणं.

LATTEN, *s.* रीति *f.*, पित्तलं.

LATTER, *a.* उत्तर, अपर, पर, अवर, अन्य, (*pron. a.*); पश्चिम, चरम, अंतिम; उत्तरोक्त, अपरोक्त; 'former and l.' पूर्वापरं; 'in the l. part of the day' पराह्णे. -LY, *adv.* अर्वाक्काले, अधुनातन-काले; *See* LATELY.

LATTICE, *s.* जालमार्गः, गवाक्षः, जालं, गवाक्षजालं, वातायनं; 'l.-work' जालकर्मन् *n.*

LAUD, *v. t.* प्रशंस् 1 P, श्लाघ् 1 A, स्तु 2 U, कृत् 10, गुणं वर्ण् 10. -*s.* प्रशंसा, श्लाघा, स्तुति *f.*, गुण-वर्णना-कीर्तनं. -ABLE, *a.* श्लाघ्य, स्तुत्य प्रशस्य, श्ला-घार्ह, प्रशंसार्ह, स्तवनोचित; *See* PRAISE,-WORTHY. -ATION, *s.* प्रशंसनं, श्लाघनं. -ATORY, *a.* प्रशंसाग-र्भ, प्रशंसक, स्तुतिरूप, प्रशंसा-श्लाघा-स्तुति-मय (यी *f.*), प्रशंसाकर (री *f.*). -ER, *s.* प्रशंसकः, स्तावकः.

LAUGH, *v. i.* हस् 1 P, प्र-वि°; स्मि 1 A (l. gently), 'l. violently' उच्चैः हस्, अट्टहासं कृ 8 U; 'l. at' अव-उप-हस्, उपहासास्पदं मन् 4 A, अव-मन्; 'l. in the sleeves' अंतर्-निभृतं-हस्. -*s.*, -ING,-LAUGHTER, *s.* हासः, हसनं, हास्यं, हसितं, वि-प्र°; स्मितं; 'a horse-l.' अट्टहासः, उच्चैर्हासः, प्र-अति-हासः; 'an inward l.' अंतर्हासः -ABLE, *a.* हासकर (री *f.*), हास्यास्पदं, हास्य. -ER, *s.* हास-कः, हासिन् *m.* -ING, *a.* हास्यमुख (खी *f.*), स्मेरमुख, हास्यवदन; 'l.-stock' उपहासास्पदं, हास्य-पात्रं. -INGLY, *adv.* सहासं, विहस्य, सस्मितं.

LAUNCH, *v. t.* (नावं जले) क्षिप् 6 P, मुच् 6 P or c.; प्रविश् c.; वह् c.; 'l. thy hundred-shafted bolt' मुंच शतशोऽशनिं (Mr. 5). 2 सहसा विसृज् 6 P or प्रक्षिप्, प्रास् 4 U. -*v. i.* जलं प्रविश् 6 P. -*s.* नौमोचनं or जले प्रवेशनं.

LAUNDRESS, LAUNDER, *s.* रजकभार्या, निर्णेजकी. -LAUNDERER, *s.* रजकः, निर्णेजकः. -LAUN-DRY, *s.* रजकगृहं, वस्त्रधावनशाला.

LAUREL, *s.* नारलं (?); 'win l. s.' ख्यातिं गम् 1 P, यशः अधिगम्; 'wear your l. s with mo-desty' लब्धेपि जये मा गर्वाऽभमातो भूः; (भाग्येषु अनु-त्सेकी भव S. 4).

LAVA, *s.* आग्नेयोद्गारः.

LAVE, *v. t.* क्षल् 10, धाव् 10; निज् 3 U; *See* WASH. -ATORY, *s.* धावनस्थानं. -ER, *s.* धावन-प्रक्षालन-पात्रं, द्रोणी. -MENT, *s.* वस्ति *m. f.*

LAVISH, *a.* अतित्यागिन्, अतिव्ययिन्, व्ययशील-पर, अ-परिमितव्यय, बहुप्रद, मुक्तहस्त. 2 अमित, अपरिमित, अ-तिरिक्त, अत्यधिक, अति pr. -*v. t.* अपरिमितं व्यय् 10 (व्यययति), मुक्तहस्तेन दा 3 U or विसृज् 6 P or त्यज् 1 P or वित् 1 P or विश्रण् 10 or अप-चि 5 U or वृष् 1 P or अवा-कृ 6 P; विक्षिप् 6 P. -ER, *s.* अति-व्ययिन् *m.*, मुक्तहस्तः, व्ययपरः. -LY, *adv.* अतिव्य-येन, मुक्तहस्तेन, अपरिमितं, अत्यंतं. -MENT,-NESS, *s.* अति-अपरिमित-व्ययः, महाव्ययः, अतित्यागः, अत्यु-त्सर्गः, मुक्तहस्तत्वं, बहुप्रदत्वं.

LAW, *s.* धर्मः, स्मृति *f.*, व्यवहारः, आचारः; धर्म-स्मृ-ति-व्यवहार-शास्त्रं. 2 विधिः, शासनं, व्यवस्था, नियमः, नि-आ-देशः, नियोगः, सूत्रं, राजाज्ञा, चोदना, व्यवस्था-शासन-पत्रं, मर्यादा, स्थिति *f.*, कार्याकार्यनियमः, विधि-निषेधनियमः. 3 न्यायः, नीति *f.*, धर्मानुसारः, व्यवहार-विधिः; 'a code of l. s' धर्मसंहिता, धर्म-स्मृति-शास्त्रं; 'criminal l.' दंडनीतिः-विधिः; 'matter recog-nizable by l.' व्यवहारविषयः-पदं; 'versed in l.' स्मृतिशास्त्रज्ञ, व्यवहारपंडित; 'common l.' स्मृतिः; 'breaking a l.' व्यवस्थातिक्रमः; 'going to l.' राजसभां-व्यवहारासनं-गत्वा विवादप्रशमनं-निर्णयः; 'to go to l.' विवद् 1 A, व्यव-हृ 1 P; 'against the l.' स्मृतिविरुद्धं; 'l.-breaker' व्यवस्थाभेदिन-लंघिन्, नियमातिक्रामिन्; 'l.-giver' स्मृति-शा-

कारः, व्यवस्थापकः, शासितृ *m.*, विधि-न्याय-प्रवर्तकः; '1.-suit' अर्थः, कार्यं, व्यवहारपदं; 'lay down a l.' व्यव-स्था c. (-स्थापयति). -FUL, *a.* न्याय्य, शास्त्रविहित, शास्त्रोक्त, धर्म्य, यथान्याय, धर्मसंमत, धर्मशास्त्रानुरूप, शास्त्रसंमत, स्मृत्युक्त, व्यवहारविधिप्रोक्त, विध्यनुसारिन्, अनिषिद्ध, धर्माविरोधिन्; '1. wife' धर्मपत्नी; '1. means' धर्मोपायः, न्यायोपायः. -FULLY, *adv.* विध्यनुसारेण, न्यायतः, धर्मेण, धर्मतः, धर्मानुसारेण, स्मृतिशास्त्रानुरूपं, यथान्यायं. -FULNESS, *s.* न्याय्यता, धर्म्यता; धर्मानुसारः, धर्माविरोधः. -LESS, *a.* विध्यपेत, स्मृति-विधि-विरुद्ध, धर्म-न्याय-विरुद्ध, अन्याय्य, अधर्म्य. 2 (Of persons) अनियंत्रण, अनियत, उच्छृंखल, स्वेच्छाचारिन्, स्वैरगति, अवश, कामचार, उद्दामवृत्ति; दुराचार, निर्मर्याद, अशिष्ट, आचार-धर्म-भ्रष्ट. -LESSLY, *adv.* अवशं, उच्छृंखलं, दुराचारवत्, धर्मविरोधेन, शास्त्रविरुद्धं. -LESSNESS, *s.* कामवृत्ति *f.*, मर्यादातिक्रमः, अनाचारः, आचारभ्रष्टता, नियमातिक्रमः; स्वेच्छाचारः. -LAWYER, *s.* विधिज्ञः, न्यायनिपुणः, व्यवहारपंडितः, धर्मशास्त्रज्ञः, धर्मज्ञः, स्मृतिपारगः; अर्थिप्रत्यर्थिपक्षसमर्थकः.

LAWN, *s.* तृणभूमि *f.*, तृणावृता भूः, शाद्वलं स्थानं, सतृण-हरित-स्थलं. 2 क्षौमं, अंशुकं, दुकूलं.

LAX, *a.* शिथिल, श्लथ, स्रस्त, विगलित. 2 मृदु, कोमल, अतीक्ष्णदंड. 3 दुराचार, भ्रष्टचरित्र, धर्म-कर्म-भ्रष्ट; '1. in bowels' मृदु-अबद्ध-कोष्ठ. -*s.* अतिसारः, प्रवाहिका. -ATIVE, *a.* सारक, रेचक. -*s.* सारकं. -ITY,-NESS, *s.* शैथिल्यं, अतीक्ष्णता; अनाचारः, मर्यादातिक्रमः; इंद्रियासंयमः, &c.

LAY, *v. t.* धा 3 U, नि-आ, न्यस् 4 U, निविश् c., स्था c. (स्थापयति); सम्-ऋ c. (अर्पयति), निक्षिप् 6 P, आरुह् c. (रोपयति); दा 3 U, धृ 1 P; क्रमेण स्था c. or नि-धा; प्रक्लृप् c., प्रयुज् 7 A, 10 (a plot, snare, &c.). 2 आ-स्तृ-स्तॄ 5, 9 U. 3 शम् c. (शमयति), प्र-उप-°; सांत्व् 10. स्थिरीकृ 8 U. 4 शी c.; निपत् c.; '1. eggs' अंडमोक्षं कृ; अंडानि सू 2, 4 A; '1. siege' रुध् 7 U, वि-ष्टंभ् 9 P; *See* BESIEGE; '1. blame on' दोषं समारुह् c. or निक्षिप्; '1. waste' उप-द्रु 1 A, उपद्रु 1 P, उद्-ध्वंस् c., निर्जनीकृ; *See* DEVASTATE; 'a sinful action, though done by others, is laid at his doors' पापं कर्म च यत् परैरपि कृतं तत्तस्य संभाव्यते (Mr. 1); '1. aside' अप-निर्-अस्, त्यज् 1 P, हा 3 P, उत्सृज् 6 P, उज्झ् 6 P; '1. it aside for a while' मुहूर्तं तत् आस्तां-तिष्ठतु तावत्; (as dress &c.) उद्-वि-मुच् 6 P, अवतॄ c., अवरुह् c.; '1. hands on' परामृश् 6 P, धृष् c.; 'laid upon him his hand' तं हस्तेन पस्पर्श or परामृशत्; '1. hold of' धृ, ग्रह् 9 P; *See* CATCH; '1. the dust' धूलिं सं-सिच् 6 P or आ-हन् 2 U; '1. open or bare' विवृ 5 U, आविष्कृ; स्फुटीकृ, वि-अंज् 7 P or c., स्पष्टी-प्रकटी-कृ, प्रकाश् c. -before, उपनि-अस्, उपक्षिप्, पुरो-नि-धा, प्रसृ c., नि-आ-विद् c. -by, सं-,रक्ष् 1 P, संचि 5 U. -down, न्यस्, निक्षिप्, नि-धा, न्यासीकृ. 2 शी c., निविश् c. 3 विमुच्, परि-,त्यज्, वि-हा 4 (Oneself) संविश् 6 P, शी 2 A. 5 प्र-णी 1 P, वि-धा (rules &c.); '1. down arms' युद्धाद्विरम् 1 P, शरणं व्रज् 1 P; '1. down life' प्राणान् त्यज्. -in, संग्रह्, संचि, संरक्ष्. -on, पत् c., प्र-युज्, सम्-ऋ c. -out, विनि-युज् 7 A, 10, प्रयुज्, व्यय् 10 (व्यययति). 2 परि-प्र-क्लृप् c., विन्यस् 4 U, विरच् 10, प्रयुज्, चिंत् 10; *See* CONTRIVE. 3 प्रसृ c., विस्तॄ c., दीर्घीकृ; प्रकाश् c., प्रकटीकृ '1. oneself out'; चेष्ट् 1 A, प्रयत् 1 A, उद्यम् 1 A. -to, आरुह् c., निक्षिप्; *See* ASCRIBE; '1. to a ship' नौगतिं रुध् or स्तंभ्. -up, नि-धा, रक्ष्, संचि; 'to be laid up' शय्याग्रस्त-*a.* भू 1 P, उत्थातुं अक्षम-*a.* भू; 'laid up with fever' ज्वरेणोत्थातुमक्षमः. -LAY, *s.* गानं, गीतं, काव्यं. 2 आस्तरः-रणं, फलकः-कं. -*a.* सामान्य, साधारण (णी *f.*), पुरोहितभिन्न. -MAN, *s.* गृहस्थः, सामान्य-साधारण-जनः, अदीक्षितः, प्राकृतः. -LAICAL, *a.* गृहस्थिन्, गार्हस्थिक (की *f.*), पुरोहितभिन्न, अदीक्षित. -LAITY, *s.* गृहस्थ-सामान्य-जनवर्गः, प्राकृत-साधारण-जनाः, पुरोहितभिन्नवर्गः.

LAYER, *s.* स्तरः; आस्तरः-रणं, फलकः-कं. 2 Twig, q. v.

LAZAR, *s.* कुष्ठिन् *m.*, श्वित्रिन् *m.*, कोठोपहतः, त्वग्रोगोपहतः; '1.-house' कुष्ठिशाला, श्वित्र्यालयः.

LAZY, *a.* अलस, तंद्रिल, जड, मंद, मंथर, तंद्रालु, मंदगति, आलस्यशील, अनुद्योगिन्, उद्योगविमुख (खी *f.*), अव्यवसायशील; शीतक, अनुष्ण, तुंदपरिमृज. -LY, *adv.* अलसवत्, जडवत्, मंदं मंदं, जाड्येन. -NESS, *s.* आलस्यं, मांद्यं, जाड्यं, जडता, तंद्रिका, तंद्रालुता, कार्यद्वेषः, अनुद्योगशीलता, उत्साहविमुखता, अलसशीलता.

LEA, *s. See* LAWN (1).

LEAD, *s.* सीसं, सीसकं, नागं, योगेष्टं, वप्रं; 'red 1.' सिंदूरं, नागसंभवं, रक्तचूर्णं, नागजं, नागगर्भं. -*s.* नायकत्वं, नेतृत्वं, अधिष्ठातृत्वं, मुख्यत्वं, अग्रगमनं-यानं, पुरःसरणं. -*v. t.* नी 1 P, वह् 1 P, प्राप् c., गम् c. (गमयति) (all with two accusatives); आ-दा 3 A. 2 (Way) दृश् c., आ-निर्-दिश् 6 P. 3 आधि-ष्ठा 1 P, अध्यास् 2 A, प्रणी, आ-निर्-दिश्; पुरस्कृ 8 U; अग्रणीः-नायकः-अग्रेसरः-भू 1 P (with gen.); वसिष्ठाधिष्ठिता देव्यः (U. 1) 'led by Vasishṭha' &c., दशरथस्य दारानधिष्ठाय (U. 4); 'led by the demon' दानवं पुरस्कृत्य. 4 आकृष् 1 P, प्र-वि-लुभ् c., प्र-वृत् c, प्रेर् c., प्रोत्सह् c., नी; मूढः परप्रत्ययनेयबुद्धिः (M. 1) 'has his mind led by the convictions of others.' 5 (Time) नी, गम् c., अतिवह् c., क्षै c. (क्षपयति), या c. (यापयति); 'led a dissolute life' विषयसुखनिरतो जीवितमत्यवाहयत्; 'l. ing a life above their station' स्वस्थानानुचितां-स्वस्थानातिरिक्तां-जीवयात्रां कल्पयंतः. —*v. i.* (On) अग्रे-पुरः-पुरतः-अग्रतः-भू or गम् 1 P or वृत् 1 A or स्था or चर् or सृ 1 P. 2 (To) (lit.) गम्, या 2 P; 'on the way l. ing to Chitrakûta' चित्रकूटयायिनि वर्त्मनि (U. 1). 3 (Cause) ex. by dat. of noun with or without भू, आवह्, उत्पद् c., जन् c. (जनयति); 'advice to fools l. s to their provocation' उपदेशो हि मूर्खाणां प्रकोपाय (भवति) (H. 3). —ED,-EN, *a.* सीसकनिर्मित, सीसकयुक्त. —ER, *s.* नायकः, नेतृ *m.*, मार्गदर्शकः, मार्गोपदेशकः (lit.); मुख्यः, मुखरः, अग्रणीः, प्रमुखः, अधिपः, ईश्वरः पतिः, अध्यक्षः, अधिपतिः, अधिष्ठातृ *m.* 2 पुरोगः-गमः, अग्रगः, अग्र(ग्रे)सरः, पुरःसरः, पुरोगामिन् *m.*; 'l. of an army' सेनानीः, चमूपतिः, योधाध्यक्षः, सेनानायकः; 'l. of a religious sect' गुरुः, आचार्यः. —ERSHIP, *s.* नायकत्वं, आधिपत्यं. —ING, *a.* अग्रग, पुरोगामिन्, पुरःसर, पुरोगम, प्राक्-अग्र-गामिन्. 2 अग्र, अग्र्य, मुख्य, उत्कृष्ट, प्रमुख, परम, उत्तम, प्रधान in comp. 3 (To) आवह, कर (री *f.*) in comp.; 'l. to happiness' कल्याणावह, कल्याणकर, कल्याणोदर्क. —*s.* नयः, नीति *f.*, नेतृत्वं; 'l.-strings' आलंबनसूत्राणि; 'hold or keep in l.-string' आत्माधीन-*a.* कृ, स्ववशं नी, नियम् 1 P. —LED, *a.* नीत, प्रेरित, अधिष्ठित, &c.; 'l. by' ex. by पुरःसर, पुरोगम, प्रमुख, आदि in comp.

LEAD-WORT, *s.* पाठिन् *m.*, चित्रकः, वह्निसंज्ञकः.

LEAF, *s.* पत्रं, पर्णं, छदः, दलः-लं, पलाशं, छदनं; (of a book) पत्रं; (of a door) कपा(वा)टः-टं-टी, अररं-री; 'fallen l.' प्रपर्णं; 'faded l.' शीर्णपर्णं; 'to strip off the leaves' निष्पत्रीकृ 8 U. —LESS, *a.* निष्पत्र, अपर्ण, निष्पर्ण, निर्दल, पत्र-पर्ण-दल-हीन. —LET, *s.* पत्रकं, सूक्ष्म-लघु-पत्रं. —Y, पर्णावृत, पर्णमय (यी *f.*), बहुपर्ण, बहुपत्र-दल, सपत्र, सपर्ण, पर्णिन्.

LEAGUE, *s.* संधिः, साहित्यं, संघातः, ऐक्यं, संयोगः, संघट्टनं, अन्योन्योपकारप्रतिज्ञा. 2 गव्यूति *f.* —*v. i.* संधा 3 U, पक्षीय-*a.* भू 1 P, संहन्-संयुज्-pass., संमिल् 6 P, संधिं कृ 8 U, संघट्ट् 1 A; 'l. ed with the enemy' शत्रुपक्षे स्थित. —ED, *a.* कृतसंधि, संधित, संहत, संघातवत्, संयुक्त, कृतसंसर्ग, संसृष्ट, मिलित; 'having l.' संभूय, मिलित्वा. —ER, *s.* संगिन् *m.*, संसर्गी, सह-संभूय-कारी.

LEAK, *s.* छिद्रं, रंध्रं, संधिः. 2 धारा, स्रवः, स्यंदः, द्रवः. —*v. i.* (अलक्षितं) स्रु 1 P; परि-स्रु, री 4 A, क्षर् 1 P, गल् 1 P, स्यंद् 1 A; आयुः परिस्रवति भिन्नघटादिवांभः (Bh. II. 109) 'like water l. ing from a broken jar' &c. —ING, *s.* स्रवः, क्षरणं, निस्यंदः, स्रयः. —Y, *a.* छिद्रपूर्ण, स्रवणशील, सच्छिद्र, सरंध्र.

LEAN, *a.* कृश, परि-,क्षाम-क्षीण, अवसन्न, तनु, क्षीणशरीर-मांस, कृशांग (गी *f.*); 'you are growing l.-er and l. er day by day' अनुदिवसं परिहीयसेऽंगैः (S. 3); 'l.ness of body' शरीरसादः. —*s.* स्नायुः, वसा. —*v. i.* अव-लंब् 1 A, आ-सं-श्रि 1 U; 'l. ing on a mango stick' अवलंब्य चूतयष्टिं; मदलेखया दत्तहस्तावलंबा (Ka. 206) 'l. ing on M.'s arm.' 2 पक्षं आश्रि or अवलंब्, प्रवण-*a.* भू 1 P. 3 आ-अव-नम् 1 P, नम्रीभू, बहिर्लंब्, तिरः-तिर्यक् लंब्. —*v. t.* उप-धा 3 U, निविश् c., न्यस् 4 U; वामहस्तोपहितवदना (S. 4) 'l. ing her face on her left hand'; also ex. by (*v. i.*). —ING, *a.* आलंबिन्, संश्रित, आनत, प्रवण, बहिर्लंब, प्रलंब, वक्र. —*s.* प्रवणता, सं-आ-श्रयः, आलंबनं. —NESS. *s.* कृशता, कार्श्यं, क्षीणता, क्षामता, अव-,सादः, शोषः, शरीरशोषणं.

LEAP, *v. i.* प्लु 1 A, उत्-प्लु, वल्ग् 1 P; नृत् 4 P; 'l. down' अवतॄ 1 P, अवप्लु; 'l. up' उत्पत्, उत्प्लु; 'l. over' लंघ् 1 A, 10, अतिक्रम् 1 U, 4 P, अती 2 P. —*s.* प्लुति *f.*, प्लुतं, प्लवः, वल्गितं. झंपः, प्लवनं; 'quick (deer's) l.' हरिणप्लुतं; 'going by l. s' प्लुतगति, प्लवग. —ING, *s.* प्लवनं, वल्गितं, प्लुतिः; 'l. over a period' मंडूकप्लुतिः.

LEARN, *v. t.* शिक्ष् 1 A, अधि-इ 2 A, पठ् 1 P, अधिगम् 1 P, अभ्यस् 4 U; अभ्यासेन विद्यां लभ् 1 A or प्राप् 5 P. —*v. i.* ज्ञा 1 U, अवगम्, विद् 2 P, बुध् 1 P, उपलभ्, श्रु 5 P, गृहीतार्थ-*a.* भू 1 P; *See* KNOW. —ED, *a.* विद्वस् (दुषी *f.*), विपश्चित्, ज्ञानिन्, विद्याविशिष्ट-संपन्न-वत्, कृत-उपात्त-विद्य, पंडित, बुध, प्रा(प्र)ज्ञ; ज्ञानवत्, व्युत्पन्न, बहुश्रुत, सूरि, विद्यावृद्ध, साक्षर. 2 अधीतिन्, विचक्षण, विज्ञ, कुशल, निपुण, प्रवीण, चतुर; कोविद, ज्ञ, विद् in comp. 3 (Of books &c.) पांडित्यस्य सूचक, ज्ञानस्य गमक; 'a l. man' पंडितः, विपश्चित्, सूरिः, बुधः, &c.; 'l. in law' स्मृतिज्ञ, न्यायविद्. —EDLY, *adv.* पंडितवत्, प्रज्ञवत्, सज्ञानं, निपुणतया, सकौशलं. —ER, *s.* शिष्यः, छात्रः, अध्येतृ *m.*, विद्यार्थिन् *m.* —ING, *s.* विद्या, विद्वत्ता, विद्वत्त्वं, ज्ञानं, पांडित्यं, व्युत्पत्ति *f.*, प्राज्ञता, विद्यासंपद् *f.* 2 (Act) अध्ययनं, शिक्षणं, अभ्यासः, विद्यार्जनं, विद्याप्राप्ति *f.*, ज्ञानागमः. 3 शास्त्रं, विद्या; 'sacred l.' श्रुति *f.*, निगमज्ञानं; 'he affects great l.' पंडितंमन्यः, पंडितायते (D.).

LEASE, *s.* पट्टः, पट्टोलिका. —*v. t.* आविहितकालात् निरूपितमूल्येन दा 3 U or विसृज् 6 P.

LEASH, *s.* चर्मबंधः, चर्मरज्जु *f.* 2 त्रयं, त्रितयं.

LEAST, *a.* अणु, अल्प, स्तोक, अत्यल्प, अल्पिष्ठ, कनिष्ठ, स्तोकतम, अल्पतम, क्षोदिष्ठ; 'the l. sorrow'

अणुरपि शोकः; 'the l. particle' लवः, लेशः, अणुः, कणः. -*adv.* स्तोकं, अल्पिष्ठं, किंचित्, कियत्; 'in the l.' मनागपि, अल्पमपि, स्तोकांशमपि, स्तोकमपि, लेशमपि, किमपि, किंचिदपि; 'at l.' ex. by अवर-*a.* in comp.; 'witnesses should be at l. three' त्र्यवराः साक्षिणो ज्ञेयाः (Y. II. 69); 'at l. 100 Rs.' शतावरा रूपकाः; oft. by तावत्, 'at l. once' सकृदपि तावत्.

LEATHER, *s.* परिष्कृतं चर्म; 'l.-bag' चर्मभस्त्रिका, चर्मप्रसेविका; 'l.-bottle' कुतू *f.*; 'a small l.-bottle' कुतुपः; 'l.-dresser' चर्मकृत्, चर्मकारः; 'l.-seller' चर्मविक्रयिन्. -LEATHERN, *a.* चर्म-कृत-निर्मित, चर्ममय (यी *f.*), चर्म in comp.

LEAVE, *s.* अनुज्ञा-ज्ञानं, अनुमति *f.*, अनुमोदनं. 2 आमंत्रणं, आप्रच्छनं; 'to take or ask l. of' आ-मंत्र् 10 A, आप्रच्छ् 6 A; *See* ADIEU; 'to give l.' अनु-ज्ञा 9 U, अनुमन् 4 A, अनुमुद् 1 A. -*v. t.* त्यज् 1 P, हा 3 P, उत्सृज् 6 P, उज्झ् 6 P, रह् 1 P, 10, परिहृ 1 P, वर्ज् 10, निर्-,मुच् 6 P. 2 निर्गम् 1 P, अपगम्, अप-इ-या 2 P, अपसृ 1 P, अपक्रम् 1 U, 4 P, (all with abl.). 3 मृत्युपत्त्रेण दा 3 U; 'estate left (after death)' रिक्थं. 3 विरम् 1 P, निवृत् 1 A (with abl.); मुच्, त्यज्, अ-पास् 4 P; oft. ex. by स्था 1 P, आस् 2 A; 'l. it now' तिष्ठतु-आस्तां तदधुना. 4 निक्षिप् 6 P, न्यस्, सम्-ऋ c. (अर्पयति); 'l. everything to him' सर्वं तदधीनं कुरु. 5 शिष् 7 P or c., अव-परि°; उद्-वृत् c., 'nothing was left' न किमप्यवशिष्टं; 'to be left' शिष् pass.; 'we being left behind' अस्मास्वव-हीनेषु (S. 2). -*v. i.* निर्गम्, अप-या, विरम्, &c. -for, प्र-स्था 1 A (with acc.). -off, विरम्, नि-वृत्, त्यज्; *See* above; 'the peacock left off dancing' परित्यक्तनर्तनो मयूरः (S. 4); 'when it left off raining' शांते पानीयवर्षे (H. 3). -out, वृज्, परित्यज्. -LEAVINGS, *s.* शेषः-षं, परि-अव°; शिष्टं, अव-परि°, शेषभागः-खंडः, उद्वर्तः, उ-च्छिष्टं. 2 मलं; 'l. of food' शेषान्नं, भक्षित-भुक्त-शेषः-षं, भुक्तावशिष्टं, उच्छिष्टं, भुक्तोज्झितं; 'one who eats l.' शेषभोजिन्, उच्छिष्टाशनः.

LEAVEN, *s.* किण्वं, नग्नहूः, कारोत्तरः, मंडः-डं. -*v. t.* दुष् c. (दूषयति); रंज् c.

LEACHER, *s.* लंपटः, कामासक्तः, कामुकः, स्त्रीपरः-लं-पटः, सुरतार्थिन् *m.* -OUS, *a.* कामुक, कामासक्त, सु-रतार्थिन्, स्त्रीपरः *See* LUSTFUL. -OUSLY, *adv.* लं-पटवत्, कामुकवत्. -OUSNESS,-Y. *s.* Lust, q. v.

LECTION, *s.* पाठः. 2 पाठांतरं, पाठभेदः.

LECTURE, *s.* प्रपाठः, व्याख्यानं, शासनं, अध्यापनं; 'it is easy to read l. s to others' सुखमुप-दिश्यते परस्य (Ka. 156) (*cf.* परोपदेशे पांडित्यं).

2 वाग्दंडः, निर्भर्त्सनवाक्यं. -*v.* पठ् c., अधि-इ c. (अ-ध्यापयति), शास् 2 P, उपदिश् 6 P. 2 निर्भर्त्स् 10 A, निंद् 1 P, गर्ह् 1, 10 A. -ER, *s.* पाठकः, अध्यापकः, शिक्षकः, उपदेशकः, प्रवक्तृ *m.*, वादिन् *m.*, व्याख्याता.

LEDGE, *s.* कटकः-कं, कूटं. 2 शिला, शिलाफलकं. 3 फलकः-कं, आस्तरः. 4 आलि-ली *f.*, आवलि-ली *f.*

LEDGER, *s.* (बृहत्) गणनापुस्तकं.

LEE, *s.* निर्वातस्थानं-देशः. 2 वाताभिमुखी दिक्. -WARD, *adv.* अनुवातं, वातानुलोमं.

LEECH, *s.* रक्तपा, जलौ(लू)का, जलौकसः (*f.* pl.): जलसर्पिणी, रक्तपायिनी, जलजंतुका. 2 भिषज् *m.*, वै-द्यः, चिकित्सकः.

LEEK, *s.* कंदः-दं.

LEER, *s.* कटाक्षः, दृष्टिविक्षेपः, दृक्पातः, अर्धवीक्षणं, साचिविलोकितं, अपांगदर्शनं. 2 कुस्मितं. -*v. t.* कटा-क्षेण ईक्ष् 1 A or दृश् 1 P, साचि-तिर्यक्-विलोक् 1 A, 10. 2 कुस्मि 1 A. -ING, *a.* अपांगदर्शिन्, साचि-तिर्यक्-दृष्टि. 2 कुस्मेर.

LEES, *s.* मलं, किट्टं, उच्छिष्टं.

LEFT, *a.* वाम, सव्य, दक्षिणेतर; 'l.-handed' वा-महस्त, सव्यसाचिन्; 'to the l.' वामेन, वामतः.

LEG, *s.* जंघा, प्रसृता, पादः; 'swelling of the l.' श्लीपदं; 'having a swelled l.' कुंभपादः-पदी; 'long-l. ed' दीर्घपाद-द्, दीर्घजंघ. -LEGGING, *s.* जंघारक्षणं.

LEGACY, *s.* उत्तरदानं, मृत्युलेखार्पितदानं.

LEGAL, *a.* धर्म्य, न्याय्य, स्मार्त (र्ती *f.*), व्यवहारानु-रूप, न्यायानुसारिन्, शास्त्रविहित, शास्त्रोक्त, स्मृत्युक्त, धर्म-न्याय-अनिषिद्ध; *See* LAWFUL. 2 स्मृति, धर्म, व्यवहार, in comp.; 'l. proceeding' व्यवहारः; 'wrong l. opinion' अव्यवस्था; 'written l. opinion' पट्टोलिका. -ITY, *s.* न्याय्यता, धर्म्यता, धर्म-शास्त्र-अनुसारः. 2 कर्ममार्गसेवा, कर्मनिष्ठा. -IZE, *v. t.* व्यव-स्था c. (स्थापयति), शास्त्रसंमत-*a.* कृ 8 U, कृ with (*a.*). -LY, *adv.* धर्मेण, न्यायेन, धर्मतः, न्यायतः, यथाधर्मं, यथान्यायं, धर्मानुसारेण.

LEGATE, *s.* दूतः, प्रणिधिः. -LEGATION, *s.* दूत-, धर्मः-क्रिया, दौत्यं.

LEGATEE, *s.* मृतरिक्थभागिन् *m.*, उत्तराधिकारी. -LEGATOR, *s.* उत्तरदानकारिन् *m.*

LEGEND, *s.* कथा, उपाख्यानं, आख्यायिका, पुरा-वृत्त-पुराण-कथा, पुरावृत्तं, लोक-जन कथा, इतिहासः, पुरा-णं. -ARY, *a.* पौराणिक (की *f.*), पुराणोक्त, पुराण-कथित. -*s.* ऐतिहासिकः, पुराणकथकः.

LEGER-DE-MAIN, *s.* हस्तलाघवं-चापल्यं, माया, कु-हका-कं, इंद्रजालं.

LEGIBLE, *a.* व्यक्ताक्षर, सुवाच्य, निर्वाच्य, सुव्यक्त, सु-

स्पष्ट, स्पष्टाक्षर.—LEGIBLY, *adv.* सुस्पष्टं, व्यक्ताक्षरैः, सुव्यक्तं.

LEGION, *s.* चमूः, सेना, वाहिनी: *See* FORCE. 2 सैन्यदलं-गुल्मः-व्यूहः-समूहः. 3 चक्रं, निवहः; 'their name is a l.' अतिसंख्याः-संख्यातीताः-ते.

LEGISLATE, *v. i.* व्यवस्थां वि-धा 3 U or कृ 8 U; विधीन् रच् 10 or प्रकृप् c. or स्था c. (स्थापयति), व्यव-स्था c. —ION, *s.* विधिप्रकल्पनं, व्यवस्था-नियमविधानं, विधि-नियम-व्यवस्था. —IVE, *a.* व्यवस्थापक, विधिकारिन्. —OR, *s.* व्यवस्थापकः, शासितृ *m.*, शास्ता, न्यायप्रवर्तकः, व्यवस्थाकारः. —URE, *s.* व्यवस्था-विधिविधायिनी सभा.

LEGITIMATE, *a.* न्याय्य, धर्म्य, उचित, यथायोग्य, यथान्याय; *See* LAWFUL, LEGAL. 2 सत्य, यथार्थ. 3 धर्मज, औरस (सी *f.*), औरस्य, उरस्य, धर्मपत्नीज, स्वजात, सुजन्मन् ; 'a l. wife' धर्मपत्नी; 'a l. son' उरस्यः, औरसः-स्यः. —*v. t.* औरसीकृ 8 U. —LY, *adv.* यथान्यायं, धर्मेण, न्यायतः, धर्मानुसारेण, यथाधर्मं; युक्तं, यथोचितं, यथार्थं. —LEGITIMACY, *s.* न्याय्यता, धर्म्यता, यथार्थता, युक्तता, औचित्यं. 2 औरसत्वं, सुजन्मन् *n.*, धर्मजत्वं, औरसजन्म.

LEGUME, LEGUMEN, *s.* शमी, शिंबा, मुद्गः, शिंबिका. 2 शमीधान्यं.

LEISURE, *s.* अवसरः, अवकाशः, विश्रामः, क्षणः, कार्यनिवृत्ति *f.*-विच्छेदः, विश्रांति *f.*; 'being at l.' लब्धावकाश, प्राप्तावकाश, प्राप्तावसर, निर्व्यापार, लब्धक्षण, कार्यरहित. —LY, *a.* मंथर, मंद, अशीघ्र, अक्षिप्र, अत्वरित, सावकाश. —*adv.* 'at leisure', मंदं मंदं, शनैः, अशीघ्रं, अक्षिप्रं, यथावकाशं, प्राप्तावसरं.

LEMON, *s.* जंबी(वि)रः, जंभः, जंभीरः, जंभरः-लः, दंतशठः, फलपूरः, बीजपूरः; रुचकः, मातुलुंगकः; (fruit) जंबीरं, जंभफलं, &c.

LEMONADE, *s.* जंबीररसः.

LEMURES, *s.* *See* DEVIL.

LEND, *v. t.* (आविहितकालात्) दा 3 U, 1 P, समृ c. (अर्पयति), निक्षिप् 6 P, न्यस् 4 U; 'l. money' ऋणं दा; 'l. money at interest' कुसीदं कृ 8 U; 'l. one's hand to' उपकृ, अनुग्रह् 9 P; *See* HELP; 'l. one's ear to' श्रु 5 P, सावधानो भूत्वा आकर्ण् 10. —ER, *s.* उत्तमर्णः, ऋणदायिन् *m.*, ऋणदः. —ING, *s.* ऋणदानं, ऋणसमर्पणं.

LENGTH,-EN, *See* under LONG.

LENIENT, *a.* सौम्य, मृदु, अतीक्ष्ण, कोमल, अतीव्र, अपरुष; क्षमावत्, क्षमिन्, सदय, कृपालु, दयार्द्र. 2 सांत्वकारिन्, साम in comp.; 'a l. measure' सामोपायः, सामोपचारः, सामप्रयोगः. —LY, *adv.* अनुग्रं, अतीक्ष्णं, सौम्यं, सदयं, अपरुषं, क्षमापूर्वं. —LENITY, —LENIENCY, *s.* सौम्यता, मृदुता, अतीक्ष्णता, अतीव्रता, कोमलता; क्षमा, क्षमाशीलता, दया, दयार्द्रभावः, कृपा; सामन् *n.*, सामबुद्धि *f.* —LENITIVE, *a.* शमक, शांतिद, शांतिकर (री *f.*). 2 स्निग्ध, चिक्कण. —*s.* प्र-उपशमनं, क्लेशापहं, शूलघ्नं.

LENS, *s.* काचः; 'convex l.' मध्योन्नतकाचः; 'concave l.' मध्यनिम्नकाचः; 'a double convex l.' यवः; 'a crystal l.' सूर्यकांतः, अर्काश्मन् *m.*, दीप्तोपलः.

LENTICULAR, *a.* मसूरोपम.

LENTIFORM, *a.* यवाकृति, यवरूप.

LENTIGO, *s.* जटु(डु)लः, कालकः, पिप्लुः. —LENTIGINOUS, *a.* जटुलिन्, कालकयुक्त.

LENTIL, *s.* मसु(सू)रः-रा.

LENTOUS, *a.* सांद्र, श्यान, घन. —LENTOR, *s.* सांद्रता, श्यानता.

LEO, *s.* सिंहः, सिंहराशिः. —LEONINE, *a.* सैंह (ही *f.*), सिंहशील-धर्मन्.

LEOPARD, *s.* चित्रकः, चित्रव्याघ्रः.

LEPER, *s.* कुष्ठिन् *m.*, श्वित्रिन् *m.*, कुष्ठरोगी, कुष्ठपीडितः. —LEPROSY, *s.* कुष्ठं, श्वित्रं, कोठः, मंडलकं, कुष्ठरोगः, त्वग्रोगः, दुश्चर्मन् *n.*; 'black l.' महारोगः, महाव्याधिः, रक्तकुष्ठं; 'wasting l.' गलत्कुष्ठं. —LEPROUS, *a.* कुष्ठिन्, श्वित्रिन्, कुष्ठपीडित.

LESION, *s.* अपकारः, पीडा, क्षति *f.*

LESS, *a.* न्यून, ऊन, अल्पतर, अल्पीयस्, क्षुद्रतर, स्तोकतर, सूक्ष्मतर. —*adv.* न्यूनं, अल्पं, &c.; 'no l. than' ex. by अवर-*a.*; अवराः साक्षिणः; 'much l.' किमुत, किं पुनः, किमु; 'a little l. than 10,000 years' किंचिदूनं शरदामयुतं (R. x. 1); (as a suffix) ex. by अ, निर्, विहीन, रहित, वर्जित, वीत, विगत, in comp. —EN, *v. t.* न्यूनीकृ 8 U, ऊन् 10, ह्रस् c., अप-चि 5 U, लघूकृ, लघयति (D.), क्षि 1, 5 P or c. —*v. i.* ह्रस् 1 P, न्यूनीभू 1 P, अल्पीभू, क्षि-अपाचि-pass. —ER, *a.* क्षुद्रतर, &c.

LESSEE, *s.* पट्टलिकाधारिन् *m.*

LESSON, *s.* पाठः, अध्यायः. 2 शासनं, उपदेशः, बोधनं, शिक्षा. 3 वाग्दंडः, भर्त्सनं: take l. from' उपदेशं ग्रह् 9 P. —*v. t.* उपदिश् 6 P, शास् 2 P.

LEST, *conj.* नोचेत्, अन्यथा; 'love not sleep l. thou come to want' तंद्रामस्को मा भव नोचेत् अकिंचनो भविष्यसि; sometimes ex. by न इति or कदाचित् with pot. or मा with simple future or imperative; मा कस्यापि तपस्विनो हस्ते पतिष्यति (S. 2) 'l. she fall into the hands &c.' मास्या विकारो वर्धतां (M. 4); 'l. he should kill us' मा नो हिंसीदिति; 'beware l. you be enticed by women' तथा प्रयतेथा यथा न प्रलोभ्यसे वनिताभिः (Ka. 109).

LET, *v. t.* अनु-ज्ञा 9 U, अनुमन् 4 A, अनुमुद् 1 A, सह् 1 A; oft. ex. by the imperative or aorist forms without अ; 'l. it not so happen' एवं मा भूत्. 2 भाटकेन दा 3 U; मूल्येन दा or विसृज् 6 P. 3 रुध् 7 U, निवार् 10; स्तंभ् 9 P. 4 (Blood) स्रु c., मोक्ष् 10; *See* BLEED; 'l. alone' न व्यपत्र् 1 P, न बाध् 1 A, oft. by आस् 2 A, स्था 1 P; 'now l. it alone' आस्तां तत्तथैव; 'l. go', 'l. loose' मुच् 6 P or c., मोक्ष्, शिथिलीकृ 8 U, शिथिलयति (D.), स्रंस् c., विसृज्, श्र-(श्रं)थ्-श्लथ् 1 P, 10; 'l. ing his hand go' मुक्त-स्रस्त-शिथिलित-हस्तः; 'l. slip' मुच्, विक्षिप् 6 P, मुधा या c. (यापयति). -down, अवतृ c., अवरुह् c. (रोपयति), अव-नि-पत् c., अवमुच्, अवसृज, अधः नि-धा 3 U or स्था c. (स्थापयति). -in, प्रविश् c.; अभ्यंतरीकृ. -off, निर्-वि-मुच्; प्रास्, क्षिप्, ईर् c., विसृज्, मोक्ष्; 'l. off with a fine' दंडदानेन विमुक्त. -out, मुच्, मोक्ष्. 2 भंज् 7 P, भिद् 7 P, प्रकाश् c. (as secrets). 3 पण्येन दा.

LETHAL, *a.* *See* DEADLY under DIE.

LETHARGY, *s.* जाड्यं, मंदता, निद्रालुता, आलस्यं, तंद्रा, तंद्रि-द्री *f*, जडबुद्धित्वं, निद्रालसता; कार्यजडता, कार्यद्वेषः, अतिमांद्यं. 2 घोर-गाढ-निद्रा, निर्भरानद्रा. -IC, *a.* निद्रालु, निद्रालस, निद्राशील, जड, मंद, जडबुद्धि, सुप्तमति; कार्यजड, कार्यविमुख (खी *f.*); आलस्यशील. -ICALLY, *adv.* जडवत्, मंदवत्. -ICALNESS, *See* (*s.*).

LETHE, *s.* विस्मृति *f.*, विस्मरणं, स्मृतिनाशः-लोपः. 2 वैतरणी.

LETTER, *s.* अक्षरं, वर्णः; 'printing l.' मुद्राक्षरं. 2 लेखः, पत्रं, लेख्यं, संदेशपत्रं; 'by l.' पत्रद्वारेण; 'l. from an inferior to a superior' विज्ञप्ति-विज्ञापना-पत्रं; 'l.-carrier' पत्रवाहः, लेखहारः. 3 शब्दार्थः, अक्षरार्थः, वाच्यार्थः, वचनं; 'obey orders to the l.' यथावचनं आज्ञामनुरुध् 4 A. 4 (Letters) विद्या, ज्ञानं; 'a man of l. s' कृतविद्यः, विद्वान्; *See* LEARNED; 'l. by l.' अक्षरशः; 'a dead l.' लुप्तार्थं वचनं. -*v. t.* अक्षरैः अंक् 10 or मुद् 10. -ED, *a.* अक्षरांकित, अक्षरमुद्रित-चिह्नित. 2 कृतविद्य, उपात्तविद्य; *See* LEARNED.

LETTUCE, *s.* हरितकं, शिग्रुः.

LEVANT, *a.* पूर्वदेशज, प्राग्भव, पौरस्त्य, पूर्वदिक्स्थ. -*s.* पूर्वदेशः, प्राग्देशः.

LEVEE, *s.* राजदर्शनं, राजदर्शनमेला, दर्शकमेला.

LEVEL, *a.* सम, समस्थ, सपाट, समरेख, समभूमिस्थित; 'lie l. with the ground' भूमिसात्कृ pass. 2 क्षितिजसमसूत्र; 'a l. ground' समभूमि *f.*, सानु *m. n.*, प्रस्थः, समस्थलं-ली. -*s.* समं, समभूमिः-स्थलं, समतलं-पृष्ठं-देशः, प्रस्थः, प्रदेशसमता, पाटः. 2 समता, तुल्यता, साम्यं, तुल्य-सम-भावः-वृत्ति *f.*; 'reduced to the l. of the poor' दरिद्रसमतां नीत-गमित; 'on a l. with' सम, तुल्य, समान; 'along the l.' अनुप्रस्थं 3 लक्ष्यसूत्रं-देशः. 4 नियमः, सूत्रं. -*v. t.* समीकृ 8 U; समस्थलीकृ. 2 लक्ष्यीकृ, उद्दिश् 6 P, सं धा 3 U, प्रेर् c, मुच् 6 P, क्षिप् 6 P. -LER, *s.* समकारिन् *m.*, विशेषनाशकः, भेद-भाव-लोपकः. -NESS, *s.* समता, साम्यं, समभूमिभावः.

LEVER, *s.* उत्तोलनदंडः; तुलायंत्रं.

LEVERET, *s.* शशशिशुः-शावकः.

LEVIATHAN, *s.* तिमिः, तिमिंगिलः.

LEVIGATE, *v. t.* चूर्ण् 10, क्षुद् 7 U, पिष् 7 P. 2 श्लक्ष्णीकृ 8 U, परिष्कृ.

LEVITICAL, *a.* याजकीय, पुरोहितसंबंधिन्.

LEVITY, *s.* लघुता, लाघवं, लघिमन् *m.*, गौरवहीनता. 2 चापल्यं, चांचल्यं, तरलता, लोलता, चापलं, लौल्यं.

LEVY, *v. t.* (Forces) समा-हृ 1 P, शस्त्राणि ग्रह् c., युद्धे व्या-पृ c. or प्रवृत् c. 2 (A tax) ग्रह् 9 P, आ-दा 3 A, दा c. (दापयति); 'l. ed taxes from them' स ताभ्यो बलिमग्रहीत् (R. I. 18). -*s.* सैन्यसमाहारः. 2 दापनं, ग्रहणं. 3 सैन्यसंग्रहः.

LEWD, *a.* कामुक, कामवश, सुरताधीन, लंपट, भोगासक्त, कामासक्त; *See* LUSTFUL. 2 दुष्ट, दुराचार, दुर्वृत्त, दुरात्मन्, पापात्मन्. -LY, *adv.* कामुकवत्, लांपट्येन. -NESS, *s.* लांपट्य, भोगासक्ति *f.*, रताधिता, व्यवायेच्छा. 2 दुष्टता, दुराचारता, दौरात्म्यं.

LEXICON, *s.* कोशः-षः; अभिधानं, शब्दसंग्रहः-कोशः, निघंटुः. -LEXICOGRAPHER, *s.* कोशकारः. -LEXICOGRAPHY, *s.* कोशरचना.

LIABLE, *a.* योग्य, अधीन, अर्ह, वश in comp.; gen. ex. by अर्ह् 1 P; पात्रं, आलु or शील in comp., or by pot. pass. part.; 'l. to punishment' दंडनीय, दंडयोग्य, दंडार्ह; 'l. to be blamed' निंदापात्रं; 'l. to fall' पतयालु, पतनशील; 'man is l. to err' मनुष्याः स्खलनशीलाः, प्रमादाधीनाः; *See* APT also. 2 अनुयोगाधीन, प्रष्टव्य, आह्वानाधीन, अभियोज्य. -NESS,-LIABILITY, *s.* अधीनता, शीलता, पात्रता, आलुता in comp.; आह्वानाधीनता, अनुयोगाधीनता. 2 (Liabilities) ऋणं, उद्धारः, पर्युदंचनं.

LIAISON, *s.* संबंधः, प्रेमबंधः.

LIAR, *s.* *See* under LIE.

LIBATION, *s.* उदकदानं-तर्पणं-पातनं-निषेकः, (देवतार्थं) पेयनिषेकः. 2 तर्पणोदकं, निषिक्तद्रव्यं-रसः, अभिधारः; 'to make l. s to' उदकादिदानेन तृप् c., उदकं पत् c. or निषिच् 6 P.

LIBEL, *s.* परि(री)वादलेखः, अपवाद-निंदा-आक्षारण-लेखः-पत्रं, पिशुनलेखः. -*v. t.* परि वद् 1 U, अप-भाष् 1 A, अभि-शंस् 1 P, निंदापत्रेण कलंकयति (D.) or आक्षर् 10; 'not only he who actually l. s great persons, but he also who countenances such l. is guilty ' न केवलं यो महतोपभाषते शृणोति तस्मादपि यः स पापभाक् (K. v. 83). -LER, *s.* अपवादकः, अभिशंसकः, परिवादकः, अभ्यसूयकः, पिशुनः. -LOUS, *a.* परिवादगर्भ, कलंकावह, अपवादक, पिशुन, कलंक-दुष्कीर्ति-कर (री *f.*).

LIBERAL, *a.* उदार, वदान्य, दानशील, अकृपण, बहुप्रद, स्थूललक्ष्य, त्यागिन्, त्यागशील, मुक्तहस्त, उदारहस्त, व्ययपर-शील. 2(L.-minded) उदारधी चेतस्-चरित, महात्मन्, महानुभाव, महेच्छ, महाशय. 3 कुलीन, महाकुल, अभिजात. 4 विपुल, बहुल, प्रचुर, परिपूर्ण, अतिरिक्त; 'l. education' सार्वविषयिकं ज्ञानं. -ITY, *s.* औदार्यं, वदान्यता, त्यागः, दानशीलता, अकार्पण्यं, बहुप्रदत्वं, दातृत्वं, अतिदानं. 2 माहात्म्यं, उदारचित्तत्वं, चित्तौदार्यं. -LY, *adv.* उदारतया, अकार्पण्येन, मुक्तहस्तेन, अतिव्ययेन-त्यागेन ; बाहुल्येन, बहुशः.

LIBERATE. *v. t.* मुच् 6 P or c., मोक्ष् 10, वि-निर्°; विसृज् 6 P, निस्तॄ c., उद्-धृ-हृ 1 P, त्रै 1 A. -ION, *s.* वि-,मुक्ति *f.*, मोचनं, मोक्षः-क्षणं, उद्धारः, त्राणं, निस्तारः. -OR, *s.* वि-,मोचकः, मोक्षकः, उद्धर्तृ *m.*, तारकः, निस्तारकः, रक्षिता.

LIBERTINE, *a.* खंडितवृत्त, व्यसनिन्, कामविषयासक्त, विषयिन्, भोग-काम-आसक्त, दुर्वृत्त, निर्-अ-मर्याद, भ्रष्टचरित्र, मुक्तमर्याद, दुराचार, व्यभिचारिन्, कामवृत्त. -*s.* लंपटः, कामुकः, कामासक्तः विटः, स्त्रीलंपटः-परः-सेवी. -ISM, *s.* व्यसनं, व्यभिचारः, लांपट्यं, विषयासक्ति *f.*, भोग-काम-आसक्तिः, दुर्वृत्तता, अमर्यादा, स्त्रीव्यसनं-व्यासंगः.

LIBERTY, *s.* स्वाधीनता, स्ववशता, स्वतंत्रता, स्वातंत्र्यं, अनायत्तता, अपारतंत्र्यं, अयंत्रणं, दास्याभावः, अदास्यं, स्वाच्छंद्यं, स्वेच्छाचारता. 2 स्वेच्छा, स्वकामः, स्वरुचि *f.*, यदृच्छा. 3 अनुज्ञा, अनुमति *f.* 4 मुक्ति *f.*, मोक्षः-क्षणं, मोचनं. 5 विरहः, अभावः, शून्यता. 6 अधिकारः, क्षमता, शक्ति *f.* 7 कर्मवशता, दैवानधीनता, अदैवपरता. 8 अमर्यादा, मर्यादातिक्रमः, अविनयः, विनयातिक्रमः, विनयोल्लंघनं; 'don't take l. with your teachers' गुरुषु अविनयं मा कार्षीः; 'your ladyship is at l. to do what befits the occasion' यदत्रावसरप्राप्तं तत्र प्रभवति भवती (Ka. 158); बंधे मोक्षे चाधुना त्वं ते प्रभवति (Ka. 354) 'she is at l. to detain or set you free'; 'to set at l.' मुच् 6 P or c. मोक्ष् 10; *See* LIBERATE; 'at l.' अयंत्रित, निरवग्रह; *See* FREE.

LIBIDINOUS, *a. See* LUSTFUL.

LIBRA, *s.* तुला, तुलाराशिः. -LIBRATE, *v. t.* तुल् 10. -ION, *s.* तोलनं.

LIBRARY, *s.* पुस्तकसंग्रहः-समूहः, ग्रंथसमुदायः-संग्रहः. 2 पुस्तकालयः, ग्रंथालयः, ग्रंथशाला, पुस्तकशाला-अगारं. -LIBRARIAN, *s.* ग्रंथशालाध्यक्षः, पुस्तकालयाधिकृतः, ग्रंथाध्यक्षः.

LICENSE, *s.* अनुज्ञा, अनुमति *f.*, आज्ञा; 'written l.' अनुज्ञापत्रं-लेखः. 2 अनियंत्रणं, मर्यादातिक्रमः, व्यतिक्रमः, उत्क्रमः, निर्यंत्रणं; 'poets have l. (in every way)' निरंकुशाः कवयः. -*v. t.* अनु-ज्ञा 9 U, आज्ञापत्रं-अनुमतिलेखं-दा 3 U, अनुमन् 4 A. -LICENTIATE, *s.* लब्धानुज्ञः-अधिकारयुक्तः, दत्ताधिकारः.

LICENTIOUS, *a.* अनियंत्रण, निर्मर्याद, स्वेच्छाचारिन्, कामवृत्त, स्वैरिन्, उच्छृंखल, अबद्ध, अनर्गल. 2 कामासक्त, उद्दामचरित, अतिक्रांतमर्याद, दुराचार, अशिष्टाचार, धर्मभ्रष्ट, व्यसनिन्, व्यसनासक्त, विषयासक्त, कामुक, दुर्वृत्त, लंपट; स्त्रीव्यसनी; *See* LIBERTINE, LUSTFUL. -LY, *adv.* उच्छृंखलं, निर्यंत्रणं, निर्मर्यादं; कामुकवत्, लंपटवत्. -NESS, *s.* व्यभिचारः, अत्याचारः, दुराचारः, दुर्वृत्तता, व्यसनिता, भ्रष्टचरित्रं-त्वं, लांपट्यं, स्त्रीसंगपरता, मर्यादातिक्रमः, व्यतिक्रमः, उत्क्रमः, निर्यंत्रणा.

LICHEN, *s.* सूकरी, सूकराक्रांता, शिलावल्का.

LICK, *v. t.* लिह् 2 U, आ-अव-सं-परि°; 'l. up' ग्रस् 1 A, गृ 6 P. 2 तड् 10, प्र-हृ 1 P; 'l. the dust (before one)' भूमौ निपत् 1 P or शी 2 A. -ING, *s.* लेहः-हनं. 2 आघातः, प्रहारः, ताडनं, दंडाघातः, वेत्रप्रहारः. -LICKERISH, *a.* सुरस, स्वादु, मिष्ट. 2 लेहोत्सुक, भोगोत्सुक.

LICORICE, *s.* यष्टिमधु *n.*, यष्टि(ष्टी)मधुकं, मधुयष्टिका, मधुकं, क्लीतकं.

LID, *s.* पिधानं, आच्छादनं, आवरणं, पटलं, पुटः-टं-टी, छदः-दनं, शरावः, मुद्रः, वर्धमानकः, उदंचनं; 'eye-l.' नेत्रच्छदः, अक्षिपुटः.

LIE, *s.* असत्यं, अनृतं, वितथं, अतथ्यं, अलीकं; मृषा-अनृत-वाक्यं-वचनं, मृषोक्ति *f.*, मृषोद्यं, मिथ्यावादः-भाषणं-वचनं-उक्तिः, मृषा-असत्य-वादः, असत्यभाषणं. -*v. i.* शी 2 A, अधि-शी (with acc.), आस् 2 A, नि-पत् 1 P, संविश् 6 P. 2 वस् 1 P, स्था 1 P, अव-स्था 1 A; gen. by भू, वृत् 1 A, अस् 2 P, विद् 4 A; 'Lanká l. s to the south of India' लंका भारतवर्षस्य दक्षिणतो अवस्थिता or वर्तते. 3 Consist in, q. v. 4 अनृतं-मिथ्या-असत्यं-वद् 1 P or वच् 2 P or भाष् 1 A, &c. (Speak, q. v.); 'thou liest in the throat' नितांतमनृतं वदसि; 'l. hard upon' पीड् 10, बाध् 1 A, आ-यस् c. -down, शी, संविश्, स्वप् 2 P, निपत्. -in, प्रसवावस्थायां वृत्; 'lying-in-chamber' अरिष्टं, सूतिकागृहं; 'l. in the wait' निभृत स्था, नि-ली 4 A; 'l. in the way' रुध् 7 U, अंतर्-इ 2 P, अंतरायो भू. -on, आ-अव-समा-लंब् 1 A, आश्रि 1 U; *See* DEPEND. 2 'Be incumbent' q. v. -with, संगम् 1 A, अनुगम्, मैथुनं कृ 8 U. 2 अधीन-*a.* भू; गम्; 'the fault l. s with you entirely' सर्वथा तवैवायं दोषः, त्वमेवात्र सर्वात्मना दोषभाक्; 'the fault l. s with my friend' सखीगामी (अयं) दोषः (S. 4) —LIAR, s. मिथ्या-मृषा-अनृत-असत्य-वादिन्-भाषिन्, असत्यवाच् m., अलीकवाच्, अनृतिन्, असत्यशीलः, मिथ्यावादशीलः. —LYING, s. असत्य-अनृत-मिथ्या-भाषणं, मृषा-मिथ्या-वादः, मिथ्यावादित्वं, असत्यता; See (s.). —a. मृषावादिन्, अनृतवाच्, असत्य; See above.

LIEF, adv. कामं, प्र-नि-कामं, कामतः, इच्छापूर्वं, संतोषेण, प्रीत्या.

LIEGE, s. प्रभुः, स्वामिन् m., ईश्वरः, पतिः; महाराजः, देवः (in addressing). —a. भक्त, सेवा-भक्ति-बद्ध, प्रभु-स्वामि-भक्त, स्वाम्यनुरक्त, प्रभुवश; 'l.-man' भक्तः, प्रभुसेवी. 2 आज्ञापक; better ex. by (s.).

LIENTERY, s. अतिसारः, आमातिसारः.

LIEU, s. स्थानं, भूमि f.; 'in l. of' स्थाने, विनिमयेन; See INSTEAD (of). —LIEUTENANT, s. प्रतिनिधिः, प्रतिपुरुषः; (lit.) सेनापतिप्रतिनिधिः; 'l. governor' प्रतिशासकः; 'lord l.' राजप्रतिनिधिः.

LIFE, s. जीवनं, जीवितं, प्राणधारण, असुधारणं. 2 जीवः, सत्त्वं, जीवितं. चैतन्यं, चेतना, प्राणवायुः, प्राणात्मन्, m., जीवात्मा; 'endowed with l.' जीविन्, प्राणिन्, सजीव, सचेतन; 'love of l.' जीविततृष्णा, जिजीविषा; 'impatience of l.' जीवितद्वेषः-त्रासः; 'deprived of l.' हतप्राण-जीवित, नष्टप्राण; 'support of l.' प्राणयात्रा-धारणं-रक्षणं; 'reckless of l.' जीवितव्ययिन्, जीवितनिरपेक्ष; 'means of l.' जीवनोपायः. 3 (Life-time) आयुस् n., जीवितं, जीवनं, जीवितकालः, आयुर्मर्यादा, आयुःपरिमाणं; 'possessed of long l.' दीर्घायुस्, आयुष्मत्, चिरायुः; 'for l.,' 'during l.', 'all one's l.' यावज्जीवं, आमरणात्; 'in all one's l.' आजन्म, जन्मतः प्रभृति or आरभ्य; 'my lamp of l. is nearly out' निर्वाणभूयिष्ठो मे जीवितप्रदीपः or अवसितप्रायो मे जीवितावधिः. 4 (fig.) जीवितं, प्राणाः, (त्वं जीवितं मे U. 3). 5 संसारः, भवः, संसृति f.. लोकयात्रा, भूलोकवासः, इहवासः. 6 वृत्ति f., आचारः. व्यवहारः, रीति f., चेष्टितं, प्रवृत्तिः, वृत्तं, आचरणं; 'leading a virtuous l.' साधुवृत्त, सदाचार; पुण्यमार्ग. 7 चरितं, चरित्रं, जीवनवृत्तांतः, चरित्ररचना-कथनं. 8 अवस्था, दशा, स्थिति f., वृत्तिः, भावः, गति f. 9 उत्साहः, वीर्य, तेजस् n.. सत्त्वं, रसः; 'bring or restore to l.' उज्जीव् c.. सोच्छ्वास-a. कृ 8 U. असून् प्राप् c., (परीक्षितं दुर्लभानसूनप्रापितवान् Ka. 175); 'come to l.' उज्जीव् 1 P; 'active l.' प्रवृत्तिः, प्रवृत्ति-संसार-मार्गः, लोकव्यवहारः;' retired l.' निवृत्तिः, निवृत्तिमार्गः; 'he entered on a military l.' योधवृत्तिमाश्रयत; 'engaging in public l.' लोकव्यवहारप्रवृत्तिः; 'in this l.' इह, इहलोके; 'the vicissitudes of l.' संसारचक्र-परिवर्तनं, दशांतराणि; 'l.-blood' प्राणः, तत्त्वं, सारभूतं द्रव्यं; 'l.-giving' प्राणद, जीवद-दायिन्; जीवद, उत्साहकर (री f.); 'l.-guard' राजपरिचरः, शरीररक्षकः; 'l.-time' जीवितावधिः, जीवितकालः; 'during one's l.-time' यावज्जीवं. —LESS, a. गतजीवित, गतासु, परासु, व्यसु, गत-नष्ट-प्राण, हतजीवित, प्राण-जीव-रहित-हीन, अचेष्ट. 2 अजीव, निर्जीव, वि-अ-चेतन, चैतन्यहीन-रहित, निश्चेतन. 3 निःसत्त्व, निरुत्साह, निस्तेजस्, सत्त्व-रस-हीन.

LIFT, v. t. उन्नम् c. (नमयति), उद्गम् c. (गमयति), उच्छ्रि 1 U, उद्यम् 1 A, उत्था c. (उत्थापयति), उत्क्षिप् 6 P, उद्धृ 1 P, उन्नी 1 P, उत्कृष् 1 P, उत्तुल् 10; oft. by उत् in comp.; 'with the neck l.-ed up' उत्कंधरः; उद्बाहुः, उद्ग्रीवः, उन्मुखः, &c. 2 (In rank) उत्कृष्टपदे नियुज् 7 A, 10, मानं संवृध् c., प्रतिपत्ति-प्रतिष्ठां-उत्कर्षं-पदवृद्धिं-लभ् c. (लंभयति); 'l. with pride' दृप् c., गर्वेण उद्धन् 2 P, दर्पेण आ-ध्मा 1 P; 'to l. up the voice' तारस्वरेण-उच्चैः-आक्रुश् 1 P. —s. उन्नमनं, उच्छ्रयः, उत्कर्षः, उत्थापनं. 2 प्रतिपत्ति f., पदवृद्धि f., उन्नति f. 3 उपकारः, साहाय्यं.

LIGAMENT, s. बंधनं, पाशः, निगडः, शृंखला-लं-लः. 2 संधिबंधः, ग्रंथि-अस्थि-बंधनं.

LIGATURE, LIGATION, s. बंधः, बंधनं, वेष्टनं, परि-आ-वेष्टनं, रज्जु f.

LIGHT, a. लघु (in all senses); अगुरु, अल्पभार, अल्पप्रमाण, लघुभार, लघुप्रमाण; सुवाह्य, सुखवाह्य, सुसह्य, अदुर्वह, अदुःसह. 2 सुख, सुकर, अकष्ट, सुसाध्य, सुगम, निरायास, अविषम, अकठिन. 3 चपल, लघु, लघुशरीर-गति. 4 सोल्लास, प्रफुल्ल, निश्चिंत. 5 चपल, चंचल, लोल, तरल, अस्थिर, अनवस्थित, लघुचित्त-स्वभाव-चेतस्, गांभीर्यहीन, निर्गौरव. 6 तुच्छ, क्षुद्र, अत्यल्प, तृणप्राय, लघ्वर्थ, अल्पार्थ, अल्प-लघु-प्रभाव; 'l.-armed' लघ्वायुध, लघुशस्त्रभृत्; 'l.-fingered' लघुहस्त, चपलपाणि; 'l.-footed' लघु-शीघ्र-गति, द्रुतगति; 'l.-headed' लघुचित्त-चेतस्, चपल-लोल-मति; भ्रांत-विक्षिप्त-बुद्धि-चित्त; बुद्धिभ्रमात् प्रलापिन्; 'l.-headedness' चित्त-बुद्धि-भ्रमः-विभ्रमः; 'l.-hearted' लघुचित्त-चेतस्, क्षुद्रमनस्; हृष्ट-प्रसन्न-हृदय, उल्लासिन्, प्रफुल्लचित्त, आनंदित, सोल्लास; 'l.-house' दीपगृहं; 'l.-minded' लघुचेतस्-चित्त, क्षुद्र-कृपण-बुद्धि-मति; 'l. spirited' हृष्टहृदय-चित्त, &c. 7 पांडु, श्वेत; oft. ex. by आ, ईषत्; 'l. red' श्वेतारुण, ईषद्रक्त; 'l. blue' श्वेतनील, आनील; 'l. food' सुपथ्य-सुपाक-अन्नं; 'to make l. of' लघूकृ 8 U, लघु मन् 4 A, न गण् 10, तृणाय मन्. —s. प्रकाशः, आलोकः, भा, प्रभा, आभा, द्युति f., कांति f., दीप्ति f., तेजस् n., ज्योतिस् n., रुचि f., भास् f., त्विष् f.; वर्चस् n. 2 दीपः, प्रदीपः; दीपिका. 3 ज्ञानं, बोधः, अव-

गमः, प्रकाशः. 4 प्रसिद्धि *f.*, प्रख्याति *f.*, प्राकाश्यं, प्रकाशता, प्राकट्यं. 5 दृष्टि *f.*; 'see or come to l.' प्रसिद्धि-प्रकाशतां-गम् 1 P, प्रकाशीभू 1 P, आविर्भू, प्रादुर्भू; 'bring to l.' प्रकाश् c., प्रकटीकृ 8 U, स्पष्टीकृ, आविष्कृ, विवृ 5 U, प्र-ख्या c. (ख्यापयति); 'to throw l. on' विशदीकृ, विवृ, प्रकाश् c.; *See* EXPLAIN; 'from the l. of utility' उपयोगदृष्ट्या; 'considered in this l.' अनया दृष्ट्या. **-*v. t.*** दीप् c., उत्-प्र-सं-°; प्र-,द्युत् c., प्रकाश् c., अव-वि-भास् c., ज्वल् c., प्र-उत्-सं; सं,-इंध् 7 A; संधुक्ष् 10; तप् c., सं-प्र-उत्°; 'to be l. ed' दीप् 4 A, ज्वल् 1 P. **-*v. i.*** आ-पत् 1 P; (अकस्मात्) आसद् c., प्राप् 5 P, आ-उपा-गम् 1 P. 2 अवतृ 1 P, अव-रुह् 1 P, अव-नि-पत्; अध्यास् 2 A, अधि-शी 2 A (with acc.), निषद् 1 P, नि-ली 4 A. **-EN,** *v. t.* प्रकाश् c., दीप् c., ज्वल् c., द्युत् c.; *See* (*v. t.*) above. 2 लघूकृ, लघयति (D.); शम् c. (शमयति), प्र-उप°. **-*v. i.*** स्फुर् 6 P, द्युत् 1 A, प्रकाश् 1 A, विलस् 1 P. **-ER,** *a.* लघुतर, लघीयस्. **-*s.*** प्रकाशकः, द्योतकः, दीपकः, द्युतिदः. 2 तरालुः, बहित्रं, टडुपं. **-LESS,** *a.* निष्प्रभ, अप्रभ, निरालोक, निस्तेजस्. **-LY,** *adv.* लघु, लाघवेन, अल्पप्रमाणेन. 2 सुखेन, अकष्टेन, अनायासेन. 3 निष्कारणं, हेतुं विना. 4 लघुगत्या, चपलं, सत्वरं. 5 लघुचेतसा, चंचलवत्, अस्थिरतया; 'to think l.' लघु मन् 4 A. **-NESS,** *s.* (lit.) लघुता-त्वं, लाघवं, अल्पभारत्वं, भाराभावः. 2 सुखं, सौकर्यं, अनायासः, सुसाध्यता, अकष्टत्वं. 3 सुवाह्यता, सुसह्यता. 4 लाघवं, चापल्यं, द्रुतगतित्वं, शरीरलघुता. 5 चापल्यं, चांचल्यं, अस्थिरता, लोलता, चपलता, अगौरवं, लघिमा, लाघवं, लघुता. 6 लघुता, तुच्छता, क्षुद्रता. **-SOME,** *a.* दीप्तिमत्, प्रकाशवत्, सुप्रभ, तेजस्विन्, सुप्रकाश, तेजोमय (यी *f.*). 2 हृष्ट, सोल्लास, प्रफुल्ल, वीतचिंत, सानंद. **-LIGHTNING,** *s.* तडित्, विद्युत्, सौदामि(म)नी, अचिरप्रभा, क्षणदा, चंचला, चपला, शतह्रदा, ह्रादिनी, शंपा, ऐरावती, क्षणप्रभा-द्युतिः (all *f.*); 'fire of l.' वैद्युतः अग्निः; 'forked l.' तडिल्लता, विद्युल्लता; 'the falling of l.' विद्युत्पातः; 'struck by l.' विद्युता उपहत.

LIGNEOUS, *a.* काष्ठ-दारु-मय (यी *f.*), काष्ठ-दारु-रूप.

LIGNIFEROUS, *a.* काष्ठद, दारुपद.

LIGNIFORM, *a.* काष्ठरूप, काष्ठाकृति.

LIKE, *a.* सदृश (शी *f.*), तुल्य, सम; समान, सन्निभ, अनुकारिन्, (with gen. or instr.); oft. by उपम, निभ, रूप, विध, प्रतिम, संकाश, नीकाश, प्रतीकाश, भूत, (all in comp.); also by स or अनु in comp.; 'of l. properties' सगुण, अनुगुण-धर्मन्, सम-तुल्य-गुण, समभाव; 'of l. form' सरूप, अनुरूप, तुल्याकृति, तुल्यरूप; 'l. a father' पितृभूतः, पितृस्थानीयः; 'of l. class' सजाति, सजातीय, सवर्ण, सवर्ग, तुल्यवर्ण; 'almost l. Hara' हरकल्प; 'l. this' ईदृश-श्, एतादृश-श्; 'l. that' तादृश्-श; 'l. what' कीदृश-श; 'l. which' यादृश्-श; 'l. me, us' मादृश, अस्मादृश, &c.; 'l. thee, you' त्वादृश, युष्मादृश, &c.; 'l. your honour' भवादृश; 'to be l.' अनुकृ 8 U (with gen.), संवद् 1 P (with instr.), अनुहृ 1 P (with acc.); *See* RESEMBLE; 'the son was l. his generating cause (father)' न कारणात् स्वाद्बिभिदे कुमारः (R. v. 57); 'these and the l.' एवमादि; 'in l. manner' तथा, एवं, तद्वत्, तथैव, एवमेव, एवंविधं. **-*s.*** समः, तुल्यः, सदृशः, तुल्यगुणः, यमकः-लः; 'his l. was and will never be seen' अनेन सदृशो न भूतो न भविष्यति. **-*adv.*** Ex. by वत् in comp., इव, यथा, निर्विशेषं in comp.; 'l. an earthen pot' मृद्घटवत्; often by Karm. or Bah. comp.; 'black l. a cloud' मेघश्याम; 'having a moon-l. face' चंद्रमुख; 'brought up l. one's own children' अपत्यनिर्विशेषं संवर्धित; 'to act l.' अनुकृ. 2 Likely, q. v. **-*v. t.*** रुच् 1 A (with dat. of person who likes); अभिनंद् 1 P, अनु-सं-अभि-मन् 4 A, अनुमुद् 1 A, प्रशंस् 1 P, प्री pass., तुष् 4 P; 'does not l. the present' उपायनं नाभिनंदति, उपायनेन न तुष्यति &c., स्निह् 4 P, अनुरंज् pass. (with loc.). **-*v. i.*** इष् 6 P, अभिलष् 1, 4 P, रुच्; oft. by काम in comp.; 'just as you l.' यस्ते छंदः (V. 3), यद्भवते रोचते; 'doing as one l. s' कामचारः, स्वैरवृत्तः, स्वच्छंदः, स्वैरिन्; 'taking what form he l. s' कामरूपः; 'do what you l.' यथाभिलषितं क्रियतां. **-ED,** *a.* मत, अभि-अनु-सं-° इष्ट, प्रिय, दयित. **-EN,** *v. t.* उप-मा 3 A, 2 P, सदृशीकृ; *See* COMPARE. **-ING,** *s.* रुचि *f.*, अभिरुचिः, कामः, इच्छा, तोषः, प्रीति *f.*, तुष्टि *f.*, प्रणयः, अनुरागः, अभिलाषः, छंदः, छंदस् *n.*, सं-अनु-मति *f.*; 'he was not to her l.' स न तस्या रुरुचे बभूव (R. VI. 44); 'of your l.' त्वदभिमत. **-NESS,** *s.* सादृश्यं, साम्यं, तुल्यत्वं, आनुरूप्यं, सारूप्यं, तुला, उपमा, अनुकारः, संवादः, आनुगुण्यं, औपम्यं, &c. 2 रूपं, आकृति *f.*, आकारः, मूर्ति *f.* 3 प्रतिमा-मानं, प्रतिरूपं-कृतिः, प्रतिमूर्तिः, प्रतिच्छंदः, चित्रं, आलेख्यं, प्रतिबिंबं; 'a speaking l.' संवादिनी आकृतिः. **-WISE,** *adv.* तथैव, तथा, तद्वत्. 2 अपि, अपि च, किं च, तथा, अपरं च. **—LIKELY,** *a.* संभाव्य, संभवनीय, उपपन्न, सत्यसंकाश; श्रद्धेय; 'it is l. that' इति संभवति or उपपद्यते. 2 (Probable) ex. by प्रायः, प्रायशः, प्रायेण, with pot. pass. part., or by अपि नाम; 'he is l. to come to-morrow' प्रायस्तेन श्व आगंतव्यं; अपि नाम तया

अभिमतः पाणिग्रहः स्यात् (Mal. 1) 'is it l. that &c.' -HOOD,-NESS, *s.* संभाव्यता, संभवः; better by (*a.*); *See* above.

LILY, *s.* नलिनी, उत्पलं, कुमुदं, पद्मं; *See* LOTUS.

LIMATION, *s.* मार्जनं, लोहमार्जनेन घर्षणं.

LIMATURE, *s.* लोहचूर्णं, लोहजं.

LIMB, *s.* अंगं, अवयवः, (lit. & fig.) ; गात्रं; 'over every l.' प्रत्यंगं, सर्वांगीण-*a.*; 'l. by l.' अवयवशः, गात्रे गात्रे. 2 प्रांतः, कोटि *f.*, सीमा. -ED, *a.* अंगिन्, सावयव; 'large-l.' बृहदवयव, महांग (गी *f.*); 'slender-l.' तन्वंग, कोमल-पेलव-अंग. -LESS, *a.* अनंग, निरवयव, अंगहीन.

LIMBER, *a.* मृदु, कोमल, शिथिल, अदृढ, नम्य.

LIMBO, *s.* नरकः, निरयः. 2 कारा, कारागारं, बंधनागारं.

LIME, *s.* (Tree) जंबीरः; *See* LEMON. 2 (Quick-l.) चूर्णः-र्णं, कर्करं; 'l.-water' सुधा, लेपः (for colouring); 'l.-stone' चूर्णखंडः, चूर्णोपलः, कर्करं. -Y, *a.* चूर्णमय (यी *f.*), सचूर्ण, कर्करमय. 2 श्यान, सांद्र, चूर्णोपम.

LIMIT, *s.* अवधिः, मर्यादा, सीमा, सीमन् *f.*, पर्यंतः, अंतः, प्रांतः, परिच्छेदः, परिमाणं, इयत्ता, अवसानं; वेला (of sea); 'of narrow l. (scope)' अल्पविषय-*a.*; 'set or fix a l. to' परिच्छिद् 7 P; 'no (definite) l. can be set to his fame' तस्य यश इयत्तया परिच्छेत्तुं नालं (R. VI. 77). -*v. t.* परिच्छिद्, परि-मा 2 P, 3 A; इयत्तया परिच्छिद्, सीमां नि-रूप् 10 or निर्धृ 10; *See* DEFINE. 2 सं-नि-यम् 1 P or c., सं-हृ 1 P, संकुच् 1 P or c., नियंत्र् 10, निबंध् 9 P, निग्रह् 9 P. -ATION, *s.* परिच्छेदः, सीमा-मर्यादा-निरूपणं. 2 परिमितता, सावधिकता, समर्यादत्वं, ससीमता. -ED, *a.* परिच्छिन्न, परिमित, मित, समर्याद, सावधिक; नियत, संहत, अल्पविषय, संकुचित, अव्यापक, संबाध; 'not through the l. nature of (your) merits' न गुणानामियत्तया (R. x. 32); 'l. meaning' नियतार्थः; 'l. knowledge' अल्पविषयं ज्ञानं; 'l. monarchy' नियंत्रितं or संयतं प्रभुत्वं. -ER, *s.* परिच्छेदकः. -LESS, *a.* अमित, अनंत, असीम, निरवधि.

LIMMER, *s.* नीचजनः, अपसदः in comp.

LIMN, *v. t.* लिख् 6 P or चित्र् 10. -ER, *s.* चित्रकरः.

LIMOUS, *a.* सकर्दम, पंकिल.

LIMP, *v. i.* खंज् 1 P, लंग् 1 P, खोड़्-खोड्-खोल् 1 P. -*s.* लंगः, लंगगति *f.* -*a.* मृदु, शिथिल, कोमल. -ER, *s.* खंजः, लंग-खंज-गतिः. -ING, *a.* खंज, खोर, खोल, खोड, लंगगति, विकलगति. -INGLY, *adv.* खंजवत्, लंगगत्या.

LIMPID, *a.* स्वच्छ, प्रसन्न, विमल, स्वच्छतोय, प्रसन्नवारि, विमलजल. -NESS, *s.* स्वच्छता, विमलता, प्रसादः.

LIN, *s.* पल्वलं, तडागः-गं, जलाशयः.

LINCH-PIN, *s.* अक्षाग्रकीलः, अ(आ)णिः, ङ्ग्रथः.

LINCTURE, *s.* अवलेहः, लेह्यं.

LINE, *s.* रे(ले)खा, रेषा. 2 पंक्तिः, पद्धतिः, सरणिः-णी, राजिः-जी, आवलिः-ली, ततिः, श्रेणिः-णी (all *f.*), माला. 3 सूत्रं, रज्जु *f.*, गुणः, तंतुः. 4 आकारः, आकृति *f.*, रूपं. 5 प्राकारः, वप्रः, परिखा, प्राचीरं. 6 (Of troops) दंडः, व्यूहः, पंक्तिः, बलविन्यासः. 7 क्रमः, अनुक्रमः, पर्यायः. 8 परिपाटि-टी *f.*, श्रेणिः-णी, पंक्तिः, परंपरा, माला, पारंपर्यं, आवलिः-ली; आनुपूर्व्यं. 9 (Of conduct) मार्गः, पथिन् *m.*, रीति *f.*, सरणिः, व्यवहारः. 10 देशः, विषयः, अंगं. 11 दिश् *f.*, दिशा, मार्गः. 12 भूचक्रं; *See* EQUATOR; 'ruled l.' रेखा, अंकः; 'in a l.' पंक्तिक्रमेण, पंक्तिशः; 'by l. and rule' यथासूत्रं; 'l. of the face' वदन-मुख-रेखा; 'printed l.' पंक्तिः; 'l. of a stanza' पादः, चरणः-णं; 'in a regular l.' अनुक्रमेण, क्रमशः, आनुपूर्व्येण, अनुपूर्वशः; 'l. of the family' वंशक्रमः-परंपरा-आवलिः; 'a good l. of conduct' सुमार्गः, सुपथः; 'a bad l. of conduct' वि-कु-पथः, विमार्गः, उन्मार्गः; 'l. of study' अध्ययनक्रमः; 'l. of posterity' वंशावली; 'fishing-l.' बडिशसूत्रं; 'to draw l. s' लिख् 6 P; 'draw l. s on the ground' भूमिं रेखाभिः वि-टन्-लिख् or अंक् 10; 'to draw the l.' वि-विच् 3, 7 U, भेदं दृश् c., or निरूप् 10. -*v. t.* अंतः आ-,छद् 10, अभ्यंतरे छद्. 2 पंक्तिक्रमेण स्था c. (स्थापयति) or निविश् c. 3 रेखाभिः अंक्; 'the streets were l. ed with guards' अनुरथ्यं पंक्तिक्रमेण रक्षिणः स्थापिताः. -AGE, *s.* अन्वयः, वंशः, कुलं, संतति *f.*, संतानः. गोत्रं, वंशावली, वंशपरंपरा; 'of royal l.' राजवंश्य, राजकुलप्रसूत; 'of high or noble l.' अभिजात, महाकुल. -AL, *a.* रेखारूप-मय (यी *f.*). 2 परंपरागत, परंपरायात-प्राप्त, क्रमप्राप्त-आगत-आयात, अन्वयागत, परंपरीण, कुलक्रमागत; 'l. descent' अन्वयागमः, क्रमागमः, कुलक्रमागमः; 'l. descendant' संतानः, संततिः, अपत्यं. -ALLY, *adv.* परंपरया, पारंपर्येण, वंशक्रमेण, कुलक्रमागमेन, 'l. descended' वंशक्रमायात; *See* above. -ING, *s.* अंतराच्छादनं, अंतःपटल-पुट-वेष्टनं, आस्तरः-रणं. -LINEAMENT, *s.* रेखा, वदन-मुख-रेखा, वदनाकारः, वदनाकृति *f.*, लक्षणं, चिह्नं. -LINEAR, *s.* पंक्ति-रेखा-रूप-मय (यी *f.*).

LINEN, *s.* क्षौमं, क्षौमपटः-वस्त्रं; शाणपटः-वस्त्रं. -*a.* क्षौम-औम (मी *f.*), शाण (णी *f.*), अतसीनिर्मित; 'l.-draper' क्षौमवस्त्रविक्रयिन् *m.*, वस्त्रविक्रयोपजीवी.

LINGER, *v. i.* वि-लंब् 1 A, मंदायते (D.), चिर(रा)यति (D.), कालं क्षिप् 6 P or हृ 1 P, मंदं मंदं चल्-र् 1 P. 2 विकृप् 1 A, विचर् c. 3 चिरं-दीर्घकालं-स्था 1 P or वृत् 1 A; 'l. ing on a sick bed' चिररोगिन्. -ER, *s.* विलंबकारिन् *m.*, विलंबी, मंदगामी, मंदगतिः, चिरक्रियः, दीर्घसूत्री. -ING, *a.* दीर्घ, चिरस्थायिन्, चिर-दीर्घ-कालीन, चिरकालस्थ. 2 विलंबिन्, विलंबित, मंदायमान. -*s.* विलंबः, कालक्षेपः-यापनं. -INGLY, *adv.* मंदं मंदं, विलंबेन, सविलंबं, मंदगत्या, कालक्षेपेण.

LINGET, *s.* धातु-लोह-पिंडः.

LINGUAL, *a.* मूर्धन्य, मूर्धस्थानीय.

LINGUIFORM, *a.* जिह्वाकृति, जिह्वारूप.

LINGUIST, *s.* भाषाकोविदः, शाब्दिकः, शब्दव्युत्पन्नः, भाषाप्रवीणः, भाषाज्ञः, बहुभाषाज्ञः, अनेकभाषानिपुणः. -IC, *a.* (*s.*) in comp.

LINIMENT, *s.* प्र-आ-वि-लेपः-पनं, उपदेहः, अभ्यंजनं, मर्दनौषधं.

LINK, *s.* संधिः, ग्रंथिः. 2 नद्धनं, बंधपाशः, शृंखला-लः-लं. 3 संयोगः, संबंधः, अन्वयः, संदर्भः, प्रबंधः. 4 उल्का, उल्मुकं; 'l. s of life' जीवितनिबंधनानि ; 'l.-boy' उल्काभृत्. -*v. t.* संयुज् 7 U. 10, सं-धा 3 U, संश्लिष् c., संबंध् 9 P, व्यति-षंज् 1 P, संग्रंथ् 9 P; *See* KNIT. -ED, *a.* संयुक्त, संश्लिष्ट, संबद्ध, अन्वित, सान्वय.

LINSEED, *s.* अतसी, उमा, क्षुमा, उमा-अतसी-बीजं, &c.

LINSEY-WOOLSEY, *a.* क्षौमौर्ण. 2 असार, निःसत्व; क्षुद्र.

LINSTOCK, *s.* ज्वलनकाष्ठं, अग्निदशलाका.

LINT, *s.* क्षौमबंधः, विकेशिका.

LINTEL, *s.* द्वाराग्रकाष्ठं, द्वारोर्ध्वदारु *n.*

LION, *s.* सिंहः, हरिः, केसरिन् *m.*, पंचास्यः, पंचाननः, हर्यक्षः, कंठीरवः, मृगरिपुः, मृगाशनः, पुंडरीकः, पंचनखः, चित्रकायः, मृगद्विट्; and comp. of इंद्रः, राजन्, पतिः, अधिपः, अधिपतिः with मृग or पशु; मृगपतिः, मृगराजः, मृगाधिपः, पशुपतिः, &c.; 'l.'s part' भूयिष्ठभागः. -ESS, *s.* सिंही. -LIKE, -LY, *a.* सिंहस्वभाव, सैंह (ही *f.*).

LIP, *s.* ओष्ठः (strictly upper), दशन-रदन-छदः, रद-दंत-छदः, दशन-दंत-वासस् *n.*, अधरः (strictly lower); 'a red or cherry l.' बिंबो(बौ)ष्ठः, बिंबाधरः; 'a woman having cherry l. s.' बिंबोष्ठी; 'drinking the l.' अधरपानं, अधरामृतसेवनं; 'l.-honeyed' मुखमधु; 'l.-loyalty' मुखभक्ति *f.*, वाग्दर्शिता भक्तिः. 2 कर्णः, पार्श्वः, कंठः, मुखं, &c. -PED, *a.* ओष्ठ in comp.

LIPOTHYMY, *s. See* FAINTING, SWOON.

LIPPITUDE, *s.* क्लिन्नाक्षता, चुल्लत्वं.

LIQUEFY, *v. i.* वि-,द्रु 1 P, वि-,ली 9 P, 4 A, जलसाद्भू 1 P, क्षर् 1 P, द्रवीभू. -*v. t.* वि-,द्रु c., वि-,ली c., द्रवीकृ 8 U, जलसात्कृ. -ACTION, *s.* द्रवीकरणं, द्रावः, विलयः-यनं, क्षरणं, द्रवीभवनं. 2 द्रवत्वं, विलीनता.

LIQUID, *s.* द्रवः, रसः, जलं, द्रववस्तु-द्रव्यं-पदार्थः. -*a.* द्रव, द्रुत, द्रवरूप, विलीन, प्रवाहिन्, तरलं; 'reduced to a l. state' द्रवतामापन्न, विलीन, जलीभूत, रसतामुपेत (Ka. 122). -ITY,-NESS, *s.* द्रवत्वं, रसता, द्रवभावः, प्रवाहधर्मः.

LIQUIDATE, *v. t.* शुध् c., अपाकृ 8 U, निस्तॄ c., अपनी 1 P, अपवृज् 10; मुच् 6 P or c., मोक्ष् 10; 'debt contracted to l. another debt' ऋणार्णं. -ION, *s.* शोधनं, शुद्धि *f.*, अपाकरणं, निस्तारः, मुक्ति *f.*, मोक्षः-क्षणं, अपनयनं.

LIQUOR, *s.* सुरा, मद्यं, हाला, वारुणी, वरुणात्मजा, मदिरा, आसवः, शी(सी)धु *m. n.*, हलिप्रिया, परिस्रुत् *f.*, गंधोत्तमा, प्रसन्ना, इरा, कादंबरी, परिस्रुता, कश्यं; 'l.-shop' शुंडापानं, मदस्थानं, शुंडा, पानं; 'round of drinking l.' मधुवारः-क्रमः; 'distilling of l.' संधानं, अभिषवः; 'l.-ferment' किण्वं, नग्नहूः, कारोत्तरः, मंडः; 'company of l.-drinkers' आपानं, पानगोष्ठिका; 'drinking l.' सरकः, अनुतर्षणं, मद्यपानं. 2 Liquid, q. v. 3 पेयं.

LISP, *v. i.* स्वरभंगेन-अस्पष्टं-वद् 1 P or वच् 2 P or उच्चर् c. or उदीर् c., अव्यक्तं वद्; अस्फुटवाचा जल्प् 1 P, स्खल् 1 P. -*s.*, -ING, *s.* गद्गदवाच् *f.*-वाक्यं, अस्फुटोच्चारणं, अव्यक्तवर्णं जल्पितं, स्खलितवाक्. -ER, *s.* अस्पष्टवाक्, गद्गदवाक्, अस्फुटवादिन् *m.* -INGLY, *adv.* अस्फुटवाचा, गद्गदवाचा.

LIST, *s.* आवलि-ली *f.*, पंक्ति *f.*, परिसंख्या, परिगणना, अनुक्रमणिका, सूचि-ची *f.*; 'a l. of names' नामावली; 'a l. of errata' शुद्धिपत्रं. 2 वस्त्रखंडः. 3 वस्त्रप्रांतः, दशाः, वस्तयः (pl.). 4 युद्ध-रण-भूमि *f.*, रंगः, रणाजिरं, मल्लभूः-भूमिः; 'enter or take the l. s' रणार्थं सज्जीभू 1 P or सन्नद्ध-*a.* भू. -*v. t.* वस्त्रखंडैः आच्छद् 10. 2 वस्त्रखंडान् संसिव् 4 P. 3 गणनापत्रे नामानि अभिलिख् 6 P or आरुह् c. (रोपयति). 4 Listen, q. v. -*v. i.* इष् 6 P, रुच् 1 A, अभिलष् 1, 4 P; *See* LIKE. 2 आ-अव-लंब् 1 A, प्रवणीभू 1 P; *See* LEAN. —LISTLESS, *a.* अनवहित, निरपेक्ष, उदासीन, प्रमादिन्, अनुत्सुक, निरुत्साह; अनिच्छु, निरीह, निरुद्योग, विरक्त, निःस्पृह. 2 जड, ग्लान; *See* LANGUID. -LY, *adv.* अनवधानेन, निरपेक्षं, उदासीनवत्, निरुत्सुकं, अनपेक्षया, जडवत्, निःस्पृहं. -NESS, *s.* अनवधानं, अनपेक्षा, औदासीन्यं, अनौत्सुक्यं, विरक्ति *f.*, अनिच्छा, अनीहा, अस्पृहा, अनुत्साहः, अनास्था, जडता, मांद्यं.

LISTEN, *v. i.* श्रु 5 P, आकर्ण् 10, नि-शम् c., कर्णं दा 3 U, अव-धा 3 U, अवहित-सावधान-*a.* भू 1 P; 'l. now' अवधीयतामधुना, कर्णं देहि. 2 अनुवृत् 1 A, अनुरुध् 4 A. -ER, *s.* श्रोतृ *m.*

LITERAL, *a.* मूल, मुख्य, प्रकृत, अरूपक; मूलार्थक, मुख्यार्थक, शब्द in comp. 2 यथाशब्द, शब्दार्थानुसा-

रिन्, मूलपदानुसारिन् 3 अक्षरमय (यी f.); 'l. meaning' प्रकृतार्थः, शब्दार्थः, मूलार्थः. -ITY, s. मुख्यार्थः, प्रकृतार्थः, शब्दार्थः, मूलार्थः, अरूपकं. -LY, adv. मूलार्थानुसारेण, शब्दतः, शब्दशः, यथाशब्दं, अक्षरशः.

LITERARY, a. विद्या-साहित्य-संबंधिन्, विद्याविषयक, शास्त्र-ज्ञान- in comp.; 'l. work' शास्त्रग्रंथः; 'l. dispute' ज्ञानसंघर्षः. 2 (Literate) विद्यावत्, विद्यासंपन्न, विद्याविशिष्ट, विद्यानुरागिन्; विद्या-शास्त्र-in comp.; *See* LEARNED. -LITERATURE, s. साहित्यं, विद्या, शास्त्रं; शास्त्रसमूहः; पुस्तकसमुदायः; 'dramatic l.' नाट्यपुस्तकसमूहः. -LITERATI, s. विद्वत्समाजः, पंडितवर्गः-गणः, विद्वद्वृंदं.

LITHE, a. शिथिल, मृदु, भिदेलिम, सुखनाम्य.

LITHOGRAPH, v. t. शिलाया उपरि लिख् 6 P, शिलां रेखादिभिः मुद्र् 10 or अंक् 10. -s. शिला-पाषाण-लेखः-मुद्रा. -ER, s. शिलालेखकः, शिलामुद्राकृत् m. -Y, s. शिलालेखनविद्या, पाषाणलेखनं.

LITHONTRIPTIC, a. अश्मरीहर, अश्मरीघ्न (घ्नी f.).

LITHOTOMY, s. मूत्राश्मोच्छेदः.

LITHOTRIPSY, s. अश्मरीसंघर्षः.

LITIGANT, a. विवदमान, विवादार्थिन्, कार्यार्थिन्, व्यावहारिक (की f.). -s. वादिन् m., कार्यार्थी, व्यवहर्तृ m., अर्थी, विवादार्थी. —LITIGATE, v. i. वि-वद् 1 A, व्यव-हृ 1 P. -v. t. विवादास्पदीकृ 8 U. -ED, a. वादग्रस्त, विवादास्पदीकृत-भूत, वादानुगत. -ION, s. वि-,वादः, व्यवहारः. -LITIGIOUS, a. विवादप्रियशील, विवादार्थिन्, विवादपर-रत-आसक्त.

LITTER, s. शिबिका, याप्ययानं. 2 तृणशय्या, तृणसंस्तरः-शयनं. 3 शावकगणः-संघः. 4 द्रव्यसंकरः, व्यस्तता. -v. t. शावकगणं सू 2, 4 A, or उत्पद् c. 2 तृणेन आवृ 5 U or आस्तृ 5 U. 3 इतस्ततः विकॄ 6 P or विक्षिप् 6 P.

LITTLE, a. अल्प, अल्पक, क्षुद्र, लघु, अणु, तनु, सूक्ष्म, ह्रस्व, श्लक्ष्ण, दभ्र, अणुक; क्षुद्र-अल्प-लघु-परिमाणः अल्पमात्र, अबहु; स्वल्प, स्तोक, अप्रचुर, ईषत् in comp. 2 क्षुद्रतनु, अल्पकाय-शरीर-तनु. 3 क्षुद्र-लघुमति, कृपणमनस्-चेतस्-बुद्धि; (as a diminutive) ex. by the suffix क; 'a l. girl' बालिका; 'a l. boy' बालकः; 'a l. cottage' कुटिका; 'very l.' अल्पिष्ठ, अत्यल्प; 'a l. wealth' द्रव्यलेशः-लवः, स्तोकं द्रव्यं; 'a l. finger' कनिष्ठांगुलि f.; 'for a l. while' कंचित्कालं. -adv. 'a l.' ईषत्, किंचित्, स्तोकं, मनाक्, अभूरि, अबहु; oft. by आ, दर, ईषत् in comp.; 'a l. split' दरदलितः 'not a l. भृशं, अत्यंतं; 'a l. distant' अनतिदूर, ईषद्दूर; 'l. less' ईषदून, किंचिन्न्यून, कल्प प्राय-in comp.; 'a l. less than dead' मृतप्राय-कल्प; 'l.-minded' कृपणबुद्धि, क्षुद्र-लघु-चेतस्. -s. अल्पं, किंचित्, स्तोकं, अल्प-स्तोक-भागः, अल्पांशः, किंचन, मात्रा, लवः, कणः, लेशः; अल्पमात्रं; 'by l. and l.' अल्पाल्पं, अल्पशः, स्तोकशः. -NESS, s. अल्पता, तनुता, लघुता, स्तोकता, &c. 2 (Of mind) दीनता, कार्पण्यं, क्षुद्रता, कदर्यता, दैन्यं.

LITTORAL, a. तटस्थ, तीरस्थ.

LITURGY, s. प्रार्थनामार्गः, भक्तिमार्गः.

LIVE, v. i. वस् 1 P, नि-प्रति-°; अधिवस्, अध्यास् 2 A, अधि-ष्ठा 1 P (with acc.). 2 जीव् 1 P, प्र-अन् 2 P, श्वस् 2 P, धृ pass. or 6A, विद् 4A, वृत् 1A; 'here I l.' एषा ध्रिये (U. 3); 'as long as you l.' यावज्जीवं, यावत्प्राणान् धारयसि or असुधारणं करोषि. 3 (On) उप-आ-जीव्, शरीरवृत्तिं-प्राणयात्रां-कॢप् c. or निर्वृत् c. or कृ 8 U; प्राणधारणं कृ, निर्वह् 1 P; 'l.-ing on fish' मत्स्याजीव, मत्स्योपजीविन्; sometimes by वृत्ति f.; 'l. ed on fruits, roots, &c.' फलमूलादिभिः वृत्तिमकरोत्; 'l. ing on the leaves of trees falling down of themselves' स्वयंविशीर्णद्रुमपर्णवृत्तिता (K. v. 28); 'l. s on wild fruits' वन्यफलैः शरीरवृत्तिं निर्वर्तयति. 4 जीवितं-कालं गम् c. (गमयति) or या c. (यापयति) or नी 1 P or अतिवह् c or वृत् c.; 'l. through time' चिरस्थायिन्-अमर-a. भू 1 P. -a. सजीव; *See* LIVING below; 'l.-long' दीर्घ-चिर-कालीन, चिरस्थायिन्; 'l-stock' जीवधनं. -ING, a. सजीव, जीविन्, प्राणभृत्, सचेतन, प्राणधारिन्, चेतनावत्, सचेष्ट, सप्रमाण; 'a l. being' प्राणी, जीवी, जंतुः, प्राणभृत्, शरीरी, जीवः, देही, चेतनः, सत्त्वं; 'world of the l.' जीवलोकः. 2 वर्तमान, ध्रियमाण, विद्यमान; 'a l. poet' वर्तमानकविः. 3 अक्षय, अनश्वर, अनपायिन्, अविनाशिन्; अजर, अमर (spring &c.). 4 आ-उप-जीविन्, आजीव or वृत्ति in comp.; 'l. by arms' शस्त्रोपजीविन्; 'l. by agriculture' कृष्याजीव; 'l. wickedly' दुर्वृत्ति, दुर्वृत्त, पापाचरित, पापवृत्ति; 'l. by beggary' याचकवृत्ति, &c.; 'within l. memory' स्मर्तें काले; 'a l. sacrifice' जीवोपहारः; 'a l. death' जीवितमरणं. -s. जीवनं, प्राणधारणं, वासः. 2 जीविका, आ-उप-°; आजीवः, वृत्ति f., जीवनं, वर्तनं, आ-उप-जीवनं, जीवनोपायः, जीवन-जीव-साधनं, प्राण-शरीर-यात्रा, निर्वाहः, प्राण-जीव-निर्वाहः, प्राण-शरीर-स्थिति f.; जीवनार्थः. 3 धर्माध्यापकवृत्तिः, धर्मदायः; 'good l.' सुभोजनं, मिष्टाहारः, परमान्नभोजनं; 'bad l.' कदन्नभोजनं. -LIVELIHOOD, s. जीविका, वृत्तिः, जीवनं, प्राणयात्रा; *See* LIVING above; 'bare l.' ग्रासाच्छादनमात्रं, अशोदकमात्रं, दिननिर्वाहः. -LIVELY, a. सोल्लास, उल्लसित्, आनंदिन्, प्रहृष्ट, उल्लसित, प्रमुदित, आनंद-उल्लास-वृत्ति. 2 स-सत्त्व, सोत्साह, उत्साहशील, तेजस्विन्, तीव्र, तीक्ष्ण; 'of a l. countenance' प्रफुल्लवदन, हास्यमुख (खी f.), सुहास्यवदन, प्रसन्नमुख. -adv. सोत्साहं, प्रफुल्लतया, सोल्लासं. -NESS, *s.* उल्लासः, प्र-,हर्षः, आनंदः, प्रफुल्लता, उत्साहः, तेजस् *n.*, सत्त्वं.

LIVER, *s.* यकृत् *n.*, कालखंडं; कालकं, कालेयं.

LIVERY, *s.* वेषः, कुल-आर्य-वेषः; 'l.-man' कुलवेशधारी; पौरवेशः; 'l.-stable' अश्वपोषणशाला, अश्वशाला.

LIVID, *a.* नील, नीलवर्ण, सीसकवर्ण, नीलकृष्ण. -ITY, -NESS, *s.* नीलवर्णः, नीलिमन् *m.*, सीसकवर्णः.

LIXIVIUM, *s.* क्षारजलं-अंबु *n.* -LIXIVIOUS, *a.* क्षाराक्त, क्षारविशिष्ट.

LIZARD, *s.* सरटः-टुः, कृक(कु)लासः-शः, प्रतिसूर्यः-र्यकः; 'house-l.' गृहगोधा-धिका, मुस(श)ली, ज्येष्ठा-ष्ठी, गृहालिका.

LO, *interj.* पश्य, प्रेक्षस्व.

LOAD, *s.* भारः, भरः; धुर् *f*, पर्याहारः. 2 बाधा, पीडा, दुःखं; कष्टं; 'the body is a l. (to me)' भारः कायः, भारभूतं शरीरं, कष्टप्रायं शरीरं; 'l. s of gold' सुवर्णभाराः; 'bearing a l.' भारवाहन, भारसह, धूर्वह, धुरंधर. -*v. t.* भारं न्यस् 4 P or नि-धा 3 U or निविश् c. or आरुह् c. (रोपयति), भारेण पूर् 10, भारेण पीड् 10 or आक्रम् 1 U, 4 P, भाराक्रांत-*a.* कृ 8 U; 'trees l. ed with fruits' फलभाराक्रांता वृक्षाः; *See* BEND (*v. i.*). 2 (A gun) आग्नेयचूर्णेन पूर्, आग्नेयचूर्णं निविश् c. -ED, *a.* सभार, भाराक्रांत, भारग्रस्त, भारवत्, आरोपित-निवेशितभार, धुरीण. 2 गर्भ in comp., पूर्ण, पूरित; 'l. with perfume' परिमलाक्रांत, वासगर्भ, वासपूर्ण. -ING, *s.* भारारोपणं. 2 भारः.

LOADSTONE, *s.* अयस्कांतः, अयोमणिः, लोहकांतः, चुंबकः, लोहचुंबकः, चुंबकप्रस्तरः-मणिः.

LOAF, *s.* अपूपः, पूपः, पिष्टकः, करंभः.

LOAM, *s.* चिक्कण-स्निग्ध-मृत्तिका. -Y, *a.* चिक्कण, मसृण.

LOAN, *s.* ऋणं, ऋणदानं, धनप्रयोगः, आविहितकालात्, द्रव्यप्रयोगः.

LOATH, *a.* अनुत्सुक, अनिच्छु, वि-पराङ्-मुख (खी *f.*), विरक्त, अनिच्छत्, अकाम, निष्काम.

LOATHE, *v. t.* गर्ह् 1, 10 A, गुप् desid. (जुगुप्सते), अत्यंतं द्विष् 2 U; *See* ABHOR. -FUL, -SOME, *a.* बीभत्स, अतिगर्हित, घृणाकारिन्, अतिगर्ह्य, कुत्सित, घृणार्ह, जुगुप्सावह. -ING, *s.* बीभत्सः, जुगुप्सा, घृणा, गर्हा, अतिनिर्वेदः-द्वेषः. -INGLY, *adv.* सबीभत्सं, घृणापूर्वं.

LOB, *s.* स्थूलकायः, स्थूलशरीरः.

LOBBY, *s.* समीपशाला, उपगृहं-शाला.

LOBE, *s.* (कर्णस्य) पालि *f.*, पालिका, लतिका. 2 भागः, अंशः. -ED, *a.* पालिविशिष्ट.

LOCAL, *a.* स्थानिक (की *f.*), स्थानीय, दैशिक (की *f.*), देश्य, देशीय, देश-स्थान-in comp.; 'l. usage' देशाचारः; 'l. news' इहवृत्तं. 2 एक-देशीय-देशिन्-स्थानिक. -ITY, *s.* स्थानं, प्र-,देशः, स्थलं. -LY, *adv.* स्थानविषयं, स्थानमुद्दिश्य.

LOCATE, *v. t.* निविश् c., नि-धा 3 U, स्था c. (स्थापयति), विन्यस् 4 U; *See* PLACE. -ION, *s.* स्थापनं, निवेशनं, विन्यासः. 2 स्थानं, प्रतिष्ठानं, अधिकरणं. -IVE, *s.* सप्तमी विभक्तिः, अधिकरणं.

LOCK, *s.* तालः-लकं, तालयंत्रं. 2 (Of hair) पाशः, कलापः, केशकलापः-पाशः, अलकः; शिखंडकः, काकपक्षः (of young persons); चूडा, शिखा. 3 जलस्तंभनी-बंधनी. 4 आलिंगनं, आश्लेषः, उपगूहनं. -*v. t.* तालेन बंध् 9 P or पि-धा 3 U or निरुध् 7 U. 2 रुध्, बंध्, संयम् 1 A. 3 गाढं आलिंग् 1 P, दृढं परिष्वंज् 1 A; *See* CLASP, EMBRACE; 'l. ed in sleep' निद्रालीढ, निद्रानिमीलितलोचन; 'l.-jaw', 'l. ed jaw' हनुस्तंभः-ग्रहः. -ER, *s.* तालकसनाथः कोष्ठः, संपुटकः.

LOCKET, *s.* कुडुपः.

LOCOMOTION, *s.* स्थानांतर-स्थलांतर-गमनं, चलनं, गमनागमनं. 2 चलन-गमनागमन-शक्ति *f.* -LOCOMOTIVE, *a.* चल, चलन, जंगम, चलनशील, गतिविशिष्ट, चलनधर्मक, संचारिन्.

LOCUS, *s.* निधिः, निधानं.

LOCUST, *s.* शल(र)भः, शिरिः.

LOCUTION, *s.* वाक्यं, उक्ति *f.*, वचनं.

LODE, *s.* धातुरेखा.

LODH, *s.* लोध्रः, गालवः, शा(सा)बरः, तिरीटः, तिल्वः, मार्जनः.

LODGE, *v. i.* निवस् 1 P, वि-श्रम् 4 P, आ-श्रि 1 U, अव-स्था 1 A, स्था 1 P, वृत् 1 A, लग् 1 P, अनुबंध्-संज् pass. -*v. t.* नि-धा 3 U, न्यस् 4 U, निविश् c., स्था c. (स्थापयति); *See* PLACE. 2 वस् c., आश्रयं दा 3 U, वासस्थानं दा; 'to l. a suit or complaint' राज्ञे निविद् c. -*s.* उपगृहं, उद्यानगृहं. 2 Lodging, q. v. -ING, *s.* वासगृहं-स्थानं, वासः, नि-आ-वासः, वसति *f.*, नि-आ-लयः, आ-सं-श्रयः, निकेतनं; *See* HOUSE. -MENT, *s.* निवेशनं, स्थापनं. 2 अव-संस्थिति *f.* 3 निवेशः-शनं, समावासः.

LOFT, *s.* अट्टः, चंद्रशाला, शिरोगृहं, उपरिकोष्ठः.

LOFTY, *a.* उन्नत, तुंग, उच्च, उत्तम, उच्छ्रित, प्रांशु, सोच्छ्राय. 2 उद्धत, मदोद्धत, दृप्त, अवलिप्त, साटोप, मदोद्धत, गर्वोद्धत; *See* HIGH. 3 प्रौढ, प्रगल्भ, धीर, गंभीर, गुरु, महत्. -LY, *adv.* उच्चैः, ऊर्ध्वं. 2 सगर्वं, साटोपं, सदर्पं, उद्धतं. -NESS, *s.* (lit.) उन्नति *f.*, उत्सेधः, उच्छ्रयः, तुंगता, उच्चत्वं, प्रांशुता. 2 औद्धत्यं, आटोपः, अवलेपः, दर्पः, गर्वः, अभिमानः. 3 प्रौढता, प्रागल्भ्यं, धीरता, गुरुत्वं, महत्त्वं, माहात्म्यं, उत्कर्षः, उन्नतत्वं, उन्नतिः.

LOG, *s.* काष्ठं, दारु-काष्ठ-खंडः-डं; स्थूल-बृहत्-काष्ठं. 2 गतिमापः.

LOGARITHM, *s.* संवर्गमानं, घातप्रमापकः.

LOGGER-HEAD, *s.* स्थूल-जड बुद्धिः, मूढः, मूर्खः, जडः; 'to be at l. s' विवद् 1 A, कलि-कलहं-प्रारभ् 1 A. —ED, *a.* स्थूल-जड-धी बुद्धि.

LOGIC, *s.* तर्कः, न्यायः, आन्वीक्षिकी, न्याय-तर्क-शास्त्रं-विद्या, युक्तिवादः. —AL, *a.* तार्किक-नैयायिक-यौक्तिक-(की *f.*), तर्कशास्त्रविषयक. 2 तर्क न्याय-युक्ति-सिद्ध, तर्क-न्याय-संमत, न्यायानुसारिन्, तर्कानुरूप; 'a l. conclusion' निगमनं. —ALLY, *adv.* न्यायतः, यथान्यायं, तर्कानुसारेण, न्यायशास्त्रानुरूपं. —IAN, *s.* नैयायिकः, तार्किकः, तर्किन् *m.*, न्यायविद् *m.*, तर्क-न्याय-शास्त्रज्ञः.

LOGOMACHY, *s.* वाग्युद्धं, वाक्कलहः, वितंडा. 2 शब्दविवादः.

LOIN, *s.* श्रोणि-णी *f.*, कटि-टी *f.*, नितंबः, जघनं, स्फिच् *f.* (hip & l. s); श्रोणिफलकं, कटी-श्रोणि-तटं; 'gird the l. s' परिकरं बंध् 9 P, कटिं बंध्; 'born from one's own l. s' अंगज, अंगजात.

LOITER, *v. i.* विलंब् 1 A, मंदायते (D.), कालं क्षिप् 6 P or हृ 1 P; 'l. about' मंदं मंदं चल्-र् 1 P, इतस्ततः मंदं भ्रम् 1, 4 P, चिरं अव-स्था 1 A. —ER, *s.* कालक्षेपकः, अलसः, विलंबिन् *m.*, मंदगतिः, चिरक्रियः. —ING, *s.* विलंबनं, मंदगमनं, कालक्षेपः; *See* LINGER,—ER.

LOLL, *v. i.* आलस्येन अवलंब् 1 A or आश्रि 1 U or संविश् 6 P or शी 2 A. —*v. t.* लल् 10 (ललयति); 'l. the tongue' जिह्वां लल् or बहिष्कृ 8 U. —ING, *s.* ललनं.

LONE, LONELY, *a.* विविक्त, निर्जन, विजन, निर्मनुष्य, निभृत, न्यून-हीन-संचार, एकांत; निर्मानुष (षी *f.*). 2 अनाथ, असहाय, एकाकिन्, एक, केवल. 3 विविक्तप्रिय, विविक्तसेविन्; 'a l. place' विविक्तं, निर्जनदेशः; 'in a l. place' विविक्ते, विजने, छन्नं, निःशलाकं, रहः, उपांशु. —LINESS, *s.* विविक्तं, निर्जनता, विजनता. 2 एकाकिता, असहायता. 3 विविक्तसेवा-रुचि *f.*-प्रीति *f.* —SOME, *a.* निर्जन, दारुण, निरानंद, घोर.

LONG, *v. i.* (for) (अत्यंतं) स्पृह् 10 (with dat.), इष् 6 P, अभिलष् 1, 4 P, वांछ् 1 P, ईह् 1 A, कांक्ष् 1 P, आशंस् 1 A; *See* WISH; लुभ् 4 P, गृध् 4 P; sometimes ex. by denom. in य or काम्य; 'l. s for a son' पुत्रीयति, पुत्रकाम्यति; पुत्रमीप्सति, &c. 2 दोहदवती भू 1 P, दोहदिनी भू. —*a.* दीर्घ, आयत, आयामवत्, लंब; दीर्घपरिमाण, दीर्घाकार; विस्तृत, विस्तीर्ण. 2 चिर in comp., दीर्घ-चिरकालीन, दीर्घ-चिर-कालिक (की *f.*), चिरंतन (नी *f.*), चिरस्थायिन्-स्थित, चिरकाल-दीर्घकाल-स्थायिन्. 3 दूर, वि-सु-दूर. 4 दीर्घसूत्र, चिरक्रिय, विलंबकारिन्. 5 परिम-माण, मात्र, मित, परिमित in comp.; 'three fingers l.' त्र्यंगुलमात्र-परिमाण, त्र्यंगुलमित, त्र्यंगुल; 'being a l. way off' दूरस्थ, दूरस्थायिन्; 'a l. period' दीर्घ-चिर-कालः; 'for a l. time' चिरं, दीर्घं, चिराय; *See* (*adv.*); 'the l. run' आयति *f.*; 'a l. vowel' दीर्घस्वरः. —*adv.* चिरं, चिरेण, चिराय, दीर्घ-चिर-काले, दीर्घं, बहुकालं, चिरदिवसं. 2 दूरं, दूरं, दूरपर्यंतं; 'l. absent' चिरप्रवासिन्, चिरगत; 'l. sick' दीर्घ-चिर-रोगिन्; 'living l.' चिरजीविन्, आयुष्मत्; 'l. since left' चिरत्यक्त, &c.; 'how l.' कियच्चिरं, कियंतं कालं, कियत्कालं यावत्; 'how l. after' कियच्चिरेण; 'not very l.' नातिचिरं; 'very l.' सुचिरं; 'l. ago' प्रागेव, पूर्वमेव, अतीतदीर्घकाले; 'not l. ago' नातिचिरात् प्राक्, अनतिपूर्वं; 'ere l.' अचिरेण, अचिरात्; 'as l. as'-'so l.' यावत्-तावत्; 'as l. as one lives' यावज्जीवं; आमरणात्; 'the whole year l.' आवर्षांतात्, वर्षपर्यंतं; 'l. after' बहोः कालात्, दीर्घकालानंतरं. In comp. words ex. by दीर्घ, चिर, लंब, दूर, आयत; 'l.-armed' दीर्घभुज, लंबहस्त; 'l.-bellied' लंबोदर; 'l.-continuing' चिरस्थायिन्; 'l.-eyed' आयताक्ष, आयतनेत्र; 'l.-headed, सूक्ष्मनिपुण-मति, विदग्ध, पटु; 'l.-lasting' चिरस्थायिन्, चिरकालिक; *See* (*a.*); 'l.-legged'. दीर्घपाद, ऊर्ध्वजानु, ऊर्ध्वज्ञु; 'l.-lived' चिर(रं)जीविन्, दीर्घायुस्, चिरायुस्, चिरायुष्य, जैवातृक, आयुष्मत्; 'l. pepper' कृष्णा, उपकुल्या, वैदेही, मागधी, चपला, कणा, उ(ऊ)षणा, पिप्पलिः-ली, शौंडी, कोला; करिपिप्पली, कपिवल्ली, कोलवल्ली, श्रेयसी, वशिरः; 'l. pepper root' ग्रंथिकं, पिप्पलीमूलं, चटकाशिरस् *n.*; 'l.-sighted' दूर-दीर्घ-दृष्टि; 'l.-suffering' सहिष्णु, सहनशील, क्षमिन्, बहुक्षम; (*s.*) क्षमा, सहिष्णुता, सहनशीलता. —ER, *a.* दीर्घतर; 'any l.' अतः परं-ऊर्ध्वं, इतः परं; 'why delay any l.' किमित्यधुना विलंब्यते. —ING, *a.* अत्यभिलाषिन्, अत्याकांक्षिन्; कुतूहलिन्, स्पृहयालु, उत्कंठित; उत्कट, लालस, अत्युत्सुक; 'a l. desire' उत्कटेच्छा; 'a l. woman' श्रद्धालुः, दोहदवती. —*s.* अत्यभिलाषः, अतिस्पृहा-वांछा, अत्याकांक्षा, उत्कंठा, लालसा, औत्सुक्यं, अतिलिप्सा; इच्छा, कामः, मनोरथः, स्पृहा, तृष्णा, आकांक्षा; 'the l. of a pregnant woman' दोहदः, गर्भदोहदः. —INGLY, *adv.* सस्पृहं, सतृष्णं, सोत्सुकं, सोत्कंठं. —LONGANIMITY, *s.* क्षमा, क्षांति *f.* —LONGEVAL,-LONGEVOUS, *a.* चिरंजीविन्; *See* LONG-LIVED.—LONGEVITY, *s.* दीर्घायुः, चिरायुः. —LONGIMETRY, *s.* दैर्घ्यमानं. —LENGTH, *s.* दैर्घ्यं, दीर्घता-त्वं, आयामः, द्राघिमन् *m.*, आरोहः, आयति *f.*, विस्तारः, आनाहः, विस्तृति *f.*, वितति *f.* 2 मात्रा, अवधिः, मर्यादा, पर्यंतः; 'my rudeness (impudence) was carried to the l. of taking up arms' आयुध-

पग्निग्रहं यावदत्यारूढो दुर्योगः (U. 6). 3 मानं, प्र-परिमाणं. 4 चिर-दीर्घ-कालः, कालदैर्घ्यं; 'to such a l.' एतावत्पर्यंतं, यावत् (with acc.); 'for a l. of time' चिरं, चिरकालं; 'to a great l.' अतिमात्रं, अतिमर्यादं; 'at l.' सविस्तरं, विस्तरेण, सुविस्तरं-रेण, विस्तरशः, असंक्षेपतः; अंतं, अंततः, शेषे, चिरकालात्, चिरस्य, अतीतदीर्घकाले; 'spread at l.' विस्तीर्ण; 'to lie at full l.' दंडवत् पत् 1 P. -EN, v. t. दीर्घीकृ 8 U, प्र-वि-तन् 8 U, विस्तॄ c., प्र-वि-सृ c., आयम् 1 A, आयती-वितती-कृ. -v. i. विस्तॄ-वितन् pass., दीर्घीभू. -WISE, adv. अन्वायामं, अनुदैर्घ्यं, अनु in comp. -Y, a. विस्तीर्ण, दीर्घ, आयत, सविस्तर, असंक्षिप्त.

LONGITUDE, s. ध्रुवकः, द्राघिमन् m. 2 रेखांशः; (of heavenly objects) भोगः; 'circle of l.' रेखांशवृत्तं.-LONGITUDINAL, a. अनुदैर्घ्यं, अन्वायाम.

LOOBY, s. स्थूलजनः, ग्राम्यः, वृषलः, प्राकृतः.

LOOK (at), v. i. दृश् 1 P, अव-वि-आ-लोक् 1 A, 10, ईक्ष् 1 A, निरूप् 10, निर्वर्ण् 10, दृष्टिं दा 3 U or क्षिप् 6 P, लक्ष् 10; 'l. intently at' नयनैः-दृष्टिभिः-पा 1 P, निध्यै 1 P, (तां राघवं दृष्टिभिरापिबंत्यः &c. R. VII. 12). 2 भा 2 P, आ-प्रति°-,लक्ष्-दृश्-pass.; oft. by वदन, मुख, आनन in comp.; 'she l. s sad' विषण्णा लक्ष्यते or आभाति, &c.; 'that l. s like wantonness' तत्साहसाभासं (Mal. 2); 'l. ing dejected' विषण्णवदन, म्लानमुख, &c.; 'l. well' शुभ् 1 A; 'l. now' ननु, पश्य. -about, परितो वीक्ष्, अनु-इष् 4 P. -after, अवेक्ष्, रक्ष् 1 P, पा c. (पालयति); *See* 'Take care' under CARE; योगक्षेमं वह् 1 U, (मुग्धाया मे जनन्या योगक्षेमं वहस्व M. 4). 2 अन्विष्; निरूप् 10, मृग् 10 A. -down, अवेक्ष्, अधो दृश्; 'l. down upon' अवमन् 4 A, उपेक्ष्; *See* CONTEMN. -for, आशंस् 1 A, अपेक्ष्, प्रति-इष् 6 P; *See* EXPECT. 2 अन्विष्, मृग्; *See* SEARCH. -in, आविर्भू 1 P, आत्मानं दृश् c., प्रकटीभू; 'l. in the face' संमुखी-अभिमुखी-भू (with gen.); *See* FACE. -into, अव-सं-निर्-परि-ईक्ष्, अनुसं-धा 3 U, निरूप्; *See* EXAMINE; 'l. into the matter very closely' अतिनिपुणमवेक्ष्यतां सोऽर्थः. -on, प्रेक्ष्, मिष् 6 P; मिषतामाच्छिनत्ति नः (K. II. 46) 'snatches (the oblation), we helplessly l.-ing on'. 2 (Upon) मन् 4 A, गण् 10; *See* CONSIDER. -out, अव-धा 3 U, सावधान-a. भू 1 P. -over, संदृश्-ईक्ष्; निरूप्, निरीक्ष्. -to, सं-विईक्ष्, अवधानं दा 3 U; ex. by 'Care' q. v. 2 आ-अव-लंब् 1 A, आश्रि 1 U. -up, ऊर्ध्वं दृश् or ईक्ष्. उदीक्ष्, उन्मुखीभू; 'l. ing up to heaven' नभोदत्तदृष्टि, गगनदृष्टि; 'l. up to' प्रतीक्ष्, उद्-दृश्; मन्, गण्, परिकॢप् c.; 'the people l. up to you as their saviour' आत्मनो रक्षकत्वेन त्वामेवामी जनाः प्रतीक्षंते, गणयंति or परिकल्पयंति. -s. दृष्टि f., दर्शनं, ईक्षणं, वीक्षणं, प्रेक्षणं, वीक्षितं, विलोकितं, आ-वि-अव-लोकनं, दृष्टिपातः, दृक्पातः. 2 रूपं, आकारः, आकृति f., दर्शनं, आलोकः, चर्या, आभा, छाया, वदनाकारः, मुखच्छाया, मुखं, वदनं; 'a l. of displeasure' अकृपादृष्टिः; 'side-l.' कटाक्षः, अपांगदर्शनं; 'l.-out' अवेक्षा, समीक्षा, अवधानं; 'to be on the l.-out' अवेक्ष्, अव-धा 3 U, अवहित-a भू. -ER, s. द्रष्टृ m., दर्शिन्, वीक्षकः. 2 (On) प्रेक्षकः, प्रेक्षमाणः. -ING, a. पश्यत्, दर्शिन्; दृष्टि, नयन in comp.; 'l. in all directions' विष्वग्दृष्टि, सर्वतोदत्तदृष्टि; 'l. up' उन्मुख, ऊर्ध्वदृष्टि; 'l. well' शुभ-सु-दर्शन, सुदृश्य, शोभनाकार, प्रेक्षणीय, शुभानन. -s. दर्शनं, विलोकनं, वीक्षणं, निर्वर्णनं, आलोकः, &c.; *See* (s.) above; 'l.-glass' आदर्शः, मुकुरः, दर्पणः.

LOOM, s. वेमन् m., वेमः, वाय(प)दंडः, तंत्रवापः. -v. i. अस्पष्टरूपेण दृश् pass., दूरे वृत् 1 A or स्था 1 P.

LOON, s. दुर्जनः, जाल्मः, कितवः, धूर्तः.

LOOP, s. शिक्यं, काचः. 2 पाशः; पुटः-टं. 3 छिद्रं, रंध्रं; 'suspended in a l.' काचित, शिक्यित; 'l.-hole' छिद्रं, रंध्रं, गवाक्षः, जालं; निर्गमः, निर्गमद्वारं, अपक्रमः; मुक्ति f., मोक्षः.

LOOSE, a. शिथिल, प्र-,श्लथ, लस्त, विगलित, चलित, मुक्त. 2 अबद्ध, उद्ग्रथित, उत्सूत्र, बंधनरहित-शून्य, उद्दाम, प्रमुक्त. 3 विरल, असंहत, अदृढसंधि. 4 अ-व्यवस्थित, अनियत, अनिर्णीत, संदिग्ध, असंक्षिप्त; अ-स्थिर. 5 असंबद्ध, निःसंग, निरन्वय. 6 उच्छृंखल, निर्मर्याद; अनवस्थ, दुर्वृत्त. व्यभिचारिन्, व्यसनिन्, दुराचार. 7 गर्ह्य, निंद्य, अश्लील; 'l. conduct' दुराचारः; व्यसनं, नीतिभ्रंशः; 'a l. man' लंपटः, व्यसनी; 'a l. woman' बंधकी, पुंश्चली, भ्रष्टा; 'let l.' मुच् 6 P; *See* (v.); 'break l.' बंधनं भिद् or छिद् 7 P, बंधनात् भ्रंश् 1 A, 4 P. -v. t., -EN, v. t. शिथिलयति (D.), शिथिलीकृ 8 U, श्र(श्रं)थ्-श्लथ् 1 P, 10 (श्लथयति), स्रंस् c., श्लथीकृ. 2 मुच् 6 P or c., वि-निर्-उत्°-; मोक्ष् 10. विसृज् 6 P or c., बंधनात् मुच्. 3 उद्-ग्रंथ् 9 P, उद्-अव-मुच्, वियुज् 7 A, 10, विश्लिष् c., विसं-धा 3 U. -v. i.,-EN, v. i. शिथिलीभू 1 P, श्र(श्र)थ् 1 A, स्रंस् 1 A, गल् 1 P, शिथिलायते (D.) -adv., -LY, adv. शिथिलं, श्लथं. अदृढं. विरलं, असंहतं, अनियतं; दुर्वृत्तवत्, निर्मर्यादं; 'l. hanging matted hair' श्लथलंबिन्यः जटाः; 'hanging l.' लम्त. -ING, -ENING, s. शिथिलीकरणं, मोचनं, मोक्षणं, मुक्ति f., श्रंथनं. -NESS, s. शैथिल्यं, प्र-,श्लथः. स्रंसः, श्लथता, लस्तता, अदृढता, अनियतता, विरलता, व्यसनिता. दुराचारः, अनवस्था, लांपट्यं, व्यभिचारः; *See* LAXITY.

Lop, *v. t.* छिद् 7 P, कृत् 6 P, लू 9 P; *See* Cut. 2 आ-अव-लंब् c. –*v. i.* आ-अव-लंब् 1 A. –per, *s.* Cutter, q. v.

Lopsided, *a.* एकपार्श्वे पतयालु.

Loquacious, *a.* वावदूक, वाचाल-ट, मुखर; *See* Garrulous. –ly, *adv.* वाचालतया. –ness, –Loquacity, *s.* वावदूकता, वाचालता, बहुभाषित्वं, जल्पकता, मौखर्यं.

Lord, *s.* ईशः, प्रभुः, ईश्वरः, स्वामिन् *m.*, अधिपः, पतिः, ईशितृ *m.*, अधिभूः, नायकः, नेता, भर्ता; नाथः; इंद्रः in comp.; राजा, परिवृढः, इभ्यः, धनी, आढ्यः; 'to be l. of' प्र-भू 1 P, ईश् 2 A, (with gen.); *See* Master; 'supreme l.' सर्वेश्वरः, अधिराजः; नरेंद्रः, क्षितिपतिः, स्वर्गाधिपः, जगन्नाथः-नायकः, &c. 2 (Title of address) देवः, महाराजः, स्वामी, आर्यपुत्रः (by wives); भर्ता (by servants &c). 3 परमेश्वरः, भगवान्, प्रभुः, ईश्वरः. –*v. i.* (सदर्पं सधर्षं) ईश् or शास् 2 P. –like,–ly, *a.* राजोचित, प्रभुयोग्य; राजसदृश (शी *f.*), राजार्ह; ईश्वरीय, ऐश्वर (री *f.*). 2 ओजस्विन्, दीप्तिमत्, तेजस्विन्; *See* Majestic. 3 धृष्ट, अवलिप्त, ऐश्वर्यमत्त, दृप्त, गर्वित, उत्सिक्त; *See* Haughty. –*adv.* सधर्षं, सदर्पं, उद्धतं, ऐश्वर्यमदेन. –ship, *s.* देवः, &c.; *See* above; 'his l.' तत्रभवान्; महाराजः; 'your l.' अत्रभवान्, देवः, &c. 2 प्रभुत्वं, स्वामित्वं, ऐश्वर्यं, अधिकारः. 3 राज्यं, विषयः.

Lore, *s.* विद्या, ज्ञानं; *See* Learning.

Loricate, *v. t.* कवचेन-पटलेन आस्तृ 5 U or आच्छद् 10. –*a.* सकवच, पटलयुक्त.

Lorn, *a.* अनाथ, अशरण; *See* Forlorn.

Lose, *v. t.* अप-,हृ c., त्यज् 1 P, हा 3 P or c. (हापयति). 2 वियुज्-विहा-परिहा-pass., विनाकृ 8 U (with instr.); भ्रंश् 1 A, 4 P, परि-प्र-°, च्यु 1 A, प्र-वि-°, (with abl.); *See* Deprived also; 'he lost his life' प्राणैर्वियुक्तः, विगतासुर्बभूव, प्राणहीनः; प्राणैरहीयत; 'lost his realm' राज्याद्भ्रष्टः-च्युतः; 'l. s his friends' मित्रैर्वियुज्यते; 'he lost his wife' तत्पत्नी मृता, पत्न्या विरहितः. 3 (Destroy) नश् c., क्षि 1, 5 P or c., अप-चि 5 U, उच्छिद् 7 P, प्र-वि-ध्वंस् c. 4 (Not to find) ex. by नश् 4 P, प्रभ्रंश्; 'have you lost a camel' अपि युष्माकमुष्ट्रो नष्टः; 'the lost ring' नष्टमंगुलीयकं; 'l. the way' मार्गात्-पथः-भ्रंश् or च्यु or विचल् 1 P; 'he lost his way' पथभ्रष्ट-नष्ट-पथः or उन्मार्गगामी अभूत्; 'lost his caste' जातिभ्रष्टः. 5 पराजि-पराभू-pass. (in battle &c.); 'l. one's wits' बुद्धिहीन-*a.* भू; 'to l. time' कालं व्यर्थं नी 1 P or विक्षिप् 6 P, कालं हृ 1 P or या c. (यापयति), कालहरणं-कालक्षेपं कृ 8 U, विलंब् 1 A; 'l. good name' चारित्र्यं-कीर्तिं कलंकयति or मलिनयति (D.) or दुष् c. (दूषयति); 'l. one's consciousness' मुह् 4 P, मुर्छ् 1 P, चेतनां-संज्ञां हा, नष्टचेतन-लुप्तसंज्ञ-*a.* भू; 'we don't l. any thing (in this way)' न नः किंचित् छिद्यते (S. B. 345), नास्माकं किमपि हीयते; 'to l. oneself in' आसक्त-निरत-*a.* भू; *See* Absorb. –er, *s.* प्राप्तापायः, अपाय-हानि-सहः, पराजितः, लब्धहानिः, प्राप्तनाशः-क्षयः. –Lost, *a.* नष्ट, भ्रष्ट, च्युत, गत, वीन, हीन, त्यक्त, हृत, हारित, क्षीण, लुप्त; 'who has l. his office' च्युताधिकारः, अधिकारभ्रष्टः; 'who has l. wealth' अर्थहीनः, गतविभवः, नष्टार्थः; 'who has l. his way' पथभ्रष्टः, उन्मार्गप्रवृत्तः, दिङ्मूढः; 'who has l. everything' हतसर्वस्वः; 'who has l. one eye' अक्ष्णा अंधः, एकाक्षिविकलः; 'l. to shame' त्यक्त-निरस्तलज्ज, व्रीडाहीन; 'l. to sense of freedom' स्वातंत्र्यरसानभिज्ञ; 'l. in meditation' ध्यानपर-परायण-निष्ठ-मग्न, चिंतासक्त; 'the bone fell and was l.' अस्थि निपतितं नयनविषयातीतं च; 'to be l.' नश्, अंतर् इ, तिरोधा pass., तिरोभू. 2 मोहित, मूढ, भ्रांतचित्त-बुद्धि. –Loss, *s* हानि *f.*, क्षयः, सं-उप-परिक्षयः, वि-,नाशः, अपायः, अपचयः, लोपः, भ्रंशः, च्युति *f.*, व्ययः, ध्वंसः, प्र-वि-ध्वंसः, वियोगः, अपहारः, अत्ययः, त्यागः, अलाभः, क्षति *f.* 2 पराजयः, पराभवः, भंगः; 'compensating l.' क्षतिपूरणं; 'profit and l.' लाभालाभौ; 'l. of time' कालहरणं-क्षेपः, विलंबः; 'l. of caste' जातिभ्रंशः; 'l. of army' सैन्यनाशः, बलव्यसनं; 'to be at a l.' मुह् 4 P; 'being at a l. what to do or say' किंकर्तव्यता-किंवक्तव्यता-मूढ.

Lot, *s.* अंशः, वि-,भागः, उद्धारः. 2 भाग्यं, दैवं, भागधेयं, दैवगति *f.*, दशा, भवितव्यता; *See* Fate. 3 गुटिका; 'fall to the l. of' आपत् 1 P, उपनम् 1 P, उप-स्था 1 U; आपतंति हि संसारपथमवतीर्णानामेते वृत्तांताः (Ka. 175); 'happiness will be your l' त्वं सुखभाग् भविष्यसि, तव सुखमुपनमेत्.

Loth, *a.* *See* Loath.

Lotion, *s.* धावनं, धावनौषधं.

Lottery, *s.* गुटिकापातः; गुटिकापातेन निर्णयः.

Lotus, *s.* पद्मं, कमलं नलिनं, अरविंदं, उत्पलं, कुवलयं, सरसिजं, अब्जं, अंभोजं, महोत्पलं, शतपत्रं, सहस्रपत्रं, कुशेशयं, पंकेरुहं, पंकजं, सरोरुहं, तामरसं, सारसं, सरसीरुहं, पुष्करं, अंभोरुहं, बिसप्रसूनं, राजीवं, अंबुजं; 'white l.' पुंडरीकं, सितांभोज; 'red l.' कोकनदं, रक्तोत्पलं; 'blue l.' इंदीवरं, नीलोत्पलं. 2 (The plant) नलिनी, कमलिनी, पद्मिनी, मृणालिनी; कुमुदिनी; 'l. stalk' नालं-लः-ली-ला; 'l. fibre or film' मृणालः-ली-लं, बिसं-शं; 'l. filament' किंजल्कः, केस(स)रः-रं; 'l. root or bulb' करहाटः,

शिफाकंदः, शालु(लु)कं; 'l. seed' कमलाक्षः, पद्मबीजं; 'seed vessel of l.' बीजकोशः, वराटकः; 'new leaf of l.' संवर्तिका, नवदलं; 'an assemblage of l. es' षंडः, खंडः, पद्मखंडः.

LOUD, *a.* उच्च, तार, महत्, गुरु, उत्ताल; महास्वन, गुरुस्वर, महाध्वनिकर (री *f.*), महा-बहु-घोष, महाशब्द, घोषण; 'a l. noise' तारस्वरः, उच्चैर्घोषः, महाशब्दः-स्वनः, प्रणादः, तुमुलरवः. —*adv.*, —LY, *adv.* उच्चैः, तार-उच्च-स्वरेण, प्रोच्चैः, महाशब्देन, महास्वनेन; 'still l. er' उच्चैस्तरां. —NESS, *s.* उच्चता, महत्त्वं, उत्तालता, &c.

LOUNGE, *v. i.* उदास् 2 A, आलस्येन कालं क्षिप् 6 P or हृ 1 P, अलसीभू. —ER, *s.* अलसजनः, कालक्षेपकः, उदासीनः, कार्यपुटः. —ING, *a.* अलस, मंद; *See* LAZY; 'l. gait' मत्तेभगति *f.*-गमनं.

LOUSE, *s.* यूकः-का, केशकीटः; 'l.-egg' लिक्षा. —Y, *a.* बहुयूक, यूकापूर्ण, यूकोपद्रुत, सयूक.

LOUT, *s.* ग्राम्यजनः; वृषलः, ग्रामीणः, स्थूलजनः. —ISH, *a.* ग्राम्य, स्थूल, अशिष्ट, असभ्य; स्थूल-बुद्धि-मति.

LOUVER, *s.* धूमरंध्रं, धूमपथः-निर्गमः.

LOVAGE, *s.* अजमोदा, उग्रगंधा, ब्रह्मदर्भा, यवा(मा)निका.

LOVE, *s.* प्रेमन् *m. n.*, अभिलाषः, स्नेहः, रागः, वात्सल्यं, अनुरागः, प्रणयः, भावः, प्रीति *f.*, प्रेम-प्रीति-स्नेह-भावः (all with loc.); 'l. for God' ईश्वरभक्ति *f.* 2 (Amorous) कामः, अनंगरागः, शृंगारः, शृंगारभावः, रति *f.*, रतिसुखं, मदनः. 3 (God of love) कामः, मदनः, स्मरः; *See* CUPID. 4 दया, अनुकंपा. 5 रुचि *f.*, अभिरुचिः, आसक्ति *f.*, व्यसनं, अभिनिवेशः, प्रीतिः. 6 (Darling) प्रियः-या, प्रियतमः-मा, दयितः-ता; 'to fall or be in l. with' स्निह् 4 P, अनुरंज् pass., भावं-अभिलाषं बंध् 9 P or निविश् c., अनुरागवत्-बद्धभाव-मोहित-*a.* भू; 'l.-affected', 'l.-stricken', 'under the influence of l.' अनंगतप्त-पीडित, कामार्त, कामवश, कामातुर, अनंगविधुर, मदनावस्थ, स्मराकुल, कामासक्त; 'to make l.' विवाहार्थं प्रार्थ् 10 A or आराध् c.; 'gestures of l.' शृंगारचेष्टा, हावः, विलासः, विभ्रमः, लीला, भावः; 'l.-knot' प्रेमग्रंथिः-बंधः; 'l.-letter' अनंग-मदन-लेखः, मन्मथलेखः; 'l.-match' प्रेम-विवाह-संबंधः; 'l.-quarrel' प्रणय-प्रेम-प्रीति-कलहः, प्रणयकोपः; 'l.-sick' कामार्त, कामातुर, कामपीडित, अनंगतप्त, विधुर, मदनविह्वल; 'l.-song' शृंगारगीतं; 'l.-tale' प्रेम-शृंगार-कथा; 'l.-token' प्रीतिलक्षणं, प्रेमाभिज्ञानं. —*v. t.* कम् 10 A (amorously); प्री-अनुरंज्-आसंज्-pass.; gen. ex. by स्निह् (with loc.); बंध्, निविश् c. with (*s.*); 'the king l. s Sâgarikâ' नृपः सागरिकायां बद्धानुरागः, आसक्तचित्तः, कृतप्रणयः, &c. 2 रुच् 1 A, आनंद् 1 P, मुद् 1 A, तुष् 4 P (with instr.); ex. by प्रिय-*a.*; *See* FOND, LIKE; 'I l. music' संगीतप्रियोस्मि; 'l. knowledge' विद्यासक्तचित्तो भव. —ABLE, *a.* स्नेहार्ह, प्रिय. —ED, *a.* प्रिय, दयित, कांत, इष्ट, अभीप्सित, स्निग्ध, हृद्य, मनीषित. —ER, *s.* (Amorous) कामुकः, कामिन् *m.*, कांतः, प्रियः, दयितः, वल्लभः, रमणः, नायकः, इष्टः, प्राणेशः, जीवितेशः. 2 प्रणयिन् *m.*, अनुरागी, निरतः, सेवी-प्रियः-in comp.; 'l. of knowledge' प्रियज्ञानः, ज्ञाननिरतः, ज्ञानेप्सुः; 'a l. of learned men' आगमवृद्धसेवी (R. VI. 41). —ING, *a.* प्रणयिन्, अनुरागवत्, सस्नेह, प्रणयवत्, प्रीतिमत्, वत्सल, अनुरक्त, अनुरागिन्, आसक्त, प्रिय, नि-,रत, सेविन् in comp; 'l. gambling' द्यूतासक्त, द्यूतसेविन्; 'a l. husband' अनुरागवान् पतिः; 'l. kindness' कृपा, दया, कारुण्यं, वात्सल्यं, प्रसादः, अनुग्रहः, स्नेहः, अनुकंपा. —INGLY, *adv.* सप्रणयं, सस्नेहं, सानुरागं, स्नेहेन, वात्सल्यात्, प्रीतिपूर्वं. —LOVELY, *a.* कांत, सुंदर (री *f.*), रुचिर, शोभन, सुभग, मनोज्ञ, मंजु, मंजुल, चारु, मनोरम, मनोहर, ललित, वाम, मुग्ध, कमनीय, अभिराम; *See* BEAUTIFUL. —LINESS, *s.* कांति *f.*, सौंदर्यं, शोभा, श्रीः, लावण्यं, सुभगता, चारुता; *See* BEAUTY.

LOW, *a.* (Of place) नीच, निम्न, नत, नीचस्थ, अधःस्थ, अधस्तन (नी *f.*), अवाच्. 2 ह्रस्व, नीच, अल्पाकार, खर्व; अनुच्च, अतुंग. 3 नीच, अप-नि-कृष्ट, अधम, हीन, जघन्य, अवर, खल, क्षुद्र, अनार्य, याप्य, गर्ह्य, अश्लील, निंद्य, (language); *See* MEAN; 'a l. man' अपसदः, नीचः, पृथग्जनः, जाल्मः, दुर्वृत्तः. 4 (Voice) नीच, मंद्र, मंद, धीर, ग(गं)भीर. 5 (Price) स्वल्प, अल्प, मित, परिमित, अल्पमूल्य. 6 (L.-spirited) अवसन्न, खिन्न, उद्विग्न, म्लान, विषण्ण, विमनस्, दीन-उद्विग्न-मनस्-चेतस्; *See* DEJECTED. 7 नम्र, विनीत, अनुद्धत, निरभिमान; *See* HUMBLE. 8 निःसत्त्व, रूक्ष, असार, अपौष्टिक (की *f.*) (as food); 'of l. rank', 'l.-born' नीच, हीनजाति, अंत्यजातीय, नीचकुलज, हीनकुल, दुष्कुलीन, अधमजन्मन्, नीचवंशप्रसूत, हीनवर्ण. —*adv.* नीचैः, अनुच्चं, नीच in comp.; 'going l.' नीचग; 'l. bending grass' नीचैः प्रणतानि तृणानि. 2 मंदं, मृदु, सौम्यं. 3 अधस्, अधोभागे, अधस्तात्. —*v. i.* रेभ् 1 A, नद् 1 P, नर्द् 1 P, गर्ज् 1 P, हंभारवं कृ 8 U. —ING, *s.* रेभणं, रेभितं, हंभा, हंभारवः. —*a.* हंभारवकारिन्, रेभमाण. —NESS, *s.* नीचता, निम्नता, अधमता, अपकर्षः, हीनता, जघन्यता, गर्ह्यता, मंद्रता, गांभीर्यं, विषादः, अवसादः, उद्वेगः, दैन्यं, दौर्मनस्यं, ग्ला-म्ला-नि *f.*, &c. —LOWER, *a.* अधर, अधरस्थ, अधस्तन, नीचस्थ, अधःस्थ, अवाच्, अधः in comp.; 'l. world' अधोलोकः; 'l. garment' अधोंशुकं; 'l. region' अधःप्रदेशः; 'the l. classes' हीन-अधम-जातीयाः,

अवरवर्णाः, अंत्यजातीयाः. -*v. t.* न्यूनीकृ 8 U, ऊन् 10, ह्रस् c., अल्पीकृ, लघूकृ, लघयति (D.), अपचि 5 U. 2 अपकृष् 1 P, अव-नम् c. (नमयति), भ्रंश् c., गौरवं-मानं-भंज् 7 P or हृ 1 P; *See* HUMBLE. 3 अवतॄ c., अधः कृ, अधः-नि-पत् c. -*v. i.* न्यूनीभू 1 P, अल्पीभू, अपाचि-क्षि- pass., ह्रस् 1 P. 2 नम्रीभू. 3 मलिनीभू, कलुषीभू, तमोवृत-मेघाच्छन्न-*a.* भू. 4 भ्रूभंगं कृ, भ्रूवौ संकुच् 1 P. -*s.* दुर्दिनं, मेघतिमिरं, तिमिरावृतत्वं, साभ्रता. 2 कालुष्यं, मुखमालिन्यं. -ING, *a.* तमोवृत, मेघाच्छन्न, साभ्र, दुर्दिनग्रस्त. 2 मलिन, कलुष. —LOWLY, *a.* नम्र, विनत, सविनय, निरभिमान, अनहंकार, अनुद्धत, अगर्व, नम्रवृत्ति, दर्पहीन; *See* HUMBLE. -*adv.*,-LY, *adv.* सविनयं, विनयेन,नम्रतया, अनुद्धतं. -NESS, *s.* विनयः, नम्रता, अनहंकारः, अगर्वः, अनभिमानः, नम्रवृत्ति *f.* —LOWLAND, *s.* निम्नदेशः-भूमि *f.*, नीचप्रदेशः, उपत्यका. -ER, *s.* निम्नदेशीयः.

LOYAL, *a.* भक्त, अनुरक्त, दृढभक्ति, भक्तियुक्त-मत्, सानुराग, आसक्त; '1. to the king' नृपानुरक्त, प्रभुभक्तिनिष्ठ, राजाज्ञानुवर्तिन्, नृपासक्त; 'a 1. wife' सती, साध्वी, पतिव्रता, एकपत्नी, सुचरित्रा; '1. husband' स्वदारनिरतः, भार्यानुरक्तः. -LY, *adv*, भक्तिपूर्वं, सानुरागं, दृढभक्तिपूर्वं, राजनिष्ठापूर्वं. -TY, *s.* भक्ति *f.*, अनुरागः, आसक्ति *f.*, प्रभु-स्वामि-भक्तिः, राजभक्तिः-अनुरागः, दृढभक्तिः, राजनिष्ठा; (in a wife) पातिव्रत्यं, सतीत्वं, &c.

LUBBER, *s.* ग्राम्यः, स्थूलजनः, स्थूलधीः-बुद्धिः. -LY, *a.* स्थूल, अदक्ष. 2 स्थलीय.

LUBRIC, LUBRICIOUS, *a.* स्निग्ध, चिक्कण, श्लक्ष्ण, मेदुर. —LUBRICATE, *v. t.* अभ्यंज् 7 P, स्निग्धीकृ 8 U, स्नेहेन अंज्. -ED, *a.* अभ्यक्त, स्नेहाक्त. -ION, *s.* अभ्यंजनं, स्निग्धीकरणं. -LUBRICITY, *s.* स्निग्धता, चिक्कणता.

LUCID, *a.* दीप्तिमत्, शोभन, सुप्रभ, तेजस्विन्, उज्ज्वल, देदीप्यमान; *See* BRIGHT. 2 विशद, स्वच्छ, निर्मल, अ-वि-मल, प्रसन्न, शुद्ध. 3 व्यक्त, सुस्पष्ट, भिन्नार्थ, स्पष्टार्थ. 4 प्रसन्नचित्त; '1. interval' चित्तप्रसादः. -LY, *adv.* स्पष्टं, सुव्यक्तं, भिन्नार्थं, स्फुटं, विशदं. -NESS, *s.* दीप्ति *f.*, कांति *f.*, शोभा, प्रभा, द्युति *f.* 2 स्पष्टता, वैशद्यं, प्रसादः, वैमल्यं.

LUCIFER, *s.* शुक्रः, भार्गवः; '1. match' अग्निशलाका.

LUCIFEROUS, *a.* प्रकाशद, दीप्तिकर (री *f.*).

LUCIFORM, *a.* तेजोमय (यी *f.*), प्रकाशविशिष्ट.

LUCK, *s.* दैवं, भाग्यं, भागधेयं, विधिः, नियति *f.*, भवितव्यता, दैवयोगः; *See* FATE; 'good 1.' सौभाग्यं, पुण्योदयः, भाग्योपचयः; 'bad or ill 1.' दैवदुर्विपाकः-विपर्यासः-विपर्ययः, मंदभाग्यं, दौर्भाग्यं, दुर्दैवं, दुर्गति *f.*, अशुभं, अमंगलं. -LESS, *a.* दैवोपहत, मंदभाग्य, अधन्य, दुर्भाग्य, अभाग्य, भाग्य-दैव-हीन, दुर्दैवग्रस्त, हीनभाग्य. -LESSLY, *adv.* दुर्दैवात्, दुर्भाग्यात्. —LUCKY, *a.* भाग्यवत्, धन्य, सौभाग्यवत्, पुण्यवत्, भाग्य-दैव-शालिन्. 2 शुभ, कल्याण (णी *f.*), भद्र, मंगल, शिव. -ILY, *adv.* दैवात्, दैवयोगात्, दिष्ट्या, दैव-भाग्य-वशात्, सौभाग्येन. -INESS, *s.* सौभाग्यं, धन्यता, पुण्यवत्ता, &c.

LUCRE, *s.* लाभः, आयः, आगमः, फलं, वृद्धि *f.*, अर्थः, फलोदयः, अर्थप्राप्ति *f.* —LUCRATIVE, *a.* लाभद, लाभकर (री *f.*), अर्थद, फलावह. -LY, *adv.* लाभपूर्वं, सफलं.

LUCUBRATE, *v. i.* रात्रौ अधि-इ 2 A or अभ्यस् 4 U. -ION, *s.* रात्र्यध्ययनं, निशाभ्यासः.

LUCULENT, *a.* *See* LUCID.

LUDICROUS, *a.* हास्य, हासकर (री *f.*), उप-अव-हास्य, असंगत. -LY, *adv.* असंगतं, हास्यरूपेण.

LUG, *v. t.* बलेन आकृष् 1 P or हृ 1 P.

LUGGAGE, *s.* परिच्छदः, उपस्करः, यात्रासामग्री, वस्त्रपात्रसंभारः.

LUGUBRIOUS, *a.* शोकात्मक, दुःखात्मक, कारुणिक (की *f.*), दुःखावेदिन्.

LUKEWARM, *a.* कोष्ण, कवोष्ण, मंदोष्ण, कदुष्ण, ईषदुष्ण, ईषत्तप्त. 2 उत्साहहीन, उदासीन, मंदोत्साह, निरुत्सुक, अतीक्ष्ण, मंदोद्योग, निरुत्साह. -LY, *adv.* ईषत्तापेन, कवोष्णं. 2 निरुत्साहं. -NESS, *s.* कवोष्णता, ईषत्तापः. 2 निरुत्सुकता, मंदोत्साहः, औदासीन्यं, मंदोद्योगः, अनौत्सुक्यं.

LULL, *v. i.* शम् 4 P, प्र-उप°, निवृत् 1 A, विरम् 1 P, निर्वा 2 P, विगम् 1 P. -*v. t.* शम् c. (शमयति), सांत्व् 10; निवृत् c. 2 प्र-सद् c., लल् 10; '1. to sleep' (गीतादिना) स्वप् c. -*s.* शांति *f.*, अक्षोभः, प्र-उप-शमः, निर्वातः, वायुनिवृत्ति *f.*-विरामः-विच्छेदः. -ER, *s.* शमकः, शांतिदः. -LULLABY, *s.* स्वापगीतं.

LUMBAGO, *s.* कटिवेदना.

LUMBER, *s.* भारः, निरर्थकद्रव्यं, निष्प्रयोजनद्रव्यं. -*v. i.* मंदं चल् 1 P. -*v. t.* संकॄ 6 P, संकुलीकृ 8 U.

LUMINARY, *s.* ज्योतिस् *n.*, प्रभावत् *m.*, ज्योतिष्मत् *m.*, तेजस् *n.*; *See* STAR.

LUMINOUS, *a.* तेजोमय (यी *f.*), सप्रकाश, तेजस्विन्, प्रभावत्, दीप्तिमत्, भास्वत्, भासुर; 'self-1.' स्वयंप्रकाश. -LY, *adv.* तेजसा.

LUMP, *s.* राशिः, संघः, गणः, समूहः, ओघः, वृंदं, संचयः, समाहारः; *See* MULTITUDE. 2 पिंडः-डं, गंडः, घनः, स्थूलभागः-अंशः. 3 साकल्यं, समासः; 'in the 1.' एकीकृत *a.*, पिंडित *a.*, साकल्येन; 'this is the meaning in the 1.' एष पिंडितार्थः (M. 1). -*v. t.* पिंडीकृ 8 U, राशीकृ, पुंजीकृ, एकीकृ, पिंड् 10. -ISH, *a.* स्थूल; स्थूलबुद्धि. -Y, *a.* सपिंड, पिंडित, पिंडीभूत.

LUNAR, *a.* चांद्र (द्री *f.*), चांद्रमस (सी *f.*), सौम्य,

ऐंदव (वी *f.*); gen. ex. by चंद्र-सोम- in comp.; '1. month' चांद्रमासः; '1. race' चंद्र-सोम-वंशः; '1. day' तिथि *m. f.*; '1. mansion' नक्षत्रं; '1. eclipse' चंद्रोपरागः.

LUNATED, *a.* अर्धचंद्राकार.

LUNATIC, *a.* उन्मत्त, सोन्माद, वातुल, भ्रांतचित्त-मति-बुद्धि, विक्षिप्तचित्त, हत-नष्ट-बुद्धि; 'a 1. asylum' वातुलालयः. –LUNACY, *s.* उन्मादः, बुद्धि-मति-भ्रंशः, चित्तविक्षेपः-विप्लवः, वातुलता, मति-बुद्धि-भ्रमः.

LUNCH, LUNCHEON, *s.* उपहारः, लघ्वाहारः.

LUNGS, *s.* तिलकं, क्लोमन् *n.*, क्लोमं, फुप्फुसः-सं.

LUNIFORM, *a.* चंद्राकृति, चंद्राकार.

LUPINE, *s.* द्विदलं, शमीधान्यं.

LURCH, *v. i.* अप-सृ 1 P, निभृतं स्था 1 P, नि-ली 4 A. 2 Disappoint, Steal, q. v. –ER, *s.* कौटिकः. 2 कौटिककुक्कुरः.

LURE, *v. t.* प्र-वि-लुभ् c., आकृष् 1 P, हृ 1 P, प्र-वृत् c., प्रोत्सह् c., प्रणुद् 6 P or c., मुह् c., प्रचुद् 10. 2 आमिषदर्शनेन आकृष्. –*s.* प्र-वि-लोभनं, आकर्षणं, प्रोत्साहनं. 2 आमिषं, आमिषदर्शनं.

LURID, *a.* वि-,पांडु, मलिन, उग्रदर्शन, घोररूप, मलिनप्रभ, तमोवृत.

LURK, *v. i.* निभृतं-प्रच्छन्नं-स्था 1 P or वृत् 1 A, नि-ली 4 A, गुप् pass.; *See* CONCEAL. –ER, *s.* निभृतस्थायिन् *m.* –ING, *s.* प्रच्छन्नवासः, गुप्ति *f.*; '1.-place' निलयः, गुप्तिः, निभृत-गूढ-स्थानं.

LUSCIOUS, *a.* ललित, सुभग, अतिमधुर, कमनीय, सुस्वादु, सुमधुर, अतिमिष्ट-स्वादु. –LY, *adv.* अतिमधुरं, सुस्वादु. –NESS, *s.* अतिमाधुर्यं, सुस्वादुता.

LUSH, *a.* सरस, रसगर्भ.

LUST, *s.* कामः, कामानलः, मैथुनेच्छा, सुरतार्थिता, मदनः, व्यवायेच्छा, रताभिलाषः, विषयसुखेच्छा, इंद्रियासक्ति *f.* 2 अतिस्पृहा-वांछा, लालसा, अतिलिप्सा, लोभः; वांछा, आकांक्षा, अभिलाषः. 3 दुर्वासना, कुवासना. –*v. i.* मैथुनं-सुरतं-इष् 6 P or अभिलष् 1, 4 P, रतार्थिन्-*a.* भू; better ex. by '1.-ful.' 2 अत्यंतं इष् or वांछ् 1 P or स्पृह् 10 or कांक्ष् 1 P, गृध् 4 P, लुभ् 4 P. –FUL, *a.* कामासक्त, कामांध, कामुक, कामिन्, इंद्रियवश, विषयनिरत, इंद्रियसुखासक्त, कामार्त, कामातुर, कामग्रस्त, कामजित, कामाविष्ट, स्मरातुर, कामवृत्ति, रतार्थिन्, मैथुनार्थिन्, मैथुनेच्छु, व्यवायिन्, लंपट, स्त्रीलंपट-पर-व्यसनिन्, कामन, अभीक, अनुक. –FULLY, *adv.* सकामं, कामुक-लंपट-वत्.

LUSTY, *a.* महाबल, सवीर्य, ससत्त्व, सबल, बल-वीर्य-वत्, मांसल, दृढांग (गी *f.*), दृढशरीर, वज्रदेह, पृथुशरीर, व्यूढोरस्क, अंसल, महाकाय. –LY, *adv.* सवीर्यं, ससत्त्वं, बलवत्, तेजसा, पौरुषेण. –NESS, *s.* वीर्यं, सत्त्वं, मांसलता, दृढांगता, &c.

LUSTRAL, *a.* पावन, पावक, शुद्धिकर (री *f.*); '1. water' पावनोदकं, शांत्युदकं. –LUSTRATE, *v. t.* पू 9 U, शुध् c. –ION, *s.* शुद्धि *f.*, शोधनं, पावनं, पवित्रीकरणं.

LUSTRE, *s.* द्युतिः, कांतिः, दीप्तिः, रुचिः, भास्, रुच्, शोभा, प्रभा, ओजस्विता (all *f.*); तेजस् *n.*, प्रकाशः, प्रतापः, उद्द्योतः. –LUSTROUS, *a.* सुप्रभ, उज्ज्वल, तेजस्विन्, शोभन, दीप्ति-कांति-मत्; *See* BRIGHT.

LUSTRUM, *s.* वर्षपंचकं.

LUTARIOUS, *a.* पंकस्थ, कर्दमवासिन्. 2 पंकिल, कार्दम (मी *f.*). 3 पंकवर्ण.

LUTE, *s.* वीणा, वल्लकी, विपंची-चिका, तंत्रीः, परिवादिनी (seven-stringed); 'bow of a 1.' कोणः, शारिकः, रणः; 'play on a 1.' वीणां वद् c.–LUTANIST, LUTER, LUTIST, *s.* वीणावादः-दकः, वैणिकः.

LUTEOUS, LUTESCENT, *a.* पीतवर्ण.

LUXATE, *v. t.* विसं-धा 3 U, अस्थिग्रंथिं भंज् 7 P or त्रुट् c. or विसं-धा. –ED, *a.* संधिच्युत-भ्रष्ट, संधिविश्लिष्ट, त्रुटितसंधि. –ION, *s.* अस्थित्रोटनं-भंगः-विश्लेषः.

LUXURY, *s.* विषयसुखं, सुखोपभोगः, सुख-भोग-आसक्ति *f.*, विषयभोगः-सेवा, विलासः, विलासित्वं, सुखसेवा-आस्वादः. 2 सुखं, भोगः, सुखसाधनं, भोगसाधनं, सुखसाहित्यं. 3 स्वाद्वन्नं, भोजनविशेषः, उत्तमान्नं, विशिष्टभोजनं. –IANCE,–CY, *s.* अति-वृद्धि-स्फीति *f.*, समृद्धि *f.*, वृद्धिबाहुल्यं, उद्रेकः. –IANT, *a.* अतिवर्धिष्णु, अतिस्फीत, अतिसमृद्ध, सुप्रचुर, अत्यंत, अतिबहुल, उद्रिक्त, अतिरिक्त, अत्यधिक. –IANTLY, *adv.* अतिसमृद्ध्या, अतिप्राचुर्येण, बाहुल्येन, अतिबहुलं, अतिरिक्तं, अतिबहुशः. –IATE, *v. i.* अत्यंतं वृध् or स्फाय् 1 A or ऋध् 4, 5 P or आ-प्यै 1 A, अतिवृद्धिं इ 1 P, अतिप्रचुरीभू 1 P. 2 अतिविलासेन वृत् 1 A or व्यव-हृ 1 P, यथेच्छं सेव् 1 A or उपभुज् 7 A. –IOUS, *a.* विलासासक्त, विषयसेविन्, विषयासक्त, सुखभोग-परायण, इंद्रियसुखनिरत, सुखास्वादतत्पर. 2 विलासयुक्त-मय (यी *f.*), सविलास, अतिसुखावह, सुखभोगकर (री *f.*), भोगानुकूल. –IOUSLY, *adv.* सविलासं, अतिसुखेन; सुखोपभोगपूर्वं, सुखासक्तवत्. –IOUSNESS, *s.* विलासित्वं &c.; *See* (*s.*).

LYE, *s.* क्षारोदकं, क्षारजलं.

LYMPH, *s.* वसा, मेदस् *n.* 2 निर्झरः, उत्सः, वारिप्रवाहः.–LYMPHATIC, *s.* मेदोवाहिनी.

LYNX, *s.* वनमार्जारः-बिडालः.

LYRE, *s.* वीणा, विपंची; *See* LUTE. –IC, –ICAL, *a.* वैणिक (की *f.*). –IST, *s.* वैणिकः.

LYTHRUM, *s.* अग्निज्वाला, सुभिक्षा, धातकी, धातु(तृ)-पुष्पिका.

M.

MACAW, *s.* वक्रतुंडः, शुकः, कीरः.

MACE, *s.* जातिपत्री, जाति-ती *f.*, जाति(ती)कोशं, जातिफलं, फलं, कोशं. 2 गदा; दंडः, यष्टि *m. f.*, वेत्रं, लगुडः, मुस(ष)लः-लं, मुद्गरः; 'm.-bearer' दंडयष्टि-धरः, वेत्रधरः, गदाहस्तः-पाणिः, याष्टिग्रहः, वेत्रपाणिः, दंडभृत्.

MACERATE, *v. t.* जलेन आर्द्र c., आर्द्रीकृ, सं-धा 3 U. -ION, *s.* संधानं, पाचनं, आर्द्रीकरणं.

MACHINATE, *v. t.* मंत्र् 10 A, (उपायं) चिंत् 10, संप्र-धृ 10, परिकृप् c., युज् 10. 2 द्रुह् 4 P, कपटप्रबंधं रच् 10, गूढमंत्रणां कृ 8 U. -ION, *s.* कुकल्पना, कुमंत्रणा, कूटप्रबंधः, गूढप्रयोगः, कपटप्रबंधः, द्रोहचिंतनं, कल्पना, चिंतनं, योजना, विधानं. -OR, *s.* कुमंत्रणाकृत् *m.*, कपटप्रबंधरचकः.

MACHINE, *s.* यंत्रं, साधनं, उपकरणं. -MACHINERY, *s.* यंत्राणि, यंत्रसामग्री, यंत्रसमुदायः. -MACHINIST, *s.* यंत्रकारः-विद्, यंत्रकलाज्ञः. —MECHANIC, *s.* शिल्पिन् *m.*, शिल्पकारः, कर्मकारः, कारुः, शिल्पोपजीवी. -*a.*,-AL, *a.* यंत्र in comp., यंत्रसंबंधिन्, यंत्रविषय, यंत्र-शिल्प-विद्यासंबंधिन्, यांत्रिक (का *f.*). 2 शिल्पविद्याकृत, यंत्रशास्त्रानुरूप; 'm. art' शिल्पं, कला. 3 यंत्रतुल्य, यंत्रवत्, अप्रबोधयुक्त. 4 यंत्रविद्या-शिल्पविद्या-निपुण; शिल्पकारिन्. -ALLY, *adv.* यंत्रविद्यानुरूपं, शिल्पशास्त्रानुसारेण. 2 यंत्रवत्, अबुद्धिपूर्वं, अमातिअप्रबोध-पूर्वं. -IAN, *s.* शिल्पशास्त्रज्ञः, यंत्रविद्याकुशलः. -MECHANICS, *s.* यंत्र-शिल्प-विद्या-शास्त्रं, यंत्रगतिशास्त्रं. -MECHANISM, *s.* यंत्ररचना, कला, युक्ति *f.*; यंत्रगति *f.*, यंत्रव्यापारः. -MECHANIST, *s.* यंत्रकारः.

MACROCOSM, *s.* विश्वं, त्रिभुवनं, अखिलं जगत्.

MACROLOGY, *s.* अतिविस्तारः, दीर्घसूत्रता.

MACULA, *s.* कलंकः, अंकः, लांछनं, लक्ष्मन् *n.* —MACULATE, *v. t.* कलंकयति-मलिनयाति (D.). -*a.*,-ED, *a.* कलंकित, कलुषित, लांछित.

MAD, *a.* उन्मत्त, वातुल, सोन्माद, हत-नष्ट-भ्रष्ट-बुद्धि, हतज्ञान, भ्रांत-विक्षिप्त-चित्त; 'make m.' उन्मादं नी 1 P, उन्मद् c.; 'to go m.' उन्मद् 4 P. 2 (Of acts) बालिश, उन्मादप्रयुक्त, असमीक्ष्य कृत, साहसिक (की *f.*); 'm.-brain,-brained' विक्षिप्तबुद्धि &c.; 'm.-cap' साहसिकः; 'm. with anger' संरब्ध, कोपाकुल, मदोदग्र; 'm.-house' वातुलालयः; 'a m. dog' अलर्कः; 'a m.-man' वातुलः, उन्मत्तः. -DEN, *v. t.* उन्मद् c., वातुलीकृ 8 U, व्यामुह् c., उन्मत्तीकृ; 'm. ed with rage' क्रोधांध; 'm. ed with liquor' सुरापानमत्त. -ING, *a.* उन्मादक, उन्मादजनन (नी *f.*). -LY, *adv.* उन्मत्तवत्, उन्मादात्, सोन्मादं, वातुलवत्, चित्तविभ्रमेण, भ्रांतचेतसा. 2 साहसिकतया. -NESS, *s.* उन्मादः, उन्मत्तता, वातुलता, मति-बुद्धि-भ्रमः, चित्तविभ्रमः-विक्षेपः, मति-बुद्धि-भ्रंशः. 2 (Fig.) व्यामोहः, मूढता, साहसं.

MADAM, *s.* आर्या, भाविनी, कुलजा; (in addressing) आर्ये, भवति.

MADDER, *s.* मंजिष्ठा, विकसा-षा, जिंगी, समंगा, कालमेशि(षि)का, मंडूकपर्णी, मंडि(डी)री, भंडी, योजनवल्ली.

MADEFY, *v. t.* क्लिद् c., आर्द्रीकृ 8 U.

MAGAZINE, *s.* नानाविषयसंबद्धं पुस्तकं; 'a m. of arms' आयुधागारं, शस्त्रास्त्रागारं. 2 भांडागारं.

MAGGOT, *s.* कृमिः, कीटः. -Y, *a.* कीटमय (यी *f.*), कीटपूर्ण.

MAGIC, *s.* इंद्रजालं, माया, अभिचारः, मंत्रयोगः, वशक्रिया, कुहका-कं, मंत्रः, कार्मणं, कुसृति *f.*, मोहः, योगः. -*a.*,-AL, *a.* ऐंद्रजालिक-आभिचारिक-मायिक-कौसृतिक- (की *f.*), मायामय (यी *f.*), मोहिन्, माया in comp. -ALLY, *adv.* इंद्रजालेन, मायया, अभिचारेण. -IAN, *s.* ऐं(इं)द्रजालिकः, मायाविन् *m.*, मायाकारः, मायी, अभिचारी, कुहकः, कुहकाजीवी, कौसृतिकः, योगी, योगेश्वरः, सिद्धः; 'm.'s brush' पिच्छिका.

MAGISTRATE, *s.* धर्माध्यक्षः, न्यायाध्यक्षः; *See* JUDGE. -MAGISTRACY, *s.* धर्माधिपत्यं, न्यायाधिकरणं, धर्माधिकारः. 2 धर्माध्यक्षगणः-समूहः. —MAGISTERIAL, *a.* (*s.*) in comp., आधिकारिक (की *f.*). 2 प्रभुत्वविशिष्ट, आज्ञापक, सावलेप, दृप्त, प्रगल्भ. -LY, *adv.* शासनरूपेण; सदर्पं, सावलेपं.

MAGNANIMOUS, *a.* महात्मन्, महामनस्, महामनस्क, महानुभाव, उदारधी-चेतस्-मति, उदार, महेच्छ, महाशय, उदारात्मन्. 2 (Of acts) अवदात, उदार, औदार्यपूर्व. -LY, *adv.* औदार्येण, माहात्म्येन, महानुभावात्, उदारचेतसा. -MAGNANIMITY, *s.* माहात्म्यं, उदारात्मता, महात्मता, औदार्यं, माहानुभावः, चित्तौदार्यं, उदारमतिता, महेच्छा, महाशयः.

MAGNATE, *s.* उत्कृष्टपदस्थः, उच्चपदस्थः, धुरंधरः, धुरीणः.

MAGNET, *s.* अयस्कांतः, अयोमणिः, लोहकांतः, चुंबकः. -IC,-ICAL, *a.* आकर्षक, आकर्षणशील, लोहचुंबकशील; 'm. needle' अयस्कांतशलाका; 'm. attraction' आकर्षः-र्षणं. -ICALLY, *adv.* आकर्षणद्वारेण. -ISM, *s.* अयस्कांतगुणः, आकर्षणशक्ति *f.*, लोहकांतधर्मः. -IZE, *v. t.* आकर्षणशक्तिं दा 3 U or संक्रम् c. or संचर् c.

MAGNIFICENT, MAGNIFIC, *a.* शोभमान, तेजस्विन्, अतिशोभन, महाप्रभ, श्रीमत्, महातेजस्, महाप्रताप, विभूतिमत्, दैदीप्यमान. 2 (Palace &c.) विशाल, तुंग, उज्ज्वल. -LY, *adv.* अतितेजसा, सप्रतापं, विभूत्या, ऐश्वर्येण. -MAGNIFICENCE, *s.* महिमन् *m.*, प्रतापः, श्रीः, शोभा, तेजस् *n.*, अतिप्रतापः-शोभा-प्रभा, ओजस्विता, महाप्रतापः, विभूति *f.*, औज्ज्वल्यं, विभवः, ऐश्वर्यं.

MAGNILOQUENT, *a.* प्रौढ-प्रगल्भ-वाच्, दृप्त-धृष्ट-वाच्. -**MAGNILOQUENCE**, *s.* प्रौढभाषणं, प्रगल्भोक्ति *f.*, गर्वोक्तिः.

MAGNIFY, *v. t.* वृध् c., उप-चि 5 U, स्फाय् c. (स्फावयति), अधिकीकृ 8 U; *See* INCREASE. 2 अत्यंतं वर्ण् 10, उत्-सं-कृत् 10. 3 अतिशयोक्त्या वृध् c. or विस्तृ c. -ER, *s.* वर्धकः. 2 बृंहणयंत्रं. -ING, *a.* वर्धिन्, बृंहणकारिन्.

MAGNITUDE, *s.* मानं, प्र-परि-माणं, आकारमानं, मात्रा in comp., इयत्ता; 'of the m. of an egg' अंडमात्र, अंडपरिमाण. 2 गुरुत्वं, महत्त्वं, बृहत्त्वं, वैपुल्यं, प्रथिमन् *m.*, गरिमा, महिमा, पृथुता, विशालता.

MAG-PIE, *s. See* JAY.

MAID, MAIDEN, *s.* कन्या, कुमारी, तरुणी, बालिका, युवतिः-ती, बाला, कन्यका, कुमारिका. 2 अनूढा, अपरिणीता, अविवाहिता, अदत्ता, अक्षत-अविद्ध-योनिः. 3 (M.-servant) दासी, चेटी, प्रेष्या, परिचारिका, कर्मकरी. -*a.* कौमार (री *f.*), कन्याविषय. 2 अभिनव, अकृतोपभोग, अक्षत, अखंड. -HOOD, *s.* कौमारं, तारुण्यं, कुमारीभावः-दशा. 2 अभिनवत्वं, अखंडता. -LY, -LIKE, *a.* कन्यकोचित, कन्या-कुमारी-योग्य.

MAIL, *s.* वर्मन् *n.*, तनुत्रं, तनुत्राणं, कवचः-चं, उरश्छदः, दंशनं, कंकटकः, ज(जा)गरः ; *See* ARMOUR; 'm.-coat' कंचुकः, वारवाणः; 'having put on a m.-coat' आ-प्रति-मुक्त, अपिनद्ध, पिनद्ध. 2 पत्र-लेख्य-वाहनं. -ED, *a.* सकवच, कवचिन्, कवचधारिन्; कृतसन्नाह, वर्मित, सन्नद्ध, सज्ज, दंशित, व्यूढकंकट.

MAIM, *v. t.* विकली-व्यंगी-कृ 8 U, हीनांगीकृ, विकलयति (D.). -*s.* अंगवैकल्यं, हीनांगता, न्यूनावयवत्वं. -ED, *a.* विकलांग (गी *f.*), व्यंग, हीनांग, विकल, अंगविकल.

MAIN, *a.* मुख्य, प्रधान, प्रमुख, परम, अग्र्य, श्रेष्ठ, उत्कृष्ट, उत्तम, विशिष्ट, मूल in comp., गुरुतम; 'm. matter' गुरुकार्यं, गुरुकं; 'm. door' सिंहद्वारं; 'm. stock' मूलधनं. -*s.* प्रधानभागः, प्रधानांशः, मुख्यांशः, बाहुल्यं, भूयिष्ठभागः. 2 महोदधिः, महार्णवः; *See* SEA. 3 बलं, शक्ति *f.*, प्रभावः, सामर्थ्यं. 4 प्राणिद्यूतं, समाह्वयः; 'in the m.' बहुशः, बाहुल्येन, भूयिष्ठं, सामान्यतः; 'with might and m.' सर्वबलेन, प्रसभं, प्रसह्य; 'm.-land' मध्य-मूल-भूमि *f.*, मुख्य-प्रधान-द्वीपः-पं. -LY, *adv.* मुख्यशः, बहुशः, प्रधानतः, मुख्यांशेन, भूयिष्ठं, बहुतरं, सामान्यतः, विशेषेण, प्राधान्येन.

MAINTAIN, *v. t.* ग्रह्, 9 P, धृ 1 P, 10. 2 पा c. (पालयति), रक्ष् 1 P, भृ 1 P, 3 U, आ-अव-लंब् 1 A, उत्तभ् 9 P or c., संस्तंभ्, संवृध् c., पुष् 1, 9 P or c., योगक्षेमं वह् 1 P, पालनं-पोषणं कृ 8 U. 3 प्रवृत् c., रक्ष्, न विच्छिद् 7 P or वि-रम् 1 P. 4 प्रति-पद् c., वद् 1 P, निर्वह् 1 P or c., समर्थ् 10, संस्तंभ्, दृढीकृ, अनु-पा c. (पालयति); *See* FULFIL also. 5 (As a theory) वद् 1 P; 'he who m. s that there is God' ईश्वरवादी ; 'one who m. s the doctrine of atheism' नास्तिकमतवादी. 6 सनिश्चयं वद् 1 P, दृढोक्त्या प्रति-पद् c.; 'to m. oneself' जीवितं धृ, शरीरवृत्तिं कृ or निर्वृत् c.; *See* LIVE (on). -ER, *s.* पालकः, पोषकः, रक्षितृ *m.*, आलंबिन्, भरः-धरः-in comp. -**MAINTENANCE**, *s.* धारणं. 2 रक्षा, रक्षणं, भरणं, भृति *f.*, आ-समा-लंबनं, पालनं, पोषणं, संवर्धनं. 3. जीविका, वृत्ति *f.*, आ-उपजीविका, आजीवः, प्राणयात्रा; *See* LIVING. 4 ग्रासाच्छादनं, अन्नवस्त्रं, अन्नाच्छादनं. 2 प्रतिपादनं, निर्वाहः.

MAIZE, *s.* शस्यं.

MAJESTY, *s.* राजश्रीः, राजप्रतापः-तेजस् *n.*, राजमहिमन् *m.*-प्रभावः-गौरवं, प्रतापः, राजत्वं, तेजः, प्रभावः, ऐश्वर्यं, महिमा, वैभवं, विभूति *f.*, गौरवं, महत्त्वं; 'your m.' देवः, महाराजः, देवपादाः, स्वामी, श्रीमद्देवपादाः, प्रभुः, प्रभविष्णुः; (in addressing) देव, महाराज, &c. -IC, -ICAL, *a.* राजयोग्य, राजतुल्य, नृपोचित, राजतेजोमय (यी *f.*), राजश्रीमत्, राजप्रतापवत्, सानुभाव, सावष्टंभ, प्रतापवत्, ऐश्वर (री *f.*), विभूतिमत्, प्रभाववत्, ओजस्विन्; उन्नत, अतिप्रौढ, उज्ज्वल, उत्तुंग; *See* LOFTY also; 'm. splendour' दीप्ति *f.*; 'm. dignity' अनुभावः, अवष्टंभः, ओजस्विता. -ICALLY, *adv.* राजसदृशं, सावष्टंभं, सानुभावं, नृपोचितं, राजप्रतापेन-तेजसा-महिम्ना, सप्रताप, सप्रभावं, ऐश्वर्येण, सगौरवं.

MAJOR, *a.* अधिक, भूयस्, अधिकसंख्य. 2 मुख्य, प्रधान, प्रमुख, गुरु, वरीयस्, वर्षीयस्. -*s.* प्राप्तव्यवहारः, व्यवहारक्षमः-योग्यः, अतीत-त्यक्त-शैशवः. 2 गुल्माध्यक्षः, सैन्यदलाध्यक्षः. -**MAJORITY**, *s.* बहु (pl.), बहुतरभागः, भूयिष्ठभागः, अधिकसंख्या; 'a m. of members have come' सभासदां मध्याद्बहवः समागताः; 'm. of votes' बहुमतं, मताधिक्यं. 2 व्यवहारः, व्यवहारक्षमता, व्यवहार्यदशा, वयस् *n.*; 'reached his m.' प्राप्तव्यवहारः, त्यक्तशैशवः; *See* GROW up.

MAKE, *v. t.* कृ 8 U, वि-धा 3 U, अनु-ष्ठा 1 P, आचर् 1 P. 2 (Create) निर्मा 3 A, 2 P, सृज् 6 P, घट् c. (घटयति), कृ, वि-धा, रच् 10, कॢप् c., उत्पद् c., जन् c. (जनयति), साध् c., निः-सं-पद् c. 3 (Produce) उत्पद् c., जन् c., कृ; *See* CAUSE. 4 (Force) ex. by causal of roots; 'm. s me question you' प्रश्नकर्मणि मां नियोजयति (Ka. 134); *See* COMPEL. 5 निर्मा, घट् c.; gen. ex. by निर्मित, घटित, रूप, मय, आत्मक in comp.; also by भू 1 P, सं-पद् 4 A; '10 repeated 2 times m. s 20' द्विरावृत्ता दश विंशतिर्भवंति or संपद्यंते. 6 आप् 5 P, विद् 6 U, लभ् 1 A;

See GET; 'm. amends for' क्षतिं पूर् 10, प्रतिफलं दा 3 U, प्रमृज् 2 P, निष्कृ; 'm. account of' मन् 4 A or c., गण् 10, अवेक्ष् 1 A; 'to m. the best of a bad matter' दोषमपि गुणत्वमापादयितुं; 'self-made man' स्वोपमलब्धप्रतिष्ठः; 'm. merry' हृष्-*a.* भू, उत्सवं कृ; 'm. much of' बहु मन्; 'm. light of' तृणाय मन् or गण्, लघूकृ, अव-ज्ञा 9 U; *See* CONTEMN; 'm. way' अंतरं दा; अप-सृ 1 P, अप-इ-या 2 P; अपक्रम् 1 U, 4 P; 'm. free with' संकोचं त्यक्त्वा आचर् or व्यवहृ 1 P; 'm. away with' नश् c., व्या-पद् c., हन् 2 P or c. (घातयति); *See* KILL; 'm. water' मूत्रोत्सर्गं कृ; 'm. good' पा c. (पालयति), पूर्, तॄ 1 P, रक्ष् 1 P (promise &c.); *See* FULFIL also; सं-पद् c., साध् 5 P or c.; (loss) पूर्, प्रतिविधा 3 U, प्रतिकृ, अपाकृ, शुध् c.; 'm. bold to say' प्रगल्भतया वद् 1 P or वचनसाहसं कृ. -for, अभि-या 2 P, प्रति-या, उपसृप्-उपगम् 1 P, अभि-उपसृ 1 P. 2 आवह् 1 P, क्लृप् 1 A. -into, निर्मा, वि-धा; 'gold is made into ornaments' सुवर्णस्यालंकाराः क्रियंते. -of, *See* MAKE (5) above; 'made of' मय (यी *f.*), घटित, निर्मित, आत्मक, रूप in comp.; or only by comp.; 'a pot made of gold' हेमनिर्मितं पात्रं, हेमपात्रं. 2 अवगम् 1 P; बुध् 1 P; 'not knowing what to m. of it' किं नु एतत्स्यादिति ज्ञातुमसमर्थाः. -off, पलाय् 1 A, अपक्रम्, अप-इ, अप-सृ-गम्-धाव् 1 P. -out, निरूप् 10, ज्ञा 9 U, अवगम्, ग्रह् 9 P, उपलभ् 1 A, विद् 2 P; *See* KNOW. 2 प्रति-पद् c., समर्थ् 10; प्रमाणीकृ, साध् c., निष्पद् c. -over, सम्-ऋ c. (अर्पयति), संक्रम् c., निक्षिप् 6 P, न्यस् 4 U, आयत्तीकृ. -up, समाह् 1 P, संकल् 10, संभृ 1 P, 3 U, समा-नी 1 P, एकीकृ. 2 (A loss) पूर्, प्रतिवि-धा; 'you should m. up for your want of beauty by being good' त्वया अलावण्यदोषः सदाचरणेन प्रतिविधेयः. 3 (A quarrel) सं-धा, प्रशम् c., (प्रशमयसि विवादं S. 5). 4 निर्णी, साध्, निष्पद् c.; 'm. up one's mind' निर्णी, निश्चि 5 U; *See* DETERMINE; 'm. up to' उपसृ, उपगम्; *See* APPROACH. -*s.* आकारः, आकृति *f.*, रूपं, विग्रहः, अंगं, वपुस् *n.*; 'handsomeness of m.' अंगसौष्ठवं. -ER, *s.* कारः, करः, कारिन्, कृत् in comp.; कर्तृ *m.*, निर्माता, विधाता, कल्पकः, रचकः, घटकः; 'm. of pots' कुंभकारः-कृत् &c. 2 Creator, q. v.; 'man is the m. of his own fortune' लोके गुरुत्वं विपरीततां वा स्वचेष्टितान्येव नरं नयंति (H. 2). -ING, *s.* करणं, विधानं, रचनं, कल्पनं, निर्माणं, &c.

MALADMINISTRATION, *s.* कुशासनं, दुर्णयः, असम्यक् निर्वाहः.

MALADY, *s.* रोगः, व्याधिः, आमयः, विकारः, रुजा, गदः; *See* DISEASE.

MALAPERT, *a.* अविनीत, धृष्ट, प्रगल्भ, प्रतिभानवत्, निर्लज्ज. -LY, *adv.* अविनयेन, धृष्टवत्, निर्लज्जं. -NESS, *s.* अविनयः, धृष्टता, प्रागल्भ्यं, प्रतिभा-भानं.

MALAPROPOS, *adv.* अस्थाने, अकाले, अनवसरं.

MALARIA, *s.* पूतिवायुः, दुर्वातः.

MALCONTENT, *a.* or *s.* असंतुष्ट, अप-वि-रक्त, राजापरक्त, राजन्यसंतुष्ट.

MALE, *s.* पुंस् *m.*, पुरुषः, नरः, नृ *m.*; 'm. and female' स्त्रीपुंसौ, स्त्रीपुरुषौ, युग्मं, मिथुनं, द्वंद्वं. -*a.* Ex. by masc. gender; पुंजातीय; 'm. sparrow' चटकः; sometimes by पुरुष-पुं-नर- in comp.; 'm. tiger' पुंव्याघ्रः; 'm. cuckoo' पुंस्कोकिलः; 'm. attire' पुरुषवेशः; 'm. child' अपत्यं पुमान्, पुत्रः, सुतः, &c.; 'm. species' पुंजाति *f.*, पुरुषजातिः.

MALEDICTION, *s.* शापः, आक्रोशः-शनं. -MALEDICTORY, *a.* अभिशापक, आक्रोशगर्भ, अमंगलाशंसिन्.

MALEFACTOR, *s.* पातकिन् *m.*, पापी, अपकारी, अपराधी, पापकर्मन् *m.*, दुष्कर्ता, दोषभाक्, कृतागस् *m.*

MALEVOLENT, *a.* अभिद्रुग्ध, द्रोहमति-बुद्धि, दुष्ट-भावमति-बुद्धि, दुरात्मन्, दुराशय, कुबुद्धि, दुर्बुद्धि, मत्सरिन्, साभ्यसूय, पापाशय, अहितैषिन्, दुर्हृद्, दुःशील, अनिष्टार्थिन्. -LY, *adv.* द्रोहबुद्ध्या, दुष्टभावेन, साभ्यसूयं, अहितेच्छया. -MALEVOLENCE, *s.* द्रोह-अहित-बुद्धि *f.*, दुष्टभावः, कुभावः, कुबुद्धिः, द्रोहमति *f.*, द्रोहः, असूया, अभ्यसूया, दौरात्म्यं, मात्सर्यं, अहितेच्छा, अपकारेच्छा, पैशुन्यं.

MALICE, *s.* वि-,द्वेषः, वैरं, द्वेष-शत्रु-भावः, द्रोहः, दुष्टभावः, द्रोहमति-बुद्धि *f.*, मात्सर्यं, असूया, अहितेच्छा, पापाशयः, दौरात्म्यं, दौर्जन्यं, पैशुन्यं. -MALICIOUS, *a.* वैर-द्वेष-पूर्वक, द्रोह-द्वेष-मूल-हेतुक. 2 अभिद्वेषिन्, द्रोहिन्, द्रोहमति-बुद्धि, दुष्टभाव-मति, द्रोहशील, अपकारेच्छु, पापात्मन्, दुरात्मन्, साभ्यसूय, मत्सरिन्, दुर्जन, खल, पिशुन ; *See* MALEVOLENT. -LY, *adv.* द्रोहबुद्ध्या, दौरात्म्येन, सद्वेषं, मात्सर्येण ; 'm. intentioned' द्रोहबुद्धि &c. -NESS, द्रोहमतित्वं, दुष्टशीलता; *See* (*s.*).

MALIGN, *v. t.* अपभाष् 1 A, परि-अप-वद् 1 U, अभिशंस् 1 P, कलंकयति (D.), वि-,द्विष् 2 U. -*a.*, -ANT, *a.* द्वेषबुद्धि, द्रोहपरायण, दुष्टबुद्धि, दुर्बुद्धि, दुराशय, नृशंस, दुर्मति; *See* MALICIOUS, MALEVOLENT. 2 (Star) अशुभ, दुष्ट, अनिष्ट, अमंगल. 3 उग्र, घोर, अतिदुष्ट, अरुंतुद, अनिनिग्म. 4 असाध्य, दुःसाध्य, दुश्चिकित्स्य, मारात्मक, सान्निपातिक (की *f.*), काल in comp. -LY, -ANTLY, *adv.* सद्रोहं, अत्युग्रं. -ER, *s.* अभिशंसकः, अपवादकः, पिशुनः. -ITY,

—MALIGNANCY, *s.* द्रोहबुद्धि *f.*, द्वेषपरायणता, परमद्वेषः, भावदुष्टता, अतिनैघृण्यं; *See* MALICE. 2 उग्रता. तिग्मता, दुष्टता. 3 असाध्यता, मारात्मकता.

MALKIN, *s.* अशुद्धा, भ्रष्टा.

MALL, *s.* महामुद्गरः, घनः. 2 जनाकीर्णमार्गः, जनसामान्यपथः.

MALLEABLE, *a.* उद्वर्तनीय. घनेन वर्धनीय, उद्वर्तनक्षम. —MALLEATE, *v. t.* मुद्गराघातेन उद्-वृत् c.

MALLET, *s.* मुद्गरः, द्रुघणः, घनः.

MALPRACTICE, *s.* दुराचारः, दुश्चरितं, कुचरितं, कुचेष्टितं.

MALT, *s.* यवपानीयबीजं; 'm.-drink' यवसुरा, यवजं, यवपानीयं; 'm.-house' यवसंधानगृहं.

MALTREAT, *v. t.* अप्रियं आचर् 1 P or वृत् 1 A, नि-अप-विप्र-कृ 8 U, पीड् 10. —MENT, *s.* अपकारः, निकारः, पीडा.

MALVERSATION, *s.* दुराचरितं, शाठ्यं, धूर्तता; *See* FRAUD.

MAMMA, *s.* माता, अंबा, जननी; *See* MOTHER.

MAMMALIA, *s.* सस्तनाः प्राणिनः.

MAMMIFEROUS, *a.* सस्तन, स्तनविशिष्ट.

MAMMIFORM, *a.* स्तनाकृति, कुचाकार.

MAMMON, *s.* धनं, लक्ष्मीः, संपद् *f.*; (the god) कुबेरः. —IST, *a.* or *s.* धनपरायण, द्रव्यार्जनतत्पर. —ISM, *s.* द्रव्यपरायणता.

MAN, *s.* मनुष्यः, मानुषः, मनुजः, नरः, नृ *m.*, मानवः, पु(पू)रुषः, मर्त्यः, पुंस् *m.* 2 (As opposed to child) मानुषः, प्रौढवयस्कः, त्यक्तशैशवः, मानुष्यप्राप्तः, प्रौढः. 3 (As opposed to woman) पुरुषः, पुमान्, नरः. 4 (M.-kind) मनुष्याः, मानवाः; मनुष्यजाति *f.*, मर्त्याः, मानुष्यं, मानुषता, जनः, लोकः, मनुष्यजीव-लोकः. 5 (In chess) शा(सा)रः-रिः; 'an eminent m.' पुरुषसिंहः-व्याघ्रः, नरवरः-शार्दूलः-पुंगवः-ऋषभः; *See* EXCELLENT; 'm.-eater' पुरुषादः, नृभुक्, नरभोजिन्; 'm.-hater' मनुष्यशत्रुः-द्रोही, मनुष्यद्वेषी; 'm. of war' बृहती युद्धनौः; 'm.-slaughter' मनुष्यवधः-घातः-हत्या, प्रमाथः; 'm.-stealing' मनुष्यापहारः. —*v. t.* पुरुषसनाथीकृ 8 U, सैन्यं निविश् c. —FUL, —LY, *a.* पौरुष (षी *f.*), पौरुषेय (यी *f.*); शूर-वीर-योग्य, महावीर्य, विक्रांत, शूर, वीर्यवत्; पुरुष-नर- in comp.; 'm. deed' पुरुषकारः, पौरुषं; 'm. office' पुरुषाधिकारः. —FULLY, *adv.* पुरुषवत्, सवीर्यं, सबलं. सपौरुषं, सविक्रमं, शूर-वीर-वत्, निर्भयं. —FULNESS,-LINESS, *s.* पौरुषं, वीर्यं, पुरुषकारः. वि-परा-क्रमः, शौर्यं, साहसं. —HOOD, *s.* मनुष्यत्वं, मानुषता, मानुष्यं, पुरुषदशा-धर्मः-भावः. 2 पुंस्त्वं, पौरुषं, ओजस्-तेजस् *n.*, वीर्यं, ऊर्जस् *n.* 3 यौवनं, तारुण्यं, यौवनावस्था, तारुण्यदशा, प्रौढता, व्यवहारदशा; 'having reached the stage of m.' प्राप्तयौवनः, आरूढयौवनः. 4 वीर्यं, वि-परा-क्रमः, शौर्यं, पौरुषं.

MANACLE, *s.* हस्तनिगडः-बंधनं-पाशः. —*v. t.* (हस्तौ) निगडेन बंध् 9 P or संयम् 1 A.

MANAGE, *v. t.* निर्वह् c., व्यव-स्था c. (स्थापयति), घट् c. (घटयति); सं-पद् c., वि-धा 3 U, प्र-वृत् c., कृ 8 U. 2 अधि-ष्ठा 1 P, अवेक्ष् 1 A; प्र-णी 1 P, शास् 2 P, नियम् 1 P, नियंत्र् 10; निग्रह् 9 P, वशीकृ, दम् c. (दमयति); *See* CONTROL. 3 विनी, अनुशास्, शिक्ष् c. 4 परिमितं व्यय् 10 (व्ययति). —*v. i.* आचर् 1 P, वृत् 1 A, घट् 1 A, उपायं युज् 10 or चिंत् 10 or कॢप् c., संवि-धा; *See* ARRANGE; यथा नौ प्रियसखी बंधुजनशोच्या न भवति तथा निर्वाहय (S. 3) 'so m. that &c.' —ABLE, *a.* प्रणेय, विधेय, विनेय, वश्य, आयत्त, शासनीय, सुकर. —ED, *a.* प्रणीत, विहित; नियत, नियंत्रित; प्रयुक्त, घटित; 'well-m.' सुघटित, सुविहित, सुप्रयुक्त. —ER, *s.* निर्वाहकः, प्रणेतृ *m.*, व्यवस्थापकः, अवेक्षकः, प्रवर्तकः, प्रयोजकः, संपादकः, घटकः, अधिकारी, अधिकृतः, नायकः, अधिष्ठाता, अध्यक्षः, चालकः; 'm. of public affairs' जनकार्याध्यक्षः, पौरकार्यावेक्षकः; जनकार्याधिकारी; 'm. of the treasury' कोशाध्यक्षः, द्रव्याधिकारी. 2 (Stage-m.) सूत्रधारः, स्थापकः. 3 परिमितव्ययिन् *m.* —ING, *a.* व्यवस्थापक, कार्याधिकारिन्, कार्यावेक्षक, चालक. —MENT, *s.* प्रणयनं, नयः, नीति *f.*, निर्वाहः-हणं, घटनं, प्रवर्तनं, करणं, विधानं; अधिष्ठानं, अवेक्षा-क्षणं, व्यवस्थापनं, चालनं. 2 अधिकारः, अधिष्ठातृत्वं, शासनं, नियमनं, अध्यक्षता, विनियमः, नियंत्रणं, वशीकरणं. 3 उपायः, प्रयोगः, युक्ति *f.*, उपायकल्पना-प्रयोगः, संविधा; 'under his m. of affairs' तस्मिन् कार्याणि अवेक्षमाणे, कार्याध्यक्षे तस्मिन्.

MANCIPLE, *s.* भोजनाधिकारिन् *m.*

MANDATE, *s.* आज्ञा, शासनं, आ-नि-देशः, नियोगः, विधिः; 'written m.' आज्ञापत्रं, शासनपत्रं. —ORY, *a.* आदेशक, आज्ञापक, शासक.

MANDIBLE, *s.* हनु *m. f.*, चिबुकं, चीचं, कुंजः.

MANDRAKE, *s.* लक्ष्मणा, पुत्रदात्री, पुत्रदा.

MANDUCATE, *v. t.* चर्व् 1 P.

MANE, *s.* केश(स)रः; सटा (of a lion). —ED, *a.* केसरिन्.

MANEGE, *s.* अश्वदमनविद्या-कला.

MANES, *s.* पितरः, स्वधा-श्राद्ध-भुजः; पिंडभाजः, पिंडाशाः (all pl.); पितृगणः-वर्गः-लोकः-जनः; 'offering oblations to the m.' पितृकर्म-कार्य-क्रिया-यज्ञः-मेधः, श्राद्धकर्म-क्रिया; 'oblation to the m.' पिंडः, स्वधा, कव्यं, श्राद्धं; 'gifts in honour of the m.' पितृदान-तर्पणं; 'a day sacred to the m.' पितृतिथि *m. f.*

MANGE, *s.* (पशूनां) सिध्मन् *m.*, पामा; *See* ITCH.

MANGER, *s.* द्रोणी, गवादनी, तृणभाजनं-पात्रं.

MANGLE, *v. t.* व्यव-च्छिद् 7 P, वि-दॄ 9 P, व्रश्च् 6 P, निकृत् 6 P, लवशः कृत् or खंड् 10 or छिद्. -*s.* वस्त्रमार्जनयंत्रं. -ED, *a.* छिन्नभिन्न, विक्षतांग (गी *f.*), व्यवच्छिन्न, क्षतविक्षत, लवशः कृत.

MANGO, *s.* आम्रं, आम्रफलं; (tree) आम्रः, चूतः-तकः, रसालः; सहकारः (very fragrant); 'm.-blossom' चूतप्रसवः; 'm.-sprout' सहकारमंजरी.

MANIA, *s.* उन्मादः, बुद्धिभ्रमः; *See* MADNESS. 2 महाव्यसनं, एकविषयासक्ति *f.* -MANIAC, *a.* उन्मत्त, वातुल. -*s.* उन्मत्तः, वातुलः; *See* MAD.

MANIFEST, *a.* स्पष्ट, स्फुट, व्यक्त, प्रत्यक्ष, प्रकाश, प्रकट, सुव्यक्त-स्पष्ट-प्रकाश, परिस्फुट, अभिव्यक्त, प्रकटित, आविर्भूत; प्रादुर्भूत; 'to become m.' प्रादुर्भू 1 P, आविर्भू, प्रकटी-स्पष्टी-भू, प्रकाश् 1 A. -*v. t.*, 'make m.' प्रकाश् c., व्यंज् 7 P or c., स्पष्टीकृ 8 U, आविष्कृ, प्रकटी-प्रत्यक्षी-स्फुटी-कृ, विशदीकृ, प्रकटयति (D.), सूच् 10, दृश् c.; आविर्भूतज्योतिषां ब्राह्मणानां (U. 4.) 'to whom the Supreme Light has m. ed itself.' -ATION, *s.* आविष्करणं, प्रकाशनं, व्यंजनं, स्फुटीकरणं, &c. 2 व्यक्ति *f.*, प्रकाशता, स्पष्टता, आविर्भावः, प्रादुर्भावः, प्रत्यक्षता, अवभासः, प्राकट्यं. -ER, *s.* प्रकाशकः, व्यंजकः. -LY, *adv.* व्यक्तं, स्पष्टं, स्फुटं, सुव्यक्तं, परिस्फुटं. -NESS, *s.* व्यक्तता, स्पष्टता, &c. -MANIFESTO, *s.* प्रकाशन-घोषणा-पत्रं, ज्ञापन-प्रसिद्धि-पत्रं.

MANIFOLD, *a.* *See* under MANY.

MANIKIN, *s.* क्षुद्रनरः, माणवकः, मनुष्यकः.

MANIPLE, *s.* मुष्टि *m. f.* 2 लघुगुल्मः.

MANIPULATE, *v. t.* हस्ताभ्यां कृ 8 U or वि-धा 3 U; हस्तौ व्याप्टृ c. or चल् c. or विक्षिप् 6 P. -ION, *s.* हस्तव्यापारः, हस्तादिचालनं-विक्षेपः.

MANNA, *s.* (Of bamboos) वंशरो(लो)चना, त्वक्क्षीरी, वंशजा, शुभ्रा, वंशक्षीरी, वैणवी.

MANNER, *s.* प्रकारः, रीति *f.*, विधा, विधिः, रूपं, मार्गः, पर्यायः, क्रमः, पद्धति *f.*, सरणि-णी *f.*; 'in this m.' इत्थं, एवं, अनेन प्रकारेण, &c.; 'in that m.' 'in such a m.' तथा, तेन प्रकारेण, एवंविधं, तथाविधं, एवंरूपेण, &c.; 'in like m.' तथा, तथैव, एवमेव, तद्वत्. 2 (Kind) भेदः, विशेषः, प्रकारः. 3 आकारः, आकृति *f.*, रूपं, मुखचर्या, वदनाकृतिः. 4 (M.s) आचारः, आचरणं, वृत्ति *f.*, वृत्तं, वर्तनं, व्यवहारः, चर्या, रीतिः; नियमः, चरितं, शीलं, मार्गः, संप्रदायः, धारा, अभ्यासः (habitual m.s); 'good m.s' सदाचारः, सद्वर्तनं, विनयः, सुनीति *f.*, शिष्टाचारः, मर्यादा, सुशीलता, शिष्टता, सभ्यता, शिष्टसंप्रदायः; 'bad m.s' अमर्यादा, दुराचारः, अनीतिः, कुरीतिः; 'm.s of a country' देशाचारः, देशव्यवहारः; 'violation of good m.s' मर्यादा-विनय-अतिक्रमः. -ED, *a.* सुशील, शिष्टाचार, विनीत; 'ill-m.' अशिष्ट, असभ्य, दुःशील, दुर्मर्याद, अविनीत. -ISM, *s.* एकरीतिसेवनं, एकरसत्वं. -LESS, *a.* अविनीत, दुराचार, अशिष्ट, अमर्याद. -LY, *a.* शिष्ट, विनीत, सभ्य, सुशील, सुजन, सदाचार, साधुवृत्त, शिष्टाचार. -*adv.* सविनयं, शिष्टवत्.

MANŒUVRE, *s.* यानप्रकारः, युद्धव्यपदेशः. 2 प्रयुक्ति *f.*, कौशलं, वैदग्ध्यं, उपायः, व्यपदेशः, माया, विदग्धप्रयोगः, कपटोपायः. -*v. t.* विदग्धोपायं रच् 10 or युज् 10, छलं-व्यपदेशं-कृ 8 U.

MANOR, *s.* ग्रामाध्यक्षभूमि *f.*-स्थानं; 'lord of the m.' ग्रामेश्वरः, ग्रामणीः.

MANSION, *s.* हर्म्यं, सौधं, गृहं, मंदिरं, भवनं, गेहं, सदनं, निकेतनं, शाला, आयतनं; *See* HOUSE; 'lunar m.' नक्षत्रं, दक्षजा, विधुप्रिया.

MANTLE, *s.* प्रावारः-रकः, अवगुंठनं, आवरणं, पिधानं. -*v. t.* आ-प्रा-वृ 5 U, समावृ 6 P, आ-च्छद् 10. -*v. i.* प्रवृध् 1 A, विस्तॄ-वितन्- pass.; प्र-वि-सृप् 1 P. 2 उद्गम् 1 P, उत्सृप्, आविर्भू 1 P. 3 उत्सिच् pass., फेनायते (D.). 4 मुद् 1 A, आनंद् 1 P, उत्सवं कृ 8 U; *See* DELIGHT.

MANTUA, *s.* स्त्रीवस्त्रं-परिधानं.

MANUAL, *a.* हस्त्य, हस्त in comp.; 'm. art' शिल्पं, कला; 'm. dexterity' हस्तकौशलं-लाघवं; 'm. labour' श्रमः, आयासः; 'sign m.' स्वाक्षरं, स्वहस्ताक्षरं. -*s.* लघुपुस्तकं, संक्षिप्तग्रंथः, सारसंग्रहः.

MANUFACTURE, *s.* निर्माणं, विरचनं-ना, घटनं-ना, उत्पादनं, शिल्पकर्मन् *n.*, शिल्पनिर्माणं. 2 शिल्पनिर्मितं द्रव्यं-वस्तु. -*v. t.* शिल्पेन निर्मा 3 A, 2 P, or क्लृप् c. or रच् 10 or वि-धा 3 U or कृ 8 U. -AL, *a.* शिल्पिक (की *f.*). -ER, *s.* शिल्पकारः, शिल्पिन् *m.*, शिल्पिकः. -MANUFACTORY, *s.* शिल्पशाला-गृहं, निर्माणशाला-गृहं.

MANUMIT, *v. t.* दास्यात् मुच् 6 P or c. or मोक्ष् 10. -MANUMISSION, *s.* दास्यमोचनं, बंधनमोक्षः.

MANURE, *s.* सारः, भूमिलेपः, पुरीषादि *n.* -*v. t.* पुरीषादिना लिप् 6 P, सारं नि-धा 3 U or निक्षिप् 6 P.

MANUSCRIPT, *s.* हस्तलेखः-लिखितं, लेख्यं, लिखितं. -*a.* लिखित, हस्तलिखित.

MANY, *a.* बहु, बहुल, अनेक, भूयिष्ठ, प्रभूत, प्रचुर, बहुसंख्यक, भूयस्, विपुल, नैक-नाना-in comp.; 'of m. kinds' अनेक-नाना-विध; 'as m. as'-'so m.' यावत्-तावत्, यावत्संख्यक-तावत्संख्यक, यति-तति; 'how m.' कियत्, कति (pl.); 'of how m. kinds' कतिविध-*a.*; 'in m. places' बहुत्र, अनेकत्र; 'in m. ways' बहुधा, अनेकधा; 'how m. times' कतिकृत्वः, कतिवारान्; 'm. times' बहुशः, भूयो भूयः, मुहुर्मुहुः, अनेकशः, अनेक-बहु-वारं, पुनःपुनः, बहुकृत्वः; 'so m.' इयत्, एतावत्. -*s.* समूहः,

समवायः, संघातः, समाजः; 'the good of the m.' समाजहितं. In comp. ex. by बहु or नाना; बहुपर्ण, नानावर्ण, बहुजिह्व, &c. —MANIFOLD, 'many-sided' *a.* नानाविध-प्रकार, बहुगुण-रूप, अनेक, अनेक-नाना-रूप, विविध, बहुविध-प्रकार; नाना in comp. —LY, *adv.* बहुधा, अनेकधा, नानाविधं. —NESS, *s.* बाहुल्यं, अनेकता.

MAP, *s.* वर्णनं. देशालिख्यं, आलेख्यपत्रं. —*v. t.* (देशादीन्) अभिलिख् 6 P, वर्ण् 10, चित्र् 10.

MAR, *v. t.* हन् 2 P, वि-,नश् c., विलुप् 6 P or c., अपकृ 8 U, क्षण् 8 P, दुष् c. (दूषयति); *See* SPOIL; 'without m. ring its beauty' लावण्यहानिं विना, रूपक्षतिं विना. —MARPLOT, *s.* कार्यविघातकः, विघ्नकरः.

MARASMUS, *s.* क्षयः, यक्ष्मन् *m.*, शोषः.

MARAUD, *v. i.* लोत्रार्थं परिभ्रम् 1, 4 P or उपद्रु 1 P or उपप्लु 1 A. —ER, *s.* उपप्लविन् *m.*, उपप्लवकारी, लुंठकः. —ING, *s.* उपप्लवः, उपद्रवः, लोत्रार्थं परिभ्रमणं.

MARBLE, *s.* मर्मरोपलः, श्लक्ष्णः प्रस्तरः, मणिशिला, शिला, पाषाणः.

MARCESCENT, *a.* विशीर्यमाण.

MARCH, *v. i.* प्र-या 2 P, प्र-गम् 1 P, प्र-सं-चल्-र् 1 P, व्रज् 1 P, प्र-स्था 1 A; *See* ADVANCE; 'm. against' अभि-या, अभिनिर्-या, प्रति-गम्-व्रज्; संमुखं या; 'who m. es slowly' मंदगामी; 'who m. es fast' जंघालः, तरस्वी, जवनः, अतिजवः. —*v. t.* प्र-स्था c. (स्थापयति), प्र-या c. —*s.* फाल्गुनचैत्रं, पूर्वचैत्रः. 2 गमनं, यानं, यात्रा, प्रस्थानं, प्रगमनं, प्रयाणं, अभिनिर्याणं; 'at a distance which is some days' m.' दिवसक्रमगम्येऽध्वनि (Ka. 258); 'going by hasty (forced) m.-es' अविच्छिन्नकैः प्रयाणकैर्वहन् (Ka. 340); 'difficult m.' दुर्गसंचरः, संक्रमः; 'm. ing with an army against the enemy' अभिषेणनं; 'a m.-ing army' प्रचक्रं, चलितं; 'a hostile m.' अभिक्रमः, आसारः. —MARCHES, *s.* देशसीमा-पर्यंतः.

MARE, *s.* वडवा, अश्वा, वामी, तुरगी, वाजिनी.

MARGIN, *s.* प्रांतः, धारः-रा, पर्यंतः, तटं, उपांतः, सीमा, परिसरः, उपकंठः, कच्छः. —AL, *a.* प्रांतस्थ, प्रांतवर्तिन्. —ALLY, *adv.* प्रांततः, अनुप्रांतं.

MARINE, *a.* सामुद्र (द्रीं *f.*), समुद्रीय, समुद्रविषयक, समुद्रज, समुद्र (Sea, q. v.) in comp.; 'm. fight' नौयुद्धं, जलसंग्रामः. —*s.* नौयोधः, समुद्रीयसैनिकः. 2 युद्धनौसमूहः. 3 नाविकप्रकरणं-विषयः.

MARINER, *s.* नाविकः, पोतवाहः, समुद्रयायिन्-गामिन् *m.*

MARITAL, *a.* पति-स्वामि-विषय.

MARITIME, *a.* समुद्रीय, समुद्र in comp. 2 नाविक (की *f.*), नाव्य. 3 समुद्रतीरस्थ.

MARJORAM, *s.* समीरणः, मरुवकः, प्रस्थपुष्पः, फणिज्जकः, जंबीरः, पर्णासः, कठिंजरः, कुठेरकः.

MARK, *s.* लक्षणं, चिह्नं, अंकः, लिंगं, लांछनं, व्यंजनं; अभिज्ञानं. 2 कलंकः, लक्ष्मन् *n.*, अंकः, बिंदुः; 'm. on the body' सामुद्रं, लक्षणं; 'whose distinctive m. is boldness' साहसलांछनः; 'freckly m.' जडुलः, कालकः, पिप्लुः, तिलकः; 'an interpreter of bodily m. s' सामुद्रिकः. 3 ले(रे)खा, अंकः. 4 लक्ष्यं, शरव्यं, वेध्यं, बाणलक्ष्यं; लक्षं; 'hitting the m.' लक्ष्यभेदः; 'hit the m.' लक्ष्यं भिद् 7 P or व्यध् 4 P; 'wide of the m.' अप्रस्तुत, अप्रास्ताविक (की *f.*). —*v. t.* अंक् 10, चिह्नयति-मुद्रयति (D.), लांछ् 1 P. 2 कलंकयति-मलिनयति (D.), मलिनी-कलुषी-कृ 8 U. 3 लिख् 6 P, रेखाः लिख्. 4 लक्ष् 10, आ-उप-°; निर्-प्र-सं-अव-ईक्ष् 1 A; अव-धा 3 U; आलोच् 10, विमृश् 6 P; निरूप् 10; 'm. out' परिच्छिद् 7 P, सीमां निर्धृ 10 or निर्दिश् 6 P, लक्ष्, बाह्यरेखां लिख्. —ED, *a.* चिह्नित, मुद्रित, अंकित, कृतलक्षण-लांछन, मुद्रांकित; 'an arm m. with the scar of the bow-string' मौर्वीकिणांकः भुजः (S. 1). —MARKSMAN, *s.* लक्ष्यभेदिन्-वेधिन् *m.*, सुसंधानी, शराभ्यासकुशलः, धनुर्विद्.

MARKET, *s.* विपणि-णी *f.*, आपणः, निषद्या, पण्यवीथी, पण्यवीथिका, हट्टः, पण्य-विक्रय-शाला-स्थानं, निगमः. 2 क्रयविक्रयः, विपणः. —*v. i.* पण् 1 A, व्यवह् 1 P; 'm.-day' हट्टदिवसः; 'm.-place' *See* (*s.*); 'm.-rate or-price' पण्यमूल्यं, अर्घबलाबलं; 'm.-town' मुख्यनगरं, कर्वटः. —ABLE, *a.* पण्य, पण्यार्ह, क्रयविक्रययोग्य.

MARKING-INK, *s.* अक्षय्यमसी.

MARL, *s.* चिक्कणमृत्तिका.

MARMALADE, *s.* मिष्टान्नं, स्वादुफलं.

MARMOREAN, *a.* पाषाणनिर्मित.

MARMOSET, *s.* क्षुद्रप्लवंगः-वानरः.

MAROON, *a.* घनारुण, घनरक्त.

MARQUEE, *s.* पटवासः-मंडपः, उपकार्या, वस्त्रगृहं.

MARROW, *s.* मेदस् *n.*, मज्जा, वपा, वसा, अस्थि-देहसारः, अस्थिजं, स्निग्धा. 2 सारः-रं, गर्भः, मुख्यांशः; 'he has knocked the m. out in no time' अचिरादेव तेन मर्मस्य सारः निष्कृष्टः-गृहीतः. —LESS, *a.* मज्जा-मेदो-हीन, अ-निः-सार. —Y, *a.* मेदस्विन्, सारवत्, ससार.

MARRY, *v. t.* वि-उद्-वह् 1 P, परि-णी 1 P, उप-यम् 1 A, प्रति-परि-ग्रह् 9 P. 2 (Take for husband) (पतिं) विद् 6 U or लभ् 1 A or अधिगम् 1 P, वृ 5 U, 10 (वरयति), वृ 9 U, पत्या संयुज् pass. 3 (Give in marriage) विवाहं कृ c., पाणिं ग्रह् c., प्र-दा 3 U, पाणिग्रहणं मं-पद् c.; विवाहेन संयुज् 7 U, 10 or संबंध् 9 P. —*adv.* नूनं, खलु; *See*

INDEED. -AGE, *s.* विवाहः, उद्वाहः, उपयमः, परिणयः, पाणिग्रहः-हणं, पाणिपीडनं, दारपरिग्रहः-अधिगमनं-क्रिया; 'give in m.' विवाहविधिना दा or प्रति-पद् c.; 'm.-contract' वाङ्निश्चयः; 'm.-price' शुल्कः-ल्कं; 'm.-gifts' यौतकं, औद्वाहिकं, पारिणाय्यं, सुदायः; 'm.-string' (विवाह-)कौतुकं, मंगलसूत्रं. -AGEABLE, *a.* विवाहयोग्य, परिणेय, विवाहवयस्क, उद्वाहोचित. -ED, *a.* ऊढ, परिणीत, उपयत, कृतविवाह, जातोपयम, निविष्ट; 'a m. man' स्त्रीमान्, कुटुंबी, सभार्यः, कृतदारः, सपत्नीकः; 'a m. woman' सभर्तृका, पतिवत्नी, सधवा, सुवासिनी; 'twice m.' पुनर्भूः, दिधिषुः-षूः; 'one m. before his elder brother' परिवेत्तृ; 'the sin of such marriage' पारिवेद्यं.

MARS, *s.* मंगलः, भौमः, अंगारकः, भू-मही-सुतः, लोहितः, रुधिरः, कुजः, लोहितांगः. 2 कुमारः, कार्तिकेयः, गुहः, स्कंदः, शक्तिधरः, षडाननः, महासेनः, शरजन्मा, सेनानीः, अग्निभूः, विशाखः, षाण्मातुरः.

MARSH, *s.* अनूपदेशः, कच्छः, कच्छभू-भूमि *f.*, सजल-जलाढ्य-भूमिः. -Y, *a.* अनूप, आनूप (पी *f.*), जलाढ्य, जलपूर्ण, सजल, जलमय (यी *f.*).

MARSHAL, *s.* बलाध्यक्षः; संविधातृ *m.*, व्यवस्थापकः. -*v. t.* विन्यस् 4 U, वि-रच् 10, व्यूह् 1 U, क्रमेण रच् or स्था c. (स्थापयति), संवि-धा 3 U.

MART, *s.* क्रयविक्रयस्थानं, आपणः; *See* MARKET.

MARTIAL, *a.* युद्ध-रण-विषयक, सांग्रामिक-सामरिक (की *f.*). 2 रणयोग्य, समरोचित. 3 रणप्रिय, समरासक्त, समर-रण-काम; 'm. music' रणवाद्यं.

MARTINET, *s.* तीक्ष्ण-उग्र-दंडः-शासनः.

MARTINGAL, *s.* तलिका, अधोबंधनं.

MARTYR, *s.* स्वधर्मार्थं-स्वमतार्थं त्यक्तप्राणः or देहत्यागी or न्यस्तजीवितः; 'a blessed m.' सुगृहीतनामा &c. -DOM, *s.* स्वधर्मार्थं-स्वमतरक्षणार्थं प्राण-जीवित-त्यागः or प्राणोत्सर्गः or देहन्यासः.

MARVEL, *s.* कौतुकं, आश्चर्यं, विस्मयहेतुः, चमत्कारः, अद्भुतं, चित्रं, चित्र-अद्भुत-वस्तु *n.* -*v. i.* वि-स्मि 1 A, साश्चर्य-सविस्मय-*a.* भू 1 P, विस्मयेन आकुलीभू or आभिभू pass. -LOUS, *a.* अद्भुत, साश्चर्य, चित्र, आश्चर्यकर (री *f.*), विस्मयावह, आश्चर्य; 'a m. tale' चित्रा कथा; 'a m. deed' अद्भुतं कर्म. -LOUSLY, *adv.* अद्भुतं, चित्रं. -LOUSNESS, *s.* चित्रता, &c.

MASCULINE, *a.* पौरुष (षी *f.*), पुंजातीय, अक्लीब, पुं-पुरुष-in comp. 2 पुरुषशील-स्वभाव, पुरुषप्रकृति; 'm. gender' पुंस्, पुल्लिंगं; 'the word दार is plural and m. (of m. gender)' दाराः पुंभूम्नि; 'a m. woman' नरस्त्री. -LY, *adv.* पुंवत्, पुरुषवत्. -NESS, *s.* पुंस्त्वं, पौरुषं.

MASH, *v. t.* संपिष् 7 P, सं-मृद् 9 P, क्षुद् 7 U, चूर्ण् 10. -*s.* संपेषः, संचूर्णनं, उदपेषः.

MASK, *s.* वर्णकः, वर्णिका, कपट-छद्म-मुखं. 2 छद्मन् *n.*, कपटः-टं, छलं, व्याजः, अप-व्यप-देशः. 3 कृत्रिम-छद्म-वेशः; 'to throw off the m.' (पूर्वं निगूढान्) निजमनोरथान् आविष्कृ 8 U or प्रकटीकृ. -*v. t.* छद्ममुखेन गुह् 1 U or प्रच्छद् 10; गुह्, अपवृ c., गुप् 1 P. -ED, *a.* छन्न-गुप्त-मुख (खी *f.*), सवर्णिक. 2 छद्मवेशिन्, कपटवेश; *See* DISGUISED. 3 गुप्त, छन्न, गूढ. -ER, *s.* छद्मवेशी, कपटरूपी &c.

MASON, *s.* लेपकः, लेपकारः, सुधाजीविन् *m.*, पलगंडः. -RY, *s.* सुधा-लेप-कर्म; इष्टकारचनं-निर्माणं.

MASQUERADE, *v. i.* छद्मवेशं धृ 10, विडंब् 10, कपटवेशं परि-धा 3 U. -*s.* छद्म-कपट-वेशधारणं, छद्मवेशक्रीडा, विडंबनक्रीडा. -ER, *s.* छद्मवेशधारिन् *m.*, कपटवेशी.

MASS, *s.* पिंडः, घनः, गंडः. 2 राशिः, नि-प्र-चयः, निकरः, समूहः, ओघः, पुंजः, संघः, गणः, समाहारः, निवहः; *See* MULTITUDE; 'in m. es' संघशः, गणशः; 'in the m.' साकल्येन. -IVE, -Y, *a.* स्थूल, गुरु, स्थूलाकार, बृहत्, बृहत्-स्थूल-परिमाण, गुरुभार, सभार; पिंडित, पिंडाकार. -IVENESS, *s.* स्थूलता, गुरुत्व, महत्त्वं, गुरुभारः.

MASSACRE, *v. t.* (क्रौर्येण) हन् 2 P, व्या-पद् c., सूद् 10, वि-शस् 1 P, प्रमंथ् 9 P, निर्दल् c. (दलयति); *See* KILL. -*s.* संहारः, विशसनं, घातः, प्रमाथः, निषूदनं, प्रमापणं; *See* KILLING.

MAST, *s.* कूपकः, कूपदंडः, गुणवृक्षकः.

MASTER, *s.* प्रभुः, ईश्वरः, ईशः, नाथः, स्वामिन् *m.*, अधिपः, अधिपतिः; भर्ता, सेव्यः; *See* LORD; 'serving two m. s' उभयवेतन, उभयस्वामिक; 'one's own m.' स्वतंत्र, स्वाधीन, अपरायत्त; 'to be m. of' ex. by (*s.*) or प्र-भू 1 P, ईश् 2 A (with gen.); 'I am not m. of myself' अप्रभुरस्मि आत्मनः (Ka. 36), न प्रभवाम्यात्मनः; गात्राणामनीशोस्मि संवृत्तः (S. 2). 2 अधिकारी, अध्यक्षः, अधिष्ठाता, अधिकृतः, अवेक्षकः, अधीशः, नायकः, पतिः, मुखरः, अग्रणीः; 'm. of a family' कुलपतिः, कौटुंबिकः, कुटुंबी; 'm. of the horse' अश्वाध्यक्षः; 'm. of sports' नर्म-केलि-सचिवः. 3 शिक्षकः, गुरुः, अध्यापकः, आचार्यः, उपाध्यायः. 4 पंडितः, कुशलः, पारंगतः, निपुणः, व्युत्पन्नः; 'm.-hand' उत्तम-परम-कर्मकारः; 'm.-workman' मुख्यशिल्पी, कर्मकाराग्रणीः; 'm.-piece' अप्रतिमं-निरुपमं-कृत्यं, अत्युत्तमं-परमं-अत्युत्कृष्टं-कर्म; 'm.-stroke' वैदग्ध्य-चातुर्य-कर्म, अत्युत्तमक्रिया. -*v. t.* अभ्यंतरीकृ 8 U, पारं गम् 1 P; 'who has m. ed all sciences' सकलशास्त्रपारंगतः. 2 वशीकृ, दम् c. (दमयति), परा-अभि-भू 1 P, जि 1 P. -LY, *a.* अनुपम, अप्रतिम, अत्युत्तम, अद्वितीय, अत्युत्कृष्ट, परम; अतुल, अतिकुशल-निपुण. -*adv.* अत्युत्कृष्टं, परमनिपुणतया.

-SHIP, *s.* प्रभुत्वं, स्वामित्वं, आधिपत्यं, ऐश्वर्यं, प्राधान्यं, &c. -Y, *s.* प्रभुत्वं, ऐश्वर्यं. आधिपत्यं, अधिकारः, अधिष्ठातृत्वं, स्वाम्यं. 2 उत्कर्षः, श्रेष्ठता, आधिक्यं, प्राधान्यं, मुख्यता, परम-उत्तम-श्रेष्ठ-पदं. 3 प्रावीण्यं, अतिनैपुण्यं, परमकौशलं-पाटवं, पारंगतता, प्रतिष्ठा; 'you have attained great m. over all sciences of arms' गतोसि सर्वास्त्रायुधविद्यासु परां प्रतिष्ठां (Ka. 77); 'to have m. over' अभि-भू, प्र-भू, ईश्, वशीकृ; *See* above.

MASTICATE, *v. t.* चर्व् 1 P, 10, संदंश् 1 P. -ION, *s.* चर्वणं, दंशनं, दंतैर्निष्पेषणं. -ORY, *a.* चर्वणोचित. -*s.* चर्व्यं.

MAT, *s.* कटः, किलिंजं, आस्तरणं, पादपाशी. -*v. t.* कटैः आस्तॄ 5 U. 2 संग्रंथ् 9 P, संश्लिष् c., जटिलीकृ 8 U; 'm. ed hair' जटा, सटा, जूटकं, जटा-सटा-जूटः; 'having m. ed hair' जटिल, जटिन्.

MATCH, *s.* समः, समानः, तुल्यः, समान-तुल्य-बलः, तुल्यशक्तिः-पराक्रमः, प्रतिद्वंद्विन् *m.*; 'let us (two) make a m.' आवां प्रतिद्वंद्विनौ भवाव. 2 (One of a pair) यमः, यमकः-लः, युग्मकः, समान-समकक्षः. 3 विवाहः, विवाह-प्रेम-संबंधः-घटना-योगः; 'bringing together a m. of equal merits' समानयंस्तुल्यगुणं वधूवरं (S. 5). 4 युद्धं; 'a m. of cocks &c.' प्राणिद्यूतं, समाह्वयः; 'boxing m.' मल्लक्रीडा-युद्धं, मुष्टीमुष्टि युद्धं. 5 अग्निशलाका; 'to be a m. for' ex. by अलं with dat.; दैत्येभ्यो हरिरलं (S. K.); 'one wrestler is a m. for another' अलं मल्लो मल्लाय, प्रभवति मल्लो मल्लाय; 'to be more than a m. for' अतीत्य-अतिक्रम्य-वृत् 1 A or स्था 1 P; अतीत्य हरितो हरींश्च वर्तंते वाजिनः (S. 1); or by अधिक-*a.* or अतिरिच्-विशिष्-pass., with abl.; सेनाशतेभ्योधिका बुद्धिः (Mu. 1). -*v. t.* तुल् 10 (तुलयति), तुल्यी-समी-कृ 8 U, उप-प्रति-मा 3 A; तुल्यतया घट् c. (घटयति) or समा-नी 1 P or संयुज् 7 U, 10. 2 समं दृश् c., प्रतिरूपं-उपमां-निर्दिश् 6 P; oft. ex. by तुल्य, सम (Equal, q. v.); 'it was a well-m. ed fight' तुल्यप्रतिद्वंद्वि बभूव युद्धं (R. VII. 37); 'palaces can m. you' प्रासादास्त्वां तुलयितुमलं (Me. 65); 'he will m. you in strength' बलविषये स त्वया तुलां समारोक्ष्यति. 3 तुल्यबलं-समं युज् or पुरस्कृ, प्रतियुध् c. 4 विवाहार्थं प्रति-पद् c. or प्र-दा 3 U, 1 P, परिणी c., उद्वह् c. 5 सं-,युज्, समा-धा 3 U, अनुरूप-*a.* कृ. -*v. i.* युज् pass., उप-मा pass., तुल्य-अनुरूप-*a.* भू; सदृशी-अनुगुणी-भू, संवद् 1 P. 2 संगम् 1 A, संमिल् 6 P, सं-इ 2 P, संगमनुव्रज् 1 P, संसज् pass. 3 विवाहार्थं दा-pass. -ED, *a.* तुल्यबल-शक्ति, समविक्रम; उपमित, &c. 2 विवाहित, कृतविवाह, कृतोपयम. -LESS, *a.* अतुल, निरुपम, अनुपम, अद्वितीय, अप्रतिरूप, अप्रतिम, अनुपमेय; अतुल्य, असदृश (शी *f.*). -LESSLY, *adv.* अनुपमं, अप्रतिरूपं. -LESSNESS, *s.* अनुपमता. &c.

MATE, *s.* सहायः, सहचरः, मित्रं, संगिन् *m.*, सखि *m.* 2 भर्ता, स्वामी, पतिः; (female) सहचरी, सखी, पत्नी, वधूः, भार्या, प्रिया, दयिता; *See* WIFE; 'an elephant's m.' वशा, करिणी, हस्तिनी. 3 सहायः, सहकारी.

MATERIAL &c., *See* under MATTER.

MATERNAL, *a.* मातृक (की *f.*), मातृसंबंधिन्; मातृ- in comp.; 'm. uncle' मातुलः (-लानी *f.*); 'm. affection' अपत्यस्नेहः, पुत्रप्रीति *f.*, वात्सल्यं; 'm. duty' मातृधर्मः.

MATHEMATICS, *s.* गणितं, गणितशास्त्रं-विद्या, संख्यापरिमाणविद्या, गणनाविद्या.—MATHEMATIC,-AL, *a.* गणितविषयक, गणितसंबंधिन्. 2 गणितशास्त्रानुरूप. -ALLY, *adv.* गणितानुसारेण. -IAN, *s.* गणितविद्याज्ञः, गणितशास्त्रज्ञः-विद्, गणितज्ञः.

MATIN, *a.* प्रातःकालीन, प्रातःकालिक (की *f.*), प्रगेतन (नी *f.*), प्रातर् in comp. -*s.* (M. s) प्रातरुपासना; प्रातःकृत्यं-कर्म.

MATRICE, *s.* गर्भाशयः, जरायुः. 2 मुद्राक्षरसंस्कारः.

MATRICIDE, *s.* मातृहत्या-वधः-घातः. 2 मातृघातिन्-मातृहन् *m.*, मातृघ्नः, मातृघातकः.

MATRICULATE, *v. t.* संस्कारपूर्वं विद्यालयं प्रविश् c. -*s.* विद्यालयप्रविष्टः.

MATRIMONY, *s.* विवाहः, परिणयः, उपयमः, उद्वाहः; *See* MARRIAGE. -IAL, *a.* वैवाहिक-औद्वाहिक (की *f.*); 'm. alliance' विवाहसंबंधः. -IALLY, *adv.* विवाहविध्यनुरूपं.

MATRON, *s.* पुरंध्री, आर्या, प्रौढा, गृहिणी, गेहिनी; पुत्रिणी, सुतिनी, कुटुंबिनी, पुत्रवती. -LY, *a.* पुरंध्रीयोग्य, गृहिणीसदृश (शी *f.*); धीर, गंभीर, प्रौढ, आर्य, विनीत.

MATTER, *s.* द्रव्यं, वस्तु *n.*, स्थूल-घन-द्रव्यं-वस्तु, भौतिकवस्तु, साकारद्रव्यं, मूर्ति *f.* 2 साधनं. प्रकृति *f.*, उपकरणं, कारणं, उपादानं. 3 द्रव्यं, वस्तु, पदार्थः; अर्थः, विषयः, प्रकरणं, पदं, आस्पदं, प्रस्तावः, प्रसंगः. 4 प्रयोजनं, हेतुः, कारणं, कार्यं, व्यापारः, अर्थः. 5 सारः, तत्त्वं, अर्थः, गुरुत्वं, गौरवं, महत्त्वं, प्रभावः. 6 पूयं, दूष्यं, क्षतजं, पूयरक्तं-शोणितं; 'm. in hand' प्रकृतं, प्रस्तुतं; 'm. of dispute' विवादवस्तु-विषयः-आस्पदं &c.; 'it is of no m.' यत्किंचित्करमेतत्, निरर्थकं, सूक्ष्मविचारस्याविषयः; 'an important m.' गुर्वर्थः; 'of no m.' निरर्थक, निःसार, अगुरु; 'what is the m. with her' किं तस्या वृत्तं, कस्तस्या वृत्तांतः. -*v. i.* Ex. by अर्थः, or by किं, कार्यं with instr.; 'what m. s it to me' किं मम तेन कार्यं, कोर्थः &c.; 'it m. s very little', 'it m. s not' लघ्वर्थमेतत्, नायं गरीयानर्थः. 2 पूयपूर्ण-*a.* भू 1 P, पूयं

उत्पद् c. -Y, *a.* पूयपूर्ण-युक्त-गर्भ, सपूय. -MATERIAL, *a.* भूतात्मक, भौतिक (की *f.*), भूतमय (यी *f*), आधि-पांच-भौतिक, मूर्त, द्रव्यमय, प्राकृतिक (की *f.*), घन, स्थूल, जड. 2 अपारमार्थिक (की *f.*), अनात्मीय. 3 सारवत्, ससार, वास्तविक (की *f.*). 4 गुरु, महत्, परमार्थ, गुर्वर्थ, आवश्यक (की *f.*), मुख्य, प्रधान, विशिष्ट; *See* PRINCIPAL; 'm. world' भूतसृष्टि *f.*, स्थूलं जगत्; 'm. body' स्थूल-जड-देहः, भौतिकपिंडः; 'm. cause' प्रकृतिः, उपादानं, उपादानकारणं; 'proximity being not m.' सन्निधानस्य अकिंचित्करत्वात् (S. B. 141). -*s.* साधनं, उपकरणं, द्रव्यं, कारणं, उपादानं, प्रकृतिः, पदार्थः, साधनवस्तु; 'all m.-s' सामग्री, सज्जा, संभारः, द्रव्य-उपकरण-सामग्री-संभारः; 'writing m. s' लिपिसज्जा, लेखनसाधनानि; 'the m. of cloth' वस्त्रयोनिः-प्रकृतिः. -ISM, *s.* लोकायतं, अनात्मवादः, चार्वाकमतं. -IST, *s.* लोकायतिकः, अनात्मवादिन् *m.*; विषयी. -ITY, *s.* भौतिकत्वं, मूर्तिमत्त्वं, &c. -LY, *adv.* अर्थतः, वस्तुतः, तत्त्वतः, परमार्थतः, सारतः, प्रकृतितः, प्रकृत्यैव.

MATTOCK, *s.* खनित्रं, टंकः, पाषाणदारणः.

MATTRESS, *s.* (मृदु-) आ-सं-स्तरः, शयनीयं, आस्तरणं, तूलिका.

MATURE, *a.* पक्व, सु-परि-पक्व, परिणत, पक्वतामापन्न, पाकोन्मुख (खी *f.*), फलोन्मुख. 2 संपन्न, सं-परि-पूर्ण, प्रौढ, सिद्ध; 'm. deliberation' सुविचारः, प्रसमीक्ष्य-सुविमृश्य-विचारः, सुसमीक्षा, सुविमर्शः. -*v. t.* परिपाकं नी 1 P, परि-णम् c. (णमयति), पक्वतां-पाकं-उत्पद् c., पच् c.; सं-पद् c., साध् c., सिद्धीकृ 8 U, कठोरीकृ; कलाकलापालोचनकठोरमतिभिः (Ka. 7) 'whose mind was m. ed by studying &c.' -*v. i.* पच् pass., परिणम् 1 P. पाकं-परिणामं-इ or या 2 P or गम् 1 P; कठोरी-प्रौढी-भू 1 P; परिणतप्रज्ञस्य कवेर्वाणीं (U. 7) 'of m. ed intellect'. -ATE, *v. t.* पच् c., परि-णम् c. -*v. i.* पच् pass., पक्वीभू, पूयपूर्ण-*a.* भू. -ATION, *s.* पाकः, विपरि°-,परिणति *f.*, परिणामः. 2 सपूयत्वं, पूयस्रावः. -ATIVE, *a.* पाकल, पाचन, पचिष्णु, पूयजनन (नी *f.*). -ITY, -NESS, *s.* पाकः, वि-परि-°, परिणामः, विपक्वता, परिणति *f.*, प्रौढ-पक्व-दशा, पक्व-परिणत-अवस्था, पक्वभावः, कठोरता, प्रौढता, सिद्धि *f.*, संपूर्णता. -LY, *adv.* सपरिणामं, सपाकं. 2 सुसमीक्ष्य, सुविमृश्य, सुविचार्य, सम्यगवधार्य. -MATURESCENT, *a* आपक्व, परिणामोन्मुख.

MATUTINAL, MATUTINE, *a.* प्रातःकालिक-प्राभातिक (की *f.*), प्रगेतन (नी *f.*), उषस्य, प्रातर् in comp.

MAUDLIN, *a.* आमत्त, मत्तप्राय-कल्प.

MAUGRE, *adv.* *See* 'In spite of' under SPITE.

MAUL, *s.* स्थूलमुद्गरः, घनः. -*v. t.* मुद्गरेण-लगुडेन प्र-हृ 1 P or तड् 10. 2 वि-रूप् 10, विकृ 8 U.

MAUSOLEUM, *s.* चैत्यं, समाधिः.

MAW, *s.* उदरं, जठरः-रं.

MAWKISH, *a.* अरस, नीरस, निःसत्त्व; बीभत्स, जुगुप्सावह.

MAXILLAR,-Y, *a.* हनुसंबंधिन्, हनु in comp.

MAXIM, *s.* सूत्रं, उक्ति *f.*, वचनं, वाक्यं, विधिः, तत्त्वं, नियमः, आ-नि-देशः, चोदना, कल्पः, सिद्धांतः; 'moral m.' नीतिवाक्यं, सदुपदेशवचनं.

MAXIMUM, *s.* उत्तम-परम-संख्या.

MAY, *s.* Gen. ex. by Potential of verbs. 2 (Showing wish or blessing) ex. by Benedictive or Imperative; 'm. god *S*iva protect you' पातु देवः शिवो वः; 'm. I be satisfied' कृतार्थो भूयासं. 3 (Liberty) gen. ex. by Pot.; *See* LIBERTY. 4 (Contingency) by Pot., with or without कदाचित्. -*s.* वैशाखज्येष्ठं.

MAYOR, *s.* नगराध्यक्षः, पुराग्रणीः. -MAYORALTY, *s.* पुराध्यक्षता, नगराधिकारः.

MAZE, *s.* गहनं, कुटिलमार्गः, सुगहनस्थानं, दुर्निर्गमं स्थानं. 2 वक्रता, गहनता, कौटिल्यं, वैषम्यं. -Y, *a.* गहन, दुर्निर्गम, कुटिल, जिह्म, अतिवक्र.

MEAD, *s.* मधु, मधुपानीयं. 2 Meadow, q. v.

MEADOW, *s.* क्षेत्रं, गोप्रचारः, केदारः. 2 स्थली, वनस्थली, शाद्वलं, यवसस्थानं; 'm. grass' यवसं. -Y, *a.* शाद्वल, यवसीय.

MEAGRE, *a.* क्षाम, कृश, क्षीण; *See* LEAN. 2 असार, विरस, नीरस, फल्गु, (style); वन्ध्यं, रूक्ष (soil). 3 अपूर्ण, स्वल्प, तनु, स्तोक. -LY, *adv.* कार्श्येन, स्वल्पं; 'm. attended' तनुपरिवार. -NESS, *s.* कृशता, क्षीणता, क्षामता, रूक्षता, तनुता, स्वल्पता, &c.

MEAL, *s.* सक्तु (*m.* pl.), क्षोदः, चूर्णं, पिष्टं. 2 भोजनं, अशनं; आहारः, आहारविधिः; 'took his m. s' आहारविधिमकरोत्, भोजनं निर्वर्तयामास, शरीरस्थितिं समपादयत्; 'good m.' सुभोजनं; 'morning m.' प्रातराशः. -Y, *a.* सचूर्ण, क्षोदमय (यी *f.*). 2 कोमल, मसृण, मृदु, चूर्णसदृश. (शी *f.*); 'm.-mouthed' मृदुभाषिन्, कोमलवाच्.

MEAN, *a.* मध्य, मध्यपरिमाण-प्रमाण, मध्यम. 2 मध्य, मध्यम, मध्यस्थित, व्यवहित, मध्यवर्तिन्, अंतर्गत; 'in the m.-while' 'in the m.-time' अत्रांतरे. 3 नीच, अप-नि-कृष्ट,अधम, जघन्य, कदर्य, कुत्सित, नि-,हीन, अनार्य, खल, दुष्ट, विवर्ण, पामर, प्राकृत, अपसद, क्षुल्लक; ग्राम्य, अवम, अवद्य, गर्ह्य, लघु, कुपूय, खेट in comp., अणक, रेफ; तुच्छ, क्षुद्र, कृपण, दीन, (mind &c.); (in birth) हीन-नीच-जाति, अंत्यजातीय, अकुलीन, कु or का in comp., 'm.-spirited' लघुचेतस्, क्षुद्रमानस, कृपणबुद्धि, कापुरुष, अधमवृत्ति. -*v. t.* उद्दिश् 6 P, इष् 6 P, अभिप्र-इ 2 P; oft. ex. by desid. forms, or by काम or मनस् in comp. with inf.; 'now what do you m. to do' अथ भवान् किं कर्तुमनाः or किं चिकीर्षति; *See* INTEND. 2 गम् c. (गमयति), बुध् c., सुत् c., अभि-धा 3 U, सूच् 10, निर्दिश्; gen. ex. by वृत् 1 A with loc., or by loc. simply; by अर्थ, पर, वाचिन् &c comp.; ज्योतिःशब्दस्तेजसि वर्तते (S. B. 146); अत्र अपचितिशब्दः पूजार्थः-पूजापरः-पूजावाची &c.; 'a speech m. ing censure' निंदापरं वचः; 'what is meant by telling a lie' असत्यमिति यदुच्यते तेन किं गम्यते, or असत्यभाषणस्य कोर्थः; 'what can all this m.' कः प्रकारः किमेतत् (Mal. 5), किं नु एतत्स्यात् (Mal. 1).—*s.* मध्यमपरिमाणं, मध्यता, मध्यं, समभागः, समपक्षः. 2 अंतरं, अभ्यंतरं, मध्यावधिः, अंतरालं. 3 परिमितता, अनतिक्रमः. 4 (Means) साधनं, उपकरणं, उपायः, करणं, द्वारं, योगः, गति *f.*, साहाय्यं, सामग्री, कारणं, हेतुः; oft. ex. by instr. 4 आयः, विभवः; द्रव्यं, धनं, सामर्थ्यं, शक्ति *f.*, धनागमः; 'don't live beyond your m.' आयमर्यादां मातिक्राम, यथाविभवं-यथाशक्ति &c. व्ययं कुरु; 'having moderate m.' नातिधन, अल्पविभव; 'by all m.' सर्वथा, सर्वप्रकारेण, अवश्यं, नूनं, खलु, अवश्यमेव; 'by no m.' न सर्वथा, न कथंचन, न कथंचित्; 'by any m.' येनकेन प्रकारेण, यथा कथंचित्, कथमपि, कथंचन, कथंचित्, कथं कथमपि; 'm. of subsistence' जीवनसाधनं-उपायः-हेतुः; उपजीविका. —ING, *s.* अभिप्रायः, उद्देशः, आशयः, अर्थः, तात्पर्यं, भावः, आकूतं, इंगितं, आकांक्षा. 2 विवक्षा, विवक्षितं, अर्थः; 'the m. of a word' पदार्थः; 'literal m.' अवयवार्थः, पदार्थः, शब्दार्थः; 'hidden m.' मर्मन् *n.*, गूढार्थः; 'what is the m. of this laughter' किंनिमित्तोयं हासः. —*a.* अर्थवत्, सार्थ, पूर्णार्थ, चरितार्थ, साकूत; 'casting at me a m. look' साकूतं मां निर्वर्ण्य. —INGLESS, *a.* निरर्थक, अनर्थक, निष्कारण, अनिमित्त. —INGLY, *adv.* सार्थं, साकूतं, सेंगितं. —LY, *adv.* कृपणवत्, अधमवत्, दीनं, &c.; सावज्ञं, सावमानं, लाघवेन; 'm. born' हीनजाति, अधमवर्ण; 'm. attired' कृपण-अनार्य-वेष. —NESS, *s.* नीचता, अधमता, कदर्यता, कुत्सितता, &c.; 'm. of birth' अकुलीनता, अपकृष्टं जन्म.

MEANDER, *v. i.* वक्रं-कुटिलं-जिह्मं-गम् or सृ 1 P or या 2 P; *See* WIND. —*v. t.* कुटिलीकृ 8 U. —*s.* वक्रता, जिह्मता, कौटिल्यं, वक्र-जिह्म-कुटिल-गति *f.*, सर्पगतिः. —ING, *a.* वक्र, कुटिल-जिह्म-सर्प-गति, विसर्पिन्, विषमगति.

MEASURE, *v. t.* मा 3 A, 2 P, प्र-परि-°; तुल् 10, मानं निरूप् 10 or ज्ञा 9 U. 2 गण् 10. 3 विभज् 1 U, परि-क्लृप् c.; *See* DIVIDE. 3 लंघ् 1 A, 10, अतिक्रम् 1 U, 4 P, अति इ 2 P. —*v. i.* Ex. by प्र-परि-माण, मात्र, मित, परिमित in comp. —*s.* मानं, प्र-परि-माणं, (fig. also); 'm. ing rod' मानदंडः; 'm. of capacity' प्रतीमानं, प्रस्थः. 2 वि-,भागः, अंशः. 3 प्रमाणं, पर्यंतः, मात्रा, मर्यादा, सीमा; 'in some m.' ईषत्, किंचित्, अल्पमात्रं; 'beyond m.' अतिमात्रं, नितांतं, अतीव, भृशं. 4 उपायः, प्रयोगः, साधनं, युक्ति *f.*, प्रवृत्ति *f.*, क्रिया, उपचारः; 'take m. s' उपायं प्रयुज् 7 A, 10 or आश्रि 1 U or अवलंब् 1 A, कार्ये प्रवृत् 1 A; 'mild m.' सामन् *n.*, सामोपायः. 5 छंदस् *n.*, वृत्तं. 6 तालः, लयः; 'the steps are in m.' पादन्यासो लयमनुगतः (M. 2); 'the m. of a vowel' मात्रा; 'in musical m.' स्वरबद्ध-*a.* 7 अपवर्तः; 'having a common m.' सापवर्त. —ED, *a.* मित, परिमित; नियत, निबद्ध; *See* LIMITED. 2 सम, समान, धीर. —ER, *s.* मापकः, माननिरूपकः. —LESS, *a.* अमित, अपरिमाण. —MENT, *s.* मापनं, मानं, प्र-परि-माणं, प्र-परि-मिति *f.*; 'rough m.' स्थूलमानं; 'accurate m.' सूक्ष्ममानं.

MEAT, *s.* आमिषं; मांसं, मांसाहारः; 'butcher's m.' सौ(शौ)नं. 2 अन्नं, भोजनं, आहारः; खाद्यं; 'seller of m.' मांसिकः, सौ(शौ)निकः, वैतंसिकः, कौटिकः.

MECHANIC, &c. *See* under MACHINE.

MEDAL, *s.* मुद्रा, कीर्तिमुद्रा, प्रतिष्ठामुद्रा. —LIST, *s.* मुद्राशास्त्रज्ञः. 2 लब्धकीर्तिमुद्रः.

MEDDLE, *v. i.* अव्यापारेषु व्यापारं कृ 8 U, (अन्यव्यापारेषु) व्यापृ 6 A, परकार्याणि निरूप् 10 or चर्च् 6 P, 10, पराधिकारचर्चां कृ, पराधिकारं प्रविश् 6 P. 2 व्यापृ, व्यापृत-*a.* भू. —ER, *s.* पराधिकारचर्चकः, परकार्यनिरूपकः-व्यापारी, अन्यव्यापारचर्चकः. —ING, —SOME, *a.* पराधिकारनिरूपक, परकार्यचर्चाशील; better by (*v.*). —*s.*, —SOMENESS, *s.* परकार्यचर्चा, पराधिकारनिरूपणं-प्रवेशः, अव्यापारेषु व्यापारः, अन्याधिकारचर्चानियोगः-निरूपणं.

MEDIAL, *a.* मध्य; *See* INTERMEDIATE.

MEDIATE, *v. i.* माध्यस्थ्यं कृ 8 U, मध्यस्थः भू 1 P, मध्ये वृत् 1 A or गम् 1 P, माध्यस्थ्येन सं-धा 3 U. —*a.* व्यवहित, मध्यवर्तिन्, मध्यस्थ, मध्यस्थित, अंतर्गत. —ION, *s.* माध्यस्थ्यं, मध्यस्थता. —LY, *adv.* माध्यस्थ्येन, अन्यद्वारेण-द्वारा. —OR, *s.* मध्यस्थः, मध्यमपुरुषः, मध्यस्थितः. —ORSHIP, *s.* मध्यस्थाधिकारः, माध्यस्थ्यं.

MEDICABLE, *a.* चिकित्स्य, उपक्रम्य, साध्य, उपचारसाध्य.

MEDICAL, *a.* वैद्य (द्यी *f.*), औषधीय, वैद्यक-आयुर्वेद-संबंधिन्, वैद्यकविषय; 'm. science' आयुर्वेदः, वैद्यशास्त्रं; 'm. treatment' वैद्य-भेषज-उपचारः;

औषध-भेषज-प्रयोगः; 'm. man' वैद्यः, भिषक्, चिकित्सकः. -LY, *adv.* वैद्यशास्त्रानुरूपं.

MEDICAMENT, *s.* Medicine, q. v.

MEDICASTER, *s.* छद्मवैद्यः, कूटचिकित्सकः.

MEDICATE, *v. t.* औषधैः मिश्र् 10 or संसृज् 6 P, औषधगुणान् दा 3 U or संक्रम् c. 2 औषधं दा; *See* CURE. -ION, *s.* औषधीयद्रव्यसंसर्गः-मिश्रणं.

MEDICINE, *s.* औषधं, भेषजं, अगदः, भैषज्यं, जायुः; 'administering of m.' औषधोपचारः, औषधोपक्रमः, भेषजप्रयोगः, चिकित्सा, रुक्प्रतिक्रिया, उपक्रमः, उपचारः, उपचर्या, वैद्यक्रिया-उपचारः-उपक्रमः. 2 (Science) आयुर्वेदः, वैद्यकं, वैद्यशास्त्रं. -AL, *a.* औषधीय, भेषज (जी *f.*), रोगघ्न (घ्नी *f.*), रोगहर, रोगहारिन्. 2 औषधविषयक.

MEDIEVAL, *a.* मध्यमकालीन.

MEDIOCRE, *a.* सामान्य, मध्यम, साधारण (णी *f.*), मध्यम-सामान्य-गुण-भाव. -*s.* सामान्यगुणः नरः. -MEDIOCRITY, *s.* सामान्याः, मध्यमाः (pl.). 2 मध्यमता, सामान्यता, मध्यम-सामान्य-भावः-दशा.

MEDITATE, *v.* ध्यै 1 P, चिंत् 10, भू c., वि-मृश् 6 P, मनसा विचर् c. or कॢप् c. or वि-भू c., समा-धा 3 U, वितर्क् 10. 2 परि-सं-कॢप् c., चिंत्, युज् 7 U, 10, मंत्र् 10 A; *See* INTEND. -ION, *s.* ध्यानं, चिंता, विमर्शः, भावनं-ना, कल्पनं; (deep) अंतर्ध्यानं, समाधिः, आत्मैकाग्रता, प्रणिधानं, प्रसंख्यानं, (हरः प्रसंख्यानपरो बभूव K. III. 40); 'religious m.' योगः, समाधिः, समाधियोगः, &c.; 'deeply absorbed in m.' ध्यानपर-मग्न-निष्ठ, समाधिस्थ. -IVE, *a.* चिंता-ध्यान-पर, चिंता-ध्यान-शील, समाधिस्थ, समाहित, सचिंत; 'by means of m. power' समाधियोगेन, प्रणिधानबलेन-योगात्, प्रणिधानतः.

MEDITERRANEAN, *a.* भूमध्यस्थ, भूवेष्टित, मध्यदेशीय, मध्यदेशस्थ.

MEDIUM, *s.* साधनं, द्वारं, द्वार् *f.*, कारणं, निमित्तं, हेतुः, करणं, अंगं, योगः, मार्गः; 'through the m. of my friend' मन्मित्रद्वारेण-द्वारा; 'through the m. of air' आकाशमार्गेण. 2 मध्यमता, सामान्य-मध्य-पक्षः.

MEDLEY, *s.* संकरः, सन्निपातः, प्र-सं-कीर्णकं, द्रव्यसंकुलं, नानाद्रव्यसंमिश्रणं-समूहः. -*a.* सं-प्र-कीर्ण, संकुल, संमिश्रित, संकरीकृत.

MEDULLAR,-Y, *a.* मज्जासंबंधिन्; मेदोमय (यी *f.*).

MEED, *s.* पारितोषिकं, प्रतिफलं.

MEEK, *a.* विनीत, सविनय, नम्र-शील-वृत्ति, अनुद्धत, अगर्व, निरहंकार, सौम्य; *See* HUMBLE. 2 दीन, कृपण. -LY, *adv.* सविनयं, नम्रतया, अनुद्धतं, नम्रचेतसा. 2 दीनवत्, कृपणं. -NESS, *s.* विनयः, सौम्यता, अगर्वः, अनौद्धत्यं, नम्रशीलता, दैन्यं, कार्पण्यं.

MEET, *v. t.* सं-इ 2 P, संगम् 1 A, आ-समा-सद् c., संमिल् 6 P, समा-उपा-गम् 1 P; oft. ex. by दृश् 1 P, नयनपथं-विषयं &c. या 2 P or गम्, प्रति-सं-अभि-मुखं या or गम् or प्राप् 5 P, अभि-सं-मुखीभू 1 P; 'I met a little cottage girl' कुटजनिवासिनी काचिद्बालिका मम नयनविषयं याता or मया दृष्टा; 'they two met each other' परस्पराभिमुखं प्राप्तौ. 2 (With) आ-सद् c., अधि-गम्, प्राप्, लभ् 1 A, अभि-या-इ-गम्; *See* FIND, GET; 'm. with calamities' संप्राप्नुवंति आपदः; 'm.s with death' मृत्युमभ्येति, निधनं याति, मरणमाप्नोति, विनाशं गच्छति &c.; 'not easy to m. with' दुर्लभ, दुष्प्राप, दुरासद, &c.; 'go out to m.' प्रत्युद्-या-व्रज्-गम्-इ; 'to rise to m.' प्रत्युत्था 1 P, अभ्युत्था. -*v. i.* संमिल्, सम्-इ, सन्नि-पत् 1 P, एकीभू, एकत्र मिल्; *See* ASSEMBLE. 2 (In battle) संयुध् 4 A, युद्धार्थं मिल्, युद्धं आरंभ् 1 A, रणे अभि-युज् pass.; 'the waters m.' आपः संप्लवंते, संगच्छंते, संभिद्यंते. -*a.* युक्त, उचित, योग्य, उपपन्न; *See* PROPER. -LY, *adv.* योग्यं, उपपन्नं. -NESS, *s.* औचित्यं, युक्तता. -ING, *s.* समागमः, संगति *f.*, संगः, संगमः, संमिलनं, संयोगः. 2 सभा, समाजः, मेला, मेलकः, सदस् *f. n.*, संसद् *f.*, परिषद् *f.*, लोक-जन-समूहः-संघः-समुदायः; गोष्ठी, आस्थानं-नी (m.-house); 'member of a m.' सभ्यः, सदस्यः, सभासद्. 3 संभेदः, व्यतिकरः, संगः-गमः.

MEGRIM, *s.* शिरोवेदना, अर्धावभेदकं. 2 Humour, q.v.

MELANCHOLY, *a.* विषण्ण, सविषाद, अवसन्न, खिन्न, उद्विग्न, दुर्मनस्, विमनस्, दीनमनस्क, चिंताशील, चिंताकुल; *See* DEJECTED. 2 सदा-नित्य-विषण्ण, खेदवृत्ति, विषादशील. 3 विषादात्मक, खेद-शोक-गर्भ; 'to be m.' अव-वि-सद् 1 P, म्लै 1 P, खिद् pass. -*s.* विषादः, अवसादः, खेदः, उद्वेगः, म्लानि *f.*, निर्वेदः, दैन्यं, चित्तोद्वेगः, वैमनस्यं, विषादवृत्ति *f.* -IC, *a.* सदाविषादिन्. -ILY, *adv.* सविषादं, सोद्वेगं, &c.

MELEE, *s.* रणसंकुलं, संकुलसंग्रामः.

MELIORATE, *v. See* IMPROVE.

MELLIFEROUS, *a.* मधुप्रद, मधुदायिन्.

MELLIFLUOUS, MELLIFLUENT, *a.* मधुर, मधुमय (यी *f.*), मधुस्यंदिन्-स्राविन्. 2 मधुराक्षर, मधुरवाच्. -LY, *adv.* मधुरं. -NESS, *s.* माधुर्यं, मधुप्रवाहः-स्रावः.

MELLOW, *a.* पक्व, परिणत, पाकमृदु. 2 मृदु, कोमल, स्निग्ध, सुखस्पर्श; 'm. to the ear' मंजुल, मंजुस्वन, मधुर-कोमल-शब्द. -*v. i.* पच् pass., पक्वदशां या 2 P or प्राप् 5 P, मृदूभू 1 P. -*v. t.* पच् 1 P or c., मृदूकृ 8 U; *See* MATURE. -NESS, *s.* पक्वता, परिपाकः, पक्वदशा; कोमलता, मार्दवं.

MELODY, *s.* सुस्वरः, स्वरमाधुर्यं, कलता, माधुर्यं, सुश्राव्यता, श्रोत्राभिरामता, सुखश्रवता, स्वरानुपूर्व्यं, तालैक्यं; 'm. of song' गीतरागः. -MELODIOUS, *a.* मधुर, सुख-

श्रव, सुश्राव्य, श्रुतिमनोहर, सुस्वर, सुस्वन, मंजुल, कल, श्रोत्राभिराम, श्रुति-श्रोत्र-सुख, मंजु-कल-स्वन, मधुरस्वर, मधुराक्षर. -LY, *adv.* मधुरं, कलं, सुस्वरेण. -NESS, *s.* माधुर्यं, कलता, &c.

MELON, *s.* स्फुटिफलं, तरंबुजं, कालिंगं, सेटुः.

MELT, *v. i.* वि-ली 9 P, 4 A, वि-,द्रु 1 P (fig. also), गल् 1 P, क्षर् 1 P, द्रवी-आर्द्री-भू 1 P. 2 दयार्द्रीभू, करुणया द्रु; 'his whole soul m. s with benevolence' अस्य सर्वात्मनि परहितबुद्धिर्निषिक्तेव, परोपकारपरवशः. -*v. t.* वि-ली c., वि-,द्रु c., गल् c. 2 दयार्द्रीकृ 8 U, करुणार्द्रीकृ, वत्सलयति (D.); 'to be m. ed' आर्द्रीभू, आर्द्र-*a.* भू, द्रु, अभि-स्यंद् 1 A; 'his heart was m. ed with affection' तस्य हृदयं स्नेहार्द्रीभूतं, स्नेहेनाभ्यष्यंदत. -ER, *s.* द्रावकः, विलयनकृत् *m.* -ING, *s.* द्रवः, द्रवणं, विलयनं, गलनं, क्षरणं. 2 द्रावणं, विलायनं.

MEMBER, *s.* अंगं, अवयवः, गात्रं, प्रतीकः, अपघनः; 'Veda with all its m. s' सांगः वेदः. 2 (Of a discourse &c.) अंगं, प्रकरणं, खंडः-डं, देशः, परिच्छेदः, विभागः, अंशः; 'm. by m.' अवयवशः, भागशः; 'becoming a m.' अंगभूत. 3 (Of an assembly &c.) सभ्यः, सभासद्, सदस्यः, पारिषदः; सभाभ्यंतरः, सामाजिकः; 'm. of an association' गणाभ्यंतरः. 4 (Of a family) कुलावयवः, कुटुंबिन् *m.*; 'm. of a compound' पदं. -ED, *a.* अंगिन्, अवयविन्, अंग in comp. -SHIP, *s.* सभ्यपदं.

MEMBRANE, *s.* त्वच् *f.*, तनुत्वक्, आवरणत्वक्, चर्मन् *n.* -OUS, *a.* तनुत्वगावृत.

MEMENTO, *s.* स्मरणं, स्मारकं.

MEMOIR, *s.* वृत्तं, चरित्रं, वृत्तांतः, इतिहासः; चरित्ररचना-लिखनं.

MEMORY, *s.* स्मृति *f.*, स्मरणशक्ति *f.*, धारणा, स्मरणं, संस्मृतिः, संस्मरणं. 2 स्मार्तकालः, स्मृतिकालः; 'retentive m.' मेधा, धारणा, धारणावती धीः; 'having retentive m.' मेधाविन्, धारणावत्; 'commit to m..' कंठस्थ-*a.* कृ 8 U, हृदये-मनसि-चित्ते-कृ, अभ्यस् 4 U; 'committed to m.' कंठस्थ, हृदयस्थ; 'store in m.' हृदये नि-उप-धा 3 U or कृ, अवधृ 10; 'to remain only in m.' स्मृतिविषयतां-स्मृतिपथं-स्मर्तव्यशेषं-कथावशेषं-गम् 1 P or प्राप् 5 P; 'loss of m.'. स्मृतिलोपः; 'time beyond m.' अस्मार्तकालः; 'within m.' स्मार्ते काले. -ABLE, *a.* स्मर्तव्य, स्मरणार्ह; प्र-वि-ख्यात, प्रसिद्ध, सुविज्ञात. -MEMORANDUM, *s.* स्मरणलेखः-पत्रं, स्मारकं पत्रं. —MEMORIAL, *s.* स्मरणचिह्नं, स्मारकं, स्मारकं कृत्यं, स्मारकविषयः. 2 आवेदनपत्रं, अभ्यर्थनालेखः, विज्ञप्ति *f.*, विज्ञापनापत्रं. -*a.* स्मारक, अनुबोधक, स्मृतिकर (री *f.*). -IST, *s.* प्रार्थकः, अर्थिन् *m.*, प्रार्थयितृ *m.*, विज्ञप्तिकृत् *m.* -IZE, *v. t.* वि-ज्ञा c. (ज्ञापयति), निवेदनपत्रेण प्रार्थ् 10 A.

MENACE, *v. t.* तर्ज् 1 P, 10 A, भी c., भर्त्स् 10 A, भयं दृश् c. ; *See* FRIGHTEN. -*s.* तर्जनं-ना, बिभीषिका, भर्त्सनं-ना, भयदर्शनं, अपकारगिर् *f.* -ER, *s.* भर्त्सनकृत् *m*, तर्जकः. -ING, *a.* भीषण, भयप्रद.

MENAGERIE, *s.* वि(वी)तंसः; पशुपक्षिसंग्रहः.

MEND, *v. t.* नवीकृ 8 U, सं-धा 3 U, समा-प्रतिसमा-धा, उद्धृ 1 P, (जीर्णं) सं-धा or साध् c. 2 शुध् c., प्रतिकृ; प्रमृज् 2 P or c. 3 प्रवृध् c., उत्कृष् 1 P, भद्रतरीकृ; *See* IMPROVE; 'm. your pace' लघु लघु गच्छ. -*v. i.* वृद्धि-उत्कर्ष-उन्नति-इ-या 2 P or गम् 1 P, भद्रतरीभू, सुस्थ-*a.* भू, वृध् 1 A. -ER, *s.* संधातृ *m.*, उद्धर्तृ *m.* -ING, *s.* संधानं, समाधानं, उद्धारः, प्रतिकरणं.

MENDACIOUS,-CITY, *See* LIAR, LYING, under LIE.

MENDICANT, *s.* भिक्षुः, भिक्षुकः, अर्थिन् *m.*, याचकः, भिक्षार्थी, भिक्षाशी, भैक्ष्यभुज् *m.*, वनीयकः, याचनकः, मार्गणः. 2 (Religious) परिव्राज् *m.*, परिव्राजकः, योगी, यतिः, संन्यासी. -MENDICANCY,-MENDICITY, *s.* भैक्ष्यं, भिक्षा, भिक्षाशित्वं, भिक्षावृत्ति *f.*, भैक्ष्याजीवः, याचना, यांचा, याचकवृत्तिः, प्रव्रज्या.

MENIAL, *s.* भृत्यः, प्रेष्यः, दासजनः, चेटः-टी, गृहदासः-सी, किंकरः, अपकृष्टः; परिजनः, दासवर्गः, भृत्यवर्गः (m. s). -*a.* (*s.*) in comp.; व्रातीन, अपकृष्ट; *See* MEAN; 'm. duties' दासकर्मन्; व्रातं, नीचकर्म.

MENISCUS, *s.* अर्धचंद्राकारः काचः.

MENOLOGY, *s.* मासपंजिका.

MENSES, *s.* ऋतुः, आर्तवं, पुष्पं, रजस् *n.*, कला; 'first appearance of m.' रजोदर्शनं.

MENSTRUAL, *a.* मासिक (की *f.*), मास्य, मासीय, प्रातिमासिक; 'm. time' ऋतुः, ऋतुकालः; 'm. discharge' रजस् *n.*, पुष्पं, ऋतुः. —MENSTRUATE, *v. i.* रजस्वला-ऋतुमती-भू 1 P. -ION, *s.* ऋतुस्रावः. -MENSTRUOUS, *a.* आर्तव (वी *f.*), ऋतु in comp. 2 रजस्वला, ऋतुमती, पुष्पवती, स्त्रीधर्मिणी, अविः, आत्रेयी; मलिनी, उदक्या, अस्पर्शा.

MENSTRUUM, *s.* द्रावणं, विद्रावकरसः.

MENSURABLE, *a.* प्रमेय, माप्य.

MENSURATE, *v. t.* मा 3 A, 2 P; *See* MEASURE. -ION, *s.* प्र-परि-माणं, मापनं, मिति *f.*

MENTAL, *a.* मानसिक (की *f.*), मानस (सी *f.*), मनःस्थ, चित्तगत, चित्तज, मनोभव; gen. by मनस् or चित्त in comp.; 'm. distress' मनस्तापः. -LY, *adv.* मनसा, बुद्ध्या.

MENTION, *v. t.* कथ् 10, आ-ख्या 2 P, नि-आ-विद् c., शंस् 1 P, अभि-धा 3 U, उदीर् c., उच्चर् c., कृत् 10, वच् 2 P, निर्दिश् 6 P; स्मृ 1 P (as precepts); 'will be m. ed further on' अग्रतो

वक्ष्यते; 'm. by name' नाम ग्रह् 9 P; 'not to m.' ex. by का कथा, का गणना (with loc.), आस्तां-तिष्ठतु-तावत्, followed by अपि; 'not to m. embodied beings (heated by affliction) even red-hot iron softens down (after a time)' अभितप्तमयोऽपि मार्दवं भजते कैव कथा शरीरिषु (R. VIII. 43); का वा गणना सचेतनेषु अपगतचेतनान्यपि संघट्टयितुमलं मदनः (Ka. 157); तिष्ठन्तु तावत्सेवापरा राजानः प्रजा अपि पृष्ठतो लगन्ति (Ka. 260). –s. अभिधानं, कथनं, आख्यानं, आ-नि-वेदनं, उच्चारणं, कीर्तनं, निर्देशः, नामग्रहणं-निर्देशः. –ED, a. कथित, उक्त, निर्दिष्ट, कीर्तित, स्मृत, &c.; 'above-m.' प्रागुक्त; 'about to be m.' वक्ष्यमाण.

MENTOR, s. उपदेशकः, उपदेष्टृ m.

MEPHITIC,-AL, a. पूतिगंधि, दुर्गंधमय (यी f.); प्राणहर, मारात्मक, जीवितापह.

MERCENARY, a. अर्थपरवश, लाभपरायण, लाभार्थिन्, धनलुब्ध, लाभदृष्टि-बुद्धि, स्वार्थपर, स्वार्थापेक्षक; 'from m. motives' लाभतृष्णया, लाभेच्छया, स्वार्थापेक्षया. 2 भृतक, वैतनिक (की f.), भृति-भरण्य-भुज्, वेतनार्थिन्. –s. भृतकः, भृति-भरण्य-भुक्, वैतनिकः, वेतनार्थी. –LY, adv. लाभतृष्णया, लाभापेक्षया, भृतकवत्, स्वार्थबुद्ध्या. –NESS, s. लाभदृष्टि f.-अपेक्षा-बुद्धि f., धनलाभलोभः, स्वार्थ-वेतन-अपेक्षा.

MERCER, s. कौशेयोर्णवस्त्रवणिज् m. –Y, s. कौशेयवस्त्रव्यवहारः.

MERCHANT, s. वणिज् m., वाणिजः, आपणिकः, नैगमः, सार्थवाहः, पण्याजीवः, क्रयविक्रयिकः, वैदेहकः, सार्थिकः, व्यवहारिन् m., वाणिज्योपजीवी, श्रेष्ठी; 'm.'s business' वाणिज्यं, वणिक्क्रिया; 'm.'s exchange' श्रेष्ठिचत्वरं; 'voyaging or seafaring m.' सांयात्रिकः, पोतवणिक्; 'company of m. s' सार्थः, निगमः. –ABLE, a. पण्य, पण्यार्ह. –MERCHANDISE, s. वाणिज्यं, व्यवहारः, क्रयविक्रयौ (du.). 2 पण्यं, भांडानि, पण्यद्रव्याणि, वाणिजद्रव्यभांडं-पण्यं. –MERCANTILE, a. वाणिज (जी f.), वाणिजिक (की f.), वाणिज्यसंबंधिन्.

MERCURY, s. पारदः, चपलः, रसः, सूतः, पारतः; 'white sublimate of m.' रसकर्पूरः; 'sulphuret of m.' कज्जली. 2 बुधः, रौहिणेयः, सौम्यः. –AL, a. पारदात्मक, पारदमय (यी f.), सपारद. 2 चपल, लघुशरीर, सोत्साह, तेजस्विन्. 3 द्रव्यपरायण, धूर्त.

MERCY, s. दया, कृपा, करुणा, अनुकंपा, अनुक्रोशः, कारुण्यं, घृणा, दया, कृपाशीलता, दयालुता, क्षमाशीलता, दया-कृपा-बुद्धि f. 2 प्रसादः, अनुग्रहः. 3 क्षमा, तितिक्षा; 'fountain of m.' करुणाकरः, दयासागरः, दयानिधिः; 'an object of m.' कृपापात्रं-भाजनं, अनुकंप्य, अनुग्राह्य, तपस्विन्; 'to show m.' दय् 1 A (with gen.), अनुकंप् 1 A (with acc.), दयां कृ 8 U (with loc.); 'm., Oh king' क्षमस्व राजन्. –FUL, a. दयालु, कृपालु, कृपा-दया-करुणा-शील, करुणार्द्र, दयार्द्र, अनुकंपिन्, सदय, सकरुण, सानुक्रोश, क्षमाशील; वत्सल, दयाबुद्धि-दृष्टि; See KIND. –FULLY, adv. सदयं, सकरुणं, सानुकंपं, दयया, करुणया, सानुक्रोशं. –FULNESS, s. दया, कृपा, घृणा, दयाशीलता, अनुकंपा, वात्सल्यं; See (s.). –LESS, a. निर्दय, निष्करुण, निर्घृण, अकरुण, कठोर, निष्कृप, निठुर, नृशंस. –LESSLY, adv. निर्दयं, निष्कृपं, निर्घृणं, निठुरं.

MERE, a. केवल, शुद्ध; gen. ex. by एव, or मात्र in comp.; 'by m. touch' स्पर्शमात्रेण; 'a m. fool' मूर्ख एव, केवलमूर्खः. –s. सरस् n., ह्रदः; See LAKE. 2 पर्यंतः, सीमा; See BOUNDARY. –LY, adv. केवलं, एव, मात्र in comp.; 'by m. advising' उपदेशमात्रात्, उपदेशादेव, &c.

MERETRICIOUS, a. कृत्रिमशोभामय (यी f.), बाह्यरुचिर, कृत्रिमरागवत्, मिथ्याशोभन. 2 पण्यांगनीय, वेश्यासंबंधिन्. –LY, adv. मिथ्याशोभया.

MERGE, v. i. नि-,मस्ज् 6 P, अव-गाह् 1 A (lit.); निपा-ग्रस्-pass., प्र-वि-ली 4 A, वि-लुप् pass., नश् 4 P, (fig.); 'one fault m. s in a collection of good qualities' एको हि दोषो गुणसन्निपाते निमज्जति (K. I. 3). –v. t. मस्ज् c., (मज्जयति), अव-गाह् c. 2 नश् c., वि-लुप् 6 P or c., ग्रस् 1 A, नि-पा 1 P, प्र-वि-ली c. –MERSION, s. मज्जनं, अवगाहः-हनं.

MERIDIAN, s. मध्याह्नः, दिनमध्यं, मध्याह्नकालः-समयः. 2 खमध्यं; 'distance from the first m.' रेखांतरं; 'the sun is on the m.' नभसो मध्यमलंकरोति भानुः. 3 परा कोटिः-काष्ठा, उत्कर्षः. –a. माध्याह्निक (की f.). 2 खमध्यसंबंधिन्. 3 उत्तम, परम; oft. ex. by परा कोटिः, परा काष्ठा.

MERIDIONAL, a. दक्षिणदेशीय; दक्षिणाभिमुख (खी f.).

MERIT, s. गुणः, योग्यता, पात्रता, उत्कर्षः, श्रेष्ठता, विशिष्टता, विशेषः, गुणोत्कर्षः, गुणवत्ता. 2 (M. s) गुणागुणौ, गुणदोषौ, धर्माधर्मौ. 3 पुण्यं, धर्मः, सुकृतं, श्रेयस् n., वृषः; 'acquired by m.' पुण्यार्जित; 'efficacy of m.' पुण्यप्रतापः-प्रभावः; 'one possessing many m. s' पुण्यनिधिः-राशिः-सागरः, पुण्यात्मा. –v. t. अर्ह् 1 P, अर्ह-योग्य-in comp.; See DESERVE; 'm. ing censure' निंद्य, गर्हणीय, निंदापात्रं. –ED, a. युक्त, उचित, योग्य; See PROPER. –MERITORIOUS, a. प्रशस्य, श्लाघ्य, प्रशस्त, श्लाघार्ह, प्रशंसार्ह. 2 गुणिन्, गुणवत्, गुणसंपन्न, गुणोपेत, गुणान्वित. 3 पुण्यवत्, पुण्यशील, पुण्यात्मन्, पुण्यात्मक, पुण्यशालिन्; पुण्य, पुण्यरूप, अवदात (deed); 'a m. deed' पुण्यं, धर्मः, सुकृतं, अवदातं कर्म. –LY, adv. श्लाघ्यतया, प्रशस्यं. –NESS, s. गुणवत्ता, पात्रता, योग्यता, &c.

MERMAID, *s.* मत्स्यांगना, मत्स्यस्त्री.

MERRY, *a.* प्र-,हृष्ट, सानंद, सोल्लास, प्रोत्फुल्ल, प्रमुदित, प्रहृष्टचित्त; आनंद-उल्लास-हास्य-वृत्ति, प्रसन्नवदन, विलासिन्, विनोदिन्, परिहासशील. 2 हास्यकर (री *f.*), विनोदक; 'to make m.' उत्सवं कृ 8 U; 'to be m.' उल्लस् 1 P, मुद् 1 A; *See* DELIGHT; 'm.-andrew' भंडः, वैहासिकः, विदूषकः; 'm.-making' आनंदोत्सवः, उत्सवकरणं. -LY, *adv.* सहर्षं, सोल्लासं, सानंदं, हृष्टमनसा. -MENT, *s.* प्र-,हर्षः, उल्लासः, प्र-,मोदः, आनंदः, आह्लादः; हास्यं, परिहासः, उत्सवः, कौतुकं, विलासः, विनोदः; लीला, खेला; 'what is said in m.' हास्यविनोदः, नर्मालापः, विनोदोक्ति *f.* -NESS, *s.* हृष्टता, सानंदता, आनंदवृत्ति *f.*

MERU, *s.* मेरुः, सुमेरुः, हेमाद्री, रत्नसानुः, सुरालयः.

MESENTERY, *s.* अंत्रपेशी.

MESH, *s.* जालरंध्रं-छिद्रं-अंतरं. -*v. t.* जाले पत् c. or बंध् 9 P. -Y, *a.* जालरूप, जालाकार.

MESLIN, *s.* मिश्रधान्यं, धान्यमिश्रणं.-*a.* मिश्रधान्यकृत.

MESS, *s.* अन्नं, अन्नपात्रं. 2 गणान्नं, सहभोजनं; सहभोजिनः, पंक्तिभोजिनः (pl.); सहभोजिपंक्ति *f.*-गणः, गणान्नपंक्तिः. 3 संकरः, प्र-सं-कीर्णकं, सन्निपातः, संमिश्रणं, संकुलं; 'm.-mate' सह-पंक्ति-भोजी. -*v. i.* सह-एकत्र-भुज् 7 A or अश् 9 P, पंक्तिभोजनं कृ 8 U. -*v. t.* संमिश्र् 10, संकॄ 6 P.

MESSAGE, *s.* संदेशः, वाचिकं, संदेशवाच् *f.*, वार्ता, शासनं; 'bearing a m.' दौत्यं, दूत्यं, प्रेष्यभावः; 'sending on a m.' प्रतिशासनं. -MESSENGER, *s.* दूतः, संदेश-वार्ता-हरः, वार्तायनः, आ-ख्यायकः, निसृष्टार्थः, प्रेष्यः; वैवधिकः; 'female m.' दूति-ती-तिका; 'who will go as a m.' कः प्रयास्यति दौत्येन.

MESSUAGE, *s.* वासगृहं, गृहवाटिका.

METACARPUS, *s.* करभः, पीलुः.

METACHRONISM, *s.* न्यूनकालनिरूपणं.

METAL, *s.* धातुः, लोहः-हं, तैजसं; 'base m.' कुप्यं; 'fused m.' रसधातुः, धातुरसः; 'inferior m.' उपधातुः. -LIC, -LICAL, *a.* धातुसंबंधिन्. 2 धातुमय (यी *f.*), धातुरूप, लौह (ही *f.*), धातु-लोह- in comp. -LIST, *s.* धातुज्ञः, धातुकर्मकारः. -METALLIFEROUS, *a.* धातुप्रद. -METALLIFORM, *a.* धातुसदृश (शी *f.*). -METALLOGRAPHY, *s.* धातुशास्त्रं-विद्या. -METALLURGY, *s.* धातुशोधनं.

METAMORPHOSE, *v. t.* रूपं परिणम् c. or परिवृत् c., रूपांतरं दा 3 U or ग्रह् c.; *See* CHANGE. -ED, *a.* परिणतरूप-शरीर-आकार. -METAMORPHOSIS, *s.* रूपपरिणामः-परिवृत्ति *f.*-भेदः, रूपांतरं, रूप-शरीर-विकारः.

METAPHOR, *s.* रूपकं, लक्षणा, आरोपः, उपचारः. 2 दृष्टांतः, निदर्शनं. -IC, -ICAL, *a.* औपचारिक-लाक्षणिक (की *f.*), सरूपक, आरोपित; 'm. use' उपचारः. -ICALLY, *adv.* लक्षणया, उपचारेण, सारोपं; 'to use m.' उपचर् 1 P; *See* FIGURATIVELY.

METAPHYSIC,-AL, *a.* आन्वीक्षिक-आध्यात्मिक (की *f.*), आत्मविषय, आत्मज्ञानपर. -ALLY, *adv.* आत्मविद्यानुसारेण. -IAN, *s.*आन्वीक्षिकीज्ञः.-METAPHYSICS, *s.* आन्वीक्षिकी, आत्म-अध्यात्म-विद्या, आत्मविषयकं ज्ञानं, आत्मतत्वविद्या-शास्त्रं.

METASTASIS, *s.* रोगस्थलांतरं.

METATARSUS, *s.* प्रपदं.

METATHESIS, *s.* अक्षर-वर्ण-विपर्यासः-व्यत्यासः-व्यत्ययः.

METE, *v. t.* परि-,मा 3 A, 2 P; *See* MEASURE.

METEMPSYCHOSIS, *s.* पुनर्जन्मन् *n.*, अन्यजन्म, जन्मांतरं, देहांतरप्राप्ति *f.*

METEOR, *s.* उल्का, उत्पातः. -IC, *a.* उल्कोद्भव, उल्कोत्पन्न. -OUS, *a.* उल्काधर्मक. -METEOROLOGY, *s.* अंतरीक्षविद्या, वायु-नभो-विद्या.

METER, *s.* मापकः.

METHINKS, *v. imp.* मन्ये, तर्कयामि, शंके; ध्रुवं.

METHOD, *s.* रीति *f.*, प्रकारः, मार्गः, विधा, विधिः; पद्धति *f.*; *See* MANNER. 2 व्यवस्था, क्रमः, अनुक्रमः, पर्यायः, आनुपूर्वी-र्व्यं, परिपाटि-टी *f.*, आवृत् *f.*, परंपरा; व्यवस्थया रचनं-ना, व्यूहनं, विन्यासः, संविधानं, क्रमेण स्थापनं, नियमः. -ICAL, *a.* व्यवस्थित, यथाक्रम, सक्रम, अनुपूर्व, सूत्रित, यथापर्याय. 2 (Of persons) क्रमानुसारिन्, क्रमानुगत, क्रम-नियम-शील. -ICALLY, *adv.* यथाक्रमं, अनुपूर्वशः, आनुपूर्व्येण, क्रमेण, क्रमशः, पर्यायेण, अनुक्रमेण, यथानियमं. -ICALNESS, *s.* व्यवस्था, क्रमशीलता, &c. -ISM, *s.* नियमनिष्ठा. -IST, *s.* नियम-कर्म-निष्ठः. -IZE, *v. t.* व्यव-स्था c. (स्थापयति), क्रमेण स्था c. or वि-धा 3 U or विरच् 10 or विन्यस् 4 U.

METRE, *s.* छंदस् *n.*, वृत्तं. -METRICAL, *a.* छंदोबद्ध, वृत्तात्मक, छांदस (सी *f.*), छंदोरूप, पद्यरूप, पद्यात्मक.

METRONOME, *s.* तालमापनी.

METROPOLIS, *s.* राजधानी. -METROPOLITAN, *a.* राजधानीय.

METTLE, *s.* तेजस् *n.*, सत्त्वं, उत्साहः, वीर्यं, ओजस् *n.*, प्रभावः, पौरुषं, ऊर्जस् *n.* -ED, -SOME, 'of great m.', 'high-m. ed' *a.* तेजस्विन्, महा-उरु-सत्व, परमोत्साह, ओजस्विन्, वीर्यवत्, सपौरुष.

MEW, *s.* पंजरं, वीतंसः. 2 बंधनं, निरोधः, बंधनागारं, गुप्ति *f.* -*v. t.* पंजरे निरुध् 7 U or बंध् 9 P. -*v. i.* पक्षान् पत् c. or मुच् c.

MEWL, *v. i.* (शिशुवत्) क्रंद् 1P, रुद् 2P, आक्रुश् 1P.

MEWS, *s.* अश्वगोष्ठं, अश्वशाला.

MIASM, *s.* पूतिबाष्पः, मारात्मकः वायुः.

MICA, *s.* अभ्रकं.

MICROCOSM, *s.* सूक्ष्मं जगत्.

MICROSCOPE, *s.* सूक्ष्मदर्शनयंत्रं.

MICTURITION, *s.* मूत्रोत्सर्गेच्छा.

MID, *a.* मध्य, मध्यम; अर्ध, in comp.; 'm.-course' अर्धमार्गः, अर्धपथः; 'm.-day' मध्याह्नः; (*a.*) माध्यंदिन (नी *f.*), माध्याह्निक (की *f.*); 'm.-heaven' खमध्यः; 'm.-land' मध्यदेशीय, देशमध्यवर्तिन्; 'm.-night' मध्यरात्रः, अर्धरात्रः, रात्रिमध्यं, निशीथः; 'm.-summer' निदाघमध्यं; 'm.-way' अर्धपथः-मार्गः; (*adv.*) अर्धमार्गे, मार्गमध्ये; 'm.-wife' सूतिका; साविका, प्रसवकारिणी; 'm.-wifery' प्रसवकार्यं-करणं, सूतिकर्म, गर्भमोचनविद्या; 'm.-winter' शिशिरमध्यं. —MIDDLE, *s.* मध्यं, मध्यभागः-देशः-स्थानं-स्थलं; अभ्यंतरं, गर्भः, अंतरं, in comp.; 'in the m. of the ocean' मध्येसमुद्रं; 'in the m. of the house' गृहाभ्यंतरे, गृहगर्भे; 'going in the m.' मध्यग. —*a.* मध्य, मध्यम, मध्यस्थ, मध्यवर्तिन्, मध्यस्थित; 'the m. classes' मध्यमजातीयाः, मध्यमवर्णाः; 'm.-aged' मध्यमवयस्क, गतयौवन; 'm. finger' मध्यमा, कर्णिका; 'm.-man' मध्यस्थः, मध्यपुरुषः. —ING, *a.* मध्य, मध्यम, मध्यपरिमाण. 2 मध्यमपदस्थ, मध्यमगुण, सामान्य, साधारण (णी *f.*). —MIDST, *s.* मध्यं; *See* MIDDLE; 'in the m.' मध्ये; 'from their m.' तेषां मध्यात्; 'in the m. of this talk' एवं वदन्नेव; 'in the m. of calamities' विपद्ग्रस्त-*a.*, दुःखमग्न-*a.*

MIEN, *s.* आकारः, रूपं, आकृति *f.*, वदनाकारः, वदनाकृतिः, मुखचर्या; 'with a dejected m.' खिन्न-म्लान-वदन.

MIGHT, *s.* बलं, शक्ति *f.*, सामर्थ्यं, तेजस् *n.*, शौर्यं, वि-परा-क्रमः, प्रभावः; *See* STRENGTH; 'with all one's m.' यथाशक्ति, यावच्छक्यं. —MIGHTY, *a.* प्रबल, शक्तिमत्, बलवत्, ओजस्विन्, ऊर्जस्वल, विक्रांत, बलिन्, दृढविक्रम; *See* STRONG. 2 महत्, विशाल, प्रतापवत्, महौजस्, विभूतिमत्; 'm. lord' महेश्वरः, अधीश्वरः. —ILY, *adv.* बलेन, विक्रमेण, शौर्येण. 2 अतीव, अत्यंतं, बलवत्, भृशं, अतिमात्रं. —INESS, *s.* सामर्थ्यं, प्रभावः, वीर्यं; *See* (*s.*)

MIGRATE, *v. i.* निर्गम् 1 P, भ्रम् 1, 4 P, देशांतरं-स्थानांतरं-गम् or अधि-वस् 1 P or अध्यास् 2 A. —ION, *s.* भ्रमणं, पर्यटनं, देशांतरगमनं. —ORY, *a.* देशभ्रमण-पर्यटन-शील.

MILCH-COW, *s.* क्षीरिणी, पयस्वती, दुग्धवती, पीनोध्नी.

MILD, *a.* मृदु, कोमल, सौम्य, अप्रखर, अचंड, अनुग्र, अपरुष, सुकुमार, शांत, अतीक्ष्ण, अतीव्र. 2 सदय, कृपालु, दयालु, दयार्द्र, क्षमाशील, अतीक्ष्ण, अतीव्र, अतीक्ष्णदंड, मृदुस्वभाव, सौम्यवृत्ति, मृदुभाव, सामोपायिन्; *See* INNOCENT also; 'm. means' सामन् *n.*, सामोपचारः, सामोपायः; 'm. speech' सांत्ववादः, मृदुभाषणं. —LY, *adv.* मृदु, कोमलं, अनुग्रं, अपरुषं, अतीव्रं, मार्दवेन, साम्ना, सामोपायेन, सामोपचारैः. —NESS, *s.* मार्दवं, मृदुता, कोमलता, सौम्यता, अतीक्ष्णता, शांति *f.* 2 प्रकृतिमृदुता, मृदुता, मृदु-कोमल-स्वभावः; कृपालुता, सदयता, सौम्यवृत्ति *f.*, दयालुता, कृपाशीलता; क्षमा, साम.

MILE, *s.* अर्धक्रोशः; '3 m. s' सार्धक्रोशः; '4 m. s' क्रोशद्वयं.

MILITANT, *a.* युद्धप्रवृत्त, रणोद्यत, युद्धोद्युक्त.

MILITARY, *a.* सांग्रामिक-सामरिक-आयुधिक (की *f.*), क्षात्र (त्री *f.*), युद्ध in comp. 2 युद्धप्रवृत्त, योधिन्, शस्त्रोपजीविन्, शस्त्रभृत् आयुधजीविन्; 'm. preparation' युद्धसामग्री; 'm. profession or life' आयुध-शस्त्र-वृत्ति *f.*, सैनिकवृत्तिः, शस्त्राजीवः; m. caste' क्षत्रियजातिः; 'a man of the m. class' क्षत्रः-त्रं, क्षत्रियः, राजन्यः, विराट्, बाहुजः, मूर्धाभिषिक्तः; 'a woman of the m. class' क्षत्रिया-याणी; 'm. man' योधः, वीरः, सैनिकः; 'm. duty' क्षात्रधर्मः, क्षत्रिय-क्षत्र-धर्मः; 'm. science' युद्धशास्त्रं, सांग्रामिकं, शस्त्रास्त्रविद्या, आयुध-रण-विद्या. —*s.* सैन्यं, सैनिकवर्गः, क्षत्रगणः.

MILITATE, *v. i.* वि-प्रति-रुध् 7 U, विरुद्ध-प्रतिकुल-*a.* भू 1 P.

MILITIA, *s.* देशरक्षिणः, रक्षकयोधाः (pl.).

MILK, *s.* पयस् *n.*, दुग्धं, क्षीरं, स्तन्यं; गोदुग्धं, गोरसः, गव्यं (cow's m.); 'fresh m.' पीयूषः-षं; 'made of m.' पयस्य; 'coagulated m.' दधि, क्षीरजं; 'giving much m.' बहुदुग्धा; 'm.-livered' कातर, क्लीबहृदय, भीरु; 'm.-maid' गोपकन्या, आभीरी, गोदोहिनी; गोपी, गोपिका; 'm.-man' दोग्धृ *m.*, दोहकः, गोपः, आभीरः, गोधुक्; 'm.-pail,-pan' दुग्ध-क्षीर-पात्रं-भांडं-भाजनं; दोहनी; 'm.-porridge' क्षैरेयी; 'm.-sop' कापुरुषः, भीरुः; 'm.-woman' गोपी, आभीरी, दोहिनी. —*v. t.* दुह् 2 U (with two acc.), दुग्धं निष्कृष् 1 P or स्नु c. —ER, *s.* दोग्धा, दोहकः, धुक्. —Y, *s.* क्षीरिन्, पयस्य, पायस (सी *f.*); (*s.*) in comp.; 'm. ocean' क्षीर-दुग्ध-सागरः. 2 क्षीरोपम, दुग्धतुल्य. 3 क्षीरद, दुग्धप्रद, बहुदुग्ध; 'm. way' वियद्गंगा; *See* GALAXY. 4 भीरु, कातर, सौम्य; *See* MILD.

MILL, *s.* चक्रं, पेषणी, पेषणयंत्रं-चक्रं. —*v. t.* पिष् 7 P, चूर्ण् 10. 2 मुष्टिना तड् 10 or प्रहृ 1 P. —ER, *s.* पेषकः, पेषणोपजीविन् *m.*

MILLENNIUM, MILLENARY, *s.* सहस्रवर्षं, सहस्रसंवत्सरं. —MILLENNIAL, —MILLENARIAN, *a.* सहस्रवर्षीय-ण, सहस्रवार्षिक (की *f.*).

MILLESIMAL, *a.* सहस्रतम (मी *f.*), सहस्रांशात्मक.

MILLET, *s.* अणुः, प्रियंगुः.

MILLINER, *s.* स्त्रीवस्त्रकृत्, स्त्रीवसनकारिणी. —Y, *s.* स्त्रीपरिच्छदः-सज्जा, स्त्रीवस्त्रसामग्री.

MILLION, *s.* नियुतं, दशलक्षं; 'ten m.' कोटि *f.*; 'hundred m.' अर्बुदः. -ARY, *a.* नियुतीय. -TH, *a.* नियुततम (मी *f.*). -MILLIONAIRE, *s.* कोटीश्वरः, लक्षाधीशः.

MILT, *s.* *See* SPLEEN.

MIME, *s.* नटः, नर्तकः, कुशीलवः, चारणः, रंगाजीवः. 2 भंडः, विदूषकः, वैहासिकः. —MIMIC,(-AL), *a.* अनुकरणशील-स्वभाव, अनुकारिन्, विडंबनकारिन्. 2 विडंबन-अनुकरण-रूप. -*s.* भंडः, वैहासिकः, विदूषकः. 2 अनुकारिन् *m.* -*v. t.* (उपहासपूर्वं) अनुकृ 8 U, विडंब् 10. -KER, *s.* अनुकारी, विडंबनकृत्. -RY, *s.* सोपहासं अनुकरणं or विडंबनं; अनुकारः, विडंबनं.

MIMOSA, *s.* नमस्कारी, गंडकारी-ली, समंगा, खदिरा, लज्जालुः.

MINARET, *s.* शिखरं, शृंगं, प्रासाद-भवन-शिखरं.

MINCE, *v. t.* खंडशः-सूक्ष्मलवशः-कृत् 6 P or छिद् 7 P or खंड् 10, शकलीकृ 8 U; 'do not m. matters' यथावृत्तं सर्वं साकल्येन निवेदय, सर्वं संपूर्णं प्रकाशय; 'm. ed meat' छिन्नमांसं. -*v. i.* ललितगत्या चल्-र् 1 P or गम् 1 P, भिन्नगत्या गम्. 2 भिन्नस्वरेण वद् 1 P. -INGLY, *adv.* खंडशः, लवशः; भिन्नगत्या, भिन्नस्वरेण.

MIND, *s.* मनस् *n.*, मानसं, चित्तं, चेतस् *n.*; बुद्धि *f.*, मति *f.*, धीः, प्रज्ञा, बोधः; *See* INTELLECT. 2 हृदयं, हृद् *n.*, अंतःकरणं, चित्तं, मनः, चेतः, अंतरं. 3 मतिः, बुद्धिः, मतं; कामः, इच्छा, वांछा, रुचि *f.*, मनोरथः, वासना, भावः, ईप्सितं, अभिलाषः. 4 अभिप्रायः, उद्देशः, संकल्पः, अभिप्रेतं, मतिः, बुद्धिः, मतं. 5 स्मरणं, स्मृति *f.*, स्मरणशक्ति *f.*, अनुबोधः; 'to give the m. to' भावं-मनो-निविश् c. or बंध् 9 P or आ-नि-धा 3 U, आसक्त-निविष्ट-चित्त-*a.* भू; *See* under SET; 'out of one's m.' भ्रांत-अव्यवस्थित-बुद्धि (*a.*); 'fixed in the m.' चित्तनिष्ठ; 'of low m.' कृपण-नीच-बुद्धि; 'working of the m.' चित्त-मनोव्यापारः-वृत्ति *f.*, मनश्चेष्टा, चेतोविकारः; 'according to one's m.' यथाकामं, यथेष्टं, यथेप्सितं, यथारुचि; 'have a m. to ask' प्रष्टुमनाः-कामः; 'to cross the m.' मनसि उद्-इ 2 P or उद्भू 1 P, बुद्धौ संजन् 4 A; *See* OCCUR; 'call to m.' स्मृ 1P, सं-अनु-°, अनुचिंत् 10; 'put in m.' स्मृ c., अनु-उद्-बुध् c.; 'of one m.' एकचित्त-*a.*; 'being of one m.' एकचित्तीभूय; 'change of m.' बुद्धि-मति-भेदः; 'flashing across the m.' स्फुरणं, सहसा आविर्भावः. -*v. t.* मन् 4 A, गण् 10, आदृ 6 A, अव-अप-ईक्ष् 1 A, आलोच् 10, अव-धा 3 U, चित्ते-मनसि-कृ 8 U, अवधृ 10, मनो दा 3 P. 2 सेव् 1 A, भज् 1 U, अनु-ष्ठा 1 P, अनुरुध् 4 A, अनुवि-धा 3 U. 3 रक्ष् 1 P, पा c. (पालयति); 'never m. the first question, answer the second' आस्तां-तिष्ठतु-तावत् प्रथमः प्रश्नः, द्वितीयस्य उत्तरं देहि; 'never m.' अगुर्वर्थमेतत्; *See* MATTER. -ED, *a.* प्रवृत्त, प्रवण, शील, मनस्, मनस्क in comp.; 'worldly-m.' संसारासक्तचित्त; धीरमनस्क, &c. -FUL, *a.* सावधान, अवहित, जागरूक, अवहितचित्त. 2 कृतादर, मन्यमान, अवेक्षक. 3 अवधारयत्, स्मरत्, चित्ते कुर्वत्; 'to be m. of' स्मृ. -FULLY, *adv.* सावधानं, सादरं, अवेक्षया. -FULNESS, *s.* अवधानं, अवेक्षा. -LESS, *a.* अनवधान, प्रमत्त, अनवेक्षक, निरपेक्ष. 2 नष्टस्मृति-बुद्धि, बुद्धिहीन.

MINE, *a.* मदीय, मामकीन, मामक (मिका *f.*), मत् in comp. -*s.* आकरः, ख(खा)नि-नी *f.*, उत्पत्तिस्थानं; 'm. for jewels' मणिभूमि *f.*, रत्नाकरः, (fig.) आकरः, निधिः, राशिः. 2 संधिः, सुरुंगा, खानिकं, कुल्या. -*v. t.* खन् 1 P, आ-नि-°, अधस्तात् खन्, उर्वीं भिद् 7 P or वि-दॄ 9 P, सुरुंगां कृ. -ER, *s.* खनकः, खातकः, आखनिकः, खनितृ *m.* 2 सुरुंगाकारः, सौरुंगिकः. —MINERAL, *s.* धातुः, खनिजं, आकरजं वस्तु. -*a.* धातुसंबंधिन्, धातु in comp. 2 खनिज, आकरज, आकरोद्भव. 3 धातुमय (यी *f.*), धातुरूप. 4 धातुसंसृष्ट, धातुधर्मोपेत. -OGY, *s.* धातुविद्या, धातुपरीक्षणविद्या-शास्त्रं. -OGIST, *s.* धातुविद्याज्ञः.

MINGLE, *v. t.* मिश्र् 10, वि-सं-व्या-°, संयुज् 7 U, 10, संसृज् 6 P, संपृच् 2 A, 7 P, संकॄ 6 P, संमिल् c., मिश्रीकृ 8 U, एकीकृ; उत्कंठासाधारणं परितोषमनुभवामि (S. 4) 'I experience pleasure m. ed with regret.' -*v. i.* संमिल् 6 P, मिश्री-एकी-भू 1 P, संकॄ-संसृज्-pass. -ED, *a.* मिश्रित, संपृक्त, संसृष्ट, सं-,मिश्र, संकीर्ण. -MENT, *s.* संमिश्रणं, संसर्गः.

MINIATURE, *a.* सूक्ष्माकार, सूक्ष्म -*s.* Ex. by ह्रस्व or सूक्ष्म; 'world in m.' ह्रस्वमानेन विश्वं.

MINIKIN, *s.* सूचिका. 2 Minion, q. v.

MINIMUM, *s.* अल्पिष्ठा-अत्यल्पा-संख्या.

MINION, *s.* वल्लभः, प्रियः, नृप-राज-वल्लभः; *See* FAVOURITE.

MINISTER, *s.* सचिवः, मंत्रिन् *m.*, अमात्यः, प्रकृतिपुरुषः, धुर्यः, धूर्वहः, धुरीणः, धुरंधरः, महामात्रः, राजसचिवः, राजामात्यः. 2 नियोगिन् *m.*, नियुक्तः, नियोज्यः, कर्मकरः, अधिकृतः. 3 उपाध्यायः, आचार्यः, पुरोहितः. 4 राजदूतः, राजप्रतिनिधिः; 'prime m.' प्रधान-मुख्य-मंत्री, प्रधानसचिवः; 'm. of counsel' धीसचिवः, अमात्यः; 'm. for ordinary affairs' कर्मसचिवः. -*v.* सेव् 1 A, परि-उप-चर् 1 P, उपास् 2 A, उपस्था 1 U, शु desid. (शुश्रूषते). 2 (उपकरणद्रव्याणि) परिक्लृप् c., संभृ 1 P, उप-पद् c., उप-स्था c. (स्थापयति). 3 (to) सं-पद् 4 A; क्लृप् 1 A; *See* TEND. -IAL, *a.* मंत्रिसंबंधिन्, नियोगसंबंधिन्, उपचारपर, सेवक, अनुवर्तिन्, gen. ex. by (*s.*) in comp.; 'm. duties' सचिवकार्याणि. -MINISTRATION, *s.* मंत्राधिकारः, साचिव्यं. 2 उपचारः, उपासना, सेवा,

शुश्रूषा, उपकारः. 3 उपाध्यायवृत्ति *f.* –MINISTRY, (Ministership), *s.* साहाय्यं, द्वारं, कर्तृत्वं, कारणत्वं. 2 साचिव्यं, मंत्रित्वं, मंत्राधिकारः, अमात्य-साचिव्य-पदवी. 3 नियोगः, अधिकारः, नियोगिपदं. 4 सचिव-मंडलं, मंत्रिगणः-मंडलं-वर्गः; मंत्रिणः, अमात्याः, सचिवाः, राज्यधुर्वहाः. 5 पौरोहित्यं, उपाध्यायपदं.

MINIUM, *s. See* 'red lead' under LEAD.

MINOR, *a.* स्वल्पतर, अल्पीयस्, कनीयस्, न्यून, अवर. 2 अप्रधान, गौण (णी *f.*), अमुख्य. 3 क्षुद्र, लघु, लघ्वर्थ, अगुरु; gen. ex. by उप pr.; 'm. portion' उपविभागः, उपांगं; उपदेवता, उपग्रहः, उपधर्मः, &c.; 'm. consideration' लघ्वर्थः-अगुरुः-क्षुद्रः-विचारः. –*s.* अप्राप्तव्यवहारः, अप्राप्तवयस्कः, व्यवहारायोग्यः, अप्राप्तव्यवहारदशः, बालः. –ITY, *s.* बालदशा, बाल्यं, बालावस्था, अप्राप्तव्यवहारता; बाल-शिशु-भावः. 2 न्यून-अल्प-पक्षः-संख्या, स्तोकसंख्या; 'being in the m.' न्यूनपक्षाश्रितः.

MINOTAUR, *s.* नृवृषः, नरवृषभः.

MINSTREL, *s.* मा(म)गधः, वैतालिकः, बंदिन् *m.*; स्तुतिपाठकः, मधुकः, संगीतकुशलः-निपुणः; 'celestial m.' गंधर्वः, चारणः. –LY, *s.* संगीतं, गीतवादनं, गांधर्वं, गंधर्व-मागध-वृत्ति *f.*

MINT, *s.* टंकशाला, मुद्रांकनशाला; (fig.) खनि *f.*; *See* MINE; 'm.-master' टंकाध्यक्षः, टंकपतिः, रूप्याध्यक्षः, नैष्किकः. –*v. t.* मुद्रादि अंक् 10. 2 Forge, Invent, q. v. –AGE, *s.* मुद्रांकनं. 2 मुद्रा, मुद्रितरूप्यं.

MINUS, *a.* न्यून, ऊन in comp.; 'm. a cubit' हस्तन्यून. 2 ऋणं, क्षयः; oft. ex. by वियुत, वर्जित, ऊन in comp.; '10 m. 1' एकवियुता दश; '100 m. 1' एकोनशतं, एकहान्या शतं.

MINUTE, *s.* क्षणः, पलं, निमि(मे)षः. 2 कला. 3 लेखः, लिखितं. –*v. t.* लिख् 6 P, स्मरणार्थं लिख्. –*a.* सूक्ष्म, अणु, अत्यल्प, अतिसूक्ष्म, अल्पिष्ठ, क्षुद्र, प्रतनु. 2 निपुण, सावधान, सूक्ष्म. 3 सूक्ष्मदृष्टि, सूक्ष्मदर्शिन्; 'after m. inquiries' निपुणं अन्विष्य; 'm. description of a woman' तरुणीपृथगवयववर्णनं or -प्रत्यवयववर्णनं. –LY, *adv.* सूक्ष्मं, लवशः, अणुशः; स्निग्धं, निपुणं, सूक्ष्मदृष्ट्या; 'while m. looking at the ring' अंगुलीयकं स्निग्धं निध्यायंती (M. 1). –NESS, *s.* सूक्ष्मता, अत्यल्पता, अतितनुता, &c. –MINUTIÆ, *s.* सूक्ष्मावयवाः, परमाणवः.

MINX, *s.* धृष्टा, अविनीता, बंधकी, भ्रष्टा, असती.

MIRACLE, *s.* अद्भुतं, अलौकिकक्रिया-कर्म, अद्भुतं-लोकोत्तरं-कर्म, आश्चर्यं; चमत्कारः, अतिमानुषं कर्म, दैवं कर्म. —MIRACULOUS, *a.* अद्भुत, लोकोत्तर, आश्चर्यभूत, आश्चर्य, अमानुष (षी *f.*), अतिमर्त्य, दिव्य, अपौरुषेय (यी *f.*). 2 अद्भुतशक्तिसंपन्न; 'm. weapon' दिव्यास्त्रं. –LY, *adv.* अद्भुततया, दिव्यशक्त्या.

MIRAGE, *s.* मृगतृष्णा-तृष्णिका, मरीचिका, मृगजलं.

MIRE, *s.* पंकः, कर्दमः, जंबालः-लं, मलः-लं; 'get into the m.' संकटे निक्षिप् pass. or पत् 1 P. –*v. t.* पंकेन दुष् c. (दूषयति) or लिप् 6 P. –Y, *a.* पंकिल, सकर्दम, सपंक, समल, कलुष, पंकक्लिन्न, पंकदूषित.

MIRROR, *s.* दर्पणः, आदर्शः, मुकुरः, आत्मदर्शः. 2 (Fig.) आदर्शः, प्रतिमा. –*v. t.* Reflect, q. v.

MIRTH, *s.* हास्यं, प्र-,मोदः, उल्लासः, आनंदः, कौतुकं, परिहासः; *See* MERRIMENT. –FUL, *a.* हृष्ट, उल्लसित, आनंदित, प्रमुदित; *See* MERRY.

MISACCEPTATION, *s.* अन्यथा-विपरीत-ग्रहणं.

MISADVENTURE, *s. See* CALAMITY.

MISANTHROPY, *s.* नर-जन-द्वेषः, विश्वशत्रुता, सर्वलोकद्वेषः. –IC, –ICAL, *a.* नर-जन-द्वेषिन्, विश्ववैरिन्-द्वेषिन्. –IST, *s.* जन-नर-द्वेषी-शत्रुः, सर्वलोकशत्रुः, विश्वशत्रुः.

MISAPPLY, *v. t.* अन्यथा-मिथ्या विनि-प्र-युज् 7 A, 10 or व्यय् 10 or निक्षिप् 6 P. –ICATION, *s.* दुर्विनियोगः, कुव्ययः, अपव्ययः.

MISAPPREHEND, *v. t.* अन्यथा-मिथ्या-ग्रह् 9 P or बुध् 1 P, विपरीतं उपलभ् 1 A. –MISAPPREHENSION, *s.* अन्यथा-विपरीत-ग्रहणं-बोधः, भ्रमः, मिथ्यामति *f.*

MISBECOME, *v. t.* न युज् pass. or उप-पद् 4 A.

MISBEGOT, *a.* विजात, कुजन्मन्.

MISBEHAVE, *v. i.* असम्यक्-अयुक्तं आचर् 1 P or वृत् 1 A. –ED, *a.* दुर्वृत्त, दुःशील, दुश्चेष्टित, दुराचार. –MISBEHAVIOUR, *s.* अविनयः, दुर्वृत्तता, दुराचारः, कुचेष्टितं, अनार्यवृत्ति *f.*

MISBELIEVE,-BELIEF, *See* DISTRUST.

MISCALCULATE, *v. t.* अन्यथा-मिथ्या-गण् 10. –ION, *s.* मिथ्यागणनं, कुगणना.

MISCALL, *v. t.* मिथ्या अभि-धा 3 U or आ-ख्या 2 P.

MISCARRY, *v. i.* गर्भः स्रु 1 P or पत् 1 P or च्यु 1 A (with gen. of woman); च्युतगर्भा भू 1 P. 2 न सिध् 4 P, विफलीभू, मोघी-वृथा-भू, प्रतिहन्-भंज्-pass. –IAGE, *s.* गर्भस्रावः-पातः-पतनं-च्युति *f.* 2 असिद्धि *f.*, वैफल्यं, भंगः; अशुभफलं, दुर्गति *f.* 3 दुराचारः, कुनीति *f.*, अविनयः; 'to cause m.' गर्भं स्रु c. or पत् c.

MISCELLANEOUS, *a.* सं-प्र-कीर्ण, नानाविध, नानाजातीय, त्रिविधप्रकार, नाना-भिन्न-जातीय, विविध. –LY, *adv.* संकीर्णं. –MISCELLANY, *s.* संकरः, प्रकीर्णकं, नानाद्रव्य-नानाविषय-संग्रहः-संनिपातः, संकीर्णवस्तुसमुदायः-संग्रहः.

MISCHANCE, *s. See* CALAMITY.

MISCHIEF, *s.* अपकारः, हानि *f.*, हिंसा, क्षति *f.*, नाशः, अनायः, ध्वंसः, दोषः, बाधा, अहितं, अनर्थः, अनिष्टं, अरिष्टं; 'm. to crops' शस्यहिंसा. 2 कुचेष्टितं,

पापं, दुराचारः, कुचेष्टा; 'm.-maker' दुर्जनः, दुर्वृत्तः, पिशुनः, कर्णेजपः, उपजापकः, कुत्र्यापारिन्, कुचेष्टः; 'm.-making' दौर्जन्यं, पैशुन्यं, कुचेष्टा, दुर्वृत्तिः, कुनीति *f.* —MISCHIEVOUS, *a.* घातुक, हिंसक, हिंसात्मक, अपकार-हिंसा-शील, हिंसारुचि, अपकारिन्, अहितकारिन्, दुष्ट, पाप, दुर्बुद्धि, दुष्टमति. 2 कुचेष्टित, कुचेष्टाप्रिय, दुर्गुणिन्, दुश्चेष्टित; 'm. trick' कुचेष्टितं; 'a m. person' लोककंटकः, कुचेष्टाप्रियः —LY, *adv.* दुष्टबुद्ध्या, सापकारं, क्षतिपूर्वं, हिंसया. —NESS, *s.* हिंसता, अपकारशीलता, हिंसारुचि *f.*, दुष्टबुद्धि *f.*, पापात्मता.

MISCOMPUTATION, *s.* मिथ्यागणना.

MISCONCEIVE, *v. t.* मिथ्या ग्रह् 9 P, अन्यथा बुध् 1 P or उपलभ् 1 A or अवगम् 1 P. —MISCONCEPTION, *s.* मिथ्या-मति-बुद्धि *f.*, मिथ्या-अन्यथा-ग्रहणं-बोधः, विपरीतार्थबोधः, भ्रमः.

MISCONDUCT, *v. t.* असम्यक् निर्वह् c. or प्र-नी 1 P or प्रवृत् c. 2 (Oneself) असम्यक् आचर् 1 P or वृत् 1 A. —*s.* दुर्नयः, असम्यक् निर्वाहः. 2 दुराचारः, दुश्चेष्टितं, कुचरितं, कुचर्या, अविनयः, मर्यादातिक्रमः, कुकृत्यं.

MISCONJECTURE, *v. t.* मिथ्या तर्क् 10 or ऊह् 1 A. —*s.* मिथ्यातर्कः, मिथ्यानुमानं.

MISCONSTRUE, *v. t.* मिथ्या-अन्यथा-अर्थं बुध् 1 P or ग्रह् 9 P, मिथ्या युज् 10 or अर्थं व्या-ख्या 2 P. —MISCONSTRUCTION, *s.* अन्यथार्थबोधः, विपरीत-मिथ्या-ग्रहणं-बोधः.

MISCREANT, *s.* पापः, खंडितवृत्तः, खलः, नरापसदः, पापिष्ठः, दुरात्मन् *m.*, दुर्वृत्तः, जाल्मः; *See* VILLAIN. 2 नास्तिकः, मिथ्यादृष्टिः.

MISDEED, *s.* दुष्कृतं, अपक्रिया, कुकर्म, कुकृत्य-क्रिया, दुष्कृति *f.*, अपचारः, कुचरितं, पापं.

MISDEMEAN, *v. i.* *See* MISBEHAVE.

MISDIRECT, *v. t.* विमार्गं दृश् c. or दिश् 6 P, विपथं दिश्. 2 'Address' (wrongly), q. v. —ION, *s.* विमार्गदर्शनं, मिथ्योपदेशः.

MISDOER, *s.* पापः, पापकर्मन् *m.*, पापकृत् *m.*, कुकर्मा. —MISDOING, *s.* Misdeed, q. v.

MISEMPLOY, *v. t.* अन्यथा विनि-युज् 7 A, 10 or व्याप्ट c. —MENT, *s.* असद्व्ययः, कुविनियोगः, अपव्ययः.

MISER, *s.* कृपणः, कदर्यः, क्षुद्रः, मितंपचः, किंपचानः, दृढ-बद्ध-मुष्टिः, अदानशीलः, दानशत्रुः-विमुखः. —ABLE, *a.* दुःखित, दुःखान्वित, अतिदुःखार्त, अनिर्वृत, निरानंद, कष्टप्राय, अतिक्लेशार्त, वि-आ-पन्न, आपद्-वि-पद्-ग्रस्त, दुर्गत, मंदभाग्य, दैवोपहत, दुर्भाग्य, दुःखापन्न, दुर्दशापन्न; 'a m. man' तपस्वी, नरहतकः. 2 कृपण, दीन, तुच्छ, गर्हणीय, गर्ह्य, कुत्सित, निंद्य, नि-अप-कृष्ट, अधम, क्षुद्र; *See* MEAN. —LY, *a.* कृपण, कदर्य, क्षुद्र, बद्ध-दृढ-मुष्टि, दानविमुख (खी *f.*), अदानशील, मितंपच, स्वल्पव्ययिन्, व्ययविमुख, अनुदार. —Y, *s.* दुःखं, विपद्-आपद् *f.*, व्यसनं, दैन्यं, निःस्वता, विपत्ति *f.*, दुर्गति *f.*, दुर्दशा; कृच्छ्रं, अनिष्टं, कष्टं, अनर्थः. 2 अतिदुःखं, गाढशोकः, दैन्यं, अनिर्वृति *f.*, क्लेशः, अतिव्यथा-बाधा-वेदना, परि-सं-तापः.

MISFORTUNE, *s.* मंदभाग्यं, दुर्दैवं, दुर्भाग्यं, दुर्जातं. 2 अनर्थः, अनिष्टं, व्यसनं, आ-वि-पद् *f.*, कृच्छ्रं, दुःखं, अत्याहितं, कष्टं, दुर्गति-विपत्ति *f.*, अपायः, अनिष्टपातः; 'm. s never come single' रंध्रोपनिपातिनोऽनर्थाः (S. 6), छिद्रेष्वनर्था बहुलीभवंति. 3 अलक्ष्मीः, निर्ऋति *f.*

MISGIVE, *v. t.* Ex. by वि-आ-शंक् 1 A, न प्रति-इ or विश्वस् 2 P, विकल्प् 1 A, वेप् 1 A; *See* DOUBT; 'my mind m. s me' उदेति मे मनसि शंका, शंकते-वेपते मे हृदयं. —ING, *s.* शंका, आ-वि-°, संदेहः, संशयः, विकल्पः, अप्रत्ययः, अविश्वासः.

MISGOTTEN, *a.* अन्यायार्जित.

MISGOVERN, *v. t.* असम्यक् शास् 2 P or पा c. (पालयति) or ईश् 2 A. —MENT, *s.* कुशासनं, असम्यक् पालनं.

MISGUIDE, *v. t.* अपथे पत् c., विमार्गेण-कुपथेन-नी 1 P or प्रवृत् c., विमार्गं दृश् c. —ED, *a.* उन्मार्गप्रवृत्त, मार्गभ्रष्ट, सत्पथभ्रष्ट, कुमंत्रित, दुर्विनीत, अपथगामिन्.

MISHAP, *s.* *See* MISFORTUNE.

MISINFORM, *v. t.* अन्यथा नि-विद् c., मिथ्या कथ् 10 or वि-ज्ञा c. (ज्ञापयति), मृषा बुध् c.

MISINTERPRET, *v. t.* *See* MISCONSTRUE.

MISJUDGE, *v. i.* मिथ्या-अन्यथा-विचर् c.

MISLAY, *v. t.* अस्थाने नि-धा 3 U or रक्ष् 1 P, नश् c.; *See* LOSE.

MISLEAD, *v. t.* प्र-लु c., वंच् 10; *See* CHEAT; विमार्गेण-उपत्थं-नी 1 P or गम् c. (गमयति), भ्रम् c. (भ्रमयति), मुह् c., भ्रमं-भ्रांतिं-उत्पद् c., विमार्गं दृश् c. or उपदिश् 6 P, अन्यथा उपदिश्. —ING, *a.* भ्रमकारिन्, मोह-भ्रांति-जनन (नी *f.*). —MISLED, *a.* विमार्ग-उन्मार्ग-गामिन्-प्रवृत्त, भ्रांत, सत्पथभ्रष्ट, कुमार्गगामिन्-प्रवृत्त, भ्रांतबुद्धि.

MISLIKE, *v. t.* *See* DISLIKE.

MISMANAGE, *v. t.* असम्यक् निर्वह् c. or प्र-नी 1 P or प्रवृत् c. —MENT, *s.* दुर्निर्वाहः, कुप्रणयनं, कुनीति *f.*, अव्यवस्था, दुर्नयः.

MISNAME, *v. t.* नामांतरेण-अन्यथा अभि-धा 3 U, मिथ्यानाम कृ 8 U.

MISNOMER, *s.* मिथ्यानामन् *n.*, मिथ्या-अन्यथा-संज्ञा-नाम, अचरितार्था संज्ञा, असंगतं-अननुरूपं नाम.

MISOGAMY, *s.* विवाहद्वेषः-निंदा. —IST, *s.* विवाहद्वेषिन् *m.*

MISOGYNY, *s.* स्त्रीद्वेषः-निंदा. —IST, *s.* स्त्रीद्वेषी.

MISPLACE, *v. t.* अस्थाने नि-धा 3 U or निविश् c. or निक्षिप् 6 P or कृ 8 U, असम्यक् प्र-विनि-युज् 7 A, 10.

MISPRINT, *s.* अशुद्धं, मुद्रणदोषः.

MISPRONOUNCE, *v. t.* अशुद्धं उच्चर् c.

MISPROPORTION, *v. t. See* DISPROPORTION.

MISQUOTE, *v. t.* अन्यथा-अयथार्थ-उद्धृ 1 P or अव-तॄ c. -ATION, *s.* अयथार्थं अवतरणं.

MISREPORT, *v. t.* मिथ्या-अन्यथा-निविद् c. or कथ् 10 or आ-ख्या 2 P. -*s.* अन्यथानिवेदनं, मृषाकथनं, अयथार्थाख्यानं.

MISREPRESENT, *v. t.* मिथ्या कथ् 10 or वर्ण् 10, असत्यं निविद् c. or ख्या 2 P, अर्थं साचीकृ 8 U or परिवृत् c. -ATION, *s.* मिथ्याकथनं-निवेदनं, मिथ्या-अन्यथा-मृषा-वादः-वर्णनं, असत्यकथनं-वर्णनं.

MISRULE, *s.* कुशासनं,दुर्णीति *f.*, असम्यक् पालनं-शासनं.

MISS, *s.* (As a prefixing title) ex. by भर्तृदारिका, कुमारी. 2 भ्रमः, दोषः, अपराधः, भ्रंशः. 3 हानि *f.*, अभावः, विरहः, नाशः, लोपः; *See* LOSS. -*v. i.* मोघी-विफली-भू 1 P, न सिध् 4 P; 'never-m. ing arrow' अमोघः बाणः. 2 भ्रम् 1, 4 P, प्र-मद् 4 P, स्खल् 1 P. 3 च्यु 1 A; *See* below. -*v. t.* भ्रंश् 1 A, 4 P, च्यु, विचल् 1 P (with abl.), हा pass. (with instr.); *See* LOSE; 'he m. ed the mark in shooting' स लक्ष्यच्युतसायकः; निमित्तादपराद्धेषुः; 'm. ed his way' मार्गाद् भ्रष्टः &c. 2 न आप् 5 P or विद् 6 U or लभ् 1 A, (Get q. v.). 3 क्षिप् 6 P, हा 3 P, त्यज् 1 P, अपास् 4 U, विसृज् 6 P; 'you have m. ed a splendid opportunity' शोभनावसरस्त्वया क्षिप्तः, न गृहीतः, त्यक्तः. 4 (Feel the absence of) अभावं ज्ञा 9 U or वि-भू c., न्यून-*a.* मन् 4 A; उत्कंठ् 1 A, उत्तम् 4 P, उत्सुकायते (D.); 'I m. him very much' तस्य बलवदुत्कंठे, तस्यासन्निधानाद् नितरां दुःखितोस्मि, तदर्शनाय उत्ताम्यामि, तद्विरहविधुरः &c. -ING, *a.* नष्ट, भ्रष्ट, स्थानभ्रष्ट-च्युत,-तिरोहित, अदृष्ट; 'one man is m.' एको नरः ऊनो दृश्यते. 2 उत्सुक, उत्कंठित, उत्कलिकाकुल.

MIS-SHAPED,-SHAPEN, *a.* वि-अप-कु-रूप, कदाकार, विकृताकार.

MISSILE, *s.* अस्त्रं, शस्त्रं, प्रहरणं, आयुधं, क्षिपणिः. 2 चक्रं. -*a.* क्षेपणीय.

MISSION, *s.* दौत्यं, प्रेरणं, प्रेषणं; 'sending on a m.' प्रतिशासनं. 2 नियुक्त-प्रेरित-गणः-जनसमूहः, नियोगिवर्गः. -ARY, *s.* धर्मार्थं प्रेरितः, धर्मप्रसारार्थं नियुक्तः or प्रेषितः.

MISSIVE, *s.* संदेशः, वाचिकं; *See* MESSAGE. 2 वार्ता-संदेश-हरः. -*a.* मुक्त, क्षिप्त, अस्त. 2 प्रेरित, प्रेषित, नियुक्त.

MIS-SPELL, *v. t.* अक्षराणि पर्यस् 4 U, अन्यथा लिख् 6 P. -ING, *s.* अक्षरविपर्यासः-व्यत्ययः.

MIS-SPEND, *v. t.* वि-क्षिप् 6 P, अपात्रे-अस्थाने-व्यय् 10 (व्यययति) or प्र-विनि-युज् 7 A, 10, असद्व्ययं कृ 8 U.

MIS-STATE, *v. t.* मिथ्या-अयथातथं-अन्यथा-कथ् 10 or नि-आ-विद् c. or ख्या 2 P. -MENT, *s.* अन्यथा-निवेदनं-विज्ञप्ति *f.*, मिथ्याकथनं-वादः.

MIST, *s*, कुहा, कुज्झटि-टी-टिका *f.*, कुहेडिका, धूमि-(पि)का, खबाष्पः, तुषारः. -Y, *a.* कुहाच्छन्न, धूमिकावृत, तुषारवृत. 2 गहन, असुगम, अस्पष्ट; *See* FAINT.

MISTAKE, *s.* भ्रमः, भ्रांति *f.*, व्या-,मोहः, मतिभ्रमः, मिथ्या-मति *f.*-बुद्धि *f.* 2 प्रमादः, दोषः, स्खलितं; 'm. in calling names' गोत्रस्खलितं. -*v. t.* अन्यथा-मिथ्या-ग्रह् 9 P or मन् 4 A or बुध् 1 P, मिथ्या ज्ञा 9 U, भ्रांत्या-संदेहेन-मन्, संदिह् 2 U; gen. ex. by बुद्धिः, धीः in comp. or by *s.* (1); 'why do you strike me, m. ing me for *Siva*' पुरारातिभ्रांत्या मां किं प्रहरासि; व्याघ्रधिया-बुद्ध्या तस्मात् पलायंते; फेनपटलैः संदेहितनूलराशिभिः (Ka. 23); 'which were m. en for heaps of cotten'; केतकशिखासंदिग्धमुग्धेंदवः (Mal. 1) 'the lovely moon being m. en for a Ketaka point.' -*v. i.* भ्रम् 1, 4 P, मुह् 4 P, प्र-मद् 4 P, स्खल् 1 P, अपराध् 4, 5 P; 'you m. in this opinion' अयं तवाभिप्रायः भ्रम एव, भ्रांतः. -ABLE, *a.* संदिग्ध; 'in no m. terms' असंदिग्धवचोभिः. -EN, *a.* भ्रांत, प्रमादिन्, मूढ, संदिग्ध. 2 अयथार्थ, अशुद्ध, मृषा-मिथ्या-अन्यथा- in comp.; 'a m. opinion' मतिभ्रमः, मिथ्यामतिः.

MISTER, *s.* आर्यः, श्री pr.

MIS-TIMED, *a. See* LATE.

MISTLE-TOE, *s.* वृक्षाश्रया, तरुरोहिणी.

MISTRESS, *s.* गृहिणी, गेहिनी, गृहस्वामिनी, कुटुंबिनी; स्वामिनी, अधिष्ठात्री, शासित्री, अध्यक्षा, सेव्या, ईश्वरी, भट्टिनी (of servants). 2 अध्यापिका, आचार्या, उपदेशिका, अध्यापयित्री, उपाध्याया-यी. 3 उपपत्नी, उपपत्नी, भुजिष्या, अवरुद्धा. 4 प्रिया, प्रियतमा, वल्लभा, कांता, दयिता, रमणी, कामिनी, प्रमदा. 5 कुशला, निपुणा,

MISTRUST, *v. t.* न विश्वस् or प्रति-इ 2 P, शंक् 1 A. -*s.* अविश्वासः, अप्रत्ययः, आ-परि-शंका, अप्रतीति *f.* -FUL, *a.* अविश्वासिन्, अप्रत्ययिन्, शंका-अश्रद्धा-शील, साशंक, आशंकित, शंकिन्, संदेहिन्. -FULLY, *adv.* साशंकं, अविश्वासेन. -FULNESS, *s.* अप्रतीतिः, आशंका.

MISUNDERSTAND, *v. t.* मिथ्या-अन्यथा समर्थ् 10 or क्लृप् c. or मन् 4 A or ग्रह् 9 P or सं-भू c. or उपलभ् 1 A or अवगम् 1 P or बुध् 1 P; 'don't m. me' अलमन्यथा गृहीत्वा (M. 1), अलमस्मानन्यथा संभाव्य (S. 1). -ING, *s.* मिथ्या-अन्यथा-ग्रहणं-संभावनं, मिथ्यामति *f.*-बोधः,अयथार्थबोधः. भ्रमः. 2 वैमत्यं, मतिभेदः, विसंवादः, द्वैधं, वि-असं-मति *f.*

MISUSE, *v. t.* मिथ्या-असम्यक् प्र-विनि-उप-युज् 7 A, 10, अनुचितं-अस्थाने व्याप्टृ c. or व्यव-हृ c, अप-व्यय् 10 (व्यययति). -*s.*, -AGE, *s.* कुप्रयोगः, असत्प्रयोगः, कु-असम्यग्-व्यापारः-व्यवहारः, अन्यथोपयोगः, असद्विनियोगः, अपव्ययः.

MITE, *s.* अणुः, लवः, कणः, लेशः, कणिका, अल्पमात्रा. 2 धनलवः-लेशः, अत्यल्पं धनं, काकिणी, कपर्दिका.

MITHRIDATE, *s.* विषनाशनं, विषघ्नं.

MITIGATE, *v. t.* शम् c. (शमयति), प्र-उप-°, लघू-कृ 8 U, लघयति (D.), न्यूनीकृ, अल्पीकृ; नि-यम् 1 P or c.; *See* MODERATE; 'to be m. ed' शम् 4 P, लघूभू 1 P. -ION, *s.* शमः, शमनं, शांति *f.*, प्र-उप-°, लघुकरणं, न्यूनता. -IVE, -MITIGANT, *a.* शमक, शांतिद, शांतिकर (री *f.*).

MIX, *v. t.* मिश्र् 10, सं-व्या-वि°-, संयुज् 7 U, 10, सं-यु 2 P; संसृज् 6 P, संश्लिष् 2 A, 7 P, प्रक्षिप् 6 P, एकीकृ 8 U, एकत्र कृ, संमिल् c. 2 संकृ 6 P, संकुलीकृ. -*v. i.* मिश्रीभू 1 P, संमिल् 6 P, संकृ-संयुज्-संसृज् pass.; संयोगं-संसर्गं-इ-या 2 P or गम् 1 P, संगम् 1 A, संगमनुव्रज् 1 P, सं-इ. -ED, *a.* मिश्रित, संयुक्त, संसृष्ट, संपृक्त, संयुत, व्या-सं-मिश्र, समवेत, संबद्ध. -ING, -TURE, *s.* मिश्रणं, संयोगः, संसर्गः, संपर्कः. 2 मिश्रता, संयुक्तता, संसृष्टता, संकीर्णता. 3 संकरः, संनिपातः, नाना-द्रव्य-संमिश्रद्रव्य-समुदायः, मिश्रद्रव्यं, मिश्रं.

MIXEN, *s.* विट्-पुरीष-राशिः.

MIZZEN-MAST, *s.* पश्चिमकूपकः.

MIZZLLE, *s.* तुषारवर्षः, शीकरासारः.

MNEMONIC, *a.* स्मृतिसहायभूत, स्मरणोपकारिन्. -*s.* (M. s) स्मरणविद्या.

MOAN, *v. i.* दीर्घं रु 2 P or निश्वस् 2 P, सशब्दं आ-क्रंद् 1 P or आक्रुश् 1 P or विलप् 1 P, आर्तरवं मुच् 6 P; *See* GROAN, LAMENT. -*s.* आर्तनादः-रवः, दीर्घनिश्वासः-रवः, क्रंदितं, विलपनं, परिदेवनं. -FUL, *a.* विलापकारिन्, परिदेविन्. -FULLY, *adv.* सनिश्वासं, सविलापं.

MOAT, *s.* परिखा, प्रतिकूपः, खातकं, उपकुल्या. -ED, *a.* परिखान्वित.

MOB, *s.* प्राकृतजनाः, जनसमूहः, अप्रबुद्धजनगणः, लोक-जन-संघः-संकुलं, जनता, बहुजनमेलकः, पृथग्जनाः, नीच-अधम-जनाः.

MOBILE, *a.* अस्थिर, चंचल, चपल, चरिष्णु, गतियोग्य, जंगम. -MOBILITY, *s.* Mob, q. v. 2 अस्थिरता, चांचल्यं, गतिक्षमता.

MOCK, *v. t.* विडंब् 10, अव-उप-हस् 1 P; सोपहासं अनुकृ 8 U. 2 गर्ह् 1, 10 A, अव-ज्ञा 9 U, अवक्षिप् 6 P, अवमन् 4 A, अवहासास्पदं मन् ; *See* CONTEMN. 3 वंच् 10, प्रतॄ c., विप्र-लभ् 1 A, मुह् c.; *See* CHEAT. -*a.* कृत्रिम, कृतक, कपट-व्याज in comp.; 'm. fight' कृत्रिमयुद्धं, व्याजयुद्धं. -ER, *s.* उप-अव-हासकः, अवक्षेपकः, विडंबनकृत् *m.* -ERY, -ING, *s.* उप-अव-हासः, अवज्ञा, विडंबनं, अवक्षेपः, गर्हणं, तिरस्कारः, अवमानः. 2 उपहासपात्रं-आस्पदं-भूमि *f.*-पदं, अवहासस्थानं-विषयः, तिरस्कारपदं-विषयः. 3 वंचनं-ना, व्याजः, कपटं, छलं, विडंबना, विडंबनहेतुः; अनर्थकारंभः, वृथोद्यमः, वृथाप्रयत्नः, निष्फलचेष्टा. -INGLY, *adv.* सोपहासं, सावहासं, सतिरस्कारं.

MODE, *s.* रीति *f.*, प्रकारः, मार्गः, पद्धति *f*; विधिः, वृत्ति *f.*, कल्पः, क्रमः, विधा, in comp.; *See* MANNER. 2 रूपं, आकारः, आकृति *f.* 3 आचारः, व्यवहारः, प्रचारः, रीतिः, संप्रदायः. 4 सभ्य-शिष्ट-मार्गः, व्यवहारः, शिष्टाचारः. 5 वाच्यं, अर्थः. 6 रागः, रागिणी. -AL, *a.* रूपविषयक. -ISH, *a.* शिष्टाचारानुरूप, सभ्यरीत्यनुसारिन्; *See* FASHIONABLE.

MODEL, *s.* आदर्शः, प्रतिरूपं, प्रतिमा-मानं, उपमा-मानं; 'a m. prince' आदर्शः सर्वनृपाणां. 2 संस्कारः, संस्थानं, आकारः, आकृति *f.* -*v. t.* संस्कृ 8 U, रूप् 10, सरूप-*a.* कृ; तक्ष् 1, 5 P; कॢप् c.

MODERATE, *a.* परि-,मित, समर्याद, नि-सं-यत, अल्प, सावधिक. 2 नियतवृत्ति, मर्यादानतिक्रामिन्; 'm. in expenses' मितव्ययिन्, अल्पव्यय; 'm. in desires' अलुब्ध, अल्पसंतुष्ट, अल्पाकांक्षिन्; 'm. in eating' मिताहार, मिताशन, स्वल्पाहार; 'm. in speech' मितवाच्-भाषिन्. 2 (Middling) मध्यम, सामान्य, अनाति-नाति- in comp.; 'trees of a m. height' नातितुंगा वृक्षाः. -*v. t.* शम् c. (शमयति), प्र-उप-°, लघयति (D.), लघूकृ 8 U, न्यूनी-अल्पी-कृ, नियम् 1 P or c.; छायाद्रुमैर्नियमितार्कमयूखतापः (S. 4) 'the heat of the sun's rays being m. ed by shady trees.' 2 नि-सं-यम्, निग्रह् 9 P, संहृ 1 P, आ-वृ 5 U. -*v. i.* शम् 4 P, निवृत् 1 A, विगम् 1 P, अल्पी-लघू-भू 1 P. -ION, *s.* लघूकरणं, प्रशमनं. 2 संयमः, निग्रहः, दमः. अनतिक्रमः, मर्यादानतिक्रमः, परि-,मितता-त्वं. 3 समता, समवृत्ति *f.*, समभावः, क्षमा, क्षांति *f.*; 'm. in desires' अलोभः, अल्पसंतोषः, अल्पाकांक्षा. -LY, *adv.* परिमितं, समर्यादं, नियतं, स्वल्पं; ईषत्, आ, मंद, नाति, अनाति in comp.; 'm. heated' ईषत्तप्त, मंदोष्ण, कोष्ण, &c.; 'm. sharp' अनतितीव्र. -OR, *s.* नियंतृ *m.*; मध्यस्थः.

MODERN, *a.* आधुनिक (की *f.*), अधुना तन-इदानींतन (नी *f.*), अर्वाचीन, अप्राचीन, अपुराण, नूतन, नव, नवीन, नूतनकालीन. -NESS, *s.* नूतनता, अप्राचीनत्वं. -MODERNS, *s.* अधुनातनाः, आधुनिकाः (pl.).

MODEST, *a.* विनीत, लज्जावत्, लज्जाशील, सलज्ज, सव्रीड, शालीन, विनयवत्, सत्रप, ह्रीमत्, लज्जा-त्रपा-व्रीडा-आन्वित-युक्त, सविनय, अप्रगल्भ, अधृष्ट. 2 (Not proud) अगर्व, नम्र, निरभिमान, निरहंकार, सविनय, अनुद्धत, विनत, नम्रशील. 3 अव्यभिचारिन्, साधुशील, सद्वृत्त. 4 परि-,मित, अल्पपरिमाण. -LY, *adv.* सविन-

पं, सव्रीडं, सलज्जं, सत्रपं. अगर्वं, अमुद्धतं, निरभिमानं. -Y, *s.* विनयः, शालीनता, लज्जा, ह्रीः, व्रीडा, त्रपा, लज्जाशीलता, अप्रागल्भ्यं, अधाष्टर्यं, मर्यादा, विनीतता. 2 नम्रता, अगर्वः, अनहंकारः, निरभिमानता, अनौद्धत्यं, नम्रशीलता, विनयः. 3 अव्यभिचारः, सद्वृत्ति *f.* 4 परिमितता.

MODICUM, *s.* अल्पांशः, अल्पभागः, लवः, लेशः, किंचित्, किंचन.

MODIFY, *v. t.* रूपं परिवृत् c. or परिणम् c. (-णमयति), विकृ 8 U or c.; रूपांतरं-रूपभेदं-कृ or वि-धा 3 U. 2 नियम् 1 P, संहृ 1 P, शम् c.; *See* LIMIT, MODERATE. -IED, *a.* विकृत, विकृतरूप, परिणतरूप, नियमित. -ICATION, *s.* रूपांतरविधानं, रूपपरिवर्तनं. 2 विकारः, विकृति *f.*, परिणामः, परिवृत्ति *f*, रूपांतरं, रूपभेदः, विशेषः. 3 भेदः, विभेदः, विशेषः.

MODULATE, *v. t.* स्वरलयं उत्पद् c., स्वरानुपूर्व्यं कृ 8 U. 2 स्वरभेदं कृ. -ION, *s.* संक्रमः, परिवर्तनं; 'm. of voice' स्वरसंक्रमः (Mr. 3). 2 स्वरभेदः-लयः-अनुक्रमः, स्वरानुपूर्व्यं. 3 Melody, q. v.

MOIETY, *s.* अर्धः-र्धं, अर्धभागः-अंशः.

MOIL, *v. t.* Dirty, q. v. -*v. i.* श्रातं कृ 8 U, देहायासेन श्रम् 4 P.

MOIST, *a.* आर्द्र, क्लिन्न, सरस, उन्न, उत्त, सद्रव, सिक्त, जलार्द्र, तिमित; 'to be m.' क्लिद् 4 P, स्तिम् 4 P. -EN, *v. t.* क्लिद् c., आर्द्रीकृ 8 U, सिच् 6 P, उंद् 7 P, उक्ष् 1 P. -ENING, *s.* क्लेदनं, उक्षणं, उंदनं. -NESS, *s.* आर्द्रता, क्लिन्नता, सरसता. -URE, *s.* क्लेदः, तेमः, स्तेमः, रसः, सजलता, आर्द्रता, क्लिन्नता; oft. ex. by जलं.

MOLAR, *s.* दंष्ट्रा, चर्वणदंतः.

MOLASSES, *s.* गुडः, इक्षुसारः, मत्स्यंडी-डिका, फाणितं.

MOLD, *s. See* MOULD.

MOLE, *s.* तिलकः, जडुलः, कालकः, पिप्लुः. 2 वप्रः-प्रं, सेतुः, चयः, पिंडलः, आलि *f.* 3 छुछुंदरी, गंधमुखी, दीर्घतुंडी, दिवांधिका; 'm.-eyed' सूक्ष्मनयन; 'm.-hill' वल्मीकः-कं, वामलूरः, कृमिशैलः, कूलकः, स्यमीकः; 'he makes mountains of m.-hills' तिले तालं पश्यति.

MOLECULE, *s.* अणुः, परमाणुः, कणः.

MOLES, *s.* व्यंगं.

MOLEST, *v. t.* बाध् 1 A, अर्द् 1 P or c., पीड् 10, उपद्रु 1 P, आ-यस् c., उपरुध् 7 U; *See* HARASS. -ATION, *s.* बाधा, पीडा, उपद्रवः, आयासः, क्लेशः. -ER, *s.* उत्पीडकः, बाधकः, आयासकः.

MOLLIENT, *a.* मृदुकारिन्, शमक, शांतिद.

MOLLIFY, *v. t.* शम् c. (शमयति), प्र-उप-°, सांत्व् 10, मृदूकृ 8 U, लघूकृ.

MOLTEN, *a.* विलीन; *See* LIQUID.

MOMENT, *s.* क्षणः, मुहूर्तः, निमि(मे)षः, पलं; 'pleasant for the m.' आपातरमणीय; 'but for a m.' क्षणमात्रं; 'this very m.' अस्मिन्नेव क्षणे; 'the m. he is here' अत्र तस्मिन्नागतमात्रे or आगत एव; 'for the present m.' आपाततः; 'in a m.' क्षणात्, क्षणेन, निमेषमात्रात्, एकपदे; 'auspicious m.' शुभमुहूर्तः, लग्नं; *See* INSTANT also. 2 गुरुत्वं, महत्त्वं, प्रभावः, गौरवं, महिमन् *m.*; *See* IMPORTANCE; 'of little m.' अगुरुक, अकिंचित्कर (री *f.*), लघ्वर्थ, क्षुद्र. -ARY, *a.* क्षणिक, क्षणस्थायिन्, अचिर, अस्थायिन्; क्षण, निमेष in comp.; 'm. flash' अचिरप्रभा, क्षणद्युति *f.*; 'm. obstacle' क्षणविघ्नः. -OUS, *a.* गुरु, गुरुप्रभाव, अलघु; *See* IMPORTANT.

MOMENTUM, *s.* जवः, वेगः, आ-सं-वेगः.

MONACHISM, *s.* मठवासः, संसारत्यागः, आरण्यकवृत्ति *f.*

MONAD, *s.* अभेद्य-अच्छेद्य-वस्तु *n.*

MONARCH, *s.* राजन् *m.*, ईशः, ईश्वरः, पतिः, अधिपः, अधीशः, स्वामिन् *m.*; *See* LORD; 'm. of the herd' यूथपतिः-पालः. 2 अधीश्वरः, नृपः, नृपालः, भूपतिः; *See* KING. -AL,-IC,-ICAL, *a.* राजकीय, राजयोग्य, राज in comp. 2 एकराभुक, एकराजायत्त, संम्राडधीन. -Y, *s.* एकराजशासनं, एकराजतंत्रं, एकराजाधिपत्यं. 2 राज्यं, विषयः, राष्ट्रं.

MONASTERY, *s.* विहारः, मठः, आश्रमः, मुनिवासः, वानप्रस्थाश्रमः. -MONASTIC,-ICAL, *a.* विहारिक, आश्रमिक (की *f.*), वैखानस (सी *f.*); 'm. vow' वैखानसं व्रतं.

MONDAY, *s.* सोमवारः-वासरः, इंदुवासरः.

MONETARY, *a.* द्रव्यसंबंधिन्, मौद्रिक (की *f.*).

MONEY, *s.* धनं, अर्थः, वित्तं, द्रव्यं, विभवः, वसु *n.*, *See* WEALTH. 2 मुद्रा, निष्कः-ष्कं, नाणकं, टंककः; 'm.-bag, कोशः-षः, मुद्राकोषः; 'm.-changer' मुद्रापरिवर्तकः; 'm.-lender' कुसीदिकः, वार्द्धुषिकः, वृद्ध्याजीवः, वार्द्धुषिः; उत्तमर्णः. -ED, *a.* धनिन्, धनिक, धनसंपन्न, धनाढ्य. -LESS, *a.* धनहीन, निर्धन, निःस्व, गतविभव, परिक्षीण; *See* POOR.

MONGER, *s.* व्यापारिन् *m.*, व्यवहारी, क्रयविक्रयिकः, वणिज् *m.*

MONGREL, *a.* संकीर्ण, संकरजातीय, संकरजः.

MONITOR, *s.* शासकः, बोधकः, उपदेशकः, शिक्षकः. 2 उपगुरुः. -Y,-MONITIVE, *a.* प्रबोधक, उपदेशक, शिक्षक, उपदेशरूप.

MONK, *s.* यतिः, संन्यासिन् *m.*, मुनिः, योगी, मठवासी, तपस्वी, वानप्रस्थः. -ISH, *a.* मुनिसंबंधिन्, यतिसदृश (शी *f.*).

MONKEY, *s.* वानरः, कपिः, मर्कटः, प्लवं(व)गः, शाखामृगः, बलीमुखः, कीशः, वनौकस् *m.*; 'm.-like' कापेय (यी *f.*).

MONOCHORD, *s.* एकतंत्रीवाद्यं.

MONOCHROMATIC, *a.* एकवर्ण-रंग.

MONOCHRONIC, *a.* समकालीन, वर्तमान.

MONOCRAT, *s.* अधीश्वरः, अनायत्तशासनः.

MONOCULAR, *a.* एकाक्ष (क्षी *f.*), एकनयन, काण. 2 एकनेत्रोपयुक्त.

MONOGAMY, *s.* सकृद्विवाहः, एकपत्नीव्रतं, एकस्त्रीविवाहः. –IST, *s.* एकपत्नीकः, एकस्त्रीकः.

MONOLOGUE, *s.* आत्म-स्व-गतभाषणं.

MONOMACHY, *s.* द्वंद्वं, नियुद्धं, द्वंद्वयुद्धं.

MONOMANIA, *s.* एकविषयासक्ति *f.*, एकविषयोन्मादः. –MONOMANIAC, *a.* एकविषयोन्मत्त.

MONOPETALOUS, *a.* एकदलविशिष्ट.

MONOPOLY, *s.* एकाधिकारः, अनन्यसाधारणः अधिकारः, एकव्यापारः-व्यवसायः. –IST,–IZER, *s.* पूर्वक्रयिन् *m.*, सर्वग्राहकः. –IZE, *v. t.* (सर्वं) पूर्वं क्री 9 U; (सर्वं) स्वायत्तीकृ 8 U, आत्मसात्कृ, अनन्यसाधारणं आत्माधीनीकृ, असामान्येन भुज् 7 A or जुष् 6 A.

MONOSYLLABLE, *s.* एकाक्षरं. –MONOSYLLABIC, *a.* एकाक्षर, एकाच् ; 'm. roots' एकाचो धातवः.

MONOTHEIST, *s.* अद्वैतवादिन् *m.* –MONOTHEISM, *s.* अद्वैतं, अद्वैतवादः.

MONOTONY, *s.* एकस्वरः-स्वनः, स्वराभेदः, एकस्वरसंतानः, स्वरसमता, स्वरभेदाभावः. 2 एक-सम-समान-रूपता, विशेषाभावः, एकव्यापारसंतति *f.* –OUS, *a.* एकस्वर-तान-स्वन, सम-अभिन्न-स्वर. 2 एक-सम-समानरूप, एकप्रकार, निर्विकार, निर्विशेष. –OUSLY, *adv* एकस्वरेण, समरूपेण, निर्विकारं. –OUSNESS, *s.* *See* (*s.*) above.

MONSOON, *s.* वर्षाः (*f.* pl.), वर्षाकालः-समयः, प्रावृष् *f.*, मेघकालः, पर्जन्यकालः.

MONSTER, *s.* राक्षसः, क्रूर-घोरकर्मन् *m.* 2 राक्षसविकट-भीम-शरीरः-विग्रहः, बृहत्परिमाणः, विकटाकारः; *See* GIANT. 3 अद्भुतं, अपूर्ववस्तु *n.*, अपरूपं, विरूपविषयः; 'm.s in the form of men' मानवराक्षसाः ; 'm.s of the deep' मकरादयः, यादांसि. —MONSTROUS, *a.* अद्भुत, विलक्षण, अपूर्व, सृष्टिक्रमबाह्य. 2 अप-वि-रूप, विकृताकृति. 3 राक्षसरूप, घोरदर्शन, विकट-भीम-कराल-रूप-शरीर, अतिमहत्, घोररूप, घोराकृति, विकटाकार, भीम-उग्र-रौद्र-दर्शन. 4 (Of acts) दारुण, घोर, अतिबीभत्स, विकट. –LY, *adv.* अद्भुतं, विकटं, दारुणं, उत्कटं, भृशं, अतीव, अत्यंतं, अतिशयेन; *See* EXCEEDINGLY. –NESS, –MONSTROSITY, *s.* अद्भुतता, घोरता, दारुणता, &c.

MONTH, *s.* मासः; 'half a m.' पक्षः; 'bright half of the m.' शुक्ल-शुद्ध-सित-पक्षः, पूर्वपक्षः; 'dark half' कृष्ण-उत्तर-तमिस्र-पक्षः, बहुलः, तमिस्रः; 'a m. old' मासजात. –LY, *a.* मासिक (की *f.*), मास्य, प्रातिमासिक ; 'half-m.' पाक्षिक (की *f.*); 'm. allowance' मासिकं. –*adv.* मासे मासे, प्रतिमासं.

MONUMENT, *s.* कीर्ति-यशः-स्तंभः, स्मारकचिह्नं. 2 चैत्यं, समाधिः; स्तूपः. –AL, *a.* स्मरणार्थक, स्मरणकारिन्. 2 चैत्यसंबंधिन्.

MOOD, *s.* भावः, वृत्तिः *f.*, प्रकृति *f.*, अवस्था, दशा, चित्तवृत्तिः, मनोभावः ; 'an angry m.' कोपवृत्तिः. 2 वाच्यं, अर्थः. –Y, *a.* रुष्ट, क्रुद्ध, वक्रभाव, उदासीन, उदासीनवृत्ति, चित्तोद्विग्न, विषण्ण, उद्विग्न, दीनमनस्क. 2 स्वच्छंद, स्वैरिन्; *See* HUMORSOME.

MOON, *s.* चंद्रः, शशिन् *m.*, इंदुः, सोमः, विधुः, चंद्रमस् *m.*, निशाकरः, रजनि(नी)करः, ग्लौः, शशधरः, शशांकः, मृगांकः, हिमांशुः, सुधांशुः, शुभ्रांशुः, ओषधीशः, ओषधीपतिः, कुमुदबांधवः, द्विजराजः, कलानिधिः-नाथः, अब्जः, जैवातृकः, नक्षत्रेशः, क्षपाकरः; and comp. of पतिः, ईशः, नाथः, पः, with words for 'Night,' 'Star,' or of 'Ray' with 'Cold' or 'Nectar,' q. v.; क्षपानाथः, शीतकरः, तारानाथः, उडुपः; 'orb of the m.' बिंबः-बं, मंडलं; 'digit of the m.' कला, रे(ले)खा; 'full m.' पूर्णिमा, पौर्णमासी; 'new m.' अमा, अमाव(वा)-सी, अमाव(वा)स्या, दर्शः, सूर्येंदुसंगमः; 'm.-beam' चंद्रपादः, शशिकरः-रश्मिः, सुधांशुः, (Ray, q. v.); 'm.-light' कौमुदी, चंद्रिका, ज्योत्स्ना, चंद्र-शशि-प्रभा, चंद्रातपः; (*a.*) ज्योत्स्नावत्, ज्योत्स्नायुक्त, चंद्रप्रकाशित; 'enjoys m.-light evenings' ज्योत्स्नावतो निर्विशति प्रदोषान् (R. VI. 34) ; 'm.-plant' सोमलता, सोमवल्ली-वल्लरी, ब्राह्मी, मत्स्याक्षी; 'm.-shine' चंद्रप्रभा-द्युति-कांति *f.*; 'm.-stone' चंद्रकांतः, सोमकांतः, चंद्रमणिः; 'm.-struck' विक्षिप्त-भ्रांत-बुद्धि, विप्लुत-हत-मति. –LESS, *a.* हत-नष्ट-चंद्र, चंद्रहीन. –Y, *a.* चंद्रतुल्य.

MOOR, *v. t.* रज्ज्वा बंध् 9 P or गतिं रुध् 7 U. –*s.* 'm.-land' कच्छः, कच्छ-अनूप-भूः. –ISH,–Y, *a.* आनूप (पी *f.*) , कच्छ, in comp., अनूप.

MOOT, *v. t.* विचर् c., परीक्ष् 1 A, वि-तर्क् 10; *See* DISCUSS. 2 उपक्षिप् 6 P, उपन्यस् 4 U ; 'm.-case', 'm.-point' विचारविषयः-पदं-आस्पदं-स्थानं, संदिग्ध-विवाद-विषयः.

MOP, *s.* संमार्जनी, शोधनी. 2 बालिका, तरुणी. –*v. t.* मृज् 2 P or c., शुध् c.

MOPE, *v. i.* वि-अव-सद् 1 P, म्लै 1 P, दुर्मनायते (D.), विषण्णीभू 1 P. –ING,-ISH, *a.* विषण्ण, अवसन्न, उद्विग्न, दुर्मनायमान, विषण्णवदन; *See* DEJECT,-ED.

MOPPET, *s.* वस्त्रपांचालिका, पटपुत्रिका.

MORAL, *a.* साधु, साधुवृत्त, सदाचार, धार्मिक-सात्विक (की *f.*) ; नीतिमत्, नयानुसारिन् ; धर्म्य, पुण्य, न्यायानुसारिन्, धर्मानुरूप, न्याय्य; gen. ex. by सत्, नीति, नय in comp. ; 'm. instruction' नयोपदेशः, नीति *f.* ; 'm. lessons' नीतिपाठाः ; sometimes by चित्त, मानस in comp. ; 'm. freedom' चित्तस्वातंत्र्यं ; 'm. advancement' मानसोन्नति

f.; 'm. science' नीतिशास्त्रं ; 'm. duties' शाश्वतधर्मः, सदाचारः. 2 नियमाधीन. 3 अनुमान-युक्ति-सिद्ध. –*s.* तात्पर्यं, अभिप्रायः, भावार्थः, तात्पर्यार्थः. –IST, *s.* नीतिशास्त्रज्ञः, नीतिज्ञः, नयज्ञः, नीत्युपदेशकः, नीतिविद्, सदसद्विवेचकः. –ITY, *s.* नीतिः, नयः, नीति-नय-विद्या-शास्त्रं, सद्व्यवहारशास्त्रं, सदसद्विवेकः-विचारः. 2 धर्मानुष्ठानं, साधुवृत्तं, पुण्यशीलता, सदाचारः, सु-सत्-चरितं, धर्मवृत्ति *f.* 3 न्याय्यता, धर्म्यता, धर्म-न्याय-अनुसारः. –IZE, *v. t.* धर्मोपदेशास्पदीकृ 8 U. –*v. i.* नीत्युपदेशं दा 3 U or लिख् 6 P. –LY, *adv.* नीतिशास्त्रानुरूपं, नयतः, नीत्या, धर्मेण, धर्मतः, न्यायेन, न्यायतः. 2 युक्त्या, मनसा, अनुमानेन. –MORALS, *s.* नीतिः, नीतिशास्त्रं-विद्या. 2 आचारः, आचरणं, वृत्तिः, चरितं, वृत्तं, व्यवहारः, रीति *f.*; 'good m.' सुशीलं, सदाचारः, साधुवृत्तं, विनयः, साधु-सु-सत्-चरितं.

MORASS, *s.* कच्छः, अनूपः, अनूपभूः.

MORBID, *a.* दूषित, उद्भ्रांत, विकृत, अस्वस्थ, असुस्थ, रोगाक्रांत, व्याधित.

MORBIFIC, *a.* रोग-व्याधि-कर (री *f.*), रोगद.

MORBOSE, *a.* रोगजनित, व्याध्युद्भव.

MORDACIOUS, *a.* दंशक. –MORDACITY, *s.* दंशकता, दंशनं.

MORE, *a.* अधिक, भूयस्, अधिकतर; उत्तर, अतिरिक्त, पर, अन्य; oft. ex. by तर or ईयस् affixed; 'm. in strength' बलीयस्, प्रबलतर; 'something m.' किंचित् अन्यदपि; 'what m.' किमपरं, किमन्यत्; after m. than three years' समधिकाद्वर्षत्रयात्; 'm. or less' न्यूनाधिक; 'for m. than 1,000 years' परःसहस्राः शरदः. –*s.* अधिकं, आधिक्यं, अतिरेकः, अतिशयः ; oft. ex. by अपरं, अन्यत् ; *See* above; 'm. or less' न्यूनातिरेकः, न्यूनाधिक्यं; 'no m. of solicitation' अलं-कृतं-अतिप्रार्थनया ; 'what m.' किमन्यत्; किं बहुना. –*adv.* (With adj.) ex. by अधिक in comp.; अधिकमनोज्ञ; or gen. by compar. degree in तर or ईयस्. 2 (With verbs) by अधिकं, अधिकतरं, अतःपरं, पुनः, भूयः; 'm. and m.' उत्तरोत्तरं, अधिकाधिकं; 'no m.' न अतः-इतः-परं or ऊर्ध्वं; अलं, कृतं; *See* ENOUGH; 'how much m.' किं पुनः, किमुत. –MOREOVER, *adv.* अन्यच्च, अपरं-अपि-च, किंच, चरं, अपितु, अपि.

MORIBUND, *a.* मृतकल्प-प्राय, मुमूर्षु.

MORINGA, *s.* सो(सौ-श्रो-शौ)भांजनः, शिग्रुः, तीक्ष्णगंधकः, अ(आ)क्षीवः, मोचकः.

MORION, *s.* शिरस्कं, शिरस्त्राणं, शीर्षकं.

MORN, MORNING, *s.* वि-प्र-भातं, प्रत्यु(त्यू)षः-षस् *n.*, उषा, उषस् *f.*, व्युष्टं, कल्यं, अरुणोदयः, प्रातर् *ind.*, अहर्मुखं, प्रभात-उषः-कालः-समयः. 2 (Opposed to afternoon) पूर्वाह्णः, प्राह्णः; 'it is broad m.' सुप्रभाता रजनी; 'in the m.' प्रातः, प्रातःकाले, प्रभाते, प्रत्यूषे, व्युष्टे, प्रगे; 'I bid you good m.', 'good m. to you' शुभस्ते प्रातःकालः (भूयात्); 'early in the m.' सुप्रातः, महति प्रत्यूषे, अतिप्रगे, प्रातरेव. –*a.* प्रातः-उषः-कालीन, प्राभातिक, औषिक (की *f.*), उषस्य, प्रभातीय; gen. ex. by प्रातर् or (*s.*) in comp. ; 'm. breeze' विभातवायुः; 'm. devotion' प्रातरुपासना; 'm. star' प्रभाततारा; 'm. twilight' प्रातःसंध्या.

MOROSE, *a.* कर्कश-कटु-वक्र-स्वभाव-प्रकृति, वाम-वक्र-भाव-शील, रूक्षस्वभाव, सदावक्र, प्रतीप, उदासीन, दुःशील, उदासवृत्ति. –LY, *adv.* वक्रभावेन, कर्कशस्वभावात्, स्वभावरौक्ष्येण. –NESS, *s.* कर्कशता, रूक्षता, वामता, वक्रता, स्वभावकटुता, वक्रशीलता, प्रतीपता, औदासीन्यं.

MORROW, *s.* पर-उत्तर-दिवसः-दिनं; 'on the m.' श्वः, परेद्युः, परेद्यवि, कल्ये, उत्तरेद्युः.

MORSEL, *s.* कवलः, ग्रासः, पिंडः. 2 खंडः, लवः, शकलः-लं, क्षुद्रभागः.

MORSURE, *s.* दंशनं.

MORTAL, *s.* मर्त्यः, मर्त्यधर्मन् *m.*, मनुष्यः, जन्मी, प्राणी, शरीरी, देही, देह-तनु-भृत्, मृत्युवशः; *See* MAN. –*a.* मर्त्य, मर्त्यधर्मन्, मरणशील, मृत्युवश, नश्वर, नाश-मरण-अधीन, मरण-काल-आयत्त, अनित्य, विनाशिन्; 'men are m.' मनुष्या मर्त्यधर्माणः. 2 प्राणहर (री *f.*), जीवितापह, प्राणांतक, मारात्मक, मर्मभेदिन्, अंतकर (री *f.*), प्राणापह, प्राणघ्न (घ्नी *f.*), मरणावह. 3 मर्त्य, मानुष (षी *f.*), मनुष्यधर्मक; *See* HUMAN. 4 अत्यंतदारुण, अतिक्लेशक; 'm. enemy' आमरणांतवैरिन् *m.*, दृढ-बद्ध-वैरः. –ITY, *s.* मर्त्यता, मरणशीलता, मृत्युवशता, मृत्यु-मरण-धर्मः, कालधर्मः, नश्वरता, अनित्यता. 2 मृत्यु, मरणं, नाशः, जीवितनाशः. 3 मानुष्यं, मानुषता. –LY, *adv.* सप्राणनाशं, ex. by *a.*; 'he was m. wounded' तस्य प्राणहरा व्रणाः संजाताः, भिन्नमर्माऽभूत्.

MORTAR, *s.* उलू(दू)खलं; 'm. and pestle' उलूखलमुसले. 2 लेपः, सुधा, चूर्णलेपः.

MORTGAGE, *s.* आधिः, क्षेत्र-स्थावर-आधिः, भूमिनिक्षेपः, बंधकः, न्यासः. –*v. t.* आ-धा 3 U, आधीकृ 8 U, बंधे दा 3 U, (स्थावरधनं) न्यासीकृ. –EE, *s.* आधिग्राहकः, आधि-बंधक-न्यास-ग्राहिन् *m.* –OR, *s.* आधाता *m.*, निक्षेप्ता.

MORTIFEROUS, *a.* मरणावह; *See* MORTAL.

MORTIFY, *v. t.* अभिभू 1 P, अवमन् c., अपकृष् 1 P, मानं-गर्वं-भंज् 7 P, खंड् 10; *See* HUMBLE. 2 निग्रह् 9 P, सं-नि-यम् 1 P, दम् c. (दमयति), वशीकृ 8 U, आवृ 5 U, जि 1 P. 3 क्लिश् 9 P, सं-परि-तप् c., आयस् c.; *See* AFFLICT. 4 चैतन्यं नश् c. or हृ c. –*v. i.* नश् 4 P; चैतन्यं नश् c. 2 तप् 4 A, तपस्तप् or चर् 1 P, तपस्याति (D.). –ED, *a.* अभिभूत, खंडित, आत्त-हृत-भग्न-गर्व, खंडितमान, भग्न-दर्प-मान. 2 दांत, वशीकृत, जित; 'whose passions are m.' जितेंद्रियः, वशी, दांतः, वीतकामः, वीतरागः, निःस्पृहः. 3 क्लिष्ट, सव्यथ, पीडित. 4 नष्टचैतन्य-मांस, कोथीभूत. -ICATION, *s.* अभिभवः, अवमानः, अपकर्षः, मान-दर्प-भंगः-खंडनं, मानहानि *f.* 2 दमः, निग्रहः, संयमः-मनं, जयः, इंद्रियदमः-जयः, कामनिरक्ति *f.*; विषयविमुखता, वैराग्यं. 3 तपश्चर्या, तपस्या, कृच्छ्रं. 4 दुःखं, क्लेशः, आयासः, व्यथा. 5 आशाभंगः-नाशः, मनोभंगः. 6 मांसपाकः, मांसकोथः, चैतन्यनाशः. -ING, *a.* मानध्वंसिन्, दर्पहारिन्, व्यथावह, क्लेशाकर (री *f.*), संतापक.

MORTISE, *s.* काष्ठसंधिः, दारुसीवनं, दारु-काष्ठ-च्छिद्रं. -*v. t.* काष्ठद्वयं सं-धा 3 U.

MORTMAIN, *s.* अन्यादेयभोगः.

MOSQUE, *s.* यावनधर्ममंदिरं, यवनीयं देवतायतनं.

MOSQUITO, *s.* मशः, मशकः.

MOSS, *s.* शैव(वा)लः, शेव(वा)लः-लं, जलनीली-लिका, 'm.-grown' रूढशैवल, शैवलावृत. -Y, *a.* शैवलवत्, शैवलिन्.

MOST, *a.* भूयिष्ठ, अधिकतम, बहु (pl.); प्रायेण सर्वे; 'm. people think so' प्रायेण सर्वे (बहवः) एवं मन्यंते. 2 निरतिशय, अत्यधिक, परम, उत्तम; 'for the m. part' भूयिष्ठं, प्रायः, प्रायेण, बहुशः. -*s.* भूयिष्ठ-परम-भागः, बहुतम-अधिकभागः, प्रायः सर्वभागः, बहुतरभागः; 'm. of the spot is green' प्रायशः सा स्थली हरिद्वर्णा; 'to the m. of one's power' यावच्छक्तिः, यावच्छक्यं. -*adv.* भूयिष्ठं, परमं, अत्यंतं, अतीव, सु-अति-अत्यंत-in comp.; gen. ex. by superlative of adj. 2 अधिकं, सर्वाधिकं (with verbs). -LY, *adv.* प्रायः, प्रायेण, प्रायशः, भूयसा, बहुशः, बहुधा, सामान्यतः, साधारणतः; gen. ex. by भूयिष्ठ affixed to adj.; 'an assembly m. composed of learned men' अभिरूपभूयिष्ठा परिषद् (S. 1).

MOTE, *s.* बिंदुः, अणुः, लवः, अणुरेणुः, परमाणुः, कणिका; 'the m. thou seest in the eyes of others, but not the beam in thine own' खलः सर्षपमात्राणि परच्छिद्राणि पश्यति । आत्मनो बिल्वमात्राणि पश्यन्नपि न पश्यति.

MOTH, *s.* शलभः, पतंगः, कीटः.

MOTHER, *s.* माता, जननी, अंबा, जनयित्री, प्रसूः, प्रसवित्री, जनी, प्रसविनी; 'm. of offspring' पुत्रवती, सुतिनी, अपत्यवती; 'm.-in-law' श्वश्रूः; 'm. of a hero' वीरसूः-माता, वीरप्रसवा ; 'born of a different m.' भिन्नोदर, अन्योदर, असोदर. -HOOD, *a.* मातृत्वं, जननीत्वं, मातृभावः-धर्मः. -LESS, *a.* अमातृक, हीन-मृत-मातृक. -LY, *a.* मातृसदृश (शी *f.*), मातृसंनिभ-अनुरूप-योग्य, मातृ in comp. -*adv.* मातृवत्, मातृभावेन, मातृस्थाने भूत्वा.

MOTION, MOTIVE, *See* under MOVE.

MOTLEY, *a.* चित्रविचित्र,नानाविध-वर्ण,बहुप्रकार,विविध.

MOTTLE, *v. t.* चित्र् 10, कर्बुरीकृ 8 U. -ED, *a.* चित्रित, कर्बुरित, कल्माषित.

MOTTO, *s.* वाक्यं, वचनं, आदर्शवाक्यं.

MOULD, *s.* संस्कारः, आकारः, आकृति *f.*, संस्थानं, रूपं, मूर्ति *f.* 2 मृद् *f.*, मृत्तिका; मृदुचूर्णं. 3 प्रकृति *f.*, कारणं. -*v. t.* संस्कृ 8 U, क्लृप् c., आकारं-रूपं-दा 3 U; प्रवृत् c., रच् 10, रूप् 10. -Y, *a.* मलिन, मलावृत, समल, कलंकमय (यी *f.*).

MOULDER, *v. i.* विशृ pass., जॄ 4 P, चूर्णीभू 1 P, अव-सद् 1 P शनैः नश् 4 P or क्षि pass.

MOULT, *v. i.* पक्षान् पत् c. or मुच् 6 P or c. -ED, *a.* मुक्त-पतित-पक्ष-पर्ण. -ING, *s.* पक्ष-पर्ण-पतनं-गलनं.

MOUND, *s.* वप्रः-प्रं, चयः, सेतुः, आलि *f.*, पिंडलः. 2 मृद्राशिः, मृत्तिकाचयः, क्षुद्रपर्वतः, वामलूरः, नाकुः, वल्मीकः-कं.

MOUNT, *v. t.* आ-अधि-रुह् 1 P, अधिक्रम् 1 U, 4 P. 2 आरुह् c. (रोपयति), ऊर्ध्वं गम् c. (गमयति), उच्चीकृ 8 U; निविश् c. 3 खच् 10 (खचयति); *See* INLAY. -*v. i.* (अश्वं, रथं, &c.) आ-अधि-रुह्, अधिक्रम्, अध्यास् 2 A. 2 ऊर्ध्वं गम् 1 P or चल् 1 P. -ED, *a.* आरूढ, आरोपित; 'a m. soldier' हयारूढः सैनिकः, सादी. -ING, *s.* आरोहः-हणं, आरोपणं.

MOUNT, MOUNTAIN, *s.* पर्वतः, अद्रिः, गिरिः, शैलः, नगः, अचलः, महीध्रः, अहार्यः, धरः, गोत्रः, ग्रावन्, शिलोच्चयः, सानुमत्, शिखरिन्; and comp. of भृत् or धर with 'Earth,' q. v.; क्ष्माभृत्, महीधरः, क्षितिधरः, &c.; 'western m.' अस्तः, अस्ताचलः, चरमक्ष्माभृत्; 'eastern m.' उदयः, उदयगिरिः-पर्वतः; 'hill near a m.' पादः, प्रत्यंतपर्वतः; 'to make m. s out of trifles' अणुमपि पर्वतीकृ 8 U, तिले तालं दृश् 1 P. -*a.* पर्वतीय, शैल (ली *f.*), (*s.*) in comp. -EER, *s.* पर्वत &c.-निवासिन् *m.*, शैलाटः. -OUS, *a.* शैलमय (यी *f.*), नगप्राय, सपर्वत, पर्वतीय. 2 (Huge) पर्वतप्रमाण.

MOUNTEBANK, *s.* मिथ्या-छद्म-वैद्यः, कूटचिकित्सकः.

MOURN, *v.* अनु-,शुच् 1 P, विलप् 1 P, परि-देव् 1 A, परिदिव् 10 A, रुद् 2 P, आक्रंद् 1 P, आक्रुश् 1P; *See* LAMENT. -ER, *s.* परिदेवकः, विलापिन् *m.*, शोचकः, विलपनकृत्. -FUL, *a.* शोकार्थक, शोक-दुःख-गर्भ, दुःखावेदिन्. 2 शोकावह, शोकप्रद, दुःखद, दुःखावह, शोच्य, शोकार्ह. 3 (Of persons) शोकार्त, शोकाकुल, सशोक, खिन्न, दुःखित, खेदयुक्त-अन्वित, उद्विग्नमनस्, विमनस्, विषण्ण, समन्यु. -FULLY, *adv.* सशोकं, सखेदं, सदुःखं, सोद्वेगं. -FULNESS, *s.* शोकः,दुःखं, उ-

द्वेगः. -ING, *s.* शोकः, खेदः, विलापः, परिदेवनं,दुःखं, उद्वेगः, आ-,क्रंदनं, रोदनं; *See* GRIEF. **2** अशौचं;'one should be in m. for 10 days' दशदिनमशौचं धारयेत्; 'm.-dress' अमंगलवेषः, शोकद्योतको वेषः.

MOUSE, *s.* मूष(षि)कः, आखुः, उंदरुः, बिलेशयः, खनकः; 'small kind of mice' गिरिका, बालमूषिका.

MOUTH, *s.* मुखं (in all senses); दरीमुखं, घटमुखं, नदीमुखं, &c.; वक्त्रं, वदनं, आननं, आस्यं; तुंडं, लपनं (of animate beings only); 'corner of the m.' सृक्कन् *n.*, सृक्कं, ओष्ठप्रांतः; 'rinsing the m.' आचमनं; 'stop the m.' वाचं स्तंभ् 9 P or c. **2** छिद्रं, रंध्रं, द्वारं, मुखं; 'm.-piece' मुखनालं; मुखं (fig.). -*v.* सगर्व-उद्धतं-वद् 1 P. **2** चर्व् 1 P, 10; ग्रस् 1 A, भक्ष् 10. -FUL, *s.* ग्रासः, कवलः, पिंडः, गंडूषः (of water). -LESS, *a.* मुखहीन, निरानन.

MOVE, *v. i.* चल्-र् 1 P, सृप् 1 P, प्र-वि-°, सृ 1 P, गम् 1 P, या 2 P, इ 1 P. **2** भ्रम् 1, 4 P, परिवृत् 1 A. **3** स्थानांतरं-गृहांतरं गम् or या. **4** चेष्ट् 1 A, यत् 1 A; 'm. on' प्र-सृ, प्र-गम, प्र-या, प्र-स्था 1 A; 'm. about' परिभ्रम्, इतस्ततः गम्; 'm. off' अप-या, अपक्रम् 1 U, 4 P, अप-सृ-गम्; 'don't m. even a step further' अस्मात्स्थानात्पदात्पदमपि न गंतव्यं (Ka. 147). -*v. t.* चल् c., प्र-वि-सं°,प्र-सृ c., ईर् c. **2** परि,-भ्रम् c. (भ्रमयति); स्थानांतरं गम् c. (गमयति). **2** कृष् 1 P, प्रेर् c., प्रवृत् c.; प्रोत्सह् c., नुद् 6 P or c., प्रचुद् 10, चेष्ट् c., उद्-प्र-युज् 10. **3** दयां-करुणां-उत्पद् c., हृदयं स्पृश् 6 P or आर्द्रीकृ 8 U, द्रु c., उपहन् 2 P; आक्षुभ् c. **4** उपन्यस् 4 U, उप-क्षिप् 6 P, उप-स्था c. (स्थापयति); 'to be m.-ed' आर्द्रीभू 1 P, (करुणया) द्रु 1 P or द्रवीभू; *See* MELT, AFFECT; 'he appears to be m. ed' द्रवीभूत इव लक्ष्यते; 'let my presence m. (you)' मामवलोक्यापि तावत्करुणार्द्रो भवत; 'she was m.-ed to tears' तथा द्रवीभूता यथा अश्रूणि व्यमुंचत्; 'he was deeply m. ed by what I said' मम वचसा तस्य चेतसि दृढं पदं चक्रे; 'm. ed with grief' शोकोपहत, दुःखाभिभूत, शोकस्पृष्ट; 'm. a chess-man' शारिं परि-णी 1 P. -*s.* गमनं, चलनं, सरणं &c.; 'm. at chess' परि(री)णायः. -ABLE, *a.* चल, चर, जंगम, चरिष्णु, चलन-गमन-शील-क्षम, अस्थावर; 'm. and im-m. world' चराचरं विश्वं, अखिलं जगत्. -ABLES, *s.* चरद्रव्याणि, अस्थावरद्रव्यजातं. -ED, *a.* चलित, प्रेरित, &c.; 'gently m.' वेल्लित, प्रेंखित, आधूत, चलित, आकंपित, धुत. -ER, *s.* चालकः, चलनः. **2** उपक्षेपकः, उपन्यासकृत् *m.* **3** प्रवर्तकः, प्रयोजकः, प्रेरकः. -ING, *a.* चर, चल, जंगम. **2** चलत्; गामिन्, यायिन्, विसर्पिन्, in comp. **3** हृदयस्पृश्, हृदयग्राहिन्, मर्मस्पृग-भिद्, हृदयंगम, दयावह, करुणात्मक, हृदयद्राविन्. -INGLY, *adv.* हृदयग्राहितया, हृदयंगमं. -MENT, *s.* चलनं, सरणं, यानं, गति *f.*, स्थानांतरगमनं. **2** व्यापारः, चेष्टा, क्रिया, कृति *f.*, चेष्टितं, प्रवृत्ति *f.*; 'graceful m.' विलासः, विभ्रमः; *See* under GRACEFUL. **3** चालनं, भ्रमणं; 'circular m.' मंडलभ्रमणं. **4** क्षोभः, कंपः. **5** ग्रामः, मूर्छना. —MOTION, *s.* गतिः, गमनं, चलनं, सर्पणं, चरणं. **2** चेष्टा, व्यापारः, अंगविक्षेपः; 'to set in m.' ईर् c., आ-धू 5, 9 U, 6 P, कंप् c. **3** क्षोभः; वेगः, सं-आ-वेगः, मनोविकारः, मनोवृत्तिः-वेगः, भावः, वासना, कल्पना. **4** प्रेरणं-णा, प्रोत्साहनं, प्रचोदना. **5** उपन्यासः उपक्षेपः, कार्योपक्षेपः, सूचना. **6** रेकः, रेचनं-ना, उच्चारः. -*v. i.* संज्ञां दा 3 U or कृ 8 U, संकेतं दा. -LESS, *a.* निश्चल, निश्चेष्ट, अचल, अचेष्ट, गतिहीन-शून्य, निष्कंप, अस्पंद, स्तब्ध, स्थिर. -MOTIVE, *a.* चालक, प्रेरक, प्रवर्तक, हेतुक in comp., कारणीभूत. -*s.* हेतुः, कारणं, निमित्तं, प्रयोजनं, कार्यं, अर्थः, निदानं, निबंधनं, प्रवर्तकं, प्रवृत्ति-निमित्त-हेतुः; 'without m. s' निष्कारणं, अनिमित्तं, अहेतुकं, निष्प्रयोजनं, अकस्मात्.

MOW, *v. t.* (दात्रेण) छिद् 7 P, लू 9 P, दो 4 P, कृत् 6 P. -*s.* तृण-धान्य-राशिः, तृणोत्करः, धान्यचयः. -ER, *s.* लावकः, तृणच्छिद् *m.* -ING, *s.* तृणच्छेदः, तृणकर्तनं.

MUCH, *a.* बहु, बहुल, प्रचुर, भूरि, विपुल, प्र-,गाढ, अत्यंत, निर्भर, महत्, अत्यर्थ, अतिरिक्त, उत्कट, अतिमात्र, नितांत, प्राज्य, पुरु, अदभ्र; gen. ex. by सु, अति pr., अतिशय in comp. -*s.* बहु *n.* or in comp., बाहुल्यं, बहुभागः, भूयिष्ठं, भूयिष्ठभागः; 'talking m.' बहुभाषिन्; 'as m. as' तावत्-यावत्; 'as m. as may lie in one's power' यथाशक्ति, यावच्छक्यं; 'how m.' कियत्; 'so m.', 'this m.' इयत्, एतावत्; तावत् (as correlative of यावत्); 'that m.' तावत्; 'm. more', 'm. less' किमुत, किमु, किंपुनः, -*adv.* बहु, भृशं, अत्यंतं, भूरि, गाढं, निर्भरं, नितांतं, अतिमात्रं, सु-नि-तरां, बलवत्, अति-सु- pr.; *See* EXCEEDINGLY.

MUCILAGE, *s.* मेदस् *n.*, वसा, वपा. **2** श्लेष्मन् *m.*, चिक्कणवस्तु. -MUCILAGINOUS, *a.* चिक्कण, स्निग्ध. **2** श्लेष्मल-ण.

MUCK, *s.* पुरीषं; *See* DUNG. **2** मलं, कर्दमः, कल्कं. अमेध्यं, कलुषं; 'm. -heap, or -hill' मलराशिः-संचयः, अवकरनिकरः; 'm.-sweat' अतिस्वेदः, अत्यंतघर्मः, 'm.-worm' पंकजः, कीटः. -*v. t.* मलेन लिप् 6 P. -Y, *a.* मलिन, समल, पंकिल, अमेध्य.

MUCUS, *s.* श्लेष्मन् *m.*, मलं, इंद्रियमलं; 'm. of the nose' सिंघाण, सिंहाण-नं, नासामलं; 'm. of the throat' कफः, श्लेष्मा; 'm. of the bowels' आमः; 'm. of the urethra' पुष्पं, कतुः -MUCOUS,

-MUCULENT, *a.* चिक्कण; श्लेष्मण-ल, कफसगुण. 2 श्लेष्म-कफ-कर (री *f.*).

MUD, *s.* पंकः-कं, कर्दमः, जंबालः-लं, शादः, निषद्वरः. -DY, *a.* पंकिल, सपंक, पंकदूषित, सकर्दम, मलिन, समल, मलीमस; 'm.-headed' स्थूल-जड-बुद्धि, मृत्पिंडबुद्धि. -MUDDLE, *v. t.* पंकिलयति-कलुषयति-आविलयति (D.), दुष् c. (दूषयति), मलिनीकृ 8 U, आविलीकृ. 2 (Fig.) आकुलयति (D.), आकुलीकृ, ईषत् मुह् c or मद् c.

MUFF, *s.* लोममयं हस्तत्राणं.

MUFFLE, *v. t.* (वस्त्रेण) अवगुंठ् 10, परि-आ-वेष्ट् 1 A or c., आच्छद् 10, अवरुध् 7 U, बंध् 9 P, प्रावृ 5 U; *See* COVER. -ER, *s.* आच्छादनं, अवगुंठनं, मुखाच्छादनं.

MUG, *s.* पानपात्रं-भाजनं, कंसः, जलपात्रं-भाजनं.

MUGGY, MUGGISH, *a.* क्लिन्न, क्लिन्ननिर्वात.

MULBERRY, *s.* तू(तू)दः, यूपः, क्रमुकः, ब्रह्मण्यः, ब्रह्मदारु.

MULCT, *s.* दंडः, अर्थ-धन-दंडः. -*v. t.* दंड् 10, दंडं दा c. (दापयति).

MULE, *s.* अश्वतरः, वेश(स)रः, वेगसरः; *See* DONKEY also; 'm.-driver (muleteer)' वेसरपालः, अश्वतरपालः.

MULIEBRITY, *s.* स्त्रीभावः, स्त्रीत्वं, नारीत्वं.

MULL, *v. t.* क्षम् 10, भू c.

MULLER, *s.* शिला, शिलापट्टः, पेषणशिला, पेषणि-णी *f.*

MULLIGRUBS, *s.* अंत्रशूलं-वेदना.

MULTANGULAR, *a.* बहुकोण, अनेकास्र.

MULTIFARIOUS, *a.* विविध, बहुप्रकार-विध, नानाविधप्रकार, नाना-बहु-रूप, अनेक, बहु.

MULTIFORM, *a.* बहु-नाना-रूप, नाना-बहु-प्रकार-विध. -ITY, *s.* बहुविधता, अनेकरूपता, नानारूपत्वं.

MULTILATERAL, *a.* अनेकभुज-पार्श्व.

MULTILINEAL, *a.* बहुरेख.

MULTIPAROUS, *a.* बहुप्रसव, बह्वपत्य, बहुप्रज.

MULTIPLE, *s.* आधारः.

MULTIPLICITY, *s.* बाहुल्यं, अनेकत्वं, प्राचुर्यं, प्रभूतत्वं; 'm. of business' अनेककार्यव्यापृतत्वं, कार्यवैविध्यं.

MULTIPLY, *v. t.* गुणयति (D.), हन् 2 P or c. (घातयति), अ-नि-°, पूर् 10; 'm. ing 4 by 3 we get 12' त्रिगुणिताः-त्रिभिराहताः-चत्वारः द्वादश संपद्यंते; त्रिभिः चतुर्णां द्वादश फलं. 2 वृध् c., उप-चि 5 U, बहुली-प्रचुरी-कृ 8 U. -*v. i.* वृध् 1 A, स्फाय् 1 A, प्र-उप-चि pass., बहुली-भू 1 P; *See* INCREASE. 2 अपत्यानि उत्पद् c., संततिं जन् c. (जनयति). -ED, *a.* गुणित, हत, गुण-घ्न- in comp. 2 वर्धित, वर्धितसंख्य. -IER, -ICATOR, *s.* गुणकः, गुणकांकः. -ICATION, *s.* गुणनं, हननं, आघातः, अभ्यासः; 'cross m.' वज्राभ्यासः, वज्राघातः; 'duodecimal m.' गोमूत्रिका. 2 वर्धनं, वृद्धि *f.*, उपचयः. -ICATIVE, *a.* गुणक. -MULTIPLICAND, *s.* गुण्यः, गुण्यांकः.

MULTIPOTENT, *a.* बहुकार्यक्षम.

MULTIRADIATE, *a.* बहुकिरण.

MULTISONOUS, *a.* बहुस्वन-ध्वनि-नाद.

MULTITUDE, *s.* समूहः, समुच्चयः, गणः, निवहः, संघातः, समुदा(द)यः, समाहारः, ओघः, प्र-नि-सं-चयः, स्तोमः, निकरः, समवायः, चयः, संहति *f.*, कदंबकं, वृंदं, संग्रहः, समाजः, व्यूहः, संदोहः, विसरः, व्रजः, व्रातः, वारः, निकुरंबं; वर्गः (of similar things); संघः, सार्थः (of animals); कुलं, यूथः-थं (of lower animals); समजः (of beasts); निकायः; पुंजः, राशिः, उत्करः, कूटः-टं (of corn &c.); जालं, मंडलं, पूगः, ग्रामः in comp. 2 जन-लोक-संमर्दः-निवहः-संघः, जनमेलकः, जनता, लोकग्रामः. 3 बाहुल्यं, बहुत्वं.

MULTITUDINOUS, *a.* बहु, बहुल, प्रचुर; *See* MANY.

MULTIVERSANT, *a.* बहुरूपधारिन्.

MULTOCULAR, *a.* बहुनेत्र-लोचन.

MUM, *a.* निःशब्द, अनालाप. -*interj.* तूष्णीं भव, निःशब्दो भव, वाचं यच्छ.

MUMBLE, *v.* अस्पष्टं वद् 1 P or उच्चर् c., अव्यक्तं उदीर् c., नीचैः वद्, जप् 1 P. -INGLY, *adv.* अस्पष्टवाचा, अव्यक्तगिरा.

MUMMER, *s.* दांभिकः, छद्मवेशिन् *m.* -Y, *s.* विडंबनं-ना, माया, छलं, व्याजः, छद्मवेशः, भंडता; *See* TRICK.

MUMMY, *s.* रक्षितं मृतशरीरं.

MUMP, *v.* अस्पष्टं वद् 1 P or उच्चर् c. 2 चर्व् 1 P, 10. 3 Cheat, q v.

MUMCH, *v. t.* चर्व् 1 P, 10.

MUNDANE, *a.* सांसारिक-लौकिक-ऐहिक-ऐहलौकिक- (की *f.*); 'm. existence' संसारः, भवः, संसृति *f.*, लोक-जीव-यात्रा.

MUNGOOSE, *s.* नकुलः, बभ्रुः, अंगूषः.

MUNICIPAL, *a.* नगरीय, नगर-पूर- in comp. -ITY, *s.* नगरपालिका, ग्रामवेक्षिका.

MUNIFICENT, *a.* उदार, वदान्य, दानशौंड, दान-त्यागशील. -LY, *adv.* उदारवत्, सौदार्यं. -MUNIFICENCE, *s.* औदार्यं, वदान्यता, अतित्यागः, दानशौंडता; *See* GENEROUS,-NESS.

MUNIMENT, *s.* दुर्गं, कोटः.

MUNITION, *s.* युद्धसामग्री-सज्जा.

MURAL, *a.* भित्ति-प्राकार-संबंधिन्.

MURDER, *s.* (सद्वेषं) वधः, हत्या, घातः, हननं, सूदनं, हिंसा. -*v. t.* हन् 2 P or c. (घातयति), व्यापद् c. -ER, *s.* घातकः, हंतृ *m.*, हन् in comp., वधकारी, वधोद्यतः, मारकः. -OUS, *a.* हंतुकाम, जिघांसु, हिंसाबुद्धि, वधोद्यत, वधैषिन्. 2 निष्ठुर, दारुण,

अतिघोर. 3 घातक, प्राणांतक, जीवितनाशिन्. 4 मारात्मक, आत्ययिक (की *f.*).

MURK,-Y, *See* DARK.

MURMUR, *s.* मंदध्वनिः-रवः, मर्मरध्वनिः, कलरवः-स्वनः-रुतं, कलकलः, गुंजितं, गंभीरनादः; 'm. of applause' प्रणादः. 2 अंतर्-गूढ-विलापः, असंतोषध्वनिः. –*v. i.* असंतोषेण-सविषादं-सनिर्वेदं-विलप् 1 P or परि-देव् 1 A or परिदिव् 10 A. 2 गुंज् 1 P, कलं-मंदं-गंभीरं-रु 2 P. 3 जप् 1 P, नीचैः वद् 1 P. –ER, *s.* असंतुष्टजनः, सदाविलापिन् *m.*

MURRAIN, *s.* मारी, महामारी.

MUSCLE, *s.* स्नायु *f.*; मांसपेशी, स्नसा, वस्नसा, पेशी, शिरा. 2 शंबूकः. –MUSCULAR,-MUSCULOUS, *a.* स्नायुसंबंधिन्. 2 मांसल, दृढांग (गी *f.*), उपचितगात्र.

MUSE, *v. i.* ध्यै 1 P, चिंत् 10, विमृश् 6 P, विचर् c., *See* MEDITATE. –*s.* ध्यानं, चिंता. 2 वाग्देवी, सरस्वती, विद्याधिष्ठात्री, विद्यादेवता. –FUL, *a.* चिंता-ध्यान-पर-शील-निष्ठ.

MUSEUM, *s.* कौतुकागारं, दुर्लभवस्तुसंग्रहः.

MUSHROOM, *s.* छत्रं, छत्रकः; *See* FUNGUS. –*a.* अचिरस्थायिन्, क्षणध्वंसिन्, उत्पत्त्यैव विलीयमान.

MUSIC, *s.* गीतं, संगीतं, संगीत-वाद्य-विद्या-शास्त्रं (science of m.). 2 (Melody) तालैक्यं, स्वरानुपूर्व्यं, सुस्वनः-स्वरः, माधुर्यं; तौर्यं, वाद्यघोषः; 'vocal m.' संगीतं; 'instrumental m.' वादनं; 'set to m.' स्वर-ताल-बद्ध; 'm.-room' संगीतशाला; 'fond of m.' नादलुब्ध. –AL, *a.* संगीतविषयक, गानीय, (*s.*) in comp. 2 सुस्वर, सुश्राव्य; *See* MELODIOUS. 3 संगीत-गान-प्रिय, नादप्रिय-लुब्ध-आसक्त, वादनशील-आसक्त; 'm. entertainment' गानोत्सवः; 'm. instrument' वादित्रं, वाद्यं; 'm. glasses' जलतरंगः. –ALLY, *adv.* सुस्वरं, संगीतशास्त्रानुरूपं. –IAN, *s.* गायकः, गातृ *m.*, गाथकः. 2 वादकः, वादित्रकुशलः, संगीतज्ञः, सुस्वराभिज्ञः.

MUSK, *s.* कस्तूरी, कस्तूरिका, मृगनाभिः, मृगमदः, नाभि *m. f.*, गंधधूलि *f.*, वातामोदा, अंडजा; 'm.-deer' गंधमृगः, कस्तूरीमृगः; 'm.-rat' गंधमूषकः, गंधाखुः. –Y, *a.* कस्तूरीयुक्त, मृगनाभिगंधि, कस्तूरीवासित.

MUSKET, *s.* आग्नेयनालि-ली *f.*, गुलिकाप्रक्षेपिणी.

MUSLIN, *s.* सूक्ष्मवस्त्रं, सूक्ष्मांशुकं, अंशुकं.

MUST, *v.* Ex. by pot. pass. part. with or without अवश्यं, नियतं, नूनं; 'I m. worship god' (अवश्यं) मयेश्वरः पूजनीयः; 'he m. have now come home' अधुना तेन गृहमागतेन भवितव्यं; oft. by अर्ह् 1 P; 'he m. be honoured' मानमर्हत्येव; 'it m. be so' एवं खलु तत्स्यात्, एवं नाम. –*s.* द्राक्षारसः. –*v. i.* विरसीभू 1 P. –Y, *a.* विरस, निःसार, दुर्गंध.

MUSTACHES, MUSTACHIO, *s.* श्मश्रु *n.*, गुंफः, ओष्ठलोमन् *n.*

MUSTARD, *s.* सर्षपः, तं(तु)तुभः कदंबकः; 'black m.' कृष्णिका, राजिका, क्षवः, क्षुता(धा)भिजननः, आसुरी, राजसर्षपः; 'white m.' सिद्धार्थः-र्थकः.

MUSTER, *v. t.* संग्रह् 9 P, समा-हृ 1 P, समा-नी 1 P, सं-ऊह् 1 U; समाह्वे 1 P, एकीकृ 8 U, संगम् c. (गमयति). 2 (सैनिकान्) परिसं-ख्या 2 P or परिगण् 10, एकत्र समा-नी. –*v. i.* सं-इ 2 P, संमिल् 6 P, संगम् 1 A; *See* ASSEMBLE; 'm.-roll' नामावलि-ली *f.*, परिसंख्या, परिगणना.

MUTABLE, *a.* विकारवत्, अस्थिर, परिवर्तनीय, विकारशील, अनियत, अनवस्थित, अस्थायिन्, व्ययिन्. 2 लोल, चंचल, तरल; *See* FICKLE. –NESS,-MUTABILITY, *s.* अस्थैर्यं, व्ययिता, विकारशीलता, परिवृत्तिक्षमता, अनवस्थिति *f.* 2 लौल्यं, चांचल्यं, तरलता. –MUTATION, *s.* परिणामः, विकृति *f.*, विकारः, विक्रिया, स्थिति-अवस्था-भेदः.

MUTE, *a.* मूक, जड, जडवाच्, वाक्शून्य, अवाच्, वाणीहीन, निःशब्द, मुद्रितमुख; 'm. with wonder' आश्चर्यजडीकृत. –*s.* मूकजनः, मूकः. 2 पक्षिपुरीषं. –LY, *adv.* निःशब्दं, मूकवत्, जडवत्. –NESS, *s.* मूकता, जाड्यं, वाग्भावः, वाक्स्तंभः, मौन-मूक-भावः.

MUTILATE, *v. t.* व्यंगीकृ 8 U, विकलीकृ; (अंगानि) खंड् 10, व्यव-च्छिद् 7 P, कृत् 6 P. –ED, *a.* विकलांग (गी *f.*), क्षतविक्षत, छिन्नभिन्न, खंडितांग, खंडितविग्रह, नष्टेंद्रिय. –ION, *s.* व्यंगीकरणं, व्यवच्छेदः-दनं, खंडनं, अंगकर्तनं. 2 न्यूनांगता, व्यंगता, वैकल्यं.

MUTINY, *s.* सैन्यद्रोहः-अपरागः-विरक्ति *f.*-क्षोभः-प्रकोपः, संक्षोभः, व्युत्थानं; 'let him raise a m. in Jambudwipa' जंबुद्वीपे कोपं जनयतु (H. 3). –*v. i.* अभि-द्रुह् 4 P, प्रकोपं दृश् c., विरागं दृश् c., क्षुभ् 4 P, व्युत्था 1 P, शासनं लंघ् 1 A, 10. –EER, *s.* प्रकोपकारिन् *m.*, आज्ञालंघी, अभि-वि-द्रोही, द्रोह-क्षोभ-कारी. –OUS, *a.* अंतःप्रकोपकर (री *f.*), आज्ञालंघिन्, क्षोभ-प्रकोप-कारिन्; प्रतीप, अवश, अनायत्त, दुःशास्य.

MUTTER, *v.* अस्फुटं-अस्पष्टं-वद् 1 P or जल्प् 1 P, अव्यक्तं उच्चर् c., नीचैः वद्; 'm. prayers' जप् 1 P. 2 गर्ज् 1 P, स्तन् 1 P, गंभीरं स्वन् 1 P. –*s.*, –ING, *s.* अस्पष्टोच्चारणं, अव्यक्तभाषणं, उपांशुवादः-भाषितं. 2 जपः, जाप्यं, स्वाध्यायः. 3 गर्जितं, स्तनितं, निर्घोषः. –ER, *s.* अस्फुटवादिन् *m.*, उपांशुवादी. –INGLY, *adv.* उपांशु, नीचैः, अस्पष्टं, अव्यक्तं.

MUTTON, *s.* मेषमांसं, अविमांसं.

MUTUAL, *a.* परस्पर, अन्योन्य, मिथः, इतरेतर, in comp.; 'm. help' अन्योन्यसाहाय्यं; oft. by प्रति pr.; 'm. obligation' प्रत्युपकारः; प्रतिघातः, प्रत्यभियोगः, &c. –ITY, *s.* परस्परयोगः-भावः-संबंधः,

व्यतिकरः, अन्योन्याश्रयः, व्यतिहारः. -LY, *adv.* परस्परं, अन्योन्यं, मिथः, इतरेतरं, (*a.*) in comp.

MUZZLE, *s.* घोणा. 2 मुखं, प्रवेशः ; छिद्रं, द्वारं. 3 मुखबंधनी-रोधनी. -*v. t.* मुखं बंध् 9 P or रुध् 7 U.

MYOGRAPHY, *s.* स्नायुवर्णनं.

MYOPE, *s.* अल्पदृश् *m.*, अदीर्घदृष्टिः.

MYRIAD, *s.* अयुतं, दशसहस्रं.

MYRMIDON, *s.* परिचरः, क्रूरपरिचरः.

MYROBOLAN, *s.* आमलकः-की-कं, तिष्यफला, अमृता, वयस्था ; (beleric m.) विभीतकः-की-कं, अक्षः, तुषः, कर्षफलः, भूतावासः, कलिद्रुमः; 'yellow m.' अव्यथा, अभया, पथ्या, कायस्था, पूतना, अमृता, हरीतकी, हैमवती, चेतकी, श्रेयसी, शिवा.

MYRRH, *s.* बोलः, गंधरसः, रसगंधः, प्राणः, पिंडः, गोपरसः, गोपः, रसः, गोसः.

MYSTERY, *s.* रहस्यं, नि-,गूढं, गुह्यं, गूढार्थः, गूढतत्त्वं गहनवस्तु-विषयः. -IOUS, *a.* नि-,गूढ, गहन, रहस्य, गुह्य, गुप्त, गूढार्थ, गुप्तार्थ, दुर्ज्ञेय, दुर्बोध, अव्यक्त,अस्पष्ट ; 'm. are the ways of Fate' कर्मणो गहना गतिः; 'a m. person' अव्यक्तकर्मा पुरुषः, गूढचरित्रो नरः -IOUSLY, *adv.* गहनं, गूढं. -IOUSNESS, *s.* गूढता, गहनता, दुर्बोधता.

MYSTIC,-AL, *a.* गूढ, गुप्त, गहन; *See* MYSTERIOUS. -ALLY, *adv.* गूढं, गहनं. -ISM,-NESS, *s.* गूढता गहनता. -MYSTIFY, *v. t.* गहनीकृ 8 U, गूढीकृ.

MYTH, MYTHE, *s.* पुराणं, पुरावृत्तं, पुराण-पुरावृत्त-कथा, पुरावृत्ताख्यानं, पौराणिकी कथा. 2 कल्पितकथा कूटार्थकथा. -IC,-ICAL, *a.* पौराणिक (की *f.*), पुराणकथित-उक्त. 2 काल्पनिक (की *f.*), कूटार्थ. —MYTHOLOGY, *s.* पुराणं, इतिहासः, पुराणशास्त्रं, देवताख्यानं. -ICAL, *s.* पौराणिक-ऐतिहासिक (की *f.*) ; *See* above. -IST, *s.* पुराविद् *m.*, पुराणविद्, इतिहासज्ञः.

N.

NAB, *v. t.* अकस्मात् धृ 1 P or ग्रह् 9 P.

NACRE, NAKER, *s.* मुक्तास्फोटः, शुक्तिपुटं.

NADIR, *s.* अधोबिंदुः.

NAG, *s.* अश्वकः, घोटकः; *See* HORSE.

NALAD, *s.* जलदेवता, अप्सरस् *f.*

NAIL, *s.* नखः-खं, नखरः-रं, कररुहः, पुनर्भवः, पुनर्नवः; 'to fight tooth and n.' अत्यावेशेन (नखानखि) विवद् 1 A or युध् 4 A. 2 कीलकः, कीलः, शंकुः, लोहकीलः-शंकुः. -*v. t.* कील् 10, (सा नभेतासि कीलितेव Mal. 5), कीलैः बंध् 9 P ; 'n. ed to the spot' तत्स्थानकीलित.

NAIVE, *a.* सरल, दक्षिण, निर्व्याज, निर्व्यलीक, ऋजु, सरलमति, सुजन; *See* FRANK. -LY, *adv.* निर्व्याजं, अमायया, सारल्येन. -NAIVETE, *s.* सारल्यं, दाक्षिण्यं, सौजन्यं, अमाया, अव्याजः, आर्जवं, निर्व्याजता.

NAKED, *a.* नग्न, विवस्त्र, निर्-अ-वस्त्र-वसन, विवसन, विवासस्, अपरिच्छन्न, दिग्वासस्, दिगंबर, वस्त्र-वसन-हीन-रहित-शून्य; विवृत, अनावृत, अनाच्छादित. 2 असज्ज, असंबद्ध, अभूषित. 3 केवल, अनावृत, शुद्ध, मात्र in comp. 4 स्पष्ट, सुप्रकाश, स्फुट; 'by the n. eye' नेत्रमात्रेण ; 'a n. woman' नग्ना, कोटवी; 'he would not have left me n. to my enemies' शत्रुप्रहारवशीशत्रुवशायत्तं-मां नाकरिष्यत् -LY, *adv.* नग्नवत्, अपरिच्छन्नं; केवलं, स्पष्टं. -NESS, *s.* नग्नता, नग्नभावः; अनावृतत्वं.

NAME, *s.* नामन् *n.* नामधेयं; अभिधा, अभिधानं, आख्या, संज्ञा, अभिधेयं, आह्वयः, आह्वा, उपाधिः, लक्षणं, व्यपदेशः; 'do you know them by n.' अपि ज्ञायंते ते नामधेयतः; 'I shall ask his mother's n.' अस्य मातरं नामतः पृच्छेयं (S. 7); 'call by n.' नाम ग्रह् 9 P, संबुध् c., नाम्ना आह्वे 1 P; 'calling by n.' नामग्रहः-हणं, संबोधनं ; 'he calls me by my n.' नामग्राहं मामाह्वयति; 'family n.' उपनाम, कुलनाम ; 'in one's n.' वचनेन, वचनात् ; 'say to the king in my n.' वाच्यस्त्वया मद्वचनात्स राजा (R. XIV. 61); 'what is the n. of the sage' किंनामधेयोसौ मुनिः; 'in the n. of' (in oaths) साक्षीकृत्य. 2 प्रतिष्ठा, कीर्ति-ख्याति-प्रसिद्धि-विश्रुति *f.*, प्र-वि-ख्यातिः, यशस् *n.*; 'who has made a n.' लब्धप्रतिष्ठः; 'good n.' सुकीर्तिः, सुख्यातिः; 'bad n.' अप-अ-कीर्तिः, दुष्कीर्तिः, अप्रतिष्ठा. -*v. t.* अभि-धा 3 U, आह्वे 1 P, आ-ख्या 2 P, आ-प्र-चक्ष् 2 A, उदाहृ 1 P, व्यप-दिश् 6 P, संज्ञां-नाम-कृ 8 U (with gen.); *See* CALL ; 'hence his father n. ed his son Aja after the creator' अतः पिता ब्रम्हण एव नाम्ना तमात्मजन्मानमजं चकार (R. v. 36). 2 नाम्ना निर्दिश् 6 P or उदा-व्या-हृ, नामतः कथ् 10 or वच् 2 P or ब्रू 2 U or कृत 10 नाम ग्रह् ; *See* TELL also. -ED, 'by name *a.* अभिहित, ख्यात, संज्ञित, कीर्तित, उदाहृत, व्यपदिष्ट gen. ex. by नाम *ind.*, or by (*s.*) in comp.; 'a son n. Râma' रामनामा or रामो नाम or रामसंज्ञः पुत्रः. 2 नामधारिन्, कृत-लब्ध-प्राप्त-नामन्. -ING, *s.* नामकरणं,नामनिर्देशः-ग्रहणं. -LESS, *a.* अनामक, नामहीन, अप्रसिद्ध. -LY, *adv.* यथा, नाम; ex. by तद्यथा, (विरक्तानां द्विविधं प्रतिविधानं तद्यथा अनुग्रहो निग्रहश्च Mu. 3). -NAMESAKE, *s.* एक-सम-नामकः, एकनामधारी, सनामन्.

NAP, *s.* अल्प-स्वल्प-निद्रा, अदीर्घनिद्रा. 2 रो(लो)-मन् *n.* 3 गंडः. -*v. i.*, 'take a n.' अल्पकालमात्रं स्वप् 2 P. -LESS, *a.* लोमहीन. -PY, *a.* लोमश,

लोममय (यी *f.*). 2 निद्रालु. 3 स्वाप-निद्रा-कारिन्-आवह.

NAPE, *s.* मन्या, घाटा, अवटुः, कृकाटिका.

NAPKIN, *s.* मुख-वदन-मार्जनं वस्त्रं, नक्तकः.

NARCOTIC, *a.* निद्रा-स्वाप-कारिन्-जनन (नी *f.*). –*s.* निद्रावहं औषधं, निद्रौषधं.

NARD, *s.* जटिला, जटामांसी, तपस्विनी, लोमशा, मिशी (षी).

NARRATE, *v. t.* वर्ण् 10, परि-कृत् 10, कथ् 10, आख्या 2 P, नि-आ-विद् c., अभि-धा 3 U, व्याह 1 P, वद् 1 P, चक्ष् 2 A ; *See* TELL. –ION, *s.* कीर्तनं, कथनं, वर्णनं, आख्यानं, निवेदनं. 2 कथा; *See* below. –IVE, *s.* कथा, आ-उपा-ख्यानं, आख्यायिका, वृत्तांतः, चरित्रं, कथाप्रबंधः; इतिहासः. –*a.* कथासंबंधिन्, कथा in comp., विवरणविषयक. –OR, *s.* निवेदकः, कथकः.

NARROW, *a.* अविस्तृत, अविस्तीर्ण, सं-नि-रुद्ध, संकट, संबाध, संकु(को)चित, संवृत, अपृथु, अविपुल, अनायत, निरायत, अल्पपरिमाण, अवितत. 2 अल्प, परि-मित, संयत, नियत, निबद्ध; *See* LIMITED; ‘a n. pass’ संकटं, संबाधः, संकटमार्गः. 3 (Fig.) क्षुद्र, अल्प, लघु, कृपण, अनुदार; ‘of n. views’, ‘n.-minded’ क्षुद्रमनस्, लघुचेतस्, कृपणबुद्धि-धी-मति-चेतस्, अनुदारशील. 4 सूक्ष्म, अतिसूक्ष्म, निपुण, सुविशुद्ध. –*v. t.* संक्षिप् 6 P, संकुच् 1 P, संबाध् 1 A, संह 1 P, संवृ 5 U, आकुंच् c., परि-मा 3 A, 2 P, सं-नि-यम् 1 P; *See* LIMIT. –*v. i.* Pass. of roots above. –LY, *adv.* अविस्तृतं, संकटं, संबाधं, अनायतं. 2 कृच्छ्रेण, कथमपि, कष्टेन, ईषदूनं; by कल्प-प्राय- in comp; ‘he n. escaped being foiled’ जितप्रायः-कल्पः. 3 सूक्ष्मं, निपुणं. –NESS, *s.* अविस्तृति *f.*, संकोचः, अल्पविस्तारः, अल्पावकाशः, मितता, कार्पण्यं, दैन्यं, अनुदारता, &c.

NASAL, *a.* अनुनासिक (की *f.*), नस्य, नासिक्य, सानुस्वार. –*s.* अनुनासिकं.

NASCENT, *a.* प्रादुर्भवत्; वर्धिष्णु.

NASTY, *a.* मलिन, अशुद्ध, समल, अपवित्र, अमेध्य; कुत्सित, गर्हित, अश्लील. –ILY, *adv.* मलिनं, कुत्सितं. –INESS, *s.* मालिन्यं, मलं, गर्ह्यता, अपवित्रता.

NATAL, *a.* जन्म in comp.; ‘n. country’ जन्मभूः.

NATION, *s.* राष्ट्रं, जनपदः, देशः, विषयः; (people) लोकः, जनाः, प्रजाः, जनता, जनः, लोकः, देशजनः-लोकः, देशवासिनः. –AL, *a.* देशीय, दैशिक (की *f.*), देश्य, राष्ट्रीय, देश in comp.; ‘n. custom’ देशाचारः; ‘n. law’ देशधर्मः ; ‘n. calamity’ उत्पातः, जनपदोद्ध्वंसः. 2 देशाभिमानिन्. 3 सामान्य, साधारण (णी *f.*), सर्वजनीन ; *See* GENERAL. –ALITY, *s.* स्वदेशाभिमानः. 2 देशीयता, देशोद्भवता. –ALLY, *adv.* सामान्यतः, जातितः.

NATIVE, *a.* देशज, देशीय, देशोद्भव, स्वदेशोत्पन्न. 2 सहज, अकृत्रिम, नैसर्गिक (की *f.*), स्वभावज; *See* NATURAL. 3 जन्मप्राप्त, जन्मसिद्ध, जन्म-स्व in comp.; ‘n. country’ जन्मभूमि *f.* -देशः, स्वविषयः-राष्ट्रं ; ‘n. place’ जन्मस्थानं, उत्पत्तिस्थानं. –*s.* देशवासिन् *m.*, देशजः, देशोद्भवः, देशीयजनः-लोकः. –ITY, *s.* उत्पत्ति *f.*, संभवः, उद्भवः, जनि *f.* 2 जन्मपत्रिका, जातकं; ‘cast one's n.’ जातकं निरूप् 10; ‘star at one's n.’ जन्मनक्षत्रं ; ‘name given at one's n.’ जन्मनाम.

NATRON, *s.* सर्जि *f.*, सर्जिका, सर्जिकाक्षारः, कापोतः, सुखवर्चकः.

NATURE, *s.* सृष्टि *f.*, जगत् *n.*, भूमंडलं, विश्वं, ब्रह्मांडं, सर्गः. 2 मार्गः, रीति *f.*, क्रमः, विधिः, नियमः, धर्मः, सृष्टिक्रमः. 3 प्रकृति *f.*, माया, शक्ति *f.*, निर्मात्री देवता, आदिशक्तिः-माया, प्रधानं (according to Sânkhyas). 4 प्रकारः, रूपं, जाति *f.*, रीतिः, विधा, in comp. 5 भावः, प्रकृतिः, स्वभावः, निसर्गः, धर्मः, तत्त्वं, सत्त्वं, गुणः, प्रकृति-निसर्ग-जाति-स्वभावः, संसिद्धि *f.*, स्वरूपं, स्वधर्मः, शीलं. 6 स्वभाव-प्रकृति-गुणः-धर्मः ; ‘properties of n.’ गुणत्रयं (सत्त्वं, रजः, तमः); ‘good n.’ सद्भावः, सुशीलं, सौजन्यं; ‘of this n.’ एवंविध ; ‘by n.’ प्रकृत्या, जात्या, जन्मतः, स्वभावतः; ‘blind by n.’ जन्मांध, जात्यंध, जनुषांध; ‘functions of n.’ देह-शरीर-धर्मः. –ED, *a.* स्वभाव, शील, प्रकृति in comp. —NATURAL, *a.* स्वाभाविक-नैसर्गिक-सांसिद्धिक-प्राकृतिक-साहजिक-औत्पत्तिक (की *f.*), सहज, स्वभाव-निसर्ग-ज, स्वभाव-प्रकृति-सिद्ध, स्व, निज, अंतर्भव, अंतर्जात, प्रकृतिस्थ ; ‘n. enemy’ जातशत्रुः, सहजारिः; ‘n. enmity’ शाश्वतिकः विरोधः; oft. ex. by (*s.*); स्वभाव एवैष परोपकारिणाम् (S. 5) ‘it is n. with the benevolent.’ 2 योग्य, यथामार्ग-न्याय, युक्त, उचित. 3 स्वभावानुगत, अनुलोम, प्रकृत्यनुसारिन्, स्वभावयोग्य. 4 अकृत्रिम, अकृतक, अयत्नकृत, अयत्ननिर्मित ; ‘n. cavity’ देवखातं; ‘n. loveliness’ अव्याजसौंदर्यं. 5 अक्लिष्ट, अयत्नकृत, सुलभ. 6 (Child) गूढज, अनौरस (सी *f.*), जारज, उपपत्नीजात, विजात; *See* ILLEGITIMATE. 7 सत्य, यथार्थ, सरल, अकृत्रिम, प्रकृत. 8 यथाकाल ; ‘n. death’ यथाकालं मरणं ; ‘n. day’ सावनदिनं; ‘n. form’ स्वरूपं ; ‘n. disposition’ स्वभावः, जन्मस्वभावः; ‘n. history’ जडाजडशास्त्रं, स्थावरजंगमशास्त्रं ; ‘n. philosophy’ पदार्थविज्ञानं ; ‘n. to’ सुलभ ; ‘levity n. to mortals’ मानुषतासुलभो लघिमा (Ka. 134). –*s.* मूढः, मूर्खः, जडः. –IST, *s.* पदार्थशास्त्रज्ञः, पदार्थविज्ञानिन् *m.* –IZE, *v. t.* अभ्यस् 4 U; *See* FAMILIARIZE. 2 देशीय-*a.* कृ 8 U. –LY, *adv.* प्रकृत्या, निसर्गेण, स्वभावतः, स्वभावेन, निसर्गतः, जात्या, (*s.*) in comp. ; ‘n.

charming' निसर्गमधुर, प्रकृतिसुभग, अव्याजसुंदर-मनोहर,&c. 2 यथाक्रमं, अनुलोमं, सृष्टिक्रमानुसारेण. 3 अकृत्रिमं, अक्लिष्टं, अयत्नतः, सहजशक्त्या-गत्या. 4 स्वतः, स्वयं, अंतःप्रवृत्त्या, अबलात्, सहजावबोधेन. 5 अवश्यं, निर्विवादं, नियतं, अनायासेनैव; नूनं, खलु. -NESS, *s.* सहजत्वं, अकृतकता, याथार्थ्यं, &c.

NAUGHT, *s.* न किमपि, न किंचिन्-किंचन. 2 शून्यं, खं; 'set at n.' अव-ज्ञा 9 U, तृणीकृ 8 U; *See* CONTEMN, DEFY. -*adv.* न किमपि, न किंचिदपि, न ईषदपि-स्तोकमपि. -*a.* असार, निर्गुण.

NAUGHTY, *a.* दुष्ट, उपद्रविन्, दुर्वृत्त, प्रतीप, अविनेय, अवश्य, हिंसाशील, अपकारप्रिय; *See* MISCHIEVOUS. -ILY, *adv.* प्रतीपं, दुष्टभावेन. -INESS, *s.* दुर्वृत्तता, प्रतीपता.

NAUMACHY, *s.* नौयुद्धं.

NAUSEA, *s.* वमनं, उत्क्लेदः, वमनेच्छा. 2 वैकृतं, बीभत्सः, कुत्सा, घृणा, निर्वेदः. -NAUSEATE, *v. i.* वम् desid. (विवमिषति). -*v. t.* Abhor, q. v. -NAUSEOUS, *a.* बीभत्सावह, बीभत्स, निर्वेदप्रद, गर्हित, कुत्सित. 2 वमनोत्पादिन्.

NAUTIC-AL, *a.* नाविक (की *f.*), नौ in comp.

NAVAL, *a.* समुद्र in comp., नाव्य, नाविक. 2 नौकात्मक, नौरूप.

NAVE, *s.* नाभि-भी *f.*, पिंडि-डी *f.*, पिंडिका. 2 (देवालयस्य) मध्यभागः.

NAVEL, *s.* नाभि-भी *f.*, तुंदः-दि-दी *f.*, तुंदिका, उदरावर्तः; 'hollow of the n.' नाभ्यावर्तः; 'having a protuberant n.' तुंदिन्, तुंदिल-भ, तुंदवत्; 'n.-string' नालः, नाभिनालः.

NAVIGABLE, *a.* नाव्य, नौतार्य, नौगम्य.

NAVIGATE, *v.* नावा तॄ 1 P or प्लु 1 A or गम् 1 P or भ्रम् 1, 4 P. 2 (A ship) चल् c., वह् c., नी 1 P, प्रेर् c. -ION, *s.* नावा तरणं-गमनं-पर्यटनं, नौयात्रा, नौभ्रमणं-गमनं, समुद्रयानं-यात्रा. 2 नौवाहनं-चालनं-नयनं. 3 नाविकविद्या, नौकागमनविद्या-शास्त्रं. -OR, *s.* नाविकः,समुद्रयायिन् *m.* 2 नौवाहः, नौनायकः.

NAVY, *s.* (युद्ध-)नौसमूहः-साधनं, पोतावलि *f.*, नौकासमूहः.

NAY, *adv.* न, नहि; 'n. more' नेदमेव, अन्यच्च, अन्यदपि, पुनः, न केवलं इदं; 'say n.' Deny, q. v.

NEAP, *a.* नीच, निम्न.

NEAR, *prep.* समीपं-पे (with gen.), आरात् (with abl.), समया, निकषा (with acc.), उप in comp.; (with verbs) ex. by उप, आ, अभि, प्रति. -*a.* आसन्न, प्रत्यासन्न, सन्निहित, समीप, निकट, समीप-निकट-स्थ, उपांत, अंतिक, समीप-निकट-वर्तिन्, उपकंठ, संनिकृष्ट, सविध, अभ्यास-श, सदेश, सवेश, अभ्यर्ण, अभ्यग्र, सनीड, समर्याद, अदूर; 'quite n.' संसक्त, अव्यवहित, अपदांतर; 'very n.' नेदिष्ठ; अंतिकतम. 2 दृढसंबद्ध-संसक्त, परिचित. 3 स्वार्थसंबंधिन्. 4 कृपण, अल्पव्ययिन्; (relation) निकट, आसन्न; 'who is n. her delivery' आसन्नप्रसवा; 'n. his death' आसन्नमृत्युः. -*adv.* समीपं-पे, अंतिकं-के, निकटं-टे, अभितः, उपांते, आरात्, निकषा, अदूरं-रे संनिधौ, सकाशे, उप in comp.; 'n. at one's side पार्श्वे, पार्श्वतः. 2 Nearly, *See* below. -*v. t.* उपगम् 1 P, उपसृ 1 P, समीपं गम्; *See* APPROACH. -LY, *adv.* प्रायः, प्रायेण, प्रायशः, ईषदूनं, कल्प-प्राय-भूयिष्ठ-उप-in comp.; 'n. like Kumâra' कुमारकल्पः; 'n. dead' मृतप्राय-कल्प; 'n. five years old' पंचवर्षदेशीय; 'n. four' उपचतुर. 2 दृढं, गाढं; 'n. connected' दृढसंबद्ध. -NESS, *s.* आसन्नता, नैकट्यं, संनिधिः, अभ्यासः, संनिकर्षः, सामीप्यं. 2 दृढसंसर्गः-संबंधः संसक्ति *f.*, परिचयः. 3 कार्पण्यं, दैन्यं.

NEAT, *a.* शुद्ध, शोभन, परिष्कृत, विनीत, परिमृष्ट, सुरेख. 2 कुशल, प्रवीण. 3 गोजातीय; 'n.-herd' गोपालः. -LY, *adv.* विनीतं, शुद्धतया, शोभनप्रकारेण. -NESS, *s.* शुद्धता, परिष्कारः, परिपाटि-टी *f.*

NEBULA, *s.* शुक्रं, शुक्लपटलं.

NEBULOUS, *a.* मेघावृत, मेघाच्छन्न; *See* CLOUDY.

NECESSARY, *a.* अवश्य, अवश्यंभाविन्, अपरिहार्य, अवश्यकरणीय, अवश्यक, आवश्यक (की *f.*), भवितव्य, भाव्य, अनिवार्य. 2 अपेक्षित, आकांक्षित. 3 विधि-दैव-वश, दैवाधीन; 'the n. result of acts' कार्य-कर्म-वशः; oft. ex. by pot. pass. part. or अर्ह् 1 P. -*s.* शौचकूपः. -IAN, *s.* दैववादिन् *m.*, दैवपरः; *See* FATALIST. -IES, अवश्यवस्तूनि, द्रव्यसंभारः, उपकरणसामग्री; 'n. of life' अन्नोदकं, अन्नाच्छादनं. -ILY, *adv.* अवश्यं, नूनं, खलु, अवश्यं-नियतं-एव.

NECESSITY, *s.* अवश्यंभाविता, अनन्यगतित्वं, आवश्यकत्वं, अवश्यकता, नियतत्वं, अवश्यकर्तव्यता, कार्यवशः. 2 दैन्यं, दीनता, दुर्गति *f.*, दारिद्र्यं, आपन्नदशा. 3 प्रयोजनं, हेतुः, कारणं, अर्थः, निमित्तं, कार्यं; अपेक्षा, आकांक्षा. 4 भवितव्यता, नियति *f.*, दैवं, विधिः, दैवाधीनता. -ATE, *v. t.* अवश्यीकृ 8 U; also ex. by अवश्यं; 'your insolence n. s your dismissal' दृप्तत्वात्त्वमवश्यं (स्वाधिकारात्) दूरीकर्तव्यः. 2 प्रवृत् c., अवश्यं कृ c.; *See* COMPEL. -OUS, *a.* दुर्गत, दीन, दरिद्र.

NECK, *s.* ग्रीवा, गलः, कंठः, कंधरा-रः, शिरोधरा; शिरोधिः; 'back of the n.' अवटुः, घाटा, कृकाटिका; 'n. of a pitcher' पात्रकंठः; 'seize by the n. and turn out' अर्धचंद्रं दत्त्वा निःसृ c.; 'n.-cloth,' 'n.-kerchief' ग्रीवावस्त्रं, गलवेष्टनं, ग्रैवेयकं; 'n.-lace' हारः, माला, सूत्रं, ग्रैवं, ग्रैवेयकं, कंठमाला-भूषा-आभरणं; 'n.-lace of jewels' मणिमाला, रत्नावलि-ली *f.*; 'n.-lace of pearls' मुक्तावलिः,

मुक्तालता, मौक्तिकसरः; 'n.-lace of gold' कनकसूत्रं.

NECROLOGY, *s.* मृतजनवृत्तांतः.

NECROMANCY, *s.* प्रेतसिद्धि *f.*, पिशाचविद्या, भूतविद्या. -ER, *s.* भूतविद्याज्ञः; *See* MAGIC,-IAN.

NECTAR, *s.* अमृतं, सुधा, पी(पे)यूषं, सुधा-अमृत-रसः; 'n. of flowers' मधु *n.*, पुष्पासवः, पुष्परसः, मकरंदः, मरंदः. -EAN,-EOUS,-INE, *a.* अमृतोपम, सुधातुल्य, अमृत-सुधा-मय (यी *f.*).

NEED, *s.* प्रयोजनं, कार्यं, अर्थः, उपयोगः, or ex. by किं (with instr.); कारणं, निमित्तं, हेतुः, अपेक्षा, आकांक्षा; 'rich persons have n. of (even) a straw' तृणेन कार्यं भवतीश्वराणां (P. I. 1); 'according to n.' यथाकार्यं, प्रयोजनवशात्. 2 व्यसनं, आपद् *f.*, कृच्छ्रं, कष्टं, दुर्गति *f.*, दुःखं, दारिद्र्यं, क्लेशः, संकटसमयः; 'times of n.' आपत्समयः; 'a friend in n. is a friend indeed' स सुहृद् व्यसने यः स्यात्. -*v. t.* अपेक्ष् 1 A, आकांक्ष् 1 P; प्रार्थ् 10 A, इष् 6 P; oft. ex. by (*s.*); 'he n. s help' तस्य साहाय्येन प्रयोजनं. 2 (Must) ex. by अवश्यं or by अर्ह् 1 P, or pot. pass. part.; 'you n. not come to me' मां प्रत्यागमनं न तेऽवश्यकं. -FUL, *a.* अपेक्षित, अपेक्षणीय, अवश्यक, आकांक्षित. -LESS, *a.* निरर्थक, व्यर्थ, निष्प्रयोजन, निरपेक्ष, निः-अ-कारण, अहेतुक. -LESSLY, *adv.* निरर्थकं, निष्प्रयोजनं, व्यर्थं, हेतुं विना. -LESSNESS, *s.* अकारणं, कारणाभावः -Y, *a.* दरिद्र, दीन, निःस्व, अकिंचन, दुर्गत; *See* POOR. -NEEDS, *adv.* अवश्यं (एव), नूनं, खलु.

NEEDLE, *s.* सूचि-ची *f.*, सेवनी; 'the eye of a n.' सूचिरंध्रं-छिद्रं; 'magnetic n.' लोहमणिशलाका; 'n.-maker' सूचिकारः; 'n.-woman' सूचिका; 'n.-work' सूचिकर्म, सूत्रकर्म.

NEFARIOUS, *a.* अतिघोर, अतिदुष्ट, निंद्य, दारुण, दुष्टतम, पापिष्ठ, महा-अति-पातकिन्. -LY, *adv.* अतिघोरं, अतिदुष्टतया. -NESS, *s.* अतिघोरता, पापिष्ठता.

NEGATIVE, *a.* अस्वीकारार्थक, निषेधार्थक, नास्तिगर्भ, निषेधद्योतिन्. 2 अभावरूप, अकरणरूप, अभावात्मक; 'n. quantity' क्षयराशिः. -*s.* नञ्, निषेधार्थक-अस्वीकारार्थक-शब्दः. 2 नास्ति-अभाव-पक्षः, निषेधवाक्यं; 'two n. s make one affirmative' द्वौ नञौ प्रकृतार्थं गमयतः; 'to reply in the n.' नेति वद् 1 P. -*v. t.* नि-प्रति-षिध् 1 P, प्रत्यादिश् 6 P, प्रत्या-ख्या 2 P, निरस् 4 U, अपलप् 1 P; *See* CONFUTE, REJECT. -LY, *adv.* नेति, नास्तीति, सनिषेधं, अस्वीकारेण. -NEGATION, *s.* प्रत्याख्यानं, प्रत्यादेशः, निषेधः, अस्वीकारः, अपलापः. 2 अभावः.

NEGLECT, *v. t.* उपेक्ष् 1 A, न अनुष्ठा 1 P or आचर् 1 P, वि-स्मृ 1 P, प्र-मद् 4 P (with abl.), न अव-धा 3 U or श्रु 5 P (words); प्रमादतः त्यज् 1 P; 'n. ed his duty' स्वाधिकारात्प्रमत्तः (Mc. 1). 2 अतिचर्, अतिवृत् 1 A, अति-व्यति-क्रम् 1 U, 4 P, उत्-, लंघ् 1 A, 10; त्यज्, हा 3 P, अपास् 4 U. 3 अव-ज्ञा 9 U, अव-मन् 4 A, अवगण् 10, अव-धीर् 10, तिरस्कृ 8 U, न गण् or आदृ 6 A; *See* CONTEMN. -*s.*,-NEGLIGENCE, *s.* उपेक्षा, अनपे(वे)-क्षा, प्रमादः, अनवधानं, विस्मरणं, असावधानत्वं. 2 त्यागः, अननुष्ठानं, लोपः, अति-व्यति-क्रमः, अतिपातः, लंघनं, उपात्ययः, उत्सर्जनं. 3 अवज्ञा, अवमानः, अनादरः, अवधीरणं-णा. -FUL,-NEGLIGENT, *a.* उपेक्षक, मंदादर, निरपेक्ष, अनवधान, प्रमत्त, अनवहित, असावधान, प्रमादिन्. -FULLY, *adv.* सोपेक्षं, निरपेक्षं, उपेक्षया, मंदादरं, अनवहितं, असावधानं, प्रमादतः, प्रमादेन, सप्रमादं, प्रमत्तवत्, असमीक्ष्य.

NEGOTIATE, *v. i.* व्यवहृ 1 P, पण् 1 A. 2 संधये संवद् 1 P. -*v. t.* संविं-धा 3 U, व्यवहारेण सं-धा. 2 वि-क्री 9 A. -ION, *s.* पणनं, व्यवहारः. 2 संधिक्रमः, सामन् *n.*, शमनं, मध्यस्थाश्रयः. -OR, *s.* व्यवहारिन् *m.*, पणिकः, व्यवहर्तृ *m.* 2 मध्यस्थः, संधि-साम-विद्, सामकुशलः.

NEGRO, *s.* श्यामदेहः, कृष्णांगः.

NEIGH, *v. i.* हेष्-ह्रेष्-रेष् 1 A. -*s.*,-ING, *s.* हे-(ह्रे)षा, हेषारवः, हेषितं, अश्वनादः-स्वनः.

NEIGHBOUR, *s.* प्रतिवेशिन् *m.*, प्रतिवेशः-श्यः, प्रतिवासी, प्रातिवेशिकः, निकट-समीप-स्थः-वर्ती-वासी, सामंतः; 'next-door n.' प्रातिवेश्यः, अनंतरवासी. -*a.* प्रतिवासिन्, समीपस्थ, &c. -*v. t.* निकटे स्था 1 P or वृत् 1 A or वस् 1 P; *See* BORDER. -HOOD, *s.* संनिधिः, उपकंठः, सांनिध्यं, सामीप्यं, संनिकर्षः, उपांतः-तं, नैकट्यं, अभ्यासः. 2 समीप-संनिहित-देशः, सामंतं, प्रतिवेशः, अधिवासः. 3 समीप-निकट-वासिनः, प्रातिवेश्याः, प्रतिवासिनः, (pl.). -ING, *a.* समीप-निकट-वर्तिन, समीप-निकट-स्थ, सामंत, संनिहित, उपांत, आसन्न; *See* NEAR. -LY, *a.* प्रतिवासयोग्य; उपकारशील, हित.

NEITHER, (-NOR) *a.*, *conj.* न-नवा, नच-नच, (न च म परिचितो न चाप्यगम्यः M. 1), or simply न-न, (मा-मा, with Imperative). 2 एक, एकतर, अन्यतर with न, or by उभौ.

NEOGAMIST, *s.* नवोढः-ढा, नवभार्या, नवपतिः.

NEOLOGY, *s.* नूतनन्यायः-मतं. 2 नूतनशब्दाश्रयः. -IST. *s.* नूतनमताश्रयिन्, नूतनन्यायसेवी.

NEOPHYTE, *s.* नवशिष्यः-छात्रः, अनभ्यस्तः, प्राथमकल्पिकः, अपरिचितः.

NEPENTHE, *s.* दुःखशमनं.

NEPHEW, *s.* भ्रात्रीयः, भ्रातृव्यः-जः, भ्रातृपुत्रः-सुतः. 2 (Sister's son) भागिनेयः, स्वस्रीयः, भगिनी-स्वसृ-पुत्रः-सुतः.

NEPHRITIC,-AL, *a.* वृक्कसंबंधिन्. 2 वृक्करोगहर(री *f.*).

Nepotism, *s.* ज्ञात्यतिस्नेहः, कुलपक्षपातः.

Nereid, *s.* जल-समुद्र-देवता.

Nerve, *s.* शिरा, वस्नसा, स्नसा: धमनि-नी *f.*, मज्जा-स्नान-तंतुः. 2 बलं, वीर्यं, तेजस्-ओजस् *n.*, शरीरदृढता. 3 धैर्यं, धृति *f.*, मनःस्थैर्यं. **–***v. t.* बलं-धैर्यं दा 3 U or वृध् c. **–less**, *a.* निर्बल, दुर्बल, शक्तिहीन. **–ous**, *a.* शिराल; मज्जातंतुगत. 2 ओजस्विन्, सबल, वीर्यवत्, ऊर्जस्वल, सुदृढ, धीर. 3 क्षिप्रक्षोभ, कंप-वेपन-शील, धैर्यहीन. **–ously**, *adv.* सवीर्यं, सबलं. 2 सकंपं, धैर्यं विना. **–ousness**, *s.* वीर्यं, ओजः, ऊर्जः, बलं. 2 स्नायुविकारः, कंपशीलता, अधृतिः.

Nescience, *s. See* Ignorance.

Nest, *s.* नीडः-डं, कुलायः, निलयः, पक्षिस्थानं-गृहं. 2 गृहं, स्थानं, आधारः, आशयः; 'find a mare's n.' शशविषाणं आसद् c. or लभ् 1 A. **–Nestle**, *v. i.* (पक्षिवत्) नीडं आश्रि 1 U or अधि-शी 2 A, सुखेन शी or संविश् 6 P or नि-ली 4 A. **–***v. t.* पुष् 1, 4, 9 P or c., पा c. (पालयति). **–ing**, *s.* नीडस्थः पक्षिशावः.

Net, *s.* जालं, पाशः, बंधनं-नी, पाशबंधः, वि(वी)तंसः; 'n. for deer' वागुरा, मृगबंधनी, मृगजालं; 'n. for fish' आनायः, जालं; 'n.-work' जाल-सूत्र-कर्मन् *n.* 2 कूटयंत्रं, उन्माथः. **–***a.* शुद्ध, अशेष, निरुद्धार, अभग्न, अखंड, अन्यून. **–***v. t.* जाले बंध् or ग्रह् 9 P. 2 जालीकृ 8 U.

Nether, *a.* अधस् in comp.; अधर, अवर, अधःस्थ, अधोभव, अधस्तन (नी *f.*); 'n. world' अधोलोकः; 'n. garment' अधोवासः. **–most**, *a.* अवरतम.

Nettle, *s.* पीतपर्णी. **–***v. t.* सं-परि-तप् c., प्रकुप् c., रुष् c.; *See* Enrage, Excite.

Neuralgia, *s.* वातशूलं.

Neurology, *s.* शिरावर्णनं.

Neurotomy, *s.* शिराच्छेदविद्या.

Neuter, *a.* नपुंसक, क्लीब, तृतीय(या)प्रकृति, षंढ; 'n. gender' क्लीबं, नपुंसकं; *See* below. **—Neutral**, *a.* मध्यस्थ, तटस्थ, उदासीन, अपक्षपातिन्, समदृष्टि, समभाव, उभयसामान्य, अपक्षपात; *See* Indifferent. **–***s.* तटस्थः, उभयसामान्यः. **–ity**, *s.* माध्यस्थ्यं, ताटस्थ्यं, अपक्षपातः, औदासीन्यं, उभयसाम्यं, समभावः, समदृष्टि *f.* **–ly**, *adv.* औदासीन्येन, उभयसामान्यं, समभावेन. **—Neutralize**, *v. t.* विशिष्टगुणान् नश् c., दुर्बलीकृ 8 U, बल-शक्ति-नश् c. 2 उदासीनीकृ. **–ation**, *s.* विशिष्टगुणनाशः-शनं, विशेषधर्मलोपः, दुर्बलीकरणं. 2 उदासीनीकरणं. **–ed**, *a.* नष्टगुण-शक्ति-बल.

Never, *adv.* न कदाचित्, न कदापि, न कदाचन, न जातु, न कर्हिचित्; 'n.-fading' अजर; 'n.-failing' अमोघ, अक्षय्य; 'n. more' न भूयः, नेतः परं न पुनः.

Nevertheless, *conj.* तथापि, किंतु, पुनः, परंतु, परं.

New, *a.* नव, नवीन, अभिनव, नूतन, प्रत्यग्र (of flowers &c.). 2 आधुनिक (की *f.*), इदानींतन-अधुनातन (नी *f.*), अर्वाचीन. 3 अपूर्व, अभूत-अदृष्ट-पूर्व, अश्रुतपूर्व. 4 अनभ्यस्त, अपरिचित, अविज्ञानिन्; 'n. comer' आगंतुकः, नवागतः; 'n.-born' नवोत्पन्न, सद्योजात; 'n.-fangled', 'n.-fashioned' नवघटित, नवकल्पित-सृष्ट; 'n. year's day' वर्षप्रतिपद् *f.* **–ly**, *adv.* नवं, प्रत्यग्रं, सद्यः, नूतनं, नव in comp.; 'n. married wife' नवोढा, नवपाणिग्रहणा वधूः; 'n. ripe (blown)' प्रत्यग्रविकसित. **–ness**, *s.* नवीनता, अपूर्वता. 2 नूतना रीतिः, नवाचारः.

News, *s.* वार्ता, वृत्तांतः, प्रवृत्ति *f.*, उदंतः, समाचारः, वृत्तं. 2 संवादः, जनवादः-श्रुति *f.*, लोकप्रवादः, किंवदंती; 'good n.' भद्रं, शुभं, शुभवार्ता; 'ill n.' अशुभं, अशुभवार्ता; 'ill n. travels fast' अशुभवार्ता सत्वरं बहुलीभवति; 'n.-monger' वार्तावृत्तिः, वार्तायनः, वार्तावहनवृत्तिः; 'n.-paper' वार्ता-समाचार-पत्रं, वृत्तपत्रं.

Newt, *s.* क्षुद्रगोधा.

Next, *a.* (Of time) आगामिन्; 'on Monday n.' आगामिनि सोमवासरे. 2 अनंतर, अव्यवहित, अव्यवधान, संसक्त, निरंतराल; 'n. to the skin' शरीरसंसक्त. 3 सन्निहित, पार्श्वस्थ, अंतिक, समीप-निकट-स्थ-वर्तिन्; *See* Near; oft. ex. by पर, अन्य, अंतरं in comp.; 'n. born' अनंतरज; 'in the absence of the first, the n. and so on' पूर्वाभावे परः परः; 'on the n. day' पराह्णे, परेद्युः; 'the n. world' परलोकः, लोकांतरं; 'n. door to' अदूर, ईषदून (with abl.), कल्प in comp.; 'in the n. world' अमुत्र, परत्र; 'n. moment' क्षणांतरं; 'n. but one' एकांतरं. **–***adv.* अनंतरं, परं, परतः (with abl.); ततः, तदनंतरं, अथ, परस्तात्, ततः-परं-ऊर्ध्वं; 'what n.' ततः किं, ततस्ततः.

Nib, *s.* चंचु *f.*, तुंडं. 2 अग्रं, अणि *f.*, अग्रभागः. **–bed**, *a.* साग्र, अणिमत्.

Nibble, *v. t.* (अल्पाल्पं) दंश् 1 P, अवकृत् 6 P, चर्व् 1 P, 10; क्रमशः-अल्पाल्पशः खाद् 1 P or कुट् or भक्ष् 10. 2 छिद्रं अन्विष् 4 P, दोषं ग्रह् 9 P, असूयति (D.) (with dat.).

Nice, *a.* ललित, शोभन, सु in comp., सुभग, रम्य, रमणीय, रुचिर, मनोहर, साधु. 2 स्वादु, सुरस, मिष्ट, आस्वादवत्, रुचिर, रुचिकर, 3 सूक्ष्मदृष्टि-दर्शिन्, कुशाग्रबुद्धि. 4 सूक्ष्म, अतिसूक्ष्म, सुपरिशुद्ध, सम्यच्. 5 अस्थूल, सूक्ष्म, विरल (cloth). 6 कोमल, मृदु, पेलव, सुकुमार. 7 अतिसूक्ष्म, अतिनिपुण. **–ly**, *adv.* सुष्ठु, सु pr., ललितं, शोभनं, सम्यक्. 2 सूक्ष्मं, सूक्ष्मत्वेन. **–ness,-ty**, *s.* लालित्यं, रम्यता;

स्वादुता, सौरस्यं ; सूक्ष्मदृष्टि *f*., सूक्ष्मदर्शिता, कुशाग्रमतित्वं, सूक्ष्मता ; युक्ति *f*., नीति *f*.

NICHE, *s.* (प्रतिमा-)आधारः, निकेतनं, स्थानं.

NICK, *s.* ग्रंथिः; अवच्छेदः. 2 शुभ-अनुकूल-समयः, युक्त-उचित-कालः, शुभयोगः-कालः-लग्नं. –*v. t.* अवच्छिद् 7 P. 2 शुभलग्ने आसद् c.

NICKNAME, *s.* संज्ञा, उपाधिः, उपाधिनामन् *n.* –*v. t.* उपाधिं दा 3 U.

NICTATE, *v. i.* निमिष् 6 P; नि-मील् 1 P. –ION, *s.* निमेषः ; निमीलनं.

NIDIFICATION, *s.* नीडकरणं, कुलायरचनं.

NIECE, *s.* भ्रातृकन्या-सुता, भ्रात्रीया. 2 (Sister's daughter) भागिनेयी, स्वस्रीया.

NIGGARD, *s.* कृपणः, क्षुद्रः, कदर्यः. –*a.*, –LY, *a.* कृपण, क्षुद्र, कदर्य, त्यागविमुख (खी *f.*), बद्धमुष्टि. –LY, *adv.* कृपणवत्, अल्पव्ययेन. –NESS, *s.* कार्पण्यं, कदर्यता; *See* MISER, &c..

NIGH, *a.*, *adv.* *See* NEAR.

NIGHT, *s.* रात्रि-त्री, रजनिः-नी, क्षपा, निशा, विभावरी, श(शा)र्वरी, यामिनी, त्रियामा, निशीथिनी, क्षणदा, तमस्विनी, तमिः-मी-मा. (all *f.*); 'a dark n.' तमिस्रा, तामसी; 'moonlight n. ज्यौत्स्नी, ज्योतिष्मती; 'by n.', 'at n.' रात्रौ, निशि, नक्तं, दोषा; 'number of n. s' गणरात्रं; 'beginning of n.' प्रदोषः, रजनीमुखं, निशामुखं; 'n. and day' रात्रिंदिवं, नक्तंदिवं; 'a n. and 2 days' पक्षिणी; 'sitting up at n.' रात्रिजागरः; 'n.-attack' सौप्तिकं, सौप्तिकाक्रमः; 'n.-blindness' रात्र्यंधता; 'n.-dress' रात्रिवेशः; 'n.-fall' प्रदोषः, निशा-रजनी-मुखं, संध्याकालः, रात्रियोगः; 'n.-hag' रात्रिचरा, रात्र्यटा; 'n.-man' खल-मल-पूः; 'n.-mare' दुःस्वप्नः, कुस्वप्नः; 'n.-shade' निदिग्धिका, स्पृशी, व्याघ्री, बृहती, कंटकारिका, प्रचोदनी, कुली, क्षुद्रा, दुःस्पर्शा, राष्ट्रिका; 'n.-wandering' निशाचर, रात्रि(त्रिं)चर ; 'n.-watch' नगररक्षिणः (pl.); यामः, प्रहरः. –LY, *a.* नैश (शी *f.*), दोषातन (नी *f.*), (*s.*) in comp.; 'n. watch' रात्रिजागरणं. –*adv.* रात्रौ, निशि, नक्तं. 2 प्रतिरात्रं, निशि-निशि, रात्रौ रात्रौ.

NIGHTINGALE, *s.* प्रियगीतः, बुल्बुलः.

NIHIL, *s.* शून्यं, अभावः. –ISM, *s.* शून्यवादः. –ITY, *s.* अभावः, शून्यता.

NIMBLE, *a.* चपल, लघु, लघुगति, लघुशरीर, चपलदेह, क्षिप्र-चपल-गति; 'n.-footed' लघुपाद्; 'n.-handed' लघुहस्त; 'n.-witted' चपल-शीघ्र-बुद्धि. –NESS, *s.* लघुता, देहचापल्यं, चापल्यं, क्षिप्रता. –NIMBLY, *adv.* लघु, लघु-द्रुत-गत्या, चपलतया, द्रुतं.

NINE, *a.*, *s.* नवन्; 'n.-fold' नवगुण. –NINTH, *a.* नवम (मी *f.*); 'n. ly', 'in the n. place' नवमस्थाने. –NINETEEN, *a.*, *s.* नवदशन्, ऊनविंशति *f.*; 'n.-th' नवदश (शी *f.*). –NINETY, *a.*, *s.* नवति *f.*

NINNY, *s.* अल्पधीः, मूर्खः, जडः.

NIP, *v. t.* नि-,कृत् 6 P, अवच्छिद् 7 P. 2 संदंश् 1 P, चर्व् 1 P, 10. 3 पीड् 10, अर्द् 1 P or c. 4 नश् c., उच्छिद्, विश् 9 P or c.; म्लानीकृ 8 U; 'n. in the bud' कलिकावस्थायां एव नश् c., जातमात्रं हन् 2 P or प्रशमं नी 1 P, (जातमात्रं न यः शत्रुं व्याधिं च प्रशमं नयेत् P. III. 1). –*s.*, –PING, *s.* निकृंतनं, अवच्छेदः. 2 हिमार्तीकरणं. –PED, *a.* छिन्न, पीडित, &c. 3 हिमार्त, हिमपीडित. –NIPPERS, *s.* संदंशः-शकः, कंकमुखं.

NIPPLE, *s.* चूचुकः-कं, स्तन-कुच-अग्रं, स्तनमुखं.

NIT, *s.* लिक्षा, यूकांडं. –TY, *a.* लिक्षापूर्ण.

NITRE, *s.* यवक्षारः, यवाग्रजः, पाक्यः. –OUS, -Y, *a.* यवक्षारमय (यी *f.*).

NO, *adv.* न, नो, नहि; 'n., n.' मा मैवं. –*a.* (Before nouns) ex. by न; अ, अन्, निर् pr. ; हीन, शून्य, रहित in comp.; 'n. one' न कोपि, न कश्चन; 'n.-body' न कश्चित्, न कश्चन; 'having n. issue' अनपत्य, वंशहीन, &c.

NOBLE, *a.* कुलीन, अभिजात, आर्य, अभिजनवत्, महाकुल, सत्कुलजात, सद्वंशज, कुलज-जात, कुलप्रसूत, वंशविशुद्ध. 2 (N.-minded) उदार, महात्मन्, महामनस्, उदात्त, उदार-धी-मति, महानुभाव, महाशय, महेच्छ. 3. महत्, धीर, श्रेष्ठ, उत्कृष्ट, विशिष्ट, उत्तम, महाभाग, उन्नत, प्रमुख, प्रशस्त, वि-प्र-ख्यात, प्रतिपत्तिमत्, सुप्रतिष्ठ, कीर्तिमत्, यशस्विन्, श्रीमत्, महाप्रताप, महातेजस्; तेजस्विन्, ओजस्विन्; *See* MAJESTIC also; oft. ex. by ऋषभः, सिंहः, व्याघ्रः, पुंगवः, शार्दूलः in comp.; *See* EXCELLENT; 'n.-looking' धीरदर्शन, महानुभावाकृति; 'n. in reason' उदात्तधी; 'n. animal' उदात्तसत्त्वं; 'n. nature' सत्त्वं. –*s.*, 'N.-man' शिष्टजनः, कुलीनः, कुलीन-उत्कृष्ट-पदस्थः, आर्यजनः, अभिजनवत् *m.* –NESS, *s.* महत्त्वं, महिमन् *m.*, उत्कर्षः, उन्नति *f.*, श्रेष्ठता &c.; प्रतापः, वैभवः ; *See* below. –NOBLY, *adv.* कुलीनवत्, आभिजात्येन; 'n. born' कुलोत्पन्न; *See* (*a.*). 2 औदार्येण, उदारतया, माहात्म्येन, उदारचेतसा, उदात्तं, धीरं. 3 सप्रतापं, अतितेजसा, महाविभूत्या, ऐश्वर्येण. –NOBILITY, *s.* कुलीनता, आर्यता, आभिजात्यं, कुलोत्कर्षः, सद्वंशता. 2 औदार्यं, माहात्म्यं, महानुभावः, उदारधीः, महाशयः, महिमन् *m.* 3 महत्त्वं, महिमा, उत्कर्षः, विशिष्टता, श्रेष्ठत्वं, प्रकर्षः, उन्नतिः, प्रतिपत्ति *f.*, प्रतिष्ठा, प्र-वि-ख्याति *f.* 4 प्रतापः, ऐश्वर्यं, विभूति *f.*, ओजस्-तेजस्- *n.*, धीरता, श्रीः. 5 शिष्ट-कुलीन-जनः, कुलीनलोकाः-जनाः. –NOBLESSE, *s.* कुलीनजनाः, कुलीनजनसमाजः.

NOCENT, *a.* *See* MISCHIEVOUS.

NOCTAVAGANT, *a.* रात्रिंचर.

NOCTURNAL, *a. See* NIGHTLY.

NOD, *s.* शिरःकंप:-चालनं, शिरःसंज्ञा-संकेतः. 2 शिरः-मस्तक-प्रणामः. —*v.* (मस्तकं, शिरः) चल् c.; 'Mâlatî n. s her head' मालती मूर्धानं चालयति (Mal. 8); शिरसा संकेतं-संज्ञां कृ 8 U or दा 3 U; 'n. consent' शिरःकंपेन अनुमन् 4 A or अनुमतिं सूच् 10. 2 (शिरः) प्र-आ-वि-अव-नम् c. (नमयति).

NODATED, *a.* ग्रंथिल, ग्रंथिमत्.

NODDLE, *s. See* HEAD.

NODDY, *s. See* IDIOT.

NODE, *s.* पातः. 2 अस्थिगुल्मः, गंडः, पिंडः.

NODOSE, *a.* ग्रंथिल, ग्रंथिमत्.

NODULE, *s.* घनः, पिंडः ; शर्करा, लोष्टः.

NOISE, *s.* नि-,नादः, ध्वनिः, शब्दः, नि-,स्वनः, घोषः, महा-उच्च-स्वरः, उत्क्रोशः, वि-,रावः, रवः, निर्ह्रादः ; 'rattling n.' रणितं,रणत्कारः; 'jingling n.' क्वणः, क्वणनं, क्वणितं; 'loud n.' कलकलः, कोलाहलः, तुमुलं, महाशब्दः-स्वनः-घोषः. 2 जनरवः-प्रवादः-श्रुति *f.*; 'make n.' नद् 1 P, ध्वन् 1 P, वि-,रु 2 P, रण् 1 P, शब्दायते (D.), कोलाहलं-कलकलं-कृ 8 U; 'shallow water makes great n.' अर्धो घटो घोषमुपैति नूनं. —*v. t.* घुष् 10, उत्-वि-°, प्रकाश् c., प्र-, ख्या c. (ख्यापयति), प्रकटीकृ. —FUL, *a.* सशब्द; *See* NOISY. —LESS, *a.* निःशब्द, नीरव, निर्घोष. —LESSLY, *adv.* निःशब्दं, नीरवं. —NOISY, *a.* महाशब्द-स्वन-नाद, तुमुल-महाशब्द-कोलाहल-कारिन्, मुखर, घोषण, घोषकारिन्, घोषकर (री *f.*), बहु-महा-घोष; बद्ध-कृत-कलकल. 2 निनादपूरित, कलकलव्याप्त, मुखर, सशब्द, नादिन्, सं-नि-न्हादिन्. —ILY, *adv.* उच्चैः-स्वरेण, महाशब्देन. —INESS, *s.* महाशब्दः-ध्वनिः.

NOISOME, *a.* दुर्गंध, पूतिगंधि, कुत्सित, दुष्ट, समल. 2 मारक, मारात्मक, क्षयकर (री *f.*), नाशावह, घातुक, बाधक. —NESS, *s.* दुर्गंधः, पूति *f.*, उग्रगंधता.

NOMAD,-IC, *a.* पशुचारणोपजीविन् ; अस्थिरवास.

NOME, *s.* प्र-,देशः, देशभागः.

NOMENCLATURE, *s.* परिभाषा, पारिभाषिकशब्दसंग्रहः.

NOMINAL, *a.* नामसंबंधिन्, नामविषयक. 2 शाब्द (ब्दी *f.*), शाब्दिक-वाचनिक-(की *f.*). 3 नाममात्र, नामधारिन्-भृत्, नाममात्रधारिन्, शब्द-नाम-in comp.; 'I am but a n. lord of the earth' ननु शब्दपतिः क्षितेरहं (R. VIII. 52); 'n. verb' नामधातुः. —LY, *adv.* शब्द-नाम-मात्रेण, नामत एव, शब्दतः.

NOMINATE, *v. t.* नाम-संज्ञां-कृ 8 U, नाम निर्दिश् 6 P; *See* CALL, NAME. 2 (To an office) नियुज् 7 A, 10 or प्रति-ष्ठा c. (-ष्ठापयति). —ION, *s.* नियोगः, नियोजनं, प्रतिष्ठापनं. —IVE, *s.* कर्ता, कर्तृवाचकः, प्रथमा विभक्तिः. —OR, *s.* नियोजकः. —NOMINEE, *s.* नियुक्तः, अधिकृतः.

NON, (a prefix) Ex. by अ, अन्; 'n.-acceptance' अपरिग्रहः, अस्वीकारः ; 'n.-appearance, -attendance' अनुपस्थिति *f.*, असंनिधानं, अदर्शनं, अविद्यमानता ; 'n.-attainment' अप्राप्ति *f.*, अलाभः ; 'n.-attention' अनवधानं, प्रमादः ; 'n.-chalant' निरुत्सुक, अनपे(वे)क्ष, उदासीन, निःस्पृह; 'n.-compliance' अननुरोधः, अननुवर्तनं, विरोधः ; 'n.-conductor' अवाहकः, अनायकः ; 'n.-conformist' अननुरोधिन् *m.*, अननुवर्तिन् ; सामान्यधर्मविरोधी, मतांतरग्राही ; 'n.-conformity' अननुरोधः, मतांतरग्रहणं ; 'n.-descript' अवर्णित, अकृतलक्षण; 'n.-resistance' अप्रतीकारः ; &c. &c.

NONAGE, *s.* बाल्यं, बाल्यदशा; *See* MINORITY.

NONAGENARIAN, *s.* नवतिवर्षीयः.

NONCE, *s.* अवसरः, कालः ; 'for the n.' अस्मिन्समये.

NONE, *a.* न कश्चित्, न कोपि, न कश्चन, न कश्चित्, &c.; oft. ex. by न with other words ; 'n. other' नान्य, नेतर ; 'n. but' एव; (with compar. adj.) न किमपि, न ईषदपि, न मनागपि, न स्तोकमपि.

NONENTITY, *s.* अभावः, असंभवः, असत्ता, असद्भावः, शून्यता. 2 शून्यं, अवस्तु *n.*; 'he is a n. in the kingdom' राज्ये अकिंचित्करः सः.

NONPAREIL, *a.* अप्रतिम, अनुपम, अद्वितीय.

NONPLUS, *v. t.* कुंठ् 10, वि-,मुह् c., आकुलीकृ 8 U, निरुत्तरीकृ. —*s.* कुंठता, वि-,मोहः, निरुत्तरता, अगति *f.*, निरुपायता. —ED, *a.* कुंठित, निरुपाय, गतिहीन, अगतिक, मूढ, निरुत्तर.

NONSENSE, *s.* असंबद्ध-अनर्थक-वाक्यं-वचनं-भाषणं, मृषाकथा-आलापः, प्रलापः, जल्पितं, असत्यं, अयाथार्थ्यं, अनर्थकं; 'to talk n.' प्रलप् 1 P, प्रजल्प् 1 P, असंबद्धं भाष् 1 A; 'talking n.' असंबद्धप्रलापिन्, वाचाल, जल्पक. —NONSENSICAL, *a.* असंबद्ध, असंगत, अनर्थक, निरर्थक, मृषार्थक, अयथार्थ. —LY, *adv.* अनर्थकं, असंबद्धं, असंगतं, मृषा, वृथा. —NESS, *s.* असंबद्धता, &c.

NONSUITED, *a.* नष्ट-हीन-वाद, अवसन्न, अर्थाद् हीन; 'to be n.' अवसद् 1 P, अर्थात्-वादाद् हा pass.

NOODLE, *s.* मूढः, मूर्खः, अल्पधीः, जडमतिः.

NOOK, *s.* कोणः, अस्रः; विविक्तस्थानं.

NOON, *s.* (N.-time) मध्याह्नः, मध्यदिनं, मध्याह्नकालः. —*a.* माध्याह्निक (की *f.*), माध्यंदिन (नी *f.*).

NOOSE, *s.* पाशः, वागुरा, बंधनं; *See* SNARE; 'n. for the neck' कंठपाशः. —*v. t.* पाशेन बंध् 9 P, पाशे ग्रह् 9 P or पत् c.

NOR, *conj.* न च, न वा; *See* NEITHER.

NORMAL, *a.* यथाक्रमं, वैधिक (की *f.*). 2 विद्यारंभ-शिक्षक.

NORTH, *s.* उत्तरा, उदीची, उत्तरदिश्-दिशा, उत्तराशा, कौबेरी; 'to the n.' उत्तरं (with abl.), उत्तरतः (with gen.); 'facing the n.' उदङ्मुख-*a.*(खी *f.*). —*a.*,-ERLY,-ERN, *a.* उत्तर, उदीचीन, उत्तरस्थ, उदीच्य, उदच्; 'in a n. direction' उत्तरेण (with acc. or gen.); 'n.-east' उत्तरपूर्वा, पूर्वोत्तरा, ऐशानी, प्रागुत्तरा, प्रागुदीची; (*a.*,-erly,-ern), प्रागुत्तर, पूर्वोत्तर, प्रागुदीचीन; पूर्वोत्तरस्थ; 'n.-pole', 'n.-star' ध्रुवः; 'n.-west' उत्तरपश्चिमा, वायवी; (*a.*,-erly,-ern) वायव, वायुदिक्स्थ. —WARD, *a.* उत्तर, उत्तरदिक्स्थ. —WARDS, *adv.* उत्तराभिमुखं, उत्तरतः, उत्तरेण, उत्तरदिशि.

NOSE, *s.* नासा, नासिका, घ्राणं, घोणा, नसा, नस्या, गंधवहा, गंधज्ञा; 'led by the n.' नस्योत, नस्तित; (fig.) यथेच्छं कृष्ट, स्वेच्छया नीत; 'aquiline n.' शुकनासा; 'having a sharp n.' खरणस्, खरणस; 'having a hoof-like n.' खुरणस्, खुरणस; 'having a flat n.' नतनासिक; *See* under FLAT; 'having a prominent n.' प्रलंबघोण, घोणोन्नत; 'breathing through the n.' नासिकंधम; 'n.-string' नास्यं; 'n.-cut' छिन्ननास; 'n.-gay' कुसुमस्तबकः, पुष्पगुच्छः, गुच्छः, गुत्सः; 'n.-ring' नासाभरणं. —LESS, *a.* अ-वि-नासिक, विग्र, विख, विख्य, गतनासिक. —NOSTRILL, *s.* नासारंध्रं-विवरं-छिद्रं-पुटं-बिलं.

NOSOLOGY, *s.* रोगनिदानशास्त्रं.

NOSTRUM, *s.* गुप्तौषधं.

NOT, *adv.* न, नो, न हि. 2 (Prohibitive) मा; oft. by अलं with instr. or gerund; 'do n. fear' अलं भयेन, मा भैषीः; 'do n. boast much' अलमलं बहु विकत्थ्य (M. 1); 'do n. do so', 'do n. say so' मा मा एवं; (rather angrily) मा तावत्. 3 (Privative) अ, निर्, अन्, वि pr.

NOTCH, *s.* छेदः, दंतः, भंगः; 'n. of a bow' अटनिनी *f.* —*v. t.* अव-,छिद् 7 P, दंतुरी-भंगुरी-कृ 8 U. —ED, *a.* दंतुर, भंगुर, दंतुरित.

NOTE, *s.* लिंगं, लक्षणं, चिह्नं, अंकः; अभिज्ञानं. 2 स्मरणचिह्नं, स्मरणं. 3 टीका, व्याख्या, भाष्यं, टिप्पनी, वृत्ति *f.*; 'edited with n. s' टिप्पनीसमवेतं प्रकाशितं (पुस्तकं). 4 स्वरः, क्वणः; 'a wrong n.' अप-वि-स्वरः; 'high n.' तारः, तारस्वरः; 'cracked n.' काकस्वरः; 'key-n.' वादिन् *m.*; (the seven n. s being निषादः, ऋषभः, गांधारः, षड्जः, मध्यमः, धैवतः, पंचमः); 'sweet n.' काकली; 'sweet indistinct n.' कलः; 'deep n.' मंद्रः; 'continued n.' एकतालः. 5 ख्याति *f.*, कीर्ति *f.*, यशस् *n.*, प्रतिष्ठा; 'of n.' विश्रुत, लब्धकीर्ति-प्रतिष्ठ. 6 वि-,रुतं, रावः, नादः, स्वनः, शब्दः, ध्वनिः. 7 अवेक्षा, अवधानं, मनोयोगः, अभिनिवेशः; 'take n. of' अवेक्ष् 1 A, अव-धा 3 U, मनसि-चित्ते-कृ 8 U, अवधृ 10. 8 पत्रं, पत्रकं, लेखः, लेख्यं; 'n.-book' स्मरण-अंकन-पुस्तकं; 'n.-worthy' स्मरणीय, स्मरणार्ह, अवेक्षणीय. —*v. t.* निर्वर्ण् 10 आलक्ष् 10, निरूप् 10, अवेक्ष्, आलोच् 10, आलोक् 1 A, 10. 2 लिख् 6 P, (लेख्ये) आरुह् c. (रोपयति), (पत्रे) निविश् c. 3 अंक् 10, चिह्नयति (D.). —ABLE, *a.* स्मरणीय, स्मरणार्ह, स्मर्तव्य. 2 विशिष्ट, उत्कृष्ट, परम; ख्यात, प्रसिद्ध, विशेष in comp.; 'a n. guest' अतिथिविशेषः. —*s.* कुलीन-विशिष्ट-जनः, आर्यः; *See* NOBLE. —ABLY, *adv.* प्रसिद्धं, विशेषेण, विशेषतः. —ARY, *s.* लेखकः, लिपिकारः, लिपिजीविन् *m.* —ATION, अंकनं, अंकविद्या. —ED, *a.* लक्षित, निरूपित, लिखित, पत्रारूढ. 2 प्र-वि-ख्यात, सुविश्रुत, प्रसिद्ध, लब्धप्रतिष्ठ, प्रथित.

NOTHING, *s.* अभावः, शून्यं, असत् *n.*, अवस्तु *n.*, असत्त्वं. 2 न किंचित्, न किमपि, न स्तोकमपि. 3 अल्प-लघु-विषयः, अल्पार्थः, अगुर्वर्थः; 'for n.' अकारणं, अनिमित्तं, वृथा, मुधा, निरर्थकं; 'good for n.' व्यर्थ, निरर्थक, अकिंचित्कर (री *f.*); 'n. but' नान्यत् किमपि (with abl.). —*adv.* न मनागपि, न किंचिदपि, न स्तोकमपि, न मनाक्, न किमपि. —NESS, *s.* अभावः, शून्यता.

NOTICE, *v. t.* लक्ष् 10, सं-आ-°, निरूप् 10, आलोक् 1 A, 10, प्र-अव-निर्-परि-ईक्ष् 1 A, दृश् 1 P, निर्वर्ण् 10. 2 मनो दा 3 U, अव-धा 3U, सावधान-*a.* भू 1 P. 3 अभि-धा, निर्दिश् 6 P, उद्दिश्, कथ् 10, वर्ण्. 4 सं-भू c., आदृ 6 A, संमन् c., सत्कृ 8 U. —*s.* आलोकनं, निरूपणं, अवेक्षा-क्षणं, परीक्षा-क्षणं. 2 निर्देशः, उल्लेखः, अभिधानं, उद्देशः, कथनं, वर्णनं. 3 अवेक्षा, मनोयोगः, अवधानं, चित्ताभिनिवेशः, विचारः, गणना; 'take n. of' आदृ, अवेक्ष्, विचर् c., आलोच् 10; *See* CONSIDER. 4 सूचना, निवेदनं, बोधनं, बोधः. 5 विज्ञापना, विज्ञप्ति *f.*, घोषणं-णा, ख्यापना; 'written n.' घोषण-विज्ञप्ति-प्रसिद्धि-पत्रं. 6 आदरः, सत्कारः, संभावना, संमानः.

NOTIFY, *v. t.* वि-,ज्ञा c. (ज्ञापयति), बुध् c., प्रकाश् c., सूच् 10, घुष् 10, प्र-ख्या c. (ख्यापयति), नि-आ-विद् c., कृत् 10. —ICATION, *s.* विज्ञापनं-ना, विज्ञप्ति *f.*, घोषणा, सूचनं-ना, ख्यापनं.

NOTION, *s.* मतिः *f.*, बुद्धि *f.*, बोधः, मनोगतं, मतं, कल्पना, भावः, अभिप्रायः, भावना, आशयः, वासना; 'under the n. that' इति बुद्ध्या. —AL, *a.* मनःसृष्ट, मनोगत, मनःकल्पित, संकल्पज; *See* IDEAL.

NOTORIOUS, *a.* प्रसिद्ध, प्र-वि-ख्यात, प्रथित, विश्रुत, विज्ञात, लोकप्रसिद्ध-विश्रुत, लौकिक (की *f.*); 'a n. report' सार्वलौकिकः प्रवादः. 2 दुर्नामन्, कुख्यातिमत्,

ख्यातगर्हेण, कुप्रसिद्ध; 'a n. thief' सर्वविज्ञातः चौरः; 'to become n.' बहुलीभू 1 P, प्रकटीभू, सर्वप्रकाशतां गम् 1 P. -LY, *adv.* सुप्रसिद्धं, प्रकटं, ख्यातगर्हेणं. -NESS,-NOTORIETY, *s.* प्र-वि-ख्याति *f.*, प्रकाशता, प्रसिद्धि *f.*, विश्रुति *f.*, प्रथा. 2 दुर्नामन् *n.*, कुकीर्ति *f.* वाच्यता, अपकीर्तिः.

NOTWITHSTANDING, *part.* तथापि, तदपि, एवं सत्यपि; gen. ex. by gen. or loc. abs.; or by अनादृत्य (with acc.); 'n. his teacher's presence' विद्यमानेपि गुरौ; *See* 'In spite of' under SPITE.

NOUGHT, *s.* *See* NAUGHT.

NOUN, *s.* नामन् *n.*, विशेष्यं, सुप्, वाचकः.

NOURISH, *v. t.* परि-,पुष् 1, 4, 9 P or c., संवृध् c., परि-,पा c. (पालयति), सं-,भृ 1, 3 U; (अन्नादिना) आप्यै c., बृंह् c., वृध् c., संतृप् c. -ER, *s.* पालयितृ *m.*, संवर्धकः. -ING, *a.* पुष्टिकर (री *f.*), पुष्टिद, पौष्टिक (की *f.*). -MENT, *s.* पोषणं, पुष्टि *f.*, पालनं, संवर्धनं, भरणं, अन्नदानं. 2 आहारः, भोजनं, भक्ष्यं, अन्नं, पौष्टिकं, जीवनसाधनं.

NOVEL, *a.* नव, नूतन, नवीन, अपूर्व, अदृष्ट-अश्रुत-पूर्व' अद्भुत; *See* NEW. -*s.* कल्पितकथा, आख्यायिका' प्रबंधकल्पना, कूटार्थकथा. -IST, *s.* आख्यायिकाकारः. -TY, *s.* पूर्वता, नवता, नूतनता. 2 अदृष्टपूर्वं वस्तु, कौतुकं, अद्भुतं.

NOVEMBER, *s.* कार्तिकमार्गशीर्षं.

NOVENNIAL, *a.* नववर्षीय.

NOVERCAL, *a.* वैमात्रीय, वैमातृक (की *f.*), विमातृयोग्य.

NOVICE, *s.* शैक्षः, प्राथमकल्पिकः, नवशिष्यः-छात्रः, अनभ्यस्तः, अलब्धकौशलः. -NOVITIATE, *s.* नवशिष्यता, अनभ्यासः, नवच्छात्रदशा. 2 नवाभ्यासकालः, विद्यारंभावधिः.

NOW, *adv.* अधुना, इदानीं, संप्रति, सांप्रतं, प्रस्तुत-वर्तमान-काले, इहसमये. 2 अथ, अथातः, अतःपरं, अतः; 'n.-n.' क्वचित्-क्वचित, कदाचित्-कदाचित, अंतराअंतरा, (अंतरा पितृसक्तमंतरा मातृसंबंधमालापं कुर्वन् Ka. 118); 'n. and then' काले काले, कदाचित, कदापि; 'till n.' अद्य यावत; 'from n.' अद्यारभ्य, अद्य प्रभृति, अतः परं; 'just n.' अधुनैव, अचिरात, इदानीमेव; 'n.-a-days' एषु दिवसेषु, संप्रति, अधुनातनकाले; 'n.-a-days people' इदानींतनाआधुनिका-जनाः.

NOXIOUS, *a.* हिंस्र, उपद्राविन्, हिंसक, दुष्ट, हिंसालु, घातुक, अपकारिन्, हिंसात्मक, अहित-अनिष्ट-कारिन्; *See* HARMFUL.

NOZZLE, *s.* नासाग्रं, प्रोथः, नस्तः; अग्रं, अग्रभागः.

NUBILOUS, *a.* मेघावृत, अभ्राच्छन्न; *See* CLOUDY.

NUCLEUS, *s.* बीजं, गर्भः; संचयास्पदं.

NUDE, *a.* नग्न, विवस्त्र; *See* NAKED. -ATION, *s.* विवस्त्रीकरणं. -ITY, *s.* नग्नता.

NUDGE, *v. t.* कूर्परेण चल् c.

NUGATORY, *a.* व्यर्थ, मोघ, निरर्थक, निष्फल, विफल, निष्प्रभाव, अप्रमाण, अनिष्पन्न.

NUISANCE, *s.* उत्पातः, कंटकः, (of persons); बाधा, पीडा, पीडा-क्लेश-हेतुः; 'public n.' लोककंटकः; 'family n.' कुलाधिः, गृहोत्पातः.

NULL, *a.* मोघ, व्यर्थ, निष्फल, विफल, निर्बल, निष्प्रभाव, अनिष्पन्न, लुप्त, वृथा-मुधा in comp. -IFY, *v. t.* मोघी-विफली-कृ 8 U, लुप् 6 P or c., खंड् 10. -ITY, *s.* मोघता, व्यर्थता, वैफल्यं. 2 अभावः, शून्यता.

NUMB, *a.* जड, सुप्त, स्तब्ध, अस्पंद, अचेतन, चैतन्यरहित, स्तब्धगति; 'n. with cold' शीताकुल. -*v. t.* जडीकृ 8 U, जडयति (D.), चैतन्यं हृ 1 P or स्तंभ् 9 P or c. -NESS, *s.* जाड्यं, स्तंभः, जडिमन् *m.*, स्वापः, त्वक्सुप्ति *f.*, चैतन्यनाशः-स्तंभः.

NUMBER, *s.* संख्या, राशिः. 2 संख्या, गणना, परिमाणं. 3 गणः, समूहः, निवहः, संघः; *See* MULTITUDE; oft. ex. by बहु, बहुल, प्रचुर, अनेक, or जनः in comp.; 'a n. of young women' युवतिजनः, तरुणीगणः; 'in n.s' संघशः, गणशः, बहुशः, अनेकशः; 'a whole n.' अभिन्नं. 4 अंकः. 5 छंदस् *n.*, पद्यं, कविता. 6 वचनं; 'science of n.' गणितं, व्यक्तगणितं, अंकविद्या; '100 in n.' शतं, शतसंख्यक. -*v. t.* सं-परिसं-ख्या 2 P, गण् 10, संकल् 10 (कलयति). 2 अंक् 10, अंकं लिख् 6 P or स्था c. (स्थापयति); oft. ex. by संख्या in comp.; 'the enemy's force n.ed 500' पंचशतसंख्यं शत्रुसैन्यं. -ER, *s.* गणकः, संख्याकृत् *m.* -ING, *s.* गणनं-ना, संख्यानं. -LESS, *a.* असंख्य, संख्यातीत, गणनातीत, अगण्य, असंख्यात.

NUMBLES, *s.* मृगांत्राणि.

NUMERAL, *s.* संख्या, अंकः. -*a.* संख्यात्मक, संख्यावाचक-विषय, संख्या in comp. -LY, *adv.* यथासंख्यं.

NUMERARY, *a.* नियतसंख्यक.

NUMERATION, *s.* संख्यानं, गणना.

NUMERATOR, *s.* अंशः, लवः.

NUMERICAL, *a.* संख्या in comp.; 'n. superiority' संख्याधिक्यं-उत्कर्षः. -LY, *adv.* संख्यामपेक्ष्यउद्दिश्य, यथासंख्यं.

NUMEROUS, *a.* बहु, बहुसंख्य, बहुल, भूरि, अनेक, प्रचुर, नैक; *See* MANY. -LY, *adv.* बहुशः, बाहुल्येन, अनेकशः.

NUMISMATICS, *s.* मुद्राविद्या.

NUMSKULL, *s.* *See* IDIOT, FOOL.

NUN, *s.* परिव्राजिका, तपस्विनी, मठवासिनी, ब्रह्मचारिणी, तपोनिष्ठा. -NERY, *s.* विहारः, मठः.

NUNCIO, *s.* धर्माध्यक्षदूतः.

Nuptial, *a.* वैवाहिक-औद्वाहिक (की *f.*), वैवाह (ही *f.*), विवाह-परिणय- in comp.; 'n. ceremony' परिणयविधिः, विवाहक्रिया; 'n. gift' यौतकं, औद्वाहिकं, पारिणाय्यं; 'n. s' विवाहः, उद्वाहः, परिणयः, पाणिग्रहणं.

Nurse, *s.* धात्री, उपमातृ *f.*, मातृका, अंकपाली. 2 परिचारिका, उपचारिका, रुग्णपालिका. 3 पालकः, पोषकः. —*v. t.* (रोगिणं) उपचर् 1 P, सेव् 1 A, परि-पा c. (पालयति); यत्नादुपचर्यतामसौ (S. 3) 'let her be carefully n. ed.' 2 पा c. (पालयति), पुष् 1,4,9 P, वृध् c., लल् 10; *See* Nourish. 3 दुग्धं पा c. (पाययति), स्तन्यं दा 3 U or धे c. (धापयति). —ery, *s.* पालन-पोषणस्थानं; बालगृहं-स्थानं; 'n. song' शिशुगीतं; 'n. man' पुष्पाजीविन् *m.* —ing, *s.* उपचारः, सेवा. 2 पालनं, पोषणं, लालनं. —ling, *s.* स्तनंधयः, स्तनपः, बालः, शिशुः.

Nurture, *v. t.* विनी 1 P, शिक्ष् c., उपदिश् 6 P. 2 पा c. (पालयति), पुष् 1, 4, 9 P or c., वृध् c.; *See* Nourish. —*s.* आहारः, भक्ष्यं. 2 शिक्षणं, विनयः, उपदेशः. 3 पोषणं, पालनं, वर्धनं.

Nut, *s.* फलं; बीजं, गर्भः (internal contents); 'cocoa-n.' नारिकेलफलं; 'n.-crackers' संदंशः-शकः; 'n.-meg' जाति(ती)कोशं-षं, जातिफलं; *See* Mace; 'n.-shell' बीजकवचः-पुटं.

Nutant, *a.* प्रणतशिरस्.

Nutrition, *s.* पोषणं, पालनं, पुष्टि *f.*, आप्यायनं.

Nutriment, *s.* आहारः, पुष्टिदं अन्नं.

Nutritious,-Nutritive, *a.* पुष्टिकर (री *f.*), पुष्टिद, पौष्टिक (की *f.*), पोषक, धातु-बल-वर्धन (नी *f.*).

Nuzzle, *v. i.* नासां अवनम् c. (नमयति).

Nymph, *s.* अप्सरस् *f.*, अप्सरा, स्वर्गस्त्री; देवता in comp.; 'wood-n.' वनदेवता; 'sea-n.' जलदेवता.

Nymphomania, *s.* उत्कटा सुरतेच्छा.

O.

O, Oh, *interj.* हे, भोः, अयि, अये, अरे; हा, अहह (sorrow). 2 अहो (joy and surprise), हंत, अहो, बत. 3 आः (anger &c.). 4 आ, आं; 'oh for' ex. by अपि नाम; 'oh for a lodge in a wilderness' अपि नाम विपिने निवासं लभेय; 'oh that' *See* Would.

Oaf, *s.* *See* Fool.

Oak, *s.* सिंदूरः.

Oakum, *s.* खंडितरज्जु *f.*

Oar, *s.* क्षे(क्षि)पणि-णी *f.*, नौ-नौका-दंडः. —*v. t.* क्षेपण्या चल् c. or वह् c.; *See* Row. —Oarsman, *s.* नौदंडधरः.

Oasis, *s.* (मरुमध्ये) शाद्वलस्थलं, रम्यस्थानं.

Oath, *s.* शपथः, अभिशापः, वचनं, प्रतिज्ञा, समयः; 'bind by an o.' शप् c.; 'to take an o.' शप् 1, 4 U, शपथं शप्; 'with an o.' सशपथं, शपथपूर्वं.

Obdurate, *a.* अनम्य, कठिन, कठिनहृदय-चित्त, अनुतापविमुख (खी *f.*), दुराग्रह; *See* Hard. —Obduracy, *s.* चित्तकाठिन्यं, कठोरहृदयता, अनुतापविमुखता; काठिन्यं, कठोरता.

Obeisance, *s.* नमस्कारः; प्रणामः, प्रणति *f.*, वंदनं, प्रणिपातः, नमस्या; अभिवादनं; 'prostrate o.' साष्टांगप्रणामः-नमस्कारः, अष्टांगपातः; 'to make an o.' प्रणम् 1 P, प्रणिपत् 1 P, नमस्कृ 8 U, अभिवद् c.

Obelisk, *s.* सूच्याकारः स्तंभः.

Obese, *a.* पीन, पीवर, स्थूल; *See* Fat.

Obey, *v. t.* (Orders) कृ 8 U, अनु-ष्ठा 1 P, अनुवृत् 1 A, अनुवि-धा 3 U, पा c. (पालयति), अनुरुध् 4 A, मन् c., प्रतिग्रह् 9 P, अभ्युप-इ 2 P or -गम् 1 P; (persons) वचनं श्रु 5 P, शासने स्था, आज्ञां-वचनं-अनुवृत्, यथादिष्टं वि-धा; श्रु desid. (शुश्रूषते), उपचर् 1 P, सेव् 1 A, उपास् 2 A, आज्ञां कृ or अनुरुध् &c. —Obedient, *a.* आज्ञानुवर्तिन्, आज्ञाकर (री *f.*), आज्ञाविधायिन्, अनुविधायिन्, अनुरोधिन्, आज्ञा-निर्देश-कारिन्, आज्ञापर, विधेय, विनयग्राहिन्, वचने स्थित, आश्रव, वश्य, प्रणेय, वशानुग, शुश्रूषु, आज्ञा-वचन-ग्राहिन्-सेविन्, आज्ञाधीन; 'o. to one's parent' पितृवश्य, पितृवचनपर. —ly, *adv.* आज्ञानुसारेण, यथाज्ञं, यथादिष्टं, निदेशानुरोधेन. —Obedience, *s.* आज्ञानुवर्तनं-अनुरोधः-अनुसारः-अनुसरणं-करणं-पालनं-सेवनं-धारणं, वश्यता, अनुविधायित्वं, शुश्रूषा, आज्ञाकरत्वं, आज्ञापरता, अनुवर्तनं, अनुरोधः.

Object, *s.* द्रव्यं, वस्तु *n.*, अर्थः, विषयः, इंद्रियार्थः; 'visible o.' चक्षुर्विषयः; (fig.) पात्रं, पदं, स्थानं, आस्पदं, भाजनं, भूमि *f.*, विषयः; 'o. of confidence' विश्वासास्पदं, विश्वासभूमिः; 'the sole o. of my affection' स्नेहस्यैकायनीभूता (M. 2): 'o. of dispute' विवादविषयः, व्यवहारास्पदं. 2 अर्थः, फलं, हेतुः; (desired o.) अभीष्टं, इष्टं, समीहितं, कांक्षितं, ईप्सितं, कामः, मनोरथः; *See* Desire. 3 निमित्तं, कारणं, प्रयोजनं, कार्यं. 4 अभिप्रायः, आशयः, तात्पर्यं, उद्देशः, लक्ष्यं; 'with what o. in view' किमपेक्ष्य फलं, केन हेतुना, किमुद्दिश्य, किंनिमित्तं, किमर्थं; 'accomplishment of one's o.' कृतार्थता, चरितार्थता, इष्टसिद्धि *f.*, फलप्राप्ति *f.*; 'highest o.' परमार्थः; 'o. of hearing' श्रुतिविषयः. 5 कर्मन् *n.*; 'a root governing 2 o. s' द्विकर्मकः धातुः. —*v.* वि-प्रति-रुध् 7 U, बाध् 1 A, खंड् 10, निरस् 4 U, अधरीकृ 8 U, अपवद् 1 A, न अनुमन् 4 A or अनुमुद् 1 A, दोषं ग्रह् 9 P; 'the sage will not o. to this'

नात्र दोषं ग्रहीष्यति कुलपतिः (S. 3); नि-प्राति-षिध् 1 P, (तदेष सर्गः न भवद्भिः प्रतिषेधनीयः R. XIV. 42); (in discussions) gen. ex. by ननु, इति चेत् or कथं तर्हि, followed by उच्यते or अत्रोच्यते (we reply); प्रत्यव-स्था 1 A, वितंड् 1 A. -ION, s. बाधः-धा, अपवादः, विरोधः, आक्षेपः, दोषः, आपत्ति f., कक्षा, उद्ग्राहः, विरुद्धहेतुः, विप्रतिषेधः, प्रत्यवायः, प्रतिबंधः, पर्युदासः; 'making an o.' दोषग्रहणं, विरोधोपन्यासः; 'settling an o.' समा-प्रतिसमा-धानं, आक्षेपपरिहारः. -IONABLE, a. बाध्य, सबाध, सदोष, निषेधार्ह, वर्ज्य, परिहार्य, आशंकनीय. -IVE, a. विषयाश्रित, पदार्थनिष्ठ, कर्मविषयक. -OR, s. बाधकः, अपवादकः.

OBJURGATE, v. t. निंद् 1 P, भर्त्स् 10 A, उपालभ् 1 A, आ-अधि-क्षिप् 6 P, तिरस्कृ 8 U. -ION, s. निंदा, भर्त्सनं-ना, उपालंभः, आक्षेपः, धिक्कारः; See CENSURE. -ORY, a. निंदक, निंदार्थक.

OBLATION, s. बलिः, उपहारः, उपायनं; हव्यं, हवनं, हुतं, आहुति f., इष्टि f., यागः, निर्वपणं; 'o. of eatables' नैवेद्यं; 'o. to all deities' वैश्वदेवः; 'to make o. s to fire' हु 3 P.

OBLIGATE, v. t. See below.

OBLIGE, v. t. Ex. by causal of verbs, gen. with बलेन or बलात्; प्रयुज् 10, प्रवृत् c.; See COMPEL. 2 नियमपूर्वं-सप्रतिज्ञं बंध् 9 P. 3 अनुग्रह् 9 P, उपकृ 8 U, उपकारेण बंध्, हितं-प्रसादं-उपकारं कृ; 'I am much o. ed to you for this reward' एतेन पारितोषिकदानेन भवता सुतरामुपकृतोस्मि-अनुगृहीतोस्मि; 'I am much o. ed' अनुगृहीतोस्मि, महानयं प्रसादः. -ATION, s. अवश्यकता, कर्तव्यता, भारः, ऋणं, बंधः, धर्मः; 'free from the o. s of debt' ऋणमुक्त, मुक्तर्णं, अनृण; 'religious o.' व्रतं, नियमः, चोदना, विधिः. 2 संविद् f., समयः, प्रतिज्ञा, नियमः, अभ्युपगमः, संधा, सं-आ-श्रवः. 3 अनुग्रहः, उपकारः, उपकृति f.-तं, हितं, प्रियं; 'under o.' उपकृत-अनुगृहीत-a.; 'my o. s to you are immense' तव मयि उपकाराः संख्यातीताः; 'to lay under o. s' उपकृ; See (v.). -ATORY, a. अवश्यक, आवश्यक (की f.), अपरिहार्य, अवश्यकर्तव्य; oft. ex. by अवश्यं; See under COMPEL. -ING, a. अनुग्रह-उपकार-शील, उपकारिन्, अनुग्राहिन्, हित-उपकार-बुद्धि, सुशील, दक्षिण, अनुकूल, सुजन. -INGLY, adv. दाक्षिण्येन, सुजनतया, सानुग्रहं, सुशीलवत्. -INGNESS, s. उपकार-अनुग्रह-शीलं, सौजन्यं.

OBLIQUE, a. वक्र, कुटिल, जिह्म, असरल, तिर्यंच्, अनृजु, विषम; 'o. speech' वक्रोक्ति f., भंगि-गी f., उपरोधवचनं; 'o. case' अप्रधानकारकं. -LY, adv. वक्रं, कुटिलं, तिर्यक्, तिरः, साचि, जिह्मं. -NESS, s. वक्रता, कौटिल्यं, अनृजुता, वैषम्यं; 'o. of sight' वक्रदृष्टि f., दृष्टिवक्रता; 'o. of conduct' विमार्ग-उत्पथ-गमनं, असदाचारः, सत्पथभ्रंशः-त्यागः.

OBLITERATE, v. t. वि-,लुप् 6 P or c., प्र-परि-अव-मृज् 2 P or c., व्यामृश् 6 P or c., वि-,नश् c., उच्छिद् 7 P, उन्मूल् 10. -ION, s. लोपः, मार्जनं, व्यामर्शः, उच्छेदः.

OBLIVION, s. अ-वि-स्मृति f., अ-वि-स्मरणं; 'to bury into o.' विस्मृ 1 P. 2 दोषविस्मरणं. -OBLIVIOUS, a. स्मृतिहर (री f.), विस्मारक, विस्मृतिकर (री f.). 2 विस्मरणशील.

OBLONG, a. दीर्घाकार, आयत, दीर्घचतुरस्र. -s. आयतः.

OBLOQUY, s. निंदा, परि(री)वादः, अपवादः, वाच्यता, भर्त्सना, गर्हा; See CENSURE, CALUMNY.

OBNOXIOUS, a. वश, अधीन, आयत्त, योग्य, अर्ह; पात्रं, आस्पदं, विषयः in comp.; ex. by pot. pass. part.; See LIABLE, APT. 2 गर्हित, द्वेष्य, द्वेषणीय, गर्ह्य; अनिष्ट, अप्रिय, निंद्य, अप्रीतिकर (री f.). -LY, adv. अप्रियं, गर्ह्यतया. -NESS, s. अधीनता, वशता, पात्रता. 2 द्वेष्यता, गर्ह्यता.

OBSCENE, a. अश्लील, ग्राम्य, अनक्षर, अवाच्य, गर्ह्य, कुत्सित, दुरुक्त, बीभत्स, अश्राव्य, वियात, व्रीडावह. 2 अशुभ, अभद्र, अमंगल, अलक्षण. -LY, adv. अश्लीलं, अवाच्यं. -ITY, -NESS, s. अश्लीलता, अवाच्यता; 'o. of language' दुरुक्ति f., दुर्वाक्यं.

OBSCURE, a. तमोवृत, सांधकार, निष्प्रभ, मलिन, सतिमिर, निस्तेजस्, तमस्विन्. 2 अप्रसिद्ध, नातिविश्रुत, अविज्ञात, अख्यात, अल्पकीर्ति, लघुप्रतिष्ठ. 3 नि-,गूढ, दुर्बोध, क्लिष्ट, दुर्ज्ञेय, गहन, दुर्गम, विषम, अप्रकाश, अस्पष्ट, अस्फुट, गूढार्थ, अव्यक्त. -v. t. (तमसा) प्र-आ-च्छद् 10, आ-वृ 5 U, उप-रुध् 7U, अंतरयति (D.), मलिनी-तिमिरी-कृ 8 U, मलिनयति-तिमिरयति (D.), प्रभां-तेजः-हृ 1 P or क्षि 1, 5 P; 'o. with clouds' मेघैः आच्छद् or आवृ. 2 गहनीकृ, गूढीकृ; ex. by (a.). 3 (Fig.) प्रत्या-दिश् 6 P, प्रत्या-ख्या 2 P, प्रच्छद्; See ECLIPSE; 'o. or of Sri' प्रत्यादेशः श्रियः (V. 1). -ATION, s. मलिनीकरणं, कांति-प्रभा-हरणं. 2 तेजः-प्रभा-क्षयः-हानि f., निष्प्रभता, सांधकारता. -ED, a. तमोवृत, नष्ट-क्षीण-मलिन-क्षत-प्रभ-कांति-प्रकाश, मलिन, निस्तेजस्, हतज्योतिस्. -ITY, -NESS, s. निष्प्रभता, तेजः-कांति-क्षयः-हानिः, तमस् n., तमिस्रं, अंधःकारः. 2 गूढता, गहनता, अस्फुटता, दुर्बोधता. 3 अप्रसिद्धि-अविख्याति f., अल्पप्रतिष्ठा-कीर्ति f. -LY, adv. निष्प्रभं, सतिमिरं, सांधकारं. 2 गूढं, दुर्बोधं, असुगमं, अस्पष्टं, अव्यक्तं.

OBSECRATE, v. t. See ENTREAT.

OBSEQUIES, s. उत्तरकार्य-क्रिया, अंत्यकृत्यं, प्रेत-कार्य-क्रिया; अंत्येष्टिक्रिया, और्ध्वदेहिकक्रिया, अंत्येष्टि f., प्रेतसंस्कारः, पारलौकिकं. -OBSEQUIAL, a. और्ध्वदेहिक-और्ध्वदैहिक (की f.), अंत्येष्टियोग्य; by (s.) in comp.

OBSEQUIOUS, *a.* छंदोनुवर्तिन्,अत्यनुवर्तिन्, अत्यनुरोधिन्, वशवर्तिन्, वशानुग, विनत, नम्र; *See* OBEDIENT. -LY, *adv.* अत्यनुरोधात्, छंदोनुवर्तनेन. -NESS, *s.* अत्यनुरोधः, अत्यनुवृत्ति *f.*, छंदोनुवर्तनं.

OBSERVE, *v. t.* दृश् 1 P, ईक्ष् 1 A, (वि-आ-अव-लोक् 1 A, 10, निरूप् 10, आ-,लक्ष् 10, निर्वर्ण् 10, आलोच् 10 (o. carefully); *See* LOOK. 2 उपलभ् 1A, वि-भू c., वि-ज्ञा 9U, अवधृ 10. 3 अनु-,पा c. (पालयति), रक्ष् 1 P, आ-अव-लंब् 1 A, आ-श्रि 1 U, आ-चर् 1 P, अनु-ष्ठा 1 P, सेव् 1 A, निषेव्, वि-धा 3 U, कृ 8 U; 'o. silence' मौनमाचर्; 'o. a fast' उपवस् 1 P; (rules) अनुवृत् 1 A, अनुसृ 1 P, अनुरुध् 4 A. 4 अभि-धा 3 U, वच् 2 P, ब्रू 2 U, वाक्यं वद् 1 P or उच्चर् c. -ABLE, *a.* दृश्य, प्रेक्षणीय, दृष्टिगोचर. 2 अनुष्ठेय, निषेव्य. -ANCE, *s.* पालनं, रक्षणं, आचरणं, सेवनं, आलंबनं, अनुसरणं, अनुवर्तनं, विधानं, अनुष्ठानं. 2 आचारः, व्यवहारः, रीति *f.*, चरितं, आचारकर्मन् *n.*; religious o.' व्रतं, नियमः, विधिः. -ANT, *a.* निरीक्षक, दर्शिन्, अवलोकिन्, सापेक्ष, अवहित, सावधान. 2 पालक, निषेवक, अनुसारिन्, आश्रित; आस्थित; 'o. of benefits' कृतज्ञ, कृतवेदिन्. -ATION, *s.* अवलोकनं, निरीक्षणं, अवेक्षणं, अवेक्षा, निरूपणं, आलोचनं. 2 वचनं, उक्ति *f.*, उदाहारः, वाक्यं; लेखः, लिखितं (in writing). -ATORY, *s.* वेधगृहं-शाला. -ER, *s.* प्रेक्षकः, अवेक्षकः, निरूपकः.

OBSOLETE, *a.* लुप्तप्रयोग, लुप्त, अप्रचलित, अप्रचल, गतव्यवहार, व्यवहारातीत, अव्यवहार्य. -NESS, *s.* लोपः, अप्रचारः, अव्यवहारः.

OBSTACLE, *s.* अंतरायः, प्रत्यूहः, व्याघातः, प्रतिबंधः, वि-प्रति-ष्टंभः, वारणं, विघ्नः, रोधः, उप-प्रति-अव-नि°-, विघातः, बाधः-धा, व्यवधानं, प्रत्यर्थिन् *m.*; 'though an o. to his meditation' प्रत्यर्थिभूतामपि समाधेः (K. I. 59).

OBSTETRIC, *a.* प्रसवसंबंधिन्. -*s.* (O. s) गर्भमोचनशास्त्रं, प्रसवकर्मन् *n.*

OBSTINATE, *a.* प्रतिनिविष्ट, अविनेय, अवश्य, अननुनेतव्य, निर्बंधवत्, निर्बंधशील, स्वैरिन्, दुर्दम, आग्रहिन्, दुराग्रह, प्रतीप, कठिन, दृढ. 2 दुःसाध्य, दुरुपचार. -LY, *adv*, निर्बंधेन, अतिदृढं, स्वैरं, साग्रहं, सनिर्बंधं, दुराग्रहेण. -NESS,-OBSTINACY, *s.* निर्बंधः, आग्रहः, स्वैरिता, दुराग्रहः. निर्बंधशीलं, दृढता, अवश्यता, प्रतिनिविष्टता, प्रतीपता.

OBSTIPATION, *s.* स्तंभनं, अवरोधः.

OBSTREPEROUS, *a.* बहुघोषकारिन्, महास्वन, तारस्वर, तुमुल, अत्युच्च, अतिपरुष (of noise). -LY, *adv.* उच्चैःस्वरेण, सकोलाहलं, तुमुलरवेण.

OBSTRUCT, *v. t.* रुध् 7 U, नि-वि-सं-प्रति-उप°-, वि-प्रति-व्या-हन् 2 P, वृ c. or वार 10 वि,-स्तंभ् 9 P, or c., प्र-सं-बाध् 1 A, विघ्नयति (D.), नि-प्रति-षिध् 1 P. -ER, *s.* विघ्नकरः, प्रतिबंधकः-रोधकः. -ION, *s.* रोधनं, वारणं, प्रतिबंधनं. 2 विघ्नः, अंतरायः, प्रत्यूहः, प्रतिबंधः, व्याघातः; *See* OBSTACLE. 3 आ-,नाहः, अवरोधः, प्रतिबंधः. -IONIST, *s.* विघ्नकारिन् *m.*, प्रतिबंधशीलः. -IVE,-OBSTRUENT, *a.* संप्रतिरोधिन्, बाधक, प्रतिबंधक, विघ्नकारिन्, विघ्नकर (री *f.*), विघातिन्, निवारक.

OBTAIN, *v. t.* आप् 5 P, लभ् 1 A, विद् 6 U, अश् 5 A, अधिगम् 1 P, अर्ज् 1 P or c., आ-समा-सद् c., आ-प्रति-पद् 4 A, सं-पद् c.; oft. by इ-या-2 P; *See* GET. -*v. i.* प्रचल्-र् 1 P, प्रवृत् 1 A, सं-स्था 1 A; *See* HOLD. -ABLE, *a.* प्राप्य, लभ्य, अधिगम्य; 'easily o.' सुलभ, सुसाध्य; 'hardly o.' दुष्प्राप, दुर्लभ, दुराप. -ER, *s.* अर्जकः, प्रापकः. -ING, *a.* प्रचलित, प्रवृत्त, स्थापित, प्रसिद्ध. -MENT, *s.* लाभः, प्राप्ति *f.*, अधिगमः, अर्जनं.

OBTEST, *v. t.* *See* ENTREAT.

OBTRUDE, *v. i.* हठात्-आगंतुकतया-बलेन-प्रविश् 6 P or गम् 1 P or आक्रम् 1 U, 4 P. -*v. t.* बलेन प्रविश् c. or प्र-सृ c. 2 अतिनिर्बंधेन ग्रह् c. or प्र-दा 3 U or उपन्यस् 4 U. -OBTRUSION, *s.* बलेन प्रवेशः, अनाहूतगमनं, सधर्ष आक्रमः, आगंतुकभावः. -OBTRUSIVE, *a.* धृष्ट, आगंतुक (की *f.*), सप्रगल्भ, बलात् प्रवेशक. -LY, *adv.* बलेन, हठात्, प्रसभं, प्रसह्य.

OBTUND, *v. t.* घनीकृ 8 U, जडीकृ, तेजः हृ 1 P. -OBTUSE, *a.* जड, मंद, स्थूल, मूढ, मंद-जड-मति-बुद्धि-धी. 2 अतीक्ष्ण, अतीव्र, अप्रखर, धाराहीन, निर्धार, घन, स्थूल, निस्तेजस्, अनिशित; 'o. angle' बहिर्लंबः-विषमः-कोणः. -LY, *adv.* जाड्येन, जडवत्, अतीव्रं, घनं, स्थूलं. -NESS, *s.* जाड्यं, मूढता, मंदता; स्थूलता, घनता, अतीक्ष्णता.

OBVERT, *v. t.* अधोमुखीकृ 8 U; अभिमुखीकृ. -OBVERSE, *s.* मुखं, अग्रभागः.

OBVIATE, *v. t.* परिहृ 1 P, नि-,वृ c., निरस् 4 U, प्रतिकृ 8 U, प्रतिवि-धा 3 U, विहन् 2 P, निवृत् c., विप्रति-रुध् 7 U; *See* OBSTRUCT.

OBVIOUS, *a.* स्पष्ट, व्यक्त, स्फुट, परिस्फुट, सुस्पष्ट-व्यक्त, सुगम, सुप्रकाश, भिन्नार्थ, स्पष्टार्थ; 'o. to the sight' दृष्टिगोचर, प्रत्यक्ष, सुलक्ष्य. -LY, *adv.* स्पष्टं, व्यक्तं, स्फुटं, सुप्रकाशं, भिन्नार्थं. -NESS, *s.* स्पष्टता, स्फुटता.

OCCASION, *v. t.* उत्पद् c., जन् c. (जनयति), आवह् 1 P, उद्भू c., भू 1 P (with dat.). -*s.* अवसरः, समयः, कालः, अवकाशः, प्रस्तावः, प्रसंगः, प्रसरः, वेला, स्थानं; 'according to the o.' यथावसरं, यथाकालं, प्रसंगानुरूपं, प्रस्तावसदृशं. 2 प्रयोजनं, अपेक्षा, आकांक्षा, उपयोगः, कार्यं, कारणं. 3 वृत्तं, संगति *f.*, घटनं-ना. 4 निमित्तं, हेतुः, प्रयोजनं, कारणं, उपाधिः. -AL, *a.* नैमित्तिक-प्रासंगिक- (की *f.*), प्रसंगागत,

कार्योपात्त, निमित्तोपनत. 2 आगंतुक-आपतिक-(की *f.*), अनियत, अनित्य, अनियतकारण, अनुकाल, विरल, कादाचित्क (की *f.*); better by 'o.-ly'. —ALLY, *adv.* कदाचित्, कदापि, क्वचित्, काले काले, अंतरा अंतरा, प्रसंगवशात्, यथासंभवं, कार्यवशात्, निमित्तेन, प्रसंगानुरूपं. —ED, *a.* उत्पादित, उत्पन्न, जनित, जात, उदित, उद्भूत; gen. ex. by ज, उद्भव, प्रभव, मूल, कारण, निमित्त, कर्तृ, हेतु in comp.; 'fever o. by fatigues' श्रमनिमित्तः ज्वरः &c.

OCCIDENT, *s.* पश्चिमा, प्रतीची, पश्चिमा दिक्. —AL, *a.* पश्चिम, प्रतीच्य, पाश्चात्य, प्रतीचीन.

OCCIPUT, *s.* मस्तक-शिरः-पृष्ठं.

OCCULT, *a.* नि-,गूढ, दुर्ज्ञेय, दुर्बोध, गहन, गुप्त, अज्ञात, गूढार्थ. —ISM,—NESS, *s.* गूढता, गहनता.

OCCULTATION, *s.* आच्छादनं, ग्रासः.

OCCUPY, *v. t.* अधि-ष्ठा 1 P, अधि-वस् 1 P, अध्यास् 2 A, आश्रि 1 U, आविश् 6 P, आ-अध्या-क्रम् 1 U, 4 P (all with acc.); व्याप् 5 P, पूर् 10, व्यश् 5 A; वृत् 1 A (with loc.), पदं कृ 8 U or वि-धा 3 U, स्था; 'o. a throne' राज्यमारुह्-राजपदमधिरुह् 1 P; 'o. ing the honorable position of a housewife' श्लाघ्ये गृहिणीपदे स्थिता (S. 4). 2 (Possess) भुज् 7 A, भृ 1 P, 10, धा. 3 प्र-नियुज् 7 A, 10, व्या-पृ c., प्रवृत् c., व्यापृत-*a.* कृ; 'o. oneself' व्यापृ 6 A, व्यापृत-निरत-आसक्त-*a.* भू 1 P, प्रवृत् (with loc.); आत्मानं व्यापृ c. —ANCY, *s.* भोगः, भुक्ति *f.*, आवेशः, आक्रमः, अधिकारः. —ANT, *s.* भोक्तृ *m.*, भोगिन्, अधिकारिन्. —ATION, *s.* वृत्ति *f.*, आ-उप-जीविका, आजीवः, जीवनसाधनं-उपायः. 2 क्रिया, कृत्यं, प्रवृत्तिः, चरितं, चेष्टा. 3 नियोगः, अधिकारः, स्वकर्म-धर्मः. 4 अधिवासः, आवेशनं, अधिष्ठानं, व्याप्ति *f.*, आक्रमणं, भोगः, भुक्तिः; 'daily o.' नित्यकृत्यं; 'to do the usual morning o. s' उचितेषु प्रभातकरणीयेषु (S. 4). —ED, *a.* आविष्ट, आक्रांत, अध्युषित, अध्यासित, अधिष्ठित, व्याप्त, भुक्त, आश्रित. 2 व्यापृत, व्यापारिन्, व्यवसायिन्, प्रवृत्त, कर्मनिष्ठरत-उद्युक्त, क्रियावत्; gen. ex. by रत, निष्ठ, मग्न, व्यापृत, पर in comp., or by व्यापृ, प्रवृत्. —ER, *s.* अधिष्ठाता, भोक्ता.

OCCUR, *v. i.* वृत् 1 A, विद् 4A; जन् 4A, उत्पद् 4A, सं-भू 1 P. 2 उप-स्था 1 U, आगम् 1 P, उप-नम् 1 P; *See* BEFALL. 3 सं-,वृत्, समा-पद्, घट् 1 A, आ-निपत् 1 P, सं-भू ; 'o. to the mind' मनसि उद्-इ 2 P or भू or जन् or स्फुर् 6 P or आविः-प्रादुः-भू ; 'this did not o. to his mind' इति तस्य बुद्धौ न संजातं, इति तस्य हृदये नापतितं (Ka. 288) ; 'the following (thoughts) o. ed to my mind' आसीत्-समभूत्-मे मनसि ; 'these two verses o. to our memory (mind)' स्मृत्युपस्थितौ इमौ द्वौ श्लोकौ (U.6). —RENCE, *s.* घटना-नं, वृत्तं, वृत्तांतः, भूतं, व्यतिकरः; संभवः, संगति *f.*, उत्पत्ति *f.*, उपस्थिति *f.*, उपागमः; 'of usual o.' नित्यसंभूत; 'of rare o.' दुर्लभ, चिरोपनत. —RENT, *s.* शत्रुः; *See* ENEMY. 2 वृत्तं, वृत्तांतः.

OCEAN, *s.* समुद्रः, सागरः, सिंधुः, उदन्वान्,अर्णवः, रत्नाकरः, अकूपारः, पारावारः; and comp. of धिः, निधिः, पतिः, राशिः with 'Water' q. v. ; वारिराशिः, जलनिधिः, अब्धिः, अंबुधिः, वार्धिः, अपांपतिः, सरित्पतिः, तोयराशिः, अंबुराशिः, &c.; 'o.-bound' सागरांत, समुद्रवलय-रसन-मेखल; 'o. of misery' दुःखसागरः, व्यसनार्णवः. —*a.*, —IC, *a.* सामुद्र (द्री *f.*), समुद्रीय, (*s.*) in comp.

OCHRE, *s.* सुवर्णगैरिकं.

OCHLOCRACY, *s.* प्राकृतजनप्रभुत्वं.

OCTAGON, *s.* अष्टास्रं, अष्टकोणाकृति *f.* —AL, —OCTANGULAR, *a.* अष्टकोण, अष्टास्र.

OCTAVE, *s.* अष्टकं. —OCTAVO, *a.* अष्टपत्रक.

OCTENNIAL *a.* अष्टवार्षिक (की *f.*), अष्टवर्षीय. 2 अष्टवर्षस्थायिन्.

OCTOBER, *s.* आश्विनकार्तिकं.

OCTOGENARIAN, *a.* अशीतिवयस्क.

OCTOPETALOUS, *a.* अष्टदल.

OCTOSYLLABLE, *s.* अष्टाक्षरं.

OCTUPLE, *a.* अष्टगुण, अष्टविध.

OCULAR, *a.* चाक्षुष (षी *f.*), प्रत्यक्ष; 'o. evidence' प्रत्यक्ष-चाक्षुष-प्रमाणं, चाक्षुषज्ञानं. —LY, *adv.* प्रत्यक्षप्रमाणेन. —OCULIST, *s.* चक्षुः-नेत्र-वैद्यः.

ODD, *a.* विषम, असम, अयुग्म. 2 विलक्षण, असाधारण (णी *f.*), अपरूप, असंगत, अपूर्व, वि-,चित्र, अद्भुत, असामान्य, लोकोत्तर ; 'game of o. and even' मुष्टिद्यूतं. —ITY,—NESS, *s.* वैषम्यं. 2 वैलक्षण्यं, वैचित्र्यं, असंगति *f.*, अपूर्वता, आचारवैलक्षण्यं. 3 कौतुकं. —LY, *adv.* विषमं, चित्रं, विलक्षणं. —ODDS, *s.* वैषम्यं, न्यूनाधिकभावः, तारतम्यं. 2 आधिक्यं, उत्कर्षः, विशेषः, श्रेष्ठता, विशिष्टता ; 'fight at o.' अधिकबलेन शत्रुणा युध् 4 A.

ODE, *s.* गीतं, गानं, गेयं.

ODIOUS, *a.* गर्हित, कुत्सित, निंद्य, गर्ह्य, द्वेष्य, अप्रिय, द्वेषपात्रं-भाजनं-आस्पदं ; कश्मल (report). 2 द्वेषावह, द्वेषोत्पादिन्. —LY, *adv.* कुत्सितं, गर्हणीयतया. —NESS, *s.* गर्ह्यता, द्वेष्यता. —ODIUM, *s.* वि-,द्वेषः, गर्हा, कुत्सनं, घृणा.

ODONTALGY, *s.* दंतशूलं-पीडा-व्यथा.

ODOUR, *s.* गंधः, वासः; 'strong or fragrant o.' सुगंधः, सुवासः, सौरभ-भ्यं, आ-,मोदः, परिमलः ; 'bad o.' दुर्गंधः, पूतिगंधः. —OUS,-ODORIFEROUS, *a.* सगंध, सुगंधि, परिमलवत्, सामोद, गंधवत्, सुरभि, सवास.

OF, *prep.* Gen. ex. by genitive or by comp.; 'o. great strength' महाबल. 2 (Showing reference) अधिकृत्य, उद्दिश्य (with acc.), or by गत in comp.; 'by thinking o. her husband' भर्तृगतया चिंतया. 3 (Made of) by Tat. comp.; or मय (यी *f.*), निर्मित in comp.; or by derivatives; 'pot o. gold' हेमपात्रं, हेममयं or हैमं पात्रं. 4 (Partitive sense) by gen. or loc., or मध्ये, मध्यात् with gen. 5 (Apposition) ex. by comp. or by नाम *ind.*; 'the island o. Ceylon' सिंहलद्वीपं, सिंहलं नाम द्वीपं. 6 (Showing cause) by instr. or abl.; 'died o. fever' ज्वरेण मृतः.

OFF, *adv.* दूरे, दूरं, दूरतः ; (with verbs) ex. by अप, वि, निः, अव, उत् ; 'o. with his head' उच्छेद्यतामस्य शिरः; 'o. with him to the prison' अपनीयतामसौ कारागृहं. –*a.*, 'far o.' दूरवर्तिन्, दूरस्थित-स्थ. –*interj.*, 'get o.', 'be o.' दूरं अपेहि, अपसर ; 'o.-hand' प्रत्युत्पन्न, अचिंतितपूर्व, आकस्मिक (की *f.*), असावधान, निरपेक्ष; 'badly o.' दुःस्थित, दुर्गत, आपन्न, कृच्छ्रगत ; 'well o.' सुस्थ, सुस्थित, संपन्न.

OFFAL, *s.* उच्छिष्टं, भुक्तावशेषः-षं, शेषान्नं, मलं, उच्छिष्टान्नं ; मांसोच्छिष्टं, अवशिष्टमांसं.

OFFEND, *v.* अपराध् 4, 5 P (with gen. or loc.), विप्रियं-अनार्यं कृ 8 U or आचर् 1 P, अप्रसादं उत्पद् c.; कास्मिन्नपि पूजार्हे अपराद्धा शकुंतला (S. 4) '*S*akuntalâ has o. ed (committed an offence against) some respectable person'. 2 पीड् 10, व्यथ् c. (व्यथयति), क्लिश् 9 P, दु 5 P, सं-परि-तप् c. 3 (Against) अतिचर्, अति-व्यति-क्रम् 1 U, 4 P, लंघ् 1 A, 10, अतिवृत् 1 A, भिद् 7 P, भंज् 7 P, लुप् c. 4 रुष् c., क्रुध् c., प्र-,कुप् c., क्षुभ् c., कुपित-क्षुब्ध-*a.* कृ, कोपं जन् c. (जनयति); अव-अप-मन् c. 5 रुध् 7 U, बाध् 1 A, स्खल् c. (स्खलयति). –ED, *a.* कुपित, क्षुब्ध, प्रकोपित, क्रुद्ध, रुष्ट, जातामर्ष, संतप्त, असंतुष्ट. 2 बाधित, व्याहत, प्रतिरुद्ध; 'to be o.' कुप्-क्रुध्-रुष् 4 P. –ER, *s.* अपराधिन् *m.*, अपराद्धः, दोषी, पापी, पातकी, कृतागस् *m.*, कृतापराधः, सदोषः, अपराधकृत्, कुकर्मन्. —OFFENCE, *s.* अपराधः, दोषः, पापं, पातकं, अघं, एनस्-आगस् *n.*, दुरितं, कुकर्म, दुष्कृति *f.* 2 कोपः, क्रोधः, रोषः, अमर्षः, मन्युः, असंतोषः ; 'easily taking o.' शीघ्रकोपिन्, सुलभकोप. 3 विप्रियं, अवमानः, अवज्ञा. 4 रोधः, बाधा-धः, स्खलनं; *See* OBSTACLE. –LESS, *a.* निर्दोष, निरपराध. —OFFENSIVE, *a.* कोपजनन (नी *f.*), रोषावह, अप्रिय, असुष्ट-अप्रीतिकर (री *f.*), असुखद, अरम्य, विरुद्ध, कटु, असभ्य; 'o. to the ear' श्रवणकटु, कुश्राव्य ; 'o. to the taste' विरस. 2 बीभत्स, जुगुप्सावह, गर्ह्य, कुत्सित, गर्हित, दुर् pr. ; 'o. smell' दुर्गंधः, पूतिगंधः. 3 पीडाकर (री *f.*), अनिष्टावह, अहित, अपकारक, उपघातिन् ; 'act on the o.' अपराधे अग्रेसरः भू 1 P ; 'o. weapon' घातोपयुक्तं शस्त्रं. 4 आक्रामक, आअभि-घातिन्. –LY, *adv.* सापकारं, अप्रियं, सापराधं, सदोषं. –NESS, *s.* अप्रियता, कटुता, गर्ह्यता, सापकारता, घातुकता.

OFFER, *v. t.* उप-नी 1 P, उप-हृ 1 P, प्र-उप-क्लृप् c., उप-स्था c. (स्थापयति); प्र-दा 3 U, 1 P, प्रति-पद् c., निविद् c., ऋ c. (अर्पयति), निक्षिप् 6 P, सृज् c., उपहारं दा, उपढौक् c. 2 उपन्यस् 4 U, उप-क्षिप्, पुरो नि-धा 3 U, अभि-धा, निर्-उद्-दिश् 6 P. 3 प्र-,दृश् c., प्रकटीकृ ; प्रस् c., प्रक्षिप्. 4 दा desid. (दित्सति-ते). 5 (As an oblation) उपहृ, निवप् 1 U, निर्वप्, उत्सृज् 6 P, ऋ c., उपहारीकृ, उपायनीकृ ; 'o. mango sprouts in memory of Smara' स्मरमुद्दिश्य निवपेः सहकारमंजरीः (K. IV. 38) ; 'water o. ed to the Manes' निवापसलिलं ; 'o. a burnt oblation' हु 3 P ; 'o. a price' मूल्यं निर्दिश् or अभि-धा ; 'o. violence' बलात्कारं कृ. –*v. i.* उप-स्था 1 U, आविः-प्रादुः-भू 1 P, उपनम् 1 P, दृश्-लक्ष् pass., आ-नि-पत् 1 P. 2 (Show willingness) ex. by desid. form, or वद् 1 P with future; 'he o.-ed to aid me' तव साहाय्यं करिष्यामीति उवाद. 3 प्रयत् 1 A, उद्यम् 1 A, चेष्ट् 1 A, उत्-जृंभ् 1 A; *See* ATTEMPT. –*s.* उपन्यासः, उपक्षेपः, प्रस्तावः, अभिधानं, निर्देशः, वचनं, निवेदनं;. sometimes प्रार्थना; 'o. for marriage' विवाहप्रार्थना; 'makes an o. of' दित्सति. 2 प्रयत्नः, उद्यमः, प्रवृत्ति *f.* –ER, *s.* उपहर्तृ *m.*, उपनेता, अर्पकः, निवेदकः, होता. –ING, *s.* उपहरण, उपनयनं, अर्पणं. 2 बलिदानं, बलिकर्म, निर्वपणं, हवनं. 3 उपायनं, उपहारः, उत्सर्गः, बलिः, दानं; *See* OBLATION, MANE. 4 (Sacrificial) हविस् *n.*, हव्यं, हुतं, आहुति *f.* 5 अर्घः, उपायनं, प्राभृतं.

OFFICE, *s.* कर्मन् *n.*, कार्यं, नियोगः, क्रिया, कृत्यं, व्यापारः, धर्मः, प्र-,वृत्ति *f.* 2 अधिकारः, पदं, पदवी, स्थानं, आस्पदं, नियोगः, अधिकारपदं. 3 विधिसंग्रहः. 4 उद्योगस्थानं, कार्यानुष्ठानगृहं, कार्यस्थानं; 'good o.' उपकारः, उपकृतं-ति *f.*, सुकृतं, अनुग्रहः, हितं; 'ill o.' अपकार, अपक्रिया, अनिष्टं; 'holding o.', 'in o.' प्राप्ताधिकार, अधिकारापन्न, पदारूढ, अधिकृत; 'dismissed from o.' च्युत-भ्रष्ट-अधिकार, पदभ्रष्टच्युत; 'permanent o.' स्थिराधिकारः; 'temporary o.' चलपदं. –OFFICER, *s.* अधिकृतः, नियुक्तः, नियोगिन्, अधिकारी, आधिकारिकः, कार्यावेक्षकः; 'o. of the king' राजपुरुषः-भृत्यः, प्रकृतिपुरुषः;

‘o. of justice’ धर्माधिकारी, न्यायाध्यक्षः ; ‘military o.’ सेनापदभाक्, सैनिकाध्यक्षः; बलाधिपः. —OFFICIAL, *s.* राजपुरुषः-भृत्यः, अधिकारी, नियोगी, पुरुषः, भृत्यः. –*a.* आधिकारिक (की *f.*), अधिकारपद-विषयक-संबंधिन्; अधिकारयुक्त. –DOM, *s.* अधिकृतवर्गः. –LY, *adv.* अधिकारपूर्वं, अधिकारवशात्. –OFFICIOUS, *a.* अनधिकारचर्चाशील, परकार्यचर्चक; *See* MEDDLESOME. 2 उपकारशील, अनुकूल, हित. 3 अत्युपचार, अत्युपकारिन्. –LY, *adv.* अधिकारचर्चया, सप्रतिभं, प्रगल्भतया. –NESS, *s.* अन्याधिकारचर्चा, परकार्यचर्चा-प्रवेशः.

OFF-SCOURING, *s.* *See* DIRT.

OFF-SET, *s.* प्ररोहः, अंकुरः. –*v. t.* समीकृ 8 U.

OFF-SHOOT, *s.* प्ररोहः, अंकुरः, शाखा (lit. and fig.).

OFFSPRING, *s.* संतानः, संतति *f.*, प्रसूति *f.*, प्रजा, अपत्यं, प्रसवः, तोकं; ‘male o.’ पुत्रः, सूनुः, पुमपत्यं, पुंसंतानः; ‘female o.’ कन्या, सुता, स्त्र्यपत्यं; ‘having no o.’ निर्वंश, निरपत्य, निःसंतान.

OFFUSCATE, *v. t.* *See* OBSCURE.

OFT, OFTEN, (O.-times), *adv.* असकृत्, बहुशः-धा, बहु-अनेक-वारं, मुहुर्मुहुः, भूयो भूयः, अनेकशः, अनेकदा, वारंवारं, अभीक्ष्णं; ‘how o.’ कतिशः, कतिवारान्; ‘as o. as-so o.’ यतिवारं-ततिवारं.

OGLE, *s.* कटाक्षः, कटाक्ष-अपांग-दर्शनं, नयनोपांतविलोकितं, अर्धवीक्षणं, भ्रूविलासः. –*v. t.* कटाक्षेण ईक्ष् 1 A or अवलोक् 1 A, 10, तिर्यक्-साचि-दृश् 1 P.

OGRE, *s.* क्रव्याद् *m.*, दैत्यः, दानवः, राक्षसः.

OIL, *s.* तैलं, स्नेहः, अभ्यंजनं ; ‘pour o. on burning fire’ क्षते क्षारं प्रक्षिप् 6 P; ‘o.-bottle’ कुतूः *f.*; ‘o.-cake’ तैलकिट्टं, पिण्याकः, तिलकल्कं; ‘o.-man’ तैलिकः, तैलिन्, तैल-स्नेह-कारः, चाक्रिकः; ‘o.-mill’ तैलपेषणी. –*v. t.* तैलेन लिप् 6 P or अंज् 7 P or दिह् 2 U. –ED, *a.* तैलाक्त, स्नेहाक्त, अभ्यक्त. –Y, *a.* तैलमय (यी *f.*), सस्नेह, सतैल, तैलयुक्त-वत्, तैलाक्त; चिक्कण, मसृण, स्निग्ध, (fig. also).

OINTMENT, *s.* अंजनं, वि-,लेपः-पनं, प्र-अनु-लेपः, अभ्यंजनं, उपदेहः; ‘perfumed o.’ गात्रानुलेपनी, वर्ति *f.*, वर्णकं.

OLD, *a.* (Person) वृद्ध, स्थविर, प्रवयस्, परिणत, परिणतवयस्, जीर्ण, वयोवृद्ध, जरठ, जरत्, जरातुर, गतवयस्क, जीन, जरण, जरंड; ‘to grow o.’ जॄ 4, 9 P, ज्या 9 P, परिणम् 1 P; ‘o. age’ जरा, परिणामः, परिणति *f.*, वार्धकं-क्यं; वृद्धावस्था, वृद्धभावः, ज्यानि *f.*, जीर्णि *f.* ; ‘o. lady’ जरती, स्थविरा, वृद्धा, पलिता, पलिक्नी; ‘o. man’ स्थविरः, जरठः, वृद्धः, जरन्, पलितः. 2 (Showing age) ex. by वर्ष, वत्सर, वर्षीण-य in comp.; ‘8 years o.’ अष्टवर्षीय, अष्टवर्ष-वर्षात्मक; ‘a year o.’ वर्षजात; ‘2 days o.’ द्व्यहजात ; ‘how o. are you’ किं ते वयःप्रमाणं, कियद्वर्षीयोसि. 3 (Not new) बहुचिर-कालिक (की *f.*), चिर-दीर्घ-कालीन, चिरकाल-चिर-स्थायिन्, चिरंतन (नी *f.*) ; oft. by चिर in comp.; ‘o. servant’ चिरसेवकः, मूलभृत्यः, मौलः; ‘o. friend’ चिरमित्रं, चिरंतनसुहृद्. 4 जीर्ण, जर्जर, जर्जरित; ‘o. cloth’ चीरं, जीर्णवस्त्रं, पटच्चरं. 5 (Ancient) पुराण, प्राचीन, पूर्व, पूर्वतन (नी *f.*), प्राक्तन, पुरातन, प्रतन, प्रत्न, पौराण (णी *f.*), प्राक्-पूर्व-कालीन, पुरावृत्त; ‘of o.’, ‘in olden times’ पुरा, पुराकल्पे, पूर्वं. –EN, *a.* पुरातन, पुराण, प्राचीन. –ISH, *a.* ईषद्वृद्ध.

OLEAGINOUS, *a.* स्निग्ध, चिक्कण, मेदुर, मसृण.

OLEANDER, *s.* प्रति(ती)हासः, करवीरः, शतप्रासः, चंडातः, हयमारकः.

OLERACEOUS, *a.* शाकविषयक.

OLFACTORY, *s.* नस्य, नासा in comp.

OLIBANUM, *s.* तुरुष्कः, पिंडकः, सिह्लः, यावनः ; *See* INCENSE also.

OLIGARCHY, *s.* अल्पजनाधिपत्यं-प्रभुत्वं. –IC, *a.* अल्प-कतिपय-स्वामिक.

OLIO, *s.* *See* MEDLEY.

OLIVE, *s.* जितवृक्षः.

OMEN, *s.* निमित्तं, शकुनः-नं, लक्षणं, चिह्नं, अजन्यं, पूर्वलक्षणं-चिह्नं, शुभाशुभलक्षणं ; ‘of good o.’ शुभ, मंगल, सुलक्षण ; ‘good o.’ सुलक्षणं ; ‘ill o.’ दुश्चिह्नं, दुर्लक्षणं, अपशकुनः, अजन्यं, अवलक्षणं, अशुभलक्षणं. —OMINOUS, *a.* अनिष्ट-अशुभ-शंसिन्-आवेदिन्, दुर्लक्षण, अलक्षण. 2 शुभ-मंगल-शंसिन्. 3 शाकुनिक (की *f.*), शकुननिमित्त in comp. –LY, *adv.* अशुभलक्षणेन, दुर्लक्षणपूर्वं.

OMIT, *v.t.* वृज् 10, वि-परि-°, परि-त्यज् 1 P, उत्-,क्षिप् 6 P, मुच् 6 P, उत्सृज् 6 P, अपास् 4 U, हा 3 P. 2 अतिक्रम् 1 U, 4 P, उपेक्ष् 1 A, लंघ् 1 A, 10, अतिचर् 1 P, अतिवृत् 1 A, लुप् c., न कृ 8 U or वि-धा 3 U or अनु-स्था 1 P. –OMISSION, *s.* वर्जनं, त्यागः, उत्सर्गः, लंघनं, अतिक्रमः, अतिचारः, लोपः, उपात्ययः ; ‘o. to do something’ अननुष्ठानं, अविधानं, उपेक्षा.

OMNIFARIOUS, *a.* सर्वविध-प्रकार.

OMNIGENOUS, *a.* सर्वप्रकार-जातीय.

OMNIPOTENT, *a.* सर्वशक्तिमत्, सर्वसमर्थ-शक्ति, अमित-अपार-शक्ति. –OMNIPOTENCE, –CY, *s.* सर्वशक्तित्वं, अपार-अमित-शक्ति *f.*, सर्वसामर्थ्यं, अनंतशक्तिः.

OMNIPRESENT, *a.* सर्वगत, सर्वात्मक, सर्व-विश्व-व्यापिन्, विश्वात्मन्, विश्वरूप. –OMNIPRESENCE, *s.* सर्व-विश्व-व्याप्ति *f.*, विश्वात्मता, विश्वरूपता, सर्व-विश्वव्यापिता.

OMNISCIENT, *a.* सर्वज्ञ, सर्वविद्-वेदिन्-बुध्, सर्वदर्शिन्-साक्षिन्, विश्वनेत्र, त्रिकालज्ञ. –OMNISCIENCE, *s.* सर्वज्ञत्वं, सर्वज्ञानं.

OMNIVAGANT, *a.* सर्वगत, सर्वगामिन्.

OMNIVOROUS, *a.* सर्वभक्ष, सर्वभोजिन्.

OMPHALIC, *a.* नाभ्य, नाभि in comp.

OMPHALOCELE, *s.* नाभिस्फोटः.

ON, *prep.* Gen. ex. by loc., अधि pr., उपरि (with gen.). 2 (Time, place) by loc. ; 'o. the shore' तीरे, तीरोपांते, उपतीरं. 3 (With verbs of motion) by loc. or instr., (स्कंधेन-स्कंधे-छागं गृहीत्वा); 'go o. foot' पद्भ्यां गम् 1 P. 4 (Direction) by loc. or by तस्, त्र affixed ; 'o. the left' वामतः ; 'o. all sides' सर्वतः, सर्वत्र, समंततः. 5 (After) ex. by abl., or loc. abs.; 'o. his arrival' तस्मिन् आगते, तदागमनात् ; or by gerund ; 'o. hearing his speech' तस्य वचः श्रुत्वा. 6 (Concerning) विषय-संबंधिन् in comp. or by comp. ; 'a work o. morals' नीतिग्रंथः; 'so o.' इत्यादि (*a.*) ; 'hence, o. thy life' स्वजीवितं यदि वांछसि तर्हि द्रागपसर, अपसरास्मात्स्थानान्नो चेत् त्वं जीवितेन वियोक्ष्यसे ; 'o. o., to the combat' ननु युद्धाय प्रयात. —*adv.* अग्रतः, अग्रे, प्र pr.; 'having clothes o.' परिहितवस्त्र. —WARD, *a.* अग्रेसर (री *f.*), अग्रगामिन्; वर्धिष्णु. —WARDS, *adv.* अग्रे, अग्रतः, पुरतः.

ON-DIT, *s.* किल *ind.*; *See* RUMOUR.

ONE, *a.* एक ; 'o. of two' एकतर ; 'o. of many' एकतम ; 'only o.' अनन्य ; 'fixed on o. object' अनन्यविषय, अनन्यवृत्ति. 2 (Any) कश्चन, कोपि. 3 (Same) एक, तद् with एव ; 'at o. time' युगपत्, समं, एककाले ; 'having o. meaning' एकार्थ. —*s.* जनः, नरः, मनुष्यः; gen. not ex.; 'o. should always protect oneself' आत्मानं सततं रक्षेत् ; 'o. by o.' एकैकशः, एकैकं प्रत्येकं, पृथक्पृथक् ; 'o. day' कदाचित्, कदापि काले ; 'young or little o.s' शिशुजनः, बालाः; 'in o. way' एकधा; 'o.-self' आत्मन् *m.*, स्वयं *ind.* ; 'o.'s own' स्व, निज, आत्मीय, स्वीय, आत्म in comp. ; 'to be at o.' संमन् 4 A ; 'o.-eyed' एकाक्ष, काण, एकाक्षिहीन ; 'o.-sided' असम, एकपक्षीय, एकदेशीय; 'o. another' अन्योन्यं, परस्परं, इतरेतरं ; 'to be o.-self again' प्रकृतिमापद् 4 A, संज्ञां लभ् 1 A; *See* 'come to senses' under SENSE ; 'to bring to o.-self' प्रकृतौ स्था c. (स्थापयति). —NESS, *s.* एकत्वं, एकभावः, अद्वैतं, अभेदः, अविशेषः —ONCE, *adv.* सकृत्, एकवारं. 2 (O. upon a time) एकदा, अथैकदा, अथ कदाचित्. 3 पुरा, पूर्वं, प्राक्काले; 'at o.' समं, युगपत्, एककाले, समकालं-लं; सद्यः, सपदि, तत्क्षणात्, तत्क्षणेन, तत्काले ; 'all at o.' अकस्मात्, एकपदे; 'o. more' पुनरपि, भूयः, पुनः.

ONEIROCRITIC,-AL, *a.* स्वप्नविचारिन्.

ONEIROMANCY, *s.* स्वप्नार्थविचारः, स्वप्नार्थज्ञापनं.

ONEROUS, *a.* दुर्भर, गुरु, गुरुभार, दुर्वह, दुःसह.

ONION, *s.* पलांडुः, सुकंदकः.

ONLY, *a.* एक, एव, एकाकिन्, केवल, मात्र-मात्रक in comp., अद्वितीय, अनन्य ; 'having that as the o. recourse' तदेकशरण, अनन्यगतिक. —*adv.* केवलं, एव, मात्र in comp.; 'not o. but' न केवलं followed by अपि or किंतु.

ONOMATOPŒIA, *s.* अनुकारः; अनुकरणं.

ONSET, *s.* आ-अभि-क्रमः-मणं, अवस्कंदः, अभिसंपातः, आपातः, अभिग्रहः, अभ्याघातः.

ONSLAUGHT, *s.* अभ्याघातः; *See* ONSET.

ONTOLOGY, *s.* सत्त्वविद्या, भूतविचारः. —IST, *s.* सत्त्वविद्याज्ञः.

OOZE, *v. i.* (शनैः) स्रु-क्षर्-गल् 1 P, स्यंद् 1 A, प्रस्नु 2 P, री 4 A. —*v. t.* स्रु c., स्यंद् c., &c. —*s.* क्षरत्पंकः, मृदुमृत्तिका. 2 स्रवः, द्रवः, धारा. —ING, *s.* स्यंदनं, क्षरणं, स्रवः. —Y, *a.* सद्रव.

OPAQUE, *a.* प्रकाशाभेद्य, किरणाभेद्य; अस्वच्छ, कलुष, निष्प्रभ, सांधकार. —NESS,-OPACITY, *s.* अस्वच्छता, निष्प्रभता, कालुष्यं. 2 शुक्रं.

OPAL, *s.* पुलकः, विमलकः.

OPEN, *v. t.* (Door &c.) अपा-वि-वृ 5 U, उद्-घट् c., निरर्गलीकृ 8 U ; (lotus) विकस् c., प्रबुध् c., भिद् 7 P or c., (सूर्यांशुभिर्भिन्नमिवारविंदं K. I. 32), स्फुट् c.; (eyes) उन्मिल् c., उत्फुल् c., उन्मिष् c.; (mouth) व्या-दा 3 P, जृंभ् c., उत्-वि-°; (hand) प्रसृ c., वितन् 8 U, विस्तृ c. 2 वि-अंज् 7 P or c., विवृ, प्रकटीकृ, आविष्कृ, व्यक्तीकृ, प्रकाश् c.; 'o. the heart', 'o. oneself' हृद्गतं निविद् c. 3 (As meaning) व्या-ख्या 2 P, व्याचक्ष् 2 A, व्याकृ, व्यक्तीकृ, विवृ. 4 छिद् 7 P, निर्भिद्. 5 शुध् c., वि-परि°. 6 प्रारभ् 1 A, प्रस्तु 2 U, प्र-उप-क्रम् 1 A. —*v. i.* उन्मील् 1 P, विकस् 1 P, स्फुट् 6 P, दल् 1 P, भिद् pass., फुल्ल् 1 P. 2 विस्तृ-विवृ pass., वि-,जृंभ् 1 A, प्रसृ c.-वितन्-pass.; (in other senses) pass. of roots in (*v. t.*). 4 (Ground) स्फुट्, विदल्, द्विधाभू, विदृ-भिद्-pass. 5 प्रवृत् 1 A, प्रारभ् pass. —*a.* वि-अपा-वृत, असंवृत, उद्घाटित; (eyes) उन्मीलित, उन्मिषित ; (hand) प्रसारित, वितत, विस्तृत, विस्तीर्ण ; (mouth) विजृंभित, सजृंभ, उज्जृंभ, व्यात्त; (letter) उन्मुद्र, निरावेष्टन, अकोशस्थ. 2 निर्यंत्रण, असंबाध, निरर्गल, अनर्गल, अरुद्ध, उत्-वि-शृंखल, निरवग्रह; वि-,शुद्ध, निर्विघ्न; *See* FREE. 3 निर्व्याज, उत्तान, निष्कपट, सरल, ऋजु, निर्माय, उदार, शुद्धमति, विमलात्मन्; *See* FRANK ; 'o.-minded person' उत्तानहृदयः जनः. 4 सु-,प्रकाश, वि-,स्पष्ट, व्यक्त, प्रकट, अगूढ, अगुप्त. 5 निर्वृक्ष, अपादप; अनाश्रय. 6 गम्य, उपसर्प-

णीय; *See* ACCESSIBLE; 'lays him o. to his enemy' शत्रुगोचरे (विषये) तं पातयति; 'o. to dispute' विवादास्पदं, विवादग्रस्त-*a.*; 'lay o.' प्रकाश् c.; *See* (*v. t.*); 'o. air' अनावृतप्रदेशः-भूभागः; 'o. at one end' एकमुख; 'having gone out into the o. air' प्रकाशं निर्गतः (S. 4); 'o.-eyed' विवृताक्ष, उत्फुल्लनयन, सचेतन (fig.); 'o.-handed' उदार, मुक्तहस्त; 'o.-hearted' उदार, उत्तानहृदय, निर्व्याज; 'o.-mouthed' व्यात्तमुख. —ER, *s.* उद्घाटकः, प्रकाशकः. —ING, *s.* विवरणं, विवृति *f.*, उद्घाटनं; उन्मीलनं, विकासः, भेदः, स्फुटनं. 2 छिद्रं, रंध्रं, द्वारं, विदरः, स्फु(स्फो)टनं, भिदा. 3 प्रारंभः, उपक्रमः, प्रस्तावः, उपोद्घातः.—*a.* विकसत्, स्फुटत्. 2 प्रथम, आद्य, आरंभक. —LY, *adv.* प्रकाशं, सुस्पष्टं, व्यक्तं, परि-,स्फुटं. —NESS, *s.* विवृतत्वं, विवृति *f.*, निर्व्याजता, सारल्यं, निष्कापट्यं, दाक्षिण्यं, शुद्धमतिता, व्यक्तता, स्पष्टता, प्रकाशता, प्राकट्यं.

OPERA, *s.* संगीतनाटकं.

OPERATE, *v. i.* गुणं आवह् 1 P, कार्यं उत्पद् c. or दृश् c., फलं सं-पद् c. or साध् c., प्र-भू 1 P, प्रबलीभू; *See* EFFECT. 2 कृ 8 U, वि-धा 3 U, चेष्ट् 1 A, प्रवृत् 1 A, प्र-,यत् 1 A, व्याप्ट 6 A. 3 शस्त्रेण उपचर् 1 P or साध् c. —ION, *s.* क्रिया, कर्मन् *n.*, कृति *f.*, कार्यं, कृत्यं. 2 चेष्टितं, प्रवृत्ति *f.*, उद्यमः, उद्योगः, प्रयत्नः, व्यापारः. 3 प्रवर्तकत्वं, हेतुता, कारणं, साधनं; 'mental o.' मनोव्यापारः; 'quick in o.' आशुकारिन्, सद्यःफल, आशुगुणावह. 4 (Surgical) शस्त्रक्रिया-कर्म, शस्त्रोपायः, शस्त्रोपचारः. —IVE, *a.* कर्मकारिन्, प्रवर्तक, प्रयोजक, कारणभूत. 2 गुणावह, गुणकारिन्, सिद्धिकर (री *f.*), प्रबल, सप्रभाव, प्रभविष्णु, कार्यक्षम. —*s.* कर्म-शिल्प-कारः, कारुः. —OR, *s.* कारकः, कर्ता, प्रवर्तकः.

OPEROSE, *a.* श्रम-कष्ट-साध्य.

OPHIOLOGY, *s.* सर्पविद्या.

OPHTHALMIA, *s.* नेत्राभिष्यंदः.

OPIATE, *a.* निद्रावह, निद्रा-स्वाप-कारिन्, स्वापन. —*s.* निद्रावहं औषधं, स्वापनं.

OPINE, *v. i.* मन् 4 A, तर्क् 10; *See* THINK. —OPINION, *s.* मतं, मति *f.*, तर्कः, बुद्धि *f.*, बोधः, अभिप्रायः, आशयः; 'such is my o.' इति मे मतिः; 'difference of o.' मति(त)भेदः, विप्रतिपत्ति *f.*, वैमत्यं; 'regard for public o.' लोकजन-लज्जा-भयं; 'secure the good o. of your husband' भर्तुर्बहुमता भव (S. 4). —ATED, -ATIVE, *a.* स्वमताभिमानिन्, मताग्रहिन्, दुराग्रहिन्.

OPIUM, *s.* अहिफेनं, अफेनं.

OPPONENT, *a.* विरुद्ध, प्रतिकूल, वि-प्रति-पक्ष, वैरिन्. —*s.* शत्रुः, अरिः, वैरी, वि-प्रति-पक्षः; प्रतियोद्धा, प्रतियोगी, प्रतिरोधकः.

OPPORTUNE, *a.* समयोचित, प्राप्तकाल, कालयोग्य, प्रस्तावसदृश (शी *f.*), प्राप्तावसर, सामयिक-प्रास्ताविक (की *f.*). —LY, *adv.* प्राप्तकाले, काले, स्थाने, यथासमयं, यथावसरं, प्रस्तावसदृशं, कालोचितं. —NESS, *s.* कालौचित्यं, प्रस्तावयोग्यता. —OPPORTUNITY, *s.* प्रस्तावः, अवकाशः, अवसरः, कालः, समयः, प्रसंगः, वेला, कार्यकालः, योगः. 2 साधनं, उपायः, प्र-युक्ति *f.*; 'lose an o.' कालं क्षिप् 6 P or ह 1 P; 'seizing an o.' अवसरं गृहीत्वा, गृहीतावसर, लब्धावकाश; 'to await an o.' अवसरं प्रति-पा c. (पालयति).

OPPOSE, *v. t.* वि-नि-प्रति-रुध् 7 U, प्रतिबंध् 9 P, प्रतिकृ 8 U, प्रतिकूलयति (D.), प्रत्यव-स्था 1 A, वि-प्रति-हन् 2 P, बाध् 1 A, निवृ c.; (in fighting) प्रतियुध् c.; संमुखी-अभिमुखी-कृ 8 U or भू. —ED, *a.* विरुद्ध, विपरीत, प्रतिकूल, विप्रतिपन्न, बाधित, वारित, असंमत, विद्विष्ट; 'o. to the practice of the world' लोकाचारविरुद्ध, लोकासंमत, लोकविद्विष्ट. 2 इतर in comp.; 'o. to false' मिथ्येतर. —ER, *s.* विरोधकः, प्रतिहंतृ *m.* —OPPOSITE, *a.* सं-प्रति-अभिमुख (खी *f.*), संमुखस्थ. 2 विरुद्ध, विरोधिन्, विपरीत, प्रतिकूल, वि-प्रति-पक्ष, प्रतिद्वंद्विन्, विपर्यस्त, व्यत्यस्त, इतर in comp.; 'o. of natural' सहजेतर; सव्येतर, &c. 3 पर, अपर, अंतर in comp.; 'the o. bank' पारं, तीरांतरं, अपरतीरं. —*s.* विपर्ययः, व्यत्यासः, विपरीतं; by (*a.*). —ION, *s.* वैपरीत्यं, प्रातिकूल्यं, विरोधः, विपक्षता, विपर्य(र्या)यः, व्यत्ययः, व्यत्यासः, विपर्यासः. 2 विरोधः, प्रतिक्रिया, प्रतिबंधः, प्रतियोगः-यत्नः, व्याघातः, बाधः-धा. 3 विरोधकजनाः, प्रतियोगिपक्षः, विरोधिजनवर्गः. 4 विरुद्ध-द्वेषभावः, वैरं. —LY, *adv.* सं-अभि-मुखं, विपरीतं, प्रतिकूलं, विपर्ययेण.

OPPRESS, *v. t.* पीड् 10, अर्द् 1 P or c., उपद्रु 1 P, बाध् 1 A, नि-अप-कृ 8 U, विप्र-कृ, उपद्रु 1 A, उपमृद् 9 P or c., कृश् c., अभिद्रुह् 4 P, अभिभू 1 P. —ION, *s.* पीडा, पीडनं, बाधः-धा, अर्दनं, उपमर्दः, उपप्लवः, उपद्रवः, नि-विप्र-अप-कारः, नैष्ठुर्यं, क्रौर्यं. —IVE, *a.* बाधक, पीडाकर (री *f.*), उपप्लविन्, उपद्रविन्, पीडाप्रद, अपकारक; निष्ठुर, अतिक्रूर, क्लेशद. 2 अतिभारवत्. —OR, *s.* प्रजापीडकः, उपप्लावकः, उपद्रविन् *m.*, अत्याचारः, निष्ठुरः, क्रूरचरितः.

OPPROBRIUM, *s.* निंदा, गर्हा, कुत्सा, तिरस्कारः, अपवादः, अवज्ञा, परिभवः, वाच्यता, धिक्कारः. —OPPROBRIOUS, *a.* गर्ह्य, निंदात्मक, गर्हारूप, निंदा-गर्हार्थक; परुष, मुखर, द्वेष्य. —LY, *adv.* सापवादं, सतिरस्कारं. —NESS, *s.* गर्ह्यता, निंदकत्वं.

OPPUGN,—ER, *See* OPPOSE &c.

OPTATIVE, *a.* इच्छार्थक.

OPTIC,-AL, *a.* चाक्षुष (षी *f.*), चक्षुः-नेत्र in comp.

2 दृक्शास्त्रसंबंधिन्. –s. चक्षुरिंद्रियं, दृगिंद्रियं. –OPTICS, s. दृग्विद्या-शास्त्रं.

OPTIMACY, s. कुलीनवर्गः-जनाः.

OPTIMISM, s. उत्तमता, उत्कृष्टता.

OPTION, s. अभि,-रुचि f., इच्छा, कामः, अभिलाषः, ईप्सितं; विकल्पः, विभाषा (in grammar); 'it is left to your o.' अत्र स्वरुच्या वर्ततां भवान्, यथाभिलाषं क्रियतां. –AL, a. वैकल्पिक-ऐच्छिक (की f.), काम्य, सविकल्प, यथाकाम, रुच्यधीन, स्वेच्छातंत्र. –ALLY, adv. विकल्पेन, अन्यतरस्यां, (इक्कोरन्यतरस्यां), वा, विभाषया.

OPULENT, a. श्रीमत्, धनिन्, धनाढ्य, वित्तवत्, धनवित्त-संपन्न, धनिक, समृद्ध, संपन्न, धनेश्वर, बहुधन. –OPULENCE, s. विभवः, ऐश्वर्यं, समृद्धि f.

OR, conj. अथवा, यद्वा, वा (never at beginning) repeated after each word, or after the last; (in questions) नु, (स्वप्नो नु माया नु मतिभ्रमो नु); उत, आहो, आहोस्वित् (correl. of किं 'whether'). 2 अन्यथा, इतरथा, अथवा, नोचेत्.

ORACLE, s. दैवी वाक्, देव-आकाश-वाणी, आकाशभवा-अशरीरिणी-सरस्वती. 2 प्रश्नदेवता-देवः. 3 प्रश्न-शकुनस्थानं. 4 प्रमाणं, आप्तः, प्रमाणपुरुषः; आप्तवचनं. –ORACULAR, a. देववाणीतुल्य, प्रमाणभूत, आप्त, प्रामाणिक (की f.).

ORAL, a. वाचिक (की f.), उक्त, अलिखित; 'o. message' वाचिकं. –LY, adv. वाचा, मुखद्वारा, अलिखितं.

ORANGE, s. नारंगः, नागरंगः, ऐरावतः, नादेयी, भूमिजंबुका; (fruit) नारंगफलं; 'o.-coloured' पिच्छिल, कौसुंभ (भी f.). –ORANGERY, s. नागरंगवाटिका.

ORATION, s. वाक्प्रबंधः, सालंकारं वचनं, प्रवचनं, सरस्वतीनिष्यंदः (fluent o.). –ORATOR, s. प्र-,वक्तृ m., वाक्शौंडः-चतुरः, प्रवचनपटुः, सद्वक्ता, वाक्पटुः, वाग्मिन् m., वागीशः, वाक्पंडितः-विशारदः, सभापंडितः. –ICAL, a. वाक्चातुर्यमय (यी f.), सालंकार, वागलंकारमय. –Y, s. वाग्मिता, वाक्पाटवं-चातुर्यं, सुवक्तृत्वं, वाक्शक्ति f., वक्तृत्वं, सभापांडित्यं. 2 प्रार्थनागारं, उपासनास्थानं, भजनालयः. –ORATORIO, s. तालबद्धं धर्मकीर्तनं. 2 Oratory, q. v.

ORB, s. मंडलः-लं, बिंबः-बं, वर्तुलं, चक्रं, वृत्तं, गोलः-लं; 'the moon with entire (undiminished) o.' पूर्ण-अविकल-मंडलः चंद्रः, अखंडकलः शशी (Mal. 2). –ED,-ORBICULAR, a. मंडलाकार, वर्तुल, गोलाकृति. –ORBICULATE, s. वर्तुलं. –a. वर्तुल; See (s.).

ORBIT, s. कक्षा-क्षः, ग्रहपथः-मार्गः.

ORCHARD, s. वाटिका, वाटः-टी, उपवनं, वृक्षोद्यानं, वृक्षवाटिका; 'fruit o.' पुष्पवाटिका.

ORCHESTRA, s. वादित्रस्थानं-स्थलं. 2 वादकसमूहः, वादित्रगणः.

ORDAIN, v. t. वि-धा 3 U, आदिश् 6 P, निर्दिश्, सं-व्यव-स्था c. (स्थापयति), प्र-परि-कॢप् c.; प्रचुद् 10, वच् 2 P, स्मृ 1 P; 'o. ed by Śāstras' शास्त्रोक्त, शास्त्रविहित-स्मृत, शास्त्रनिर्दिष्ट, &c. 2 (अधिकारे) नियुज् 7 A, 10, अधिकृ 8 U, or c., अभिषिच् 6 P, व्या-दिश्; (religiously) दीक्ष् 1 A, धर्मकर्मणि नियुज्. –ER, s. प्रकल्पकः, संस्थापकः, प्रचोदकः.

ORDEAL, s. दिव्यं, सत्यं, परीक्षा, प्रमाणं; 'o. by fire' कोशः-षः, तप्तदिव्यं; 'subjecting oneself to o.' दिव्यग्रहणं; 'trying o.' (fig.) तत्त्वनिकषा आपद्.

ORDER, v. t. आदिश् 6 P, निर्-नि-समा-व्या-दिश्, शास् 2 P, आ-ज्ञा c. (ज्ञापयति), प्रचुद् 10. 2 वि-धा 3 U, प्रणी 1 P, निर्वह् c.; See MANAGE. 3 परि-कॢप् c., क्रमेण विन्यस् 4 U or c. or स्था c. (स्थापयति) or नि-धा, संवि-धा, व्यव-स्था c., वि-,रच् 10; व्यूह् 1 U. 4 Ordain, q. v. –s. आज्ञा, आ-नि-देशः, निर्देशः, शासनं, नियोगः; 'written o.' आज्ञापत्रं; 'what are your o. s' को नियोगोऽनुष्ठीयतां; 'your Majesty's o. s will be obeyed' यथाज्ञापयति देवः. 2 प्र-,चोदनं-ना, विधिः, नियमः, विधानं, प्रेरणा, वचनं. 3 क्रमः, अनुक्रमः, परिपाटि-टी f., आनुपूर्व्यं-र्वी, पर्यायः, परंपरा, पारंपर्यं, आवृत् f.; व्यवस्था, विन्यासः, विरचनं-ना, संविधानं; 'natural o.' आनुलोम्यं; 'inverted o.', 'reverse o.' प्रातिलोम्यं, व्युत्क्रमः, व्यतिक्रमः, विपर्ययः, विपर्यासः, व्यत्यासः, व्यत्ययः; 'o. of battle' व्यूहः, सैन्यरचना, बलविन्यासः; 'natural o. of words' अन्वयः; 'in natural or direct o.' अनुलोम-मतः; 'in inverted o.' प्रतिलोम-मतः; 'in good o.' सुस्थित, सुरक्षित, सुविहित; 'in o.' सुविन्यस्त, सुविरचित, व्यवस्थित, क्रमेण स्थापित; (adv.) क्रमेण, क्रमशः, यथाक्रमं, क्रमानुरूपं, अनुपूर्वशः, आनुपूर्व्येण, परिपाट्या; 'in o. to' ex. by अर्थे-र्थं in comp.; by dat. or by inf.; 'out of o.' अव्यवस्थित, भग्नक्रम, असुस्थ. 4 मार्गः, स्थिति f., रीति f., पद्धति f., आचारः, नियमः; 'not breaking the (established) o.' स्थितेरभेत्ता (R. III. 27); स्थित्यै दंडयतो दंड्यान् (R. I. 25) 'for maintaining o. &c.'; 'breaking the o.' स्थितिभेदः, अतिपातः, पर्ययः, उपात्ययः. 5 गणः, वर्गः, वर्णः, जाति f.; 'the lower o. s' अवर-अधमवर्णाः, अंत्यवर्गः, अधमजातीयाः. 6 आश्रमः, वर्णाश्रमः; 'head of a religious o.' आश्रमगुरुः. –ER, s. आज्ञापकः, आदेष्टृ m.; शास्ता. –LESS, a. क्रमहीन-शून्य, अक्रम, अनवस्थित. –LY, a. व्यवस्थित, यथाक्रम, क्रमानुगत, सक्रम, अनुपूर्व. –adv. यथाक्रमं, पर्यायेण, क्रमशः.

ORDINAL, *a.* क्रमवाचक. –*s.* क्रमिकसंख्या. 2 विधिसंहिता.

ORDINANCE, *s.* विधिः, मर्यादा, कल्पः, प्र-,चोदनं-ना, स्थिति *f.*, धर्मशास्त्रविधिः-मर्यादा, नियमः, सूत्रं. 2 नि-आ-देशः, शासनं, नियोगः.

ORDINARY, *a.* प्रचलित, प्रसिद्ध, प्रायिक (की *f.*), लोकप्रसिद्ध. 2 साधारण (णी *f.*), सामान्य, व्य(व्या)-वहारिक-आचारिक-नैयमिक (की *f.*), नित्य, यथाव्यवहार, यथापद्धति; ' something more than o. ' विशेषः. 3 सामान्य, मध्यम, प्राकृत, अवर, नीतिविशिष्ट; ' an o. woman ' नातिरूपवती स्त्री, सामान्यलावण्योपेता. –*s.* धर्माध्यक्षः. 3 साधारणभोजनस्थानं. –ILY, *adv.* सामान्यतः, साधारणतः, प्रायः, प्रायेण, प्रायशः.

ORDINATE, *a.* यथानुक्रम, अनुपूर्व. –ION, *s.* विधानं, कल्पनं, नियोगः. 3 दीक्षा; *See* ORDAIN.

ORDNANCE, *s.* युद्धास्त्रसामग्री, युद्धयंत्रसमूहः.

ORDURE, *s.* पुरीषं, विष्ठा, उच्चारः; *See* DUNG; ' to void o. ' पुरीषं उत्सृज् 6 P or उच्चर् 1 P.

ORE, *s.* धातुः, खनिज-असंस्कृत-धातुः.

ORGAN, *s.* इंद्रियं, करणं, हृषीकं, विषयिन् *n.*; (of action) साधनं, करणं, उपकरणं, कर्मसाधनं, कर्मेंद्रियं; ' intellectual or internal o. ' धींद्रियं, अंतरिंद्रियं. 2 द्वारं, मुखं, साधनं. 3 वंशी. –IC, –ICAL, *a.* इंद्रियसंबंधिन्, इंद्रियमय (यी *f.*) -विशिष्ट, इंद्रियोत्पन्न, सकरण; इंद्रिय in comp. –ISM, *s.* रचना, घटना. –IST, *s.* वंशीवादकः. —ORGANIZE, *v. t.* निर्मा 3 A, 2 P, सृज् 6 P, क्लृप् c., विं-रच् 10, घट् c. (घटयति). 2 वि-धा 3 U, संवि-धा, विन्यस् 4 U, क्रमेण स्था c. (स्थापयति), व्यव-स्था c., व्यूह् 1 U. 3 इंद्रियैः संयुज् 7 U, 10. –ATION, *s.* निर्माणं, सृष्टि *f.*, घटनं-ना, विन्यासः, व्यूहः-हनं, संविधानं. 2 भागविरचनं-कल्पना-विन्यासः. 3 सेंद्रियता.

ORGASM, *s.* आ-सं-वेगः, क्षोभः, उत्तापः, अत्यंतावेगः.

ORGY, *s.* रात्र्युत्सवः, नैशोत्सवः, प्रहर्षः, प्रमोदः.

ORIENT, *a.* उज्ज्वल, भास्वत् ; *See* BRIGHT. 2 उद्यत्, उदयमान. –*s.* प्राची, पूर्वदेशः. –AL, *a.* पौरस्त्य, प्राच्य, पूर्वदेशीय, पूर्व, प्राचीन. –*s.* पूर्वदेशवासिन् *m.* –ALIST, *s.* पूर्वदेशीयभाषाज्ञः.

ORIFICE, *s.* मुखं, छिद्रं, रंध्रं, द्वारं, सुषिरं, विवरं; ' o. of the ear ' कर्णमः.

ORIGIN, *s.* मूलं, प्रभवः, आ-प्रा-रंभः, उत्पत्ति *f.*, उद्भवः, उद्गमः, संभवः, जन्मन् *n.*, जाति *f.*, आदिः, योनि *f.*, बीजं, हेतुः, आदिकारणं, उत्पत्तिस्थानं. 2 प्रयोजकः, प्रवर्तकः ; ' of low o. ' हीनजाति-जन्मन्, दुर्योनि ; 'of good o. ' मौल (ली *f.*), उत्कृष्टजाति. –AL, *a.* मौल, प्रथम, आदिम, आद्य, पूर्व, आदि-मूल-in comp.; ' o. passage ' मूलं, मूलवचनं. 2 अपूर्व, अपूर्वकल्पित, अचिंतितपूर्व, स्वतः-स्वयं-कल्पित. 3 अपूर्वरचक, स्वतः-कल्पक. –*s.* मूलं, आदर्शः, मूलपत्रं-ग्रंथः-लेखः; *See* (*s.*). –ALITY, *s.* अपूर्वरचनाशक्ति *f.*, कल्पकत्वं-ता, अपूर्वकल्पनासामर्थ्यं, कल्पनाशक्तिः. 2 अपूर्वता. –ALLY, *adv.* आदौ, प्रथमं, प्रथमतः, प्रारंभे, मूलतः. –ATE, *v. t.* (प्रथमं) उत्पद् c., जन् c. (जनयति), उद्भू c., सृज् 6 P, क्लृप् c., प्रवृत् c., निर्मा 3 A ; प्रारभ् 1 A, उपक्रम् 1 A. –*v. i.* (प्रथमं) उत्पद् 4 A, जन् 4 A, प्र-उद्-सं-भू 1 P, प्रसृ 1 P; उद्-इ 2 P, उद्-गम् 1 P, प्रवृत् 1 A, उत्था 1 P; ex. by (*s.*) or by ' Arise ', q. v. – ATION, *s.* प्रारंभः, प्रथमोद्भवः. –ATOR, *s.* प्रवर्तकः, उत्पादकः, कल्पकः, योजकः, आरंभकः, निर्माता ; also ex. by (*s.*).

ORION, *s.* मृगशीर्षं.

ORISON, *s.* प्रार्थना, स्तवः, स्तुति *f.*, उपासना, स्तोत्रं.

ORNAMENT, *s.* अलंकारः वि-भूषणं, आभरणं, मंडनं ; (decoration) अलंकरणं, भूषा, अलंक्रिया, संस्कारः, परिष्कारः, परिकर्मन् *n.*, प्रतिकर्म, प्रसाधनं, कल्पना, लज्जा, नेपथ्यं, शोभा ; (fig.) ललामं, अवतंसः, अलंकारः, तिलकः; ' o. to the Kshatriya family ' क्षत्रियकुलावतंसः; आश्रमललामभूता ; पंडितकुलतिलकः &c.–*v. t.* अलंकृ 8 U, परिष्कृ, मंड् 10; भूष् 10, प्रसाध् c., शुभ् c., रंज् c. –AL, *a.* शोभावह, वि-, भूषक, शोभाप्रद, शोभा-भूषा-कर (री *f.*), अलंकरिष्णु; or by (*s.*). –ALLY, *adv.* विभूषणार्थं. —ATION, *s.* अलंकरणं, मंडनं; रंजनं.

ORNATE, *a.* कांतिमत्, विचित्र, शोभित, वि-,भूषित; सालंकार, अलंकारमय (यी *f.*), अलंकृत, कृतालंकार. –LY, *adv.* सालंकारं, शोभापूर्वं.

ORNITHOLOGY, *s.* पक्षिविद्या. –IST, *s.* पक्षिविद्याज्ञः.

ORPHAN, *s.*, *a.* अनाथः, मातापितृरहितः-हीनः, गतमातृकः, गतपितृकः. –AGE, *s.* अनाथता. 2 अनाथाश्रयः, अनाथालयः.

ORPIMENT, *s.* (Yellow) पिंजरं, पीतनं, तालं, आ-(अ)लं, हरितालकं.

ORRIS, *s.* वचा, उग्रगंधा, षड्ग्रंथा, गोलोमी, शतपर्णिका; (white) हैमवती, श्वेतवचा.

ORTHODOX, *a.* शास्त्रीय, शास्त्रसंमत, शास्त्रमतानुसारिन्, धर्मपरायण, सत्यधर्मानुरोधिन्. –Y, *s.* शास्त्रानुसारः, शास्त्रमार्गावलंबनं, धर्मपरायणता.

ORTHOEPY, *s.* शुद्धोच्चारः-रणं. –IST, *s.* शुद्धोच्चारणविद् *m.*

ORTHOGON, *s.* समचतुरस्रं. –AL, *a.* समकोणाकृति.

ORTHOGRAPHY, *s.* अक्षर-वर्ण-विन्यासः, वर्णविन्यासशास्त्रं-विचारः.

ORTS, *s.* *See* OFFAL.

OSCILLATE, *v. i.* दोलायते (D.), प्रेंख् 1 P, इतस्ततः चल् 1 P or कंप् 1 A or स्फुर् 6 P or स्पंद् 1 A; *See* WAVER. –ION, *s.* आंदोलनं, प्रेंखणं, इतस्ततः चलनं, गतागतं. –ING, -ORY, *a.* दोलायमान, स्पंदमान, स्फुरित.

Oscitant, *a.* वि-,जृंभमाण, जृंभित. 2 निद्रालु, तंद्रालु. —**Oscitate**, *v. i.* वि-,जृंभ् 1 A.

Osprey, *s.* कुररः-री, उत्क्रोशः.

Osseous, *a.* अस्थिमय (यी *f.*). —**Ossicle**, *s.* अस्थिकं. —**Ossify**, *v. t.* अस्थिसात्कृ 8 U. —*v. i.* अस्थिसात् भू 1 P. —**Ossuary**, *s.* अस्थिस्थानं.

Ostensible, *a.* व्यक्त, सुप्रकाश, प्रकट, प्रसिद्ध, अगूढ. —**Ostensibly**, *adv.* प्रकाशं-शतः, प्रकटं, अगूढं.

Ostentation, *s.* आडंबरः, दंभः, दर्पः, विकत्थनं, आत्मश्लाघा. —**Ostentatious**, *a.* आडंबरप्रिय-शील, दंभशील, दांभिक (की *f.*); आत्मश्लाघिन्. —**ly**, *adv.* साडंबरं, दंभपूर्वं, सदंभं.

Osteocope, *s.* अस्थिवेदना.

Osteology, *s.* अस्थिवर्णनं-विद्या.

Ostler, *s.* *See* Groom.

Ostracism, *s.* विवासनं, निर्वासनं.

Other, *a.* अन्य, अपर, इतर, पर, अन्यतर (*pron. a.*) अंतरं in comp. 2 भिन्न, व्यतिरिक्त. 3 अव-,शिष्ट 'the o. s' अपरे, अन्ये, इतरे, शिष्टजनाः; 'at o. times' अन्यदा; 'the o. day' अन्येद्युः, नातिचिरं. —**wise**, *adv.* अन्यथा, इतरथा. 2 वा, न-नो-चेत्, अन्यथा, अथवा.

Otter, *s.* उद्रः, जलमार्जारः.

Ought, *v.* Ex. by अर्ह् 1 P; gen. by pot. pass. part. or by pot.; *See* Must.

Ounce, *s.* टंकद्वयं, पणार्धं. 2 द्वीपिन् *m.*

Oust, *v. t.* निःसृ c., निष्कस् c., अपास् 4 U, निराकृ 8 U, बहिष्कृ; *See* Dispel, Drive out.

Out, *adv.* बहिः (with abl.); 'gone o.' बहिर्गत; (with verbs) ex. by निर्, वि, अप, प्र, बहिः; 'to be o.' प्रकाशतां गम् 1 P, प्रकाशीभू 1P; 'the secret is o.' रहस्यं भिन्नं. 2 निर्वापित-*a.*; 'to be o.' प्रशम् 4 P, निर्वा 2 P; 'the lamp was o.' दीपः प्रशशाम-निर्ववौ. 3 क्षीण-विगत-अवसित-*a.* 4 अंतं-शेषं-यावत्, आ-अवसानात्; 'hear me o.' शृणु मे सावशेषं वचः (M. 4); 'let me speak o.' वचः समापयानि तावत्. 5 उच्चैः, उच्च-तार-स्वरेण, मुक्तकंठं. 6 व्यक्तं, प्रकटं, स्पष्टं, स्फुटं; 'o. upon (with) the thief' दूरीक्रियतां-निःसार्यतां-असौ चौरः; 'o. of' बहिः with abl., or by abl. ; (among) मध्यात् with gen., or by gen. or loc.; (exclusion) ex. by अ, निर्, वि, अप, गत, नष्ट, त्यक्त in comp.; 'o. of the road' त्यक्त-भ्रष्ट-मार्ग; 'o. of one's mind' हत-नष्टबुद्धि, बुद्धिभ्रष्ट; 'o. of place' अस्थान, अनुचित; 'o. of order' उत्सूत्र, क्रमहीन, विधिविरुद्ध, अव्यवस्थित; 'o. of tune' अप-वि-स्वर; (showing motive) ex. by instr. or abl.; (beyond) अतीत, अगोचर in comp., अति pr.; 'o. of sight' नयनविषयातीत, दृगगोचर, अंतर्हित; 'o. of one's reach' अविषय, अप्राप्य; 'o. of one's power' अतिशक्ति; 'o. of use' गत-लुप्त-व्यवहार, अव्यवहारित; 'o. of fashion' लोकाचारविरुद्ध; 'o. of time' गतकाल, कालातीत; 'o. of hope' गताश, निराश; 'o. of man's strength' अतिमानुष; 'to pass o. of sight' नयनविषयं अति-इ 2 P or अतिक्रम् 1 U, 4 P; 'stand o. of hearing' श्रवणागोचरस्तिष्ठ; 'o. of employment' क्षीणवृत्ति, निर्व्यापार, नियोगहीन; 'o. of office' भ्रष्ट-च्युत-अधिकार, अधिकारभ्रष्ट-च्युत; 'o. of hand' सद्यः, सपदि; 'o.-door' द्वारबहिःस्थ, बहिःप्रदेशकृत; 'o.-house' उपगृहं, बहिर्गृहं. —*interj.* अपेहि, अपसर, धिक् (with acc.). —**er**, —**ermost**, *a.* बाह्य, बहिःस्थ, बहिर्भव, बहिर्वर्तिन्, बहिः in comp. —**most**, *a.* अतिबाह्य. —**ward**, *a.* बाह्य, बहिः in comp. 2 दृश्य, आविर्भूत, प्रकट, प्रकाश. 3 अवास्तव (वी *f.*), मिथ्या-मृषा in comp. —*adv.* (O. s) बहिः, बहिर्भागे-देशे. —**wardly**, *adv.* बाह्यतः, बहिः, बहिर्भागे. 2 अवस्तुतः, मृषा, मिथ्या, कृतकं, कृत्रिमं.

Out-act, *v. t.* अत्याचर् 1 P, अतिकृ 8 U.

Out-balance, *v. t.* *See* Outweigh.

Out-bid, *v. t.* अधिकमूल्यदानेन अभि-भू 1 P.

Outbreak, **Outburst**, *s.* उद्भेदः, निर्गमः, प्रादुर्भावः, उदयः, आस्फोटः.

Outcast, *s.* निष्कासितः, बहिष्कृतः, जातिबाह्यः-भ्रष्टः, जाति-वर्ण-पतितः, अपांक्तः, अपांक्तेयः, पतितः. 2 चं-(चां)डालः, अपसदः, हीनजातिः-वर्णः, विहीनः, विवर्णः, नीच-अधम-वर्णः; *See* Mean.

Outcry, *s.* उत्क्रोशः, आक्रोशः, कोलाहलः, कलकलः, तुमुलं, संहूति *f.*, उद्घोषः; 'popular o.' जनरवः-संहूतिः. 2 आर्तनादः-रवः.

Outdo, *v. t.* अति-शी 2 A, अतिक्रम् 1 U, 4 P; *See* Excel.

Outfit, *s.* सज्जा, सामग्री, उपकरणसंभारः, परिच्छेदः.

Outgo, *v. t.* अति-इ 2 P, अतिचर् 1 P, अतिगम् 1 P. —**ing**, *s.* व्ययः, अपचयः, क्षयः, विनियोगः.

Outgrow, *v. t.* अतीत्य वृध् 1 A, अति-वृधं.

Outlandish, *a.* विजातीय, विदेशीय, विदेशज, पर-अन्य-देशीय. 2 असंगत, ग्राम्य, अशिष्ट, असभ्य.

Outlaw, *s.* निषिद्धाभ्युदकः, न्यायरक्षणबाह्यः. —*v. t.* न्यायाद् बहिष्कृ 8 U, अभ्युदकदानं निषिध् 1 P.

Outlay, *s.* (द्रव्यादेः) व्ययः, अपचयः, विनियोगः; धनोत्सर्गः, द्रव्यव्ययः.

Outlet, *s.* द्वारं, मुखं, निर्गमः, परि(री)वाहः, जलोच्छ्वासः, निर्गमद्वारं; स्वजनस्य हि दुःखमग्रतो विवृतद्वारमिवोपजायते (K. iv. 26) 'finds an o.' &c.

Outline, *s.* बाह्यले(रे)खा, आकारमात्रं, वस्तुमात्रं. 2 पांडुलेख्यं, चित्रारंभः. 3 स्थूलवर्णनं, असूक्ष्मविचारः.

Outlive, *v. t.* अति-जीव् 1 P.

Outlook, *s.* अवेक्षणं, अवेक्षा.

OUTMARCH, *v. i.* अग्रे या 2 P, अति-या.

OUTNUMBER, *v. t.* संख्यया अति-शी 2 A, आधिकसंख्य-*a.* भू 1 P, अधिकीभू.

OUTPOUR, *v. t.* वृष् 1 P, निषिच् 6 P, उत्सृज् 6 P. –*s.*, –ING, *s.*, वर्षः,-र्षणं, उत्सर्गः.

OUTRAGE, *s.* साहसं, आधर्षः-र्षणं, बलात्कारः, अन्यायः, अत्याचारः, उपमर्दः, उपद्रवः, अभि-,द्रोहः, उपघातः, प्रमाथः, मर्यादातिक्रमः. 2 न्यक्कारः, धिक्कारः; अवलेपः, उत्सेकः. –*v. t.* कलंकयति (D.); (a woman) सतीत्वाद् भ्रंश् c. or च्यु c., दुष् c. (दूषयति), आधृष् c.; उपमृद् c., प्रमंथ् 9 P or c., उप-द्रु 1 P, अभिद्रुह् 4 P, न्यक्कृ 8 U, धिक्कृ; *See* INSULT also. –OUS, *a.* दारुण, घोर, उग्र, अतिदुष्ट, उद्दंड, प्रमाथिन्, अतिसाहसिक (की *f.*), राक्षस (सी *f.*), निर्लज्ज, वीतत्रप, अतिदुराचार. –OUSLY, *adv.* घोरं, दारुणं, अन्याचारपूर्वं, अतिसाहसेन. –OUSNESS, *s.* दारुणता, &c.

OUTREACH, *v. t.* अतिगम् 1 P, अति-इ 2 P.

OUTRIDER, *s.* अश्वारूढः परिचरः.

OUTRIGHT, *adv.* सद्यः, सपदि, तत्क्षणं-णे, अविलंबितं. 2 सर्वथा, सार्वतं, सम्यक्, सु-अति pr. 3 स्पष्टं, व्यक्तं, अवक्रं.

OUTROOT, *v. t.* *See* ERADICATE.

OUTRUN, *v. t.* अतिधाव् 1 P, धावने अति-शी 2 A.

OUTSET, OUTSTART, *s.* प्रारंभः, उप-प्र-क्रमः, आदिः, उपोद्घातः; 'at the very o.' प्रथममेव, आदावेव, उपोद्घातरूपेण.

OUTSHINE, *v. t.* आधिकं प्रकाश् 1 A or द्युत् 1 A, अतिशुभ् 1 A or रुच् 1 A.

OUTSIDE, *s.* बहिर्भागः, बहिःप्रदेशः, बाह्यभागः; oft. by बहिः; 'charming on the o. only' बहिरेव मनोरम. 2 परमावधिः. –*adv.* बहिः (with abl.), बहिर्भागे. –*a.* बाह्य, बहिस्थ, बहिः in comp. –ER, *s.* बहिर्देशवासिन् *m.*, अन्यदेशीयः, पारदेशिकः; *See* FOREIGNER.

OUTSKIRT, *s.* उपांतः, पर्यंतः, सीमा, परिसरः, प्रांतः, उत्संगः; 'o. of a village' ग्रामांतः, उपकंठं; 'o of a forest' वनांतः.

OUTSPOKEN, *a.* स्पष्ट-स्फुट-वादिन्, स्फुटवक्तृ; *See* CANDID, FRANK.

OUTSPREAD, *v. t.* विस्तॄ c., प्र-वि-सृ c., वितन् 8 U.

OUTSTANDING, *a.* अशोधित, अनिष्पन्न, अनिस्तीर्ण.

OUTSTRETCH, *v. t.* प्र-सृ c., उच्छ्रि 1 U or c.; oft. by उत् in comp.; 'with the neck o. ed' उत्कंधर; 'with hands o. ed as far as the wrist' आपूर्वभागोत्थितैः करतलैः (S. 4).

OUTSTRIP, *v. t.* अति-इ 2 P, अतिक्रम् 1 U, 4 P अतिवृत् 1 A, अतिचर् 1 P, लंघ् 1 A, 10; oft. by अति in comp.; 'o. s the senses' इंद्रियगोचरो न वर्तते, अतींद्रियः.

OUTVIE, *v. t.* *See* EXCEL.

OUTWEIGH, *v. t.* भारेण-भारतः-अतिरिच् pass. (with abl.), अधिकभारीभू 1 P, (Excel, q. v.).

OUTWIT, *v. t.* प्र-तॄ c., वंच् 10, वि-प्र-लभ् 1 A; *See* CHEAT.

OVAL, OVATE, *a.* अंडाकार, अंडाकृति. –*s.* अंडाकारः, अंडाकृति *f.*, कक्षा-क्षः.

OVARIOUS, *a.* अंडयुक्त, अंडरूप. –OVARY, *s.* अंडाशयः.

OVEN, *s.* चुल्लि-ल्ली *f.*, कंदु *m. f.*, आपाकः, उखा.

OVER, *prep.* उपरि (with gen.) or in comp., अधि-ऊर्ध्वं in comp.; अधिक in comp.; 'o. 20' विंशत्यधिक; gen. ex. by अति, अधि, अभि, उत्, सं, with verbs; 'cross o. a river' नदीपारं गम् 1 P. 2 (Superiority), प्र, अधि, वि in comp.; 'wander o.' परिभ्रम् 1, 4 P, पर्यट् 1 P; 'o. against' अभि-सं-मुखं, अभि-प्रति pr. –*adv.* परपारं, अन्यतीरं, पारं-रे. 2 प्रति, सं, नि, with verbs; 'hand o. to another' अन्यस्मिन् निक्षिप् 6 P or संक्रम् c. 3 अधिकं, भूयः, अतिरिक्तं. 4 (Beyond) अति pr. 5 अव-,शिष्ट, उद्वृत्त, अंतरित (*a.*); अधिक in comp. 6 सांतं, शेषं यावत्, ex. by पार; 'to read o.' अधि-इ 2 A, पारं गम्. 7 अत्यंतं, अति-सु-pr., अधिकं, अतिशय-एकांत in comp.; as a prefix of verbs, ex. by अति, अत्यंत. 8 अतीत, गत, अतिक्रांत, वृत्त, भूत; 'o. again' पुनरपि; 'o. and o. again' पुनःपुनः, मुहुर्मुहुः, वारंवारं; 'o. and above' अपरं च, अवशिष्ट- *a.*; 'to be o.' ex. by अवसित-अतीत-समाप्त-*a.*; *See* FINISH; 'my work is o.' समाप्तकार्योस्मि; 'in a moment all will be o. with him' क्षणेन स समाप्तजीवितः-परासुः-भवेत्.

OVERACT, *v. t.* अतिशयेन कृ 8 U, अत्याचर् 1 P.

OVERAWE, *v. t.* आकुलीकृ 8 U, भयेन उपहन् 2 P or अभिभू 1 P. –ED, *a.* संभ्रमाकुल, भयोपहत.

OVERBALANCE, *v. t.* *See* OUTWEIGH. –*s.* अति-अधिक-भारः.

OVERBEAR, *v. t.* वशीकृ 8 U, दम् c. (दमयति); नि-पत् c., धृष् c. –ING, *a.* धृष्ट, उद्धत, दृप्त, अवलिप्त, गर्वित, उत्सिक्त; *See* HAUGHTY. –INGLY, *adv.* सावलेपं, सदर्पं, उद्धतं.

OVERBOARD, *adv.* नौपृष्ठात्, नौकाया बहिः, मध्येसमुद्रं, अर्णवमध्ये.

OVERBURDEN, *v. t.* अतिभारं न्यस् 4 U, अतिभारेण पीड् 10 or अर्द् 1 P or c. –ED, *a.* अतिभाराक्रांत.

OVERCAST, *v. t.* (मेघैः) आ-वृ 5 U, प्र-आ-च्छद् 10; कलुषीकृ 8 U, तिमिरीकृ, साभ्र-*a.* कृ. –*a.* मेघावृत, मेघाच्छन्न, तमोवृत, साभ्र, सतिमिर, घनावरुद्ध.

OVER-CAUTIOUS, *a.* अत्यवहित.

OVERCHARGE, *v. t.* अतिमूल्यं अर्थ् 10 A. 2 Overload, q. v. –*s.* अतिमूल्यप्रार्थनं.

OVERCLOUD, *v. t. See* OVERCAST.

OVERCOME, *v. t.* अतिक्रम् 1 U, 4 P, तॄ 1 P, पारं गम् 1 P, आ-अधि-रुह् 1 P, अति-इ 2 P; अति-शी 2 A, अतिरिच् pass. 2 जि 1 P, पराजि (A), परा-अभि-भू 1 P, वशीकृ 8 U, दम् c. (दमयति). 3 प्रधृष् c., पर्यामृश् 6 P; (with fatigue &c.) आकुलीकृ, आक्रम्, खिद् c., अव-सद् c., better by (*a.*); 'o. by the force of truth' सत्यबलेनाभिभूत, भूतार्थवचनेन कुंठितमति or किंकर्तव्यतामूढ; 'I am o. by sleep caused by fatigue' अपह्रियै परिश्रमजनितया निद्रया (U. 1). –*a.* परा-, जित, दांत, वशीकृत &c. 2 अभिभूत, व्याकुल, पर्याकुल, आकुल, आर्त, आतुर, ग्रस्त, आक्रांत, आविष्ट, परिगत, gen. in comp.

OVERDO, *v. t.* अतिशयेन कृ 8 U. 2 अति-पच् 1 P. –OVERDONE, *a.* अतिपक्व. 2 अतिश्रांत, परिक्लांत.

OVEREAT, *v. t.* अति-खाद् 1 P or अद् 2 P.

OVER-ESTIMATE, *v. t.* अति-गण् 10 or मन् 4 P. –*s.* अतिगणना.

OVERFATIGUE, *v. t.* अति-खिद् c. or श्रम् c. –*s.* अतिखेदः, अतिश्रमः.

OVERFLOOD, OVERFLOW, *v. t.* जलेन आ-सं-प्लु c., परिवह् c., उपरि स्रु c., उत्सिच् 6 P or c. –*v. i.* परिवह् 1 P; उत्सिच् pass., प्रवृध् 1 A, स्फाय् 1 A; gen. ex. by अति-,पूर्ण, उत्सिक्त, आ-सं-प्लुत, स्फीत-वृद्ध-जल, प्रचुर, उपचित, आढ्य, घन, अतिरिक्त, उद्रिक्त, वृद्ध, स्फीत; 'with an eye o. ing with joy' आनंदपरिवाहिणा चक्षुषा (S. 4); 'a heart o. ing with kindness' दयाघनं हृदयं; 'my curiosity first o. ed' प्रथमं कुतूहलं सपरिवाहमासीत् (S. 2); 'her eyes o. ed with tears' अश्रुपरिप्लुतेक्षणा सा, अश्रुजलेनाप्लुते नेत्रे. –*s.* पूरोत्पीडः, आस्रावः, उत्सेकः, जलवृद्धि *f.*, तोयास्रावः, जलोत्सेकः. 2 उद्रेकः, अतिरेकः, वृद्धि *f.*, स्फीति *f.*, उपचयः, आधिक्यं, प्राचुर्यं. –ING, *a.* उत्सिक्त, अति-परि-पूर्ण, अति-, बहुल, प्रचुर, आ-सं-प्लुत, उपचित, उद्रिक्त, अतिरिक्त; 'o. with water' जलप्लावित, आप्लुतोदक; 'o. the boundary' अतिवेल. –*s.*, *See* (*s.*); 'to fill to o.' आ-परि-प्लु c.

OVERGROW, *v.* अतिरुह् 1 P, अतिवृध् 1A, अत्यंतं-वृध्.

OVERHANG, *v. t.* उपरि लंब् 1 A, अव-प्र-लंब्, बहिः लंब् or स्था 1 P.

OVERHASTY, *a.* अतिसाहसिन्, साहसपरायण.

OVERHAUL, *v. t.* पुनः पुनः परीक्ष् 1 A or निरूप् 10.

OVERHEAD, *adv.* ऊर्ध्वं, उपरि, उपरिस्थाने; मस्तकोपरि, अधिशीर्षं; 'the sun being o.' नभोमध्यारूढे सवितरि, मध्याह्नकाले.

OVERHEAR, *v. t.* अलक्षितं-निभृतं श्रु 5 P, प्रच्छन्नं आकर्ण् 10.

OVERJOY, *v. t.* प्रहृष् c., अत्यंतं आनंद् c. –*s.* प्रहर्षः, अत्यंतप्रमोदः. –ED, *a.* प्रहृष्ट, परममुदित, हर्षाकुल, आनंदपुलकित, उल्लसित, हृष्टचित्त.

OVERLAP *v. t.* अतिव्याप् 5 P.

OVERLARGE, *a.* अतिविपुल, अतिमहत्.

OVERLAND, *a.* स्थल in comp.; 'o. route' स्थलवर्त्मं, (प्रतस्थे स्थलवर्त्मना R. IV. 60).

OVERLAY, *v. t.* आ-,छद् 10, आ-वृ 5 U, पि-धा 3 U, पि-नह् 4 P. 2 अतिभारेण पीड् 10.

OVERLEAP, *v. t.* उत् लंघ् 1 A, 10, उत्प्लु 1 A.

OVER-LENIENT, *a.* एकांत-अति-मृदु.

OVERLOAD *v. t.* अतिपूर् 10, अतिभारं न्यस् 4 U or आरुह् c. (रोपयति) ; अतिभारेण आक्रम् 1 U, 4 P or पीड् 10. –ED, *a.* अतिपूरित-पूर्ण, अतिभाराक्रांत. –ING, *s.* अतिभारारोपणं, अतिभारन्यासः.

OVERLOOK, *v. t.* उपेक्ष् 1 A, न गण् 10 or दृश् 1 P, न आदृ 6 A, क्षम् 1 A, 4 P, अवसृज् 6 P, मुच् 6 P. 2 अवेक्ष्, अधि-ष्ठा 1 P, अध्यक्षः भू 1 P. 3 आ-अव-लोक् 1 A, 10; *See* COMMAND.

OVERMUCH, *a.* अतिमात्र, अत्यंत, अत्यधिक, एकांत, अतिरिक्त, अति pr. –*s.* आधिक्यं, अतिबाहुल्यं, अतिरेकः. –*adv.* अत्यंतं, अतिमात्रं, अति-सु pr.

OVERNIGHT, *adv.* अतीतरात्रौ, गतनिशायां.

OVERPASS, *v. t.* अतिचर् 1 P, अतिगम् 1 P.

OVERPAY, *v. t.* अधिकमूल्यं दा 3 U.

OVERPEOPLED, *a.* अतिजनाकीर्ण.

OVERPLUS, *s. See* SURPLUS.

OVERPOWER, *v. t.* परा-अभि-भू 1 P, पराजि 1 A, आक्रम् 1 U, 4 P; *See* OVERCOME.

OVERPRIZE, OVERRATE, *v. t.* अधिकं मन् 4 A or c., अतिमूल्यं स्था c. (स्थापयति).

OVERREACH, *v. t.* प्र-तॄ c., वंच् 10, विप्र-लभ् 1 A. –ING, *s.* प्रतारणं-णा, वंचनं; *See* CHEAT.

OVERRIDE, *v. t.* अति-धाव् 1 P. 2 Overrule, q. v.

OVERRULE, *v. t.* अधः क्षिप् 6 P, निराकृ 8 U, अधरीकृ, प्रत्यादिश् 6 P; *See* REJECT. 2 प्र-भू 1 P, ईश् 2 A (with gen.), अधि-ष्ठा 1 P, शास् 2 P, नियम् 1 P.

OVERRUN, *v. t.* उप-द्रु 1 A, आक्रम् 1 U, 4 P, उप-अभि-द्रु 1 P, व्याप् 5 P, आकॄ 6 P; *See* HARASS, OPPRESS.

OVERSEE, *v. t.* अवेक्ष् 1 A, अधि-ष्ठा 1 P. –ER, *s.* अवेक्षकः, अधिष्ठातृ *m.*, अध्यक्षः, अधिकृतः, अधिकारिन् *m.*

OVERSET, *v. t.* वि-,पर्यस् 4 U, परिवृत् c.; अधरीकृ 8 U, निपत् c., अधः क्षिप् 6 P. –*v. i.* परिवृत् 1 A, नि-पत् 1 P.

OVERSHADOW, *v. t.* आ-,छद् 10, छायया आवृ 5 U.

OVERSHOOT, *v. t.* लक्ष्यं अतिक्रम् 1 U, 4 P, लक्ष्याद् भ्रंश् 1 A, 4 P or च्यु 1 A.

OVERSIGHT, *s.* अनवेक्षा, प्रमादः, भ्रमः; भ्रांति *f.*, स्खलितं, दृष्टिदोषः.

OVERSLEEP, *v. i.* अति-दीर्घं-स्वप् 2 P.

OVERSPREAD, *v. t.* आच्छद् 10; आ-वृ 5 U, आस्तृ 5 U, आस्तॄ 9 U, पूर् 10, आक्रम् 1 U, 4 P, आ-सं-कॄ 6 P, वि-अव-तन् 8 U, व्याप् 5 P. —*a.* आच्छन्न, आच्छादित, आवृत, आस्तीर्ण, आक्रांत, आकीर्ण' व्याप्त, पूरित, पूर्ण.

OVERSTATE, *v. t.* अतिशयेन वच् 2 P; *See* EXAGGERATE.

OVERSTEP, *v. t.* अतिक्रम् 1 U, 4 P, लंघ् 1 A, 10.

OVERSTOCK, *v. t.* अति-पूर् 10 or संग्रह् 9 P or उपक्लृप् c., प्र-सं-चि 5 U. —*s.* अतिसंचयः-संग्रहः-संभारः.

OVERSTRAIN, *v. i.* अत्यंतं यत् 1 A or उद्यम् 1 A.

OVERT, *a.* प्रकाश, स्फुट, व्यक्त, स्पष्ट, अगूढ, प्रकट, प्रत्यक्ष. —LY, *adv.* प्रकाशं, स्पष्टं, प्रत्यक्षं, प्रकटं —NESS, *s.* स्फुटता, व्यक्तता.

OVERTAKE, *v. t.* आ-सद् c., (पूर्वप्रस्थितं वैनतेयमप्यासादयेयं V. 1), लंघ् 1 A, 10; आत्मोद्धतैरपि रजोभिरलंघनीयाः (S. 1); 'not to be o.-n' &c.; सं-,प्राप् 5 P, आक्रम् 1 U, 4 P, ग्रह् 9 P. 2 अभि-भू 1 P, धृ 1 P, 10, ग्रस् 1 A; सहसा-अकस्मात्-आपत् 1 P or आक्रम्; *See* ATTACK, OVERCOME; 'o. business' कार्यं समाप् c.

OVERTASK, OVERTAX, *v. t.* अतिभारं-अतिकरं-न्यस् 4 U or निक्षिप् 6 P.

OVERTHROW, *v. t.* नश् c., वि-प्र-°, क्षि 1, 5 P, ध्वंस् c., प्र-वि-उत्°, उच्छिद् 7 P, अव-उत्-सद् c. 2 परिवृत् c., परि-विपरि-अस् 4 U, पराक्षिप् 6 P or c., अधोमुखीकृ 8 U, निपत् c. 3 जि 1 P, पराजि (A.), अभि-परा-भू 1 P, दम् c. (दमयति), वशीकृ 8 U, परास् 4 U, भंज् 7 P, पराहन् 2 P. —*s.* नाशः, ध्वंसः, प्र-वि-°,उच्छेदः, उत्सादः, क्षयः. 2 घातः, भंगः, भेदः, परा-अभि-भवः, पराजयः, व्यसनं. 3 परिवर्तनं, पर्यासः, निपातनं.

OVERTOP, *v. t.* मूर्ध्नि-शिखरे-स्था 1 P, अति-शी 2 A, अभि-भू 1 P; *See* EXCEL.

OVERTURE, *s.* प्रस्तावः, उपन्यासः, उपक्षेपः, निवेदनं, प्रार्थना, वचनं ; 'secret o.' उपजापः. 2 प्रस्तावना, उपोद्घातः.

OVERTURN, *v. t.* परि-विपरि-अस् 4 U, परिवृत् c., निपत् c., अधोमुखीकृ 8 U, अधरोत्तरीकृ. 2 Overthrow, q. v.

OVERVALUE, *v. t.* अधिकं मन् 4 A or c., बहु मन्, अधिकमूल्यं कृ 8 U or स्था c. (स्थापयति).

OVERWEENING, *a.* अत्यभिमानिन्, अतिदृप्त, अत्यवलिप्त, अतिश्लाघिन्.

OVERWHELM, *v. t.* अभि-भू 1 P, आकुलीकृ 8 U, ग्रस् 1 A, आक्रम् 1 U, 4 P; अव-सद् c., अव-सं-मृद् 9 P or c., अव-नि पत् c., निक्षिप् 7 P. 2 आ-वृ 5 U, आस्तृ-स्तॄ 5, 9 U, आच्छद् 10, आकॄ 6 P. 3 नि-,मस्ज् c. (मज्जयति), गाह् c., अव-वि-°, प्लु c., आ-सं-परि-°. —ED, *a.* अभिभूत, ग्रस्त, आक्रांत, मग्न, आकीर्ण, उपप्लुत, उपद्रुत, आकुल; *See* OVERCOME; 'o. with grief' शोकसमाकुल; 'o. with a flood of tears' बाष्पपूरपरिप्लुत.

OVERWORK, *v. t.* अधिकं कर्म कृ c., अत्यंतं आयस् c. or खिद् c.; (oneself) अत्यंतं परिश्रम् 4 P. —अत्यायासः, अतिक्लेशः-श्रमः.

OVERWROUGHT, *a.* अतिपरिष्कृत.

OVERZEAL, *s.* अत्यौत्सुक्यं, अत्युत्कंठा. —OUS, *a.* अत्युत्सुक, अत्यासक्त, अतिव्यग्र.

OVIFORM, *a.* अंडाकृति, कोशाकार.

OVIPAROUS, *a.* अंडज, द्विज, द्विजन्मन्, अंडोत्पन्न.

OWE, *v. t.* धृ 10 (with dat. of creditor). 2 ऋणबद्ध-*a.* भू 1 P, अनुगृहीत-*a.* भू; oft. ex. by pot. pass. part.; 'you o. respect to your elders' गुरुजनस्त्वया पूज्यः. —ING, *a.* देय, दातव्य, शोधनीय, निस्तार्य. 2 जनित, जात, उद्भूत, प्रयुक्त, कारण-प्रभव-हेतु- in comp.; 'o. to' ex. by abl. or instr.; 'to whom is your deliverance o.' कस्त्वन्मुक्तिहेतुः-कारणं, केन त्वं मोचितः.

OWL, *s.* कौशिकः, उलूकः, पेचकः, दिवाभीतः, दिवांधः, घूकः, निशाटनः, वायसारातिः; 'o.-light' मंदप्रभा, ईषत्प्रकाशः.

OWN, *a.* स्वीय, स्वकीय, आत्मीय, स्वक, निज, आत्मभूत; स्व, आत्मन् in gen. or in comp.; 'my o.' मदीय; so त्वदीय, तदीय, युष्मदीय, अस्मदीय; 'of one's o. accord' स्वयं, स्वेच्छया; 'to make one's o.' आत्मसात् कृ 8 U. —*v. t.* स्वीकृ, अंगीकृ, प्रति-पद् 4 A, अभ्युप-गम् 1 P or इ 2 P, ग्रह् 9 P, *See* ACKNOWLEDGE. 2 (To be master of) ex. by स्वामी, ईश्वरः, पतिः, अधिकारी, with gen. or by (*a.*) ; or by gen. alone; 'I o. much land' विपुलभूमेः स्वाम्यहं; 'who o. s this treasure' कोऽस्य वित्तस्य स्वामी-पतिः, कस्येदं वित्तं. 3 स्वत्वं प्रति-पद् c. or बुध् c., स्वीय-*a.* इति वद् 1 P; *See* CLAIM. —ED, *a.* स्वीकृत; स्वत्वविशिष्ट; 'o. by me' मत्स्वत्वविशिष्ट, मत्स्वामिक, मदधीन. —ER, *s.* स्वामी, ईश्वरः, पतिः, अधिकारी, ईशः, प्रभुः; *See* LORD. —ERSHIP, *s.* स्वत्वं, स्वामित्वं, स्वाम्यं, प्रभुत्वं, अधिकारः. —ING, *s.* स्वीकारः, अभ्युपगमः.

OX, *s.* वृषभः, वृषः, उक्षन् *m.*, बली(री)वर्दः, ऋषभः, अनडुह् *m.*, गौः, भद्रः, सौरभेयः; 'a herd of oxen ' औक्षकं; ' a large o. ' महोक्षः; ' an old o. ' वृद्धोक्षः, जरद्गवः; ' head of a herd of oxen ' आर्षभ्यः; ' an o. allowed to go at liberty ' षंडः, गोपतिः, इट्चरः; ' his shoulder ' वहः; ' the dewlap of an o.' सास्ना, गलकंबलः; ' who bears the yoke ' युग्यः; धूर्वोढा; ' who draws a cart ' शाकटः; ' who draws a plough ' हालिकः, सैरिकः; ' who bears a burden ' धूर्वहः, धूर्यः, धुरीणः, धौरेयः, धुरंधरः.

OXIDIZE, *v. t.* जॄ c. –OXIDATION, *s.* जारणं, आतंचनं.

OYSTER, *s.* शुक्ति *f.*, शुक्तिका, मुक्तास्फोटः; ' o.-shell ' शुक्तिपुटं.

P.

PABULUM, *s.* भोजनं, आहारः, पौष्टिकं. –PABULAR, *a.* पौष्टिक (की *f.*).

PACE, *s.* पदं, चरणन्यासः, पदविक्षेपः-पातः-क्रमः, पादविक्षेपः-न्यासः, विक्रमः. 2 गति *f.*, गमनं, अयनं, चलनं, चारः. 3 गतिवेगः-क्रमः; 'a quick p.' द्रुतपदं; 'at a rapid p.' द्रुतगत्या. 4 (Of horses) धारा, गतिः; *See* under HORSE ; ' a horse with a good p. ' सुखायनः, सुखचारः; ' keep p. with ' सह गम् or चल् 1 P. –*v. i.* परि-अति-क्रम् 1 U, 4 P; क्रमेण क्रमेण गम्-व्रज्-चल् 1 P; ' p. up and down ' इतस्ततः चल् or भ्रम् 1, 4 P; ' p. ing to and fro ' इतस्ततः परिक्रम्य. –ED, *a.* गति in comp.; ' slow-p. ' मंदगति, मंदगामिन्.

PACIFY, *v. t.* सां(शां)त्व् 10, शम् c. (शमयति), प्र-उप-°, प्र-सद् c., सं-परि-तुष् c , आराध् c. –IED, *a.* शांत, प्रसादित, शांतक्रोध; ' to be p. ' शम् 4 P, प्रसद् 1 P, तुष् 4 P, शमं इ-या 2 P. –IER, *s.* शमकः, सांत्वकः. –IC, *a.* शांत, प्रशमित, निरुद्वेग. 2 सांत्व-प्रशम-शील; सांत्वनकारिन्, साम in comp.; ' p. words ' सामवादः. –ICATION, *s.* शमः, शमनं, शांति *f.*, प्र-उप-°, सांत्वनं, सामन् *n.*, प्रसादनं. 2 संधानं, संधिकरणं. –ICATORY, *a.* शांतिद, शांतिकर (री *f.*), शमक, सामोपायक, साम in comp.

PACK, *s.* भारः, कूर्चः, भांडं, गुच्छः, पोटलिका, पटलं. 2 गणः, संघः, वर्गः, समूहः, वृंदं, संचयः; *See* MULTITUDE; ' p. of hounds' श्वगणः, कुक्कुरसंघः; ' a p. of persons ' मंडलं, जनसमूहः; ' p.-horse ' पृष्ठ्यः, स्थौरिन्; ' p.-saddle ' पर्याणं, पल्ययनं; ' p.-thread ' शणसूत्रं; ' p.-cloth ' वेष्टनं, पटः. –*v. t.* पटलीकृ 8 U, पुटीकृ, पुटयति (D.), सपिंड् 10, कूर्चीकृ; ' p. in a box ' समुद्गके नि-धा 3 U or निविश् c. 2 कुकर्मार्थं-उपदंशपूर्वं-संमिल् c. or समाहृ 1 P or एकीकृ or संयुज् 7 U, 10. 3 (Off) अप-निः-सृ c., सहसा अपगम् c. (गमयति) or प्र-स्था c. (स्थापयति). –*v. i.* पुटीभू 1 P, पिंडीभू, एकीभू. 2 सहसा अपगम् 1 P or प्र-स्था 1 A. –AGE, *s.* भांडं, कूर्चः, वस्त्रादिगुच्छः. –PACKET, *s.* पोटलिका, लघुकूर्चः, लघुवेष्टनं; पत्रवेष्टनं. 2 पत्रवाहिनी नौः.

PACT, *s. See* CONTRACT.

PAD, *s.* कूर्चः. 2 उपधानं, उपबर्हः. 3 सुखायनः, सुखचारः. 4 पादविक्रमः. 5 मृदुवस्तु *n.*, तुलादिद्रव्यं. –*v. t.* मृदुवस्तुना आ-स्तृ 5 U or युज् 7 U, 10. –*v. i.* मंदं-शनैः-गम् or व्रज् 1 P.

PADDLE, *s.* क्षेपणि-णी *f.*, नौदंडः ; ' p.-box ' क्षेपण्याधारः ; ' p.-wheel ' नौचालनी. –*v. t.* नौदंडेन प्रेर् c. or चल् c. or प्रणुद् 6 P or c. –*v. i.* क्षेपण्या जलं चल् c. or आहन् 2 U or तड् 10. 2 जले क्रीड् 1 P.

PADDOCK, *s.* वाटः, वाटिका.

PADDY, *s.* धान्यं.

PADLOCK, *s.* तालकं.

PÆAN, *s.* जयशब्दः-ध्वनिः-घोषः.

PAGAN, *s.* देवता-प्रतिमा-पूजकः. –ISM, *s.* देवतार्चनं, प्रतिमापूजा-उपासना; *See* IDOLATER,-TRY.

PAGE, *s.* पृष्ठं, पत्रं. 2 चेटः, किंकरः, भृत्यः, पार्श्वानुचरः, परिचरः, बालानुचरः.

PAGEANT, *s.* आडंबरः, शोभा; चमत्कारः. कौतुकं. –*a.* Ex. by (*s.*). –RY, *s.* आडंबरः; *See* (*s.*).

PAGODA, *s. See* TEMPLE.

PAIL, *s.* भांडं, पात्रं, भाजनं.

PAIN, *s.* दुःखं, वेदना, पीडा, व्यथा, आतंकः, रुज् *f.*, रुजा, अ-आर्ति *f.*, सं-परि-तापः, बाधा, यातना, क्लेशः, कष्टं, कृच्छ्रं, उद्वेगः, खेदः; ' bodily p. ' व्याधिः; ' mental p. ' आधिः, मनस्तापः, मनोव्यथा, चित्तोद्वेगः ; ' causing p. ' पीडा-दुःख-कर (री *f.*); ' suffering p. ' दुःखभाक्, दुःखित ; ' sharp p. ' शूलः-लं, तीव्रवेदना. 2 (Pains) परि-,श्रमः, प्र-,यत्नः, उद्योगः, व्यवसायः, उद्यमः, उत्साहः, आ-प्र-यासः, कष्टं; ' to take p. s ' प्रयत् 1 A, उद्यम् 1 A, चेष्ट् 1 A, घट् 1A, व्यव-सो 4 P. 3 दंडः, साहसं. –*v. t.* पीड् 10, दु 5 P, व्यथ् c. (व्यथयति), तप् c., सं-परि-उप-°, बाध् 1 A, क्लिश् 9 P, अर्द् 1 P or c., दुःखयति (D.). –ED, *a.* पीडित, दून, दुःखित, व्यथित, तापित, सं-परि-तप्त, आर्त, दुःखार्त, दुःखातुर, सवेदन, कृच्छ्रगत, सव्यथ ; ' to be p. ' व्यथ् 1 A, पीड्-क्लिश्-तप्-pass. –FUL, *a.* सरुज, रुजावत्, दुःखित, सव्यथ, दुःखार्त ; *See* PAINED. 2 दुःखद, कष्ट, पीडा-दुःख-कष्ट-व्यथा-कर (री *f.*), दुःखावह, कष्ट-क्लेश-द-प्रद, बाधक, संतापक. 3 श्रम-कष्ट-साध्य, दुष्कर, कठिन. –FULLY, *adv.* सव्यथं, कष्टं, सदुःखं, सोद्वेगं. 2 सश्रमं, सायासं, कृच्छ्रेण, कष्टेन. –LESS, *a.* दुःख-व्यथा-

हीन-रहित. –PAINSTAKING, *a.* व्यवसायिन्, उद्यमिन्, उद्योगिन्, उद्यम-उत्साह-शील; *See* INDUSTRIOUS.

PAINT, *v. t.* आ-लिख् 6 P, चित्र् 10. 2 रंज् c., वर्ण् 10, रंगेण लिप् 6 P, वर्णैः शुभ् c. 3 वर्ण्; *See* DESCRIBE. –*s.* वर्णकः-कं, वर्णिका, रंगः, लेपः; 'p.-brush' वर्तिका, तूलिका, तूलि *f.*, वर्णतूली, ईषिका. –ED, *a.* चित्रित, वर्णित; (in a picture) चित्र-आलेख्य-गत, चित्रार्पित, आलिखित. –ER, *s.* चित्रक-(का)रः, रंगाजीवः, चित्रकृत्-लिख् *m.*, रंजकः, चित्रकः, आलेखकः, तौलिकः. –ING, *s.* (Art) चित्रकर्मन् *n.*, चित्रक्रिया-विद्या. 2 आलेखनं, वर्णनं, रंजनं, चित्रलेखनं. 3 आलेख्यं, चित्रं; 'drawn in a p.' आलेख्यगत; 'p. on the body' पत्ररेखा, पत्ररचना, पत्रावलि-ली *f.*

PAIR, *s.* युगं, युगलं, युग्मं, द्वितयं, द्वयं, यमलं-कं, युतकं; द्वंद्वं, मिथुनं, दंपती in comp. (of animate beings only); 'a p. of swans' हंसदंपती; 'a married p.' भार्यापती, जायापती, दंपती, जंपती, स्त्रीपुरुषौ. –*v. t.* संयुज् 7 U, 10; oft. ex. by 'Match' q. v.; 'well-p. ed rivals' तुल्यप्रतिद्वंद्विनौ. –*v. i.* मैथुनं आचर् 1 P or कृ 8 U, स्त्रीपुरुषवत् संगम् 1 A.

PALACE, *s.* प्रासादः, हर्म्यं, सौधः-धं, राजकुलं, राज-नृप-गृहं-भवनं-मंदिरं (House, q. v). –PALATIAL, *a.* महत्, विशाल, राजयोग्य; 'p. building' महाभवनं.

PALÆSTRA, *s.* मल्लभूमि *f.*

PALANQUIN, *s.* नरयानं, शिविका, चतुरस्रयानं, याप्ययानं.

PALATE, *s.* तालु *n.*, काकुदं; 'soft p.' शुंडिका, अलिजिह्वा. 2 रुचि *f.*, अभिरुचिः. –ABLE, *a.* आस्वाद्य, सुरस, स्वादु, रुच्य, रुचिकर (री *f.*), सरस, रसिक. –AL,-IAL, *a.* तालव्य.

PALAVER, *See* FLATTER,-Y.

PALE, *a.* पांडु, पांडुर, विवर्ण, गतवर्ण, नीरक्त, मंदच्छाय, गतश्रीक; 'he grew or turned p.' विवर्णभावं प्रपेदे, पांडुच्छायो बभूव. 2 मंदप्रभ, मंदद्युति-कांति, हततेजस्, निस्तेजस्, मलिन-म्लान-प्रभ-कांति. 3 (Of colours) श्वेत, ईषत्, आ, in comp.; 'p. blue' आनील, श्वेतनील. –*s.* शलाका, शल्यं, शूलः-लं, शंकुः, स्थाणुः. 2 वृति *f.*, आवरणं, वेष्टनं, वरणः. –*v. t.* (शंकुपंक्त्या) आ-परि-वृ 5 U or c., परिवेष्ट् 1 A or c., अवरुध् 7 U. –ING, *s.* शंकुपंक्ति *f.*, आवरणं. –ISH, *a.* आपांडु, आपांडुर. –NESS, *s.* पांडुता, वैवर्ण्यं, पांडुवर्णः-रागः. 2 तेजः-प्रभा-हानि *f.*, कांतिक्षयः; न्यूनप्रभा.

PALFREY, *s.* लघुवाजिन् *m.*, क्षुद्रघोटकः.

PALINDROME, *s.* मुरजबंधः.

PALISADE, *s.* स्तंभ-शंकु-पंक्ति *f.*-वलयः-यं, अवरोधकं.

PALL, *s.* वासस् *n.*, प्रावारः, प्रच्छदपटः. 2 प्रेतपटः, प्रेतवासस् *n.*, शवाच्छादनं. –*v. t.* विरसीकृ 8 U, अरुचिं उत्पद् c. –*v. i.* विरसीभू 1 P.

PALLADIUM, *s.* पुर-नगर-देवता, रक्षादेवता. 2 रक्षालक्षणं.

PALLET, *s.* खट्वा, लघुतल्पः. 2 वर्ण-रंग-पत्रं.

PALLIATE, *v. t.* (दोषं) लघूकृ 8 U, प्र-उप-शम् c. (शमयति), लंघयति (D.), प्रमृज् 2 P, क्षल् 10, आच्छद् 10. –ION, *s.* प्र-उप-शमः-शांति *f.*, लघूकरणं, दोष-पाप-मार्जनं-क्षालनं-शमः. –IVE, *a.* उपशमन (नी *f.*), शांतिप्रद, शमक. –*s.* पाप-दोष-शमनं. 2 उपशमनं, शूलघ्नं, क्लेशापहं.

PALLID, PALLOR, *See* PALE,-NESS.

PALM, *s.* तलः-लं, प्रहस्तः, प्रपाणिः, प्रतलः, चपेटः, चर्पटः, करतलः; 'the p. s joined' संहततलः, संतलः; 'the hollowed p.' प्रसृतः-तिः, चुलुकः; 'joining the p. s together' बद्धांजलि, कृतांजलि, अंजलिपुटं कृत्वा. 2 (Tree) तालः, तृणद्रुमः, द्रुमेश्वरः; (the fruit) तालं; 'p. of victory' जयध्वजः-लक्षणं; 'p. of superiority' गुणाधिक्यपताका. –*v. t.* करतले गुप् 1 P or गुह् 1 U. 2 (Off) प्रत्ट् c., वंच् 10; *See* CHEAT; 'the trick was p. ed off upon him' तेन छद्मना असौ सम्यग् विप्रलब्धः. –ATE, –ATED, *a.* करतलाकृति. –Y, *a.* तालावृत, तालसंकीर्ण. 2 समृद्ध, श्रीमत्, विभव-भूतिं in comp.; 'p. days' विभवकालः, विभवः.

PALMA-CHRISTI, *s.* एरंडः, उरुबूकः, रूबू(बु)कः, रुचकः, चित्रकः, चंचुः, पंचांगुलः, मंडः, वर्धमानः, व्यडंबकः.

PALMISTER, *s.* सामुद्रज्ञः, सामुद्रिकः. –PALMISTRY, *s.* सामुद्रिकं, सामुद्रविद्या.

PALMIPED, *a.* जालपाद (पदी *f.*).

PALMYRA, *s.* *See* PALM (2).

PALPABLE, *a.* स्पर्शेंद्रिय-गोचर, स्पृश्य. 2 स्थूल, घन, गाढ, निबिड. 3 स्पष्ट, सुविज्ञेय, प्रत्यक्ष, व्यक्त. –PALPABLY, *adv.* स्फुटं, व्यक्तं, प्रत्यक्षं.

PALPITATE, *v. i.* वेप् 1 A, कंप् 1 A, स्पंद् 1 A, स्फुर् 6 P, उच्छ्वस् 2 P. –ION, *s.* स्पंदनं, कंपः, स्फुरणं, स्फुरितं, वेपनं, वेपथुः.

PALSY, *s.* स्तंभः, सं-वि-°, स्वापः, सुप्ति *f.* 2 पक्षाघातः, पक्षवायुः. –*v. t.* स्तंभ् 9 P or c., जडीकृ 8 U, स्वप् c., चैतन्यं नश् c. –IED,–ICAL, *a.* पक्षवायुग्रस्त.

PALTER, *v.* *See* PREVARICATE.

PALTRY, *a.* क्षुद्र, लघु, तुच्छ, असार, अपकृष्ट, अधम, कु pr., कुत्सित.

PAMPER, *v. t.* (अत्यंतं) स्फाय् c. (स्फावयति), संवृध् c., आप्यै c., परि-,पुष् c., संतृप् c., पूर् 10. –ED, *a.* स्फात, परिपुष्ट, हृष्टपुष्ट, आपीन, आप्यायित. –ER, *s.* अतिपोषकः, आप्यायकः. –ING, *s.* स्फीति *f.*, परिपोषणं, आप्यायनं.

PAMPHLET, *s.* पत्रिका, लघुपुस्तकं. –EER, *s.* पत्रिकाकार:, लघुपुस्तककृत् *m.*

PAN, *s.* भाजनं, पात्रं, भांडं, आधार:; ' frying p. ' अंबरीषं, भ्राष्ट्र:; *See* under FRY; ' p.-cake ' भृष्टापूप:.

PANACEA, *s.* सर्वरोगघ्नं औषधं, त्रैलोक्यचिंतामणि:.

PANCRATIUM, *s.* मल्लयुद्धं-क्रीडा. –PANCRATIC, *a.* मल्लक्रीडानिपुण.

PANDECT, *s.* विद्यासंग्रह:. 2 स्मृतिसंहिता.

PANDEMIC, *a.* सर्वजनीन, सार्वलौकिक (की *f.*), सर्वसामान्य; ' p. disease ' जनपदोद्ध्वंस:.

PANDEMONIUM, *s.* रक्ष:सभा, पिशाचसभा.

PANDER,-ER, *s.* नर्मसचिव:, विट:, सुरतदूत:, कुंडाशिन् *m.*, संचारक:. –*v. t.* सुरतकामान् सं-पद् c., लांपट्यं प्रयुज् 7 A, 10. –ING,–ISM, *s.* कौट्टिन्यं, विटकार्य.

PANDICULATION, *s.* *See* STRETCHING.

PANE, *s.* काचफलक:-शिला.

PANEGYRIC, *s.* स्तुति *f.*, श्लाघा, प्रशंसा. स्तुतिवाद:-पाठ:, गुणवर्णनं-कीर्तनं. –AL, *a.* स्तुतिमय (यी *f.*), प्रशंसात्मक. –PANEGYRIZE, *v. t.* स्तु 2 U, श्लाघ् 1 A, प्रशंस् 1 P; *See* PRAISE. –PANEGYRIST, *s.* संस्तावक:, वैतालिक:, वंदिन् *m.*, मागध:, स्तुतिपाठक:.

PANEL, *s.* कपाट:-टं, अरर:-री-रं; शाखा, भाग:. 2 स्थेयगण:,-पत्रं.

PANG, *s.* वेदना, यातना, व्यथा, पीडा; (extreme) कारणा, अतिव्यथा; *See* PAIN.

PANIC, *s.* संत्रास:, समुद्वेग:, महासाध्वसं, विभ्रव:, आकस्मिकभयं, त्रास:; ' p.-struck or -seized ' संत्रस्त, भयविप्लुत, विद्रावित; ' p. in an army ' पिंजल:, समुत्पिंज:. 2 अणु:, प्रियंगु:.

PANNEL, *s.* पर्याणं.

PANNIER, *s.* कंडोल:, पिट:, पे(पि)टक:, करंड:.

PANOPLY, *s.* सर्वांगत्रं, सर्वांगकवच:. –IED, *a.* संवर्मित, कृतसन्नाह.

PANORAMA, *s.* विश्वदृश्यं.

PANT, *v. i.* वेप् 1 A, स्पंद् 1 A, कंप् 1 A, उद्-ध्मा 1 P, स्फुर् 6 P, उच्छ्वस् 2 P. 2 कृच्छ्रेण निश्वस्, दीर्घ-स्थूलस्थूलं-निश्वस्. 3 सोत्कंठं स्पृह् 10 or अभिलष् 1, 4 P; *See* LONG. –*s.*,–ING, *s.* कंप:, स्फुरणं; कृच्छ्रोच्छ्वास:, उच्छ्वास:, स्थूलस्थूलनिश्वास:.

PANTALOON, *s.* जंघावस्त्रं-परिधानं. 2 भंड:, विदूषक:, वैहासिक:.

PANTHEIST, *s.* विश्वदेवतावादिन् *m.* –PANTHEISM, *s.* विश्वदेवतावाद:, वैश्वदेवमतं. –PANTHEON, *s.* विश्वदेवतागण:, विश्वदेवकुलं.

PANTHER, *s.* द्वीपिन् *m.*

PANTOMIME, *s.* मुग्धनर्तक:, केवलं अभिनेतृ *m.*, मूकाभिनेता. 2 मुग्धाभिनय:, लास्यं, नि:शब्दलास्यं-हाव:.

PANTRY, *s.* अन्नकोष्ठ:, भक्ष्यागारं.

PAP, *s.* चूचुकं, स्तनाग्रं. 2 स्तन:, कुच:. 3 मृदु खाद्यं.

PAPA, *s.* तात:, पिता; *See* FATHER.

PAPER, *s.* पत्रं, पत्रकं; ' written p. ' लेख:, लिखितं, पत्रिका, लेख्यं. –*v. t.* पत्रेण आच्छद् 10 or आस्तृ 5 U.

PAPPY, *a.* मज्जायुक्त, मृदु, कोमल.

PAPULÆ, *s.* वि-,स्फोट:, पिटि(ट)का.

PAR, *s.* समता, तुल्यता, साम्यं, सम-तुल्य-भाव:; ' at p. ' सम, तुल्य. –ITY, *s.* साम्यं; तुल्यत्वं.

PARABLE, *s.* उपमा, दृष्टांत:, निदर्शनं. –PARABOLIC, *a.* दृष्टांतरूप.

PARABOLA, *s.* अनुवृत्तं.

PARADE, *s.* आडंबर:, दंभ:, बाह्यशोभा. 2 यात्रा, सैन्ययात्रा. 3 शस्त्राभ्यास:, अस्त्र-रण-शिक्षा, युद्धाभ्यास:, व्यायाम:, योग्या; ' p.-ground ' व्यायामभूमि *f.* –*v. t.* सदंभं-साडंबरं-दृश् c. 2 सैनिकान् व्यायम् c. or शस्त्रव्यापारं शिक्ष् c. –*v. i.* सदंभं पर्यट् 1 P or भ्रम् 1, 4 P.

PARADIGM, *s.* निदर्शनं, रूपनिदर्शनं; ' p. of verbs ' धातुरूपादर्श:.

PARADISE, *s.* वैकुंठं, स्वर्ग:, स्वर्लोक:, सुखभवनं; *See* HEAVEN. 2 नंदनवनं. –PARADISIACAL, *a.* स्वर्गीय, स्वर्ग्य.

PARADOX, *s.* असत्याभास:, विरुद्धमतं. –ICAL, *a.* अयुक्ताभास, लोकविरुद्ध.

PARAGON, *s.* प्रतिमा, उपमा, आदर्श:, प्रतिरूपं; *See* MODEL. 2 अनुपमं वस्तु.

PARAGRAPH, *s.* परिच्छेद:, खंड:, भाग:, वाक्यखंड:-विच्छेद:.

PARALLAX, *s.* लंबनं.

PARALLEL, *a.* समांतर. 2 सदृश (शी *f.*), समान, सम, तुल्य, संवादिन्, समरूप, अनुरूप. –*s.* समांतररेखा; ' p. of latitude ' अक्षवृत्तं. 2 सादृश्यं, साम्यं, समता, आनुरूप्यं, उपमा, प्रतिमा, प्रतिरूपं; having no p. ', ' un-p.ed ' अनुपम, अद्वितीय; *See* MATCHLESS. –*v. t.* समांतरीकृ 8 U. 2 उप-प्रतिमा 3 A, 2 P, तुल् 10. 3 समीभू 1 P, संवद् 1 P. –ISM, *s.* समांतरं, सादृश्यं.

PARALLELOGRAM, *s.* समांतरचतुर्भुज:.

PARALLELOPIPED, *s.* समांतरखात:.

PARALYSIS, *s.* स्तंभ:, स्वाप:, जाड्यं, साद:, पक्षाघात:; ' p. of limbs ' अंगभंग:, गात्रोपघात:, गात्रसाद:. –PARALYTIC, *a.* सुप्तत्वच्, स्तब्धगात्र, पक्षवायुग्रस्त. –PARALYZE, *v. t.* संस्तंभ् 9 P, जडीकृ 8 U, अव-,सद् c., स्वप् c.; ' my limbs are p.-ed ' सीदंति मम गात्राणि.

PARAMOUNT, *a.* प्रधानतम, सर्वाधीश, परम, विं-

शिष्ट, प्रमुख, प्रधान; 'p. lord' अधीश्वरः, सम्राट्, सर्वेशः, सार्वभौमः; 'p. sway' साम्राज्यं.

PARAMOUR, *s.* भुजंगः, जारः, विटः, उपपतिः. 2 (Female) उपपत्नी, उपस्त्री.

PARAPET, *s.* वक्षोदघ्नः प्राकारः.

PARAPHERNALIA, *s.* सामग्री, परिच्छदः, उपकरणं; 'royal p.' छत्रचामरादि राजचिह्नं, राजलक्षणानि; 'woman's p.' स्त्रीधनं, यौतकं.

PARAPHRASE, *v. t.* विस्तरेण व्या-ख्या 2 P, अनुवद् 1 P, शब्दांतरेण विपरि-णम् c. (णमयति). –*s.* अनुवादः, मूलशब्दविस्तारः-विवरणं. –PARAPHRASTIC, *a.* मूलाधिकशब्द, विस्ताररूप.

PARASITE, *s.* परान्नभोजिन् *m.*, परान्नपुष्टः, परपिंडादः, पात्रेसमितः. 2 विटः, चाटुकारः; *See* FLATTERER. 3 वंदा, वृक्षादनी, वृक्षरुहा, जीवंतिका. –IC, -ICAL, *a.* परान्नपुष्ट, पराश्रय, परोपजीविन्; वृक्ष-तरु-रोहिन्-रुह.

PARASOL, *s.* छत्रं, आतपत्रं.

PARBOIL, *v. t.* ईषत् क्वथ् 1 P.

PARCEL, *s.* पोटली, पोटलिका, कूर्चः, भांडं. 2 भागः, अंशः, खंडः, उद्धारः. 3 राशिः, चयः, संघः, गणः, समूहः, वृंदं; 'part and p.' अंगभूत *a.*, शरीरावयवभूत *a.*; 'she forms, as it were, part and p. of my body' अव्यतिरिक्तेयमस्मच्छरीरात् (Ka. 151); मेनकासंबंधेन शरीरभूता मे शकुंतला (S. 6). –*v. t.* (Out) विभज् 1 U, विभागशः विन्यस् 4 U or क्लृप् c.

PARCENER, *s.* समांशिन् *m.*, समाधिकारी. –PARCENARY, *s.* समाधिकारः.

PARCH, *v. t.* तप् c., दह् 1 P, शुष् 1 P, भ्रस्ज् 6 P; उद्-,शुष् c. (throat &c.). –ED, *a.* तप्त, दग्ध, भृष्ट, शुष्क, उच्छोषित, निर्जल, शोषितजल, क्षाम; having his throat p. up with thirst' पिपासाक्षामकंठः.

PARCHMENT, *s.* चर्मपटः-पत्रं.

PARDON, *v. t.* क्षम् 1 A, 4 P, सह् 1 A, मृष् 4 P, 10, मुच् 6 P, अव-सृज् 6 P, तिज् desid. (तितिक्षते). –*s.* क्षमा, क्षांति *f.*, तितिक्षा, मर्षणं, मोचनं, दोषमुक्ति *f.*, अपराधक्षमा; 'I beg your p.' क्षंतव्योहं भवता; 'to beg p. of' क्षमां प्रार्थ् 10 A. –ABLE, *a.* क्षंतव्य, मर्षणीय, क्षमार्ह, सोढव्य, क्षमोचित. –ED, *a.* क्षांत, मर्षित, दोष-दंड-मुक्त, मुक्तदंड-दोष.

PARE, *v. t.* तनूकृ 8 U, अवकृत् 6 P, तक्ष् 1, 5 P, त्वक्ष् 1 P, अवच्छिद् 7 P, खंड् 10, उल्लिख् 6 P, वि-लू 9 U. 2 (Skin) निस्त्वचीकृ, निस्तुषीकृ, त्वचयति (D.), त्वचं निष्कुष् 1 P; 'having p. ed nails' कृत्तनखः. –ER, *s.* तष्टृ *m.*, खंडकः. –ING, *s.* तक्षणं, कर्तनं, तनूकरणं 2 तष्टं, खंडः, भिन्नं, विदलं, शकलः-लं.

PARENT, *s.* मातृ *f.*, पितृ *m.*; *See* MOTHER, FATHER; 'p. s' मातापितरौ, पितरौ, मातरपितरौ, प्रसूजनयितारौ; 'p. institution' उत्पादिका-पितृभूता-शाला; 'p. tree' उत्पादकः-जन्मदः-वृक्षः. 2 प्रभवः, कारणं, बीजं, हेतुः, उत्पादकः, जन्महेतुः. –AGE, *s.* अन्वयः, जाति *f.*, कूलं, वंशः, जन्मन् *n.*, उत्पत्ति *f.*; 'of royal p.' राजवंश्य, नृपबीज; 'of noble p.' महाकुल, कुलजन्मन्, अभिजनवत्. –AL, *a.* पितृ, मातृ in comp., पैतृक (की *f.*), मातापितृयोग्य, पित्रुचित, पित्रनुरूप; 'p. affection' वात्सल्यं, अपत्यस्नेहः, पुत्रप्रीति *f.*

PARENTHESIS. *s.* निक्षेपचिह्नं; निक्षिप्तवाक्यं-वचनं, उप-अनन्वित-वाक्यं, प्रासंगिक-अप्रधान-वचनं. –PARENTHETICAL, *a.* प्रासंगिक (की *f.*), निक्षिप्त, निवेशित, मूलानन्वित, अप्रधान. –LY, *adv.* निक्षिप्य, मूलानन्वयेन.

PARHELION, *s.* सूर्याभासः, मिथ्यासूर्यः.

PARISH, *s.* पौरोहित्यभूमि *f.*-प्रदेशः; 'p. priest' ग्रामयाजकः-पुरोहितः. –PARISHIONER, *s.* ग्रामिकः, ग्रामस्थः, ग्रामवासिन् *m.*

PARK, *s.* उपवनं, कृत्रिमवनं; क्रीडा-प्रमद-वनं, आक्रीडः, मृगयास्थानं-भूमि *f.* –ER, (P.-keeper) *s.* वनपालः, उद्यानरक्षकः.

PARLEY. *v. i.* संभाष् 1 A, संवद् 1 P, संलप् 1 P. –*s.*,-PARLANCE, *s.* संभाषणं, संवादः, संकथा, संलापः. 2 संधिप्रसंगः.

PARLIAMENT, *s.* विचार-मंत्रण-सभा, प्रतिनिधिसभा.

PARLOUR, *s.* आलाप-संकथा-स्थानं, संलापकोष्ठः.

PAROCHIAL, *a.* ग्राम्य, ग्रामीय, ग्रामिक (की *f.*).

PARODY, *s.* अनुकरणकाव्यं. –*v. t.* शब्दान् परिवृत् c.

PAROLE, *s.* उक्ति *f.*, वचनं, प्रतिज्ञा.

PARONOMASIA, *s.* श्लेषः.

PARONYCHIA, *s.* चिप्यं.

PAROTIS, *s.* लालाधारः.

PAROXYSM, *s.* वेगः, सं-आ-वेगः, आवेशः, आक्रमः; 'p. of rage' क्रोधावेशः; 'in a p. of rage' क्रोधावेशवशात्.

PARRICIDE, *s.* पितृहत्या-वधः-घातः. 2 पितृहन् *m.*, पितृघातिन् *m.*, पितृघ्नः. –AL, *a.* पितृहन्. 2 पितृवधात्मक.

PARROT, *s.* शुकः, कीरः, किंकिरातः, वक्रतुंडः-चंचुः.

PARRY, *v. t.* नि-वृ c., परिहृ 1 P, प्रति-हन् 2 P.

PARSE, *v. t.* (पदानि) भंज् 7 P, छिद् 7 P. –ING, *s.* पदभंजनं-छेदः.

PARSIMONY, *s.* अल्प-मित-व्ययः. –IOUS, *a.* अल्प-मित-व्ययिन्, कृपण, व्ययपराङ्मुख (खी *f.*), दृढबद्ध-मुष्टि. –IOUSLY, *adv.* कार्पण्येन, मितव्ययेन. –IOUSNESS, *s.* *See* (*s.*).

PARSLEY, *s.* अजमोदा.

PARSON, *s.* ग्रामपुरोहितः, ग्रामोपाध्यायः, ग्रामगुरुः. –AGE, *s.* ग्रामगुरुगृहं.

PART, *s.* वि-,भागः, अंशः, खंडः-डं, शकलः-लं, लवः, वि-,दलं, भिन्नं, कला. 2 प्र-,देशः, एकदेशः, अवयवः, अंगं. 3 (Allotted) वि-,भागः, अंशः, उद्धारः, वंटः. 4 कर्मन् *n.*, कार्यं, नियोगः, धर्मः, स्वकर्तव्यं-धर्मः ; 'perform one's p.' कर्म निर्वह् c., नियोगमनुष्ठा 1 P. 5 भूमिका ; पात्रं ; 'assignment of p. s' भूमिकाकल्पनं. 6 अंगं, अवयवः, घटकः, घटकावयवः ; 'consisting of 4 p. s' चतुरंगं (बलं). 7 वारः, पर्यायः; *See* TURN. 8 पक्षः. 9 संबंधः, अनुषंगः ; 'to have a p. in' संबंध्-अनुषंज्-pass. 10 (P.-s) मति *f.*, मतिगुणः, बुद्धि *f.*, धीशक्ति *f.* ; *See* INTELLECT; (region) प्र-,देशः; 'for (on) one's p.' तावत्, अपि; 'for the most p.' प्रायः, बहुशः, प्रायशः, प्रायेण, भूयिष्ठं; *See* MOSTLY, 'by p. s', 'in p. s' भागशः, अंशशः; 'in p.' अंशतः, ईषत्, किंचित्; 'in good p.' संप्रीतमनसा, प्रियं, अनुकूलं, प्रसन्नं; प्रसन्नमनसा; 'in ill p.' दुष्ट-खिन्न-मनसा ; 'in four p. s' चतुर्धा; 'in many p. s' बहुधा. —*v. t.* विभज् 1 U, परि-कृप् c., विभागशः विन्यस् 4 U, वंट् 10; *See* DIVIDE. 2 वि-युज् 7 A, 10, विश्लिष् c., पृथक् कृ 8 U, वि-भिद् 7 P or c., विच्छिद् 7 P; (the hair) सीमंतयति (D.). —*v. i.* वियुज्-विभिद्-विच्छिद्-pass., विगम् 1 P, विश्लिष् 4 P, अप-या 2 P, अपगम्. 3 वि-,दल् 1 P, स्फुट् 6 P, वि-दॄ pass., शकलीभू. 4 (With) आ-मंत्र् 10 A, आपृच्छ् 6 A; त्यज् 1 P, क्षिप् 6 P (place) ; 'let me now p. with you' अनुजानीहि मामधुना गमनाय. —ING, *a.* प्रास्थानिक (की *f.*), प्रस्थान-प्रयाण in comp. ; 'p. ceremony' प्रस्थानकौतुकं. —*s.* वियोगः, विश्लेषः, विरहः, विभेदः. 2 वि-अप-गमः, प्रस्थानं, प्रयाणं, अपयानं ; 'p. of the hair' सीमंतः, सीमंतरचनं. —LY, *adv.* अंशतः, भागतः, किंचित्, ईषत्, स्तोकं, कियत्, अल्पं, स्तोकांशेन, खंडतः. —PARTAKE, *v.* अंशभाज्-*a.* भू 1 P, अंशं-भागं-ग्रह् 9 P or हृ 1 P, भज् 1 A, अंशं भज्, भागिन्-*a.* भू; *See* SHARE. 2 भुज् 7 A, सेव् 1 A. —ER, *s.* अंशिन् *m.*, भागी, अंश-भाग-ग्राही-हारी-हरः, सहभाक्-भोगिन्, भुज्-भाज्- in comp. —PARTIAL, *a.* अव्यापक, असार्वत्रिक-आंशिक (की *f.*), असमग्र, असंपूर्ण, असकल, एकदेश-खंड- in comp. ; 'p. eclipse' खंडग्रासः; 'p. rent' एकदेशच्छिद्रं. 2 पक्षपातिन्, पक्षस्नेहिन्, पक्षानुकूल, पक्षानुरागिन्, एकदेशीय, सपक्षपात, संगिन्, असमदृष्टि, असमदर्शिन्. —ITY. *s.* पक्षपातः, पक्षपातिता, पक्षस्नेहः-आनुकूल्यं-अनुरागः, असमता, असमदृष्टि *f.*-बुद्धि *f.*, संगः. 2 स्नेहः, अनुरागः, प्रणयः, प्रेमन् *m. n.*; 'speak without any p.' मध्यस्थतां गृहीत्वा भण (M. 3). —LY, *adv.* अंशतः, असमग्रं, असकलं, असंपूर्णं, क्वचित् क्वचित्, असर्वत्र, खंडतः, एकदेशे, ईषत्, स्तोकं, खंड-एकदेश-in comp.; 'p. broken' खंडभग्न; *See* PARTLY. —PARTICIPATE, *v. t.* भागं-अंशं-ग्रह् 9 P, संविभज् 1 U. —ION, *s.* अंश-भाग-ग्रहणं, संविभागः, सहभोगः-भुक्ति *f.* —PARTICIPANT, *a.*, *s.* भागिन्, अंशिन् ; *See* PARTAKER. —PARTICLE, *s.* कणः, अणुः, लवः, क्षुद्रांशः, कणिका, लेशः, कला, परमाणुः. 2 निपातः, अव्ययः-यं. —PARTITION, *s.* परिच्छेदः, वियोजनं. 2 वि-,भागः, विभागकल्पनं-ना, विभजनं, वंटनं, व्यंशनं. 3 व्यवच्छेदनं, भित्ति *f.*, व्यवधा-धानं, कोष्ठः, संधिः. —*v. t.* विच्छिद् 7 P, विभज् 1 U, अंशांशि दा 3 U; *See* (*v. t.*). —PARTNER, *s.* अंशिन् *m.*, भागी, समांशी, सहभोगी-भागी; संगी, सहायः, सहकारी, संभूयकारी, संसर्गी, अनुषंगी; 'p. of joys and sorrows' समदुःखसुखः (S. 3). 2 Husband, Wife, q. v. —SHIP. *s.* सहकारिता, संभूयकारित्वं, समांशिता, संभूयसमुत्थानं.

PARTERRE. *s.* पुष्पवाटी-टिका, कुसुमाकरः.

PARTICIPLE. *s.* कृदंतः; 'present p.' शतृ, शानच् ; 'past p.' निष्ठा; 'potential passive p.' कृत्यः (all being names of terminations).

PARTICULAR, *a.* विशिष्ट, सविशेष, विशेषक, अव-परिच्छेदक, विशेष in comp. 2 व्यक्त, विभिन्न, विविक्त, उद्दिष्ट, पृथगात्मक, अमुक in comp. 3 अव्यापक, अनौत्सर्गिक (की *f.*); विशिष्ट, not 'General' q. v. 4 असाधारण (णी *f.*), असामान्य, लोकोत्तर, अप्राकृत (ती *f.*). 5 विलक्षण, अपूर्व. 6 सूक्ष्म, सूक्ष्मदृष्टि, सूक्ष्मदर्शिन्; 'at a p. time' विशिष्टसमये, समयविशेषे; 'a p. rule' विशेषविधिः; 'he is very p. about his dress' वेषक्रियायां सोऽतीव सूक्ष्मदृष्टिः. —*s.* विशेषः, अव-परि-च्छेदः; 'give p. s of the man' तस्य नरस्य विशेषं ब्रूहि ; 'he told all the p. s of the battle' युद्धं स विस्तरेण अवर्णयत्, अखिलं युद्धवृत्तांतं अकथयत् ; 'in p.' विशेषतः, विशेषेण. —ITY, *s.* विशेषनिर्देशः-कथनं, एकैकशः निर्देशः. 2 असामान्यता, अव्यापकत्वं. 3 पार्थक्यं, भिन्नता, व्यक्ति *f.*, विशिष्टता. 4 विवरणं, विस्तरः. —LY, *adv.* विशेषतः, सविशेषं, प्रधानतः. 2 विस्तरेण, सविस्तरं ; सूक्ष्मतया, अतिसूक्ष्मं. 3 पृथक्, अवयवशः, एकैकशः. —PARTICULARIZE, *v. t.* विशिष् 7 P, एकैकशः निर्दिश् 6 P or अभि-धा 3 U. सविशेषं वर्ण् 10 or कथ् 10, व्यवच्छिद् 7 P. —ATION, *s.* विशेषवर्णनं-ना, विशेषनिर्देशः-कथनं, व्यवच्छेदः. —ED, *a.* विशेषित, एकैकशः निर्दिष्ट, व्यवच्छिन्न.

PARTRIDGE, *s.* तित्तिरः-रिः, चकोरः-रकः.

PARTURIENT, *a.* आसन्नप्रसवा, प्राप्तप्रसववेदना. —PARTURITION, *s.* प्रसवः, जननं, जन्मन् *n.*, उत्पत्ति *f.*

PARTY, *s.* पक्षः ; 'one's own p.' स्व-आत्म-पक्षः ; 'of one's p.' स्वपक्षावलंबिन् . स्वपक्षपातिन् ; 'of the opposite p. ' वि-प्रति-पक्षः. 2 संसर्गः, सपक्षाणां गणः-संघः, कृतसंसर्गा जनाः, शाखा, पक्षः. 3 गणः, समूहः, दलं, संघः, वृंदं, मंडलं, गुल्मः-ल्मं, पंक्ति *f.* 4 अर्थिन् *m.*, प्रत्यर्थी, वादी, प्रतिवादी. 5 सभा, समाजः, पंक्तिः, गणः ; ' dinner (convivial) p. ' सग्धि *f.*, सह-सं-भोजनं ; सपीति *f.*, तुल्यपानं (drinking p.). 6 विशिष्टजनः, व्यक्ति *f.*, विवक्षितपुरुषः. 7 संबंधिन् *m.*, अनुषंगी, भागी, अंशी, सहकारा, सहायः; ' a p. to a plot ' कूटसहायः. –*a.* पाक्षिक (की *f.*), पक्ष in comp., by (*s.*); ' p.-coloured ' चित्रविचित्र, नानावर्ण-रंग, विचित्र ; ' p.-man ' पक्षपाती, पाक्षिकः ; ' p.-spirit ' पक्षपातः; *See* PARTIALITY; ' p-wall ' भित्ति *f.*, संधिः; कुड्यं. —PARTISAN, *s.* पक्षपाती, पक्षावलंबी, पक्ष्यः, एकपक्षः, सपक्षः, सहोन्थायी, अनु-,संगी, पार्श्व(र्श्वि)कः, पक्षधरः. –SHIP, *s.* पक्षपातः-ग्रहणं-अवलंबनं.

PARVENU, *s. See* UPSTART.

PASQUINADE, *s.* निंदात्मको लेखः, उपहासलेखः.

PASS, *v. t.* अति-व्यति-इ 2 P, अतिक्रम् 1 U, 4 P ; ' they two p. ed each other ' परस्परमतीत्य-उल्लंघ्य-तौ निर्गतौ; तॄ 1 P, सं-उत्-निः-°, उत्-,लंघ् 1 A, 10, पारं गम् 1 P, अतिगम् ; ' p. ed his examination ' परीक्षापारं गतः, परीक्षामुत्ततार. 2 (Time) गम् c. (गमयति), नी 1 P, अति-वह् c., क्षै c. (क्षपयति), या c. (यापयति) ; ' he with difficulty p. ed eight years ' तेनाष्टौ परिगमिताः समाः कथंचित् (R. VIII. 92) ; ' p. ing (staying for) three nights ' तिस्रो वसतीरुषित्वा (R. VII. 33). 3 सं-,चर्-ल् c., संक्रम् c. 4 निष्पद् c., व्यव-स्था c. (स्थापयति), सिध् c. (साधयति); स-अनु-मन् 4 A, परिग्रह् 9 P (bill &c.) ; ' p. sentence ' निर्णयं दा 3 U, दंडं आदिश् 6 P ; 'this p. es conception ' विचारविषयातिक्रांतमेतत् , धियः पथि न वर्तते. –*v. i.* गम् , इ-या- 2 P, चल्-चर् 1 P, प्र-,सृ 1 P, अति-व्यति-इ, अतिक्रम्; ' let it p. now' तिष्ठतु तदधुना, यातु, किमनेन. 2 प्र-चल्-र्, प्रचलित-*a.* भू 1 P, प्र-सृ, प्रचलीभू. 3 सिध् 4 P, निष्पन्नी-सिद्धीभू,अनु-सं-मन् pass., परिग्रह् pass. 4 उप-,संक्रम्, संचर्. 5 संवृत् 1 A, समा-पद् 4 A, सं-,भू, आ-पत् 1 P, घट् 1 A; *See* HAPPEN, OCCUR. –away, अति-व्यति-इ, गम् , या, अतिक्रम्, अतिवृत्. 2 प्र-, नश् 4 P, प्र-वि-ली 4 A, तिरोभू , क्षि pass., क्षर् 1 P. –by, अतिक्रम्, अति-इ, अतिचर्, उल्लंघ्. 2 उपेक्ष् 1 A, न गण् 10, त्यज् 1 P, अपास् 4 U; *See* NEGLECT. –for, Ex. by denominatives; एरंडोपि द्रुमायते ' p. es for a tree '; मन्-गण्-pass.; ' he p. s for a learned man ' पंडित इति मन्यते (जनैः).–into, निविश्-प्रविश्- 6 P. –off, अप-इ, अप-या-गम् , विगम्. –(*v. t.*) वि-भू c., संदृश् c., आकल् 10 ; ' tried to p. the matter off with a joke ' तं वृत्तांतं परिहासमिव गणयितुं-आकलयितुं-येते ; हृदयवल्लभोऽभिलिख्य कामदेवव्यपदेशेन सखीपुरतोऽपह्नुतः (Rat. 2) ' p. ed off the picture of her beloved upon her friend as that of Cupid.' –on, प्र-वृत्, प्र-या-गम्-सृ. –over, उपेक्ष्, उत्सृज् 6 P, त्यज्, न गण् , लंघ् , अति-इ, अतिक्रम् , अतिक्रम्य गम्, तॄ; *See* (*v. t.*); अंतरयति (D.), मध्यमांबावृत्तांतोंऽतारित आर्येण (U. 1) ' is p.ed over ' &c ; oft. by स्था, आस् 2 A with तावत्; 'let us p. over this sad tale ' तिष्ठतु-आस्तां-तावदयं दुःखवृत्तांतः. –through, निर्भिद् 7 P, प्रविश्य निर्गम्; (thoughts &c.) *See* OCCUR. –*s.* संकटं, संक्रमः, संचरः, संकट-संबाध-पथः-मार्गः, दुर्गसंचरः. 2 दरी, विदरः, रंध्रं. 3 (Passport) अनुज्ञा, अनुमति *f.*, अनुज्ञापत्रं, मुद्रा; ' why do you leave the camp without (taking) a p. ' किमर्थमगृहीतमुद्रः कटकान्निष्क्रामसि; ' without a p.' अमुद्रालांछितः (Mu. 2). 4 प्रहारः, आघातः, ताडनं. 5 दशा, अवस्था, स्थिति *f.*, दुर्दशा, दुर्गति *f.*, कष्टं, कृच्छ्रं, कष्टावस्था. –ABLE, *a.* गम्य, तार्य, सुगम, उल्लंघ्य ; ' not p. ' दुर्गम, अगम्य. 2 सह्य, सोढव्य, उपेक्षणीय, विगुण. –AGE, *s.* गमनं, तरणं, यानं ; ' p. through the world ' लोकयात्रा, संसारपथः ; ' p. to and fro ' गमनागमनं, यातायातं. 2 मार्गः; *See* WAY. 3 संक्रमः, संचारः, अतिक्रमः, पारगमनं, उल्लंघनं; *See* (*s.*). 4 गमनसंक्रमण-कालः. 5 संचरः, संक्रमः, दुर्गसंचरः. 6 गमनाधिकारः, अनुज्ञा, पत्रं, मुद्रा; *See* PASS. 7 वचनं. स्थानं, स्थलं, देशः. 8 वृत्तं, भूतं, वृत्तांतः; 'p.-money' आता(त)रः, तरमूल्यं-पण्यं, तारिकं, तार्यं. –ED, *a.* अतीत, गत, संक्रांत, वीत, तीर्ण, सिद्ध. 2 (As excrement) उच्चारित, हन्न, गून. –ER, *s.* (p.-by), पथिकः, अध्वगः, पांथः; *See* TRAVELLER. –ING, *s.* तरणं, गमनं, चलनं. –*a.* गामिन्, यायिन् in comp. 2 अतिक्रामक. 3 उत्तम, परम, श्रेष्ठ, विशिष्ट. –*adv.* अतीव, अतिमात्रं, नितांतं, अति pr., अतिशय in comp. –PASSENGER, *s.* तरः, तरितृ *m.*, उत्तरणकृत्. 2 नौ-पोत-गामी-यायी. 3 पथिकः, यात्रिकः, पांथः; *See* TRAVELLER. –PAST, *a.* गत, अतीत, भूत, व्यतीत, अतिक्रांत, वृत्त, परोक्ष ; ' p. time ' भूतकालः. 2 पूर्व, पूर्वतन (नी *f.*) ; ' in p. times ' पुरा, पूर्वं, पुराकल्पे. 3 सिद्ध, निष्पन्न, समाप्त, कृत. –*s.* भूतं, अतीतं, समतीतं, अतिक्रांतं, गत-अतीत-भूत-कालः. –*prep.*, अति pr., अतीत, अतिक्रांत, नष्ट, हीन in comp., अ-निर्-pr.; ' p. cure ' असाध्य, निरुपचार ; ' p. the range of sight ' चक्षुर्विषयातिक्रांत, नयनपथातीत ; ' p. all shame ' निर्लज्ज, नष्ट-त्यक्तलज्ज ; ' p. human strength ' अतिमानुषशक्ति ; *See* BEYOND also.

PASSION, *s.* भावः, विकारः, विकृति *f.*, वृत्ति *f.*, रागः, रसः, मनोविकारः-धर्मः-भावः-वृत्तिः-रागः, इंद्रियवृत्तिः. 2 इंद्रियं; 'the p. s' इंद्रियाणि, इंद्रियवर्गः; 'subduing the p. s' इंद्रियनिग्रहः; 'p. of love' कामविकारः, शृंगारभावः; 'void of p. s' वीतराग, विरक्त; 'absence of p. s' विरागः, विरक्ति *f.* 3 प्रकोपः, संरंभः, क्रोधः, रोषः, अमर्षः, उत्-सं-तापः; चंडता, उग्रता, क्षोभः, व्या-सं-क्षोभः, चित्तक्षोभः-तापः-वेगः. 4 लालसा, लोभः, लोलुपता, औत्सुक्यं, उत्कंठा, उत्कंटेच्छा, गाढाभिलाषः, व्यसनं, आसक्ति *f.*; 'quality of (tendency to) p.' रजोगुणः, रजस् *n.* 5 कामः, मदनः, स्मरः, कामविकारः, स्मरमोहः, रजः, रजोवृत्तिः, मदः, कामुकत्वं, अभिलाषः, अनुरागः; *See* LOVE, LUST. 6 दुःखानुभवः, दुःखभोगः. 7 सहनं, कर्माश्रयता, ग्रहणं. -ATE, *a.* क्रोधन, कोपन, क्रोधिल, शीघ्रकोपिन्, सुलभकोप, संरंभिन्, ससंरंभ, रोष-कोप-क्रोध-शील, अमर्षण, रोषण, क्रोधिष्ठ, चंडचित्त-स्वभाव, आवेशवत्, चंड-उत्ताप-संताप-शील, तिग्म, उष्ण. 2 तीव्र, तीक्ष्ण, उग्र, अत्युत्कट, उच्चंड, प्रखर, अतिरिक्त, परम, नितांत, गाढ, उत्कट; 'p. love for gambling' द्यूते गाढाभिनिवेशः; 'p. lover of music' नितांतं संगीतप्रियः. 3 रागयुक्त, विकाराधीन, "राग, रागान्वित, उत्कंठित, सानुराग, रजोगुणिन्, कामार्त; 'a. p. woman' भामिनी, कोपना. -ATELY, *adv.* सकोपं, सक्रोधं, ससंरंभं, सामर्षं. 2 चंडं, अत्युत्कटं, तीक्ष्णं, बलवत्. 3 सरागं, सानुरागं, रागपूर्वं. -ATENESS, *s.* चंडस्वभावः, सुलभकोपित्वं, रोषणता, &c. -LESS, *a.* विरक्त, रागहीन, शांत-वीत-राग, निःसंग.

PASSIVE, *a.* कर्मवाच्यं (p. voice); 'impersonal p.' भाववाच्यं. 2 सहन, सहिष्णु, सहनशील-वृत्ति-धर्मक, तितिक्षु, अनिवारक; oft. ex. by सह् 1 A. 3 निश्चेष्ट, निष्क्रिय, अप्रवर्तक, कर्माश्रय, कर्मपात्र. -LY, *adv.* सहिष्णुतया, निश्चेष्टं, अप्रतिकारेण. -NESS, *s.* सहनशीलं-धर्मः-वृत्तिः, सहिष्णुता. 2 निश्चेष्टता, कर्माश्रयता, कर्मपात्रता.

PASTE, *v. t.* (उदपेषं) वि-,लिप् 6 P, बंध् 9 P, आ-संज् c. -*s.* उदपेषः, जलपेषः; 'p.-board' संसृष्टपत्रं.

PASTERN, *s.* अश्वखुरसंधिः.

PASTIME, *s.* क्रीडा, विनोदः, लीला, केलि *f.*, विहारः, खेला, खेलनं, विलासः, कौतुकं.

PASTOR, *s.* अवि-अजा-पालः, मेषपालः. 2 आचार्यः, गुरुः, उपाध्यायः. -AL, *a.* Ex. by (*s.*) in comp.; 'p. life' अविपालवृत्ति *f.*; 'p. duties' धर्मकार्याणि; 'p. office' आचार्यकर्म. -*s.* 'p. poem' गोपकाव्यं.

PASTRY, *s.* मिष्टान्नं, आपूपिकं, पिष्टकाः (pl.); 'p.-cook' आपूपिकः, भक्ष्यंकारः.

PASTURE, *s.* शाद्वलं, शाद्वल-तृणावृत-भूमि *f.*, यवसक्षेत्रं, गोप्रचरः. 2 तृणं, यवसं, घासः, पशव्यं, गवादनं, पशुभोजनं. -*v. i.* चर् 1 P, तृणं खाद् 1 P or भक्ष् 10. -*v. t.* चर् c., तृणं भुज् c. or खाद् c. -AGE, *s.* प्रचारभूमिः, गोप्रचरः. 2 शस्यं, घासः, यवसं; *See* (*s.*).

PASTY, *s.* मांसपूपः.

PAT, *a.* युक्त, उचित. -*adv.* युक्तं, उचितं, सम्यक्. -*v. t.* हस्तेन स्पृश् 6 P or परामृश् 6 P; लघु प्र-हृ 1 P or तड् 10. -*s.* लघ्वाघातः, लघुप्रहारः.

PATCH, *v.* सं-ग्रंथ् 9 P, वस्त्रखंडान् निविश् 4 P or सं-धा 3 U; 'p. ed up garment' नानाखंडैर्ग्रथितं वस्त्रं, कर्पटः, कंथा ; 'wearing p. ed garment' कंथाधारिन्, कार्पटिक. -*s.* खंडः-डं, शकलः-लं, वस्त्रपट-खंडः, ग्रथितखंडः; 'p.-work' संग्रंथनं, खंडकर्म, कंथाकरणं. 2 भूभागः, प्रदेशः, भूमि *f.*, क्षेत्रं. -ED, *a.* संग्रथित, खंडमय (यी *f.*), खंडरूप.

PATE, *s.* मुंडं, मस्तकाग्रं; *See* HEAD.

PATENT, *a.* स्पष्ट, व्यक्त, स्फुट, सुप्रकाश, सुव्यक्त, सुस्पष्ट, प्रत्यक्ष. -*s.* असामान्याधिकारः, विशिष्टाधिकारपत्रं. -EE, *s.* असामान्याधिकारिन् *m.*

PATER-FAMILIAS, *s.* कुलपतिः, कौटुंबिकः.

PATERNAL, *a.* पैतृक (की *f.*), पैत्र (त्री *f.*), पित्र्य, पितृ in comp., पित्रागत, पितृप्राप्त; 'p. estate' पैतृकी भूमिः; 'p. aunt' पितृष्वसा. 2 पितृतुल्य, पितृतुल्य-सन्निभ. -LY, *adv.* पितृवत्, पित्रेव, पितृसंनिभं.

PATERNITY, *s.* पितृत्वं, पितृधर्मः. 2 प्रभवः, प्रसूति *f.*

PATH, *s.* (P.-way) पथिन् *m.*, मार्गः, पद्धति *f.*, सरणि-णी *f.*, वर्त्मन् *n.*, पदवि-वी *f.* ; *See* WAY; 'the p. of a planet' कक्षा-क्षः ; 'the wrong p.' उत्पथः, कापथः, विमार्गः; 'good p.' सुपथः ; 'to seduce from the right p.' उत्पथं नी 1 P. -LESS, *a.* निष्पथ, अगम्य, दुर्गम.

PATHETIC,-AL, *a.* करुण, हृदयद्राविन्-ग्राहिन्, हृदिस्पृश्, हृदयंगम, करुणात्मक. -ALLY, *adv.* करुणं, हृदयग्राहितया ; 'a speech p. worded' करुणार्थग्रथितं वचः. -PATHOS, *s.* करुणो रसः, कारुण्यरसः, करुणारसः; रागः, रसः, कारुण्यं.

PATHOLOGY, *s.* रोगनिदानशास्त्रं.

PATIENT, *a.* क्षमिन्, सहिष्णु, तितिक्षु, सहन-क्षमा-शील, सहन, क्षमावत्, मर्षिन्, क्षमायुक्त, क्षम-सह in comp. 2 धीर, शांत, धृतिमत् ; 'very p.' बहुसह ; 'p. of labour' क्लेशसह-क्षम ; 'to be p.' सह् 1 A, क्षम् 1 A; *See* ENDURE. -*s.* आतुरः, रुग्णः, रोगिन् *m.* -LY, *adv.* क्षांत्या, क्षमापूर्वं, धीरतया. -PATIENCE, *s.* क्षमा, तितिक्षा, क्षांति *f.*, सहिष्णुता. 2 धीरता, प्रशांति *f.*, धृति *f.*, धैर्यं, उत्साहः.

PATRIARCH, *s.* कुलपतिः, आदि-मूल-पुरुषः. 2 वृद्ध-गुरु-जनः. -AL, *a.* (*s.*) in comp.

PATRICIAN, *s.* कुलीनः, अभिजातः, कुलीनजनः, शिष्टः. - *a.* कुलीन, शिष्ट, सद्वंशज, अभिजात.

PATRIMONY, *s.* पैतृकरिक्थं-धनं, प्राप्तिरिन्नं, पैतृकं,

दायः, पित्रागतधनं. -IAL, *a.* पितृप्राप्त-आगत, दायलब्ध, पैतृक (की *f.*).

PATRIOT, *s.* स्वदेशानुरागिन् *m.*, स्वदेशहितपरायणः, स्वदेशाभिमानी, स्वदेशभक्तः. -IC, *a.* स्वदेशानुरागिन्, स्वभूम्यनुरक्त, स्वदेशाभिमानिन्, स्वदेशभक्त-आसक्त. -ICALLY, *adv.* स्वदेशहितेच्छया. -ISM, *s.* स्वदेशप्रीति *f.*-अनुरागः, जन्मभूमिवात्सल्यं, स्वदेशाभिमानः.

PATROL, *v. i.* (रक्षणार्थं) रात्रौ परिक्रम् 1 U, 4 P or परिभ्रम् 1, 4 P. -*s.* रक्षिणः, नागारिकाः (pl.), रक्षकः, रक्षिन् *m.*, रात्रिपरिचरः.

PATRON, *s.* संभावयितृ *m.*, पालकः, उपकारकः, संवर्धकः, आश्रयः, पुरस्कर्ता, रक्षकः, शरणं; नाथः, पोषकः, पिंडदः. -AGE, *s.* संभावना, आश्रयः, साहाय्यं, अनुग्रहः, उपकारः, पालनं, पोषणं, रक्षणं, संवर्धनं, अवलंबः, पुरस्कारः. -AL, *a.* रक्षक, वर्धक. -IZE, *v. t.* सं-भू c., आश्रयं दा 3 U, प्रति-अनु-पा c. (पालयति), अनुग्रह् 9 P, अवलंब् 1 A, संवृध् c.; oft. by (*s.*) with भू 1 P. -LESS, *a.* निराश्रय, अनाथ, अशरण, निरवलंब, निराधार.

PATRONYMIC, *s.* पैतृकनामन् *n.*, गोत्रनाम, अपत्यवाचकः; 'chapter treating of Taddhita p. terminations' तद्धितापत्याधिकारप्रकरणं.

PATTEN, *s.* काष्ठपादुका.

PATTER, *v. i.* पटपटायते (D.). -*s.* पटपटाशब्दः.

PATTERN, *s.* आदर्शः, निदर्शनं, उपमा, प्रतिमा, प्रतिरूपं-कृति *f.* 2 आकारः, रूपं, संस्कारः; *See* MODEL.

PAUCITY, *s.* अल्पता, स्तोकता, ex. by 'few' q. v.

PAUNCH, *s.* पिचिंडः, उदरं, जठरः-रं, तुंदं, लंबोदरं; 'having a p.' लंबोदर, तुंदिन्, पिचिंडिल; *See* CORPULENT. -*v. t.* निरंत्रीकृ 8 U.

PAUPER, *s.* अनाथः, अकिंचनः, दरिद्रः, भिक्षुः, भिक्षाजीविन्; *See* BEGGAR, POOR. -ISM, *s.* भिक्षावृत्ति *f.*, भिक्ष्याजीवः, भैक्ष्यं.

PAUSE, *v. i.* वि-उप-रम् 1 P, निवृत् 1 A; विश्रम् 4 P, शम् 4 P, विच्छिद् pass.; 'p. upon' सं-,चिंत् 10; *See* CONSIDER. -*s.* विरामः, विरति *f.*, निवृत्ति *f.*, विच्छेदः, विश्रामः, प्र-उप-शमः. 2 अंतरं, व्यवधानं, अवकाशः, अंतरालं. 3 अवसानं, यतिः (in poetry).

PAVE, *v. t.* प्रस्तरैः-इष्टकाभिः-खच् 10 (खचयति) or आस्तॄ 9 U,-स्तृ 5 U, (भूमिं) निबंध् 9 P. -ER, *s.* शिलास्तरणकृत् *m.* -MENT, *s.* कुट्टिमः-मं, निबद्धभूः, शिलास्तरः-फलकं.

PAVILION, *s.* मंडपः-पं, पटमंडपः-वासः; *See* TENT.

PAW, *s.* पादः, सनखः पादः. 2 हस्तः, करः, चपेटः. -*v.* पादेन-खुरेण (भूमिं) अभिहन् 2 P or विलिख् 6 P. 2 करेण स्पृश् or परामृश् 6 P.

PAWN, *v. t.* निक्षिप् 6 P, न्यस् 4 U, आ-धा 3 U, न्यासीकृ 8 U, आधीकृ. -*s.* न्यासः, निक्षेपः, आधिः, बंधकः, पणः; *See* PLEDGE. 2 (At chess) शा-(सा)रः-रिः; 'p.-broker' निक्षेपव्यवसायिन् *m.*

PAY, *v. t.* दा 3 U, 1 P. 2 सं-पद् c., संवृ c., साध् c.; (a person) वेतनं-मूल्यं-दा ; (debt) परि-, शुध् c., अपाकृ 8 U, अपवृज् 10, प्रतिकृ ; 'p. for' निस्तॄ 1 P, निष्कृ ; 'he paid for the book' तस्य पुस्तकस्य मूल्यं स ददौ ; 'they paid for their offence with their lives' जीवितव्ययेन स्वापराधस्य निष्क्रयः कृतः ; *See* COST. -*s.* वेतनं, भृति *f.*, मूल्यं, निर्वेशः; *See* HIRE ; 'p.-day' वेतनदानदिवसः ; 'p.-master' वेतनाध्यक्षः. -EE, *s.* परि-, ग्रहीतृ *m.* -ER, *s.* दाता, शोधकः. -MENT, *s.* दानं, शोधनं, निराकरणं, निस्तारः, साधनं; 'p. of a debt' ऋणमुक्ति *f.*-शोधनं, आनृण्यं.

PEA, *s.* कलायः, स(सा)तीनकः, सतीलकः, हरेणुः, रेणुकः.

PEACE, *s.* संधिः, संधानं; 'to make p.' सं-धा 3 U. 2 शमः, प्र-उप-शमः-शांति *f.*, निर्वृति *f.*, स्वास्थ्यं, स्वस्थता, शांतता, सुखं ; निरुद्वेगः, उपप्लवाभावः. 3 ऐक्यं, सख्यं, मैत्री, अविरोधः, संवादः. 4 मौनं, तूष्णींभावः ; 'p. of mind' स्वास्थ्यं, चित्तप्रसादः, मनःशांतिः ; 'hold p.' तूष्णीं भू, वाचं यम् 1 P, मौनीभू; 'p.-maker' संधाता ; 'p.-offering' शांतिहोमः. -*interj.* शांतं, तूष्णीं भव. -ABLE, *a.* प्र-,शांत, शांतप्रकृति-स्वभाव, अक्षुब्ध, प्रसन्न, निराकुल, अव्यग्र, अनुद्विग्न, स्वस्थ. 2 शांतिप्रिय, युद्ध-कलह-विमुख (खी *f.*). -ABLENESS, *s.* शांतता, स्वास्थ्यं. 2 युद्धद्वेषः, कलहविमुखता. -FUL, *a.* प्र-,शांत, निरुपद्रव, निरुपप्लव, निष्कंटक, विग्रह-संग्राम-हीन. 2 (Life &c.) निर्वृत, स्वस्थ, निरुद्वेग, सुख in comp.; *See* PEACEABLE. -FULLY, *adv.* शांतं, निरुद्वेगं, स्वस्थं, शांत-प्रसन्न-चेतसा. 2 युद्धं विना, साम्ना, सामोपायेन.

PEACOCK, *s.* मयूरः, नीलकंठः, शिखंडिन् *m.*, शिखी, बर्ही, बर्हिणः, शिखावलः, केकी, भुजंगभुक्, कलापी, मेघनादानुलासी, प्रचलाकी ; 'p.'s tail' शिखंडः, बर्हः, पिच्छं, कलापः ; 'p.'s crest' शिखा, चूडा ; 'eye in the tail' चंद्रकः ; मेचकः ; 'p.'s cry' केका. —PEAFOWL, *s.* मयूरः-री, मयूरजाति *f.* -PEAHEN, *s.* मयूरी, शिखंडिनी, बर्हिणी.

PEAK, *s.* शिखरः-रं, शृंगं, कूटः-टं, सानु *m. n.*, चूडा, ककुदः-दं, पर्वताग्रं. 2 (Generally) अग्रं, शिखरं, शिखा, चूडा. -ED, *a.* शिखरिन्, शृंगिन्, सकूट, ककुद्मत्. 2 तीक्ष्णाग्र, सूच्यग्र.

PEAL, *s.* ध्वनिः, रवः, नि-,नादः, महाध्वनिः, निर्घोषः; *See* NOISE ; 'p. of thunder' घनगर्जितं, मेघनिर्घोषः, स्तनितं ; 'p. of bells' घंटानादः, क्वणितं. -*v. i.* नद्, स्वन्, क्वण्, ध्वन् 1 P ; स्तन्, गर्ज् 1 P (of thunder).

PEARL, *s.* मुक्ता, मुक्ताफलं, मौक्तिकं, शुक्तिजं ; 'p.-shell' शुक्ति *f.*, मुक्तास्फोटः, शुक्तिका, मुक्तागारं, -Y, *a.* मुक्तामय (यी *f.*), मुक्तापूर्ण. 2 मुक्तोपम, मुक्ताभ.

PEASANT, *s.* कृषकः, कृषीवलः, क्षेत्रिकः, ग्राम्यः, ग्रामीणः, जानपदः; *See* FARMER. -RY, *s.* कृषीवलाः, कृषकवर्गः.

PEASE, *s.* pl. *See* PEA.

PEBBLE, *s.* उपलः, दृषत्कणः, चूर्णखंडः, शर्कराखंडः. -Y, *a.* प्रचुरोपल, उपलसंकीर्ण, शर्करिल, सशर्कर, शार्करीय.

PECCABLE, *a.* पापवश-अधीन.

PECCADILLO, *s.* स्खलितं, अल्प-क्षुद्र-दोषः-अपराधः.

PECCANT, *a.* पापिन्, अपराधिन्, दोषिन्, सदोष, पापशील. 2 दुष्ट, दूषित, विकृत. -PECCANCY, *s.* विकारः, दोषः.

PECCAVI, *s.* दोषस्वीकारः.

PECK, *v.* (चंचुपुटेन) अभिहन् 2 P, तुद् 6 P, प्र-हृ 1 P, वि-,लिख् 6 P, दंश् 1 P, तुंडेन खंड् 10, चंचुप्रहारं कृ 8 U, चंचुप्रहारेण जर्जरीकृ. 2 (Grain) चंच्वा ग्रह् 9 P or आ-दा 3 A or लिह् 2 U; 'p. at' सततं प्रहृ 1 P, निंद् 1 P; *See* CENSURE. -*s.* द्रोणपादः. -ER, *s.* प्रतुदः.

PECTORAL, *a.* उरस्य. 2 कासघ्न (घ्नी *f.*). -*s.* कासघ्नं, कफ-श्लेष्म-घ्नं.

PECULATE, *v. i.* छलेन आत्मसात्कृ 8 U or ग्रस् 1 A, or मुष् 9 P or अपहृ 1 P. -ION, *s.* छलेन अपहारः, ग्रसनं, मोषणं. -OR, *s.* मोषकः.

PECULIAR, *a.* विशेष in comp.; विशिष्ट, असाधारण (णी *f.*), असामान्य, अव्यापक; आत्मीय, स्वीय; *See* PARTICULAR. -*s.* असाधारणधनं, स्वीयं धनं. -ITY, *s.* विशेषधर्मः-लक्षणं-चिह्नं-गुणः, विशेषः, धर्मः, गुणः. -LY, *adv.* विशेषतः, विशेषेण, सविशेषं.

PECUNIARY, *a.* अर्थ-धन-द्रव्य-in comp.; 'p. loss' अर्थहानिः; 'p. difficulty' अर्थकृच्छ्रं. 2 धन-द्रव्यरूप, अर्थात्मक.

PEDAGOGUE, *s.* बालशिक्षकः-पाठकः. 2 Pedant, q. v.

PEDAL, *a.* पादविषयक, पादसंबंधिन्.

PEDANT, *s.* पंडितंमन्यः, पंडितमानिन् *m.*, विद्यागर्वितः. -IC,-ICAL, *a.* पांडित्यदर्शिन्, समुद्धत. -ICALLY, *adv.* विद्याभिमानेन. -RY, *s.* विद्यावलेपः, पांडित्यदर्पः, दंभार्थं पांडित्यदर्शनं.

PEDDLER, *s.* *See* PEDLER.

PEDESTAL, *s.* (स्तंभादेः) पादः, आधारः; स्तंभतलं फलकः.

PEDESTRIAN, *s.* पदातिः, पादचारिन् *m.*, प(पा)दगः, पादातः; *See* FOOT-SOLDIER. -*a.* पादग, पादचारिन्-गामिन्, पाद in comp. -ISM, *s.* पादचारः, पादगमनं.

PEDICLE, PEDICEL, *s.* मंजरि-री *f.* 2 वृंतं, प्रसवबंधनं.

PEDICULAR, *a.* यूकापूर्ण.

PEDIGREE, *s.* वंशावलि-ली *f.*, अन्वयः, वंशः, कुलं. 2 वंशावलिपत्रं, वंशचरितं.

PEDLER, *s.* (भ्रमन्) भांडवाहः, क्षुद्रद्रव्यविक्रयी.

PEDUNCLE, *s.* वृंतं, प्रसव-पुष्प-बंधनं.

PEEL, *s.* त्वच् *f.*, वल्कं, चर्मन् *n.*, शल्कं. -*v. t.* त्वचं अप-नी 1 P or निष्कृष् 1 P or निर्हृ 1 P, त्वचयति (D.), निस्त्वचीकृ 8 U, त्वक्ष् 1 P. -*v. i.* निस्त्वचीभू 1 P. -ING, *s.* त्वक्षणं, त्वग्निष्कर्षः.

PEEP, *v. i.* जालमार्गेण दृश् 1 P or वीक्ष् 1 A, प्रच्छन्नं ईक्ष्, सूक्ष्मं निरूप् 10; जालांतरप्रेषितदृष्टिरन्या (R. VII. 9) 'another p. ing through a window.' 2 शनैः उद्-गम् 1 P or उद्-इ 2 P or प्र-निर्-भा 2 P, प्रकाश् 1 A, दृश्-लक्ष्-pass., प्रादुः-आविः-भू 1 P. -*s.* जालमार्गेण वीक्षणं, सूक्ष्मनिरूपणं-वीक्षणं-दृष्टिः *f.* 2 पूर्व-प्रथम-दर्शनं-आलोकः-प्रकाशनं; 'p.-hole' जालमार्गः-रंध्रं, सूक्ष्मरंध्रं, जालांतरं.

PEER, *s.* वयस्यः, सहायः, तुल्यः, तुल्य-सम-पदस्थः. 2 कुलीनः, अभिजातः, शिष्टजनः. -*v. i.* Appear, q. v. 2 Peep, q. v. -ER, *s.* सूक्ष्मनिरूपकः. -ESS, *s.* कुलीना. -LESS, *a.* अतुल, अनुपम, अप्रतिम; *See* MATCHLESS.

PEEVISH, *a.* पिशुन, प्रतीप, वक्र, वक्र-वाम-शील, दुःशील, कर्कश, रूक्षभाव, दुष्टप्रकृति. 2 कलहप्रिय, कोपन. -LY, *adv.* प्रतीपं, वक्रभावेन. -NESS, *s.* पैशुन्यं, वक्रभावः-शीलं, रूक्षस्वभावः, दुःशीलता, कार्कश्यं.

PEG, *s.* नागदंतः, भारयष्टि *f.*, विहंगिका; 'p. of a lute' कूणिका; 'iron p.' कालः-लकः. -*v. t.* नागदंते अवलंब् c. or बंध् 9 P.

PELF, *s.* अन्यायार्जितं धनं.

PELLET, *s.* *See* PILL.

PELLICLE, *s.* तनुत्वच् *f.*, सूक्ष्मचर्मन् *n.*, पटलं, पुटः-टं.

PELL-MELL, *adv.* संकुलं, संकीर्णं, क्रमं विना.

PELLUCID, *a.* स्वच्छ, निर्-वि-मल, विशद, प्रसन्न, शुद्ध. -ITY,-NESS, *s.* स्वच्छता, निर्मलता, वैशद्यं, प्रसादः.

PELT, *v. t.* (लोष्टैः) प्रहृ 1 P, तड् 10, अभि-,हन् 2 P, आहन् 2 U; 'he was p. ed to death' लोष्टघातं हतः. 3 तीव्रं-बलवत्-वृष् 1 P, धारासारेण वृष्; 'there was a p. ing shower of rain' धारासारैः महती वृष्टिर्बभूव (H. 3). -*s.* चर्मन् *n.*, दृति *f.*, कृत्ति *f.* 2 प्रहारः, आघातः.

PELVIS, *s.* वस्तिदेशः.

PEN, *v. t.* लिख् 6 P, पत्रे निविश् c. 2 (व्रजे) नि-अव-रुध् 7 U. -*s.* लेखनी, कलमः, अक्षरतूलिका, तूलिका, वर्णिका (painter's p.). 2 व्रजः, अवरोधः; 'cow-p.' गोशाला, गोष्ठं; 'p.-man' लिपिज्ञः, लेखकः, लेखनकुशलः; 'p.-manship' लिपि *f.*, लेखनविद्या, लेखनचातुर्यं-कौशलं. -PENT, (up) *a.* नि-अव-रुद्ध; 'p. house' उपगृहं.

PENAL, *a.* दंडार्ह, दंडनीय, दंड्य. 2 दंडविषयक. -TY, *s.* दंडः, निग्रहः, शासनं. 2 साहसं, अर्थ-धन-दंडः.

PENANCE, *s.* तपस् *n.*, तपस्या, तपश्चर्या, कृच्छ्रं,

यमः, कायक्लेशः; 'imposed p.' प्रायश्चित्तं; 'practise p.' तपः तप् 4 A or आचर् 1 P, तपस्यति (D.).

PENCHANT, *s. See* INCLINATION.

PENCIL, *s.* तूलिका, तूलि *f.*, वर्तिका, ईषिका; लेखनी. —*v. t.* लिख् 6 P, वर्तिकया लिख् or अंक् 10.

PENDANT, *s.* कर्णावतंसः, कुंडलं, प्रालंबः, लोलकः.

PENDENT, *a.* वि-,लोल, चल, प्रलंबमान, प्रलंब, आलंबिन्, आ-प्र-लंबित.

PENDING, *a.* अनिर्णीत, अनिश्चित, अनिष्पन्न; 'p. the decision' यावन्निर्णयो न कथ्यते.

PENDULOUS, *a.* प्र-,लंब, लंबिन्, लंबित, लोल.

PENDULUM, *s.* लोलकः, लोलदंडः.

PENETRATE, *v. t.* प्र-आ-विश् 6 P, निर्-,भिद् 7 P, व्यध् 4 P, छिद् 7 P, गाह् 1 A (forest &c.); निखन् 1 P. 2 व्याप् 5 P, मूर्छ् 1 P, (छाया न मूर्छति मलोपहतप्रसादे दर्पणतले S. 7). 3 अर्थं बुध् 1 P or ज्ञा 9 U, आशयं ग्रह् 9 P. —ION, *s.* प्रवेशः-शनं, भेदः-दनं, वेधः-धनं. 2 व्याप्ति *f.*, मूर्च्छनं. 3 अर्थबोधः, अर्थ-आशय-ज्ञानं. 4 (Power of p.) ग्रहणसामर्थ्यं, कुशाग्र-सूक्ष्म-मति *f.*-बुद्धि *f.*, तीक्ष्ण-सूक्ष्म-बुद्धित्वं-मतित्वं, वैदग्ध्यं ; 'a man of p.' सूक्ष्ममतिः, कुशाग्रबुद्धिः. विदग्धः, मर्मज्ञः, मार्मिकः. —ING, —IVE, *a.* प्रवेशक, भेदिन्, वेधिन्, भेदक. 2 व्यापक, व्यापिन्. 3 सूक्ष्म-तीक्ष्ण-मति-बुद्धि, कुशाग्रमति-बुद्धि, विदग्ध, मर्मज्ञ, मर्मवेदिन्.

PENINSULA, *s.* द्वीपकल्पः-ल्पं. —R, *a.* द्वीपकल्परूप ; द्वीपकल्पस्थ.

PENIS, *s.* लिंगं, उपस्थः, शिश्नः, मेढ्रः, मेहनं, शेफस् *n.*, चर्मदंडः.

PENITENT, *a.* अनुशयिन्, अनुतापदग्ध, जात-कृत-अनुताप. —IAL, *a.* अनुतापजनित, अनुशयार्थक, पश्चात्तापरूप. —IARY, *s.* प्रायश्चित्तागारं, कारावासः. —LY, *adv.* सानुशयं, सपश्चात्तापं. —PENITENCE, *s.* अनुतापः, पश्चात्तापः, अनुशयः, अनुशोकः; *See* REPENTANCE.

PENNANT, PENNON, *s.* ध्वजः, पताका, केतुवसनं; *See* BANNER. —PENNATE, *a.* सपक्ष, पक्षयुक्त.

PENNY, *s.* मुद्रा. —PENNILESS, *a.* अकिंचन, निर्धन; *See* POOR.

PENSILE, *a. See* PENDENT.

PENSION, *s.* (भूत-पूर्व-सेवार्थं) वृत्ति *f.*, वेतनं, वार्षिकं. —*v. t.* (भूत-पूर्व-सेवार्थं) वृत्तिं दा 3 U. —ER, *s.* वृत्तिभुज् *m.*, वृत्तिभोगी.

PENSIVE, *a.* चिंता-ध्यान-पर-परायण, सचिंत, चिंताक्रांत, उन्मनस्क. उदासीन ; 'in a p. mood' सचिंतवृत्त्या, गंभीरं. —LY, *adv.* सचिंतं, ध्यानपूर्वं. —NESS, *s.* ध्यानपरता, विषादः, खेदः.

PENTACHORD, *s.* पंचतंत्रीवाद्यं.

PENTAGON, *s.* पंचभुजः. —AL, *a.* पंचकोण, पंचभुज.

PENTANGULAR, *a.* पंचकोण, पंचास्र.

PENULTIMATE, *a.* उपांत्य; 'p. letter' उपधा, उपांत्यं.

PENUMBRA, *s.* खंडच्छाया.

PENURY, *s.* दारिद्र्यं, निर्धनता, दुर्गति *f.* —IOUS, *a.* दीन, निर्धन, निःस्व; *See* POOR. 2 कृपण, क्षुद्र, कदर्य; *See* MISERLY.

PEON, *s.* भृत्यः, पदातिः; *See* SERVANT.

PEOPLE, *s* जनः, लोकः, प्रजा, (pl. also); जनता, देशवासिनः, प्रकृतयः (pl.); 'country p.' ग्रामीणाः, ग्रामीयजनः, जानपदाः; 'common p.' प्राकृताः, इतरे-पृथग्-जनाः, सामान्य-प्राकृत-जनाः-लोकाः. 2 वर्गः, गणः, वर्णः, जनः, लोकः. 3 सेवकजनः-गणः, परिवारः. —*v. t.* जनैः पूर् 10 or आकॄ 6 P, वस् c.

PEPPER, *s.* मरी(रि)चं, कालकं, वेल्लजं, कृष्णं, ऊषणं, धर्मपत्तनं; 'long p.' पिप्पली; *See* under LONG. —*v. t.* अवकॄ 6 P.

PEPTIC, *a.* पाचक, पाचन, दीपन, अग्निद.

PERACUTE, *a.* अतितीक्ष्ण, अतितीव्र.

PERADVENTURE, *adv.* कदापि, कदाचित्, दैवात्, दैववशात्.

PERAMBULATE, *v. t.* परि-इ 2 P, परिक्रम् 1 U, 4 P, परिभ्रम् 1, 4 P, पर्यट् 1 P, परि-सृ-गम् 1 P; इतस्ततः चल्-चर् 1 P. —ION, *s.* परिक्रमः-मणं, परिभ्रमणं, पर्यटनं.

PER ANNUM, *adv.* प्रतिवर्षं, प्रतिवत्सरं.

PERCEIVE, *v. t.* उपलभ् 1 A, ज्ञा 9 U, वि-भू c., बुध् 1 P, ग्रह् 9 P, अवगम् 1 P, अव-इ 2 P, अनुभू 1 P, विद् 2 P; *See* KNOW. 2 (By the eye) दृश् 1 P, ईक्ष् 1 A, निरूप् 10, आ-,लक्ष् 10, आलोक् 1 A, 10; *See* SEE. —ED, *a.* ज्ञात, विदित, उपलब्ध, गोचर; 'p. by the senses' इंद्रियगोचर. —ER, *s.* लक्षकः. —PERCEPTIBLE, *a.* वेद्य, उपलभ्य, प्रत्यक्ष, दृष्टिगोचर, व्यक्त, परिस्फुट, सुस्पष्ट; oft. by विषय, गोचर, ग्राह्य in comp.; 'p. by the eye' प्रत्यक्ष, चक्षुर्ग्राह्य, दृष्टिगोचर ; कर्णविषय, इंद्रियगोचर, &c —PERCEPTIBLY, *adv.* प्रत्यक्षं, प्रत्यक्षतः. —PERCEPTION, *s.* उपलब्धि *f.*, ग्रहणं, बोधः, अवगमनं, अनुभवः, वेदनं, विभावनं, ज्ञानं, व्यक्ति *f.* 2 (Power of p.) ग्राहकत्वं, ग्रहण-वेदन-शक्ति *f.*, विषयानुभवः, चैतन्यं, चिच्छक्ति *f.* —PERCEPTIVE,-PERCIPIENT, *a.* ग्रहणक्षम, ग्राहिन्, ग्राहक. विषयग्रहणसमर्थ, चेतन.

PER CENT, *adv.* Ex. by उत्तर in comp.; '5 p.' पंचोत्तरं शतं.

PERCH, *s.* वासयष्टि *f.*, संडीनयष्टिः, यष्टिः, दंडः. —*v. i.* अध्यास् 2 A (with acc.), नि-ली 4 A, निषद् 1 P (with loc.) ; सं-डी 1 A (of birds.).

PERCHANCE, *adv. See* PERHAPS.

PERCOLATE, *v. i.* कणशः-लवशः स्रु-क्षर्-गल्- 1 P or स्यंद् 1 A. —*v. t.* शुध् c., बिंदुक्रमेण-लवशः-स्रु-

c. or गल् c. -ION, *s.* लवशः क्षरणं-स्रवणं-गलनं.

PERCUSSION, *s.* समाघातः, संघट्टः, आ-प्रति-घातः.

PERDITION, *s.* उच्छेदः, क्षयः, वि-प्र-नाशः. 2 अधोगति *f.*, अधःपातः, नरक-निरय-पातः; 'p. (ruin) seize thee' (cf. 'Murrain take thee') अकरणिः-अजीवनिः-अवग्राहः-निग्राहः-ते भूयात्.

PERDUE, *a.* प्रच्छन्न, गूढ.

PEREGRINATE,-ION, *See* TRAVEL.

PEREMPTORY, *a.* सुनिश्चित, निर्णीत, नियत; अविशंक्य, अवैकल्पिक(की *f.*), परिच्छिन्न, अवश्यक. 2 स्पष्ट, परिस्फुट, सुव्यक्त, भिन्नार्थ; 'p. order' अलंघनीयः-अनतिक्रमणीयः-आदेशः; 'the command of elderly persons is (to be considered as) p.' आज्ञा गुरूणां ह्यविचारणीया (R. XIV. 46). 3 दृढ-स्थिर-मति, सकृद्वादिन्, दृढसंकल्प. -ILY, *adv.* सुनिश्चितं, सुव्यक्तं, भिन्नार्थं, सुस्पष्टं; दार्ढ्येन, दृढनिश्चयपूर्वं. -INESS, *s.* स्पष्टता, दृढनिश्चयः, दृढता, अविशंक्यता.

PERENNIAL, *a.* वर्षावधि, वर्षस्थायिन्. 2 नित्य, अक्षय्य, निरंतर, अविरत.

PERFECT, *a.* सिद्ध, संपन्न, निष्पन्न, समाप्त, परिणत. 2 अशेष, समग्र, सकल, सं-परि-पूर्ण, समस्त, अविकल, अखंड, अक्षत, अन्यून, निर्दोष. 3 परम, उत्कृष्ट, विशिष्ट, उत्तम; निपुण, कुशल, अभिज्ञ, पारंगत, विशारद, प्रवीण, परिपक्व, संपन्न. 4 (In grammar) लिट्. -*v. t.* साध् c., सिध् c. (साधयति), सं-निः-पद् c., परि-सं-पूर् 10, समाप् c., निर्वृत् c.; ex. by कृ 8 U with (*a.*). -ER, *s.* संपादकः, साधकः. -ION, -NESS, *s.* सिद्धि *f.*, संपन्नता, समग्रता, अखंडता, सं-परि-पूर्णता. निष्पत्ति-समाप्ति *f.* 2 परि-,पाकः, परिणति *f.*, पक्वावस्था, उत्कृष्टता, उत्कर्षः, विशिष्टता, प्रकर्षः. परा कोटिः-काष्ठा. 3 नैपुण्यं, संपन्नता, कौशलं, विज्ञानं, प्रावीण्यं. 4 गुणः, परम-उत्तम-गुणः, विशेषः, प्र-उत्-कर्षः. -IVE, *a.* साधक, संपादक, समापक, सिद्धिकर (री *f.*). -LY, *adv.* सर्वथा, सर्वशः, साकल्येन, समग्रं, संपूर्णं, अशेषतः, निःशेषं.

PERFIDY, *s.* विश्वासघातः-भंगः-भेदः, असत्यसंधता, प्रतिज्ञा-समय-भंगः; शत्रुसेवा, कापट्यं, वंचनं-ना. -IOUS, *a.* असत्यसंध, विश्वास-विश्रंभ-घातिन्-भेदिन्, भग्नप्रतिज्ञ; वंचक, शठ, मिथ्याचार, शत्रुसेविन्. 2 (Of acts) अनार्य. -IOUSLY, *adv.* विश्वासघातेन, शठवत्, कैतवेन.

PERFORATE, *v. t.* आ-,व्यध् 4 P, छिद्रयति (D.), निर्भिद् 7 P, उत्-समुत्-कृ 6 P, (मणौ वज्रसमुत्कीर्णे R. I. 4); 'un-p. ed jewel' अनाविद्धं रत्नं (S. 2). -ED, *a.* विद्ध, सच्छिद्र, उत्कीर्ण, सरंध्र, सुषिर. -ION, *s.* वेधः-धनं, निर्भेदः. 2 छिद्रं, रंध्रं, विवरं, सुषिरं. -OR, *s.* वेधनिका, आविधः, आस्फोटनी.

PERFORCE, *adv.* बलात्, बलेन, प्रसभं, प्रसह्य, बलवत्, बलात्कारेण.

PERFORM, *v. t.* कृ 8 U, निर्वृत् c., आचर् 1 P, सं-निः-पद् c., साध् 5 P or c., वि-धा 3 U, अनु-ष्ठा 1P, निर्वह् c.; (promise) पूर् 10, तृ 1 P, शुध् c., अपवृज् 10; (a sacrifice) आतन् 8 U, आह् 1 P. 2 (On the stage) नट् 10, अभि-नी 1 P, प्रयुज् 7 A, 10; *See* ACT,; 'has not been (seen) p. ed on the stage' न प्रयोगतो दृष्टं (Rat. 1). -ANCE, *s.* संपादनं, साधनं, करणं, विधानं, निर्वर्तनं, अनुष्ठानं, आचरणं. 2 कार्यं, कर्मन् *n.*, क्रिया, कृति *f.*, व्यापारः, चेष्टा, चेष्टितं, प्रवृत्ति *f.*, चरितं. 3 प्रयोगः, अभिनयः, नाटनं. -ER, *s.* कर्तृ *m.*, संपादकः, निर्वर्तकः, अनुष्ठाता, निर्वाहकः. 2 (In dramas) अभिनेतृ *m.*, नटः; प्रयोजकः. 3 वादकः.

PERFUME, *v. t.* अधि-,वास् 10, धूप् 1 P, 10, धूपेन वास्, सुरभीकृ 8 U, परिमलयति-आमोदयति- (D.) भू c. -*s.* परिमलः, आमोदः, सुगंधः, सु-,वासः, सौरभं-भ्यं. 2 (Thing scented) गंधः, गंधद्रव्यं, गांधिकं. 3 (For the person) गात्रानुलेपनी; वर्ति *f.*, अनु-वि-लेपनं, वर्णकं; 'p. artificially made' कृत्रिम-वृक-धूपः. -ED, *a.* सुवासित, सवास, सुरभीकृत, सामोद, धूपित, भावित. -ER, *s.* गांधिकः, गंधोपजीविन् *m.*, गंधविक्रयी, गंधवणिज् *m.*, गंधाजीवः. -ERY, *s.* गंधद्रव्यं, गंधव्यापारः-विक्रयः. -ING, *s.* वासनं, भावनं. 2 (With unguents) चर्चा, चार्चिक्यं, अनु-वि-लेपनं, स्थासकः, अंगरागः.

PERFUNCTORY, *a.* अनवहित, निरुत्साह, प्रमत्त, अनुत्कंठ; *See* NEGLIGENT. -ILY, *adv.* अनवधानेन, निरुत्साहं. -INESS, *s.* अनवधानं, अनास्था, निरुत्साहता.

PERHAPS, *adv.* कदाचित्, दैवात्, कदापि, नु वा, किंस्विद्, स्यात्, or by pot.

PERIAPT, *s.* रक्षाकरंडः.

PERICARDIUM, *s.* हृदयकोशः, हृदाशयः.

PERICARP, *s.* बीजकोशः-गुप्ति *f.*

PERICRANIUM, *s.* कपालावरणं.

PERIGEE, *s.* नीचतमं-नेदिष्ठं-स्थानं.

PERIL, *s.* भयं, शंका, संदेहः, संशयः. -*v. t.* संशये पत् c. -OUS, *a.* संदिग्ध, सशंक, भयहेतुक; *See* DANGER, HAZARD.

PERIOD, *s.* समयः, कालः, वेला, कालावधिः, अंतरं, अवधिः, नियतकालः. 2 कालचक्रं-पर्यायः-आवर्तः, वर्षचक्रं, युगं. 3 अंतः, अवसानं, विरामः. 4 पूर्णवाक्यं, वाक्योच्चयः; पूर्णविरामः; 'p. of life' वयः, वयोवस्था; 'last p.' चरमवयः, अंत्यावस्था. -IC,-ICAL, *a.* नित्य, अनुकालिक-नियतकालिक-सामयिक-(की *f.*). -*s.* सामयिकपुस्तकं; 'a monthly p.' मासिकपुस्तकं. -ICALLY, *adv.* काले काले, समयतः, कालानुरूपं, नियतकाले.

PERIOSTEUM, *s.* अस्थित्वच् *f.*

PERIPHERY, *s.* परिवेशः-षः, परिधिः, परिणाहः. 2 नेमि-मी *f.*, प्रधिः.

PERIPHRASE, PERIPHRASIS, *s.* वागुपचयः, वाग्विस्तरः, वाग्बाहुल्यं-प्रपंचः. –*v. t.* प्रपंचयति (D.), वाग्विस्तरेण वर्ण् 10 or व्या-ख्या 2 P. –PERIPHRASTIC, *a.* बहुवाक्य, बहुपद; 'p. future' लुट्.

PERISH, *v. i.* नश् 4 P, प्र-वि-°, क्षि-pass.; प्रमी 4 A, ध्वंस् 1 A, क्षयं-नाशं-लयं-गम् 1 P or इ-या 2 P, प्र-वि-ली 4 A; मृ 6 A, व्यापद् 4 A; *See* DIE. –ABLE, *a.* वि,-नश्वर (री *f.*), विनाशधर्मन्, भंगुर, क्षयिन्, वि,-ध्वंसिन्, क्षयिष्णु, क्षय-नाश-शील, लयाधीन; 'p. in a moment' क्षणिक, क्षणभंगुर.

PERISTYLE, *s.* स्तंभपंक्ति-श्रेणी *f.*

PERITONEUM, *s.* अंत्रवेष्टनं.

PERJURE, *v. t.* साक्ष्ये मिथ्या-अनृतं वद् 1 P, मिथ्या शप् 1, 4 U, कूटसाक्ष्यं कृ 8 U. –ED, –ER, *a.*, *s.* कूटशपथकारिन्, मिथ्याशपक, कूटसाक्षिन्. –Y, *s.* कूट-मिथ्या-साक्ष्यं-शपनं.

PERMANENT, *a.* नित्य, स्थिर, नित्य-चिर-स्थायिन्, ध्रुव, अक्षय, स्थायिन्; *See* LASTING. –LY, *adv.* नित्यं, स्थिरं, ध्रुवं, शाश्वतं, सर्वकालं. –PERMANENCE, -CY, *s.* स्थिरता, स्थायित्वं, ध्रुवता, नित्यता, अक्षयता, अनपायः, सनातनत्वं. 2 प्रतिष्ठा, स्थिति *f.*, (कुलस्य स्थितये K. I. 18), (दशरथस्य कुलं प्रतिष्ठां गतं U. 5).

PERMEATE, *v. t.* व्याप् 5 P, व्यश् 5 A; *See* PERVADE. 2 प्र-विश् 6 P, भिद् 7 P, गाह् 1 A. –ION, *s.* व्याप्ति *f.*, प्रवेशः, भेदनं. –PERMEABLE, *a.* व्याप्य, भेद्य, प्रवेश्य.

PERMIT, *v. t.* अनु-ज्ञा 9 U, अनुमन् 4 A, अनुमुद् 1 A, आज्ञां दा 3 U; *See* ALLOW. –*s.* अनुज्ञा-अनुमति-पत्रं, अनुज्ञा. –PERMISSIBLE, *a.* अनुज्ञेय, अनुमंतव्य, अनुज्ञार्ह. 2 धर्म्य, न्याय्य, ग्राह्य, युक्त; *See* LAWFUL. –PERMISSION, *s.* अनुज्ञा, अनुमति *f.* -तं, अनुमोदनं; आदेशः, आज्ञा. –PERMISSIVE, *a.* अनुज्ञाप्रद, अनुमोदक; अनवश्यक.

PERMUTATION, *s.* वि-,निमयः, परिवर्तः, परिवृत्ति *f.*, व्यतिहारः. 2 अंकपाशः.

PERNICIOUS, *a.* घातक, अपकारक, वि-,नाशक, हिंस्र, हिंसक, अपकारिन्, दुष्ट, गर्ह्य; *See* INJURIOUS.–LY, *adv.* सापकारं, सापायं, सनाशं.

PERORATION, *s.* उपसंहारः.

PERPENDICULAR, *a.* लंब, लंबरूप; सरल, ऋजु, अकुटिल. –*s.* लंबः. –LY, *adv.* लंबरूपेण, सरलं, ऋजु.

PERPETRATE, *v. t.* कृ 8 U, वि-धा 3 U, आचर् 1 P; *See* COMMIT.

PERPETUAL, *a.* नित्य, सतत, शाश्वत (ती *f.*), अविच्छिन्न, अविरत, संतत, निरंतर, सनातन (नी *f.*), अनंत, नित्य-चिर-स्थायिन्. –LY, *adv.* नित्यं, सदा, नित्यशः, शाश्वतं, शश्वत्, सततं, अविरतं. –PERPETUITY, *s.* अविच्छेदः, नित्य-चिर-स्थायिता, आनंत्यं, नित्यता, अविरामः, नैरंतर्यं, अक्षयस्थिति *f.*, सनातनत्वं; 'to p.' शाश्वतीः समाः. –PERPETUATE, *v. t.* स्थिरीकृ 8 U, कृ with (*a.*).

PERPLEX, *v. t.* मुह् c., आकुलीकृ 8 U, सं-वि-भ्रम् c. (भ्रमयति), मोहं-संभ्रमं-उत्पद् c. 2 संकुलीकृ, संकीर्णीकृ, क्लिश् 9 P; *See* EMBARRASS, CONFUSE. –ED, *a.* आ-व्या-कुल, संभ्रांत, वि-,मूढ, कातर, व्यग्र, उद्विग्न, अधीर; व्याकुलचित्त, संभ्रांतमनस्, व्यस्त-मूढ-विक्षिप्त-चित्त. –ING, *a.* मोहक, संदिग्ध, भ्रम-मोह-कारिन्, मोहकर (री *f.*), मोहन, भ्रांतिजनन (नी *f.*); विषम. –ITY, *s.* व्या,-मोहः, आ-व्या-कुलत्वं-ता, संभ्रमः, व्यग्रता, चित्तविक्षेपः, व्यस्तचित्तत्वं, चित्तवैक्लव्यं, संशयः, संदेहः.

PERQUISITE, *s.* अधिकलाभः, पुरस्कारः; *See* GIFT.

PERSECUTE, *v. t.* प्र-सं-बाध् 1 A, उप-द्रु 1 A, पीड् 10, उप-द्रु 1 P, क्लिश् 9 P, पीडार्थं अनुसृ 1 P, अभि-,द्रुह् 4 P. –ION, *s.* बाधा, उपद्रवः, उपप्लवः, पीडनं, अभिद्रोहः. –OR, *s.* बाधकः, उपद्रवकारिन् *m.*

PERSEVERE, *v. i.* मनः-चित्तं-अभिनिविश् c., सदा प्रवृत् 1 A, अभियुज् pass., अभिनिवेशेन सं-पद् c., सततं प्रयत् 1 A, अनवरतं चेष्ट् 1 A, निर्बंधं कृ, साग्रहं प्रवृत्; 'p. in your opposition' स्थिरप्रतिबंधो भव (S. 2); 'he who p. s in good actions' सदाचारप्रवृत्तः, सदा सन्मार्गयायी. –ANCE, *s.* अभिनिवेशः, अध्यवसायः, उद्यमसातत्यं, दीर्घप्रयत्नः-उद्यमः-उद्योगः-उत्साहः, अतिनिर्बंधः, सदाभियोगः. 2 अनवरतचेष्टा-प्रवृत्ति *f.*, प्रसक्ति *f.*, धैर्यं, आग्रहः, उद्योगः, उद्यमः, व्यवसायः. –ING, *a.* अभियोगवत्, उद्यमिन्, अभिनिविष्ट, अध्यवसायिन्, दीर्घोद्योगिन्, सदाप्रवृत्त, उत्साहवत्, आग्रह-निर्बंध-शील, प्रसक्त, प्रसित. –INGLY, *adv.* अभिनिवेशेन, दीर्घोद्योगेन, प्रसक्तं, सोत्साहं, सनिर्बंधं.

PERSIST, *v. i.* साग्रहं प्रवृत् 1 A, अतिनिर्बंधेन आचर् 1 P, पर्यव-स्था 1 A; *See* below; 'do not p. in your wickedness' दुराचरितेषु मा ते निर्बंधो भूत्; *See* PERSEVERE. –ENCE,-CY *s.* निर्बंधः, आग्रहः, अभिनिवेशः, पर्यवस्थानं, दृढाग्रहः. –ENT, *a.* निर्बंधपर, साग्रह; *See* OBSTINATE. –ENTLY, *adv.* साग्रहं, निर्बंधेन.

PERSON, *s.* पुरुषः, नरः, जनः, व्यक्ति *f.*; 'this p.' अयं जनः (referring to the speaker); 'a female p.' स्त्रीजनः, अंगनाजनः. 2 शरीरं, अंगं, वपुस् *n.*, देहः, कायः, तनु *f.*, गात्रं; *See* BODY. 3 रूपं, आकारः, आकृति *f.*, मूर्ति *f.*; 'an enemy in the p. of Krishna' कृष्णरूपः शत्रुः. 4 पात्रं, भूमिका. 5 पुरुषः (in grammar); 'in p.' स्वयं, स्वतः, आत्मना, साक्षात्, प्रत्यक्षं. –ABLE, *a.* सुरूप, सुगात्र (त्री *f.*), शोभनाकार. –AGE, *s.* पुरुषः, जनः, नरः, व्यक्तिः. 2 श्रेष्ठ-विशिष्ट-जनः. –AL, *a.* व्यक्तिगत, पुरुषविशेषानुबद्ध, विशिष्टजनोद्दिष्ट. 2 शारीरिक-दैहिक-

(की *f.*), शरीर-अंग in comp.; 'p. beauty' अंगसौष्ठवं; 'p. graces' शरीरलावण्यं; 'p. union' शरीरसंबंधः; 'p. attendant' आसन्नपरिचारकः; 'p. attendance' शरीरचर्या-शुश्रूषा. 3 स्वयंकृत, स्व-आत्म-कृत, साक्षात्कृत. 4 आत्मन्, स्व, निज in comp.; 'for p. profit' आत्म-स्व-हिताय; 'p. experience'. स्वानुभवः. 5 पुरुष-व्यक्ति-वाचिन्, पुरुष in comp. 6 अस्थावर, जंगम. -ALITY, *s.* व्यक्तिगताक्षेपः; विशेष-व्यक्ति-निर्देशः, व्यक्त्युद्देशः, व्यक्तिसंस्पर्शः. 2 व्यक्तिः, पृथक्त्वं, स्वत्वं. -ALLY, *adv.* स्वयं, स्वतः, प्रत्यक्षं-क्षतः, साक्षात्. 2 व्यक्तितः, पृथक्. —PERSONATE, *v. t.* रूपं-वेषं ग्रह् 9 P or धृ 1 P, 10 or आ-स्था 1 U (with gen.), छद्म-कूटं-कृ 8 U; oft. ex. by वेश or रूप in comp., or by denom.; 'p. ing Nala' नलरूपमास्थाय, नलरूपः, नलवेशधारिन्; 'p. s a king' नृपायते, राजानति. 2 अभि-नी 1 P, नट् 10, रूप् 10. -ION, *s.* रूप-वेश-धारणं-ग्रहणं. 2 अभिनवः, नाटनं. -OR, *s.* वेशधारिन्-भृत् *m.* 2 अभिनेतृ *m.* —PERSONIFY, *v. t.* चेतनत्वं-चेतनभावं-आरुह् c. (रोपयति), (अचेतने) चेतनवदुपचर् 1 P, (अचेतनेपि चेतनवदुपचारदर्शनात् S. B. 99). -ED, *a.* Ex. by मूर्ति *f.*, मूर्तशरीरिन्-*a.*, इव or साक्षात्. -ICATION, *s.* चेतनत्वारोपः, चेतनधर्मारोपः; मनुष्यगुणारोपः, उपचारः; oft. by इव, साक्षात्; 'p. of virtue' साक्षात्-मूर्तिमान्-धर्मः; *See* EMBODIED.

PERSPICACIOUS, *a.* तीक्ष्ण-सूक्ष्म-दृष्टि, सूक्ष्मदर्शिन्. 2 तीक्ष्ण-सूक्ष्म-बुद्धि-मति, कुशाग्रबुद्धि. -NESS, -PERSPICACITY, *s.* सूक्ष्मदृष्टित्वं, दृष्टिसूक्ष्मता, दृक्पाटवं. 2 सूक्ष्ममतित्वं.

PERSPICUOUS, *a.* स्पष्ट, विशद, प्रसन्न, व्यक्त, सुप्रकाश, सुबोध. -LY, *adv.* स्पष्टं, विशदं, भिन्नार्थं. -NESS, -PERSPICUITY, *s.* स्पष्टता, प्रसादः, वैशद्यं.

PERSPIRE, *v. i.* प्र-,स्विद् 4 P, स्वेदं-घर्मं-स्रु c. -*v. t.* रोमद्वारा निःसृ c. or स्रु c., स्विद् c. -ATION, *s.* स्वेदनं, घर्म-स्वेद-स्रावः. 2 स्वेदः, घर्मः, स्वेद-घर्मजलं-बिंदुः-उदकं; 'excessive p.' प्रस्वेदः. -ING, *a.* सस्वेद, सघर्म, स्वेद-घर्म-स्राविन्, स्वेदित, स्विन्न; 'violently p.' प्रस्विन्न, भृशस्विद्.

PERSUADE, *v. t.* अनु-नी 1 P, प्रबुध् c., अनुशास् 2 P, प्र-वृत् c., नियुज् 10, प्रोत्सह् c., आकृष् 1 P; oft. by causal of roots. 2 प्रति-इ c., प्रतीति-विश्वासं जन् c. (जनयति), संशयं-संदेहं-छिद् 7 P; *See* CONVINCE. -ED, *a.* अनुनीत; जातनिश्चय-विश्वास, प्रतीत, छिन्नसंशय, जातप्रत्यय; 'I feel p.' इति मे प्रतीतिः, इति दृढं मन्ये. -ER, *s.* प्रवर्तकः, प्रोत्साहकः, नियोजकः. -PERSUASION, *s.* अनुनयः, अनुशासनं, उपदेशः, प्रवर्तनं, नियोजनं, प्रबोधः-धनं, प्रोत्साहनं. 2 संदेह-संशय-च्छेदः, शंकानिवृत्ति *f.*, दृढनिश्चयः, प्रत्ययः, निर्णयः. 3 मतं, मार्गः, पथिन् *m.*, संप्रदायः. —PERSUASIVE, PERSUASORY, *a.* सानुनय, प्रवर्तक, प्रबोधक, अनुनयिन्, हृदयग्राहिन्, आकर्षिन्. 2 प्रत्ययकारिन्, संशयच्छिद्.

PERT, *a.* चपल, लघु; *See* LIVELY. 2 धृष्ट, प्रगल्भ, अविनीत. -LY, *adv.* चापल्यात्, धृष्टतया, अविनयेन. -NESS, *s.* चापल्यं, धाष्टर्यं, अविनयः.

PERTAIN, *v. i.* संबंध् pass., संबंधिन्-*a.* भू 1 P; *See* BELONG.

PERTINENT, *a.* प्रास्ताविक (की *f.*), युक्त, यथायोग्य, उपपन्न, योग्य, प्रस्तावसदृश (शी *f.*); 'to be p.' उप-पद् 4 A, युज् pass. -LY, *adv.* युक्तं, उपपन्नं, यथोचितं, प्रसंगानुरूपं, प्रस्तावसदृशं. -PERTINENCE,-CY, *s.* युक्तता, उपपत्ति *f.*, योग्यता, प्रसंगसंगति *f.*, याथार्थ्यं, प्रस्तुतानुसारः.

PERTINACIOUS, *a.* निर्बंधशील, आग्रहिन्, स्थिर-दृढप्रतिज्ञ; धीर, दृढ. -LY, *adv.* सनिर्बंधं, साग्रहं. -NESS, -PERTINACITY, *s.* निर्बंधः, आग्रहः, अभिनिवेशः, दार्ढ्यं, धैर्यं; *See* OBSTINATE, -CY.

PERTURB, *v. t.* सं,-क्षुभ् c., आकुलीकृ 8 U, उपहन् 2 P, वि-मुह् c., व्यग्रीकृ, व्यस् 4 A, संकरीकृ ; *See* CONFUSE. -ATION, *s.* सं-,क्षोभः, व्यग्रता, उपप्लवः, व्या-,मोहः, आकुलत्वं, वैक्लव्यं, उद्वेगः. -ED, *a.* क्षुब्ध, आ-व्या-कुल, विक्लव, व्यग्र, परिप्लव, उद्विग्न, पर्याकुल.

PERUSE, *v. t.* समग्रं पठ् 1 P or अधि-इ 2 A, निपुणं वच् c.; *See* READ.-AL, *s.* अध्ययनं, पठनं, पारायणं.

PERVADE, *v. t.* अभि-,व्याप् 5 P, वि-अश् 5 A, सर्वतः आक्रम् 1 U, 4 P or प्रविश् 6 P, वि-गाह् 1 A, मुर्छ् 1 P; मूर्च्छंत्यमी विकाराः ऐश्वर्यमत्तेषु (S. 5) 'p. (the minds of) those' &c., '(the freshness of) youth has p. ed her limbs' यौवनमंगेषु सन्नद्धं (S. 1). -ING, -PERVASIVE, *a.* व्यापक, व्यापिन् ; 'p. all things' सर्वग, सर्वव्यापिन् ; 'p. the whole body' सर्वांगीण. -PERVASION, *s.* अभिव्यापनं-व्याप्ति *f.*, आक्रमणं; मूर्च्छनं.

PERVERSE, *a.* वाम, कुटिल, प्रतीप, विपरीत, वक्र, प्रतिकूल, वि-प्रति-लोम, वक्र-वाम-शील, कुटिलमति, पिशुन; *See* OBSTINATE. -LY, *adv.* वामतया, कौटिल्येन, प्रतीपं, विपरीतं, वामशीलतया. -NESS, *s.* प्रतीपता, वामता, वैपरीत्यं, कौटिल्यं, दुष्टता, दौरात्म्यं, दुःशीलं.

PERVERT, *v. t.* वि-कृ 8 U, परिवृत् c., साचीकृ, विरूप् 10, विलोमीकृ, अन्यथा कृ; भ्रंश् c., विपर्यस् 4 U or c., कलुषयति (D.), कलुषीकृ; दुष् c. (दूषयति), विपारि-णम् c. (णमयति). -ER, -ING, *s.*, *a.* विकारिन्, विपरिणामिन्, विपर्यासकारिन्. -PERVERSION, *s.* विकारः, विकृति *f.*, विक्रिया, विलोमत्वं, प्रतीपता, विपरिणामः, विपर्यासः, विपर्ययः, दूषणं, भ्रंशनं, साचीकरणं, कालुष्यं.

PERVIOUS, *a.* व्याप्य, भेद्य, प्रवेश्य.

PESTER, *v. t.* बाध् 1 A, पीड् 10, उपद्रु 1 A; *See* HARASS.

PEST, PESTILENCE, *s.* मारि-री *f.*, म(मा)रकः; (fig.) आधिः, कंटकः, उत्पातः, शल्यं; त्रामाः कुलस्याधयः (S. 4) 'are a p. to the family'; 'p. of the people' लोककंटकः. -PESTIFEROUS,

PESTILENTIAL, *a.* मरकावह, मारात्मक, घातुक, विनाशक, दूषक, बाधक, अपकारक, अपकारिन्, अनिष्टकर (री *f.*).

PESTLE, *s.* मुस(श)लः-लं, अयोग्रं.

PET, *s.* प्रेम-प्रीति-पात्रं, प्रेमास्पदं; क्रीडामृगः. 2 ईषत्कोपः, कोपावेशः. -*a.* प्रिय, प्रेमास्पदीभूत, वल्लभ; *See* FAVOURITE. -*v. t.* लल् 10; *See* FONDLE.

PETAL, *s.* दलं, पत्रं. -ED, -OUS, *a.* सदल, दलवत्.

PETITION, *v. t.* अर्थ् 10 A, प्र-अभि-°, याच् 1 A; निविद् c., वि-ज्ञा c. (ज्ञापयति). -*s.* प्रार्थना, याच्ञा, निवदनं, विज्ञप्ति *f.*, विज्ञापना. 2 (Written) विज्ञप्तिः, प्रार्थना-निवेदन-पत्रं. -ER, *s.* प्रार्थकः, प्रार्थयितृ *m.*, अर्थिन् *m.*, याचकः, निवेदकः; 'ascertain who are the p. s' ज्ञायतां कः कः कार्यार्थीति (Mr. 9).

PETRIFY, *v. t.* पाषाणी-प्रस्तरी-कृ 8 U, कठिनीकृ, जडीकृ, संस्तंभ् c.; 'p. ed with astonishment' आश्चर्यजडीकृत. -*v. i.* पाषाणीभू 1 P. -ACTION, *s.* पाषाणीकरणं; पाषाणीभूतद्रव्यं.

PETROLEUM, *s.* शिलातैलं-रसः.

PETTICOAT, *s.* शाटी, शाटकः, चंडातकं, अर्धोरुकं (girl's); 'under p. government' स्त्रीजितः, स्त्रीवश्यः; 'p. government' स्त्रीशासनं.

PETTIFOGGER, *s.* क्षुद्र-अधम-वृत्तिः.

PETTISH, *a.* कर्कश, वक्रशील-भाव, परुषस्वभाव, प्रतीप; *See* PEEVISH. -LY, *adv.* कर्कशं, परुषं. -NESS, *s.* कार्कश्यं, स्वभावपारुष्यं.

PETTY, *a.* लघु, क्षुद्र, अल्प; *See* SMALL; oft. by उप or कल्प in comp.; 'a p. king' उपराजा, नृपकल्पः.

PETULANT, *a.* कर्कश, प्रतीप, दुःशील, वाम; *See* PEEVISH. 2 अविनीत, प्रगल्भ, धृष्ट. -LY, *adv.* प्रतीपं, धृष्टवत्.-PETULANCE, *s.* प्रतीपता, दुःशीलं, धृष्टता.

PEWTER, *s.* कांस्यं, पीतलोहं. -ER, *s.* कांस्यकारः.

PHALANX, *s.* व्यूहः; पंक्ति *f.*

PHANTASM, *s.* आ-,भासः, छाया, माया, मनोरथसृष्टि *f.*

PHANTASMAGORIA, *s.* मायाजालं.

PHANTASY, *s.* *See* FANCY.

PHANTOM, *s.* भूतः, वेतालः, पिशाचः, रात्रिचरः. 2 आ-,भासः, मनोरथसृष्टि *f.*, माया, कल्पना.

PHARISEE, PHARISAIC, *s.*, *a.* *See* HYPOCRITE.

PHARMACOPÆIA, *s.* औषधतत्त्वशास्त्रं, भेषजसंस्कारग्रंथः.

PHARMACY, *s.* औषधक्रिया-संस्कारः-विद्या.

PHAROS, *s.* दीपस्थानं-गृहं.

PHASE, PHASIS, *s.* दर्शनं, वस्तु *n.*; 'p. s of the moon' चंद्रस्य क्षयवृद्धी. 2 (Point of view) दृष्टि *f.*; *See* VIEW.

PHEASANT, *s.* वीजनः, जीवंजीवः.

PHENOMENON, *s.* दृग्विषयः, गोचरवस्तु *n.*, दर्शनं, आलोकः. 2 उत्पातः, अद्भुतं.

PHIAL, *s.* लघुकूपी, काचकूपी-पात्रं.

PHILANTHROPY, *s.* लोकहितेच्छा, लोक-जन-प्रीति *f.*, सर्वभूतदया, विश्वप्रीतिः, विश्वसौहृदं. -IC,-ICAL, *a.* लोकहितैषिन्, जनहितकाम; जगन्मित्रं, विश्वमित्रं, विश्वसुहृद्. -IST, *s.* जनहितैषी, विश्वसुहृद्.

PHILIPPIC, *s.* भर्त्सनवाक्यं, निंदात्मकः प्रबंधः.

PHILOLOGY, *s.* भाषाविज्ञानं-तत्त्वं, शब्दव्युत्पत्तिशास्त्रं-विद्या. -ER,-IST, *s.* शाब्दिकः, भाषातत्त्वज्ञः. -ICAL, *a.* शाब्दिक (कीं *f.*), शब्दशास्त्रीय.

PHILOMATH, *s.* विद्याप्रियः-भक्तः, ज्ञानसेविन् *m.* -Y, *s.* विद्यासेवनं.

PHILOSOPHY, *s.* दर्शनं; 'six systems of p.' षड्दर्शनं. 2 तत्त्वज्ञानं, विज्ञानं, तत्त्वविद्या-शास्त्रं; तत्त्वं, ज्ञानं, विद्या, शास्त्रं in comp.; 'moral p.' नीतिशास्त्रं; 'logical p.' तर्कशास्त्रं-विद्या, &c. -ER, *s.* दर्शनज्ञः, तत्त्वविद् *m.*, तत्त्वज्ञः-ज्ञानी, तात्त्विकः, ज्ञानी, पंडितः, प्राज्ञः, ज्ञाननिष्ठः; 'p.'s stone' चिंतामणिः. स्पर्शमणिः. -IC,-ICAL, *a.* तत्त्व-दर्शन in comp., दार्शनिक (की *f.*). 2 विज्ञ, तत्त्वज्ञानपर, ज्ञान-विद्यापर. -ICALLY, *adv.* दर्शनानुसारेण, तत्त्वतः. -IZE, *v. i.* तत्त्वं निरूप् 10 or आलोच् 10 or अन्वीक्ष् 1 A

PHILTRE, *s.* मंत्रौषधं, वशीकरणचूर्णं.

PHIZ, *s.* *See* FACE.

PHLEBOTOMY, *s.* शिरावेधः-मोक्षः-छेदः, रक्तमोक्षणं-स्रावः.

PHLEGM, *s.* कफः, श्लेष्मन् *m.*, सिंघाणकं. 2 मांद्यं, जाड्यं; 'a medicine removing p.' (phlegmagogue) श्लेष्मघ्नं, कफनाशनं. -ATIC, *a.* कफिन्, श्लेष्मल-ण, बहुकफ. 2 कफकर (री *f.*), श्लेष्मजनन (नी *f.*). 3 श्लेष्मज. 4 जड, मंद, शीत; *See* INDIFFERENT.

PHONETIC, *a.* स्वरसंवादिन्, ध्वनि-स्वर- in comp. -PHONETICS, PHONICS, *s.* स्वर-ध्वनि-विद्या-शास्त्रं.

PHOTOGRAPH, *s.* आलोकलेख्यं. -ER, *s.* आलोकलेख्यकारः.

PHRASE, *s.* वाक्यं, उक्ति *f.*, वचनं. -*v. t.* अभि-धा 3 U, उद्दिश् 6 P; *See* CALL. -PHRASEOLOGY, *s.* वाक्यबंधः-रचना, भाषासरणि *f.*, वाक्प्रकारः, वाग्रीति *f.*-व्यापारः-व्यवहारः; 'dramatic p.' नाट्योक्तिः, नाट्यपरिभाषा.

PHRENETIC, *a.* उन्मत्त; *See* FRANTIC. -PHRENITIS, *s.* सन्निपातज्वरः, उन्मादः; *See* FRENZY.

PHRENOLOGY, *s.* मस्तिष्कविद्या.

PETHISIC, PETHISIS, *s.* श्वासावरोधः, श्वासकृच्छ्रं;

क्षयः, क्षयरोगः, शोषः, यक्ष्मन् *m.*, राजयक्ष्मा. —PHTHISICAL, *a.* क्षयिन्, क्षयरोगिन्.

PHYLACTERY, *s.* रक्षाकरंडः.

PHYSIC, *s.* चिकित्सा, उपचारः, वैद्यक्रिया, औषधोपचारः. 2 औषधं, भेषजं, अगदः. —*v. t.* कित् desid. (चिकित्सति-ते), उपचर् 1 P, भेषजं दा 3 U. —IAN, *s.* वैद्यः, भिषज् *m.*, चिकित्सकः, अगदंकारः, रोगहारी-हृत्. —PHYSICAL, *a.* साकार, स्थूल, जड; *See* MATERIAL. 2 अंग, विग्रह, शरीर in comp.; 'p. strength' शारीरबलं; 'p. substance' स्थूलद्रव्यं-वस्तु. 3 Medicinal. q. v.; 'p. science (physics)' पदार्थविज्ञानं,-शास्त्रं. —LY, *adv.* प्रकृत्या, स्वभावतः, जातितः, जन्मतः; *See* NATURALLY.

PHYSIOGNOMY, *s.* आकृति *f.*, वदनाकृतिः, मुखं, वदनं. 2 वदनलक्षणनिरूपणं. —IST, *s.* मुखसामुद्रिकः.

PIACULAR, *a.* अघ-पाप-नाशिन्.

PICAROON, *s.* समुद्रीयदस्युः.

PICK, *v. t.* चि 5 U, ग्रह् 9 P, समाहृ 1 P, आ-दा 3 A, उद्-धृ 1 P, 10, लू 9 U, छिद् 7 P, (flower &c.). 2 शुध् c., मृज् 2 P or c., परिष्कृ 8 U. 3 (Up) वृ 5 U, उद्धृ 1 P, उद्ग्रह्; पृथक् कृ; 'p. a bone' अस्थिमांसं चर्व् 1 P, 10; 'p. out' उत्पट् 10, निष्कृष् 1 P; 'p. a quarrel' कलहं उत्-स्था c. (उत्थापयति); 'p. holes' (in another's coat) परस्य छिद्राणि दृश् 1 P, रंध्राणि-छिद्राणि-अन्विष् 4 P; 'p. the pocket' ग्रंथिं छित्त्वा अपहृ. —*s.* Pick-axe, q. v. 2 उद्धारः, वरणं. 3 विशिष्टभागः, उत्कृष्टभागः; 'ear-p.' कंडूयनकं; 'tooth-p.' दंतोल्लेखनी; 'p.-axe' टंकः, पाषाणभेदनी, पाषाणदारणः; 'p.-pocket' ग्रंथिच्छेदकः-चौरः. —ING, *s.* उद्धरणं, उद्ग्रहणं.

PICKET, *s.* सेनारक्षः, रक्षकदलं. 2 शंकुः, स्थाणुः.

PICKLE, *s.* संधितं, संधानं, संधितद्रव्यं. 2 लवणं. —*v. t.* सं-धा 3 U, उपस्कृ 8 U.

PICNIC, *s.* विहरणं, वनभोजनं.

PICTORIAL, *a.* सचित्र, चित्रोपेत, चित्रलिखित.

PICTURE, *s.* चित्रं, आलेख्यं, प्रतिमा, प्रतिकृति *f.*, प्रतिरूपं, प्रतिच्छेदः-दकं, प्रतिच्छाया; 'as if drawn in a p.' आलिखित इव; 'p.-board' चित्रफलकः; 'p.-frame' चित्राधारः, चित्रावरणं; 'p.-gallery' चित्रावली, चित्रशाला; 'p.-maker' चित्रक(का)रः. —*v. t.* मनसि कृ 8 U, आलोच् 10, मनसा कृप् c. or विचर् c. or वि-भू c. 2 चित्र् 10, आलिख् 6 P, वर्ण् 10. —ED, *a.* चित्रगत, आलेख्यगत, चित्रार्पित, आलिखित. 2 मनसा, कल्पित. —PICTURESQUE, *a.* चित्रोपम, वि-,चित्र, शबल.

PIEBALD, *a. See* VARIEGATED.

PIECE, *s.* खंडः-डं, विभागः; अंशः, लवः, शकलः-लं, वि-,दलं, भित्तं. 2 रचना, प्र-,बंधः; 'to break in p. s' शकलीकृ 8 U. खंडशः कृ, खंड् 10; 'to fall to p. s' वि-,दल् 1 P; 'p. of poetry' काव्यप्रबंधः, कविता; 'p. of work' कार्यं; 'p. of money' मुद्रा; 'p. of water' जलाधारः, जलाशयः; 'in p. s' खंडशः, लवशः; 'p. at chess' शा(सा)रिः-रः; 'a p. to each' एकैकं, प्रत्येकं, पृथक् पृथक्; 'what a p. of work is man' अहो निर्माणविशेषः नरजीवः; 'of a p.' एकरूप-प्रकार; 'of a p. with' सदृश (शी *f.*), अनुरूप; *See* LIKE. —*v. t.* संयुज् 7 U, 10, संधा-समाधा- 3 U. —LESS, *a.* अखंड. —PIECEMEAL, *adv.* खंडशः, लवशः, भागशः, खंडे खंडं, पृथक् पृथक्. —*a.* भागिन्, खंड in comp.

PIED, *a. See* VARIEGATED.

PIER, *s.* सेतुबंधः. 2 स्तंभः. वप्रः-प्रं.

PIERCE, *v. t.* व्यध् 4 P, निर्-भिद् 7 P, प्र-भंज् 7 P, छिद् 7 P; *See* PERFORATE. 2 आ-उप-हन् 2 U; शीतवातोपहतः 'p. ed by cold winds'. —ED, *a.* विद्ध, निर्भिन्न, छिद्रित; 'p. ed through the heart' भिन्नहृदय; 'having the ears p.' विद्ध-छिद्रित-कर्ण. —ER, *s.* वेधकः, भेदकः. 2 वेधनिका, वेधनी. —ING, *a.* वेधक; वेधिन्, भेदिन्, भिद्-छिद्-in comp.; 'p. the vital parts of the heart' हृदयमर्मभिद्-छिद्; (sound) परुष, कर्कश. —*s.* वेधः-धनं, निर्भेदः, छेदः-दनं.

PIETY, *s. See* under PIOUS.

PIG, *s.* शूकरशावः-वकः, शूकरः; *See* HOG. 2 कुशी, लोहपिंडः; 'p.-iron' असंस्कृतं अयः; 'p.-headed' स्थूल, स्थूलधी. —GISH, *a.* शूकरोपम. —PIGGERY, *s.* शूकरालयः.

PIGEON, *s.* कपोतः, पारावतः, कलरवः; 'wood p.' हारि(री)तः; 'p.-hearted' भीरुहृदय, कातर; 'p.-whole' कपोतबिलं; 'p.-house,-cot' कपोतपालिका, विटंकः.

PIGMENT, *s.* वर्णकः, वर्णः, रंगः.

PIGMY, *s.* वामनः, ह्रस्वः, खर्वः. —*a.* वामन, ह्रस्व, खर्व, लघुतनु, अल्पमूर्ति.

PIKE, *s.* प्रासः, कुंतः, शूलः-लं; *See* LANCE; 'p.-man' प्रासिकः, कौंतिकः, शाक्तीकः, शूली.

PILE, *s.* राशिः, चयः, निकरः, पुंजः, पूगः, स्तोमः, समूहः. 2 चिता, चिति *f.*, चित्या. 3 स्थूणा, स्तंभः, शंकुः, कीलः. 4 हर्म्यं, भवनं, महामंदिरं. —*v. t.* समाचि 5 U, राशीकृ 8 U.

PILES, *s.* अर्शस् *n.*, दुर्नामकं, अर्शोरोगः, गुदकीलकः, गुदांकुरः; 'affected by p.' अर्शस.

PILFER, *v. t.* मुष् 9 P, चुर् 10, अपहृ 1 P. —ER, *s.* चौरः, मोषकः; *See* ROB,-BER.

PILGRIM, *s.* यात्रिकः, तीर्थसेविन् *m.* —AGE, *s.* तीर्थयात्रा, यात्रा, यात्राप्रसंगः, तीर्थाटनं-सेवा; 'on a p.

to Garuda' गरुडस्य यात्राप्रसंगेन; 'place of p.' तीर्थः-र्थं, पुण्यस्थानं.

PILL, s. वटिका, गुटिका, गुलिका.

PILLAGE, v. t. वि-,लुंट्-ठ् 1 P, 10, अपहृ 1 P. -s. विलुंटनं, लोप्त्रं, लोत्रं, अपहारः. -ER, s. लुंठकः, अपहारकः.

PILLAR, s. स्तंभः, स्थाणुः, स्थूणा, अवष्टंभः; यूपः (sacrificial); 'p. of state' राज्यस्य आधारस्तंभः; 'p. s of justice' न्यायाधाराः, धर्मावष्टंभाः.

PILLOW, s. उपधानं, उपबर्हः, बालिशं; 'p.-case' उपधानकोशः-आवेष्टनं; 'I slept, making my left arm serve as a p.' वामभुजमुपधाय अशयिषि (D. K. II. 5). -v. t. उप-धा 3 U, उपधानीकृ 8 U.

PILOUS, a. लोमश, प्रचुरलोमन्. -PILOSITY, s. लोमशत्वं, लोमप्राचुर्यं.

PILOT, s. कर्णधारः-ग्राहः, कार्णिकः, कर्णिन् m., नाविकः, नौवाहः. 2 Guide, q. v. -v. t. मार्गं दृश् c., प्रणी 1 P, वह् c. -AGE, s. कर्णिकवेतनं.

PIMP, s. विटः, संचारकः; See PANDER.

PIMPLE, s. पिटिका, स्फोटः, क्षुद्र-तनु-व्रणः, रक्तस्फोटः-गंडः, रक्तवटी. -ED,-Y, a. सस्फोट, व्रणिन्, दद्रुण, पिटिकावृत.

PIN, s. सूचि f., कीलः-लकः-कं, शलाका, शंकुः, शल्यं. 2 (Of a carriage) अणिः-णी, अक्षाग्रकीलः; 'p.-maker' सूचिकारः. -v. t. सूच्या बंध् 9 P, कील् 10.

PINCERS, s. संदंशः-शकः, कंकमुखं.

PINCH, v. t. पीड् 10, बाध् 1 A, क्लिश् 9 P, संकुच् 1 P (the body), आतंक् 8 U; 'p. ed with cold' शीतार्त, हिमपीडित; 'p. ing poverty' दुःसहं दारिद्र्यं. 2 अंगुल्यग्रेण पीड्. 3 मुष्टिना संग्रह् 9 P, संग्रह्; 'none but the wearer knows where the shoe p. es' न हि वंध्या विजानाति गुर्वीं प्रसववेदनां. -s. अंगुलिपीडनं; संग्राहः, ग्रहणं; 'p. of snuff' नस्यकूर्चः. 2 संकटावस्था, दुर्गति f., कष्टं, कृच्छ्रं; 'p.-fist' बद्ध-दृढ-मुष्टिः, अमुक्तहस्तः.

PINE, s. देवदारुः-रु, पीतद्रुः, सरलः, पूतिकाष्ठं; See FIR also. -v. i. (Away) अवसद् 1 P, परि-, म्लै-ग्लै 1 P, क्षि-pass., खिद्-म्ली 4 A. 2 (For) उत्तम् 4 P, उत्कंठ् 1 A, उत्सुकायते (D.); oft. by उत्क, उत्सुक, उत्कंठ in comp.; 'a heart p. ing away in absence' विरहोत्कंठं हृदयं; 'p. ed for his home' गृहं गंतुमुदताम्यत्; अद्रिसुतासमागमोत्कः (K. VI. 95) 'p. ing to be united with Pàrvati'; अंतःपुरविरहपर्युत्सुकस्य राजर्षेः (S. 3) 'who is p. ing by separation' &c. -ING, s. म्लानि f., अवसादः, उत्कंठा. -a. म्लान, क्षीण, विषण्ण, उत्क, उत्सुक, सोत्कंठ.

PINION, s. पक्षः, पर्णं. 2 बाहुपाशः-बंधः. -v. t. पक्षौ बंध् 9 P, बाहू बंध्.

PINK, s. पाटलवर्णः, पाटलः. 2 अग्रं, शिखरं, परा काष्ठा. -a. पाटल, पाटलवर्ण; 'p.-eyed' गज-सूक्ष्म-नेत्र. -v. t. व्यध् 4 P; See PERFORATE.

PINNACE, s. क्षुद्र-लघु-नौका.

PINNACLE, s. अट्टः, प्रासादाग्रं-शृंगं, प्रोच्छ्रितं हर्म्यं. 2 शिखरं, शृंगं, अग्रं.

PIONEER, s. आटविकः, काष्ठ-तरु-छिद् m. 2 मार्गदर्शकः, अग्रेसरः, अग्रयायी; See FORERUNNER. -v. t. सैन्यमार्गं शुध् c.

PIOUS, a. धार्मिक (की f.), पुण्य-धर्म-शील, धर्मात्मन्, पुण्य, पुण्यात्मन्, भक्तिमत्, शुचिव्रत, भक्ति-धर्म-निष्ठ-परायण, धर्माचार; 'led a p. life' धर्माचरणेन आयुरपक्षयत्; 'p. action' धर्म्यक्रिया; 'for p. purpose' धर्मार्थं. 2 धर्म-भक्ति-मूलक. -LY, adv. भक्त्या, धार्मिकवत्. -NESS,-PIETY, s. धर्मनिष्ठा-परता-आसक्ति f., धर्मात्मता, पुण्यशीलं, ईश्वर-धर्म-भक्ति f., ईश्वरनिष्ठा-सेवा, पुण्यता, भक्तिः; 'distinguished for p.' धर्मप्रधान. 2 पितृसेवा, पुत्रधर्मः.

PIP, s. बीजं. 2 बिंदुः, अंकः.

PIPE, s. वंशः, वेणुः, सुषिरं. 2 नालः, नाडि-डी-लि-ली f., प्रणालः-ली; 'water-p.' सारणि f., प्रणालिका. -v. i. वेणुं वद् c. or ध्मा 1 P. -ER, s. वांशिकः, वेणुध्मः.

PIQUANT, a. उग्र, तिग्म, कटु, तीक्ष्ण, प्र-,खर. 2 मिष्ट, स्वादु, सरस.

PIQUE, s. कलिः, कलहः; ईषत्कोपः. -v. t. ईषत् कुप् c. or रुष् c. 2 उत्तिज् c., उत्पद् c., प्रोत्सह् c., प्र-वृत् c. 3 (Oneself) अभि-मन् 4 A; विकत्थ् 1 A; 'he p. s himself upon his learning' पंडितंमन्योऽसौ.

PIRATE, s. समुद्रदस्युः. 2 साहसिकनौका. 3 शब्दचौरः. -v. t. अपहृ 1 P, लुंट्-ठ् 1 P, 10. -PIRACY, s. समुद्रीयचौर्यं-लुंठनं. -PIRATICAL, a. साहसिन्, साहसिक (की f.).

PISCES, s. मीनः, मीनराशिः.

PISCIVOROUS, a. मत्स्याशन, मत्स्याद.

PISMIRE, s. See ANT.

PISS, s. मूत्रं, मेहः. -v. t. मूत्रं उत्सृज् c., मिह् 1 P, मूत्र् 10.

PISTIL, s. गर्भकेसरः-रं.

PIT, s. गर्तः-र्ता, विवरं, बिलं, अवटः; 'p.-coal' आकरांगारः; 'p.-fall' गूढ-छन्न-कूपः-गर्तः, अंधकूपः. -v. t. सूक्ष्मगर्तैः अंक् 10 or चिह्नयति (D.). 2 योद्धुं प्रोत्सह् c., प्रतियुध् c.

PITCH, v. t. रच् 10, प्रतिवि-धा 3 U; रुह् c. (रोपयति), स्था c. (स्थापयति), निविश् c. 2 क्षिप् 6 P, प्र-, अस् 4 P, नि-,पत् c. 3 अरालेन अंज् 7 P. -v. i. आ-अव-पत् 1 P, अवरुह् 1 P, अव-तॄ 1 P, अध्यास् 2 A. 2 निविश् 6 A, शिबिरं अध्यास्. 3 अधोमुखेन पत्, अवाङ् गम् 1 P. 4 (Upon) वृ 5 U; See CHOOSE. -s. सिंदुः, रालः, अरालः, यक्षधूपः, सर्ज-

रसः, सर्वरसः, बहुरूपः. 2 कोटि *f.*, काष्ठा, अग्रं; शिखरं; 'highest p.' परा काष्ठा-कोटिः. 3 परिमाणं, पर्यंतः; *See* DEGREE. 4 उत्संगः, कटकः-कं. 5 स्वरः; 'mineral p.' शिलाजतु *n.* -Y, *a.* तिंदुलित. 2 सुचिभेद्य, अंध, अतिकृष्ण.

PITCHER, *s.* कुंभः, घटः, घटी, कलसः-शः, पुटग्रीवः; *See* JAR.

PITH, *s.* मज्जा, गर्भः, सारः. 2 सारः, सारांशः, सत्त्वं, तत्त्वं. 3 निर्यासः, रसः. 4 सत्त्वं, वीर्यं, बलं, उत्साहः. -LESS, *a.* असार, निःसार, फल्गु, निःसत्त्व, विरस. -Y, *a.* ससार, सत्त्वपूर्ण, सरस, ससत्त्व, सारवत्, सारगर्भ. 2 सप्रभाव, तेजस्विन्, वीर्यवत्, ससत्त्व.

PITTANCE, *s.* स्तोकांशः, अत्यल्पभागः; अल्पमूल्यं-वेतनं, ग्रासाच्छादनमात्रं.

PITY, *s.* दया, अनुकंपा, करुणा, घृणा, कृपा, अनुक्रोशः; 'in p. to my passion' (रागजनितं) दुःखं मे निरवेक्ष्य (Mr. 5); 'what a p. it is' अहो नु कष्टमेतत्. -*v. t.* 'take p. on' दय् 1 A (with gen.); अनुकंप् 1 A, दयां कृ 8 U (with loc.); प्रसद् 1 P. —PITEOUS, PITIABLE, *a.* अनुकंप्य, करुणा-अनुकंपा-योग्य, दयाविषयः-भाजनं-पात्रं, करुण, दीन; 'in p. accents' करुणस्वनैः. 2 वराक (की *f.*), तपस्विन् (of persons). -LY, *adv.* करुणं, दीनं. -NESS, *s.* अनुकंप्यता, कारुण्यं; दैन्यं. —PITIFUL, PITYING, *a.* करुणार्द्र, करुणामय (यी *f.*), करुणा-दया-शील, सदय, सानुकंप, दयालु, कृपालु; *See* KIND; 'a p. person' दयानिधिः-सागरः, दीनबंधुः-वत्सलः. 2 करुण, दीन शोच्य. 3 Contemptible, q. v. -LY, *adv.* सदयं, सानुकंपं, सकरुणं. -NESS, *s.* दयालुता, कारुण्यं, दयार्द्रता. —PITILESS, *a.* निर्दय, निरनुक्रोश, निर्घृण, निष्कृप, क्रूर, निष्ठुर, कठोर, अकरुण. -LY, *adv.* निर्दयं, क्रूरं, निष्ठुरं.

PIVOT, *s.* विवर्तनकीलः.

PLACARD, *s.* घोषणापत्रं. -*v. t.* घोषणापत्रेण प्रकाश् c.

PLACATE, *v. t.* Appease, q. v. —PLACABLE, *a.* क्षमाशील; सांत्वनीय, आराध्य, प्रसाद्य.

PLACE, *s.* स्थानं, स्थलं, प्र-,देशः, स्थली, भू-भूमि *f.*, धिष्ण्यं. 2 पदं, आस्पदं, विषयः. 3 पदं, पदवि-वी *f.*, अधिकारः, नियोगः, अधिकारपदं; *See* OFFICE. 4 अवकाशः, अवसरः, प्रसरः; 'p. of honour' संमानपदं, गौरवपदं; 'in one p.' एकत्र; 'in many p. s' बहुत्र; 'p. of residence' निवासस्थानं; वसति *f.*; 'p. for dancing' नृत्यशाला-स्थानं; 'out of p.' अस्थाने, अनुचितं; 'in the p. of a father' पितृस्थाने-भूमौ; 'p. for fear' भयस्थानं-कारणं-हेतुः; 'in one p.- in another p.' क्वचित्-क्वचित्, इतः-इतः, एकत्र-अन्यत्र; 'in the first p.' प्रथमं, प्रथमतः, प्रथमं तावत्; 'in the next p.' अपरंच, पुनः, पुनश्च; 'to give p.' स्थानं त्यज् 1 P, अप-सृप् 1 P, अपसृ 1 P; 'to take p.' *See* HAPPEN, OCCUR. -*v. t.* स्था c. (स्थापयति), धा 3 U, नि-आ-°, वि-, न्यस् 4 U, निक्षिप् 6 P, आ-नि-विश् c., आरुह् c. (रोपयति), धृ 10; oft. by कृ 8 U, दा 3 U, व्यापृ c., (व्यापारयामास करं किरीटे R. VI. 19); 'p. over' अधिकृ, अधि-ष्ठा 1 P; 'p. in an office' पदे नियुज् 7 A, 10 or आरुह् c.

PLACID, *s.* शांत, प्र-उप-°, प्रसन्न, निराकुल, अनुद्विग्न, जितक्रोध, असंभ्रम, शांतात्मन्, प्रसन्नचित्त. -LY, *adv.* प्रसन्नं, शांत्या, शांतचेतसा, निराकुलं. -ITY, -NESS, *s.* शमः, शांति *f.*, प्रसादः, अक्रोधः, असंभ्रमः, अक्षोभः.

PLAGIARISM, *s.* शब्दचौर्यं, वागपहारः —PLAGIARIST, *s.* शब्द-ग्रंथ-चौरः.

PLAGUE, *s.* मारी, महामारी, म(मा)रकः. 2 उत्पातः, अरिष्टं, अनर्थः, शल्यं, उपद्रवः, कंटकः, उपप्लवः; *See* PEST. -*v. t.* मार्या ग्रस् 1 A or आक्रम् 1 U, 4 P. 2 बाध् 1 A, पीड् 10, तप् c., दु 5 P; *See* HARASS. -ING, *a.* बाधक, पीडक, क्लेशद, पीडाप्रद.

PLAIN, *s.* समभूमि *f.*-देशः-स्थलं-ली, समभूभागः; *See* LEVEL. -*a.* सम, सपाट. 2 विनीत, निरलंकार, अभूषित, निर्भूषण. 3 स्पष्ट, व्यक्त, विशद, परि-,स्फुट, सुबोध, स्पष्टार्थ, भिन्नार्थ, प्रकाश, प्रत्यक्ष, प्रकट. 4 केवल, मात्र in comp. 5 (Style) अनलंकृत, शुद्ध, अनलंकार, अव्यंजन. 6 (Food) उपस्करहीन-शून्य, असंस्कृत. 7 अमाय, दक्षिण, निष्कपट, निर्व्याज, सरल, कपट-माया-हीन, निर्व्यलीक, अकृत्रिम, ऋजु; *See* FRANK. 8 सामान्य, साधारण (णी *f.*); मध्यमरूप, नातिसुंदर (री *f.*); 'a p. woman', 'one p. in person' सामान्यलावण्योपपन्ना, नातिसुभगा, अनतिसुंदरी; 'p. dealing' न्यायाचार, शुद्ध-सरल-मति, निर्व्यलीक, दक्षिण, अमाय, ऋजु; (*s.*) सारल्यं, निष्कापट्यं. -*v. t.* समीकृ 8 U. -LY, *adv.* स्पष्टं, व्यक्तं, स्फुटं, स्पष्टार्थं, सुबोधं, प्रकाशं, प्रकटं, प्रत्यक्षं. 2 निर्व्याजं, निर्व्यलीकं, अवक्रं, सारल्येन, अमायया, निष्कपटं. 3 विनीतं, अनलंकार; 'p. dressed' विनीतवेष. -NESS, *s.* समता, विनीतत्वं, भूषणाभावः, व्यक्तता, स्पष्टता, वैशद्यं, सुबोधता, प्राकाश्यं, अव्याजः, निर्व्याजता, अकापट्यं, सारल्यं, अमाया, आर्जवं, &c.

PLAINT, *s.* प्रतिज्ञा, अभियोगः, भाषापादः; भाषा, पूर्वपक्षः, पक्षः. 2 विलापः, विलपनं, परिदेवनं-ना, शोकः. —PLAINTIFF, *s.* अर्थिन् *m.*, वादी, अभियोगी, कार्यार्थी, अभियोक्तृ *m.*, सूचकः. —PLAINTIVE, *a.* परिदेविन्, विलापिन्. 2 शोकावह, शोकार्थक, शोकदुःख-गर्भ; करुण, दीन, सकरुण; 'in p. words' परिदेविताक्षरैः. -LY, *adv.* करुणं, दीनं.

PLAIT, *s.* भंगि-गी *f.*, भंगः, ऊर्मि *f.*, पुटः, चूणः. 2 वेणि-णी *f.*, कबरी, धम्मिल्लः. -*v. t.* ग्रंथ् 9 P, व्या-वृह् c., पुटीकृ 8 U, संवे 1 P, वेणीकृ, वेणीरूपेण ग्रंथ्.

PLAN, *s.* उपायः, प्रयोगः, प्र-,युक्ति *f.*, कल्पना. 2

सूत्रपातः, चित्रलेखनं; आलेख्यं, स्थूलवर्णनं. —*v. t.* प्र-सं-क्लृप् c., प्र-,युज् 10, चिंत् 10, मंत्र् 10 A, अनुसंधा 3 U, आलोच् 10, मनसा विचर् c. or वि-भू c. 2 आलिख् 6 P, सूत्रपातं कृ 8 U. —NING, *s.* उपायकल्पना-योजना.

PLANCH, *See* PLANK.

PLANE, *a.* सम, समस्थ. —*s.* समं, समक्षेत्रं, धरातलं. 2 तक्षणी, त्वक्षणी. —*v. t.* समीकृ 8 U. 2 तक्ष् 1, 5 P.

PLANET, *s.* ग्रहः, ज्योतिस् *n.*; 'minor p.' उपग्रहः; 'passage of a p.' संक्रमः, संक्रांति *f.*; 'aspect of a p.' ग्रहदशा ; 'influence of a p.' ग्रहावेशः. —ARY, *a.* ग्रह in comp.

PLANK, *s.* फलकः-कं; दारु-काष्ठ-फलकः. —*v. t.* फलकैः आस्तॄ 9 U or आच्छद् 10.

PLANT, *s.* ओषधि *f.*, लता; तरुः, वृक्षः. —*v. t.* (Seeds) आ-,रुह् c. 2 प्रति-,स्था c. (स्थापयति), वि-,न्यस् 4 U, निविश् c., नि-खन् 1 P, नि-धा 3 U, रुह् c. 3 अधि-,वस् c. —ATION, *s.* रोपणं. 2 क्षेत्रं, in comp., वाटः-टी, वाटिका; शाकटं-शाकिनं in comp., वृक्षवाटिका; 'sugar-p.' इक्षुशाकटं-वाटिका. 3 Colony, q. v. —ER, *s.* रोपयितृ *m.*, रोपकः. 2 वाटिकेश्वरः.

PLANTAIN, *s.* कदली-लः, रंभा, वारणबुसा-षा, मोचा, अंशुमत्फला, काष्ठीला; 'p. fruit' कदलीफलं, मोचं; 'wild p.' काष्ठकदली.

PLASH, *s.* आघातः, आस्फालनं. 2 क्षुद्रजलाशयः. —*v. t.* जले क्रीड् 1 P, जलं आस्फल् c. —*v. t.* अवच्छिद् 7 P, लू 9 U, कृत् 6 P. 2 संग्रंथ् 9 P. —Y, *a.* जलाढ्य.

PLASTER, *s.* लेपः, सुधा, चूर्णलेपः. 2 उपनाहः, उपदेहः. —*v. t.* लिप् 6 P, वि-अनु-प्र°-, दिह् 2 U, उपनह् 4 P. —ER, *s.* लेपकः, पलगंडः. —ING, *s.* वि-प्र-लेपः-पनं.

PLASTIC, *a.* आकारद, कल्पक. 2 नम्य, सुखनम्य.

PLAT, *s.* Plot. q. v. —*v. t.* Weave, q. v.

PLATE, *s.* पात्रं, भाजनं. 2 कोशः-षः, हेमरूप्यं. 3 फलकः-कं, पत्रं; पट्टः-ट्टं, पट्टिका; 'copper-p.' ताम्रपट्टः, ताम्रपत्रं; 'p. s of grant' शासन-नियम-पत्राणि. —*v. t.* रजतपत्रेण आवृ 5 U or आच्छद् 10; रजतेन अलंकृ 8 U. —ED, *a.* रजतपत्रावृत, रूप्यनिबद्ध.

PLATEAU, *s.* समस्थली, अधित्यका; *See* LEVEL.

PLATFORM, *s.* वेदि *f.*, वेदिका, उन्नतस्थानं.

PLATOON, *s.* गुल्मः-ल्मं.

PLATTER, *s.* पात्रं, भाजनं.

PLAUDIT, *s.* प्रशंसा, धन्यवादः, जयघोषः.

PLAUSIBLE, *a.* सत्याभास, सत्यसंकाश, बाह्यतः रमणीय.

PLAY, *v. i.* क्रीड् 1 P, रम् 1 A, वि-हृ 1 P, विलस् 1 P, खेल् 1 P. 2 (At dice) दिव् 4 P, क्रीड्, ग्लह् 1 A; 'p. s at dice' अक्षैः-अक्षान्-दीव्यति. 3 वद् c. (instrument). 4 चेष्ट् 1 A, वृत् 1 A, चल् 1 P. —*v. t.* रूप् 10, नट् 10, अभिनी 1 P, ex. by denom.; 'p.s the king' नृपायते; 'p. s the woman' स्त्रीवाचरति. 2 प्र-,चल्-र् c., प्रवृत् c., प्रसृ c. 3 वि-धा 3 U, कृ 8 U, अनु-ष्ठा 1 P. —*s.* क्रीडा, खेला-लनं, लीला, केलि *f.*, विनोदः, विलासः, विहारः, कौतुकं, परिहासः; 'in p.' लीलया, परिहासेन. 2 नाटकं. 3 अक्षक्रीडा, द्यूतं, देवनं. 4 अभिनयः, गति *f.* 5 आचरणं, चेष्टितं, वृत्ति *f.*, व्यापारः, कृत्यं, चेष्टा; 'foul p.' दुश्चेष्टितं. 6 चलनं, सरणं. 7 प्रसरः, अवकाशः, अवसरः; 'p.-day' अनध्यायदिवसः-तिथिः, विश्रामदिवसः; 'p.-house' नाटक-रंग-शाला; 'p.-thing' क्रीडनकं, क्रीडाद्रव्यं-वस्तु. —ER, *s.* क्रीडकः; (at dice) अक्ष-,देविन् *m.*, अक्षक्रीडकः, अक्षधूर्तः. 2 नटः, कुशीलवः, नर्तकः, अभिनेतृ, पात्रं. —FUL, *a.* क्रीडासक्त, क्रीडापर-मग्न, केलि-क्रीडा-लीला-शील, लीला-खेला-पर, विलासिन्, विनोदिन् ; (of things) सलील क्रीडा-केलि in comp.; 'p. anger' प्रणयक्रीडा-कोपः, केलिकोपः. —FULLY, *adv.* क्रीडापूर्वं, परिहासेन (jokingly); लीलया, सकौतुकं, सविलासं, सखेलं. —FULNESS, *s.* क्रीडासक्ति *f.*, लीलापरता, सलीलत्वं, क्रीडाशीलता.

PLEA, *s.* कारणोत्तरं, उत्तरं, उत्तरपादः. 2 व्यपदेशः, छद्मन् *n.*, अपदेशः, निमित्तं, कारणं, मोचनहेतुः. 3 वादः, व्यवहारः, कार्यं. 4 प्रार्थना ; 'raising a p.' स्वजीकरणं. —PLEAD, *v.* उत्तरं दा 3 U or प्रतिपद् 4 A or वद् 1 P, निमित्तं दृश् c., वि-,अप-दिश् 6 P; 'p. guilty' अपराधी अस्मीति वद् or प्रतिपद् ; 'tears shall p. in vain' अश्रुपातो निर्गुणो भवेत्. 2 विनयेन प्रार्थ् or अभ्यर्थ् 10 A, सविनयं याच् 1 A ; 'p. ed for his life' जीवितदानार्थं प्रार्थयामास. 3 उप-क्षिप् 6 P, उपन्यस् 4 U, व्यपदेशार्थं पुरः क्षिप्. 4 (Cause) प्रति-पद् c., परार्थं उत्तरं वद्, परपक्षं समर्थ् ; 'p. ing head-ache as an excuse' शिरःशूलस्पर्शं व्यपदिशन् ; 'p. ing illness' अस्वास्थ्यव्याजेन-व्यपदेशेन. —ER, *s.* अभिभाषकः, उत्तरवादी, समर्थकः, हेतुवादी. —ING, *s.* हेतु-उत्तर-वादः, व्यपदेशनं, हेतूपन्यासः.

PLEASE, *v. t.* प्री 9 P, 10 (प्रीणयति), तृप् c., सं-परि-°, रम् c. (रमयति), प्रमुद् c., सुखयति (D.), आ-नंद् c., सं-,तुष् c., प्रसद् c., आह्लाद् c., हृष् c., आराध् c., अनुरंज् c.; oft. by इच्छा, प्रसादः, कृपा ; विषमप्यमृतं क्वचिद्भवेदमृतं वा विषमीश्वरेच्छया (R. VIII. 46) 'if it p. God to do so' &c.; 'he was p. ed to accept my presents' ममोपायनानि स सुप्रीतमनसा-सुप्रसन्नं-स्वीचकार ; 'may it p. your ladyship' प्रसीदतु भट्टिनी (M. 4). 2 (Like) *See* below. —*v. i.* 'to be p. ed' तुष् 4 P, तृप् 4 P ; रम्-मुद् 1 A, नंद् 1 P. 2 अर्ह् 1 P or प्रसद्

1 P, with inf., or simply by Imperative ; 'p. sit here' अत्रोपविशत्वार्यः; 'worthy Sir, p. to wait for 2 or 3 days' द्वित्राण्यहान्यर्हसि सोढुमर्हन् (R. v. 25). 3 रुच् 1 A, इष् 6 P; See LIKE; 'just as my friend p. s' यदभिरोचते वयस्याय ; 'do as you p.' यथाभिलषितं क्रियतां. -ANT, *a.* सुखकर (री *f.*), मधुर, सुखद-प्रद, सुखावह, रम्य, रमणीय, प्रिय, मनोहर-रम, अभिराम, सुभग, अभिमत, सुख, काम्य, कांत, हर्षावह, रुचिर, हृद्य, हृदयंगम, प्रीति-तुष्टि-कर, मनोज्ञ, मंजुल, चारु ; 'a p. joke' हृदयंगमः परिहासः (Mal. 3). -ANTLY, *adv.* सुखं, रम्यं, मधुरं, प्रियं, रुचिरं. -ANTRY, *s.* परि(री)हासः, नर्मभाषितं, विनोदः, नर्मालापः, विनोदनर्म-उक्ति *f.* -ING, *a.* सुख in comp., रम्य, कांत; See PLEASANT ; 'p. to the ear' सुखश्रव, श्रुतिसुख, मंजुलस्वन, सुश्राव्य ; 'p. to the eye' प्रेक्षणीय, नयनाभिराम, सुदृश्य ; 'p. language' चाटु *m. n.*, चाटूक्तिः. -INGLY, *adv.* सुभगं, सुखं, सुख-चारु in comp. -PLEASURE, *s.* सुखं, सं-परि-तोषः, आनंदः, प्रीति *f.*, सौख्यं, तुष्टि *f.*, प्र-,मोदः, आह्लादः, हर्षः, मुदा. 2 अभि-,रुचि *f.*, इच्छा, अभिलाषः, छंदः-दस् *n.*, कामः; 'at one's p.' स्वेच्छया, कामतः, यथाकामं, यदृच्छया, स्वैरं; 'wandering at p.' कामचारिन्, स्वच्छंदगामिन्; 'sensual p.' भोगः, विषयसुखं, विषयानुरागः; 'sexual p.' रति *f.*, रतिसुखं, सु-,रतं; 'p.-boat' केलि-क्रीडा-नौका; 'p.-ground' आरामः, क्रीडा-केलि-विलास-वनं-काननं, प्रमदवनं, क्रीडोद्यानं; 'p.-mansion' केलिगृहं-भवनं, लीलागारं, विलासमंदिरं. 3 प्रसादः, अनुग्रहः. -ABLE, *a.* रम्य, रमणीय, सुखद, सुख; See PLEASANT. -IST, *s.* विषयिन् *m.*, विषयासक्तः, भोगासक्तः, भोगपरायणः.

PLEBIAN, *a.* प्राकृत (ती *f.*), सामान्य, साधारण (णी *f.*), अवरवर्ण, अकुलीन. -*s.* प्राकृतः, प्राकृतजनः, पृथग्जनः; नीच-अधर-जनः.

PLECTRUM, *s.* कोणः, शारिका.

PLEDGE, *s.* न्यासः, निक्षेपः, आधिः, उपनिधिः, उपन्यासः-निक्षेपः, पणः. 2 अभिज्ञानं; 'p. of love' प्रीत्यभिज्ञानं. 3 प्रतिज्ञा, क्षणः, परिपणः-णनं; 'I have given a p.' विहितप्रतिज्ञः-गृहीतक्षणः-अहं. 4 प्रतिभूः, लग्नकः, बंधकः. -*v. t.* न्यस् 4 U, निक्षिप् 6 P, आ-नि-धा 3 U, परि-,पण् 1 A, आधी-न्यासी-कृ 8 U. 2 (One's word) प्रति-श्रु 5 P, प्रति-ज्ञा 9 A, (with dat. of person), उरीकृ, वचनेन बंध् 9 P; ex. by (*s.*); अस्मत्सौदामिनीसमक्षमनयोर्वृत्तेयं प्रतिज्ञा (Mal. 1) 'they two p. ed their word' &c.; 'he has p. ed his virtue (honor) that he would not harm you' तव विरूपकरणे तेन सुकृतमंतरे धृतं (P. IV. 1); 'he who has p. ed his word' कृत-विहित-प्रतिज्ञः, प्रतिज्ञा-वचन-बद्धः, दत्तवचनः-प्रतिज्ञः, गृहीतक्षणः.

PLEDGET, *s.* पट्टः, आवेष्टनं.

PLEIADES, *s.* कृत्तिकाः.

PLENARY, *a.* सं-परि-पूर्ण, समग्र.

PLENIPOTENT, *a.* पूर्णशक्तियुक्त. -PLENIPOTENCE, *s.* पूर्णसामर्थ्य-शक्ति *f.* -PLENIPOTENTIARY, *s.* पूर्णशक्तियुक्तः, महादूतः.

PLENIST, *s.* पूर्णतावादिन् *m.*

PLENITUDE, *s.* पूर्णता, प्राचुर्यं, वैपुल्यं, समृद्धि *f.*, अतिरेकः, उत्सेकः, परा कोटिः-काष्ठा.

PLENTY, *s.* बाहुल्यं, प्राचुर्यं, वैपुल्यं, बहुत्वं, समृद्धि *f.*, उद्रेकः, अतिरेकः, उत्सेकः, स्फीति-वृद्धि *f.* —PLENTEOUS, PLENTIFUL, *a.* प्रभूत, प्रचुर, विपुल, बहु, बहुल, भूरि, भूयिष्ठ, पुष्कल, समृद्ध, सं-परि-पूर्ण, उद्रिक्त, स्फीत, उत्सिक्त, उपचित. -LY, *adv.* बाहुल्येन, बहुशः, भूयिष्ठं, भूरि, प्रभूतं, विपुलं, अतिरिक्तं. -NESS, *s.* बाहुल्यं, प्राचुर्यं; See (*s.*).

PLEONASM, *s.* अधिकपददोषः ; शब्दाधिक्यं, शब्दातिशयः. -PLEONASTIC, *a.* अधिकशब्द, बहुपद.

PLETHORA, *s.* रक्तपित्तं. 2 बाहुल्य, प्राचुर्यं, अतिवृद्धि *f.* -PLETHORIC, *a.* रक्तपित्तरोगिन्.

PLEURISY, *s.* पार्श्वशूलं.

PLIANT, PLIABLE, *a.* आ-,नम्य, सुखनम्य, मृदु, शिथिल, अदृढ, आयम्य.

PLIGHT, *s.* दशा, अवस्था, स्थिति *f.*, भावः, वृत्ति *f.*, गति *f.*; 'sorry p.' दुर्दशा, दुर्गतिः. 2 Pledge, q. v. -*v. t.* प्रति-ज्ञा 9 A, न्यस् 4 U; See PLEDGE. -ED, *a.* प्रतिज्ञात, न्यस्त ; 'p. word' विहितप्रतिज्ञा, संगरः, अभिसंधिः.

PLINTH, *s.* स्तंभमूलं-तलं ; प्राकारमूलं.

PLOD, *v. i.* अविरतं श्रम् 4 P or आयासं कृ 8 U, मंदं मंदं आयस् 1, 4 P. -DER, *s.* मंदं मंदं निरंतरायासिन् *m.*, नित्योद्योगी, पिपीलिकाधर्मी. -DING, *s.* अतिमांद्येन निरंतरश्रमः-नित्यायासः.

PLOT, *s.* भू-भागः-प्रदेशः, क्षेत्रं, स्थलं-ली, भू-भूमि *f.* 2 कपटप्रबंधः, कूटप्रबंधः, कपटोपायः, मंत्रणा, कु-संकल्पः-मंत्रणा-कल्पना, कूटोपायः, उपजापः; (generally) उपायः, संकल्पः, प्रयोगः. 3 कथा, वस्तु *n.*; 'arrangement of p.' वस्तुरचना-विन्यासः ; 'the p. of which is composed by Kâlidâsa' कालिदासग्रथितवस्तु नाटकं (S. 1). -*v. i.* कपटप्रबंधान् चिंत् 10 or युज् 10, उपायान् क्लृप् c. or निरूप् 10 or अनुसं-धा 3 U ; 'p. against' द्रुह् 4 P (with dat.), अभिद्रुह् (with acc.); 'p. against one's life' जीवितापहरणाय कपटप्रबंधान्रचयति. -TER, *s.* कुमंत्रणाकृत् *m.*, अभिद्रोग्धा.

PLOUGH, *s.* हलं, लांगलं, सी(सी)रः, हालः, गोदारणं ; 'body of a p.' निरीशं-षं ; कुटकं, फालः,

कृषकः ; 'pole of a p.' ईषा-शा, (लांगलीषा), लांगलदंडः ; 'handle of p.' ईषादंडः ; 'furrow made by a p.' सीता, लांगलपद्धति *f.*; 'p.-boy' बालकर्षकः ; 'p.-gear' हलसज्जा-उपकरणं; 'p.-land' सीत्यं, हल्यं, फालकृष्टं, हल्यक्षेत्रं ; 'p.-man' हालिकः, लांगलिन् *m.*, हली, लांगलिकः, सैरिकः, हलधरः-भृत्, कृषकः, कर्षकः; 'p.-share' कुशी, फालः, कृषकः. —*v. t.* कृष् 1 P, 6 U, भिद् 7 P, विद् 9 P or c., उत्कृष् 1 P, (सद्यः सीरोत्कषणसुरभि Me. 16). —*v. i.* हलं वह् c. or चल् c. —ED, *a.* कृष्ट, हल्य, सीत्य; 'twice, thrice, p.' द्वि-त्रि-हल्य ; 'p. after sowing' बीजाकृत, उत्कृष्ट. —ER, *s.* कर्षकः, हालिकः. —ING, *s.* कर्षणं, उत्कर्षणं, भूमिदारणं.

PLUCK, *v. t.* (Off) लू 9 U, निष्कुष् 1 P; 'crows with feathers p. ed off' लूनपक्षाः काकाः; (out) उत्पट् 10, सं-,उद्धृ 1 P, निर्हृ; (hair) लुंच् 1 P, अव-उत्-°, उत्पट् c.; (up) उन्मूल् 10, उत्-खन् 1 P, उच्छिद् 7 P, उत्पट्, उद्धृ, कृष्. 2 (Gather) चि 5 U, अव-सं-°,लू, छिद्, आ-दा 3 A, ग्रह् 9 P. —*s.* सत्त्वं, वीर्यं, पौरुषं, उत्साहः; *See* COURAGE. —ING, *s.* उत्पाटनं, उद्धरणं, उल्लुंचनं, अव-,चयः.

PLUG, *s.* रोधनी, स्तंभनी. —*v. t.* पि-धा 3 U, स्तंभ् 9 P.

PLUM, *a.* कर्कंधूः,-फलं; *See* JUJUBE.

PLUMAGE, *s.* पक्षाः (pl.), पिच्छकलापः, बर्हभारः, पक्षः, पर्णं, पतत्रं, गरुत् *n.*

PLUMB, *s.* लंबः,-सूत्रं. —*a.* लंब, ऋजु, लंबरूप. —*v. t.* सूत्रेण समायुज् 7 U, 10. 2 वेधं परि-मा 3 A, 2 P. —ER, *s.* सीसकारः.

PLUME, *s.* पक्षः, पर्णं, पिच्छं; *See* FEATHER. 2 शिखा, चूडा, शेखरः. —*v. t.* पर्णानि रच् 10. 2 पक्षान् निर्हृ 1 P or उत्पट् 10. 3 (Oneself upon) आत्मानं श्लाघ् 1 A, विकत्थ् 1 A; 'p. s himself upon his learning' ज्ञानेन आत्मानं अतीव श्लाघते-विकत्थते, पंडितंमन्यः, पंडितमानी. —LESS, *a.* पक्षहीन. —OUS,-OSE, —Y, PLUMIGEROUS, *a.* सपक्ष, पक्षवत्, पक्षविशिष्ट.

PLUMMET, *s.* लंबः, लंबसूत्रं, लंबसीसकं, सीसकसूत्रं.

PLUMP, *a.* पीन, पीवर, पुष्ट, स्थूल, उच्छून, आप्यान, स्फीत; *See* FAT. —*adv.* अकस्मात्. —*v. t.* आप्यै c., श्वि c., स्फाय् c. (स्फावयति). —LY, *adv.* व्यक्तं, स्पष्टं. —NESS, *s.* पीनता, पुष्टि *f.*, स्फीति *f.*

PLUNDER, *v. t.* (धनादि) अप-,हृ 1 P, मुष् 9 P, चुर् 10, वि-,लुंट्-ठ् 1 P, 10. —*s.* विलुंठनं, लोत्रं, लोप्त्रं, अपहारः, अपहृतं धनं. —ER, *s.* अपहारकः, विलुंठकः, मोषकः. —ING, *s.* अपहारः, अपहरणं, मोषणं.

PLUNGE, *v. i.* मस्ज् 6 P, नि-अव-°, आप्लु 1 A, गाह् 1 A, वि-अव-°, प्रविश् 6 P. —*v. t.* Causal of roots above. —*s.* अवगाहः-हनं, नि-,मज्जनं, आप्लवः, प्रवेशः. —ED, *a.* मग्न, अवगाढ, आप्लुत, लीन, प्रनि-विष्ट.

PLUNGEON, *s.* प्लवः, प्लाविन् *m.*

PLURAL, *a.* (Number) बहुवचनं. 2 अनेक, बहु. —ITY, *s.* बहुत्वं, अनेकता; ex. by 'Many' q. v.

PLUS, *s.* धनं; सहित, संकलित in comp.

PLUVIOUS, *a.* वृष्टिमत्, प्रचुर-बहु-वृष्टि.

PLY, *v. t.* पत् c., धा 3 U, व्यस् 4 U, प्रयुज् 7 A, 10; पुनः पुनः प्रयुज् or व्याप् c., सततं व्याप् c.; 'p. thy work' कार्यव्यापृतो भव, कार्यं निर्वाहय; 'p. thy needle' सूच्या कार्यं प्रवर्तस्व. 2 (प्रयत्नेन) चल् c., संचर्-ल् c. 3 आग्रहेण उप-स्था 1 U, अनु-निर्बंध् 9 P; *See* IMPORTUNE; 'p. with entreaties' अतिप्रार्थनया उद्विज् c. —*v. i.* अविरतं व्याप् 6 A or प्रवृत् 1 A or उद्यम् 1 A or चेष्ट् 1 A. —*s.* पुटः, भंगः; *See* FOLD.

PNEUMATIC, *a.* वायुरूप, वायुमय (यी *f.*), वायव (वी *f.*), वायु in comp. —*s.* (P. s) वायुविद्या-शास्त्रं.

PNEUMONIA, *s.* क्लोमपाकः.

POACH, *v. t.* ईषत् पच् 1 P. 2 (Game) कूटोपायेन ग्रह् 9 P or अपहृ 1 P or चुर् 10. 3 ग्रहणार्थं अनुसृ 1 P or अनुगम् 1 P; *See* PURSUE. —ER, *s.* मृगयाचौरः, जांगलचौरः. —ING, *s.* मृगया-जांगलचौर्यं, पक्षिग्रहणं.

POCK, *s. See* PIMPLE.

POCKET, *s.* कोषः, आधारः. —*v. t.* कोषे नि-धा 3 U, (छलेन) आत्मसात्कृ 8 U. 2 (Insult) सह् 1 A; *See* BEAR. —ED, *a.* कोषगुप्त, कोषांतर्गत, अंतर्हित.

POD, *s.* बीजकोशः-गुप्ति *f.*, शिंबा, शिंबि-बी *f.*, शिंबिका.

PODAGRICAL, *a.* वातकिन्, वातरोगिन्.

POET, *s.* कविः, सूरिः; 'a ready p.' शीघ्रकविः. —IC,-ICAL, *a.* Ex. by कविता-काव्य in comp.; 'p. genius' कवित्वशक्तिः. 2 श्लोक-कविता-रूप-बद्ध, पद्यमय (यी *f.*), छंदोबद्ध-रूप, पद्यात्मक; 'p. work, पद्यात्मको ग्रंथः. —ICALLY, *adv.* पद्यरूपेण, छंदोरूपेण. —POETICS, *s.* काव्यशास्त्रं, पद्यशास्त्रं; साहित्यं. —POETRY, *s.* काव्यं, कविता. 2 पद्यं (opp. of prose). 3 काव्यरचना, कवित्वं, कविताक्रिया. —POETASTER, *s.* कुकविः, कविदेश्यः. —POEM, *s.* काव्यं, काव्यप्रबंधः, काव्यबंधः, कविता; 'a p. interspersed with prose' खंडकाव्यं. —POESY, कवित्वं-ता. 2 काव्यरचना, कविताशक्ति *f.*

POIGNANT, *a.* उग्र, तीक्ष्ण, तीव्र, तिग्म, अरुंतुद, मर्मस्पृश्-भिद्. —POIGNANCY, *s.* तीक्ष्णता, तीव्रता.

POINT, *s.* अग्रं, अणिः-णी *f.*, धारा, कोटि *f.*, अश्रि *f.*, पालि-ली *f.*; शिखा, शिखरं. 2 (Of land) उदग्रस्थलं, भूनासिका. 3 मर्मन् *n.*, रहस्यं, रसः. 4 दिश्-शा, ककुभ्, आशा, हरित्, काष्ठा, (all *f.*). 5 बिंदुः, चिह्नं अंकः. 6 आशयः, अभिप्रायः, उद्देशः, अर्थः, लक्ष्यं. 7

पर्यंतः, अंतः; अवधिः, परिमाणं. 8 विषयः, पदं, वस्तु *n.*, अर्थः, स्थानं, स्थलं, आस्पदं, प्रकरणं, प्रस्तावः; 'p. at issue' विवादवस्तु-विषयः. 9 लक्षणं, विशेषचिह्नं, विशेषणं, विशिष्टगुणः. 10 प्रसंगः, कालः, समयः; 'being to the p.' प्रास्ताविक (की *f.*), प्रकृत, प्रस्तुत; 'to such a p.' एतावत्, एतावत्पर्यंतं; 'come to the p.' प्रस्तुतमनुसंधीयतां; 'on the p. of' ex. by उन्मुख (खी *f.*), उद्युक्त, उद्यत, by desid. or by fut. part., आसन्न in comp.; 'on the p. of death' मरणोन्मुख, आसन्नमृत्यु, मुमूर्षु; 'on the p. of departing' निर्गंतुमुद्यत, निर्जिगमिषु; 'on the p. of delivery' प्रसवोन्मुखी, आसन्नप्रसवा; 'gain a p.' अभीष्टं साध् 5 P; 'p. of view' दृष्टि *f.*; *See* under VIEW. —*v.* नि-शो 4 P, तिज् c., तीक्ष्णीकृ 8 U. 2 उद्दिश् 6 P, सं-धा 3 U, लक्षीकृ, अभि-प्रेर् c.; 'p. ing to it' तदुद्दिश्य, तदधिकृत्य. 3 (Out) प्र-उप-आ-दिश् (as a way); (at) अंगुल्या निर्दिश् or आ-ख्या 2 P, (मामंगुलीदलविलासेनाख्यातवत्य: Mal. 1); 'p. ing towards the north' उदङ्मुख, उत्तराभिमुख; 'p. blank' स्पष्ट, असंदिग्ध. —ED, *a.* नि-,शित, तीक्ष्णाग्र, साग्र, सधार; oft. by सूचि *f.*; 'pricked by the p. Kusa grass' कुशसूचिविद्ध (S. 4); *See* SHARP. 2 मार्मिक (की *f.*), अरुंतुद, मर्मस्पृश्-भिद्; सरस, रसिक, रसपूर्ण. 3 निर्दिष्ट, सूचित &c. —EDLY, *adv.* उद्दिश्य, उद्देशपूर्वं, मर्मभेदपूर्वं, स्पष्टं, भिन्नार्थं. —ER, *s.* निर्-प्रदेशकः, प्र-,दर्शकः, सूचकः. 2 (Of a dial) प्रदेश(शि)नी. —ING, *s.* निर्देशः, सूचनं, अंगुलिनिर्देशः. —LESS, *a.* धाराहीन, अनिशित, अतीक्ष्ण, निरग्र. 2 रसहीन, अरसिक, फल्गु. 3 अप्रकृत, अप्रस्तुत.

POISE, *v. t.* तुल् 10, तुल्यी-समीकृ 8 U, समभारीकृ. —*s.* भारः, तोलः. 2 भारतुल्यता-साम्यं, समभारता, समतोलः, तुल्यता.

POISON, *s.* विषः-षं, गरलं, क्ष्वेडः, जांगुलं; 'administering p.' विषप्रयोगः-दानं; 'curing p.' विषघ्न (घ्नी *f.*), विषापह, विषहर (री *f.*); 'curer of p.' विषवैद्यः, जांगुलिकः. —*v. t.* विषेण दिह् 2 U or अंज् 7 P or मिश्र् 10. 2 विषं दा 3 U, विषदानेन हन् 2 P or मृ c. or नश् c.; (oneself) विषं भक्ष् 10 or सेव् 1 A or भुज् 7 A. 3 कलुषीकृ 8 U, दुष् c. (दूषयति). —ED. *a.* विषाक्त, विषदिग्ध, विषलिप्त; 'p. arrow' विषाक्तः, दिग्धः, लिप्तकः. 2 विषनाशित. —ER, *s.* विषघातिन् *m.*, विषदायी. —OUS, *a.* विषमय (यी *f.*), सविष, विषालु, सगर, विषपूर्ण, गरविशिष्ट, विष in comp.

POKE, *v. t.* (Fire) चल् c., उत्तिज् c. 2 तड् 10, आहन् 2 U; प्रह 1 P. 3 (दंडादिना) परामृश् 6 P, अन्विष् 4 P. —*v. i.* Grope, q. v. —*s.* ताडनं, प्रहारः, आघातः. —ER, *s.* उत्तेजनी (शलाका); अंगारान्धापकः.

POLE, *s.* यष्टि *f.*, दंडः, काष्ठं; 'raised on a p.' उदंड. 2 (Of a carriage) धुर् *f.*, धुरा; कूबरः, युगंधरः. 3 दंडः. 4 ध्रुवः-वकः; 'p.-axe' परशुः, कुठारः, परश्वधः; 'p.-cat' गंधमार्जारः; 'p.-star' ध्रुवः, उत्तानपादजः, नक्षत्रनेमिः, ज्योतीरथः; ध्रुवतारा. —POLAR, *a.* ध्रुव in comp.; 'p. longitude' ध्रुवः. —ITY, *s.* ध्रुवाभिमुखता, ध्रुवाभिसारिता. —Y, *a.* ध्रुवाभिसारिन्, ध्रुवाभिगामिन्.

POLEMICS, *s.* वादानुवादः. —POLEMIC, —AL, *a.* विवादात्मक, वादानुवादार्थक, वादकुशल. —*s.* विवादकुशलः, वादानुवादशीलः.

POLICE, *s.* रक्षापुरुषाः, नगररक्षिणः, नगरपालाः (pl.), रक्षिगणः-दंडः; 'rural p.' ग्रामरक्षिणः, ग्रामपालाः; 'p.-man', 'p. officer' नगररक्षी, नागरिकः, रक्षी, राजपुरुषः; 'p. magistrate' दंडाधिकारी.

POLICY, *s.* नीति *f.*, नयः, नीतिक्रमः-मार्गः, राजनीतिः-नयः, राज्यशासनरीतिः-मार्गः. 2 नीतिचातुर्यं, वैदग्ध्यं, राज्यशासनकौशलं, नीतिज्ञता. 3 युक्ति *f.*, प्रयोगः, उपायः, व्यवहारः, रीतिः; 'prudential p.' समीक्षा, समीक्ष्यकारित्वं; 'bad p.' कुप्रयोगः, कुयुक्तिः. —POLITIC, *a.* नीतिज्ञ, नीतिविद्-कुशल, नयविद्-ज्ञ, नीतिचतुर-निपुण. 2 व्यवहारकुशल-दक्ष, विचक्षण, कुशल, चतुर, निपुण. 3 सुप्रयुक्त, सुघटित, सुनीत, समीक्ष्य कृत, हित, सु pr. —AL, *a.* नीति-राज in comp.; 'p. affairs' राजकार्याणि; 'p. science' राजनीतिशास्त्रं; 'p. economy' अर्थशास्त्रं, अर्थविज्ञानं; 'he led a p. life' राजकार्यव्यापृतो जीवितमत्यवाहयत्; 'p. institutions' राज्यतंत्राणि; 'p. rights' राज्यनिर्वाहाधिकाराः. —IAN, *s.* नीतिज्ञः, नीतिविद्-कुशलः, नयज्ञः-विद्, राजनीतिनिपुणः, राजकार्यधुरंधर. —POLITICS, *s.* नीतिः-नयः, राजनीतिः, राज्यशासनशास्त्रं. 2 राजकार्याणि, राजव्यवहाराः. —POLITY, *s.* राजनीतिः-रीतिः-व्यवस्था, दंडनीतिः; (generally) नीतिः, व्यवस्था, विधिः.

POLISH, *v. t.* तिज् c., धाव् 10, निः-तप् c., प्र-,मृज् 2 P or c., परिष्कृ 8 U, श्लक्ष्णीकृ, कांतिं दा 3 U. 2 परिष्कृ, वि-नी 1 P, उपस्कृ 8 U, संस्कृ (lit. also); आदर्शो निघर्षणक्रियया संस्क्रियमाणे (S. B. 72). —*s.* कांति *f.*, शोभा, तेजस् *n.*, स्निग्धता, श्लक्ष्णता. 2 संस्कारः, परिष्कारः, सभ्यता, शिष्टता, सौजन्यं. —ED, *a.* निर्मृष्ट, परिष्कृत, प्रमृष्ट, निर्धौत, उत्तेजित. 2 शिष्ट, संस्कृत, सभ्य, परिष्कृत, विनीत, अग्राम्य. —ER, *s.* तेजकः. कांतिदः, मार्जकः, परिष्कारकः; *See* FURBISHER.

POLITE, *a.* दक्षिण, सौजन्यवत्, सुजन, विनीत, शिष्ट, सभ्य, संस्कृत, सभ्यशील, शिष्टाचार, सुशील, आदरशील, प्रियंवद. —LY, *adv.* सौजन्येन, दाक्षिण्येन, सविनयं, शिष्टवत्. —NESS, *s.* शिष्टता, सभ्यता, सौजन्यं, विनयः, दाक्षिण्यं, सुशीलता. 2 शिष्टाचारः, सुशीलवृत्ति *f.*

POLL, *s.* शीर्षं, शिरस् *n.*; *See* HEAD. 2 नामावलि-

ली *f.*; नामलिखनं, नामारोपणं. —*v. t.* (केशान्) लू 9 U, छिद् 7 P, आवप् 1 P. 2 नामानि लिख् 6 P or निविश् c.

POLLARD, *s.* लूनाग्रवृक्षः.

POLLEN, *s.* रेणुः, परागः, रजस् *n.*, पांशुः, पुष्परजः-परागः.

POLLUTE, *v. t.* कलंकयति-मलिनयति-कलुषयति-(D.), दुष् c. (दूषयति), मलिनी-कलुषीकृ 8 U, मलेन लिप् 6 P or दिह् 2 U. 2 भ्रंश् c., दुष् c., आधृष् c., सतीत्वं भ्रंश् c. or नश् c. —ER, *s.* दूषकः, आधर्षकः. —ION, *s.* दूषणं, कलुषीकरणं. 2 मालिन्यं, अमेध्यता, कालुष्यं, मलं, कलंकः, अशौचं. 3 Emission, q. v.

POLTROON, *s. See* COWARD.

POLYANDRY, *s.* अनेकभर्तृकता. —IST, *s.* अनेकपतिका, बहुभर्तृका.

POLYGAMY, *s.* अनेकपत्नीकता, बहुभार्यत्वं. —IST, *s.* बहु-अनेक-भार्यः. 2 बहुपत्नीवादिन् *m.*

POLYGENOUS, *a.* बहु-विध-प्रकार-जाति.

POLYGLOT, *a.* बहुभाषामय (यी *f.*).

POLYGON, *n.* बहुभुजः, बह्वस्रं. —AL, *a.* बहुकोण-भुज-अस्र.

POLYMATHY, *s.* बहुशास्त्रज्ञानं.

POLYPETALOUS, *a.* बहु-अनेक-पर्ण.

POLYPHONOUS, *a.* बहुस्वर-स्वन.

POLYPUS, *s.* अनेकपादः, बहुमूलः.

POLYSYLLABIC, *a.* बह्वक्षर, अनेकाच्.

POLYTHEIST, *s.* अनेकदेववादिन् *m.* —POLYTHEISM, *s.* बहुदेववादः.

POMADE, *s. See* PERFUME.

POMEGRANATE, *s.* (Fruit) दाडि(लि)मं, दाडिमफलं; (tree) दाडि(लि)मः, डालिमः, दाडिंबः, करकः.

POMMEL, *s.* गुल्मः, पिंडः, गंडः. —*v. t.* तड् 10, प्रहृ 1 P.

POMP, *s.* आडंबरः, शोभा, श्रीः, प्रतापः, ऐश्वर्यं, वैभवं. —OUS, *a.* विभ्राजमान, शोभन, सश्रीक, साडंबर, अतिशोभन, महाप्रताप. 2 दांभिक (की *f.*), साटोप, गर्वित, दर्पाध्मात; (style) सालंकार, अलंकृत. —OUSLY, *adv.* साडंबरं, अतिशोभया, अतिप्रतापेन. 2 सदंभं, साटोपं, सगर्वं. —OUSNESS, *s.* ऐश्वर्यं, &c. 2 दंभः, आटोपः.

POND, *s.* तडागः-गं, जलाशयः, कासारः, जलाधारः, पद्माकरः, सरसी, सरस् *n.*; 'deep p.' ह्रदः; 'small p.' पल्वलः-लं, वेशंतः, अल्पसरः; (for drinking water) आहावः, निपानं.

PONDER, *v.* चिंत् 10, ध्यै 1 P, विचर् c., विमृश् 6 P, मनसा क्लृप् c. or भू c. or विगण् 10; *See* MEDITATE.

PONDEROUS, *a.* अतिगुरु, भारवत्, अतिभारिन्, सभार. —LY, *adv.* अतिभारेण. —PONDEROSITY, *s.* भारवत्त्वं, अतिगुरुता.

PONIARD, *s.* कृपाणिका, छुरिका, असिपुत्रिका, असिधेनुका.

PONTAGE, *s.* सेतुसंधानशुल्कं.

PONTIFF, *s.* प्रधानधर्माध्यक्षः, मुख्यपुरोहितः. —PONTIFICATE, *s.* धर्माध्यक्षाधिकारः.

PONY, *s.* अश्वशावः, क्षुद्रघोटकः.

POOL, *s.* जलाशयः, जलाधारः, कुंडं, पल्वलं, निपानं; *See* POND.

POOP, *s.* नौपृष्ठं, नौपश्चाद्भागः.

POOR, *a.* दरिद्र, निर्धन, निःस्व, दीन, अधन, अकिंचन, धन-द्रव्य-अर्थ-हीन, अल्प-धन-विभव, दुर्गत, परिक्षीण, क्षीणधन; 'to be p.' दरिद्रा 2 P. 2 दीन, तपस्विन्, वराक (की *f.*), कृपण, अनुकंप्य. 3 कुत्सित, अपकृष्ट, तृणप्राय, तुच्छ, गर्हित, अधम, विगुण; oft. ex. by कु, कद्, दुर्, अप, in comp.; 'p. food' कदन्नं; *See* BAD, MEAN; 'p. soil' निर्गुणा-असारा-भूमिः, ईरिणा-रूक्षा-भूमिः; 'p. house', 'p. asylum' दरिद्रालयः, अनाथालयः, दरिद्रगृहं; 'p.-spirited' दीन-कृपण-बुद्धि, कृपण, अल्पसत्त्व, क्षुद्रमति. —LY, *adv.* दरिद्रवत्, दीनं, निर्धनवत्; 'p. dressed' दीनवेषं दधान. 2 निष्फलं, व्यर्थं, सिद्धिं विना. —NESS, POVERTY, *s.* दारिद्र्यं, दैन्यं, निर्धनता, निःस्वता, दुर्गति *f.*, दरिद्रदशा-अवस्था, अकिंचनत्वं; 'reduced to p.' नष्ट-गत-विभव-धन, दुर्गत; *See* (*a.*); 'struck with p.' दारिद्र्योपहत, दारिद्र्यग्रस्त.

POP, *s.* आकस्मिकध्वनिः-शब्दः. —*v. i.* अकस्मात् प्रविश् 6 P. 2 सहसा निर्गम् or निःसृ 1 P. 3 सहसा क्वण्-स्वन् 1 P. —*v. t.* Causal of roots above.

POPINJAY, *s. See* PARROT.

POPPY, *s.* खसतिलः.

POPULACE, *s.* लोकः, जनः, सामान्य-प्राकृत-जनाः; *See* PEOPLE. —POPULAR, *s.* लोक-जन-प्रिय, सर्वप्रिय. 2 लौकिक (की *f.*), लोकप्रसिद्ध, लोकरूढ-संमत, जन-लोक in comp.; 'p. scandal' लोकापवादः; 'seeking p. favor' लोक-जन-रंजनं; 'p. usage' रूढि *f.*, जनव्यवहारः, लोकाचारः, लोकमर्यादा-रीति *f.*; 'p. report' जनप्रवादः, लोक-जन-वार्ता-श्रुति *f.*, किंवदंती; 'p. tumult' प्रकृतिक्षोभः; 'conformity to p. opinion' लोकानुसरणं. 3 सामान्य, साधारण (णी *f.*). —ITY, *s.* लोकप्रियता, लोक-जन-प्रीति *f*-अनुरागः-संमानः. —LY, *adv.* लोके, लौकिकतया, साधारणतः, सामान्यतः, लोकरंजनार्थं. —POPULATE, *v. t.* वस् c., जनैः आक्रम् 6 P or पूर् 10. —*v. i.* प्रजां उत्पद् c., प्रजन् 4 A, प्रजावृद्धिं कृ 8 U. —ION, *s.* प्रजा, प्रजा-लोक-संख्या, जनाः, लोकाः. —POPULOUS, *a.* जनाकीर्ण, जनसंकुल-पूर्ण, बहु-प्रचुर-जन-प्रज, जनसंबाध. —NESS, *s.* लोक-प्रजा-बाहुल्यं.

PORCELAIN, *s.* (चीनदेशीय) मार्तिकं, कौलालकं, मृद्भांडानि.

PORCH, *s.* प्रघाणः, प्रघणः, अ(आ)लिंदः, द्वारप्रकोष्ठः.

PORCUPINE, *s.* शल्यः-ल्यकः, श्वाविध् *m.*; 'quill of a p.' शलं, शललं-ली.

PORE, *s.* रो(लो)मरंध्रं-कूपः. 2 (सूक्ष्म) रंध्रं, कूपः. —*v. i.* अनन्यदृष्ट्या-साभिनिवेशं-अधी 2 A or वच् c. —OUS, *a.* बहुरंध्र, रंध्रबहुल, रंध्रपूर्ण-विशिष्ट, सरंध्र. 2 रोमकूपमय (यी *f.*), स्वेदमार्गविशिष्ट, विरलावयवक. —OUSNESS, POROSITY, *s.* रंध्रबाहुल्यं, रंध्रविशिष्टता.

PORK, *s.* शूकर-वराह-मांसं. —ER, *s.* शूकरः, वराहः.

PORPOISE, *s.* शिशुकः, शिशुमारः, उलूपिन् *m.*

PORRIDGE, *s.* यूषं, जूषं.

PORRINGER, *s.* यूषपात्रं-भाजनं.

PORT, *s.* नौकाशयः, नौकाश्रयः, उत्तरणस्थानं, आश्रयः, रक्षणस्थानं, आशयः; 'arrived at the wished-for p.' इष्टदेशं जगाम. 2 द्वारं; *See* DOOR. —ABLE, *a.* वहनीय, लघुभार, सुवाह्य, लघु, सुखवाह्य, हस्तवाह्य. —ER, *s.* द्वाःस्थः, द्वारपालः, प्रतीहारः, दौवारिकः. 2 भारवाहः, भारहरः, वोढृ *m.*, भारिकः. —ERAGE, *s.* भारवहनं. 2 वहनमूल्यं. —PORTAL, *s.* द्वारं, मुखं, प्रवेशद्वारं; *See* DOOR.

PORTEND, *v. t.* अग्रे (अनिष्टं) सूच् 10 or निविद् c. or शंस् 1 P. —PORTENT, *s.* उत्पातः, दुर्निमित्तं, अशुभलक्षणं, अजन्यं, उपसर्गः, दुर्लक्षणं, दुश्चिह्नं, अपशकुनं, कुलक्षणं; अत्याहितं, उपद्रवः, अरिष्टं, अद्भुतं. 2 पूर्व-चिह्नं-लक्षणं. —OUS, *a.* उत्पात-अनिष्ट-अशुभ-शंसिन्, अद्भुत; अत्याहित, औपसर्गिक-औत्पातिक (की *f.*). —OUSLY, *adv.* सोत्पातं, दुर्लक्षणपूर्वं.

PORTFOLIO, *s.* पत्राधारः.

PORTHOLE, *s.* नौपार्श्वमुखं.

PORTICO, *s.* *See* PORCH.

PORTION, *s.* अंशः, वि-,भागः, खंडः-डं, छेदः, शकलः-लं. 2 अंशः, वंटः, उद्धारः, वि-,भागः; 'p. of an estate' दायः, रिक्थभागः, उद्धारः; 'wife's p.' स्त्रीधनं, यौतकं, औद्वाहिकं. —*v. t.* विभज् 1 U, वंट् 10, विभागशः क्लृप् c. 2 शुल्कं-वृत्तिं दा 3 U. —ING, *s.* विभागः, भागकल्पनं, वंटनं. —LESS, *a.* अनंश, अंशहीन.

PORTLY, *a.* गौरवगति-वृत्ति, उदात्त, धीर, धीरदर्शन, गंभीराकृति. 2 स्थूल, बृहत्, स्थूलकाय, पृथूदर, पीन, पीवर. —INESS, *s.* स्थूलकायत्वं, शरीरगौरवं.

PORTMANTEAU, *s.* चर्ममंजूषा-पेटकः.

PORTRAY, *v. t.* आ-,लिख् 6 U, चित्र् 10, वर्ण् 10. 2 उप-,वर्ण्, कृत् 10. —PORTRAIT, *s.* चित्रं, आलेख्यं, प्रतिकृति *f.*, प्रतिमा; *See* PICTURE; 'p.-painter' चित्रक(का)रः.

POSE, *v. t.* स्तंभ् 9 P, मुह् c., निरुत्तरीकृ 8 U, कुंठ् 10.

POSITION, *s.* प्रतिज्ञा, उक्ति *f.*, हेतुः, पक्षः, उपन्यासः; 'wrong p.' पक्षाभासः, हेत्वाभासः. 2 स्थिति *f.*, स्थानं, पदं, आस्पदं, पदवि-वी *f.* 3 प्रतिष्ठा, गौरवं. 4 अवस्था, दशा, आकारः, संस्थानं, भावः, वृत्ति *f.*; 'attain the p. of' पदं या 2 P, (यान्त्येवं गृहिणीपदं युवतयः S. 4); 'holding the p. of mistress of the house' गृहिणीपदभाक्, गृहिणीपदे स्थिता; 'give the p. of' पदं ग्रह् c., भावं गम् c., (महिषीपदं ग्राहिता, देवीभावं गमिता); 'p. in life' स्थितिः, निसर्गजातिः, अवस्थानं.

POSITIVE, *a.* स्पष्ट, असंदिग्ध, अगूढ, प्रत्यक्ष, व्यक्त, अवक्र, परिस्फुट, साक्षात् *ind.*; 'reply in the p.' भवतु-बाढं-तथा-इति वद् 1 P. 2 अवश्यक, अवैकल्पिक (की *f.*), अविशंक्य; *See* PEREMPTORY. 3 सु-,नियत, निश्चित, निर्णीत, निर्दिष्ट. 4 सत्य, तथ्य, यथार्थ, वास्तविक-तात्त्विक (की *f.*). 5 विविक्त, केवल, अनन्यसंबद्ध. 6 दृढ-कृत-निश्चय, दृढमति-संकल्प, निर्विकल्प, निःसंदेह; मताभिमानिन्, स्वमताग्रहिन्, दृढोक्ति; 'a p. quantity' धनं (opposed to ऋणं क्षयः, व्ययः, हानिः). —LY, *adv.* स्पष्टं, व्यक्तं, असंदिग्धं, साक्षात्. 2 अवश्यं, निर्विकल्पं, अविचार्य. 3 सुनिश्चितं, नियतं, नूनं, खलु. 4 वस्तुतः, तत्त्वतः, परमार्थतः, सत्यं, यथार्थतः. 5 सुनिश्चयेन, दृढनिश्चयपूर्वं. 6 मताग्रहेण, मताभिमानेन, दृढोक्त्या. —NESS, *s.* स्पष्टता, असंदिग्धता, दृढनिश्चयः-निर्णयः, तथ्यता, याथार्थ्यं, मताग्रहः, दृढोक्ति *f.*, &c.

POSSESS, *v. t.* धृ 1 P, 10, धा 3 U, भृ 3 U. 2 भुज् 7 U, अधि-ष्ठा 1 P, अध्यास् 2 A, सेव् 1 A; better by वत्, मत्, इन् &c.; *See* below. 3 आप् 5 P, लभ् 1 A, अधिगम् 1 P; *See* GET. 4 अधिकृ 8 U, प्रभू 1 P, अधि-ष्ठा, पदं कृ. 5 आविश् 6 P, आक्रम् 1 U, 4 P, उपसृज् 6 P, बाध् 1 A, उपहन् 2 P, ग्रस् 1 A, व्याप् 5 P, oft. ex. by 'p. ed'. —ED, *a.* धृत, भुक्त, अधिष्ठित, अध्यासित, अधीन, हस्तगत. 2 प्राप्त, लब्ध, अधिगत. 3 आविष्ट, आक्रांत, उपसृष्ट, ग्रस्त, उपहत. 4 (By spirits) भूताविष्ट, भूतोपसृष्ट, वेतालोपहत, भूतग्रस्त. 5 (Having) युक्त, युत, उपेत, संपन्न, उपपन्न, अन्वित, सनाथ, शालिन् in comp.; by वत्, मत्, इन्, विन् affixed, or by Bah. comp. —ION, *s.* भोगः, भुक्ति *f.*, अधिकारः, आवेशः, आक्रमः-मणं, आत्मसात्करणं; 'to take p. of' आक्रम्, आविश्, स्वायत्तीकृ, आत्मसात्कृ; पदं कृ or वि-धा; *See* ENTER; 'to put in p.' अधिकृ c., अधिकारं दा, नियुज् 7 A, 10; 'being in one's p.' स्वाधीन, हस्तगत, वशवर्तिन्. 2 संपन्नता, युक्तत्वं, सनाथता; वत्त्वं, शालिता in comp.; 'p. of wealth' धनवत्त्वं, सधनता. 3 आवेशः, उपसर्गः, बाधा, पीडा; भूतावेशः, भूतपीडा-बाधा-संचारः. 4 द्रव्यं, स्वं वस्तु, स्वाधीनं द्रव्यं; (p. s) द्रव्यजातं, वस्तुजातं, द्रव्याणि, वस्तूनि, वित्तं, विभवः, द्रविणं, अर्थः; क्षेत्रादि, भूमि *f.*, (landed). —IVE, *a.* संबंध in comp.; 'p. case

षत्री. -OR, *s.* भोक्तृ *m.*, भोगिन् *m.*, स्वामी, अधिकारी, शाली-धारी- in comp.

POSSIBLE, *a.* शक्य, साध्य, संभाव्य; gen. ex. by pot. pass. part.; 'not p. to be united' दुःसंधेय; 'p. to be done' करणीय, संपाद्य, साध्य; oft. by शक् pass.; 'to be p.' संभू 1 P, (सर्वं सौदामिन्यां संभाव्यते Mal. 1), उपपद् 4 A, घट् 1 A; उभयथापि घटते (V. 3) 'it is p. in both ways' (both sides are p.); 'as far as p.' यावच्छक्यं, यथाशक्ति. -POSSIBILITY, *s.* संभवः, शक्यता, संभाव्यता, उपपत्ति *f.*, घटना, संगति *f.* -POSSIBLY, *adv.* Ex. by शक्यं or शक् pass. 2 कदाचित्, कदापि, नाम, by pot. mood ; *See* PERHAPS. 3 (In questions) इव, नाम, वा; 'who p. that is dead, is not born again' मृतः को वा न जायते (P. I. 1).

POST, *s.* स्तंभः, स्थाणुः, स्थूणा, उपस्तंभः; 'p. for securing an elephant' आलानं, बंधस्तंभः; 'p. for tethering cattle' शिवकः, कीलकः, मेधिः-थिः, खलेदारु *n.* 2 पदं, अधिकारः, नियोगः, अधिकारपदं. 3 स्थानं, स्थलं, आस्पदं, अवस्थानं, स्थिति *f.*, पदवी. 4 गुल्म-सैन्य-स्थानं. 5 पत्रवाहः, पत्रवाहनसाधनं; 'p.-boy' जवाश्वपालः ; 'p.-chaise' जवरथः-वाहनं ; 'p.-haste' सवेगं, अतिजवेन, जवाश्ववत्; 'p.-horse' जवाश्वः, जवतुरंगः; 'p.-man' पत्र-लेख-वाहः-हारः; 'p.-master' पत्रस्थानाधिकारी, पत्रवाहाध्यक्षः; 'p. office' पत्रस्थानं-गृहं. -*v. t.* स्था c. (स्थापयति), सं-प्रति-°, नियुज् 7 A, 10. 2 स्तंभे बंध् 9 P. 3 पत्रस्थाने निविश् c. or क्षिप् 6 P. 4 प्रकाश् c., आसंज् c. -*v. i.* जवेन गम् or व्रज् 1 P; 'p. up' अवबुध् c.; 'p. off' व्याक्षिप् 6 P, विलंब् c. -AGE, *s.* पत्रवाहनमूल्यं. -ER, *s.* जवनः, जवः, जवाश्वः, प्रजवी. -POSTILION, *s.* जवाश्वारूढः.

POST-DATE, *v. t.* पश्चात् तिथिं लिख् 6 P.

POST-DILUVIAN, *a.* प्रलयोत्तरकालीन.

POSTERIOR, *a.* पश्चात्-उत्तर-कालीन, उत्तर, अपर अवर, अर्वाच्. -ITY, *s.* परता, उत्तरता. -LY, *adv.* पश्चात्, उत्तरं-रतः, परतः, परस्तात्. -POSTERIORS, *s.* नितंबः; गुदप्रदेशः.

POSTERITY, *s.* संतति *f.*, अपत्यं, संतानः, वंशः, प्रजा, पुत्रपौत्रादयः.

POSTERN, *s.* पक्षद्वारं, पक्षकः.

POSTHUMOUS, *a.* मरणादनंतरं प्रकाशित, मृत्यूत्तरजात.

POST-MERIDIAN, *a.* अपराह्णतन (नी *f.*), पराह्णकालिक (की *f.*).

POST-MORTEM, *a.* मरणोत्तर, मृत्यूत्तर.

POST-NATAL, *a.* जन्मोत्तर.

POSTPONE, *v. t.* व्याक्षिप् 6 P, विलंब् c.; (नियतकालं यावत्) त्यज् 1 P, विसृज् 6 P. -MENT, *s.* व्याक्षेपः, विलंबः.

POST-SCRIPT, *s.* अनुलेखः.

POSTULATE, *s.* स्वीकृतपक्षः, गृहीतपदं, परिग्रहः. -*v. t.* परिग्रह् 9 P, स्वीकृ 8 U.

POSTURE, *s.* सं-,स्थिति *f.*, संस्थानं, संस्था, अंगविन्यासः-स्थितिः; आसनं, बंधः; वीरासनं, कमलबंधः &c.; 'in a sitting p.' आसीन, उपविष्ट. 2 Condition, q. v.

POSY, *s.* कुसुमस्तबकः, पुष्पगुच्छः. 2 अंगुलीयकलेखः.

POT, *s.* घटः, कलसः-शः, कुंभः, पात्रं, भाजनं, भांडं; 'cooking-p.' स्थाली, उखा, पिष्टपचनं, ऋजीषं, पिठरः; 'p.-bellied' तुंदिल, लंबोदर, पिचिंडिल, तुंदिन्; 'p.-belly' पिचिंडः, लंबोदरं; 'p.-companion' पानमित्रं-सुहृद्, सहपायी; 'p.-house' शुंडा, पानं; 'p.-sherd' घटशकलं, भिन्नपात्रं. -TER, *s.* कुंभकारः, कुलालः, घटकारः, चक्रिन् *m.* -TERY, *s.* कुंभ-घट-स्थानं. 2 कौलालकं, मार्तिकं, मृद्भांडानि.

POTASH, *s.* सर्जिका, क्षारः; *See* NATRON.

POTATION, *s.* पानं, सपीति *f.*, तुल्यपानं.

POTATO, *s.* गोलालुः.

POTENT, *a.* प्रबल, सप्रभाव, वीर्यवत्, सप्रताप, शक्तिमत्, प्रभविष्णु; *See* STRONG.-ATE, *s.* अधिपतिः, नरेश्वरः, प्रभुः; *See* KING. -LY, *adv.* प्रबलं, सप्रतापं, बलवत्.

POTENTIAL, *a.* शक्य, उपपन्न, संभवनीय; (mood) विधिलिङ्. -ITY, *s.* शक्यता, संभाव्यता.

POTHER, *See* BUSTLE, PERPLEX.

POTHERB, *s.* शाकः, हरितकं, शिग्रुः.

POTION, *s.* अगदः, पानं, पेयौषधं.

POTTAGE, *s.* जूषं.

POTULENT, *a.* आमत्त. 2 पानयोग्य.

POUCH, *s.* स्यूतः, प्रसेवः, कोशः-षः. 2 लंबोदरं. 3 पेशि-शी *f.*, उपजठरं. -*v. t.* कोशे निविश् c. or नि-धा 3 U.

POULTERER, *s.* वैतंसिकः, शौनिकः, पक्षिविक्रयी.

POULTICE, *s.* उपनाहः, प्र-,लेपः. -*v. t.* उपनाहं दा 3 U.

POULTRY, *s.* गृहपक्षिणः; 'p. yard' कुक्कुटादिस्थानं.

POUNCE, *v. i.* अवपत्य ग्रह् 9 P, सहसा अवपत् 1 P or अवस्कंद् 1 P or आक्रम् 1 U, 4 P. -*s.* नखः, नखरः. 2 मसीशोषणचूर्णं.

POUND, *s.* (For cattle) अवरोधः, अवरोधस्थानं, व्रजः, गोष्ठं. -*v. t.* सं-, चूर्ण् 10, मृद् 9 P, पिष् 7 P, क्षुद् 7 P, खंड् 10; 'p. to dust' चूर्णशः कृ, चूर्णपेषं पिष्, चूर्णीकृ 8 U. 2 (व्रजे) नि-अव-रुध् 7 U, or बंध् 9 P. 3 तड् 10, तुद् 6 P, प्रह् 1 P. -AGE, *s.* शुल्कं, राजस्वं. -ER, *s.* पेष्टृ *m.*, पेषणः. 2 मुसलः-लं, अयोग्रं, मुद्गरः. -ING, *s.* चूर्णनं, पेषणं, मर्दनं, खंडनं.

POUR, *v. t.* पत् c., नि-,सिच् 6 P, प्र-,स्रु c.; 'p.

water in' जलेन पॄ 3, 9 U, सिच्. 2 (Out, forth) प्र-निर्-मुच् 6 P, उत्-वि-सृज् 6 P, अवपत् c., अवतॄ c., निःसृ c., उत्क्षिप् 6 P, उद्-गॄ 6 P, उदीर् c., उद्वम् 1 P, वृष् 1 P, प्र-वि-कॄ 6 P; निर्वृ, निर्गल् c.; 'which has p.ed out its watery contents' निर्गलितांबुगर्भः, पानीयरिक्तोदरः (घनः); 'p. out the water from the pot' पात्रं जलरिक्तं कुरु; 'p. ed forth arrows' शरवृष्टिं मुमोच; 'p. one's soul to another' अन्यस्मै स्वमनोगतं सर्वात्मना निविद् c. —*v. i.* स्रु 1 P, प्र-परि-°, प्र-,स्यंद् 1 A, च्युत् 1 A, जलं स्रु c. or प्रवह् 1 P. 2 वृष्, निर्गल् 1 P. 3 निःसृ 1 P, निर्गम् 1 P, निः-स्रु; 'rain p. ed down in torrents' धारासारैर्महती वृष्टिर्बभूव (H. 3); 'p. in upon' समापत् 1 P, अभिद्रु 1 P बहुशः आपत् or आक्रम् 1 U, 4 P. —ER, *s.* स्रावकः, सेचकः, सेक्तृ *m.* —ING, *s.* सेकः, स्रावः, स्रवः, स्रोतः

POUT, *v. i.* (क्रोधात्) ओष्ठौ प्रसृ c. or दृश् c. 2 उन्नत-उच्छ्रित -*a.* भू 1 P. —*s.* क्रोधावेशः.

POVERTY, *See* under POOR.

POWDER, *s.* चूर्णं, पिष्टं, क्षोदः; 'gun-p.' आग्नेयचूर्णं 'perfumed p.' वासयोगः, पिष्टातः-तकः, पटवासकः —*v. t.* 'to reduce to p.' चूर्ण् 10, क्षुद् 7 P, चूर्णीकृ, पिष् 7 P; *See* POUND. 2 चूर्णेन लिप् 6 P or भू c. or मिश्र् 10. —Y, *a.* पांसुल, चूर्णवत्, चूर्णमय (यी *f.*), सचूर्ण, सक्षोद.

POWER, *s.* शक्ति *f.*, सामर्थ्यं, बलं, प्रभावः, वीर्यं ऊर्जः, सहस्-ओजस् *n.*, विभवः (वाग्विभवः); (martial) तेजस् *n.*, वि-परा-क्रमः, शौर्यं. 2 (Ability) शक्तिः, क्षमता, धीशक्तिः; 'p. of thinking' विचारणाशक्तिः; 'according to one's p.' यथाशक्ति-बलं, यावच्छक्यं. 3 (Influence) प्रभुत्वं, प्रभावः वशः-शं, बलं, गौरवं, अधिकारः; आधिपत्यं, ईशत्वं, सत्ता, ऐश्वर्यं, अधीनता. 4 अधिपः-पतिः, अधीशः प्रभुः. 5 (Legal) अधिकारः, or by अर्ह् 1 P. 6 अधिकारिजनः, अधिकृतः. 7 घातः. 8 सेना, बलं पृतना; 'have or exercise p. over' प्रभू 1 P, ईश् 2 A (with gen.), वशीकृ, आयत्तीकृ, आत्मवशं नी 1 P; 'in (under) the p. of' वश' अधीन, आयत्त, तंत्र in comp.; 'fallen into another's p.' परहस्तगत ; 'to be in one's p.' ex. by शक् 5 P or by (*s.*). —FUL, *a.* बलसामर्थ्य-वत्, शक्त, बलिन्, सबल, प्रबल, ऊर्जस्वल, ओजस्विन्, शक्तिमत्, ऊर्जितसत्त्व, बलाढ्य, सप्रभाव, प्रभविष्णु. 2 शूर, वीर, विक्रांत, तेजस्विन्, महाप्रताप, प्रतापवत्, धामवत्, उरुविक्रम. 3 (Medicine) वीर्यवत्, अमोघ, गुणावह, प्रबल, अलंतम. 4 दृढ, प्रतीतिकारिन्, प्रबल. —FULLY, *adv.* बलवत्, प्रबलं, सप्रभावं, अत्यंतं. —FULNESS, *s.* प्राबल्यं, शक्तत्वं. —LESS, *a.* निर्बल, शक्तिहीन, अशक्त, अबल, निष्प्रभाव, असमर्थ, अक्षम. —LESSNESS, *s.* अशक्ति *f.*, असामर्थ्यं.

POX, *s.* Small-pox, q. v. 2 उपदंशः.

PRACTICE, *s.* प्र-आ-चारः, संप्रदायः, व्यवहारः, रीति *f.*, मार्गः, पद्धति *f.*, क्रमः, वृत्तिः *f.* 2 अभ्यासः, क्रिया प्रबंधः-सातत्यं, नित्यप्रवृत्तिः-चर्या-अनुष्ठानं, अनुशीलनं,-निरंतरप्रवृत्तिः, आवृत्तिः; 'does not require p.' नाभ्यासक्रममीक्षते. 3 क्रिया, आचारः, आचरणं, कर्म, कृति *f.*, व्यापारः, व्यवसायः; करणं, विधानं, अनुष्ठानं; (execution) प्रवृत्तिः, प्रचारः, व्यवहारः; 'bring or put into p.' प्रवृत् c., व्यवहृ c.; 'has long been in p.' चिरप्रवृत्त. 4 (Opp. of theory) प्रयोगः. 5 छलं, व्याजः, कैतवं ; *See* FRAUD; 'ancient p.' वृद्धाचारः, वृद्धपरंपरा; 'family p.' कुलसंप्रदायः, कुलधर्मः, कुलाचारः; 'local p.' देशाचारः ; 'good p.' सदाचारः ; 'following good p.s' सदाचार, सद्वृत्ति, सद्वृत्त, साधुवृत्त; 'bad p.' दुराचारः, कुमार्गः, दुर्वृत्तिः; 'following bad p. s' दुर्वृत्त, दुराचार; 'p. of medicine' वैद्यक्रियाउपचारः, चिकित्सा, भेषजप्रयोगः, उपक्रमः; 'p. of arms' शस्त्राभ्यासः, शस्त्रचर्या; 'p. of law' व्यवहारः, व्यवहाराभ्यासः; 'p. in archery' शराभ्यासः, उपासनं. —PRACTISE, *v. t.* अभ्यस् 4 U, नित्यं कृ 8 U, &c. 2 आचर् 1 P, अनु-ष्ठा 1P, कृ, वि-धा 3U, आ-स्था 1 U. 3 प्र-उप-युज् 7 A, 10, प्रवृत् c., व्यवहृ c., सेव् 1 A, आश्रि 1 U, आ-अव-लंब् 1 A; 'what profession do you p.' कां वृत्तिमुपजीवत्यार्यः (Mr. 2). —*v. i.* शाठ्येन आचर् or व्यवहृ 1 P, छलं-कपटं-कृ. —ED, *a.* अभ्यस्त, आचरित, अनुष्ठित, कृत, सेवित, &c. 2 अभिज्ञ, परिचयवत्, बहुदृष्ट, व्यवहारज्ञ, दृष्टकर्मन्, पक्वबुद्धि, ज्ञानवृद्ध, जाताभ्यास; also ex. by (*s.*). —ING, *a.* अभ्यासिन्, सेविन्, शालिन्, in comp.; आस्थित, आश्रित. —PRACTICABLE, *a.* करणीय, कर्तुं शक्य, साध्य, संभाव्य, शक्य, सुकर, सुखसाध्य, उपपाद्य. —PRACTICAL, *a.* अभ्यासिक-व्यावहारिक (की *f.*), अभ्याससिद्ध-प्राप्त, आचार-व्यवहार in comp.; 'p. knowledge' व्यवहारज्ञानं, लौकिकज्ञानं. 2 अभ्यासक्षम, व्यवहार्य, प्रयोज्य, प्रवर्तनीय, व्यवहारोचित; 'a p. scheme' व्यवहारोचित उपायः; 'he is a p. teacher' स शिक्षाप्रयोगनिपुणः. 3 व्यवहारज्ञ, दृष्टकर्मन्, अभिज्ञ ; *See* PRACTISED. —LY, *adv.* कार्यतः, अर्थतः, वस्तुतः, परमार्थतः, व्यवहारतः. फलापेक्षया. 2 अभ्यासेन, व्यवहारेण. —PRACTITIONER, *s.* सेविन्, व्यवसायी, व्यापारिन्, वृत्ति, आजीव in comp. 2 वैद्यः, वैद्यवृत्तिः, चिकित्सकः. 3 व्यवहारज्ञः, व्यवहारदर्शिन्-निपुणः.

PRAGMATIC,-AL, *a.* परकार्यचर्चक, अनधिकारव्यापारिन् ; *See* MEDDLE, &c.

PRAISE, *v. t.* प्रशंस् 1 P, श्लाघ् 1 A, ईड् 2 A, नु 2 P, स्तु 2 U, वर्ण् 10, गै 1 P, कृत् 10, वि-प्र-°

ख्या 2 P or c. (ख्यापयति), पन् 1 P, नू 6 P. –*s.* प्र-,शंसा, श्लाघा, स्तुति *f.*, स्तवः, वर्णनं-ना, कीर्तनं, नुति *f.*, ईडा, स्तोत्रं. –ER, *s.* प्रशंसकः, स्तावकः, वर्णकः, वंदारुः. –PRAISEWORTHY, *a.* प्रशस्य, प्रशंसार्ह, श्लाघ्य, स्तुत्य.

PRANCE, *v. i.* प्लु 1 A, वल्ग् 1 P, नृत् 4 P. –ING, *s.* प्लुतं, वल्गितं, प्लवनं.

PRANK, *s.* क्रीडा, चेष्टा, चापलं, लीला, छंदः-दस् *n.*; ' idle p. ' वानर-मर्कट-चेष्टा-क्रीडा ; ' mischievous p. ' कु-दुः-चेष्टितं. –*v. t.* दंभार्थं भूष् 10 or अलंकृ 8 U. –ISH, *a.* कुचेष्ट, चपल, क्रीडाशील.

PRATE, PRATTLE, *v. i.* प्र-,लप् 1 P, प्र-,जल्प् 1 P, अनर्थकं वद् 1P or भाष् 1 A. –ER, *s.* वाचाटः, वाचालः, जल्प(ल्पा)कः, वावदूकः, बहुभाषिन्. –ING, *s.* प्रलापः, प्रलपितं, प्र-,जल्पः-ल्पितं-ल्पनं; बालालापः, बालभाषणं-प्रलापः.

PRAVITY, *s.* भ्रष्टता, विक्रिया, विकारः.

PRAY, *v.* (A deity) स्तु 2 U, प्र-अभि-सं-°, नमस्यति (D.), अभिवद् c., आराध् c., प्रणम् 1 P; (मनसा) पूज् 10, उपास् 2 A, ध्यै 1 P, चिंत् 10. 2 आशंस् 1 A. 3 याच् 1 A, प्र-अभि-अर्थ् 10 A; विज्ञा c. (ज्ञापयति); gen. ex. by अर्ह् 1 P with inf.; *See* PLEASE; ' I p. you tell me ' मह्यं कथयितुमर्हति भवान्. 4 (Lowly) जप् 1 P. –ER, *s.* स्तवः, स्तोत्रं, प्रार्थना-नं, नमस्या, उपासना, पूजा; (mental) ध्यानं, आवाहनं; (low) जपः, स्वाध्यायः. 2 याच्ञा, प्रार्थना, अभ्यर्थना, विज्ञप्ति *f.*, विज्ञापना. –FUL, *a.* प्रार्थनाशील, भजनपरायण.

PREACH, *v. t.* उदार् c., उद्-घुष् 10, उच्चर् c., प्र-ख्या c. (ख्यापयति), प्रकाश् c., प्रवद् 1 P, कॄत् 10. –*v. i.* धर्मं प्रवच् 2 P or शास् 2 P or उपदिश् 6 P. –ER, *s.* उपदेशकः, प्रवक्तृ *m.*, प्रचारकः, धर्मशासकः, धर्मोपदेशी. 2 घोषकः, प्रख्यापकः. –ING, *s.* वि-,घोषणं-णा, प्रख्यापनं, धर्मोपदेशः, धर्मशासनं, प्रवचनं, उपदेशः.

PREAMBLE, *s.* उपोद्घातः; *See* INTRODUCTION.

PREBEND, *s. See* CANON.

PRECARICOUS, *a.* संदिग्ध, अनिश्चित, अनिर्णीत, अनियत, अस्थिर, अध्रुव. 2 पराधीन, परायत्त, अस्वतंत्र; *See* DOUBTFUL, DANGEROUS. –LY, *adv.* संदिग्धं, अनियतं. –NESS, *s.* अनियतत्वं, अन्याधीनता.

PRECATIVE, PRECATORY, *a.* याचक, प्रार्थनात्मक; ' p. mood ' आशीर्लिङ्.

PRECAUTION, *s.* पूर्वोपायः, निवारणोपायः, पूर्व-समीक्षा-चिंता, पूर्वावधानं, पूर्वप्रबोधः; ' take p. s ' पूर्वमेव उपायं समीक्ष् 1 A or चिंत् 10; ' hence I give you this p. ' अतस्त्वामेवं प्रबोधयामि. –ARY, *a.* पूर्वोपायरूप; by (*s.*).

PRECEDE, *v. t.* पूर्वं-अग्रे-पुरतः गम्-सृ-चर् 1 P or इ-या 2 P or वृत् 1 A or स्था 1 P ; oft. ex. by पूर्वं, प्राक्, प्रथमं, ततः, अनंतरं ; ' the flower p. s the fruit ' उदेति पूर्वं कुसुमं ततः फलं, so घनोदयः प्राक् तदनंतरं पयः (S. 7.); ' visarga p. ed by अ ' अपूर्वः विसर्गः; ' many kings p. ed Râma ' रामात् पूर्वं बहवो नृपाः समजायंत. 2 (In rank) अग्रपदे वृत्, अग्रमानं अर्ह् 1 P. –ENCE, *s.* अग्रगमनं, पुरःसरणं. 2 अग्र-श्रेष्ठ-पदं, पुरस्कारः, उत्कर्षः, प्राधान्यं, अग्रत्वं, अग्रणीत्वं, आग्रमानः-पूजा, मुखरता, श्रेष्ठत्वं, प्राथम्यं. –ENT, *s.* (पूर्वं) निदर्शनं, उदाहरणं, आदर्शः, प्रतिमा, प्रमाणं, दृष्टांतः; ' having no p. ' अप्रतिम. –*a.*, –ING, *a.* पूर्व-अग्र-गामिन्, अग्रग, पूर्वग, पूर्व, अग्र, प्रथम, अग्र-पुरः-सर. –ENTED, *a.* भूत-दृष्ट-पूर्व, दृष्टप्रतिम; ' un-p. ' अप्रतिरूप, निरुपम, अतुल.

PRECENTOR, *s.* मुख्यगायकः, गायकाग्रणीः.

PRECEPT, *s.* नियोगः, आ-नि-देशः, अनु-,शासनं, अनुज्ञा, विधिः, नियमः, प्र-,चोदनं-ना, कल्पः, आज्ञा, स्थिति *f.*, मर्यादा. 2 वचनं, उपदेशः; ' moral p. s ' नीतिवचनानि; ' religious p. ' धर्मानुज्ञा, धर्मशासनं; ' example is better than p. ' शासनात् करणं श्रेयः, वाचः कर्मातिरिच्यते. –IAL, -IVE, *a.* वैधिक-नैयमिक (की *f.*), विधिरूप, (*s.*) in comp. –OR, *s.* गुरुः, शिक्षकः, उपदेशकः, आचार्यः, अध्यापकः, उपाध्यायः.

PRECESSION, *s.* अग्रगति *f.*; ' p. of the equinoxes ' अयनचलनं. क्रांतिपातगति *f.*

PRECINCT, *s.* सीमा, पर्यंतः, मर्यादा, अवधिः, परिसरः, उपांतं, उपकंठं, समंतदेशः.

PRECIOUS, *a.* महार्ह-र्घ, महा-बहु-मूल्य, अनर्घ्य, अमूल्य, उत्कृष्ट, बहुमत, गुरु, परम; ' p. stone ' उपलरत्नं, अमूल्यरत्नं, रत्नं, मणिः. –NESS, *s.* महार्घता, बहुमूल्यं.

PRECIPICE, *s.* प्रपातः, भृगुः, अतटः. –PRECIPITOUS, *a.* पातुक, विषम, प्रवण, अवसर्पिन्. 2 Rash, q. v.

PRECIPITATE, (PRECIPITANT) *a.* अवाङ्मुख (खी *f.*), अधोमुख, अवाक्शिरस्. 2 असमीक्ष्य-क्षिप्र-अविमृश्य-कारिन्, साहसिन्, साहसिक (की *f.*); (act) सरभस, अविमृष्ट, अतिक्षिप्र, साहस in comp. –*v. t.* रभसा अधः क्षिप् 6 P or पत् c. 2 सरभसं प्रवृत् c. or प्रोत्सह् c., त्वर् c. (त्वरयति). –*v. i.* अव-अधः-पत् 1 P, नि-सद् 1 P. 2 (Fig.) अविचार्य-सरभसं-व्याप्तृ 6 A or c. –LY, *adv.* अवाक्, अवाक्शिरसा, अधोमुखेन. 2 अविमृश्य, असमीक्ष्य, सहसा, साहसेन, अतिक्षिप्रं, सरभसं. –ION, –NESS, *s.* अधःपातनं-क्षेपणं, अवपातनं. 2 साहसं, साहसिकता, क्षिप्रकारिता, असमीक्ष्य-अविमृश्य-कारिता. –PRECIPITANCE, *s.* साहसं ; *See* above.

PRECIS, *s.* सारः, संक्षेपः, संग्रहः.

PRECISE, *a.* नियत, निर्दिष्ट, निश्चित, परिच्छिन्न, यथार्थ, विशेष in comp. ; *See* EXACT. 2 व्यक्त, स्फुट,

सूक्ष्म. 3 (Of persons) सामयिक (की *f.*), समयानुवर्तिन्, संकेतानुरोधिन्, सूक्ष्मनियमनिष्ठ. -LY, *adv.* नियतं, यथार्थं, सूक्ष्मतया ; oft. by एव ; 'at noon p.' मध्याह्नसमये एव ; 'p. so' एवमेव. -ION, -NESS, *s.* नियतत्वं, निर्देशः, सूक्ष्मता, सुनिश्चितता, याथार्थ्यं, व्यक्तता, &c.

PRECLUDE, *v. t.* निवृ c., नि-प्रति-षिध् 1 P, नि-प्रति-रुध् 7 U, बाध् 1 A, प्रतिबंध् 9 P; *See* OBSTRUCT. -PRECLUSION, *s.* प्रतिबंधः, निवारणं, नि-प्रति-षेधः, निरोधः. -PRECLUSIVE, *a.* निवारक, प्रतिबंधक, निरोधक.

PRECOCIOUS, *a.* अकालपक्व-परिणत-प्रौढ. 2 बालप्रौढ-पक्व. -NESS,-PRECOCITY, *s.* अकालपरिणति *f.* -प्रौढता, बालप्रौढि. *f.*

PRECOGITATE, *v. i.* पूर्वं-अग्रे चिंत् 10 or विचर् c. or विमृश् 6 P.

PRECOGNITION, *s.* पूर्वज्ञानं-बोधः.

PRECONCEIVE, PRECONCERT, *v. t.* पूर्वं चिंत् 10 or क्लृप् c. or वि-भू c. -ED, *a.* पूर्वकल्पित-निर्धारित, पूर्वघटित-निर्णीत. -ION, *s.* अग्र-पूर्व-कल्पना-बोधः-ज्ञानं ; पूर्वघटनं-संकेतः.

PRECURSOR, *s.* पूर्वगः, अग्रेसरः, अग्रयायी, पुरःसरः; *See* HARBINGER. 2 पूर्वलक्षणं-चिह्नं-लिंगं. -Y, *a.* पूर्वग, पुरःसर, अग्रवर्तिन्.

PREDATORY, *a.* दस्युवृत्ति, अपहारक, उपद्रविन्, लुंटक, चौर in comp.

PREDECESSOR, *s.* पूर्वगः, पूर्वाधिकारिन् *m.*

PREDESTINATE, PREDESTINE, *v. t.* पूर्वं-अग्रे-निरूप् 10 or प्रक्लृप् c. or निर्दिश् 6 P. -ED, *a.* अग्र-पूर्वं-निर्दिष्ट-निरूपित, भाविन्, दैवाधीन, दैवायत्त, दैष्टिक (की *f.*). -ION, *s.* अग्रनिरूपणं-निर्देशः. 2 दैववादः, दैवपरता, अदृष्टप्रारब्ध-वादः, दैष्टिकता. -PREDESTINARIAN, *s.* दैवपरः, दैव-अदृष्ट-वादी, यद्भविष्यः, दैवायत्तः, दैष्टिकः.

PREDETERMINE, *v. t.* पूर्वं-अग्रे-निश्चि 5 U or निर्णी 1 P. -ATE,-ED, *a.* पूर्वनिश्चित-निर्णीत. -ATION, *s.* पूर्वं-अग्र-निश्चयः-संकल्पः-निर्णयः.

PREDIAL, *a.* क्षेत्र, भूमि in comp.

PREDICAMENT, *s.* पदार्थः ; वर्गः, जाति *f.* 2 अवस्था, दशा, वृत्ति *f.*, भावः, स्थिति *f.* ; कष्टावस्था, दुःस्थितिः, कृच्छ्रं.

PREDICATE, *v. t.* उद्दिश्य वद् 1 P or वच् 2 P or कथ् 10 or अभि-धा 3 U ; विशिष् 7 P or c., वि-धा, निर्दिश् 6 P. -*s.* विधेयं, वाच्यं, विशेषणं. -ION, *s.* विधानं, विशेषणं, निर्देशः, अभिधानं. -PREDICABLE, *a.* वाच्य, अभिधेय.

PREDICT, *v. t.* पूर्वं-अग्रे-कथ् 10 or वच् 2 P or निरूप् 10, आ-समा-दिश् 6 P; कथ्, वद् 1 P, with words for 'Future,' q. v.; 'p. ed that she would be the sole wife of Hara' तां समादिदेशैकवधूं भवित्रीं...हरस्य (K. I. 51); कथयत्यागामिनमर्थं (Ka. 46) 'p. s (unforeseen) events'. -ION, *s.* अनागतकथनं, भाविकथनं, आ-समा-देशः, भविष्यद्वादः. -OR, *s.* पूर्वादिन् *m.*, अग्रनिरूपकः, सिद्धः. आदेष्टा.

PREDILECTION, *s.* पक्षपातः, पूर्वस्नेहः, अनुरागः; *See* PARTIALITY.

PREDISPOSE, *v. t.* पूर्वं प्रवृत् c. or प्र-उद्-युज् 7 A, 10, प्रवणीकृ 8 U; ex. by प्रवण, उद्यत, उन्मुख, शील in comp.; 'p. ed to anger' क्रोधप्रवणशील. -ITION, *s.* प्रावण्यं, प्रवृत्ति *f.*, शीलं.

PREDOMINATE, *v. i.* प्र-भू 1 P, प्रबल-अधिक-वरीयस्- *a.* भू 1P, अतिरिच्-विशिष्-pass.; *See* EXCEL. -PREDOMINANT, *a.* प्रबल, अतिरिक्त, प्रधान, विशिष्ट, अधिक, प्रभविष्णु. -LY, *adv.* प्राधान्येन, प्रबलं, विशिष्टतया. -PREDOMINANCE, *a.* प्राबल्यं, प्राधान्यं, आधिक्यं, अतिरेकः.

PRE-EMINENT, *a.* सर्वप्रधान, श्रेष्ठ, सर्वोत्कृष्ट, अग्रगण्य, परम, उत्तम, विशिष्ट, प्रमुख, अग्रणी, अग्रीय, वरेण्य; oft. by व्याघ्रः, शार्दूलः, पुंगवः, ऋषभः, प्रकांडः, &c. in comp.; *See* EXCELLENT. -LY, *adv.* परमं, प्रधानतः, विशिष्टं, सातिशयं, अत्यंतं, सविशेषं. -PRE-EMINENCE, *s.* उत्कर्षः, प्राधान्यं, प्रमुखता, श्रेष्ठता, उत्तमता, अग्रगण्यत्वं, वैशिष्ट्यं.

PRE-EMPTION, *s.* पूर्वक्रयः, पूर्वक्रयाधिकारः.

PRE-ENGAGE, *v. t.* पूर्वं प्रतिज्ञा 9 A, पूर्वं संक्लृप् c. -MENT, *s.* पूर्वसंकेतः-प्रतिज्ञा.

PRE-EXIST, *v. i.* पूर्वं भू 1 P ('Be.' q. v.). -ENCE, *s.* प्राग्भावः-जन्मन् *n.* -जीवनं. -ENT, *a.* पूर्वभव-भूत.

PREFACE, *s.* आमुखं, प्रस्तावना, मुखबंधः, उपोद्घातः, वाङ्मुखं, उपन्यासः, प्रारंभः. -*v. t.* प्रस्तु 2 U, प्रस्तावनां लिख् 6 P or कृ 8 U. -PREFATORY, *a.* प्रस्तावना-उपोद्घात-रूप.

PREFER, *v. t.* उन्नम् c. (नमयति), उत्कर्षं नी 1 P or प्राप् c., पुरस्कृ 8 U, उत्कृष्टपदे नियुज् 7 A, 10, प्रतिपत्तिं प्राप् c. 2 अधिकं रुच् 1 A or मन् 4 A or c. or प्रशंस् 1 P: वृ 5 U or 10 (वरयति); gen. ex. by वरं-न with पुनः, च, तथापि; 'I p. death to disgrace' वरं मृत्युः न पुनरपमानः; वरं वंध्या भार्या न चाविद्वान् तनयः &c. 3 सम्-ऋ c. (अर्पयति), निविद् c., उपह 1 P; *See* OFFER. -ABLE, *a.* वरीयस्, श्रेयस्, गरीयस्; better ex. by (*v.*). -ENCE, *s.* अभिरुचि *f.*, अधिकानुरागः. 2 आदराधिक्यं, अधिकमानः; 'in p. to' विहाय, अतीत्य, अपेक्ष्य in comp. -MENT, *s.* उन्नति *f.*, पदोत्कर्षः, प्रतिपत्ति *f.*, उत्कर्षः; स्थानोन्नतिः, प्रतिष्ठापदं, गौरवास्पदं.

PREFIGURE, *v. t.* प्रतिबिंबं दृश् c. -ATION, *s.*

पूर्वलक्षणं-दर्शनं.

PREFIX, *s.* उपसर्गः.—*v. t.* पूर्वं आ-प्र-युज् 7 A, 10, पूर्वं-अग्रे-विन्यस् 4 U or नि-आ-धा 3 U or लिख् 6 P.

PREGNANT, *a.* गर्भिणी, गर्भवती, सगर्भा, अंतर्वत्नी, आपन्नसत्त्वा, ससत्त्वा, धृत-रूढ-गृहीत-गर्भा, गर्भधारिणी; 'to be p.' गर्भं-आधा 3 U or धृ 1 P, 10, भृ 1 P with (*a.*); 'a p. woman longing for things' श्रद्धालुः, दोहदवती. 2 अर्थयुक्त-गर्भ. 3 सं-परि-पूर्ण, आढ्य-गर्भ in comp. —PREGNANCY, *s.* गर्भः, दौर्हृदं, गर्भधारणं-ग्रहणं, गर्भिणीभावः ; 'showed signs of p.' दौर्हृदलक्षणं दधौ (R. III. 1); 'advanced in p.' कठोरगर्भा.

PREJUDGE, *v.* पूर्वं निर्णी 1 P or विचर् c. or निश्चि 5 U. —MENT, *s.* पूर्वनिर्णयः-निश्चयः.

PREJUDICE, *s.* दुराग्रहः, आ-,ग्रहः, चेतोविकारः-विक्रिया, वक्रीभावः; अविचारमति *f.*, अविचारपूर्वः निर्णयः. 2 पक्षपातः, संगः. 3 नाशः, क्षति *f.*, हानि *f.*, अपायः, अपकारः; *See* HARM. —*v. t.* विकृ 8 U, साचीकृ, आवृज् 10, पूर्वं प्रवृत् c. 2 अपकृ, नश् c., क्षण् 8 P; *See* INJURE. —IAL, *a.* हानि-क्षय-कर (री *f.*), अहित, अननुकूल, अपकारक. —IALLY, *adv.* सापायं, सापकारं.

PRE-KNOWLEDGE, *s.* पूर्वज्ञानं-बोधः.

PRELATE, *s. See* BISHOP.

PRELECTION, *s. See* LECTURE.

PRELIBATION, *s.* पूर्वास्वादः, पूर्वभुक्ति *f.*

PRELIMINARY, *a.* पूर्व-आदि-प्रथम in comp. ; प्राथमिक (की *f.*). 2 पारिभाषिक (की *f.*), प्रस्तावनारूप. —*s.* (pl.) पूर्वकार्याणि, पूर्वविषयः. 2 Preface, Introduction, q. v.

PRELUDE, *s.* प्रस्तावना, आमुखं, पूर्वरंगः. 2 आ-प्रारंभः, उपक्रमः. —*v. t.* प्रस्तु 2 U, प्रारभ् 1 A, उपक्रम् 1 A.

PREMATURE, *a.* अकालपरिणत-पक्व, अपूर्णकाल, अपूर्णकालज, असामयिक-अ(आ)कालिक-(की *f.*), अकाल-असमय in comp.; 'p. death' अकालमृत्युः. 2 साहसिन्, अकालसह; *See* RASH. —LY, *adv.* अपूर्णकालं, अकाले, असमये ; 'p. born' अपूर्णकाल ; 'p. bald' युवखलतिः. —NESS, *s.* अकालिकत्वं.

PREMEDITATE, *v. i.* पूर्वं संकृप् c. or विचर् c. or चिंत् 10. —ED, *a.* पूर्वसंकल्पित-चिंतित, मति-बुद्धि-पूर्व, सांकल्पिक-सांकेतिक (की *f.*), बुद्धिकृत. —ION, *s.* पूर्वसंकल्पः-विचारः-घटना.

PREMIER, *s.* प्रधानामात्यः, मुख्यमंत्रिन् *m.*, प्रधानसचिवः. —*a.* प्रधान, मुख्य, प्रमुख. —SHIP, *s.* प्रधानमंत्रिपदं.

PREMISE, *v. t.* उपन्यस् 4 U, उपक्षिप् 6 P, पूर्वं कथ् 10 or ब्रू 2 U or वद् 1 P, प्रस्तु 2 U or c., प्रस्तावनारूपेण कथ् or ख्या 2 P, प्र-उप-क्रम् 1 A. —*s.*, —PREMISS, *s.* पक्षः, प्रतिज्ञा; 'major p.' उदाहरणं ; 'minor p.' उपनयः. —PREMISES, *s.* गृहक्षेत्रादि, गृहपरिसरः.

PREMIUM, *s.* लाभः, फलं, अधिकमूल्यं, पारितोषिकं.

PREMONISH, *v. t.* पूर्वं सूच् 10 or उपदिश् 6 P, प्रबुध् c. —PREMONITION, *s.* पूर्वबोधः, प्रबोधनं. —PREMONITORY, *a.* पूर्वबोधक, प्रबोधक.

PREOCCUPY, *v. t.* पूर्वं ग्रह् 9 P or भुज् 7 A or आक्रम् 1 U, 4 P. —ATION, *s.* पूर्वभोगः-आक्रमः.

PREORDAIN, *v. t.* पूर्वं प्रकॢप् c. or निर्दिश् 6 P.

PREPARE, *v. t.* प्र-उप-परि-कॢप् c., सज्जीकृ 8 U, सं-,विधा 3 U, निर्मा 3 A, 2 P, घट् c. (घटयति), उप-प्र-युज् 7 A, 10 (medicines) ; संभृ 1, 3 U, उपकरणद्रव्यैः संयुज् ; oft. by कृ ; (food) प्रसाध् c., सिध् c. (साधयति), संस्कृ, पच् 1 P, निष्पद् c. ; (army) सन्नह् 4 P or c., आयुधैः उपकॢप् c. ; (a book &c.) प्रणी 1 P, निर्मा, प्र-नि-बंध् 9 P, वि-,रच् 10; (lesson) शिक्ष् 1 A, पठ् 1 P, अधि-इ 2 A, पारं गम् 1 P; तॄ 1 P (p. well). —*v. i.* उपकरणानि-द्रव्याणि-संभृ or कॢप् c. 2 सज्जीभू 1 P, उद्यत-उद्युक्त-सज्ज-सिद्ध-*a.* भू. —ATION, *s.* उपकल्पनं, योजनं, साधनं, विधानं, सज्जीकरणं, वि-,रचनं-ना, करणं. 2 संभारः, संविधा, संविधानं, सिद्धि *f.*, सिद्धता, सामग्री ; 'marriage-p. s' विवाहसंभाराः ; 'war-p. s' युद्धसामग्री ; तदुत्तिष्ठ गच्छावो गमनसंविधानाय वत्सस्य (Ka. 294) 'come, let us go to make p. s' &c. 3 योगः. 4 संस्कारः, निष्पत्ति *f.*, सिद्धि *f.* —ATIVE,-ATORY, *a.* उपक्रमोपकारिन्, उपक्रमानुकूल ; उपकल्पक, प्रथम, आद्य. —*s.* उपक्रमसाधनं, सिद्धिसाधनं ; better ex. by (*v. t.*). —ED, *a.* कृत, निर्मित, घटित, रचित, उपकृत, कल्पित, निष्पन्न, &c. 2 सिद्ध, सन्नद्ध, सज्ज, उद्यत, उद्युक्त. —EDNESS, *s.* सिद्धता, सज्जता. —ER, *s.* उपकल्पकः, साधकः, रचकः, संस्कर्तृ *m.*

PRE-PAYMENT, *s.* पूर्वदानं-शोधनं.

PREPENSE, *a.* चिंतितपूर्व, मतिपूर्व; *See* PREMEDITATED ; 'malice p.' द्रोहचिंता.

PREPONDERATE, *v. i.* अतिरिच्-विशिष्-pass., भारेण-गौरवेण-अतिरिच् or वृध् 1 A, प्र-भू 1 P, अधिक-गुरुतर- *a.* भू. —PREPONDERANCE, *s.* आधिक्यं, अतिरेकः, प्राबल्यं, प्राधान्यं, प्रभावः, गौरवं. 2 अधिकभारः, भाराधिक्यं.

PREPOSITION, *s.* उपसर्गः. —AL, *a.* औपसर्गिक (की *f.*).

PREPOSSESS, *v. t.* (चित्तं) आवृज् 10, प्रह्वीकृ 8 U, आकृष् 1 P, साचीकृ. 2 पूर्वं अधि-ष्ठा 1 P or भुज् 7A. —ED, *a.* (सद्यः) आकृष्टचित्त, ससंग, जातानुराग. —ING, *a.* (सद्यः) हृदयग्राहिन्, चित्ताकर्षिन्. —ION, *s.* पक्षपातः, संगः, ग्रहः, प्रावण्यं, चित्ताकर्षणं. 2 पूर्वभोगः.

PREPOSTEROUS, *a.* विपरीतक्रम, विपर्यस्त. 2 (अतीव) अयुक्त, असंगत, अनुपपन्न, असंबद्ध, अनर्थक. -LY, *adv.* अयुक्तं, असंगतं. -NESS, *s.* वैपरीत्यं, क्रमविपर्यासः, अयुक्तता, असंगति *f.*, असंबंधः.

PREPUCE, *s.* शिश्नाग्रत्वच् *f.*

PRE-REQUISITE, *a.* पूर्वाकांक्षित. -*s.* पूर्वाकांक्षा.

PREROGATIVE, *s.* असाधारणाधिकारः, विशेषाधिकारः, विशेषशक्ति *f.*, सत्ता.

PRESAGE, *v. t.* पूर्वं सूच् 10 or आदिश् 6 P; *See* FOREBODE, PREDICT. -*s.* पूर्वसूचनं-ना, पूर्वलक्षणं-चिह्नं; *See* OMEN.

PRESCIENCE, *s.* पूर्वज्ञानं, भविष्यद्विज्ञानं, भावि-अनागत-ज्ञानं, समवेक्षणं. -PRESCIENT, *a.* भाविज्ञानिन्, अनागतवेदिन्; gen. ex. by पूर्वं ज्ञा 9 U or बुध् 1 P.

PRESCRIBE, *v. t.* निर्दिश् 6 P, वि-धा 3 U, प्रक्लृप् c., प्र-चुद् 10, शास् 2 P, आ-ज्ञा c. (ज्ञापयति), नियम् 1 P. -ED, *a.* निर्दिष्ट, विहित, प्र-,चोदित, विध्यनुरूप, वैधिक (की *f.*). -ER, *s.* निर्देशकः, शास्तृ *m.* -PRESCRIPT, *s.* आदेशः, विधिः, आज्ञा, चोदनं-ना. -*a.* निर्दिष्ट, प्रकल्पित. -ION, *s.* कल्पः, योगः, अगद-निर्देशः, उपचार-औषध-विधिः. 2 विधिः, निर्देशः, आज्ञा, प्र-,चोदनं-ना, शासनं, वचनं. 3 चिर-बहुकाल-भोगः-भुक्ति *f.*, अनादिपरंपरा, अस्मार्तभोगः -IVE, *a.* चिरकालभुक्त, अनादिपरंपराप्राप्त, चिरव्यवहारसिद्ध.

PRESENT, *v. t.* उपहृ 1 P, उपहारं दा 3 U, प्र-उप-दा 3 U, ऋ c. (अर्पयति), वितॄ 1 P, वि-श्रण् 10, उपढौक् c., प्रति-पद् c.; (oblation) निर्वप् 1 P, निविद् c., उत्सृज् 1 P; *See* OFFER. 2 उपन्यस् 4 P, उपक्षिप् 6 P, पुरो निधा 3 U. 3 (Oneself) आविर्भू 1 P, उप-स्था 1 P, प्रादुर्भू, दृश्-लक्ष्- pass., प्रविश् 6 P, आत्मानं दृश् c. 4 दर्शनं कृ c., प्रविश् c.; दृश् c., पुरस्कृ 8 U, समक्षं नी 1 P; सकाशं नी; 'p. me to the king' मां राजदर्शनं कारय. 5 प्र-दृश् c., आविष्कृ, व्यंज् 7 P or c., प्रकटयति (D.), प्रकटीकृ, सूच् 10; oft. ex. by 'Appear' q. v.; 'the court p. ed a gay scene' अधिकरणमंडपः सुतरां रमणीयो बभौ, रम्यालोक आसीत्; 'what a charming sight do these girls p.' अहो मधुरमासां (कन्यकानां) दर्शनं (S. 1), अहो मनोज्ञदर्शनः कन्यकाजनः; 'p. an appearance of' विडंब् 10, अनुकृ (with gen.). -*a.* प्रस्तुत, प्रकृत. 2 (Mind) सावधान, अभ्रांत, अव्यग्र, अशून्य, समाहित, अव्याकुल, निराकुल, असंभ्रम; प्रत्युत्पन्न. 3 विद्यमान, वर्तमान, आधुनिक-सांप्रतिक (की *f.*), अधुनातन-इदानींतन (नी *f.*). 4 सद्यस्क, तात्कालिक (की *f.*); अविलंबित; 'in the p. state' अस्यामवस्थायां; 'at p.', 'for the p. time' अधुना, सांप्रतं इदानीं; *See* Now. 5 उपस्थित, सन्निहित, प्रत्यक्ष, सं-अभि-मुख (खी *f.*), समीपवर्तिन्; *See* NEAR; 'to be p.' उप-स्था 1 P, सन्निधा- pass., समीपं वृत् 1 A; 'you should be p.' त्वयोपस्थातव्यं, सन्निहितेन भाव्यं; 'to be p. in one's thoughts' हृदये-चित्ते-वस् 1 P. -*s.* भवत् *n.*; समतीतं च भवच्च भावि च (R. VIII. 78) 'the past, p. and future.' 2 वर्तमान-प्रस्तुत-कालः, तत्कालः, तत्क्षणः, आपातः. 3 (In grammar) लट्. 4 उपायनं, उपहारः, उपदा, प्र-,दानं, वितरणं, पारितोषिकं, उपग्राह्यं, प्राभृतं, प्रदेशनं, प्रीतिदानं; 'p. of money' दक्षिणा; *See* GIFT. -ABLE, *a.* उपहार्य, देय, दर्शनीय, प्रवेश्य. 2 पांक्तेय, पांक्त्य, सभ्य. -ATION, *s.* उपहरणं, अर्पणं, प्रतिपादनं, दानं; 'p. of an oblation' बलिदानं, निर्वपणं. -LY, *adv.* अधुना, संप्रति, सांप्रतं. 2 सपदि, अनंतरं, द्राक्, तत्क्षणं-णे, तत्काले, सद्यः, अचिरात्, शीघ्रं, आशु, झटिति. -PRESENCE, *s.* संनिधिः, समुपस्थिति *f.*, उपस्थानं, सांनिध्यं, सन्निधानं, प्रत्यक्षता, समक्षता, आभिमुख्यं; 'in the p. of' समक्षं, प्रत्यक्षं, संमुखं, साक्षात्, in comp. or with gen.; in the p. of fire' अग्निसाक्ष्ये आधाय (R. VII. 20); 'into the p. of' सकाशं-शे, समीपं-पे, अंतिकं, in comp. or with gen. 2 आकारः, आकृति *f.*, रूपं, शरीरसंस्था. 3 (Of mind) प्रत्युत्पन्नमति *f.*, प्रतिभा, प्रतिभानं, प्रतिभानवत्त्वं, समाहितत्वं, अव्यग्रता, असंभ्रमः, निराकुलत्वं; 'p.-chamber' दर्शनशाला, आस्थानं-नी.

PRESENTIMENT, *s.* पूर्वज्ञानं-बोधः-कल्पना; 'my mind has a p. of evil' मम मनः किमप्यशुभमाशंकते.

PRESERVE, *v. t.* रक्ष् 1 P, त्रै 1 A, पा c. (पालयति), उद्-धृ 1 P, 10, गुप् 1 P, पा 2 P, तॄ c., अव् 1 P, परि-आप् desid. (ईप्सति), (इमां परीप्सुः दुर्जाते: M. 5). 2 सं-,भृ 3 U, पुष् c., संवृध् c., पा c. (पालयति). 3 सं-धा 3 U, उपस्कृ 8 U. -*s.* संधितं, उपस्करः, मिष्टसंधित-फलं-द्रव्यं. 2 वि(वी)तंसः, विहगस्थानं. -ATION, *s.* सं-,रक्षा-क्षणं, त्राणं, स्थितिपालनं, गोपनं, तारणं. -ATIVE, *s.* रक्षा, रक्षणं, रक्षण-त्राण-साधनं, त्रं-त्राणं in comp. -*a.* रक्षक, पालक, तारक.

PRESIDE, *v. i.* (Over) अधि-ष्ठा 1 P, अध्यास् 2 A (with acc.); अधीश् 2 A, प्र-भू 1 P (with gen.); अवेक्ष् 1 A, अध्यक्षः-अधिपतिः-भू, अभिमन् 4 A; अग्न्यायभिमानिनीभिर्देवताभिः (S. B. 725) 'p.-ing over fire &c.' -ENCY, *s.* अध्यक्षता, अधिष्ठानं, अधिकारः. 2 आधिपत्यं, अधिष्ठातृत्वं, अध्यक्षपदं, अधीशत्वं, better by (*v.*); 'during his p.' तस्मिन्नधितिष्ठति. 3 मंडलं, भागः, देशविभागः. -ING, *a.* अध्यक्ष, अधिष्ठातृ, अभिमानिन्, अधि pr.; 'the p. deity' अधिदेवता, अधिष्ठात्री देवता; 'the soul p. over the body' शरीराभिमानी आत्मा. -PRESI-

DENT, *s.* अध्यक्षः, अधिष्ठाता, अधीशः, अधि-,पतिः, अध्यासीनः, अधिकारी, प्रभुः, नायकः. -SHIP, *s.* आधिपत्यं, अध्यक्षता; *See* PRESIDENCY.

PRESS, *v. t.* पीड् 10, निः-आ-°, निष्कृष् 1 P, निर्ह 1 P, निर्दुह् 2 U; (together) संपीड्, संहन् 2 P, संह, संकुच् 1 P, संपिड् 10, संघट्ट c. 2 Clasp, q. v.; 'p. ing him to the bosom' तं वक्षसा परिरभ्य ; भुजाभ्यां आपीड्य 'p. ing in the arms' &c. 3 प्रेर् c., प्रचुद् 10, प्रणुद् 6 P or c., आकृष् 1 P, आकृ c. 4 निर्बंध् 9 P, अनु-अनुनिर्बंध्, साग्रहं-निर्बंधेन-प्रच्छ् 6 P or याच् 1 A or अर्थ् 10 A, पुनः पुनः प्रच्छ् ; *See* IMPORTUNE. 5 बलेन प्रवृत् c. or नियुज् 7 A, 10 or व्याप् c. 6 बाध् 1 A, पीड्, क्लिश् 9 P, उद्विज् c., सं-परि-तप् c., व्यथ् c. (व्यथयति). 7 मुहुर्मुहुः-पुनःपुनः-उपदिश् 6 P or कथ् 10 or अनुशास् 2 P. -*v. i.* समापत् 1 P, आ-अधि-क्रम् 1 U, 4 P, अभिद्रु 1 P ; (against) संघट्ट् 1 A, प्रतिहन् 2 P, अभ्याहन् ; संघट्टयन्नंगदमंगदेन (R. VI. 73) ; 'making his Angada ornament p. against Indra's.' 2 सवेगं प्रगम् or प्रसृ 1 P, सरभसं उपसृप् 1 P or संगम् 1 A ; 'p.-ing close to the rock' शिलायामात्मानं निबिडं-निरंतरं-संसंजयन्. 3 प्र-,बाध् 1 A; 'my time p. es' कालातिपातो मया नैव कर्तुं शक्यते ; 'p. through' अतीत्य-अतिक्रम्य-गम्, उल्लंघ् 1 A, 10, निस्तॄ 1 P. -*s.* पीडनं, निष्कर्षः. 2 मुद्रण-मुद्रा-यंत्रं. 3 पीडन-पेषण-यंत्रं. 4 जनसंकुलं-संमर्दः, लोकनिवहः. 5 निर्बंधः, पीडा, अतिभारः. -ER, *s.* पीडकः, बाधकः. -ING, *a.* अतिनिर्बंधक, बाधक, अत्यवश्यक, अविलंब्य, अव्याक्षेप्य, विलंबाक्षम, अनतिपात्य ; 'p. business of state' आशुसंपादनीयं-विलंबाक्षमं-राजकार्यं. -INGLY, *adv.* निर्बंधेन, सनिर्बंधं, साग्रहं. -URE, *s.* पीडनं. 2 बलं, शक्ति *f.*, प्रभावः, वेगः, प्रवर्तनं, प्रेरणा, प्रणोदः, प्रोत्साहः. 3 भारः, पीडा, बाधा, क्लेशः ; 'p. of business' कार्यभारः ; 'having much p. of work' कार्यसमाकुल.

PRESTIGE, *s.* दीर्घरूढा प्रतिष्ठा, चिरप्रतिष्ठितं गौरवं. 2 माया, इंद्रजालं.

PRESTO, *adv. See* QUICKLY.

PRESUME, *v. t.* (अविचार्य-अनिश्चित्य) तर्क् 10, सं-भू c., अनु-मा 3 A, 2 P. 2 धृष् 5 P, धैर्येण आक्रम् 1 U, 4 P, उत्सह् 1 A, प्र-भू 1 P ; प्रगल्भ् 1 A, दृप् 4 P, साहसं कृ 8 U ; कः पतिदेवतामन्यः परिमार्ष्टुमुत्सहेत (S. 6) 'p to lay hands on &c.' ; तद्दोषनिरूपणरूपं साहसं मा कुरु 'do not p. to find fault with him'. -PRESUMPTION, *s.* तर्कः, कल्पना, भावना, अनुमानं, ग्रहणं. 2 साहसं, धाष्टर्यं, प्रागल्भ्यं. 3 अवलेपः, दर्पः, अभिमानः, अहंकारः, गर्वः. 4 संभाव्यता, संभवः. -PRESUMPTIVE, *a.* आनुमानिक (की *f.*), अनुमानसिद्ध, संभावित ; 'p. proof' अनुमाननिर्णयः. —PRESUMPTUOUS, *a.* साहसिक (की *f.*), धृष्ट, धृष्णु, प्रगल्भ. 2 अवलिप्त, अत्यभिमानिन् ; 'a p. statement' साहसोक्ति *f.*, साहसं. -LY, *adv.* साहसेन, धृष्टवत्, प्रगल्भं, सावलेपं, सगर्वं. -NESS, *s.* धृष्टता, प्रागल्भ्यं; प्रतिभा, प्रतिभानं.

PRESUPPOSE, *v. t.* पूर्वं क्लृप् c. or भू c. -ITION, *s.* पूर्वकल्पना-भावना.

PRETEND, *v.* अप-व्यप-दिश् 6 P, छलं-कपटं-व्याजं कृ 8 U, ध्वजीकृ ; gen. ex. by मिथ्या, कृतक, कपट, व्याज, छद्म in comp. or by भू c., दृश् c.; 'p. ing to be asleep' सुप्तमिव आत्मानं संदर्श्य, व्याजसुप्त, सुप्तलक्षण, मिथ्यासुप्त ; 'p. ing to be affected by poison' भावितविषवेगः ; 'p. s not to hear' अश्रुतिमभिनयति ; 'p. ing to be just' आर्यध्वजिन्-लिंगिन् ; 'p. ed weeping' कपट-व्याज-रोदनं. 2 अभिमन् 4 A, मिथ्या मन् ; 'he p. s to know everything' अहं सर्वज्ञोस्मीति तस्याभिमानः (अवलेपः). 3 मिथ्याहेतुं दृश् c. or वद् 1 P. -ED, *a.* छाद्मिक-कौटिक (की *f.*), व्याज-कपट-छद्म-कूट-मिथ्या in comp.; 'p. ascetic' छद्मतापसः, तापसध्वजीलिंगी ; *See* HYPOCRITE ; *See* (*v.*) also. -EDLY, *adv.* सकपटं, सव्याजं, छलेन, मिथ्या. -ING, *a.* -ER, *s.* छाद्मिकः, कापटिकः, अभिमानी-ध्वजी-लिंगी-मन्यः-अभियोगी in comp. ; 'p. in learning' पंडितंमन्यः, विद्याभिमानी ; 'p. in religion' धर्मध्वजी, आर्यलिंगी, धार्मिकवेशधारी, कपटधर्मी ; 'p. to the throne' राज्याभियोगी. -PRETENCE, PRETEXT, *s.* व्याजः, अप-व्यप-देशः, छद्मन् *n.*, उपधिः, कपटं, छलं, उपधा, कूटः-टं, कैतवं, मिषं, मिथ्याहेतुः, निमित्तं. 3 अभिमानः, अभियोगः. -PRETENSION, *s.* अभिमानः, अभियोगः, स्वत्वप्रतिपादनं ; 'lay p. s to' *See* CLAIM. 2 महात्वाकांक्षा, यशोलिप्सा, लोभः ; 'p. s to the throne' राज्यं मदीयमिति प्रतिपादनं, राज्याभियोगः.

PRETERITE, *a.* भूत, परोक्ष ; 'p. tense' लङ्.

PRETERITION, *s.* अतिक्रमः-मणं, अत्ययः.

PRETERMIT, *v. t. See* OMIT.

PRETERNATURAL, *a.* अद्भुत, विलक्षण, निसर्ग-प्रकृति-बाह्य. -LY, *adv.* अद्भुतं, वैलक्षण्येन.

PRETTY, *a.* सु in comp., चारु, शोभन, कमनीय, वाम, सुंदर ; *See* BEAUTIFUL, LOVELY. -*adv.* ईषत्, स्तोकं, अल्पं ; आ, कल्प, देश्य, देशीय in comp. ; 'p. warm' मंदोष्ण, कोष्ण, कदुष्ण; 'p. clear' शुद्धकल्प-प्राय ; 'p. ripe' आपक्व, पक्वप्राय. 2 (P. nearly) प्रायेण, प्रायशः, बहुशः, कल्प-भूयिष्ठ-प्राय in comp.; 'p. nearly furnished' समाप्तभूयिष्ठ &c. -LY, *adv.* चारु, सुंदरं, चारु-सु in comp. -NESS, *s.* चारुता, सौंदर्यं, लावण्यं.

PREVAIL, *v. i.* अभिभू 1 P, प्र-भू, पराभू, पराजि 1 A, आक्रम् 1 U, 4 P; अति-शी 2 A, अतिरिच् pass., प्रबल-क्षम-*a.* भू; *See* EXCEL. 2 (In) प्रचलित-प्रवृत्त-*a.* भू, प्र-चल्-र् 1 P, प्रवृत् 1 A; 'darkness p. ed everywhere' सर्वं तमोवृतं आसीत्. 3 सिध् 4 P, निष्पद् 4 A; 'p. with, on, or upon' अनुनी 1 P, प्रवृत् c., प्रोत्सह् c.; *See* PERSUADE; 'p. against' मुच्छ् 1 P, (मारुतस्य रंहः शिलोच्चये न मूर्च्छति R. II. 34). -ING,-PREVALENT, *a.* प्रचलित, साधारणी-बहुली-भूत, प्रसिद्ध, प्रचल, प्रवृत्त, साधारण (णी *f.*); 'universally p.' सर्वत्र प्रचलित, सर्वप्रवृत्त; 'long since p.' चिरप्रवृत्त. 2 प्रबल, प्रधान, अतिरिक्त, अधिकबल, प्रभविष्णु, सप्रभाव. -INGLY, *adv.* प्राबल्येन, सप्रभावं.—PREVALENCE, *s.* प्रचारः, प्रवृत्ति *f.*, प्रचलनं, प्रसिद्धि *f.*, साधारण्यं. 2 प्राबल्यं, प्राधान्यं, आधिक्यं, अतिरेकः.

PREVARICATE, *v. i.* सापह्नवं मिथ्योत्तरं दा 3 U, अप-व्यप-दिश् 6 P, छलं कृ 8 U, अपलप् 1 P, अपनि-ह्नु 2 A, वाक्छलं कृ; 'when he p. ed' यदा वाक्यभेदान् बहूनकथयत् (Mu. 2). -ING, *a.* अपलापिन्, निह्नवकारिन्, व्यपदेशिन्. -ION, *s.* वाक्छलं, अपलापः, अप-नि-ह्नवः, व्यप-अप-देशः, वक्रोक्ति *f.*, छद्मवादः, उत्तराभासः.

PREVENT, *v. t.* वृ c., नि-विनि-°, रुध् 7 U, प्रति-अवनि°, प्रति-नि-षिध् 1 P, प्रतिकृ 8 U, बाध् 1 A, प्रतिबंध् 9 P, प्रतिष्टंभ् 9 P, प्रति-व्या-हन् 2 P, प्रत्या-ख्या 2 P, निवृत् c., अंतरायःभू- परिपंथीभू 1 P; 'do not p. me from fighting' युध्यमानं मां मा रुन्धि, युध्यमानस्य मेऽन्तरायो मा भूः. -ION, *s.* प्रति-,रोधः, नि-, वारणं, प्रतिबंधः, प्रतिकारः, व्याघातः, प्रतिषेधः; 'p. is better than cure' प्रक्षालनाद्धि पंकस्य दूरादस्पर्शनं वरं. -IVE, *a.* हर (री *f.*), घ्न (घ्नी *f.*) in comp., निवारक, प्रतिबंधक, निरोधक. -*s.* वारणं, प्रतिबंधकं.

PREVIOUS, *a.* पूर्व, प्राग्भूत, भूत, गत, अतीत, पूर्ववृत्तगत, प्राक् in comp. -LY, *adv.* पूर्वं, प्राक्, पुरस्तात्, पूर्वं in comp.

PREVISION, *s.* अग्रनिरूपणं-दृष्टि *f.*

PREY, *s.* आमिषं (fig. also); मांसं, भक्ष्यं, अन्नं, खाद्यं, भोज्यं; 'fell a p. to enemies' द्विषामामिषतां ययौ (R. XII. 11). -*v. i.* भक्ष्यं आ-अप-हृ 1 P. 2 (Upon) भक्ष् 10; संतप् c., बाध् 1 A, क्रमशः नश् c.

PRICE, *s.* मूल्यं, अर्घः, पण्यं, अवक्रयः, वस्नं; 'high p.' महार्घः, बहुमूल्यं. -*v. t.* मूल्यं स्था c. (स्थापयति) or संक्लृप् c. -ED, *a.* कृतमूल्य; 'high-p.' महार्घ-र्ह, बहुमूल्य, दुर्मूल्य; 'low-p.' अल्पमूल्य. -LESS, *a.* अनर्घ-र्घ्य, अमूल्य.

PRICK, *v. t.* व्यध् 4 P, निर्-,भिद् 7 P, तुद् 6 P, पीड् 10; व्यथ् c. (व्यथयति), क्लिश् 9 P or c. 2 प्रेर् c., उत्तिज् c., प्रोत्सह् c., प्रणुद् 6 P or c. 3 (Ears) उन्नम् c. (नमयति), उच्छ्रि 1 U, स्तब्धीकृ 8 U; 'with ears p. ed' स्तब्धकर्ण. -*s.*, -ING, *s.* प्रतोदः, तोत्रं, तोदनं; सूचि *f.*, शल्यं, कंटकः. 2 वेधः-धनं, तोदनं. 3 यातना, तीव्रव्यथा, आतंकः, शूलः-लं. -ED, *a.* विद्ध, भिन्न, शल्य-सूचि-विद्ध-भिन्न; 'p. at heart' भिन्न-विद्ध-मर्मन्. -ER, *s.* वेधकः. 2 तोत्रं; *See* (*s.*).

PRICKLE, *s.* कंटकः, सूचि-ची *f.*, शल्यं, शूकं. -Y, *a.* सकंटक, सशूक, बहुकंटक-शूक.

PRIDE, *s.* (Good) अभिमानः. 2 अहंकारः, गर्वः, उत्सेकः, अवलेपः, दर्पः, औद्धत्यं, मदः, मादः, आटोपः, अहंमानः, मानः, चित्तसमुन्नति *f.*, अवष्टंभः, चित्तोद्रेकः, स्मयः; (impudent) प्रागल्भ्यं, धृष्टता, प्रतिभा-मानं. 3 अलंकारः, अवतंसः, ललामं, अभिमानास्पदं-भूमिः. -*v. t.* (Oneself upon) आत्मानं श्लाघ् 1 A or विकत्थ् 1 A, अभिमन् 4 A, or ex. by (*s.*); 'p.-ing himself on his learning' पंडितमानी, पंडितंमन्यः, विद्याभिमानी, जातज्ञानावलेपः; 'p. ing herself upon her beauty' रूपगर्विता. —PROUD, *a.* (In a good sense) अभिमानिन्. 2 दृप्त, गर्वित, अवलिप्त, सगर्व, सदर्प, उत्सिक्त, उद्धत, उत्सेकिन्, अभिमानिन्, साटोप, साहंकार; अहंमानिन्, उन्-,मत्त, समुन्नद्ध; प्रगल्भ, धृष्ट, प्रतिभावत्, गर्वितचित्त, मदोद्धत; दर्पाध्मात, स्मयाकुल. 3 (Building &c.) उत्तुंग, प्रोच्छ्रित, विशाल, सप्रताप; 'p. of one's birth' कुलाभिमानिन्; रूपगर्वित, यौवनोन्मत्त, &c.; 'to be p.' दृप् 4 P, गर्व् 1 P, प्रगल्भ् 1 A. -LY, *adv.* सदर्पं, सगर्वं, सावलेपं, साटोपं, साहंकारं, उद्धतं.

PRIEST, *s.* (Family) पुरोहितः, पुरोधस् *m.*, कुलाचार्यः. 2 (Sacrificial) ऋत्विज् *m.*, याजकः, अध्वर्युः, होता, याज्ञिकः. 3 (Vedic) श्रोत्रियः, मंत्रविद् *m.*, ब्राह्मणः, द्विजः, विप्रः. 4 आचार्यः, गुरुः, उपाध्यायः, पुरोहितः, धर्माचार्यः, धर्माध्यक्षः. 5 (Of a deity) पूजकः, उपासकः, अर्चकः; 'p.-craft' उपाध्यायछलं-कैतवं; 'p.-ridden' पुरोहिताधीन. -ESS, *s.* होत्री, याजिका. -HOOD, *s.* पौरोहित्यं, उपाध्यायपदं-वृत्ति *f.* 2 पुरोहिताः, पुरोहित-याज्ञिक-गणः-वर्गः, पौरोहित्यं. -LY, *a.* याजकीय, पौरोहित्यसंबंधिन्, (*s.*) in comp.

PRIG, *s.* दांभिकः, दंभिन् *m.*, रूपगर्वितः. -GISH, *a.* दांभिक (की *f.*), आत्माभिमानिन्.

PRIM, *a.* अतिविनीत, अतिसूक्ष्म.

PRIME, *s.* आदिः, आरंभः, पूर्व-प्रथम-भागः. 2 उत्तमदशा, प्रौढता, उत्तमभागः-अंशः; 'in the p. of youth' प्रथमे वयसि; 'the p. of youth' प्रथमं वयः, नव-अक्षत-यौवनं, यौवनश्रीः; 'being in the p. of youth' अक्षत-नव-यौवन. -*a.* प्रथम, आद्य. 2 मुख्य, प्रधान, प्रमुख, अग्र्य; 'p. minister' मुख्यमंत्री, प्रधानामात्यः, महामंत्री. 3 उत्कृष्ट, श्रेष्ठ, परम,

उत्तम, विशिष्ट ; *See* PRINCIPAL. —LY, *adv.* प्रथमं, श्रेष्ठं. —NESS, *s.* उत्तमता, विशिष्टता. —PRIMARY, *a.* प्रथम, आद्य, आदिम, पूर्व, मौल (ली *f.*), मूल-आदि in comp. ; ' p. cause ' आदिकारणं-बीजं, निदानं, मूलहेतुः ; ' p. sense ' मूलार्थः. 2 प्रधान, मुख्य, प्रमुख, अग्र्य; *See* PRIME. —ILY, *adv.* प्रथमं-मतः, आदौ, पूर्वं, मुख्यशः, प्राधान्येन. —INESS, *s.* प्रथमता, प्राधान्यं. —PRIMATE, *s.* प्राधानोपाध्यायः. —PRIMER, *s.* प्रथम-आरंभ-पुस्तकं. —PRIMEVAL, *a.* आद्य, आदिम, प्राक्कालीन, पूर्वकालीन, प्राक्तन (नी *f.*), मौलिक-प्राथमिक- (की *f.*). —PRIMITIVE, *a.* प्राथमिक, प्रथम, आद्य ; *See* PRIMEVAL. 2 मूल in comp., अव्युत्पन्न ; *See* PRIMARY. 3 प्राक्तनमार्गसेविन्. —LY, *adv.* आदौ, आरंभे, प्रथमं-मतः. 2 प्राक्तनव्यवहारानुसारेण.

PRIMOGENIAL, *a.* प्रथम-आदि-जात, मूल in comp.

PRIMOGENITOR, *s.* प्रथम-कुल-पुरुषः. —PRIMOGENITURE, *s.* पूर्वजत्वं, ज्येष्ठत्वं, अग्रजत्वं, वयोज्येष्ठता.

PRIMORDIAL, *a.* आद्य ; बीजभूत, मौल (ली *f.*); *See* PRIMEVAL.

PRINCE, *s.* कुमारः, राजपुत्रः-सुतः, युवराजः. 2 नृपः, राजन् *m.*, पार्थिवः ; *See* KING. 3 भर्तृदारकः, कुमारः, (in dramas). —DOM, *s.* राज्यं, राष्ट्रं, विषयः. 2 यौवराज्यं. —LIKE,-LY, *a.* राजयोग्य-सदृश (शी *f.*), राजार्ह, नृपोचित; नृपोपम, राजकीय, प्रतापवत्, ऐश्वर्यवत्; प्रताप-वैभव-शालिन्. 2 राजवंश्य, राजकुलज ; ' p. birth ' राजवंशप्रसूतिः; ' p. merits ' राजोचिता गुणाः —PRINCESS, *s.* कुमारी, राजपुत्री, नृपात्मजा, नृपसुता ; भर्तृदारिका.

PRINCIPAL, *s.* अध्यक्षः, अधि-,पतिः नायकः, मुख्यः ; *See* LEADER. 2 मूलं, मूलधनं, नीवि-वी *f.*, परिपणः. —*a.* मुख्य, परम, प्रधान-वर in comp., प्रमुख, अग्र, अग्र्य, प्रवर, श्रेष्ठ, विशिष्ट, उत्कृष्ट, उत्तम, अनुत्तम, वर्य, वरेण्य, परार्ध्य, अग्रि(ग्री)य, प्राग्रहर ; नायक, अग्रणी, मुखर, धुर्य, धुरीण, धूर्वह, धुरंधर ; oft. ex. by व्याघ्र, पुंगव, ऋषभ, कुंजर, सिंह, शार्दूल, नाग, प्रकांड, in comp.; *See* EXCELLENT ; ' p. door ' सिंहद्वारं ; ' p. queen ' अग्र-पट्ट-महिषी; ' p. minister ' प्रधानामात्यः. —ITY, *s.* राष्ट्रं, प्रदेशः, मंडलं, राज्यं. —LY, *adv.* प्रधानतः, प्राधान्येन, मुख्यशः, विशेषतः, विशेषेण.

PRINCIPLE, *s.* तत्त्वं, मूलतत्त्वं, बीजं, सारः. 2 कारणं, हेतुः, आदिबीजं-हेतुः, मूलं, अंगं, अवयवः, साधनं, मूलांगं-द्रव्यं. 3 नियमः, विधिः, सूत्रं, उत्सर्गः, स्थिति *f.*, व्यवस्था. 4 गुणः, भावः, धर्मः, स्वभावः. 5 क्रमः, रीति *f.*, मार्गः, मर्यादा, धारा, पद्धति *f.* 6 आधारः, आश्रयः, उपष्टंभः, मूलं ; (opp. of practice) आगमः, शास्त्रं ; ' grounded in p. s ' आगमिन्, शास्त्रनिपुण ; ' having good p. s ' सुनियमनिष्ठ, सुवृत्त; ' of bad p. s ' खंडितवृत्त, भ्रष्टचरित.

PRINT, *v. t.* मुद्रयति (D.), अंक् 10, मुद्राक्षरैः अंक्. —*s.* चिह्नं, अंकः, मुद्रा ; ' foot-p. ' पदं, पदमुद्रा-चिह्नं. 2 मुद्रणयंत्रं. 3 मुद्रणं ; ' in p. ' मुद्र्यमाण. —ED, *a.* मुद्रित, मुद्रांकित, मुद्राक्षरांकित. —ER, *s.* मुद्रकः, मुद्रणकृत् *m.* —ING, *s.* मुद्रणं, मुद्रांकनं ; ' p.-house ' मुद्रणयंत्रालयः, मुद्रणशाला ; ' p.-press ' मुद्रणयंत्रं.

PRIOR, *a.* प्रधान, गरीयस्, गुरुतर, पूर्व, अग्र्य, आदिम, आद्य, पूर्व-आदि-प्राक् in comp. ; ' p. existence ' प्राग्भावः, पूर्व जन्म ; ' p. and subsequent ' पूर्वापर, परापर, परावर. —*s.* मठाध्यक्षः, मठाधिपतिः, विहारपालः. —ITY, *s.* पूर्वता, प्रथमता. 2 (Of rank) अग्रपदं-मानः, श्रेष्ठपदं, प्राधान्यं. —Y, *s.* मठः, विहारः, आश्रमः.

PRISM, *s.* क्रकचायतं. —PRISMATIC, *a.* क्रकचायत.

PRISON, *s.* कारा, बंदिशाला-गृहं, बंधनालयः, कारागृहं, चारः-रकः, गुप्तिस्थानं; 'escaped from the p.' बंधनं भित्त्वा पलायांचक्रे ; ' keep in p.' बंधने निरुध् 7 U. —ER, *s.* बंदि-दी *f.*, कारागुप्तः, रुद्धः, कारागारस्थः. 2 (Of war) युद्धगृहीतः.

PRISTINE, *a.* प्राक्तन (नी *f.*), पुराण, पूर्व, पूर्वकालिक (की *f.*), प्राचीन, प्राक्कालीन.

PRIVATE, *a.* विजन, विविक्त, निर्जन, एकांत, निभृत, निःशलाक. 2 स्व, आत्मीय, असाधारण (णी *f.*), असामान्य, विविक्त, स्व-आत्म in comp. 3 गुप्त, गूढ, रहस्य, प्र,-छन्न, अप्रकट, अव्यक्त, रहस्-मिथः-अंतः- in comp. 4 अनधिकारिन्, अनधिकारिक (की *f.*); ' p. profit ' आत्महितं, स्वलाभः; ' p. road ' गूढ-प्रच्छन्नमार्गः; ' p. door ' अंतर्द्वारं, गूढद्वारं, प्रच्छन्नं; ' p. apartments ' अंतःपुरं, अवरोधगृहं, अंतर्गृहं; ' now is the time to be p. ' रहस्यमधुना (Bh. II. 97); ' p. talk ' रहःसंकथा, मिथोजल्पः; ' p. parts ' गुह्यं, उपस्थः; ' p. room ' अंतःशाला-कोष्ठः, उपरोधकं. —*s.* सैनिकः. —LY, ' in p. ' *adv.* रहः, रहसि, मिथः, रहस्ये, निभृतं, विविक्ते, एकांते, विजने, उपांशु, गूढं, प्रच्छन्नं, गुप्तं, अप्रकाशं, अप्रकटं. —NESS, -PRIVACY, *s.* रहस् *n.*, विविक्तं, विजनं, रहोभावः, विविक्त-एकांत-वासः; रहस्यं, गुप्तता, छन्नता, अप्राकाश्यं. 2 रहःस्थानं-स्थलं, विविक्त-निर्जन-स्थानं, निर्जनदेशः.

PRIVATION, *s.* अभावः, विरहः, राहित्यं, हानि *f.* क्षयः, लोपः, नाशः. 2 कष्टं, कृच्छ्रं, आपद्-विपद् *f.* 3 आहारविरहः, आहाराभावः, सुखसाधनलोपः, अन्नवस्त्रहानिः. —PRIVATIVE, *a.* हानि-क्षय-लोप-कर (री *f.*). 2 अभावात्मक, अभावरूप, अभाववाचिन्. —*s.* अभावशब्दः, नञ्पदं. —LY, *adv.* अभावरूपेण.

PRIVILEGE, *s.* विशेषाधिकारः, असामान्याधिकारः, स्वाधिकारः, अधिकारः, स्वत्वं. —*v. t.* विशेषाधिकारं दा 3 U. —ED, *a.* अधिकारविशिष्ट, साधिकार, विशेषाधिकारयुक्त.

PRIVY, *a.* गूढ, प्रच्छन्न, विविक्त, रहः in comp.; *See* PRIVATE. 2 (To) संसर्गिन्, सहाय, सहकारिन्; सहज्ञानिन्, सहवेदिन्; 'p. council' गूढसभा; 'p. councillor' गूढसभासद्. —*s.* शौचस्थानं-कूपः, उच्चारप्रस्रावस्थानं. —LY, *adv.* रहसि, गूढं; *See* PRIVATELY.—PRIVITY, *s.* सहकारिता, सहायता, संसर्गः, सहज्ञानं. 2 गुह्य-गुप्त-स्थानं-इंद्रियं, अधोंगं.

PRIZE, *s.* पारितोषिकं, उपायनं, प्रतिफलं. 2 रत्नं, बहुमूल्यं वस्तु, महार्घद्रव्यं. 3 युद्धजितं धनं-द्रव्यं. 4 जय-सिद्धि-फलं-लाभः. 5 स्पर्धा-पण-जेयं, पणः; 'p.-fighter' मल्लः; 'p.-fighting' मल्लयुद्धं, स्पर्धायुद्धं. —*v. t.* बहु मन् 4 A, अवेक्षया पा c. (पालयति), संमन् c. 2 मूल्यं-अर्घं-निरूप् 10 or निर्णी 1 P. —ED, *a.* बहुमत, अभीप्सित, इष्ट.

PRO, PREFIX, प्र, अग्रे; 'p. s and cons' विधिनिषेधपक्षौ.

PROBABLE, *a.* संभाव्य, सत्यसंकाश; gen. ex. by सं-भू 1 P, उप-पद् 4 A, युज् pass. or by (*adv.*); 'it is p.' एतत् उपपद्यते, संभवति, युज्यते, स्यान्नाम एवं. —PROBABLY, *adv.* प्रायेण, प्रायः, प्रायशः, किल, नाम, स्यात्; by pot. pass. part. of भू; एतेन मम प्रियमित्रेण भाव्यं 'he is p. my dear friend.' —PROBABILITY, *s.* संभवः, संभाव्यता, अनुमानं, better by (*adv.*).

PROBATE, *s.* मृतलेखप्रमाण.

PROBATION, *s.* परीक्षा-क्षणं. —ARY, *a.* परीक्ष्यमाण. —ER, *s.* परीक्ष्यमाणः; अंतेवासिन् *m.*, नवशिष्यः, प्राथमकल्पिकः.

PROBE, *s.* शलाका, एषणी. —*v. t.* शलाकया परीक्ष् 1 A. 2 निपुणं-सूक्ष्मं-परीक्ष् or आलोच् 10. —ATOR, *s.* परीक्षकः. —ING, *s.* क्षतपरीक्षणं.

PROBITY, *s.* *See* HONESTY.

PROBLEM, *s.* प्रश्नः, विकल्प-विवाद-प्रश्न-विषयः. 2 कृत्यं, उपपाद्यं. 3 (Question) उद्देशकः (in Math.); 'its solution' न्यासः (Lit.) —ATICAL, *a.* संदिग्ध, अनिश्चित, वैकल्पिक (की *f.*).

PROBOSCIS, *s.* प्रोथः; करः, शुंडा, हस्तः.

PROCEED, *v. i.* प्रचल् 1 P, प्र-या 2 P, प्रगम्-सृ 1 P, अग्रे गम्, प्र-स्था 1 A. 2 प्रवृत् 1 A, न विरम् 1 P; 'the play still p. s' क्रीडा अद्यापि प्रवर्तते एव. 3 पुनः वक्तुं प्रवृत्. 4 प्रवृत्, आरभ् 1 A, प्र-उप-क्रम् 1 A; (with) प्रस्तु 2 U or c., प्रवृत् c.; (प्रारब्धं) सं-पद् c., निष्पद् c., निर्वह् c.; 'p. with your tale' तत-स्ततः, ततः, परं कथय; 'p. with the matter at issue' प्रस्तूयतां विवादवस्तु (M. 2); 'you may p. with your dinner preparations in honor of the worthy Brâhmaṇas' प्रवर्त्यतां भगवतो ब्राह्मणानुद्दिश्य पाकः (Mu. 1). 5 प्र-उत्-सं-भू 1 P, प्रवृत्, उत्पद् 4 A, प्र-,जन् 4 A, उद्-इ 2 P, निःसृ, निर्गम्; oft. ex. by कारणं, मूलं, निमित्तं, हेतुः; 'from what cause does thy disorder p.' किंनिमित्तं ते संतापः (S. 3). 6 (Against) अभियुज् 7 A, 10, राजकुले निविद् c. —ING, *a.* उत्पन्न, जात, प्रभव, उद्भव, उत्थित, मूल, कारण, निमित्त, हेतु in comp.; *See* (*v.*).—*s.*,—PROCEDURE, *s.* कार्यं, व्यवहारः, व्यापारः, चरितं, चेष्टितं, आचारः, वृत्तं, कृति *f.*, विधानं, अनुष्ठानं. 2 रीति *f.*, क्रमः, संप्रदायः, मार्गः, पर्यायः; 'legal p.' व्यवहारविधिः, व्यवहारक्रमः. —PROCEEDS, *s.* उत्पन्नं, उदयः, लाभः, फलं. —PROCESS, *s.* प्रसरः, प्रगमः, प्रवृत्तिः, प्रयाणं. 2 क्रमः, रीतिः, मार्गः, पर्यायः, विधिः, गतिः, परिपाटि-टी *f.*, सरणि-णी *f.*, पद्धति *f.* 3 व्यवहारः, कार्यं; 'in p. of time' कालक्रमेण, दिनेषु गच्छत्सु, गच्छता कालेन. —PROCESSION, *s.* यात्रा, जन-लोक-यात्रा-श्रेणी. 2 प्रगमनं, प्रस्थानं, प्रचलनं, प्रवृत्तिः. —AL, *a.* यात्रारूपं.

PROCLAIM, *v. t.* घुष् 10, उत्-वि-°, प्र-ख्या c. (ख्यापयति), प्रकाश् c., प्रकटयति (D.), प्रकटीकृ, कृत् 10, उच्चर् c. 2 Outlaw, q. v. —ER, *s.* घोषकः, प्रख्यापकः. —PROCLAMATION, *s.* घोषः-षणं-णा, ख्यापनं, प्रकाशनं, उत्कीर्तनं; 'written p.' घोषणपत्रं, राजाज्ञापत्रं.

PROCLIVITY, *s.* प्रावण्यं, प्रवृत्ति *f.*, शीलता in comp. —PROCLIVIOUS, *a.* प्रवण, शील in comp.

PROCRASTINATE, *v.* विलंब् 1 A, व्याक्षिप् 6 P, कालं क्षिप् or हृ 1 P, चिर(रा)यति (D.), मंदायते (D.). —ION, *s.* विलंबः, दीर्घसूत्रता, व्याक्षेपः, कालयापनं-हरणं-क्षेपः. —OR, *s.* दीर्घ-सूत्रः-त्री, चिरक्रियः.

PROCREATE, *v. t.* प्र-सू 2, 4 A, उत्पद् c., जन् c. (जनयति). —ION, *s.* प्रसवः, प्रसूति *f.*, जननं, उत्पत्ति *f.*, प्रजोत्पादनं. —IVE, *a.* उत्पादक, सावक, जनयितृ. —OR, *s.* जनकः, उत्पादयिता.

PROCTOR, *s.* प्रतिहस्तः, प्रतिनिधिः.

PROCUMBENT, *a.* शयान, पतित.

PROCURE, *v. t.* आ-नी 1 P, संपद् c., घट् c. (घटयति). 2 लभ् 1 A, आप् 5 P, अधिगम् 1 P, विद् 6 U, आ-समा-सद् c.; *See* GET. —ER, *s.* प्रापकः, संपादकः. 3 विटः, नर्मसचिवः, संचारकः, कुंडाशिन् *m.* —ESS, *s.* कुट्ट(ट्टि)नी, शंभली, दूती-तिका, संचारिका, सु-,रततालौ.

PRODIGAL, *a.* मुक्तहस्त, अति-अमित-बहु-व्ययिन्, उत्सर्गिन्, अतिव्ययशील-पर, अतित्यागिन्.—*s.* मुक्तहस्तः, व्ययपरः. —ITY, *s.* अतिव्ययः, अपचयः, बहु-अमितव्ययः, अतित्यागः, अत्युत्सर्गः, अर्थोत्सर्गः, मुक्तहस्तत्वं. —LY, *adv.* महाव्ययेन, मुक्तहस्तेन, अत्युत्सर्गेण.

PRODIGY, *s.* अद्भुतं, अद्भुत-अपूर्व-विषयः-वस्तु, उत्पातः, महाश्चर्यं, अनन्यसाधारणं वस्तु. 2 (Of persons) अद्भुतशक्ति, अद्भुतबुद्धिसंपन्न. —IOUS, *a.* महाप्रमाण, अतिमहत्-बृहत्, विकट-राक्षस-शरीर, अद्भुताकार; *See* GIANT. 2 अद्भुत, अपूर्व, विलक्षण, विचित्र, आश्चर्य.

—IOUSLY, *adv.* अद्भुतं, साश्चर्यं. —IOUSNESS, *s.* अद्भुतता, अतिमहत्त्वं.

PRODUCE, *v. t.* निर्मा 3 A, 2 P, सृज् 6 P, उत्पद् c., जन् c. (जनयति), उत्-सं-भू c., साध् 5 P or c., कृ 8 U, वि-धा 3 U, क्लृप् c., घट् c. (घटयति), वि-, रच् 10. 2 प्र-,सू 2, 4 A, उत्पद् c., सं-प्र-जन् c. 3 प्र-,दृश् c., आ-उपा-नी 1 P, प्रसृ c., पुरस्कृ, पुरो नि-धा, अग्रे स्था c. (स्थापयति) or निविश् c., आविष्कृ, प्रकटीकृ, निष्कृष् 1 P. 4 प्र-,दा 3 U. 5 वृध् c. —*s.* फलं, उत्पन्नं, लाभः, उत्पत्ति *f.*, प्रसवः. —ED, *a.* उत्पन्न, उत्पादित, निर्मित, घटित, सृष्ट, जनित, जात, उद्भूत ; 'to be p.' जन् 4 A, उत्पद् 4 A, उत्था 1 P, सं-उद्-भू 1 P; *See* ARISE ; gen. ex. by ज, जात, जन्य, प्रभव, उद्भव, हेतु, प्रवृत्त, प्रयुक्त in comp.; 'p. from water' अंभोज, जलोद्भव, &c. ; 'p. from flowers' कुसुमभव &c. —ER,-ING, *s.*, *a.* उत्पादक, प्रसविन्, प्रद, द, दायिन्, आवह, कारिन्, कर (री *f.*), in comp. —PRODUCT, *s.* फलं, उत्पन्नं, लाभः. 2 परिणामः, फलं, उत्तरफलं. 3 गुणनफलं, वधः, घातः, फलं, गुणाकारः. —ION, *s.* उत्पादनं, निर्माणं, सृष्टि *f.*, घटनं, विधानं, निष्पादनं. 2 जननं, उत्पत्तिः, प्रसवः, उद्भवः, संभवः, जन्मन् *n.* 3 निर्मितद्रव्यं-वस्तु, शिल्पनिर्माणं. —IVE, *a.* शस्यप्रद-दायिन्, सफल, अवंध्य. 2 उत्पादक ; दायिन्, द, प्रद, कारिन्, आवह in comp. ; 'p. of gain' लाभप्रद, लाभावह. 3 लाभफल-प्रद-कर.

PROEM, *s. See* PREFACE.

PROFANE, *v. t.* अपवित्रीकृ 8 U, दुष् c. (दूषयति). 2 लंघ् 1 A, 10, अतिक्रम् 1 U, 4 P, अतिचर् 1 P. 3 Contemn, q. v. —*a.* अपवित्र ; अपुण्य, अमेध्य, अशुद्ध ; not 'Holy' q. v. 2 अधार्मिक (र्का *f.*), धर्म-ईश्वर-द्वेषिन्, धर्म-ईश्वर-निंदारूप. 3 असंस्कृत, अप्रतिष्ठित, संस्कारहीन. 4 लौकिक-सांसारिक-प्रापंचिक (की *f.*) —ATION, *s.* दूषणं, अपवित्रीकरणं, अतिक्रमः-मणं. —LY, *adv.* धर्मनिंदापूर्वं, अधार्मिकवत्. —NESS, *s.* धर्म-ईश्वर-निंदा-द्वेषः, धर्म-ईश्वर-अवज्ञा-अतिक्रमः.

PROFESS, *v. t.* प्रति-ज्ञा 9 A, प्रकाश् c., प्रतिज्ञापूर्वं कथ् 10 or वद् 1 P, स्वी-अंगी-कृ 8 U, उ(ऊ)रीकृ, अभ्युपगम् 1 P. 2 छद्म-छलं-कृ. दृश् c., भू c.; *See* PRETEND ; oft. by नाम ; तव कन्या नाम भवेयं (D. K. II. 5) 'I shall p. myself to be your daughter'. 3 उद्यम् 1 A, चेष्ट् 1 A. —ED, *a.* स्वीकृत, अंगीकृत, प्रकाशित, प्रकटित, व्यक्तोदित, प्रकाश. —EDLY, *adv.* प्रतिज्ञापूर्वं, प्रकाशमेव, सप्रतिज्ञं. —ION, *s.* प्रतिज्ञा, उक्ति *f.*, वचनं, अंगी-स्वी-कारः, प्रकाशवादः-वचनं, ख्यापनं. 2 Pretension, q. v. ; 'p. s of love' कृत्रिमप्रीतिः, अलीकः रागाविर्भावः. 3 वृत्ति *f.*, आ-उप-जीविका, आजीवः, व्यवसायः, व्यापारः; 'military p.' शस्त्राजीवः, क्षत्रवृत्तिः. —IONAL, *a.* वृत्तिमत्, व्यवसायिन्, (*s.*) in comp. —OR, *s.* अध्यापकः, गुरुः. 2 ख्यापकः, प्रकाशकः, प्रतिज्ञातृ *m.*, स्वीकर्ता. —ORSHIP, *s.* अध्यापकपदं-पदवी.

PROFFER, *v. See* OFFER.

PROFICIENT, *a.* प्रवीण, कुशल, निपुण, अभिज्ञ, विचक्षण, पारंगत, अभ्यंतर, निष्णात, व्युत्पन्न, लब्धप्रतिष्ठ, पटु. —PROFICIENCE,-CY, *s.* प्रावीण्यं, वैचक्षण्यं, प्रतिष्ठा, कौशलं, पाटवं ; 'has attained p. in all sciences' सर्वशास्त्रेषु परां प्रतिष्ठां गतः, परं कौशलमवाप, सकलशास्त्रपारंगतः.

PROFILE, *s.* पार्श्वदृश्यं, अर्धमुखदर्शनं.

PROFIT, *s.* लाभः, हितं, उपकारः, अर्थः, कल्याणं. 2 फलं, लाभः, आयः, उदयः, वृद्धि *f.*, कलांतरं, लभ्यं ; 'p. and loss' लाभालाभौ ; 'capital with p. thereon' मूलकलांतरं. —*v. t.* हितमावह् 1 P, उपकृ 8 U, हिताय भू 1 P. —*v. i.* (Oneself) फलंलाभं-प्राप् 5 P or विद् 6 U. 2 वृध् 1 A, उन्नतिंउत्कर्षं-या 2 P, प्र-उप-चि pass. ; *See* IMPROVE. —ABLE, *a.* लाभ-अर्थ-कर(री *f.*), लाभप्रद,लाभफल-द, फल-लाभ-आवह. 2 हित, हितकर, हितावह, उपयुक्त, उपकारिन्, सोपकार. —ABLENESS, *s.* साफल्यं, फलदता, उपयुक्तता. —ABLY, *adv.* सलाभं, सफलं, सहितं, अमुधा. —LESS, *a.* निष्फल, अफल, अहित, व्यर्थ, निरर्थक.

PROFLIGATE, *a.* खंडितवृत्त, दुश्चरित्र, दुराचार, पापनिरत-अभिनिविष्ट, व्यसनिन्, दुर्वृत्त, भ्रष्ट-नष्ट-चरित्र, भोगविषय-आसक्त. —*s.* व्यसनी, लंपटः, विषयी, भोगासक्तः. —LY, *adv.* सव्यसनं, दुर्वृत्ततया. —PROFLIGACY, *s.* व्यसनिता, भ्रष्टचरितं, दुराचारः, भ्रष्टता, भोगासक्ति *f.*, दुर्वृत्तता.

PROFOUND, *a.* प्र-,गाढ, अतिग(गं)भीर, घन, अगाध. 2 परम, गाढ, घन, अत्यंत, सु-अति-pr. ; 'p. respect' परमादरः, आदरातिशयः. 3 गहन, नि-, गूढ, गूढार्थ, दुर्बोध, दुर्ज्ञेय, परमगहन. 4 (Of persons) निष्णात, पारंगत, परम, व्युत्पन्न, अभिनिविष्ट, गूढतत्वज्ञ. —LY, *adv.* गंभीरं, गाढं, अत्यंतं, भृशं, सु-अति pr. —NESS,-PROFUNDITY, *s.* गांभीर्यं, अगाधता. 2 घनता, गाढता. 3 गहनता, गूढता. 4 अभिनिवेशः.

PROFUSE, *a.* प्रचुर, प्रभूत, अपरिमित, विपुल, बहु, अत्यधिक, अतिरिक्त, समृद्ध, उद्रिक्त, अतिशय-सु-अति in comp. 2 मुक्तहस्त, अतिव्ययिन्, व्ययपर ; *See* PRODIGAL; 'he is a p. writer' वाग्प्रपंचप्रियः, प्रचुरवाक्यानि लेखे प्रयोजयति. —LY, *adv.* प्रचुरं, भृशं, भूरि, बाहुल्येन, अत्यंतं, सु-अति pr. ; अतिव्ययेन, अपरिमितं. —NESS,-PROFUSION, *s.* अतिव्ययः, अमितव्ययः, अत्युत्सर्गः. 2 समृद्धि *f.*, प्राचुर्यं, उद्रेकः, अतिरेकः, उपचयः, बाहुल्यं.

PROG, *s.* भोजनं, अन्नं, भैक्ष्यं.

PROGENITOR, *s.* पिता, प्रजापतिः, पूर्वजः, पूर्व-कुल-पुरुषः, जन्मदः, जनयिता; *See* ANCESTOR.

PROGENY, *s.* संतानः, अपत्यं, संतति *f.*, प्रजा.

PROGNOSTIC, *s.* निमित्तं, अजन्यं, शकुनः-नं, लक्षणं; *See* OMEN. -*a.* प्र-उद्-बोधक, अग्रसूचक. -ATE, *v. t.* पूर्व-अग्रे-सूच् 10 or दृश् c.; *See* FOREBODE. -ATION, *s.* पूर्वसूचनं-ना. -ATOR, *s.* पूर्वलक्षणज्ञः, अग्रसूचकः.

PROGRAMME, *s.* सूचिपत्रं; कार्यक्रमः-परिपाटी.

PROGRESS, *s.* प्र-,वृद्धि *f.*, उत्कर्षः, क्रमशः वृद्धिः, उत्कर्षक्रमः. 2 प्राप्ति *f.*, आगमः; 'p. in learning' विद्यागमः, विद्याभिनिवेशः. 3 प्र-गमनं, प्रयाणं, यानं, यात्रा, प्रस्थानं, प्रसरः, क्रमः-मणं, अयनं; *See* MARCH; 'difficult p.' संक्रमः, दुर्गसंचरः. -*v. i.* उत्कृष् pass., वृद्धि-उन्नति-या 2 P, प्र-,वृध् 1 A, प्र-उप-चि-pass.; *See* IMPROVE. 2 प्रगम्-चल्-सृ 1 P, प्रया 2 P, प्र-स्था 1 A; *See* ADVANCE. -ION, *s.* श्रेढी, श्रेढीव्यवहारः; 'first term' मुखं, वदनं, आदिः; 'common difference' चयः; 'geometric mean' चयो गुणः; 'sum' श्रेढीफलं; 'number of terms' गच्छः. -IVE, *a.* आनुक्रमिक (की *f.*), क्रमिक, अधिकाधिक, उत्तरोत्तर, क्रमशः वर्धमान. -IVELY, *adv.* क्रमशः, अनुक्रमेण, उत्तरोत्तरं, अधिकाधिकं.

PROHIBIT, *v. t.* नि-प्रति-षिध् 1 P, प्रत्यादिश् 6 P, निवृ c., प्रत्या-ख्या 2 P, नि-अव-रुध् 7 U. -ION, *s.* नि-प्रति-षेधः, प्रत्यादेशः, निरोधः, निवारणं, बाधा. -OR, *s.* निवारकः, निषेधकः. -IVE, -ORY, *a.* निषेधक, निवारक, नि-प्रति-षेधिन्, निषेधार्थक, निषेधवाचिन्.

PROJECT, *s.* उपायः, प्र-,युक्ति *f.*, कल्पना, प्रयोगः, संकल्पः, प्रबंधः. 2 अभिप्रायः, आशयः, उद्देशः. -*v. i.* प्रलंब् 1 A, बहिर्लंब्, उपरि लंब्. बहिः स्था 1 P or भू 1 P or वृत् 1 A. -*v. t.* प्र-,क्षिप् 6 P, प्रास् 4 U, निपत् c., प्रमुच् 6 P; *See* THROW. 2 (मनसा) क्लृप् c., निरूप् 10, चिंत् 10, युज् 10, आलोच् 10, अनुसं-धा 3 U. -ILE, *a.* प्रक्षेपणीय, दूरवेधिन्. -*s.* अस्त्रं; *See* MISSILE. -ING, *a.* प्र-,लंब, उन्नत, उदग्र, उत्तुंग, बहिर्वर्तिन्; oft. by उत्सेध, उत्सेधिन्; 'with a p. nose' प्रलंबनास, घोणोन्नत, उन्नस; 'having p. teeth' उदग्रदत्, करालदंत; 'having p. breasts' स्तनाभोगवती, उन्नतस्तनी; 'shattered by falling over (her) p. breasts' पयोधरोत्सेधनिपातचूर्णिताः (K. v. 24). -ION, *s.* प्रलंबता, उदग्रता. 2 आभोगः, उत्सेधः; निर्यूहः, दंतकः. 3 छेयकं. -OR, *s.* चिंतकः, योजकः.

PROLAPSE, PROLAPSUS, *s.* भ्रंशः. -*v. i.* भ्रंश् 1 A, 4 P.

PROLATED, *a.* प्लुत (vowel), दीर्घोच्चारित.

PROLEGOMENON, *s.* प्रस्तावना, उपोद्घातः.

PROLEPSIS, *s.* पूर्वग्रहणं, पूर्वादानं.

PROLIFIC, *a.* अवंध्य, बहुप्रज-प्रसव-अपत्य, प्रसवशील, सुतिन्, बहुसंतान. 2 बहुफलप्रद, बहुफल; *See* PRODUCTIVE. -ALLY, *adv.* प्राचुर्येण, विपुलं.

PROLIX, *a.* सु-अति-विस्तर, प्रपंचित, सुदीर्घ, दीर्घसूत्रिन्, अत्यायत. -ITY, *s.* अतिविस्तरः, प्रपंचः, वाग्विस्तरः-प्रपंचः, वागुपचयः; दीर्घसूत्रता, अतिविस्तारः. -LY, *adv.* विस्तरशः; अतिविस्तरेण, सप्रपंचं.

PROLOGUE, *s.* प्रस्तावना, आमुखं, प्रास्ताविकी विज्ञप्तिः; 'benedictory p.' नांदी.

PROLONG, *v. t.* दीर्घीकृ 8 U, प्र-वि-तन् 8 U, वि-प्र-सृ c., विस्तृ c., आयम् 1 A or c. 2 व्याक्षिप् 6 P or विलंब् c.; 'a p. ed note' तानः. -ATION, *s.* विस्तारः, वितति *f.*, आयतिः, दीर्घीकरणं.

PROLUSION, *s.* *See* PRELUDE.

PROMENADE, *v. t.* विहृ 1 P, विचर् 1 P, विहारार्थं परिभ्रम् 1, 4 P. -*s.* विहारः, परिभ्रमणं. 2 विहारस्थानं.

PROMINENT, *a.* प्रधान, प्रमुख, श्रेष्ठ, मुख्य, विशिष्ट, परम; *See* PRINCIPAL. 2 सुस्पष्ट, सुप्रकाश, सुव्यक्त, सुदृश्य. 2 उन्नत, उदग्र, उत्तुंग, प्रलंब, साभोग, उत् pr.; *See* PROJECTING. -LY, *adv.* प्राधान्येन, विशेषतः, सुप्रकाशं, सुस्पष्टं, उन्नतं. -PROMINENCE, *s.* प्राधान्यं, विशिष्टता, श्रेष्ठता, उत्कर्षः, परमपदं. 2 उन्नति *f.*, उत्सेधः, उत्तुंगता, आभोगः.

PROMISCUOUS, *a.* प्र-सं-कीर्ण, संकुल, अविविक्त, निर्विशेष, अपरिच्छेद, अभेद, संमिश्रित; 'p. union' संकरः, सांकर्य. -LY, *adv.* निर्विशेषं-षेण, संकीर्णं, अभेदेन, अक्रमेण, अपरिच्छेदेन. -NESS, *s.* संकीर्णता, संकुलता, अभेदः, संकरः.

PROMISE, *v. t.* सं-प्रति-आ-श्रु 5 P, प्रति-ज्ञा 9 A, (with dat. of persons); स्वी-अंगी-कृ 8 U, अभ्युपगम् 1 P, अभ्युप-इ 2 P, संविद् 2 A, संगॄ 6 A, उ(ऊ)रीकृ, उररीकृ, परि-,पण् 1 A; 'the plan p. s to succeed' उपायः सफलो भवेदित्यनुमीयते or अहं आशंसे; 'a p. ing boy' वर्धिष्णुर्बटुः, आशानिबंधनं. -*s.* प्रतिज्ञा, समयः, सं-प्रति-श्रवः, वचनं, संविद् *f.*, नियमः, संगरः, संकेतः, अभिसंधा, अभ्युपगमः, स्वीकारः, उरीकारः, अंगीकारः, परिपणनं. 2 आशा, आशंसा; 'hollow p.' मुधावचनं, शब्दपांडित्यं; 'breaking a p.' प्रतिज्ञा-वचन-भंगः, संविद्-व्यतिक्रमः, विसंवादः; 'keep or fulfil a p.' प्रतिज्ञां पा c. (पालयति) or शुध् c.; *See* KEEP, FULFIL; 'p-breaker' प्रतिज्ञालंघिन्-व्यतिक्रमिन्, विसंवादिन्; 'give a p. orally' वाचा प्रतिज्ञा, वाग्दानं कृ. -ORY, *a.* प्रतिज्ञाविशिष्ट.

PROMONTORY, *a.* उदग्रभूमि *f.*, भूशिरस्-नासिका.

PROMOTE, *v. t.* वि-,वृध् c., उपकृ 8 U, पुरस्कृ, प्रवृत् c., साध् c., उपचि 5 U, प्रयुज् 10; (a person)

सं-,उन्नम् c. (नमयति). उन्नतिं नी 1 P or प्राप् c., पदं वृध् c., पदोत्कर्ष-प्रतिपत्ति-प्राप् c., अधिकपदे नि-युज्. 3 Prompt, q. v. —ER, s. प्रवर्तकः, उपकर्ता; *See* PATRON. —ION, s. उपकारः, पुरस्कारः, प्रवर्तनं, साहाय्यं, वर्धनं, वृद्धि *f*., उपचयः, उन्नतिः, उत्कर्षः, पदवृद्धिः, पदोन्नतिः, प्रतिपत्ति *f*., श्रेष्ठपदावाप्ति *f*. —IVE, *a*. प्रवर्तक, साधक, उपकारिन्.

PROMPT, *a*. सत्वर, अविलंब ; क्षिप्र, अविलंबित, अदीर्घसूत्र ; (of persons) उद्यत, उद्युक्त, अविलंबिन्, आशुकारिन्, प्रत्युत्पन्नमति, सप्रतिभ, पटु, उद्यमिन्, उद्योगिन्. —*v. t*. प्र-उत्सह् c., प्रणुद् 6 P or c., प्रचुद् 10, प्रवृत् c., प्र-उद्-युज् 10, उत्तिज् c., प्र-इष् c., आक्रु c., उद्दीप् c., उत्था c. (उत्थापयति), प्र-उद्-बुध् c.; 'p. ed by hunger' क्षुद्बोधित. 2 प्र-अनु-बुध् c., सूच् 10. —ER, s. प्रोत्साहकः, प्रवर्तयितृ *m*., प्रयोजकः, &c. 2 अनु-प्र-बोधकः, सूचकः; 'who seldom wanted a p.' यः सदा प्रत्युत्पन्नमतिः, प्रबोधननिरपेक्षः. —ING, s. प्रेरणं, प्रोत्साहनं, उत्तेजनं, &c. 2 सूचना, प्रबोधनं. —NESS, —ITUDE, s. औत्सुक्यं, अविलंबः, उत्साहः, क्षिप्रता. 2 प्रतिभा, प्रत्युत्पन्नमति *f*., पटुता. 3 उद्यमः, उद्योगः. —LY, *adv*. सत्वरं, अविलंबेन, क्षिप्रं, सद्यः, आशु, अचिरात्, सप्रतिभं.

PROMULGATE, *v. t*. प्रकाश् c., वि-,घुष् 10, कृत् 10, प्र-ख्या c. (ख्यापयति); *See* PROCLAIM. —ION, s. प्रकाशनं, घोषणं, कीर्तनं. —OR, s. प्रकाशकः, घोषकः.

PRONE, *a*. प्रवण, शील, आलु in comp., उद्यत, उन्मुख ; *See* INCLINED, APT; 'p. to fall' पतयालु, पातुक, पतनशील. 2 (Bent) नत, नम्र, अधोवदन, अधोमुख-अवाङ्मुख- (खी *f*.). —NESS, s. प्रावण्यं, प्रवृत्ति *f*.; उन्मुखता, शीलता, आलुता in comp. 2 अधोमुखता, नम्रता.

PRONG, s. शूलः-लं, कंटकः, अग्रं, शिखा.

PRONOUN, s. सर्वनामन् *n*.

PRONOUNCE, *v. t*. उच्चर् c., उदीर् c., उदा-व्या-हृ 1 P, गद् 1 P, वद् 1 P, प्र-,वच् 2 P, प्र-ख्या 2 P, कृत् 10; 'p. judgment' निर्णयं कथ् 10; उत्तरं दा 3 U, &c. 2 निश्चयेन वद्, दृढं प्रति-ज्ञा 9 A; 'imperfectly p. ed' ग्रस्त, असंपूर्णोच्चारित, लुप्तवर्ण-पद. —PRONUNCIATION, s. उच्चारणं, उदाहरणं, उदीरणं; 'science of p.' शिक्षा; 'easy of p.' सुखोच्चार्य.

PROOF, s. *See* under PROVE.

PROP, s. आश्रयः, शरणं, आधारः, अवष्टंभः. आ-अवलंबः-बनं, उपघ्नः. —*v. t*. धृ 1 P. 10. आ-अव-लंब् 1 A, अवष्टंभ् 9 P; 'a tree that p. s another creeper' उपघ्नतरुः.

PROPAGATE, *v. t*. विस्तृ c., प्रवृध् c., वि-प्र-तन् 8 U, वि-प्र-सृ c.; (opinions) प्रचर्-सृ c., प्रवृत् c., संचर् c., प्रचलीकृ, प्रसृ c. 2 परंपरया उत्पद् c. or प्र-सू 2 A, प्रसवपरंपरया जातिं वृध् c., शावकान् प्रभू or जन् c. or उत्पद् c. —ION, s. प्र-,वर्धनं, प्रसारः, विस्तारः, विततिः *f*., प्र-,वृद्धि *f*., प्रचारः-रणं. 2 परंपरोत्पत्ति *f*., प्रसूतिपारंपर्य-क्रमः; प्रजा-संतान-वृद्धि *f*. —OR, s. प्रचारकः, प्रवर्तकः.

PROPEL, *v. t*. प्रेर् c., प्र-,नुद् 6 P or c., सं-चल् c., प्रचुद् 10, सं-,चर् c., कृष् 1 P; *See* PROMPT.

PROPENSE, *a*. प्रवण, उन्मुख, आसन्न, उद्यत. —ITY, s. प्रवणता, प्रवृत्ति *f*., उन्मुखता, प्रावण्यं, प्रवाहः, शीलता-आलुता in comp.; 'p. to fall' पतयालुता; 'good p.' सुशीलं, साधुवृत्तिः; 'evil p.' व्यसनं, दुर्गुणः, दुःशीलं.

PROPER, *a*. स्वीय, निज, आत्मीय, स्व-आत्म in comp. 2 युक्त, योग्य, उचित, उपपन्न, अनुरूप, न्याय्य, संगत, सदृश (शी *f*.), यथार्ह, यथोचित, समंजस, पर्याप्त, सांप्रतिक (की *f*.); oft. ex. by pot. pass. part.; 'to be p.' युज् pass., उपपद् 4 A; 'it is p.' स्थाने; स्थाने व्रीडिता अप्सरसः (V. 1), स्थाने भवान् अकिंचनत्वं व्यनक्ति (R. v. 16). —LY, *adv*. युक्तं, उचितं, यथार्हं सम्यक्, स्थाने, न्यायतः, सांप्रतं, यथायोग्यं, धर्मेण. 2 यथार्थतः, परमार्थतः; तत्त्वतः, वस्तुतः ; 'p. speaking' वस्तुतः, यथार्थदृष्ट्या. —TY, s. धर्मः, गुणः, लक्षणं, स्वभावः, विशेषः, रूपं, स्वरूपं-धर्मः, सहज-प्रकृति-गुणः. 2 स्वत्वं, स्वाम्यं, अधिकारः, प्रभुत्वं. 3 संपत्ति *f*., द्रव्यं, अर्थः, धनं, वित्तं, वसु *n*., विभवः; द्रव्य-अर्थ-जातं, रिक्थं; 'woman's p.' स्त्रीधनं ; 'landed p.' भूमिधनं, भूमिः, स्थावरं धनं ; 'public p.' गण-सामान्य-द्रव्यं ; 'p. in cattle' गोधनं. —PROPRIETY, s. युक्तता, औचित्यं, उपपत्ति *f*., न्यायः, सामंजस्यं, योग्यता, यथार्थता, पात्रता, संगति *f*.; 'p. of conduct' विनयः, मर्यादा, अनतिक्रमः, सुचरितं.

PROPHESY, *v. t*. भावि कथ् 10 or सूच् 10 or प्रदृश् c., अनागतं नि-आ-विद् c. ; *See* PREDICT. —PROPHECY, s. भाविकथनं-सूचनं, भविष्यद्वादः, आदेशः, भविष्यार्थः, सिद्धादेशः. —PROPHET, s. सिद्धः, भविष्यद्वादिन् *m*., अग्रनिरूपकः, भाविकथकः, अनागतविद्-दर्शिन्; 'saying of a p.' सिद्धादेशः. —ESS, s. अनागतदर्शिनी, भविष्यद्वादिनी. —IC,-ICAL, *a*. (s.) in comp.

PROPHYLACTIC, *a*. रोगहारिन्-हृत्.

PROPINQUITY s. सन्निधिः, संनिकर्षः, सामीप्यं ; *See* NEARNESS.

PROPITIATE, *v. t*. प्रसद् c., आराध् c., अनुरंज् c., सांत्व् 10, अनुनी 1 P, प्र-,शम् c. (शमयति), सं-परि-तुष् c. —ION, s. प्रसादनं, आराधनं, अनुरंजनं, सांत्वनं, अनुनयः; प्र-उप-शमः-मनं. —OR, s. प्रसादकः, आराधयिता, अनुरंजकः &c.—ORY, *a*. शमक, सांत्वक, शांतिकर (री *f*.), शांतिप्रद ; 'p. rite' शांतिक्रिया. —PROPITIOUS, *a*. सु-प्रसन्न, सदय, अनुकूल, हितकाम-

बुद्धि, अभिमुख (खी *f.*). प्रवर्णाकृत, अनुग्राहिन्, वरद. 2 शुभ, मंगल, कल्याण (णी *f.*), शर्मद, शुभंकर. -LY, *adv.* प्रसन्नं, अनुकूलं, सदयं, सानुग्रहं. -NESS, *s.* प्रसादः, आनुकूल्यं, आभिमुख्यं; शुभता.

PROPORTION, *s.* प्रमाणं, परिमाणं; आनुगुण्यं, आनुरूप्यं, परस्पर-अन्योन्य-संबंधः-अन्वयः-अनुषंगः-सादृश्यं-समता; अन्वयः, संबंधः; संधानं, संयोगः, संमिति *f.* (of limbs &c.). 2 अंशः, विभागः; *See* PART. 3 अनुपातः, संबंधसाम्यं; 'in p. to' ex. by अनुगुण, अनुरूप, सदृश, प्रमाणतः, अनुसारेण, यथा in comp.; 'in p. to one's strength' यथाशक्ति, शक्त्यनुसारेण, शक्तितः; 'spend in p. to your gains' आयप्रमाणेन व्ययं कुरु; 'p. of limbs' अंगसंयोगः, अवयवसंगतिः. -*v. t.*, -ATE, *v. t.* अनुरूपी-सदृशी-कृ 8 U, समीकृ, संमा 3 A, 2 P. -AL, *a.* समप्रमाण, परस्परानुगुण. -ATE,-ABLE,-ED, *a.* अनुरूप, अनुगुण, सदृश, संमित, सम, तुल्य, अनुसारिन्; 'with jars p. to their size (strength)' स्वप्रमाणानुरूपैर्घटैः (S. 1); 'her body beautiful, being p.' चतुरश्रशोभि तस्या वपुः (K. I. 32). -ATELY, -ABLY, *adv.* अनुरूपं-पेण, अनुगुणं, अनुसारेण, सदृशं, यथाप्रमाणं, यथाभागशः.

PROPOSE, *v. t.* प्र-स्तु 2 U, उपन्यस् 4 U, उपक्षिप् 6 P, प्रति-ज्ञा 9 A, सूच् 10, कर्तव्यं निर्दिश् 6 P or अभि-धा 3 U. 2 उद्दिश्, आकांक्ष् 6 P; *See* INTEND. -AL, *s.* प्रस्तावः, उपन्यासः, उपक्षेपः, अभिधानं, प्रतिज्ञा, वचनं, कर्तव्यनिर्देशः. -ITION, *s.* Proposal, q. v. 2 प्रतिज्ञा, सिद्धांतः, प्रमेयं.

PROPOUND, *v. t.* प्रति-पद् c., उपन्यस् 4 U, उपक्षिप् 6 P, निर्दिश् 6 P, प्रति-ज्ञा 9 A.

PROPRIETOR, *s.* स्वामी, प्रभुः, ईशः, पतिः, अधिकारी; *See* OWNER. -SHIP, *s.* स्वाम्यं, प्रभुत्वं, स्वामित्वं, अधिकारः. -PROPRIETARY, *a.* स्वाम्यधीन, प्रभुनिष्ठ, स्वामिगत; 'p. right' स्वाम्यं, अधिकारः, स्वत्वं.

PROROGUE, *v. t.* व्याक्षिप् 6 P, (नियतकालं यावत्) विसृज् 6 P or त्यज् 1 P. -PROROGATION, *s.* कार्यत्यागः-निवृत्ति *f.*, व्याक्षेपः.

PROSCRIBE, *v. t.* घोषणापूर्वं दंडं आदिश् 6 P or बहिष्कृ 8 U or निर्वस् c.; 'here is Jivasiddhi being disgraced and p. ed from the city' एष जीवसिद्धिः सनिकारं नगरान्निर्वास्यते (Mu. 1). 2 निषिध् 1 P, निवृ c. -PROSCRIPTION, *s.* सघोषण दंडाज्ञा.

PROSE, *s.* गद्यं. -*a.* गद्यात्मक, गद्यरूप, गद्य in comp. -PROSAIC, *a.* गद्यरूप, गद्यात्मक, गद्य in comp. 2 नीरस, विरस, रस-सत्त्व-हीन.

PROSECUTE, *v. t.* (नित्यं-अनवरतं) प्रवृत् c., अनुसृ 1 P, अनु-ष्ठा 1 P, अनु-सेव् 1 A, निर्वह् c., अनुशील् 10; 'p. studies' अध्ययनक्रममनुसृ; 'p. one's efforts' अनवरतं उद्यम् 1 A, or प्रयत् 1 A; 'p. one's undertaking' प्रारब्धं उद्वह् 1 P, प्रतिपन्नं निर्वह् c. 2 अभियुज् 7 A, 10, अभिशंस् 1 P; सूच् 10, निविद् c. -ION, *s.* अनुशीलनं, प्रवर्तनं, नित्यानुष्ठानं, नित्यप्रवृत्ति *f.*, निर्वाहणं, अविरतानुसरणं. 2 अभियोगः, निवेदनं; 'p. of effort' नित्योद्योगः; 'p. of study' नित्याध्ययनं, अध्ययनक्रमः. -OR, *s.* निर्वाहकः. 2 अभियोक्तृ *m.*, वादी, अर्थी, अभिशंसकः.

PROSELYTE, *s.* परधर्माश्रयिन्, स्वधर्मत्यागिन्, पक्षांतर-मतांतर-ग्राहिन्; *See* CONVERT. -IZE, *v. i.* स्वधर्मं ग्रह् c. -ISM, *s.* मतांतरग्रहणं, धर्मांतरस्वीकारः.

PROSODY, *s.* छंदस् *n.*, छंदःशास्त्रं. -AL,-ICAL, *a.* छांदस (सी *f.*), छंदः in comp. -IAN, *s.* छंदःशास्त्रज्ञः.

PROSPECT, *s.* आलोकः, दर्शनं, चक्षुर्विषयः, दृग्गोचरप्रदेशः-विषयः. 2 आयति *f.*, उत्तरापेक्षा; 'he has good p. s before him' शुभा तस्यायतिः. 3 आशा, प्रत्याशा, आशंसा, अपेक्षा. -IVE, *a.* उत्तर, उत्तरकालीन, भाविकालप्राप्य, उत्तरकालसापेक्ष; *See* FUTURE. -IVELY, *adv.* उत्तरकालापेक्षया.

PROSPER, *v. i.* सं-,ऋध् 4, 5 P, प्र-वि-वृध् 1 A, स्फाय् 1 A, एध् 1 A, प्र-उप-चि pass., समृद्धि-वृद्धिं या 2 P or उप-इ 2 P; 'I hope your (commercial) business is p. ing' अपि प्रचीयंते संव्यवहाराणां लाभा वः (Mu. 1). 2 सिध् 4 P, सं-पद् 4 A, सफलीभू 1 P, कृतार्थीभू. -*v. t.* वृध् c., प्र-उप-चि 5 U, एध् c., उपकृ 8 U, अनुग्रह् 9 P, सफलीकृ, साध् c., सिद्धिं नी 1 P. -ITY, *s.* सं-,ऋद्धि *f.*, संपद् *f.*, संपत्ति *f.*, अभ्युदयः, श्रीः, लक्ष्मीः, वि-,भूति *f.*, सौभाग्यं, वैभवं, पुण्योदयः, ऐश्वर्यं; 'time of p.' संपत्-समृद्धि-उदय-कालः-समयः. 2 समृद्धिः, उत्कर्षः, उन्नति *f.*, उदयः, प्र-उप-चयः, वि-सं-वृद्धि *f.*, साफल्यं, कृतार्थता, सिद्धि *f.* 3 क्षेमः-मं, कौशल्यं, कल्याणं, शुभं, शिवं, हितं, भद्रं. -OUS, *a.* समृद्ध, श्रीमत्, समृद्धिमत्, लक्ष्मीवत्, सश्रीक, ऐश्वर्यशालिन्; (state &c.) वर्धिष्णु, प्र-उप-चीयमान, एधमान, वर्धमान; 'in p. days' संपत्सु, अभ्युदयकाले, भूतिसमये, समृद्धिकाले. 2 सफल, सिद्ध, कृतार्थ, सिद्धार्थ; (happy) सुस्थ, निरापद्, क्षेम, कुशल, कल्याण (णी *f.*), शिव, भद्र, मंगल, शुभ, सौभाग्यवत्, धन्य. -OUSLY, *adv.* समृद्ध्या, अभ्युदयेन, सुसंपदा, सौभाग्येन, शुभं, भद्रं.

PROSTITUTE, *s.* वेश्या, वेशवधूः, गणिका, वार-पण्य-स्त्री-अंगना-योषित्, भोग्या, सामान्यस्त्री, रूपाजीवा; (false to her husband) पुंश्चली, बंधकी, असती, कुलटा, स्वैरिणी, पांसु(शु)ला, धर्षिणी, इत्वरी. -*v. t.* नियकर्मार्थं प्र-उप-विनि-युज् 7 A, 10 or व्याप्टृ c. -ION, *s.* वेश्याजीवः, वेश्या-गणिका-वृत्ति *f.*, वारसेवा, बंधकीत्वं, पौंश्चल्यं, &c.

PROSTRATE, *a.* प्रणत, भूमिगत, साष्टांगप्रणत-पतित; 'lie or fall p.' *See* (*v.*); 'p. on the bed' शयनगत, शयने अवमूर्धशय: 'lying p. at the feet' चरण-पाद-पतित-प्रणत. 2 अवसन्न, क्षीण. –*v. t.* (Oneself) दंडप्रणामेन-साष्टांगपातं-नम् 1 P or प्रणिपत् 1 P, दंडवत् पत्; नीचैः प्रणम् or प्रणिपत्. 2 नि-अव-पत् c.; भूमिं गम् c. (गमयति). 3 (Strength) अवसद् c.; ध्वंस् c., प्र-वि-नश् c., हृ 1 P; क्षि 1, 5 P. –ED, *a.* प्रणिपतित, भूमिगत, निपतित, &c. 2 क्षीणबल-शक्ति, हत-नष्ट-शक्ति-ओजस्. –ION, *s.* दंडप्रणामः अष्टांगप्रणामः-प्रणिपातः, साष्टांगप्रणामः-वंदनं; प्रणिपातः, प्रणामः. 2 (Of spirits) अवसादः, ग्लानि *f.*, विषण्णता, उद्वेगः; 'p. of strength' शक्तिपातः-क्षयः, सत्त्वहानि *f.*

PROTECT, *v. t.* रक्ष् 1 P, अव् 1 P परि-,त्रै 1 A, गुप् 1 P, पा 2 P, पा c. (पालयति), परि-प्रति°-; तृ c. 2 संवृध् c., परि-,पुष् c. –ION, *s.* गोपनं, गुप्ति *f.*, पालनं, त्राणं, रक्षा, रक्षणं, अभ्युपपत्ति *f.*, संवर्धनं, परिपोषणं. 2 शरणं, आ-संश्रयः, आ-अव-लंबः, आधारः; 'go for p.' आश्रि 1 U, आलंब् 1 A, शरणं गम् 1 P or प्रपद् 4 A; 'paper granting p.' अभयपत्रं. –OR, *s.* रक्षकः, गोप्तृ *m.*, पालयिता, रक्षिता, रक्षिन्, पालकः, त्राता, शरणं, शरण्यः, आश्रयः, पः-पालः in comp. –PROTEGE, *s.* आश्रितः, पालितः, उपजीविन् *m.*, पोष्यः, शरणं गतः.

PROTEND, *v. t.* विस्तृ c., प्रसृ c.; *See* EXTEND.

PROTEST, *v. i.* दृढं-दृढोक्तिपूर्वं-वद् 1 P or आ-ख्या 2 P; 'p. against' दृढं विरुद्धं वद्, दृढोक्तिपूर्वं नि-प्रति-षिध् 1 P, दृढं असंमतिं प्रकाश् c. or ज्ञा c.; 'I strongly p. against this order' अयमादेशोऽन्याय्य इति सनिश्चयं वदामि; 'p. in writing' असंमतिलेखं-विप्रतिपत्तिपत्रं-प्रकाश् c. –*s.* दृढनिषेधवाक्यं, अस्वीकार-असंमति-वादः, विरुद्धवादः, अस्वीकारप्रकाशनं; 'written p.' असंमतिपत्रं. –ANT, *s.* रोमीयमतविरुद्धः. –ATION, *s.* दृढवचनं-उक्तिः-वादः, विरुद्धवचनं, निषेधोक्तिः.

PROTEUS, *s.* कामरूपः.

PROTOTYPE, *s.* आदर्शः, मूलं, मूलप्रतिमा.

PROTRACT, *v. t.* विलंब् c., व्याक्षिप् 6 P; *See* DELAY. 2 प्र-,तन् 8 U; प्रसृ c., दीर्घीकृ 8 U. –ED, *a.* सुदीर्घ, विलंबित, चिरस्थित, चिर in comp.; 'p. note' तानः; 'p. sound' प्लुतः. –ION, *s.* विलंबः, व्याक्षेपः.

PROTRUDE, *v. i.* प्र-निः-सृ 1 P, निर्गम् 1 P, उद्भिद् pass., प्रलंब् 1 A, बहिर्वृत् 1 A or स्था 1 P. –*v. t.* Causal of roots above. –ING, *a.* बहिर्लंब, बहिःस्थ. –PROTRUSION, *s.* निःसरणं, उद्भेदः, प्रलंबनं. –PROTUBERANCE, *s.* वि-,स्फोटः, गंडः, शोथः, शोफः, श्वयथुः, (on the skin). 2 प्रलंबनं, उत्सेधः, उत्तुंगता, आभोगः, उन्नति *f.* –PROTUBERANT, *a.* उन्नत, उत्तुंग, उच्छ्रित, उच्छून, प्रलंब; 'having p. breasts' तुंग-उन्नत-स्तनी, घट-कुंभ-स्तनी; oft. ex. by उत्सेधः; पयोधरोत्सेधविशीर्णसंहति (K. v. 8) 'the continuity being broken by her p. breasts.' –PROTUBERATE, *v. i.* प्रलंब् 1 A; *See* PROJECT.-ING &c.

PROUD, *a.* *See* under PRIDE.

PROVE, *v. t.* उप-प्रति-पद् c., साध् c., वि-भू c., प्र-मा 3 A, 2 P, प्रमाणीकृ 8 U, सत्याकृ, स्था c. (स्थापयति). 2 प्र-,दृश् c., सूच् 10, निर्दिश् 6 P, प्रकाश् c., व्यंज् 7 P or c.; 'he was p. ed guilty' अपराधी स्थापितः; 'good men p. their usefulness by deeds, not by words' ब्रुवते हि फलेन साधवो न तु कंठेन निजोपयोगितां (N. II. 48), कर्मणा न तु वाङ्मात्रेण दर्शयंति. 3 परीक्ष् 1 A, निरूप् 10, निर्णी 1 P, निश्चि 5 U, प्रति-इ c.; *See* TEST. –*v. i.* सं-उत्-पद् 4 A, वृत् 1 A, सं-,भू 1 P; निर्णी-निश्चि-प्रती-pass.; 'the tilled ground p. ed a treasure indeed' कृष्टा भूमिरेव कोषस्थाने बभूव, कोषत्वमापद्यत. –ER, *s.* साधकः, विभावकः. –PROOF, *s* साधनं, प्रमाणं, उपपत्ति *f.*, उप-प्रतिपादनं; 'written p.' लेखप्रमाणं, साधनपत्रं; 'burden of p.' साधनधर्मः, क्रियानिर्णयः; 'the burden of p. lies on both parties' द्वयोरपि वादिनोः क्रिया प्राप्नोति (V. M. 6). 2 लक्षणं, चिह्नं. 3 परीक्षणं, निर्णयः, निश्चयः; 'to put to the p.' परीक्ष्. 4 स्थूल-प्रथम-मुद्रणं. 5 अभेद्यता, अहार्यता, अविकार्यता; 'p. against advice' उपदेशाहार्य; 'water-p.' जलेनाभेद्य. –LESS, *a.* निष्प्रमाण, साधनहीन.

PROVENDER, *s.* पाथेयं; खाद्यं, पशुभोज्यं, शुष्कतृणादि *n.*

PROVERB, *s.* जनप्रवादः, लोकवादः, आभाणकः, जनोक्ति *f.*, न्यायः, वचनं, उक्तिः. –IAL, *a.* लौकिक (की *f.*), लोकप्रसिद्ध-प्रचलित, लोक-जन in comp., न्यायरूप. –IALLY, *adv.* लोके, जनरूढ्या.

PROVIDE, *v. t.* (पूर्वं) सं-,युज् 7 U, 10, संभृ 3 U, प्र-उप-कॢप् c., सनाथीकृ 8 U, द्रव्यसामग्रीं उपपद् c. or वि-धा 3 U or कृ; *See* PREPARE. 2 (पूर्वं) नियम् 1 P, प्रति-ज्ञा 9 A, परिपण् 1 A, संकेतं-समयं-कृ; निर्दिश् 6 P; *See* ENJOIN, ORDAIN; (for, against) gen. ex. by अर्थे-अर्थं in comp.; 'should p. wealth against times of want' आपदर्थं धनं रक्षेत्; 'who p. s for the future' अनागतविधाता; 'p. against' निवारणाय सज्जीभू, प्रतिकारोपायं कॢप् c. –ED, *a.* (पूर्वं) संभृत, परिकल्पित; युक्त, उपेत, सहित, अन्वित, सनाथ, सनाथीकृत; 'he is duly p. for' तस्य सम्यक्ता: संविधाः कृताः; उपकरणसामग्रीयुक्तः, अन्नवस्त्रादियुक्तः.

2 पूर्वं निर्दिष्ट, परिपणित, पूर्वं संकेतित; 'p. that' यदि, चेत्, एतेन समयेन. -ENCE, *s.* विधिः, परमेश्वरः; *See* GOD. 2 सुविमर्शः, दूरदर्शित्वं, पर्यवेक्षणं, पूर्वविवेकः-विचारः, सुसमीक्षा, दूर-दीर्घ-दृष्टि *f.* -ENT, *a.* दूरदर्शिन्, विमृश्यकारिन्, विवेकिन्, दूर-दीर्घ-दृष्टि. -ENTIAL, *a.* ईश्वर-विधातृ-कृत-प्रयुक्त-घटित. -ENTIALLY, *adv.* विधिवशात्, ईश्वरेच्छया, दैवात्, दिष्ट्या. -ENTLY, *adv.* सविवेकं, सुसमीक्ष्य, सुविमृश्य, दूरदृष्ट्या. —PROVISION, *s.* परिकल्पनं, विधानं, उपपादनं. 2 पूर्वोपायः, पूर्वकल्पना, संविधा-धानं. 3 समयः, संकेतः, प्रतिज्ञा, पणः, नियमः, अभिसंधिः. 4 (P. s) सामग्री, संभारः, संचयः, संग्रहः. साहित्यं, संविधा, उपस्करः, उपकरणजातं; (for journey) पाथेयं, भोज्यं, भक्ष्यं, भक्ष्यादिसामग्री, गमनसंविधा; (for army) वीवधः. -*v. t.* Provide, q. v. -AL, -ARY, *a.* सामयिक (की *f.*), अल्पकालस्थायिन्, आपात in comp., आपाततः नियुक्त. -ALLY, *adv.* आपाततः, समयानुरूपेण, स्तोककालं. -PROVISORY, *a.* सप्रतिज्ञ, सामयिक. -PROVISO, *s. See* (*s.*) (3).

PROVINCE, *s.* विषयः, राष्ट्रं, देशः, चक्रं, मंडलं. 2 नियोगः, कार्यं, कर्म, कर्तव्यं, अधिकारः. 3 प्रकरणं, अंगं, विषयः (fig. also), (सर्वत्रौदरिकस्याभ्यवहार्यमेव विषयः V. 3). -IAL, *a.* देशीय, देश्य, राष्ट्रीय, राष्ट्रिक-दैशिक (की *f.*), देश-राष्ट्र in comp. -*s.* देशस्थः, ग्रामस्थः. -IALISM, *s.* ग्रामीणभाषा, असंस्कृतभाषा.

PROVOKE, *v. t.* प्र-,कुप् c., क्रुध् c., क्रोधं-कोपं-उत्पद् c. or उद्दीप् c. or उत्तिज् c. 2 उत्पद् c., जन् c. (जनयति), प्रवृत् c., उत्तिज् c.; *See* EXCITE, CAUSE. 3 धृष् 5 P, आह्वे 1 A. -ING, *a.* प्रकोपक, उद्दीपक, उत्तेजक, क्रोधावह, संतापकारिन्, संतापक. -INGLY, *adv.* Ex. by (*v.*). -PROVOCATION, *s.* प्रकोपः, क्रोधोद्दीपनं, कोपोत्तेजनं; कोपकारणं-हेतुः. 2 उद्दीपनं, उद्बोधनं. -PROVOCATIVE, *a.* उद्दीपक, उद्बोधक. -*s.* दीपनं, अग्निवर्धनं, क्षुदुबोधनं, प्ररोचनं.

PROVOST, *s.* अध्यक्षः, अधिकारिन् *m.*, अधीशः.

PROWESS, *s.* शौर्यं, वीर्यं, वि-परा-क्रमः, पौरुषं, ओजस् *n.*, रणोत्साहः-शौर्यं; 'personal p.' बाहुवीर्यं, भुजबलं.

PROW, *s.* पोताग्रभागः.

PROWL, *v. i.* (भक्ष्यार्थं) परि-,भ्रम् 1, 4 P, पर्यट् 1 P. -ING, *s.* परिभ्रमणं, पर्यटनं.

PROXIMATE, *a.* समीप, निकट, आसन्न, संसक्त, सन्निकृष्ट. -LY, *adv.* समीपं, संसक्तं. -PROXIMITY, *s.* सन्निधिः, सन्निकर्षः, सान्निध्यं, नैकट्यं, संसक्ति *f.*; *See* NEARNESS.

PROXY, *s.* प्रतिनिधिः-पुरुषः, प्रतिहस्तः; 'by p.' प्रतिनिधिद्वारा.

PRUDE, *a.* (Woman) अतिविनीता, विनयाभिमानिनी, सूक्ष्माचारनिष्ठा. -ERY, *s.* अतिविनीतता, विनयाभिमानः, मिथ्याविनयः. -ISH, *a. See* (*a.*).

PRUDENT, *a.* दूरदर्शिन्, विमृश्य-समीक्ष्य-कारिन्, विवेकिन्, दूर-दीर्घ-दृष्टि, परिणामदर्शिन्, सदसद्विवेकिन्; बुध, मनस्विन्, नीतिज्ञ, विज्ञ, प्र(प्रा)ज्ञ, मनीषिन्, सावधान, कृतधी; *See* WISE also. 2 (Of acts) समीचीन, श्रेयस्, वरं *ind.* -IAL, *a.* सविवेक, विवेकसमीक्षा-प्रयुक्त. -LY, *adv.* विमृश्य, समीक्ष्य, सविवेकं, दूरदर्शितया, परिणामदृष्ट्या, प्राज्ञवत्. -PRUDENCE, *s.* दूरदर्शिता, दूर-दीर्घ-दृष्टि *f.*, विवेकः, प्रसमीक्षा, समीक्ष्य-विमृश्य-कारित्वं, सदसद्विवेकः, नीति *f.*, मनीषा, मति-बुद्धि *f.*

PRUNE, *v. t.* अग्राणि लू 9 U or अव-छिद् 7 P or निकृत् 6 P. -ING, *s.* अवच्छेदः, निकृंतनं; 'p.-knife' विटपच्छेदनी छुरिका.

PRURIGO, PRURIENT, *See* ITCH,-Y.

PRY, *v.* (Into) सूक्ष्मं निरीक्ष् 1 A or निरूप् 10 or दृश् 1 P; निपुणं अनुसं-धा 3 U or अन्विष् 4 P or चर्च् 6 P. -ING, *s.* सूक्ष्मनिरूपणं-अन्वेषणं, सूक्ष्मचर्चा.

PRYTHEE, *adv.* अयि, ननु, (ननु मां प्रापय पत्युरंतिकं K. IV. 32).

PSALM, *s.* स्तोत्रं, गेयं, गीतं, भक्ति-धर्म-गीतं. -IST, *s.* गीत-स्तोत्र-कारः. -PSALTER, *s.* गीतसंहिता-संग्रहः.

PSEUDO, prefix, Ex. by मिथ्या, कपट, कूट, छद्म, कृत्रिम in comp.; *See* FALSE.

PSHAW, *interj.* धिक्, अपेहि.

PSYCHOLOGY, *s.* अध्यात्मविद्या, आन्वीक्षिकी.

PUBERTY, *s.* यौवनं, वयस् *n.*, तारुण्यं, यौवनदशा-अवस्था, प्रौढदशा; 'a woman attained to p.' स्त्रीधर्मिणी, उदक्या; *See* under MENSTRUAL. -PUBESCENT, *a.* प्राप्तयौवन, प्रौढ, तरुण.

PUBLIC, *s.* लोकाः, जनाः, प्रजाः, प्रकृतयः, (pl.); लोकः, जनः, प्रजा; 'in p.' प्रकाशं, लोकसमक्षं, प्रकटं, सर्वप्रत्यक्षं. -*a.* प्रजा-लोक-संबंधिन्; साधारण (णी *f.*), सामान्य, सर्वजनीन-य, सार्वलौकिक (की *f.*), लोक-जन-गण in comp.; 'p. odium' जनद्वेषः; 'p. good' लोकहितं ;'p. property' गणद्रव्यं. 2 प्रसिद्ध, लोक-जन-प्रसिद्ध, सर्वत्र प्रचलित, बहुलीभूत, लोकविश्रुत, प्रकाशीभूत, सार्वलौकिक (की *f.*). 3 प्रकाश, अगूढ, अच्छन्न, अविविक्त, सर्वप्रकाश, राज in comp.; 'p. road' राजमार्गः; 'p. sale' प्रकाशविक्रयः; 'p. house' शुंडा, पानं, शुंडापानं, सुरालयः, सुरापणः; *See* under LIQUOR; 'p.-minded', 'p.-spirited' उपकारशील, जनहितबुद्धि, सर्वजनहितपरायण, लोकहित, जनहितैषिन्. -AN, *s.* शौंडिकः, सुराजीविकः. 2 कर-शुल्क-ग्राहिन् *m.* -ITY, *s.* प्रकाशता, प्राकाश्यं, प्रख्याति *f.*, प्रसिद्धि *f.*, विश्रुति *f.*, जन-लोक-प्रसिद्धिः, स्पष्टता; 'give p.' Publish, q. v. -LY, *adv.* प्रकाशं-शतः, प्रसिद्धं, प्रकटं, सर्वप्रकाशं-संमुखं-समक्षं; अगूढं, अच्छन्नं, सुव्यक्तं, स्पष्टं. —PUBLISH, *v. t.* प्रकाश् c., प्रथ् 10, ख्या c. (ख्यापयति), प्र-वि-घुष् 10, ज्ञा c. (ज्ञापयति), प्रचर् c., बुध् c., प्रकाशीकृ 8 U, प्रकटीकृ, आविष्कृ, प्रकटयति (D.), प्रकटी-प्रसिद्धी-कृ; (books &c.) प्रकाश् c. —ER, *s.* प्रकाशकः, प्रकाशयितृ *m.*, ख्यापकः. —PUBLICATION, *s.* प्रकाशनं, घोषणं, ख्यापनं. 2 प्रकाशितपुस्तकं-ग्रंथः.

PUCKER, *v. t.* संकुच् 1 P, आकुंच् c., संहृ 1 P, पुटीकृ 8 U. —*s.*, —ING, *s.* संकोचः, पुटः, वलि-ली *f.* —ED, *a.* संकुचित, पुटीकृत. 2 Wrinkled, q. v.

PUDDLE, *s.* पंकिलजलं, पंकगुल्मः, पंकजलाशयः. —*v. t.* आविली-कलुषी-कृ 8 U; *See* SPOIL.

PUDENCY, *s. See* MODESTY.

PUDENDUM, PUDENDA, *s.* योनि *f.*; भगं, उपस्थः.

PUERILE, *a.* बालिश, बालोचित, बालेय, बाल-शिशुयोग्य. —ITY, *s.* बालिश्यं, बालधर्मः.

PUERPERAL, *a.* प्रसव-प्रसूति in comp. —PUERPEROUS, *a.* बालप्रसविनी.

PUFF, *v. t.* ध्मा 1 P, आ-उप-°, उत्-,श्वि c., (lit. & fig.); वातेन पूर् 10, उद्-हन् 2 P, स्फाय् c. (स्फावयति). —*v. i.* श्वस् 2 P, कृच्छ्रेण श्वस्, उद्-ध्मा. 2 वा 2 P. 3 फूत्कृ 8 U, मारुतं निःसृ c. 4 श्वि-उद्धन्-ध्मा-pass., स्फीत-आध्मात-उच्छून- *a.* भू 1 P; 'do not p. up, when praised' स्तूयमाना नोत्सिच्यंते (Ka. 329). —*s.* श्वासः, मुखमारुतः. 2 फूत्कारः, फूत्कृतं. 3 वात्या, वातवेगः; *See* GUST. 4 अतिप्रशंसा. —ED, *a.* आध्मात, उच्छून, स्फीत, उद्धत, मारुतपूर्ण, श्वासपूरित; 'p. up with pride' दर्पाध्मात, उत्सिक्त, मदोद्धत, उद्धत. —ING, *s.* उत्सेकः; *See* PRIDE.

PUG-FACED, *a.* वानरवदन, कपिमुख.

PUG-NOSE, *s. See* under FLAT.

PUGILIST, *s.* मुष्टियोधः, मल्लः. —PUGILISM, *s.* मुष्टि-मल्ल-युद्धं, मुष्टीमुष्टि युद्धं.

PUGNACIOUS, *a.* कलह-युद्ध-प्रिय, रणोत्सुक, युयुत्सु, रण-युद्ध-कलह-काम. —PUGNACITY, *s.* युयुत्सा, कलहेच्छा, कलह-युद्ध-कामः.

PUISNE, *a.* अवर, अवरपदस्थ.

PUISSANT, *a.* शूर, विक्रांत, वीर्यवत्, प्रबल. —PUISSANCE, *s.* शौर्यं, वि-परा-क्रमः, वीर्यं; *See* BRAVERY.

PUKE, *v. i.* वम् 1 P, छर्द् 10. —*s.* (वांतिकृत) औषधं.

PULCHRITUDE; *s. See* BEAUTY.

PULE, *v. i.* बालकवत् रु 2 P or कूज् 1 P.

PULL, *s.* कर्षणं, आकर्षः; ग्रहणं, धरणं. —*v. t.* कृष् 1 P, आ-सं-°. 2 ग्रह् 9 P, आ-दा 3 A, धृ 1 P, 10. —down, नि-,पत् c., अधः पत् c., अवकृष्; (in strength) अव-सद् c., अप-चि 5 U, क्षि 5 P, अपकृष्. —off, अप-नी 1 P, अप-उत्-कृष्, अवहृ c., उन्मुच् 6 P, अपहृ 1 P; निष्कृष्, निर्हृ. —out, उद्धृ, निष्कृष्, वि-उत्-पट् 10, उत्खन् 1 P, निर्हृ; (hair) उत्-,लुंच् 1 P. —towards, आ-सम-कृष्. —up, उन्मूल् 10, उद्धृ, उच्छिद् 7 P, उत्पट्; *See* ERADICATE. —ING, *s.* आकर्षणं, ग्रहणं, &c.; 'p. by the hair' केशग्रहः-हणं; 'mutual p. of the hair' केशाकेशि युद्धं.

PULLET, *s.* कुक्कुटशावः.

PULMONARY, *a.* तिलक-फुप्फुस in comp.

PULP, *s.* मज्जा, सारः, वसा. 2 गर्भः, बीजं. —OUS,-Y, *a.* मज्जाबहुल, मज्जागुणक; मांसल, मज्जोपम, कोमल.

PULPIT, *s.* पीठं, आसनं.

PULSE, *s.* नाडि-डी *f.*; (beating) नाडीस्फुरणं-स्पंदनं; 'feel the p.' नाडीं दृश् 1 P or स्पृश् 6 P or परीक्ष् 1 A; 'the p. is quick' लघुगतिः नाडी; 'the p. is slow on account of phlegm' कफान्मंदगतिर्नाडी (नाडी). 2 वैदलः, शमी-शिंबीधान्यं; शमीजः. —PULSATE, *v. i.* स्पंद् 1 A, स्फुर् 6 P; *See* THROB. —ION, *s.* गति *f.*, स्फुरणं, आघातः, स्पंदनं; 'p. of the heart' हृदयोद्वर्षः.

PULVERIZE, *v. t.* चूर्ण् 10, क्षुद् 7 P, पिष् 7 P. —PULVERULENT, *a.* चूर्ण-क्षोद-मय (यी *f.*).

PUMMEL, *s.* वंका.

PUMP, *s.* उत्तोलनयंत्रं, जलोत्क्षेपणं. —*v. t.* (जलादि) उत्तुल् 10, उत्क्षिप् 6 P. 2 (Out) निष्कृष् 1 P, रिच् 7 P or c., रिक्तीकृ 8 U.

PUMPKIN, *s.* कूष्मांडः-डकः, कर्कारुः.

PUN, *s.* श्लेषः —*v. t.* श्लेषं प्रयुज् 7 A, 10.

PUNCH, *s.* प्रहारः, आ-अभि-घातः. 2 विदूषकः, भंडः. 3 वेधनिका. —*v. t.* तड् 10 or प्रहृ 1 P. 2 Perforate, q. v.

PUNCHY, *a.* स्थूलकाय; *See* FAT.

PUNCTILIO, *s.* सूक्ष्मता, अतिसौक्ष्म्यं; सूक्ष्मविषयः-नियमः.—PUNCTILIOUS, *a.* सूक्ष्मनियमनिष्ठ-निरत, सूक्ष्माचारनिष्ठ, अतिसूक्ष्मदृष्टि. —NESS, *s.* सूक्ष्मनियमनिष्ठा, अतिसूक्ष्मदृष्टि *f.*

PUNCTUAL, *a.* सामयिक (की *f.*), संकेत-समय-निष्ठ-अनुवर्तिन्; 'let us be p.' सामयिका भवामः (M. 1). —ITY,-NESS, *s.* समय-संकेत-पालनं-निष्ठा-अनुवर्तनं, सामयिकता. —LY, *adv.* यथासमयं, यथासंकेतकालं.

PUNCTUATE, *v. t.* विरामचिह्नानि लिख् 6 P; चिह्नैः अंक् 10.

PUNCTURE, *v. t.* कीलाग्रेण व्यध् 4 P or भिद् 7 P. —*s.* वेधः-धनं; *See* PRICK.

PUNGENT, *a.* तीव्र, तीक्ष्ण, प्रखर, तिग्म, उग्र, चंड. 2 मर्मभिद्, अरुंतुद, मर्मविध्, कटु. 3 (To the taste) तीक्ष्ण, तीव्र, तिक्त, कटु, उष्ण. —PUNGENCY, *s.* प्रखरता, उग्रता, चंडता, तीक्ष्णता, कटुता, तीव्रता, &c.

PUNISH, *v. t.* दंड् 10, शास् 2 P, (with two acc.); निग्रह् 9 P, दम् c. (दमयति); तड् 10 (by beating); 'p. ed him by an unjust death' अन्यायेन तं जघान, अन्याय्यवधं तमदंडयत्; 'should p. as a thief' चौरदंडेन दंडयेत् (Y. II. 269). **2** Pain, q. v. —ER, *s.* शास्तृ *m.*, शासकः. दंडयिता. —MENT, *s.* दंडः, शासनं, निग्रहः; साहसं; दमः. —PUNITIVE, PUNITORY, *a.* दंड in comp.

PUNT, *s.* तरालुः, तरांधुः.

PUNY, *s.* क्षुद्र, अल्पाल्प, अतिलघु.

PUPIL, *s.* शिष्यः, छात्रः, अंतेवासिन् *m.*, अध्येतृ *m.*, विद्यार्थी. **2** कनीनिका, तारा, तारका. —AGE, *s.* शिष्यदशा-अवस्था, अंतेवासित्वं.

PUPPET, *s.* पुत्रिका, पांचालिका; *See* DOLL; 'p.-show' पुत्रिकाक्रीडा.

PUPPY, PUP, *s.* कुक्कुरशावः-शिशुः.

PURBLIND, *a.* हतदृष्टि, ईषदंध.

PURCHASE, *v. t.* क्री 9 U. **2** व्ययेन-श्रमेण प्राप् 5 P or लभ् 1 A. —*s.* क्रयः. **2** क्रीतद्रव्यं. **3** संग्रहणं, ग्राहः; 'p.-money' क्रयमूल्यं. अर्घः. मूल्यं. —ER, *s.* क्रयिन् *m.*, क्रेतृ *m.*

PURE, *a.* वि-,शुद्ध, शुचि (in all senses); स्वच्छ, विशद, निर्-वि-अ-मल, प्रसन्न, अनाविल, अकलुष. **2** पुण्य, अनघ, निष्पाप, साधु, अपाप, अलिप्त, निष्कलंक, अकल्मष. **3** पवित्र, पावन, मेध्य, परि-,पूत, प्रयत, तीर्थ in comp. **4** केवल, शुद्ध, मात्र in comp. **5** अदुष्ट, अभ्रष्ट, असंसृष्ट, अविकृत. **6** (Language) अपशब्दहीन-रहित, असंकीर्ण. **7** (Woman) सती, साध्वी, अज्ञातव्यवाया, सुरतानभिज्ञा, अस्पृष्टा, अक्षतयोनिः, पुरुषास्पृष्टा; 'of p. descent' सद्वंशज, शुद्धान्वय; 'of p. heart', 'p.-minded' शुद्धात्मन्, विमलात्मन्, शुद्धमति, शुद्धहृदय; प्रयतात्मन्; 'to be p.' शुध् 4 P. —LY, *adv.* निर्मलं, विशुद्धं, शुचि; निष्पापं, &c.; मात्रं, केवलं &c. —NESS,-PURITY, *s.* वैमल्यं, वि-,शुद्धि *f.*, शुद्धता, प्रसादः, वैशद्यं, शुचिता, शौचं, पुण्यता, साधुता, अपापता, पवित्रता, पूतता, साध्वीत्वं, &c. —PURIFY, *v. t.* परि-,पू 9 U or c., शुध् c., वि-परि-,° शुचीकृ 8 U, निर्मलीकृ, पवित्रीकृ, संस्कृ; प्र-,मृज् 2 P, निर्णिज् 3 U, प्रक्षल् 10, धाव् 10. —ED, *a.* परि-,पूत, शुद्ध, शोधित, प्रक्षालित, धौत, निर्णिक्त, &c.; 'p. by penance' प्रयतात्मन्. —ICATION, *s.* परि-,पूति *f.*, वि-परि-शुद्धि *f.*, शौचं, संस्कारः, पावनं, शोधनं, निर्मलीकरणं, प्रक्षालनं, धावनं, मार्जनं. —ICATIVE, -ICATORY, *a.* पावन, पवित्र, पावक, तीर्थ in comp.; अघ-पाप-नाशिन्, अघमर्षण; *See* PURE; 'p. rites' शांतिक्रिया, संस्कारः. —ING, *a.* पावन, पावक, पवित्र, &c.

PURGE, *v. t.* शुध् c., वि-,रिच् 7 P or c., मलं निःसृ c. or शुध् c. **2** परि-,पू 9 U, शुध् c., पापं-अघं-शुध्; *See* PURIFY. —*s.* वि-,रेचनं-कं; उदरशोधनं. —ATION, *s.* वि-,रेचनं. वि-,रेकः, शोधनं, शुद्धि *f.* —ATIVE, *a.* वि-,रेचक-न, सारक. शोधन. —*s.* वि-,रेचनं-कं, सारकं. —ATORY, *s.* शोधक, पावन, अघनाशन-मर्षण. —*s.* पापमोचनस्थानं.

PURLIEU, *s. See* BORDER.

PURLOIN, *v. See* ROB, STEAL.

PURPLE, *a.* धूम्र, धूमल, नीललोहित, धूम्रवर्ण. —*s.* धूम्रः, धूमलः, धूम्रवर्णः, नीललोहितः. —*v. t.* धूम्रीकृ 8 U. —ISH, *a.* आधूम्र, ईषद्धूमल.

PURPORT, *s.* भावः, अभिप्रायः, तात्पर्यं, अर्थः. आशयः, भावार्थः, तात्पर्यार्थः. —*v. t.* अभिप्र-इ 2 P, उद्दिश् 6 P; *See* INTEND, MEAN.

PURPOSE, *s.* हेतुः, अभिप्रायः, आशयः, अर्थः, संकल्पः, उद्देशः, तात्पर्यं, चिकीर्षितं, इच्छा, आकूतं, आकांक्षा, कार्यं, मति-बुद्धि *f.*, धीः; *See* INTENTION; 'fixed p.' स्थिर-दृढ-संकल्पः-निश्चयः; 'of unfailing p.' दृढ-सत्य-संकल्प, स्थिरधी-मति; 'to no p.' निरर्थकं, वृथा, मुधा, व्यर्थं, निर्गुणं; 'who has effected his p.' कृती, कृतार्थः. कृतकृत्यः; 'for the p. of' ex. by अर्थं-अर्थे, हेतोः, निमित्तं-त्ते, in comp., कृते (with gen. or by dat.); 'for what p.' किमर्थं, किमुद्दिश्य, केन हेतुना. —*v. t.* अभिप्र-इ 2 P. उद्दिश् 6P, संकृप् c., इष् 6 P; *See* INTEND. —LY, 'on p.' *adv.* कामतः, बुद्धि-बोध-पूर्वं, ज्ञानतः, बुद्ध्या. साभिप्रायं.

PURSE, *s.* धनभस्त्रिका-कोषः, ग्रंथिः. **2** धनं; *See* WEALTH; 'p.-cutting' ग्रंथिच्छेदः-भेदः; 'p.-pride' धनगर्वः-दर्पः-अभिमानः; 'p.-proud' धनोन्मत्त, वित्तगर्वित; धनदृप्त, —*v. t.* कोषे नि-धा 3 U or निविश् c. **2** Contract, q. v.

PURSUE, *v. t.* अनुसृ 1 P, अनुगम्-धाव्-व्रज् 1 P, अनु-या 2 P, अनुवृत् 1 A, अनुक्रम् 1 U, 4 P. **2** अनु-स्था 1 P, आचर् 1 P, नि-,सेव् 1 A, आश्रि 1 U, आ-स्था 1 P. **3** प्रवृत् c., निर्वह् c., सततं प्रणी 1 P; *See* PROSECUTE. **4** आप् desid. (ईप्सति), लभ् desid. (लिप्सते); 'p. one's way' मार्गं आक्रम्, वह् 1 P; *See* FOLLOW. —ER, *s.* अनुसारिन् *m.*, अनुधावकः, अनुगामी. —PURSUIT, *s.* अनुसरणं-धावनं-गमनं; अन्वेषणं, मार्गणं. **2** अनुष्ठानं, आचरणं, निषेवणं, अभिनिवेशः, अनुशीलनं; प्रवृत्ति *f.*, लिप्सा, अर्जनप्रयत्नः. निरतता-रतता in comp. **3** व्यापारः. व्यवसायः, उद्योगः, उद्यमः, आरंभः, व्यवहारः, कार्यं, प्र-,वृत्तिः; 'literary p. s.' विद्यागमकार्याणि, ज्ञानसंपादनारंभाः. —PURSUANT, *a.* अनुवर्तिन्, अनुसारिन्, अनुरोधिन्, अनुरूप. —LY, *adv.* अनुरूपं, अनुसारेण-तः, अनुरोधेन, यथा in comp. —PURSUANCE, *s.* अनुसरणं-वर्तनं-गमनं-रोधः; 'in p. of' अनुरूपं, अनुसारेण, &c. —PURSUIVANT, *s.* अनुचरः, दूतः.

PURSY, *a.* स्थूलन्हस्व, उच्छून, स्फीत. 2 दुःश्वासिन्, कृच्छ्रश्वास.

PURULENT, *a.* पूयपूर्ण-मय (यी *f.*), पूयस्राविन् सपूय. -PURULENCE, *s.* पूयपूर्णता, सपूयता.

PURVEY, *v. t.* उपकरणानि उपक्लृप् c., सं-भृ 1, 3 U or संयुज् 7 U, 10; *See* PROVIDE. -ANCE, *s.* भोजनपरिकल्पनं-संभार:-सामग्री. 2 परिकल्पनं, संभार:, संनिधा-धानं. -OR, *s.* भोजनाधिकारी, आहाराधिकृत:.

PUS, *s.* पूय:-यं, दूष्यं, पूयरक्तं.

PUSH, *v.* (हस्तादिना) प्रसृ c., संचल् c., प्रक्षिप् 6 P, प्रचुद् 10, प्रेर् c., प्रणुद् 6 P or c.; *See* DRIVE. 2 तड् 10, प्र-हृ 1 P; आ-व्यध् 4 P, प्रति-अभि-हन् 2 P, आहन् 2 U; 'p. aside' अपसृ c., बहिष्कृ 8 U, निःसृ c.; 'p. forward' प्रणुद् c., प्रचल् c., प्रसृ c.; 'p. afar' उत्सृ c. -*s.*, -ING, *s.* प्रसारणं, प्रक्षेप:, प्रेरणं-णा, प्रचोदना. 2 ताडनं, आघात:, प्रहार:, अभ्याघात:. 3 वेग:, प्रयत्न:. -ING, *a.* उद्यमिन्, उद्योगिन्, साहसशील, प्रगल्भ, साहसिन्.

PUSILLANIMOUS, *a.* कृपण, दीन, क्षुद्रमनस्, कृपणबुद्धि-मति, लघुचेतस्, पामर, भीरुहृदय, कातर, कापुरुष, क्लीब. -PUSILLANIMITY, *s.* कार्पण्यं, दैन्यं, क्लीबता, कातर्यं, भीरुता, कृपणमतित्वं, क्षुद्रता.

PUSS, PUSSY, *s. See* CAT.

PUSTULE, *s.* Pimple, q. v. -OUS, *a.* स्फोटपूर्ण.

PUT, *v. t.* स्था c. (स्थापयति), नि-आ-धा 3 U, आरुह् c., दा 3 U, कृ 8 U, ऋ c. (अर्पयति), निविश् c., वि-,न्यस् 4 P. 2 आ-समा-युज् 7 U, 10. 3 Incite, q. v.; 'p. to death' हन् 2 P or c., मृ c., व्या-पद् c.; *See* KILL; 'p. to flight' वि-द्रु c.; 'p. in mind' स्मृ c., प्र-अनु-बुध् c.; 'p. in order' यथाक्रमं-यथातथं-रच् 10 or स्था c. or विन्यस्, सज्जीकृ; 'p. in writing' पत्रे निविश् c., लेख्ये आरुह् c. -about, परिवृत् c. -aside, by, अपास् 4 U, मुच् 6 P, त्यज् 1 P; *See* ABANDON. 2 परि-,रक्ष् 1 P, सं-चि 5 U. -away, अप-निः-सृ c., निष्कस् c., बहिष्कृ, व्याक्षिप् 6 P, विलंब् c. -down, भूमौ निधा, अवतॄ c., निक्षिप्. 2 नश् c., विलुप् c., उच्छिद् 7 P ; *See* DESTROY, OVERTHROW. 3 (In writing) पत्रे लिख् 6 P or निविश् c. or आरुह् c. -forth, प्रसृ c. 2 आविष्कृ, अंज् 7 P, व्यक्तीकृ, प्रकाश् c., प्र-,दृश् c. 3 उत्क्षिप्, उपानी, उपन्यस्, उदाहृ 1 P. 4 उद्-भिद् c.; 'a creeper having p. forth foliage' संजातपत्रा लता (R. III. 7). -off, व्याक्षिप्, विलंब् c., अतिपत् c. 2 उन्मुच्, अवतॄ c., अपनी, उच्छद् 10, अपनह् 4 P. 3 निराकृ, निःसृ c.; *See* DISCARD, DISCHARGE. 4 (From land) अपगम्, अप-या, अपसृ 1 P; 'the boat p. off' मुक्ता नौः (D. K. II. 6). -on, वस् 2 A, परि-धा; धृ 1 P, 10, संव्ये 1 P; प्रसाध् c., आच्छद्; प्रा-आ-वृ 5 U; 'p. on armour' संनह् 4 P. 2 ग्रह् 9 P, स्वीकृ, धृ, दृश् c. 3 संक्रम् c., संचर् c. 4 आसंज् c.; निविश् c. -out, विस्तॄ c., प्रसृ c., वितन् 8 U. 2 (Eyes &c.) सं-, उद्धृ, वि-उत्-पट् 10. 3 निर्वा c. (वापयति), प्र-उपशम् c. (शमयति). 4 विलक्षीकृ, व्रीडया आकुलीकृ, *See* EMBARRASS. 5 निःसृ c., बहिष्कृ. 6 प्र-विनि-युज् 7A, 10; 'p. out at interest' वृद्धिलाभाय विनियोजित. -over, अधिकृ c., अधि-ष्ठा c. 2 Put off, q. v. -to, Expose, q. v.; 'p. to the sword' खड्गेन छिद् 7 P or हन् 2 P; 'p. to sea' नावं मुच्; 'p. to a stand' स्तंभ् 9 P. -together, संयुज्; संधा, सं-ग्रंथ् 9 P. -up, उत्तॄ 1 P, वस् 1 P; *See* LODGE. 2 (with) सह् 1 A, क्षम् 1 A; *See* BEAR. 3 व्यक्तीकृ, प्रकाशं स्था c., प्रदृश् c.; 'an article p. up for sale' क्रय्यं द्रव्यं; 'p. up to' प्रणुद् c., प्रोत्सह् c.

PUTATIVE, *a.* प्रसिद्ध, अभिमत.

PUTRIFY, *v. i.* पूतीभू 1 P, पूय् 1 A, दुर्गंध-*a.* भू; वि-,गल् 1 P, वि-ली 4 A. -*v. t.* पूतीकृ 8 U, गल् c., विली c. -ACTION, *s.* पूति *f.*, दुर्गंधता, पूतिगंध:, गलनं, विलय:. —PUTRID, PUTRESCENT, *a.* पूतिगंधि, उग्रगंध, दुर्गंध, विगलित, विलीयमान. -NESS, PUTRESCENCE, *s.* पूति:, दुर्गंध:, पूतिगंध:.

PUZZLE, *v. t.* व्या-,मुह् c., सं-वि-भ्रम् c. (भ्रमयति), आकुलीकृ 8 U, व्यस् 4 U ; *See* CONFUSE, PERPLEX. -*s.* कूटं, प्रहेलिका, प्रवह्लिका. 2 व्या-मोह:, भ्रांति *f.*, संभ्रम:, वैक्लव्यं, व्याकुलता, व्यग्रता. -ED, *a.* मूढ, भ्रांत, व्यसनखिन्न, आकुलमनस्, किंकर्तव्यतामूढ. -ING, *a.* भ्रम-मोह-कारिन्, संभ्रमप्रद.

PYGMY, *s.* ह्रस्व:, खर्व:, वामन:. -*a.* ह्रस्व, खर्व, वामनमूर्ति.

PYRAMID, *s.* सूच्यग्रस्तंभ: -AL, *a.* सूच्याकार ; सूच्यग्र, शिखरिन्, शुंडाकृति.

PYRE, *s.* चिता, चित्या, चिति *f.*

PYRITES, *s.* स्वर्णमाक्षिकं.

PYRRHONIST, *s.* नास्तिक:, मिथ्यादृष्टि:.

Q.

QUACK, *s.* कुवैद्य:, दांभिक:, छद्मवैद्य:, मिथ्याचिकित्सक:. 2 हंसनाद:-रव:. -*v. t.* हंसवत् नद् 1 P or रु 2 P. -ERY, *s.* दुश्चिकित्सा ; मिथ्याभिमान:. 2 Boast, q. v.

QUADRANGLE, *s.* चतुर्भुज:, चतुष्कोण: ; (of a house) प्रकोष्ठ:,चत्वरं, संजवनं, चतु:शालं. -QUADRANGULAR, *a.* चतुष्कोण, चतुरस्र.

QUADRANT, *s.* चतुर्थभाग:, पाद:. 2 वृत्तपाद:.

QUADRATE, *s. See* SQUARE.

QUADRATIC, *a.* चतुरस्रीय. 2 (Equation) वर्गसमीकरणं.

QUADRATURE, *s.* पदसंस्थानं.

QUADRENNIAL, *a.* चातुर्वार्षिक (की *f.*).

QUADRILATERAL, *a.* चतुर्भुज, चतुःपार्श्व.

QUADRIPARTITE, *a.* चतुर्विध.

QUADRISYLLABLE, *s.* चतुरक्षरं.

QUADRUPED, *s.* चतुष्पदः (दी *f.*), चतुष्पाद्.

QUADRUPLE, *a.* चतुर्गुण. —*v. t.* चतुर्गुणीकृ 8 U.

QUAFF, *v. t.* (सतृष्णं) पा 1 P, उत्-चुलुंप् 1 P. —ER, *s.* अतिपायिन् *m.*

QUAGMIRE, *s. See* MARSH.

QUAIL, *s.* वर्तकः, वर्तिका, लावः. —*v. i.* कंप् 1 A, वेप् 1 A. 2 वि-अव-सद् 1 P, क्षि pass. ; प्रली 4 A.

QUAINT, *a.* अपरूप, विलक्षण, असंगत. 2 विदग्ध, चतुर, अतिसूक्ष्म. —LY, *adv.* विलक्षणं, असंगतं.

QUAKE, *v. i.* कंप् 1 A, उद्विज् 6 A, त्रस् 1, 4 P; (with abl.). —*s.* कंपः-पनं, उत्-प्र-कंपः, वेपथुः.

QUALIFY, *v. t.* योग्य-उचित-क्षम-*a.* कृ 8 U ; ex. by ' q. ed. ' 2 नियम् 1 P, परिच्छिद् 7 P, परि-मा 3 A, 2 P, निबंध् 9 P. 3 Moderate, q. v. —ED, *a.* योग्य, क्षम, समर्थ, पर्याप्त, कर्मक्षम, अलंकर्मीण. 2 गुणिन्, गुणोपेत, गुणसंपन्न. 3 नियत, परिच्छिन्न, समर्याद ; *See* LIMITED. —ICATION, *s.* योग्यता, क्षमता, पात्रता, औचित्यं, गुणविशिष्टता. 2 गुणः, पात्रत्वं, विशिष्टगुणः. 3 परिच्छेदः, मर्यादा, नियमनं, नियतत्वं, परिमाणं. —QUALITY, *s.* गुणः. 2 भावः, धर्मः, गुणः, स्वभावः, प्रकृति *f.*, स्व-,रूपं, लक्षणं, विशेषभावः-धर्मः-लक्षणं, शीलं; शक्ति *f.* 3 कुलीनता, श्रेष्ठ-विशिष्ट-पदं, प्रतिष्ठा, गौरवं, उत्कृष्टपदं. 4 प्रकारः, जाति *f.*; *See* KIND; ' good q. ' गुणः, सद्गुणः, सद्भावः, ' having good q. es ' गुणिन्, गुणवत्, गुणोपेत, गुणयुक्त, सद्गुण; ' bad q. ' दुर्गुणः, अवगुणः; ' inherent q. of a thing ' निसर्गधर्मः, वस्तुशक्तिः; ' men of q. ' कुलीनजनाः, अभिजात-कुलीन-वर्गः.

QUALM, *s.* वमनेच्छा, विवमिषा. 2 मनस्तापः, अनुशयः, अनुतापः. —ISH, *a.* विवमिषु.

QUANDARY, *s. See* DIFFICULTY.

QUANTITY, *s.* परिमाणं, प्रमाणं, मानं, मात्रा, अंशः, भागः. 2 मात्रा. 3 राशिः. 4 (Large) संचयः, ओघः, पूगः, पुंजः, राशिः, संग्रहः; ' a great q. of ' प्रभूत, प्रचुर, बहु, विपुल; ' great q. ' बाहुल्यं, प्राचुर्यं, बहुभागः, भूयिष्ठांशः; ex. by बहु, प्रचुर, विपुल (Much, q. v.); ' in large q. es ' बहुशः, बाहुल्येन, प्राचुर्येण; ' small q. ' स्तोकांशः, अल्पभागः, अल्पं, स्तोकं, अल्पमात्रं; ' in small q. es ' अल्पशः, स्तोकांशेन; ' long q. ' दीर्घः; ' short q. ' ह्रस्वः; ' known q.' व्यक्तराशिः; ' unknown q.' अव्यक्तराशिः; ' positive, negative, q. ' धन-ऋण-राशिः; ' what q. of ' कियत्.

QUANTUM, *s.* परिमाणं, मात्रा, कल्पितभागः.

QUARANTINE, *s.* गमनागमन-संसर्ग-निषेधः.

QUARREL, *s.* कलहः, कलिः, विवादः, विसंवादः, विप्रतिपत्ति *f.*, वाक्कलहः, वाग्युद्धं, विगलापः; द्वंद्वं, वैरं. —*v. i.* विवद् 1 A, विप्रलप् 1 P, विसंवद् 1 P, विप्रतिपद् 4 A, वैरायते-कलहायते (D.), कलहं कृ 8 U, युध् 4 A. —ER, *s.* विवादिन् *m.*, कलहकारी. —SOME, *a.* कलह-कलि-प्रिय, विवादशील, विसंवादिन्, कलहकलि-पर, कलहकारिन्, युयुत्सु, विवादार्थिन्.

QUARRY, *s.* आकरः, ख(खा)नि-नी *f.*, पाषाणस्थानं-भूमि *f.* 2 आमिषं, मार्गितजंतुः. —*v. t.* खन् 1 P; *See* DIG.

QUARTAN, *a.* चातुर्थिक.

QUARTER, *s.* पादः, तुर्यः, तुरीयः, अर्धार्धं, तुरीय-चतुर्थ-भागः; ' a rupee and a q. ' सपादरूपकः. 2 दिश्-शा, आशा, काष्ठा, ककुभ्, हरित्; *See* DIRECTION; ' in intermediate q.' अपदिशं; ' guardian of a q. ' दिक्पालः, लोकपालः ; ' guardian elephant of the q. ' दिग्गजः. 3 प्र-,देशः, उद्देशः, स्थानं, दिक्-शा, दिग्भागः, दिग्देशः, दिगंतः; ' from various q. s ' नानादिग्देशात्, नानादिगंतेभ्यः, नानादिग्भ्यः; ' in every q.' चतुर्दिक्षु. 4 (Q. s) वासः, वसति *f.*, निकेतनं, वासस्थानं, निवेशः, कटकः-कं; ' head q. s ' सेनापतिनिवेशः, कटकः. 5 दया, कृपा, जीव-प्राण-दानं; ' give q. ' दयां कृ 8 U, अभयं दा 3 U. 6 (Of night) यामः, प्रहरः. 7 मासत्रयं, त्रिमासं, वत्सरपादः; ' to close q. s ' बाहूबाहवि, हस्ताहस्ति, मिथःप्रत्यासन्न- *a.*; ' they two came to close q. s ' तौ बाहूबाहवि व्यासजेताम् (Si. XVIII. 12). —*v. t.* चतुर्धा विभज् 1 U or खंड् 10 or छिद् 7 P. 2 वस् c., निविश् c. —*v. i.* निवस् 1 P, निविश् 6 A, अध्यास् 2 A. —LY, *a.* त्रैमासिक (की *f.*), पादिक (की *f.*). —*adv.* मासत्रयांते, प्रतित्रिमासं.

QUARTO, *s.* चतुःपत्रकं.

QUASH, *v. t.* मृद् 9 P, पराजि 1 A, पराभू 1 P. 2 खंड् 10, निवृत् c., विलुप् 6 P or c., उच्छिद् 7 P, निरस् 4 U.

QUASI, Ex. by कु, कल्प, देशीय, in comp.

QUATERNION, *s.* चतुष्टयं, चतुष्कं.

QUATRAIN, *s.* चतुष्पदश्लोकः.

QUAVER, *v. i.* Tremble, q. v. 2 भग्नस्वरेण गै 1 P. —*s.* स्वरभंगः, कंपस्वरः.

QUAY, *s.* घट्टः, घट्टी, तीर्थं, उत्तरणस्थानं.

QUEAN, *s. See* PROSTITUTE.

QUEEN, *s.* राज्ञी, महिषी, देवी (title of address),

राजपत्नी-महिषी; 'q.'s metal' कांस्यं. -LIKE, -LY, *a.* राज्ञीसदृश (शी *f.*)-अनुरूप.

QUEER, *a.* विलक्षण, असंगत, अपरूप, अद्भुत; *See* ODD.

QUELL, *v. t.* शम् c. (शमयति), प्र-उप-,° निवृत् c., विनश् c., उच्छिद् 7 P. 2 दम् c. (दमयति), वशीकृ 8 U, परा-अभि-भू 1 P, पराजि 1 A.

QUENCH, *v. t.* (Thirst) शम् c. (शमयति), प्र-उप-,° छिद् 7 P, निवृत् c., अपनी 1 P. 2 निर्वा c. (वापयति), प्र-उप-शम् c. -ING, *s.* शमनं, शांति *f.*, वि-,च्छेदः.

QUERULOUS, *a.* दुःखित, परिदेवनाकुल, विलापिन्, परिदेविन्, विलापशील, शोकगर्भ, दुःखात्मक. -LY, *adv.* सविलापं. -NESS, *s.* विलपनशीलता.

QUERY, *s. See* QUESTION.

QUEST, *s.* अन्वेषणं, अनुसंधानं, मार्गणं, निरूपणं; 'in q. of prey' भक्ष्यार्थं.

QUESTION, *s.* प्रश्नः, अनुयोगः, पृच्छा; 'put a question to' प्रच्छ् 6 P, अनुयुज् 7 A; 'you have put me a good q.' सम्यक् पृष्टोस्मि भवता. 2 जिज्ञासा, निरूपणं, परीक्षा-क्षणं, अनुसंधानं, विचारः-रणा. 3 संदेहः, संशयः, वितर्कः, विकल्पः, आ-,शंका; 'here a q. arises' अत्रेदं प्रष्टव्यं. 4 वि-,वादविषयः-पदं-वस्तु-आस्पदं; विचारविषयः, &c.; 'call in q.' विचर् c., (आज्ञा गुरूणां ह्यविचारणीया R. XIV. 46); 'the topic in q.' प्रस्तुत-प्रकृत-विषयः; 'the q. arose as to &c.' इति-विवादः-प्रश्नः-समुपस्थितः. -*v. t.* प्रच्छ्, अनुयुज्, ज्ञा desid. (जिज्ञासते); 'ascetics may be q. ed without reserve' अनियंत्रणानुयोगस्तपस्विजनः (S. 1). 2 परीक्ष् 1 A, निरूप् 10, अनुसं-धा 3 U, विचर् c. 3 आशंक् 1 A, न प्रति-इ 2 P, न विश्वस् 2 P, वितर्क् 10, विक्लृप् 1 A; *See* DOUBT. -ABLE, *a.* विचार्य, विशंक्य, शंकनीय, संदिग्ध, शंकार्ह, संदेह-शंका-पदं. -ABLY, *adv.* साशंकं, संदिग्धं. -ARY, *a.* प्रश्नात्मक. -ER, *s.* पृच्छकः, प्रष्टृ *m.*, अनुयोक्ता, अनुयोगी, जिज्ञासुः. -LESS, *adv.* निःसंशयं, निःशंकं.

QUIBBLE, *s.* वाक्छलं, वक्रोक्ति *f.*, वक्रभणितं, कैतववादः, अप-व्यप-देशः, अपलापः, अपह्नवः. -*v. i.* अपलप् 1 P, वक्रं भण् or वद् 1 P, अपदिश् 6 P, वाक्छलं कृ 8 U. -ER, *s.* अपलापिन् *m.*, वक्रोक्तिवादी. -ING, *s. See* (*s.*).

QUICK, *a.* शीघ्र, त्वरित, द्रुत, क्षिप्र, सत्वर, अविलंबित, तूर्णं; 'q.-wit' प्रत्युत्पन्नधीः-मतिः &c.; 'q. as thought' मनोजवेन, संकल्पस्य त्वरयेव. 2 तीक्ष्ण, सूक्ष्म, तीव्र, शीघ्रग्राहिन्, आशुकारिन्. 3 शीघ्र, शीघ्र-द्रुत-गति, सवेग, चपल; *See* SHARP. 4 सजीव, चल, स्पंदमान; 'q. with child' चलितगर्भा, आपन्नसत्त्वा, *See* PREGNANT; 'be q.', 'q., q.' त्वरस्व, त्वरस्व; 'q.-lime' चूर्णजलं, ततचूर्णं; 'q.-sight' तीक्ष्ण-सूक्ष्म-दृष्टि *f.*; 'q.-silver' पारदः; *See* MERCURY; 'q.-witted' शीघ्र-तीक्ष्ण-बुद्धि-मति, प्रत्युत्पन्नमति. -*adv.* Quickly, q. v. -*s.* मर्मन् *n.*, मर्मस्थानं-देशः; 'piercing to the q.' मर्मस्पृश्-भिद्-च्छिद्-आविध्. -EN, *v. t.* त्वर् c. (त्वरयति), गतिं वृध् c. 2 जीव् c., सोच्छ्वास- *a.* कृ 8 U, जीवं दा 3 U. 3 उद्दीप् c., उत्तिज् c., शो 4 P, प्ररुष् c., वृध् c.; *See* SHARPEN. -*v. i.* त्वर् 1 A, द्रुततरं गम् or चल् 1 P. 2 जीवित्वं-चैतन्यं-प्राप् 5 P, सजीवीभू. 3 स्पंद् 1 A, चल् 1 P, स्फुर् 6 P. -ENING, *a.* जीवद, उद्दीपक. -LY, *adv.* शीघ्रं, सत्वरं, त्वरितं, तूर्णं, लघु, आशु, क्षिप्रं, द्रुतं, अविलंबं, अविलंबितं, चपलं, अरं, शीघ्र-क्षिप्र-द्रुत in comp.; 'going q.' द्रुतगामिन्, शीघ्रगति. 2 अह्नाय, सपदि, सद्यः, झटिति, अचिरात्, अचिरेणैव. -NESS, *s.* शीघ्रता, तीक्ष्णता, &c.

QUIESCENT, *a.* निश्चल, निश्चेष्ट, स्थिर, अचल, विरत, शांत. -QUIESCENCE, *s.* निश्चलता, चेष्टाभावः, शांति *f.*, &c.

QUIET, *a.* शांत, प्र-उप-°, निश्चल, अचल, स्थिर, निष्कंप; अक्षुब्ध, अव्याकुल, स्तिमित, निर्वात, निवृत्तवायु, (sea); विरत, विश्रांत. 2 सौम्य, मृदु, अचंड, अनुग्र; *See* MILD. 3 स्वस्थ, निर्विघ्न, अबाध, निरुपद्रव, निरुपप्लव, निरुद्वेग, अभंग. 4 निःशब्द, तूष्णीक; 'keep q.' मौनमवलंबस्व, जिह्वां धारय, तूष्णीं भव, जोषमास्स्व. -*s.* स्थिरता, निश्चलत्वं, शांति *f.*, शमः, प्र-उप-°, विश्रामः, स्वास्थ्यं, निरुपद्रवता, निर्वातत्वं, अक्षोभः, निरुपप्लवता, &c. -*v. t.* सांत्व् 10, प्र-उप-शम् c. (शमयति), निवृत् c., विरम् c., विश्रम् c., स्थिरीकृ 8 U. -ISM, *s.* शमः, वैराग्यं, निवृत्तिमार्गः. -IST, *s.* विरागी. -LY, *adv.* शांतं, शांत्या, निराकुलं, अव्याकुलं, अक्षुब्धं, स्वास्थ्येन, अनुग्रं, अचंडं; तूष्णीं, निःशब्दं. -NESS, -ITUDE, *s.* शमः; *See* (*s.*).

QUILL, *s.* पक्षः, पर्णं; (for writing) कलमः, लेखनी; (of a lute) रणः, शारिका, कोणः; (of a porcupine) शलं, शललं-ली.

QUILT, *s.* तूला, तूलिका, तूलिकाप्रच्छदः-संस्तरः; प्रच्छदपटः. -*v. t.* तूलादिना निषिव् 4 P.

QUINARY, *s.* पंचकं. -*a.* पंचरूप, पंचक.

QUINDECAGON, *s.* पंचदशभुजः.

QUINQUENNIAL, *s.* पंचवार्षिक (की *f.*), पंचवर्षीय.

QUINSY, *s.* श्लेष्मजा रोहिणी; कंठपाकः.

QUINTESSENCE, *s.* सारः, तत्त्वं; *See* ESSENCE.

QUINTUPLE, *a.* पंचगुण; पंचविध.

QUIP, *See* TAUNT.

QUIRE, *s.* गायकगणः.

QUIRK, *s.* Quibble, q. v. 2 उपालंभः, अवक्षेपः, धिक्कारः. 3 छंदस् *n.*, मनोलौल्यं; *See* FANCY. -ISH, *a.* चपल, लोलमति.

QUIT, *v. t.* त्यज् 1 P, हा 3 P, अपास् 4 U, वि-उत्-सृज् 6 P ; *See* ABANDON ; अप-सृप् 1 P, निर्गम् 1 P, अप-या 2 P, व्यप-इ 2 P, (with abl.). 2 (Debt) वि-मुच् 6 P or c., शुध् c., निस्तॄ c., भिरा-अपा-कृ 8 U. -*a.* वि-,मुक्त, शोधित, निस्तीर्ण. -TANCE, *s.* निष्कृति *f.*, मोक्षः, शुद्धि *f.*, निस्तारः, मुक्ति *f.*, साधनं; 'q. of a spite' वैरशुद्धिः-साधनं.

QUITE, *adv.* सर्वथा, सर्वशः, साकल्येन, निःशेषं. 2 सु-अति pr.; अत्यंतं, अतीव, भृशं; *See* EXCEEDINGLY.

QUIVER, *s.* तूणः-णी, तूणीरः, निषंगः, इषुधिः, उपासंगः. -*v. t.* स्फुर् 6 P, कंप् 1 A, स्पंद् 1 A, वेप् 1 A. -ED, *a.* तूणिन्, तूणीरभृत्. -ING, *a.* कंपमान, वेपमान, कंपित, स्फुरित, सकंप, चंचल, लोल, चपल. -*s.* स्फुरणं, स्पंदनं, कंपः-पनं.

QUIZ, *s.* उपहासकः, अवक्षेपकः. -*v. t.* उप-अव-हस् 1 P, अवक्षिप् 6 P.

QUOIT, *s.* चक्रं, वलयः-यं. -*v.* चक्रैः क्रीड् 1 P.

QUONDAM, *a.* पूर्व; *See* FORMER.

QUORUM, *s.* निर्दिष्टसंख्या, कार्यनिर्वाहक्षमा संख्या.

QUOTA, *s.* अंशः, भागः.

QUOTE, *v. t.* उद्-हृ 1 P, अवतॄ c., उपन्यस् 4 U, उद्-गॄ 6 P, उदा-हृ, उप-नी 1 P. -ATION, *s.* उद्धारः, अवतरणं, उद्धरणं, उपन्यासः, उद्धृत-अवतारित-वाक्यं-लेखः.

QUOTH, *v.* आह, वदति, &c.

QUOTIDIAN, *a.* दैनंदिन (नी *f.*), प्रात्याहिक (की *f.*); अन्येद्युष्क.

QUOTIENT, *s.* फलं, गुण्यः; 'by dividing is obtained the q.' भजनेन लब्धो गुण्यः.

R.

RABBIT, *s.* शशः, शशकः.

RABBLE, *s.* प्राकृताः, पृथक्-प्राकृत-जनाः, नीचाः, प्राकृतगणः.

RABID, *a.* उन्मत्त, संभ्रांत, विक्षिप्तचित्त, वातुल. -LY, *adv.* सोन्मादं, उन्मत्तवत्. -NESS, *s.* उन्मादः, वातुलता.

RACE, *s.* अन्वयः, कुलं, वंशः, संतानः, संतति *f.*, वंशावलि-ली *f.*, गोत्रं. 2 जाति *f.* वर्गः. 3 March, q. v. 4 चर्या, धावनं. 5 मूलं; 'to run a r.' अहमहमिकया-परस्परजिगीषया-धाव् 1 P ; 'slow and steady wins the r.' मंदोप्यविरतोयोगः सदा विजयभाग्भवेत्, (कूर्मवृत्तिं समास्थाय सर्वत्र विजयी भवेत्); 'r.-course' चर्याभूमि *f.*; 'r.-horse' जवाश्वः, जवनः. -*v. i.* धाव् 1 P; *See* RUN.

RACK, *s.* तीव्रवेदना, यातना, अतिव्यथा; 'put to the r.' अर्द् 1 P or c., संपीड् 10. 2 गवादनी, द्रोणि-णी *f.* 3 संपीडनयंत्रं, प्रमाथ-यातना-यंत्रं; 'r. and ruin' उच्छेदः. -*v. t.* अत्यंतं पीड् or व्यथ् c. (व्यथयति), यातनायंत्रेण पीड् or प्रमथ् c.

RACKET, *s.* कोलाहलः, कलकलः, तुमुलरवः. 2 गुलिकाताडनी. -Y, *a.* तुमुलकारिन्.

RACY, *a.* सरस, रसवत् ; तीक्ष्ण-उग्र-रस.

RADIATE, *v. i.* निर्गम् 1 P, समंततः प्रसृ 1 P or उद्-इ 2 P (rays) ; स्फुर् 6 P, किरणान् विकॄ 6 P or प्रसृ c., दीप् freq. (देदीप्यते). -ION, *s.* अंशुप्रसरणं-स्फुरणं, किरणपातनं-विकिरणं. —RADIANT, *a.* उज्ज्वल, दीप्तिमत्, सुप्रभ, देदीप्यमान, तेजस्विन् ; *See* BRIGHT. -LY, *adv.* सुप्रभं, अतितेजसा, उज्ज्वलं. -RADIANCE, *s.* प्रभा, दीप्ति *f.*, कांति *f.*, तेजस् *n.*, औज्ज्वल्यं ; *See* LUSTRE, LIGHT.

RADICAL, *a.* मूलं in comp., मौलिक (की *f.*) ; मौल (ली *f.*). 2 निसर्गज, स्वाभाविक-नैसर्गिक (की *f.*); *See* NATURAL. -LY, *adv.* समूलं, मूलतः, आमूलं. 2 स्वभावतः, प्रकृत्या, जातितः.

RADISH, *s.* मूलकः-कं.

RADIUS, *s.* त्रिज्या, जीवा ; व्यासार्धं, विष्कंभार्धं. 2 (Of a wheel) अरः.

RAFF, *s.* *See* RABBLE.

RAFT, *s.* उडुपं, प्लवः, कोलः, तरंडः.

RAFTER, *s.* तुला, दीर्घस्थूणा-काष्ठं, दीर्घदारु, गृहस्थूणा.

RAG, *s.* वस्त्रखंडः-डं, पटखंडः, चीरं, चीवरं, कर्पटः, न-(ल)क्तकः. 2 जर्जर-जीर्ण-वस्त्रं, पटच्चरं ; 'dressed in r. s' चीरवासस्, परिहितचीर, कर्पटिक. -GED, *a.* जीर्ण, जर्जर.

RAGE, *s.* संरंभः, मन्युः, रोषः, क्रोधः, प्रकोपः, उत्तापः, संतापः, क्रोधावेशः, अमर्षः. 2 उत्कटेच्छा, लालसा, तीक्ष्णता, उचंडता, तीव्रता, उग्रता, तिग्मता. -*v. i.* नितरां क्षुभ् 4 P, 1 A, क्रुध्-रुष्-कुप् 4 P, संरंभ-मन्यु-वशं-गम् 1 P or प्राप् 5 P, क्रोधाकुल- *a.* भू 1 P. 2 उग्र-चंड-तीक्ष्ण- *a.* भू ; 'r. on (oh ? cloud)' गर्ज्, गर्जस्तिष्ठ. -FUL, *a.* क्रोधान्वित, कोपाकुल, रुष्ट, कुपित, जातामर्ष, संरंभित. -ING, *a.* संरंभिन्, उग्र, तीक्ष्ण, तीव्र, उचंड, वेगवत्.

RAIL, *v. i.* अव-आ-अधि-क्षिप् 6 P, अप-भाष् 1 A, अपवद् 1 A, आक्रुश् 1 P, शप् 1, 4 U, गर्ह् 1, 10 A, निंद् 1 P, भर्त्स् 10 A; 'r. ing words' आक्षेपवादः, गर्हणा, निंदावचः. -*v. t.* लोहस्तंभैः परिवृ 5 U or परिवेष्ट् 1 A or c., निरुध् 7 U. -*s.* लोहशंकुः-शलाकाक्रुला; 'r.-way,' 'r.-road' लोहपथः-मार्गः. -ER, *s.* अवक्षेपकः, निंदकः, निर्भर्त्सकः, अपवादकः, आक्रोशकः. -ING, *s.* लोहावरणं, लोहशलाकावृति *f.* 2 अव-आ-क्षेपः, आक्रोशः, निंदा, निर्भर्त्सना, गर्हणा, अपवादः, उपालंभः, अपभाषणं, तिरस्कारः.

RAIMENT, *s.* वस्त्रं, वसनं, वासस् *n.*, अंबरं, आच्छादनं, वेशः-षः, परिच्छदः; *See* CLOTH, GARMENT ; 'food and r.' ग्रासाच्छादनं, अन्नवस्त्रं.

RAIN, *s.* वृष्टि *f.*, वर्ष:-र्षं, पर्जन्यः ; 'gentle r.' शीकरासारः ; 'heavy r.' अतिवृष्टिः ; 'shower of r.' धारासंपातः, धारासारः ; (r. s) वर्षाः *f.* (pl.), प्रावृष् *f.*, वर्ष-मेघ-घन-समयः-कालः, मेघागमः, तपात्ययः, वर्षाकालः ; 'r.-bow' इंद्रधनुस् *n.*, इंद्रचापं, and similar comp. ; सुरधनुः, इंद्रायुधं ; 'r.-fall' वर्ष-वृष्टि-पातः ; 'r.-water' वृष्टि-वर्ष-जलं. -*v. i.* वृष् 1 P, (the subject being 'Indra' 'Sky' or 'Cloud'), जलं सृ or पत् 1 P; 'when it was r. ing gently' मंदं मंदं वर्षति जलधरे-गगने-वासवे, &c. ; 'it r. ed in torrents' धारासारैर्वृष्टिर्बभूव ; 'to r. off', 'cease to r.' विवृष्. -*v. t.* वृष्, जलं सृ c. -Y, *a.* वृष्टिमत्, वर्षिन्, प्रावृषिक (की *f.*) ; 'a r. day' दुर्दिनं ; 'r. season' वर्षाः, प्रावृट् ; *See* (*s.*).

RAISE, *v. t.* उत्-स्था c. (उत्थापयति), in all senses ; उत्तुल् 10, उन्नी 1 P, उच्छ्रि 1 U, उत्कृष् 1 P ; उत्क्षिप् 6 P, उद्यम् 1 A, उन्नम् c. (नमयति), उद्-ह्-धृ 1 P, उद्-हन् 2 P ; आत्मोद्धतैरपि रजोभिः (S. 1) 'r. ed by themselves' ; आ-अधि-रुह् c.; oft. ex. by उत् in comp. ; 'having r. ed his neck' उत्कंधरः ; उन्मुखः &c.; 'r. ing both his arms' बाहू उद्यम्य. 2 उन्नम् c., उत्कृष्, उच्छ्रि, पदवृद्धिं कृ 8 U, प्रतिपत्तिं प्राप् c., उत्कृष्टपदे नियुज् 7 A, 10. 3 (Doubt, anger, &c.) उत्पद् c., जन् c., प्रवृत् c., उत्था c.; *See* CAUSE. 4 वृध् c., *See* INCREASE ; (building) निर्मा 3 A, 2 P, रच् 10 ; (tax) ग्रह् 9 P; *See* LEVY; 'to r. one's voice' उच्चैः-तारस्वरेण-वद् 1 P; 'r. a cry' उत्क्रुश् 1 P, उद्-घुष् 10 ; 'r. dust' रजः उद्धन्, उद्-धू 5, 9 U, 6 P ; 'r. a siege' अवरोधं त्यज् 1 P or मुच् 6 P. -ED, *a.* उत्थापित, उच्छ्रित, उन्नत, उन्नामित, उद्यत, उत्थित, उद्धत ; उत्पन्न, जात, जनित; oft. by उत्, उद्यत, उच्छ्रित in comp.; 'having the arms r.' उद्बाहुः &c. -ING, *s.* उत्थापनं, उन्नयनं, उन्नति *f.*, उत्क्षेपः, &c.

RAISIN, *s.* शुष्कद्राक्षा.

RAKE, *s.* विटः, लंपटः, व्यसनिन् *m.*, खंडितवृत्तः ; *See* LIBERTINE. 2 दंतच्छुरिका-कर्तरिका. -*v. t.* समाहृ 1 P, संग्रह् 9 P, सं-चि 5 U. 2 पुनर्जीव् c.; उज्जीव् c. -*v. i.* व्यभिचर् 1 P, लंपटवत् आचर् 1 P, भोगासक्त्या आयुः गम् c. -ISH, *a.* व्यसनिन्, लंपट, भोगासक्त, विषयसुखनिरत.

RALLY, *v. i.* एकत्र-सं-भू 1 P, संमिल् 6 P, व्यूहीभू; *See* ASSEMBLE. 2 (Fig.) सुस्थ-*a.* भू ; प्रकृतिं आ-पद् 4 A, प्रकृतौ स्था 1 P, समुत्था, बलं लभ् 1 A. -*v. t.* एकत्र आनी or समाहृ 1 P, पुनः व्यूह् 1 U or क्रमेण विन्यस् 4 U or विरच् 10. 2 Jest, q. v.

RAM, *s.* मेषः, उरभ्रः, उरणः, अविः, एडकः, मेढ्रः, ऊर्णायुः, वृष्णिः, हुडुः, लोमशः ; 'a flock of r. s' औरभ्रं. 2 (Sign) मेषः, मेषराशिः. -*v. t.* बलात् अतिबलेन प्र-नि-विश् c. or प्रणुद् c., or संपीड् 10 'R.-rod', 'battering-r.' चूर्णप्रणोदनी यष्टिः.

RAMBLE, *v. i.* परि-अट् 1 P, परिभ्रम् 1, 4 P; विहृ 1 P, इतस्ततः चर् 1 P or भ्रम् ; 'r. ing from the subject' अप्रस्तुतालापः. -*s.* परिभ्रमणं, पर्यटनं, विहारः, विहरणं. -ER, *s.* पर्यटनशीलः, पथिकः, भ्रमणकारिन्.

RAMIFY, *v. i.* शाखाप्रतिशाखारूपेण विस्तॄ pass., उपशाखारूपेण विभिद् pass. -*v. t.* बहुशाखीकृ 8 U. -IED, *a.* शाखिन्, सूक्ष्मशाखामय (यी *f.*), शाखाप्रतिशाखारूपेण विस्तीर्ण. -ICATION. *s.* प्र-प्रति-शाखा, सूक्ष्म-उप-शाखा.

RAMMER, *a.* मुद्गरः, घनः, अयोघनः.

RAMMISH, *a.* उग्र-तीक्ष्ण-गंध.

RAMOUS, *a.* शाखिन्, शाखाबहुल.

RAMP, *v. i.* प्लु 1 A, वल्ग् 1 P. -*s.* प्लुति *f.*, प्लुतं, वल्गितं; *See* LEAP. —RAMPANT, *a.* अनियंत्रित, निरवग्रह, निर्यंत्रण, उच्छृंखल. 2 अतिरिक्त, उद्रिक्त, उत्सिक्त, अतिमर्याद. 3 पश्चात्पादयोः स्थित. -RAMPANCY, *s.* अनियंत्रणा, अतिरेकः, उत्सेकः, अतिक्रमः, उत्क्रमः.

RAMPART, *s.* प्राकारः, वप्रः-प्रं, वरणः, सालः ; *See* FENCE.

RANCID, *a.* उग्र-तीक्ष्ण-रस-गंध, विरस, पूतिगंधि.

RANCOUR, *s.* अभिद्रोहः, विद्वेषः, अतिद्वेषः-द्रोहः, अतिमात्सर्यं; *See* MALICE. -OUS, *a.* अभिद्रुग्ध, विद्वेषिन्, अति-दीर्घ-द्वेषिन्-द्रोहिन्, द्रोह-मत्सर-बुद्धि. 2 जिघांसु; विषपूर्ण, दंशशील. -OUSLY, *adv.* सद्वेषं, अतिद्रोहेण.

RANDOM, *a.* आकस्मिक-यादृच्छिक (की *f.*), अनियत, अयंत्रित, संधानहीन, दैवादागत, अतर्कितोपनत, सहसा उत्पन्न; 'at r.' अकस्मात्, यदृच्छया, निःसंधानं, अविचार्य, सहसा, असंबद्धं, अनियतं, उच्छृंखलं; अव्यवस्थया, अक्रमेण; 'talk at r.' अक्रमेण जल्प् or वद् 1 P, (जल्पतोरक्रमेण U. 1); 'oh ! how he lies at r. carelessly diffused on the ground' हा हा कथं धरणीपृष्ठे निरुत्साहनिःसहं विपर्यस्तः (U. 3).

RANDY, *a. See* DISORDERLY.

RANGE, *s.* राजिः, श्रेणिः-णी, माला, पंक्तिः, ततिः, आवलिः-ली, आलिः-ली, वीथिः-थी, (all *f.*). 2 गणः, वर्गः, वर्णः. 3 परिभ्रमणं, पर्यटनं. 4 सोपानं, आरोहणं. 5 विषयः, पथिन् *m.*, गोचरः in comp.; 'beyond the r. of sight' चक्षुर्विषयं-नयनगोचरं अतीत्य or अतीत; 'within the r. of hearing' श्रुतिपथे-विषये-गोचरे; 'beyond the r.' अविषये, अविषय-विषयातीत- *a.*; 'r. of an arrow' शरपातः, बाणविषयः. -*v. i.* परिभ्रम् 1, 4 P, विचर् 1 P, विहृ 1 P (for diversion); 'r. about' इतस्ततो भ्रम्,

पर्यट् 1 P. 2 स्था 1 P, वृत् 1 A; *See* BE. –*v. t.* विन्यस् 4 U, क्रमेण रच् 10, व्यूह् 1 U. –ER, *s.* लुब्धकः, व्याधः. 2 वनग्राहिन् *m.*, वनपालः.

RANK, *s.* श्रेणि-णी *f.*, पंक्ति *f.*, राजि *f.*; *See* RANGE, LINE. 2 (Of an army) व्यूहः, दंडः, सैन्यपंक्तिः-विन्यासः. 3 वर्गः, वर्णः, गणः. 4 पदं, स्थानं, आस्पदं, वृत्ति *f.*, स्थिति *f.* 5 प्रतिष्ठा, मानः, गौरवं, उत्कर्षः, उन्नति *f.*, प्रतिपत्ति *f.*, प्राधान्यं, उच्च-परम-पदं-पदवी, कुलोत्कर्षः, आभिजात्यं; 'a man of high r.' प्रतिपत्तिमत्, अभिजात, कुलीन, उच्चपदभाक्. –*v. i.* समान-तुल्य- *a.* वृत् 1 A or स्था 1 P; पंक्तिक्रमेण स्था. –*v. t.* पंक्तिक्रमेण न्यस् 4 U or रच् 10, वर्गक्रमेण रच्; oft. ex. by वर्ग-पक्ष-स्था c. or गण्-कृत्-10, (दृष्टिपातमप्युपकारपक्षे स्थापयंति Ka. 108); 'fit to be r. ed first' धुरि प्रतिष्ठापयितव्य or कीर्तनीय. 2 तुल्य-सम- *a.* मन् 4 A. –*a.* प्रभूत, प्रचुर, विपुल, अतिस्फीत, अतिरिक्त, उद्रिक्त. 2 उग्रगंध, पूतिगंधि, तीक्ष्णगंध. –NESS, *s.* उद्रेकः, अतिस्फीति-वृद्धि *f.*, अतिरेकः, प्रचुरवृद्धिः. 2 उग्रता, तीक्ष्णता.

RANKLE, *v. i.* उद्दीप् 4 A; उग्रतर-तीक्ष्णतर- *a.* भू 1 P; oft. ex. by शल्यं; 'those words r. in my heart' तद्वचो मम हृदये शल्यं जातं, शल्यमिव हृदये प्रत्युप्तं; 'I r. in his eyes' अक्षिगतोहं तस्य. 2 अंतः पूय् 1 A or पूतीभू; 'the wound r. ed' स प्रहारः करालतां गतः (P. IV. 3).

RANSACK, *v. t.* लुंट्-ठ् 1 P, 10; *See* PLUNDER. 2 निपुणं-सूक्ष्मं-आन्विष् 4 P or मृग् 10 A.

RANSOM, *s.* निष्क्रयः; उद्धारः, निस्तारः, मुक्ति *f.*, मोक्षः; निस्तार-परिक्रय-मूल्यं. –*v. t.* मूल्यं-धनं-दत्वा मुच् c. or उद्धृ 1 P or निस्तृ c., निष्क्री 9 U, परिक्री 9 A. –ER, *s.* निस्तारकः, निष्क्रेतृ *m.*

RANT, *s.* निरर्थक-निरर्गल-प्रलापः, शब्दमात्रं वाक्यं. –*v. i.* उच्चैः स्वरेण प्रलप् 1 P, शब्दपांडित्यं कृ 8 U. –ER, *s.* प्रलापिन् *m.*

RAP, *v. t.* तीव्रं प्रहृ 1 P or तड् 10 or अभिहन् 2 P. 2 अप-,हृ 1 P; ग्रह् 9 P, चित्तं-मनः-आकृष् 1 P or ग्रह्. –*s.* तीव्रप्रहारः-आघातः. —RAPACIOUS, *a.* अति-,लुब्धक, अपहारिन्, अपहरणशील, ग्रसनबुद्धि, सर्वहारिन्-ग्राहिन्, साहसिक (की *f.*). –LY, *adv.* प्रसह्य, प्रसभं, बलात्; अपहारबुद्ध्या, अतिलोभेन. –NESS,-RAPACITY, *s.* साहसिकता, आततायित्वं, अपहारशीलता, अपहरणबुद्धि *f.* 2 लुब्धता, अतिलोभः. –RAPT, *a.* हर्षोन्मत्त ; परमहृष्ट, अत्यानंदित; (for 'wrapt') पर, लीन, निमग्न in comp. —RAPTURE, *s.* हर्षोन्मादः, आनंदातिरेकः, हर्षावेशः, अत्यंतहर्षः, प्रहर्षः, उन्मादः. –ED, *a.* हर्षोन्मत्त, उन्मत्त. –OUS, *a.* उन्मत्त, परमहर्षद, मोहन; 'r. joy' परमानंदः. –OUSLY, *adv.* सोन्मादं, परमहर्षेण; *See* ECSTASY.

RAPE, *s.* अप-,हरणं, 2 दूषणं, बलात्कारेण-बलात्-रतं-संभोगः; हठसंभोगः, आधर्षः-र्षणं, बलात्कारः, स्त्रीसंग्रहः; 'to commit r.' बलात्कारेण रम् 1 A or अभिगम् 1 P or संगम् 1 A, आधृष् c.

RAPID, *a.* शीघ्र, द्रुत, क्षिप्र, लघु. –ITY,-NESS, *s.* त्वरा, वेगः, तरस् *n.*; द्रुतता. –LY, *adv.* शीघ्रं, सत्वरं, द्रुतं. *See* QUICK,-LY &c.

RAPIER, *s.* छुरिका, कर्तरिका, क्षुद्रकृपाणः.

RAPINE, *s.* *See* PLUNDER, PILLAGE.

RARE, *a.* विरल, दुर्लभ, दुष्प्राप, अप्राप्य, असुलभ; 'of r. occurrence' विरल, विरलदृष्ट. 2 अपूर्व, अदृष्टपूर्व, परम, अत्युत्तम, अतुल्य, अत्युत्कृष्ट. 3 विरल. सूक्ष्म, अघन. –LY, *adv.* विरलं, क्वचित्, कृच्छ्रेण, कथमपि, कष्टेन, दुर् pr.; oft. ex. by (*a.*); 'r. to be found' दुष्प्राप, दुर्लभ ; 'r. to be seen' दुर्लभदर्शन. –NESS, *s.* विरलता, दुष्प्रापता, दुर्लभत्वं. 2 अपूर्वता, अत्युत्तमता. 3 सूक्ष्मता. –RARITY, *s.* अपूर्वं वस्तु, चमत्कारः, कौतुकं, दुर्लभवस्तु. 2 Rareness, q. v. –RAREFY, *v. i.* सूक्ष्मी-तनू-विरली-भू 1 P. –*v. t.* तनूकृ 8 U, विरलीकृ.

RASCAL, *s.* धूर्तः, दुर्जनः, जाल्मः, शठः, कितवः, दुरात्मन् *m.*, दुर्वृत्तः, खलः, पापात्मा, निंद्यचरितः, अधम-जघन्य-वृत्तिः. –ITY, *s.* धूर्तता, दौर्जन्यं, दौरात्म्यं, कैतवं, शाठ्यं, खलता, पापवृत्ति *f.*, अधम-नीच-वर्तनं. –LY, *a.* *See* (*s.*).

RASE, *v. t.* प्रमृज् 2 P or c., विलुप् c. ; घृष् 1 P, उल्लिख् 6 P. 2 भूमिसात्कृ 8 U; *See* RAZE, ERASE. –URE, *s.* प्रमार्जनं, विलोपनं.

RASH, *a.* क्षिप्र-अविमृश्य-असमीक्ष्य-कारिन्, अविवेकिन्, अपरिणामदर्शिन्, साहसिन्, साहसिक (की *f.*), अदूरदर्शिन्, असावधान. 2 (Of acts) असमीक्ष्य &c. कृत; अविमृष्ट, सरभस, साहसिक, अविचार-असमीक्षा-पूर्व ; better ex. by 'r.-ly.' –*s.* Eruption, Pimple, q. v. –LY, *adv.* असमीक्ष्य, अविमृश्य, सहसा, अविवेकेन, अविचार्य, अनालोच्य, अनवेक्षा-अविवेक-पूर्वं, सरभसं, क्षिप्रं, उत्तापेन, सावेगं. –NESS, *s.* असमीक्ष्य-अविमृश्य-कारिता, साहसं, अविवेकः, अविचारः, असमीक्षा, अनवेक्षा, रभसः, आवेगः, उत्तापः.

RASHER, *s.* (वल्लूर) खंडः, छेदः.

RASP, *s.* सं-,घर्षणी. –*v. t.* घर्षण्या घृष् 1 P.

RAT, *s.* आखुः, मूष(षि)कः, बिलेशयः, छुंदुरः, खनिकः ; 'I smell a r.' किमप्यनिष्टं-अशुभं-आशंकते मे मनः. –*v. i.* कार्यात् अन्यपक्षं अवलंब् 1 A or आश्रि 1 U.

RATAN, *s.* वेतसः, वेणुः, वेत्रः-त्रं, वानीरः, वंजुलः ; 'crackling r.' कीचकः.

RATE, *s.* मूल्यं, अर्घः, मूल्य-अर्घ-प्रमाणं, वस्नः, अवक्रयः. 2 मानं, प्र-परि-°. 3 वेगः, गति *f.*, गतिमानं-प्रमाणं. 4 नियत-निरूपित-मूल्यं-वेतनं. 5 करः, शुल्कं,

बलि: ; 'at any r.' येन केन प्रकारेण ; तावत् ; 'market-r.' आपणिक:; अर्घबलाबलं. -*v. t.* अर्घ-मूल्यं-निर्णी 1 P or सं-स्था c. (स्थापयति) or निरूप् 10 or सं-ख्या c. 2 प्रमाणं निरूप् ; oft. ex. by गण् 10, मन् 4 A ; *See* CONSIDER. 3 निंद् 1 P, उपालभ् 1 A ; *See* REPROACH.

RATHER, *adv.* Ex. by वरं with न च-न पुन: ; for 'than' ; *See* PREFER ; 'I would r. die than be disgraced' वरं मृत्युर्न पुनरपमान: ; 'I had r. not go there' वरं तत्र न गत एव, यदि न गच्छेयं तर्हि वरं-श्रेय:-स्यात्. 2 ईषत्, किंचित्, किमपि, किंचिदिव ; 'r. less' ईषदून, किंचिन्न्यून.

RATIFY, *v. t.* स्थिरीकृ 8 U, दृढीकृ, सत्याकृ, द्रढयति-सत्यापयति (D.), संस्तंभ् 9 P or c., प्रमाणीकृ. -IER, *s.* सत्यापक:, संस्तंभक:. -ICATION, *s.* स्थिरी-दृढी-करणं, संस्तंभनं, सत्यापनं, सत्यंकार:.

RATIO, *s.* संबंध:, प्रमाणं.

RATIOCINATE, *v. i.* युक्तिपूर्वं-सहेतुकं-उपपद् c. or विचर् c. or वितर्क् 10 ; *See* ARGUE. -ION, *s.* वितर्क:, विचार:, युक्तिवाद:.

RATION, *s.* अन्नपरिमाणं, आहारांश:, निरूपिताहारभाग:.

RATIONAL, *a.* विचारवत्, सचेतन, सचेतस्, विवेकिन्, सज्ञान, व्युत्पत्तिमत्, व्युत्पन्न, प्रतिबोधवत्, चिच्छक्ति-ज्ञानशक्ति-संपन्न. 2 युक्त, उपपन्न, सयुक्तिक, न्याय्य, यथोचित, यथायोग्य, न्यायानुरूप, युक्तिसिद्ध, उपपत्तिमत्, न्यायानुसारिन्. -ISM, *s.* हेतु-कारण-वाद:, हैतुकत्वं. -IST, *s.* हेतु-न्याय-वादी, हैतुक:. -ITY,-NESS, *s.* ज्ञानशक्ति *f.*, चिच्छक्ति:, ज्ञानं, अव-प्रति-बोध:, चेतनत्वं, तर्क-विचार-शक्ति:. 2 युक्तता, न्याय्यता, उपपत्ति *f.* -LY, *adv.* न्यायत:, युक्तिपूर्वं, न्यायानुसारेण, तर्क-विवेक-द्वारेण. -RATIONALE, *s.* उपपत्ति:.

RATTLE, *v. i.* क्वण्-ध्वन्-स्वन्-रण् 1 P, शिंज् 2 A, वि-रु 2 P, झणझणायते (D.); (as a wheel) संक्रीड् 1 P, (संक्रीडति चक्रं S. K.). 2 प्रजल्प् 1 P, प्रलप् 1 P. -*v. t.* Causal of roots above. -ING, *s.* क्वणनं, शिंजितं, ध्वनि:, क्वणितं, वि-,राव:, झणझणायितं ; संक्रीडितं. 2 प्रलपितं, प्रजल्पनं. 3 (Instrument) शिंजिनी, क्वणनी.

RAVAGE, *v. t.* वि-उप-प्लु 1 A, उप-द्रु 1 P, प्र-सं-बाध् 1 A, अव-मृद् 9 P, उच्छिद् 7 P, विनश् c., उद्-ध्वंस् c. -*s.* वि-उप-प्लव:, संबाधा, उपद्रव:, अवमर्द:, उच्छेद:, विनाश:, उद्ध्वंस:. -ER, *s.* उपप्लवकारिन् *m.*, प्र-सं-बाधक:, अवमर्दक:, उच्छेदक:.

RAVE, *v. i.* (भ्रमात्-उन्मत्तवत्) प्रलप् 1 P, प्रजल्प् 1 P, बुद्धिभ्रमेण वद् 1 P. 2 उन्मद् 4 P, नष्टचेतन-बुद्धिभ्रष्ट-*a.* भू 1 P. -ING, *s.* वि-भ्रमप्रलाप:; चित्तविप्लव:-विभ्रम:, चैतन्यनाश:. -INGLY, *adv.* उन्मत्तवत्, भ्रांतचेतसा, बुद्धिभ्रमेण.

RAVEL, *v. t.* संग्रंथ् 9 P, संश्लिष् c., जटिलीकृ 8 U; *See* ENTANGLE. 2 विश्लिष् c., उद्-ग्रंथ्. -ING, *s.* विश्लिष्टतंतु:.

RAVEN, *s.* द्रोणकाक:, काकोल:. -*v.* गृध् 4 P, अतिलोभेन भक्ष् 10 or ग्रस् 1 A. -OUS, *a.* घस्मर, अतिक्षुधार्त-क्षुधातुर, अतिलोलुप, आमिषलोलुप, अतिबुभुक्षु. -OUSLY, *adv.* अतिघस्मरवत्, अतिलोलुपतया.

RAVINE, *s.* कंदर:, दरीभू:, दरी, द्रोणी.

RAVISH, *v. t.* प्रसह्य-बलात्कारेण-अभिगम् 1 P or भुज् 7 A or रम 1 A, आ-प्र-धृष् c., दुष् c. (दूषयति), परा-परि-मृश् 6 P; *See* RAPE. 2 बलाद् अपहृ 1 P or नी 1 P. 3 (चित्तं) हृ, आकृष् 1 P, मुह् c., वि-लुभ् c., अत्यंतं-परमं-आनंद् c. or हृष् c.; *See* ATTRACT. -ER, *s.* आ-,धर्षक:, हठदूषक:, अपहर्ता. -ING, *s.* धर्षणं, बलसंभोग:, संग्रह:; *See* RAPE. -*a.* हारिन्, मोहिन्, चित्ताकर्षिन् ; हारिणा गीतरागेण (S. 1) 'by the r. melody of song'. -MENT, *s.* अपहरणं. धर्षणं, दूषणं, &c. 2 हर्षोन्माद:, चित्तमोह:, मनोहरणं.

RAW, *a.* आम, अपक्व, असिद्ध, असंस्कृत. 2 (Fruit) आम, अपक्व, अपरिणत, अकठोर, अप्रौढ. 3 (Mind) अपरिणत, अपरिपक्व, अपक्व; (person) अपरिणत-अकठोर-अपक्व-मति-बुद्धि ; अदृष्टकर्मन् ; not 'Mature' q. v. 4 निश्चर्मन्, त्वग्रहित. 5 आर्द्रशीतल. 6 जलामिश्रित, असंसृष्ट; 'r. flesh' क्रव्यं; आमामिषं; 'smell of r. flesh' विस्रं, आमगंध:; 'r. fruit' शलाटु *m. f. n.* -NESS, *s.* अपाक:, आमता, अपरिणाम:, अपरिपाक:; अपक्वबुद्धित्वं, मत्यपरिपाक: &c.

RAY, *s.* किरण:, कर:, रश्मि:, अंशु:, उस्र:, पाद:, मयूख:, मरीचि:, दीधिति:, गभस्ति:, धामन् *n.*, घृणि:, भानु:, अभीशु:-षु:; 'a pencil of r. s' अंशुजालं.

RAZE, *v. t.* उच्छिद् 7 P, अवसद् c., निपत् c., ध्वंस् c., विनश् c.; उन्मूल् 10, उद्धृ 1 P; *See* ERASE also; 'r. to the ground' भूमिसात्कृ 8 U. -URE, *s.* उच्छेद:, विनाश:, विध्वंस:.

RAZOR, *s.* क्षुर:; 'r.-case' क्षुरभांडं; 'r.-strop' क्षुरतेजनी.

RE, as a prefix of verbs, ex. by पुनर् or प्रति; 're-consider' पुन: विचर् c. ; 're-fill' पुन: पूर् 10, &c.

REACH, *v. t.* आप् 5 P, आ-समा-सद् c., उपा-आ-गम् 1 P or या 2 P, प्रति-प्र-पद् 4 A; *See* ARRIVE. 2 अधिगम्, अश् 5 A, विद् 6 U, लभ् 1 A; *See* GET. 3 (Hand) प्र-सृ c., दा 3 U, उच्छ्रि 1 U. 4 (Extend to) व्याप्, या, गम्; प्रसृ 1 P, विस्तृ-वितन्- pass.; oft. ex. by पर्यंत, प्रमाण, in comp.; (in height) मात्र (त्री *f.*), दघ्न (घ्नी *f.*), द्वयस (सी *f.*); वृत्तांतेन श्रवणविषयप्रापिणा (R. XIV. 87) 'by the account r. ing (her) ears'; इदं प्रायेण कल्याणाभिनिवेशिन: श्रुतिविषयमापतितमेव (Ka.

136) 'must have probably r. ed the ears of' &c. **—***s.* गोचरः, विषयः, पथिन् *m.* **2** प्रसरः, पर्यंतः, प्रमाणं; 'the utmost r.' पारः; 'within the r. of' गम्य, ग्राह्य, लभ्य, विषय in comp.; धी-गम्य, हस्तप्राप्य, प्रांशुलभ्य, &c.; 'beyond the r. of' अविषय, अतीत, अतिग, विषयातीत, अगोचर, अ-ग्राह्य, अगम्य in comp.; अति pr.; बोधातीत, नयना-गोचर, बोधविषय, अतिमानुष, &c. **—ING,** *a.* गामिन्, प्रापिन्, ग in comp.; better by (*v.*).

REACT, *v. i.* प्रति-कृ 8 U, प्रतिहन् 2 P, प्रत्याहन्. **—ION,** *s.* प्रतिक्रिया, प्रतिकारः; प्रतिघातः, प्रत्याघातः.

READ, *v.* पठ् 1P, वच् c.; अधि-इ 2 A, अधिगम् 1 P; 'r. out' निर्वच् c., श्रु c.; 'r. to oneself' अनु-वच् c.; 'r. through' अशेषतः पठ्, पारं गम् or दृश् 1 P, सार्वतं पठ्, तॄ 1 P; 'he who has r. through the Vedas' श्रुतिपारदृश्वा, वेदपारंगत; 'well-r.' अधीतिन्, (अधीती चतुर्ष्वाम्नायेषु D. K. II. 5), स्वधीत, विद्यासंपन्न; *See* LEARNED. **—ER,** *s.* वाचकः, पठितृ *m.*, अध्येता, अधीयानः, अध्ययन-पठन-कृत् *m.* **—ING,** *s.* पाठः, पठनं, अध्ययनं, अधि-गमनं, वाचनं, अनुवाचनं, श्रावणं; 'this is a various r.' इति वा पाठः, पाठांतरमेतत्, पाठभेदोयं; 'r. through' पारायणं, अशेषपठनं; 'suspension of r.' अनध्यायः, अनध्ययनं.

READY, *a.* सज्ज, सिद्ध, उपकृत, सज्जीभूत-कृत, आ-योजित, उपस्थित; सन्नद्ध; उप-परि-कल्पित; 'to get r.' सज्जीकृ 8 U, उप-परि-क्लृप् c., उप-स्था c., (स-बाणासनं रथमुपस्थापय S. 2), सन्नह् 4 P or c.; *See* PREPARE; 'to be r.' सज्जीभू; (food) सिद्ध, संस्कृत, निष्पन्न. **2** (Of persons) उद्यत, सिद्ध, सज्ज, सन्नद्ध, उद्युक्त, उन्मुख, अभिमुख; oft. by desid.; कूलं पिपतिषति 'is r. to drop down'; 'r. to go' गंतुमुद्यत, गमनोद्यत, गमनोन्मुख; 'stands r. to burst forth' भेदोन्मुखं तिष्ठति (V. 2). **3** प्रत्युत्पन्न, तीक्ष्ण, कुशाग्र, सूक्ष्म, समयोपयुक्त, का-लोचित. **4** शीघ्र, त्वरित, द्रुत, अविलंबित, क्षिप्र; कुशल, निपुण, दक्ष, पटु, लघु. **5** सुकर, सुगम, सुख, अनायासि-न्. **6** उत्सुक, इच्छु, सकाम, oft. ex. by मनः or काम with inf.; 'r. at hand' उपस्थित, हस्तगत, निकटवर्तिन्; 'having r. wit', 'r.-witted' प्र-त्युत्पन्नमति-धी-बुद्धि, विदग्ध. **—ILY,** *adv.* कामं, का-मतः, प्रकामं, इच्छापूर्वं, सोत्साहं, सोत्सुकं. **2** झटिति, शीघ्रं, सपदि, अचिरात्, आशु, अविलंबितं; *See* QUICK-LY. **3** सुखेन, अनायासेन, सुखं, अयत्नेन, अक्लेशेन, सुख in comp. **—INESS,** *s.* सिद्धता, सज्जता, सिद्धि *f.* **2** सकामत्वं, इच्छा, औत्सुक्यं, उत्साहः. **3** अविलंबः, शीघ्र-ता, तीक्ष्णता, सूक्ष्मता, प्रत्युत्पन्नता; दक्षता, &c.

REAL, *a.* सत्य, अवितथ, वास्तविक-तात्विक-(की *f.*), अ-कृत्रिम, परमार्थ, यथार्थ, तथ्य, अकल्पित, अकपट, अ-न्वर्थ. **2** (Property) स्थावर; 'to take to be r.' परमार्थेन ग्रह् 9 P; *See* EARNEST. **—ITY,** *s.* सत्यता, याथार्थ्यं, सत्यं, तथ्यं, तत्त्वं; 'un-r.' मिथ्यात्वं, अ-सारता-त्वं, निःसारता; 'a r.' सत्यं, तत्त्वं, वस्तु *n.*; 'in r.' वस्तुतः, तत्त्वतः, परमार्थतः. **—LY,** *adv.* व-स्तुतः, परमार्थतः, तत्त्वतः, यथार्थं, सत्यमेव, नूनं खलु; 'r. speeking' वस्तुवृत्तेन, परमार्थदृष्ट्या, तत्त्वतः, वस्तुतः. **—REALIZE,** *v. t.* साध् c.; परि-,पूर् 10, सं-पद् c.; *See* GET. **2** प्रत्यक्षीकृ 8 U, सत्याकृ, प्रत्यक्षं अनुभू 1 P. **—ATION,** *s.* साधनं, सिद्धि *f.*, निष्पत्ति *f.*, संपादनं, पूरणं, प्रत्यक्षीकरणं; 'r. of an object' कृतार्थता, इष्टसिद्धिः.

REALM, *s.* राष्ट्रं, विषयः, राज्यं; *See* KINGDOM. **2** प्र-,देशः, लोकः, भुवनं; 'r. s below the earth' अधोलोकः, पाताललोकः, अधोभुवनं.

REAP, *v. t.* (Corn) लू 9 U, छिद् 7 P, अव-कृत् 6 P, दो 4 P; छित्त्वा संग्रह् 9 P or सं-चि 5 U. **2** लभ् 1 A, आप् 5 P, भुज् 7 A, भज् 1 A, अनुभू 1 P, आ-स्वाद् 1 A; स्वकर्मफलभाग् भवतु (Mu. 1) 'let him r. the fruit of his own deeds'; 'as you sow, so you r.' यथा बीजं तथांकुरः. **—ER,** *s.* लवितृ *m.*, लवकः, शस्यच्छिद्, शस्यसंग्रही-संचयी. **—ING,** *s.* लवनं, छेदनं, संग्रहः, संचयः; 'r.-hook' लवित्रं, दात्रं, शस्यकर्तनी.

REAR, *s.* पृष्ठं, पार्ष्णिः, पृष्ठभागः-देशः; 'in the r.' पृष्ठतः, पश्चात्; 'we having fallen in the r.' अस्मास्ववहीनेषु (S. 2). **2** (Of an army) पृष्ठं, पार्ष्णिः, प्रत्यासा (स)रः, सैन्यपृष्ठं, परि-प्रतिं-ग्रहः, पतद्ग्रहः; 'one who attacks the r.' पार्ष्णिग्राहः; 'r.-guard' पार्ष्णित्रं. **—***v. t.* उत्-स्था c. (उत्थाप-यति), उच्छ्री 1 P, उच्छ्रि 1 U, उद्यम् 1 A, उन्नम् c. (उन्नमयति); *See* RAISE. **2** परि-सं-वृध् c., परि-,पुष् 1, 4, 9 P, or c., वि-नी 1 P, प्रति-परि-पा c. (पाल-यति) संभृ 3 U; *See* NOURISH. **—ING,** *s.* उत्था-पनं, उच्छ्रयः, उन्नमनं. **2** पोषणं, भरणं, संवर्धनं, पाल-नं, विनयः.

REASON, *s.* (The faculty) मति-बुद्धि-व्युत्पत्ति *f.*, विवेकः, प्रज्ञा, विचारणाशक्ति *f.*, ज्ञानं, चिच्छक्तिः, तर्क-अनुमान-शक्तिः; *See* INTELLECT. **2** उपपत्ति *f.*, युक्ति *f.*, युक्तता, न्यायः, नाय्यता, सामंजस्यं, याथार्थ्यं, हेतुः. **3** हेतुः, कारणं, निमित्तं, प्रयोजनं, (gen. with loc.); 'for what r.' किंनिमित्तं, कुतः, केन हेतुना, कस्य हेतोः, किमर्थं; 'for this r.' अतः, अनेन हेतुना, अस्मात्कारणात्; 'by reason of' ex. by abl. or instr.; हेतुना, कारणात्, अर्थं; 'for some r.' केनापि कारणेन. **—***v. i.* वि-,तर्क् 10, ऊह् 1 A, अनु-मा 3 A, 2 P, युक्तिवादेन साध् c. or प्रति-पद् c.; विचर् c.; *See* ARGUE; 'r. ing faculty' विवेकः, धीशक्ति *f.*, विचारः. **—ABLE,** *a.* Rational, q. v. **2** युक्त, न्याय्य,

उचित, योग्य, उपपन्न, यथार्थ, न्याय-युक्ति-सिद्ध, यथान्याय; *See* JUST also; 'to be r.' घट् 1 A, उपपद् 4 A, युज् pass. 3 परि-,मित, नियत, अनातिमहत्, नातिगुरु, मर्यादानतिक्रांत. —ABLENESS, *s.* न्याय्यता, औचित्यं, युक्ति *f.*, उपपत्तिः, याथार्थ्यं, युक्तता; परिमितता अनतिक्रमः, &c. —ABLY, *adv.* न्यायतः, युक्तिपूर्वं, सोपपत्तिकं, युक्तितः, यथान्यायं, यथोचितं, न्यायानुसारेण. 2 परिमितं, नियतं. —ER, *s.* तार्किकः, तर्की, नैयायिकः, हेतुवादी, ऊही, विचारकः, न्यायविद्. —ING, *s.* वि-,तर्कः, विचारः, ऊहः-हनं, अध्याहारः, ऊहापोहः, न्यायः, अनुमानं; 'art of r.' तर्कशास्त्रं-विद्या. —LESS, *a.* निर्बुद्धि, ज्ञानहीन. 2 अहेतुक, निष्कारण, अनिमित्त.

REBATE, *v. t. See* BLUNT.

REBEL, *s.* राजद्रोहिन् *m.*, राजापथ्यकारी, राजद्रुह् *m.*, राजप्रतिरोधी. —*v. i.* (राज्ञे) द्रुह् 4 P, अभिद्रुह् (with acc.); व्युत्था 1 A, प्रतियुध् 4 A, राजशासनं लंघ् 1 A, 10 or अतिक्रम् 1 U, 4 P. —LION, *s.* प्रकृतिकोपः, राजाभिद्रोहः, प्रजा-प्रकृति-क्षोभः-प्रकोपः, आज्ञा-शासन-अतिक्रमः-उल्लंघनं. —LIOUS, *a.* राजद्रुह्, राजापथ्यकारिन्, राजाभिद्रोहिन्, &c.; *See* MUTINY,-EER, &c.

REBOUND, *v. t.* उत्पत् 1 P, (पातितोपि कराघातैरुत्पतत्येव कंदुकः); उत्प्लु 1 A, प्रतिहन् pass. —*s.* उत्पतनं, प्रतिघातः.

REBUFF, *v. t.* प्रति-परा-हन् 2 P; पराभू 1 P, पराजि 1 A. 2 प्रत्यादिश् 6 P, निराकृ 8 U. —*s.* प्रतिघातः; पराभवः; पराजयः; प्रत्यादेशः; *See* REPULSE.

REBUKE, *v. t.* निंद् 1 P, उपालभ् 1 A, आक्रुश् 1 P, गर्ह् 1, 10 A, निर्-,भर्त्स् 10 A. —*s.* निंदा, उपालंभः, निर्भर्त्सना, आक्रोशः; वाग्दंडः; *See* CENSURE.

REBUT, *v. t. See* REFUTE, REPEL.

RECALL, *v. t.* प्रत्याह्वे 1 P, नि-प्रत्या-वृत् c., प्रत्यानी 1 P, प्रत्यादा 3 A. 2 (To mind) स्मृ 1 P, अनुचिंत् 10. 3 वि-लुप् 6 P or c., निवृत् c., प्रत्यानी, खंड् 10, निरस् 4 U, प्रत्यादिश् 6 P. —*s.* प्रत्याह्वानं, निवर्तनं, प्रत्यानयनं, प्रत्यादानं.

RECANT, *v. t.* प्रत्या-ख्या 2 P, प्रत्यादिश् 6 P, खंड् 10, विलुप् c. —ATION, *s.* प्रत्याख्यानं, प्रत्यादेशः, खंडनं, विलोपः, विपरीतवादः.

RECAPITULATE, *v. t.* संक्षेपतः कथ् 10 or वर्ण् 10, विषयसारं वर्ण्, भाषणसारं अनुवद् 1 P. —ION, *s.* संक्षेपतः वर्णनं, संक्षेपेण अनुवादः; (of past events) सिंहावलोकनं.

RECEDE, *v. i.* अपसृ 1 P, अपा-परा-नि-वृत् 1 A, अपसृप् 1 P, अपक्रम् 1 U, 4 P, अपगम् 1 P, अप-याइ 2 P. —ING, *s.* अपसरणं, अपक्रमणं, अपयानं, &c.

RECEIVE, *v. t.* आ-दा 3 A, प्रति-इष् 6 P, ग्रह् 9 P, प्रति-परि-°, प्रति-आ-पद् 4 A, स्वीकृ 8 U, अंगीकृ. 2 आप् 5 P, अधिगम् 1 P, लभ् 1 A; *See* GET. 3 प्रविश् c.; *See* ADMIT. 4 (A guest) प्रत्युद्-गम्-व्रज् 1 P, प्रत्युद्-इ-या 2 P, सं-मन् c., सं-भू c., सत्कृ, आदृ 6 A, स्वागतं वद् 1 P or व्याह् 1 P. 5 आ-धा 3 U, ग्रह्, आ-दा, धृ 1 P, 10. —ED, *a.* आदत्त, आप्त, गृहीत, लब्ध, सत्कृत, संभावित, &c. 2 लोकप्रसिद्ध, अभिमत, प्रचलित, अभ्युपेत; 'r. practice' लोकाचारः, प्रचलितो व्यवहारः; 'r. doctrine' आम्नायः, संप्रदायः. —ER,-RECIPIENT, *s.* प्रतिग्राहकः, परि-प्रति-ग्राहिन्, ग्रहीता, आदाता, प्रतीच्छकः. 2 आशयः, आधारः, भाजनं, नि-आ-धानं. —RECEIPT, *s.* आदानं, ग्रहणं, प्राप्ति *f.* 2 आयः, लाभः, उदयः, फलं, आगमः, आदायः. 3 स्वीकारपत्रं, अभ्युपगमलेखः, प्रतिग्रहपत्रं-लेखः; 'or the creditor shall give a r. in his own hand' धनी वोपगतं दद्यात् (धनं) स्वहस्तपरिचिह्नितं (Y. II. 93). 4 (Recipe) योगः, कल्पः, संस्कारलेखः. —RECEPTACLE, *s.* आधारः, आ-नि-धानं, भाजनं, आशयः, पात्रं, निधिः, आश्रयः, आस्पदं, पदं; 'r. of bile' पित्ताशयः; आमाशयः, &c. —RECEPTION, *s.* परि-प्रति-ग्रहः, आदानं, ग्रहणं, स्वी-अंगी-कारः, प्रवेशः-शनं. 2 संभावना, उपचारः, प्रत्युद्गमः, सत्कारः, संमानः, आदरः.

RECENT, *a.* नव, अभिनव, नूतन, प्रत्यग्र, अचिर, अप्राचीन, अदीर्घकालीन. —LY, *adv. See* LATELY.

RECESS, *s.* विविक्तं स्थानं, निगूढस्थानं; कोणः, निभृत-गुप्त-स्थानं. 2 निर्वृति-विश्राम-स्थानं, आरामः. 3 विरामः, विश्रांति *f.*, क्षणः, कार्यत्यागः-निवृत्ति *f.*, विश्रामः, विश्रामकालः.

RECIPROCAL, *a.* अन्योन्य, परस्पर, इतरेतर, व्यतिकर, मिथः, in comp.; oft. ex. by व्यति pr.; *See* MUTUAL. 2 अन्योन्यानुगामिन्, परस्परानुवर्तिन्, अनुपूर्व. —LY, *adv.* परस्परं, इतरेतरं, मिथः. —NESS, —RECIPROCITY, *s.* परस्परता, व्यतिकरः, व्यतिषंगः, व्यति(ती)हारः, विनिमयः, परि(री)वर्तः. —RECIPROCATE, *v. t.* परस्परं परिवृत् c., विनि-मे 1 A, व्यतिहृ 1 P; 'to r. assistance' प्रत्युपकृ 8 U; *See* EXCHANGE. —ION, *s.* विनिमयः, व्यतिहारः, परिवर्तः.

RECITE, *v. t.* पठ् 1 P, उदीर् c. उच्चर् c., अनुवद् 1 P, उदाहृ 1 P, उद्-गृ 6 P. 2 वर्ण् 10, कथ् 10, आ-ख्या 2 P, व्याहृ; *See* TELL. —AL,-ATION, *s.* पठनं, उदाहारः, उद्गारः, उच्चारणं, अनुवादः. 2 कथनं, आख्यानं, वर्णनं. —ER, *s.* पठकः, अनुवादकः, उच्चारकः, आख्यायकः.

RECK, *v. i.* गण् 10, अवेक्ष् 1 A; *See* CARE. —LESS, *a.* प्रमत्त, अनवहित, असावधान, निरपे(वे)क्ष, साहसिन्. —LESSLY, *adv.* असावधानं, प्रमादेन, निःशंकं, अविचार्य. —LESSNESS, *s.* प्रमादः, अनवधानं, साहसं, साहसशीलता.

RECKON, *v. t.* गण् 10, परि-,सं-ख्या 2 P, कल् 10 (कलयति). 2 मन् 4 A, गण्, भू c. –*v. i.* वि-,तर्क् 10, अनु-मा 3 A, 2 P, ऊह् 1 A. 2 मन्, बुध् 1 P, *See* CONSIDER; 'r. upon' आ-अव-लंब् 1 A, आश्रि 1 U, विश्वस् 2 P; 'r. with' देयं परिशुध् c. –ER, *s.* गणकः, गणयितृ *m.* –ING, *s.* गणनं-ना, परि-,संख्यानं. 2 गणनापत्रं. 3 व्ययपत्रं. 4 मानं, गणना, मात्रा.

RECLAIM, *v. t.* सत्पथे-सन्मार्गे-प्रवृत् c. or नी 1 P, or नियुज् 7 A, 10, दुर्मार्गात्-दुष्कर्मणः-नि-परा-वृत् c. or विरम् c., दुर्मार्गं त्यज् c. 2 कृषियोग्य- *a.* कृ 8 U. 3 पुनः लभ् 1 A or ग्रह् 9 P. –RECLAMATION, *s.* पापनिवृत्ति *f.*, दुर्मार्गपरावर्तनं; कुपथत्यागः. 2 पुनर्ग्रहणं, पुनर्लाभः-अवाप्ति *f.*

RECLINE, *v. i.* अव-आ-लंब् 1 A, समा-आ-श्रि 1 U. 2 शी 2 A, सं-उप-विश् 6 P, आस् 2 A; अध्यास्, अधिशी (with acc.); निषद् 1 P, विश्रम् 4 P; *See* LIE. –*v. t.* नि-धा 3 U, उप-धा; *See* LEAN. –ING, *a.* आलंबिन्, आश्रित, अवलंबित. 2 आ-अव-नम्र; शयान; संविष्ट, निषण्ण.

RECLUSE, *s.* परिव्राज् *m.*, संन्यासिन् *m.*, विविक्त-एकांत-वासी-सेवी, वानप्रस्थः; 'female r.' परिव्राजिका. –*a.* विविक्त, निर्जन; *See* LONELY. –NESS, *s.* आरण्यकवृत्तं, विविक्तसेवा, परिव्रजनं.

RECOGNIZE, *v. t.* प्रति-,अभि-ज्ञा 9 U, संविद् 2 A, परिच्छिद् 7 P, अनु-स्मृ 1 P, निश्चि 5 U, निर्णी 1 P; 'not properly r. ed' न तत्त्वतः परिच्छिन्नः. 2 स्वी-अंगी-कृ 8 U, प्रति-पद् 4 A, अभ्युपगम् 1 P, अभ्युप-इ 2 P, ग्रह् 9 P, प्रमाणीकृ. –ANCE, *s.* अंगीकारपत्रं, प्रातिभाव्यं, दर्शनप्रातिभाव्यं (r. bond); 'entered into a r. bond' दर्शनप्रतिभुवं ददौ. –RECOGNITION, *s.* प्रति-,अभिज्ञा-ज्ञानं, परिच्छेदः. 2 अंगी-स्वी-कारः, प्रतिपत्ति *f.*, अभ्युपगमः.

RECOIL, *v. i.* वि-परा-वृत् 1 A, व्यपवृत्; परापत् 1 P. –*s.* (अकस्मात्) परा-वि-वर्तः-र्तनं, परापतनं.

RECOLLECT, *v. t.* स्मृ 1 P, अनु-सं-°, अनु-ध्यै 1 P, अनुचिंत् 10, अनुबुध् 4 A, 1 P. 2 (Oneself) धैर्यं अवष्टंभ् 9 P or अवलंब् 1 A; *See* COURAGE; 'he tries to r.' सुस्मूर्षते. –ION, *s.* स्मृति *f.*, स्मरणं, अनुचिंतनं, अनुबोधः; 'I am a sage having r. of my former birth' अहं जातिस्मरः मुनिः (Ka. 355).

RECOMMEND, *v. t.* श्लाघ् 1 A, प्रशंस् 1 P; *See* PRAISE. 2 निक्षिप् 6 P, सं-,ऋ c. (अर्पयति); *See* ENTRUST; स्तुतिपूर्वकं निक्षिप् or उपन्यस् 4 U; or gen. ex. by स्तु 2 U, प्रशंस्; गुणान् प्रशंस्; 'I r. this boy to your care' अयं बालको भवतावेक्षणीय इति मे विनतिः; 'I shall, therefore, r. you to Damayanti' तदहं विदधे तव स्तवं दमयंत्याः सविधे (N. II. 47); 'I beg to r. him to your kind notice' तस्मिन् कृपादृष्टिं पातयतु or तं स्निग्धदृष्ट्या पश्यतु भवान् इति मे प्रार्थना. –ATION, *s.* गुणवर्णनं-प्रशंसा-कीर्तनं. 2 गुणवर्णनपत्रं, प्रशंसालेखः. 3 उपदेशः, अनुशासनं, प्रबोधनं. 4 अनुग्रह-प्रसाद-कारणं, आदरहेतुः 'a fair face is a good r.' आकृतिविशेषेष्वादरः पदं करोति (M. 1). –ATORY, *a.* गुणश्लाघिन्, प्रशंसाकारिन्.

RECOMPENSE, *v. t.* शुध् c., निष्कृ 8 U, प्रतिकृ, प्रतिफलं-निष्कृतिं दा 3 U, निस्तॄ c.; (क्षतिं) पूर् 10 &c.; *See* COMPENSATE. 2 मूल्यं दा; परितुष् c., सं-भू c.; *See* REWARD. –*s.* पारितोषिकं, मूल्यं, प्रतिफलं; निष्कृति *f.*, निस्तारः, शुद्धि *f.*, निर्यातनं, प्रतिक्रिया; पूरणं; क्षतिनिष्कृतिः-पूरणं.

RECONCILE, *v. t.* सं-धा 3 U, सं-घट् c. (घटयति), संमिल् c., द्वेषं-वैरं शम् c. (शमयति), सख्यं कृ 8 U; प्रसद् c., अनुनी 1 P, सांत्व् 10, सं-परि-तुष् c.; 'you are not yet r. ed' नाद्यापि प्रसादं गृह्णासि (M. 4), न अनुनीयसे, प्रसन्ना न भवसि; 'easy to be r. ed' आशुसंधेय. 2 (Statement &c.) विसंवादं-विरोधं-अपनी 1 P or अपा-निरा-कृ, ऐक्यतां-एकवाक्यतां-संगतिं-कृ, समा-धा, प्रतिसमा-धा. 3 (Quarrels &c.) प्रशम् c., सं-धा, निराकृ. –ED, *a.* कृतसंधि, शांतवैर, प्रसादित, एकीकृत; 'to be r.' प्रसद् 1 P, मैत्र्यं गम् 1 P, प्रसादं ग्रह् 9 P, तोषं गम्, संमिल् 6 P. –ER, *s.* संधातृ *m.*, समाधाता, संधिकृत् *m.* –MENT, –RECONCILIATION, *s.* संधान, संघटनं, प्रसादनं, संमेलनं, वैरशमनं, सख्यकरणं. 2 संधिः, सामन् *n.*, वैरशांति *f.*, पुनः सख्यं-मैत्री, सांत्वनं, अनुनयः, ऐक्यं. 3 समाधानं, संगति *f.*, एकवाक्यता, विरोधशमनं.

RECONDITE, *a.* गहन, नि-,गूढ, गूढार्थ, दुर्बोध, रहस्य, दुर्ज्ञेय, गहनार्थ.

RECONNOITRE, *v. t.* निपुणं-सूक्ष्मं-परीक्ष् 1 A or निरूप् 10 or अनुसं-धा 3 U, गवेष् 10.

RECORD, *s.* लेख्यं, लेखः, पत्रं, पत्रकं, पट्टः, लेखप्रमाणं (evidence on r.). –*v. t.* अभि-,लिख् 6 P, लेख्य-पत्रे-आरुह् c. or निविश् c. or ऋ c. (अर्पयति); *See* COMMIT. –ER, *s.* लेखकः, लिपिकारः, कायस्थः (court-officer).

RECOUNT, *v. t.* कथ् 10, आ-ख्या 2 P, वर्ण् 10, निविद् c., परि-,कृत् 10; *See* TELL.

RECOURSE, *s.* आ-सं-उपा-श्रयः. आ-अव-लंबः. 2 शरणं, गति *f.*, (श्रीहरिमें गतिः); 'have r. to' श्रि 1 U, आ-उपा-समा-सं°, आ-स्था 1 P, आ-अव-लंब् 1 A; उपगम् 1 P.

RECOVER, *v. i.* आरोग्यं लभ् 1 A, रोगाद् विमुच् pass.; oft. by निर्, वि, गत in comp.; निर्विषः गौतमः (M. 4.) 'has r. ed from (the effects of) poison'; प्रकृतिं आपद् 4 A, सुस्थ-प्रकृतिस्थ-

a. भू 1 P, रोगमुक्त-निरामय- *a.* भू; पूर्वस्थितिं प्राप् 5 P. 2 (From fainting) संज्ञां-चेतनां-लभ्; *See* below. –*v. t.* (पुनः) लभ्, प्राप्, विद् 6 U, प्रति-आ-पद्; प्रत्यवाप्, प्रत्या-दा 3 A, प्रतिग्रह् 9 P, प्रत्याहृ 1 P, प्रत्युज् 1 P; 'r. consciousness' संज्ञां-चेतनां-लभ् or प्राप्, प्रकृतिं-संज्ञां प्रति-आ-पद्, प्रकृतिस्थ-*a.* भू. 2 रोगं हृ or नश् c. or साध् c. or शम् c., नीरुज-स्वस्थ-*a.* कृ 8 U; *See* CURE; 'she r. ed him from poison' सा तं निर्विषं चकार. –ED, *a.* प्रतिलब्ध, प्रत्याहृत, पुनर्गृहीत, &c. 2. (From sickness) गत-नष्ट-शांत-रोग, नीरोग, निरामय, रोगमुक्त, स्वस्थ, प्रकृतिस्थ, उत्थित; oft. by मुक्त, गत, in comp.; 'r. from fever' ज्वरमुक्त; 'r. from swooning' नष्ट-गत-मोह ; 'r. from poison' निर्विष, &c. 3 (From fainting) लब्ध-संज्ञ-चेतन, प्रकृतिमापन्न, प्रकृतिस्थ, चेतनापन्न. –Y, *s.* पुनर्लाभः, पुनःप्राप्ति *f.*, पुनरादानं, प्रतिपत्ति *f.*, अधिगमनं, प्रत्युद्धारः. 2 स्वास्थ्यलाभः आरोग्यप्राप्तिः, प्रकृतिलाभः, स्वास्थ्यं, निरामयत्वं, आरोग्यं, रोगमुक्ति *f.*

RECREANT, *a.* धर्मभ्रष्ट, त्यक्त-लंघित-स्वधर्म, पतित. 2 कातर, भीरु, क्लीब; *See* COWARD.

RECREATE, *v. t.* (Oneself) विश्रम् 4 P, विहृ 1 P, रम् 1 A, क्रीड् 1 P. 2 आ-समा-प्रत्या-श्वस् c., आनंद् c., विनुद् c., रम् c. (रमयति), सं-परि-तुष् c.; *See* PLEASE, REFRESH. –ION, *s.* विश्रामः, विनोदः-दनं, विहारः, विहरणं, क्रीडा, कौतुकं, मनोरंजनं. –IVE, *a.* सुखकर (री *f.*), मनोरंजन (नी *f.*), विनोदशील.

RECREMENT, *s.* *See* DROSS.

RECRIMINATE, *v.* प्रत्यभियुज् 7 A, 10, प्रत्यभिशंस् 1 P. –ION, *s.* प्रत्यभियोगः, प्रत्यारोपः; 'crimination and r.' परस्परदोषारोपः. –IVE,-ORY, *a.* प्रत्यभियोगिन्.

RECRUIT, *v. t.* शक्तिं वृध् c., प्रबलीकृ 8 U, आश्वस् c., आप्यै c., समा-प्रतिसमा-धा 3 U, सुस्थ-*a.* कृ; 'to r. the strength of' वाजीकृ. 2 नवसैनिकैः पूर् 10. –*v. i.*, 'r. one's strength' बलं-सत्त्वं लभ् 1 A, स्वतेजः-वीर्यं प्राप् 5 P, सुस्थ-*a.* भू. –*s.* नूतन-नव-सैनिकः. –ED, *a.* लब्ध-प्राप्त-बल, वर्धितसत्त्व, आप्यायित, प्रत्याश्वस्त. 2 नवसैनिकयुक्त-पूर्ण.

RECTANGLE, *s.* समकोणः, समचतुरस्रं. –RECTANGULAR, *a.* समकोण, समचतुरस्र.

RECTIFY, *v. t.* समा-प्रतिसमा-धा 3 U, शुध् c. –ICATION, *s.* समाधानं, शोधनं.

RECTILINEAL, *a.* सरलरेखाविशिष्ट.

RECTITUDE, *s.* सारल्यं, आर्जवं, दाक्षिण्यं, न्यायिता, शौचं, सत्यशीलता, सद्वर्तनं, सदाचारः; 'path of r.' सन्मार्गः, सुपथः, नीतिमार्गः-पथः; 'deviation from the path of r.' सत्पथत्यागः-भ्रंशः, उत्पथगमनं.

RECTOR, *s.* नायकः, अध्यक्षः. 2 ग्रामाचार्यः.

RECUMBENT, *a.* पार्श्वशय, अर्धकायेन शयान, कुक्षिशय, संविष्ट.

RECUR, *v. i.* प्रति-,आ-वृत् 1 A, पुनर् आगम् 1 P or आपत् 1 P or सं-पद् 4 A or सं-भू 1 P or घट् 1 A or उप-स्था 1 P; (to the mind) आविः-प्रादुः-भू, उद्-इ 2 P, स्फुर् 6 P, स्मृ pass. 2 शरणं गम् or प्रपद्. –RENCE,-RENCY, *s.* प्रत्यावृत्ति *f.*, पुनर्वर्तनं, पुनर्घटनं-आपातः-उपस्थानं-संभवः. 2 स्मरणं, स्फुरणं, प्रादुर्भावः, उदयः. –RENT,-RING, *a.* आवर्तक, प्रत्यावर्तिन्.

RECUSANT, *a.* प्रतीप; *See* OBSTINATE.

RED, *a.* रक्त, लोहित, शोण (blood-r.), रक्त-लोहित-वर्ण, अरुण (dark r.), कषाय, शोणित; 'r.-hot' उत्तप्त, ज्वलत्, अभि-सं-तप्त, अग्निवर्ण; 'r.-lead' सिंदूरं; *See* under LEAD. –*s.* (R. colour) रक्तवर्णः, अरुणिमन् *m.*, लोहितः, रक्तः. –DEN, *v. t.* लोहितीकृ 8 U, रक्तीकृ, &c. –*v. i.* रक्तीभू 1 P, लोहितायते (D.). –DISH, *a.* आरक्त-लोहित, ईषद्रक्त, &c. –NESS, *s.* रक्तत्वं, लौहित्यं, रक्तिमा, अरुणिमा.

REDEEM, *v. t.* अव-हृ 1 P, निष्क्री 9 U, परिक्री 9 A, धनं दत्त्वा मोक्ष् 10; मुच् c., मोक्ष्, वि-निर्-°, प्रत्या-दा 3 A, उप-नी 1 U; 'a pledge to be r. ed at a fixed time' कृतकालोपनेयः आधिः (V. M. 66). 2 परि-,त्रै 1 A, उद्-धृ 1 P, 10, निस्तॄ c. 3 पूर् 10, प्रतिकृ 8 U; *See* ATONE for; 'he has this r.-ing virtue in him' अयं तस्य गुणोऽन्यान्दोषान् प्रमार्ष्टि-लोपयति. –ER, *s.* परिक्रेतृ *m.*, निष्क्रयिन् *m.* 2 त्राता, मोक्षकः, उद्धर्ता, तारकः. –REDEMPTION, *s.* निष्क्रयः, परिक्रयः-यणं. 2 परि-,त्राणं, उद्धारः, मोक्षः-क्षणं, मुक्ति *f.*, तारणं.

REDOLENT, *a.* सुगंधि, सपरिमल, सुरभि; *See* FRAGRANT; 'to make r.' वास् 10, सुरभीकृ 8 U.

REDOUBLE, *v. t.* द्विगुणीकृ 8 U, पुनः पुनः कृ; अविरतोद्यमेन वृध् c. –ED, *a.* विवृद्ध, द्विगुणित, पुनः पुनः कृत.

REDOUBTABLE, *a.* भीम, विक्रांत, महापराक्रम, महाप्रताप, उरुविक्रम.

REDOUND, *v. i.* साध् c., आवह् 1 P, सं-पद् c.; कॢप् 1 A, सं-पद् 4 A (with dat.), भू with dat. ; 'will r. to thy glory' तव यशसे भवेत्-कल्पेत &c. 2 अव-सो 4 P; परिणम् 1 P; oft. ex. by अंतः, परिणामः. 3 Overflow, q. v.

REDRESS, *v. t.* प्रतिकृ 8 U, निराकृ, समा-धा 3 U; उद्धृ 1 P, मुच् c. (persons); 'r. one's grievances' दुःखाद्-मुच् c. or उद्धृ. –*s.* प्रति(ती)कारः, प्रतिक्रिया, समाधानं; उद्धारः.

REDUCE, *v. t.* पूर्वस्थितिं नी 1 P, प्रत्यादिश् 6 P. 2 (Bring to a state) ex. by नी, गम् c., कृ 8 U or सात्कृ; 'r. to subjection' आत्मवशं नी, वशीकृ; 'r. to ashes' भस्मसात्कृ, भस्मीकृ, भस्मावशेषं नी or कृ; 'r. to a wretched state' दीनावस्थां नी; 'r. ed to a skeleton of bones' अस्थिमात्रावशिष्ट, कंकालशेष; 'who has r. ed kings to the state of tributaries' करदीकृतभूपालः. 3 न्यूनीकृ, अल्पीकृ, ह्रस् c., लघयति (D.), लघूकृ; वि-प्र-कृष् 1 P, (विप्रकर्षत्यलक्ष्मीं U. 5); अपकृष्; 'r. in price' अर्घतः पत् c.; 'r. the strength' बलं शिथिलीकृ or अपचि 5 U or क्षि 1, 5 P. 4 (Person) कृशीकृ, क्षीणीकृ, क्षै-क्षि c. (क्षपयति), शक्तिं अप-चि or अवसद् c. 5 वशीकृ, जि 1 P, पराजि 1 A, स्ववशं नी. 6 (In Math.) रूपं दा 3 U, रूपेण कथ् 10; 'r. to a system' व्यव-स्था c., क्रमेण विन्यस् 4 U or विरच् 10. -ED, *a.* पूर्ववद्भूत; कृत, भूत, गमित, आपन्न, गत; 'r. to misery' कृच्छ्रगत, कृच्छ्रापन्न, कष्टापन्न; 'r. to ashes' भस्मीकृत, भस्मीभूत. 2 वशीकृत, न्यूनीकृत; क्षीणबल &c.; 'you appear to be much r.' अतीव क्षामः-कृशगात्रः-दृश्यसे; अपचितं गात्रं (S. 2) 'a body r. in bulk'; 'r. in strength' क्षीणबल, शिथिलबल, क्षीण, कृश. -REDUCTION, *s.* करणं, नयनं, गमनं,&c. 2 ह्रासः, अपविप्र-कर्षः, अपचयः, न्यूनीकरणं, न्यूनता, शैथिल्यं. 3 पराजयः, वशीकरणं, पराभवः.

REDUNDANT, *a.* अतिरिक्त, समधिक, उद्रिक्त, उत्सिक्त, अत्यंत; व्यर्थ, पुनरुक्तभूत, अति-अतिशय in comp. -LY, *adv.* सातिशयं, उद्रिक्तं. -REDUNDANCY, *s.* आधिक्यं, अतिरेकः, उत्सेकः, उद्वर्तः; पौनरुक्त्यं, व्यर्थता; *See* EXCESS,-IVE.

REDUPLICATE, *v. t.* द्विगुणीकृ 8 U. 2 (In grammar) अभ्यस् 4 P (syllable); आम्रेडयति (D.) (word). -ION, *s.* अभ्यासः, आम्रेडितं, आम्रेडनं, द्विरुक्ति *f.*

REED, *s.* नडः-लः, धमनः, पोटगलः; वेतसः, वेत्रं, वेणुः, वंशः; 'r. for writing', 'r.-pen' कलमः. -Y, *a.* नड्वल, नल-वेत्र-मय (यी *f.*), वेतसपूर्ण.

REEF, *s.* शिलासंघातः, शिलोच्चयः-श्रेणी, शैलसेतुः. -*v. t.* संहृ 1 P; *See* CONTRACT.

REEK, *v. i.* बाष्पं उद्-गृ 6 P or उद्गम् c. or उद्गम् 1 P or उत्क्षिप् 6 P, बाष्पायते (D.). -*s.* बाष्पः, धूमिका. -ING,-Y, *a.* बाष्पोद्गारिन्, बाष्पमय (यी *f.*).

REEL, *v. i.* प्र-,स्खल् 1 P, पार्श्वे पत् 1 P, सं-विचल् 1 P. -*s.* स्खलनं, विचलनं. 2 आवापनं.

REFECTION, *s.* अल्प-लघु-आहारः-भोजनं, उपाहारः. -REFECTORY, *s.* उपाहारशाला.

REFER, *v. i.* उद्दिश् 6 P, अधिकृ 8 U, लक्ष्यीकृ; *See* ALLUDE, ADVERT; आश्रि 1 U, अपेक्ष् 1 A, संबंध्-अनुषंज्-pass.; 'it does not r. to me' न मत्संबद्धं तत्; oft. by विषय, पर, in comp.; ब्रह्मविषयाणि वाक्यांतराणि (S. B. 114) 'r. ing to Brahman'; संदिह्यमानानि वाक्यानि ब्रह्मपरतया निर्णीतानि (S. B. 166) 'have been proved to r. to Brahman.' -*v. t.* Ex. by दृश् 1 P, निरूप् 10, प्रच्छ् 6 P, ऋ c. (अर्पयति), प्रति-पद् c.; निर्दिश् 6 P; 'I r. you to the sage about it' तद्विषये मुनिमेव पृच्छ; 'r. the word to the dictionary' कोशे तं शब्दं निरूपय; 'the matter must be r.-ed to the judge for opinion' अयमर्थः अभिप्रायार्थं प्राड्विवाकाय निवेदनीयः-प्रतिपादनीयः-निर्देष्टव्यः. 2 आरुह् c.; आसंज् c.; संबंध् 9 P. -EE, *s.* प्रमाणपुरुषः, मध्यस्थः, निर्णेतृ *m.* -ENCE, *s.* अर्पणं, निवेदनं, निर्देशः &c. 2 उद्देशः, संबंधः, अनुषंगः, अपेक्षा, आश्रयः, विषयः, संपर्कः, अन्वय, अनुसंधानं; 'a r. is here made to a mythological story' अत्र पुरावृत्तकथा अनुसंधेया (Mallinátha on K. I. 21); oft. ex. by आलोकनं, आलोचनं; 'on a r. to the book again' पुनः पुस्तकं आलोक्य &c.; भवन्निर्दिष्टस्थलं पुनरालोच्य &c.; 'in or with r. to' अधिकृत्य, उद्दिश्य, आश्रित्य, अपेक्ष्य, अपेक्षया-संबंधेन-विषये in comp.

REFINE, *v. t.* वि-,शुध् c., विमलीकृ 8 U, प्र-,मृज् 2 P. 2 संस्कृ, परिष्कृ, उपस्कृ, विनी 1 U. -*v. i.* शुध् 4 P, विमलीभू 1 P. -ED, *a.* वि-,शुद्ध, शोधित, हतमल; 'r. gold' प्रमृष्ट-संस्कारशुद्ध-हेम. 2 संस्कृत, संस्कारवत्, परिष्कृत, प्रबुद्ध; विनीत, शिष्ट, सभ्य. 3 अति-,सूक्ष्म. -MENT, *s.* शोधनं, वि-,शुद्धि *f.*, शुद्धता, प्रमार्जनं. 2 संस्कारः, परिष्कारः, शिष्टता, सौजन्यं, चित्तप्रबोधः, शुद्धिः; 'r. of manners' विनयः, आचारसौजन्यं, सभ्याचारत्वं; 'a man of r.' शिष्टाचारः, विनीतः. 3 अति-,सूक्ष्मता. -ER, *s.* सं-,शोधकः, शोधयितृ *m.*, मलहारी.

REFIT, *v. t.* *See* REPAIR.

REFLECT, *v. i.* चिंत् 10, ध्यै 1 P, विचर् c., विगण् 10, भू c., तर्क् 10, विमृश् 6 P, आलोच्-पर्यालोच् 10. 2 (On) आ-अधि-क्षिप् 6 P, निंद् 1 P, अव-ज्ञा 9 U; *See* CENSURE. -*v. t.* प्रतिक्षिप्, परा-प्रत्यावृत् c., प्रतिबिंबयति (D.); 'a lake r. ing stars' ताराप्रतिबिंबं सरः; 'this action r. s great credit on you' इदं ते चरितं अतीव प्रशस्यं. -ED, *a.* प्रतिबिंबित, परावर्तित, संक्रांत, प्रतिफलित; 'to be r.' मूर्च्छ् 1 P, संक्रम् 1 U, 4 P, परावृत् 1 A, प्रतिफल् 1 P; हर्म्येषु मूर्च्छंति न चंद्रपादाः (R. XVI. 18); मणिकुट्टिमसंक्रांतप्रतिबिंबतया (Ka. 9). -ING, *a.* परावर्तनकारिन्, परावर्तिन्. 2 चिंता-ध्यान-शील, विचारशील. -ION, *s.* चिंता; विचारः, विमर्शः, भावना, ध्यानं. 2 आ-अधि-क्षेपः, आक्षारणं. 3 परावर्तनं, प्रतिक्षेपः, संक्रांति *f.* 4 प्रतिबिंबः-बं, प्रतिच्छाया, प्रतिफलं; छाया, प्रतिमा, प्रतिमूर्ति *f.*-रूपं. -OR, *s.* आदर्शः, दर्पणः-णं,

प्रतिक्षेपकः, परावर्तकः. 2 विचारकः. -REFLEXIBLE, *a.* परावर्तनीय. —REFLEXIVE, *a.* पूर्वसंबंधिन्; 'a r. verb' कर्मकर्तृवाच्यं. -LY, *adv.* कर्मकर्तरि.

REFLUENT, *a.* परावर्तिन्. -REFLUX, REFLUENCE, *s.* परावर्तः, प्रतिस्पंदः.

REFORM, *v. t.* दोषं अपनी 1 P or खंड् 10 or अपाकृ 8 U or निवृत् c.; पापात् निवृत् c. or विरम् c.; दुर्मतिं नश् c., (of persons). 2 शुध् c., परि-वि-सं-°, समा-प्रतिसमा-धा 3 U, प्रतिकृ. 3 पुनः कृ or कॢप् c. or वि-धा. -*v. i.* पापात् नि-परा-वृत् 1 A or विरम् 1 P, पापमार्गं त्यज् 1 P. -*s.*, -ATION, *s.* पाप-दोष-निवृत्ति *f.*-त्यागः, दोषच्छेदः-खंडनं-शोधनं-समाधानं; पापप्रतिकारः, संशोधनं, परिवर्तनं; (religious) धर्मपरिवर्तनं-क्रांति *f.* -ATORY, *s.* शोधनालयः. -ED, *a.* निवृत्त-त्यक्त-पाप-दोष, विरत-हत-दोष, संशोधित. -ER, *s.* निवर्तकः, संशोधकः, दोष-पाप-च्छिद्. 2 धर्मप्रवर्तकः.

REFRACT, *v. t.* परावृत् c., वक्रीकृ 8 U; 'to be r.-ed' वक्रीभू 1 P, परावृत् 1 A. -ION, *s.* वक्रीभवनं-करणं, परावर्तनं, वक्रीभावः. —REFRACTORY, *a.* वि-, प्रतीप, अविधेय, अविनेय, अवश्य, अनिवार्य, शासनलंघिन्; *See* PERVERSE; 'do not show a r. spirit towards thy husband' भर्तुः प्रतीपं मा स्म गमः (S. 4); 'to be r.' प्रतीपायते (D.). -INESS, *s.* प्रतीपता, वक्रता, दुःशीलं, वक्रभावः, अविधेयता.

REFRAGABLE, *a.* छेद्य, खंडनीय, भेद्य.

REFRAIN, *v. t.* नि-सं-यम् 1 P, निग्रह् 9 P, निवृ 5 U or c., संहृ 1 P; *See* CONTROL. -*v. i.* निवृत् 1 A, विरम् 1 P, (with abl.); परिहृ 1 P, वि-,वृज् 10, त्यज् 1 P; *See* ABSTAIN, CEASE, FORBEAR.

REFRANGIBLE, *a.* परावर्तनीय.

REFRESH, *v. t.* समा-प्रत्या-आ-श्वस् c., आनंद् c., जीव् c.; आ-प्र-ह्लाद् c., सुखयति (D.). 2 नवीकृ 8 U, (एते वयं पुनर्नवीकृताः स्मः S. 5); श्रमं अपहृ 1 P or छिद् 7 P or अपनी 1 P, विश्रम् c.; बलं-सत्त्वं वृध् c., आप्यै c. 3 निर्वा c. (वापयति), शीतलयति (D.), शीतलीकृ; *See* COOL. -ED, *a.* हृत-गत-क्लम-श्रम, विश्रांत, आप्यायित, आश्वासित, नवीकृत, छिन्न-श्रम. -ING, *a.* आह्लादन (नी *f.*), क्लम-श्रम-विनोदिन्, आनंद-सुख-प्रद, श्रम-क्लम-च्छिद्, श्रमापह, क्लांतिहर. -MENT, *s.* आह्लादनं, श्रम-क्लम-अपहारः-विनोदनं, आश्वासनं, श्रम-क्लांति-च्छेदः; विश्रांति *f.*, विश्रामः. 2 अभ्यवहारः, लघ्वाहारः, उपाहारः; 'morning r.' प्रातराशः, कल्यवर्तः.

REFRIGERATE, *v. t.* तापं-दाहं-हृ 1 P or नश् c. or छिद् 7 P, निर्वा c. (वापयति), शीतलीकृ 8 U; *See* COOL. -ION, *s.* ताप-दाह-च्छेदः, निर्वापणं. -REFRIGERANT, *a.* निर्वापक, ताप-दाह-हर. -*s.* उष्ण-निर्वापणं, तापशमनं.

REFUGE, *s.* आश्रयः, संश्रयः, शरणं, गति *f.*; (person) शरण्यः, आश्रयभूतः, पालकः, रक्षकः, त्राता. 2 उपायः, प्र-,युक्ति *f*, गतिः, साधनं; 'giving r.' शरण्यः &c; 'take r. with' शरणं या 2 P or गम् 1 P or प्रपद् 4 A, उपा-आ-सं-श्रि 1 U, अवलंब् 1 A, शरणार्थं गम् &c; 'seeking r.' शरणार्थिन्; 'come for r.' शरणं प्रपन्न, शरणागत; 'having only one r.' अनन्यगतिक. —REFUGEE, *s.* शरणं प्रपन्नः, शरणागतः, शरणार्थी, आश्रितः, अवलंबितः.

REFULGENT, *a.* देदीप्यमान, विभ्राजमान, भास्वत्, उज्ज्वल, अतितेजस्विन्, प्रद्योतमान; *See* BRIGHT. -REFULGENCE, *s.* अतिप्रभा-तेजस् *n.*, औज्ज्वल्यं.

REFUND, *v. t.* प्रतिदा 3 U, प्रति-ऋ c. (अर्पयति.)

REFUSE, *v. t.* प्रत्या-ख्या 2 P, नि-प्रति-षिध् 1 P, प्रत्याचक्ष् 2 A, निराकृ 8 U, प्रत्यादिश् 6 P, निर्-अप-अस् 4 U, वि-प्रति-हन् 2 P, न संमन् 4 A or ग्रह् 9 P or अंगीकृ or प्रतीष् 6 P, अवधीर् 10; 'pray, do not r. my request' नार्हसि मे प्रणयं विहंतुं (R. II. 58). 2 (Followed by inf.) Ex. by a sentence with वच्, वद् &c. (Say, q. v.). -*s.* उच्छिष्टं, अवशिष्टं, अवशेषः, शेषः-षं; असारः, मलं. -*a.* उच्छिष्ट, असार, अवशिष्ट.

REFUTE, *v. t.* निराकृ 8 U, निरस् 4 U, प्रतिक्षिप् 6 P, खंड् 10, बाध् 1 A, अधरीकृ, प्रत्या-ख्या 2 P, प्रत्यादिश् 6 P, अपवद् 1 U, निर्धू 5, 9 U, 6 P. -ATION, *s.* निरासः, निरसनं, खंडनं, निराकरणं, प्रतिक्षेपः, प्रत्याख्यानं.

REGAIN, *v. t.* पुनः लभ् 1 A or प्राप् 5 P, प्रतिपद् 4 P; *See* RECOVER.

REGAL, *a.* राजकीय, राजार्ह, राजोचित.

REGALE, *v. t.* संतृप् c., संतुष् c., आह्लाद् c., आनंद् c. 2 आश्वस् c., आप्यै c, संवृध् c.; *See* REFRESH; 'r. oneself' उत्तमान्नेन संतुष् 4 P or संतृप् 4 P or आत्मानं संतुष् c., उत्सवं कृ 8 U.

REGALIA, *s* राजचिह्नानि-लक्षणानि-लिंगानि, राजोपचारः.

REGARD, *v. t.* आदृ 6 A, प्रति-अव-ईक्ष् 1 A, सं-, मन् c., पूज् 10, नि-,सेव् 1 A. 2 ईक्ष्, दृश् 1 P, आ-अव-लोक् 1 A, 10, आ-,लक्ष् 10; *See* LOOK. 3 मन् 4 A, वि-,गण् 10. 4 अव-धा 3 U; अवेक्ष्, सावधान- *a.* भू, विगण्, आदृ. 5 सेव्, पा c. (पालयति), अनु-ष्ठा 1 P; *See* OBSERVE. 6 उद्दिश् 6 P, अपेक्ष्; संबंध् 9 P. -*s.* आदरः, संमानः, पूजा, अवेक्षा. 2 अवधानं, मनोयोगः, अवेक्षा. 3 दृष्टि *f.*, ईक्षणं; *See* LOOK. 4 स्नेहः, प्रणयः, अनुरागः, प्रीति *f.* 5 विचारः, अवेक्षा, अपेक्षा, अनुसंधानं, गणना, उ-

देशः, संबंधः, अन्वयः, विषयः ; 'having r. to the result' फलापेक्षया ; 'with r. to' उद्दिश्य, अधिकृत्य, अंतरेण, अपेक्ष्य, (with acc.) ; अपेक्षया, विषये, गत-*a.* in comp.; 'a scandal with r. to Mâlavikâ' मालविकागतं कौलीनं (M. 3); भर्तृगता-विषया-चिंता &c. -FUL, *a.* अवे(पे)क्षक, अवहित, सावधान, सापेक्ष. -FULLY, *adv.* सापेक्षं, सावधानं. -ING, *a.* सापेक्ष, संबंधिन्, गत-विषय- in comp.; *See* (*s.*). -LESS, *a.* निरपेक्ष, अनपेक्ष, उदासीन, विरक्त, अनुत्सुक, in comp. gen.; oft. by अनादृत्य, अनवेक्ष्य, अगणयित्वा. -LESSLY, *adv.* निरपेक्षं, उपेक्षया. -LESSNESS, *s.* अनपेक्षा, उपेक्षा.

REGATTA, *s.* नौकाक्रीडा.

REGENERATE, *v. t.* पुनर् जन् c. (जनयति) or जीव् c. or उद्-धृ 1 P, 10 or उत्था c. (उत्थापयति). -*a.*,-ED, *a.* पुनर्जात, पुनर्भव, पुनर्जन्मन्, पुनरुज्जीवित. -ION, *s.* पुनरुज्जीवनं, पुनरुत्पत्ति *f.*, पुनर्जन्मन् *n.*; उत्थापनं, उद्धारः.

REGENT, *s.* पालः in comp.; शासकः, अधिपतिः, शास्ता; 'r. s of the eight quarters' अष्ट दिक्पालाः. 2 शून्यपालः; राजप्रतिनिधिः. -REGENCY, *s.* शासनं. 2 राजप्रतिनिधिमंडलं.

REGICIDE, *s.* राजवधः-हत्या-हिंसा-घातः. 2 (Person) राजहन् *m.*, राजघातकः, राजघः.

REGIME, *s.* *See* GOVERNMENT.

REGIMEN, *s.* अन्नपानविधिः, पथ्यापथ्यनियमः; 'one observing r.' पथ्याशिन्.

REGIMENT, *s.* सैन्यदलं-गुल्मं-गणः-व्यूहः. -REGIMENTALS, *s.* सैनिकवेषः.

REGION, *s.* प्र-,देशः, लोकः, भुवनं; विषयः, राष्ट्रं, चक्रं, मंडलं; (of the sky) दिश् *f.*, काष्ठा, आशा; *See* DIRECTION; 'r. of the heart' हृदयदेशः; नाडीचक्रं &c.

REGISTER, *s.* लेख्यं, लेखः, पत्रिका, पंजिका; गणनापत्रं. -*v. t.* पत्रिकायां लिख् 6 P or निविश् c. -REGISTRAR, *s.* लेखकः, पंजिकाधिकृतः. -REGISTRY, REGISTRATION, *s.* नामालिखनं, पत्रिकायां निवेशनं or आरोपणं. 2 लिखनस्थानं.

REGNANT, *a.* शासक, अधिकारिन्, राज्याधिकारिन्.

REGORGE, *v. t.* उद्वम् 1 P, उद्-गॄ 6 P, निःसृ c.

REGRESS, *s.* प्रतीपगति *f.*, परावर्तनं. -*v. i.* परावृत् 1 A, प्रत्यावृत्. -ION, *s.* प्रतीपगमनं, प्रत्यावर्तनं.

REGRET, *v. t.* अनुशुच्, 1P, अनुतप् 4 A; *See* LAMENT; 'he died r. ed by all' मृतः सर्वैरनुशोचितश्च; न वाप्यनुशोचिता (U. 3) 'nor was she (her absence) r. ed;' oft. ex. by दुःखित *a.* or दुःखं; 'I r. I cannot go with you' त्वया सह गंतुमसमर्थोऽस्मीति दुःखितोऽहं. 2 Repent, q. v. -*s.* दुःखं, अनुशोकः, अनुतापः, खेदः, मनस्तापः, उद्वेगः; *See* GRIEF. -FUL, *a.* दुःखित, दुःखाकुल, अनुतप्त, अनुशोकार्त, उद्विग्न, खिन्न, सोत्कंठ.

REGULAR, *a.* नियत, नियमानुसारिन्, नैयमिक-वैधिक (की *f.*), विध्यनुरूप, सूत्र-विधि-अनुसारिन्; 'not at r. hours' अनियतवेले (S. 2). 2 अनुपूर्व, अनुक्रमागत, यथाक्रम, क्रमानुगत, अनुलोम, क्रमानुसारिन्. 3 नियतकालिक (की *f.*) नियतवेल. 4 व्य(व्या)वहारिक-आचारिक (की *f.*), नित्य, यथामार्ग, यथारीति. 5 (Of persons) नियमानुसारिन्, नियमनिष्ठ-पर-शील, विधि-नियम-अनुवर्तिन्; व्यवस्थित, अत्यक्तक्रम, अव्यभिचारिन्, नियतवृत्ति. -ITY, *s.* नियतत्वं, विध्यनुसारः, नियमः, सूत्रानुसारः, नैयमिकत्वं. 2 पर्यायः, अनुक्रमः, परिपाटि-टी *f.*, व्यवस्था, परंपरा, आनुपूर्व्यं, आनुलोम्यं;, *See* ORDER. 3 विधि-नियम-निष्ठा, नियमानुसारित्वं, विध्यनुवर्तनं, क्रमात्यागः, व्यवस्थिति *f.*, विधि-नियमपरता. 4 (Of arrangement) विरचनं-ना, व्यूहः-हनं, विन्यासः. -LY, *adv.* यथा-अनु-क्रमं, अनुपूर्वशः, आनुपूर्व्येण, अनुलोमं, आनुलोम्येन, क्रमशः, क्रमेण, पर्यायेण. 2 यथाविधि, विधिवत्, विधितः, यथानियमं, यथासूत्रं, विधिपूर्वकं, विधि-नियम-अनुसारेण. 3 नित्यं, अनुज्झितक्रमं, नियतक्रमेण, नियतवेलायां.

REGULATE, *v. t.* सं-,वि-धा 3 U, परिक्लृप् c., क्रमेण विन्यस् 4 U, विरच् 10, व्यव-स्था c. (स्थापयति). 2 वि-,नियम् 1 P, वि-धा; अनुशास् 2 P, नि-,यंत्र् 10; *See* RULE, CONTROL; ये द्वे कालं विधत्तः (S. 1) 'who r. time.' 3 यथाविधि व्यव-स्था c. or वि-धा, प्रमाणं निरूप् 10. -ION, *s.* विधानं, व्यवस्थापनं, यंत्रणं, शासनं, &c. 2 व्यवस्था, वि-,नियमः, शासनं, विधिः, स्थिति *f.*, मर्यादा, क्रमः. -OR, *s.* शासकः, संविधातृ *m.*, वि-,नियंता, शास्ता.

REHEARSE, *v. t.* पठ् 1 P, अनुवद् 1 P. 2 कथ् 10, वर्ण् 10; *See* NARRATE. 3 प्रयोगात् पूर्वं अभिनी 1 P or नट् 10. -AL, *s.* पठनं, अनुवादः; कथनं, आख्यानं, पूर्वप्रयोगः, पूर्वाभिनयः.

REIGN, *v. i.* प्र-,शास् 2 P, राज्यं-महीं &c. शास् or अव् 1 P or भुज् 7 U. 2 Prevail, q. v. -*s.* शासनं, राज्यपालनं, आधिपत्यं, अधिकारः; better by (*v.*) with loc. abs.; 'during Râma's r.' रामे महीं शासति; 'after a r. of 12 years' द्वादशाब्दान् भुक्तक्षितौ तस्मिन्. 2 राज्यशासनकालः, राज्यकालः. -ING, *a.* राजपदारूढ, शासत्, राज्याधिकारिन्.

REIMBURSE, *v. t.* प्रतिदा 3 U, निष्कृ 8 U, अपाकृ, पूर् 10, शुध् c.

REIN, *s.* अभीशुः-षुः, प्रग्रहः, रश्मिः; 'by drawing in the r. s' रश्मिसंयमनात् (S. 1); 'give the r. s to' वशं या 2 P; आयत्तीभू 1 P, अधीन-*a.* भू; 'r. s of government' राज्यसूत्राणि. -*v. t.* नि-

सं-यम् 1 P, नि-प्र-ग्रह् 9 P; *See* CONTROL; 'r. in the horses' प्रगृह्णंतां वाजिनः (S. 1).

REINS, *s.* कटि-टी *f.*, कटि-श्रोणी-देशः. 2 वृक्कौ.

REINFORCE, *v. t.* Recruit, q. v. —MENT, *s.* सैन्यं, सेनासामग्री.

REINSTATE, *v. t.* प्रति-ष्ठा c. (-ष्ठापयति), पुनः स्था c. or नियुज् 7 A, 10. —MENT, *s.* प्रतिष्ठापनं, पुनर्नियोगः, पुनःस्थापनं.

REITERATE, *v. t.* Repeat, q. v. 2 पुनः पुनः कृ 8 U. —ED, *a.* पुनःपुनरुक्त; पौनःपुनिक (की *f.*). —ION, *s.* पुनर्वचनं, आमेडनं, पुनरुक्ति *f.*, पौनःपुन्यं.

REJECT, *v. t.* अवधीर् 10, निराकृ 8 U, प्रत्या-ख्या 2 P, वि-हन् 2 P, प्रत्याचक्ष् 2 A; प्रत्यादिश् 6 P, निर्-अप-अस् 4 U, निर्धू 5, 9 U, प्रति-अप-क्षिप् 6 P, त्यज् 1 P; *See* REFUSE. —ION, *s.* अवधीरणं-णा, निराकरणं, प्रत्यादेशः, प्रत्याख्यानं, निरसनं.

REJOICE, *v. i.* प्री pass., मुद् 1A, आनंद् 1P, सं-परि-तुष् 4P, हृष् 4P, रम् 1A, उल्लस् 1P; *See* DELIGHT; 'I r. to see you' प्रीतोस्मि ते दर्शनात्, त्वद्दर्शनेन मुदितोस्मि; 'this is to be r. ed at' एतदभिनंदनीयं ((S. 5). —*v. t.* Causal of roots above. —ING, *a.* आनंदद, हर्षावह, हर्षकर (री *f.*). 2 प्रीयमाण, मुदित, हृष्ट. —*s.* आनंदः, हर्षः, प्रमोदः, उत्सवः.

REJOIN, *v. See* ANSWER. —REJOINDER, *s.* प्रतिवचनं, उत्तरं, प्रत्युक्ति *f.*

RELAPSE, *v. i.* पुनः पत् 1 P or आगम् 1 P or प्राप् 5 P; oft. ex. by पुनः with other words; 'r.-ed into a feverish state' ज्वरेण पुनरभ्यभूयत, पुनः ज्वरातुरो बभूव; 'r. ed into vice' पुनर्दुर्मार्गं गंतुं प्रचक्रमे, सत्पथात् भ्रष्टः, सन्मार्गं अत्यजत्; 'r. ed into his natural joviality' सहजामानंदवृत्तिं प्रत्यपद्यत. —*s.* पुनः पतनं, आवृत्ति *f.*, प्रत्यागमनं, पूर्वावस्थाप्राप्ति *f.*

RELATE, *v. i.* (To) उद्दिश् 6 P, अपेक्ष् 1 A, अनु-षंज्-संबंध् pass.; by deriv. in ईय, or विषय in comp.; 'r. ing to *S*ástras' शास्त्रीय, शास्त्रविषय; 'news r. ing to the king's murder' राजघातविषयकः-संबद्धः-वृत्तांतः; *See* REFER. —*v. t.* कथ् 10, आ-ख्या 2 P, वर्ण् 10, शंस् 1 P, चक्ष् 2 A, आ-नि-विद् c.; *See* TELL. —ED, *a.* कथित, ख्यात, वर्णित, &c. 2 सं-अनु-बद्ध, अनुषक्त, अन्वित, संसक्त, संयुक्त, संबंधिन्, संपर्किन्, in comp. 3 संबंधिन्, सजाति, स-जातीय, एक-स-गोत्र, सकुल्य, गोत्रज, एकशरीरावयव. —ER, *s.* आख्यायकः, कथयितृ *m.* —ING, *a.* (To) संबंधिन्, विषय in comp.; *See* REFER. —ION, *s.* संबंधः, अन्वयः, संदर्भः, संसर्गः, संपर्कः, अनुषंगः, भावः; 'mutual r.' व्यतिषंगः, अन्योन्यसंबंधः, आकांक्षा (between a word and its meaning); 'intimate r.' समवाय-नित्य-संबंधः; 'the r. of the container and the thing contained' आधाराधेयभावः. 2 बंधुता, ज्ञातिभावः, शरीरसंबंधः, शरीरान्वयः, सजातित्वं, सगोत्रता, सपिंडता. 3 बंधुः, बांधवः, ज्ञातिः, गोत्रजः, सगोत्रः, सकुल्यः, संबंधी, सपिंडः (to the 7th degree), समानोदकः (8th to 14th degree); सनाभिः, सोदर्यः, समानोदरः (by blood); 'r. s collectively' बांधवगणः-जनः, बंधु-ज्ञाति-वर्गः. 4 आ-उपा-ख्यानं, वर्णनं, कथनं, निरूपणं, कीर्तनं. —IONSHIP, *s.* बंधुता, सनाभिता, ज्ञातिभावः, संबंधः; 'near r.' प्रत्यासन्नता; 'distant r.' व्यवहितता. —IVE, *s.* सगोत्रः, सकुल्यः, बांधवः, बंधुः, ज्ञातिः; *See* RELATION. —*a.* सापेक्ष, अविविक्त, अन्यसापेक्ष, अ-केवल; 'r. importance' तारतम्यं. 2 अन्योन्यान्वित. 3 संबंधिन्, विषयक, in comp.; अनुविद्ध, अनुषक्त, संबद्ध, सान्वय, उद्दिष्ट. 4 संबंधवाचिन्. —IVELY, *adv.* अन्यापेक्षया, अन्यसापेक्षं, अपेक्ष्य; *See* COMPARATIVE.

RELAX, *v. t.* शिथिलीकृ 8 U, शिथिलयति (D.), श्रथ्-श्रंथ् 1, 9 P, 10, वि-,स्रंस् c., वि-गल् c. 2 मुच् 6 P, or c., विसृज् 6 P. 3 शिथिलीकृ, प्र-शम् c. (शमयति), न्यूनीकृ, लघूकृ, मंदीकृ, (मंदीचकार मरणव्यवसायबुद्धिं K. IV. 45); 'r. ing their efforts' शिथिलितप्रयत्नाः. 4 उद्-ग्रंथ् 9 P, विसं-धा 3 U; 'r. the bowels' विरिच् 7 P or c.; *See* PURGE; 'r. the mind' मनः विनुद् c., or विश्रम् c. —*v. i.* शिथिलीभू 1 P, श्लथ् 1 P, श्रथ् 1 A, स्रंस् 1 A, शिथिलायते-मंदायते (D.). 2 प्र-उप-शम् 4 P, न्यूनी-भू. —ATION, *s.* शैथिल्यं, विस्रंसः, प्रश्रथः, मुक्ति *f.* 2 प्र-उप-शमः-शांति *f.*, न्यूनीभावः. 3 विनोदः, विश्रामः, उद्योगविरति *f.*-निवृत्ति *f.* -शैथिल्यं. —ED, *a.* शिथिलित, शिथिल, प्र-,श्लथ, मुक्त, स्रस्त, विगलित; 'having r. his hold' मुक्त-शिथिलित-ग्रहः-हस्तः.

RELAY, *s.* विश्रामदायी जवाश्वगणः or सेवकगणः.

RELEASE, *v. t.* मोक्ष् 10, मुच् 6 P or c., वि-निर्-°, उद्धृ 1 P, निस्तॄ c., विसृज् 6 P; *See* FREE. —*s.* वि-मुक्ति *f.*, मोक्षः, मोचनं, उद्धारः, निस्तारः. —ER, *s.* मोचकः, मोक्षकः, उद्धर्ता.

RELENT, *v. i.* करुणामृदु-करुणार्द्र-मृदुचित्त- *a.* भू 1 P; अनुकंप् 1 A, दयार्द्रीभू, करुणया द्रु 1 P; 'his heart r. ed' तस्य मनो मार्दवमभजत, कठिनतामजहात्; 'being appeased, he r. ed' स चानुनीतो मृदुतामगच्छत् (R. v. 54); किमपि सानुक्रोशः कृतः (S. 4) 'somewhat r. ed'. —LESS, *a.* निर्दय, निष्करुण, निरनुक्रोश, क्रूर, कठोर, कठिन-पाषाण-हृदय, निर्घृण; *See* CRUEL. —LESSLY, *adv.* निर्दयं, निष्करुणं, कठोरं.

RELEVANT, *a.* प्रास्ताविक (की *f.*), प्रस्तुत, प्रस्तुतानुषंगिन्, प्रासंगिक (की *f.*), प्रस्तावसदृश (शी *f.*)-उचित-अनुरूप, प्रसंगोचित. —LY, *adv.* प्रस्तावसदृशं,

प्रासंगिक. —RELEVANCE,-CY, *s.* प्रस्तावौचित्यं, प्रस्तावसंगति *f.*, प्रस्तुतानुसारः-अन्वयः, प्रकरणानुसारः, प्रास्ताविकत्वं.

RELIC, *s.* अव-शिष्टं-शेषः-षं, शेषभागः ; शवः-वं, मृतशरीरं.

RELICT, *s. See* WIDOW.

RELIEVE, *v. t.* (Persons) (दुःखात् &c.) मुच् 6 P or c., मोक्ष् 10, उद्धृ 1 P ; दुःखं &c. अपनी 1 P or शम् c. (शमयति) or परिहृ. 2 (Pain &c.) प्र-शम् c., परिहृ, दूरीकृ ; लघयति (D.), विश्रम् c., लघूकृ ; *See* ALLEVIATE ; 'I feel myself to be r. ed' ममात्मा विशदः जातः (S. 4), निश्चितोहं. 3 उपकृ, साहाय्यं दा 3 U, अनुग्रह् 9 P. 4 (Guard &c.) विश्रम् c., नियोगात् विश्रामं दा. —ED, *a.* उद्धृत, मुक्त, शांत, शमित &c. ; 'r. of anxiety' वीतचिंत, निश्चित, निःशल्य (मनः) ; 'r. of pain' शांतदुःख. —RELIEF, *s.* (दुःखात्) मोचनं, मोक्षः, उद्धारः, शमनं, मुक्ति *f.*, अपहरणं, अपनयनं, परिहारः. 2 सुखं, उप-प्र-शमः, निर्वापणं, चिंताप्रशमः-शांति *f.*, स्वास्थ्यं, निर्वृत्तिः, विश्रामः, निश्चितता; एकपदे एव दुःखविश्रामं ददाति (U. 6) 'gives r. to my sorrow'; कर्तव्यानि दुःखितैर्दुःखनिर्वापणानि (U. 3). 3 उपकारः, साहाय्यं; 'she brought her lovely limbs into r.' पुपोष लावण्यमयान् विशेषान् (K. I. 25).

RELIGION, *s.* धर्मः. 2 Piety, q. v. —RELIGIOUS, *a.* धर्म्य, धर्म-देव- in comp.; 'r. rites' धर्मक्रियाः. 2 धर्मात्मन्, पुण्यशील, धर्मोचारिन्, व्रतिन्, धर्मनिष्ठ, धार्मिक (की *f.*); *See* PIOUS. —LY, *adv.* धार्मिकवत्, ईश्वरभक्त्या. —NESS, *s.* धार्मिकत्वं, धर्मनिष्ठा, धर्मपरता.

RELINQUISH, *v. t.* त्यज् 1 P, उत्-वि-सृज् 6 P, हा 3 P, मुच् 6 P. —MENT, *s.* त्यागः, उत्सर्गः, मोचनं; *See* ABANDON,-MENT.

RELIQUARY, *s.* अवशिष्टाधारः-भाजनं.

RELISH, *v. t.* स्वाद् c., रस् 10, सुरसीकृ 8 U, स्वादूकृ. 2 आस्वाद् 1 A. 3 अभि-,रुच् 1 A, अभिनंद् 1 P; *See* LIKE, *s.* रसः, आ-,स्वादः-दनं, रुचिः; 'has lost r. for dates' पिंडखर्जूरैरुद्वेजित (S. 2). 2 अभि-,रुचिः, अभिलाषः, इच्छा. 3 अव-उप-दंशः.

RELUCTANT, *a.* अनिच्छत्, विमनस्, अनिच्छु, असंतुष्ट, अकाम, निष्काम, वि-पराङ्-मुख, विमत. —LY, *adv.* बलात्, अनिच्छया, अकामं-मतः-मेन, by (*a.*), 'he went out r.' अनिच्छन्नपि निर्जगाम. —RELUCTANCE, *s.* अनिच्छा, अकामः, असंतोषः, वैमनस्यं, विमुखता, अरुचि *f.*

RELY, *v. i.* (On) विश्वस् 2 P, प्रति-इ 2 P, विश्रंभ् 1 A; श्रद्धा 3 U. 2 आ-अव-लंब् 1 A, आ-सं-श्रि 1 U; oft. ex. by आयत्त, अधीन, तंत्र in comp.; 'I r. on you alone' भवानेव ममाश्रयः, शरणं. —IANCE, *s.* विश्वासः, प्रत्ययः, विश्रंभः, श्रद्धा. 2 अवलंबः-बनं, आ-सं-श्रयः, शरणं. —ING, *a.* अवलंबिन्, आश्रित, विश्वासिन्, जातप्रत्यय.

REMAIN, *v. i.* अव-स्था 1 A, स्था 1 P, आस् 2 A, वृत् 1 A; *See* CONTINUE. 2 नि-,वस् 1 P, स्था, अधि-ष्ठा. 3 शिष् pass., अव-परि-उत्°-, उद्-वृत्; 'he r. ed only in memory (his name only r. ed)' स्मर्तव्यशेषं नीतः; 'r. ing after what is eaten' भुक्तावशिष्टं, भुक्तशेषं (अन्नं); 'those who r. ed alive' हतशेषाः. —ING, *a.* अव-,शिष्ट-शेष, उद्वृत्त; 'pass the r. months' शेषान्मासान्गमय; 'during the r. part of his life' आयुःशेषे. —REMAINS, *s.* अस्थ्यादिशेषः, अस्थीनि. —REMAINDER, *s.* अव-,शेषः-षं-शिष्टं, उद्वर्तः, शेषभागः; (in arithmetic) शेषं, अंतरं; (of men) ex. by अन्य, इतर; *See* OTHER; 'subtracting 4 from 10 the r. is 6' दशसु चतुर्भिर्विवर्जितेषु षट् शेषं or षट् अवशिष्यंते.

REMAND, *v. t.* पुनः प्र-हि 5 P or आह्वे 1 P.

REMARK, *v. t.* लक्ष् 10, अवेक्ष् 1 A, निरूप् 10. 2 अभि-धा 3 U, वच् 2 P, वद् 1 P; *See* OBSERVE. —*s.* उक्ति *f.*, वचनं, अभिधानं, वचस् *n.*, भाषणं; (written) लिखितं, लेखः. 2 अवेक्षणं, निरूपणं. 3 चर्चा, अनुशासनं. —ABLE, *a.* अपूर्व, अद्भुत, आश्चर्यभूत. 2 विख्यात, विश्रुत, अलौकिक (की *f.*), लोकोत्तर, प्रसिद्ध, विशिष्ट, उत्कृष्ट, स्मरणार्ह, विशेष in comp. —ABLY, *adv.* सातिशयं, विशेषेण, विशेषतः, अद्भुतं, विशिष्टप्रकारेण.

REMARRIED, *a.* पुनरूढ, पुनर्भू.

REMEDY, *v. t.* प्रतिकृ 8 U, प्रतिवि-धा 3 U, प्रतिसमा-समा-धा; परिहृ 1 P; प्र-उप-शम् c. (शमयति), साध् c., कित् desid. (चिकित्सति-ते); उप-चर् 1 P. —*s.* औषधं; भेषजं, अगदः; *See* MEDICINE. 2 प्रतिक्रिया, प्रति(ती)कारः, उपशमः, उपायः, उपचारः, प्रतिविधानं, उपक्रमः, चिकित्सा, प्रतिसमाधानं. —IABLE, *a.* प्रतिकार्य, प्रतिविधेय, चिकित्स्य, शक्यप्रतिकार, शक्योपचार. —IAL, *a.* प्रतिकारक, प्रतिकारिन्, (*s.*) in comp.; 'a r. measure proves effective' प्रतिकारविधानं फलाय कल्पते (R. VIII. 40). —LESS, *a.* अप्रतिकार्य, अप्रतिविधेय, निरुपाय, अप्रतिकार, दुरुपचार.

REMEMBER, *v. t.* स्मृ 1 P, सं-अनु-,° (with gen. when regret is shown), अनुचिंत् 10, अनु-बुध् 1 P, 4 A. 2 (Keep in mind) स्मृ, हृदये-चित्ते नि-उप-धा 3 U, मनसि कृ 8 U, अव-धृ 10; 'please, r. these words well' हृदि एनां (भारतीं) उपधातुमर्हसि (R. VIII. 77); 'r. me to your brother' स्मर्तव्योहं तव भ्रातुः. —REMEMBRANCE, *s.* स्मरणं, स्मृति *f.*, अनुचिंतनं, अवधारणं-णा. 2 स्मा-

रकं, स्मारणं, स्मरणवस्तु, अभिज्ञानं; 'r. of love' प्रीत्यभिज्ञानं. -ER, s. स्मारकः, उद्‌बोधकः.

REMIND, v. t. स्मृ c., अनु-सं-°, उद्-प्र-अनु-बुध् c.; 'this group of gallants, as if, r. s me to-day of Pátála' पातालं मामद्य संस्मरयतीव भुजंगलोकः (Rat. 1); 'Oh, I am well r. ed' अये सम्यगनुबोधितोस्मि (S. 1). -ER, s. उद्बोधकः, अनुबोधकः.

REMINISCENCE, s. स्मृति f., स्मरणं; See MEMORY.

REMISS, a. अनवधान, असावधान, प्रमत्त, निरपेक्ष, उपेक्षक, मंदादर, शिथिलोद्यम; 'to be r.' प्रमद् 4 P (with abl.). -LY, adv. अनवधानेन, उपेक्षया, निरपेक्षं, प्रमादेन. -NESS, s. अनवधानं, उपेक्षा, निरपे(वे)क्षा, प्रमादः, शैथिल्यं.

REMIT, v. t. प्र-हि 5 P, प्रेष् c., प्रति-ऋ c. (अर्पयति); संचर् c., संक्रम् c. 2 शिथिलीकृ 8 U, मुच् 6 P, वि-उत्-सृज् 6 P, त्यज् 1 P; विरम् 1 P, निवृत् 1 A, (with abl.). 3 क्षम् 1 A, निवृत् c., मुच्, अवसृज्, त्यज्. 4 प्र-उप-शम् c. (शमयति), लघूकृ, न्यूनीकृ. -v. i. प्र-उप-शम् 4 P, शिथिलीभू 1 P, विरम्. -TANCE, s. प्रेषणं, संक्रामणं; प्रेषितधनसंख्या. -TENT, a. संतत, अविसर्गिन्. -TING, a. विरत, विसर्गिन्, शिथिलित. -REMISSION, s. शैथिल्यं, प्र-उप-शमः-शांति f., विरामः. 2 मोचनं, मुक्ति f., निस्तारः, उद्धारः. 3 मार्जनं, क्षमा, विच्छेदः, निवृत्ति f., उत्सर्गः.

REMNANT, s. अव-,शेषः-षं; See REMAINDER.

REMONSTRATE, v. i. (With) निवारणार्थं उपदिश् 6 P, निवारयितुं यत् 1 A, प्रत्यादिश्, प्रत्या-ख्या 2 P; See DISSUADE.-REMONSTRANCE, s. प्रत्यादेशः, प्रबोधवचनं, निवारणोपदेशः, निवर्तनं.

REMORSE, s. अनुतापः, अनुशयः, अनुशोकः, पश्चात्तापः. -FUL, a. अनुतप्त, अनुशयार्त; See REPENTANCE, &c. -LESS, a. कठिन, निर्दय; See CRUEL.

REMOTE, a. दूर, दूरस्थ, दूरवर्तिन्, असन्निहित, विप्रकृष्ट; See DISTANT. -LY, adv. दूरं, विप्रकृष्टं; 'he is r. connected with me' स मम विप्रकृष्टः . बंधुः. -NESS, s. विप्रकर्षः, असन्निकर्षः, दूरता.

REMOVE, v. t. स्थानांतरं नी 1 P or गम् c., अप-सृ c., वि-,चल् c. 2 दूरीकृ 8 U, निरस् c., निष्कस् c., अप-निः-उत्-सृ c., बहिष्कृ; (from office) प्र-,भ्रंश् c., च्यु c.; See DISMISS, DISCHARGE; (of things) अपनी, विनुद् c., अपहृ 1 P, अप-अव-कृष् 1 P, अप-अपा-नुद् 6 P or c., अप-व्यप-ऊह् 1 U, निर्-अप-अस् 4 U, निराकृ, अपाकृ, उच्छिद् 7 P, विनश् c., प्रतिकृ, खंड् 10, वि-प्रति-हन् 2 P, भंज् 7 P, निर्-अव-धू 5, 9 U, 6 P. -v. i. स्थानांतरं गम् 1 P or या-इ- 2 P; अपसृ 1 P, अपगम्-या. -s. पुरुषः (in geneology); 'separated by one r. from the creator' स्रष्टुरेकांतरं (द्वंद्वं) (S. 7). 2 पदं, पदवी, क्रमः. 3 अपगमः, अपसरणं, &c.; See below. -AL, s. अपनयनं, उत्सारणं, दूरीकरणं, विचालनं, स्थानांतरीकरणं. 2 अपसरः-रणं, अपयानं, अपगमः-गमनं, स्थानांतरं, स्थलभेदः. 3 निरासः, निराकरणं, प्रभ्रंशनं, अप-परि-हारः-हरणं, उच्छेदः, विनाशः-शनं, अपनोदः, अपोहः, प्रतिघातः, प्रति(ती)-कारः, खंडनं, भंगः, &c. -ER, s. अपनेतृ m., अपहर्ता, नाशकः, उच्छेत्ता; gen. ex. by हारः, हारी, अपहः, हा, घ्नः, अंतकः in comp., also हृत्, नुद् in comp.; 'r. of darkness' तमोनुत्, तमोहृत्, तमश्छिद् &c.

REMUNERATE, v. t. मूल्यं-वेतनं-प्रतिफलं दा 3 U, See RECOMPENSE, REWARD. -ION, s. मूल्यं, वेतनं, प्रतिफलं, पारितोषिकं.

RENCOUNTER, s. संमर्दः, द्वंद्वं, संघट्टः, अभिघातः; See BATTLE, COLLISION.

REND, v. t. दॄ 9 P or c., भिद् 7 P, छिद् 7 P, व्यध् 4P, विशॄ 9P; वि-उद्-दल् c. (दलयति), खंड् 10; See TEAR; 'heart-r. ing' हृदयस्पृश्, हृदिस्पृश्, हृदयमर्मच्छिद्. -ER, s. विदारकः, भेदकः. -ING, s. विदारणं, भिदा, स्फुटनं, भेदः, भंगः. -RENT, a. विदीर्ण, स्फुटित, भिन्न, &c. -s. छिद्रं, रंध्रं, भेदः, विदरः, स्फुटनं, भिदा, भंगः.

RENDER, v. t. प्रति-दा 3 U, प्रति-ऋ c. (अर्पयति), प्रति-पद् c., निर्यत् c. 2 दा, कृ 8 U, उपक्लृप् c. 3 जन् c., उत्पद् c., कृ; by the causal of roots; 'r. help' साहाय्यं कृ or दा; 'to r. proud' दृप् c.; 'r. unfriendly' विकृ c., विरंज् c., &c. 4 Translate, q. v.

RENDEZVOUS, s. समागम-संकेत-स्थानं, संकेतगृहं-स्थलं.

RENEGADE, s. धर्मभ्रष्टः, पतितः, पाखंडः, स्वधर्म-स्वपक्ष-त्यागी.

RENEW, v. t. नवीकृ 8 U, प्रतिसमा-धा 3 U, उद्धृ 1 P, पूर्वावस्थां नी 1 P or प्राप् c. or गम् c. 2 पुनः कृ; gen. ex. by पुनः आरभ् 1 A with other words; 'r. s studies' पुनः अध्ययनं प्रारभते; 'they r. ed hostilities' पुनः वैरं प्रारेभिरे. -AL, s. नवीकरणं, पूर्ववत्करणं, प्रतिसमाधानं, उद्धारः, पुनःकरणं, पुनः प्रारंभः.

RENOUNCE, v. t. न स्वीकृ or अंगीकृ 8 U, प्रत्याख्या 2 P, प्रत्यादिश् 6 P, प्रत्याचक्ष् 2 A; See REFUSE. 2 त्यज् 1 P, अपास् 4 U, वि-उत्-सृज् 6 P, हा 3 P; See ABANDON; 'to r. the world' संन्यस्, सर्वसंगं परित्यज्. -RENUNCIATION, s. प्रत्यादेशः, प्रत्याख्यानं, परित्यागः, उत्सर्गः, परिहारः; 'r. of the world' संन्यासः, सर्वसंगपरित्यागः.

RENOVATE, v. t. नवीकृ 8 U, पुनः कृ. -ION, s. नवीनता, नूतनावस्था, उद्धारः; See REFRESH, RENEW.

RENOWN, s. कीर्ति f., यशस् n., प्र-वि-ख्याति f.,

विश्रुति *f.* -ED, *a.* प्र-वि-ख्यात, विश्रुत, प्रथित, लब्ध-कीर्ति, प्रसिद्ध, लब्धप्रतिष्ठ; *See* FAME,-OUS.

RENT, *s.* करः, बलिः, राजस्वं. -*v. t.* भाटकेन दा 3 U; भद् c., भाटकेन-मूल्यदानेन-ग्रह् 9 P or सेव् 1 A or भुज् 7 A. -AL, *s.* 'r.-bill' करपत्रिका.

REPAIR, *v. t.* नवीकृ 8 U, सं-धा 3 U, प्रतिसमा-समा-धा, उद्धृ 1 P, पूर्ववत्कृ, पुनः स्वस्थीकृ, सुस्थित *a.* कृ. 2 (Loss &c.) पूर् 10, प्रमृज् 2 P, निष्कृ, शुध् c., प्रतिकृ, सं-धा. -*v. i.* आश्रि 1 U, प्रपद् 4 A, गम्-व्रज् 1 P, शरणं प्रपद् or गम् or या 2 P or अभ्युप-इ 2 P. -*s.* प्रति-,समाधानं, संस्कारः, संधानं, उद्धारः, नवीकरणं, पूर्वावस्थापापणं. -REPARABLE, *a.* पूरणीय; उद्धार्य, प्रतिसमाधेय; 'loss not r.' अपूरणीया हानिः. -REPARATION, *s.* Repair, q. v. 2 क्षति-हानि-पूरणं-निष्कृति *f.*, शोधनं, प्रतिफलं.

REPARTEE, *s.* क्षिप्रोत्तरं, व्यंगोक्ति *f.*, भंगिभाषणं, सरसोक्तिः.

REPAST, *s.* भोजनं, अन्नं, आहारः, अशनं, अभ्युपहारः.

REPAY, *v. t.* प्रतिदा 3 U, प्रति-ऋ c. (अर्पयति), निर्यत् 10, प्रति-पद् c., निवृत् c., प्रतिकृ 8 U. 2 प्रति-फलं-निष्कृतिं-दा, निष्कृ, अपाकृ, शुध् c., अपवृज् 10, oft. by प्रति; 'r. kindness' प्रत्युपकृ; 'r. an injury' प्रत्यपकृ, वैरं साध् c. -MENT, *s.* प्रतिदानं, प्रत्यर्पणं, निर्यातनं, शोधनं, शुद्धि *f.*, प्रतिफलं.

REPEAL, *v. t.* खंड् 10, निरस् 4 U, वि-,लुप् c., नि-परा-वृत्-c., उच्छिद् 7 P. -*s.* वि-,लोपः, निवर्तनं, खंडनं, निरसनं, प्रचारलोपः-भंगः. -ER, *s.* निवर्तकः, विलोपकः,

REPEAT, *v. t.* पुनः वद्-गद् 1 P, or उदीर् c. or व्याहृ 1 P, (Say, q. v.); अभ्यस् 4 U, (a letter) आम्रेडयति (D.). 2 आवृत् c., पुनः-मुहुः-कृ 8 U or आचर् 1 P or अनु-ष्ठा 1 P; 'ten r. ed two times' द्विरावृत्ता दश, द्विदशाः. 3 पठ् 1 P, व्याहृ, अनुवद्, उद्गृ 6 P, आ-ख्या 2 P, कथ् 10, उदीर्. -ED, *a.* पुनरुक्त, पुनर्भणित, पुनः पुनः कृत, आवृत्त, आवर्तित; 'with r. exertions' पुनः पुनः कृतैः प्रयत्नैः; 'in r. birth' परिवर्तिनि जन्मनि, जन्मनि जन्मनि. -EDLY, *adv.* वारं वारं, भूयो भूयः, पुनः पुनः, मुहुर्मुहुः, अभीक्ष्णं, असकृत्, बहुशः, अनेकशः. -REPETITION, *s.* पुनरुक्ति *f.*, पुनर्वादः, पुनर्वचनं-कथनं, पौनरुक्त्यं; 'made as a r.' पुनरुक्त, पुनरुक्ततां नीत; *See* SUPERFLUOUS. 2 पठनं, समभिव्याहारः, अनुवादः, अनुलापः. 3 आवृत्ति *f.*, आवर्तनं, पुनः विधानं-अनुष्ठानं-आवृत्तिः, पौनःपुन्यं, अभ्यासः; आम्रेडितं, द्विरुक्तिः (of a word &c.).

REPEL, *v. t.* अपास् 4 U, प्रति-व्या-हन् 2 P, प्रतिसृ c., निरस्, प्रतिक्षिप् 6 P, प्रतिवृ c., अपानुद् 6 P, नि-परा-वृत् c., प्रत्यादिश् 6 P; *See* DISPEL, DRIVE. -LENT,-LING, *a.* प्रतिघातिन्, प्रतिकारक, अपानोदिन्. -*s.* प्रति(ती)कारः, प्रतिघातः, प्रतिवारणं.

REPENT, *v. i.* अनु-पश्चात्-तप् 4 A, अनुशी 2 A, अनुशुच् 1 P, अनुतापं वह्-व्रज्-गम् 1 P, पश्चात् पीड्-खिद् pass. -ANCE, *s.* अनु-पश्चात्-तापः, अनुशयः, अनुशोकः, पश्चात्खेदः, मनस्तापः, विप्रतीसारः, पाप-दुष्कृत-खेदः. -ANT, *a.* सानुशय, सानुताप, संजातानुताप, अनुशयविधुर-पीडित, अनुतप्त, जातानुशय, जातखेद, अनुतापार्त.

REPERCUSSION, *s.* प्रतिघातः, प्रतिपतनं.

REPERTORY, *s.* *See* TREASURY.

REPINE, *v. i.* व्यथ् 1 A, शुच् 1 P, अवसद् 1 P, खिद्-पीड्-दु-संतप्-pass.; *See* FRET. -ING, *s.* मनस्तापः, मनोव्यथा, शोकः.

REPLACE, *v. t.* (स्थाने) पुनः आ-नि-धा 3 U or निविश् c. or न्यस् 4 U or स्था c. (स्थापयति); पूर् 10, स्थाने निविश् c., प्रतिनिधिं दा 3 U; 'one servant was r. ed by two' किंकरस्थाने किंकरद्वयं निवेशितं; *See* SUBSTITUTE.

REPLENISH, *v. t.* (पुनः) संपूर् 10 or उपक्लृप् c.

REPLETE, *s.* सं-परि-पूर्ण, सं-आ-कीर्ण, परिपूरित, आ-नि-चित, आढ्य, मय (यी *f.*) in comp. -ION, *s.* पूर्णता, पर्याप्ति *f.*; परि-,पूर्ति *f.*

REPLY, *s.* उत्तरं, प्रतिवचनं-वाक्यं-वाच् *f.*-उक्ति *f.* 2 उत्तरपक्षः, प्रतिवादः; 'leave no room for r.' निरुत्तरीकृ 8 U. -*v. i.* दा 3 U with (*s.*), उत्तरं प्रति-पद् 4 A, प्रतिवच् 2 P, प्रतिवद् 1 P, -भाष् 1 A. 2 Echo, q. v. -REPLICANT, *s.* उत्तरवादिन् *m.*, प्रतिवादी.

REPORT, *v. t.* आ-नि-विद् c., आ-ख्या 2 P or c. (ख्यापयति), विज्ञा c. (ज्ञापयति), बुध् c., वृत्तांतं लिख् 6 P, श्रु c.; 'he is r. ed to be dead' स मृत इति श्रूयते, इति जनश्रुतिः-प्रवादः. -*s.* नि-आ-वेदनं, विज्ञापना, विज्ञप्ति *f.*, कथनं; 'written r.' आवेदनपत्रं, विज्ञप्तिलेखः. 2 ख्याति *f.*, विश्रुति *f.*, कीर्ति *f.*; 'evil or bad r.' कौलीनं, अकीर्तिः. 3 वार्ता, वृत्तांतः,-प्रवादः, जन-लोक-वादः-प्रवादः-श्रुतिः-वार्ता, उपश्रुति, जनरवः; किंवदंती; 'there goes a r.' इति जनप्रवादः &c. श्रूयते, इति प्रवादः. 4 ध्वनिः, नादः, शब्दः; *See* NOISE. -ER, *s.* वृत्तांतनिवेदिन् *m.*

REPOSE, *v. i.* विश्रम् 4 P, संविश् 6 P, शी 2 A. 2 विश्वस् 2 P, प्रति-इ 2 P. 3 आ-अव-लंब् 1 A, आ-सं-श्रि 1 U; 'r. ing in confidence' विश्वासप्रतिपन्न, सविश्वासं स्थित. -*v. t.* विश्रम् c., संविश् c. 2 निक्षिप् 6 P, स्था c. (स्थापयति), नि-आ-धा 3 U. -*s.* विश्रा(श्र)मः, विश्रांति *f.*, विरामः, उप-प्र-शमः, प्र-शांति *f.*, श्रमच्छेदः-निवृत्ति *f.*, निर्वृति *f.*

REPOSIT, *v. t.* नि-आ-धा 3 U, न्यस् 4 U, रक्ष् 1 P. -ORY, *s.* निधिः, आगारं, निधानं, पात्रं, भाजनं, आश्रयः, आशयः, आधारः, कोष्ठः, रक्षणस्थानं.

REPREHEND, *v. t.* भर्त्स् 10 A, परुषं निंद् 1 P or उपालभ् 1 A; *See* CENSURE. –REPREHENSIBLE, *a.* निंद्य, उपालभ्य, गर्हित, गर्हणीय, दूषणीय. –REPREHENSION, *s.* निंदा, गर्हा, भर्त्सनं-ना, दूषणं, उपालंभः.

REPRESENT, *v. t.* वर्ण् 10, वि-वृ 5 U, निरूप् 10; oft. ex. by स्था c.; 'r. even vices as virtues' दोषानपि गुणपक्षमध्यारोपयंति, गुणपक्षे स्थापयंति (Ka. 108); 'r. in writing' अभि-,लिख् 6 P, लेख्ये निविश् c. or आरुह् c. 2 प्र-,दृश् c., सूच् 10, आविष्कृ 8 U, निरूप्. 3 नि-आ-विद् c., वि-ज्ञा c. (ज्ञापयति); *See* INFORM. 4 भूमौ-स्थाने-स्था 1 P or वृत् 1 A; प्रतिनिधिः भू; 'you r. the queen' भवान् राज्ञीस्थाने वर्तते, राज्ञीप्रतिनिधिः. 5 रूपं-वेषं-ग्रह् 9 P or धृ 1 P, 10; *See* PERSONATE; (a play &c.) प्रयुज् 10; 'have not seen it r. ed' न प्रयोगतो दृष्टं (Rat. 1); नाटकं प्रयोगेणाधिक्रियतां (S. 1) 'let it be r. ed on the stage'; 'r. a character' भूमिकायां वृत्; 'Urvaśí r. ing Lakshmi' उर्वशी लक्ष्मीभूमिकायां वर्तमाना (V. 3). –ATION, *s.* वर्णनं, निवेदनं, विज्ञापना, प्रदर्शनं, निरूपणं, विज्ञप्ति *f.* 2 प्रयोगः, अभिनयः. 3 प्रतिकृति *f.*, प्रतिरूपं, आलेख्यं, प्रतिच्छंदः, प्रतिमा, प्रतिमूर्ति *f.*; *See* PICTURE. –ATIVE, *s.* प्रतिनिधिः, प्रतिभूः, प्रतिपुरुषः. –*a.* प्रतिनिधीभूत; आदर्शभूत.

REPRESS, *v. t.* प्रति-नि-रुध् 7 U, सं-नि-यम् 1 P, नियंत्र् 10, नि-ग्रह् 9 P, प्रशम् c.; *See* CHECK. –ION, *s.* निरोधः, नियमः, निग्रहः, नियंत्रणं. –IVE, *a.* निरोधिन्, निग्रहकारिन्.

REPRIEVE, *s.* विश्रामः, विरति *f.* 2 दंडव्याक्षेपः-विलंबः. –*v. t.* दंडं व्याक्षिप् 6 P or विलंब् c., व्यवहारदर्शनं व्याक्षिप्.

REPRIMAND, *v. t.* निंद् 1 P, भर्त्स् 10 A, उपालभ् 1 A, वाचा दंड् 10, अव-अधि-क्षिप् 6 P. –*s.* निंदा, भर्त्सना-नं, उपालंभः, वाग्दंडः, वाक्ताडनं; *See* CENSURE.

REPRISAL, *s.* प्रत्यपहरणं, प्रतिपीडनं.

REPROACH, *v. t.* (परुषं) निंद् 1 P, गर्ह् 1, 10 A, उपालभ् 1 A, आक्रुश् 1 P, अप-परि-वद् 1 A, निर्-, भर्त्स् 10 A, आ-अधि-क्षिप् 6 P, दुष् c. (दूषयति), कुत्स् 10; सावज्ञं निंद्, तिरस्कृ 8 U, धिक्कृ, अवमन् 4 A. –*s.* धिक्कारः, निंदा, गर्हा, तिरस्कारः, आ-अधिक्षेपः, परि(री)वादः, उपालंभः, आक्रोशः, भर्त्सनं-ना, परुषोक्ति *f.*, वाक्पारुष्यं, दुरुक्तं, वाग्दंडः, निंदा-भर्त्सनावाक्यं. 2 दूषणं, कलंकः, अ-अप-कीर्ति *f.*; लज्जास्पदं. –FUL, *a.* निंदागर्भ; निंदात्मक, परिवादक; better by (*s.*) in comp.; 'r. words' निंदावचनानि. 2 गर्हित, निंद्य, गर्हणीय, लज्जाप्रद. –FULLY, *adv.* साधिक्षेपं, सोपालंभं.

REPROBATE, *v. t.* धिक्कृ 8 U, न्यक्कृ, दुष् c. (दूषयति), गर्ह् 1, 10 A; *See* REPROACH. –*a.*, *s.* दुर्वृत्त, दुराचार, पाप-खंडित-वृत्त, दुष्ट, पापात्मन्, दुःशील, दुरात्मन्; (of acts) दुष्ट, निंद्य, गर्ह्य. –ION, *s.* गर्हा, गर्हणं, अतिदुष्टता.

REPRODUCE, *v. t.* पुनः कृ 8 U or उत्पद् c. or जन् c.; 'he r. ed the whole speech' समग्रमेव भाषणं स यथातथमुदीरयामास. –REPRODUCTION, *s.* प्रत्युत्पत्ति *f.*, पुनर्जननं.

REPROVE, REPROOF, *See* REPROACH.

REPTILE, *s.* सरीसृपः, सर्पणशीलः, उरगः, उरोगःगामी, उरंगमः, सर्पः. –*a.* सर्पिन्, सर्पणशील.

REPUBLIC, *s.* प्रजासत्ताकं-प्रजातंत्रं-राज्यं, लोक-प्रजाप्रभुत्वं. –AN, *a.* प्रजाप्रभुत्वविशिष्ट, लोकप्रभुत्वसंबंधिन्, (*s.*) in comp. –*s.* प्रजाप्रभुत्ववादी, प्रजापक्षवादी. –ANISM, *s.* प्रजाप्रभुत्ववादः, प्रजातंत्रपक्षः.

REPUDIATE, *v. t.* प्रत्यादिश् 6 P, निराकृ 8 U, निर्-अप-अस् 4 U, निः-सृ c., परित्यज् 1 P, प्रत्या-ख्या 2 P, अपध्वंस् c., अव-निर्-धू 5, 9 U, 6 P; *See* REJECT also. –ION, *s.* प्रत्यादेशः, निराकरणं, प्रत्याख्यानं, परित्यागः, अपासनं. 2 विवाहसंबंधत्यागः, दांपत्यभ्रेषः.

REPUGNANT, *a.* प्रतीप, विरुद्ध, प्रतिकूल, विपरीत, अत्यंतविमुख-विरक्त. –REPUGNANCE, *s.* विरोधः, प्रातिकूल्यं, वैपरीत्यं, विरागः, विद्वेषः, अनिच्छा, वैमुख्यं, विमति *f.*, विरक्ति *f.*

REPULSE, *v. t.* निराकृ 8 U, निः-प्रति-सृ c., अवधीर् 10; प्रत्यादिश् 6 P, प्रत्या-ख्या 2 P, परा-प्रति-हन् 2 P, भंज् 7 P, वि-द्रु c. (army). –ION, *s.* निराकरणं, निःसारणं, प्रत्यादेशः, अवधीरणं-णा, प्रतिघातः, प्रतिहननं; विद्रावणं, पराजयः, भंगः. –IVE, *a.* अप्रिय, द्विष्ट, निंद्य, बीभत्स, बीभत्सावह; *See* HIDEOUS. 2 प्रतिघातिन्, प्रतिसारिन्.

REPUTE, *v. t.* मन् 4 A, अभि-सं-°,गण् 10; *See* CONSIDER; 'r. ed as authors' कर्तृत्वेनाभिमताः. –*s.*,-ATION, *s.* कीर्ति *f.*, ख्याति *f.*, प्र-वि-°, यशस् *n.*, प्रतिष्ठा, प्रथा, प्रतिपत्ति *f.*, गौरवं, प्रसिद्धि *f.*; 'of established r.' लब्धप्रतिष्ठ; 'good r.' सुख्यातिः; 'bad r.' दुष्कीर्तिः, अप-अ-कीर्तिः, वाच्यता, कौलीनं, दुर्नाम. –ABLE, *a.* सं-,मान्य, प्रशस्य, माननीय, आदरणीय. 2 यशः-कीर्ति-कर (री *f.*), कीर्ति-मान-प्रद. –ED, *a.* अभिमत, जन-लोक-विश्रुत, सर्वज्ञात, जनप्रसिद्ध.

REQUEST, *v. t.* याच् 1 A, अर्थ् 10 A, प्र-अभि-,° वि-ज्ञा c. (ज्ञापयति), सविनयं नि-आ-विद् c. –*s.* प्रार्थना, अभ्यर्थना, याचना, विज्ञापना, विज्ञप्ति *f.*, नि-आ-वेदनं, याच्ञा. 2 आकांक्षा, इच्छा, अभिलाषः, अपेक्षा; 'in general r.' सर्वाभीप्सित, बहुशः इष्ट.

REQUIRE, *v. t.* प्रार्थ् 10 A, प्रच्छ् 6 P, याच् 1 A,

2 (Need) वि-,अपेक्ष् 1 A, आकांक्ष् 1 P; oft. ex. by उपयोगः, प्रयोजनं, कार्यं, with instr.; or अर्ह् 1 P; or by pot. pass. part.; 'that it is affection and should r. a cause is a contradiction' स्नेहश्च निमित्तसव्यपेक्ष इति विप्रतिषिद्धमेतत् (Mal. 1); 'I do not r. his help' न मम तस्य साहाय्येन प्रयोजनं; 'r. s a careful consideration' निपुणमवेक्षणीयः, निपुणावेक्षणमर्हति. -MENT, s. Ex. by (v.); 'all the r. s of man' यद्यन्नरैरपेक्ष्यते or इष्यते. -REQUISITE, a. आवश्यक (की f.), अवश्यक, आकांक्षित, अपेक्षित. -s. अवश्यकवस्तु-द्रव्यं, अपेक्षितं. -REQUISITION, s. प्रार्थना-नं, अपेक्षा, आकांक्षा.

REQUITE, v. t. प्रति-दा 3 U, प्रतिफलं दा, प्रत्युपकृ 8 U, निस्तॄ c.; See RECOMPENSE, REPAY; (grudge &c.) प्रतिकृ, निर्यत् 10, शुध् c., साध् c. -AL, s. प्रतिदानं, प्रतिफलं, निस्तारः, निष्कृति f., प्रत्युपकारः, पारितोषिकं, निर्यातनं. 2 प्रति(ती)कारः, प्रतिक्रिया, शुद्धि f.; साधनं.

RESCIND, v. t. विलुप् c., खंड् 10, निरस् 4 U, निवृत् c. -RESCISSION, s. वि-,लोपः, खंडनं, निरसनं; See REPEAL.

RESCRIPT, s. See COUNTERPART.

RESCUE, v. t. मुच् 6 P or c., मोक्ष् 10, वि-निर्-°, निस्तॄ c., उद्-हृ 1 P or धृ 10; परि-त्रै 1 A, रक्ष् 1 P; See PROTECT. -s. वि-,मुक्ति f., मोचनं, मोक्षः-क्षणं, उद्धारः; परि-,त्राणं, रक्षणं, निस्तारः, तारणं; 'on, on, to the r.' सत्वरं परित्रायध्वं. -ER, s. उद्धर्तृ m., त्राता, रक्षकः, मोक्षकः.

RESEARCH, s. अन्वेषणं-णा, निरूपणं, अनुसंधानं, जिज्ञासा, मार्गणं, विचारणा.

RESEMBLE, v. t. सं-वद् 1 P (with instr.), अनुकृ 8 U (with gen.), अनुहृ 1 P (with acc.); 'the characters r. each other' संवदंत्यक्षराणि (Mu. 5); gen. by तुल्य, सदृश, समान, उपम, अनुरूप in comp., ('Like', q. v.); भव पितुरनुरूपो गुणैः (V. 5) 'r. your father in qualities'; देहबंधेन स्वरेण च रामभद्रमनुहरति, अस्य मुखं वध्वा मुखचंद्रेण संवदत्येव (U. 4). 2 उप-प्रति-मा 3 A, 2 P, समीकृ. -ANCE, s. सादृश्यं; सारूप्यं, तुल्यत्वं, संवादः, साम्यं, औपम्यं, उपमा, अनुकारः, अनुहारः, तुला; साधर्म्यं (in qualities); 'to bear r.' सादृश्यं-तुलां-अधिरुह् or समारुह् 1 P; See (v.); (तुलां यदारोहति दंतवाससा K. v. 34). 2 प्रतिकृति f., प्रतिरूपं, आलेख्यं; See PICTURE. -ING, a. संवादिन्, (न केवलमस्मदंगसंवादिनी आकृतिः U. 6); अनुरूप, तुल्य, सम, समान, अनुकारिन्, अनुहारिन्;

RESENT, v. i. अभि-प्रति-क्रुध् 4 P (with acc.), क्रुध्-कुप्-रुष् 4 P, अपकारापेक्षया कुप्. -FUL, a. क्रोधिल, क्रोधशील, समन्यु, सासूय, प्रत्यपकारबुद्धि. -MENT, s. कोपः, क्रोधः, रोषः, अमर्षः, मन्युः; See INDIGNANT, &c.

RESERVE, v. t. सं-प्रतिसं-हृ 1 P, निग्रह् 9 P. 2 (आकालांतरात्) सं-चि 5 U, नि-धा 3 U, संग्रह्, रक्ष् 1 P, अवशिष् 7 P or c., त्यज् 1 P (temporarily); आपदर्थे धनं रक्षेत् 'should r. his money for times of want.' 3 गुप् 1 P, सं-वृ 5 U, अप-ह्नु 2 A, न स्पष्टीकृ, न विशदीकृ. -s. संवरणं, संवृति f., नि-अप-ह्नवः, मनोगुप्ति f. 2 नि-,यंत्रणं-णा, निग्रहः, निरोधः; 'without any r.' विवृतं, निर्व्याजं, अनियंत्रणं, निर्यंत्रणं. 3 (Of disposition) वाग्यंत्रणं, कथा-आलाप-विरक्ति f.-पराङ्मुखता, अल्पभाषणं, वाग्यतत्वं. 4 संचयः, संग्रहः. 5 (Of an army) प्रति-परिग्रहः, प्रत्यासा(स)रः, पार्ष्णित्रं सैन्यं. -ATION, s. गोपनं, निग्रहः, संहारः, गुप्तिः, अपवारणं. 2 नि-अप-ह्नवः, मनोगुप्तिः, संतरणं, संवृतिः. 3 परिवर्जनं, अपवादः, व्यावृत्ति f.; 'with this r. only' अयमेव तस्यापवादः. 4 संग्रहः-हणं, संचयः. -ED, a. रक्षित, गुप्त, अवशेषित. 2 संवृतिमत्, गूढभाव, गुप्तांतःकरण, अनुत्तानहृदय, संवरणशील; वाग्यत, यंत्रितवाक्, कथा-आलाप-विरक्त-विमुख, अल्पभाषिन्, अल्पालापिन्. -EDLY, adv. गूढभावेन, संवृतचेतसा. -RESERVOIR, s. जलाशयः, तडागः-गं, जलाधारः, तोयाधारः, वापी.

RESIDE, v. i. वस् 1 P, नि-प्रति-°; अधि-ष्ठा 1P, अधिवस् (with acc.); निली 4 A; आश्रि 1 U, वृत् 1 A; See DWELL. 2 सद् 1 P; अवशिष् pass. -ENCE, s. स्थिति f., वसति f., वर्तनं, अधिष्ठानं, वासः; 'r. abroad' प्रवासः. 2 वसतिः, वासस्थानं, नि-,वासः, गृहं, आ-नि-लयः, आश्रयः, अधिष्ठानं, स्थानं, निकेतनं; See HOUSE; 'change of r.' स्थलांतरगमनं. -ENT, s. नि-,वासिन्, or by deriv.; 'r. of this or that place' अत्रत्यः; तत्रत्यः; आयोध्यिकः, कौशांबीयः, &c. -a. नि-,वासिन्, स्थ, वर्तिन् in comp.; आश्रित, कृतालय. —RESIDUE, s. अव-,शेषः-षं-शिष्टं. -AL,-ARY, a. अव-शिष्ट, शेष in comp.

RESIGN, v. t. परि-,त्यज् 1 P, उत्-वि-सृज् 6 P, हा 3 P, प्रत्यादिश् 6 P, पराक्षिप् 6 P; See ABANDON. 2 सं-,कृ c. (अर्पयति), आयत्तीकृ, आ-नि-विश् c., समा-धा 3 U, न्यस् 4 U, निक्षिप्, प्राति-पद् c. 3 क्षम् 1 A, सह् 1 A ; 'of those who r. themselves to you' त्वय्यावेशितचित्तानां, त्वत्समाहितचेतसां; 'r. one's claims' स्वत्वं निवृत् c., अधिकारं त्यज्; 'r. oneself to his fate' दैवाधीनीभू. -ATION, s. परि-,त्यागः, उत्सर्गः, प्रत्यादेशः, पराक्षेपः; 'r. of one's claim' स्वत्वनिवृत्तिः; 'written r.' त्यागपत्र-लेखः. 2 समर्पणं, निक्षेपणं, न्यसनं, निवेशनं. 3 क्षमा, क्षांति f., संतोषवृत्ति f.; 'r. to God' ईश्वराधीनता; ईश्वरेच्छानुवर्तनं. -ED, a. त्यक्त, अर्पित

न्यस्त, &c. 2 क्षमावत्, तितिक्षु, शांत, ईश्वरेच्छाधीन, ईश्वरन्यस्तचित्त.

RESIN, *s.* अ-,राल:, सर्जरस:, यक्षधूप:; *See* PITCH.

RESIST, *v. t.* प्रति-बंध् 9 P, प्रति-वि-रुध् 7 U, नि-, वार् 10, प्रत्यव-स्था 1 A; प्रतिकृ 8 U, प्रत्या-व्या-हन् 2 P; बाध् 1 A, निग्रह् 9 P, प्रतिष्टंभ् 9 P, परिपंथी-भू; *See* OPPOSE. —ANCE, *s.* प्रति-वि-रोध:, प्रतिबंध:, प्रति(ती)कार:, प्रतियोग:, पर्यवस्थानं, प्रतिष्टंभ:, प्रतियत्न:, प्रत्याघात:. —ER, *s.* प्रतियोगी, प्रतिबंधक:. —LESS, *a.* अनिवार्य, दुर्निवार, अप्रतिकार, अनवग्रह, दुर्निग्रह.

RESOLVE, *v. i.* निश्चि 5 U, निर्णी 1 P, व्यव-सो 4 P, अध्यव-सो, संक्लृप् c., मति-बुद्धि-कृ 8 U; *See* DETERMINE. —*v. t.* वि-ली c., वि-द्रु c. (melt); गल् c., क्षर् c.; सागरे नद्यो विलीयंते 'rivers are r. ed into the sea.' 2 वि-युज् 7 A, 10, विश्लिष् c., व्याकृ, विभिद् c., पृथक् कृ; *See* SEPARATE. 3 (Doubts) छिद् 7 P, अपाकृ, अपनी 1 P, निरस् 4 U; *See* DISPEL. —*s.* Resolution, q. v. —ED, *a.* विश्लेषित, व्याकृत, &c. 2 कृतनिश्चय-संकल्प-मति-बुद्धि, व्यवसित, निश्चित, निर्णीत, संकल्पित. —ENT, *s.* द्रावणं, शोथहृत्. —ER, *s.* निभेत्तृ *m.*, छेत्ता, छिद् *m.* in comp. —RESOLUTE, *a.* दृढ-स्थिर-निश्चय-संकल्प, स्थिरधी-मति, धीर, धृतिमत्; *See* RESOLVED also. —LY, *adv.* दृढं, सनिश्चयं, स्थिरचेतसा. —NESS, *s.*; *See* below. —RESOLUTION, *s.* निश्चय:, निर्णय:, संकल्प:, व्यवसाय:, सर्ग:, अध्यवसाय:; स्थिर-दृढ-निश्चय:-संकल्प:, मति *f.*, संप्र-अव-धारणा. 2 स्थिरता, स्थैर्यं. धैर्यं, धृति *f.*, निर्बंध:, स्थिरमतित्वं, अभिनिवेश:. 3 विश्लेषणं, वियोजनं, विभेदनं. 4 उपन्यास:, प्रतिज्ञा, उपक्षेप:.

RESONANT, *a.* मुखरित, प्रतिध्वनित, प्रतिनादित, अनुनादिन्, संघुष्ट. —RESONANCE, *s.* अनु-प्रति-नाद:, प्रतिध्वनि:-स्वन:.

RESORT, *v. i.* (To) सेव् 1 A, नि-पारि-°, श्रि 1 U, आ-सं-समा-उपा-°, उप-अभि-गम् 1 P or इ-या 2 P, अभि-उप-सृ 1 P; जुष् 6 A (frequently). —*s.* आश्रयणं, सेवनं, गमनं, &c. 2 आश्रय:, शरणं, आयतनं, अभिगमनस्थानं. 3 गति *f.*, उपाय:, शरणं.

RESOUND, *v. i.* प्रति-नद्-स्वन्-ध्वन् 1P, अनु-रस् 1P; *See* ECHO. —*v. t.* प्रतिध्वन् c. &c.; निनादेन पूर् 10; 'r. ing the directions' दिश: प्रतिनिनादेन पूरयन्, दिश: प्रतिध्वानयन्. —ING, *a.* Resonant, q. v.

RESOURCE, *s.* उपाय:, गति *f.*, प्रयुक्ति *f.*, कल्पना, साधनं; 'having no other r.' अनन्यगतिक. 2 (r. s) विभव:, द्रव्यसाधनं, आय:, वित्त-द्रव्य-सामग्री, अर्थ:, धनं; 'of small r. s' अल्पविभव.

RESPECT, *v. t.* पूज् 10, अर्च् 1 P, 10; संमन् c., आदृ 6 A, सेव् 1 A, भज् 1 U, सं-भू c., सत्कृ 8 U, पुरस्कृ. 2 अपेक्ष् 1 A, उद्दिश् 6 P; *See* REFER, RELATE. —*s.* अपेक्षा, उद्देश:, संबंध:, अनुषंग:, विषय:; 'with r. to the result' फलापेक्षया, फलमुद्दिश्य. 2 सं-,मान:, पूजा, अभि-,अर्चनं, आदर:, संभावना, प्रश्रय:, गौरवं, पुरस्कार:, सत्कार:, अर्हणा, अर्चा, भक्ति *f.* 3 दृष्टि *f.*, अवेक्षा. 4 विषय:, प्रकरणं, वस्तु *n.*, अर्थ:. 5 (r. s) नमस्कार:, प्रणाम:, प्रणति *f.*, अभिवंदनं, प्रणिपात:, सभाजनं; 'in this r.' अत्र विषये; 'in all r. s' सर्वथा; 'pay one's r. s' प्रणम् 1 P, सभाज् 10, प्रणिपत् 1 P. —ABLE, *a.* पूज्य, माननीय, &c.; विशिष्ट, आर्य, सप्रतिष्ठ, गुरु; 'a r. person' आर्य-सु-जन:; 'of a r. family' अभिजात, अभिजनवत्, कुलीन. 2 मध्यम, सामान्य, नातिगुरु. —ABLY, *adv.* आर्यं, उदार, in comp.; आर्यवत्, शिष्टवत्, सगौरवं; 'r. dressed' उदारनेपथ्यभृत्, आर्यवेषधारिन्. —FUL, *a.* सादर, सप्रश्रय, सगौरव, सविनय, आदर-मर्यादा-शील, मानपुर:-सर, आदर-मान-पूर्व. —FULLY, *adv.* सादरं, सप्रश्रयं, सविनयं. —ING, *a.* उद्दिश्य, अधिकृत्य, अपेक्ष्य; *See* REGARDING. —IVE, (Own) *a.* Ex. by स्व-स्व, ('Own' q. v.); 'they went to their r. houses' स्वं स्वं गृहं ते जग्मु:; 'in their r. places' स्वेषु स्वेषु स्थानेषु. 2 सापेक्ष, अकेवल, अविविक्त, अन्यसंबद्ध; इतरेतर-अन्योन्य in comp. —IVELY, *adv.* यथाक्रमं, यथानुक्रमं, पौर्वापर्येण, प्रत्येकं प्रत्येकं.

RESPIRE, *v. i.* उत्-नि-श्वस् 2 P, प्र-अन् 2 P. —ATION, *s.* श्वास:, श्वासोच्छ्वास:, प्राण:. —ATORY, *a.* श्वास in comp.; 'r. organ' श्वासेंद्रियं.

RESPITE, *s.* विराम:, विश्राम:, विरति *f.*, अवकाश:, विलंब:, विच्छेद:, प्र-उप-शम:. —*v. t.* विश्रामं-अवकाशं-दा 3 U.

RESPLENDENT, *a.* देदीप्यमान, विभ्राजमान, अतितेजस्; *See* BRIGHT, SPLENDID.

RESPOND, *v. i.* प्रति-वच् 2 P, प्रति-वद् 1 P, उत्तरं दा 3 U; *See* REPLY. —ENT, *s.* प्रतिवादिन् *m.*, प्रत्यर्थिन्, उत्तरवादी. —RESPONSE, *s.* उत्तरं, प्रतिवचनं, प्रतिवाक्यं. 2 प्रतिवाद:, उत्तरं. —RESPONSIBLE, *a.* अनुयोगाधीन, अनुयोज्य, आह्वानाधीन, प्रष्टव्य; oft. by उत्तरं दा; 'you are r. for this act' अस्य त्वयैवोत्तरं दातव्यं. 2 धूर्वह, धूर्वोढृ, धुरंधर, धुरीण. —RESPONSIBILITY, *s.* भार:, भर:, धुर् *f.*; 'the whole r. of the kingdom' राज्यस्य समस्तो भर:, राज्यधुरा. 2 अनुयोगाधीनता, प्रष्टव्यता. —RESPONSIVE, *a.* उत्तरदायिन्. 2 संवादिन्.

REST, *v. i.* विश्रम् 4 P, वि-आ-रम् 1 P, (कार्यात्) निवृत् 1 A; निश्चलीभू 1 P, स्थिरीभू, निश्चेष्टीभू. 2 (Lean against) आलंब् 1 A, उपा-समा-आ-श्रि 1 U; नि-उप-धा pass.; 'with her face r. ing on her left hand' वामहस्तोपहितवदना (S. 4);

oft. by भरं कृ 8 U (with loc.); 'r. ing on his three hoofs (legs)' खुरत्रये भरं कृत्वा (H. 2); दंडं भारं निधाय, यष्टिमवलंब्य, &c. 3 प्र-उप-शम् 4 P, सुखिन्-निर्वृत-स्वस्थ- a. भू. 4 शी 2 A, स्वप् 2 P, सं-विश् 6 P, नि-द्रा 2 P, नि-ली 4 A. 5 स्था 1 P, भू, वृत्; 'r. with' अवलंब्, अपेक्ष् 1 A, अधीन-आयत्त- a. भू; *See* DEFEND (on); 'further than this r. s with fate' भाग्यायत्तमतः परं (S. 4). –*v. t.* विश्रम् c., शी c., संविश् c. 2 निविश् c., न्यस् 4 U, अवलंब् c., स्था c., आ-नि-धा 3 U; चापे विजयाशंसां निदधौ 'r. ed his hope of victory on his bow'; सकलरिपुजयाशा यत्र बद्धा सुतैस्ते (Ve. 5) 'on whom your sons had r.-ed their hopes of overthrowing all enemies'. –*s.* विश्रा(श्र)मः, विश्रांति *f.*, कार्य-व्यापार-निवृत्तिः. 2 (Of a boby) स्थिरता, निश्चलता, निश्चेष्टता, अचलता. 3 सुखं, सौख्यं, स्वास्थ्यं, निर्वृति *f.*, प्र-उप-शमः-शांति *f.*; *See* EASE. 4 अवलंबनं, आधारः, स्थानं. 5 निद्रा, शयनं, संवेशः-शनं. 6 अव-,शेषः-शिष्टं; अन्य, इतर, अपर (*a.* pl.) (of persons); आदि, प्रभृति, in comp. 7 यति *f.*, अवसानं; 'at r.' निश्चल, निश्चेष्ट, अचल, स्थिर; सुस्थ, प्र-उप-शांत, निर्वृत, विश्रांत; निर्व्यापार, निरुद्योग. –ING, *a.* आलंबित, आश्रित, नि-उप-हित, स्थित; स्थ, वर्तिन् in comp.; 'r.-place' शयन-विश्राम-स्थानं. –LESS, *a.* व्याकुल, पर्या-समाकुल, पारिप्लव, अशांत, विह्वल, अस्वस्थ, व्यग्र, अनिर्वृत, उद्विग्न. 2 चपल, चंचल, चल; सदागति, सास्पंद. 3 उन्निद्र, विनिद्र, निर्णिद्र; 'passes r. nights' उन्निद्रा रजनीं गमयति (Mal. 3). –LESSLY, *adv.* अनिर्वृतं, व्यग्रं; चंचलतया. –LESSNESS, *s.* अनिर्वृतिः, अस्वास्थ्यं, उद्वेगः, व्यग्रता, चापल्यं, चांचल्यं, &c.

RESTITUTION, *s.* प्रतिदानं, प्रत्यर्पणं, प्रत्यानयनं.

RESTIVE, RESTIFF, *a.* दुष्ट, दुर्मार्गप्रस्थित, अदम्य, दुर्दम, प्रतीप, दुर्वृत्त, दुर्विनीत, उद्धत.

RESTORE, *v. t.* पुनर्-प्रति-दा 3 U or ऋ c. (अर्पयति), प्रति-पद् c., निर्यत् 10, परावृत् c., प्रत्यानी 1 P; पुनर्लभ् 1 A, प्रति-पद् 4 A, प्राप् 5 P, (when passively used); प्रत्यर्पितस्वांगः 'with his body r. ed to him'; स्मरं वपुषा स्वेन नियोजयिष्यति (K. IV. 42) 'will r. to Cupid his body'; 'r. ed the universe to the rule of Indra' पुनरपि त्रिभुवनमिंद्रवशमगात् or नीतं, इंद्रशासनायत्तं कृतं; 'r. ed to its pristine splendour' पुराणशोभामधिरोपितायां (वसतौ) (R. XVI. 42); 'r. to life' जीव् c., सोच्छ्वास- *a.* कृ 8 U, असून् प्राप् c.; 'r. ed to consciousness' लब्धसंज्ञ, प्राप्तचैतन्य. –ATION, *s.* प्रतिदानं, प्रत्यर्पणं, प्रतिपादनं, निर्यातनं, परावर्तनं, प्रत्यानयनं, उद्धारः, पूर्वावस्थाप्रापणं, &c. –ATIVE, *a.* अग्निवर्धन (नी *f.*), सत्व-बल-वर्धन. –*s.* बलवर्धनं, बल्यं, वाजीकरणं. –ER, *s.* प्रतिदातृ *m.*, प्रत्यर्पयिता.

RESTRAIN, *v. t.* सं-अव-नि-रुध् 7 U, निग्रह् 9 P, नि-सं-यम् 1 P, नि-प्रति-बंध् 9 P, आ-वृ 5 U, संह् 1 P, नि-,यंत्र् 10; *See* FORBID, CONTROL also. 2 (Legally) आसिध् 1 P, रुध्. –ER, *s.* नियंता, निग्रहीता, निरोधकः. –RESTRAINT, *s.* निग्रहः, नि-अव-रोधः, सं-नि-यमः, नि-,यंत्रणं-णा, प्रतिबंधः, स्तंभः, प्रतिरोधः, बाधा, यमः, जयः, दमः (of the senses). 2 आसेधः ; 'r. of speech' वाग्यमः, वाक्संयमः.

RESTRICT, *v. t.* निरुध् 7 U, नियंत्र् 10, अवधृ 10, नि-सं-यम् 1 P, निबंध् 9 P, परि-मा 3 A, 2 P, निग्रह् 9 P; 'my actions being thus r. ed on all sides' एवं सर्वतो निरुद्धचेष्टाप्रसरस्य मे (Mu. 3); बाध् 1 A, व्यावृत् c. (scope); अपवाद इवोत्सर्गं व्यावर्तयितुमीश्वरः (R. XV. 7) 'can r. the scope of a rule'. –ED, *a.* नियत, समर्याद, सावधिक, परिमित, &c.; *See* LIMITED. –ION, *s.* सीमा, इयत्ता, नियमः, मर्यादा, अवधिः, परिच्छेदः, निर्बंधः, निरोधः, अवधारणा, व्यावृत्ति *f.*, यंत्रणा ; 'without r.' स्वैरं, यथेच्छं, अनियंत्रणं. –IVE, *a.* व्यावर्तक, नियामक, परिच्छेदक, अवधारण; तुशब्दोऽवधारणार्थः, व्यावृत्त्यर्थकः (S. B.) 'has a r. sense.'

RESULT, *v. i.* अव-पर्यव-सो 4 P, वि-,परिणम् 1 U; *See* END. 2 उत्पद्-निष्पद् 4 A, प्र-सं-उद्-भू 1 P, जन् 4 A, प्रवृत् 1 A; *See* PRODUCE; gen. ex. by (*s.*); 'it will r. in nothing' तन्निरर्थकं भवेत् ; 'it will r. in his destruction' तस्य नाश एव फलं भवेत्. –*s.* परिणामः, फलं. 2 अर्थः, गुणः, निष्पन्नं, सिद्धि *f.*; अंतः, अवसानं, शेषः, उदर्कः; पाकः; 'good r.' शुभफलं. 3 सिद्धांतः, मथितार्थः, निश्चितार्थः; 'producing no r.' निष्फल, निर्गुण, व्यर्थ. –ING, *a.* ज, जन्य, उद्भव, फल in comp.; *See* PRODUCED.

RESUME, *v. t.* पुनः-भूयः-आदा 3 A or ग्रह् 9 P or आप् 5 P or लभ् 1 A, प्रत्याह् 1 P; 'let us r. (the thread of) our discourse' प्रकृतं-प्रस्तुतविषयं-अनुसंदधाम or अनुसराम; oft. by पुनः-भूयः-आरभ् 1 A or कृ, with other words; 'r. ed their fighting' पुनर्योद्धुमारेभिरे; अतः परं पुनः कथयिष्यामि (M. 4) 'I shall r. my story from this point afterwards'; 'he r. ed his discourse' पुनर्वक्तुं प्रचक्रमे. –*s.* सारः, संग्रहः, सारार्थः. –RESUMPTION, *s.* प्रत्यादानं, पुनर्ग्रहणं, प्रत्याहारः.

RESURRECTION, *s.* पुनरुज्जीवनं, मृतोत्थापनं.

RESUSCITATE, *v. t.* पुनर्जीव् c. or उत्था c. (उत्थापयति), उज्जीव् c., प्रत्युद्-जीव् c. –ION, *s.* पुनर्जीवनं, उत्थापनं, उज्जीवनं, प्रत्युज्जीवनं.

RETAIL, *s.* अल्पशः विक्रयः, पण्यक्रयः. –*v. t.* अल्पशः विक्री 9 A or पण् 1 A. –ER, 'r.-dealer' *s.* अल्पशः पण्यविक्रयिन्, खंडवणिक्.

RETAIN, *v. t.* धृ 1 P, 10, रक्ष् 1 P, धा 3 U; ग्रह् 9 P. 2 (Servants) वेतनं दत्त्वा नियुज् 7 A, 10, व्या-पृ c., उप-नी 1 A, (कर्मकरानुपनयते S. K.); (in memory) चित्ते-मनसि कृ 8 U or नि-धा or निविश् c., अवधृ. –ER, *s.* अनुयायिन् *m.*, अनुगः, अनुचरः, पार्श्वकः, अनुगामी, अनुजीवी, सेवकः, भृत्यः, किंकरः, आश्रितः; *See* SERVANT; 'body of r.s' परिवारः, भृत्य-अनुयायि-वर्गः. –RETENTION, *s.* धारणा-णं, ग्रहणं. 2 (Faculty) *See* below; 'r. of urine' मूत्रसंगः. –RETENTIVE, *a.* धारणावत्, धारणक्षम; 'r. faculty' धारणाशक्ति *f.*, धारणा, मेधा, धारणावती धीः, ग्रहणसामर्थ्यं. 2 धर, ग्राहिन् in comp., धारक.

RETALIATE, *v. t.* प्रति-कृ 8 U, प्रत्यपकृ; (वैरं) निर्यत् 10, शुध् c., साध् c.; प्रति-हिंस् 7 P. –TION, *s.* प्रतिक्रिया, प्रति(ती)कारः, प्रत्यपकारः, प्रतिहिंसा, वैरसाधनं-शुद्धिः-निर्यातनं.

RETARD, *v. t.* प्रति-नि-रुध् 7 U, स्तंभ् 9 P, प्रतिबंध् 9 P, बाध् 1 A, नि-वृ c.; *See* OBSTRUCT. 2 विलंब् c., व्याक्षिप् 6 P, गतिं अवरुध् or स्तंभ्. –ATION, *s.* निरोधः, प्रतिबंधः, वेग-गति-रोधः, विलंबः, व्याक्षेपः. –ED, *a.* निरुद्ध, विलंबितगति, अवरुद्धवेग.

RETICENCE, *s.* मौनं, संवृति *f.*, मूकभावः, वाग्यमः. –RETICENT, *a.* मौनावलंबिन्, संवृतिमत्, यंत्रितवाच्, वाग्यत; *See* RESERVED.

RETICULAR, *a.* जालाकार, जालरूप. –RETICULATION, *s.* जालकर्म.

RETINUE, *s.* परिजनः, परिवारः, परिबर्हः, परिच्छदः, अनुयायि-भृत्य-वर्गः, परिचराः, अनुचराः.

RETIRE, *v. i.* अपक्रम् 1 U, 4 P, अपगम् 1 P, अप-या-इ 2 P, चल् 1 P, परावृत् 1 A; एकपार्श्वे स्था 1 P. 2 विश्रामार्थं उद्योगाद्-विरम् 1 P or कार्य-अधिकारं-त्यज् 1 P, विविक्तवृत्तिं सेव् 1 A, सेवां त्यज्; 'r. from the world' सर्वसंगं परित्यज्, संन्यस् 4 U, विविक्ते वस्; शांतिमार्गोत्सुकोभत् (R. VII. 71) 'wished to r. from the world'. –ED, *a.* विविक्त, गुप्त, विजन, गूढ, प्रच्छन्न, एकांत, निभृत, निर्जन; *See* LONELY; 'a r. spot' रहःस्थानं, विविक्तं. 2 (Disposition) संवृतिमत्, गूढ, अनुत्तान; *See* RESERVED. 3 त्यक्तकर्मन्, विविक्तसेविन्, त्यक्ताधिकार; 'a r. person' संन्यासी, मुक्तसंगः. –MENT, *s.* अपसरणं, अपक्रमणं, अपगमनं, &c. 2 निर्जन-विविक्त-स्थानं, रहःस्थानं. 3 विविक्तवृत्ति *f.*, अधिकार-कार्य-त्यागः; विविक्तसेवनं; संन्यासः. –ING, *a.* अपक्रामिन् &c. 2 विविक्त-प्रिय-सेविन्, अधृष्ट; *See* RESERVED.

RETORT, *v. i.* प्रत्युत्तरं दा 3 U, प्रत्यवस्कंद् 1 P, प्रत्याक्षिप् 6 P, प्रतिकृ 8 U, प्रत्यभि-युज् 7 A, 10. –*s.* प्रत्युत्तरं, प्रत्यवस्कंदनं, प्रत्यपवादः, प्रत्यभियोगः, प्रत्यारोपः. 2 बकयंत्रं.

RETRACE, *v. t.* (One's steps) प्रत्यावृत्, निवृत्, 1 A; *See* RETURN.

RETRACT, *v. t.* प्रत्या-ख्या 2 P, प्रत्यादिश् 6 P, (word, promise, &c.); निवृत् c., निवृत् 1 A (with abl.); व्यतिक्रम् 1 U, 4 P, अतिचर् 1 P. –ION, *s.* प्रत्याख्यानं, प्रत्यादेशः, निवर्तनं, उक्त-त्यागः-व्यतिक्रमः.

RETREAT, *v. i.* अप-या 2 P, -गम्-सृ 1 P, अपक्रम् 1 U, 4 P, प्रतिनि-नि-प्रत्या-वृत् 1 A; *See* RETIRE. 2 प्र-वि-द्रु 1 P, अपधाव् 1 P, पलाय् 1 A. –*s.* अपसरणं, अपक्रमः-मणं, अपयानं, परावर्तनं, परावृत्ति *f.*, अपगमः, प्रतिनिवृत्तिः. 2 पलायनं, प्र-वि-द्रावः. 3 शरणं, आश्रयस्थानं, निलयः, विविक्त-निर्जन-देशः-स्थानं.

RETRENCH, *v. t.* न्यूनीकृ 8 U, ह्रस् c., अल्पीकृ, अवच्छिद् 7 P, अवकृत् 6 P, खंड् 10, अप-चि 5 U. –MENT, *s.* अवच्छेदः, खंडनं, व्यवच्छेदः, न्यूनव्ययः. व्ययापचयः.

RETRIBUTION, *s.* प्रति(ती)कारः, प्रतिफलं; *See* REVENGE. –RETRIBUTIVE, –RETRIBUTORY, *a.* प्रतिकारिन्, प्रतिकार in comp.

RETRIEVE, *v. t.* पुनः प्राप् 5 P or लभ् 1 A, प्रत्याहृ 1 P, उद्धृ 1 P, प्रति-,समा-धा 3 U; *See* RECOVER; 'irretrievably gone' असन्निवृत्तये गतं.

RETROCEDE, *v. i.* परावृत् 1 A; *See* RETURN.

RETROGRADE, *a.* प्रतीप, प्रतिलोम, वक्र, परावृत्त, विपरीत, प्रतीपगामिन्; 'in a r. direction' वि-,प्रतीपं; 'turn in a r. direction' प्रतीपयति (D.), परावृत् c. –*v. i.* परावृत् 1 A, प्रतीपं गम् 1 P; विपरीतं या-इ 2 P. 3 Decline, Decay, q. v. –ATION, RETROGRESSION, *s.* प्रतीपगमनं, विपरीतगमनं-गति *f.*

RETROSPECT, *s.* अतीतपर्यालोचनं, सिंहावलोकनं, अनुदर्शनं, भूतावलोकनं.–IVE, *a.* अनुदर्शिन्, गतावलोकिन्. 2 भूतापेक्ष, गतकालसापेक्ष.

RETURN, *v. i.* नि-प्रत्या-प्रतिनि-वृत् 1 A, प्रति-या 2 P, पुनर्या, पुनर्-इ 2 P, प्रत्यागम्-परापत् 1 P, प्रति with words for 'Come', 'Go', q. v.; 'it is gone never to r.' असन्निवृत्त्यै तदतीतमेव (S. 6); 'r. to life' चेतनां लभ् 1 A or प्रतिपद् 4 A, सोच्छ्वास- *a.* भू. 2 Answer, q. v. –*v. t.* प्रति-दा 1 P, 3 U, प्रति-ऋ c. (अर्पयति), निर्यत् 10, प्रति-पद् c. 2 पुनः आनी; 'r. good for good' प्रत्युपकारं कृ 8 U; 'r. an injury' प्रत्यपकृ, प्रतिहिंस् 7 P. –*s.* निवृत्ति *f.*, प्रत्यागमनं, प्रत्यावृत्तिः, परापतनं, पुनरागमनं, निवर्तनं, प्रत्यायानं, &c.; 'on your r.' प्रतिनिवृत्ते त्वयि. 2 प्रत्यर्पणं, प्रतिदानं, नि-र्यातनं, प्रतिकारः, प्रत्युपकारः. 3 परिवर्तः, परिवृत्ति *f.*, पर्यायः, आवर्तः. 4 फलं, लाभः, प्राप्ति *f.*, उदयः, उ-त्पन्नं ; 'in r.' प्रति in comp. ; 'injury in r.' प्रत्यपकारः ; 'benefit in r.' प्रत्युपकारः ; 'in r. for' विनिमयेन, परिवर्तनेन.

RE-UNITE, *v. t.* पुनः संयुज् 7 U, 10 or सं-धा 3 U. —RE-UNION, *s.* पुनः संयोगः-समागमः-संसर्गः.

REVEAL, *v. t.* वि-वृ 5 U, प्रकाश् c., व्यंज् 7 P or c., आविष्कृ 8 U, व्यक्तीकृ, प्रकटीकृ ; दृश् c., ज्ञा c. (ज्ञापयति); 'the missiles r. ed themselves to us' स्वतःप्रकाशान्यावयोरस्त्राणि (U. 6); 'the sacred hymns were r. ed to the sages' ऋषयः मंत्राणां द्रष्टारः, मंत्रान् स्वयं ददृशुः; 'r. a secret' रहस्यं प्र-काश् c. or भिद् 7 P &c. —ER, *s.* प्रकाशकः, व्यंजकः, भेदकः —REVELATION, *s.* विवरणं, प्रकाशनं, व्यक्ती-करणं, आविष्करणं. 2 श्रुतिप्रकाशः; ऐशोन्मेषः.

REVEL,-RY, *s.* निर्भरं पानगोष्ठीसुखं, संप्रीति *f.*, तुमुलः पानमहोत्सवः. —*v. i.* अनु-भू 1 P or सेव् 1 A with (*s.*).

REVENGE, *s.* प्रत्यपकारः, प्रति(ती)कारः, प्रति-हिंसा, प्रतिद्रोहः, वैरसाधनं-निर्यातनं-शुद्धि *f.*, प्रतिक्रिया. 2 (Desire for r.) जिघांसा, प्रत्यपकारबुद्धि *f.* —*v. t.* (Persons) वैरनिर्यातनं or वैरसाधनं-शुद्धि कृ 8 U (with gen.); प्रतिहिंस् 7 P, प्रतिद्रुह् 4 P, प्रत्यपकृ. 2 (Insult &c.) निर्यत् 10, साध् c., शुध् c., प्रतिकृ, निस्तॄ c. —ER, *s.* प्रत्यपकारकः, प्रतिहिं-सकः. —FUL, *a.* प्रतिकारपरायण, प्रत्यपकार-प्रति-हिंसा-शील-बुद्धि, प्रत्यपकारेच्छु, अक्षमिन्, अमर्षण. —FULLY, *adv.* प्रत्यपकारबुद्ध्या.

REVENUE, *s.* करः, बलिः, आयः, उदयः, भागधेयः, राजस्वं.

REVERBERATE, *v. i.* प्रतिध्वन्-नद् 1 P, अनुनद्-गर्ज् 1 P. —*v. t.* प्रतिध्वन् c. &c. 2 प्रतिक्षिप् 6 P, प्रतिहन् 2 P. —ION, *s.* प्रतिध्वनिः-नादः-शब्दः. 2 प्रतिक्षेपः.

REVERE, *v. t.* सं-,मन् c., पूज् 10, सं-भू c., पुर-स्कृ 8 U, सत्कृ, भज् 1 U, उपास् 2 A, आदृ 6 A, अर्च् 1 P, 10. —ENCE, *s.* सं-,मानः, अर्चना, प्रश्रयः, पूजा, सत्कारः, आदरः, सपर्या, पुरस्कारः, उपासना; अर्हणा, भक्ति *f.*; 'his r.' तत्रभवान्, भगवान्, 'your r.' अत्रभवान्; 'act of r.' नमस्कारः, नम-स्या, प्रणिपातः, प्रणामः, अभिवंदनं. —*v. t. See* (*v.*). —ED, *a.* पूज्य, अर्चनीय, सं-,मान्य, आर्य, पूजार्ह, नमस्य, उपास्य; oft. ex. by सुगृहीतनामन् (when dead), पूज्यपाद; 'r. sir' भगवन्. —ENT,-ENTIAL, *a.* भक्तिमत्, सादर, सप्रश्रय, मानपुरःसर, भक्तिपूर्व; 'with a r. bow' भक्तिप्रणामं कृत्वा. —ENTLY, *adv.* भक्त्या, भक्तिपुरःसरं, सादरं, सप्रश्रयं.

REVERIE, *s.* ध्यानं, चिंतनं, भावना.

REVERSE, *s.* पृष्ठं, पृष्ठभागः. 2 परिणामः, विकारः, परिवृत्ति *f.*; 'r. s of fortune' दैवदुर्विपाकः, भाग्य-विपरिणामः, अत्याहितं, आपद्-विपद् *f.*; *See* MIS-FORTUNE. 3 विपर्ययः, व्यत्ययः, व्यत्यासः, वि-पर्यासः, व्यतिक्रमः, वैपरीत्यं, वि-प्रति-पक्षः; 'if r. be the case' विपर्यये तु; 'r. of' ex. by इतर in comp. ; 'r. of red' रक्तेतर, &c. —*a.* विपरीत, व्यत्यस्त, वि-प्रति-लोम, प्रतीप, विपर्यस्त, विरुद्ध, व्य-तिक्रांत, वि-प्रति-पक्ष; 'r. order' विपर्ययः, व्यति-क्रमः, प्रातिलोम्यं; 'in the r. order' वि-प्रति-लोमं, विपर्यासेन, व्यत्यासेन. —*v. t.* परिवृत् c., विपर्यासं नी 1 P, परावृत् c., विपर्यस् 4 U, व्यत्यस्; अधोमुखीकृ 8 U; *See* OVERTURN, CHANGE; (in law) प्रत्यादिश् 6 P, परावृत् c., अधरीकृ, खंड् 10, प्रतिक्षि-प् 6 P. —AL, *s.* परा-परि-वृत्ति *f.*-वर्तनं. —ED, *a.* विपर्यस्त, परिवृत्त, वि-प्रति-लोम, अधरोत्तर, अधोमुख, &c.; *See* (*a.*); 'my fortune being r.' परि-वृत्तभाग्यतया, भाग्यविपर्यासात्, &c. —ION, *s.* परा-प्रत्या-वृत्तिः-वर्तनं, विपर्यासः. —LY, *adv.* विपर्ययेण, वि-प्रति-लोमं, व्यतिक्रमेण, व्यत्यासेन.

REVERT, *v. i.* प्रत्या-परा-नि-वृत् 1 A, प्रत्यागम् 1 P. —*v. t.* Reverse, q. v. —REVERSION, *s.* प्रत्यावृत्ति *f.*, परावर्तनं, पुनरागमनं. 2 उत्तराधिकारः. —ARY, *a.* उत्तरभोग्य; 'r. right' शेषभोगाधिकारः; 'r. heir' उत्तराधिकारिन्.

REVIEW, *v. t.* (Book) गुणदोषं वि-विच् 3, 7 U or निरूप् 10 or परीक्ष् 1 A. 2 पुनः ईक्ष् or दृश् 1 P or आ-अव-लोक् 1 A, 10, पुनः विचर् c. or परीक्ष् or निरूप् 10 or अनुसं-धा, प्रत्यालोच् 10. —*s.* गुणदो-षविवेचनं, गुणागुणविचारः-निरूपणं-परीक्षा; परीक्षा-क्षणं, निरूपणं. 2 पुनरीक्षणं, पुनर्दर्शनं, प्रत्यालोचनं, पु-नः विचारः-निरूपणं-परीक्षा. —ER, *s.* गुणदोषविवेचकः.

REVILE, *v. t.* निर्-,भर्त्स् 10 A, गर्ह् 1, 10 A, आ-अधि-क्षिप् 6 P, अप-वद् 1 A, निंद् 1 P, आक्रुश् 1 P. —ER, *s.* निर्भर्त्सकः, निंदकः, अपवादकः. —ING, *s.* निर्-,भर्त्सनं-ना, गर्हणं-णा, अपवादः, आ-क्रोशः, आ-अधि-क्षेपः; उपालंभः, वाक्पारुष्यं; *See* ABUSE, REPROACH.

REVISE, *v. t.* पुनः दृश् 1 P or ईक्ष् 1 A or विचर् c.; *See* REVIEW. 2 (पुनः) शुध् c., सं-वि-परि-शुध् c. —AL,-ION, *s.* पुनर्दर्शनं, पुनः परीक्षा, संशोधनं.

REVIVE, *v. t.* जीव् c., प्रत्युत्-उत्-सं-°, (fig. also); पुनः जीव् c., प्र-वि-बुध् c., चेतनां-संज्ञां लभ् c. (लं-भयति) or प्राप् c., प्रत्या-समा-श्वस् c., पुनः उत्-स्था c. (उत्थापयति), उद्-धृ 10. 2 पुनः प्रवृत् c., नवी-कृ 8 U. —*v. i.* प्रत्युत्-उत्-सं-जीव् 1 P, पुनः जीव्; संज्ञां-चेतनां लभ् 1 A or प्राप् 5 P or आ-प्रति-पद् 4 A; प्र-वि-बुध् 4 A, सं-उत्था 1 A, प्रत्या-समा-श्वस्

2 P. 2 पुनः प्रवृत् 1 A. -AL, *s.* संजीवनं, प्रत्युत्-उत्-जीवनं, (fig. also); संज्ञाप्राप्ति *f.*, चेतनागमः, चेतनालाभः, प्र-अव-बोधः. 2 पुनरुत्थानं, समुत्थानं, पुनः स्वास्थ्यं, पुनः स्वास्थ्यप्राप्तिः. 3 उद्धारः, पुनःप्रवृत्तिः.

REVOKE, *v. t.* निवृत् c., खंड् 10, निरस् 4 U. -REVOCATION, *s.* निवर्तनं, खंडनं, प्रत्यादेशः ; *See* REPEAL.

REVOLT, *v. i.* अभि-,द्रुह् 4 P, व्युत्था 1 A, कोपं उत्पद् c., शासनं अति-इ 2 P or उल्लंघ् 1 A, 10. -*s.* राजद्रोहः; प्रकृतिकोपः; *See* REBELLION, MUTINY; 'fall into r.' (fig.) विसंवादिन्-विरोधिन्- *a.* भू 1 P. -ING, *a.* बीभत्स, अतिगर्ह्य, अतिद्वेष्य; 'a r. scene' बीभत्सालोकः.

REVOLVE, *v. i.* परिवृत् 1 A ; वि-व्या-आ-वृत्, परि-भ्रम् 1, 4 P, घूर्ण् 6 P, 1 A, वि-परि-°, लुट् 6 P; 'that matter (idea) constantly r. ing in his mind' तस्य चार्थस्य सततं मनसि विपरिवर्तमानत्वात् (Ka. 67). -*v. t.* Causal of roots above. 2 (मनसा) विचर् c., वितर्क् 10, विमृश् 6 P, आलोच् 10; *See* CONSIDER. -ING, *a.* परिवर्तिन्, परि-,भ्रमिन्. —REVOLUTION, परिवर्तः-र्तनं, परिवृत्ति *f.*, आवर्तः, आवृत्तिः, घूर्णनं. 2 (Of time &c.) परि-आ-वर्तः, पर्यायः, चक्रं, भ्रमणं, भ्रांति *f.*, युगशतपरिवर्तान् 'for r. s of ages;' 'r. of time' कालचक्रं, कालावर्तः. 3 गति *f.*, प्रवृत्तिः; 'r. of a planet' (time) भगणः. 4 राज्यपरिवर्तः-परिवृत्तिः. -ARY, *a.* (*s.*) in comp. -IST, *s.* राज्यपरिवृत्तिवादिन्. -IZE, *v. t.* सर्वथा-साकल्येन-परिवृत् c. -REVULSION, *s.* विरागः, विरक्ति *f.*

RAWARD, *s.* पारितोषिकं, प्रतिफलं, प्रतिदानं ; दक्षिणा, मूल्यं, वेतनं; 'the r. due to a spiritual teacher' गुरुदक्षिणा ; 'deserving a r.' दक्षिण्य, दक्षिणीय. -*v. t.* पारितोषिकं &c. दा 3 U, परितुष् c., दानेन संतुष् c. or सं-भू c., मूल्यं दा. 2 सफलीकृ 8 U, कृतार्थयति (D.) ; 'his labour was r. ed' तस्य प्रयत्नः सफलो बभूव.

RHAPSODY, *s.* असंगतप्रबंधः, असंबद्धकविता. -IC, -ICAL, *a.* असंगत, असंबद्ध, निरन्वय, अनन्वित.

RHETORIC, *s.* अलंकारशास्त्रं-विद्या, साहित्यशास्त्रं. -AL, *a.* आलंकारिक (की *f.*), अलंकाररूप, अलंकार in comp. ; 'r. style' अलंकारयुता-आलंकारिकी-भाषासरणिः; 'r. expression' अलंकारः, वाक्यालंकारः. -IAN, *s.* अलंकारशास्त्रज्ञः. 2 वाग्मिन् *m.*, प्रवक्तृ *m.* ; *See* ORATOR.

RHEUM, *s.* (Of the eye) दूषि-षी *f.*, दूषिका. 2 श्लेष्मन् *m.*, कफः ; क्लेदनः, क्लेदकः. -Y, *a.* (Eye) क्लिन्नाक्षि *n.*, चुल्लः, चिल्लः, पिल्लः ; 'having r. eyes' क्लिन्नाक्ष, चुल्ल, चिल्ल, पिल्ल. 2 श्लेष्मल-ण, कफिन्. -RHEUMATIC, *a.* वातीय, वात in comp. 2 वातकिन्, वातुल, वातग्रस्त, वातोपहत, वात-वायु-ग्रस्त. -RHEUMATISM, *s.* संधिवातः-वायुः (of the joints) ; वातः, वायुः, वातव्याधिः-रोगः.

RHINOCEROS, *s.* गंडः, गंडकः, खड्गिन् *m.* ; 'the female r.' खड्गधेनुः.

RHOMBUS, *s.* तुल्यचतुर्भुजः.

RHYME, *s.* यमकः-कं, मित्राक्षरं. 2 पद्यं, कविता. -ER, *s.* कविता-पद्य-कारः, कुकविः.

RHYTHM, *s.* तालः, लयः. -ICAL, *a.* लय-ताल-अनुगत ; तालबद्ध.

RIB, *s.* पर्शुका, पार्श्वकं, पार्श्वास्थि *n.*; 'the r. s taken together' पंजरः-रं. 2 पोलिंदः. 3 शलाका (of umbrellas). 4 रेखा.

RIBALD, *a.* *See* OBSCENE &c.

RIBBON, RIBAND, *s.* पट्टबंधः, दुकूलपट्टः.

RICE, *s.* (Plant) शालिः, कलमः, नीवारः, व्रीहिः (various kinds). 2 तंडुलः, धान्यास्थि *n.* 3 (Boiled) अन्नं, ओदनः-नं, भक्तं; *See* FOOD; 'r. with milk and sugar' पायसं, परमान्नं; 'scum of r.' मासरः, आचामः, निस्र(स्रा)वः, भक्तमंडः ; 'scorched r.' भिस्सटा, दग्धिका; 'fried r.' धानाः (*f.* pl.); 'ear of r.' कणिशः-शं, धान्यशीर्षकः.

RICH, *a.* धन-वित्त-द्रव्य-वत्, धनिन्, धन-वित्त-शालिन्, सधन, महा-बहु-धन, अर्थवत्, धानिक, धनाढ्य, विभवसंपन्न, धनसमृद्ध, श्रीमत्, लक्ष्मीवत्; समृद्ध, धनेश्वर, लक्ष्मीश ; संपन्नवत्, शालिन्, युक्त in comp. with 'Wealth' q. v. 2 (Costly) महार्ह-र्घ, बहुमूल्य, महामूल्य, अतिप्रतापवत्. 3 आढ्य, बहुल, प्रचुर, पूर्ण, बहु, समृद्ध, संपन्न, मय in comp. ; 'r. perfume' बहलामोदः ; 'r. in beauty' रूपाढ्य ; गुणाढ्य, बहुलरत्न, &c. 4 सत्व-सार-गुण-वत्, स्फीत, बहुफलप्रद, उर्वरा (भूमिः), सस्याढ्य. 5 उज्ज्वल, सुप्रकाश, अतिशोभन (colours). 6 घृतप्लुत-पूर्ण. -ES, *s.* धनं, अर्थः, विभवः, वित्तं, द्रव्यं ; *See* WEALTH. 2 धनाढ्यता, सधनता, धनबाहुल्यं. -LY, *adv.* बहुधनेन, प्रभूतं, भूरि, महामूल्येन, अतिशोभया, अतिप्रतापेन, सश्रीकं ; 'r. decorated' अतिशोभया प्रसाधित, सविशेषमंडित. -NESS, *s.* धनाढ्यता, सश्रीकता, सधनता, स्फीतता, महार्घता, अतिशोभा, प्रतापः; बाहुल्यं, समृद्धि *f.*, संपद् *f.*; 'r. of beauty' रूपसंपद्, लावण्यातिशयः; 'r. of expression' वचसामुदारता (Mal. 1).

RICKETS, *s.* बालग्रहः.

RICKETY, *a.* शिथिलसंधि, अस्थिर, अदृढसंधि; (building) जीर्ण, अजर्जरित.

RID, *v. t.* मुच् 6 P or c., मोक्ष् 10, वि-,शुध् c., उद्धृ 1 P; 'to get r. of' अप-नी 1 P, निराकृ, त्यज् 1 P, अप-हा 3 P, निः-सृ c., अपास् 4 U; oft. by निर् pr.; 'r. of thorns' निष्कंटकीकृ; 'r. of difficulties' निर्विघ्नीकृ. -a. वि-,मुक्त, वर्जित, हीन, रहित, गत, वीत, हत, निर्, अ in comp.; कंटकहीन, निःशल्य, &c. -DANCE, s. मुक्ति f., मोक्षः, उद्धारः, शोधनं.

RIDDLE, s. प्रहेलिका, प्रवह्लिका, प्रश्नदूती; गूढं, कूटप्रश्नः. 2 शोधनी, चालनी. -v. t. शुध् c. 2 व्यध् 4 P; See PERFORATE.

RIDE, v. i. अश्वेन संचर् 1 A or गम् 1 P or या 2 P or चल् 1 P, अश्वेन &c. वह् pass. -v. t. (अश्वं &c.) आ-अधि-समा-अध्या-रुह् 1 P, अध्या-आ-क्रम् 1 U, 4 P, अधि-ष्ठा 1 P, अध्यास् 2 A. -s. अश्वेन संचरणं or विहरणं. -ER, s. अश्वारोहः, अश्वारोहिन् m., अश्वारूढः. 2 आरोही, आरूढः. -ING, s. अश्वारोहणं. -a. आरूढ, आरोहिन्, आरोह, आश्रयिन् in comp.

RIDGE, s. कटकः-कं, उत्संगः. 2 पृष्ठं. 3 सेतुः, धरणः, आलि f., पिंडलः. -Y, a. सकटक.

RIDICULE, v. t. उप-अव-हस् 1 P, उपहास्यतां नी 1 P, उपहासास्पदं कृ 8 U, अवहासास्पदीकृ, आ-अव-क्षिप् 6 P; See CONTEMN also; 'I shall be r.-ed' गमिष्याम्युपहास्यतां (R. I. 3); 'to be r. ed' उपहास्यतां गम् 1 P or या 2 P. -s. उप-अव-हासः-हसनं, आ-अव-क्षेपः, अवज्ञा, अवहेलना, उपहास्यता. -OUS, a. अव-उप-हास्य, हासास्पदीभूत, हासयोग्य, उपहासार्ह, हासास्पदं, हासकर (री f.), हासोत्पादक.

RIFE, a. सर्वत्र प्रचलित, प्रवृत्त, प्रचल, बहुल.

RIFF-RAFF, s. अधमाः, प्राकृत-पृथग्-जनाः.

RIFLE, s. आग्नेयास्त्रं. -v. t. अप-हृ 1 P; See ROB.

RIFT, s. See FISSURE.

RIG, v. t. सज्जीकृ 8 U, उपकरणैः उपक्लृप् c. -GING, सज्जा, सामग्री, परिच्छदः, रज्ज्वादिसाधनं; पोतसज्जा.

RIGHT, a. दक्षिण, वामेतर, सव्येतर, अपसव्य; 'to the r.' दक्षिणतः; दक्षिणेन; 'r. hand' अग्रहस्तः-करः, दक्षिणपाणिः. 2 उचित, न्याय्य, युक्त, उपपन्न, सम्यच्, यथान्याय, धर्म्य, साधु, समंजस, सत्-सु in comp.; 'r. path' सन्मार्गः, सुपथः. 3 सत्य, यथार्थ, अवितथ, तथ्य; See True; 'Priyamvadá is r.' or 'says r.-ly' अवितथमाह प्रियंवदा (S. 1); 'you are r.' सत्यं-यथार्थं-आह-भवान्. 4 सरल, ऋजु, अवक्र; 'r. angle' समकोणः, ऋजुकोणः. -s. दक्षिणपार्श्वः-दिक्; दक्षिणः, अपसव्यं; 'on the r.' दक्षिणतः, दक्षिणस्यां दिशि. 2 न्यायः, धर्मः, न्याय्यता, न्यायिता, औचित्यं, याथार्थ्यं, नीति f., युक्तता. 3 सत्यता, तथ्यता, शुद्धता. 4 अधिकारः, स्वत्वं, स्वाम्यं, सत्ता; oft. ex. by अर्ह् 1 P; 'a woman has no r. to independence' न स्त्री स्वातंत्र्यमर्हति. -adv. युक्तं, न्यायतः, स्थाने, साधु, उचितं, यथोचितं, यथान्यायं, उपपन्नं, सम्यक्; 'I acted r. in delivering her into the charge of the queen' एनां देवीहस्ते निक्षिपता मया युक्तमेवानुष्ठितं (Rat. 1). 2 सत्यं, यथार्थं; सरलं, ऋजु; सु-अति pr. -interj. साधु, सुष्ठु, भद्रं, बाढं. -v. t. ऋजूकृ 8 U, सुस्थीकृ, समा-प्रतिसमा-धा 3 U. -v. i. सरल-ऋजु- a. भू 1 P. -EOUS, a. न्यायपरायण-पर, साधुवृत्त, पवित्र, न्यायाचार, सुशील; (of acts) न्याय्य, युक्त; See JUST. -EOUSLY, adv. न्यायतः, धर्मेण. -EOUSNESS, s. सदाचारः, साधुवृत्तं. -FUL, a. अधिकारिन्, स्वत्वविशिष्ट. 2 Just, q. v. -FULLY, adv. साधिकारं. -LY, adv. उचितं, सत्यं, यथार्थतः, परमार्थतः, यथार्थं, स्थाने, युक्तं, यथाधर्मं, यथान्यायं, न्यायतः, सम्यक्. 2 सत्यं; See TRULY.

RIGID, a. कठोर, कर्कश, उग्र, दारुण, परुष. 2 दृढ, घन, कठिन, अशिथिल, अमृदु. -ITY,-NESS, s. कठोरता, कठिनता, दृढता, घनता, काठिन्यं. -LY, adv. दृढं, कठिनं, अशिथिलं; See STRICT.

RIGMAROLE, s. अनर्थककथा.

RIGOUR, s. दृढता, काठिन्यं, अशैथिल्यं. 2 उग्रता, कठोरता, कर्कशता, निष्ठुरता. -OUS, a. कठोर, निष्ठुर, उग्र, परुष, तीक्ष्णदंड, असौम्य, कर्कश, कठिन. 2 सूक्ष्म; See STRICT. -OUSLY, adv. उग्रं, निष्ठुरं, परुषं.

RILL, s. कुसरित् f., क्षुद्रनदी, कुल्या.

RIM, s. प्रांतः, अंतः, धारा, कर्णः (of ships).

RIME, s. See HOAR-FROST.

RIND, s. त्वच् f., वल्कः-ल्कं, वल्कलः-लं, शल्कं, चर्मन् n., कंचुकः.

RING, v. i. रण्-क्वण् 1 P, वि-रु 2 P, शिंज् 2 A. -v. t. चल् c., वद् c., आहन् 2 U, नद् c., क्वण् c.; 'r. the bell' घंटां वादय, घंटानादं कुरु. -s. अंगुली(री)यं-यकं, ऊर्मिका; 'signet. r.' अंगुलिमुद्रा, मुद्रा. 2 वलयः-यं, मंडलं, चक्रं; 'dancing in a r.' मंडलनृत्यं. 3 मंडलं (of persons). 4 रंगः. 5 शिंजितं, क्वणितं, क्वणनं, नि-,क्वा(क)णः, रवः, नादः; 'r.-leader' नायकः, अग्रणीः, मुख्यः, प्रवर्तकः, मुखरः, प्रधानराजद्रोहिन् m. (of conspirators); 'r.-worm' दद्रुमंडलं, मंडलकुष्ठं; 'having r.-worm' दद्रु(द्रू)णः, दद्रुरोगिन्.

RINGLET, s. अलकः, चूर्णकुंतलः, कुरलः.

RINSE, v. t. जलेन प्रक्षल् 10, (जलं) उपस्पृश् 6 P, आचम् 1 P. -ING, s. आचमनं, उपस्पर्शः.

RIOT, s. संमर्दः, संक्षोभः, तुमुलं, कोलाहलः, विप्लवः. 2 यथेच्छपानोत्सवः, विषयसुखातिरेकः, तुमुलोत्सवः. 3 सं-अव-मर्दः (संभूय कृतः); राजाभिद्रोहः, प्रजाक्षोभः, प्रकृतिकोपः; 'to run r.' मर्यादां अतिक्रम् 1 U, 4 P or अति-इ 2 P. -v. i. संक्षोभं इ 2 P, संरंभं गम् 1 P, तुमुलं कृ 8 U. 2 सुखोपभोगे निमग्न- a. भू 1 P, तुमुलरवेण उत्सवं सेव् 1 A or कृ. -ER, s. तुमुलसंक्षोभकारिन् m. -OUS, a. तुमुल-क्षोभ-कारिन्, तुमुलोत्सवकारिन्. -OUSLY, adv. तुमुलशब्देन, सकोलाहलं.

RIP, *v. t.* वि-,दृ 9 P or c., विपट् 10, निर्भिद् 7 P, निकृत् 6 P; *See* TEAR. —*s.* विदरः, विपाटनं.

RIPE, *a.* पक्व, परि-वि-सु-°, पक्वतां आपन्न, परिणत, पाकोन्मुख (खी *f.*), फलोन्मुख, प्रौढ ; 'r. in years' परिणतवयस्, प्रवयस्, प्रवृद्ध, वयोवृद्ध ; 'r. to meet one's doom' विनाशोन्मुख, पक्व. 2 सिद्ध, संपन्न; *See* PERFECT. 3 सिद्ध, सज्ज, सन्नद्ध; *See* READY. —RIPEN, *v. i.* पाकं इ 2 P or व्रज् 1 P, पाकाभिमुख-पाकोन्मुख- *a.* भू 1 P, पच् pass., उपचि pass.; 'coldness r.ed into downright hatred' अनादरः (कालक्रमेण) उपचीयमानः साक्षाद्द्वेषस्य परां कोटिं इयाय. —*v. t.* पच् 1 P, कृ with (*a.*); *See* MATURE. —NESS, *s.* परि-वि-पाकः, परिणति *f.*, परिणामः, पक्वावस्था, पक्वदशा.

RIPPLE, *s.* तरंगः, वीचि-ची *f.*, ऊर्मि *f.*, भंगः. —*v. i.* क्षुभ् 4 P, 1 A, चलोर्मि-सतरंग- *a.* भू 1 P. —ING, *a.* चलोर्मि, क्षुब्ध, प्रचलदूर्मि, सतरंग, तरंगाकुल, उत्तरंग.

RISE, *v. i.* उत्था 1 P, समुत्था 1 A, (in all senses); 'r. ing from the bed' समुत्थित, मुक्तशयन; 'do not r. to receive their elders' नाभ्युत्तिष्ठंति गुरून् (Ka. 108). 2 उद्गम् 1 P, उद्-इ 2 P, उदय् 1 A, उत्पत् 1 P, ऊर्ध्वं गम् or व्रज् 1 P, उद्वृत् 1 A; आ-अधि-रुह् 1 P, आक्रम् 1 A (पूर्वे दिशं); उद्गम् 1 P. 3 प्रति-भा 2 P निर्भा, प्रादुर्भू 1 P, आविर्भू, दृश्-लक्ष्- pass. 4 प्र-,जन् 4 A, उत्पद् 4 A, प्रवृत्, उद्-सं-प्र-भू, निः-प्र-सृ 1 P, निर्गम्. 5 (Advance) उत्था, प्र-,वृध्, 1 A, उपचि- pass., अधिकीभू, प्रबलतर- *a.* भू; 'r. ing enemy' उत्तिष्ठमानः शत्रुः. 6 प्रतिपत्ति-उन्नति-प्राप् 5 P, उन्नम्, उत्कृष् pass. 7 (Against) अभिद्रुह् 4 P (with acc.), द्रुह् (with dat.), व्युत्था 1 A. 8 (As sea) क्षुभ् 1 A, 4 P, ऊर्मिमालाकुल-क्षुब्ध- *a.* भू. —*s.* सं-,उत्थानं (fig. also). 2 उदयः, उद्गमः-मनं, उत्पातः, ऊर्ध्वगतिः; 'he owes his r. to me' मत्तः लब्धोदयः; 'r. and fall' पातोत्पातौ. 3 उत्पत्ति *f.*, प्रभवः, उद्भवः, संभवः, उद्गमः, प्रवृत्ति *f.* प्र-उपक्रमः, आरंभः. 4 वृद्धि *f.*, उपचयः, आधिक्यं. 5 उन्नति *f.*, उत्कर्षः, प्रतिपत्ति *f.*, पदवृद्धिः, उदयः; 'to give r. to' उत्पद् c., जन् c. —ING, *s.* उत्थानं, उदयः, उद्गमः &c.; 'r. to receive another' अभ्युत्थानं, प्रत्युद्गमः. 2 प्रजा-प्रकृति-क्षोभः-प्रकोपः; *See* MUTINY. 3 Tumour, q. v.; 'r. ground' उन्नतभूमिः, उच्चस्थानं, उत्सेधः.

RISIBLE, *a.* हासजनन (नी *f.*), हास्यास्पदं, हासकर (री *f.*), हासोत्पादक.

RISK, *s.* संशयः, संदेहः, शंका, भयं, संकटं; 'run the r. of losing all' सर्वनाशसंशये आत्मानं पत् c. —*v. t.* संशये निक्षिप् 6 P or पत् c.; *See* DANGER.

RITE, *s.* क्रिया, विधिः, कर्मन् *n.*, कार्यं, आचारः, संस्कारः, नियमः, कल्पः; 'scriptural r.' शास्त्रविधिः-कर्म, शास्त्रोक्तक्रिया. —RITUAL, *a.* वैधिक-नैयमिक (की *f.*). विध्यनुरूप, शास्त्रोक्त, विधि-क्रिया in comp. —*s.* क्रियासंस्कारः-विधिः-पद्धतिः-शास्त्रं. —IST, *s.* संस्कारशास्त्रज्ञः.

RIVAL, *v. t.* स्पर्ध् 1 A, प्रति-परि-°, (with instr.), संघृष् 1 P, अहमहमिकया-परस्परजिगीषया-यत् 1 A, वि-,जि desid. (जिगीषति); oft. by प्रतिद्वंद्विन्, प्रतिस्पर्धिन्; 'with hands r. ing young foliage (in beauty)' किसलयोद्भेदप्रतिद्वंद्विभिः करतलैः (S. 4); चंद्रच्छायाप्रतिस्पर्धी or-प्रतिद्वंद्वी &c. —*a.*, —*s.* प्रति-,स्पर्धिन्, प्रतियोगिन्, वि-,जिगीषु, प्रतिपक्ष, सपत्न, परस्परसंघर्षिन्, अभिभवेच्छु; by प्रति in comp.; 'r. combatant' प्रतियोधः; 'r. army' प्रतिबलं &c.; 'r. woman' सपत्नी; 'a r. Kesava' अपरः केशवः, प्रतिकेशवः; 'a r. to Srí' प्रत्यादेश इव श्रियाः (V. 1). —RY, *s.* प्रतिस्पर्धा, प्रतियोगिता, वि-,जिगीषा, अहमहमिका, प्रतिद्वंद्विता, संघर्षः, सापत्न्यं, प्रतिपक्षता; विरोधः, वैरं.

RIVE, *v. See* TEAR.

RIVER, *s.* नदी, सरित्, सिंधुः, आ(अ)पगा, निम्नगा, तरंगिणी, स्रोतोवहा, तटिनी, ह्रादिनी, स्रोतस्विनी, धुनी, शैवलिनी, द्वीपवती, स्रवंती, निर्झरिणी ; 'a small r.' कुल्या, अल्प-कृत्रिम-सरित् ; 'confluence of r. s' संभेदः, सिंधुसंगमः; 'watered by r. s' नदीमातृक.

RIVET, *v. t.* कील् 10, कीलेन बंध् 9 P, दृढं बंध् ; अभिनि-विश् c., सञ्ज् c.; 'to be r. ed' कीलित-दृढबद्ध- *a.* भू, सञ्ज् 1 U (sight); स्थाने खलु सज्जति दृष्टिः (M. 1); 'all eyes were r. ed on him' नेत्रव्रजाः तस्मिन्निपेतुः (R. VI. 7), तस्मिन् दृष्टिः सक्ताभूत्; बध्नाति मे चक्षुः चित्रकूटः (R. XIII. 47), दयिते मय्युत्सस्य चक्षुषः (U. 3); आलिखित इव रंगः (S. 1) 'the audience is r. ed (to the spot) with attention'. —*s.* कीलः-लकः-कं, शलाका.

RIVULET, *s.* क्षुद्र-कु-सरित् *f.*, अल्प-क्षुद्र-नदी.

ROAD, *s.* मार्गः, पथिन् *m.*, अध्वन् *m.*, वर्त्मन् *n.*, वीथि-थी *f.*, रथ्या, सरणि-णी *f.*, पदवी, पद्धति-ती *f.*; 'high r.' राजमार्गः-पथः; 'common r.' प्रचारः; 'difficult r.' दुर्गसंचरः, संक्रमः, दुर्गमार्गः; 'dreary, lonely r.' प्रांतरं, शून्यमार्गः; 'crossing of r. s' चतुष्पथं, शृंगाटकं; *See* WAY.

ROAM, *v. i.* परि-,अट् 1 P, परि-,भ्रम् 1, 4 P, वि-संचर् 1 P ; 'r. about' इतस्ततः वि-हृ 1 P or चर् or भ्रम्. —ING, *s.* परि-,अटनं, परि-,भ्रमणं, विचरणं.

ROAR, *v. i.* गर्ज् 1 P, स्तन् 1 P, नर्द् 1 P, रस् 1 P, रु 2 P, नद् 1 P, अनु-हुंकृ 8 U (of lion) ; 'a r. ing river' घर्घररवा सरित्. 2 वि-आ-उत्-,व्या-क्रुश् 1 P, प्रणद्, घुष् 10; 'r. ing with pain' आर्तनादं मुंचत्. —*s.*, —ING, *s.* गर्जितं, स्तनितं, गर्जनं-

ना, नर्दनं, विरावः, महा-दीर्घ-गंभीर-शब्दः-नादः; घनध्वनिः, दीर्घरावः-घोषः; हुंकारः. 2 नादः, वि-आ-क्रोशः, निर्घोषः, शब्दः, स्वरः, ध्वनिः.

ROAST, *v. t.* भ्रस्ज् 6 P; 'r. on a spit' शूलाकृ 8 U. 2 तप् 1 P or c., दह् 1 P. -ED, *a.* भ्रष्ट, भृष्ट; 'r. on a spit' शूल्य, शूलाकृत, भटित्र, शूलसंस्कृत.

ROB, *v. t.* चुर् 10, मुष् 9 P, लुंट्-ठ् 1 P, 10, अपहृ 1 P, (with gen. of person). -BER, *s.* दस्युः, चोर(चौ)रः, स्तेनः, तस्करः, लुंटाकः, मोषकः; *See* THIEF. -BERY, *s.* अपहरणं, मोषणं, स्तेयं, चौर्यं, स्तैन्यं, अपहारः, लुंठनं.

ROBE, *s.* वसनं, वस्त्रं. -*v. t.* वसनं परि-धा 3 U, वस् 2 A; *See* DRESS.

ROBUST, *a.* दृढदेह, व्यूढोरस्क, दृढांग (गी *f.*), वज्रदेह, मांसल, सवीर्य, ससत्त्व, उपचित; 'r. body' उपचितं गात्रं, सिंहसंहननं. -LY, *adv.* सवीर्यं, ससत्त्वं. -NESS, *s.* दृढांगता, वीर्यं, मांसलता.

ROCK, *s.* स्थूलशिला, शिलोच्चयः, बृहदुपलः, महाप्रस्तरः, शैलः; शिला, पाषाणः, ग्रावन् *m.*, उपलः, अश्मन् *m.*, प्रस्तरः, (small); *See* STONE; 'r.-salt' सैंधवः-वं, शीतशिवं, सिंधुजं, माणिमंथं. -*v. t.* दोलनेन स्वप् c. (rock to sleep); दोलयति-आंदोलयति (D.), इतस्ततः प्र-वि-सं-चल् c. -*v. i.* दोलायते (D.), इतस्ततः वि-प्र-चल् 1 P; *See* WAVER. -Y, *a.* शिलामय (यी *f.*), शिलापूर्ण, अश्मर, औपल (ली *f.*), (*s.*) in comp.

ROCKET, *s.* हंबतारा, अग्निबाणः.

ROD, *s.* दंडः, शलाका (of metal), यष्टि *f.*, वेत्रं (of cane).

RODOMONTADE, *s.* गर्वितवाक्यं, उद्धतवचनं.

ROE, *s.* मीनांडं, मत्स्यांडं, मत्स्यगर्भः. 2 मृगी, हरिणी.

ROGUE, *s.* धूर्तः, कितवः, जाल्मः, शठः, खलः, वंचकः, प्रतारकः, कापटिकः, कूटकः, कूटकारः, दुर्जनः, दुरात्मन् *m.*, कुहकः. -ERY, -ISHNESS, *s.* कैतवं, शाठ्यं, दौर्जन्यं, वंचनं, &c. -ISH, *a.* धूर्त, शठ, कितव; *See* (*s*). -ISHLY, *adv.* धूर्ततया, शाठ्यात्, सकैतवं.

ROLL, *v. i.* वि-लुठ् 6 P, वि-लुट् 1, 4 P. 2 परि-व्या-वि-वृत् 1 A, परि-भ्रम् 1, 4 P, घूर्ण् 6 P, 1 A; (about) प्र-वि-चल् 1 P, घूर्ण्, वि-लुल् 1 P; 'with eyes r. ing about' घूर्णल्लोचन, लोलाक्ष, विलोलदृष्टि. 3 (On, by &c.) व्यति-इ 2 P, गम् 1 P, अति-व्याति-क्रम् 1 U, 4 P, परि-आ-वृत्, परि-इ; 'as days r. ed on' दिनेषु गच्छत्सु, गच्छता कालेन; 'a cloud r. s on through the air' मेघः खमाक्रमितुं प्रवृत्तः (Mr. 5); 'which has r. ed out at the feet of the Vindhya' विंध्यपादे विशीर्णा (Mc. 19). -*v. t.* व्या-परि-वृत् c., घूर्ण् c., भ्रम् c., &c.; 'r. down' रयेण नी 1 P; 'r. ing down corpses' प्रेतवाहिनी (नदी). 2 लुट्-ठ् c., वि-प्र-°. 3 पिंडीकृ 8 U, संपुटीकृ, संपिंड् 10. 4 आ-परि-वेष्ट् c., अवगुंठ् 10, आ-आ-वृ 5 U. -*s.* लुठनं, परिवर्तनं, &c. 2 पिंडः, गोलः-लकः, नाली. 3 नामावलि-ली *f.* -ER, *s.* परि-,वर्तनी, वर्तनयंत्रं-चक्रं. 2 वेलनं-नी (for flour). 3 पटः. -ING, *s.* लोठनं, परि-व्या-वर्तनं, घूर्णनं, परि-,भ्रमणं, &c. -*a.* घूर्णत्, वि-,लोल, प्रचलित.

ROMANCE, *s.* आख्यायिका, कल्पितकथा. -*v. i.* आख्यायिकां लिख् 6 P or प्रबंध् 9 P. -ROMANTIC, *a.* अद्भुत, विचित्र, आश्चर्यभूत. 2 शूर, विक्रांत; अद्भुतप्रिय, अशृंखलवृत्ति. 3 असंभव, कल्पित.

ROMP, *v. i.* प्रगल्भं क्रीड् 1 P, उद्धतं खेल् 1 P, (U. 4). -*s.* उद्धतखेलनं, प्रगल्भ-अविनीत-क्रीडा. 2 प्रगल्भा, अविनीता, निर्लज्जा; क्रीडाशीला.

ROOF, *s.* छदिस् *f.*, पटलं; 'the wooden frame of a r.' गोपानसी, वल(ड)भी; 'the edge of a r.' वलीकं, नीध्रं. 2 तालु *n.* (of the mouth). -*v. t.* पटलेन आच्छद् 10. -ED, *a.* सपटल, पटलाच्छन्न. -LESS, *a.* निष्पटल; (fig.) निराश्रय.

ROOK, *s.* काकः, वायसः. -ERY, *s.* काकाश्रयः.

ROOM, *s.* वेश्मन् *n.*, प्र-,कोष्ठः, शाला, कक्षः-क्षा, कुटी, गृहं; 'upper r.' चंद्रशाला, शिरोगृहं; 'inner r.' गर्भागारं, वासगृहं, अंतःकोष्ठः. 2 प्र-,देशः, स्थानं, आस्पदं, भूमि *f.*, पदं; स वासवेन इतो निर्षादेति विसृष्टभूमिः (K. III. 2) 'Vāsava made r. for him' &c.; 'there is r. for doubt here' शंकास्थानमेतत्. 3 अवकाशः, अवसरः, प्रसरः, विषयः, अंतरं, स्थलं; 'want of r.' अनवकाशः, स्थलसंकोचः; 'giving no r. for envy' अदत्तावकाशो मत्सरस्य; 'make r.' अंतरं दीयतां, अपसर. 4 (Stead) स्थानं, भूमिः; *See* INSTEAD of. -Y, *a.* विशाल, विस्तीर्ण, विपुल, असंबाध, सावकाश.

ROOST, *s.* वासयष्टि *f.*, यष्टिनिवासः, निलयन-शयनदंडः-स्थानं. -*v. i.* शी 2 A, स्वप् 2 P, निली 4 A, निषद् 1 P, आश्रि 1 U.

ROOT, *s.* मूलं, in all senses; तरुमूलं, कलहमूलं &c.; अंघ्रिः, पादः (Foot, q. v.); बु(ब्र)ध्नः; शिफा, जटा (fibrous); 'bulbous r.' कंदः-दं; 'to the r. s' आमूलं, मूलतः, समूलं; 'the r. of a branch' अवरोहः. 2 अधोभागः-देशः, तलं, मूलं, जाहं in comp. (of animals only). 3 मूलं, बीजं, योनि *f.*, आदिः, निदानं, कारणं, आदिबीजं-कारणं-हेतुः, प्रकृति *f.*; 'having for its r.' मूल, हेतु, &c. in comp.; वित्तमूलः कलहः, &c. 4 (Of a word) मूलं, प्रकृतिः, शब्दयोनिः; 'r.-meaning' मूलार्थः, यौगिकार्थः, व्युत्पत्तिसिद्धः. 5 (Of numbers) मूलं, पदं; 'to extract a r.' मूलीकृ 8 U. -*v. i.*, 'take r.' मूलं बंध् 9 P. -*v. t.* दृढं निखन् 1 P or रुह् c.; ex. by 'r. ed'. 2 (Up) उन्मूल् 10, समूलं उद्-हृ 1 P, उत्पट्

10, उत्खन्, व्यपरुह् c., उच्छिद् 7 P. –ED, *a.* दृढ-बद्ध-मूल, रूढ-धृत-मूल.

ROPE, *s.* रज्जु *f.*, गुणः. दामन् *f. n.*, शुल्वं, वराटकः-कं, संदानं, वटः-टी-टं; 'the rope and bucket of a well' उद्घाटनं, घटीयंत्रं; 'r.-dancer' सूत्रायणः-कलायणः; 'r.-ladder' रज्जुसोपानं; 'r.-maker' रज्जुकारः. –Y, *a.* रज्जुधर्मन्; श्यान, सांद्र.

ROSARY, *s.* अक्षमाला, अक्षसूत्रं, जपमाला-सूत्रं.

ROSE, *s.* जपापुष्पं, ओड्रपुष्पं; (tree or flower) जपा-वा; सेवती, शतपत्री; 'r.-apple' जंबु-बू *f.*; (fruit) जंबुफलं, जांबवं. –Y, *a.* पाटल, जपावर्ण. 2 जवारूप. –ROSEATE, *a.* 'r.-coloured' पाटल, जपासवर्ण. 2 बहिः रमणीय, दृष्टिमनोहर.

ROT, *v. i.* पूतीभू 1 P, वि-,गल् 1 P, विली 4 A, दुर्गंध- *a.* भू. –*v. t.* गल् c., विली c., पूतीकृ 8 U. –ROTTEN, *a.* पूतिगंधि, दुर्गंध, विगलित, विलीन; पूतीभूत, दुष्ट, दूषित. 2 क्षीणसत्त्व, असार, निःसत्त्व.

ROTATE, *v. i.* भ्रम् 1, 4 P, चक्रगत्या भ्रम्, परि-वृत् 1 A; *See* REVOLVE. –ION, *s.* भ्रमणं, भ्रांति *f.*, आ-परि-वर्तः-वृत्ति *f.*, चक्रावर्तः, चक्रगतिः. 2 पर्यायः, क्रमः, आनुपूर्व्यं; 'in r.' पर्यायेण, पर्यायवृत्त्या, चक्रवत्, पर्यायानुसारेण, अनुपूर्वं. –ORY,-ROTARY, *a.* चक्रावर्तिन्, चक्रगति.

ROTE, *s.* आवृत्ति *f.*, अभ्यासः, आवर्तनं; 'learn by r.' (अर्थज्ञानं विना) कंठस्थ- *a.* कृ 8 U, अभ्यस् 4 U; 'learnt by r.' कंठस्थ, अभ्यस्त.

ROTUND,-ITY, *See* ROUND,-NESS.

ROUGH, *a.* नतोन्नत, विषम, असम, अश्लक्ष्ण. 2 रु(रू)-क्ष, परुष, कर्कश, कठिन, अमसृण, असौम्य, अमृदु, दुःस्पर्श; (in disposition) निष्ठुर, उग्र, कटु, कठोर; (in manners) असभ्य, अशिष्ट, असंस्कृत, स्थूल, घन; 'r. measurement' स्थूलमानं. 3 अपटु, अदक्ष, अनिपुण, अकुशल, स्थूल. 4 (Sea) क्षुब्ध, तरंगाकुल, उत्तरंग, वायुक्षुब्ध, पवनाहत. 5 लोमश, लोमावृत, स्थूललोमन्; 'r.-cast' स्थूलं क्लृप् c. or वि-धा 3 U; 'r.-draw' स्थूलं लिख् 6 P; 'r.-hew' स्थूलं तक्ष् 1, 5 P or छिद् 7 P; 'r.-rider' अ-श्वशिक्षकः. –EN, *v. t.* रूक्षी-स्थूली-कृ 8 U. –LY, *adv.* रूक्षं, परुषं, कर्कशं, स्थूलं, निष्ठुरं, &c. –NESS, *s.* वैषम्यं, रूक्षता, पारुष्यं, कर्कशत्वं, उग्रता, कठोरता, स्थूलता, अदक्षता; संक्षोभः, ऊर्मिप्रलोटनं, &c.

ROUND, *a.* वर्तुल, गोल, वृत्त, वृत्ताकार, निस्तल, मंडलाकार, चक्राकृति, वृत्त-गोल-रूप, वलयाकार. 2 पीन, पीवर, उन्नत. 3 अवक्र, असंदिग्ध, परिस्फुट, निश्चित, परिच्छिन्न, व्यक्त; *See* DECIDED. 4 (Number) समग्र; शून्यांतक. –*s.* मंडलं, चक्रं, वर्तुलं, गोलः, वलयः-यं. 2 परिभ्रमणं, परिवर्तः, पर्यायः, आवृत्ति *f.*, आवर्तः. 3 वक्रमार्गः-गतिः *f.*; (of a ladder) भंगि *f.*, आरोहणं, सोपानं. –*prep.* परितः, अभितः, (with acc.); समंततः, समंतात् (with gen.). –*adv.* परि in comp. (with verbs). 2 चक्रवत्, मंडलाकारेण, वलयरूपेण, चक्ररूपेण; 'turn r.' परि-वृत् c., परिभ्रम् c.; 'turning r.' चक्रभ्रांतिः, परिभ्रमणं, मंडलावृत्तिः; 'to get r.' मतं परिवृत् c. 3 सर्वतः, समंततः, समंतात्, विश्वतः, सर्वदिक्षु; 'the whole year r.' समग्रवर्षं. –*v. t.* वर्तुलीकृ 8 U, गोलीकृ. 2 परिगम् 1 P, परि-या-इ 2 P. 3 समा-धा 3 U; संस्कृ; 'well-r. ed' सुवृत्त; (fig.) सुसमाहित, सुसंस्कृत; 'r.-about' वक्र, कुटिल, असरल; समंततः, अभितः, &c. –LY, *adv.* अवक्रं, सपरिच्छेदं, सुव्यक्तं, स्पष्टार्थं. –NESS, *s.* वृत्तता, गोलत्वं, वर्तुलता, पीनता, अवक्रता, स्पष्टता, &c.

ROUSE, *v. t.* (From sleep) वि-प्र-बुध् c., जागृ c., उत्था c. (उत्थापयति), निद्रां भंज् 7 P or भिद् 7 P. 2 उत्पद् c., जन् c., उद्-प्र-बुध् c., उत्तिज् c., उद्युज् 10, उत्था c., उद्दीप् c., प्रोत्सह् c.; 'r. to action' क्षुभ् c., चेष्ट् c., प्रचुद् 10, कार्ये प्रवृत् c. –*v. i.* A-wake, q. v. –*s.* पानोत्सवः, सग्धि *f.*, सपीति *f.*

ROUT, *v. t.* भंज् 7 P, वि-द्रु c., प्र-वि-ध्वंस् c., प्र-पलाय् c. –*s.* भंगः, विध्वंसः, विद्रावः, सैन्यभंगः, व्यूहभेदः, बलव्यसनं. 2 जनसंमर्दः; *See* MOB. 3 कोलाहलः, तुमुलरवः, कलकलः. –ED, *a.* विद्रावित, भग्न, प्रपलायित; भग्नव्यूह, उत्यिजल, समुत्पिंज, कांदिशीक.

ROUTE, *s.* *See* ROAD.

ROUTINE, *s.* क्रमः, पर्यायः, अभ्यासः; 'daily r.' दिनक्रमः, दैनिककार्यपरिपाटी-परंपरा; 'r. work' नित्यकर्म; 'usual r.' नित्यक्रमः, नित्याभ्यासः.

ROVE, *v. i.* पर्यट् 1 P, परि-,भ्रम् 1, 4 P, प्र-वि-चर् 1 P. –ER, *s.* परिभ्रमकः, पर्यटनकृत् *m.*, भ्रमणशीलः. 2 दस्युः, चौरः. –ING, *s.* परि-,भ्रमणं-अटनं, विचरणं.

ROW, *v. t.* (नौदंडेन) वह् c., प्रेर् c., संचल् c., प्रचुद् 10, प्रणुद् c. –*v. i.* नौकां वह् c. or प्रेर् c. &c. –*s.* राजिः, पंक्तिः, श्रेणिः-णी, आवलिः-ली, ततिः, माला, (all *f.*); *See* LINE. 2 कलहः, संमर्दः, तुमुलरवः, कोलाहलः. –ER, *s.* नाविकः, पोतवाहः, क्षेपणिधरः, दंडधरः.

ROWEL, *s.* कंटकः.

ROYAL, *a.* राजकीय, राजयोग्य, राजार्ह, नृपोचित; राज-नृप in comp. –IST, *s.* राजपक्षीयः, राजपक्षावलंबी. –LY, *adv.* राजवत्, नृपोचितं. –TY, *s.* राजत्वं, राजमहिमन् *m.*, राजाधिकारः, नृपत्वं, प्रभुत्वं, आधिपत्यं, ऐश्वर्यं.

RUB, *v. t.* घृष् 1 P, मृद् 9 P or c. 2 प्र-परि-मृज् 2 P or c., प्रक्षल् 10, निज् 3 U, परिष्कृ, श्लक्ष्णीकृ 8 U. 3 चूर्ण् 10, पिष् 7 P, क्षुद् 7 P. 4 अभि-,अंज् 7 P, दिह् 2 U, लिप् 6 P, मृद्. 5 (Feet) संवह् c., मृद्; 'r. together' संपिष्, संघृष्; 'r. the teeth together' दंतैर्दंतान् घृष् or निष्पिष्; 'r.

out' आ-व्या-मृज्, व्यामृश् 6 P or c., विलुप् c., उच्छिद् 7 P. –*v. i.* सं-घट् 1 A, संघृष्. 2 संघर्षणेन अपघि-क्षि-pass. or अवसद् 1 P. 3 कृच्छ्रेण सं-उत्-तॄ 1 P, अति-इ 2 P. –*s.* घर्षणं, अभ्यंजनं, संवाहनं, मर्दनं, &c. 2 संघट्टः, समाघातः, संमर्दः. 3 कृच्छ्रं, कष्टं; *See* DIFFICULTY. –BER, *s.* घर्षकः, मार्जकः, मर्दकः. 2 (Substance) घर्षकः. –BING, *s.* घर्षणं, मर्दनं, &c.

RUBBISH, *s.* अवस्करः, उच्छिष्टं, मलं, तुच्छ-निःसार-द्रव्यं.

RUBICUND, *a.* आरक्त, पाटल.

RUBRIC, *s.* व्यवस्था, विधिः.

RUBY, *s.* माणिक्यं, पद्मरागः, शोणरत्नं, लोहितकः. –*a.* रक्त, पाटल, रक्तवर्ण.

RUDDER, *s.* केनिपातः-तकं, अरित्रं, कर्णः.

RUDDY, *a.* रक्त, अरुण; *See* RED.

RUDE, *a.* अविनीत, अविनय, वियात, धृष्ट, अमर्याद, उद्धत, सप्रतिभ, असभ्य, अशिष्ट, अनार्य, दुःशील, नष्टविनय, निर्लज्ज, प्रगल्भ. 2 असंस्कृत, अशिष्ट, ग्राम्य, अकृतविद्य, अप्रबुद्ध, अनक्षर, अशिक्षित, विद्याहीन-शून्य. 3 स्थूल, अदक्ष, अनिपुण, अपटु, रूक्ष. –LY, *adv.* अविनयेन, धृष्टवत्, प्रगल्भं, स्थूलं, अशिष्टतया, &c. –NESS, *s.* अविनयः, वैयात्यं, धाष्टर्यं, अमर्यादा, प्रागल्भ्यं, प्रतिभा, अनार्यता, अदाक्षिण्यं. 2 असंस्कारः, अशिष्टता, ग्राम्यता. 3 स्थूलता, अदाक्ष्यं, &c.

RUDIMENT, *s.* उपक्रमः, प्रारंभः, मूलं, प्रथम-मूल-तत्त्वं; 'r. s of knowledge' ज्ञानतत्त्वानि, ज्ञानमूलं, उपक्रमणिका. 2 मूलांगं, बीजं, मूलं, मूलवस्तु-द्रव्यं. –AL, –ARY, *a.* प्राथमिक-मौलिक (की *f.*), मूल-प्रथम-आदि in comp.

RUE, *v. t.* अनुशुच् 1 P, अनुतप् 4 A; *See* REPENT, REGRET. –*s.* ब्राह्मी. –FUL, *a.* अनुशोकाकुल, अनुतापार्त, शोकार्त, विषण्ण, उद्विग्न.

RUFFIAN, *s.* आततायिन् *m.*, साहसिकः, वधोद्यतः.

RUFF, RUFFLE, *v. t.* संकुच् 1 P, आकुंच् c., पुटीकृ 8 U, चूर्ण् 10; 'r. up' प्र-सं-क्षुभ् c., प्रकुप् c., व्याकुलीकृ, उद्विज् c.; 'not r. ed in disposition' प्रकृतिगंभीर, शांतात्मन्. –*s.* भंगि *f.*, ऊर्मि *f.*, पुटः, चूर्णः. 2 प्र-सं-वि-क्षोभः, प्रकोपः, व्याकुलत्वं, उद्वेगः, संभ्रमः, अशांति *f.* –ED, *a.* सं-,क्षुब्ध, क्षोभित, प्रकोपित, आकुल, व्याकुल, व्यग्र, अस्थिर, संभ्रांत, अशांत, उद्विग्न, कातर, पर्याकुल.

RUG, *s.* कंबलः, रल्लकः; आस्तरः-रणं.

RUGGED, *a.* विषम, नतोन्नत. 2 रु(रू)क्ष, कर्कश; *See* HARSH. –NESS, *s.* वैषम्यं, कार्कश्यं.

RUIN, *v. t.* नश् c., वि-प्र-°, प्र-वि-ध्वंस् c., क्षि 5, 9P or c., वि-,लुप् 6 P or c., उच्छिद् 7 P, हन् 2 P or c. (घातयति); उत्-अव-सद् c., नि-अव-पत् c., उद्-ह 1 P, (building); 'r. a man' संपत्ति-विभवं-नश् c., परिक्षीण- *a.* कृ. –*s.* वि-,नाशः, प्र-वि-ध्वंसः, क्षयः, लोपः, विघातः, उच्छेदः, अवसादः, निपातनं, उत्सन्नता, जीर्णता (of a house); 'in r. s' जीर्ण, विशीर्ण, उत्सन्न, जर्जर, जर्जरित. 2 अनिष्टं, अपायः, हानि *f.*, क्षति *f*, अनर्थः. 3 (Of fortune) परिक्षयः, वित्त-विभव-नाशः, भाग्यक्षयः, ऐश्वर्यनाशः-भंगः-लोपः, परिक्षीणता; 'r. of an army' बलव्यसनं, भंगः, पराभवः, पराजयः; 'to go to r.' परिक्षि-pass., क्षयं-नाशं-या 2 P or -इ 2 P, प्र-वि-ली 4 A; ध्वंस् 1 A; 'r. seize thee' अजीवनिः ते भूयात्; *See* under PERDITION. –ED, *a.* नष्ट, ध्वस्त, क्षीण; अवसन्न, उच्छिन्न, जीर्ण, विशीर्ण, जर्जर, &c. 2 परिक्षीण, नष्टविभव, गतश्रीक, नष्ट-गत-धन-ऐश्वर्य, प्रचलितविभव, क्षीणधन. –OUS, *a.* उत्सन्न, क्षीण, जीर्ण &c. 2 वि-,नाशिन्, नाशावह, नाश-क्षय-कर (री *f.*), घातुक, अनिष्टोत्पादक. –OUSLY, *adv.* सनाशं, सक्षयं, सापायं.

RULE, *v.* प्र-,शास् 2P, नि-विनि-यम् 1 P, परिपा c. (पालयति), विनी 1 P, गुप् 1 P, ईश् 2 A (with gen.); अध्यास् 2 A, अधि-ष्ठा 1 P; तंत्र् 10; 'r. ing subjects like one's own children' प्रजाः प्रजाः स्वा इव तंत्रयित्वा (S. 5). 2 आदिश् 6 P, वि-धा 3 U, नियमं-निधि-कृ 8 U, व्यव-स्था c. (स्थापयति); gen. ex. by (*s.*). 3 निग्रह् 9 P, सं-नि-यम् ; *See* CONTROL. 4 रेखाभिः अंक् 10. –*s.* शासनं, अधिकारः, प्रभुत्वं, आधिपत्यं, स्वाम्यं, ईशत्वं, ऐश्वर्यं, राजपालनं. 2 विधिः, नियमः, सूत्रं, व्यवस्था; (moral &c.) मर्यादा, क्रमः, निर्देशः, आ-नि-देशः, प्रचोदनं-ना, शासनं, मार्गः, कल्पः; तत्त्वं (of science); न्यायः. 3 प्रमाणं, मानं; 'general r.' उत्सर्गः, सामान्यविधिः; 'r. of action' क्रियाविधिः-मार्गः; 'r. of judicature' व्यवहारविधिः-मार्गः; 'according to the r.' यथाविधि, विधितः; यथान्यायं; 'r. of three' त्रैराशिकं. –ER, *s.* शासितृ *m.*, पालयिता, शास्ता, शासकः, पालकः, अधिष्ठाता, अधिपतिः, अधीशः, नियंता, स्वामी, प्रभुः, ईश्वरः; 'under one r.' एकस्वामिक. 2 रेखालेखनी. –ING, *a.* शासत्, नियंतृ, पालक &c. 2 प्रबल, गरिष्ठ, प्रधान, बलिष्ठ; 'r. deity' अधिदेवता, अधिष्ठात्री देवता.

RUM, *s.* सीधु *m. n.*, आसवः, मैरेयं. –*a.* असंगत, अपरूप.

RUMBLE, *v. i.* रस् 1 P, नद् 1 P, गर्ज् 1 P, गंभीरं स्वन् 1 P or घुष् 1 P. –ING, *s.* गर्जनं, नर्दनं, दीर्घ-गंभीर-नादः-ध्वनिः-घोषः, निर्घोषः, (of clouds) स्तनितं, घनध्वनिः, मेघनादः, &c.

RUMINATE, *v. i.* रोमंथायते (D.), रोमंथं अभ्यस् 4 U, (S. 2). 2 पुनः पुनः ध्यै 1 P or विचर् c., निध्यै desid. (निदिध्यासति). –ION, *s.* रोमंथः; अभीक्ष्णचिंता, निदिध्यासनं. –RUMINANT, *a.* रोमंथकर (री *f.*).

RUMMAGE, *v. t.* अस्ताव्यस्तीकृत्य सूक्ष्मं अन्विष् 4 P or निरूप् 10.

RUMOUR, *s.* जनप्रवादः, किंवदंती, प्रवादः, जनश्रुति *f.*, लोकवादः-वार्ता; *See* REPORT, –*v. t.* Ex. by (*s.*); 'it is r. ed' इति किंवदंती श्रूयते, इति जनप्रवादः.

RUMP, *s.* *See* HIP.

RUMPLE, *See* FOLD.

RUN, *v. i.* धाव् 1 P, द्रु 1 P, प्र-वि-°, शीघ्रं-द्रुतं गम्-चल्-चर् 1 P or या-इ 2 P, रंह् 1 P; (as a fluid) क्षर् 1 P, प्र-,स्यंद् 1 A, गल् 1 P, द्रु, प्र-,स्रु; (as rivers) वह् 1P, अवतॄ 1 P, गम् (सागरं); 'how much has the night yet to r.' कियदवशिष्टं रजन्याः (S. 4). 3 प्र-वि-ली 4 A, द्रवीभू, द्रु. 4 प्रवृत् 1 A, प्रगम्, प्रसृ; *See* PROCEED. 5 अति-इ 2 P, अतिक्रम् 1 U, 4 P, या 2 P, गम्; *See* PASS. 6 (Away) प्र-, पलाय् 1 A, अपसृ 1 P, अपक्रम्; अपया गम्-धाव्-सृ 1 P, प्र-वि-द्रु. 7 (As a sore) पूयं स्रु c. or मुच् 6 P. 8 वितन्-विस्तृ pass.; प्रसृ; *See* EXTEND; 'r. to waste' परि-,क्षि pass; 'r. riot' मर्यादां अति-इ or अतिक्रम्. –*v. t.* धाव् c.; चल् c.; वह् c. –about, इतस्ततो धाव्, वि-परि-धाव्. –after, अनुधाव्-द्रु-गम्-सृ &c. –against, at, towards, अभि-प्रति-उप-धाव्-द्रु, संमुखं गम्. –down, (*v. t.*) गुणान् अपलप् 1 P, अवमृद् 9 P; *See* DECRY, DEPRECIATE. 2 Chase, q. v. –in, आ-प्र-विश् 6 P. –into, उप-गम्, आ-पद् 4 A, ग्रस् pass.; 'ran into debt' ऋणग्रस्तो बभूव. –off, अपसृ, अपक्रम्, अपया; 'till the brook has r. off' यावन्निर्झरस्रोतो नापक्रामति, न तिरोभवति, न क्षीयते. –on, (of water) प्र-,वह्. 2 प्रवृत्, प्रसृ. 3 Prate, q. v. –out, क्षि-अपचि-pass., अवसो-समाप्- pass. –over, परिवह्, उपरि स्रु; *See* OVERFLOW. –up, वृध् 1 A; *See* INCREASE. –*s.* धावनं, द्रवणं, विद्रवः, पलायनं. 2 गति *f.*; क्रमः, मार्गः, प्रवृत्ति *f.* 3 प्रवाहः, स्रावः, प्र-नि-स्यंदः. 4 प्रचारः, प्रसिद्धि *f.*; प्रचलनं. 5 पर्यंतः, परिमाणं. 6 जलयात्रा, समुद्रपर्यटनं; 'in the long r.' अंते, दीर्घकालादूर्ध्वं; 'the ordinary r. of people' सामान्याः, पृथग्जनाः, प्राकृताः, साधारणजनः. –NER, *s.* धावकः. 2 जांघिकः, जंघाकारिकः, प्र-,जविन् *m.*, तरस्वी, त्वरितः, वेगी, जवनः, जवः. –NING, *s.* *See* (*s.*). –*a.* धावत्, स्रवत् &c. 2 सपूय, पूयस्राविन् (sore). 3 यथाक्रमं, अनुपूर्वशः. –RUNAWAY,-RUNAGATE, *s.* प्रपलायितः, अपधावितः. 2 युद्धत्यागी, रणविमुखः.

RUNDLE, *s.* सोपानं, आरोहणं.

RUPTURE, *s.* भेदः, स्फोटनं, भंगः. 2 भेदः, कलहः, स्नेहभंगः, भेदः, सुहृद्भेदः. 3 अंत्रवृद्धि *f.*-स्रंसः. –*v. t.* भंज् 7 P, भिद् 7 P, स्फुट् c.

RURAL, *a.* ग्राम्य, जानपद (दी *f.*), ग्रामीय, ग्रामीण, ग्राम-जनपद in comp.; 'r. pleasures' ग्रामवाससौख्यं.

RUSE, *s.* *See* PRETEXT.

RUSH, *v. i.* वेगेन-तरसा-धाव् 1 P or गम्-पत्-चल् 1 P, सवेगं प्रया 2 P or प्रसृ 1 P; 'r. upon' आक्रम् 1 U, 4 P, आ-अव-स्कंद् 1 P, सवेगं अभिद्रु or आपत्, अभिसृ ; युद्धाभिसारिणः चमूपतयः (U. 5) 'r. ing upon (me) for fighting'; 'r. forth' निर्गम्, बहिर्गम्, निःसृ ; 'r. headlong' अतिवेगेन-साहसपूर्वं-प्रविश् 6 P. –*s.* महावेगः, जवः, आवेगः, संरंभः. 2 अतिवेगेन धावनं-आपातः, सवेगावस्कंदः, सरभसाक्रमः; 'I do not care a r.' अणुमात्रमपि नोत्सुकः.

RUSH-LIGHT, *s.* तृणप्रकाशः, तृणालोकः.

RUSSET, *a.* कपिश, श्याव.

RUST, *s.* किट्टं, मंडूरं, सिंहा(घा)णं-नं, मलं, अयोमलं ; कलंकः. –*v.* कलंकेन-मलेन-आवृ 5 U. –Y, *a.* मलित, मलीमस ; मलावृत, समल, कलंकावृत.

RUSTIC, *a.* ग्राम्य, ग्रामीय-ण, ग्रामिक (की *f.*), जानपद (दी *f.*), असभ्य, अशिष्ट, अविनीत, प्राकृत. –*s.* ग्राम्यः, ग्रामीणः, वृषलः, जानपदः. –ALLY, *adv.* ग्रामिकवत्, ग्राम्यजनवत्. –ITY, *s.* ग्राम्यता, अशिष्टता, असभ्यता.

RUSTICATE, *v. t.* निर्वस् c., प्र-वि-वस् c. –*v. i.* प्र-वि-वस् 1 P.

RUSTLE, *v. i.* मर्मररवं कृ 8 U. –ING, *s.* मर्मरशब्दः, मर्मरः, वस्त्र-पर्ण-स्वनितं.

RUT, *s.* गर्तः-र्ता, चक्रांकः, चक्रमार्गः. 2 मदः, मदजलं; 'in r.' मदजलस्यंदिन्. –TISH, *a.* मत्त, मदोत्कट.

RUTHLESS, *a.* निर्दय, निर्घृण, क्रूर, निष्कृप; *See* CRUEL.

RYOT, *s.* कृषकः, कर्षकः, कृषीवलः.

S.

SABBATH (day), *s.* विश्रामवासरः-दिवसः.

SABLE, *a.* श्याम, कृष्ण, कृष्णवर्ण. –*s.* श्यामकः. 2 कृष्णवेषः.

SABOT, *s.* काष्ठपादुका.

SABRE, *s.* खड्गः, निस्त्रिंशः, चंद्रहासः, कृपाणः.

SABULOUS, *a.* *See* SANDY.

SACCHARINE, *a.* शार्कर (री *f.*), मिष्ट, मधुर.

SACERDOTAL, *a.* पुरोहित in comp. ; याजकीय, पौरोहित (ती *f.*).

SACHEL, *s.* क्षुद्रकोषः, पुस्तकाधारः, भस्त्रा.

SACK, *s.* स्यूतः, प्रसेवः, स्योतः, स्यूनः, शाणपुटः-कोषः, गोणी. 2 लुंठनं, अपहारः, धनादेः अपहरणं ; 's.-cloth' शाणपटः-वस्त्रं, वराशिः, स्थूलशाटकः, शाणं. –*v. t.* लुंठ् 1 P, 10, उपप्लु 1 A, सर्वस्वं अपहृ 1 P.

SACRAMENT, *s.* संस्कारः. –AL, *a.* संस्काररूप.

SACRED, *a.* पुण्य, पवित्र, परि-,पूत, मेध्य, शुचि. 2 अलौकिक-असांसारिक-वैदिक-(की. *f.*), (opposed to profane). 3 पूज्य, पूजार्ह; भावितात्मन्. 4 पुण्यार्थक, सुप्रतिष्ठित. 5 अनतिक्रमणीय, अलंघ्य, अभेद्य; दुर्धर्ष, अवध्य (person); 'an ambassador, being considered s., never tells an untruth' सदैवावध्यभावेन दूतो वदति नान्यथा (H. 3); 's. spot' क्षेत्रं, पुण्यस्थानं, तीर्थं; 's. grove' पुण्यवनं, तपोवनं; 's. knowledge' निगम-वेद-ज्ञानं,'श्रुतिबोधः; 's. writing' वेदः, निगमः, श्रुति *f.*

SACRIFICE, *s.* यज्ञः, क्रतुः, अध्वरः, यागः, इज्या, मखः, सवः, होमः, हवनं, इष्टि *f.*, मेधः in comp.; 'horse-s.' अश्वमेधः; 'human s.' नरमेधः-यज्ञः &c.; 'imperial s.' राजसूयः; 'fit for a s.' यज्ञिय, मेध्य. 2 आलंभः, उत्सर्गः, बलिः, उपहारः. 3 व्ययः, उत्सर्गः, परि-,त्यागः, विनियोगः, समर्पणं; 'even at the s. of one's life' जीवितव्ययेनापि, प्राणपरित्यागेनापि; oft. by instr. alone (आत्मानं सततं रक्षेत् दारैरपि धनैरपि). -*v. t.* यज् 1 U; हु 3 U, उपहृ 1 P, उत्सर्गार्थं हन् 2 P or बलिं दा 3 U, समा-आ-लभ् 1 A (animal); 'he s. a beast to Rudra' पशुना रुद्रं यजते; 'he s. ed a horse' अश्वमेधं ततान, अश्वमेधेन ईजे. 2 परि-,त्यज् 1 P, उत्-सृज् 6 P, हा 3 P, सं-ऋ c. (अर्पयति), विनियुज् 7 A, 10; 's. ing their own interests' स्वार्थं परित्यज्य; 'without s. ing their interests' स्वार्थाविरोधेन (Bh. I. 74). -ER, *s.* यजमानः, यष्टृ *m.*, याजकः, यज्वन् *m.*, याज्ञिकः, होता. -SACRIFICIAL, *a.* याज्ञिय, वैतान (नी *f.*), मेध्य; यज्ञ in comp.; 's. work' यज्ञकर्म; 's. fire' होमाग्निः, समूह्यः, परिचाय्यः, उपचाय्यः; 's. priest' ऋत्विज् *m.*; *See* PRIEST; 's. session' सत्रं.

SACRILEGE, *s.* देवतादूषणं, देवस्वापहरणं, देवस्वचौर्यं, पुण्यवस्तुदूषणं; धर्मलंघनं-लोपः. -SACRILEGIOUS, *a.* देवस्वापहारिन्; पुण्यद्रव्यदूषिन्.

SAD, *a.* विषण्ण, म्लान, शोकाकुल, सोत्कंठ, अवसन्न, उद्विग्न, उत्कंठासंस्पृष्ट, उदासीन, खिन्न, दुर्मनस्, विमनस्. 2 शोचनीय, शोकावह, दुःखद, क्लेशकर (री *f.*), क्लेशप्रद. 3 गंभीर; *See* GRAVE;'to be s.' खिद्-pass., अव-वि-सद् 1 P, शुच् 1 P, दुर्मनायते (D.). -DEN, *v. t.* विषण्णीकृ 8 U, अव-वि-सद् c., खिद् c.; *See* GRIEVE. -LY, *adv.* सशोकं, सविषादं, सखेदं, सोद्वेगं, म्लानमुखेन.-NESS, *s.* विषादः, उद्वेगः, अवसादः, उत्कंठा, औदासीन्यं, ग्लानि *f*, खेदः.

SADDLE, *s.* पर्याणं, पल्ययनं, पर्ययणं. -*v. t.* पर्याणं आरुह् c. or निविश् c., सज्जीकृ 8 U; 'mounting the s. ed Indrāyudha' दत्तपर्याणमिंद्रायुधमारुह्य (Ka. 126); (fig.) भारं नि-धा 3 U or न्यस् 4 U; 's.-horse' वाहाश्वः. -ER, *s.* पर्याणकारः.

SAFE, *a.* सुरक्षित, निराबाध; सुस्थ, क्षेम, अक्षत, निर्व्रण, अजातापाय. 2 निर्भय, अकुतोभय, अभय, निःशंक, भयातीत, आपद्-भय-मुक्त. 3 अलंघ्य, दुरासद, दुर्धर्ष; 's. against enemies' दुरासदः परैः (R. VIII. 4). 4 क्षेम्य, भयरहित, क्षेम, निर्भय; 'a s. place' निर्भयस्थानं, अभयंकरं स्थलं; 'sound and s.' कुशलिन्, निरामय, सुस्थ, अक्षत. -*s.* लोहपेटिका, लोहमंजूषा; 's. conduct' अभयदानं-पत्रं; 's.-guard' रक्षा, गुप्ति *f.*, रक्षणं; 'Pass', q. v. -LY, *adv.* क्षेमेण, निराबाधं, अक्षतं, सक्षेमं, निर्भयं; 'when she is s. brought to bed' यदा अनघप्रसवा भवति (S. 4). -TY, *s.* क्षेमः-मं, स्वास्थ्यं, क्षेमता, अक्षतं, कुशलं, अनामयं. 2 रक्षा-क्षणं, निर्भयत्वं, अभयं, निर्भयं, भय-आपद्-मुक्ति *f.*; 'to promise s.' अभयवचनं दा 3 U.

SAFFLOWER, *s.* कुसुंभं, वह्निशिखं, महारजनं, कमलोत्तरं.

SAFFRON, *s.* कुंकुमं, अग्निशिखं, वरं, बाह्लि(ह्री)कं, पीतनं, रक्तं, संकोचं, पिशुनं, धीरं, लोहितचंदनं, काश्मीरजन्म. -*a.* कुंकुमवर्ण-राग, अरुण; 'dyed with s.' कुंकुमाक्त.

SAGACIOUS, *a.* चतुर, विदग्ध, दूरदृष्टि, मेधाविन्, सूक्ष्मधी, तीक्ष्ण-कुशाग्र-मति-बुद्धि. -LY, *adv.* चतुरं, सूक्ष्मधिया, विदग्धतया. -SAGACITY, *s.* वैदग्ध्यं, चातुर्यं, तीक्ष्णमतित्वं, सूक्ष्मधीः-मति *f.*

SAGE, *s.* प्र(प्रा)ज्ञः, विपश्चित् *m.*, तत्त्वविद् *m.*, बुधः, पंडितः, ज्ञानी. 2 ऋषिः, मुनिः. 3 सिद्धः, साधुः, यतिः, सिद्धजनः-पुरुषः, आत्मज्ञः, मुमुक्षुः, ब्रह्मज्ञः. -*a.* प्राज्ञ, पंडित, ज्ञानिन्; *See* WISE. -LY, *adv.* पंडितवत्. -NESS, *s.* प्राज्ञता, पांडित्यं.

SAGITTARIUS, *s.* धनुः, धनूराशिः.

SAIL, *s.* वातवस्त्रं-वसनं, नौवसनं-वस्त्रं; 'set s.' नावं-पोतं-मुच् 6 P or चल् c. -*v. i.* (Of a boat &c.) वायुना नुद्-चुद्-वह्-प्रेर्-pass. 2 (Of persons) पोतमारुह्य or अध्यास्य प्र-स्था 1 A; नावा-पोतेन गम्-चल् 1 P, नावा तॄ 1 P or प्लु 1 A, जलवर्त्मना गम्-या &c. 3 चल्, सं-वि-सृप् 1 P; 's. ing in the air' विहायसा-नभोवर्त्मना-गच्छन्, नभसि संसर्पन्. -ING, *s.* समुद्रयानं. -OR, *s.* नाविकः, पोतवाहः, नौवाहः, समुद्रगः.

SAINT, *s.* मुनिः, साधुः, सिद्धः, सिद्धजनः, ऋषिः, पुण्यजनः; *See* SAGE. -LY, *a.* विमल, पवित्र, पुण्यात्मन्, परिपूत, अतिपुण्य, सिद्धतुल्य.

SAKE, *s.* कारणं, निमित्तं, हेतुः, प्रयोजनं; 'for the s. of' अर्थे or अर्थं in comp., हेतोः, निमित्तं, कारणात्, with gen. or in comp., कृते (with gen.); *See* FOR.

SAL, *s.* सालः, श्यालः, सर्जः, कार्श्यः, अश्वकर्णकः, सस्यसंबरः.

SALACIOUS, *a. See* LUSTFUL.

SALARY, *s.* वेतनं, वृत्ति *f.*, भृति *f.*, मूल्यं; *See* HIRE;

'monthly s.' मासिकं; 'annual s.' वार्षिकं. -IED, *a.* वृत्ति-वेतन-भुज्, कृतवेतन.

SALE, *s.* *See* under SELL.

SALIENT, *a.* प्रलंब, प्रोच्छ्रित. 2 प्रवण, द्रुतगामिन्. 3 (fig.) मुख्य, प्रधान, विशिष्ट, पुरःस्फुरत्.

SALINE, *a.* लवण, क्षार, लवणगुणविशिष्ट; 's. taste' लवणरसः; 's. soil' ऊषः, क्षारमृत्तिका; 'having s. soil' ऊषर, ऊषवत्.

SALIVA, *s.* लाला, सृणि(णी)का, स्यंदिनी; 'his mouth emits s.' वक्त्रं लालायते. -SALIVARY, -SALIVAL, *a.* लालास्राविन्. -SALIVATE, *v. t.* लालां स्रु c. or निःसृ c.

SALLOW, *a.* आपीत, पांडुर, विवर्ण; *See* PALE.

SALLY, *v. i.* निर्गम् 1 P, निष्पत् 1 P, निष्क्रम् 1 U, 4 P, जवेन बहिर्गम्, अभ्यव-स्कंद् 1 P, अभ्या-सद् c. -*s.* निर्गमः, निष्क्रमः-मणं, निःसरणं, आपातः, अभ्यासादनं, अभ्यवस्कंदनं, अवपातः. 2 स्फुरणं, उत्प्लवनं, उत्पतनं. 3 विलासः, विलसितं, विभ्रमः; 's. es of wit' बुद्धिविलासाः; विदग्धालापाः, नर्मालापविभ्रमाः; 's. of levity' बुद्धिचापल्यं-चांचल्यं; 's.-port' निर्गमद्वारं.

SALOON, *s.* (सुप्रसाधित-) शाला, कोष्ठः.

SALT, *s.* लवणं; (fig.) पिंडः; सफलीकृतभर्तृपिंडः (M. 5) 'who showed that he had not eaten his master's s. in vain'; 'rock-s.' सैंधवः-वं, शीतशिवं; *See* under ROCK; 'sea-s.' अक्षी(क्षि)वं, वशि(सि)रं; 'black s.' पाक्यः, बिडं; क्षारं; 'sambhar s.' रौमकं, वसुकं; 'sochal s.' सौवर्चलः, अक्षं, रुचकं; 's.-petre' यवजः, यवक्षारः, पाक्यः; यवाग्रजः. -*a.* लवण, लवण-क्षारयुक्त-मय (यी *f.*); लवणगुणविशिष्ट, क्षारधर्मक, लवण-क्षार in comp. -*v. t.* लवणीकृ 8 U, लवणेन सिच् 6 P or अंज् 7 P. -ED, *a.* लवणान्क, लवणसंसृष्ट, लवणित. -ISH, *a.* ईषल्लवण. -NESS, *s.* लवणत्वं, क्षारता.

SALUBRIOUS, *a.* हित-स्वास्थ्य-कर (री *f.*), आरोग्यावह, पथ्य, अनामयकर, क्षेम्य, पुष्टिद, हित. 2 Salutary, q. v.

SALUTARY, *a.* हित, हित-कल्याण-कर (री *f.*),-आवह, उपकारिन्, श्रेयस्कर, शुभंकर. 2 पथ्य; *See* SALUBRIOUS.

SALUTE, *v. t.* अभि-,वंद् 1 A, अभिवद् 10 A, प्रणिपत् 1 P, प्रणम् 1 P, नमस्कृ 8 U, नमस्यति (D.), सभाज् 10; अभिनंद् 1 P, उप-स्था 1 A; 's. in return' प्रतिनंद्; प्रत्यभिनंद्. 2 Kiss, q. v. -*s.*, -ATION, *s.* प्रणामः, प्रणति *f.*, प्रणिपातः, अभि-,वंदनं, अभिवादः-दनं, नमस्कारः, नमस्क्रिया, सभाजनं; 'a s. to thee' नमस्तुभ्यं. -ER, *s.* अभिवादकः, अभिवंदकः.

SALVAGE, *s.* सं-,उद्धृतं; उद्धारः.

SALVATION, *s.* तारणं, उद्धारः, मुक्ति *f.*, मोक्षः, निस्तारः, पापमुक्तिः, ऊर्ध्व-परम-गति *f.* 2 (Generally) परि-,त्राणं, रक्षणं, रक्षा; 'devotional way of s.' भक्तिमार्गः.

SALVE, *s.* अंजनं, प्र-अनु-लेपः, उपदेहः. -*v. t.* अंज् 7 P.

SALVER, *s.* रजतभाजनं, रूप्यपात्रं.

SALVO, *s.* *See* EXCUSE.

SAME, *a.* तद् (*pron. a.*) with or without एव; अभिन्न, निर्विशेष, अनन्य; सम, समान, तुल्य; *See* LIKE; 'it is the s. Vásanti' सैव वासंती; ते एव पादपाः; तदेव वनं &c. (U. 3); gen. by एक, स, सम, समान in comp.; 'of the s. family' सगोत्र; 'sitting in the s. car' एकस्यंदनमास्थितौ; 'of the s. age' समवयस्क; एकरूप, समानजाति, सोदर &c.; 'at the s. time' एकदैव, युगपत्, एकसम-काले, समं, यौगपद्येन; 'in the s. way' तद्वत्, तथैव, तथा, एवं; 'he is the s. as a father to me' मां प्रति स पितृस्थाने-भूमौ वर्तते, पितृनिर्विशेषः. -NESS, *s.* ऐक्यं, साम्यं, एकरूपत्वं, सादृश्यं, संवादः, अभेदः, समभावः; 's. of class' सवर्णता, सावर्ण्यं, एकवर्णता.

SAMPLE, *s.* आदर्शः, प्रतिमा, प्रतिरूपं. -SAMPLER, *s.* सूचिकर्मादर्शः.

SANATIVE, SANATORY, *a.* स्वास्थ्यकारिन्, रोगघ्न (घ्नी *f.*), रोगापह.

SANCTIFY, *v. t.* पवित्रीकृ 8 U, पुण्यीकृ, पापमलं हृ 1 P or क्षल् 10, परि-,पू 9 U, शुध् c., शुचीकृ, पापं-कल्मषं- निर्धू 5, 9 U, 6 P. 2 अनुमंत्र् 10 A, पुण्यकर्मणि विनियुज् 7 A, 10 or निक्षिप् 6 P. -ICATION, *s.* पापहरणं-नाशनं, पवित्रीकरणं. 2 Sanctity, q. v. -ING, *a.* शोधक, पावन. -SANCTITY, *s.* निर्मलता, पवित्रता, पुण्यता, वि-,शुद्धि *f.*, पाप-कल्मषनाशनं-हरणं, अंतःशुद्धिः-शौचं.

SANCTIMONY, *s.* दंभः, धर्माभिमानः, पुण्यवेशधारणं, बकवृत्ति *f.* -IOUS, *a.* दंभिन्, दांभिक (की *f.*), पवित्रंमन्य, बकवृत्ति, धर्माभिमानिन्, कपटधर्मिन्. -IOUSNESS, *s.* दंभः; *See* (*s.*).

SANCTION, *v. t.* अनु-ज्ञा 9 U, अनुमन् 4 A, अनुमुद् 1 A; अनुशास् 2 P, आदिश् 6 P; प्रमाणीकृ 8 U, दृढीकृ, सत्यापयति-द्रढयति (D.), सत्याकृ. -*s.* अनुज्ञा, अनुमति *f.*, अनुशासनं, अनुमोदनं, प्रामाण्यं, प्रमाणं, दृढीकरणं, सत्यापनं.

SANCTUARY, *s.* शरणं, आश्रय-शरण-स्थानं. 2 पुण्यालयः, देवतागारं, पुण्य-पवित्र-स्थानं. 3 गर्भः, गर्भागारं, गर्भगृहं.

SAND, *s.* वालुका, सिकताः (pl.); 's.-bank' पुलिनं, सैकतं; 's.-glass' वालुकायंत्रं. -*v. t.* सिकताभिः आवृ 5 U or आकृ 6 P. -Y, *a.* वालुकामय (यी *f.*), वालुकाकीर्ण, सिकतिल, सैकत (ती *f.*), बहुसिकत; 's. desert' मरुः, धन्वन् *m.* 2 वालुकानिभ; (fig.) अस्थिर, भंगुर, क्षणस्थायिन्, अदृढ.

SANDAL, *s.* चंदनः (tree), चंदनं (wood); गंधसारः, मलयजः, भद्रश्रीः; 'white s. wood' तैलपर्णिकं; 'red s.' रक्तचंदनं, तिलपर्णी, पत्रांगं, रंजनं, कुचंदनं. 2 कोशा-षी, पादुका.

SANDARAC, *s.* मसीशोषणचूर्णं.

SANDERS, *s.* (Yellow) पीतद्रुमः, कालीयकः, हरिद्रुः, दार्वी, पचंपचा, दारुहरिद्रा, पर्जनी. 2 (Red) *See* 'red sandal' under SANDAL.

SANE, *a.* सुस्थ, निरामय, स्वस्थ, प्रकृतिस्थ, कल्य. 2 (In mind) अनु-मत्त, प्रकृतिस्थ, अवातुल, अनुपहतचित्त, अविभ्रुत, अविक्षिप्तचित्त. –ITY,-NESS, *s.* स्वास्थ्यं, अनुन्मादः.

SANGUIFEROUS, *a.* असृग्वाहिन्.

SANGUINARY, *a.* (Of person) रक्त-रुधिर-प्रिय, जिघांसु, मारात्मक, क्रूरचित्त, निष्ठुरचेतस्. 2 रुधिरपातदूषित, रक्तस्रावयुत, बहुरक्त.

SANGUINE, *a.* गाढ, उत्कट; *See* INTENSE; चंड, तीक्ष्ण, चंड-तीक्ष्ण-स्वभाव. 2 (Of persons) आशावत्, सुप्रत्याशिन्, अत्याशान्वित, दृढप्रत्यय, जातविश्वास; 'I feel quite s. that' इति मे गाढाशंसा; 's. hope' सुप्रत्याशा, गाढाशंसा, उत्कटेच्छा. –NESS, *s.* अत्याशा, अत्याशंसा, &c.

SANIES, *s.* पूयं; *See* PUS.–SANIOUS, *a.* पूयस्राविन्.

SANITARY, *a.* स्वास्थ्यहित, स्वास्थ्य in comp., आरोग्यकर (री *f.*), आरोग्यावह.

SAP, *s.* सारः, रसः, द्रवः, सत्त्वं, निर्यासः. –*v. t.* उत्खन् 1 P, समूलं उच्छिद् 7 P or नश् c. –PER, *s.* खनकः, सौरंगिकः. –LESS, *a.* असार, निःसार, विरस, नीरस, निःसत्त्व. –PY, *a.* रसाढ्य, सरस, आर्द्र, ससत्त्व, रसवत्. –SAPID, *a.* सुरस, मिष्ट, स्वादु.

SAPLING, *s.* बालवृक्षः, वृक्षकः.

SAPIENT, *a.* प्राज्ञ, प्रज्ञ, ज्ञानपूर्ण; *See* WISE.

SAPONACEOUS, *a.* चिक्कण, मेदुर.

SAPOR, *s.* *See* FLAVOUR.

SAPPHIRE, *s.* महानीलः, इंद्रनीलः, नीलः, नीलोपलः.

SARCASM, *s.* अव-आ-क्षेपः, निंदागर्भं वचः, परिभाषणं, सनिंद उपालंभः; कटुः उपहासः. –SARCASTIC,-AL, *a.* साक्षेप; निंदागर्भ, अरुंतुद, उग्र, कटु, तीक्ष्ण, सावहास, परिभाषिन्, सोपालंभ. –ALLY, *adv.* साक्षेपं, सोपालंभं.

SARCOMA, *s.* *See* TUMOUR.

SARCOPHAGOUS, *a.* मांसाशिन्, मांसभुज्.

SARDONIC, *a.* विकृत, कराल.

SARDONYX, *s.* गोमेदः-दकः.

SASH, *s.* (अलंकारार्थं) परिकरः, मेखला, कटिसूत्रं. 2 वातायनकाष्ठं.

SATAN, *s.* पिशाचाग्रणीः, पिशाचनाथः. –IC, *a.* पैशाच (ची *f.*).

SATELLITE, *s.* उपग्रहः. 2 (सदा-) पार्श्वचरः, अनुयायिन् *m.*, अनुषंगी; नित्यपार्श्ववर्ती.

SATE, SATIATE, *v. t.* सं-परि-तृप् 5 P or c., अत्यंतं तृप् c., अतितृप्ति-सौहित्यं-उत्पद् c., परिपूर् 10. –ED, *a.* अतितृप्त, परिपूर्णकाम, पर्याप्तकाम, संतर्पित, संपरि-पूर्ण; सुहित; 'to be s.' सं-परि-तृप् 4 P or तुष् 4 P. –SATIETY, *s.* तृप्ति *f.*, तर्पणं, सौहित्यं, अतितुष्टि *f.*,-सौहित्यं-तृप्तिः; पूर्णकामता, वितृष्णता, परिपूर्ति *f.*

SATIN, *s.* चीनांशुकं (s.-cloth).

SATIRE, *s.* आक्षेपगर्भं पद्यं-गीतं, अवगीतं, संक्षेपकविता. 2 Sarcasm, q. v. –ICAL, *a.* उपहासात्मक, सोपहास, साधिक्षेप; *See* SARCASTIC. –IST, *s.* आक्षेपवादिन् *m.* –IZE, *v. t.* साक्षेपं वर्ण् 10, अवगै 1 P, काव्यद्वारा आ-अधि-क्षिप् 6 P.

SATISFY, *v. t.* (Persons) सं-परि-तृप् c.,-तुष् c., कामं-इच्छां-पूर् 10 or निवृत् c., तृप्तिं-तुष्टिं-उत्पद् c., सुखयति (D.), प्री 9 P, आराध् c.; सांत्व् 10, प्रसद् c.; (hunger, desire, &c.) शम् c. (शमयति), प्र-उप-°, छिद् 7 P, परि-पूर्, निराकृ 8 U, निवृत् c.; 'child, s. your curiosity' पूरयत् कुतूहलं वत्सः (U. 4). 2 संदेहं अपनी 1 P, संशयं छिद् or हृ 1 P or निरस् 4 U, निरुत्तरीकृ. –ACTION, *s.* सं-परि-तोषः-तुष्टि *f.*, पर्याप्ति *f.*, इच्छापूर्ति *f.*, सौहित्यं, काम-इच्छा-तृप्तिः-निवृत्तिः-शांति *f.* 2 शांतिः, शमनं, निराकरणं, परि-,पूरणं, छेदः, निवृत्तिः, पूर्तिः, तर्पणं. 3 संशयच्छेदः, संदेहनिवृत्तिः-परिहारः. 4 प्रतिफलं, निस्तारः, शुद्धि *f.* –IED, *a.* तृप्त, तुष्ट, तोषित, तर्पित, पूर्ण-निवृत्त-काम, पर्याप्तकाम, प्रीत, कृतिन्, कृतार्थ, चरितार्थ. 2 छिन्न, पूर्ण, शांत, निवृत्त. 3 छिन्नसंशय, हत-निरस्त-संदेह; 'to be s.' तुष्-तृप् 4 P, प्री pass. –ING, *a.* संतर्पक, संतोषक, तुष्टि-तृप्ति-कर (री *f.*), संशयच्छिद्. –SATISFACTORY, *a.* युक्त, समर्थ, (समर्थमुत्तरं), पर्याप्त, संशयच्छिद्, संदेहच्छेदिन्. 2 तुष्टिप्रद, संतोष-तृप्ति-तुष्टि-कर. 3 (Atoning) Ex. by प्रमृज् 2 P, निस्तृ c.; *See* ATONE. –ILY, *adv.* सम्यक्कृतया, वैशद्येन, संशयच्छेदितया, सम्यक्.

SATRAP, *s.* मंडलेशः, भोगपतिः.

SATURATE, *v. t.* अत्यंतं पर् 10, आ-परि-पूर्; नि-सिच् 6 P, अतिक्लिद् c. –ED, *a.* अति-सिक्त, परिपूर्ण; *See* IMPREGNATE. –ION, *s.* अतिसेकः-क्लेदः, परिपूरणं.

SATURN, *s.* शनिः, शनैश्चरः, रविसुतः, सौरः-रिः. –SATURNINE, *a.* मंद, जड-मंद-शांत-प्रकृति, जडस्वभाव. –SATURNALIA, *s.* शनिमहोत्सवः.

SATYR, *s.* वनदेवता, वन-अरण्य-चरः.

SAUCE, *s.* सूपः, तेमनं, निष्ठानं; उपदंशः, व्यंजनं, उपस्करः; 's.-pan' उखा, पिठरः; *See* FRYING-PAN. –SAUCER, *s.* शरावः, पात्रं, आधारः.

SAUCY, *a.* धृष्ट, निर्व्रीड, निर्लज्ज, प्रगल्भ, अविनीत; सप्रतिभ. –ILY, *adv.* अविनयेन, धृष्टवत्. –INESS, *s.* अविनयः, धाष्टर्यं, प्रतिभा-भानं.

SAUNTER, *v. i.* मंदं मंदं परिक्रम् 1 U, 4 P or परि-

भ्रम् 1, 4 P, शनैः शनैः विचर् 1 P. -ING, s. मंदं परिक्रमणं.

SAVAGE, a. वन्य, जांगल (ली *f.*), अरण्यज, वन-अरण्य in comp. 2 असभ्य, अशिष्ट, अविनीत, असंस्कृत, आचारहीन, अनाचार. 3 क्रूर, हिंस्र, निष्ठुर, निर्दय, दारुण, क्रूरकर्मन्, आपद (दी *f.*); 'all of man is s.' पुरुषा नाम निष्ठुराः (Mr. 5). -s. अशिष्ट-असभ्यजनः. 2 क्रूरकर्मा, राक्षसः, दैत्यः, नरपशुः 3 म्लेच्छः, किरातः, शबरः, यवनः, भिल्लः &c. -LY, *adv.* अशिष्टवत्, निष्ठुरं. -NESS, s. अशिष्टता, क्रौर्यं, दारुणता, &c.

SAVANT, s. बुधजनः, पंडितः, विद्वज्जनः; *See* LEARNED.

SAVE, v. t. रक्ष् 1 P, in all senses, परि-,त्रै 1 A, उद्-समुद्-हृ 1 P, धृ 1 P, तॄ c., उत्-सं-निः-°, मुच् c., मोक्ष् 10, पापात् मुच् &c. 2 सं-चि 5 U, संरक्ष्, नि-धा 3 U, संग्रह् 9 P, अवशिष् c. 3 निवृत् c., निवृ c., निरुध् 7 U, परिहृ; 'those that were s. ed out of the slain' हतशेषाः, हतावशिष्टाः. -*prep.* विहाय, मुक्त्वा, वर्जयित्वा; *See* EXCEPT. -ING, a. अव्ययशील, अल्पव्ययिन्, मितव्यय, अमुक्तहस्त. 2 उद्धारक, मुक्तिदायिन्; मोक्षप्रद. 3 विमोचक, विमोचनहेतुः. -s. रक्षणं, संचयः, संग्रहः, निधानं. 2 संचित-रक्षित-धनं, संचयः. -SAVIOUR, s. तारकः, त्रायकः, परि-,त्राता, रक्षिता, उद्धर्ता, उद्धारकः.

SAVOUR, s. स्वादः, रसः, रुचि *f.* 2 गंधः, वासः. -v. i. सरसी-सगंधी-भू 1 P. 2 (Appear like) Ex. by कल्प, प्राय in comp., ईषदून with abl.; by आ-अव-भास् 1 A; 'it s. s of falsehood' तत् असत्यकल्पं, अनृताभासं, असत्यसंकाशं, असत्यवदाभासते. -Y, a. सरस, सुरस, स्वादु; मिष्ट, रसवत्, रुचिकर. 2 सुरभि, सुगंधि.

SAW, s. करपत्रं, क्रकचः-चं, पत्रदारणः. -v. t. क्रकचेन पट् 10 or दॄ 9 P or c. or छिद् 7 P or अवकृत् 6 P; 's.-dust' काष्ठविदलं; 's.-pit' काष्ठविपाटनमार्गः. -SAWYER, s. क्राकचिकः, दारुदारणः.

SAY, v. t. वद्-गद्-भण् 1 P, वच् 2 P, ब्रू 2 U, भाष् 1 A, उदा-व्या-हृ 1 P; उच्चर् c., उदीर् c., आलप् 1 P (words &c.); मंत्र् 10 A; (tell) कथ् 10, आचक्ष् 2 A. आ-,शंस् 1 P, अभि-धा 3 U, आ-ख्या; *See* TELL; 'I say' ननु भणामि, ननु ब्रवीमि, ननु simply, (ननु पदे परिवृत्य भण Mr. 5); 'they s.' ex. by किंवदंती, जनप्रवादः, इति श्रूयते; *See* REPORT; 'that is to s.' ex. by नाम. -ING, s. वचनं, वाक्यं, वचस् *n.*, उक्तं, &c.; भाषितं, भाषणं, उक्ति *f.*, भणितं. 2 आभाणकः, प्रवादः; 'popular s.' जनप्रवादः; 'so runs the popular s.' तथा च लौकिकानामाभाणकः; *See* PROVERB.

SCAB, s. कच्छु-च्छू *f.*, पामन् *f.*, पामा; *See* ITCH; (white eruption) सिध्मं, किलासं. 2 अधमजनः, नराधमः, हीनः, अपकृष्टः. -BY, a. कच्छुर, वामन, सिध्मल.

SCABBARD, s. कोशः-षः, पिधानं, आधारः.

SCAFFOLD, s. मंचः, इंद्रकोषः. 2 प्रेक्षामंचः. 3 वध्यशिला-स्थानं-काष्ठं, घातस्थानं. -ING, s. मंचः.

SCALD, v. t. तप्तजलादिना दह् 1 P. -s. दाहः.

SCALE, s. तुला, धटः, तुलायंत्रं; 's.-pan' शिक्यं, पार्श्वः. 'goldsmith's s.' एषणी-णिका, नाराची. 2 (Of fishes &c.) वल्कः-ल्कं, वल्कलः-लं, शल्कं, शल्कलं; कवचः-चं. 3 फलकः-कं, पत्रं. 4 नि(निः)श्रेणी, अधिरोहि(ह)णी, सोपानपद्धति *f.*-परंपरा. 5 श्रेणी, परंपरा, आवलि-ली *f.*, माला, पंक्ति *f.* 6 प्रमाणं, परिमाणं; 'on a large scale' स्थूलपरिमाणेन. 7 ग्रामः. -v. t. आ-अधि-रुह् 1 P, आ-अधि-क्रम् 1 U, 4 P, लंघ् 1 A, 10, अवस्कंद् 1 P. 2 वल्कं निष्कृष् 1 P or निर्हृ 1 P. -Y, a. सशल्क, वल्कावृत; सवल्क, शल्किन्, वल्किन्.

SCALENE, a. विषमत्रिभुज.

SCALL, s. *See* SCAB, ITCH.

SCALP, s. मस्तकत्वच् *f.*, शिरोग्रत्वक्, शिरोस्थिचर्मन्. -v. t. मस्तकत्वचं अवच्छिद् 7 P or निर्हृ 1 P.

SCAMP, s. *See* RASCAL.

SCAMPER, v. i. वि-द्रु 1 P, जवेन-वेगात्-द्रु or धाव् 1 P or पलाय् 1 A, सवेगं गम् 1 P.

SCAN, v. t. निपुणं-सूक्ष्मं-निरूप् 10 or निरीक्ष् 1 A or अवलोक् 1 A, 10. 2 (Verses) मात्राः-गणान् गण् 10 or विभज् 1 U. -SCANSION, s. गण-मात्रागणनं-विभागः.

SCANDAL, s. निर्वादः, परि(री)वादः, अपवादः, असूया, अवर्णः, दुर्वर्णः, कौलीनं, अक्षेपः, उपक्रोशः, जुगुप्सा, कुत्सा, निंदा, वाच्यं, वाच्यता, गर्हणं-णा, पैशुन्यं, पिशुनवाक्यं. 2 कलंकः, दूषणं, अपमान-अपकीर्तिहेतुः. -IZE, v. t. (s.) with प्रकाश् c.; अप-परिवद् 1 A, परि-अप्-भाष् 1 A; *See* LIBEL. 2 Offend, q. v. -OUS, a. परि-अप-वादक, आक्षेपगर्भ, परिवादात्मक, असूयक, (s.) in comp. 2 गर्हित, निंद्य, कलंककर-अकीर्तिकर-(री *f.*), दूषणीय, कुत्सित. 3 बीभत्स, घृणावह. -OUSLY, *adv.* गर्ह्यं, कुत्सितं.

SCANT, SCANTY, a. अपर्याप्त, अप्रचुर, स्वल्प, अविपुल, न्यून, अबहुल, अभूयिष्ठ. 2 संबाध, अविस्तीर्ण, संकट; *See* NARROW. 3 Miserly, q. v. -LY, *adv.* अपर्याप्तं, स्वल्पं, अप्रचुरं, अल्पमात्रं, स्तोकं. -NESS, s. अप्राचुर्यं, अपर्याप्ति *f.*, स्वल्पता.

SCAPE-GOAT, s. बलिः.

SCAR, s. किणः, अंकः, चिह्नं, क्षतचिह्नं, क्षतांकः, व्रणः-णं, क्षतं; (fig.) कलंकः. -v. t. क्षतेन-किणेन अंक् 10. -RED, a. क्षतांकित, किणांक.

SCARAMOUCH, s. भंडः, वैहासिकः.

SCARCE, a. अबहुल, अप्रचुर, अप्रभूत, अपर्याप्त, अवि-

पुल, न्यून, अभूयिष्ट, स्वल्प. 2 विरल, दुर्लभ, दुष्प्राप, असुलभ; *See* RARE. -LY, *adv.* कष्टेन, कथमपि, कृच्छ्रेण, दुःखेन, सकृच्छ्रं, आयासेन, दुर् pr.; oft. by (*a.*); 'one s. gets a good son' दुर्लभो गुणवान् पुत्रः; by न, स्तोकं; 's. touches (walks on) the ground' स्तोकमुर्व्यां प्रयाति (S. 1); 's. a day passed' नैकमपि दिनं व्यतीतं; 's.-when' ex. by एव with loc. abs.; मात्र affixed to *adj.*, or यावत्-तावत्; उपस्थितेयं कल्याणी नाम्नि कीर्तिते एव (R. I. 87); प्रविष्टमात्र एवाश्रमं तत्रभवति निरुपप्लवानि नः कर्माणि संवृत्तानि (S. 3); एकस्य दुःखस्य न यावदंतं गच्छामि तावद् द्वितीयं समुपस्थितं (P. II. 6); oft. by च-च; आपूर्णश्च कलाभिरिंदुरमलो यातश्च राहोर्मुखं &c. (Mal. 9). -ITY,-NESS, *s.* दुर्लभता, दुष्प्रापता, विरलता, अप्राचुर्यं, अपर्याप्ति *f.*, स्वल्पता, न्यूनता, अबाहुल्यं, &c. 2 दुर्भिक्षं, अभावः, दुष्कालः, प्रयामः, नीवाकः.

SCARE. *v. t.* त्रस् c., सं-वि-,° भी c., उद्विज् c.; 's. away' भयदर्शनेन वि-द्रु c.; 's.-crow' बिभीषिका, संत्रासनं, भयहेतुः.

SCARF, *s.* चेलकः, सिचयः; उत्तरीयं, चेलं; 's.-skin' बाह्यत्वच् *f.*-चर्मन् *n.*

SCARIFY, *v. t.* त्वचं-चर्म-उल्लिख् 6 P or छिद् 7 P. -ICATION, *s.* त्वगुल्लिखनं, चर्मच्छेदः.

SCARLET, *a.* शोण, अरुण, सिंदूरवर्ण; 's. fever' उदर्धः.

SCARP, *s.* लंबः. -*v. t.* लंबरूपेण निकृत् 6 P.

SCATE, *See* SKATE.

SCATH, SCATHE, *v. t.* क्षण् 8 P, अर्द् 1 P or c.; *See* HARM, INJURE. -LESS, *a.* अक्षत, अपरिक्षत, क्षतहीन, असंजातव्यथ, निर्व्रण.

SCATTER, *v. t.* कॄ 6 P, वि-आ-अवा-प्र-°, प्रसृ c., विक्षिप् 6 P; (away) विक्षिप् c., निर्धू 5, 9 U, विभिद् c.; निरस्, 4 U, अपनुद् 6 P; वि-द्रु c. (army); *See* DISPEL, DISPERSE. -*v. i.* विकॄ pass., दिशि दिशि निर्गम् 1 P or प्र-या 2 P, बहुधा विक्षिप् pass. -ED, *a.* प्र-वि-आ-कीर्ण, विक्षिप्त, व्यस्त, प्रसृत, प्रसारित, विनिर्धूत, असंहत, विश्लिष्ट, विभिन्न. -ING, *s.* विकिरणं, विक्षेपणं, &c.

SCAVENGER, *s.* संमार्जकः, खलपूः, बहुकरः, मल-अवकर-वाहः.

SCENE, *s.* स्थलं, स्थानं, भूमि *f.*; 'the s. lies in Hastinâpura' स्थलं हास्तिनापुरं. 2 अपटी; य(ज)-वनिका, नेपथ्यं, रंगसज्जा. 3 प्रवेशः. 4 रंगः,-भूमिः,-शाला. 5 दृश्यं, दृग्गोचरं स्थानं, आलोकः, दृक्पातविषयः; oft. by स्थानं, आलोकः, or other words; 'this is indeed a lamentable s.' नन्वनुशयस्थानमेतत् (Mal. 8); रमणीयालोकं तत्स्थानं, &c.; अहो अधिकरणमंडपस्य परा श्रीः (Mr. 9) 'how splendid the s. of (presented by) the Court of Justice'; *See* PRESENT also. -SCENERY, *s.* Ex. by भूमिः, स्थानं; *See* above. 2 गृहवृक्षादिरचना, कृत्रिमरचना.

SCENT, *s.* गंधः, अधिवासः; 'sweet s.' आमोदः, परिमलः (arising from trituration) सौरभं; *See* FRAGRANCE; 'diffusing s.' निर्हारी, समाकर्षी; 'having a sweet s.' सुगंधि, इष्टगंध, सुरभि, घ्राणतर्पण. 2 (Organ) घ्राणं घ्राणेंद्रियं, घ्राणशक्ति *f.*; 'having a quick s.' तीक्ष्णघ्राण. -*v. t.* घ्रा 1 P, उप-आ-°. 2 वास् 10, सुरभीकृ 8 U, भु c., धूप् 1 P, 10. -ED, *a.* सु-,वासित, सुरभि, सुगंधि, सुरभीकृत, सामोद, भावित, सगंध. -LESS, *a.* निर्गंध, गंधहीन.

SCEPTIC, *s.* संदेहभृत् *m.*, हैतुकः, अप्रत्ययिन् *m.*, अविश्वासी. -AL, *a.* हैतुक, अप्रत्ययिन्, संशयात्मन्. -ISM, *s.* संदेहः, हैतुकता, अविश्वासः.

SCEPTRE, *s.* दंडः, राजदंडः-वेत्रं-यष्टि *f.* 2 राजाधिकारः, प्रभुत्वं, आधिपत्यं; 'hold the s.' महीं शास् 2 P; *See* REIGN. -ED, *a.* दंडधर, दंडभृत्; 's. king' अभिषिक्तो राजा.

SCHEDULE, *s.* पत्रं, लेख्यं. 2 परिसंख्या, परिशिष्टं.

SCHEME, *s.* उपायः, कल्पना, प्रयोगः, संकल्पः, प्रबंधः, प्र-,युक्ति *f.* 2 पद्धति *f.*, व्यवस्था; 'secret s.' गूढमंत्रणा, कपटप्रबंधः, कुटिलनयः. -*v.* (मनसा) परि-, क्लृप् c., उपायं चिंत् or युज् 10. -ING, *a.* कुटिलनयनिष्णात, युक्तिमत्, विदग्ध; अनुसंधायिन् (in a good sense).

SCHISM, *s.* भेदः, शाखा, धर्म-मत-भेदः. -ATIC, *a.* मतभेदमूलक.

SCHOLAR, *s.* शिष्यः, छात्रः, अंतेवासिन् *m.*; *See* PUPIL; 's. of a s.' प्रशिष्यः. 2 वृत्तिभुज् *m.*, वृत्तिभाक्. 3 पंडितः, कृतविद्यः, विद्वान्; *See* LEARNED, WISE. -LY, *a.* पंडितोचित, पांडित्ययोगिन्. -SHIP, *s.* पांडित्यं, वैदुष्यं, विद्या. 2 वृत्ति *f.*, वेतनं.

SCHOLIAST, *s.* टीकाकारः, टीकाकृत् *m.*, वृत्ति-भाष्य-कारः. -SCHOLIUM, *s.* टीका, भाष्यं, वृत्ति *f.*

SCHOOL, *s.* विद्यालयः, विद्यागारं-गृहं-मंदिरं, पाठशाला, अध्ययनस्थानं. 2 शिष्य-छात्र-समूहः. 3 शाखा, संप्रदायः; 's. of philosophy' दर्शनं; 's.-boy' बालशिष्यः, युवच्छात्रः; 's.-fellow' सहाध्यायिन् *m.*, सतीर्थः-र्थ्यः, एकगुरुः; 's.-man' तार्किकः, नैयायिकः; 's.-master' आचार्यः, गुरुः. उपदेशकः, उपाध्यायः, पाठशालाधिकृतः-अध्यक्षः. -*v. t.* शिक्ष् c., वि-नी 1 P, अधि-इ c. (अध्यापयति); *See* INSTRUCT. -ING, *s.* शिक्षणं, अध्यापनं, उपदेशः. 3 गुरुदक्षिणा, शिक्षामूल्यं.

SCHOONER, *s.* द्विकूपका नौः.

SCIATICA, *s.* कटिशिरावेदना.

SCIENCE, *s.* वि-,ज्ञानं; *See* KNOWLEDGE. 2 विद्या, शास्त्रं.-SCIENTIFIC,-AL, *a.* शास्त्रानुरोधिन्, विज्ञान-शा-

क in comp. 2 कृतविद्य, विद्वस्, आगमिन्, विज्ञानविद्.
SCIMITAR, *s.* खड्गः, असिः; निस्त्रिंशः, करवालः; *See* SWORD.
SCINTILLATE, *v. i.* स्फुलिंगान् मुच् 6 P or उत्क्षिप् 6 P; 'a blazing fire will s. in all directions' अग्नेर्ज्वलतः सर्वा दिशो विस्फुलिंगा विप्रतिष्ठेरन् (S. B. 109). 2 स्फुर् 6 P, भ्राज् 1 A, प्रकाश् 1 A; *See* SHINE. -ION, *s.* स्फुरणं; अग्निकणः, स्फुलिंगनिर्गमः; 'in the state of s.' स्फुलिंगावस्थ *a.*
SCIOLIST, *s.* पल्लवग्राहिपंडितः, किंचिज्ज्ञः, (शास्त्र-) चुंबकः. -SCIOLISM. *s.* पल्लवग्राहिज्ञानं, किंचिज्ज्ञता.
SCION, *s.* नवपल्लवः, किसलयः, अंकुरः, प्ररोहः. 2 वंश्यः, वंशजः; 'the s. of the family of some one' कस्यापि कुलांकुरः (S. 7).
SCIRRHUS, *s.* मांसग्रंथिः.
SCISSORS, *s.* कर्तरी, खंडधारा, कर्तरिका, कृपाणी, छेदनी.
SCOFF (at), *v.* अव-उप-हस् 1 P, अव-आ-अधि-क्षिप् 6 P, अव-ज्ञा 9 U, तिरस्कृ 8 U, धिक्कृ, अवमन् 4 A, परिभू; *See* CONTEMN, MOCK. -ING, *s.* अव-उपहासः, अव-अधि-क्षेपः, अवज्ञा, अवमानः, धिक्कारः. -INGLY, *adv.* सोपहासं, साक्षेपं.
SCOLD, *v. t.* निर्-,भर्त्स् 10 A, परुषं निंद् 1 P, आक्रुश् 1 P, आ-अधि-क्षिप् 6 P, गर्ह् 1, 10 A, अप-परिभाष् 1 A, उपालभ् 1 A; *See* REPROACH. -*s.* कर्कशा, दुर्मुखी, कैकेयी, वक्रशीला. -ER, *s.* निंदकः, भर्त्सकः. -ING, *s.* भर्त्सनं,-ना, निंदा, उपालंभः, आक्रोशः, परिभाषणं, &c.
SCONCE, *s.* दंडः. 2 आश्रयस्थानं, शाला, आश्रयः. 3 Fort, q. v. 4 दीपाधारः. -*v. t.* दंड् 10; *See* FINE.
SCOOP, *s.* दर्वी, कंबि-वी *f.*; *See* LADLE. 2 कोटरः-रं, पुटं. 3 खनित्रं. -*v. t.* दर्व्या अवपत् c. or अवतृ c. 2 उत्खन् 1 P, खनित्रेण पुटीकृ 8 U.
SCOPE, *s.* आशयः, अभिप्रायः, हेतुः, अर्थः, तात्पर्यं, उद्देशः. 2 विषयः, प्रसरः, परिमाणं, पर्यंतः, अवधिः, सीमा; 'mind of limited s.' अल्पविषया मतिः (R. I. 2). 3 अवसरः, अवकाशः; लब्धावकाशा मे प्रार्थना (S. 1) 'has found a s. (for itself)'.
SCORCH, *v. t.* अभि-सं-तप् 1 P or c., निर्-परि-दह् 1 P, प्लुष् 1 P, भ्रस्ज् 6 P, (in a pan); 's. ed with heat' आतपाक्रांत; 's. ed with the fire of missiles' अस्त्रपावकप्लुष्ट. -ING, *a.* दाहक, तापक, अत्युष्ण, अतितिग्म, उग्र, प्रखर, नैदाघ (घी *f.*).
SCORE, *s.* विंशति *f.* 2 अव-,च्छेदः, भंगः, दंतः. 3 रेखा, चिह्नं. 4 गणना, गणनापत्रं-लेखः. 5 विन्यासः (in music). 6 हेतुः, कारणं, निमित्तं; विषयः, अर्थः; 'on that s.' तस्मिन्विषये, तदर्थं; 'on the s. of friendship' सख्यहेतोः &c. -*v. t.* अवच्छिद् 7 P, दंतुरीकृ 8 U, भंगं कृ. 2 अंक् 10; रेखाभिः अंक्. 3 अभि-,लिख् 6 P, गण् 10; (ऋणं or देयं) गण् or पत्रे लिख् 6 P.
SCORIA, *s.* *See* DROSS.
SCORN, *v. t.* निर्-अव-धू 5,9 U, तिरस्कृ 8 U, अवज्ञा 9 U, अवमन् 4 A, उपेक्ष् 1 A, परिभू 1 P, न्यक्कृ, धिक्कृ, परुषं निंद् 1 P. -*s.* (अत्यंत) अवज्ञा, अवमानः, तिरस्कारः, धिक्कारः, परिभवः, उपेक्षा; *See* CONTEMN, CONTEMPT. 2 अवलेपः, दर्पः; *See* PRIDE. -ER, *s.* अवमंतृ *m.*, तिरस्कर्तृ, निंदकः. -FUL, *a.* सावमान, सावज्ञ; तिरस्कारिन्, अवमानिन्, निंदात्मक; अवज्ञागर्भ; सावलेप, दृप्त. -FULLY, *adv.* सावज्ञं, सावमानं, सावलेपं.
SCORPIO, *s.* वृश्चिकः.
SCORPION, *s.* वृश्चिकः, अ(आ)लिः, द्रु(द्रो)णः; 'the sting of a s.' लूमं.
SCOT, *s.* करः, देयभागः; 's.-free' अक्षत, अविकल, निर्व्रण.
SCOTCH, *v. t.* छेदैः अंक् 10, ईषत् छिद् 7 P.
SCOUNDREL, *s.* खंडितवृत्तः, जाल्मः, दुरात्मन् *m.*, अधमः, नरापसदः, निकृष्टः, खलः, दास्याः पुत्रः; (in voc.) काणेलीमातः; *See* RASCAL.
SCOUR, *v. t.* सं-परि-मृज् 2 P or c., निर्णिज् 3 U, घर्षणेन शुध् c., निर्घृष् 1 P. 2 Purge, q. v. -*v. i.* (Off, along) द्रुतं-जवेन-शीघ्रं-अपक्रम् 1 U, 4 P or धाव् 1 P or पलाय् 1 A, द्रुतं द्रु 1 P or अतिक्रम्. -ER, *s.* निर्णेजकः, वस्त्रधावकः. -ING, *s.* मार्जनं, निर्णेजनं.
SCOURGE, *s.* कशा-षा, प्रतिष्कशः-षः, प्रतोदः, ताडनरज्जु *f.*; (fig.) धूमकेतुः, उपद्रवः, उत्पातः, कृतांतः, कालः, पीडकः. -*v. t.* कशया हन् 2 P or तड् 10 or प्रह् 1 P; 'fit to be s. ed' कश्य. 2 अत्यंतं पीड् 10 or अर्द् 1 P or c., उप-द्रु 1 A. -ING, *s.* कशाघातः, कशाताडनं-प्रहारः.
SCOUT, *s.* चारः, चरः, प्रणिधिः, अपसर्पः, गूढचरः; *See* SPY. -*v. i.* संचर् 1 P, गूढं-प्रच्छन्नं परचेष्टां निरूप् 10. -*v. t.* अव-उप-हस् 1 P, सहासं निरस् 4 U or निराकृ 8 U or प्रत्यादिश् 6 P.
SCOWL, *s.* भ्रूभंगः, भ्रु(भ्रू)कुटि-टी *f.* -*v. i.* भ्रुकुटिं बंध् 9 P, कृ 8 U with (*s.*), भ्रुवौ संकुच् 1 P, भ्रूभंगेन दृश् 1 P; *See* FROWN. -ING, *a.* सभ्रूभंग; 'with a s. look' सभ्रूभंगं, भ्रूवोर्भेदात्.
SCRAGGY, *a.* रूक्ष, कर्कश; *See* ROUGH, HARD. 2 कृश, क्षाम, क्षीण; *See* LEAN.
SCRAMBLE, *v. i.* हस्ताभ्यां धृत्वा-मंदंमंदं आरुह् 1 P. 2 संमर्दं-कलहं-कृ 3 U (with dat.); झटिति संग्रह् 9 P, ग्रहीतुं उद्यम् 1 A; 's. ed for water' जलादानार्थं परस्परं संमर्दमकुर्वन्. -*s.*,-ING, *s.* मंदं मंदं आरोहणं. 2 सरभसग्रहणं, संमर्दः.
SCRAP, *s.* खंडः, शकलः-लं, लवः, अंशः; 's. s of

what is eaten' फेला, भुक्तसमुज्झितं; उच्छिष्टं, पिंड:; 's.-book' खंडाधार:, द्रव्यखंडाधार:.

SCRAPE, *s.* कृच्छ्रं, संकटं, आपद् *f.*, दुर्गं, कष्टं, दुःखं, दुर्गति *f.*, दुर्दशा; 'got into a s.' कृच्छ्रगत, आपद्गत, दुःस्थित. 2 घर्षणं. –*v. t.* घृष् 1 P; लिख् 6 P, उत्-वि-°, तक्ष् 1, 5 P, त्वक्ष् 1 P, खुर् 6 P. 3 घर्षणेन प्रमृज् 2 P or निर्णिज् 3 U or अप-नी 1 P or शुध् c.; (with feet) अपस्कृ 6 P. 4 (Together) (कष्टेन or महाप्रयत्नेन) समाहृ 1 P, संचि 5 U, संग्रह् 9 P, एकीकृ. –ER, *s.* उल्लेखनी, निर्घर्षणी, निर्घर्षणक:. 2 काष्ठकुद्दाल:. –ING, *s.* घर्षणं, उल्लेखनं, तक्षणं, क्षुरणं. 2 विदलं, तष्टं; अव(प)स्कर:, अवकर:, मलं.

SCRATCH, *v. t.* वि-उत्-प्रोत्-लिख् 6 P, वि-अव-दृ 9 P or c.; छिद् 7 P, निर्भिद् 7 P, खुर् 6 P; 's. with the nail' नखेन क्षण् 8 P or अंक् 10 or लिख्. 2 कंडूयति-ते (D.); नखैः घृष् 1 P. 3 (As birds) विष्कृ 6 P, अपस्कृ. 4 ईषत् क्षण् or उल्लिख्. 5 Scrawl, q. v. 6 (Out) प्रमृज् 2 P, विलुप् 6 P or c., निर्घृष्, उच्छिद् 7 P, विनश् c.; *See* ERASE. –*s.* (त्वच:) उल्लेखनं, दारणं, छेद:, भेद:; क्षतं, घर्षणं; व्रण:; 's. with the nail' नखक्षतं, नखांक:-व्रण:-पदं. 2 ईषत्क्षतं, त्वग्व्रण:; 'hard s.' ओरंफ:. –ER, *s.* उल्लेखक:, विदारक:, कंडूयनक:; विष्किर:. –ING, *s.* उल्लेखनं, विदारणं, छेद:, &c.; कंडूयनं, कंडूया, कंडूति *f.*

SCRAWL, *v. t.* अस्पष्ट-स्थूलं-लिख् 6 P, स्थूलाक्षरै:-अतिक्षिप्रं-लिख्. –*s.*, –ING, *s.* अस्पष्ट-स्थूल-लेख:.

SCREAM, *v. i.* आ-उत्-वि-क्रुश् 1 P, उच्चैः नद् 1 P or वि-,रु 2 P, वाश् 4 A (of birds); रवं मुच् 6 P, उच्चैः आक्रंद् 1 P, चीत्कारशब्दं कृ 8 U; 's. with pain' आर्तवत् रु, आर्तनादं मुच्. –*s.*,–ING, *s.* आक्रंदनं, उत्क्रोश:, चीत्कार:, उच्चनाद:-रव:, कोलाहल:, विक्रुष्टं; 's. of pain' आर्तरव:-नाद:,

SCREECH, *See* SCREAM; 's.-owl' नक्तरावी उलूक:, कालपेचक:.

SCREEN, *s.* आवरणं, व्यवधा-धानं, तिरस्करिणी, ज-(य)वनिका; अंतर्धा-र्धानं, प्रतिसीरा. –*v. t.* प्र-,छद् 10, निगुह् 1 U, गुप् 1 P, (crime &c.); नि-आ-सं-वृ 5 U or c., व्यव-धा 3 U, पिधा, अंतर्धा. 2 रक्ष् 1 P; आश्रयं दा 3 U, आश्रयदानेन प्रच्छद्, &c.

SCREW, *s.* कर्षणी, व्यावर्तनकील:. 2 कृपण:, बद्धमुष्टि:. –*v. t.* कर्षण्या-कीलकेन-बंध् 9 P. 2 व्या-परिवृत् c. 3 (Out) निष्पीड् 10, निर्हृ 1 P, निष्कृष् 1 P, निर्दुह् 2 U. 4 पीड्, अर्द् 1 P or c., बाध् 1 A, उपद्रु 1 A.

SCRIBBLE, *See* SCRAWL.

SCRIBE, *s.* लेखक:, लिपिकार:, अक्षरचण:, कायस्थ:.

SCRIP, *s.* पुट:, पुटी, क्षुद्रकोष:. 2 लेख:, पत्रं, लेख्यं.

SCRIPTURE, *s.* वेद:, श्रुति *f.*, आम्नाय:, निगम:. 2 शास्त्रं; 'religious s.' धर्मशास्त्रं; 'authority of the s. s' शास्त्रप्रमाणं. –AL, *a.* शास्त्रसिद्ध-उक्त, श्रुतिबोधित, शास्त्र in comp.; 's. prohibition' शास्त्रप्रतिषेध:.

SCRIVENER, *s.* कुसीद:; *See* USURER. 2 लेखक:, लिपिकार:, लेखकवृत्ति:.

SCROFULA, *s.* गंड-कंठ-माला. –SCROFULOUS, *a.* गंडमालिन्.

SCROLL, *s.* पट्ट:, लेख्यं, दीर्घपत्र-पट:.

SCROTUM, *s.* मुष्क:, अंड:, फलं, कोश:-ष:, अंड-मुष्क-फल-कोश:-ष:, वृषण:.

SCRUB, *v. t.* अत्यंतं मृज् 2 P or c. or प्रक्षल् 10 or निर्णिज् 3 U or घृष् 1 P. –*s.* व्रातीन:, अधम-नीच-जघन्य-वृत्ति:. –SCRUBBY, *a.* तुच्छ, निकृष्ट, हीन; *See* MEAN.

SCRUPLE, *s.* संदेह:, आ-,शंका, संशय:, विकल्प:.–*v.i.* विकृप् 1 A or c., संदिह् 2 U, शंक् 1 A, वि-आ-परि-°; ex. by 'Doubt', q. v.–SCRUPULOUS, *a.* सरल, ऋजु. 2 सूक्ष्म, निपुण, आत्मसूक्ष्म, अतिसूक्ष्मदृष्टि. 3 साशंक, शंकाशील, आ-,शंकित.

SCRUTINY, *s.* निपुणपरीक्षणं, सूक्ष्मनिरूपणं-परीक्षा-दर्शनं, अनुसंधानं, निरूपणं. –EER, *s.* सूक्ष्मनिरूपक:. –IZE, *v. t.* सूक्ष्मं-निपुणं-दृश् 1 P or परीक्ष् 1 A or निरूप् 10, निपुणं अनुसं-धा 3 U or अनुयुज् 7 A or अभिवृ 4 P. –IZER, *s.* सूक्ष्मनिरूपक:, निपुणपरीक्षक:, सूक्ष्मदर्शिन्.

SCUD, *v. i.* अतिवेगेन-सहसा-गम् 1 P or चल् 1 P.

SCUFFLE, *s.* तुमुलं, नियुद्धं, कलह:, बाहूबाहवियुद्धं, द्वंद्वं. –*v. i.* बाहूबाहवि युध् 4 A.

SCULK, *v. i.* निभृते-गूढस्थाने-वृत् 1 A or स्था 1 P, गुप् pass.; 's. off' व्यपसृप् 1 P, पलाय् 1 A, अपक्रम् 1 U, 4 P. –ER, *s.* गुप्तवर्तिन् *m.*

SCULL, *s.* कपाल:-लं, शिरोस्थि *n.*, करोटि-टी *f.*, कर्पर:. 2 क्षुद्रक्षेपणि *f.*; 's.-cap' शिरस्कं, मस्तकावरणं.

SCULLION, *s.* पात्रक्षालक:-मार्जक:.

SCULPTOR, *s.* त्वष्टृ *m.*, तक्षक:, तष्टा, तक्षन् *m.* –SCULPTURE, *v. t.* तक्ष् 1, 5 P, त्वक्ष् 1 P, उल्लिख् 6 P, प्रतिमां कृ 8 U or निर्मा 3 A. –*s.* तक्षणं, त्वक्षणं, प्रतिमा-मूर्ति-करणं. 2 प्रतिमा, मूर्ति *f.*

SCUM, *s.* मंड:-डं; फेन:-ण:; 's. of boiled rice' निस्राव:, आचाम:; *See* under RICE. 2 मलं, उच्छिष्टं, अवस्कर:, अवकर:, कल्कं, असारद्रव्यं, किट्टं; (fig.) मलं; मलं पृथिव्या वाहीकं (Mah. VIII. 45. 23) 'are the s. of the (whole) world.'

SCURF, *s.* शुष्कचर्मन् *n.*; किलासं, सिध्मं; *See* ITCH (dry).

SCURRILOUS, *a.* परुष, तीक्ष्ण; दुरुक्त, अश्लील, अदक्षिण, दुर्वाच. 5 कटुभाषिन्, दुर्मुख, मुखर, वाग्दुष्ट. –SCURRILITY, *s.* पारुष्यं, मौखर्यं, दुरुक्तं, &c.

SCURVY, *s.* शीताद:, लवणरक्तं. –*a.* कुत्सित, गर्ह्य, तुच्छ, नीच; *See* MEAN.

SCUTCHEON, *s.* कुलीनचिह्नगर्भं, कौलीनकोशः.

SCUTTLE, *s.* करंडः, मंजूषा. 2 छिद्रं.

SCYTHE, *s.* लवित्रं, दात्रं, खड्गीकं, शस्यकर्तरिका.

SEA, *s.* सागरः, समुद्रः, उदधिः, अर्णवः, जलधिः, वारिधिः, अपांपतिः; *See* OCEAN; 'a rough s.' क्षुब्धार्णवः; 's. of worldly existence' भवसागरः, संसारार्णवः; 's. of troubles' क्लेशसागरः, दुःखार्णवः, &c.; 'go to s.' नाविकः-सांयात्रिकः-भू 1 P, नाविकवृत्तिं सेव् 1 A; 'beyond the s. s' द्वीपांतरे; 's.-beat' तरंगाहत; 's.-faring' समुद्रग-यायिन्, सांयात्रिक; 's.-fight' नौयुद्धं; 's.-girt' *See* Girt; 's.-green' श्यामहरित, सागरवर्ण; 's.-gull' करटः; 's.-man' नाविकः, समुद्रगः, पोतवाहः; 's.-port' पोताश्रयस्थानं, पोतशरणं, नौकाश्रयः; 's.-shore' समुद्रतटं-तीरं, वेला, रोधस् *n.*; 's.-sick' समुद्रच्छर्दिग्रस्त; 's.-side' समुद्रवेला &c.

SEAL, *s.* मुद्रा, (fig. also); 'opening the s. of sleep' क्षिपन्निद्रामुद्रां (Mal. 2); 'open it, preserving the s. and show me' मुद्रां परिपालयन् उद्घाट्य दर्शय (Mu. 5); 's. of the lips' ओष्ठमुद्रा. 2 मकरः, नक्रः —*v. t.* मुद्रयति (D.). 2 निर्णी 1 P, स्थिरीकृ 8 U, दृढीकृ, दृढयति (D.); 'the defeat in that battle s. ed his fate' पराजयेन तस्य भाविगतिः एकांततः निर्णीता. 2 मुद्रया अंक् 10 or चिह्नयति (D.). 3 (मुद्रया) पि-धा 3 U, बंध् 9 P; मुखं बध्नाति 's. s the lips'. —ED, *a.* मुद्रित, कृतमुद्र, मुद्रांकित, मुद्राबद्ध; 's. ing wax' ला(रा)क्षा; *See* LAC.

SEAM, *s.* संधिः; सीवनं; 's. of planks' काष्ठसंधिः. 2 शुष्कव्रणः. —Y, *a.* संधियुक्त; 'turn the s. side within' स्वदोषान् प्रच्छादय-निगूह. —SEAMSTRESS, *s.* सूचिका, सूचिकर्मोपजीविनी.

SEAR, *v. t.* निर्दह् 1 P, मुष् 1 P; दहनेन दृढीकृ or शुष्कीकृ 8 U. —*a.* संशुष्क, विशीर्ण, म्लान.

SEARCH, *v.* (For) अन्विष् 4 P, निरूप् 10, अनुसंधा 3 U, मृग् 10 A, मार्ग् 1 P, 10, विचि 5 U, निर्-अव-ईक्ष् 1 A; (fig.) निपुणं परीक्ष् or निरूप्; 's. into' निरूप्, परीक्ष्; 's. out' अन्विष्य &c. उपलभ् 1 A or प्राप् 5 P. —ING, *s.* अन्वेषणं-णा, मार्गणं, निरूपणं, अनुसंधानं, निरीक्षणं, अन्वीक्षणं; विचयः, जिज्ञासा. —ER, *s.* अन्वेषकः, अन्वेष्टृ *m.*, निरूपकः, निरीक्षकः; 's. of the human heart' पुरुषांतरविद्. —ING, *a.* निपुण, सूक्ष्म, अवहित; 'casting at me a s. look' सुनिपुणं मां विलोक्य.

SEASON, *s.* ऋतुः, कालः, समयः; (in general) कालः, वेला, समयः, अवसरः, अवकाशः, प्रस्तावः; 'auspicious s.' लग्नं, मुहूर्तः, शुभवेला,-लग्नं; 'in due s.' काले ; 'pertaining to the s.' आर्तव (र्वी *f.*); 'out of s.' अकाले, अनवकाशे; 'in s. and out of s.' कालेऽकाले वा, औचित्यानौचित्यमविचार्य; 'wrong s.' अकालः, अनवकाशः. —*v. t.* अधि-,वास् 10, उपस्कृ 8 U or स्वादूकृ. 2 पच् 1 P, परिपाकं उत्पद् c., पक्वीकृ; *See* MATURE. 3 (Accustom) ex. by परिचय, सहिष्णु, &c.; 's. ed to heat' रविकिरणसहिष्णु (S. 2); 's. s the body to exertions' श्रमजयात् तनुं प्रगुणां करोति (R. IX. 49); 's. ed to exertions' जितश्रम, श्रमसहिष्णु. —ABLE, *a.* समयोचित, कालानुरूप, प्रस्तावसदृश (शी *f.*), प्राप्तकाल, कालोचित, and sim. comp. 2 कालकृत, काल in comp. ; 's. efforts' कालकृतोद्योगाः. 3 आर्तव (वी *f.*), कालोद्भव, ऋतुज, ऋतव्य. —ABLENESS, *s.* कालौचित्यं, प्रस्तावसादृश्यं, &c. —ABLY, *adv.* यथाकालं-समयं-अवसरं, काले, समये, प्रस्तावसदृशं, प्राप्तकालं, कालानुरूपं. —ING, *s.* उपस्करः, व्यंजनं.

SEAT, *s.* आसनं, पीठः-ठं; 'take a s. here' अत्र आसनपरिग्रहं करोतु भवान्; पर्यंकः (s. on a sofa), विष्टरः (cane-s.); आस्तरः-रणं; 'raised s.' वितर्दि-र्दी *f.*, वेदिका. 2 स्थानं, आयतनं, आस्पदं, धामन् *n.*, अधिष्ठानं, निकेतनं, नि-आ-लयः, आगारं, पदं, आशयः; 'capital s.' राजधानी-नगरं; 's. of justice' न्यायासनं, धर्मासनं, व्यवहारासनं; 's. of blood' रक्ताशयः; क्रोधस्थानं; विद्यागारं, &c. —*v. t.* (Oneself) आसने उपविश् 6 P, निषद् 1 P, आसनपरिग्रहं कृ 8 U; (another) (आसने) उपविश् c., आसनं ग्रह् c., अध्यास् c., अधि-ष्ठा c. (-ष्ठापयति). 2 प्रति-ष्ठा c., अधिकृ, अधि-आ-रुह् c., निविश् c.; 'he was s. ed on the throne' राजपदमधिरोपितः, सिंहासने प्रतिष्ठापितः. —ED, *a.* आसीन, उपविष्ट, निषण्ण, अध्यासीन; आसनस्थ, आसनस्थित-उपविष्ट-आरूढ-गत-आश्रित, पीठस्थ; 's. at ease' सुखासीन, सुखोपविष्ट; 'be s.' गृह्यतां आसनं, क्रियतामासनपरिग्रहः. 2 प्रतिष्ठित, निविष्ट, स्थित, गत-स्थ-निष्ठ in comp.; 's. in the heart' हृदयनिष्ठ, हृत्स्थ; कंठगत, अस्थिनिष्ठ, &c.

SECEDE, *v. i.* अपसृ 1 P, अपगम् 1 P, अप-या-इ 2 P, अपक्रम् 1 U, 4 P; व्यपसृ &c.; (to) आश्रि 1 U, अव-आ-लंब् 1 A; (from) (धर्म &c.) त्यज् 1 P, उत्सृज् 6 P; मतांतरं ग्रह् 9 P or आश्रि &c. —ER, *s.* भिन्नमताश्रितः; मतांतरग्राही. —SECESSION, *s.* अपसरणं, अपगमः-मनं, अपक्रमः-मणं, &c. 2 मतांतरस्वीकारः-ग्रहणं, स्वधर्मत्यागः.

SECLUDE, *v. t.* नि-अव-रुध् 7 U, गुप् 1 P. 2 विविक्ते वस् c., पृथक् कृ 8 U ; वि-विच् 3, 7 U or c. 3 (Oneself) विविक्तं आश्रि 1 U or सेव् 1 A, विविक्ते-एकांते-वस् 1 P, जनसंसर्गं त्यज् 1 P or परिहृ 1 P or वृज् 10. —ED, *a.* विविक्त, निर्जन, विजन, निभृत; *See* LONELY. 2 (Of persons) त्यक्त-मुक्तसंग, विविक्तसेविन्-वासिन्-वृत्ति. —SECLUSION, *s.*

रहस् *n.*, विविक्तता, एकांतता, विविक्तदशा-स्थिति *f.*; रहःस्थानं, विविक्तं, एकांतवासः.

SECOND, *a.* द्वितीय ; 's. to none', 'without a s.' अद्वितीय, अनुत्तर, अत्युत्तम; 's. in rank' द्वितीयपदभाज्. 2 Secondary, q. v.; 's.-hand' भुक्तपूर्व, अन्यभुक्त-व्यवहारित, अन्योपयुक्त; अन्यकथित, अन्यसृष्ट; 's.-hand information' अन्यस्मादधिगता वार्ता; 's.-hand witness' श्रुतसाक्षी; 's.-rate' मध्यम, सामान्य; 's.-sight' दिव्यचक्षुः-दृष्टि *f.* –*s.* विपलं; विकला; क्षणः, निमि(मे)षः. 2 सहायः, सहकारिन् *m.*, उपकारी. –*v. t.* अनुमुद् 1 A, अनुग्रह् 9 P, उपकृ 8 U, अभिनंद् 1 P. –ER, *s.* अनुमोदी, समर्थयिता, पक्षोद्ग्राही. –LY, *adv.* द्वितीयतः, द्वितीयस्थाने. —SECONDARY, *a.* अप्रधान, गौण (णी *f.*), अमुख्य, अनुषंगिन्, उपसर्जन, उपसृष्ट, अप्रथम; oft. by उप pr.; 'a s. planet' उपग्रहः; 'a s. rank' अप्राधान्यं. 2 मध्यम, सामान्य, सामान्यगुणक. –LY, *adv.* अप्राधान्येन, गौणतः, अप्रधानतः, अनुषंगतः.

SECRET, *a.* नि-,गूढ, गुप्त, प्र-,छन्न, निभृत, संवृत, अव्यक्त, अप्रकाश, अविदित; 's. door' प्रच्छन्नं, अंतर्द्वारं. 2 गुह्य, गोप्य, रहस्य, संवरणीय. 3 गुह्यभेदिन्, रहस्यभेदिन्. 4 गहन, गूढ, अव्यक्त, गूढार्थ, गहनार्थ. 5 रहस् in comp., विविक्त, निर्जन, निभृत; 'keep s.' गुह् 1 U, छद् 10 ; *See* CONCEAL. –*s.* रहस्यं; गुह्यं, गोप्यं, मर्मन् *n.*; 'have you kept the s. entrusted to you' रक्ष्यते भवता रहस्यनिक्षेपः (V. 2); 'the s. of one's power' शक्तेः रहस्यं; 'the s. of good men (of their conduct)' साधूनां रहस्यं (U. 2); 'in s.' रहसि, रहः, मिथः ; 's. counsel' मंत्रः, गूढमंत्रः ; 'knowing s. s' रहस्यज्ञ, अंतर्वेदिन् ; मर्मविद् ; 'the matter is no longer a s.' बहुलीभूतः-प्रकाशतां गतः-सोऽर्थः; 'diving into the s. s of others' परमर्मभेदिन्, मर्मान्वेषिन्, पररहस्यविद्. –LY, *adv.* प्र-,छन्नं, गूढं, निभृतं, गुप्तं, अव्यक्तं, उपांशु, गूढ-गुप्त in comp.; 'walking s.' गूढाचार, गुप्तसंचारिन्. –NESS,-SECRECY, *s.* गुप्तता, गूढता, प्रच्छन्नता, गुप्ति *f.*, गुप्त-निभृत-भावः. 2 संवृत्ति *f.*, गुप्तिः, गुह्य-रहस्य-रक्षणं, गोपनं, रहस्याभेदः-पालनं, मौनं, अप्रकाशनं. 3 विविक्तता; रहः, रहोवासः, विविक्तवासः-भावः.

SECRETARY, *s.* कार्याधिकृतः, सचिवः.

SECRETE, *v. t.* स्नु c., प्र-निः-परि°-, निर्गम् c., निःसृ c., उद्वम् 1 P, उद्-गृ 6 P, उत्सृज् 6 P ; (bile &c.) उत्-,रिच् 7 P or c.; उत्पद् c., जन् c.; 'the mouth frequently s. s saliva' मुहुर्वक्त्रं लालायते, लालां स्रावयति. 2 गुप् 1 P, गुह् 1 U, संवृ 5 U, अप-नि-ह्नु 2 A ; *See* CONCEAL. –ION, *s.* स्रावः-वणं, उद्रेचनं, उत्सर्गः, उत्पादनं. 2 मलं ; 's. of the throat' कफः, श्लेष्मा ; 's. of the bowels' पुरीषं, विष्ठा ; *See* DUNG.

SECT, *s.* शाखा, पथिन् *m.*, मार्गः, पक्षः, मतं, संप्रदायः, गणः. –ARY,-ARIAN, *a.* शाखागत, सांप्रदायिक (की *f.*); स्वपक्षानुसारिन्, शाखावलंबिन्, शाखाश्रित.

SECTION, *s.* वि-,भागः, छेदः, परिच्छेदः ; खंडः-डं, पर्वन् *n.*, प्रकरणं, उल्लासः, उच्छ्वासः, स्कंधः, कांडः-डं, पादः (of different compositions); 'sub-s.' अधिकरणं.

SECTOR, *s.* वृत्तखंडं.

SECULAR, *a.* लौकिक-ऐहलौकिक-सांसारिक-ऐहिक-प्रापंचिक-व्यावहारिक- (की *f.*). –ITY,-NESS, *s.* ऐहिकत्वं; संसारासक्ति *f.*, प्रपंचानुरागः.

SECURE, *a.* सुरक्षित, अकुतोभय, अभय, निर्भय, वीतभय, अनापद्, निराबाध, निर्विघ्न; (of persons) निःशंक, अशंक, निश्चिंत, निरातंक, निरपेक्ष, स्वस्थ. –*v. t.* रक्ष् 1 P, भयं निवृ c., or निवृत् c. or निरस् 4 U, निर्भयीकृ 8 U; ex. by (*a.*) with कृ. 2 स्थिरीकृ, दृढीकृ, निर्णी 1 P. 3 दृढं बंध् 9 P; 's. ed with a bolt' अर्गलाबद्धं (द्वारं). 4 आक्रम् 1 U, 4 P, ग्रह् 9 P. –ITY, *s.* रक्षा-क्षणं, गुप्ति *f.*, स्थैर्यं, परि-,त्राणं, गोपनं, क्षेमः-मं, निर्भयत्वं, अहार्यता, शंकाभावः, अभयं. 2 अभयवाच् *f.*, अभयदानं-दक्षिणा. 3 रक्षकः, शरणं, आश्रयः. 4 प्रतिभूः, बंधकः, लग्नकः (persons); प्रातिभाव्यं, आधिः, न्यासः, निक्षेपः ; *See* PLEDGE. –LY, *adv.* निःशंकं, निर्भयं, क्षेमेण, निराबाधं.

SEDAN, *s.* शिबिका.

SEDATE, *a.* धीर, शांत, स्तिमित, गंभीर, निरुद्वेग, अनाकुल, अक्षुब्ध, अचंचल. –LY, *adv.* धीरवत्, शांतं, अनाकुलं, निरुद्वेगं. –NESS, *s.* धीरता, शांतता, गांभीर्यं, अनुद्वेगः, अक्षोभः, स्थैर्यं, गौरववृत्ति *f.* –SEDATIVE, *a.* शांतिकर (री *f.*), शीतल, शांतिद, शमक. –*s.* लंघनं, अप-,कर्षणं.

SEDENTARY, *a.* निरुद्योग, अचपल, अव्यवसायिन्, अनुद्योगशील, अव्यायामिन्, चलन-गति-हीन.

SEDIMENT, *s.* मलं, खलं, कल्कं, किट्टं, उच्छिष्टं, शेषः-षं.

SEDITION, *s.* राजद्रोहः, प्रजाप्रकोपः -संक्षोभः, प्रकृतिक्षोभः, भेदः, कलहः; 'fomenting s.' उपजापः, भेदजननं. —SEDITIOUS, *a.* राजद्रोहिन् ; (causing s.) प्रजासंक्षोभजनन (नी *f.*), प्रजा-प्रकृति-क्षोभकर (री *f.*), भेदकर, उपजापक. –LY, *adv.* राजद्रोहपूर्वं, सोपजापं.

SEDUCE, *v. t.* दुष् c. (दूषयति), वि-,मुह् c., विलोभ् अपह् 1 P, सत्पथात् प्रभ्रंश् c. or च्यु c. ; प्र-विलुभ् c., आ-वि-कृष् 1 P, आक्षिप् 6 P ; (a woman) दुष् c., सतीत्वात् भ्रंश् c., चारित्र्यं नश् c.; पापमार्गे प्रवृत् c. ; अभिगम् 1 P. –ER, *s.* दूषकः, प्रलोभयितृ *m.*, प्र-वि-लोभकः, आकर्षकः, वि-,मोहकः. –SEDUCTION, *s.* प्र-वि-लोभनं, आकर्षणोपायः ; विमोहनं, आकर्षणं. 2 प्रतारणं-णा, वंचनं-ना, विप्रलंभः. 3

दूषणं, शीलपातनं, सतीत्वनाशः, चारित्र्यभ्रंशः, संग्रहणं. –SEDUCTIVE, *a.* प्र-वि-लोभक, आकर्षक, वि-,मोहिन्.

SEDULOUS, *a.* उद्यमिन्, उद्योगासक्त, उद्यमतत्पर, कार्यव्यापृत, अभिनिविष्ट. –LY, *adv.* आसक्तिपूर्वं, साभिनिवेशं, सोद्यमं. –NESS, *s.* कार्यासक्ति *f.*, उद्योगशीलता, उद्यमपरता ; *See* INDUSTRY-OUS &c.

SEE, *s.* धर्माध्यक्षाधिकारः. –*v. t.* दृश् 1 P, ईक्ष् 1 A, वि-सं-अव-प्र-निर्°-; लक्ष् 10, अव-वि-आ-लोक् 1 A, 10, निरूप् 10, निर्वर्ण् 10 (carefully), आलोच् 10; 's. with one's own eyes' प्रत्यक्षीकृ 8 U, (कदाचिदस्याः प्रत्यक्षीकृता विक्रिया S. 7). 2 ज्ञा 9 U, बुध् 1 P, अवगम् 1 P, अव-इ 2 P, उपलभ् 1 A. 3 Beware, q. v. ; 's. ing that' यतः, यस्मात्, यत्. –ER, *s.* द्रष्टृ *m.*, दर्शिन् *m.* 2 सिद्धः, भविष्यद्वादी. –SIGHT, *s.* दर्शनं, विलोकनं, वीक्षणं, आलोकः &c. 2 (View) दृष्टिपथः-विषयः-गोचरः. 3 (Eye) दृष्टि *f.*, दृश् *f.*, चक्षुस् *n.*, नेत्रं, नयनं, दृक्शक्ति *f.* 4 आलोकः, कौतुकं, चमत्कारः ; 'being within s.' दृश्य, दृग्गोचर, दृष्टिविषय ; 'out of one's s.' परोक्षं-क्षे, अगोचरं-रेण ; 'gone out of s.' अंतरित, अंतर्हित, तिरोहित ; 'in s. of' समक्षं, प्रत्यक्षं, साक्षात्, with gen. or in comp. ; 'at the very first s.' प्रथमदर्शनादेव, आप्रथमदर्शनात्; 'charming the s.' दृष्टिमोहः-बंधः. –LY, *a.* सुदृश्य, प्रेक्षणीय, ललित ; *See* PLEASANT.

SEED, *s.* बीजं, in all senses ; 'growing from s.' बीजप्ररोह-रुह, बीज्य. 2 मूलं, आदिः, प्रभवः, उद्भवः ; *See* ORIGIN. 3 प्रजा, अपत्यं, वंशः, संतानः, संतति *f.* 4 शुक्रं, रेतस् *n.*; *See* SEMEN; 's.-corn' बीजधान्यं; 's.-time' बीज-वाप-कालः; 's.-vessel' बीजकोशः-गुप्ति *f.* –*v. t.* बीजं आरुह् c., बीजयति (D.). –*v. i.* बीजं प्रदा 3 U or उत्पद् c. –LESS, *a.* निर्बीज. –LING, *s.* बीजप्ररोहः, बीजांकुरः. –Y, *a.* बीजिन्, बीजपूर्ण, बहुबिज. –SEEDSMAN, *s.* बीजिन् *m.* 2 बीजविक्रयिन् *m.*

SEEK, *v.* अन्विष् 4 P, मृग् 10 A, निरूप् 10, विचि 5 U ; *See* SEARCH. 2 कम् 1 A, आ-अभि-कांक्ष् 1 P, इष् 6 P ; प्रार्थ् 10 A, अभ्यर्थ्, याच् 1 A ; 's. ing to get heaven' स्वर्गकामः. 3 प्र-,यत् 1 A, घट् 1 A, चेष्ट् 1 A, उत्-ज़ृंभ् 1 A; *See* ATTEMPT. –ER, *s.* अन्वेष्टृ *m.*, निरूपकः, प्रार्थकः. –ING, *s.* अन्वेषणं, मार्गणं, निरूपणं.

SEEM, *v. i.* भा 2 P, आ-प्रति-,° दृश्-लक्ष्-pass., आभास् 1 A ; *See* APPEAR ; 'it s. s to me' मन्ये, शंके, इति मे मतिः. –ING, *a.* बाह्य, बहिः in comp., कृतक, कृत्रिम. –*s.* आभासः, बाह्यरूपं, आकारः. –INGLY, *adv.* बहिः, बाह्यतः, आभासेन; 's. true' सत्याभास, सत्यसंकाश. –LY, *a.* विनीत ; युक्त, उचित, संगत, उपपन्न; *See* PROPER.

SEE-SAW, *s.* उन्नतानतं, निम्नोन्नतं.

SEETHE, *v. t.* क्वथ् 1 P, पच् 1 P. –*v. i.* पच् pass. –R, *s.* स्थाली, उखा, पिठरः, ऋजीषं.

SEGMENT, *s.* खंडः-डं, वि-,च्छेदः; (of a circle) वृत्तखंडं.

SEGREGATE, *v. t.* वियुज् 7 A, 10, विश्लिष् c. –*v. i.* विश्लिष् 4 P, विभिद् pass ; *See* SEPARATE. –ION, *s.* वियोगः, विश्लेषः.

SEIZE, *v. t.* सं-ग्रह् 9 P, धृ 1 P, 10, परामृश् 6 P, कल् 10 (कलयति); ग्रस् 1 A; 's. ing by the hair' केशेषु-केशैः-गृहीत्वा. 2 अप-,हृ 1 P, बलेन ग्रह् or धृ. 3 आपत् 1 P, अभिद्रु 1 P; *See* ATTACK. 4 आक्रम् 1 U, 4 P, अभिभू 1 P, उपसृज् 6 P, ग्रस्, उपहन् 2 P, आविश् 6 P; 's. ed with deep sleep' गाढनिद्राक्रांत; 's. ing an opportunity' गृहीतावसर, प्राप्तकाल, प्राप्तावसर, अवसरं प्राप्य-गृहीत्वा. –ER, *s.* हर्तृ, हारिन्-ग्राहिन् in comp. –URE, *s.* ग्रहणं, धारणं, हरणं, सं-,ग्राहः, ग्रहः, ग्रसनं, आकलनं. 2 आक्रमः, आवेशः, अभिभवः, ग्रासः.

SELDOM, *adv.* क्वचित्, कदाचित्, विरलं, दुर् pr.; 's. to be found' दुर्लभ.

SELECT, *v. t.* वृ 5 U or 10 (वरयति), वृ 9 U, उद्-हृ 1 P, उद्-ग्रह् 9 P, विशिष् 7 P or c. 2 संग्रह्, समुद्धृ, संकल् 10 (कलयति). –*a.* विशिष्ट, उत्तम, उत्कृष्ट; *See* CHOICE. –ED, *a.* वृत, वृत्त, व्यावृत्त, उद्धृत. –ION, *s.* वरणं, उद्धरणं, वरः, वृति *f.* 2 संग्रहः, सारः; 's. of poetical pieces' काव्यसंग्रहः.

SELENITE, *s.* चंद्रकांतः.

SELF, *a.* आत्मन्, स्व in comp., स्वीय, निज; *See* OWN; 's.-interest' आत्महितं; 's.-destroyer' आत्मघातकः; (with pronouns) स्वयं, स्वतः. –*s.* आत्मन् (sing. and *m.*); देवी प्राप्तप्रसवमात्मानं गंगादेव्यां विमुंचति (U. 7). In comp. ex. by आत्म, स्व, or स्वयं, स्वतः ; 's.-accomplished' आत्मोपार्जित, स्वतः अर्जित; 's.-command' आत्मसंयमः, दमः, इंद्रियजयः; 's.-conceit' अहंकारः, ममत्वं, स्वाभिमानः; 's.-denying' आत्मसंयमिन्; 's.-evident' स्वतःसिद्ध, स्वयंप्रकाश, प्रत्यक्ष ; 's.-existent' स्वयंभू, आत्मभू ; 's.-interested' स्वार्थपर, स्वार्थबुद्धि ; 's.-love' ममता, अहंमानः, स्वानुरागः ; 's.-possessed' अव्यग्र, स्थिरात्मन्, स्वस्थचित्त, धृतिमत् ; 's.-possession' धृति *f.*, स्वास्थ्यं, आत्म-स्व-निष्ठा ; *See* PRESENCE (of mind) ; 's.-sufficient' स्वाभिमानिन्; 's.-will' स्वेच्छा, स्वैरिता, स्वाच्छंद्यं ; 's.-willed' स्वैर, स्वैरिन्, स्वच्छंद, काम-स्वेच्छा-चारिन्, कामवृत्ति, स्वैरगति. –ISH, *a.* स्वार्थपर-निष्ठ-परायण ; उदरंभरि, स्वार्थदृष्टि-बुद्धि, स्वहितपर-निष्ठ, स्वहितैषिन्, स्वलाभनिष्ठ-तत्पर, &c. –ISHLY, *adv.* स्वार्थदृष्ट्या, आत्महितबुद्ध्या,

स्वलाभेच्छया. -ISHNESS, *s.* स्वार्थ-स्वलाभ-स्वहित-परता-निष्ठा-बुद्धि *f.*-दृष्टि *f.*, स्वलाभेच्छा, ममता.

SELL, *v. t.* वि-क्री 9 A (rarely P also). -*v. i.* मूल्येन विक्री pass.; 'this picture will s. for a large price' महता मूल्येनेदमालेख्यं विक्रेष्यते. -ER, *s.* विक्रेतृ *m*, विक्रयिन् *m.*, विक्रयिकः, पणायिता. -ING, -SALE, *s.* विक्रयः; पणनं; 'exposed for s.' क्रय्य, क्रयार्थं प्रसारित; 'an article for s.' पण्यं, पण्यद्रव्यं; 'underhand s.' अवक्रयः. -SALE-ABLE, *a.* विक्रेय.

SELVAGE, *s. See* BORDER.

SEMBLANCE, *s.* आभासः, आभा, औपम्यं, सादृश्यं, आकारः, रूपं; 'it has a s. of truth' सत्यमिवावभासते, सत्यसंकाशं; 'to wear the s. of displeasure (anger)' कृतककोपं दर्शयितुं.

SEMEN, *s.* शुक्रं, रेतस् *n.*, बीजं, वीर्यं, तेजस् *n.*, इंद्रियं. -SEMINAL, *a.* (*s.*) in comp.; 's. discharge' रेतःस्रावः-क्षरणं, निषेकः.

SEMI, *a.* अर्ध or सामि in comp.; 's.-circle' वृत्तार्धं, अर्धवर्तुलं; 's.-form' अर्धाकृति &c. &c.

SEMINARY, *s.* बीजारोपणस्थलं. 2 शिक्षणालयः, विद्यामंदिरं.

SEMI-VOWEL, *s.* अंतस्थः.

SEMPITERNAL, *a. See* ETERNAL.

SEMPSTRESS, *s.* सूचिका.

SENATE, *s.* वृद्ध-शिष्ट-सभा; मंत्रि-सचिव-सभा. -OR, *s.* सभासद् *m.*, वृद्धसदस्यः.

SEND, *v. t.* प्र-हि 5 P, सं-,प्रेष् c., सं-,प्रेर् c., विसृज् 6 P or c., (with acc. of place and dat. of person); 's. away' प्र-स्था c. (स्थापयति), विसृज्; 's. for' आह्वे 1 P, आनी c.; आगम् c., आहृ c.; 's. for a doctor' भिषजमाह्वातुं कमपि प्रेषय; 's. forth' नि-प्र-सृ c., उदीर् c., उत्क्षिप् 6 P, उद्वम् 1 P, उद्-गॄ 6 P; (as a missile) प्र-,मुच् 6 P, प्रक्षिप्, मास् 4 P. -ER, *s.* प्रेषकः, प्रेरकः.

SENILE, *a.* वृद्ध, जराजन्य. -ITY, *s.* वृद्धत्वं, जरा, वार्धक्यं.

SENIOR, *a.* ज्येष्ठ, वरिष्ठ, ज्यायस्, वरीयस्, वर्षीयस्; (in age) कालज्येष्ठ, वयोज्येष्ठ; 's. in office' अधिकारज्येष्ठ. -*s.* ज्येष्ठः, अग्रजः, &c. 2 गुरुः, गुरुजनः, आर्य-वृद्ध-जनः. -ITY, *s.* ज्येष्ठता, ज्यैष्ठ्यं, वरिष्ठता; वयोज्येष्ठता, &c.; 'according to s.' अनुज्येष्ठं.

SENNIGHT, *s.* सप्तरात्रं, सप्ताहः.

SENSE, *s.* इंद्रियं, हृषीकं, विषयिन् *n.*; 's.s collectively' इंद्रियवर्गः-गणः, पंचेंद्रियं; 's. s of perception or knowledge' ज्ञानेंद्रियाणि; 's. s of action' कर्मेंद्रियाणि;, करणानि, कर्मसाधनानि; 'evident to the s.' प्रत्यक्ष, इंद्रियग्राह्य-गोचर; 'pleasures of s.' विषय-इंद्रिय-सुखं; 'object of s.' विषयः, इंद्रियार्थः, इंद्रियविषयः. 2 उपलब्धि *f.*, वेदनं-ना, बोधः, ज्ञानं, अनुबोधः, ग्रहणं, संवेदनं, इंद्रियबोधः-ग्रहणं. 3 बुद्धि *f.*, मति *f.*, धीः, चित्शक्तिः, प्रज्ञा; *See* INTELLECT. 4 चेतना, संज्ञा, चैतन्यं, ज्ञानं, बोधः, अनुभवः, संवेदनं; 's. of obligation' कृतज्ञता, कृतवेदित्वं; 's. of pleasure' सुखबोधः-अनुभवः; 'come to s. s', 'recover one's s. s' संज्ञां-चेतनां-लभ् 1 A or आ-प्रति-पद् 4 A, प्रकृतिं आ-पद्, प्रकृतिस्थ- *a.* भू 1 P; 'loss of s. s' मतिभ्रंशः, बुद्धि-मति-नाशः, विभ्रमः; 'common s.' विवेकः; 'good s.' सुबुद्धिः, सद्भावः, सौजन्यं; 'out of s. s' विगतचेतन, लुप्तसंज्ञ, नष्ट-हत-ज्ञान, बुद्धिभ्रष्ट, नष्टेंद्रिय-बुद्धि; 'who has lost all s. of honour and dishonour on account of old age' जरावलुप्तमानावमानचित्तः. 5 मतं, अभिप्रायः, उद्देशः, आशयः, आकांक्षा. 6 अर्थः, भावः (purport); 'understanding the literal s.' शाब्दबोधः; 'literal s.' शब्दार्थः, अक्षरार्थः; 'in its true s.' अन्वर्थ-यथार्थ- *a.*, यथार्थतः, परमार्थतः, अर्थतः; 'else this repetition has no s.' अन्यथा एषा वीप्सा न चरितार्था भवति (Ka. 320), निरर्थका भवेत् &c.; *See* SIGNIFICANT. -IBLE, *a.* इंद्रियगोचर-ग्राह्य-गम्य-ज्ञेय, प्रत्यक्ष. 2 विषय-इंद्रियार्थ-ग्राहिन्, ग्रहणसमर्थ. 3 अभिज्ञ, ज्ञ, वेदिन् in comp.; 's. of your service' त्वत्सेवाभिज्ञ; उपकारज्ञ-वेदिन् 's. of obligations'. 4 संज्ञावत्, चेतनोपपन्न, सचेतन, चेतन, चेतनावत्, वेदन-ज्ञान-क्षम; लब्ध-प्राप्त-संज्ञ-चैतन्य, आपन्नचेतन. 5 मति-बुद्धि-मत्, सज्ञान, ज्ञानवत्, विवेकिन्, ज्ञान-बुद्धि-शालिन्, मनस्विन्, धीसंपन्न; *See* RATIONAL also. 6 विचक्षण, सुधी, सुमेधस्, प्राज्ञ. 7 उपपन्न, युक्त, उचित, संगत, समंजस, सयुक्तिक, युक्तिपूर्व. -IBILITY, *s.* ग्रहणसामर्थ्य-शक्ति *f.* 2 सूक्ष्म-शीघ्र-चैतन्य-बोधः; वेदनं-ना, बोधः, ज्ञानं, अनुभवः, चेतना; चैतन्यं; संज्ञा. -IBLY, *adv.* प्रत्यक्षं-क्षतः, &c. 2 सुबुद्ध्या, सुबुद्धिपूर्वं, बोध-ज्ञान-पूर्वं, चेतनवत्, अभ्रमेण. -LESS, *a.* अचेतन, विषयग्रहणाक्षम. 2 अ-विगत-चेतन, निःसंज्ञ, लुप्तसंज्ञ, नष्टचैतन्य, सुप्तबुद्धि, संज्ञा-चैतन्य-हीन. 3 दुर्बुद्धि, मति-बुद्धि-हीन, मूढ, मूर्ख, अनात्मज्ञ, निर्बोध; *See* FOOLISH. 4 अयुक्त, असमंजस, अनुपपन्न, अनुचित. 5 निरर्थक, असंगत, असंबद्ध. -LESSLY, *adv.* मूर्खवत्, मूढवत्, &c. —SENSITIVE, *a.* सचेतन, चेतनावत्, विषयग्रहणक्षम-समर्थ. 2 सूक्ष्म-शीघ्र-वेदिन्-ग्राहिन्, शीघ्रचेतन; चलेंद्रिय, अनायासेन संक्षोभ्य, मृदुप्रकृति, कोमलहृदय. 3 लज्जालु, लज्जावत्; *See* MODEST; 's. plant' लज्जालुः, नमस्कारी. -LY, *adv.* शीघ्रज्ञानेन, सूक्ष्मचैतन्येन. -NESS, *s.* सूक्ष्मचैतन्यं, शीघ्रबोधः, &c. —SENSUAL, *a.* इंद्रिय, विषय in comp.; 's. pleasures' विषयसुखानि, इंद्रियोपभोगः, विषयासक्ति *f.* 2 (Of persons) इंद्रियसुखानिरत, विषयासक्त, विषयपरायण-

पर-निरत-अधीन-वश, इंद्रियवश, &c.; विषयिन्, विषयोपसेविन्, विषयसुखासक्त, भोग-काम-आसक्त. -IST, *s.* विषयी, विषयासक्तः, भोगासक्तः ; *See* above. -ITY,-NESS, *s.* विषयासक्तिः, इंद्रियसुखोपभोगः, विषयवशता-परायणता &c., भोगासक्तिः, कामासक्तिः, इंद्रिय-विषय-सुखानिरतिः. -SENTIENT, *a.* सचेतस, सचेतन, चेतनावत्, चैतन्य-प्राण-विशिष्ट; *See* SENSIBLE; 'a s. being' प्राणी, देही, शरीरी, जीवः, प्राणभृत्, चेतनः. -SENSATION, *s.* प्रत्यक्षं. 2 सं-वेदनं-ना, बोधः, ज्ञानं, उपलब्धिः, चेतना, प्रत्यक्षज्ञानं, अनुभवः. 3 विकारः, विक्रिया ; 'produced a great s. among the people' जनमनांसि भृशं समक्षोभयत्-आकुलीचकार.

SENTENCE, *s.* निर्णयः, दंडाज्ञा, दंडादेशः, आधर्षणं ; 's. of death' प्राणदंडाज्ञा. 2 विचारः, निश्चयः, निर्णयः, संकल्पः. 3 वाक्यं, वचनं, उक्ति *f.*, वचस् *n.*, पदसमूहः. 4 सूत्रं. -*v. t.* दंडं आदिश् 6 P or निर्णी 1 P or कथ् 10 or निविद् c.; 's. ed him to death' तस्य वधदंडमादिशत्, वध्यतामसौ इति आज्ञापयत्. -SENTENTIOUS, *a.* लाघवयुक्त, लाघवगुणोपेत, सूत्रमय (यी *f.*), सूत्रप्राय.

SENTIMENT, *s.* मतं, अभिप्रायः, बुद्धि *f.*, मति *f.* 2 संकल्पः, कल्पना. 3 अर्थः; *See* SENSE, IDEA. 4 भावः, रसः, रागः; 's. of love' शृंगाररसः; करुणारसः &c. -AL, *a.* रसिक, रसमय (यी *f.*), सरस, रसात्मक, सराग, रसभूयिष्ठ. 2 काल्पनिक (की *f.*), भावित.

SENTINEL, SENTRY, *s.* रक्षिन् *m.*, रक्षापुरुषः, रक्षकः.

SEPARATE, *v. t.* वियुज् 7 A 10, वि-,रह् 1 P, 10 (रहयति), विनाकृ 8 U, (with instr.); 'Rati s. ed from Madana' मदनेन विनाकृता रतिः. 2 पृथक् कृ, विश्लिष् c., वि-,भिद् 7 P or c. विभज् 1 U, विच्छिद् 7 P, विघट् c., विगम् c. (गमयति); व्यासंज् c., व्यतिरिच् 7 P or c.; (distinguish between) वि-विच् 3, 7 U, विशिष् 7 P or c.; 's.-ing milk from water' दुग्धजलभेदविधिः. -*v. i.* पृथग्भू 1 P, विश्लिष् 4 P, विघट् 1 A, अपया 2 P, व्यप-इ 2 P, वियुज्-विच्छिद्-भिद्-pass.; 'the brothers have s. ed' विभक्ता भ्रातरः. -*a.*,-ED, *a.* वि-,भिन्न, विभक्त, वियुक्त, विच्छिन्न ; न जाने कियताऽध्वना विच्छिन्नमितो बलमनुयायि मे (Ka. 120) 'by what distance s.' &c.; पृथक् *ind.*, असंलग्न, असंसृष्ट, व्यतिरिक्त, व्यस्त. -ION, *s.* वियोगः, विरहः, विप्रयोगः, विश्लेषः, विभेदः, व्यतिरेकः, विच्छेदः, (with instr. for 'from'); भिन्नता, पार्थक्यं, पृथग्भावः. 2 पृथक्करणं, विभागः, वि-,भेदः-दनं, व्यासंगः, विगमः, विघटनं; विवेकः; 'afflicted by s.' विरहातुर, विरहपर्युत्सुक, विधुर. -LY, *adv.* पृथक्, वि-,भिन्नं; 'taken s.' एकैक- *a.*, व्यस्त- *a.*; सर्वाविनयानामेकैकमप्येषामायतनं (Ka. 103), तदस्ति किं व्यस्तमपि त्रिलोचने (K. v. 72) 'even one, taken s.' &c. -NESS, *s.* पृथग्भावः, पार्थक्यं. -SEPARABLE, *a.* विभाज्य, वियोज्य, विच्छेद्य; 'not s.' नित्यस्थायिन्, नित्य, प्रकृतिस्थ.

SEPTANGULAR, *a.* सप्तकोण, सप्तास्र.

SEPTEMBER, *s.* भाद्रपदाश्विनं.

SEPTENARY, *s.* सप्तकं. -*a.* सप्तन्.

SEPTENNIAL, *a.* सप्तवार्षिक (की *f.*).

SEPTIC,-AL, *a.* विलयनकारिन्.

SEPTILATERAL, *a.* सप्तभुज, सप्तपार्श्व.

SEPTAGENARIAN, *a.* सप्ततिवर्षीय.

SEPTUM, *s.* महाबीज्यं, विटपः.

SEPULCHRE, *s.* समाधिः, प्रेतवासः, श्मशानं, शवस्थानं-मंदिरं-गर्तः. -SEPULCHRAL, *a.* (*s.*) in comp. -SEPULTURE, *s.* निखननं, भूमौ निगूहनं. 2 प्रेतकर्मक्रिया; *See* FUNERAL.

SEQUEL, *s.* उत्तरं, उत्तरभागः, शेषः, शेषभागः, परिशिष्टं. 2 परिणामः, अंतः.

SEQUENCE, *s.* अनु-,क्रमः, अन्वयः, आनुपूर्व्यं, परंपरा.

SEQUESTER, SEQUESTRATE, *v.* वियुज् 7 A, 10, पृथक् कृ 8 U. 2 Seclude, q. v. -ED, *a.* विविक्त; *See* SECLUDED.

SERAGLIO, *s.* अंतःपुरं, अवरोधः, शुद्धांतः, अंतर्गृहं; *See* HAREM.

SERE, *a.* शुष्क, म्लान, विशीर्ण.

SERENE, *a.* प्र-,शांत, प्रसन्न, अक्षुब्ध, स्तिमित, स्थिर, निरुद्वेग, निराकुल, अनुद्विग्न; (sky) निरभ्र, वितिमिर, प्रसन्न; (water) विशद, स्वच्छ, शुद्ध, निर्-वि-अमल, प्रसन्न. -LY, *adv.* प्रसन्नं, सप्रसादं, शांत-प्रसन्न-चेतसा. -ITY,-NESS, *s.* प्रशांति *f.*, प्रसादः, अनुद्वेगः, असंभ्रमः, अक्षोभः, प्रसन्नता, निरभ्रता, निर्मलता.

SERF, *s.* दासः, कृषकदासः. -DOM, *s.* दास्यं, दासवृत्ति *f.*

SERIATIM, *adv.* यथाक्रमं, अनुपूर्वशः, अनु-,क्रमशः, आनुपूर्व्येण.

SERIES, *s.* माला, परंपरा, राजिः, श्रेणिः-णी, आवलिः-ली, पंक्तिः, (all *f.*); दामन् *f. n.*, पर्यायः, परिपाटिः-टी *f.*, आनुपूर्वी-र्व्यं. -SERIAL, *a.* क्रमिक, यथाक्रम, क्रमानुसारिन्.

SERIOUS, *a.* ग(गं)भीर, धीर; गंभीरवृत्ति-शील-स्वभाव; 'a s. look' धीरविलोकितं. 2 गुरु, अलघु, अनुपेक्ष्य, अनतिपात्य, गुर्वर्थ. 3 अपरिहासिन्, अविनोदशील; 'this is, in truth, a s. matter' न खलु अयं परिहासस्य विषयः (Mal. 9); *See* EARNEST. -LY, *adv.* गंभीरं, धीरं, सधैर्यं, गौरवेण. 2 अपरिहासेन, सत्यं; 'I tell you s.' न परिहसामि, नायं विनोदः, न परिहासः. -NESS, *s.* गांभीर्यं, धीरता, धैर्यं, गौरवं, गुरुता; अपरिहासः, अविनोदः, &c.

SERMON, *s.* धर्मोपदेशः, धर्मव्याख्यानं.

Serous, *a.* मेदस्विन्, मेदुर.

Serpent, *s.* सर्पः, भुजगः, भुजंगः-गमः, अहिः, पन्नगः, नागः, उरगः; *See* Snake. **-ine**, *a.* (*s.*) in comp.; वि-,सर्पिन्, वक्र, कुटिल; 's. course' भुजंगगतिः, वक्रा-कुटिला-गतिः.

Serrate,-ed, *a.* करपत्रनिभ, क्रकचतुल्य; अनुक्राकच, क्रकचधार, दंतुर, सच्छेद.

Serried, *a.* संहत, संश्लिष्ट.

Serum, *s.* मेदस् *n.*, वसा, वपा.

Serve, *v. t.* सेव् 1 A, श्रु desid. (शुश्रूषते), उपास् 1 A, उप-स्था 1 A, उपचर् 1 P, परि-अनु-चर्; 'he who s. s not another's will' परेच्छानुरूपं न वर्तते, परच्छंदानुवर्ती न भवति, अन्यभावं न अनुप्रविशति. 2 अनुवृत् 1 A, अनुरुध् 4 A, अनुवि-धा 3 U; *See* Obey. 3 उपकृ 8 U, अनुग्रह् 9 P, उपचर्, साहाय्यं कृ; श्रेयः सं-पद् c. 4 (अर्थं) साधु c., प्रवृत् c., सं-पद् c., निर्वृत् c. 5 पर्याप्त-उचित-*a.* भू 1 P, अलं with dat. or inf., कृप् 1 A (with dat.); 'this will s. to rouse his anger' तस्य कोपमुद्दीपयितुं-कोपोद्दीपनाय-अलं or पर्याप्तमिदं. 6 उप-परि-कृप् c., उप-स्था c. (स्थापयति). 7 स्थाने-भूमौ-वृत् or भू or प्रयुज् pass. 8 प्र-उप-युज् 7 A, 10, विनि-युज्, निक्षिप् 6 P. 9 वृत्, आचर्, व्यव-हृ 1 P, (with loc. of person); *See* Act, Behave; 's. the purpose of', 's. as' उपयोगं व्रज् 1 P, स्थाने-भूमौ-भू; भूर्जत्वचः व्रजंति विद्याधरसुंदरीणामनंगलेखक्रिययोपयोगं (K. i. 7) 's. as love-letters' &c.; 's. up meals' परिविष् c., अन्नं उप-स्था c.; 'the gods s. ed up food' मरुतः परिवेष्टारः आसन्; 's. out' प्रतिकृ, वैरं &c. निर्यत् 10. **-v. i.** सेवां-कार्यं-कृ; नियोगमनुष्ठा 1 P; कार्यं सं-पद् c.; 'this will s. as water to wash his feet with' इदं पादोदकं भविष्यति (S. 1). **-ant**, *s.* भृत्यः, सेवकः, किंकरः, अनु-उप-जीवी, दासः, चेटः, प्रेष्यः, अनु-परि-चरः, परिजनः, परिचारकः, नियोज्यः, भुजिष्यः, शुश्रूषकः, उपासकः, सेवाजीवी; वैतनिकः, भृतिभुक्, भरण्यभुक्, भृतकः; कर्मक (का)रः, (labourer); 'female s.', 's.-maid' चेटी, दासी, भुजिष्या, प्रेष्या, कर्मकरी, सैर(रं)ध्री. **—Service**, *s.* सेवा, शुश्रूषा, उपचारः, उप-परि-चर्या, उपासनं-ना; आ-सं-श्रयः; 's. of kings' नृपसंश्रयः, राजाश्रयः. 2 (State) दास्यं, दासवृत्ति *f.*, प्रेष्य-भृत्य-भावः. सेवा; 'he lives in my s.' स मामनुजीवति, मदाश्रितः. 3 अनुवर्तनं, अनुवृत्तिः, आराधनं; *See* Obedience. 4 वृत्तिः, नियोगः, कार्यं, व्यवसायः; व्यापारः, कर्मन् *n.*, व्यवहारः. 5 उपकारः, साहाय्यं, उपकृतं-ति *f.*, अनुग्रहः, हितं, अर्थः. 6 उपयोगः, व्यवहारः. 7 सपर्या, उपासना, पूजा, उपचारः, पूजोपचारः. 8 भोजनपात्रगणः; 'I am entirely at your s.' सर्वथा त्वदधीनोहं, भवता यथेच्छं नियुज्यतामयं दासः; 'in whose s. are you' कस्य सेवया जीवसि, केन नियुक्तस्त्वं; 'to keep in s.' सेवायां नियुज् 7 A, 10, (कर्मणि) व्यापृ c. **-able**, *a.* उपयुक्त, उपयोगिन्, उपकारिन्, सहायभूत, प्र-उप-योज्य. 2 कार्यक्षम, कर्मकुशल, अलंकर्मीण. **-ably**, *adv.* सोपयोगं, सलाभं, सोपकारं. **—Servile**, *a.* दासेय (यी *f.*), दासोचित, दास-दास्य in comp.; 's. state' दासभावः, दास्यं, प्रेष्यभावः, दास्यवृत्तिः. 2 अतिचाटुपर, अत्यनुरोधिन्, श्ववृत्ति, अतिलालनपर. **-ity**, *s.* दास्यं, दास्यभावः. 2 चरणावपातः, श्ववृत्तिः, अतिलालनं, अत्यनुरोधः, छंदोनुवर्तनं. **-ly**, *adv.* दासवत्, अत्यनुरोधेन, अतिलालनपूर्वं. **-Servitor**, *s.* सेवकः, भृत्यः, &c.; *See* Servant. **-Servitude**, *s.* दास्यं, भृत्यभावः, किंकरत्वं, सेवा, प्रेष्यभावः, श्ववृत्तिः, सेवाधर्मः, सेवकदशा.

Sesame, **Sesamum**, *s.* तिलः, सारालः, सुबंधः; 'sowed with s.' तिल्य.

Session, *s.* उपवेशनं; 'sacrificial s.' सत्रं; 's. s judge' दंडाधिकरणिक. 2 (Time) सत्रकालः, कार्यनिर्वाहकालः.

Set, *s.* अस्तमयः, अस्तमनं, अस्तः. 2 जातं, जाति *f.*, गणः, संघः, श्रेणी, पंक्ति *f.*, समूहः, संयोगः; 's. s of ornaments fitting all parts of the body' सर्वांगिका आभरणसंयोगाः (Mal. 6). 3 (Of persons) वर्गः, गणः, संघः. **-v. t.** आ-नि-धा 3 U, वि-, न्यस् 4 U, स्था c. (स्थापयति), निविश् c., अवरुह् c.; oft. by कृ 8 U, दा 3 U, ऋ c. (अर्पयति); (in the ground) रुह् c., निखन् 1 P. 2 प्र-परिकृप् c., व्यव-स्था c. 3 प्रणि-धा, प्रतिबंध् 9 P, (यदि मणिस्त्रपुणि प्रतिबध्यते P. i. 1), उत्-खच् 10 (खचयति), अनु-व्यध् 4 P; 's. with jewels' रत्नानुविद्ध. 4 नि-,शो 4 P, उत्-,तिज् c., तीक्ष्णीकृ. 5 युज् 7 U, 10, सं-आ-°, समा-धा, सं-,वि-धा (limb &c.); 's. one's foot in' पदं कृ (lit. and fig.), करिष्यसि पदं पुनराश्रमेस्मिन् (S. 4), कृतं मे वपुषि नवयौवनेन पदं (Ka. 137); 's. a trap' पाशं युज्; 's. in motion' चल् c., संचर् c., ईर् c.; 's. the heart on' मनः-धियं-चित्तं, &c. ('Mind,' q. v.) बंध् or आ-धा or संनि-विश् c. or युज्, आसक्त-*a.* भू 1 P (with loc.); 's. your heart on religious duties' आधीयतां धर्मे धीः (Ka. 63); 's. not your heart on transient objects' विनाशधर्मसु विषयेषु मनो मा संनिवेशय, विनाशिविषयासक्तो मा भूः; 's. the teeth on edge' दंतहर्षं जन् c.; 's. right', 's. in order' समीकृ, व्यव-स्था c., विन्यस्, विरच् 10; 's. to rights' प्रति-,समा-धा, सुस्थीकृ; प्रतियुज्, (प्रतियोजयितव्यवल्लकी R. viii. 41); 's. free' मुच् 6 P or c.; *See* Free; 's. at naught' तृणाय-तृणवत्-मन् 4 A, तृणीकृ; ex. also by का मात्रा-गणना; 's. to music' स्वर-ताल-बद्ध *a.* कृ. –*v. i.* अस्तं गम्-व्रज् 1 P or या-इ 1 P, अस्ताचलं-अस्तशिखरं-अवलंब् 1 A or आप् 5 P, सागरे मस्ज् 6 P. **2** संहन्-बंध्-pass. –about, आरभ् 1 A, प्र-वृत् 1 A. –against, विरुध् 7 U, प्रत्यव-स्था c., प्रतियुध् c. ; *See* OPPOSE. –apart, पृथक् रक्ष् 1 P or स्था c, पृथक् कृ. –aside, अवक्षिप् 6 P, मुच्, त्यज् 1 P, oft. by आस् 2 A, स्था 1 P; 's. aside that point' आस्तां-तिष्ठतु-तावद्दूरे स विषयः ; *See* REJECT, OMIT. –before, उप-स्था c., उपानी 1 P, उपाहृ 1 P; 's. food before a person' परिविष् c. –down, न्यस्, भूमौ न्यस् or नि-धा. **2** आ-अधि-क्षिप्, भर्त्स् 10 A, अपकृष् 1 P, अवमन् c., अव-ज्ञा 9 U. **3** गण् 10, मन् 4 A. **4** (In writing) लिख् 6 P, निर्दिश् 6 P. –forth, उपनि-विनि-अस्, वर्ण् 10, उपक्षिप्, निर्दिश्, अभि-धा. –forward, प्रया, प्रगम्, प्रस्थ; (*v. t.*) पुरस्कृ, उन्नम् c., वृध् c. –in, समुपा-गम्, उप-स्था, प्रवृत्, अवतॄ 1 P; 'summer which has just s. in' अचिरप्रवृत्तं ग्रीष्मसमयं (S.1), वसंतावतारसमये &c.; (*v. t.*) अंतर् ग्रह् 9P. –off, Set out, q. v.; (*v. t.*) शुभ् c., प्रकाश् c.; शोभां पुष् 4, 9 P, लक्ष्मीं तन् 8 U, (मलिनमपि हिमांशोर्लक्ष्म लक्ष्मीं तनोति S. 1); oft. by शुभ् 1 A, गुणा विनयेन शोभंते 'are s. off by modesty'; 's. off against' तुल् 10 (तुलयति), प्रतिगण्. –on, प्रवृत् c., प्रयुज्, (अथावमानेन पितुः प्रयुक्ता K. I. 21), प्रेर्, प्रोत्सह् c.; *See* PROMPT; 's. on foot' प्रति-ष्ठा c., प्रवृत् c., आरभ्; 's. on fire' दह् c., ज्वलनाय कृ c. or विसृज् 6 P; 's. on guard' अवहित *a.* कृ. –out, प्र-स्था 1A, प्र-या, प्रगम्, प्रचल्, निर्गम्. –over, नियुज्, अधिकृ, अधि-ष्ठा c. –to, मनः बंध् or युज् or निविश् c., आसक्त-*a.* भू; 'they s. to their work' कार्यव्यापृता बभूवुः &c. –up, बंध्, उत्था c. ; सं-अव-प्रति-स्था c.; *See* RAISE, 'the people s. up a howl' बद्धकोलाहला जनाः; उत्थितो निनादः 'a scream was s. up'; (*v. i.*) वृत्ति-व्यवहारं-आरभ् or प्रवृत् c.; 's. up for' अभिमन् 4 A; *See* PRETEND, PROFESS. –upon, आक्रम्, आ-अव-स्कंद् 1 P, सहसा ग्रह्. –*a.* नियत, परिकल्पित, एकरूप; विन्यस्त, सुविरचित. **2** स्थापित, न्यस्त, निहित, निवेशित, &c. **3** खचित, छुरित, अनुविद्ध, प्रणिहित, प्रतिबद्ध, प्रत्युप्त, करंब, करंबित. –TER, *s.* योजयितृ *m.*, प्रतिष्ठापकः, &c. **2** मृगयाकुक्कुरः, विश्वकद्रुः. –TING, *s.* योजना, सन्निवेशः, स्थापनं-ना, अर्पणं, रोपणं, &c. **2** अस्तमनं, अस्तं. –SET-DOWN, *s.* अपकर्षणं, अभिभवः, मानखंडनं. –SET-OFF, *s.* परिवर्तः, तुल्यमूल्यं वस्तु.

SETATEOUS, *a.* शूकयुक्त, बहुशूक.

SETTLE, *v. t.* स्था c. (स्थापयति), प्रति-अव-°, नि-आ-रुह् c. **2** सं-व्यव-स्था c., व्यवसो 4 P, निर्-अव-धृ 10, संकॢप् c., साध् c.; 's. ing what to say' व्यवस्थापितवाक्, वार्थ व्यवस्थाप्य; अस्याः पितुः समीपनयनमवस्थितमेव (S. 5) 'is but s. ed &c.' **3** (Lands &c.) दा 3 U, युज् 10 (with instr. of grant); त्वां शासनशतेन योजयिष्यामि (P. I. 4). **4** अधिवस् c. **5** स्थिरीकृ 8 U, स्वस्थ-निर्वृत-*a.* कृ. **6** प्र-,शम् c (शमयति), सं-धा 3 U, समा-धा. **7** सं-, वि-धा, वि-,रच्, विन्यस् 4 U; 's. in marriage' निविश् c., (तनयं निवेश्य S. 4); 's. a debt' ऋणं शुध् c. or अपाकृ. **8** अधः पत् c. or गम् c., अवसद् c. –*v. i.* अव-व्यव-स्था 1 A, स्थिरीभू 1 P, निवासं स्थिरीकृ. **2** प्रशम् 4 P, विश्रम् 4 P. **3** तलं पत् 1 P, सद् 1 P, अव-नि-°, अधः गम् 1 P; प्रसद् (for becoming clear). **4** अधः पत् c. **5** घनीभू, संहन् pass., संहतीभू ; 's. ed amongst themselves' मिथः प्रशमं याताः, परस्परसंधानमकुर्वन् ; 's. in life' विवह् pass., निविश् 6 A (संसारपथे), विवाहं कृ, प्रतिष्ठित-*a.* भू. –ED, *a.* स्थापित, रोपित, प्रतिष्ठित &c. **2** नियत, निश्चित, निर्णीत, व्यवस्थित, सिद्ध, नि[illegible]त. –ING,-MENT, *s.* स्थापनं, सं-प्रति-अव-°. **2** निर्णयः, निश्चयः, निर्धारणं-णा, अवधारणं. **3** संधानं, प्र-,शमः-मनं, संधिः, समाधानं. **4** अधिवासनं. **5** अधिवासितदेशः; 's. in life' विवाहः, संसारप्रतिष्ठा; 'marriage-s.' शुल्कः-ल्कं. –ER, *s.* अधिवासिन् *m.*

SEVEN, *a.* सप्तन्. –FOLD, *a.* सप्तगुणं. –*adv.* सप्तधा, सप्तगुणं. –TH, *a.* सप्तम (मी *f.*). —SEVENTEEN, *a.* सप्तदशन्. –TH, *a.* सप्तदश (शी *f.*). –SEVENTY, *a.* सप्तति *f.*

SEVER, *v. t.* अव-वि-च्छिद् 7 P or c., अवकृत् 6 P or c., वियुज् 7 A, 10, विश्लिष् c., विभिद् c. –AL, *a.* भिन्न, पृथक् in comp., पृथगात्मक. **2** अनेक, बहु; *See* MANY. **3** स्व, आत्म in comp. **4** स्व-स्व; *See* RESPECTIVE. –ANCE, *s.* विच्छेदः, विश्लेषः, विभेदः, पृथक्करणं. –ALLY, *adv.* पृथक्, पृथक् पृथक्, प्रत्येकं, अवयवशः, व्यक्तिशः. –ALTY, *s.* भिन्नता, पार्थक्यं, पृथग्भावः.

SEVERE, *a.* खर, परुष, तीक्ष्ण, निष्ठुर, कठोर, चंड, तीव्र, उग्र, असौम्य, उग्रशासन, तीक्ष्णदंड. **2** (Of things only) दुःसह, दुर्विषह; तुमुल, घोर, (of fight); अत्यंत, अतिमात्र; सु-अति pr. –ITY, *s.* पारुष्यं, कठोरता, नैष्ठुर्यं, काठिन्यं, उग्रदंडता; तीव्रता, दुःसहता, &c. **2** तीक्ष्णदंडः. –LY, *adv.* परुषं, कठोरं, निष्ठुरं, उग्रं, तीव्रं, तीक्ष्णं, चंडं, बलवत्.

SEW, *v. t.* सिव् 4 P, वि-नि-° (together); वे 1P, प्र-वि-°. –ED, SEWN, *a.* स्यूत-न, उत, प्रोत. –ING, *s.* सीवनं, सेवनं, स्यूति *f.*

SEWER, *s.* प्रणाली-लः, परि(री)वाहः, जलोच्छ्वासः, मलनिर्गमः, संकरः, मलपथः.

SEX, *s.* Ex. by स्त्री or पुंस्-पुरुष: ('Man' q. v.), द्वंद्वं, मिथुनं. 2 जाति *f.*, लिंगं; 'the male s.' पुंजातिः; स्त्रीजातिः &c. -UAL, *a.* स्त्रीपुंस, स्त्रीपुरुष in comp.; 's. intercourse' सु-,रतं, मैथुनं, संगमः, व्यवायः, संगः, संभोगः.

SEXAGENARIAN, *a.* षष्टिवर्षीय.

SEXANGULAR, *a.* षडस्र, षट्कोण.

SEXENNIAL, *a.* षड्वार्षिक (की *f.*).

SEXTANT, *s.* वृत्तषड्भागः.

SHABBY, *a.* कुत्सित, कृपण, तुच्छ, निंद्य, अपकृष्ट, अधम, जघन्य; *See* MEAN. 2 मलिन; सूत्रदरिद्र, जर्जरित, पाश in comp. -ILY, *adv.* कुत्सितं, कृपणं. मलिनं. -INESS, *s.* कार्पण्यं, मालिन्यं &c.

SHACKLE, *s.* निगडः, शृंखला-लः, बंधनं, पाशः.-*v.t.* निगडैः बंध् 9 P or संयम् 1 A; *See* FETTER.

SHADE, *s.* छाया, in all senses ; 'the dense s. of sugarcanes' इक्षुच्छायं; 'full of s.' प्रच्छायं; अनातपः, अप्रकाशः, निरातपस्थानं. 2 अंधकारः, तिमिरं, तमस् *n.* 3 व्यवधा-धानं, तिरस्करिणी, वितानं. 4 क्रमः, भागः. 5 Ghost, q. v.; 's. of difference' सूक्ष्मभेदः, स्वल्पांतरं; 's. of meaning' अर्थस्य सूक्ष्मभेदः; 'like a picture with all its s. s painted by a pencil' उन्मीलितं तूलिकयेव चित्रं (K. I. 32); 'cast into s.' तिरस्कृ 8 U, प्रत्यादिश् 6 P; *See* BACK-GROUND. -*v. t.* छद् 10, प्र-आ-°, वितन् 8 U. 2 आतपं निवार् 10, अनातप-*a.* कृ. -Y, *a.* प्रच्छाय, सच्छाय, छायाबहुल-आवृत-युक्त-सनाथ; निरातप, आतपरहित, छाया in comp. ; 'a s. tree' छायावृक्षः. —SHADOW, *s.* छाया , प्रतिच्छाया, प्रतिबिंबं, प्रतिमा, प्रतिरूपं, प्रतिमूर्ति *f.* 2 आश्रयः, शरणं. 3 तमस् *n.*, अंधकारः; 'deep s. s' गाढतमः-पटलानि. 4 गंधः, लेशः, आभासः. -*v. t.* प्र-आ-च्छद् 10. 2 आभासं दृश् c., प्रतिबिंबयति (D.). -Y, *a.* छायारूप, असार, छायात्मक, अवास्तविक (की *f.*), मिथ्यामृषा in comp. 2 मंदच्छाय, मंदकांति-प्रभ, मंद-न्यूनतेजस्; *See* DIM, FAINT.

SHAFT, *s.* कांडः (of arrows). 2 बाणः, शरः, इषुः; *See* ARROW; शल्यः-ल्यं. 3 दंडः; (of a carriage) धुर् *f.*, कूबरः; (of a plough) ईषा-शा; (of a mine) कूपः, गर्तः, अवटः.

SHAG, *s.* दृढ-स्थूल-लोमन् *n.* -GY, *a.* लो(रो)मश, लोमावृत, स्थूललोमन्. 2 रूक्ष, मलिन.

SHAKE, *v. i.* प-,कंप्-वेप्-1 A, वि-प्र-चल् 1 P, वेल्ल् 1 P, सं-प्र-क्षुभ् 4 P, 1 A; (fig.) अभिभू-बाध्-pass. -*v. t.* कंप् c., धू 5, 9 U, 6 P, वि-आ-,° चल् c., सं-वि-प्र-°; क्षुभ् c.; ध्वनिना सर्वतः प्रचलितमिव तदरण्यमभवत् (Ka. 29) 'was, as if, s. en by the sound'. 2 अभिभू 1 P, आकुलीकृ 8 U; 'this position would be s. en' इति प्रतिपादितमाकुलीभवेत् (S. B. 335); 's. one's confidence' साशंक-शंकान्वित-*a.* कृ; 's. about' प्रेंख् c., आंदोलयति (D.); 's. off' निर्धू, निरस् 4 U, निराकृ, अपास्, त्यज् 1 P, अपानुद् 6 P, प्रतिक्षिप् c.; *See* DISPEL; 's. hands with each other' अन्योन्यं हस्तौ स्पृशतः. -*s.*,-ING, *s.* कंपः, धूननं, विं-,धु-(धू)ति *f.*, विचलनं, वेपनं, सं-,क्षोभः. -ING, *a.* चल, सकंप, चलन, लोल, तरल, चंचल, पारिप्लव. 2 क्षोभकारिन्. -Y, *a.* अस्थिर, चल, लोल; *See* FICKLE.

SHALLOW, *a.* गाध, उत्तान; अग(गं)भीर, गाधजल, अल्पजल; 's. knowledge' पल्लवग्राहि पांडित्यं; 's. person' अल्पमतिः-बुद्धिः, गाधज्ञानः. -*s.* सैकतं, पुलिनं, गाधस्थलं.

SHAM, *s.* व्यपदेशः, छद्मन् *n.*, व्याजः, छलं; *See* PRETEXT. -*a.* छाद्मिक-कापटिक (की *f.*), कपट-व्याज-कूट-मिथ्या in comp.; कृतक, अश्रद्धेय, अनृत. -*v. i.* अप-व्यप-दिश् 6 P; *See* PRETEND.

SHAMBLES, *s.* शू(सू)ना, सौनस्थानं.

SHAMBLING, *a.* वक्र, विरूप. 2 चंचल, चपल, विषम.

SHAME, *s.* लज्जा, ह्रीः, त्रपा, व्रीडा. 2 अपमानः, दुष्कीर्ति *f.*, कलंकः, लज्जास्पदं, अकीर्तिहेतुः; 'to feel s.' लज्ज् 6 A; 's., for s.!' धिक् (with acc.). -*v. t.* 'put to s.' ह्री c. (ह्रेपयति), त्रप् c., व्रीड् c., लज्ज् c. 2 अपमन् c., कलंकयति (D.); *See* DISGRACE. 3 अवमन् 4 A, लघूकृ 8 U, अव-ज्ञा 9 U. -ED, 's.-faced' *a.* लज्जित, त्रपित, व्रीडित, लज्जा-व्रीडा-शील. -FUL, *a.* लज्जाकर (री *f.*), ह्रेपण (णी *f.*), लज्जा-त्रपा-जनन (नी *f.*), अपकीर्तिकर, गर्ह्य. -LESS, *a.* निर्लज्ज, निर्व्रीड, निर्ह्रीक, अपत्रप, लज्जाहीन, त्यक्त-निरस्त-लज्ज, वियात, धृष्ट, सप्रतिभ. -LESSLY, *adv.* निर्लज्जं, लज्जां विहाय-विजित्य.

SHAMPOO, *v. t.* संवह् c., मृद् 9 P or c. -ER, *s.* संवाहकः. -ING, *s.* संवाहनं, अंगमर्दनं.

SHANK, *s.* जंघास्थि *n.* 2 जंघा, दीर्घभागः-अंशः; 'having long s. s' दीर्घजंघ, ऊर्ध्वज्ञु, ऊर्ध्वजानु.

SHAPE, *s.* आकारः, रूपं, आकृति *f.*, मूर्ति *f.*, संस्कारः, संस्थानं. -*v. t.* आकारं वि-धा 3 U or दा 3 U, रूप् 10, कॢप् c., घट् c. (घटयति), रच् 10. -ED, *a.* साकार, सरूप, रूपिन्, (*s.*) in comp.; 'moon-s.' चंद्राकृति &c. -LESS, *a.* निराकार, अमूर्त, निराकृति, अरूप. 2 अप-वि-कु-रूप. -LY, *a.* सुरूप, सुरेख, शस्ताकार.

SHARD, *s.* मृत्पात्रखंडः.

SHARE, *v. t.* सं-,विभज् 1 U, परिकॢप् c., अंश् 10, वंट् 10; अंशांशि दा 3 U; 'sorrow s. ed by dear friends' स्निग्धजनसंविभक्तं दुःखं (S. 3); 'with whom else shall I s. my grief' केन वान्येन सह

साधारणीकरोमि दुःखं (Ka. 233). 2 भागं-अंशं-ह 1 P or लभ् 1 A or ग्रह् 9 P, अन्येन सह भुज् 7 A; 'the demons shall s. the labour of churning' दानवा अपि मंथनश्रमभाजः भवेयुः, (युष्माभिः सार्धं) मंथनश्रममनुभवेयुः, &c.; 's. ing equally pleasure and pain' समदुःखसुख, -s. अंशः, भागः, वंटः, उद्धारः (of an estate); 'he is to have a s.' अंशभाग्भवेत्; 'he has a s. in the plot' कपटप्रबंधे सहकारी असौ. 2 (Of a plough) फालः, कुशी. -ER, s. अंशहरः, अंशिन् m., भागिन्-भाक् in comp. -SHARE-HOLDER, s. अंशभागी, अंशग्राही, भागहारी-ग्राही.

SHARK, s. ग्राहः, नक्रः, अवहारः, मकरः; (fig.) बकवृत्तिः, धूर्तः; *See* ROGUE.

SHARP, a. तीक्ष्ण, in all senses; तीक्ष्णा बुद्धिः, तीक्ष्णा वर्षधारा, तीक्ष्णो दंडः &c.; नि-,शात, नि-,शित, प्र-,खर, तिग्म, तीव्र, तीक्ष्ण-शित-धार, सूच्यग्र, तीक्ष्णाग्र; 's. descending arrows' निशितनिपाताः शराः (S. 1). 2 (Intellect) अतिप्रदीप्त, सूक्ष्म, तीक्ष्ण, सूक्ष्म-शीघ्र-ग्राहिन्; (of persons) तीक्ष्णमति, कुशाग्रबुद्धि-मति, सूक्ष्म-शीघ्र-तीव्र-मति, प्रदीप्तप्रज्ञ, विदग्ध, निपुण, पटु, चतुर, कुशल; (in action) शीघ्र, आशु-क्षिप्र-कारिन्, तीक्ष्णकर्मन्. 3 सरस, विदग्ध, रसिक. 4 अम्ल, शुक्त. 5 कटु, उग्र, (smell &c.). 6 कटु, उग्र, तीव्र, तीक्ष्ण, परुष, अरुंतुद, मर्मस्पृश्-भिद्; 's. pain' तीव्रवेदना; 's. language' परुषवचनं, वागसिः; 's. sound' कर्कशध्वनिः; 's.-edged' तीक्ष्ण, निशितधार, धारासनाथ; 's.-pointed' तीक्ष्णाग्र, सूच्यग्र; 's.-set' तीव्रक्षुधाग्रस्त, अतिप्रबलक्षुधावसन्न; 's.-shooter' लक्ष्यवेधिन्; 's.-sighted' तीक्ष्ण-सूक्ष्म-दृष्टि, &c. -s. उदात्तः, उदात्त-उच्च-स्वरः. -EN, v. t. नि-,शो 4 P, उत्तिज् c., शाणयति (D.), तीक्ष्णीकृ 8 U, क्ष्णु 2 P; (appetite) उत्-,बुध् c., प्र-,रुच् c., दीप् c. -ER, s. वंचकः, धूर्तः; *See* ROGUE. -LY, adv. तीक्ष्णं, तीव्रं, प्रखरं, उग्रं, परुषं, &c. -NESS, s. तीक्ष्णता, कुशाग्रमतित्वं, मतिप्रकर्षः, पाटवं, पारुष्यं, कार्कश्यं &c.

SHATTER, v. t. वि-,शॄ 9 P, वि-,दॄ 9 P or c., खंडशः-लवशः-भंज् 7 P, लवशः चूर्ण् 10 or निष्पिष् 7 P; 'why am I not s. ed into a thousand pieces?' दीर्यें किं न सहस्रधाहं (U. 6); यथा यथायं वैनाशिकसमय उपपत्तिमत्त्वाय परीक्ष्यते तथा तथा विदीर्यत एव (S. B. 580) 'the more is this V. theory put to a logical test, the more is it s. ed to pieces (does it give way).' -v. i. विदॄ &c. pass.

SHAVE, v. t. मुंड् 1 P, 10, क्षुरेण कृत् 6 P or छिद् 7 P or लू 9 U, आ,वप् c., क्षुर्-खुर् 6 P. 2 तक्ष् 1, 5 P; *See* PARE. -ER, s. क्षौरिकः, नापितः, क्षुरिन् m., मुंडकः. -ING, s. क्षौरं, मुंडनं. 2 तष्टं, विदलं, शकलं, खंडः.

SHE, pron. सा; in comp. ex. by f. terminations, 's.-goat' अजा, 's.-sparrow' चटका &c.

SHEAF, s. (शस्य-) मुष्टि m. f., स्तंबः, गुच्छः, स्तबकः.

SHEAR, v. t. लू 9 U, कृत् 6 P, छिद् 7 P, आवप् c., मुंड् 1 P, 10, वि-,शॄ 9 P. 2 अपहृ 1 P, निर्हृ; 'shorn of' वीत, हत, निर्, हीन in comp.; *See* DESTITUTE; 'was shorn of his arms' छिन्नबाहुः कृतः or तस्य बाहू व्यशीर्येताम्. -ER, s. लोमच्छिद् m.-च्छेदिन्, छिद् in comp. -ING, s. लवनं, कर्तनं, वपनं, छेदः-दनं. -SHEARS, s. खंडधारा, कर्तरिका, कर्तरी, कृपाणी.

SHEATH, s. कोशः-षः, पिधानं, आधारः; आ-,वेष्टनं, पुटः-टं, आच्छादनं. 2 दलं. -SHEATHE, v. t. कोशे नि-धा 3 U or निविश् c. 2 आ-परि-वेष्ट् 1 A or c., पि-धा, आवृ 5 U, आच्छद् 10.

SHED, v. t. नि-,पत् c., वि-,मुच् 6 P or c., विसृज् 6 P, गल् c.; 's. tears' बाष्पं विहा 1 P, अश्रूणि वि-,मुच् or पत् c. 2 (Blood) स्रु c., पत् c., मुच्, मोक्ष् 10; 's. influence' फल् 1 P; 'the moon s. s her white glory' इंदुर्धवलरश्मिजालं विकिरति. 3 (Light) क्षिप् 6 P, विसृज्, प्रकॄ 6 P, प्रसृ c. -s. शाला; 's. for cattle' गोशाला, गोष्ठं. -DER, s. स्रावकः, मोचकः, पातकः.

SHEEN, a. उज्ज्वल, दीप्तिमत्; *See* BRIGHT. -s. प्रभा, तेजस् n.

SHEEP, s. मेषः, अविः, उरभ्रः, ऊर्णायुः; *See* RAM; 'a female s.' मेषी, एडका; 'goats and s.' अजाविकं; 'flock of s.' औरभ्रं. -ISH, a. अप्रतिभ, लज्जाशील, जनभीत; निस्तेजस्, निष्प्रभ, हत-नष्ट-गत-वीर्य, मेषस्वभाव-शील.

SHEER, a. शुद्ध, केवल, मात्र in comp.; *See* BARE, MERE. -v. i. वि-,अपसृ-सृप् 1 P.

SHEET, s. उत्तरच्छदः, प्रच्छदः, प्रच्छदपटः-वस्त्रं, शय्याच्छादनं. 2 (Of paper) पत्रं, फलकं, खंडः, एकभागः. 3 पत्रं, फलकः-कं (of metal); 'winding-s.' प्रेत-शव-वस्त्रं; 's. of water' जलसंघातः, तोयराशिः.

SHELF, s. काष्ठफलकः.

SHELL, s. कोशः-षः, कंचुकः, कवचः-चं, त्वच् f. (of fruit &c.); पुटः-टं; 'bivalve s.', कंबुः-बु; 'conch-s.' शंखः, कंबुः; 'oyster-s.' शुक्ति f.; 'dealer in s. s' शंखकारः, शांखिकः; कांबविकः; 's. of a pea' शिंबा, बीजकोशः; तुषः (of rice). 2 आ-परि-वेष्टनं, पुटः, कोशः (envelope). 3 बहिर्भागः; 's.-cutter' कांबविकः; 's.-fish' कंबुस्थः, शंखस्थः. -v. t. कोषं-त्वचं &c. अपनी 1 P or निर्हृ 1 P, निस्त्वचीकृ 8 U. -Y, a. शंखिन्, कंबुमय (यी f.),-पूर्ण.

Shelter, *s.* सं-आ-श्रयः, शरणं, निवासस्थानं. 2 रक्षणं, त्राणं; 'able to give s.' शरण्य; 'take s. with' आ-समा-श्रि 1 U, शरणं या 2 P or गम् 1 P, शरणार्थं या. –*v. t.* 'give s.' रक्ष् 1 P, त्रै 1 A; *See* Protect; प्र-,छद् 10, व्यव-धा 3 U; आश्रयं दा 3 U, शरणं भू; 's. ed from the wind' निर्वात. –less, *a.* निराश्रय, निरालंब, अशरण.

Shelve, *v. i.* अवसृप् 1 P, प्रवणीभू 1 P. –*v. t.* निष्कस् c., निराकृ 8 U. –ing, *a.* अवसर्पिन्, प्रवण.

Shepherd, *s.* अविपालः, मेषपालः. –ess, *s.* मेषपाली, मेषरक्षिणी.

Sherd, *s.* खंडः-डं, शकलः-लं.

Shew, *v. t. See* Show.

Shield, *s.* चर्मन् *n.*, फलकः-कं, फलं; 'armed with a s.' चर्मिन्, फलकपाणि, फलभृत्; 'having sword and s.' खड्गचर्मधर. 2 आश्रयः, शरणं, रक्षणं, गुप्ति *f.* –*v. t.* रक्ष् 1 P, त्रै 1 A, आ-, छद् 10; *See* Protect.

Shift, *s.* उपायः, प्र-,युक्ति *f.*, गति *f.*, साधनं, प्रयोगः. 2 छलोपायः, कपटं; छद्मन् *n.*, छलं, अप-व्यप-देशः. 3 अंतरीयं, अधोंशुकं, अधोवसनं. –*v. i.* परि-व्या-वृत् 1 A. 2 वि-,चल् 1 P, स्थानांतरं गम् 1 P or चल्. 3 वस्त्रांतरं परि-धा 3 U; 's. for oneself' वृत्तिं-जीविकां-उपपद् c. or प्रक्लृप् c. –*v. t.* परि-व्या-वृत् c., अन्यथा कृ 8 U, विकृ. 2 विचल् c., स्थानांतरं गम् c. or चल् c. –y, *a.* छल-कपट-प्रिय.

Shin, *s.* अग्रजंघा, पादः; *See* Leg.

Shine, *v. i.* प्रकाश् 1 A, प्र-,भा 2 P, वि-,द्युत् 1 A, शुभ् 1 A, दीप् 4 A, राज् 1 U, भास् 1 A, स्फुर् 6 P, भ्राज्-भ्राश्-भ्लाश् 1 A, चकास् 2 P, प्र-,रुच् 1 A, ज्वल् 1 P, विलस् 1 P; 'stars s. by their own light' स्वतःप्रकाशाः तारकाः. –*s.* प्रकाशः, द्युति *f.*, प्रभा; *See* Light. –ing, *a.* भास्वत्, द्युति-दीप्ति-मत्, भासुर, रुचिर, तेजस्विन्, कांतियुक्त, भ्राजमान, द्योतमान, &c. –y, *a.* भास्वत्; *See* above.

Shingle, *s.* शर्करा, शिलाखंडः. 2 फलकः-कं.

Ship, *s.* पोतः; यानं, प्रवहणं, (the sense being clear); बृहन्नौका-तरणि-णी *f.*; 's.-master' नौकाधिपतिः, पोताध्यक्षः. –*v. t.* (Off) पोतेन प्र-स्था c. or प्र-हि 5 P, पोतं आरुह् c., नौकायां प्रविश् c. 2 स्वस्थाने निविश् c. –Shipwreck, *s.* यान-पोत-भंगः, नौव्यसनं-भंगः-भेदः; (fig.) विध्वंसः, उच्छेदः, प्रणाशः; 'suffered a s.' यानभंगेन सागरे निमग्नः. –*v. t.* नावं-पोतं-भंज् 7 P or नश् c.; 'her hopes were s. ed' सर्वा आशा उन्मूलिताः, मूलच्छिन्ना इव.

Shirk, *v.* सव्यपदेशं-छलेन-परिहृ 1 P or त्यज् 1 P or हा 3 P; अप-व्यप-दिश् 6 P, छलं-छद्म-कृ 8 U; व्यपसृप् 1 P, व्यपक्रम् 1 U, 4 P, पलाय् 1 A. –er, *s.* कार्यत्यागिन् *m.*

Shirt, *s.* युतकं, चोलः, अधोवसनं-वस्त्रं.

Shiver, *v. i.* कंप्-वेप्- 1 A, सीत्कारं मुच् 6 P; 's.-ing with cold' शीतकंपिततनु, शीतार्तत्वात् कंपमान; 'with s. ing force' सतरलवेगं. 2 बहुखंडशः भिद्-विद्-pass., शकलीभू 1 P. –*v. t.* शकलीकृ 8 U, बहुखंडशः भिद् 7 P or विद् 9 P or c., सहस्रधा भंज् 7 P. –*s.* प्र-,कंपः, वेपथुः, सीत्कारः, देह-गात्र-कंपः. 2 शकलः-लं, खंडकः, सूक्ष्मलवः, दलं, छेदः, भिन्नं; 'went to a hundred s. s' शतखंडीभूतः, शतधा भिन्नः.

Shoal, *s.* गाधस्थलं, सैकत, पुलिनं. 2 संघः (मत्स्यादीनां), संघातः; 's. of fish' पोताधानं.

Shock, *s.* आ-अभि-घातः, निर्घातः, सं-वि-क्षोभः, संघट्टः, आकस्मिकक्षोभः; 'Oh hard s. of fate' अहह दारुणो दैवनिर्घातः (U. 2). 2 भयावेशः, साध्वसाक्रमः. 3 राशिः, उत्करः, चयः. –*v. t.* उप-अभि-हन् 2 P, वज्रेण व्यध् 4 P or तड् 10, अकस्मात् उद्विज् c. or त्रस् c.; 'I am s. ed to hear this from you' एतत्त्वन्मुखाच्छ्रुत्वा वज्रताडित इवास्मि-प्रचकितोस्मि. 2 सं-वि-क्षुभ् c., संघट्ट् c. –ed, *a.* आकस्मिकसाध्वसोपहत. –ing, *a.* उद्वेगकर (री *f.*), साध्वसकारिन्, बीभत्स.

Shoe, *s.* उपानह् *f.*, पादुका, पादूः, पादत्रं; (for horses &c.) खुरत्रं-त्राणं. –*v. t.* पादुकया तड् 10 or प्र-हृ 1 P. 2 खुरत्रेण सनाथीकृ 8 U, खुरत्रं बंध् 9 P; 's.-black,-cleaner' पादुकामार्जः; 's.-maker' चर्मकारः, पादूकृत्; 's.-string' पादुकाबंधनी.

Shoot, *s.* पल्लवः-वं, किस(श)लयः-यं, प्रवालः; प्ररोहः, अंकुरः, नवपल्लवः; उद्भिद् *m.*, उद्भिज्जं. –*v. i.* आग्नेयास्त्रं-शरं &c. मुच् 6 P or अस् 4 P. 2 (Forth) निर्गम् 1 P, अंकुरयति (D.), उद्भिद् pass., प्ररुह् 1 P, स्फुट् 6 P, सहसा प्रादुर्भू 1 P; 'the bud though long shot forth' चिरनिर्गतापि कलिका (S. 6); better ex. by (*s.*); 'the seed has not (yet) shot forth' अंकुरोदयो नास्ति, प्ररोहाभिमुखमपि न दृश्यते बीजं (after K. v. 60). 3 निः-सृ 1 P, प्रवृत् 1 A. 4 मर्माणि भिद् 7 P or व्यध् 4 P. –*v. t.* प्र-,मुच्-क्षिप् 6 P, प्रास्, विसृज् 6 P, पत् c., ईर् c. 2 आग्नेयास्त्रेण-गुलिकाक्षेपेण-शरेण &c. हन् 2 P or प्रहृ 1 P or क्षण् 8 P or क्षि 5 P, हत्वा निपत् c.; 'shot (at) them only' तौ शरव्यमकरोत् स नेतरान् (R. xi. 27); 'shot in the eye' (गुलिका-)विद्धनयनः. 3 उत्-वि-सृज्, निरस्, निः-सृ c. –er, *s.* भेत्तृ *m.*, वेधिन् *m.* –ing, *a.* उद्भिद्-ज्ज, प्ररोहिन्. –*s.* शरप्रक्षेपः, शरासनं, बाणमोक्षणं. 2 गुलिकाप्रक्षेपः. 3 तीक्ष्ण-तीव्र-वेदना; 'one skilled in s.' कृतहस्तः, कृतपुंखः, सुप्रयोगविशिखः. –Shot, *s.* क्षेपः, प्रहारः, ताडनं &c. 2 अस्त्रं, मुक्तं, आग्नेयास्त्रं, गुलिका. 3 शरपातः, शरायणं. 4 विषयः, गोचरः. 5 लक्ष्यभेदप्रवीणः, लक्ष्यवेधी.

SHOP, *s.* शाला, पण्य-विक्रय-शाला-गृहं ; आपणः, विपणि *f.*; 'work-s.' उद्योगशाला ; 's.-keeper' आपणिकः, पण्याजीवः, विपणिन् *m.*, क्रयविक्रयिकः.

SHORE, *s.* कूलं, तीरं, तटं, वेला, रोधस् *n.*; 'brought on the s.' उत्कूलित.

SHORT, *a.* (Of time) अल्प, स्तोक, स्वल्प; 'of s. duration' अल्पकालीन-कालिक (की *f.*), अचिरस्थायिन्. 2 (In size &c.) ह्रस्व, खर्व, वामन; अतुंग, नीच, क्षुद्र, लघु; ह्रस्वपरिमाण, अल्प-क्षुद्र-प्रमाण; क्षुद्रतनु, अल्पमूर्ति, पृश्नि. 3 अविस्तीर्ण, लघु, संक्षिप्त. 4 अपूर्ण, अपर्याप्त, ऊन, न्यून. 5 अनायत, अदीर्घ. 6 हीन, विकल, रहित. 7 (Vowel) ह्रस्व, लघु ; 'in a s. time' अचिरेण, अचिरात्; 'for a s. time' कंचित्कालं, अल्पकालं-मात्रं ; 'in s.' किं बहुना, समासेन, संक्षेपतः, संक्षेपेण, समासतः; 's. of' विना, अंतरेण, मुक्त्वा, ऋते; 'I shall be satisfied with nothing s. of Râma's banishment' नान्येन तुष्येयमृते रामविवासनात्; 'cut s.' आक्षिप् 6 P; संहृ 1 P, संक्षिप्; 'come or fall s.' न्यूनीभू 1 P, क्षि-अपचि- pass.; *See* FAIL; 'a s. cut' अवक्रः-सरलः-मार्गः; 'stop s.' अकस्मात् स्था 1 P, मार्गमध्ये स्था ; 's.-coming' दोषः, प्रमादः, स्खलितं, छिद्रं, वैकल्यं, न्यूनता, अतिपातः, अपराधः; 's.-hand' संक्षिप्तलिपि *f.*; 's.-lived' क्षणध्वंसिन्-स्थायिन्-जीविन्-भंगुर, अचिरस्थायिन्, अल्पायुस् ; 's.-sighted' अदूरदर्शिन्, अदीर्घदर्शिन्, ह्रस्वदृष्टि; 's.-winded' श्वासकृच्छ्राभिभूत, दुःश्वासिन्. -EN, *v. t.* संक्षिप् 6 P, ह्रस् c., न्यूनी-अल्पीकृ 8 U, संकुच् 1 P, संहृ. 2 खर्वी-वामनीकृ. -*v. i.* ह्रस्वीभू 1 P, ह्रस् 1 P. 2 तनुतां गम् 1 P, क्षि pass., न्यूनीभू, अल्पीभू. -LY, *adv.* अचिरात्, अचिरेण, शीघ्रं, सपदि, झटिति; *See* QUICKLY. 2 संक्षेपतः, संक्षेपेण, समासतः; अविस्तरेण, आविस्तरशः. -NESS, *s.* ह्रस्वता, क्षुद्रता, लघुता, अल्पता, खर्वता; अविस्तरः, संक्षेपः, न्यूनता, अपर्याप्ति *f.*, &c.

SHOULD, Ex. by pot. pass. part.; 'I s. think so' अहं तावदेवं मन्ये, इति मम मतिः.

SHOULDER, *s.* स्कंधः, अंसः, भुजशिरस् *n.* -*v. t.* स्कंधे कृ 8 U or स्था c. (स्थापयति), स्कंधेन वह् 1 P. 2 स्कंधेन तड् 10 or प्रहृ 1 P.

SHOUT, *s.* रवः, कलकलः, उत्क्रोशः, निनादः, महाशब्दः-स्वनः-नादः, प्रणादः, घोषः-षणा, कोलाहलः, संहूति *f.*; (of victory) जयघोषः-ध्वनिः-शब्दः, हर्षनादः, सिंहनादः. -*v. i.* आ-वि-उत्-क्रुश् 1 P, उच्चैःस्वन्-नद् 1 P or क्रुश्, मुच् 6 P or कृ with (*s.*), उद्-घुष् 10, मुक्तकंठं रु 2 P.

SHOVE, *v. t.* प्र-सृ c., संचल् c.; *See* PUSH; 's. off' अपसृ c. -*s.* प्रसारणं, अपसारणं.

SHOVEL, *s.* खनित्रं, अभ्रि *f.*, काष्ठकुद्दालः.

SHOW, *v. t.* दृश् c. (with acc. or dat. of person'; प्र-सं-°. 2 निर्दिश् 6 P, सूच् 10, प्रकाश् c., व्यंज् 7 P or c., व्यक्तीकृ 8 U; आविष्कृ, प्रकटीकृ ; आ-उप-दिश् 6 P or c. (way). 3 कथ् 10, आ-, ख्या 2 P, बुध् c., ज्ञा c. (ज्ञापयति), आ-नि-विद् c.; 's. me the way' आदेशय मे मार्गं; 's. a favour' उपकृ, अनुग्रह् 9 P ; 's. off' दंभार्थं दृश् c.; 's. to be true' प्रति-पद् c. -*v. i.* Appear, q. v. -*s.* दर्शनं, आलोकः, प्रेक्षास्थानं, कौतुकं. 2 दृश्यं, स्थानं. 3 आभासः; by अव-आ-भा 2 P or भास् 1 A. 4 व्यपदेशः, व्याजः; *See* PRETEXT. 5 आडंबरः, दंभः. -ER, *s.* प्र-, दर्शकः. -Y, *a.* दृष्टिहारिन्, सुभगालोक; अतिदर्शनीय, एकांतशोभन.

SHOWER, *s.* वृष्टि *f.*, वर्षः, आसारः; धारासंपातः, धारासारः; 's. of arrows' शरवृष्टिः, इषुवर्षः; 's. of tears' अश्रुधारा, बाष्पासारः-धारा; 's.-bath' धारागृहं, धारायंत्रगृहं. -*v. t.* वृष् 1 P, (fig. also). -Y, *a.* वृष्टिमत्, बहुधार, वर्षुक.

SHRED, *s.* खंडः-डं, शकलः-लं; वस्त्र-पट-खंडः. -*v. t.* खंडशः व्यवच्छिद् 7 P.

SHREW, *s.* वक्र-वाम-शीला, कर्कशा, उग्र-कटु-शीला, कैकेयी. 2 छुछुंदरी, गंधमुखी (s.-mouse). -ISH, *a.* वक्र-वाम-कटु-शील, कर्कश, कर्कशस्वभाव.

SHREWD, *a.* चतुर, विदग्ध, विचक्षण, निपुण, सूक्ष्मधीमति. 2 वैदग्ध्यप्रयुक्त, विदग्ध in comp. -LY, *adv.* चातुर्येण, विदग्धवत्. -NESS, *s.* वैदग्ध्यं, चातुर्यं, &c.

SHRIEK, *v. i.* परुषं आक्रंद् 1 P, वि-उत्-आ-क्रुश् 1 P, उच्चैः रु 2 P, आरट् 1 P, कर्कशं क्रुश्. -*s.* आ-,क्रंदितं, क्रंदनं, रावः, रवः, उत्क्रोशः, कर्कशनादः-रवः; *See* SCREAM.

SHRIKE, *s.* कलिंगः, धिंगः, धूम्या(मा) टः.

SHRILL, *a.* कर्कश, परुष, तीव्र, पटु, कर्णकटु, कर्णवेधिन्. -NESS, *s.* कार्कश्यं, कटुता.

SHRIMP, *s.* इंचाकः, जलवृश्चिकः.

SHRINE, *s.* पुण्यस्थानं, देवायतनं, तीर्थं.

SHRINK, *v. i.* संकुच्-आकुंच्-संहृ-संक्षिप्- pass., संकोचं इ-या 2 P, निमील् 1 P (lotus). 2 (Withdraw) सकंप-सभयं-परावृत् 1 A, वित्रस् 1, 4 P, उद्विज् 6 A, भयेन-सहसा-अपसृ 1 P or अपक्रम् 1 U, 4 P; (into) गात्रसंकोचेन प्रविश् 6 P. -*v. t.* संकुच् 1 P, आकुंच् c., संहृ 1 P. -ING. *s.* संकोचः, आकुंचनं.

SHRIVEL, *v. i.* संकुच्-आकुंच्-विशॄ- pass. -*v. t.* संकुच् 1 P, विशॄ 9 P or c.; better by 's.-ed'. -LED, *a.* संकुचित, आ-कुंचित, विशीर्ण ; (into wrinkles) वलिपूर्ण, वलिमत्, वलिन-भ.

SHROUD, *s.* आच्छादनं, आवरणं, पिधानं. 2 शव-प्रेत-वस्त्रं-वसनं-आच्छादनं. -*v. t.* आ-,छद् 10 ; पि-धा 3 U, गुह् 1 U, गुप् 1 P; *See* COVER, CONCEAL.

SHRUB, *s.* गुल्मः-ल्मं, विटपिन् *m.*, स्तंबः, क्षुपः, वी-

लवृक्षः. –BY, *a.* गुल्मावृत. –SHRUBBERY, *s.* गुल्मवाटिका.

SHRUG, *v.* (असंतोषदर्शनार्थं स्कंधौ) धू 5, 9 U, संकुच् 1 P, संचल् c. –*s.* स्कंधधूननं-संकोचः.

SHUDDER, *v. i.* वेप्-कंप् 1 A, प्र-वि-°, वि-प्र-स्फुर् 6 P. –*s.*,–ING, *s.* प्र-,कंपः, वेपथुः, अंगकंपः-स्फुरणं-वेपनं. –ING, *a.* संजातवेपथु, सकंप.

SHUFFLE, *v. i.* नि-अप-ह्नु 2 A, अप-व्यप-दिश् 6 P, छद्म-छलं-कृ 8 U; *See* PREVARICATE. 2 वंच् 10; *See* CHEAT. –*v. t.* इतस्ततः संचल् c. or विक्षिप् 6 P. 2 संमिश्र् 10, बहुधा विकृ 6 P, संकरीकृ 8 U, संकुलीकृ. –*s.*,–ING, *s.* वंचना, छलं, छद्मन् *n.*, अप-व्यप-देशः, अप-नि-ह्नवः, निह्नवोक्ति *f.* 2 संचालनं, विक्षेपः, संमिश्रणं. –ER, *s.* छद्म-कपटवृत्तिः, छलिन् *m.*

SHUN, *v. t.* परि-हृ 1 P, वृज् 10, परि-वि-°,परि-,त्यज् 1 P, हा 3 P; न उपगम् or उपसृ 1 P, संगमं परिहृ (a person).

SHUT, *v. t.* अपि-पि-धा 3 U, सं-आ-वृ 5 U, नि-अव-रुध् 7 U, बंध् 9 P, (book, hand &c.); (eye) नि-,मील् 1 P or c., मुकुलयति (D.). 2 संहृ 1 P, संकुच् 1 P, संवृ, संहन् 2 P, संपीड् 10. 3 रुध्, स्तंभ् 9 P or c., प्रतिबंध्. –*v. i.* नि-,मील् pass., मुकुलायते (D.). –in, निरुध्; बंध् &c.–out, निवार् 10, निषिध् 1 P, बहिष्कृ 8 U, निराकृ, व्यावृत् c. –up, संनि-रुध्, पि-धा. 2 मुखं स्तंभ्; 's. up in a box' संपुटीकृ, मंजूषायां निविश् c. –TER, *s.* कपा (वा)टः-टी-टं; अवरोधकं, आच्छादनं.

SHUTTLE, *s.* मल्लिकः, सूत्रवेष्टः-ष्टनं, त(त्र)सरः.

SHY, *a.* सलज्ज, शालीन, विनीत, सव्रीड. 2 कातर, भीरुस्वभाव; लोक-जन-भीत, भीरु, आलापविरक्त. –*v. i.* भी 3 U; 'the horse s. ed at a rock' पाषाणं दृष्ट्वाऽश्वः सहसा भीतः-चकितः. –NESS, *s.* शालीनता, कातर्यं, भीरुता, भीति *f.*

SIBILANT, *s.* ऊष्मन् *m.*, ऊष्मवर्णः.

SIBYL, *s.* सिद्धा, सिद्धस्त्री.

SICK, *a.* आतुर, पीडित, व्याधित, रुजार्त, रोगार्त, रुग्ण, रोगिन्, विकृत, अस्वस्थ, सामय, अभ्यांत, आमयाविन्, अपटु, अभ्यमित. 2 (Mentally) संतप्त, पीडित, व्यथित, उपतप्त. 3 विवमिषु, वमनोन्मुख, वमनेच्छु. 4 निर्विण्ण, विरक्त, वितृष्ण, वीतस्पृह, द्वेषिन्; 's. of eating flesh' मांसाशनेन निर्विण्ण; 's. of the world' संसारविरक्त, उदीर्णवैराग्य; 'a man on a s.-bed' शय्यागतो रोगी; 'to be s.' वम् 1 P, छर्द् 10. –EN, *v. t.* निर्वेदं-वितृष्णां-विरक्ततां-उत्पद् c. 2 वम् c.; रोगार्तीकृ 8 U. –*v. i.* व्याधिना अभिभू-pass., भू with (*a.*). 2 बध् desid. (बीभत्सते); *See* ABHOR. –ENING, *a.* बीभत्स, बीभत्सावह. –LY, *a.* रुग्ण, अस्वस्थ, अशक्त; गदोपसृष्ट; *See* (*a.*). 2 नित्य-सदा-रोगिन्, रोगशील; 's. by nature' जन्मप्रकृति-रोगिन्. –NESS, *s.* व्याधिः, रोगः, गदः, रुज् *f.*, अस्वास्थ्यं, आमयः, विकारः, उपतापः. 2 विवमिषा, वमनेच्छा, प्रच्छर्दिका, छर्दि-र्दी *f.*, वमः-मि *f.*

SICKLE, *s.* दात्रं, लवित्रं, शस्यकर्तनी.

SIDE, *s.* पार्श्वः-र्श्वं; पक्षः, in all senses; कुक्षिः, पार्श्व-पक्ष-भागः; 'left s.' वामांगं, वामपार्श्वः; 'opposite s.' वि-प्रति-पक्षः; 'first s.' (of arguments) पूर्वपक्षः; उत्तरपक्षः, &c.; 'at one's s.' पार्श्वतः, पार्श्वे; 'staying at the s.' पार्श्वगत-स्थित. 2 प्रांतः, सीमा, उपांतं, अंतः. 3 (Of a mountain) उत्संगः, कटकः-कं, नितंबः. 4 भागः; 'outer s.' बाह्यभागः; पूर्वभागः, &c. 5 (Direction) दिश्-शा; gen. ex. by त्र, तः affixed; 'on both s. s' उभयतः, उभयत्र; 'on the other s.' परतः, पारे; 'on the left s.' वामतः; 'on all s. s' सर्वत्र, सर्वतः, विश्वतः, समंतात्, समंततः, चतुर्दिक्षु; 's. by s.' पार्श्वापार्श्वि. 6 (Party, faction) पक्षः; 'one of the opposite s.' वि-प्रति-पक्षः; 'of the same s.' सपक्षः, स्वपक्षीयः, स्वपक्षावलंबी; 'relations on the father's s.' पितृपक्षाः बांधवाः. 7 (In geometry) भुजः, पार्श्वः, दोस् *m. n.*, बाहुः; (of a river) पारः-अवारः; 's.-long'; वक्र, तिरश्चीन, अपांग-साचि-तिर्यक् in comp.; (*adv.*) पार्श्वतः, तिर्यक्, साचि, तिरः; 's.-long look' नयनोपांतविलोकितं, साचिवीक्षणं, अपांगदृष्टि *f.*, तिर्यग्दृष्टिः, कटाक्षः; 's.-look' अपांगदर्शनं, कटाक्षः, &c.; 's.-ways', 's.-wise' तिरश्चीनं, तिर्यक्, तिरः. –*a.* पार्श्व, पक्ष in comp.; पार्श्वस्थ, पार्श्विक-पाक्षिक (की *f.*); 's. breeze' पक्षवातः; पक्षद्वारं, &c. –*v. i.* 'to be on the s. of' पक्षे भू, पक्षं ग्रह् 9 P or अधि 1 U or आ-अवलंब् 1 A; 'one who s. s' पक्ष्यः. –ER, SIDESMAN, *s.* पक्षपातिन् *m.*, पक्षीयः, पक्षोद्ग्राही; *See* PARTIZAN.

SIDEREAL, *a.* तारा, नक्षत्र in comp.

SIDLE, *v. i.* तिर्यक् गम् 1 P or या 2 P. –ING, *a.* तिर्यग्गति *f.*

SIEGE, *s.* उप-,अव-,रोधः, परिवेष्टनं; 'lay s. to' उप-अव-रुध् 7 U.

SIEVE, *s.* चालनी, तितउः.

SIFT, *v. t.* पृथक् कृ; वि-,शुध् c., तितउना शुध् c., निर्गल् c. 2 सूक्ष्मं-निपुणं-निरूप् 10 or परीक्ष् 1 A or आलोच् 10 or अनुसं-धा 3 U. –ING, *s.* शोधनं, निर्गलनं.

SIGH, *s.* नि(निः)श्वासः, उच्छ्वासः, उच्छ्वसितं, दीर्घश्वासः-निश्वासः &c. –*v. i.* दीर्घं नि-उत्-श्वस् 2 P, निश्वासं मुच् or सृज् 6 P; 's. ing deep and hot' दीर्घं उष्णं च निश्वस्य. 2 शुच् 1 P, रुद् 2 P; *See*

LAMENT. —ING, *a.* निश्वासिन्, उच्छ्वासिन्, दीर्घनिश्वासिन्, सनिश्वास.

SIGHT, *s. See* under SEE.

SIGN, *s.* चिह्नं, लक्षणं, लिंगं, अभिज्ञानं, लांछनं, व्यंजनकं ; 'a bad s.' अव-दुर्-लक्षणं. 2 संज्ञा, संकेत:, इंगितं. 3 Portent, q. v. 4 राशि:. 5 चिह्नं (in Math. &c.) ; 's. manual' स्वहस्त:, स्वाक्षरं, स्वहस्ताक्षरं; 'under one's own s. manual' स्वहस्तपरिचिह्नित (Y. II. 93). 6 ध्वज:; 's.-post' ध्वजस्तंभ:. —*v.*; 'make a sign' संज्ञां दा 3 U ; 'understand the s.' संज्ञां ग्रह् 9 P; 'makes a s. to Vidûshaka' विदूषकं संज्ञां लंभयति; 's. ed to him by her eyes to come' नेत्रसंज्ञया तं आह्वयत्; गुरुं नेत्रसहस्रेण नोदयामास वासव: (K. II. 29) 's. ed to speak &c.'. 2 नाम लिख् 6 P or निविश् c. (with loc.); स्वाक्षरेण अंक् 10 or चिह्नयति (D.). —ATURE, *s.* नामलेखनं-निवेशनं. 2 नामाक्षरं, हस्ताक्षरं. —SIGNAL, *s.* संज्ञा, संकेत:. —*a.* अपूर्व, अनन्यसाधारण (णी *f.*), विशिष्ट, स्मरणार्ह, अत्युत्कृष्ट, विशेष in comp. —IZE, *v. t.* प्रसिद्धी-विश्रुती-कृ 8 U; (oneself) कीर्ति-प्रतिष्ठां-यश:-प्राप् 5 P or लभ् 1 A. —LY, *adv.* अति, नितरां, अत्यंतं, अपूर्वतया. —SIGNET, *s.* मुद्रा ; 's.-ring' मुद्रासनाथमंगुलीयं, अंगुलिमुद्रा. —SIGNIFY, *v. t.* बुध् c., गम् c., सुत् c., अभि-धा 3 U; *See* INDICATE, MEAN; oft. ex. by अर्थ: ; 'what does it s.' अस्य कोर्थ:, किमनेन गम्यते, &c.; 'it s.es much' गुर्वर्थमेतत् 2 by गौरवं, महत्त्वं, भार:; 3 by शक्ति *f.*, बलं. —ICANT, -ICATIVE, *a.* सार्थ, चरितार्थ, अर्थयुक्त, समर्थ, अर्थान्वित, अर्थवत्, पूर्णार्थ. 2 हेतुगर्भ, साकूत, अभिप्रायगर्भ ; 'casting at me a s. look' साकूतं मां निर्वर्ण्य. 3 वाचक, अभिधायक, [illegible]चक. 4 गुरु, महत. —ICANTLY, *adv.* अर्थदर्शक, [illegible] सार्थं, पूर्णार्थत:. —ICATION, *s.* अर्थ:. 2 वत्, साकूतं, [illegible] शक्ति:.

SIGNIOR, *s.* आर्य:.

SILENT, *a.* तूष्णीक, अन[illegible]षिन्, मूक, मौनिन्, नि:शब्द, नीरव. 2 रुद्ध-बद्ध-मुख, नि[illegible]त्तर, अनुत्तर ; 'habitually s.' तूष्णींशील, अल्पभा[illegible]षिन्, वाग्यत, वाचंयम ; 'when the lute was s.' वीणायां मूकीभूतायां ; 'become or remain s.' ([illegible]fter speaking) उपशम् 4 P, विरम् 1 P ; एवमुक्त्वा उपशशाम, उपशांतवचसि तस्मिन् &c. —LY, *adv.* तू[illegible]र्णीं, जोषं, नि:शब्दं, निभृतं, मौनीभूय. —SILENCE, *s.* मौनं, मूकभाव:, नि:शब्दता; अनालाप:, तूष्णींभाव:, अभाषणं ; 'keeping s.' वाक्स्तंभ:-रोध:-यमनं, मु[illegible]बंधनं ; 'one who holds s.' वाचंयम:, मौनव्रती; 'keep s.' तूष्णीं-जोषं-आस् 2 A or स्था 1 P; मौनं आस्था-[illegible] 1 A, वाचं यम् 1 P or निरुध् 7 U, मुखं बंध् 9 P. 2 प्र-, शांति *f.*, स्तिमितता ; 'in the s. of night' प्रशांतायां रात्रौ. —*interj.* तूष्णीं भव, मौनं कुरु. —*v. t.* मौनं लभ् c. (लंभयति) or अवलंब् c., विरम् c., प्र-उप-शम् c. 2 निरुत्तरीकृ 8 U, अधरीकृ, मुखं बंध्. —ED; *a.* निरुत्तर, अनुत्तर, निरुत्तरीकृत, रुद्ध-बद्ध-मुख.

SILK, *s.* कौशेयं, कौशं, कीटसूत्रं ; पट्ट:, क्षौमं, दुकूलं कौशांबरं, कौशिकं (s.-cloth) ; 'China s.' चीनांशुकं ; 'bleached s.' पत्रोर्णं, धौतकौशेयं; 's.-cotton tree' शाल्मलि:-ल:, शाल्मलिवृक्ष:, पिच्छिला; 's.-worm' कोश(ष)कार:, पट्टकीट:, तंतुकीट:-कृमि:, कोशस्थ:. —EN, *a.* कौशेय (यी *f.*), क्षौम (मी *f.*), कौशिक (की *f.*), कौश (शी *f.*) ; 's. cloth' दुकूलं, कौशांबरं, क्षौमं, &c. 2 मृदु, कोमल.

SILL, *s.* देहली, शिला, गृहावग्रहणी.

SILLY, *a.* मूर्ख, बालिश, मूढ, अल्पधी-मति, दुर्मति, निर्बुद्धि ; *See* FOOLISH ; 'what a s. boy' अहो मूढो बालक:.

SILT, *v. t.* (up) अवरुध् 7 U, अवष्टंभ् 9 P.

SILVAN, *a.* वन in comp., वन्य, वनस्थ, अरण्यज ; 's. goddess' वनदेवता; 's. scenery' वनशोभा-श्री:.

SILVER, *s.* रूप्यं, रजतं, श्वेतं, दुर्वर्णं, खर्जूरं, कलधौतं; 's.-leaf' रूप्यपत्रं ; 's.-smith' रूप्यकार:, स्वर्णकार:. —*a.* राजत (ती *f.*) (*s.*) in comp., रजतनिर्मितकृत, रौप्य (प्यी *f.*). —*v. t.* रूप्येण आच्छद् 10, रजतयति (D.), श्वेतवर्णीकृ 8 U. —Y, *a.* रजतोपम, रूप्यवर्ण, श्वेत-शुक्ल-वर्ण, अतिधवल.

SIMILAR, *a.* सम, समान, तुल्य, अनुगुण, अनुरूप, सधर्मन्; *See* LIKE. —ITY, *s.* साम्यं, सादृश्यं, तुल्यत्वं. —LY, *adv.* तद्वत्, तथैव, एवं.

SIMILE, *s.* उपमा, निदर्शनं. —SIMILITUDE, *s.* औपम्यं, सादृश्यं. 2 आकार:, रूपं, मूर्ति *f.*

SIMMER, *v. i.* शनै: पच्-क्वथ् pass.

SIMPER, *v. i.* विकृतं स्मि 1 A, कुस्मितं कृ 8 U, अनर्थकं हस् 1 P.

SIMPLE, *a.* निरवयव, असंकीर्ण, असमस्त, शुद्ध, केवल, अमिश्र. 2 सरल, ऋजु, अमाय, शुद्धात्मन्, अवक्र, निर्व्याज, निष्कपट, मायाहीन. 3 (Dress) विनीत, (विनीतवेषेण प्रवेष्टव्यानि तपोवनानि S. 1). 4 स्पष्ट, व्यक्त, सुगम, सुबोध, भिन्नार्थ, अगूढार्थ ; *See* PLAIN. 5 मुग्ध, बालिश, मूढ, दुर्मति. —*s.* ओषधिधी *f.* —SIMPLETON, *s.* मूढ:, मूढधी:, सुविश्वास्य:, क्षुद्र:, क्षुद्रमति:. —SIMPLICITY, *s.* शुद्धता, अमिश्रता, सरलता, आर्जवं, सारल्यं, निर्व्याजता, अनुपधित्वं, अमाया, अव्याज:, निष्कापट्यं. 2 विनीतत्वं, शुद्धता. 3 स्पष्टता, सुबोधता, सुगमत्वं. 4 बालिश्यं, मूढता. —SIMPLIFY, *v. t.* ऋजूकृ 8 U, विशदीकृ, सुगमीकृ, व्यक्तीकृ; *See* EXPLAIN. —SIMPLY, *adv.* एव, केवलं, मात्र in comp.

SIMULATE, *v. t. See* PRETEND.

SIMULTANEOUS, *a.* एक-सम-कालिक (की *f.*), यौ-

गपदिक. -LY, *adv.* समं, युगपत्, एक-सम-कालं-ले, यौगपद्येन, एकदैव, सममेव. -NESS, *s.* यौगपद्यं, एक-सम-कालता, युगपद्भावः.

SIN, *s.* पापं, पातकं, एनस् *n.*, कल्मषं, दुरितं, अघं, दुष्कृतं, वृजिनं, अंहस् *n.*, किल्बिषं, पंकः-कं, पाप्मन् *m.*, कलुषं; दोषः, अपराधः, पाप-अप-कर्म, कुकर्म, दुष्कृति *f.* -त्यं; 'heinous s.' महा-घोर-पातकं; 'destroying s.' पापनाशन-नाशिन्, अघमर्षण, पापापह. -*v. i.* पापं &c. आचर् 1 P or कृ, अपराध् 4, 5 P, दुष् 4 P.-NER, *s. See* SINFUL below ; 'an atrocious s.' महा-घोर-पातकिन्-पापिन्, पापराशिः-निधिः. -FUL, *a.* पापिन्, पातकिन्, पापकर (रीf.), पाप्मन्, पापकृत्, पापात्मन्, कुकर्मन्, दुष्कर्मन्, एनस्विन्, पाप-दुष्ट-कर्मन्, अपराधिन्, किल्बिषिन्, पापनिरत-बुद्धि-मति, पापात्मक. 2 (Of acts) पाप in comp., दुष्ट; कलुष; 's. act' पापं, दुष्कर्म; *See* (*s.*). -FULLY, *adv.* पापवत्, सपापं, दुष्टवत्. -FULNESS, *s.* सपापता, पापमति-निरति *f.*, दुष्टता, &c. -LESS, *a.* अनघ, निष्पाप, अपाप, अकल्मष, पापरहित, निर्दोष, निरपराध, and sim. comp.

SINCE, *prep.* प्रभृति, आरभ्य, (with abl.), आ with abl. or in comp.; sometimes also ex. by gen. abs.; अस्य कतिपये संवत्सरास्तपस्तप्यमानस्य (U. 4) 'it is several years s. he began to practise penance'; 's. then' तदाप्रभृति; '4 years s.' इतः पूर्वं चतुर्वर्षं; 'long s.' चिरं; 'ever s.' यतः-प्रभृति. 2 पूर्वं, प्राक्, गत-पूर्व-काले. -*conj.* यतः, यस्मात्, यत्, हि (not at beginning); by abl. of abstract noun; *See* BECAUSE.

SINCERE, *a.* अकृत्रिम, निर्व्याज, निष्कपट, निर्व्यलीक, दक्षिण, ऋजु, सरल, विशुद्ध, अमाय; यथार्थ, सत्य, तात्त्विक-वास्तविक (की *f.*) ; (of persons only) शुद्धमति-भाव, शुद्धात्मन्, विमलात्मन्, शुचि, सत्यशील-व्रत-वादिन्; *See* FRANK, HONEST. -LY, *adv.* निर्व्याजं, निर्व्यलीकं, अमायया, शुद्धहृदयेन-भावेन, विमलात्मना. -ITY, -NESS, *s.* सारल्यं, दाक्षिण्यं, आर्जवं, निष्कापट्यं, अमाया, विमलात्मता, शौचं, यथार्थता, &c.

SINE, *s.* ज्या, ज्यापिंडः.

SINECURE, *a.* अकर्माधिकृत, कर्मशून्याधिकारिन्.

SINEW, *s.* स्नायु *f.*, स्नसा; (s. s) बलं, शक्ति *f.*, सामर्थ्यं. -Y, *a.* स्नायुमय (यी *f.*). 2 प्र-स-बल.

SING, *v. i.* गै 1 P; (of birds) कूज् 1 P, रु 2 P. -*v. t.* गै; गानेन वर्ण् or कृत् 10, उत्कृत्, अभिगै; 'they sang his praises' तं स्तुतिभिरुपतस्थिरे. -ER,-SONGSTER, *s.* गायकः, गातृ *m.*, गायकः. -ING,-SONG, *s.* गीतं, गीति *f.*, गेयं, गानं. 2 कूजनं, रुतं, रावः, रवः.

SINGE, *v. t.* ईषद् दह् 1 P, अग्निना स्पृश् 6 P.

SINGLE, *a.* एक, एकाकिन्, अद्वितीय, केवल, असहाय; अद्वैध (धी *f.*). 2 भिन्न, व्यक्त, अविभक्त. 3 Simple, q. v. 4 अनूढ, अविवाहित, अकृतोद्वाह, निःसंग; 's. combat' द्वंद्वयुद्धं, नियुद्धं, बाहुयुद्धं ; 's.-handed' एक, एकाकिन्, बाहुसहाय, भुजमात्रसहाय; 's.-hearted' अनन्यवृत्ति, एकचित्त ; 's. stick' यष्टि *f.*, दंडः. -*v. t.* (Out) (बहूनां मध्यात्) वृ 5 U, उद्धृ 1 P, उद्-ग्रह् 9 P; निरूप् 10, निर्दिश् 6 P. -NESS, *s.* कैवल्यं, अद्वितीयता, &c. 2 शुद्धि *f.*, अनन्यता, अनन्यभावः. -SINGLY, *adv.* Ex. by (*a.*). 2 एकैकं, एकैकशः, प्रत्येकं, एकशः, पृथक्, पृथक् पृथक्; *See* SEPARATELY.

SINGULAR, *a.* अपूर्व, अप्रतिम, अद्वितीय, अप्रतिरूप, अनुपम. 2 अनन्यसाधारण (णी *f.*), लोकोत्तर, अनन्यसामान्य; अपरूप, विलक्षण, अद्भुत, लोकबाह्य, अलौकिक (की *f.*); 's. number' एकवचनं. -ITY, *s.* अपूर्वता, अप्रतिमता, असामान्यता, वैलक्षण्यं, वैचित्र्यं, असंगति *f.*, लोकोत्तरता. -LY, *adv.* अपूर्वं, विशेषतः, अद्भुतं, लोकोत्तरप्रकारेण.

SINISTER, *a.* अमंगल, अशुभ, अकल्याण (णी *f.*), अभद्र. 2 दुष्ट, वक्र, वाम, कुटिल, अनृजु. 3 वाम, सव्य; 'of s. motives' दुराशय, पापमति; उमां स पश्यन्नृजुनैव चक्षुषा (K. v. 32) 'looking at Umâ with no s. eye'. -SINISTRALLY, *adv.* वामतः, वामदिशि. -SINISTROUS, *a.* वामस्थ, वामपार्श्ववर्तिन्.

SINK, *v. i.* नि-,मस्ज् 6 P; 'sank in deep mire' महापंके निमग्नः; सद् 1 P, अव-नि-°, अधः गम् 1 P or पत् 1 P or या 2 P, अवपत्. 2 ह्रासं-क्षयं या-इ 2 P, क्षि pass., ध्वंस् 1 A; *See* DECAY, DECLINE. 3 (Down) अव-वि-सद्, परि-,म्लै-ग्लै 1 P, स्रंस् 1 A; *See* DROOP; 'my heart s. s down' सीदति मे हृदयं; 'limbs, s. ing down through excessive thirst' प्रबलपिपासावसन्नानि अंगकानि (Ka. 36); 'his heart sank within him' तस्य धैर्यमहीयत; स लुप्त-स्खलित-धैर्यः. -*v. t.* नि-मस्ज् c. (मज्जयति); अधः गम् c. or पत् c. 2 (A well &c.) खन् 1 P. 3 अवसद् c., परि-,म्लै c. (spirits &c.). 4 न्यूनीकृ 8 U, अल्पीकृ, लघयति (D.), ह्रस् c., अपचि 5 U; क्षि 5 P. -*s.* जलनिर्गमः, गुप्तनाली.

SINUOUS, *a.* कुटिल, वक्र, अराल, जिह्म. -SINUOSITY, *s.* वक्रिमन् *m.*; कौटिल्यं.

SINUS, *s.* नाडि-डी-लि-ली *f.*

SIP, *v. t.* आचम् 1 P; उपस्पृश् 6 P, ईषत्-अल्पशः-पा 1 P. -*s.* आचमनं, उपस्पर्शः, ईषत्पानं.

SIPHON, *s.* उत्क्षेपणी, वक्रनाली.

SIR, (Voc.) आर्य; भवन्, भोः; 'holy s.' भगवन्; 'gentle or good s.' भद्र, भद्रमुख.

SIRE, *s.* (In addressing) देव, भीमदेव, महाराज,

राजन्. 2 भगवन् (of holy men). 3 तातः, जनकः, पिता.

SIREN, *s.* वि-,मोहिनी, (गानेन) लोभयित्री, मायिनी.

SIRRAH, *interj.* रे, अरे, अरेरे.

SIRRUP, *s.* स्वादु-मधुर-रसः-पेयं.

SISTER, *s.* स्वसृ, भगिनी, सोदर्या, जा(या)मिः-मी. 2 धर्मभगिनी; 'elder s.' अग्रजा; 'younger s.' अवरजा; 's.'s son' भागिनेयः, स्वस्रेयः; 's.'s daughter' स्वस्रीया, भागिनेयी; 's.'s husband' आवुत्तः; 's.-in-law' यातृ, ननांदृ, श्याली, भ्रातृजाया, प्रजावती (expressing different relations). -HOOD, *s.* भगिनीत्वं, भगिनीसंबंधः. 2 भगिनीसमाजः, स्त्रीगणः. -LY, *a.* भगिन्यनुरूप, स्वस्रीय, स्वसृयोग्य.

SIT, *v. i.* आस् 2 A, नि-,सद् 1 P, उपविश् 6 P; 'please s. here' अत्रास्यतां, इदमासनमलंकरोतु भवान्. 2 कार्यं निर्वह् c. 3 (Fit) Ex. by शुभ् 1 A; 'this crown s. s well on you' नितरां तवेदं मुकुटं शोभते, शोभसे एतेन मुकुटेन; 's. by' उपास्, अन्वास्; 's. up' स्था 1 P, सम्यक् (अनतकायं) स्था; 'half s. ing up in the bed' पूर्वार्धविसृष्टतल्पः (R. XVI. 6); जागृ 2 P.

SITE, *s.* सन्निवेशः, सं-,स्थिति *f.*, स्थानं, पदं, स्थलं, आस्पदं, भूमि *f.*; (of a house) वास्तु *m. n.*, वेश्मभूः, गृहपोटः; 'purificatory ceremony of a s.' वास्तुशमनं.

SITUATE,-ED, *a.* अव-,स्थित, निविष्ट; दिश्य, स्थ, वर्तिन् in comp.; 's. to the east' पूर्वदिश्य, पूर्वस्थ; (of persons) स्थ, स्थित, अवस्थ in comp., अवस्थापन्न; 'so s.' एतदवस्थ; 'badly s.' दुःस्थ, दुःस्थित, कृच्छ्रगत, कष्टदशापन्न. -ION, *s.* सन्निवेशः, अवस्थानं, अव-,स्थितिः. 2 पदं, नियोगः, अधिकारः, पदवि-वी *f.* 3 अवस्था, दशा, स्थितिः, भावः, वृत्ति *f.*, आस्पदं.

SIX, *a.* षष्; 's.-fold' षड्गुण; 's.-faced' षण्मुखः, षडाननः; 'having s. mothers' षाण्मातुरः; 'collection of s.' षट्कं; 'in s. ways' षड्धा, षोढा; 'of s. months standing' षाण्मासिक (की *f.*), षण्मास्य. -TH, *a.* षष्ठ (ष्ठी *f.*) —SIXTEEN, *a.* षोडशन्. -TH, *a.* षोडश (शी *f.*). —SIXTY, *a.* षष्टि *f.* -IETH, *a.* षष्टितम (मी *f.*).

SIZE, *s.* प्र-परि-माणं, मानं; 'of great s.' महाप्रमाण, पृथु; 'of a big s.' बृहत्प्रमाण. 2 आकारः, आकृति *f.*, रूपं, आकारमानं; 'of the s. of' ex. by (*s.*) or मात्र in comp.; 'of the s. of a mustard seed' सर्षपमात्रं (छिद्रं); बिल्वमात्रं, अंडपरिमाणं, &c.

SKAIN, SKEIN, *s.* पं(पिं)जि-जी *f.*-जिका.

SKATE, *s.* हिमविसर्पणपादुका.

SKELETON, *s.* कंकालः; 'mules reduced to s. s' कंकालशेषाः खराः (U. 3); अस्थिपंजरः. 2 आकारः, संस्थानं. 3 वस्तुमात्रं.

SKETCH, *v. t.* वर्ण् 10, आलिख् 6 P, स्थूलवर्णनं-पांडुलेख्यं-कृ 8 U. -*s.* वर्णनं; आलेख्यं; 'rough s.' स्थूललेख्यं, पांडुलेखः; 's. of a painting' पांडुचित्रं, चित्रारंभः, रेखामात्रं. 2 वस्तुमात्रं.

SKEWER, *s.* शलाका, कीलः-लकः, शंकुः.

SKIFF, *s.* तरीः, नौ *f.*, लघुनौका.

SKILFUL, SKILLED, *a.* कुशल, निपुण, प्रवीण, पटु, विचक्षण, दक्ष, विदग्ध, चतुर, विशारद, पेशल, युक्तिमत्, कृतिन्, विज्ञ, अभिज्ञ-ज्ञ-विद् in comp. -LY, *adv.* सपाटवं, सनैपुण्यं, दक्षतया, चतुरं, कुशलतया, विज्ञवत्, सवैदग्ध्यं, &c. -NESS, SKILL, *s.* कौशलं, नैपुण्यं, पटुता, पाटवं, प्रावीण्यं, चातुर्यं, वैदग्ध्यं, युक्ति *f.*, विज्ञता, &c.

SKIM, *s.* मंडः-डं, फेनः-णः. -*v. t.* फेनं गल् c. or अपनी 1 P or निर्हृ 1 P. -*v. i.* जवेन-वेगात् परिसृप् 1 P or परि-द्रु 1 P, लघुगत्या विसृप्. -MED, *a.* हृत-मंड-फेन; 's. milk' घोलं, मथिततक्रं. -MER, *s.* झर्झरी-रं, खजः-कः.

SKIN, *s.* चर्मन् *n.* (of animals), त्वच् *f.*; (hide) अजिनं, दृतिः, कृत्ति *f.*; (of snakes) निर्मोकः, कंचुकः; 'reduced to mere s. and bones' त्वगस्थिमात्रशेष. 2 Rind, q. v.; 's.-deep' चर्मगत; *See* SUPERFICIAL; 's.-flint' अतिकृपणः, कदर्यः; *See* MISER. -*v. t.* चर्म-त्वचं-अपनी 1 P or निर्हृ 1P or उल्लिख् 6 P, निस्त्वचीकृ 8 U. -NY, *a.* चर्मभूत, त्वङ्मात्र, चर्ममात्रावशेष, क्षीण, कृश; *See* LEAN.

SKIP, *v. i.* प्लु 1 A, वल्ग् 1 P, नृत् 4 P. -*s.*,-PING, *s.* प्लुतं-ति *f.*, प्लवनं, प्लुतगति *f.* -PING, *a.* प्लुतगतिगामिन्.

SKIRMISH, *s.* डिंबाहवः, डिंबः, डिंबयुद्धं. -*v. i.* कृ 8 U with (*s.*).

SKIRT, *s.* प्रांतः, पर्यंतः, अंतः, प्रांत-पर्यंत-भागः, परिसरः, सीमा, धारा; 's. s of a mountain' पर्यंतभूः. 2 अंचलः, दशा-वस्ति *m. f.* (pl.); वस्त्रांचलः, वसनांतः. -*v.* Ex. by (*s.*), प्रांतयति (D.); *See* BORDER.

SKITTISH, *a.* चंचल, चपल, तरल. 2 क्रीडा-खेला-शील-पर.

SKULK, *v. i.* निभृतं-अलक्षितं-स्था 1 P or वृत् 1 A, प्रच्छन्नं आस् 2 A.

SKULL, *s.* कपालः-लं, कर्परः, शिरोस्थि *n.*; 's. for alms' भिक्षाकपालं; *See* SCULL.

SKY, *s.* नभस् *n.*, वियत् *n.*, व्योमन् *n.*, गगनं-णं, आकाशः-शं, अंबरं, अंतरि(री)क्षं, खं, नाकः, दिव् *f.*, द्यो *f.*, विहायस् *m. n.*, विहायसः, अभ्रं, पुष्करं, अनंतं, सुरवर्त्मन् *n.*, विष्णुपदं, तारापथः; 'roaming through the s.' नभश्चरः, खेचरः, &c.; 's.-

coloured' व्योम-नील-वर्ण ; 's.-lark' भ(भा)रद्वाज:; व्याघाट:; 's.-light' आकाशप्रकाश:; 's.-touching' अभ्रंलिह्-लिख्, नभोलिह्, व्योमस्पृश्, गगनचुंबिन्.

SLAB, *s.* शिला, शिलातलं-पट्ट:-फलक:.

SLABBER, *v. i.* लालायते (D.), लालां स्रु c.

SLACK, *a.* शिथिल, प्र-,श्लथ, स्रस्त, गलित. 2 मंद, अतीव्र, अतीक्ष्ण, प्रमत्त, अनवहित; *See* REMISS. -EN, *v.t.* शिथिलयति (D.), श्लथ् 10, शिथिली-श्लथी-कृ 8U, मंदीकृ; रथस्य मंदीकृतो वेग: (S. 1) 'I have s.-ed the speed' &c.; प्र-शम् c. (शमयति); 'will not s. (the bonds of) her love' न अनुरागं शिथिलयति (V. 2); 's. your pace a little' गतिवेगं किंचित् शिथिलय; 'who have s. ed their efforts' शिथिलितप्रयत्नाः, श्लथोद्यमा:. -*v. i.* शिथिली-श्लथी-भू, शिथिलायते (D.), मंदीभू; *See* RELAX. -ENED, *a.* शिथिलित, शांतवेग-रय. -LY, *adv.* शिथिलं, प्रमादत:, अनवधानेन. -NESS, *s.* शैथिल्यं, &c.

SLAKE, *v. t.* प्र-,शम् c. (शमयति), छिद् 7 P, (thirst). 2 जलेन संमिश्र् 10 or संसृज् 6 P. -*v. i.* प्र-,शम् 4 P.

SLAM, *v. t.* (Door) तीव्राघातेन पि-धा 3 U or बंध् 9 P.

SLANDER, *s.* अप-परि-वाद:, पैशुन्यं, पिशुनवचनं, अभि-, असूया, निर्वाद:; *See* SCANDAL. -*v. t.* परि-अप-वद् 1 A, असूयति (with dat.); अपभाष् 1 A, कलंकयति (D.), अभिशंस् 1 P; *See* DEFAME, LIBEL. 2 सूच् 10, उपजप् 1 P, कर्णे जप्. -ER, *s.* परि-अप-वादक:, अभि-,असूयक:, पिशुन:, सूचक:, कर्णेजप:, उपजापक:. -EROUS, *a.* पिशुन, साभ्यसूय, सपरिवाद, सापवाद, परिवाद-अपवाद-गर्भ, परिवादात्मक. -EROUSLY, *adv.* सापवादं, पिशुनं, सपरिवादं.

SLANG, *s.* प्रलाप:, अपभाषा, अश्लीलं,-भाषणं, खलोक्ति *f.*

SLANT,-ING, *a.* तिर्यंच्, वक्र, कुटिल, तिरश्चीन; अवसर्पिन्, प्रवण; 'striking s.-ly with the tusks' तिर्यग्दंतप्रहारिन्; 's. blow' तिर्यक्प्रहार:. -*v. t.* आवृज् 10, वक्रीकृ 8 U, प्रवणीकृ. -*v. i.* वक्रीभू, अवसृप् 1 P, प्रवणीभू, आनम् 1 P. -INGLY, *adv.* तिर्यक्, तिर:, साचि, तिरश्चीनं.

SLAP, *s.* चपेटिका, चपेट:, तल-चपेट-प्रहार:-आघात:, आस्फोटनं. -*v. t.* चपेटेन प्रह् 1 P or तड् 10 or आहन् 2 U, आस्फुट् c.

SLASH, *v. t.* दीर्घं छिद् 7 P or कृत् 6 P, व्यवच्छिद्, विनि-कृत्, क्षतविक्षतीकृ 8 U. -*s.* दीर्घ-महा-छेद:,महाक्षतं-ति *f.* -ING, *a.* दीर्घच्छेदकारिन्; (fig.) अरुंतुद, मर्मच्छिद्-भिद्, तीक्ष्ण; *See* SHARP.

SLATTERN, *s.* वेशप्रमत्ता, अपरिष्कृतवेशा.

SLAUGHTER, *v. t.* विशस् 1 P, हन् 2 P or c. (घातयति), व्या-पद् c., प्र-मी 9 U, आलभ् 1 A (beast); *See* KILL. -*s.* विशसनं, वैशसं, घातनं, प्रमाथ:, कंदनं, संहार:, प्रमापणं; *See* KILLING; 's.-house' सू(शू)ना, वध्यस्थानं, वधभूमि *f.*, घातस्थानं. -ER, *s.* घातक:, विशसितृ *m.*, सौ(शौ)निक:.

SLAVE, *s.* दास:, प्रेष्य:, चेट:, किंकर:, भृत्य:, दासेय:-र:, भुजिष्य:; *See* SERVANT; 'born a s.' गर्भदास:; 'domestic s.' गृहदास:; 'a female s.' दासी, चेटी, भुजिष्या; 's.-trade' दासविक्रय:; 's.-dealer' दासविक्रयी; (fig.) दास:, or ex. by वश, अधीन in comp.; 'a s. to carnal passions' इंद्रियसुखवशग:, विषयसुखाधीन:; 's. to love' कामपरवश:. -RY, *s.* दास्यं, दासत्वं, दासभाव:, दास्यवृत्ति *f.* -ISH, *a.* दासवत् *adv.*, दास in comp., दासोचित; *See* SERVILE.

SLAVER, *s.* *See* SALIVA.

SLAY, *v. t.* विशस् 1 P, हन् 2 P, व्या-पद् c., मृ c. -ER, *s.* घातक:, हंतृ *m.*, हन् in comp.; *See* KILL,-ER.

SLEDGE, *s.* अचक्रयानं.

SLEDGE-HAMMER, *s.* मुद्गर:, महाघन:.

SLEEK, *a.* मृदु, श्लक्ष्ण, स्निग्ध, सुखस्पर्श.

SLEEP, *v. i.* स्वप् 2 P, शी 2 A, संविश् 6 P, नि-द्रा 2 P, निद्रायते (D.); 'I also do not s. over this matter' मयाप्यस्मिन् वस्तुनि न शयानेन स्थीयते (Mu. 1). -*s.* निद्रा, स्वप्न:, स्वाप:, सुप्ति *f.*, शयनं, संवेश:; 'go to s.' निद्रां या 2 P; *See* (*v.*); 'fall into s.' निद्रया अभिभू pass. or आक्रम् pass.; 'he fell into a deep s.' गाढनिद्राभिभूत:-विधेय:-बभूव; 'death-s.' घोर-काल-निद्रा; 'roused from s.' विनिद्र, भग्ननिद्र, प्रबोधित. -ER, *s.* निद्रालु:, शयालु:, better by (*v.*). -ING, *s.* शयनं, निद्रा, &c.; 's.-house' शयनमंदिरं-गृहं. -*a.* निद्राण, शयित, शयान, सुप्त; 's. draught' निद्राकरमौषधं. -LESS, *a.* नष्टनिद्र, उन्निद्र, अ-वि-निद्र, निर्निद्र; 'passes s. nights' उन्निद्रा:-उत्सन्ननिद्रा:-क्षपा गमयति. -LESSNESS, *s.* निद्रानाश:, निर्निद्रता, निद्राभाव:. -Y, *a.* निद्रालु, शयालु, तंद्रालु, निद्राशील. 2 निद्राक्रांत, निद्रापर-वश-विधेय-अभिभूत-आकुल-ग्रस्त. 3 निद्राप्रद-जनन (नी *f.*), स्वापकर (री *f.*). 4 सुषुप्सु, शिशयिषु, शयनेच्छु; 'to feel s.' स्वप्-शी- desid.; 'I feel s.' निद्रयाऽपह्रिये-पराभूये, सुषुप्सामि.

SLEET, *s.* शीकर:, तुषार-शीकर-वर्ष:-आसार:.

SLEEVE, *s.* पिप्पल:; 'to laugh in one's s.' अंतर् हस् 1 P.

SLEIGHT, *s.* (Of hand) हस्तलाघवं-कौशलं, माया, इंद्रजालं.

SLENDER, *a.* प्र-,तनु, कृश, क्षीण, क्षाम; 'having a s. waist', 's.-waisted' क्षीण-तनु-मध्य-मध्यम, कृशोदर, मृग-सिंह-कटि-मध्य; 's.-waisted woman'

सुमध्यमा, कृशोदरी, तनुमध्या, वेदिविलग्नमध्या. 2 अल्प, क्षुद्र, लघु, तनु; 'possessed of s. means' क्षीणविभव. -NESS, *s.* तनुता, कृशता, कार्श्यं, तानवं, अल्पता.

SLICE, *s.* खंडः-डं, शकलः-लं, छेदः, भागः, लवः. -*v. t.* खंड् 10, छिद् 7 P, खंडशः छिद्.

SLIDE, *v. i.* अव-वि-सृप् 1 P; 's. up and down' आरोहावरोहं कृ 8 U. 2 च्यु 1 A, स्खल् 1 P, भ्रंश् 1 A, 4 P. -ING, *s.* विसर्पः, अवसर्पणं, स्खलनं.

SLIGHT, *a.* सु-,अल्प, स्तोक, क्षुद्र, तनु, लघु, ईषत् in comp.; 'a s. blow' लघुप्रहारः, ईषदाघातः; 'in a s. degree' ईषत्, किंचित्, मनाक्, स्तोकं, कियत्; 'not in the s. est degree' न मनागपि-किंचिदपि-स्तोकमपि. -*v. t.* उपेक्ष् 1 A, अवधीर् 10, अव-ज्ञा 9 U, तृणीकृ 8 U, तृणाय मन् 4 A, अवमन् 4 A, अवगण् 10; *See* CONTEMN. -*s.* उपेक्षा, अवधीरणं-णा, अवज्ञा, अवमानः, अनादरः, अवगणनं-ना. -ER, *s.* उपेक्षकः, मंदादरः. -ING, *a.* सावज्ञ, अनादरपूर्वक, सावमान. -INGLY, *adv.* सोपेक्षं, अनादरेण. -LY, *adv.* ईषत्, मनाक्, किंचित्, स्तोकं, अल्पमात्रं, by आ pr.; 's. blue' आनील, ईषन्नील.

SLIM, *a. See* SLENDER.

SLIME, *s.* पंकः, श्यानकर्दमः, सांद्र-श्यान-पंकः. -Y, *a.* श्यान, पंकिल, चिक्कण, सांद्र.

SLING, *s.* क्षेपणः, भिंदि(द)पालः, गोफणा. 2 दोला, काचः, शिक्यं, भारयष्टि *f.* -*v. t.* क्षेपणेन क्षिप् 6 P or प्रास् 4 P. 2 उद्-बंध् 9 P, काचयति-आंदोलयति (D.).

SLINK, *v. i.* अलक्षितं-निभृतं-अपया 2 P or अपगम् 1 P or अपसृप् 1 P or अपक्रम् 1 U, 4 P, छलेन अप-या, &c.

SLIP, *v. i.* प्र-,स्खल् 1 P, (fig. also); वचनानि स्खलयन् पदे पदे (K. IV. 12) 'making their words s.' &c.; चल् 1 P. 2 सहसा-अलक्षितं-अज्ञानतः-निर्गम् 1 P or अपसृप् 1 P. 3 (Off) च्यु 1 A, प्र-,भ्रंश् 1 A, 4 P, स्रंस् 1 A, निर्-,गल् 1 P, पत् 1 P; 's. away' अप-या 2 P, अपसृप्-गम्; *See* SLINK; 's. in' अलक्षितं आ-प्र-विश् 6 P; 'let s. an opportunity' अवसरं-समयं न ग्रह् 9 P or अवक्षिप् 6 P. -*v. t.* अलक्षितं नि-धा 3 U or प्र-नि-विश् c. 2 वि-,मुच् 6 P, क्षिप्, भ्रंश् c.; अवगण् 10, उपेक्ष् 1 A, च्यु c., त्यज् 1 P, *See* NEGLECT. 3 शिथिलीकृ 8 U, स्रंस् c., शिथिलयति (D.); *See* LOOSE. -*s.* स्खलनं, स्खलितं, (fig. also); 's. as to names' गोत्रस्खलितं; प्र-,भ्रंशः, च्युति *f.*, पतनं. 2 दोषः, प्रमादः, अपराधः, भ्रमः, स्खलितं. 3 विटपः, शाखा, पल्लवः, कांडः. 4 खंडः-डं. -PERY, *a.* पिच्छिल, मेदुर, चिक्कण, स्निग्ध, श्लक्ष्ण; 's. ground' निपत्या, पिच्छिलभूमिः. 2 अस्थिर, चल, लोल, तरल, अनवस्थित, चपल, चंचल; *See* FICKLE.

SLIPPER, *s.* (लघु) पादुका, पादत्रं, उपानह् *f.*

SLIT, *s.* दीर्घच्छेदः-वेधः-छिद्रं.

SLOBBER, *v. i.* लालां स्रु c.

SLOP, *s.* (S. 8) अधोंशुकं, अधोवसनं. 2 अमेध्यं-अपवित्र-जलं, मलिनं-समलं-जलं. 3 कर्दमः, पंकः. -*v. t.* इतस्ततः प्रमादात् पत् c. or क्षिप् 6 P. -PY, *a.* पंकिल, अनूप, सकर्दम.

SLOPE, *v. i.* अवसृ 1 P, प्रवणीभू 1 P, क्रमशः निम्नीभू. -*v. t.* आवृज् 10, प्रवणीकृ 8 U. -*s.* प्रावण्यं; प्रवणभूमिः, अवसर्पिणी भूमिः; क्रमशः निम्नता. 2 (Of a mountain) नितंबः, उत्संगः, कटकः-कं; 'mountain s.' गिरिनितंबः; अवसर्पिणी भूः. -ING, *a.* प्रवण, अवसर्पिन्, क्रमशः निम्न, पातुक.

SLOTH, *s.* तंद्रा, आलस्यं, तंद्रि-द्री *f.*, तंद्रिका, कार्यविमुखता. -FUL, *a.* अलस, तंद्रिल, तंद्रालु; *See* LAZY.

SLOUCH, *v. i.* अलसं चल् or गम् 1 P. -ING, *a.* प्रलंब, निम्न.

SLOUGH, *s.* निर्मोकः, कंचुकः, अहि-भुजंग-त्वच् *f.* 2 महापंकः, पंकिलस्थानं, पंकाढ्यस्थलं.

SLOVENLY, *a.* मलिन, अव्यवस्थित; अविनीत, अपरिष्कृत, अविनीत-अपरिष्कृत-वेश. -INESS, *s.* अव्यवस्था, अपरिष्कारः, मालिन्यं.

SLOW, *a.* मंद, (in all senses); मंदाग्निः, मंदगतिः, मंदमतिः, मंदविषं, &c.; मंदगति-गामिन्, अद्रुत; अक्षिप्र, अशीघ्र; मंथर; 'a mind s. to discriminate' मंथरविवेकं चेतः; 's. in recognizing' प्रत्यभिज्ञानमंथर (S. 4). 2 विलंबित; कालातीत, अतीतसमय; *See* LATE. 3 मंदमति-धी-बुद्धि, जड-स्थूल-बुद्धि-मति, &c.; *See* DULL. 4 दीर्घसूत्र-त्रिन्, चिरक्रिय; 's. time' विलंबितवृत्ति *f.*; 's. fever' जीर्णज्वरः. -LY, *adv.* मंदं, मंदं मंदं, मंथरं; शनैः, शनैः शनैः, अशीघ्रं, अद्रुतं, विलंबेन. -NESS, *s.* मांद्यं, मंदता; विलंबः, दीर्घसूत्रता, &c.

SLUGGARD, *s.* मंदः, अलसः, जडः, तुंदपरिमृजः, शीतकः, आलस्यशीलः, तंद्रालुः, स्थूल-जड-मतिः. —SLUGGISH, *a.* मंद, अलस, तंद्रालु, मंदगति, आलस्यशील; *See* DULL. -LY, *adv.* मंदं, अलसवत्. -NESS, *s.* मांद्यं, आलस्यं, तंद्रा, जाड्यं.

SLUICE, *s.* (जल-) प्रवाहः, प्रपातः. 2 द्वारं, परि(री)-वाहः, जलनिर्गमः.

SLUMBER, *v. i.* प्र-,स्वप् 2 P; अनिर्भरं स्वप्; (fig.) अनुपयुक्त-अव्यापृत-*a.* स्था or भू 1 P. -*s.* लघु-अल्प-अगाढ-निद्रा.

SLUR, *s.* कलंकः, दूषणं, अकीर्तिचिह्नं. -*v. t.* 'cast a s. on' कलंकयति-मलिनयति-(D.), मलिनीकृ 8 U, दुष् c. (दूषयति). 2 प्र-,छद् 10, गुह् 1 U.

SLUSH, *s.* कर्दमः, सजलपंकः.

SLUT, *s.* बंधकी, अविनीता, पुंश्चली; *See* PROSTITUTE. -TISH, *a.* अविनीत, अपरिष्कृतवेश.

SLY, *a.* धूर्त, कितव, कापटिक-छाद्मिक (की *f.*), समाय,

सव्याज, वंचन-कपट-पटु. 2 चतुर, विदग्ध; 's. laugh' अंतर्हासः. -LY, *adv.* चतुरं, धूर्ततया, वैदग्ध्येन, सव्याजं, समायं. 2 निभृतं, अलक्षितं. -NESS, *s.* व्याजः, छलं, छद्मन् *n.*, कापट्यं, माया, धूर्तता, वैदग्ध्यं, चातुर्यं.

SMACK, *v. t.* Ex. by गंध, स्वाद in comp.; आ-अव-भास् 1 A; *See* SAVOUR. -*v. t.* आ-,स्फुट् c.; आस्फल् c. 2 सशब्दं चुंब् 1 P. -*s.* आ-,स्वादः, रसः, गंधः. 2 आस्फोटनं, आस्फालनं; चपेटाघातः. 3 सशब्द-चुंबनं.

SMALL, *a.* अल्प, स्तोक, (of quantity). 2 लघु, तनु, अणु, क्षुद्र; अल्प-क्षुद्र-तनु, अल्पशरीर, अगुरु, अबृहत्, अमहत्; oft. ex. by क affixed; *See* LITTLE; 's. tree' वृक्षकः; 's. boy' बालकः &c. 3 (Voice) नीच, अगुरु; 's.-pox' मसूरी-रिका, विस्फोटकः; शीतला, वसंतरोगः (modern names).

SMART, *a.* तीक्ष्णमति, कुशाग्रबुद्धि, प्रदीप्तप्रज्ञ, चतुर; विदग्ध. 2 तीव्र, तीक्ष्ण, शीघ्र, द्रुत, लघु; आशु-शीघ्रकारिन्. 3 (Speech &c.) सरस, मार्मिक (की *f.*), रसिक, रसगर्भ. 4 शोभन, सुवेश, प्रफुल्ल, सु pr. 5 (Pain &c.) तीव्र, तीक्ष्ण, उग्र, दुर्विषह; वेगवत्. -*s.* तीव्रवेदना, तीक्ष्णव्यथा-वेदना; शूलः-लं. -*v. i.* व्यथ् 1 A, तप् pass., तीक्ष्णव्यथां अनुभू 1 P; 'I am s.ing under the defeat' पराभवो मम हृदि प्रत्युप्तं शल्यमिव; न्यक्कारो हृदि वज्रकील इव मे तीव्रं परिस्पंदते (Vi. 5). -LY, *adv.* तीक्ष्णं, तीव्रं, शीघ्रं, द्रुतं; लाघवेन, शोभनं, सु pr. -NESS, *s.* तीव्रता, तीक्ष्णता; शीघ्रमतित्वं, मार्मिकता, सरसता; शोभा, &c.

SMASH, *v. t.* चूर्ण् 10, वि-,मृद् 9 P, निष्पिष् 7 P, भंज् 7 P, प्रमंथ् 9 P, निर्दल् c. (दलयति); *See* BREAK. -*s.* प्रमाथः, निर्दलनं, विमर्दः, चूर्णनं, निष्पेषः-षणं.

SMATTERER, *s.* चुंबकः, पल्लवग्राहिपंडितः. -SMATTERING, *s.* पल्लवग्राहि पांडित्यं; oft. ex. by किंचित्, अल्पमात्र; 's. of knowledge' अत्यल्पं ज्ञानं.

SMEAR, *v. t.* लिप् 6 P, वि-प्र-आ-अव-°, अभि-,अंज् 7 P or c., दिह् 2 U. -ING, *s.* लेपः-पनं, अंजनं.

SMELL, *s.* घ्राणं; 'sense of s.' घ्राणेंद्रियं, घ्राणशक्ति *f.*, गंधग्रहणशक्तिः. 2 आ-,घ्राणं, गंधग्रहणं. 3 गंधः, वासः, आमोदः; *See* ODOUR, FRAGRANCE. -*v. t.* घ्रा 1 P, आ-उपा-° -*v. i.* Ex. by गंध in comp. or सगंध-तुल्यगंध- *a.*; 's.ing of honey' मधुगंधि; 's.ing like fat' वसागंधि; 'the flower s.s sweet' मधुरोस्य कुसुमस्य गंधः; 'it s.s of smoke' धूमसगंधमेतत्. -ING, *a.* गंधग्राहिन्. 2 गंधयुत, सगंध, वासयुक्त.

SMELT, *v. t.* वि-ली c., वि-द्रु c. -ER, *s.* लोहद्रावकः; लोहकारः.

SMILE, *v. i.* स्मि 1 A, मंदं विहस् 1 P, ईषद् हस्, मंदस्मितं-मंदहास्यं-कृ 8 U; 's. on' अनुग्रह् 9 P; प्र-सद् 1 P, प्रसन्न-कृपार्द्रदृष्टि- *a.* भू (with loc.); 'fortune s. s on you' भाग्यशाली भवान्. -*s.* स्मितं, मंदहासः-हास्यं-स्मितं, विहसितं, विहसनं; 'speaking with a s.' स्मितपूर्वाभिभाषिन्; 'with a s.' सस्मितं. -ING, *a.* स्मेर, सस्मित, स्मयमान, प्रसन्न, प्रफुल्ल; 's. sweetly' शुचिस्मित, चारुहासिन्; 'a s. countenance' स्मेर-हास्य-मुखं, प्रसन्न-प्रफुल्ल-वदनं. -INGLY, *adv.* सस्मितं, विहस्य.

SMIRCH, *v. t.* मलिनीकृ 8 U.

SMIRK, *s.* विकृतहासः, विलक्षस्मितं. -*v. i.* कृ 8 U with (*s.*).

SMITE, *v. t.* हन् 2 P, प्र-हृ 1 P, तड् 10, नि-अप-कृ 8 U, तुद् 6 P; व्यथ् 4 P; 's.en with anxiety' संप्रहृष्टमुत्कंठया (S. 4); 's.en by love' मदनबाणहत, कामोपहत, कामार्त, मदनसंतप्त, अनंगपीडित. 2 हन्, मृ c., सूद् 10; *See* KILL. -ER, *s.* हंता, सूदनः, घातकः.

SMITH, *s.* शिल्पिन् *m.*, कारः in comp.; 'iron. s.' लोहकारः, अयस्कारः; स्वर्णकारः, &c. -ERY,-Y, *s.* शिल्प-कर्म-शाला, लोहकारशाला.

SMOCK, *s.* (स्थूल) शाटकः, अधोवसनं.

SMOKE, *s.* धूमः-मिका, धूपः-पिका; 'a quantity of s.' धूम्या; 'cloud of s.' धूमपटलं-ओघः. -*v. t.* (धूमनालीं) पा 1 P, सेव् 1 A. 2 धूमेन शुध् c. or शुचं c., धूप् 1 P, 10, धूमयति-धूपयति (D.). -*v. i.* धूमायते (D.), धूमं उत्क्षिप् 6 P or उद्-गॄ 6 P or निः-सृ c. or उत्सृज् 6 P; 's. ing food' धूमं विसृजत् (मोष्णं) अन्नं. 2 धूमनालीं पा. -ER, *s* धूमपाः, धूमपायिन्-सेविन् *m.* -ING, *s.* धूमपानं. 2 धूमोत्क्षेपः-पणं. -LESS, *a.* निर्धूम, धूमहीन-रहित. -Y, *a.* सधूम, धूमावरुद्ध, धूमबहुल. 2 धूम्र, धूमाभ, धूमल, धूमाकार. 3 धूमगंध-स्वाद.

SMOOTH, *a.* सम; श्लक्ष्ण, मृदु (fig. also); स्निग्ध, मसृण, अरूक्ष; अपरुष, अकटु, अकर्कश (sound); 'by s. words' श्लक्ष्णया गिरा, सान्त्ववादेन, मृदुभिर्वचोभिः; 'by s. remedies' सामोपायैः. 2 धारावाहिन्, विसारिन्, सततप्रवाहिन्; निरुपद्रव, निर्विघ्न, निरंतराय, निर्बाध, (business &c.); शांत, अक्षुब्ध, प्रसन्न, अनुत्तरंग, निर्वात (water). -*v. t.* समीकृ 8 U, श्लक्ष्णीकृ. 2 अविघ्न- *a.* &c. कृ, निर्विघ्नीकृ. -LY, *adv.* सुखेन, निर्विघ्नं, निरंतरायं, अनायासेन. -NESS, *s.* श्लक्ष्णता, स्निग्धता, मृदुता, अक्षोभः, प्रसादः, &c.

SMOTHER, *v. t.* श्वासं अव-नि-रुध् 7 U, श्वासावरोधं कृ 8 U. 2 प्रति-,स्तंभ् 9 P, निग्रह् 9 P, नियंत्र् 10, नियम् 1 P -ED, *a.* रुद्धश्वास-प्राण.

SMOULDER, *v. i.* अंतर् ज्वल् 1 P or स्फुर् 6 P or दह् pass., better by 's. ing'; 'just as a s.-ing tree bursts into flame' अंतःप्रसुप्तदहनो ज्वलतीव वनस्पतिः (U. 4). -ING, *a.* अंतर्दाहिन्-ज्वालिन्, गूढदाहवत्, प्रसुप्तदहन.

SMUGGLE, *v. i.* प्रतिषिद्धानि भांडानि आह् 1 P or आनी 1 P.

SMUT, *s.* मसी, मलं. 2 अश्लीलवाच् *f.*, दुरुक्तं, दुर्वचनं. –*v. t.*, SMUTCH, *v. t.* मलिनीकृ 8 U, मलीमसीकृ, मलिनयति (D.). –TY, *a.* मलिन, मलीमस. 2 अश्लील, दुरुक्त, अवाच्य.

SNACK, *s. See* SHARE, REPAST.

SNAFFLE, *s.* लघुवल्गा.

SNAIL, *s.* शंबूकः, कोष-कवच-स्थः. 2 मंथरः.

SNAKE, *s.* सर्पः, भुजगः, भुजंगः-गमः, पन्नगः, अहिः, नागः, उरगः, उरंगमः, विषधरः, भोगी, व्यालः, आशीविषः, फणी, दर्वीकरः, जिह्मगः, पवनाशनः, कुंभीनसः, दंदशूकः, चक्री, द्विजिह्वः, द्विरसनः, सरीसृपः, कुंडली, गूढपाद्, चक्षुःश्रवस्, काकोदरः, दीर्घपृष्ठः, बिलेशयः; ‘hooded s.’ फणभृत्, भोगधरः, भोगी ; ‘s. without poison’ राजि(जी)लः, डुंडुभः ; ‘s. with a spotted skin’ मालुधानः, मातुलाहिः ; चित्रसर्पः ; ‘that has cast off his slough’ निर्मुक्तः, मुक्तकंचुकः ; ‘his venom’ क्ष्वेडः, गरलं, विषं ; ‘his hood’ स्फटा, फटा, फणा, स्फोटा, दर्वी ; ‘charmer of s. s’ अ(आ)हितुंडिकः, व्यालग्राही. –Y, *a.* (*s.*) in comp.; आहेय (यी *f.*).

SNAP, *v. t.* (अकस्मात्) त्रुट् c., भंज् 7 P, खंड् 10, छिद् 7 P. 2 आ-,स्फल् c., सहसा ग्रह् 9 P or उद्-हृ 1 P. 3 अकस्मात् दंश् 1 P; ‘s. the fingers’ अंगुली स्फुट् c., छोटिकां दा 3 U or कृ 8 U. –*v. i.* (सहसा) त्रुट् 4, 6 P, दल् 1 P, स्फुट् 6 P, भंज्-भिद्-pass. 2 क्रण् 1 P. 3 भष् 1 P. 4 दंश् 1 P, दंतैः ग्रह् 9 P. –*s.*,–PING, *s.* त्रोटनं, आस्फालनं, आस्फोटनं, आकस्मिकभंगः. 2 छोटिका, त्रुकु(चु)टी, अंगुलिभंगः. 3 आकस्मिकदंशः. –PISH, *a.* दंशनशील, दिदंक्षु. 2 कर्कश, परुष, दुःशील, कुक्कुरस्वभाव.

SNARE, *s.* पाशः, वागुरा, जालं ; ‘take in a s.’ जाले बंध् 9 P ; (fig.) उन्मार्गेण-अपथेन-प्रवृत् c. or गम् c. (गमयति). –*v. t.* पाशे पत् c., पातयित्वा बंध् 9 P, पाशीकृ 8 U, जाले बंध्.

SNARL, *v. i.* भष् 1 P, रै 1 P; गर्ज् 1 P. 2 परुषं-कर्कशं-वद् 1 P. –ER, *s.* भषकः, कर्कशः, श्वशीलः-स्वभावः.

SNATCH, *v. t.* (away) आच्छिद् 7 P, (कृपाणपातविषयात् आछिदतः प्रेयसीं Mal. 5); आक्षिप्य ग्रह् 9 P, झटिति ग्रह् or कृष् 1 P or हृ 1 P or धृ 1 P, 10 or आ-कल् 10 (कलयति). –at, ग्रहीतुं प्रवृत् 1 A, सवेगं ग्रह् desid. (जिघृक्षति). –off, अपहृ, मुष् 9 P, चुर् 10. –out, उत्-कृष्, निर्हृ, उद्धृ, उन्मूल् 10, वि-उत्-पट् 10. –up, उत्क्षिप् 6 P, (उत्क्षिप्यैनां ज्योतिरेकं जगाम S. 5). –*s.*,–ING, *s.* आकस्मिकग्रहणं-धरणं; आच्छेदः, सहसा आकलनं. 2 अल्पांतरं, अल्पावकाशः. 3 क्षण-आकस्मिक-प्रवृत्ति *f.*; ‘by s. es’ खंडशः; ‘s. es of moonlight’ कादाचित्कः चंद्रप्रकाशः. –ING, *a.* लोलुप, गृध्नु ; *See* GREEDY.

SNEAK, *v. i. See* SLINK. –ING, *a.* कुत्सितवृत्ति, अधम, कापुरुषवृत्ति; *See* MEAN.

SNEER, *v. i.* (at) अव-उप-हस् 1 P (with acc.), सहासं अवज्ञां सूच् 10; अव-ज्ञा 9 U, अवमन् 4 A; *See* DERIDE. –*s.* अव-उप-हासः ; अवज्ञाहासः. –INGLY, *adv.* सोपहासं, सावज्ञं.

SNEEZE, *v. i.* क्षु 2 P, कृ 8 U with (*s*). –*s.*, –ING, *s.* क्षुतं, क्षवः, क्षवथुः, क्षुत् *f.*, हंजिः, छिक्का.

SNICKER, SNIGGER, *v. i.* अंतर् हस् 1 P.

SNIFF, *v. t.* नासाद्वारेण निश्वस् 2 P.

SNIP, *v. t.* अग्रभाग-अग्रं-लू 9 U; *See* NIP.

SNIPE, *s.* दीर्घचंचुः. 2 Fool, q. v.

SNIVEL, *s.* नासामलं, सिंहा(घा)णं-नं. –*v. i.* मलं स्रु c.; ‘he s. s’ तस्य नसः मलं स्रवति.

SNOB, *s.* सभ्यंमन्यः, भद्रमानिन् *m.*

SNOOZE, *See* NAP.

SNORE, *v. t.* घर्घरायते (D.), घर्घररवं कृ 8 U. –ING, *s.* घर्घरः, घर्घररवः, क्रथनं.

SNORT, *s.* फू(फु)त्कारः. –*v. i.* फूत्कृ 8 U, फुत्कारं मुच् 6 P.

SNOT, *See* SNIVEL.

SNOUT, *s.* प्रोथः, नासा, पोत्रं.

SNOW, *s.* हिमं, तुषारः, तुहिनं, प्रालेयं, अवश्यायः, नीहारः, मिहिका ; ‘flow of s.’ तुषारस्रुति *f.*, हिमनिष्यंदः ; ‘s.-drift’, ‘mass of s.’ हिमानी, हिमसंहति *f.*, हिमराशिः ; ‘s.-capped’ हिमावृतशिखर; ‘s.-storm’ हिमवर्षः-संपातः. –*v. i.* हिमं वृष् 1 P, हिमकणान् मुच् 6 P. –Y, *a.* हिमवत्, हैम (मी *f.*) ; तुषार-हिम-मय (यी *f.*), हिमावृत, (*s.*) in comp. ; ‘s. mountain’ हिमाद्रिः, तुहिनाचलः, &c. 2 हिमाभ, हिमवर्ण.

SNUB, *v. t.* पराभू 1 P, अधिक्षिप् 6 P;; प्रत्यादिश् 6 P, अधरीकृ 8 U, अपकृष् 1 P, वाचं रुध् 7 U; ‘s. nose’ चिपिटनासा, नतनासिका ; ‘s.-nosed’ अवटीट, अवनाट, अवभ्रट, नतनासिक, चिपिट.

SNUFF, *s.* नस्यं, नासाचूर्णं, क्षुत्करी ; ‘s.-box’ नस्यधानी, नस्याधारः. 2 दग्धवर्ति *f.* -तूला, छत्रं. –*v. t.* निश्वस् 2 P, अंतर् ग्रह् 9 P. 2 दग्धवर्तिं अवच्छिद् 7 P, छत्रं अपनी 1 P ; ‘s. out’ निर्वा c.; *See* EXTINGUISH. –ERS, *s.* वर्तिकर्तनी-छेदनी. –Y, *a.* नस्यदूषित-मलिन.

SNUFFLE, *See* SNORT.

SNUG, *a.* सु-,संहत, सु-,प्रच्छन्न, सुगुप्त, आवृत, सुगूढ, सुसंश्लिष्ट, सुरक्षित. 2 सुखावह, हितकर (री *f.*), सुस्थ, सुस्थित, सुख, स्वस्थ. 3 निकटशायिन्. –LY, *adv.* सुखेन, यथासुखं; सुसंहतं, सुसंश्लिष्टं, सुगुप्तं. –SNUGGLE, *v. i.* निकटे-पार्श्वतः-शी 2 A.

So, *adv.* तथा, एवं, तद्वत्, एवंविधं; इति, इत्थं. 2 ईदृक्, एतावत्, इयत्, तथा, एतादृशं. 3 तत्, तेन, तस्मात्, ततः 'as—s.' यथा-तथा; 's.-that' तथा-यथा; 's. and so' अमुक (की *f.*); मया अमुकसूनुना लिखितं अमुकेन (Y. II. 88) 'written by me s. and s., the son of s. and s.'; 's.-called' नाम, नामन् in comp.; 's. far' एतावत्, एतदवधि; एतावत्पर्यंतं; 's. far as' तावत्, oft. ex. by इति; *See* As; 's. forth' इत्यादि, एवमादि; 's. long' एतावत्कालं यावत्, इयतो दिवसान्, इयंतं कालं; 's. long as' यावत्-तावत्; 's. many' इयत्, एतावत्; 'as many' 's. many' यावत्-तावत्; 's. much' (*adv.*) तादृक्, ईदृक्, तथा; (*a.*) एतावत् इयत्; 's. that' येन, यथा; 's. then' एवं तर्हि, एतावता, एवं च; 's. much as' अपि, अपि तावत्; 'could not s. much as wet the tip of his bill' चंच्वग्रमपि तावत् जलक्लिन्नं कर्तुं नाशकत्.

Soak, *v. t.* (चिरं) मस्ज् c. (मज्जयति), जलेन सिच् 6 P, क्लिद् c., आ-द्रु c., अभ्युक्ष् 1 P. -ed, *a.* जलसिक्त-क्लिन्न, अभ्युक्षित.

Soap, *s.* मार्जनलेपः; perhaps अरिष्टः, फेनिलः (s.-berry plant). -y, *a.* चिक्कण, स्निग्ध.

Soar, *v. i.* उत्पत्-उद्भ्रम् 1 P, उड्डी 1 A, ऊर्ध्वं विसृप् 1 P or डी; 'the aspirations of the great s. high' उत्सर्पिणी महतां प्रार्थना (S. 7); 'high-s. ing hope' दूराधिरोहिणी आशा (S. 5) -er, *s.* उड्डयनकृत् *m.* -ing, *s.* ऊर्ध्वगमनं, उड्डयनं, ऊर्ध्वारोहणं, दूराधिरोहणं.

Sob, *v. i.* सगद्गदं रुद् 2 P or क्रंद् 1 P, फु(फू)-त्कृ 8 U. -bing, *s.* फु(फू)त्कारः, गद्गदः, सगद्गदाक्रंदनं. -bingly, *adv.* सगद्गदं, गद्गदगिरा.

Sober, *a.* शांत, धीर, गंभीर, स्थिर, स्थिरमति-बुद्धि, विचारशील. 2 अमत्त, अक्षीव, निर्मद. 3 (In drinking) पानाप्रसक्त, पानसंयमिन्, अनतिपायिन्. 4 मित, परिमित, नियत, समर्याद. -*v. t.* निर्मदीकृ 8 U, स्थिरीकृ, मदं अपनी 1 P, स्थैर्यं आ-पद् c. -ed, *a.* विगतमद, निर्मद, नष्टमद. -ly, *adv.* धीरवत्, गंभीरं, शांतचेतसा, विचारपूर्वं; सविवेकं. -ness, Sobriety, *s.* धीरता, गांभीर्यं, स्थैर्यं, विचारशीलता, सुविचारः; शांति *f.*, अनुद्वेगः, अरभसः. 2 अमत्तता, मदाभावः. 3 संयमः, निग्रहः, पानाप्रसक्ति *f.*, मितपानं.

Sobriquet, *s.* उपाधिः, उपनामन् *n.*

Sociable, *a.* संगमप्रिय, संसर्गप्रिय-शील, जनसंगशील, संवासप्रिय-शील. 2 सुजन, मधुरालाप, सुशील, संलापप्रिय, स्नेहबुद्धि. -ness, Sociability, *s.* संसर्गशीलता, जनसंगमप्रीति *f.*; सौजन्यं, सुशीलं, संलापप्रियता-शीलता.

Society, *s.* संगमः, संगः, संसर्गः, समागमः, सहवासः, संगति *f.*, संवासः, साहचर्यं. 2 श्रेणी, संघः. 3 समाजः, लोक-जन-समूहः-संघः, पंक्ति *f.*, सभा, संसद्-परिषद् *f.*; 'admissible into s.' पांक्तेय, पांक्त्य, सभ्य. -Social, *a.* सामाजिक, सांसर्गिक (की *f.*); oft. ex. by (s.) in comp.; 's. interest' समाजहितं; 's. intercourse' अन्योन्यसंघट्टनं, परस्परसंसर्गः-व्यवहारः. 2 Sociable, q. v. 3 संसर्ग-संगम-रूप-आत्मक.

Sock, *s.* पादत्रं, (और्ण) पादत्राणं.

Socket, *s.* आधारः, पात्रं, भाजनं.

Sod, *s.* शाद्वलं, तृणावृतभूभागः.

Sodomy, *s.* पुंमैथुनं, पुरुषमेहः, पायु-गुद-मैथुनं. -Sodomite, *s.* पुरुषमेहिन् *m.*, गुदमैथुनकृत्.

Sofa, *s.* पर्यंकः, मंचः, शय्या, शयनं, आसनं.

Soft, *a.* मृदु (in all senses); प्रकृत्या मृदुः, मृदुगीः, मृदु पुष्पं, मृदुरुपायः &c.; 'even red-hot iron becomes s.' अभितप्तमयोपि मार्दवं भजते (R. VIII. 43); 'neither very severe nor very s.' न खरो न च भूयसा मृदुः (R. VIII. 9); कोमल, मृदुल, पेलव, सुकुमार, अप्रखर, अपरुष, अकठोर, अनुग्र, अकठिन, अकर्कश, सौम्य (disposition). 2 स्निग्ध, श्लक्ष्ण, मसृण, मृदु-सुख-स्पर्श; अशिथिल, अदृढ, अघन; (voice) मधुर, मृदु, मंजुल; (in mind) सुप्रतार्य, अल्पबुद्धि, बालिश. -*interj.* तूष्णीं भव, तूष्णीं, शांतं, नीचैः. -en, *v. t.* मृदूकृ 8 U, कृ with (*a.*); (with pity) दयार्द्रीकृ, वि-,द्रु c., करुणया द्रु c. 2 शम् c. (शमयति), प्र-,उप-°, सांत्व् 10, लघूकृ, लघयति (D.); *See* Alleviate. -*v. i.* मार्दवं भज् 1 A, भू 1 P with (*a.*); मृदूभू, दयार्द्रीभू; प्र-,शम् 4 P; *See* Melt. -ening, *a.* शांतिद, शांतिकर (री *f.*). शमक-न. -ly, *adv.* मृदु, कोमलं, समार्दवं, &c. 2 लघुगत्या, चपलं. 3 निःशब्दं, निभृतं, मंदं, शनैः, शनैः शनैः. -ness, *s.* म्रदिमन् *m.*, मार्दवं, सौकुमार्यं, कोमलता, शैथिल्यं, मसृणता, माधुर्यं, &c.

So-ho, *interj.* हंहो, भो भोः.

Soil, *s.* भूः, भूमि *f.*, प्र-,देशः, स्थलं-ली; (earth) मृद् *f.*, मृत्तिका; 'native s.' जन्मभूमिः; 'fertile s.' उर्वरा, सर्वसस्याढ्या; 'dry s.' मरुः, धन्वन् *m.*; 'barren and salt s.' ई(इ)रिणं; 'waste s.' खिलं, अप्रहतभूमिः; 'stony s.' शर्करिलभूमिः. 2 मलः-लं, कल्कं. कलुषं, किट्टं, कलंकः. -*v. t.* मलिनीकृ 8 U, कलुषयति-मलिनयाति-कलंकयति (D.), दुष् c. (दूषयति). -ed, *a.* मलिनित; कलुषित, &c.; कल्किन्, मलिन, समल, लिप्त.

Sojourn, *v. i.* अव-स्था 1 A, स्वल्पकालं निवस् 1 P, प्रवस्, देशांतरं अधि-आ-वस्, प्रवासं-यात्रां-कृ 8 U. -*s.*, -ing, *s.* अवस्थानं, अवस्थिति *f.*, यात्रा, प्रवासः, अल्पकालनिवासः; 'the s. of life' संसारवृत्तिः, संसारयात्रा. -er, *s.* आगंतुकः, अवस्थायिन् *m.*, प्रवासी, यात्रिकः, परदेशसेवी.

Solace, *v. t.* सां(शां)त्व् 10, आ-समा-श्वस् c.; प-

रितुष् c.; (oneself) विनुद् c., वि-हृ 1 P. —s. सांत्वनं-ना, आश्वासनं, विनोदः-दनं, क्लेश-शोक-शांति *f.*-अपहरणं; *See* COMFORT, CONSOLE.

SOLAR, *a.* सौर (री *f.*), सावन (नी *f.*); सूर्य, अर्क (Sun, q. v.) in comp.; 's. heat' सूर्यातपः; सूर्यवंशः, सूर्यग्रहणं, अर्कबिंबं, &c.

SOLDER, *v. t.* सं-धा 3 U. —*s.* संधिः, धातुलेपः.

SOLDIER, *s.* सैनिकः, योधः, भटः, आयुधिकः, योद्धा, शस्त्र-अस्त्र-धरः-भृत्-जीवी-आजीवः, शस्त्र-युद्ध-उपजीवी. —LIKE,-LY, *a.* सैनिकवत्, सैनिक इव, सैनिकयोग्य. 2 शूर, विक्रांत; *See* BRAVE. —Y, *s.* सेना, बलं, सैन्यं, योध-सैनिक-समूहः, भटगणः.

SOLE, *a.* एक with एव; एकाकिन्, केवल. —*s.* तलं, पादतलं; (of shoe) पादुकातलं. —LY, *adv.* एक-*a.* with एव or simply एव; केवलं.

SOLECISM, *s.* संस्कारच्युति *f.*; अपप्रयोगः, अशुद्धप्रयोगः, म्लेच्छितं.

SOLEMN, *a.* पुण्य, पवित्र; विधिपूर्व, संस्कारसहित, धर्मसंस्कारयुक्त. 2 गुरु, गंभीर, धीर, उदात्त; (occasion) अलघु, गुर्वर्थ; oft. ex. by उत्सव in comp.; 's. occasions' उत्सवदिवसाः; 's. procession' यात्रोत्सवः. 3 दृढ, दृढप्रतिज्ञापूर्व, सुनिश्चय, स्थिरनिश्चयात्मक; 'a s. promise' दृढप्रतिज्ञा. —ITY,-NESS, *s.* क्रिया, संस्कारः, धर्म-पुण्य-क्रिया, विधिः, उत्सवः. 2 गांभीर्यं; गुरुत्वं, गौरवं. 3 आडंबरः. —IZE, *v. t.* यथाविधि अनु-ष्ठा 1 P or सं-पद् c., यथाशास्त्रं निर्वह् c. 2 गौरवं उत्पद् c. or आ-हृ 1 P. —LY, *adv.* यथाविधि, विधिवत्, यथाशास्त्रं, विधिपूर्वं. 2 साडंबरं; धीरं, गौरवेण, सगौरवं, गंभीरं, &c.

SOLICIT, *v. t.* याच् 1 A, प्र-अभि-अर्थ् 10 A, सविनयं याच् or प्रच्छ् 6 P. —ATION, *s.* याञ्चा, प्रार्थनं-ना, याचना, सविनयप्रार्थना. —OR, *s.* याचकः, अर्थिन् *m.*, प्रार्थयितृ *m.*, प्रार्थकः. —OUS, *a.* उत्सुक, सचिंत, सोत्कंठ, व्यग्र, उत्क in comp.; उद्विग्न, चिंताक्रांत. —OUSLY, *adv.* उत्सुकं, सोत्कंठं. —UDE, *s.* व्यग्रता, चिंता, उत्कंठा, औत्सुक्यं, उद्वेगः.

SOLID, *a.* ससार, सारवत्, वास्तविक (की *f.*). 2 अशून्य, सगर्भ, पूर्णगर्भ. 3 घन, सु-,दृढ, दृढसंधि; सु-,संहत, स्थूल, कठिन, संघातवत्; अद्रव; अग्निसंयोगाद् द्रवभावापत्त्या काठिन्यविनाशो भवति (S. B. 545) 'lose their s. state' &c. 4 (Knowledge) अगाध, परिपक्व, सुदृढ, सुपरिणत. —*s.* घनः; 's. contents' घनफलं. 2 संघातः, घन-अद्रव-द्रव्यं. —IFY, *v. t.* घनीकृ 8 U, कठिनीकृ. —ITY,-NESS, *s.* घनता, काठिन्यं, दृढता, &c.

SOLILOQUY, *s.* स्वगत-आत्मगत-भाषणं-वचः. —SOLILOQUIZE, *v. i.* स्वगतं &c. वच् 2 P, ('Say' q. v.).

SOLITARY, *a.* विविक्त, निर्जन, विजन, निभृत, एकांत; (of persons) विविक्त-एकांत-वासिन्-सेविन्, विविक्तप्रिय, एकचर, निःसंग; एक, एकाकिन्, असहाय. 2 Single, q. v. —*s.* विविक्तवासी, परिव्राज् *m.* —ILY, *adv.* विविक्तं, निभृतं, रहः, उपांशु. —INESS, *s. See* below. —SOLITUDE, *s.* विविक्तं, निर्जनं-विजनं-स्थानं, रहःस्थानं, विजनं, अरण्यं. 2 विजनता, निर्जनता, विविक्तता. 3 विविक्ताधिवासः, विविक्तवृत्ति *f.*-सेवा, संसर्गाभावः.

SOLSTICE, *s.* अयनांतः, अयनं, अयनकालः-संधिः, क्रांति *f.*,-कालः; 'summer s.' कर्कसंक्रांतिः, उत्तरायणं; 'winter s.' मकरसंक्रांतिः, दक्षिणायनं. —SOLSTITIAL, *a.* (*s.*) in comp.; 's. point' अयनांतः.

SOLVE, *v. t.* व्याकृ 8 U, विवृ 5 U; शुध् c., वि-प्रि-,° व्या-ख्या 2 P, विशदीकृ, साध्-सिध् c. (साधयति), उप-प्रति-पद् c.; 's. s the difficulties' विषमपदानि शोधयति-विमर्शयति. 2 (Question) उत्तरं दा 3 U or वद् 1 P; 's. doubt' संशयं छिद् 7 P or निराकृ or निरस् 4 U or अपनी 1 P. 3 वि-,द्रु c.,वि-,ली c. —ENCY, *s.* समृद्धता, ऋणशोधनक्षमता. —ENT, *a.* समृद्ध, सधन, ऋणशोधनक्षम. 2 द्रावण (णी *f.*), द्रावक. —*s.* द्रावणं. —SOLUBLE, *a.* वि-,द्राव्य, विलाप्य, द्रवार्ह. —SOLUTION, *s.* साधनं, विवरणं, &c.; व्याख्या, व्याख्यानं, सिद्धि *f.*, उपपत्ति *f.* 2 द्रावणं, विलयनं. 3 सं-,योगः.

SOMBRE, *a.* श्याम, मलिन, धूसर, मंद-मलिन-प्रभ.

SOME, *a.* किम् (कः-का-किं) with चित्, चन, अपि, or अमुक in comp.; 'the son of s. one' अमुकसूनुः. 2 (Quantity) किंचित्, कियत्, ईषत्, अल्प, स्वल्प, स्तोक; 'to s. extent' किंचित्, ईषत्, कियतांशेन,स्तोकांशेन; 's.-others' एके or केचित्-अन्ये-अपरे. 3 (Number) कतिचित्, कतिपय (यी-या *f.*); 'going s. steps' कतिचित् पदानि गत्वा; 's. how' कथमपि, केनापि प्रकारेण, कथं कथमपि, कथंचित्, यथाकथंचित्; 's. how or other' येन केन प्रकारेण; 's. one,' 's.-body' कश्चित्, कोपि, यःकश्चन; अमुकः, &c.; 's.-thing' यत्किंचित्, किमपि, किंचन, किंचित्; 's.-thing is better than nothing' बधिरान्मंदकर्णः श्रेयान्; 's.-time' पूर्वं, एकदा, पुरा, प्राक्, गतकाले, पूर्वकाले; 's.-times' क्वचित्, कदाचित्, कदापि, कर्हिचित्; कदा कदा, काले काले; 's.-what' किंचित्; किंचन, अल्पं, स्तोकं; (*adv.*) किंचित्, ईषत्, स्तोकं, आ pr., देश्य-देशीय-कल्प in comp.; or by doubling *adj.*; 's.-what red' आताम्र, ताम्रकल्प, ईषद्रक्त; 's.-what afraid' भीतभीत इव; 's.-where' क्वापि, कुत्रचित्, कुत्रापि, यत्र कुत्रचित्, यत्र कुत्रापि.

SOMER-SAULT,-SET, *s.* ऊर्ध्वपादलंघनं.

SOMNAMBULISM, *s.* निद्राचारः-भ्रमणं, स्वप्नचारः. —SOMNAMBULIST, *s.* निद्राचारः, स्वप्नचारी.

SOMNIFEROUS, *a.* स्वाप-निद्रा-जनन (नी *f.*), निद्राकृत्, स्वापकर (री *f.*).

SOMNILOQUIST, *s.* निद्रालापिन् *m.*, निद्राभाषी.

SOMNOLENT, *a.* निद्रालु, निद्रालस; *See* SLEEPY.

SON, *s.* पुत्रः, सुतः, तनयः, सूनुः, आत्मजः, आत्मसंभवः, नंदनः, अंगजः, तनु(नू)जः, दारकः, कुमारः; oft. ex. by deriv.; 's. of Dasaratha' दाशरथिः; गांगेयः, पांडवः, &c.; 's.-in-law' जामातृ *m.* -LESS, *a.* अपुत्र, निपुत्रिक, निःसंतान.

SONG,-STER, *s. See* under SING.

SONNET, *s.* गीतिका, गाथा, लघुगीतं-काव्यं.

SONOROUS, *a.* मधुर, मंजुल. 2 व्यक्त, स्पष्ट, परिस्फुट, व्यक्तवर्ण. 3 विराविन्, उच्च, मुखर, शब्दन, घोषण, शब्द-ध्वनि-कर (री *f.*). -LY, *adv.* मधुरं, स्पष्टं; उच्चैः; महाशब्देन. -NESS, *s.* माधुर्यं, स्पष्टता, उच्चता, मुखरता.

SOON, *adv.* अचिरेण, अचिरात्, अविलंबं, आशु, सद्यः, झटिति, सपदि; द्राक्, द्रुतं; *See* QUICKLY; 'as s. as' (so s.), 'no s.-er than' ex. by यावत्-तावत्, च-च, मात्र in comp.; *See* SCARCELY. -ER, *adv.* वरं; शीघ्रं; 's. or later' अद्य श्वो वा; 'this is s. said than done' वक्तुं सुकरमिदं न तु कर्तुं.

SOOT, *s.* कज्जलं, किट्टं, मसी-षी. -Y, *a.* कज्जलमय (यी *f.*), धूमश्याम.

SOOTH, *s.* सत्यं, तथ्यं; 'in s.' सत्यं, नाम, यत्सत्यं, नूनं खलु, सत्यमेव; 's.-sayer' दैवज्ञः, गणकः, मौहूर्तिकः; 's.-saying' शुभाशुभकथनं, दैवपरीक्षा-चिंतनं.

SOOTHE, *v. t.* शम् c. (शमयति), प्र-उप-°, लघूकृ 8 U, लघयति (D.), निर्वा c. (वापयति); (persons) लल् 10, अनुनी 1 P, सांत्व् 10, प्र-सद् c., परितुष् c., आराध् c.. परामृश् 6 P (by stroking), आश्वस् c. -ING, *a.* शमन (नी *f.*), शांतिकर (री *f.*), शांतिप्रद, निर्वापयितृ, तापहर-हारिन्. 2 सांत्वक, आश्वासनशील; 'by s. words' सांत्वनगिरा, सामवचोभिः. -*s.* प्र-उप-शमनं, निर्वापणं, सांत्वनं, अनुनयः, लालनं.

SOP, *s.* पिंडः, अन्नं, पिष्टकखंडः.

SOPHISM, SOPHISTRY, *s.* हेत्वाभासः, युक्त्याभासः, पक्षाभासः, आभासः, सत्याभासः, वाक्छलं. -SOPHIST,-ER, *s.* हेत्वाभासवादिन् *m.*, तार्किकः. -IC, -ICAL, *a.* आभासरूप, हेत्वाभासरूप, सत्याभास. -SOPHISTICATE, *v. t.* Adulterate, q. v.

SOPORIFIC, SOPORIFEROUS, *a.* निद्राजनन-स्वापन-(नी *f.*), निद्रा-स्वाप-कर (री *f.*), निद्रावह.

SORCERY, *s.* ऐंद्रजालं, माया, कुहति *f.*, योगः, अभिचारः (black art). -ER, *s.* ऐंद्रजालिकः, मायाकरः, अभिचारविद्. -ESS, *s.* योगिनी, मायिनी, अभिचारिणी.

SORDID, *a.* नीच, कृपण, कुत्सित, अधम, दीन, जघन्य, निंद्य; *See* MEAN. 2 मलिन, मलीमस.

SORE, *s.* क्षतं, व्रणः-णं, अरुस् *n.*, ईर्मं. -*a.* सरुज, जातव्यथ, दुःखित, क्षत, सव्रण; सवेदन, सव्यथ, स्पर्शासह. 2 पीडाकर (री *f.*), कष्ट-क्लेश-प्रद, दुःखद. 3 उग्र, तीव्र, दारुण, गुरु; 's. (throat)' कंठपाकः, कंठरुज् *f.* -LY, *adv.* भृशं, अतीव, नितांतं, उग्रं, दारुणं, सुतरां, बलवत्.

SORREL, *s.* चुक्रः, सहस्रवेधिन् *m.*, अम्लवेतसः, शतवेधी.

SORROW, *s.* शोकः, शुच् *f.*, दुःखं, खेदः, क्लेशः, आधिः, संतापः, आर्ति *f.*, व्यथा; *See* GRIEF. -*v. i.* शुच् 1 P, खिद् pass., व्यथ् 1 A; *See* GRIEVE. -FUL, *a.* सशोक, शोकार्त-आकुल-अन्वित-उपहत-आविष्ट, दुःखित, संतप्त, दुःखिन्, दुःखार्त, उद्विग्न, विषण्ण, दीन, दुर्मनस्, खिन्न, अवसन्न, म्लान, विमनस्. 2 शोच्य, शोचनीय, शोकास्पदीभूत, दुःखावह. -FULLY, *adv.* सशोकं, सखेदं, सोद्वेगं, सदुःखं. -SORRY, *a.* दुःखित, दुःखिन्, खिन्न, कष्टापन्न, &c.; *See* SORROWFUL. 2 दीन, अनु-,शोच्य, कृपण, अनुकंप्य; 's. for one's past conduct' सानुशय, अनुतप्त; 'I am s. to hear this' इदं श्रुत्वा दुःखितोस्मि; 'I am s. to inform you' &c. इति भवते निवेदनं मे दुःखमावहति, निवेदयन्नहं कष्टापन्नोस्मि; 's. horse' कदश्वः; 's. fare' कदन्नं.

SORT, *s.* प्रकारः; विशेषः, भेदः in comp.; जाति *f.*, विधा in comp.; *See* MANNER; 'a s. of tree' वृक्षविशेषः-भेदः; 'out of s. s' असुस्थ-अस्वस्थ-शरीर. -*v. t.* यथाक्रमं-यथावर्गं रच् 10 or विन्यस् 4 U, वर्गक्रमेण न्यस्. -*v. i.* युज्-उपपद्-pass., ex. by अनुरूप, युक्त; *See* BECOMING, PROPER.

SORTIE, *s.* अवस्कंदः, अवपातः; *See* SALLY.

SOT,-SOTTISH, *a.* पानमूढ, पानासक्त, मदोन्मत्त, सदापानरत. 2 Foolish, q. v.

SOUL, *s.* आत्मन् *m.*; 'individual s.' प्रत्यगात्मा, विज्ञानात्मा; 'rational s.' चिदात्मा; 'supreme s.' परमात्मा, ब्रह्मन् *n.*; 'animating s.' जीवात्मा, प्राणः, चेतनः, जीवः; 'embodied s.' देही, शारीरात्मा, शारीरी, प्राणात्मा, क्षेत्रज्ञः. 2 आत्मा, चेतस् *n.*, चित्तं, मनस् *n.*, हृदयं; *See* MIND; 'possessed of a large s.' महात्मन्, उदारचेतस्; 'oneness of s.' चित्तैक्यं, ऐक्यभावः; 'the whole s.' सर्वात्मा, सर्वभावः. 3 जीवनं, सारः; तत्त्वं, सार-तत्त्व-भागः-अंशः, सारभूतः. 4 (Self) आत्मा, स्वः. 5 वीर्यं, बलं, उत्साहः, तेजस्. 6 Person, q. v.; 'the departed s.' प्रेतः, प्रेतनरः; 'heart and s.' प्र-नि-कामं, सर्वात्मना, सर्वभावेन; *See* HEART; 'he throws his heart and s. into the work' सुसमाहितेन चेतसा-सर्वात्मना-कार्ये प्रवर्तते-व्याप्रियते.

SOUND, *s.* शब्दः, नि-,नादः, ध्वनिः, नि-,स्व(स्वा)नः, निर्ह्रादः, स्वरः, निनदः, निर्-,घोषः, रावः, रवः, वि-संरावः, नि-,स्वा(ध्व)नः, स्वनितं; 'musical s.' नि-, क्वा(क्व)णः, क्वणितं; 'confused s.' कोलाहलः, क-

लकलः, तुमुलरवः; 'rattling s.' रणः, रणितं. 2 संधिसागरः. –*a.* सुस्थ, अव्रण, कल्य, निरामय, अनामय, नीरोग, नीरुज, प्रकृतिस्थ, व्याधिरहित; (in body) अक्षतशरीर, अविकलेंद्रिय; (in mind) अनुपहतचित्त, अविप्लुत, अवातुल, अविक्षिप्त. 2 अक्षत, अजातक्षत, अ-निर्-व्रण, क्षत-व्रण-हीन. 3 ससार, सारवत्, सारगर्भ. 4 अविकल, अन्यून, अखंड, अभिन्न. 5 तीक्ष्ण, तीव्र; निर्भर, प्र-,गाढ, सु-अति pr.; 's. sleep' गाढनिद्रा; 's. beating' तीक्ष्णदंडः, अतिताडनं. 6 निर्दोष, निश्छिद्र, विशुद्ध, दोषहीन. 7 गाढ, ग(गं)भीर, अगाध, सुपरिणत, परिपक्व. 8 (Argument &c.) अखंड्य, सप्रमाण, दृढ-सु-प्रमाण, न्याय्य, धर्म्य, युक्तिसिद्ध. 9 (In views) विशुद्धाचार; सत्यमार्गानुयायिन्. –*v. i.* नि-,नद् 1 P, ध्वन् 1 P, स्वन् 1 P, क्वण् 1 P, ह्राद् 1 A, वि-,रु 2 P, स्तन्-रस्-1 P, शब्दं कृ 8 U, शब्दायते (D.). –*v. t.* ध्वन् c., स्वन् c., नद् c.; वद् c., आ-,ध्मा 1 P, मुखमारुतेन पूर् 10, (trumpet, conch &c.); (drum) तड् 10, आहन् 2 U; 'the drum being s.ed' आहतायां भेर्यां; (bow) आस्फल् c. 2 परीक्ष् 1 A, सूक्ष्मं-निपुणं-निरूप् 10 or अनुसं-धा 3 U, ज्ञा desid. (जिज्ञासते). 3 उद्-घुष् 10, प्र-ख्या c. (ख्यापयति), प्रकाश् c., प्रकटीकृ; 's. the depth' तलं अवगाह् 1 A; 's. the depth of water' जलवेधं परि-मा 3 A, 2 P. –ING, *a.* शब्दन, मुखर, शब्दायमान, निनादिन्, निनदत्, घोषण, गर्जत्, निर्ह्रादिन्, शब्दकर (री *f.*); 's.-lead' लंबः, लंबसीसकं. –*s.* ध्वाननं, शब्दनं, वादनं. 2 वेधपरिमाणं, तलावगाहनं. –LY, *adv.* तीव्रं, तीक्ष्णं, अत्यंतं, प्र-,गाढं; निर्भरं, दृढं, सुखेन, सु-अति pr. –NESS, *s.* स्वास्थ्यं, कल्यता, आरोग्यं, अक्षतत्वं, निर्व्रणत्वं, अवैकल्यं, अन्यूनता, अखंड्यता, निर्दोषता, &c; 's. of mind' चित्तस्वास्थ्यं, अविभ्रवः.

SOUP, *s.* जू(यू)षः-षं.

SOUR, *a.* अम्ल, शुक्त, अम्लरस; 's. to the teeth' दंतशठ. 2 कर्कश, परुष, दारुण, रूक्ष, अरुंतुद; सदावक्र, वक्र-वाम-शील, कर्कशस्वभाव, दुष्प्रकृति. –*v. t.* अम्लीकृ 8 U. 2 कर्कशीकृ, वक्रीकृ. –*v. i.* अम्लीभू 1 P, कर्कशीभू. –NESS, *s.* अम्लता, कार्कश्यं &c.

SOURCE, *s.* प्रभवः, योनिf., मूलं, कारणं, हेतुः, प्रसूतिf., उद्भवः, संभवः, आदिः, उद्गमस्थानं; *See* ORIGIN; 'to have s. in' प्र-भू 1 P, प्र-,जन् 4 A, उत्पद् 4 A (with abl.); लोभात्क्रोधः प्रभवति, लोभात्कामः प्रजायते (H. 1); 'the s. of the Ganges is in the Himálaya' हिमवतो गंगा प्रभवति (S. K.).

SOUSE, *v. t.* सहसा मस्ज् c. or मस्ज् c. (मज्जयति) or जलेन सिच् 6 P. –*v. i.* Pounce, q. v.

SOUTH, *s.* दक्षिणा, दक्षिणदिक्-दिशा-आशा, अवाची; 'to the s.' दक्षिणतः, (with gen.). –*a.*, –ERN, –ERLY, *a.* दक्षिण, अवाच्, अवाचीन, अवाच्य, दाक्षिणात्य; 'in a s. direction' दक्षिणेन (with acc. or gen.); 's. country' दक्षिणापथः; 's.-east' दक्षिणपूर्वा, आग्नेयी; (*a.*,–ern,–erly,) दक्षिणपूर्व, आग्नेय; 's.-west' दक्षिणपश्चिमा, नैर्ऋती; (*a.*,–ern, –erly) दक्षिणपश्चिम, नैर्ऋत. –WARD,-WARDS, *adv.* दक्षिणाभिमुखं, दक्षिणतः, दक्षिणस्यां दिशि.

SOUVENIR, *s. See* MEMORIAL.

SOVEREIGN, *s.* स्वर्णमुद्रा. 2 अधिराजः, अधीश्वरः, अधिपतिः, महाराजः, अधीशः, सार्वभौमः, नृपतिः, सम्राज् *m.*, oft. by राजा, पालः, नाथः, &c.; *See* KING. –*a.* परम, श्रेष्ठ, मुख्य, प्रमुख; *See* PRINCIPAL. 2 उत्कृष्ट, गुणावह (medicine &c.); 's. medicine' परमौषधं, महौषधं. –TY, *s.* प्रभुत्वं, राज्यं, आधिपत्यं, साम्राज्यं, ऐशत्वं, स्वाम्यं, ऐश्वरत्वं, इंद्रता in comp.; 's. of beasts' मृगेंद्रता. 2 (Authority) मुख्य-श्रेष्ठ-अधिकारः, प्रधानाधिकारः.

SOW, *s.* सू(शू)करी, वराही, कोली. –*v. t.* वप् 1 P, आ-नि-°, (बीजानि) विकॄ 6 P, आरुह् c.; 's. dissensions' भेदं जन् c., भेदबीजानि वप्; 's. dragon's teeth' कलहबीजं वप्; 'as you s., so you reap' यो यद्वपति बीजं हि सोपि तल्लभते फलं; *See* also REAP. –ER, *s.* वप्तृ *m.*, वापिन् *m.*, वापकः. –ING, *s.* वपनं, वापः, उप्ति *f.*, बीजारोपणं.

SPACE, *s.* आकाशः-शं, शून्यं, दिगंतरं, रिक्तं, अंतरिक्षं, नभोमंडलं; 'infinite s.' अनंतं, महाकाशं; 'finite s.' घटाकाशं. 2 (Intervening s.) अंतरालं, मध्यं, अभ्यंतरं, अंतरं, अभ्यंतरावकाशः, व्यवधानं. 3 अवकाशः, अवसरः, प्रसरः, विषयः, स्थानं, स्थलं, भूमि *f.* 4 प्र-,देशः, दिश्-शा, दिग्भागः; 'pervading all s.' सर्वदिग्व्यापिन्, अभिव्यापिन्. 5 अंतरं, अध्वन् *m.*, देशः; 's. of time' अंतरं, अवधिः, कालावधिः, कालांतरं; oft. ex. by अभ्यंतरं; 'in the s. of six months' षण्मासाभ्यंतरे. —SPACIOUS, *a.* विस्तीर्ण, विशाल, विपुल, विस्तृत, पृथु; *See* LARGE. –NESS, *s.* विस्तारः, विस्तृति *f.*, वैपुल्यं.

SPADE, *s.* खनित्रं, अवदारणं, स्तंबघ्नः.

SPAN, *s.* किष्कु-वितस्ति-*m. f.*; 'life's s.' जीवितावधिः; gen. ex. by words for 'Transitory' q. v.; 'the s. of life is short' आयुः कल्लोललोलं (Bh. II. 82), कतिपयनिमेषायुषि जने (सति) (Bh. II. 40); जीवितं तरलं &c. –*v. t.* प्र-परि-मा 3 A, 2 P.

SPANGLE, *s.* रजतपत्रं; धातुतारा. –*v. t.* Adorn, q. v.

SPANK, *v. t.* चपेटेन प्रह् 1 P or तड् 10. –*v. i.* सवेगं चल् 1 P or विसृप् 1 P.

SPAR, *s.* स्फटिकमृत्तिका. 2 दीर्घयष्टि *f.*-काष्ठं, दारुखंडः, –*v. i.* परिहासेन मुष्टीमुष्टि युध् 4 A.

SPARE, *v. t.* रक्ष् 1 P, सं-धि 5 U, (money); न व्यय् 10 (व्यययति) or विक्षिप् 6 P, परिमितं प्र-विनि-युज् 7 A, 10; 'does not s. time' कालं विक्षिपति.

हराति; 'will you s. three hours for me' अपि भवान्मदर्थं प्रहरमेकं विनियोजयिष्यति. 2 मुच् 6 P, (वधात्, छेदात् &c.), त्यज् 1 P, हा 3 P, वि-उत्-सृज् 6 P. 3 उपेक्ष् 1 A, न अपेक्ष्, सुखेन त्यज्; oft. ex. by 'not' with other words; 'but s. this tree' इमं वृक्षं तावन्मा छिन्द्धि; 's. him' मुच्यतामसौ, न हंतव्यः; 'he can now be s.ed from my service' तस्य सेवया न मे प्रयोजनमधुना, तस्य सेवां नापेक्षे; *See* DISPENSE. 4 अव-,शिष् c., उद्-वृत् c. —*a.* उद्वृत्त, अभ्याशत, अधिक, अतिरिक्त, अव-, शिष्ट. 2 अल्प, स्तोक, परि-,मित, अबहुल. 3 क्षाम, कृश, परि-,क्षीण, निर्मांस, शुष्क; *See* LEAN. —ING, *a.* मितव्यय, अल्प-परिमित-व्ययिन्; परिमित, अल्प; 's. of words' अल्पभाषिन्; परिमितालाप. —INGLY, *adv.* मितं, अल्पं, मितव्ययेन, अल्पशः, स्तोकशः; 'eating s.' मिताहार, मितभुज्. —NESS, *s.* कृशता, क्षीणता.

SPARK, *s.* वि-,स्फुलिंगः, अग्नि-ज्वलन-कणः-कणिका; कणः, कणिका, लवः, लेशः, अणुः. 2 Fop, q. v. —SPARKLE, *v. i.* स्फुर् 6 P, प्र-वि-°, तेजःकणान्-स्फुलिंगान्-उत्क्षिप् 6 P or विकॄ 6 P; *See* SHINE also; 's.-ing fitfully' क्षणनष्टदृष्टाः (Mr. 5). —ING, *a.* स्फुरत्, स्फुरितप्रभ, दीप्तिमत्, &c.; 's. wit' पुरःस्फुरंती मतिः, मतिविलासः.

SPARRING, *s.* मुष्टियुद्धं, मुष्टीमुष्टि युद्धं. 2 विचारः.

SPARROW, *s.* चटकः, कलविंकः; 'female s.' चटका.

SPARSE, *a.* विरल, अबहुल, अनिबिड.

SPASM, *s.* (अंग) संकोचः, आक्षेपः, आकर्षः, उद्वेष्टनं, व्यासः; 's. in the leg' पिंडिकोद्वेष्टनं; शूलं (with pain). —SPASMODIC, *a.* सोद्वेष्टन, आकर्षिन्, आक्षेपक, by (*s.*); 's. contraction' आकर्षः, संकोचः.

SPATTER, *v. t.* अवसिच् 6 P or अवकॄ 6 P, (पंकादिना).

SPATTLE, SPATULA, *s.* प्र-वि-लेपनी.

SPAVIN, *s.* संधिशोथः.

SPAWL, *s.* निष्ठ्यूतं; *See* SALIVA.

SPAWN, *s.* अंडं, मीनांडं, भेकांडं, &c. —*v.* अंडानि मोक्ष् 10 or प्रसू 2, 4 A.

SPEAK, *v. t.* वद् 1 P, वच् 2 P, भण्-गद् 1 P, भाष् 1 A, ब्रू 2 U, आलप् 1 P; *See* SAY; वाचं-गिरं-उदीर् c. or उद्-गॄ 6 P; 's. of' अभि-धा 3 U, कथ् 10, निर्दिश् 6 P, वर्ण् 10; 's. ill of' अपभाष्, परि-अप-वद् 1 A, निंद् 1 P; 's. out' स्पष्टं-स्फुटं-वद्, प्रकाशं ब्रू; 's. well of' प्रशंस् 1 P; *See* PRAISE; 's. with,' 's. together' संवद्, संभाष्, संमंत्र् 10 A. —ER, *s.* प्र-,वक्तृ *m.*, वाग्मिन् *m.*, वादी. —ING, *s.* भाषणं, भाषितं, वचस् *n.*, उक्ति *f.*, व्याहारः; *See* SPEECH below. —SPEECH, *s.* वाच् *f.* वाक्शक्ति *f.*, वाणी, गिर् *f.* 2 वाक्, वचः, गीः, वाणी, उक्तिः, व्याहारः, भाषणं, वचनं, आलापः, वाक्यं, भारती, सरस्वती, व्याहृति *f.* 3 भाषा, उक्तिः; 'eloquence of s.' शब्द-पद-लालित्यं; 'covert s.' भंगिभाषणं, व्याजोक्तिः; 'opening of s.' वाङ्मुखं; 'goddess of s.' वाग्देवी, भारती, सरस्वती; 'part of s.' शब्दजातिः-भेदः. —IFY, *v. i.* Harangue, q. v. —LESS, *a.* मूक, वाग्हीन, स्तंभितवाक्; *See* MUTE.

SPEAR, *s.* शूलः-लं, कुंतः, प्रासः, तोमरः, शक्ति *f.*, शल्यं; 'head of a s.' फलं, शूलाग्रं; 's.-man' शूलिन् *m.*, शूलधरः-भृत्, शूलपाणिः, प्रासिकः, कौंतिकः, शाक्तीकः, शक्तिधरः-ग्रहः. —*v. t.* शूलेन व्यध् 4 P.

SPECIE, *s.* मुद्रा, नाणकं.

SPECIES, *s.* जाति *f.*, प्रकारः, भेदः, विशेषः; 'of the same s.' स-एक-जातीय; 'a s. of animal' प्राणिविशेषः-भेदः; 'genus and s.' सामान्यविशेषौ. —SPECIAL, *a.* विशेष in comp., असामान्य, असाधारण (णी *f.*), अव्यापक, वैशेषिक (की *f.*), विशिष्ट, अवच्छेदक; 's. duty' विशेषधर्मः; विशेषनियमः, समयविशेषः, &c. 2 लोकोत्तर, लोकबाह्य. 3 तद्धेतुक, तन्निमित्तक, तदुद्दिष्ट. 4 जातिवाचिन्, जाति in comp.; 's. characteristic' जातिधर्मः-लक्षणं. —LY, *adv.* विशेषतः, विशेषेण; सविशेषं, कार्यतः, प्रयोजनापेक्षया. —ITY,-TY, *s.* विशेषः, विशेषधर्मः, विशिष्टता. —SPECIFIC,-AL, *a.* विशेष, जाति in comp.; विशिष्ट, असामान्य, जाति-व्यक्ति-गत; 's. gravity' विशिष्टगुरुत्वं; 's. character' जाति-विशेष-धर्मः-लक्षणं. —*s.* 's. medicine' अमोघगुणमौषधं, विशिष्टौषधं. —ICALLY, *adv.* जातितः, विशेषतः, सविशेषं. —SPECIFY, *v. t.* (सविशेषं) निर्दिश् 6 P, कथ् 10, अभि-धा 3 U, उदाहृ 1 P, विशिष् 7 P or c., एकैकशः परिसं-ख्या 2 P or कथ्; विशेषं कथ् or ब्रू 2 U, अवच्छिद् 7 P. —IED, *a.* निर्दिष्ट, अवच्छिन्न, निर्दिष्ट-उक्त-लक्षण &c.; 'will be s. further on' अग्रे वक्ष्यते. —ICATION, *s.* विशेषनिर्देशः-कथनं-वर्णनं, व्यवच्छेदः, परिसंख्या, विशेषः.

SPECIMEN, *s.* आदर्शः, प्रतिमा, प्रतिरूपं.

SPECIOUS, *a.* सत्यसंकाश-आभास-सन्निभ, आपातरमणीय, बहिः रमणीय, सुदृश्य, बहिरेव मनोरम. —LY, *adv.* सत्याभासपूर्वं. —NESS, *s.* सत्याभासः.

SPECK, SPECKLE, *s.* बिंदुः, चिह्नं, अंकः, कलंकः; तिलकः-कं. 2 शकलः-लं, कणः, लवः, अणुः, सूक्ष्मबिंदुः; 's. s of clouds' मेघशकलानि. —*v. t.* चित्र् 10, चित्री-कर्बुरी-कृ 8 U; बिंदुभिः चित्र्. —ED, *a.* चित्र, चित्रित-कर्बुरित, चित्रविचित्र, बिंदुचित्रित-चिह्नित, शबलीकृत, चित्रांग (गी *f.*); 'having a s. belly' चित्रोदर, पृषदुदर.

SPECTACLE, *s.* दृश्यं, कौतुकं, आलोकः, चमत्कारः, स्थानं, दृष्टिविषयः. 2 (S. s) उपनेत्रं-त्रे, दृष्टिसहायौ.

SPECTATOR, *s.* प्रेक्षकः, प्रेक्षकजनः-लोकः, द्रष्टृ *m.*; (in an audience &c.) पारिषद्यः, सामाजिकः, पार्षदः.

SPECTRE, *s.* भूतः, पिशाचः, छाया, वेतालः, प्रेतः; 'to raise a s.' वेतालं उत्था c., छायां उद्धृ c.

SPECULAR, *a.* आदर्शगुणक.

SPECULATE, *v. i.* विचर् c., वितर्क् 10, विमृश् 6 P; *See* CONSIDER. 2 बहुलाभापेक्षया क्री 9 U; अविचारेण दैवाधीनं कर्म कृ 8 U. -ION, *s.* विचारः, वितर्कः, विमर्शः, परिकल्पना. 2 कल्पना, प्र-,युक्ति *f.*, उपायः. -IVE, *a.* विचारवत्, विचार-ध्यान-शील. 2 काल्पनिक-मानसिक (की *f.*), अव्यवहार्य, अप्रवर्तनीय, अव्यवहारानुरूप, व्यवहारायोग्य. -OR, *s.* कल्पकः, विचारकः. 2 Philosopher, q. v.

SPECULUM, *s.* *See* MIRROR.

SPEED, *s.* वेगः, प्र-,जवः, रंहस् *n.*, रयः, जवनं, त्वरा, रभसः, तरस् *n.*, शीघ्रता, तूर्णि *f.* -*v. i.* त्वर् 1 A, शीघ्रं-सवेगं गम् or चल् 1P. 2 सिध् 4P, सफलीभू 1P; *See* PROSPER, SUCCEED. 3 Fare, q. v. -*v. t.* त्वर् c. (त्वरयति). 2 पुरस्कृ, उपकृ, सिध् c. (साधयति); शुभं-कल्याणं-कृ 8 U. 3 Ruin, Kill, q. v.; 'God s. !' शिवास्ते पंथानः संतु (P. I. 1), शिवस्ते पंथाः भूयात् (S. 4); विजयी भव. —SPEEDY, *a.* शीघ्र, त्वरित, सत्वर, अविलंबित, द्रुत, सजव, वेगवत्, जवन, महावेग, शीघ्रगति; *See* PROMPT also; better by 's.-ly'. -ILY, *adv.* आशु, शीघ्रं, सत्वरं, झटिति, त्वरितं, तूर्णं, अविलंबं, सपदि. 2 सरभसं, सवेगं. -INESS, *s.* जवनता, वेगवत्त्वं, शीघ्रता &c.

SPELL, *s.* मंत्रः, अभिचारमंत्रः (magic); मोहनं, आकर्षणं; 's.-bound' अभिमंत्रित, मंत्ररुद्धवीर्य -*v. t.* अभिमंत्र् 10 A, अभिचर् c., मंत्रैः वशीकृ 8 U, वि-,मुह् c. 2 अक्षराणि निर्दिश् 6 P, यथाक्षरं सं-ख्या 2 P or पठ् 1 P or लिख् 6 P. -ING, *s.* वर्ण-अक्षर-विन्यासः-रचना; 'having a double s.' द्विरूप; 'variation in s.' पाठांतरं, पाठभेदः.

SPEND, *v. t.* उत्-वि-सृज् 6 P, परि-,त्यज् 1 P, व्यय् 10 (व्यययति), विनि-युज् 7 A, 10; 'good men, like clouds, take (things) for s.ing (them)' आदानं हि विसर्गाय सतां वारिमुचामिव (R. IV. 86); 's.-ing on proper objects' पात्रे व्ययः. 2 अव-,सद् c., क्षि 5 P or c., नश् c., अप-चि 5 U, क्षीणीकृ 8 U, विक्षिप् 6 P; *See* EXHAUST; 'spent with toil' श्रमखिन्न, श्रमावसन्न. 3 (Time) क्षै c. (क्षपयति), गम् c., नी 1 P, या c., अतिवह् c.; *See* PASS; 's. in vain' क्षिप्, हृ 1 P. -ING, *s.* व्ययः, वि-उत्-सर्गः, त्यागः, विनियोगः; यापनं, हरणं, विक्षेपः -SPENDTHRIFT, *s.* अतिव्ययिन् *m.*, त्यागशीलः, मुक्तहस्तः, अर्थनाशिन्.

SPERM,-ATIC, *See* SEMEN &c.

SPEW, *v. t.* वम् 1 P, छर्द् 10, नि-,ष्ठिव् 1, 4 P.

SPHERE, *s.* गोलः-लं, वर्तुलं, मंडलं; *See* ORB; 'celestial s.' व्योम-नभो-मंडलं. 2 नियोगः, विषयः, अधिकारः, धर्मः, प्रकरणं. 3 सं-,स्थिति *f.*, अवस्था, दशा, (in life). -SPHERICAL, *a.* गोलाकार, वर्तुल, गोल. —SPHEROID, *s.* उपगोलः; अंडाकृतिः. -AL, *a.* गोलप्राय-कल्प, उपगोल. -SPHERULE, *s.* गोलकः, लघु-क्षुद्र-गोलः.

SPICE, *s.* गंधद्रव्यं; 'the three s. s' त्रिजातकं. -*v. t.* वास् 10, अधि-सु-°. -ED,-Y, *a.* वासित, सगंध, सुगंध, मिष्ट, सुरस.

SPIDER, *s.* तंतुवायः, तंतुनाभः, तंत्रवायः, ऊर्णनाभः, लूता, मर्कटकः, जालिकः, कोश(ष)कारः, अष्टापदः.

SPIKE, *s.* शस्यमंजरी; कणिशं-षं, धान्यशीर्षकं. 2 महाकीलः, शंकुः, शूलः-लं, कंटकः. -*v. t.* कील् 10. -ED, *a.* शंकुयुक्त; कीलित, शंकुबद्ध. -Y, *a.* तीक्ष्णाग्र, सूच्यग्र, कीलनिचित.

SPIKENARD, *s.* जटामांसी, तपस्विनी, जटिला, लोमशा, म(मि)सि-सी-षि-षी *f.*, नलदा.

SPILL, *s.* शलाका. -*v. t.* (अकस्मात्) अधः क्षिप् 6 P; अव-,पत् c., निः-,स्रु c.; 's. blood' रुधिरं स्रु c., रक्तस्रावं कृ 8 U. -*v. i.* स्रु 1 P, पत् c. pass.

SPIN, *v. t.* (तंतून्) कृ 8 U, जन् c., तन् 8 U, सृज् 6 P, वे 1 P, कृत् 6 P; 'the spider s. s out its web (threads) from itself' तंतुनाभः स्वत एव तंतून् सृजति (S. B. 477). 2 निष्कृष् 1 P, निर्गम् c. 3 परिवृत् c., परि-,भ्रम् c., घूर्ण् c. -*v. i.* भ्रम् 1, 4 P, परिवृत् 1 A. -NER, *s.* तंतुवायः-पः, कर्तकः. -NING, *s.* तंतुवायः-वापः, तांतवं, तंतुकरणं. -SPINDLE, *s.* तर्कु *f.*, तर्कुटी-टं ; 's.-shanked' क्षामजंघ, पृश्नि, दीर्घजंघ. -SPINSTER, *s.* सूत्रकर्तिका. 2 अनूढा, अविवाहिता.

SPINE, *s.* पृष्ठवंशः, कशेरु *m. n.*, कशेरुका, पृष्ठास्थि *n.*

SPINOUS,-SPINY, *a.* सकंटक.

SPIRACLE, *s.* छिद्रं, सूक्ष्मरंध्रं, वायुमार्गः.

SPIRE, *s.* व्या-आ-वर्तनं, आवर्तः, व्यावर्तनरेखा. 2 शिखरं, शृंगं, शिखा. -AL, *a.* वि-,आवर्तिन्, चक्राकार. -ALLY, *adv.* चक्राकारेण.

SPIRIT, *s.* प्राणाः, असवः, (pl.). 2 आत्मन् *m.*, देही, क्षेत्रज्ञः; *See* SOUL; 'the supreme s.' परमात्मा, ब्रह्म. 3 चित्तं, मनस्-चेतस् *n.*, वृत्ति *f.*, भावः; 'low-s.-ed' लघुचेतस्, क्षुद्रमनस्; 'proudness of s.' चित्तसमुन्नति *f.*, चित्तोद्रेकः; *See* PRIDE; 'in good s. s', 'in high s. s' सोल्लास, प्रहृष्ट, प्रमुदितचित्त; हर्षवृत्ति; 'high s. s' उत्साहः, उल्लासः, प्रफुल्लता, प्रहर्षः; 'low s. s' विषादः, उद्वेगः; 'in low s. s' उद्विग्न, विषण्ण, उदासीन; *See* DEJECTED. 4 सत्त्वं, तेजस् *n.*, वीर्यं, प्रभावः, ऊर्जः, उत्साहः. 5 भावः, भावार्थः, उद्देशः; 'he obeyed my order in s. only' भावार्थमेव गृहीत्वा ममाज्ञामनुष्ठितवान्. 6 सारः, तत्त्वं, सत्त्वं, सारांशः, जीवितं; जीवनं; 'Ojas is the s. (soul) of prose' ओजः गद्यस्य जीवितं (Kav.).

7 प्रकृति *f.*, शीलं, स्वभावः, वृत्तिः; 'gentle s.' स्वभावसौजन्यं, शांतशीलता; 'of a noble s.' उदारप्रकृति. 8 भूतः, वेतालः; 'evil s.' रक्षस् *n.*, राक्षसः, पिशाचः, अपदेवता. 9 प्रेतः, परेतः, छाया. 10 (Of style) ओजस् *n.*, ऊर्जः; रसः. 11 (S. s) सुरा, मद्यं; *See* LIQUOR. –*v. t.* (up) आश्वस् c., उज्जीव् c., उत्तिज् c. –ED, *a.* सत्त्ववत्, सोत्साह, तेजस्विन्, वीर्यवत्, ससत्त्व; 'a s. speech' ऊर्जिताश्रयं वचनं. 2 ओजस्विन्, सरस. –EDLY, *adv.* सोत्साहं, ससत्त्वं. –LESS, *a.* निःसत्त्व, तेजोविहीन; निस्तेजस्, निर्वीर्य, नीरस. –UOUS, *a.* मादिन्, मादक; 's. liquor' सुरा, मदिरा, &c. —SPIRITUAL, *a.* अध्यात्म in comp., (अध्यात्मज्ञानं), आध्यात्मिक (की *f.*); निरवयव, निराकार, चिद्रूप, अमूर्त, परम. 2 पारत्रिक-पारलौकिक-पारमार्थिक-(की *f.*), मानसिक-सात्त्विक-(की *f.*). 3 धार्मिक (की *f.*), धर्म in comp.; असांसारिक-अलौकिक (की *f.*); 's. preceptor' उपाध्यायः; 's. father' धर्मतातः-पिता. –ISM, *s.* ब्रह्मवादः, ज्ञान-निवृत्ति-मार्गः. –IST, *s.* ब्रह्मवादिन् *m.* –ITY, अमूर्तता, असांसारिकता, परमार्थनिष्ठा. –LY, *adv.* परमार्थदृष्ट्या, परमार्थतः; 's. minded' परमार्थदृष्टि-बुद्धि, परमार्थासक्त, ब्रह्मनिष्ठ, संसारव्यावृत्त.

SPIT, *v. t.* नि-,ष्ठिव् 1, 4 P, उद्वम् 1 P, निःसृ c., उद्-गॄ 6P. 2 शूला कृ 8 U, शूलं आरुह् c.–*v. i.* ष्ठिव्, श्लेष्माणं-लालां निःसृ c. –*s.*, –TING, *s.* निष्ठ्यूति *f.*, नि-,ष्ठीवः-वनं, उद्वमनं, उद्गिरणं; 's. ing-pit, spittoon' प्रतिग्राहः, पतद्ग्रहः. 2 शूलः-लं; 'roasted on a s.' शूल्य, शूलाकृत, भटित्र. –SPITTLE, *s.* नि-,ष्ठ्यूतं,-ष्ठीवनं, मुखस्रावः, लाला; *See* SALIVA.

SPITE, *s.* वि-,द्वेषः, ईर्ष्या, असूया, द्रोहः, मात्सर्यं; 'in s. of' अनादृत्य (with acc.), gen. ex. by gen. or loc. abs.; पश्यतोपि गुरोः, तिष्ठत्सु लोकपालेषु वव्रे इति नलं पतिं; 'snatches away, in s. of our looking on' मिषतां नः आच्छिनत्ति (K. II. 46). –*v. t.* वि-,द्विष् 2U; द्रुह् 4P, ईर्ष्य् 1P (with dat.). –FUL, *a.* सासूय, विद्वेषिन्, मत्सरिन्, सेर्ष्य, द्रोहबुद्धि, दुष्टभाव; *See* MALICIOUS. –FULLY, *adv.* सासूयं, द्वेषात्, द्वेष-द्रोह-बुद्ध्या, सेर्ष्यं, मात्सर्यात्.

SPLASH, *v.* आस्फल् c., (आस्फालितं यत्प्रमदाकराग्रैः R. XVI. 13), क्रीडायां तड् 10; इतस्ततः विक्षिप् 6 P. –*s.*,-ING, *s.* आस्फालनं, विक्षेपः, आस्फालन-शब्दः-नादः; 'the log fell down with a s.' काष्ठखंडः पतितो जलमास्फालयन्.

SPLEEN, *s.* प्लीहन् *m.*; प्लीहा, गुल्मः; 'enlargement of the s.' प्लीहाभिवृद्धि *f.*, प्लीहोदरं. 2 संरंभः, मन्युः; 's.-wort' प्लीहघ्नः, प्लीहशत्रुः. –SPLENETIC, *a.* प्लीहरोगिन्. 2 वक्र-कर्कश-शील, पिशुन, कर्कश.

SPLENDID, *a.* भासुर; उज्ज्वल, भास्वत, अतितैजस (सी *f.*), अतिशोभन, सुप्रभ, अतिप्रभ, अतिदीप्तिमत्; महातेजस्; 'a s. dress' उज्ज्वलवेशः, उदारनेपथ्यं. 2 श्रेष्ठ, प्रशस्य, परम, विशिष्टतम, अभिनंद्य, (success). 3 महाप्रताप, प्रतापवत्; *See* MAJESTIC. –LY, *adv.* उज्ज्वलं, सुप्रभं, अतिशोभया, अतिप्रतापेन; 's. dressed' उज्ज्वलवेशधारिन्. –SPLENDOUR, *s.* शोभा, तेजस् *n*, भाः, प्रभा, औज्ज्वल्यं, भासुरत्वं, अतिशोभा-कांति-दीप्ति *f.*, महातेजः, प्रतापः, विभूति *f.*, वैभवं.

SPLICE, *v. t.* संयुज् 7 U, 10.

SPLINTER, *s.* (काष्ठ-) खंडः, शकलं, विदलं, भिन्नं. –*v. t.* वि-दॄ 9 P or c.; *See* TEAR. –*v. i.* वि-दल् 1 P, स्फुट् 6 P, विभिद् pass.

SPLIT, *v. i.* स्फुट् 6 P, वि-,दल् 1 P, भंज्-विभिद्-विदॄ-pass., भ्रंश् 4, 6 P, शकलीभू 1 P. –*v. t.* स्फुट् c., वि-,दॄ 9 P or c., वि-,पट् 10, वि-,भिद् 7 P or c., भंज् 7 P, खंड् 10, वि-,छिद् 7 P, भ्रंश् c., विदल् c. (दलयति), शकलीकृ 8 U. –*s.* वि-,भेदः, भंगः, विदरः, स्फु(स्फो)टनं, भिदा, छिद्रं, रंध्रं. –TING, *s.* विदारणं, विपाटनं, विदलनं, &c.

SPOIL, *v. t.* मलिनीकृ 8 U, कलुषी-आविली-कृ, मलिनयति-कलुषयति-आविलयति-(D.), दुष् c. (दूषयति), (fig. also), विकृ, विप्रकृ; भ्रंश् c. (सत्पथात्). 2 अत्यंतं लल् 10, अत्यंतं छंदं अनुवृत् 1 A or अनुरुध् 4 A. 3 लुंट् 1 P, 10, अप-हृ 1 P. 4. नश् c., उद्-वि-ध्वंस् c., उच्छिद् 7 P, दुष् c. –*v. i.* दुष् 4 P, नश् 4 P. –*s.* युद्धलब्धं धनं, लुंटितं लोत्रं,लोप्त्रं, अपहारः; 's. of cattle' गोग्रहः. –ED,–SPOILT, *a.* दूषित, मलिनीकृत, नाशित, उच्छिन्न. 2 अतिलालित, दुर्ललित; लालनात् दूषित. –ER, *s.* अपहारकः, लुंटाकः, दूषकः, उच्छेदकः. –SPOLIATION, *s.* अपहारः-हरणं, लुंटनं.

SPOKE, *s.* अरः-रं, सक्थि *n.*; 's. s are fixed on to the nave' नाभौ अराः प्रतिष्ठिताः; 'a wheel having long s. s' दीर्घसक्थि चक्रं.

SPOKESMAN, *s.* मुखं, (त्वं मम मुखं भव V. 1), वक्तृ.

SPONGE, *s.*. Sponger, q. v. –Y, *a.* विरल-शिथिल-अवयव. –SPONGER, *s.* परान्नपुष्टः, परपिंडादः, पात्रेसमितः.

SPONSOR, *s.* धर्मप्रतिभूः-प्रतिनिधिः.

SPONTANEOUS, *a.* यादृच्छिक-ऐच्छिक (की *f.*), स्वेच्छानुरूप, स्वतःप्रवर्तित, यदृच्छा-स्वेच्छा-मूलक-पूर्वक, कामहेतुक, अयत्नकृत-भूत, यदृच्छा-स्वेच्छा-काम- in comp. –LY, *adv.* स्वेच्छातः, स्वेच्छया, यदृच्छया, स्वेच्छानुसारेण, स्वयं, स्वतः, स्वेच्छापूर्वं, कामतः, अंतःप्रवृत्त्या, अयत्नेन, सहजावबोधेन. –NESS, –SPONTANEITY, *s.* यदृच्छा, स्वेच्छा, कामः, रुचि *f.*

SPOON, *s.* चमसः-सं, कंबि-बा *f.*, दर्वि-र्वी *f.*, शलाका; *See* LADLE; 'wooden s.' दारुहस्तकः, तर्दू *m.* –FUL, *s.* Ex. by (*s.*); 'two s. s' दर्वीद्वयं, चमसद्वयमात्रं.

SPORADIC, *a. See* SINGLE.

SPORT, *v. i.* वि-हृ 1 P, क्रीड् 1 P, विलस् 1 P, रम् 1 A, खेल् 1 P. 2 मृगयां कृ 8 U, आच्छोदनं कृ. 3 परिहस् 1 P. –*s.* विहारः, क्रीडा, खेला, केलि *m. f.*, लीला, विलासः; 'boys' s.' कूर्दनं, क्रीडा, लीला. 2 मृगया, आच्छोदनं; आखेटः; 'to make the better s.' मृगयारसं वर्धयितुं, मृगयां अधिकफलदां कर्तुं. 3 अव-उप-हासः; विडंबना; *See* MOCKERY. 4 परिहासः, लीला, केलिः, नर्मन् *n.*; 'in s.' परिहसिन, लीलया; 'uttered in s.' नर्मालापः, परिहासजल्पितं. –IVE, *a.* (Of persons) क्रीडाशील-पर, विलासपर, खेलनपर, विहारिन्, विहार-केलि-प्रिय; *See* PLAYFUL. 2 उपहासगर्भ, नर्मप्राय, सपरिहास. 3 सविलास, सलील, सहेल, सखेल, उल्लसित. –IVELY, *adv.* सखेलं, लीलया, सलीलं, सविलासं. –SPORTSMAN, *s.* मृगया-सेविन् *m.* विहारी-शीलः, मृगयुः, व्याधः, लुब्धकः, शकुनिलुब्धकः.

SPOT, *s.* स्थानं, स्थलं, पदं, प्र-,देशः, आस्पदं, भूमि *f.*, क्षेत्रं; 'on the spot' तत्रैव. 2 बिंदुः, अंकः, लांछनं, चिह्नं, लक्षणं, पदं; 's. on the body' तिलकः-कं; 's. on the moon' लक्ष्मन् *n.*, अंकः. 3 कलंकः, दूषणं. –*v. t.* बिंदुभिः चित्र् 10 or चिह्नयति (D.), कर्बुरीकृ 8 U, शबलीकृ, कल्माषयति (D.); oft. by चित्र-*a.*; 's.-ted deer' चित्रो मृगः, बिंदुलांछितो मृगः, चित्रांगः, कर्बुरितगात्रः, &c. 2 कलंकयति (D.), दुष् c. (दूषयति). 3 Soil, SPOIL, q. v. –LESS, *a.* निष्कलंक, अकलंक, विशुद्ध, निष्कल्मष, निर्मल, अकलुष, अमलिन; अनिंद्य, निरवद्य, अनघ.

SPOUSE, *s.* परिग्रहीतृ *m.*, परिणेता, वरः, भर्ता, पतिः. 2 भार्या, वधूः; *See* WIFE. –AL, *s.* विवाहः, परिणयः, पाणिदानं-ग्रहणं; *See* MARRIAGE.

SPOUT, *s.* नाली, प्रणालः-ली. –*v. t.* उत्क्षिप् 6 P, उदस् 4 U, बलवत् निरस् or निःसृ c. or उत्क्षिप्; (fig.), उद्-गॄ 6 P, उद्वम् 1 P, निः-सृ c., विसृज् 6 P. –*v. i.* सवेगं उद्वम् 1 P or निर्गम्, निःसृ 1 P, उत्सिच्-उत्क्षिप्-pass.

SPRAIN, *v. t.* अतियत्नेन (संधीन् &c.) वितन् 8 U, आक्षिप् 6 P, अभिहन् 2 P. –*s.* संध्यभिघातः, स्नायुवितानः, अतिवितानः.

SPRAT, *s.* नल-तल-मीनः.

SPRAWL, *v. i.* सांगविक्षेपं स्वप् 2 P.

SPRAY, *s.* शी(सी)करः, तुषारः; 'bearing s.s' शीकरिन्, शीकरासारवाहिन्. 2 विटपः, शाखा, प्रशाखिका.

SPREAD, *v. i.* प्र-वि-सृप् 1 P, प्र-वि-सृ 1 P, वितन्-विस्तृ-विस्तॄ-pass., व्याप् 5 P, विजृंभ् 1 A, प्रचर् 1 P; (disease) संक्रम् 1 U, 4 P, संचर्, वि-सृप्; प्ररुह् 1 P, वृध् 1 A. –*v. t.* स्तृ 5 U, स्तॄ 9 U or c., वि-सं-आ-°; अव-वि-कॄ 6 P, (net &c.); वि-प्र-सृप् c., वि-प्र-सृ c., तन् 8 U, प्र-वि-सं-आ-°, प्रवृध् c. 2 (Opinions &c.) प्र-सृ c., सं-प्र-चर् c., प्रवृत् c., प्रकाश् c., बहुलीकृ 8 U. –*s.* प्रसारः, प्रसरः, अभि-, वृद्धि *f.*, प्रवर्तनं, विस्तारः. –ING, *a.* प्र-वि-सारिन्, प्रसर्पिन्, प्रतानिन्, प्ररोहिन्; 'a s. creeper is वीरुध्' लताप्रतानिनी वीरुत्. –*s.* प्रसरः, विसर्पणं, वितति *f.*, प्रतानः, प्रवर्धनं.

SPRIG, *s.* विटपः, शाखा, पल्लवः-वं, दलं, उपशाखा.

SPRIGHTLY, *a.* उत्साहवत्, प्रफुल्ल, सोत्साह, सोल्लास, प्रमुदित, उल्लसित, उल्लासवृत्ति. –INESS, *s.* उल्लासः, प्रहर्षः, प्रफुल्लता.

SPRING, *s.* वसंतः,-कालः,-समयः, सुरभिः, मधुः, पुष्पसमयः-कालः, मधुमासः; 's. of life' प्रथमं वयः, अक्षतं यौवनं, अयातयामं वयः. 2 उत्सः, निर्झरः. स्रोतस् *n.*, वारिप्रवाहः, प्रस्रवणं; 's.-water' नैर्झरं जलं, निर्झरवारि. 3 प्रभवः, उद्भवः, मूलं, उत्पत्तिस्थानं, योनि *f.*; *See* ORIGIN. 4 उत्प्लवः, प्लवः, प्लुतं-ति *f.*, उत्प्लुतिः, वल्गितं. 5 स्थितिस्थापकत्वविशिष्टः पदार्थः. –*v. i.* उद्भिद् pass.; प्ररुह् 1 P, स्फुट् 6 P, अंकुरयति (D.), *See* SHOOT. 2 उत्पद् 4 A, प्र-,जन् 4 A, प्र-,सं-उद्-भू 1 P, प्रवृत् 1 A, उद्-इ 2 P, निःसृ 1 P; also by भव, संभव, उद्भव, जात, ज in comp.; 'sprung from a noble family' कुलज, कुलोद्भव, कुलसंभव, &c.; 'sprung from a royal family' राजवंश्य, राजवंशज. 3 परावृत्, परापत् 1 P, उत्पत्. 4 प्लु 1 A, वल्ग् 1 P; 's. up' उत्पत्, उत्प्लु; 's. over' लंघ् 1 A, 10, उत्प्लुत्य अति-इ; 's. upon' सवेगं आपत् 1 P or आक्रम् 1 U, 4 P, सरभसं आस्कंद् 1 P. 5 Split, Start, q. v. –*v. t.* उत्था c. (उत्थापयति), प्रबुध् c. 2 उद्-भू c., उत्पद् c., जन् c. 3 Burst, Split, q. v.

SPRINGE, *s.* पाशः; *See* SNARE.

SPRINKLE, *v. t.* सिच् 6 P, आ-नि-अव-°, सं-प्र-अभि-उक्ष् 1 P; अवकॄ 6 P. –ER, *s.* सेक्तृ *m.*, सेचकः, प्रोक्षकः. –ING, *s.* प्रोक्षणं, आ-अव-सेकः; 's. of' ex. by विरल-*a.*, (विरलतुषारकणाः).

SPRITE, *s. See* GHOST.

SPROUT, *s.* मंजरी. 2 पल्लवः-वं, किस(श)लयः-यं; अंकुरः, प्ररोहः, उद्भिद्-अभिनवोद्भिद् *m.*, उद्भिज्जः. –*v. i.* उद्भिद् pass., प्ररुह् 1 P, स्फुट् 6 P, उत्-,फुल्ल् 1 P, विकस् 1 P. –ED, *a.* उद्भिन्न, अंकुरित, पल्लवित, स्फुटित. –ING, *a.* उद्भिद्-ज्ज-द, प्ररोहिन्, अंकुरित. –*s.* उद्भेदः, प्ररोहः.

SPRUCE, *a.* विनीत, विनीतवेश; *See* NEAT.

SPUME,-Y, *See* FROTH,-Y.

SPUR, *s.* कंटकः. 2 नखः-खं (of a cock). 3 प्रोत्साहनं, उत्तेजनं, प्रचोदनं, उत्साहहेतुः-कारणं; *See* INCITEMENT, INCENTIVE; 'on the s. of the moment' पूर्वं अविचार्य or अनालोच्य, अविचारपूर्वं. –*v. t.* कंटकेन उत्सह् c., प्रतुद् 6 P. 2 (On) प्रोत्सह् c., प्रचुद् 10; *See* PROMPT.

SPURIOUS, *a.* कृत्रिम, कल्पित, कपट-कूट-मिथ्या in comp.; *See* COUNTERFEIT, FALSE.

SPURN, *v. t.* (Away) लत्ताप्रहारेण प्रत्या-ख्या 2 P or निः-सृ c. or प्रत्यादिश् 6 P. 2 प्रत्या-ख्या, अवधीर् 10, तिरस्कृ 8 U, निर्-अव-धू 5, 9 U, निराकृ, धिकृ, सावज्ञं प्रत्यादिश्; *See* SCORN, CONTEMN.

SPURT, *s.* हठोद्यमः, महाप्रयत्नः. 2 सवेगः जलोत्क्षेपः. –*v. t.* सवेगं उत्क्षिप् 6 P or उदस् 4 U. –*v. i.* सवेगं निःसृ 1 P or निःस्रु 1 P.

SPUTTER, *v.* अंबूकृ 8 U, सनिष्ठीवं वद् 1 P or उच्चर् c. –*s.*,-ING, *s.* अंबूकृतं, निष्ठीवनं.

SPY, *s.* चारः, चरः, अप(व)सर्पः, स्पशः, प्रणिधिः, गूढ-गुप्त-चरः-गतिः, गूढ-गुप्त-पुरुषः ; पिशुनः, सूचकः, कर्णेजपः, रहस्याख्यायी (slanderous); 'see as a s.' अपसृप् 1 P, (स मया पौरजानपदानपसर्पितुं प्रयुक्तः U. 1); 'the king sees by s. es' चारचक्षुर्महीपालः. –*v. t.* दृश् 1 P, ईक्ष् 1 A; *See* SEE. 2 निरूप् 10, निरीक्ष्, अवेक्ष्, अनुसं-धा 3 U.

SQUAB, *a.* ह्रस्वस्थूल.

SQUABBLE, *See* QUARREL.

SQUAD, *s.* नवसैन्यदलं.

SQUADRON, *s.* (सैन्य-) गणः, गुल्मः-ल्मं, दलं, व्यूहः. 2 पोतावली, नौसमूहः.

SQUALID, *a.* मलिन, कुत्सित, अमेध्य, अप-नि-कृष्ट, अधम, जघन्य; *See* DIRTY.

SQUALL, *s.* चीत्कारः, चंडरवः, कलकलः, उत्क्रोशः, उच्चनादः-रवः. 2 (Of wind) चंडवातः, प्रभंजनः, प्रकंपनः. –*v. i.* उत्-व्या-क्रुश् 1 P, उच्चैः हृ 2 P or घुष् 10; *See* SCREAM.

SQUANDER, *v. t.* अप-व्यय् 10(व्ययति), विक्षिप् 6P, मुधा क्षै c. (क्षपयति) or हृ 1 P, अमितं व्यय्, अतिव्ययं कृ. –ER, *s.* अपव्ययकारिन्, अमितव्ययकारी, विक्षेपी. –ING, *s.* अपव्ययः, विक्षेपः ; अति-अमित-व्ययः.

SQUARE, *s.* (In Arith.) वर्गः, कृति *f.*, द्विघातः ; 's. root' वर्गमूलं, पदं ; 'the root of the sum of their s. s' तत्कृत्योर्योगपदं ; 'take the s. root' पदीकृ, (Li.). 2 (In geometry) वर्गः, समचतुरस्रः, समचतुर्भुजः. 3 चत्वरं, अंगनं-णं ; *See* COURTYARD ; 's. formed by 4 houses' संजवनं, चतुःशालं. –*v. t.* वर्गीकृ 8 U, वर्गयति (D.), द्विः हन् 2 P or गुणयति (D.). 2 समीकृ, शुध् c.; समा-धा 3 U, प्रति-सं-आ-युज् 7 U, 10. –*v. i.* संवद् 1 P, युज्-उपपद्-pass.; *See* SUIT. –*a.* समचतुर्भुज, समचतुरस्र. 2 Just, q. v.

SQUASH, *v. t.* संमृद् 9 P, संपीड् 10, संपिष् 7 P, चूर्ण् 10. –*s.* संमर्दः, संपीडनं, चूर्णनं.

SQUAT, *v. i.* उत्कटुकासनं कृ 8 U, अवसक्थिकासनं कृ ; अवनतसक्थि आस् 2 A or उपविश् 6 P. 2 Cower, q. v.

SQUEAK, SQUEAL, *v. i.* कर्कशं हृ 2 P or नद् 1 P, वाश् 4 A. –*s.* कर्कशरवः-नादः, वाशितं, चीत्कारः.

SQUEAMISH, *a.* विवमिषु, वमनोन्मुख (खी *f.*). 2 Fastidious, q. v. –NESS, *s.* विवमिषा.

SQUEEZE, *v. t.* नि-सं-पीड् 10, संमृद् 9 P, निष्पिष् 7 P; (out) निर्गल् c., निष्कृष् 1 P, निर्दुह् 2 U; *See* CRUSH, PRESS. –ING, *s.* संपीडनं, संमर्दः-र्दनं, निर्गालनं, निष्पेषः, निष्कर्षः.

SQUIB, *s.* *See* SATIRE.

SQUINT, *v. i.* तिर्यक् दृश् 1 P or प्रेक्ष् 1A, वक्रं वीक्ष्. –*s.* तिर्यक्-वक्र-दृष्टि *f.*; 's.-eyed' वक्रदृष्टि, वलिर, केकर, केदर; तिर्यग्दृष्टि.

SQUIRE, *s.* महाजनः, आर्यः, श्री pr. 2 सान्निहनिकः.

SQUIRREL, *s.* काष्ठमार्जारः-बिडालः, वृक्षशायिका, चमरपुच्छः.

SQUIRT, *s.* धारायंत्रं. –*v. t.* उदस् 4 U, उत्क्षिप् 6 P, बलेन निःसृ c. or निरस्.

STAB, *v. t.* (छुरिकया &c.) व्यध् 4 P, भिद् 7 P, क्षण् 8 P, छुर् 1 P; 's. in the secret' परोक्षे मर्मभेदं कृ 8 U. –*s.* क्षतं, वेधः, त्वग्भेदः.

STABLE, *a.* स्थिर, निश्चल, अचल, दृढ, स्थावर; *See* FIRM. –*s.* मंदुरा, वाजि-अश्व-शाला; (for elephants) वारी, गजबंधनी; (for cattle) गोशाला, गोष्ठं; 's.-keeper' अश्वपालः, मंदुरापालः. –STABILITY, *s.* स्थैर्यं, दृढता, सं-,स्थिति *f.*, स्थायित्वं, प्रतिष्ठा; *See* PERMANENCE.

STACK, *s.* राशिः, सं-,चयः, संघः, उत्करः, चिति *f.* –*v. t.* राशीकृ 8 U, समाहृ 1 P, आ-सं-चि 5 U.

STAFF, *s.* दंडः, यष्टि *f.*, वेत्रं (cane), लगुडः (wooden). 2 आलंबः-बनं, आधारः, आश्रयः. 3 वर्गः, गणः, अधिकारिगणः &c.; 's. of teachers' शिक्षकवर्गः-समुदायः.

STAG, *s.* हरिणः, मृगः, कुरंगः-गमः, एणः.

STAGE, *s.* रंगः,-भूमि *f.*, शाला; नाट्यशाला; नेपथ्यं; 'behind the s.' नेपथ्ये. 2 मंचः-चकः. 3 (On a journey) वसति *f.*, (तिस्रो वसतीरुषित्वा R. VII. 33), प्रयाणकं; विश्रामस्थानं, अवस्थानं. 4 पदं, स्थानं, आस्पदं, वृत्ति *f.*, दशा, अवस्था. 5 (State of existence) आश्रमः, (वानप्रस्थाश्रमः); 'last s.' चरमावस्था; 'first s.' उपक्रमः, प्रथमारंभः; 's.-coach' अध्वगयानं, पथिकयानं; 's.-manager' सूत्रधारः; 's.-player' रंगोपजीविन् *m.*, नटः, नर्तकः.

STAGER, *s.* ज्ञानवृद्धः, वृद्धः.

STAGGER, *v. i.* प्रस्खल् 1 P, विचल् 1 P, भ्रम् 1, 4 P, घूर्ण् 1 A, 6 P, दोलायते (D.); सभयं-सचकितं-परावृत् 1 A. 2 विशंक् 1 A, विक्लृप् 1 A. –*v. t.* विचल् c., भ्रम् c., शंका-विकल्पं-उत्पद् c.

STAGNANT, *a.* स्थिर, निश्चल, निष्प्रवाह, निश्चेष्ट, गतिप्रवाह-हीन-रहित. –STAGNATE, *v. i.* स्थिरीभू 1 P, ex. by (*a.*) with भू; 'when the stream of knowledge s.s' यदा ज्ञानस्रोतसो गतिरोधः भवति, ज्ञानस्रोतोगतिः कुंठिता भवति. –ION,-STAGNANCY, *s.* अप्रवाहः, निश्चलता, गति-प्रवाह-अभावः, निश्चलता, स्थैर्यं.

STAID, *a.* धीर, ग(गं)भीर, स्थिर ; *See* SERIOUS.

STAIN, *v. t.* (lit. and fig.) दुष् c. (दूषयति), कलंकयति-मलिनयति-आविलयति-कलुषयति (D.), मलिनी-कलुषी-कृ 8 U, लिप् 6 P, लांछ् 1 P, समलीमलीमसी-कृ; 'what is the use of life s. ed by infamy (ignominy)' उपक्रोशमलीमसैः प्राणैः किं (R. II. 53); 's. ed by blood' रक्तमलिन; 'with s. ed hands' लिप्तहस्त. 2 रंज् c. –*s.* कलंकः, अंकः, दूषणं, लांछनं, चिह्नं, कलुषं, मलं, मालिन्यं. 2 निंदा, उपक्रोशः, वाच्यता, वचनीयं, गर्हा. –LESS, *a.* निष्कलंक, निर्मल, अदूषण, अकलुष, कलंक-लांछन-हीन, निर्दोष, निरवद्य.

STAIR, *s.* सोपानं, आरोहणं, पर्वन् *n.*, भंगिः-गी *f.*; 'flight of s. s,' 's.-case,' 's.s' सोपानपथः-मार्गः-पद्धति *f.*-परंपरा-पदवी-पंक्ति *f.*, निश्रेणी, अधिरोहिणी.

STAKE, *s.* ग्लहः, पणः 2 कीलः, शंकुः, शूलः-लं; स्थाणुः, स्थूणा, शलाका. 3 संशयः, संदेहः; 'his life was at s.' संशयस्थं जीवितं तस्य, संशयितजीवित आसीत्, जीवितं संशयदोलाधिरूढं. –*v. t.* पण् 1 A, (with gen. of thing staked); शतस्य पणते 's. s a hundred'. 2 शूलेन-कीलेन व्यध् 4 P or बंध् 9 P, कील् 10.

STALE, *a.* यातयाम, परि-,उषित, रात्र्यंतरित; निःसार, नीरस, असत्त्व; दुष्ट (जलं). 2 जीर्ण, पुराण, उच्छिष्ट. –*v. i.* मिह् 1 P, मूत्र् 10.

STALK, *s.* कांडः-डं, नालः-लं-ली; बंधनं, वृंतं, प्रसव-शस्य-बंधनं. 2 साटोपगति *f.*, धीरोद्धता गतिः. –*v. i.* साटोपं परिक्रम् 1 U, 4 P, उद्धतं-सगर्वं-चल् or गम् 1 P, धीरोद्धतं गम्; 's. ing-horse' Pretext, q. v.

STALL, *s.* पण्यवीथिका, पण्यगेहं, आपणः, विपणि *f.*; *See* SHOP. 2 शाला, स्थानं; (for horses) मंदुरा, अश्वस्थानं; (for cattle) गोष्ठं, गो-शाला-स्थानं.

STALLION, *s.* बीजाश्वः, सवृषणः अश्वः.

STAMEN, *s.* केसरः, पुंकेसरः. –STAMINA, *s.* (fig.) सारः, सत्त्वं, तेजस् *n.*, बलसाधनं-हेतुः.

STAMMER, *v. i.* स्खल् 1 P, असमंजसं जल्प् 1 P, स्खलद्वाक्येन--अस्पष्टवर्णैः--अस्फुटस्वरेण-गद्गदवाचा--वद् 1 P, अस्पष्टं-अस्फुटं-वच् 2 P. –ER, *s.* अव्यक्त-अस्पष्ट-वादिन् *m.*, स्खलत्-गद्गद-वादी, स्खलितस्वरः. –ING, *s.* स्खलनं, अस्पष्ट-अव्यक्त-भाषणं.

STAMP, *s.* मुद्रा, मुद्रिका, मुद्रायंत्रं. 2 मुद्रा, चिह्नं, अंकः, न्यासः, पदं. 3 पादप्रहारः,-आघातः-विष्टंभः. 4 स्व-रूपं, आकारः, आकृति *f.*, प्रकृति *f.*, संस्कारः; 'of the common s.' सामान्यप्रकृति, प्राकृत ; 'of high s.' महाप्रभाव, महानुभाव ; 'of the same s.' समानरूप, तुल्य-स्वभाव-प्रकृति. –*v.* पादेन-पादतलेन-प्रह् 1 P or आ-अभि-हन् 2 U, पादप्रहारं कृ 8 U. 2 अंक् 10, मुद्रयति-चिह्नयति- (D.), लांछ् 1 P; 's.-ed with infamy' दुष्कीर्तिचिह्नित, उपक्रोशमलीमस, अपयशोंकित. 3 कृप् c., रच् 10, संवि-धा 3 U. 4 पादतलेन मृद् 9 P or चूर्ण् 10 or पिष् 7 P. –ED, *a.* अंकित, लांछित, समुद्र, कृतमुद्र, मुद्रांकित.

STANCH, *a.* दृढ, स्थिर, धीर, अचल; 'a s. adherent' बद्धानुरागः सहायः, दृढपक्ष्यः; *See* FIRM. –*v. t.* प्रवाहं-प्रस्रावं स्तंभ् 9 P or रुध् 7 U, शुष् c. –*v. i.* शुष् 4 P, स्तब्धप्रवाह-*a.* भू 1 P.

STANCHION, *s.* क्षुद्रस्तंभः-स्थाणुः.

STAND, *v. i.* स्था 1 P, पद्भ्यां स्था. 2 वृत् 1 A, विद् 4 A, अव-स्था 1 A; *See* REMAIN. 3 भू 1 P, अस् 2 P, वृत्. 4 निवृत्, विरम् 1 P, स्तंभ् pass., स्थिर-रुद्धगति-कुंठित- *a.* भू; 'this will remain a s.-ing stigma (on me)' वचनीयमिदं व्यवस्थितं (K. IV. 21); 'this argument will not s. long' इयं युक्तिर्न चिरं स्थास्यति, अचिरात् खंडयिष्यते. –*v. t.* सह् 1 A, मृष् 4 P, 10; *See* BEAR ; 'to s. the test' निकषपरीक्षां तॄ 1 P, निकषे परीक्ष् pass. 2 उप-नि-रुध् 7 U; प्रति-वि-रुध्. –against, प्रत्यव-स्था, बाध् 1 A; विरुध्; *See* OPPOSE. –by, -near, साहाय्यं कृ, संरक्ष् 1 P, परि-,त्रै 1 A, उपकृ; अनुग्रह्. 2 स्था, अव-स्था, अनुरुध् 4 A, अनुवृत्; 's. by your lord's orders' शासने तिष्ठ भर्तुः (V. 5); *See* OBEY. –for, स्थाने-भूमौ स्था or वृत्. 2 पदं आप् desid. (ईप्सति). –off, अप-सृ 1 P, दूरतः स्था. –on, आ-अव-लंब् 1 A, आ-स्था (A), आश्रि 1 U. –out, प्रलंब्, उन्नम् 1 P; *See* PROJECT. 2 Persist, q. v. –over, व्याक्षिप् pass. 2 अधि-ष्ठा, अध्यास् 2 A; 'his name s.s over all' स सर्वेषां मूर्ध्नि तिष्ठति. –to, संवद् 1 P; 'does not s. to reason' सयुक्तिकं-सोपपत्तिकं न भाति. –up, उत्था. –*s.* आधारः, भाजनं, पात्रं, उपष्टंभः, आश्रयः ; 'ink-s.' मसीपात्रं-धानी ; 's. of a lamp' दीपाधारः-वृक्षः. 2 मंचः. 3 अव-,स्थानं, पदं, स्थिति *f.*, अव-,स्तंभः; गतिरोधः-स्तंभः, कुंठनं ; 'come to a s.' स्तब्ध-शांत- *a.* भू; 'bring to a s.' स्तंभ् 9 P or c., गतिं रुध् or वृ c.; 'at a s.-still' कुंठित, प्रतिहत-रुद्ध-गति ; 'make a s. against' प्रतिबंध् 9 P, प्रत्यव-स्था (A), प्रति-वि-रुध्. –ING, *s.* अव-,स्थितिः, अवस्थानं, स्थायित्वं; 'of long s.' चिरस्थायिन्, दीर्घकालीन, पुराण; *See* OLD. 2 स्थानं, पदं, आस्पदं, पदवी, प्रतिष्ठा ; 'high s.' उच्चपदं, महती प्रतिष्ठा ; 'who has obtained a s.' लब्धप्रतिष्ठः. –*a.* सनातन, चि-

र-नित्य-स्थायिन् ; *See* LASTING. 2 स्थित, उत्थित, दंडवत् स्थित. 3 स्थ, स्थायिन्, वर्तिन्, अव-,स्थित in comp.; 'with the hair s. on their end' पुलकित, रोमांचित, कंटकित.

STANDARD, *s.* ध्वजः, पताका, केतुः, केतनं, वैजयंती; 's.-bearer' ध्वजिन्, पताकिन्. 2 मानं, प्र-परि-°, सूत्रं, विधिः, नियमः; 'a s. person' प्रमाणपुरुषः, प्रमाणं; 's. authors' प्रमाणभूताः (विशिष्टाः) ग्रंथकृतः.

STANZA, *s.* श्लोकः.

STAPLE, *a.* प्रधान, मुख्य, विशिष्ट. —*s.* Market, q. v. 2 लोहपुटः.

STAR, *s.* तारा, तारका, नक्षत्रं, ज्योतिस् *n.*, उडुः, भं, ऋक्षं; 'the s. s collectively' उडुगणः, भगणः; 'shooting s.' नक्षत्रपतनं, उल्का; 's. under which one is born' जन्मनक्षत्रं; 's.-light' ताराप्रकाश, तारकित; (*s.*) ताराप्रकाशः. —*v. t.* तारासनाथ-*a.* कृ 8 U, तारकयति (D.); 'the breast s. ed with drops of tears' अश्रुबिंदुतारकितपयोधरा; 'the s.-red heaven' तारासनाथं-तारकितं-नभः. —RY, *a.* तारासंकुल-मय (यी *f.*)-आकीर्ण-सनाथ, तारकित. 2 तारानिभ, तारा in comp.; 's. firmament' नभोमंडलं, नक्षत्रमंडलं.

STARBOARD, *s.* नौदक्षिणपार्श्वः.

STARCH, *s.* मंडः-डं. —*v. t.* मंडयति (D.), मंडेन लिप् 6 P.

STARE, *v. i.* सूक्ष्मं-बद्धलक्ष्यं-स्थिरदृष्ट्या-अनिमेषलोचनाभ्यां-प्रेक्ष् 1 A or दृश् 1 P or आलोक् 1 A, 10, अनन्यदृष्ट्या निरीक्ष्, स्निग्धं निर्वर्ण् 10. —*s.* स्थिरदृष्टि *f.*, बद्ध-अनिमेष-दृष्टिः, अनन्यदृष्टिः. —ING, *a.* बद्ध-स्थिर-अनन्य-अनिमेष-दृष्टि, बद्धलक्ष्य, विवृत-उत्फुल्ल-नयन-लोचन &c., उन्मीलिताक्ष.

STARK, *a.* समग्र, पूर्ण, केवल, अत्यंत, अशेष. 2 रूक्ष, विषम. —*adv.* केवलं, अत्यंतं.

START, *v. i.* प्र-स्था 1 A, प्र-या 2 P, प्र-,चल् 1 P; यात्राभिमुखं प्रवृत् 1 A 's. on a journey' (Mal. 6). 2 स्फुर् 6 P, सहसा कंप् 1 A or स्पंद् 1 A; 's. back' ससाध्वसं परावृत् or अपसृ 1 P, सचकितं व्यपसृ, चकित-*a.* भू; संत्रस्त-भयचकित- *a.* भू; 's. aside' स्वस्थानात् विचल् or भ्रंश् 1 A, 4 P or च्यु 1 A; अभिन्नगतयः शब्दं सहंते (S. 1) 'not s. ing aside &c.; 's. up' सहसा उत्था; (in sleep) सहसा अवबुध् 4 A.; (an idea) सहसा उद्भू or उत्पद् 4 A. —*v. t.* प्रवृत् c., प्र-स्तु c., संचल् c., प्रचर् c. 2 उद्विज् c., संत्रस् c., चकित-*a.* कृ 8 U, उत्था c. (उत्थापयति), भी c.; अकस्मात् त्रस् c. or कंप् c. 3 Propose, q. v. —*s.* प्रस्थानं, प्रस्थानारंभः. 2 कंपः-पनं, स्फुरणं, साध्वसोत्कंपः, सहसाकर्षः, आकस्मिकप्रकंपः; चकितं; 'gave a sudden s.' (सहसा) ससाध्वसं चकितो बभूव; 'with a s.' चकितं, सचकितं. 2 प्रवर्तनं, आरंभः, प्रचारः; 'to get or have the s. of' पूर्वं (with abl.) प्र-स्था or प्रारभ् 1 A; 'by s. s' सातत्यं विना, सुप्तैरिव, आकस्मिकयत्नैः.

STARTLE, *v. See* START; 's. ing news' उद्वेगकरी वार्ता; 'in a very s. ed manner' चकितचकितं.

STARVE, *v. i.* क्षुधया पीड् or अर्द् pass., आहाराभावात् मृ 6 A or अव-,सद् 1 P or नश् 4 P, क्षुधया अवसद्; (oneself) आहारं-अशनं-त्यज् 1 P, प्रायोपवेशनं कृ 8 U; 'likely to s.' आसन्नमृत्युरिव, अनशनेन मुमूर्षुरिव; (fig.) अव-,सद्. —*v. t.* अनशनेन मृ c. or नश् c.; 'be sure, I shall s. myself (to death)' मया प्रायोपवेशनं कृतं विद्धि (P. IV. 1). —ATION, *s.* अनशनं, अनाहारः, आहाराभावः, क्षुधावसादः, क्षुत्क्षामता. —ED, -ING, *a.* क्षुधापीडित-अर्दित-आर्त, क्षुधावसन्न, निराहार, निरन्न.

STATE, *s.* अवस्था, दशा, भावः, स्थिति *f.*, वृत्ति *f.*, गति *f.*; त्वं-ता affixed. 2 राज्यं, राष्ट्रं, राजन् in comp.; 's. affairs' राजकार्याणि; 's.-servant' राजसेवकः. 3 ऐश्वर्यं, आडंबरः, आटोपः, प्रतापः, वैभवं, विभूति *f.*; श्रीः, गौरवं. —*v. t.* कथ् 10, आचक्ष् 2 A, वच् 2 P, वद् 1 P, नि-आ-विद् c., निर्दिश् 6 P, वि-ज्ञा c. (ज्ञापयति), वर्ण् 10, उपन्यस् 4 U; *See* TELL, SAY. —ED, *a.* कथित, उक्त, निर्दिष्ट, वर्णित, &c.; 'as above s.' यथानिर्दिष्ट. 2 नियत, व्यवस्थित. —LY, *a.* सप्रताप, सश्रीक, सवैभव, उज्ज्वल; *See* MAJESTIC, GRAND. 2 साटोप, उद्धत, सखेल; 's. in gait' साटोपगामिन्, खेलगति-गामिन्, हंसगामिन्. —*adv.* साटोपं, उद्धतं, सखेलं, सलीलं, सप्रतापं. —MENT, *s.* कथनं, आ-नि-वेदनं, उक्ति *f.*, वचनं, उपन्यासः, निर्देशः, विज्ञापना; 'clearness of s.' उपन्यासशुद्धिः. —STATESMAN, *s.* नीतिज्ञः-विद् *m.*-विशारदः, राजकार्यकुशलः-धुरंधरः, राजनीतिनिपुणः. —SHIP, *s.* नीतिज्ञता, नीति *f.*

STATION, *s.* स्थानं, अव-,स्थिति *f.*, आस्पदं, स्थलं, पदं, अवस्थानं. 2 दशा, पदं, अवस्था, वृत्ति *f.*, पदवी *f.*; 'high s.' उन्नतपदं, परमस्थानं, उन्नतावस्था; 's. of life' जाति *f.* 3 अधिकारः, नियोगः, पदं, पदविः-वी. 4 निवेशः. —*v. t.* स्था c. (स्थापयति), अव-सं-प्रति-°, निविश् c.; 's. in any post' पदे-अधिकारे-नियुज् 7 A, 10. —ARY, *a.* स्थिर, अचल, निश्चल, अचर, स्थावर; अजंगम. 2 अवर्धिष्णु, अवर्धमान.

STATIONER, *s.* लेखनसाधनविक्रयिन् *m.* —Y, *s.* लेखलिपि-साधनं-सज्जा-सामग्री.

STATUE, *s.* प्रतिमा, प्रतिकृति *f.*, मूर्ति *f.*; *See* IMAGE. —STATUARY, *s.* कारः in comp. with (*s.*), तक्षकः. 2 मूर्तिविधानं-करणं.

STATURE, *s.* प्रमाणं, परिमाणं, उच्चता, मूर्ति *f.*, आकृति *f.*, आकारः; 'of low s.' अल्पप्रमाण; 'of dwarfish s.' वामनाकृति, खर्व, ह्रस्व; 'short in s.' ह्रस्व-अल्प-मूर्ति.

STATUTE, *s.* विधिः, नियमः, व्यवस्था; *See* LAW, RULE. —STATUTORY, *a.* विधिप्रोक्त, व्यवस्थाकल्पित, नियत.

STAVE, *s.* काष्ठखंडः-डं, फलकः-कं. —*v. t.* स्फुट् c., छिद्रयति (D.).

STAY, *v. i.* वस् 1 P, स्था 1 P, वृत् 1 A, अध्यास् 2 A; *See* DWELL. 2 विरम् 1P; अलं with instr. or gerund. —*v. t.* स्तंभ् 9 P, प्रतिबंध् 9 P, उप-नि-रुध् 7 U, विलंब् c., नि-प्रति-वृ c.; नि-प्रति-षिध् 1 P; 's. one's progress' मार्गं निरुध् (Mr. 5.). 2 आ-अव-लंब् 1 A, आश्रि 1 U, आधृ 10, अव-उप-स्तंभ्; *See* PROP. —*s.*,-ING, *s.* नि-,वासः, अवस्थानं, अव-,स्थिति *f.* 2 आलंबः, आधारः, आश्रयः, उपघ्नः, उप-अव-ष्टंभः. 3 प्रतिष्टंभः, निरोधः, गतिरोधः, प्रतिबंधः. —STAYS, *s.* अंगिका, चोलः-लं, कूर्पासकः.

STEAD, *s.* स्थानं, भूमि *f.*; *See* INSTEAD (of).

STEADFAST, *a.* स्थिर, दृढ, सतत, अचल; निश्चल, धीर, स्थिरबुद्धि-वृत्ति, अचंचलवृत्ति; 's. in friendship' दृढसौहृद. —LY, *adv.* दृढं, स्थिरं. —NESS, *s.* स्थैर्यं, धैर्य, धृति *f.*

STEADY, *a.* स्थिर, दृढ, अचल, निश्चल, धीर, अस्खलित, धृतिमत्; सतत, अविश्रांत, अविरत; अविरतोद्योग, सदोद्यमिन्; 'of s. action' स्थिरकर्मा; 's. in resolution' स्थिर-दृढ-निश्चय-संकल्प. 2 अनुद्विग्न, अक्षुब्ध, अनाकुल, प्रशांत. —*v. t.* स्थिरीकृ 8 U, दृढयति (D.), दृढीकृ, व्यव-स्था c. (स्थापयति). —ILY, *adv.* स्थिरं, दृढं, धीरं, अनवरतं, अविरतं, नित्यं, सदा, अविश्रांतं. —INESS, *s.* स्थैर्यं, धैर्यं, अचापल्यं, नित्यता, सातत्यं, अविच्छेदः, अविरति *f.*; 's. of conduct' अव्यभिचारः, आचारमर्यादा.

STEAL, *v. t.* चुर् 10, मुष् 9 P, अपहृ 1 P, स्तेन् 10. —*v. i.* चुर्, स्तेयं वि-धा 3 U. 2 (Away) अलक्षितं-निभृतं-गम् 1 P or अपक्रम् 1 U, 4 P or अपसृ 1 P; निःशब्दं चल् 1 P; 'the night, the quarters of which (gradually) stole away' अविदितगतयामा रात्रिः (U. 1); 's. over,-upon' अलक्षितं समाक्रम् or अभिभू or ग्रस् 1 A; 'sleep gently stole upon my eyes' शनैर्निद्रा निमीलितलोचनं मामकार्षीत्. —ER, *s.* अपहर्तृ *m.*, अपहारकः, स्तेनः, स्तेयकृत्, चो(चौ)रः, मोषकः, तस्करः, हारी in comp.; 's. of hearts' हृदयचौरः. —ING, *s.* स्तेयं, चौरकर्मन् *n.*, स्तैन्यं, चौर्यं, मोषः, अपहारः. —TH, *s.* अपहारः &c. 2 छलं, गूढं कर्म, चोरिका, निह्नवः, निभृत-प्रच्छन्न-कर्म; 'marriage by s.' चोरिकाविवाहः. —THILY, 'by s.' *adv.* छलेन, निभृतं, प्रच्छन्नं, अलक्षितं, अप्रकाशं, सुगूढं, रहसि. —THY, *a.* निभृत, प्रच्छन्न, गुप्त, गूढ, रहस्य, अलक्षित, अप्रकाश, अव्यक्त.

STEAM, *s.* बाष्पः; 's.-boat', 'steamer' अग्निनौका, बाष्पीयनौः. —*v. i.* बाष्पायते (D.), बाष्पं उत्-सृज् or उत्क्षिप् 6 P or उद्-गॄ 6 P. —*v. t.* बाष्पेण व्याप् c., स्विद् c.

STEED, *s.* अश्वः, तुरगः, वाजिन् *m.*; *See* HORSE.

STEEL, *s.* चित्रायसं, सारलोहं, पिंडायसं, तीक्ष्णायसं, शस्त्रकं. 2 शस्त्रं, शस्त्रकं; 's.-yard' तुलादंडः, मापनदंडः. —*a.* तीक्ष्णायस (सी *f.*). —*v. t.* कठिनीकृ 8 U, दृढी-निर्दयी-कृ.

STEEP, *a.* दुरारोह, उत्सर्पिन्, पातुक, प्रवण, अतट. —*s.* प्रपातः, भृगुः, अतटः. —*v. t.* नि-,मस्ज् c. (मज्जयति), स्ना c. (स्न-स्ना-पयति), जलेन आप्लु c. or सिच् 6 P. 2 सं-धा 3 U, वास् 10, भू c.; 's.ing indigo' नीलीसंधानं-पाचनं; 's.ed in perfumes' वासित, भावित.

STEEPLE, *s.* शिखरं, शृंगं, (of a palace &c.).

STEER, *s.* वत्सतरः, दम्यः. —*v. t.* चल् c., वह् c., मार्गं उपदिश् 6 P (with gen.); नी 1 P, मार्गं निश्चि 5 U or निर्णी ; 's. one's course' स्वमार्ग-कर्तव्यं-निर्णी; 'he who s. s the vessel of state' (बिभर्ति) राज्यधूर्वहः, भुवनराज्यभारनौकर्णधारः (Ka. 56). —ER,-STEERSMAN, *s.* कर्णधारः-ग्राहः, कर्णिन् *m.*, नाविकः.

STELLAR, *a.* तारा in comp.; *See* STARRY. —STELLATE,-ED, *a.* तारोपम.

STEM, *s.* बंधनं, वृंतं, प्रसवबंधनं. 2 प्र-,कांडः-डं; स्तंभः, नालं-लः. —*v. t.* प्रतिबंध् 9 P, प्रति-वि-रुध् 7 U, प्रतिष्टंभ् 9 P, प्रत्यव-स्था 1 A, प्रतिकूलयति-प्रतीपयति (D.); *See* OPPOSE.

STENCH, *s.* पूति *f.*, पूतिगंधः; दुर्गंधः.

STENTORIAN, *a.* अतितार, अत्युच्च, उरुस्वन.

STEP, *s.* पदं, पद-पाद-न्यासः-विक्षेपः, क्रमः, पद-चरणपातः, विक्रमः (as in त्रिविक्रमः); 'Vishnu took 3 s.s' विष्णुस्त्रीणि पदानि विचक्रमे. 2 पदं, क्रमः, (distance also); पर्यायः, परिपाटी; 'at every s.', 's. by s.' प्रति-अनु-पदं, पदे पदे, पदात्पदं, क्रमशः, पदशः; 'by s. s' क्रमशः, शनैः शनैः, क्रमेण; 'the first s.' प्रथमारंभः, उपक्रमः, प्रथमचरणः. 3 (Of a ladder) भंगि *f.*, सोपानं, आरोहणं ; 'flight of s. s' अधिरोहिणी; *See* LADDER, STAIRCASE. 4 उपायः, प्रतिपत्ति *f.*, क्रिया; वयस्य कात्र प्रतिपत्तिः (Mal. 3); 'not knowing what s. s to take' प्रतिपत्तिमूढः, विषादलुप्तप्रतिपत्ति (R. III. 40); 's.-brother' वैमात्रः-त्रेयः, विमातृजः, अन्योदर्यः;'s.-child' अन्योदर्यं अपत्यं; 's.-daughter' सपत्नीसुता; 's.-father' मातुः पतिः; 's.-mother' विमाता, सपत्नीमाता; 's.-sister' वैमात्री-त्रेयी, विमातृजा, अन्योदर्या; 's.-son' सपत्नीसुतः. —*v.* पादं विन्यस् 4 U or निक्षिप् 6 P, पादन्यासं-पदविक्षेपं-कृ 8 U; 's. ing over his body' तच्छरीरे पादन्यासं

कृत्वा. 2 क्रमशः चल् 1 P or गम् 1 P; (over) आक्रम् 1 U, 4 P; व्याप् 5 P; 'as much space as I can s. over in three steps' यावतीं भूमिं त्रिपदैनाहं व्याप्नुयां-आक्रमेयं-तावतीं; 's. in between' अंतरा आगम् or पत् 1P; 's. towards' प्रतिपद् 4 A —PING, s. पादन्यासः &c.; 's.-stone' सोपानशिलाप्रस्तरः.

STEREOTYPED, a. स्थिर, अपरिवर्तनीय, दृढसंकल्पित.

STERILE, a. वंध्य, अफल, निष्फल. —ITY, s. वंध्यता, निष्फलत्वं.

STERLING, a. यथार्थ, परमार्थ, वास्तविक (की f.); अकृत्रिम, सारभूत.

STERN, s. पृष्ठभागः. —a. निष्ठुर, रूक्ष, दारुण, परुष, कठिन, कठोर, उग्र; निर्दय, क्रूर; 'in a decisive and s. tone' परिच्छेदनिष्ठुर; 'of s. stuff' अभेद्यसार. —LY, adv. निष्ठुरं, कठोरं, दारुणं, उग्रं —NESS, s. नैष्ठुर्य, कठोरता, पारुष्यं.

STERNUM, s. उरोस्थि n.

STERNUTATION, s. See SNEEZE. —STERNUTATORY, s. नस्यं.

STEWARD, s. परिचारकः. 2 अर्थाधिकारी, कार्याधीशः. —SHIP, s. कार्याधीशत्वं.

STIBIUM, s. सौवीरं, कापोतं, स्रोतोंजनं, यामुनं.

STICK, s. दंडः, यष्टि f.; वेत्रं, वेत्रयष्टिः (cane); काष्ठं, काष्ठखंडः, लगुडः. —v. i. सं-लग् 1 P, संश्लिष् 4 P, संज् pass., आ-सं-अनु-°, आसज् 1 P, अनुबंध् 9 P, संसक्ती-संलग्नी-भू 1 P. 2 मस्ज् 6 P, निरुध्-स्तंभ् pass.; 'the wheels stuck fast into the mire' पंके गाढं निरुद्धानि चक्राणि. 3 विक्लृप् 1 A, विशंक् 1 A; See DOUBT; 's. out' प्रलंब् 1 A; See PROJECT. —v. t. निविश् c., अनुबंध्, आ-सं-संज् c., संलग्नीकृ 8 U. 2 प्रसृ c. —Y, a. स्निग्ध, चिक्कण, श्यान, सांद्र, संलग्नशील.

STICKLE, v. i. पक्षं ग्रह् 9 P. 2 Contend, q. v.

STIFF, a. कठिन, संहत; दृढ, घन, अनम्य, अशिथिल, स्तब्ध. 2 परुष, रुक्ष, कर्कश. 3 असुगम, दुर्बोध, दुर्ज्ञेय, गहन; 's.-hearted,-necked' प्रतिनिविष्ट, स्तब्ध, दृढनिश्चय. —EN, v. t. कठिनीकृ 8 U, घनीकृ, स्तंभ् 9 P or c. —v. i. कठिनीभू 1 P; 'remain with your body s. ed' स्तंभितगात्रस्तिष्ठ. —LY, adv. दृढं, कठिनं. —NESS, s. काठिन्यं, दृढता, &c.

STIFLE, v. t. श्वासं नि-,रुध् 7 U, श्वासरोधं कृ. 2 स्तंभ् 9 P or c., निग्रह् 9 P, नियम् 1 P, नियंत्र् 10; See CHOKE, SUPPRESS; 'with s.ed words' स्तंभितवाक्.

STIGMA, s. कलंकः, अंकः, लांछनं, दूषणं. —TIZE, v.t. निंद् 1 P, परिवद् 1 A, दुष् c. (दूषयति); कलंकयति (D.), अपकीर्त्या अंक् 10; See STAIN.

STILE, s. सोपानमार्गः-पद्धति f.

STILETTO, s. See DAGGER..

STILL, s. अधोयंत्रं, बकयंत्रं, संधानपात्रं. —a. निःशब्द, नीरव, मूक; See SILENT. 2 निष्कंप, निश्चल, अचल, स्थिर, निश्चेष्ट. 3 प्र-उप-शांत, स्तिमित; निर्वात, अक्षुब्ध; See QUIET; 'heart, be s.' हृदय मा उन्माम्य (S. 1); 'in the s. midnight' स्तिमितेऽर्धरात्रे; 'to be s.' प्र-उप-शम् 4 P; 's.-born' मृतजात; 'a s.-born child' मूढगर्भः, मृतजातः. —adv. तथापि. 2 अद्यापि; अद्य यावत्. 3 सदा, सर्वदा. 4 शांतं, तूष्णीं, निःशब्दं. —v. t. शम् c. (शमयति), प्र-उप-°, निःशब्दीकृ 8 U. 2 Stop, q. v. —NESS, s. निःशब्दता, निश्चलता, शांतता, अक्षोभः.

STILT, s. पादयष्टि f.

STIMULATE, v. t. उत्तिज् c., प्रोत्सह् c., प्रचुद् 10, प्रवृत् c., प्रचुद् c., उद्दीप् c., (शक्ति-तेजः-) वृध् c. —ING,-STIMULANT, a. दीपक-न, उत्तेजक, प्ररोचक, तेजोवर्धन; प्रवर्तक, प्रोत्साहक.—s. दीपनं-कं, प्र-, रोचनं, जीवनीयं, उत्तेजकं, प्रवर्तकं, &c. —ION, s. प्र-उद्-दीपनं, प्रोत्साहः-हनं. —STIMULUS, s. दीपनं, प्रोत्साहः-हनं, प्रचोदनं, उत्तेजनं, &c.; 'give s. to' वृध् c. &c.

STING, v. t. दंश् 1 P. 2 अत्यंतं पीड् 10 or व्यथ् c. (व्यथयति), मर्माणि भिद्-छिद् 7 P or स्पृश् 6 P. —s. दंशः; दंशचंचु f., कंटकः, शंकुः; (of a scorpion) अलं. 2 मर्मन् n., रसः. —ING, a. कटु, दंशक, मर्मस्पृश्, अरुंतुद.

STINGY, a. कृपण, बद्धमुष्टि, दानविरक्त, अमुक्तहस्त, क्षुद्र, कदर्य. —ILY, adv. कृपणं, बद्धमुष्ट्या. —INESS, s. कार्पण्यं.

STINK, s. पूति f.,-गंधः, दुर्गंधः. —v. i. Ex. by 's. ing' with भू. —ING, a. पूतिगंधि, दुर्गंध, कुत्सितगंध, पूति.

STINT, v. t. नियम् 1 P, निबंध् 9 P, निग्रह् 9 P, संहृ 1 P, परि-मा 3 A,2 P, परिच्छिद् 7 P. —s. परिमाणं, परिमिति f., नियमः-मनं, इयत्ता, मर्यादा; See LIMIT.

STIPEND, s. वेतनं, वृत्ति f., वर्तनं, भृति f. —STIPENDIARY, s. वृत्ति-वेतन-भुज् m., वृत्तिग्राही, वैतनिकः.

STIPULATE, v. i. समयं-संविदं-कृ 8 U, नियम् 1 P; प्रतिपद् 4 A, परि-,पण् 1 A, प्रति-ज्ञा 9 A, अभ्युपगम् 1 P, -इ 2 P. —ED, a. नियत, नैयमिक-सामयिक-(की f.), प्रतिज्ञात, संकेतित, निरूपित, निर्दिष्ट. —ION, s. समयः, संविद् f., अभिसंधिः, नियमः, पणः, संकेतः, प्रतिज्ञा.

STIR, v. t. चल् c., सं-वि-°; See MOVE; 'when the fuel is s.ed, the fire blazes up' ज्वलति चलितेंधनोऽग्निः (S. 6). 2 आ-वि-लुड् c., क्षुभ् c., (of water); मंथ् 9 P or c., आ-धू 5, 9 U; (up) सं-,क्षुभ् c., उत्तिज् c., प्रकुप् c.; उद्दीप् c., प्रवृत् c., प्रणुद् c.; See EXCITE, PROMPT. —v. i.

क्षुभ् 4 P, 1 A, चल् 1 P, उद्विग्न-संक्षुब्ध- *a.* भू 1 P. —*s.* संक्षोभः, संभ्रमः, चलनं, धूननं, विप्लवः, तुमुलं. —RING, *a.* प्रक्षोभिन्, प्रकोपक, उद्दीपक.

STIRRUP, *s.* पादग्रहणी-धारणी.

STITCH, *v. t.* सिव् 4 P; *See* SEW; संश्लिष् c. —*s.* गुणः, सूचिमार्गः-अंकः. 2 शूलः-लं; 'a s. in time saves nine' स्वल्पोपि कालकृतो यत्नः महांतं उत्तरकरणीयं यत्नं व्यावर्तयति. —ING, *s.* सी(से)वनं, स्यूति *f.*

STOCK, *s.* मूलं, मूलधनं, पण्यिणः; नीवि-वी *f.*; 'common s.' गणद्रव्यं. 2 स्तरुः, दंडः, वारंगः, मुष्टि *m. f.* 3 संचयः, राशिः, संभारः, सामग्री; 's. in cattle' गोधनं, पशुसंपत्ति *f.* 4 मूलं, प्रसूति *f.*, वंशः, कुलं, अन्वयः. 5 प्र-,कांडः-डं, स्कंधः. 6 स्तंभः, स्थाणुः. 7 (S.s) निगडः, हडिः; 's.-dove' कपोतः; *See* DOVE; 's.-still' स्थिर, स्थाणुरिव अचल. —*v. t.* सं-भृ 1, 3 U, संचि 5 U, समाहृ 1 P, राशीकृ 8 U, उपक्लृप् c., परि-,पूर् 10. —*a.* मूल in comp., प्रधान, विशिष्ट; 's. instance' मूर्धाभिषिक्तमुदाहरणं. —STOCKADE, *s.* स्तंभपंक्ति *f.*, शंकुवरणः.

STOCKING, *s.* चरणच्छदः, पादावरणं, पादत्रं-त्राणं.

STOIC,-AL, *a.* निःस्पृह, जितेंद्रिय, निःसंग, समबुद्धिचित्त, सुखदुःखानधीन, समसुखदुःख, इंद्रियानायत्त. —ALLY, *adv.* औदासीन्येन, निःसंगं, वीतस्पृहं. —ISM, *s.* निःस्पृहता, औदासीन्यं, आत्मसंयमः, इंद्रियजयः, सुखदुःखसमता.

STOLID, *a.* *See* STUPID.

STOMACH, *s.* जठरः-रं, पक्वाशयः, कोष्ठः, अन्नाशयः, आमाशयः; उदरं, पिचं(चिं)डः. 2 रुचि *f.*, ex. by Like, q. v. 3 औद्धत्यं, दर्पः; *See* HAUGHTINESS. —*v. t.* वि-,सह् 1 A, मृष् 4 P, 10. —IC, *a.* अग्निदीपन-वर्धन (नी *f.*), उत्तेजक, अग्निद, दीपक, रुचक, पाचक. 2 जाठर (री *f.*). —*s.* दीपनं, रुचकं, अग्निवर्धनं.

STONE, *s.* शिला, पाषाणः, अश्मन् *m.*, प्रस्तरः, उपलः, ग्रावन् *m.*, दृषद् *f.*, शर्करा. 2 (Of fruits) अस्थि *n.*, अष्ठि *f.*, अष्ठीला. 3 (In the bladder) अश्मरी, मूत्रकृच्छ्रं. 4 Testicle, q. v.; 's.-blind' घनांध; 's.-cutter' औपलिकः, आश्मिकः, पाषाणदारकः; 's.-hearted' पाषाणहृदय, अश्महृदय, निर्दय, कठोर; 's.-horse' बीजाश्वः; 's.-pit,' 's.-quarry' प्रस्तरखनि *f.*-आकरः. —*a.* Stony, q. v. —*v. t.* लोष्टघातं-उपलैः-हन् 2 P or व्या-पद् c. —Y, *a.* उपलसंकुल-बहुल-आकीर्ण. 2 औपल (ली *f.*), शिला-प्रस्तरमय (यी *f.*), शार्कर (री *f.*), आश्मिक (की *f.*). शर्करिल, श(शा)र्करिक (की *f.*), (*s.*) in comp.: 's. seat' शिलासनं. 3 प्रस्तरनिभ-तुल्य-समान.

STOOL, *s.* पीठः-ठं, आसनं, पाद-चरण-पीठं. 2 उच्चारः, रेकः, मलोत्सारः, पुरीषोत्सर्गः; 'to pass s.s' उच्चर् 1 P, पुरीषं उत्सृज् 6 P.

STOOP, *v. i.* गात्रं नम् c. or आवृज् 10, नम् 1 P, अव-आ-प्र-°, प्रह्वीभू 1 P, नम्रीभू, प्रवणीभू. 2 Condescend, q. v. —*v. t.* आवृज्, नम् c., नम्रीकृ 8 U, प्रह्वीकृ. —*s.*,-ING, *s.* नति *f.*, नमनं, आ-अव-प्र-°. —ING, *a.* नत, प्रवण, प्रणतिप्रवण; अव-,नम्र, प्रह्व, नतांग, अवनतकाय, प्रणतशिरस्; 'a s. posture' नतिः, वैतसी वृत्तिः.

STOP, *v. t.* वि-,स्तंभ् 9 P or c., अव-स्था c. (स्थापयति), रुध् 7 U, नि-प्रति-अव-सं-°, प्रति-बंध् 9 P; पि-धा 3 U (ears &c.); 's.s the chariot' रथं स्थापयति. 2 निवृ c., बाध् 1 A, प्रति-वि-हन् 2 P, प्रति-नि-षिध् 1 P, विच्छिद् 7 P. 3 निवृत् c., विरम् c., विश्रम् c., प्र-उप-शम् c. —*v. i.* प्र-उप-शम् 4 P, विरम् 1 P, निवृत् 1 A; स्था 1 P, अव-स्था (A), निश्चल-स्थिर-स्तब्ध-रुद्ध-गति-*a.* भू 1 P; *See* CEASE, END. 2 विश्रम् 4 P (rest); 'the evil does not s. here' नैतावता पीडा निष्क्रामति (S. 2). —*s.*,-PING, *s.* स्तंभः, स्तंभनं, प्रतिष्टंभः, प्रतिबंधः, अव-नि-प्रति-रोधः, पिधानं; विष्टंभः, यानिवृत्ति *f.*, विरामः; 'put a s. to' *See* (*v.*), often by विरम् with abl. 2 अव-,स्थिति *f.*, विरामः, प्रशांति *f.*, विश्रांति *f.*, वि-,निवृत्तिः, विच्छेदः, भंगः, विरति *f.* 3 (In music) यति *f.*, अवसानं, विरामः. 4 विरामः,-चिह्नं,-बिंदुः, अवसानचिह्नं. —PAGE, *s.* प्रतिबंधः, प्रतिष्टंभः; *See* (*s.*); 's. of any organic function' अव-,रोधः, आ-,नाहः, बंधः. —PER, -STOPPLE, *s.* रोधः, अवष्टंभः.

STORAX, *s.* शिलाजं, शिलाकुसुमं-पुष्पं.

STORE, *v. t.* संभृ 1, 3 U, समाहृ 1 P, संचि 5 U, संग्रह् 9 P, संपूर् 10, पृ c. —*s.*,-AGE, *s.* संभारः, संचयः, राशिः, संग्रहः, समाहारः, सामग्री, निधिः, निधानं, कोशः-षः, संघातः. 2 Store-house, q. v.; 's.-house' कोषः, भांडारं; कोष्ठः; 's.-keeper' कोषाध्यक्षः-पालः; 's.-house of corn' कुशूलः, धान्यकोष्ठः.

STORK, *s.* सारसः, बकः, बलाकः, क्रौंचः.

STORM, *s.* वात्या, चंडवातः, प्रभंजनः, महा-अति-वातः, वात्यावेगः, प्रकंपनः, दुर्दिनं, झंझावातः (with showers). 2 संरंभः, संक्षोभः. 3 लंघनं, अवस्कंदः-दनं. —*v. t.* आ-अव-स्कंद् 1 P, लंघ् 1 A, 10, सहसा आपत् 1 P or ग्रह् 9 P or रुध् 7 U. —*v. i.* Rage, q. v. —Y, *a.* प्रचंडवात, वात्याकुल, वाताहत, पवनक्षुब्ध, अतिवातविशिष्ट; ex. by (*s.*); 'it is s. weather to-day' अद्य प्रभंजनः सर्वतो वाति, दुर्दिनमद्य; 's. sea' क्षुब्धार्णवः. 2 संरब्ध, संक्षुब्ध, संक्षोभित.

STORY, *s.* कथा, वृत्तांतः, आख्यानं, उपाख्यानं, उप-परि-कथा, आख्यायिका; 'historical s.' इतिहासः, चरित्रं-तं; 'remaining only in s.' कथीकृत, कथावशेषीकृत, कथाशेष. 2 वस्तु *n.*, कथानकं (of dramas &c.). 2 भूमि *f.*; सप्तभूमिकः प्रासादः 'a palace having 7 s.es'; 'ground s.' तलं; 's.-teller' कथकः.

STOUT, *a.* महा-स्थूल-काय, बृहच्छरीर, मांसल, स्थूलशरीर, प्रबल, महाबल, बलवत्. 2 धीर, विक्रांत, शूर, प्रगल्भ (heart). -NESS, *s.* शरीरस्थूलता, मांसलता.

STOVE, *s.* चुल्लि-ल्ली *f.*, अधिश्रयणी, अग्निकुंडं, अश्मंतं, उद्धानं, अंतिका.

STOW, *v. t.* (कोशे) निविश् *c.*, नि-धा 3 U, स्था *c.* (स्थापयति); *See* STORE also.

STRADDLE, *v. i.* प्रगतजंघ-*a.* स्था 1 P.

STRAGGLE, *v. i.* व्यभिचर् 1 P, विभ्रम् 1, 4 P, मार्गात् प्र-वि-चल् 1 P or च्यु 1 A or भ्रंश् 1 A, 4 P. -ER, *s.* भ्रष्ट-भ्रांत-पथः, व्यभिचारिन् *m.*, नष्टपथः.

STRAIGHT, *a.* सरल, ऋजु, अजिह्म, अकुटिल, अभुग्न, अवक्र, समरेख, अनराल, प्रगुण, अंजस; 'the s.-stemmed lotus' अनरालनालनलिनी. -*adv.*, 's.-way' सपदि, अनंतरमेव; सद्यः, तत्कालं, अविलंबितं. 2 सरलं, अवक्रं, ऋजु. -EN, *v. t.* ऋजूकृ 8 U, सरलीकृ. -LY, *adv.* सरलं, अवक्रं, ऋजुतया, &c. -NESS, *s.* सारल्यं, आर्जवं, अकौटिल्यं.—STRAIGHTFORWARD, *a.* ऋजु, सरल, शुचि, ऋजु-सरल-प्रकृति; *See* HONEST. -LY, *adv.* सरलं, अवक्रं, ऋजुतया; स्पष्टं, व्यक्तं. -NESS, *s.* आर्जवं, सारल्यं, दाक्षिण्यं.

STRAIN, *v. t.* आयम् *c.*, अत्यंतं आकृष् 1 P; 's. every nerve' सर्वात्मना प्रयत् 1 A. 2 अत्यंतं तन् 8 U, अतितानेन अभिहन् 2 P; *See* SPRAIN. 3 (Juice) निष्पीड् 10, निर्गल् *c.*, निष्कृष्. 4 (Filter) शुध् *c.*, पू 9 U, विमलीकृ 8 U, स्रु *c.*; 'should s. through a cloth' स्रावयेत् पटात्. 5 (To the bosom) *See* CLASP; 'this is not the time to s. courtesies' अत्युपचारपूर्वकं-यथाचारं-व्यवहर्तुं नायं समयः.-*v. i.* अत्यंतं प्रयत् or उद्यम् 1 A or आयस् 1, 4 P or व्यव-सो 4 P. 2 निर्गल् 1 P, स्रु 1 P. -*s.* आयासः, अतियत्नः-श्रमः. 2 प्रवहणं, अत्यंताकर्षः; *See* SPRAIN. 3 तानः, संततस्वरः. 4 आ-, कर्षणं, विततिः *f.* 5 रीति *f.*, प्रकारः. 6 विषयः. -ED, *a.* वितत, आ-, कृष्ट &c. 2 (Meaning) क्लिष्ट, नेयार्थ. -ER, *s.* गालनी, चालनी, शोधनी.

STRAIT, *a.* संकट, संबाध, अनायत, संकुचित; *See* NARROW. -*s.* कृच्छ्रं, कष्टं, संकटं, दुर्दशा, कष्टावस्था, संकटावस्था; 'in s. s' कृच्छ्रगत, कष्टापन्न. 2 सामुद्रधुनी, संकटमार्गः. -EN, *v. t.* पीड् 10, सं-, बाध् 1 A, संकुच् 1 P; 's.ed circumstances' (अर्थ-) कृच्छ्रं, कष्टं, दुर्गति *f.*

STRAND, *s.* तीरं, तटं, कूलं. -*v. t.* उत्कूलयति (D.). -*v. i.* तीरं प्राप् 5 P.

STRANGE, *a.* अपूर्व, वि-, चित्र, अद्भुत, आश्चर्यभूत; 'what is s. in this' किमत्र चित्रं. 2 विदेशीय, परकीय; *See* FOREIGN. 3 अप-वि-रूप, विलक्षण, असंगत, असंबद्ध, अलौकिक (की *f.*), असंभव. 4 अपरिचित, असंस्तुत, अज्ञातपूर्व. -*interj.* चित्रं, अहो बत चित्रं, आश्चर्यं. -ER, *s.* आगंतुकः, अभ्यागतः. 2 वैदेशिकः, विदेशीयः, वैदेश्यः. 3 परः, परपुरुषः, पारक्यः, अपरिचितः, अन्यजनः. 4 (*a.*) अपरिचित, अनभ्यस्त, अनभिज्ञ, अज्ञात; 'we are s. s to the use of chariots' वयं अनभ्यस्तरथचर्याः (U.5). -LY, *adv.* अद्भुतं, चित्रं. -NESS, *s.* अपूर्वता, वैचित्र्यं, वैलक्षण्यं, &c.

STRANGLE, STRANGULATE, *v. t.* कंठं निपीड्य-श्वासं निरुध्य-मृ *c.* or व्यापद् *c.*, गलहस्तयति (D.); श्वासं अव-नि-रुध् 7 U. -ING,-ION, *s.* गलपीडनं, गलहस्तः, श्वासावरोधः.

STRANGURY, *s.* अश्मरी, मूत्रकृच्छ्रं.

STRAP, *s.* चर्मपट्टः-बंधः, वरत्रा, वर्ध्री, नध्री. -*v. t.* चर्मपट्टेन ग्रह् 1 P or तड् 10.

STRATAGEM, *s.* उपायः, कल्पना, युक्ति *f.*, अप-व्यपदेशः, छलं, कपटोपायः, छद्मन् *n.*

STRATEGY, *s.* युद्धकौशलं, समरपाटवं, व्यूहरचनाविद्या-नैपुण्यं.

STRATUM, *s.* स्तरः, फलकः-कं, आ-सं-स्तरः.

STRAW, *s.* पलः, पलालः-लं, नालः-लं, तृणं (fig. also), शुष्कधान्यं; 'to make s. of', 'not to care a s. for' तृणाय-तृणं-मन् 4 A; 'a man of s.' तृणमूर्ति *f.*; कल्पितपुरुषः.

STRAY, *v. i.* (यूथात् &c.) भ्रंश् 1 A, 4 P, व्यभिचर् 1 P, (मार्गात्) प्र-, विचल् 1 P, प्र-, भ्रंश्. 2 प्रमद् 4 P, स्खल् 1 P; *See* ERR, MISTAKE. -ED, *a.* प्र-, भ्रष्ट, च्युत, विचलित, भ्रांत, मार्गभ्रष्ट, नष्टपथ, यूथभ्रष्ट. 2 (Thoughts) निरन्वय.

STREAK, *s.* रे(ले)खा, राजि *f.*; 's. of lightning' विद्युल्लेखा. -*v. t.* रेखाभिः अंक् 10, चित्रीकृ 8 U; 's. ed with gold' कनकरेखाभिः सनाथीकृत, हेमरेखांकित. -ED,-Y, *a.* रेखांकित-चिह्नित, चित्र, चित्रित, शबल.

STREAM, *s.* स्रोतस् *n.*, सरित् *f.*, नदी. 2 स्रोतः, प्रवाहः, रयः, ओघः, प्रवृत्ति *f.*, वेला, वेगः, प्लावः, धारा-रः; 's. of rain' पर्जन्यधारा. -*v. i.* वृष् 1 P, सततं प्रवह् 1 P or प्रस्रु 1 P. 2 Radiate, Extend, q. v. -ER, *s.* पताका, केतुवसनं. -ING, *a.* संतत-निरंतरप्रवाहिन्-स्राविन्. -LET, *s.* क्षुद्र-कु-सरित्; अल्पस्रोतः.

STREET, *s.* पथिन् *m.*, मार्गः; वीथि-थी *f.*, रथ्या, प्रतोली, विशिखा; 'royal s.' राजमार्गः-पथः, महापथः, संसरणं.

STRENGTH, *s.* *See* under STRONG.

STRENUOUS, *a.* सोत्साह, सोद्यम, सोद्योग, महोद्यम; अविरत, अविश्रांत, अभिनिविष्ट, संतत. -LY, *adv.* सोत्साहं, प्रयत्नैः, अविरतं. -NESS, *s.* उत्साहः, उद्योगः, उद्यमः, उद्यमसातत्यं; *See* ENERGY, INDUSTRY.

STRESS, *s.* भारः, भरः; गुरुत्वं, माहात्म्यं, गौरवं, प्रभावः, बलं; 'I lay s. on this point' इममर्थं गुरुप्रयोजनं-गुरुं-मन्ये.

STRETCH, *v. t.* विस्तृ-स्तृ c., प्र-वि-तन् 8 U, आयम् 1 P, दीर्घीकृ 8 U ; (hand) प्रसृ c., लंब् c. —*v. i.* प्र-वि-तन् pass., विस्तॄ pass., प्र-सृ 1 P, प्र-,लंब् 1 A; *See* EXTEND also. 2 Exaggerate, q. v. —*s.* विततिः *f.*, विस्तारः, विस्तृतिः, आयामः, प्रसारः-रणं. 2 प्रयत्नः, प्रयासः, उद्यमः. 3 विषयः, प्रसरः. 4 वागुपचयः, अत्युक्ति *f.* —ER, *s.* शिबिका.

STREW, *v. t.* अव-प्र-वि-कॄ 6 P, स्तॄ 9 U, सं-आ-परि-°, आच्छद् 10.

STRICT, *a.* अशिथिल, दृढ, नियत. 2 अनतिक्रमणीय, अनुल्लंघ्य; *See* PEREMPTORY. 3 परुष, निष्ठुर, कठिन, कठोर, तीक्ष्ण, तीव्र. 4 सूक्ष्म, निपुण; 'on the s.-est search' अतिनिपुणमन्विष्यापि. —LY, *adv.* अशिथिलं, परुषं, सनिर्भयं, परिच्छेदनिष्ठुरं, दृढं; 's. true' सर्वथा सत्य. —NESS, *s.* अशैथिल्यं, सूक्ष्मता, काठिन्यं, &c.

STRICTURE, *s.* निंदा, भर्त्सना, आक्षेपः; *See* CENSURE. 2 मलावरोधः, मूत्रग्रंथिः.

STRIDE, *s.* विक्रमः, पादन्यासः, दीर्घविक्रमः. —*v.* वि-परि-क्रम् 1 U, 4 P, लंघ् 1 A, 10, आ-अध्या-रुह् 1 P, आ-अध्या-क्रम्.

STRIFE, *s.* कलिः, विवादः, कलहः, विप्रतिपत्ति *f.*, विरोधः, द्वंद्वं.

STRIKE, *v. t.* हन् 2 P, प्र-अभि-उप-°, आहन् 2 U, तुद् 6 P, प्रहृ 1 P (with loc.), तड् 10 ; आस्फल् c. (water) ; 's. on the face' मुखे चपेटां दा 3 U, हस्ततलेन प्रहृ. 2 विधुृ c., पीड् 10, अर्द् 1 P or c. ; 'famine-s.en' दुर्भिक्ष-पीडित-विधुत. 3 (With wonder &c.) उपहन्, चकित-*a.* कृ; oft. by चकित-सविस्मय ; 'was struck with the beauty of his horns' शृंगशोभां दृष्ट्वा विस्मयमापेदे. 4 वद् c., नद् c., ध्वन् c. (lute &c.). 5 जन् c., उत्पद् c.; 's.s fear in the mind' चित्ते भयं जनयति ; 's. ing deep root' स्थिरबद्ध-प्ररूढ-मूल ; 's. sail' वातवस्त्रं अवपत् c. or अवतॄ c., निभृलीस्तब्धी-भू ; 's. blind' अंधीकृ ; 's. accounts' गणनां समीकृ ; 'it struck me as wonderful' तदद्भुतमिव मां प्रतिबभौ ; 'he was struck with wonder' तस्य हृदयं पस्पर्श विस्मयः (Ka. 80), आश्चर्यचकितो बभूव ; 'being used in its most general sense, it easily s. s the mind' तद्धि प्रसिद्धतरेण प्रयोगेण शीघ्रं बुद्धिमारोहति, प्रसिद्धिबलेन प्रथमतरं प्रतीयते (S. B. 135, 137). —*v. i.* (Against) संघट्ट् 1 A or c., आस्फल् 1 P; *See* DASH. 2 संभूय कर्म परित्यज् 1 P ; कार्यनिवृत्तिसंकेतं कृ. —down, नि-अव-पत् c., शद् c. (शातयति), आहत्य भूमौ पत् c. —for, प्र-स्था 1 A, प्र-या 2 P, निर्गम् 1 P; *See* START. —off, वि-,नश् c., वि-,लुप् c.; अप-व्या-मृज् 2 P or c., उच्छिद् 7 P. —out, (Fire) घर्षणेन-संघट्टनेन जन् c. 2 लुप् 6 P or c., नश् c., उच्छिद्, व्यामृज्; *See* EFFACE. 3 क्लृप् c., चित्र् 10, मुज् 7 U, 10, निरूप् 10. 4 मुद्रयति (D.). —through, निर्भिद् 7 P, प्रविश् 6 P, प्रविश्य निर्गम्. —up, आरभ् 1 A, प्रस्तु 2 U; *See* BEGIN. —*s.* युगपत् or संभूय कार्यनिवृत्तिसंकेतः. —ING, *a.* वि-,चित्र, आश्चर्यजनन (नी *f.*), अद्भुत, विस्मयावह, आश्चर्यभूत, हृदयग्राहिन्, चित्तहारिन्. —INGLY, *adv.* मनोहरं, विचित्रतया, अद्भुतं, अतीव, हृदयग्राहितया. —STROKE, *s.* आ-अभि-घातः, आहति *f.*, प्रहारः, ताडनं, पातः; 's. of a thunder-bolt' वज्रपातः, अशनिपातः. 2 रेखा, लेखा. 3 आक्रमः, अवतारः, आवेशः, लंघनं; 'sun-s.' आतपलंघनं, सूर्याभिघातः. 4 प्रयत्नः, आकस्मिकयत्नः; 's. of policy' नीत्युत्कर्षः, नयनिपुणता. —*v. t.* (पाणिना-हस्तेन) परामृश् 6 P, स्पृश् 6 P; (परामृशन् हर्षजडेन पाणिना R. III. 68); शनैः मृज् 2 P or समालभ् 1 A, हस्तेन लल् 10.

STRING, *s.* रज्जु *f.*, गुणः, तंत्रं-त्री (of lutes &c.), तंतुः, सूत्रं, दामन् *f. n.*, शुल्बं; *See* ROPE; (of a bow) ज्या, गुणः, मौर्वी, शिंजिनी. 2 परंपरा, माला, पंक्ति *f.*, श्रेणि-णी *f.*, आवलि-ली *f.*; 's. of pearls' मुक्तावली, मुक्ताहारः-सरः. 3 (Human) शिरा. —*v. t.* सं-ग्रंथ् 9 P, गु(गु)फ् 6 P, वि-,रच् 10, सं-,दृभ् 6 P, 10, सूत्र् 10. 2 तंत्रीभिः-गुणैः-बंध् 9 P; (a bow) अधिज्यं कृ; धनुषि ज्यां आरुह् c. or आतन् 8 U; 'a bow strung' अधिज्यं-आततज्यं-आरोपितज्यं-धनुः; 'a string strung tight on a bow' धनुषि आतता मौर्वी (R. I. 19). —ED, *a.* तंत्रिन्, तंत्री-गुण-विशिष्ट, तंतुयुक्त. —Y, *a.* सूत्रिन्, सूत्र-तंतु-मय (यी *f.*).

STRINGENT, *a.* तीक्ष्ण, कठोर, दृढ, अशिथिल.

STRIP, *v. t.* अप-,हृ 1 P, अप-नी 1 P निर्-हृ; gen. by अप, निर्, वि in comp.; 's. of clothes' विवस्त्रयति (D.), निर्वस्त्रीकृ 8 U, उच्छद् 10; 's. of bark' विवल्कयति (D.); निष्पत्रयति, निर्दलीकृ, &c. —*s.* खंडः-डं, पट्टः. —PED, *a.* अप-,हृत, अपनीत. 2 विवस्त्र, विवस्त्रीकृत, नग्नीकृत; हृतवस्त्र-वेश; 's. of one's all' हृतसर्वस्व.

STRIPE, *s.* रे(ले)खा. 2 दीर्घखंडः. 3 कशाघातः-प्रहारः. —*v. t.* रेखाभिः चित्रयति (D.) or अंक् 10. 2 कशया तड् 10 or प्रहृ 1 P.

STRIPLING, *s.* शिशुः, अर्भकः, डिंभः, बालः, किशोरः.

STRIVE, *v. i.* प्र-,यत् 1 A, घट् 1 A, उद्यम् 1 A, चेष्ट् 1 A, व्यव-सो 4 P, प्रवृत् 1 A. 2 स्पर्ध् 1 A. 3 (Against) विवद् 1 A, विरुध् 7 U, कलहं कृ 8 U; *See* CONTEND.

STROKE, *s. See* under STRIKE.

STROLL, *v. i.* (आलस्येन) विचर् 1 P, परिक्रम् 1 U, 4 P, विहृ 1 P, परिभ्रम् 1, 4 P. —*s.* परिक्रमः-मणं,

विहारः, परि-,भ्रमणं, यथेष्टचारः. -ER, *s.* पथिकः, यथेष्टविहारिन् *m.*

STRONG, *a.* बलिन्, बलवत्, सबल, वीर्यवत्, शक्तिमत्, समर्थ, ऊर्जस्वल, ओजस्विन्, प्रबल, ऊर्जित; 's.-minded' मनस्विन्, धीरप्रकृति. 2 क्षम, दक्ष, कुशल. 3 दृढ, स्थिर (resolution); उग्र (smell). 4 तीव्र, तीक्ष्ण, चंड, प्रखर, अति pr. 5 गाढ, उत्कट, प्रबल; *See* INTENSE. 6 वीर्यवत्, प्रतापवत्, गुणावह, गुणकारिन् (medicine); 'to grow s.' प्रबलीभू, मुर्च्छ् 1 P; '10000 s.' अयुतसंख्याक; 's.-bodied,' 's.-built' उपचितगात्र, मांसल, दृढांग, दृढावयव; 's.-hold' दुर्गं, कोटः. -LY, *adv.* बलवत्, दृढं, गाढं, परमं, उग्रं, उत्कटं, &c. -STRENGTH, *s.* बलं, वीर्यं, शक्ति *f.*, सामर्थ्यं, तेजस् *n.*, प्रभावः, ओजस् *n.*, ऊर्जः, सत्त्वं; वि-परा-क्रमः; क्षमता, बलवत्ता, प्राबल्यं, विभवः; 'the s. of mind' धीशक्तिः, बुद्धिप्रभावः, मतिविभवः; 'what is the s. of the enemy' कियत्संख्यकाः शत्रवः; 'on the s. of' अवलंब्य. -EN, *v. t.* प्रबलीकृ 8 U, बलं दा 3 U or वृध् c. 2 दृढीकृ, द्रढयति (D.); *See* CONFIRM, ESTABLISH; निवेशः शैलानां तदिदमिति बुद्धिं द्रढयति (U. 2) 's.s the belief that it is the same'; 'Sringâra s.ed by Karu*n*a' करुणानुप्राणितः शृंगाररसः -*v. i.* प्रबलीभू 1 P, प्र-उप-चि-pass.; वि-प्र-वृध् 1 A; प्ररुह् 1 P. -ING, *a.* बलवर्धन (नी *f.*), बलप्रद.

STRUCTURE, *s.* निर्माणं, संस्थानं, विधानं, रचनं-ना. 2 आकारः, रूपं. 3 मंदिरं, भवनं.

STRUGGLE, *v. i.* प्रयत् 1 A, प्रयासं-यत्नं-कृ, चेष्ट् 1 A; शार्दूलः पशुमिव हन्मि चेष्टमानं (S. 6) 'an animal s.-ing, while being killed' &c. 2 युध् 4 A, संयत्; *See* FIGHT. -ING, *s.* प्रयासः, प्रयत्नः, वि-चेष्टा-चेष्टितं, अतियत्नः; मुक्तप्रयत्नं मां सलिलबिंदुनपाययत् (Ka. 38) 'me who had ceased s.' &c. 2 युद्धं, कलहः, विवादः, द्वंद्वं.

STRUMPET, *s. See* PROSTITUTE.

STRUT, *v. i.* साटोपं-उद्धतं-धीरोद्धतं-परिक्रम् 1 U, 4 P, सगर्वं चल् 1 P. -*s.* साटोप-उद्धत-सगर्व-गति *f.* -TING, *a.* सगर्वगति, साटोपगामिन्.

STUBBLE, *s.* नालः-ली, लूनशस्यनालः.

STUBBORN, *a.* दुर्दांत, दुर्दम, प्रतिनिविष्ट, अवश्य, अविनेय, प्रतीप; *See* OBSTINATE.

STUCCO, *s.* सुधा, चूर्णलेपः. -*v. t.* सुधया लिप् 6 P. -ED, *a.* सुधालित.

STUD, *s.* गंडः; (of horses) अश्वाः, आश्वं, अश्वीयं, वाडवं; (place) अश्वशाला, मंदुरा. -*v. t.* खत्-,खच् 10 (खचयति), प्रतिबंध् 9 P, प्रतिवप् 1 P, अनुव्यध् 4 P; 'sky s. ed with stars' तारकितं नभः; 's. ed with gems' रत्नखचित, रत्नानुविद्ध-प्रत्युप्त &c.

STUDY, *v. t.* अधि-इ 2 A, अधिगम् 1 P, (acquire by s.); शिक्ष् 1 A; पठ् 1 P; आवृत् c., अभ्यस् 4 U. 2 ध्यै 1 P, चिंत् 10, क्लृप् 10; प्रयत् 1 A, विमृश् 6 P. -*s.* अध्ययनं, अभ्यासः, अभ्यसनं, शिक्षणं, पठनं, पाठः, अधिगमः-मनं; 's. of the Vedas' वेदाध्ययनं, उपाकरणं; 'close s.' अविरताभ्यासः, अनुपरि-शीलनं; 'desultory s.' चंक्रमणं. 2 अध्ययनशाला-आगारं, ग्रंथकुटी. 3 पाठः, अध्ययनविषयः. 4 चिंतनं, कल्पना, विचारः. -ENT, *s.* अध्येतृ *m.*, छात्रः, शिष्यः, आधीयानः, विद्यार्थी; 'a religious s.' ब्रह्मचारी, व्रती, लिंगी. -IED, *a.* पूर्वपठित, सुनिश्चित, पूर्वनिर्णीत, चिंतित-निर्णीत-पूर्वं, कामतः कृत. -IOUS, *a.* अध्ययनपरायण-तत्पर-शील-आसक्त, विद्याप्रसित-अभिनिविष्ट. 2 उत्सुक, व्यवसायपर, अध्यवसायिन्; 'of s. habits' व्यवसायशील. -IOUSLY, *adv.* विद्याभ्यासंगेन; संकल्प-निर्णय-पूर्वं, कामतः. -IOUSNESS, *s.* अध्ययन-विद्या-आसक्ति *f.*-अभिनिवेशः, विद्याभ्यासंगः.

STUFF, *s.* वस्तु *n.*, द्रव्यं, प्रकृति *f.*, पदार्थः. 2 पटः, वस्त्रं, वसनं; *See* CLOTH. 3 गृहोपस्करः, गृहसामग्रीद्रव्याणि-भांडानि. 4 तुच्छ-कुत्सित-द्रव्यं. 5 अनर्थकप्रलापः. -*v. t.* अत्यंतं पूर् 10, अतिशयेन तृप् c. 2 Crowd, Cram, q. v.; 's.-ed with cotton' कार्पासपूरित. -*v. i.* आतृप्ति पृ pass. -ING, *s.* पूरणं &c.

STULTIFY, *v. t.* मूढीकृ 8 U, मूर्खवत् आचर् c.; (oneself) मूर्खवत् आचर् 1 P.

STUMBLE, *v. i.* प्र-,स्खल् 1 P, विषमीभू, (मार्गे पदानि खलु ते विषमीभवंति S. 4); प्र-वि-चल् 1 P, च्यु 1 A. -*v. t.* प्र-,स्खल् c. (स्खलयति). -*s.*,-ING, *s.* स्खलनं, स्खलितं; 's. ing-block' गतिकुंठनस्थानं; 'this is a s. ing-block to all' अत्र सर्वे स्खलंति; अत्र सर्वेषां गतिः कुंठिता भवति.

STUMP, *s.* कंदः-दं, स्थाणुः. -Y, *a.* ह्रस्वस्थूल.

STUN, *v. t.* बधिरीकृ 8 U. (आक्रोशेन दिशो बधिरीकृताः); (persons) आघातेन-प्रहारेण-जडीकृ 8 U, मूर्च्छां प्राप् c. or जन् c.; 's. the ears' कर्णविवरंकर्णपुटं जर्जरीकृ or जर्जरयति (D.) or स्फुट् c. or उपहन् 2 P, जर्जरितकर्णविवरः (Ka. 27), जर्जरीकृतकर्णपुटः 'the ears being s.ed' &c.; 'he was s.ed by the noise' निनादश्रवणेनामूर्च्छत्. -NED, *a.* आघात-प्रहार-मूढ-जड-मोहित, जर्जरितकर्ण, बधिरीकृत. -NING, *a.* कर्णोपघातिन्, श्रवणशक्तिहारिन्.

STUNT, *v. t.* (वृद्धिं) स्तंभ् 9 P or c., रुध् 7 U, वामनी-खर्वी-कृ 8 U. -*s.* वृद्धिरोधः-स्तंभः. -ED, *a.* पृश्नि, अल्पतनु, वामनाकृति, रुद्धवृद्धि.

STUPEFY, *v. t.* जडीकृ 8 U, जडयति (D.), मुह् c., सं-ज्ञा-°, निष्पंदीकृ, सं-,स्तंभ् c. -ACTION, STUPOR, *s.* जाड्यं, जडिमन् *m.*, जडता-त्वं, मोहः, सं-ज्ञा-°, इंद्रियस्वापः-मोहः-स्तंभः. -ING, *a.* ज्ञा-, मोहिन्, मोहकारिन्, स्तंभक. —STUPID, *a.* जड, मूढ,

मूर्ख, मंद, मूढ-स्थूल-जड-मंद-धी-मति-बुद्धि, निर्बुद्धि, दुर्बुद्धि, अविज्ञ, अज्ञ; 'a s. mistake' अतिगर्हणीयः प्रमादः. -ITY,-NESS, *s.* जाड्यं, मौर्ख्यं, मूढता, जडिमन् *m.*, अज्ञानं &c. -LY, *adv.* जाड्येन, मूर्खतया, मूढवत्.

STUPENDOUS, *a.* अतिविशाल, अद्भुत, आश्चर्य विस्मयकर (री *f.*), विस्मयोत्पादक.

STURDY, *a.* कठिन, कठोर; दृढांग, प्रबल; *See* STOUT.

STUTTER, *v. i. See* STAMMER.

STY, *s.* शूकरशाला.

STYLE, *s.* रीति *f.*, प्रकारः, पद्धति *f.*, वृत्ति *f*, सरणि *f.* 2 भाषासरणिः, लेखनपद्धतिः; (of speaking) वाग्वृत्तिः-व्यापारः-सरणिः. 3 संज्ञा, आख्या, ख्याति *f.* 4 लेखनी, कलमः. 5 शलाका, कीलः; शंकुः (of a dial). -*v. t.* अभि-धा 3 U, वच् 2 P, संज्ञां दा 3 U, कृत् 10; *See* NAME, CALL; 's. ed Kakutstha' ककुत्स्थ इत्याहितलक्षण (R. VI. 71), ककुत्स्थसंज्ञ &c. -ISH, *a.* शिष्टजनमत, सभ्याचारानुरूप.

STYPTIC, *a.* रक्तस्तंभन, रक्तस्रावरोधिन्. -*s.* रक्तस्तंभनं-अवरोधः.

STYX, *s.* वैतरणी, प्रेतनदी.

SUAVITY, *s.* माधुर्यं, मनोज्ञता, स्वादुता.

SUBACID, *a.* ईषदम्ल.

SUBDIVIDE, *v. t.* प्रतिभज् 1 U, अंशांशान् कृ 8 U. -SUBDIVISION, *s.* प्रभागः, प्रविभागः, उपशाखा, प्रति-प्र-शाखा, उपांगं, अवयवः.

SUBDUE, *v. t.* वशं नी 1 P, वशीकृ 8 U, वि-परा-जि 1 A, अभि-परा-भू 1 P, दम् c. (दमयति), स्वायत्तीकृ, स्ववशे स्था c. (स्थापयति). 2 (Passions) जि, सं-नि-यम् 1 P, निग्रह् 9 P, दम् c., वशं नी; *See* CONTROL. -ER, *s.* जेतृ *m.*, दमनकारिन्. 2 वशिन् *m.* -ING, *s.* वि-,जयः, दमः-मनं, अभिभवः, नि-संयमः, निग्रहः, &c.

SUBJACENT, *a.* अधोवर्तिन्.

SUBJECT, *s.* प्रजा, प्रकृति *f.* (usually in pl.). 2 विषयः (विषयिन् *m.*, as opp. to object); प्रकरणं, प्रस्तावः, प्रसंगः, अर्थः, पदं, स्थानं, आस्पदं, भूमि *f.*, अधिष्ठानं, आधारः, आश्रयः, आशयः, भाजनं. 3 नायकः, कथापुरुषः-नायकः. 4 कर्ता (in grammar). 5 साध्यं; 's. in hand' प्रकृतं, प्रस्तुतं, प्रस्तुतार्थः; 'this chapter is on the s. of Sânkhya doctrines' सांख्यवादविषयकोऽयमध्यायः. -*a.* वशवर्तिन्, वशग, उपजीविन्, आश्रित; निघ्न, वश, अधीन, आयत्त, तंत्र in comp. 2 (Liable) अधीन, आयत्त, &c., अर्ह, पात्रं, आस्पदं in comp.; *See* LIABLE; 'one that is born is s. to death' जातेन खलु मर्तव्यं, जातस्य हि ध्रुवो मृत्युः; 'not s. to anger' अनायत्तो रोषस्य (Ka. 45); so अवशो विषयाणां, अदत्तावकाशो मत्सरस्य (*ibid.*); 's. to disease' रोगाधीन, नित्य-सदा-रोगिन्, रोगपात्रं, &c. -*v. t.* वशीकृ 8 U, अभिभू 1 P; *See* SUBDUE. 2 पदं नी 1 P, अधीनी-आयत्ती-आस्पदीकृ; 'you have s.-ed yourself to trouble' क्लेशस्यात्मा पदमुपनीतः (S. 1); 'you have s. ed yourself (soul) to great penance' आयोजितस्तपसि महत्यात्मा (Ka. 173);अयत्नेनैवोपहासास्पदतामीश्वरो नयति जनं (Ka. 151) 'easily s. s to ridicule' &c.; उपहासास्पदं कृ, &c. -ION, *s.* वशः-शं, वशता, निघ्नता, तंत्रता, आश्रितत्वं, अधीनता, &c. in comp.; 's. to another' परवशता, पराधीनता, परवत्ता, &c.-IVE, *a.* विषयिन्, अधिकरणनिष्ठ.

SUBJOIN, *v. t.* अनुबंध् 9 P, आयुज् 7 U, 10; अधः लिख् 6 P or निर्दिश् 6 P.

SUBJUGATE, *v. t.* वशीकृ 8 U, अभिभू 1 P, परा-वि-जि 1 A, भंज् 7 P, करदीकृ; *See* SUBDUE. -ION, *s.* दमः-मनं, जयः, परा-अभि-भवः, भंगः, नियमः, निग्रहः; *See* CONTROL also.

SUBLIMATE, *s.* रसकर्पूरः-पुष्पं. -*v. t.* बाष्पीकृ 8 U.

SUBLIME, *a.* उन्नत, अत्युच्छ्रित, उत्कृष्ट, विशिष्ट, गुरु; *See* LOFTY; उदात्त, प्रौढ (sentiment &c.). -*v. t.* Exalt, q. v. -ITY,-NESS, *s.* तुंगता, उन्नति *f.*, अनुभावः, प्रौढि *f.*, अत्युत्कर्षः, गौरवं; 's. of meaning' अर्थगौरवं, उदात्तार्थः.

SUBLUNARY, *a.* ऐहिक-सांसारिक (की *f.*); *See* WORLDLY.

SUBMARINE, *a.* समुद्रस्थ-गत; 's. fire' और्वः, वडवानलः, वाडवः.

SUBMERGE, *v. t.* नि-,मस्ज् c. (मज्जयति), आप्लु c -*v. i.* नि-,मस्ज् 6 P, अवगाह् 6 A; *See* PLUNGE. -SUBMERSION, *s.* निमज्जनं, आप्लावः, प्लावनं.

SUBMIT, *v. i.* प्रणम् 1 P, वशं गम् 1 P, शरणं गम् or या 2 P or प्रपद् 4 A; (to order &c.) अनुरुध् 4A, अनुवृत् 1 A, अनुपा c. (पालयति); *See* OBEY; सह् 1 A, क्षम् 1 A, मृष् 4 P, 10; oft. ex. by प्रमाणं; आर्यमिश्राः प्रमाणं (M. 1) 'I s. to your honor's opinion (decision)'. 2 सविनयं वद् 1 P or प्रार्थ् 10 A. -*v. t.* सविनयं ऋ c. (अर्पयति) or निक्षिप् 6 P or निर्दिश् 6 P; *See* REFER. -SUBMISSION, *s.* प्रणति *f.*, वशता-त्वं. 2 अनुवृत्ति *f.*, अनुवर्तनं, अनुरोधः. 3 क्षमा, क्षांति *f.*, सहिष्णुता. -SUBMISSIVE, *a.* वश्य, प्रणतिप्रणव, वशग, वशवर्तिन्, विधेय, अनुविधायिन्, आज्ञाकर (री *f.*). 2 सविनय, नम्र, दीन. -LY, *adv.* सविनयं, नम्रतया, प्रार्थनापूर्वं, प्रणतिपूर्वं.

SUBORDINATE, *a.* अधीन, आयत्त. 2 अप्रधान, गौण (णी *f.*), अमुख्य; 'any thing s. to another' अप्रधानं, उपसर्जनं. -*v. t.* (to) अन्यापेक्षया गौण-अप्रधान- *a.* मन् 4 A. -ION, *s.* अधीनता, वशता, वश्यता, परवशता, पारतंत्र्यं, पराधीनता. 2 अप्राधान्यं,

गौणता. -LY, *adv.* गौणतः, अप्राधान्येन, अमुख्यतः.

SUBORN, *v. t.* (धनदानादिना) कूटसाक्ष्यं दा c. (दापयति).

SUBPŒNA, *s.* आह्वानपत्रं. -*v. t.* आह्वे 1 P.

SUBSCRIBE, *v.* (अधः) नाम लिख् 6 P or निविश् c., हस्ताक्षरेण अंक् 10 or चिह्नयति (D.); *See* SIGN. 2 Agree, q. v. 3 (द्रव्यं) दातुं प्रतिज्ञा 9 A, अंशं दा desid. (दित्सति-ते). -ER, *s.* अंशदायिन् *m.* -SUBSCRIPTION, *s.* नामलिखनं-निवेशनं. 2 अंश-उद्धार-दानं; स्वांशः, उद्धारः. 3 (Of a paper) मूल्यं.

SUBSEQUENT, *a.* उत्तरगामिन्, उत्तर, पश्चात् in comp.; पर, पश्चात्कालीन; अनु pr.; 's. rites' अनुकर्माणि; अनुगमनं, &c.; 's. mention' वक्ष्यमाणता. -LY, *adv.* तत ऊर्ध्वं; अनंतरं, तत उत्तरं; पश्चात्; (to) परं; ऊर्ध्वं, अनंतरं, परतः (with abl.); अनु pr.; 's. to the marriage' अनुविवाहं, विवाहात्परं, &c. -SUBSEQUENCE, *s.* अनुगमनं-यानं.

SUBSERVE, *v. i.* पुरस्कृ 8 U, वृध् c., उपकृ; *See* PROMOTE. -SUBSERVIENT, *a.* आयत्त, अधीन, वश, निघ्न, तंत्र in comp. 2 उपयुक्त, उपकारिन्, सहयोगिन्. -SUBSERVIENCE,-CY, तंत्रता, अधीनत्वं. 2 उपयोगः, उपकारः.

SUBSIDE, *v. i.* शम् 4 P, प्र-उप-°, निवृत् 1 A, विरम् 1 P, वि-गम् 1 P; प्रसद् 1 P. 2 अधस्तले आसद्, अधः गम् or पत् 1 P.

SUBSIDY, *s.* (धनरूपं) साहाय्यं, करः. -SUBSIDIARY, *a.* सहकारिन्, साहाय्यकारिन्, अनुकूल, मित्रभावापन्न. 2 Subordinate, q. v.; 'something s.' अप्रधानं, उपसर्जनं, गौणार्थः.

SUBSIST, *v. i.* भू 1 P, वृत् 1 A, विद् 4 A, अस् 2 P, स्था 1 P. 2 जीव् 1 P, आ-उप-°, प्राणयात्रां कृ, जीवितं-प्राणान् धृ 1 P, 10; *See* LIVE. -ENCE, *s.* सत्ता, अस्तित्वं, भावः, वृत्ति *f.* 2 आजीवः, वृत्तिः, आ-उप-जीविका, प्राण-शरीर-यात्रा; *See* LIVING. -ENT, *a.* जीविन्, सत्त्ववत्.

SUBSTANCE, *s.* सारः, सत्त्वं, तत्त्वं; भावः, भावार्थः, सारांशः, तात्पर्यं, तात्पर्यार्थः; 'sum and s.' पिंडितः-निर्गलितः-अर्थः, निष्कर्षः, भावः; 'they are the same in s.' वस्तुतः समाः, अर्थतः तुल्याः. 2 (In Philosophy) द्रव्यं, पदार्थः. 3 वस्तु *n.*, द्रव्यं, अर्थः, मूर्तद्रव्यं. 4 संपत्ति *f.*, द्रव्यं, धनं, अर्थः, वित्तं, विभवः, वैभवं; *See* WEALTH. — SUBSTANTIAL, *a.* सारवत्, ससार, सगर्भ, घन. 2 तात्त्विक-सात्त्विक-वास्तविक-(की *f.*), यथार्थ, सत्य, वास्तव (वी *f.*). 3 धनिन्, सधन, समृद्ध, धनवत्; *See* WEALTHY.-LY, *adv.* वस्तुतः, अर्थतः, तत्त्वतः, सारतः. —SUBSTANTIATE, *v. t.* साध् c., उप-प्रति-पद् c., प्रमाणयति (D.), प्रमाणीकृ 8 U, सत्यापयति (D.), सत्याकृ, वि-भू c.; *See* PROVE. -ION, *s.* उपपादनं, साधनं, सिद्धि *f.* -SUBSTANTIVE, *s.* विशेष्यं, सत्त्वं; 'dependent on the gender of the s.' विशेष्यनिघ्न, वाच्यलिंग. -*a.* सत्त्ववाचिन्.

SUBSTITUTE, *s.* प्रतिनिधिः, प्रतिहस्तः-स्तकः, प्रतिपुरुषः; oft. by स्थानीय- *a.* or स्थाने वृत् 1 A. 2 (In grammar) आदेशः. -*v. t.* स्थाने-पदे-सं-,निविश् c. or प्र-नि-उप-युज् 7 A, 10 or उपकृप् c.; तत्पदे धातोः स्थान इवादेशं सुग्रीवं संन्यवेशयत् (R. XII. 58) 's. ed Sugriva in his place' &c.; 'Adeśa is one word s.-ed for another' आदेशो नाम शब्दांतरस्य स्थाने विधीयमानं शब्दांतरमभिधीयते (M. N. on *ibid.*). 2 परिवृत् c., उपसृज् 6 P. -ION, *s.* स्थाने निवेशनं-उपकल्पनं-विधानं.

SUBSTRATUM, *s.* स्तरः, फलकः-कं. 2 आधारः, आश्रयः, स्थानं.

SUBTEND, *v. t.* अभिमुखं-संमुखं-वृत् 1 A or स्था 1 P (with gen.).

SUBTERFUGE, *s.* छलं, छद्मन् *n.*, अप-व्यप-देशः.

SUBTERRANEAN, *a.* आंतर्भौम (मी *f.*), भूमि in comp.; भूम्यंतर्गत, गूढ; 's. place' भूमिगृहं, अंतर्भूमिः; 's. passage' सुरुंगा, गूढमार्गः.

SUBTILE, SUBTLE, *a.* अतिसूक्ष्म; अणु, अतिलघु, निरवयव. 2 चतुर, विदग्ध, सूक्ष्मदर्शिन्, सूक्ष्म-कुशाग्र-मति-बुद्धि, मार्मिक (की *f.*), मर्मविद्. 3 Roguish, Sly, q. v. -LY, *adv.* सूक्ष्मं, सूक्ष्ममत्या. -NESS, -TY, *s.* सूक्ष्मता, अणिमन् *m.*, अतिलाघवं. 2 वैदग्ध्यं, चातुर्यं.

SUBTRACT, *v. t.* वियुज् 10, वियु 2 P, व्यव-कल् 10 (कलयति); विवृज् 10, (with instr.); शुध् c.; एतानयुतवियुतान् (Li. 13) 'these s. ed from 10,000;' अयुताच्छोधिते जातं &c. (*ibid.*). 2 उद्हृ 1 P. -ION, *s.* वियोजनं, वियोगः, व्यवकलितं, व्यवकलनं, शोधनं, वि-,वर्जनं. 2 उद्धारः. -SUBTRAHEND, *s.* ऋणं, शोधकः.

SUBURB, *s.* (नगर-) परिसरः, उपकंठं, पर्यंतभूमि *f.*, उपशल्यं, उपांतं, शाखानगरं, उपनगरं.-AN, *a.* नगरोपांतस्थ-वर्तिन्, उपकंठ.

SUBVERT, *v. t.* उद्-,ध्वंस् c., उन्मूल् 10, विनश् c., उच्छिद् 7 P or c., अवसद् c , खंड् 10, नि-अव-पत् c. -SUBVERSION, *s.* ध्वंसः, उच्छेदः, वि-,नाशः, &c. -SUBVERSIVE, *a.* विनाशिन्, ध्वंस-नाश-कर (री *f.*), उच्छेदिन्; better ex. by (*v.*); 'it is s. of happiness' सुखं उच्छिनत्ति, सुखांतकरं.

SUCCEED, *v. i.* (Of things) निष्पद् 1 A, सं-पद्, सफलीभू 1 P; फल् 1 P; सिध् c. (साधयति), जयं आप् 5 P, विजयिन्-*a.* भू (of persons); सिध् 4 P (of both); 'he s. ed in all his attempts' सर्वे तस्य प्रयत्ना निष्पन्नाः-सफला बभूवुः &c. -*v. t.* Ex. by 'Go' q. v., with अनंतरं (with abl.), पश्चा-

त् (with gen.); अनु pr.; 's. ing his father as sovereign of the North Kosala' पितुरनंतरमुत्तरकोशलासमधिगम्य (R. IX. 1); 's. to the throne' राजपदं-सिंहासनं-आरुह् 1 P, राजपदं आप् 5 P, राजपदभाग् भू; 's.-ed his brother' भ्रातुः पश्चात् राज्यमवाप; 's. ed the General' सेनापतेः पश्चात् तत्पदमवाप, (lit.) सेनापतिमन्वगच्छत्; *See* FOLLOW; 'joy s.-ed by fear' भयोत्तरः हर्षः. –ING, *a.* पर, उत्तर, आगामिन्, अनुयायिन्-गामिन्; 's. generations' पुत्रपौत्रादयः, उत्तरकालीना जनाः. —SUCCESS, *s.* सिद्धि *f.*, साफल्यं, अर्थ-साध्य-सिद्धिः, कृतार्थता, जयः, संपद् *f.*, श्रीः, उदयः. –FUL, *a.* कृतिन्, कृतार्थ, सिद्धार्थ, विजयिन्, चरितार्थ, कृतकृत्य, प्राप्त-पूर्ण-लब्ध-काम, संपन्नमनोरथ. 2 (Of things) सिद्ध, सफल, निष्पन्न, फलवत्. –FULLY, *adv.* सफलं, अमृथा, अमोघं, सिद्ध्या. –ION, *s.* अनु-,क्रमः, परंपरा, आनुपूर्व्यं, पर्यायः, अन्वयः, श्रेणी; *See* ORDER; 'in s.' अनुक्रमं-क्रमेण, यथाक्रमं, अनुपूर्वशः, निरंतरास्वंतरवातवृष्टिषु (K. v. 25) 'coming in s.'. 2 श्रेणी, आवलि-ली *f.*, माला; *See* SERIES. 3 उत्तराधिकारः-रिता, दायाधिकारः. –IVE, *a.* क्रमबद्ध, आनुक्रमिक (की *f.*), यथाक्रम, अनुपूर्व, परंपरा-क्रम-आगत-आयात, क्रमानुसारिन्. 2 निरंतर, सतत, अविरत. –IVELY, *adv.* क्रमशः, क्रमेण, अनुक्रमशः, अनुपूर्वशः, आनुपूर्व्येण, यथाक्रमं. –OR, *s.* प्रत्यनंतरः, उत्तराधिकारिन् *m.*, अनंतरागामी.

SUCCINCT, *a.* संक्षिप्त, लघु, अविस्तीर्ण. –LY, *adv.* संक्षिप्तं, समासतः.

SUCCOUR, *s.* साहाय्यं, शरणं. –*v. t.* दा 3 U with (*s.*), उपकृ 8 U.

SUCCULENT, *a.* सरस, आर्द्र, रसमय (यी *f.*), सद्रव, सजल.

SUCCUMB, *v. i.* वशं गम् 1 P or इ-या 2 P, वशीभू 1 P, अव-,सद् 1 P; *See* 'Give way' under GIVE.

SUCH, *a.* ईदृश्-श (शी *f.*), तादृश्-श, एतादृश्-श, तथाविध, एवंविध; 's. as myself,-yourself' मादृश्-श, मद्विध; भवादृश्-श, त्वादृश &c.; 's. and s.' अमुक; 'as s.' एवं सति; परमार्थतः प्रेम 'affection as s.'

SUCK, *v. t.* आ-,चूष् 1 P, पा 1 P. 2 (As children) धे 1 P, स्तनं-स्तन्यं-पा; 'a child that s.-s the breast' स्तनंधयः शिशुः. 3 (up) उत्-, शुष् c., आ-नि-पा, आचम् 1 P, (रसं) आदा 3 A. –ING, *s.* स्तनपानं, चूषणं. 2 स्तन्यं, दुग्धं; चूष्यं; 'who gives s.' स्तन्यदायिनी. —SUCKLE, *v. t.* स्तन-स्तन्यं पा c. or दा 3 U, स्तनं धे c. (धापयति), स्तन्यद नेन पुष् c. –ING, *s.* स्तन्यदानं. 2 स्तनंधयः (यी *f.*), स्तन्यपायिन्. –SUCTION, *s.* आ-, चूषणं.

SUDDEN, *a.* आकस्मिक (की *f.*), अकांड, अलक्षित, अतर्कित-अचिंतित-पूर्व, अकल्पित, अकस्माद्भूत. 2 चल, चंचल, लोल; *See* FICKLE. –LY, 'on a s.' *adv.* अकस्मात्, सहसा, एकपदे, अकांडं-डे, काकतालीयन्यायेन, अतर्कितं, असमर्थितं; 'befalling s.' अतर्कितोपनत.

SUDORIFIC, *a.* स्वेदजनन (नी *f.*), स्वेदकर (री *f.*).

SUE, *v.* प्र-अभि-अर्थ् 10 A, सविनयं याच् 1 A. 2 अभियुज् 7 A, 10, निविद् c. (राजकुले); 'if he s. me in a court of law' यद्यसौ राजकुले मां कथयति (Mr. 4).

SUET, *s.* वसा, मेदस् *n.*

SUFFER, *v. t.* अनुभू 1 P, उपगम् 1 P, उप-,भुज् 7 A, प्राप् 5 P, ज्ञा 9 U ('Experience', q. v.). 2 अनु-ज्ञा, अनुमन् 4 A, अनुमुद् 1 A, न प्रतिबंध् 9 P or प्रतिषिध् 1 P. 3 वि-,सह् 1 A, क्षम् 1 A, मृष् 4 P, 10. –*v. i.* (from) क्लिश्-तप्-पीड्-pass., व्यथ् 1 A; 'is s. ing from an injury' (कृत-) निकृत्या पीड्यते; ex. by भाज् in comp., (दुःखभाक्); दुःखं-पीडां-अनुभू; परार्थे यः पीडामनुभवति 'who s. s for others'; 'if any important duty should not s. thereby' यदि नावसीदति गुरु प्रयोजनं (Ka. 181); 'a wicked person commits a fault and a good man s. s for it' खलः करोति दुर्वृत्तं नूनं फलति साधुषु. –ANCE, *s.* अनुज्ञा, अनुमति *f.*, क्षमा. –ER, *s.* दुःखितः, दुःखभाक्, दुःखी. –ING, *s.* पीडा, क्लेशः, दुःखं, व्यथा, परि-,सं-,तापः, वेदना, कृच्छ्रं. 2 दुःखानुभवः-वेदनं &c. –*a.* क्लिष्ट, दुःखभाक्-भागिन्.

SUFFICE, *v. i.* क्लृप् 1 A (with dat.), पर्याप्त-*a.* भू 1 P; *See* below; 's. it to say' इति कथनं पर्याप्तं भवेत्. –SUFFICIENT, *a.* पर्याप्त, उपयुक्त, उचित, समर्थ, gen. by अलं (with dat.); 'this (cow) will be s. to satisfy my hunger' तस्यालमेषा क्षुधितस्य तृप्त्यै (R. II. 39), क्षुधाशांतये कल्पेत, पर्याप्ता भवेत्. 2 यथेष्ट, प्रचुर, विपुल; 'you cannot do him s. honour' तद्विषये अपर्याप्तिर्बहुमानस्य. –LY, *adv.* पर्याप्तं, यथेष्टं, प्रचुरं. –SUFFICIENCY, *s.* पर्याप्ति *f.*, औचित्यं, यथेष्टता. 2 स्वशक्त्यभिमानः.

SUFFIX, *See* AFFIX.

SUFFOCATE, *v. t.* श्वासं-कंठं-रुध् 7 U or स्तंभ् 9 P; *See* CHOKE. –ED, *a.* रुद्धश्वास-प्राण-कंठ. –ION, *s.* श्वास-प्राण-रोधः, कंठस्तंभनं.

SUFFRAGE, *s. See* VOTE.

SUFFUSE, *v. t.* आ-परि प्लु c., व्याप् 5 P, व्यश् 5 A, आ-सं-कॄ 6 P; 'eyes s. ed with tears' बाष्पपरिप्लुत-अश्रुप्लावित-बाष्पसमाकुल-नयने; 's. ed with blushes' व्रीडापरिगत; सव्रीड, व्रीडाविलक्ष. –ION, *s.* आप्लावः-वनं, व्यापनं.

SUGAR, *s.* शर्करा, सिता, खंडविकारः; 'coarse s.' गुडः; 'raw s.' मत्स्यंडी, फाणितं. -*v. t.* मिष्टी-मधुरी-कृ 8 U, शर्करान्वित-*a.* कृ. -ED,-Y, *a.* मधुमय (यी *f.*), मधुस्यंदिन्, शर्करावगुंठित; सशर्कर, मिश्र, शर्करायुक्त; 's.-candy' सिताखंडः, खंडमोदकः; 's.-cane' इक्षुः, रसालः.

SUGGEST, *v. t.* सूच् 10, उपन्यस् 4 U, उपक्षिप् 6 P, उद्दिश् 6P, प्रस्तु c., समुप-स्था c. (स्थापयति); व्यंज् c. 2 उपदिश्, प्रबुध् c., मंत्र् 10 A; 's. ed sense' ध्वनितः-व्यंग्यः-अर्थः; 'such is the s. ed sense' इति ध्वनिः; 'this plan s. ed itself to my mind' अयमुपायो मे मनसि प्रादुर्बभूव, एनमुपायमहमचिंतयम्. -ION, *s.* सूचना, उपन्यासः, उपक्षेपः, प्रस्तावः 2 मंत्रणं, उपदेशः, बुद्धि *f.* -IVE, *a.* व्यंजक, सूचक, प्र-, बोधक.

SUICIDE, *s.* आत्महत्या-घातः-वधः, प्राण-जीवित-त्यागः, हिंसा. 2 आत्मघातकः-घाती-हन् *m.*; 'commit s.' प्राणान् उत्सृज् 6 P, आत्महत्यां कृ. -AL, *a.* आत्मघातिन्, आत्मनाशिन्, स्वनाशावह.

SUIT, *v.* युज् pass. (with loc. of person), शुभ् 1 A (with gen. of person), उपपद् 4 A, (with gen. or loc.); ननु रामभद्र इत्येव मां प्रत्युपचारः शोभते तातपरिजनस्य (U. 1); द्युमर्यादत्वं ब्रह्मणो नोपपद्यते, ते गुणाः परस्मिन् ब्रह्मणि उपपद्यंते (S. B. 147, 170), oft. ex. by words for 'proper' q. v. -*s.* प्रार्थना, प्रणयः, विज्ञप्ति *f.*, विज्ञापना. 2 कार्यं, अभियोगः, व्यवहारः, अक्षः; 'file a s.' अभियुज् 7 A; *See* SUE. 3 (Of clothes &c.) युगलं, युग्मं, युतकं, युगं, संयोगः, समूहः; *See* SET. 4 परिजनः; परिवारः; *See* RETINUE. -ABLE, *a.* अनुरूप, युक्त, उचित, योग्य, उपपन्न, अनुगुण, सदृश (शी *f.*); *See* BECOMING, PROPER. -ABLY, *adv.* यथोचितं, अनुरूपं, यथायोग्यं, यथार्हं, युक्तं. 2 अनुगुणं, अनुसारेण, अनुरोधेन. -OR, *s.* प्रार्थयितृ *m.*, प्रार्थकः; आवेदकः. 2 अर्थिन् *m.* 3 विवाहार्थी, पाणिग्रहणार्थी.

SUITE, *s.* परिच्छदः, परिवारः, परिजनगणः. 2 (Of rooms) समष्टि *f.*, संयोगः.

SULKY, SULLEN, *a.* रूक्ष, प्रतीप, विषण्ण, उदासीन, उद्विग्न, अंतःकुपित. -LY, *adv.* उदासीनवत्, सोद्वेगं. -NESS, *s.* औदासीन्यं, अंतःकोपः, उद्वेगः.

SULLY, *v. t.* दुष् c. (दूषयति), आविलयति-कलंकयति (D.), मलिनीकृ 8 U; *See* STAIN.

SULPHATE, *s.* (Of copper) तुत्थं; 'red s. of iron' काशी(सी)शं; 'green s. of iron' धातुशेखरः.

SULPHUR, *s.* गंधिकः, गंधकः, गंधाश्मन् *m.*, सौगंधिकः. -ATED,-EOUS, *a.* गंधकसंश्लिष्ट-युक्त, गंधकगुणविशिष्ट, गंधकगर्भ.

SULPHURET, *s.* (Of iron) ताप्यं; (of mercury) कज्जली.

SULTRY, *a.* प्रखर, तिग्म, प्रवृद्धताप, अत्युष्ण, निर्वात; 's. season' निदाघः, ग्रीष्मः.

SUM, *s.* योगः, संकलनं, संयोजनं (in Math.). 2 साकल्यं, समाहारः, समवायः. 3 सारः, तात्पर्यं, सारांशः. 4 राशिः. 5 समासः, संक्षेपः. 6 (Of money) राशिः, धनभागः-अंशः, oft. not ex.; 'spending a large s. of money' भूरिद्रव्यव्ययः; 'small s. of money' अल्पधनं; बहुधनं &c. 7 परा कोटिः, सारः; 's. and substance'; *See* SUBSTANCE. -*v. t.* संयुज् 10, सं-कल् 10 (कलयति). 2 (up) संक्षेपेण कथ् 10, समासतो वद् 1 P, (उक्तं) उपसं-हृ 1 P. —SUMMARY, *a.* संक्षिप्त, सामासिक (की *f.*). 2 क्षिप्र, अविलंबित. -*s.* संक्षेपः, सारः, संग्रहः. -ILY, *adv.* संक्षेपतः, संक्षेपेण, समासतः.

SUMMER, *s.* ग्रीष्मः, निदाघः, घर्मः, तपः, उष्णः, उ-(ऊ)ष्मागमः, उ(ऊ)ष्मकः, ग्रीष्ममयः-कालः &c.; 's.-house' केलि-विलास-गृहं-मंदिरं; 's.-house with fountains &c.' जलमंदिरं, धारायंत्रगृहं.

SUMMIT, *s.* शिखरः-रं, शृंगं, सानु *m. n.*, चूडा, शिखा, अग्रं, कूटः-टं; 'reclining on the s. of the western mountain' अस्ताचलचूडावलंबिन्. 2 (fig.) परा काष्ठा-कोटिः.

SUMMON, *v. t.* आह्वे 1 P, आकृ c., आनी c., आवह् c.; 'to s. up courage'; *See* COURAGE. -SUMMONS, *s.* आह्वानं; 'written s.' आह्वानपत्रं; 'he who disobeys a s.' आहूतोऽनागच्छन् (V. M. 4).

SUMMUN-BONUM, *s.* निःश्रेयसं, परमार्थः, अपवर्गः.

SUMPTER,-HORSE, *s.* स्थू(स्थौ)रिन् *m.*, पृष्ठ्यः.

SUMPTUARY, *a.* व्ययविषयक, व्ययनियमसंबंधिन्.

SUMPTUOUS, *a.* महार्ह-र्घ, बहुव्ययसाध्य, महा-बहु-मूल्य. 2 विशिष्ट; 's. feast' भोजनविशेषः. -LY, *adv.* अतिव्ययपूर्वं, महार्घ्येण. -NESS, *s.* महा-अति-व्ययः.

SUN, *s.* रविः, सूर्यः, आदित्यः, भानुः, सवितृ, अर्कः, भास्करः, दिनकरः, दिवाकरः, मार्तंडः, मरीचिन्, विवस्वत्, मित्रः, खगः, पूषन्, भास्वत्, and comp. of 'Hot' with 'Ray', 'Ray' with सहस्र, पतिः with 'Day'; उष्णरश्मिः, सहस्रकिरणः, सहस्रधामा, दिनपतिः &c. 2 आतपः; 'morning s.' बालातपः, बालार्कः; 'exposed to the sun' आतपे दत्तं, आतपायोज्झितं (धान्यं); 's.-beam' सूर्यकिरणः, अंशुः; *See* RAY; 's.-day' रविवारः-वासरः, भानुवासरः; 's.-dial' सूर्यघटी; 's.-rise' सूर्योदयः, उदयः; 's-set' अस्तमनं, अस्तः, दिनांतः; 'at s.-set' अस्तं गते रवौ; समुदिते रवौ 'at s.-rise'; 'from, s-stroke' आतपलंघनात् (S. 3); 's-shine' सूर्यातपः, प्रकाशः, सूर्यालोकः. -NY, *a.* सौर (री *f.*)

(*s.*) in comp. 2 सूर्यतप्त, आतपव्याप्त, आतपाक्रांत; आतपवत्, सातप.

SUNDER, *See* SEPARATE.

SUNDRY, *a.* बहुविध, नानाविध, विविध, अनेक-नाना in comp.

SUP, *v. i.* रात्रौ भुज् 7 A. —SUPPER, *s.* रात्रिभोजनं.

SUPER, A prefix rendered by अति, अधिक, अतिशय in comp.; 's.-abound' अतिबहुलीभू; 's.-abundant' अतिबहुल, उपचित.

SUPER-ANNUATED, *a.* वयोधिक, वार्धक्येन कार्योक्षम.

SUPERB, *a.* अतिशोभन; *See* MAGNIFICENT.

SUPERCILIOUS, *a.* अवलिप्त, अत्युद्धत, अतिदृप्त.

SUPEREROGATORY, *a.* विध्यतिरिक्त, नियमातिरिक्त. —SUPEREROGATION, *s.* नियमातिरेकः, अत्याचारः.

SUPERFICIES, *s.* तलं, पृष्ठं. —SUPERFICIAL, *a.* बाह्य, बहिःस्थ, बहिः-पृष्ठ in comp.; 's. contents' पृष्ठफलं; 's. view' बाह्यालोकः. 2 गाध, पल्लवग्राहिन्, अल्प, असूक्ष्म, अनिपुण, अगाढ; 's. scholar' अल्पज्ञः, चुंबकः. —LY, *adv.* बाह्यतः, बहिः.

SUPERFINE, *a.* अतिसूक्ष्म, सर्वोत्कृष्ट.

SUPERFLUOUS, *a.* अधिक, अतिरिक्त, व्यर्थ, अपेक्षातिरिक्त; oft. ex. by पुनरुक्त; 'render s.' पुनरुक्ततां नी 1 P, (इदमुत्पाद्य सरःसलिलं अमृतरसमुत्पादयता पुनरुक्तनामिव नीता स्वसृष्टिः Ka. 124); 'when there is clear moonlight, torches are s.' अभिव्यक्तायां चंद्रिकायां किं दीपिकापौनरुक्त्येन (V. 3); आशास्यमन्यत्पुनरुक्तभूतं (R. v. 34). —NESS,-SUPERFLUITY, *s.* आधिक्यं, पुनरुक्तता, अतिरेकः,वैयर्थ्यं.

SUPERHUMAN, *a.* अ-अति-मानुष (षी *f.*), अतिमर्त्य, अपौरुष (षी *f.*), मानुषातिग.

SUPERINCUMBENT, *a.* उपरिस्थित, अधिशयान, उपरिवर्तिन्.

SUPERINDUCE, *v. t.* अध्यारुह् c., आधिनि-विश् c.

SUPERINTEND, *v. t.* पर्यवेक्ष् 1 A, अधि-ष्ठा 1 P, अध्यास् 2 A. —ENCE, *s.* अधिष्ठानं, अवेक्षा, अधिकारः, अध्यक्षता, अवेक्षणं, कार्यदर्शनं. —ENT, *s.* पर्यवेक्षकः, अधीशः, अध्यक्षः, अधिकारी.

SUPERIOR, *a.* (To) ज्यायस्, गरीयस्, श्रेयस्, वरीयस्; अधिक, श्रेष्ठ, वरिष्ठ, गरिष्ठ, विशिष्ट, प्रमुख; oft. by अतिरिच्-विशिष्-pass.; *See* EXCEL; 'truth is s. to thousands of horse-sacrifices' अश्वमेधसहस्रेभ्यः सत्यमेवातिरिच्यते-विशिष्यते (H. 4); 'of s. merits' गुणाधिक, विशिष्टगुण. —*s.* गुरुः, ज्येष्ठः, श्रेष्ठः, वरिष्ठः, अध्यक्षः. —ITY, *s.* आधिक्यं, ज्येष्ठता, श्रेष्ठता, विशिष्टता, उत्कर्षः, प्राबल्यं, प्राग्भावः.

SUPERLATIVE, *a.* सर्वोत्कृष्ट; परम, अत्युत्तम, अतिशय in comp. —LY, *adv.* अत्यंतं, परमं.

SUPERNATURAL, *a.* अलौकिक (की *f.*), अ-अति-मानुष- (षी *f.*), प्रकृतिबाह्य, मानुषातिग. —LY, *adv.* अलौकिकतया.

SUPERNUMERARY, *a.* अतिरिक्त; अधिक, संख्यातिरिक्त.

SUPERSCRIBE, *v. t.* बाह्यनाम लिख् 6 P or दा 3 U. —SUPERSCRIPTION, *s.* बाह्यनाम; (fig.) बहिर्देशः, बाह्यभागः.

SUPERSEDE, *v. t.* उल्लंघ् 1 A, 10, अतिक्रम् 1 U, 4 P, निरस् 4 U, निराकृ 8 U; 's. ed him in the office' तमतिक्रम्य तत्पदमवाप. 2 वि-,लुप् c., खंड् 10, निवृत् c. —ED, *a.* निरस्त, विलोपित; 'a s. wife' अधिविन्ना, अध्यूढा.

SUPERSTITION, *s.* मूढविश्वासः, अतिविश्वासः-भक्ति *f.*, मिथ्याधर्मः; अविधिनिष्ठा-श्रद्धा. —SUPERSTITIOUS, *a.* मूढ, विश्वासनिष्ठ; असत्य-मिथ्या-धर्मिन्, अत्याचारनिष्ठ. 2 मूढविश्वासमूलक.

SUPERSTRUCTURE, *s.* भवनं, मंदिरं; *See* BUILDING.

SUPERVENE, *v. i.* अकस्मात् उप-स्था 1 P, or उपनम् 1 P.

SUPERVISE, *v. t.* पर्यवेक्ष् 1 A. —ER, *s.* पर्यवेक्षकः; *See* SUPERINTEND.

SUPINE, *a.* उत्तानशय, अवाङ्मुखशायिन्, उत्तान, ऊर्ध्वमुख (खी *f.*). 2 अलस, निरीह, उदासीन. —NESS, *s.* आलस्यं, तंद्रा.

SUPPLANT, *v. t.* निष्कस् c., स्थानं व्याप् 5 P or अधि-ष्ठा 1 P, अप-निः-सृ c., निराकृ 9 U, निरस् 4 U.

SUPPLE, *a.* कोमल, सुनम्य, अदृढ, मृदु, चपल, लघु, नमनशील.

SUPPLEMENT, *s.* परिशिष्टं, परिपूरणं, उत्तरखंडः, शेषपूरणं. —*v. t.* पूर् 10, न्यूनतां निराकृ 8 U. —AL, —ARY, *a.* परिशिष्ट in comp.

SUPPLIANT, SUPPLICANT, *s.* अर्थिन् *m.*, प्रणयिन्, प्रार्थकः, शरणागतः; 'service to s. s' प्रणयिक्रिया. —*a.* प्रणत, नम्र, कृतांजलि, बद्धांजलि, शरणार्थिन्. —LY, *adv.* सानुनयं, प्रणतिपूर्वं, कृतांजलि.

SUPPLICATE, *v. t.* अनु-नी 1 P, अर्थ् 10 A, सांजलि याच् 1 A. —ION, *s.* प्रार्थना-नं, अनुनयः, सविनयप्रार्थना. —ORY, *a.* सानुनय, सविनय, प्रणतिपूर्व.

SUPPLY, *v. t.* उपाहृ 1 P, परि-उप-क्लृप् c., संयुज् 10; 'he was s. ed with food' अन्नमुपकल्पितं तस्य; सं-भृ 3 U, उप-स्था c. (स्थापयति), परि-,पूर् 10. 2 (An ellipsis) अध्याहृ, अभ्यूह् 1 U, पूर्. —*s.* संभारः, संचयः, सामग्री, उपकल्पनं. 2 (S. s) वीवधः; *See* PROVISION.

SUPPORT, *v. t.* उप-सं-अव-उत्-स्तंभ् 9 P or c., आ-अव-लंब् 1 A, सं-,धृ 1 P, 10, आलंबं-अवलंबं-दा 3 U; 'how shall I s. my life' कथं जीवितं धारयिष्यामि (S. 4); 's. by the hand' हस्तं दा, (सेवाविचक्षणहरीश्वरदत्तहस्तः R. XIII. 69); *See* LEAN. 2 भृ 1, 3 U, ग्रासाच्छादनं दा 3 U, पुष् 1, 9P or c., (अत्रादिना) पा c. (पालयति), संवृध् c.; ' s. oneself ' उदरपूरणं कृ. 3 वि-,सह् 1 A; *See* BEAR. 4 उपकृ 8 U, अनुग्रह् 9 P, साहाय्यं कृ. 5 समर्थ् 10, दृढयति (D.); *See* PROVE; न ह्ययं मंत्रः स्वातंत्र्येण कंचिदपि वादं समर्थयितुमुत्सहते (S. B. 356) ' cannot, by itself, s. any theory '. 6 अभिनंद् 1 P, अनुमुद् 1 A, अनुकूलयति (D.). –*s.* आ-अव-लंबः-लंबनं, धारणं; ' s. of life असुधारणं, प्राणयात्रा. 2 अवष्टंभः, आश्रयः, आधारः, आ-अव-लंबः, उपस्तंभः, उपघ्नः; ' a tree of s. ' संश्रय-आश्रय-द्रुमः, उपघ्नतरुः. 3 भरणं, पोषणं, पालनं, संवर्धनं. 4 (Means) आजीवः; उपजीविका; *See* LIVING. 5 साहाय्यं, अनुग्रहः, आनुकूल्यं; अभिनंदनं. –ED, *a.* साधार, सावष्टंभ, उत्तंभित, दत्तहस्त (with the hand). 2 सप्रमाण. –ER, *s.* आधारः, अवष्टंभः, आलंबी, उद्वहः. 2 पोषकः, वर्धयितृ *m.*, पालकः.

SUPPOSE, *v. t.* वि-सं-भू c., क्लृप् c., उपन्यस् 4 U. 2 मन् 4 A, ऊह् 1 A, अनु-मा 3 A, अवगम् 1 P, वि-, तर्क् 10; *See* INFER; ' s. ing that ' ex. by अथ, यदि, (अथ मरणमवश्यमेव जंतोः Ve. 3). –ITION, *s.* सं-,भावना, कल्पना, उपन्यासः; तर्कः, ऊहः, अनुमानं; ' on this s. only ' एवं कल्पिते एव, अनेन एव उपन्यासेन. –SUPPOSITITIOUS, *a.* कूट in comp., कृत्रिम, कल्पित; ' s. child ' पुत्रप्रतिनिधिः, कूटपुत्रः.

SUPPRESS, *v. t.* सं-नि-यम् 1 P, निग्रह् 9 P, अव-सं-नि-रुध् 7 U, नि-वृ c., नियंत्र् 10; धृ 10, स्तंभ् 9 P or c., प्र-,शम् c. (शमयति), निवृत् c.; ' s. ing the emotions of sorrow ' नियम्य शोकावेगं; अंतर् in comp.; ' who s. es his tears ' अंतर्बाष्पः; अंतःकोपः &c.; ' s. ing disturbance ' संक्षोभशमनं-निवारणं; (the passions) जि 1 P, दम् c. (दमयति), नि-सं-यम् , निग्रह्; *See* CONTROL. 2 गुह् 1 U, छद् 10, गुप् 1 P, संवृ 5 U, अपलप् 1P; *See* CONCEAL. –ION, *s.* सं-नि-यमः-मनं, निग्रहः, अव-नि-रोधः, नियंत्रणं, स्तंभनं, निवारणं, प्र-,शमनं, अवष्टंभः; (of the passions) दमः-मनं, जयः, निग्रहः, &c. 2 गूहनं, गोपनं, छादनं.

SUPPURATE, *v. i.* पाकं व्रज् 1 P, पच् pass., सपूय-*a.* भू. –ION, *s.* परि-,पाकः, सपूयत्वं.

SUPREME, *s.* परम, अतिश्रेष्ठ, निरतिशय; ' s. soul ' परमात्मा, परब्रह्म, जगदात्मा. 2 मुख्य, प्रभविष्णु, प्रधान, विशिष्ट; *See* PRINCIPAL; ' s. power ' साम्राज्यं, पारमेष्ठ्यं, प्रधानाधिकारः, ऐकपत्यं; ' s. monarch ' अधीश्वरः, सम्राट्, परमराजः; ' be s. to ' अतिरिच्-विशिष्-pass., (with abl.); *See* EXCEL. –LY, *adv.* परमं, अत्यंतं, परं, अति-सु pr. –SUPREMACY, *s.* आधिपत्यं, प्रभुत्वं, प्रभविष्णुता, स्वाम्यं; प्राधान्यं, मुख्यता, श्रेष्ठता, विशिष्टता.

SURCHARGE, *v. t.* अत्यंतं पूर् 10. –ED, *a.* अतिभाराक्रांत, पूर्णगर्भ.

SURD, *s.* करणी.

SURE, *a.* निश्चित, असंदिग्ध, ध्रुव, निःसंशय, स्थिर, नियत; *See* CERTAIN; (of persons) दृढनिश्चय, जातप्रत्यय, संशयहीन; ' I am s. ' दृढं मन्ये, मम दृढप्रत्याशा विद्यते, नूनं खलु, or एव with verbs; ' he is s. of success ' सिद्धिं ध्रुवां मन्यते; ' she is s. of heaven ' तस्याः स्वर्गवासोऽवस्थित एव; तं हतं विद्धि ' be s. that he will be killed '. 3 निर्भय; अकुतोभय; *See* SECURE, SAFE. –LY, *adv.* नियतं, नूनं, खलु, ध्रुवं, अवश्यं, निश्चितं, निःसंदेहं, निःसंशयं ; *See* CERTAINLY. –TY, *s.* प्रतिभूः, बंधकः, लग्नकः; ' s. for recognizance ' दर्शनप्रतिभूः. 2 प्रत्ययः, निर्णयः, निश्चयः. –TYSHIP. *s.* प्रातिभाव्यं.

SURF, *s.* लहरी, तरंगः, कल्लोलः.

SURFACE, *s.* तलं, पृष्ठं, मुखं, दृश्यांगं, तल-पृष्ठ-भागः, पीठं ; ' s. of the earth ' क्षितितलं, धरापीठं, &c.

SURFEIT, *v. t.* अतिपूर् 10, अतिभोजनं कृ c., अत्यंतं तृप् c., सौहित्यं-निर्वेदं-जन् c.; *See* GLUT. –*s.* अतिभोजनं, अतिपूरणं, अतितृप्ति *f.*-सौहित्यं.

SURGE, *v. i.* उद्वल् 1 P, उद्भ्रम् 1 P, उत्क्षिप् pass.; ' s. ing waters ' कल्लोलाकुलं-तरंगक्षुभितं-जलं. –*s.* कल्लोलः, महोर्मि *f.*

SURGEON, *s.* शल्यतंत्रविद्, शस्त्रवैद्यः. –SURGERY, *s.* शल्यं, शल्यतंत्रं-शास्त्रं, शस्त्रविद्या. –SURGICAL, *a.* (*s.*) in comp.

SURLY, *a.* कर्कश, रूक्ष, परुष, प्रतीप, वक्र, दुःशील.

SURMISE, *v.* आ-,शंक् 1 A, तर्क् 10, सं-भू c. –*s.* वि-,तर्कः, आ-,शंका.

SURMOUNT, *v. t.* तॄ 1 P, सं-उत्-,° अतिक्रम् 1 U, 4 P, लंघ् 1 A, 10, पारं गम् 1 P.

SURNAME, *s.* उपनामन् *n.*, कुलनाम. –*v. t.* Ex. by (*s.*) ; ' s. ed Vyâsa ' व्यासकुलोत्पन्नः, व्यासोपनामा.

SURPASS, *v. t.* अति-शी 2 A, अतिक्रम् 1 U, 4 P, अतिरिच्-विशिष्- pass., जि 1 P ; *See* EXCEL. –ING, *a.* अति in comp. ; ' s. the strength of man ' अतिमानुष; *See* BEYOND.

SURPLICE, *s.* धौतावारः, उपरिच्छदः.

SURPLUS, *s.* उद्-वृत्तं, उद्वर्तः, अतिरिक्तभागः.

SURPRISE, *v. t.* वि-स्मि c. (स्माययति, स्मापयते), साश्चर्य- *a.* कृ, विस्मयेन उपहन् 2 P, विस्मयाकुल-आश्चर्यचकित- *a.* कृ. 2 अतर्कितं-सहसा-आपत् 1 P or आसद् c. or अवस्कंद् 1 P ; सहसैवाभियुक्तः (U. 3) ' was s. ed and attacked.' –*s.*,-AL, *s.* विस्मयः, आश्चर्यं, चमत्कारः, चमत्कृति *f.*, अद्भुतं. 2 अतर्कितः आपातः-अवस्कंदः, सहसाक्रमः-अवस्कंदनं. –ED, *a.* विस्मित, विस्मापित, विस्मयाकुल, साश्चर्य, आश्चर्यचकित,

विस्मयोपहत-अन्वित-आपन्न; 'to be s.' विस्मि 1 A. 2 सहसाक्रांत. -ING, *a.* आश्चर्य-विस्मय-कर (री *f.*), अद्भुत, वि-,चित्र, आश्चर्य-विस्मयावह.

SURRENDER, *v. t.* उपा-हृ 1 P, उपा-नी 1 P, सं-,ऋ c. (अर्पयति), निक्षिप् 6 P, प्र-दा 3 U, प्रति-पद् c. 2 परि-,त्यज् 1 P, उत्सृज् 6 P, हा 3 P, संन्यस् 4 U. 3 (Oneself) शरणं गम् 1 P or या 2 P or प्र-पद् 4 A, वशं गम्-या. -*s.* समर्पणं, प्रदानं, परि-,त्यागः, उत्सर्गः. 2 प्रणति *f.*, वशीभवनं.

SURREPTITIOUS, *a.* मोषेण-चौर्येण-छलेन-कृत-प्रकाशित-निवेशित, &c. -LY, *adv.* छलेन, सकपटं.

SURROUND, *v. t.* परि-वृ 5 U or c., परिक्षिप् 6 P, परि-इ 2 P, परिगम् 1 P, परि-,वेष्ट् 1 A or c., परिसृ 1 P; oft. by मेखला, रसना, वलय in comp.; 'the earth s. ed by ocean' समुद्ररसना-उदधिवलया-रत्नाकरमेखला-उर्वी. -ING, *a.* समंततः वर्तिन्, आभोग-पर्यंत-वर्तिन्; परिसरस्थ; *See* NEAR. -*s.* परिवेष्टनं, संवलनं.

SURTOUT, *s.* उत्तरीयं, प्रावारः.

SURVEILLANCE, *s.* अवेक्षा-क्षणं, निरूपणं.

SURVEY, *v. t.* प्र-,परि-,मा 3 A or c. (मापयति). 2 (With the eye) संदृश् 1 P, परि-अव-ईक्ष् 1 A, विलोक् 1 A, 10, निरीक्ष्, निरूप् 10. -*s.* अव-आ-लोकः-कनं, निरीक्षा, निरीक्षणं. 2 मापनं. -OR, *s.* क्षेत्र-भू-मापकः.

SURVIVE, *v. t.* अति-जीव् 1 P; जीव् with पश्चात् (with gen.) or उत्तरं (with abl.); 's. danger' आपदं उत्तॄ 1 P. -*v. i.* धृ pass., अव-स्था 1 A. -AL, *s.* अतिजीवनं, अवस्थानं. -ING, *a.*,-OR, *s.* शेष, अवशिष्ट, अतिजीविन्, ध्रियमाण, अवस्थित.

SUSCEPTIBLE, *a.* योग्य, उचित, ग्राहिन्, ग्रहण-वेदन-क्षम-शक्त, गमनीय, ग्राहक; *See* ADMIT (of); 'I am made s. of an emotion' विकारस्य गमनीयास्मि संवृत्ता (S. 1); 'youth is s.' विकारि यौवनं (Mal. 1); 's. of anger' सुलभकोप, क्रोधशील, शीघ्रकोपिन्. -SUSCEPTIBILITY, *s.* ग्राहकत्वं, ग्रहण-वेदन-शीलता-क्षमता.

SUSPECT, *v. t.* शंक् 1 A, वि-आ-परि-°, सं-शी 2 A, न प्रति-इ 2 P or विश्वस् 2 P; 'excessive affection s. s evil' अतिस्नेहः पापशंकी (S. 4). 2 मन् 4 A, वि-,तर्क् 10. -SUSPICION, *s.* आ-,शंका, संदेहः, संशयः, विकल्पः, वि-,तर्कः. -SUSPICIOUS, *a.* आ-,शंकिन्, आतशंक, शंका-संशय-शील-बुद्धि, साशंक, संदिग्धचित्त-मति, अविश्वासिन्. 2 आ-,शंक्य, शंकावह, शंकास्थानं-आस्पदं-पात्रं.

SUSPEND, *v. t.* उद्-,बंध् 9 P, प्र-अव-लंब् c., वि-अव-संज् c.; विटपविषक्तवल्कलेषु (S. 1) 'the bark-garments s. ed from the branches'; आंदोलयामि (D.). 2 व्याक्षिप् 6 P, विलंब् *c.* 3 (From office) नियतकालं यावत् अधिकारात् निष्कस् c. or प्रच्यु c. or भ्रंश् c. -ED, *a.* उद्बद्ध, प्र-अव-लंबित, विषक्त, आंदोलित, &c.; 's. ed in a loop' काचित, शिक्यित; 's. ed from the neck' कंठलंबिन्-लग्न. -SUSPENSE, *s.* अनिश्चयः, संदेहः, संशयः, विकल्पः, दोलावृत्ति *f.*, द्वैधीभावः; धृतद्वैधीभावकातरं मे मनः (S. 1) 'my mind is held in s. and hence anxious'; 'being in s.' दोलायमान, संशयदोलारूढ, संदेहदोलास्थ. -SUSPENSION, *s.* उद्बंधनं, अवलंबनं. 2 विलंबनं, व्याक्षेपः. 3 विच्छेदः, निवृत्ति *f.*, निरोधः.

SUSTAIN, *v. t.* भृ 3 U, सं-वृध् c., पा c. (पालयति) &c. 2 सं-,धृ 10, (शोकक्षोभे हृदयं प्रलापैरेव धार्यते U. 3); सं-स्तंभ् 9 P or c.; *See* SUPPORT; 's. life' प्राणधारणं-प्राणयात्रां-कृ 8 U, जीवितं धृ, प्राणसारं भृ; *See* LIVE, MAINTAIN. 3 प्रवृत् c. 4 प्रति-उप-पद् c.; *See* PROVE. 5 सह् 1 A, अनु-भू 1 P. -SUSTENANCE, *s.* जीवनं, उपजीविका, वृत्ति *f.*, अन्नं, आहारः; *See* MAINTENANCE, LIVING.

SUTURE, *s.* संधिः, सीवनं.

SWADDLE, *v. t.* क्षौमेण परिवृ c. or परि-वेष्ट् c.; 's.-ing clothes' बालपरिवेष्टनं.

SWAGGER, *v. i.* प्र-,गल्भ् 1 A, विकत्थ् 1 A; *See* BOAST.

SWAIN, *s.* ग्रामिकः, असभ्यः, ग्रामीणः. 2 Agriculturist, q. v.

SWALLOW, *v. t.* ग्रस् 1 A, नि-,गॄ 6 P. -*s.* ग्रासः, गिलनं. 2 निगरणस्रोतस् *n.*, अन्नमार्गः; 's.-wort' अर्कः, वसु(सू)कः, आस्फोटः, गणरूपः, विकी(कि)रणः, मंदारः, अर्कपर्णः.

SWAMP, *s.* कच्छभूः, अनूपो देशः, अनूपभूः. -*v. t.* आ-प्लु c.; *See* PLUNGE. -Y, *a.* कच्छ, अनूप.

SWAN, *s.* मरालः, राजहंसः, श्वेतगरुत् *m.*

SWARD, *s.* शाद्वलं, सतृणभूमि *f.*

SWARM, *s.* संघः, समूहः, गणः, वृंदं, कुलं; *See* MULTITUDE. -*v. i.* गणशः संनिपत् 1 P or संमिल् 6 P, संघशः गम् 1 P or या 2 P. -ING, *a.* (with) व्याप्त, संकुल, आ-सं-कीर्ण, जुष्ट, उपसेवित.

SWARTHY, *a.* श्याम, कृष्ण, कृष्णवर्ण.

SWATH, *s.* पट्टः, दीर्घखंडः. -*v. t.* (पट्टेन) वेष्ट् 1 A or c., परि-वृ c., परिच्छद् 10.

SWAY, *s.* शासनं, आधिपत्यं, ईश्वरत्वं, प्रभुत्वं, वशः-शं, अधीनता. -*v. t.* शास् 2 P. 2 प्रवृत् c., प्र-,नी 1 P, प्रेर् c., प्रयुज् 10, प्रचुद् 10; *See* INFLUENCE, SUBJECT; 'not s. ed by avarice' अवशो लोभस्य, अनाकृष्टः लोभेन, लोभाप्रेरित, &c. -*v. i.* प्रेंख् 1 P, इतस्ततः चल् 1 P or कंप् 1 A; नम् 1 P, आ-प्र-लंब् 1 A.

SWEAR, *v. i.* शप् 1, 4 U, शपथं शप्. -*v. t.* शप्

c., शपथं ग्रह् c. –ER, *s.* शपथकृत् *m.* –ING, *s.* शपथं, शापः.

SWEAT, *v. i.* प्र-,स्विद् 4 P; *See* PERSPIRE. 2 परिश्रम् 4 P; तम् 4 P (tire). –*v. t.* स्विद् c.–*s.* स्वेदः, घर्मः, स्वेदजलं. 2 परिश्रमः, आयासः; 'by the s. of thy brow' आत्मनः परिश्रमेण. –ING,–Y, *a.* सस्वेद, घर्मेलिप्त, स्वेदवत्.

SWEEP, *v. t.* मृज् 2 P or c., सं-परि-प्र-°; 's. away' अव-अप-मृज्, अपवह् c., (रयेण) अपनी; 's. across', 's. over' जवेन अतिक्रम् 1 U, 4 P or अति-इ 2 P. –*s.* प्रसरः, गोचरः, विषयः; *See* RANGE. –ER, *s.* संमार्जकः, खलपूः, बहुकरः. –ING, *s.* सं-,मार्जनं-ना, मलापहरणं. –INGS, *s.* अवकरः, अव(प)स्करः, मलं, संकरः, उच्छिष्टं.

SWEET, *a.* मधुर; मिष्ट, सुरस, स्वादु, मधुमय (यी *f.*), (of taste only). 2 चारु, मंजुल, ललित, कोमल, मनोज्ञ; *See* PLEASANT; 's. smile' चारु-मधुर-स्मितं; 's. song' चारुगीतं, &c. –*s.* मधु *n.*, मिष्टं, आस्वादः. 2 सुखं, सौख्यं; 's. s of royalty' राज्य-सुखानि; 's.-heart' वल्लभ, प्रणयिन्, दयित, कांत, रमण (णी *f.*), प्रियतम; 's.-meat' मिष्टान्नं, मोदकः, वायनं; 's.-smelling' सुगंधि, सुरभि; 's.-speaking, -toned,-voiced' मंजुलस्वन, चारुभाषिन्, प्रियंवद, मधुरवाक्. –EN, *v. t.* मधुरीकृ 8 U, मिष्टीकृ, स्वादूकृ. –*v. i.* मधुरीभू. –LY, *adv.* मधुरं, चारु, मधुर in comp.; 'smiling s.' चारुहासिन्. –NESS, *s.* माधुर्यं, स्वादुता, &c.

SWELL, *v. i.* श्वि 1 P or pass., प्र-उत्-°, स्फाय् 1 A, वृध् 1 A, उत्सृप् 1 P; प्र-उप-चि pass., बहुलीभू 1 P; 'a heart s. ing with joy' हर्षोत्फुल्लं हृदयं; *See* INCREASE. –*v. t.* श्वि c., स्फाय् c. (स्फावयति), वृध् c. (with air), उद्-प्र-आ-ध्मा 1 P; *See* PUFF. –*s.*, -ING, *s.* स्फीति *f.*, वृद्धि *f.*, उपचयः. 2 श्वयथुः, शोथः; शोफः, गंडः. 3 (Of the sea) ऊर्मिप्रलोठनं, संक्षोभः. –ING, *a.* शूयमान, उत्सर्पिन्; 'a s. sea' प्रचलदूर्मिमालाकुल. –SWOLLEN, *a.* शून, स्फीत, प्रवृद्ध, &c.

SWERVE, *v. i.* प्र-वि-चल् 1 P, भ्रंश् 4 P, 1 A, पराङ्मुखीभू 1 P, च्यु 1 A, व्यति-इ 2 P, व्यतिक्रम् 1 U, 4 P, (with abl.); अतिचर् 1 P, अति-वृत् 1 A (with acc.); *See* DEVIATE; 's. ing from the right path' सन्मार्गभ्रष्ट, &c.

SWIFT, *a.* जवन, वेगवत्, त्वरित, सत्वर, शीघ्र-द्रुत-लघु-गामिन्, प्र-,जविन्, शीघ्रग, प्रजवन, तरस्विन्, महावेग; 's. of foot' धावने महाजव; 'as s. as the wind' वायुगति, वायुवेग. –LY, *adv.* शीघ्रं, जवेन, सवेगं, सत्वरं. –NESS, *s.* शीघ्रता, वेगः, तरस् *n.*

SWIG, SWILL, *v.* अतिपानं कृ 8 U.

SWIM, *v. t.* प्लु 1 P; प्लु 1 A; 'swam across the sea with their arms' पयः अतारिषुर्भुजैः (Si. XII. 77); 's. ing against the waves' बाहुभ्यां लहरीश्छिंदन्; 'the Earth s. s in blood' रुधिराप्लाविता मही. –*v. t.* तॄ (with acc.), पारं गम् 1 P. –MER, *s.* तरण-प्लवन-कृत् *m.* –MING, *s.* तरणं, प्लवनं; 's. against the current' प्रतीपतरणं.

SWINDLE,-ER, *See* CHEAT.

SWINE, *s.* शू(सू)कराः, वराहाः. –ISH, *a.* सौकर (री *f.*), सूकरशील-वृत्ति.

SWING, *s* दोला-ली, प्रेंखा, प्रेंखोलनं, हिंदोलः; काचं, शिक्यं (with a loop). 2 दोलनं, प्रेंखणं. 3 रयः, वेगः, गति *f.* –*v. t.* प्रेंख् 1 P, दोलायते (D.), इतस्ततः सं-वि-चल् 1 P. –*v. t.* प्रेंख् c., आंदोलयति-प्रेंखोलयति (D.), इतस्ततः सं-वि-चल् c. –ING, *a.* प्रेंखत्, दोलायमान; काचित, शिक्यित.

SWINGE, *v. t.* बलवत् तड् 10, प्रतुद् 6 P, परुषं प्रह् 1P.

SWIRL, *v. i.* घूर्ण् 6 P, 1 A, भ्रम् 1, 4 P.

SWITCH, *s.* पिंजा; पल्लवः.

SWOON, *v. i.* मुह् 4 P, प्र-वि-ध्या-°, मुर्छ् 1 P. – *s* मूर्च्छा, मोहः; 'he fell in a s.' मोहपरायणो बभूव, मूर्च्छापन्नः. –ING, *a.* मूढ, मुग्ध, मूर्च्छापन्न, मोहवश.

SWOOP, *s.* अवपातः, सहसाक्रमणं-आपतनं. –*v. i.* सहसा अवपत्य ग्रह् 9 P or आक्रम् 1 U, 4 P.

SWORD, *s.* असिः, खड्गः, निस्त्रिंशः, कृपाणः, करवा(पा)लः, चंद्रहासः, रिष्टिः, मंडलाग्रः, कौक्षेयकः; 's.-belt' त्सरुबंधनं; 's.-stick' कूटासिः; 's.-man' खड्गिन्, खड्गधरः, आसिकः.

SYCOPHANT, *s.* चाटुकारः-पटुः, अतिलालनपरः, अत्यनुरागिन् *m.* –SYCOPHANCY, *s.* चाटूक्ति *f.*, चाटुकारित्वं; *See* FLATTER,-Y.

SYLLABLE, *s.* अक्षरं; 'of one s.' एकाच्, एकाक्षर; 'of many s. s' अनेकाच्, बह्वक्षर.

SYLLABUS, *s.* सारः, संक्षेपः, सारांशः.

SYLLOGISM, *s.* न्यायः. –SYLLOGISTIC, *a.* न्यायसंगत, न्याय्य, न्याय in comp.

SYLPH, *s.* तन्वंगी, तनुगात्री. 2 विद्याधरी, दिव्यांगना.

SYMBOL, *s.* चिह्नं, लक्षणं, लिंगं, संज्ञा, प्रतिरूपं. –IC, *a.* लाक्षणिक-सांकेतिक (की *f.*), संकेतरूप.

SYMMETRY, *s.* सौष्ठवं, चतुरस्रता, यथाप्रमाणता, अंगसंयोगः, अवयवसंगति *f.* –ICAL, *a.* सम, चतुरस्र, सम-यथा-स-प्रमाण, संगतावयव.

SYMPATHY, *s.* सहानुभवः, संवेदनं, अनुकंपा, समदुःखता, समदुःखिता; समसुखिता, oft. by समदुःख-सुख; 'the birds even screamed as if out of s.' विहगाः समदुःखा इव चुक्रुशुः (R. VIII. 39). 2 स्वभाव-प्रकृति-साम्यं, आनुगुण्यं, साधर्म्यं, आनुरूप्यं. –ETIC, *a.* समदुःख-दुःखिन्, सदय, स्निग्ध, सहदुःखिन्,-सुखिन्. –IZE, *v. i.* सह-सम-दुःखिन्- *a.* भू &c.; *See* (*s.*); 'I s. with you in your distress' त्वद्दुःखदुःखितोऽहं, त्वत्समदुःखभागहं; 'many s. with us in our success' बहवः अस्मदभ्युदयेन सुखभाजो भवंति-मोदंते-मोदंते &c.

SYMPHONY, *s.* एकतानता, स्वरैक्यं, साम्यं; *See* HARMONY. -IOUS, *a.* सम-संगत-स्वर-तान.

SYMPTOM, *s.* लिंगं, लक्षणं; *See* INDICATION. -ATIC, *a.* सूचक, बोधक.

SYNAGOGUE, *s.* समाजः, सभागृहं.

SYNCHRONOUS, *a.* एक-सम-कालीन. -SYNCHRONISM, *s.* यौगपद्यं, समकालीनता. -SYNCHRONIZE, *v. i.* युगपत्-एककाले-वृत् 1 A or भू 1 P or जन् 4 A.

SYNCOPE, *s.* मूर्छा.

SYNOD, *s.* समाजः, सभा, परिषद् *f.* -IC, *a.* चंद्र in comp.; (चंद्रमासः).

SYNONYM, *s.* पर्यायः, तुल्यार्थशब्दः, पर्यायशब्दः. -OUS, *a.* समानार्थ, तुल्य-एक-अर्थ, सहार्थ.

SYNOPSIS, *s.* सारसंग्रहः-पत्रकं. -SYNOPTICAL, *a.* सारभूत.

SYNTAX, *s.* कारकप्रक्रिया, वाक्यरचनाविचारः.

SYNTHESIS, *s.* संयोगः, संकलनं. -SYNTHETICAL, *a.* सांयोगिक (की *f.*); संयोग in comp., संयोगात्मक.

SYPHILIS, *s.* उपदंशः.

SYRINGE, *s.* शृंग-नकं, वस्ति *m. f.*

SYSTEM, *s.* पद्धति *f.*, रीति *f.*, सरणि-णी *f.*, क्रमः, पर्यायः; *See* MANNER. 2 कल्पना, प्रयोगः. 3 शाखा. 4 (Of the body) कायव्यूहः. 5 (Of philosopy) दर्शनं; 'the solar s.' सौरं जगत्. -ATIC, *a.* अनुज्झितक्रम, यथापद्धति, यथाक्रम, क्रमानुगत. -ATICALLY, *adv.* यथाक्रमं, यथापद्धति. -ATIZE, *v. t.* व्यव-स्था c. (स्थापयति), यथाक्रमं रच् 10 or विन्यस् 4 U; *See* METHOD, -IZE, &c.

T.

TABARD, *s.* तनुत्राणारः.

TABASHEER, *s. See* MANNA.

TABBY, *a.* चित्र, शबल, कर्बुरित.

TABERNACLE, *s.* पटवेश्मन् *n.*, पटमंडपः, दूष्यं; (fig.) अचिरस्थायी आवासः.

TABES, *s.* क्षयः, क्षयथुः.

TABLATURE, *s. See* PICTURE.

TABLE, *s.* फलकः-कं, आधारः, मंचः; 't. for writing' लिखनाधारः, लिपिसज्जाधारः. 2 पत्रं. 3 (Of metal &c.), पत्रं, फलकं; 'sitting at the same t.' सहभोजिन्, पांक्तेयः; 't. of contents' सूची-निर्घंट-पत्रं, सूचि-ची *f.*, अनुक्रमणिका; 't. of numbers' अंकपत्रं-जालं; 'be at t.' भुज् 7 A; 'to keep good t.' भोजनविशेषान् उपकृ c.; 't.-land' अधित्यका, ऊर्ध्वभूमि *f.*, मालं क्षेत्रं, सानु *m. n.*, प्रस्थः; 't.-talk' विश्रंभालापः-कथा. -TABLET, *s.* पट्टिका, पट्टः, फलकः, पत्रं; 'on the t. of your heart' हृत्पट्टिकायां. -TABULAR, *a.* पत्राकार.

TABOO, *See* INTERDICT.

TABOR, *s.* मुरजः, मृदंगः.

TACIT, *a.* तूष्णीं दत्त, मानस (सी *f.*); 't. consent' मानसाज्ञा; 't. obedience' निर्विकल्प-निर्विवाद-आज्ञापालनं. -LY, *adv.* तूष्णीं, जोषं, मूकभावेन, मनसा; निर्विकल्पं.

TACITURN, *a.* संवृतिमत्, मौनिन्, अनालापशील, तूष्णीक, तूष्णींशील, भाषणविरक्त, मितवाक्-कथ. -ITY, *s.* संवृति *f.*, मौनं, मूकभावः, अनालापः, मितवाक्, कथाविरक्ति *f.*, वाग्यमः.

TACK, *v. t.* आ-बंध् 9 P, पि-आ-नह् 4 P. 2 (a vessel) नौमार्गं परि-व्या-वृत् c. -*s.* कीलकः, गुणः. -ING, *s.* नौमार्गपरिवृत्ति *f.*

TACKLE,-ING, *s.* (नौ-)सज्जा, रज्ज्वादिसामग्री. -*v. t.* सज्जीकृ 8 U, संनह् c.

TACT, *s.* कौशलं, नैपुण्यं, वैदग्ध्यं, युक्ति *f.*, चातुर्यं; *See* SKILL. -TACTICS, *s.* युक्तिकौशलं; (of war) बलविन्यासकौशलं, व्यूहरचनाविद्या. -TACTICIAN, *s.* युक्तिकुशलः, व्यूहपंडितः.

TACTILE, *a. See* TANGIBLE.

TADPOLE, *s.* भेकशिशुः-शावकः.

TAG, *s.* अग्रं.

TAIL, *s.* लांगू(गु)लं, पुच्छः-च्छं, लूमं; बालहस्तः, बालधिः (bushy end). -ED, *a.* पुच्छिन्, लांगूलयुक्त.

TAILOR, *s.* सौचिकः, तुन्नवायः, सूचिकः; 't.'s work' सूच्या सेवनं, सूचिकर्मन् *n.*

TAINT, *v. t.* दुष् c. (दूषयति), लिप् 6 P, कलंकयति (D.). -*s.* दूषणं, कलंकः, दोषः; *See* STAIN.

TAKE, *v. t.* ग्रह् 9 P, प्रति-परि-° (in all senses); अगृहीते राक्षसे (Mu. 1); उपदेशं गृहाण &c.; आ-दा 3 A, प्रति-इष् 6 P; स्वी-अंगी-कृ 8 U. 2 धृ 1 P, 10, आ-अव-लंब् 1 A. 3 (A word in a sense) परि-,ग्रह्; तत्राथशब्द आनंतर्यार्थः परिगृह्यते (S. B. 23) 'is t. en in the sense of' &c. 4 नी 1 P, वह् 1 P, हृ 1 P. 5 उपलभ् 1 A, अवगम् 1 P. 6 अनुभू 1 P; *See* SUFFER, AFFECT. 7 लभ्, प्राप् 5 P, अधिगम्, आ-सद् c.; *See* GET. 8 Captivate, q. v.; 't. food' आहारं सेव् 1 A; 't. the field' रणभूमिं अवतॄ 1 P, रणांगणे युध् 4 A; 't. rest' विश्रम् 4 P; 't. root' मूलं बंध् 9 P; 't. heart' समाश्वस् 2 P, धैर्यं अवलंब्-अवष्टंभ् 9 P; *See* COURAGE; 't. fire' दह् pass., अग्निं उप-इ 2 P; 't. in hand' प्रतिपद् 4 A, उ(ऊ)रीकृ;

't. place'; *See* HAPPEN; 't. part in' हस्तं दा 3 U, संगिन्-सहकारिन्-सहाय- *a.* भू; 'took part in the massacre' विशसनं सहायो बभूव; 't. aim' सं-धा 3 U; 't. one's way' सिध्-साध् c. (साधयति). साधयामो वयं (S. 1); 't. effect' फल् 1 P, सफलीभू 1 P; 't. possession of' आक्रम् 1 U, 4 P, आविश् 6 P; 't. to task' निर्भर्त्स् 10 A, परुषं निंद् 1 P. -*v. i.* सिध् 4 P, संपद् 4 A, गुणं आवह् 2 आश्रि 1 U, व्रज् 1 P. -away, अप-वि-नी 1 P, अप-,हृ 1 P, अप-उह् 1 U, विरुद् c.; *See* REMOVE. -back, सं-प्रतिसं-हृ, प्रत्या-दा, प्रत्या-नी. -down, अवरुह् c., नि-अव-पत् c., अधो नी. 2 लिख् 6 P. -for, मन् 4 A; *See* CONSIDER; 'mischievousness is t. en for assiduity' चापल्यमनुयोगितां भजते. -in, ग्रह्, सेव्; (in the stomach) ग्रस् 1 A, नि-,गॄ 6 P. 2 विप्र-लभ् 1 A; *See* CHEAT. -off, अपनी, अवतॄ c., उन्मुच् 6 P, अवकृष्. -out, बहिर्नी, अपनी. -to, सेव्, आश्रि, अवलंब्. -up, प्रतिपद्, अंगी-स्वी-कृ. 2 आरभ् 1 A, प्रवृत् c. 3 Occupy, Engross, q. v. -upon, (oneself) अंगीकृ, प्रति-पद्, उ(ऊ)रीकृ; (निर्वाहः प्रतिपन्नवस्तुषु Mu. 2). -ER, *s.* ग्रहीतृ *m.*, ग्राहिन्-हारिन्-हृत् in comp. -ING, *a.* मोहिन्, मनोहारिन्, चित्ताकर्षिन्, मनोज्ञ; *See* CHARMING. 2 ग्राहिन्, &c. -*s.* आदानं, ग्रहणं, स्वीकारः.

TALE, *s.* कथा, उप-,आख्यानं, आख्यायिका. 2 परि-,गणना, संख्यानं; 't.-bearer' सूचकः, कर्णेजपः; 't.-bearing' पैशुन्यं, उपजापः.

TALENT, *s.* मति *f.*, बुद्धि *f.*, धीशक्ति *f*, प्रज्ञा, बुद्धिमति-प्रभावः-विभवः, बुद्धिकौशलं. 2 गुणः. -ED, *a.* धीमत्, प्रज्ञ, सुधी, गुणिन्, गुणवत्.

TALISMAN, *s.* कवचः-चं, माया, रक्षाकरंडकः.

TALK, *v. i.* आ-सं-लप् 1 P, सं-,भाष् 1 A, संवद् 1 P, संमंत्र् 10 A; *See* CONVERSE. -*s.* आलापः, संवादः, सं-,कथा, सं-,भाषणं, कथाप्रसंगः. 2 किंवदंती, प्रवादः; *See* REPORT; 'idle t.' प्र-,जल्पितं, प्रलापः; 'popular t.' जनप्रवादः; 'fine t.' शाब्दपांडित्यं; 'mere t.' वाङ्मात्रं. -ATIVE, *a.* बहुभाषिन्, जल्पनशील, जल्प(ल्पा)क, वावदूक. -ATIVENESS, *s.* वावदूकता, जल्पकता, बहुभाषित्वं. -ER, *s.* कथकः, वक्तृ *m.*, आलापिन् *m.*

TALL, *a.* उच्च, तुंग, उन्नत, उच्छ्रित, प्रांशु; 't. in stature' उच्च-दीर्घ-देह-मूर्ति; 't. person' प्रांशुः. -NESS, *s.* उच्चता, उत्तुंगता, उन्नति *f*, उच्छ्रायः; 't. of stature' देहदीर्घता-उच्चता.

TALLOW, *s.* (मेषादीनां) वसा, वपा; 't.-chandler' वसाविक्रयिन् *m.*

TALLY, *v. i.* सं-वद् 1 P, तुल्य-अनुरूप-अनुगुण-*a.* भू 1 P; 't.-ing of hands' अक्षरसंवादः. -*s.* Match, q. v.

TALON, *s.* नखः-खं नखरः-रं.

TAMARIND, *s.* चिंचा, तिंतिडी-डिका, अम्लिका, आम्लि-(म्ली)का.

TAMARIX, *s.* पिचुलः, भानुकः.

TAMBOURINE, *s.* *See* DRUM.

TAME, *v. t.* वि-नी 1 P, दम् c. (दमयति), निग्रह् 9 P, वशीकृ 8 U; (fury) शम् c. (शमयति). -*a.* विनीत, दांत, वशग, अधीन. 2 ग्राम्य, गृहपुष्ट, गृह्य, गृह-ग्राम- in comp; 't. dove' गृहकपोतः; 't. hog' ग्राम्यशूकरः, विड्वरः. 3 निस्तेजस्, नष्टवीर्य; नीरस, निःसत्त्व; *See* SPIRITLESS. -ED, *a.* दांत, शांतशौर्य, विनीत. -ER, *s.* विनेतृ *m.*, दमयिता. -ING, *s.* दमनं. -LY, *adv.* नष्टवीर्यवत्-कापुरुषवत्, क्लीबवत्. -NESS, *s.* वशता, गृह्यता, &c.

TAMPER, (with) *v. i.* Meddle, q. v. 2 (Witness &c.) कपटेन-उत्कोचेन-वशीकृ 8 U; दुष् c. (दूषयति), अन्यथा कृ, विकृ.

TAN, *v. t.* श्यामीकृ 8 U, सं-धा 3 U, शुध् c; परिष्कृ c. -NER, *s.* चर्मकारः, चर्मशोधनकृत् *m.*

TANGENT, *s.* स्पर्शः, स्पर्शरेखा.

TANGIBLE, *a.* स्पर्शनीय, स्पृश्य. 2 स्पर्शनीय, प्रकट, सुस्पष्ट, विभाव्यमान.

TANGLE, *v.* Entangle, q. v. -ED, *a.* जटिल, संमिश्र, संकुल, संकीर्ण.

TANK, *s.* तडागः-गं, जलाशयः, कासारः, वापी, दीर्घिका (large t.); *See* POND.

TANKARD, *s.* चषकः.

TANTALIZE, *v. t.* आशां-तृष्णां-वृध् c., आशां वर्धयित्वा विप्रलभ् 1 A, जाताशाः खड् 10 or भंज् 7 P. 2 (general) Cheat, q. v.

TANTAMOUNT, *a.* सम, तुल्य, समार्थक, तुल्यार्थक.

TAP, *v. t.* लघु आ-अभि-हन् 2 U or प्र-हृ 1 P. 2 छिद्रयति (D.), छिद्रं कृ 8 U. -*s.* मृदु-लघु-चपेटः, लघ्वाघातः-प्रहारः.

TAPE, *s.* दीर्घपट्टः-बंधनी.

TAPER, *s.* दीपिका, क्षुद्रदीपः.

TAPERING, *a.* वृत्तानुपूर्व (K. I. 35); गोपुच्छाकार, सुंडाकृति.

TAPESTRY, *s.* चित्रयवनिका.

TAPEWORM, *s.* कृमिः, अंत्रकीटः.

TAR, *s.* अ-,रालः, सर्जरसः; *See* PITCH.

TARDY, *a.* चिरक्रिय, दीर्घसूत्रिन्, मंद; *See* SLOW.

TARGET, *s.* क्षुद्रचर्मन् *n.* 2 शरव्यं, लक्ष्यं-क्षं. -EER, *s.* चर्मधरः.

TARIFF, *s.* (पण्य-) शुल्कपत्रिका.

TARNISH, *v. t* दुष् c. (दूषयति). कलंकयति (D.); *See* STAIN. -*v. i.* मलिनीभू 1 P, क्षुद् 4 P.

TARRY, *v. i.* विलंब् 1 A, चिर(रा)यति (D.); अव-स्था 1 A.

TART, *a.* अम्ल, शुक्त. –*s.* अम्लीयं.

TARTAR, *s.* दंतशर्करा, मल, [illegible].

TASK, *s.* कार्य, नियुक्तं कर्म, कर्तव्य, कार्यभा(भ)-रः, व्रतं; 'one who does a t. imposed' व्रातीनः; 'to take to t.' आधाक्षिप् 6 P, निर्भर्त्स् 10 A; *See* REPROACH. –*v. t.* कार्यभारं न्यस् 4 U, गुरुकार्ये नियुज् 7 A, 10.

TASTE, *v. t.* आ-,स्वाद् 1 A or c., रस् 10, प्राश् 9 P, लिह् 2 U. –*v. i.* Oft. by (*s.*). –*s.* आ-, स्वादः, रसः. 2 आ-,स्वादनं, रसनं. 3 (Sense of t.) रसनं, रसनेंद्रियं, रुचि *f.* 4 अभि-,रुचिः, प्रवृत्ति *f.*, शीलं, व्यसनं; 't.s differ', 'different men have different t.s' भिन्नरुचिर्हि लोकः; 'he was not to her t.' स न तया रुच्यं बभूव (R. VI. 44); 'of like t.s' समानशील. 5 रसज्ञता, रसिकता; 'devoid of t.' अरसिक, अरसज्ञ. –ER, *s.* आस्वादकः. –Y, -FUL, *a.* रुचिकर(री *f.*), स्वादु, मिष्ट, सरस, सुरस, रुच्य. 2 हृद्य, मनोहर, हृदयग्राहिन्. –FULLY, *adv.* सकौशलं; रसज्ञतया, यथारुचि, –LESS, *a.* नीरस, विरस, रसहीन.

TATTER, *s.* चीरं, चीरचीरं, नक्तकः, कर्पटः; *See* RAG. –ED, *a.* जीर्ण, जर्जरित.

TATTLE,-ER, *See* BABBLE,-ER.

TATTOO, *v. t.* रंज् c. –*s.* पटहप्रणादः.

TAUNT, *v. t.* आ-अधि-क्षिप् 6 P, निंद् 1 P, उपालभ् 1 A; *See* CENSURE. 2 सोलुंठनं-सोपहासं-वद् 1 P; 'enough of t.ing' अलमलमुपालभ्य. –*s.* आ-अधि-क्षेपः, उपालंभः, सोलुंठनोक्ति *f.* –ING, *a.* साक्षेप, सोपालंभ, आक्षेपगर्भ; *See* SARCASTIC.

TAURUS, *s.* वृषभः,-राशिः.

TAUTOLOGY, *s.* पुनरुक्ति *f.*, पुनरुक्तत्वं, पौनरुक्त्यं. –OUS, *a* पुनरुक्त, पुनरुक्तभूत.

TAVERN, *s.* गंजा, शुंडागारं, शुंडा; पथिकाश्रमः; 't.-keeper' शौंडिकः.

TAWDRY, *a.* बहिरुज्ज्वल, बाह्यशोभन, मिथ्याशोभायुक्त.

TAWNY, *a.* पिंग, पिंगल, पिशंग (गी *f.*), कपिल, कडार, कद्रु.

TAX, *s.* करः, बलिः; शुल्कः-ल्कं, राजस्वं. 2 भारः. –*v. t.* करं न्यस् 4 P (with loc.) or दा c. (दापयति) or ग्रह् 9 P (with abl.). 2 आयम् c., अत्यंतं पीड् 10. 3 निंद् 1 P, दोषं ग्रह् 9 P: *See* CENSURE. –ABLE, *a.* करार्ह, शुल्क-कर-अधीन. –ATION, *s.* करग्रहणं-आधानं, शुल्कसंस्थापनं.

TEACH, *v. t.* अधि-इ c. (अध्यापयति), शिक्ष् c., पठ् c., उपदिश् 6 P, शास् 2 P. –ER, *s.* अध्यापकः, शिक्षकः, गुरुः, उपदेष्टा, शास्ता; 'religious t.' उपाध्यायः, आचार्यः. –ING, *s.* अध्यापनं, शिक्षा-क्षणं, उपदेशः.

TEAK *s.* अर्जुनः; 't.-wood' अर्जुं, अर्जुनकाष्ठं.

TEAM, *s.* युग्मं or by pl.

TEAR, *s.* अश्रु-स्र *n.*, बाष्पः, अस्रं, नेत्रांबु *n.* -जलं-उदकं, नयनवारि, and sim. comp.; 'with t.s in eyes' सबाष्पं, सास्रं, बाष्पाकुलनयन- *a.*; 'starting of t.s' बाष्पोद्गमः, उद्बाष्पत्वं; 'flood of t.s' धारास्र, अश्रुधारा; 'having the eyes filled with t.s' बाष्पाकुल, अश्रुनयन, सास्र, अश्रुमुख, अश्रुपरिप्लुतेक्षण, पर्यश्रु. 2 छिद्रं, विदरः, भिदा; *See* RENT. –*v. t.* वि-,दॄ 9 P or c., वि-,शॄ 9 P, विदल् c., भिद्-निर्भिद्- 7 P; 'she tore her hair for grief' विललाप विकीर्णमूर्धजा (K. IV. 4); 't. to pieces' शकलीकृ, चूर्ण् 10. –down, अवकृष् 1P, निकृष्. –off, आच्छिद् 7 P, अप-नी 1 P, व्यपह 1 P, निर्ह 1 P; 't. off the hair' केशान् उल्लुंच् 1 P; *See* PULL also; 'I am unable to t. myself off from the cane-bower' निर्गंतुं सहसा न वेतसगृहाच्छक्तोऽस्मि (S. 3). –up, उन्मूल् 10, उत्-वि-पट् 10, उद्-धृ 1 P, उच्छिद्, उत्खन्, व्यपरुह् c. –*v. i.* विदॄ-विभिद्-pass. 2 सवेगं चल् 1 P. –FUL, *a.* सबाष्प, साश्रु, अश्रु-संकुल-पूर्ण-परिप्लुत. –FULLY, *adv.* सास्रं, सबाष्पं, साश्रु. –ING, *s.* वि-,दारणं, विभेदनं, पाटनं, &c.

TEASE, *v. t.* दु 5 P, क्षम् c., अर्द् 1 P or c., बाध् 1 A, पीड् 10; *See* INJURE.

TEAT, *s.* वृंतं. 2 चूचकं, स्तनाग्रं.

TECHNICAL, *a.* पारिभाषिक-सांकेतिक (की *f.*). –ITY, *s.* पारिभाषिकशब्दः, परिभाषा. 2 पारिभाषिकत्वं. –LY, *adv.* परिभाषानुसारेण.

TECHNOLOGY, *s.* परिभाषा. 2 शिल्प-कला-विज्ञानं; 'school for t.' शिल्पशाला.

TEDIOUS, *a.* अतिदीर्घ, दीर्घसूत्र, दीर्घतर; 'passes the night grown t. by sorrow' गमयति रजनीं विषाददीर्घतरां (S. 4). 2 श्रमावह, क्लांति-खेद-कर (री *f.*). 3 मंद, मंथर, दीर्घसूत्रिन्, चिरक्रिय. –LY, *adv.* अति-सु-दीर्घ. –NESS, *s.* अतिदैर्घ्यं, श्रमावहता; दीर्घता: ex. by (*a.*).

TEEM, *v. i.* Abound, q. v. 2 बाहुल्येन उत्पद् c. or प्र-सू 2, 4 A. –ING, *a.* परिपूर्ण, पूर्णगर्भ, आढ्य, समाकुल, आकीर्ण, प्रचुर; *See* ABUNDANT.

TEGUMENT, *s.* आवेष्टनं, आवरणं, कवचः-चं, पुटः-टं.

TELEGRAM, *s.* विद्युत्प्रेरितवार्ता, विद्युत्संदेशः-वार्ता. –TELEGRAPH, *s.* विद्युद्यंत्रं, विद्युद्वार्तावहः.

TELEOLOGY, *s.* मीमांसा, हेतुविद्या.

TELESCOPE, *s.* दूरदर्शनयंत्रं.

TELL, *v. t.* कथ् 10, आचक्ष् 2 A, शंस् 1 P, आ-नि-विद् c., आ-,ख्या 2 P or c. (ख्यापयति), (with dat.); वर्ण् 10, कृत् 10, श्रु c., नि-,गद् 1 P, व्या-उदा-हृ 1 P, अभि-धा 3 U, निरूप् 10; *See* SAY also. 2 गण् 10, सं-परिसं-ख्या; 't. beads' जप् 1 P. **–***v. i.* सिध् 4 P, सफलीभू 1 P, गुणं-कार्यं-कृ, यशः-सिद्धिं-दा 3 U. 2 (upon) गुणं-कार्यं-जन् c. or उत्पद् c.; अवसद् c., अप-चि 5 U, क्षि 5 P or c. 2 दुर्बलीकृ; *See* IMPAIR; 't.-tale' सूचकः, पिशुनः, कर्णेजपः. **–ER,** *s.* कथकः, आख्यायकः. **–ING,** *s.* कथनं, शंसनं, &c.

TEMERITY, *s.* साहसं, क्षिप्रकारिता, असमीक्ष्य-अविमृश्य-कारिता; *See* RASHNESS.

TEMPER, *v. t.* संमिश्र् 10, संयुज् 10, संसृज् 6 P. 2 मृदूकृ 8 U, स्निग्धीकृ, प्र-,शम् c. (शमयति), लघूकृ, लघयति (D.), नियम् 1 P; *See* MODERATE. **–***s.* शीलं, प्रकृति *f.*, स्व-,भावः; 'good t.' सुशीलं, सद्भावः, सौजन्यं; *See* under GOOD. 2 समता, अक्षोभः, असंभ्रमः, संयमः, रोषाभावः, चित्तस्वास्थ्यं,-समता; 'to lose t.' क्षुभ् 4 P, क्रुध्-कुप् 4 P. 3 Anger, q. v. **–TEMPERAMENT,** *s.* प्रकृतिः, स्वभावः. देह-शरीर-प्रकृति-स्वभावः; 'of a choleric t.' पित्तप्रकृति. **–TEMPERATE,** *a.* परि-,मितं, समर्याद, नियत. 2 प्र-,शांत, अक्षुब्ध, धीर, अकोपन, अचंड. 3 संयत, संयमिन्, संयतवृत्ति, संयमशील; 't. in eating' मिताहार, अल्पाहार, मिताशिन्, संयताहार; 't. in drinking' &c.; *See* MODERATE. 4 समशीतोष्ण, मंदोष्ण. **–LY,** *adv.* धीरं, शांत्या, अक्षोभेण, निरुद्वेगं, शांतचेतसा. **–TEMPERANCE,** *s.* संयमः, निग्रहः, परिमितता, नियमः, नियतत्वं, मिताहारः, मिताशनं, मितपानं, पानाप्रसक्ति *f.*, &c.

TEMPERATURE, *s.* उष्ण-घर्म-परिमाणं.

TEMPEST,-OUS, *See* STORM,-Y.

TEMPLE, *s.* देवालयः, देवतायतनं-निकेतनं, सिद्धायतनं, देवगृहं-भवनं-मंदिरं; and sim. comp.; मठः, विहारः (Jaina t.); 'endowment of a t.' देवस्वं. 2 कुंभः, कपोलः, शंखः.

TEMPORAL, *a.* ऐहिक-सांसारिक-ऐहलौकिक-प्रापंचिक-लौकिक- (की *f.*).

TEMPORARY, *a.* अचिरस्थायिन्, अचिर- अल्प-कालिक (की *f.*), अशाश्वत (ती *f.*), असनातन (नी *f.*), अचिर, अनित्य, क्षणिक. **–ILY,** *adv.* स्वल्पकालं, अचिरं, अशाश्वतं.

TEMPORIZE, *v. i.* यथाकालं-यथासमयं-व्यवहृ 1 P; छंदोनुवृत् 1 A. **–ING,** *a.* समयानुवर्तिन्, कालानुरोधिन्.

TEMPT, *v. t.* प्र-वि-लुभ् c., नि-आ-कृष् 1 P, वि-,मुह् c.; *See* ALLURE. 2 परीक्ष् 1 A. **–ATION,** *s.* प्र-वि-लोभनं, आकर्षणं, विकारहेतुः, विकारहेतौ सति विक्रियंते येषां न चेतांसि त एव धीराः (K. I. 59) 'there being t. s &c.'; 'liable to t. s' प्रलोभनाप्पद. **–ER,** *s.* प्र-वि-लोभकः, मोहकः. **–ING,** *s.* आकर्षिन्, वि-,मोहिन्, प्रलोभिन्.

TEN, *a.* दशन्; 'in t. ways' दशधा; 't. times' दशकृत्वः. **–TH,** *a.* दशम (मी *f.*).

TENABLE, *a.* रक्षणीय, प्रतिपादनीय.

TENACIOUS, *a.* ग्राहिन्, संलग्नशील. 2 धारणावत्; *See* RETENTIVE. 3 साग्रह, प्रतिनिविष्ट, आग्रहिन्, दृढसंकल्प, स्वमताग्रहिन्; *See* OBSTINATE. 4 श्यान, सांद्र, चिक्कण. **–NESS,-TENACITY,** *s.* ग्राहकत्वं, धारणाशक्ति *f.* 2 ग्राहः, (एको ग्राहस्तु मीनानां), आ-,ग्रहः, अभिनिवेशः, दृढता, श्यानता.

TENANT, *s.* भूम्यधिवासिन् *m.*; (in general) गृहनिवासिन्. **–***v. t.* परभूमिं अधिवस् 1 P or अधि-ष्ठा 1 P.

TEND, *v. i.* प्रवणी-भू 1 P, प्रवृत् 1 A, प्रवह् 1 P, उद्दिश् 6 P, अभिसं-धा 3 U; oft. by आलु, शील in comp.; 't. ing to fall' पतयालु, पतनशील, पिपतिषु; 't. ing to the same object' तदुद्दिष्ट; 't. s to the centre' केंद्राभिमुखीभवति. 2 (to) आवह् 1 P; कॢप् 1 A, संपद् 4 A (with dat.), (शिष्यजनप्रायमपि प्रभुप्रयोजनं न मे धृतिमावहति Rat. 1); कल्पते रक्षणाय &c.; oft. by dat. with or without भू; *See* LEAD. **–***v. t.* चर् c., पा c. (पालयति), रक्ष् 1 P (of cattle only). **–ENCY,** *s.* प्रवृत्ति *f.*, प्रवणता, प्रावण्यं, स्वभावः, शीलता-आलुता in comp.

TENDER, *a.* सुकुमार, कोमल मृदु, पेलव; *See* DELICATE, SOFT. 2 सुलभवेदन-दुःख, दुःखज्ञ, मृदु. 3 बाल, कौमार (री *f.*). 4 सदय, करुणार्द्र, करुण, स्निग्ध, दयालु; 't.-hearted' करुणात्मक, कोमलमृदु-चित्त, क्लिन्नहृदय, दयार्द्रचित्त. **–***v. t.* उपानी 1 P, उपहृ 1 P. 2 उपक्षिप् 6 P, उपन्यस् 4 U. **–***s.* उपन्यासः, प्रस्तावः. **–LY,** *adv.* सकरुणं, सदयं, सानुकंपं, सादरं, करुणार्द्रदृष्ट्या. **–NESS,** *s.* मार्दवं, कोमलता, स्निग्धता, कारुण्यं, दयालुता, वात्सल्यं, &c.

TENDON, *s.* शि(सि)रा; स्नायु *f.*, स्नसा. **–TENDINOUS,** *a.* शिरालु; स्नायुमय (यी *f.*).

TENDRIL, *s.* तंतुः; (of creepers) प्रतानं, किसलयः-यं; *See* SHOOT.

TENEMENT, *s.* भवनं, आयतनं; 'earthly t.' देहः. 2 स्थावरं.

TENET, *s.* मतं, अभिप्रायः.

TENOUR, *s.* भावः, भावार्थः, अभिप्रायः, तात्पर्यं. 2 क्रमः, अन्वयः.

TENSE, *s.* कालः.

TENSION, *s.* आ-,तति *f.*

TENT, *s.* वस्त्र-पट-वेश्मन् *n.*, दूष्यं-श्यं, पटमंडपः-गृहं; 'royal t.' उपकार्या, उपकारिका; 'pitch a t.' दूष्यं रच् 10 or उप-कॢप् c.

TENUOUS, *a.* *See* THIN.

TEPID, *a.* कोष्ण, कवोष्ण, ईषदुष्ण, मंदोष्ण.

TERGIVERSATION, *s.* वाकछलं, अपलाप: ; *See* PREVARICATION.

TERM, *s.* पर्यंत:, अंत:. 2 मर्यादा, अवधि:, सीमा; 'the utmost t.' परमावधि:; 't. of life' आयुर्मर्यादा, आयु:सीमा; 'the t. of life is small' स्वल्पं आयु:. 3 कार्यनिर्वाहसमय:-काल:. 4 पदं, शब्द:, संज्ञा. 5 व्यवहार:, वृत्ति *f*, भाव:; 'on friendly t. s' मित्रभावेन, सद्भावेन, प्रीत्या, सुखेन; 'ill t. s' अप्रीति *f.*, विरोध:, असंतोष:. 6 (Math.) पदं. 7 अवयव: (of a syllogism). 8 (T. s) समय:, संकेत:, संविद् *f.*, प्रतिज्ञा. —*v. t.* आ-ख्या 2 P, अभि-धा 3 U, आह्वे 1 P; *See* CALL, NAME. —LESS, *a.* निरवधि, अनंत. —TERMINABLE, *a.* अंत्य, सीमा in comp. —TERMINATE, *v. t.* अव-सो 4 P, समाप् c. —*v. i.* समाप् pass. —ION, *s.* अंत:, अवसानं, परिणाम:, निष्ठा, समाप्ति *f.*, निवृत्ति *f.* 2 प्रत्यय:.

TERMAGANT, *s.* अतिकलहप्रिया, कर्कशा, चंडी; *See* SHREW, SCOLD.

TERMINOLOGY, *s.* परिभाषा.

TERRACE, *s.* अलिंद:,-भूमि *f.*, प्रघा(घ)ण:. 2 Roof, q. v. 3 वितर्दि *f.*, वेदिका.

TERRAQUEOUS, *a.* जलस्थलात्मक.

TERRENE, TERRESTRIAL, *a.* पार्थिव (वी *f.*), भौमिक (की *f.*), भौम (मी *f.*), भू in comp. 2 लौकिक, ऐहिक (की *f.*); *See* WORLDLY. 3 भूचर, स्थलज, भूलोकस्थ; 't. globe' भूगोल:.

TERRITORY, *s.* प्र-,देश:, राष्ट्रं, राज्यं, भूमि *f.* —IAL, *a.* राष्ट्रीय; by (*s.*) in comp.

TERROR, *s.* सं-,त्रास:, भयं, साध्वसं, शंका. 2 भयहेतु:-स्थानं, शंकास्थानं; 'a t. to the wicked' शठानां व्यथयिता (Mr. 9). —TERRIBLE,-TERRIFIC, *a.* घोर, दारुण, भीषण, भीम, उग्र, कराल, विकट. —TERRIBLY, *adv.* दारुणं, बलवत्, घोरं, उग्रं. —TERRIFY, *v. t.* सं-,त्रस् c., भी c.; *See* FRIGHT, -FUL, &c.

TERSE, *a.* लाघवान्वित, संक्षिप्त, लघुपद. —NESS, *s.* लाघवं, संक्षेप:.

TERTIAN, *s.* तृतीयक:,-ज्वर:, त्र्यैहिकविषम: (t. ague).

TEST, *v. t.* परीक्ष् 1 A, (मायां मयोद्भाव्य परीक्षितोसि R. II. 62), विमृश् 6 P, (शास्त्रं प्रयोगे च मां विमृशतु M. 1). —*s.* परीक्षा, विमर्श:, प्रतीति *f.* 2 प्रमाणं; (something whereby to t.) निकष:, निकषग्रावन् *m.*; 'this should be put to t.' एतत्प्रतीतिरुत्पाद्या; *See* TOUCH.

TESTACEOUS, *a.* कंबुविशिष्ट, शंखवासिन्.

TESTAMENT, *s.* मृत्युलेख:-पत्रं, इच्छापत्रं. 2 संहिता. —ARY, *a.* मृत्युपत्रदत्त.

TESTICLES, *s.* अंड:,-कोष:-श:, मुष्क:, वृषण:, फलं (in dual).

TESTIFY, *v. t.* साक्ष्यं दा 3 U, प्रमाणयति (D.), प्रमाणीकृ 8 U. 2 प्रकाश् c., विद् 5 U, व्यंज् 7 P or c., प्रकटीकृ, आविष्कृ; (by words) ब्रू 2 U, वच् 2 P, &c.

TESTIMONY, *s.* साक्ष्यं, प्रमाणं, प्रामाण्यं. —TESTIMONIAL, *s* प्रमाणपत्रं-लेख:.

TESTY, *a.* *See* FRETFUL.

TETANUS, *s.* धनुर्वात:.

TETE-A-TETE, *s.* रह:-संलाप:-प्रत्यासत्ति *f.*

TETHER, *s.* बंधनरज्जु *f.* -सूत्रं. —*v. t.* (रज्ज्वा) बंध् 9 P.

TETRAD, *s.* चतुष्टयं, चतुष्कं.

TETRAGON, *s.* चतुर्भुज:, चतुरस्रं. —AL, *a.* चतुरस्र, चतुष्कोण.

TEXT, *s.* मूलं, मूलपंक्ति *f.*, मूलग्रंथ:. 2 उक्ति *f.*, सूत्रं, वचनं, वाक्यं. —UAL, *a.* मौलिक (की *f.*), मौल (ली *f.*).

TEXTILE. *a.* तांतव (वी *f.*), तंतुनिर्मित.

TEXTURE, *s.* विन्यास:, वि-,रचना-नं, ऊति *f.*, वाप:-य:. 2 तंतु-सूत्र-गुण:. 3 तांतवं.

TEW, *v. t.* *See* PLY.

THAN, *conj.* Ex. by abl. of word following it; मतिरेव बलाद्गरीयसी &c.; with 'better' ex. by न च, न तु, न पुन:; *See* PREFER, BETTER; oft. ex. by अपेक्ष्य (with acc.), अपेक्षया in comp.

THANK, *v. t.* उपकृत-अनुगृहीत- *a.* अस्मि इति वद् 1 P, ('Say', q. v.); कृतज्ञतां दृश् c. or आविष्कृ 8 U, कृतोपकारं स्तु 2 U or प्रशंस् 1 P; 't.-ed his deliverer' भवतानुगृहीत:-उपकृत:-अस्मि इति रक्षितारमुवाद; '(I) t. you', 'thanks' अनुगृहीतोस्मि, महाननयं प्रसाद:. 't. God' दिष्ट्या. —*s.* (Thanks) कृतज्ञतादर्शनं-प्रकाशनं, उपकारस्तुति *f.*, धन्यवाद:; better ex. by (*v.*); 'accept my t. s' by (*v.*). —FUL, *a.* कृतज्ञ, कृतवेदिन्, उपकारज्ञ, कृतज्ञतादर्शिन्. —FULLY, *adv.* कृतज्ञतापूर्वं, कृतज्ञतया. —LESS, *a.* अकृतज्ञ, कृतघ्न. —THANKSGIVING, *s.* *See* (*s.*).

THAT, *a.* तद् (स:-सा-तत्). 2 यत् (य:-या-यत्), oft. by comp.; 'he t. has strength' सबल, बलिन् &c. —*conj.* इति (after assertions), यथा, यत् (at beginning) with or without इति; sometimes not ex. 2 (Purpose) इति with pot. mood or अर्थे-र्थं in comp.; 'Oh t.' *See* WOULD.

THATCH, *s.* छदिस् *f.*, पटलं, तृणपटलं-छदि:. —*v. t.* तृणादिना आ-,छद् 10. —ER, *s.* तृणपटलकार:.

THAW, *v. i.* द्रु 1 P, वि-ली 4 A. —*v. t.* द्रु c., द्र-

वीकृ, वि-ली c.; *See* MELT. —*s.* हिम-तुषार-स्राव *f.* -स्रावः.

THE, (Article) Ex. by तद् (सः-सा-तत्) or अदस् (असौ-अदः); gen. not ex. 2 (With comp. adj.) by यथा यथा-तथा तथा; यथा यथा यौवनमतिचक्राम तथा तथा अनपत्यताजन्मा अवर्धतास्य संतापः (Ka. 59) 't. older he grew, t. greater his torment' &c.; 't. sooner, t. better' यथा यथा लघु कार्यं संपाद्यते तथा तथा अधिकं श्रेयो भवेत्; 't. more so' विशेषतः, विशेषेण.

THEATRE, *s.* रंगः,-भूमि *f.*,-शाला, नृत्य-नाट्य-शाला, नाटकगृहं. —THEATRICAL, *a.* नाटक, नाट्य in comp.; 't. performance' नाटकप्रयोगः.

THEFT, *s. See* under THIEVE.

THEISM, *s.* ईश्वरवादः, आस्तिकवादः, आस्तिक्यं. —THEIST, *s.* ईश्वरवादिन् *m.*, आस्तिकः.

THEME, *s.* विषयः, प्रकरणं, वस्तु *n.*, प्रबंधः.

THEN, *adv.* तदा, तदानीं, तस्मिन्काले. 2 ततः, अनंतरं, अथ. 3 तर्हि; तत्; 'now and t.' कदापि, कदाचित्; 'so t.' एवं, तर्हि; 'what t.' ततः किं. —THENCE, *adv.* ततः, तस्मात्, तस्मात् स्थानात्; 't.-forth', 't.-forward' ततः प्रभृति-आरभ्य, तदाप्रभृति.

THEOCRACY, *s.* ईश्वरप्रभुत्वं, ईश्वरकर्तृत्वं.

THEOGONY, *s.* देवोत्पत्ति *f.*-वंशः.

THEOLOGY, *s.* ईश्वर-ब्रह्म-ज्ञानं, परमार्थविद्या, अध्यात्मज्ञानं-विद्या. —IAN, *s.* परमार्थविद् *m.*, ईश्वरज्ञानविशारदः, ब्रह्म-विद्-ज्ञानिन्, वेदांती, अध्यात्मवादी. —ICAL, *a.* Ex. by (*s.*) in comp., आध्यात्मिक-पारमार्थिक- (की *f.*).

THEOREM, *s.* प्रमेयोपपाद्यं.

THEORY, *s.* मतं, सिद्धांतः; वादः; 't. of evolution' परिणामवादः; नास्तिकमतं &c. 2 कल्पना, तर्कः, मनःसृष्टि *f.* 3 आगमः, शास्त्रं, उपपत्ति *f.* (as opp. to 'practice' प्रयोगः), द्वावेवाप्यागमिनौ प्रयोगनिपुणौ च (M. 3) 'well-versed in t. and practice'; oft. मंत्रतंत्रं 't. and practice'. —THEORETICAL, *a.* व्यवहारायोग्य, काल्पनिक-अव्यावहारिक (की *f.*). —ALLY, *adv.* कल्पनापूर्वं. —THEORIZE, *v. t.* मतं उपक्लृप् c.

THEOSOPHY, *s.* ईश्वरवादः-ज्ञानं.

THERAPEUTIC, *a.* शांतिकर (री *f.*), रोगघ्न (घ्नी *f.*); 't. s' भेषजशास्त्रं.

THERE, *adv.* तत्र, तस्मिन्स्थाने, तत्स्थले. 2 (Expletive) by अस्ति. —*interj.* पश्य, पश्य; 'here and t.' इतस्ततः; 't.-about,' (t. s) तत्रैव क्वापि; तत्स्थानसमीपे; (with number) उप-आसन्न in comp.; *See* NEARLY, ABOUT; '20 or t.-abouts' उप-आसन्न-विंशाः (नराः) &c.; 't.-after' ततः, तदनु, ततः परं, तदनंतरं; 't-at' तेन, तत्र; तदुपरि; ततः; 't.-by' तेन; तेनोपायेन, तद्द्वारेण; 't.-fore' अतः, तस्मात्, तस्मात् कारणात्-हेतोः, ततः, तत्; इति हेतोः, अनेन कारणेन-हेतुना; 't.-in' तस्मिन्विषये; 't.-of' तदीय, तत्संबंध्य, तत्र थ (*a.*); तस्य, अस्य, तदीय; 't.-upon' ततः, &c.

THERMOMETER, *s.* उष्णमापनयंत्रं.

THESIS, *s.* प्रतिज्ञा, पूर्वपक्षः. 2 प्रबंधः.

THICK, *a* घन, निबिड, अविरल, सांद्र, गाढ; नीरंध्र-स्थान. 2 स्थूल, महत्, विपुल; *See* LARGE. 3 मंद, जड, स्थूल; *See* DULL; 't.-headed' मंदधी; 't.-skinned' कठिन, मसृण; मंद, स्थूल. 4 पंकिल, कलुषित, आविल. 5 (Of a solid body) घन. —*s.* तुमुलं, शिरस् *n.*, मूर्धन् *m.*, संकुलं; 'in the t of the fight' रणशिरसि, रणसंमर्द-मूर्ध्नि. —*adv.* अविरतं, निरंतरं, अविरलं, निबिडं, by (*a.*) in comp.; 't.-sown' घनोप्त; सांद्राच्छादित &c; 't.-set' घन-,संहत, उपचित. —EN *v. t.* घनीकृ 8 U. निबिडीकृ &c. —*v. i.* घनीभू 1 P, निबिडीभू; 'the horizon t. ed' दिङ्मंडलं (अभ्रपटलैः) घनीभूतं, अभ्रपटलाकीर्णं. —ET, *s.* गहनं, गुल्मः-ल्मं, निबिडारण्यं, वृक्ष-तरु-गहनं. —LY, *adv.* निरंतरं, अविरलं, निबिडं, गाढं. —NESS, *s.* घनता, सांद्रता, संहति *f.*, &c. 2 वैधः, घनता, पिंडत्वं. 3 (Of voice) स्वरभंगः.

THIEVE, *v. t.* चुर् 10, मुष् 9 P, स्तेन् 10. —ISH, *a.* अपहरण-चौर्य-शील-वृत्ति. चौर्यासक्त. —ISHNESS, *s.* चौर्यासक्ति *f.* —THIEF, *s.* स्तेनः, चोरः, चौरः, तस्करः, दस्युः, मोषकः, कुम्भीलकः, पा(प)टच्चरः, प्रतिरोधिः, परास्कंदिः, मालिम्लुचः, ऐकागारिकः. —THEFT, *s.* स्तेयं, मोषः, चौर्यं, चो(चौ)रिका, स्तैन्यं.

THIGH, *s.* ऊरुः (*m.*), सक्थि *n.*; 'having beautiful t. s' वामोरुः-रू.

THIMBLE, *s.* अंगुलित्राणं, अंगुलिमुखत्रं.

THIN, *a.* प्र-,तनु, सूक्ष्म, विरल, अस्थूल, श्लक्ष्ण. 2 कृश, क्षीण, शात; 'grown t.' तन्वंग-कृशतांग (गी *f.*); 'having a t. waist' तनुमध्यम, क्षीणमध्यम; *See* SLENDER. —*v. t.* विरलयति (D.), ऊनी-विरली-कृ 8 U, संक्षि अप-चि 5 U or क्षि 5 P or c. 2 तनूकृ. तक्ष् 1, 5 P, उल्लिख् 6 P. —LY, *adv.* विरलं, असंहतं. —NESS, *s.* तनुता, सूक्ष्मता, वैरल्यं, कार्श्यं; क्षीणता.

THING, *s.* वस्तु *n.*, द्रव्यं, पदार्थः, अर्थः. 2 विषयः, अर्थः.

THINK, *v.* चिन्त् 10, ध्यै 1 P, विमृश् 6 P, आ-पर्यालोच् 10, वि-,तर्क् 10, वि-चर् c., मनसा कृ c., सं-, भू c. 2 मन् 4 A, गण् 10; *See* CONSIDER; 't. much of' बहु मन्; 'I t. so' इति मे मतिः; 'does not t. of going to his capital' नगरगमनाय मतिं न करोति (S. 2); 't. of' स्मृ 1 P, मनसि कृ;

'I never thought of winter' हेमंतः समुपस्थास्यति इति चिंता नैव मनसि कृता, इति नैवालोचितं. —ER, *s.* सूरिः, मुनिः; (lit.) चिंतकः; *See* PHILOSOPHER. —THOUGHT, *s.* (act) चिंता, ध्यानं, आलोचनं; (result also) विचारः, विमर्शः, विचारणं-णा, भावना, मनोव्यापारः, चित्तचेष्टा. 2 मतं, अभिप्रायः, मनोरथः. 3 मति *f.*, बुद्धि *f.*, कल्पना विचारः, संकल्पः, मनोगतं, चित्त, मनस् *n.*, तर्कः, चित्त-मनो-वृत्ति *f.*, भावना; 'one's inmost t.s' अंतर्गतं मनः; 'evil t.' कुमतिः; 'benevolent t.' परहितबुद्धिः; 'swift as t.' मनोजव; 'beyond t.' अचिन्त्य; 'in t., word or (actual) deed' मनोवाक्कायकर्मभिः. —FUL, *a.* चिंताशील, विचार-विवेकशील, विमृश्य-समीक्ष्य-कारिन्, असाहसिक (की *f.*), सावधान, अप्रमत्त. 2 चिंता-कुल-पर-निमग्न, ध्यानपर. —FULLY, *adv.* विचिंत्य, विमृश्य, विचार्य, समीक्ष्य, सविवेकं, पर्यालोच्य. —FULNESS, *s.* सविचारता, विवेकिता, समीक्ष्यकारिता. —LESS, *a.* प्रमत्त, अनवहित, असावधान *See* NEGLIGENT. 2 निश्चिंत, वीतचिंत. 3 अनवीक्ष्य-अविमृश्य-कारिन्, क्षिप्रकारिन्, विवेक-विचार-हीन, सरभस, मूढ. —LESSLY, *adv.* मोहात्, रभसा, अविमृश्य, अविवेकेन, अविचारेण. —LESSNESS, *s.* अविवेकः, अविचारः, रभसः, मोहः

THIRST, *v. t.* तृष् 4 P, (fig. also); पा desid. (पिपासति), उदन्यति (D.). —*s.* तृष्णा, (fig. also); द्रव्यतृष्णा, जीवितृष्णा &c.; पिपासा, तृषा, तृष् *f.*, उदन्या, पानेच्छा. —Y, *a.* तृषित, पिपासित, तृषार्त-आकुल-आतुर, सतृष्ण, पिपासु, उदकार्थिन्, तृष्णाविष्ट-आक्रांत.

THIRTEEN, *a.* त्रयोदशन्. —TH, *a* त्रयोदश (शी *f.*).

THIRTY, *a.* त्रिंशत् *f.* —IETH, *a.* त्रिंश (शी *f.*), त्रिंशत्तम (मी *f.*).

THIS, *pron. a.* एतद् (एषः-एषा-एतत्), इदं (अयं-इयं-इदं); 't. way', 't. way' इतः इतः.

THISTLE, *s.* गोक्षुरः-रकः, गोकंटकः, वनशृंगाटः, स्वादुकंटकः; पलंकषा, इक्षुगंधा, श्वदंष्ट्रा, (plant).

THITHER, *adv.* तत्र. —WARD, *adv.* तं देशं प्रति.

THONG, *s.* वरत्रा, नद्धी, वर्धी, चर्मरज्जु *f.*

THORAX, *s.* उरः-वक्षः *n.*,-स्थलं.

THORN, *s.* कंटकः-कं, शल्यं; शिखाग्रः, तरु-द्रुम-नखः; (fig.) कंटकः, शल्यं; 'he is a t. in your side' अंतःप्रसृतं शल्यं-कंटकं-इव स त्वां पीडयति; 'there is no rose without a t.' सुखं नाम दुःखमिश्रितमस्त्येव, दुःखासंमिश्रं सुखं नैव प्राप्यते. 2 कंटकलता-वृक्षः; 't.-apple' धत्तूरः, धुस्तरः, उन्मत्तः, कितवः, धूर्तः, कनकाह्वयः, मातुलः, मदनः; (fruit) मातुलपुत्रकः. —LESS, *a.* निष्कंटक. —Y, *a.* कंटकावृत, कंटकाकीर्ण, कंटाकित, सकंटक.

THOROUGH, *a.* संपूर्ण, सम्यच्, सायंत, पर्याप्त; *See* COMPLETE; 't.-bred' अभिजात, अतिकुलीन; (horse) आजानेयः, कुलीनः; 't-fare' राजमार्गः, घंटापथः, संसरणं; सर्वसाधारणपथः, सर्वगम्यमार्गः. —LY, *adv.* सम्यक्, संपूर्णं, सायंतं; by पार in comp.; 'who has t. learnt the lores' विद्यानां पारदृश्वनः (R. I. 23); 't. mastered all lores' ततार सर्वा विद्याः (R. III. 30). —NESS, *s.* पूर्णता, परिपूर्ति *f.*, निःशेषता.

THOU, *pron.* त्वं; 'to t. and thee' त्वंकृ 8 U; 'do not t. your elders' गुरुषु त्वंकारं न प्रयोजयेत्. —THINE, *a.* त्वदीय, तावक (की *f.*), तावकीन, त्वत्क, भवदीय, त्वत् in comp.

THOUGH, *adv.* अपि, यद्यपि; 'as t.' इव.

THOUSAND, *a.*, *s.* सहस्रं, दशशतं; 't.s of times' सहस्रशः-वारं; 'in a t. ways or parts' सहस्रधा; 'ten t.' अयुतं; 'hundred t.' लक्षं; 'by t.s' सहस्रशः. —TH, *a.* सहस्रतम (मी *f.*).

THRALL, *s.* दासः. —DOM, *s.* दास्यं, दासवृत्ति *f.*, दासत्वं; *See* SLAVE,-ERY. 2 वशता, पारतंत्र्यं, अधीनता.

THRASH, *v. t.* प्रहृ बलवत्-तड् 10 or प्र-हृ 1 P. 2 निस्तुषीकृ 8 U, पू 9 U; *See* THRESH.

THREAD, *s.* सूत्रं, तंतुः, (fig. also), (आशातंतुः), गुणः. तंत्रं; 't. of a story' कथाप्रबंधः-अनुबंधः-संदर्भः-अन्वयः, अनु-,संधानं, प्रबंधार्थः; 't.-bare' सूत्रदरिद्र; अयं पटः सूत्रदरिद्रतां गतः (Mr. 2), सूत्रशेष; जर्जर. —*v. t.* सूत्र् 10; गु(गुं)फ् 6 P, ग्रंथ् 9 P; 't. one's way' मंदं मंदं प्रसृ 1 P. —Y, *a.* सूत्र-तंतु-मय (यी *f.*).

THREAT, *s.* तर्जनं, तर्जितं, भर्त्सनं, अपकारगिर् *f.* —EN, *v. t.* सं-,तर्ज् 1 P, 10 A, निर्-,भर्त्स् 10 A, भी c. —*v. i.* प्रत्या-सद् 1 P, अभ्- *a.* संपद् 4 A, उपक्रम् 1 P; 'war t. s' प्रत्यासीदति रणप्रसंगः; *See* IMPEND. —ENING, *a.* भर्त्सनकृत्; अनिष्टवेदिन्; प्रत्यासन्नभय, विभीषक. —ENINGLY, *adv.* तर्जयत्-*a.*

THREE, *a.* त्रि (तिसृ *f.*); 'aggregate of t.' त्रयं, त्रितयं, त्रिकं, त्रयी; 't. months' त्रिमासं, मासत्रयं; 'two or t.' द्वित्र, त्रिचतुर, &c.; 't.-cornered' त्रिकोण; 't.-eyed' त्रिलोचनः, त्रिनयनः; &c.; 't.-fold' त्रिगुण; 't.-fourths' त्रिपादः, पादत्रयं; '2 and t.-fourths' पादोनत्रयं. —THIRD, *a.* तृतीय. —*s.* तृतीयभागः-अंशः. —LY, *adv.* तृतीयस्थाने. —THRICE, *adv.* त्रिः, त्रिवारं.

THRESH, *v. t.* मृद् 9 P, परि-,पू 9 U, निस्तुषीकृ 8 U. कंड् 10. 2 तड् 10, प्र-हृ 1 P. —ED, *a.* निस्तुषित, निस्तुष, पूत, बहुलीकृत. —ING, *s.* पावनं, बहुलीकरणं, कंडनं, निस्तुषीकरणं; 't. floor' खलधान्यं; 't. instrument' मुसलः-लं, अयोग्रं, कंडनी.

THRESHOLD, *s.* देहली, द्वारपिंडी, महावप्रहणी; (fig.) प्रारंभः.

THRIFT, *s.* मितव्ययः-व्ययिता. 2 सं-वि-वृद्धि *f.* –Y, *a.* मितव्ययिन्, अल्पव्यय ; *See* FRUGAL.

THRILL, *s.* प्र-,कंपः, स्फुरणं, हर्षः; (of joy, horror, &c.) रोमांचः, पुलकः; उद्धर्षः ; 't. of joy' हर्षरोमांचः, पुलकोद्गमः, रोमहर्षः; 'a t. came over her body' तस्या गात्रं रोमांचितं-पुलकितं-कंटकितं-बभूव; 'with a t. of horror' सात्वसरोमांचितगात्रः. –*v.* स्फुर् 6 P, हृष् 4 P, प्र-,कंप् 1 A ; gen. ex. by पुलकित, रोमांचित, कंटकित, (*a.*); 'he t.ed with joy' आनंदपुलकिततनुर्बभूव. –ING, *a.* लो-(रो)महर्षण (णी *f.*), पुलकित, रोमांचित, &c.

THRIVE, *v. i.* प्र-,वृध् 1 A, प्र-उप-चि pass., सं-ऋध् 4, 5 P, उन्नतिं-उत्कर्षं-प्राप् 5 P ; *See* PROSPER, FLOURISH. –ING, *a.* वर्धिष्णु, प्र-उप-चीयमान, समृद्ध.

THROAT, *s.* कंठः, गलः, कृकः, निगरणः; 'relating to t.' कंठ्य; 'up to the t.' आकंठं, आकंठात्.

THROB, *v. t.* प्र-,स्पंद् 1 A, स्फुर् 6 P, वेप् 1 A; कंप् 1 A. –BING, *s.* स्पंदः, स्पंदनं; स्फुरणं, स्फुरितं, कंपः.

THROE, *s.* यातना, वेदना, व्यथा ; (of delivery) प्रसववेदना, प्रसवकालव्यथा.

THRONE, *s.* सिंहासनं, नृपासनं, &c.; भद्रासनं ; 'ascended the ancestral t.' भेजे पैतृकमासनं (R. XVII. 28) ; 'getting the t.' राजपदप्राप्ति *f.* ; 'having lost his t.' छत्रभ्रष्टः. –*v. t.* अभिषिच् 6 P, राज्ये अभिषिच्, सिंहासनं आरुह् c. ; 't. ed king' अभिषिक्तो राजा.

THRONG, *s.* जनसंमर्दः-संकुलं; लोकनिवहः. –*v. t.* आ-समा-कॄ 6 P, संबाध् 1 A. –*v. i.* जनाकीर्ण-जनसंबाध-*a.* भू; *See* CROWD. –ED, *a.* आ-समा-कीर्ण, जनसंकुल-संबाधित.

THROTTLE, *v. t.* गलं निष्पीड् 10, गलनिष्पीडनेन व्या-पद् c., गलहस्तयति (D.).

THROUGH, *prep.* Ex. by instr. or abl. 2 मध्येन, अंतरेण; 't. the branches' विटपांतरेण. 3 पारं, तीरांतरं यावत्. 4 मुखेन, द्वारेण, द्वारा, in comp.; सखीमुखेनोचे 'spoke t. her friend'. –*adv.* समग्रं, साद्यंतं, शेषं यावत्, आसमाप्तेः; oft by पारं गम् or दृश् 1 P; 'he has learnt the Vedas t.' श्रुतिपारं गतः, श्रुतिपारदृश्वा; 'to get t.' तीरयति-पारयति (D.), समाप् c. –THROUGHOUT, *prep.* Ex. by सर्व, समस्त; *See* ALL; आ or यावत् in comp.; 't. one's life' यावज्जीवं-वेन, आजीवितांतात्; 't. the town' अखिले नगरे, नगरे सर्वत्र. –*adv.* सर्वत्र, अशेषतः; सर्वत्र वैतालीयं छंदः 'the metre is Vaitâliya t.'

THROW, *v. t.* प्र-,क्षिप् 6 P, प्र-,अस् 4 P, पत् c., प्र-,मुच् 6 P, विसृज् 6 P, ईर् c., प्रेष् c., (with loc. of place); 't. a glance' दृष्टिं-चक्षुः-क्षिप् or दा 3 U or पत् c.; 't. into disorder' पिंजरी-आकली-कृ 8 U, व्यूहं भंज् 7 P; 't. dice' अक्षान् आवप् 1 P or पत् c. –about, उत्-वि-क्षिप्, इतस्ततः चल् c.; बाहूत्क्षेपं 't. ing about the arms.' –away, निः-वि-क्षिप्, अपास्, अप-हा 3 P, अपव्यध् 4 P, त्यज् 1 P; (time) क्षिप्, हृ 1 P, या c. (यापयति). 2 निरस्, प्रत्याख्या 2 P; *See* REJECT; 'it was t. ing words away' निरर्थकं-मोघं-एव तद् भाषणं, वागायासमात्रकं भाषणं; 'kindness was not thrown away upon him' सोऽनुग्रहं कृतज्ञतयास्मरत् ; 'to be thrown away upon' विफलीभू 1 P, विफलतां गम् 1 P, लयं-क्षयं-नाशं-गम्-या &c.; गता नाशं तारा उपकृतमसाधाविव जने (Mr. 5); असत्पुरुषसेवेव दृष्टिविफलतां गता (Mr. 1). –down, पत् c., अधः क्षिप् or पत्; प्र-भ्रंश् c., प्र-च्यु c. –off, निः-प्र-क्षिप्, अव-निर्-धू 5, 9 U, निराकृ, अपव्यध्, अप-सृ c. ; 't. one off his guard' असावधान- *a.* कृ; 't. off the veil or mask' स्वरूपं प्रकटीकृ or वि-वृ 5 U or प्रकाश् c. –out, Reject. q. v. 2 निः-,सृ c., अपास्. 3 (Hints) सूच् 10, उप-क्षिप्, उपन्यस्, व्यंज् c. –up, उदस्, उत्क्षिप् &c.; (from the stomach) उद्वम् 1 P, उद्-गॄ 6 P; 'I have thrown a wall around' उत्क्षिप्तो मया भित्तिबंधः (M. 5). –*s.* प्र-,क्षेपः-पणं, प्रासनं, प्रेरणं; &c. –ER, *s.* क्षेप्तृ *m.*, प्रासकः.

THRUM, *s.* दशाः-वस्तयः (pl.).

THRUSH, *s.* सारिका, शारिः *f.*

THRUST, *v. t.* अवव्यध् 4 P, प्र-सृ c., प्र-क्षिप् 6 P; 't. away', 't. out' निरस् 4 U, निः-सृ c., बहिष्कृ 8 U; (the hand &c.) प्र-सृ c.; 't. into' प्र-नि-विश् c.; 't. on' प्रचुद् c., प्रचल् c. –*s.* आघातः, प्रहारः, ताडनं; (with fist) मुष्टिप्रहारः-आघातः.

THUMB, *s.* अंगुष्ठः; 'under one's t.' आयत्त, वश्य. –*v. t.* अंगुष्ठेन परामृश् 6 P or स्पृश् 6 P or अंक् 10.

THUMP, *v. t.* आहन् 2 U, तड् 10, प्र-हृ 1 P. –*s.* आ-अभि-घातः, प्रहारः.

THUNDER, *s.* मेघगर्जनं, घनध्वनिः, जीमूतस्तनितं, मेघगर्जितं; and sim. comp.; वि-,स्फूर्जथुः-थूः, स्फूर्जितं, स्तनितं, रसितं; गर्जितं, गर्जनं-ना ; 't.-bolt' वज्रः-ज्रं, कुलिशं, भिदुरं, पविः, अशनि *m. f.*, शतकोटिः, स्वरुः, शंबः, ह्रादिनी, दंभोलिः; 't.-clap' वज्रनिर्घोषः-निर्घातस्वनः-निष्पेषः; *See* (*s.*); 't.-storm' अशनिवर्षः-पातः; 't.-struck' अशनिताडित, वज्राहत; *See* ASTOUNDED. –*v.* गर्ज् 1 P, स्तन् 1 P, वि-स्फूर्ज् 1 P; 'shouldst t. reproof' यस्त्वं (साक्षेपमिव) नदसि सिंहनादैः (Mr. 5). –ER, *s.* वज्रिन् *m.*, कुलिशभृत्, वज्रपाणिः.

THURSDAY, *s.* गुरुवासरः.

THUS, *adv.* एवं, इत्थं, इति, अनेन प्रकारेण, अनया रीत्या.

THWACK, *See* SMACK.

THWART, *v. t.* खंड् 10, वि-प्रति-हन् 2 P, मोघीकृ 8 U, नि-प्रति-वि-रुध् 7 U; प्रतिकूलयति-प्रतीपयति (D.); क ईप्सितार्थस्थिरनिश्चयं मनः प्रतीपयेत् (K. v. 5); *See* FRUSTRATE, BAFFLE.

TIARA, *s.* मुकुटं, किरीटः, मौलिः.

TICK, *s.* यूका. 2 Credit, q. v.

TICKET, *s.* निर्देशनी, अभिज्ञानपत्रं.

TICKLE, *v.* कुतकुतयाति (D.), कंडूयाति (D.); (fig.) Please, Gratify, q. v. -ER, *s.* कडूयनकः.

TIDE, *s.* वेला (of the sea). 2 स्रोतस् *n.*, ओघः, वेगः, रयः; *See* STREAM. -*v. t.* (over) तॄ 1 P, सं- उत्-°.

TIDY, *a.* Neat, q. v.

TIDINGS, *s.* वार्ता, प्रवृत्ति *f.*; *See* NEWS.

TIE, *v. t.* नि-,बंध् 9 P, पिनह् 4 P; (together) योक्त्रयति (D.), संबंधु, संश्लिष् c., संसंज् c., सं-युज् 7 U, 10, सं-धा 3 U; (flowers &c.) गुंफ् 6 P, सं-ग्रंथ् 9 P. -*s.* निबंधनं, (द्वितीयं मनसो निबंधनं); संश्लेषणं, बंधः-धनं-नी, ग्रंथिः; 't. of a yoke' योक्त्रं, आबंधः; 'this (child) is the mutual t. of parents' एतदन्योन्यसंश्लेषणं पित्रोः (U. 3). 2 दामन् *f. n.*, गुणः, तंतुः. 3 Fetter, q. v. 4 संगः, बंधः; 'worldly t. s' संसारबंधः; 'free from t. s' निःसंग, मुक्तसंग. -ER, *s.* पंक्ति-श्रेणि *f.*; *See* LINE.

TIGER, *s.* व्याघ्रः, शार्दूलः, द्वीपिन् *m.*

TIGHT, *a.* अशिथिल, दृढ, गाढ, ससक्त, सुसंहत. 2 अतिपिनद्ध, गाढ-दृ-बद्ध, संनिबद्ध; 'I am chained down by this t. bark-garment' अतिपिनद्धेन वल्कलेन नियंत्रितास्मि (S. 1); 'the coat sits t. on your body' अंगानंतरवर्ती-अंगसंसक्तः-कंचुकः. 3 आतत. 4 संबाध. -EN, *v. t.* दृढीकृ 8 U, नियम् 1 P, दृढयति (D.). -LY, *adv.* दृढं, प्र-,गाढं, अशिथिलं; 'tied t.' दृढबद्ध &c. -NESS, *s.* दृढता, घनता, सुसंसक्ति *f.*, संहति *f.*, आनंतर्यं.

TILL, *adv.*, *prep.* यावत् (with acc. of noun) or यावत् न (followed by तावत्); 't. now' अद्यावधि, अद्य यावत्; gen. by आ in comp. or with abl.; 't. death' आमरणं, आमृत्योः; 't. the learned are satisfied' आपरितोषाद्विदुषां (S. 1). -*v. t.* कृष् 1 P, 6 U. -AGE, *s.* कृषिकर्मन् *n.*, कृषि *f.* -ER, *s.* कृषकः, कर्षकः, कृषीवलः, क्षेत्राजीवः.

TILT, *s.* वितानं, उल्लोचः. 2 प्रासक्रीडा-युद्धं. -*v. t.* आवृज् 10. 2 प्रासयुद्धे प्रवृत् 1 A. -*v. i.* आ-अवनम् 1 P, भुज् 6 P.

TIMBER, *s.* काष्ठं, दारु *n.*

TIMBEREL, *s.* *See* DRUM.

TIME, *s.* कालः, समयः, वेला. 2 (Occasion) अवसरः, प्रसंगः, प्रस्तावः. 3 वारः, वासरः. 4 अवधिः, मर्यादा. 5 तालः, लयः. 6 (Personified) कालः. 7 (With numerals) गुणं, कृत्वः, वारं, in comp.; '10 t. s' दशकृत्वः; सहस्रगुणं, त्रिवारं, &c.; 'from t. to t.' काले काले; 'losing or wasting t.' कालहरणं, कालक्षेपः-हानिः; 'by this t.' अनेन समयेन, इयता कालेन; 'after a long t.' चिरात्, बहोः कालात्; 'for a long t.' चिरं, महांतं कालं; 'of the same t.' समकालीन, समकालिक (की *f.*); 'at the right t.' काले, यथावसरं, प्राप्तकालं; 'in time' यथासमयं-अवसरं, काले; 'in a short t.' अचिरेण-रात्; 'at the t. when' यदा-तदा; 'at the same t.' सह, एकावसरं, तत्कालं, तत्क्षणं; 'at all t. s' सदा, सर्वदा; 'at other t.' अन्यदा; 'at t. s' काले काले, अंतरा अंतरा; 'at this, that, t.' अधुना, तदा; 'at any t.' यदा कदा; 'come at any t.' यदा इच्छसि तदा-यथेष्टकाले-आगच्छ; 'of our, those, t. s' इदानींतन-तदानींतन (नी *f.*); 'high t.' उचितः समयः; 'it is high t. to bathe and take our meals' समयः स्नानभोजनं सेवितुं (V. 2); 'good for the t. being' आपातरमणीय, आपाततो रम्य; 'hard t. s' आपत्कालः; विपत्समयः, आपद् *f.*; 'dark t. s' कलिकालः; from t. to t.' अनुवेलं, वारंवारं; 'many t. s' बहुशः, बहुवारं, काले काले; 't.-server', 't.-serivng' कालानुवर्तिन्, समयानुरोधिन्; 'I shall not do so next t.' नैवं वारांतरं विधास्यामि; 'what is the t. now' का वेला अधुना वर्तते; 'begging is out of t.' अनवसरग्रस्तोऽर्थिभावः (Mal. 9); 'sign of the t.' कालधर्मः; 'without loss of t.' अकालक्षेपेण, अविलंबितं; 'one keeping or beating t. with the hands' पाणिघः, पाणिवादः; करकिसलयतालैर्मुग्धया नर्त्यमानः (U. 3) 'by keeping t. with her hands' &c.; quick, mean, slow, t.' द्रुतं, मध्यं, विलंबितं; 'out of t.' विताल, वैतालिक (की *f.*). -*v. t.* कालं निर्णी 1 P or परिक्लृप् c., कालानुरूप *a.* कृ 8 U. -LY, *a.* Ex. by (*s.*) in comp.; 'showering t.' काल-समय-वर्षिणः; सामायिक (की *f.*); कालकृतोद्योगात् 'by t. attempts.'. -*adv.* काले, यथासमयं-कालं.

TIMID, TIMOROUS, *a.* भीरु, कातर, ससाध्वस, त्रस्त, सभय, दीन, भीरुहृदय, चकित. -ITY,-NESS, *s.* सं-,त्रासः, कातर्यं, साध्वसं, &c., भीरुता-त्वं, चित्तवैक्लव्यं. -LY, *adv.* ससाध्वसं, चकितं, सभयं.

TIN, *s.* त्रपु *n.*, वंगं, रंगं, पिच्चटं; 't.-man' वंग-त्रपुकारः; 'calx of t.' त्रपुभस्मन् *n.*

TINCTURE, *s.* आभा, छाया, आभासः; ईषन्मिश्रणं-संसर्गः. 2 औषधाधिवासितो मद्यार्कः; निर्यासः, (extract). -*v.* (lit.) ईषत् मिश्र् 10 or अधिवास् 10; (fig.) ex. by (*s.*); 't. ed with truth' सत्याभास.

TINDER, *s.* इंधनं, एधस् *n.*, वह्निप्रदाहं.

TINGE, *s.* रंगः, रागः; आभा, छाया, आभासः; 'speech with a t. of falsehood' असत्याभासं वचनं -*v. t.* रंज् c. -ED, *a.* सराग.

TINGLE, *v. i.* रणत्कारं कृ 8 U, रणरणायते (D.), सशूलं स्फुर् 6 P; 'making the ears t.' श्रवणाविदारणं (वचः). -*s.* सशूलस्फुरणं, रणरणायितं.

TINKER, *s.* कांस्यकारः.

TINKLE, *v. i.* क्वण् 1 P, शिंज् 2 A, झणझणायते (D.); वि-हृ 2 P. -ING, *s.* क्वणितं, शिंजितं, झणझणध्वनिः.

TINSEL, *s.* मिथ्याशोभनं वस्तु, बाह्यशोभनं द्रव्यं. -*a.* बाह्यशोभ, कृत्रिमशोभि, मिथ्याशोभन.

TINT, *s.* रागः, रंगः, छाया. -*v. t.* रंज् c.

TINY, *a.* क्षुद्र, अतिलघु, प्रतनु; 't. spark' तनुप्रकाशः.

TIP, *s.* अग्रं, शिखरं, अग्रभागः, प्रांतः, मुखं, अणि *m. f.*; 't. of the foot' प्रपदं, पादाग्रं; 'learning danced on the t. of his tongue' अमुष्य विद्या रसनाग्रनर्तकी (N. I), समस्ता एव विद्या जिह्वाग्रेऽभवन् (Ka. 346); 't.-toe' पादाग्रं, प्रपदं, अग्रपादः; 'from head to t.-toe' आपादमस्तकं, नखशिखांतं. -*v. t.* Ex. by अग्र, मुख in comp.; 't. ed with silver' रजताग्र, रजताश्लिष्टकोटि; 't. ed with iron' अयोग्र, लोहाग्र, अयोमुख. 2 Top, q. v.

TIPPET, *s.* ग्रैवेयं-यकं, ग्रीवाच्छादनं.

TIPPLE, *v. t.* अतिपानं कृ 8 U, नित्यशः मद्यं पा 1 P. -ER, *s.* अतिपानासक्तः, मद्यपः.

TIPSY, *a.* क्षीब, प्रमत्त, मदविह्वल, मदवश.

TIRADE, *s.* आक्षेपः, निंदावचः-लेखः, उपालंभलेखः.

TIRE, *s.* उष्णीषः-षं, शिरोवेष्टनं; 't. ing room' नेपथ्यं,-शाला. 2 लोहवलयः-यं. -*v. t.* खिद् c., क्लम् c., श्रम् c.; 'to be t. ed' क्लम् 1, 4 P, परि-,श्रम् 4 P, आयस् 1, 4 P, खिद् pass., निर्विद् pass. (राज्ञां वयस्यभावेन निर्विण्णोस्मि S. 2); *See* FATIGUE. -ING,-SOME, *a.* कष्ट-खेद-कर (री *f.*), आयासक, कष्टावह.

TISSUE, *s.* जालं, क्रमः, रचना; 't. of falsehood' अनृतवाग्जालं.

TITAN, *s.* दानवः, दैत्यः; *See* DEMON.

TITHE, *s.* दशांशः, दशमभागः.

TITILLATE, *v. i.* *See* TICKLE.

TITLE, *s.* नामन् *n*, संज्ञा, लक्षणं, आख्या; *See* NAME; 't. of honor' उपाधिः, उपपदं, मानपदं, कीर्तिचिह्नं; 'distinguished by the t. of *Srikantha*' श्रीकंठपदलांछनः (U. 1). 2 अधिकारः, आगमः, स्वत्वं. 3 उपाधिः, उपपदं. 4 स्थानं, पदं, विषयः; 't.-page' मुखपृष्ठ-पत्रं; 't.-deed' आगमः,-पत्रं.-TITULAR, *a.* नाममात्र; *See* NOMINAL.

TITTLE, *s.* लवः, लेशः, अणुमात्रं.

TITTLE-TATTLE, *s.* विजल्पितं.

TO, *prep.* (With verbs of motion) ex. by acc.; वाचयतां याति, इमाख्यां जगाम &c. 2 (As indirect object) by dat. of person. 3 (Up to) आ in comp. or with abl., यावत् with acc.; अंत-पर्यंत in comp.; 'from one to ten' एकादिदशांताः (संख्याः). 4 (Possession) by gen. 5 (Purpose) by dat. or inf., or अर्थे-र्थं in comp. 6 (Consequence) by circum.; by dat.; 'he was stoned to death' लोष्टघातं हतः; 'he, to my great delight, soon recovered' सोऽचिरात्सुरथोऽभवद्यनाहं प्रमुदितोऽभवम्; 'tortured to death' तथा पीडितो यथा विगतासुरभूत्; 'went to his ruin' स्वनाशायैव जगाम; 'was frightened to death' भीत्या मृतकल्पो बभूव; 'she accompanies the movements of her feet to the musical time' पादन्यासो लयमनुगतः (M. 2); 'to the number of 10' दशसंख्य- *a.*; 'face to face' समक्षं, संमुखं; 'ten to one' प्रायः, भूयसा; भूयिष्ठं; 'take to wife' पत्नीस्थाने मन् 4 A; 'to a man' निःशेषं, अशेषेण.

TOLL, *v. t.* (घंटां &c.) वद् c., क्वण् c.; *See* SOUND. -*v. i.* शनैः क्वण् 1 P. -*s.* शुल्कः-ल्कं, करः; 't.-collector' शौल्किकः, शुल्कग्राही.

TOMB, *s.* समाधिः,-स्थानं; 't.-stone' चैत्यं.

TO-MORROW, *adv.* श्वः, परेद्युः, परेद्यवि; 'day after t.' परश्वः; 'of t.' श्वस्तन (नी *f.*).

TON, *s.* शिष्टाचारः.

TONE, *s.* स्वरः, स्वनः, नादः, ध्वनिः, रवः, शब्दः; *See* SOUND. 2 भावः, चेष्टा, चेष्टितं. 3 (In music) स्वरः; 'long t.' तानः; 'keep a protracted t.' तानं प्रदा 3 U, (उद्गास्यतामिच्छति किन्नराणां तानप्रदायित्वमिवोपगंतुं K. I. 8). 4 (Of body) बलं, आरोग्यं, स्वास्थ्यं, सुस्थता, आग्नः. -*v. t.* (down) मृदूकृ 8 U, स्निग्धीकृ; पारुष्यं अप-नी 1 P. -TONIC, *s.* बल्यं, वाजीकरणं, बलवर्धनं, आग्नेदं, रोचकं, दीपनं; क्षीणबलायवाजीकरणचिकित्सा 'administering t.s to persons reduced in strength'. -*a.* वाजीकर (री *f.*), बलवर्धन.

TONGS, *s.* कंकमुखं, संदंशः.

TONGUE, *s.* जिह्वा, रस(श)ना, रसज्ञा; 'hold the t.' *See* HOLD; 't. of a bell' लोला. 2 वाणी, भाषा; *See* LANGUAGE; 't.-tied' बद्ध-नियंत्रित-जिह्व.

TO-NIGHT, *adv.* अद्य रात्रौ, नक्तं.

TONSURE, *s.* क्षौरं, मुंडनं, केशवपनं, चूडासंस्कारः, शिरोमुंडनं; 't.-ceremony' चौलं.

TOO, *adv.* अपि, तथा, चैव. 2 अति or सु pr.; अत्यंतं, अतीव, भृशं; *See* EXCEEDINGLY; सुदीर्घ, दीर्घतर 't. long' &c.

TOOL, *s.* उपकरणं, साधनं, यंत्रं; 'a mere t.' यं-

भ्रमात्रं; 'you are a t. in the minister's hands' त्वं सर्वथा सचिवाज्ञानुवर्ती तेन यंत्रवत् चाल्यसे.

TOOTH, *s.* दंतः, दशनः, रदः, रदनः, दंशः, दंष्ट्रा, द्विजः, जंभः; 'two middle fore-teeth' राजदंतौ; 'double teeth' माढि *f.* 2 (Of a saw) दंतः; 't.-picker' दंतस्य निष्कोषणं, दंतोल्लेखनी; शोधनी, निर्घर्षणकं; 't.-powder' दंतशोधनचूर्णं, दंतपवनं; 't.-brush' दंतपवनं,-कूर्चकं; 'having good teeth' सुदत्; 'in the teeth of' अनादृत्य (with acc.) or by abs. constr.; *See* ' In spite of ' under SPITE; 'in the teeth of the Vedas' वेदेषु जागरूकेषु सत्सु अपि. -ED, *a.* दंत, दत् in comp. -LESS, *a.* दंतहीन, गलितदंत, निर्दंत, नीरद, भग्नदंष्ट्र, उद्धृत-दंष्ट्र. -SOME, *a.* स्वादु. -TEETHING, *s.* दंतोद्भेदः, दंतोद्गमः.

TOP, *s.* अग्रं, शिखरं, शृंगं, सानु *m. n.*, शिखा, चूडा, शिरस् *n.*, शीर्षकं, मूर्धन् *m.*, मस्तकं. 2 भ्रमरं. 3 पिधानं, आच्छादनं, पुटं. 4 मुख्य-श्रेष्ठ-स्थानं; 'he stands at the t. of the class' सर्वेषां बालकानां मूर्ध्नि तिष्ठति; 't.-heavy' ऊर्ध्वगुरु; 't.-knot' चूडा, शिखा, शिखंडः, शेखरः. -*a.* मुख्य, श्रेष्ठ, उपरिस्थ, अग्र in comp.; 't.-most branch' अग्रशाखा. -*v. t.* Ex. by (*s.*); 't. ed with snow' तुहिनावृतशिखर. 2 Excel, q. v.; *See* (*s.*) also.

TOPAZ, *s.* पीताश्मन् *m.*, पुष्परागः.

TOPE, *s.* स्तूपः.

TOPIC, *s.* विषयः, अर्थः, प्रस्तावः; प्रकरणं, वस्तु *n.*

TOPOGRAPHY, *s.* स्थानवर्णनं.

TOPPLE, *v. i.* (शिखरात्) सहसा पत् 1 P or अवपत्.

TOPSYTURVY, *adv.* विपर्यस्त *a.*, अधरोत्तर *a.*

TORCH, *s.* उल्का, उल्मुकं, दीपिका, अग्निकाष्ठं.

TORMENT, *v. t.* (अत्यंतं) अर्द् 1 P or c., पीड् 10, संतप् c., सं-,बाध् 1 A, क्लिश् 9 P, आयस् c., विप्र-कृ 8 U, प्रमंथ् 9 P; *See* AFFLICT. -*s.* (अत्यंत-) आतंकः, संतापः, व्यथा, पीडा, दुःखं, वेदना, यातना; कारणा, दारुण-तीव्र-तिग्म-यातना-वेदना. -ING, *a.* प्रमाथिन्, अरुंतुद, आयासकारिन्. -OR, *s.* अतिपीडकः, प्रमाथिन् *m.*, आयासकः, संतापकः.

TORNADO, *s.* घूर्णवायुः.

TORPID, *a.* जड; सुप्त, विचेतन. 2 मंद, जड; *See* DULL, SLOW. -ITY, TORPOR, *s.* जाड्यं, सुप्ति *f.*, चैतन्यनाशः, स्वापः, मांद्यं, तंद्रा, जडिमन् *m.*

TORRENT, *s.* स्रोतस् *n.*, रयः, वेगः, ओघः. 2 जलप्रवाहः-प्रपातः, निर्झरः, प्रस्रवणं; नदी. 3 धारा, आसारः; 't. s of rain' धारासंपातः, धारासारः, वृष्टिधारा; धारासारैर्महती वृष्टिर्बभूव 'it rained in t. s'.

TORRID, *a.* उष्ण; *See* HOT.

TORTOISE, *s.* कूर्मः, कमठः, कच्छपः; 'female of a t.' कूर्मी, कमठी, डुलिः.

TORTUOUS, *a.* वक्र, कुटिल, जिह्म, तिर्यच्. -LY, *adv.* वक्रं, तिर्यक्-कुटिल in comp.

TORTURE, *v. t.* यत् c., अत्यंतं पीड् 10, प्र-मंथ् 9 P; *See* TORMENT.

TOSS, *v. t.* उत्-वि-क्षिप् 6 P, व्युदस् 4 U, उद्-धू 5, 9 U, संक्षुभ् c.; *See* THROW. -*v. i.* विक्षिप्-उद्धू-pass., इतस्ततः विचल् 1 P or लुठ् 6 P or लुल् 1 P or प्लु 1 A, घूर्ण् 6 P, 1 A. -*s.* उत्-क्षेपः-पणं; सं-व्या-क्षोभः.

TOTAL, *a.* सकल, सर्व, समग्र, संपूर्ण, &c.; *See* WHOLE; 't. rout' अत्यंतनाशः, सुपलायितं; 't. disorder' अत्यंतमाकुलं. -ITY, *s.* साकल्यं, समष्टि *f.*, ऐक्यं, कार्त्स्न्यं; 'what is the t.' एवं सर्वं (पिंडीकृत्य) कति संपद्यंते. -LY, *adv.* संपूर्णं, साकल्येन, सर्वथा-तः, अशेषेण, निःशेषं.

TOTTER, *v.* प्र-,स्खल् 1 P, कंप् 1 A, वि-चल् 1 P; *See* SHAKE. -ING, *a.* स्खलित, स्खलित-विह्वल-गति.

TOUCH, *v. t.* सं-,स्पृश् 6 P, (fig. also); परामृश् 6 P, हस्तेन आलभ् 1 A; शतसंख्या तु मामियं स्पृशति (Ve. 2) 't. es me home'; 'was t.ed to the heart' हृदये (दिग्धशरैरिव) आहतः (K. IV. 25); 'heart t. ed with anxiety' हृदयं संस्पृष्टमुत्कंठया (S. 4). 2 (on, upon) उद्दिश्य-अधिकृत्य-वद् 1 P ('Say', q. v.). -*v. i.* संसर्गं-संपर्कं-इ 2P or गम् 1P. -*s.* सं-,स्पर्शः-र्शनं, परामर्शः, आलंभनं, संसर्गः, संपर्कः. 2 स्पर्शबोधः-ज्ञानं. 3 स्पर्शः, स्पर्शेंद्रियं; 't.-stone' नि-,कषः, निकषग्रावन् *m.*-पाषाणः-उपलः, शाणः; 'adversity is the t.-stone of (the sincerity of) friendship' तेषां (मित्राणां) तत्त्वनिकषग्रावा विपत् (H. 1). -ING, *prep.* उद्दिश्य, अधिकृत्य; *See* ABOUT. -*a.* हृदयंगम, हृदिस्पृश्; *See* PATHETIC. -Y, *a.* कोपन, चंडकोप, शीघ्र-सुलभ-कोप.

TOUGH, *a.* कठिन, दृढ, दुर्भेद्य.

TOUR, *s.* परि-,भ्रमणं; पर्यटनं; 'he is on t.' स्वमंडले चरति-भ्रमति; 'make a t.' परिभ्रम् 1, 4 P. -IST, *s.* पर्यटकः.

TOURNAMENT, *s.* सादिक्रीडा-युद्धं.

TOW, *v. t.* कृष् 1 P, आकृष्य संचल् c. -*s.* स्थूलशाणं, शाणसूत्रं.

TOWARD, TOWARDS, *prep.* प्रति (with acc.), अभि in comp; by अभिमुख- *a.* (खी *f.*) or अभिमुखं-*adv.* in comp., (गृहाभिमुखं प्रतस्थे), उद्दिश्य (with acc.). 2 (With words of direction) by loc. also, उपरि (with gen.): 't. the north' उत्तरस्यां दिशि, उत्तराभिमुखं; 't. me' ममोपरि, मां प्रति, मामुद्दिश्य, मयि. 3 प्रायः; 't. evening' अभिसायं, सायाह्नकल्पं. -*a.* *See* FORWARD; 'un-t.' अतर्कित' असमर्थितोपनत.

TOWEL, *s.* गात्रमार्जनी, मार्जनवस्त्रं.

TOWER, *s.* अट्टः, उत्सेधः; क्षौमः-मं (room on the t.). –*v. i.* मूर्ध्नि वृत् 1 A or स्था 1 P. –ING, *a.* प्रोन्नत, प्रोच्छ्रित, उत्तुंग.

TOWN, *s.* पुरं, पुर् *f.*, पुरी, नगरं-री, पत्तनं(small t.), पुटभेदनं, स्थानीयं, निगमः. –TOWNSMAN, *s.* नागरिकः, पौरः,-जनः (पौरी, पौरवधू *f.*).

TOY, *s.* क्रीडनकं, क्रीडाद्रव्यं-वस्तु. –*v. i.* क्रीड् 1 P; *See* PLAY.

TRACE, *s.* चिह्नं, अंकः, अभिज्ञानं; *See* MARK. 2 (Of foot-steps) पदवी, पदपद्धति *f.*; *See* FOOTSTEP. 3 (Of carts) प्रग्रहः, चर्मबंधः. –*v. t.* आलिख् 6 P, बाह्यरेखां लिख्. 2 अनु-सृ 1 P, अनु-धाव् 1 P; मृग् 10 A, अनुपदं या or गम्. 3 (Out) आ-सद् c., ग्रह् 9 P; ग्राहकैर्गृह्यते चौरो लोप्त्रेणाथ पदेन वा (Y. II. 266) 'or is t.ed out' &c.; oft. by प्रभवः ('Source', q. v.); 'his sudden affluence has been t.ed out' तस्याकस्मिकविभूतेः प्रभव उपलब्धः. 4 (Word) व्युत्पद् c.; 'when the word *Brahman* is t.ed (to its root)' ब्रह्मशब्दस्य व्युत्पाद्यमानस्य (S. B. 33).

TRACHEA, *s.* श्वास-प्राण-मार्गः.

TRACK, *v. t.* अनु-सृ 1 P, अनु-धाव् 1 P, मार्ग् 10; *See* FOLLOW. –*s.* मार्गः, पदचिह्नं-पंक्ति *f.*; *See* WAY. 2 चिह्नं, अंकः. –LESS, *a.* निःसंचार, निर्जन, पादास्पृष्ट.

TRACT, *s.* प्र-,देशः, भूभागः. 2 प्रबंधः, ग्रंथः, लघुलेखः,-ग्रंथः.

TRACTABLE, *a.* विधेय, विनीत; वश्य; *See* DOCILE.

TRADE, *s.* वाणिज्यं, वणिक्कर्मन् *n.*, व्यापारः, क्रयविक्रयः. 2 व्यवसायः, व्यवहारः, वृत्ति *f.*, व्यापारः. –*v. i.* वाणिज्यं कृ 8 U, व्यव-हृ 1 P, पण् 1 A, क्रयविक्रयं कृ; oft. by (*s.*); 'went out to t.' वाणिज्येन गतः; 't. ing by sea' समुद्रव्यवहारी (S. 6). –ER, *s.* वणिज् *m.*, वाणिज्यकारिन्; *See* MERCHANT. –TRADESMAN, *s.* पण्यविक्रयिन् *m.*

TRADITION, *s.* संप्रदायः, आम्नायः. 2 ऐतिह्यं, लोककथा, पारंपरीयकथा, पारंपर्यं; 'there runs a t. to this effect' इति ऐतिह्यं. –AL,-ARY, *a.* परंपरागत-प्राप्त, पारंपरीण, क्रमागत-आयात, सांप्रदायिक-पौराणिक (की *f.*); 't. knowledge' संप्रदायः, (कुमारस्य पुनः कुतः संप्रदाय इति पृच्छामि U. 6). –ALLY, *adv.* संप्रदायतः, पारंपर्येण.

TRADUCE, *v. t.* आक्षर् c., अभिशंस् 1 P, अप-परि-वद् 1 A; *See* CALUMNIATE. –ER, *s.* आक्षारकः, अपवादकः.

TRAFFIC, *See* TRADE.

TRAGEDY, *s.* शोकपर्यवसायि नाटकं. –TRAGIC, –TRAGICAL, *a.* शोकपर्यवसायिन्, दुरंत. 2 करुणरसप्रधान.

TRAIL, *s.* गंधः. 2 पदवी, पादचिह्नं, पदं. –*v. t.* वि-आ-कृष् 1 P; *See* DRAG. –*v. i.* कृष् pass.

TRAIN, *s.* परंपरा, श्रेणी, माला; *See* SERIES. 2 परिवारः, परिबर्हः, परिजनः 3 (Of dress) पुच्छं, वसनांतः. 4 परिपाटी, अनु-,क्रमः, प्रबंधः; 't. of reasoning' ऊहक्रमः, तर्कप्रबंधः; 't. of a peacock' बर्हः, पुच्छं.–*v. t.* वि-नी 1 P, (animal also), अधि-इ c. (अध्यापयति); अनु-,शास् 2 P, शिक्ष् c.; दम् c. (दमयति). 2 परिचयं-अभ्यासं-कृ c.; 'a t.ed soldier' कृतशस्त्रपरिचयः पदाती. –ING, *s.* शिक्षा, विनयः-यनं; शिक्षणं, अभ्यासः; 'military t.' रणअस्त्र-शिक्षा, युद्धाभ्यासः.

TRAIT, *s.* लक्षणं, चिह्नं.

TRAITOR,-OUS, *s.*, *a.* विश्वास-विश्रंभ-घातिन्, मिथ्याप्रतिज्ञ, शत्रु-द्विट्-सेविन्; 't. to the king' राजात्ययकारिन्, राजद्रोहिन्; 't. to the country' स्वदेशशत्रुः-घातकः; 'act the t.' द्रुह् 4 P.

TRAMMEL, *See* FETTER.

TRAMP, *v. i.* चरणं-पादं-न्यस् 4 P or क्षिप् 6 P. –*s.* पादशब्दः, चरणविक्षेपः.

TRAMPLE, *v. t.* मृद् 9 P, सं-अव-°, अभिहन् 2 P; (under foot) पादतलेन आहन् 2 U or आ-समाक्रम् 1 U, 4 P or क्षुद् 7 P; 't. to dust' चूर्ण् 10; निष्पिष् 7 P. –ED, *a.* सं-अव-मर्दित, पादतलाहत, पादाक्रांत, पादक्षुण्ण. –ING, *s.* मर्दनं, पादाघातः, पादाक्रमणं, प्रमथनं.

TRANCE, *s.* समाधिः, लयः, तन्मयावस्था, देहातीतवृत्ति *f.*; 'being in a t.' लीनवृत्ति, समाधिस्थ.

TRANQUIL, *a.* प्र-,शांत, स्तिमित, निश्चल, स्वस्थ, अक्षुब्ध, शांतात्मन्; *See* CALM. –LITY, *s.* शमः-शांति *f.*, प्र-,उप-°, अक्षोभः, निर्वृति *f.*, निरुपद्रवत्वं, धैर्यं, अनुद्वेगः, स्वास्थ्यं, स्थैर्यं. –LIZE, *v. t.* सां(शां)त्व् 10, शम् c. (शमयति), प्र-उप-°,-आ-समा-श्वस् c.; *See* CALM, COMPOSE; 't. yourself' समाश्वसिहि.

TRANSACT, *v. t.* सं-निः-पद् c., साध् 5 P or c., विधा 3 U, कृ 8 U, अनु-ष्ठा 1 P; निर्वह् c., प्रवृत् c., आ-समा-चर् 1 P; (a business) पण् 1 A, व्यव-हृ 1 P. –ION, *s.* करणं, अनुष्ठानं, विधानं, निर्वाहः, आचरणं &c. 2 कार्यं, कृत्यं, कर्म, व्यापारः, व्यवहारः, पणाया.

TRANSCEND, *v. t.* अति-इ 2 P, अति-शी 2 A; अतिक्रम् 1 U, 4 P; *See* EXCEL; 't. s definition' अपरिच्छेद्य, परिच्छेदातीत; 't. s description' सकलवचनानामविषयः (Mal. 1), वर्णनाविषयातिक्रांतः; *See* PASS. –ENT, –ENTAL, *a.* सर्वातिरिक्त, सर्वातिशायिन्, अत्युत्तम. –ENTLY, *adv.* सविशेषं, परमं, अत्युत्तमं.

TRANSCRIBE, *v. t.* लिख् 6 P. –ER, *s.* लिपिकारः, लेखकः. –TRANSCRIPT, *s.* प्रतिलेखः, प्रति-,लिपि *f.*

TRANSFER, *v. t.* स्थानांतरं नी 1 P or गम् c. 2 सं-क्रम् c. (with loc. for 'to') संचर् c., सं-, ऋ c. (अर्पयति), निक्षिप् 6 P, अध्यारुह् c.; तनयलेहं तरुषु संक्रमय्य (Ka. 345), (पुत्रसंक्रांतलक्ष्मीकैः U. 1). –ENCE, *s.* स्थानांतरप्रापणं-नयनं, स्थान-स्थल-परिवृत्ति *f.* 2 संक्रांति *f.*, संक्रमणं, संचारः, परहस्तसमर्पणं.

TRANSFIGURE, *v. t. See* TRANSFORM.

TRANSFIX, *v. t.* व्यध् 4 P, निर्भिद् 7 P. 2 जडीकृ 8 U, कील् 10, निखन् 1 P, कीलितेव चारिमन्नेव स्थाने तनुः (Ka. 278) 'as if t ed to this very spot'; 't. ed through the belly' निर्भिन्नोदर.

TRANSFORM, *v. t.* परिणम् c. (परिणमयति), रूपांतरं वि-धा 3 U, आकारं-रूपं-परिवृत् c.; 'to be t. ed' परिणम् 1 U, रूपांतरेण परिणता &c. (V. 4). 2 विडंब् 10, विकृ 8 U. –ATION, *s.* रूपांतरपरिणामः, परिवर्तः, रूपांतरं, विकृति *f.*, विडंबनं.

TRANSFUSE, *v. t.* अन्यपात्रे संक्रम् c. or निविश् c. –ION, *s.* संक्रामणं.

TRANSGRESS, *v. t.* वि-,अतिक्रम् 1 U, 4 P, अति-इ 2 P, उद्-,लंघ् 1 A, 10, भंज् 7 P; व्यभि-आति-चर् 1 P, अतिवृत् 1 A, लुप् 6 P or c. –*v. i.* अ-,पराध् 4 P (with loc. of person); *See* OFFEND. –ION, *s.* अतिक्रमः, उल्लंघनं, व्यतिक्रमः, अत्याचारः, अत्ययः, भंगः, लोपः, अतिपातः. 2 अपराधः, दोषः, पापं. –OR, *s.* अतिक्रामिन्, अत्याचारी, अपराधी.

TRANSIENT, *a.* चंचल, लोल, क्षणभंगुर, अस्थिरस्थायिन्, अस्थायिन्, चपल, विनश्वर, अनित्य, क्षणिक, असार, अशाश्वत (ती *f.*), क्षणविध्वंसिन्. –NESS, *s.* अनित्यता, अस्थायित्वं.

TRANSIT, *s.* क्रांति *f.*, संक्रमः. –ION, *s.* संक्रांति *f.*, परिवर्तः, विकारः; (state) स्थित्यंतरं, अवस्थांतरं. –IVE, *a.* सकर्मक. –ORY, *a.* क्षणभंगुर, असार; *See* TRANSIENT.

TRANSLATE, *v. t.* भाषांतरेण वि-परिणम् c. or परिवृत् c.; 'boys should t. Sanskrit sentences into English' बालकाः संस्कृतवाक्यानि आंग्लभाषया विपरिणमयेयुः. 2 Transform, q. v. 3 (To the skies) (सशरीरं) लोकांतरं नी 1 P or प्राप् c. or गम् c.; 't. ed to the skies' सशरीरमुक्तः. –ION, *s.* विपरिणामः, विपरिणमनं; भाषांतरं, अनुवादः. 2 लोकांतरनयनं, स्वर्गारोपणं, सशरीरमुक्ति *f.* –OR, *s.* भाषांतरकृत् *m.*

TRANSLUCENT, *a. See* CLEAR.

TRANSMIGRATE, *v. i.* पुनर्जन्म प्राप् 5 P, देहांतरं गम् 1 P. –ION, *s.* पुनर्जन्म, पुनर्जननं, देहांतरप्राप्ति *f.*-गमनं, योन्यंतरं.

TRANSMIT, *v. t. See* SEND, REMIT. –TRANSMISSION, *s.* प्रापणं, वाहनं, प्रेषणं, संचारणं.

TRANSMUTE, *v. t. See* CHANGE, TRANSFORM.

TRANSPARENT, *a.* शुद्ध, स्वच्छ, प्रसन्न, विशद, निर्-वि-अ-मल, स्फटिकप्रभ. 2 प्रकाश-किरण-भेद्य, पारदर्शिन्. –TRANSPARENCY, *s.* स्वच्छता, प्रसादः, नैर्मल्यं, &c.

TRANSPIRE, *v. i.* प्रकाशतां गम् 1 P, प्रचली-प्रकाशीभू 1 P, (कथं प्रकाशतां गतोयमर्थः पौरेषु Mu. 1), प्रसिद्धीभू, निः-प्र-सृ 1 P.

TRANSPLANT, *v. t.* स्थानांतरे रुह् c.

TRANSPORT, *v. t.* नी-वह्-1 P; तॄ c. 2 द्वीपांतरे निर्वस् c. or विवस् c., स्वदेशात् दूरीकृ 8 U. 2 अत्यंतं प्रमुद् c.; 'Delight' excessively, q. v.; 't. ed with joy' हर्षनिर्भर, आनंदस्य परां कोटिं गत. –*s.* नयनं, वाहनं. 2 प्रवहणं. 3 हर्षोन्मादः, हर्षनिर्भरः; हर्षावेशः.

TRANSPOSE, *v. t.* विपर्यस् 4 U, स्थानं परिवृत् c., वि-नि-मे 1 A; *See* EXCHANGE. –ITION, *s.* (स्थान-) व्यत्ययः, व्यत्यासः, विनिमयः, विपर्यासः, परिवृत्ति *f.*

TRANSVERSE, *a.* व्यत्यस्त, तिर्यक्; 'with legs t.' व्यत्यस्तपाद-*a.* –LY, *adv.* व्यत्यासेन, तिर्यक्, व्यत्यस्तं.

TRAP, *s.* उन्माथः, कूटयंत्रं, कूटं; 't.-door' कूटद्वारं, छन्नमार्गः. –*v. t.* कूटे निक्षिप् 6 P.

TRAPEZIUM, *s.* अतुल्यलंबकः.

TRAPEZOID, *s.* समलंबकः.

TRAPPINGS, *s.* सज्जा, भूषा, परिकर्म, परिच्छदः; 't. of an elephant' परिस्तोमः, आदानं; *See* HOUSINGS.

TRASH, *a.* असार, निरर्थक, निःसार. –*s.* असार-निरर्थक-द्रव्यं.

TRAVAIL, *See* LABOUR.

TRAVEL, *v. i.* परि-भ्रम् 1, 4 P, परि-,अट् 1 P, वि-चर् 1 P; *See* JOURNEY. –*s.*,-LING, *s.* पर्यटनं, परि-,भ्रमणं, विचरणं, यात्रा, प्रवासः, अध्वगमनं. –LER, *s.* पांथः, पथिकः, अध्वगः, अध्वनीनः, अध्वन्यः, यात्रिकः, पादविकः, सारणिकः.

TRAVERSE, *v. t.* आक्रम् 1 U, 4 P, तॄ 1 P, सं-अति-उत्-°, पारं गम् 1 P.

TRAY, *s.* भाजनं, आधारः, पात्रं.

TREACHERY, *s.* विश्वासभंगः-घातः, विश्रंभभंगः, असत्यसंधता, प्रतिज्ञा-समय-भंगः; *See* PERFIDY. –OUS, *a.* विश्वासघातिन्, अविश्वास्य, असत्यसंध. 2 मिथ्यावभास, असार, मायाबहुल. –OUSLY, *adv.* विश्वासघातेन, शाठ्येन. –OUSNESS, *s. See* (*s.*).

TREACLE, *s.* गुडः; *See* MOLASSES.

TREAD, *v.* क्षुद् 7 P, आ-समा-क्रम् 1 U, 4 P, पादाभ्यां पीड् 10 or आक्रम् or मृद् 9 P; 'from the trodden path' क्षुण्णाद्वर्त्मनः, (क्षुद्रजनक्षुण्ण एष मार्गः Ka. 146); 'trod one of them to death' तेषामेकतमः पादाक्रांतोऽम्रियत, एकं पादतलेन अवामृद्गात्; 't. in the footsteps of' पदं अनुवि-धा 3 U,

पदवीं प्रतिपद् 4 A, (पदवीं तरुवल्कवाससां प्रपेदिरे R. VIII. 11). 2 क्रम्, पदं-चरणं-विन्यस् 4 P or क्र c. (अर्पयति). –s. चरणपातः, पादन्यासः-विक्षेपः, विक्रमः.

TREASON, *s.* राजद्रोहः, राजाभिद्रोहः-अपकारः, राजापथ्यकारित्वं. –ABLE,-OUS, *a.* राजद्रोहिन्, राजापथ्यकारिन्.

TREASURE, *s.* कोशः-षः, निधिः निधानं, द्रव्यसंचयः-राशिः-संग्रहः. 2 वित्तं, धनं, भांडं, द्रविणं; *See* WEALTH. –*v. t.* सं-चि 5 U, राशीकृ 8 U, नि-उप-धा 3 U; *See* STORE; 't. in the heart' हृदि उप-नि-धा, अवधृ 10, चित्ते कृ. –ER, *s.* कोशाध्यक्षः-अधीशः, कोषगृहे नियुक्तः, अर्थाधिकारिन् *m.*, धनाध्यक्षः, कनकाध्यक्षः, भौरिकः (gold t.); रूप्याध्यक्षः, नैष्किकः (silver t.). –Y, *s.* कोषागारं, कोशः-षः, भांडागारं, कोशगृहं.

TREAT, *v. t.* Ex. by 'Act' (towards) q. v.; पुत्रे मित्रवदाचरेत् 'should t. a son like a friend'; 't. your rivals as dear friends' कुरु प्रियसखीवृत्तिं सपत्नीजने (S. 4); 't. with honour' पूज् 10, पुरस्कृ, सत्कृ, सेव् 1 A; *See* HONOUR; 't. hospitably' आतिथ्यं कृ, अतिथिसत्कारं कृ. 2 (A subject) निरूप् 10, विचर् c., वर्ण् 10, प्र-स्तु 2 U; 't. at length' प्रपंचयति (D.) 3 उप-उपा-चर् 1 P, कित् desid. (चिकित्सति-ते). 4 संतृप् c.; 'gave a good t.' भोजनविशेषैः संतर्पयांचकार; 't. with' सं-धा 3 U. –*s.* भोजनविशेषः, उत्तमात्रतर्पणं. –MENT, *s.* आचरणं, व्यवहारः, वृत्ति *f.*, आचारः, नयः; 'ill-t.' अपकारः, अपक्रिया. 2 चिकित्सा, उपचारः, उपक्रमः. 3 वर्णनं-ना, निरूपणं, विवेचनं, विचारणा. –Y, *s.* संधिः, संधानं 2 संधिपत्रं, नियम-समय-पत्रं. –TREATISE, *s.* नि-प्र-बंधः, लेखः.

TREBLE, *a.* त्रिगुण, त्रिविध. –*s.* (In music) तारः; उच्चस्वनः. –*v. t.* त्रिगुणीकृ 8 U. –TREBLY, *adv.* त्रिगुणं, त्रिधा, त्रेधा.

TREE, *s.* वृक्षः, तरुः, द्रुमः, पादपः, वनस्पतिः, शाखिन् *m.*, अनोकहः, विटपिन्, कुटः, सालः. पलाशिन्, द्रुः, अगमः, अगः; and रुह-ह् with 'Earth,' q. v., क्षिति-मही-पृथिवी-रुहः-ह् *m.* &c.

TREFOIL, *a.* त्रिपर्ण, त्रिदल.

TRELLIS, *s.* जालं, गवाक्षजालं.

TREMBLE, *v. i.* वि-त्रस् 1, 4 P, (with fear) प्रवेप् 1 A, कंप् 1 A, स्फुर् 6 P, प्र-वि-°, स्पंद् 1 A; प्र-वि-चल् 1 P. –ING,-TREMULOUS, *a* कंपमान, वेपथुमत्, सकंप, तरल, विलोल, चपल, चंचल; उत्त्रस्त, कातर (with fear); भग्न, गद्गद (voice); 'in a t. voice' स्वरभंगेन, सगद्गदं. –TREMOR, *s.* प्र-,कंपः, साध्वसं, वेपथुः, वेपनं, स्फुरणं, उत्त्रासः, कातरता, &c.

TREMENDOUS, *a.* महाप्रमाण, अतिबृहत्; घोर, दारुण, अतिगुरु.

TRENCH, *s.* खातं, परिखा; नाली, प्रणाली; आलवालं (of a tree). –*v. t.* खन् 1 P; 't. upon' आक्रम् 1 U, 4 P; *See* ENCROACH. –ER, *s.* खनकः. 2 काष्ठपात्रं-भाजनं.

TREPIDATION, *s.* उद्वेगः, संक्षोभः, साध्वसोत्कंपः, भयकंपः.

TRESPASS, *v.* अति-उत्-क्रम् 1 U, 4 P, अतिचर् 1 P, अनधिकारं प्रविश् 6 P; *See* TRANSGRESS, INTRUDE, OFFEND. –*s.* अतिक्रमः, मर्यादातिक्रमः, अमर्यादा, अपराधः, दोषः.

TRESS, *s.* कबरी, केशकलापः; अलकः, चूर्णकुंतलः.

TRIAD, *s.* त्रिकं, त्रयं, त्रितयं.

TRIANGLE, *s.* त्रिभुजः, त्रिकोणः, त्र्यस्रं. –TRIANGULAR, *a.* त्रिकोण, त्र्यस्र, त्रिभुजाकार, त्रिकोणाकृति.

TRIBE, *s.* जाति *f.*; वर्गः, वर्णः (caste).

TRIBULATION, *s.* दुःखं, क्लेशः, कष्टं; *See* DISTRESS.

TRIBUNAL, *s.* धर्म-न्याय-आसनं, व्यवहारासनं; 'sat on the t.' व्यवहारासनमादद. 2 धर्म-न्याय-सभा.

TRIBUTE, *s.* करः, शुल्कः-ल्कं; (fig.) उपहारः; *See* PRESENT. –ARY, *a.*, *s.* करद; सामंत; 'rendered t.' करदीकृत. 2 (Of a river) शाखा.

TRICE, *s. See* TWINKLING.

TRICK, *s.* छलं, छद्मन् *n.*, कपटं, कूटोपायः-कल्पना-प्रबंधः, अप-व्यप-देशः, व्याजः, कैतवं. 2 माया, हस्तलाघवं (juggler's t.). 3 कुचेष्टा, चेष्टितं; लीला, खेलनं, दुर्लक्षणं. –*v. t.* वंच् 10, प्र-तॄ c.; *See* CHEAT. –ERY, *s. See* DECEIT. –STER, *s.* वंचकः, कितवः, प्रतारकः.

TRICKLE, *v. i.* मंदं मंदं स्रु 1 P, परि-स्रु, कणशः-शनैः शनैः-क्षर् 1 P or स्यंद् 1 A.

TRIDENT, *s.* त्रिशूलं; त्रिशिखं, त्रिशीर्षकं; पिनाकः,-कं (of Siva).

TRIDUAN, *a.* त्र्याहिक (की *f.*).

TRIENNIAL, *a.* त्रैवार्षिक (की *f.*).

TRIFLE, *v. i.* बालकवत् आचर् 1 P or वृत् 1 A; खेल् 1 P; 't. with' परिहस् 1 P; *See* JEST; 't. away' अव-,क्षिप् 6 P; *See* SPEND. –*s.* अणुः, लेशः, लवः. 2 अल्प-स्वल्प-विषयः, लघ्वर्थः. –ING, *a.* लघु, निरर्थक, तुच्छ, क्षुद्र, लघ्वर्थ, सु-,अल्प, तृणप्राय, अकिंचित्कर (री *f.*).

TRIFOLIATE, *a.* त्रिदल, त्रिपर्ण.

TRIGONOMETRY, *s.* त्रिकोणमिति *f.*

TRILATERAL, *a.* त्रिभुज, त्रिपार्श्व.

TRILITERAL, *a.* त्र्यक्षर.

TRILLION, *s.* दशपरार्धं.

TRIM, *v. t.* क्लृप् c., वि-,रच् 10; परिष्कृ 8 U. –*a.* क्लृप्त, सु-,रचित, विनीत, परिष्कृत. –*s.*,-MING, *s.* परिकल्पः, भूषा-णं, सज्जा; 'the body is not in good t.' शरीरमसौष्ठवं (Mal. 1). 2 अवस्था, दशा.

TRINITY, *s.* त्रिमूर्ति.

TRINKET, *s.* कंकण:-णं; अलंकार:; *See* ORNAMENT.

TRINOMIAL, *a.* त्रिपद.

TRIO, *s.* त्रयी, त्रयं, त्रितयं, त्रिकं.

TRIP, *v. i.* प्र-,स्खल् 1 P; वि-,भ्रम् 1, 4 P, वि-चल् 1 P. 2 लघु चल्-र् 1 P. —*v. t.* प्र-,स्खल् c. —*s.* स्खलितं, स्खलनं, भ्रमणं, पर्यटनं.

TRIPARTITE, *a.* त्रिभाग, त्रिखंड.

TRIPE, *s.* जठरं, उदरं; अंत्राणि (pl.).

TRIPLE, *a.* त्रिगुण, त्रिविध, त्रिधा-त्रेधा *ind.* —*v. t.* त्रिगुणीकृ 8 U. —TRIPLICITY, *s.* त्रैविध्यं, त्रैगुण्यं.

TRISYLLABLE, *s.* त्र्यक्षरं, त्रिकं.

TRIPED, *s.* त्रिपदी.

TRITE, *a.* क्षुण्ण, जीर्ण, उच्छिष्ट, सुप्रसिद्ध, सदाव्यवहारित.

TRITURATE, *v. t.* संघृष् 1 P, निष्पिष् 7 P; *See* GRIND.

TRIUMPH, *v. i.* वि-परा-जि 1 A, पराभू 1 P. 2 विजयोत्सवं कृ 8 U. —*s.* वि-,जय:; 2 विजयोत्सव:, जययात्रा. 3 जयहर्ष:-उल्लास:; आनंदहेतु:. —AL, *a.* जय in comp.; जयतोरणं 't. arch'; 't. column' जयस्तंभ:. —ANT, *a.* जैत्र (त्री *f*), जयशालिन्, जेतृ, जिष्णु, वि-,जयिन्, प्राप्तजय, क्षतारि. —ANTLY, *adv.* सजयं, सजयघोषं.

TRIUMVIRATE, *s.* त्रिनरप्रभुत्वं.

TRIVIAL, *a.* *See* TRIFLING.

TROOP, *s.* (T. s) सैनिका:, पदातय:, सैन्यं; *See* FORCE. 2 गुल्म:-ल्मं, दलं. 3 यूथं, गण:, कदंबं:, वृंदं, कुलं; *See* HERD. —ER, *s.* सादिन् *m.*, अश्वारोह:.

TROPE, *s.* रूपकं.

TROPHY, *s.* जयस्तंभ:-चिह्नं.

TROPIC, *s.* अयनवृत्तं, क्रांतिवलयं-मंडलं. —AL, *a.* Ex. by (*s.*) in comp.

TROT, *s.* धो(धौ)रितं-तकं. —*v. i.* धोरितेन या 2 P or गम् 1 P.

TROTH, *s.* विश्वास:, प्रत्यय:; 'by my t.' सत्यमेव, यदि तव मयि विश्वास:.

TROUBLE, *s.* कष्टं, दु:खं, पीडा, क्लेश:, प्र-आ-यास:, खेद:, कृच्छ्रं; आ-वि-पद् *f.*, दुर्दशा, बाधा, उपरोध:. 2 यत्न:, उद्यम:; *See* PAINS. 3 कंटक:, आयासक:, शल्यं. —*v. t.* बाध् 1 A, पीड् 10, क्लिश् 9 P, उपरुध् 7 U, आयस् c., सं-परि-तप् c.; *See* AFFLICT; 't. ed at heart' खिन्नांत:करण, उद्विग्नचित्त and sim. comp.; 'Oh ! do not t. yourself' अलमात्मानमायास्य, कृतं कृतं आयासेन. —ED, *a.* बाधित, पीडित &c., व्यग्र, उद्विग्न, कातर, विह्वल, आर्त, विक्लव. —SOME, *a.* कष्ट-पीडा-कर (री *f.*), पीडाप्रद, क्लेशावह, दु:खावह, दुष्ट, आयासहेतुक; 'a t. fellow' कंटक:. —TROUBLOUS, *a.* क्षुब्ध, सोपप्लव.

TROUGH, *s.* द्रोणि-णी *f.*

TROWEL, *s.* कर्णी *f.*

TROWSERS, *s.* जंघात्राणं-वस्त्रं.

TRUANT, *a.* कार्यपराङ्मुख (खी *f.*); अलस; 'to be t.' अलसवत् आचर् 1 P.

TRUCE, *s.* युद्धविश्राम:, युद्धनिवृत्ति *f.*, अवहार:; 't. to' ex. by विरम् 1 P, अलं (with instr.); 't. to your jest' अलं परिहासेन; 't. to your impudence' विरमातिप्रसंगात् (U. 5).

TRUCK, *s.* शकट:-टं; *See* CART.

TRUCKLE, *v. i.* *See* FLATTER.

TRUCULENT, *a.* क्रूर, निष्ठुर, निर्दय.

TRUDGE, *v. i.* शनै:-मंदं-व्रज् or चल् 1 P, पद्भ्यां चल्.

TRUE, *a.* सत्य, तथ्य, अवितथ, ऋत, यथार्थ, वास्तविक (की *f.*), सत् pr.; अकृत्रिम, अकृतक (not feigned). 2 युक्त, उपपन्न; 'what you say is t.' युक्तं आह भवान्; 't. to one's engagements' सत्यसंध-प्रतिज्ञ-व्रत. —LY, *adv.* सत्यं, वस्तुत:, यथार्थत:, परमार्थत:, तत्त्वत:; 'affection t. so called' परमार्थत: प्रेम; 'Parantapa t. so called' परंतपो नाम यथार्थनामा (R. VI. 21); ध्रुवसिद्धेरपि यथार्थनाम्न: सिद्धिं न मन्यते (M. 4) 'true to his name', 't. so called.' —TRUISM, *s.* सत्यं, स्वत:सिद्धवचनं. —TRUTH, *s.* तथ्यं, सत्यं, अवितथं, ऋतं, तत्त्वं, भूतार्थ:, परमार्थ:, तत्त्वार्थ:. 2 सत्यता, यथार्थता, याथार्थ्यं; 'in t.' सत्यमेव, खलु, नूनं; 'to tell you the t.' यत्सत्यं, वस्तुत:. —FUL, *a.* सत्य; *See* (*a.*). 2 (Of persons) सत्यवादिन्, यथार्थवक्तृ-वादिन्, तथ्यभाषिन्.

TRUMP, *v. t.* क्लृप् c., सकूटं निर्मा 3 A; *See* FABRICATE. —TRUMPERY, *a.* असार, कृत्रिम, कूट in comp. —*s.* असार-तुच्छ-द्रव्यं.

TRUMPET, *s.* तूर्यं, तूरी. 2 (Flower) पाटला-लि:, मोघा, काचस्थाली, फलेरुहा, कृष्णवृंता, कुबेराक्षी. —*v. t.* उद्-घुष् 10, प्रकाश् c., उच्चै: प्र-ख्या c. (ख्यापयति). —ER, *s.* तूर्यवादक:. 2 उद्घोषक:.

TRUNCATE, *v. t.* लू 9 U, अवच्छिद् 7 P.

TRUNCHEON, *s.* यष्टि *f.*, दंड:, गदा.

TRUNDLE, *See* ROLL.

TRUNK, *s.* (Of the body) कबंध:, अपमूर्धकलेवरं. 2 (Of trees) स्कंध:, प्र-,कांड:-डं; 't. with the branches lopped off' स्थाणु:. 3 (Of elephants) शुंड:, शुंडा,-दंड:, हस्त:, कर:. 4 भांडं. 5 अग्र-मुख्य-भाग:.

TRUSS, *s.* पट्ट:, बंधनं. 2 (तृण-) कूर्च:, भार:. —*v. t.* कील् 10, संबंध् 9 P, संसंज् c.

TRUST, *v. t.* विश्वस् 2 P, प्रति-इ 2 P; *See* BELIEVE. 2 निक्षिप् 6 P, सं-,ऋ c. (अर्पयति), न्यस् 4 U; *See* ENTRUST. —*v. i.* Ex. by 'Sure,' q. v.; 'learn to t. in God' ईश्वरासक्त-ईश्वराधीन-चित्तो भव, ईश्वरं शरणं प्रपद्यस्व; 't. to' आ-अव-लंब् 1 A, आश्रि 1 U. -s. विश्वासः, विश्रंभः, प्रत्ययः. 2 निक्षेपः, न्यासः. 3 कालिका, उद्धारः. -EE, s. निक्षेपधारिन् m. -ING, a. विश्वासिन्, विश्वस्त; 't. to the strength of his own arms' स्वभुजबलमवलंब्य. -WORTHY, -Y, a. विश्वसनीय, विश्वास्य, विश्वासार्ह, विश्वासयोग्य, विश्रंभास्पदं-पात्रं-भूमिः, आप्त.

TRY, v. t. परीक्ष् 1 A, अनु-भू 1 P; 'to t. their strength upon a traveller' पथिकमात्मशक्तिनिकषं कर्तुं. 2 (Cases) दृश् 1 P, वि-चर् c., अनुसं-धा 3U, वि-विच् 3, 7 U; *See* JUDGE; 't. ing cases' व्यवहारदर्शनं; ददर्श संशयच्छेद्यान्व्यवहारान् (R. XVI. 39) 'tried contested cases'. -v. i. प्र-यत् 1 A, उद्यम् 1 A, व्यव-सो 4 P, प्रवृत् 1 A; *See* ATTEMPT; oft. ex. by desid. forms. -ING, a. कष्ट-पीडा-कर (री f.), (heat &c.). -TRIAL, s. परीक्षा-क्षणं; 'to make a t. of' परीक्ष्; अनुभवः; 'under t.' अनुभूयमान. 2 व्यवहारदर्शनं, विचारः. 3 कृच्छ्रं, वि-आ-पद् f.; *See* CALAMITY, MISFORTUNE. 4 प्र-,यत्नः, उद्यमः, उद्योगः.

TUB, s. द्रोणि-णी f.

TUBE, s. नालः-ली-लं, न(ना)लिका, नाडि-डी f., सुषिरं, प्रणालः-ली. -TUBULAR, a. नालाकृति, नाडीरूप.

TUBER, s. कंदः-दं. -OUS, a. ग्रंथिल, ग्रंथिमत्, कंदिन्.

TUBERCLE, s. सूक्ष्मव्रणः, ग्रंथिः.

TUCK, *See* FOLD.

TUESDAY, s. मंगलवासरः.

TUFT, s. चूडा, शिखा, शिखरः-रं, शेखरः; 'having a t.' शिखिन्. 2 पक्षवः; स्तवकः, गुच्छः, अवतंसः. -ED, a. शिखिन्, शेखरित.

TUG, v. t. आ-कृष् 1 P. प्रयत्नेन कृष्; *See* PULL.

TUITION, s. शिक्षणं, अध्यापनं, उपदेशः.

TUMBLE, v. i. अवपत् 1 P, स्खल् 1 P. -s. अवपातः, स्खलनं.

TUMBLER, s. काचपात्रं. 2 कलायनः, सूत्रायणः.

TUMID, a. स्फीत, आध्मात.

TUMOUR, TUMEFACTION, s. वि-,स्फोटः-टकः, शोफः, श्वयथुः, व्रणः-णं, मांसार्बुदं, ग्रंथिः; 'fatty t.' मेदोर्बुदं.

TUMULT, s. तुमुलं, संकुलं, अत्यंतमाकुलं; 't. in the army' पिंजलः. 2 कोलाहलः, कलकलरवः. -UOUS, a. तुमुल, संकुल, क्षुब्ध, अव्यवस्थित.

TUNE, s. रागः; तालः. 2 तालैक्यं, स्वरैक्यं; 'out of t.' विस्वर-a.; 'in t.' श्लिष्टस्वर, युक्तस्वर- a. -v. t. स्वरैक्यं कृ 8 U. -FUL, a. सुस्वर, मधुर, संगतस्वर; *See* HARMONIOUS.

TUNIC, s. चोलः-ली, कूर्पासकः-कं.

TUNNEL, s. कुल्या, सुरुं(रं)गा, गूढ-आंतर्भौम-मार्गः. -v. t. उत्खन् 1 P, सुषिरीकृ 8 U.

TURBAN, s. उष्णीषः-षं, शिरोवेष्टनं.

TURBID, a. कलुष, आविल, पंकिल, सपंक, पंकदूषित, मलिन.

TURBULENT, a. पीडाकर (री f.). दुर्दांत, कलहतुमुल-कारिन्, अवशवर्तिन्; अनवस्थित.

TURF, s. शाद्वलं, सतृणभूमि f.

TURGID, s. स्फीत, उच्छून.

TURMERIC, s. हरिद्रा, कांचनी, पीता, निशा, वरवर्णिनी.

TURMOIL, s. संक्षोभः, उपद्रवः, तुमुलं; 't. of war संग्रामतुमुलं.

TURN, v. i. परि-,भ्रम् 1, 4 P, घूर्ण् 1 A, 6 P, व्यापरि-वृत् 1 A. 2 परिवृत्; oft. by भू 1 P, जन् 4 A. 3 अम्लीभू, अम्लतां गम् 1 P; 'food t. s into blood' अन्नं रुधिरभावेन परिणमति; *See* CHANGE; 't. into white' श्वेतीभवति; 't. to nothing' निरर्थक-व्यर्थ- a. भू. 4 भू with संमुख-अभिमुख- (खी f.) in comp. or with gen.; 't. ing to the hero' नायकाभिमुखी भूत्वा. -v. t. परि-,भ्रम् c., (fig. also), घूर्ण् c.; परि-वि-व्या-वृत् c. 2 परिवृत् c., आ-,वल् c., (आवलितवदनं राजकमासीत् Ka. 10); परिवृत्तार्धमुखी (V. 1) 'with her face half-t.-ed'. 3 विपर्यस् c. 4 साचीकृ 8 U; *See* BEND. 5 अम्लीकृ; 't. to account'; *See* under ACCOUNT; 't. to use' उपयुज् 10; 't. into ashes' भस्मसात्-भस्मी-कृ or भू; 't. the back' पृष्ठं दृश् c., पराङ्मुखीभू; 't. s a single fault to two' एकापराधं द्विगुणीकरोति. -about, वि-परि-वृत्; परिक्रम् 1 U, 4 P. -against, प्रतीपयति (D.); (v. i.) प्रतिकूलीभू, प्रत्यर्थिन्- a. भू, विरुद्ध- a. भू. -away, अपनी 1 P, दूरीकृ; अपास्, निःसृ c., निराकृ; *See* DISMISS, DISCHARGE. 2 (aside) नि-व्या-वृत् c., सं-हृ 1 P; साचीकृ, तिर्यग्-वल्; (अभिमुखे मयि संहृतमीक्षितं S. 2); 'shall t. away his mind (in another direction)' अन्यतः एनं क्षिपामि-संचारयामि; (v. i.) व्यावृत् 1 A, (व्यावर्तमाना ह्रिया), पराङ्मुखी-विमुखी-भू; मुखं परिवृत्. -back, परि-परा-वृत्; (v. t.) परि-परा-वृत् c. -into, कृ, (तपोवनमुपवनं कृतं S. 2). 2 परिणम् c. with भावेन; आखुं बिडालभावेन पर्यणमयत् 't. ed the rat into a cat'; *See* CHANGE. -off, दूरीकृ, निवृत् c., अपास् &c.; (v. i.) अप-सृ 1 P, निर्गम् 1 P. -out, (v. t.) निः-सृ c., निष्कस् c., बहिष्कृ; *See* DISCHARGE; (v. i.) संपत् 1 P; *See* HAPPEN. 2 अस् 4 A, भू 1 P; 't. ed out pale' विवर्णीभूतः, सहसा विवर्णभावं प्रपेदे; 'the words of the great never t. out untrue' न हीश्वरव्याहृतयः कदाचित्पुष्णंति लोके विपरीतमर्थं (K. III. 63). -over, उत्क्षिप् 6P. 2 परिवृत् c., चल् c.; 't. ing over the pages' पृष्ठानि चालयित्वा-समालोक्य. -round, परि-परा-वृत्

–to, दृश् 1 P, ईक्ष् 1 A; by प्रति with acc. –towards, अभिमुखी-संमुखी-भू (with gen.). –up, सहसा आविर्भू or प्रादुर्भू. 2 Happen, q. v. –s. आवर्तः-र्तनं, आवृत्ति f. 2 परिवृत्तिः, परिवर्तः, विकारः. 3 पर्यायः, परिवृत्तिः ; 'by t. s.' पर्यायेण, पर्याय in comp.; 'service by t. s.' पर्यायसेवा. 4 वारः, (शशकस्य वारः समायातः P. I. 8). 5 प्र-,वृत्तिः, भावः, दशा; 't. of mind' चित्तवृत्तिः, मनःस्वभावः. 6 आकारः, स्वरूपं; 'matters took a different t.' वस्तुस्थितेरवस्थांतरं अदृश्यत, सकलार्थः परिवृत्तः. 7 गति f., क्रमः; 'mysterious is the t. of fate' कर्मणो गहना गतिः; 't. of fortune' दैवगतिः. 8 परिक्रमः; (walk) ईषद्विहारः. 9 अवसरः, समयः, कालः. 10 वंकः (of rivers); 'a good t.' उपकारः; 'ill t.' अपकारः; 'one good t. deserves another' उपकारः प्रत्युपकारेण निर्यातयितव्यः. –ER, s. चक्रिन् m., कुंदिन् m. –TURNCOAT, s. स्वपक्षत्यागिन् m., समयानुरोधिन्.

TURNIP, s. शिखामूलं.

TURPENTINE, s. देवदारुतैलं, सरलद्रवः.

TURPITUDE, s. दुष्टता, दोषः.

TURQUOISE, s. वैदूर्यं, हरिताश्मन् m.

TURRET, s. शिरोगृहं; प्रासादशृंग-शिखरं.

TURTLE, s. कूर्मः; *See* TORTOISE.

TUSK, s. दंतः, दंष्ट्रा, रदः, रदनः.

TUTELAGE, s. बालावस्था, बाल्यं.

TUTELARY, a. रक्षक, रक्षा in comp.; 't. deity' इष्ट-कुल-देवता.

TUTENAG, s. तुत्थं, तुत्थांजनं.

TUTOR, s. गुरुः, अध्यापकः, आचार्यः, शिक्षकः. –SHIP, s. आचार्यत्वं.

TWADDLE, *See* PRATE.

TWAIN, s. (In t.) द्विधा, द्वेधा.

TWANG, v. t. (A bow) आ-स्फल् c.; टंकृ 8 U, ज्यां घुष् 10; (a lute) क्वण् c., नद् c. –v. i. क्वण् 1 P, टंकारं कृ 8 U. –s. टंकारः, ज्या-शब्दः-घोषः, धनुरास्फालनं. 2 क्वणितं, झणत्कारः.

TWEAK, *See* PINCH.

TWEEZER, s. संदंशः, कंकमुखं.

TWELVE, a. द्वादशन्. –TWELFTH, a. द्वादश (शी f.). –s. द्वादशांशः.

TWENTY, a. विंशति f. –TWENTIETH, a. विंश (शी f.), विंशतितम (मी f.).

TWIG, s. विटपः, शाखा, प्रशाखा.

TWILIGHT, s. संध्या, संधिप्रकाशः, संध्याकालः-समयः, निशादिः.

TWIN, a., s. यम, यमज, यमल; 'we are t. brothers' भ्रातरावावां यमजौ (U. 6); oft. by यमलं, युगं, द्वंद्वं, मिथुनं, युगलं; 't. stars' मिथुनं; 'one of t.' यमः, यमलः.

TWINE, s. सूत्रं, तंतुः. –v. t. उद्-ग्रंथ् 9 P, उत्खच् 10, (कुसुमोत्खचितान्वलीभृतश्चलयत् अलकान् R. VIII. 53). 2 (Itself) आ-परि-वेष्ट् c., आ-परि-वृत् c.

TWINGE, s. व्यथा, पीडा, वेदना, शलः-लं, तीव्रवेदना. –v. t. Ex. by कृ with (s.).

TWINKLE, v. i. (Of the eye) नि-,मिष् 6 P, उन्मिष्, निमील् 1 P, उन्मील्, निमेषोन्मेषं कृ. 2 स्फुर् 6 P, तरलं-सकंपं-प्रभा 2 P or प्रकाश् 1 A or द्युत् 1 A. –s.,-ING, s. निमि(मे)षः, निमेषोन्मेषौ; 'within the t. of the eye' निमेषमात्रात्, निमेषेण. 2 स्फुरणं, स्फुरितं, तरलज्योति n. -प्रभा; 'the eyes knowing no t.' (पपौ) निमेषालसपक्ष्मपंक्तिः (R. II. 19), अनिमेषलोचनो ददर्श (Ka. 11).

TWIRL, v. t. त्वरितं भ्रम् c. or परि-वृत् c. –v. i. परि-वृत् 1 A, भ्रम् 1, 4 P. –s. त्वरितपरिवृत्ति f.

TWIST, v. t. परि-व्या-वृत् c., आकुंच् c., मुद्-ड् 10. –v. i. व्यावृत् 1 A, आकुंच् pass. –s. व्यावर्तनं, आ-,कुंचनं, मोटनं.

TWIT, v. t. *See* CENSURE, TAUNT.

TWITCH, v. t. (सहसा) आकृष् 1 P, आ-क्षिप् 6 P. –v. i. स्फुर् 6 P, स्पंद् 1 A, प्र-,कंप् 1 A. –s. सहसाकर्षः-आक्षेपः, स्फुरणं, स्पंदनं.

TWITTER, v. i. प्र-जल्प् 1 P, प्र-लप् 1 P. –s. प्रलापः, प्रजल्पः; *See* CHATTER.

TWO, a. द्वि (द्वौ, द्वे f. n.), द्वि pr.; द्वयं affixed ; 't. years' द्विवर्ष, वर्षद्वयं; 't. or three' द्वित्राः; 't.-fold' द्विगुण; 't.-handed' द्विहस्त; द्विजिह्व &c.; 'in t. ways' द्विधा. –TWICE, adv. द्विः, द्विवारं; 't. married' पुनरूढा, पुनर्भूः (widow remarried); '20 is t. 10' द्विरावृत्ता दश विंशतिः संपद्यते.

TYPE, s. आदर्शः; प्रतिरूपं; *See* MODEL. 2 चिह्नं, लक्षणं, व्यंजनं. 3 मुद्राक्षरं. 4 प्रकारः, रीति f. –ICAL, a. Ex. by (s.) in comp.; आदर्शभूत, प्रतिरूपक. –TYPEFY, v. t. आदर्शीकृ 8 U, प्रतिरूपेण दृश् c. –TYPOGRAPHY, s. मुद्रांकनं.

TYRANNY, s. प्रजापीडनं, लोकोपद्रवः, जनमर्दनं, निष्ठुरशासनं. –IC,-ICAL, a. प्रजोपमर्दिन्, प्रजोपद्रविन्. –IZE, v. t. (भृशं) पीड् 10, उप-द्रु 1 A, विप्रकृ 8 U, उपद्रु 1 P. –TYRANT, s. प्रजापीडकः, लोकोपद्रावकः, उपद्रवी, निष्ठुरशासनः.

TYRO, s. नवच्छात्रः-शिष्यः, अनभ्यस्तः.

U.

UBIQUITOUS, a. सर्वगत, सर्वव्यापिन्.

UDDER, s. ऊधस् n., आपीनं, स्तनं (mostly human); 'having pot-like u.s' घटोध्नी; 'having large u.s' पीनोध्नी.

UGLY, *a.* कु-वि-अप-रूप, विकृत, कदाकार; दुर्दर्शन, विकृताकार. 2 कुत्सित, निंद्य. -INESS, *s.* वैरूप्यं, अपरूपता, कदाकारः.

ULCER, *s.* पूयव्रणः-णं, विद्रधिः, नाडीव्रणः-णं, पूयक्षतं. -ATE, *v. t.* व्रणं उत्पद् c. -*v. i.* सक्षतीभू 1 P, व्रणं बंध् 9 P. -ATED,-OUS, *a.* पूयव्रणिन्, सव्रण, सक्षत, उपहत in comp. with (*s.*).

ULTERIOR, *a.* उत्तर, अपर; *See* DISTANT.

ULTIMATE, *a.* चरम, अंतिम; *See* LAST. -LY, *adv.* अंते, शेषे, अंततः. -ULTIMATUM, *s.* चरमाभिसंधिः, अंत्यप्रतिज्ञा.

ULTRA, *a.* Ex. by अति in comp.

UMBILICAL, *a.* नाभ्य, नाभि in comp.; 'u. cord' नाभि *f.*,-नालः.

UMBRAGE, *s.* छाया. 2 अप्रीति *f.*, कोपः, असंतोषः, अपराधः; 'take u.' प्र-,कुप् 4 P, 'Angry', q. v.; 'give u.' विरागं नी 1 P; *See* INSULT.

UMBRELLA, *s.* छत्रं, आतपत्रं, घर्मवारणं, जलत्रं.

UN, A prefix, ex. by अ (अन् before vowels), sometimes by निर्, वि, दुस् pr., हीन, रहित in comp.; 'unaided' असहाय, साहाय्यहीनः; 'undaunted' निर्भीक, अभय; 'unmixed' अमिश्र; 'unwelcome' अप्रिय, अनभिमत &c.; 'unattainable' दुष्प्राप. (In cases where the word formed with 'un' is not given, the student should take the simple word or form it, and use the above prefixes. With nouns the sense of 'un' may be expressed by अप-नी 1 P, or हृ 1 P; *e. g.* 'unbar' अर्गलं अपनी, निरर्गलीकृ &c.)

UNACCUSTOMED, *a.* अपरिचित, अनभ्यस्त, अननुभूत.

UNAFFECTED, *a.* अकृत्रिम, सहज, अव्याज; *See* ARTLESS.

UNANIMOUS, *a.* एकमत-चित्त. -LY, *adv.* एकचित्तीभूय, ऐकमत्येन. -UNANIMITY, *s.* ऐकमत्यं, चित्त-मत-ऐक्यं, एकचित्तता; अस्मिन् विषये सर्वेषामैकमत्यं 'there is a u. on this point'.

UNARMED, *a.* विशस्त्र, निरायुध, असज्ज.

UNASSAILABLE, *a.* दुष्प्रधर्ष, अधृष्य, दुरासद.

UNASSUMING, *a.* अविकत्थन, अदृप्त, विनीत; *See* HUMBLE.

UNAVAILING, *a.* निरर्थक, निर्गुण, निष्फल.

UNAWARES, *adv.* अतर्कितं, अलक्षितं, निभृतं, अकस्मात्; *See* SUDDENLY also.

UNBAR, UNBOLT, *v. t.* निरर्गलयति (D.).

UNBELIEVER, *s.* नास्तिकः,-बुद्धिः, पाखंडः, मिथ्यादृष्टिः.

UNBEND, *v. t.* शिथिलीकृ 8 U; *See* RELAX. -ING, *a.* Cruel, q. v.

UNBIND, *v. t.* उद्-ग्रंथ् 9 P, शिथिलीकृ 8 U.

UNBLEMISHED, *a.* निष्कलंक, निरवद्य, अक्षत.

UNBOSOM, *v. t.* विवृ 5 U; *See* DISCLOSE; 'u. oneself' हृदयं-मनोगतं-विवृ.

UNBOUNDED, *a.* अनंत, अमित.

UNBRIDLED, *a.* उच्छृंखल, उद्दाम, निमर्याद, अनर्गल.

UNBURDEN, *v. t.* भारमपनी 1 P; *See* ALLEVIATE also.

UNCEREMONIOUS, *a.* अनादर, मंदादर. -LY, *adv.* मंदादरेण.

UNCERTAIN, *a.* संदिग्ध, संशयग्रस्त; *See* DOUBTFUL. -TY, *s.* अनिश्चयः, अनिर्णयः.

UNCHAIN, *v. t.* निगडान् अपनी 1 P, मुच् c.; *See* FREE, LIBERATE.

UNCHARITABLE, *a.* दोषदृष्टि, असूयक, छिद्रान्वेषिन्.

UNCHASTE, *a.* अविनीत, पांसुल, &c.; *See* PROSTITUTE.

UNCLAIMED, *a.* अस्वामिक, अनाधिकृत.

UNCLE, *s.* पितृव्यः. 2 मातुलः (maternal u.)

UNCLOSE, *v. t.* Open. q. v.

UNCLOTHE, *v. t.* Strip, q. v. -ED, *a.* विवस्त्र, नग्न; *See* NAKED.

UNCLOVEN, *a.* एकशफ, एकखुर.

UNCOMMON, *a.* असामान्य, अपूर्व, अलौकिक (की *f.*). -LY, *adv.* अपूर्वं; *See* EXCEEDINGLY.

UNCONCERN,-ED, *a.* Indifferent, &c., q. v.

UNCONTROLLED, *a.* अप्रतिबंध, निरर्गल, निर्यंत्रण.

UNCOUPLE, *v. t.* Separate, q. v.

UNCOUTH, *a.* Ugly, Strange, q. v.

UNCOVER, *v. t.* उच्छद् 10, अपा-वि-वृ 5 U; *See* STRIP; 'they u. ed their heads' शिरोवेष्टनमपनिन्युः.

UNCTION, *s.* अभि-,अंजनं, आ-वि-लेपः-पनं. -UNCTUOUS, *a.* स्निग्ध, मसृण, चिक्कण, सांद्र.

UNDECEIVE, *v. t.* भ्रमं निरस् 4 U or अपाकृ 8 U or छिद् 7 P.

UNDECIDED, *a.* अनिश्चित; (of persons) Irresolute, q. v.

UNDENIABLE, *a.* निर्विवाद, निःसंदेह.

UNDER, UNDERNEATH, *prep.* अधः, अधस्तात् (with gen.); *See* BELOW; तले in comp. or with gen. 2 अधीन, आयत्त, वशग; *See* SUBJECT. 3 (Age &c.) ऊन in comp.; 'u. 16' ऊनषोडशवर्षे; 'u. age' अप्राप्तवयस्क, अप्राप्तव्यवहार; 'should bury one who is u. two years' ऊनद्विवर्षं निखनेत् (Y. III. 1). 4 काले, समये or ex. by 'Reign', q. v.; 'u. the Moghuls' मोंगलेषु महीं शासत्सु; gen. ex. by loc. or instr.; 'u. this condition' अनेन समयेन; 'u. misfortunes' आपदि, आपत्काले; 'u. your favour' भवदनुग्रहेण,

–*a.* अधर, अधः in comp.: 'u.-garment' अधोंशुकं, अधोवासः; *See* GARMENT; oft. by उप pr.

UNDERGO, *v. t.* अनुभू 1 P, सह् 1 A, उपगम् 1 P; *See* SUFFER; 'u. examination' परीक्ष् pass.; 'u. change' परिवृत् 1 A, विकृ pass.

UNDERGROUND, *a.* आंतर्भौम, भूम्यधस्तात्.

UNDERHAND, *a.* गूढ, प्रच्छन्न, परोक्षकृत, छलेन कृत; निंद्य, गर्हणीय.

UNDERLIE, *v. t.* ली 4 A, निगृह् pass. (with loc.).

UNDERLINE, *v. t.* अधोरेखया अंक् 10.

UNDERLING, *s.* अनुजीविन् *m.*

UNDERMINE, *v. t.* सुरंगां कृ 8 U, उत्खन् 1 P, अधस्तात् विनश् c. 2 विनश् c, अवसद् c., उच्छिद् 7 P, कष् 1 P; 'a river u. ing its banks' कूलंकषा सिंधुः.

UNDERRATE, UNDERVALUE, *v. t.* न्यूनमूल्यं कृप् c., अर्धतः पत् c. 2 लघु मन् 4 A, अवमन्, लघूकृ, अपकृष् 1 P.

UNDERSTAND, *v. t.* बुध् 1 P, ज्ञा 9 U, अवगम् 1 P, ग्रह् 9 P, उपलभ् 1 A, वि-भू c., अव-इ 2 P, अवधृ 10; *See* KNOW. 2 (Words &c.) अध्याहृ 1 P, ऊह् 1 A, (इदं पदमत्राध्याहर्तव्यं). –ING, *s.* मतिः, बुद्धिः, धीः, मेधा, ग्रहण-ज्ञान-शक्तिः, प्रज्ञा; *See* INTELLECT. 2 भावः, वृत्ति *f.*; 'good u.' सद्भावः, मित्रभावः; 'come to an u.' *See* SETTLE.

UNDERTAKE, *v. t.* आरभ् 1 A, उपक्रम् 1 A; *See* BEGIN. 2 व्यवसो 4 P, ईह् 1 A; *See* ATTEMPT, INTEND. 3 स्वी-अंगी-कृ 8 U, उ(ऊ)रीकृ, अभ्युपगम् 1 P, अभ्युप-इ 2 P, प्रति-पद् 4 A. –ER, *s.* आरंभकः, अनुष्ठातृ *m.* 2 प्रेतकर्मनिर्हारकः. –ING, *s.* कार्यं, व्यवसायः, कर्म, आरंभः, व्यापारः, प्रवृत्ति *f.*

UNDESERVING, *a.* अनर्ह, अगुणवत्, अपात्र, निर्गुण.

UNDESIGNED, *a.* अनभिप्रेत, अबुद्धिपूर्व. –LY, *adv.* अज्ञानतः, अबोधपूर्वं, अकामतः.

UNDESIGNING, *a.* Sincere, q. v.

UNDIMINISHED, *a.* अक्षत, अन्यून, अनपाय, अलुप्त, अक्षीण.

UNDISGUISED, *a.* Frank, q. v.

UNDIVIDED, *a.* अभिन्न; (attention) एकाग्र, अनन्य, अनन्यासक्त, सुसमाहित; *See* FIXED.

UNDO, *v. t.* उन्मुच् 6 P, उद्-घट् c., उद्-ग्रंथ् 9 P. 2 व्या-परा-वृत् c.; 'able to do, not to do, or u. things' कर्तुमकर्तुमन्यथा कर्तुं क्षमः. 3 हन् 2 P, नश् c.; 'Oh! I am undone' हा हतास्मि (मंदभाग्यः), दैवेन मुषितोस्मि.

UNDRESS, *v. t.* वासः-वस्त्रं-अपनी 1 P or अवतॄ c. or उन्मुच् 6 P or अपनह् 4 P. –*s.* लघुवासस् *n.* –ED, *a.* (food) असंस्कृत, अपक्व, आम. 2 विवस्त्र, विवसन, उन्मुक्तवसन.

UNDULATE, *v. i.* तरंगायते (D.), उत्प्लु 1 P; better by 'u. ing.' –ING,-ORY, *a.* ऊर्मिमत्, तरंगित, उन्नतावनत, भंगुर, उत्सर्पिन्. –ION, *s.* भंगुरता, ऊर्मिमत्ता, &c.

UNEARTH, *v. t.* उत्खन् 1 P.

UNEQUALLED, *a.* Matchless, q. v.

UNERRING, *a.* अमोघ, अभ्रांत, अवंध्यपात; 'took an u. aim on his bow' धनुषि अमोघं समधत्त बाणं; *See* FIX.

UNEVEN, *a.* विषम, उन्नतानत.

UNEXPECTED, *a.* असमर्थित, अतर्कित, आकस्मिक (की *f.*), अकांड, अनपेक्षित, अचिंतितपूर्व. –LY, *adv.* अकस्मात्, अकांडे, अतर्कितं.

UNFAITHFUL, *a.* Faithless, q. v.

UNFASTEN, *v. t.* Loose, q. v.

UNFATHOMABLE, *a.* अगाध, अतलस्पर्श.

UNFAVOURABLE, *a.* प्रतिकूल, वि-पराङ्-मुख (खी *f.*), विरक्त, अननुकूल; विषम, अप्रिय, अप्रसन्न.

UNFEELING, *a.* निर्दय, क्रूर; *See* CRUEL.

UNFIT, *a.* अयोग्य, अक्षम, &c. –*v. t.* Disable, q. v.

UNFOLD, UNFURL, *v. t.* विस्तृ-स्तॄ c. 2 विवृ 5 U; *See* DISCLOSE.

UNFORESEEN, *a.* Unexpected, q. v.

UNFORTUNATE, *a.* अधन्य, दुर्दैव, मंद-हत-भाग्य, दैवोपहत, आपद्ग्रस्त. 2 अमंगल, अभद्र, अशुभ. –LY, *adv.* मंदभाग्यतया, दुर्दैवात्.

UNFOUNDED, *a.* अमूलक, निर्मूल, मिथ्या in comp.

UNFRUITFUL, *a.* Fruitless, q. v.

UNGAINLY, *a.* Clumsy, q. v.

UNGOVERNABLE, *a.* अवश्य, अविधेय, अनिवार्य, दुर्निवार, दुर्निग्रह, उद्दाम, निर्यंत्रण, उच्छृंखल.

UNGRATEFUL, –NESS, *See* INGRATE &c.

UNGUENT, *s.* अभ्यंजनं, अनु-वि-लेपः-पनं, समालंभः-भनं.

UNHAPPY, *a.* अधन्य, मंदभाग्य, दुःखभाज्, अनिर्वृत; *See* MISERABLE.

UNHARMED, UNHURT, *a.* अक्षत, निर्व्रण.

UNHARNESS, *v. t.* मुच् c.

UNHINGE, *v. t.* विसंधीकृ 8 U, अपसंधीकृ.

UNICORN, *s.* एकशृंगः.

UNIFORM, *a.* सरूप, एक-समान-विध, एक-समान-रूप, एकप्रकार, एकाकार; सम, समान, अविशेष. –*s.* निर्विशेषः वेषः. –ITY, *s.* सारूप्यं, ऐकविध्यं, साम्यं, एकरूपता. –LY, *adv.* नियतं, अभ्रांतं, अविरतं, एकरूपेण, सदा.

UNIMPEDED, UNINTERRUPTED, *a.* निर्विघ्न, निरंतर, अनंतराय, अविच्छिन्न, अविरत.

UNIQUE, *a.* अपूर्व, अद्वितीय, अप्रतिरूप.

UNISON, *s.* एकतानः, स्वरैक्यं.

UNIT, *s.* एकः, एकांकः. –UNITY, *s.* एकता-त्वं, अद्वैतं; 'doctrine of u.' अद्वैतवादः, अभेदः. 2 ऐक्यं, एकचित्तता. –UNITARIAN, *s.* अद्वैतवादिन् *m.*

UNITE, *v. t.* युज् 7 U, 10, सं-समा-°, संगम् c., संहन् 2 P, समानी 1 P, सं-घट् c., सं पृच् 7 P, 2 A, सं-धा 3 U; 'seems u. ed' भवति कृतसंधानामिव (S. 1). –*v. i.* घट् 1 A, (तदेन तनमयसा घटनाय योग्यं V. 2), संयुज् pass.; एकत्र भू, सं-,मिल् 6 P; *See* ASSEMBLE. –ED, *a.* संहत; मिलित; संयुक्त. –EDLY, *adv.* संभूय, मिलित्वा, एकीभूय, संहत- *a.* –UNION, *s.* संगः, संगमः, समागमः, संगतं-ति *f.*, संहति *f.*, समवायः, सं-,योगः, संधिः; 'u. is strength' समवायो हि दुस्तरः; (*cf.* बहूनामप्यसाराणां संहतिः कार्यसाधिका 'weak faggots make a strong bundle').

UNIVERSE, *s.* विश्वं, सर्वं जगत्, त्रिभुवनं; *See* WORLD. –AL, *a.* विश्व, सार्वलौकिक-सार्वत्रिक-(की *f.*); सर्वगत, सर्व; 'u. spirit' विश्वात्मा, जगदात्मा, ब्रह्म. –ALITY, *s.* सर्वगतत्वं, अभिव्यापित्वं. –ALLY, *adv.* सर्वतः, सर्वत्र, विश्वतः, विष्वक्.

UNIVOCAL, *a.* एकार्थ, ऐकतानिक (की *f.*).

UNKIND, *a.* अस्निग्ध, विप्रिय, निर्दय, क्रूर. –NESS, *s.* निर्दयता, &c. 2 अपकारः, अहितं.

UNLACE, *v. t. See* FREE.

UNLAWFUL, *a.* Illegal, q. v.

UNLEARN, *v. t.* स्मृतेः अपास् 4 U, वि-स्मृ 1P. –ED, *a.* अज्ञान, अकृतविद्य.

UNLESS, *conj.* न-नो-चेत्, यदि न.

UNLOAD, *v. t.* भारं अप-नी 1 P or अव-तॄ c. or अवरुह् c.; *See* DISBURDEN.

UNLOCK, *v. t.* उद्-घट् c., उन्मुद्रयति (D.).

UNLOOSE, *See* LOOSE,-EN.

UNMAN, *v. t.* पौरुषं नश् c. or हृ 1 P. –LY, *a.* क्लीब, पौरुषहीन, पुरुषानर्ह.

UNMASK, *v. t.* छद्मवेशं अपहृ 1 P; (fig.) निजरूपं प्रकटीकृ 8 U; 'he was u. ed' तस्य वास्तविकं स्वरूपमाविष्कृतं.

UNMEANING, *a.* अनर्थक, असंगत, अपार्थ.

UNMOOR, *v. t.* उन्मुच् 6 P or c.

UNMOVED, *a.* स्थिर, अविचलित, निर्विकार.

UNNATURAL, *a.* निसर्ग-सृष्टिक्रम-विरुद्ध-बाह्य.

UNNECESSARY, *a.* निष्प्रयोजन, वृथा in comp.

UNNERVE, *v. t.* Enfeeble, q. v.

UNPACK, *v. t.* उद्-घट् c., कोशात् निष्कृष् 1 P.

UNPRINCIPLED, *a.* दुर्वृत्त, विचारहीन, सदसद्विवेकहीन.

UNRAVEL, *v. t.* उद्-ग्रंथ् 9P, व्याकृ 1U, व्या-ख्या 2P.

UNREAL, *a.* असार, मायात्मक, अतथ्य.

UNRELENTING, *a. See* CRUEL.

UNRESERVED, *a.* अशेष, निःशेष, सं-,पूर्ण.

UNRESTRAINED, *a.* निरवग्रह, उच्छृंखल, उद्दाम, नियंत्रण, अनर्गल, निरंकुश.

UNRIVALLED, UNPARALLELED, *a.* अप्रतिम, अद्वितीय, अतुल, अप्रतिरूप; अनुपम.

UNROLL, *v. t. See* OPEN.

UNRULY, *a.* Ungovernable, q. v.

UNSADDLE, *v. t.* पर्याणं अपनी 1 P.

UNSCRUPULOUS, *a.* निःशंक, शंकाहीन.

UNSEAL, *v. t.* मुद्रां अपनी 1 P, उद्-घट् c., उन्मुद्रयति (D.).

UNSETTLE, *v. t.* आकुलीकृ 8 U, क्षुभ् c., आकुलयति (D.); *See* AGITATE. –ED, *a.* अस्थिर, आकुल, क्षुब्ध.

UNSHAKLE, *v. t. See* FREE.

UNSHEATHE, *v. t.* कोशात् उद्-हृ 1 P or निष्कृष् 1 P. –ED, *a.* विकोश, उल्लसित.

UNSIGHTLY, *a.* अप्रिय-विरूप-दर्शन, कुरूप; *See* UGLY.

UNSOUND, *a.* असार, अयुक्तिसिद्ध.

UNSTEADY, *a. See* FICKLE.

UNSTRING, *v. t.* (A bow) ज्यां अपनी 1 P or शिथिलयति (D.); 'a bow unstrung' शिथिलज्याबंधं धनुः (S. 2).

UNTIE, *v. t.* उत्-मुच् c., मोक्ष् 10, उद्-ग्रंथ् 9 P, शिथिलयति (D.).

UNTIL, *prep. See* TILL.

UNTIMELY, *a.* अकाल in comp.; oft. अप pr.

UNTO, *prep. See* TO.

UNTWIST, UNTWINE, UNVEIL, UNWRAP, *v. t. See* OPEN.

UNUSUAL, *a.* अपूर्व, असामान्य, अलौकिक (की *f.*).

UNWHOLESOME, *a.* अपथ्य, अहितावह.

UNWIELDY, *a.* स्थूल, अतिमहत्, अनुत्थानयोग्य.

UNWORTHY, *a.* अनर्ह, अयोग्य, निर्गुण; oft. by अ; 'u. object' अपात्रं; अकार्य, &c.

UNYOKE, *v. t.* मुच् c., मोक्ष् 10. 2 वियुज् 10.

UP, *prep.*, *adv.* उत् prefixed; ऊर्ध्वं, उपरि, उच्चैः; 'up to' *See* TILL; आप्रदानात् 'up to being given away'; आफलोदयकर्मणां &c.; 'be up and doing' कार्योद्यमी भव; 'ups and downs' पातोत्पाताः; *See* DOWN. –PER, *a.* उपरितन (नी *f.*), उपरिस्थ, ऊर्ध्व, उत्तर; 'to get the u. hand' अभि-भू 1 P, अतिरिच् pass; *See* EXCEL.

UPBRAID, *v. t.* निर्भर्त्स् 10 A; *See* REPROACH.

UPHOLD, *v. t.* समर्थ् 10, दृढयति (D.), उत्तंभ् 9 P, सं-धृ 10, आ-अव-लंब् 1 A; *See* SUPPORT.

UPHOLSTERER, *s.* गृहोपस्करविक्रयिन् *m.*

UPLAND, *s.* उपरिभूमि *f.*, अधित्यका.

UPLIFT UPRAISE, *v. t.* उद्यम् 1 A, उत्था c., (उत्थापयति), उच्छ्रि 1 U; *See* RAISE.

UPON, *prep. See* ON.

UPRIGHT, *a.* उन्नत, उच्छ्रित, दंडवत् *ind.*, ऋजु. 2 सरल, सत्यात्मन्, ऋजु; *See* HONEST. -LY, *adv.* दंडवत्; ऋजु, सारल्येन.

UPROAR, *s.* कोलाहलः, कलकलः, तुमुलं.

UPROOT, *v. t.* उन्मूल् 10, मूलात् छिद् 7 P, उत्पट् 10, उद्धृ 1 P; *See* ERADICATE.

UPSET, *v. t.* परिवृत् c., पर्यस् 4 U.-*s.* पर्यासः, परिवर्तनं; *See* OVERTURN.

UPSHOT, *s.* परिणामः, पर्यवसानं.

UPSIDE, *s.* अधरांशः; 'u.-down' अधरोत्तर-*a.*, अधोमुख-*a.*; 'turn u.-down' अधोमुखीकृ.

UPSTART, *s.* नवोदयः, नवोत्थानः, नवर्द्धिः, आगंतुकः.

UPWARD, UPWARDS, *adv.* ऊर्ध्वं, उपरि. 2 अधिक in comp.; अधिकत्रिंशा नराः 'u. of 30'; परं, परः in comp. (परःसहस्राः शरदः U. 1).

URBAN, *a.* पौर (री *f.*), नागरिक (की *f.*). 2 सुजन, सुशील, दक्षिण. -ITY, *s.* दाक्षिण्यं, नागरिकवृत्ति *f.*, सौजन्यं.

URCHIN, *s.* (दुष्ट-) बटुः, माणवकः.

URETHRA, *s.* मूत्रमार्गः-द्वारं.

URGE, *v. t.* प्रोत्सह् c., प्रचुद् 10, उत्तिज् c., प्रणुद् 6 P or c., प्रवृत् c.; *See* PROMPT. 2 निर्बंधेन प्रच्छ् 6 P, अनुनिर्बंध् 9 P; *See* IMPORTUNE. -ENCY, *s.* गौरवं, गुरुता, भारः. 2 निर्बंधः, आग्रहः. -ENT, *a.* गुरु, आवश्यक (की *f.*), अपरिहार्य, अविलंब्य. -ENTLY, *adv.* निर्बंधेन. 2 आशु, अपरिहार्यतया.

URINE, *s.* मूत्रं, प्रस्रावः, मेहः. -*v. i.* मूत्र् 10. -AL, *s.* मूत्रपात्रं-भाजनं. -ARY, *s.* मूत्रस्थानं. -*a.* मूत्र in comp.

URN, *s.* (जल-) कुंभः, कलसः-शः, भाजनं.

URSA-MAJOR, *s.* सप्तर्षयः.

USE, *v. t.* प्र-उप-युज् 7 A, 10, व्यव-हृ c., व्याप् c., उप-,भुज् 7 U, सेव् 1 A; धृ 10 (clothes &c.). 2 प्र-युज्; 'is used in the sense of *Light*' तेजसि प्रयुज्यते; 'for it is found to be so used' इति प्रयोगदर्शनात्; 'to be used (conventionally or by popular acceptance)' ex. by रूढ, प्रसिद्ध; ज्योतिःशब्दो ज्वलन एव रूढः (S. B. 104); दाक्षिण्यरूढेन नाम्ना (R. I. 31). 3 आचर् 1 P, व्यव-हृ 1 P, वृत् 1 A (with loc.); *See* ACT. 4 अभ्यस्त-परिचित-*a.* कृ 8 U. 5 (With inf.) By present tense simply; पातुं न प्रथमं व्यवस्यति, नादत्ते &c. (S. 4) or by पूर्वं, पुरा; 'I used to sing' पुरा गायकवृत्तिरासं; 'it used to be so' एवं पूर्वं आचार आसीत्; 'to be used to' अभिज्ञ, परिचित, अभ्यस्त, अनुभूत, उपभुक्त; अनभ्यस्तरथचर्याः (U. 5) 'not used to sit in chariots'; 'used to pain' दुःखाभिज्ञ, अनुभूतदुःख; 'not used to ornaments' अनुपभुक्तभूषणः (S. 4). -*s.* उपयोगः, प्रयोजनं, अर्थः, फलं, कार्यं; किं with instr.; किं तेन जातेन, कोर्थस्तेन जातेन &c.; *See* WANT. 2 प्रयोगः, व्यवहारः, व्यापारः, उपभोगः, सेवनं; 'to apply to one's own u.' स्वयं उपयुज्; 'in general u.' रूढ, प्रसिद्ध, सर्वप्रयुक्त. -AGE, *s.* प्रयोगः. 2 व्यवहारः, आचारः, आचरणं, वृत्ति *f.*; 'conventional u.' रूढि *f.* -FUL, *a.* उपयुक्त, हित, सोपकार, उपयोगिन्, उपकारिन्, हितकर (री *f.*). -FULLY, *adv.* अवृथा, सफलं, सोपयोगं, अमुधा. -FULNESS, *s.* उपयोगः-गिता, हितकारित्वं. -LESS, *a.* निष्प्रयोजन, निरर्थक, विफल, निष्फल, निर्गुण, निरुपयोग, व्यर्थ, अनुपयोगिन्, वृथा-मुधा in comp. -LESSLY, *adv.* वृथा, व्यर्थं, मुधा, निष्फलं. -LESSNESS, *s.* अनुपयोगः, वैयर्थ्यं. —USUAL, *a.* साधारण (णी *f.*), सामान्य, व्य(व्या)वहारिक-प्रायिक-लौकिक-सांप्रदायिक (की *f.*), प्रसिद्ध; oft. by 'u.-ly.' -LY, *adv.* प्रायः, प्रायेण, प्रायशः, साधारण्येन, सामान्यतः, बहुशः.

USUFRUCT, *s.* फल-फलभोग-अधिकारः.

USURP, *v. t.* बलाद् ग्रह् 9 P or आत्मसात्कृ 8 U, अनधिकारेण आक्रम् 1 U, 4 P. -ATION, *s.* बलाद् आक्रमणं-ग्रहणं, बलापहारः. -ER, *s.* बलाद् ग्राहिन्; 'u. to the throne' राज्यापहारी.

USURY, *s.* कुसीदं, कौसीद्यं; अर्थप्रयोगः, वृद्धिजीविका. -ER, *s.* कुसीदकः, वृद्ध्याजीवः, वार्धुषिकः, वार्धुषिः. -OUS, *a.* कौसीद (दी *f.*), सवृद्धिक.

UTENSIL, *s.* भांडं, पात्रं, उपकरणं, भाजनं.

UTERUS, *s.* गर्भकोशः, गर्भाशयः, योनि *f.* -UTERINE, *a.* सहोदर, सोदर, समानोदर, सनाभि.

UTILITY, *s.* उपयोगः; *See* USE.

UTMOST, *a.* परम, पर; 'to the u. of one's power' यावच्छक्यं, यावच्छक्तितः; 'do or try one's u.' यावच्छक्यं प्रयत् 1 A; 'u. limit' परा काष्ठा, परा कोटिः; 'this is the u. that I can do' एष मे परमो विभवः (Ka. 159).

UTOPIAN, *a.* काल्पनिक (की *f.*), मनःसृष्ट; 'u. scheme' कल्पना-मनः-सृष्टिः.

UTTER, *a.* संपूर्ण; *See* COMPLETE. 2 केवल, मात्र in comp.; (मौर्ख्यमात्रमिदं). -*v. t.* उदीर् c., व्या-हृ 1 P, उदाहृ, उद्-गृ 6 P, उच्चर् c.; *See* SAY also. -ANCE, *s.* उच्चारः-रणं, उद्गारः, व्याहारः, उदीरणं; 'easy of u.' सुखोच्चार्य, सुखोद्य. -LY, *adv.* सर्वथा, अशेषेण, साकल्येन, संपूर्णं.

UVULA, *s.* अलि-प्रति-जिह्वा.

UXORIOUS, *a.* स्त्रीवश्य, भार्यासक्त, स्त्रीविधेय, दारनिरत, कामवश. -NESS, *s.* भार्यासक्ति *f.*, भार्याधीनता.

V.

VACANT, *a.* शून्य, (fig. also), रिक्त; 'with v. looks' शून्येक्षण *a.*; 'v.-minded' शून्यहृदय. 2 अस्वामिक; 'a v. throne' अराजक. —VACANCY, *s.* शून्यं, रिक्तं. 2 शून्यं; अस्वामिकं अधिकारपदं. —VACATE, *v. t.* उत्सृज् 6 P, रिच् 7 P, परि-, त्यज् 1 P. —ION, *s.* अनध्ययनं, अध्ययनविश्राम:-निवृत्ति *f.*, विश्रामकाल:.

VACCINE, *a.* गव्य.

VACCINATE, *v. t.* गोबीजं निविश् c.

VACILLATE, *See* WAVER.—ION, *s.* अस्थिरता, अनिश्चय:, चांचल्यं.

VACUITY, VACUUM, *s.* शून्यं, खं, रिक्तं, आकाशं.

VAGABOND, VAGRANT, *a.*, *s.* स्वेच्छाचारिन्, परिभ्रमिन्; यथेच्छविहारिन्. 2 अज्ञातनिवास, गूढचारिन्.

VAGARY, *s.* वि-,भ्रम:, छंद:-दस् *n.*, मनोलौल्यं, बुद्धिचापल्यं.

VAGUE, *a.* अनिश्चित, संदिग्ध, अनियत, अनिर्णीत, अपरिच्छिन्न. —NESS, *s.* अनिश्चय:, अपरिच्छेद:, अनिर्णय:, संदेह:, संशय:.

VAIN, *a.* व्यर्थ, निष्फल, विफल, निरर्थक, मोघ, मुधा-वृथा in comp. ; 'v. thoughts' वृथामनोरथा:. 2 असार, नि:सार, शून्य. 3 (Vainglorious) वृथाभिमानिन्, अहंकारिन्, वृथावलेप, गर्वित; *See* PROUD. —LY, 'in v.' *adv.* वृथा, मुधा, निरर्थकं, व्यर्थं, निष्फलं. —VANITY, *s.* वृथाभिमान:, मिथ्यागर्व:, अहंकार:; *See* PRIDE. 2 असारत्वं, नि:सारता, अवलेप:, वैयर्थ्यं, मोघता. 3 असारद्रव्यं.

VALEDICTION, *s.* आमंत्रणं, आपृच्छा, आप्रच्छनं; स्वस्तिवाद:. —VALEDICTORY, *a.* स्वस्तिवाचनिक (की *f.*).

VALET, *s.* चेट:, दास:, पार्श्वचर:.

VALETUDINARIAN, *a.*, *s.* रोगिन्, दुर्बल, व्याधिपीडित, सदारोगिन्.

VALIANT, *a.* विक्रांत, पराक्रमवत्, उरुविक्रम, शूर, वीर; *See* BRAVE. —LY, *adv.* सविक्रमं, सपराक्रमं, शूर-वीर-वत्, साहसपूर्वकं.

VALID, *a.* सबल, प्रबल, सप्रमाण; सयुक्तिक (की *f.*), अखंड्य, न्याय्य, धर्म्य. —ITY, *s.* प्राबल्यं, सिद्धि *f.*

VALLEY, VALE, *s.* दरी, उपत्यका, अद्रिद्रोणी.

VALOR, *s.* वि-परा-क्रम:, शौर्यं, वीर्यं. —OUS, *a.* शूर, वीर, विक्रांत; *See* BRAVE.

VALUE, *v. t.* मूल्यं-अर्घं-निरूप् 10 or स्था c. (स्थापयति) or सं-ख्या c. 2 मन् 4 A, वि-गण् 10, आ-कल् 10 ; 'v. highly' बहु मन्, संमन् c. —*s.* मूल्यं, अर्घ:; *See* PRICE. 2 माहात्म्यं, गरिमन् *m.*, ससारता. 3 महार्घ:, बहु-महा-मूल्यं. 4 अर्घप्रमाणं; 'fixing the v.' अर्घसंस्थापनं. —ABLE, *a.* महार्ह-र्घ, महा-बहु-मूल्य, मूल्यवत्, गुणवत्. —*s.* बहुमूल्यद्रव्यं. —ATION, *s.* मूल्यनिरूपणं-संख्यापनं-निर्णय:.

VALVE, *s.* कपा(वा)ट:-टी-टं; पिधानं.

VAMPIRE, *s.* भूत:, प्रेत:, पिशाच:.

VAN, *s.* (सेना-) मुखं, अग्रभाग:, अग्रं, मूर्धन् *m.*, नासीरं, शिरस् *n.*; 'in the v.' अग्रे, पुरस्तात्, अग्रत:. 2 यानं; *See* CART; 'v.-guard' अग्रानीकं, सेनामुखं, नासीरचरा: (pl.).

VANE, *s.* वायुगतिदर्शि यंत्रं.

VANISH, *v. i.* तिरोभू 1 P, तिरोधा-अंतर्धा-pass.; *See* DISAPPEAR. 2 वि-नश् 4 P, प्र-वि-ली 4 A.

VANQUISH, *v. t.* पराजि 1 A, पराभू 1 P, वशं नी 1 P; *See* HUMBLE, SUBDUE. —ER, *s.* जेतृ *m.*

VANTAGE,-GROUND, *s.* अग्रभूमि *f.* 2 उत्कर्ष:, श्रेष्ठपदं.

VAPID, *a.* विरस, नीरस, रसहीन.

VAPOUR, *s.* बाष्प:, धूम:; 'v. of the sky' खबाष्प:, अभ्रं ; 'v.-bath' उष्णस्वेद:. —*v. i.* वि-,कत्थ् 1 A; *See* BOAST. —OUS,-Y, *a.* बाष्पमय (यी *f.*), बाष्परूप. 2 असार, नि:सार.

VARIEGATE, *v. t.* चित्र् 10, चित्रीकृ 8 U, कर्बुरीकृ, शबलीकृ; कल्माषयति (D.). —ED, *a.* चित्र, कर्बुर, कर्बुरित, कि(क)र्मीर, किर्मीरित, शबल, कल्माष, कल्माषित, एत, शार; 'v. colour' कर्बुर:, किर्मीर:, शबल:.

VARNISH, *s.* कुकुभ:. —*v. t.* कुकुभेन लिप् 6 P, स्निग्धीकृ ; (fig.) बाह्यशोभां दा 3 U.

VARY, *v. t.* परिवृत् c., विपर्यस् 4 U or c., अन्यथाकृ 8 U, नानाविध-विविध- *a.* कृ; विपर्यासं नी 1 P; *See* CHANGE. —*v. i.* भिद् pass., परिवृत् 1 A; विरुध् pass.; oft. ex. by भिन्न, भिन्नरूप ; प्रयोजनापेक्षितया प्रभूणां प्रायश्चलं गौरवमाश्रितेषु (K. III. 1) 'v. es with the object in view' &c. —IABLE, *a.* अस्थिर, चंचल, परिवृत्तिशील, अनित्य, अनवस्थित. —IANCE, *s.* भेद:, विरोध:, विप्रतिपत्ति *f.*; विवाद:, कलह:, वैरं, द्वंद्वं; 'to be at v.' विप्रति-पद् 4 A; (अत्र स्मृतय: विप्रतिपद्यंते) ; 'at v.' विमत, विप्रतिपन्न, परस्परविरुद्ध. —IATION, *s.* परिवृत्ति *f.*, विकार:, भेद:, —IETY, *s.* विचित्रता; भेद:, विशेष: in comp.; शमीवृक्षविशेष:-भेद:. 2 शबलता, चित्रता, (of colours); 'v. of' Various, q. v. —VARIED, VARIOUS, *a.* विविध, नानाविध-रूप-प्रकार-जातीय, अनेक-नाना in comp.; बहुविध; 'v. talks' उच्चावचा: प्रलापा:; 'in v. ways' अनेकधा, बहुविधं, नाना. —LY, *adv.* बहुधा, विविधं, नाना, नानाप्रकारं, अनेकविधं.

VASCULAR, *a.* नाडीविशिष्ट-संबंधिन्.

VASE, *s.* कुंभ:, कलस:-श:, पात्रं, भाजनं; 'a golden v.' भृंगार:, कनकालुका.

VASSAL, *s.* प्रजा, वशवर्ती, आयत्त:, परतंत्र:; *See* DEPENDENT.

VAST, *a.* विशाल, विस्तीर्ण, विपुल, अपरिमित, सुमहत्, अतिबृहत्.

VAT, *s.* कुंडं, (बहत्) भांडं.

VAULT, *s.* गुप्ति *f.*, विवरं, भूमिगृहं. 2 खोडकशीर्षं; 'v. of heaven' नभोमंडलं. 3 वल्गितं. –*v. i.* वल्ग् 1 P, प्लु 1 A.

VAUNT,-ER, *See* BOAST; 'v. ing of his might' अतिदर्पितबलः (Mr. 5), स्वबलावलितः.

VEAL, *s.* गोवत्समांसं.

VEER, *v.* परिवृत् 1 A, भिन्नदिशं या 2 P or गम् 1 P.

VEGETATE, *v. i.* उद्भिद् pass., स्फुट् 6 P, प्र-रुह् 1 P. –ION, *s.* उद्भिद्, उद्भेदः, तृणादि, तृणजाति *f.* –VEGETABLE. *a.* उद्भिद्-द, उद्भिज्ज, औद्भिद (दी *f.*). –*s.* (Eatable) शाकः-कं; हारितकं, शिग्रुः. –*s.* उद्भिद्-ज्जं, ओषधि *f.*, तृणादि.

VEHEMENT, *a.* प्रचंड, तीव्र, तीक्ष्ण, बलवत्, उग्र, सरभस, सवेग; परुष, रूक्ष (of tone, speech &c.). –LY, *adv.* बलवत्, चंडं, तीव्रं. –VEHEMENCE, *s.* चंडता, तीक्ष्णता, रभसः, वेगः, तरस् *n.*, संरंभः.

VEHICLE, *s.* यानं, प्रवहणं, वाहनं, रथः, वाहः, पत्रं. 2 द्वारं.

VEIL, *v. t.* छद् 10, आ-प्र-सं-°, अवगुंठ् 10, सं-वृ 5 U, व्यव-धा 3 U; *See* COVER. –*s.* अवगुंठनं, आवरकं, आवरकः, तिरस्करिणी. 2 आवरणं, व्यवधानं, आच्छादनं, संवरणं ; 'throw the v. off' स्वरूपं प्रकटीकृ or आविष्कृ, वि-वृ 5 U, विशदीकृ.

VEIN, *s.* शि(सि)रा, धमनी, नाडि-डी *f.* ; (of stones) रे(ले)खा. 2 वृत्ति *f.*, भावः, मनोवृत्तिः; 'angry v.' कोपवृत्तिः. –Y, *a.* शिराल.

VELOCITY, *s.* जवः, वेगः, रंहस् *n.*, रभसः, तरस् *n.*

VENAL, *a.* धनभेद्य, उत्कोचदानवश्य. 2 पण्य in comp ; 'a v. woman' पण्यस्त्री.

VEND, *v. t.* वि-क्री 9 A, पण् 1 A. –ER, *s.* विक्रयिन् *m.* –IBLE, *a.* पण्य, विक्रेय.

VENERATE, VENERABLE, *See* REVERE,-ED.

VENERY, *s.* मैथुनं, रति *f.*, संभोगः. –VENEREAL, *a.* (*s.*) in comp.; 'v. disease' उपदंशः. 2 वाजीकर (री *f.*).

VENESECTION, *s.* शिराच्छेदः.

VENGEANCE, *s.* प्रतिहिंसा, प्रत्यपकारः, वैरनिर्यातनं-शुद्धि *f.*; *See* REVENGE.

VENIAL, *a.* मर्षणीय, क्षंतव्य, लघु, उपेक्ष्य, अल्प; oft. by उप pr.

VENISON, *s.* मृग-हरिण-मांसं.

VENOM, *s.* विषं, गरलं, गरं, क्ष्वेडः. –OUS, *a.* सविष, विषाक्त, दंदशूक, विष in comp.

VENT, *v. t.* उत्-वि-सृज् 6 P, उत्क्षिप् 6 P, निः-सृ c., उद्वम् 1 P, उद्-गॄ 6 P ; *See* EMIT. –*s.* छिद्रं, रंध्रं, द्वारं; 'give v. to' उदीर् c., प्रकटयति (D.), आविष्कृ 8 U.

VENTILATE, *v. t.* वीज् 10 ; *See* FAN. 2 प्रचर् c., प्रं सृ c. –ED, *a.* प्रवात, वायव्याप्त; 'a bed in a v. place' प्रवातशयनं (M. 4). –OR, *s.* वीजनं, व्यजनं.

VENTRAL, *a.* उदर in comp.

VENTRICLE, *s.* कोशः-षः, द्वारं.

VENTRILOQUIST, *s.* गारुडवादिन् *m.* –VENTRILOQUISM, *s.* गारुडवादः.

VENTURE, *s.* साहसं, साहसक्रिया. 2 संकटं, संशयः; *See* DANGER. –*v. i.* संशये निक्षिप् 6 P. 2 उत्सह् 1 A, साहसं कृ 8 U, धृष् 5 P; 'we cannot v. to state this' इति कथनरूपं साहसं कर्तुं न शक्नुमः, इति कथयितुं नोत्सहामहे; 'nothing v., nothing gain' साहसे श्रीः प्रतिवसति. –OUS, -SOME, *a.* साहसिक (की *f.*), साहसबुद्धि.

VENUS, *s.* शुक्रः, भार्गवः, कविः, उशनस् *m.*, काव्यः, दैत्यगुरुः.

VERACIOUS, *a.* सत्यवाच्, सत्यगिर्, सत्यवादिन्, सत्यशील. –VERACITY, *s.* सत्यवादित्वं, सत्यशीलता.

VERANDA, *s.* *See* PORCH.

VERB, *s.* क्रिया,-पदं. –AL, *a.* शाब्दिक (की *f.*), शाब्द (ब्दी *f.*), शब्दरूप. 2 (Oral) वाचिक-वाचनिक (की *f.*); (वाचिकमिदानीं श्रोतुमिच्छामि Mu. 5). –ALLY, *adv.* वाचा. 2 शब्दतः, यथाशब्दं. –ATIM, *adv.* यथाव्याहृतं, पदानुपदं, शब्दशः, यथाशब्दं. –OSE, *a.* वाग्बहुल, अतिविस्तीर्ण; *See* PROLIX. –OSITY,-IAGE, *s.* वाग्विस्तरः, वाक्प्रपंचः, वागुपचयः.

VERDANT, *a.* हरित, शाद्वल.

VERDURE, *s.* हरितत्वं, हारित्यं; शादः, शाद्वलता; 'clothed in fresh v. of sprouts' नवहरितसस्यांकुरवती.

VERDICT, *s.* निर्णयः; विचारः; दंडनिर्णयः.

VERDIGRIS, *s.* ताम्रकिट्टं-मलं, कलंकः.

VERGE, *s.* प्रांतः, पर्यंतः, धारा; 'on the v. of' उन्मुख (खी *f.*), आसन्न in comp.; 'on the v. of ruin' विनाशोन्मुख, आसन्नलय. 2 दंडः, यष्टि *f.* –*v. i.* अव-,लंब् 1 A; by (*s.*); 'is v. ing on ruin' आसन्ननाशो वर्तते; 'when it was v. ing towards sunset' परिणतप्राये अहनि; 'v. ing on 18' अष्टादशवर्षदेशीय; *See* BORDER. –ER, *s.* दंडिन् *m.*, दंड-वेत्र-धरः.

VERIFY, *v. t.* प्रमाणीकृ 8 U, प्रमाणयति (D.), समर्थ् 10, सत्याकृ, सत्यापयति (D.), निर्णी 1 P. –ICATION, *s.* सत्यापनं, सत्याकारः.

VERILY, *adv.* सत्यं, नूनं, नियतं, नाम, खलु.

VERITABLE, VERITY, *See* TRUE, TRUTH.

VERMICULAR, *a.* कृमिसदृश (शी *f.*).

VERMIFUGE, *a.* कृमिहर, कृमिघ्न (घ्नी *f.*)

VERMILION, *s.* सिंदूरं. –*a.* शोण, रक्त. –*v. t.*, 'cover with v.' सैंदूरीकृ, सिंदूरेण रंज् c.

VERMIN, *s.* कृमय: (pl.), कृमिगण:.

VERNACULAR, *a.* जन्म in comp.; 'v. dialects' भाषा, प्राकृतभाषा. –*s.* जन्मभाषा, मातृभाषा.

VERNAL, *a.* वासंत (ती *f.*), वासंतिक (की *f.*), वसंत in comp.

VERSATILE, *a.* चपल, लोल, लोल-मति-बुद्धि, चंचल; *See* FICKLE. –ITY, *s.* (बुद्धि-) चापल्यं, लौल्यं.

VERSE, *s.* कविता, पद्यं, काव्यं; 'syllabic v.' वृत्तं; 'blank v.' मुक्तप्रास:. 2 श्लोक:. 3 (Portion of v.) चरण:, पाद:, पदं. —VERSIFY, *v. t.* पद्यानि रच् 10 or निबंध् 9P, कवयति (D.). –IER, *s.* कवि:, कविंदेश्य:.–ICATION, *s.* श्लोक-पद्य-रचना, छंदोबंध:.

VERSED, *a.* अभिज्ञ, कुशल, निपुण, प्रवीण, सुप्रतिष्ठित, अभ्यंतर, विशारद; *See* SKILFUL.

VERSION, *s.* Translation, q. v. 2 पाठांतरं, पाठभेद:.

VERTEBRA, *s.* पृष्ठवंशास्थि *n.* –ATE,-TED, *a.* पृष्ठवंशयुत-विशिष्ट.

VERTEX, *s.* शीर्षं, अग्रं, शिखरं ; *See* TOP also.

VERTICAL, *a.* ऊर्ध्व-उपरि-तन (नी *f.*), लंबरूप. –LY, *adv.* अधोमुखं, ऊर्ध्वाधरं.

VERTIGO, *s.* भ्रमरं ; *See* GIDDINESS.

VERY, *adv.* अति-सु pr., सातिशयं, अतीव, भूरि, नितु-तरा, अत्यंतं ; *See* EXCEEDINGLY ; 'v. deceitful' भूरिमाय. –*a.* Ex. by demonstrative pron. with एव ; 'the v. hills' त एव गिरय: ; 'this v. day' अद्यैव. 2 सत्य, तथ्य. 3 मात्रं in comp., केवल.

VESICLE, *s.* त्वक्-चर्म-स्फोट:.

VESPER, *s.* संध्या, संध्योपासनं.

VESSEL, *s.* पात्रं, भाजनं, भांडं, आधार:. 2 पोत:, समुद्रयानं, जलयानं, वहित्रं, नौ:. 3 नाडी ; *See* VEIN.

VEST, *s.* वस्त्रं, वेश:-ष:, वसनं. –*v. t.* वेष् c., परि-धा c.; *See* DRESS. –ED, *a.* (in) व्यवस्थित; 'are warlike qualities v. (in any one)' किं व्यवस्थितविषया: क्षात्रधर्मा इति (U. 5). 2 अधीन, आयत्त. –VESTMENT, VESTURE, *s.* वासस् *n.*, वस्त्रं ; *See* DRESS.

VESTAL, *a.* शुद्ध, पवित्र ; *See* CHASTE.

VESTIBULE, *s.* देहलि-ली *f.* ; *See* PORCH.

VESTIGE, *s.* चिह्नं, अंक:, लक्षणं, पदांक:, पदपंक्ति *f.*, पदवी.

VETERAN, *a.*, *s.* जातानुभव, ज्ञानवृद्ध, अभ्यासवृद्ध.

VETERINARY, *s.* पशुचिकित्सक:, पशुवैद्य:; (art) पशुचिकित्सा.

VETO, *v. t.* प्रति-नि-षिध् 1 P, प्रत्या-ख्या 2 P; *See* CONTRADICT. –*s.* प्रति-नि-षेध:, प्रत्यादेश:.

VEX, *v. t.* बाध् 1 A, पीड् 10, क्लिश् 9 P, संतप् c., उद्विज् c., अर्द् 1 P or c. 2 प्रकुप् c., क्रोधं उद्दीप् c. –ATION, *s.* क्लेश:, दु:खं, पीडा, कष्टं, बाधा, आयास:, संताप:. 2 प्रकोपनं, क्रोधोद्दीपनं. –ATIOUS, *a.* कष्टद, क्लेशकर-पीडाकर (री *f.*), उद्वेगकर, संतापक. –ED, *a.* दु:खित, संतापित, अर्दित, &c. –EDLY, *adv.* सक्रोधं, सोद्वेगं.

VIAND, (V. s) *s.* अन्नं, भक्ष्यं, सिद्धान्नं.

VIATICUM, *s.* पाथेयं, पथि भोज्यं.

VIBRATE, *v. i.* दोलायते (D.), कंप् 1 A, स्फुर् 6 P, भ्रम् 1, 4 P. –*v. t.* भ्रम् c., इतस्तत: चल् c., वि-धू 5, 9 U. –ION, *s.* आंदोलनं, दोलायितं, स्फुरणं, कंप:, भ्रमणं.

VICAR, *s.* प्रतिनिधि:. –IOUS, *a.* प्रतिनिधिरूप.

VICE, *s.* अधर्म:, पापं, पापाचरणं, असदाचार:, व्यभिचार:. 2 दोष:, दुर्गुण:, व्यसनं. 3 (Instead of) Ex. by स्थाने or प्रतिनिधि:, oft. by उप pr.; 'viceroy' राजप्रतिनिधि:, राजस्थाने स्थित: ; 'v.-president' उपाध्यक्ष:. —VICIOUS, *a.* दुष्ट, दुराचार, अपथप्रवृत्त, व्यसनिन्, दुरात्मन्, पापवृत्त; दुर्वृत्त, दुश्चरित, खंडितवृत्ति. –LY, *adv.* दुष्टतया, दुर्वृत्ततया, दुष्टभावेन.

VICINAGE, VICINITY, *s.* संनिधि:, संनिधानं, संनिकर्ष:.

VICISSITUDE, *s.* आ-परि-वृत्ति *f.*, विपर्यय:, परिवर्त:, अनुक्रम:; 'Oh ! how rarely seen (by mortal prescience) the strange v. s of human life' अहो अलक्षितोपनिपाता: पुरुषाणां समविषमदशाविभागपरिणतयो भवंति (Mu. 6).

VICTIM, *s.* बलि:, उपहार:, वध्य:, यज्ञपशु:; (fig.) *See* PREY. –IZE, *v. t.* उपहारीकृ 8 U ; *See* SACRIFICE.

VICTOR, VICTORIOUS, *s.*, *a.* वि-,जयिन्, जैत्र (त्री *f.*), जित्वर (री *f.*), जिष्णु, प्राप्तजय. 2 जयप्रद, जयावह. –IOUSLY, *adv.* सविजयं, जयपूर्वं. –Y, *s.* वि-,जय: ; 'gain v.' विजयं लभ् 1 A or प्राप् 5 P, वि जि 1 A ; 'v. to your Majesty' जयतु जयतु देव:.

VICTUAL, *v. t.* खाद्यसामग्रीं उपक्लृप् c. –*s.* (V. s) खाद्य-भक्ष्य-सामग्री, भक्ष्यसंभार:. –LER, *s.* भक्ष्यविक्रयिन् *m.* –LING, *s.* अन्नविक्रय:, भक्ष्यव्यवहार:.

VIE, (with) *v. i.* स्पर्ध् 1 A, जि desid. (जिगीषति); *See* RIVAL ; अहमहमिकया प्रणामलालसा: (Ka. 81) 'v. ing with each other for saluting'.

VIEW, *v. t.* सं-,ईक्ष् 1 A, निर्वर्ण् 10, आ-अव-लोक् 1 A, 10, निरीक्ष् ; *See* SEE. –*s.* आलोकनं, समीक्षणं, दर्शनं, दृष्टि *f.* ; 'point of v.' दृष्टि:, पक्ष: ; 'from a worldly (practical) point of v.' लोक-व्यवहार-दृष्ट्या; शास्त्रदृष्ट्या &c.; इत्येतल्लोकदृष्ट्या निदर्शितं शास्त्रदृष्ट्या न पराणुयते (S. B. 503); 'from this point of v.' अस्मिन् पक्षे. 2 मतं, बुद्धि *f.*, मति *f.*, दृष्टि:. 3 हेतु:, आशय:, अभिप्राय:, उद्देश: ;

'with what v.' किमुद्दिश्य, केन हेतुना, किमाभिप्रेत्य; 'with this v.' अस्माद्धेतोः, एतदर्थं; 'of narrow v. s' कृपणबुद्धि-दृष्टि; 'of liberal v. s' उदारधीः. 4 दृक्पातः-विषयः, नयनगोचरः प्रदेशः; 'having in v.' दृग्गोचरवर्तिन्. -LESS, *a.* अदृश्य.

VIGIL, *s.* जागरणं, प्र-,जागरः, रात्रिजागरः. -ANCE, *s.* अवधानं, अवहितता, दक्षता, जागरूकता. -ANT, *a.* जागरूक, अवहित, दक्ष, सावधान, अप्रमत्त. -ANTLY, *adv.* अप्रमादेन, सावधानं.

VIGOUR, *s.* वीर्यं, बलं, शक्ति *f.*, ओजस् *n.*, सत्त्वं, तेजस् *n.*, प्रभावः, पौरुषं; *See* STRENGTH. -OUS, *a.* प्रबल, ओजस्विन्, महासत्त्व, ऊर्जस्वल, वीर्यवत्; *See* STRONG; सोत्साह, सप्रयत्न. -OUSLY, *adv.* चंडं, बलवत्, तरसा, ओजस्वितया; सवीर्यं, महाप्रयत्नेन, सोद्यमं, सोत्साहं.

VILE, *a.* अधम, नीच, जघन्य, नि-अप-कृष्ट. -NESS, *s.* नीचता &c.; *See* MEAN &c. —VILIFY, *v. t.* परि-वद् 1 A, कुत्स् 10, आक्षर् c.; *See* TRADUCE, LIBEL. -ER, -ICATION; *See* under CALUMNY.

VILLA, *s.* ग्राम्यं गृहं, विनोदस्थानं.

VILLAGE, *s.* ग्रामः; निवसथः; 'head of a v.' ग्रामणीः, ग्रामेशः, ग्रामाध्यक्षः. -*a.* ग्राम्य, ग्रामीय, ग्रामीण, ग्राम in comp. -ER, ग्रामिन् *m.*, ग्रामिकः, ग्रामवासी, ग्रामीणः, ग्रामस्थः, ग्राम्यजनः.

VILLAIN, *s.* दुर्वृत्तः, अपसदः affixed, (नरापसदः), चांडालः, खलः, अधमः, दुरात्मन् *m.*; *See* RASCAL also. -OUS, *a.* दुर्वृत्त, दुष्टतम, अधम &c.

VILLEIN, *s.* दासः, प्रजा.

VINDICATE, *v. t.* रक्ष् 1 P, प्रमाणीकृ 8 U, समर्थ् 10, प्रति-पद् c., स्था c. (स्थापयति); (from blame) शुध् c., निर्दोषीकृ. 2 निर्वह् 1 P or c.; निर्व्यूढस्तेपत्यस्नेहः (U. 3) 'thy parental affection has been v.ed'. -ION, *s.* रक्षणं, प्रतिपादनं; स्थापनं; निर्वाहः; दोषमुक्ति *f.*, परिशोधनं. -OR, *s.* रक्षकः, समर्थयितृ *m.*

VINDICTIVE, *a.* प्रतिकारपरायण-शील, वैरसाधनपर, वैरनिर्यातनोत्सुक; क्रोधन, क्रोधिल; अक्षमिन्, असहिष्णु.

VINE, *s.* द्राक्षा,-लता. -OUS, *a.* सुरामय (यी *f.*). -VINEGAR, *s.* शुक्तं, शौक्तिकं. -VINEYARD, *s.* द्राक्षाक्षेत्रं-वाटिका. -VINTAGE, *s.* द्राक्षाः, द्राक्षाफलं; 'v.-time' द्राक्षावचयकालः. -VINTNER, *s.* शौंडिकः, सुराजीविन् *m.*

VIOLATE, *v. t.* धृष् c. (a woman). 2 अतिक्रम् 1 U, 4 P, उल्लंघ् 1 A, 10, अतिचर् 1 P, व्याहन् 2 U, लुप् c., भंज् 7 P; 'for fear of v. ing your word' प्रतिज्ञाभंगभीरुणा (त्वया). 3 भंज्, पराजि 1 A. -ION, *s.* अतिक्रमः, भंगः, उल्लंघनं, लोपः,-पनं. 2 आ-,धर्षणं-णा. -OR, *s.* धर्षकः. 2 उल्लंघकः.

VIOLENT, *a.* प्रचंड, प्रबल, तीव्र, गुरु, महावेग, उग्र. 2 साहसिन्, साहसिक (की *f.*), तीक्ष्णकर्मन्; 'a v. death' अपमृत्युः. -LY, *adv.* प्रसह्य, प्रसभं, तरसा, वेगेन, बलात्कारेण, बलवत्, उच्चंडं, तीव्रं, गाढं, अति-सुpr.; 'v. in love' गाढानुरागः. -VIOLENCE, *s.* बलं, तरस् *n.*, जवः, वेगः. 2 बलात्कारः; साहसं, प्रमाथः, प्रसभं.

VIOLET, *s.* पाटलं. 2 (Colour) नीललोहितः.

VIOLIN, *s.* सा(शा)रंगी, पिनाकी.

VIPER, *s.* दंदशूकः, अहिः; *See* SNAKE.

VIRAGO, *s.* स्त्रीयोधी, पुरुषवृत्तिः, ऋषभी.

VIRGIN, *s.* कुमारी, कन्या, तरुणी, अक्षता, अक्षत-अविद्ध-योनिः, पुरुषास्पृष्टा. -*a.* कौमार (री *f.*), (*s.*) in comp. 2 वि-,शुद्ध, अक्षत. -ITY, *s.* कौमारं, कुमारीत्वं; पुरुषास्पर्शः. 2 विशुद्धता.

VIRGO, *s.* कन्या,-राशिः.

VIRILE, *a.* पौरुष (षी *f.*), पौरुषेय (यी *f.*), पुरुष in comp. -ITY, *s.* पुंस्त्वं, पुरुषत्वं, पौरुषं.

VIRTUE, *s.* धर्मः, पुण्यं; सुकृतं, सदाचारः, साधुता, धर्माचरणं, नीति *f.* 2 गुणः, सद्गुणः. 3 शक्ति *f.*, बलं, प्रभावः, सामर्थ्यं; 'by v. of' वशात्, बलेन, प्रभावेण. —VIRTUAL, *a.* वास्तविक (की *f.*), better by 'v.-ly'. -LY, *adv.* वस्तुतः, यथार्थतः, अर्थतः. —VIRTUOUS, *a.* धार्मिक (की *f.*), पुण्य-धर्म-शील, धर्मपर-परायण, साधु, पुण्यात्मन्, सुकृतिन्, पुण्यभाज्, न्यायाचार, साधुवृत्त, सदाचार, सच्चरित; oft. by सत्; सती, सज्जनः &c. 2 (Of acts) धर्म्य, पुण्य, साधु. -LY, *adv.* धर्मतः, धर्मेण, सदाचारतः.

VIRULENT, *a.* उग्र, कटु, तीक्ष्ण, चंड; *See* MALIGNANT, SHARP.

VIRUS, *s.* विषं.

VISAGE, *s.* आस्यं, आननं, वदनाकृति *f.*, वदनच्छाया; 'with sad v.' विषण्णवदन.

VISCERA, *s.* अंत्राणि (pl.).

VISCID, VISCOUS, *a.* सांद्र, श्यान, शीन; चिक्कण, स्निग्ध; 'v. fluid' दानजलं, दानं (of an elephant).

VISIBLE, *a.* दृश्य, दृग्गोचर, प्रत्यक्ष, दृष्टिविषय, नयनपथवर्तिन्, नेत्रविषयगत, व्यक्त, सुप्रकाश, चक्षुर्ग्राह्य, and sim. comp. -VISIBLY, *adv.* प्रत्यक्षं, प्रत्यक्षतः, साक्षात्.

VISION, *s.* दृष्टि *f.*, चक्षुरिंद्रियं. 2 छाया, आभासः, माया, मनःसृष्टि *f.*, कल्पना. 3 स्वप्नः, स्वप्नदर्शनं. -ARY, *a.* अवास्तव (वी *f.*), मानसिक-काल्पनिक (की *f.*), मनःसृष्ट-कल्पित.

VISIT, *s.* दर्शनं, अभ्यागमः. 2 साक्षात्कारः; 'pay a v. to' द्रष्टुं अभ्यागम् 1 P. -*v. t.* दृश्, अभि-इ 2 P, अभ्युपगम्, द्रष्टुं गम् or या 2 P. 2 साक्षात्कृ 8 U. 3 (With punishment) दंड् 10; 'v. a lover' अभि-सृ 1 P (कामुकं). -ANT,-OR,

s. अभ्यागतः, गृहागतः. -ATION, s. अभ्यागमनं. 2 दुर्विपाकः.

VISTA, s. वीथि-थी f., तरुपंक्ति-श्रेणी f.

VISUAL, a. चाक्षुष (षी f.), दृष्टिगत, चक्षुस्-नेत्र in comp.; 'v. organ' चक्षुरिंद्रियं.

VITAL, a. आवश्यक (की f.). 2 प्राणभूत, जीव-प्राण in comp.; 'v. air' प्राणवायुः; 'v. principle' जीवात्मा; 'v. part' मर्मन् n.; 'v. s' मर्माणि; 'touching (rending, piercing,) the v. s' अरुंतुद, मर्मस्पृश्, मर्माणि कृंतत्. -ITY, s. जीवनं, चेतनत्वं, सजीवत्वं, चेतना; प्राणः, जीवः, जीव-प्राण-शक्ति f.

VITIATE, v. t. Corrupt, q. v. -ION, s. दूषणं, भ्रंशनं.

VITRIOUS, a. काचज, काचाभ, काचमय (यी f.). -VITRIFY, v. t. काचसात्कृ 8 U.

VITRIOL, s. (Blue) तुत्थांजनं, शिखिग्रीवं, वितुन्नकं, मयूरकं, कर्परी; (green) कासीसं.

VITUPERATE,-ION, *See* CENSURE.

VIVACIOUS, a. प्रफुल्ल, सोत्साह, सतेजस्. -NESS, -VIVACITY, s. उत्साहः, तेजस्विता, प्रफुल्लता, उल्लासः.

VIVA-VOCE, *See* ORALLY.

VIVID, a. सुस्पष्ट, विशद, परिस्फुट.

VIVIFY, v. t. जीव् c., सजीवीकृ 8 U.

VIVITAROUS, a. जरायुज, जीवज. 2 सचेतनप्रज.

VIXEN, s. कलहप्रिया, कर्कशा, चंडी.

VOCABLE, s. शब्दः, वाक्यं, वचनं.

VOCABULARY, s. अभिधानं, कोशः, शब्दार्णवः, शब्दसंग्रहः-कोशः.

VOCAL, a. वाचिक (की f.), वाङ्मय (यी f.), वाग्जात. 2 वाणीयुक्त, वाग्विशिष्ट. 3 सुस्वर, मधुर; 'v. music' कंठगीतं.

VOCATION, s. वृत्ति f., व्यवसायः, नियोगः, व्यापारः.

VOCATIVE, s. संबोधनं, संबुद्धि f.

VOCIFERATE, v. i. उच्चैः आक्रंद् 1 P, उत्क्रुश् 1 P, उद्-घुष् 10. -ION, s. आक्रोशः, उद्घोषः. —VOCIFEROUS, a. महाशब्द, सकोलाहल, उद्घोषण. -LY, *adv.* महाशब्देन, उद्घोषेण.

VOGUE, s. व्यवहारः, प्रवृत्ति f., प्रचारः, रीति f., क्षुण्णा पद्धतिः; 'it is not in v. here' अत्र नेदृशो व्यवहारः; 'being long in v.' चिरप्रवृत्त.

VOICE, s. स्वरः, स्वनः, नादः, शब्दः, वाणी, वचनं, वाच् f., कंठध्वनिः-रवः. 2 मतं, अभिप्रायः; 'with one v.' एकचित्तीभूय, ऐकमत्येन; 'cracked v.' भग्नस्वरः; 'active v.' कर्तृवाच्यं; 'passive v.' कर्मवाच्यं; 'neuter v.' भाववाच्यं.

VOID, a. शून्य, रिक्त. 2 असिद्ध, अप्रमाण, आकिंचित्कर (री f.), निरर्थक. 3 Destitute, Devoid of, q. v. -s. शून्यं, शून्यस्थानं. -v. t. रिच् 7 P or c., शून्यीकृ 8 U. 2 निष्फलीकृ. 3 (Excrement) उत्सृज् c., वि-उत्-सृज्, उद्-गॄ 6 P. -ABLE, a. विवर्जनीय, परित्यक्तव्य.

VOLATILE, a. वायुपरिणामशील. 2 चंचल, लोल; *See* FICKLE. -ITY, s. चापल्यं, चांचल्यं.

VOLCANO, s. ज्वालामुखः, आग्नेयगिरिः.

VOLITION, s. संकल्पः, इच्छा; *See* WILL.

VOLLEY, s. वर्षः, (शिलावर्षः, शरवर्षः &c.), वृष्टि f.,-पातः.

VOLUBLE, a. चंचल, चपल. 2 (Of tongue) वाचाल, चपलजिह्व. -VOLUBILITY, s. वाक्चापल्यं.

VOLUME, s. खंडः-डं, भागः, पुस्तकं (when the sense is clear). 2 अंतर्गतं घनफलं. 3 आवलि-ली f., पटलं, राशिः, संहति f. -VOLUMINOUS, a. विस्तीर्ण, बहुपुस्तक.

VOLUNTARY, a. ऐच्छिक-यादृच्छिक (की f.), इच्छामति-पूर्व; better ex. by 'v.-ily'. -ILY, *adv.* यदृच्छया, इच्छापूर्वकं, स्वेच्छातः, प्र-नि-कामं, आत्मसंतोषेण. -VOLUNTEER, v. t. अयाचितं उपानी 1 P or ऋ c. (अर्पयति) or दा 3 U or कृ 8 U. -s. यादृच्छिकः युयुत्सुः, स्वेच्छासैनिकः.

VOLUPTUARY, VOLUPTUOUS, s., a. विषयासक्त, भोगनिरत, इंद्रियसुखासक्त, विषयिन्; *See* SENSUAL.

VOMIT, v. उद्-,वम् 1 P, उद्-गॄ 6 P, छर्द् 10, उत्क्षिप् 6 P. -s. वांतं. 2 वमनं (emetic). -ING, s. वमनं, वमः-मि f., वमथुः, प्रच्छर्दिका. -IVE, a. वमन (नी f.), वांतिकर (री f.), वांतिकृत्.

VORACIOUS, a. घस्मर, गृध्नु, अतिलोलुप, औदरिक (की f.); *See* GLUTTONOUS.

VORTEX, s. भ्रमि f., आवर्तः.

VOTARY, s. भक्तः, उपासकः, पूजकः; आश्रितः.

VOTE, s. संमति f., संमतं. -v. t. संमतिं-अनुमोदनं-दा 3 U, मतं प्रकाश् c.; संमतिपूर्वं वृ 5 U or नियुज् 7 A, 10 or दा.

VOUCH, v. t. साक्षीकृ 8 U, प्रमाणीकृ, प्रमाणं दा 3 U. 2 दृढीकृ, द्रढयति (D.). -ER, s. प्रमाणपत्रं-लेखः, साधनपत्रं-लेखः, आगमः.

VOUCHSAFE, v. t. वि-तॄ 1 P, कृपया दा 3 U; (with inf.) प्र-सद् 1 P; *See* CONDESCEND, PLEASE; भगवान् मारीचस्ते दर्शनं वितरति (S. 7) 'v. s thee an audience' 2 अनु-ज्ञा 9 U.

VOW, s. व्रतं, संकल्पः, प्रतिज्ञा, शपथः, नियमः; 'under a v.' व्रतबद्ध, धृतव्रत, संकल्पबद्ध. -v. प्रतिज्ञा 9 A, प्रतिज्ञां कृ 8 U or आरुह् 1 P, सशपथं-सप्रतिज्ञं वद् 1 P or अभि-धा 3 U, ('Say', q. v.); 'he has v. ed to destroy us' अस्मद्विनाशे कृतसंकल्पोसौ.

VOWEL, s. स्वरः, अच् m., अज्वर्णः.

VOYAGE, s. जलयात्रा-यानं, समुद्रयानं, संयात्रा. -v.

Ex. by कृ with (*s.*), पोतेन गम् 1 P, जलवर्त्मना गम्. -ER, *s.* सांयात्रिकः, जलयात्रिकः.

VULGAR, *a.* ग्राम्य, असभ्य, अश्लील, अशिष्ट; प्राकृत, लौकिक (की *f.*). -ISM, *s.* ग्राम्या रीतिः. 2 ग्राम्यशब्दप्रयोगः. -ITY, *s.* असभ्यता, अश्लीलता. -LY, *adv.* साधारणतः, लौकिकरीत्या. 2 असभ्यरीत्या, ग्राम्यतया. -IZE, *v. t.* ग्राम्यीकृ.

VULNERABLE, *a.* भेद्य, धृष्य; वेध्य; 'v. point' रंध्रं, छिद्रं, मर्मन् *n.*; आवृणोदात्मनो रंध्रं रंध्रेषु प्रहरन् रिपून् (R. XVIII. 61) 'guarded against his own v. points' &c.

VULPINE, *a.* धूर्त, शृगालवत्.

VULTURE, *s.* गृध्रः, दाक्षाय्यः.

W.

WAD, *s.* चूर्णरोधनी.

WADDLE, *v. i.* हंसवत् गम् 1 P or चर् 1 P.

WADE, *v. i.* तॄ 1 P, कष्टेन गम् 1 P, कृच्छ्रेण पारं गम्.

WAFT, *v. t.* वह् 1 P or c., उत्क्षृ 6 P; कणवाही मालिनीतरंगाणां (S. 3); पुष्परेणूत्किरैर्वातैः (R. I. 38); (boat &c.) वह् c., प्रणुद् c., प्रचुद् 10, प्रेर् c.; *See* DRIVE. -*v. i.* प्लु 1 A, वायुना वह्-नी pass.

WAG, *v. t.* सं-,चल् c., वि-,धू 5, 9 U, वि-क्षिप् 6 P; 'w. ging the tail' लांगूलचालनं-विक्षेपः-विधूति *f.* -*v. i.* चल् 1 P, धू pass. -*s.* परिहासवादिन् *m.* -GISH, *a. See* WITTY.-WAG-TAIL, *s.* खंजनः.

WAGE, *v. t.* (War) विग्रह् 9 P, युद्धं आरभ् 1 A.

WAGER, *s.* ग्लहः, पणः. -*v.* ग्लह्-पण् 1 A, (with gen. of thing staked).

WAGES, *s.* वेतनं, भृति *f.*, मूल्यं, निर्वेशः, पणः; *See* HIRE.

WAGON, *s.* प्रवहणं, यानं, शकटः-टं, चातुरं. -ER, *s.* शाकटिकः, शकटवाहः, चातुरिकः.

WAIF, *s.* अज्ञातस्वामिकं द्रव्यं.

WAIL,-ING, *See* LAMENT,-ATION.

WAIN, *s.* गोवहनं, शकटः-टं.

WAINSCOT, *s.* भित्तिपटलं.

WAIST, *s.* मध्यः-ध्यं, मध्यमः-मं, कटि-टी *f.*, कटिदेशः; 'w.-coat' कटिवस्त्रं.

WAIT, *v. i.* स्था 1 P; (for) प्रति-ईक्ष् 1 A, अनु-प्रतिपा c. (पालयति) (of time and persons); 'w. for some time' कालः कश्चित्प्रतीक्ष्यतां (K. II. 54); मां प्रतिपालय &c.; सह् 1 A, स्था, (of time only) (द्वित्राण्यहान्यर्हसि सोढुमर्हन् R. v. 25); स्फुलिंगावस्थया वह्निरेधापेक्ष इव स्थितः (S. 7) 'here is fire in the state of a spark (only) w. ing for fuel (to blaze up)'; (on or upon) उप-स्था 1 A, उप-अनु-आस् 2A, उप-सेव् 1A, उप-चर् 1 P; 'w. at table' परिविष् c. -ER, *s.* सेवकः, परिवेषकः, परिवेष्टृ *m.* (at table).

WAIVE, *v. t.* परि-,त्यज् 1 P; *See* ABANDON.

WAKE, *v. t.* प्र-बुध् c., जागृ c.-*v. i.* प्र-वि-बुध् 4 A, जागृ 2 P. -*s.* जागरणं, जागरः, प्र-बोधः-धनं. 2 पदवी; 'follow in the w. of' पदवीं प्रतिपद् 4 A; *See* TREAD. -FUL, *a.* (lit.) रात्रिजागर, निद्राविमुख, विनिद्र, उन्निद्र; जागरूक, दक्ष, अवहित, सावधान. -FULNESS, *s.* जागरः-रणं, अस्वापः, अस्वप्नः, अनिद्रा, प्रबोधः, जाग्रदवस्था. 2 दक्षता, अवधानं, &c.

WALK, *v. i.* (पद्भ्यां) चर्-चल्- गम् 1 P, परि-, क्रम् 1 U, 4 P, पादाभ्यां या 2 P &c.; 'w. about', 'w. to and fro' परिक्रम्, इतस्ततः भ्रम् 1, 4 P; (for pleasure) वि-हृ 1 P; 'w. away,-off' अपसृ 1 P, अप-या-क्रम्-गम् &c. -*s.*-ING, *s.* पादचारः-गमनं; 'w. about' परिक्रमः-मणं; 'taking a w.' विहारः, विहरणं, (वायुसेवनार्थं) परिक्रमणं. 2 गमनागमनस्थानं; अध्वगमार्गः. -ER, *s.* पादचारिन्, पा(प)दगः.

WALL, *s.* भित्ति *f.*, कुड्यं; 'enclosing w.' प्राकारः, वरणः, सालः, प्राचीरं; 'take the w. of' अग्रस्थानं आ-सद् c.; 'go to the w.' अव-सद् 1 P, अवसन्न-उच्छिन्न- *a.* भू 1 P; 'drive to the w.' अव-सद् c., उच्छिद् 7 P. -*v. t.* प्राकारेण आ-वृ 5 U.

WALLET, *s.* भस्त्रा; क्षुद्रकोषः.

WALLOW, *v. i.* लुठ् 6 P, लुट् 4 P; क्रीड् 1 P.

WALNUT, *s.* अक्षोटः; अक्षोटं (fruit).

WAN, *a. See* PALE.

WAND, *s.* दंडः, यष्टि *f.*

WANDER, *v. i.* परि-,भ्रम् 1, 4 P, अट् 1 P, वि-चर् 1 P, परि-,क्रम् 1 U, 4 P; 'w. from' भ्रंश् 1 A, 4 P, च्यु 1 A. -*s.*, -ING, *s.* परि-,भ्रमणं-अटनं. -ER, *s.* परिभ्रमकः, भ्रमिन् *m.*

WANE, *v. i.* परि-,क्षि 1 P or pass., ह्रस् 1 P; *See* DECAY, DECLINE. -*s.* क्षयः, ह्रासः. -ED, *a.* परि-क्षीण, क्षीणकल, प्राप्तक्षय, निष्कल, कलाशेष (चंद्रः). -ING, *a.* क्षयिन्, क्षय in comp.; 'w. period' क्षयकालः, कृष्णपक्षः, बहुलः, तमिस्रपक्षः.

WANT, *v.* अपेक्ष् 1 A, आ-,कांक्ष् 1 P, इष् 6 P; gen. ex. by कार्यं, प्रयोजनं, अर्थः, किं, (with gen. of that which wants and instr. of thing wanted); 'I do not w. this house' ममानेन गृहेण न कार्यं, न प्रयोजनं &c.; 'why do you w. to see her' किं तया दृष्टया (S. 2). 2 Wish, q. v. 3 परि-,हा pass.; हीन, रहित, निर् in comp.; आर्यस्य सुविहितप्रयोगतया न किमपि परिहास्यते (S. 1) 'nothing will be w. ing' &c.; 'w. ing in courage' शौर्यहीन, निर्वीर्य, &c.; 'he w. s wisdom' स निर्बुद्धिः, ज्ञानरहितः. -*s.* अपेक्षा, प्रयोजनं, कार्यं,

आकांक्षा. 2 अभावः, विरहः, अप्राप्ति *f.*, राहित्यं, हीनता. 3 न्यूनता, ऊनत्वं, अपचयः. 4 दारिद्र्यं, धनाभावः, दुर्गति *f.*, कृच्छ्रं; 'come to or reduced to w.' दारिद्र्योपहत, भाग्यक्षयपीडितां दशां प्रपन्न (Mr. 1). -ING, *a.* ऊन, न्यून, विकल; *See* DEFICIENT.

WANTON, *a.* विलासवत्, विलासिन्; 'w. sport' विलसितं; *See* PLAYFUL. 2 अनियंत्रित, निर्मर्याद, स्वेच्छाप्रवृत्त, लोल, (स्वभावलोल); स्वैरिन्, स्वेच्छाचारिन्; काम in comp.; 'a w. woman' पुंश्चली, स्वैरिणी, बंधकी. 3 ज्ञानतः-कामतः-कृत, बोधपूर्वं कृत. 4 प्रचुर, विपुल. -*v. i.* विलस् 1 P, क्रीड् 1 P, वि-भ्रम् 1, 4 P. -LY, *adv.* सविलासं; निर्यंत्रणं, स्वैरं, स्वेच्छया, यथाकामं; कामतः. -NESS, *s.* विलासः, कामचारः; न कामचारो मयि शंकनीयः 'do not suspect me of w.'

WAR, WARFARE, *s.* विग्रहः, संप्रहारः, वैरारंभः, वैरं, संग्रामः, युद्धं, रणं, (a particular battle); 'w.-cry' सिंहनादः, क्ष्वेडा; 'w.-horse' वारकीरः. -*v. i.* विग्रह् 9 P, युध् 4 A, कृ with (*s.*). -LIKE, *a.* रणप्रिय, युयुत्सु, युद्धदुर्मद; रणोत्सुक, रणवीर-शूर; 'w. qualities' क्षात्रधर्माः; 'w. tribe' क्षत्रियजातिः. 2 सांग्रामिक-सामरिक (की *f.*).

WARBLE, *v.* कूज् 1 P, वि-रु 2 P.

WARD, *s.* रक्षा. 2 रक्षितः पुरुषः, आश्रितः, रक्षकाधीनः, रक्ष्यः. 3 विभागः. -*v. t.* वार् 10 or वृ c., नि-प्रति-°, निरुध् 7 U, निरस् 4 U, नि-प्रति-षिध् 1 P, प्रति-हन् 2 P, अप-ऊह् 1 U. -EN, *s.* रक्षकः, रक्षापुरुषः. -ER, *s.* रक्षकः, दौवारिकः, द्वाःस्थः.

WARDROBE, *s.* वासांसि (pl.); वस्त्रसमूहः. 2 वस्त्राधानं-आधारः.

WARE, WARES, *s.* पण्यं, पण्यद्रव्यं; 'w.-house' पण्यागारं, पण्याधानं, पण्यशाला.

WARM, *a.* तप्त, उष्ण, चंड, घर्म in comp.; (fig.) तीक्ष्ण, चंड, सोत्साह. 2 घर्मार्त, आतपाक्रांत; 'grown w.' Angry, q. v. -*v. t.* तप् c., ईषत् तप्; 'w. oneself' (in the sun) सूर्यातपं सेव् 1A, (सेवयेत्सृष्टतो ह्यर्कं H. 2); 'w. oneself at the fire' अग्न्यातपं सेव्. -LY, *adv.* सोत्साहं, सस्नेहं, उष्णं &c. -NESS, -TH, *s.* तापः, उत्तापः, उष्मन् *m.*; 'w. of wealth' वित्तोष्मा. 2 चंडता, तीक्ष्णता. 3 उत्साहः; 'w. of affection' स्नेहातिशयः.

WARN, *v. t.* (पूर्वं) प्र-अनु-बुध् c., उप-दिश् 6 P, अनु-शास् 2 P. 2 सूच् 10, निर्दिश्, वि-ज्ञा c. (ज्ञापयति); 'I w. ed him of the impending danger' प्रत्यासन्नापदं तं प्राबोधयं; oft. by 'Beware', q. v.; अवहिता भव यदापत्प्रत्यासन्ना. -ING, *s.* प्रबोधनं, उपदेशः.

WARP, *v. t.* आ-वृत् c., संकुच् 1 P; (fig.) कलुषीकृ, दुष् c. (दूषयति). -*v. i.* आवृत् 1 A, संकुच् pass.

WARRANT, *s.* प्रमाणं, अधिकारः; (written) अनुज्ञा-अधिकार-पत्रं. -*v. t.* प्रमाणं दा 3 U, प्रमाणीकृ 8 U, अधिकृ c.; *See* SANCTION. -ED, *a.* सप्रमाण, साधार. -Y, *s.* प्रमाणपत्रं.

WARREN, *s.* शशकनिलयः.

WARRIOR, *s.* भटः, योधः, योद्धृ *m.*, वीरः, रथी, विक्रांतः; *See* HERO, SOLDIER; 'w. s on the enemy's side' प्रतिभटाः.

WART, *s.* किणः, चर्मकीलः-लं, अधिमांसं.

WARY, *a.* सावधान, अप्रमत्त, दक्ष; *See* CAREFUL.

WASH, *v. t.* प्र-,क्षल् 10, प्र-मृज् 2 P or c., निज् 3 U, अव-निर्-°, धाव् 1 U, 10; 'w. the mouth (after meals)' उपस्पृश् 6 P. -*s.*,-ING, *s.* धावनं, प्र-,क्षालनं, मार्जनं, अवसेकः, निर्णेकः. 2 आलेपः, वि-प्र-लेपः-पनं. -ED, *a.* प्रक्षालित, निर्णिक्त, धौत, धावित, मार्जित &c. -Y, *a.* जलधर्मक.-WASHERMAN, *s.* रजकः, धावकः, निर्णेजकः, (रजकी, रजकवधू *f.*).

WASP, *s.* वरटा, गंधोली. -ISH, *a.* कर्कशस्वभाव, वरटाशील.

WASTE, *v. t.* क्षि 1, 5 P or c., अव-सद् c., नश् c., क्षै c. (क्षपयति), न्हासं-क्षयं-नी 1 P, अप-चि 5 U, व्यय् 10 (व्ययति). 2 (Away) मुधा-व्यर्थं-हृ 1 P or गम् c., वि-क्षिप् 6P. -*v. i.* परि-,क्षि-परिहा-अपचि- pass., क्षयं-नाशं-लयं या 2 P or गम् 1 P, विनश् 4 P, अवसद् 1 P, न्हस् 1 P; क्षै 1 P; (in strength) अंगैः परिहा pass.; *See* LEAN. -*s.* क्षयः, नाशः, अपचयः, व्ययः, न्हासः, अवसादः. 2 अपव्ययः, वि-,क्षेपः, हरणं; 'w. of time' कालक्षेपः-नाशः-हरणं-यापनं; 'w. of breath' वाग्व्ययः-क्षेपः. 3 (Land) खिलंभूमि *f.*, मरुभूः. -*a.* उच्छिष्ट, निःसार, निर्गुण. 2 निर्जन, शून्य, खिल, अप्रहत, जंगल; 'lay w.' उप-क्षु 1 A, उप-द्रु 1 P, बाध् 1 A, पीड् 10. -ED, *a.* परि-,क्षीण, क्षाम, अपचित, &c. -FUL, *a.* अपव्ययिन्, वृथाव्ययिन्, व्ययशील. -ING, *a.* क्षीयमाण, क्षयिन्. -WASTEPIPE, *s.* उच्छिष्टजलनाली, परि(री)वाहः.

WATCH, *v. t.* रक्ष् 1 P, प्रति-,पा c. (पालयति); *See* PROTECT. 2 निरूप् 10, निरीक्ष् 1 A, अवेक्ष्. 3 उपास् 2 A, उप-स्था 1 A; 'w. over' अधि-ष्ठा 1 P. -*v. i.* जागृ 2 P, (fig. also), रक्षार्थं जागृ. 2 अव-धा 3U, अवहित-सावधान-*a.* भू; 'w. for' अपेक्ष्, प्रतीक्ष्. -*s.* रक्षा, निरूपणं. 2 रक्षिन् *m.*, रक्षापुरुषः, रक्षितृ *m.* 3 जागरणं, जागरूकत्वं, दक्षता. 4 प्रहरः, यामः; 'w.-house' उद्घाटः; 'w.-man' रक्षिन् *m.*, रक्षकः; प्रहरिन् *m.*, वैबोधिकः, वैतालिकः; 'w.-word' प्रत्ययवाच् *f.* -FUL, *a.* जागरूक, दक्ष, सावधान, अप्रमत्त. 2 प्रजागर in comp., उन्निद्र.

WATER, *s.* जलं, अंबु-अंभस् *n.*, उदकं, वारि; पयस् *n.*, तोयं, सलिलं, नीरं, पानीयं, वार् *f.*, अप् *f.* (pl.),

पाथस् *n.*; 'land and w.' स्थलजले; 'place where w. is distributed' प्रपा, पानीयशालिका; 'by w.' जलेन, जलवर्त्मना; 'of first w.' अनर्घ्य; 'it can hold w.' प्रमाणकोटिं प्रवेष्टुमर्हति. 2 मूत्रं, प्रस्राव:; 'make w.' मूत्रोत्सर्गं कृ; 'w.-carrier' जलवाह:, उदवाह:, दृतिहार:; 'w.-closet' शौचकूप:; 'w.-course' जलमार्ग:, परि(री)वाह:; 'w.-fall' जलप्रपात:, निर्झर:; 'w.-ing place' प्रपा; 'w.-man' नाविक:, उदवाह:; 'w.-melon' गोडुंबं, सेटु *n.*, तरंबुजं, कालिंगं; 'w.-mill' जलचाल्यचक्रं, जलयंत्रं; 'w.-pot' घट:, कुंभ:, कलस:-श: ; *See* JAR ; 'w.-proof' जलाभेद्य; 'w.-snake' जलसर्प:; राजिल:; 'w.-spout' जलवज्र:; 'w.-wheel' घटीयंत्रं, उदंचनयंत्रं. –*v. t.* (जलेन) सिच् 6 P, प्लु c., उक्ष् 1 P. 2 जलं पा c. or दा 3 U. –*v. i.* जलं मुच् 6 P or स्रु c. or पत् c.; 'my eyes are w. ing' जललवस्यंदिनी नेत्रे. 2 लालायते (D.). –ED, *a.* जलभूयिष्ठ, अनूप; जलसिक्त; 'w. by rivers' नदीमातृक; 'w. by rain' देवमातृक. –Y, *a.* जलमय (यी *f.*), जलात्मक, जलरूप; 'w. shafts' वर्षशरा:, धाराशरसंपाता:. 2 जलाढ्य, बहूदक, जलभूयिष्ठ, अनूप, जलप्राय.

WAVE, *s.* तरंग:, ऊर्मि *f.*, वीचि-ची *f.*, कल्लोल:, भंग:, भंगि-गी *f.* –*v. t.* धू 5, 9 U or c. (धूनयति), वि-आ-°, चल् c., सं-,ईर् c. 2 उत्सृज् 6 P, परित्यज् 1 P. –*v. i.* इतस्तत: प्र-वि-चल् 1 P, धू pass. –Y, *a.* तरंगित, ऊर्मिमत्, कल्लोलमय (यी *f.*), भंगिमत्, भंगुर, उन्नतानत.

WAVER, *v. i.* दोलायते (D.), द्वैधीभू 1 P, सं-शी 2 A, विकृप् 1 A; 'his mind w. ed being at a loss which course to follow' इत्येकपक्षाश्रयाविक्लवत्वादासीत्स दोलाचलचित्तवृत्ति: (R. XIV. 34); oft. by अनवस्थित, अकृतनिश्चय also. –ING, *a.* अनिश्चित, दोलायमान, संदिग्ध, अनवस्थित.

WAX, *s.* लाक्षा (for sealing). 2 सि(शि)क्थं, सिक्थकं, मधूच्छिष्टं, मधुजं. 3 कर्णमलं, तोक्मं. –*v. i.* वृध् 1 A; 'w. ing and waning' वृद्धिक्षयौ; 'the moon w. ed' कलावृद्धो बभूव; 'w. ing hot' क्रोधेद्धो भूत्वा. 2 सिक्थकेन लिप् 6 P or अंज् 7 P. –EN,-Y, *a.* सिक्थमय (यी *f.*), शिक्थाक्त.

WAY, *s.* मार्ग:, पथिन् *m.*, अध्वन् *m.*, वर्त्मन् *n.*, पदवि-वी *f.*, अयनं, सरणि-णी *f.*, पद्धति-ती *f.*, पया; 'step in a wrong w.' अपथे पदमर्पयंति (R. IX. 74). 2 अंतरं, मार्गं, पर्यंत:; 'a little w.' ईषद्दूरं, स्तोकांतरं. 3 उपाय:, युक्ति *f.* 4 प्रकार:, विधि:, रीति *f.*, क्रम:, मार्ग:; 'a good way' अतिपंथा:, सुपंथा:, सत्पथ:, सुपथ:; 'a bad or wrong w.' अपंथा:; अपथ:, व्यध्व:, दुरध्व:, विमार्ग:, विपथ:, कदध्वा, का(कु)पथ:; 'a place where four w. s meet' शृंगाटक:, चतुष्पथं; 'a dreary w.' प्रांतरं, दूरशून्योऽध्वा; 'difficult w.' कांतार:-रं, दुर्गमं वर्त्म, दुर्गसंचर:, संक्रम:. 5 (With numerals) Ex. by धा; 'in two w. s' द्विधा; शतधा &c.; 'a long w. off' सुदूरं; 'on the w.' अंतरा, अंतरे; 'stand or come in the (one's) w.' परिपंथीभू, अंतराय: &c. ('Obstacle', q. v.) भू; (lit.) नयनपथं-विषयं-या 2 P; 'in this, that w.' इत्थं-एवं, तथा; 'by w. of example' निदर्शनद्वारा-रूपेण ; 'lead the w.' मार्गं आदिश् 6 P or दृश् c.; 'this w.' 'this w.' इत इत:; 'by w. of' द्वारेण, रूपेण ; 'make w.' अपसर, अपेहि, अंतरं दीयतां; 'in every w.' सर्वथा; 'in another w.' अन्यथा; 'w.-farer' पथिक:; *See* TRAVELLER; 'w.-lay' पथि निभृतं प्रतीक्ष् 1 A, (लुंठनार्थं, वधार्थं), पथि अवस्कंद् 1 P; 'w.-ward' प्रतीप, स्वैरिन्, दुर्ललित; *See* OBSTINATE; 'w.-worn' अध्वश्रांत, अध्वसंजातखेद.

WEAK, *a.* दुर्बल, अशक्त, अबल, क्षीणबल, बल-शक्तिहीन, नि:सत्त्व, निस्तेजस्, निर्वीर्य, अल्प-बल-शक्ति. 2 (In mind) मंद, अल्पधी, विकलचित्त; 'w. point or side' छिद्रं, रंध्रं, दोष:, मर्मस्थानं. –EN, *v. t.* दुर्बलीकृ 8 U, शक्ति-बलं ह्र 1 P, शक्तिं अव-सद् c. or अपचि 5 U; 'to be w. ed' अपचि pass.; *See* WASTE, LEAN. –ED, *a.* हतबल, क्षीणशक्ति, ह्रस्व (form). –NESS, *s.* दौर्बल्यं, बल-शक्ति-क्षय:-नाश:, असामर्थ्यं, बल-सत्त्व-हानि *f.* 2 दोष:, (यौवनदोषा:); छिद्रं.

WEAL, *s.* हितं, कल्याणं, क्षेमं, श्रेयस् *n.*, भद्रं, कुशलं; 'w. and woe' शुभाशुभं.

WEALTH, *s.* धनं, द्रव्यं, वसु:, *n.*, अर्थ:, वित्तं, द्रविणं, संपद्, हिरण्यं, विभव:, वैभवं, संपत्ति *f.*, ऐश्वर्यं, रै *f.*, रि(रु)क्थं, द्युम्नं, स्वापतेयं; 'w. in cattle' गोधनं. –Y, *a.* धनिन्, धनिक, धन-वित्त-वत् &c., सधन, वित्तसंपन्न, सश्रीक, वसुमत्, अर्थयुक्त, विभवशालिन् and sim. comp.

WEAN, *v. t.* स्तन्यं त्यज् c. or हा c. (हापयति) or विसृज् c. 2 विरक्तीं-विमुखी-कृ 8 U; *See* SEPARATE. –ING, *s.* स्तन्यत्याग:. 2 विरक्ति *f.*, वैराग्यं, संगत्याग:.

WEAPON, *s.* शस्त्रं, अस्त्रं, आयुधं, प्रहरणं, हेति *f.*

WEAR, *v. t.* परि-धा 3 U, धृ 1 P, 10, भृ 3 U, वस् 2 A. 2 (Away) क्षि 5 P, नश् c., विलुप् c., प्रमृज् 2 P or c.; घर्षणेन नश् c. 3 जीर्णीकृ 8 U. 4 अव-,सद् c., खिद् c., क्लम् c., ग्लै c.; *See* FATIGUE. –*v. i.* (Away) क्षि pass., अवसद् 1 P, अपचि pass. 2 (By use) जॄ 4 P, जर्जरीभू 1 P; 'when the night had almost worn away' क्षीणभूयिष्ठायां क्षपायां; 'w. off' अपगम् 1 P, नश् 4 P, क्षि pass.; 'w. out' जीर्णी-जर्जरी-कृ, अपचि; (*v. i.*) जॄ, ज्या 9 P, जर्जरीभू. –*s.* परि-,क्षय:, अ-

पचय:, उपयोग:. 2 घर्षणं. 3 सेतु:, आलि *f.* -ER, *s.* धारिन्, भृत् in comp. -ING, *a.* धारिन्, भृत्, धर in comp. 2 परिधानयोग्य.

WEARY, *v. t.* आयस् c., क्लम् c., खिद् c. -*v. i.* आयस् 1, 4 P, क्लम् 1, 4 P. -IED, *a.* खिन्न, क्लांत, परिश्रांत, म्लान, जातखेद; 'w. of' निर्विण्ण, निर्वेदमापन्न; *See* DISGUSTED; 'w. of life' जीविताद्‌द्विजमान: (Mal. 3). -INESS, *s.* क्लम:, श्रम: खेद:, आयास:; *See* FATIGUE,-ED &. -ISOME, *a.* श्रमखेद-जनन (नी *f.*), आयासकर (रीं *f.*), श्रमावह, कष्टप्रद.

WEASEL, *s.* नकुल:, बभ्रु:, अंगूष:.

WEATHER, *s.* काल:, दिनं; 'bad w.' दुर्दिनं; 'good w.' सुदिनं; 'if the w. be fine' यदि दुर्दिनं न स्यात्; 'w.-beaten' वाताहत, प्रभंजनोपहत; 'w.-wise' वातादिलक्षणविद्, कालविद्. -*v. t.* तॄ 1 P, प्रत्यव-स्था 1 A; पारं गम् 1 P.

WEAVE, *v. t.* वे 1 P; वप् 1 P, गुं(गु)फ् 6 P, वि-,रच् 10. -ER, *s.* तंतुवाय:-प:, कुविंद:, पटकार:. -ING, *s.* वाय:-प:, तंतु-तंत्र-वाय:, ऊति-स्यूति *f.*, पटनिर्माणं, पटकर्म.

WEB, *s.* जालं, तंत्र-तंतु-संतति *f.*; (of the eye) पटलं; 'w.-footed' जालपाद.

WED, *v. t.* वि-उद्-वह् 1 P, परि-णी 1 P. -DED, *a.* ऊढ, परिणीत. 2 आसक्त, अवलंबिन्, रक्षिन्, (to an opinion); 'w.-lock' विवाह:; 'a wife married in w.-lock' धर्मपत्नी, सहधर्मचारिणी; *See* MARRIAGE.

WEDGE, *s.* कील:, शंकु:. -*v. t.* संपीड् 10, संबाध् 1 A, संमृद् 9 P.

WEDNESDAY, *s.* बुधवासर:.

WEED, *s.* कक्ष:, तृणादिकं, स्तंब:; (fig.) गतिरोधनं, प्रसरस्तंभनं. 2 (W. s) वासस् *n.*; *See* GARMENT; 'widow's w. s' क्लिष्टनिवसनं, चीरं. -*v. t.* (Out) (कक्षं) उद्-हृ 1 P, निर्दो 4 P, उत्पट् 10. -ER, *s.* निर्दातृ *m.*, कक्षोद्धारिन्. -Y, *a.* कक्षपूर्ण-बहुल.

WEEK, *s.* सप्ताह:, सप्तदिनं; 'w.-day' वार:. -LY *a.* साप्ताहिक (की *f.*), सप्तदैनिक (की *f.*). -*adv.* प्रतिसप्ताहं.

WEEN, *v. i.* मन् 4 A ; *See* THINK; 'over w.-ing' अत्यंताभिमानिन्.

WEEP, *v. i.* रुद् 2 P, वि-लप् 1 P, अश्रूणि पत् c. or विमुच् 6 P, आ-,क्रंद् 1 P; *See* CRY, LAMENT -ING, *s.* रुदितं, रोदनं, विलाप:, आक्रंदनं, क्रंदितं, अश्रुपात:. -*a.* साश्रु, अश्रुलोचन.

WEIGH, *v. t.* तुल्-तूल् 10, तुलायां धृ 10. 2 (In mind) वि-मृश् 6 P, आलोच् 10, वि-चर् c., वि-गण् 10; *See* THINK. 3 (Anchor) उत्तुल्; 'w. down' अभि-भू 1 P, आकुलीकृ; 'w. duly' परिच्छिद् 7 P, सूक्ष्मं निरूप् 10. -*v. i.* Ex. by 'Weight' q. v.; 'what does it w.' किंभारमिदं; किं भारपरिमाणं; 'w. upon' पीड् 10, बाध् 1 A; *See* AFFLICT; 'w. with' मन् pass.; 'dress w. s much with them' वेषस्तैर्बहु मन्यते. -ING, *s.* तोलनं, विगणनानं. —WEIGHT, *s.* मानं, भार:, तोल:, परिमाणं, भारपरिमाणं, गुरुत्वं. 2 गुरुत्वं, गौरवं, प्रभाव:, भार:. 3 भार:, धुर् *f.*; 'of little w.' लघ्वर्थ, लघुप्रभाव, अगुरु. -Y, *a.* गुरु, महत्, सप्रभाव; सप्रमाण.

WEIR, *s.* बंध:, योग:.

WELCOME, *a.* स्वागत. 2 शुभ, इष्ट, हित; प्रिय, अभिमत, सुखद. -*v. t.* स्वागतं व्याहृ 1 P, सभाज् 10, अभिनंद् 1 P, सत्कृ 8 U, पूज् 10; (आश्रममृगैरभिनंदितागमनेषु समीरेषु Ka. 49). -*interj.* स्वागतं (with dat.). -*s.* स्वागतं, सभाजनं, अभिनंदनं.

WELD, *v. t. See* UNITE.

WELFARE, *s.* हितं, कल्याणं, क्षेमं, कुशलं, श्रेयस् *n.*, भद्रं, मंगलं, सुखं, भूति *f.*, शिवं, सुस्थिति *f.*

WELKIN, *s.* नभस् *n.*; *See* SKY.

WELL, *s.* वापी, कूप:, प्रहि:, अंधु:, दीर्घिका (large w.), उदपानं; 'covering of a w.' वि(वी)नाह:; 'reservoir near a w.' आहाव:, निपानं, उपकूपजलाशय:. 2 गुप्ति *f.* -*a.* कुशलिन्, स्वस्थ, सुस्थशरीर, निरामय, नीरोग, कल्य; *See* HEALTHY. 2 कुशल, क्षेम, सुखिन्; oft. by कुशलं; अपि कुशलमस्या: प्रजापालस्य मातु: (U. 4) 'is she w.'; 'got w. again' पुन: प्रकृतिस्थोऽभवत्, प्रकृतिमापन्न:; 'know that we are doing w. in every respect' सर्वत्र नौ वार्तमवेहि (R. v. 13). -*adv.* सु pr., (सुकृत, सुदर्शन &c.); सुष्ठु, साधु, सम्यक्; 'w. said' साधूक्त, सूक्त; 'w. off' सुस्थित *a.*, वित्तवत्, सुस्थ; 'you might as w. have kept all (fruits)' सर्वेषां रक्षणेपि न तव कश्चिद्दोषोऽभविष्यत्. -*interj.* बाढं; तथा; 'saying very w.' युज्यते, बाढं, तथेति उक्त्वा; 'very w.' भवतु; 'w. then' तेन हि. 2 (As expletive) भवतु, अस्तु, gen. by तावत्; 'w. we go away now' साधयामस्तावदधुना; 'w.-behaved' साधुशील, सुवृत्त; 'w.-being' हितं, कुशलं; *See* WELFARE; 'w.-born' कुलीन, सत्कुलजात; 'w.-done' साधु साधु; 'w.-informed' बहुज्ञ, बहुश्रुत; 'w.-meaning' सदाशय, हितबुद्धि; 'w. nigh; *See* NEARLY; 'w.-read' अधीतिन्, शास्त्रपारंगत, बहुदृश्वन्; 'w.-wisher' हितकाम:, हितैषिन् *m.*, प्रियैषी.

WELTER, *v. i.* लुट् 6 P, लुट् 4 P; *See* ROLL.

WEN, *s.* मांसार्बुदं.

WENCH, *s.* बंधकी, पुंश्चली, दुर्वृत्ता. 2 कन्या, तरुणी. -*v. i.* Fornicate, q. v.

WEND, *v. t.* (One's way) गम् 1 P, चल् 1 P; *See*

Go; 'here he w. s his way' इत एवाभिवर्तते.

WEST, *s.* प्रतीची, पश्चिमा, वारुणी. –*a.*,-ERLY, –ERN, *a.* पाश्चात्य, प्रतीच्य, चरम, अपर. 2 पश्चिमाभिमुख (खी *f.*). –WARDS, *adv.* प्रतीचीमभि, प्रतीच्यभिमुखं, पश्चिमादिशि.

WET, *a.* आर्द्र, क्लिन्न, सिक्त, उक्षित, उन्न, जलार्द्र. –*v. t.* क्लिद् c., आर्द्रीकृ 8 U, आर्द्रयति (D.); *See* MELT. –*s.* आर्द्रता, तेमः, क्लेदः. 2 दुर्दिनं; 'w.-nurse' स्तन्यदायिनी, धात्री, उपमाता.

WETHER, *s.* छिन्नवृषणो मेषः.

WHACK, *v. t. See* STRIKE.

WHALE, *s.* तिमिः, तिमिंगिलः.

WHARF, *s.* घट्टः, तरस्थानं. –AGE, *s.* तरपण्यं-मूल्यं, घट्टदेयं शुल्कं.

WHAT, *pron.* किं (कः-का-किं), किं in comp.; 'w. then' ततः किं, किं तर्हि; 'w. is he doing now' स (राजा) किमारंभः संप्रति (U. 2); 'w. is his name' किंनामासौ ; 'w. else' अथ किं; 'w. is that to me' किं मम तेन; 'w. though' यद्यपि. 2 यद्यद्. –*interj.* कथं, आः, किं, ननु. –EVER,-SOEVER, *a.* यद्-यद्. 2 यत्किम्, यत्किंचित् ; 'to w. person' यस्मै कस्मैचित्पुरुषाय; यो वा को वा भवाम्यहं, &c.

WHEAT, *s.* गोधूमः, सुमनः. –EN, *a.* गोधूममय, (*s.*) in comp.

WHEEDLE, *v. t.* चाटूक्तिभिः प्र-नृ c. or वंच् 10 or लल् 10; *See* FLATTER.

WHEEL, *s.* चक्रं, रथांगं, मंडलं. –*v. i.* परि-भ्रम् 1, 4 P, परा-परि-आ-वृत् 1 A, मंडलाकारेण भ्रम्. –*v. t.* व्यावृत् c., भ्रम् c. –ED, *a.* चक्रिन्, चक्रयुक्त. –WHEEL-WRIGHT, *s.* रथकारः, चक्रकारः.

WHEEZE, *v. i.* कृच्छ्रेण श्वस् 2 P.

WHELP, *s.* शावः-वकः, शिशुः, किशोरः.

WHEN, *adv.* यदा; by loc. abs.; 'w. the speech was over' वचस्यवसिते तस्मिन्. 2 कदा; 'w.-ever,-soever' यदा यदा, यदा कदाचित्. –WHENCE, *adv.* यतः, यस्मात्. 2 कुतः, कस्मात्.

WHERE, *adv.* क्व, कुत्र. 2 यत्र; 'w.-ever' यत्र यत्र; यत्र कुत्रापि, यत्र कुत्राचित्; 'w.-as' यतः, विपर्यये तु; 'w.-by' येन; 'w.-fore' यदर्थं, यतः, येन, किमर्थं, कस्य हेतोः; 'w.-in', 'w.-to' यत्र; 'w.-upon' यदनंतरं, तदनु.

WHET, *v. t.* तिज् c., नि-,शो 4 P, क्ष्णु 2 P. –*s.*, –STONE, *s.* शाणः-णी, शाणाश्मन् *m.*

WHETHER, *pron.* कतरः-रा-रत्. –*conj.* किं followed by वा, उत, आहो or आहोस्वित् (for 'or'), 'w. he do that or not' स तत्करोतु न करोतु वा.

WHEY, *s.* मस्तु *n.*, दधिमंडं.

WHICH, *pron. a.* यत् (यः-या-यत्). 2 किं (कः-का-किं); 'w. of two' यतर, कतर; 'w. of many' यतम, कतम; 'w.-ever' ex. by repeating (1).

WHIFF, *s.* फूत्कारः, फूत्कृतं.

WHILE, *s.* क्षणः, मुहूर्तः, कालः, समयः; 'for a w.' कंचित्कालं, क्षणं; 'after a long w.' चिरेण; 'not worth w.' निष्फल, निरर्थक, न उपयुक्त; 'worth w.' उपयुक्त. –*conj.*, WHILST, यदा, यावत् (followed by तावत्); gen. by pres. part.; ग्रामं गच्छंस्तृणं स्पृशति 'w. going' &c. –*v. t.* (away) क्षिप् 6 P, गम् c., हृ 1 P, वि-नुद्.

WHIM, *s.* कामचारः, कामवृत्ति *f.*, छंदः, छंदस् *n.*, चापल्यं, मनोलौल्यं, लहरी, चित्ततरंगः; 'at one's w.' स्वच्छंदेन, स्वेच्छया; 'acting according to another's w.' छंदोनुवृत्ति *f.* —WHIMSICAL, *a.* कामचारिन्, स्वैरिन्, स्वैर, स्वच्छंदानुवर्तिन्, स्वच्छंद; चपल, लोल, अनवस्थित.

WHIMPER, *v. i.* बालकवत् रुद् 2 P or क्रंद् 1 P.

WHINE, *v. i. See* MURMUR.

WHIP, *s.* कशा-षा, प्रतोदः, प्रतिष्कषः-शः. –*v. t.* कशया प्र-हृ 1 P or तड् 10 or चुद् 10 or दंड् 10 or आहन् 2 U. –PING, *s.* कशाघातः-ताडनं-प्रहारः; 'deserving w.' कश्य, कशार्ह.

WHIRL, *v. i.* घूर्ण् 6 P, 1 A, परि-,भ्रम् 1, 4 P. –*v. t.* घूर्ण c., भ्रम् c. (भ्रमयति). –*s.*,-ING, *s.* भ्रमणं, घूर्णनं, भ्रमि *f.*, आवृत्ति *f.*; 'w.-pool' आवर्तः, भ्रमिः, भ्रमः, जलावर्तः, जलगुल्मः; 'w.-wind' चक्रवातः, वातावर्तः; वात्या, वातभ्रमः.

WHISK, *v. t.* अतिशीघ्रं चल् c. or विक्षिप् 6 P. –*s.* लघुक्षेपः. 2 चामरं (for flies).

WHISKERS, *s.* गंडलोमन् *n.*, गुंफः.

WHISPER, *v.* नीचैः-उपांशु-वद् 1 P; कर्णे जप् 1 P or कथ् 10 or ख्या 2 P; कर्णे उप-जप्; 'w. aside' जनांतिकं वद्. –*s.*,-ING, *s.* कर्णवादः, उपांशुवादः, कर्णेजपः; जपः-पनं; 'in a w.' उपांशु, जनांतिकं, नीचस्वरेण. –ER, *s.* कर्णे(र्ण)जपः-कथकः.

WHISTLE, *s.* शीशशब्दः. 2 वंशः-शी. –*v. i.* शीशशब्दं कृ 8 U.

WHIT, *s.* लेशः, लवः, गंधः, अणुः; 'not a w.' न मनागपि, न स्तोकमपि, नाल्पमपि.

WHITE, *a.* शुक्ल, श्वेत, धवल, शुभ्र, सित, गौर (री *f.*), शुचि, अवदात, विशद; धौत, पांडुर, अ-वि-मल. –*s.* श्वेतवर्णः, शुक्लवर्णः, शुक्लः; श्वेतः, सितः, &c. ; 'dressed in w.' श्वेतवासो दधानि. –EN, *v. t.* धवलीकृ 8 U, धवलयति (D.) &c. –*v. i.* धवलीभू 1 P, धवलायते (D.). –ISH, *a.* आपांडु. –NESS, *s.* शुक्लता, धावल्यं, शुभ्रता, धवलिमन्-शुक्लिमन् *m.* –WHITE-WASH, *v. t.* सुधया लिप् 6 P or धवलीकृ; 'a house w. ed' सुधाभवनं. –*s.* सुधा, सुधालेपः. –WHITES, *s.* श्वेतप्रदरः.

WHITHER, *adv.* कुत्र, क्र. 2 यत्र.

WHITLOW, *s.* नखंपचः, चिप्यं, नखव्रणं.

WHO-EVER, &c. *See* WHICH &c.

WHOLE, *a.* सकल, समग्र, कृत्स्न, अखिल, समस्त, सर्व, अखंड, निखिल, विश्व, अशेष, निःशेष, पूर्ण, अनून. 2 (Number) अभिन्न. -*s.* साकल्यं, कात्स्न्यं, सामग्र्यं, समासः; 'on the w.' एवं च, एतावता, समासतः, समासेन; 'the w. of' ex. by (*a.*). -LY, *adv.* समग्रं, साकल्येन, अशेषेण, निरवशेषं. सर्वथा, सर्वतः-शः, सर्वभावेन, एकांततः. -WHOLESALE, *a.* Ex. by स्तूप in comp., समस्त (विक्रयः); 'w. dealer' स्तूपविक्रयिन् ; 'w. buying' समस्तराविक्रयः.

WHOLESOME, *a.* पथ्य, आरोग्यावह; हितावह; *See* SALUTARY.

WHOOP, *s.* सिंहनादः, क्ष्वेडा.

WHORE, *s. See* PROSTITUTE; 'w.'s son' वेश्यापुत्रः; 'w.-monger' भुजंगः, विटः. -DOM, *s.* वेश्यावृत्ति *f.*-प्रसक्ति *f.*

WHY, *adv.* किं, कुतः, कस्मात्, किमर्थं, किन्निमित्तं, केन हेतुना; 'w. do you do so' एवं करणे कस्तव हेतुः. 2 ननु; 'w. you yourself are before me' ननु भवानेव ममाग्रे वर्तते (S. 2).

WICK, *s.* दशा, वर्ति *f.*, वर्तिका, तैलिनी.

WICKED, *a.* (Of persons) दुष्ट, दुर्जात, दुरात्मन्, पाप, शठ, दुराचार, खल, पापकर्मन्, दुर्वृत्त, नृशंस, पापात्मन्, पापचरित, अधार्मिक (की *f.*), दुश्चरित्र. 2 (Of things) दुष्ट, पाप in comp., दुर् pr.; 'w. policy' दुर्णीतिः; *See* SINFUL. -LY, *adv.* दुष्टतया, दुर्वृत्ततया, खलवत्. -NESS, *s.* दुष्टता, दौर्जन्यं, दौरात्म्यं, पापं, दुष्कृतं-ति *f.*, पापकर्म, दुराचारः, अनाचारः.

WICKER, *a.* वैणव (वी *f.*), वैदल (ली *f.*); 'w.-work' वैदलं.

WIDE, *a.* विस्तीर्ण, विशाल, उरु, विपुल, पृथु; *See* BROAD; 'w. of the mark' लक्ष्यभ्रष्ट-च्युत, अप्रास्ताविक (की *f.*). -*adv.*, -LY, *adv.* विपुलं, सर्वत्र, सु-अति-बहु pr.; 'w. known' सुविख्यात; 'w. awake' सुप्रबुद्ध; 'with eyes w. open' उत्फुल्लनयन. -EN, *v. t.* पृथूकृ 8 U, विशालीकृ, प्रथ् 10. -WIDTH, *s.* विस्तारः, व्यासः, परिणाहः, विशालता.

WIDOW, *s.* विधवा, अ-गत-भर्तृका, विश्वस्ता, अनाथा, रंडा; 'child-w.' बालविधवा. -ED, *a.* अनाथा, नष्टभर्तृका. -ER, *s.* मृतपत्नीकः, गतभार्यः. -HOOD, *s.* वैधव्यं, वैधव्यदशा.

WIELD, *v. t.* (हस्तेन) भृ 3 U, धृ 1 P, 10, प्र-उप-युज् 7 A, 10. 2 (A state &c.), प्र-,शास् 2 P, निर्वह् c. ; राज्यधुरां वह् 1 P. -Y, *a.* सुप्रयोज्य ; (body) उत्थानयोग्य (S. 2).

WIFE, *s.* भार्या, पत्नी, जाया, वधूः, कलत्रं, दार *m.* (pl.), स्त्री, परिग्रहः, गृहिणी, गेहिनी, सहधर्मिणी, दयिता, वल्लभा, प्रिया, कांता, रमणी, क्षेत्रं, गृहाः (pl.); 'a rival w.' सपत्नी ; 'taking a w.' दारपरिग्रहः-क्रिया ; 'a w. whose husband has gone abroad' प्रोषितभर्तृका.

WIG, *s.* उपकेशः, कृत्रिमकेशः.

WIGHT, *s.* माणवकः, जंतुः, प्राणिन् *m.*

WILD, *a.* वन्य, वनजात, आरण्यक, वन-अरण्य in comp.; 'a w. mountain' कांतारमध्यवर्ती-वनांतर्गतः-पर्वतः; वनपशुः, वनगजः, वनपुष्पं &c. 2 हिंस्र, क्रूर, क्रव्याद्. 3 उन्मत्त, अतिव्याकुल ; 'w. with anger' क्रोधोन्मत्त; 'w. with joy' हर्षोन्मत्त, हर्षनिर्भर. 4 प्रचंड, तीव्र ; दुर्दांत, अनियंत्रण, उद्दामवृत्ति, उच्छृंखल ; 'w. storm' प्रचंडप्रकंपनः. 5 अयुक्तिक, अनुपपन्न, निरर्थक ; *See* ABSURD. -ERNESS, *s.* वनं, अरण्यं ; *See* FOREST. 2 मरुः-,भूमि *f.*, धन्वन् *m.* -LY, *adv.* उन्मत्तवत्, प्रचंडं, सोन्मादं, उच्छृंखलं. -NESS, *s.* वन्यता, रौद्रता, उन्मादः, &c.

WILE, *s.* छलं, कपटं, वंचनं, माया, छद्मन् *n.* -WILY, *a.* भूरिमाय, मायाविन्, समाय, छद्मपर, कापटिक-छाद्मिक (की *f.*), सकपट.

WILL, *v.* संक्लृप् c., निर्दिश् 6 P, निश्चि 5 U, निर्णी 1 P. 2 Wish q. v. 3 (As auxiliary) by Futures or Pot. mood. -*s.* संकल्पः, संकल्प-इच्छा-शक्ति *f.* 2 कामः, इच्छा, अभिलाषः, आकांक्षा, इष्टं; 'god's w. be done' ईश्वरेच्छा बलीयसी, प्रभवति भगवान् विधिः; 'against one's w.' बलात्, हठात्, अकामतः; 'would have her w.' आत्माभिप्राये निर्बंधपरासीत्; 'at w.' स्वेच्छया, यथाकामं, स्वैरं, काम in comp.; 'subject to the w. of another' परतंत्रवश. 3 इच्छापत्रं. -FUL, *a.* कामतः कृत. 2 स्वैरिन्, काम-स्वेच्छा-चारिन्, स्वैरवृत्त-गामिन्, *See* WANTON.-FULLY, *adv.* कामतः, इच्छापूर्वकं, स्वैरं, बुद्ध्या, जानत्- *a.* अपि. -FULNESS, *s.* कामचारः, स्वेच्छाचारः, यदृच्छा, स्वैरिता, स्वाच्छंद्यं.-ING, *a.* इच्छु, सकाम, उद्यत; oft. by desid. 2 इष्ट, अनुमत, यथेप्सित. -INGLY, *adv.* प्रकामं, स्वेच्छया, कामतः, स्वेच्छापूर्वं. -WOULD (that) Ex. by अपि नाम; अपि नामाहमप्यात्मनोनुरूपं वरं लभेयेति (S. 1); 'w. I had loved him more' वरं तस्मिन्नहमधिकतरं स्निग्धोऽभूवं; यदि...अभविष्यं तर्हि अहो शोभनमापतिष्यत्.

WIN, *v. t.* वि-जि 1 A, विजयिन् *a.* भू; 'won the battle' युद्धे जयमाप, समरविजयी बभूव; 'who is said to w.' यो विजयीति गण्यते-मन्यते. 2 लभ् 1 A, प्राप् 5 P; *See* GET. 3 आकृष् 1 P, प्र-विलुभ् c., *See* ATTRACT; 'w. over' स्वपक्षं ग्रह् c., अनुयायिन् *a.* कृ.-NER, *s.* जयिन् *m.*,जेतृ *m.*-NING, *s.* जयः. 2 लाभः, अर्जितं.-*a.* हृदयहारिन्, चित्ताकार्षिन्.

WINCE, *v. i.* वि-,कंप् 1 A, स्फुर् 6 P ; 'he did

not w.' स भयचकितो नाभवत्; *See* START.

WIND, *s.* वातः, वायुः, पवनः, पवमानः, अनिलः, समीरणः, मारुतः, मरुत् *m.*, मातरिश्वन्, श्वसनः, स्पर्शनः, गंधव(वा)हः, आशुगः. 2 (In stomach) वातः, वायुः. 3 श्वासः; 'w.-fall' वायुपातः; (fig.) अलभ्यलाभः; 'w.-lass' उत्तोलनी; 'w.-mill' वायुचाल्यं चक्रं, वायुपेषणी. —*v. i.* वक्र-कुटिलं-गम् or सृप् 1 P, जिह्मं-या 2 P; 'the river runs w. ing for a koss' क्रोशं कुटिला नदी (S. K.). 2 Turn, q. v. —*v. t.* परि-आ-वृत् c. 2 पूर् 10 (मारुतेन), ध्मा 1 P. 2 (Up) संपुटीकृ 8 U, पिंडीकृ, उप-, सं-हृ 1 P; अव-सो 4 P; (hair) सं-हृ, सं-यम् c., (संयमय केशपाशं Ka. 84.). —ING, *a.* वक्र, कुटिल, जिह्म. —*s.* वक्रं, वंकः, पुटभेदः. —WARD, *adv.* वाताभिमुखं. —Y, *a.* वातमय (यी *f.*), वातुल. —WINDOW, *s.* वातायनं, जालं, गवाक्षः.

WINDPIPE, *s.* श्वासनालिका.

WINE, *s.* मद्यं, द्राक्षारस-आसवः; मधु *n.*, माध्वीकं; मदिरा, सुरा; 'w.-bibber' मद्यपः, सुरापः; 'w.-seller' मद्यविक्रयिन्, शौंडिकः.

WING, *s.* पक्षः, पत्रं, पतत्रं, गरुत् *m.*, छदः, पक्ष्मन् *n.*; 'root of a w.' पक्षति *f.*, पक्षमूलं; 'to be on the w.' डी 1 A; 'under the w. of' आश्रित- *a.* 2 (Of army &c.) पक्षः, दलं, पार्श्वदलं. —*v. t.*, 'w. the way' अध्वक्रमणं कृ 8 U. —ED, *a.* पक्षिन्, पतत्रिन्.

WINK, *v. i.* नि-मिष् 6 P, नि-मील् 1 P, पक्ष्म संकुच् 1 P. 2 संकेतं-संज्ञां-कृ 8 U (नेत्रेण); 'w. at' उपेक्ष् 1 A, न गण् 10. —*s.* निमि(मे)षः, निमीलनं, पक्ष्मसंकोचः. 2 नेत्रसंज्ञा, अक्षिसंकेतः.

WINNOW, *v. t.* वि-, शुध् c., पू 9 U, बहुलीकृ 8 U, प्रस्फुट् c.; (fig.) परीक्ष् 1 A; *See* DISCRIMINATE. —ER, *s.* पावकः. —ING, *s.* पवनं, प्रस्फोटनं; 'w. ing basket' शूर्पः-र्पं, प्रस्फोटनं.

WINTER, *s.* हेमंतः, शिशिरः, तुषारकालः, हिमागमः, हिम-शीत-कालः. —WINTRY, *a.* (*s.*) in comp.; हैमंत (ती), हैम (मी *f.*). 2 शीत, शिशिर.

WIPE, *v. t.* प्र-परि-मृज् 2 P or c., प्र-क्षल् 10, निर्घृष् 1 P, सं-मृद् 9 P; *See* WASH; 'w.-away,' 'w. out' प्रमृज्, (स्वभावलोलेत्ययशः प्रमृष्टं R. VI. 41), अप-अव-मृज्. —*s.* मार्जनं, प्रक्षालनं. 2 प्रहारः. —ER, *s.* मार्जनी, प्रक्षालनी.

WIRE, *s.* तंत्रं, तंत्री, तारः-रा, धातुसूत्रं, लोहतारा-सूत्रं-तंतुः. —*v. t.* तारायंत्रेण प्रेष् c. —Y, *a.* तंत्रमय (यी *f.*).

WISE, *a.* प्र(प्रा)ज्ञ, विज्ञ, विदग्ध, ज्ञानवत्, पंडित, प्रज्ञावत्, धीमत्, विवेकिन्, सुधी, धीर, मति-बुद्धि-मत्, मनीषिन्, विद्वस्; *See* LEARNED also. 2 (Of acts) सु in comp.; ज्ञानप्रयुक्त, वैदग्ध्यमूलक; 'w. saying' सुभाषितं; 'w. step' साधुमार्गः. —*s.* प्रकारः; *See* MANNER; 'in this w.' एवं, इत्थं. —LY, *adv.* प्रज्ञया, ज्ञानेन, सविवेकं, सम्यक्, सुसमीक्ष्य, सुष्ठु, प्राज्ञवत्. —WISDOM, *s.* प्रज्ञा, ज्ञानं, वैदग्ध्यं, बुद्धि *f.*, धीः, विवेकः, वैदुष्यं, पांडित्यं, धीरता, मनीषा. —WISEACRE, *s.* पंडितंमन्यः.

WISH, *v. t.* इष् 6 P, स्पृह् 10 (with dat.), सं-ईह् 1 A, वांछ् 1 P, आ-कांक्ष् 1 P, अभिलष् 1, 4 P, कम् 1 A, वश् 2 P; oft. by desid. forms; जिगमिषति 'w. es to go;' जिघृक्षति &c.; 'w. ill to' असूयति (D.) (with dat.); अमंगलं आशंस् 1 A; 'I w. no evil to any' न मे कस्मिन्नपि द्रोहबुद्धिः-द्वेषभावः; 'I w. I could see him again' अपि नाम तं पुनरपि पश्येयं; 'he had nothing left to w. for' न किमपि तस्य स्पृहणीयमासीत्. —*s.* इच्छा, मनोरथः, स्पृहा, ईहा, कामः, इष्टं, वांछितं, अभिलाषः; वांछा, कांक्षा.

WIST, *s.* शुष्कतृणकर्षकः.

WISTFUL, *a.* *See* EAGER.

WIT, *s.* बुद्धि-मति *f.*, मेधा, धीः; *See* INTELLECT. 2 बुद्धितीक्ष्णता, बुद्धिविलासः-चातुर्यं; 'was at his w.'s end' किंकर्तव्यतामूढः-कुंठितमतिः-आसीत्, निरुत्तरीकृतः. 3 (Person) वाक्चतुरः, नर्मज्ञः, परिहासकथः, नर्मभाषी. 4 रसः, नर्मन् *n.*, वैदग्ध्यं, सारस्यं, नर्म-रसिक-उक्ति *f.*, नर्मालापः-भाषणं; 'to w.' तद्यथा. —TY, *a.* नर्मवेदिन्, नर्मभाषिन्, सरस, विदग्ध, रसयुक्त; परिहासजनन (नी *f.*); 'w. speech' परिहासालापः, नर्मवाक्यं, नर्मालापः.

WITCH, *s.* डाकिनी, मायाविनी, कुहकिनी, मायिनी. —ERY, 'w.-craft', *s.* माया, अभिचारः.

WITH, *prep.* Gen. ex. by instr. 2 (Manner) by instr. प्रीत्या 'w. affection'; by comp. with स; सहर्षं, सभयं &c.; पूर्व, पूर्वकं in comp.; 'w. respect' मानपुरःसरं, आदरपूर्वकं. 3 (Accompaniment) by Bah. comp.; 'Madana w. Rati' रतिसहायो मदनः; सकृष्णो रामः; gen. by समं, साकं, सार्धं, सह, सहितं, with instr.; 'send the book w. Rama' रामहस्ते पुस्तकं प्रेषय. 4 (With verbs) सं; 'to live w.' सं-वस्. 5 (On the side of) पक्षे. 6 (In the opinion of) मतेन, मते, (तव मतेनाकिंचित्करमिदं); 'w. all' अनादृत्य; *See* 'in spite of' under SPITE. —AL, *adv.* समं, तथा च, अपि च, तथैव.

WITHDRAW, *v. t.* प्रति-, सं-हृ 1 P, अपाकृष् 1 P, अप-नी 1 P, प्रत्यव-हृ; 'w. s the world into himself' आत्मन्येवाखिलं विश्वं संहरति. —*v. i.* अप-क्रम् 1 U, 4 P, अप-सृ 1 P, अप-गम् 1 P, परावृत् 1 A; *See* RETIRE. —AL, *s.* संहारः, संहरणं, अपनयनं, अपक्रमः-मणं.

WITHER, *v. i.* म्लै 1 P, ग्लै 1 P, वि-शॄ pass., मद

1 P, क्षि pass. –*v. t.* नश् c., शॄ c.; *See* FADE. –ED, *a.* म्लान, ग्लान, विशीर्ण, शुष्क, जीर्ण.

WITHERS, *s.* स्कंधदेशः, स्कंधः.

WITHHOLD, *v. t.* नि-ग्रह् 9 P, अव-नि-रुध् 7 U, नियम् 1 P, प्रति-,सं ह 1 P, अपसं-ह, वि-धृ 10; न दा 3 U.

WITHIN, *adv.* अंतर् in comp.; अंतर्वर्तिन्. 2 चित्तोद्भूत, आंतर. (*a.*). –*prep.* अंतरे, अभ्यंतरे, मध्ये, अंतर् in comp.; 'w. the house' गृहाभ्यंतरे, अंतर्गृहं &c.; 'w. six months' षण्मासाभ्यंतरे, षण्मासमध्ये; अर्वाक् (with abl.). 2 (In the reach of) गोचर, विषय, ग्राह्य, in comp.; 'w. hearing' कर्णगोचरीभूत; 'w. the reach of eyes' नयनगोचरे, नयनविषये &c.; 'w. the reach of the hand' हस्तप्राप्य-ग्राह्य.

WITHOUT, *prep.* विना (with acc., instr., abl.), अंतरेण (with acc.), ऋते (with abl.), वर्जयित्वा, मुक्त्वा, विहाय (with acc.); by अ-निर्-pr., हीन, रहित, वर्जित, व्यतिरेकेण, व्यतिरिक्तं in comp.; 'w. delay' अविलंबं; 'w. doubt' निःसंशयं, असंशयं; 'w. money' धनहीन-रहित, निर्धन. 2 (Before participles) By अ (अन्); 'w. burning' अदहन्, अदग्ध्वा; 'w. being marked' अलक्षित. 3 बहिः (with abl.), बहिर्भागे. –*adv.* बहिः, बाह्यतः; 'lying w.' बहिःस्थित.

WITHSTAND, *v. t.* निरा-प्रति-कृ 8 U, प्रतिकूलयति (D.), वि-रुध् 7 U, परिपंथीभू 1 P, (बद्धपरिकरस्य तेन त्रैलोक्यमपि क्षमं परिपंथीभवितुं Ve. 3); प्रत्यव-स्था 1 A; *See* OPPOSE.

WITNESS, *s.* साक्षिन् *m.*; 'w. es for prosecution' पूर्ववादिनः साक्षिणः; 'ear-w.' श्रुतसाक्षी; 'eye-w.' दृष्टसाक्षी. 2 साक्षात् द्रष्टृ *m.* 3 साक्ष्यं, प्रमाणं. –*v. t.* प्रत्यक्षीकृ 8 U, प्रत्यक्षं दृश् 1 P; *See* SEE. 2 साक्ष्येण प्रमाणीकृ. –*v. i.* साक्ष्यं दा 3 U, साक्षीभू 1 P.

WIZARD, *s.* मायाकारः; *See* MAGICIAN.

WOE, *s.* दुःखं, शोकः; *See* SORROW, GRIEF. –*interj.* हा, धिक्, (with acc.); अहो बत, हा कष्टं. –FUL, *a.* Sorrowful, q. v.; 'is in a w. plight' कष्टमभ्यापन्नः (U. 3).

WOLF, *s.* वृकः, कोकः, ईहामृगः.

WOMAN, *s.* स्त्री, नारी, अंगना, अबला, योषित्, वनिता, ललना, योषा, सीमंतिनी, वधूः, वामा, महिला; 'nobly-born w.' कुलांगना, कुलजा; 'young w.' युवतिः-ती, यूनी, तरुणी, प्रमदा, बाला; 'beautiful w.' सुंदरी, प्रमदा, सुभगा, नितंबिनी, वामलोचना; 'an excellent w.' वरारोहा, मत्तकाशिनी, उत्तमा, वरवर्णिनी; 'passionate w.' कोपना, भामिनी; 'old w.' स्थविरा, वृद्धा, जरती; 'virtuous w.' सती, साध्वी, पतिव्रता, सुचरित्रा, कुलस्त्री, कुलपालिका. –HOOD, *s.* यौवनं. –ISH, *a.* स्त्रीवत् *ind.*, स्त्रैण (णी *f.*). –KIND, *s.* स्त्रीजनः, अबलाजनः, स्त्रैणं. –LY, *a.* (*s.*) in comp.; 'with w. timidity' स्त्रीस्वभावसुलभकातरतया.

WOMB, *s.* गर्भः, गर्भाशयः, गर्भस्थानं.

WONDER, *s.* विस्मयः, चमत्कारः. आश्चर्यं, कौतुकं. 2 अद्भुतं, चित्रं, अद्भुतवस्तु; 'it is no w. that' नैतच्चित्रं यद् &c., किमत्र चित्रं; 'w.-struck' विस्मयाकुल-उपहत-आपन्न. –*v. i.* वि-स्मि 1 A, by (*s.*) in comp. ; w. ed at hearing the news' वार्ताश्रवणेन संजातविस्मयः-सविस्मयः-बभूव. –FUL, WONDROUS, *a.* अद्भुत, आश्चर्यभूत, विस्मयकर (री *f.*), आश्चर्य, वि-,चित्र, विस्मापक. –FULLY, *adv.* अद्भुतं, साश्चर्यं. –INGLY, *adv.* सविस्मयं, साश्चर्यं.

WONT, *s.* अभ्यासः, रीति *f.*, संप्रदायः, आचारः, नित्यव्यवहारः. –ED, *a.* परिचित, नित्य, अभ्यस्त; 'w. nature' स्वभावः, प्रकृति *f.*; *See* NATURE; 'to bring to one's w. nature' प्रकृतौ स्था c., प्रकृतिस्थ-*a.* कृ.

WOO, *s.* (विवाहार्थं) याच् 1 A, अर्थ् 10 A, आराध् c. –ER, *s.* विवाहकामः, विवाहार्थी.

WOOD, *s.* काष्ठं, दारु *n.* 2 वनं, अरण्यं; *See* FOREST; 'w.-apple' कपित्थः; 'w.-cock' काष्ठ-वनकुक्कुटः; 'w.-cutter' काष्ठच्छिद्, काष्ठिकः; 'w.-land' वृक्ष-वृक्षावृत-भूमि *f.*; 'w.-man' आटविकः, वनजीविन् *m.*, 'w.-cutter', q. v.; 'w.-nymph' वनदेवता; 'w.-pecker' काष्ठकूटः, दार्वाघाटः; 'w.-pigeon' हारीतः; 'w.-sorrel' चुक्रिका, दंतशठा. –ED, *a.* वृक्षावृत, सवृक्ष. –EN, *a.* काष्ठ-दारु-मय (यी *f.*), काष्ठ-दारु in comp. –Y, *a.* वृक्षाकीर्ण, द्रुमभूयिष्ठ, द्रुमावृत. 2 Silvan, q. v.

WOOF, *s.* प्रतितंतुः, वाणि-णी *f.*

WOOL, *s.* लो(रो)मन् *n.*, ऊर्णा (of sheep). –LEN, *a.* लोमज, और्ण (णी *f.*), ऊर्णामय (यी *f.*); मेषलोमज; 'w. cloth' और्णवस्त्रं-पटः. –LY, *a.* लोमश, रोमवत्.

WORD, *s.* शब्दः, नामन् *n.*, पदं, वाचकः; 'w. for w.' यथाशब्दं. 2 वचनं, संगरः, प्रतिज्ञा; *See* PROMISE, ; 'true to, or keeping, one's w.' सत्यपालित-संगरः; 'you have given your w.' विहितप्रतिज्ञः-दत्तवचनः-असि; 'to break one's w.' विसं-वद् 1 P, प्रतिज्ञां लुप् c. 3 वाक्यं, वचस् *n.*, वाच् *f.*, उक्ति *f.*, वचनं; 'whose w. can be trusted' आप्तः, आप्तवाक्; यथार्थवक्ता; 'war of w. s' वाग्युद्धं, वाक्कलहः; 'a man of few w. s' मितवाक्, अल्पभाषी. 4 संदेशः, वार्ता; 'in a w.' किं बहुना; 'in a few w. s' समासतः, समासेन; 'upon my w.' (I tell you &c.) यदि मद्वचः श्रद्धेयं मन्यसे, यदि

ते मद्वचने विश्वासः. –*v. t.* शब्दान् रच् 10 or युज् 10 or ग्रंथ् 9 P; gen. ex. by (*s.*); 'a briefly w. ed message' लघुसंदेशपदा सरस्वती; 'well-w. ed' सम्यग्ग्रथित, साधुविन्यस्तशब्द; 'pathetically w.-ed' करुणार्थग्रथित (संदेश &c.). —WORDY, *a.* बहुशब्द, विस्तीर्णवाच्, बहुवाङ्मय (यी *f.*), उपचितवाक्. –INESS, *s.* शब्द-वाक्य-विस्तरः, वागुपचयः, बहुशब्दत्वं.

WORK, *s.* कर्मन् *n.*, कृति *f.*, कार्यं, व्यापारः, व्यवसायः, नियोगः; क्रिया. 2 Labour, q. v.; उद्यमः, उद्योगः. 3 ग्रंथः, क्रिया, कृतिः; 'at w.' कर्मव्यग्र *a.*, कार्यव्यापृत *a.*; 'had hard w. to go' गच्छन्नतीवायासितः. 'w.-house' कर्मशाला; 'w.-shop' कर्म-शिल्प-उद्योगशाला. –*v. i.* परिश्रमं-कर्म-कृ 8 U, व्या-पृ 6 A (with loc.), कार्यासक्त,-कार्यव्यापृत्- *a.* भू 1 P, परि-, श्रम् 4 P, उद्यम्. 2 फल्, गुणं आवह् 1 P or दा 3 U, oft. by गुणः; अतिवीर्यवतीव भेषजे बहुरल्पीयसि दृश्यते गुणः (Ki. II. 4) 'w. s well or efficaciously'. –*v. t.* सं-,चल् c., प्र c. 2 कृ 8 U, वि-धा 3 U, निर्मा 3 A, 2 P, रच् 10, घट् c. (घटयति), कॢप् c. 3 उत्पद् c., जन् c., आवह्. 4 आयस् c., परि-श्रम् c., क्लिश् c. 5 Manage, q. v.; 'w. out' परि-उप-कॢप् c., साध् 5 P or c.; 'w. up,' Excite, q. v.; उप-प्र-युज् 7 A, 10. –ING, *s.* चेष्टा, व्यापारः, प्रवृत्ति *f.*, क्रिया; *See* (*s.*). –WROUGHT, *a.* कृत, विहित &c. 2 संस्कृत, परिष्कृत, कृत; 'w. gold' कृतहेम; 'w. iron' कुशी. —WORKMAN, *s.* कर्मकरः-री *f.*, कर्मकारः, कर्मकारिन्-णी, कारुः, शिल्पकारः. –LIKE, *a.* दक्ष, कर्मठ. –SHIP, *s.* कर्मकौशलं, हस्तक्रिया. 2 कर्म, निर्माणं, घटना, आकृतिः.

WORLD, *s.* विश्वं, जगत् *n.*, भुवनं, लोकः, चराचरं, त्रिविष्टपं, अखिलं जगत्, ब्रह्मांडं; 'three w. s' त्रिभुवनं, त्रिलोकी, त्रैलोक्यं. 2 Earth, q. v.; 'end of the w.' कल्पांतः. 3 लोकः, जनः, (pl. also). 4 संसारः, भवः, संसृति *f.*, प्रपंचः, जीवयात्रा. 5 लोकाचारः-मार्गः, जनरीति *f.*, रूढि *f.*, लौकिकं, लोकः; 'in this w.' इह; 'in the next w.' अमुत्र, परत्र, प्रेत्य; 'the next w.' पर-प्रेत-लोकः, लोकांतरं; 'of this w.' ऐहिक; 'of the next w.' पारत्रिक-आमुष्मिक-पारलौकिक- (की *f.*); 'you are my all the w.' त्वं मम जीवितसर्वस्वीभूतः; 'renounce the w.' संन्यस् 4P, वैराग्यं भज् 1U; 'aversion to w.' वैराग्यं; 'knowing the ways of the w.' लौकिकज्ञ (S. 4); 'snares of the w.' मोहपाशः, मायाजालं-चक्रं. —WORLDLY, *a.* लौकिक; 'w. sages' लौकिकाः साधवः; (*s.*) in comp; 'w. tie' संसारतंतुः-निबंधनं, भवपाशः. 2 ऐहिक, सांसारिक, ऐहलौकिक, प्रापंचिक. 3 (W.-minded), ऐहिकदृष्टि-बुद्धि, संसारनिष्ठ, विषयासक्तचित्त, प्रपंचासक्त; 'w. wise' संसारज्ञानिन्; 'w. wisdom' संसारज्ञानं, व्यवहारज्ञानं. –INESS, *s.* संसारनिष्ठा, प्रपंच-विषय-आसक्ति *f.* –WORLDLING, *s.* *See* above; SENSUALIST also.

WORM, *s.* कृ(क्रि)मिः (in the stomach also), कीटः-टकः; 'w.-disease' कृमिरोगः; 'destroying w. s' कृमिहर, कृमिघ्न. –Y, *a.* कृमिल, कृमिमय (यी *f.*), कृमिकुलचित. 2 कृमिभक्षित-निष्कुषित.

WORRY, *v. t.* प्र-,बाध् 1 A, अर्द् 1 P or c., आयस् c., क्लिश् c., पीड् 10, प्र-हृ 1 P.

WORSE, *a.* निकृष्टतर, अधिकदुष्ट, पापीयस्, दुष्ट-खलतर. 2 अधिकरुग्ण, or by वृध् 1 A; 'she is getting w. day by day' अनुदिवसं तस्या विपर्ययो दृश्यते or तस्या विकारो वर्धते एव; 'you are none the w. for it' न तर्हि प्रागवस्थायाः परिहीयसे (Mal. 4). –*adv.* कु, दुष्टतया; ex. by (*a.*).

WORSHIP, *v. t.* पूज् 10, उपास् 2 A, उप-स्था 1 A, अभि-,अर्च् 1 P, 10, आ-राध् c., भज् 1 U, सेव् 1 A, नमस्यति (D.). –*s.* पूजा, उपासना-नं, अर्चा, अर्चनं-ना, आराधनं, नमस्या, सपर्या, अपचिति *f.*, अर्हणा. 2 (As a title) देवः, महाराजः. –PER, *s.* पूजकः, अर्चकः, उपासकः, भक्तः,-जनः, आराधकः, सेवकः; 'w. of *S*iva' शैवः; 'w. of Vishnu' वैष्णवः.

WORST, *a.* दुष्टतम, पापिष्ठ, निकृष्टतम, कष्टतम. –*s.* कष्टतमावस्था, कष्टतमो भागः. –*v. t.* Humble, Subdue, q. v.

WORSTED, *s.* और्णसूत्रं-तंतुः.

WORTH, *s.* अर्घः, मूल्यं; *See* VALUE. 2 गुणः, उत्कर्षः, सारवत्ता. –*a.* अर्घ, मूल्य, अर्ह in comp.; ex. by pot. pass. part. or अर्ह् 1 P; 'w. considering' विचारार्ह, विचारमर्हति, विचार्य; 'w. much' बहुमूल्य; 'w. little' अल्पार्घ; 'w. while' सांप्रत, उचित, श्रमार्ह. –LESS, *a.* निर्गुण, गुणहीन, निरर्थक, असार, अकिंचित्कर (री *f.*), सार-गुण-हीन, अल्पमूल्य, तृणप्राय, अधम, कुत्सित; *See* MEAN; oft. by अ in comp., अद्रव्यं, अपात्रं 'a w. object'. —WORTHY, *a.* योग्य, उचित, अर्ह, सदृश, अनुरूप, or by pot. pass. part. or अर्ह; 'a pupil w. of the name' परमार्थतः यः शिष्यः, यः शिष्यनामार्हः; 'having a husband w. of her' अनुरूपभर्तृगामिनी (S. 1); 'a w. object' पात्रं, सत्पात्रं, गुणास्पदं. 2 आर्य, मान्य, पूज्य, भगवत्. 3 गुणिन्, गुणवत्, गुणोपेत. –*s.* मान्यजनः, आर्यः, जनः, सज्जनः. –ILY, *adv.* योग्यतया, उचितं, यथार्थं, उपपन्नं. –INESS, *s.* योग्यता, अर्हता, गुणः, पात्रता.

WOULD, *See* under WILL.

WOUND, *s.* व्रणः, क्षतं, क्षति *f.*; अरुस् *n.*, ईर्मं, आघा-

तः; प्रहारः; 'a w. in the flesh' त्वग्व्रणः; 'fresh w.' आर्द्रक्षतं, सद्योव्रणः. —*v. t.* व्यथ् 4 P, क्षण् 8 P, तुद् 6 P, आ-अभि-हन् 2 U, क्षि 5 P, व्रण् 10, भिद्-छिद् 7 P, वि-दॄ 9 P; *See* OFFEND, HURT. —ED, *a.* क्षत, व्रणित, भिन्न, विद्ध, भिन्नदेह; 'greatly w.' क्षतविक्षत; 'mortally w.' भिन्नमर्मन्.

WRANGLE, *v. i. See* QUARREL.

WRAP, *v. t.* आ-वृ 5 U, आ-परि-वेष्ट् 1 A or c., अव-गुंठ् 10, आच्छद् 10. —PED, *a.* वेष्टित &c.; कोशीकृत, कोशस्थ. —PER, *s.* प्रावारः, प्रावरणं, अवगुंठनं, आ-, वेष्टनं, पुटः-टं, कोशः-षः, आच्छादनं, पिधानं.

WRATH, -FUL, *See* INDIGNANT &c.

WREAK, *v. t.* (revenge) सिध् c.-साध् c. (साधयति), युध् c., निर्यत् 10; 'w. ing revenge' वैरसाधनं-निर्यातनं; 'w. anger upon one' कोपसंदीपनं कृ, क्रोधं शम् c.

WREATH, *s.* माला, स्रज् *f.*, माल्यं, हारः, उत्पीडः, दामन् *f. n.*, आवलि-ली *f.*; *See* GARLAND; 'w. of smoke' धूमस्य उत्पीडः. —WREATHE, *v. t.* ग्रंथ् 9 P, सूच् 10, गु(गुं)फ् 6 P, सं-दृभ् 6 P, 10. —ED, *a.* स्रगन्वित, माल्यवत्, सूत्रित.

WRECK, *v. t.* (नावं &c.) भंज् 7 P, नश् c., उच्छिद् 7 P, भिद् 7 P. —*v. i.* भंज् pass. —*s.* पोतभंगः, यानभंगः, नौव्यसनं. 2 भग्नपोतः (portion w.-ed) भिन्ननौः. 3 उच्छेदः, भंगः, नाशः.

WRENCH, WREST, *v. t.* संपीड्य ग्रह् 9 P, बलात् आकृष् 1 P or आच्छिद् 7 P, अप-हृ 1 P, आच्छिद्य ग्रह्. —*s.* बलादाकर्षणं.

WRESTLE, *v. i.* मल्लयुद्धं-बाहुयुद्धं-कृ 8 U, बाहू-बाहवि युध् 4 A. —ER, *s.* मल्लः, बाहुयोधः-धी. —ING, *s.* बाहु-मल्ल-युद्धं, मल्लक्रीडा-युद्धं.

WRETCH, *s.* दुरात्मन् *m.*, दुर्जातः, पापः, पापिष्ठः, जाल्मः, हताशः, नराधमः, चंडालः, खलः. 2 मंद-हतभाग्यः, वराकः, अधन्यः, दीनः, तपस्विन्. —ED, *a.* दीन, वराक (की *f.*), अधन्य; gen. ex. by हतक affixed, दग्ध pr.; दग्धोदरं, मदनहतकः &c.; हताश; दुर् pr.; 'w. state' दुर्दशा. 2 निकृष्टतम, अधम. 3 दुःखभाज्, अतिदुःखित. —EDLY, *adv.* दीनवत्, दीन in comp.; 'w. dressed' दीनवेष; *See* MISERABLE.

WRIGGLE, *v. t.* इतस्ततः चल् c.

WRING, *v. t.* (बलवत्) आकुंच् c., सं-पीड् 10; 'w.-ing his hands in grief' दुःखात् हस्तं हस्तेन निष्पिषन्; 'w. off' बलात् निष्कृष् 1 P or निर्हृ 1 P; 'w. out' निष्पीड्य ग्रह् 9 P, निष्कृष्; बलवत् निःसृ c. or निर्गम् c.

WRINKLE, *s.* वलि-ली *f.*, भंगः, रे(ले)खा, चर्मलेखा-भंगः, चर्मसंकोचः. —*v. t.* चर्म-त्वचं-संकुच् 1 P or सं-हृ 1 P. —*a.* वलिभ-न, वलीमत्. —ED, -Y, *a.* रेखांकित, भंगवत्.

WRIST, *s.* मणिबंधः-धनं, प्रकोष्ठः.

WRITE, *v. t.* लिख् 6 P, (in all senses), पत्रे आरुह् c. or नि-विश् c. 2 प्रणी 1 P, रच् 10; ग्रंथ् 9 P, निर्मा 3 A, 2 P, नि-प्र-बंध् 9 P. —ER, *s.* लेखकः, लिपिकारः, लिख् in comp. 2 प्रणेतृ *m.*, ग्रंथकृत्-कारः, रचकः, निर्माता. —ING, *s.* लेखः, लेख्यं, लिखितं, पत्रं, लेख्यपत्रं; 'committed to w.' पत्रारूढ, लेख्यार्पित, पत्रे-निवेशित. 2 (Art of w.) लिपि-वि *f.*, लि(ले)खनं. 3 रचना, निर्माणं, प्रणयनं. 4 अक्षरसंस्थानं-रचना-विन्यासः.

WRITHE, *v. i.* (दुःखात्) संकुच् 1 P (limbs &c.) or आकृष् 1 P; *See* SMART.

WRONG, *a.* अन्याय्य, अधर्म्य, न्यायविरुद्ध, अयथान्याय्य; oft. by उत्-कु pr.; 'w. road' विमार्गः, उत्पथः, कुमार्गः. 2 अयुक्त, अनुचित. अनुपपन्न, अनर्ह. 3 भ्रांत, मिथ्या, अयथार्थ, सदोष, वितथ, असत्य, अनृत; 'you are w.' मिथ्या-अनृतं-भ्रांतिमूलकं-ते वचः; 'this is not w.' नैष दोषः. —*s.* अन्यायः, अधर्मः. 2 अपकारः, निकृति *f.*, अपराधः. 3 भ्रांति *f.*, भ्रमः, अयाथार्थ्यं, असत्यता. 4 दोषः; 'in the w.' सदोष, भ्रांत, भ्रांतियुक्त; 'yourself are in the w. here' अत्र तवैव दोषः. —*v. t.* नि-अप-कृ, वि-प्र-कृ, अपराध् 4 P, (with gen. or loc.). 2 मिथ्यादोषं निक्षिप् 6 P or न्यस् 4 P; 'w.-doer' अपराधिन्, अपकारकः. —FUL, *a.* अन्याय्य, दुष्ट. —FULLY, *adv.* अन्यायतः, अन्यायेन. 2 दुष्टतया. —LY, *adv.* मिथ्या, अयुक्तं, अन्यथा, अवितथं. 2 अन्यायतः, अयथान्यायं, अन्यायेन, अधर्मेण; भ्रांत्या, &c.

WROTH, *a. See* ANGRY.

WRY, *a.* वक्र. —NESS, *s.* वक्रता. 2 विकृतं, विकृति *f.*

X

XANTHIPPE, *s.* कैकेयी, कर्कशा, वक्रशीला.

Y.

YACHT, *s.* केलिपोतः, क्रीडानौ *f.*

YAK, *s.* चमरः (री *f.*).

YAM, *s.* आलु(रु)कं.

YARD, *s.* अंगनं, प्रांगणं, चत्वरं, अजिरं. 2 गजः. 3 कूपकाष्ठं.

YARN, *s.* सूत्रं, (और्ण-) सूत्र-तंतुः.

YAWN, *v. i.* वि-, जृंभ् 1 A, ज(जं)भ् 1 A.

—ING, *s.* जृंभः-भा, वि-,जृंभणं, वि-,जृंभिका-जृंभितं. —ER, *s.* वि-,जृंभकः.

YEA, *adv.* बाढं, ओम्; *See* YES. 2 अपरं च, अपि च.

YEAR, *s.* वर्षः-र्षं, सं-,वत्सरः, अब्दः, हायनः, समा *f.* (pl.), शरद् *f.*, संवत् *ind.*; '12 y.s old' द्वादशवार्षिक (की *f.*); '2 y.s old' द्विहायनी (बाला), 'approached their 16th y.' षोडशवर्षात्मका बभूवुः, षोडशवर्षवयोवस्थामस्पृशन्; 'this or current y.' वर्तमानवर्षं, ऐषमस्; 'last y.' गतवर्षं, परुत् *ind.*; 'the y. before last' परारि *ind.*; 'next y.' उत्तर-आगामि-वत्सरः; परवर्षं; 'half-y.' षण्मासं, वर्षार्धं; 'throughout the y.' आवर्षांतात्; 'y. after y.' प्रतिवर्षं, वत्सरे वत्सरे. —LY, *a.* वार्षिक-सांवत्सरिक-आब्दिक-(की *f.*), प्रति°; 'half-y.' अर्धवार्षिक-षाण्मासिक (की *f.*). —*adv.* वर्षे वर्षे, प्रतिवर्षं, प्रतिसंवत्सरं &c.

YEARN, *v. i.* स्पृह् 10; स्निह् 4 P; *See* LONG; उत्कंठ् 1 A (उत्कंठते च युष्मत्सन्निकर्षस्य U. 6), उत्सुकायते-वत्सलायते (D.); नूनमनपत्यता मां वत्सलयति (S. 7) 'causes me to y. towards the child'. —ING, *s.* स्पृहा, उत्कंठा, औत्सुक्यं, वात्सल्यं.

YEAST, *s.* सुरामंडः, कारोत्तरः; किण्वं, नग्नहूः (*m.*).

YELL, *v. i.* आ-उत्-क्रुश् 1 P, उच्चैः आ-क्रंद् 1 P; *See* SCREAM. —*s.* उत्क्रोशः, चीत्कारः,-शब्दः, महा-दीर्घ-शब्दः.

YELLOW, *a.* पीत, पीतल, हरिद्राभ, गौर (री *f.*), पीतवर्ण. —ISH, *a.* आपीत, हरिद्राभ; 'y.-white' पांडुर, आपांडु. —NESS, *s.* पीतवर्णः, पीतता.

YELP, *See* BARK.

YEOMAN, *s.* क्षेत्रपालः, गृहपतिः; 'y.-ly service' उपयुक्ता-बहुमाननीया-सेवा.

YES, *adv.* बाढं, ओं, अथ किं, तथा, एवं; एवमेव; sometimes by repeating verbs; 'saying y.' तथेति उक्त्वा.

YESTER, *a.* ह्यस्तन (नी *f.*), ह्यस्त्य. —YESTERDAY, *adv.* ह्यः, पूर्वेद्युः; 'of y.' ह्यस्तन (नी *f.*). —YESTERNIGHT, *s.* गतरात्रिः. —*adv.* अतीतायां रात्रौ.

YET, *conj.* तथापि (correl. of यद्यपि), not ex. when y. comes after अपि (पुष्पवत्यपि पवित्रा). —*adv.* अद्यापि, अधुनापि, इदानीमपि. 2 (With adjectives) by अधिकं, परं in comp.; 'y. more glorious' अतोधिकतरं तेजस्विन्.

YIELD, *v. t.* प्र-,दा 1 P, 3 U; 'y.ing fruits and flowers' फलपुष्पदा (भूः); प्र-,सू 2, 4 A, उत्पद् c., जन् c. (जनयति). 2 त्यज् 1 P, उत्-वि-सृज् 6 P, हा 3 P. 3 प्र-दा, वि-तॄ 1 P, (with loc.). —*v. i.* वशं गम् 1 P or या-इ 2 P, वशीभू 1 P. 2 शरणं प्रपद् 4 A or गम् &c. 3 (To another's opinion) अनु-मन् 4 A, निर्बंधं-स्वाग्रहं-त्यज्, अनुरुध् 4 A; 'y. to a superior foe' वैतसीं वृत्तिं आश्रि 1 U (R. IV. 35); 'y. ed to his prowess' विक्रमशालिनस्तस्य वशं ययौ; 'does not y. to Sachî in majestic splendour' ओजस्वितया न परिहीयते शच्याः (V. 3). —*s.* उत्पन्नं, फलं, लाभः. —ING, *a.* फलद-प्रद-दायिन्. 2 अनुरोधिन्, अनुवर्तिन्, अनुकूल.

YOKE, *s.* युगः-गं, धुर् *f.*, (धुरा in comp.); 'fit for the y.' युग्य, धुर्य, प्रासंग्य; (fig.) 'being under a foreign y.' परवशता, पारतंत्र्यं. 2 युगं, युगलं, युग्मं. 3 योक्त्रं बंधनं, आबंधः. —*v. t.* युज् 10, योक्त्रयति (D.), सं-गम् c.; 'y. ed to an unfit husband' अननुरूपपतिसंगता; 'y.-fellow' सहचरः (री *f.*).

YOLK, *s.* अंडमध्यं, पेशीगर्भः.

YON, YONDER, *a.* अदस्, इदम्, (*pron. a.*) पुरो दृश्यमान, नातिदूरस्थ. —*adv.* नातिदूरं-रे, स्तोकांतरे, अग्रतः.

YORE, (of) पुरा, पूर्वं; *See* FORMERLY.

YOU, यूयं. —YOUR, *a.* त्वदीय, युष्मदीय, तावक-यौष्माक (की *f.*), यौष्माकीण.

YOUNG, *a.* युवन् (यूनी-युवति-ती *f.*), तरुण-(णी *f.*), बाल (of trees &c. also), अल्पवयस्, कौमार (री *f.*), अभिनववयस्क; (of men) oft. ex. by दारकः, कुमारः in comp.; 'y. sage' मुनिकुमारः-रकः, ऋषिदारकः; 'y. warrior' वीरपोतः, बालवीरः, oft. by (*s.*) in comp., *See* below. —*s.*, 'y. one' शावः-वकः, अर्भकः, अपत्यं, पोतः-तकः, शिशुः, डिंभः, पृथुकः; 'y. of an elephant,' 'y. elephant' गजशिशुः, कलभः. —ER, *a.* यवीयस्, कनीयस्, अनुजन्मन्; 'y. brother or sister' अनुजः-जा, अवरजः-जा, अनंतरजः-जा. —YOUNGSTER, *s.* बटुः, अर्भकः, कुमारकः, बालः. —YOUTH, *s.* यौवनं, तारुण्यं, पूर्वं-नवं-प्रथमं-वयः, कौमारं-रकं; 'being in the prime or heyday of her y.' प्रथमे वयसि वर्तमाना, नवयौवना; (state of y.) यौवनदशा-पदवी, तारुण्यावस्था, यौवनकालः &c. 2 (Young man) युवन् *m.*, तरुणः, बालः, कुमारः-रकः बालजनः, किशोरः. —FUL, *a.* तरुणवयस्क; by पोतः, बालः, in comp., *See* (*a.*). —FULNESS, *s.* तारुण्यं.

Z.

ZANY, *s.* भंडः, वैहासिकः, विदूषकः.

ZEAL, *s.* उत्साहः, औत्सुक्यं, सोत्साहता, व्यग्रता, आस्था, अत्युत्कंठा, उद्योगः, उत्तापः, उत्कंठा, अत्यनुरा-

ग्र:. -ous, *a.* सोत्साह, अति-,उत्सुक, उत्साहवत्, व्यग्र, चंड, तीक्ष्ण, अत्यासक्त, उद्युक्त, तीक्ष्णकर्मन् *m.* -OUSLY, *adv.* औत्सुक्येन, सोत्साहं, व्यग्रतया. -ZEALOT, *s.* अतिव्यग्र:, सोत्साह:.

ZEBRA, *s.* वनगर्दभ:-रासभ:.

ZENITH, *s.* खमध्यं, शिरोबिंदु:, खस्वस्तिकं; (fig.) 'z. of prosperity' ऐश्वर्यस्य परा काष्ठा-परा कोटि:; 'z. distance' नतं.

ZEPHYR, *s.* मंदवायु:-वात:, मृदु-सुखस्पर्श-पवन:.

ZERO, *s.* शून्यं, खं, बिंदु:.

ZEST, *s.* आ-,स्वाद:, अभिरुचि *f.* 2 Zeal, q. v.

ZIGZAG, *a.* वक्र, कुटिल, जिह्म, कुटिलगति.

ZINC, *s.* दस्ता.

ZODIAC, *s.* ज्योतिश्चक्रं, भूचक्रं, मंडलं, राशिचक्रं; 'a sign of the z.' राशि:, लग्नं.

ZONE, *s.* मेखला, रश(स)ना, कांची; *See* GIRDLE. 2 मंडलं, (भू-)वलय:-यं, कटिबंध:.

ZOOGRAPHY, *s.* प्राणिवर्णनं.

ZOOLOGY, *s.* प्राणिविद्या-शास्त्रं, जीवादिशास्त्रं.

ZOOTOMY, *s.* प्राणिव्यवच्छेद:.

FINISH.